April 2005

Jack —

May you never be at
a loss for words.

Happy Birthday,
Love, Jane

WEBSTER'S
CROSSWORD PUZZLE
DICTIONARY

WEBSTER'S
CROSSWORD
PUZZLE
DICTIONARY

GRAMERCY BOOKS
NEW YORK

This 2004 edition is published by Gramercy Books, an imprint of Random House Value Publishing,
by arrangement with Random House Reference, divisions of Random
House, Inc., New York.

Gramercy is a registered trademark and the colophon is a trademark of Random House, Inc.

Random House
New York • Toronto • London • Sydney • Auckland
www.randomhouse.com

Printed and bound in the United States of America

A catalog record for this title is available from the Library of Congress.

ISBN 0-375-42584-5

9 8 7 6 5 4 3 2

Preface

Although various word games and puzzles have existed almost since the beginnings of language, the modern crossword puzzle is a 20th-century innovation. The first newspaper crossword appeared on December 21, 1913, in the *New York World*, and this new type of word puzzle quickly captured the public's fancy. Within a decade, crossword puzzles were featured in most American newspapers, and they soon became the rage in England as well. Since the 1920s, crossword puzzles have been a standard feature of daily newspapers and have proved enormously popular when collected in book form.

Now found in almost every language and in variations ranging from theme puzzles to diagramless puzzles, crosswords are available for almost any age and vocabulary level. Those who solve crossword puzzles invariably relish the challenge of completing a puzzle, of "getting it right." When faced with a clue they cannot answer, they resist "cheating"—looking at the puzzle's solution. One way out of this difficulty is to consult a reference work—just as the puzzle's creator may have done in finding words or crafting clues. Yet neither a dictionary nor an encyclopedia nor an almanac contains the necessary information in a useful, quick-reference format. A standard dictionary might give a few synonyms for a word, an encyclopedia would give information about countries or historical figures, and an almanac usually has information about sports figures or the Academy Awards, but only a crossword puzzle dictionary combines in one handy volume the information that might be found in all three. Equally important, it does so without extraneous information and with the convenience of an arrangement by the number of letters in each word, and it includes the many words that are common in crossword puzzles but too obscure to be in other references.

Webster's Crossword Puzzle Dictionary, drawing on the resources of the Random House dictionaries and thesauruses, with research into a host of other topics, answers the need of crossword puzzlers for one single-purpose reference work. In addition to general vocabulary and synonyms, there are entries covering history; the natural and physical sciences; literature; music, painting, and other arts; religion; mythology; sports; popular culture; and current affairs, among others. Longer items provide easy-to-find detailed information on the continents and countries of the world, states of the United States, U.S. presidents, the months of the year, and other facts of special interest. This Third Edition has been fully updated, with special emphasis placed on the pop cultural questions that are now such an important part of puzzledom—sports teams, TV characters, even sneaker manufacturers.

While *Webster's Crossword Puzzle Dictionary*'s primary purpose is to meet the needs of the growing numbers of people who find crosswords both relaxing and challenging, even a cursory glance will demonstrate the book's usefulness as a reference for trivia buffs. From who won the Academy Award for best actress in 1970 (Glenda Jackson) to the name of a coffee grown in Jamaica (Blue Mountain), it's all here.

How To Use This Book

The main entries in *Webster's Crossword Puzzle Dictionary* are words or phrases likely to appear as crossword puzzle clues. Each entry consists of a clue word or phrase and a list of answer words, arranged first by the number of letters in each word and then alphabetically. For example, if the main entry—**banal**—is the clue for a five-letter answer, the answer—"trite"—will be found alphabetically listed under the five-letter answer words. For phrases, such as **contracted form,** the answer could be "digest," "summary," or "synopsis." Entries may also contain indented subheads and secondary subheads. If, for instance, the clue is a phrase, like **cotton fabric,** the word **cotton** will be found as a main entry in the dictionary, and **fabric** will be found as a subhead under it, with such possible answer words as "terry," "poplin," and "gingham." In some cases, the answer can be found in more than one place. For example, if the clue is **Mexican coin,** the answer could be found by looking under the main entry **Mexico** and the subhead **monetary unit,** or by looking under the main entry **coin/currency** and the subhead **of Mexico.**

There are also cross references for alternate spellings and very closely related items. Many terms that do not have explicit cross references may still have valuable additional answers at related entries. The reader is encouraged to look up synonyms even when there is no explicit cross reference. To take one example, the clue **canine** has a short entry in this book, but **dog** has a much longer list that could be examined as well.

The main entries, subheads, secondary subheads, and numbers all appear in boldface type; the answer words are in regular roman type. Most punctuation and accent marks have been omitted, since they are not used in puzzle answers; occasionally, apostrophes and other marks have been included in answers to make them more readable.

WEBSTER'S
CROSSWORD PUZZLE
DICTIONARY

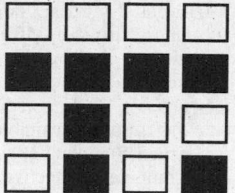

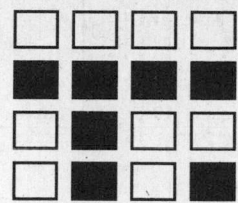

aardvark
  also: 7 ant bear 8 anteater
  native to: 6 Africa
  food: 4 ants 8 termites
  name comes from: 9 Africaans
    meaning: 8 earth hog, earth pig

Aaron
  brother: 5 Moses
  father: 5 Amram
  mother: 8 Jochebed
  sister: 6 Miriam
  son: 5 Abihu, Nadab 7 Eleazar, Ithamar
  wife: 8 Elisheba
  successor: 7 Eleazar
  Aaron's Rod 21 miraculously blossomed
    yielded: 7 almonds
  deathplace: 3 Hor 8 Mount Hor
  priestly descendant of: 8 Aaronite
  set up: 10 golden calf

Aaron, Henry (Hank)
  sport: 8 baseball
  position: 10 outfielder
  record: 8 homeruns
  team: 13 Atlanta Braves 15 Milwaukee Braves 16 Milwaukee Brewers

Aaron's Rod 21 miraculously blossomed
  yielded: 7 almonds

Aatam *see* 4 Pima

Ab 16 fifth Hebrew month

Abaddon 4 hell 8 Appolyon

abaft 6 behind 11 to the rear of 12 to the stern of

Abagtha 6 eunuch
  served: 9 Ahasuerus

abandon 4 dash, drop, elan, jilt, junk, quit, stop 5 ardor, cease, forgo, gusto, leave, let go, scrap, verve, waive 6 desert, give up, spirit 7 discard, forfeit, forsake, freedom 8 abdicate, evacuate, forswear, get rid of, renounce, run out on 9 animation, cast aside, repudiate, surrender 10 depart from, enthusiasm, exuberance, relinquish, wantonness 11 discontinue, impetuosity, leave behind, spontaneity, unrestraint 12 immoderation, intemperance, recklessness, withdraw from 13 impulsiveness

abandoned 4 lewd, wild 5 loose 6 impure, jilted, sinful, vacant, wanton, wicked 7 debased, immoral 8 cast away, degraded, deserted, desolate, forsaken, marooned, rejected, un-

chaste 9 cast aside, debauched, discarded, dissolute, neglected, reprobate, shameless 10 dissipated, left behind, licentious, profligate, unoccupied 11 unrepentant 12 disreputable, incorrigible, irreformable, relinquished, unprincipled 13 irreclaimable

abandon oneself to 7 yield to 8 give in to, give up to 9 indulge in

Abaris
  origin: 5 Greek
  form: 4 sage

Abas
  mentioned in: 5 Iliad
  king of: 7 Argolis
  father: 6 Celeus 7 Lynceus 9 Eurydamas
  mother: 8 Metanira 12 Hypermnestra
  wife: 6 Aglaia
  son: 7 Proetus 8 Acrisius
  daughter: 7 Idomene
  changed into: 4 bird 6 lizard
  mocked: 7 Demeter
  protected by: 11 magic shield
  companion: 8 Diomedes
  killed by: 8 Diomedes

a bas 8 down with 11 to the bottom

abase 4 mock 5 shame 6 debase, defame, demean, humble, malign, vilify 7 cheapen, degrade, mortify, put down, vitiate 8 badmouth, belittle, besmirch, bring low, cast down, disgrace, dishonor 9 denigrate, devaluate, discredit, downgrade, humiliate 13 bring down a peg, cut down to size

abash 3 awe, cow 4 dash, faze 5 daunt 6 deject, dismay 7 depress 8 dispirit 9 discomfit, embarrass 10 discompose, disconcert, discourage, dishearten

abashed 3 shy 5 cowed, fazed 7 ashamed, bashful, crushed, daunted, humbled, subdued 8 confused, dismayed, overawed 9 chagrined, mortified 10 bewildered, confounded, humiliated, nonplussed, taken aback 11 dumbfounded, embarrassed, intimidated 12 disconcerted, disheartened 13 self-conscious

abate 3 ebb 4 cool, dull, ease, fade, slow, wane 5 allay, blunt, lower, quell, quiet, slack 6 dampen, go down, lessen, pacify, recede, reduce, soften, soothe, temper, weaken 7 assuage, curtail, decline, dwindle, fall

off, lighten, mollify, relieve, slacken, subside 8 decrease, diminish, fade away, fall away, mitigate, moderate, palliate, restrain, restrict, slack off, slow down, taper off 9 alleviate

Abba
  means: 6 father
  statesman: 4 Eban

abbey 6 cenoby, chapel, church, friary, priory 7 convent, nunnery 8 cloister, seminary 9 cathedral, hermitage, monastery

Abbott, Bud
  real name: 14 William A Abbott
  partner: 11 Lou Costello
  born: 12 Asbury Park NJ
  roles: 11 Who's on First 12 Buck Privates 13 Hold that Ghost 33 Abbott and Costello Meet Frankenstein

abbreviate 3 cut 4 clip, trim 6 reduce 7 abridge, curtail, cut down, shorten 8 boil down, compress, condense, contract, cut short, diminish, truncate 9 summarize, synopsize

abbreviated 5 brief, short 7 limited, summary 8 abridged 9 condensed, curtailed, shortened 10 compressed, summarized

abbreviation 5 brief 6 digest 7 cutting, pruning, summary 8 abstract, clipping, synopsis, trimming 9 lessening, reduction, short form 10 abridgment, diminution, shortening 11 abstraction, compression, contraction, curtailment, cut-down form, reduced form 12 condensation 13 condensed form, shortened form 14 compressed form, contracted form

abdicate 4 cede, quit 5 forgo, waive, yield 6 abjure, give up, resign 7 abandon 8 abnegate, renounce 9 surrender 10 relinquish 15 vacate the throne

abdomen 3 gut, pot 5 belly, tummy 6 paunch, venter 7 stomach 8 pot belly 9 bay window 11 breadbasket

abduct 5 seize, steal 6 kidnap 7 bear off 8 carry off, take away 10 run off with 11 make off with

Abduction from the Seraglio, The
  also: 25 Die Entfuhrung aus dem Serail
  opera by: 6 Mozart
  character: 5 Osmin 6 Blonde 8 Belmonte, Pedrillo 9 Constanze 10 Pasha Selim

Abdul-Jabbar, Kareem
 formerly: 11 Lew Alcindor
 sport: 10 basketball
 position: 6 center
 team: 8 LA Lakers 10 UCLA Bruins
  14 Milwaukee Bucks 16 Los Angeles
  Lakers
 shot: 7 sky hook

Abednego
 companion: 6 Daniel
 friend: 8 Meschach, Shadrach
 former name: 7 Azariah

Abel
 father: 4 Adam
 mother: 3 Eve
 brother: 4 Cain, Seth
 killer: 4 Cain

Abel, Walter
 field: 9 film actor

Abe Lincoln in Illinois
 author: 14 Robert Sherwood
 director: 12 John Cromwell
 cast: 10 Alan Baxter, Mary Howard,
  Ruth Gordon (Mary Todd Lincoln)
  11 Dorothy Tree, Minor Watson 12
  Gene Lockhart 13 Howard da Silva,
  Raymond Massey (Abraham Lincoln)

aberrant 3 odd 7 unusual 8 abnormal,
 atypical, peculiar, uncommon 9
 anomalous, eccentric, irregular

aberration 5 lapse, quirk 6 lunacy,
 oddity 7 anomaly, madness 8 delusion, illusion, insanity, mutation, rambling, straying 9 aberrance, aberrancy,
 curiosity, departure, deviation, exception, wandering 10 digression, distortion, divergence 11 abnormality, derangement, incongruity, mental lapse,
 peculiarity, singularity, strangeness

abet 3 aid 4 back, goad, help, spur,
 urge 5 egg on 6 assist, incite, lead on,
 second, uphold, urge on 7 advance,
 endorse, promote, support, sustain 8
 advocate, join with, sanction 9 encourage, instigate

abettor 4 ally 6 cohort 7 partner 9 accessory, associate, colleague 10 accomplice 11 confederate 12 collaborator

abeyance 5 delay, on ice, pause 6 hiatus, recess 7 latency 8 deferral, dormancy, inaction 9 cessation, remission 10 quiescence, suspension 11
 adjournment 12 intermission, postponement 13 in cold storage, on a
 back burner, waiting period 14 discontinuance

abhor 4 hate, shun 5 scorn 6 detest,
 eschew, loathe 7 despise, disdain, dislike 8 execrate, recoil at 9 abominate,
 can't stand, shudder at 10 shrink
 from 11 can't stomach 12 be revolted
 by 13 be nauseated by, find repulsive

abhorrence 4 hate 5 odium, scorn 6
 hatred 7 disdain, disgust, dislike 8
 aversion, contempt, distaste, loathing
 9 antipathy, revulsion 10 repugnance
 11 abomination

abhorrent 4 foul, vile 6 odious 7
 hateful 8 accursed 9 execrable, loathsome, repellent, repugnant, repulsive,
 revolting 10 abominable, despicable,
 disgusting, nauseating

abide 3 sit 4 bear, last, live, stay, stop
 5 brook, dwell, stand, tarry, visit 6
 accept, endure, linger, remain, reside,
 suffer 7 sojourn, stomach 8 stand for,
 submit to, tolerate

abide by 4 obey 6 follow 8 accede to,
 adhere to, submit to 9 conform to 10
 comply with 11 go along with

abiding 4 fast, firm 6 steady 7 durable, eternal, lasting 8 constant, enduring, unending 9 immutable, permanent, steadfast 10 changeless,
 continuing, unchanging, unshakable
 11 everlasting 12 indissoluble, wholehearted 13 unquestioning

Abidjan
 capital of: 10 Ivory Coast

Abigail
 husband: 5 David, Nabal
 brother: 5 David

Abihu
 father: 5 Aaron
 mother: 8 Elisheba
 brother: 5 Nadab 7 Eleazar, Ithamar
 killed with: 5 Nadab
 accompanied to Mt Sinai: 5 Moses

Abijah
 father: 8 Rehoboam
 grandfather: 7 Solomon
 grandmother: 6 Naamah

ability 4 bent, gift 5 flair, knack,
 power, skill 6 acumen, genius, talent
 7 faculty, knowhow, mind for 8 aptitude, capacity, facility 9 adeptness,
 expertise, potential 10 adroitness, capability, competence 11 proficiency
 12 potentiality 13 qualification

Abimelech
 king of: 5 Gerar
 means: 15 the father is king
 father: 6 Gideon 8 Abiathar
 brother: 6 Jotham
 army commander: 7 Phichol

Abinoam
 father: 4 Saul
 son: 5 Barak

abject 3 low 4 base, mean, vile 6 sordid 7 ignoble 8 complete, cringing,
 hopeless, horrible, terrible, thorough,
 wretched 9 groveling, miserable 10
 deplorable, despicable, spiritless 11
 inescapable 12 contemptible

abjure 6 desert, give up, recant, reject
 7 abandon, disavow 8 disallow, disclaim, forswear, renounce 9 repudiate
 10 relinquish

ablaze 5 afire, eager, fiery 6 aflame,
 alight, ardent, fervid, on fire, red-hot
 7 blazing, burning, excited, fervent,
 flaming, flushed, glowing, ignited,
 zealous 8 feverish, hopped-up, in
 flames, turned-on 10 passionate,
 switched-on 11 conflagrant, impassioned, intoxicated

able 3 apt, fit 4 good 5 adept 6 adroit,
 expert, fitted 7 capable, equal to,
 learned 8 adequate, skillful, talented
 9 competent, effective, efficient, masterful, practiced, qualified 10 proficient 11 experienced 12 accomplished

able-bodied 5 beefy, hardy, husky,
 lusty, thewy 6 brawny, hearty, robust,
 rugged, strong, sturdy 8 athletic, muscular, powerful, stalwart, vigorous 9
 herculean, strapping, well-built 15
 broad-shouldered

ablution 4 bath, wash 7 bathing,
 washing 8 cleaning, lavation 9 cleansing 12 purification 13 ritual washing

Abnaki (Wabanaki)
 language family: 9 Algonkian 10 Algonquian
 tribe: 6 Micmac 8 Malecite 9 Penobscot 13 Norridegewock, Passamaquoddy
 location: 5 Maine 6 Canada, Quebec
 7 Old Town 9 Norumbega 10 New
 England 12 New Brunswick

abnegate 5 forgo, waive 6 abjure, eschew, give up, refuse 7 abstain, forbear 8 renounce 9 repudiate 10 relinquish 11 deny oneself

abnegation 7 refusal 8 eschewal, giving up 9 rejection, sacrifice, surrender
 10 abstinence, continence, forbearing,
 self-denial, temperance 11 forbearance, resignation 12 renunciation 14
 relinquishment

Abner
 commanded: 9 Saul's army
 father: 3 Ner
 cousin: 4 Saul

abnormal 3 odd 4 rare 5 queer, weird
 7 bizarre, curious, deviant, strange,
 unusual 8 aberrant, atypical, deformed, freakish, peculiar, uncommon
 9 anomalous, eccentric, grotesque, irregular, monstrous, unheard of, unnatural 10 inordinate, outlandish, unexpected 11 exceptional 12
 unaccustomed 13 extraordinary 14
 unconventional

abnormality 6 oddity 7 anomaly 9
 aberrance, curiosity, deformity, deviation 10 aberration, perversion 11 peculiarity 12 eccentricity, idiosyncrasy,
 irregularity, malformation, unconformity

abode 3 pad 4 home, nest 5 house 7
 address, habitat, lodging 8 domicile,
 dwelling 9 residence 10 habitation 13
 dwelling place 14 living quarters

abolish 3 end 5 annul, erase, quash 6
 cancel, repeal, revoke 7 blot out, nullify, rescind, squelch, vitiate, wipe out
 8 abrogate, set aside, stamp out 9
 eliminate, eradicate, extirpate, repudi-

ate, terminate **10** annihilate, do away with, extinguish, invalidate, obliterate, put an end to **11** exterminate **18** declare null and void

abolition 6 ending, repeal **9** annulment, vitiation **10** abrogation, extinction, rescinding, retraction, revocation **11** abolishment, dissolution, elimination, eradication, recantation, repudiation, termination **12** cancellation, invalidation **13** nullification

abominable 4 base, evil, foul, vile **5** awful, lousy **6** cursed, horrid, odious **7** hateful, heinous, hellish **8** accursed, damnable, horrible, infamous, terrible, wretched **9** abhorrent, atrocious, execrable, loathsome, miserable, repellent, repugnant, repulsive, revolting **10** deplorable, despicable, detestable, disgusting, unsuitable, villainous **11** ignominious **12** contemptible, disagreeable **13** reprehensible

abominate 4 hate **5** abhor, scorn **6** detest, loathe **7** despise **8** execrate **9** can't stand **10** recoil from, shrink from **11** can't stomach **12** be revolted by **13** find repugnant, find repulsive

abomination 4 evil, hate **6** hatred, horror, plague **7** bugbear, disgust, torment **8** anathema, aversion, disgrace, loathing **9** annoyance, antipathy, bete noire, obscenity, revulsion **10** abhorrence, affliction, defilement, repugnance **11** detestation

aboriginal 5 first, prime **6** native **7** ancient, endemic, primary **8** earliest, original, primeval **9** primitive **10** indigenous, primordial **13** autochthonous

aborigine 6 native **16** indigenous person **18** original inhabitant **19** primitive inhabitant

abort 3 end **4** fail, halt, stop **7** call off **8** miscarry **9** terminate

abortion 6 ending, fiasco **7** failure, halting **8** disaster **10** calling off **11** miscarriage, termination **16** fruitless attempt **19** unsuccessful attempt

abortive 4 vain **6** futile **7** sterile, useless **8** bootless **9** fruitless, nonviable, worthless **10** profitless, unavailing, unfruitful **11** ineffective, ineffectual, unrewarding **12** unproductive, unprofitable, unsuccessful **13** inefficacious

abound 4 gush, teem **5** swarm **6** thrive **7** run wild **8** be filled, be rich in, flourish, overflow **9** be flooded, luxuriate, spill over **10** be numerous **11** be plentiful, superabound, proliferate

abounding 4 rich, rife **5** ample **6** lavish, plenty **7** profuse, replete, teeming **8** abundant, brimming, swarming **9** bounteous, bountiful **11** overflowing, running over **14** more than enough

about 2 in, of, on **4** inre, near **5** astir, circa **6** abroad, almost, around, cir-

cum, nearby, nearly **7** close to **9** proximate, regarding **10** concerning, in regard to **13** approximately

about-face 5 shift **6** switch **7** reverse **8** reversal **9** disavowal, turnabout, volte-face **10** retraction, rightabout, turnaround **11** recantation **13** change of heart **14** tergiversation

above 4 atop, over **5** aloft, north, supra **6** before, beyond, dorsal, excess, heaven, higher **7** earlier **8** in heaven, overhead, superior, upstairs **9** exceeding **10** surpassing

aboveboard 4 just, open **5** blunt, frank, legal, legit, licit, moral, overt, plain **6** candid, direct, honest, public, square **7** artless, ethical, sincere, upright **8** revealed, straight, truthful, virtuous **9** disclosed, guileless, ingenuous, righteous **10** forthright, foursquare **11** unconcealed **12** on the up and up, plain-dealing, out in the open **13** square-dealing, undissembling **15** straightforward **16** straight-shooting

ab ovo 10 from the egg **16** from the beginning

abracadabra 5 charm, magic, spell **6** voodoo **7** sorcery **8** exorcism **10** hocus-pocus, invocation, magic spell, mumbo-jumbo, open sesame, witchcraft **11** incantation

abrade 3 rub **4** file, fray, sand **5** chafe, erode, grate, scour, scuff **6** scrape **7** scratch

Abraham
  former name: **5** Abram
  founded: **12** Hebrew nation
  father: **5** Terah
  wife: **5** Sarah, Sarai **7** Keturah
  brother: **5** Haran, Nahor
  son: **5** Isaac **6** Midian **7** Ishmael
  nephew: **3** Lot
  birthplace: **15** Ur of the Chaldees
  received: **17** law of circumcision
  sacrificed Isaac at: **6** Moriah
  burial place: **6** Hebron
  tomb in: **9** Machpelah

Abraham Lincoln
  author: **12** Carl Sandburg

Abraham's bosom 6 heaven

Abram see **7** Abraham

Abrams, Creighton
  served in: **4** WWII **10** Vietnam War
  rank: **16** army chief of staff

abrasive 5 harsh, nasty, rough, sharp **6** biting, coarse **7** caustic, chafing, cutting, galling, grating, hurtful, rasping **8** annoying **10** irritating **11** excoriating **16** grinding material, scouring material, scraping material

abreast 6 in rank **7** aligned **8** arm in arm **10** side by side **11** in alignment

abridge 3 cut **4** trim **6** limit **7** digest, lessen, reduce **7** curtail, cut down, shorten **8** compress, condense, decrease, diminish, pare down, restrict,

take away, truncate **9** scale down, telescope **10** abbreviate

abridgment 6 digest **8** decrease **9** lessening, reduction, restraint **10** diminution, limitation, truncation **11** curtailment, diminishing, restriction **12** abbreviation, condensation

abroad 3 out **4** rife **5** astir, forth **7** at large, outside **8** overseas **9** all around **10** out of doors **13** in circulation, out of the house, round and about **15** making the rounds, out in the open air, out of the country

abrogate 3 end **4** junk, undo, void **5** annul, quash **6** abjure, cancel, negate, recall, repeal, revoke **7** abolish, nullify, rescind, retract, reverse, vitiate **8** dissolve, override, renounce, set aside, throw out, withdraw **9** repudiate, terminate **10** do away with, invalidate, put an end to **11** countermand

abrupt 4 curt, rude **5** blunt, brisk, crisp, gruff, hasty, quick, rapid, rough, sharp, sheer, short, steep, swift **6** sudden **7** brusque, uncivil **8** impolite **9** impulsive **10** unexpected, unforeseen, ungracious **11** precipitate, precipitous, unannounced, unlooked for **12** discourteous **13** instantaneous, unanticipated, unceremonious

Absalom
  father: **5** David
  mother: **6** Maacah
  half-sister: **5** Tamar
  brother: **7** Solomon **8** Adonijah
  half-brother: **5** Amnon
  defeated at: **6** Gilead
  killed by: **4** Joab

Absalom, Absalom!
  author: **15** William Faulkner
  character: **5** Henry **6** Judith **10** Charles Bon **13** Rosa Coldfield **14** Quentin Compson, Shreve McCannon **16** Goodhue Coldfield **19** Colonel Thomas Sutpen **20** Ellen Coldfield Sutpen

Absalom and Achitophel
  author: **10** John Dryden

abscond 3 fly **4** flee, skip **5** split **6** escape, run off, vanish **7** make off, run away, take off **8** steal off **9** disappear, steal away **10** take flight

absence 3 cut **4** lack, want **6** dearth **7** truancy **8** scarcity **10** deficiency, scantiness **11** absenteeism, nonpresence

absent 3 cut, out **4** away, AWOL, gone **5** blank, empty, vague **6** dreamy, musing, truant, vacant **7** faraway, missing, out of it, removed, unaware **8** heedless, keep away, stay away, tuned out **9** not appear, not show up, oblivious **10** distracted, nonpresent, not present, out to lunch, play truant, unthinking **11** inattentive, preoccupied, unconscious **12** nonattendant

absentee 6 no show, truant **10** nonpresent **11** nonattendee, nonpresence **12** nonattendant **13** nonattendance

absenteeism 5 hooky **7** truancy **11** nonpresence **13** nonappearance **19** absence without cause

absent-minded 5 blank, vague **6** dreamy **9** oblivious **10** abstracted, distracted **11** preoccupied **14** out in left field **17** out of it

Absent Without Leave
  author: **12** Heinrich Boll

absinthe
  ingredient: **8** licorice, wormwood **9** aromatics, star anise
  color: **11** yellow green
  substitute: **4** Ouzo **6** Pastis, Pernod **8** Anisette

absolute 4 full, pure, real, sure **5** sheer, total, utter **7** certain, genuine, perfect, supreme **8** complete, decisive, definite, outright, positive, reliable, thorough **9** confirmed, out-and-out, unbounded, unlimited **10** conclusive, consummate, infallible, undeniable

Absolute, Sir Anthony
  character in: **9** The Rivals
  author: **8** Sheridan

absolutely 3 yes **4** sure **5** truly **6** indeed, really, wholly **7** utterly **8** entirely **9** certainly, decidedly **10** completely, definitely, positively, thoroughly **11** indubitably, undoubtedly

absolution 5 mercy **6** pardon **7** amnesty, release **9** acquittal, clearance, quittance, remission **10** indulgence, liberation **11** deliverance, exculpation, exoneration, forgiveness, vindication **12** dispensation

absolve 4 free **5** clear, loose **6** acquit, exempt, pardon, shrive **7** deliver, forgive, release, set free **9** discharge, exculpate, exonerate, vindicate **10** excuse from **13** find not guilty, judge innocent

absolved 5 freed **6** exempt, spared **7** cleared, excused **8** forgiven, innocent, not guilty, pardoned, released, relieved **9** acquitted **10** discharged, exonerated, vindicated **9** found innocent

absorb 3 fix, get **5** grasp, rivet, sop up **6** arrest, digest, engage, enwrap, ingest, occupy, soak up, suck up, take up **7** consume, drink in, engross, immerse **8** sponge up **9** fascinate, preoccupy, swallow up **10** assimilate, understand **11** incorporate

absorbed 4 deep, rapt **8** immersed, involved, soaked up, sucked up **9** blotted up, engrossed

absorbent 6 porous, spongy **7** osmotic, thirsty **8** bibulous, pervious **9** permeable **10** absorptive, penetrable **12** assimilative

absorbing 8 engaging, exciting **9** thrilling **10** engrossing, intriguing **11** captivating, fascinating, interesting

abstain 5 avoid, forgo **6** desist, eschew, refuse, resist **7** decline, forbear, refrain

abstainer 3 dry **7** ascetic **10** nondrinker, self-denier, teetotaler

abstemious 3 dry **5** sober **7** ascetic, austere, sparing, spartan **8** teetotal **9** abstinent, continent, temperate **10** forbearing **11** abstentious, self-denying, straitlaced, teetotaling **12** nonindulgent **15** self-disciplined

abstention 7 refusal **8** eschewal **9** avoidance, desisting, eschewing **10** abstaining, refraining, resistance **11** forbearance, holding back **13** nonindulgence **14** denying oneself **16** nonparticipation

abstinence 8 chastity, sobriety **10** abstention, continence, discipline, self-denial, temperance **11** forbearance, self-control **13** nonindulgence, self-restraint

abstinent 3 dry **5** sober **6** chaste **8** celibate, virginal **9** continent **10** abstemious, forbearing

abstract 4 take **5** brief **6** arcane, digest, precis, remote, remove, resume, subtle **7** abridge, extract, general, isolate, obscure, outline, summary, take out **8** abstruse, compress, condense, esoteric, profound, separate, synopsis, withdraw **9** imaginary, recondite, summarize, synopsize, theoretic, unapplied, visionary **10** abridgment, conceptual, dissociate, indefinite, intangible **11** generalized, impractical, nonspecific, theoretical **12** condensation, hypothetical, intellectual **14** recapitulation

abstruse 4 deep **6** arcane, remote, subtle **7** complex, obscure **8** abstract, esoteric, profound, puzzling **9** enigmatic, recondite **10** perplexing **11** complicated **12** unfathomable **16** incomprehensible

absurd 4 wild **5** crazy, funny, inane, kooky, silly **6** screwy, stupid **7** asinine, comical, foolish, idiotic **8** farcical **9** illogical, laughable, ludicrous, senseless **10** irrational, ridiculous **11** nonsensical **12** preposterous, unreasonable

absurdity 6 drivel, idiocy **7** fallacy, inanity **8** delusion, nonsense **9** asininity, falsehood, silliness **10** buffoonery **11** comicalness, foolishness **13** irrationality **14** ridiculousness **15** unbelievability **16** unreasonableness

Absyrtus see **8** Apsyrtus
Abu Dhabi
  capital of: **18** United Arab Emirates
Abuja
  capital of: **7** Nigeria
abundance 4 glut, heap **5** flood **6** bounty, excess, plenty, wealth **7** surfeit, surplus **8** plethora, richness **9** plenitude, profusion, repletion **10** cornucopia **11** copiousness, full measure, sufficiency

abundant 4 rich, rife **5** ample **6** enough, galore, lavish, plenty **7** copious, profuse, replete, teeming **8** brimming, prolific **9** abounding, bounteous, bountiful, luxuriant **10** sufficient

ab urbe condita 24 from the founding of the city

abuse 4 harm, hurt, slur **5** curse, scold **6** berate, carp at, defame, deride, illuse, injure, injury, insult, malign, misuse, rail at, revile, tirade, vilify **7** assault, bawl out, beating, carping, censure, cruelty, cursing, exploit, harming, insults, railing, slander, torment, upbraid **8** badmouth, belittle, berating, denounce, derision, diatribe, ill-treat, maltreat, mistreat, reproach, ridicule, scolding, sneering, torments **9** castigate, criticism, criticize, denigrate, disparage, excoriate, invective **10** belittling, defamation, impose upon, imposition, oppression, speak ill of, upbraiding **11** castigation **12** exploitation, maltreatment, mistreatment, vilification **13** disparagement, misemployment, tongue-lashing **14** inveigh against, misapplication **15** take advantage of

abusive 4 rude, vile **5** cruel, gross, harsh **7** harmful, hurtful, obscene **8** critical, improper, reviling, scornful **9** injurious, insulting, maligning, offensive, vilifying **10** censorious, defamatory, derogatory, scurrilous, slanderous **11** acrimonious, castigating, deprecatory, disparaging, foulmouthed **12** vituperative

abusive word 5 curse **6** insult **7** epithet **9** blasphemy, expletive, invective, obscenity

abut 4 join, meet **5** touch **6** adjoin, border

abutment 4 prop, stay **5** brace, union **7** contact, meeting, support **8** buttress, junction, shoulder, touching **9** adjacency

abutting 6 next to **7** joining, meeting **8** adjacent, touching **9** bordering **10** contiguous, juxtaposed **12** conterminous

abysmal 4 deep, vast **7** endless, extreme, immense **8** complete, enormous, profound, thorough, unending **9** boundless **10** bottomless, incredible, stupendous **12** unfathomable, unbelievable, unimaginable

abyss 4 gulf, void **5** depth, gorge, gully, nadir **7** fissure **8** crevasse **9** vast chasm **13** bottomless pit

Abyssinia see **8** Ethiopia
Acacallis
  father: **5** Minos

mother: 8 Pasiphae
son: 11 Amphithemis
acacia 9 gum arabic
also called: 5 thorn **6** mimosa, wattle
academic 4 moot **6** remote, school **7** bookish, erudite, general, learned **8** abstract, educated, pedantic, studious **9** scholarly **10** collegiate, scholastic, university **11** conjectural, educational, liberal-arts, presumptive, speculative, theoretical **12** hypothetical, ivory-towered, nontechnical, not practical **13** nonvocational, suppositional **14** nonspecialized **18** college-preparatory
Academus
origin: 8 Arcadian
owned: 6 estate
located in: 6 Athens
served as meeting place for: 12 philosophers
Academy Award
also called: 5 Oscar
1927-28:
actor: 12 Emil Jannings
actress: 11 Janet Gaynor
director: 12 Frank Borzage **14** Lewis Milestone
picture: 5 Wings
1928-29:
actor: 12 Warner Baxter
actress: 12 Mary Pickford
director: 10 Frank Lloyd
picture: 14 Broadway Melody
1929-30:
actor: 12 George Arliss
actress: 12 Norma Shearer
director: 14 Lewis Milestone
picture: 25 All Quiet on the Western Front
1930-31:
actor: 15 Lionel Barrymore
actress: 13 Marie Dressler
director: 12 Norman Taurog
picture: 8 Cimarron
1931-32:
actor: 12 Fredric March
actress: 10 Helen Hayes
director: 12 Frank Borzage
picture: 10 Grand Hotel
1932-33:
actor: 15 Charles Laughton
actress: 16 Katharine Hepburn
director: 10 Frank Lloyd
picture: 9 Cavalcade
1934:
actor: 10 Clark Gable
actress: 16 Claudette Colbert
director: 10 Frank Capra
picture: 18 It Happened One Night
1935:
actor: 14 Victor McLaglen
actress: 10 Bette Davis
director: 8 John Ford
picture: 17 Mutiny on the Bounty
1936:
actor: 8 Paul Muni
actress: 11 Luise Rainer
director: 10 Frank Capra

picture: 16 The Great Ziegfeld
1937:
actor: 12 Spencer Tracy
actress: 11 Luise Rainer
director: 10 Leo McCarey
picture: 15 Life of Emile Zola
1938:
actor: 12 Spencer Tracy
actress: 10 Bette Davis
director: 10 Frank Capra
picture: 20 You Can't Take It with You
1939:
actor: 11 Robert Donat
actress: 11 Vivien Leigh
director: 13 Victor Fleming
picture: 15 Gone with the Wind
1940:
actor: 12 James Stewart
actress: 12 Ginger Rogers
director: 8 John Ford
picture: 7 Rebecca
1941:
actor: 10 Gary Cooper
actress: 12 Joan Fontaine
director: 8 John Ford
picture: 19 How Green Was My Valley
1942:
actor: 11 James Cagney
actress: 11 Greer Garson
director: 12 William Wyler
picture: 10 Mrs Miniver
1943:
actor: 9 Paul Lukas
actress: 13 Jennifer Jones
director: 13 Michael Curtiz
picture: 10 Casablanca
1944:
actor: 10 Bing Crosby
actress: 13 Ingrid Bergman
director: 10 Leo McCarey
picture: 10 Going My Way
1945:
actor: 10 Ray Milland
actress: 12 Joan Crawford
director: 11 Billy Wilder
picture: 14 The Lost Weekend
1946:
actor: 12 Fredric March
actress: 17 Olivia de Havilland
director: 12 William Wyler
picture: 22 The Best Years of Our Lives
1947:
actor: 12 Ronald Colman
actress: 12 Loretta Young
director: 9 Elia Kazan
picture: 19 Gentleman's Agreement
1948:
actor: 15 Laurence Olivier
actress: 9 Jane Wyman
director: 10 John Huston
picture: 6 Hamlet
1949:
actor: 17 Broderick Crawford
actress: 17 Olivia de Havilland
director: 17 Joseph L Mankiewicz

picture: 14 All the King's Men
1950:
actor: 10 Jose Ferrer
actress: 12 Judy Holliday
director: 17 Joseph L Mankiewicz
picture: 11 All About Eve
1951:
actor: 14 Humphrey Bogart
actress: 11 Vivien Leigh
director: 13 George Stevens
picture: 17 An American in Paris
1952:
actor: 10 Gary Cooper
actress: 12 Shirley Booth
director: 8 John Ford
picture: 19 Greatest Show on Earth
1953:
actor: 13 William Holden
actress: 13 Audrey Hepburn
director: 13 Fred Zinnemann
picture: 18 From Here to Eternity
1954:
actor: 12 Marlon Brando
actress: 10 Grace Kelly
director: 9 Elia Kazan
picture: 15 On the Waterfront
1955:
actor: 14 Ernest Borgnine
actress: 11 Anna Magnani
director: 11 Delbert Mann
picture: 5 Marty
1956:
actor: 10 Yul Brynner
actress: 13 Ingrid Bergman
director: 13 George Stevens
picture: 26 Around the World in Eighty Days
1957:
actor: 12 Alec Guinness
actress: 14 Joanne Woodward
director: 9 David Lean
picture: 23 The Bridge on the River Kwai
1958:
actor: 10 David Niven
actress: 12 Susan Hayward
director: 16 Vincente Minnelli
picture: 4 Gigi
1959:
actor: 14 Charlton Heston
actress: 14 Simone Signoret
director: 12 William Wyler
picture: 6 Ben-Hur
1960:
actor: 13 Burt Lancaster
actress: 15 Elizabeth Taylor
director: 11 Billy Wilder
picture: 12 The Apartment
1961:
actor: 16 Maximilian Schell
actress: 11 Sophia Loren
director: 10 Robert Wise **13** Jerome Robbins
picture: 13 West Side Story
1962:
actor: 11 Gregory Peck
actress: 12 Anne Bancroft
director: 9 David Lean

picture: **16** Lawrence of Arabia
1963:
actor: **13** Sidney Poitier
actress: **12** Patricia Neal
director: **14** Tony Richardson
picture: **8** Tom Jones
1964
actor: **11** Rex Harrison
actress: **12** Julie Andrews
director: **11** George Cukor
picture: **10** My Fair Lady
1965:
actor: **9** Lee Marvin
actress: **13** Julie Christie
director: **10** Robert Wise
picture: **15** The Sound of Music
1966:
actor: **12** Paul Scofield
actress: **15** Elizabeth Taylor
director: **13** Fred Zinnemann
picture: **17** A Man for All Seasons
1967:
actor: **10** Rod Steiger
actress: **16** Katharine Hepburn
director: **11** Mike Nichols
picture: **19** In the Heat of the Night
1968:
actor: **14** Cliff Robertson
actress: **15** Barbra Streisand **16**
Katharine Hepburn
director: **12** Sir Carol Reed
picture: **6** Oliver!
1969:
actor: **9** John Wayne
actress: **11** Maggie Smith
director: **15** John Schlesinger
picture: **14** Midnight Cowboy
1970:
actor: **12** George C Scott
actress: **13** Glenda Jackson
director: **17** Franklin Schaffner
picture: **6** Patton
1971:
actor: **11** Gene Hackman
actress: **9** Jane Fonda
director: **15** William Friedkin
picture: **19** The French Connection
1972:
actor: **12** Marlon Brando
actress: **11** Liza Minnelli
director: **8** Bob Fosse
picture: **12** The Godfather
1973:
actor: **10** Jack Lemmon
actress: **13** Glenda Jackson
director: **13** George Roy Hill
picture: **8** The Sting
1974:
actor: **9** Art Carney
actress: **12** Ellen Burstyn
director: **18** Francis Ford Coppola
picture: **12** The Godfather (Part II)
1975:
actor: **13** Jack Nicholson
actress: **14** Louise Fletcher
director: **11** Milos Forman
picture: **25** One Flew Over the
Cuckoo's Nest

1976:
actor: **10** Peter Finch
actress: **11** Faye Dunaway
director: **13** John G Avildsen
picture: **5** Rocky
1977:
actor: **15** Richard Dreyfuss
actress: **11** Diane Keaton
director: **10** Woody Allen
picture: **9** Annie Hall
1978:
actor: **9** Jon Voight
actress: **9** Jane Fonda
director: **13** Michael Cimino
picture: **13** The Deer Hunter
1979:
actor: **13** Dustin Hoffman
actress: **10** Sally Field
director: **12** Robert Benton
picture: **14** Kramer vs Kramer
1980:
actor: **12** Robert De Niro
actress: **11** Sissy Spacek
director: **13** Robert Redford
picture: **14** Ordinary People
1981:
actor: **10** Henry Fonda
actress: **16** Katharine Hepburn
director: **12** Warren Beatty
picture: **14** Chariots of Fire
1982:
actor: **11** Ben Kingsley
actress: **11** Meryl Streep
director: **19** Richard Attenborough
picture: **6** Gandhi
1983:
actor: **12** Robert Duvall
actress: **15** Shirley MacLaine
director: **12** James L Brooks
picture: **17** Terms of Endearment
1984:
actor: **14** F Murray Abraham
actress: **10** Sally Field
director: **11** Milos Forman
picture: **7** Amadeus
1985:
actor: **11** William Hurt
actress: **13** Geraldine Page
director: **13** Sydney Pollack
picture: **11** Out of Africa
1986:
actor: **10** Paul Newman
actress: **12** Marlee Matlin
director: **11** Oliver Stone
picture: **7** Platoon
1987:
actor: **14** Michael Douglas
actress: **4** Cher
director: **18** Bernardo Bertolucci
picture: **14** The Last Emperor
1988:
actor: **13** Dustin Hoffman
actress: **11** Jodie Foster
director: **13** Barry Levinson
picture: **7** Rain Man
1989:
actor: **14** Daniel Day-Lewis
actress: **12** Jessica Tandy

director: **11** Oliver Stone
picture: **16** Driving Miss Daisy
1990:
actor: **11** Jeremy Irons
actress: **10** Kathy Bates
director: **12** Kevin Costner
picture: **16** Dances With Wolves
1991:
actor: **14** Anthony Hopkins
actress: **11** Jodie Foster
director: **13** Jonathan Demme
picture: **20** The Silence of the
Lambs
1992:
actor: **8** Al Pacino
actress: **12** Emma Thompson
director: **13** Clint Eastwood
picture: **10** Unforgiven
1993:
actor: **8** Tom Hanks
actress: **11** Holly Hunter
director: **15** Steven Spielberg
picture: **14** Schindler's List
1994:
actor: **8** Tom Hanks
actress: **12** Jessica Lange
director: **14** Robert Zemeckis
picture: **11** Forrest Gump
1995:
actor: **11** Nicolas Cage
actress: **13** Susan Sarandon
director: **9** Mel Gibson
picture: **10** Braveheart
1996:
actor: **12** Geoffrey Rush
actress: **16** Frances McDormand
director: **16** Anthony Minghella
picture: **17** The English Patient
1997:
actor: **12** Jack Nicholson
actress: **9** Helen Hunt
director: James Cameron
picture: **7** Titanic

Accad
kingdom of: **6** Nimrod
location: **13** Plain of Shinar
captured by: **6** Sargon (I)

Acca Larentia
form: **7** goddess
corresponds to: **6** Dea Dia

accede 5 admit, grant **6** accept, permit
7 abide by, agree to, approve, concede, defer to, endorse, inherit, yield
to **8** assent to, submit to **9** acquiesce,
conform to, consent to, succeed to **10**
comply with, concur with **11** acknowledge, subscribe to, surrender to

accede to the throne 4 keep **5**
claim, usurp **6** ascend **7** possess, succeed **8** take over **9** be crowned **15** ascend the throne

accelerando
music: **15** becoming quicker

accelerate 4 rush, spur **5** hurry, impel
6 hasten, step up **7** advance, augment, further, promote, quicken,
speed up **8** expedite **9** intensify **10** fa-

cilitate, to go faster **11** pick up speed, precipitate

accelerator 3 gas **4** goad, prod, spur **8** gas pedal **13** encouragement

accent 4 hint, tone **5** drawl, touch, twang **6** detail, stress **7** feature **8** emphasis, ornament, tonality, trimming **9** adornment, emphasize, highlight, punctuate, spotlight, underline **10** accentuate, inflection, intonation, modulation, underscore **11** enunciation **12** articulation **13** embellishment, primary stress, pronunciation

accentuate 6 accent, stress **7** feature, point up **9** emphasize, punctuate, underline **10** underscore

accentuation 6 accent, stress **8** emphasis

accept 3 buy **4** avow, bear **5** admit **6** assume **7** agree to, fall for, swallow **8** accede, assent to **9** consent to, undertake **11** acknowledge, go along with

acceptable 4 fair, good, so-so **6** proper, worthy **8** adequate, passable, suitable **9** agreeable, allowable, tolerable **10** admissible **12** satisfactory

acceptable person
Latin: **12** persona grata

acceptance 6 belief, taking **7** consent, receipt **8** approval, sanction **9** accepting, agreement, receiving, reception **10** concession, permission **11** affirmation, approbation, endorsement, recognition **12** acquiescence, confirmation **14** acknowledgment **15** stamp of approval

accepted 5 usual **6** common, normal **7** regular **8** approved, standard **9** confirmed, customary, universal **10** acceptable, agreed upon **11** established, time honored **12** acknowledged, conventional

access 3 way **4** door, gate, path, road **5** entry **6** avenue, course, entree **7** gateway, passage **8** entrance **10** admittance

accessible 5 handy, on tap, ready **6** at hand, nearby, on hand **8** possible **9** available, reachable **10** attainable, obtainable **11** within reach **12** approachable

accession 7 seizure **9** induction **10** arrogation, assumption, investment, taking over, usurpation **11** inheritance **12** inauguration, installation

accessory 4 plus **6** accent, cohort, detail **7** adjunct, partner **8** addition **9** adornment, assistant, associate, auxiliary, colleague, component, extension **10** accomplice, attachment, complement, decoration, supplement **11** confederate, contributor **13** accompaniment

accident 4 fate, luck **5** crash, fluke, wreck **6** chance, mishap **7** smashup **8** fortuity **9** collision, mischance **10** mis-

fortune **11** good fortune, serendipity **12** happenstance, misadventure

accidental 6 chance, random **9** haphazard, unplanned, unwitting **10** fortuitous, incidental, unexpected, unforeseen

acclaim 4 hail, laud **5** cheer, exalt, extol, honor, kudos **6** bravos, praise, salute **7** applaud, commend, ovation **8** applause, cheering, eulogize, plaudits **9** celebrate, rejoicing **10** compliment, enthusiasm **11** acclamation, endorsement

acclamation 6 cheers, homage **7** acclaim, hurrahs, ovation, tribute **8** cheering, hosannas, plaudits **9** adulation **10** salutation **11** approbation

acclimate 5 adapt, enure, inure **6** adjust, orient **8** accustom **9** get used to, habituate, reconcile **11** accommodate **16** become seasoned to

acclimation 9 seasoning **10** adaptation, adjustment **11** habituation

acclivity 4 hill, ramp, rise **5** slope **6** ascent **9** elevation **11** upward slope

accolade 5 award, honor, prize **6** praise, trophy **7** acclaim, tribute **8** applause, citation **10** admiration, compliment, decoration **11** recognition, testimonial **12** commendation

accommodate 3 aid, fit **4** help, hold **5** adapt, board, house, lodge, put up **6** adjust, assist, billet, modify, oblige, supply **7** bed down, conform, contain, furnish, provide, quarter, shelter **8** accustom **9** acclimate, entertain, get used to, harmonize, lend a hand, reconcile

accommodating 4 kind **6** polite **7** helpful **8** friendly, gracious, obliging, yielding **9** courteous **10** hospitable, neighborly **11** considerate **12** conciliatory

accommodation 5 rooms **7** concord, housing **8** lodgings, quarters **9** agreement **10** adjustment, compromise, settlement **12** arrangements **14** reconciliation

accompaniment 6 escort **7** support **8** ornament **9** accessory, adornment **10** incidental

accompany 5 guard, usher **6** attend, back up, convoy, escort, follow **7** conduct, support **8** chaperon

accomplice 4 aide, ally **5** crony **6** cohort, helper, stooge **7** abettor, comrade, partner **8** henchman, sidekick **9** accessory, assistant, associate, colleague, supporter **11** confederate, participant, subordinate **12** collaborator **13** co-conspirator **14** partner-in-crime

accomplish 2 do **6** attain, finish **7** achieve, execute, fulfill, get done, perform, produce, realize **8** carry out, complete, expedite, knock off **9** succeed at **10** bring about

accomplished 3 apt **4** able, deft, fine **6** adroit, expert, gifted, proved, proven **7** capable, eminent, skilled **8** accepted, effected, existing, finished, masterly, polished, realized, seasoned, skillful, talented **9** brilliant, completed, concluded, practiced, qualified **10** cultivated, proficient **11** consummated, established, experienced, welltrained

accomplishment 3 act **4** deed, feat, gest, gift **5** skill, geste **6** talent **7** exploit, success, triumph, victory **9** execution **10** attainment, capability **11** achievement, carrying out, culmination, fulfillment, proficiency, realization, tour de force **12** consummation

accord 4 cede, give, jibe **5** agree, allow, award, grant, match, tally **6** bestow, concur, render, square, tender, unison **7** concede, concert, conform, entente, harmony, present, rapport **8** be in tune, bequeath, sympathy **9** agreement, harmonize, unanimity, vouchsafe **10** accordance, be in unison, comply with, conformity, consonance, correspond, uniformity **11** concurrence, go along with **19** mutual understanding

accordant 4 like **7** similar **8** parallel **10** consistent **11** homogeneous

accordingly 2 so **4** ergo, then, thus **5** hence **6** thence, whence **8** suitably **9** as a result, therefore, wherefore, whereupon **11** conformably, in due course, in which case **12** consequently **15** correspondingly

accost 3 nab **4** hail, halt, stop **5** greet **6** call to, salute, waylay **7** address, solicit **8** approach, confront **10** buttonhole **11** proposition

accouchement 10 childbirth **11** confinement

accoucheur 12 obstetrician **25** assistant during childbirth

accoucheuse 7 midwife **25** assistant during childbirth

account 3 IRA, use **4** deem, hold, note, rank, rate, sake, tale **5** basis, books, cause, count, gauge, honor, judge, merit, score, story, think, value, weigh, worth **6** esteem, import, reason, reckon, record, regard, report, repute, view as **7** believe, clarify, dignity, explain, grounds, history, justify, recital, version **8** appraise, consider, estimate, megillah, standing **9** calculate, chronicle, narration, narrative, statement **10** accounting, commentary, illuminate, importance

accountable 6 guilty, liable **7** at fault, to blame **8** beholden, culpable **9** obligated **10** answerable, chargeable **11** blameworthy, responsible

accountant 3 CPA **7** actuary, auditor **10** bookkeeper **25** certified public accountant

account for 6 excuse 7 explain, justify 9 answer for

accounting 5 cause 6 answer, motive, reason 7 warrant 10 motivation 11 explanation

account rendered
French: 11 compte rendu

accoutrements 4 gear 7 apparel 8 supplies 9 equipment, trappings 11 accessories, furnishings 13 paraphernalia

Accra, Akkra
capital of: 5 Ghana

accredit 6 assign, credit 7 ascribe, certify, empower, endorse, license 8 sanction 9 attribute, authorize, guarantee 10 commission 19 officially recognize 22 furnish with credentials

accredited 8 ascribed, assigned, endorsed, licensed 9 authentic, certified, empowered 10 attributed, authorized, recognized, sanctioned 12 commissioned 20 officially recognized

accretion 4 rise 6 growth 7 accrual 8 addition, increase 9 expansion, extension, increment 10 supplement 11 enlargement 12 accumulation, augmentation 13 amplification

accrue 4 grow 5 add up, amass 6 pile up 7 build up, collect 8 increase 10 accumulate

accumulate 4 grow 5 amass, hoard 6 accrue, garner, gather, heap up, pile up, save up 7 collect, store up 8 assemble, cumulate 9 aggregate 10 congregate 14 gather together

accumulation 4 heap, mass, pile 5 hoard, stack, stock, store 6 pile-up, supply 7 accrual 8 amassing, hoarding 9 acquiring, gathering, stockpile 10 assemblage, collecting, collection 11 aggregation 13 agglomerating 14 conglomeration

accuracy 5 truth 6 verity 8 fidelity 9 exactness, precision 10 exactitude 11 correctness 12 accurateness, faithfulness

accurate 4 true 5 exact, right 7 careful, correct, perfect, precise 8 faithful, truthful, unerring 9 authentic, faultless 10 meticulous, scrupulous 11 punctilious 12 without error

accursed 4 base, foul, vile 6 cussed, horrid, odious 7 hellish 8 damnable, horrible, infamous 9 abhorrent, atrocious, execrable, loathsome, revolting 10 abominable, despicable, detestable, disgusting 12 contemptible

accusation 6 charge 8 citation 9 complaint 10 allegation, imputation, indictment 11 insinuation 13 incrimination

accuse 4 cite 5 blame 6 charge, indict 7 arraign, upbraid 8 reproach 10 take to task 13 call to account 22 lodge a complaint against

accuser 8 attacker 11 complainant 13 finger pointer

accustomed 3 set 5 fixed, prone, trite, usual 6 cliche, common, inured, normal, used to, wonted 7 general, given to, regular, routine 8 everyday, expected, familiar, habitual, hardened, ordinary, seasoned 9 customary, hackneyed, ingrained, prevalent, well-known 10 acclimated, habituated, prevailing 11 commonplace, established 12 conventional, familiarized

ace 2 A-1 3 top, one 4 A-one, star, tops 5 crack, pilot, super 6 expert, master, tip-top, victor, winner 7 one-spot 8 champion, medalist, terrific, top-notch, top-rated, 9 excellent, first-rate, headliner 10 first-class 11 crackerjack, outstanding 12 front-ranking

Aceldama
means: 12 field of blood
purchased by: 5 Judas

Acerbas see 8 Sychaeus

acerbity 7 acidity, sarcasm 8 acridity, acrimony, pungency, sourness, tartness 9 nastiness, sharpness 10 bitterness 11 astringency, brusqueness 12 irascibility

aces 2 A-1 4 fine, tops 5 great, prime, super 6 grade-A, superb, tip-top 8 peerless, superior, terrific, top-notch 9 excellent, first-rate, marvelous, matchless, superfine, wonderful 10 first-class, tremendous 11 outstanding, superlative 13 extraordinary

Acesius
epithet of: 6 Apollo
means: 6 healer

Achaeus
founder of: 6 Achaea
father: 6 Xuthus
mother: 6 Creusa
brother: 3 Ion

Achan
punishment: 13 stoned to death

ache 4 hurt, need, pain, pang, want 5 covet, crave, mourn, smart, throb, yearn 6 be sore, desire, grieve, hanker, hunger, lament, sorrow, suffer, twinge 7 agonize, long for 8 soreness 10 discomfort

Achech
origin: 8 Egyptian
form: 8 creature
body of: 4 lion
wings of: 4 bird

Achelous
form: 3 god
habitat: 5 river
father: 7 Oceanus
mother: 6 Tethys
daughter: 6 Sirens 8 Castalia 10 Callirrhoe
defeated by: 8 Hercules
struggled over: 8 Deianira

Acheron
river in: 5 Hades

ferryman: 6 Charon
carries: 4 dead

Acheson, Dean
Secy. of State 6 Truman
author of: 20 Present at the Creation

a cheval 7 by horse 11 on horseback

achieve 2 do 3 get, win 4 earn, gain 5 reach 6 attain, effect, finish, obtain 7 acquire, fulfill, procure, realize 8 arrive at, carry out, complete, dispatch 9 succeed in 10 accomplish, bring about, effectuate 11 bring to pass

achievement 3 act 4 coup, deed, fear 5 skill 6 effort 7 command, exploit, mastery 9 expertise 10 attainment 11 acquirement, fulfillment, realization, tour de force 14 accomplishment

achieve recognition 6 arrive, make it 7 succeed 8 make good 10 be somebody 11 reach the top

Achilles
mentioned in: 5 Iliad
father: 6 Peleus
mother: 6 Thetis
foster father: 7 Phoenix
grandfather: 6 Aeacus
teacher: 6 Chiron
charioteer: 9 Automedon
friend: 9 Patroclus
warrior in: 9 Trojan War
vulnerability: 4 heel
killed: 6 Hector
killed by: 5 Paris

acid 4 sour, tart 5 acrid, harsh, nasty, sharp 6 biting, bitter, ironic 7 acerbic, caustic, crabbed, cutting, pungent 8 scalding, scathing, stinging, vinegary 9 acidulous, irascible, sarcastic, satirical, vitriolic 10 astringent, vinegarish 11 acrimonious

acidity 8 acerbity, pungency, sourness, tartness 9 sharpness 10 bitterness 11 astringency 13 nonalkalinity

Acis
lover: 7 Galatea
killed by: 10 Polyphemus

Acis and Galatea
opera by: 6 Handel

Acis et Galatee
opera by: 5 Lully

acknowledge 3 own 5 admit, allow, grant, yield 6 accede, accept, answer, assent, concur 7 concede, confess, own up to, reply to 8 call upon, thank for 9 recognize, respond to

acknowledgment 5 reply 6 answer, credit, thanks 8 response 9 admission, gratitude 10 concession, confession 11 affirmation, recognition 12 appreciation, recognizance

acme 3 top 4 apex, peak 5 crest, crown 6 apogee, climax, height, heyday, summit, zenith 8 pinnacle 9 flowering, high point 11 culmination 12 highest point
Latin: 11 ne plus ultra

Acmon
  companion: 8 Diomedes
  changed into: 4 bird
  defied: 9 Aphrodite

acolyte 3 fan 6 helper, novice 7 admirer, devotee, groupie 8 adherent, altar boy, follower 9 assistant, attendant

Acoma
  language family: 6 Pueblo
  location: 3 Ako 4 Acus 8 Valencia 9 New Mexico
  noted for: 7 pottery

acorn
  from: 3 oak
  shape: 8 balanoid

a couvert 9 sheltered 10 under cover

acquaint 4 meet, tell 6 advise, inform, notify, reveal 7 apprise 8 disclose 9 divulge to, enlighten, introduce, make aware 11 familiarize

acquaintance 8 dealings 9 awareness, knowledge 10 cognizance, friendship 11 association, conversance, familiarity 12 relationship

acquiesce 5 admit, agree, allow, bow to, grant, yield 6 accede, assent, comply, concur, give in, submit 7 concede, conform, consent 10 capitulate, fall in with 13 resign oneself 16 reconcile oneself

acquiescence 5 leave 7 consent 8 approval, giving in, sanction 10 permission, submission 11 concurrence

acquiescent / willing 8 amenable, yielding 9 agreeable 10 submissive

acquire 3 get, win 4 earn, gain 6 attain, obtain, pick up, secure 7 achieve, capture, procure, realize 9 cultivate

acquisition 4 gain 5 prize 8 property, purchase 10 attainment, obtainment, possession 11 achievement, acquirement, procurement

acquisitive 6 greedy 7 selfish 8 covetous, grasping 10 avaricious, possessive 13 materialistic

acquit 3 act 5 clear 6 behave, excuse, exempt, let off, pardon 7 absolve, comport, conduct, deliver, release, relieve, set free 8 liberate, reprieve 9 discharge, exculpate, exonerate, vindicate

Acraea
  epithet of: 9 Aphrodite
  means: 6 height

acre
  one-fourth: 4 rood
  one-half: 3 erf 5 erven
  two-thirds: 5 cover
  ten: 6 decare 7 furlong
  one hundred: 7 hectare
  one hundred twenty: 4 hide

Acres, Bob
  character in: 9 The Rivals
  author: 8 Sheridan

acrid 4 acid 5 harsh, nasty, sharp 6 biting, bitter, ironic, smelly 7 burning, caustic, pungent 8 stinging 9 sarcastic, satirical, vitriolic 10 irritating, malodorous 11 acrimonious 12 foul-smelling

acrimonious 4 sour 5 nasty, testy 6 biting, bitter 7 caustic, cutting, peevish 8 venomous, spiteful 9 corrosive, irascible, rancorous, sarcastic, splenetic, vitriolic 10 ill-natured

acrimony 5 anger, scorn, spite 6 animus, malice, rancor, spleen 7 ill will 8 asperity, derision 9 animosity, hostility, malignity 10 antagonism, bitterness, malignancy 12 hard feelings, spitefulness

Acrisius
  king of: 5 Argos
  father: 4 Abas
  mother: 6 Aglaia
  twin brother: 7 Proetus
  daughter: 5 Danae
  grandson: 7 Perseus
  killed by: 7 Perseus

acrophobia
  fear of: 7 heights

acrostic 6 cipher, puzzle 7 acronym

act 2 do 3 bit, gig, law 4 bill, deed, do it, fake, feat, move, play, pose, show, skit, step, work 5 edict, enact, feign, front, order, put-on 6 action, affect, behave, decree, stance 7 execute, exploit, go about, mandate, measure, operate, perform, portray, posture, press on, routine, statute 8 carry out, function, pretense, put forth, simulate 9 enactment, ordinance, represent 10 pretension, resolution 11 achievement, affectation, counterfeit, impersonate, legislation, performance, pretend to be 14 accomplishment

Actaeon
  form: 6 hunter
  father: 9 Aristaeus
  mother: 7 Autonoe
  changed into: 4 stag
  transformed by: 5 Diana
  killed by: 6 hounds
  killed at: 9 Gargaphia

acting 5 drama 6 deputy, ersatz, pro tem 7 interim, theater 8 the stage 9 dramatics, simulated, surrogate, temporary 10 dramaturgy, stagecraft, substitute, the theater 11 dramatic art, officiating, provisional, thespianism 12 stage playing

actinium *see* 8 elements

action 3 act 4 deed, feat, move, step, suit, work 5 force, power 6 battle, combat, effect, effort, motion 7 exploit, process, warfare 8 activity, conflict, endeavor, exertion, fighting, movement, progress 9 adventure, execution, influence, operation 10 enterprise, excitement, performing, production 11 achievement, functioning,

performance, prosecution 14 accomplishment

Actis
  father: 6 Helius
  mother: 5 Rhoda
  crime: 10 fratricide
  taught: 9 astrology
  fled to: 5 Egypt
  memorial: 16 Colossus of Rhodes

activate 4 stir 5 drive, impel, start 6 prompt, propel, turn on 7 actuate 8 energize, mobilize, motivate, vitalize 9 stimulate

activated 5 began 7 started 8 impelled, in action, in effect, turned on 9 effective, energized, mobilized, operative, vitalized 10 stimulated 11 in operation

active 4 busy, spry 5 agile, alert, alive, peppy, quick 6 acting, at work, frisky, lively, nimble 7 engaged, in force, on the go, working, zealous 8 animated, diligent, forceful, occupied, spirited, vigorous 9 ambitious, assertive, effectual, energetic, go-getting, operative, sprightly, strenuous 10 aggressive, productive 11 functioning, imaginative, industrious 12 enterprising 13 indefatigable

active person 4 doer 6 beaver, dynamo 7 hustler 8 activist, go-getter

activist 4 doer 6 zealot 7 apostle 8 advocate, exponent 9 proponent, supporter

activity 4 fuss, stir, to-do 6 action, bustle, flurry, hustle, tumult 7 project, pursuit, venture 8 endeavor, exercise, exertion, function, goings on, movement, vivacity 9 agitation, animation, avocation, commotion 10 assignment, enterprise, hurly-burly, liveliness, occupation 11 undertaking 13 sprightliness

act of the faith
  Spanish: 8 auto da fe, auto de fe

act of war 4 raid 6 attack, strike 7 assault, offense 8 invasion 10 aggression, hostile act

actor 3 ham 4 doer, star 6 player, walk on 7 starlet, trouper 8 thespian 9 bit player, performer 11 functionary, participant, perpetrator 14 dramatic artist 15 supporting actor
  type: 4 hero 5 cameo 7 feature, leading 9 character 10 supporting
  hint: 3 cue

Actor
  king of: 6 Phthia
  father: 8 Myrmidon
  mother: 8 Pasidice
  brother: 6 Augeas
  son: 7 Cteatus, Eurytus

actual 4 real, sure, true 7 certain, current, factual, genuine, present 8 bona fide, concrete, existent, existing, physical, tangible 9 authentic, confirmed, corporeal **10** legitimate, prevailing, true-to-life, verifiable

actual being 4 esse

actuality 4 fact, life **5** being, truth **6** effect, living, verity **7** reality **8** existing **9** existence, plain fact, substance **10** brutal fact **11** point of fact

actually 5 truly **6** indeed, in fact, really, verily **9** genuinely, literally **Latin: 7** ex facto

actually existing Latin: 6 in esse **7** de facto

actuary 5 clerk **9** tabulator **12** statistician

actuate 4 move, stir **5** cause, drive, impel, rouse **6** arouse, excite, incite, induce, prompt **7** animate, inspire, trigger **8** activate, motivate **9** influence, instigate, stimulate **10** bring about

acumen 6 wisdom **7** insight **8** keenness, sagacity **9** acuteness, ingenuity, smartness **10** astuteness, cleverness, perception, shrewdness **11** discernment **12** intelligence, perspicacity **13** sound judgment **15** clearheadedness

acute 4 keen **5** sharp **6** clever, fierce, peaked, severe **7** intense, very bad **8** critical, piercing, powerful **9** agonizing, ingenious, intuitive, sensitive, very great **10** discerning, perceptive **11** distressing, penetrating **12** excruciating, needle-shaped **14** discriminating

acute suffering 5 agony **7** anguish, torment, torture **8** distress

A.D. *see* **10** anno Domini

adage 3 saw **4** quip, wise **5** axiom, maxim, motto **6** cliche, dictum, old saw, saying, truism **7** epigram, precept, proverb **8** aphorism **9** platitude **11** observation

adagio music: 4 slow

Adah also: 9 Bashemath **husband: 4** Esau **6** Lamech **son: 5** Jabal, Jubal **7** Eliphaz

Adam wife: 3 Eve **son: 4** Abel, Cain, Seth **home: 4** Eden **grandson: 4** Enas **5** Enoch

adamant 3 set **4** firm **5** fixed, rigid, tough **7** uptight **8** obdurate, resolute, stubborn **9** immovable, insistent, unbending **10** determined, hard as rock, inexorable, inflexible, unyielding **12** intransigent **14** uncompromising

Adam Bede author: 11 George Eliot **character: 8** Seth Bede **11** Dinah Morris, Hetty Sorrel **12** Martin Poyser **17** Arthur Donnithorne

Adams, Henry author of: 6 Esther **9** Democracy **14** Chapters of Erie **24** History of the United States (Under the Jefferson and Adams Administration), The Education of Henry Adams **26** Mont-Saint Michel and Chartres **34** The Degradation of the Democratic Dogma

Adams, John nickname: 19 Atlas of Independence **presidential rank: 6** second **party: 10** Federalist **state represented: 2** MA **defeated: 9** Jefferson **vice president: 9** Jefferson **cabinet:** **state: 8** (John) Marshall **9** (Timothy) Pickering **treasury: 6** (Samuel) Dexter **7** (Oliver) Wolcott **war: 6** (Samuel) Dexter **7** (James) McHenry **attorney general: 3** (Charles) Lee **navy: 8** (Benjamin) Stoddert **born: 2** MA **9** Braintree **town now called: 6** Quincy **died/buried: 6** Quincy **education: 7** Harvard **religion: 9** Unitarian **author: 18** Discourses on Davila **20** Thoughts on Government **political career: 13** vice president **24** First Continental Congress **25** Second Continental Congress **minister: 11** Netherlands **12** Great Britain **civilian career: 6** lawyer **notable events of lifetime/term: 9** XYZ Affair **act: 9** Judiciary **16** Alien and Sedition **father: 4** John **mother: 7** Susanna (Boylston) **siblings: 5** Elihu **13** Peter Boylston **wife: 7** Abigail (Smith) **children: 7** Charles, Susanna **10** John Quincy (6th president) **13** Abigail Amelia **14** Thomas Boylston

Adams, John Quincy nickname: 14 Old Man Eloquent **presidential rank: 5** sixth **party: 4** Whig **10** Federalist **20** Democratic-Republican **state represented: 2** MA **defeated: 4** (Henry) Clay **7** (Andrew) Jackson **8** (William H) Crawford **vice president: 7** (John C) Calhoun **cabinet:** **state: 4** (Henry) Clay **treasury: 7** (Richard) Rush **war: 6** (Peter Buell) Porter **7** (James) Barbour **attorney general: 4** (William) Wirt **navy: 8** (Samuel Lewis) Southard **born: 2** MA **9** Braintree **town now called: 6** Quincy **died: 2** DC **10** Washington **buried: 2** MA **6** Quincy **education:** **studied in: 5** Paris **9** Amsterdam **11** Latin School **University of: 6** Leyden **College: 7** Harvard **religion: 9** Unitarian **author: 7** Memoirs **14** Eulogy to Monroe, The Adams Papers **17** Eulogy to Lafayette **18** Letters from Silesia **political career: 8** US Senate **19** Massachusetts Senate **24** US House of Representatives **secretary of: 5** state **minister: 6** Russia **7** Prussia **8** Portugal **11** Netherlands **12** Great Britain **civilian career: 6** lawyer **notable events of lifetime/term: 19** Pan-American Congress **20** Tariff of Abominations **father: 4** John **mother: 7** Abigail (Smith) **siblings: 7** Abigail, Charles, Susanna **14** Thomas Boylston **wife: 6** Louisa (Catherine Johnson) **children: 4** John **14** Charles Francis **15** Louisa Catherine **16** George Washington

Adams, Parson character in: 13 Joseph Andrews **author: 8** Fielding

Adams, Richard author of: 4 Maia **7** Shardik **12** Girl in a Swing **13** The Plague Dogs, Watership Down

Adam's Rib director: 11 George Cukor **script by: 10** Ruth Gordon **11** Garson Kanin **cast: 8** Tom Ewell **9** Jean Hagen **10** David Wayne **12** Judy Holliday, Spencer Tracy **16** Katharine Hepburn

adapt 3 fit **4** suit **5** alter, frame, shape **6** adjust, change, modify, rework **7** conform, convert, fashion, make fit, remodel, reshape **8** attune to **9** acclimate, harmonize, recompose, reconcile, transform **10** assimilate, coordinate **11** accommodate, acculturate **12** make suitable

adaptable 6 pliant, usable **7** unrigid **8** amenable, flexible, obliging **9** alterable, compliant, easygoing, malleable, tractable **10** adjustable, applicable, changeable, open- minded **11** conformable, serviceable **13** accommodating, accommodative

adaptation 5 shift **6** change **8** revision **9** refitting, reshaping, reworking **10** adjustment, alteration, conversion, remodeling **12** modification **13** metamorphosis

Adar 18 twelfth Hebrew month

add 4 join **5** affix, sum up, total **6** append, attach, join on, reckon, tack on **7** combine, compute, count up, enlarge, include **8** figure up, increase **9**

calculate, enlarge by **10** increase by, supplement

Addams, Frankie
character in: **19** A Member of the Wedding
author: **15** Carson McCullers

Addams Family, The
character: **5** Gomez, Lurch **7** Pugsley **8** Morticia **9** Cousin Itt, Grandmama, Wednesday **11** Uncle Fester
cast: **9** John Astin **10** Lisa Loring, Ted Cassidy **11** Blossom Rock **12** Carolyn Jones, Jackie Coogan **13** Ken Weatherwax

add details 6 expand **7** clarify **9** elaborate, embellish **13** particularize

added 5 bonus, extra **6** joined **7** totaled **8** appended, attached, computed, included, joined on, reckoned, summed up, tacked on **9** counted up **10** additional, enlarged by, enumerated **11** increased by **13** supplementary

addendum 7 codicil **8** addition **9** appendage **10** attachment, postscript, supplement **12** afterthought

addict 3 fan, nut **4** buff, head, hook, user **5** freak, hound **6** junkie, submit, turn on, votary **7** acolyte, devotee, druggie, habitue **8** adherent **9** dope fiend, indulge in, surrender

addiction 5 craze, mania, quirk **6** fetish, hangup **8** fixation **9** cocainism, obsession **10** alcoholism, compulsion, dipsomania, morphinism **11** barbiturism, enslavement **12** addictedness, enthrallment **13** preoccupation

adding machine
invented by: **6** Pascal **9** Burroughs

Addis Ababa
capital of: **8** Ethiopia

Addison, Joseph
author of: **4** Cato **9** The Tatler **12** The Spectator **13** The Freeholder
co-author: **13** Richard Steele

addition 4 wing **5** annex, extra **6** adding **7** adjunct, joining **8** addendum, additive, annexing, increase, totaling **9** adjoining, appendage, appending, attaching, embracing, expansion, extending, extension, including, increment, reckoning, summation, summing up **10** counting up, increasing **11** enlargement, enumeration **12** appurtenance, augmentation, encompassing

additional 5 added, extra, spare **7** added on **8** appended **12** over-and-above **13** supplementary

additional feature 5 extra **7** adjunct **10** attachment, complement, supplement **12** appurtenance **13** accompaniment

additive 5 extra **8** addition **10** adulterant, supplement **12** augmentation, preservative

addle 5 mix up **6** muddle **7** confuse, nonplus, stupefy **8** befuddle

addled 5 silly **7** foolish, mixed-up, muddled **8** confused **9** befuddled, nonplused **10** nonplussed

add on 5 affix **6** append, attach, tack on **7** include **10** increase by

address 4 talk **5** greet, orate **6** salute, speech, talk to **7** lecture, oration, speak to, write to **8** dwelling, locality, location **9** discourse, statement

Address to the Deil
author: **11** Robert Burns

add to 6 expand, extend, pad out **7** amplify, augment, bolster, enlarge **8** compound, increase, lengthen **10** strengthen, stretch out, supplement

Ade, George
author of: **13** Fables in Slang **15** The College Widow **17** The County Chairman

Aden
seaport of: **5** Yemen
Gulf in: Arabian Sea

adept 3 apt **4** able, good **6** adroit, expert, gifted, master **7** skilled **8** skillful **9** dexterous, ingenious, masterful, practiced **10** proficient **12** accomplished

adequacy 7 fitness **11** sufficiency **16** satisfactoriness

adequate 3 fit **4** so-so **5** ample **6** enough **7** fitting **8** passable, suitable **9** tolerable **10** sufficient **12** satisfactory

a deux 6 for two **10** two at a time

ad extremum 6 at last **7** finally **12** to the extreme

ad fin 8 at the end **12** toward the end

adhere 3 fix **4** glue, hold, keep **5** cling, paste, stick **6** be true, cement, cleave, fasten, glue on, keep to **7** abide by, be loyal, stand by **8** maintain **9** stick fast **10** be constant, be faithful

adherence 6 fealty **7** loyalty **8** adhesion, devotion, fidelity **9** constancy, keeping to, obedience **10** allegiance, attachment, observance, stickiness **12** adhesiveness, faithfulness

adherent 3 fan **4** ally **5** gummy, pupil **6** sticky, viscid **7** acolyte, devotee, viscous **8** adhering, adhesive, advocate, champion, clinging, disciple, follower, partisan, sticking, upholder **9** supporter

adhesion 9 adherence **10** attachment, sticking to

adhesive 4 glue **5** epoxy, gummy, paste **6** cement, gummed, mortar, solder, sticky **7** stickum **8** adherent, adhering, clinging, sticking **12** mucilaginous, rubber cement

ad hoc 17 with respect to this **18** for this purpose only

ad hominem 8 to the man **17** against an opponent **20** appealing to prejudice

adieu 4 by-by, ciao, ta-ta **5** adios,

aloha **6** bye-bye, goodby, so long **7** a demain, cheerio, goodbye, good day **8** a bientot, au revoir, farewell, godspeed, toodle-oo **10** take it easy **11** leavetaking, see you later, valediction **14** Auf Wiedersehen

ad infinitum 9 endlessly **10** infinitely, to infinity, unendingly **11** boundlessly, ceaselessly, limitlessly, unceasingly **12** continuously, interminably, without limit

ad initium 14 at the beginning

ad interim 13 in the meantime

adios 4 by-by, ciao, ta-ta **5** adieu, aloha **6** bye-bye, goodby, so long **7** a demain, cheerio, goodbye, good day **8** a bientot, au revoir, farewell, godspeed, toodle-oo **10** take it easy **11** leavetaking, see you later, valediction **14** Auf Wiedersehen

adjacent 6 beside, next to **8** abutting, touching **9** bordering, proximate **10** contiguous, juxtaposed, next door to, tangential **12** conterminous

adjoining 6 joined **7** joining **8** nextdoor, touching **9** connected **10** contiguous **14** interconnected

adjourn 3 end **4** move **5** close **6** put off, recess, remove, repair **7** dismiss, suspend **8** break off, dissolve, postpone, withdraw **9** depart for, interrupt **11** discontinue

adjournment 6 recess **7** removal **8** abeyance **9** dismissal **10** suspension **12** postponement

adjudge 4 deem, rule **5** judge **6** decide, decree, ordain, rule on, settle, umpire **7** referee **8** consider **9** arbitrate, determine, pronounce **10** adjudicate

adjudicate 4 rule **5** judge **6** settle **7** adjudge **9** arbitrate

adjunct 9 accessory, auxiliary, secondary **10** complement, incidental, subsidiary, supplement **12** appurtenance

adjuration 4 oath, plea, suit **6** appeal **8** advising, entreaty **12** supplication

adjure 3 beg **5** plead **6** charge, enjoin, exhort **7** beseech, command, entreat, implore, solicit **8** appeal to, petition **9** importune **10** supplicate

adjust 3 fix, set **4** move **5** adapt, alter, order, reset **6** attune, change, modify **7** conform **8** accustom, regulate **9** acclimate, reconcile **11** accommodate

adjustable 7 movable **9** adaptable, alterable **11** rectifiable, regulatable **12** controllable

adjusting 8 adapting, altering **9** modifying **10** regulating **11** acclimating, controlling

adjusting device 5 lever, tuner, valve **6** handle **7** adapter **8** governor **9** modulator, regulator **11** control knob

adjustment 6 fixing **7** control, setting **8** adapting, focusing **9** adjusting, alignment, regulator **10** alteration, regulating, regulation, settlement, settling in **11** acclimation, orientation **12** modification **13** justification, rectification, straightening **14** reconciliation

adjutant 3 ADC **4** aide **9** assistant, right hand **10** aide-de-camp **12** right-hand man

ad-lib 6 make up **9** improvise **11** extemporize **13** improvisation **14** speak impromptu **15** speak off the cuff **21** speak extemporaneously **23** extemporaneous wisecrack

ad loc, ad locum 10 at the place, to the place

ad majorem Dei gloriam 23 for the greater glory of God

Admete
    father: 10 Eurystheus
    received: 12 golden girdle
        belonged to: 4 Ares
        received from: 8 Hercules
        stolen from: 9 Hippolyte

Admeto, Re di Tessaglia
    also: 21 Admetus King of Thessaly
    opera by: 6 Handel

Admetus
    king of: 8 Thessaly
    member of: 9 Argonauts
    father: 6 Pheres
    wife: 8 Alcestis

administer 3 run **4** boss, give **5** apply **6** direct, govern, manage, tender **7** oversee **8** dispense **9** supervise **11** preside over, superintend **12** administrate

administering 7 bossing, running, tending **8** managing **9** directing, executing **10** dispensing, governance, overseeing **11** carrying out, supervising, supervision **14** administration, superintending

administration 5 brass **8** officers **9** execution, governing, tendering **10** executives, government, leadership, management, overseeing **11** application **12** dispensation, distribution **13** administering, governing body **15** superintendence

administrative 9 executive **10** management, managerial **11** supervisory **14** organizational

administrative head 3 CEO **7** manager **8** chairman, director **9** executive, president **10** supervisor **13** administrator **14** superintendent

admirable 6 worthy **8** laudable **9** estimable, venerable **11** commendable **12** praiseworthy

Admirable Crichton, The
    author: 12 James M Barrie

admiration 5 honor **6** esteem, praise **7** respect **8** approval **10** high regard, veneration **11** high opinion **12** commendation

admire 5 prize, value **6** esteem, praise **7** respect

admirer 3 fan **5** swain **6** suitor, votary **7** acolyte, devotee, groupie **8** adherent, advocate, champion, disciple, follower, partisan **9** attendant **10** aficionado

admissible 7 allowed **8** passable **9** allowable, permitted, tolerable, tolerated **10** acceptable, admittable, legitimate **11** permissible

admission 3 fee **5** entry **6** access, assent, charge, entree, tariff, ticket **8** entrance **10** admittance, concession, confession, profession **11** affirmation, declaration, entrance fee **14** acknowledgment

admit 3 let **5** allow, grant, let in, own up **6** induct, invest, permit **7** appoint, concede, confess, declare, profess, receive, welcome **8** let enter **11** acknowledge

admittable 7 allowed **9** allowable, permitted, tolerable, tolerated **10** acceptable, admissible **11** permissible

admittance 5 entry **6** access, entree **7** ingress **8** entrance **9** admission

admixture 4 mess, olio **5** blend **6** jumble, medley **7** amalgam, melange, mixture **8** compound, mishmash **9** composite, confusion, potpourri **10** commixture, hodgepodge, salmagundi **11** combination, commingling, gallimaufry **12** amalgamation, intermixture **13** intermingling **14** conglomeration

admonish 4 warn **5** chide, scold **6** advise, enjoin, rebuke, tip off **7** caution, censure, chasten, counsel, reprove, upbraid **8** reproach **9** criticize, reprimand **10** put on guard, take to task **11** remonstrate **13** call to account **16** rap on the knuckles

admonition 6 advice, rebuke **7** chiding, warning **8** reproach, scolding **9** reprimand **11** mild reproof **12** remonstrance **16** rap on the knuckles

Adnah
    deserted from: 4 Saul
    deserted to: 5 David
    fought against: 10 Amalekites
    commander for: 10 Jehosaphat

ado 4 fuss, stir, to-do **5** furor **6** bother, bustle, flurry, fracas, furore, hubbub, pother, racket, tumult, uproar **7** flutter, trouble, turmoil **9** agitation, commotion, confusion **10** hurlyburly

adobe 3 mud **4** clay, silt, tile **5** brick, marly **6** earthy **7** clayish **13** sun-dried brick

adolescence 5 teens, youth **7** puberty **10** pubescence

adolescent 3 lad **4** lass, teen **5** minor, youth **6** boyish, callow, lassie **7** babyish, girlish, puerile **8** childish, immature, juvenile, teenager, young man, youthful **9** fledgling, pubescent, schoolboy, stripling, young teen **10** schoolgirl, sophomoric, young woman **11** undeveloped

Adolf Hitler 9 der Fuhrer **10** der Fuehrer

Adonai 3 God **6** my Lord

Adonijah
    father: 5 David
    mother: 7 Haggith
    brother: 5 Amnon **7** Absalom, Chileab
    executed by: 7 Solomon
    conspired to overthrow: 5 David

Adonis
    represents: 15 vegetation cycle
    father: 7 Cinyras
    mother: 6 Myrrha, Smyrna
    favorite of: 9 Aphrodite
    killed by: 4 boar
    festival in honor of: 6 Adonia

adopt 3 use **4** take **6** accept, affect, assume, choose, employ, follow, take up **7** approve, embrace, espouse, utilize **9** conform to **11** acknowledge, appropriate

adorable 4 cute **6** divine **7** darling, likable, lovable, winsome **8** charming, engaging, fetching, pleasing, precious **9** appealing **10** delightful **11** captivating **12** irresistible

adoration 5 honor **7** worship **8** devotion **9** adulation, reverence **10** exaltation, veneration, worshiping **11** idolization **13** glorification, magnification

adore 4 like, love **5** exalt, fancy, prize **6** admire, dote on, revere **7** cherish, glorify, idolize, worship **8** hold dear, venerate

adorer 3 fan **5** lover **7** admirer **8** follower **9** worshiper

adorn 5 array **6** bedeck **7** bejewel, deck out, furbish **8** beautify, decorate, ornament **9** embellish

adornment 6 attire, finery **7** jewelry **8** ornament **10** decoration **13** embellishment, ornamentation

ad patres 4 dead

Adrammelech 13 Sepharvite god
    father: 11 Sennacherib
    killed: 11 Sennacherib

Adrastea
    also: 7 Nemesis
    origin: 5 Greek
    goddess of: 17 divine retribution
    father: 9 Melisseus
    reared: 4 Zeus
    entrusted by: 4 Rhea

Adrastus
    also: 8 Adrastos
    king of: 5 Argos
    son: 8 Aegialus
    leader of: 18 Seven against Thebes
    companions: 6 Tydeus **8** Capaneus **9** Polynices **10** Amphiaraus, Hippomedon **13** Parthenopaeus
    horse: 5 Arion

ad rem 9 pertinent **15** straightforward **17** without digression

Adrian, Edgar Douglas
field: **8** medicine **10** physiology
nationality: **7** British
discovered function of: **10** nerve cells
awarded: **10** Nobel Prize

Adriana
character in: **17** The Comedy of Errors
author: **11** Shakespeare

adrift 4 lost **5** at sea **6** afloat, aweigh **8** confused, drifting, unmoored, unstable **9** perplexed, uncertain, unsettled **10** bewildered, irresolute, unanchored

adroit 3 apt **4** deft **5** slick **6** artful, clever, expert, facile, nimble **7** cunning, skilled **8** skillful **9** dexterous, masterful **10** proficient

adroitness 7 aptness **8** deftness, facility **9** dexterity, handiness **10** cleverness **11** proficiency **12** skillfulness
French: **11** savoir-faire

adulation 7 fawning **8** flattery **9** adoration **11** fulsomeness **13** fulsome praise

adulatory 7 fulsome **8** admiring **10** flattering **13** complimentary

adult 3 big, man **5** elder, of age, woman **6** father, granny, mature, mother, parent, senior, x-rated **7** grandma, grandpa, grownup, oldster **8** seasoned **9** developed, full-grown **11** experienced, grandfather, grandmother **13** senior citizen

adulterate 3 cut **4** thin **5** water **6** dilute **9** water down **10** depreciate **11** contaminate

adulterated 3 cut **6** impure, watery **7** debased, diluted, thinned, watered **8** doctored, weakened **11** watered down

adultery 3 sin **9** carnality, cuckoldry **10** unchastity **11** fornication, promiscuity **14** unfaithfulness **17** marital infidelity **18** illicit intercourse **21** extramarital relations

adulthood 8 maturity, ripeness **10** full growth **11** age of reason

adumbrate 3 dim **6** darken, sketch **7** obscure, outline **8** intimate **9** prefigure **10** foreshadow, overshadow

adumbrated 3 dim **5** murky **7** shadowy **8** darkened **9** intimated **10** indistinct, prefigured **12** foreshadowed, overshadowed

advance 3 pre **4** gain, lend, loan, pass, step **5** add to, offer, prior **6** assign, binder, growth, move up, pay now, propel, send up **7** bring up, forward, further, improve, in front, lay down, press on, proffer, promote, upgrade, up front **8** foremost, increase, multiply, overture, previous, progress **9** go forward, promotion **10** furthering, move onward, prepayment, put up

front **11** advancement, down payment, improvement, preliminary, proposition **12** breakthrough, bring forward, pay on account

advanced 7 extreme, far gone, radical **10** avant-garde **12** farther along, further along **14** industrialized

advanced in years 3 old **4** aged **5** hoary, older **7** ancient, antique, elderly **8** outmoded **9** senescent, venerable **10** antiquated, gray-haired

advancement 4 rise **5** boost **9** bettering, elevation, promotion **10** betterment, forwarding **11** improvement, progression

Advancement of Learning
author: **12** Francis Bacon

advance slowly 4 inch **5** crawl, creep

advantage 3 aid **4** boon, edge, help **5** asset, clout **6** profit **7** benefit, comfort, service, success, support **8** blessing **9** dominance, upper hand **10** precedence **11** convenience, superiority

advantageous 6 useful **7** helpful **8** enviable, superior, valuable **9** favorable, fortunate **10** auspicious, beneficial, dominating, profitable

advent 5 onset, start **6** coming **7** arrival **9** appearing, beginning, emergence, opening up **10** appearance, occurrence **12** commencement

adventitious 5 alien **6** exotic **7** foreign, strange **9** adventive, extrinsic **10** accidental

adventure 5 geste, quest **7** emprise, venture **8** escapade **10** enterprise **11** undertaking

adventurer 4 hero **7** heroine, upstart **8** romantic, vagabond **9** buccaneer, daredevil **11** giant-killer **12** dragon-slayer, swashbuckler **16** soldier of fortune

Adventures of Robin Hood, The
director: **13** Michael Curtiz **15** William Keighley
cast: **8** Alan Hale (Little John) **10** Errol Flynn (Robin Hood) **11** Claude Rains (Prince John) **13** Basil Rathbone **17** Olivia de Havilland (Lady Marion)
Oscar for: **5** score (Erich Wolfgang Korngold)

Adventures of Sherlock Holmes
author: **16** (Sir) Arthur Conan Doyle
character: **9** Mrs Hudson **10** Irene Adler **12** Dr John Watson **13** Mycroft Holmes **14** Sherlock Holmes **17** Inspector Lestrade, Professor Moriarty **21** Baker Street Irregulars

adventuresome 4 bold **6** daring **9** audacious, daredevil **11** adventurous

adventurous 4 bold **5** brave, risky **6** daring **7** valiant **8** intrepid, perilous **9** audacious, dangerous, hazardous **10**

courageous **11** challenging, venturesome

ad verbum 8 verbatim **9** to the word

adversary 3 foe **5** enemy, rival **8** opponent **10** antagonist, competitor

adverse 3 ill **4** evil **7** harmful, hostile **8** contrary, inimical, negative, opposing **9** difficult, injurious **10** pernicious, unfriendly **11** detrimental, unfavorable **12** antagonistic, unpropitious

adversity 3 woe **4** ills **5** trial **6** mishap **7** bad luck, trouble **8** calamity, disaster, distress, hardship **9** suffering **10** affliction, ill-fortune, misfortune **11** catastrophe, tribulation

advertise 4 show, tout **5** vaunt **6** reveal **7** display **8** proclaim **9** broadcast, publicize **11** noise abroad

advertisement 4 spot **5** blurb, flier, pitch, promo **6** notice, poster, want ad **7** leaflet, placard, trailer **8** circular, handbill **9** billboard, broadside, throwaway **10** commercial **12** announcement, classified ad, public notice

advice 4 news, view, word **6** report **7** account, counsel, message, opinion, tidings **8** guidance **10** advisement, suggestion **11** information **12** intelligence, notification **13** communication **14** recommendation

advisable 3 fit **4** best, wise **5** smart, sound **6** proper, seemly **7** fitting, prudent **8** a good bet, suitable **9** expedient, judicious **13** recommendable

advise 4 tell, urge, warn **6** enjoin, exhort, inform, notify, report **7** apprise, caution, commend, counsel, suggest **8** admonish **9** encourage, make known, recommend, suggest to **10** give notice **11** communicate

advise against 5 deter **8** dissuade **10** discourage, disincline

advisement 5 study **7** thought **12** deliberation **13** consideration

adviser, advisor 4 aide **5** coach, guide, tutor **6** egeria, mentor, nestor **7** monitor, teacher **8** Dear Abby, director **9** admonitor, assistant, counselor, preceptor, surrogate **10** Ann Landers, consultant, idea person, instructor

advisory 7 caution, guiding, warning **10** admonitory, cautionary, counseling **11** informative, instructive **12** consultative, consultatory **13** informational

advisory board 7 cabinet, council **8** ministry

advocaat
type: **7** liqueur
origin: **7** Holland

advocacy 4 egis **5** aegis **7** backing, defense, support **8** auspices, espousal **9** patronage, promotion **10** furthering, supporting **11** advancement, endorsement, pressing for, propagation, spon-

sorship 12 championship **14** campaigning for, recommendation

advocate 4 back, urge **5** favor **6** advise, backer, lawyer, patron **7** advance, apostle, counsel, endorse, espouse, further, pleader, promote, propose, push for, support **8** argue for, attorney, believer, champion, defender, press for, promoter, upholder **9** apologist, barrister, counselor, encourage, prescribe, propagate, proponent, recommend, solicitor, spokesman, supporter **10** mouthpiece, stand up for **11** campaign for, speak out for **12** legal adviser, propagandist, spokesperson **13** attorney-at-law

advocatus diaboli 14 devil's advocate

adz or **adze 2** ax **3** axe **5** addis **7** hatchet

Aeacus
  descendants of: 8 Aeacides
  form: 5 judge
  habitat: 5 Hades
  father: 4 Zeus
  mother: 6 Aegina
  brother: 12 Rhadamanthys
  wife: 6 Endeis
  son: 6 Peleus, Phocus **7** Telamon
  grandson: 8 Achilles

Aeetes
  king of: 7 Colchis
  custodian of: 12 Golden Fleece
  father: 6 Helios
  mother: 5 Perse
  sister: 5 Circe **8** Pasiphae
  wife: 5 Idyia **9** Asterodea
  son: 8 Absyrtus, Apsyrtus
  daughter: 5 Medea **9** Chalciope

Aegaeon see **8** Briareus

Aegean Sea
  branch of: 13 Mediterranean
  islands: 5 Chios, Crete, Samos **6** Euboea, Lesbos, Rhodes **8** Cyclades **10** Dodecanese **16** Northern Sporades
  rivers into: 6 Struma, Vardar **7** Maritsa **8** Menderes
  surrounding countries: 6 Greece, Turkey

Aegeon
  character in: 17 The Comedy of Errors
  author: 11 Shakespeare

Aegeria see **6** Egeria

Aegesta see **6** Egesta

Aegeus
  king of: 6 Athens
  son: 6 Medeus **7** Theseus

Aegimius
  king of: 5 Doris **7** Dorians
  father: 5 Dorus
  son: 5 Dymas **9** Pamphylus

Aeginaea
  epithet of: 7 Artemis
  means: 11 goat goddess

Aegir
  origin: 6 Nordic

form: 5 giant
god of: 3 sea
wife: 3 Ran

aegis 4 wing **5** favor, guard **6** surety **7** backing, shelter, support **8** advocacy, auspices, guaranty **9** patronage **10** protection **11** sponsorship **12** championship, guardianship

Aegis
  form: 6 shield
  shield of: 4 Zeus **6** Athena

Aegisthus
  father: 8 Thyestes
  mother: 7 Pelopia
  cousin: 9 Agamemnon
  daughter: 7 Erigone
  seduced: 12 Clytemnestra
  killed by: 7 Orestes

Aegle
  member of: 8 Heliades **10** Hesperides
  mother of: 6 Graces

Aegyptus
  king of: 5 Egypt
  father: 5 Belus
  twin brother: 6 Danaus
  number of sons: 5 fifty

Aella
  form: 6 Amazon
  gift: 9 swiftness
  killed by: 8 Hercules

Aello
  member of: 7 Harpies

aelurophobia
  fear of: 4 cats

Aemilia
  character in: 17 The Comedy of Errors
  author: 11 Shakespeare

Aeneas
  hero of: 4 Troy
  father: 8 Anchises
  mother: 5 Venus
  grandfather: 5 Capys
  son: 5 Iulus **7** Silvius **8** Ascanius
  ancestor of: 6 Romans

Aeneas Silvius
  king of: 9 Alba Longa

Aeneid
  author: 6 Virgil
  character: 4 Gyas **5** Amata, Dares, Nisus **6** Arruns, Iarbas, Lausus, Pallas, Salius, Turnus **7** Acestes, Allecto, Camilla, Celaeno, Drances, Evander, Harpies, Helenus, Juturna, Latinus, Lavinia, Tarchon, Trojans, Venulus, Virbius **8** Ascanius, Entellus, Euryalus, Messapus **9** Cloanthus, Mezentius, Mnestheus, Palinurus, Sergestus **10** Andromache **12** Cumaean Sibyl
    gods: 4 Juno **5** Diana, Venus **6** Vulcan **7** Jupiter, Neptune
    Queen of Carthage: 4 Dido
    Aeneas' father: 8 Anchises
    Aeneas' mother: 9 Aphrodite
    Aeneas' wife: 6 Creusa
    Aeneas' son: 5 Iulus

Aeneas meets in underworld: 6 Charon **8** Cerberus **9** Palinurus
parts of the underworld: 7 Elysium **8** Tartarus **9** Ivory Gate
  river: 4 Styx **5** Lethe
Aeneas plucks: 11 Golden Bough
Aeneas visits: 5 Crete, Delos **6** Latium, Sicily, Thrace **8** Carthage

Aeolus
  other name: 5 Eolis
  ruler of: 5 winds
  founder of: 8 Aeolians
  father: 6 Hellen
  mother: 6 Orseis
  brother: 5 Dorus **6** Xuthus
  wife: 7 Enarete
  son: 5 Deion **6** Magnes **7** Athamas, Misenus **8** Cretheus, Macareus, Perieres, Sisyphus **9** Salmoneus
  daughter: 6 Calyce, Canace **7** Alcyone **8** Cleobule, Perimede, Pisidice

aerate 3 air **9** ventilate **10** mix with air **11** expose to air

aerial 3 air **4** airy **5** by air, lofty **6** dreamy, flying, unreal **7** antenna, elusive, soaring, tenuous **8** airborne, ethereal, fanciful, in the air **9** ephemeral, imaginary, visionary **10** by aircraft, from the air, of aircraft **11** atmospheric, impractical, wind-created **13** unsubstantial **15** capable of flight

aerobatic group 10 Blue Angels

aeronautics 6 flight, flying **8** aviation

Aerope
  father: 7 Catreus, Cerheus
  husband: 6 Atreus **10** Plisthenes
  sister: 9 Clymene
  son: 8 Menelaus **9** Agamemnon

aerophobia
  fear of: 6 flying

aeroplane 5 plane **8** aircraft, airplane

Aeschylus
  author of: 8 Oresteia **9** Agamemnon, Choephori (The Libation-bearers), Eumenides **11** The Persians **13** The Suppliants **15** Prometheus Bound **16** The House of Atreus **18** Seven Against Thebes

Aesculapius
  origin: 5 Roman
  god of: 7 healing **8** medicine
  corresponds to: 9 Asclepius

Aesir
  also: 4 Asar
  means: 9 chief gods
  origin: 12 Scandinavian
  leader: 4 Odin **5** Othin
  home: 6 Asgard
  conflicting with: 5 Vanir

aesthetic see **8** Esthetic

Aethalides
  member of: 9 Argonauts
  father: 6 Hermes
  trait: 6 memory

Aether
  origin: 5 Greek
  personifies: 3 air, sky

Aethra
  father: **8** Pittheus
  son: **7** Theseus

Aethylla
  brother: **5** Priam

Afars and the Issas *see* **8** Djibouti

affability 9 geniality **10** amiability, cordiality **11** sociability **12** friendliness, pleasantness **13** compatibility

affable 4 open, warm **5** civil **6** genial **7** amiable, cordial **8** friendly, gracious, mannerly, pleasant, sociable **9** agreeable, congenial, courteous, easygoing **10** compatible **11** good-humored, good-natured

affair 5 amour, event, party **6** effort, matter **7** concern, episode, liaison, pursuit, romance, shindig **8** activity, business, function, incident, interest, intrigue, occasion **9** adventure, festivity, happening, operation **10** love affair, occurrence, proceeding **11** celebration, transaction, undertaking **12** circumstance, relationship **14** social function **15** social gathering

affaire d'honneur 4 duel **13** affair of honor

affect 4 fake, move, stir **5** act on, adopt, alter, fancy, feign, put on, touch **6** assume, change, modify, regard **7** embrace, concern, imitate, impress **8** interest, relate to, simulate **9** impinge on, influence, pertain to, pretend to **10** tend toward **11** counterfeit

affectation 4 airs, sham **5** put-on **6** facade **8** false air, pretense **10** pretension **11** insincerity **13** artificiality, false mannerism

affected 4 vain **5** moved, phony, sorry, upset **6** harmed, la-di-da, unreal **7** assumed, changed, grieved, injured, pompous, stirred, studied, touched **8** impaired, mannered, troubled **9** acted upon, afflicted, concerned, conceited, contrived, impressed, pertinent, sorrowful, unnatural **10** artificial, distressed, influenced, interested, not genuine **11** pretentious **12** vainglorious

affectedness 4 airs **7** hauteur, tension **9** formality **10** constraint **11** haughtiness, pretensions **12** affectations **15** pretentiousness

affection 4 love **6** liking, malady, warmth **7** ailment, disease, illness **8** disorder, fondness, sickness **10** proclivity, tenderness

affectionate 4 fond, warm **6** ardent, caring, doting, loving, tender **10** lovey-dovey **11** warmhearted **13** demonstrative, tenderhearted

affectionate term 3 hon **4** dear **5** cheri, honey, sugar **7** pet name, sweetie, darling, dearest **8** nickname **9** sobriquet **10** endearment

Affery

character in: **12** Little Dorrit
author: **7** Dickens

affettuoso
  music: **8** tenderly

affiance 6 engage, pledge **7** betroth **13** engage to marry **15** solemnly promise

affiancing 5 troth **8** pledging **9** betrothal **10** engagement

affiche 6 poster **12** public notice

affidavit 4 oath **8** document **11** affirmation **14** sworn statement

affiliate 3 arm **4** ally, join, part **5** merge, unite **6** branch **7** chapter, connect, consort **8** division **9** associate, colleague **10** amalgamate, fraternize **11** incorporate, subdivision **12** band together

affiliated 6 allied, joined, united **9** connected **10** associated **12** incorporated

affiliation 5 union **8** alliance **10** connection **11** association **12** relationship

affinity 4 bent **5** fancy **6** liking **7** leaning, rapport **8** fondness, homology, likeness, penchant, relation, sympathy, tendency **10** connection, partiality, proclivity, propensity, similarity **11** inclination, parallelism **13** compatibility

affirm 4 aver, avow, hold **5** claim **6** allege, assert, ratify, uphold **7** approve, confirm, contend, declare, endorse, profess, support, sustain, warrant **8** maintain, proclaim, validate

affirmation 6 avowal **7** consent **8** approval **11** declaration, endorsement **12** confirmation, ratification **13** certification

affirmative 3 yes **8** emphatic, positive **9** affirming, approving, assenting, ratifying **10** conclusive, concurring, confirming **11** affirmatory, categorical **12** confirmatory **13** corroborative

affix 3 fix, tag **4** glue, seal **5** add on, paste, put on, set to, stick **6** attach, fasten, tack on

afflict 5 beset **6** plague **7** oppress, torment **8** distress

afflicted 6 cursed **7** plagued **8** affected, troubled **9** tormented **10** distressed

affliction 4 pain **5** curse, trial **6** misery, ordeal **7** anguish, torment, trouble **8** calamity, distress, hardship **9** adversity **10** misfortune, oppression **11** tribulation **12** wretchedness

affluence 5 money **6** plenty, riches, wealth **7** success **10** prosperity **14** prosperousness, successfulness

affluent 4 rich **6** loaded **7** moneyed, wealthy, well-off **8** well-to-do **9** well-fixed **10** prosperous, well-heeled

afford 4 bear, give, lend, risk **5** grant, offer, yield **6** chance, impart, manage, supply **7** command, furnish, provide, support, sustain

affray 4 fray **5** brawl, melee **6** fracas **7** contest, scuffle **8** conflict **9** encounter **11** altercation

affright 4 fear **5** alarm, dread, panic, scare **6** dismay, fright, horror, terror **8** frighten

affront 4 slur **5** abuse, wrong **6** injury, insult, offend, slight **7** offense, outrage, provoke, put-down **8** disgrace, dishonor, ignominy, rudeness **9** indignity, insolence **11** discourtesy, humiliation **12** ill-treatment, impertinence **13** mortification **16** contemptuousness

afghan 5 shawl, throw **7** blanket **8** covering, coverlet

Afghanistan
  other name: **6** Ariana, Aryana
  capital/largest city: **5** Kabul
  others: **3** Rui **4** Jurm, Nani, Wama **5** Asmar, Balkh, Doshi, Farah, Herat, Kunar, Makur, Maruf, Matun, Pahra, Tagab, Tulak, Urgan **6** Chaman, Gardez, Ghazni, Haibak, Kunduz, Nauzad, Panjao, Rustak, Sangan, Sarobi, Tukzar, Washir **7** Andkhui, Baghlan, Bamiyan, Dilaram, Ghurian, Girishk **8** Charikar, Faizabad, Kandahar **9** Jalalabad **10** Daulatabad, Pul-i-Khumri, Shibarghan **12** Mazar-i-Sharif
  government:
    parliament: **10** Loya-Jirgah
    radical group: **7** Taliban
  leader: **4** amir, emir **5** ameer, emeer **6** sharif, sherif
  measure: **3** paw, sir **5** jerib, karoh **6** khurds **7** kharwar
  monetary unit: **3** pul **5** abaze, riyal, rupee **6** abbasi, amania **7** afghani
  weight: **3** pau, paw, ser, sir
  lake: **13** Hamud-i-Helmand
  mountain: **3** Koh **5** Safeo **6** Chagai, Pamirs **7** Nowshak **8** Koh-i-Baba, Safed Koh, Sulaiman **9** Himalayas, Hindu Kush **11** Khwaja Amran, Paropamisus
  highest point: **9** Istoro Nal
  river: **4** Lora, Oxus **5** Cabul, Indus, Kabul, Kunar **6** Kokcha, Kunduz **7** Hari Rud, Helmand, Helmund, Murghab, Taleqan **8** Amu Darya, Farah Rud, Harut Rud, Khash Rud **9** Arghandab
  sea: **5** Darya
  physical feature:
    desert: **8** Registan
    panhandle: **6** Wakhan
    pass: **6** Khyber
    wind: **9** Afghanets
  people: **5** Aimak, Aymak, Kafir, Nuris **6** Baloch, Baluch, Chahar, Durani, Hasara, Hazara, Kaffir, Kirgiz, Pathan, Tajiks, Uzbeks **7** Beluchi, Belucki, Ghilzai, Pakhton, Pakhtun, Pashtun, Pukhtun, Pushtun, Sistani, Taimani, Taimuri **8** Jamshidi, Siah Push **9** Firuzkuhi, Safed Push, Safid Push

dynasty: 8 Barakzai
leader: 5 Najib **7** Mohmand **10** Najibullah **12** Babrak Karmal **14** Hafizullah Amin **17** Mohammad Zahir Shah, Mohammed Daoud Khan **18** Burhanuddin Rabbani Noor Mohammed Taraki
language: 4 Dari **5** Farsi **6** Afghan, Pashto, Pushtu **7** Balochi, Baluchi, Persian
religion: 5 Islam
place:
  dam: 6 Boghra **7** Kajakai **9** Arghandab
  feature:
  clothing: 7 chaderi
  coat: 6 chapan
  dance: 5 attan
  game: 8 buz-kashi
  guest room: 5 hujra
  hat: 7 karakul
  head-cloth: 7 chawdar
  house with tower: 4 qala
  medicinal plant: 9 asafetida
  wrestling: 6 ghosai
  food:
  potluck meal: 6 sulibat
aficionado 3 fan, nut **5** freak, pupil **7** devotee, pursuer, student **8** disciple
afield 5 amiss **6** abroad, astray **10** off the mark **11** out of the way **16** off the right track
afire 5 fiery **6** ablaze, aflame, alight, ardent, fervid, fuming, on fire **7** blazing, burning, fervent, flaming, flaring, glowing, ignited, smoking, zealous **8** aflicker, in flames, inspired **10** flickering, smoldering
afloat 5 at sea **6** adrift, wafted **7** sailing, wafting **8** drifting, floating
afoot 5 astir **8** underway **10** in the works
a fortiori 10 all the more
afraid 5 sorry **6** scared **7** alarmed, anxious, chicken, fearful, panicky, unhappy **8** cowardly, timorous **9** regretful, terrified **10** apologetic, frightened **11** lily-livered **12** apprehensive, disappointed, fainthearted **13** anxiety-ridden, panic-stricken **14** chicken-hearted, chicken-livered, terror-stricken
Afreet
  also: 5 Afrit
  origin: 7 Arabian
  form: 5 demon
afresh 4 anew **5** again **11** from scratch **16** from the beginning
  Latin: 6 de novo
Africa
  country: 4 Chad, Mali, Togo **5** Benin, Congo, Egypt, Gabon, Ghana, Kenya, Libya, Niger, Sudan, Zaire **6** Angola, Gambia, Guinea, Malawi, Rwanda, Uganda, Zambia **7** Algeria, Burundi, Comoros, Eritrea, Lesotho, Liberia, Morocco, Namibia, Nigeria, Reunion, Senegal, Somalia, Tunisia **8** Botswana, Cameroon, Djibouti, Ethiopia, Tanzania, Zimbabwe **9** Cape Verde, The Gambia, Mauritius, Swaziland **10** Ivory Coast, Madagascar, Mauritania, Mozambique, Seychelles **11** Burkina Faso, Sierra Leone, South Africa **12** Guinea-Bissau **13** Canary Islands, Western Sahara **15** South-West Africa **16** Equatorial Guinea **18** Sao Tome and Principe **22** Central African Republic
  people: 2 Ga **3** Ibo, Kru, Luo, San, Tiv, Yao **4** Arab, Beja, Bobo, Boer, Fang, Hutu, Kota, Kuba, Luba, Nuba, Nuer, Nupe, Teda, Tibu, Zulu **5** Bemba, Dinka, Galla, Hausa, Kamba, Makua, Masai, Mende, Mongo, Negro, Pygmy, Rundi, Serer, Shona, Sotho, Swazi, Temne, Tigre, Tutsi, Wolof, Xhosa **6** Bateke, Berber, Fulani, Herero, Ibibjo, Kikuyu, Mau Mau, Nubian, Ovambo, Rwanda, Senufo, Sidamo, Somali, Tswana, Tuareg, Yoruba, Watusi **7** Ashanti, Baganda, Bambara, Bushmen, Chaamba, Makonde, Mashoma, Ndebele, Nilotic, Oshogbo, Songhai, Turkana **8** Khoikhoi, Mangbetu, Matabele **9** Africaner, Afrikaner, Hottentot
  desert: 5 Namib **6** Sahara **8** Kalahari
  island: 5 Bioko, Pemba **6** Canary **7** Comoros, Madeira, Mayotte, Reunion **8** St Helena, Zanzibar **9** Ascension, Cape Verde, Mauritius **10** Madagascar, Seychelles
  ancient people/empire: 3 Oyo **4** Kush, Mali, Toro **5** Aksum, Benin, Ghana, Kongo, Mossi, Nubia, Wadai **6** Ankole, Tekrur **7** Ashanti, Buganda, Bunyoro, Dahomey, Songhai **8** Baguirmi, Carthage **10** Kanem-Bornu, Monomotapa **11** Ife and Benin
  ancient city: 5 Kilwa, Meroe **8** Timbuktu
  language: 4 Afar, Peul, Teda **5** Bantu, Bemba, Click, Hausa, Masai, Wolof **6** Arabic, Berber, French, Kanuri, Tsonga **7** Amharic, Khoisan, Lingala, Nilotic, Songhai, Swahili, Turkana **8** Cushitic, Mandingo **9** Afrikaans
  river: 4 Juba, Nile, Sudd **5** Congo, Kasai, Niger **6** Kwango, Orange, Ubangi **7** Senegal, Zambezi **8** Blue Nile **9** White Nile
  lake: 4 Chad, Kivu, Tana **5** Assal, Nyasa **6** Albert, Edward, Kariba, Malawi, Nassar, Red Sea, Rudolf **8** Victoria **10** Tanganyika **12** Chott Melrhir
  falls: 8 Victoria
  mountain/mountain range: 3 Air **4** Bihu, Meru **5** Atlas, Elgon, Kenya **6** Hoggar **7** Ahaggar, Crystal, Tibesti, Toubkal **8** Cameroon **9** Emi Koussi, Munchinga, Ruwenzori **10** Futa Jallon **11** Drakensberg, Kilimanjaro **13** Tibesti Massif
  lowest point: 17 Qattari Depression
  mineral/natural resource: 3 oil, tin **4** gold **5** ivory **6** cloves, copper, rubber **7** diamond, palm oil, uranium
  disease: 4 AIDS **5** Ebola **7** malaria **9** bilharzia **11** yellow fever **16** sleeping sickness
  homeland: 5 Venda **6** Ciskei **8** Transkei **14** Bophuthatswana
  game reserve: 5 Tsavo **6** Kruger **8** Amboseli **9** Serengeti
  tree: 4 cork, teak **5** cedar, ebony, olive **6** acacia, baobab, okoume, rubber **7** juniper, oil palm **8** date palm, mahogany, tamarisk **10** silk-cotton
  animal: 4 lion **5** bongo, hippo, hyena, zebra **6** jackal, monkey **7** buffalo, cheetah, giraffe, gorilla, leopard, wild pig **8** aardvark, antelope, elephant **9** crocodile **10** chimpanzee, rhinoceros **11** wildebeeste **12** hippopotamus
  bird: 5 heron, stork **6** falcon **7** bustard, ostrich, pelican **8** flamingo, hornbill **10** kingfisher
  fly: 6 tsetse
  snake: 5 cobra, mamba **6** python
Africaine, L'
  also: 14 The African Girl
  opera by: 9 Meyerbeer
African Queen, The
  director: 10 John Huston
  cast: 12 Robert Morley **14** Humphrey Bogart **16** Katharine Hepburn
  setting: 5 Congo
  Oscar for: 5 actor (Bogart)
Afrit see **6** Afreet
after 4 next, post **5** later **6** behind **9** afterward, following **10** conclusion, subsequent, succeeding
aftereffect 6 result **11** consequence
After Hours
  director: 14 Martin Scorsese
  cast: 12 Griffin Dunne **15** Rosanna Arquette
Afterlife
  god of: 4 Gwyn
aftermath 6 payoff, result, sequel, upshot **7** outcome **8** follow-up, offshoot **9** byproduct **11** consequence
afterpart 4 back, tail **5** stern **6** far end **7** back end, rear end, tail end **8** backside, hind part **9** posterior
after the fact 4 late **5** tardy **7** belated, delayed, too late **10** behindhand, behind time
After the Fall
  author: 12 Arthur Miller
after this, therefore because of it
  Latin: 21 post hoc ergo propter hoc
  describes: 14 logical fallacy
afterword 4 coda **8** addendum, epilogue **10** conclusion
Agacles
  king of: 9 Myrmidons

Agag
king of: **10** Amalekites
captured by: **4** Saul
killed by: **6** Samuel

again 3 bis **4** also, anew, more **6** encore **7** besides **8** moreover, once more **10** in addition, repetition **11** another time, duplication, furthermore **12** additionally
Latin: **6** de novo

against 7 adverse, opposed **8** conflict, contrary, opposite **10** opposition **11** unfavorable

against an opponent
Latin: **9** ad hominem

Against Our Will
author: **16** Susan Brownmiller

against the property
Latin: **5** in rem
describes: **15** legal proceeding

against the thing
Latin: **5** in rem

Agamemnon
author: **9** Aeschylus
mentioned in: **5** Iliad
king of: **7** Mycenae
leader of: **6** Greeks
fought in: **9** Trojan War
father: **6** Atreus
brother: **8** Menelaus
sister: **8** Anaxibia
wife: **12** Clytemnestra
daughter: **7** Electra **9** Iphigenia **12** Chrysothemis
son: **7** Orestes
cousin: **9** Aegisthus
captive: **9** Cassandra
Clytemnestra's lover: **9** Aegisthus
killed by: **12** Clytemnestra

Aganippe 8 fountain
location: **6** Greece **7** Helicon
sacred to: **5** Muses

Aganus
father: **5** Paris
mother: **5** Helen

agape 4 agog **6** amazed, gaping **8** wide open **9** awestruck, stupefied **10** astonished, dumbstruck, spellbound **11** dumbfounded **12** wonderstruck **13** flabbergasted

Agassiz, Jean Louis Rodolphe
field: **7** zoology
worked on: **7** fossils **8** glaciers **14** classification

agate
species: **6** quartz
variety of: **10** chalcedony
type: **3** eye **4** moss, onyx, ring **9** landscape **13** fortification
source: **4** Ider **6** Brazil **7** Uruguay **9** Oberstein **14** Rio Grande de Sul

Agathon
father: **5** Priam

Agathyrsus
father: **8** Hercules

Agave

father: **6** Cadmus
mother: **8** Harmonia
sister: **3** Ino **6** Semele **7** Autonoe
husband: **6** Echion
son: **8** Pentheus

age 3 eon, era **4** date **5** epoch, phase, ripen **6** mature, mellow, period, season **7** develop, forever, make old **8** life span, lifetime **9** adulthood, a long time, grow older, seniority **10** generation, millennium **11** stage of life, stage of time
French: **6** siecle

aged 3 old **4** ripe **6** mature, mellow **7** ancient, as old as, elderly, ripened **8** enduring, grown old **9** developed, full-grown, long-lived

Agee, James
author of: **10** Agee on Film **17** A Death in the Family **23** Let Us Now Praise Famous Men
screenwriter for: **15** The African Queen **19** The Night of the Hunter

Agelaus
mentioned in: **5** Iliad **7** Odyssey
occupation: **8** herdsman
father: **8** Hercules, Phradmon
mother: **7** Omphale
courted: **8** Penelope
raised: **5** Paris
employer: **5** Priam

ageless 7 classic, eternal **8** enduring, timeless

agency 5 force, means, power **6** action, bureau, charge **8** activity **9** influence, mediation, operation **10** department, instrument **12** intervention **15** instrumentality

agenda 6 docket **7** program **8** schedule **9** timetable

agent 4 doer **5** cause, envoy, force, means, mover, power **6** agency, author, deputy, worker **7** vehicle **8** advocate, emissary, executor, operator **9** go-between, performer **10** instrument, negotiator **11** perpetrator **12** intermediary, practitioner **14** representative

Age of Innocence, The
author: **12** Edith Wharton
character: **10** May Welland **12** Ellen Olenska **13** Newland Archer

age-old 4 aged **7** ancient, antique, very old **9** venerable

agglomerate 4 clot, mass **5** amass, bunch, clump, rally **6** gather, heap up, muster, pile up **7** cluster, collect **8** assemble, condense, mobilize **10** accumulate, collection **12** accumulation, conglomerate, heap together, lump together **14** conglomeration **15** gather into a mass

agglomeration 4 heap, mass, pile **5** bunch, clump **7** cluster **10** collection **12** accumulation **14** conglomeration

aggrandize 5 bloat, exalt, widen **6** beef up, blow up, dilate, expand, extend, puff up, step up **7** amplify,

broaden, build up, distend, enhance, enlarge, inflate, magnify, stretch **8** escalate, increase **9** intensify **10** strengthen

aggrandizement 8 increase, widening **9** expansion, extension **10** broadening, escalation, exaltation, stepping up **11** enhancement, enlargement **13** amplification, magnification **15** intensification

aggravate 3 vex **4** rile **5** anger, annoy **6** nettle, worsen **7** affront, inflame **8** heighten, increase, irritate **9** intensify, make worse **10** exacerbate, exasperate

aggravating 7 irksome **9** inflaming, vexatious, worsening **10** irritating **11** heightening **12** exacerbating, exasperating, intensifying

aggregate 3 mix **4** mass **5** blend, union **7** mixture **8** amassing, compound **9** composite, gathering, summation **10** collection **11** combination **12** accumulation, conglomerate **14** conglomeration

aggregation 3 mob **4** army, band, bevy, crew, gang, host, mass, pack **5** crowd, horde, swarm **6** throng **7** cluster **9** multitude **10** collection

aggression 4 raid **7** assault, offense **8** act of war, invasion **9** hostility, pugnacity **11** viciousness **12** belligerence **13** combativeness

aggressive 4 bold **5** harsh, pushy **7** dynamic, hostile, intense, vicious, warlike, warring, zealous **8** forceful, militant **9** ambitious, assailant, assertive, attacking, combative, energetic **10** pugnacious **11** belligerent, competitive, contentious, quarrelsome **12** antagonistic, enterprising **13** self-assertive **15** tending to attack

aggressiveness 9 hostility, pugnacity **10** antagonism **12** belligerence **13** combativeness

aggressor 7 invader **8** attacker **9** assailant **11** belligerent **12** antagonistic

aggrieved 3 sad **4** hurt **5** stung **6** abused, pained **7** injured, put upon, tearful, wounded, wronged **8** grieving, mournful, offended, saddened, troubled **9** affronted, disturbed, sorrowful **10** distressed, ill-treated, maltreated, persecuted **11** imposed upon **13** grief-stricken

aghast 6 amazed **7** shocked, stunned **8** appalled **9** astounded, horrified, terrified **10** astonished, fear-struck, frightened **12** horror-struck **13** thunderstruck

agile 4 keen, spry **5** alert, fleet, lithe, quick, swift **6** active, clever, limber, nimble, supple **8** athletic, graceful **9** dexterous

agility 8 alacrity, spryness **9** dexterity, quickness, swiftness **10** limberness, nimbleness **12** gracefulness

agitate 3 jar, mix **4** beat, goad, rock,

stir 5 alarm, churn, shake, upset **6** excite, foment, stir up, work up **7** disturb, provoke, shake up, trouble **8** disquiet

agitated 5 tense **6** uneasy **7** anxious, frantic, nervous, uptight **8** confused, seething **9** disturbed, perturbed, unsettled **10** disquieted, distracted, distraught **11** discomfited, discomposed **12** disconcerted

agitation 7 anxiety **9** confusion **10** discomfort, uneasiness **11** disquietude, distraction, nervousness **12** discomfiture, discomposure, perturbation

agitato
music: **8** agitated

agitator 7 inciter **8** fomentor, inflamer, provoker **9** firebrand **10** incendiary, instigator **11** provocateur **12** rabble-rouser, troublemaker **13** mischiefmaker, revolutionary **16** agent provocateur

Aglaia
member of: **6** Graces
father: **7** Jupiter
mother: **8** Eurynome
sister: **6** Thalia **10** Euphrosyne
husband: **4** Abas
son: **7** Proteus **8** Acrisius
daughter: **7** Idomene

aglow 4 warm **5** fiery **6** ablaze, redhot **7** blazing, glowing, radiant, shining

Agnes Grey
author: **10** Anne Bronte
character: **8** Mr Weston **13** Rosalie Murray

agnostic 5 pagan **7** atheist, doubter, heathen, heretic, infidel, skeptic **10** empiricist, free spirit, secularist, unbeliever **11** disbeliever, freethinker, nonbeliever **14** doubting Thomas

ago 4 gone, over, past **5** since **6** gone by **7** earlier **8** backward **15** retrospectively

agog 5 astir **7** excited **8** thrilled, worked up **9** awestruck **10** enthralled **11** openmouthed

Agon
ballet by: **10** Stravinsky

agonize 5 labor, sweat, worry **6** strain, suffer **7** anguish, wrestle **8** struggle

agonizing 6 severe **7** painful, racking **8** grievous, worrying **9** suffering, torturous **10** tormenting, unbearable **11** distressing, intolerable, unendurable **12** excruciating, insufferable

agony 3 woe **4** pain **5** trial **6** effort, misery, sorrow, strain, throes **7** anguish, anxiety, torment, torture **8** distress, striving, struggle **9** suffering **10** affliction **11** tribulation

Agony and the Ecstasy, The
author: **11** Irving Stone
about: **12** Michelangelo

Agoraea

epithet of: 6 Athena
means: **16** of the marketplace

agoraphobia
fear of: **10** open spaces

Agraeus
epithet of: **6** Apollo
means: **6** hunter

agrarian 5 rural **7** farming **8** pastoral **11** agronomical, crop-raising **12** agricultural

agree 4 jibe **5** admit, allow, chime, grant, match, tally **6** accede, accept, accord, assent, concur, settle, square **7** concede, conform, consent, support **8** coincide, side with **9** harmonize, subscribe **10** correspond, think alike

agreeable 4 nice **7** fitting **8** amenable, amicable, in accord, pleasant, pleasing, suitable **9** approving, complying, congenial **10** acceptable, concurring, consenting, gratifying **11** appropriate
German: **9** gemutlich

agreeableness 7 amenity **9** geniality **10** amiability **11** sociability **12** pleasantness

agreed
French: **7** d'accord

agreed upon 6 common, normal **8** accepted, approved **9** confirmed, customary **10** acceptable **11** established **12** acknowledged

agreement 4 deal, pact **6** accord **7** analogy, bargain, compact, concert, concord, harmony, promise **8** affinity, alliance, contract, covenant **10** accordance, compliance, conformity, settlement, similarity **11** arrangement, concordance, conformance **13** compatibility **14** correspondence

agricultural 4 farm **5** rural **7** farming **8** agrarian **9** gardening **11** agronomical, crop-raising **13** nonindustrial

agriculture 7 farming, tillage **8** agronomy **9** geoponics, husbandry **10** agronomics **11** crop-raising, cultivation **15** market gardening

Agriculture
god of: **4** Dago **5** Dagan, Dagon, Picus **6** Saturn **12** Bonus Eventus
goddess of: **5** Ceres **6** Brigit, Dea Dia, Vacuna **7** Demeter

Agriope see **8** Eurydice

Agrius
member of: **8** Gigantes
form: **7** centaur
mother: **5** Circe
father: **8** Odysseus
son: **9** Thersites
attacked: **8** Hercules

agronomics 7 farming, tillage **8** agronomy **9** geoponics **11** agriculture, crop-raising

agronomy 7 farming **9** gardening, husbandry **11** agriculture, cultivation

aground 5 stuck **6** ashore **7** beached **8** grounded, stranded **9** foundered

ague 5 chill, fever **7** malaria, shivers **12** sweating fits

Aguecheek, Sir Andrew
character in: **12** Twelfth Night
author: **11** Shakespeare

Agyius
epithet of: **6** Apollo
means: **15** god of the streets

Ah, But Your Land Is Beautiful
author: **9** Alan Paton

Ah! Wilderness
author: **12** Eugene O'Neill

Ahab
character in: **8** Moby Dick
author: **8** Melville
rank: **7** captain
feature: **6** pegleg

Ahab
father: **4** Omri
wife: **7** Jezebel
son: **7** Ahaziah
daughter: **8** Athaliah
opposed: **6** Elijah
killed by: **4** Aram

Ahasuerus
known as: **6** Xerxes **8** Cyaxares
wife: **6** Esther
divorced: **6** Vashti
son: **6** Darius
eunuchs: **6** Biztha, Carcas, Zethar **7** Abagtha, Harbona, Mehuman
servant: **7** Abagtha
courtier: **5** Haman
conqueror of: **7** Nineveh

ahead of time 5 early **6** before, in time, sooner **7** betimes, earlier **9** before now, in advance **10** beforehand, in good time **13** before the fact

Ahib 16 first Hebrew month

Ahithophel
counseled: **5** David
rebelled with: **7** Absalom
granddaughter: **9** Bathsheba

aid 4 abet, alms, dole, help **5** serve **6** assist, foster, relief **7** advance, charity, further, promote, subsidy, support, sustain **8** donation, minister **9** allowance **10** assistance, contribute, facilitate **11** accommodate, helping hand **12** contribution

Aida 17 Ethiopian princess
opera by: **5** Verdi
character: **4** Aida **6** Ramfis **7** Amneris, Radames **8** Amonasro, Rhadames
set in: **5** Egypt

aide 5 gofer **6** deputy, helper **7** abettor, acolyte **8** adherent, adjutant, follower, retainer, sidekick **9** assistant, associate, auxiliary, man Friday **10** aide-de-camp, apprentice, girl Friday, lieutenant **11** helping hand, subordinate **12** right-hand man

aide-de-camp 3 ADC **4** aide **6** helper **8** adjutant **9** assistant, man Friday, right hand **12** right-hand man

aide memoire 4 memo, note **10** memorandum

aider 4 aide **6** helper **7** abettor **9** assistant **11** helping hand

Aiken, Conrad Potter
author of: **6** Ushant **10** Blue Voyage **12** Reviewer's ABC **14** The Charnel Rose **15** Earth Triumphant

Aiken, Howard H
field: **11** mathematics
designed: **15** digital computer

ail 4 pain **5** annoy, be ill, upset, worry **6** be sick, bother, sicken **7** afflict, make ill, trouble **8** be infirm, be unwell, distress **12** be indisposed, fail in health

ailing 3 ill **4** sick **6** infirm, sickly, unwell **8** delicate

ailment 6 malady **7** disease, illness **8** disorder, sickness, weakness **9** complaint, infection, infirmity **10** affliction, disability, discomfort **13** indisposition

ailurophobia
fear of: **4** cats

aim 3 end, try **4** beam, goal, mean, plan, seek, want, wish **5** essay, focus, level, point, sight, slant **6** aiming, design, desire, direct, intend, intent, object, scheme, strive, target **7** attempt, be after, purpose, take aim, train on **8** ambition, aspire to, endeavor **9** intention **10** aspiration, have in mind, have in view, work toward **11** have an eye to, line of sight **12** marksmanship

aim at 4 seek **6** pursue, target **8** aspire to, shoot for

aimless 6 chance, random **7** erratic, wayward **8** unguided **9** frivolous, haphazard, hit-or-miss, pointless, unfocus(s)ed **10** accidental, rudderless, undirected **11** purposeless, unorganized **12** inconsistent, unsystematic **13** directionless, unpredictable **14** indiscriminate

aine 5 elder **6** eldest

Ainsworth, William Harrison
author of: **8** Boscobel, Crichton, Rookwood **9** Guy Fawkes **10** Old St Paul's **12** Jack Sheppard **13** Windsor Castle **16** The Flitch of Bacon, The Tower of London **17** The Miser's Daughter, The South Sea Bubble **20** The Lancashire Witches

Ainu
language spoken in: **8** Hokkaido, Sakhalin
native of: **5** Japan

air, airs 3 lay, sky **4** aura, look, mood, puff, song, tell, tone, tune, vent, waft, wind **5** blast, carol, ditty, draft, ozone, style, swank, utter, voice, whiff **6** aerate, ballad, breath, breeze, expose, manner, melody, reveal, spirit, strain, zephyr **7** declare, display, divulge, exhibit, express, feeling, hauteur, quality **8** ambience, disclose,

pretense, proclaim **9** arrogance, publicize, ventilate **10** appearance, atmosphere, make public **11** haughtiness, pretensions **12** affectations, affectedness, stratosphere **16** superciliousness
god of: **5** Enlil
goddess of: **6** Ninlil

airborne 5 aloft **6** aerial, Eolian **8** in flight **12** off the ground

aircraft 3 jet, SST **4** bird **5** blimp, crate, plane **6** copter, glider **7** balloon, chopper, prop-jet **8** airplane, jumbo jet, zeppelin **10** helicopter, whirlybird

air current 4 puff, wind **5** blast, draft, whiff **6** breeze, zephyr **11** breath of air

airdrome, aerodrome 7 airbase, airport, jet base **8** airfield **11** flying field **12** landing field

airfield 7 air base, airport, jet base **8** airstrip **11** flying field **12** landing field, landing strip

airfoil
insect: **4** wing

airless 8 stifling **10** overheated, sweltering **16** poorly ventilated

airlines, American 3 TWA **4** Reno, Mesa **5** Aloha, Delta, Pan Am, USAir **6** United, Alaska **7** Eastern, Simmons, ValuJet **8** American, Hawaiian, Carnival, TowerAir **9** Southwest, Northwest **10** Transworld, Horizon Air **11** Continental, America West, Trans States **12** Air Wisconsin **14** Western Pacific **16** American Trans Air **17** Atlantic Southeast **18** Continental Express **21** Continental Micronesia

airplane 3 jet **4** bird **5** crate, plane **7** airship, prop-jet **8** aircraft **9** aeroplane **11** flying jenny **19** heavier-than-air craft **20** propeller-driven plane
invented by:
automatic pilot: **6** Sperry
jet engine: **5** Ohain
with motor: **12** Wilbur Wright **13** Orville Wright **14** Wright Brothers
hydro: **7** Curtiss
first: **5** Flyer
part: **3** fin **4** flap, nose, tail, wing **5** cabin, cargo, pylon **6** rudder **7** aileron, cockpit, turbine **8** elevator, fuel tank, fuselage, throttle, turbofan, turbojet **9** empennage, propeller, turboprop **10** flight deck, power plant, stabilizer **11** landing gear **13** undercarriage
kind: **3** MIG **4** Zero **5** Eagle, Gotha, Piper, Sabre **6** Boeing, Cessna, Fokker, Mirage **7** Concorde, Piper Cub **10** Beechcraft, Dornier Do-X **11** Piper Navajo **12** Lockheed Vega, Sopwith Camel **13** Boeing Clipper, Messerschmitt, Piper Cherokee, Super Fortress **14** Cessna Citation, Flying Fortress, Grumman Hellcat, Stratofortress **15** Hawker Hurrican **16** De Havilland Comet

variation: **3** SST **4** STOL, VTOL **5** blimp, drone, VSTOL **6** bomber, glider **7** airship, fighter **8** zeppelin **10** hang glider, helicopter, supersonic
battle: **8** dog fight

airport 5 field **7** air base, jet base **8** airdrome, airfield, airstrip **9** aerodrome **11** flying field **12** landing field, landing strip
Paris: **4** Orly
Chicago: **5** O'Hare
New York: **3** JFK
London: **8** Heathrow
Boston: **5** Logan
Airport Abbreviations:
Atlanta: **3** ATL (Hartsfield International)
Boston: **3** BOS (Logan International)
Chicago: **3** ORD (O'Hare)
Dallas/Ft. Worth: **3** DFW
Denver: **3** DEN
Detroit: **3** DTW
Honolulu: **3** HNL
Houston: **3** IAH
Las Vegas: **3** LAS (McCarren International)
Los Angeles: **3** LAX
Miami: **3** MIA
Minneapolis/St. Paul: **3** MSP
Newark: **3** EWR
New York: **3** JFK, LGA (John F. Kennedy International, LaGuardia)
Orlando: **3** MCO
Phoenix: **3** PHX (Sky Harbor International)
St. Louis: **3** STL (Lambert St. Louis International)
San Francisco: **3** SFO
Seattle/Tacoma: **3** SEA

airship 5 blimp **7** balloon **9** dirigible **19** lighter-than-air craft

airship, rigid dirigible
invented by: **8** Zeppelin

airstrip 6 runway **12** landing field, landing strip

air weapon
German: **9** Luftwaffe

airy 5 light, merry, sunny, windy **6** breezy, cheery, drafty, dreamy, jaunty, lively **8** cheerful, ethereal, fanciful, gossamer, illusory, spacious **9** idealized, imaginary, sprightly **10** frolicsome, immaterial **11** unrealistic **12** lighthearted, light-of-heart **13** unsubstantial **14** well-ventilated

aisle 3 way **4** lane, path, walk **5** alley **6** avenue **7** passage, walkway **8** cloister, corridor **10** ambulatory, passageway

Aius Locutius
form: **5** voice
warned: **6** Romans
warned of: **14** Gallic invasion

ajar 4 open **5** agape **6** gaping **8** unclosed **10** partly open

Ajax
also: 4 Aias
called: 9 Great Ajax **10** Oilean Ajax **11** Locrian Ajax **13** Ajax the Lesser **14** Telamonian Ajax
king of: 7 Locrius
father: 6 Oileus **7** Telamon
mother: 8 Periboea
brother: 6 Teucer
author: 9 Sophocles
character: 8 Achilles, Odysseus **9** Agamemnon
  son: 9 Eurysaces
  slave: 8 Tecmessa
  seer: 7 Calchas
rescued body of: 8 Achilles
violated shrine of: 6 Athena
killed in: 9 shipwreck

Akela
character in: 14 The Jungle Books
author: 7 Kipling

Akh
origin: 8 Egyptian
transfiguration of: 4 dead

Akihito
position: 7 emperor **11** crown prince
reign name: 6 Heisei **17** Establishing Peace
family:
  father: 5 Showa **8** Hirohito
  mother: 6 Nagako
  wife: 7 Michiko
  children: 4 Hito **8** Narahito
schools: 6 Oxford **9** Gakushuin

akin 3 kin **4** like **5** alike **6** allied **7** kindred, related, similar, uniform **8** agreeing, parallel **9** analogous, congenial, connected, identical **10** affiliated, comparable, resembling **11** correlative **13** corresponding **14** consanguineous

Akkad *see* **5** Accad

Akutagawa, Ryunosuke
author of: 5 Kappa **8** Rashomon **13** The Hell Screen

a la 9 in honor of **13** in the manner of

Alabama
abbreviation: 2 AL **3** Ala
nickname: 6 Cotton **12** Heart of Dixie, Yellowhammer
capital: 10 Montgomery
largest city: 10 Birmingham
others: 5 Selma **6** Athens, Dothan, Marion, Mobile **7** Decatur, Gadsden **8** Anniston **9** Huntsville, Tuscaloosa
colleges: 5 Miles **6** Auburn **7** Alabama **8** Tuskegee **9** Talladega **10** Huntingdon
explorer: 12 Herman DeSoto
feature:
  festival: 11 Azalea Trail
  statue: 6 Vulcan
tribe: 5 Creek **6** Tohome **7** Alabamu, Alibamu, Koasati **8** Tuskegee
people: 8 Joe Louis **9** Hank Aaron, Hugo Black **10** Willie Mays **11** Helen Keller, Nat King Cole **13** George Wallace, William C Handy, William Gorgas
lake: 12 Guntersville
land rank: 11 twenty-ninth
physical feature:
  gulf: 6 Mexico
  highest point: 6 Cheaha
  highlands: 11 Appalachian
river: 3 Pea **5** Coosa **6** Mobile **7** Alabama **9** Tombigbee, Tennessee **10** Tallapoosa **13** Chattahoochee
state admission: 12 twenty-second
state bird: 7 flicker **12** yellowhammer
state fish: 6 tarpon
state flower: 8 camellia **9** goldenrod
state motto: 21 We Dare Defend Our Rights
state song: 7 Alabama
state tree: 20 southern longleaf pine

Alabama, Alibamu
language family: 9 Muskogean
location: 5 Texas **9** Louisiana **10** Polk County **12** Alabama River
related to: 7 Koasati

alacrity 4 zeal **5** speed **6** fervor **7** agility, avidity **8** dispatch **9** alertness, briskness, eagerness, readiness **10** enthusiasm, liveliness, nimbleness, promptness **11** willingness **13** sprightliness

Aladdin
character in: 27 Arabian Nights' Entertainments
character: 13 Chinese sailor

Al Aiun, El Aaiun
capital of: 13 Western Sahara

a la mode 12 in the fashion, in the style of **13** in the manner of

Alarcon, Pedro Antonio de
author: 10 The Scandal **12** Captain Venom **14** El Nino de la Bola **19** The Three-Cornered Hat

alarm 4 fear **5** alert, panic, scare **6** appall, dismay, fright, terror, war cry **7** agitate, disturb, terrify, trouble, unnerve, warning **8** affright, distress, frighten **9** agitation, hue and cry, misgiving **11** trepidation **12** apprehension, perturbation **13** consternation

alarmed 6 afraid, scared **7** anxious, fearful, panicky, worried **8** dismayed **9** concerned, terrified **10** frightened **12** apprehensive **13** panic-stricken **14** terror-stricken

alarming 5 awful, dread, scary **7** fearful **8** dreadful **10** horrifying, terrifying **11** frightening, hair-raising

alas
expresses: 4 pity **5** grief **6** sorrow **7** concern **9** weariness **11** unhappiness **12** wretchedness
phrase: 7 woe is me

Alaska
abbreviation: 2 AK **4** Alas
nickname: 9 Great Land, Sourdough **12** Last Frontier **20** Land of the Midnight Sun
capital: 6 Juneau
largest city: 9 Anchorage
others: 4 Nome **5** Sitka **6** Barrow, Kodiak **7** Cordova, Douglas, Skagway **9** Fairbanks, Ketchikan
feature: 5 Alcan **13** Alaska Highway
  national park: 13 Mount McKinley
tribe: 3 Han **5** Aleut, Haida, Inuit **6** Ahtena, Akkhas, Eskimo, Karluk, Tetlin **7** Amerind, Ingalik, Kayukon, Khotana, Kutchin, Tanaina, Tlingit, Tlinkit, Venetie **9** Tsimshian, Unakalett
island: 4 Adak, Atka **5** Aleut **6** Kodiak, Unimak **7** Diomede, Nunivak **8** Aleutian, Pribilof **9** Alexander
lake: 6 Naknek **7** Iliamna **8** Becharof **9** Teshekpuk
land rank: 5 first
mountain: 3 Ada **4** Muir **5** Coast **6** Alaska, Brooks **7** Foraker, St Elias **8** Aleutian, Wrangell **9** Blackburn
  highest point: 8 McKinley
physical feature:
  bay: 7 Glacier, Prudhoe
  channel: 9 Gastineau
  glacier: 9 Malaspina
  pass: 8 Chilkoot
  peninsula: 5 Kenai **6** Alaska, Seward
  rapids: 10 Whitehorse
  sea: 6 Arctic **8** Beaufort
  strait: 6 Bering
river: 5 Kobuk, Yukon **6** Copper, Noatak, Tanana **7** Koyukuk, Susitna **8** Colville **9** Kuskokwim, Matanuska, Porcupine
sled race: 8 Iditarod
state admission: 10 forty-ninth
state bird: 15 willow ptarmigan
state fish: 10 king salmon
state flower: 11 forget-me-not
state motto: 16 North to the Future
state song: 11 Alaska's Flag
state symbol: 9 bald eagle
state tree: 11 sitka spruce

Alaskan Adventures
author: 8 Rex Beach

Albania
other name: 8 Shqiperi **9** Shqiprija, Shqyptare
capital/largest city: 6 Tirana, Tirane
others: 3 Opp **4** Fier, Klos, Puka, Puke **5** Berat, Dukat, Korce, Kruje, Pecin, Peqin, Qukes, Rubic, Spash, Vlore **6** Avlona, Bitsan, Dardhe, Durres, Karaje, Preshe, Valona **7** Chimara, Coritza, Durazzo, Elbasan, Koritsa, Preyesa, Scutari, Shkoder **8** Tepeleni **11** Gjirokaster
monetary unit: 3 lek **5** franc **6** qintar **7** quintar
island: 6 Saseno
lake: 4 Ulze **5** Matia, Ohrid **6** Prespa **7** Ochrida, Scutari, Shkoder **8** Ohridsko
mountain: 5 Shala **6** Pindus **8** Koritnjk **12** Albanian Alps

highest point: 10 Mount Korab
river: 3 Mat **4** Arta, Drin **5** Byene, Er-
zen, Seman **6** Bojana, Bojane, Vijosa,
Vijosa, Vijose **7** Drin-i-ci, Shkumbi
sea: 6 Ionian **8** Adriatic
physical feature:
  bay: 5 Vlore
  cape: 6 Glossa
  gulf: 4 Drin
  lagoon: 10 Kara Vastas
  peninsula: 6 Balkan
  promontory: 13 acroceraunium
  strait: 7 Otranto
  wind: 4 bora
people: 3 Geg **4** Cham, Gheg, Gueg,
Tosk **6** Arnaut, Arnout **8** Illyrian,
Skipetar
  king: 3 Zog **9** Ahmet Zogu
  leader: 4 Alia **5** Hoxha **7** Berisha
10 Scanderbeg, Skenderbeg **13**
Bishop Fan Noli
language: 3 Geg **4** Cham, Gheg,
Hish, Tosk **5** Greek **8** Albanian
religion: 5 Islam **7** Bektash **13** Roman Catholic **15** Eastern Orthodox
place:
  square: 10 Skenderbeg
feature:
  lute: 6 luhata
  soldier: 7 palikar
  stone house: 4 kula
food:
  cheese: 8 kackaval

Albanian
language family: 12 Indo-European
spoken in: 7 Balkans

Albee, Edward
author of: 3 Box **7** All Over **8** Seascape, Zoo Story **9** Tiny Alice **10**
The Sandbox **13** A Delicate Balance,
The American Dream **18** The Lady
from Dubuque **21** The Ballad of the
Sad Cafe, The Death of Bessie Smith
25 Who's Afraid of Virginia Woolf?
identified with: 18 theater of the absurd

Albeniz, Isaac
born: 5 Spain **9** Camprodon
composer of: 6 Iberia **12** The Magic
Opal **13** Henry Clifford

Alberich
origin: 8 Teutonic
king of: 6 dwarfs
possessed treasure of: 8 Niblungs **9**
Nibelungs
also possessed: 9 Tarnkappe

Albert, Eddie
real name: 21 Eddie Albert Heimberger
wife: 5 Margo
born: 12 Rock Island IL
roles: 8 Oklahoma **10** Brother Rat,
Green Acres **11** Room Service **12** Roman Holiday **13** The Longest Day **16**
The Heartbreak Kid **19** The Boys
from Syracuse

Alberta
abbreviation: 4 Alta

capital/largest city: 8 Edmonton
others: 7 Calgary, Reddeer **10** Leth-
bridge **11** Medicine Hat
lakes: 5 Banff, Claire **6** Jasper **8**
Waterton **9** Athabasca **11** Lesser
Slave
rivers: 3 Bow **4** Milk **6** Oldman, Wapiti **9** Athabasca **12** Saskatchewan
religion: 13 Roman Catholic **20**
United Church of Canada **22** Anglican Church of Canada
people: 5 Dutch **6** French, German **7**
British, English **9** Ukrainian **12** Scandinavian

Albert Herring
opera by: 7 Britten

Alberti, Leon Battista
architect of: 15 Palazzo Rucellai **18**
Church of Sant' Andrea, Temple Ma-
latestiano **20** Church of San Sebastian **25** Church of Santa Maria No-
vello

Albertson, Jack
born: 8 Malden MA
roles: 14 Chico and the Man **15** The
Sunshine Boys **18** Days of Wine and
Roses, The Subject Was Roses
album 2 LP **4** book **6** record **8** register
9 portfolio, scrapbook

Alceste
opera by: 5 Gluck

Alcestis
author: 9 Euripides
character: 6 Apollo **7** Admetus **8** Heracles, Thanatos

Alcestis
father: 6 Pelias
mother: 8 Anaxibia **10** Phylomache
husband: 7 Admetus
son: 7 Eumelus **8** Hippasus
returned from: 5 Hades
returned by: 8 Hercules

Alchemist, The
author: 9 Ben Jonson
character: 4 Face **5** Surly **6** Dapper,
Subtle **7** Ananias, Drugger, Kastril,
Love-wit **9** Dol Common **10** Dame
Pliant **16** Sir Epicure Mammon **20**
Tribulation Wholesome
alchemy 5 magic **7** sorcery **8** wizardry
10 conversion, witchcraft **11** magic
appeal **13** transmutation **17** medieval
chemistry
god of: 6 Hermes
purpose: 12 lead into gold

Alcimede
father: 8 Phylacus
mother: 7 Clymene
husband: 5 Aeson
son: 5 Jason

Alcimedon
origin: 8 Arkadian
mentioned in: 5 Iliad
father: 7 Laerces
daughter: 6 Philao
captain of: 9 Myrmidons

Alcina

opera by: 6 Handel
character: 6 Alcina **8** Ruggiero

Alcindor, Lew
former name of: 17 Kareem Abdul-
Jabbar

Alcmaeon
father: 10 Amphiaraus
mother: 8 Eriphyle
brother: 11 Amphilochus
wife: 10 Callirrhoe
son: 7 Acarnan **10** Amphoterus
daughter: 9 Tisiphone
commanded: 7 Thebans

Alcmene
father: 9 Electryon
mother: 5 Anaxo
husband: 10 Amphitryon **12** Rhadamanthys
twin sons: 8 Hercules, Iphicles
alcohol 3 ale **4** beer, wine **5** drink **6**
liquor **7** whiskey **9** the bottle
Latin: 9 aqua vitae
alcoholic 3 sot **4** hard, lush, soak **5**
drunk, rummy, souse, toper **6** barfly,
boozer, strong **7** guzzler, imbiber, tippler **8** drunkard **9** distilled, fermented,
inebriate **10** spirituous **11** dipsomaniac, hard drinker, inebriating, ine-
briative, whiskey head **12** intoxicating
alcoholism 3 DT's **9** oenomania **10**
dipsomania **12** intemperance **15** delirium tremens

Alcon
form: 6 archer, Trojan **7** warrior
aided: 8 Hercules
wounded: 8 Odysseus
abducted: 13 Geryons cattle
killed by: 8 Odysseus

Alcott, Louisa May
author of: 7 Jo's Boys **9** Little Men
11 Little Women **12** Eight Cousins,
Flower Fables **15** Aunt Jo's Scrap-
Bag **18** An Old-Fashioned Girl
alcove 3 bay **4** nook **5** niche **6** corner,
recess **7** cubicle, opening **11** compartment

Alcyoneus
form: 5 giant
hurled: 5 stone
killed by: 8 Hercules

Alda, Alan
born: 9 New York NY
father: 10 Robert Alda
  real name: 15 Alfonso D'Abruzzo
roles: 4 MASH **8** A New Life **9** Paper
Lion, Playmates, White Nile **12**
Sweet Liberty **13** Betsy's Wedding,
Hawkeye Pierce, The Glass House **14**
The Four Seasons **16** Same Time
Next Year, The Mephisto Waltz

Alden, Roberta
character in: 17 An American Tragedy
author: 7 Dreiser
al dente 10 to the tooth
alder 5 Alnus
varieties: 3 Red **5** Black, Hazel,

White, Witch **6** Oregon, Smooth, Yellow **7** Italian, Seaside **8** Japanese, Mountain, Speckled **9** Caucasian **10** Manchurian **13** American green, European green

Aldiss, Brian W
author of: **7** Non-Stop **9** Greybeard **13** The Saliva Tree **19** Frankenstein Unbound, The Billion Year Spree, The Eighty Minute Hour **20** The Trillion Year Spree

ale 4 beer, brew **5** stout **12** malt beverage **15** English festival

Alea
epithet of: **6** Athena
means: **9** sanctuary

Alecto
member of: **6** Furies

alehouse 3 pub **6** saloon, tavern **7** taproom **11** public house

Aleichem, Sholom
author of: **12** The Great Fair **14** Tevye's Daughter

Alembert, Jean le Rond d'
field: **11** mathematics
nationality: **6** French
studied: **13** fluid dynamics **18** celestial mechanics **28** partial differential equations

Aleph and Other Stories
author: **15** Jorge Luis Borges

alert 4 warn, wary **5** alarm, aware, quick, siren **6** active, inform, lively, nimble, notify, signal **7** careful, heedful, on guard, warning **8** diligent, forewarn, keen-eyed, vigilant, watchful **9** attentive, observant, sprightly, wideawake **10** perceptive **11** intelligent

alertness 8 alacrity, dispatch **9** awareness, readiness, vigilance **10** liveliness **12** watchfulness

Aleut
language family: **6** Eskimo
tribe: **4** Atka **8** Unalaska
location: **6** Alaska **15** Shumagin Islands **17** Aleutian Peninsula
noted for: **7** hunting

Aleutians
islands: **3** Fox, Rat **4** Attu, Near **5** Kiska **9** Andreanof **25** Islands of the Four Mountains
state: **6** Alaska
people: **6** Aleuts
language: **5** Atkan **9** Unalaskan

Alexander, Jane
real name: **11** Jane Quigley
born: **8** Boston MA
roles: **9** Testament **17** The Great White Hope **18** Eleanor and Franklin **19** All the President's Men

Alexander's Feast
author: **10** John Dryden

Alexander the Great
battle: **5** Issus **9** Gaugamela
birthplace: **5** Pella

conquered: **6** Darius, Persia
father: **8** Philip II
founded: **10** Alexandria
friend: **11** Hephaestion
general: **7** Cleitus **8** Philotas **9** Parmenion
horse: **10** Bucephalus
mother: **8** Olympias
nationality: **10** Macedonian
tutor: **9** Aristotle
wife: **6** Roxana

alexandrite
species: **11** chrysoberyl
source: **8** Sri Lanka
color: **3** red **5** green

Alfheim
origin: **12** Scandinavian
dwelling place of: **5** elves
location: **11** above ground

Alfie
director: **12** Lewis Gilbert
based on play by: **12** Bill Naughton
cast: **12** Michael Caine **14** Shelley Winters

alga, algae 6 fungus **8** pond scum
contains: **4** agar **5** algin **11** carrageenan, chlorophyll
type: **3** red **5** brown, green **9** blue-green, euglenids **11** golden-brown, yellow-green **15** dinoflagellates
forms: **4** kelp **5** dulse **7** diatoms, seaweed **8** plankton, rockweed **9** Irish moss, stonewort

Alger, Horatio
author of: **10** Ragged Dick **11** Tattered Tom **12** Luck and Pluck

Algeria
other name: **7** Algerie, Numidia, Pomaria **9** al-Djazair
capital/largest city: **7** Algiers
others: **4** Bona, Bone, Oran **5** Aflou, Arzew, Batna, Blida, Medea, Saida, Setif, Tenes **6** Abadla, Annaba, Aumale, Barika, Bechar, Bejaia, Benoud, Biskra, Bougie, Dellys, Djanet, Djelfa, Dzioua, Eloued, Frenda, Guelma, Skikda **7** Boghari, Mascara, Miliana, Negrine, Nemours, Ouargla, Tebessa, Tlemcen **8** Ghardaia, Laghouat **9** Touggourt **11** Constantine **12** Sidi-bel-abbes
division: **4** Oran **6** Annaba **7** Algiers **11** Constantine
leader: **3** bey, dey **6** disawa **9** beylerbey
measure: **3** pik **5** rebis, tarri **6** termin
monetary unit: **5** dinar **7** centime
weight: **4** rotl
lake: **5** Hodna **6** Sabkha **7** Cherqui, Fedjadj, Meirhir **10** Azzel Matti, Mekerrhane
mountain: **5** Aissa, Atlas, Aures, Dahra **6** Chelia **7** Ahaggar, Kabylia, Mouydir **8** Djurjura **9** Djurdjura, Tell Atlas **12** Saharan Atlas
highest point: **5** Tahat
river: **6** Shelif **7** Cheliff **8** Medjerda **15** Cheliffmedjerda

sea: **13** Mediterranean
physical feature: **14** Tropic of Cancer
desert: **6** Sahara
giant sand dune: **3** erg
grass: **4** diss **7** esparto
hill: **4** tell
oasis: **4** Mzab
oil field: **7** Edjeleh, El Gassi **10** Zarzaitine **13** Hassi Messaoud (happy spring), Tiguentourine
plain: **7** Cheliff, Mitidja
rocky plateau: **7** hammada
salt basin: **5** chott, shatt
wind: **7** sirocco
people: **4** Arab **6** Berber, Kabyle, Shawia, Tuareg **7** Haratin
author: **3** Dib **5** Camus, Fanon **6** Yacine
leader: **9** Bendjedid **10** Abd al-Qadir, Abd-al-Kadir, Abd- el-Kader **11** Boumedienne **13** Ahmed Ben Bella
ruler: **8** Jugurtha **9** Masinissa
language: **6** Arabic, Berber, French, Zenata **7** Senhaja
religion: **5** Islam
place:
monastery: **5** Ribat
ruins: **7** Djemila
feature:
camel: **6** mehari
cavalry man: **5** spahi **6** spahee
commune: **5** setif
dwelling: **6** gourbi
French settler/landowner: **5** colon **8** piednoir
holy man: **8** marabout
kingdom: **7** Numidia
native quarter: **6** casbah, kasbah
pirate: **7** corsair
ship: **5** xebec, zebec
slum: **10** bidonville
food:
dish: **8** couscous
fruit drink: **5** syrop
seasoning: **4** mint **5** anise, cumin **6** cloves, fennel, ginger, pepper **7** parsley, pimento **8** cinnamon **9** coriander

Algiers
Arabic: **8** al-Jazair
building: **11** Great Mosque
capital of: **7** Algeria
center of city: **6** Casbah
French: **5** Alger
hills: **5** Sahel
Roman: **7** Icosium
ruled by: **5** Turks **6** French **7** Berbers **10** Free French **14** Barbary Pirates
sea: **13** Mediterranean

Algonkian-Ritwan
language family: **14** Algonkian-Mosan
subgroup: **3** Fox **4** Cree, Sauk **5** Wiyot, Yurok **6** Ojibwa **7** Abenaki, Arapaho, Mohican **8** Cheyenne, Delaware, Menomini **9** Blackfoot

Algonkin, Algonquin

language family: 9 Algonkian **10** Algonquian

tribe: 7 Abitibi **8** Algonkin **9** Nipissing **11** Temiscaming

location: 6 Canada **11** Ottawa River

spirit of nature: 7 Manitou

Algonquian, Algonkin

tribe: 3 Fox, Sac **4** Cree, Innu, Sauk **5** Miami **6** Abnaki, Atsina, Micmac, Ojibwa, Ottawa, Pequot **7** Arapaho, Mahican, Mohegan, Mohican, Ojibway, Shawnee **8** Algonkin, Cheyenne, Chippawa, Delaware, Haaninin, Iliniwek, Illinois, Kickapoo, Menomini, Merrimac, Powhatan, Puyallop **9** Algonquin, Blackfeet, Blackfoot, Massasoit, Menominee, Menomonie, Mesquakie, Pennacook, Penobscot, Pokanoket, Twightwee, Wampanoag **10** Leni-Lenape, Potawatomi **11** Gros Ventres **12** Narragansett **17** Montagnais-Naskapi

algophobia

fear of: 4 pain

Algum 13 red sandalwood

Ali, Muhammad

formerly: 11 Cassius Clay

sport: 6 boxing

class: 11 heavyweight

won: 8 Olympics **16** heavyweight title

alias 9 pseudonym **11** assumed name, nom de guerre

Ali Baba

character in: 27 Arabian Nights' Entertainments

alibi 3 out **6** excuse **7** pretext **11** explanation **13** justification

Alice Adams

author: 15 Booth Tarkington

character: 6 Mr Lamb **11** Virgil Adams, Walter Adams **13** Arthur Russell, Mildred Palmer

Alice's Adventures in Wonderland

author: 12 Lewis Carroll **22** Charles Lutwidge Dodgson

character: 5 Alice **7** Duchess **9** Mad Hatter, March Hare **10** Mock Turtle **11** Cheshire Cat, White Rabbit **13** Knave of Hearts, Queen of Hearts

Alice Sit-by-the-Fire

author: 12 James M Barrie

alien 6 exotic, remote, unlike **7** distant, foreign, opposed, strange **8** contrary, newcomer, outsider, stranger **9** different, estranged, foreigner, immigrant, not native, outlander, separated, unrelated **10** dissimilar, outlandish **11** conflicting, incongruous, unconnected **12** incompatible, inconsistent **13** contradictory

German: 9 Auslander

alienate 7 divorce **8** estrange, separate, turn away

alienation 5 exile **7** divorce **9** isolation **10** separation, withdrawal **13** repulsiveness

alight 4 land **6** get off **7** deplane, descend, detrain, get down **8** come down, dismount **9** climb down, disembark, thump down, touch down

align 4 ally, even, join, side **6** even up, line up **9** affiliate, associate **10** straighten

alignment 7 allying, evening **9** evening up **13** straightening

alike 4 akin, even, same **5** equal **6** evenly **7** equally, kindred, uniform **8** of a piece, parallel **9** analogous, identical, similarly, uniformly **10** equivalent, synonymous **11** homogeneous, identically **13** corresponding

Allsande (Sandy)

character in: 36 A Connecticut Yankee in King Arthur's Court

author: 5 Twain

alive 4 spry **5** alert, aware, eager, quick, vital **6** active, extant, lively, living, viable **7** animate, in force, not dead **8** animated, possible, spirited, vigorous **9** breathing, energetic, operative, vivacious **10** subsisting, unquenched **11** above ground, in existence, in operation **14** unextinguished

alive to 5 alert, awake, aware **7** heedful, mindful **8** watchful **9** attentive, conscious, wide-awake

alkaline 3 lye **5** salty **7** antacid **9** non-acidic

alkaloid 7 alkaline, codeine, quinine **8** morphine, nicotine **16** colorless complex

all 4 each, full, very **5** any of, every, fully, total, utter, whole **6** each of, entire, to a man, utmost, wholly **7** highest, perfect, totally, utterly **8** any one of, complete, entirely, everyone, greatest, the sum of, the total, the whole **9** every item **10** altogether, completely, every one of, everything, the total of, the whole of **11** every member, every part of, exceedingly, the entirety

All About Eve

director: 17 Joseph L Mankiewicz

cast: 10 Anne Baxter, Bette Davis **11** Celeste Holm, Gary Merrill **12** Thelma Ritter **13** George Sanders, Marilyn Monroe

Oscar for: 7 picture **8** director **10** screenplay **15** supporting actor (George Sanders)

Allan-a-Dale, Alan-a-Dale

character in: 9 Robin Hood

allargando

music: 13 getting slower

all around 6 abroad **7** all over **10** everywhere, far and wide **15** making the rounds

all-around 5 broad **6** adroit, gifted **8** flexible **9** adaptable, many-sided, versatile **11** well-rounded **12** ambidextrous, multifaceted **13** comprehensive

allay 4 calm, dull, ease, hush **5** blunt, check, quell, quiet, slake **6** lessen, pacify, quench, reduce, smooth, soften, soothe, subdue **7** appease, assuage, lighten, mollify, relieve, slacken **8** diminish, mitigate, moderate **9** alleviate, put to rest **14** cause to subside

all but 6 almost, nearly **7** close to **8** not quite **10** not far from, very nearly **14** except everyone, within an inch of **16** everything except

all by oneself 5 alone **7** unaided **9** on one's own **10** unassisted **13** unaccompanied

all-consuming 3 hot **5** fiery **6** ardent, fervid, raging, red-hot **7** burning, fanatic, fervent, frantic, glowing, intense, zealous **8** frenzied **10** passionate **11** impassioned

allegation 5 claim **6** avowal, charge **9** assertion, statement **10** accusation, contention, indictment, profession **11** declaration

allege 3 say **4** aver, avow **5** claim, state **6** accuse, affirm, assert, charge, impugn, impute **7** contend, declare, profess **8** maintain

allegiance 6 fealty, homage **7** loyalty **8** devotion, fidelity **9** adherence, constancy, deference, obedience **12** faithfulness

allegory 5 fable **7** parable

allegro

music: 4 fast

all-embracing 5 broad **6** all-out **7** general, overall **8** complete, sweeping, thorough **9** expansive, extensive, universal, unlimited **10** exhaustive, widespread **11** far-reaching, wide-ranging **12** all-inclusive, encyclopedic **13** comprehensive

Allen, Arabella

character in: 14 Pickwick Papers

author: 7 Dickens

Allen, Ethan

served in: 16 Revolutionary War

commander of: 17 Green Mountain Boys

captured: 15 Fort Ticonderoga

state: 7 Vermont

Allen, Fred

real name: 20 John Florence Sullivan

born: 11 Cambridge MA

roles: 11 What's My Line **16** The Fred Allen Show

Allen, Steve

real name: 12 Stephen Allen

wife: 12 Jayne Meadows

nickname: 10 Mr Midnight

born: 9 New York NY

roles: 13 I've Got a Secret **14** The Tonight Show

Allen, William Hervey

author of: 7 Israfel **14** Anthony Adverse

Allen, Woody

author of: 11 Getting Even, Side Effects **15** Without Feathers

real name: 22 Allen Stewart Konigsberg

wife: 12 Louise Lasser, Soon-Yi Previn

born: 10 Brooklyn NY

films: 5 Alice, Zelig **7** Bananas, Sleeper **9** Annie Hall, Interiors, Manhattan, Radio Days **12** Casino Royale, Love and Death **14** New York Stories **15** Mighty Aphrodite, Scenes from a Mall **16** Husbands and Wives, Stardust Memories **17** Broadway Danny Rose **19** Bullets over Broadway, Hannah and Her Sisters **20** The Purple Rose of Cairo **21** Crimes and Misdemeanors **22** Manhattan Murder Mystery

alleviate 4 dull, ease, quit **5** abate, allay, blunt, check, slake **6** lessen, quench, reduce, soften, subdue, temper **7** assuage, lighten, mollify, relieve, slacken **8** diminish, mitigate, moderate

alleviation 6 easing, relief **9** lessening **10** palliation

alley 4 lane **5** byway **7** passage, pathway **10** passageway **16** narrow back street

Alley Oop
   creator: 14 Vincent T Hamlin
   character:
      girlfriend: 5 Ooola
      dinosaur: 5 Dinny
      king: 6 Guzzle
      scientist: 8 Dr Wonmug
   place:
      kingdom of: 3 Moo

All for Love
   author: 10 John Dryden
   character: 6 Antony, Caesar **7** Octavia **9** Cleopatra, Dolabella, Ventidius

All God's Chillun Got Wings
   author: 12 Eugene O'Neill
   character: 6 Mickey **9** Jim Harris **10** Ella Downey

alliance 4 pact **5** union **6** league, treaty **7** compact, company **9** agreement, coalition, concordat **10** federation **11** affiliation, association, confederacy, partnership **13** confederation **15** entente cordiale

allied 4 akin, like **5** alike, joint **6** united **7** cognate, kindred, related, similar **8** combined **9** corporate, federated **10** affiliated, associated, resembling **11** amalgamated **12** incorporated

all in 4 beat **5** spent, tired, weary **6** bushed, done in, pooped **7** drained, wearied, worn out **8** dog tired, fatigued, tired out **9** bone weary, dead tired, exhausted, played out

all in all 5 in sum **10** on the whole **20** when all is said and done

all-inclusive 5 broad **6** all-out, entire **7** general, overall **8** absolute, com-

plete, sweeping, thorough **9** expansive, extensive, universal, unlimited **10** altogether, exhaustive, widespread **11** far-reaching, wide-ranging **12** all-embracing **13** comprehensive

All in the Family
   character: 10 Joey Stivic, Mike Stivic (Meathead) **11** Edith Bunker (Dingbat) **12** Archie Bunker **18** Gloria Bunker Stivic
   cast: 9 Rob Reiner **13** Jean Stapleton **14** Carroll O'Connor, Sally Struthers
   spinoffs: 5 Maude **12** Archie's Place **13** The Jeffersons

allocate 5 allot, allow **6** assign, budget **7** earmark **8** set aside **9** apportion, designate **11** appropriate

allocation 5 quota, share **7** measure, portion **8** division **9** allotment, meting out **10** dealing out **11** consignment, designation **12** apportioning, dispensation, distribution **13** apportionment

allot 4 dole, mete **5** allow, grant **6** assign **7** appoint, consign, dole out, earmark, give out, mete out, provide **8** allocate, dispense, divide up **9** apportion, parcel out **10** distribute, portion out

allotment 5 grant, quota, share **6** ration **7** measure, portion **9** allowance **10** allocation **11** consignment **12** dispensation **13** apportionment, appropriation

all-out 5 broad, total **7** full-out, maximum **8** complete, sweeping, thorough **9** extensive, full-scale **11** unqualified, unremitting **12** all-embracing, all-inclusive **13** comprehensive, thoroughgoing

all over 4 done **5** ended, kaput **8** finished **9** concluded **10** everywhere **11** universally

All Over
   author: 11 Edward Albee

allow 3 let **4** give **5** allot, grant **6** assign, permit **7** agree to, approve, concede, provide **8** allocate, sanction **9** authorize

allowable 7 allowed **8** accepted **9** permitted, tolerable, tolerated **10** acceptable, admissible, admittable, authorized, sanctioned **11** permissible

allowance 5 grant **6** bounty, income, ration **7** annuity, payment, pension, stipend, subsidy **8** discount **9** allotment, deduction, reduction **10** concession **11** subtraction

allow to go 4 free **5** let go **6** excuse, parole **7** dismiss, release, set free **8** liberate **9** discharge

allow to pass
   French: 13 laissez passer

alloy 3 mix **5** admix, blend **6** commix, dilute, fusion, impair **7** amalgam, combine, mixture **8** compound, intermix **9** admixture, composite, synthesis

10 adulterate, commixture, interblend **12** conglomerate

alloyed 5 mixed **6** impure **7** debased

All Quiet on the Western Front
   author: 18 Erich Maria Remarque
   character: 6 Muller, Tjaden **10** Paul Baumer **11** Albert Kropp, Haie Westhus **20** Stanislaus Katczinsky (Kat)
   director: 14 Lewis Milestone
   cast: 8 Lew Ayres **12** Louis Wolheim **14** Russell Gleason
   setting: 3 WWI
   Oscar for: 7 picture

all right 2 OK **3** yes **4** fair, hale, safe, sure, well **6** hearty **7** healthy **8** properly, unharmed **9** certainly, correctly, uninjured **10** absolutely, acceptably, unimpaired **14** satisfactorily
   Spanish: 5 bueno

All Said and Done
   author: 16 Simone de Beauvoir

allspice
   botanical name: 7 pimenta, p dioica **12** p officinalis
   also called: 7 pimento
   origin: 7 Jamaica **16** Caribbean Islands
   flavor: 5 clove **6** nutmeg **8** cinnamon
   use: 6 baking

Allston, Washington
   born: 10 Waccamaw SC
   artwork: 9 The Deluge **13** Uriel in the Sun **16** Belshazzar's Feast, Moonlit Landscape **20** Spanish Girl in Reverie

All's Well That Ends Well
   author: 18 William Shakespeare
   character: 5 Diana **6** Helena **7** Bertram **8** Parolles **12** King of France **14** Duke of Florence **19** Countess of Rousillon

All That Jazz
   director: 8 Bob Fosse
   cast: 9 Ben Vereen **11** Ann Reinking, Cliff Gorman, Roy Scheider **12** Jessica Lange, Leland Palmer

All the King's Men
   author: 16 Robert Penn Warren
   character: 10 Jack Burden, Judge Irwin, Sadie Burke **11** Adam Stanton, Willie Stark **12** Annie Stanton
   director: 12 Robert Rossen
   cast: 9 Joanne Dru, John Derek **11** John Ireland **17** Broderick Crawford **19** Mercedes McCambridge
   Oscar for: 5 actor (Crawford) **7** picture **17** supporting actress (McCambridge)

all the more
   Latin: 9 a fortiori

All the President's Men
   author: 11 Bob Woodward **13** Carl Bernstein
   subject: 16 Watergate scandal
   newspaper: 14 Washington Post
   director: 11 Alan J Pakula

cast: 10 Jack Warden **11** Hal Holbrook **12** Jason Robards, Martin Balsam **13** Dustin Hoffman (Carl Bernstein), Jane Alexander, Robert Redford (Bob Woodward)
Oscar for: 12 screenwriter **15** supporting actor (Robards)

all the same 5 alike **7** however, uniform **8** unvaried **9** identical **11** homogeneous

all together 7 en masse, in a body **8** as a group, in a group, in unison
French: 12 tout ensemble

all told 5 in sum, total **6** in toto **7** totally **8** as a whole **10** altogether

allude 4 hint **5** refer **7** mention, speak of, suggest **8** intimate **9** touch upon

allure 4 bait, lure **5** charm, tempt **6** entice, lead on, seduce **7** attract, beguile, enchant, glamour **8** intrigue **9** captivate, fascinate **10** attraction, enticement, temptation **11** enchantment, fascination

allurement 4 draw, lure **5** charm **9** magnetism **10** attraction **11** fascination

alluring 4 sexy **8** charming, enticing, magnetic **10** attractive **11** fascinating

allusion 4 hint **7** mention **9** reference **10** suggestion

Allworthy, Squire
character in: 8 Tom Jones
author: 8 Fielding

ally 5 unite **6** league **7** combine, partner **8** confrere **9** accessory, affiliate, associate, colleague **10** accomplice, join forces **11** confederate **12** band together, bind together, collaborator, join together

Ally McBeal
creator/writer: 11 David E Kelly
actor (role): 16 Calista Flockhart (10 Ally McBeal) **19** Courtney Thorne-Smith (7 Georgia) **11** Greg Germann (11 Richard Fish) **16** Lisa Nicole Carson (11 Renee Radick) **13** Jane Krakowski (12 Elaine Vassal) Peter MacNicol (8 John Cage) **10** Gil Bellows (15 Billy Alan Thomas)
music: 13 Vonda Sheppard
setting: 6 Boston

Allyson, June
real name: 11 Ella Geisman
husband: 10 Dick Powell
born: 9 New York NY
roles: 8 Good News **9** Interlude, The Shrike **11** Little Women **12** My Man Godfrey **16** The Stratton Story **19** The Glenn Miller Story

Almagest
author: 7 Ptolemy
title means: 11 the greatest
subject: 9 astronomy

Al Maghrib see **7** Morocco
almandite

species: 6 garnet
color: 3 red

Almaviva, Count and Countess
author: 12 Beaumarchais
characters in: 18 The Barber of Seville **19** The Marriage of Figaro

Almayer's Folly
author: 12 Joseph Conrad

almighty 7 supreme **8** absolute, infinite **9** sovereign, unlimited **10** invincible, omnipotent **11** all-powerful **12** transcendent

Almira
opera by: 6 Handel

almond 12 Prunus dulcis
varieties: 4 Wild **5** Earth, Green, Sweet **6** Bitter, Desert, Indian **8** Tropical **9** Flowering **12** Dwarf Russian
candy: 8 marzipan
liqueur: 6 orgeat **7** ratafia

almost 5 about **6** all but, nearly **7** close to **8** not quite, well-nigh **9** just about **10** not far from, very nearly **11** practically, on the verge of **13** approximately **14** within an inch of

almost alike 5 close **7** similar **10** resembling **11** approaching, much the same **15** nearly identical

alms 3 aid **4** dole, gift **5** mercy **6** relief **7** charity, handout, largess, present, subsidy, tribute **8** donation, gratuity, offering, pittance **9** baksheesh **10** assistance **11** benefaction, beneficence **12** contribution

almshouse 6 asylum **9** poorhouse, workhouse

almsman 5 tramp **6** beggar **9** mendicant **10** panhandler

Almug 13 red sandalwood

aloe 4 balm **9** succulent
full name: 8 aloe vera
in: 6 lotion **7** shampoo

aloft 2 up **5** above, way up **6** high up, on high **7** skyward **8** in the air, in the sky, overhead **10** heavenward

Aloha State
nickname of: 6 Hawaii

alone 4 only, sole **6** lonely, single, singly, solely, unique **7** forlorn, unaided **8** deserted, desolate, forsaken, isolated, lonesome, peerless, singular, solitary, uniquely **9** abandoned, matchless, nonpareil, separated, unmatched, unrivaled **10** friendless, separately, singularly, solitarily, unassisted, unattended, unequalled, unescorted **11** unsurpassed, without help **12** incomparable, unchaperoned, unparalleled, without peers **13** unaccompanied, without others **14** single-handedly
Latin: 4 sola **5** solus
French: 4 seul

along 2 on **4** over **6** beside, during, onward **7** abreast, forward, through

alongside 2 at, by **6** beside, next to **7** abreast, close by **9** at the side **10** parallel to **12** collaterally, parallelwise **13** equidistantly

aloof 3 icy **4** cold, cool **5** above, apart **6** chilly, formal, remote **7** distant, haughty, high-hat **8** detached, reserved **10** unsociable **11** at a distance, indifferent, standoffish, unconcerned **12** uninterested, unresponsive **13** unsympathetic **14** unapproachable

aloofness 7 reserve **8** coldness, coolness **9** formality **10** detachment, remoteness **11** haughtiness **12** indifference **13** unsociability **15** standoffishness

aloud 7 audibly

alphabet 4 ABCs **6** schema **7** grammar, letters **8** elements **9** rudiments, tablature **10** characters, principles **13** writing system

Alphesiboea
also: 7 Arsinoe
form: 5 nymph
father: 4 Bias **7** Phegeus **9** Leucippus
mother: 9 Philodice
husband: 8 Alcmaeon
son: 6 Adonis
rejected: 8 Dionysus
nurse for: 7 Orestes

Alpheus
father: 7 Oceanus
mother: 6 Tethys
loved: 8 Arethusa
changed into: 5 river

Alphonse and Gaston
creator: 14 Frederick Opper
saying: 22 After you my dear Alphonse, No after you my dear Gaston

alpine 5 alpen, lofty **6** aerial **8** elevated, snow-clad, towering **9** subalpine **10** alpestrine, sky-kissing, snow-capped **11** cloud capped, mountainous **13** cloud-piercing, cloud-touching **14** heaven-touching

Alps, Alpine
country: 5 Italy **6** France **7** Austria, Germany **10** Yugoslavia **11** Switzerland **13** Liechtenstein
range: 6 Carnic, Graian, Julian, Otztal **7** Bernese, Cottian, Pennine **8** Bavarian, Ligurian, Maritime, Rhaetian **9** Dolomites, Lepontine **10** Hohe Tauern
peak: 4 Rosa **5** Eiger, Monch **8** Jungfrau **10** Karawanken, Matterhorn, Piz Bernina **13** Grossglockner
highest point: 5 Blanc
pass: 7 Brenner, Simplon, Splugen, Stelvio **9** Semmering **10** St Gotthard **14** Great St Bernard
lake: 4 Como **6** Alpine, Geneva **7** Lucerne **8** Maggiore **9** Constance
phenomenon: 4 echo
resort: 7 Zermatt **8** Chamonix, Salzburg, St Moritz **9** Innsbruck **13**

Berchtesgaden

singing: 5 yodel
wind: 5 foehn

already 5 early, so far **6** before **8** formerly, hitherto, until now **10** heretofore, previously

already seen
French: 6 deja vu

also 3 and, too **4** more, plus **5** extra **6** as well **7** besides **8** moreover **9** including **10** in addition **12** additionally

Altaic
language branches: 6 Turkic **8** Tungusic **9** Mongolian

altar 5 bomos **6** hestia, scribis **7** eschara **8** credence **9** holy table, prothesis **10** Lord's table

Altar
constellation of: 3 Ara

Altdorfer, Albrecht
born: 7 Germany **10** Regensburg
artwork: 16 Susanna at the Bath **20** St George and the Dragon, Susannah and the Elders **24** Landscape with a Footbridge **39** The Battle of Alexander and Darius on the Issus

alter 4 vary **5** amend **6** change, modify, recast, revise **7** convert, remodel **9** transform **13** make different

alterable 7 unfixed **8** variable **9** adaptable **10** adjustable, changeable, modifiable **11** convertible

alteration 6 change **10** adjustment, conversion, remodeling **12** modification **13** transmutation **14** transformation

altercation 3 row **4** spat, tiff **5** brawl, broil, fight, melee, scene **6** affray, fracas, rumpus, scrape **7** discord, dispute, quarrel, scuffle **8** argument **9** bickering, wrangling **10** falling-out **11** controversy **12** disagreement

alter ego 4 twin **5** match **6** double **9** duplicate, other self, semblable **10** complement, other image, second self, simulacrum **11** counterpart **12** Doppelganger

alternate 3 sub **4** vary **5** alter, proxy **6** backup, change, deputy, rotate, second **7** another, standby, stand-in **9** surrogate, take turns **10** every other, reciprocal, substitute, successive, understudy **11** alternating, consecutive, every second, interchange, intersperse, pinch hitter

alternative 6 choice, option, way out **8** recourse **9** selection **10** substitute **11** other choice

although 3 but, yet **4** even **5** still **7** however **11** nonetheless **12** nevertheless **15** notwithstanding

altitude 4 apex **6** height, vertex, zenith **8** eminence, tallness **9** elevation, loftiness, sublimity **10** prominence

Altman, Robert
director of: 4 Aria, MASH **6** Popeye

8 A Wedding **9** Short Cuts, The Player, Streamers, Nashville **10** Kansas City **11** Ready to Wear **14** The Long Goodbye **17** The James Dean Story

altogether 5 fully, in all, in sum, quite **6** in toto, wholly **7** all told, totally, utterly **8** all in all, as a whole, entirely **9** in general, out and out, perfectly **10** absolutely, completely, in sum total, on the whole, thoroughly **12** all inclusive, collectively

altruism 7 charity **10** generosity **11** benevolence **12** philanthropy, public spirit **13** unselfishness **14** bigheartedness, charitableness **15** humanitarianism

altruistic 8 generous **9** unselfish **10** benevolent, charitable **12** humanitarian, largehearted **13** philanthropic **14** public-spirited

aluminum
chemical symbol: 2 Al

alumni 5 grads

alumnus, alumna 4 grad **8** graduate **13** former student

Alverio, Rosita Dolores
real name of: 10 Rita Moreno

always 7 forever **8** evermore **9** eternally, every time, regularly **10** for all time, invariably **11** continually, incessantly, perpetually, unceasingly **12** consistently **13** everlastingly, unremittingly **14** forever and ever

Amadan
origin: 5 Irish
form: 5 fairy

Amadeus
director: 11 Milos Forman
cast: 8 Tom Hulce (Wolfgang Amadeus Mozart) **14** F Murray Abraham (Antonio Salieri)
choreography: 10 Twyla Tharp
Oscar for: 5 actor (Abraham) **7** picture **8** director

Amadis of Gaul
author: 16 Garcia de Montalvo
character: 6 Oriana, Perion **7** Elisena **8** Garinter, Lisuarte

Amado, Jorge
author of: 14 Tent of Miracles **15** Home Is the Sailor **19** Shepherds of the Night **24** Gabriela Clove and Cinnamon **25** Dona Flor and Her Two Husbands **30** The Two Deaths of Quincas Wateryell

Amahl and the Night Visitors
opera by: 7 Menotti

Amalek
father: 7 Eliphaz
mother: 6 Timnah
grandfather: 4 Esau
descendant of: 9 Amalekite

amalgam 5 alloy, blend, combo, union **6** fusion, league, merger **7** joining, mixture **8** alliance, compound, mish-

mash **9** admixture, composite **10** assemblage, commixture **11** combination **12** amalgamation, intermixture

amalgamate 3 mix **4** fuse **5** blend, merge, unify, unite **7** combine **8** coalesce, federate **9** commingle, integrate **10** synthesize **11** consolidate, incorporate **12** join together

Amarcord
director: 15 Federico Fellini
cast: 10 Bruno Zanin, Magali Noel **13** Pupella Maggio

amaretto
type: 7 liqueur
origin: 5 Italy
flavor: 6 almond
with vodka: 9 Godmother

Amaryllis
character in: 9 Ecologues
author: 6 Virgil
represented: 11 shepherdess

amass 6 gather, heap up, pile up **7** acquire, collect, compile, round up **8** assemble **10** accumulate

amateur 4 tyro **6** novice, non-pro **7** dabbler **8** beginner, hobbyist, inexpert, neophyte **9** greenhorn, unskilled **10** dilettante, unpolished **13** inexperienced **14** unprofessional **15** nonprofessional

amateurish 5 inept **6** clumsy **7** awkward **8** inexpert, mediocre **9** unskilled, untrained **10** unskillful **11** incompetent, ineffective, unpracticed **13** inexperienced **14** unaccomplished, unprofessional

amatory 3 hot **4** fond, sexy **6** ardent, doting, erotic, loving, sexual, steamy, tender **7** adoring, amorous, devoted, fervent, sensual, sexed-up **8** lovesick, romantic, yearning **9** libidinal, loverlike, rapturous **10** infatuated, lascivious, passionate **11** impassioned, languishing

amaxophobia
fear of: 7 driving **8** vehicles

amaze 3 awe **4** daze, stun **5** shock **7** astound, stagger, stupefy **8** astonish, surprise **9** dumbfound **11** flabbergast

amazement 3 awe **5** shock **6** wonder **8** surprise **9** disbelief **11** incredulity **12** astonishment, bewilderment, stupefaction

Amazon
occupation: 7 warrior
sex: 6 female
queen: 9 Hippolyta
river: 6 Brazil

amazonite
species: 8 feldspar

Amazonomachia
battle between: 6 Greeks **7** Amazons

ambassador 5 agent, envoy **6** consul, deputy, legate, nuncio **7** attache, courier **8** diplomat, emissary, minister **9** go-between **11** diplomatist **12** intermediary **13** consul general **14** representative

Ambassadors, The
author: **10** Henry James
character: **8** Strether, Waymarsh **10** Mrs Newsome **11** Mamie Pocock, Sarah Pocock **12** Maria Gostrey **15** Chadwick Newsome **17** Comtesse de Vionnet

amber
formed from: **5** resin
color: **6** yellow
Greek: **8** elektron

ambiance 3 air **4** aura, mood, tone **5** tenor **6** spirit, flavor, milieu, temper **7** climate, setting **9** character **10** atmosphere **11** environment **12** surroundings

ambiguity 9 vagueness **11** uncertainty **12** abstruseness, doubtfulness, equivocation **14** indefiniteness
French: **13** double entente

ambiguous 5 vague **7** cryptic, unclear **8** doubtful, puzzling **9** enigmatic, equivocal, uncertain **10** indefinite, misleading

ambition 3 aim **4** goal, hope, plan, push, zeal **5** dream, drive **6** design, desire, intent **7** longing, purpose **8** striving, yearning **9** objective **10** aspiration

ambitious 4 avid **5** eager **6** ardent, intent **7** arduous, zealous **8** aspiring, desirous **9** difficult, energetic, grandiose, strenuous **10** determined **11** industrious **12** enterprising

ambivalent 5 mixed **7** warring **8** clashing, confused, opposing, wavering **9** equivocal, undecided, unfocused **10** wishy-washy **11** conflicting, fluctuating, vacillating **13** contradictory

amble 6 ramble, stroll **7** meander, saunter **15** wander aimlessly

Ambler, Eric
author of: **11** The Levanter **12** A Kind of Auger **13** The Care of Time **14** The Night-Comers, Uncommon Danger **15** Journey Into Fear, The Dark Frontier **16** The Light of the Day **19** A Coffin for Dimitrios **22** The Siege of the Villa Lipp

Ambling Alp, The
nickname of: **12** Primo Carnera

ambrosial 5 balmy **8** fragrant, luscious, perfumed **9** delicious **13** sweet-smelling

ambrosia of the gods 4 food **5** drink **6** nectar **7** perfume

ambulance chaser 4 beak **6** lawyer **8** attorney **9** counselor **10** mouthpiece **12** legal advisor

ambulatory 6 mobile, moving **7** walking **10** up and about **11** peripatetic

ambush 4 trap **5** blind, cover **6** attack, entrap, hiding, lay for, waylay **7** assault **8** hideaway, surprise **9** ambus-

cade **11** concealment, hiding place **13** stalking-horse

Ameche, Don
real name: **17** Dominic Felix Amici
born: **9** Kenosha WI
roles: **4** Pais **5** Folks (Oscar) **6** Cocoon (Oscar) **12** Things Change **13** Heaven Can Wait, Moon Over Miami, Silk Stockings, Trading Places **14** That Night in Rio **16** Down Argentine Way **18** The Three Musketeers **21** Harry and the Hendersons **29** The Story of Alexander Graham Bell

Amelia
author: **13** Henry Fielding
character: **10** Dr Harrison **11** Mrs Atkinson **12** Miss Matthews **19** Captain William Booth

ameliorate 4 heal, help, mend **5** amend, fix up **6** better, perk up, pick up, reform, remedy, revise **7** advance, correct, improve, patch up, promote, rectify **8** palliate, progress **9** come along, get better **10** grow better **11** improve upon

ameliorative 8 remedial **9** improving **10** corrective, palliative **11** therapeutic **12** compensatory

amen 5 truly **6** it is so, so be it, verily **8** hear hear **9** let it be so, yes indeed **11** so shall it be **17** would that it were so

Amen
also: **4** Amon **5** Ammon
origin: **8** Egyptian
king of: **4** gods
worshiped at: **6** Thebes
personifies: **3** air **6** breath
represented by: **3** ram **5** goose
patron of: **6** Thebes
corresponds to: **4** Jove, Zeus **6** Amen Ra, Amon Ra **7** Jupiter

amenable 4 open **7** cordial, willing **8** obliging, yielding **9** agreeable, tractable **10** open-minded, responsive, submissive **11** acquiescent, complaisant, cooperative, persuadable, sympathetic **17** favorably disposed

amend 3 fix **4** mend **5** alter, emend **6** better, change, modify, polish, reform, remedy, revise **7** correct, develop, enhance, improve, perfect, rectify

amendment 6 change, reform **7** adjunct **8** addition, revision **10** alteration, correction, emendation **11** improvement **12** modification **13** rectification

amends 7 apology, defense, payment, redress **8** requital **9** atonement, expiation **10** recompense, reparation **11** explanation, restitution, restoration, retribution, vindication **12** compensation, satisfaction **13** justification, peace offering **14** acknowledgment **15** indemnification

amenity, amenities 8 civility, mild-

ness, niceties **9** geniality, gentility **10** affability, amiability, courtesies, gentleness, politeness, refinement **11** gallantries, good manners **12** friendliness, graciousness, pleasantness **13** agreeableness

Amen Ra
also: **6** Amon Ra, Amen Re
origin: **8** Egyptian
god of: **8** universe
corresponds to: **4** Amen, Amon, Jove, Zeus **5** Ammon **7** Jupiter

America
author: **19** Stephen Vincent Benet

America, North
country: **4** Cuba **5** Haiti **6** Belize, Canada, Mexico, Panama **8** Honduras **9** Costa Rica, Guatemala, Nicaragua **10** El Salvador **12** United States **17** Dominican Republic
island: **5** Banks **6** Baffin, Kodiak **7** Bahamas, Bermuda **8** Victoria **9** Alexander, Anticosti, Ellesmere, Greenland, Vancouver **10** Aleutians, Cape Breton, Long Island, West Indies **11** Southampton **12** Newfoundland, Prince Edward **13** Prince of Wales **14** Queen Charlotte
mountain: **5** Coast, Rocky **6** Brooks **7** Cascade **9** Mackenzie **10** Bitterroot **11** Appalachian **12** Sierra Nevada
highest point: **8** McKinley
lowest point: **11** Death Valley
river: **3** Red **4** Ohio **5** Yukon **6** Copper, Fraser, Hudson, Nelson **8** Arkansas, Colorado, Columbia, Delaware, Missouri **9** Mackenzie **10** Coppermine, Sacramento, San Joaquin, St Lawrence **11** Connecticut, Mississippi
lake: **4** Erie **5** Huron **6** Carson, Walker **7** Nipigon, Ontario **8** Manitoba, Michigan, Reindeer, Superior, Winnipeg **9** Athabasca, Champlain, Great Bear, Great Salt **10** Great Slave **11** Yellowstone
animal: **3** bat, rat **4** bear, lynx, puma, wolf **5** bison, moose, skunk **6** beaver, musk ox **7** bighorn, caribou **8** sewellel **9** pronghorn, white goat
bird: **4** hawk **5** eagle, snipe **8** bobwhite, woodcock, wood ibis **9** blue heron, ptarmigan
sea: **6** Bering **7** Chukchi, Lincoln **8** Beaufort **9** Caribbean
religion: **7** Judaism **10** Protestant **13** Roman Catholic **27** Eastern Orthodox Christianity
people: **6** Eskimo **8** European **12** African Negro **14** American Indian
language: **6** French **7** English, Spanish

America, South
country: **4** Peru **5** Chile **6** Brazil, Guyana **7** Bolivia, Ecuador, Uruguay **8** Colombia, Paraguay, Suriname **9** Argentina, Venezuela
city: **4** Lima **5** Quito **6** Bogota, Recife

7 Caracas **8** Salvador, Santiago, Sao Paulo **10** Montevideo **11** Buenos Aires, Porto Alegre **12** Rio de Janeiro **13** Belo Horizonte

island: 6 Chiloe, Chonos, Marajo **9** Galapagos **10** Wellington **11** Madre de Dios **13** Juan Fernandez, Reina Adelaida **14** Tierra del Fuego

sea: 9 Caribbean

lake: 5 Patos, Poopo, Mirim **6** Viedma **8** Titicaca **9** Maracaibo, San Martin **10** Concepcion

mountain: 6 Andes **9** Pakaraima **12** Monte Fitz Roy **14** Cerro Aconcagua, Monte Sarmiento **15** Serra dos Parecis **16** Monte San Valentin, Serra do Espinhaco

highest point: 9 Aconcagua

lowest point: 15 Peninsula Valdes

river: 3 Ica **4** Beni, Iaco, Jari, Meta, Napo **5** Abuna, Cauca, Chico, Iriri, Ituxi, Jurua, Jutai, Negro, Palma, Pardo, Purus, Tiete, Tigre, Xingu **6** Amazon, Arauca, Branco, Chubut, Cumina, Curaco, Cuyuni, Grande, Gurupi, Iguacu, Japura, Javari, Mamore, Maroni, Mortes, Parana, Salado, Vaupes **7** Bermejo, Caqueta, Deseado, Guapore, Jamunda, Juruena, Madeira, Mapuera, Maranon, Orinoco, Oyapock, Ucayali, Vichada **8** Amazonas, Araguaia, Colorado, Guaviare, Jamachim, Paraguay, Parnaiba, Putumayo, Tapajoz, Urubamba, Uruguay **9** Essequibo, Jaguaribe, Paranaiba, Saladillo, Sao Manuel, Tocantins **10** Courantyne **12** Sao Francisco

animal: 3 bat **4** bear, deer **5** llama, sloth, tapir **6** alpaca, monkey, ocelot, weasel **7** opossum, peccary, raccoon **8** capybara, javelina **9** armadillo

bird: 3 owl **4** hawk, rhea **5** eagle **6** condor, falcon, jabiru **7** hoatzin **8** flamingo **11** hummingbird

people: 6 Indian **7** African, Chibcha, Mestizo, Mulatto, Spanish **10** Araucanian, Portuguese

religion: 7 Judaism **10** Protestant **13** Roman Catholic

language: 5 Dutch **7** English, Spanish **10** Portuguese

American, The
　author: 10 Henry James
　character: 8 Mrs Bread **10** Mr Tristram **11** Mrs Tristram **12** Noemie Nioche **13** Count Valentin **14** Claire de Cintre **17** Christopher Newman **25** Marquis Urbain de Bellegarde
　setting: 5 Paris

American Caesar
　author: 17 William Manchester

American Claimant, The
　author: 9 Mark Twain

American Dreams
　author: 11 Studs Terkel

American Graffiti
　director: 11 George Lucas

cast: 9 Paul Le Mat, Ron Howard **10** Candy Clark **11** Wolfman Jack **12** Harrison Ford **13** Cindy Williams **15** Richard Dreyfuss **17** MacKenzie Phillips

American Indian *see under* **14** Native American

American in Paris, An
　director: 16 Vincente Minnelli
　cast: 8 Nina Foch **9** Gene Kelly **11** Leslie Caron, Oscar Levant **14** Georges Guetary
　score: 14 George Gershwin
　Oscar for: 7 picture

Americanization of Emily
　director: 12 Arthur Hiller
　script by: 14 Paddy Chayefsky
　cast: 11 James Coburn, James Garner **12** Julie Andrews **13** Melvyn Douglas

American Tragedy, An
　author: 15 Theodore Dreiser
　character: 12 Roberta Alden **14** Clyde Griffiths, Sondra Finchley **15** Samuel Griffiths
　movie: 14 A Place in the Sun

America's Sweetheart
　nickname of: 12 Mary Pickford

amethyst
　species: 6 quartz
　color: 6 purple
　month: 8 February

Amfortas
　leader of: 7 knights
　in search of: 9 holy grail

ami, amie 6 friend

amiability 10 good nature, kindliness **12** agreeability, friendliness, pleasantness

amiable 6 genial, kindly, polite **7** affable, cordial, winning **8** amicable, charming, engaging, friendly, gracious, obliging, pleasant, pleasing, sociable **9** agreeable, congenial **10** attractive **11** good-natured

amicability 5 amity **7** concord **8** good will **9** affection **10** cordiality, friendship **12** friendliness **14** neighborliness

amicable 4 kind **5** civil **6** kindly, polite **7** amiable, cordial **8** amenable, friendly, sociable **9** agreeable, courteous, peaceable **10** benevolent, harmonious, neighborly **11** kindhearted

Amici, Dominic Felix
　real name of: 9 Don Ameche

amicus curiae 17 a friend of the court

amigo, amiga 6 friend

Amis, Kingsley
　author of: 8 Ending Up, Lucky Jim **10** Colonel Sun, Jake's Thing **11** I Like It Here, The Green Man **16** One Fat Englishman, Take A Girl Like You **18** Russian Hide-and-Seek, The Anti-Death League **20** That Uncertain Feeling
　father of: 10 Martin Amis

amiss 4 awry **5** askew, false, wrong **6**

astray, faulty **7** falsely, mixed-up, off base, wrongly **8** faultily, improper, mistaken, untoward **9** erroneous, incorrect, out of line **10** fallacious, improperly, mistakenly, out of order, unsuitable, unsuitably, untowardly **11** erroneously, incorrectly **12** inaccurately **13** inappropriate **15** inappropriately

Amittai
　son: 5 Jonah

amity 6 accord **7** concord, harmony **8** good will, sympathy **9** agreement **10** cordiality, fellowship, fraternity, friendship **11** brotherhood, cooperation **13** understanding

Ammishaddai
　son: 7 Ahiezer

Ammon
　father: 3 Lot
　descendants: 9 Ammonites

Ammonite god 6 Molech, Moloch

ammunition 4 ammo, arms **5** shell **6** bullet, rocket **7** missile, torpedo **9** artillery, cartridge, small arms **11** iron rations **13** powder and shot

ammunition dump 7 arsenal **8** magazine **18** military storehouse, munitions warehouse

amnesia 4 daze **5** fugue **6** stupor **7** agnosia **8** blackout **9** memory gap **11** anterograde, trance state

amnesty 6 pardon **8** immunity, reprieve **10** absolution **11** forgiveness **14** reconciliation

amoeba, ameba 4 dyad, germ, mold **5** spore, virus **6** fungus **7** ciliate, microbe **8** bacteria, reovirus **9** bacterium, echovirus **13** microorganism
　part: 7 nucleus **8** membrane **9** pseudopod **10** protoplasm **11** food vacuole **18** contractile vacuole
　reproduction by: 7 fission

amok *see* **5** amuck

Amon *see* **4** Amen

among 2 at **3** mid **4** amid, with **6** amidst **7** amongst, between, betwixt **12** in the midst of

among other persons
　Latin: 10 inter alios

among others 8 attended, escorted, in a crowd, in a group, together **11** accompanied

among other things
　Latin: 9 inter alia

among themselves
　Latin: 7 inter se

Amon Ra *see* **6** Amen Ra

Amor *see* **5** Cupid

Amore dei Tre Re, L'
　opera by: 10 Montemezzi

Amoretti
　author: 13 Edmund Spenser

amoretto
　art figure: 5 Cupid

amorous 4 fond **6** ardent, doting, loving, tender **8** enamored, lovesick **10** passionate **11** impassioned **12** affectionate

amorousness 4 love **5** ardor **6** warmth **7** passion

amor patriae 10 patriotism **13** love of country

amorphous 5 vague **8** formless, unshapen **9** anomalous, shapeless, undefined **11** nondescript **12** undelineated **13** characterless, indeterminate

Amos
   father: **4** Naum

Amos 'n' Andy
   character: **8** Lightnin' **9** Amos Jones, Andy Brown **13** George (the King Fish) Stevens **15** Sapphire Stevens
   cast: **8** Tim Moore **13** Ernestine Wade, Horace Stewart **14** Alvin Childress **15** Spencer Williams

amount 3 sum **4** bulk, mass **5** total **6** extent, volume **7** measure **8** quantity, sum total **9** aggregate, magnitude

amour 6 affair **7** liaison, romance **8** intrigue **10** love affair

amour propre 8 self-love **10** self-esteem **11** self respect

Ampelos
   form: **5** satyr

Ampere, Andre-Marie
   field: **7** physics **11** mathematics
   nationality: **6** French
   founded: **15** electrodynamics **16** electromagnetism

amphibian 8 seaplane **10** hydroplane, vertebrate **14** aerohydroplane
   kind: **4** frog, newt, toad **9** caecilian **10** salamander
   young: **6** larvae **7** tadpole **8** polliwog

Amphisbaena
   form: **7** serpent
   number of heads: **3** two

amphitheater 4 bowl **5** arena **7** gallery, stadium **8** coliseum **10** auditorium
   Roman: **9** Colosseum

Amphitrite
   origin: **5** Greek
   goddess of: **3** sea
   father: **6** Nereus
   mother: **5** Doris
   husband: **8** Poseidon

Amphitruo (Amphitryon)
   author: **7** Plautus
   character: **4** Zeus **7** Alcmena, Jupiter, Mercury **10** Amphitryon

Amphitryon
   father: **7** Alcaeus
   grandfather: **7** Perseus
   uncle: **9** Electryon, Sthenelus
   wife: **7** Alcmene
   son: **8** Iphicles
   daughter: **8** Perimede

Amphitryon 38
   author: **13** Jean Giraudoux

amphora 3 jar, jug, urn **4** vase

ample 3 big **4** huge, vast, wide **5** broad, large, roomy **6** enough, plenty **7** copious, immense, liberal, profuse **8** abundant, adequate, extended, generous, spacious **9** bountiful, capacious, expansive, extensive, outspread, plentiful **10** commodious, sufficient, voluminous **11** substantial **12** satisfactory **14** more than enough

amplification 7 raising **8** increase, widening **9** expansion, extension **10** developing, filling out, increasing **11** added detail, development, elaboration, enlargement, expatiation, fleshing out, heightening, lengthening, rounding out **12** augmentation **13** magnification **14** aggrandizement **15** supplementation

amplify 5 add to, raise, widen **6** deepen, expand, extend **7** augment, broaden, develop, enlarge, fill out **8** complete, heighten, increase, lengthen **9** elaborate (on), expatiate, intensify **10** illustrate, strengthen, supplement

amplitude 4 bulk, mass, size **5** range, reach, scope, sweep, width **6** extent, volume **7** bigness, breadth, compass, expanse **8** fullness, plethora, richness, vastness **9** abundance, dimension, largeness, magnitude, plenitude, profusion **11** copiousness **12** completeness, spaciousness **13** capaciousness

amply 5 fully **6** richly **8** lavishly **9** copiously, liberally, profusely **10** abundantly, adequately, completely, generously, thoroughly **11** bountifully, plentifully **12** sufficiently, unstintingly **14** satisfactorily

amputate 5 sever **6** cut off, excise, lop off, remove **9** dismember

Amram
   father: **4** Bani **6** Dishon
   son: **5** Aaron, Moses
   daughter: **6** Miriam

Amsterdam
   airport: **8** Schiphol
   canal: **11** Herengracht **13** Keizersgracht, Prinsengracht
   capital of: **7** Holland **11** Netherlands
   landmark: **8** Oude Kerk **10** Nieuwe Kerk
   museum: **7** Van Gogh **9** Stedelijk **11** Rijksmuseum
   nickname: **16** Venice of the North
   waters: **6** Amstel **7** Ij River **9** Zuiderzee **10** Ijsselmeer **13** North Sea

amuck 4 amok, nuts **6** wildly **7** berserk, bonkers **8** crackers, insanely **9** in a frenzy **10** frenziedly, maniacally **11** ferociously, murderously **14** uncontrollably

amulet 5 charm **6** fetish **8** talisman **10** lucky piece

amuse 5 cheer **6** absorb, divert, oc-

cupy, please **7** beguile, engross, enliven, gladden **8** interest **9** entertain

amusement 3 fun **4** game, play **5** hobby, revel **7** delight, pastime **8** pleasure **9** avocation, diversion, enjoyment, merriment **10** recreation **11** distraction **13** entertainment

amusing 5 droll, funny, witty **7** comical, waggish **8** cheering, farcical, humorous, pleasant, pleasing **9** absorbing, beguiling, diverting **10** delightful, engrossing **11** interesting, pleasurable **12** entertaining

Amy, Gilbert
   composer of: **9** Alpha-Beth **10** Epigrammes, Mouvements **11** Antiphonies **12** Trajectories

anagram 4 code **6** cipher

Anakim 11 giant people

analects 8 extracts **9** gleanings **10** miscellany, selections **11** collectanea, miscellanea

Analects of Confucius, The
   author: **9** Confucius

analeptic 9 stimulant **11** restorative

analgesic 4 drug **6** opiate **7** anodyne **8** narcotic **10** anesthetic, painkiller

analogous 4 akin, like **7** similar **8** parallel **10** comparable, equivalent **11** correlative **13** corresponding

analogy 6 simile **8** likeness, metaphor **10** comparison, similarity, similitude **11** correlation, equivalence, parallelism, resemblance **14** correspondence

analysis 4 test **5** assay, brief, study **6** digest, precis, review, search **7** breakup, inquiry, outline, summary, therapy **8** abstract, judgment, synopsis, thinking **9** appraisal, breakdown, diagnosis, partition, reasoning, reduction **10** dissection, estimation, evaluation, resolution, separation **11** examination, observation, speculation **12** dissociation **13** investigation, psychotherapy **14** interpretation, psychoanalysis

analyst 5 judge **6** shrink, tester **8** examiner, observer **9** appraiser, estimator, evaluator **12** headshrinker, investigator **13** psychoanalyst

analytic, analytical 7 logical, testing **8** rational, studious **9** inquiring, organized, searching **10** diagnostic, systematic **14** problem-solving

analyze 5 assay, judge, study **6** search **7** examine **8** appraise, consider, diagnose, evaluate, question **9** reason out **11** investigate **12** think through

Ananais
   father: **8** Nebedeus
   wife: **8** Sapphira
   sent to: **4** Paul, Saul
   lied to: **5** Peter
   same as: **4** liar

anarchist 5 rebel **8** mutineer, nihilist **9**

insurgent, terrorist **11** syndicalist **13** revolutionary

anarchy 5 chaos **6** utopia **8** disorder **11** lawlessness **13** the millennium **19** absence of government

Anastasia
director: **13** Anatole Litvak
cast: **10** Helen Hayes, Yul Brynner **12** Akim Tamiroff **13** Ingrid Bergman (Oscar)

anathema 3 ban **5** curse, taboo **7** censure **11** abomination, malediction **12** condemnation, denunciation, proscription **13** unmentionable **15** excommunication

Anathema
author: **14** Leonid Andreyev

anathematize 4 damn **7** accurse, condemn **8** execrate, maledict **9** abominate **13** excommunicate **17** hold in abomination

Anatolia see **7** Armenia

Anatolian
language family: **12** Indo-European
includes: **6** Luwian Lycian Lydian **7** Hittite
spoken in: **9** Asia Minor
spoken by: **8** Hittites

anatomist 12 morphologist
American: **5** Allen, Evans **7** Herrick **8** Stockard
Arabian: **8** Avicenna
British: **4** Owen **5** Hooke **6** Harvey
Dutch: **10** Swammerdam
French: **6** Buffon, Cuvier
German: **5** Wolff **7** Schwann
Greek: **5** Galen **9** Aristotle **10** Herophilus **12** Erasistratus
Italian: **8** Malpighi
Scottish: **5** Brown

anatomize 7 analyze, dissect **18** separate into pieces

anatomy 4 body **8** analysis **9** structure **10** dissection **11** examination

Anatomy Lesson, The
author: **10** Philip Roth

Anatomy of a Murder
director: **13** Otto Preminger
cast: **8** Eve Arden **9** Lee Remick **10** Ben Gazzara **12** George C Scott, James Stewart, Kathryn Grant **14** Arthur O'Connell
score: **13** Duke Ellington

Anatomy of Melancholy, The
author: **12** Robert Burton

Anatosaurus
type: **8** dinosaur **10** ornithopod
period: **10** Cretaceous
characteristic: **10** duck-billed
location: **12** North America

Anaxibia
father: **6** Atreus
mother: **6** Aerope
brother: **8** Menelaus **9** Agamemnon
husband: **6** Nestor **9** Strophius
son: **7** Pylades

Anaximander
field: **11** mathematics
nationality: **5** Greek
doctrine: **11** single-world
first: **22** geometric universe model

ancestor 8 begetter, forebear **9** precursor, prototype **10** antecedent, forefather, forerunner, procreator, progenitor **11** predecessor

ancestry 4 line, race **5** house, stock **6** family, origin **7** descent, lineage **8** heredity, pedigree **9** ancestors, blood line, genealogy, parentage **10** derivation, extraction, family tree **11** progenitors

Anchisaurus
type: **8** dinosaur
location: **17** Connecticut Valley

Anchises
prince of: **4** Troy
father: **5** Capys
mother: **8** Themiste
grandfather: **9** Assaracus
uncle: **8** Laomedon
brother: **7** Laocoon
son: **5** Lyrus **6** Aeneas

anchor 3 fix **4** hook, moor **5** affix, basis **6** fasten, secure **7** bulwark, defense, mooring, support **8** mainstay, security **9** safeguard **10** foundation **12** ground tackle

anchorage 3 key **4** bund, dock, pier, port, quay, slip **5** berth, haven, jetty, wharf **6** harbor, marina **7** dockage, mooring, seaport **9** harborage, roadstead

ancient 3 old **4** aged **5** early, hoary, Greek, olden, passe, Roman **6** age-old, bygone, old hat, remote **7** antique, archaic, classic, very old **8** long past, obsolete, outmoded, primeval, timeworn **9** classical, out-of-date, primitive **10** antiquated, fossilized, Greco-Roman **11** obsolescent, prehistoric **12** old-fashioned, out-of-fashion

ancientness 8 great age **9** antiquity **11** advanced age

ancient times 9 antiquity **10** days of yore **12** the Golden Age

ancillary 5 minor **7** adjunct **8** inferior **9** accessory, auxiliary, dependent, secondary **10** additional, subsidiary **11** subordinate, subservient **12** contributory **13** supplementary

Ancius
form: **7** centaur

Ancus Marcius
king of: **4** Rome

and 3 too **4** also, more, plus **8** as well as **10** in addition **11** furthermore

andante
music: **4** even **14** moderately slow

Andean
language family: **16** Andean-Equatorial

group: **3** Ona **6** Aymara, Yahgan, Zaparo **7** Quechua **10** Araucanian

Andean-Equatorial
language branch: **6** Andean **10** Equatorial

and elsewhere 4 et al **7** et alibi

Andersen, Hans Christian
known for: **10** fairy tales
born: **7** Denmark
author of: **10** Thumbelina **11** The Red Shoes **12** The Snow Queen, The Swineherd, The Tinder Box **14** The Nightingale **15** The Ugly Duckling **16** The Little Mermaid **18** The Little Match Girl **20** The Princess and the Pea **21** The Emperor's New Clothes **22** The Steadfast Tin Soldier **25** The Shepherdess and the Sweep
played by: **9** Danny Kaye

Anderson, Frances Margaret
real name of: **14** Judith Anderson

Anderson, Judith
real name: **23** Frances Margaret Anderson
born: **8** Adelaide **9** Australia
roles: **5** Medea **6** Hamlet, Salome **7** Macbeth, Rebecca **8** Kings Row **16** Cat on a Hot Tin Roof

Anderson, Maxwell
author of: **7** High Tor **8** Key Largo **9** Winterset **11** Valley Forge **14** Both Your Houses, Lost in the Stars, Mary of Scotland, What Price Glory? **17** Elizabeth the Queen **20** Knickerbocker Holiday

Anderson, Sherwood
author of: **9** Poor White **12** Beyond Desire, Dark Laughter, Horses and Men **13** Many Marriages, Winesburg Ohio **15** Death in the Woods **18** The Triumph of the Egg

Anderson, Sparky (George Lee)
sport: **8** baseball
position: **7** manager
team: **9** Minnesota **14** Cincinnati Reds

Andersonville
author: **15** MacKinlay Kantor

Andersson, Bibi
born: **6** Sweden **9** Stockholm
roles: **14** The Seventh Seal **16** Wild Strawberries **19** Scenes from a Marriage **20** Smiles of a Summer Night

Andes
Spanish: **20** Cordillera de los Andes
peak: **6** Pissis, Sajama, Sorata **7** Illampu **8** Cotopaxi, Illimani **9** Huascaran **10** Chimborazo **14** Cristobal Colon
highest point: **9** Aconcagua
volcano: **6** Sangay, Tolima **8** Cotopaxi **10** Tungurahua
country: **4** Peru **5** Chile **6** Panama **7** Bolivia, Ecuador **8** Colombia **9** Argentina, Venezuela
river: **5** Cauca **6** Amazon, Parana **7** Orinoco, Ucayali **9** Magdalena

lake: 5 Poopo **8** Titicaca
animal: 5 llama **6** alpaca, condor, huemul **10** chinchilla

And I Worked at the Writer's Trade
author: 13 Malcolm Cowley

Andorra
other name: 13 Valls d'Andorra **16** Valleys of Andorra
capital/largest city: 14 Andorra-la-Vella
others: 3 Pal **5** Ramio **6** Ordino, Soldeu **7** Canillo, Certers **9** La Massana **11** Les Escaldes **16** San Julian de Loria
division: 6 Encamp, Ordino **7** Andorra, Camillo **9** La Massana, Sant Julia
heads of state: 13 Bishop of Urgel (Spain) **17** President of France
head of government: 11 First Syndic
monetary unit: 5 franc **6** peseta
lake: 11 Engolasters
location: 8 Pyrenees
mountain: 6 d'Etats **8** l'Estanyo, Pyrenees **10** Cataperdis
highest point: 11 Como Pedrosa
neighbors: 5 Spain **6** France
river: 6 Ariege, Valira
people: 7 Catalan **8** Andosian
language: 6 French **7** Catalan, Spanish
religion: 13 Roman Catholic
place: 12 Casa de la Vall
    Moorish ruin: **4** Ceca, Meka
feature:
    co-princes' representative: 7 vigueer, viguier
    fiesta: 13 Bal de Morratxa
    food payment to bishop: 9 la quistia

Andorra-la-Vella
capital of: 7 Andorra

and others 3 etc **4** et al **6** et alii **7** and so on **8** et cetera **10** and so forth, and the rest

And Quiet Flows the Don
author: 15 Mikhail Sholokov
character: 6 Piotra **7** Bunchuk, Natalia **14** Gregor Melekhov **16** Aksinia Astakhova

Andrea del Sarto
real name: 32 Andrea Domenico d'Agnolo di Francesco
born: 5 Italy **8** Florence
artwork: 7 Caritas **9** A Young Man **16** Birth of the Virgin, Journey of the Magi **19** Madonna of the Harpies, Portrait of a Sculptor

Andrea del Sarto
author: 14 Robert Browning

Andress, Ursula
husband: 9 John Derek
born: 5 Bern **11** Switzerland
roles: 3 She **4** Dr No **12** Casino Royale, Four for Texas

Andrew 7 apostle
brother: 5 Peter, Simon

Andrews, Dana
real name: 17 Carver Dana Andrews
brother: 12 Steve Forrest
born: 9 Collins MS
roles: 5 Laura **9** State Fair **12** Elephant Walk **13** A Walk in the Sun, Ox-Bow Incident **15** Two for the Seesaw **22** The Best Years of Our Lives

Andrews, Julie
real name: 19 Julia Elizabeth Wells
husband: 12 Blake Edwards
born: 7 England **14** Walton-on-Thames
roles: 10 My Fair Lady **11** Mary Poppins (Oscar) **14** Victor Victoria **15** The Sound of Music

Andreyev, Leonid Nikolaevich
author of: 3 S O S **5** Savva **7** Lazarus, Silence **8** Anathema **10** To the Stars **11** The Red Laugh **12** The Life of Man **16** He Who Gets Slapped **18** Love of One's Neighbor **19** Seven That Were Hanged

Andria
author: 7 Terence

Androcles
origin: 5 Roman
position: 5 slave

Androcles and the Lion
author: 17 George Bernard Shaw
removed: 5 thorn

androgenous 8 bisexual **14** hermaphroditic

Andromache
father: 6 Eetion
husband: 6 Hector
son: 6 Pielus **8** Astyanax, Molossus, Pergamus **9** Cestrinus
author: 9 Euripides
character: 6 Peleus, Thetis **7** Orestes **8** Menelaus
    mistress of: 11 Neoptolemus
    rival: 8 Hermione
    son: 8 Molossus
setting: 8 Thessaly

Andromaque
author: 18 Jean Baptiste Racine
character:
    son: 8 Astyanax
    king: 7 Pyrrhus
setting: 6 Epirus

Andromeda
astronomy: 13 constellation
father: 7 Cepheus
mother: 10 Cassiopeia
husband: 7 Perseus
son: 6 Mestor, Perses **7** Alcaeus, Heleius **9** Electryon, Sthenelus
daughter: 10 Gorgophone
rescued from: 10 sea monster
rescued by: 7 Perseus

Andromeda Strain, The
author: 15 Michael Crichton

androphobia
fear of: 3 men

Androsphinx
form: 6 sphinx
head of: 3 man

and so forth 3 etc **7** and so on **8** et cetera **9** and others **10** and the rest

and so on 3 etc **8** et cetera **9** and others **10** and so forth, and the rest

And Then There Were None
director: 9 Rene Clair
based on novel by: 14 Agatha Christie
cast: 11 Roland Young **12** Louis Hayward, Walter Huston **15** Barry Fitzgerald
remade as: 16 Ten Little Indians

and thou, Brutus
Latin: 9 et tu Brute
spoken by: 12 Julius Caesar

Andvari
origin: 6 Nordic
form: 5 dwarf

Andy Capp
creator: 14 Reginald Smythe
character: 5 Vicar
    wife: 3 Flo
plays: 7 snooker

Andy Griffith Show, The
character: 10 Andy Taylor, Barney Fife, Goober Pyle, Helen Crump, Opie Taylor **11** Floyd Lawson **12** Otis Campbell **13** Aunt Bee Taylor, Howard Sprague
cast: 8 Hal Smith **9** Don Knotts, Ron (Ronny) Howard **10** Jack Dodson **12** Andy Griffith, Anita Corsaut, Howard McNear **13** Frances Bavier, George Lindsey
setting: 8 Mayberry
Andy's job: 7 sheriff

anecdote 4 tale, yarn **5** story **6** sketch **12** brief account, reminiscence
collection: 3 ana

anemic, anaemic 3 wan **4** dull, pale, weak **5** quiet **6** feeble, pallid **7** subdued **9** colorless **11** thin-blooded **13** characterless

anemone 4 lily **5** plant **6** flower

anesthesia, anaesthesia, anesthesis 6 stupor **8** numbness **11** insentience **13** loss of feeling **15** unconsciousness

anesthetic, anaesthetic 4 drug **5** ether, local **6** caudal, opiate, spinal **7** general **8** narcotic, procaine **9** analgesic, enflurane, halothane, lidocaine, peridural **10** chloroform, isoflurane, painkiller, tetracaine, thiopental **11** acupuncture, laughing gas **12** nitrous oxide **15** sodium pentothal

anesthetize 4 dope, drug, numb **6** deaden, sedate

anew 5 again, newly **6** afresh **8** once more **9** over again **11** from scratch
Latin: 6 de novo

a new order of the ages is born
Latin: 17 novus ordo seclorum

author: 6 Virgil
  work: 8 Eclogues
  motto of: 11 US great seal

angel 3 gem **4** doll **5** jewel, power, saint **6** cherub, patron, seraph, throne, virtue **7** sponsor **8** cherabim, seraphim, treasure **9** archangel **10** benefactor, domination **11** underwriter **12** principality **14** celestial being, heavenly spirit, messenger of God **15** financial backer

Angel, fallen 5 Satan **6** Azazel **7** Lucifer

angelic 4 good, pure **5** ideal **6** divine, lovely **7** saintly **8** adorable, beatific, cherubic, ethereal, heavenly, innocent, seraphic **9** angel-like, beautiful, celestial, rapturous, spiritual **10** entrancing **11** enrapturing

Angelic Doctor
  nickname of: 15 St Thomas Aquinas

Angelico, Fra
  real name: 13 Guido di Pietro
  born: 7 Vicchio **14** Castell Vecchio
  artwork: 12 Annunciation **15** Madonna Annalena **19** Descent from the Cross **21** Coronation of the Virgin **29** Madonna of the Linen Drapers' Guild

Angelo
  character in: 17 Measure for Measure
  author: 11 Shakespeare

Angel of Fire, The
  also: 13 The Fiery Angel
  opera by: 9 Prokofiev

anger 3 ire, vex **4** bile, fury, gall, rage, rile **5** annoy, chafe, pique, wrath **6** choler, dander, enmity, enrage, hatred, madden, nettle, rankle, ruffle, spleen, temper **7** incense, inflame, outrage, provoke, umbrage **8** acrimony, embitter, irritate, vexation **9** animosity, annoyance, displease, hostility, hot temper, ill temper, infuriate, petulance **10** antagonism, antagonize, exacerbate, exasperate, irritation, resentment **11** displeasure, indignation **12** exasperation, make bad blood **14** disapprobation **15** get one's dander up **16** cause ill feelings **18** ruffle one's feathers

Anger
  author: 9 May Sarton

Angerboda
  also: 9 Angrbodha, Angurboda
  origin: 12 Scandinavian
  form: 8 giantess
  children: 3 Hel **6** Fenrir, Fenris **11** Iormungandr, Jormungandr **14** Midgard Serpent

angle 4 bend, cusp, edge, side, turn **5** focus, slant **6** aspect, corner **7** outlook **8** position **9** viewpoint **10** divergence, standpoint **11** perspective, point of view
  kind: 5 acute, right **6** obtuse **8** straight

  point: 6 vertex
  measure: 7 degrees

angled 4 bent **6** fished **7** crooked, slanted **8** diverged

Anglo-Frisian
  language family: 12 Indo-European
  branch: 8 Germanic
  group: 15 Western Germanic
  language: 7 English, Frisian

Angola
  other name: 7 Bakongo **20** Portuguese West Africa
  capital/largest city: 6 Luanda
  others: 5 Dundo **6** Ambriz, Huambo, Lobito **7** Cabinda, Kampala, Malange, Malanje, Salazar **8** Benguela, Cassinga, Vila Luso **9** Ambrizete, Mocamedes **10** Mossamedes, Nova Lisboa, Silva Porto
  division: 3 Bie **4** Uige **5** Huila, Lunda, Zaire **6** Cunene, Huambo, Luanda, Moxico **7** Cabinda, Malanje **8** Benguela **9** Cuanza Sul, Mocamedes **11** Cuanza Norte **13** Cuando Cubango
  monetary unit: 6 escudo, macuta, macute **7** angolar, centavo
  mountain: 5 Chela **6** Loviti **16** Humpata Highlands
  highest point: 4 Moco
  river: 4 Cuvo **5** Congo, Cuito, Longa **6** Cassai, Coanza, Cuando, Cuanza, Cunene, Kunene, Kwango, Kwanza, Luando **7** Chiumbe, Cubango, Zambezi **11** Lungue-Bungo
  sea: 6 Indian **8** Atlantic
  physical feature:
    basin: 8 Okavango
    desert: 9 Mocamedes
    falls: 15 Catarata Ruacana, Duque de Braganca
    plain: 8 Planalto
    plateau: 4 Rand **5** Huila **11** Benguela Bie, Lunda Divide
  people: 5 Bantu, Kongo, Lundu **6** Chokwe, Herero, Mbundu, Ovambo **7** Bakongo, Kangela, Kikongo **8** Kimbundu, Kwangare **9** Ovinbundu **12** Nyaneka-Humbi
    leader: 13 Agostinho Neto **20** Jose Eduardo dos Santos
  language: 5 Bantu **8** Kimbundu, Oumbundu **9** Ovimbundu **10** Portuguese
  religion: 7 animism **10** Protestant **13** Roman Catholic
  place:
    fortress: 9 Sao Miguel
  feature:
    mahogany: 5 khaya
    weed: 6 archil

angry 3 mad **5** huffy, irate, riled, vexed **6** fuming, galled, piqued, raging **7** annoyed, boiling, burnt up, enraged, furious, hateful, hostile, nettled **8** incensed, inflamed, offended, outraged, petulant, provoked **9** affronted, indignant, irascible, irritated, resent-

ful, splenetic, turbulent **10** displeased, embittered, infuriated **11** acrimonious, exasperated, ill-tempered **12** antagonistic

angst 5 dread **6** unease **7** anxiety **10** foreboding, uneasiness **12** apprehension

angstrom
  abbreviation: 1 A

Angstrom, Anders Jon
  field: 7 physics **9** astronomy
  founded: 12 spectroscopy
  mapped: 11 solar system
  angstrom unit: 17 wavelength of light

Angstrom, Harry see **6** Updike

anguish 3 woe **4** pain **5** agony, grief **6** misery, sorrow **7** anxiety, despair, remorse, torment **8** distress **9** heartache, suffering

Anguish
  goddess of: 8 Angerona

anguished 6 pained **7** anxious, fearful **9** tormented **10** distressed **11** heartbroken

angular 4 bent, bony, lank, lean **5** gaunt, lanky, spare **6** jagged **7** crooked, scrawny **8** rawboned **13** sharp-cornered

Angus Og
  origin: 5 Irish
  god of: 4 love **5** youth **6** beauty

animadversion 4 flak **7** nagging, quibble **9** aspersion, criticism, pestering **12** faultfinding **14** censoriousness

animal 3 pet **5** beast, brute **6** mammal **8** creature, nonhuman, organism **9** quadruped
  group: 4 bird, fish, worm **6** insect, mammal, sponge **7** primate, reptile, rotifer **8** ruminant **9** amphibian **10** vertebrate **12** invertebrate

Animal Crackers
  director: 13 Victor Heerman
  cast: 5 Chico, Harpo, Zeppo **7** Groucho **11** Lillian Roth **12** Marx Brothers **14** Margaret Dumont
  song: 25 Hooray for Captain Spaulding

Animal Farm
  author: 12 George Orwell
  character: 5 Boxer **7** Mr Jones **8** Napoleon, Snowball

Animals in That Country, The
  author: 14 Margaret Atwood

animate 4 fire, goad, move, stir, urge, warm **5** alive, impel, liven, set on **6** arouse, excite, fire up, incite, moving, prompt, spur on, vivify, work up **7** actuate, enliven, inspire, provoke, quicken **8** activate, energize, vitalize **9** instigate, make alive, stimulate **10** invigorate, make lively **11** add spirit to **12** give energy to

animated 3 gay, hot **4** airy **5** brisk, quick, vivid **6** active, ardent, blithe, breezy, bright, elated, lively **7** buoyant, dynamic, fervent, glowing, vibrant, zealous, zestful **8** exciting, spirited, sportive, vigorous **9** ebullient, energetic, sprightly, vivacious **10** passionate **12** invigorating

animation 3 vim **4** fire, glow, life, zest **5** ardor, verve, vigor **6** action, gaiety, spirit **7** elation **8** activity, alacrity, buoyancy, vibrancy, vitality, vivacity **9** alertness, briskness, eagerness, good cheer **10** brightness, ebullience, enthusiasm, excitement, liveliness **12** exhilaration, sportiveness **13** sprightliness

animosity 4 hate **5** anger **6** enmity, hatred, malice, rancor, strife **7** dislike, ill will **8** acrimony **9** antipathy, hostility, malignity **10** antagonism, bitterness, resentment **11** malevolence **14** unfriendliness

animus 5 anger, spite, venom **6** enmity, hatred, malice, rancor **7** disdain, dislike, ill will **8** acrimony, bad blood **9** animosity, antipathy, hostility **10** antagonism, bitterness, ill feeling, resentment **12** hard feelings

anise
  botanical name: 16 Pimpinella Anisum
  origin: 5 Egypt, India **13** Mediterranean
  flavor: 8 licorice
  use: 5 cakes, fruit, rolls **7** cookies
  plant with similar flavor: 9 star anise
  legend:
    safeguards against: 7 evil eye **10** nightmares **11** indigestion
    antidote to: 12 scorpion bite

anisette
  type: 7 liqueur
  origin: 6 France
  flavor: 5 anise
  drink: 17 Suissesse cocktail
  with gin: 8 Snowball **11** Bachio Punch
  substitute for: 8 Absinthe

Ankylosaurus
  type: 8 dinosaur **10** ornithopod
  location: 12 North America
  period: 10 Cretaceous
  characteristic: 7 armored

Anna
  husband: 5 Tobit
  daughter: 4 Mary
  sister: 4 Dido
  corresponds to: 11 Anna Perenna
  died by: 8 drowning

Annabel Lee
  author: 13 Edgar Allan Poe

Anna Christie
  author: 13 Eugene O'Neill
  character: 6 Marthy **8** Mat Burke **19** Chris Christopherson
  ship: 14 Simeon Winthrop

Anna Karenina
  author: 10 Leo Tolstoy
  character: 12 Count Vronsky **13** Alexei Karenin **15** Konstantin Levin **19** Kitty Shcherbatskaya **20** Prince Stepan Oblonsky
  setting: 6 Moscow, Russia **12** St Petersburg
  director: 13 Clarence Brown
  cast: 9 May Robson **10** Greta Garbo (Anna Karenina) **13** Basil Rathbone (Karenin), Frederic March (Vronsky) **16** Maureen O'Sullivan **18** Freddie Bartholomew
  earlier film version: 4 Love

annals 7 history, minutes, records **8** archives **9** registers **10** chronicles, chronology **13** yearly records **15** historical rolls **20** chronological records

Annam *see* **7** Vietnam

Anna Marie
  character in: 16 Giants of the Earth
  author: 7 Rolvaag

Anna of the Five Towns
  author: 13 Arnold Bennett

anneal 6 harden, temper **7** toughen

Anne of Geierstein (or, The Maiden of the Mist)
  author: 14 Sir Walter Scott

annex 3 add **4** grab, join **5** affix, merge, seize **6** adjoin, append, attach, tack on **7** acquire, connect, subjoin **8** addition **9** appendage **10** attachment **11** appropriate, expropriate, incorporate

Annfwn
  also: 5 Annwn
  origin: 5 Welsh
  means: 8 paradise

Annie Hall
  director: 10 Woody Allen
  cast: 9 Carol Kane, Paul Simon **10** Woody Allen **11** Diane Keaton, Tony Roberts **13** Shelley Duvall **15** Colleen Dewhurst
  Oscar for: 7 actress (Keaton), picture **8** director (Allen) **10** screenplay

annihilate 3 end **5** erase, waste **7** abolish, destroy, wipe out **8** decimate, demolish, lay waste **9** eradicate, extirpate, liquidate **10** extinguish, obliterate **11** exterminate

annihilation 9 abolition, wiping out **11** destruction, extirpation, laying waste, liquidation **12** obliteration **13** extermination

anniversary 4 fete **7** holiday, name day **8** birthday, feast day **9** centenary **10** centennial **11** bicentenary, celebration **12** bicentennial **13** commemoration, golden jubilee **16** sesquicentennial

Ann-Margret
  real name: 16 Ann-Margret Olsson
  husband: 10 Roger Smith
  born: 6 Sweden **9** Valsjobyn
  roles: 5 Tommy **8** Scarlett **12** Bye-Bye Birdie **15** Carnal Knowledge, Grumpy Old Men **21** A Streetcar Named Desire

anno Domini 18 in the year of our Lord
  abbreviation: 2 AD
  alternative: 2 CE Common Era

anno mundi 19 in the year of the world

anno regni 19 in the year of the reign

annotate 5 gloss **6** remark **7** comment, explain, expound **8** construe, footnote **9** elucidate, explicate, interpret **10** commentate

annotation 4 note **5** gloss **6** remark **7** comment **8** exegesis, footnote **10** commentary, marginalia **11** elucidation, explication, observation

announce 5 augur **6** herald, reveal, signal **7** betoken, declare, divulge, give out, portend, presage, publish, signify, trumpet **8** disclose, foretell, proclaim **9** advertise, broadcast, harbinger **10** promulgate **11** disseminate

announcement 9 broadcast, statement **11** declaration **12** proclamation

annoy 3 irk, nag, tax, vex **4** gall, rile **5** harry, tease, worry **6** badger, bother, harass, heckle, hector, nettle, pester, plague, ruffle **7** disturb, provoke, torment, trouble **8** distract, irritate **10** exasperate **13** inconvenience

annoyance 6 bother **8** irritant, nuisance, vexation **10** irritation **11** distraction, disturbance

annoyed 5 irked, upset, vexed **9** disturbed, irritated, perturbed **11** discomposed **12** disconcerted

annual 4 weed **5** plant **6** flower, serial **7** gazette, journal, reports **8** bulletin, magazine, notebook, periodic **9** vegetable **10** periodical, record book

annuity 6 income **7** pension, stipend **9** allowance

annul 4 undo, void **6** cancel, negate, recall, repeal, revoke **7** abolish, nullify, rescind, retract, reverse **8** abrogate, dissolve **10** invalidate

annulment 6 recall, repeal **7** undoing, voiding **8** reversal **9** abolition **10** abrogation, retraction, revocation **11** dissolution, repudiation **12** cancellation, invalidation **13** nullification

annus mirabilis 13 year of wonders

anodyne 4 balm **6** solace **7** comfort **9** comforter **10** palliative

anoint 3 oil **5** crown **6** ordain **8** put oil on **9** pour oil on

Anointed One 5 Jesus **7** Messiah

anomalous 3 odd **7** bizarre, strange **8** abnormal, atypical, peculiar **9** irregular, monstrous **11** incongruous **12** out of keeping

anomaly 6 oddity, rarity **9** deviation **10** aberration **11** abnormality, incongruity, peculiarity **12** eccentricity, irregularity **18** exception to the rule

anon 4 soon, then 5 again, later 7 by and by, shortly 8 tomorrow 9 afterward, presently 10 before long 11 immediately, in the future

anonymous 7 unnamed 8 nameless, unsigned 12 unidentified 13 bearing no name 14 unacknowledged 19 of unknown authorship

another 4 else, more 5 extra, other 7 further, renewed 9 accessory, otherwise 10 additional 12 supplemental 13 something else, supplementary 14 different thing

Anouilh, Jean
author of: 6 Becket 8 Antigone, Eurydice, Leocadia, L'hermine 11 Dear Antoine 14 Time Remembered 15 Le Bal des Voleurs, Thieves' Carnival 16 Point of Departure, Ring Round the Moon 19 Waltz of the Toreadors 20 L'Invitation au Chateau 23 Traveller Without Luggage

ansate 7 handled

anser 5 goose 6 stupid 7 foolish 8 anserine

answer 3 say 4 fill, meet, suit 5 reply, serve, solve, write 6 be like, rejoin, retort 7 conform, fulfill, react to, resolve, respond 8 be enough, response, solution 9 be similar, rejoinder 10 be adequate, correspond, pass muster, resolution 11 acknowledge, explanation 12 be correlated, be equivalent, be sufficient, do well enough 14 acknowledgment, be satisfactory

answerable 6 liable 8 beholden 10 chargeable 11 accountable, responsible

Answer as a Man
author: 14 Taylor Caldwell

ant
caste: 4 male 5 queen 6 worker 7 soldier
kind: 3 red 4 army, fire 5 dairy, thief 6 beggar, farmer, velvet, weaver 7 formica, janitor, pharaoh 8 honeypot, mushroom 9 Argentine, carpenter, cornfield, harvester, legionary 10 leaf cutter 11 little black 12 fungus grower, odorous house, southern fire 13 mound building 14 Texas harvester
group of: 6 colony

antagonism 5 spite 6 animus, enmity, hatred, rancor, strife 7 discord, dislike, rivalry 8 aversion, clashing, conflict, friction 9 animosity, antipathy, hostility 10 bitterness, dissension, opposition, resentment 11 detestation

antagonist 3 foe 5 enemy, rival 7 opposer 8 attacker, opponent 9 adversary, assailant, disputant 10 competitor, contestant

antagonistic 7 hostile 8 contrary, inimical 9 rancorous 10 antisocial, unfriendly 11 belligerent 12 antipathetic, disputatious

antagonize 5 repel 6 offend 8 alienate, estrange

Antananarivo, Tananarive
capital of: 10 Madagascar

Antarctica
division: 10 Wilkes Land 13 Marie Byrd Land, Queen Maud Land 14 Edith Ronne Land 17 Ellsworth Highland
island: 4 Ross 5 Peter, Scott 6 Biscoe, Hearst 7 Ballery, Charcot 8 Adelaide, Elephant 9 Alexander, Joinville, Roosevelt 10 Coronation, King George 11 South Orkney 13 South Shetland
mountain: 8 Sentinel 9 Pensacola 14 Transantarctic 23 Executive Committee Range
valley: 6 Wright
river: 4 Onyx
natural resource/mineral: 4 coal
plant life: 4 moss 5 algae, fungi 6 lichen, pollen 8 bacteria
animal: 4 lice, mite, tick 5 whale 7 fur seal 8 ross seal 9 crabeater 11 weddell seal, wingless fly
bird: 4 skua 6 fulmar, petrel 7 penguin 10 cape pigeon
sea: 4 Ross 5 Davis 6 Scotia 7 Weddell 8 Amundsen 14 Bellingshausen

ante 3 bet, pot 5 stake, wager 12 beginning bet

anteater 5 sloth 7 echidna 8 aardvark 9 armadillo

antecede 7 precede, predate 8 go before, preexist 10 anticipate

ante Christum 12 before Christ
abbreviation: 2 AC

antedate 7 precede, predate 8 antecede, go before 9 come first 10 anticipate 12 happen before

Antediluvian 14 before the flood

antediluvian 7 antique, archaic 8 obsolete 10 antiquated

antelope 8 ruminant
family: 7 Bovidae
kind: 3 doe, gnu 4 buck, deer, fawn, kudu, oryx, roan 5 bongo, eland, moose, sable 6 dik-dik, duiker, impala, lechwe, nilgai 7 gazelle, gemsbok, gerenuk 8 bluebuck, bontebok, steinbok 9 blackbuck, sitatunga, springbok, waterbuck 10 four-horned 12 Klipspringer
habitat: 4 Asia 6 Africa

Antelope State
nickname of: 8 Nebraska

antenna 6 aerial, feeler

anterior 5 front, prior 7 forward, in front 8 previous 9 precedent 10 antecedent 12 placed before

Anteros
brother: 4 Eros
avenger of: 14 unrequited love

Anthea
epithet of: 4 Hera
means: 7 flowery

Antheil, George
born: 9 Trenton NJ
autobiography: 13 Bad Boy of Music
composer of: 7 Volpone 12 Helen Retires, Jazz Symphony 13 Sonata Sauvage, Transatlantic 14 Airplane Sonata 15 Ballet Mecanique

anthem 4 hymn, song 5 carol, ditty, music, paean, psalm 6 ballad, sacred 7 cantata 8 doxology 11 church music

Anthesteria
origin: 5 Greek
festival of: 4 wine 6 spring 7 flowers

anthology 6 choice, digest 7 garland 8 analects, chapbook, extracts, treasury 9 gleanings, scrapbook 10 collection, compendium, miscellany, selections 11 collectanea, compilation, florilegium, miscellanea 15 commonplace book

Anthony, Susan B.
leader in: 14 women's suffrage

Anthony Adverse
author: 18 William Hervey Allen

anthophobia
fear of: 7 flowers

anthropologist
American: 4 Boas, Mead 5 Lowie, Sapir 6 Geertz, Linton, Morgan 7 Kroeber 8 Benedict
British: 5 Leach, Tylor 6 Fortes, Leakey, Rivers 14 Evans-Pritchard, Radcliffe-Brown
French: 5 Mauss 8 Durkheim 11 Levi-Strauss
Polish: 10 Malinowski

anthropology
term: 4 myth 6 custom, ritual 7 culture, kinship 8 artifact 9 ethnology, evolution, field work 11 ethnography 16 natural selection
type/related study: 5 legal, urban 6 social 7 applied, medical 8 cultural, economic, physical 9 political 11 linguistics 12 human ecology 13 psychological 19 structural-symbolist
famous study: 3 San 4 Kung 7 Eskimos, Samoans, Tasaday 10 Aborigines 16 Pacific Islanders

anthropophobia
fear of: 6 people

antibiotic 4 drug 5 venom 6 poison 8 curative 9 antidotal, antitoxic, pesticide 10 wonder drug 11 insecticide, miracle drug
kind: 8 neomycin, subtilin 9 mycomycin 10 ampicillin, penicillin 12 erythromycin

antic, antics 5 larks, sport 6 pranks, tricks 9 escapades 10 buffoonery, skylarking, tomfoolery 11 shenanigans 12 clownishness, monkeyshines 14 practical jokes

anticipate 5 await 6 expect 7 count on, foresee, long for, look for, predict 8 envision, forecast, foretell 9 pin hope on **10** look toward **13** look forward to

anticipation 4 hope **10** expectancy **11** expectation, preparation

anticlimax 7 letdown **8** comedown **14** disappointment

antidote 4 cure **6** remedy **9** antitoxin **10** antipoison, corrective **12** counteragent, countervenom **13** counterpoison **14** countermeasure

Antigone
author: **9** Sophocles **11** Jean Anouilh
character: **6** Ismene **8** Tiresias
   father: **7** Oedipus
   mother: **7** Jocasta
   brother: **8** Eteocles **9** Polynices
   sister: **6** Ismene
   uncle: **5** Creon
   cousin/lover: **6** Haemon
defied: **5** Creon

Antigua and Barbuda
capital/largest city: **7** St John's
government:
   member of: **26** West Indies Associated States
head of state: **14** British monarch **15** governor-general
island: **4** Long **5** Guana **7** Antigua, Barbuda, Redonda
highest point: **9** Boggy Peak
sea: **9** Caribbean
physical feature:
   cove: **5** Royal
   harbor/harbour: **7** English
people: **7** African, British **8** Lebanese **10** Portuguese
language: **7** English
religion: **8** Anglican, Moravian **13** Roman Catholic
feature: **15** Nelson's Dockyard

anti-intellectual 5 yahoo **7** lowbrow **9** ignoramus, vulgarian **10** illiterate, philistine

antimony
chemical symbol: **2** Sb

Antinous
suitor of: **8** Penelope
killed by: **8** Odysseus

antipathetic 6 averse **7** hostile **8** inimical **9** rancorous **11** ill-disposed

antipathy 6 enmity, rancor **7** disgust, dislike, ill will **8** aversion, distaste, loathing **9** animosity, hostility, repulsion **10** abhorrence, antagonism, repugnance **14** unfriendliness

Antiphas
father: **7** Laocoon

Antipholus
character in: **17** The Comedy of Errors
author: **11** Shakespeare

antiphony 6 chorus **7** refrain **8** response

antipode 8 contrary, opposite **10** antithesis

Antiquary, The
author: **14** Sir Walter Scott

antiquated 5 dated, passe **7** antique, archaic **8** obsolete, outdated, outmoded **9** out-of-date **11** obsolescent **12** old-fashioned

antique 3 old **5** curio, relic **6** rarity **7** bibelot, trinket **9** objet d'art **10** antiquated, memorabile **11** memorabilia

antiquities 6 relics **8** artifact **9** monuments

antiquity 7 oldness **8** great age **11** ancientness **12** ancient times

antiseptic 6 iodine **7** aseptic, sterile **8** germ-free **9** germicide **10** germ killer **11** bactericide **12** disinfectant, prophylactic

antisocial 7 asocial, hostile **8** menacing, retiring, unsocial **9** alienated **10** disruptive, rebellious, unfriendly, unsociable **11** belligerent, sociopathic **12** antagonistic, misanthropic

antithesis 7 inverse, reverse **8** antipode, contrary, contrast, converse, opposite

antithetical 8 contrary, opposing, opposite **10** discrepant, refutatory **11** conflicting, disagreeing **13** contradictory **14** countervailing, irreconcilable

antitoxin 5 serum **8** antidote **9** antivenom **12** counteragent **13** counterpoison

antler 4 horn, knob, rack **5** spike **6** shovel **8** deerhorn, troching
part: **3** bay **4** brow **5** crown, royal

ant lion
also: **8** lacewing **9** doodlebug
kind: **6** owlfly **9** dusty wing, mantidfly **12** spongillafly **13** brown lacewing, giant lacewing, green lacewing **14** beaded lacewing **15** ithonid lacewing **16** pleasing lacewing

Antonello da Messina
born: **5** Italy **7** Messina
artwork: **8** Ecce Homo **11** Three Angels **13** Il Condottiere (Portrait of a Man), Salvador Mundi **21** Saint Jerome in his Study

Antonio
character in: **12** Twelfth Night **19** The Merchant of Venice
author: **11** Shakespeare

Antonioni, Michelangelo
director of: **6** Blowup **8** The Night **10** The Eclipse **12** The Adventure, The Passenger **14** Zabriskie Point

Antony, Mark
also: **14** Marcus Antonius
member of: **11** triumvirate
other triumvirs: **7** Lepidus **8** Octavian (Caesar Augustus)
lover: **9** Cleopatra
cousin: **12** Julius Caesar
wife: **7** Octavia
battle: **6** Actium **8** Philippi **9** Pharsalus

invaded: **7** Parthia
died by: **7** suicide

Antony and Cleopatra
author: **18** William Shakespeare
character: **7** Octavia **9** Cleopatra **10** Mark Antony **14** Octavius Caesar
setting: **5** Egypt
Cleopatra bitten by: **3** asp

antonym 8 opposite **10** antithesis
abbreviation: **3** ant

Antrodemus
type: **8** dinosaur, therapod
also called: **10** Allosaurus
period: **8** Jurassic **10** Cretaceous

Anu
origin: **8** Akkadian
god of: **6** heaven
corresponds to: **2** An

Anubis
origin: **8** Egyptian
god of: **5** tombs **9** embalming
weigher of: **15** hearts of the dead
represented by head of: **6** jackal

anvil 5 block, incus **9** converter **11** transformer

anxiety 4 fear **5** alarm, angst, dread, worry **6** unease **7** anguish, concern, tension **8** disquiet, distress, suspense **9** misgiving **10** foreboding, solicitude, uneasiness **11** disquietude, fretfulness **12** apprehension

anxiety-ridden 7 anxious, fearful, nervous **10** distraught **11** worried sick **12** apprehensive

anxious 4 avid, keen **5** eager, tense **6** ardent, intent, uneasy **7** alarmed, earnest, fearful, fervent, fretful, itching, uptight, wanting, worried, zealous **8** desirous, troubled, yearning **9** anguished, concerned, disturbed, expectant, impatient **10** disquieted, distressed **11** overwrought **12** apprehensive

any 3 all, one **4** each, lone, sole, some **5** every **6** single, unique **8** anything, singular, solitary **9** something **10** individual, quantifier

anybody 3 any **6** anyone **8** anything

anyhow see **6** anyway

anything 3 any **4** some **5** aught **6** anyone **7** anybody

anyway 6 anyhow **8** sloppily **9** at any rate, in any case **10** carelessly, in any event, regardless **11** haphazardly, just the same, nonetheless **12** nevertheless **13** indifferently **14** without concern

anywhere 8 anyplace, wherever **11** wheresoever

A-1 3 ace **4** aces, fine, tops **5** great, prime, super **6** choice, grade-A, superb, tip-top **7** capital **8** sterling, superior, top-notch **9** excellent, first-rate, superfine **10** first-class, tremendous **11** crackerjack, outstanding, superlative

Aornis
  tributary of: **4** Styx
Aornum
  entrance to: **5** Hades
  used by: **7** Orpheus
apace 4 fast **7** flat-out, hastily, quickly, rapidly, swiftly **8** speedily **9** posthaste **10** at top speed **11** double-quick, on the double **12** lickety-split **13** expeditiously, precipitately **18** hell bent for leather
Apache
  language family: **10** Athabascan, Athapaskan
  band: **9** Jacarilla, Mescalero, San Carlos **13** White Mountain
  location: **7** Arizona **8** Oklahoma **9** New Mexico
  leader: **7** Cochise **8** Geronimo
  noted for: **8** basketry
apart 4 afar **5** alone, aloof, aside **6** cut off **7** asunder, distant **8** by itself, divorced, isolated, separate **9** by oneself, into parts, to one side **10** into pieces, separately
apartment 3 pad **4** flat **5** rooms, suite
Apartment, The
  director: **11** Billy Wilder
  cast: **10** Jack Lemmon, Ray Walston **13** Fred MacMurray **15** Shirley MacLaine
  Oscar for: **7** picture
apathetic 4 cold **7** unmoved **9** impassive, unfeeling **10** disengaged, impossible, phlegmatic, spiritless **11** emotionless, indifferent, passionless, uncommitted, unconcerned, unemotional **12** uninterested, unresponsive
apathy 8 coolness, lethargy, numbness **9** lassitude, unconcern **11** impassivity, inattention, passiveness **12** indifference **13** impassibility, lack of feeling **14** lack of interest **15** emotionlessness **16** unresponsiveness
apatite
  source: **5** Burma, Mogok
Apatosaurus *see* **12** Brontosaurus
ape 4 copy, echo, mock **5** mimic **6** follow, mirror, monkey, parody, parrot **7** emulate, imitate, primate **8** travesty **9** burlesque **10** caricature
  family: **8** Pongidae
  combining form: **8** pithecus
  study of: **11** pithecology
  kind: **6** gibbon **7** gorilla, siamang **9** orangutan **10** chimpanzee
  famous: **8** Godzilla, King Kong
apercu 6 glance **7** glimpse, insight, outline, summary
aperture 3 gap **4** hole, rent, rift, slit, slot **5** chink, cleft, space **6** breach **7** fissure, opening, orifice **10** interstice
apex 3 cap, tip **4** acme, peak **5** crest, crown **6** apogee, climax, height, summit, vertex, zenith **8** pinnacle **11** culmination **12** consummation, highest point **13** crowning point

aphasic 4 dumb, mute **12** inarticulate **17** incapable of speech
aphid
  variety: **3** pea **4** pine, rose **5** apple, grape, peach, tulip **6** cereal, cotton, potato, spruce **7** adelgid, cabbage **8** pear root **9** elm woolly, plant lice, water lily **10** gall-making, phylloxera
aphorism 3 saw **5** adage, axiom, maxim **6** dictum, old saw, saying, slogan, truism **7** epigram, proverb **8** apothegm
aphrodisiac 4 sexy **6** carnal, erotic, turn-on **7** fleshly, philter, raunchy **8** prurient **9** cantharis **10** love potion **11** cantharides, magic potion, stimulating
Aphrodite
  also: **6** Urania **7** Cyprian, Paphian **8** Cytherea **10** Anadyomene
  origin: **5** Greek
  goddess of: **4** love **6** beauty
  husband: **10** Hephaestus
  lover: **4** Ares
  son: **5** Lyrus **6** Deimos, Phobus, Rhodus **7** Priapus
  daughter: **8** Harmonia
  corresponds to: **5** Venus
  epithet: **6** Acraea, Scotia **7** Doritis, Erycina, Limenia **8** Melaenis, Nymphaea, Pandemos **9** Migonitis **11** Aphrogeneia, Apostrophia
Apia
  capital of: **12** Western Samoa
apiary 4 hive **7** beehive
apiece 4 each **9** severally **12** individually, respectively
a pied 6 on foot **7** walking
Apis
  origin: **8** Egyptian
  also: **3** Hap **4** Hapi
  form: **4** bull
  from: **7** Memphis
  father: **6** Apollo **9** Phoroneus
  mother: **8** Teledice
  sister: **5** Niobe
  nephew: **5** Argus
  rld Argos of: **8** serpents
  killed by: **7** Aetolus
  worshipped at: **7** Memphis
aplomb 5 poise **7** balance **8** calmness, coolness **9** composure, sang-froid, stability **10** confidence, equanimity **11** intrepidity, savoir faire **13** self-assurance, self- composure **14** self-confidence, self-possession **15** level-headedness **16** imperturbability
Apocalypse Now
  director: **18** Francis Ford Coppola
  based on: **15** Heart of Darkness
    novel by: **12** Joseph Conrad
  cast: **11** Martin Sheen **12** Marlon Brando, Robert Duvall **16** Frederick Forrest
  setting: **7** Vietnam
apocalyptic 4 dire **7** ominous **8** oracular **9** far-seeing, ill- boding, ill-omened, prescient, prophetic, reveal-

ing **10** disclosing, eye-opening, foreboding, portentous, predictive, revelatory **11** prophetical **12** inauspicious, revelational **15** prognosticative
apocryphal 7 dubious **8** disputed, doubtful, mythical, spurious **10** fabricated, fictitious, unofficial, unverified **11** unauthentic, uncanonical **12** questionable, unauthorized **14** probably untrue **15** unauthenticated, unsubstantiated
apogee 3 top **4** acme, apex, peak **5** crest, crown **6** climax, summit, vertex, zenith **8** meridian, pinnacle **9** high point **11** culmination **12** highest point
Apollo
  also: **7** Phoebus, Pythius **9** Musagetes
  origin: **5** Greek, Roman
  god of: **5** light, music **6** beauty, poetry **7** healing **8** prophecy
  father: **4** Zeus
  mother: **4** Leto
  twin sister: **7** Artemis
  sons: **3** Ion **5** Iamus **8** Laodocus **9** Aristaeus, Asclepius, Philammon **10** Polypoetes
  corresponds to: **5** Paeon **8** Hyperion
  epithet: **6** Loxias **7** Acesius, Agraeus, Agyieus, Carneus, Phyteus, Spodius **8** Grynaeus **9** Parnopius, Smintheus **10** Alexicacus, Archegetes, Boedromius, Delphinius **11** Argyrotoxus, Epibaterius **12** Platanistius
Apollyon 4 hell **7** Abaddon
apologetic 5 sorry **8** contrite, penitent **9** defensive, regretful **10** excusatory, mitigatory, remorseful **11** exonerative, extenuatory, vindicatory **12** apologetical **13** justificatory, making excuses **15** self-reproachful
Apologia pro Vita Sua
  author: **15** John Henry Newman (Cardinal)
Apologie for Poetrie (Defense for Poetry)
  author: **15** Sir Philip Sidney
apologist 7 pleader **8** advocate, defender **9** supporter
apologize 9 beg pardon **11** make apology **13** express regret
apology 6 excuse **7** defense **11** explanation, vindication **13** begging pardon, justification
Apophis
  also: **5** Apepi
  form: **7** serpent
  habitat: **8** darkness
  destroyed daily by: **4** Dawn
Apophthegms New and Old
  author: **12** Francis Bacon
apostasy 7 atheism, perfidy **8** unbelief **9** defection, disbelief, recreancy **10** disloyalty, infidelity, irreligion **11** godlessness **13** double-dealing
apostate 6 bolter **7** heretic, seceder, traitor **8** defector, deserter, recanter,

recusant, renegade, turncoat **9** dissenter, dissident, turnabout **10** backslider **13** nonconformist, tergiversator

apostle 5 envoy **6** zealot **7** pioneer, witness **8** activist, advocate, disciple, emissary, exponent, preacher **9** messenger, proponent, supporter **10** evangelist, missionary, propagator **12** propagandist, proselytizer, spokesperson

Apostle, The
author: **10** Sholem Asch
film by: **12** Robert Duvall

Apostles 4 John, Jude, Levi, Paul **5** Jacob, James, Peter, Simon **6** Andrew, Philip, Thomas **7** Matthew **8** Barnabas, Matthais **9** Nathanael, Thaddaeus **11** Bartholomew **12** James the Less **13** Judas Iscariot
apostle to the Gentiles: **4** Paul
apostle to the English: **9** Augustine
apostle to the Irish: **7** Patrick
apostle to the Goths: **7** Ulfilas
apostle to the Germans: **8** Boniface
apostle to the French: **5** Denis
apostle to the American Indians: **9** John Eliot

apothegm 3 saw **5** adage, axiom, maxim, motto **6** dictum, slogan **7** epigram, proverb **8** aphorism **9** catchword, watchword

apotheosis 7 epitome, essence **9** elevation **10** embodiment, exaltation **11** deification **12** canonization, consecration, enshrinement, idealization, quintessence **13** dignification, glorification, magnification **15** immortalization

Appalachian Spring
ballet by: **7** Copland

appall 4 stun **5** abash, alarm, repel, shock **6** dismay, offend, revolt, sicken **7** disgust, horrify, outrage, terrify, unnerve **8** frighten, nauseate **10** dishearten

appalled 6 aghast **7** alarmed, shocked **8** dismayed, outraged, repelled, revolted **9** disgusted, horrified, nauseated

appalling 4 dire, grim **5** awful **6** horrid **7** fearful, ghastly **8** alarming, dreadful, horrible, horrific, shocking, terrible **9** dismaying, frightful, repellent, repulsive, revolting, sickening **10** abominable, disgusting, horrifying, nauseating, outrageous, terrifying **11** frightening, intolerable **12** insufferable **13** disheartening

apparatus 4 gear **5** gismo, setup, tools **6** device, gadget, outfit, system, tackle **7** machine **8** material, utensils **9** appliance, equipment, machinery, materials, mechanism **10** implements **11** contraption, contrivance, instruments **12** organization **13** paraphernalia

apparel 4 duds, garb, gear, togs **5** array, dress, habit, robes **6** attire **7** clothes, costume, raiment, threads, vesture **8** clothing, garments **9** equipment, trappings, vestments **13** accoutrements

appareled 4 clad **5** robed **6** garbed, suited **7** attired, clothed, covered, dressed

apparent 4 open **5** clear, overt, plain **6** likely, marked, patent **7** blatant, evident, obvious, seeming, visible **8** clear-cut, distinct, manifest, probable **10** clear as day, ostensible, presumable **11** conspicuous, discernible, perceivable, perceptible, self-evident, unequivocal **12** unmistakable **14** understandable

apparently
Latin: **7** ex facie

apparition 5 ghost, shade, spook **6** spirit, wraith **7** phantom, specter **8** phantasm, presence, revenant **10** phenomenon **13** manifestation **15** materialization

appeal 3 beg, SOS **4** plea, pull, suit **5** apply, charm, plead, sue to, tempt **6** adjure, allure, engage, entice, excite, invite, invoke **7** attract, beseech, entreat, implore, request, solicit **8** call upon, charisma, entreaty, interest, petition **9** fascinate **10** adjuration, attraction, supplicate **11** fascination **12** solicitation, supplication

appealing 7 likable, lovable **8** adjuring, charming, engaging, enticing, fetching, inviting, pleading, pleasing, tempting **10** attractive, entreating, requesting, soliciting **11** charismatic, petitioning **12** irresistible, supplicating

appear 4 look, seem, show **5** arise **6** crop up, emerge, loom up, show up, turn up **7** be clear, be plain, come out, perform, surface **8** be patent **9** be evident, be obvious **10** be apparent, be manifest **11** be published, come to light, materialize

appearance 4 look **5** guise, image **6** advent, aspect, coming **7** arrival, pretext **8** pretense **9** appearing, emergence, showing up, turning up **10** impression **11** outward show **13** manifestation **15** materialization

appear at 6 attend, show up **9** perform at

appease 4 calm, dull, ease, lull **5** abate, allay, blunt, quell, quiet, slake, still **6** pacify, quench, solace, soothe, temper **7** assuage, compose, mollify, placate, relieve, satisfy **8** mitigate **9** alleviate **10** conciliate, propitiate **11** accommodate

appeasement 6 easing **7** abating, dulling **8** allaying, blunting, giving in **9** abatement, assuasion, quenching **10** mitigation, submission **11** alleviation, assuagement **12** conciliation, pacification, propitiation, satisfaction **13** accommodation, gratification, mollification

appellation 3 tag **4** name **5** title **6** handle **7** epithet, moniker **8** cognomen **9** sobriquet **11** designation, nom de guerre

append 3 add **4** join **5** affix **6** attach, hang on, tack on **7** subjoin, suspend **10** supplement

appendage 3 arm, leg **4** limb, tail **6** branch, feeler, member **7** adjunct **8** addition, offshoot, tentacle **9** accessory, auxiliary, extension, extremity **10** attachment, supplement

appendix 7 codicil **8** addendum, addition **10** back matter, postscript, supplement

appertain 7 apply to, concern, refer to **8** bear upon, be part of, belong to, inhere in, relate to **9** touch upon

appetite 4 zest **5** gusto **6** desire, hunger, liking, relish, thirst **7** craving, passion, stomach **8** fondness, penchant, yearning **10** proclivity **11** inclination

appetizer 6 canape, dainty, savory, tidbit **8** aperitif, cocktail, delicacy **9** antipasto **11** bonne bouche, hors d'oeuvre

appetizing 6 savory **8** alluring, enticing, inviting, tempting **9** appealing, palatable, succulent **10** attractive **11** tantalizing **13** mouth-watering

applaud 4 clap, hail, laud **5** extol **6** praise **7** acclaim, commend **8** eulogize **10** compliment **12** congratulate

applaudable 8 laudable **9** admirable, desirable, excellent **11** commendable, meritorious, outstanding **12** praiseworthy

applause 5 kudos **6** praise **7** acclaim, ovation **8** approval, clapping, plaudits **9** accolades **11** compliments

apple 5 Malus **15** Malus Sylvestris
varieties/fruit: **4** Crab, Lodi **6** Pippin **7** Baldwin, Stayman, Winesap **8** Ben Davis, Cortland, Jonathan, McIntosh **9** Delicious **10** Rome Beauty **11** Granny Smith, Gravenstein, Northern Spy, Summer Rambo **12** Grimes Golden, York Imperial **13** Yellow Newtown **14** Stayman Winesap **15** Yellow Delicious **17** Esopus Spitzenberg, Yellow Transparent **19** Rhode Island Greening
varieties/tree: **2** Wi **3** Kai, Kau, Sea, Wax **4** Cane, Java, Jew's, Pond, Rose, Star **5** Adam's, Baked, Belle, Blade, Chess, Conch, Malay, Melon, Thorn **6** Balsam, Indian, Mammee, Possum **7** Chinese, Custard, Dead Sea, Mexican **8** Elephant, Kangaroo, Otaheite, Paradise, Peruvian **11** Soulard crab, Toringo crab **12** Siberian crab
beverage: **5** cider **8** Calvados **9** Applejack

apple brandy
   drink: **8** Jack Rose **12** Jack-in-the-Box
   with rum: **6** Bolero **8** Apple Pie

applejack
   type: **6** brandy
   origin: **6** Canada **10** New England
   flavor: **10** apple cider
   drink: **11** Frozen Apple **13** Harvard
   Cooler

Apple of discord
   color: **6** golden
   thrown by: **4** Eris
   awarded to: **9** Aphrodite
   awarded by: **5** Paris
   inscription: **13** for the fairest

apple of one's eye 11 pride and joy
15 light of one's life

applesauce 3 rot **4** bull, bunk **5** hokum, hooey **6** bunkum **7** baloney,
hogwash, spinach **8** tommyrot **9** poppycock **12** fiddlesticks **13** horsefeathers **16** stuff and nonsense

Apples of the Hesperides
   color: **6** golden
   given to: **4** Hera
   kept by: **5** Ladon **10** Hesperides

appliance 4 gear **6** device **7** fixture,
machine **9** apparatus, equipment, implement, mechanism **11** contraption,
contrivance

applicable 3 apt, fit **6** useful **7** apropos, fitting, germane **8** relevant, suitable **9** adaptable, befitting, pertinent

applicant 7 hopeful **8** aspirant, claimant **9** candidate, job seeker, suppliant
10 petitioner

application 4 balm, form, suit, wash
5 claim, salve **6** appeal, lotion **7** request, unguent **8** dressing, entreaty,
industry, ointment, petition, poultice,
solution **9** assiduity, attention, diligence, emollient, putting on, relevance **10** commitment, dedication,
pertinence **11** germaneness, persistence, requisition, suitability **12** appositeness, perseverance, solicitation **13**
attentiveness

Appling, Luke (Lucius Benjamin)
   nickname: **16** Old Aches and Pains
   sport: **8** baseball
   position: **9** shortstop
   team: **15** Chicago White Sox

apply 3 fit, use **4** suit **5** adapt, lay on,
put on, refer **6** devote, direct, employ,
relate **7** address, pertain, request, utilize **8** dedicate, exercise, petition,
practice, spread on **9** implement

apply oneself 6 attend **10** buckle
down **13** give oneself to **15** give it all
one has **16** put one's heart into

appoint 3 fix, set **4** name **5** equip **6**
assign, choose, engage, fit out, select,
settle, supply **7** arrange, furnish, provide **8** decide on, delegate, deputize,
nominate **9** designate, determine, establish, prescribe **10** commission

appointment 3 job **4** date, post, spot

5 berth, place **6** naming, office **7**
meeting, station **8** choosing, position
9 placement, selection, situation **10**
assignment, engagement, nomination,
rendezvous **11** designation, meeting
time **13** commissioning

Appointment in Samarra
   author: **9** John O'Hara
   character: **8** Al Grecco, Caroline **11**
   Harry Reilly **13** Julian English

appointments 4 gear **6** outfit **8** equipage **9** equipment, furniture **11**
furnishings **13** accoutrements

apportion 5 allot, share **6** divide, ration **7** consign, deal out, dole out,
mete out, prorate **8** allocate, disperse
9 parcel out, partition **10** measure out

apportioning 8 alloting, dividing **9**
doling out, meting out **10** allocating,
consigning, dealing out, dispensing **12**
distributing

apportionment 5 quota **6** ration **7**
measure, portion **8** division **9** allotment **10** allocation **11** consignment
12 distribution, pro rata share

apposite 3 apt **7** apropos, fitting, germane **8** material, relevant, suitable **9**
pertinent **10** applicable **11** appropriate

appositeness 9 relevance **10** pertinence **11** germaneness **15** appropriateness

appraisal 8 estimate, judgment **9** valuation **10** assessment, evaluation **14**
estimated value

appraise 5 assay, judge, value **6** assess, review, size up **7** examine, inspect **8** evaluate

appreciable 7 evident, obvious **8**
clear-cut, definite **10** detectable, noticeable, pronounced **11** discernible,
perceivable, perceptible, significant,
substantial **12** recognizable **13** ascertainable

appreciate 4 like **5** prize, savor, value
6 admire, esteem, relish **7** cherish, enhance, improve, inflate, realize, respect **8** perceive, treasure **9** recognize
10 comprehend, sympathize, understand **11** acknowledge

appreciation 4 rise **6** growth, liking,
regard, relish, thanks **7** advance **8**
sympathy **9** awareness, elevation,
gratitude **10** admiration, cognizance
12 gratefulness, thankfulness **13** comprehension, understanding

apprehend 3 bag, nab, see **4** know **5**
catch, grasp, seize, sense **6** arrest, collar **7** capture, discern, realize **8** perceive **9** recognize **10** comprehend, understand **12** take prisoner **15** take into
custody

apprehension 4 fear **5** alarm, dread,
worry **6** arrest, dismay **7** anxiety, capture, concern, seizure **8** disquiet, distress, mistrust **9** misgiving, suspicion
10 foreboding, perception, uneasiness
11 premonition **12** presentiment **13**

comprehension, understanding **16** apprehensiveness

apprehensive 6 afraid, scared, uneasy
7 alarmed, anxious, fearful, jittery,
nervous, worried **9** concerned, misgiving **10** disquieted, distressed, suspicious **11** distrustful

apprehensiveness 5 dread, worry **6**
dismay **7** anxiety **9** misgiving **10** foreboding, uneasiness **12** apprehension

apprentice 4 tyro **5** pupil **6** novice **7**
learner, student **8** beginner, neophyte
19 indentured assistant

apprise 4 tell **6** advise, inform, notify
8 disclose **9** enlighten, make aware

approach 3 way **4** come, near, road **5**
begin, equal, match **6** access, avenue,
be like, method, system **7** advance,
compare, passage, solicit **8** attitude,
come near, draw near, embark on,
gain upon, initiate, resemble, set
about, sound out **9** come close, enter
upon, procedure, technique, undertake **10** move toward, passageway **11**
approximate

approachable 9 available, reachable
10 accessible

approbation 6 praise **7** acclaim, support **8** applause, approval, sanction **9**
laudation **10** acceptance, compliment
11 endorsement **12** commendation,
ratification **14** congratulation

appropriate 3 apt **4** take **5** allot, seize
6 assign, proper, seemly **7** apropos,
correct, earmark, fitting, germane **8**
allocate, relevant, set apart, suitable **9**
apportion, befitting, belonging, congruous, opportune, pertinent **10** confiscate, to the point, well-chosen,
well-suited **11** expropriate **12** to the
purpose **14** characteristic

appropriateness 7 aptness, fitness **9**
congruity, propriety, relevance **10** pertinence **11** correctness, suitability

appropriation 6 taking **9** allotment
10 allocation, arrogation, usurpation
12 confiscation **13** expropriation,
money set aside **16** misappropriation

approval 5 favor, leave **6** esteem, liking, regard **7** acclaim, consent, license, mandate, respect **8** sanction **9**
agreement **10** acceptance, admiration,
compliance, permission **11** approbation, concurrence, countenance, endorsement, good opinion **12** acquiescence, appreciation, confirmation **13**
authorization **14** acknowledgment

approve 4 like, pass **5** allow **6** accept,
affirm, defend, esteem, permit, praise,
ratify, second, uphold **7** condone,
confirm, endorse, respect, sustain **8**
accede to, advocate, assent to, concur
in, sanction **9** authorize, consent to
10 appreciate **11** countenance, go
along with, rubber-stamp, subscribe to

approved 8 official **9** canonical **10** authorized, sanctioned

approving 9 endorsing, favorable **10** concurring **11** affirmative, sanctioning **12** appreciative

approximate 5 guess, rough **6** reckon **7** inexact, verge on **8** approach, border on, estimate, look like, relative, very near **9** estimated

approximately 5 circa **6** almost, around **7** close to **9** generally, just about **10** more or less, not far from, very nearly

appurtenance 4 wing **5** annex, extra **7** adjunct **8** addendum, addition **9** accessory, appendage, extension **10** attachment

APR
abbreviation for: **14** above prime rate **20** annual percentage rate

Apres-midi d'un Faune, L' (The Afternoon of a Faun)
author: **16** Stephane Mallarme
(prelude) ballet music: **7** Debussy

April
event: **11** Black Monday (13)
flower: **5** daisy **8** sweet pea
French: **5** Avril
gem: **7** diamond
German: **5** April
holiday: **6** Easter **11** All Fool's Day (1) **13** April Fool's Day (1)
Italian: **6** Aprile
Latin: **7** Aprilis
number of days: **6** thirty
origin of name: **4** aper (wild boar) **6** aparae (following) **7** aperire (to open) **9** Aphrodite
place in year:
  Gregorian: **6** fourth
  Roman: **6** second
saying: **24** April is the cruellest month **27** April showers bring May flowers
Spanish: **5** Abril
zodiac signs: **5** Aries **6** Taurus

April Fool's Day
French: **9** April Fish

a priori 6 theory **7** opinion **11** of reasoning

apron 3 bib **5** smock **8** covering **10** stagefront

apropos 3 apt **6** seemly **7** correct, fitting, germane, related **8** relevant, suitable **9** befitting, congruous, opportune, pertinent **10** applicable, to the point, well-suited **11** appropriate **12** just the thing

apry
type: **7** liqueur
origin: **6** France
flavor: **7** apricot

Apsyrtus
also: **8** Absyrtus
father: **6** Aeetes
sister: **5** Medea
killed by: **5** Medea

apt 5 prone **6** bright, clever, gifted, liable, likely, proper, seemly **7** apropos, fitting, germane, given to **8** inclined, relevant, suitable **9** befitting, congruous, opportune, pertinent **10** disposed to, well-suited **11** appropriate, intelligent, predisposed

aptitude 4 bent, gift, turn **5** flair, knack, skill **6** genius, talent **7** ability, faculty, leaning **8** capacity, facility, penchant, tendency **9** endowment, proneness, quickness **10** capability, cleverness, proclivity, propensity **11** inclination, proficiency **12** predilection **14** predisposition

aptness 4 bent, gift **5** flair, knack **6** talent **7** ability, faculty **8** aptitude, facility **11** suitability **15** appropriateness

Apuleius
author of: **12** The Golden Ass **13** Metamorphoses

aqua 4 blue **5** water **6** bluish **9** turquoise **10** aquamarine **12** greenish-blue

aquamarine 4 aqua, blue **5** beryl **9** turquoise **12** greenish-blue
color: **9** blue-green

aquaphobia
fear of: **5** water

aquarelle 10 watercolor

Aquarius
symbol: **11** water bearer **12** water-carrier
planet: **6** Saturn, Uranus
rules: **5** hopes **7** friends
born: **7** January **8** February

aquatic 6 marine **7** abyssal, fluvial, neritic, oceanic, pelagic **8** littoral **9** thalassic **10** fluviatile, lacustrine

aquavit
type: **6** spirit
origin: **11** Scandinavia
flavor: **4** dill **7** caraway **9** coriander
drink: **5** Glogg

aqua vitae 7 alcohol **11** water of life

aqueduct 4 duct, race **7** channel, conduit **11** watercourse **18** artificial waterway

aqueous 4 damp **5** moist **6** liquid, serous, watery **7** hydrous **8** waterish **9** lymphatic

Aquinas, St Thomas
nickname: **13** Angelic Doctor
followers: **8** Thomists
author of: **15** Summa Theologica **21** Summa Totius Theologiae **34** Summa Catholicae Fidei contra Gentiles

Arab
clothing: **3** fez **4** veil
country: **4** Iraq, Oman **5** Egypt, Libya, Qatar, Sudan, Syria, Yemen **6** Jordan, Kuwait **7** Algeria, Bahrain, Lebanon, Morocco, Tunisia **11** Saudi Arabia **18** United Arab Emirates
demon: **5** afrit **6** afreet
habitat: **6** desert
Holy City: **5** Mecca **6** Medina

language: **6** Arabic
people: **7** Semitic
religion: **6** Muslim **7** Islamic
tribe: **4** Kurd **6** Berber, Nubian, Tuareg

Arabella
opera by: **7** (Richard) Strauss

Arabia
ancient name: **14** Jazirat al-Arab
ancient people: **6** Sabean **8** Egyptian **10** Babylonian
bounded by: **5** Syria **6** Jordan, Red Sea **10** Gulf of Aden, Gulf of Oman **11** Indian Ocean, Persian Gulf
country: **4** Oman **5** Qatar, Yemen **6** Kuwait **11** Saudi Arabia **18** United Arab Emirates
highest peak: **11** Jabal Shayib
holy book: **5** Koran
Holy City: **5** Mecca **6** Medina
island: **7** Bahrain, Socotra **9** Laccadive
language: **6** Arabic
mineral/natural resource: **3** oil **4** goat **5** sheep, wheat **6** barley, millet **7** iron ore, granite **8** porphyry **9** manganese, petroleum
nomadic tribe: **5** Maaza **6** Ababda
prophet: **8** Muhammad
religion: **6** Muslim **7** Islamic
river: **4** Nile, Oxus **5** Indus **6** Tigris **9** Euphrates
sea: **3** Red **7** Arabian **11** Persian Gulf **13** Mediterranean

Arabian Nights
director: **17** Pier Paolo Pasolini
based on: **20** Thousand and One Nights
cast: **11** Franco Citti **13** Ninetto Davoli **14** Ines Pellegrina

Arabian Nights' Entertainments, The (The Thousand and One Nights)
author: **7** unknown
storyteller: **12** Scheherazade
character: **3** Roc **5** Ahmed **6** Fatima, Sinbad **7** Aladdin, Ali Baba, Sindbad **9** Abu Hassan

Arabic
national language in: **4** Iraq **5** Syria **6** Jordan **7** Lebanon **11** North Africa **16** Arabian Peninsula
also spoken in: **6** Israel **12** North America, South America **17** Soviet Central Asia, Sub-Saharan Africa
language of: **5** Koran

arable 6 fecund **7** fertile **8** farmable, fruitful, plowable, tillable **10** cultivable, productive

Arachne
origin: **6** Lydian
challenged: **6** Athena
contest: **7** weaving
changed into: **6** spider

arachnid
class: **4** mite, tick **6** spider **8** scorpion **13** daddy-long-legs

phylum: **9** Arthropod
pairs of legs: **4** four
respiratory organ: **12** pulmonary sac, tracheal tube
dwelling: **4** land **5** water
body part: **15** anterior prosoma **20** posterior opisthosoma
way of feeding: **8** parasite, predator **9** scavenger

arachnophobia
fear of: **7** spiders

Aram *see* **5** Syria

Aramis
character in: **18** The Three Musketeers
author: **5** Dumas (pere)

Arapaho
language family: **9** Algonkian **10** Algonquian
tribe: **6** Atsine **11** Gros Ventres **15** Northern Arapaho, Southern Arapaho
location: **6** Plains **8** Colorado, Red River
related to: **8** Cheyenne
ceremony: **8** sun dance

Arawak
language family: **8** Arawakan
tribe: **5** Taino **6** Igneri, Lucayo
location: **4** Cuba **5** Haiti **6** Guyana **8** Antilles, Colombia **9** Venezuela **12** South America

Arawakan
tribe: **6** Arawak **8** Boriquen **9** Borinquen

arbiter 5 judge **6** pundit, umpire **7** referee **9** authority **10** arbitrator **11** connoisseur

arbitrary 6 chance, random **7** summary, willful **8** absolute, despotic, fanciful, personal **9** frivolous, imperious, unlimited, whimsical **10** autocratic, capricious, peremptory, subjective **12** inconsistent, uncontrolled, unrestrained

arbitrate 5 judge **6** decide, settle, umpire **7** adjudge, mediate, referee **9** reconcile **10** adjudicate **12** bring to terms **13** sit in judgment

Arbitration, The
author: **8** Menander

arbitrator 5 judge **6** umpire **7** arbiter, referee **8** mediator **9** go-between, moderator **10** negotiator **11** adjudicator **12** intermediary

arbor 5 bower, folly, kiosk **6** gazebo, grotto **7** pergola **8** pavilion **9** belvedere **10** shaded walk **11** summerhouse

arc 3 bow **4** arch **5** curve **8** crescent, half-moon **10** semicircle

arcade 6 loggia, piazza **7** archway, areaway, gallery, skywalk **8** cloister, overpass **9** breezeway, colonnade, peristyle, underpass

Arcadia, The

author: **15** Sir Philip Sidney
character: **5** Mopsa **6** Pamela **7** Dametas, Gynecia, Zelmane **8** Basilius, Cecropia, Pyrocles **9** Amphialus, Musidorus, Philoclea, Plexistus

Arcadian stag *see* **8** Cerynean

Arcanan
father: **8** Alcmaeon
mother: **10** Callirrhoe
brother: **10** Amphoterus

arcane 6 mystic, occult **7** obscure **8** abstruse, esoteric, hermetic, mystical **9** enigmatic, recondite **10** mysterious

arch 3 arc, bow, sly **4** bend, dome, main, span, wily **5** chief, curve, major, saucy, vault **7** cunning, primary, roguish **8** bow shape **9** curvature, designing, principal **10** curved span **11** mischievous

archaeologist
American: **7** Bingham **8** Douglass, Stephens
British: **5** Evans **6** Carter, Childe, Layard, Leakey, Petrie, Wooley **7** Lubbock, Ventris, Wheeler **9** Rawlinson **10** Pitt-Rivers **13** Caton-Thompson
Danish: **7** Thomsen, Worsaae
French: **5** Botta **8** Cousteau **11** Champollion
German: **5** Conze **7** Curtius **8** Dorpfeld, Koldewey **9** Grotefend **10** Schliemann **11** Winckelmann
Italian: **8** Fiorelli
Swedish: **4** Geer **9** Montelius

archaic 5 passe **6** bygone **7** ancient, antique **8** obsolete **9** out-of-date **10** antiquated **11** obsolescent **12** old-fashioned

archangel 5 Satan, Uriel **7** Gabriel, Michael, Raphael

arched 4 bent **5** bowed **6** curved

archenemy 3 foe **7** archfoe, bugbear, nemesis, scourge **8** opponent **9** adversary, assailant, bete noire, combatant, disputant **10** antagonist

archeology
term: **3** dig **6** midden **9** earthwork **11** burial mound **17** aerial photography
type: **7** salvage **8** American, medieval **9** classical, text- aided **10** Egyptology, industrial, underwater **11** Assyriology, prehistoric **12** Mesopotamian
ages: **4** Iron **6** Bronze
　Old Stone Age: **11** Paleolithic
　Middle Stone Age: **10** Mesolithic
　New Stone Age: **9** Neolithic
dating method: **5** cross **8** absolute, carbon-14 **13** geochronology **16** dendrochronology **18** thermoluminescence **28** potassium-argon varved deposits
site/artifact: **2** Ur **4** Giza, Troy **5** Copan, Crete, Delos, Minos **6** Amarna, Carnac, Nimrud, Nippur, Tiryns **7** Alalakh, Babylon, Ephesus, Knossos, Mycenae, Nineveh, Olympia, Pom-

peii, Rio Azul **8** Behistun, Kuyunjik, Pergamum, pyramids **9** Arikamedu, Hissarlik, Khorsabad, New Grange, Tarquinia, Woodhenge **10** Carchemish, Persepolis, Samothrace, Stonehenge **11** Herculaneum, Machu Picchu, Mohenjodaro **12** Easter Island, Hadrian's Wall, Olduvai Gorge, Rosetta Stone **13** Avebury Circle, Zimbabwe Ruins **14** Dead Sea Scrolls, Laocoon statues **15** temple of Artemis **16** Valley of the Kings **18** Ostrava-Petrokovice, Royal Palace of Minos
tomb: **11** Tutankhamen **15** Ch'in Shih Huang Ti

archer 6 bowman **8** spearman
famous: **5** Cupid **9** Robin Hood **11** William Tell

Archer
constellation of: **11** Sagittarius

Archer, Isabel
character in: **18** The Portrait of a Lady
author: **5** James

Archer, Lew
created by: **13** Ross Macdonald
role: **10** private eye
played by: **10** Paul Newman (as Harper)
on TV: **10** Brian Keith

Archer, Miles
character in: **16** The Maltese Falcon
author: **7** Hammett

Archer, Newland
character in: **17** The Age of Innocence
author: **7** Wharton

Archer in Jeopardy
author: **13** Ross MacDonald

archery
athlete: **10** Linda Myers, Luanne Ryon **11** Darrell Pace

archetypal 5 model **7** classic **8** original **9** classical, exemplary **10** definitive, prototypal, protypical

archetype 5 model **7** classic **8** exemplar, original **9** prototype **12** prime example

Archias
founder of: **8** Syracuse
location: **6** Sicily
descendant of: **8** Hercules

Archie
creator: **10** Bob Montana **13** John Goldwater
character: **5** Betty, Moose **6** Reggie **7** Sabrina **8** Big Ethel, Veronica **11** Mr Weatherby **12** Jughead Jones
place: **9** Riverdale

Archimago
character in: **15** The Faerie Queene
author: **7** Spenser

Archipenko, Alexsandr
born: **4** Kiev **6** Russia
artwork: **8** Medranos **9** Gondolier, Medrano II, Pregnancy, The Bather

11 Boxing Match **12** Archipentura, Walking Woman **15** Geometric Statue **18** Wilhelm Furtwangler **19** Woman Combing Her Hair

architect 6 author, shaper **7** creator, deviser, founder, planner **8** designer, engineer **9** artificer, contriver, draftsman, innovator **10** instigator, originator, prime mover **13** master builder **16** building designer
  name 3 Pei **4** Hunt, Mead, Pope, Root, Wren **5** Hoban, IM Pei, Jones, Le Vau, McKim, Mills, Roche, Stone, Tange, White, Wyatt **6** Breuer, Fuller, Owings, Smirke, Wright **7** Bernini, Burnham, Gilbert, Gropius, Johnson, Latrobe, Mansart, Merrill, Renwick **8** Bramante, Harrison, Palladio, Saarinen, Skidmore, Sullivan, Yamasaki **9** Jefferson **10** Richardson **11** Le Corbusier **12** Brunelleschi, Michelangelo **14** Mies van der Rohe **15** Hardouin-Mansart
  legendary first: 8 Daedalus
    designed: 18 Minotaur's Labyrinth
  Roman: 9 Vitruvius

architecture 5 style **6** design **11** structuring **12** construction **14** architectonics **16** structural design

archives 6 annals, museum, papers **7** library, records **9** documents **10** chronicles, depository **11** memorabilia

arctic 3 icy **5** gelid, polar **6** bitter, frigid, frozen **7** glacial, ice-cold **8** freezing, icebound **9** North Pole **10** frostbound **11** far-northern, hyperborean **13** septentrional

Arden, Eve
  real name: 13 Eunice Quedens
  born: 12 Mill Valley CA
  roles: 13 Mildred Pierce, Our Miss Brooks

ardent 4 keen **5** eager, fiery, lusty **6** fierce **7** earnest, fervent, intense, zealous **8** feverish, spirited, vehement **10** passionate **11** impassioned, tempestuous **12** enthusiastic

ardor 4 love, zeal **5** gusto, verve, vigor **6** fervor, spirit **7** feeling, passion, rapture **8** devotion **9** eagerness, intensity, vehemence **10** enthusiasm, excitement, fierceness **11** amorousness **12** feverishness

Ardrey, Robert
  author of: 17 The Social Contract

arduous 4 hard **5** heavy, tough **6** severe, tiring, trying **7** onerous **8** toilsome, vigorous **9** difficult, energetic, fatiguing, Herculean, laborious, strenuous, wearisome **10** burdensome, exhausting, formidable **11** troublesome

arduousness 5 trial **8** tough job **10** difficulty, rough going, uphill work **12** hard sledding, toilsomeness **13** laboriousness, wearisomeness

area 4 turf, zone **5** arena, field, range, realm, scope, space, tract **6** domain, extent, region, sphere **7** expanse, portion, section, stretch, terrain **8** district, locality, precinct, province **9** territory

Areithous
  origin: 5 Greek
  mentioned in: 5 Iliad
  king of: 7 Arcadia
  son: 10 Menesthius
  nickname: 7 maceman
  weapon: 8 iron mace
  killed by: 8 Lycurgus

Areius see **5** Areus

arena 4 area, bowl, ring **5** field, lists, realm, scene, stage **6** circus, domain, sector, sphere **7** stadium, theater **8** coliseum, platform, province **9** gymnasium, territory **10** hippodrome **11** battlefield, marketplace **12** amphitheater, battleground, playing field

Arendt, Hannah
  author of: 10 On Violence **12** On Revolution **13** Life of the Mind **17** The Human Condition **19** Crises of the Republic, Eichmann in Jerusalem **27** The Origins of Totalitarianism

Arene
  son: 4 Idas **7** Lynceus

Arensky, Anton Stepanovich (Antony)
  born: 6 Russia **8** Novgorod
  composer of: 7 Tempest **13** Egyptian Night **18** Variations on Legend

Areopagitica
  author: 10 John Milton

Ares
  also: 8 Theritas
  origin: 5 Greek
  god of: 3 war
  father: 4 Zeus
  mother: 4 Hera
  sister: 4 Hebe
  son: 5 Molus **6** Cycnus, Deimos, Phobos, Tereus **8** Diomedes, Eurytion, Meleager, Oenomaus, Phlegyas, Thestius **10** Ascalaphus
  daughter: 7 Alcippe **8** Harmonia **9** Melanippe **11** Penthesilea
  nurse: 5 Thero
  corresponds to: 4 Mars
  epithet: 8 Enyalius **14** Gynaecothoenas

Arete
  father: 8 Rhexenor
  husband: 8 Alcinous
  daughter: 8 Nausicaa
  personifies: 7 courage

Arethusa
  form: 5 nymph
  changed into: 6 spring
  saved from: 7 Alpheus

Aretus
  father: 5 Priam
  killed by: 9 Automedon

Areus
  also: 6 Areius
  father: 4 Bias
  mother: 4 Pero
  brother: 6 Talaus **8** Leodocus
  member of: 9 Argonauts
  epithet of: 4 Zeus
  means: 7 warlike

Are You There, God? It's Me, Margaret
  author: 9 Judy Blume

Argades
  father: 3 Ion

Argeiphontes
  also: 11 Argiphontes
  epithet of: 6 Hermes
  means: 13 slayer of Argus

argent 5 white **6** silver **7** shining, silvery

Argentina
  name means: 6 silver
  capital/largest city: 11 Buenos Aires
  others: 4 Acha, Azul, Goya, Oran, Puan, Rosa **5** Jujuy, Junin, Lanus, Lujan, Metan, Monte, Salta, Tigre **6** Parana, Rufino, Zarate **7** Bolivar, Cascros, Cordoba, Dolores, Formosa, LaBanda, LaPlata, LaRioja, Mendoza, Neuquen, Posadas, Quilmes, Rafaela, Rosario, San Juan, Santa Fe, Tucuman **9** Catamarca, Rio Cuerto **10** Avellaneda, Corrientes **11** Bahai Blanca, Mar del Plata, Resistencia **17** Santiago del Estero **20** San Carlos de Bariloche
  division: 5 Andes, Chaco, Pampa **9** Patagonia **11** Mesopotamia **14** Tierra del Fuego
  measure: 4 sino **5** legua **6** cuadra, lastre **7** manzana
  monetary unit: 4 peso **7** centavo **9** argentino
  weight: 4 last **5** libra **7** quintal **8** tonelada
  island: 14 Tierra del Fuego
  lake: 6 Viedma **7** Cardiel, Fagnano, Musters **11** Buenos Aires, Mar Chiquita, Nahuel Huapi
  mountain: 4 Toro **5** Andes, Chato, Laudo, Potro **6** Bonete, Conico, Pissis, Rincon **8** Famatina, Murallon, Olivares, Tronador, Zapaleri **9** Aconcagua, Tupungato **13** Cordillera **15** Ojos del Salado **15** Cerro Mercedario, Sierra de Cordoba
  highest point: 9 Aconcagua
  river: 4 Sali **5** Atuel, Chico, Coyle, Dulce, Limay, Negro, Plata, Teuco **6** Blanco, Chubut, Cuarto, Flores, Grande, Iguazu, Parana, Quinto, Salado **7** Bermejo, Deseado, Iguassu, Mendoza, Tercero, Tunuyan, Uruguay **8** Colorado, Paraguay, Picomayo, Senguerr **9** Pilcomayo
  sea: 8 Atlantic
  physical feature:
    falls: 6 Grande, Iguazu **7** Iguassu
    lowland: 5 chaco
    plains: 6 pampas
    plateau: 4 Puna **6** Parana
    salt flat: 14 Salinas Grandes
    volcano: 5 Lanin, Maipo **6** Domuyo

7 Peteroa
wind: 5 Zonda **7** Pampero
people: 3 Api **4** Lule **5** Vejoz **6** Abipon, Vilela **7** Guarani, Puelche, Ranquel, Taluhet **8** Querandi, Querendy
  artist: 6 Borges
  author: 4 Wast **6** Banchs, Borges **7** Lugones **9** Guiraldes, Hernandez **10** Echeverria
  leader: 4 Roca **5** Illia, Menem, Mitre, Peron, Rosas **6** Videla **7** Urquiza **8** Aramburu, Belgrano, Eva Peron (Evita), Frondici, Galtieri **9** San Martin, Sarmiento **11** Isabel Peron
language: 7 Spanish
religion: 13 Roman Catholic
place:
  opera house: 11 Teatro Colon
  world's southernmost town: 7 Ushuaia
  feature:
  bird: 6 chunga
  cowboy: 6 gaucho **7** vaquero
  dance: 5 samba, tango, zamba **6** cuando, gaucho **7** milonga **9** chacarera
  farm: 6 quinta
  knife: 5 facon
  metal straw: 8 bombilla
  ranch: 8 estancia
  school smock: 9 delantale
  shawl: 6 poncho
  trousers: 9 bombachas
  weapon: 4 bola
  food:
  cocktail: 7 clarito
  dish: 4 luna **7** criollo, puchero **8** chivitos, empanada **10** parrillada

Arges
  member of: 8 Cyclopes

Argia
  also: 5 Aegia
  father: 7 Oceanus
  mother: 6 Tethys
  husband: 7 Polybus
  son: 5 Argus

Argiope
  form: 5 nymph
  father: 8 Teuthras
  husband: 6 Agenor **8** Telephus
  son: 6 Cadmus
  daughter: 6 Europa

Argiphontes see **12** Argeiphontes

Argive
  pertaining to: 5 Argos

Argo
  built by: 5 Argus
  ship of: 4 Argo

argon
  chemical symbol: 2 Ar

Argonauts
  crew: 6 Castor, Mopsus, Peleus, Pollux **7** Acastus, Orpheus, Telamon **8** Atalanta, Heracles, Hercules, Melampus, Meleager **10** Polydeuces

searchers for: 12 Golden Fleece
  leader: 5 Jason
  ship: 4 Argo
  sailed to: 7 Colchis
  pilot: 6 Tiphys

argot 4 cant **5** idiom, lingo, slang **6** jargon, patois **10** vernacular

arguable 7 at issue **9** debatable **10** disputable **12** questionable **13** controversial, problematical

argue 4 hold, show **5** claim, imply, plead **6** assert, bicker, debate, denote, evince, reason **7** contend, display, dispute, exhibit, express, point to, quarrel, quibble, wrangle **8** indicate, maintain, manifest **11** demonstrate, expostulate, remonstrate

argument 3 row **4** case, gist, plot, spat, tiff **5** clash, fight, story **6** debate, reason **7** dispute, outline, quarrel, summary **8** abstract, contents, squabble, synopsis **9** bickering, imbroglio **10** war of words **11** altercation, central idea, controversy, embroilment **12** disagreement

argumentation 6 debate **7** dispute **8** argument **10** discussion

argumentative 5 testy **7** peevish, scrappy **8** contrary, petulant, snappish **9** combative, fractious, litigious, querulous **11** belligerent, contentious, quarrelsome **12** cantankerous, disputatious

aria 3 air **4** solo, song, tune **6** melody, number **7** arietta, excerpt, section **9** selection **10** canzonetta **13** aria cantabile

Ariadne
  also: 7 Ariadna
  father: 5 Minos
  mother: 8 Pasiphae
  husband: 8 Dionysus
  son: 8 Oenopion
  gave thread to: 7 Theseus
  deserted by: 7 Theseus

Ariadne auf Naxos
  also: 14 Ariadne on Naxos
  opera by: 7 (Richard) Strauss
  character: 7 Bacchus, Theseus **8** Composer **10** Zerbinetta

Ariana see **11** Afghanistan

Ariane et Barbe-Bleu
  also: 19 Ariadne and Bluebeard
  opera by: 5 Dukas
  character: 7 Ariadne **9** Bluebeard

Arianrhod
  origin: 5 Welsh
  form: 7 goddess
  brother: 7 Gwydion
  mistress of: 7 Gwydion
  son: 14 Llew Llew Gyffes
  cursed: 14 Llew Llew Gyffes

arid 3 dry **4** dull **5** vapid **6** barren, dreary, jejune **7** dried-up, parched, tedious **8** lifeless, pedantic **9** colorless, dry as dust, waterless **10** desertlike,

uninspired **13** unimaginative, uninteresting **15** drought-scourged

aridity 6 dearth **7** drought, dryness **8** aridness, dullness **10** barrenness **12** lifelessness, rainlessness **17** unimaginativeness

aridness 6 dearth **7** aridity, drought, dryness **8** dullness **10** barrenness **12** lifelessness, rainlessness **17** unimaginativeness

arid region 6 desert **9** wasteland **16** barren wilderness

Ariel
  author: 11 Shakespeare, Sylvia Plath
  character in: 10 The Tempest

Aries
  symbol: 3 ram
  planet: 4 Mars
  rules: 11 personality
  born: 5 April, March

Arimaspians
  member of: 9 Scythians
  number of eyes: 3 one

Arion
  form: 11 winged horse
  father: 8 Poseidon
  mother: 7 Demeter

Ariosto, Ludovico
  author of: 14 Orlando Furioso

arise 4 dawn, go up, rise, wake **5** awake, begin, climb, ensue, get up, mount, occur, set in, start **6** appear, ascend, crop up, emerge, result, wake up **7** emanate, stand up **8** commence, spring up, stem from **9** originate **11** come to light

arista 3 awn **7** bristle

aristocracy 5 elite **6** gentry **7** peerage, society **8** nobility **9** beau monde **10** patricians, upper class, upper crust **11** high society

aristocrat 4 duke, earl, lady, lord, peer **5** noble **7** Brahmin, duchess, grandee, marquis **8** countess, marquess, nobleman **9** blue blood, gentleman, patrician **10** noblewoman **11** gentlewoman **12** silk stocking

aristocratic 5 noble, regal, royal **6** lordly, titled **7** courtly, genteel, refined **8** highborn, highbred, wellborn **9** dignified, patrician **10** of high rank, upper-class **11** blue- blooded, gentlemanly **12** silk-stocking **13** of gentle blood

Aristophanes
  author of: 6 Plutus **8** The Birds, The Frogs, The Peace, The Wasps **9** The Clouds **10** Lysistrata, The Knights **13** Ecclesiazusae, The Acharnians

Aristotle
  author of: 7 Physics, Poetics **8** On Plants, Politics, Rhetoric, Sophisms **9** On the Soul **10** Generation **11** Metaphysics **12** On the Heavens **14** Parts of Animals, Prior Analytics **17** Ni-

comachean Ethics **18** Posterior Analytics **23** On Beginning and Perishing

Arizona
abbreviation: 2 AZ **4** Ariz
nickname: 11 Grand Canyon
capital/largest city: 7 Phoenix
others: 3 Ajo **4** Eloy, Mesa, Naco, Yuma **5** Globe, Leupp, Tempe **6** Bisbee, McNary, Salome, Toltec, Tucson **7** Cortaro **8** Chandler, Glendale, Prescott **9** Flagstaff **10** Scottsdale
college: 11 Grand Canyon **12** Southwestern
explorer: 8 Coronado **12** Marcos de Niza
feature:
   dam: 6 Hoover **8** Coolidge **9** Roosevelt
   national park: 11 Grand Canyon **15** Petrified Forest
tribe: 4 Hano, Hopi, Pima **6** Apache, Navaho, Navajo, Papago
people: 7 Cochise **8** Geronimo **14** Barry Goldwater
lake: 4 Mead **6** Havasu, Mohave, Mormon, Powell **9** Roosevelt
land rank: 5 sixth
mountain: 5 White **6** Lemmon **7** Hualpai **8** Mazatzal **9** Baldy Peak **13** Santa Catalina
   highest point: 13 Humphreys Peak
physical feature:
   canyon: 5 Grand
   desert: 6 Sonora **7** Painted
   forest: 9 Petrified
river: 4 Gila, Salt, Zuni **5** Verde **6** Puerco **8** Colorado **12** Bill Williams **14** Little Colorado
state admission: 11 forty-eighth
state bird: 10 cactus wren
state flower: 13 saguaro cactus
state motto: 11 God Enriches
state song: 7 Arizona
state tree: 9 palo verde
ark 3 box **4** ship **5** barge, chest **8** flatboat **9** houseboat **10** Noah's boat

Ark
built by: 4 Noah
landing place: 6 Ararat
groups: 5 pairs

Arkansas
abbreviation: 2 AR **3** Ark
nickname: 4 Bear **9** Bowie Land **17** Land of Opportunity
capital/largest city: 10 Little Rock
others: 3 Coy, Cuy, Keo, Ola, Roe, Ulm **4** Alma, Bono, Casa, Dell, Diaz, Moro **5** Enola, Perla, Rondo **6** Alicia, Camden **8** El Dorado **9** Fort Smith, Jonesboro, Pine Bluff, Texarkana **10** Hot Springs **11** Blytheville **12** Fayetteville
feature:
   national park: 10 Hot Springs
tribe: 5 Caddo, Osage **6** Quapaw **7** Choctaw, Wichita **8** Cherokee
people: 8 Alan Ladd **10** Dick Powell **11** Bill Clinton **16** Douglas Mac-

Arthur
lake: 6 Beaver, Chicot, Conway, Nimrod **7** Greeson, Norfork **8** Maumelle, Ouachita **10** Bull Shoals **11** Greers Ferry **12** Blue Mountain
land rank: 13 twenty-seventh
mountain: 4 Blue **5** Ozark **6** Boston, Gaylor **7** Fourche **8** Magazine, Ouachita
   highest point: 8 Magazine
river: 3 Red **5** Black, White **6** Saline **7** Buffalo, Current **8** Arkansas, Cossatot, Ouachita **9** St Francis **11** Mississippi
state admission: 11 twenty-fifth
state bird: 11 mockingbird
state flower: 12 apple blossom
state motto: 13 (Let) The People Rule
state song: 8 Arkansas
state tree: 13 shortleaf pine

Arkin, Alan
born: 9 New York NY
roles: 5 Simon **6** Havana **7** Catch-22 **9** The In-Laws, Rocketeer **12** Indian Summer, The **13** Wait Until Dark **16** Grosse Point Blank **17** Glengarry Glen Ross **21** Last of the Red-Hot Lovers **23** The Heart Is a Lonely Hunter **40** The Russians Are Coming The Russians Are Coming

Ark of the Covenant
gold covering: 9 mercy seat **12** propitiatory
arm, arms 4 guns **5** brace, crest, equip, prime **6** branch, outfit, sector **7** forearm, fortify, prepare, protect, section, weapons **8** armament, blazonry, division, firearms, insignia, materiel, offshoot, ordnance, weaponry **9** appendage, make ready, upper limb **10** coat of arms, department, detachment, obtain arms, projection, strengthen, take up arms **12** anterior limb **13** prepare for war **14** heraldic emblem **18** furnish with weapons
armada 4 navy **5** fleet **8** flotilla, squadron **10** escadrille
armadillo 4 a par
family: 11 Dasypodidae
order: 8 Edentata
body: 5 armor **6** plates
habitat: 12 South America, United States **14** Central America
habit: 9 nocturnal
Armageddon 8 doomsday **11** final battle **13** great conflict
author: 8 Leon Uris
armagnac
type: 6 brandy **7** liqueur
origin: 6 France **7** Gascony
armament 4 arms, guns **7** weapons **8** ordnance, weaponry **9** equipment, munitions **10** outfitting **13** military might **16** war-making machine

Armenia
other name: 5 Minni **6** Urartu **8** Ana-

tolia
former name: 31 Armenian Soviet Socialist Republic
capital/largest city: 6 Erivan **7** Yerevan
ancient capital: 3 Ani **8** Artashat, Artaxata
others: 3 Van **5** Sivas **7** Trabzon **9** Kirovakan, Leninakan, Trabizond **13** Bitlisarzurum
head of state: 9 President
monetary unit: 5 ruble
lake: 3 Van **5** Sevan, Urmia **8** Urumiyah
mountain: 6 Ararat, Taurus **7** Aladagh **8** Karabakh
highest peak: 12 Mount Aragats
river: 3 Ara **4** Aras, Kura **5** Araks, Cyrus, Halys, Zanga **6** Araxes, Razdan, Tigris **9** Euphrates **10** Kizil-Irmak
physical feature:
   volcano: 7 Aragats
people: 5 Armen, Ermyn, Gomer, Hadji
   apostle: 7 Gregory
   gypsy: 5 bosha
   hero: 4 haik **6** vartan
   leader: 26 Levon Akopovich Ter Petrosyan
   me: 3 ara
   saint: 5 Sahak **6** Mesrop
language: 7 Russian **8** Armenian
religion: 16 Armenian Orthodox
feature:
   cap: 6 calpac
   fortress: 7 erebuni
   game: 7 barbout
   kingdom: 6 Urartu, Vannic **7** Cilicia, Sophene **8** Ardsruni
food:
   bread: 4 peda
   cucumber: 4 guta
   dish: 7 lahvosh **9** paraghatz, soubeoreg

Armenian
language family: 12 Indo-European
spoken in: 4 USSR **6** Russia **7** Armenia

Armida
opera by: 5 Gluck, Haydn, Lully **6** Dvorak **7** Rossini **10** Eszterhazy
Armies 7 Sabaoth

Armies of the Night
author: 12 Norman Mailer
armistice 5 peace, truce **9** cease-fire **23** suspension of hostilities
armlet 6 bangle **8** bracelet, ornament
arm of the sea 5 bight, firth, fjord (fiord), inlet **6** strait **7** channel, estuary, narrows
armoire 8 cupboard, wardrobe **12** clothespress
armor 4 mail **5** chain **6** shield **7** bulwark **10** coat of mail, protection **11** suit of armor **18** protective covering

armorial bearings 4 arms **5** crest **10** coat of arms, escutcheon

armory 7 arsenal **9** arms depot **13** ordnance depot

Arms and the Man
author: **17** George Bernard Shaw

arms depot 6 armory **7** arsenal **13** ordnance depot **18** military storehouse

Armstrong, Henry
sport: **6** boxing
class: **11** lightweight **12** welterweight

army 3 mob **4** band, bevy, crew, gang, host, mass, pack **5** crowd, force, horde, swarm **6** legion, throng, troops **7** legions, militia **8** military, soldiers, soldiery **9** land force, multitude **10** land forces **11** aggregation, fighting men **12** congregation **13** military force **15** military machine

Arnaeus
also: **4** Irus
origin: **5** Greek
mentioned in: **7** Odyssey
form: **6** beggar **9** errandboy
errandboy for: **16** Penelope's suitors

Arne
author: **20** Bjornstjerne Bjornson

Arne
son: **6** Aeolus **7** Boeotus
foster father: **9** Desmontes

Arne, Thomas Augustine
born: **6** London **7** England
composer of: **6** Alfred, Judith **8** Rosamond, Tom Thumb **10** Artaxerxes **13** Rule, Britannia **14** Love in a Village, Thomas and Sally

Arness, James
real name: **12** James Aurness
brother: **11** Peter Graves
born: **13** Minneapolis MN
roles: **8** Gunsmoke **10** Matt Dillon

Arnold, Matthew
author of: **7** Thyrsis **10** Dover Beach **15** Sohrab and Rustum, The Scholar-Gypsy **16** Empedocles on Etna **17** Culture and Anarchy, Essays in Criticism **18** On Translating Homer

aroma 4 odor **5** savor, scent, smell **7** bouquet **9** fragrance, redolence

aromatic 5 spicy **7** odorous, piquant, pungent, scented **8** fragrant, perfumed, redolent **11** odoriferous

around 4 near **5** about, circa **10** encircling, on all sides, roundabout **11** surrounding

Around the World in Eighty Days
author: **10** Jules Verne
director: **15** Michael Anderson
character: **11** Phileas Fogg **12** Passepartout
cast: **10** Cantinflas, David Niven **12** Robert Newton **15** Marlene Dietrich, Shirley MacLaine
score: **11** Victor Young
Oscar for: **5** score **7** picture

arouse 3 fan **4** goad, move, spur,

warm, whet **5** pique, rouse, waken **6** awaken, bestir, excite, foment, foster, heat up, incite, kindle, stir up, wake up **7** provoke, quicken, sharpen **8** summon up **9** stimulate

Arowhena
character in: **7** Erewhon
author: **6** Butler

arpeggio 5 chord, scale **8** flourish **13** musical device

arraign 6 accuse, charge, impute, indict **7** censure **8** denounce **9** criticize

arrange 4 file, plan, plot, pose, rank, sort **5** adapt, array, fix up, group, order, range, score **6** assort, design, devise, lay out, line up, map out, set out, settle **7** agree to, marshal, prepare, provide **8** classify, contrive, organize, schedule **9** methodize **11** orchestrate, systematize

arrangement 5 order **8** arraying, disposal, grouping, ordering **10** assortment **12** distribution, organization **13** methodization **14** categorization, classification **15** systematization
German: **9** Ausgleich
flower: **7** ikebana

arrangements 5 plans, score, terms **7** compact **8** measures **9** agreement **10** adaptation, provisions, settlement **12** preparations **13** orchestration

arrant 4 rank **5** utter **7** extreme **8** flagrant, outright, thorough **9** confirmed, downright, egregious, notorious, out-and-out **11** undisguised, unmitigated **13** thoroughgoing

array 4 deck, garb, pose, rank, robe, show, wrap **5** adorn, align, dress, group, order, place, range **6** attire, bedeck, clothe, deploy, finery, fit out, outfit, parade, set out, supply **7** apparel, arrange, display, marshal, raiment **8** clothing, garments, organize **9** pageantry **10** assortment, collection, exhibition, marshaling **11** arrangement, disposition

arrears 5 debit **9** liability **10** balance due, obligation, unpaid debt **11** overdue debt **12** indebtedness **15** outstanding debt

arrest 3 end, fix, nab **4** bust, halt, hold, slow, stay, stop **5** block, catch, check, delay, pinch, rivet, roust, seize, stall **6** absorb, collar, detain, engage, hinder, occupy, retard, secure **7** attract, capture, engross, inhibit, seizure, slowing, staying **8** blocking, checking, hold back, restrain, stoppage, stopping, suppress **9** apprehend, interrupt, retention **10** inhibiting **11** holding back **12** apprehension, take prisoner

Arrhenius, Svante August
field: **7** physics **9** chemistry
nationality: **7** Swedish
theory of: **24** electrolytic dissociation

arriere pensee 12 hidden motive **17** mental reservation

arrival 5 comer **6** advent, coming **7** entrant, visitor **8** approach, arriving, entrance, newcomer, visitant **10** appearance

arrive 4 come, near **5** get to, occur, reach **6** appear, befall, happen, show up, turn up **7** succeed **8** approach, make good

arrivederci, a rivederci 7 goodbye **8** farewell **16** until we meet again

arrogance 5 scorn **6** egoism, vanity **7** bluster, conceit, disdain, swagger **8** contempt **9** assurance, insolence, loftiness, vainglory **10** lordliness, pretension **11** braggadocio, haughtiness, presumption **13** imperiousness **14** self-importance

arrogant 4 vain **6** lordly **7** haughty, pompous **8** insolent, scornful **9** conceited, imperious **10** disdainful, egoistical, swaggering **11** egotistical, overbearing, overweening, pretentious **12** contemptuous, presumptuous, self-assuming, supercilious, vainglorious **13** high-and-mighty, self-important

arrogate 5 adopt, claim, seize, usurp **6** assume **7** preempt **8** take over **10** commandeer **11** appropriate

arrogation 6 taking **7** seizure **10** assumption, usurpation **12** confiscation **13** appropriation, expropriation

arrow 3 bow **4** bolt, dart, nock **5** shaft **7** pointer **9** direction **12** pointed shaft

Arrow
constellation of: **7** Sagitta

Arrowsmith
author: **13** Sinclair Lewis
character: **10** Leora Tozer **11** Max Gottlieb **12** Terry Wickett **14** Capitola McGurk **15** Gustaf Sondelius **16** Martin Arrowsmith **18** Dr Almus Pickerbaugh

arroyo 4 wadi **5** gorge, gully **6** ravine, trench

arsenal 6 armory **7** weapons **8** magazine **9** arms depot **11** arms factory **13** ordnance depot **14** ammunition dump

arsenic
chemical symbol: **2** As

Arsenic and Old Lace
director: **10** Frank Capra
cast: **9** Cary Grant **10** Jack Carson, Peter Lorre **13** Josephine Hull, Priscilla Lane, Raymond Massey

Arsinoe see **11** Alphesiboea

Arsinous
son: **8** Aecamede

Arsippe
father: **6** Minyas
mocked: **8** Dionysus

ars longa, vita brevis 18 art is long, life short

Ars Poetica
author: **5** Homer

art, arts 5 craft, knack, skill 6 genius 7 finesse, mastery, methods 8 artistry, facility, strategy 9 dexterity, expertise, technique 10 fine points, humanities, principles, subtleties, virtuosity
  goddess of: 6 Athena, Athene, Pallas, Saitis 7 Minerva 11 Tritogeneia 12 Pallas Athena 18 Alalcomenean Athena

Artegall
  character in: 15 The Faerie Queene
  author: 7 Spenser

Artemis
  also: 7 Cynthia 9 Astrateia
  origin: 5 Greek
  form: 6 virgin 7 goddess 8 huntress
  habitat: 4 moon
  mother: 4 Leto
  twin brother: 6 Apollo
  companion: 4 Opis 5 Oread
  corresponds to: 5 Diana 6 Phoebe, Selene 11 Britomartis
  epithet: 6 Orthia 7 Eurippa, Laphria, Limnaea, Pyronia 8 Aeginaea, Agrotera, Calliste, Caryatis, Daphnaea 9 Hemerasia, Lygodesma 10 Polymastus 11 Leucophryne

artery 3 way 4 path, road, vein 5 aorta 6 street 7 channel, highway 11 blood vessel

artful 3 apt, sly 4 able, deft, foxy, wily 5 adept, quick, sharp, smart 6 adroit, astute, clever, crafty, gifted, shifty, shrewd, subtle, tricky 7 cunning, knowing, politic 8 masterly, scheming, skillful, talented 9 deceitful, deceptive, designing, dexterous, ingenious, inventive, strategic, underhand 10 contriving, diplomatic, proficient 11 imaginative, machinating, maneuvering, resourceful 12 disingenuous

artfulness 5 guile 6 deceit 7 cunning, slyness 8 artifice, foxiness, scheming, subtlety, trickery, wiliness 10 craftiness 11 machination

Arthur
  director: 11 Steve Gordon
  cast: 11 Dudley Moore, John Gielgud 12 Liza Minnelli 19 Geraldine Fitzgerald
  Oscar for: 15 supporting actor (Gielgud)

Arthur
  began: 10 Round Table
  buried: 6 Avalon
  chronicler: 4 Wace 6 Malory 8 Chretien
  father: 14 Uther Pendragon
  half-sister: 11 Morgan le Fay
  home: 7 Camelot
  island: 6 Avalon
  knights: 3 Kay 6 Gareth, Gawain 7 Geraint 8 Bedivere, Lancelot, Percival, Tristram 9 Launcelot
  knights sought: 9 Holy Grail
  mother: 7 Igraine, Ygaerne
  nephew: 6 Modred 7 Mordred
  sword: 9 Excalibur
    given by: 13 Lady of the Lake
  wife: 9 Guinevere
  wizard: 6 Merlin
  women, Arthurian: 4 Anna, Enid 5 Nimue 6 Elaine, Gyneth, Iseult, Isolde 7 Igraine, Ygaerne 9 Bellicent, Guinivere 11 Morgan le Fay

Arthur, Chester Alan
  nickname: 4 Chet 16 The Gentleman Boss
  presidential rank: 11 twenty-first
  party: 10 Republican
  state represented: 2 NY
  defeated: 5 no-one
    succeeded upon death of: 8 Garfield
  vice president: 4 none
  cabinet:
    state: 6 (James Gillespie) Blaine 13 (Frederick Theodore) Frelinghuysen
    treasury: 6 (Charles James) Folger, (William) Windom 7 (Walter Quintin) Gresham 9 (Hugh) McCulloch
    war: 7 (Robert Todd) Lincoln
    attorney general: 8 (Benjamin Harris) Brewster, (Isaac Wayne) MacVeagh
    navy: 4 (William Henry) Hunt 8 (William Eaton) Chandler
    postmaster general: 4 (Timothy Otis) Howe 5 (Thomas Lemuel) James 6 (Frank) Hatton 7 (Walter Quinton) Gresham
    interior: 6 (Henry Moore) Teller 8 (Samuel Jordan) Kirkwood
  born: 2 VT (or Canada) 9 Fairfield
  died: 2 NY 11 New York City
  buried: 2 NY 6 Albany
  education:
    college: 5 Union
    studied: 3 law
  religion: 12 Episcopalian
  interests: 8 good food (an epicure) 13 salmon fishing
  political career: 13 vice president 26 customs collector for New York
  civilian career: 6 lawyer 7 teacher
  military service: 8 Civil War
    quartermaster general of: 12 state militia (New York)
  notable events of lifetime/term: 5 Panic (of 1883)
    Act: 9 Pendleton 16 Chinese Exclusion 19 Edmunds Anti-Polygamy
  father: 7 William
  mother: 7 Malvina (Stone)
  siblings: 4 Jane, Mary 6 Almeda, George, Regina 7 Malvina, William 8 Ann Eliza
  wife: 5 Ellen (Lewis Herndon)
    nickname: 4 Nell
  children: 11 Chester Alan 12 Ellen Herndon 19 William Lewis Herndon

artichoke 14 Cynara Scolymus
  varieties: 5 Globe 7 Chinese 8 Japanese 9 Jerusalem 14 White Jerusalem

article 4 item, part, term 5 count, essay, paper, piece, point, story, theme, thing 6 clause, detail, matter, object, review, sketch 7 portion, product, proviso, write-up 8 division 9 commodity, condition, paragraph, provision, substance 10 commentary, particular 11 proposition, stipulation

articulate 4 join 5 hinge, state, utter, voice 6 convey, facile, fluent, hook up 7 connect, enounce, express 8 eloquent, organize 9 enunciate, formulate, pronounce 10 enunciated, expressive, meaningful, speechlike 12 intelligible

articulation 5 hinge, joint 7 diction 8 juncture 9 elocution, utterance 10 connection 11 enunciation 13 pronunciation

artifact 4 tool 7 manmade 9 arrowhead

artifice 4 hoax, ruse, trap, wile 5 blind, dodge, feint, guile, trick 6 deceit, device, tactic 7 cunning, slyness 8 foxiness, intrigue, maneuver, scheming, trickery, wiliness 9 deception, duplicity, falsehood, imposture, ingenuity, invention, stratagem 10 artfulness, cleverness, craftiness, subterfuge 11 contrivance, machination 13 inventiveness

artificer 7 artisan, deviser 9 contriver, craftsman

artificial 4 fake, mock, sham 5 bogus, false, phony, stagy 6 ersatz, forced 7 feigned, labored, manmade, stilted 8 affected, mannered, specious, spurious 9 imitation, insincere, pretended, simulated, synthetic, unnatural 10 factitious, non-natural, theatrical 11 counterfeit 12 manufactured

artillery 6 cannon 7 big guns 8 ordnance 11 mounted guns

artisan 6 master 9 craftsman 10 technician 14 handicraftsman

art is long, life short
  Latin: 18 ars longa vita brevis

artist 6 expert, master 8 virtuoso

artistic 7 elegant, stylish 8 graceful, handsome, tasteful 9 aesthetic, exquisite 10 attractive

artistic ability 6 talent 7 mastery 8 artistry 10 virtuosity

artistry 5 taste, touch 6 talent 7 mastery 10 virtuosity 11 proficiency, sensibility 14 accomplishment

artless 4 naif, open, pure, true 5 crude, frank, naive, plain 6 candid, honest, humble, simple 7 natural, sincere 8 innocent, trusting 9 guileless, ingenuous, primitive, unadorned 10 inartistic, lacking art, unaffected, untalented 11 open-hearted, undesigning

13 unpretentious 15 straightforward, unselfconscious, unsophisticated

artlessness 6 candor 7 honesty, naivete 8 openness 9 frankness, sincerity 10 simplicity 11 naturalness 13 guilelessness, ingenuousness 14 unaffectedness

art object
  French: 9 objet d'art

Art of Living, The
  author: 11 John Gardner

Art of Love, The (Ars Amatoria)
  author: 4 Ovid

arty 6 dainty 7 foppish 8 affected, high- brow, overnice, precious 9 dandified, overblown 10 effeminate 11 overrefined, pretentious 12 artsy-craftsy, bluestocking, high-sounding

Aryan
  modern name: 13 Indo-European
  origin: 10 North India 11 Central Asia
  family of languages: 5 Hindi 7 Bengali, Panjabi 9 Sinhalese
  religion: 8 Hinduism
  originated: 11 caste system

Aryana *see* 11 Afghanistan

as 4 that, when 5 while 7 because, equally

Asa
  father: 6 Abijah
  grandfather: 8 Rehoboam
  grandmother: 6 Maacah
  deposed: 6 Maacah
  defeated: 6 Baasha

as above
  Latin: 7 ut supra

as a group 7 en masse, in a body 8 as a whole, together 11 all together

as a matter of form
  Latin: 8 pro forma

Asar *see* 5 Aesir

as a result 2 so 5 due to 7 because 9 therefore, wherefore, whereupon 11 accordingly 12 consequently 13 in consequence

as a whole 6 in toto 8 all in all 10 altogether 19 all things considered
  French: 6 en bloc

as below
  Latin: 7 ut infra

Ascalaphus
  occupation: 6 sentry 8 gardener
  location: 10 underworld
  father: 4 Ares
  brother: 8 Ialmenus
  member of: 9 Argonauts
  killed by: 9 Deiphobus
  changed into: 3 owl
  changed by: 7 Demeter

Ascanius
  also: 5 Iulus
  father: 6 Aeneas
  mother: 6 Creusa
  founder of: 9 Alba Longa

ascend 4 rise 5 climb, mount, scale 7 inherit 9 succeed to

ascendancy, ascendance 4 edge, rule, sway 5 power, reign 7 command, control, mastery 8 whip hand 9 advantage, authority, dominance, influence, supremacy, upper hand 10 domination, leadership 11 preeminence, sovereignty, superiority 12 predominance

ascension 6 ascent, rising 7 scaling 8 climbing, mounting 10 ascendancy

ascent 4 rise 5 climb, grade, slope 6 rising 7 advance, incline, scaling, upgrade 8 climbing, gradient, mounting, progress 9 ascension 11 advancement, progression

ascertain 5 learn 6 detect, verify 7 certify, find out, unearth 8 discover 9 determine, establish, ferret out

ascertainable 10 detectable 11 discernible, perceivable, perceptible

ascetic 3 nun 4 monk, yogi 5 fakir, stern 6 essene, hermit, strict 7 austere, dervish, eremite, recluse, Spartan 8 celibate, cenobite, rigorous, solitary 9 abstainer, anchorite, religious 10 abstemious, flagellant, self-denier 11 self- denying 13 self-mortifier 14 self-mortifying

Asch, Sholem
  author of: 4 Mary 5 Moses 8 A Village 10 The Apostle, The Prophet 11 The Nazarene, Three Cities 15 Song of the Valley 17 The God of Vengeance

Asclepius
  origin: 5 Greek
  god of: 7 healing 8 medicine
  father: 6 Apollo
  mother: 7 Coronis
  wife: 6 Epione
  son: 7 Machaon 10 Podalirius
  daughter: 4 Iaso 6 Hygeia
  nurse: 6 Trygon
  corresponds to: 11 Aesculapius
  epithet: 8 Cotyleus

ascribe 6 assign, credit, impute, relate 7 trace to 8 accredit, charge to 9 attribute

asea 4 lost 6 addled, adrift 7 puzzled 8 confused 10 bewildered

Asgard
  home of: 4 Asar 5 Aesir
  origin: 12 Scandinavian
  connected to earth by: 7 bifrost 13 rainbow bridge
  location of: 8 Valhalla

ash 4 dust 6 cinder 7 residue 12 powdered lava
  family: 5 olive
  genus: 8 Fraxinus
  climatic zone: 17 northern temperate
  varieties: 3 Pop, Red, Sea 4 Blue 5 Black, Green, Manna, Texas, Wafer, Water, White 6 Alpine, Ground, Shamel, Syrian, Velvet 7 Arizona,

Modesto, Prickly 8 Carolina, Stinking 9 Evergreen, Flowering 10 Manchurian, Montebello 18 Yellow-topped mallee
  use: 4 fuel 6 timber 7 barrels 8 landscape 9 furniture 10 motor parts, sport goods
  most common species: 8 white ash

ashamed 3 shy 7 abashed, bashful, prudish 9 chagrined, mortified, squeamish 10 chapfallen, distressed, humiliated, shamefaced 11 crestfallen, discomfited, embarrassed 12 disconcerted 13 guilt-stricken 18 conscience-stricken

Ashby, Hal
  director of: 10 Being There, Coming Home

ashen 3 wan 4 gray, pale 5 livid, pasty 6 anemic, leaden, pallid 8 blanched

Asher
  father: 5 Jacob
  mother: 6 Zilpah
  brother: 3 Dan, Gad 4 Levi 5 Judah 6 Joseph, Reuben, Simeon 7 Zebulun 8 Benjamin, Issachar, Nephtali
  sister: 5 Dinah
  city in: 8 Manasseh
  descendant of: 8 Asherite

Ashkenaz
  father: 6 Japhet
  mother: 5 Gomer

Ashley, Lady Brett
  character in: 15 The Sun Also Rises
  author: 9 Hemingway

ashore 6 on land 7 aground 9 on dry land

Ashton-Warner, Sylvia
  author of: 5 Three 6 Myself 7 Teacher 8 Spinster 10 Greenstone

Ashtoreth
  origin: 7 Semitic
  corresponds to: 6 Inanna, Ishtar 7 Astarte, Mylitta

Ash Wednesday
  author: 7 T S Eliot

ashy 3 wan 4 pale 5 ashen, pasty, white 6 pallid, sallow 7 ghastly, ghostly 8 blanched 9 colorless

Asia
  country: 4 Iran, Iraq, Laos, Oman 5 Burma, China, India, Japan, Macao, Nepal, Qatar, Syria, Yemen 6 Bhutan, Brunei, Cyprus, Israel, Jordan, Russia, Sikkim, Taiwan, Turkey 7 Armenia, Bahrain, Georgia, Kashmir, Lebanon, Myanmar, Vietnam 8 Cambodia, Hong Kong, Malaysia, Maldives, Mongolia, Pakistan, Sri Lanka, Thailand 9 East Timor, Indonesia, Kirghizia, Singapore 10 Azerbaijan, Bangladesh, Kazakhstan, Kyrgyzstan, North Korea, South Korea, Tajikistan, Uzbekistan 11 Afghanistan, Saudi Arabia 12 North Vietnam, South Vietnam, Turkmenistan 13 Inner Mongolia 14 Papua New

Guinea **15** Sinkiang-Uighur **18** United Arab Emirates

desert: 4 Gobi, Thar **6** Syrian **7** Arabian, Karakum **8** Kyzylkum **10** Takla Makan

island: 5 Kuril, Japan **6** Taiwan **7** Hai-nan **8** Sri Lanka **9** Indonesia: **3** Aru **4** Java, Sulu **5** Ceram, Sumba, Timor **6** Borneo, Flores **7** Celebes, Sumatra **8** Moluccas, Tanimbar **9** Halmahera, New Guinea **11** Philippines

ancient people/empire: 4 Elam, Thai **5** Akkad, Aryan, Indus, Khmer, Media, Shang **6** Mongol, Ohoman, Semite **7** Amorite, Assyria, Hwang Ho, Parthia, Persian **8** Sumerian **9** Babylonia, Dravidian, Sassanian **11** Hephthalite, Mesopotamia

ancient city: 2 Ur **5** Pagan, Sumer **6** Anyang **7** Ayuthia, Harappa **8** Mandalay **12** Mohenjo-daro

ancient leader: 5 Asoka, Kassi **6** Darius **9** Anawratha, Zoroaster **13** Cyrus the Great **17** Alexander the Great

religion: 5 Islam **6** Muslim, Shinto, Taoism **7** Jainism, Judaism **8** Buddhism, Hinduism **12** Christianity, Confucianism **13** Protestantism **16** Roman Catholicism

language: 5 Hindi, Malay **6** Arabic, French, Korean **7** Chinese, English, Russian, Spanish **8** Japanese **10** Indonesian, Portuguese

  Chinese dialects: 2 Wu **3** Min **5** Hakka **8** Mandarin **9** Cantonese

river: 2 Ob **3** Amu, Hsi, Syr **4** Amur, Lena **5** Indus **6** Ganges, Mekong, Tigris **7** Hwang Ho, Salween, Yangtze, Yenisei **9** Euphrates, Irrawaddy **11** Brahmaputra **16** Tigris-Euphrates

lake: 6 Baikal **7** Aral Sea **8** Balkhash **10** Caspian Sea

mountain/mountain range. 5 Altai, Urals **6** Kunlon, Pamirs, Taurus, Zagros **8** Caucasus, Sulaiman, Tien Shan **9** Himalayas, Hindu Kush, Karakoram **10** Arakan Yoma

highest point: 12 Mount Everest

lowest point: 7 Dead Sea

mineral/natural resources: 3 oil, tin **4** coal, mica, talc, zinc **7** bauxite, iron ore, mercury **8** chromium, graphite, selenium, tungsten **9** manganese **10** natural gas

largest city: 8 Shanghai

vegetation: 3 fir, sal **4** moss, pine, teak **5** larch **6** bamboo, lichen, spruce **8** ironwood

animal: 3 elk, yak **4** bear, wolf **5** camel, panda, sable, takin, tiger **6** ermine, kuland **7** markhor **8** antelope, elephant, reindeer **9** arctic fox, polar bear

people: 4 Huis, Kurd, Thai, Turk **5** Aryan, Khmer, Malay, Tungu **6** Buryat, Chuang, Kalmyk, Mongol, Semite, Vighor **7** Baluchi, Burmese, Chi-

nese, Chukchi, Persian, Russian, Tadzhik, Tibetan **8** Armenian, Filipino, Japanese **9** Dravidian **10** Han Chinese, Indonesian, Vietnamese

aside 4 away **5** apart **6** aslant, beside **7** whisper

As I Lay Dying
  author: 15 William Faulkner
  character:
    Bundren family: 4 Anse, Cash, Darl **5** Addie, Jewel **9** Dewey Dell

Asimov, Isaac
  author of: 6 I Robot **10** Foundation (trilogy) **12** Caves of Steel, Robots of Dawn **17** The Gods Themselves
  character: 12 Elijah Bailey **13** R Daneel Olivaw

asinine 5 silly **6** absurd, insane, stupid **7** foolish, idiotic, moronic, witless **9** brainless, imbecilic, senseless **10** half-witted, irrational, muddlehead, ridiculous **11** lamebrained, thickheaded, thick-witted **12** dunderheaded, feebleminded, simpleminded, thick-skulled

asininity 5 folly **8** dumbness **9** silliness, stupidity **10** imbecility **11** doltishness, foolishness **16** simplemindedness

as it should be
  French: 11 comme il faut

Asius
  origin: 5 Greek
  mentioned in: 5 Iliad
  king of: 7 Percote
  father: 8 Hyrtacus
  killed by: 9 Idomeneus

ask 3 beg, bid, sue **4** call, pump, quiz, seek, urge **5** apply, claim, grill, plead, press, query **6** appeal, charge, demand, desire, expect, invite, summon **7** beseech, entreat, implore, inquire, request, solicit **8** petition, question, sound out **10** supplicate **11** interrogate

askance 11 skeptically **12** disdainfully, suspiciously **13** distrustfully, mistrustfully **14** disapprovingly

askew 4 awry **6** aslant **7** crooked **8** cockeyed, lopsided, sleeping **9** crookedly

Askkimey see **6** Eskimo

aslant 4 awry **5** askew **7** crooked **8** cockeyed, lopsided **9** crookedly, obliquely, slantwise

asleep 6 dozing **7** napping **10** slumbering **13** taking a siesta **14** dead to the world

as much as this
  Latin: 8 quoad hoc

Asner, Ed
  born: 12 Kansas City KS
  roles: 5 Roots **6** Daniel **8** El Dorado, Lou Grant **12** A Case of Libel, The Gathering, Silent Motive **14** Rich Man Poor Man **18** Mary Tyler Moore Show

asocial 8 unsocial **9** nonsocial, reclusive **10** antisocial **12** misanthropic

Asopus
  form: 3 god
  habitat: 5 river
  father: 7 Oceanus
  mother: 6 Tethys
  wife: 6 Metope
  son: 7 Ismenus, Pelagon
  number of daughters: 6 twenty

asparagus
  varieties: 4 Cape **6** Common, Garden, Smilax **7** Cossack **8** Prussian, Sprenger

aspect 3 air **4** look, side **5** angle, facet, point **7** feature **10** appearance **13** consideration

aspen 7 Populus
  varieties: 7 Chinese, Quaking **8** European, Japanese **9** Trembling **12** Large-toothed

asperity 5 rigor **6** rancor **8** acrimony, hardship, severity **9** harshness, hostility, roughness **10** difficulty

Aspern Papers, The
  author: 10 Henry James

aspersion 4 slur **5** abuse, smear **7** calumny, censure, obloquy, railing, slander **8** reproach, reviling **10** defamation, detraction **11** deprecation **12** vilification **13** disparagement

Asphodel Fields
  meadow of: 10 dead heroes

asphyxiate 5 choke **6** stifle **7** smother **9** suffocate **11** strangulate

aspirant 7 hopeful, nominee **9** applicant, candidate **10** competitor, contestant

aspiration 3 end **4** hope, mark, wish **6** design, desire, intent, object **7** craving, longing, purpose **8** ambition, daydream, endeavor, yearning **9** hankering, intention, objective

aspire 4 seek **5** aim at, covet, crave **6** desire, pursue **7** hope for, long for, pine for, wish for **8** yearn for **9** pant after **10** hunger over **11** hanker after, thirst after

ass 3 oaf **4** dolt, fool, jerk **5** booby, burro, dunce, idiot, moron, ninny **6** donkey, dum-dum, nitwit **7** half-wit, jackass **8** bonehead, imbecile, lunkhead, numskull **9** blockhead, lamebrain **10** dunderhead, nincompoop

assail 5 fly at **6** attack **7** assault, lunge at, set upon **9** pitch into **11** descend upon

assailant 6 mugger **8** assailer, attacker, molester **9** aggressor, assaulter

assailer 8 attacker **9** aggressor, assailant, assaulter

Assamese
  language family: 12 Indo-European
  branch: 11 Indo-Iranian
  group: 5 Indic
  spoken in: 5 (northern) India

Assaracus
origin: **5** Greek
mentioned in: **5** Iliad
father: **4** Tros
son: **5** Capys
founder of: **10** royal house

assassin 6 hit man, killer, slayer **8** murderer **11** executioner

assassinate 4 kill, slay **6** murder, rub out **7** bump off **9** do to death, liquidate **10** put to death **11** exterminate

assault 4 push, raid **5** drive, fly at, foray, lunge, sally, siege, storm **6** assail, attack, charge, invade, strike, thrust **7** besiege, bombard, lunge at, offense, set upon **8** fall upon, invasion, storming, strike at, thrust at **9** assailing, lash out at, onslaught **10** aggression **11** bombardment

assaulter 6 mugger **8** assailer, attacker **9** aggressor, assailant

assay 3 try **4** rate, test **5** essay, prove **6** assess **7** analyze, attempt **8** appraise, endeavor, estimate, evaluate **9** undertake

assemblage 4 body, heap, herd, mass, pack, pile **5** batch, bunch, clump, flock, group, stock, store **6** throng **7** cluster, company **8** assembly, conclave **9** aggregate, amassment, gathering **10** collection **11** aggregation **12** accumulation, congregation

assemble 4 join, meet **5** amass, flock, rally **6** gather, heap up, muster, pile up, summon **7** collect, compile, connect, convene, convoke, marshal, round up **8** construct, fabricate **10** accumulate, congregate **11** fit together, put together **12** call together, come together **13** bring together, group together

assembly 4 body, herd, mass, pack **5** crowd, flock, group, troop **6** throng **7** cluster, company, council **8** conclave, congress **9** aggregate, gathering **10** assemblage, collection **11** aggregation, convocation, legislature **12** congregation

assembly hall 8 auditory **10** auditorium **11** concert hall, lecture hall, meeting hall

assent 5 agree, allow, grant, yield **6** accept, accord, comply, concur, permit **7** approve, concede, consent, defer to **8** approval, sanction **9** acquiesce, admission, agreement **10** acceptance, compliance, concession, fall in with **11** affirmation, approbation, concurrence, endorsement, recognition, subscribe to **12** acquiescence, confirmation, ratification, verification **13** corroboration **14** acknowledgment

assent to 4 okay **5** allow **6** accept, permit **7** approve **8** sanction, say yes to **9** agree with, authorize **11** acquiesce to, go along with

assert 4 aver, avow **5** argue, claim, state, swear **6** accent, affirm, avouch, insist, stress, uphold **7** advance, contend, declare, profess **8** advocate, maintain, propound, set forth **9** emphasize **10** put forward

assertion 5 claim **6** avowal, dictum **8** argument, averment **9** statement, upholding **10** allegation, contention **11** declaration, maintaining **12** protestation

assertive 5 pushy **8** cocksure, decisive, emphatic, forceful, positive **9** confident, insistent, outspoken **10** aggressive **11** domineering, self-assured **12** strong-willed

assertiveness 10 insistence **11** forwardness **12** cocksureness, forcefulness, positiveness **13** agressiveness, outspokenness **14** self-confidence

assess 3 tax **4** levy **5** judge, value **6** charge **8** appraise, consider, estimate, evaluate, look over

assessment 3 fee, tax **4** dues, fine, rate, toll **6** charge, impost, tariff **8** judgment **9** appraisal **10** estimation, evaluation

asset 3 aid **4** boon, help, plus **7** benefit, service **9** advantage

assets 4 cash **5** goods, means, money **6** wealth **7** capital, effects **8** property, reserves **9** resources **10** belongings **11** possessions

asseverate 4 aver, avow **5** state, swear **6** affirm, assert, attest, avouch, insist **7** certify, contend, declare, protect **8** maintain, proclaim **9** emphasize, pronounce

as shown below
Latin: **7** ut infra

assiduity 8 industry, tenacity **9** diligence **10** dedication, doggedness **11** application, persistence **13** determination

assiduous 6 dogged **7** earnest **8** constant, diligent, sedulous, tireless, untiring **9** laborious, steadfast, tenacious **10** determined, persistent, unflagging **11** hardworking, industrious, persevering, unremitting **13** indefatigable

assign 3 fix, set **4** give, name **5** allot, grant **6** charge, choose, invest **7** appoint, consign, entrust, mete out, specify **8** allocate, delegate, dispense, set apart **9** apportion, designate, determine, prescribe, stipulate **10** commission, distribute

assignation 4 date **5** tryst **7** meeting **10** rendezvous **11** appointment

assignment 3 job **4** duty, post, task **5** chore **6** lesson **8** exercise, homework **9** allotment **10** allocation, commission **11** appointment, designation **12** distribution **13** apportionment

assimilate 6 absorb, digest, imbibe, in-gest, take in **9** integrate **10** metabolize **11** incorporate

Assiniboine, Assiniboin
language family: **6** Siouan
location: **9** Minnesota **12** Lake Winnipeg, Saskatchewan
related to: **7** Dakotas

assist 3 aid **4** abet, hand, help **5** boost, serve **6** back up, uphold, wait on **7** benefit, support, sustain **9** cooperate, lend a hand, reinforce **11** accommodate, collaborate, helping hand

assistance 3 aid **4** alms, help **6** relief **7** charity, service, stipend, subsidy, support **10** sustenance **11** cooperation, helping hand **12** contribution **13** collaboration, reinforcement **16** financial support

assistant 3 aid **4** aide, ally **5** aider **6** helper **7** partner **8** adjutant, coworker, sidekick **9** accessory, associate, auxiliary, colleague, subaltern, supporter **10** accomplice, apprentice, cooperator, lieutenant **11** confederate, helping hand, subordinate **12** collaborator **15** second-in-command

associate 3 mix, pal, tie **4** ally, bind, chum, club, join, link, mate, pair, peer, yoke **5** buddy, crony, merge, unite **6** allied, couple, fellow, friend, hobnob, league, mingle, relate **7** combine, comrade, connect, consort, hang out, partner, related **8** confrere, coworker, identify, intimate, sidekick **9** affiliate, colleague, companion, confidant, correlate, pal around, rub elbows, run around **10** accomplice, affiliated, fraternize **11** confederate, subordinate **12** collaborator

associated 6 allied, joined, united **9** connected **10** affiliated **11** amalgamated

association 3 tie **4** body, bond, club, meld **5** blend, group, union **6** clique, league **7** combine, company, linkage, mixture, society **8** alliance, intimacy, mingling, relation **9** coalition, community, relations, syndicate **10** assemblage, connection, federation, fellowship, fraternity, friendship, membership **11** affiliation, camaraderie, combination, confederacy, corporation, correlation, familiarity, partnership **12** acquaintance, friendliness, organization, relationship **13** collaboration, companionship, confederation, participation **14** fraternization, identification

assorted 5 mixed **6** motley, sundry, varied **7** diverse, various **9** different **11** diversified **13** heterogeneous, miscellaneous

assortment 5 array, stock, store **6** medley, motley **7** melange, mixture, sorting, variety **8** grouping, quantity **9** arranging, assorting, diversity, potpourri, selection **10** collection, hodgepodge, miscellany **11** arrangement, classifying, disposition **14** classification, conglomeration

assuage 4 calm, ease **5** allay, quiet, still **6** lessen, pacify, soften, soothe, temper **7** appease, lighten, mollify, relieve **8** mitigate, tone down **9** alleviate **14** take the edge off

assuagement 6 easing, relief, solace **7** comfort **8** blunting, easement **9** abatement, lessening, tempering **10** mitigation **11** appeasement **13** mollification

assume 4 take **5** fancy, guess, infer, judge, seize, think, usurp **6** accept, deduce, gather, take on, take up **7** believe, imagine, presume, suppose, surmise, suspect **8** arrogate, shoulder, take over, theorize **9** postulate, speculate, undertake **10** commandeer, conjecture, understand **11** appropriate, expropriate, hypothesize **14** take for granted

assumed 4 fake **5** bogus, false, phony **6** made-up **8** presumed, supposed **9** falsified **10** fictitious **11** make-believe, presupposed, pseudonymic **12** pseudonymous

assumed name 5 alias **7** pen name **9** pseudonym **13** false identity
French: 10 nom de plume **11** nom de guerre

assuming 4 bold **5** nervy, pushy **6** brazen, cheeky **7** forward, haughty **8** arrogant, insolent **9** audacious, presuming **11** overbearing **12** presumptuous **13** self-assertive

assumption 6 belief, taking, theory **7** premise, seizure **8** assuming, taking on, taking up **9** accepting, postulate **10** acceptance, arrogation, hypothesis, usurpation **11** postulation, presumption, shouldering, supposition, undertaking **13** appropriating **14** presupposition

assurance 3 vow **4** oath **5** poise **6** binder, pledge **7** promise **8** averment, boldness, coolness, sureness, warranty **9** certainty, certitude, guarantee **10** confidence, profession **11** affirmation, assuredness, word of honor **12** self-reliance **14** aggressiveness, self-confidence, self-possession

assure 5 vow to **6** clinch, ensure, secure **7** confirm, promise **8** pledge to **9** guarantee **11** make certain **14** give one's word to

assured 4 sure **5** fixed **6** poised, secure **7** certain, settled **8** positive **9** confident, undoubted **10** dependable, guaranteed **11** indubitable, irrefutable **12** indisputable **13** self-confident, self-possessed **14** unquestionable

Astaire, Fred
real name: 19 Frederick Austerlitz
partner: 12 Ginger Rogers
born: 7 Omaha NE
roles: 6 Top Hat **9** Funny Face, Let's Dance, Swing Time **10** Holiday Inn **12** Easter Parade, Royal Wedding, Shall We Dance **14** The Gay Divorcee

Astarte
origin: 7 Semitic
goddess of: 9 fertility **12** reproduction
habitat: 4 moon
corresponds to: 6 Inanna, Ishtar **7** Mylitta **9** Ashtoreth

aster 12 Callistephus
varieties: 4 Tree **5** Black, China, Heath **6** Annual, Golden, Mojave, Stoke's **7** Italian **8** Blue-wood **9** Tartarian, White wood **10** New England **11** White upland

Asteria
form: 8 Titaness
father: 5 Coeus
mother: 6 Phoebe
sister: 4 Leto
husband: 6 Perses
son: 8 Paropeus
daughter: 6 Hecate
changed into: 5 Delos **6** island

Asterius
also: 8 Asterion
form: 5 giant **8** minotaur
king of: 5 Crete
father: 4 Anax **8** Tectamus **10** Cretan Bull, Hyperasius
mother: 8 Pasiphae
wife: 6 Europa
adopted sons: 5 Minos **8** Sarpedon **12** Rhadamanthys
daughter: 5 Crete
member of: 9 Argonauts

astern 3 aft **5** abaft **6** behind

asteroid 6 debris **9** planetoid

Asteropaeus
origin: 5 Greek
mentioned in: 5 Iliad
father: 7 Pelegon
ally of: 4 Troy
killed by: 8 Achilles

Asterope *see* **7** Sterope

astir 2 up **5** afoot, awake **6** active, roused **8** in motion, out of bed **10** up and about

astonish 4 daze, stun **5** amaze, shock **6** dazzle **7** astound, confuse, perplex, stagger, startle, stupefy **8** bewilder, confound, dumfound, surprise **9** electrify, overwhelm, take aback **10** strike dumb **11** flabbergast **15** make one's eyes pop **18** take one's breath away

astonishing 7 amazing **8** dazzling, shocking, striking **9** confusing, startling **10** astounding, impressive, perplexing, staggering, stupefying, surprising **11** bewildering, confounding **12** breathtaking, electrifying, overpowering, overwhelming

astonishment 3 awe **5** shock **6** wonder **8** surprise **9** amazement, confusion **10** perplexity, wonderment **12** bewilderment, stupefaction

Astor, Mary
real name: 28 Lucille Vasconcellos Langhanke
born: 8 Quincy IL
roles: 6 Marmee **11** Little Women, The Great Lie **15** Meet Me in St Louis **16** The Maltese Falcon **17** The Palm Beach Story **18** The Prisoner of Zenda

astound 4 daze, stun **5** amaze, shock **6** dazzle **7** stagger, startle, stupefy **8** astonish, dumfound, surprise, take back **9** electrify, overwhelm **10** strike dumb **11** flabbergast **15** make one's eyes pop **18** take one's breath away

Astrabacus
origin: 5 Greek **7** Spartan
form: 6 prince
found: 11 wooden image
hidden by: 7 Orestes
co-finder: 8 Alopecus

Astraea
also: 6 Astrea
goddess of: 7 justice
father: 4 Zeus
mother: 6 Themis

Astraeus
form: 5 Titan
consort of: 3 Eos
father of: 4 wind **5** stars

astral 6 starry **9** celestial **12** astronomical

Astrateia *see* **/** Artemis

astray 3 off **5** amiss **6** afield **10** off the mark **12** off the course **16** off the right track

Astrea *see* **7** Astraea

astringent 4 acid, keen, sour, tart **5** brisk, sharp, stern, tonic **6** biting, severe **7** acerbic, austere, bracing, puckery, styptic **8** curative, incisive, piercing, salutary, stabbing, vinegary **10** antiseptic, salubrious **11** contracting, penetrating, restorative **12** invigorating

astrology 6 Zodiac **9** horoscopy, starcraft **10** astromancy, astrometry, stargazing **11** genethliacs **13** mathematicals **14** astrodiagnosis
belief in: 8 siderism
term: 4 sign **5** house, trine **6** alnath, apheta, aspect **7** almuten, anareta, mansion, mundane, sextile **8** alkahest, nativity, quartile, synastry **9** planetary **10** opposition **11** conjunction

astronomer 4 Bode, Bopp, Gold, Hale **5** Adams, Baade, Bayer, Bethe, Gould, Hoyle, Royer **6** Bessel, Halley, Hubble, Jansky, Kepler, Newton, Piazzi **7** Bradley, Celcius, Galileo, Huggins, Huygens, Kapteyn, Laplace, Ptolemy, Russell, Shapley, Slipher **8** Angstrom, Einstein, Herschel, Hevelius, Lacaille, Lemaitre, Mercator **9** Eddington, Le-

verrier 10 Copernicus, Hipparchus, Tycho Brahe **11** Aristarchus, Hertzsprung **13** Petrus Apianus

astronomy
  term: 5 comet, orbit **6** apogee, meteor, nebula, parsec, quasar **7** azimuth, eclipse, equinox, perigee, transit **8** aphelion, asteroid, ecliptic, meridian, solstice **9** meteorite, satellite **10** perihelion, precession **11** declination, occultation **12** perturbation, spectroscopy **16** celestial equator
  type/related study: 9 cosmogony, cosmology **10** astrometry, photometry **12** astrophysics **18** celestial mechanics
  see also **4** star

Astrophel and Stella
  author: 15 Sir Philip Sidney

astute 3 sly **4** able, foxy, keen, wily **5** acute, sharp, smart **6** adroit, artful, bright, clever, crafty, shrewd, subtle **7** cunning, knowing, politic **9** designing, sagacious **10** discerning, keen-minded, perceptive **11** calculating, intelligent, penetrating **13** Machiavellian, perspicacious

astuteness 6 acumen **8** keenness **9** acuteness, smartness **10** cleverness, shrewdness **12** perspicacity

Astyanax
  also: 11 Scamandrius
  father: 6 Hector **9** Strophius
  mother: 10 Andromache
  thrown from: 11 Trojan walls
    thrown by: 6 Greeks
  slain by: 8 Menelaus

Asuncion
  capital of: 8 Paraguay

asunder 4 rent **5** apart **8** in pieces, to shreds **9** torn apart **11** broken apart

asylum 4 home **5** haven **6** harbor, refuge **7** retreat, shelter **8** madhouse, preserve **9** almshouse, orphanage, poorhouse, sanctuary **10** sanatorium, sanitarium **11** institution **13** children's home, state hospital **14** mental hospital **15** place of immunity **17** mental institution **23** eleemosynary institution

Asynjur
  origin: 12 Scandinavian
  goddesses of: 4 Asar **5** Aesir
  leader: 3 Fri **5** Frigg, Frija **6** Frigga

As You Like It
  author: 18 William Shakespeare
  character: 5 Celia (Aliena) **6** Audrey, Jaques, Oliver **7** Orlando **8** Rosalind (Ganymede) **9** Frederick **10** Touchstone

Atabyrian *see* **4** Zeus

at a distance 4 afar, away **5** above, aloof, apart **6** far off **9** separated

Atala
  author: 21 Francois Chateaubriand

Atalanta
  also: 8 Atalante
  form: 6 virgin **8** huntress

father: 5 Iasus
mother: 7 Clymene
son: 13 Parthenopaeus
wounded: 14 Calydonian boar
lost race to: 10 Hippomenes

Atalanta in Calydon
  author: 24 Algernon Charles Swinburne

at any rate 6 anyhow, anyway **9** in any case **10** in any event

at cross purposes 7 counter, opposed **8** contrary, converse, inimical, opposite **9** disparate **10** at variance, discordant **11** conflicting **12** antithetical, incompatible **13** contradictory

Ate
  origin: 5 Greek
  form: 7 goddess
  personifies: 12 recklessness **16** divine punishment

at ease 4 calm, cool **6** at rest, serene **7** content, relaxed, unmoved **8** composed **9** at leisure, confident, unruffled **10** complacent, nonchalant, unbothered, untroubled **11** comfortable, unconcerned

a tergo 9 at the back **10** from behind

at fault 6 guilty **8** culpable **10** implicated **11** blameworthy, responsible

at full length
  Latin: 9 in extenso

Athabascan, Athapascan (Slave Indians)
  language family: 10 Athabascan, Athapaskan
  location: 6 Canada **14** Great Slave Lake
  dominated by: 4 Cree
  related to: 4 Chipewyan
  tribe: 4 Dine **5** Slave **6** Apache, Navaho, Navajo **9** Mescalero **10** Athabascan

Athalie
  author: 18 Jean Baptiste Racine

Athamas
  king of: 6 Thebes
  father: 6 Aeolus
  wife: 3 Ino **7** Nephele
  son: 5 Ptous **6** Leucon **7** Phrixus **8** Learchus **10** Melicertes
  daughter: 5 Helle

at hand 4 near, nigh **5** close, handy, on tap, ready **6** nearby **7** close by **8** imminent **9** available, impending **10** accessible, convenient **11** at one's elbow, forthcoming **14** at one's disposal **15** within arm's reach

atheism 8 apostasy, unbelief **9** disbelief **10** irreligion **11** godlessness

atheist 7 infidel **10** unbeliever **11** disbeliever, nonbeliever

Athena
  also: 6 Athene, Pallas, Saitis **11** Tritogeneia **12** Pallas Athena **18** Alalcomenean Athena
  origin: 5 Greek

goddess of: 4 arts **6** wisdom **7** warfare **9** fertility
father: 4 Zeus **6** Triton
mother: 5 Metis
sprang from head of: 4 Zeus
raised by: 12 Alalcomeneus
symbol: 3 owl
corresponds to: 7 Minerva
epithet: 4 Alea **5** Meter, Xenia **6** Ergane, Itonia, Polias **7** Agoraea, Cissaea, Paeonia, Pronaus, Pronoea **8** Anemotis, Poliates, Zosteria **9** Oxyderces, Parthenia, Poliuchus, Promachus **10** Axiopoenus, Chalinitis, Cyparissia **11** Promachorma

Athens
  capital of: 6 Greece
  Greek: 7 Athinai
  hills: 9 Acropolis **14** Hagios Georghis
  landmark: 4 Stoa **9** Areopagus, Parthenon **10** Erechtheum, Propylaeum **17** Theater of Dionysus
  marketplace: 5 Agora
  mountain: 6 Parnes **8** Aigaleos, Hymettus **10** Pentelikon
  named for: 6 Athena
  port: 7 Piraeus
  river: 7 Ilissus
  sea: 6 Aegean **11** Saronic Gulf
  square: 8 Syntagma (Constitution)

Athens Graces 4 Auxe **8** Hegemone

athirst 4 avid, keen **5** eager **6** raring **7** longing, panting **8** yearning

athlete 4 jock **8** champion **9** contender, sportsman **10** contestant, game player

athletic 5 burly, hardy, husky, manly **6** brawny, robust, strong, sturdy, virile **8** muscular, powerful, stalwart, vigorous **9** masculine, strapping **10** able-bodied

athletics 5 games **6** sports **8** exercise **9** exercises **10** gymnastics

at home 6 at ease, inside, shut in **7** indoors **8** confined **10** in the house **11** comfortable
  French: 4 chez

Athos
  character in: 18 The Three Musketeers
  author: 5 Dumas (pere)

athwart 6 across **7** astride **8** sideways, sidewise **9** crossways, crosswise **12** transversely

Atlanta
  baseball team: 6 Braves
  basketball team: 5 Hawks
  football team: 7 Falcons
  hockey team: 9 Thrashers

Atlantean
  pertaining to: 5 Atlas

Atlantic City
  director: 10 Louis Malle
  cast: 8 Kate Reid **13** Burt Lancaster, Michel Piccoli, Susan Sarandon

at large 5 astir, loose **6** abroad **8** as a whole, at length **9** at liberty, in general **10** on the loose, unconfined **11** out and about **13** in circulation **14** around and about **15** making the rounds

Atlas
form: **5** Titan
father: **7** Iapetus
mother: **7** Clymene
brother: **9** Menoetius **10** Epimetheus, Prometheus
wife: **7** Pleione
daughters: **6** Hyades **7** Calypso **8** Pleiades **10** Hesperides
supported: **3** sky
identified with: **14** Atlas Mountains

Atlas Shrugged
author: **7** Ayn Rand
character: **8** John Galt **11** Hank Reardon **12** Dagny Taggart, James Taggart

at last
Latin: **10** ad extremum

at leisure 4 idle **7** off duty **8** inactive **9** at liberty **10** unemployed, unoccupied

Atli
origin: **12** Scandinavian
sister: **8** Brynhild
wife: **6** Gudrun, Kudrun **7** Guthrun
killed by: **6** Gudrun, Kudrun **7** Guthrun
represents: **6** Atilla

atmosphere 3 air **4** aura, feel, mood, tone **5** color **6** spirit **7** feeling, quality **8** ambience **11** environment **12** surroundings

atmospheric 3 air **4** airy **8** ethereal

at odds 6 unlike **8** contrary **9** different **10** at variance, discordant, discrepant, dissimilar **11** contrasting

at odds with 9 counter to **10** contrary to **14** at variance with

atoll 6 island
made of: **5** coral
pool: **6** lagoon
famous: **6** Bikini **8** Eniwetok

atom 3 bit, dot, jot **4** iota, mite, mote, whit **5** crumb, grain, scrap, shred, speck, trace **6** morsel, tittle **7** smidgen **8** fragment, particle **9** scintilla **10** smithereen

atomic 6 cobalt **7** fission, neutron, nuclear, uranium **8** hydrogen **9** molecular, plutonium, subatomic, unseeable **10** impalpable **11** fissionable, microcosmic, microscopic, superatomic **13** imperceptible, indiscernible, infinitesimal, thermonuclear

atom part 6 proton **7** neutron **8** electron

at once
French: **11** tout de suite

atone 6 pay for, redeem, repent, shrive **7** expiate **9** make up for **10** compensate, recompense, remunerate **12** do penance for **13** make amends for **17** make reparation for

atonement 6 amends, shrift **7** penance, redress **9** expiation **10** recompense, redemption, reparation, repentance **12** compensation, satisfaction **14** penitential act

at one's disposal 5 handy **6** at hand, on hand **9** available **10** accessible, convenient **11** at one's elbow, ready for use **13** at one's service

at one's elbow 5 handy **6** at hand, nearby **9** available **10** accessible, convenient

at rest 5 quiet, still **6** asleep, at ease, serene **7** at peace, content **8** in repose **9** quiescent **10** motionless

Atreus
father: **6** Pelops
mother: **10** Hippodamia
sister: **7** Nicippe
wife: **6** Aerope
son: **8** Menelaus **9** Agamemnon **10** Plisthenes
daughter: **8** Anaxibia
killed: **6** Aglaus

Atridae
descendants of: **6** Atreus
family name of: **8** Anaxibia, Menelaus **9** Agamemnon **10** Plisthenes

atrium 4 hall **6** cavity **7** auricle **8** entrance **13** Roman entrance

atrocious 3 bad, low **4** dark, evil, rude, vile **5** black, cruel **6** brutal, savage, tawdry, vulgar **7** heinous, hellish, inhuman, uncouth, vicious **8** dreadful, enormous, fiendish, flagrant, grievous, horrible, infamous, infernal, pitiless, ruthless, terrible **9** barbarous, execrable, merciless, monstrous, nefarious, tasteless **10** diabolical, outrageous, villainous

atrociousness 6 infamy **7** cruelty **8** enormity, vileness **9** barbarity, brutality, depravity **11** heinousness, viciousness **13** monstrousness, offensiveness **14** outrageousness

atrocity 6 horror **7** outrage **8** enormity, savagery, villainy **9** barbarism, barbarity, brutality **10** inhumanity **11** heinousness

atrophy 7 decline **8** decaying, drying up **9** lack of use, withering **10** emaciation, shriveling **11** wasting away **12** degeneration **13** deterioration

Atropos
member of: **5** Fates
cuts thread of: **4** life

Atsina (Gros Ventres, Haaninin)
language family: **9** Algonkian **10** Algonquian
location: **6** Canada **7** Montana **9** Milk River **12** Saskatchewan **13** Missouri River
related to: **7** Arapaho

attach 3 fix **4** join **5** affix, allot, annex **6** append, assign, couple, detail, secure **7** connect, destine, earmark **8** allocate, be fond of, fasten to, make fast **9** affiliate, associate, designate

attache 4 aide **5** envoy **6** consul **8** adjutant, diplomat, emissary, minister **9** assistant **10** ambassador, vice consul **11** diplomatist, subordinate **12** ambassadress **13** consul general

attachment 4 bond, love **6** fixing, liking, regard **7** adjunct, fixture, respect **8** addendum, addition, affinity, affixing, appendix, coupling, devotion, fondness, securing **9** accessory, affection, appendage, attaching, fastening **10** connection, friendship, supplement, tenderness **12** predilection

attack 3 fit **4** damn, go at **5** abuse, blame, fault, fly at, onset, spasm, spell **6** assail, charge, impugn, strike, stroke, tackle **7** assault, censure, lunge at, offense, seizure **8** denounce, fall upon, invasion, paroxysm **9** criticism, criticize, denigrate, disparage, incursion, offensive, onslaught, pitch into, undertake **10** aggression, impugnment **11** denigration **13** disparagement

attacker 6 mugger **7** accuser **8** assailer, opponent **9** adversary, aggressor, assailant **10** antagonist **11** belligerent

attain 3 win **4** earn, gain, reap **5** reach **6** effect, obtain, secure **7** achieve, acquire, procure, realize **10** accomplish

attainable 6 at hand **9** available, reachable **10** accessible, achievable, realizable **11** within reach

attainment 5 skill **6** talent **7** earning, gaining, getting, mastery, success, winning **8** securing **9** acquiring, attaining, obtaining, procuring **10** competence **11** achievement, acquirement, acquisition, fulfillment, procurement, proficiency, realization **14** accomplishment

attempt 3 aim, try **4** seek **5** essay **6** attack, effort, hazard, strive, tackle, work at **7** assault, venture **8** endeavor **9** have a go at, onslaught, undertake **11** undertaking **12** make an effort, take a crack at, take a whack at

Attenborough, Richard
director of: **6** Gandhi (Oscar) **7** Chaplin **10** Cry Freedom **11** A Chorus Line, Shadowlands **12** In Love and War, Young Winston **13** A Bridge Too Far
roles: **10** Wavelength **12** Jurassic Park **14** The Great Escape **15** Doctor Doolittle **16** Ten Little Indians

attend 4 go to, heed, mark, mind, note **5** serve, usher, visit **6** convoy, escort, follow, show up, squire, tend to **7** care for, conduct, observe, oversee, service **8** appear at, consider, frequent, harken to, listen to, wait upon **9** accompany **11** superintend

French: **4** oyez
cry used by: **10** court crier
preceded: **12** proclamation

attendance 4 gate **5** crowd, house **8** audience, presence **10** appearance, assemblage, being there

attendant 3 aid **6** escort, flunky, helper, lackey, menial **7** related, servant **8** adherent, chaperon, follower **9** accessory, assistant, companion, underling **10** associated, consequent **12** accompanying

attention 4 care, heed, mind, note, suit **5** court **6** homage, notice, regard, wooing **7** concern, respect, service, thought **8** civility, courtesy, devotion, wariness **9** alertness, deference, diligence, vigilance **10** observance, politeness **11** assiduities, compliments, gallantries **12** deliberation **13** concentration, consideration, contemplation **14** thoughtfulness

attentive 5 alert, awake **6** intent, polite **7** devoted, heedful, mindful, zealous **8** diligent, obliging **9** courteous, dedicated, listening, observant, wide awake **10** respectful, thoughtful **11** considerate, deferential, painstaking **13** accommodating

attentiveness 7 concern **8** devotion, industry **9** alertness, attention, diligence **10** commitment, dedication **11** application, devotedness, heedfulness, mindfulness **14** thoughtfulness

attenuate 6 dilute, impair, lessen, reduce, weaken **7** draw out, spin out **8** decrease, diminish, enervate, enfeeble **9** water down **10** adulterate

attest 4 show **5** prove **6** affirm, assert, assure, evince, verify **7** bear out, certify, confirm, declare, display, exhibit, support, swear to, testify, warrant **8** vouch for **11** bear witness, corroborate, demonstrate **12** substantiate

attestation 9 testimony **10** deposition **11** declaration

at the back
Latin: **6** a tergo

at the beginning
Latin: **9** ad initium

at the bottom
French: **6** au fond

at the end
Latin: **5** ad fin

at the place
Latin: **5** ad loc **7** ad locum

At the Sign of the Reine Pedauque
author: **13** Anatole France

attic 4 loft **6** garret **7** mansard **8** cockloft **10** clerestory
French: **7** grenier
German: **9** Dachboden
Spanish: **9** guardilla

attire 3 don **4** duds, garb, gown, robe, togs **5** array, dress **6** bedeck, clothe,

finery, fit out, invest, outfit, rig out **7** apparel, clothes, costume, deck out, raiment, turn out **8** clothing, garments, glad rags, wardrobe **9** vestments **11** habiliments

Attis
also: **4** Atys
form: **5** youth
home: **7** Phrygia
loved: **6** Cybele
driven mad by: **6** Cybele

attitude 3 air **4** pose **6** manner, stance **7** outlook, posture **8** demeanor, position **11** disposition, frame of mind, perspective, point of view

attorney 4 beak **6** lawyer **7** counsel **8** advocate **9** barrister, counselor, solicitor **10** mouthpiece **12** legal adviser **14** member of the bar **15** ambulance chaser

attract 4 draw, lure, pull **5** cause, charm, evoke **6** allure, beckon, entice, induce, invite **7** bewitch, enchant, provoke **8** appeal to, interest **9** captivate, fascinate **11** precipitate

attraction 4 lure, pull **5** charm **6** allure, appeal **7** glamour **8** affinity, charisma, tendency **9** magnetism **10** enticement, inducement, temptation **11** captivation, enchantment, fascination **12** drawing power

attractive 4 chic, fair, foxy, sexy **6** lovely, pretty **7** elegant, likable, sightly, winning **8** alluring, becoming, charming, engaging, enticing, fetching, handsome, inviting, pleasant, pleasing, tasteful, tempting **9** agreeable, appealing, beautiful, seductive **10** bewitching, delightful, enchanting **11** captivating, charismatic, fascinating

attractiveness 5 charm **6** beauty **9** good looks **11** pulchritude **12** handsomeness

attribute 4 gift **5** facet, grace, lay to, trait **6** aspect, assign, credit, impute, talent, virtue **7** ability, ascribe, blame on, cause by, faculty, feature, quality, trace to **8** charge to, property **9** character, endowment, set down to **10** account for, attainment, derive from, saddle with **11** acquirement, bring home to, distinction **14** accomplishment, characteristic

attrition 4 loss **7** erosion **8** abrasion, decrease, friction, grinding, scraping **9** reduction **10** decimation **11** wearing away, wearing down **14** disintegration

attune 5 adapt **6** adjust, tailor **8** accustom **9** acclimate **11** acclimatize

attune to 3 fit **5** adapt **6** adjust **7** conform **9** harmonize **11** accommodate

at variance 7 counter, opposed **8** contrary, converse, inimical, opposite **9** disparate **10** discordant **11** conflicting **12** antithetical, incompatible **13** contradictory **15** at cross purposes

Atwood, Margaret

author of: **7** Cat's Eye **8** Survival **9** Surfacing **10** Alias Grace, Bodily Harm, Lady Oracle **11** Second Words **13** Bluebeard's Egg, Life Before Man, Power Politics, The Circle Game **14** The Robber Bride **16** The Handmaid's Tale

at work 4 busy **5** in use **6** active **7** engaged, working **8** occupied

Atymnius
mentioned in: **5** Iliad
companion of: **8** Sarpedon
killed by: **10** Antilochus

atypical 7 unusual **8** abnormal, contrary, uncommon **9** anomalous, irregular, unnatural, untypical **10** nontypical **11** uncustomary, unlooked for **12** out of keeping **16** unrepresentative

Atys see **5** Attis

Auber, Daniel Francois Esprit
born: **4** Caen **6** France
composer of: **6** Haydee **7** La Macon **10** Fra Diavolo **12** Le Domino Noir **14** The Bronze Horse **16** Le Cheval de Bronze, The Crown Diamonds **17** La Muette de Portici **19** La Bergere Chatelaine **20** The Dumb Girl of Portici **22** Le Premier Jour de Bonheur

auberge 3 inn **6** tavern

auburn 5 henna, tawny **6** russet **8** cinnamon, nutbrown **11** golden-brown, rust-colored **12** reddish-brown **13** copper-colored **15** chestnut-colored

Aucassin and Nicolette
author: **7** unknown

Auchincloss, Louis
author of: **10** Watchfires **11** The Dark Lady, The Partners **12** Second Chance, The Embezzler **14** A World of Profit **16** Powers of Attorney, Tales of Manhattan, The Country Cousin **17** The Rector of Justin **19** The Winthrop Covenant **20** Portrait in Brownstone

au contraire 13 on the contrary

au courant 8 up-to-date

auction 3 sale **7** bidding **8** offering

Auction Block, The
author: **8** Rex Beach

audacious 4 bold, pert, rash, rude, wild **5** bossy, brave, fresh, gutsy, risky, saucy **6** brazen, cheeky, daring, plucky **7** defiant, forward, valiant **8** assuming, fearless, heedless, impudent, insolent, intrepid, reckless, stalwart, unafraid, valorous **9** breakneck, daredevil, dauntless, desperate, foolhardy, hotheaded, imprudent, shameless, unabashed **10** courageous, outrageous, self-willed **11** adventurous, impertinent, injudicious, lionhearted, venturesome **12** death-defying, devil-may-care, discourteous, enterprising, presumptuous, stouthearted **13** disrespectful

audaciousness 6 daring **8** audacity,

boldness **11** forwardness **13** assertiveness **14** aggressiveness **15** adventurousness

audacity 4 gall, grit, guts **5** brass, cheek, nerve, pluck, spunk, valor **6** daring, mettle **7** bravery, courage **8** backbone, boldness, chutzpah, rashness, temerity **9** brashness, derring-do, impudence, insolence **10** brazenness, effrontery **11** forwardness, presumption **12** fearlessness, impertinence, recklessness **13** bumptiousness, foolhardiness, shamelessness **15** venturesomeness

Auden, W H
author of: **11** Another Time, Thank You Fog **12** Homage to Clio, The Dyer's Hand **13** About the House, Journey to a War **15** For the Time Being, The Age of Anxiety **16** City Without Walls, Epistle to a Godson **17** In Memory of W B Yeats, Musee des Beaux Arts **20** The Dog Beneath the Skin **22** Forewords and Afterwords

Audhumbla
also: **8** Audhumla
origin: **12** Scandinavian
form: **3** cow
owner: **4** Ymir
birth from: **3** ice
uncovered: **4** Buri

audible 5 clear, heard **8** distinct **11** discernible, perceptible

audience 4 talk **5** house **6** market, parley, public **7** hearing, meeting **8** assembly, audition **9** following, interview, listeners, onlookers, reception **10** conference, discussion, readership, spectators **12** congregation, constituency, consultation

audit 5 check **6** go over, review, verify **7** balance, examine, inspect **10** inspection, scrutinize **11** examination, investigate, take stock of **12** scrutinizing, verification **13** investigation

audition 6 tryout **7** hearing **15** test performance

auditor 8 listener **10** accountant, bookkeeper **11** comptroller **17** financial examiner

auditorium 4 hall **5** arena **7** theater **8** auditory, coliseum **11** concert hall, lecture hall, meeting hall **12** assembly hall

Audrey
character in: **11** As You Like It
author: **11** Shakespeare

Audubon, John James
born: **8** Les Cayes **12** Santo Domingo
artwork: **14** Birds of America **34** Viviparous Quadrupeds of North America

Auel, Jean M
author of: **15** Plains of Passage **17** The Mammoth Hunters, The Valley of Horses **20** The Clan of the Cave Bear

Auerbach, Arnold (Red)
sport: **10** basketball
position: **5** coach
team: **13** Boston Celtics

au fait 6 expert, versed **11** experienced **13** knowledgeable

Aufklarung 13 enlightenment **16** the Enlightenment

au fond 9 basically, in reality **11** at the bottom

auf Wiedersehen 7 goodbye **8** farewell **16** until we meet again

Auge
priestess of: **6** Athena
father: **9** King Aleus
mother: **6** Neaera
son: **8** Telephus
assaulted by: **8** Hercules

Augean stables
owned by: **10** King Augeas
number of oxen: **13** three thousand
cleaned by: **8** Hercules
river running through: **7** Alpheus

auger 4 bore **5** drill **6** pierce **10** boring tool

aught 3 all, zip **4** love, nada, null, zero **6** naught **7** a cipher, nothing **8** goose egg **11** horse collar

augment 5 add to, boost, raise, swell, widen **6** deepen, expand, extend **7** amplify, build up, enlarge, inflate, magnify **8** flesh out, heighten, increase, lengthen **9** intensify

augmentation 5 boost, extra, raise **8** addition, increase, swelling, widening **9** deepening, expansion, extension, inflation **10** supplement **11** elaboration, enlargement, heightening, lengthening **13** amplification, magnification **15** intensification

augur 4 bode, seer **6** herald, oracle **7** diviner, portend, predict, presage, promise, prophet, signify **8** forecast, foretell, forewarn, intimate, prophesy **9** be a sign of **10** be an omen of, foreshadow, soothsayer **13** prognosticate **14** prognosticator

augury 4 omen, sign **5** token **6** herald **7** auspice, portent, promise, warning **8** prophecy **9** harbinger, precursor, sortilege **10** divination, forerunner, indication **11** forewarning, soothsaying **14** fortunetelling **15** prognostication

august 5 grand, lofty, noble, regal **6** solemn, superb **7** eminent, exalted, stately, sublime, supreme **8** glorious, imposing, majestic **9** dignified, estimable, grandiose, venerable **10** impressive, monumental **11** high-ranking, illustrious, magnificent **12** aweinspiring **13** distinguished

August
Anglo-Saxon: **10** Weod-Monath
characteristic: **7** dog days
flower: **5** poppy
French: **4** Aout
gem: **7** peridot **8** sardonyx **9** carnelian
German: **6** August
holiday:
England/Scotland: **11** Harvest Home (1)
Italian: **6** Agosto
number of days: **9** thirty-one
original name: **8** Sextilis **12** Metageitnion
origin of name: **6** Augere (Latin to open) **8** Augustus (Roman emperor)
place in year:
Roman: **5** sixth
Gregorian: **6** eighth
Spanish: **6** Agosto
zodiac sign: **3** Leo **5** Virgo

Augustine, St (of Hippo)
author of: **10** Civitas Dei **11** Confessions, Enchiridion **12** The City of God

augustness 7 dignity, majesty **8** eminence, nobility **9** loftiness **11** distinction **13** monumentality **15** illustriousness

August 1914
author: **23** Aleksandr Solzhenitsyn Jr

au naturel 4 nude **8** uncooked **15** in a natural state

Auntie Mame
author: **13** Patrick Dennis

Aunt Jo's Scrap-Bag
author: **15** Louisa May Alcott

Aunt Julia and the Scriptwriter
author: **16** Mario Vargas Llosa

au pair 4 maid **5** nanny **9** governess **13** mother's helper

aura 3 air **4** feel, mood **5** aroma **7** essence, feeling, quality **8** ambience **9** character, emanation **10** atmosphere, suggestion

Aura
companion of: **7** Artemis
bore: **5** twins
fathered by: **9** Dionysius
changed into: **6** spring
changed by: **4** Zeus

au revoir 7 goodbye **8** farewell **16** until we meet again

Aurora
origin: **5** Roman
goddess of: **4** dawn
corresponds to: **3** Eos

Aurora Leigh
author: **24** Elizabeth Barrett Browning

Ausgleich 10 compromise **11** arrangement **12** equalization

Auslander 5 alien **9** foreigner, outlander

auspice 4 omen, sign **6** augury **7** portent, warning **10** indication **15** prognostication

auspices 4 care, egis **5** aegis **6** charge **7** control, support **8** advocacy, guidance **9** authority, influence, patronage **10** protection **11** countenance, sponsorship **12** championship

auspicious **4** good **5** happy, lucky **6** benign, timely **7** hopeful **9** favorable, fortunate, opportune, promising, red-letter **10** felicitous, heartening, propitious, reassuring, successful **11** encouraging

Austen, Jane
author of: **4** Emma **10** Persuasion **13** Mansfield Park **15** Northanger Abbey **17** Pride and Prejudice **19** Sense and Sensibility

austere **5** rigid, spare, stark, stern **6** chaste, severe, simple, strict **7** ascetic, Spartan **8** rigorous **10** abstemious, forbidding **11** self-denying, strait-laced

Austerlitz, Frederick
real name of: **11** Fred Astaire

Australia
other name: **9** Down Under
name means: **19** unknown southern land
capital: **8** Canberra
largest city: **6** Sydney
others: **3** Ayr **4** Yass **5** Dubbo, Perth **6** Albury, Cairns, Casino, Coburg, Darwin, Hobart **7** Bendigo, Geelong, Kogarah, Mildura, Mitcham, Whyalla **8** Adelaide, Ballarat, Bathurst, Brighton, Brisbane, Essendon, Randwick, Ringwood **9** Melbourne, Newcastle, Port Pirie, Toowoomba **10** Broken Hill, Kalgoorlie, Waggawagga, Wollongong **11** Collingwood, Rockhampton **12** Alice Springs
division: **8** Tasmania, Victoria **10** Queensland **13** New South Wales **14** South Australia **16** Western Australia **17** Northern Territory **26** Australian Capital Territory
head of state: **14** British monarch **15** governor general
measure: **4** arna, naut, saum
monetary unit: **4** dump, tray, zack **5** pound **6** dollar **8** shilling
island: **4** Cato, King **5** Cocos, Green, Timor **6** Barrow, Koolan **7** Coringa, Keeling, Neptune, Norfolk **8** Flinders, Kangaroo, Lacepede, Melville, Rottnest, Tasmania, Thursday **9** Admiralty
lake: **4** Eyre **5** Carey, Cowan, Frome, Moore, Wells **6** Austin, Barlee, Bulloo, Dundas, Harris, Mackay **7** Amadeus, Blanche, Everard, Torrens **8** Carnegie, Gairdner **9** MacDonald **10** Yammayamma **14** Disappointment
mountain: **3** Ise **4** Blue, Olga, Ossa, Zeil **5** Bruce, Snowy **6** Cradle, Doreen, Garnet, Gawler, Magnet, Morgan **7** Bongong, Gregory, Herbert **8** Augustus, Brockman, Cuthbert, Jusgrave, Mulligan, Surprise **9** Murchison, Woodroffe **14** Australian Alps

15 New England Range **18** Great Dividing Range
highest point: **9** Kosciusko
river: **3** Hay **4** Avon, Daly, Swan, Yule **5** Bullo, Comet, Drava, Naomi, Paroo, Roper, Yarra **6** Barcoo, Barwon, Bulloo, Culgoa, Degrey, Hunter, Isaacs, Murray, Norman **7** Darling, Derwent, Fitzroy, Georges, Gilbert, Lachlan, Staaten, Warrego **8** Belyando, Brisbane, Burdekin, Clarence, Drysdale, Flinders, Gascoyne, Georgina, Mitchell, Thompson, Victoria, Weeribee, Wooramel **9** Ashburton, Fortescue, Hawksbury, MacKenzie, Macquarie, Murchison, Saltwater **10** Diamantina, Shoalhaven **12** Murrambidgee
sea: **5** Coral, Timor **6** Indian, Tasman **7** Arafura, Pacific
physical feature:
   bay: **5** Bight, Shark **6** Botany **7** Moreton **11** Port Phillip
   cape: **4** Howe, York **5** Byron **9** Southeast
   channel: **5** Cowal **9** Anabranch, Billabong
   desert: **6** Arunta, Gibson, Stuart, Tanami **7** Simpson **10** Great Sandy **13** Great Victoria
   gulf: **8** Spencers **9** Van Dieman **11** Carpentaria **15** Joseph Bonaparte **20** Great Australian Bight
   peninsula: **4** Eyre
   reef: **12** Great Barrier
   strait: **4** Bass
people: **3** Abo **4** Koko, Mara, Wong **5** Anzac, Binge, Dieri, Maori, Myall **6** Aranda, Arunta, Aussie, Binghi, Digger, Kipper, Papuan **7** Arawong, Ilpirra **8** Antipode, Barkinji, Billijim, Euahlayi, Warragal, Warrigal **9** Aborigine **10** Australoid, Melanesian, Sandgroper
   actor: **9** Judy Davis, Mel Gibson, Paul Hogan **10** Bryan Brown
   author: **4** West **5** White **7** Russell **10** Richardson
   explorer: **4** Bass, Cook **6** Mawson, Tasman **7** Wilkins
   leader: **4** Holt **5** Hawke **7** Keating, Menzies, Whitlam
   nurse: **11** Sister Kenny
language: **7** English
religion: **7** Judaism **8** Anglican **10** Protestant **13** Roman Catholic
place: **7** outback **9** billabong **11** back country
   aborigine area: **9** Arhemland
   beach: **5** Manly
   dam: **4** Hume
possession: **12** Cocos Islands **13** Norfolk Island **16** Christmas Islands
feature:
   animal: **5** dingo **6** kelpie **7** wallaby **8** anteater, kangaroo **9** koala bear **18** duckbilled platypus
   bird: **3** emu **10** kookaburra

   cowboy: **6** waddie **8** jackaroo
   dance: **6** dreher
   flower: **7** boronia, fuchsia, waratah **9** coachwood **12** kangaroo paws
   game: **3** sye **10** tambaroora
   tree: **3** gum **10** eucalyptus
   weapon: **5** kiley, kyley **7** wommera **9** boomerang
food: **3** kai **6** tucker
   cake: **6** damper **7** brownie
   dish: **8** coolamon
   drink: **9** arkaloola
   fruit: **5** nonda **7** kumquat **11** desert-lemon

Austria
other name: **10** Osterreich
name means: **12** eastern state
capital/largest city: **6** Vienna
others: **4** Enns, Graz, Lech, Linz, Ried, Wels **5** Krems, Steyr, Traun **6** Leoben **7** Bregenz, Modling, Spittal, Villach **8** Bad Ischl, Dornbirn, Salzburg **9** Innsbruck, Semmering **10** Kapfenberg, Klagenfurt **11** Sankt Polten **14** Wiener Neustadt
division: **5** Tirol, Tyrol **6** Istria, Styria, Triest **7** Bohemia, Galicia, Moravia, Silesia **8** Bukowina, Dalmatia, Earniola, Gradisca **9** Earinthia **10** Burgenland, Vorarlberg **12** Lower Austria, Upper Austria
   Roman province: **6** Raetia **7** Noricum **8** Pannonia
government:
   legislature: **9** Bundesrat, Reichsrat **10** Herrenhaus, Reichsrath
head of government: **10** Chancellor
other leader: **7** emperor **12** burgomeister
measure: **4** fass, fuss, joch, mass, muth, yoke **5** halbe, linie, meile, metze, pfiff, punkt **6** achtel, becher, leipoa, seidel **7** dlafter, viertel **8** dreiling **12** futtermassel
monetary unit: **4** lira **5** crown, ducat, krone **6** florin, gulden, heller, zehner **8** albertin, groschen, kreutzer **9** schilling
weight: **4** marc, unze **5** denat, karch, stein **7** centner, pfennig **8** vierling **9** quantchen
lake: **6** Almsee **7** Fertoto, Mondsee **8** Bodensee, Traunsee **9** Constance **10** Neusiedler
mountain: **4** Alps **6** Stubai, Tirols, Tyrols **8** Eisenerz, Rhatikon **9** Dolomites, Kitzbuhel **10** Hohe Tauern **14** Silvretta Group
highest point: **13** Grossglockner
river: **3** Inn, Mur **4** Drau, Elbe, Enns, Iser, Kamp, Lech, Murz, Raab **5** Donau, Drava, Drave, March, Salza, Thaya, Traun **6** Danube, Moldau
physical feature:
   basin: **7** Styrian
   canal: **6** Danube
   mountain pass: **7** Brenner
   wind: **6** Foehen

woods: 6 Vienna
people: 5 Poles **6** Croats, Czechs **7** Germans, Gypsies **8** Slovenes **10** Hungarians
  botanist: 6 Mendel
  composer: 5 Haydn **6** Czerny, Mahler, Mozart, Webern **7** Amadeus, Strauss **8** Bruckner, Schubert **9** Beethoven **10** Schoenberg
  emperor: 7 Charles, Francis **9** Ferdinand, Habsburgs, Hapsburgs **10** Franz Josef
  philosopher: 12 Wittgenstein
  psychiatrist: 5 Adler, Freud, Reich
  statesman: 10 Metternich **12** Kurt Waldheim
language: 5 Czech **6** German, Magyar **8** Croatian **9** Slovenian
religion: 7 Judaism **10** Protestant **13** Roman Catholic
place:
  boulevard: 3 Kai **11** Ringstrasse
  cathedral: 9 St Stephen
  city hall: 7 Rathaus
  fortress: 13 Hochosterwitz, Hohensalzburg
  imperial palace: 7 Hofburg
  monastery: 4 Melk **8** Gottweig **14** Klosterneuburg
  museum: 6 Mozart **9** Johanneum
  people's garden: 11 Volksgarten
  resort: 5 Baden **7** Bregenz **8** Bad Ischl **9** Innsbruck, Semmering
feature: 8 yodelers **11** ice grottoes
  clothing: 5 loden **10** lederhosen
  dance: 5 waltz **6** dreher **7** landler **13** schuhplattler **14** grand polonaise
  festival: 8 Salzburg
  horse: 10 Lippizaner
  pastry shop: 12 konditoreien
food:
  breaded veal cutlet: 15 Wiener schnitzel
  cake: 11 linzer torte, sacher torte
  cookie: 7 kipferl
  roll: 10 golatschen
Austroasiatic
  language subfamily: 5 Khasi, Munda **8** Annamite, Mon-Khmer **9** Palaung-Wa **10** Nicobarese **11** Semang-Sakai **13** Annamite-Muong
  spoken in: 5 Burma, India **7** Nicobar, Vietnam **8** Cambodia, Malaysia **9** Kampuchea
authentic 4 pure, real, true **5** valid **6** actual **7** factual, genuine **8** accurate, attested, bona fide, faithful, original, reliable, verified **9** veritable **10** accredited, dependable, legitimate **11** trustworthy **12** unquestioned **13** authoritative, unadulterated
authenticate 6 attest, avouch, verify **7** certify, confirm, endorse, warrant **8** document, validate, vouch for **9** guarantee **11** corroborate **12** substantiate
authenticated 7 genuine **8** attested,

verified **9** validated **10** accredited, vouched for **13** substantiated
authentication 7 voucher **10** validation **11** certificate **12** verification **13** authorization, certification
author 4 poet **5** maker **6** father, framer, writer **7** creator, founder, planner **8** essayist, inventor, novelist, producer **9** initiator, innovator, organizer **10** originator, playwright, prime mover **16** short-story writer
  see author under each country
authoritarian 5 harsh **6** severe, strict, tyrant **7** austere, fascist **8** autocrat, dogmatic, martinet **9** by the book, by the rule **10** inflexible, tyrannical, unyielding **11** dictatorial, doctrinaire **12** disciplinary, rule follower **14** disciplinarian, little dictator, uncompromising
authoritative 5 sound, valid **6** lordly, ruling **7** factual, learned **8** arrogant, decisive, dogmatic, imposing, official, reliable **9** authentic, masterful, scholarly, sovereign **10** autocratic, commanding, definitive, dependable, imperative, impressive, peremptory, sanctioned, tyrannical **11** dictatorial, trustworthy **14** administrative
authoritativeness 6 belief **9** authority **10** conviction **11** credibility **14** conclusiveness
authorities 6 expert, police, pundit **7** scholar **10** mastermind, specialist **11** connoisseur, officialdom **12** powers that be
authority 4 rule, sway **5** clout, force, might, power **6** esteem, weight **7** command, control, respect **8** dominion, prestige, strength **9** influence, supremacy **10** domination, importance **12** jurisdiction **14** administration
authorization 7 license **8** approval, sanction **10** commission, imprimatur, permission **11** entitlement **12** confirmation, legalization **13** accreditation, certification
authorize 5 allow **6** enable, invest, permit **7** approve, certify, charter, confirm, empower, entitle, license, warrant **8** accredit, sanction, vouch for **9** give leave **10** commission
authorized 8 approved, official **9** canonical **10** sanctioned
Autobiography of Alice B Toklas
  author: 13 Gertrude Stein
Autobiography of Miss Jane Pittman, The
  author: 13 Ernest J Gaines
autochthonous 5 first **6** native, primal **7** ancient **8** earliest, original, primeval **10** aboriginal, indigenous, primordial
autocracy 7 czarism, tyranny **8** autarchy, monarchy **9** Caesarism, despotism, Hitlerism, kaiserism, monocracy, Stalinism **10** absolutism **11** Bonapart-

ism **12** dictatorship **14** tyrannical rule **15** totalitarianism
autocrat 5 ruler **6** despot, tyrant **7** monarch **8** dictator, overlord **13** absolute ruler
autocratic 8 despotic **9** czaristic, imperious, tyrannous **10** iron-handed, oppressive, repressive, tyrannical **11** dictatorial, monarchical **13** authoritarian
auto da fe, auto de fe 13 act of the faith **17** burning of heretics
  from: 18 Spanish Inquisition
autograph 4 mark, sign **5** x-mark **9** John Henry, signature **11** endorsement, handwriting, inscription, John Hancock **16** countersignature
Autolycus
  character in: 14 The Winter's Tale
  author: 11 Shakespeare
Autolycus
  form: 5 thief
  father: 6 Hermes
  mother: 6 Chione
  half-brother: 9 Philammon
  wife: 9 Amphithea
  daughter: 8 Anticlea
  grandson: 8 Odysseus
  gift: 12 invisibility **13** shape changing
automated 9 automatic **10** mechanical, mechanized **15** machine-operated
automatic 6 reflex **7** natural, routine **8** electric, habitual, inherent, unwilled **9** automated **10** mechanical, pushbutton, self-acting, self-moving **11** instinctive, involuntary, spontaneous, unconscious **12** uncontrolled **13** nonvolitional, self-operating **14** self-propelling
automaton 4 pawn, tool **5** golem, patsy, robot **6** puppet, stooge **7** android, cat's-paw, fall guy, machine **10** fantoccino, marionette
automobile
  invented by:
    differential gear: 4 Benz
    electric: 8 Morrison
    gasoline: 6 Duryea **7** Daimler
    muffler: 5 Maxim
    self-starter: 9 Kettering
  see also car
automobiles
  Buick: 7 LeSabre
  Chevrolet: 6 Lumina **7** Beretta, Corsica
  Chrysler-Plymouth: 7 LeBaron
  Dodge: 4 Neon **8** Intrepid
  Ford: 5 Tempo **6** Escort, Taurus **7** Mustang
  Honda: 5 Civic **6** Accord
  Lexus
  Mercury: 5 Sable
  Nissan: 6 Altima, Maxima, Sentra
  Oldsmobile: 5 Ciera **7** Achieva **11** Ninety-Eight
  Pontiac: 7 Grand Am, Trans Am **8** Firebird

Saturn
Toyota: 5 Camry 7 Corolla

Autonoe
father: 6 Cadmus
mother: 8 Harmonia
sister: 3 Ino 5 Agave 6 Semele
husband: 9 Aristaeus
son: 7 Actaeon
daughter: 6 Macris

autonomous 4 free 9 sovereign 11 independent, self-reliant 13 self-governing 14 self-determined, self-sufficient

autonomy 7 freedom 8 home rule, self-rule 10 liberation 11 sovereignty 12 independence 14 self-government 17 self-determination

auto racing
driver: 6 A J Foyt 7 Al Unser 8 Tom Sneva 9 Niki Lauda 10 Bobby Unser, Jeff Gordon, Juan Fangio 11 Jack Brabham 12 Bobby Allison, Janet Guthrie, Richard Petty 13 Jackie Stewart, Mario Andretti 14 Barney Oldfield, Cale Yarborough, Craig Breedlove 16 Johnny Rutherford

Autry, Gene
horse: 8 Champion
born: 7 Tioga TX
roles: 11 Melody Ranch 16 The Singing Cowboy 19 Tumbling Tumbleweeds 22 Springtime in the Rockies

autumn 4 fall 11 harvest time 12 Indian summer 15 autumnal equinox

auxiliary 6 backup, helper 7 partner, reserve 9 accessory, ancillary, assistant, associate, companion, emergency, secondary 10 accomplice, subsidiary, supplement 11 subordinate 13 supplementary

avail 3 aid, use 4 help 5 serve 6 assist, profit 7 benefit, purpose, service, success, utilize 9 advantage

available 4 free, open 5 handy, on tap 6 at hand, on hand 9 in reserve 10 accessible, convenient, obtainable

avalanche 4 heap, mass, pile 5 flood 6 deluge 7 barrage, cascade, torrent 8 blizzard 9 cataclysm, rockslide, snowslide 10 earthslide, inundation 11 bombardment

Avalon
island of: 8 Paradise
burial place for: 6 heroes 10 King Arthur

avant-garde 7 leaders 8 pioneers, vanguard 10 innovators 11 forerunners, originators, tastemakers 12 advance guard, trailblazers, trendsetters

avarice 5 greed 6 penury 8 rapacity, venality 9 parsimony 10 greediness, stinginess 11 miserliness 12 covetousness, graspingness 13 moneygrubbing, niggardliness, pennypinching 15 close-fistedness

Ave Maria 8 Hail Mary

avenge 5 repay 6 injure, punish 7 revenge 9 retaliate

Avengers, The
character: 8 Emma Peel, Tara King 9 John (Jonathan) Steed
cast: 9 Diana Rigg 12 Linda Thorson 13 Patrick Macnee
movie cast: 10 Uma Thurman 12 Ralph Fiennes

avenue 3 way 4 gate, path, road 5 means, route 6 access, chance, course, outlet 7 gateway, parkway, passage, pathway 8 approach 9 boulevard, concourse, direction, esplanade 10 passageway 11 opportunity 12 thoroughfare

aver 4 avow 5 state, swear 6 affirm, assert, avouch, insist, verify 7 certify, contend, declare, profess, protest 8 maintain, proclaim 9 emphasize, guarantee, pronounce, represent 10 asseverate

average 3 par 4 fair, mean, norm, so-so 5 ratio, usual 6 common, medial, median, medium, normal, not bad 7 the rule, typical 8 mediocre, midpoint, moderate, ordinary, passable, standard, standing, the usual 9 tolerable 10 mean amount 11 indifferent, rank and file 12 run-of-the-mill

averment 5 claim 6 avowal 8 argument 9 assertion, assurance 10 allegation, contention, profession 11 affirmation

averse 5 loath 7 opposed 8 inimical 9 reluctant, unwilling 10 indisposed, unamenable 11 disinclined, ill-disposed, unfavorable 12 antipathetic, recalcitrant

aversion 6 hatred, horror 7 disgust, dislike 8 distaste, loathing 9 animosity, antipathy, hostility, prejudice, repulsion, revulsion 10 abhorrence, opposition, reluctance, repugnance 11 detestation 13 unwillingness 14 disinclination

avert 4 turn 5 avoid, deter, shift 7 beat off, deflect, fend off, keep off, prevent, ward off 8 preclude, stave off, turn away 9 forestall, frustrate, keep at bay, sidetrack 11 nip in the bud

aviary 4 cage 5 birdhouse, enclosure

aviation 6 flight, flying 11 aeronautics 12 aerodynamics

aviator, aviatrix 4 bird 5 flyer, pilot 6 airman, fly-boy 7 birdman

avid 4 keen 5 eager, rabid 6 ardent, greedy, hungry 7 anxious, devoted, fanatic, intense, zealous 8 covetous, desirous, grasping 9 rapacious, voracious 10 avaricious, insatiable 11 acquisitive 12 enthusiastic

avidity 4 zeal 5 greed 6 fervor, hunger 8 rapacity, voracity 9 eagerness 10 enthusiasm, fanaticism, greediness 12 covetousness 15 acquisitiveness

Avignon Papacy 15 Babylonian Exile 19 Babylonian Captivity

avocado 9 dark green 13 alligator pear, tropical fruit
origin: 6 Mexico 12 South America 14 Central America
family: 9 Lauraceae
used to make: 9 guacamole

avocation 5 hobby 7 pastime 8 sideline 9 diversion 10 recreation 11 distraction 13 entertainment

Avogadro, Amedeo
field: 7 physics 9 chemistry
nationality: 7 Italian
formulated: 19 molecular hypothesis

avoid 4 shun 5 avert, dodge, elude, evade, skirt 6 escape, eschew 7 boycott, forbear, forsake 8 sidestep 10 fight shy of 11 refrain from 12 steer clear of

avoidance 7 eluding, evasion 8 shirking, shunning, skirting

avoid the issue 4 duck 5 dodge, evade, hedge, stall 10 equivocate 17 beat around the bush

a votre sante 5 toast 12 to your health

avouch 5 argue, swear 6 affirm 7 declare 8 advocate, maintain

avow 3 own 4 aver 5 admit, state, swear 6 affirm, assert, reveal 7 confess, declare, profess 8 announce, disclose, proclaim 11 acknowledge

avowal 4 word 8 averment 9 admission, assertion, assurance, statement 10 confession, profession 11 affirmation, declaration 12 proclamation, protestation 14 acknowledgment

avowed 5 sworn 8 admitted, declared 9 confessed, professed 12 acknowledged, self-declared 14 self-proclaimed

await 6 attend, expect 7 look for 10 anticipate

awake 5 alert, aware, spark 6 arouse, awaken, bestir, excite, incite 7 alive to, heedful, inspire, mindful, provoke 8 open-eyed, vigilant, watchful 9 attentive, conscious, stimulate

Awake and Sing!
author: 13 Clifford Odets

awaken 3 fan 4 fire 6 arouse, excite, kindle, revive, stir up 9 stimulate

awakening 7 arising, arousal 8 sparking, stirring 11 stimulation

award 4 give 5 allot, allow, grant, honor, medal, prize 6 accord, assign, bestow, decree, trophy 7 appoint, concede, laurels, tribute 8 citation, confer on 10 decoration

aware 6 with it 7 alert to, alive to, awake to, mindful 8 apprised, informed, sensible, sentient 9 cognizant, conscious, tuned in to 10 conversant 11 enlightened 12 familiar with 13 knowledgeable

awareness 9 acuteness, alertness, appraisal, knowledge 10 cognizance, perception 11 familiarity, information, mindfulness, realization, recognition, sensibility 12 acquaintance 13 consciousness, understanding

away 3 far 4 gone 6 absent, at once, way off 8 distance 9 elsewhere

awe 3 cow 4 fear 5 abash, alarm, amaze, dread, panic, shock 6 dismay, fright, horror, terror, wonder 7 perturb, quaking, respect, terrify 8 astonish, disquiet, frighten 9 abashment, adoration, amazement, quivering, reverence, solemnity, trembling 10 exaltation, intimidate, veneration 11 disquietude, trepidation 12 apprehension, astonishment, perturbation 13 consternation

awe-inspiring 5 giant, grand, great, noble 6 august, mighty 7 eminent, exalted, mammoth, sublime, supreme, titanic 8 colossal, enormous, gigantic, glorious, imposing, majestic, wondrous 9 excessive 10 impressive, incredible, monumental, prodigious, stupendous, tremendous 11 astonishing, extravagant, illustrious, magnificent, spectacular 12 breathtaking, overwhelming

awesome 6 solemn 7 amazing, fearful 8 alarming, dreadful, fearsome, majestic, wondrous 9 inspiring 10 formidable, perturbing, stupefying, terrifying 11 astonishing, disquieting, frightening, magnificent 12 breathtaking, intimidating, overwhelming

awestruck 6 humble 8 overcome 11 reverential

awful 3 bad, low 4 base, dire, mean, ugly 5 lousy 6 solemn 7 amazing, awesome, fearful, ghastly, heinous, hideous 8 alarming, dreadful, fearsome, gruesome, horrible, majestic, shocking, terrible, wondrous 9 appalling, frightful, monstrous, revolting 10 deplorable, despicable, formidable, horrendous, horrifying, stupefying, terrifying, unpleasant 11 displeasing, disquieting, distressing; redoubtable 12 awe-inspiring, contemptible, disagreeable 13 reprehensible

awfully 4 very 5 quite 8 horribly, terribly 9 extremely, immensely 10 dreadfully 11 excessively 13 exceptionally

awkward 5 inept 6 clumsy, touchy, trying 7 unhandy 8 bungling, delicate, inexpert, ticklish, ungainly, unwieldy 9 difficult, graceless, maladroit 10 blundering, cumbersome, unpleasant, unskillful 11 troublesome 12 embarrassing, inconvenient, unmanageable 13 disconcerting, uncomfortable, uncoordinated
French: 6 gauche

Awkward Age, The
author: 10 Henry James

awkwardness 9 gaucherie 10 clumsiness, difficulty, ineptitude 12 ungainliness, unwieldiness 13 embarrassment, inconvenience

awl 4 nail 6 gimlet 11 leather tool, sharp device

awning 4 hood 6 canopy 7 marquee 8 covering, sunshade

awry 5 amiss, askew, wrong 6 astray, uneven 7 crooked, twisted 8 unevenly 9 crookedly, obliquely 11 out of kilter

axe, ax 3 can 4 chop, fire, oust, sack 5 let go, split 6 bounce, cut out, delete, remove 7 cut down, dismiss 8 get rid of, tomahawk 9 discharge, terminate 11 send packing
type: 4 pick 6 poleax 7 hatchet 8 tomahawk

Axelrod, Julius
field: 9 chemistry
studied: 24 nerve-impulse transmission
awarded: 10 Nobel Prize

axiom 3 law 5 basic 7 precept 9 postulate, principle 10 assumption 14 fundamental law

axiomatic 5 banal, given 6 cliche 7 assumed 8 accepted, manifest 9 apodictic 10 aphoristic 11 self-evident 12 demonstrable, epigrammatic, indisputable, unquestioned 13 incontestable, platitudinous

axis 4 stem 5 pivot, shaft 7 compact, entente, spindle 8 alliance 9 alignment, coalition 10 center line 11 affiliation 12 pivotal point 13 confederation 14 line of rotation, line of symmetry

axle 3 bar, pin 5 shaft, wheel 7 spindle 8 crossbar 10 turning bar

ayah 4 maid 5 nurse

aye 3 yea, yes 11 affirmative

Aykroyd, Dan
born: 6 Canada, Ottawa 7 Ontario
roles: 6 My Girl 7 Dragnet 8 Sgt. Bilko 9 Coneheads 11 Spies Like Us 12 Ghostbusters 13 Doctor Detroit, Trading Places 16 The Blues Brothers, Driving Miss Daisy, The Great Outdoors, Grosse Point Blank 17 Saturday Night Live

Aymara
location: 4 Peru 7 Bolivia 12 South America

Ayres, Lew
wife: 8 Lola Lane 12 Ginger Rogers
born: 13 Minneapolis MN
roles: 7 Holiday, The Kiss 9 Dr Kildare 25 All Quiet on the Western Front

azalea 12 Rhododendron
varieties: 4 Cork, Mock, Snow 5 Coast, Dwarf, Early, Flame, Hiryu, Hoary, Luchu, Royal, Sims's, Swamp, Sweet, Torch 6 Alpine, Balsam, Clammy, Indian, Korean, Kurume, Kyushu, Oconee, Pontic, Smooth, Spider, Summer, Yellow 7 Alabama, Chinese, Maries's, Mt Amagi, Oldham's, Western 8 Fiveleaf, Japanese, Piedmont, Rusticum, Yodogawa 9 Kirishima, Mayflower, Pink-shell, Rose-shell, Wild-thyme 10 Cumberland, Macranthum, Plumleaved, White swamp 11 Gable hybrid, Ghent hybrid, Molle hybrid 12 Arnold hybrid, Florida flame, Sander hybrid 13 Indicum hybrid 15 Glenn Dale hybrid, Kaempferi hybrid, Knapp Hill hybrid 16 Rutherford hybrid 24 Rusticum Flore Pleno hybrid

Azan
father: 5 Arcas
mother: 5 Erato

Azariah
also: 6 Uzziah
father: 4 Jehu 5 Ethan 6 Nathan 7 Hilkiah, Jehoram, Johanan 11 Jehoshaphat
son: 4 Joel
known as: 8 Abednego
companion: 6 Daniel
friend: 7 Meshach 8 Shadrach
succeeded: 5 Zadok

Azazel 9 scapegoat 11 fallen angel

Azerbaijan
capital/largest city: 4 Baku
others 9 Kirovabad
division 14 Nagorno-Karabakh Territory 29 Nakhichevan Autonomous Republic
head of state: 9 president
government: 8 republic
monetary unit: 5 manat
mountain: 8 Caucasus
sea: 7 Caspian
people: 5 Azeri 11 Azerbaijani
language: 6 Turkic
religion: 6 Muslim

Aziz, Dr
character in: 15 A Passage to India
author: 7 Forster

Aztec (Nahua, Mexica)
language family: 7 Nahuatl 10 Uto-Aztecan
location: 6 Mexico, Puebla 8 Guerrero, Veracruz 9 Guatemala, Michoacan 11 Lake Texcoco 14 Central America
leader: 9 Montezuma
worshipped: 12 Quetzalcoatl
capital: 12 Tenochtitlan
conquerer: 6 Cortes, Cortez

Azuela, Mariano
author of: 8 The Flies 9 The Bosses 12 The Underdogs 26 Trials of a Respectable Family

azure 4 blue 5 lapis 6 cobalt 7 sky blue 8 cerulean 9 clear blue, cloudless 11 lapis lazuli

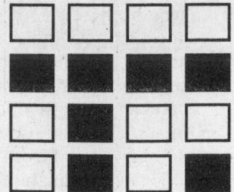

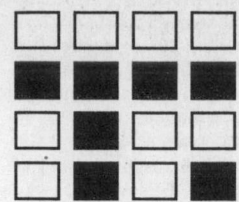

Baade, Walter
field: **9** astronomy
discovered: **15** Hidalgo asteroid

Baal 3 god **5** deity

Baal Merodach *see* **6** Marduk

Babbage, Charles
field: **11** mathematics
nationality: **7** British, English
first: **15** actuarial tables
inventor of: **13** adding machine **18** calculating machine
invented forerunner of: **15** digital computer
planned: **10** calculator

Babbitt 9 bourgeois **10** contormist, middlebrow, philistine

Babbitt
author: **13** Sinclair Lewis
character: **11** Myra Babbitt, Seneca Deane **12** Paul Riesling **15** Mrs Tanis Judique **22** George Folansbee Babbitt

babble 3 coo, din, gab, hum **4** blab, talk **5** prate **6** burble, clamor, drivel, gabble, gibber, gurgle, hubbub, jabber, murmur **7** blabber, blather, chatter, prattle, twaddle **8** chitchat, rattle on **9** jabbering, murmuring **14** chitterchatter

babbling 6 drivel, hubbub **7** blabber, twaddle **8** burbling, gabbling, gurgling, nonsense **9** clamoring, gibberish, jabbering, murmuring

babe 3 tot **4** baby **5** child **6** infant

babe in arms 4 baby **6** infant **7** neonate, newborn

babe in the woods 8 innocent **9** fledgling, greenhorn **10** tenderfoot

babel, Babel 3 din **6** bedlam, clamor, hubbub, tumult, uproar **7** turmoil **9** confusion **10** hullabaloo **11** pandemonium

Babel, Isaac
author of: **9** Benia Krik **11** Odessa Tales **13** The Red Cavalry

Babe Ruth
nickname of: **16** George Herman Ruth

Babe the Blue Ox
character in: **10** Paul Bunyan

baboon 6 monkey
breeding: **9** year round
characteristic: **4** mane, pads **6** muzzle
diet: **6** plants **8** scorpion **12** small animals
dwelling: **5** Egypt, Sudan **6** Africa, Arabia **7** Somalia **8** Ethiopia
family: **15** cercopithecidae
habitat: **5** hills **6** plains
largest genus: **6** Chacma
most sacred: **6** Anobis
smallest genus: **7** Western

babushka 4 baba, veil **5** scarf, stole **8** kerchief **11** grandmother

baby 3 wee **4** babe, tiny **5** dwarf, humor, pygmy, small, spoil, young **6** bantam, coddle, coward, infant, little, midget, minute, pamper, petite **7** crybaby, indulge, neonate **8** dwarfish, sniveler **9** miniature, youngster **10** babe in arms, diminutive **11** mollycoddle, overindulge, pocket-sized

Baby
nickname of: **12** Lauren Bacall

baby carriage 4 cart, pram **6** cradle **12** perambulator

babyish 7 puerile **8** childish, immature, juvenile **9** infantile

babylike 3 wee **4** tiny **5** small **9** infantile **10** diminutive

Babylonian Captivity 13 Avignon Papacy **15** Babylonian Exile

Babylonian god 3 Bel **6** Marduk

Babylonian Mythology
chief of gods: **6** Marduk **8** Merodach **12** Baal Merodach
demon: **6** Namtar
goddess of air: **6** Ninlil
goddess of death: **10** Ereshkigal
goddess of love/war/ fertility: **6** Ananna, Inanna, Ishtar **7** Astarte, Mylitta **9** Ashtoreth
god of air: **5** Enlil
god of dead: **6** Nergal
god of fire: **5** Ishum
god of heaven: **2** An **3** Anu
god of moon: **3** Sin
god of pastures/vegetation: **6** Dumuzi
god of pestilence: **4** Irra
god of shepherds: **6** Tammuz
god of sun: **3** Utu **7** Shamash
god of wisdom: **4** Enki
hero: **5** Ninib **7** Ninurta
king: **9** Gilgamesh
king of gods: **5** Enlil
mother of gods: **5** Nammu
queen of heaven: **6** Ishtar
world of dead: **3** Kur

Baby Roo
character in: **13** Winnie-the-Pooh

author: **5** Milne
mother: **5** Kanga

Baby Snooks 10 Fanny Brice

Baby Snookums
character in: **12** The Newlyweds

Bacall, Lauren
real name: **15** Betty Joan Perske
husband: **12** Jason Robards **14** Humphrey Bogart
nickname: **4** Baby
born: **9** New York NY
roles: **8** Applause, Key Largo **11** Dark Passage, The Big Sleep **12** Cactus Flower **16** To Have and Have Not **22** How to Marry a Millionaire

Bacchae
form: **11** priestesses
attendants of: **7** Bacchus
participants in: **11** Bacchanalia

Bacchae, The
author: **9** Euripides
character: **4** Zeus **5** Agave **6** Cadmus, Semele **8** Dionysus, Pentheus, Tiresias

bacchanal 4 orgy **5** feast, revel, spree **6** frolic **7** carouse, debauch, revelry, wassail **8** carnival, carousal, festival **10** debauchery, Saturnalia **11** merrymaking

Bacchanalia
festival honoring: **7** Bacchus

Bacchant
priest who worships: **7** Bacchus

Bacchante
also: **6** Thyiad
priestess who worships: **7** Bacchus

Bacchus
also: **5** Evius **8** Dionysus
god of: **4** wine **5** drama **9** fertility
father: **4** Zeus
mother: **6** Semele
son: **6** Phlias **7** Narcaus, Priapus **8** Oenopion
epithet: **6** Lyaeus **7** Bromius, Cresius **8** Thyoneus, Triambus **9** Pyrigenes **11** Dithyrambus, Mitrephorus

Bach, Carl (Karl) Philipp Emanuel
born: **6** Weimar **7** Germany
father: **19** Johann Sebastian Bach
composer of: **14** Prussian Sonata **19** Wurtembergian Sonata

Bach, Johann Sebastian
born: **7** Germany **8** Eisenach
composer of: **8** Chaconne **10** Giant Fugue, Inventions, Magnificat,

Wedge Fugue **11** Dorian Fugue, Fiddle Fugue, Little Fugue **12** Corelli Fugue, French Suites, Fuga alla Giga, German Suites, St Anne's Fugue **13** Coffee Cantata, English Suites, St John Passion **14** Alla Breve Fugue, Easter Oratorio, Peasant Cantata, Wedding Cantata **15** Jesu Meine Freude, Musical Offering **16** St Matthew Passion, The Art of the Fugue **17** Christmas Oratorio **18** Goldberg Variations **20** Brandenburg Concertos **22** The Well-Tempered Clavier **24** The Wise and Foolish Virgins **30** The Dispute Between Phoebus and Pan

Bach, Richard
   author of: **25** Jonathan Livingston Seagull

bachelor 6 single **9** single man, unmarried **12** unmarried man

Bachelor Father
   character: **9** Peter Tong **10** Kelly Gregg **12** Bentley Gregg **13** Ginger Farrell
   cast: **10** Sammee Tong **12** John Forsythe **14** Noreen Corcoran **17** Bernadette Withers

bachelorhood 8 celibacy **13** baccalaureate **14** unmarried state

bacillus 3 bug **4** germ **7** microbe **8** pathogen **9** bacterium **13** microorganism

back 3 aid, ebb **4** abet, gone, help, hind, late, past, rear, tail **5** after, guard, minor, rural, spine, tardy **6** affirm, assist, attest, behind, bygone, caudal, dorsal, dorsum, far end, former, hinder, hold up, praise, recede, recoil, remote, retire, return, revert, second, succor, tergal, uphold, verify **7** belated, bolster, certify, confirm, delayed, distant, earlier, elapsed, endorse, expired, far side, finance, not paid, overdue, promote, protect, rear end, rebound, retract, retreat, reverse, sponsor, support, sustain, tail end, warrant **8** advocate, backbone, hind part, hindmost, maintain, move away, obsolete, previous, sanction, secluded, turn tail, validate, vouch for, withdraw **9** afterpart, encourage, in arrears, out-of-date, patronize, posterior, reinforce, subsidize **10** retrogress, testify for, underwrite, untraveled **11** bear witness, corroborate, countenance, countrified, countryside, farthermost, furthermost, reverse side, undeveloped, unimportant, unpopulated **12** beat a retreat, hindquarters, spinal column, substantiate **13** take sides with

back away from 7 back off **11** retreat from **12** draw back from, withdraw from

backbiter 5 scold **6** carper, critic **7** reviler **8** vilifier **9** slanderer

backbiting 5 abuse, catty **6** gossip,

malice **7** abusive, calumny, gossipy, hurtful, obloquy, slander **8** libeling, reviling **9** aspersion, cattiness, censuring, contumely, injurious, invective, malicious, maligning, vilifying **10** belittling, bitchiness, calumnious, defamation, defamatory, derogating, detracting, detraction, scandalous, scurrility, slanderous, traduction **11** badmouthing, denigrating, deprecating, disparaging, traducement **12** backstabbing, calumniation, vilification, vituperation **13** disparagement, maliciousness **16** scandal-mongering

backbone 4 grit, guts, sand **5** basis, chine, nerve, pluck, spine, spunk **6** dorsum, mettle, spirit **7** bravery, courage, resolve **8** firmness, mainstay, strength, tenacity **9** character, fortitude, manliness, vertebrae **10** foundation, resolution **11** intrepidity **12** resoluteness, spinal column **13** dauntlessness, steadfastness **15** vertebral column **19** strength of character

back-country 4 farm **5** rural **6** rustic **7** farming **10** provincial

back down 7 back off **8** draw back, move away **9** withdrawn

backdrop 4 flat **7** curtain, scenery **10** background

backer 4 ally **5** angel **6** patron **7** sponsor **8** adherent, advocate, champion, follower, investor, promoter **9** financier, guarantor, supporter **10** well-wisher **11** underwriter

backfire 4 flop, miss **5** crash **6** fizzle, go awry **8** backlash, lay an egg, miscarry, ricochet **9** boomerang **10** bounce back, disappoint **11** come to grief, fall through **12** come to naught **13** come to nothing

background 3 set **4** past, rear **5** flats **6** milieu **7** context, history, rearing, setting **8** backdrop, breeding, distance, heritage, training **9** education, grounding, landscape, life story **10** experience, upbringing **11** antecedents, credentials, environment, mise-en-scene, preparation **13** circumstances

backhanded 7 awkward **8** reversed **9** insincere

backing 3 aid **4** core, help **5** aegis **6** succor **7** support **8** advocacy, interior, sanction **9** patronage, prompting **10** assistance, inner layer, sustenance **11** championing, cooperation, endorsement, helping hand, sponsorship **13** encouragement

backlash 4 flop, snag **5** crash, ravel **6** fizzle, go away, recoil **7** rebound **8** backfire, kick back, miscarry, ricochet, snap back **9** animosity, boomerang, hostility, reversion **10** antagonism, bounce back, opposition, resistance **11** come to grief, fall through **12** come to naught **13** come to nothing, counteraction, recalcitrance

backlog 5 hoard, stock, store **6** assets, excess, supply **7** nest egg, reserve, savings **9** abundance, amassment, inventory, reservoir, stockpile **12** accumulation **13** reserve supply **14** super-abundance

back matter 5 index **8** addendum, appendix **10** supplement **12** bibliography

back off 7 retreat **8** back down, pull back, withdraw

backpack 4 hike, load **5** pouch **6** bundle **8** knapsack

backside 3 can **4** buns, butt, duff, prat, rear, rump, seat, tail **5** fanny **6** behind, bottom, settee, setter, sitter **7** keister, rear end **8** buttocks, derriere **9** fundament, posterior

backslide 5 lapse **6** revert **7** relapse **10** recurrence, regression **11** deteriorate **14** slip from virtue

back street 5 alley, byway **8** alleyway **13** secondary road

Back Street
   director:
      1941 version: 15 Robert Stevenson
      1961 version: 11 David Miller
   based on story by: **11** Fannie Hurst
   cast:
      1932 version: 9 John Boles **10** Irene Dunne
      1941 version: 12 Charles Boyer **16** Margaret Sullavan
      1961 version: 9 John Gavin, Vera Miles **13** Susan Hayward

back talk 3 jaw, lip **4** gall, guff, rude, sass **5** cheek **8** pertness, rudeness **9** impudence, insolence, sassiness, sauciness **12** impertinence

Back to the Future
   director: **14** Robert Zemeckis
   cast: **11** Lea Thompson, Michael J Fox **16** Christopher Lloyd

backup 6 second **7** reserve, standby, stand-in **9** alternate, auxiliary, emergency, secondary **10** substitute, understudy **11** pinch-hitter **13** supplementary

back up 4 abet **6** assist, uphold **9** reinforce **11** corroborate

backward, backwards 3 shy **4** dull, slow **5** dense, tardy, timid, wrong **6** behind, ebbing, remiss, toward **7** bashful, impeded, laggard, messily, reverse, the rear **8** inverted, rearward, receding, reserved, retarded, reticent, reversed, sluggish **9** in retreat, in reverse, inside out, returning, slow-paced, to the past, to the rear, withdrawn **10** disorderly, improperly, regressive, retreating, retrograde, slow-witted, topsy-turvy, upside down **11** chaotically, undeveloped, withdrawing **12** wrong side out **13** retrogressive **15** uncommunicative
   French: **9** en arriere

backwash 4 burg, wake **6** result,

sticks, upshot **7** boonies, outcome **8** frontier, tank town **9** aftermath, backwater, boondocks, provinces, upcountry **10** hinterland **11** aftereffect, backcountry, consequence

backwater 3 ebb **5** slack **7** retreat, reverse **8** holdback, stagnant, withdraw

backwoods 5 rural, wilds **6** rustic, simple, sticks **7** boonies, country **8** woodland **9** boondocks, rural area **10** hinterland, provincial **11** backcountry, countryside, hinterlands **15** unsophisticated

bacon 3 pig **4** pork **6** gammon **8** porkslab **10** smoked pork **11** porkbellies
measure: 6 rasher

Bacon, Francis
author of: 6 Essays **11** New Atlantis **12** Novum Organum **14** Maxims of the Law **16** Instauratio Magna **17** History of Henry VII **18** De Sapientia Veterum **20** Apophthegms New and Old **21** Advancement of Learning **25** Reading on the Statute of Uses

Bacon, Francis
born: 6 Dublin **7** Ireland
artwork: 15 Henrietta Moraes **35** Three Studies at the Base of a Crucifixion **44** Studies After Velazquez' Portrait of Pope Innocent X

Bacon, Henry
architect of: 15 Lincoln Memorial

bactericide 9 germicide **10** antiseptic, germ killer **12** disinfectant

bacteriologist
American: 4 Reed
British: 7 Fleming
German: 4 Koch **7** Behring, Ehrlich **10** Wassermann
Japanese: 7 Noguchi **8** Kitasato

bacterium 3 bug **4** germ **5** virus **7** microbe **8** bacillus, pathogen **13** microorganism

bad 3 ill, sad, sin **4** base, dire, evil, foul, glum, grim, mean, poor, rank, sick, sour, vile **5** acrid, acute, angry, awful, cross, false, fetid, grave, harsh, lousy, moldy, nasty, risky, sorry, unfit, wrong **6** ailing, bitter, crimes, faulty, gloomy, guilty, infirm, odious, putrid, rancid, rotten, severe, sickly, sinful, touchy, tragic, turned, unwell, wicked, wrongs **7** baneful, beastly, corrupt, decayed, harmful, hurtful, immoral, joyless, lacking, naughty, not good, noxious, painful, searing, serious, spoiled, tainted, unsound, useless **8** below par, contrite, criminal, dreadful, grievous, inferior, menacing, mildewed, offenses, polluted, terrible, troubled, villainy, wretched **9** agonizing, dangerous, defective, deficient, erroneous, frightful, hazardous, imperfect, incorrect, injurious, irascible, irritable, loathsome, miserable, nefarious, obnoxious, offensive, regretful, repugnant, repulsive, revolting, sad events,

sickening, troubling, unethical, unhealthy, unnerving, unwelcome, valueless **10** calamitous, decomposed, deplorable, detestable, disastrous, disgusting, distressed, disturbing, fallacious, immorality, inadequate, indisposed, melancholy, misfortune, nauseating, not correct, perfidious, putrescent, remorseful, second-rate, unpleasant, villainous, wickedness **11** detrimental, discouraged, distasteful, distractive, distressing, ineffective, inefficient, opprobrious, regrettable, substandard, troublesome, unpalatable **12** contaminated, disagreeable, discouraging, disreputable, excruciating, questionable, unprincipled, unproductive **13** below standard, disappointing, disheartening, harmful things, nonproductive, reprehensible, short-tempered **14** disappointment **15** disadvantageous, under the weather **18** conscience-stricken

bad faith 7 perfidy, treason **8** betrayal **9** falseness, treachery, two timing **10** disloyalty **11** double-cross **13** breach of faith, double-dealing **14** unfaithfulness

badge 4 mark, seal, sign, star **5** brand, stamp, token **6** device, emblem, ensign, shield, symbol **7** earmark **8** hallmark, insignia **9** medallion

badger 3 nag, vex **4** bait, goad **5** annoy, beset, bully, chafe, harry, hound, tease **6** coerce, harass, hector, nettle, pester, plague **7** provoke, torment, trouble **8** irritate **9** persecute
group of: 4 cete

Badger State
nickname of: 9 Wisconsin

badinage 5 chaff **6** banter, joking **7** jesting, joshing, kidding, ragging, ribbing, waggery **8** chaffing, raillery, repartee, word play

bad judgment 5 folly **10** imprudence **11** foolishness **12** carelessness **13** senselessness **15** thoughtlessness **16** shortsightedness, unperceptiveness

bad luck 6 mishap **7** ill wind **8** bad break **9** adversity, mischance **10** ill fortune, misfortune

badly 3 ill **5** wrong **6** basely, poorly, sorely, vilely **7** acutely, greatly, ineptly, not well, wrongly **8** faultily, horribly, severely, shoddily, sinfully, sloppily, terribly, very much, wickedly **9** corruptly, extremely, immorally, intensely, unsoundly **10** carelessly, criminally, dreadfully, improperly, wretchedly **11** defectively, deficiently, desperately, erroneously, exceedingly, frightfully, imperfectly, incorrectly, nefariously, offensively, unethically **12** disreputably, inadequately, villainously **13** incompetently, in the worst way **16** unsatisfactorily

bad manners 8 rudeness **9** surliness

10 incivility **11** boorishness, discourtesy **12** impoliteness

bad mark 4 blot **7** demerit **9** poor grade

badminton
racket: 10 battledore
racket used to hit: 4 bird **7** shuttle **11** shuttlecock
Indian version: 5 poona
stroke: 4 drop **5** clear, smash **7** service **13** backhand drive, forehand drive

badmouthing 5 barbs **7** dissing, insults, slander **9** criticism, insulting **10** slandering **11** criticizing

bad taste 9 crudeness, vulgarity **10** coarseness, garishness, tawdryness

bad tasting 4 sour **5** nasty **6** bitter **7** spoiled **9** medicinal, revolting **10** disgusting **11** unpalatable

bad-tempered 5 cross, testy **6** grumpy **7** grouchy **8** choleric, churlish **9** difficult, irascible, irritable **10** ill-natured **11** acrimonious **12** disagreeable

bad times 4 bust **5** slump **9** hard times, recession **10** depression

bad turn 4 harm, hurt **5** wrong **6** injury **7** ill turn **8** disfavor **9** injustice **10** disservice **11** discourtesy

Baekleland, Leo Hendrik
field: 9 chemistry
invented: 8 Bakelite **32** artificial light photographic paper

Baer, Max (Maximillian Adalbert)
nickname: 17 Livermore Larruper
sport: 6 boxing
class: 11 heavyweight

Baeyer, Johann Friedrich Wilhelm Adolph von
field: 9 chemistry
nationality: 6 German
synthesized: 6 indigo
discovered: 13 phthalein dyes
awarded: 10 Nobel Prize

baffle 3 bar **4** daze, dull, foil, stop **5** amaze, check, stump **6** deaden, muddle, puz- zle, reduce, thwart **7** astound, confuse, inhibit, mystify, nonplus, perplex **8** astonish, befuddle, bewilder, confound, dumfound, minimize, restrain, surprise **10** disconcert

baffling 7 elusive **8** puzzling **9** confusing, enigmatic **10** mysterious, mystifying, perplexing **11** confounding **16** incomprehensible

bag 3 get, sag **4** hunt, kill, sack, take, trap **5** bulge, catch, droop, pouch, purse, shoot, snare **6** bundle, entrap, obtain, packet **7** acquire, capture, collect, ensnare **8** paper bag, protrude, suitcase **10** receptacle

bagatelle 6 trifle **7** nothing, trinket **10** knickknack, light music **11** unimportant

baggage 4 bags, gear **5** grips **6** trunks

7 bundles, effects, luggage, valises **8** movables, packages **9** apparatus, equipment, suitcases, trappings **10** belongings **11** impedimenta **13** accoutrements, paraphernalia

baggy 4 limp **5** loose, slack **6** droopy, flabby, puffed **7** bloated, bulbous, flac- cid, paunchy, sagging, swollen **9** unpressed, unshapely **12** loose-fitting

Baghdad
　capital of: **4** Iraq
　founder: **8** (Caliph) al-Mansur
　landmark:
　　minaret: **10** Suq al-Ghazi
　　mosque: **8** Madrasah **14** al-Mustansiriya
　means: **8** God-given
　river: **6** Tigris

Bagheera
　character in: **14** The Jungle Books
　author: **7** Kipling

bagnio 4 bath, stew **5** house **6** bordel, prison **7** brothel **8** bordello, cathouse **10** bawdy house, fancy house, whorehouse **13** sporting house **14** house of ill fame **16** house of ill repute **19** house of prostitution

Bagnold, Enid
　author of: **14** National Velvet, The Chalk Garden **23** The Chinese Prime Minister

Bagstock, Joe
　character in: **12** Dombey and Son
　author: **7** Dickens

Bahamas
　capital/largest city: **6** Nassau
　others: **8** Freeport **9** Rock Sound **10** George Town **11** Mastic Point **12** Spanish Wells
　head of state: **14** British monarch **15** governor general
　island: **3** Cat **4** Long **5** Berry, Exuma **6** Andros, Bimini, Caicos, Rum Cay **7** Crooked, Harbour, Watling **9** Eleuthera, Mayaguana **10** Great Abaco **11** Grand Bahama, Great Inagua, Great Ragged, San Salvador **13** New Providence
　sea: **8** Atlantic **9** Caribbean
　physical feature:
　　strait: **7** Florida
　　swamp: **8** mangrove
　people: **5** black **7** Haitian
　language: **6** Creole **7** English
　religion: **12** Christianity
　place:
　　harbor: **9** Governors
　　naval base: **9** Mayaguana
　feature:
　　key: **3** cay
　　native: **5** conch

Bahrain
　capital/largest city: **6** Manama
　others: **5** Rifaa **7** Jidhafs **8** Muharraq
　head of state/government: **4** emir
　monetary unit: **4** fils **5** dinar
　island: **5** Hawar, Jidda **6** Sitrah **7**

Bahrain **9** Umm Nassan **10** al-Muharraq **11** An Nabi Salih
　physical feature:
　　gulf: **7** Bahrain, Persian
　people: **4** Arab **6** Indian **7** Persian **8** American, European **9** Pakistani
　　ruling family: **9** al-Khalifa
　language: **4** Urdu **5** Farsi **6** Arabic **7** English, Persian
　religion: **5** Islam

bail 3 dip **4** bond, lade **5** ladle, scoop, spoon **6** surety **9** guarantee **11** post bond for

bailiff 6 deputy **8** marshall, overseer **9** assistant, constable **12** court officer

bailiwick 4 area, beat, turf **5** arena, orbit, place, realm **6** domain, sphere **7** compass **8** dominion, province **9** territory **10** department **12** neighborhood

Baird, Spencer Fullerton
　field: **7** zoology
　authority on: **5** birds **7** mammals
　established: **30** US Commission of Fish and Fisheries
　laboratory at: **11** Woods Hole MA

bait 3 vex **4** lure, ride, worm **5** annoy, bribe, harry, hound, tease, worry **6** allure, bad- ger, come-on, harass, heckle, hector, magnet, needle **7** provoke, torment **9** put bait on, tantalize **10** allurement, antagonize, attraction, enticement, inducement, temptation

bake 3 fry **4** boil, burn, cook, sear, stew **5** grill, roast, saute, toast **6** braise, pan-fry, scorch, simmer **7** parboil, swelter

Baked Bean State
　nickname of: **13** Massachusetts

Baker, Norma Jean Mortenson
　real name of: **13** Marilyn Monroe

Balaam
　father: **4** Beor
　brother: **4** Bela
　lived at: **4** Aram **6** Pethor
　commanded by: **5** Balak
　killed by: **6** Israel
　rebuked by: **3** ass

Balak
　father: **6** Zippor
　commanded: **6** Balaam

Balakiref, Mily
　born: **6** Russia **13** Nijni-Novgorod
　member of: **7** Kutchka, The Five
　composer of: **6** Russia, Tamara, Thamar **7** Islamey **8** King Lear (overture)

balance, balances 3 pay **4** cool, mean, rest **5** poise, ratio, scale, sum up, tally, total, tot up, weigh **6** aplomb, equate, offset, parity, ponder, reckon, scales, set off, square, steady, weight **7** compare, compute, harmony, opinion, reflect, remnant, residue **8** cogitate, consider, contrast, coolness, equality, estimate, evaluate, judgment, leftover, level off, parallel, presence, symmetry **9** appraisal,

calculate, composure, equipoise, juxtapose, make level, remainder, stability, stabilize **10** amount owed, comparison, counteract, deliberate, equanimity, evaluation, keep steady, neutralize, proportion, steadiness **11** equilibrium **12** counterpoise, equalization, middle ground **13** compensate for, consideration, judiciousness **14** amount credited, self-possession, unflappability **15** level-headedness **16** imperturbability
　constellation of: **5** Libra

balanced 4 fair, just **9** equitable, impartial **12** unprejudiced **13** disinterested

balance out 6 cancel, offset **9** make up for **10** neutralize **13** compensate for **14** counterbalance

Balanchine, George
　choreographer of: **4** Agon **6** Jewels **8** Episodes, Ivesiana, Serenade **15** Concerto Barocco **16** Allegro Brillante

balcony 4 deck **5** boxes, foyer, loges **6** loggia **7** portico, terrace, veranda **9** mezzanine

bald 4 bare, flat, open **5** blunt, naked, plain, stark, utter **6** barren, simple, smooth **7** denuded, obvious **8** flagrant, glabrous, hairless, outright, treeless **9** depilated, out- and-out, unadorned **11** categorical, undisguised, unqualified, unvarnished **12** without cover **13** unembellished, unequivocable **15** straightforward

Balder
　also: **5** Baldr **6** Baldur
　origin: **6** Nordic
　god of: **6** beauty **8** radiance
　father: **4** Odin **5** Othin
　mother: **3** Fri **5** Frigg, Frija **6** Frigga
　twin brother: **5** Hoder, Hodur
　killed by: **5** Hoder, Hodur

balderdash 3 rot **4** bosh, bull, bunk **5** crock, trash **6** bunkum, drivel, hot air **7** twaddle **8** buncombe, claptrap, flummery, nonsense, tommyrot **9** gibberish, poppycock **10** double-talk, tomfoolery **11** obfuscation **16** stuff and nonsense

baldheaded 8 hairless **9** baldpated, depilated **10** skin- headed **11** chromedomed

Baldr
　see: **6** Balder

Baldung Grien, Hans
　born: **6** Alsace **10** Weyersheim
　artwork: **9** Todentanz **17** Death and the Maiden **19** Death Kissing a Maiden **21** The Bewitched Stable Boy **24** Rest on the Flight into Egypt

Baldur
　see: **6** Balder

Baldwin, James
　author of: **13** Giovanni's Room, The Amen Corner **14** Another Country **15**

Just Above My Head, The Fire Next Time **17** Going to Meet the Man, Nobody Knows My Name, No Name in the Street **21** Blues for Mister Charlie, Go Tell It on the Mountain
bale 4 case, load, pack **6** bundle, packet, parcel **7** package **11** bound bundle
balefire 6 beacon **9** watchfire **10** signal fire
baleful 3 icy **4** cold, dire, evil **6** deadly, malign **7** baneful, furious, harmful, hurtful, ominous **8** sinister, spiteful, venomous **9** malicious, malignant **10** malevolent **11** cold-hearted, threatening
Balfe, Michael William
  born: 6 Dublin **7** Ireland
  composer of: 15 The Bohemian Girl, The Maid of Artois **17** I rivali di se stessi **18** The Siege of Rochelle
Balfour, David
  character in: 9 Kidnapped
  author: 9 Stevenson
Bali
  province of: 9 Indonesia
  capital: 8 Denpasar
  city: 10 Singaraja
  island: 11 Lesser Sunda
  highest peak: 6 Agoeng
  climate: 3 dry **7** monsoon
  tree: 8 waringin
  animal: 4 deer **5** tiger
  people: 7 Malayan
  religion: 8 Hinduism
  agriculture: 3 pig **4** corn, rice **6** cattle, coffee **7** tobacco
Balius
  horse of: 8 Achilles
  gift: 11 immortality
balk 3 bar **4** foil, shun **5** block, check, demur, evade, shirk, spike, stall **6** baffle, defeat, derail, eschew, hinder, impede, recoil, refuse, resist, stymie, thwart **7** inhibit, prevent **8** draw back, hang back, hesitate, obstruct **9** forestall, frustrate **10** shrink from
Balkan 16 Forested mountain
  agriculture: 5 grain **6** cotton, grapes, olives **7** tobacco
  ancient people: 4 Slav **5** Greek, Roman **8** Illyrian, Thracian
  language: 9 Slovenian **10** Macedonian **14** Serbo-Croatian
  mountain: 6 Balkan, Massif **7** Rhodope **10** Carpathian **11** Dinaric Alps **13** Transylvanian
  religion: 5 Islam **8** Orthodox **13** Roman Catholic
  river: 6 Danube, Morava, Vardar
  sea boundary: 5 Black **6** Aegean, Ionian **8** Adriatic **13** Mediterranean
  state: 6 Greece, Turkey **7** Albania, Romania **8** Bulgaria **10** Yugoslavia
balky 6 mulish, ornery, unruly **7** restive, wayward, willful **8** contrary, perverse, stubborn **9** fractious, obstinate,

pigheaded **10** rebellious, refractory **11** disobedient, intractable **12** recalcitrant, unmanageable
ball 3 hop, orb **4** prom, shot **5** dance, globe **6** pellet, soiree, sphere **7** bullets, globule **8** spheroid **9** cotillion, promenade **11** projectiles
Ball, Lucille
  husband: 9 Desi Arnaz
  children: 4 Desi **5** Lucie
  born: 11 Jamestown NY
  roles: 9 Here's Lucy, I Love Lucy **11** The Lucy Show
Balla, Giacomo
  born: 5 Italy, Turin
  artwork: 8 The Sewer **11** The Mad Woman **18** Speeding Automobile **20** Rhythm of the Violinist **22** Dynamism of a Dog on a Leash **26** The Street Light Study of Light **29** Mercury Passing in Front of the Sun **40** Swifts Paths of Movement and Dynamic Sequences
ballad 3 lay **4** song **5** carol, ditty **6** chanty **8** folk song **12** rhyming story **13** narrative poem **14** narrative verse
Ballad of Reading Gaol, The
  author: 10 Oscar Wilde
Ballads and Poems
  author: 19 Stephen Vincent Benet
ballast 6 weight **7** balance, control **9** equipoise **10** ballasting, dead weight, makeweight, stabilizer **12** counterpoise **13** counterweight **14** counterbalance **19** stabilizing material
Ballesteros, Severiano
  nickname: 4 Seve
  sport: 4 golf
  nationality: 7 Spanish
ballet 4 Agon **5** Manon, Rodeo **6** Apollo, Parade **7** Giselle, Orpheus **8** Coppelia, Episodes, Ivesiana, Les Noces, Serenade, Swan Lake, The Doves **9** Anastasia, Fancy Free, Interplay, Petrushka, The Jewels **10** La Sylphide, Petrouchka **11** Billy the Kid, Lilac Garden, Soccer Dance, Symphony in C, The Firebird **12** Pillar of Fire, Sailor's Dance, Spring Waters, The Partisans **13** The Nutcracker **14** Romeo and Juliet **15** Concerto Barocco, Fall River Legend, The Rite of Spring **16** Allegro Brillante, La Fille Mal Gardee, Specter of the Rose **17** The Sleeping Beauty **18** Raymonda Variations **19** The Afternoon of a Faun, The Four Temperaments **24** Stravinsky Violin Concerto
  ballet company: 5 Kirov, Royal **7** Bolshoi, Joffrey **9** Mariinsky, Maryinsky **11** New York City **13** Ballets Russes **20** Dance Theater of Harlem **21** American Ballet Theater **22** National Ballet of Canada
  choreographer: 9 Hanya Holm, Lev Ivanov **10** John Weaver **11** Jules Perrot **12** Agnes de Mille, Igor Moi-

seyev, Marius Petipa, Michel Fokine **13** Jean Dauberval, Jerome Robbins, Leonid Massine **15** Arthur Saint-Leon **16** George Balanchine, Kenneth MacMillan **18** August Bournonville, Bronislava Nijinska, Jean Georges Noverre, Sir Frederick Ashton
  chorus: 8 ensemble **13** corps de ballet
  dancer: 9 Karen Kain **10** Anton Dolin, Marie Lieta, Serge Lifar **11** Allegra Kent, Anna Pavlova, Anthony Blum, Lucile Grahn, Lynn Seymour, Nadia Nerina **12** Fanny Cerrito, Marie Camargo, Peter Martins **13** Alicia Markova, Andre Eglevsky, Anthony Dowell, Carlotta Grisi, Frank Augustyn, Galina Ulanova, Margot Fonteyn, Marie Taglioni, Melissa Hayden, Patricia Neary, Rudolf Nureyev **14** Arthur Mitchell, Cynthia Gregory, Edward Villella, Gelsey Kirkland, Leonide Massine, Maria Tallchief, Suzanne Farrell, Vaslav Nijinsky **15** Jacques D'Amboise, Martine Van Hamel, Maya Plisetskaya, Natalia Makarova, Patricia McBride, Tamara Karsavina **16** Antoinette Sibley, Olga Spessivtseva **17** Alexandra Danilova, Marina Kondratieva **18** Mikhail Baryshnikov
  fast movement: 7 allegro
  first ballet: 22 Ballet Comique de la Reine
  impresario: 12 Marie Rambert **15** Ninette de Valois, Sergei Diaghilev
  kick: 9 battement
  modern dancer/choreographer: 8 Ted Shawn **9** Eliot Feld **10** Mary Wigman, Paul Draper, Twyla Tharp **11** Anna Sokolow, Antony Tudor, Eric Hawkins, Ruth St Denis **12** Martha Graham **13** Alwin Nikolais, Doris Humphrey, Isadora Duncan **14** Charles Weidman **15** Merce Cunningham
  position/step: 4 jete, plie, tour **5** saute **6** releve **7** en avant, fouette, on point, pas seul, turnout **8** batterie, cabriole, en dedans, en dehors, glissade **9** arabesque, developpe, en arriere, entrechat, pas de chat, pas-de-deux, pirouette **10** demipointe, port de bras, tour en l'air **11** rond de jambe, terre-a-terre **12** pas de bourree, saut de basque **17** changement de pieds
  principal female dancer: 6 etoile **9** ballerina **14** prima ballerina
  principal male dancer: 12 danseur noble
  skirt: 4 tutu
  slow movement: 6 adagio
  term: 4 coda **5** barre **6** ballon **14** divertissement
Ball of Fat
  author: 15 Guy de Maupassant
balloon 4 grow **5** belly, bloat **6** billow, blow up, dilate, expand **7** distend,

enlarge, fill out, inflate, puff out **8** increase, swell out

ballot 4 poll, vote **5** slate **6** ticket, voting **7** polling **13** round of voting **16** list of candidates

ballyhoo 4 hype, puff, push, tout **6** herald, hoopla **7** buildup, promote, puffery, trumpet **8** proclaim **9** advertise, promotion, publicity, publicize **10** hullabaloo, propaganda **11** advertising **15** public relations

balm 5 cream, salve **6** balsam, lotion, solace **7** anodyne, comfort, unguent **8** curative, narcotic, ointment, sedative **9** comforter, emollient **10** palliative **11** restorative **12** tranquilizer

balmy 3 odd **4** calm, fair, mild, soft, warm **5** bland, kooky, weird **6** easing, gentle **7** calming, clement, summery **8** aromatic, fragrant, perfumed, pleasant, redolent, soothing **9** agreeable, ambrosial, eccentric, temperate **10** refreshing, salubrious

Balnibari
 fictional land in: **16** Gulliver's Travels
 author: **5** Swift

baloney 3 rot **4** bull, bunk **5** hokum, hooey, stuff **6** bunkum, hot air, humbug **7** hogwash, sausage, spinach **8** claptrap, nonsense, tommyrot **9** poppycock **10** applesauce **11** foolishness

Baloo
 character in: **14** The Jungle Books
 author: **7** Kipling

balsam 3 fir **4** balm **5** cream, salve **7** unguent **8** ointment **9** Impatiens
 varieties: **2** He **3** Fir, She **4** Rose, Wild **6** Garden **8** Zanzibar

Balsam, Martin
 born: **9** New York NY
 roles: **6** Psycho **7** Catch-22 **15** A Thousand Clowns, On the Waterfront

Baltic
 language family: **12** Indo-European
 group: **11** Balto-Slavic
 subgroup: **7** Latvian **10** Lithuanian
 canal: **4** Kiel
 port: **4** Kiel, Riga **6** Danzig, Gdansk **7** Tallinn

Baltimore
 baseball team: **7** Orioles
 football team: **5** Stars **6** Ravens

Baltimore, David
 field: **12** microbiology
 studied: **11** animal cells **13** viral genetics
 awarded: **10** Nobel Prize

Balto-Slavic
 language family: **12** Indo-European
 branch: **6** Baltic, Slavic

baluster 4 post, rail **6** column, pillar **7** support, upright **8** pilaster

balustrade 7 railing **8** baluster, banister, handrail

Balzac, Honore de

author of: **7** Gobseck **10** La Vendetta **11** Cousin(e) Bette **12** Father Goriot, Le Cousin Pons, Le Pere Goriot **13** Lost Illusions **14** Eugenie Grandet, The Human Comedy **15** The Wild Ass's Skin **16** La Comedie Humaine **23** The Physiology of Marriage

Bamako
 capital of: **4** Mali

Bambi
 author: **11** Felix Salten
 character: **3** Ena **6** Faline, Flower **7** Thumper
 film made by: **6** Disney
 directed by: **9** David Hand

bamboo 4 Sasa **7** Bambusa **9** Shibataea **10** Pseudosasa **11** Arundinaria **13** Phyllostachys **14** Chimonobambusa **15** Semiarundinaria
 varieties: **4** Moso **5** Arrow, Black, Dwarf, Giant, Hardy, Hedge, Henon, Meyer, Pygmy, Simon, Stake **6** Buddha, Common, Forage, Oldham, Sacred, Sickle, Square, Tonkin **7** Allgold, Beechey, Mexican **8** Calcutta, Feathery, Heavenly, Narihira **9** Canebrake, Castillon **10** Red- berried, Square-stem **11** Punting-pole **12** Alphonse Karr, Yellow-groove **13** Dwarf fern-leaf, Fern-leaf hedge, Oriental hedge **14** Chinese goddess **16** Dwarf white-stripe **17** Silver-stripe hedge **18** Stripe-stem fern- leaf

bamboozle 3 con, gyp **4** coax, dupe, fool, gull, hoax, lure, rook, take **5** cheat, coz- en, trick **6** delude **7** beguile, deceive, defraud, mislead, swindle **8** hoodwink **9** victimize

ban 3 bar **5** debar, taboo **6** banish, enjoin, forbid **7** barring, embargo, exclude **8** disallow, prohibit, stoppage, suppress **9** exclusion, interdict, proscribe, restraint **10** banishment, censorship **11** forbiddance, prohibition, restriction **12** interdiction, proscription

banal 4 dull **5** corny, stale, stock, tired, trite, vapid **6** jejune **7** humdrum, insipid, prosaic **8** bromidic, everyday, ordinary, shopworn **9** hackneyed **10** pedestrian, threadbare, unexciting, unoriginal **11** commonplace, stereotyped **12** cliche-ridden, conventional **13** platitudinous, unimaginative, uninteresting

banality 6 cliche **7** bromide **9** platitude, staleness, triteness **10** insipidity

banana 4 Musa
 varieties: **3** Fe'i **4** Fehi, Koae **5** Dwarf **6** Edible **7** Chinese **9** Flowering **10** Abyssinian, Ladyfinger **12** Canary Island, Chinese dwarf
 similar to: **8** plantain

Bananas
 director: **10** Woody Allen
 cast: **10** Woody Allen **12** Howard Cosell, Louise Lasser **15** Carlos Montalban

Bancroft, Anne
 real name: **23** Anna Maria Louise Italiano
 husband: **9** Mel Brooks
 born: **7** Bronx NY
 roles: **11** Mrs Robinson, The Graduate **15** The Pumpkin Eater, The Turning Point, Two for the Seesaw **16** The Miracle Worker (Oscar)

band 3 set **4** belt, body, club, crew, gang, hoop, join, pack, ring, sash **5** bunch, crowd, group, junta, party, strap, strip, swath, thong, troop, unite **6** caucus, circle, clique, collar, fillet, gather, girdle, league, ribbon, streak, stripe, throng **7** bandeau, binding, circlet, company, society **8** assembly, cincture, ensemble **9** multitude, orchestra, surcingle **10** fellowship, sisterhood **11** association, brotherhood, confederacy, consolidate **13** confederation

bandage 4 bind **5** dress **7** binding, plaster **8** compress, dressing

bandanna, bandana 5 scarf **8** kerchief **10** silk square **11** neckerchief **12** handkerchief

Bandar Seri Begawan
 capital of: **6** Brunei

bandeau 3 bra **4** band **6** fillet **7** binding, circlet **9** brassiere

bandit 4 thug **5** crook, thief **6** badman, outlaw, robber **7** brigand, burglar, footpad, ladrone **8** blackleg **9** desperado, road agent **10** highwayman

bandleader 6 master **7** maestro **8** director **9** conductor
 famous: **11** Glenn Miller, Tommy Dorsey **12** Lawrence Welk

Band of Merry Men
 followers of: **9** Robin Hood

band together 5 unify, unite **6** league **7** combine **10** join forces **11** consolidate

bandy 4 swap **5** trade **6** barter **7** shuffle **8** exchange **9** toss about **11** interchange **16** toss back and forth

bandying 4 swap **5** trade **8** exchange **9** tit for tat **10** quid pro quo **11** give and take

bane 3 woe **4** ruin **5** curse, toxin, venom **6** blight, burden, canker, plague, poison **7** scourge, torment, tragedy **8** calamity, disaster, downfall, nuisance **9** destroyer, detriment, ruination **10** affliction **13** pain in the neck **14** thorn in the side **16** fly in the ointment

baneful 4 evil **6** deadly, malign, woeful **7** harmful, noxious **8** venomous **9** injurious, malignant, poisonous **10** malevolent **11** destructive

bang 3 box, hit, pop, rap, tap **4** beat, blow, boom, clap, cuff, kick, lick, slam, slap, sock **5** burst, clout, crash, knock, smack, thump, whack **6** buffet, charge, report, thrill, thwack, wallop **7** delight **8** good time, headlong, pleasure, suddenly **9** enjoyment, explosion **10** crashingly, excitement

Bangkok
also: 9 Krung Thep
capital of: 8 Thailand
landmark: 5 Wat Po **11** Grand Palace **16** Wat Emerald Buddha
means: 12 City of Angels
nickname: 15 Venice of the East
port: 8 Klongtoi
river: 10 Chao Phraya

Bangladesh
other name: 10 East Bengal **12** East Pakistan
capital/largest city: 5 Dacca
others: 6 Khulna, Sylhet **7** Comilla, Jessore, Rangpur, Saidpur **8** Jamalpur, Rajshahi **9** Madaripur **10** Chittagong **11** Narayanganj **12** Brahmanbaria
monetary unit: 4 taka **5** paisa
island: 10 Sundarbans
mountain: 15 Chittagong Hills
highest point: 10 Keokradong
river: 5 Padna **6** Ganges, Meghna **10** Burhi Ganga, Karnaphuli **11** Brahmaputra
physical feature:
  bay: 6 Bengal
people: 7 Bengali
  guerrillas: 11 muktibahini
  leader: 6 Ershad **11** Ziaur Rahman **19** Sheikh Mujibur Rahman
language: 6 Bihari **7** Bengali, English
religion: 5 Hindu, Islam
feature:
  clothing: 4 sari **5** lungi

bangle 3 fob **5** chain, charm **6** armlet, bauble, gewgaw, tinsel **7** bibelot, fribble, trinket **8** bracelet, gimcrack, ornament, wristlet **10** knickknack **11** junk jewelry **14** costume jewelry

Bangui
capital of: 22 Central African Republic

banish 3 ban, bar **4** drop, oust **5** eject, erase, evict, exile, expel **6** deport, dispel, outlaw, reject, remove **7** cast out, discard, dismiss, exclude, put away, shut out, turn out **8** cast away, dislodge, drive out, get rid of, send away, shake off **9** discharge, eliminate, eradicate, extradite **13** excommunicate **14** send to Coventry

banished person 5 exile **6** emigre, pariah **7** outcast **8** deportee, expellee **10** expatriate **14** deported person **15** displaced person

banishment 3 ban **5** exile **6** ouster **7** removal **8** eviction **9** dismissal, exclusion, expulsion **11** deportation **12** expatriation **14** transportation **15** excommunication

Banjo Eyes
nickname of: 11 Eddie Cantor

Banjul, Bathurst
capital of: 6 Gambia

bank 3 bar, row, tip **4** dike, dune, edge, file, flat, fund, heap, hill, keep, line, mass, pile, rank, reef, rise, save, side, tier, tilt **5** amass, array, brink, chain, knoll, mound, ridge, shelf, shoal, shore, slant, slope, stack, store, train **6** barrow, line up, margin, pile up, series, strand, string, supply **7** deposit, parapet, reserve, savings, shallow, terrace **8** keyboard, sandbank **9** exchequer, reservoir, stockpile **10** depository, embankment, repository, storehouse, succession **12** accumulation, trust company **14** savings and loan

Bank Dick, The
director: 10 Eddie Cline
cast: 8 W C Fields **9** Una Merkel **15** Cora Witherspoon

Bankhead, Tallulah
father: 16 William B Bankhead
born: 12 Huntsville AL
roles: 8 Lifeboat **14** The Little Foxes **17** The Skin of Our Teeth

banknote 4 bill **9** greenback **11** certificate, legal tender **12** currency note, treasury note **17** silver certificate

bank of pity
French: 11 mont-de-piete
literal name for: 10 pawnbroker

bankrupt 5 broke **6** busted, failed, ruined **8** depleted, indigent, in the red, wiped out **9** destitute, exhausted, insolvent, penniless **12** impoverished, without funds

Bankruptcy, A
author: 20 Bjornstjerne Bjornson

Banks, Ernie
nickname: 5 Mr Cub
sport: 8 baseball
noted for: 7 hitting
team: 11 Chicago Cubs

banner 4 flag **6** burgee, colors, ensign, record **7** leading, notable, pendant, pennant, winning **8** standard, streamer **9** red-letter **10** profitable **11** outstanding **14** most successful

Bannock
language family: 10 Shoshonean
location: 5 Idaho

banquet 4 dine **5** feast, revel **6** dinner, repast **9** symposium

Banquo
character in: 7 Macbeth
author: 11 Shakespeare

bantam 3 hen, wee **4** cock, fowl, tiny **5** dwarf, pygmy, runt, small, teeny, weeny **6** little, midget, minute, petite **7** chicken, dwarfed, rooster, stunted **9** miniature **10** diminutive, pocket-size, teeny-weeny **11** Lilliputian, pocket-sized

banter 3 kid, rib **4** dish, josh, mock, ride, twit **5** chaff, jolly, taunt, tease **6** joking, needle **7** jesting, joshing, kid-

ding, rag- ging, ribbing, teasing, waggery **8** badinage, chaffing, raillery, repartee, word play

Banting, Frederick Grant
field: 8 medicine
nationality: 8 Canadian
extracted: 7 insulin
awarded: 10 Nobel Prize

Bantu
means: 9 the people
dwelling: 6 Africa
tribe: 5 Xosas, Zulus **6** Swazis **7** Basutos, Kalanga

baptism 9 beginning, immersion, sacrament **10** initiation, sprinkling **11** christening **12** introduction, purification **13** rite of passage **16** spiritual rebirth

baptize 3 dub **4** name **8** christen

bar 3 ban, pub, rib, rod **4** band, bank, beam, belt, bolt, cake, curb, flat, line, lock, oust, pale, pole, rail, reef, snag, spar, spit, stay, stop **5** block, catch, check, court, debar, eject, evict, exile, expel, forum, ingot, jimmy, lever, limit, shelf, shoal, slice, sprit, stake, stick, strip, taboo **6** banish, enjoin, fasten, forbid, impede, lounge, paling, ribbon, saloon, secure, streak, stripe, stroke, tavern **7** barrier, block up, canteen, cast out, close up, crowbar, exclude, grating, lock out, measure, prevent, sandbar, shallow, shut out, taproom **8** alehouse, crossbar, disallow, judgment, obstacle, obstruct, preclude, prohibit, restrain, restrict, tribunal **9** barricade, blackball, blacklist, hindrance, long table, lunchroom, restraint, speakeasy **10** constraint, crosspiece, impediment, injunction, limitation **11** obstruction, public house, restriction **14** cocktail lounge, serving counter, stumbling block **15** legal profession

Bara, Theda
real name: 16 Theodosia Goodman
nickname: 7 The Vamp
born: 12 Cincinnati OH
roles: 6 Carmen, Salome **7** Camille **8** The Vixen **9** Cleopatra **13** A Fool There Was, Madame Du Barry

Barabbas 6 robber **8** murderer

Barak
father: 7 Abinoam
summoned by: 7 Deborah
defeated: 6 Sisera

barb 3 cut, dig, nib **4** cusp, jibe, snag, spur, tine **5** point, prong, spike **6** insult **7** affront, barbule, bristle, prickle, putdown, sarcasm, spicule **9** complaint, criticism **11** badmouthing

Barbados
capital/largest city: 10 Bridgetown
others: 7 Oistins **8** Boscabel, Crab Hill, Hastings, Holetown, Portland, Worthing **9** Bathsheba **10** Martin's Bay **11** Belleplaine **12** Speightstown

school: 10 Codrington
head of state: 14 British monarch **15** governor general
mountain: 6 Chalky
highest point: 7 Hillaby
river: 12 Constitution
sea: 8 Atlantic **9** Caribbean
physical feature:
   bay: 4 Foul, Long **8** Carlisle
   beach: 5 Crane
   gully: 12 Welchman Hall
   hill: 10 Cherry Tree
   point: 5 North, South **6** Ragged **8** Harrison, Kitridge
people: 5 Bajan **9** Barbadian
   leader: 5 Adams
language: 7 English
religion: 8 Anglican
place:
   airport: 7 Seawell
   castle: 8 Sam Lords
   church: 7 St Johns
feature:
   sea crab: 7 shagger
barbarian 4 boor, hood, lout, punk **5** alien, bully, crude, rowdy, tough, yahoo **6** savage, vandal **7** boorish, hoodlum, lowbrow, peasant, ruffian, uncouth **8** hooligan **9** ignoramus, outlander, roughneck, vulgarian **10** delinquent, illiterate, philistine, provincial, troglodyte, uncultured **11** knownothing **12** uncultivated **15** unsophisticated **16** anti-intellectual
barbaric 4 rude, wild **5** crude **6** coarse, savage, vulgar **7** boorish, uncouth, untamed **9** barbarian, barbarous **10** unpolished **11** ill-mannered, uncivilized
barbarism 7 cruelty **8** savagery **9** brutality **10** inhumanity **11** viciousness
barbarity 7 cruelty **9** brutality **10** savageness **12** ruthlessness
barbarous 4 mean **5** crass, crude, cruel, harsh, rough **6** brutal, coarse, vulgar **7** inhuman, vicious **8** barbaric, impolite **10** outrageous
barber 3 cut **4** trim **5** dress, shave, style **6** Figaro **7** arrange, stylist, tonsure **10** haircutter **11** hairdresser
Barber, Samuel
   born: 13 West Chester PA
   composer of: 7 Vanessa **10** Dover Beach **16** Adagio for Strings **17** Capricorn Concerto **19** Anthony and Cleopatra, The School for Scandal
Barber of Seville, The
   author: 12 Beaumarchais
   opera by: 7 Rossini
   character: 6 Bazile, Figaro, Rosine, Rosina **8** Almaviva, Bartholo **9** Dr Bartolo **13** Count Almaviva
barbette 5 mound **7** bastion, rampart **8** platform **9** earthwork **10** breastwork
barbiturate 8 euphoria, hypnotic, sedative **10** depressive **13** anesthesiatic **14** barbituric acid

kind: 7 seconal **10** thiopental **11** amobarbital **12** secobarbital **13** phenobarbital
barbule 4 barb **11** feather part
Barchester Towers
   author: 15 Anthony Trollope
   sequel to: 9 The Warden
   character: 7 Mr Slope, Mrs Bold **8** Mr Arabin **9** Dr Proudie, Mr Harding **10** Mrs Proudie **11** Mr Quiverful **13** Canon Stanhope **17** Archdeacon Grantly **18** Signora Vesey-Neroni
bard 4 poet **6** rhymer, writer **8** epic poet, minstrel, poetizer **9** poetaster, rhymester, troubador, versifier **10** poet- singer **13** narrative poet
Bardell, Mrs
   character in: 14 Pickwick Papers
   author: 7 Dickens
Bardot, Brigitte
   husband: 10 Roger Vadim
   born: 5 Paris **6** France
   roles: 18 And God Created Woman
bare 4 bald, mere, nude, open, show, thin, void, worn **5** basic, blank, empty, naked, offer, plain, scant, stark, strip **6** denude, divest, expose, meager, peeled, reveal, simple, unclad, unmask, unveil, vacant **7** austere, exposed, hapless, uncover, undrape, undress, unrobed **8** disrobed, in the raw, marginal, stripped **9** endurable, essential, unadorned, unclothed, uncolored, uncovered, undressed, unsheathe **10** elementary, just enough, threadbare **11** fundamental, supportable, undecorated, undisguised, unvarnished **12** unelaborated, unornamented **13** unembellished **15** straightforward
barefaced 4 bald, bold, flip **5** brash, fresh, sassy **6** brazen, cheeky, snotty **7** forward **8** flippant, impudent, insolent, palpable **9** shameless, unabashed **11** transparent
barefoot 6 unshod **8** shoeless **9** discalced **10** unsandaled **11** discalceate
Barefoot Boy
   author: 21 John Greenleaf Whittier
Barefoot in the Park
   director: 8 Gene Saks
   based on play by: 9 Neil Simon
   cast: 9 Jane Fonda **12** Charles Boyer **13** Robert Redford
barely 4 just **6** almost, hardly **7** faintly, scantly **8** meagerly, only just, scarcely, slightly **9** almost not, just about, sparingly **10** no more than **20** by the skin of one's teeth
bareness 6 nudity **9** bleakness, emptiness, nakedness **10** barrenness
Baresark
   origin: 12 Scandinavian
   form: 7 warrior
   trait: 7 courage
Baretta
   character: 7 Rooster **11** Billy Truman,

(Det) Tony Baretta, (Lt) Hal Brubaker
   cast: 8 Tom Ewell **11** Robert Blake **12** Edward Grover **15** Michael D Roberts
   Tony's pet: 8 cockatoo
      named: 4 Fred
barfly 3 sot **4** lush, soak **5** drunk, rummy, souse, toper **7** tippler **8** drunkard **9** alcoholic **11** dipsomaniac
bargain 4 deal, pact **5** steal **6** accord, barter, dicker, haggle, higgle, pledge, treaty **7** compact, entente, good buy, promise **8** contract, covenant, good deal **9** agreement, negotiate **10** settlement **11** arrangement, transaction **13** understanding
   French: 9 bon marche
bargain for 6 expect **7** foresee **8** envision, reckon on **11** contemplate
barge 4 bust, scow, ship **6** launch, vessel **7** freight, intrude
barium
   chemical symbol: 2 Ba
bark 3 bay, cry, rub, yap, yip **4** flay, hide, howl, hull, husk, peel, rind, roar, skin, woof, yell, yelp **5** crust, scale, shout, strip **6** abrade, arf-arf, bellow, bow wow, casing, cry out, holler, scrape **7** howling **8** covering, periderm **9** sheathing
Barker, Lex
   real name: 25 Alexander Crichlow Barker Jr
   wife: 10 Arlene Dahl, Lana Turner
   born: 5 Rye NY
   roles: 6 Tarzan **11** La Dolce Vita
Barkis
   character in: 16 David Copperfield
   author: 7 Dickens
Barkley, Catherine
   character in: 15 A Farewell to Arms
   author: 9 Hemingway
Barlach, Ernst
   born: 5 Wedel **7** Germany **8** Holstein
   artwork: 9 Expellees **10** Seated Girl, Singing Man **11** Man in a Stock **13** Mater Dolorosa **14** Crippled Beggar, The Hovering One **16** Man Drawing a Sword **25** The Community of the Holy Ones
barn 4 mews **6** corral, stable
Barnabas
   companion: 4 Paul
Barnaby Jones
   character: 7 J R (Jedediah Romano) Jones **8** Lt Biddle **10** Betty Jones
   cast: 9 Mark Shera **10** Buddy Ebsen, John Carter **13** Lee Meriwether
Barnaby Rudge
   author: 14 Charles Dickens
   character: 8 Mrs Rudge **9** Miss Miggs **10** John Willet **11** Dolly Varden **12** Emma Haredale **13** Edward Chester, Gabriel Varden **14** Reuben Haredale, Simon Tappertit, Sir John Chester **16** Dennis the Hangman, Geoffrey

Haredale
subject: **11** Gordon riots
Barnard, Christiaan
field: **7** surgery **8** medicine
nationality: **12** South African
performed first: **15** heart transplant
Barnard, Edward Emerson
field: **9** astronomy
named for him: **12** red dwarf star
Barnes, Jake
character in: **15** The Sun Also Rises
author: **9** Hemingway
Barney Google
creator: **11** Billy DeBeck
character: **11** Snuffy Smith
baby: **5** Bunky
horse: **9** Spark Plug
Barney Miller
character: **8** (Det) Phil Fish **9** (Det)
Ron Harris **10** (Det Wojo) Wojo-
howicz, (Det) Nick Yamana, (Officer)
Carl Levitt **14** Inspector Luger, (Det)
Arthur Dietrich
cast: **7** Jack Soo **8** Ron Carey, Ron
Glass **9** Abe Vigoda, Hal Linden **11**
Maxwell Gail **12** James Gregory **15**
Steve Landesberg
Barnstock see **9** Branstock
Baroja y Nessi, Pio
author of: **15** Caesar or Nothing **23**
The Struggle for Existence **26** Mem-
orias de un Hombre de Accion
barometer
invented by: **10** Torricelli
baroque **6** florid, ornate **10** flamboyant
11 extravagant
Barrack-Room Ballads
author: **14** Rudyard Kipling
barracks **3** BOQ **4** base, camp **7** lodging **8** garrison
barrage **5** blast, burst, salvo, spray **6**
ack-ack, deluge, shower, stream, vol-
ley **7** battery, torrent **8** shelling **9** cannonade, fusillade **10** outpouring **11**
bombardment
barrel **3** keg, tub, tun, vat **4** butt, cask,
drum, tube **8** hogshead
abbreviation: **3** bar, bbl
barren **3** dry **4** arid, dull **5** stale, waste
6 farrow, futile **7** austere, prosaic,
sterile, useless **8** depleted, desolate,
infecund **9** fruitless, infertile **10** lackluster, unfruitful **11** ineffectual, uninspiring, unrewarding **12** unproductive
13 uninformative, uninstructive, uninteresting
barrenness **8** bareness **9** bleakness,
emptiness **10** desolation
barren wilderness **6** desert **9** wasteland
barricade **5** block, fence **7** barrier, bulwark, rampart **8** blockade, obstacle,
obstruct **10** impediment **11** obstruction
Barrie, Sir James M
author of: **7** The Will **8** Mary Rose,

Peter Pan **10** Dear Brutus **13** Quality
Street **15** Margaret Ogilvie, The Wedding Guest **17** Alice Sit-By-the-Fire,
The Little Minister **18** A Kiss for Cinderella, The Twelve- Pound Look **19**
What Every Woman Knows **20** Shall
We Join the Ladies?, The Admirable
Crichton
character: **8** Peter Pan **10** Tinkerbell
11 Captain Hook
Darling children: **4** John **5** Wendy
7 Michael
nurse/Newfoundland dog: **4** Nana
setting: **14** Never-Never Land
barrier **3** bar **4** moat, wall **5** ditch,
fence, hedge **6** hurdle, trench **7** rampart **8** blockade, handicap, obstacle **9**
barricade, hindrance **10** difficulty, impediment, limitation **11** obstruction,
restriction **13** fortification **14** stumbling block
Barrier, The
author: **8** Rex Beach
barring **3** but **4** save **6** except, saving
7 besides **9** excepting, excluding,
other than **11** exclusive of
barrister **6** lawyer **7** counsel **8** advocate, attorney **9** counselor **10** mouthpiece **13** attorney-at-law
barroom **3** bar, pub, **6** bistro, lounge,
saloon, tavern **7** taproom
barrow **4** heap, pile **5** mound **7** tumu-
lus **8** handcart, pushcart **11** wheelbarrow
Barrow, Joe Louis
real name of: **8** Joe Louis
Barry, Gene
real name: **11** Eugene Klass
born: **9** New York NY
roles: **9** Burke's Law **11** Thunder
Road **12** Bat Masterson **16** The
Name of the Game **17** The War of
the Worlds
Barry, John
served in: **16** Revolutionary War
commander of ship: **7** Raleigh **8** Alliance **9** Effingham, Lexington
ship captured: **6** Edward
Barry, Redmond
character in: **11** Barry Lyndon
author: **7** Thackeray
Barry, Sir Charles
architect of: **8** Cliveden **14** City Art
Gallery (Manchester) **18** Houses of
Parliament (London)
Barry Lyndon
author: **25** William Makepeace
Thackeray
character: **12** Redmond Barry **14** Lord
Bullingdon **17** Lady Honoria Lyndon
(Countess of Lyndon) **19** Chevalier
de Balibari
director: **14** Stanley Kubrick
cast: **9** Ryan O'Neal **11** Hardy Kruger
12 Patrick Magee **14** Marisa Berenson
Barrymore, Ethel

real name: **14** Ethel Mae Blythe
brother: **4** John **6** Lionel
born: **14** Philadelphia PA
roles: **11** A Doll's House **14** The Corn
Is Green **16** Portrait of Jennie **19**
Trelawney of the Wells **21** None But
the Lonely Heart, Rasputin and the
Empress
Barrymore, John
real name: **10** John Blythe
brother: **6** Lionel
sister: **5** Ethel
son: **17** John Drew Barrymore
daughter: **14** Diana Barrymore
granddaughter: **4** Drew
nickname: **12** Great Profile
born: **14** Philadelphia PA
roles: **6** Hamlet **7** Don Juan **8** Moby
Dick, Svengali **9** Richard IV **10**
Grand Hotel **11** Beau Brummel **13**
Dinner at Eight **17** Dr Jekyll and Mr
Hyde **21** Rasputin and the Empress
Barrymore, Lionel
real name: **12** Lionel Blythe
brother: **4** John
sister: **5** Ethel
born: **14** Philadelphia PA
roles: **7** The Jest **9** A Free Soul (Oscar), (friend of) Dr Kildare **11** Dr Gillespie **13** Peter Ibbitson, The Copperhead **21** Rasputin and the Empress
Barsabbas see **6** Joseph
Barstad, John
character in: **16** A Tale of Two Cities
author: **7** Dickens
Bart, Lily
character in: **15** The House of Mirth
author: **7** Wharton
barter **4** swap **5** trade **8** exchange **11**
interchange
Bartered Bride, The
opera by: **7** Smetana
character: **5** Jenik, Kecal, Micha,
Vasek **7** Marenka
Barth, John
author of: **7** Chimera **12** Giles Goat-
Boy **15** The End of the Road **16** The
Floating Opera, The Sot-Weed Factor
17 Lost in the Funhouse
Barthelme, Donald
author of: **7** Sadness **8** City Life **9**
Great Days, Snow White **12** Sixty
Stories **13** The Dead Father **15** Guilty
Pleasures **18** Come Back Dr Caligari
33 Unspeakable Practices Unnatural
Acts
Bartholdi, Frederic-Auguste
born: **6** Alsace, Colmar
artwork: **13** Lion of Belfort **26** Liberty
Enlightening the World (Statue of
Liberty)
Bartholo, Dr
character in: **18** The Barber of Seville
19 The Marriage of Figaro
author: **12** Beaumarchais
Bartholomew **7** apostle
also called: **9** Nathanael

Bartholomew Fair
author: 9 Ben Jonson

Bartok, Bela
born: 7 Hungary 15 Nagyszentmiklos
composer of: 9 Wrestling 11
Mikrokosmos 12 Divertimento 14
Cantata Profana 15 The Wooden
Prince 20 Duke Bluebeard's Castle
21 The Miraculous Mandarin

Bartolommeo, Fra
born: 5 Italy 8 Florence
real name: 31 Bartolommeo di Pagolo
del Fattorino
artwork: 5 Jonah 6 Isaiah 13 Salvator Mundi 15 The Last Judgment 17
Vision of St Bernard 24 Madonna
della Misericordia 30 The Mystic
Marriage of St Catherine

Barton, Benjamin Smith
field: 6 botany
noted for first American: 14 botany
textbook

Bartram, John
field: 6 botany
noted for first American: 12 hybrid
plants

Baruch
father: 5 Judah 6 Neriah
friend and scribe of: 8 Jeremiah

Baruch, Bernard 9 statesman, financier

basal 3 key 4 easy 5 basic, vital 6 simple 7 initial, minimal, primary 8 cardinal 9 beginning, essential, intrinsic,
necessary 10 elementary, lower-level,
simplified 11 fundamental, rudimentary 12 prerequisite 13 indispensable

bas bleu 12 bluestocking

base 3 bad, bed, key, low 4 camp,
core, foul, mean, post, root, vile 5 basis, dirty, gross, heart, petty, place,
stand 6 abject, billet, bottom, craven,
ground, impure, locate, scurvy, sinful,
sneaky, sordid, source, vulgar, wicked
7 alloyed, corrupt, debased, essence,
found on, ignoble, immoral, install,
model on, scrubby, situate, station,
support 8 backbone, cowardly, degraded, depraved, garrison, infamous,
inferior, pedestal, rudiment, shameful,
spurious, unworthy 9 dastardly, dissolute, establish, faithless, insidious, nefarious, principle 10 degenerate, derive from, despicable, detestable, evil-minded, foundation, groundwork,
iniquitous, villainous 11 adulterated,
disgraceful, ignominious, poor quality,
scoundrelly 12 black-hearted, contemptible, dishonorable, disreputable,
installation, substructure, underpinning, unprincipled 13 discreditable,
reprehensible

baseball
term: 3 bag, ERA, fan, RBI, run 4
balk, base, bunt, bush 5 choke,
curve, error, fungo, liner, pop-up,
slide 6 assist, bat-ter, cellar, double,
dugout, duster, inning, on deck, relief (pitcher), rookie, single, slider,
triple, umpire, windup 7 blooper,
bullpen, catcher, cleanup, fly ball,
home run, infield, pickoff, pitcher,
rhubarb, rundown, shutout, slugger
8 bean ball, changeup, grounder,
keystone, no hitter, outfield, pitchout, southpaw, spitball 9 bleachers,
brushback, grand slam, hot corner,
infielder, line drive, sacrifice, shortstop 10 bush league, gopher ball, infield fly, outfielder, passed ball 11
bases loaded, knuckleball, pinch hitter, triple crown, World Series 12
Texas leaguer 16 designated hitter,
earned run average

Hall of Fame:
1936: 4 Cobb (Ty), Ruth (Babe) 6
Wagner (Honus) 7 Johnson (Walter) 9 Mathewson (Christy)
1937: 4 Mack (Connie) 5 Young
(Cy) 6 Lajoie (Nap), McGraw
(John), Wright (George) 7 Johnson (Ban), Speaker (Tris) 8 Bulkeley (Morgan)
1938: 8 Chadwick (Henry) 9 Alexander (Grover) 10 Cartwright (Alexander)
1939: 5 Anson (Cap), Ewing (Buck)
6 Gehrig (Lou), Keeler (Willie),
Sisler (George) 7 Collins (Eddie) 8
Comiskey (Charlie), Cummings
(Candy), Spalding (Albert) 9 Radbourne (Old Hoss)
1942: 7 Hornsby (Rogers)
1944: 7 Kenesaw (M. Landis)
1945: 5 Duffy (Hugh), Kelly (King)
6 Clarke (Fred) 7 Collins (Jimmy),
O'Rourke (Jim) 8 Jennings
(Hughey), Robinson (Wilbert) 9
Bresnahan (Roger), Brouthers
(Dan), Delahanty (Ed)
1946: 5 Evers (Johnny), Plank (Eddie), Walsh (Ed) 6 Chance
(Frank), Tinker (Joe) 7 Burkett
(Jesse), Chesbro (Jack), Waddell
(Rube) 8 Griffith (Clark),
McCarthy (Tommy) 9 McGinnity
(Joe)
1947: 5 Grove (Lefty) 6 Frisch
(Frankie) 7 Hubbell (Carl) 8 Cochrane (Mickey)
1948: 7 Pennock (Herb), Traynor
(Pie)
1949: 5 Brown (Mordecai) 7
Nichols (Kid) 9 Gehringer (Charlie)
1951: 3 Ott (Mel) 4 Foxx (Jimmie)
1952: 5 Waner (Paul) 8 Heilmann
(Harry)
1953: 4 Dean (Dizzy), Klem (Bill) 6
Barrow (Ed), Bender (Chief),
Wright (Harry) 7 Simmons (Al),
Wallace (Bobby) 8 Connolly
(Tom)
1954: 5 Terry (Bill) 6 Dickey (Bill)
1955: 5 Baker (Frank), Lyons

(Ted), Vance (Dazzy) 6 Schalk
(Ray) 8 DiMaggio (Joe), Hartnett
(Gabby) 10 Maranville (Rabbit)
1956: 6 Cronin (Joe) 9 Greenberg
(Hank)
1957: 8 Crawford (Sam), McCarthy
(Joe)
1959: 5 Wheat (Zach)
1961: 5 Carey (Max) 8 Hamilton
(Billy)
1962: 5 Roush (Edd) 6 Feller (Bob)
8 Robinson (Jackie) 9 McKechnie
(Bill)
1963: 4 Rice (Sam), Eppa (Rixey) 5
Flick (Elmer) 8 Clarkson (John)
1964: 4 Ward (Monte) 5 Faber
(Red), Keefe (Tim) 6 Grimes (Burleigh), Manush (Heinie) 7 Appling
(Luke), Huggins (Miller)
1965: 6 Galvin (Pud)
1966: 7 Stengel (Casey) 8 Williams
(Ted)
1967: 5 Waner (Lloyd) 6 Rickey
(Branch) 7 Ruffing (Red)
1968: 6 Cuyler (Kiki), Goslin
(Goose) 7 Medwick (Joe)
1969: 4 Hoyt (Waite) 6 Musial
(Stan) 9 Coveleski (Stan) 10 Campanella (Roy)
1970: 5 Combs (Earle), Frick (Ford)
6 Haines (Jesse) 8 Boudreau (Lou)
1971: 5 Paige (Satchel), Hafey
(Chick), Weiss (George) 6 Hooper
(Harry), Kelley (Joe) 7 Beckley
(Jake) 8 Bancroft (Dave), Marquard (Rube)
1972: 4 Wynn (Early) 5 Berra
(Yogi), Gomez (Lefty) 6 Gibson
(Josh), Koufax (Sandy), Youngs
(Ross) 7 Leonard (Buck) 8 Harridge (Will)
1973: 5 Evans (Billy), Irvin
(Monte), Kelly (George), Spahn
(Warren), Welch (Mickey) 8 Clemente (Roberto)
1974: 4 Bell (Cool Papa), Ford
(Whitey) 6 Conlan (Jocko), Mantle
(Mickey) 8 Thompson (Sam) 9
Bottomley (Jim)
1975 5 Kiner (Ralph) 6 Harris
(Bucky), Herman (Billy) 7 Averill
(Earl), Johnson (Judy)
1976: 5 Lemon (Bob) 6 Connor
(Roger) 7 Hubbard (Cal), Roberts
(Robin) 9 Lindstrom (Fred) 10
Charleston (Oscar)
1977: 5 Banks (Ernie), Lloyd (Pop),
Lopez (Al), Rusie (Amos) 6 Dihigo (Martin), Sewell (Joe)
1978: 4 Joss (Addie) 7 Mathews
(Eddie) 8 MacPhail (Larry)
1979: 4 Mays (Willie) 5 Giles
(Warren) 6 Wilson (Hack)
1980: 5 Klein (Chuck) 6 Kaline
(Al), Snider (Duke), Yawkey
(Tom)
1981: 4 Mize (Johnny) 6 Foster
(Rube), Gibson (Bob)

1982: 5 Aaron (Hank) **7** Jackson (Travis) **8** Chandler (Happy), Robinson (Frank)
1983: 4 Kell (George) **6** Alston (Walter) **8** Marichal (Juan), Robinson (Brooks)
1984: 5 Reese (Pee Wee) **7** Ferrell (Rick) **8** Aparicio (Luis), Drysdale (Don) **9** Killebrew (Harmon)
1985: 5 Brock (Lou) **7** Vaughan (Arky), Wilhelm (Hoyt) **9** Slaughter (Enos)
1986: 5 Doerr (Bobby) **7** McCovey (Willie) **8** Lombardi (Ernie)
1987: 6 Hunter (Jim "Catfish") **8** Williams (Billy) **9** Dandridge (Ray)
1988: 8 Stargell (Willie)
1989: 5 Bench (Johnny) **7** Barlick (Al) **11** Yastrzemski (Carl) **12** Schoendienst (Red)
1990: 6 Morgan (Joe), Palmer (Jim)
1991: 5 Carew (Rod), Perry (Gaylord), Veeck (Bill) **7** Jenkins (Ferguson), Lazzeri (Tony)
1992: 6 Seaver (Tom) **7** Fingers (Rollie), McGowan (Bill) **9** Newhouser (Hal)
1993: 7 Jackson (Reggie)
1994: 7 Carlton (Steve), Rizzuto (Phil "Scooter") **8** Durocher (Leo)
other player/coach: 7 Jim Rice **8** Pete Rose, Vida Blue **9** Alvin Dark, Bowie Kuhn, Gil Hodges, Hank Bauer, Luis Tiant, Nellie Fox, Nolan Ryan, Ralph Houk, Ron Guidry, Ted Turner, Tommy John **10** Boog Powell, Earl Weaver, Maury Wills, Roger Maris, Sparky Lyle **11** Billy Martin, Dave Kingman, Frank Thomas, George Brett, Mark Fidrych, Mike Schmidt, Rich Gossage **12** Graig Nettles, Dave Winfield, Dennis McLain, Dick Williams, Elston Howard, Ken Griffey Jr, Tommy Lasorda **13** Rocky Colavito, Thurman Munson, Walter O'Malley **14** Keith Hernandez, Peter Ueberroth, Sparky Anderson **15** Rickey Henderson **16** Darryl Strawberry **18** Fernando Valenzuela, George Steinbrenner

baseball leagues
National: 11 Chicago Cubs, New York Mets **13** Atlanta Braves, Houston Astros, Montreal Expos **14** Cincinnati Reds, Florida Marlins, San Diego Padres **15** Colorado Rockies **16** Milwaukee Brewers, St Louis Cardinals **17** Los Angeles Dodgers, Pittsburgh Pirates **18** San Francisco Giants **19** Arizona Diamondbacks **20** Philadelphia Phillies
American: 9 Oakland A's **12** Boston Red Sox, Texas Rangers **13** Anaheim Angels, Detroit Tigers **14** Minnesota Twins, New York Yankees **15** Chicago White Sox, Seattle Mariners,

Toronto Blue Jays **16** Baltimore Orioles, Cleveland Indians, Kansas City Royals, Oakland Athletics **17** Tampa Bay Devil Rays

baseball team
Anaheim: 6 Angels
stadium: 11 Edison Field **7** Anaheim
Atlanta: 6 Braves
stadium: 11 Turner Field
Arizona 12 Diamondbacks
stadium: 15 Bank One Ballpark
Baltimore: 7 Orioles
stadium: 11 Camden Yards
Boston: 6 Red Sox
stadium: 10 Fenway Park
Chicago: 4 Cubs
stadium: 12 Wrigley Field
Chicago: 8 White Sox
stadium: 12 Comiskey Park
Cleveland: 7 Indians
stadium: 11 Jacobs Field
Cincinnati: 4 Reds
stadium: 10 Riverfront **12** Cinergy Field
Colorado: 7 Rockies
stadium: 8 Mile High **10** Coors Field
Detroit: 6 Tigers
stadium: 5 Tiger
Florida: 7 Marlins
stadium: 9 Joe Robbie, Pro Player
Houston: 6 Astros
stadium: 9 Astrodome
Kansas City: 6 Royals
stadium: 8 Kauffman
Los Angeles: 7 Dodgers
stadium: 6 Dodger **18** Los Angeles Coliseum
Milwaukee: 7 Brewers
stadium: 6 County
Minnesota: 5 Twins
stadium: 12 Metropolitan **24** Hubert H Humphrey Metrodome
Montreal: 5 Expos
stadium: 7 Olympic
New York: 4 Mets
stadium: 4 Shea
New York: 7 Yankees
stadium: 6 Yankee
Oakland: 2 A's
stadium: 7 Oakland **8** Coliseum
Philadelphia: 8 Phillies
stadium: 8 Veterans
Pittsburgh: 7 Pirates
stadium: 11 Three Rivers
St Louis: 9 Cardinals
stadium: 13 Busch Memorial
San Diego: 6 Padres
stadium: 8 Qualcomm **10** Jack Murphy
San Francisco: 6 Giants
stadium: 7 3Com Park **15** Candlestick Park
Seattle: 8 Mariners
stadium: 8 Kingdome
Tampa bay: 9 Devil Rays
stadium: 14 Tropicana Field

Texas: 7 Rangers
stadium: 11 The Ballpark
Toronto: 8 Blue Jays
stadium: 7 Sky Dome

baseless 7 unsound **9** unfactual, unfounded **10** groundless, ungrounded **11** unjustified, unsupported **12** without basis **13** unjustifiable **14** uncorroborated **15** unsubstantiated
basement 5 below **6** bottom, cellar **15** underground room
baseness 7 lowness **8** meanness, vileness **9** depravity **11** ignobleness **14** iniquitousness **16** contemptibleness
base of operations
Greek: 6 pou sto
bash 4 blow **5** blast, clout, crack, knock, party, whack **7** clopper **8** wingding **9** bacchanal
Bashemath *see* **4** Adah
bashful 3 shy **5** timid **6** demure, modest **8** blushing, reserved, reticent, retiring, sheepish, skittish, timorous **9** diffident, shrinking, uncertain **10** shamefaced **11** constrained, unconfident
bashfulness 7 shyness **10** diffidence **12** sheepishness **14** self-effacement **15** unassertiveness
basic 3 key **4** base, core **5** prime, vital **7** bedrock, primary **8** rudiment **9** essential, intrinsic **10** elementary, foundation **11** fundamental, rudimentary **12** foundational, prerequisite, underpinning
basically
French: 6 au fond
basic ideas 6 basics **7** essence, factors, origins **8** elements, features **9** rudiments **10** principles **11** foundations
basic need 9 essential, necessity, requisite, vital part **10** key element, sine qua non
basic part 4 unit **7** element **9** component **10** ingredient **11** constituent **13** building block
basic quality 6 nature **7** essence **9** principle, substance **12** quintessence
basics 4 ABCs **8** elements **9** rudiments **10** principles **11** nitty- gritty **12** fundamentals
basil
also called: 6 tulasi
botanical name: 6 Ocimum **8** O minimum **10** O basilicum
means: 5 royal **6** kingly, lizard (basilisk)
nickname: 14 kiss-me-Nicholas
origin: 5 India
sacred to: 6 Vishnu **7** Krishna, Lakshmi
symbol of: 4 hate, love
use: 5 pasta, pesto, sauce **10** vegetables

basilica 6 church 10 house of God 14 house of worship

Basilisk
form: 6 dragon

basin 3 pan, tub, vat 4 bowl, dale, dell, font, glen, sink 5 gulch, gully, stoup 6 crater, hollow, lavabo, ravine, tureen, valley 7 dishpan, washtub 8 lavatory, sinkhole, washbowl 9 porringer, washbasin, washstand 10 depression, finger bowl

basis, bases 4 base, root 6 ground 7 bedrock 9 essential, principle 10 foundation, touchstone 11 cornerstone, fundamental 12 underpinning 13 starting point

bask 5 revel, savor 6 relish, wallow 7 delight 8 sunbathe 9 luxuriate 11 warm oneself 12 soak up warmth, toast oneself

basket 5 cesta, crate 6 barrel, hamper 7 carrier, pannier 8 bassinet, canister

basketball
term: 3 key 4 dunk, hoop, pick, post, trap, zone 5 court, guard, lay-up, pivot, point, press, steal 6 assist, basket, center 7 dribble, forward, palming, rebound, referee 8 charging, hook shot, jump shot, sixth man, turnover 9 backboard, backcourt, fast break, field goal, free throw, give-and-go, traveling 11 goal tending, pick-and-roll 12 three-pointer

Hall of Fame:
1959: 5 Allen (Phog; Forrest Clare), Hyatt (Charles), Mikan (George), Olsen (Harold), Stagg (Amos Alonzo), Tower (Oswald) 6 Gulick (Luther), Hickox (Edward), Morgan (Ralph) 7 Carlson (Henry), Kennedy (Matthew) 8 Luisetti (Hank), Meanwell (Walter E), Naismith (James), Schommer (John) 15 Original Celtics
1960: 5 Blood (Ernest) 6 Hanson (Victor), Keaney (Frank), Murphy (Charles), Porter (Henry), Wooden (John) 7 Hepbron (George), Lambert (Ward) 8 Macauley (Ed) 9 McCracken (Branch)
1961: 4 Hoyt (George) 5 Sachs (Leonard), Tobey (David), Walsh (David) 6 Keogan (George), O'Brien (John), Roosma (John) 7 Kurland (Bob), Phillip (Andy), Quigley (Ernest), Trester (Arthur), Wachter (Edward) 8 Borgmann (Bernhard) 9 Steinmetz (Christian) 10 DeBernardi (Forrest), Schabinger (Arthur) 14 Buffalo Germans
1962: 4 Page (Harlan) 6 Sedran (Barney), St John (Lynn) 8 Thompson (John) 9 McCracken (Jack) 10 Morgenweck (Frank)
1963: 4 Reid (William) 7 Gruenig (Robert) 11 New York Rens
1964: 4 Bunn (John) 5 Irish (Ned),

Jones (R William) 6 Foster (Harold), Holman (Nat) 7 Russell (John) 8 Loeffler (Kenneth)
1965: 5 Brown (Walter) 6 Hinkle (Paul), Hobson (Howard), Mokray (William)
1966: 4 Dean (Everett) 8 Lapchick (Joe)
1967: 3 Bee (Clair) 4 Cann (Howard), Gill (Amory) 6 Julian (Alvin)
1968: 3 Iba (Hank; Henry P) 4 Rupp (Adolph F) 6 Taylor (Charles H) 7 Denhart (Henry G) 8 Auerbach (Red; Arnold J)
1969: 6 Davies (Bob) 9 Carnevale (Bernard L)
1970: 5 Cousy (Bob) 6 Pettit (Bob) 10 Saperstein (Abe)
1971: 5 Wells (W R Clifford) 6 Diddle (Edgar A) 7 Douglas (Robert L) 8 Endacott (Paul), Friedman (Max), Gottlieb (Edward)
1972: 5 Drake (Bruce) 6 Ripley (Elmer H), Wooden (John) 7 Beckman (John), Lonborg (Arthur C), Schayes (Dolph)
1973: 6 Fisher (Harry A) 7 Schmidt (Ernest) 8 Podoloff (Maurice)
1974: 6 Liston (Emil) 7 Brennan (Joseph), Russell (Bill) 9 Vandivier (Robert)
1975 4 Gola (Tom) 6 Krause (Edward W) 7 Litwack (Harry), Sharman (Bill)
1976: 4 Gale (Lauren) 6 Baylor (Elgin), Cooper (Charles T) 7 Johnson (Wiliam C), McGuire (Frank)
1977: 5 Fulks (Joe), Hagan (Cliff) 6 Arizin (Paul) 7 Pollard (Jim) 8 Nucatola (John P)
1978: 5 Barry (Sam; Justin M), Meyer (Raymond J) 6 Hickey (Edgar S), Newell (Peter F) 7 Enright (James E) 8 McLendon (John B) 11 Chamberlain (Wilt)
1979: 4 West (Jerry) 5 Lucas (Jerry) 7 Shelton (Everett), Shirley (J Dallas) 8 Harrison (Lester) 9 Robertson (Oscar)
1980: 4 Hepp (Ferenc) 6 Barlow (Thomas B) 7 Kennedy (J Walter) 9 McCutchan (Arad A)
1981: 4 Case (Everett N), Duer (Alva O), Reed (Willis) 5 Greer (Hal) 6 Gaines (Clarence E), Martin (Slater), Ramsey (Frank)
1982: 5 Leith (Lloyd R), Smith (Dean E), Wilke (Louis G) 6 Twyman (Jack) 7 Bradley (Bill) 11 DeBusschere (Dave)
1983: 5 Fagan (Clifford B), Jones (Sam) 6 Steitz (Edward S) 7 Gardner (Jack) 8 Havlicek (John)
1984: 4 Wade (L Margaret) 5 Cervi (Al) 6 Abbott (Senda Berenson), Teague (Bertha F) 8 Anderson (W Harold), Harshman (Marv K), Thurmond (Nate)

1985--1986: 5 Watts (Stanley H) 6 Taylor (Fred R) 7 Holzman (Red), Mihalik (Red) 8 Heinsohn (Tom) 10 Cunningham (Billy)
1986--1987: 5 Barry (Rick) 6 Wanzer (Bobby) 7 Frazier (Walt) 8 Houbregs (Robert J), Maravich (Pete)
1987--1988: 6 Miller (Ralph H), Unseld (Wes) 9 McDermott (Robert), Lovelette (Clyde)
1988--1989: 5 Gates (William "Pop"), Jones (K C) 7 Wilkens (Lenny)
1989--1990 4 Bing (Dave) 5 Hayes (Elvin) 6 Monroe (Earl) 8 Johnston (Neil)
1990--1991: 6 Cowens (Dave), Knight (Bobby), O'Brien (Lawrence F) 8 Fleisher (Lawrence), Gallatin (Harry) 9 Archibald (Nate), Stankovic (Borislav)
1991--1992: 5 Belov (Sergei), White (Nera) 6 Lanier (Bob), Ramsay (Jack) 7 Hawkins (Connie), McGuire (Al) 8 Woolpert (Phillip) 10 Carnesecca (Louie) 13 Harris-Stewart (Lucia)
1992--1993: 5 Issel (Dan) 6 Erving (Julius), Meyers (Ann), Murphy (Calvin), Walton (Bill) 7 Bellamy (Walter), McGuire (Dick) 9 Semjonova (Uljana)
1994: 4 Crum (Denny), Daly (Charles J) 6 Rubini (Cesare) 9 Jeannette (Buddy) 11 Blazejowski (Carol)

other player/coach: 8 Pat Riley 9 Bob McAdoo, Larry Bird 10 Danny Ainge, Kobe Bryant 11 Alex English, Bernard King, Bill Lambeer, Dick Barnett, James Worthy, Kevin McHale, Lew Alcindor, Moses Malone 12 Clyde Drexler, George Gervin, Isaiah Thomas, Larry Johnson, Patrick Ewing, Robert Parish 13 David Robinson, Earvin (Magic) Johnson, Michael Jordan, Scottie Pippen, Terry Cummings 14 Charles Barkley, Hakeem Olajuwon, Shaquille O'Neal 17 Kareem Abdul-Jabbar

basketball team
league: 3 NBA 29 National Basketball Association
Atlanta: 5 Hawks
Boston: 7 Celtics
Charlotte: 7 Hornets
Chicago: 5 Bulls
Cleveland: 9 Cavaliers
Dallas: 9 Mavericks
Denver: 7 Nuggets
Detroit: 7 Pistons
Golden State: 8 Warriors
Houston: 7 Rockets
Indiana: 6 Pacers
Los Angeles: 6 Lakers 8 Clippers
Miami: 4 Heat

Milwaukee: 5 Bucks
Minnesota: 12 Timberwolves
New Jersey: 4 Nets
New York: 14 Knickerbockers
Orlando: 5 Magic
Philadelphia: 5 76ers **13** Seventy-Sixers
Phoenix: 4 Suns
Portland: 12 Trail Blazers
Sacramento: 5 Kings
San Antonio: 5 Spurs
Seattle: 11 SuperSonics
Toronto: 7 Raptors
Utah: 4 Jazz
Vancouver: 9 Grizzlies
Washington: 7 Wizards
WNBA
Charlotte: 5 Sting
Cleveland: 7 Rockers
Detroit: 5 Shock
Houston: 6 Comets
Los Angeles: 6 Sparks
New York: 7 Liberty
Phoenix: 7 Mercury
Sacramento: 8 Monarchs
Utah: 6 Starzz
Washington: 7 Mystics

Basque
language spoken in: 5 Italy, Spain **6** France

bas-relief
Italian: 12 basso-rilievo

bass 3 low **4** alto **5** basso **7** harmony **8** baritone, bass clef

bass
types: 3 sea **4** rock **5** black **6** calico **7** striped, sunfish **10** largemouth, smallmouth
characteristic: 10 forked-tail **12** spiny-finned

Bassanio
character in: 19 The Merchant of Venice
author: 11 Shakespeare

basso-rilievo 9 bas-relief

Bast, Jacky and Leonard
characters in: 10 Howards End
author: 9 E M Forster

bastard 6 impure **8** inferior, spurious **9** imperfect, irregular, love child **12** natural child **17** illegitimate child

bastardize 6 debase, weaken **7** degrade **9** downgrade

baste 3 sew **4** drip **5** roast **6** cudgel, flavor, stitch, thrash **7** moisten **15** temporary stitch

bastinado 4 beat, blow, cane, drub **5** whale **7** beating **8** drubbing

bastion 4 fort **5** tower **6** pillar **7** bulwark, citadel, rampart **8** barbette, fortress **10** breastwork, stronghold

bat 3 hit, rod **4** cane, clip, club, cuff, mace, slug, sock **5** baton, billy, knock, smack, staff, stick, whack **6** buffet, cudgel, mallet, strike, thwack, wallop **7** clobber **8** bludgeon **9** blackjack, truncheon **10** shillelagh

batch 3 lot **5** bunch, crowd, group, stock **6** amount, number **8** quantity **9** aggregate **10** collection

Bates, Alan
born: 7 England **9** Allestree **10** Derbyshire
roles: 6 Hamlet **8** The Fixer **10** Duet for One, Georgy Girl **12** King of Hearts **13** A Kind of Loving, The Collection, Zorba the Greek **16** An Unmarried Woman **18** An Englishman Abroad, A Prayer for the Dying **22** Far From the Madding Crowd

Bates, Kathy
born: 7 Memphis
roles: 6 Misery **7** Titanic **10** Diabolique, Used People **12** The Late Shift, Men Don't Leave **18** Fried Green Tomatoes

Bates, Miss
character in: 4 Emma
author: 6 Austen

Bateson, William
field: 7 biology
nationality: 7 British
founded: 8 genetics

bath 3 dip, tub **4** wash **5** sauna **6** douche, shower **7** washing **8** ablution, lavement **9** cleansing, immersion, steam bath **10** irrigation
type: 3 hip, mud **4** sitz **5** steam **6** shower, sponge **7** Turkish bath

bathe 3 dip, tub, wet **4** lave, soak, wash **5** douse **6** douche, shower, sponge **7** cleanse **8** irrigate

bathing 3 dip, tub **6** laving, plunge **7** washing **8** swimming **9** ablutions, immersion

bathos 4 corn, mush **5** slush **8** schmaltz **9** mushiness, soppiness **10** maudlinism, slushiness **11** false pathos, mawkishness **14** sentimentalism, sentimentality

bathroom 2 W C **3** can, loo **4** head, john **5** biffy **6** toilet **7** commode, latrine **8** facility, lavatory, men's room, restroom, washroom **10** ladies' room, powder room **11** water closet **14** little boys' room **15** little girls' room

Bathsheba
also: 8 Bathshua
father: 5 Eliam
husband: 5 David, Uriah
son: 7 Solomon
grandfather: 10 Ahithophel

Batman
character: 6 Alfred **7** Egghead, King Tut **8** Catwoman, The Joker **10** Bruce Wayne (Batman), Chief O'Hara, The Penguin, The Riddler **11** Dick Grayson (Robin) **13** Barbara Gordon (Batgirl) **17** Aunt Harriet Cooper **24** Police Commissioner Gordon
cast: 8 Adam West, Burt Ward **9** John Astin **10** Alan Napier, Eartha Kitt, Madge Blake **11** Cesar Romero, Julie Newmar, Victor Buono, Yvonne

Craig **12** Frank Gorshin, Neil Hamilton, Stafford Repp, Vincent Price **13** Lee Meriwether **15** Burgess Meredith
city: 10 Gotham City
nickname: 9 Boy Wonder **10** Dynamic Duo **13** Caped Crusader
gimmick: 6 Batlab **8** Batphone **9** Batmobile, Batsignal

Bat Masterson
cast: 9 Gene Barry

baton 3 bat, rod **4** club, mace, wand **5** billy, crook, staff, stick **6** cudgel, fasces **7** crosier, scepter, war club **8** bludgeon, caduceus **9** billy club, truncheon **10** nightstick, shillelagh

batter 4 beat, lash, maul **5** break, crush, pound, smash, smite **6** beat up, buffet, mangle, pummel **7** clobber, shatter

battercake 6 waffle **7** biscuit, pancake

battered 4 shot **6** beat-up, ruined, shabby **8** decrepit **11** dilapidated **12** disreputable

battery 3 set **4** army, band, pack, team **5** block, cadre, force, group, suite, troop **6** caning, cannon, convoy, legion, lineup, outfit, series **7** beating, brigade, company, hitting, hurting, maiming, phalanx, section **8** armament, cannonry, clubbing, division, drubbing, flogging, ordnance, squadron, whipping, wounding **9** cudgeling, spearhead, strapping, thrashing

battle 3 war **4** bout, duel, feud, fray, meet **5** argue, brawl, clash, fight, siege **6** action, affray, combat, debate, engage, tussle **7** contend, contest, crusade, dispute, quarrel, warfare **8** campaign, conflict, skirmish, struggle **9** agitation, encounter, firefight **10** engagement **11** altercation, controversy **13** confrontation

Battle, final
place: 10 Armageddon

battle cry 6 war cry **8** Geronimo, war whoop **9** Rebel yell

Battle Cry
author: 8 Leon Uris

battlefield 5 arena, lists **8** the front, war arena **9** front line **10** battle line, no man's land **11** battlefront **12** battleground

battleground 5 arena, lists **11** battlefield, battlefront

Battle of the Books
author: 13 Jonathan Swift

battle-ready 5 armed **7** arrayed **8** prepared **9** fortified

battleship 4 Iowa **5** Maine **6** Oregon **7** carrier, warship **8** Missouri **9** Ironsides, New Jersey, Wisconsin **10** bluish-gray **11** Dreadnought **12** Constitution
first: 7 Gloire
largest: 6 Yamato
German: 8 Graf Spee

Battus
  ruler of: 5 Libya
  form: 7 peasant
  witness to: 11 cattle theft
  thief: 6 Hermes
  turned to: 5 stone
  cured of: 16 speech impediment
batty 4 nuts **5** crazy, loony, queer, wacko, wacky **6** cuckoo, crazed **7** bat-like, cracked
bauble 3 toy **4** bead **6** geegaw, trifle **7** trinket **8** gimcrack, ornament
Baucis
  form: 7 peasant
  home: 7 Phrygia
  husband: 8 Philemon
  offered hospitality to: 4 Zeus **6** Hermes
Baudelaire, Charles
  author of: 13 Flowers of Evil **14** Les Fleurs du Mal
Baugh, Sammy
  nickname: 13 Slinging Sammy
  sport: 8 football
  position: 11 quarterback
  team: 18 Washington Redskins
Baum, Lyman Frank
  author of: 13 The (Wonderful) Wizard of Oz **18** Father Goose His Book, Mother Goose in Prose
Baum, Vicki
  author of: 8 Shanghai **10** Grand Hotel, Grand Opera **12** Men Never Know **13** A Tale from Bali, And Life Goes On
Baumer, Paul
  character in: 25 All Quiet on the Western Front
  author: 8 Remarque
Baumgarner, James
  real name of: 11 James Garner
bawdy 4 blue, lewd, sexy **5** dirty, gross, lusty **6** coarse, earthy, ribald, risque, sexual, vulgar **7** raunchy **8** immodest, improper, indecent, off-color **10** indecorous, indelicate, licentious, suggestive
bawdy house 7 brothel **8** bordello, cathouse **10** fancy house, whorehouse **13** sporting house **14** house of ill fame **16** house of ill repute **19** house of prostitution
bawl 3 cry **4** call, howl, roar, wail, weep, yell, yowl **5** shout **6** bellow, clamor, cry out, squall **7** blubber, call out
bawling out 6 rebuke **7** censure, chiding, reproof **8** reproach, scolding **9** reprimand **10** chewing out, upbraiding **11** castigation, reprobation **12** dressing-down, remonstrance **13** tongue-lashing
bawl out 5 scold **6** berate, rail at, rebuke, yell at **7** censure, chew out, reprove, upbraid **8** admonish, reproach **9** castigate, dress down, reprimand **10**

take to task, tongue-lash **14** read the riot act
Bax, Arnold Edward Trevor
  born: 6 London **7** England
  composer of: 8 Tintagel **13** November Woods **14** Mater Ora Filium **15** The Garden of Fand **27** Overture to a Picaresque Comedy
Baxter, Anne
  grandfather: 16 Frank Lloyd Wright
  born: 14 Michigan City IN
  roles: 8 Applause **11** All About Eve **13** The Razor's Edge
Baxter, Jody
  character in: 11 The Yearling
  author: 8 Rawlings
Baxter, William Sylvanus
  character in: 9 Seventeen
  author: 10 Tarkington
bay 3 cry, yap **4** bank, bark, cove, gulf, howl, nook, road, yelp **5** basin, bayou, bight, fiord, firth, inlet, niche, sound **6** alcove, bellow, clamor, lagoon, recess, strait **7** barking, estuary, howling, narrows, yapping, yelling, yelping **9** bellowing **11** compartment **13** natural harbor
bay (at bay) 7 trapped **8** cornered
bay leaf
  botanical name: 12 Pimenta acris
  expression: 16 to win one's laurels
  from tree: 9 bay laurel
    transformation of: 6 Daphne
    tree sacred to: 6 Apollo
    laurel berries called: 10 bacca lauri
    source of: 13 baccalaureate
  gives gift of: 8 prophecy
  helps girls win back: 12 errant lovers
  origin: 5 Italy
  protects against: 5 death **6** poison **7** sorcery **11** evil spirits
  symbol of: 7 victory (laurel wreath)
  use: 4 fish, fowl, meat, soup, stew
bayou 4 slew **5** creek, inlet, marsh, river, swamp **6** outlet, slough, stream **9** backwater **13** stagnant marsh
Bayou State
  nickname of: 9 Louisiana **11** Mississippi
Bay Psalm Book
  author: 9 John Eliot
Bay State
  nickname of: 13 Massachusetts
bazaar 4 fair, mart **6** market **8** carnival, exchange **11** charity fair, charity sale, marketplace
Bazile
  character in: 18 The Barber of Seville
  author: 12 Beaumarchais
Bazzard, Deputy
  character in: 22 The Mystery of Edwin Drood
  author: 7 Dickens
BC *see* **12** before Christ
B C

  creator: 10 Johnny Hart
  character: 3 Tor **4** Grog **5** Peter **8** anteater **10** Clumsy Carp **11** the Fat Broad
  poet: 5 Wiley
  era: 11 Neanderthal, prehistoric
BCE 15 before Common Era
be 4 last, live, stay **5** exist, occur **6** befall, endure, happen, remain **7** persist, subsist **8** continue **9** be present, take place **10** come to pass
be absent 4 miss **12** fail to attend
beach 5 coast, shore **6** strand **8** littoral, seashore **10** water's edge
Beach, Rex
  author of: 6 The Net **7** Oh Shoot **8** Pardners **9** Going Some **10** Jungle Gold, The Barrier **11** Don Careless, The Spoilers **12** Son of the Gods **13** The Goose Woman, The Ne'er-do-well **15** The Auction Block **17** Alaskan Adventures
beached 7 aground **8** grounded, stranded **11** shipwrecked **12** washed ashore
beacon 4 beam **5** light **6** pharos, signal **7** seamark **8** bale-fire, landmark **9** watch fire **10** lighthouse, watchtower **11** lighted buoy
bead 3 dot **4** blob, drop, pill **5** speck **6** bubble, pellet **7** droplet, globule **8** particle, spherule
be adequate 2 do **6** answer **8** be enough **10** pass muster **12** be sufficient, do well enough **14** be satisfactory
be afraid of 4 fear **5** dread **7** cower at **8** cringe at **10** shrink from
beak 3 neb, tip **4** bill, nose, pike, prow **5** lorum, snout, spout **7** process, rostrum, snozzle **8** hooknose **9** headmaster, proboscis **10** magistrate
beaker 3 cup **5** glass **6** vessel **9** container
beam 3 ray **4** emit, glow, prop, spar, stud **5** brace, glare, gleam, glint, joist, shine, width **6** girder, rafter, streak, stream, timber **7** breadth, expanse, glimmer, glitter, radiate, trestle **8** transmit **9** broadcast, radiation
bean 9 Phaseolus
  varieties: 3 goa, pea, soy, wax, yam **4** fava, jack, lima, moth, mung, rice, seim, snap, soja, soya, tick, wild **5** azuki, black, broad, civet, coral, field, green, horse, lubia, pinto, salad, screw, sewee, sieva, snail, sword, tonka **6** butter, castor, common, French, Indian, kaffir, kidney, lablab, locust, manila, mescal, nicker, potato, romano, runner, sacred, string, tepary, velvet, winged, wonder **7** cluster, English, sarawak, Windsor **8** Bovanist, Bush lima, Carolina, Cherokee, European, Egyptian, hyacinth, yard-long **9** algarroba, asparagus, bonavista, dwarf lima, Java

glory **10** dwarf sieva, giant stock, Hottentot's **12** Italian queen, scarlet flame **13** African locust, Florida velvet, Scarlet runner **14** Dutch case-knife **16** white Dutch runner
bean curd: 4 tofu

be a party to 3 aid **4** abet **7** support **9** connive in **11** cooperate in **13** be accessory to, participate in

be apparent 6 appear **7** be clear, be plain **8** be patent **9** be evident, be obvious **10** be manifest

bear 4 bend, drop, give, haul, have, lead, push, show, take, tend, tote, turn, wear **5** abide, admit, allow, apply, brace, brave, bring, brook, carry, curve, drive, force, hatch, press, refer, spawn, stand, whelp, yield **6** affect, aim for, convey, convoy, create, endure, escort, go with, harbor, invite, permit, relate, render, suffer, take on, uphold **7** bolster, cherish, concern, conduct, contain, deliver, develop, deviate, display, diverge, exhibit, pertain, possess, produce, stomach, support, sustain, undergo, warrant **8** bear down, engender, generate, maintain, manifest, shoulder, submit to, tolerate, transfer, underpin **9** accompany, appertain, encourage, germinate, hold close, propagate, put up with, reproduce, touch upon, transport **10** bring forth, keep in mind **11** give birth to, hold up under

bear
combining form: 4 arct, ursi **5** arcto
constellation: 4 ursa **9** ursa major, ursa minor
family: 7 Ursidae
group of: 6 sleuth
kind: 3 sun **5** black, brown, koala, malay, panda, polar, sloth **6** kodiak, wombat **7** grizzly **9** roachback, silvertip **10** spectacled, thalarctos
male: 4 boar
mythological: 8 Callisto
order: 9 carnivora
young: 3 cub
famous: 6 Smokey

beard 4 dare, defy, face, trap **5** brave **6** corner **7** stubble **8** bristles, confront, whiskers **10** bring to bay **16** five- o'clock shadow

bearded 5 bushy, hairy **6** shaggy **7** bristly, hirsute **8** unshaven **9** whiskered **11** bewhiskered

bear down 4 push **5** press **13** apply pressure

bear down upon 6 assail, attack, come at **7** assault **11** descend upon

Beardsley, Aubrey Vincent
born: 7 England **8** Brighton
artwork: 6 Salome **10** Lysistrata **12** Morte d'Arthur

Beard's Roman Women
author: 14 Anthony Burgess

bearer 5 Atlas **6** holder, porter **7** carrier **8** conveyer, producer **9** messenger **13** beast of burden **16** one holding a check
Spanish: 8 escudero, portador

bear fruit 4 bear **6** mature **7** develop, prosper **8** fructify

bearing 3 air **4** mien, port **5** sense **6** import, manner **7** concern, meaning **8** attitude, behavior, breeding, carriage, demeanor, presence, relation **9** producing, reference, relevance **10** conception, connection, deportment, importance, pertinence **11** application, association, comportment, germination, giving birth, procreation, propagation, reproducing **12** relationship, reproduction, significance **13** applicability

bearing no name 7 unnamed **8** unsigned **9** anonymous

bearings 3 way **6** course **8** position **9** direction **11** orientation **16** sense of direction

bearish 5 cross, gruff, surly, testy **6** crusty, sullen **7** brusque, crabbed, grouchy **8** churlish **9** crotchety, irascible **10** ill-humored, out of sorts **11** ill-tempered, pessimistic **12** cantankerous

bear off 5 seize, steal **6** abduct, convey, kidnap

bear out 5 prove **6** verify **7** confirm **11** corroborate **12** substantiate

Bear State
nickname of: 8 Arkansas

bear up under 4 bear, take **5** abide, brave, brook, stand **6** endure, suffer **7** stomach, undergo, weather **9** go through, withstand

bear witness 4 back **6** attest **7** confirm, testify **11** corroborate, demonstrate **12** give evidence, substantiate

beast 3 cad, cur, pig, rat **4** ogre **5** brute, swine **6** animal, mammal, savage **8** creature **9** barbarian, quadruped

beastly 3 bad **4** vile **5** awful, cruel, gross, lousy, nasty **6** brutal, coarse, savage **7** bestial, brutish, inhuman, swinish **8** degraded, dreadful, terrible **9** barbarous, loathsome, monstrous **10** abominable, deplorable, disgusting, unpleasant **12** contemptible, disagreeable

beat 3 bat, hit, mix, rap, tap, way **4** area, bang, best, blow, cane, club, drub, flap, flog, flop, lick, maul, path, rout, slap, time, whip, zone **5** clout, count, crush, flail, knock, meter, outdo, pound, pulse, punch, quake, quell, realm, repel, route, shake, smack, smite, strap, throb, whack **6** accent, batter, course, defeat, domain, hammer, master, pummel, quiver, rhythm, rounds, stress, strike, stroke, subdue, switch, thrash, thwack, twitch, wallop **7** cadence, circuit, clobber, conquer, destroy, eclipse, flutter, pulsate, put down, repulse, scourge, shellac, surpass, trounce, vibrate, win over **8** overcome, vanquish **9** excel over, fluctuate, go pit-a-pat, overpower, palpitate, pulsation, territory **10** win out over **11** predominate, prevail over, triumph over **14** stir vigorously

beat a retreat 6 beat it **7** back off **8** turn tail, withdraw **10** high tail it

beat around the bush 5 dodge, evade, hedge, stall **10** equivocate, mince words

beatific 4 rapt **6** divine, serene **7** angelic, exalted, saintly, sublime **8** blissful, ecstatic, glorious, heavenly **9** rapturous **10** enraptured **14** transcendental

beat it 2 go **3** out **4** away, scat, shoo **5** be off, leave, scram **6** begone, cut out, depart, get out, go away **7** get lost, vamoose **10** hit the road, make tracks

beatitude 5 bliss **7** ecstasy, rapture **8** euphoria, felicity **10** exaltation **11** blessedness, exaltedness, saintliness **13** transcendence **15** transfiguration

Beatles 10 John Lennon, Ringo Starr **13** Paul McCartney **14** George Harrison
Songs: 6 Taxman **7** Hey Jude, Get Back **10** Nowhere Man, Drive My Car, Revolution **12** Come Together, Dear Prudence, Eleanor Rigby, Rocky Raccoon **13** Twist and Shout **14** A Hard Day's Night, Eight Days A Week **23** Strawberry Fields Forever **24** Lucy in the Sky with Diamonds
albums: 4 Help **7** Hey Jude, Let It Be **8** Revolver **9** Abbey Road **10** Rubber Soul, White Album **14** A Hard Day's Night, Meet the Beatles **15** Yellow Submarine **17** Yesterday...and Today **18** Magical Mystery Tour **30** Sgt. Pepper's Lonely Hearts Club Band

be at loggerheads 5 clash **7** quarrel **8** disagree

be at odds 6 differ **7** dispute, diverge **8** conflict, disagree

beat rhythmically 3 rap, tap **4** drum **6** tattoo **7** pulsate

Beatrice
character in: 12 Divine Comedy
author: 5 Dante

Beatrice
character in: 19 Much Ado About Nothing
author: 11 Shakespeare

Beatrice et Benedict
opera by: 7 Berlioz

Beat the Clock
host: 10 Bud Collyer

Beattie, Ann
author of: 11 Distortions **14** Falling in Place **15** The Burning House **19** Secrets and Surprises **20** Chilly Scenes of Winter

Beatty, Ned
born: 10 Louisville
roles: 3 Spy 4 Rudy 9 The Affair 10 The Big Easy, Black Water, Hear My Song 11 Deliverance 14 Prelude to a Kiss

Beatty, Warren
real name: 11 Warren Beaty
sister: 15 Shirley MacLaine
born: 10 Richmond VA
wife: 13 Annette Bening
roles: 4 Reds 5 Bugsy 6 Ishtar 8 Bulworth 9 Dick Tracy 10 Love Affair 11 All Fall Down 13 Heaven Can Wait 14 Bonnie and Clyde 18 Splendor in the Grass 24 The Roman Spring of Mrs Stone
director of: 4 Reds (Oscar) 8 Bulworth

beat up 3 mug 4 lick, maul, whip 6 batter, pummel 7 assault, clobber

beat-up 4 shot 6 shabby 7 worn-out 8 battered 10 broken-down 11 dilapidated

Beaty, Shirley MacLean
real name of: 15 Shirley MacLaine

Beaty, Warren
real name of: 12 Warren Beatty

beau, beaux 3 fop, guy, nob 4 buck, dude, love, stud, toff 5 blade, dandy, flame, lover, Romeo, spark, swain, swell, wooer 6 adorer, escort, fellow, fiance, garcon, squire, steady, suitor 7 admirer, beloved, courter, coxcomb, cupidon, Don Juan, gallant, playboy 8 cavalier, courtier, gay blade, Lothario, paramour, popinjay, true love, young man 9 betrothed, boyfriend, courtesan, gentleman, inamorato, ladies' man 10 sweetheart, young blood 15 gentleman caller, gentleman friend
nickname of: 14 George Brummell

Beauchamp's Career
author: 14 George Meredith

Beau Geste
author: 6 P C Wren 15 Christopher Wren
director: 14 William Wellman
cast: 10 Gary Cooper, Ray Milland 12 Brian Donlevy, Susan Hayward 13 Robert Preston
silent version starred: 12 Ronald Colman
setting: 19 French Foreign Legion

Beaumarchais, Pierre Augustin Caron de
author of: 18 The Barber of Seville 19 The Marriage of Figaro

beau monde 5 elite 6 gentry 7 society 10 upper class, upper crust 11 aristocracy, high society 15 beautiful people

Beaumont, Ned
character in: 11 The Glass Key
author: 7 Hammett

Beauregard, P G T (Pierre Gustave Toutant)
served in: 8 Civil War

side: 11 Confederate
rank: 7 general
ordered firing on: 8 Ft Sumter
battle: 7 Bull Run

beaut 4 lulu, oner 5 daisy, dandy 6 beauty 7 stunner 8 knockout 10 good-looker

beautification 9 adornment 10 decoration 13 embellishment, ornamentation

beautiful 4 fair, fine 5 bonny, great 6 comely, lovely, pretty, seemly, superb, worthy 7 radiant 8 alluring, gorgeous, handsome, pleasing, splendid, very good 9 admirable, beauteous, enjoyable, estimable, excellent, exquisite, first-rate, ravishing, wonderful 10 attractive, stupendous 11 captivating, commendable, fine-looking, good-looking, resplendent 15 pulchritudinous

beautify 4 do up 5 adorn, grace 7 dress up, enhance, gussy up, improve 8 ornament 9 embellish, glamorize

beauty 4 boon, doll 5 asset, beaut, belle, grace, Venus 6 eyeful, looker 7 benefit, feature, goddess, splendor 8 knockout, radiance, splendor 9 advantage, good looks, good thing 10 attraction, excellence, good-looker, loveliness 11 pulchritude 12 handsomeness, magnificence, resplendence 14 attractiveness
goddess of: 6 Graces 7 Gratiae 9 Aphrodite, Charites
god of: 5 Baldr 6 Apollo, Balder, Baldur 7 Angus Og, Phoebus, Pythias 9 Musagetes

Beauvoir, Simone de
author of: 12 The Mandarins, The Second Sex 14 A Very Easy Death, All Said and Done, The Coming of Age, The Prime of Life 17 Ethics of Ambiguity 22 The Force of Circumstance 25 Memoirs of a Dutiful Daughter 34 Brigitte Bardot and the Lolita Syndrome

beaver
young: 3 kit

Beaver State
nickname of: 6 Oregon

be blessed with 3 own 4 have 5 enjoy 7 possess 16 have the benefit of

because 2 so 3 for 4 that, then, thus 5 cause, hence, since 6 whence 7 whereas 8 inasmuch 9 therefore 10 seeing that 11 considering

Bechuanaland
now called: 8 Botswana

Bechuanland see 8 Botswana

beck 3 bid 4 call 7 bidding, summons 9 summoning

Becket
author: 11 Jean Anouilh 18 Alfred Lord Tennyson
director: 14 Peter Glenville
cast: 11 John Gielgud, Peter O'Toole

(King Henry II) 13 Richard Burton (Becket)

Beckett, Samuel
author of: 4 Not I, Play, Watt 6 Embers, Molloy 7 Endgame 8 That Time 9 Footfalls, Happy Days 10 Malone Dies 11 All that Fall, The Lost Ones 13 The Unnameable 15 Waiting for Godot 16 Mercier and Camier 20 Murphy Krapp's Last Tape 25 Stories and Texts for Nothing

Beckmann, Max
born: 7 Germany, Leipzig
artwork: 6 Kasbek 7 Perseus 8 Acrobats, The Night 9 The Actors 11 View of Genoa 12 Charnel House, The Argonauts, The Departure 13 Blindman's Buff, Family Picture 14 Double Portrait 17 David and Bathsheba 18 Odysseus and Calypso 19 Sinking of the Titanic 20 Destruction of Messina 22 The Descent from the Cross

beckon 4 call, coax, draw, lure, pull 6 allure, entice, invite, motion, signal, summon, wave at, wave on 7 attract, gesture 11 gesticulate 14 crook a finger at

be clear 6 appear 7 be plain 8 be patent 9 be evident, be obvious 10 be apparent, be manifest

becloud 3 fog 4 blur, hide, veil 5 befog, cloud 6 muddle, screen, shroud 7 confuse, cover up, eclipse, obscure 8 confound, make hazy, overcast 9 obfuscate 10 camouflage, overshadow 14 make indistinct

become 3 get 4 grow, suit, turn 6 go with 7 enhance, flatter, get to be 8 come to be 9 agree with, begin to be 10 complement 11 be reduced to, turn out to be

become apparent 4 dawn, loom 5 arise 6 appear, crop up, emerge, turn up 7 develop, surface

become bigger 4 grow 5 swell 6 expand 7 develop, enlarge, inflate 8 increase

become irrational 5 break, crack 7 crack up 9 break down, fall apart, go berserk 10 go to pieces 11 lose control 12 lose one's mind

become one 3 wed 4 fuse 5 blend, marry, merge, unite 7 combine 8 coalesce 10 amalgamate 11 consolidate

become seasoned to 5 adapt, inure 6 adjust 8 accustom 9 acclimate, get used to, habituate 15 learn to live with

become smaller 6 lessen, shrink 7 decline, dwindle, shrivel 8 decrease, diminish

become visible 4 loom, show 6 appear, crop up, emerge, show up, turn up 7 surface 11 come to light 12 come into view

becoming 3 apt, fit 4 meet 6 pretty, proper, seemly, worthy 7 fitting 8 suitable 9 befitting, congenial, congruous, enhancing, in keeping 10 attractive, compatible, consistent, flattering, harmonious 11 appropriate, good-looking

Becquerel, Antoine Henri
 field: 7 physics
 nationality: 6 French
 discovered: 13 radioactivity
 awarded: 10 Nobel Prize

bed 3 cot, hay 4 band, bank, base, belt, bunk, crib, lode, plot, sack, seam, zone 5 berth, floor, layer, patch 6 bottom, cradle, pallet 7 deposit, stratum 8 bedstead 10 foundation

bedazzle 4 daze 6 dazzle 7 astound, confuse, enchant, fluster, nonplus, stagger, stupefy 8 befuddle, bewilder, confound, dumfound 9 captivate, overpower, overwhelm 10 disconcert 11 flabbergast 19 sweep one off one's feet

bed chamber 7 bedroom, boudoir

bed down 5 sleep 7 lie down, sack out 8 doss down 10 hit the hay, settle down 11 accommodate, hit the sack

bedeck 4 deck, trim 5 adorn, array 7 garnish 8 decorate, ornament 9 embellish

be deficient in 4 fail, lack, want 7 be scant 9 be short of 10 have too few

be deprived of 4 lack, lose, want

be deserving of 4 earn, rate 5 merit 7 deserve 10 be worthy of 12 be entitled to

bedevil 3 dog 5 annoy, hound, worry 6 badger, harass, pester, plague 9 beleaguer

be devoted to 4 love 5 adore 6 dote on 7 cherish 8 be fond of

bedim 4 blur 6 darken 7 obscure

Bedivere
 character in: 16 Arthurian romance

bedizen 5 adorn, array 6 bedeck, rig out 7 bejewel, costume

bedlam 5 chaos 6 tumult, uproar 7 turmoil 8 madhouse 11 pandemonium

bed of justice
 French: 12 lit de justice

Bedouin, Beduin
 also: 4 Absi, Arab 5 nomad 7 bedawee
 Arabic: 6 badawi
  means: 13 desert dweller
 found in: 5 Egypt, Syria 6 Arabia 11 North Africa
 religion: 5 Islam

bedraggled 4 limp 5 dirty, dowdy, messy, seedy, soggy, tacky, tatty 6 blowsy, frowsy, frumpy, matted, ragtag, sloppy, soiled, untidy 7 unkempt 8 frumpish, sluttish, tattered 10 disarrayed, disordered, disheveled, slatternly, threadbare 11 disarranged 13

draggletailed 14 down-at-the-heels, out-at-the-elbows

bedridden 7 invalid 8 disabled, immobile 13 incapacitated

bedroom 7 boudoir, chamber 10 bedchamber

bedspread 5 quilt 8 bedcover, coverlet 9 comforter

bedstead 3 bed 8 bed frame 10 four poster

bee
 caste: 5 drone, queen 6 worker
 classification: 6 social 8 solitary
 communication: 13 dance language
 family: 6 Apidae 7 Apoidea 8 Bombidae 10 Andrenidae, Halictidae 11 Meliponidae, Xylocopidae 12 Megachilidae
 group of: 5 grist, swarm
 order: 11 Hymenoptera
 scent: 10 pheromones
 variety: 5 mason, miner 6 alkali, cuckoo 8 burrower, honeybee 9 bumblebee, carpenter, plasterer 10 leaf-cutter 11 yellow-faced

beech 5 Fagus
 varieties: 4 Blue 5 Water 6 Copper, Purple 7 Cut-leaf, Weeping 8 American, European, Fern-leaf, Japanese

Beedle, William Franklin, Jr,
 real name of: 13 William Holden

beef 4 heft, kick, meat 5 brawn, gripe, steer 6 cattle, grouch, grouse 7 grumble 8 complain 9 bellyache, complaint, criticize, find fault

Beef State
 nickname of: 8 Nebraska

beefy 5 bulky, burly, hefty 6 brawny, robust 8 thickset 9 strapping

beehive 4 hive 6 apiary 9 busy place 10 powerhouse

Beehive State
 nickname of: 4 Utah

Beekeeping
 god of: 9 Aristaeus

Beelzebub
 character in: 12 Paradise Lost
 author: 6 Milton

be enough 2 do 6 answer 7 suffice

be entitled to 4 rate 5 merit 7 deserve 10 be worthy of 13 be deserving of

beer 3 ale, keg, mum 4 bier, bock, brew, dark, faro, flip, gail, grog, gyle, hops, kvas, malt, mild, quas, scud, suds 5 chang, chica, draft, grout, kvass, lager, light, quass, scuds, stout, weiss 6 bitter, chicha, double, gatter, porter, spruce, stingo, swanky, swipes, wallop, zythum 7 bottled, cerveza, pangasi, pharaoh, Pilsner, tankard, taplash, tapwort 8 bock beer, cervisia, near beer, pilsener 9 microbrew 10 malt liquor
 add to beer: 7 krausen
 bad/inferior beer: 4 tack 5 belch 6

swanky 7 taplash
 brand: 3 Bud 5 Beck's, Coors, Pabst, Piels 6 Corona, Miller, Molson, Stroh's 7 Schlitz 8 Bud Light, Michelob 9 Budweiser, Lowenbrau 10 Miller Lite, Molson Gold 11 Samuel Adams 13 Guinness Stout 14 Pete's Wicked Ale 15 Pabst Blue Ribbon
 cask: 4 butt
 cup: 3 mug 4 toby 5 glass, stein 6 flagon, seidel 7 tankard 8 schooner 9 blackjack
 hot beer and gin: 4 purl
 ingredient: 4 hops, malt 5 yeast 6 barley
 maker: 6 brewer 8 brewster, maltster
 mythological inventor: 9 Gambrinus
 quantity of: 3 keg 4 case 7 six-pack
 small beer: 4 tiff 5 grout
 sour beer: 4 kuas, kvas 5 quash, quass 8 beeregar
 thin beer: 6 pritch, swipes
 Tibetan beer: 5 chang
 warm beer and oatmeal: 6 storry
 with whiskey: 11 Boilermaker

beer-bust 4 toot 5 binge, drunk, spree 6 bender 8 carousal 9 bacchanal

Beery, Noah
 brother: 7 Wallace
 son: 6 Noah Jr
 born: 12 Kansas City MO
 roles: 7 Lord Jim, The Dove 9 Beau Geste 10 The Sea Wolf 14 The Mark of Zorro

Beery, Wallace
 brother: 4 Noah
 nephew: 6 Noah Jr
 wife: 13 Gloria Swanson
 born: 12 Kansas City MO
 roles: 8 The Champ (Oscar) 9 The Bowery, Viva Villa 10 Grand Hotel 11 The Big House 13 Dinner at Eight 14 Treasure Island 15 The Mighty Barnum 16 A Message to Garcia

beet 12 Beta vulgaris
 varieties: 3 Red, Sea 4 Leaf, Wild 5 Sugar 6 Garden, Yellow 7 Spinach
 base for: 6 borsch 7 borscht

Beethoven, Ludwig van
 born: 4 Bonn 7 Germany
 composer of: 5 Laube (sonata) 6 Egmont, Eroica (symphony no 3), Spring (sonata) 7 Fidelio, Leonore 8 Coriolan, Dramatic (sonata), Kreutzer (sonata), Pastoral (symphony no 6), The Storm 9 Moonlight (sonata), Pastorale (sonata), Waldstein (sonata) 10 Bagatellen, Great Fugue (no 133), Pathetique (sonata), Spirit Trio 11 Grosse Fugue (no 133), Harp Quartet (no 74), Namensfeier 12 Appassionata (sonata), Archduke Trio, Konig Stephan 13 Hammerklavier (sonata), Missa Solemnis 15 Emperor Concerto (No 5) 16 Christus am Olberg, The Mount of Olives, The Ruins of Athens 17 Die Ruinen von Athen, Die Weihe des Hauses 18 An

die ferne Geliebte, Rage over a Lost Penny **20** Rasoumoffsky Quartets (no 59) **24** The Creatures of Prometheus **25** Die Geschopfe des Prometheus

beetle
variety: 3 bog, may, sap **4** bark, bean, flea, leaf, mold, moss, pill, rove, sand, stag **5** cedar, click, flour, grain, marsh, penny, tiger, water **6** beaver, diving, flower, fungus, ground, hister, lizard, scarab, spider, weevil **7** bessbug, blister, burying, carrion, firefly, goldbug, goliath, lady- bug, soldier **8** elephant, glow-worm, hercules, Japanese, ladybird, tortoise **9** ant loving, bombadier, burrowing, checkered, fruitworm, goldsmith, grassroot, scavenger, tumblebug, whirligig **10** deathwatch, false clown, longhorned, mammal nest, shiptimber **11** reticulated, trout stream **12** antlike stone, lightning bug **13** feather winged, horseshoe crab

Beetle Bailey
creator/artist: 9 Dik Browne **10** Mort Walker **12** Bob Gustafson
character: 5 Cosmo, Plato **6** Killer, Lt Flap, Lt Fuzz **10** Miss Buxley **12** Gen Halttrack **17** Sgt Orville Snorkel
chef: 6 Cookie
place: 10 Camp Swampy

be evident 6 appear **7** be clear, be plain **8** be patent **9** be obvious **10** be apparent, be manifest

befall 5 ensue, occur **6** betide, chance, follow, happen **10** come to pass **11** materialize

befitting 3 apt, fit **5** right **6** decent, proper, seemly **8** becoming, relevant, suitable **11** appropriate

be fond of 6 dote on **11** be devoted to **12** be in love with

before 3 ere, yet **5** afore, ahead, prior **6** rather, sooner **7** already, earlier, vis-a-vis **8** erewhile, until now **9** in advance, in front of, in sight of **10** face-to-face, previously

before Christ
abbreviation: 2 BC
alternative: 3 BCE **15** before Common Era
Latin: 2 AC **12** ante Christum

beforehand 6 in time, sooner **7** earlier **9** in advance **11** ahead of time

before now 6 in time, sooner **7** earlier **9** in advance

before the fact 6 in time **9** in advance **10** beforehand **11** ahead of time

before the public
Latin: 11 coram populo

befoul 4 soil **5** dirty, smear, stain, sully, taint **6** defile, poison **7** blacken, corrupt, pollute, tarnish **8** besmirch **9** desecrate **11** contaminate

befriend 4 help **6** assist, defend, suc-

cor, uphold **7** comfort, embrace, help out, protect, stand by, stick by, support, sustain, welcome **8** side with **9** give aid to, look after **10** minister to **11** consort with **13** associate with **14** fraternize with, sympathize with **17** take under one's wing

be friends 7 consort **9** associate, pal around **10** fraternize

befringe 3 hem **4** bind, edge, trim **6** border **7** festoon **8** decorate

befuddle 4 daze **5** addle, mix up **6** baffle, muddle, puzzle, rattle **7** confuse, fluster, perplex, stupefy **8** bewilder, confound, unsettle **9** disorient, inebriate, make drunk, make tipsy **10** intoxicate, make groggy **11** disorganize

beg 3 bum, sue **4** pray, shun **5** avert, avoid, cadge, dodge, evade, mooch, parry, plead, shirk **6** escape, eschew, hustle, sponge **7** beseech, entreat, fend off, implore, solicit **8** appeal to, petition, sidestep **9** importune, panhandle **10** supplicate

beg, bey 4 lord **6** prince **8** governor

beget 3 get **4** sire **5** breed, cause, spawn **6** effect, father, lead to **7** produce **8** engender, generate, occasion, result in **9** call forth, procreate, propagate **10** bring about, give rise to

begetter 4 sire **6** father **7** creator **9** generator **10** progenitor

beggar 3 bum, guy **4** chap **5** devil, tramp **6** baffle, fellow **7** almsman, moocher, sponger, surpass **8** be beyond **9** challenge, mendicant **10** panhandler

Beggar 7 Lazarus

Beggar's Opera, The
author: 7 John Gay
form: 11 ballad opera
character: 6 Lockit **10** Lucy Lockit **12** Polly Peachum **15** Captain Macheath

begin 5 arise, found, start **6** be born, crop up, emerge, launch, set out **8** break out, commence, embark on, initiate **9** establish, institute, introduce, originate, undertake **10** burst forth, inaugurate **11** set in motion **16** take the first step

beginner 4 babe, tyro **6** author, father, novice, rookie **7** creator, founder, learner, starter, student **8** freshman, neophyte **9** fledgling, greenhorn, initiator, organizer **10** apprentice, originator, prime mover, tenderfoot **11** inaugurator **14** babe in the woods

beginning 3 new **4** germ, seed **5** birth, onset, start **6** embryo, novice, origin, outset, source, spring **7** kickoff, student, untried **8** neophyte, zero hour **9** embryonic, inception, incipient, launching **10** foundation, wellspring **11** preliminary, springboard **12** commencement, fountainhead, inauguration, introduction **13** inexperi-

enced, starting point
Latin: 12 terminus a quo

Beginning of Wisdom, The
author: 19 Stephen Vincent Benet

Beginnings
god of: 5 Janus

begone 3 out **4** away, scat, shoo **5** be off, leave, scram **6** beat it, depart, get out, go away **7** get lost, vamoose

begonia
varieties: 3 Rex, Wax **4** Fern, King, Star, Wild **5** Hardy, Trout **6** Bamboo, Kidney, Shrimp, Winter, Zigzag **7** Bedding, Dewdrop, Elm-leaf, Eyelash, Fuchsia, Leopard, Lily-pad, Swedish **8** Climbing, Fern-leaf, Fire-king, Lorraine, Palm-leaf, Pond-lily, Star-leaf, Trailing **9** Alder- leaf, Angel-wing, Beefsteak, Calla-lily, Christmas, Crazy-leaf, Grape-leaf, Grapevine, Hollyhock, Holly- leaf, Honeybear, Iron-cross, Maple-leaf, Miniature, Pennywort, Trout-leaf, Whirlpool **10** Bronze-leaf, Castorbean, Finger-leaf, Guinea-wing, Seersucker, Strawberry **11** Fairy-carpet, Lettuce-leaf, Painted-leaf **12** Blooming-fool, Elephant's Ear, Metallic-leaf **13** Peanut-brittle **14** Hybrid tuberous, Nasturtium-leaf, Youth-and-old-age **15** Winter-flowering **16** Manda's woolly-bear, Philodendron-leaf **17** Miniature pond-lily **18** Trailing watermelon

beg pardon 6 excuse **9** apologize **13** express regret, say one is sorry

be grateful 9 be obliged **10** appreciate, be beholden, be thankful **11** be obligated

begrime 4 soil **5** dirty, muddy, smear, stain, sully **6** smudge, soot up **7** besmear, tarnish

begrimed 5 dirty, grimy, muddy **6** filthy, grubby, soiled **7** unclean **8** unwashed **9** tarnished

begrudge 4 envy **5** covet **6** grudge, resent **11** be jealous of, hold against

beguile 4 dupe, hoax, lull, lure **5** amuse, charm, cheat, cheer, trick **6** delude, divert, occupy, please **7** bewitch, deceive, enchant, ensnare **8** distract, hoodwink **9** bamboozle, captivate, entertain **10** lead astray

beguiling 7 winning, winsome **8** charming, magnetic **9** appealing, disarming **10** bewitching, entrancing **11** captivating **12** ingratiating, irresistible

behalf 3 aid, for **4** part, side **5** favor **7** benefit, by proxy, defense, in aid of, support **8** interest

Behan, Brendan
author of: 10 Borstal Boy, The Hostage **12** The Scarperer **14** The Quare Fellow **25** Confessions of an Irish Rebel

be handed down 4 pass **7** descend **11** be inherited

behave 3 act **13** acquit oneself, deport oneself **14** comport oneself, conduct oneself, control oneself

behavior 4 acts **5** deeds **6** action, habits, manner **7** actions, bearing, conduct, control **8** activity, attitude, demeanor, practice, reaction, response **9** operation **10** deportment **11** comportment, functioning, performance, self-control

behead 9 decollate **10** decapitate, guillotine **15** bring to the block

behest 4 fiat **5** edict, order, say-so **6** charge, decree, ruling **7** bidding, command, dictate, mandate **9** direction, ultimatum **10** injunction **11** instruction

behind 4 rump, seat, slow **5** abaft, after, fanny **8** backward, buttocks, in back of **9** fundament, in arrears **11** to the rear of **12** hindquarters

behind closed doors 7 sub rosa **8** in secret, secretly **9** in private, privately

behindhand 4 late, slow **5** tardy **7** belated **8** backward **10** unpunctual

behind the times 5 passe **7** archaic **9** out-of-date **10** antiquated **12** old-fashioned

behind time 4 late, slow **5** tardy **7** belated, delayed **12** after the fact

behold 3 see **4** heed, look, mark, note, scan, view **5** watch **6** attend, gaze at, look at, notice, regard, survey **7** discern, examine, inspect, observe, stare at, witness **8** look upon **10** scrutinize **11** contemplate **12** pay attention

beholden 5 bound **6** liable **7** obliged **8** indebted **9** obligated **10** answerable, in one's debt **11** accountable, responsible **15** under obligation

behold the man
Latin: **8** ecce homo
said by: **13** Pontius Pilate
spoken of: **6** Christ

behoove 4 suit **5** be apt, befit **6** become, be wise **7** benefit **8** be proper **9** be fitting **11** be advisable, be necessary **13** be appropriate **14** be advantageous

Behring, Emil Adolph von
field: **12** bacteriology
nationality: **6** German
developed: **19** diphtheria antitoxin
awarded: **10** Nobel Prize

beige 3 tan **4** ecru, fawn **6** greige **8** brownish

be ill 3 ail **6** be sick **8** be unwell **12** be indisposed **13** be in ill health

be in a class with 5 equal, match **6** be up to **7** compare **8** approach **10** be as good as **11** compete with **12** be comparable, be on a par with **13** hold a candle to **14** bear comparison

being 4 core, life, soul **5** human **6** living, mortal, nature, person, psyche, spirit **7** essence, persona, reality **8** creature, existing **9** actuality, existence **10** individual, occurrence **11** subsistence

be inherited 4 pass **7** descend **12** be handed down

be in short supply 4 lack, want **8** be scanty, be scarce **9** fall short

be intemperate 7 carouse, debauch **9** dissipate **11** overindulge

be in tune 4 jibe **5** agree, match, tally **6** accord, square **7** conform **9** harmonize

Beirut, Beyrouth
capital of: **7** Lebanon
Phoenician name: **7** Berytus
sea: **13** Mediterranean
settled by: **11** Phoenicians
square: **15** Place des Martyrs

be jealous of 4 envy **6** resent **8** begrudge

Bekesy, Georg von
field: **7** physics
researched: **3** ear **7** cochlea, hearing
awarded: **10** Nobel Prize

Bel 3 god **5** deity

belabor 6 rehash, repeat **7** dwell on **9** reiterate **11** pound away at **12** hammer away at, recapitulate **14** beat a dead horse, go on and on about

Bel-Ami
author: **15** Guy de Maupassant

Belarus
other name: **10** Belorussia **11** Byelorussia, White Russia
capital/largest city: **5** Minsk
head of state: **9** president
government: **8** republic
monetary unit: **5** ruble
river: **5** Dvina **7** Dnieper
physical feature: **13** Pripet Marshes
people: **12** Byelorussian

Belasco, David
author of: **7** DuBarry **15** Madame Butterfly **21** The Return of Peter Grimm **22** The Girl of the Golden West

belated 4 late, slow **5** tardy **6** behind **7** delayed, overdue, past due **8** deferred **9** behindhand, behind time, unpunctual **12** after the fact

belch 4 burp, emit, gush, spew, vent **5** eject, eruct, erupt, expel, issue, spout, spurt, vomit **7** cough up, issuing **8** disgorge, ejection, emission, eruption **9** discharge, roar forth, send forth **10** eructation

Belch, Sir Toby
character in: **12** Twelfth Night
author: **11** Shakespeare

beleaguer 3 vex **5** annoy **6** assail, badger, bother, harass, hector, pester, plague **7** besiege, bombard **8** blockade, surround

bel-esprit 3 wit **12** intellectual

belfry 4 dome **5** spire **7** steeple **9** bell tower, campanile

Belgian Congo see **5** Congo

Belgium
other name: **13** Gallia Belgica **15** Cockpit of Europe **16** Koninkrijk Belgie **17** Royaume de Belgique
capital/largest city: **8** Brussels **9** Bruxelles
others: **2** As **3** Aat, Ans, Ath, Hal, Huy, Mol, Spa **4** Aath, Amay, Asse, Boom, Bree, Doel, Gaud, Geel, Genk, Gent, Hoei, Lier, Looz, Mons, Vise, Waha, Zele **5** Aalst, Alost, Arlon, Ciney, Ecklo, Essen, Eupen, Evere, Genck, Ghent, Heist, Ieper, Jette, Jumet, Liege, Namur, Ronse, Tielt, Uccle, Vorst, Wezet, Ynoir, Ypres **6** Aarlen, Anvers, Bergen, Bilzen, Bruges, Deurne, Izegem, Leuven, Lierre, Merxem, Opwijk, Ostend **7** Antwerp, Ardooie, Berchem, Brabant, Hainaut, Herstal, Hoboken, Ixelles, Leliven, Limburg, Louvain, Malmedy, Mechlin, Roulers, Seraing, Tournai **8** Bastogne, Courtrai, Doorwick, Flanders, Kortrijk, Mouscron, Turnhout, Verviers, Waterloo **9** Antwerpen, Charleroi **10** Anderlecht, Borgerhout, Luxembourg, Quatrebras, Schaerbeek
school: **7** Louvain
division: **5** Liege, Namur **7** Antwerp, Brabant, Hainaut, Limburg **8** Flanders, Wallonia
head of state: **4** king
measure: **3** vat **4** aune, pied **5** carat **6** perche **8** boisseau
monetary unit: **5** belga, franc **7** brabant, centime, crocard
weight: **4** last **5** carat, livre **6** charge **7** chariot **8** esterlin
mountain: **8** Ardennes
highest point: **16** Signal de Botrange
river: **3** Lys **4** Dyle, Leie, Maas, Mark, Yser **5** Boucq, Demer, Lesse, Meuse, Nethe, Rupel, Senne **6** Dender, Escaut, Manjel, Ourthe, Sambre, Semois, Vesdre, Warche **7** Ambleve, Schelde, Scheldt
sea: **5** North
physical feature:
canal: **4** Yser **5** Union **6** Albert **7** Campine
cave: **7** Furfooz **8** Grenelle
forest: **8** Ardennes
plateau: **8** Hohevenn
people: **4** Remi **6** Nervii **7** Belgian, Fleming, Flemish **8** Walloons **9** Bellovaci
artist: **5** Ensor **6** Rubens **7** Delvaux, Van Dyke, Van Eyck **8** Brueghal, Magritte
author: **6** Coster **7** Simenon **9** Verhaeren **10** Conscience, Ghelderode **11** Maeterlinck
composer: **6** Franck
king: **6** Albert **7** Leopold **8** Baudouin
leader: **5** Spaak **9** Tindemans
language: **5** Dutch **6** French, German

7 Flemish
religion: 13 Roman Catholic
place:
  battleground: 5 Bulge **8** Waterloo
  breadhouse: 9 Broodhuis
  castle: 5 Steen
  cathedral: 5 Ghent **13** Saint Rombauts
  city hall: 12 Hotel de Ville
  home for elderly women: 9 Beguinage
  museum: 9 Beaux Arts
  palace: 10 Gruuthuuse
features:
  horse: 9 Brabancon
  lace: 5 fichu **6** Bruges **7** Malines, Mechlin **8** Brussels
  lawn bowling: 6 boules
  linen: 7 brabant
  musical instrument: 8 carillon
  religious procession: 9 Holy Blood
  tapestry: 9 oudenarde
food:
  cheese: 9 Limburger
  gingerbread: 12 pain d'espices
  raisin bread: 8 cramique
  soup: 9 Waterzooi
Belgrade, Beograd
  capital of: 10 Yugoslavia
  landmark:
    fortress: 10 Kalemegdan
    parliament house: 9 Skupstina
  name means: 11 white forest
  river: 4 Sava **6** Danube
  Roman fort: 10 Singidinum
  Serbian: 7 Beograd
Belial
  character in: 12 Paradise Lost
  author: 6 Milton
belie 4 defy, deny, mask **5** cloak **6** betray, negate, refute **7** conceal, falsify, gainsay **8** disguise, disprove **9** repudiate **10** camouflage, contradict, controvert, invalidate **12** misrepresent
belief 4 view **5** faith, guess, trust **6** theory **7** feeling, opinion **8** judgment, reliance **9** assurance, certitude, deduction, inference **10** assumption, conclusion, confidence, conviction, firm notion, hypothesis, impression, persuasion **11** expectation, presumption, supposition
beliefs 5 canon, creed, dogma, faith, tenet **6** ethics, gospel, morals **8** doctrine, morality **9** principle, teachings **10** conviction, persuasion
believable 8 credible, knowable, possible **9** plausible, thinkable **10** acceptable, convincing, imaginable, supposable **11** conceivable, perceivable
believe 4 hold **5** guess, infer, judge, think, trust **6** assume, credit, deduce, rely on **7** count on, fall for, imagine, presume, suppose, surmise, suspect, swallow, swear by **8** be sure of, consider, depend on, maintain, theorize **9**

speculate **10** conjecture, presuppose, put faith in **11** hypothesize
believe in 5 trust **6** accept, esteem **7** approve, go in for, respect **11** have faith in **16** have confidence in
Believe It or Not
  author: 13 Robert L Ripley
believer 7 admirer **8** advocate, disciple, partisan **9** supporter **16** faithful adherent
be like 5 equal, match **8** approach, resemble
Bel-Imperia
  character in: 17 The Spanish Tragedy
  author: 3 Kyd
Belinda
  character in: 16 The Rape of the Lock
  author: 4 Pope
belittle 5 knock, scorn **6** deride, malign **7** disdain, put down, run down, sneer at **8** minimize, mitigate, play down, pooh-pooh **9** deprecate, disparage, underrate **10** depreciate, undervalue **11** make light of **13** underestimate **16** cast aspersions on
belittling 5 snide **10** derogatory **11** deprecating, disparaging, unfavorable **12** depreciating **15** uncomplimentary
Belize
  other name: 15 British Honduras
  capital: 8 Belmopan
  largest city/former capital: 10 Belize City
  head of state: 13 prime minister **14** British monarch **15** governor-general
  monetary unit: 6 dollar
  island: 8 Turneffe
  mountain range: 4 Maya
  highest point: 12 Victoria Peak
  river: 3 New **4** Moho **6** Belize, Monkey
  sea: 9 Caribbean
  physical feature:
    gulf: 8 Honduras
    peninsula: 7 Yucatan
    swamp: 8 mangrove
  people: 5 Mayan **6** Indian, Syrian **7** African, Chinese **15** Spanish-American
  language: 7 English, Spanish
bell 4 gong, peal **5** chime **6** tocsin **7** ringing **8** carillon **16** tintinnabulation
Bell, Alexander Graham
  born: 8 Scotland
  inventor of: 9 telephone **14** record cylinder
  saying: 24 Mr Watson come here I want you
Bellamann, Henry
  author of: 8 King's Row
Bellamy, Edward
  author of: 8 Equality **15** Looking Backward
Bellamy, Ralph
  born: 9 Chicago IL
  roles: 11 Ellery Queen, Mike Barnett **13** The Awful Truth **14** Detective

Story **15** Man Against Crime, State of the Union **19** Sunrise at Campobello
Bellarius
  character in: 9 Cymbeline
  author: 11 Shakespeare
Bellaston, Lady
  character in: 8 Tom Jones
  author: 8 Fielding
bell buoy 5 float **6** signal **13** channel marker
belle 4 star **5** queen **6** beauty **7** charmer **12** heart-stopper
Belle Dame Sans Merci, La
  author: 9 John Keats
Bellefleur
  author: 15 Joyce Carol Oates
Belle Helene, La
  also: 14 Beautiful Helen
  operetta by: 9 Offenbach
Bellerophon
  form: 4 hero
  brother: 8 Deliades
  son: 11 Hippolochus
  home: 7 Corinth
  rode: 7 Pegasus
  killed: 7 Chimera
Bell for Adano, A
  author: 10 John Hersey
  director: 9 Henry King
  cast: 10 John Hodiak **11** Gene Tierney **13** William Bendix
bellicose see **11** belligerent
belligerence, belligerency 9 animosity, hostility, pugnacity **10** aggression, antagonism **11** bellicosity **12** warmongering **13** combativeness **14** aggressiveness, unfriendliness
belligerent 7 fighter, hostile, martial, warlike, warring **8** attacker, inimical **9** adversary, aggressor, bellicose, combatant, combative, irascible, irritable, truculent **10** aggressive, antagonist, pugnacious, unfriendly **11** bad-tempered, contentious, quarrelsome **12** antagonistic, cantankerous
belligerent state 3 foe **5** enemy **9** aggressor **13** hostile nation
Bellini, Gentile
  born: 5 Italy **6** Venice
  father: 6 Jacopo
  brother: 8 Giovanni
  artwork: 24 The Miracle of the True Cross **26** A Procession in St Mark's Square, The Miracle at Ponte di Lorenzo **27** St Mark Preaching in Alexandria **38** A Procession of Relics in the Piazza San Marco
Bellini, Giovanni (Giambellino)
  born: 5 Italy **6** Venice
  father: 6 Jacopo
  brother: 7 Gentile
  artwork: 8 St Jerome **16** Venus with a Mirror **18** St Francis in Ecstasy, The Madonna and Child **19** Allegory of Purgatory, The Agony in the Garden, The Barberini Madonna

Bellini, Jacopo
  born: 5 Italy 6 Venice
  son: 7 Gentile 8 Giovanni
  artwork: 11 Crucifixion 16 Christ on
    the Cross 35 The Madonna and
    Child with Lionello d'Este
Bellini, Vincenzo
  born: 5 Italy 7 Catania
  composer of: 5 Norma, Zaira 8 Il
    Pirata 9 I Puritani 11 La Straniera 12
    La Sonnambula 15 Bianca e Fer-
    nando
Bell Jar, The
  author: 11 Sylvia Plath
bellow 4 bawl, roar, yell 5 shout,
  whoop 6 holler, scream, shriek
Bellow, Saul
  author of: 6 Herzog 13 Dean's De-
    cember, Humboldt's Gift, Mosby's
    Memoirs 15 The Last Analysis 16 Mr
    Sammler's Planet 18 To Jerusalem
    and Back 25 The Adventures of Au-
    gie March
Bellows, George Wesley
  born: 10 Columbus OH
  artwork: 8 Lady Jean 11 Billy Sun-
    day, Edith Cavell, Floating Ice, Up
    the Hudson 12 Forty-Two Kids 13
    Men of the Docks 14 Rain on the
    River, Stag at Sharkey's 16 The Cliff
    Dwellers 18 Emma and her Children
    21 Both Members of This Club
Bells Are Ringing
  music: 5 Styne
  lyric: 5 Green 6 Comden
  director: 16 Vincente Minnelli
  cast: 9 Fred Clark 10 Dean Martin 12
    Judy Holliday
  song: 10 Just in Time 13 The Party's
    Over
Bells in Winter
  author: 13 Czeslaw Milosz
Bells of St Mary's, The
  director: 10 Leo McCarey
  cast: 10 Bing Crosby (Father
    O'Malley) 12 Henry Travers 13 In-
    grid Bergman
  sequel to: 10 Going My Way
  song: 20 Aren't You Glad You're You
bell tower 5 spire 6 belfry 7 steeple 9
  campanile
Belluschi, Pietro
  architect of: 21 Bank of America
    Building (San Francisco) 22 Juilliard
    School of Music (NYC) 31 Pan
    American World Airways Building
    (NYC, with Gropius)
bellwether 4 lead 5 doyen, guide, pilot 6 leader 8 director, shepherd 9
  conductor, guidepost, precursor 10
  forerunner, pacesetter 14 standard-
  bearer
belly 3 abs, gut, yen 4 guts 5 taste,
  tummy 6 bowels, depths, desire, hunger, liking, paunch, vitals 7 abdomen,
  insides, midriff, stomach 8 appetite,
  interior, recesses 11 breadbasket

bellyache 4 beef, kick 5 gripe 6
  grouch, grouse, squawk 7 grumble 8
  complain 9 tummy ache 11 stomach
  ache 12 upset stomach
belong 6 go with 7 concern 8 attach
  to, be held by, be part of 9 be owned
  by, pertain to 10 be allied to 11 be a
  member of 12 be included in 15 be
  connected with, be the property of
belongings 4 gear, junk 5 goods, stuff
  6 things 7 effects 8 movables 11
  possessions 13 accoutrements, paraphernalia 16 personal property
Beloved
  author: 12 Toni Morrison
beloved 4 beau, dear, love, wife 5
  loved, lover 6 adored, fiance, spouse,
  steady 7 admired, darling, dearest, fiancee, husband, revered 8 endeared,
  esteemed, loved one, precious 9 betrothed, boyfriend, cherished, respected, treasured 10 girlfriend,
  sweetheart
below 4 less 5 lower, under 6 in hell
  7 beneath, on earth, short of 8 inferior, unworthy 9 at a low ebb, down-
  wards 10 downstairs, downstream,
  second-rate, underneath 11 at a discount, at the foot of, indifferent, subordinate, underground
below par 3 bad 4 poor 8 inferior 9
  imperfect 10 second-rate 12 below average, not up to snuff
below standard 3 bad 4 poor 5 lousy
  6 faulty, shoddy 8 below par, inferior,
  slipshod, terrible 9 imperfect 10 second-rate 12 not up to snuff
belt 4 area, band, land, sash, zone 5
  cinch, layer, strip 6 circle, girdle, region, stripe 7 country 8 district, encircle 9 waistband 10 cummerbund
Belushi, James
  born: 7 Chicago
  roles: 8 Curly Sue 9 Mr. Destiny 13
    Working Stiffs 14 About Last Night
    15 Jumpin' Jack Flash 19 Little Shop
    of Horrors
Belushi, John
  born: 9 Chicago IL
  roles: 9 Neighbors 11 Animal House
    16 The Blues Brothers 17 Saturday
    Night Live
be manifest 6 appear 7 be clear, be
  plain 8 be patent 9 be evident, be obvious 10 be apparent
bemoan 3 rue 5 mourn 6 bewail, lament, regret 7 cry over 8 weep over
  9 whine over 10 grieve over
bemused 5 dazed, fuzzy 7 muddled,
  stunned 8 confused 9 engrossed, stupefied 10 bewildered, dull- witted,
  thoughtful 11 preoccupied 12 absent-
  minded
be nauseated by 4 hate 5 abhor 6
  detest, loathe 7 despise 8 execrate 9
  abominate 11 can't stomach 13 be

disgusted by, find repulsive, find revolting, find sickening
Benbow, Horace
  character in: 9 Sanctuary
  author: 8 Faulkner
Ben Casey
  character: 12 Dr David Zorba, Dr Ted
    Hoffman 13 Nick Kanavaras 14 Dr
    Maggie Graham
  cast: 8 Sam Jaffe 10 Nick Dennis 12
    Harry Landers, Vince Edwards 14
    Bettye Ackerman
bench 3 pew 4 banc, seat 5 board,
  court, stool, table 6 settee 7 counter,
  take out, trestle 8 sideline, tribunal 9
  judiciary, workbench, worktable 10
  second team 11 judge's chair, substitutes 12 second string
Benchley, Peter
  author of: 4 Jaws 7 The Deep
Benchley, Robert
  author of: 14 From Bed to Worse 21
    Benchley Beside Himself, My Ten
    Years in a Quandary
benchmark 4 norm 5 gauge, guide,
  model 7 example, measure 8 exemplar, paradigm, standard 9 criterion,
  principle, prototype, reference, yardstick 10 touchstone
bend 3 arc, bow 4 flex, hook, lean,
  loop, mold, sway, turn, warp, wind 5
  crook, curve, defer, force, shape,
  stoop, twist, yield 6 accede, attend,
  buckle, coerce, compel, crouch, give
  in, relent, submit 7 bow down, contort, control, succumb 9 genuflect, influence, surrender 10 buckle down,
  capitulate 11 make crooked
Bend in the River, The
  author: 9 V S Naipaul
Bendix, William
  born: 9 New York NY
  roles: 8 Hostages, Lifeboat 11 The
    Hairy Ape 13 A Bell for Adano 14
    The Life of Riley 16 Guadalcanal Di-
    ary, The Babe Ruth Story
bend to one's own will 4 tame 5
  break, train 6 master, subdue 8 overcome 10 discipline 12 show who's
  boss 18 have under one's thumb
beneath 5 below, lower, under 9 covered by 10 inferior to, underneath,
  unworthy of 11 subordinate, underground 16 below one's dignity
Benedick
  character in: 19 Much Ado About
    Nothing
  author: 11 Shakespeare
Benedict 5 groom 8 newlywed
benedictine
  type: 6 brandy, cognac 7 liqueur
  flavor: 4 herb
  with brandy: 5 B and B
  with bourbon: 9 Twin Hills 13
    Brighton Punch
  with whiskey: 10 Frisco Sour

benediction 6 prayer 7 benison 8 blessing 10 invocation 12 consecration 13 closing prayer

benefaction 4 alms, gift 5 grant 7 charity 8 bestowal, donation, offering 9 endowment 10 almsgiving 12 contribution, dispensation, philanthropy

benefactor 5 angel, donor 6 backer, friend, helper, patron 7 sponsor 8 upholder 9 supporter 11 contributor 14 fairy godmother

beneficent 6 benign, kindly 7 liberal 8 generous, salutary 10 beneficial, benevolent, charitable 11 magnanimous 13 philanthropic

beneficial 6 useful 7 good for, healing, helpful 8 valuable 9 favorable, healthful 10 productive, profitable, propitious 12 advantageous, contributive

beneficiary 4 heir 7 grantee, heiress, legatee 8 receiver 9 inheritor, recipient

benefit 3 aid, use 4 gain, good, help 5 asset, avail, serve, value, worth 6 assist, behalf, better, profit 7 advance, be aided, service 8 be helped, be served, blessing, interest 9 advantage, do good for 10 be useful to, betterment, profit from 13 charity affair 18 charity performance

Benet, Stephen Vincent
author of: 7 America 8 Tiger Joy 11 Western Star 14 John Brown's Body, Thirteen O'Clock, Young Adventure 16 Five Men and Pompey 19 Tales Before Midnight, The Headless Horseman 20 The Beginning of Wisdom 24 The Devil and Daniel Webster

benevolence 7 charity 8 good will, kindness 9 benignity 10 compassion, generosity, kindliness, liberality 13 bountifulness 14 charitableness 15 humanitarianism, kindheartedness

benevolent 3 kin 6 benign, humane, tender 7 liberal 8 generous 9 benignant, bounteous, bountiful, unselfish 10 bighearted, charitable 11 considerate, kindhearted, warmhearted 12 humanitarian 13 compassionate, philanthropic

Bengali
language family: 12 Indo-European
branch: 11 Indo-Iranian
group: 5 Indic
spoken in: 5 (northern) India

Ben-Hur
author: 10 Lew Wallace
character: 4 Iras, Isas 5 Jesus 6 Esther 7 Messala 9 Balthasar, Simonides 11 Judah Ben-Hur
director: 12 William Wyler
cast: 11 Jack Hawkins, Stephen Boyd 12 Hugh Griffith 14 Charlton Heston (Judah Ben-Hur)
setting: 9 Palestine

Oscar for: 5 actor (Heston) 7 picture 8 director 14 cinematography 15 supporting actor (Griffith)

benighted 4 dumb 5 crude, unhip 8 backward, ignorant, untaught 9 primitive, untutored 10 illiterate, uncultured, uneducated, uninformed, unlettered, unschooled 11 empty-headed, know-nothing, uncivilized 12 uncultivated 13 unenlightened

benign 4 good, kind, mild, nice, soft 5 balmy, lucky 6 genial, gentle, humane, kindly, tender 7 affable 8 gracious, harmless, pleasant, salutary 9 favorable, healthful, innocuous, temperate 10 auspicious, benevolent, propitious 11 encouraging, kindhearted, soft-hearted 13 tender-hearted

benignant 4 kind 6 benign, humane, kindly, tender 9 forgiving 10 benevolent 11 kindhearted 13 compassionate, tenderhearted

benignity 8 good will, kindness 10 compassion, kindliness 11 benevolence 15 kindheartedness

Benin
other name: 17 Republic of Dahomey
capital: 9 Porto-Novo
largest city: 7 Cotonou
others: 4 Pobe 5 Kandi, Kerou, Ketou, Porga 6 Abomey, Ouidah 7 Parakou, Savalou 8 Aplahoue
government: 30 Military Council of the Revolution
monetary unit: 5 franc 7 centime
lake: 5 Aheme 6 Nokoue
mountain: 7 Atakora
river: 4 Mono 5 Niger, Oueme 6 Couffo
sea: 8 Atlantic
physical feature:
    gulf: 6 Guinea
    plains: 6 Borgou
people: 3 Fon, Pla 4 Adja, Aizo, Mina, Peul 5 Pedah, Peuhl, Somba 6 Bariba, Fulani, Yoruba 8 Pilapila 9 Dahomeyan
language: 3 Fon 5 Dendi 6 Bariba, French, Fulani, Yoruba
religion: 5 Islam 6 tribal 7 animism 13 Roman Catholic
food:
    tapioca: 4 gari

Benito Cereno
author: 14 Herman Melville

Benjamin
father: 5 Jacob
mother: 6 Rachel
also known as: 6 Benoni
brother: 3 Dan, Gad 4 Levi 5 Asher, Judah 6 Joseph, Reuben, Simeon 7 Zebulun 8 Issachar, Naphtali
sister: 5 Dinah
descendant of: 11 Benjaminite

Bennet family
characters in: 17 Pride and Prejudice
members: 4 Jane, Mary 5 Kitty, Lydia

9 Elizabeth
author: 6 Austen

Bennett, Arnold
author of: 8 Accident 10 Clayhanger, Lord Raingo, Milestones, These Twain 11 Buried Alive 13 Hilda Lessways, Riceyman Steps 15 The Old Wives' Tale 18 Anna of the Five Towns

Benny, Jack
real name: 16 Benjamin Kubelsky
born: 10 Waukegan IL
roles: 12 Charley's Aunt 13 Jack Benny Show, To Be or Not To Be 16 Artists and Models

Benoni see 8 Benjamin

Benson
character: 5 Kraus 12 (Lt Gov) Benson DuBois 13 (Gov) Eugene Gatling
cast: 10 James Noble 11 Inga Swenson 15 Robert Guillaume

bent 4 bias, gift, mind 5 bowed, flair, knack 6 angled, arched, curved, genius, liking, talent 7 ability, aptness, crooked, faculty, hunched, leaning, stooped, twisted 8 aptitude, capacity, facility, fondness, penchant, tendency 9 contorted, endowment 10 attraction, partiality, proclivity, propensity 11 disposition, inclination 12 predilection 14 predisposition

bent into folds 6 fluted, ridged 7 creased, grooved, pleated 8 crinkled, furrowed, puckered, wrinkled 10 corrugated

Benton, Robert
director of: 14 Kramer vs Kramer (Oscar) 16 Places in the Heart

Benton, Thomas Hart
born: 8 Neosho MO
artwork: 7 Bubbles 8 Boomtown 9 Homestead 12 American Life 13 Arts of the West, Cotton Pickers 14 Threshing Wheat 19 Louisiana Rice Fields, The Lord Is My Shepherd

Benue-Congo
language family: 16 Niger-Kordofanian
group: 10 Niger-Congo
includes: 3 Tiv 4 Zulu 5 Bantu, Jukun 6 Chwana, Nyanja 7 Kikongo, Luganda, Swahili

benumb 4 daze, dull 5 blunt 6 deaden 7 stupefy 15 make insensitive

Benvolio
character in: 14 Romeo and Juliet
author: 11 Shakespeare

Benz, Karl
nationality: 6 German
inventor of: 22 electric ignition engine 26 differential gear automobile
built first practical: 10 automobile

be obvious 6 appear 7 be clear, be plain 8 be patent 9 be evident 10 be apparent, be manifest

be off 2 go 5 leave, scram 6 beat it, begone, cut out, depart, go away, set

be of one mind (continued)
out **8** set forth, withdraw **10** make tracks

be of one mind 5 agree **6** accord, concur **10** think alike **11** see eye to eye

be of use 3 aid **4** help **5** serve **6** assist **7** benefit

be on a par with 5 equal **6** be up to **7** compare **10** be as good as **12** be comparable **14** be in a class with

be on the sick list 3 ail **5** be ill **6** be sick **8** be unwell **12** be indisposed **13** be in ill health **17** be under the weather

Beor
son: **4** Bela **6** Balaam

Beothuk (Red Indians)
location: **6** Canada **12** Newfoundland
intermixed with: **7** Naskapi

Beowulf
author: **7** unknown
character: **4** Finn **5** Breca, Hnaef, Oslaf, Scyld **6** Wiglaf **7** Guthlaf, Hengest, Higelac, Hrethel, Unferth **8** Aeschere, Heardred, Hondscio, Hrothgar **9** Hildeburh
great hall: **6** Heorot
monster: **7** Grendel **14** Grendel's mother
tribe: **5** Danes, Geats **8** Frisians
Beowulf tears from Grendel: **3** arm

be part of 4 form **6** make up **8** belong to **9** appertain, pertain to **10** constitute

be patent 6 appear **7** be clear, be plain **9** be evident, be obvious **10** be apparent, be manifest

be pertinent to 4 bear **5** apply, refer **6** affect, relate **7** concern, pertain **9** appertain, touch upon

be plain 6 appear **7** be clear **8** be patent **9** be evident, be obvious **10** be apparent, be manifest

be pleased with 4 like **5** favor **7** approve

bequeath 4 will **5** endow, leave **6** impart **7** consign **8** hand down

bequest 6 legacy **8** bestowal **9** endowment **10** settlement **11** inheritance

berate 5 scold **6** rail at, rebuke **7** bawl out, chew out, reprove, upbraid **8** reproach **9** castigate, criticize, reprimand **10** take to task, tongue-lash

Berber
language family: **11** Afro-asiatic **13** Hamito-Semitic
spoken in: **6** Sahara **11** North Africa

bereave 3 rob **5** strip **6** divest **7** deprive **10** dispossess

Berenice's Hair
constellation of: **13** Coma Berenices

be resigned to 6 accept **8** tolerate

Beret
character in: **16** Giants of the Earth
author: **7** Rolvaag

be revolted by 4 hate **5** abhor **6** detest, loathe **7** despise **8** execrate **9** abominate **10** recoil from, shrink from **11** can't stomach **13** find repulsive

berg 4 floe **7** glacier, iceberg, icefloe
South African: **8** mountain
French: **4** neve **5** serac

Berg, Alban
born: **6** Vienna **7** Austria
composer of: **4** Lulu **7** Wozzeck

Bergen, Candace
father: **11** Edgar Bergen
born: **14** Beverly Hills CA
roles: **8** The Group **11** Murphy Brown **15** Carnal Knowledge
husband: **10** Louis Malle

Berger, Thomas
author of: **7** The Feud **9** Neighbors **10** Vital Parts **11** Killing Time **12** Little Big Man, Sneaky People **15** Regiment of Women

Bergman, Ingmar
director of: **14** The Seventh Seal **16** Cries and Whispers, Wild Strawberries **17** Fanny and Alexander **19** Scenes from a Marriage **20** Smiles of a Summer Night

Bergman, Ingrid
born: **6** Sweden **9** Stockholm
children: **12** Pia Lindstrom **18** Isabella Rossellini
roles: **8** Gaslight (Oscar) **9** Anastasia (Oscar), Golda Meir, Joan of Arc, Notorious **10** Casablanca, Intermezzo, Spellbound **17** A Woman Called Golda, The Bells of St Mary's **19** For Whom the Bell Tolls **24** Murder on the Orient Express **25** The Inn of the Sixth Happiness

Berith, Berit, Bris, Brith, Brit 8 covenant **12** circumcision

Berle, Milton
real name: **15** Milton Berlinger
nickname: **11** Uncle Miltie **12** Mr Television
born: **9** New York NY
roles: **17** The Texaco Star Hour **18** Who's Minding the Mint **23** Always Leave Them Laughing

Berlin (East, West)
landmark: **14** Humboldt Castle **15** Gruenwald Castle **16** Berlin Opera House, Markisches Museum **21** Scharlottenburg Castle **29** Kaiser-Wilhelm-Gedachtniskirche
river: **5** Spree
square: **14** Alexander-Platz

Berlin, Elaine
real name of: **9** Elaine May

Berlinger, Milton
real name of: **11** Milton Berle

Berlioz, (Louis) Hector
born: **6** France **13** La Cote St Andre
composer of: **6** Rob Roy, Te Deum **7** Requiem, **8** Herminie, King Lear, Waverley **9** Cleopatra, Nuits d'Ete **10** Le Corsaire, Les Troyens, The Trojans **11** Sardanapale **13** Harold in Italy **14** Les Francs Juges, Romeo and Juliet **16** Benvenuto Cellini, Damnation of Faust, Le Carnaval Romain, L'Enfance du Christ **18** Beatrice et Benedict **20** Symphonie Fantastique **28** Symphonie Funebre et Triomphale

Bermuda
other name: **13** Somers Islands
capital/largest city: **8** Hamilton
others: **8** St George
head of state: **14** British monarch **15** governor general
island: **4** Boaz **5** Coney **7** Bermuda, Ireland, Watford **8** Somerset, St Davids **9** St Georges
highest point: **8** Town Hill
sea: **8** Atlantic
physical feature:
  harbor: **6** Castle
  hill: **5** Gibbs
people:
  discoverer: **14** Juan de Bermudez
language: **7** English
religion: **8** Anglican **10** Protestant **15** Church of England
feature:
  dancers: **6** Gombey

Bermuda Triangle
bounded by: **7** Bermuda, Florida **9** Melbourne **10** Puerto Rico
site of: **24** mysterious disappearances
of: **5** ships **9** airplanes

Bern, Berne
capital of: **11** Switzerland
landmark: **10** Clock Tower **12** Nydegg Church
river: **3** Aar **4** Aare

Bernard, Henriette-Rosine
real name of: **14** Sarah Bernhardt

Bernhardt, Sarah
real name: **22** Henriette-Rosine Bernard
nickname: **11** Divine Sarah
born: **5** Paris **6** France
roles: **6** Phedre **7** Hernani, Ruy Blas **8** King Lear **14** Queen Elizabeth **17** La Dame aux Camelias

Bernini, Gianlorenzo (Giovanni Lorenzo)
born: **5** Italy **6** Naples
father: **6** Pietro
artwork: **7** Montoya **8** Louis XIV, Vigevano **10** Bellarmine, St Longinus **13** Cathedra Petri, Francis I d'Este, The Assumption **15** Apollo and Daphne **18** Costanza Buonarelli **19** The Rape of Proserpina **21** Saints Andrew and Thomas, The Ecstasy of St Theresa **24** Blessed Lodovica Albertoni **25** Aeneas Anchises and Ascanius
architect of: **12** Santa Bibiana **16** Piazza of St Peter's (Rome) **19** Palazzo Montecitorio **21** Sant' Andrea al Quirinale **22** Palazzo Chigi-Odescalchi **23** Fountain of the Four

Rivers **24** Santa Maria dell' Assunzione

Bernoulli, Daniel
  field: 11 mathematics
  nationality: 5 Swiss
  theory of: 5 gases **6** fluids **18** Bernoulli's Equation

Bernstein, Carl
  author of: 12 The Final Days (with Bob Woodward) **19** All the President's Men (with Bob Woodward)
  newspaper reporter for: 14 Washington Post
  ex: 10 Nora Ephron

Bernstein, Leonard
  born: 10 Lawrence MA
  composer of: 4 Mass **7** Candide, Kaddish **8** Jeremiah **9** Facsimile, Fancy Free, On the Town **13** West Side Story, Wonderful Town **15** The Age of Anxiety, Trouble in Tahiti **16** Chichester Psalms

Beroe
  father: 6 Adonis
  mother: 9 Aphrodite
  nurse of: 6 Semele

Berowne
  character in: 16 Love's Labour's Lost
  author: 11 Shakespeare

Berra, Yogi (Lawrence Peter Berra)
  sport: 8 baseball
  position: 5 coach **7** catcher
  team: 14 New York Yankees

berry **3** egg **4** seed **5** fruit, grain, grape **6** dollar, kernel, tomato, banana **7** currant **8** allspice, bayberry, mulberry **9** blueberry, cranberry, raspberry **10** blackberry, gooseberry, peppercorn, strawberry **11** boysenberry, huckleberry, pomegranate **12** checkerberry
  poisonous: 9 baneberry

Berryman, John
  author of: 8 Recovery **9** Delusions **11** Love and Fame **12** 77 Dream Songs **13** The Dream Songs **16** Berryman's Sonnets **19** The Freedom of the Poet **21** His Toy His Dream His Rest **26** Homage to Mistress Bradstreet

berserk **4** amok, wild **5** crazy **6** insane **7** frantic, violent **8** demented, deranged, frenzied, maniacal, wild-eyed **9** desperate **10** distracted, distraught **12** out of control

Berserker
  origin: 6 Nordic
  form: 7 warrior

berth **3** bed, job **4** bunk, dock, pier, post, quay, slip, spot **5** haven, niche, place, wharf **6** billet, employ, office **8** position **9** anchorage, situation **11** appointment **12** resting place **13** sleeping place

Berthollet, Claude Louis
  field: 9 chemistry
  nationality: 6 French
  researched: 7 ammonia **8** chlorine

Bertram
  character in: 20 All's Well That Ends Well
  author: 11 Shakespeare

Bertram family
  characters in: 13 Mansfield Park
  members: 3 Tom **5** Julia, Maria **6** Edmund **9** Sir Thomas
  author: 6 Austen

beryl
  color: 5 green **6** yellow

Berzelius, Jons Jakob
  field: 9 chemistry
  nationality: 7 Swedish
  developed: 15 chemical symbols
  discovered: 6 cerium **7** silicon, thorium **8** selenium, titanium **9** zirconium
  founded: 15 modern chemistry

be satisfactory **2** do **6** answer **7** suffice **8** be enough **10** be adequate, pass muster **12** be sufficient, do well enough

be scant **4** lack, want **8** be skimpy **9** fall short **14** be insufficient **15** be in short supply

beseech **3** beg **4** pray **6** adjure **7** entreat, implore **9** plead with **10** supplicate

beset **3** dog, set **4** bead, deck, stud **5** annoy, array, hem in, hound, worry **6** assail, badger, harass, pester, plague **7** bedevil, besiege, set upon **8** surround **9** beleaguer, embellish

be sick **3** ail **5** be ill **8** be unwell **12** be indisposed **13** be in ill health

beside **2** by **4** near **5** saved **6** except, nearby, unless **7** abreast, barring, without **8** let alone **9** adjoining, alongside, aside from, other than **10** on a par with, side by side **12** compared with, in addition to

beside oneself **4** wild **6** elated, joyful, joyous, raging **7** berserk, exalted, frantic, furious, ranting **8** agitated, blissful, distrait, ecstatic, frenetic, frenzied **9** delirious, in a frenzy, overjoyed, rapturous **10** distracted, distraught, distressed, enraptured **11** carried away, overwrought, transported **13** out of one's wits

besides **3** but **4** also, save **6** as well, except, saving **8** barring **8** moreover **9** excepting, excluding, other than **11** exclusive of, furthermore

besiege **3** dog **5** annoy, beset, hound **6** assail, badger, harass, pester, plague **7** assault, bedevil **9** beleaguer **10** lay siege to

besmear **4** soil **5** dirty, muddy, smear, stain, sully **6** mess up, slop up, smudge **7** begrime, tarnish **8** besmirch

besmeared **5** dirty, grimy, messy **6** grubby, smudgy **7** muddied, sullied **8** begrimed **10** besmirched

besmirch **4** soil **5** smear, stain, sully,

taint **6** defame, defile **7** blacken, corrupt, debauch, degrade, slander, tarnish **8** discolor, disgrace, dishonor **9** discredit

besotted **5** drunk **6** sodden, soused, wasted, zapped, zonked **7** smashed **9** plastered **10** inebriated, infatuated **11** intoxicated **17** under the influence **20** three sheets to the wind

bespangle **3** dot **4** gild, star, stud **5** adorn, jewel **6** bedeck **7** dress up, festoon, garnish **8** decorate, ornament **9** embellish **10** illuminate

bespatter **4** blot, soil, spot **5** decry, dirty, libel, smear, stain, sully, taint **6** debase, defame, defile, smudge, splash **7** condemn, slander, smotter, tarnish **8** denounce, reproach **9** deprecate, fling dirt **10** calumniate, disapprove

Bessemer, Sir Henry
  nationality: 7 English
  inventor of manufacturing process for: 5 steel

best **3** top **4** most, pick **5** cream, elite **6** choice, finest, nicest, utmost **7** hardest, largest **8** foremost, greatest, superior, topnotch **9** greetings, loveliest, most fully, most of all, unequaled, unrivaled **10** unexcelled **11** compliments, unsurpassed **13** most competent, most desirable, most excellent **14** highest quality, kindest regards

Best, Charles Herbert
  field: 10 physiology
  nationality: 8 Canadian
  discovered: 7 insulin

best group **3** top **5** cream, elite **6** choice **9** chosen few **10** select body **14** cream of the crop, creme de la creme

bestial **5** cruel **6** brutal, savage **7** beastly **8** barbaric, depraved, inhumane, ruthless **9** barbarous, merciless

bestir **4** goad, spur, stir, urge **5** rouse, speed **6** arouse, excite, hasten **7** quicken **8** activate **9** get moving

bestir oneself **5** rouse **8** be active **9** make haste **10** get up early, lose no time **11** keep moving **15** make short work of **19** seize the opportunity

bestow **3** use **4** give, mete **5** apply, award, grant, lay on, spend **6** accord, confer, devote, donate, employ, expend, impart, occupy, render **7** consign, consume, deal out, deliver, hand out, present, utilize **8** dispense, give away **9** apportion **10** settle upon, turn over to

bestowal **4** alms, gift **5** bonus, favor, grant **6** reward **7** charity, present, tribute **8** donation, gratuity, offering **9** endowment **10** conferment, recompense **11** benefaction **12** contribution, dispensation

best society
French: 10 grand monde

Best Years of Our Lives, The
director: 12 William Wyler
based on story by: 15 MacKinlay
Kantor
script: 14 Robert Sherwood
cast: 8 Myrna Loy 11 Dana Andrews
12 Teresa Wright, Virginia Mayo 13
Frederic March, Harold Russell 15
Hoagy Carmichael
Oscar for: 5 actor (March) 7 picture
8 director

be sufficient 6 answer 7 suffice 8 be
enough 10 be adequate, pass muster
12 do well enough 14 be satisfactory

bet 4 ante, risk 5 stake, wager 6
chance, gamble, hazard, plunge 7
venture 8 make a bet 9 speculate 11
speculation

bete noir 5 bogey 6 plague 7 bugaboo, bugbear 8 anathema, bogeyman
9 annoyance 10 black beast

be thankful 8 thank God 10 appreciate 11 thank heaven 19 thank one's
lucky stars

Bethe, Hans Albrecht
field: 7 physics
developed: 8 atom bomb
awarded: 10 Nobel Prize

be the same 5 agree, equal, match 6
equate 7 balance 11 be identical

betide 4 fall 5 occur 6 befall, chance,
happen 10 come to pass

betimes 5 early 10 in good time

betoken 4 show 5 augur 6 attest, denote 7 portend, presage, signify 8
foretell

betray 4 dupe, fink, jilt, show, tell 5
rat on, trick 6 expose, reveal, squeal,
tell on, unmask 7 abandon, deceive,
divulge, lay bare, let down, let slip,
sell out, two-time, uncover, violate 8
blurt out, disclose, give away 9 play
Judas 10 be disloyal 11 double-cross
12 be unfaithful 13 inform against,
play false with 14 break faith with

betrayal 7 perfidy, telling, treason 8
bad faith, sedition, trickery 9 chicanery, deception, duplicity, falseness,
treachery, two-timing, violation 10
disclosure, disloyalty, divulgence, revelation 11 double-cross 13 breach of
faith, double-dealing 14 unfaithfulness

betrayal of trust 7 falsity, perfidy 8
apostasy, cheating 9 falseness, recreancy 10 disloyalty, infidelity 11 inconstancy 13 deceitfulness, double-
dealing, faithlessness 14 unfaithfulness

Betrayer 13 Judas Iscariot

betroth 6 commit, engage, pledge 7
espouse, promise 8 affiance, contract

betrothal 5 troth 8 espousal 10 affiancing, betrothing, engagement

betrothed 6 fiance 7 engaged, fiancee
8 promised 9 affianced

Bettelheim, Bruno
author of: 15 Love Is Not Enough 16
The Informed Heart 20 The Uses of
Enchantment

better 3 top 4 more 5 finer, outdo,
raise 6 bigger, enrich, exceed, fitter,
larger, longer, refine, uplift 7 advance,
elevate, enhance, farther, forward,
further, greater, improve, mending,
promote, surpass, upgrade 8 heighten,
improved, increase, outstrip, stronger,
superior 9 cultivate, healthier, improving 10 preferable, recovering,
strengthen 11 more healthy, progress-
ing

bettering 9 elevation 10 betterment
11 advancement, improvement

betterment 4 good 6 reform 7 benefit
8 revision 9 advantage, amendment,
promotion 10 correction, enrichment
11 advancement, improvement 12
amelioration, regeneration 13 rectification 14 reconstruction

better than average 2 A-1 3 A-OK 4
aces, a-one, fine, good, tops 5 great,
prime, super 6 choice, grade-A, superb 7 capital, special 8 peerless, sterling, superior, terrific, top-notch 9 excellent, first-rate, marvelous,
matchless, wonderful 10 first-class, inimitable, preeminent, remarkable, tremendous 11 exceptional, outstanding,
superlative 12 incomparable 13 extraordinary

between 4 amid 5 among, entre 6
amidst, atwixt, shared 7 betwixt, joining 9 in the midst 10 connecting

between ourselves
French: 9 entre nous
Latin: 8 inter nos

Between the Battles
author: 20 Bjornstjerne Bjornson

between themselves
Latin: 7 inter se

between us 9 entre nous, privately 14
confidentially 15 between you and me
16 between me and thee, between
ourselves

betwixt and between 4 so-so 7 average 8 confused 9 in between, undecided 14 halfway between 21 neither
one nor the other

Beulah, Land of
place in: 16 Pilgrim's Progress
author: 6 Bunyan

be unlike 4 vary 6 differ 7 deviate, diverge 9 conflict, disagree 12 be at
variance, be discordant, be dissimilar

be unwell 3 ail 5 be ill 6 be sick 12
be indisposed 13 be in ill health

be unwilling to pursue
Latin: 13 nolle prosequi

bevel 4 blow, cant, ream, tool 5 angle,
bezel, miter, mitre, slant, slope,

snape, splay 6 aslant 7 incline,
oblique 8 slanting

beverage 3 ade, ale, cup, nog, pop,
tea 4 beer, brew, cafe, dram, grog,
milk, soda, soup, wine 5 broth, caffe,
cider, cocoa, draft, drink, juice, julep,
lager, latte, leban, punch, toddy, water 6 bishop, coffee, cordial, eggnog,
liquid, liquor, potion 7 limeade, seltzer, spirits, wassail 8 aperitif, cocktail,
espresso, expresso, highball, lemonade, libation, potation 9 champagne,
chocolate, orangeade 10 cappuccino

Beverley, Constance de
character in: 7 Marmion
author: 5 Scott

Beverly Hillbillies, The
character: 11 Jed Clampett 12 Jane
Hathaway, Jethro Bodine 14 Granny
Clampett, Milton Drysdale 16 Ellie
May Clampett
cast: 9 Irene Ryan, Max Baer Jr,
Nancy Kulp 10 Buddy Ebsen 12
Donna Douglas 13 Raymond Bailey

Beverly Hills Cop
director: 11 Martin Brest
cast: 11 Eddie Murphy 13 Judge
Reinhold, Lisa Eilbacher

bevy 4 band, body, herd, host, pack 5
brood, covey, crowd, drove, flock,
group, horde, party, shoal, swarm 6
clutch, flight, gaggle, school, throng 7
company, coterie 9 gathering, multitude 10 assemblage, collection

bewail 3 rue 5 mourn 6 bemoan, lament, regret 7 cry over, deplore 8
moan over, weep over 10 grieve over

beware 4 mind 6 be wary 7 look out
8 take care, take heed 9 be careful 11
take warning, watch out for 12 be on
the alert, guard against 15 take pre-
cautions

beware of the dog
Latin: 9 cave canem

bewhiskered 5 bushy, hairy 6 shaggy
7 bearded, bristly, hirsute 8 unshaven
11 mustachioed

bewilder 5 addle, mix up 6 baffle, be-
muse, muddle, puzzle 7 confuse, fluster, mystify, nonplus, perplex, stupefy
8 befuddle 10 disconcert

bewildered 7 at a loss, up a tree 8 all
at sea, confused 9 perplexed 10 confounded, nonplussed 12 disconcerted

bewilderment 9 confusion 10 perplexity, puzzlement 11 frustration 13
mystification

bewitch 4 jinx 5 charm, spook 6 turn
on 7 bedevil, beguile, delight, enchant
8 entrance 9 captivate, enrapture, fascinate 12 cast a spell on 14 put under
a spell

bewitched 7 charmed, seduced 8 beguiled 9 bedeviled, enchanted, entranced 10 captivated, enraptured,
fascinated, spellbound 11 under a
spell

Bewitched
  character: **6** Endora, Serena **7** Maurice **9** Aunt Clara, Esmerelda, Larry Tate **11** Uncle Arthur **12** Abner Kravitz **13** Gladys Kravitz **14** Darrin Stephens **15** Tabitha Stephens **16** Samantha Stephens
  cast: **8** Dick York **9** Paul Lynde **10** David White **11** Dick Sargent, Marion Lorne, Sandra Gould **12** George Tobias, Maurice Evans **13** Alice Ghostley **14** Agnes Moorehead **19** Elizabeth Montgomery
bewitching 8 alluring, charming, enticing, fetching, tempting **9** appealing, beguiling, disarming, seductive **10** enchanting, entrancing **11** captivating, fascinating **12** irresistible
be worthy of 4 earn, rate **5** merit **7** deserve
bey, beg 4 lord **6** prince **8** governor
beyond 2 by **4** over, past **5** above, later, ultra **6** abroad, except, yonder **7** beneath, besides, farther, further, outside, passing **8** superior **9** exceeding, hereafter **10** out of range, out of reach **11** at a distance, in addition to
Beyond Desire
  author: **15** Maxwell Anderson
beyond hope 8 hopeless **9** desperate **10** despairing
Beyond Human Power
  author: **20** Bjornstjerne Bjornson
beyond one's means 10 immoderate **11** extravagant **15** too high on the hog
beyond question 4 sure **6** surely **7** certain, decided, settled **9** certainly, decidedly **10** absolutely, positively **12** without doubt
Bharat (Varsha) *see* **5** India
Bhot *see* **5** Tibet
Bhutan
  other name: **7** Druk-Yul **15** Kingdom of Bhutan, Land of the Dragon
  capital/largest city: **6** Thimbu **7** Thimphu
  others: **4** Paro **12** Phuntsholing **14** Wangdu Phedrang
  government:
    assembly: **7** Tsongdu
  head of state/ government:
    hereditary king: **10** dragon king, druk gyalpo
  other leader:
    spiritual leader: **10** dharma raja
    temporal ruler: **7** deb raja
  monetary unit: **5** paisa, rupee **8** chetrums, ngultrum
  mountain: **5** Black **9** Himalayas **10** Chomo Lhari
  highest point: **10** Kula Kangri
  river: **4** Kuru, Paro **5** Machu, Manas, Pachu, Torsa **6** Amochu, Raidak, Tongsa **7** Sankosh, Thinchu
  physical feature:
    plain: **5** Duars

people: **5** Monpa **6** Bhutia **7** Tibetan **8** Assamese, Nepalese
  dragon people: **7** Drukpas
language: **5** Hindi, Lhoke **7** Tibetan **8** Dzongkha, Nepalese
religion: **15** Tibetan Buddhism
place:
    fortress (dzong): **4** Paro **6** Bya Kar, Tongsa **8** Tashi Cho
feature:
    pony: **6** Tangun
Bianca
  character in: **10** Kiss Me Kate **19** The Taming of the Shrew
  author: **11** Shakespeare
Bianchi, Mose
  born: **5** Italy, Milan
  artwork: **11** Snow in Milan **21** Return from the Festival
bias 4 bent, sway **5** angle, slant **7** bigotry, feeling, leaning **8** tendency **9** fixed idea, prejudice, proneness **10** narrow view, partiality, predispose, proclivity, propensity, unfairness **11** inclination, intolerance **12** diagonal line, one-sidedness, predilection **13** preconception **16** narrow-mindedness, preconceived idea
biased 6 unfair, unjust **7** bigoted, slanted **8** inclined **9** arbitrary **10** intolerant, prejudiced **11** close-minded, opinionated **12** narrow-minded
bibelot 5 curio **7** trinket **8** ornament **9** objet d'art
Bible 5 guide **6** manual **8** handbook **9** authority, guidebook **13** reference book
Bible 6 Gospel **7** the Book **8** good book, Holy Writ **10** Scriptures **11** bibliotheca, the Good Book **13** holy scripture **14** Holy Scriptures, sacred writings
Bible, books of
  Old Testament: **3** Job **4** Amos, Ezra, Joel, Osee, Ruth **5** Hosea, Jonah, Jonas, Josue, Kings, Micah, Nahum, Tobit **6** Abdias, Aggeus, Baruch, Daniel, Es- dras, Esther, Exodus, Haggai, Isaiah, Isaias, Joshua, Judges, Judith, Psalms, Samuel, Sirach, Tobias, Wisdom **7** Ezekiel, Genesis, Habacuc, Malachi, Micheas, Numbers, Obadiah **8** Ezechiel, Habakkuk, Jeremiah, Jeremias, Nehemiah, Proverbs **9** Leviticus, Maccabees, Machabees, Malachias, Sophonias, Zacharias, Zechariah, Zephaniah **10** Chronicles **11** Deuteronomy, Song of Songs **12** Ecclesiastes, Lamentations **13** Paralipomenon, Song of Solomon **14** Ecclesiasticus **19** Canticle of Canticles
  New Testament: **4** Acts, John, Jude, Luke, Mark **5** James, Peter **6** Romans **7** Hebrews, Matthew, Timothy **9** Ephesians, Galatians **10** Colossians, Revelation **11** Corinthians,

Philippians **13** Thessalonians, Titus Philemon
  first five books called: **3** Law **5** Torah **10** Pentateuch
  first seven books called: **10** Heptateuch
Bible scholar 7 biblist **9** biblicist
Bible version 5 Douay **6** The Way **7** Vulgate **8** Peshitta **9** Gutenberg, Jerusalem, King James **10** Authorized, New English **11** New American, Rheims-Douay **14** The Living Bible **15** American revised, revised standard
Biblical animal 7 unicorn
Biblical gemstone 6 ligure **7** sardius **8** sardonyx
Biblical instrument 7 sackbut
Biblical length
  reed: **9** six cubits
Biblical measure 3 cab, cor **4** epah, omet, reed, seah **5** cubit, epheh, homer **6** shekel **9** half homer
Biblical personage 9 patriarch
Biblical plant 6 hyssop **12** Rose of Sharon
Biblical precept
  Hebrew: **7** mitsvah, mitzvah
Biblical tree 5 algum, almug **6** storax **7** juniper **8** sycamire **10** gopherwood **11** shittim wood **12** opobalsammum **13** red sandalwood
Biblical weed 4 tare **6** darnel
Biblical weight 6 talent
Biblicist 12 Bible scholar
Bibliotheca 5 Bible **14** sacred writings
Biblist 12 Bible scholar
Bickel, Ernest Frederick McIntyre
  real name of: **13** Frederic March
bicker 4 spar, spat **5** argue, fight **6** haggle **7** dispute, quarrel, wrangle **8** disagree, squabble
bickering 4 spat **5** fight **7** arguing, dispute, quarrel **8** argument, fighting **9** wrangling **10** quarreling, squabbling **12** disagreement
Bickford, Charles
  born: **11** Cambridge MA
  roles: **12** Anna Christie **13** Johnny Belinda **16** Song of Bernadette **18** The Farmer's Daughter
bicycle 4 bike, ride **5** cycle, moped **10** two-wheeler
  invented by: **7** Starley
Bicycle Thief, The
  director: **14** Vittorio De Sica
  cast: **14** Lianella Carell **18** Lamberto Maggiorani
bid 3 ask, say, try **4** call, tell, wish **5** greet, offer, order **6** beckon, charge, demand, direct, effort, enjoin, insist, invite, ordain, summon, tender **7** attempt, command, proffer, propose, request, require **8** call upon, endeavor, instruct, offering, proposal **10** invitation

bidding 4 beck, call 5 offer, order 6 behest, charge, demand, offers 7 command, dictate, mandate, request, summons 8 offering, proposal 9 direction, summoning, tendering 10 injunction, invitation, proffering 11 instruction

bide 4 stay, wait 5 abide, dwell, stand, tarry 6 endure, linger, remain, suffer 8 tolerate 9 put up with

Bierce, Ambrose
author of: 15 Can Such Things Be? 16 In the Midst of Life 19 The Devil's Dictionary

Bierstadt, Albert
born: 7 Germany 8 Solingen
artwork: 11 Laramie Park 13 Mount Corcoran 17 The Rocky Mountains 20 Discovery of the Hudson, Storm on the Matterhorn 21 Sunrise Yosemite Valley 22 Settlement of California 31 Thunderstorm in the Rocky Mountains

bifocal lenses
invented by: 8 Franklin

Bifrost
origin: 12 Scandinavian
form: 6 bridge
bridge of: 4 gods
made of: 7 rainbow
from: 6 Asgard
to: 5 earth

bifurcate 4 fork 5 split 6 branch, divide 7 diverge 8 separate

big 3 top 4 head, high, huge, just, kind, main, vast 5 adult, ample, bulky, chief, great, grown, heavy, husky, large, major, noble, prime, vital 6 heroic, humane, mature 7 eminent, grown-up, haughty, hulking, immense, leading, liberal, mammoth, massive, notable, pompous, sizable, weighty 8 abundant, arrogant, boastful, bragging, colossal, enormous, generous, gigantic, gracious, princely 9 conceited, grandiose, honorable, important, momentous, prominent, strapping 10 benevolent, chivalrous, high-minded, monumental, prodigious 11 magnanimous, pretentious, significant, substantial 12 considerable 13 consequential

Big Apple
nickname of: 11 New York City

Big Bend State
nickname of: 9 Tennessee

Big Chill, The
director: 14 Lawrence Kasdan
cast: 8 Meg Tilly 10 Glenn Close, Kevin Kline 11 Tom Berenger, William Hurt 12 Jeff Goldblum

Big Daddy
character in: 16 Cat on a Hot Tin Roof
author: 8 Williams
played by: 8 Burl Ives

Big E
nickname of: 10 Elvin Hayes

Bigfoot 4 Yeti 9 Sasquatch 17 Abominable Snowman

big guns 4 VIPs 5 brass 6 cannon 7 bigwigs, top dogs 8 big shots, ordnance 9 artillery 14 heavy artillery, high mucky-mucks 15 important people

bighearted 6 lavish 7 liberal 8 generous, handsome, princely, prodigal 9 bounteous, bountiful, unselfish 10 beneficent, benevolent, charitable, free-handed, open-handed, unstinting 11 magnanimous, open-hearted 12 humanitarian

bight 3 bay 4 bend, cave, road

Biglow Papers
author: 18 James Russell Lowell

Big Money, The
author: 13 John Dos Passos

bigness 4 bulk 8 enormity, hugeness 9 amplitude, great size, greatness, largeness, magnitude 11 massiveness

Big O, The
nickname of: 14 Oscar Robertson

bigoted 6 biased 10 intolerant, prejudiced 12 closed-minded, narrow-minded

bigotry 4 bias 6 racism 9 prejudice 10 unfairness 11 intolerance 14 discrimination 16 closed-mindedness, narrow-mindedness

Big Parade, The
director: 9 King Vidor
cast: 11 John Gilbert, Renee Adoree 14 Hobart Bosworth

big shot 3 VIP 4 name 5 mogul, nabob, wheel 6 big gun, bigwig, fat cat, tycoon 7 big deal, magnate, notable 8 somebody 9 big cheese, dignitary, personage 13 high-muck-a-muck, wheeler-dealer

Big Six
nickname of: 16 Christy Mathewson

Big Sky, The
author: 11 A B Guthrie Jr

Big Sky State
nickname of: 7 Montana

Big Sleep, The
author: 15 Raymond Chandler
hero: 13 Philip Marlowe
director: 11 Howard Hawks
cast: 12 Elisha Cook Jr, Lauren Bacall 13 Dorothy Malone, Martha Vickers 14 Humphrey Bogart (Philip Marlowe)
setting: 10 Los Angeles

Big Train
nickname of: 13 Walter Johnson

Big Valley, The
character: 11 Nick Barkley 12 Audra Barkley, Heath Barkley 13 Jarrod Barkley 15 Victoria Barkley
cast: 9 Lee Majors 10 Linda Evans, Peter Breck 11 Richard Long 15 Barbara Stanwyck

bigwig 3 VIP 7 big shot, notable 9 dignitary, personage

bikini 8 two-piece 11 bathing suit
top: 3 bra
bottom: 5 thong
topless: 8 monokini
type: 6 string

Bikini 5 atoll 9 Namu islet 10 West Pacific 15 Marshall Islands

bile 4 gall, rage 5 anger, venom, wrath 6 choler, spleen

bilge 3 rot 4 bosh, bull, bunk, tosh 5 hooey, tripe 6 drivel, humbug, jabber, piffle 7 baloney, hogwash, rubbish, twaddle 8 malarkey, nonsense 9 gibberish 10 balderdash 11 foolishness, jabberwocky 13 horsefeathers 16 stuff and nonsense

bilious 4 sick 5 angry, cross, huffy, nasty, testy 6 crabby, cranky, grumpy, queasy, sickly, touchy 7 grouchy, peevish 8 bile-like, greenish, nauseous, petulant, snappish 9 irritable, sickening 10 ill-humored, out of sorts 11 ill-tempered 12 cantankerous 13 short-tempered 15 green at the gills

bilk 3 gyp 4 dupe, gull, rook, take 5 cheat, cozen, trick 6 fleece, rip off 7 deceive, defraud, swindle 8 hoodwink 9 bamboozle, victimize

bill 3 act, fee, law 4 card, chit, list 5 tally 6 agenda, charge, decree, docket, poster, roster, ticket 7 account, catalog, charges, invoice, leaflet, measure, placard, program, statute 8 banknote, brochure, bulletin, calendar, circular, handbill, proposal, register, schedule 9 greenback, inventory, ordinance, reckoning, statement 10 regulation 12 treasury note 13 advertisement 17 silver certificate

billet 3 job 4 base, bunk, camp, digs, note, post 5 berth, house, lodge, place, put up 6 letter, office 7 bed down, lodging, quarter, shelter 8 domicile, dwelling, lodgment, position, quarters 9 residence, situation 11 accommodate, appointment 13 accommodation

billfold see 6 wallet

billiards
player: 11 Willie Hoppe 13 Minnesota Fats, Willie Mosconi

Bill of Divorcement, A
director: 11 George Cukor
cast: 11 Billie Burke 13 John Barrymore 16 Katharine Hepburn

billow 4 roll, wave 5 belly, cloud, crest, surge, swell 6 puff up 7 balloon, breaker

Billy Budd
author: 14 Herman Melville
character: 8 Claggart 11 Captain Vere
opera by: 7 Britten

billyclub 3 bat 5 billy, stick 8 bludgeon 9 truncheon

bin 3 box **4** cart, crib, silo **5** crate, frame, hatch **6** barrel, basket, bunker, hamper, holder, trough, vessel **9** container, inclosure **10** receptacle

binate 4 dual **6** double **7** coupled, twofold **14** growing in pairs

bind 3 rim, tie **4** edge, gird, glue, join, lash, rope, trim, wrap **5** affix, chafe, cover, cramp, force, frame, hitch, paste, stick, strap, tie up, truss **6** attach, border, coerce, compel, encase, fasten, fringe, oblige, secure, swathe **7** bandage, confine, require **8** encumber, obligate **9** prescribe **11** necessitate

binder 4 glue, roux **5** paste **6** cement **8** notebook **9** assurance, guarantee **11** down payment **12** earnest money **17** looseleaf notebook

binding 4 band, face, tape **5** valid **6** edging, ribbon **7** styptic **8** fastener, ligative **9** stringent **10** compulsory, obligatory, peremptory **12** constricting

binge 3 jag **4** bust, orgy, tear, toot **5** blast, drunk, fling, revel, spree **6** bender **7** carouse **8** beer-bust, carousal **11** bacchanalia **12** drunken spree

Bingham, George Caleb
born: 15 Augusta County VA
artwork: 13 Stump Speaking **17** The Trapper's Return **18** Verdict of the People **19** The Jolly Flatboatman **20** Raftsmen Playing Cards **31** Fur Traders Descending the Missouri

Dingley, Mr
character in: 17 Pride and Prejudice
author: 6 Austen

biochemist 17 biological chemist
American: 4 Cori **5** Bloch, Moore, Ochoa **7** Axelrod, Lipmann **8** Kornberg
English: 5 Krebs **6** Porter, Sanger **8** Mitchell
French: 5 Monod **7** Duclaux
German: 5 Lynen

biogenesis
discoverer: 12 Louis Pasteur

biography 3 bio **4** life, vita **6** memoir **7** account, history **9** life story

biologist
American: 6 Carson, Yerkes **7** Burbank **8** Delbruck
British: 6 Darwin, Huxley **7** Bateson, Medawar
French: 5 Jacob, Monod **7** Lamarck
German: 7 Schwann
Swiss: 6 Haller

biology
branch: 6 botany **7** zoology
classification: 15 Carolus Linnaeus

birch 6 Betula
varieties: 3 Low, Red **4** Fire, Gray **5** Black, Canoe, Dwarf, Paper, River, Swamp, Sweet, Water, White **6** Cherry, Yellow **7** Monarch **8** Mahogany, Old-field **10** West Indian **13** European white, Japanese white, Young's weeping **14** Japanese cherry

Birches
author: 11 Robert Frost

bird
anatomy: 3 bec, neb, nib **4** beak, bill, cere, crop, lora, lore, mala, nape, rump, tail, tuft, wing **5** alula, crest, crown, flank, larum, lorum, pilea, rosta **6** breast, gullet, pecten, pileum, pinion, syrinx, tarsus **7** ambiens, crissum, gizzard, rostrum **8** gigerium, pectines, scapular **9** auchenium, gastraeum **10** cordylanus
aquatic/water: 3 auk, cob, ern, mew **4** cobb, coot, duck, erne, gony, gull, ibis, loon, rail, shag, skua, sora, swan, teal, tern **5** booby, cahow, crane, diver, goose, grebe, heron, murre, ousel, rotch, snipe, solan, stilt, stork **6** avocet, curlew, cygnet, dipper, fulmar, gannet, godwit, hagdon, jabiru, jacana, osprey, petrel, plover, puffin, rotche, scoter, wigeon **7** anhinga, bidcock, bittern, bustard, dovekey, dovekie, finfoot, mallard, moorhen, pelican, penguin, seriema, skimmer, widgeon **8** alcatras, baldpate, dabchick, flamingo, murrelet, umbrette **9** albatross, baptornis, cormorant, gallinule, guillemot, kittiwake, phalarope, snakebird, spoonhill **10** gaviformes, kingfisher, shearwater, sheathbill, yellowlegs **13** whooping crane
bird cage/home: 4 cote, mews, nest **5** roost **6** aviary, volary, volery **7** rookery
bird of freedom: 9 bald eagle
bird of ill-omen: 5 raven
bird of Jove: 5 eagle
bird of June: 7 peacock
bird of Minerva: 3 owl
bird of peace: 4 dove
bird of prey: 3 owl **4** gled, hawk, kite **5** buteo, eagle, glead, glede, harpy, saker **6** condor, elanet, elenet, falcon, musket, osprey, raptor **7** buzzard, goshawk, harrier, kestrel, stooper, vulture **8** caracara **9** accipiter, gyrfalcon, peregrine **11** accipitrine, lammergeier
bird of wonder/rebirth: 7 phoenix
carrion-eater: 4 aura **5** urubu **6** condor **7** buzzard, vulture
class: 4 Aves
combining form: 3 avi **4** orni **5** ornis **6** ornith **7** ornitho **8** ornithes
crow family: 3 daw, jay, kae **4** crow, rook **5** crake, raven **6** chough, corbie, magpie **7** corvine, jackdaw
duck family: 4 clee, coot, lory, smew, teal, wood **5** eider, goose **6** scoter **7** gadwall, mallard, Muscovy, pintail, pochard **8** baldpate, redshank, shoveler **9** merganser **10** bufflehead, canvasback
extinct: 3 auk, jib, moa **4** dodo, jibi, mamo **5** didus **8** Diatryma **9** aepyornis, apatornis, gastornis, hespornis, solitaire **11** archaeornis
flightless: 3 emu, ihi, moa **4** dodo, gorb, kagu, kiwi, rhea, weka **5** nandu **6** callow, kakapo, moorup, ratite, takahe **7** apteryx, horling, ostrich, peacock, penguin, roatelo **8** notornis **9** cassowary
game: 4 duck, guan, rail, sora, teal **5** brant, goose, quail, snipe **6** chukar, colima, grouse, pigeon, plover, turkey **7** bustard, chicken, flapper, gadwall, mallard, pintail, prairie, widgeon **8** baldpate, bobwhite, moorfowl, pheasant, shoveler, tragopan, wildfowl, woodcock **9** merganser, partridge, ptarmigan **10** canvasback
group of birds: 3 nye **4** bank, bevy, cast, nide, sord **5** aerie, brood, covey, drove, flock, plump **6** covert, flight, gaggle, litter, spring
largest: 7 ostrich **11** lammergeier
legendary: 3 roc **6** simurg **7** phoenix, simurgh **9** feng- huang, feng-hwang
loss of feathers: 7 molting
smallest: 11 hummingbird
nocturnal: 3 owl **5** cahow, owlet, potoo **7** bullbat, dorhawk **8** guacharo, nightjar **9** nighthawk, thickknee **10** goatsucker **11** nightingale
pet: 4 myna **5** mynah **6** canary, parrot, pigeon **8** cockatoo, lovebird, parakeet
plumage: 8 ptilosis
poultry: 3 hen **4** duck **5** goose **6** pigeon, turkey **7** chicken, rooster **8** pheasant **14** Cornish game hen
talking: 4 myna **5** mynah **6** parrot
wingless: 4 kiwi, weka **7** apteryx
young: 4 eyas, gull **5** chick, piper, poult, squab **6** gorlin, pullus **7** flapper, nestler **8** birdikin, nestling **9** fledgling
of Africa: 4 coly, fink, taha, tock **5** crane, paauw **6** barbet, bulbul, cuckoo, jabiru, quelea, whidah **7** courser, finfoot, marabou, ostrich, touraco **8** hornbill, oxpecker, parakeet, umbrette **9** beefeater, broadbill, francolin, napecrest, trochilus **10** hammerhead, weaverbird
of Antarctic/Arctic: 3 auk **4** gull, knot, skua, xema **5** brant, murre, rotch **6** dunlin, falcon, fulmar, jaeger, rotche **7** dovekey, dovekie, penguin **8** grayling **9** guillemot, gyrfalcon, ptarmigan **10** sheathbill
of Asia: 4 kora, myna, ruff, smew **5** mynah, pewit, pitta **6** bulbul, chukar, drongo, dunlin, hoopoe, linnet **7** boobook, courser, hill tit, lapwing, peacock, sirgang **8** accentor, dotterel, hornbill, leaf bird, parakeet, tragopan, wheatear **9** brambling, francolin, muted swan
of Australia: 3 emu **4** kahu, kiwi, koel, koil, lory **5** arara, galah, lowan,

pitta **6** drongo, leipoa **7** boobook, bustard, figbird, grinder, waybung **8** bellbird, bushlark, cockatoo, gang-gang, lorikeet, lyrebird, megapode, manucode, morepork, parakeet, platypus **9** bowerbird, cassowary, coachwhip, cockatiel, frogmouth, pardalote, thornbird **10** kookaburra

of Central America: 4 guan, ibis **5** booby, macaw **6** barbet, jabiru, quezal, toucan **7** bittern, cotinga, jacamar, quetzal, tinamou **8** curassow, puffbird, troupial

of Cuba: 6 trogon **8** tocororo **14** bee hummingbird

of England: 4 kite, rook **9** cormorant **11** carrion crow

of Europe: 3 dar, mag, mew, nun **4** clee, gled, mall, merl, pope, rook, ruff, shag, smew, wren **5** amsel, crake, egret, finch, glede, merle, ousel, ouzel, pewit, pipit, stilt, stork, swift, tarin, terek, whaup **6** cuckoo, dunlin, godwit, grouse, hoopoe, linnet, martin, merlin, missel, redleg, roller, siskin, thrush **7** bittern, bustard, jackdaw, kestrel, lapwing, martlet, ortolan, redwing, ruddock, skylark, sparrow, starnel, wagtail, wryneck **8** bee eater, blackcap, brantail, daychick, dotterel, garganey, nightjar, nuthatch, peesweep, redstart, reedling, starling, throstle, wheatear, whimbrel, whinchat, whinshat, woodcock **9** brambling, chaffinch, crossbill, field fare, gallinule, sheldrake, stonechat **10** chiffchaff, goatsucker, kingfisher, lammergeir, turtledove **11** lammergeier, nightingale, wallcreeper **12** capercaillie

of Hawaii: 2 io **3** ava, ioa, iwa, poe **4** nene, iiwi, koae, mamo, moho, omao **6** parson **7** frigate

of India: 4 baya, kala, koel, koil **5** sarus, shama **6** argala, bulbul, homrai, luggar **7** peacock **8** adjutant, amadavat, pheasant, tragopan **11** red hornbill

of Jamaica: 7 vervain

of Java: 7 sparrow **8** rice bird **9** fruit dove

of Madagascar: 6 drongo **7** anhinga, kirombo, roatelo

of Mexico: 6 jacana

of New Guinea: 9 cassowary **14** bird of paradise

of New Zealand: 3 ihi, kea, moa, poe, tui **4** huia, kaka, kaki, kiwi, koko, kuku, ruru, titi, weka **6** kakapo **7** apteryx **8** morepork, notornis

of North America: 3 ani, auk, tit **4** coot, crow, dove, ibis, lark, loon, pape, rook, sora, stib, swan, tern, wamp, wren **5** booby, brant, colin, crane, egret, finch, grebe, junco, murre, quail, robin, snipe, swift, veery, vireo **6** chebec, cuckoo, cur-

lew, darter, dunlin, fulmar, grouse, hagdon, magpie, martin, oriole, phoebe, plover, shrike, thrush, towhee, turkey, verdin, willet **7** anhinga, bittern, blue jay, catbird, flicker, goshawk, grackle, lapwing, pelican, sparrow, swallow, tanager, warbler **8** bluebird, bobolink, bobwhite, cardinal, grosbeak, killdeer, nuthatch, poorwill, starling, thrasher, titmouse, wheatear **9** blackbird, chickadee, crossbill, goldfinch, gyrfalcon, nighthawk, partridge, sandpiper, snakebird **10** bufflehead, kingfisher, meadowlark, woodpecker **11** hummingbird, mockingbird **12** whippoorwill

of South America: 3 ara, hia **4** anna, guan, jacu, loro, mitu, rhea, soco, toco, yeni **5** egret, macaw, potoo, sylph **6** barbet, chatja, chunga, cracid, jabiru, motmot, sappho, toucan **7** cariama, cotinga, hoatzin, jacamar, limpkin, manakin, seriema, tinamou, warrior **8** boatbill, caracara, curassow, guacharo, hoactzin, screamer, tapacolo, tapaculo, terutero, troupial **9** campanero, trumpeter **11** scarlet ibis

of West India: 3 ani **4** tody

Bird, Larry
sport: 10 basketball
position: 5 coach **7** forward
team: 13 Boston Celtics
from: 7 Indiana

Birdman of Alcatraz
director: 17 John Frankenheimer
cast: 10 Karl Malden **12** Edmond O'Brien, Neville Brand, Thelma Ritter **13** Burt Lancaster (Robert Stroud)

Bird of Paradise
constellation of: 4 Apus

Birds, The
author: 12 Aristophanes
character: 4 Iris **5** Meton **8** Basileia, Cinesias **9** Euelpides **10** King Tereus, Prometheus **12** Peithetairos

Birds, The
director: 15 Alfred Hitchcock
based on story by: 15 Daphne du Maurier
cast: 9 Rod Taylor **11** Tippi Hedren **12** Jessica Tandy **16** Suzanne Pleshette
setting: 10 California

Birds Fall Down, The
author: 15 Dame Rebecca West

Birkin, Rupert
character in: 11 Women in Love
author: 8 Lawrence

Birmingham
football team: 9 Stallions

Birmingham, Stephen
author of: 8 Our Crowd **11** The Grandees **14** The Right People **15** Life at the Dakota

Birnbaum, Nathan
real name of: 11 George Burns

birth 5 blood, start, stock **6** family, origin, source, strain **7** bearing, descent, genesis, lineage **8** ancestry, breeding, delivery **9** beginning, being born, emergence, genealogy, inception, parentage **10** background, beginnings, childbirth, derivation, extraction **11** confinement, parturition **12** commencement

Birth of a Nation, The
director: 10 D W Griffith
cast: 8 Mae Marsh **11** Lillian Gish **14** Henry B Walthall

Birth of Tragedy, The
author: 18 Friedrich Nietzsche

birthstones
January: 6 garnet
February: 8 amethyst
March: 6 jasper **10** aquamarine, bloodstone
April: 7 diamond **8** sapphire
May: 5 agate **7** emerald
June: 5 pearl **7** emerald **9** moonstone **11** alexandrite
July: 4 onyx, ruby **8** star ruby
August: 7 peridot **8** sardonyx **9** carnelian
September: 8 sapphire **10** chrysolite **12** star sapphire
October: 4 opal **5** beryl **10** aquamarine, tourmaline
November: 5 topaz
December: 4 ruby **6** zircon **9** turquoise

biscuit 3 bun **4** cake, roll **5** cooky, scone, wafer **6** bisque, cookie, muffin, parking, simnel **7** cracker, dogbone **8** hardtack, zwieback **9** pale-brown **10** crisp bread, quick bread **15** unglazed pottery

bisect 5 cross, split **8** cut in two **9** cut in half, intersect

bishop 4 abba, pope **5** punch **6** cleric, despot, priest **7** pontiff, prelate, primate **8** overseer **9** clergyman, patriarch **10** chesspiece, high priest
of Rome: 4 pope
Greek: 9 episkopos
means: 8 overseer
district: 7 diocese
headdress: 5 miter, mitre

Bismarck, Otto von
nickname: 14 Iron Chancellor
unified: 7 Germany
chancellor/minister for: 15 Emperor William I
policy: 12 "iron and blood"

bison 4 urus **6** wild ox, wisent **7** aurochs, buffalo
native to: 6 Europe **12** North America

Bissau
capital of: 12 Guinea-Bissau

Bisset, Jacqueline
real name: 22 Jacqueline Fraser Bis-

set
born: 7 England **9** Weybridge
roles: 5 Class **7** Airport, The Deep **11** Day for Night **12** Anna Karenina **16** The Mephisto Waltz **24** Murder on the Orient Express
bistro 3 bar **4** cafe **6** tavern **7** cabaret **9** nightclub **10** supper club
French: 9 estaminet
bit 3 dab **4** chip, drop, iota, mite, snip, whit **5** crumb, grain, pinch, scrap, shred, speck, spell, trace **6** dollop, moment, morsel, paring, trifle **7** droplet, granule, shaving, smidgen **8** fragment, particle **9** short time **10** short while, small piece, smithereen, sprinkling
type: 5 auger, drill **6** gimlet, wimble **7** bradawl **11** brace and bit
bitch 3 nag **5** botch, brood, cheat, fault, shrew, spoil, witch, whine **6** kvetch, virago **7** blunder, bungle, grouse **8** complain, harridan **9** complaint, female dog, termagant
bitchy 4 mean **5** catty, cruel, nasty **6** wicked **7** hateful, vicious **8** spiteful **9** heartless, malicious **10** backbiting, malevolent, vindictive
bite 3 bit, dab, dig, nip **4** gnaw, grip, snip **5** champ, crumb, gnash, prick, scrap, shred, smart, speck, sting, taste **6** morsel, nibble, pierce **7** eat into **8** mouthful, stinging, take hold **10** small piece, tooth wound **12** small portion
biting 5 harsh, sharp **6** bitter **7** caustic, cutting, mordant, nipping **8** piercing, scathing, smarting, stinging **9** sarcastic, trenchant, withering **12** sharp-tongued
bit player 5 extra **6** walk on **14** minor character
bitte 6 please **12** you're welcome **14** I beg your pardon
bitter 4 acid, mean, sour, tart **5** acrid, angry, cruel, harsh, sharp **6** biting, morose, severe, sullen **7** acerbic, caustic, crabbed, painful **8** grievous, piercing, scornful, smarting, spiteful, stinging, wretched **9** rancorous, resentful **10** astringent **11** distressing
bitterness 5 anger, scorn, spite **6** animus, rancor, spleen **7** ill will **8** acerbity, acrimony, sourness **9** animosity, harshness, hostility, malignity, sharpness **10** antagonism, malignancy **11** astringency **12** hard feelings, spitefulness **14** unpleasantness
bitters
type: 6 spirit
flavor: 6 orange **7** gentian
brand: 9 Angostura, Peychaud's
bivalve 4 clam **5** pinna **6** cockle, mussel, mollusk, scallop **8** mollusca **9** pelecypod **13** lamellibranch
bivouac 4 camp **5** tents **10** campground, encampment
bizarre 3 odd **5** kinky, kooky, queer,
weird **7** strange, unusual **8** freakish **9** fantastic, grotesque **10** outlandish

Bizet, Georges
real name: 26 Alexandre Cesar Leopold Bizet
born: 5 Paris **6** France
composer of: 4 Roma (suite) **6** Carmen, Patrie **8** Djamileh **11** Don Procopio, L'Arlesienne **12** Jeux d'enfants, Pearl Fishers **14** Children's Games **15** Ivan the Terrible **16** Le Docteur Miracle **18** The Fair Maid of Perth

Bjornson, Bjornstjerne
author of: 4 Arne **7** The King **8** Magnhild **9** A Happy Boy, In God's Way, Lame Hulda, The Editor **10** King Sverre **11** A Bankruptcy, The Bankrupt **12** Sigurd Slembe **14** Arnljot Gelline, Beyond Our Power **15** The Fisher Maiden, The Newly Married **16** Beyond Human Might, Sigurd the Bastard **17** Between the Battles **20** Mary Stuart in Scotland **24** Paul Lange and Tora Parsberg **27** Flags Are Flying in Town and Port

blab 3 rat **6** babble, tattle **7** blabber, prattle **9** tell tales **13** spill the beans **20** let the cat out of the bag
blabber 3 gab, gas, yak **4** blab, bull **5** prate **6** babble, drivel, gabble, gibber, gossip, jabber **7** blather, chatter, palaver, prattle, twaddle **8** blah-blah, chitchat, idle talk **9** jabbering **10** mumbo-jumbo **12** gobbledegook **14** chitter-chatter
blabbermouth 6 gabber, gossip, prater **7** blabber **8** bigmouth, busybody, gossiper, informer, jabberer, liverlip, prattler, quidnunc **9** chatterer **10** chatterbox, talebearer, tattletale **11** rumormonger **12** gossipmonger **13** scandalmonger
black, Black 3 bad, dim, jet **4** dark, evil, grim, inky **5** angry, ebony, murky, Negro, raven, sable **6** dismal, gloomy, somber, sullen, wicked **7** colored, furious, hostile, stygian, sunless, swarthy **8** moonless, coal-black, lightless, nefarious, unlighted **10** calamitous **11** dark-skinned, threatening **12** Afro-American **13** unilluminated

Black Arrow, The
author: 20 Robert Louis Stevenson
blackball 3 ban, bar, cut **4** snub **5** debar **6** banish, outlaw, reject **7** boycott, exclude, keep out, shut out **8** pass over, turndown **9** blacklist, ostracize, proscribe **11** vote against **12** coldshoulder **14** send to Coventry
black beast
French: 9 bete noire
blackberry 5 Rubus
variety: 4 Sand **5** Swamp **7** Cut-leaf, Pacific, Running, Sow-teat **9** Evergreen **13** Parsley-leaved **18** Evergreen thornless

Blackberry Winter
author: 12 Margaret Mead
blackbird 3 ani **4** crow, rook **5** raven, slave **6** thrush **7** cowbird, grackle, redwing **8** song bird **9** slave ship **11** slave trader **17** kidnapped islander, plantation laborer
kind: 9 red-winged **12** yellow-headed
family: 8 Turdidae **9** Icteridae
Blackboard Jungle, The
director: 13 Richard Brooks
based on novel by: 10 Evan Hunter
cast: 9 Glenn Ford, Vic Morrow **11** Anne Francis **12** Louis Calhern, Paul Mazursky, Richard Kiley **13** Sidney Poitier **14** Warner Anderson
Black Boy
author: 13 Richard Wright
blacken 5 libel, smear, stain, sully **6** befoul, darken, defame, defile, revile, vilify **7** slander, tarnish **8** besmirch, disgrace, dishonor **9** denigrate, discredit **10** stigmatize
Blackfoot, Blackfeet
language family: 9 Algonkian **10** Algonquian
tribe: 6 Bloods, Kainah, Piegan, Pikuni **7** Siksika
location: 6 Canada **7** Alberta, Montana **12** Saskatchewan
blackguard 3 cad, rat, SOB **5** knave, louse, rogue, scamp **6** rascal **7** bastard, villain **9** miscreant, scoundrel
blackhearted 4 base, vile **6** sinful, wicked **7** ignoble **10** despicable, evil-minded, villainous **11** scoundrelly **12** unprincipled **13** reprehensible
blackjack
also known as: 9 twenty-one
French: 9 vingt-et-un
play against: 6 dealer
additional card: 3 hit
Black Lamb and Grey Falcon
author: 15 Dame Rebecca West
Black Land, The *see* **5** Egypt
blackleg 7 cheater **8** swindler **9** trickster
blacklist 3 ban, bar **4** shun **5** debar **6** reject **7** exclude, lock out, shut out **8** preclude **9** blackball, ostracize
blacklisting 7 boycott **8** spurning **9** exclusion, ostracism, rejection **12** blackballing
black magic 7 sorcery **10** witchcraft
blackmail 5 force **6** coerce, extort, payoff **7** squeeze, tribute **8** threaten **9** extortion, hush money, shakedown
black mark 4 blot **5** stain **6** bruise **7** blemish, demerit **9** contusion
Blackmore, Richard Doddridge
author of: 10 Lorna Doone **11** Springhaven **13** The Maid of Sker
black mountain *see* **10** Montenegro
Black Narcissus
author: 11 Rumer Godden
director: 13 Michael Powell **17**

Emeric Pressburger
cast: 4 Sabu **11** David Farrar, Deborah Kerr, Jean Simmons
setting: 9 Himalayas
blackness 4 dark **5** gloom, shade **7** dimness **8** darkness
Blackpool, Stephen
character in: **9** Hard Times
author: **7** Dickens
Black Prince, The
author: **11** Iris Murdoch
Blackstone, Sir William
author of: **12** Commentaries (on the Laws of England)
Black Uhlan
nickname of: **12** Max Schmeling
Blackwater State
nickname of: **8** Nebraska
Blackwell, Elizabeth
first American: **11** woman doctor
bladder 3 bag, sac **4** cyst **5** pouch **7** blister, pustule, saccule, utricle **10** receptacle
blade 4 epee, leaf **5** frond, knife, razor, saber, sword **6** cutter, needle, switch **7** scalpel **10** sled runner **11** cutting edge, skate runner
blah 4 bosh, dull, flat, guff, so-so **5** bland, ho-hum, hooey, vapid **6** boring, bunkum, dreary, hot air, humbug **7** blather, eyewash, humdrum, nothing, tedious, twaddle **8** claptrap, lifeless, listless, nonsense **9** gibberish **10** balderdash, monotonous, pedestrian **11** uninspiring **13** characterless, unimaginative, uninteresting, unstimulating
Blaik, Earl H
sport: **8** football
position: **5** coach
team: **4** Army **9** Dartmouth
military rank: **7** colonel
Blair, Eric Arthur
real name of: **12** George Orwell
Blake, Robert
real name: **28** Michael James Vijencio Gubitosi
born: **8** Nutley NJ
roles: **7** Baretta, Our Gang **8** Red Ryder **11** In Cold Blood **12** Little Beaver **23** Tell Them Willie Boy Is Here **24** The Treasure of Sierra Madre
Blake, William
born: **6** London **7** England
author of: **6** Milton, Tiriel **9** Jerusalem **13** The Book of Thel **14** Prophetic Books **15** The Book of Urigen **16** Songs of Innocence **17** Songs of Experience **21** Little Lamb Who Made Thee **23** Marriage of Heaven and Hell, Tiger Tiger Burning Bright
artwork: **6** Milton **9** Book of Job, Jerusalem **11** The Four Zoas **12** Book of Urizen, Divine Comedy **16** Songs of Innocence **17** Songs of Experience **23** Marriage of Heaven and Hell

blamable 10 censurable, deplorable, punishable, reprovable **11** blameworthy **12** reproachable **13** reprehensible
Blamauer, Karoline
real name of: **10** Lotte Lenya
blame 4 onus **5** fault, guilt **6** accuse, burden, charge, rebuke **7** censure, condemn, reproof, reprove **8** reproach **9** castigate, criticism, criticize, liability **10** accusa- tion, disapprove **11** castigation, culpability **12** condemnation, denunciation, remonstrance **13** find fault with, recrimination **14** accountability, responsibility **15** hold responsible
blameless 5 clear **8** innocent, spotless **9** guiltless, not guilty, unspotted, unstained, unsullied, untainted **10** inculpable, not at fault, unblamable **11** unblemished, uncorrupted **13** unimpeachable **14** irreproachable, not responsible
blameless in life
Latin: **12** integer vitae
blame on 7 trace to **8** charge to **9** set down to **11** attribute to **14** lay at the door of
blameworthy 8 blamable **10** censurable, deplorable, punishable, reprovable **12** reproachable **13** reprehensible
blanch 4 fade **6** bleach, whiten **7** lighten **8** turn pale
blanched 3 wan **4** pale **5** ashen, faded **6** chalky, pallid **8** bleached **9** bloodless
bland 4 blah, calm, dull, even, flat, mild **5** balmy, quiet, vapid **6** benign, smooth **7** calming, humdrum, nothing, prosaic, tedious **8** moderate, peaceful, soothing, tiresome, tranquil **9** peaceable, temperate, unruffled **10** monotonous, unexciting, untroubled **11** uninspiring **13** nonirritating, uninteresting, unstimulating
blandish 4 coax, lure, urge **5** charm, tempt **6** cajole, entice, prompt **7** blarney, flatter, wheedle **8** inveigle, persuade
blandishment, blandishments 7 blarney, coaxing **8** cajolery, flattery **9** sweet talk, wheedling **12** ingratiation, inveiglement
Blandois, Monsieur
character in: **12** Little Dorrit
author: **7** Dickens
blank 3 gap **4** dull, idle, void **5** clean, clear, empty, inane, plain, space **6** futile, hollow, unused, vacant, vacuum, wasted **7** useless, vacancy, vacuous **8** unmarked **9** emptiness, fruitless, valueless, worthless **10** empty space, hollowness, profitless **11** meaningless, thoughtless, unrewarding **12** inexpressive **14** expressionless
blanket 4 coat, film **5** cloak, cover, quilt, throw **6** afghan, carpet, mantle,

veneer **7** coating, overlay **8** covering, coverlet **9** comforter
blare 4 honk, peal, roar **5** blast **6** bellow, scream **7** resound, trumpet
blarney 4 fibs, line **5** pitch, spiel **6** hot air **7** coaxing, fawning, snow job, stories **8** cajolery, flattery **9** hyperbole, wheedling **10** inveigling, overpraise, sweet words **12** exaggeration, honeyed words **13** blandishments, overstatement
blase 4 full **5** bored, jaded **6** gorged **7** glutted **9** apathetic, satisfied, saturated, surfeited, unexcited, unmovable **10** insouciant, nonchalant, spiritless, world-weary **11** indifferent, unconcerned **12** uninterested **14** unenthusiastic
Blasko, Bela
real name of: **10** Bela Lugosi
blaspheme 5 curse, swear **6** revile **7** profane **10** take in vain
blasphemous 7 godless, impious, profane, ungodly **10** irreverent **11** irreligious **12** sacrilegious
blasphemy 7 cursing, impiety **8** swearing **9** profanity, sacrilege **11** impiousness, irreverence, profanation
blast 4 bomb, boom, bore, gale, gust, honk, peal, roar, rush, toot **5** blare, bleat, burst, level, shell, surge **6** bellow, blow up, report, scream, shriek **7** explode, resound, torpedo **8** dynamite, eruption **9** discharge, explosion, loud noise **10** detonation **11** sound loudly
blasting material 3 TNT **8** dynamite **9** explosive
blatant 4 loud **5** cheap, clear, crass, crude, gross, harsh, noisy, overt **6** brazen, coarse, tawdry, vulgar **7** blaring, glar- ing, obvious, uncouth **8** flagrant, piercing, unsubtle **9** clamorous, deafening, obtrusive, offensive, prominent, tasteless, ungenteel, unrefined **10** indelicate, unpolished **11** conspicuous, ill-mannered, undignified **12** earsplitting, unmistakable
blather 4 stir **7** chatter, prattle **8** nonsense **9** commotion
Blatty, William P
author of: **11** The Exorcist
Blaue Reiter 10 Blue Riders
group of: **13** German artists
blaze 3 ray **4** beam, burn, fire, glow, rush **5** blast, burst, flame, flare, flash, glare, gleam, shine **6** flames **7** glisten, glitter, shimmer, torrent **8** eruption, outbreak, outburst, radiance **9** explosion **10** brightness, brilliance, effulgence **12** resplendence **13** conflagration
blazer 4 coat **6** jacket **12** sports jacket
blazing 3 hot **5** fiery, afire **6** firing, on fire **7** burning, flaming, flaring, glaring, glowing, intense, shining **8** burst-

ing, bleaming, shooting, shouting **9** brilliant

Blazing Saddles
director: **9** Mel Brooks
cast: **9** Mel Brooks **10** Alex Karras, Dom DeLuise, Gene Wilder **11** Slim Pickens **12** Harvey Korman, Madeline Kahn **13** Cleavon Little, John Hillerman **15** David Huddleston

blazon 5 blare, boast **7** trumpet **8** proclaim **10** coat of arms, make public **16** armorial bearings

blazonry 4 arms **5** crest **6** blazon **8** insignia **10** coat of arms **14** heraldic emblem **16** heraldic bearings

bleach 4 fade **6** blanch, whiten **7** lighten, wash out **8** make pale

bleak 3 icy, raw **4** bare, cold, grim **5** chill **6** barren, biting, bitter, dismal, dreary, frosty, gloomy, somber, wintry **7** nipping **8** desolate, piercing **9** cheerless, windswept **10** depressing, forbidding **11** distressing, unpromising **13** weather-beaten

Bleak House
author: **14** Charles Dickens
character: **2** Jo (the crossing sweeper) **4** Nemo **5** Guppy, Krook **6** Bucket, Guster **7** Snagsby **8** Ada Clare, Chadband **9** Miss Flite **10** Mrs Jellyby, Turveydrop **11** Dr Woodcourt, Lady Dedlock, Tulkinghorn **12** John Jarndyce **13** Captain Rawdon **14** Harold Skimpole **15** Esther Summerson, Richard Carstone **19** Sir Leicester Dedlock
satire of: **3** law **6** courts **8** chancery
case: **19** Jarndyce and Jarndyce

bleakness 8 bareness, grimness **10** barrenness, desolation, dreariness, gloominess **13** cheerlessness

bleat 3 baa, cry, maa **5** whine **7** whimper

bleb 6 bubble **7** blister

bleed 3 run, tap **4** leak, soak **5** drain, valve **6** fleece, suffer **7** diffuse, extract, **8** let blood **9** draw blood, sacrifice **10** hemorrhage, overcharge **12** phlebotomize

Blefuscu
fictional land in: **16** Gulliver's Travels
author: **5** Swift

blemish 3 mar, zit **4** blot, blur, flaw, mark, spot **5** spoil, stain, sully, taint **6** blotch, defect, smirch, smudge **7** tarnish **9** disfigure **12** imperfection **13** disfigurement

blend 3 mix **4** fuse **5** merge, unite **6** fusion, go well, merger, mingle **7** amalgam, combine, mixture **8** coalesce, compound, mergence, mingling **9** harmonize **10** amalgamate, complement, concoction **11** combination, incorporate, intermingle

bless 4 give **5** endow, favor, grace, guard, honor **6** anoint, bestow, hallow, oblige, ordain **7** baptize, benefit, protect, support **8** dedicate, sanctify **9** watch over **10** consecrate

blessed 4 holy **5** happy, lucky **6** adored, graced, joyful, joyous, sacred **7** endowed, favored, revered **8** blissful, hallowed **9** fortunate, venerated, wonderful **10** felicitous, sanctified **11** consecrated

Blessed Damozel, The
author: **20** Dante Gabriel Rossetti

blessedness 5 bliss **8** felicity **9** beatitude **11** saintliness

blessing 4 boon, gain, gift, good **5** favor, grace, leave **6** bounty, profit, regard **7** backing, benefit, consent, support **8** approval, sanction **9** advantage, hallowing **10** dedication, good wishes, invocation, permission **11** benediction, concurrence, good fortune **12** consecration, thanksgiving **14** sanctification

blessings 4 joys **5** gifts **6** favors **7** success **8** benefits, delights **10** advantages **11** good fortune

Blifil, Master
character in: **8** Tom Jones
author: **8** Fielding

Bligh, Captain William
character in: **17** Mutiny on the Bounty
authors: **4** Hall **8** Nordhoff

blight 3 pox, rot **4** harm, kill, ruin, rust **5** blast, crush, curse, decay, smash, spoil, wreck **6** cancer, canker, dry rot, fungus, injure, mildew, plague, thwart, wither **7** cripple, destroy, scourge, shrivel **8** demolish **9** frustrate **10** affliction, corruption, pestilence **12** plant disease **13** contamination

Blimber, Dr
character in: **12** Dombey and Son
author: **7** Dickens

blind 4 dull, ruse **5** cover, dodge, front, shade **6** hidden, insane, obtuse, screen **7** obscure, pretext, unaware **8** disguise, heedless, ignorant, mindless, unseeing **9** concealed, deception, senseless, sightless, sun shield, unfeeling, unknowing, unmindful, unnoticed **10** camouflage, insouciant, irrational, masquerade, neglectful, subterfuge, unthinking **11** inattentive, incognizant, indifferent, insensitive, smoke screen, unconcerned, unconscious, unobservant, unobserving **12** imperceptive, uncontrolled, undiscerning, uninterested, unnoticeable, unperceptive, unreasonable **13** unenlightened **14** uncontrollable **15** uncomprehending

blind alley 7 closure, dead-end, impasse **8** blockade, cul-de-sac, dead lock, no escape **9** hindrance, stone wall **10** impassable, standstill **11** obstruction

blinder 4 hood **5** blind, shade **6** screen **7** blinker **9** blindfold

blindfold 6 darken **7** bandage, blinder, obscure **8** covering heedless, reckless **11** strike blind

blind seer 8 Tiresias

blink 4 wink **5** flash, shine, waver **6** fal- ter, flinch, squint **7** flicker, glimmer, shimmer, sparkle, twinkle **9** nictitate, vacillate

blinker(s) 3 eye **6** peeper **7** blinder, flasher, goggles **8** black eye **13** warning signal

blintz, blintze 4 blin **5** crepe **6** blints **7** pancake

blip 3 dot, tap **4** spot **5** bleep, image **6** censor **7** replace

bliss 3 joy **4** glee **6** heaven, luxury **7** delight, ecstasy, rapture **8** gladness, paradise **9** cloud nine, happiness **10** exaltation, jubilation **12** exhilaration

blissful 5 happy **6** divine, joyful, joyous **7** blessed, sublime **8** beatific, ecstatic, glorious, heavenly **9** rapturous

blithe 3 gay **4** airy, glad **5** blind, happy, jolly, merry, sunny **6** casual, cheery, jaunty, jovial, joyous, lively **7** gleeful, radiant **8** carefree, careless, cheerful, debonair, exaltant, heedless, mirthful, uncaring **9** ebullient, sprightly, unfeeling, unmindful **10** blithesome, frolicking **11** indifferent, insensitive, thoughtless, unconcerned, unconscious **12** light-hearted **13** inconsiderate

Blithedale Romance, The
author: **18** Nathaniel Hawthorne

blithesome 3 gay **5** light, merry, sunny **6** breezy, jaunty, lively **7** buoyant **8** animated, carefree, cheerful **11** free and easy

Blixen-Finecke, Karen
real name of: **11** Isak Dinesen

blizzard 4 blow, gale **5** blast **6** flurry, squall **7** tempest **8** snowfall **9** snowstorm **11** winter storm

Blizzard State
nickname of: **11** South Dakota

bloat 5 swell **6** blow up, dilate, expand, puff up **7** balloon, distend, enlarge, inflate

blob 3 dab **4** daub, drop, glob, mass **7** globule, splotch

bloc 4 body, ring, wing **5** cabal, group, union **6** clique **7** combine, faction **8** alliance **9** coalition **11** combination

Bloch, Ernest
born: **6** Geneva **11** Switzerland
composer of: **7** Macbeth, Solomon **8** Baal Shem, Schelomo **13** Sacred Service **14** Avodath Hakdesh, Israel Symphony **16** American Symphony **19** Concerto Symphonique **20** Voice in the Wilderness

block 3 bar, jam **4** cube, form, halt, mold **5** brick, check, choke, shape **6**

hinder, impede, re-form, square, stop up, thwart **7** barrier, prevent, reshape **8** blockade, blockage, obstacle, obstruct **9** hindrance **10** impediment **11** obstruction **12** interference

blockade 3 bar, dam **4** dike **5** block, check, levee **6** hurdle **7** barrier, parapet, rampart **8** blockage, obstacle, obstruct, stockade, stoppage **9** barricade, hindrance, roadblock **10** checkpoint, earthworks, impediment **11** obstruction, restriction **13** fortification

blockage 3 jam **8** obstacle **9** hindrance **10** impediment **11** obstruction

blockhead 3 ass, oaf **4** clod, dolt, dope, fool, yutz **5** booby, dummy, dunce, idiot, klutz, moron, ninny **6** dum-dum, nitwit **7** fathead, half-wit, jackass **8** bonehead, dumb-dumb, dummkopf, imbecile, lunkhead, mushhead, numskull **9** harebrain, lamebrain, simpleton **10** chowerhead, dunderhead, nincompoop, noodlehead **12** featherbrain

block out 3 hew **5** carve **6** chisel, devise, map out, sculpt, sketch **7** outline **8** indicate **9** formulate

block up 3 bar **4** clog **6** stop up **7** brick up **9** barricade

blond, blonde 4 fair, gold, pale **5** light **6** flaxen, golden, yellow **8** light tan **9** yellowish **10** fair-haired **11** fair-skinned **12** light-colored

Blonde Bombshell
nickname of: **10** Jean Harlow

Blondell, Joan
husband: **8** Mike Todd **10** Dick Powell
born: **9** New York NY
roles: **8** The Champ **11** Blonde Crazy, Gold Diggers, The Blue Veil **14** Blondie Johnson, The Public Enemy **20** A Tree Grows in Brooklyn

Blondie
creator: **9** Chic Young
character:
 husband: **15** Dagwood Bumstead
 children: **6** Cookie **9** Alexander **12** Baby Dumpling
 boss: **6** Julius **9** Mr Dithers
 boss's wife: **4** Cora
 neighbor: **11** Herb Woodley **14** Tootsie Woodley
 dog: **5** Daisy

blood 4 gore **5** birth, stock **6** family, source, spirit, temper **7** descent, lineage, passion **8** ancestry, heritage, vitality **9** lifeblood **10** extraction, family line, vital fluid, vital force **11** temperament **13** consanguinity **14** vital principle

Blood, field of 8 Aceldama

bloodless 4 pale **5** ashen **6** anemic, pallid **7** insipid **8** blanched, lifeless, peaceful **9** colorless, deathlike, washed out

bloodline 6 family **8** ancestry, pedigree **9** genealogy **10** family tree

Bloodline
author: **13** Sidney Sheldon

bloodshed 4 gore **6** murder, pogrom **7** carnage, killing, slaying **8** butchery, massacre **9** blood bath, blood feud, slaughter **10** mass murder **12** bloodletting, manslaughter **15** spilling of blood

Bloodsmoor Romance, A
author: **15** Joyce Carol Oates

bloodstone
month: **5** March

Blood, Sweat and Tears
author: **17** Winston S Churchill

blood system
part: **5** blood, liver **6** spleen **9** lymph node **10** bone marrow

bloodthirsty 5 cruel **6** bloody, brutal, fierce, savage **7** bestial, demonic, inhuman, vicious **8** barbaric, demoniac, fiendish, pitiless, ruthless **9** atrocious, barbarous, cutthroat, heartless, homicidal, merciless, murdering, murderous **10** demoniacal, sanguinary **11** sanguineous

blood vessel 4 vein **5** aorta **6** artery **7** carotid **9** capillary
prefix: **5** angio

Blood Wedding
author: **19** Federico Garcia Lorca

bloody 3 red **4** gory, rude, vevy **5** cruel, lurid **6** cursed, damned **7** crimson, scarlet **8** bleeding **9** merciless, murderous **10** sanguinary

Bloody Shame see **10** Virgin Mary (drink)

bloom 3 bud **4** glow, grow, zest **5** flare, flush, prime, shine, vigor **6** beauty, flow- er, heyday, luster, sprout, thrive **7** blossom, burgeon, develop, prosper, succeed **8** fare well, flourish, fructify, radiance, rosiness, strength **9** bear fruit, flowerage, flowering, germinate **10** blossoming **11** florescence, flourishing

Bloom, Claire
real name: **11** Claire Blume
husband: **10** Rod Steiger
born: **6** London **7** England
roles: **6** Charly **9** Limelight **10** Richard III **15** Look Back in Anger **26** The Spy Who Came in from the Cold

Bloom, Leopold and Molly
characters in: **7** Ulysses
author: **5** Joyce

bloomers 8 knickers, trousers **9** plus fours, underwear **10** underpants **15** knickerbockers

blooming 3 fit **4** pert, rosy **5** utter **6** abloom, robust, strong **7** healthy **8** vigorous **9** healthful **10** blossoming **11** flourishing **12** efflorescent, fit as a fiddle **15** picture of health

blooper 4 goof, slip **5** boner, botch, er-

ror, fluff, gaffe, lapse **6** bobble, booboo, slip-up **7** blunder, mistake, screwup

blossom 4 grow **5** bloom **6** flower, thrive **7** burgeon, develop **8** flourish, progress

Blossomed miraculously 9 Aaron's rod

blossoming 5 bloom **8** blooming, thriving **9** flowering **10** burgeoning, developing **11** florescence, flourishing

blot 3 dry **4** flaw, mark, spot **5** smear, stain, taint **6** absorb, blotch, remove, smirch, smudge, soak up, stigma, take up **7** bad mark, blemish, splotch **8** besmirch **13** discoloration

blotch 4 blot, mark, spot **7** splotch

Blot on the 'Scutcheon, The
author: **14** Robert Browning

blot out 5 erase **6** remove, rub out **7** abolish, eclipse, expunge **9** eliminate, eradicate **10** obliterate

blotting out 7 eclipse, erasing **9** expunging, wiping out **11** eradicating, eradication **12** annihilation, obliterating, obliteration **13** overshadowing

blouse 4 coat **5** drape, tunic, shirt, smock **6** camise, billow **7** blouson **8** casaquin

blow 3 box, hit, jab, pop **4** bang, bash, belt, cuff, gale, gust, honk, jolt, play, puff, sock, toot, wind **5** blast, burst, clout, crack, knock, punch, shock, smack, sound, storm, thump, upset, whack **6** exhale, rebuff, squall, wallop **7** breathe, explode, tempest, tragedy, whistle **8** calamity, disaster, expel air, reversal **9** detriment, windstorm **10** affliction, misfortune **11** catastrophe **14** disappointment

blow from the hand
French: **10** coup de main

blowhard 6 gascon **7** boaster, bragger, egotist **8** braggart **9** big talker **11** braggadocio

blow of mercy
French: **11** coup de grace

blow out 5 burst **7** rupture **10** extinguish

blowsy, blowzy 5 messy **6** frowzy, mussed, sloppy, untidy **7** unkempt **10** disarrayed, disheveled, disordered, disorderly, in disorder **11** disarranged

blow up 5 bloat, burst **6** billow, dilate, expand **7** balloon, distend, enlarge, explode, inflate, puff out **8** dynamite, swell out **12** lose one's cool **14** lose one's temper

Blowup
director: **21** Michelangelo Antonioni
cast: **8** Verushka **10** Sarah Miles **13** David Hemmings **15** Vanessa Redgrave

blowy 5 gusty, windy **6** breezy **7** squally **8** blustery

blubber 3 cry, fat, sob 4 bawl, flab, wail, weep 6 boohoo

Blubber
  author: 9 Judy Blume

bludgeon 3 bat, hit 4 club 5 billy, clout, stick 6 cudgel 7 clobber 9 billy-club, truncheon

blue 3 low, sad 4 aqua, down, navy 5 azure 6 bluish, cobalt, gloomy, indigo, morose 7 doleful 8 cerulean, dejected, downcast, sapphire 9 depressed, turquoise 10 aquamarine, despondent, melancholy 11 down-hearted, lapis lazuli, ultra-marine 12 disconsolate 14 down in the dumps, down in the mouth

Blue Angel, The
  director: 17 Josef von Sternberg
  based on novel by: 12 Heinrich Mann
  cast: 10 Kurt Gerron 12 Emil Jannings 15 Marlene Dietrich (Lola-Lola)
  song: 18 Falling in Love Again

Bluebeard
  characteristic: 9 many wives

bluebell 9 Mertensia 18 Mertensia Virginica 21 Campanula rotundifolia
  variety: 7 English, Spanish 8 Virginia 10 Australian, California 11 Clanwilliam

blueberry 9 Vaccinium
  variety: 3 Low 4 Male 5 Swamp 7 Lowbush, Sourtop, Western 8 Creeping, Elliott's, Highbush, Low sweet 9 Late sweet, Rabbit-eye 10 Velvet-leaf 13 Black highbush

blueblood 4 peer 5 noble 8 nobleman 9 patrician, socialite 10 aristocrat, noblewoman 14 peer of the realm

blue-blooded 5 noble, regal, royal 6 titled 7 courtly 8 highbred, wellborn 9 patrician 10 upper-class 12 aristocratic, of royal blood

blue bloods 5 elite, toffs 8 nobility 9 haut monde 10 patricians 11 aristocracy, high society 14 creme de la creme

bluegrass 3 Poa
  varieties: 3 Big 4 Wood 5 Rough, Texas 6 Annual, Canada 7 Bulbous, English 8 Kentucky, Sandberg 10 Rough-stalk

Bluegrass State
  nickname of: 8 Kentucky

Blue Hen State
  nickname of: 8 Delaware

Blue Knight, The
  author: 14 Joseph Wambaugh

Blue Law State
  nickname of: 11 Connecticut

blue-pencil 3 cut 4 edit, trim 6 censor, cut out, delete, digest, reduce 7 abridge, shorten 8 boil down, condense, pare down 9 expurgate 10 abbreviate

blueprint 4 plan 5 chart 6 design, scheme 7 diagram 9 schematic

Blue Riders
  German: 11 Blaue Reiter
  group of: 7 artists

blues 5 dumps 8 doldrums 10 depression, low spirits, melancholy 11 despondency

bluestocking
  French: 7 bas bleu

bluff 3 lie 4 bank, bold, crag, curt, dupe, fake, fool, hoax, liar, open, peak, sham 5 blunt, boast, cliff, faker, frank, fraud, ridge, rough 6 abrupt, candid, crusty, delude, direct, humbug 7 bluffer, boaster, brusque, deceive, fake out, mislead, pretend 8 bragging, headland, headlong, palisade, pretense 9 bamboozle, deception, idle boast, outspoken, precipice, pretender 10 escarpment, forthright, promontory, subterfuge 11 braggadocio, counterfeit, plainspoken 13 unceremonious, straightforward

bluffer 5 bluff, faker, fraud, phony 6 humbug 9 pretender

bluish 7 off-blue 12 somewhat blue

Blume, Claire
  real name of: 11 Claire Bloom

Blume, Judy
  author of: 5 Wifey 6 Deenie 7 Blubber, Forever 19 Then Again Maybe I Won't 22 It's Not the End of the World 26 Tales of a Fourth Grade Nothing 27 Are You There God? It's Me Margaret

Blumenbach, Johann Friedrich
  field: 7 anatomy 10 physiology
  nationality: 6 German
  father of: 20 physical anthropology

blunder 4 goof, slip 5 boner, error, gaffe 6 boo-boo, bumble, bungle, slip up 7 faux pas, mistake, stagger, stumble 8 flounder 9 gaucherie 11 impropriety, make a booboo 12 indiscretion

blunt 4 curt, dull, numb, open 5 frank, rough, thick 6 abrupt, benumb, candid, deaden, dulled, soften, weaken 7 brusque, lighten, stupefy 8 edgeless, explicit, mitigate, moderate, tactless 9 outspoken, unpointed 10 to the point 11 insensitive, unsharpened 15 straightforward

bluntness 6 candor 10 directness 14 forthrightness 15 plainspokenness

blur 3 dim, fog, run 4 blot, haze, veil 5 bedim, befog, cloud, smear 6 blotch, darken, smudge, spread 7 becloud, obscure, splotch 9 confusion, obscurity

blurb 2 ad 4 rave, spot 5 brief 10 commercial 13 advertisement

blurred 3 dim 5 vague 6 blurry 7 smeared 10 ill-defined, indefinite, indistinct

blurt out 4 blab, sing 7 confess, divulge, let slip 8 give away 9 come clean

blush 5 color, flush 6 redden 7 grow red, turn red 8 rosy tint 9 reddening

blushing 3 coy, red 4 rosy 5 fresh, timid 6 demure, modest 7 colored, bashful, flushed, glowing 8 blooming, sheepish 9 rosaceous 10 embarrassed 11 flourishing

bluster 4 brag, crow, rant 5 bluff, boast, bully, gloat, noise, storm 7 bombast, bravado, crowing, protest, ranting, swagger 8 boasting, gloating, threaten 9 noisy talk 10 swaggering 14 boisterousness

blustery 5 blowy, gusty, windy 6 breezy 7 squally

Blythe, Ethel Mae
  real name of: 14 Ethel Barrymore

Blythe, John
  real name of: 13 John Barrymore

Blythe, Lionel
  real name of: 15 Lionel Barrymore

Boadicea
  Latin name: 8 Boudicca
  queen of: 5 Iceni
  husband: 10 Prasutagus
  ruled: 7 Norfolk (England)
  fought: 6 Romans
  died: 7 suicide

Boanerges
  means: 13 sons of thunder
  name given to: 4 John 5 James

boar
  group of: 7 sounder

board 3 bed 4 deal, feed, food, slat 5 enter, get on, house, lodge, meals, panel, plank, put up 6 batten, billet, embark, go onto 7 council, quarter 8 tribunal 9 clapboard, directors 10 daily meals

board game 4 Clue, Life, ludo 5 chess 7 Othello 8 checkers, cribbage, dominoes, draughts, fanorona, Monopoly, Scrabble 9 Alquerque 10 backgammon 14 Trivial Pursuit 15 Chinese checkers
  Egyptian: 5 Senat
  Korean: 5 Nyout, Pa-tok
  Indian: 7 pachisi 8 parchesi, shatranj 9 ashtapada 10 shaturanga
  Japanese: 2 Go 3 I-go 5 Sho-gi
  Chinese: 6 Ma-jong, wei-ch'i 7 Mah-jong, Ma-jongg 8 Mah-jongg
  Swedish: 5 tablut

boast 4 brag, crow, have 5 vaunt 6 flaunt 7 contain, exhibit, possess, show off, talk big 15 blow one's own horn

boaster 6 gascon 7 bragger, egotist 8 blowhard, braggart 9 big talker 11 braggadocio

boastful 5 cocky 7 crowing, pompous, swollen 8 bragging, cocksure, inflated, puffed up, vaunting 9 conceited 11 braggadocio, exaggerated, pretentious **12** vainglorious

boastfulness 7 conceit, egotism **8** bragging **9** cockiness, immodesty, pomposity, vainglory **10** self-praise **11** braggadocio **12** cocksureness

boastful soldier
Latin: **14** miles gloriosus

boat 4 ship **5** craft **6** vessel

Boaz
father: **5** Salma **6** Salmon
wife: **4** Ruth
son: **4** Obed
kinsman of: **5** Naomi **9** Elimelech

bob 3 cut, hop, nod **4** clip, crop, dock, duck, leap, trim **5** dance, shear **6** bounce **7** shorten

Bobadill
character in: **19** Every Man in His Humour
author: **6** Jonson

bobbin 3 pin **4** coil, cord, reel **5** quill, spool **6** piping **7** ratchet, spindle, torchon **8** cylinder

bobcat 3 cat **4** lynx **7** wildcat

Bob Cummings Show, The
later name: **11** Love That Bob
character: **10** Bob Collins **14** Chuck MacDonald **15** Charmaine (Shultzy) Shultz **17** Margaret MacDonald
cast: **9** Ann B Davis **11** Bob Cummings **13** Dwayne Hickman **14** Rosemary DeCamp

Bob Newhart Show, The
character: **12** Elliot Carlin, Emily Hartley, Howard Borden **13** Jerry Robinson, Robert (Bob) Hartley **20** Carol Kester Bondurant
cast: **9** Bill Daily, Jack Riley **11** Peter Bonerz **13** Marcia Wallace **16** Suzanne Pleshette

Boccaccio, Giovanni
author of: **10** Filostrato, Filocopo **11** Life of Dante **12** The Decameron

Boccherini, Luigi
born: **5** Italy, Lucca
composer of: **8** La Divina **9** The Aviary **10** Clementina **11** L'Uccelliera

Boccioni, Umberto
born: **5** Italy **12** Reggio Emilia **16** Reggio di Calabria
artwork: **10** Elasticity **12** The City Rises **15** Charge of Lancers **18** Dynamism of a Cyclist, The Forces of a Street **21** Fusion of Head and Window **30** Unique Forms of Continuity in Space

Bock, Hier
field: **6** botany
nationality: **6** German
founded: **12** modern botany
classified: **6** plants
author of: **15** Neu Kreutterbuch

Bocklin, Arnold
born: **5** Basel **7** Germany

artwork: **13** Pan in the Reeds **16** The Isle of the Dead

Bod see **5** Tibet

bode 4 omen **5** augur **6** herald **7** betoken, ominate, point to, portend, predict, presage, signify **8** forecast, foretell, precurse **9** foreshadow, prefigure

bodega 9 warehouse **12** grocery store

bodice 3 top **5** stays, waist **6** bolero, corset, girdle **7** corsage **8** camisole, corselet **9** stomacher **10** underwaist

bodily 8 corporal, physical

Bodily Harm
author: **14** Margaret Atwood

bodkin 3 awl **4** pick, tool **5** auger, borer, drill, point, probe **6** dagger, lancet, needle, reamer **7** hair pin, piercer **8** puncheon, stiletto

body 3 mob **4** bloc, bulk, form, mass **5** being, build, force, frame, group, shape, stiff, thing, torso, trunk **6** corpse, corpus, figure, league, person, throng **7** cadaver, carcass, combine, council, faction, remains, society **8** assembly, cohesion, congress, deceased, main part, majority, physique, quantity **9** coalition, multitude, stiffness, thickness **10** federation **11** brotherhood, consistency **13** confederation

Body and Soul
director: **12** Robert Rossen
cast: **10** Anne Revere **11** Hazel Brooks, Lilli Palmer **12** John Garfield **13** William Conrad

bodybuilder 12 Charles Atlas **20** Arnold Schwarzenegger

Boeotus
father: **8** Poseidon
mother: **4** Arne

Boer, Boor 6 farmer **9** Afrikaner
language: **9** Afrikaans
ancestry: **5** Dutch
inhabitants of: **9** Transvaal **11** South Africa **15** Orange Free State

Boffin
character in: **15** Our Mutual Friend
author: **7** Dickens

bog 3 fen **4** mire, sink **5** marsh, swamp **6** morass **7** be stuck **8** quagmire, wetlands **9** marshland, swampland

Bogaerde, Derek Van den
real name of: **11** Dirk Bogarde

Bogarde, Dirk
real name: **19** Derek Van den Bogaerde
born: **6** London **7** England **9** Hampstead
roles: **6** Victim **7** Darling **10** The Servant **13** Death in Venice **14** Song Without End, The Night Porter **16** A Tale of Two Cities

Bogart, Humphrey
nickname: **5** Bogie
wife: **12** Lauren Bacall
born: **9** New York NY

roles: **8** Key Largo **10** Casablanca, High Sierra **11** The Big Sleep **14** The Caine Mutiny **15** The African Queen (Oscar) **16** The Maltese Falcon, To Have and Have Not **18** The Petrified Forest **27** The Treasure of the Sierra Madre

Bogdanovich, Peter
director of: **4** Mask **7** Targets, The Trip **9** Paper Moon, Saint Jack **10** Texasville **14** They all Laughed, Picture Windows **18** The Last Picture Show
roles: **7** Targets, The Trip **9** Saint Jack

bogey
term in: **4** golf
song: **18** Colonel Bogey's March

boggle 3 shy **4** balk, muff **5** botch, demure, hover, waver **6** bungle, shrink, wobble **7** blunder, stumble **8** flounder, frighten, hesitate, hold back **9** overwhelm **11** make a mess of

boggy 3 wet **4** soft **5** foggy, mossy, soggy **6** marshy, spongy, swampy **7** squashy

Bogie
nickname of: **14** Humphrey Bogart

Bogota
capital of: **8** Colombia

bogus 4 fake, sham **5** dummy, false, phony **6** ersatz, forged, pseudo **7** feigned, pretend **8** spurious **9** imitation, simulated, synthetic **10** artificial, fraudulent **11** counterfeit, make-believe

Boheme, La
also: **12** Bohemian Life
opera by: **7** Puccini
character: **4** Mimi **7** Colline, Musetta, Rodolfo **8** Marcello **9** Schaunard

bohemian, Bohemian 6 hippie **7** beatnik **10** unorthodox **13** nonconformist **14** unconventional

Bohr, Niels
field: **7** physics
nationality: **6** Danish
developed: **8** atom bomb **13** quantum theory, uranium theory

Boiardo, Matteo Maria
author of: **17** Orlando Innamorato

boil 4 brew, burn, foam, fume, rage, rant, rave, sore, stew, toss **5** chafe, churn, froth, storm **6** bubble, fester, quiver, seethe, simmer, sizzle, well up **7** abscess, bristle, parboil, pustule, smolder **8** furuncle **9** carbuncle, fulminate

boil down 3 cut **6** reduce **7** abridge, cut down, shorten **8** condense, contract **10** abbreviate

boiler 6 copper, geyser, heater, kettle **7** alembic, caldron, furnace

Boilermaker, the
nickname of: **20** James Jackson Jeffries

boisterous 4 loud, wild **5** noisy, rowdy **6** unruly **9** clamorous, out-of-hand **10** disorderly, uproarious **12** obstreperous, uncontrolled, unrestrained

boite, boite de nuit 7 cabaret **9** nightclub

Bojer, Johan
  author of: 12 Folk by the Sea, The Emigrants **14** The Great Hunger, The Power of a Lie **16** Last of the Vikings

bold 3 hot **4** loud, rude **5** brash, brave, fiery, fresh, saucy, vivid **6** brazen, cheeky, daring, flashy, heroic **7** defiant, forward, valiant **8** colorful, creative, fearless, impudent, insolent, intrepid, spirited, stalwart, striking, unafraid, valorous **9** audacious, daredevil, dauntless **10** courageous **11** eye-catching, imaginative, impertinent, indomitable, lionhearted, unshrinking **12** stouthearted **13** adventuresome

boldfaced 5 brash, saucy **6** brassy, brazen **7** forward **8** immodest, impudent, insolent **9** audacious, barefaced, shameless, unabashed

boldness 4 grit **5** nerve, pluck, spunk **6** daring, mettle **7** bravery, courage **8** audacity **9** brashness, hardihood **10** brazenness **13** audaciousness, determination, self- assurance **14** courageousness **15** adventurousness

Bolger, Ray
  born: 12 Dorchester MA
  roles: 9 Scarecrow **10** On Your Toes **13** The Wizard of Oz, Where's Charley

Bolivia
  named for: 12 Simon Bolivar
  capital:
    administrative: 5 La Paz
    legal: 5 Sucre
  largest city: 5 La Paz
  others: 3 Ivo **4** Icla, Itau, Mojo, Saya, Yaco, Yato, Yura **5** Cliza, Llica, Oruro, Quime, Uyuni, Zongo **6** Guaqui, Potosi, Tiraja, Tupiza **8** Pulacayo **9** Santa Cruz **10** Chuquisaca, Cochabamba **11** Vallegrande, Villa Montes
  school: 6 Xavier **8** St Andrew **12** San Francisco
  division: 6 Valles **7** Oriente, Valleys **8** Montanas **9** Altiplano
  measure: 6 league **7** celemin
  monetary unit: 7 centavo **13** peso boliviano
  weight: 5 libra, marco
  lake: 5 Poopo **7** Allagas, Coipasa, Rogagua **8** Titicaca **10** Desaguader
  mountain: 4 Jara **5** Andes, Cusco, Cuzco **6** Pupuya, Sajama, Sorata, Sunsas **7** Illampu **8** Illimani, Mururata, Sansimon, Santiago, Zapaleri **12** Eastern Range, Western Range **18** Cordillera Oriental **20** Cordillera Occidental

  highest point: 8 Ancohuma
  river: 4 Beni, Yata **5** Abuna, Lauca, Orton **6** Blanco, Ichilo, Itenez, Madidi, Mamore, Mizque, Yacuma **7** Guapore, Machupo **8** Inambari, Itonamas **9** Pilcomayo, Rio Grande, San Miguel **11** Desaguadero, Madre de Dios
  physical features:
    lowlands: 6 Llanos
    plateau: 9 Altiplano
    swamp: 6 Izozog
    valley: 5 Yunga
    volcano: 7 Ollague
  people: 6 Aymara **7** mestizo, Quechua
    author: 7 Mendoza **8** Arguedas **11** Costa du Rels
    leader: 5 Busch, Sucre **6** Candia, Ortuno, Zamora **7** Bolivar **9** Melgarejo, Paz Zamora, Santa Cruz **10** Barrientos, Estenssoro
  language: 6 Aymara **7** Quechua, Spanish
  religion: 13 Roman Catholic
  place:
    church: 9 St Francis, St Michael **10** San Lorenzo
    monument: 11 La Coronilla
    ruins: 10 Tiahuanaco
    tower: 6 Chulpa
  feature:
    animal: 5 llama **6** alpaca, vicuna
    bar/club: 7 boliche
    boat: 5 balsa
    dance/song: 5 cueca **7** huainos, pasillo **8** morenada **9** taquirari **10** palla-palla **11** cacharpayas, wakatokonis
    devil dance: 8 Diablado
    guitar: 8 charango
    skirt: 7 pollera
    wind instrument: 4 kena, sicu **5** erque, quena, tarka **6** pututu **9** pinquillo
  food:
    chicken dish: 14 picante de pollo
    corn: 4 mote
    corn drink: 3 api **14** chicha taratena
    dish: 11 plato paceno **14** sajta de gallina
    dried meat: 7 charque
    pancakes: 7 bunulos
    potato: 5 chuno

Bolkonsky, Andrei
  character in: 11 War and Peace
  author: 7 Tolstoy

Boll, Heinrich
  author of: 8 The Clown **12** The Safety Net **18** Absent Without Leave **21** Group Portrait With Lady **27** The Lost Honor of Katharina Blum **28** Missing Persons and Other Essays

bolster 3 aid **4** help **5** add to, brace **6** assist, cradle, hold up, pillow, prop up, uphold **7** cushion, shore up, support, sustain **8** buttress, maintain, shoulder **9** reinforce **10** strengthen

bolster one's spirits 5 cheer **7** cheer up, comfort, hearten **8** inspirit **9** buoy one up, encourage

bolt 3 bar, fly, peg, pin, rod, run **4** dart, dash, flee, gulp, jump, leap, lock, roll, rush, tear, wolf **5** bound, brand, catch, dowel, flash, hurry, latch, rivet, scoot, shaft, speed **6** fasten, gobble, hasten, hurtle, length, secure, spring, sprint, stroke **8** fastener **12** swallow whole

bolt down 4 wolf **5** scarf **6** devour, gobble **8** gulp down

bomb 3 dud, egg **4** bust, fail, flop, mine **5** lemon **6** fiasco, fizzle, turkey **7** bombard, grenade, failure, washout

bombard 5 beset, hound, shell, worry **6** assail, attack, batter, harass, pepper, pester, strafe **7** assault, barrage, besiege **8** fire upon **9** cannonade

bombardment 5 blitz, siege **7** air raid, assault, barrage, bombing **10** blitzkrieg

bombast 3 pad **4** puff, rant **6** cotton **7** bluster, fustian, palaver **8** boasting, flummery, rhapsody, tall talk, verbiage **9** bavardage **10** balderdash **12** braggadocio, exaggeration **13** magniloquence, overstatement **14** grandiloquence **17** sesquipedalianism

bombastic 5 tumid, windy, wordy **6** padded, turgid **7** pompous, verbose **8** inflated **12** magniloquent **13** grandiloquent

Bombay
  area: 7 Trombay **8** Salsette **12** Bombay Island
  called: 14 Gateway to India
  creek: 7 Bassein
  landmark: 9 High Court **13** Taj Mahal Hotel **14** Gateway of India **16** Victoria Terminus **17** Rajabai Clock Tower
  rock formation: 10 Deccan Trap
  sea: 7 Arabian

Bona Dea
  also: 5 Fauna
  origin: 5 Roman
  goddess of: 8 chastity **9** fertility
  worshipped by: 5 women
  father: 6 Faunus
  brother: 6 Faunus
  husband: 6 Faunus

bona fide 4 real, true **5** legal **6** actual, honest, lawful **7** genuine, sincere **9** authentic, honorable **10** legitimate **11** in good faith

bon ami 5 lover **8** cleanser. **10** good friend

bonanza 8 gold mine, windfall

Bonanza
  character: 3 Ben **4** Adam, Hoss **5** Candy **7** Hop Sing **9** Little Joe
  family: 10 Cartwright
  cast: 10 Dan Blocker **11** David Ca-

nary, Lorne Greene **13** Michael Landon, Victor Sen Yung **14** Pernell Roberts
ranch: **9** Ponderosa
Bonanza State
nickname of: **7** Montana
bon appetit 14 hearty appetite
Bonario
character in: **7** Volpone
author: **6** Jonson
bonbon 5 candy, sweet **7** fondant **9** sweetmeat **10** confection, sugar candy **13** confectionery **14** chocolate cream
bond, bonds 3 tie **4** cord, knot, link, rope **5** irons, scrip, union **6** chains, pledge **7** compact, fetters, promise **8** affinity, bindings, manacles, security, shackles **9** agreement, guarantee, handcuffs **10** allegiance, attachment, connection, fastenings, obligation **11** certificate, stipulation
Bond, James
actor: **10** Roger Moore **11** Sean Connery **12** Peter Sellers **13** George Lazenby, Pierce Brosnan, Timothy Dalton
appears in: **4** Dr No **9** Golden Eye, Moonraker, Octopussy **10** Goldfinger **11** Thunderball **12** A View To A Kill **13** Licence to Kill, Live and Let Die **15** For Your Eyes Only **16** The Spy Who Loved Me, You Only Live Twice **17** Tomorrow Never Dies **18** Diamonds Are Forever, From Russia with Love, Never Say Never Again, The Living Daylights **22** The Man with the Golden Gun **26** On Her Majesty's Secret Service
author: **10** Ian Fleming
drink: **12** vodka martini **16** shaken not stirred
employer: **3** MI-6 **20** British Secret Service
foe: **7** Blofeld, SPECTRE
office staff: **1** M, Q **14** Miss Moneypenny
university: **6** Oxford
wife: **5** Tracy
bondage 4 yoke **6** chains **7** fetters, serfdom, slavery **8** shackles **9** captivity, servitude, vassalage **11** enslavement
bone
comprise: **8** skeleton
contain: **6** marrow **9** cartilage **11** blood vessel
fitted together by: **5** joint
held by: **8** ligament
pulled by: **6** muscle
specific: **3** rib **4** ulna **5** femur, skull, tibia **6** carpal, fibula, pelvis, radius, sacrum, tarsal **7** humerus, patella, scapula, sternum **8** clavicle, vertebra **9** vertebrae
bone chilling 3 icy **4** cold **5** harsh, sharp **6** arctic, biting, bitter, frigid **7**

cutting, glacial **8** piercing, stinging **11** penetrating **15** teeth-chattering
bonehead 3 ass **4** clod, dolt, fool **5** booby, dunce, idiot, moron, ninny **6** dimwit, nitwit **7** fathead, half-wit **8** dumb- dumb, imbecile, lunkhead **9** blockhead, lamebrain, numbskull **10** dunderhead, nincompoop **11** chowderhead
boner 4 goof, slip **5** error **6** boo-boo, slip-up **7** blooper, blunder, mistake
boneyard 4 dump **7** ossuary **8** Boot Hill, cemetery, junkyard **9** graveyard **10** churchyard **12** burial ground **13** burying ground
Bonheur, Rosa
real name: **19** Marie Rosalie Bonheur
born: **6** France **8** Bordeaux
artwork: **12** The Horse Fair **23** Ploughing in the Nivernais
bonjour 5 hello **7** good day
Bonjour Tristesse
author: **14** Francoise Sagan
bon marche 7 bargain
bon mot 4 quip **7** epigram **9** witticism
Bonn
former capital of: **11** West Germany
landmark: **10** Bundeshaus **11** Munsterkerk
museum: **18** Ludwig van Beethoven
river: **5** Rhine
Roman fort: **15** Castra Bonnensia
Bonnard, Pierre
born: **6** France **16** Fontenay-aux-Roses
artwork: **8** Intimist, Luncheon **9** The Review **13** Nude in the Bath, The Open Window, Women with a Dog **14** After the Shower, Farm at Le Cannet **16** The Breakfast Room **17** The Terrasse Family **22** Figure Before a Fireplace
bonne amie 5 lover **6** friend **10** good friend
bonne nuit 9 good night
bonnet 3 cap, hat **4** cowl, hood, sail **5** cover, toque **7** chapeau, commode **8** headgear **9** headdress
Bonnie and Clyde
director: **10** Arthur Penn
cast: **11** Faye Dunaway (Bonnie Parker), Gene Hackman **12** Warren Beatty (Clyde Barrow) **15** Michael J Pollard
bonny 4 fair **6** comely, lovely, pretty, seemly **7** winning, winsome **8** engaging, fetching, handsome, pleasing **9** beautiful, exquisite, ravishing **10** attractive
bon soir 9 good night **11** good evening
bonus 4 gift **5** prize **6** bounty, reward **7** benefit, premium **8** dividend, gratuity **10** honorarium
Bonus Eventus
also: **7** Eventus
origin: **5** Roman

god of: **4** luck **10** prosperity **11** agriculture
bon vivant 7 epicure, gourmet **8** gourmand, sybarite **10** gastronome
bony 4 lean **5** gaunt, lanky, spare **6** skinny **7** angular, scrawny **11** full of bones **12** skin-and-bones
boo 3 pan **4** hiss **5** taunt **6** deride, heckle, revile **7** catcall **8** ridicule **9** criticize, shout down **11** give the bird **16** give the raspberry
boo-boo 4 goof, slip **5** boner, error **6** slip-up **7** blunder, mistake
boobtube 2 TV **3** box **5** telly **8** idiot box **13** television set
booby 4 bird, dope, fool **5** dummy, dunce, idiot, moron, ninny **6** dimwit, gannet, nitwit **7** fathead, halfwit **8** bonehead, dumb-dumb, imbecile, lunkhead, numskull **9** blockhead, lamebrain, simpleton **10** nincompoop **11** chowderhead
Booby, Lady
character in: **13** Joseph Andrews
author: **8** Fielding
boodle 4 loot, swag **5** booty, bribe, crowd, graft, group **7** plunder **10** collection **11** stolen goods
Boog
nickname of: **10** John Powell
boohoo 3 cry, sob **4** bawl, weep **7** blubber **9** shed tears
book 4 bill, file, list, note, opus, post, tome **5** album, enter, index, slate **6** accuse, charge, engage, enroll, indict, insert, line up, record, tablet, volume **7** catalog, procure, program, put down, reserve **8** mark down, notebook, register, schedule, treatise **9** bound work, write down **10** arrange for **11** publication, written work **16** make reservations
bookish 7 erudite, learned, stilted **8** academic, educated, informed, literary, pedantic, studious, well-read **9** scholarly **11** pedagogical, impractical **12** intellectual
bookkeeper 5 clerk **7** auditor **10** accountant **11** comptroller
booklet 5 folio **7** leaflet, program **8** brochure, circular, pamphlet
Book of Common Prayer
author: **10** Joan Didion
Book of Lights, The
author: **10** Chaim Potok
Book of Manuel
author: **13** Julio Cortazar
Book of Odes
author: **9** Confucius
Book of psalms 12 psalter
Book of Sand, The
author: **15** Jorge Luis Borges
Book of the Duchess, The
author: **15** Geoffrey Chaucer
boom 3 bar **4** bang, beam, gain, grow,

push, roar, spar **5** blast, boost, shaft, spurt **6** growth, rumble, thrive, thrust, upturn **7** advance, develop, prosper, thunder, upsurge **8** flourish, increase **9** expansion, good times

Boom Boom
  nickname of: **15** Bernie Geoffrion

boomerang 5 kalie, kiley, kylie, wango **6** atlatl, recoil **7** rebound, womerah, woomera **8** backfire, ricochet, trombush **9** bound back, solitaire **10** projectile

Boomer State
  nickname of: **8** Oklahoma

boon 3 fun, gay **4** gift **5** favor, jolly, merry **6** kindly **7** benefit, bequest **8** blessing, donation, offering, pleasant **9** advantage, congenial, convivial, endowment **11** full of cheer, good-natured

boon companion 3 pal **4** chum **5** buddy, crony **6** friend **7** comrade **8** confrere, intimate **9** confidant **10** bosom buddy

boondocks 4 bush, veld **6** Podunk, sticks **7** boonies, country, outback **8** frontier **9** backwater, backwoods, provinces **10** hinterland **11** backcountry, countryside **12** squaresville **13** nowheresville **14** wide open spaces

Boone, Richard
  born: **12** Los Angeles CA
  roles: **5** Medic **6** Hombre **7** Paladin **8** The Alamo **11** The Shootist **12** Ten Wanted Men, The Desert Fox **17** Have Gun Will Travel

boonies 6 sticks **7** country **9** backwoods, boondocks, provinces **10** hinterland **11** countryside

boor 3 oaf **4** hick, lout, rube **5** brute, churl, yokel **6** rustic **7** bumpkin, hayseed, peasant **9** vulgarian **10** clodhopper, philistine **11** guttersnipe

boorish 4 rude **5** crude **6** coarse, gauche, oafish, rustic, vulgar **7** loutish, uncouth **9** unrefined **10** unpolished **11** peasantlike

boorishness 8 rudeness **9** surliness, vulgarity **10** bad manners, coarseness, incivility, oafishness **12** churlishness, impoliteness

boost 4 hike, laud, lift, plug, push, rise **5** add to, extol, heave, hoist, pitch, raise, shove, steal, swipe **6** expand, foster, free ad, growth, pickup, praise, upturn, urge on **7** acclaim, advance, develop, elevate, enlarge, forward, further, improve, nurture, promote, root for, support, sustain, upsurge, upswing **8** addition, applause, good word, increase, propound, shoplift **9** expansion, incre- ment, promotion **10** compliment, give a leg up, stick up for **11** development, enlargement, improvement, speak well of

boot
  French: **9** chaussure

booth 3 pen **4** coop, nook, tent **5** hutch, stall, stand, table **7** counter **9** cubbyhole, enclosure **11** compartment

Booth, Shirley
  real name: **15** Thelma Booth Ford
  born: **9** New York NY
  roles: **5** Hazel **13** The Matchmaker **19** Come Back Little Sheba (Oscar)

bootleg 5 hooch **7** illegal, illicit **8** unlawful **9** moonshine **12** football play

bootless 6 futile **7** useless **11** ineffective, ineffectual **12** unproductive, unprofitable

bootlick 4 fawn **5** toady **6** cringe, grovel **7** flatter, truckle

bootmaker 7 cobbler **9** shoemaker

booty 4 gain, loot **5** prize **6** boodle, spoils **7** pillage, plunder, takings **8** pickings, winnings

booze 4 bout, soak **5** drink, hooch, spree **6** guzzle, liquor, tipple **7** alcohol, spirits, swizzle **8** cocktail **10** intoxicant **14** drink like a fish
  type: **3** gin, rum, rye **4** beer, wine **5** vodka **6** scotch **7** bourbon, whiskey

boozer 3 sot **4** lush **5** drunk, souse, toper **7** tippler **8** drunkard **9** alcoholic, inebriate **11** hard drinker

bordello, bordel 4 stew **5** house **6** bagnio **7** brothel **8** cathouse **10** bawdy house, fancy house, whorehouse **13** sporting house **14** house of ill fame **16** house of ill repute **19** house of prostitution

border 3 hem, rim **4** abut, bind, brim, curb, edge, join, line, pale, trim **5** brink, flank, frame, limit, skirt, touch, verge **6** adjoin, fringe, margin **8** befringe, be next to, boundary, frontier, outskirt **9** extremity, perimeter, periphery **13** circumference

borderline 4 open **5** vague **7** halfway, inexact, obscure, unclear **8** marginal **9** ambiguous, equivocal, uncertain, undecided, unsettled **10** ambivalent, indefinite **11** indefinable, problematic **13** indeterminate

bore 4 drag, drip, sink, tire **5** drill, drive, weary **6** burrow, pierce, tunnel **7** caliber, exhaust, fatigue, wear out **8** gouge out **9** hollow out **10** wet blanket **14** inside diameter

Boreal
  pertaining to: **6** Boreas

Boreas
  origin: **5** Greek
  personifies: **9** north wind
  father: **8** Astraeus
  mother: **3** Eos
  twin sons: **5** Zetes **6** Calais
  daughter: **6** Chione **9** Cleopatra

bored 5 jaded **7** wearied **12** discontented, uninterested

boredom 5 ennui **6** tedium **8** doldrums, dullness, monotony **9** weariness **11** tediousness

Borges, Jorge Luis
  author of: **8** The Aleph **10** Labyrinths **11** Dreamtigers **13** The Book of Sand **18** A Personal Anthology, In Praise of Darkness **19** Doctor Brodie's Report, Fervor of Buenos Aires **25** A Universal History of Infamy
  nationality: **9** Argentina

Borghild
  origin: **12** Scandinavian
  mentioned in: **8** Volsunga
  husband: **7** Sigmund

Borgia, Alfonso de 16 Pope Callistus III

Borgia, Rodrigo de 15 Pope Alexander VI

Borglum, (John) Gutzon
  born: **10** Bear Lake ID
  artwork: **7** Lincoln **18** Mt Rushmore Memorial, The Mares of Diomedes

Borgnine, Ernest
  real name: **18** Ermes Effron Borgnine
  wife: **11** Ethel Merman
  born: **8** Hamden CT
  roles: **5** Marty (Oscar) **8** Barabbas **11** McHale's Navy **12** The Wild Bunch **13** The Dirty Dozen **17** Bad Day at Black Rock **18** From Here to Eternity **20** The Poseidon Adventure

boring 4 dull, flat **5** stale **6** tiring **7** humdrum, insipid, tedious **8** tiresome **9** wearisome **10** monotonous, unexciting **11** repetitious **13** uninteresting

boring tool 3 bit **5** auger, drill **11** brace and bit

Borinquen see **10** Puerto Rico

Boriquen, Borinquen
  language family: **8** Arawakan
  location: **10** Puerto Rico
  related to: **5** Taino

Boris Godunov
  author: **16** Alexander Pushkin
  opera by: **10** Mussorgsky **12** Shostakovich **14** Rimsky Korsakov
  role: **4** czar, tsar
  character: **6** Dmitri, Feodor, Maryna **7** Gregory, Grigory **8** Basmanov, Otrepyev

born 6 innate **7** natural **9** delivered, intuitive **12** brought forth

Born, Max
  field: **7** physics
  nationality: **7** British
  worked on: **13** quantum theory
  awarded: **10** Nobel Prize

borne 6 afloat, braved **7** carried, endured **9** put up with, tolerated **11** gone through, went through **12** given birth to

Borneo
  other name: **10** Kalimantan
  largest city: **12** Bandjermasin
  others: **5** Kumai **6** Sambas, Sampit **7** Malinau, Pagatan, Sanggau, Sintang, Tarakan **8** Ketapang **9** Pontianak **10** Balikpapan
  division of island:

independent: 6 Brunei
Malaysian state: 5 Sabah **7** Sarawak
part of Indonesia: 10 Kalimantan
measure: 7 gantang
weight: 4 para **6** chapah
mountain: 4 Iran, Raja **5** Saran **6** Kapuas, Muller, Nijaan, Tebang **8** Kinibalu, Schwaner
highest point: 8 Kinabalu
river: 4 Arut, Iwan **5** Bahau, Berau, Kajan, Padas, Pawan **6** Barito, Kapuas, Rajang, Sebuku **7** Kahajan, Mahakam, Mendawi **8** Pembuang
sea: 4 Java, Sulu **7** Celebes **10** South China
physical feature:
  bay: 5 Adang, Kumai **6** Sampit
  cape: 3 Aru **4** Datu **5** Lojar **6** Puting, Sambar **7** Selatan
  port: 4 Miri **5** Balik, Papan **6** Brunei **9** Pontianak **12** Bandjermasin
  strait: 8 Macassar
people: 4 Iban **5** Bukat, Dajak, Dayak, Dusan, Malay, Punan **6** Illano **7** Bakatan, Chinese, Illanum
language: 5 Malay **6** tribal **7** Chinese, English
religion: 5 Islam **7** animism **12** Christianity
feature:
  tree: 5 kapor, kapur **7** billian

Born Yesterday
director: 11 George Cukor
cast: 12 Judy Holliday **13** William Holden **17** Broderick Crawford
Oscar for: 7 actress (Holliday)

Borodin, Alexander
born: 6 Russia **12** St Petersburg
member of: 7 The Five
composer of: 8 Bogatyri **10** Prince Igor **25** In the Steppes of Central Asia

boron
chemical symbol: 1 B
compound: 5 borax

borough 4 burg, town **5** borgo, shire **6** county, parish **7** village **8** district, precinct, province, township **12** municipality
  of New York City: 5 Kings, Bronx **6** Queens **8** Brooklyn, Richmond **9** Manhattan **12** Staten Island

Borromini, Francesco
architect of: 10 San Carlino **17** Palazzo Falconieri **20** Sant' Ivo della Sapienza **23** Oratory of San Filippo Neri **24** Collegio di Propaganda Fide **26** San Carlo alle Quattro Fontane (Rome)

borrow 3 get, use **4** copy, take **5** filch, steal, usurp **6** obtain, pilfer, pirate **7** acquire **10** commandeer, plagiarize, take on loan **11** appropriate

Borrow, George Henry
author of: 8 Lavengro **9** Romany Rye, Wild Wales **10** The Zincali **15** The Bible in Spain

Bors, Sir
character in: 16 Arthurian romance

Bosch, Hieronymus
real name: 13 Jerome van Aken **14** Jerome van Aeken **17** Jeroen Anthoiszoon
artwork: 7 Hay-Wain **11** Ship of Fools **14** The Crucifixion **19** Adoration of the Kings **21** The Crowning with Thorns **26** The Garden of Earthly Delights

bosh 3 rot **4** bunk **6** bunkum, drivel **7** twaddle **8** claptrap, nonsense, tommyrot **10** balderdash, tomfoolery **11** foolishness **16** stuff and nonsense

bosky 5 bushy, drunk, shaded, tipsy, treed **6** wooded

Bosnia-Herzegovina
capital/largest city: 8 Sarajevo
others: 4 Neum **5** Tuzla **6** Citluk, Kupres, Lenica, Mostar **8** Prijedor **9** Banja Luka, Bijeljina **10** Srebrenica **12** Bosanski Brod, Siroki Brijeg
head of state: 9 president
monetary unit: 5 dinar
mountain: 11 Dinaric Alps
river: 3 Una **4** Sava **5** Bosna, Drina, Vrbas **7** Neretva
sea: 8 Adriatic
people: 4 Serb **5** Croat **6** Muslim **8** Yugoslav
language: 13 Serbo Croatian
religion: 11 Sunni Muslim **15** Serbian Orthodox

bosom 4 bust, core, dear, soul **5** chest, close, heart, midst **6** breast, center, spirit **7** beloved, nucleus **8** intimate **9** cherished **11** inner circle

bosom buddy 4 chum **5** crony **6** cohort **7** best pal, comrade **8** alter ego, intimate, sidekick **9** companion, confidant **10** best friend

bosomy 5 busty, buxom **6** zaftig **11** full-figured **13** large- breasted

boss 4 head, push **5** chief, order **6** leader, master **7** command, foreman, kingpin, manager **8** employer **9** big cheese, executive **10** supervisor **13** administrator **14** superintendent

bossy 3 cow **9** imperious **10** commanding, tyrannical **11** dictatorial, domineering

Boston
airport: 5 Logan
area: 7 Back Bay **10** Bunker Hill, Fenway Park **11** Faneuil Hall **14** Kennedy Library, Old North Church
baseball team: 6 Red Sox
basketball team: 7 Celtics
dish: 10 baked beans
hockey team: 6 Bruins
landmark: 10 Beacon Hill
leader: 7 Brahmin
nickname: 8 Bean town
river: 7 Charles

Bostonians, The
author: 10 Henry James

Boston Strong Boy
nickname of: 13 John L Sullivan

Boswell, James
author of: 22 The Life of Samuel Johnson

botanist
American: 6 Barton, Carver, Torrey **7** Bartram
Austrian: 6 Mendel
Dutch: 7 DeVries
German: 4 Bock, Cohn
Scottish: 5 Brown
Swedish: 8 Linnaeus
Swiss: 6 Bauhin

botch 3 err, mar **4** blow, fail, flop, flub, goof, hash, mess, muff, ruin **5** spoil **6** bungle, foul up, fumble **7** blunder, butcher, failure, louse up **8** butchery **9** mismanage **11** make a mess of

bother 3 ado, irk, nag, tax, try, vex **4** care, drag, fret, fuss, load, onus, stir **5** annoy, harry, trial, upset, worry **6** dismay, flurry, harass, pester, racket, rumpus, strain, stress, tumult **7** attempt, disturb, problem, trouble **8** disquiet, distress, hardship, headache, irritate, nuisance, vexation **9** aggravate, commotion, hindrance **10** affliction, difficulty, impediment, irritation **11** aggravation, disturbance, encumbrance **12** make an effort **13** inconvenience, pain in the neck **14** responsibility

bothersome 6 taxing, vexing **8** annoying **9** worrisome **10** disturbing **11** aggravating, disquieting, distressing, troublesome **12** inconvenient

Botswana
other name: 12 Bechuanaland
capital/largest city: 8 Gaborone **9** Gaberones
others: 5 Kanye, Orapa, Tsane **6** Serowe **7** Lobatse, Lobotsi, Mochudi, Palapye, Thamaga **10** Molepolole **11** Francistown, Selebi-Pikwe
monetary unit: 4 pula, rand
lake: 3 Dow, Xau **5** Ngami
highest point: 11 Tsodilo Hill
river: 4 Nata, Okwa **5** Chobe, Nosob **6** Cuando, Molopo, Shashi **7** Cubango, Limpopo **8** Botletle, Okovango **9** Okovanggo
physical feature:
  desert: 8 Kalahari
  salt pans: 10 Makarikari
  swamp: 8 Okavango
people: 5 Bantu **6** Tswana **7** Bakatla, Bakwena, Bushman **8** Bamalete, Baralong, Batawana, Batlokwa, Botswana **10** Bamangwato **11** Bangwaketse
language: 5 Bantu, Click **6** Tswana **7** English, Khoisan **8** Setswana

religion: 7 animism **10** Protestant **12** Christianity

Botticelli, Sandro
real name: 30 Alessandro di Mariano dei Filipepi
born: 5 Italy **8** Florence
artwork: 12 Birth of Venus **14** Mystic Nativity **16** Calumny of Apelles **18** Adoration of the Magi **22** Pallas Subduing a Centaur **25** The Madonna of the Magnificat

bottle 3 jar **4** vial **5** flask, phial **6** carafe, flagon, vessel **7** canteen

bottleneck 3 bar, jam **4** clog, stop **5** block **6** detour **7** barrier, embolus **8** blockage, embolism, gridlock, obstacle, stoppage, thrombus **10** congestion, impediment, infarction **11** costiveness, obstruction

bottom 3 can **4** base, core, foot, gist, root, rump, seat, sole **5** basis, belly, cause, fanny, heart, lower **6** center, deeper, depths, ground, lowest, origin, source, spring **7** deepest, essence **8** backside, buttocks, pedestal, riverbed **9** beginning, fundament, principle, rudiments, substance, underpart, underside **10** foundation, mainspring, wellspring **12** quintessence

Bottom
character in: 21 A Midsummer Night's Dream
author: 11 Shakespeare
turned into: 3 ass

bottomless 4 deep **7** abysmal **8** profound **11** measureless **12** immeasurable, unfathomable

Boucher, Francois
born: 5 Paris **6** France
artwork: 9 The Rising **13** Madame Boucher, Reclining Girl **16** Evening Landscape, Rinaldo and Armida, The Toilet of Venus **17** Chinese Tapestries, The Triumph of Venus **18** The Setting of the Sun

boudoir 7 bedroom **10** bedchamber **12** dressing room

bough 4 limb **6** branch

bougie 3 dip, wax **5** light, taper **6** candle, cierge, tallow

boulder, bowlder 3 nob **4** crag, knob, rock **5** block, stone **6** gibber **7** dornick **8** megalith

boulevard 6 avenue **7** parkway **9** concourse

bouleversement 7 turmoil **9** confusion, upsetting **11** overturning

bounce 3 bob, hop, pep **4** bump, life **5** bound, thump, verve, vigor **6** energy, jounce, recoil, spirit **7** rebound **8** dynamism, ricochet, vitality, vivacity **9** animation **10** liveliness

bouncing 3 big **4** full **5** jolly, large, lusty, plump **6** chubby, lively, robust, strong **7** healthy **8** animated, vigorous **12** in good health

bound 3 bob, orb, rim **4** area, edge, jump, leap, line, mark, pale, romp, sure, tied **5** dance, fated, hedge, limit, orbit, range, realm, vault **6** border, bounce, define, domain, doomed, forced, fringe, gambol, liable, prance, region, spring, tied up **7** certain, compass, confine, covered, encased, enclosed, flounce, going to, in bonds, limited, obliged, rebound, secured, trussed, wrapped **8** beholden, boundary, confined, destined, district, encircle, fastened, province, required, resolute, resolved, surround, tethered **9** bailiwick, committed, demarcate, extremity, periphery, territory **10** determined, restrained **11** demarcation **12** circumscribe

boundary 3 rim **4** edge, line, pale **6** border, margin **7** barrier **8** frontier, landmark **9** extremity, periphery **11** demarcation **12** dividing line

boundary line 4 edge **5** bound **6** border **8** sideline

bounder 3 cad, rat **4** heel **5** knave, louse, rogue **6** rascal, rotter **7** caitiff, dastard, villain **9** scoundrel **10** blackguard

Bounderby, Mr
character in: 9 Hard Times
author: 7 Dickens

boundless 4 vast **7** endless, immense **8** infinite, unending **9** limitless, perpetual, unbounded, unlimited **10** without end **11** everlasting, measureless **12** immeasurable, incalculable, unrestricted **13** inexhaustible

bounteous, bountiful 4 free, full, rich **5** ample, large **6** lavish **7** copious, liberal, profuse, teeming **8** abundant, generous, prolific **9** abounding, plenteous, plentiful, unsparing **10** beneficent, benevolent, charitable, munificent, unstinting **11** magnanimous, overflowing

Bountiful, Lady
character in: 17 The Beaux Stratagem
author: 8 Farquhar

bountifulness 10 liberality, generosity **11** benevolence, magnanimity, munificence **14** charitableness **15** humanitarianism

bounty 3 aid **4** gift, help **5** bonus, favor, grant **6** giving, reward **7** charity, present, tribute **8** bestowal, donation, gratuity **9** endowment **10** almsgiving, assistance, generosity, liberality, recompense **11** benefaction, benevolence, munificence **12** contribution, philanthropy **14** charitableness, openhandedness

bouquet 4 odor **5** aroma, scent, spray **7** essence, garland, nosegay, perfume **9** fragrance **11** boutonniere

bouquet garni
ingredient: 5 basil, thyme **6** celery,

savory **7** bay leaf, chervil, parsley **8** rosemary, tarragon

bourbon
variety of: 7 whiskey
origin: 7 America
ingredient: 4 corn
type: 7 blended **8** straight
drink: 9 Mint Julep **10** Boston Sour **11** John Collins **12** Old Fashioned
with Benedictine: 9 Twin Hills
with brandy and Benedictine: 13 Brighton Punch
with Cointreau: 10 Temptation
with rum: 14 Artillery Punch
with sloe gin: 9 Black Hawk
with Southern Comfort: 14 Blended Comfort
with triple sec: 10 Chapel Hill
with vermouth: 9 Allegheny

bourgeois 6 square **7** Babbitt, burgher **8** commoner, ordinary **11** middle-class **12** conventional **13** unimaginative

Bourgeois Gentleman, The
author: 7 Moliere
character: 6 Lucile, Nicole **7** Cleonte, Dorante **8** Coville, Dorimene **14** Madame Jourdain **16** Monsieur Jourdain

Bourget, Charles Joseph Paul
author of: 11 The Disciple **12** A Cruel Enigma **14** The Night Cometh

Bourgh, Lady Catherine de
character in: 17 Pride and Prejudice
author: 6 Austen

Bourjaily, Vance
author of: 11 The Violated **14** The End of My Life **18** Brill Among the Ruins **22** Now Playing at Canterbury

Bourne Identity, The
author: 12 Robert Ludlum

bout 4 fray, term, tilt, turn **5** brush, clash, cycle, fight, match, set-to, siege, spell, spree **6** affair, battle, course, period, series **7** contest, go-round, scuffle, session, tourney **8** conflict, interval, skirmish, struggle **9** encounter **10** contention, engagement **11** boxing match, embroilment

boutonniere 4 posy **7** nosegay **16** buttonhole flower

bow 3 arc **4** bend, knot, prow, stem **5** agree, curve, defer, front, stoop, yield **6** archer, comply, curtsy, give in, kowtow, relent, salaam, submit, weapon **7** concede, succumb, crescent **9** acquiesce, genuflect, surrender **10** capitulate, forward end **12** genuflection, knuckle under

Bow, Clara
nickname: 6 It Girl
born: 10 Brooklyn NY
roles: 2 It **7** Mantrap **12** The Wild Party

bowdlerize 6 censor **9** expurgate **10** blue-pencil

bow down 5 yield **6** give in, submit **9**

surrender **10** capitulate **12** knuckle under

bowed 4 bent **6** arched, curved, nodded **7** hunched, stooped

bowels 3 gut, pit **4** core, guts, womb **5** abyss, belly, bosom, heart, midst **6** depths, hollow, vitals **7** innards, insides, stomach, viscera **8** entrails, interior, recesses **10** intestines **11** vital organs **13** innermost part

Bowen, Elizabeth
author of: **8** Eva Trout, The Hotel **10** To the North **11** Bowen's Court, Little Girls, The Cat Jumps **12** A World of Love **15** The Heat of the Day, The House in Paris **18** The Death of the Heart

Bowen's Court
author: **14** Elizabeth Bowen

bower 4 jack, joker, nook **5** arbor **6** alcove, anchor, pandal **7** bedroom, chamber, cottage, enclose, retreat, sanctum, shelter **8** dwelling, snuggery

Bowie, David
real name: **16** David Robert Jones
born: **6** London **7** England
roles: **9** Cat People, Labyrinth, The Hunger **20** The Man Who Fell to Earth **24** Merry Christmas Mr Lawrence
wife: **4** Iman
Personae: **11** Aladdin Sane **13** Ziggy Stardust

Bowie Land, Bowie State
nickname of: **8** Arkansas

bowl 4 boat **5** arena, basin **6** cavity, hollow, tureen, valley, vessel **7** dishful, helping, portion, stadium **8** coliseum, deep dish **9** container, porringer **10** depression, receptacle **12** amphitheater

bowler 11 Earl Anthony

bowling
variation: **7** tenpins **8** duckpins, fivepins **10** candlepins
term: **4** miss **5** frame, spare, split **6** strike **10** gutterball
perfect score: **12** three hundred

bow-shape 3 arc **4** arch, bend **5** curve **9** curvature

bow to 5 yield **6** give in, give up, submit **9** acquiesce

box 3 bat, hit, rap **4** belt, cuff, slap, spar **5** booth, caddy, chest, crate, fight, punch, stall, whack **6** buffet, carton, coffer, strike, thwack **8** thumping **9** container **10** receptacle **11** compartment **13** exchange blows

boxer 7 Max Baer **8** Joe Louis **9** Mike Tyson **10** Barney Ross, Gene Tunney, Joe Frazier, Joe Walcott, Leon Spinks **11** Archie Moore, Jack Dempsey, Jack Johnson, Jake LaMotta, Larry Holmes, Muhammad Ali, Sonny Liston **12** Benny Leonard, James Corbett, John Sullivan, Johnny Dundee, Max Schmeling, Mickey Walker, Primo Carnera,

Roberto Duran, Thomas Hearns **13** Carmen Basilio, Ezzard Charles, George Foreman, Hector Camacho, James Jeffries, Rocky Graziano, Rocky Marciano **14** Bob Fitzsimmons, Floyd Patterson, Henry Armstrong **15** Maxie Rosenbloom, Sugar Ray Leonard **16** Evander Holyfield, Sugar Ray Robinson

boy 3 lad **5** youth **8** man child **9** male child, stripling, youngster
French: **6** garcon

Boy
character in: **6** Tarzan
author: **9** Burroughs

boycott 5 spurn **6** reject **7** exclude **8** spurning **9** blackball, blacklist, exclusion, ostracism, ostracize, rejection **12** blackballing, blacklisting

Boyd, James
author of: **5** Drums **8** Long Hunt **9** Roll River **10** Marching On

Boyd, William
born: **13** Hendrysburg OH
roles: **15** Hopalong Cassidy

Boyer, Charles
born: **6** Figeac, France
roles: **7** Algiers **8** Conquest, Gaslight **10** Back Street **11** Lost Horizon **16** The Garden of Allah **19** All This and Heaven Too

boyfriend 3 man **4** beau, date **5** flame, lover, swain, wooer **6** escort, fellow, old man, squire, steady, suitor **7** admirer, beloved, Don Juan **8** cavalier, Lothario, paramour, truelove, young man **9** companion, inamorato **10** sweetheart **15** gentleman caller

boyish 5 boyey, fresh **6** callow, tender **7** boylike, puerile **8** childish, immature, innocent, juvenile, youthful **9** childlike **10** sophomoric

Boylan, Blazes
character in: **7** Ulysses
author: **5** Joyce

Boyle, Robert
field: **9** chemistry
nationality: **7** British
father of: **9** chemistry
advocated: **20** experimental approach
established: **9** Boyle's Law

boylike 5 fresh, young **6** boyish, callow **7** puerile **8** childish, immature, innocent, juvenile, youthful **9** childlike

Boys Town
director: **12** Norman Taurog
cast: **9** Henry Hull **12** Mickey Rooney, Spencer Tracy (Father Flanagan)
Oscar for: **5** actor (Tracy)
sequel: **13** Men of Boys Town
near: **5** Omaha

Boy Wonder
nickname of: **5** Robin **6** Mel Ott

brace 3 duo **4** pair, prop, stay **5** shore, strut, truss **6** bracer, couple, hold up, prop up, steady **7** bolster, bracket,

fortify, prepare, shore up, support, sustain, twosome **8** buttress **9** reinforce, stanchion **10** strengthen **13** reinforcement

bracelet 6 armlet, bangle

bracer 10 stiff drink, stimulator, wristguard **11** invigorator **12** strengthener, strong drink

Brachiosaurus
type: **8** dinosaur, sauropod
location: **10** East Africa **12** United States
period: **8** Jurassic

bracing 8 arousing, reviving **10** energizing, fortifying, refreshing **11** restorative, stimulating **12** exhilarating, invigorating **13** strengthening

Brack, Judge
character in: **11** Hedda Gabler
author: **5** Ibsen

bracken 4 fern **5** brake, brush, ferns **10** underbrush **11** undergrowth

bracket 4 prop, rank, stay **5** brace, class, group, range, shore, strut, truss **6** prop up, status **7** shore up, support **8** category, classify, division, grouping **9** designate, stanchion **10** categorize **11** designation **14** classification

brackish 4 salt **5** briny, salty **6** saline

Bracknell, Lady Augusta
character in: **27** The Importance of Being Earnest
author: **5** Wilde

bract 4 leaf

Bradbury, Ray
author of: **13** Dandelion Wine, Fahrenheit 451 **17** The Illustrated Man **20** The Martian Chronicles **27** Something Wicked This Way Comes

Bradford, Barbara Taylor
author of: **17** A Woman of Substance

Bradford, Richard
author of: **15** Red Sky at Morning

Bradley, Bill (William Warren)
nickname: **10** Dollar Bill
sport: **10** basketball
team: **13** New York Knicks
elected: **7** Senator
from: **9** New Jersey

Bradstreet, Anne
author of: **35** The Tenth Muse Lately Sprung Up in America

Brady Bunch, The
character: **3** Jan **4** Greg **5** Alice, Bobby, Cindy, Peter **6** Marcia **9** Mike Brady **10** Carol Brady
cast: **8** Eve Plumb **9** Ann B Davis **10** Robert Reed, Susan Olsen **13** Barry Williams **14** Mike Lookinland **16** Maureen McCormick **17** Christopher Knight, Florence Henderson

brag 4 crow **5** boast, vaunt **7** big talk, crowing, talk big **8** boasting, bragging **10** exaggerate, self-praise **12** boastfulness, exaggeration **15** blow one's own horn **19** pat oneself on the back

Brage *see* 5 Bragi

Bragg, William Henry and William Lawrence
field: 7 physics
nationality: 7 British
determined: 16 crystal structure
  by: 15 X-ray diffraction
established: 9 Bragg's Law
awarded: 10 Nobel Prize

braggadocio 5 pride 6 egoism, vanity 7 bluster, conceit, swagger 9 cockiness, vainglory 10 pretension 14 self-importance

braggart 7 boaster, bragger 8 blowhard 9 big talker

Bragi
also: 5 Brage
origin: 6 Nordic
god of: 5 music 6 poetry
father: 4 Odin 5 Othin
wife: 4 Idun 5 Iduna, Ithun 6 Ithunn
mother: 3 Fri 5 Frigg, Frija 6 Frigga

Brahe, Tycho
field: 9 astronomy
nationality: 6 Danish
built: 11 observatory

Brahman
country: 5 India
religion: 8 Hinduism
system: 5 caste
rank: 7 highest
function: 6 leader, priest 7 teacher

Brahms, Johannes
born: 7 Germany, Hamburg
composer of: 7 Rinaldo 10 Rain Sonata 11 Triumphlied, Volksleder 12 Thuner-Sonate 13 German Requiem, Song of Destiny, Song of Triumph 14 Schicksalslied, Song of the Fates, Tragic Overture 15 Gesang der Parzen, Hungarian Dances 19 Liebeslieder Waltzes, Meistersinger Sonata 24 Academic Festival Overture 31 Variations on the St Anthony Chorale

braid 4 knit, lace 5 plait, ravel, twine, twist, weave 7 entwine, wreathe 9 interlace 10 intertwine

brain
part: 7 medulla 8 cerebrum 9 pituitary 10 cerebellum

brainchild 8 creation 9 invention 12 original work 15 imaginative work

braininess 6 genius 9 smartness 10 brightness, brilliance, cleverness 12 intelligence

brainless 4 dumb 6 stupid 7 asinine, foolish, idiotic, moronic, witless 8 mindless 9 imbecilic 10 half-witted 11 lamebrained 12 feeble-minded, simple-minded

brain power 4 mind 9 intellect 12 intelligence 14 mental capacity

Brainworm
character in: 19 Every Man in His Humour
author: 6 Jonson

brainy 5 smart 6 bright, clever 9 brilliant 11 intelligent

brainy group 5 mensa

brake 4 curb, drag, halt, rein, slow, stay, stop 5 check 6 arrest 7 control 9 restraint 10 constraint 11 reduce speed

Bramante, Donato
architect of: 9 Tempietto 14 Belvedere Court (the Vatican), Palazzo Caprini 19 Santa Maria della Pace 21 Santa Maria della Grazie

bramble 4 bush, vine 5 rough, shrub 7 thicket 8 prickers 13 raspberry bush 14 blackberry bush

Bramble, Matthew
character in: 14 Humphry Clinker
author: 8 Smollett

Bran
origin: 5 Welsh
giant king of: 7 Britain
habitat: 3 sea
saint in: 12 Christianity
brother: 9 Evnissyen 10 Manawyddan
sister: 7 Branwen
head buried in: 6 London

branch 3 arm, leg 4 fork, limb, part, wing 5 bough, prong, spray 6 agency, bureau, divide, feeder, member, office, ramify 7 channel, chapter, diverge, radiate, section, segment 8 division, offshoot, separate, shoot off 9 bifurcate, component, extension, tributary 10 department 11 subdivision 12 ramification

branched 6 forked, parted 7 divided 8 extended 9 spread out

Brancusi, Constantin
born: 7 Romania 13 Pestisani Gorj
artwork: 4 Fish 7 Chimera, The Kiss, The Seal 9 Sorceress 10 Adam and Eve, Prometheus 11 Bird in Space, Prodigal Son 12 Flying Turtle, Sleeping Muse 13 Endless Column 20 Sculpture for the Blind

brand 4 blot, kind, make, mark, sear, sign, slur, sort, spot, type 5 class, grade, label, smear, stain, stamp, taint 6 burn in, emblem, smirch, stigma 7 blemish, quality, variety 8 besmirch, disgrace 9 discredit, trademark 10 imputation, stigmatize 11 manufacture

brandish 4 wave 5 shake, swing, wield 6 flaunt, waggle 7 display, exhibit, show off 8 flourish

brand new 4 mint 5 fresh, young 6 unused

Brando, Marlon
born: 7 Omaha NE
roles: 8 Sayonara 10 The Wild One, Viva Zapata 12 Julius Caesar, The Godfather (Oscar refused) 13 Apocalypse Now 15 On the Waterfront (Oscar) 16 Last Tango in Paris 17 Mutiny on the Bounty 21 A Streetcar Named Desire

brandy 6 cognac, grappa, kahlua, kirsch, metaxa 8 Armagnac, Calvados, Tia Maria 9 applejack, Slivovitz 12 Grand Marnier, Peter Heering 14 forbidden fruit
French: 8 eau de vie

Brangwen, Ursula and Gudrun
characters in: 11 Women in Love
author: 8 Lawrence

Branstock
also: 9 Barnstock
origin: 12 Scandinavian
mentioned in: 8 Volsunga
form: 3 oak 4 tree
location: 7 Volsung
house of: 7 Volsung
Odin (Othin) thrusts: 4 Gram 5 sword

Brant, Captain Adam
character in: 22 Mourning Becomes Electra
author: 6 O'Neill

Branwen
origin: 5 Welsh
brother: 4 Bran
husband: 10 Matholwych
son killed by: 9 Evnissyen

Braque, Georges
born: 6 France 18 Argenteuil sur Seine
artwork: 7 Atelier, Grand Nu (Great Nude), The Echo 8 The Table 13 The Portuguese 14 Man with a Guitar 16 Violin and Palette, Violin and Pitcher 19 Woman with a Mandolin

brash 4 bold, rash, rude 5 fresh, hasty, sassy 6 brazen, cheeky, madcap 7 forward 8 careless, heedless, impudent, reckless 9 foolhardy, impetuous, imprudent, know-it-all 10 incautious 11 impertinent, precipitous, smart alecky 12 unconsidered 13 overconfident

brashness 4 gall 5 brass, cheek, nerve 8 audacity, boldness, chutzpah, temerity 10 brazenness, effrontery 11 forwardness, presumption

Brasilia
capital of: 6 Brazil

brass 4 gall, sand, VIPs 5 cheek, nerve 8 audacity, boldness, chutzpah, officers, temerity 9 impudence 10 brazenness, effrontery 11 forwardness, presumption

Brass, Sampson
character in: 19 The Old Curiosity Shop
author: 7 Dickens

brass instrument 4 tuba 5 bugle 6 cornet 7 trumpet 8 trombone 9 euphonium 10 French horn, sousaphone
ancient: 3 lur 7 Alphorn, buisine, serpent 10 ophicleide

brass tacks 4 crux, meat 7 details 9 realities, substance 10 essentials 11 nitty-gritty 15 sum and substance

brassy 4 bold, loud 5 brash, cheap, cocky, sassy, saucy, showy 6 brazen

7 blaring, forward **8** arrogant, impudent, insolent, overbold **9** barefaced, outspoken, shameless, unabashed **10** unblushing **11** impertinent

brat 3 imp **4** chit **5** whelp **6** hoyden, rascal **9** rude child **10** holy terror **12** spoiled child

Brauhaus 6 tavern **7** brewery

Brautigan, Richard
   author of: **15** Sombrero Fallout **18** The Hawkline Monster **21** Trout Fishing in America **38** The Pill Versus the Springhill Mine Disaster

bravado 7 big talk, blowing, bluster, bombast, bravura, crowing, puffery, swagger **8** boasting, bragging **9** cockiness **10** swaggering **11** braggadocio **12** boastfulness **13** show of courage

brave 4 bear, dare, defy, face, game, take **5** abide, brook, gutsy, stand **6** breast, endure, gritty, heroic, plucky, spunky, suffer **7** doughty, stomach, sustain, undergo, valiant, weather **8** confront, fearless, intrepid, stalwart, tolerate, unafraid, valorous **9** challenge, dauntless, outbrazen, put up with, stand up to, undaunted, withstand **10** courageous **11** lionhearted, unflinching, unshrinking **12** stouthearted

brave deed 4 feat, gest **5** geste **7** exploit **9** heroic act **11** achievement

Brave New World
   author: **12** Aldous Huxley
   character: **4** John **11** Bernard Marx **12** Lenina Crowne, Mustapha Mond

bravery 4 grit **5** pluck, spunk, valor **6** daring, mettle, spirit **7** courage, heroism **8** audacity, boldness **11** intrepidity **12** fearlessness **13** dauntlessness

Bravo, The
   author: **19** James Fenimore Cooper

brawl 3 row **4** fray, tiff **5** broil, clash, fight, melee, scrap, set-to **6** battle, fracas, ruckus, rumpus, uproar **7** dispute, quar- rel, scuffle, wrangle **8** squabble **9** imbroglio **11** altercation, embroilment

brawn 5 might, power **7** muscles, stamina **8** strength **9** beefiness, huskiness **10** robustness, ruggedness, sturdiness **19** muscular development

brawny 5 burly, husky **6** mighty, robust, rugged, strong, sturdy **8** muscular, powerful **9** strapping

Bray, Madeline
   character in: **16** Nicholas Nickleby
   author: **7** Dickens

brazen 4 bold, open **5** brash, saucy **6** brassy, cheeky **7** forward **8** arrogant, immodest, impudent, insolent **9** audacious, barefaced, boldfaced, shameless, unabashed

brazenness 4 gall **5** brass, cheek, nerve **8** audacity, boldness, chutzpah

9 impudence **10** effrontery, fowardness **11** presumption

Brazil
   capital: **8** Brasilia
   former capital: **12** Rio de Janeiro
   largest city: **8** Sao Paulo
   others: **5** Bahia, Belem **6** Recife, Sabara, Santos **7** Vitoria **8** Salvador **9** Ouro Preto, Paranagua **10** Diamantina **11** Porto Alegre **13** Belo Horizonte, Cruzeiro do Sul
   school:
     junior high: **7** ginasio
     senior high: **7** colegio
   measure: **2** pe **4** moio, sack, vara **5** braca, legoa, milha, tonel **6** canada, cuarto, quarto, tarefa **7** garrafa **8** alqueire
   monetary unit: **3** joe **4** reis **5** dobra **7** centara, halfjoe, milreis **8** cruzeiro
   weight: **3** bag **4** onca **5** libra **6** arroba, oitava **7** quilate, quintal **8** tonelada
   island: **6** Maraca, Marajo **7** Bananal, Cardoso, Caviana, Mexiana **8** Comprida
   lake: **4** Aima, Feia **5** Mirim **13** Logo dos Platos
   mountain: **3** Mar **5** Geral, Organ, Piaui **6** Acarai, Gurupi, Parima, Urucum **7** Amambai, Carajas, Gradaus, Oragaos, Roraima **8** Bandeira, Itatiaja, Roncador, Tombador **9** Pacaraima, Sugar Loaf **10** Tumuc-Humac
   highest point: **7** Neblina
   river: **3** Apa, Ica **4** Doce, Geio, Ivai, Jari, Para, Paru, Sono, Tefe **5** Abuna, Anaua, Apore, Capim, Claro, Corua, Icana, Iriri, Itapi, Jurua, Jutai, Manso, Negro, Pardo, Piaui, Preto, Tiete, Turvo, Urubu, Verde, Xingu **6** Ajuana, Amazon, Arinos, Balsas, Branco, Canuma, Contas, Cuiaba, Demini, Grajau, Grande, Gurupi, Ibicui, Iguacu, Japura, Javari, Mearim, Mortes, Mucuri, Parana, Purpus, Ronuro, Sangue, Tacutu, Tibagi, Uatuma, Uaupes **7** Corumba, Iguassu, Madeira, Madiera, Orinoco, Paraiba, Sucuriu, Tapajos, Taquari, Teodoro, Uruguai, Uruguay, Velhass **8** Araguaia, Padauiri, Paracatu, Paraguay, Parnaiba, Solimoes, Tarauaca **9** Tocantins **12** Sao Francisco
   sea: **8** Atlantic
   physical feature:
     bay: **9** All Saints
     cape: **4** Frio **6** Blanco, Buzios, Gurupy, Orange **7** Saotome **8** Saoroque
     dam: **6** Furnas **7** Peixoto
     estuary: **4** Para
     rain forest: **5** selva
     waterfall: **6** Guaira, Iguacu **7** Iguassu **11** Paulo Afonso
   people: **2** Ge **4** Anta **5** Acroa, Arara, Araua, Bravo, Carib, Guana, Negro **6**

Arawak, Caraja **7** Carayan, Javahai, Tariana **8** Botocudo, Chambioa **9** Caucasian, mamelucos, mulattoes **10** Portuguese **11** Tupi-Guarani
   architect: **8** Niemeyer
   artist: **6** Segall **9** Portinari **10** Cavalcenti
   author: **5** Amado, Bilac, Ramos **6** Freyre
   composer: **10** Villalobos
   discoverer: **6** Cabral
   leader: **6** Aranha, Branco, Collor, Franco, Geisel, Medici, Vargas **7** Goulart
   sculptor: **11** Aleijadinho
   language: **10** Portuguese
   religion: **10** Protestant **13** Roman Catholic
   place:
     beach: **7** Ipanema **9** Boa Viagem **10** Copacabana
   feature:
     bird: **4** mitu **5** mitua
     dance: **5** frevo, samba **6** maxixe **9** bossa nova
     fish: **7** piranha
     gourd: **4** cuia
     plantation: **7** fazenda
     slums: **7** favelas
     tree: **5** icica **6** ucuuba **7** arariba
   food:
     dish: **6** vatapa **8** feijoada
     dried salted beef: **7** charque
     drink: **4** acai **9** cafezinho
     tea: **4** mate
     turtle soup: **16** cas quinho de mucua

Brazil
   director: **12** Terry Gilliam
   cast: **8** Ida Lowry **9** Kim Greist **12** Robert De Niro **13** Jonathan Pryce

Brazilian Bombshell
   nickname of: **13** Carmen Miranda

Brazzaville
   capital of: **5** Congo

breach 3 gap **4** gash, hole, rent, rift, slit **5** break, chink, cleft, crack, split **7** crevice, failure, fissure, neglect, opening, rupture **8** defiance, trespass **9** disregard, violation **10** infraction **11** dereliction **12** disobedience, infringement **13** noncompliance, nonobservance, transgression

breach of faith 7 perfidy **8** bad faith, betrayal **9** falseness, treachery, two-timing **10** disloyalty **11** double-cross **13** double-dealing

breach of order 4 riot **6** fracas, mutiny, ruckus, uproar **7** turmoil **8** uprising **9** commotion, rebellion **10** dissension **11** disturbance, pandemonium **18** disturbance of peace

breach of trust 7 falsity, perfidy **9** falseness, treachery **10** disloyalty, infidelity **13** deceitfulness, double-dealing

bread 3 rye **4** food, pita **5** bucks, dough, money, wheat, white **6** staple

9 sourdough **10** livelihood, sustenance **11** staff of life **12** pumpernickel

bread and butter 3 job **6** career, living **7** calling **8** business, vocation **9** life's work **10** livelihood **14** means of support

Bread and Wine
author: **13** Ignazio Silone

breadbasket 3 gut **5** belly, tummy **6** paunch **7** abdomen, labonza, midriff, Midwest, stomach **11** solar plexus

breadth 4 area, size, span **5** range, reach, scope, width **6** extent, spread **7** compass, expanse, measure, stretch **8** latitude, wideness **9** broadness **10** dimensions **13** extensiveness

break 3 cap, end, fly, gap, off, run, top **4** beat, bust, chip, dash, defy, flee, gash, halt, hole, rend, rent, rest, rift, rive, ruin, snap, stop, tame, tear, tell **5** burst, cease, cleft, crack, crush, erupt, excel, lapse, occur, outdo, pause, sever, shirk, smash, split, train **6** appear, better, breach, chance, cleave, detach, divide, escape, exceed, happen, hiatus, ignore, inform, lessen, master, powder, recess, reveal, soften, subdue, sunder, weaken **7** control, cushion, destroy, disobey, divulge, eclipse, fissure, fortune, give out, lighten, neglect, opening, pull off, respite, run away, rupture, shatter, surpass, suspend, tear off, violate, wipe out **8** announce, bankrupt, burst out, cracking, demolish, diminish, disclose, disjoint, division, fracture, fragment, go beyond, interval, outstrip, overcome, proclaim, renege on, separate, shut down, slip away, splinter **9** dismember, disregard, granulate, interlude, interrupt, make a dash, pulverize, splitting, transcend **10** discipline, disconnect, fall back on, fly the coop, fracturing, impoverish, infringe on, make public, overshadow, separation, shattering, take flight, wrench away **11** discontinue, get away from, opportunity, pay no heed to **12** be derelict in, disintegrate, intermission, interruption, make a getaway, stroke of luck **13** strap for funds **14** bend to one's will, take the force of **15** take to one's heels

breakable 5 frail, shaky **6** flimsy **7** brittle, crumbly, fragile **8** delicate

break apart 7 crumble, shatter **8** collapse **9** fall apart **12** disintegrate, fall to pieces

breakdown 6 mishap **7** crackup, decline, failure **8** analysis, collapse, disorder, division **12** detailed list **13** deterioration **14** categorization

break down 6 divide **7** dissect **8** collapse, separate **9** decompose **11** deteriorate

breaker 4 cask, wave **6** comber **7** crusher **8** boat cask **9** destroyer

break faith with 6 betray **7** do wrong **9** play false **11** double-cross **12** be unfaithful **13** be treacherous **16** sell down the river

Breakfast at Tiffany's
author: **12** Truman Capote
director: **12** Blake Edwards
cast: **10** Buddy Ebsen **12** Mickey Rooney, Patricia Neal **13** Audrey Hepburn (Holly Golightly), George Peppard
score: **12** Henry Mancini
song: **9** Moon River

Breakfast Club, The
director: **10** John Hughes
cast: **10** Ally Sheedy, Judd Nelson **13** Emilio Estevez, Molly Ringwald **18** Anthony Michael Hall

Breakfast of Champions
author: **12** Kurt Vonnegut

break free 4 bolt, flee, skip **6** escape **7** get away, make off, run away **9** cut and run **10** fly the coop **12** make a getaway

breakfront 5 hutch **7** cabinet **8** bookcase, cupboard **12** china cabinet

break in 5 train **7** intrude **8** accustom, initiate **9** acclimate, interrupt **10** burglarize **12** indoctrinate

break-in 5 theft **7** robbery **8** burglary, stealing **12** burglarizing **13** housebreaking **19** breaking and entering

Breaking Away
director: **10** Peter Yates
screenplay: **11** Steve Tesich
cast: **10** Paul Dooley **11** Daniel Stern, Dennis Quaid **13** Barbara Barrie **16** Jackie Earle Haley **17** Dennis Christopher
setting: **7** Indiana **11** Bloomington

break loose 4 bolt, flee, skip **6** escape **7** get away, make off **9** cut and run **10** fly the coop **12** make a getaway

breakneck 4 rash **5** risky **8** reckless, very fast **9** dangerous, daredevil **12** death-defying

break of day 4 dawn **5** sunup **7** dawning, sunrise **8** daybreak **11** crack of dawn

break off 3 end **4** halt **5** cease **6** recess **7** adjourn, snap off, suspend **8** conclude, shut down **11** discontinue

breakout 6 escape, flight **7** getaway **10** decampment

break out 4 bolt, skip **5** begin, erupt **6** escape **7** bust out, get away **10** burst forth, fly the coop **12** make a getaway

Break the Bank
host: **9** Bert Parks **10** Bud Collyer

break the habit 4 kick, quit, stop **6** eschew, give up **8** renounce, withdraw **14** quit cold turkey

breakthrough 7 advance **11** advancement, improvement, penetration, step forward

breakup 5 split **7** crackup **9** dispersal,

splitting **10** separation **14** disintegration

break with 5 leave **8** be untrue, part from **10** be disloyal **11** divorce from **12** fall away from, separate from

breast 4 bust, core **5** bosom, chest, heart **10** very marrow
Italian: **5** petto

breastwork 7 bastion, rampart **8** barbette **9** earthwork **13** fortification

breath 4 wind **6** spirit **9** animation, breathing, lifeblood, life force **10** exhalation, inhalation, vital spark **11** divine spark, respiration, vital spirit **12** vitalization

breathe 4 gasp, huff, pant, puff **5** utter **6** impart, murmur **7** respire, whisper **9** draw in air **10** draw breath **15** inhale and exhale

breathe in 6 inhale **7** inspire, respire

breathe out 4 huff, pant, puff **6** exhale, expire **7** respire

breathing 4 live **5** alive **6** living **7** animate **11** respiratory **13** drawing breath

Breathless
director: **14** Jean-Luc Goddard
written by: **16** Francois Truffaut
cast: **10** Jean Seberg **16** Jean-Paul Belmondo
setting: **5** Paris

breathtaking 7 amazing, awesome **8** exciting **9** startling **10** surprising **11** astonishing

Brecht, Bertolt
author of: **13** Mother Courage **15** Drums in the Night **18** The Threepenny Opera **21** St Joan of the Stockyards **23** The Caucasian Chalk Circle **27** The Resistable Rise of Arturo Ui **29** The Private Life of the Master Race

Breck, Alan
character in: **9** Kidnapped
author: **9** Stevenson

breech 4 rump, seat **6** behind **8** buttocks, haunches, hind part **9** fundament, posterior **12** hindquarters

breeches 5 pants **8** trousers

breed 4 bear, grow, kind, race, sire, sort, type **5** beget, cause, order, raise, spawn, stock **6** family, father, foster, lead to, mother, strain **7** develop, nurture, pro- duce, promote, species, variety **8** generate, multiply, occasion **9** cultivate, give forth, procreate, propagate, reproduce **10** bring forth, give rise to **11** proliferate **16** produce offspring

breeding 4 line **5** grace **6** mating, polish **7** bearing, descent, growing, lineage, manners, raising, rearing **8** ancestry, courtesy, hatching, heredity, pedigree, spawn- ing, training **9** begetting, bloodline, genealogy, gentility, parentage, producing **10** background, extraction, family tree, generation, politeness, production, refinement, upbringing **11** cultivation, germination, multiplying, procreation, propagation **12** reproduction

breeze 4 flit, pass, sail, snap, waft **5** coast, float, glide, sweep **6** zephyr **9** light gust, light wind **10** gentle wind, puff of wind

breezy 3 gay **4** airy, pert, spry **5** blowy, brisk, fresh, gusty, light, merry, pep- py, sunny, windy **6** bouncy, casual, frisky, jaunty, lively **7** buoyant, squally **8** animated, blustery, carefree, cheerful, debonair, spirited **9** energetic, resilient, sprightly, vivacious, windswept **10** blithesome **11** free and easy

Brennan, Walter
   born: 12 Swampscott MA
   roles: 8 Kentucky **12** Come and Get It, The Westerner **13** The Real McCoys **16** To Have and Have Not

Brent, George
   real name: 18 George Brendan Nolan
   wife: 11 Ann Sheridan **14** Ruth Chatterton
   born: 7 Ireland **14** Shannonsbridge
   roles: 7 Jezebel **11** Dark Victory, The Great Lie **17** Forty- Second Street

Bres
   origin: 5 Irish
   king of: 7 Ireland

Breton, Andre
   author of: 5 Nadja **21** Manifesto of Surrealism

Breuer, Marcel
   architect of: 17 IBM Research Center (La Gaude France) **18** UNESCO headquarters (Paris) **25** St John's Abbey and University (Collegeville MN) **26** Whitney Museum of American Art (NYC)
   designed: 5 chair

brevity 9 briefness, pithiness, quickness, shortness, terseness **10** transience **11** conciseness **12** ephemerality, impermanence, succinctness

brew 3 ale **4** beer, boil, cook, form, make, plan, plot, soak, suds **5** begin, drink, hatch, ripen, start, steep, stout **6** cook up, devise, foment, gather, porter, scheme, seethe **7** arrange, brewski, concoct, ferment, mixture, prepare, produce, think up **8** beverage, contrive, initiate **9** formulate, germinate, originate **10** concoction, malt liquor

brewery
   German: 8 Brauhaus

Brian de Bois, Sir
   character in: 7 Ivanhoe
   author: 5 Scott

bribe 3 sop **5** graft **6** buy off, grease, pay off, payola, suborn **9** hush money **10** inducement **11** illegal gift **15**

grease the hand of, grease the palm of
   French: 7 douceur

bric-a-brac 7 baubles, gewgaws **8** bibelots, trinkets **9** gimcracks, kickshaws, ornaments **11** knickknacks

Brick
   character in: 16 Cat on a Hot Tin Roof
   author: 8 Williams

Bricks
   god of: 5 Kulla

bridal 7 nuptial, wedding **8** marriage **11** matrimonial

Bridehead, Sue
   character in: 14 Jude the Obscure
   author: 5 Hardy

Bride of Lammermoor, The
   author: 14 Sir Walter Scott
   character: 10 Lady Ashton, Lucy Ashton, Ravenswood **14** Laird of Bucklaw **16** Sir William Ashton

Brideshead Revisited
   author: 11 Evelyn Waugh
   character: 5 Celia, Julia **8** Cordelia **9** Sebastian **10** Brideshead (Bridey), Rex Mottram **12** Boy Mulcaster, Charles Ryder **13** Lady Marchmain, Lord Marchmain **14** Anthony Blanche

bridge 3 tie **4** band, bind, bond, link, span **5** cross, unify, union **6** go over **7** catwalk, connect, liaison, viaduct **8** alliance, overpass, traverse **9** cross over **10** connection, passageway **11** association, reach across **12** extend across

bridge
   derived from: 5 whist
   type: 7 auction **8** contract
   partnership: 9 East/West **11** North/South
   cards/hand: 8 thirteen
   no cards of a suit: 4 void
   one card of a suit: 9 singleton
   two cards of a suit: 9 doubleton
   rule book by: 5 Goren
   position: 4 east
   action: 3 bid **4** pass
   term: 4 slam **5** trump **6** double, renege, tenace

Bridge of San Luis Rey, The
   author: 14 Thornton Wilder
   character: 5 Clara, Jaime **6** Manuel, Pepita **7** Esteban, Viceroy **8** Uncle Pio **11** La Perichole **14** Brother Juniper **20** Marquesa de Montemayor

Bridge on the River Kwai, The
   director: 9 David Lean
   based on story by: 12 Pierre Boulle
   cast: 11 Jack Hawkins **12** Alec Guinness **13** William Holden **14** Sessue Hayakawa
   Oscar for: 5 actor (Guinness) **7** picture

Bridges, Beau
   real name: 21 Lloyd Vernet Bridges III

father: 5 Lloyd
brother: 4 Jeff
born: 12 Los Angeles CA
roles: 5 Space **8** Norma Rae **11** Signs of Life, The Landlord, The Wild Pair **17** The Fifth Musketeer **20** The Fabulous Baker Boys **25** The Other Side of the Mountain

Bridges, Jeff
   father: 5 Lloyd
   brother: 4 Beau
   born: 12 Los Angeles CA
   roles: 4 Tron **7** Starman **8** King Kong **10** Jagged Edge **12** The Vanishing **13** Kiss Me Goodbye, The Fisher King **14** Against All Odds **18** The Last Picture Show **20** The Fabulous Baker Boys

Bridges, Lloyd
   sons: 4 Beau, Jeff
   born: 12 San Leandro CA
   roles: 7 Sea Hunt **8** Airplane, High Noon

Bridges at Toko-ri, The
   author: 13 James Michener

Bridget
   character in: 19 Every Man in His Humour
   author: 6 Jonson

Bridge Too Far, A
   author: 13 Cornelius Ryan

Bridgetown
   capital of: 8 Barbados

bridle 3 gag **4** curb, rule **5** check **6** arrest, direct, draw up, flinch, hinder, manage, master, muzzle, rear up, recoil **7** con- trol, harness, inhibit, repress **8** draw back, restrain, restrict, suppress **9** constrain, restraint **11** bit and brace, head harness

brief 4 case **5** hasty, pithy, quick, short, swift, terse **6** advise, inform, precis, resume **7** capsule, compact, concise, defense, limited, prepare, summary **8** abridged, abstract, argument, fill in on, fleeting, instruct, succinct **9** condensed, curtailed, momentary, shortened, temporary, thumbnail, transient **10** abridgment, compressed, contention, describe to, short-lived, summarized, transitory **11** abbreviated **12** legal summary

brief account 6 precis, sketch **7** outline, summary **8** anecdote

brier, briar 4 Rosa **5** Rubus, thorn **6** Smilax **7** bramble
   varieties: 3 Cat, Dog, Hag, Saw **4** Bull **5** Green, Horse, Sweet **7** Jackson **8** Austrian **9** Sensitive **14** Austrian copper

brigade 4 crew, team, unit **5** corps, force, group, squad **6** legion, outfit **7** company **9** regiments, squadrons **10** army groups, battalions, contingent, detachment

Brigadoon
   director: 16 Vincente Minnelli

based on Broadway hit by: 14 Lerner and Loewe
cast: 9 Gene Kelly **10** Van Johnson **11** Cyd Charisse
setting: 8 Scotland

brigand 5 thief **6** bandit, gunman, looter, outlaw, pirate, robber, vandal **7** corsair, hoodlum, ruffian, rustler, spoiler **8** marauder, pilferer, pillager **9** buccaneer, cutthroat, desperado, despoiler, plunderer, privateer **10** highwayman

bright 3 gay **4** glad, good, keen, rosy, sage, warm, wise **5** acute, alert, aware, grand, great, happy, jolly, merry, quick, sharp, smart, sunny, vivid **6** astute, blithe, brainy, clever, gifted, joyful, joyous, lively, shrewd **7** beaming, blazing, capable, glowing, healthy, hopeful, intense, lambent, radiant, shining **8** cheerful, dazzling, exciting, gleaming, luminous, lustrous, profound, splendid, talented **9** brilliant, competent, effulgent, excellent, favorable, ingenious, inventive, masterful, promising, sagacious, sparkling, wide-awake **10** auspicious, discerning, glittering, optimistic, perceptive, proficient, propitious, prosperous, remarkable, shimmering, successful **11** clearheaded, illuminated, illustrious, intelligent, light-filled, magnificent, outstanding, quick-witted, resourceful, resplendent **12** exhilarating

brighten 4 lift **5** boost, cheer, light **6** buoy up, lift up, perk up **7** animate, enliven, gladden, lighten **9** make happy, stimulate **10** illuminate

bright-eyed 5 alert, awake **9** wideawake **12** on the qui vive

Bright Flows the River
author: 14 Taylor Caldwell

brightness 4 glow **5** glare, gleam, shine **6** dazzle, luster **7** glitter, sparkle **8** radiance **9** lightness **10** brilliance, luminosity **12** intelligence

bright spot 3 joy **6** solace **7** comfort **8** pleasure **13** consolation

Brigit
origin: 5 Welsh
goddess of: 4 fire **6** wisdom **9** fertility, household **11** agriculture

Brigitte Bardot & the Lolita Syndrome
author: 16 Simone de Beauvoir

Brill Among the Ruins
author: 14 Vance Bourjaily

brilliance, brilliancy 4 gift, glow **5** blaze, eclat, gleam, sheen, shine **6** acuity, dazzle, genius, luster, talent, wisdom **7** glitter, shimmer, sparkle **8** grandeur, keenness, radiance, sagacity, splendor **9** alertness, awareness, greatness, ingenuity, intensity, quickness, sharpness, smartness, vividness **10** braininess, brightness, capability, cleverness, competence, effulgence,

excellence, luminosity, perception, profundity, shrewdness **11** discernment, distinction, proficiency **12** intelligence, magnificence, resplendence **13** inventiveness, masterfulness **15** clearheadedness, illustriousness, resourcefulness

brilliant see **6** bright

brim 3 fill, lip, rim **5** brink, flood, ledge, verge **6** border, fill up, margin, well up **8** overflow

brimless hat 3 cap **5** beret **6** beanie **11** stocking cap, tam o'shanter

brimming 4 full **7** flooded, teeming **8** overfull, swarming **11** overflowing

Brimo
origin: 5 Greek
form: 7 goddess
corresponds to: 6 Hecate **7** Demeter **10** Persephone

brine 6 the sea **8** sea water **9** salt water **12** salt solution **14** saline solution **16** pickling solution

bring 4 bear, make, take, tote **5** begin, carry, cause, fetch, force, start **6** compel, convey, create, effect, induce **7** deliver, produce, sell for, usher in **8** convince, engender, generate, initiate, persuade, result in **9** accompany, institute, originate, transport **10** bring about

bring about 2 do **4** form, open **5** begin, cause, found, set up, start **6** attain, create, effect, lead to **7** achieve, execute, produce **8** carry out, generate, initiate, organize **9** establish, institute, succeed at **10** accomplish, effectuate, inaugurate **11** bring to pass, precipitate **18** bring into existence

bring back 6 return **7** restore **8** recreate **9** surrender **10** return with

bring down a peg 5 abase **6** humble **7** mortify **9** humiliate **13** cut down to size

bring down to earth 10 disenchant **11** disenthrall, disillusion, open the eyes **13** break the spell **14** burst the bubble **20** shatter one's illusions

bring forth 4 bear **5** breed, elicit, evoke, hatch, spawn, whelp **7** deliver, produce **9** reproduce **10** make appear **11** give birth to

bring home to 7 blame on, clarify **11** attribute to **15** place emphasis on

bringing together 7 joining, wedding **8** amassing **9** combining, gathering, including **10** assembling, collecting **12** accumulating **13** incorporating

Bringing Up Baby
director: 11 Howard Hawks
cast: 9 Cary Grant **14** Charlie Ruggles **16** Katharine Hepburn
"Baby": 7 leopard

Bringing Up Father
creator: 13 George McManus
character: 5 Jiggs **6** Maggie

daughter: 5 Rosie
brother-in-law: 5 Bimmy
place: 11 Dinty Moore's
favorite dish: 20 corned beef and cabbage

bring into being 4 bear, form, make **5** erect, hatch, spawn, whelp **6** create, design, devise, invent, render **7** concoct, deliver, develop, fashion, produce **8** contrive, generate **9** construct, fabricate, formulate, originate **10** bring forth **11** give birth to

bring into existence 4 form **5** begin, set up, start **6** create **8** organize **9** establish, institute **10** bring about, inaugurate

bring into line 5 adapt **6** adjust **7** conform, shape up **9** harmonize, reconcile **10** discipline **11** accommodate **13** whip into shape

bring into question 11 cast doubt on **18** throw suspicion upon

bring into relief 6 accent, stress **7** dwell on, feature, point up **9** emphasize, press home, underline **10** accentuate, underscore

bring low 5 abase, shame **6** humble **8** cast down **9** denigrate, humiliate

bring off 4 gain **6** attain, effect, secure **7** achieve **10** accomplish

bring to an end 5 cease **6** finish **8** break off, conclude **9** call a halt, terminate **11** discontinue

bring to a standstill 3 end **4** halt, stay, stop **5** block, check **6** arrest **12** bring to a halt

bring to bay 4 trap, tree **6** corner **8** confront, hunt down

bring to bear 5 apply **6** employ **7** utilize **9** implement

bring together 5 amass **6** gather, muster **7** collect, marshal, round up **8** assemble **10** accumulate

bring to light 6 expose, reveal, unveil **7** clarify, divulge, explain, uncover **8** disclose **9** explicate, make known, make plain **10** illuminate, make public

bring to one's senses 3 jar **5** alarm, alert, shock **9** make aware

bring to pass 5 cause **6** create, effect **8** carry out **10** bring about, effectuate

bring to terms 6 settle **7** mediate **9** arbitrate, reconcile

bring to view 5 dig up **6** reveal **7** exhibit, uncover, unearth **8** disclose, retrieve **10** come up with

bring word 4 tell **6** advise, convey, inform, notify, relate, reveal **7** divulge, publish **8** announce, disclose, proclaim **9** apprise of, broadcast, make known, publicize **11** communicate

brink 3 rim **4** bank, brim, edge **5** point, shore, skirt, verge **6** border, margin **9** threshold

briny 4 salt 5 salty 6 saline
brio, con
  music: 9 with vigor 10 with spirit
Briseis
  origin: 5 Greek
  mentioned in: 5 Iliad
  father: 18 Briseus of Lyrnessus
  husband: 5 Mynes
  captured by: 8 Achilles
  caused: 7 quarrel
    between: 8 Achilles 9 Agamemnon
Briseus
  origin: 5 Greek
  mentioned in: 5 Iliad
  daughter: 7 Briseis
  death by: 7 suicide
Brisingamen 8 necklace
  origin: 12 Scandinavian
  trait: 5 magic
  owned by: 5 Freia, Freya
brisk 4 busy, spry 5 alert, fresh, peppy, quick, swift 6 active, breezy, lively, snappy 7 bracing, chipper, dynamic, rousing 8 animated, bustling, spirited, stirring, vigorous 9 energetic, sprightly, vivacious, vivifying 10 refreshing 11 stimulating 12 exhilarating, invigorating
briskness 3 pep 5 vigor 6 energy 8 alac-rity, spryness 9 quickness, swiftness 13 sprightliness
bristle 4 hair, seta 5 quill 7 stiffen, whisker
bristles 5 barbs, setae 6 quills 7 stubble 8 prickles, whiskers
bristletail
  variety: 7 jumping 8 firebrat 9 primitive 10 nicoletiid, silverfish
bristly 5 rough 6 barbed, coarse 7 prickly, stubbly 8 unshaven 9 whiskered 11 bewhiskered
Britannia *see* 7 England
British 6 Breton, Briton 7 English 8 Brittany
British Columbia
  bordered by: 5 Idaho, Yukon 6 Alaska 7 Montana 10 Washington 12 Pacific Ocean, United States 20 Northwest Territories
  country: 6 Canada
  Indian: 5 Haida 6 Nootka, Salish 8 Kwakiutl 9 Tsimshian 10 Bella Coola
  island: 9 Vancouver 14 Queen Charlotte
  mountain: 5 Coast, Rocky 7 Cascade 8 Columbia 11 Cordilleran 14 Cassiar Omineca
  nickname: 2 BC
  park: 7 Glacier
  rank in size: 5 sixth
  river: 6 Fraser
  section: 8 province
British Guiana *see* 6 Guyana
British Honduras *see* 6 Belize
British Mythology
  god of rebirth/afterlife: 4 Gwyn

  chief of gods: 5 Woden
  island of paradise: 6 Avalon
Britomart
  character in: 15 The Faerie Queene
  author: 7 Spenser
Britomartis
  origin: 6 Cretan
  goddess of: 7 hunters, sailors 9 fishermen
  father: 4 Zeus
  mother: 5 Carme
  corresponds to: 7 Artemis 8 Dictynna
Briton 4 Celt 6 Celtic 7 British
Brittany
  coast: 5 Armor
  country: 6 France
  inhabitant: 5 Celts 6 French, Romans
  interior: 6 Argoat
  land form: 9 peninsula
  language: 6 Breton
  other name: 5 Breiz 6 Breton 8 Bretagne
Britten, (Edward) Benjamin
  born: 7 England 9 Lowestoft
  composer of: 8 Gloriana 9 Billy Budd 10 Paul Bunyan, War Requiem 11 Curlew River, Peter Grimes, Winter Words 12 Owen Wingrave, The Poet's Echo 13 Albert Herring, Death in Venice 14 The Prodigal Son, Turn of the Screw 15 Phantasy Quartet 17 A Ceremony of Carols, A Charm of Lullabies, Sinfonia da Requiem, The Rape of Lucretia 18 Holderlin Fragments 20 Cantata Misericordium 21 A Midsummer Night's Dream, Sonnets of Michelangelo 22 The Burning Fiery Furnace
brittle 7 crumbly, fragile, friable 9 breakable, frangible
broach 4 pose 6 launch, open up, submit 7 advance, bring up, mention, propose, suggest, touch on 9 institute, introduce
broad 4 full, open, wide 5 ample, clear, large, plain, rangy, roomy, thick 7 general, immense, obvious, sizable 8 extended, spacious, sweeping 9 capacious, expansive, extensive, inclusive, outspread, universal, unlimited 10 undetailed 11 far-reaching, nonspecific, wide-ranging 12 all-embracing, encyclopedic 13 comprehensive
broadcast 4 beam, show, talk 5 cable, radio, relay 7 program, send out 8 televise, transmit 9 statement 10 distribute 11 disseminate, put on the air 12 announcement
broaden 5 boost, raise, swell, widen 6 dilate, expand, extend 7 advance, amplify, augment, build up, develop, distend, enlarge, improve, stretch 8 increase 9 intensify, reinforce, spread out 10 strengthen, supplement
broadened 7 dilated, swelled, swollen,

widened 8 enlarged, expanded, extended 9 distended, spread out
broad-minded 7 liberal 8 amenable, catholic, flexible, tolerant, unbiased 9 receptive, unbigoted 10 charitable, open-minded, undogmatic 11 magnanimous 12 unprejudiced, unprovincial
Broadway Joe
  nickname of: 9 Joe Namath
Brobdingnag
  fictional land in: 16 Gulliver's Travels
  author: 5 Swift
Brobdingnagian 4 huge 5 giant 7 immense, mammoth 8 colossal, enormous, gigantic 10 gargantuan, tremendous 11 elephantine
broccoli 9 vegetable 12 Brassica rapa 16 Brassica oleracea (Botyris Group) 17 Brassica septiceps
  variety: 6 Turnip 7 Italian 9 Asparagus, Sprouting
brochure 5 flier 6 folder 7 booklet, leaflet 8 circular, handbill, pamphlet 9 throwaway
Brockton Blockbuster
  nickname of: 13 Rocky Marciano
Broglie, Louis Victor de
  field: 7 physics
  nationality: 6 French
  developed: 13 wave mechanics
  awarded: 10 Nobel Prize
broil 3 fry 4 bake, burn, cook, sear 5 parch, roast, toast 6 scorch 7 blister
broiler 3 hot, pan 4 rack 5 grill 6 cooker 8 scorcher 12 young chicken
broke 8 bankrupt, strapped, wiped out 9 insolvent, penniless 10 down and out 12 impoverished, on one's uppers, without funds 16 strapped for funds
broken 4 torn 5 rough, split, tamed 6 ruined, uneven 7 crushed, damaged 8 bankrupt, in pieces, ruptured 9 fractured, separated, shattered 10 incomplete 11 fragmentary, interrupted
Broken Commandment, The
  author: 14 Toson Shimazaki
broken-down 6 beat-up, ruined 7 rickety, worn-out 8 battered, decrepit 10 ramshackle 11 dilapidated 12 deteriorated
broken-hearted 3 sad 6 gloomy, woeful 7 crushed, doleful, forlorn, unhappy 8 dejected, desolate, downcast, mournful, wretched 9 depressed, long-faced, miserable, sorrowful, woebegone 10 despairing, despondent, melancholy 11 heartbroken 12 disconsolate, inconsolable
Brom Bones
  also: 12 Brom Van Brunt
  character in: 23 The Legend of Sleepy Hollow
  author: 6 Irving
Bromfield, Louis

author of: 11 Early Autumn, Malabar Farm **12** The Rains Came **13** Mrs Parkington, Night in Bombay **14** Wild Is the River **15** The Green Bay Tree **31** The Strange Case of Miss Annie Spragg

bromide 6 cliche **8** banality **9** platitude **10** stereotype **11** trite phrase **19** hackneyed expression

bromidic 4 dull **5** banal, corny, stale, tired, trite, vapid **6** jejune **7** humdrum, insipid **8** ordinary **9** hackneyed **10** pedestrian, unexciting, unoriginal **13** platitudinous, unimaginative

bromine
    chemical symbol: 2 Br

Bromius
    epithet of: 8 Dionysus
    means: 7 thunder

Bronson, Charles
    real name: 16 Charles Buchinsky
    wife: 11 Jill Ireland
    born: 11 Ehrenfeld PA
    roles: 9 Death Wish **13** The Dirty Dozen **14** The Great Escape **16** Battle of the Bulge, The Valachi Papers **19** The Magnificent Seven

Bronte, Anne
    author of: 9 Agnes Grey **23** The Tenant of Wildfell Hall
    pseudonym: 9 Acton Bell

Bronte, Charlotte
    author of: 7 Shirley **8** Jane Eyre, Villette **12** The Professor
    pseudonym: 10 Currer Bell

Bronte, Emily
    author of: 16 Wuthering Heights
    pseudonym: 9 Ellis Bell

Brontes
    member of: 8 Cyclopes

brontophobia
    fear of: / thunder

Brontosaurus
    also: 11 Apatosaurus
    type: 8 dinosaur, sauropod
    period: 8 Jurassic

Bronx Bull
    nickname of: 11 Jake La Motta

bronze 3 tan **5** metal **8** brownish, chestnut **10** reddish- tan **12** reddish-brown **13** copper-colored

brooch 3 pin **5** clasp

brood 4 chew, fret, mope, mull, sulk **5** cover, dwell, hatch, spawn, worry, young **6** chicks, family, litter **7** agonize, sit upon **8** children, incubate **9** offspring **10** hatchlings

brook 3 run **4** bear, rill, take **5** abide, allow, creek, stand **6** accept, endure, stream, suffer **7** rivulet, stomach **8** tolerate **9** put up with, streamlet

Brooks, Gwendolyn
    author of: 4 Riot **10** Annie Allen **14** Family Pictures

Brooks, James L

director of: 13 Broadcast News **17** Terms of Endearment (Oscar)

Brooks, Mel
    real name: 14 Melvin Kaminsky
    wife: 12 Anne Bancroft
    born: 10 Brooklyn NY
    director of/roles: 10 Life Stinks, Spaceballs **11** High Anxiety, Silent Movie **12** The Producers **14** Blazing Saddles **17** Young Frankenstein **20** The History of the World

Brooks, Richard
    director of: 10 Fever Pitch **11** Elmer Gantry, In Cold Blood **16** Cat on a Hot Tin Roof, Sweet Bird of Youth **19** Looking for Mr. Goodbar, The Blackboard Jungle **20** The Brothers Karamazov, The Last Time I Saw Paris

broom 4 bush **5** besom, brush, whisk **7** sweeper

broth 5 stock **8** bouillon, consomme **9** clear soup

brothel 4 stew **5** house **6** bagnio, bordel **8** bordello, cathouse **10** bawdy house, fancy house, whorehouse **11** maison close **13** maison de passe, sporting house **14** house of ill fame **16** house of ill repute **19** house of prostitution

brother 3 pal **4** chum, monk, peer **5** buddy, friar **6** cleric **7** comrade, kinsman, part- ner, sibling **8** confrere, landsman, monastic, relative, relation **9** associate, colleague, companion, fellowman **10** countryman **11** male sibling **12** fellow member **13** fellow citizen
    French: 5 frere

brotherhood 4 club **5** amity, lodge **10** fellowship, fraternity, friendship **11** association

Brother Juniper
    character in: 21 The Bridge of San Luis Rey
    author: 6 Wilder

Brothers Karamazov, The
    author: 10 Dostoevsky **17** Fyodor Dostoyevsky
    character: 4 Ivan **6** Dmitri **7** Alyosha (Alexey), Zossima **8** Katerina **9** Grushenka **10** Smerdyakov **15** Fyodor Karamazov

brougham 3 car **8** carriage **10** automobile

brought 6 caused **7** carried, fetched, sold for **8** conveyed **9** conducted, convinced, persuaded

brow 3 rim **4** brim, edge, side **5** brink, verge **6** border, margin **8** boundary, forehead **9** periphery

browbeat 3 cow **5** abash, bully, cower **6** badger, harass, hector **7** henpeck **8** bulldoze, domineer, frighten, threaten **9** terrorize, tyrannize **10** intimidate

browbeater 5 bully **6** despot **7** co-

ercer **9** oppressor, tormenter, tormentor **11** intimidator, petty tyrant

browbeating 8 bullying **11** threatening, tyrannizing **12** intimidation

brown 3 bay, dun, fry, tan **4** buff, cook, drab, fawn, puce, roan, rust **5** beige, camel, cocoa, hazel, khaki, saute, taw- ny, toast, umber **6** auburn, bronze, brunet, coffee, copper, ginger, russet, sorrel, walnut **8** brunette, chestnut, cinnamon, mahogany **9** chocolate, olive drab **10** terra- cotta **11** dirt-colored, sand-colored **12** liver-colored

Brown, Angeline
    real name of: 14 Angie Dickinson

Brown, Berenice Sadie
    character in: 19 A Member of the Wedding
    author: 9 McCullers

Brown, Charles Brockden
    author of: 6 Ormond **7** Wieland **11** Edgar Huntly **12** Arthur Mervyn

Brown, Claude
    author of: 16 The Children of Ham **25** Manchild in the Promised Land

Brown, Dee
    author of: 15 Creek Mary's Blood **24** Bury My Heart at Wounded Knee

Brown, Helen Gurley
    author of: 19 Sex and the Single Girl
    editor of: 12 Cosmopolitan

Brown, Helen Hayes
    real name of: 10 Helen Hayes

Brown, Jim (Jimmy)
    sport: 8 football
    position: 8 fullback
    team: 15 Cleveland Browns
    actor in: 10 Dirty Dozen

Brown, Robert
    field: 6 botany
    nationality: 8 Scottish
    established: 16 Brownian movement

Brown Bomber
    nickname of: 8 Joe Louis

Browne, Dik
    creator/artist of: 9 Hi and Lois **12** Beetle Bailey **16** Hagar the Horrible

Browne, Sir Thomas
    author of: 9 Urn Burial **12** Hydriotaphia **13** Religio Medici **16** The Garden of Cyrus

brownie 3 elf **4** cake, puck **5** fairy, pixie **6** sprite **9** girl scout **10** leprechaun

Browning, Elizabeth Barrett
    author of: 11 Aurora Leigh **14** How Do I Love Thee **16** Casa Guidi Windows **24** Sonnets from the Portuguese

Browning, Robert
    author of: 8 Sordello **10** Paracelsus **11** Pippa Passes **13** Fra Lippo Lippi, My Last Duchess **14** Andrea del Sarto **17** The Ring and the Book **20** The Pied Piper of Hamlin **29** Solilo-

quy of the Spanish Cloister **30** Childe Roland to the Dark Tower Came

brownish 3 tan **5** taupe **6** bronze **8** chestnut **13** copper- colored

Brownlow, Mr
  character in: 11 Oliver Twist
  author: 7 Dickens

Brownmiller, Susan
  author of: 14 Against Our Will

Brown's Descent
  author: 11 Robert Frost

browse 3 eat **4** feed, scan, skim, surf **5** graze **6** nibble, peruse, survey **7** dip into, pasture **8** look over **9** check over **11** look through **13** glance through

Bruckner, Anton
  born: 7 Austria **9** Ansfelden
  composer of: 6 Te Deum **7** Psalm CL **11** Grosse Messe **16** Romantic Symphony **26** Intermezzo for String Quartet

Brueghel, Pieter (the Elder)
  born: 5 Breda **8** Flanders
  nickname: 14 Peasant Bruegel
  sons: 3 Jan **6** Pieter
  artwork: 9 Blue Cloak, The Months **10** Dulle Griet (Mad Meg) **12** Fall of Icarus, Peasant Dance, Tower of Babel **14** Children's Games, The Misanthrope **15** Return of the Herd **16** Hunters in the Snow **17** The Triumph of Death **19** Peasant Wedding Dance **21** Peasant Wedding Banquet, The Magpie on the Gallows **22** Massacre of the Innocents **23** The Blind Leading the Blind, The Fall of the Rebel Angels

Brueghel, Jan
  born: 8 Brussels, Flanders
  nickname: 6 Velvet
  father: 13 Pieter Bruegel
  artwork: 12 Four Elements **13** Village Street **15** The Garden of Eden (with Rubens) **17** The Battle of Arbela

Brueghel, Pieter (the Younger)
  born: 8 Brussels, Flanders
  nickname: 12 Hell Brueghel **19** The Infernal Brueghel
  father: 13 Pieter Bruegel (the Elder)
  artwork: 11 Village Fair **14** The Crucifixion **16** The Burning of Troy

Brugh, Spangler Arlington
  real name of: 12 Robert Taylor

bruise 3 mar **4** hurt, mark **5** abuse, wound **6** damage, injure, injury, offend **7** blacken, blemish **8** discolor **9** black mark, contusion **13** discoloration

bruit 3 din **5** noise, rumor **6** clamor, hubbub, racket, report, uproar **7** clangor **10** clattering, noise about **11** voice abroad

Brunei
  capital/largest city: 17 Bandar Seri Begawan
  others: 4 Labi **5** Badas, Danau, Muara, Seria **6** Bangar, Tutong **7**

Kampong **10** Kuala Abang, Kuala Balai **11** Kuala Belait
  head of state/government: 6 sultan
  island: 6 Borneo **8** Sipitang
  mountain: 6 Teraja **9** Ulu Tutong
  highest point: 10 Pagon Priok
  river: 6 Belait, Brunei, Tutong **9** Temburong
  sea: 10 South China
  physical feature:
    bay: 6 Brunei
  people: 4 Iban **5** Dayak, Malay **7** Chinese, Kadazan
  language: 4 Iban **5** Malay **7** Chinese, English
  religion: 5 Islam **6** Taoism **7** animism **8** Buddhism **12** Christianity
  feature: 3 oil

Brunelleschi, Filippo
  architect of: 10 San Lorenzo **11** Pazzi Chapel (Santa Croce), Pitti Palace **12** Santo Spirito **14** Badia Fiesolana **15** Duomo of Florence **16** Palazzo Quaratesi **21** Santa Maria degli Angeli **22** Ospedale degli Innocenti **23** Dome of Florence Cathedral

brunet, brunette 4 dark **5** black **9** brown-eyed, dark brown **10** dark-haired **11** brown-haired, dark-skinned **12** olive-skinned **16** dark-complexioned

Brunhild
  origin: 8 Germanic
  Scandinavian: 8 Brynhild
  character in: 14 Nibelungenlied
  queen of: 8 Isenland
  husband: 7 Gunther
  won by: 9 Siegfried

brunt 5 force **6** impact, stress, thrust **8** violence **9** full force, main shock

brush 4 bush, dust, fern, wash **5** clean, copse, flick, graze, groom, paint, run-in, scrub, sedge, set-to, shine, sweep, touch, whisk **6** battle, bushes, caress, duster, forest, fracas, polish, shrubs, stroke **7** bracken, cleanse, dusting, grazing, meeting, scuffle, thicket, varnish **8** skirmish, woodland **9** encounter, shrubbery, woodlands **10** engagement, underbrush, whisk-broom **11** bush country, undergrowth **12** bristled tool **13** confrontation
  type: 4 hair, nail, shoe, wash **5** paint, scrub, tooth **7** clothes

brush aside 6 slight **7** neglect **8** pass over **9** disregard

brush-off 3 cut **4** snub **5** brush **6** rebuff, slight **7** put-down, squelch **9** disregard, rejection **11** repudiation **12** cold shoulder

brusque 4 curt, rude, tart **5** bluff, blunt, gruff, harsh, rough, short **6** abrupt, crusty **7** bearish **8** impolite, ungentle **10** ungracious **12** discourteous **13** unceremonious

Brussels
  canal: 9 Charleroi **10** Willebroek

  capital of: 7 Belgium
  cathedral: 26 Saint Michel and Sainte Gudule
  early name: 10 Bruoc-sella
    means: 16 marshy settlement
  Flemish: 7 Brussel
  French: 9 Bruxelles
  headquarters of: 3 EEC **4** NATO **12** Common Market **25** European Economic Community
  landmark: 11 Royal Palace **15** Palace of Justice **17** Palace of the Nation
  province: 7 Brabant
  river: 5 Senne, Zenne
  square: 11 Grande Place

brutal 5 crude, cruel, harsh **6** bloody, coarse, fierce, savage **7** brutish, hellish, inhuman, vicious **8** barbaric, pitiless, ruthless **9** atrocious, barbarous, heartless, merciless, unfeeling **10** demoniacal **11** hardhearted, remorseless **12** bloodthirsty

brutality 7 cruelty **8** ferocity, savagery **9** barbarity, harshness **10** inhumanity, savageness **11** brutishness, viciousness **12** ruthlessness

brute 5 beast, demon, devil, fiend, swine **6** animal, savage **7** monster **9** barbarian **10** wild animal **11** cruel person **12** dumb creature

brutish 5 cruel, feral **6** bloody, brutal, fierce, savage **7** inhuman **8** barbaric **9** barbarous, ferocious, unfeeling **11** remorseless

brutishness 8 ferocity, savagery **9** barbarity, brutality **10** bestiality, coarseness, inhumanity, savageness **11** viciousness **15** remorselessness

Brutus
  also: 12 Marcus Brutus
  character in: 12 Julius Caesar
  author: 11 Shakespeare

Bruxelles see **8** Brussels

Bryan, C D B
  author of: 12 Friendly Fire **24** Ugly Scenes Beautiful Women

Bryant, Bear (Paul)
  sport: 8 football
  position: 5 coach
  team: 7 Alabama **11** Crimson Tide

Brynhild
  origin: 12 Scandinavian
  Germanic: 8 Brunhild
  husband: 6 Gunnar
  won by: 6 Sigurd
  position: 8 Valkyrie

Brynhildr Sigrdrifa see **9** Sigrdrifa

Brynner, Yul
  real name: 10 Taidje Khan
  born: 14 Sakhalin Island
  roles: 9 Anastasia, West World **11** The King and I (Oscar) **18** The Ten Commandments **19** The Magnificent Seven **20** The Brothers Karamazov **23** Invitation to a Gunfighter

Brythonic
  language family: 12 Indo-European

group: 5 Welsh **6** Breton **7** Cornish, Pictish

Bschliessmayer, Oskar Josef
  real name of: **11** Oskar Werner

Bubba Smith
  nickname of: **17** Charles Aaron Smith

bubble, bubbles 4 bleb, boil, fizz, foam **5** froth **6** burble, fizzle, gurgle, seethe **7** air ball, blister, droplet, globule, sparkle **9** percolate **10** effervesce **13** effervescence

bubbliness 9 fizziness, foaminess **10** ebullience, enthusiasm, frothiness, liveliness **11** high spirits **13** effervescence

bubbling 5 fizzy, foamy **6** frothy **7** fizzing, foaming **9** sparkling **12** effervescent

bubbly 5 fizzy, foamy **6** frothy, lively **7** fizzing, foaming **9** champagne, sparkling **12** effervescent, high-spirited

buccaneer 6 pirate **7** corsair **9** privateer **10** freebooter

Buchan, John (Baron Tweedsmuir)
  author of: **10** John Macnab **11** Greenmantle, Pilgrim's Way **17** John Burnet of Barns **18** The Thirty-Nine Steps

Buchanan, Daisy
  character in: **14** The Great Gatsby
  author: **10** Fitzgerald

Buchanan, Edgar
  born: **13** Humansville MO
  roles: **5** Shane, Texas **7** Arizona **8** Cimarron **9** McLintock **13** Penny Serenade **17** Petticoat Junction **18** Ride the High Country

Buchanan, James
  nickname: **7** Old Buck
  presidential rank: **9** fifteenth
  party: **8** Democrat
  state represented: **2** PA
  defeated: **7** (John Charles) Fremont **8** (Millard) Fillmore
  vice president: **12** (John Cabell) Breckinridge
  cabinet:
    state: **4** (Lewis) Cass **5** (Jeremiah Sullivan) Black
    treasury: **3** (John Adams) Dix **4** (Howell) Cobb **6** (Philip Francis) Thomas
    war: **4** (Joseph) Holt **5** (John Buchanan) Floyd
    attorney general: **5** (Jeremiah Sullivan) Black **7** (Edwin McMasters) Stanton
    navy: **6** (Isaac) Toucey
    postmaster general: **4** (Horatio) King, (Joseph) Holt **5** (Aaron Venable) Brown
    interior: **8** (Jacob) Thompson
  born: **11** Cove Gap PA (near Mercersburg)
  died/buried: **11** Lancaster PA
  education:
    Academy: **8** Old Stone

    College: **9** Dickinson
    studied: **3** law
  religion: **12** Presbyterian
  political career: **13** state assembly **24** US House of Representatives
    secretary of: **5** State
    minister: **6** Russia **12** Great Britain
  civilian career: **6** lawyer
  notable events of lifetime/term: **5** Panic (of 1857) **11** English Bill, Pony Express
    raid by: **9** John Brown
    raid on: **12** Harper's Ferry
    Supreme Court case: **9** Dred Scott
  father: **5** James
  mother: **9** Elizabeth (Speer)
  siblings: **4** Jane, John, Mary **5** Maria, Sarah **7** Harriet **9** Elizabeth **11** Edward Young **12** William Speer **16** George Washington
  wife: **4** none
  children: **4** none

Bucharest
  capital of: **7** Romania, Rumania
  founder: **5** Bucur
  landmark: **8** Scinteia **13** Village Museum
  river: **9** Dimbovita
  Rumanian: **9** Bucuresti

Buchinsky, Charles
  real name of: **14** Charles Bronson

buck 3 man **4** beau, deer, dude, kick, male **5** dandy **6** dollar, oppose **7** coxcomb **8** cavalier, gay blade **9** go against **10** young blood

Buck
  character in: **16** The Call of the Wild
  author: **6** London

Buck, Pearl S
  author of: **8** The Exile **9** Other Gods **10** Dragon Seed **12** The Good Earth **13** A House Divided

bucket 3 can, hod, tub **4** cask, pail **5** scoop **6** vessel **7** pailful, pitcher, scuttle **9** container **10** receptacle

Buckeye State
  nickname of: **4** Ohio

buckle 3 sag **4** bend, clip, curl, hasp, hook, warp **5** bulge, catch, clasp **6** cave in, couple, fasten, secure **7** contort, crinkle, crumple, distort, wrinkle **8** belly out, collapse, fastener

buckle down 6 attend **12** apply oneself

Buckley, William F Jr
  author of: **11** Who's on First? **15** God and Man at Yale, God Save the Queen
  editor of: **14** National Review
  wife: **3** Pat
  son: **11** Christopher

Buck Rogers
  creator: **14** Richard Calkins
  character: **5** Alura, Buddy, Dercu, Kayla, Wilma **6** Ardala **10** Killer Kane

bucolic 4 idyl, poem **5** idyll, rural **6** poetic, rustic **7** eclogue, idyllic, peasant **8** pastoral, shepherd

bud 4 open **5** shoot **6** flower, sprout **7** blossom, burgeon, develop

Bud, Rosa
  character in: **22** The Mystery of Edwin Drood
  author: **7** Dickens

Budapest
  area: **4** Buda, Pest **5** Obuda
  capital of: **7** Hungary
  cathedral: **13** Saint Matthias
  hill: **10** Castle Hill
  island: **6** Csepel
  river: **6** Danube
  Roman town: **8** Aquincum

Buddenbrooks
  author: **10** Thomas Mann

Buddha
  also called: **5** Butsu
  born: **11** Kapilavastu
  father: **11** Suddhodhana
  founded: **8** Buddhism
  means: **15** enlightened one
  message: **6** dharma
  name for: **17** Siddhartha Gautama
  son: **6** Rahula
  tree: **2** bo **5** bodhi
  wife: **9** Yasodhara

Buddhism
  action: **5** karma
  branch: **3** Zen **8** Mahayana **9** Theravada **12** Great Vehicle **14** way of the elders
  doctrine: **6** duhkha **7** nirvana **9** suffering **13** eightfold path **15** four noble truths **17** pratityasamutpada
  founded by: **6** Buddha **17** Siddhartha Gautama
  monk: **7** bhikshu
  nun: **9** bhikshuni
  rebirth: **7** samsara
  religious community: **6** sangha

buddy 3 pal **4** chum, mate **5** amigo, crony **6** cohort, fellow, friend **7** brother, comrade, partner **8** confrere, intimate, playmate, sidekick **9** associate, colleague, companion, confidant **10** playfellow **11** confederate

buddy-buddy 5 close, palsy **6** chummy **8** friendly, intimate **10** palsy-walsy

budge 4 move, push, roll, stir, sway **5** shift, slide **6** change **8** convince, dislodge, persuade **9** dislocate, influence

budget 4 cost, plan **5** funds, means **6** moneys, ration **7** arrange **8** allocate, schedule **9** allotment, allowance, apportion, resources **10** allocation, portion out **12** spending plan **13** financial plan

budgetary 6 fiscal **8** economic, monetary **9** financial, pecuniary

buenas noches 9 good night

bueno 4 good

Buenos Aires
  capital of: **9** Argentina

landmark: 11 Teatro Colon **16** Saavedra Monument, San Martin Theater **17** Wildestein Gallery, Witcomb Art Gallery **18** Church of El Salvador **27** Christopher Columbus Monument
park: 7 Palermo
people: 8 portenos
    means: 15 people of the port
river: 12 Rio de la Plata

buff 3 bug, fan, nut, rub, tan **4** swab **5** freak, hound, maven, mavin, sandy, straw, tawny **6** addict, dauber, polish, smooth, the raw **7** admirer, burnish, devotee, leather **8** bare skin, follower, polisher **9** nakedness, yellowish **10** aficionado, enthusiast **11** buffalo hide, connoisseur **14** yellowish-brown

buffalo 5 bison **6** puzzle **7** mystify **10** intimidate
kind: 7 African **10** Asian water
African: 14 syncerus caffer
Asian water: 14 bubalus bubalis

Buffalo
    football team: 5 Bills
    hockey team: 6 Sabres

buffer 6 bumper, fender, shield **7** cushion **9** protector

buffet 3 box, hit, jab, rap **4** bang, beat, bump, cuff, meal, push, slap **5** baste, knock, pound, shove, thump **6** pum- mel, strike, supper, thrash, thwack, wallop **7** cabinet, counter **8** credenza **9** cafeteria, sideboard **11** smorgasbord

Buffone, Carlo
    character in: 22 Every Man out of His Humour
    author: 6 Jonson

buffoon 3 wag **4** fool, zany **5** clown, comic, joker, mimic, Punch **6** jester, madcap **7** Pierrot **8** comedian, funnyman **9** harlequin, pantaloon, prankster, trickster **10** Scaramouch, silly-billy **11** merry-andrew, punchinello, Scaramouche

buffoonery 6 antics, comedy **7** foolery, inanity **8** zaniness **9** asininity, horseplay, silliness, slapstick **10** tomfoolery **11** foolishness, loutishness **12** clownishness, monkeyshines, prankishness **14** clowning around, playing the fool

bug 3 nag **4** flaw, germ **5** annoy, fault, virus **6** badger, bother, defect, insect, pester **7** wiretap **8** drawback, listen in, weakness **9** eavesdrop, Hemiptera **11** Heteroptera
variety: 3 bat, bed, red **4** gnat, lace, leaf, seed, toad **5** negro, plant, shore, stilt, stink, water **6** ambush, damsel, fungus, pirate, ripple **7** boatman, stainer **8** assassin, burrower, creeping **9** royal palm **10** leaf footed **11** ashgray leaf, backswimmer, broadheaded, jumping tree, velvet water **12** velvety shore, water strider, water treader **13** jumping

ground, water measurer, water scorpion **14** scentless plant **17** terrestrial turtle

bugaboo 4 ogre **5** scare **6** fright **7** anxiety

bugbear 4 ogre **5** bogey **6** goblin **7** bugaboo **8** bogeyman **9** bete noire

buggy 4 cart **5** wagon **7** vehicle **8** carriage **10** conveyance

bugle 4 horn **10** instrument

Bugs Bunny
    creator: 15 Leon Schlesinger
    character: 9 Elmer Fudd
    voice of: 8 Mel Blanc
    saying: 10 what's up doc

build 4 body, form, make, mold, open **5** begin, brace, erect, forge, found, put up, raise, renew, set up, shape, start, steel **6** create, extend, figure, harden, launch **7** amplify, augment, develop, enhance, enlarge, fashion, greaten, improve, produce **8** embark on, increase, initiate, multiply, physique **9** construct, establish, fabri- cate, institute, intensify, originate, reinforce, structure, undertake **10** inaugurate, strengthen, supplement **11** manufacture, put together **12** construction

building 7 edifice **9** structure **12** construction

building front 6 facade **8** frontage

build up 5 amass **7** develop, promote **8** increase **10** accumulate

Bujold, Genevieve
    born: 6 Canada **8** Montreal
    roles: 4 Coma **9** Monsignor, Obsession **12** King of Hearts **21** Anne of the Thousand Days

Bujumbura
    capital of: 7 Burundi

Bul 17 eighth Hebrew month

bulb 3 bud **4** corm, seed **5** plant, tuber **8** swelling

Bulfinch, Charles
    architect of: 7 Capitol (Washington DC) **16** Hartford City Hall (CT) **23** Massachusetts State House (Boston)
    style: 7 Federal

Bulgakov, Mikhail
    author of: 9 Black Snow **13** The White Guard **14** The Heart of a Dog **19** The Days of the Turbins **21** The Master and Margarita

Bulgaria
    capital/largest city: 5 Sofia
    others: 3 Lom **4** Rila, Ruse **5** Aytos, Butan, Byclu, Elena, Iskra, Stara, Varna **6** Bleven, Burgas, Devnia, Dulovo, Levsky, Pernik, Pleuna, Pleven, Plevna, Shumen, Shumla, Sliven, Slivno, Widden, Yambol, Zagora **7** Gabrovo, Karlovo, Plovdiv, Sistova, Tirnova **8** Khaskovo, Rustchuk, Svishtov **9** Ruse Vidin, Silistria **11** Kolorovgrad **12** Dimitrovgrad

school: 5 Sofia **7** Plovdiv **13** Veliko Turnovo
measure: 3 oka, oke **5** krine, lekhe, likhe
monetary unit: 3 lev **8** stotinki
weight: 3 oka, oke **5** tovar
mountain: 3 Kom **5** Botev, Pirin, Sapka **6** Balkan, Sredna **7** Vikhren **11** Rila-Rhodope
highest point: 6 Musala **8** Musallah
river: 3 Lom, Vit **4** Arda, Osma **5** Isker, Iskur, Mesta **6** Danube, Marica, Ogosta, Struma, Yantra **7** Maritsa, Stryama, Tundzha
sea: 5 Black
physical feature:
    cape: 5 Emine, Sabla **7** Kuratan
    gulf: 5 Burga
    plateau: 6 Danube
    resort: 9 Pyassatzi **13** Slunchev Bryay
    valley: 7 Maritsa
people: 4 Slav, Turk **5** Gypsy, Pomak, Tatar **6** Bulgar, Slavic **7** Chuvash **9** Cheremiss **10** Macedonian
language: 9 Bulgarian
religion: 5 Islam **24** Bulgarian Eastern Orthodox
place:
    church: 9 St Nedelja
    monastery: 4 Rila **6** Rilski
    monument: 7 Red Army
    mosque: 10 Banya Bashi
    museum: 21 Revolutionary Movement
    square: 5 Lenin
    valley of roses: 8 Kazanluk
feature:
    dance: 4 horo
    holiday: 12 St Georges Day
    newspaper: 17 Rabot Nichesko Delo
food:
    stew: 8 giuvetch

bulge 3 bag, sag **4** bump, lump **5** curve, swell **6** excess **7** distend, project, puff out, sagging **8** protrude, stand out, stick out, swelling, swell out **9** bagginess **10** projection, prominence, protrusion **12** protuberance

bulk 4 body, mass, most, size **6** extent, volume, weight **7** bigness, measure **8** enormity, hugeness, main part, majority, quantity **9** amplitude, greatness, largeness, magnitude, major part, plurality, substance **10** better part, dimensions, lion's share **11** greater part, massiveness, proportions **13** preponderance

bulky 3 big **4** huge **5** large **6** clumsy **7** awkward, hulking, immense, lumpish, massive, sizable, unhandy **8** enormous, ungainly, unwieldy **9** capacious, extensive **10** cumbersome, voluminous **12** unmanageable

bull 2 ox **4** male
    male of the: 3 elk **4** seal **5** moose, whale **6** bovine **8** elephant

constellation of: 6 Taurus
Spanish: 4 toro

bulldoze 3 cow **4** bump, fell, push, rage, raze **5** abash, bully, drive, force, level, press, shove **6** coerce, hector, jostle, propel, subdue, thrust **7** buffalo, dragoon, flatten **8** bludgeon, browbeat, domineer, shoulder **9** push about, tyrannize **10** intimidate

Bullen, Frank T
author of: 19 Told in the Dry Watches **22** The Cruise of the Cachalot

bullet 4 ball, lead, shot, slug **7** missile **8** buckshot

bulletin 4 note **6** report **7** account, message, release **8** dispatch **9** statement **10** communique, news report **12** notification **13** communication

Bullet Park
author: 11 John Cheever

bullfighter 6 torero **7** matador, picador **8** Manolete, toreador **9** Escamillo **10** El Cordobes (Manuel Benitez Perez) **15** Miguel Dominguin

Bullion State
nickname of: 8 Missouri

Bullitt
director: 10 Peter Yates
cast: 9 Don Gordon **12** Robert Duvall, Robert Vaughn, Steve McQueen **16** Jacqueline Bisset
setting: 12 San Francisco

bullock 2 ox **4** beef, bull **5** steer

bullocks 4 kine, oxen **5** beefs, bulls **6** beeves, cattle, steers

bull session 3 rap **4** talk **7** gabfest, palaver **8** dialogue **9** discourse **10** discussion **12** conversation **13** confabulation

bull's-eye 5 black **6** center **7** exactly **8** on target **9** dead center, precisely

bully 3 cow **4** good **5** annoy, swell, tough **6** cheers, coerce, despot, harass, hurrah, hurray **7** coercer, right on, ruffian, tread on **8** browbeat, bulldoze, domineer, frighten, ride over, well done **9** oppressor, terrorize, tormentor, tyrannize **10** browbeater, intimidate **11** intimidator

bullying 7 torment **8** coercion **9** despotism **10** harassment, tormenting **11** browbeating, domineering, tyrannizing **12** intimidation

bulrush 5 plant, sedge **7** cattail, papyrus

bulwark 5 guard **7** barrier, parapet, rampart, support, defense **8** mainstay **9** earthwork **10** embankment

Bulwer-Lytton, Edward
author of: 6 Harold, Pelham, Rienzi **9** Richelieu **13** The Coming Race **16** Kenelm Chillingly **18** The Last of the Barons **20** The Last Days of Pompeii

bum 3 beg **4** grub, hobo **5** cadge, idler, mooch, tramp **6** borrow, loafer,

sponge **7** drifter, vagrant **8** derelict, vagabond

bumble 6 bungle **7** blunder, stagger, stumble **8** flounder

Bumble
character in: 11 Oliver Twist
author: 7 Dickens

bumcombe, bunkum 3 rot **4** bosh, bunk **6** drivel **7** twaddle **8** nonsense, tommyrot **10** balderdash **16** stuff-and-nonsense

bump 3 hit, jar, rap **4** bang, blow, butt, hump, jolt, knob, knot, lump, node, poke, slam, slap, sock **5** bulge, clash, crack, crash, gnarl, knock, punch, shake, smack, smash, thump, whack **6** bounce, buffet, impact, jostle, jounce, nodule, rattle, strike, wallop **7** collide, run into **8** swelling **9** collision, crash into, smash into **11** excrescence **12** protuberance

bump into 4 meet **7** collide, run into **9** encounter

bumpkin 3 oaf **4** boor, lout **5** churl, yokel **8** ship beam **10** clodhopper

bump off 4 do in, kill, slay **6** murder, rub out **7** execute, gun down **8** dispatch **11** assassinate **12** take for a ride

bumptious 4 bold **5** cocky, pushy **6** brazen **7** forward, haughty **8** arrogant, boastful, cocksure, impudent, insolent **9** bodacious, conceited, obtrusive **10** aggressive, swaggering **11** impertinent, overbearing **12** presumptuous **13** overconfident, self-assertive

bumptiousness 4 gall **5** cheek **8** audacity, boldness **9** impudence **11** forwardness, presumption **12** impertinence **13** obtrusiveness **17** self-assertiveness

bumpy 5 lumpy, rocky, rough **6** uneven **10** undulating

bun 4 coil, knot, roll **8** soft roll **9** sweet roll

Bunaea
epithet of: 4 Hera
refers to: 6 temple

bunch 3 lot, mob **4** band, bevy, gang, heap, herd, host, knot, mass, pack, pile, team **5** array, batch, clump, crowd, flock, group, shock, stack, tribe, troop **6** amount, bundle, gather, huddle, number, string **7** cluster, collect, company **8** assemble, assembly, quantity **9** gathering, multitude **10** assortment, collection, congregate **12** accumulation

bundle 3 lot **4** bale, bind, heap, mass, pack, pile, wrap **5** array, batch, bunch, group, sheaf, stack, truss **6** amount, packet, parcel **7** package **8** quantity **9** multitude **10** assortment, collection **11** tie together **12** accumulation

Bundren family

characters in: 11 As I Lay Dying
member: 4 Anse, Cash, Darl **5** Addie, Jewel **9** Dewey Dell
author: 8 Faulkner

bungalow 5 cabin, house, lodge **7** cottage

bungle 3 mar **4** flub, goof, miff, ruin **5** botch, spoil **6** foul up, mess up, muddle **7** blunder, butcher, do badly, louse up, screw up **8** misjudge **9** mismanage, misreckon **10** miscompute **11** make a mess of, misestimate **12** miscalculate

Bunin, Ivan Alekseyevich
author of: 10 The Village **15** The Elagin Affair **17** The Life of Arseniev **28** The Gentleman from San Francisco

bunk 3 bed, cot, rot **4** bull **5** berth, hokum, hooey, stuff **6** bunkum, hot air, humbug, pallet **7** baloney, blather, bombast, hogwash, inanity, malarky, spinach **8** claptrap, nonsense, tommyrot **9** poppycock **10** applesauce, balderdash **11** foolishness **16** stuff and nonsense

Bunsen, Robert Wilhelm
nationality: 6 German
inventor of: 9 gas burner **10** photo meter **12** Bunsen burner, spectroscope **24** electromechanical battery

Bunshaft, Gordon
architect of: 10 Lever House (NY) **23** Beinecke Rare Book Library (Yale) **33** Hirshhorn Museum and Sculpture Garden (Washington DC) **34** Lyndon Baines Johnson Memorial Library (Austin TX)

Bunyan, John
author of: 10 The Holy War **16** Pilgrim's Progress **25** The Life and Death of Mr Badman **33** Grace Abounding to the Chief of Sinners

buona notte 9 good night

buona sera 11 good evening

buon giorno 7 good day **11** good morning

Buono, Victor
born: 10 San Diego CA
roles: 11 The Stranger **12** Four for Texas **22** Hush Hush Sweet Charlotte **26** Whatever Happened to Baby Jane

buoy 4 bell, lift **5** boost, cheer, float, raise **6** beacon, uplift **7** cheer up, elevate, gladden, lighten **8** brighten **10** keep afloat **14** floating marker

buoyancy, buoyance 4 glee **6** gaiety **7** jollity **8** gladness, vivacity **9** animation, good humor, joviality, lightness, sunniness **10** brightness, cheeriness, enthusiasm, floatiness, joyousness **11** good spirits **12** cheerfulness, exhilaration, floatability **14** weightlessness **16** lightheartedness

buoyant 3 gay **4** glad **5** happy, jolly, light, merry, peppy, sunny **6** afloat, breezy, bright, elated, joyful, joyous, lively **7** hopeful **8** animated, carefree, cheerful, floating, sportive **9** energetic, floatable, sprightly, vivacious **10** blithesome, optimistic, weightless **11** exhilarated, free and easy **12** enthusiastic, lighthearted

buoyed 6 elated **7** exalted, pleased **8** elevated **9** confident, heartened, reassured **10** inspirited

buoy up 4 warm **6** assure, uplift **7** comfort, hearten, inspire **8** inspirit, reassure **9** encourage

Burbank, Luther
field: **7** biology
developed: **13** plant breeding

burble 6 babble, bubble, gurgle, murmur **8** babbling

Burce, Suzanne
real name of: **10** Jane Powell

Burchill, Mr
character in: **19** The Vicar of Wakefield
author: **9** Goldsmith

burden 3 tax, try, vex **4** care, load, onus, pack **5** cargo **6** hamper, hinder, strain, stress, weight **7** afflict, anxiety, freight, oppress, trouble **8** encumber, handicap, hardship, load with, obligate, overload **9** press down, weigh down **10** saddle with **11** encumbrance **14** responsibility

Burden, Jack
character in: **14** All the King's Men
author: **6** Warren

burden of proof
Latin: **12** onus probandi

burdensome 4 hard **5** heavy **6** tiring **7** arduous, onerous **8** wearying **9** Herculean, laborious **10** exhausting

bureau 6 agency, branch, office **7** cabinet, commode, dresser, service, station **8** division **10** chiffonier, department **14** administration, chest of drawers

bureaucrat 8 mandarin, official, politico **9** penpusher **10** politician **11** apparatchik, functionary, rubber stamp **12** civil servant, officeholder **13** public servant

burgee 4 flag **6** banner, colors, ensign **7** pennant

burgeon 3 wax **4** blow, grow, open **5** bloom **6** expand, flower, spread, thrive **7** augment, blossom, develop, enlarge, prosper, shoot up, succeed **8** escalate, flourish, fructify, increase, mushroom, spring up **9** bear fruit **10** effloresce **11** proliferate

Burgess, Anthony
author of: **2** MF **13** Man of Nazareth, Time for a Tiger **14** Enderby Outside, The Wanting Seed **16** A Clockwork Orange, Beard's Roman Women **17** Nothing Like the Sun **20** The End of the World News

burgher 7 citizen **9** bourgeois **11** townsperson

burglar 3 cat **4** yegg **5** thief **6** robber **7** prowler **8** pilferer **9** cracksman, purloiner **12** housebreaker **14** second-story man

burglary 5 theft **6** felony **7** break-in, larceny, robbery **8** filching, stealing **9** pilfering **10** purloining **13** housebreaking **19** breaking and entering

burgundy 3 red **4** wine **5** color **13** reddish-purple

Burgundy
ancient city: **5** Autun
city: **5** Dijon
district: **5** Youne **6** Nievre **7** Cote d' Or **12** Saone-et-Loire
French: **9** Bourgogne
location: **6** France
river: **5** Rhone, Saone
tribe: **9** Burgundii

Buri
origin: **12** Scandinavian
first: **3** god
revealed by: **8** Audhumla **9** Audhumbla

burial 5 rites **7** funeral **9** interment, obsequies **10** entombment, inhumation

burial ground 7 ossuary **8** boneyard, Boot Hill, catacomb, cemetery **9** graveyard **10** churchyard, necropolis **12** potter's field

buried 4 laid, sunk **6** hidden **7** covered, inhumed, immured **9** concealed, deep sixed **10** laid to rest **11** underground

Burke, Francis
character in: **21** The Master of Ballantrae
author: **9** Stevenson

Burkina Faso *see* **10** Upper Volta

burlap 3 bag **4** hemp, jute **5** cloth **6** fabric **8** material

burlesque 5 farce, spoof **6** comedy, parody, satire **7** mockery, takeoff **8** ridicule, travesty **10** buffoonery, caricature **15** slapstick comedy

burly 3 big **5** beefy, bulky, hefty, large **6** brawny, stocky, strong, sturdy **7** hulking, sizable **8** thickset **9** ponderous, strapping

Burma *see* **7** Myanmar

burn 3 nip, tan **4** bite, char, fire, glow, hurt, pain, sear, skin **5** be hot, blaze, brown, chafe, flame, flare, flash, parch, prick, scald, singe, smart, smoke, sting **6** abrade, bronze, flames, ignite, kindle, nettle, scorch, scrape, suntan, tingle, wither **7** blister, consume, cremate, flicker, oxidize, prickle, shrivel, smolder, sunburn, swelter **8** abrasion, be ablaze, be on fire, charring, irritate, kindling **9** be flushed, reddening, set fire to, set on fire, use as fuel **10** be feverish,

be in flames, blistering, incandesce, incinerate, irritation, smoldering **12** incineration **13** reduce to ashes

burnable 9 flammable, ignitable **10** combustive **11** combustible, inflammable **13** conflagrative

Burne-Jones, Sir Edward Coley
born: **7** England **10** Birmingham
artwork: **11** Laus Veneris **15** The Golden Stairs **16** The Mirror of Venus **18** The Star of Bethlehem **28** King Cophetua and the Beggar Maid

burner, gas
invented by: **6** Bunsen

Burnett, Carol
born: **12** San Antonio TX
roles: **14** The Four Seasons **19** The Carol Burnett Show

Burnett, Frances H
author of: **20** Little Lord Fauntleroy

Burney, Fanny
author of: **7** Camilla, Diaries, Evelina

Burnham, Daniel Hudson
partner: **16** John Wellborn Root
architect of: **7** Rookery **12** Union Station (Washington DC) **15** Calumet Building **16** Flatiron Building (NYC), Reliance Building **17** Monadnock Building **25** World's Columbian Exposition

burning 3 hot **5** acrid, afire, aglow, eager, fiery, sharp **6** aflame, ardent, biting, fervid, heated, raging, red-hot **7** blazing, boiling, caustic, earnest, fanatic, fervent, flaming, flaring, frantic, glowing, ignited, intense, kindled, painful, pungent, sincere, smoking, zealous **8** flashing, frenzied, piercing, resolute, sizzling, smarting, stinging, tingling **9** corroding, prickling **10** astringent, compelling, flickering, irritating, passionate, smoldering **11** impassioned **12** all-consuming

burnish 3 wax **4** buff **5** rub up, shine **6** polish, smooth

burnished 5 shiny **6** bright, buffed, shined **8** lustrous, polished, smoothed

burnoose 4 cape, robe **5** cloak **6** mantle **7** pelisse

burn out 3 pop **4** blow **7** exhaust **10** exhaustion, extinguish

Burns, George
real name: **14** Nathan Birnbaum
wife: **11** Gracie Allen
born: **9** New York NY
roles: **5** Oh God **12** Going in Style **15** The Sunshine Boys **17** Burns and Allen Show

Burns, Robert
author of: **8** To a Louse, To a Mouse **11** A Red Red Rose, Tam O'Shanter **12** Auld Lang Syne **16** Address to the Deil, Coming Thro the Rye **17** Holy Willie's Prayer **20** Flow Gently Sweet Afton **22** My Heart's in the Highlands **23** The Cotter's Saturday

Night **32** Poems Chiefly in the Scottish Dialect

Burnt Norton
author: **7** T S Eliot

burp 5 belch, eruct **10** eructation

burr 4 buhr, rock **5** notch, stone **9** whetstone **13** pronunciation

Burr
author: **9** Gore Vidal

Burr, Aaron 13 vice president
event: **4** duel
victim: **17** Alexander Hamilton

Burr, Raymond
born: **6** Canada **14** New Westminster **15** British Columbia
roles: **8** Ironside **10** Perry Mason, Rear Window

burro 3 ass **4** mule **6** donkey, onager **7** jackass

Burroughs, Edgar Rice
author of: **15** Tarzan of the Apes

Burroughs, William S
author of: **5** Junky, Queer **6** Junkie **13** The Naked Lunch
member of: **14** Beat Generation

Burroughs, William Seward
nationality: **8** American
inventor of: **13** adding machine
grandson: **17** William S Burroughs (author)

burrow 3 den, dig **4** cave, hole, lair **6** covert, dugout, furrow, tunnel **8** excavate, scoop out **9** hollow out

Burrows, Abe
author of: **41** How to Succeed in Business without Really Trying

bursa 3 bag, sac **5** pouch, purse **6** cavity

bursar 6 purser **7** cashier **9** paymaster, treasurer **10** cashkeeper

burst 3 fly, pop, run **4** bang, bust, rend, rush **5** barge, blast, break, crack, erupt, split, spout **6** blow up, detach, divide, sunder **7** disjoin, explode, rupture, shatter, torrent **8** breaking, break out, cracking, crashing, detonate, eruption, fly apart, fracture, fragment, outbreak, separate, splinter **9** break open, discharge, explosion, gush forth, pull apart, splitting, tear apart **10** detonation, disconnect, outpouring, shattering **11** spring forth **12** disintegrate

burst forth 5 arise, begin, erupt, start **6** arrive, emerge **8** break out, commence

Burstyn, Ellen
real name: **14** Edna Rae Gillooly
born: **9** Detroit MI
roles: **11** The Exorcist **16** Same Time Next Year **18** The Last Picture Show **26** Alice Doesn't Live Here Anymore (Oscar)

Burton, Richard
real name: **22** Richard Walter Jenkins Jr
wife: **15** Elizabeth Taylor
born: **5** Wales **11** Pontrhydfen Wales
roles: **6** Becket, Hamlet **7** Camelot, The Robe **9** Cleopatra **14** My Cousin Rachel **19** The Night of the Iguana, The Taming of the Shrew **21** Anne of the Thousand Days **25** Who's Afraid of Virginia Woolf **26** The Spy Who Came in from the Cold

Burton, Robert
author of: **22** The Anatomy of Melancholy

Burundi
capital/largest city: **9** Bujumbura
others: **5** Ngozi **6** Bururi, Gitega, Kitega, Rutana, Ruyigi **7** Kibumbu, Muyinga
monetary unit: **5** franc **7** centime
lake: **7** Rugwero **8** Tshohoha **10** Tanganyika
mountain: **9** Nyamisana
highest point: **8** Nyarwana
river: **6** Akanya, Ruvuvu, Ruzizi **8** Rukagera **10** Malagarasi
people: **3** Twa **4** Hutu **5** Bantu, Batwa, Pygmy, Tutsi **6** Bahutu, Watusi **7** Barundi
language: **6** French **7** Kirundi, Swahili
religion: **5** Islam **7** animism **10** Protestant **13** Roman Catholic
feature:
  king: **4** mwami
food:
  coffee: **7** Arabica

Burushaski
language spoken in: **7** Kashmir

bury 4 hide **5** cache, cover, inter **6** encase, engulf, entomb, inhume **7** conceal, cover up, enclose, immerse, secrete **8** submerge, submerse **13** lay in the grave **17** consign to the grave

Bury My Heart at Wounded Knee
author: **8** Dee Brown

bush 4 veld **5** brush, hedge, plant, shrub, woods **6** forest, jungle **7** barrens **9** shrubbery, woodlands

Bush, George Herbert Walker
presidential rank: **10** forty-first
party: **10** Republican
state represented: **2** TX **5** Texas
defeated: **7** (Michael) Dukakis
defeated by: **7** (Bill) Clinton
vice president: **6** (James Danforth) Quayle
born: **8** Milton MA
education: **4** Yale **7** Andover
religion: **12** Episcopalian
vacation spot: **5** Maine **13** Kennebunkport
political career: **13** vice president **14** representative **21** Ways and Means Committee
  ambassador to: **2** UN **13** United Nations
  chairman of: **27** Republican National Committee

head of: **3** CIA
  liaison with: **5** China
civilian career: **3** oil **14** Zapata Offshore
military career: **5** pilot **6** US Navy
vice president under: **12** Ronald Reagan
notable events of lifetime/term: **7** Gulf War **14** Persian Gulf War **20** Operation Desert Storm
  Supreme Court appointments: **11** David Souter **14** Clarence Thomas
  invasion of: **6** Panama
father: **15** Prescott Sheldon
mother: **13** Dorothy Walker
wife: **13** Barbara Pierce
children: **4** John, Neil **5** Robin (died 1953) **6** George, Marvin **7** Dorothy

bush country 5 scrub, wilds **7** outback **10** wilderness

bushed 4 beat **5** all in, spent, tired, weary **6** done it, pooped **7** drained, wearied, worn out **8** dog tired, fatigued, tired out **9** dead tired, exhausted, played out

bushel
abbreviation: **2** bu **4** bush

bushes 5 brush **6** shrubs **9** brushwood, shrubbery **10** underbrush **11** undergrowth

bushy 5 hairy **6** fluffy, shaggy **7** hirsute **9** overgrown

business 3 job **4** case, duty, firm, line, shop, task, work **5** chore, field, place, point, store, topic, trade **6** affair, career, living, matter, office, racket **7** affairs, calling, company, concern, dealing, factory, mission, problem, pursuit, subject, venture **8** activity, commerce, function, industry, position, province, question, vocation **9** procedure, situation, specialty **10** assignment, bargaining, employment, enterprise, livelihood, occupation, profession, walk of life **11** corporation, negotiation, partnership, transaction, undertaking **13** establishment, manufacturing, merchandising **14** bread and butter, responsibility

businesslike 7 careful, correct, orderly, regular, serious **8** diligent, sedulous, thorough **9** assiduous, efficient, organized, practical **10** methodical, systematic **11** industrious, painstaking **12** professional

Busiris
king of: **5** Egypt
father: **8** Poseidon
mother: **10** Lysianassa

Busoni, Ferruccio
born: **5** Italy **6** Empoli
composer of: **8** Turandot **10** Arlecchino **11** Doctor Faust, Doktor Faust **12** Die Brautwahl **14** Comedy Overture **25** Fantasia Contrappuntistica

bus station 5 depot **8** terminal, terminus

Bus Stop
  director: **11** Joshua Logan
  cast: **9** Don Murray **10** Betty Field **13** Eileen Heckart, Marilyn Monroe **14** Arthur O'Connell

bust 3 nab **4** head, raid **5** bosom, chest, seize **6** arrest, breast, collar **7** capture **9** apprehend, sculpture **12** take prisoner **15** take into custody

Buster Brown
  creator: **10** RF Outcault
  bulldog: **4** Tige
  trademark: **9** sailor hat **10** wide collar

bustle 3 ado, fly **4** dash, flit, fuss, rush, stir, tear, to-do **5** hurry **6** bestir, flurry, hustle, pother, scurry, tumult **7** be quick, fluster, flutter, press on, scamper, scuttle **8** activity, be active, scramble **9** agitation, commotion, make haste **10** excitement, hurly-burly

busy 4 full **6** active, employ, engage, intent, occupy, on duty, work at **7** engaged, labor at, slaving, toiling, working **8** absorbed, bustling, employed, laboring, occupied **9** engrossed, in harness, strenuous **10** hard at work **11** industrious **12** be absorbed in, keep occupied **13** be engrossed in

busybody 3 pry **5** snoop **6** gossip **7** blabber, meddler, Paul Pry **8** telltale **10** chatterbox, newsmonger, talebearer, tattletale **12** blabbermouth **13** scandalmonger

busy place 4 hive **6** warren **7** anthill, beehive

but 3 yet **4** save, than that **5** if not, still **6** except, saving, unless **7** however, outside, that not **9** excepting, other than, otherwise **10** except that **14** on the other hand

Butch Cassidy and the Sundance Kid
  director: **13** George Roy Hill
  cast: **10** Paul Newman (Butch) **13** Katharine Ross (Etta Place), Robert Redford (The Kid)
  score: **13** Burt Bacharach
  Oscar for: **5** score
  song: **27** Raindrops Keep Fallin' on My Head

butcher 4 goof, kill, muff, ruin, slay **5** botch, purge, spoil **6** boggle, bungle, fumble, hack up, hit man, killer, mess up, murder **7** louse up, screw up **8** assassin, decimate, homicide, massacre, murderer **9** liquidate, manhandle, mishandle, slaughter **10** annihilate, hatchet man, liquidator **11** assassinate, exterminate, make a mess of, slaughterer **12** exterminator, mass-murderer **15** homicidal maniac

butchery 4 flop, mess **5** botch **8** massacre **9** slaughter

Butes
  father: **6** Boreas **7** Pandion

  mother: **8** Zeuxippe
  brother: **8** Lycurgus **10** Erechtheus
  sister: **6** Procne **9** Philomela
  son: **4** Eryx
  priest of: **6** Athena **8** Poseidon
  member of: **9** Argonauts
  stricken with: **8** insanity
  enticed by: **6** Sirens
  leaped into: **3** sea
  rescued by: **9** Aphrodite

Butkus, Dick (Richard Marvin)
  sport: **8** football
  position: **10** linebacker
  team: **12** Chicago Bears

Butler, Rhett
  character in: **15** Gone With the Wind
  author: **8** Mitchell

Butler, Samuel
  author of: **7** Erewhon **8** Hudibras **16** The Way of All Flesh **20** The Elephant in the Moon

butt 3 end, hit, jab, ram, rap **4** buck, bump, bunt, dupe, goat, mark, push, slap, stub **5** knock, shank, shove, smack, stump, thump **6** bottom, buffet, jostle, object, strike, target, thrust, thwack, victim **8** blunt end **13** laughingstock

buttercup 10 Ranunculus
  variety: **4** Tall **5** Early **6** Common **7** Bermuda, Bulbous, Persian **8** Colombia, Creeping **11** Yellow water

butterfingered 5 inept **6** clumsy **7** awkward **8** bungling **9** maladroit **10** ungraceful

butterfly
  pupa: **9** chrysalis **10** chrysalids **11** chrysalides
  variety: **4** blue **5** giant, nymph, satyr, snout, tiger, zebra **6** alpine, apollo, arctic, kalima **7** alfalfa, budwing, dogface, monarch, peacock, viceroy **9** Baltimore, bathwhite, brimstone, christmas, metalmark, orange tip, wood nymph **10** Parnassian **11** painted lady, spring azure **12** blue mountain, cabbage white, clouded white, silver stripe, white admiral **13** chalkhill blue, mourning cloak, pearl crescent **14** American copper, gulf fritillary, tailed birdwing **15** longtail skipper, regal fritillary **16** black swallowtail, black veined white, camberwell beauty, green veined white, Leonardus skipper, red-spotted purple **18** orchard swallowtail **19** European swallowtail **20** spicebush swallowtail, variegated fritillary **21** great purple hairstreak, questionmark anglewing, white admiral wood nymph

butter up 4 coax **6** cajole **7** flatter, wheedle **8** soft-soap

buttocks 4 buns, butt, rear, rump, seat **5** fanny, nates **6** behind, bottom **7** keister, rear end **8** backside, derriere, haunches **9** fundament, posterior **12** hindquarters

buttonhole 4 halt, slit, stop **6** accost, waylay **7** solicit **8** approach, confront

button one's lip 7 keep mum **10** keep silent **16** keep one's trap shut **18** keep one's lips sealed

Buttons, Red
  real name: **11** Aaron Chwatt
  born: **9** New York NY
  roles: **8** Sayonara **13** The Longest Day **20** The Poseidon Adventure **23** They Shoot Horses Don't They

buttress 4 arch, prop, stay **5** boost, brace, shore, steel **6** prop up **7** bolster, shore up, support **8** abutment, shoulder **9** reinforce, stanchion **10** strengthen

buxom 5 plump **6** bosomy, chesty, robust, zaftig **9** strapping **10** voluptuous **13** large-breasted, well-developed

buy 3 get **4** deal, gain **5** bribe **6** buy off, obtain, pay for, suborn **7** acquire, bargain, corrupt, procure **8** invest in, purchase **9** influence

buy and sell 4 deal **5** trade **6** market

buy off 5 bribe **6** pay off **13** grease the palm

Buzi
  son: **7** Ezekiel

Buz Sawyer
  creator: **8** Roy Crane
  sidekick: **7** Sweeney

Buzuhov, Pierre
  character in: **11** War and Peace
  author: **7** Tolstoy

buzz 3 hum **4** whir **5** drone **6** murmur **7** whisper

by 4 near, over, past **5** along **6** beside, beyond, during, toward **7** through **9** alongside **10** concerning, on or before **11** according to, no later than

by air
  French: **8** par avion

Byam, Roger
  character in: **17** Mutiny on the Bounty
  authors: **4** Hall **8** Nordhoff

Byblis
  father: **7** Miletus
  mother: **6** Cyanea
  twin brother: **6** Caunus
  loved: **6** Caunus
  changed into: **8** fountain

by few words
  Latin: **12** paucis verbis

bygone 4 past **5** olden **6** former, gone by, of yore **7** ancient, earlier **8** departed, obsolete, previous **10** antiquated

by horse
  French: **7** a cheval

Byington, Spring
  born: **17** Colorado Springs CO
  roles: **7** Jezebel **11** Little Women **13** December Bride, Heaven Can Wait **17** Mutiny on the Bounty **20** The Devil and Miss Jones, You Can't

Take It with You **26** The Charge of the Light Brigade

by itself 4 solo **5** alone, aloof, apart **8** isolated **13** unaccompanied

Byng, Admiral
character in: **7** Candide
author: **8** Voltaire

by oneself 4 solo **5** alone, aloof **8** isolated **10** solitarily **13** unaccompanied
Latin: **4** sola **5** solus

by operation of law
Latin: **8** ipso jure

bypass 4 go by **5** avert, avoid, dodge **8** go around **10** circumvent **12** detour around

bypath 3 way **4** lane **5** alley, byway, track, trail **6** bypass **7** footway, pathway, towpath, walkway **8** back road, dirt road, footpath, shortcut, side road **10** beaten path, bridle path, garden path

by-product 8 offshoot **9** aftermath **16** incidental result

by right
Latin: **6** de jure

Byron, Lord (George Gordon)
author of: **7** Don Juan, Manfred **10** The Corsair **19** The Vision of Judgment **20** The Prisoner of Chillon **23** Childe Harold's Pilgrimage

byrrh
type: **8** aperitif
origin: **6** France
flavor: **6** orange **7** quinine

bystander 6 viewer **7** watcher, witness **8** attender, beholder, looker-on, observer, onlooker, passerby **9** spectator

by the book 9 by the rule **13** authoritarian **16** according to Hoyle

by the fact itself
Latin: **9** ipso facto

by the grace of God
Latin: **9** Dei gratia

by the law itself
Latin: **8** ipso jure

by the month
Latin: **9** per mensem

by the rule 9 by the book **11** as specified **13** authoritarian

by the skin of one's teeth 6 barely, hardly **8** only just, scarcely **11** by an eyelash

by the very nature of the deed
Latin: **9** ipso facto

by the way
French: **9** en passant

by virtue and arms
Latin: **13** virtute et armis
motto of: **11** Mississippi

byway 4 lane **5** alley **6** detour, street **8** shunpike

by what right?
Latin: **7** quo jure

byword 3 law, saw **4** rule **5** adage, axiom, maxim, motto, truth **6** dictum, saying, slogan **7** precept, proverb **8** aphorism, apothegm **9** catchword, pet phrase, principle, watchword **10** shibboleth

Byzantine 6 complex **8** scheming **9** expedient, intricate **13** Machiavellian

Byzas
founder of: **9** Byzantium
father: **8** Poseidon

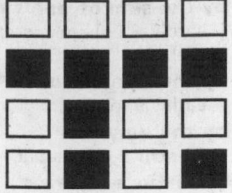
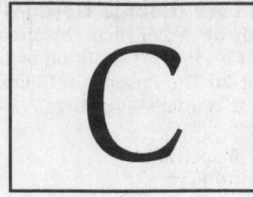
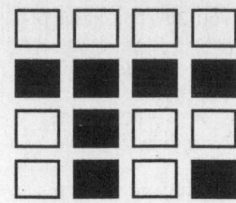

C

Caan, James
born: 9 New York NY
roles: 6 Misery 9 Dick Tracy, Funny
Lady 10 Brian's Song, For the Boys,
Rollerball 11 Bulletproof, The Gamblers 12 Brian Piccolo, The Godfather 13 Sonny Corleone 17 Cinderella Liberty

cab 4 hack, taxi 7 taxi cab

Cab 15 Biblical measure

cabal 4 band, plan, plot, ring 5 junta 6
design, league, scheme 7 faction 8 intrigue 10 connivance, conspiracy 11
combination, machination

cabalistic 6 arcane, mystic, occult, secret 7 cryptic, obscure, strange 8 abstruse, esoteric, mystical 10 mysterious, unknowable 11 inscrutable 12
impenetrable, supernatural, unfathomable 16 incomprehensible

cabaret 4 cafe, club 6 bistro 9 nightclub 10 supper club
French: 5 boite 11 boite de nuit

Cabaret
director: 8 Bob Fosse
based on stories by: 20 Christopher
Isherwood
cast: 8 Joel Grey 11 Fritz Wepper,
Helmut Griem, Michael York 12 Liza
Minnelli (Sally Bowles) 14 Marisa
Berenson
Oscar for: 7 actress (Minnelli) 8 director 15 supporting actor (Grey)
song: 12 The Money Song

cabbage 16 Brassica oleracea (Capitata
Group)
varieties: 3 Cow 4 Deer, Head, Wild
5 John's, Savoy, Skunk 6 Celery 7
Chinese 9 Flowering, Tronchuda 10
Portuguese 11 Yellow skunk 12
Western skunk

Cabecar
language family: 10 Talamancan
location: 9 Costa Rica 12 Sixaola
River 14 Central America, Talamanca
Plain
intermixed with: 6 Bribri

Cabell, James Branch
author of: 6 Jurgen 12 The High
Place 14 Figures of Earth 17 The
Cream of the Jest

cabin 3 hut 4 room 5 hutch, lodge,
shack 6 shanty 7 cottage 8 bungalow,
log cabin, quarters 9 stateroom 11
compartment

cabinet 3 box 4 case, file 5 chest 6
bureau 7 council 8 advisors, cupboard, ministry 10 breakfront, counse-
lors, receptacle 11 china closet 13 advisory board 14 chest of drawers

cable 4 cord, line, rope, wire 5 chain,
wires 6 hawser 7 mooring 8 wire
line, wire rope 12 electric wire 16
overseas telegram

Cable, George W
author of: 8 Dr Sevier 13 Old Creole
Days 15 The Grandissimes

cablegram 4 wire 5 cable 7 message
8 wireless 16 overseas telegram

Cabot, Ephraim
character in: 18 Desire Under the
Elms
author: 6 O'Neill

Caca
origin: 5 Roman
goddess of: 6 hearth
corresponds to: 5 Vesta

Cacambo
character in: 7 Candide
author: 8 Voltaire

cache 4 heap 5 hoard, stock, store 8
hideaway 9 stockpile 11 hiding place,
secret place

cachet 4 mark, seal 5 stamp, wafer 6
design, slogan 7 capsule

cackle 7 chatter 10 harsh laugh 11
shrill laugh
sound made by: 3 hen 4 chicken

cacophonous 5 harsh 6 off-key 7
grating, jarring, raucous 8 off-pitch,
screechy, strident 9 dissonant, out of
tune, unmusical 10 discordant 11 unmelodious 12 inharmonious, nonme-
lodious 13 disharmonious

cacophony 3 din 5 noise 7 discord 9
harshness 10 disharmony, dissonance

cactus
varieties: 3 Cob, Sun 4 Ball, Cane,
Chin, Claw, Club, Comb, Crab,
Hook, Lace, Leaf, Moon, Rose, Star,
Toad, Vine, Yoke 5 Agave, Apple,
Brain, Chain, Coral, Crown, Devil,
False, Giant, Leafy, Melon, Paper,
Plain, Prism, Snake, Spice, Torch 6
Barrel, Button, Cholla, Dagger, Dol-
lar, Easter, Hatpin, Hot-dog, Myrtle,
Nipple, Old-man, Orchid, Peanut,
Pencil, Ribbon, Spider 7 Cushion,
Eve's pin, Feather, Hatchet, Hat-rack,
Jumping, Old-lady, Popcorn, Rain-

bow, Rattail, Redbird, Serpent, Thim-
ble, Whisker 8 Cinnamon, Dumpling,
Fishbone, Fishhook, Flapjack, Gold
lace, Golf-ball, Hedgehog, Old-
woman, Polka-dot, Pond-lily, Snowball, Snowdrop, Starfish, Tortoise,
Turk's-cap 9 Bird's nest, Chain-link,
Christmas, Cow-tongue, Electrode,
Fire-crown, Hairbrush, Lamb's-tail,
Mistletoe, New old-man, Organ-pipe,
Porcupine, Red orchid, Sea-urchin,
Spineless, Teddy-bear, Toothpick,
Totem-pole, Turk's-head, White chin
10 Bluebarrel, Candelabra, Cotton-
pole, Easter-lily, Golden ball, Golden-
star, Living-rock, Powder-puff, Silver
ball, Strawberry, Unguentine, White
torch, Wickerware 11 Frilled lace,
Grizzlybear, Joseph's coat, Large bar-
rel, Scarlet ball, Woolly torch 12
Dancing-bones, Golden barrel, Mule-
crippler, Scarlet crown, Thanksgiving
13 Colombian ball, Creeping-devil,
Dutchman's pipe, Peruvian apple,
Peruvian torch, Silver cluster 15
Golden bird's nest 16 Mexican dwarf
tree 17 Burbank's spineless 18 Fishhook pincushion

Cacus
form: 5 giant
father: 6 Vulcan
eats: 3 men
killed by: 8 Hercules

cad 3 cur, rat 4 heel, lout 5 churl,
knave, louse, rogue 6 rascal, rotter 7
bounder, caitiff, dastard, villain 9
scoundrel

cadaver 4 body 5 stiff 6 corpse 7
remains 8 dead body, deceased

cadaverous 4 pale 5 ashen, gaunt 6
chalky, pallid 7 deathly, ghastly 8
blanched 9 bloodless, deathlike 10
corpselike

caddisfly
variety: 5 micro 8 northern 9 finger-
net, primitive, snailcase 10 long-
horned, trumpetnet, tubemaking 11
netspinning

Caddoan
tribe: 6 Pawnee 14 Chahiksichhiks

caddy 3 box, can, tin 5 chest 6 coffer

cadence 4 beat, lilt 5 meter, pulse,
swing, tempo, throb 6 accent, rhythm
7 measure

Caderousse
character in: 21 The Count of Monte

Cristo
author: 5 Dumas (pere)
cadet 5 plebe **7** recruit, student **11** youngest son **14** military student
cadge 3 beg, bum **5** mooch **6** hustle, peddle, sponge **7** solicit, scrounge **9** panhandle
cadmium
  chemical symbol: 2 Cd
Cadmus
  form: 6 prince
  realm: 9 Phoenicia
  father: 6 Agenor
  mother: 10 Telephassa
  brother: 5 Cilix **7** Phoenix
  sister: 6 Europa
  wife: 8 Harmonia
  son: 8 Illyrius **9** Polydorus
  daughter: 3 Ino **5** Agave **6** Semele **7** Autonoe
  introduced to the Greeks: 7 writing
  founded: 6 Thebes
  planted: 12 dragons teeth
Caduceus
  staff of: 7 Mercury
Caeneus
  also: 6 Caenis
  member of: 9 Argonauts
  gift: 15 invulnerability
  former identity: 6 Caenis
Caenis
  also: 7 Caeneus
  father: 6 Elatus
  violated by: 8 Poseidon
  changed into: 3 man
  subsequent identity: 7 Caeneus
caesar, Caesar 5 ruler **6** despot, kaiser, tyrant **7** emperor **8** autocrat, dictator
Caesar, Julius
  adopted son: 8 Octavian **14** Caesar Augustus
  author of: 13 On the Civil War **14** On the Gallic War
  battle: 4 Zela **5** Munda **7** Durazzo, Thapsus **8** Mytilene **9** Pharsalus **11** Dyrrhachium
  conquered: 4 Gaul
  crossed: 7 Rubicon (river)
  defeated: 6 Pompey
  lover: 9 Cleopatra
  member of: 16 First Triumvirate
  murdered by: 5 Casca **6** Brutus **7** Cassius
  murdered on: 11 Ides of March
  other triumvirs: 6 Pompey **7** Crassus
  saying: 9 Et tu Brute? (Even you Brutus?) **12** Veni vidi vici (I came I saw I conquered)
  wife: 7 Pompeia **8** Cornelia **9** Calpurnia
Caesar, Sid
  partner: 11 Imogene Coca
  born: 9 Yonkers NY
  roles: 15 Your Show of Shows
Caesar and Cleopatra
  author: 17 George Bernard Shaw

Caesar or Nothing
  author: 9 Pio Baroja
caesura 5 break, pause **6** hiatus **12** interruption
cafe 3 bar, inn **5** diner **6** bistro, eatery, nitery, tavern **7** automat, beanery, cabaret **9** cafeteria, chophouse, hash house, lunchroom, nightclub **10** restaurant, supper club **11** bar and grill, coffeehouse, discotheque **12** luncheonette
  French: 9 estaminet
cafe au lait 10 light brown **14** coffee with milk
cafe noir 11 black coffee
cage 3 pen **4** coop **5** pen in **6** coop up, encage, lock up, shut in **7** confine, impound **8** imprison, restrain, restrict **9** enclosure
cagey 3 sly **4** foxy, keen, wary, wily **5** alert, chary, leery, sharp **6** artful, crafty, shifty, shrewd **7** careful, cunning, heedful, prudent **8** cautious, discreet, watchful
Cagliari
  capital of: 8 Sardinia
Cagney, James
  nickname: 5 Jimmy
  born: 9 New York NY
  roles: 7 Ragtime **14** The Public Enemy **17** Yankee Doodle Dandy (Oscar) **19** Man of a Thousand Faces
Cagney and Lacey
  cast: 8 Tyne Daly **11** Sharon Gless
Cain
  father: 4 Adam
  mother: 3 Eve
  brother: 4 Abel, Seth
  home: 4 Eden
  son: 5 Enoch
  killed: 4 Abel
  traveled to: 3 Nod
Caine, Michael
  real name: 24 Maurice Joseph Micklewhite
  born: 6 London **7** England
  roles: 4 Zulu **5** Alfie **6** Sleuth **9** Deathtrap **13** Educating Rita, Jekyll and Hyde **14** The Ipcress File **17** A Shock to the System **19** Hannah and Her Sisters **20** The Man who would be King **21** Dirty Rotten Scoundrels
Caine Mutiny, The
  author: 10 Herman Wouk
  director: 13 Edward Dmytryk
  cast: 7 May Wynn **9** Lee Marvin **10** E G Marshall, Jose Ferrer, Van Johnson **13** Fred MacMurray, Robert Francis **14** Humphrey Bogart (Captain Queeg)
Caingua see **7** Guarani
Cairo
  Arab camp: 8 al-Fustat
  Arabic: 9 al-Qahirah
  capital of: 5 Egypt
  island: 5 Rodah **7** Zamalik
  landmark:

  mosque: 7 al-Azhar **11** Muhammed Ali
  statue: 8 Ramses II
  museum: 8 Egyptian
  river: 4 Nile
  Roman fortress: 7 Babylon
  rulers: 5 Turks **7** British, Saladin **8** Fatimids **9** Mamelukes **11** Ismail Pasha, Muhammed Ali **12** Ottoman Turks
  university: 7 Al-Azhar **8** Ain Shams, American
Cairo, Joel
  character in: 16 The Maltese Falcon
  author: 7 Hammett
  played by: 10 Peter Lorre
caitiff 3 cad, cur, rat **4** heel **5** churl, knave, louse, rogue **6** rascal, rotter **7** bounder, dastard, villain **9** scoundrel **10** blackguard
cajole 4 coax **7** beguile, deceive, flatter, wheedle **8** blandish, inveigle, persuade
cajolery 7 blarney, coaxing, fawning **8** flattery, promises, soft soap **9** adulation, sweet talk, wheedling **10** enticement, inveigling, persuasion **11** beguilement **12** blandishment
cake 3 bar, bun, dry **4** lump, mass **5** block, crust, tort **6** cookie, eclair, gateau, harden, pastry **7** congeal, cupcake, thicken **8** compress, solidify **9** coagulate, sweet roll **11** consolidate
Cakes and Ale
  author: 16 W Somerset Maugham
cakewalk 5 cinch, dance **9** promenade **12** dance contest
calaboose 3 pen **4** jail, stir **6** prison **7** slammer **8** hoosegow
Calah
  founder: 6 Nimrod
Calais
  origin: 5 Greek
  member of: 9 Argonauts
  father: 6 Boreas
  mother: 8 Orithyia
  twin brother: 5 Zetes
calamitous 5 fatal **6** tragic, woeful **7** adverse, baleful, harmful, ruinous, unlucky **8** dreadful **9** blighting **10** disastrous, pernicious **11** cataclysmic, deleterious, destructive, detrimental, distressful, unfortunate **12** catastrophic
calamity 3 ill, woe **4** blow, ruin **5** trial **6** misery, mishap **7** bad luck, failure, ill wind, reverse, scourge, tragedy, trouble, undoing **8** disaster, distress, downfall, hardship **9** adversity, cataclysm, mischance **10** affliction, ill fortune, misfortune **11** catastrophe, tribulation **13** sea of troubles **15** stroke of ill luck
calando
  music: 22 getting weaker and slower
calcium
  chemical symbol: 2 Ca

calculate 4 mean, plan **5** add up, aim at, count, judge, sum up **6** design, devise, figure, intend, reckon **7** compute, measure, predict, project, surmise, work out **8** estimate **9** ascertain, determine **10** conjecture

calculated 7 planned **10** deliberate, purposeful, thought out **11** intentional, prearranged **12** premeditated

calculating 3 sly **4** foxy, wily **6** artful, crafty, shrewd, tricky **7** cunning, devious **8** plotting, scheming **9** designing **10** contriving, intriguing **12** manipulative **13** Machiavellian

calculating machine
  invented by: 7 Babbage

calculation 6 answer, result **8** figuring, judgment **9** reckoning **10** estimation **11** computation

calculator 6 abacus **7** counter, thinker **8** computer, reckoner

Calcutta
  captured by: 5 Clive
  founded by: 23 British East India Company
  landmark: 10 Jain Temple **12** Howrah Bridge, Indian Museum **16** Botanical Gardens, Victoria Memorial **17** Zoological Gardens **18** Dakshineswar Temple
  opposite city: 6 Howrah
  river: 7 Hooghly
  state: 10 West Bengal

Calder, Alexander
  born: 14 Philadelphia PA
  sculptures also called: 7 mobiles **8** stabiles
  artwork: 3 Man **5** Whale **6** Spiral **10** Teodelapio **12** Ticket Window **13** La Grande Voile **14** The Brass Family **23** Lobster Traps and Fish Tail

Calderon de la Barca, Pedro
  author of: 12 Life Is a Dream

caldron, cauldron 3 pot **6** boiler, kettle

Caldwell, Erskine
  author of: 10 Georgia Boy **11** Tobacco Road **14** God's Little Acre

Caldwell, Taylor
  author of: 12 Answer as a Man **13** A Pillar of Iron **14** Great Lion of God **17** Testimony of Two Men, The Devil's Advocate **19** Bright Flows the River **20** Glory and the Lightning **22** The Captains and the Kings **24** Dear and Glorious Physician

Caleb Williams
  author: 13 William Godwin

Caledonia *see* **8** Scotland

calendar 4 list **5** chart, diary, table **6** agenda, docket **7** day book, program **8** register, schedule

calf 4 veal **5** dogie **6** weaner **7** leg part
  young of: 3 cow **4** bull, seal **5** whale **8** elephant

Calgary
  hockey team: 6 Flames

Calhern, Louis
  real name: 13 Carl Henry Vogt
  born: 10 Brooklyn NY
  roles: 8 King Lear **12** Julius Caesar **15** Annie Get Your Gun **16** The Asphalt Jungle **20** The Magnificent Yankee

Calhoun, Rory
  real name: 20 Francis Timothy Durgin
  born: 12 Los Angeles CA
  roles: 8 The Texan **21** Treasure of Pancho Villa **22** How to Marry a Millionaire, Requiem for a Heavyweight

Caliban
  character in: 10 The Tempest
  author: 11 Shakespeare

caliber 4 bore, rank **5** gifts, merit, place, power, scope, skill, worth **6** repute, talent **7** ability, quality, stature **8** capacity, diameter, eminence, position, prestige **10** capability, competence, estimation, excellence, importance, prominence, reputation **11** achievement, distinction

California
  abbreviation: 2 CA **3** Cal **5** Calif
  nickname: 6 Golden **8** Eldorado **12** Promised Land
  capital: 10 Sacramento
  largest city: 10 Los Angeles
  others: 4 Lodi **5** Azusa, Chico, Chino, Indio **6** Blythe, Carmel, Covina, Eureka, Fresno, Lompoc, Merced, Oxnard, Pomona, Sonoma, Tulare **7** Alameda, Anaheim, Burbank, Gardena, Needles, Oakland, Salinas, Vallejo, Visalia **8** Altadena, Berkeley, Palo Alto, Pasadena, Redlands, San Diego, Stockton **9** Cucamonga, Long Beach **11** Palm Springs, Santa Monica **12** Beverly Hills, San Francisco, Santa Barbara
  college: 3 USC **4** UCLA **5** Mills **6** Pitzer, Pomona **7** Caltech, Chapman, Scripps **8** Stanford, Whittier **10** Occidental, Pepperdine
  explorer: 6 Cortez
  feature:
    amusement park: 10 Disneyland **15** Knotts Berry Farm
    area: 9 Hollywood **15** Fishermans Wharf
    dam: 6 Hoover, Shasta **7** Boulder
    island prison: 8 Alcatraz
    mill: 7 Sutters
    national park: 7 Redwood, Sequoia **8** Yosemite **11** Kings Canyon **14** Channel Islands, Lassen Volcanic
    parade: 4 Rose
    prison: 6 Folsom **10** San Quentin
  tribe: 4 Hupa, Pomo, Yana, Yuki **5** Karok, Maidu, Miwok, Wappo, Wiyot, Yurok **6** Patwin, Shasta, Tolowa, Yokuts **7** Chumash, Luiseno, Salinan, Serrano **8** Diegueno

  people: 6 Sutter **10** Earl Warren **11** Robert Frost **13** George S Patton, John Steinbeck **14** William Saroyan
  island: 4 Goat, Mare **7** Anacapo, Channel **8** Alcatraz, Catalina, Coronado **9** Farallone
  lake: 4 Mono, Soda **5** Clear, Eagle, Owens, Tahoe **6** Salton, Tulare **7** Almanor **8** Elsinore **9** Berryessa
  land rank: 5 third
  mountain: 4 Muir **5** Coast **6** Lassen, Shasta, Wilson **7** Cascade, Klamath, Palomar, Whitney **10** Peninsular, Transverse **12** Sierra Nevada
    highest point: 7 Whitney
  physical feature:
    bay: 8 Monterey, San Diego **12** San Francisco
    cape: 9 Mendocino
    desert: 6 Mohave, Mojave **8** Colorado
    fault: 10 San Andreas
    glacier: 8 Palisade
    sea: 6 Cortez **7** Pacific
    tree: 7 redwood
    valley: 5 Death
    volcano: 6 Lassen
    wind: 7 Collada **8** Santa Ana
  president: 13 Richard M Nixon, Ronald W Reagan
  river: 3 Eel, Mad, Pit **4** Kern **5** Kings, Owens, Putah, Smith, Stony **6** Little, Merced, Salmon **7** Feather, Klamath, Rubicon, Russian, Salinas, Trinity, Truckee **10** Sacramento, San Jacinto, San Joaquin, Stanislaus
  state admission: 11 thirty-first
  state bird: 21 California Valley quail
  state fish: 21 California golden trout
  state flower: 11 golden poppy
  state motto: 6 Eureka (I have found it)
  state song: 18 I Love You California
  state symbol: 11 grizzly bear
  state tree: 17 California redwood
  baseball team: 6 Angels, Giants, Padres **7** Dodgers **9** Athletics
  basketball team: 6 Lakers **8** Clippers **19** Golden State Warriors
  football team: 7 Raiders **8** Chargers **11** Forty-Niners

Calinieff, Martin
  real name of: 13 Michael Callan

Calinky State
  nickname of: 13 South Carolina

calisay
  type: 7 liqueur
  origin: 5 Spain **9** Catalonia
  flavor: 5 herbs **7** quinine

Calkins, Richard
  creator/artist of: 10 Buck Rogers

call 3 ask, bid, cry, dub, tag **4** bawl, buzz, hail, name, need, plea, ring, roar, stop, term, yell **5** cause, claim, label, order, phone, rally, right, shout, style, title, visit **6** appeal, ask for, bellow, charge, clamor, cry out, decree, demand, direct, drop in, excuse, gather, halloo, holler, invite, invoke, know as, muster, notice, outcry, pray to, reason, scream, stop by, summon **7** collect, command, contact, convene, convoke, declare, entitle, entreat, grounds, refer to, request, require, specify, stop off, summons, warrant **8** announce, appeal to, assemble, christen, entreaty, identify, instruct, look in on, occasion, petition, proclaim **9** crying out, designate, direction, pay a visit, telephone **10** describe as, invitation, supplicate **11** declaration, instruction **12** announcement, call together, characterize, proclamation, supplication **13** justification

Callan, Michael
real name: **15** Martin Calinieff
born: **14** Philadelphia PA
roles: **9** Cat Ballou **10** The Interns **18** Gidget Goes Hawaiian, The Flying Fontaines **23** The Magnificent Seven Ride

call for 4 need **6** demand, pick up **7** request, require

call forth 4 spur **5** evoke, raise **6** arouse, awaken, excite, incite, invoke, kindle, stir up **7** command, conjure, provoke **8** summon up **9** make aware, stimulate **10** make appear

calling 3 job **4** line, work **5** craft, field, forte, trade **6** career, crying, living, metier, outcry **7** hailing, mission, passion, yelling **8** activity, business, devotion, function, province, shouting, vocation **9** bellowing, crying out, first love, hallooing, life's work, screaming, specialty **10** assignment, attachment, dedication, employment, enthusiasm, livelihood, occupation, profession, walk of life **14** bread and butter, means of support, specialization

calling off 6 ending **7** halting **8** giving up **11** termination **12** backing out of, cancellation

calling oneself thus
French: **9** soi-disant

Calliope
member of: **5** Muses
presided over: **10** epic poetry
father: **4** Zeus
mother: **9** Mnemosyne
son: **7** Orpheus

Callisto
form: **5** nymph
attended: **7** Artemis
loved: **4** Zeus
changed into: **4** bear
killed by: **7** Artemis

call off 3 end **4** halt **5** abort **6** cancel, give up **8** postpone **9** back out of, terminate **10** summon away **12** dispense with

Call of the Wild, The
author: **10** Jack London
dog: **4** Buck
master: **12** John Thornton

callous 4 cold, hard **5** cruel, horny, tough **6** inured **8** hardened, uncaring **9** apathetic, heartless, unfeeling **11** hard-hearted, indifferent, insensitive **12** thick-skinned, unresponsive **13** dispassionate, unsympathetic **14** pachydermatous

call out 3 cry **4** bawl, hail, yell **5** shout **6** bellow, cry out, holler, summon **9** challenge

callow 3 raw **5** crude, green, naive **7** artless, awkward, puerile, shallow, untried **8** childish, ignorant, immature, juvenile **9** infantile **10** sophomoric, uninformed, unschooled, unseasoned **11** uninitiated **13** inexperienced **15** unsophisticated

call to 4 hail **5** greet **6** accost, salute **7** address, shout at

call to account 5 chide, scold **6** accuse, charge, rebuke **7** arraign, bawl out, censure, chasten, reprove, upbraid **8** admonish, denounce, reproach **9** criticize, dress down, reprimand **10** take to task **11** remonstrate

call to arms 6 war cry **9** battle cry **11** rallying cry

call to order 4 open **6** muster **7** convene, convoke

call upon 3 ask, bid **4** urge **5** visit **6** charge, enjoin, exhort, invite, invoke **7** beseech, entreat, request, require **8** appeal to, petition, summon up **9** encourage **11** acknowledge

callused 4 hard **5** horny, tough **8** hardened **12** thick- skinned **14** pachydermatous

calm 4 cool, ease, mild **5** allay, balmy, bland, quell, quiet, still **6** becalm, gentle, lessen, pacify, placid, reduce, repose, sedate, serene, smooth, soothe, subdue **7** assuage, collect, compose, cool off, halcyon, mollify, pacific, placate, relaxed, relieve **8** composed, coolness, diminish, mitigate, moderate, peaceful, serenity, tranquil, unshaken **9** alleviate, collected, composure, impassive, placidity, quietness, stillness, unexcited, unruffled **10** cool-headed, motionless, simmer down, smoothness, unagitated, untroubled **11** impassivity, passionless, restfulness, self-control, tranquility, tranquilize, undisturbed, unflappable, unperturbed **12** peacefulness, tranquillity, windlessness **13** imperturbable, self-possessed, stormlessness **14** self- possession **16** imperturbability

calmness 5 poise **6** aplomb **8** coolness, serenity **9** composure, placidity, sangfroid, stillness **10** equanimity, steadiness **11** self-control, tranquility **12** peacefulness, tranquillity **14** presence of mind, self-possession **16** imperturbability

Calpurnia

character in: **12** Julius Caesar
author: **11** Shakespeare

calumnious 8 libelous **9** maligning, vilifying **10** defamatory, derogatory, slanderous **11** disparaging

calumny 4 barb, slur **5** libel, smear **6** malice **7** slander **8** innuendo **9** aspersion **10** backbiting, defamation, derogation, revilement **11** denigration, deprecation, insinuation **12** backstabbing, calumniation, depreciation, vilification **13** animadversion, disparagement, malicious lies

calvados
type: **6** brandy
origin: **6** France **8** Normandy
flavor: **5** apple
aged in: **3** oak

Calvary 8 Golgotha
means: **10** skull place

Calydonian boar
sent by: **5** Diana
killed by: **8** Meleager

Calydonian hunt
pursuit of: **4** boar

Calypso
form: **5** nymph
home: **6** Ogygia
father: **10** Titan Atlas
detained: **8** Odysseus
for: **10** seven years

calyx 4 husk **5** sepal

cam 3 cog **4** disk **8** cylinder **10** projection
located on: **5** shaft, wheel
motion: **7** rocking **8** circular **12** back and forth

camaraderie 7 jollity **8** bonhomie, good will **10** affability, clubbiness, fellowship, friendship **11** brotherhood, comradeship, sociability **12** congeniality, conviviality, friendliness **13** companionship, esprit de corps **14** good-fellowship

Camarasaurus
type: **8** dinosaur, sauropod
location: **12** United States
period: **8** Jurassic

Cambodia
other name: **7** Camboja **8** Cambodge **9** Kampuchea
capital/largest city: **8** Pnom-Penh
others: **3** Som **4** Ream **5** Takeo **6** Kampot, Kratie, Pursat **7** Kohnieh, Kompong, Kracheh, Rovieng, Samrong **8** Siem Reap, Sisophon **10** Battambang, Stung Treng **11** Kompong Cham **12** Krungkoh Kong **13** Sihanoukville
head of state: **4** King
monetary unit: **3** sen **4** quan, riel **6** puttan **7** piaster
weight: **4** mace, tael
island: **4** Kong, Rong
lake: **8** Tonle Sap
mountain: **3** Pan **7** Dangrek, Dong Rek **8** Cardamom, Elephant

highest point: 10 Phnom Aoral, Phnom Aural
river: 3 San, Sen **5** Sreng **6** Bassac, Chinit, Mekong, Porong, Pursat, Srepok **7** Kamlong, Sekhong **8** Tonle Sap
physical feature:
  bay: 10 Kompongsom
  cape: 5 Samit
  gulf: 4 Siam **8** Thailand
people: 4 Cham, Thai **5** Khmer **7** Chinese **10** Vietnamese
  leader: 6 Pol Pot **8** Sihanouk
language: 5 Khmer **6** French **9** Cambodian **10** Vietnamese
religion: 7 animism **8** Buddhism **12** Christianity
places:
  ruins/temple: 6 Angkor **9** Angkor Wat
feature:
  Communist group: 10 Khmer Rouge
Cambria see **5** Wales
cambric 5 cloth, linen **6** cotton, fabric **8** material
camel
  called: 13 beast of burden **15** ship of the desert
  chews: 3 cud
  group: 4 herd
  habitat: 5 Asia **6** Africa, desert
  kind: 7 Arabian **8** Bactrian **9** dromedary
  number of humps: 3 one, two
  species: 6 mammal
  type of: 8 ruminant
  young: 4 calf
camellia
  varieties: 5 Silky **6** Common **8** Mountain, Sasanqua
Camenae
  means: 11 foretellers
  form: 6 nymphs **7** deities
  gift: 8 prophecy
  names: 6 Egeria **8** Carmenta **9** Antevorta, Postvorta
  habitat: 8 fountain
  correspond to: 5 Muses
camera 3 APS, SLR **4** 35mm, view **6** manuel **7** plastic **8** panorama, Polaroid, twin lens **9** automatic **11** large format, range finder **12** medium format **13** point-and-shoot
  brand: 4 Fuji **5** Canon, Kodak, Leica, Nikon, Ricoh **6** Konica, Pentax, Rollei **7** Bronica, Minolta, Olympus **8** Polaroid **10** Hasselblad
  invented by:
    Kodak: 6 Walker **7** Eastman
    Polaroid: 4 Land
    photography: 6 Niepce, Talbot **8** Daguerre
    film, celluloid: 6 Edison **11** Reichenbach
    film, transparent: 7 Eastman, Goodwin
    color photo: 4 Ives

Cameroon
  capital: 7 Yaounde
  largest city: 6 Douala
  others: 3 Wum **4** Bali, Buea, Edea, Tiko **5** Kumba, Lomie, Mamfe **6** Garona, Maroua **7** Batouri, Dschang, Ebolowa, Foumban **8** Victoria **10** N'Gaoundere, N'Kongsamba
  monetary unit: 5 franc **7** centime
  island: 5 Nanny **8** Fernando
  lake: 4 Chad
  mountain: 5 Mbabo **7** Bambuto, Kapsiki, Mandara **8** Batandji **9** Atlantika
  highest point: 8 Cameroon
  river: 3 Dja, Lom **4** Faro, Mbam, Vina **5** Benue, Campo, Cross, Kadei, Mbere, Nyong, N'Goko, Sanga, Shari **6** Djerem, Ivindo, Logone, Sanaga
  sea: 8 Atlantic
  physical feature:
    cape: 10 Debundscha
    gulf: 6 Guinea
    plateau: 7 Adamawa **8** Mambilla
  people: 3 Abo, Edo, Ibo **4** Beti, Bulu, Ekoi, Ijaw, Sara **5** Bantu, Bassa, Kirdi, Pygmy, Tikar **6** Bamoun, Donala, Ewondo, Fulani, Ibibio **7** Bakweri **8** Bamileke
    Fulani chief: 7 Lamidos
  language: 4 Bulu **5** Bantu, Bassa, Hausa **6** Douala, Ewondo, French, Fulani **7** English **8** Bamileke, Fulfulde
  religion: 5 Islam **7** animism **12** Christianity
  places:
    home of prime minister: 7 Schloss
Camille
  also: 17 La Dame aux camelias
  author: 14 Alexander Dumas (fils)
  character: 6 Nanine **11** Armand Duval **17** Marguerite Gautier (Camille)
  director: 11 George Cukor
  cast: 10 Greta Garbo (Camille) **12** Henry Daniell, Robert Taylor (Armand) **14** Elizabeth Allan, Laura Hope Crews **15** Lionel Barrymore
Camillo
  character in: 14 The Winter's Tale
  author: 11 Shakespeare
Camirus
  origin: 5 Greek
  grandfather: 6 Helios, Helius
camisole 3 top **4** slip **6** jacket **10** underwaist
camouflage 4 hide, mask, veil **5** blind, cloak, cover, front **6** screen, shroud **7** conceal, cover up **8** disguise **10** masquerade, subterfuge **11** concealment
camouflaged 6 hidden, masked **7** cloaked **8** shrouded **9** concealed, disguised
camp 4 tent **5** tents **7** bivouac, lodging, rough it **8** army base, barracks, quarters **10** pitch a tent
campaign 3 run **4** push **5** drive,

stump **6** action, effort **7** crusade **8** endeavor, movement **9** offensive, operation **11** electioneer, whistle-stop **12** battle series, beat the drums, solicit votes
campanile 6 belfry **9** bell tower
campari
  type: 7 bitters **8** aperitif
  origin: 5 Italy
campground 7 bivouac **8** tent city **16** temporary shelter
Campin, Robert
  born: 8 Flanders
  also known as/identified with: 14 Master of Merode **16** Master of Flemalle
  artwork: 10 St Veronica, The Trinity **13** The Entombment **16** Merode Altarpiece (Merode Triptych) **17** The Virgin and Child **18** The Thief on the Cross
Camptosaurus
  type: 8 dinosaur **10** ornithopod
  location: 12 North America
  period: 8 Jurassic
  characteristic: 10 duck-billed
Camus, Albert
  author of: 4 L'ete **6** Summer **7** The Fall **8** Caligula, The Rebel **9** The Plague **11** A Happy Death, The Stranger **12** Cross Purpose **17** The Myth of Sisyphus
can 3 tin **4** buns, fire, rump, seat **5** fanny, put up **6** bottom **8** backside, buttocks, preserve **9** container, fundament, give the ax
Canaan
  father: 3 Ham
  brother: 4 Cush
  grandfather: 4 Noah
  known as: 12 promised land
  see also **6** Israel
Canada
  capital: 6 Ottawa
  largest city: 8 Montreal
  others: 4 Hull **5** Banff, Laval **6** Dawson, Guelph, London, Oshawa, Quebec, Regina, Sarnia, Val d'or **7** Calgary, Halifax, Moncton, Nanaimo, Sudbury, Toronto, Welland, Windsor **8** Edmonton, Hamilton, Kingston, Moose Jaw, Victoria, Winnipeg **9** Saskatoon, Vancouver **10** Port Arthur, Sherbrooke **11** Fredericton **12** Niagara Falls, Peterborough, Prince Albert, Prince George **13** Charlottetown **21** St Catherines Stratford
  school: 3 UBC **5** Laval **6** McGill, Queens **7** Toronto **8** McMaster, Montreal **9** Concordia, Dalhousie **11** Simon Fraser
  division: 5 Yukon **6** Quebec **7** Alberta, Ontario **8** Manitoba **10** Nova Scotia **12** Newfoundland, New Brunswick, Saskatchewan **15** British Columbia **18** Prince Edward Island **20** Northwest Territories

New division: 7 Nunavut
head of state: 14 British monarch **15** governor general
measure: 3 ton **5** minot, perch, point **6** arpent **7** chainon
island: 4 Read **5** Banks, Bylot, Coats, Devon, Grand, Manan, Parry, Sable **6** Baffin, Breton, Mansel, Middle **7** Belcher **8** Bathurst, Magdalen, Victoria **9** Anticosti, Ellesmere, Vancouver **10** Campobello, Manitoulin **11** Southampton **14** Queen Charlotte
lake: 4 Cree, Erie, Gras, Seul **5** Garry, Huron, Rainy **6** Louise, St John **7** Abitibi, Dubawnt, Nipigon, Ontario, Testlin **8** Kootenay, Manitoba, Okanagan, Reindeer, Superior, Winnipeg **9** Athabaska, Great Bear, Nipissing **10** Great Slave, Mistassini **12** Winnipegosis
mountain: 5 Coast, Royal **6** Robson, Skeena **7** Cariboo, Cascade, Purcell, Rockies, Selkirk, St Elias **8** Columbia, Hazelton, Monashee **9** Mackenzie, Notre Dame, Tremblant **10** Laurentian, Richardson, Shickshock **14** Jacques Cartier
highest point: 5 Logan
river: 3 Hay, Red **4** Peel **5** Liard, Peace, Slave, Yukon **6** Albany, Fraser, Nelson, Nicola, Ottawa, Skeena, St John, Thames, Thelon **7** St Marys **8** Columbia, Gatineau, Kootenay, Petawawa, Saguenay **9** Athabasca, Athapaska, Churchill, Mackenzie, Richelieu **10** Coppermine, St Lawrence **11** Assiniboine, **12** Saskatchewan
sea: 6 Arctic **7** Pacific **8** Atlantic, Labrador
physical features:
  bay: 5 Basin, Fundy, Hecla, James, Minas **6** Baffin, Gilper, Hudson, Ungava **8** Georgian
  canal: 3 Soo **7** Welland **10** Wellington
  cape: 5 Canso
  falls: 7 Niagara **9** Horseshoe
  gulf: 10 St Lawrence
  pass: 8 Chilkoot
  peninsula: 5 Gaspe **7** Boothia **8** Labrador, Melville
  plain: 11 Barren lands
  port: 6 Quebec **7** St Johns **8** Hamilton, Victoria **9** Churchill
  strait: 5 Cabot, Davis, Dease **6** Hecate, Hudson **7** Georgia **9** Belle Isle **10** Juan de Fuca
people: 5 Inuit **6** Canuck, Eskimo, French **7** English
  explorer: 5 Cabot **6** Fraser, Joliet **7** Cartier, LaSalle, Selkirk **8** Thompson **9** Champlain, MacKenzie, Marquette
  leader: 4 King, Riel **5** Clark **6** Borden **7** Laurier, Trudeau **8** Campbell, Chretien, Mulroney **9** Macdonald, St Laurent **11** Diefenbaker

language: 6 Eskimo, French **7** English
religion: 8 Anglican **13** Roman Catholic **20** United Church of Canada
places:
  battlefield: 15 Plains of Abraham
  national park: 4 Yoho **5** Banff **6** Jasper **7** Glacier **8** Kootenay **9** Elk Island **10** La Mauricie, Revelstoke **11** Wood Buffalo **12** Prince Albert **13** Waterton Lakes
  resort: 5 Banff **10** Lake Louise
feature:
  airport: 6 Gander
  emblem: 9 maple leaf
  fish: 5 charr, trout
  flower: 10 Juneflower
  police: 8 Mounties **12** Royal Mounted
food:
  soup: 7 rubaboo
canaille 6 proles, rabble **8** riffraff **9** commoners, hoi polloi **11** proletariat **13** great unwashed
canal 4 duct, Erie, Kiel, Suez, tube **5** Grand **6** Panama **7** channel, conduit, passage **8** aqueduct
Canaletto
  real name: 20 Giovanni Antonio Canal
  born: 5 Italy **6** Venice
  artwork: 18 The Stonemason's Yard
canard 4 hoax **5** rumor **7** slander **9** falsehood **12** exaggeration
Canary Islands
  other name: 14 Fortunate Isles **15** Isles of the Blest
  named for: 3 dog **5** canis **6** canine
  capital: 9 Las Palmas **19** Santa Cruz de Tenerife
  largest city: 9 Las Palmas
  others: 4 Icod **6** Laguna **7** Orotava **8** Arrecife, Valverde **12** San Sebastian
  government: 16 overseas province of: **5** Spain
  measure: 8 fanegada
  monetary unit: 6 peseta
  island: 4 Roca **5** Clara, Ferro, Lobos, Rocca **6** Gomera, Hierro **7** Inferno, La Palma **8** Graciosa, Tenerife **9** Lanzarote **10** Lanzarotte **11** Gran Canaria **13** Fuerteventura
  mountain: 6 La Cruz **8** El Cumbre, Tenerife
  highest point: 5 Teide, Teyde
  sea: 8 Atlantic
  people: 7 Spanish
  language: 7 Spanish
  religion: 13 Roman Catholic
canasta
  number of players: 4 four
  cards/hand: 8 eleven
  meld: 12 three of a kind
  wild card: 5 deuce, joker
Canberra
  capital of: 9 Australia
  territory: 13 New South Wales **26** Australian Capital Territory
  lake: 13 Burley Griffin
cancel 4 undo, void **5** abort, annul, erase, quash, scrub **6** delete, offset, recall, recant, repeal, revoke **7** abolish, call off, nullify, rescind, retract, vitiate **8** abrogate, call back, set aside **9** repudiate **10** balance out, bluepencil, do away with, invalidate, neutralize **11** countermand **12** dispense with **13** compensate for **14** counterbalance **18** declare null and void
cancellation 6 repeal **9** abolition **10** abrogation, effacement, rescinding, revocation **11** abolishment, eradication, repudiation, termination
cancer 3 rot **4** crab **6** plague **7** sarcoma, scourge **8** neoplasm, sickness **9** carcinoma **10** malignancy **14** malignant tumor **15** malignant growth
Cancer
  symbol: 4 crab
  planet: 4 Moon
  rules: 4 home **6** family
  born: 4 July, June
Cancer Ward, The
  author: 21 Aleksandr Solzhenitsyn
candelabrum 7 menorah **8** dikerion **9** girandole, trikerion **11** candlestick **12** candleholder
Candia *see* **5** Crete
candid 4 fair, free, just, open **5** blunt, frank, plain **6** direct, honest **7** genuine, natural, relaxed, sincere, unposed **8** informal, outright, truthful **9** downright, impromptu, outspoken **10** forthright **11** plain spoken, spontaneous, unvarnished **14** extemporaneous **15** straightforward
Candida
  author: 17 George Bernard Shaw
candidate 7 hopeful, nominee **8** aspirant, eligible **9** applicant, contender, job seeker **10** competitor, contestant **11** possibility **12** office seeker
Candid Camera
  host: 9 Allen Funt
  co-host: 11 Bess Myerson **12** Durward Kirby **13** Arthur Godfrey
  tag: 5 smile
Candide
  author: 8 Voltaire
  character: 6 Martin **7** Cacambo **8** Pangloss **9** Cunegonde **10** Admiral Byng **17** Thunder-ten-Tronckh
candidness 6 candor **7** honesty, openess **9** frankness, sincerity **10** directness **12** truthfulness **13** guilelessness
candle 3 dip, wax **5** light, taper **6** bougie, cierge, tallow **9** rush light
candleholder, candlestick 6 sconce **7** menorah **8** dikerion **9** girandole, trikerion **10** chandelier **11** candelabrum
candor 7 honesty **8** fairness, justness, openness **9** bluntness, frankness, sin-

cerity **10** directness **11** artlessness **12** impartiality, truthfulness **14** forthrightness **15** plainspokenness **19** straightforwardness

candy 3 bar **4** kiss **5** cream, fudge, jelly, sweet, taffy **6** bonbon, comfit, dainty, nougat, sweets, toffee **7** brittle, caramel, fondant, gumdrop, praline **8** lollipop **9** chocolate, jellybean, sweetmeat **10** confection **12** all-day sucker **13** confectionery, peanut brittle

cane 3 hit, rap, rod, tan **4** beat, drub, flog, lash, whip **5** baste, flail, smite, staff, stick, whack **6** strike, switch, thrash, wallop **7** trounce **12** walking stick

cane 11 Arundinaria
varieties: 4 Dumb, Wild **5** Arrow, Sugar **6** Rattan, Switch, Tobago, Tonkin **7** Tsingli **8** Southern **11** Spotted dumb **12** Chinese sweet **14** Yellow-leaf dumb

Canea
capital of: 5 Crete

Canetti, Elias
author of: 8 Auto da Fe **12** Tower of Babel **14** Crowds and Power **15** The Torch in My Ear **16** Kafka's Other Trial, The Tongue Set Free

Caniff, Milton
creator/artist of: 10 Dickie Dare **11** Steve Canyon **14** The Gay Thirties **18** Terry and the Pirates

canine 3 cur, dog, fox, pup **4** mutt, wolf **5** hound, hyena, puppy, tooth **6** coyote, cuspid, jackal **7** mongrel **8** eyetooth

canker 4 sore **5** ulcer **6** blight, cancer, lesion **9** mouth sore **12** inflammation

Cannibal Galaxy, The
author: 12 Cynthia Ozick

cannon 3 bit, gun **4** bone **5** carom **6** mortar **7** battery **8** field gun, howitzer, ordnance **9** artillery **10** field piece, mounted gun, pickpocket

Cannon
character: 11 Frank Cannon
cast: 13 William Conrad

Cannon, Dyan
real name: 19 Samille Diane Friesen
husband: 9 Cary Grant
born: 8 Tacoma WA
roles: 6 Shamus **9** Deathtrap **10** Ally McBeal **13** Heaven Can Wait **15** Such Good Friends **19** Bob & Carol & Ted & Alice **23** Revenge of the Pink Panther

cannonade 5 burst, salvo **6** volley **7** barrage, battery **8** shelling **9** fusillade **11** bombardment

canny 4 foxy, wary, wily, wise **5** cagey, sharp **6** artful, astute, clever, crafty, shrewd, subtle **7** careful, cunning, knowing **8** skillful **9** judicious, sagacious **10** convincing **11** circumspect, intelligent **13** perspicacious

Cano, Alonso
born: 5 Spain **7** Granada
artwork: 16 Granada Cathedral (facade) **18** Madonna of the Rosary **20** Immaculate Conception **23** The Seven Joys of the Virgin

canoe 4 boat **5** bungo, kayak **6** dugout **7** pirogue

canoeing
athlete: 11 Marcia Smoke

canon 3 law **4** code, rule **5** dogma, edict, model, order **6** decree **7** pattern, precept, statute **8** doctrine, standard **9** bench mark, criterion, ordinance, principle, yardstick **10** regulation, touchstone

canonical 6 proper **8** accepted, approved, official orthodox **9** authentic, customary **10** authorized, legitimate, recognized, sanctioned **12** conventional **13** authoritative

Canonization, The
author: 9 John Donne

canopy 4 hood **5** cover **6** awning, tester **8** covering

Canova, Antonio
born: 5 Italy **8** Possagno
artwork: 7 Perseus **12** Venus Victrix (Pauline Bonaparte Borghese) **14** Cupid and Psyche **16** Letizia Bonaparte **17** Daedalus and Icarus

Cansino, Margarita Carmen
real name of: 12 Rita Hayworth

cant 4 sham, talk **5** argot, lingo, slang **6** humbug, jargon **8** parlance, pretense **9** hypocrisy **10** lip service, vernacular **11** insincerity **15** pretentiousness **17** sanctimoniousness

cantabile
music: 7 flowing, singing **8** songlike

cantaloupe 5 fruit, melon **9** muskmelon

cantankerous 4 mean **5** cross, huffy, short, sulky, surly, testy **6** crabby, cranky, crusty, grumpy, morose, ornery, sullen, touchy **7** bearish, crabbed, fretful, grouchy, peevish, waspish **8** choleric, churlish, contrary, snappish **9** irascible, irritable, splenetic **10** ill-humored, ill-natured **11** contentious, ill-tempered, quarrelsome **12** disagreeable **13** argumentative

cantatrice 6 singer **9** chanteuse **10** songstress **18** professional singer

canteen 2 PX **4** club **5** flask **6** bottle **10** commissary **11** pocket flask **12** post exchange

canter 4 gait, lope, pace, trot **6** gallop, singer, whiner

Canterbury Tales, The
author: 15 Geoffrey Chaucer
starting point: 9 Southwark, Tabard Inn
goal:
tomb of: 6 Becket
character/tale: 3 Nun **4** Cook, Dyer,

Monk **5** Canon, Friar, Reeve, Webbe **6** Knight, Miller, Parson, Squire, Yeoman **7** Shipman, Tapicer **8** Franklin, Manciple, Merchant, Pardoner, Prioress, Summoner **9** Carpenter, Ploughman **10** Wife of Bath **11** Haberdasher **13** Clerk of Oxford, Sergeant of Law **14** Doctor of Physic

Cantor, Eddie
real name: 21 B Edward Israel Iskowitz
nickname: 9 Banjo Eyes
wife: 9 Ida Tobias
born: 9 New York NY
roles: 7 Whoopee **8** Kid Boots **9** Banjo Eyes

cantor of a synagogue
Hebrew: 5 hazan **6** chazan

Cantos
author: 9 Ezra Pound

can't stand 4 hate **5** abhor **6** detest, eschew, loathe **7** despise **8** execrate **9** abominate, can't abide **11** can't stomach **14** hate the sight of

canvas 4 duck **7** painting **8** painting **9** sailcloth, tarpaulin, tent cloth

canvass 4 poll, scan, sift **5** study, tally **6** survey **7** analyze, discuss, examine, explore, inquiry, inquire, inspect, solicit **8** analysis, campaign, scrutiny **10** evaluation, scrutinize **11** enumeration, exploration, inquire into, investigate, take stock of **13** give thought to, investigation

canyon 3 col, cut, gap **4** draw, pass, wadi, wash **5** break, chasm, cleft, crack, gorge, gulch, gully, notch **6** arroyo, coulee, defile, divide, ravine, valley **7** fissure, opening **8** corridor, crevasse, water gap

cap 3 fez, lid, tam, top **4** acme, seal **5** beret, cover, limit, outdo **6** better, exceed, top off **7** surpass **8** headgear, out-strip **9** headdress **10** visored hat

capability 3 art **4** gift **5** flair, knack, power, skill **6** talent **7** ability, faculty, know-how **8** capacity, efficacy, facility **9** potential **10** attainment, competence, competency **11** proficiency **12** potentiality **13** qualification

capable 3 apt **4** able, deft **5** adept **6** adroit, artful, clever, expert, gifted **7** skilled **8** masterly, skillful, talented **9** competent, effective, ingenious **10** proficient **11** efficacious, intelligent **12** accomplished

capable of assuming legal responsibility
Latin: 8 sui juris

Capable of Honor
author: 10 Allan Drury

capable of managing one's own affairs
Latin: 8 sui juris

capacious 3 big **4** huge, vast, wide **5** ample, broad, large, roomy **7** mammoth, massive **8** gigantic, spacious **9**

expansive, extensive **10** commodious, expandable, tremendous, voluminous **13** amplitudinous

capaciousness 9 amplitude, roominess **12** spaciousness **14** commodiousness

capacitate 5 allow **6** enable, permit **7** empower, qualify **8** make able

capacity 4 mind, role, room, size **5** gifts, limit, might, power, range, scope, space **6** extent, talent, volume **7** ability, faculty **8** aptitude, facility, function, judgment, position, sagacity, strength **9** amplitude, endowment, intellect, potential **10** brain power, capability **11** discernment **12** intelligence, perspicacity **15** maximum contents

caparison 5 adorn, equip **6** bedeck **9** equipment, trappings

cape 4 spit **5** cloak, manta, point, shawl **6** mantle, poncho, serape, tabard, tongue **7** pelisse **8** headland **9** peninsula **10** promontory

Capek, Karel
author of: **3** R U R **8** Hordubal, Krakatit **9** The Mother **13** Power and Glory **18** The War with the Newts

caper 3 hop **4** jape, jump, lark, leap, romp, skip **5** antic, bound, fling, frisk, prank, spree, stunt, trick **6** bounce, cavort, frolic, gambol, prance **7** caprice **8** escapade **9** adventure, high jinks **10** carrying on **11** shenanigans **14** monkey business

capital 4 cash, fine **5** great, money, super **6** center, riches, superb, wealth **7** supreme **9** excellent, financing, first-rate, majuscule, matchless, principal, resources **10** cash on hand, first class **11** large letter, wherewithal **12** headquarters **13** working assets **14** available means **15** investment funds, upper-case letter

capital city (of countries)
of **Afghanistan: 5** Kabul
of **Albania: 6** Tirana, Tirane
of **Algeria: 7** Algiers
of **Andorra: 14** Andorra-la-Vella
of **Angola: 6** Luanda
of **Antigua and Barbuda: 7** St John's
of **Argentina: 11** Buenos Aires
of **Armenia: 6** Erivan **7** Yerevan
of **Australia: 8** Canberra
of **Austria: 6** Vienna
of **Azerbaijan: 4** Baku
of **the Bahamas: 6** Nassau
of **Bahrain: 6** Manama
of **Bangladesh: 5** Dacca
of **Barbados: 10** Bridgetown
of **Belarus: 5** Minsk
of **Belgium: 8** Brussels **9** Bruxelles
of **Belize: 8** Belmopan
of **Benin: 9** Porto-Novo
of **Bermuda: 8** Hamilton
of **Bhutan: 6** Thimbu **7** Thimphu
of **Bolivia: 5** La Paz, Sucre
of **Bosnia-Herzegovina: 8** Sarajevo

of **Botswana: 8** Gaborone **9** Gaberones
of **Brazil: 8** Brasilia
of **Brunei: 17** Bandar Seri Begawan
of **Bulgaria: 5** Sofia
of **Burkina Faso: 11** Ouagadougou
of **Burundi: 9** Bujumbura
of **Cambodia: 8** Pnom-Penh
of **Cameroon: 7** Yaounde
of **Canada: 6** Ottawa
of **the Canary Islands: 9** Las Palmas **19** Santa Cruz de Tenerife
of **Cape Verde: 5** Praia
of **the Central African Republic: 6** Bangui
of **Chad: 8** Fort-Lamy, N'Djamena
of **Chile: 8** Santiago
of **China: 6** Peking
of **Colombia: 6** Bogota
of **Comoros: 6** Moroni
of **the Congo: 11** Brazzaville
of **Costa Rica: 7** San Jose
of **Crete: 5** Canea **8** Iraklion
of **Croatia: 6** Zagreb
of **Cuba: 6** Havana **8** La Habana
of **Cyprus: 7** Nicosia
of **Czechoslovakia/ Czech Republic: 6** Prague
of **Denmark: 10** Copenhagen
of **Djibouti: 8** Djibouti
of **the Dominican Republic: 12** Santo Domingo **14** Ciudad Trujillo
of **Ecuador: 5** Quito
of **Egypt: 5** Cairo
of **El Salvador: 11** San Salvador
of **England: 6** London
of **Equatorial Guinea: 6** Malabo
of **Eritrea: 6** Asmara
of **Estonia: 7** Tallinn
of **Ethiopia: 8** Addis Ababa
of **Fiji: 4** Suva
of **Finland: 8** Helsinki **11** Helsingfors
of **France: 5** Paris
of **the Gabon Republic: 10** Libreville
of **The Gambia: 6** Banjul **8** Bathurst
of **Georgia: 7** Tbilisi
of **Germany (East): 10** East Berlin
of **Germany (West): 4** Bonn
of **Germany (reunited): 5** Berlin
of **Ghana: 5** Accra, Akkra
of **Greece: 6** Athens
of **Greenland: 3** Nuk **8** Godthaab, The Point
of **Grenada: 9** St Georges
of **Guatemala: 13** Guatemala City
of **Guinea: 7** Conakry
of **Guinea-Bissau: 6** Bissau
of **Guyana: 10** Georgetown
of **Haiti: 12** Port-au-Prince
of **Honduras: 11** Tegucigalpa
of **Hong Kong: 8** Victoria
of **Hungary: 8** Budapest
of **Iceland: 9** Reykjavik
of **India: 8** New Delhi
of **Indonesia: 7** Jakarta **8** Djakarta
of **Iran: 6** Tehran **7** Teheran
of **Iraq: 7** Baghdad
of **Ireland: 6** Dublin

of **Israel: 9** Jerusalem
of **Italy: 4** Roma, Rome
of **the Ivory Coast: 7** Abidjan
of **Jamaica: 8** Kingston
of **Japan: 3** Edo **5** Tokyo
of **Java: 7** Jakarta **8** Djakarta
of **Jordan: 5** Amman
of **Kazakhstan: 7** Alma-Ata
of **Kenya: 7** Nairobi
of **Kiribati: 6** Tarawa
of **Korea (North): 9** Pyongyang
of **Korea (South): 5** Seoul
of **Kuwait: 10** Kuwait City
of **Kyrgyzstan: 7** Bishkek (Frunze)
of **Laos: 9** Viengchan, Vientiane
of **Latvia: 4** Riga
of **Lebanon: 6** Beirut **8** Beyrouth
of **Lesotho: 6** Maseru
of **Liberia: 8** Monrovia
of **Libya: 7** Tripoli
of **Liechtenstein: 5** Vaduz
of **Lithuania: 5** Vilna **6** Kausas **7** Vilnius
of **Luxembourg: 10** Luxembourg
of **Macedonia: 6** Skopje
of **Madagascar: 10** Tananarive **12** Antananarivo
of **Malawi: 8** Lilongwe
of **Malaysia: 11** Kuala Lumpur
of **Maldives: 4** Male
of **Mali: 6** Bamako
of **Malta: 8** Valletta
of **Mauritania: 10** Nouakchott
of **Mauritius: 9** Port Louis
of **Mexico: 10** Mexico City
of **Moldova: 16** Chisinau, Kishinev
of **Monaco: 11** Monaco-Ville
of **Mongolia: 9** Ulan Bator
of **Montenegro: 7** Cetinje **8** Titograd **9** Podgorica
of **Morocco: 5** Rabat **6** Rabbat
of **Mozambique: 6** Maputo **15** Lourenco Marques
of **Myanmar: 6** Yangon **7** Rangoon
of **Namibia: 8** Windhoek
of **Nauru: 13** Yaren District
of **Nepal: 8** Katmandu **9** Kathmandu
of **Netherlands: 8** The Hague **9** Amsterdam
of **New Guinea: 11** Port Moresby
of **New Zealand: 10** Wellington
of **Nicaragua: 7** Managua
of **Niger: 6** Niamey
of **Nigeria: 5** Abuja, Lagos
of **Northern Ireland: 7** Belfast
of **Norway: 4** Oslo **11** Christiania
of **Oman: 6** Masqat, Muscat
of **Pakistan: 9** Islamabad
of **Panama: 10** Panama City
of **Paraguay: 8** Asuncion
of **Peru: 4** Lima
of **the Philippines: 6** Manila
of **Poland: 6** Warsaw
of **Portugal: 6** Lisbon
of **Puerto Rico: 7** San Juan
of **Qatar: 4** Doha **7** al-Dawha
of **Romania: 9** Bucharest
of **Russia: 6** Moscow

of Rwanda: 6 Kigali
of Samoa (American): 8 Pago Pago
of Samoa (Western): 4 Apia
of San Marino: 9 San Marino
of Sao Tome and Principe: 7 Sao Tome
of Sardinia: 8 Cagliari
of Saudi Arabia: 6 Riyadh
of Scotland: 9 Edinburgh
of Senegal: 5 Dakar
of Seychelles: 8 Victoria
of Sicily: 7 Palermo
of Sierra Leone: 8 Freetown
of Sikkim: 7 Gangtok
of Singapore: 9 Singapore
of Slovakia: 10 Bratislava
of Slovenia: 9 Ljubljana
of the Solomon Islands: 7 Honiara
of Somalia: 9 Mogadishu **10** Mogadiscio
of South Africa: 8 Cape Town, Pretoria **12** Bloemfontein
of Spain: 6 Madrid
of Sri Lanka: 7 Colombo
of the Sudan: 8 Khartoum
of Suriname: 10 Paramaribo
of Swaziland: 7 Mbabane
of Sweden: 9 Stockholm
of Switzerland: 4 Bern
of Syria: 8 Damascus
of Taiwan: 6 Taipei
of Tajikistan: 8 Dushanbe
of Tanzania: 11 Dar es Salaam
of Thailand: 6 Bankok **7** Bangkok **8** Thonburi **9** Ayutthaya
of Tibet: 5 Lassa, Lhasa
of Togo: 4 Lome
of Tongo: 9 Nukualofa
of Trinidad and Tobago: 11 Port of Spain
of Tunisia: 5 Tunis
of Turkey: 6 Ankara
of Turkmenistan: 9 Ashkhabad
of Tuvalu: 8 Funafuti
of Uganda: 7 Kampala
of Ukraine: 4 Kiev
of United Arab Emirates: 8 Abu Dhabi
of United States: 12 Washington DC
of Uruguay: 10 Montevideo
of Uzbekistan: 8 Tashkent
of Vanuatu: 4 Vila
of Venezuela: 7 Caracas
of Vietnam: 5 Hanoi **6** Saigon
of Wales: 7 Cardiff
of Western Sahara: 6 Al Aiun **7** El Aaiun
of Western Samoa: 4 Apia
of Yemen: 4 Sana, Aden **5** Sanaa
of Yugoslavia: 7 Beograd **8** Belgrade
of Zaire: 8 Kinshasa
of Zambia: 6 Lusaka
of Zimbabwe: 6 Harare **9** Salisbury
capital city (of states) *see state capitals*
capitalism 14 free enterprise
capitalist 5 mogul **6** tycoon **8** investor

9 financier, plutocrat **14** businessperson
capitalize 4 back, fund **5** stake **7** exploit, finance, support, trade on, utilize **8** bankroll, cash in on, profit by **9** subsidize **11** foot the bill **13** make the most of **17** turn an honest penny **23** strike while the iron is hot **24** make hay while the sun shines
capitalize on 7 exploit, utilize **8** profit by **13** turn to account **14** use to advantage
capitol 10 statehouse **11** legislature **15** government house
capitulate 5 yield **6** accede, give in, give up, relent, submit **7** succumb **8** cry quits **9** acquiesce, surrender **11** come to terms, sue for peace **15** lay down one's arms **17** acknowledge defeat, hoist the white flag
capitulation 8 giving in, giving up, quitting, yielding **9** surrender **10** submission
Capote, Truman
    author of: 11 In Cold Blood **12** A Tree of Night **19** Breakfast at Tiffany's **21** other voices other rooms
    character: 14 Holly Golightly
Capp, Al
    real name: 18 Alfred George Caplin
    creator/artist of: 13 Li'l Abner Yokum
Cappotas
    epithet of: 4 Zeus
    means: 8 reliever
Capra, Frank
    director of: 11 Lady for a Day, Lost Horizon **15** State of the Union **17** Arsenic and Old Lace, It's a Wonderful Life, Mr Deeds Goes to Town (Oscar) **18** It Happened One Night (Oscar) **20** You Can't Take It with You (Oscar) **23** Mr Smith Goes to Washington
caprice 3 fad **4** lark, whim **5** antic, caper, craze, fancy, fling, prank, quirk, spree, stunt **6** notion, oddity, vagary **7** impulse **8** crotchet, escapade **10** erraticism **11** peculiarity **12** eccentricity, idiosyncrasy
capricious 6 fickle, fitful, quirky, uneven **7** erratic, faddish, flighty **8** fanciful, skittish, unstable, unsteady, variable, wavering **9** eccentric, impulsive, mercurial, uncertain, undecided **10** changeable, indecisive, irresolute **11** vacillating **12** inconsistent **13** irresponsible **15** shilly-shallying
capriciousness 7 caprice **10** fickleness **11** instability **12** irresolution **13** impulsiveness, inconsistency **15** shilly-shallying
Capricorn
    symbol: 4 goat
    planet: 6 Saturn
    rules: 6 career
    born: 7 January **8** December

capsicum peppers
    origin: 15 tropical America
    color: 3 red **5** green, white **6** violet, yellow
    variety: 5 ancho, chile **7** cayenne, paprika, serrano **8** chipotle, habanero, jalapeno **9** red pepper **11** chili pepper, chili powder, curry powder, sweet pepper
    flavor: 3 hot
    use: 5 chili, curry, pizza **8** barbecue **9** paprikash
capsize 5 upset **6** invert **7** tip over **8** flip over, keel over, overturn, turn over **10** turn turtle
capsule 4 case, pill **6** ampule **7** cockpit **8** covering **9** spore case **12** condensation
captain 4 boss, head **5** chief, pilot **6** leader, master, old man **7** headman, skipper **9** chieftain, commander **10** commandant **12** chief officer **16** company commander **17** commanding officer
    famous: 4 Ahab, Andy, Hook, Kirk, Nemo
Captain Blood
    director: 13 Michael Curtiz
    cast: 10 Errol Flynn **12** Lionel Atwill **13** Basil Rathbone **17** Olivia de Havilland
Captain Carpenter
    author: 15 John Crowe Ransom
Captain Craig
    author: 22 Edwin Arlington Robinson
Captain Hook
    character in: 8 Peter Pan
    author: 6 Barrie
    henchman: Smee
Captain Horatio Hornblower
    author: 10 C S Forester
Captains Courageous
    author: 14 Rudyard Kipling
    director: 13 Victor Fleming
    cast: 12 Mickey Rooney, Spencer Tracy **13** John Carradine, Melvyn Douglas **15** Lionel Barrymore **18** Freddie Bartholomew
    Oscar for: 5 actor (Tracy)
Captain's Daughter, The
    author: 16 Alexander Pushkin
Captain Video and His Video Rangers
    character: 7 Dr Pauli **9** The Ranger **12** Captain Video
    cast: 7 Al Hodge **10** Hal Conklin **11** Don Hastings **13** Richard Coogan
    slogan: 29 Guardian of the Safety of the World
    villain: 4 Atar **7** Nargola **8** Dahoumie, Kul of Eos **9** Dr Clysmok **12** Heng Foo Seeng **14** Mook the Moon Man
    gimmick: 5 Tobor **9** Discatron **11** Atomic Rifle **16** Barrier of Silence, Radio Scillograph **17** Cosmic Ray Vibrator **18** Opticon Scillometer **19** Cloak of Invisibility, Trisonic Com-

pensator

spaceship: 6 Galaxy

caption 5 title **6** legend **7** heading, subhead **8** headline, subtitle **11** explanation

captious 4 mean **5** picky, testy **6** ornery **7** carping, cutting, peevish **8** caviling, contrary, niggling, perverse, petulant, picayune, snappish **9** fractious, querulous **10** belittling, censorious, nitpicking **11** deprecating **12** cantankerous, faultfinding **13** hypercritical

captivate 4 lure **5** charm **6** dazzle, enamor, seduce **7** attract, bewitch, delight, enchant, win over **8** enthrall **9** carry away, enrapture, fascinate, hypnotize, infatuate, mesmerize, transport **13** turn the head of **14** take the fancy of

captivated 7 charmed, pleased **9** delighted, enchanted **10** enraptured, enthralled, spellbound

captivating 7 winning, winsome **8** adorable, charming, dazzling, engaging, fetching, magnetic **9** appealing, beguiling, disarming **10** attractive, bewitching, delightful, enchanting, entrancing **11** enthralling, fascinating, mesmerizing **12** ingratiating, irresistible

captive 3 POW **5** caged **6** penned **7** hostage **8** confined, enslaved, interned, locked up, prisoner **9** oppressed **10** imprisoned, subjugated **12** incarcerated

captivity 7 bondage, holding, slavery **9** servitude **10** detainment **12** imprisonment

capture 3 bag, nab **4** bust, grab, snag, take, trap **5** catch, grasp, pinch, seize, snare **6** arrest, collar, taking **7** bagging, ensnare, procure, seizure, snaring **8** catching, trapping **9** apprehend, collaring, ensnaring, lay hold of **12** apprehension, laying hold of, take prisoner **14** taking prisoner **15** take into custody

Capulet family
  characters in: 14 Romeo and Juliet
  author: 11 Shakespeare

Capys
  father: 9 Assaracus
  son: 7 Laocoon **8** Anchises
  grandson: 6 Aeneas
  founded: 5 Capua
  warned against: 11 Trojan horse

car 4 auto, heap **5** buggy, coach, diner, motor **6** boxcar, hot rod, jalopy, wheels **7** flivver, machine, sleeper, vehicle **8** carriage **9** tin lizzie **10** automobile **12** motor vehicle
  kind: 4 coal **5** cable, horse, motor **6** cattle, dining, parlor, street **7** baggage, freight, Pullman, railway **8** sleeping

carabiniere 9 policeman

Caracas
  birthplace of: 12 Simon Bolivar
  capital of: 9 Venezuela
  founder: 13 Diego de Losada
  museum: 7 Bolivar **8** Criolan **11** Colonial Art, Raul Santana
  river: 6 Guaire

carafe 5 flask **6** bottle, vessel **9** container

carapace 4 case **5** shell **6** lorica, shield **7** carapax **8** calipash, covering **11** turtle shell

Caravaggio, Michelangelo Merisi da
  born: 5 Italy **10** Caravaggio
  artwork: 12 Young Bacchus **14** Burial of St Lucy **16** Raising of Lazarus **17** The Supper at Emmaus **18** Calling of St Matthew, The Life of St Matthew **20** St Matthew and the Angel **21** The Conversion of St Paul **23** The Crucifixion of St Peter **30** The Beheading of St John the Baptist

caravan 4 band, file, line **5** queue, train, troop **6** coffle, column, convoy, parade, string **7** company, cortege, retinue, trailer **9** cavalcade, chain gang, entourage, motorcade **10** procession, wagon train

caravansary 3 inn **5** hotel **8** hostelry

caraway
  botanical name: 10 Carum carvi
  origin: 6 Europe **9** Asia Minor **14** the Netherlands
  liqueur: 6 Kummel
  candy-covered caraway seeds: 6 comfit **12** whisky-killer
  use: 4 pork, soup, stew **8** rye bread

carbohydrate
  consists of: 5 water **6** carbon, oxygen **8** hydrogen **13** carbon dioxide
  kinds: 5 sugar **6** simple, starch, xylose **7** complex, glucose, lactose, maltose, sucrose **8** dextrose, fructose **9** cellulose

carbon 4 coal, coke, copy **8** charcoal **9** lampblack
  chemical symbol: 1 C

carbon copy 5 clone **7** replica **9** duplicate, facsimile **12** reproduction

carbonize 4 burn, char, sear **5** singe **6** scorch **10** incinerate

carbuncle 4 boil, sore **11** excrescence **12** inflammation

carcass 4 body, bouk, husk, wall **5** shell, stiff, trunk **6** corpse **7** cadaver, carrion, remains **8** dead body, fireball, skeleton **9** framework

carcinoma 5 tumor **6** cancer **8** neoplasm **10** malignancy **15** malignant growth

card 4 bill **6** ticket **7** program **8** postcard
  kind: 7 calling, get-well, playing **8** birthday, business, greeting **9** Christmas, Valentine

cardamon
  botanical name: 19 Elettaria cardamomum
  origin: 4 Asia **5** India **13** southeast Asia
  related to: 6 ginger
  color: 5 black
  use: 5 curry **7** dessert **12** Danish pastry

Cardew, Cecily
  character in: 27 The Importance of Being Earnest
  author: 5 Wilde

card game 3 loo, war **4** brag, faro, fish, skat, vint **5** ombre, poker, rummy, whist **6** boston, bridge, casino, chemmy, ecarte, euchre, go fish, hearts, memory, piquet, pocher **7** bezique, canasta, cooncan, Old Maid, plafond, primero **8** baccarat, conquian, cribbage, gin rummy, napoleon, patience, pinochle, slapjack **9** blackjack, pelmanism, solitaire, spoil five, twenty-one, vingt-et-un **11** chemin de fer, crazy eights **13** concentration **14** contract bridge **16** beggar-my-neighbor, trente et quarante
  card names: 3 ace **4** fool, jack, king, trey **5** deuce, joker, queen
  combination of cards: 4 meld
  one hand or round: 5 trick
  rulebook by: 5 Hoyle
  suits: 4 club **5** heart, spade **7** diamond
    French: 5 coeur, pique **6** trefle **7** carreau
    German: 4 grun, herz, piks **5** karos, treff **6** eichel **7** schelle
    Italian: 5 coppa, cuori, fiori, spada **6** denaro, picchi, quadri **7** bastone
    Spanish: 3 oro **4** copa **5** basto **6** espada

Cardiff
  capital of: 5 Wales

Cardiff Giant 4 hoax **5** relic

cardigan 5 corgi **6** jacket, wampus **7** sweater **10** Welsh corgi

cardinal 3 key, top **4** head, main **5** basic, chief, first, prime, vital **6** cherry, claret, red hat **7** carmine, central, deep-red, highest, leading, primary, scarlet **8** blood-red, dominant, foremost, greatest **9** essential, intrinsic, necessary, paramount, principal, uppermost **10** elementary, preeminent, underlying **11** fundamental, outstanding, predominant, wine-colored **13** indispensable, most important
  number suffix: 3 eth

care 3 TLC **4** heed, load, mind, want, wish **5** grief, pains, worry **6** bother, charge, desire, effort, misery, regard, sorrow, strain, stress **7** anguish, anxiety, caution, concern, control, custody, keeping, sadness, thought, trouble **8** distress, give a rap, hardship, nuisance, pressure, vexation **9** annoyance, attention, be worried, diligence, exactness, give a hoot, heartache, vigilance **10** affliction, management, precaution, protection, solicitude **11** application, be concerned, bother about, carefulness, supervision, tribulation, unhappiness **12** ministration, trouble about, watchfulness **13** attentiveness, consideration **14** be interested in, circumspection, discrimination, fastidiousness, meticulousness, responsibility, scrupulousness **17** conscientiousness

Careas 6 eunuch

careen 3 tip, yaw **4** lean, list, sway, tilt, veer **5** heave, slant, slope **7** capsize **8** lean over, overturn

career 3 job **4** line, work **7** calling, pursuit **8** activity, business, lifework, vocation **10** employment, livelihood, occupation, profession, walk of life

care for 4 like, mind, tend **5** fancy **7** oversee **8** attend to, wait upon **9** look after, watch over **10** minister to, provide for

carefree 3 gay **4** glad **5** happy, jolly, sunny **6** breezy, elated, jaunty, joyous **7** buoyant, gleeful, radiant, relaxed, smiling **8** careless, cheerful, jubilant, laughing **9** easygoing **10** full of life, optimistic, untroubled **11** free-and-easy **12** happy-go-lucky, light-hearted, without worry **13** in high spirits **23** without a worry in the world
French: 9 sans souci

careful 4 fine, nice, wary **5** alert, chary, exact, fussy **7** correct, guarded, heedful, mindful, on guard, precise, prudent, tactful **8** accurate, cautious, diligent, discreet, vigilant, watchful **9** attentive, concerned, judicious, observant, regardful **10** fastidious, meticulous, particular, scrupulous, solicitous, thoughtful **11** circumspect, painstaking, punctilious **13** conscientious

carefulness 7 caution **10** steadiness **12** deliberation **14** circumspection

careless 3 lax **4** rash **5** messy, slack **6** casual, sloppy, untidy **7** inexact, offhand **8** heedless, mindless, slapdash, slipshod, slovenly **9** forgetful, imprecise, incorrect, negligent, unmindful **10** disorderly, inaccurate, neglectful, nonchalant, unthinking, untroubled **11** indifferent, thoughtless, unconcerned **12** absent-minded, devilmay-care **13** inconsiderate, lackadaisical

carelessness 6 laxity **7** neglect **9** messiness, slackness **10** inaccuracy, negligence, sloppiness, untidiness **11** imprecision, inexactness **12** heedlessness, indiscretion, slovenliness **13** unmindfulness **14** disorderliness **15** thoughtlessness **16** absentmindedness, irresponsibility

Care of Time, The
  author: 10 Eric Ambler

caress 3 hug, pat, pet **5** clasp, touch **6** cuddle, fondle, stroke **7** embrace, petting, toy with **8** fondling, stroking **11** gentle touch

caretaker 6 keeper, porter, warden **7** curator, janitor, steward **8** overseer, watchman **9** concierge, custodian **10** gatekeeper **14** superintendent

careworn 7 haggard, worried **8** fatigued, troubled **11** pessimistic

cargo 4 load **5** goods **6** burden, lading **7** freight **8** shipment **11** consignment, merchandise

Carib
  language family: 7 Cariban
  location: 7 Guianas **9** Caribbean, Venezuela **12** South America
  alleged custom: 11 cannibalism

Cariban
  tribe: 5 Carib **6** Acawai, Akawai

Caribbean 3 sea
  channel: 7 Yucatan
  city: 6 Havana **7** San Juan **8** Santiago **10** Guantanamo **12** Port au Prince **13** Santo Domingo **15** Charlotte Amalie
  Indian: 5 Carib **6** Arawak
  island: 4 Cuba **5** Aruba, Haiti, Nevis **6** Cayman, Nassau, Tobago, Virgin **7** Antigua, Bahamas, Barbuda, Curacao, Grenada, Jamaica, Leeward **8** Anguilla, Dominica, Trinidad, Windward **9** Saint John **10** Guadeloupe, Hispaniola, Martinique, Montserrat, Puerto Rico, Saint Kitts, Saint Lucia **11** Saint Thomas **12** Saint Vincent **14** Lesser Antilles **15** Greater Antilles **19** Dominican Republic, Netherlands Antilles
  language: 6 gullah **10** papiamento
  product: 3 rum **5** fruit, spice, sugar **6** coffee

caricature 4 mock **6** parody, satire **7** lampoon, mockery, takeoff **8** satirize, travesty **9** absurdity, burlesque **10** distortion **12** exaggeration

Carker
  character in: 12 Dombey and Son
  author: 7 Dickens

Carlisle, Kitty
  real name: 13 Katherine Conn
  husband: 8 Moss Hart
  born: 12 New Orleans LA
  roles: 13 She Loves Me Not **14** To Tell the Truth **16** A Night at the Opera **19** Murder at the Vanities

Carlton, Steve (Steven Norman)
  nickname: 5 Lefty
  sport: 8 baseball
  position: 7 pitcher
  team: 20 Philadelphia Phillies

Carlyle, Thomas
  author of: 8 Cromwell **14** Sartor Resartus **17** Frederick the Great **19** The

French Revolution **20** Heroes and Hero-Worship

Carmen
  author: 14 Prosper Merimee
  opera by: 5 Bizet
  setting: 7 Seville
  character: 7 Don Jose **9** Escamillo, Frasquita
  song: 8 Habanera

Carmen Jones
  director: 13 Otto Preminger
  based on opera by: 5 Bizet (Carmen)
    adaptation by: 18 Oscar Hammerstein II
  cast: 11 Pearl Bailey **14** Harry Belafonte **16** Dorothy Dandridge

carmine 3 red **6** cherry **7** crimson, deep red, scarlet **8** blood red **9** bright red

carnage 8 butchery, massacre **9** blood bath, slaughter

carnal 4 lewd **6** erotic, impure, sexual, sinful, wanton **7** fleshly, immoral, lustful, sensual **8** prurient, sensuous, unchaste, venereal **9** lecherous, salacious **10** lascivious, libidinous, voluptuous

Carnegie, Dale
  author of: 33 How To Win Friends and Influence People

carnelian
  species: 6 quartz

Carnera, Primo
  nickname: 13 the Ambling Alp
  sport: 6 boxing
  class: 11 heavyweight

Carney, Art
  real name: 26 Arthur William Matthew Carney
  partner: 13 Jackie Gleason
  born: 13 Mount Vernon NY
  roles: 8 Ed Norton **13** Harry and Tonto (Oscar) **15** The Honeymooners

carnival 4 fair, fete, gala **6** circus **7** holiday, jubilee **8** festival, jamboree, sideshow **9** Mardi Gras **11** celebration

carnivore 3 cat, dog, fox **4** bear, lion, lynx, mink, puma, wolf **5** civet, dingo, fossa, hyena, otter, panda, skunk, tayra, tiger **6** badger, bobcat, coyote, ferret, grison, hyaena, jackal, jaguar, marten, olingo, weasel **7** polecat, raccoon, suricat **8** aardwolf, kinkajou, mongoose **9** meat eater, wolverine **10** cacomistle, coatimundi, flesh eater

carnivorous 9 predatory **10** meateating, predaceous **11** flesh-eating

carol 4 hymn, noel, sing **5** paean **6** warble **8** canticle **9** song of joy **12** song of praise

Caroline Islands
  district: 3 Yap **4** Truk **5** Palau **6** Ponape
  inhabitant: 10 Polynesian **11** Micronesian
  island: 3 Yap **6** Ponape, Ulithi **8**

Nukuroro **10** Babelthuap **14** Kapina-marangi
language: 7 English **10** Polynesian **11** Micronesian
ocean: 7 Pacific

carom 6 bounce, strike **7** collide, rebound, **8** billiard, ricochet **9** bounce off

Caron, Leslie
born: 6 France **19** Boulogne-Billancourt
roles: 4 Gaby, Gigi, Lili **5** Fanny **11** Father Goose **13** Daddy Longlegs **14** The L-Shaped Room **17** An American in Paris

Carothers, Wallace Hume
field: 9 chemistry
discovered: 5 nylon

carousal 4 orgy **5** binge, drunk, spree **7** debauch **9** bacchanal **10** debauchery, saturnalia

carouse 5 drink, party, quaff, revel **6** guzzle, imbibe, tipple **7** roister, wassail **8** live it up **9** make merry **10** go on a binge **11** make whoopee

Carousel (film)
director: 9 Henry King
based on: 6 Liliom
  adaptation by: 21 Rodgers and Hammerstein
cast: 12 Gordon MacRae (Billy Bigelow), Shirley Jones **15** Cameron Mitchell
song: 9 Soliloquy **11** If I Loved You **19** You'll Never Walk Alone

carp 3 nag **5** cavil, chide, decry, knock **6** deride, impugn, jibe at, pick on **7** censure, condemn **8** belittle, complain, reproach **9** criticize, deprecate, disparage, fault-find, find fault **10** disapprove

Carpaccio, Vittore
born: 5 Italy **6** Venice
artwork: 13 Two Courtesans **18** The Dream of St Ursula **19** The Legend of St Ursula **21** St Augustine in his Study **24** St George Killing the Dragon **28** St Augustine's Vision of St Jerome **29** The Arrival of St Ursula at Cologne

carpal
bone of: 5 wrist

carpe diem 11 seize the day **15** enjoy the present

carpenter 6 fitter, joiner **7** builder **8** repairer **10** woodworker **12** cabinet-maker
ant: 10 camponotus
bee: 8 xylocopa
bird: 10 woodpecker
fish: 10 hammerhead
moth: 10 prinoxysus

Carpenter, Harlean
real name of: 10 Jean Harlow

carper 6 critic **7** caviler **9** nit-picker **11** fault-finder

carpet 3 mat, rug **4** shag **5** cover,

layer, sheet **7** blanket, matting **8** covering

Carpetbaggers, The
author: 13 Harold Robbins

Carr, Emily
born: 6 Canada **8** Victoria **15** British Columbia
artwork: 3 Sky **8** Big Raven **14** Blunden Harbour, Kispiax Village **15** Woods and Blue Sky **17** Forest Landscape II **36** Cape Mudge An Indian Family with Totem Pole

Carra, Carlo
born: 5 Italy **9** Quargneto
artwork: 13 Lot's Daughters **16** Metaphysical Muse **20** Patriotic Celebration **29** The Funeral of the Anarchist Galli

Carradine, David
father: 4 John
half-brothers: 5 Keith **6** Robert
born: 11 Hollywood CA
roles: 6 Kung Fu **13** Bound for Glory **14** The Serpent's Egg

Carradine, John
real name: 21 Richmond Reed Carradine
son: 5 David, Keith **6** Robert
born: 18 Greenwich Village NY
roles: 9 Cleopatra, Kidnapped **10** Stagecoach **12** Count Dracula **15** The Invisible Man **18** Captains Courageous, The Three Musketeers

Carradine, Keith
father: 4 John
brother: 6 Robert
half-brother: 5 David
born: 10 San Mateo CA
roles: 9 Nashville **10** Pretty Baby

Carraway, Nick
character in: 14 The Great Gatsby
author: 10 Fitzgerald

Carrere, John Merven
partner: 14 Thomas Hastings
architect of: 19 House Office Building (Washington DC) **20** New York Public Library, Senate Office Building (Washington DC) **21** Henry Clay Frick mansion (now Frick Collection NYC)
style: 18 French neo-classical, Spanish Renaissance

carriage 3 air, rig **4** mien **5** buggy, coach, poise, wagon **6** aspect, manner **7** bearing, posture, vehicle **8** attitude, behavior, demeanor, presence **10** appearance, conveyance, deportment **11** comportment

Carrie
author: 11 Stephen King

carried away 7 excited, frantic, seduced **8** ecstatic, frenzied, overcome **9** delirious **10** fascinated, infatuated **11** transported

carrier 3 bus, car **4** rack, wave **5** agent, barge, plane, coach, drain, ferry, train, truck, wagon **6** bearer,

boxcar, pigeon, porter **7** airline, channel, mailman, postman, trucker, vehicle **8** airplane, aircraft, carriage, catalyst, railroad **9** messenger **11** transmitter, wheelbarrow

carrion 5 bones, offal, waste **6** corpse, refuse **7** cadaver, carcass, garbage, remains, wastage **8** crowbait, dead body, leavings

Carroll, Leo G
born: 6 Weedon **7** England
roles: 6 Topper **7** Rebecca **9** Suspicion **10** Spellbound **11** Cosmo Topper **15** A Christmas Carol, The Man from UNCLE, The Paradine Case **16** Father of the Bride, North by Northwest

Carroll, Lewis
real name: 22 Charles Lutwidge Dodgson
author of: 11 Jabberwocky **20** The Hunting of the Shark **22** Through the Looking Glass **28** Alice's Adventures in Wonderland

carrousel 4 ride, tray **8** conveyor **9** quadrille, whirligig **10** tournament **12** merry-go-round

carry 3 lug, run **4** bear, cart, haul, lift, move, prop, ship, take, tote **5** brace, bring, fetch, offer, print, shift, stock **6** convey, hold up, supply, uphold **7** conduct, deliver, display, publish, release, support, sustain **8** displace, maintain, shoulder, transfer, transmit **9** broadcast, transport **10** keep on hand **11** communicate, disseminate

carry away 4 lure **6** abduct, kidnap, seduce **7** attract **9** captivate, fascinate, infatuate, transport

carry off 5 seize, steal **6** abduct, kidnap **7** bear off **9** succeed at **11** get away with

carry out 2 do **6** effect, wind up **7** achieve, execute, fulfill, perform, realize **8** complete, conclude, dispatch **9** discharge, dispose of, succeed at **10** accomplish, bring about **11** bring to pass

carry through 6 effect, finish **7** achieve, develop, execute, fulfill, perform, realize **8** complete, conclude **9** discharge **10** accomplish, consummate, effectuate, perpetuate **13** put into effect

Carson, Rachel Louise
field: 7 biology
studied: 9 pollution
author of: 12 Silent Spring **14** The Sea Around Us **15** The Edge of the Sea

Carstone, Richard
character in: 10 Bleak House
author: 7 Dickens

cart 3 gig, lug **4** bear, dray, haul, move, take, tote, trap **5** bring, carry, fetch, truck, wagon **6** barrow, convey **7** schlepp, trundle, tumbrel **8** curricle, transfer, transmit **9** transport **10** handbarrow, transplant, two-wheeler **11** wheelbarrow

kind: 2 go **3** dog, tip **4** dump, hand, push

carte blanche 7 license **9** a free hand, free reign **10** blank check **12** open sanction **13** full authority **18** unconditional power

cartel 4 OPEC, pool **5** chain, trust **7** combine **8** monopoly **9** syndicate **10** consortium, federation **11** corporation

Carter, Charles
   real name of: 14 Charlton Heston

Carter, James Earl, Jr
   nickname: 3 Hot **5** Jimmy **7** Hotshot
   presidential rank: 11 thirty-ninth
   party: 10 Democratic
   state represented: 2 GA **7** Georgia
   defeated: 4 (Gerald R) Ford **8** (Eugene) McCarthy
   vice president: 7 (Walter Frederick "Fritz") Mondale
   cabinet:
      state: 5 (Cyrus R) Vance **6** (Edmund S) Muskie
      treasury: 6 (G William) Miller **10** (W Michael) Blumenthal
      defense: 5 (Harold) Brown
      attorney general: 4 (Griffin B) Bell **9** (Benjamin R) Civiletti
      interior: 6 (Cecil D) Andrus
      agriculture: 8 (Robert S) Bergland
      commerce: 5 (Juanita Morris) Kreps **9** (Philip M) Klutznick
      labor: 8 (F Ray) Marshall
      HEW: 6 (Patricia Roberts) Harris **8** (Joseph A) Califano (Jr)
      HUD: 6 (Patricia Roberts) Harris **8** (Moon) Landrieu
      transportation: 5 (Brockman) Adams **11** (Neil E) Goldschmidt
      education: 10 (Shirley) Hufstedler
   born: 2 GA **6** Plains
   education: 14 US Naval Academy **26** Georgia Southwestern College **28** Georgia Institute of Technology
   religion: 15 Southern Baptist
   interests: 5 track **6** tennis **7** fishing, hunting **8** football, softball **10** basketball **12** cross country **13** square dancing **17** collecting bottles
      music: 8 folk rock **9** classical
   author: 11 Living Faith **12** Keeping Faith **13** Why Not the Best? **16** Everything to Gain **17** The Blood of Abraham
   political career: 12 state senator
      governor of: 7 Georgia
   civilian career: 12 peanut farmer
   military service: 6 US Navy
   notable events of lifetime/term: 6 SALT II **9** Love Canal, recession **18** Habitat for Humanity
      deaths at: 9 Jonestown
      eruption of: 13 Mount St Helens
      first baby from: 8 test tube
      hostages taken in: 4 Iran

nuclear accident: 15 Three Mile Island

pipeline: 5 Alcan

scandal/investigation: 6 Abscam **9** Bert Lance, Koreagate **11** Billy Carter

Supreme Court case: 5 Bakke

treaty: 11 Panama Canal **16** Camp David Accords

father: 11 James Earl Sr

mother: 7 Lillian (Gordy)
   nickname: 11 Miss Lillian

siblings: 6 Gloria **17** William "Billy" Alton **19** Ruth Carter Stapleton

wife: 8 Rosalynn (Smith)

children: 7 Amy Lynn **11** John William (Jack) **12** James Earl III (Chip) **13** Donnel Jeffrey (Jeff)

first lady: 36 Presidential Commission on Mental Health
   author: 19 First Lady from Plains

Carthage *see* **7** Tunisia

carton 3 box **4** case **5** crate **9** container **11** packing case **12** cardboard box, packing crate **18** cardboard container

Carton, Sydney
   character in: 16 A Tale of Two Cities
   author: 7 Dickens

cartoon 5 comic **6** design, satire, sketch **7** drawing, funnies, picture **8** animated **10** caricature, comic strip

cartoonist 6 artist, drawer **7** gagster **12** caricaturist
   famous: 6 Al Capp, C C Beck, Ted Key **7** Bob Kane, Stan Lee **8** Herblock (Herbert L. Block), Jim Davis, Roy Crane **9** Bud Fisher, Chic Young, Dik Browne, Frank King, Hal Foster, Ham Fisher, Walt Kelly **10** Bob Montana, Gary Larson, Harold Gray, Jimmy Hatlo, Johnny Hart, Joe Shuster, Mort Walker, Paul Conrad, Thomas Nast, Walt Disney **11** Alex Raymond, Bill Mauldin, Dale Messick, David Levine, Ding Darling, Elzie C. Segar, Hank Ketcham, Max Beerbohm, Rollin Kirby **12** Al Hirschfeld, Brad Anderson, Chester Gould, Garry Trudeau, James Thurber, Jeff MacNelly, Jules Feiffer, Milton Caniff, Rube Goldberg, Rudolph Dirks, Virgil Partch **13** Bill Watterson, Charles Addams, Charles Schulz, George McManus, Honore Daumier, Joseph Keppler, Saul Steinberg **14** Homer Davenport, William Hogarth **15** Ernie Bushmiller, Patrick Oliphant, Richard Outcault **16** Benjamin Franklin, George Cruikshank

cartridge 3 dud **4** case, tape **5** blank, shell **6** holder **7** capsule, package **8** cassette, cylinder **9** container

Cartwright, Edmund
   nationality: 7 English
   inventor of: 9 power loom **18** wool-combing machine

carve 3 hew, saw **4** etch, form, hack, mold, rend, turn, work **5** allot, cleve, cut up, model, shape, slash, slice, split **6** chisel, divide, incise, sculpt **7** engrave, fashion, pattern, quarter **8** block out, dissever **9** apportion, sculpture

Carver, George Washington
   field: 9 chemistry
   worked in: 11 agriculture
   studied: 6 peanut **7** soybean **11** sweet potato

carving 5 cameo **8** intaglio, triptych **9** sculpture

caryatid 6 column
   shape of: 12 female figure

Casablanca
   director: 13 Michael Curtiz
   cast: 10 Peter Lorre **11** Claude Rains (Louis), Conrad Veidt, Paul Henreid (Victor Laslo) **12** Dooley Wilson (Sam), **13** Ingrid Bergman (Ilsa Lund) **14** Humphrey Bogart (Rick) **17** Sydney Greenstreet
   Oscar for: 7 picture
   song: 12 As Time Goes By

Casanova 3 cad, rip **4** beau, lech, roue, wolf **5** lover, Romeo, swain, wooer **6** chaser, lecher, suitor **7** admirer, bounder, Don Juan, gallant, rounder **8** cavalier, Lothario, lover boy, paramour **9** ladies' man, libertine, womanizer **10** lady-killer, profligate **11** philanderer

Casby
   character in: 12 Little Dorrit
   author: 7 Dickens

cascade 4 fall, gush, pour, rush **5** chute, falls, surge **6** plunge, rapids, tumble **7** Niagara **8** cataract **9** waterfall

Cascade Range
   location: 9 northwest
   highest peak: 9 Mt. Rainier

case 3 bin, box **4** plea, suit, tray **5** cause, chest, cover, crate, event **6** action, affair, appeal, carton, debate, injury, jacket, matter, sheath, victim **7** cabinet, concern, disease, dispute, episode, example, hearing, housing, inquiry, invalid, lawsuit, overlay, patient, wrapper **8** argument, business, covering, envelope, incident, instance, sufferer **9** condition, container, happening, incidence, sheathing, situation **10** litigation, occurrence, proceeding, protection, receptacle, sick person **11** controversy **12** circumstance, illustration

case in point 7 example **8** instance **12** illustration

Case of Sergeant Grischa, The
   author: 11 Arnold Zweig

Casey
   nickname of: 20 Charles Dillon Stengel

team: **7** Yankees
role: **7** manager
Casey at the Bat
  author: **6** Thayer
  town: **8** Mudville
Casey Jones 8 engineer, folksong, railroad
cash 5 bills, bread, coins, dough, money **6** change, redeem **8** currency, exchange **9** bank notes **10** paper money **11** legal tender **13** turn into money **14** coin of the realm
cashier 6 banker, bursar, purser, teller **9** treasurer **10** bank teller
cash register
  invented by: **4** till **5** Ritty
  sign: **6** no sale
casing 4 skin **5** frame **9** sheathing
Casino Royale
  author: **10** Ian Fleming
cask 3 keg, tub, tun, vat **4** butt, pipe **6** barrel **8** hogshead
casket 4 case, pall **5** chest **6** coffer, coffin **8** jewel box **11** sarcophagus
Cask of Amontillado, The
  author: **13** Edgar Allan Poe
  character: **9** Fortunato, Montresor
Cassandra 7 seeress
  also: **9** Alexandra
  father: **5** Priam
  mother: **6** Hecuba
  brother: **5** Paris
  concubine of: **9** Agamemnon
  son: **6** Pelops **9** Teledamus
  cursed by: **6** Apollo
  violated by: **4** Ajax
  killed by: **12** Clytemnestra
Cassatt, Mary
  born: **15** Allegheny City PA
  artwork: **6** La Loge **7** The Bath **11** The Cup of Tea **12** After the Bath, Woman Bathing **14** Gathering Fruit **15** Reading Le Figaro **20** Girl Arranging Her Hair, Woman and Child Drawing
Cassavetes, John
  wife: **12** Gena Rowlands
  born: **9** New York NY
  roles/films: **8** Husbands **10** The Tempest **13** Rosemary's Baby, The Dirty Dozen **23** A Woman Under the Influence
casserole 4 dish, food, mold **6** tureen, vessel **8** saucepan
Cassio
  character in: **7** Othello
  author: **11** Shakespeare
Cassiopeia 13 constellation
  husband: **7** Cepheus
  daughter: **9** Andromeda
  offended: **7** Nereids
Cassius
  also: **12** Caius Cassius
  character in: **12** Julius Caesar
  author: **11** Shakespeare
Cass Timberlane

author: **13** Sinclair Lewis
character: **11** Bradd Criley **24** Jinny Marshland Timberlane
cast 3 set, sow **4** fire, form, hurl, look, mien, mint, mold, pick, shed, toss **5** fling, heave, model, pitch, shape, shoot, sling, stamp, throw **6** actors, assign, casing, choose, direct, launch, let fly, propel, sculpt, spread, troupe **7** appoint, company, deposit, diffuse, pattern, players, project, scatter **8** catapult, disperse **9** broadcast, circulate, discharge, launching, semblance **10** appearance, distribute, impression, performers, propulsion **11** disseminate, give parts to **16** dramatis personae
Castalia
  origin: **5** Greek
  sacred: **6** spring
  location: **14** Mount Parnassus
  sacred to: **5** Muses **6** Apollo
  source of: **11** inspiration
cast aside 4 junk, shed **6** desert, reject **7** abandon, discard, forsake, neglect **8** get rid of, renounce, throw out **9** repudiate, throw away **11** discontinue
cast a spell on 3 hex **4** jinx **5** charm **7** bewitch, conjure, enchant **8** entrance **11** work magic on
cast aspersions on 5 knock, scorn **6** deride, malign **7** disdain, put down, run down, sneer at **8** belittle, poohpooh **9** criticize, disparage **13** find fault with
castaway 3 bum **4** hobo, waif **5** exile, leper, nomad, rover, stray **6** outlaw, pariah **7** Ishmael, outcast, vagrant **8** deportee, derelict, renegade, unperson, vagabond, wanderer **9** foundling, nonperson **10** expatriate **11** beachcomber, offscouring, untouchable **12** down-and-outer **15** knight-of-the-road
cast away 4 junk **6** launch, propel, reject **7** abandon, discard, toss out **8** get rid of, pitch out, throw out **9** throw away
cast down 5 abase, droop, lower **6** abased, deject, droopy, humble, sadden **7** depress, humbled, lowered **8** bring low, dejected, disgrace, saddened **9** depressed, disgraced, humiliate **10** brought low, dishearten, humiliated **11** crestfallen **12** disheartened
caste 4 rank **6** status **7** lineage, station **8** position **9** condition
  Hindu: **5** sudra, varna **6** vaisya **7** brahman **9** kshatriya
castigate 5 chide, scold **6** berate, punish, rebuke **7** bawl out, censure, chasten, chew out, correct, reprove, upbraid **8** admonish, chastise, penalize, reproach **9** criticize, dress down, reprimand **10** discipline, take to task **15** call on the carpet **16** haul over the coals

castigation 9 reprimand **10** chastening, correction, discipline, penalizing, punishment **12** chastisement
Castiglione, Baldassare
  author of: **20** The Book of the Courtier
castle 4 hall, keep, rook **5** manor, tower, villa **6** palace **7** chateau, citadel, mansion **8** fortress **10** stronghold
Castle, Vernon[1]
  wife: **5** Irene **15** ballroom dancers
  invented: **10** Castle Walk
Castle, The[2]
  author: **10** Franz Kafka
  character: **1** K
Castle of Otranto, The
  author: **13** Horace Walpole
  character: **6** Conrad **7** Alfonso, Manfred, Matilda **8** Isabella, Theodore **12** Father Jerome
Castle Rackrent
  author: **14** Maria Edgeworth
cast off 4 shed **6** reject **7** discard, set sail, toss out **8** throw off, throw out **9** repudiate, throw away **11** weigh anchor
Castor and Pollux
  also: **6** Gemini **8** Dioscuri **10** Polydeuces, Tyndaridae
  form: **8** twin sons
  mother: **4** Leda
  father: **4** Zeus
  sister: **5** Helen **12** Clytemnestra
  members of: **9** Argonauts
  protectors of: **6** seamen
cast out 4 oust **5** eject, evict, exile, expel **6** banish, reject **7** discard, dismiss, turn out **8** drive out, send away, throw out
cast up 4 spew **5** eject, expel, vomit **6** spew up **7** cough up, throw up **8** disgorge
casual 4 cool, so-so **5** blase, vague **6** chance, random, sporty **7** offhand, passing, relaxed **8** informal **9** easygoing, haphazard, non-dressy, unplanned **10** accidental, fortuitous, incidental, nonchalant, unarranged, undesigned, undirected, unexpected, unforeseen **11** half-hearted, indifferent, unlooked for **13** lackadaisical, serendipitous, unintentional **14** indiscriminate, unpremeditated
Casuals of the Sea
  author: **12** William McFee
casualty 4 loss **6** injury, victim **7** injured **8** fatality
casuistry 5 guile **6** deceit **7** fallacy, sophism **8** subtlety **9** Jesuitism, quibbling, sophistry **10** nitpicking **12** equivocation, pettifoggery, speciousness **13** deceptiveness, hair-splitting **14** sophistication
casus belli 10 cause of war
Casy, Jim

character in: 16 The Grapes of Wrath
author: 9 Steinbeck

cat 3 pet **4** puss, whip **5** kitty, pussy, tabby **6** feline, kitten, mouser, tomcat
anatomy: 3 paw **4** loin, nape, rump, tail **5** break, flank, shank **6** feeler **7** dewclaw, leather, whisker **8** vibrissa **10** metatarsus
breed/kind: 3 tom **4** coon, Eyra, lion, lynx, Manx, puma **5** alley, civet, hyena, kitty, Korat, tabby, tiger **6** Angola, angora, bobcat, cougar, jaguar, ocelot, serval **7** Burmese, caracal, cheetah, leopard, linsang, Maltese, panther, Persian, polecat, Siamese, Turkish, wildcat **8** Balinese, Cheshire, Egyptian, ringtail **9** Himalayan, shorthair **10** Abyssinian, chinchilla **11** Russian blue **13** tortoise-shell
combining form: 5 aelur, ailur, felin **6** aeluro, ailuro, felino
Egyptian goddess of: 4 Bast
extinct: 10 saber-tooth
family: 7 Felidae
famous: 6 Morris **8** Cheshire, Garfield, Kilkenny **9** Mehitabel **10** Heathcliff
fastest: 7 cheetah
fear of: 12 aelurophobia, ailurophobia
female: 5 queen **7** lioness, tigress **8** wheencat **9** grimalkin
genus: 5 Felis
grinning: 8 Cheshire
group: 7 clowder, clutter
group of kittens: 6 kendle, kindle
lover: 11 aelurophile, ailurophile
male: 3 gib, tom **6** tomcat
ring-tailed: 6 serval **10** cacomistle
tailless: 4 Manx
young: 6 kitten

cataclysm 4 blow **7** debacle **8** calamity, disaster, upheaval **11** catastrophe, devastation
cataclysmic 4 dire **6** tragic **7** ruinous **10** calamitous, disastrous **12** catastrophic, earth-shaking
catacomb 4 tomb **7** ossuary **8** cemetery **10** passageway **12** burial ground
catafalque 3 box **4** pall **6** casket, coffin
catalog, catalogue 4 file, list, post, roll **5** index **6** record, roster **7** listing **8** classify, register, syllabus, tabulate **9** directory, enumerate, inventory, mail order
Catamitus *see* **8** Ganymede
Cat and Mouse
author: 11 Gunter Grass
catapult 4 cast, hurl, toss **5** fling, heave, pitch, shoot, sling, throw **6** hurtle, onager, propel **9** slingshot **13** hurling engine
cataract 5 falls, flood **6** deluge, rapids **7** cascade, torrent **8** downpour **9** lens cover, waterfall **10** inundation
catastrophe 4 blow **5** havoc **6** mis-

hap, ravage **7** debacle, scourge, tragedy **8** calamity, disaster **9** cataclysm **10** affliction, misfortune **11** devastation
catastrophic 6 tragic **7** ruinous **10** calamitous, disastrous **11** cataclysmic
catcall 3 boo **4** gibe, hiss, hoot, jeer, razz **7** whistle **8** heckling **9** raspberry **10** Bronx cheer
catch 3 bag, bat, get, hit, nab **4** bait, bang, belt, bump, bust, dupe, feel, find, fool, grab, hasp, haul, hoax, hook, lock, lure, make, snag, snap, spot, take, trap **5** booty, break, charm, clasp, crack, get to, grasp, hitch, latch, prize, reach, seize, sense, smack, smite, snare, trick, whack, yield **6** allure, arrest, betray, buffet, collar, corner, corral, dazzle, deceit, delude, descry, detect, expose, fasten, fathom, kicker, snatch, strike, take in, turn on, unmask **7** attract, bewitch, capture, closure, deceive, delight, discern, enchant, ensnare, find out, gimmick, mislead, rasping, seizure **8** catching, come upon, contract, coupling, discover, drawback, enthrall, hoodwink, overtake, perceive, pickings, surprise **9** apprehend, bamboozle, captivate, carry away, enrapture, fastening, intercept, lay hold of, play false, recognize, transport **10** comprehend, understand **11** take captive **12** break out with, come down with, disadvantage, seize and hold, take off guard **14** stumbling block **15** take into custody **18** become infected with
catch-as-catch-can 7 cursory **9** haphazard, hit-or-miss, unplanned **10** disorderly, incomplete **11** superficial, unorganized **12** disorganized, unsystematic
Catcher in the Rye, The
author: 10 J D Salinger
character: 15 Holden Caulfield Phoebe Caulfield
catching 10 contagious, infectious **12** communicable **13** transmittable
catch on to 3 get **5** grasp, savvy **6** absorb, digest, fathom, pick up **10** assimilate, comprehend, get the idea, understand
catch sight of 3 see **4** espy **6** behold, descry, detect, notice **7** discern, make out, observe, pick out **8** perceive
Catch-22
author: 12 Joseph Heller
character: 9 Yossarian
means: 7 paradox
catchword 5 motto **6** byword, cliche, slogan, war cry **8** password **9** battle cry, guide word, pet phrase, watchword **10** shibboleth
categorical 4 flat, sure **7** certain, express **8** absolute, definite, emphatic, explicit **10** pronounced, unreserved

11 unequivocal, unqualified **12** unmistakable **13** unconditional
categorically 10 absolutely, definitely, positively **12** conclusively
categorization 5 order **11** arrangement **14** classification
category 5 class, group **8** division, grouping **14** classification
cater 5 humor **6** pamper, pander, please **7** gratify, indulge, satisfy
caterpillar 4 moth, worm **5** larva **7** cutworm, tractor, webworm **8** hangworm, silkworm, wortworm **9** butterfly, woolybear **10** astragalus
caterwaul 3 cry **4** bawl, howl, wail, yelp **5** whine **6** clamor, scream, shriek, squawk, squeal **7** screech **10** rend the air
catfish 4 barb **5** banjo **6** dorado, madtom, mudcat, sucker **7** ariidae, bluecat **8** bagridae, bullhead, claridae, electric, flathead **9** siluridae **10** channel cat, cuttlefish, mochocidae, plotosidae, spotted cat **11** ictaluridae, pimelodidae, schilbeidae **12** aspredinidae, ostariophysi **14** malapteruridae **16** trichomycteridae
Catfish
nickname of: 9 Jim Hunter
Catfish Row
setting of: 12 Porgy and Bess
catharsis 7 purging, release, venting **9** cleansing **12** purification
Catharsius
epithet of: 4 Zeus
means: 8 purifier
cathartic 5 purge **6** physic **8** aperient, evacuant, laxative **9** castor oil, purgative, purifying
cathedral 3 see **6** church, temple **7** lateran **8** basilica, official **9** authority **10** pontifical
Italian: 5 duomo
Cather, Willa
author of: 9 A Lost Lady, My Antonia, One of Ours, O Pioneers! **13** My Mortal Enemy **16** Shadows on the Rock, The Song of the Lark **18** The Professor's House **23** Sapphira and the Slave Girl **26** Death Comes for the Archbishop
cathode ray tube
abbreviation: 3 CRT
invented by: 7 Crookes
catholic, Catholic 5 broad **7** liberal **9** universal, worldwide **12** all-embracing, all-inclusive **13** comprehensive
cathouse 4 stew **5** house **6** bagnio, bordel **7** brothel **8** bordello **10** bawdy house, fancy house, whorehouse **13** sporting house **14** house of ill fame **16** house of ill repute **19** house of prostitution
Cat Jumps, The
author: 14 Elizabeth Bowen

catlike 5 catty, lithe **7** sinuous **8** stealthy **14** light on the feet

Catlin, George
 born: 13 Wilkes-Barre PA
 artwork: 16 Gallery of Indians

catnap 3 nap **4** doze **6** siesta, snooze **10** forty winks, light sleep

Cato 5 Roman
 Elder: 6 Censor
 younger (grandson): 5 Stoic

Cato
 author: 13 Joseph Addison

Cat on a Hot Tin Roof
 author: 17 Tennessee Williams
 director: 13 Richard Brooks
 cast: 8 Burl Ives (Big Daddy) **10** Jack Carson, Paul Newman (Brick) **14** Judith Anderson **15** Elizabeth Taylor (Maggie)

cats-eye
 species: 11 chrysoberyl
 source: 8 Sri Lanka

cat's paw 4 dupe, pawn, tool **5** patsy **7** fall guy

cattle 4 cows, kine, oxen **5** beefs, bulls, stock **6** beeves, calves, dogies, steers **8** bullocks, milk cows **9** livestock
 family: 7 Bovidae
 group of: 5 drove
 kind: 2 ox **3** yak **4** Zebu **5** Angus **6** Ankole, Jersey **7** Brahman **8** Ayrshire, Guernsey, Hereford, Highland, Holstein **9** Charolais **12** water buffalo **13** Texas Longhorn **16** English Shorthorn, Holstein-Friesian
 young: 4 calf **6** heifer **8** yearling

Catton, Bruce
 author of: 22 A Stillness at Appomattox

catty 4 mean **7** catlike **8** spiteful **9** malicious, malignant **10** malevolent

catwalk 6 bridge **7** walkway **10** passageway

Caucasian
 language branch: 5 Ubykh **9** Daghestan **10** Circassian **11** Khartvelian

Caucon
 brought mysteries to: 8 Messenia

caucus 6 parley, powwow **7** council, meeting, session **8** assembly, conclave **10** conference

caudal 4 back, tail **7** tail-end

cauldron *see* **7** caldron

Caulfield, Holden
 character in: 18 The Catcher in the Rye
 author: 8 Salinger

Caulfield, Joan
 real name: 21 Beatrice Joan Caulfield
 born: 8 Orange NJ
 roles: 8 Dear Ruth **17** My Favorite Husband

causation 4 root **5** cause **6** author, origin, reason, source **7** creator, genesis **8** etiology, inventor, stimulus **9** generator, invention **10** antecedent, conception, mainspring, originator **11** determinant, inspiration, origination

cause 4 goal, make, root, side **5** ideal, impel, tenet **6** belief, create, effect, incite, lead to, motive, object, origin, reason, source, spring, stir up **7** genesis, grounds, incline, inspire, produce, provoke, purpose **8** etiology, generate, motivate, occasion, stimulus **9** incentive, principle, stimulate **10** aspiration, bring about, conviction, foundation, give rise to, inducement, initiation, mainspring, motivation, persuasion, prime mover **11** bring to pass, inspiration, instigation, precipitate, provocation

cause of war
 Latin: 10 casus belli

cause to appear 6 expose, reveal **7** uncover **8** disclose **12** bring to light **13** bring into view

caustic 3 lye **4** tart **5** acrid, harsh, sharp **6** biting, bitter **7** burning, cutting, erosive, gnawing **8** scathing, stinging **9** corroding, corrosive, sarcastic **10** astringent **11** acrimonious

caution 4 care, heed, warn **5** alarm, alert **6** advise, caveat, exhort, notify, regard, tip-off **7** concern, thought, warning **8** admonish, forewarn, prudence, wariness **9** alertness, restraint, vigilance **10** admonition, discretion, precaution **11** carefulness, forewarning, guardedness, heedfulness, mindfulness **12** deliberation, watchfulness **14** circumspection, put on one's guard

cautionary 7 warning **8** advisory **10** admonitory **11** admonishing

cautious 4 wary **5** alert, cagey **7** careful, guarded, prudent **8** discreet, vigilant, watchful **9** attentive, judicious **11** circumspect

cavalcade 5 troop **6** column, parade **7** caravan, retinue **10** procession

Cavalcade
 director: 10 Frank Lloyd
 based on play by: 10 Noel Coward
 cast: 10 Clive Brook **11** Ursula Jeans **12** Diana Wynyard **13** Herbert Mundin **15** Margaret Lindsay
 Oscar for: 7 picture

cavalier 3 fop **4** beau **5** blade, cocky, dandy, swell **6** hussar, lancer **7** cursory, dragoon, gallant, haughty, offhand, playboy **8** arrogant, courtier, gay blade, horseman, uncaring **9** easygoing **10** cavalryman, disdainful, nonchalant **11** indifferent, thoughtless

cavalry 7 hussars, lancers **8** dragoons **10** mounted men **11** horse troops **13** horse soldiers, mounted troops

cavalryman 6 hussar, lancer **7** dragoon **8** cavalier, horseman **12** horse soldier, horse trooper **14** mounted soldier

cave 3 den **4** lair, sink **6** burrow, cav-

ern, cavity, dugout, grotto, hollow
 growth: 10 stalactite, stalagmite
 explorer: 9 spelunker

caveat 5 alarm, alert, aviso **6** tip-off **7** caution, red flag, warning **8** high sign, red light **10** admonition, danger sign, yellow jack **11** forewarning **12** admonishment, flea in the ear **13** word to the wise **20** handwriting on the wall

caveat emptor 17 let the buyer beware

cave canem 14 beware of the dog

cave in 6 buckle, fall in, give up, submit **7** crumple, give way, implode **8** collapse **10** capitulate **12** fall to pieces

Cavendish, Henry
 field: 7 physics **9** chemistry
 nationality: 7 British
 discovered: 8 hydrogen
 determined composition of: 3 air **5** water **10** nitric acid
 method: 19 Cavendish experiment

cavernous 4 huge, vast **5** roomy **6** gaping **7** chasmal, immense, yawning **8** cavelike, enormous, spacious **10** tremendous

cavil 6 deride **7** nitpick, quibble **8** belittle, complain **9** criticize, deprecate, discredit, disparage, faultfind, find fault **12** pick to pieces

cavity 3 dip, pit **4** bore, dent, hole, sink **5** basin, niche **6** burrow, crater, hollow, pocket, tunnel **7** opening, orifice, vacuity **8** aperture **9** concavity **10** depression, excavation

cavort 4 play, romp **5** bound, caper, frisk **6** frolic, gambol, prance

Cawdor
 author: 15 Robinson Jeffers

Caxtons, The
 author: 12 Bulwer Lytton

Cayuga
 language family: 9 Iroquoian
 location: 4 Ohio **6** Canada **7** New York **8** Oklahoma **9** Wisconsin
 branch of: 10 Six Nations **19** Iroquois Confederacy, League of the Iroquois

CE 9 Common Era

cease 3 end **4** halt, pass, quit, stop **5** abate, pause **6** desist, finish **7** adjourn, die away, forbear, suspend **8** break off, conclude, leave off **9** terminate **11** abstain from, discontinue, refrain from **12** bring to an end

cease-fire 5 truce **9** armistice

ceaseless 7 endless, eternal **8** constant, enduring, unending **9** continual, incessant, permanent, perpetual, unceasing **10** continuous, protracted **11** everlasting, never-ending, unremitting **12** interminable **13** uninterrupted

cease to be 3 die, end **6** die out, expire, vanish **9** disappear, evaporate **13** become extinct

Cecilia (Memoirs of an Heiress)
author: **11** Fanny Burney

Cecrops
also: **8** Cecropia
form: **3** man **6** dragon
founder of: **6** Attica
king of: **6** Attica
father: **14** King Erechtheus
brother: **6** Metion, Orneus
wife: **8** Aglaurus
son: **11** Erysichthon
daughter: **5** Herse **8** Aglaurus **9** Pandrasos
renamed Attica: **8** Cecropia

cedar 6 Cedrus
varieties: **3** red **4** pink, salt **5** Atlas, giant, white **6** Alaska, Cyprus, ground, Mlanje **7** Bermuda, incense, Russian, Spanish **8** Barbados, cigarbox, creeping, Japanese, stinking **10** Ozark white, Port Orford, swamp white, western red, West Indian, Willowmore **11** Clanwilliam, Colorado red, southern red **13** Atlantic white, southern white **14** Chilean incense, Formosa incense **17** California incense

cede 4 give **5** grant, leave, yield **6** tender **7** abandon, deliver, release **8** hand over, transfer **9** deliver up, surrender **10** relinquish

cedez
music: **8** slow down

Cedric the Saxon
character in: **7** Ivanhoe
author: **5** Scott

ceiling 3 top **4** roof **5** cover, limit **6** canopy, cupola, lining **7** maximum **8** altitude **10** upperlimit

Celebes
also: **8** Sulawesi
bordered by: **6** Borneo **8** Moluccas **10** Celebes Sea, Kalimantan **12** Flores Strait **14** Makassar Strait
city: **4** Poso **6** Manado **7** Kendari, Madjene **8** Bonthain, Donggala, Makassar **9** Gorontalo
location: **9** Indonesia
people: **4** Bugi, Laki, Mori, Muna, Napu, Palu, Peso, Seko, Wana **5** Besoa, Buton, Toala **6** Bungku, Butung, Parigi, Sadang, Sangir, Toland **7** Banggai, Bolaang, Kabaena, Loinang, Toradja **8** Balantak, Buginese, Mongondu, Rongkong, Sanghike **9** Gorontalo **11** Makassarese
province: **13** North Sulawesi, South Sulawesi **15** Central Sulawesi **17** Southeast Sulawesi

Celebes ox 4 anoa

celebrate 4 laud **5** bless, cheer, exalt, extol, honor **6** hallow, praise, revere **7** acclaim, applaud, commend, glorify, observe **8** proclaim, sanctify, venerate **9** broadcast, ritualize, solemnize **10** consecrate **11** commemorate **13** ceremonialize

celebrated 5 famed, feted, noted **6** famous, prized **7** eminent, honored, notable, revered **8** lionized, renowned **9** acclaimed, important, prominent, respected, treasured, venerable, wellknown **11** illustrious, outstanding **13** distinguished

Celebrated Jumping Frog of Calaveras County, The
author: **9** Mark Twain

celebration 4 fete, gala **5** feast, party **6** ritual **7** jubilee, revelry **8** carnival, ceremony, festival **9** festivity, hallowing **10** ceremonial, observance **13** commemoration, solemnization **14** sanctification **15** memorialization

celebrity 3 VIP **4** fame, name, note, star **5** glory, wheel **6** bigwig, renown **7** big shot, notable, stardom **8** eminence, luminary **9** dignitary, notoriety, personage **10** notability, popularity, prominence **11** distinction, personality **12** famous person, person of note

celerity 5 haste, hurry, speed **6** hustle **8** alacrity, dispatch, fast clip, fastness, legerity, rapidity **9** briskness, quickness, swiftness **10** expedition, snappiness, speediness **12** precipitance **14** lightning speed **15** expeditiousness

celery seed
also called: **8** smallage
origin: **13** Mediterranean
use: **4** soup **5** salad, sauce **6** pickle **10** vegetables

celestial 3 sky **5** solar **6** astral, divine **7** angelic, elysian, stellar, sublime **8** beatific, blissful, empyrean, ethereal, hallowed, heavenly, seraphic **9** planetary, unearthly **12** astronomical, otherworldly, paradisiacal

celestial being 3 god **5** angel, deity **7** goddess **8** divinity **11** divine being

Celestial City
place in: **16** Pilgrim's Progress
author: **6** Bunyan

Celia (Aliena)
character in: **11** As You Like It
author: **11** Shakespeare

celibacy 6 purity **8** chastity **9** virginity **10** abstinence, continence **12** bachelorhood, spinsterhood

celibate 4 pure **5** unwed **6** chaste, single **8** bachelor, spinster, virginal **9** abstinent, continent, unmarried

Celine, Louis-Ferdinand
author of: **12** Guignol's Band **25** Death on the Installment Plan, Journey to the End of the Night

cell
part: **7** nucleus **8** membrane **9** cytoplasm
made of: **3** fat **4** salt **5** water **7** protein **9** compounds **12** carbohydrate
theory of: **7** (Rudolf) Virchow, (Theodor) Schwann

cellar 3 den **4** cave **6** dugout **8** basement **10** downstairs **14** wine collection

Cellini, Benvenuto
born: **5** Italy **8** Florence
artwork: **7** Cosimo I, Perseus **13** Bindo Altoviti **18** The Crucified Christ **20** Nymph of Fontainebleau
autobiography: **22** Life of Benvenuto Cellini

Celsius
abbreviation of: **1** C

Celt 4 Gaul, Kelt, Manx, Pict, Scot **5** Irish, Welsh **6** Breton, Briton, chisel **8** Scottish **10** Highlander

Celtic 4 Erse
language group: **6** Gaelic **9** Brythonic
family: **12** Indo-European
language of: **5** Gauls

cement 3 fix, set **4** bind, fuse, glue, join, seal, weld **5** paste, stick, unite **6** mortar, secure **8** concrete

cemetery 7 ossuary **8** boneyard, Boot Hill, catacomb **9** graveyard **10** churchyard, necropolis **12** burial ground, memorial park, potter's field **13** burying ground

Cenci, The
author: **18** Percy Bysshe Shelley

cenobite 4 monk **7** ascetic **8** celibate **9** religious

censor 4 blip, edit **5** amend, bleep, judge, purge **6** critic, delete, excise **7** amender, Bowdler, clean up **8** black out, examiner, reviewer, suppress **9** expurgate, inspector **10** blue-pencil, bowdlerize, expurgator, suppressor **11** bowdlerizer, faultfinder, scrutinizer **12** investigator **17** custodian of morals **25** guardian of the public morals

censorious 5 picky **7** abusive, carping **8** critical **10** defamatory **12** faultfinding

censurable 8 blamable **10** deplorable, punishable, reprovable **11** blameworthy **12** reproachable **13** reprehensible

censure 3 pan, rap **5** chide, scold **6** berate, rebuke **7** bawl out, chew out, chiding, condemn, reproof, reprove, upbraid **8** admonish, denounce, reproach, scolding **9** castigate, complaint, criticism, criticize, reprehend, reprimand **10** admonition, bawlingout, chewing-out, disapprove, upbraiding **11** castigation, disapproval, reprobation **12** condemnation, dressing-down, remonstrance **13** tonguelashing **14** disapprobation **16** rap on the knuckles, take over the coals
god of: **5** Momos, Momus

census 3 tax **4** data, list, poll **5** count **6** amount, number **11** enumeration **12** registration

Centaur
form: **3** man **5** horse **7** monster **16** half-man half-horse
constellation of: **9** Centaurus

famous: 6 Chiron
represents: 11 Sagittarius
Centennial
author: 13 James Michener
Centennial State
nickname of: 8 Colorado
center, centre 3 fix, hub, mid **4** axis, core, crux **5** focus, heart, pivot, point **6** direct, gather, middle **7** address, essence, nucleus **8** converge, interior **9** middle **10** focal point **11** concentrate
centered 4 even, true **5** right **7** focused **8** straight **10** pinpointed **12** concentrated
centigrade 5 scale **6** degree **7** celcius **11** thermometer
centigram
abbreviation of: 2 cg
centiliter
abbreviation of: 2 cl
centimeter
abbreviation of: 2 cm
centipede 4 boat **5** shrub **6** earwig, insect **8** chilopod, multiped **9** arthropod **13** muehlenbeckia
central 3 key **4** core, main **5** basic, chief, focal, inner, major, prime **6** inmost, middle **7** leading, midmost, pivotal, primary **8** dominant, foremost, interior **9** essential, paramount, principal **10** middlemost **11** fundamental, predominant **13** most important
Central African Republic
other name: 11 Ubangi-Chari **20** Central African Empire
capital/largest city: 6 Bangui
others: 3 Obo **4** Bria, Ippy **5** Birao, Bouar, Kembe, Ndele, Ngoto, Paoua, Rafai, Zemio **6** Baboua, Bakala, Bozoum, Mbaiki **7** Bambari, Grimari, Zemongo **9** Bangassou, Berberati, Bossangoa, Fort Sibut
monetary unit: 5 franc **7** centime
lake: 4 Chad
mountain: 5 Karre, Tinga **6** Mongos **9** Dar Challa
highest point: 11 Kayagangiri
river: 4 Bomu, Nana **5** Chari, Kotto, Mbari, Mpoko, Ouaka **6** Chinko, Lobaye, Mbomou, Ubangi **11** Upper Sangha
people: 4 Baya, Sara **5** Banda, Bwaka, Sango **6** Azande, Yakoma **7** Banziri, Mandjia, Nzakara
language: 5 Sango, Zande **6** French
religion: 5 Islam **7** animism **12** Christianity **13** Roman Catholic
place:
plaza: 13 Edouard Renard
food:
tapioca: 6 manioc **7** cassava
Central America
land form: 7 isthmus
countries: 6 Belize, Panama **8** Honduras **9** Costa Rica, Guatemala, Nicaragua **10** El Salvador
bordered by: 6 Mexico, **8** Colombia

12 Caribbean Sea, North America, Pacific Ocean, South America
capital city: 7 Managua, San Jose **8** Belmopan **10** Panama City **11** San Salvador, Tegucigalpa **13** Guatemala City
river: 3 New **4** Axul, Coco, Sico, Tuma, Ulua, Wawa **5** Aguan, Chepo, Hondo, Lempa, Wauks **6** Chixoy, Grande, Pasion, Patuca, Sulaco, Waspuk **7** Motagua, Paulaya, San Juan, Sarstun, Segovia **8** Kukalaya **9** Choluteca, Escondido **10** Chucunague **11** Prinzapolca
lake: 5 Gatun, Guija, Yojoa **7** Atitlan, Managua **9** Nicaragua, Peten Itza
mountain: 4 Maya, Pija **5** Colon, Huapi, Minas, Pando **6** Blanco **7** Dipilto, Gongora, San Blas **8** Brewster, Dariense, Isabelia, San Pablo, Santa Ana **9** Esperanza **14** Chirripo Grande
people: 3 Mam **5** Zambo **6** Indian, Ladino, Quiche **7** mestizo **8** Miskitas **10** Black Carib, Cakchiquel
animal: 5 tapir **6** agouti **7** opossum, peccary **8** anteater, kinkajou, marmoset **9** armadillo, porcupine, tree sloth **12** howler monkey, spider monkey **14** capuchin monkey
Central Amerind
language branch: 9 Oto-Mangue **10** Uto-Aztecan **11** Kiowa-Tanoan
central city 8 core city, downtown **9** inner city, urban area **10** metropolis **16** business district, metropolitan area
central idea 3 nut **4** core, crux, gist, meat **5** heart, theme **6** kernel **7** essence **9** main point
centralization 5 focus **11** convergence **13** concentration, consolidation
centralize 5 focus, unify **6** center, gather **7** collect, compact **8** center on, coalesce, converge, pinpoint **9** integrate **10** congregate **11** concentrate, consolidate
central part 4 core, crux, gist, pith **5** heart **6** center, kernel **7** nucleus
century
abbreviation of: 4 cent
French: 6 siecle
cephalopod 5 squid **7** mollusk, octopus **8** nautilus **10** cuttlefish
ceramic ware 5 china, glass **7** pottery **8** crockery **9** chinaware, glassware, porcelain, stoneware **10** enamelware **11** earthenware
ceratopsid
type of: 8 dinosaur
member: 10 Torosaurus **11** Monoclonius, Triceratops **13** Protoceratops, Styracosaurus **14** Psittacosaurus
Ceratosaurus
type: 8 dinosaur
period: 8 Jurassic
Cerberus
form: 3 dog

father: 6 Typhon
mother: 7 Echidna
sibling: 5 Hydra **7** Orthrus **8** Chimaera **10** Nemean lion **12** Theban Sphinx
number of heads: 5 three
guarded: 10 Underworld
Cercopes
race of: 6 Gnomes
cereal 4 bran, corn, oats, rice, seed **5** grain, grass, gruel, plant, wheat **6** barley, pablum **7** oatmeal, pabulum **8** porridge
cerebellum
part of: 5 brain
controls: 7 balance **8** movement
cerebrum
part of: 5 brain
controls: 6 seeing **7** hearing, tasting **8** deciding, feelings, learning, smelling, thinking, touching **9** awareness **11** remembering
ceremonial 4 rite **6** formal, ritual **7** liturgy, service **8** ceremony **9** formality, sacrament **10** liturgical, observance **11** celebration, ritualistic
ceremonialize 7 observe **9** celebrate, ritualize **11** commemorate
ceremonious 5 exact, fussy, rigid, stiff **6** formal, proper, solemn **7** careful, correct, pompous, precise **8** starched **9** dignified **10** methodical, meticulous **11** punctilious
ceremony 4 rite **6** custom, nicety, ritual **7** amenity, decorum, pageant, service **8** function, protocol **9** etiquette, formality, propriety **10** observance, politeness **11** celebration, formalities **13** commemoration
Cerenkov, Pavel Alekseevich
field: 7 physics
nationality: 7 Russian
discovered: 12 cause of light **14** Cerenkov effect
Ceres
origin: 5 Roman
goddess of: 11 agriculture
corresponds to: 7 Demeter
certain 4 sure **5** valid **6** secure **7** assured, express, settled, special **8** absolute, cocksure, definite, positive, reliable, specific **9** confident, convinced, satisfied **10** conclusive, individual, inevitable, particular, undeniable, undisputed, undoubtful, undoubting, unshakable **11** indubitable, inescapable, irrefutable, unalterable, unequivocal, unqualified **12** indisputable, unchangeable, unmistakable, wellgrounded **13** bound to happen, incontestable **14** unquestionable **16** incontrovertible
certainly 5 truly **6** indeed, surely **7** for sure **8** of course **9** decidedly **10** absolutely, definitely, positively **11** indubitably, undoubtedly **13** unequivocally,

without a doubt **14** unquestionably
21 beyond a shadow of a doubt

Certain Smile, A
author: **14** Francoise Sagan

certainty 4 fact **5** faith, trust **6** belief,
surety **7** reality, sure bet **8** sureness **9**
actuality, assurance, certitude, sure
thing **10** confidence, conviction **11**
presumption **12** positiveness **13** inevitability **14** conclusiveness, inescapability **17** authoritativeness

certificate 4 deed **6** permit **7** diploma,
license, voucher **8** document, warranty **9** affidavit **10** credential **11** testimonial **13** authorization **14** authentication

certification 7 voucher **8** approval **10**
validation **11** endorsement **12** confirmation, ratification, verification
13 authorization, corroboration **14** authentication, substantiation

certify 4 aver **5** swear, vouch **6** assure,
attest, ratify, second, verify **7** confirm,
declare, endorse, support, warrant,
witness **8** notarize, sanction, validate
9 authorize, guarantee, testify to **10**
underwrite **11** corroborate **12** authenticate, give one's word, substantiate

certitude 5 faith, trust **6** belief, surety
8 reliance, sureness **9** assurance, certainty **10** confidence **12** positiveness
14 conclusiveness

cerulean 4 blue **5** azure **6** cobalt **7** sky
blue **9** clear blue

Cervantes Saavedra, Miguel de
author of: **20** Don Quixote de la
Mancha

Cesar Birotteau
author: **14** Honore de Balzac

cessation 3 end **4** halt, stay, stop **5**
pause **6** ending, recess **7** ceasing,
halting, respite **8** quitting, stopping,
surcease **9** desisting **10** concluding,
leaving off, suspension **11** adjournment, breaking off, termination **12** interruption **13** coming to a halt, dis-
continuing **14** discontinuance

c'est la vie 9 that's life **10** such is life

Cestus
girdle of: **5** Venus

cetacean 4 apod, orca **5** whale **6** beluga, mammal **7** cetacea, dolphin,
dowfish, grampus, narwhal **8** porpoise, sturgeon **9** blue whale **11** baleen whale, killer whale

Cetinje
capital of: **10** Montenegro

Ceylon see **8** Sri Lanka

Cezanne, Paul
born: **6** France **13** Aix-en-Provence
artwork: **7** Bathers **11** Card Players
13 The Black Clock, The Railway
Out **14** Uncle Dominique **15** La Maison du Pendu **16** The Suicide's
House **17** Grandes Baigneuses **19**

Woman with a Coffee Pot **36** Mont-
Sainte-Victoire with Large Pine Trees

Chabrier, (Alexis) Emmanuel
born: **6** Ambert, France
composer of: **6** Espana **7** L'Etoile **10**
Gwendoline **13** Marche Joyeuse **14**
Le Roi Malgre Lui **18** King Despite
Himself **19** Une Education Manquee

Chad
other name: **5** Tchad
capital/largest city: **8** Fort-Lamy,
N'Djamena
others: **3** Ati, Bol, Lai, Mao **4** Fada,
Faya, Sarh **5** Mongo **6** Abeche, Bon-
gor **7** Largeau, Moundou **8** Moussoro
monetary unit: **5** franc **7** centime
lake: **4** Chad
mountain: **7** Tibesti, Touside
highest point: **9** Emi Koussi
river: **5** Chari **6** Logone **8** Bahraouk
physical feature:
plateau: **6** Ennedi
people: **4** Arab, Daza, Maba, Sara,
Teda, Tubu **5** Barma, Hakka, Kreda,
Massa **6** Fulani, Kotoko, Toubou,
Wadaii **7** Kamadja, Kanembu, Moun-
dan
language: **4** Sara **5** Turku **6** Arabic,
French
religion: **5** Islam **7** animism **12** Christianity

Chadband
character in: **10** Bleak House
author: **7** Dickens

Chadic
language family: **11** Afroasiatic **13**
Hamito-Semitic
includes: **5** Hausa
spoken in: **6** Africa **8** Lake Chad

Chadwick, James
field: **7** physics
nationality: **7** British
discovered: **7** neutron
awarded: **10** Nobel Prize

chafe 3 rub **4** boil, burn, foam, fume,
rage, rasp **6** abrade, rankle, scrape,
seethe **7** scratch **9** be annoyed **11** be
irritated

chaff 3 bug, kid, rag, rib **4** josh, junk,
pods, razz, ride, slag, twit **5** dross,
hulls, husks, jolly, trash, waste **6** banter, debris, litter, refuse, rubble,
shells, shoddy, shucks **7** kidding, ragging, remnant, residue, ribbing, rubbish, waggery **8** badinage, chaffing,
leavings, raillery, ridicule **9** sweepings
9 give and take

chaffing 6 banter **7** jesting, joshing,
kidding, ragging, ribbing, waggery **8**
badinage, raillery

chafing 5 harsh **6** fuming **7** rasping,
rubbing **8** abrading, abrasive **10** irritating

Chagall, Marc
born: **6** Liosno, Liozno, Russia
artwork: **8** Birthday, Cockcrow **9** The
Circus, The Red Sun **10** The Juggler

11 Over Vitebsk **12** The Violinist **14**
Double Portrait, I and the Village **16**
The Jewish Wedding **17** Lovers with
Rooster **20** Paris Through My Win-
dow

chagrin 5 shame **6** dismay **8** distress
11 humiliation **13** embarrassment,
mortification

chagrined 7 abashed, ashamed **9** mortified **10** humiliated **11** embarrassed

Chahiksichhiks see **6** Pawnee

chain 3 fob **5** cable, links **7** shackle **8**
necklace **10** metal links **11** linked cable
abbreviation: **2** ch

Chain, Ernst Boris
field: **12** biochemistry
nationality: **7** British
discovered: **10** penicillin
worked with: **6** Florey **7** Fleming
awarded: **10** Nobel Prize

Chained Lady
constellation of: **9** Andromeda

chains 3 tie **4** bind, lash, moor **5**
bonds, irons, tie up, train **6** fasten,
fetter, secure, series, string, tether **7**
bondage, fetters, manacle, serfdom,
shackle, slavery **8** leg irons, manacles,
sequence, shackles **9** handcuffs, servitude, thralldom **10** put in irons, succession **11** enslavement, subjugation

chair 4 seat **5** bench, couch, sedan
stool **6** chaise, lounge, rocker, settee,
throne **7** conduct, ottoman **11** preside
over **16** presiding officer

chairman 4 head **5** chair, emcee **6**
leader **7** manager, preside, speaker **8**
director **9** chairlady, executive, moderator **10** chairwoman, supervisor **11**
chairperson, toastmaster **13** administrator **16** presiding officer **18** master
of ceremonies

Chair of Forgetfulness
form: **4** seat
made of: **5** stone
location: **10** Underworld

chaise 3 gig **4** shay **5** chair **6** daybed,
longue, lounge **7** calesin **8** carriage,
duchesse

chalcedony 3 gem **4** onyx, opal, sard
5 agate, prase **6** jasper, plasma,
quartz, silica **7** catseye, mineral, opal-
ine, sardius **8** hematite, sardonyx **9**
carnelian **10** bloodstone, heliotrope
11 chrysoprase **12** semiprecious **14**
silicon dioxide

Chaldean 4 seer **5** magic **6** Syriac **7**
Aramaic, semitic **8** magician **9** astrology, enchanter, Nabonidus **10** astrologer, Babylonian, soothsayer **12** Nabopolassar **14** Nebuchadnezzar

chalice 3 cup **5** grail **6** goblet, vessel

chalk 4 draw **6** crayon, pastel, sketch **9**
limestone

chalk up 4 earn **5** score **6** attain,
charge, credit **7** achieve, ascribe

chalky 3 wan **4** pale **5** ashen, white **6** pallid **7** powdery **8** blanched **9** bloodless

challenge 3 bid, tax, try **4** dare, defy, gage, test **5** doubt, trial **6** demand, impute, summon **7** defiant, dispute, summons **8** question **15** take exception to **20** fling down the gauntlet

chamber 4 diet, hall, room **5** board, court, house, salon **6** office, parlor **7** bedroom, boudoir, council **8** assembly, congress **9** apartment

Chamberlain, Owen
  field: **7** physics
  developed: **8** atom bomb
  awarded: **10** Nobel Prize

Chamberlain, Richard
  real name: **24** George Richard Chamberlain
  born: **12** Los Angeles CA
  roles: **6** Shogun **9** Dr Kildare **10** Wallenberg **13** The Thorn Birds **17** The Bourne Identity **21** The Count of Monte Cristo

Chamberlain, Wilt (Wilton Norman)
  nickname: **6** Dipper **12** Wilt the Stilt
  sport: **10** basketball
  position: **5** coach **6** center
  team: **16** Los Angeles Lakers **17** Philadelphia 76ers **20** Philadelphia Warriors, San Francisco Warriors **21** San Diego Conquistadors

chambermaid
  French: **14** femme de chambre

chambord
  type: **7** liqueur
  origin: **6** France
  flavor: **14** black raspberry

chameleon 4 newt **6** lizard **8** renegade, turncoat **10** fickleness **14** changeableness

champ 4 bite, chew, gnaw **5** chomp, crush, grind, munch **6** crunch **8** champion

champagne 4 fizz **6** bubbly
  type: **4** wine
  drink: **7** the Pope
  with white wine: **8** Cold Duck
  with orange juice: **6** Mimosa
  measure: **6** magnum **8** jeroboam, rehoboam **9** balthazar **10** methuselah, salmanazar **14** Nebuchadnezzar

Champaigne, Philippe de
  born: **7** Belgium **8** Brussels
  artwork: **6** Ex Voto **17** Cardinal Richelieu **26** The Adoration of the Shepherds

champion 3 aid **4** abet, back **6** backer, defend, master, uphold, victor, winner **7** espouse, paladin, paragon, promote, support **8** advocate, defender, fight for, laureate, promoter, speak for, upholder **9** battle for, conqueror, protector, supporter **10** stand up for, vanquisher **11** protagonist, title holder

Champion
  constellation of: **7** Perseus

championship 3 cup **5** crown, title **7** backing, defense, support, winning **8** advocacy, espousal

Chan, Charlie
  creator: **15** Earl Derr Biggers
  actors: **7** E. L. Parks **10** George Kuwa **11** Warner Oland, Sidney Toler **13** Roland Winters, Kamiyama Sojin
  films: **7** The Trap **8** Jade Mask **11** Dead Men Tell **13** Shanghai Cobra, The Chinese Cat, The Black Camel **16** House Without a Key **17** Castle in the Desert, Behind that Curtain

chance 3 try **4** fall, fate, luck, risk **5** lucky, occur **6** befall, danger, gamble, happen, hazard, random **7** attempt, destiny, fortune, turn out, venture **8** accident, jeopardy, occasion **9** come about, fortunate, unplanned **10** accidental, fortuitous, likelihood, likeliness, providence, undesigned, unexpected, unforeseen **11** opportunity, possibility, probability, speculation, unlooked for **12** happenstance **13** unintentional **14** unpremeditated

chance upon 4 find, meet **7** learn of, run into **8** come upon, discover **9** encounter, light upon **10** happen upon **11** stumble upon

chancy 4 iffy **5** dicey, risky **6** touchy, tricky **7** dubious, erratic, unsound **8** doubtful **9** hazardous, uncertain, whimsical **10** capricious, precarious **11** speculative, venturesome **13** problematical, unpredictable

chandelier 11 hanging lamp **12** candleholder **15** lighting fixture

Chandler, Jeff
  real name: **10** Ira Grossel
  born: **10** Brooklyn NY
  roles: **7** Cochise **11** Broken Arrow **17** Merrill's Marauders

Chandler, Raymond
  author of: **11** The Big Sleep **14** The Long Goodbye **16** Farewell My Lovely
  born: **7** England
  character: **13** Philip Marlowe
  screenplay: **13** The Blue Dahlia **15** Double Indemnity **17** Strangers on a Train

Chaney, Lon
  real name: **12** Alonso Chaney
  son: **9** Creighton (Lon Chaney Jr)
  nickname: **19** Man of a Thousand Faces
  born: **17** Colorado Springs CO
  roles: **14** The Unholy Three **18** Tell It to the Marines **20** Hunchback of Notre Dame, The Phantom of the Opera

Chaney, Lon Jr
  real name: **9** Creighton
  father: **3** Lon
  born: **14** Oklahoma City OK

  roles: **6** Lennie **8** The Mummy **10** The Wolf Man **12** Of Mice and Men, Son of Dracula **20** Frankenstein's Monster

change 4 swap, turn, vary **5** alter, coins, shift, trade **6** modify, mutate, recast, reform, silver, switch **7** convert, novelty, remodel, replace, restyle, shuffle, variety, veering **8** pin money, swapping, transfer **9** deviation, diversion, exception, restyling, transform, transmute, turn about, variation **10** alteration, conversion, difference, remodeling, reorganize, revolution, small coins, substitute **11** fluctuation, pocket money, reformation **12** metamorphose, modification, substitution, transmogrify **13** make different, metamorphosis, revolutionize, transmutation, transposition **14** reorganization, transformation **15** transfiguration

changeable 6 fickle, fitful **7** erratic, flighty, mutable, varying **8** unstable, unsteady, variable, volatile **9** deviating, irregular, mercurial, uncertain **10** capricious, inconstant, modifiable, reversible **11** alternating, convertible, fluctuating, vacillating **13** transformable

change in plan
  French: **8** demarche

changeless 4 fast **5** fixed **6** stable **7** abiding, certain, durable, eternal, lasting **8** constant, enduring **9** immutable, steadfast, unvarying **10** unshakable **11** everlasting, unalterable **12** indissoluble

changelessness 9 certainty, constancy, stability **10** durability, permanence **12** immutability **13** steadfastness

change of heart 10 conversion **16** change of attitude

changeover 10 conversion

channel 3 cut **4** gash, lead, send **5** guide, route, steer **6** convey, course, direct, furrow, groove, gutter, strait, trough **7** narrows, passage **11** watercourse **21** avenue of communication

Channing, Carol
  born: **9** Seattle WA
  roles: **10** Hello Dolly **22** Gentlemen Prefer Blondes, Thoroughly Modern Millie

chanson 4 song

Chanson de Roland
  also: **12** Song of Roland
  author: **7** unknown
  character: **4** Aude **6** Turpin **7** Ganelon, Marsile, Olivier **11** Charlemagne, Twelve Peers
  foe: **8** Saracens
  knight: **7** paladin

chant 2 om **3** ode **4** hymn, lied, sing, song **5** carol, croon, dirge, elegy, psalm, theme, trill, troll **6** chorus, intone, melody, monody, strain **7** chanson, chorale, descant **8** canticle, doxology, threnody, vocalize **9** homophony, monophony, offertory, plainsong **11** Gloria Patri **14** Gregorian chant

chanteuse 6 singer (female)

Chants de Maldoror, Les
author: **18** Comte de Lautreamont

chaos 4 mess **5** furor **6** bedlam, jumble, muddle, tumult, uproar **7** turmoil **8** disarray, disorder, upheaval **9** agitation, commotion, confusion **10** turbulence **11** pandemonium **12** discomposure **14** disarrangement **15** disorganization

Chaos
origin: **5** Greek
personifies: **9** confusion

chaotic 7 jumbled, mixed-up, muddled, tangled **8** confused **9** confusing, illogical, turbulent **10** disjointed, incoherent, in disarray **11** unorganized **12** disorganized **13** disharmonious

chap 3 boy, dry, guy, jaw, lad, man, rap **4** chop, gent **5** bloke, buyer, crack, knock, split **6** fellow, redden, split, stroke **7** fissure, roughen **8** customer **9** purchaser

chapbook 7 garland **8** treasury **9** anthology **10** collection **11** florilegium

chapeau 3 hat

chapel 6 church, shrine **7** oratory **9** sanctuary **10** house of God, tabernacle **14** place of worship

chaperon, chaperone 5 guard, watch **6** duenna, escort **7** oversee **8** guardian, shepherd **9** accompany, attendant, custodian, protector, safeguard **11** keep an eye on

chaperoned 7 oversaw **8** attended, escorted **10** supervised **11** accompanied

chapfallen 6 droopy **8** cast down, dejected **9** depressed

chaplain 4 abbe **5** padre, rabbi, vicar **6** cleric, curate, father, parson, pastor, priest, rector **7** Holy Joe **8** minister, preacher, reverend, sky pilot **9** churchman, clergyman **12** ecclesiastic

chaplet 4 band **6** fillet, wreath **7** circlet, coronet

Chaplin, Charlie
real name: **24** Sir Charles Spencer Chaplin
nickname: **14** the Little Tramp
wife: **10** Oona O'Neill **15** Paulette Goddard
daughter: **9** Geraldine
born: **6** London **7** England
director of/roles: **6** The Kid **8** The Tramp **9** Limelight **10** City Lights **11** Modern Times, The Gold Rush **15** Monsieur Verdoux **16** The Great Dictator

Chaplin, Geraldine
father: **14** Charlie Chaplin

mother: 17 Oona O'Neill Chaplin
born: **13** Santa Monica CA
roles: **12** The Hawaiians **13** Doctor Zhivago

chapter 3 era **4** body, part, span, unit **5** group, phase **6** branch, clause, period **7** episode, portion, section **8** division **9** affiliate **11** subdivision

Chapters of Erie
author: **10** Henry Adams

char 4 burn, sear **5** singe **6** scorch **9** carbonize **10** incinerate

character 4 part, role, self **5** being, honor **6** makeup, nature, person, traits, weirdo **7** honesty, oddball, persona **8** goodness, morality, original, specimen **9** eccentric, integrity, odd person, qualities, rectitude **10** attributes, individual, one-of-a-kind **11** personality, uprightness **13** individuality, moral strength **15** distinctiveness **16** dramatis personae

characteristic 4 mark **5** trait **6** aspect **7** earmark, feature, quality, typical **8** property, symbolic **9** attribute, mannerism, specialty, trademark **10** emblematic, indicative **11** distinctive, peculiarity **14** distinguishing, representative

characterization 8 portrait **9** depiction, picturing, portrayal **11** delineation, description **12** representing **14** representation

characterize 4 mark **5** class **6** define, depict, typify **7** earmark, portray **8** classify, describe, indicate **9** designate, represent **11** distinguish

characterless 4 weak **5** vague **6** anemic **11** nondescript **13** indeterminate **14** expressionless

Characters of Shakespeare's Plays, The
author: **14** William Hazlitt

Charcot, Jean Martin
nationality: **6** French
father of: **9** neurology

Chardin, Jean Baptiste Simeon
born: **5** Paris **6** France
artwork: **7** The Kiss **8** The Grace **14** Young Governess **16** The Copper Cistern **17** Attributes of Music **19** Attributes of the Arts **28** Rayfish Cat and Kitchen Utensils

charge 3 ask, bid, fee **4** care, cost, duty, fill, heap, lade, levy, load, pack, pile, rate, rush, toll **5** beset, blame, debit, exact, onset, order, price, stack, storm, stuff **6** accuse, advice, amount, assail, assess, assign, attack, come at, demand, direct, enjoin, impute, indict, sortie, summon **7** ascribe, assault, bidding, command, control, custody, dictate, expense, keeping, payment, require **8** call upon, instruct, storming **9** attribute, complaint, direction, enjoining, onslaught **10** accusation, allegation, assessment, indictment, in-

junction, management, protection **11** arraignment, incriminate, instruction, safekeeping, supervision **12** delay payment, guardianship, jurisdiction **14** administration, lay the blame for, request payment **15** superintendence **16** put on one's account

chargeable 6 liable **10** answerable **11** responsible

charged 5 taxed, tense **6** blamed, filled, levied, loaded, priced **7** accused, ordered, uptight **8** assessed, attacked, exhorted, mandated, prepared **9** commanded, entrusted **10** accusation, allegation, indictment

Charge of the Light Brigade, The
author: **18** Alfred Lord Tennyson
director: **13** Michael Curtiz
cast: **10** David Niven, Errol Flynn, Nigel Bruce **11** Donald Crisp **13** Patric Knowles **15** Henry Stephenson **17** Olivia de Havilland
setting: **6** Russia

charger 5 horse, mount, steed **6** vessel **7** accuser, platter **8** warhorse

charge with 5 trust **6** assign, commit **7** consign, entrust **8** delegate, hand over, turn over **9** authorize

chariot 3 car **5** buggy **7** phaeton, vehicle **8** carriage

Charioteer
constellation of: **6** Auriga

Chariots of Fire
director: **10** Hugh Hudson
cast: **7** Ian Holm **8** Ben Cross (Harold Abrahams) **11** John Gielgud, Nigel Havers **12** Ian Charleson (Eric Liddell)
Oscar for: **5** score (Vangelis) **6** script **7** picture

charisma 5 charm **6** allure, appeal **7** glamour **8** presence, witchery **9** magnetism, sex appeal **10** bewitchery **11** enchantment, fascination **14** attractiveness

charitable 4 kind **6** giving, kindly **7** lenient, liberal **8** generous, gracious, tolerant **9** bounteous, bountiful, forgiving, indulgent **10** almsgiving, benevolent, munificent, open-handed **11** considerate, kindhearted, magnanimous, sympathetic, warmhearted **12** eleemosynary, sympathizing **13** philanthropic, understanding

charitableness 10 liberality **11** benevolence, generousity **12** philanthropy **13** bountifulness **14** openhandedness **15** humanitarianism

Charites see **6** Graces

charity 3 aid **4** alms, fund, gift, help, love **6** bounty, giving **7** handout **8** altruism, donating, good will, goodness, humanity, kindness, offering, sympathy **9** benignity, donations, endowment, tolerance **10** alms-giving, assistance, compassion, generosity **11** benefaction, benevolence, fundraising, munificence **12** graciousness, philanthropy **13** contributions, financial help, love of mankind **14** openhandedness

charlatan 4 fake **5** cheat, fraud, quack **7** cozener **8** deceiver, imposter, impostor, swindler **9** trickster **10** mountebank **16** confidence artist

Charles, Nick and Nora
characters in: **10** The Thin Man
author: **7** Hammett
pet dog **4** Asta

Charles O'Malley
author: **12** Charles Lever

Charleston 5 dance **13** ballroom dance
capital of: **9** W Virginia

Charlie's Angels
character: **10** Jill Monroe, John Bosley, Kris Munroe **12** Kelly Garrett **13** Sabrina Duncan **15** Charlie Townsend
cast: **10** Cheryl Ladd, David Doyle **11** Jaclyn Smith, Kate Jackson **18** Farah Fawcett-Majors
voice of Charlie: **12** John Forsythe

Charlotte's Web
author: **7** E B White
Charlotte: **6** spider
saved: **6** Wilbur (piglet)

Charly
director: **11** Ralph Nelson
based on story by: **11** Daniel Keyes (Flowers for Algernon)
cast: **10** Leon Janney, Lilia Skala **11** Claire Bloom **13** Dick van Patten **14** Cliff Robertson
Oscar for: **5** actor (Robertson)

charm 4 draw, grip, lure, take **5** magic, spell **6** allure, amulet, bauble, cajole, engage, please, seduce, turn on **7** attract, beguile, bewitch, conjure, delight, enchant, gratify, sorcery, trinket, win over **8** charisma, enthrall, entrance, ornament, talisman **9** captivate, enrapture, fascinate, magnetism **10** allurement, attraction, cast a spell, lucky piece **11** conjuration, enchantment, fascination, incantation, work magic on

charmer 4 vamp **5** belle, siren **9** enchanter, temptress **11** enchantress, femme fatale, spellbinder

charming 6 lovely **7** likable, winning, winsome **8** alluring, engaging, enticing, fetching, graceful, magnetic, pleasing **9** agreeable **10** attractive, bewitching, delightful, enchanting, entrancing **11** captivating, charismatic, enthralling, fascinating **12** irresistible

charmless 4 dull **5** blunt **6** dreary **9** repulsive, unlikable, unlovable **10** unpleasant **12** disagreeable, unattractive

Charon
father: **6** Erebus
mother: **3** Nyx
occupation: **8** ferryman
river: **4** Styx

Charops
epithet of: **8** Hercules
means: **14** with bright eyes

Charpentier, Gustave
born: **6** Dieuze, France
composer of: **6** Julien, Louise **18** Impressions of Italy

chart 3 map, pie **4** plan, plot **5** draft, graph, table **6** design, draw up, lay out, map out, scheme, sketch **7** diagram, outline **8** tabulate **9** blueprint, delineate **10** tabulation

charter 3 let **4** deed, hire, rent **5** grant, lease **6** employ, engage, permit **7** compact, license **8** contract, covenant, sanction **9** agreement, authority, authorize, franchise **10** commission, concession

Charterhouse of Parma, The
author: **23** Marie Henri Beyle Stendhal
character: **8** Marietta **10** Count Mosca **11** Clelia Conti **14** Gina Pietranera **16** Fabrizio del Dongo

chartreuse
type: **7** liqueur
origin: **6** France **15** Carthusian monks
flavor: **4** herb
color: **5** green **6** yellow
with apricot brandy: **13** Golden Slipper
with gin: **5** Bijou **9** Green Lady

chary 3 shy **4** wary **5** alert, cagey, leery **7** careful, guarded, heedful, prudent, sparing **8** cautious, hesitant, vigilant, watchful **10** economical, suspicious **11** circumspect, distrustful

Charybdis
form: **7** monster
father: **8** Poseidon
mother: **4** Gaea
identified with: **9** whirlpool

chase 3 dog **4** hunt, oust, rout, shoo, tail **5** drive, evict, hound, quest, stalk, track, trail **6** dispel, follow, pursue, shadow **7** cast out, go after, hunting, pursuit, repulse, scatter **8** pursuing, run after, send away, stalking, tracking **9** drive away, following **11** put to flight, send packing

Chase, Chevy
real name: **19** Cornelius Crane Chase
born: **9** New York NY
roles: **4** Hero **6** Fletch **8** Foul Play, Vacation **10** Caddyshack **11** Spies Like Us, Three Amigos **17** Saturday Night Live

chasm 3 gap, pit **4** gulf, hold, rift **5** abyss, break, cleft, crack, gorge, gulch, split **6** breach, cavity, crater, divide, ravine **7** fissure **8** crevasse

chasseur 6 hunter

chaste 4 pure **5** clean **6** decent, modest, severe, strict **7** austere, classic, precise, sinless **8** virginal, virtuous **9** continent, righteous, unadorned, unsullied, untainted, wholesome **10** im-

maculate, restrained **11** clean-living, uncorrupted **12** unornamented **13** unembellished

chasten 5 chide, scold **6** berate, punish, rebuke **7** censure, reprove, upbraid **8** admonish, chastise, reproach **9** reprimand **10** discipline, take to task

chastened 7 humbled **8** contrite, penitent **9** repentant **10** remorseful **18** conscience-stricken

chastise 4 beat, flog, whip **5** chide, roast, scold, spank, strap **6** berate, punish, rebuke, thrash **7** censure, chasten, correct, reprove, scourge, upbraid **8** admonish, call down, penalize, reproach **9** castigate, criticize, reprimand **10** discipline, take to task, tongue-lash **15** call on the carpet **16** fulminate against, haul over the coals

chastisement 10 correction, discipline, punishment **11** castigation **12** reprimanding

chastity 6 purity **8** celibacy **9** innocence, virginity **10** abstinence, continence, singleness **12** bachelorhood, spinsterhood **14** abstemiousness
goddess of: **5** Diana, Fauna **7** Artemis, Bona Dea

chasuble 6 casual **7** garment **8** vestment

Chasuble, Reverend Canon
character in: **27** The Importance of Being Earnest
author: **5** Wilde

chat 3 gab, rap **4** talk **5** prate **7** chatter, palaver, prattle **8** chitchat, converse **10** chew the fat, chew the rag, rap session **11** talk session **12** conversation **13** confabulation **16** heart-to-heart talk

chateau 4 wine **6** castle, estate **7** mansion **8** chatelet **12** country house

Chateaubriand, Francois Rene
author of: **4** Rene **5** Atala **10** Los Natchez, The Martyrs **19** Memoires d'Outre-tombe **24** Memoirs from Beyond the Tomb

Chateau d'If
prison in: **21** The Count of Monte Cristo
author: **5** Dumas (pere)

Chateaupers, Phoebus de
character in: **23** The Hunchback of Notre Dame
author: **4** Hugo

chattel 4 gear **6** things **7** effects **8** movables **9** trappings **10** belongings **13** accoutrements, paraphernalia **15** personal effects **19** personal possessions

chatter 3 gas **4** blab, talk **5** clank, click, prate **6** babble, gabble, gibber, gossip, jabber, patter **7** blabber, blather, clatter, palaver, prattle, talking, twaddle **8** blabbing, chitchat, idle talk, talk idly **11** confabulate **14** chitterchatter

chatterbox 6 gabber, gasbag, gossip, talker **7** babbler, tattler, windbag **8** jabberer, prattler, tell tale **9** chatterer **10** talebearer, tattle tale **12** blabbermouth, blatherskite, hot-air artist **13** chatterbasket

chatty 5 gabby, gassy, gushy, talky, windy **7** gossipy, gushing, prating, verbose, voluble **8** babbling, chatting, effusive **9** garrulous, jabbering, talkative **10** blabbering, long-winded, loquacious **11** loose-lipped **12** loose-tongued **13** tongue-wagging

Chaucer, Geoffrey
  author of: **18** The Canterbury Tales, Troilus and Criseyde **19** The Book of the Duchess **20** The Legend of Good Women, The Parlement of Fowles

Chauchoin, Claudette Lily
  real name of: **16** Claudette Colbert

chauffeur 6 driver

chaussure 4 boot, shoe **8** footwear

chauvinism 8 jingoism **10** flag-waving, militarism, patriotism **11** nationalism **15** ethnocentricity, superpatriotism

cheap 4 base, easy, mean, poor **5** close, gaudy, petty, tacky, tight **6** common, flashy, meager, paltry, shabby, shoddy, sordid, stingy, tawdry, trashy, two-bit, vulgar **7** ignoble, immoral, miserly **8** costless, gimcrack, indecent, inferior, wretched **9** inelegant, low-priced, penurious, worthless **10** despicable, economical, effortless, in bad taste, reasonable, second-rate **11** inexpensive, tightfisted **12** contemptible

Cheaper by the Dozen
  author: **14** Frank B Gilbreth (with Ernestine Gilbreth Carey)

cheat 3 con, gyp **4** bilk, dupe, fake, foil, fool, gull, hoax, rook, take **5** cozen, crook, fraud, quack, shark, trick **6** baffle, betray, defeat, delude, dodger, escape, fleece, humbug, outwit, thwart **7** deceive, defraud, mislead, swindle **8** chiseler, deceiver, hoodwink, imposter, impostor, swindler **9** bamboozle, charlatan, con artist, frustrate, trickster, victimize **10** circumvent, mountebank **11** shortchange **13** break the rules, double-crosser

check 3 bar, end, fit, gag, tab **4** curb, halt, hold, jibe, mesh, rein, slow, stay, stop, test **5** agree, block, brake, chime, choke, limit, probe, stall, study, tally **6** arrest, bridle, impede, look at, muzzle, peruse, rein in, retard, review, search, survey, thwart **7** barrier, conform, control, examine, explore, harness, inhibit, inspect, perusal, prevent, smother **8** hold back, look into, look over, obstacle, obstruct, restrain, scrutiny, stoppage,

suppress **9** cessation, constrain, frustrate, harmonize, hindrance, restraint **10** circumvent, constraint, correspond, impediment, inspection, limitation, prevention, repression, scrutinize **11** examination, exploration, investigate, obstruction, prohibition, restriction, take stock of **13** investigation **18** bring to a standstill

checkered 4 pied **6** fitful, motley, seesaw, uneven, varied **7** checked, dappled, mottled, piebald **9** irregular, up-and-down **10** inconstant, variegated **11** fluctuating, vacillating **12** particolored

checkmate 4 rout, stop **6** corner, defeat, outwit, stymie, thwart **8** chess win, deadlock **9** frustrate, overthrow **11** countermove

cheder, heder 12 Jewish school

cheek 4 jowl **5** brass, nerve **8** audacity, boldness, temerity **9** arrogance, brashness, impudence, insolence **10** brazenness, effrontery **11** forwardness **12** impertinence

cheep 4 peep **5** chirp, tweet **7** chirrup, chitter, twitter

cheer 3 cry, fun, joy, ole, rah **4** glee, hail, hope, root, warm, yell **5** bravo, shout **6** assure, buoy up, gaiety, hooray, hurrah, huzzah, shriek, uplift **7** acclaim, animate, comfort, delight, enliven, fortify, gladden, hearten, inspire, revelry **8** brighten, buoyance, buoyancy, gladness, optimism, pleasure, reassure, vivacity **9** animation, assurance, encourage, festivity, geniality, joviality, merriment, rejoicing **10** joyfulness, jubilation, liveliness **11** acclamation, high spirits, hopefulness, merrymaking, reassurance **13** encouragement

cheerful 3 gay **4** airy, glad **5** happy, jolly, merry, sunny **6** blithe, breezy, bright, cheery, elated, jaunty, jovial, joyful, joyous, lively **7** buoyant, gleeful **8** gladsome, pleasant **9** agreeable, sparkling, sprightly **10** optimistic **11** in high humor **12** high-spirited, lighthearted

cheerfulness 5 gaity **7** jollity **8** buoyancy, optimism **9** joviality, merriment **10** brightness, cheeriness **11** high spirits **16** lightheartedness

cheerless 3 sad **4** dull, glum, gray, grim **5** bleak **6** dismal, dreary, gloomy, morose, rueful, solemn, somber, sullen, woeful **7** austere, doleful, forlorn, joyless, sunless, unhappy **8** dejected, desolate, dolorous, downcast, funereal, mournful **9** miserable, saturnine, woebegone **10** depressing, despondent, dispirited, lugubrious, melancholy, spiritless, uninviting **11** comfortless, downhearted **12** disconsolate, heavy-hearted

Cheers

location: **3** bar **6** Boston
character: **4** Norm **5** Cliff, Coach, Woody **5** Lilith **7** Rebecca **9** Sam Malone **13** Carla Tortelli, Diane Chambers
cast: **9** Ted Danson **11** George Wendt, Rhea Perlman, Shelley Long **12** Kirstie Alley **13** Kelsey Grammer **14** Woody Harrelson **16** John Ratzenberger

cheer up 5 elate, pep up **6** buoy up **7** comfort, enliven, hearten **8** brighten, inspirit **9** bolster up, encourage **18** bolster one's spirits

cheery 3 gay **5** happy, jolly, merry, sunny **6** bright, joyful **9** sprightly **12** lighthearted

Cheeryble Brothers
  nephew: **5** Frank
  characters in: **16** Nicholas Nickleby
  author: **7** Dickens

cheese
  French: **7** fromage
  kind: **4** bleu, blue, brie, edam, feta, jack **5** brick, colby, cream, gouda, Swiss **6** romano, samsoe **7** cheddar, cottage, fontina, gjetost, gruyere, limburg, munster, ricotta, sapsago, stilton **8** American, bel paese, cheshire, emmental, muenster, parmesan, port wine, raclette **9** camembert, jarlsberg, limburger, port salut, provolone, roquefort **10** caerphilly, Danish blue, Gloucester, gorgonzola, mozzarella, neufchatel **11** emmenthaler, liederkranz, petit suisse, port du salut, wensleydale **12** monterey jack

Cheever, John
  author of: **8** Falconer **10** Bullet Park **16** The Enormous Radio, The World of Apples **17** The Wapshot Scandal **19** The Wapshot Chronicle **20** The Way Some People Live **22** Oh What a Paradise It Seems

Chekhov, Anton
  author of: **6** Ivanov **10** The Sea Gull, Uncle Vanya **15** The Three Sisters **16** The Cherry Orchard

chemical compound 4 acid, base, enol **5** amide, amine, ester, imide **6** isomar, ketone **8** aldehyde

chemical symbols
  actinium: **2** Ac
  aluminum: **2** Al
  antimony: **2** Sb
  argon: **2** Ar
  arsenic: **2** As
  barium: **2** Ba
  boron: **1** B
  bromine: **2** Br
  cadmium: **2** Cd
  calcium: **2** Ca
  carbon: **1** C
  chlorine: **2** Cl
  chromium: **2** Cr
  cobalt: **2** Co
  columbium: **2** Cb

copper: 2 Cu
fluorine: 1 F
gold: 2 Au
hafnium: 2 Hf
helium: 2 He
hydrogen: 1 H
iodine: 1 I
iron: 2 Fe
krypton: 2 Kr
lead: 2 Pb
lithium: 2 Li
magnesium: 2 Mg
manganese: 2 Mn
mercury: 2 Hg
molybdenum: 2 Mo
neon: 2 Ne
nickel: 2 Ni
nitrogen: 1 N
oxygen: 1 O
phosphorus: 1 P
platinum: 2 Pt
plutonium: 2 Pu
potassium: 1 K
radium: 2 Ra
radon: 2 Rn
rhodium: 2 Rh
rubidium: 2 Rb
silicon: 2 Si
silver: 2 Ag
sodium: 2 Na
sulfur: 1 S
thorium: 2 Th
tin: 2 Sn
titanium: 2 Ti
tungsten: 1 W
uranium: 1 U
xenon: 2 Xe
zinc: 2 Zn
zirconium: 2 Zr
chemise 4 slip **5** dress, shift, shirt, smock **6** blouse **7** garment **8** camisole, lingerie, unbelted **12** undergarment
chemist
  American: 4 Urey **5** Tatum **6** Carver **7** Axelrod, Lipmann, Pauling **8** Kornberg, Langmuir, McMillan **9** Carothers **10** Baekleland
  British: 4 Davy **5** Boyle, Chain, Soddy **6** Dalton, Ramsay **7** Faraday **8** Smithson **9** Cavendish, Priestley, Wollaston
  Dutch: 4 Hoff
  French: 5 Curie, Le Bel **6** Cuvier, Dulong **7** Pasteur **9** Gay-Lussac, Lavoisier **10** Berthollet **11** Joliot-Curie
  German: 4 Hahn **5** Krebs **6** Baeyer, Wohler **9** Glauber, Ostwald
  Italian: 8 Avogadro
  Russian: 9 Mendeleev **10** Mendeleyev
  Scottish: 5 Dewar
  Swedish: 7 Scheele **9** Arrhenius, Berzelius
  Swiss: 6 Muller
Chemosh 10 Moabite god
Chennault, Claire L
  served in: 4 WWII **15** Sino-Japanese War

commander of: 12 Flying Tigers
  general in: 12 Army Air Force
  air advisor to: 13 Chiang Kai-shek
cherchez la femme 15 look for the woman
cheri, cherie 4 dear **10** sweetheart
cherish 4 love **5** honor, nurse, prize, value **6** dote on, esteem, revere, succor **7** care for, idolize, nourish, nurture, shelter, sustain **8** hold dear, treasure, venerate **10** appreciate, take care of
cherished 4 dear **5** loved **7** beloved, darling, dearest **8** favorite, held dear, precious **9** treasured
Cherokee
  language family: 9 Iroquoian
  location: 7 Alabama, Georgia **8** Oklahoma, Virginia **9** Tennessee **13** North Carolina, South Carolina
  associated with: 12 Trail of Tears
  scholar: 7 Sequoya
cherry
  varieties: 3 pie, pin, rum **4** bing, bird, duke, fire, sand, sour, wild **5** black, brush, choke, dwarf, Higan, Naden, sweet **6** bitter, Brazil, ground, Indian, Madden, Oregon, Taiwan, winter **7** bastard, Cayenne, Morello, Nanking, Potomac, prairie, rosebud, sargent, Spanish, St Lucie, wild red, Windsor, Yoshino **8** Barbados, Catalina, oriental, perfumed, Suriname **9** christmas, cornelian, ever green, Jerusalem, wild black **10** west indian **11** downy ground, Hansen's bush, holly-leaved, western sand **12** clammy ground, European bird, Japanese bush, purple ground **13** European dwarf **14** European ground, false Jerusalem, purple-leaf sand **15** Australian brush **17** Japanese cornelian, Japanese flowering, north Japanese hill
  drink: 6 kirsch
cherry brandy 6 kirsch **12** Peter Heering
Cherry Orchard, The
  author: 12 Anton Chekhov
  character: 4 Anya, Gaev **5** Fiers, Varya, Yasha **7** Pischin **8** Dunyasha, Lopakhin, Trofimov **9** Charlotta **16** Madame Ranevskaya
cherub 4 amor **5** angel, child, cupid, youth **6** moppet **8** amoretto, cherubim **13** heavenly being
cherubic 7 angelic **8** innocent **9** spiritual
Cherubin
  character in: 19 The Marriage of Figaro
  author: 12 Beaumarchais
chervil
  botanical name: 20 Anthriscus cerefolium
  origin: 6 Europe, Russia

use: 4 soup **5** salad **11** fines herbes, potato salad
Chesapeake
  author: 13 James Michener
Cheshire Cat
  character in: 28 Alice's Adventures in Wonderland
  author: 7 Carroll
chess
  also called: 9 Royal Game
  chess champion: 3 Tal **4** Euwe, Fine **6** Karpov, Lasker, Morphy **7** Fischer, Kashdan, Smyslov, Spassky **8** Alekhine, Kasparov, Philador, Steinitz **9** Anderssen, Botvinnik, Petrosian, Reshevsky **10** Capablanca
  French: 6 echecs
  German: 11 schachspiel
  horizontal rows: 4 rank
  international chess federation: 4 FIDE
  patron goddess/muse: 6 Caissa
  piece: 4 king, pawn, rook **5** queen **6** bishop, castle, knight **8** chessman, material
  Russian: 8 shakhmat
  Spanish: 7 Ajedrez
  term: 3 pin **4** fork, hole **5** check, tempo **6** center **7** isolani, outpost **8** castling, majority, open file, queening, zugzwang **9** checkmate, en passant, promotion **10** fianchetto **11** zwischenzug
  tied game: 4 draw **9** stalemate
  vertical rows: 4 file
chest
  Italian: 5 petto
Chester, Edward
  character in: 12 Barnaby Rudge
  author: 7 Dickens
chesterfield 4 coat, sofa **5** couch **8** overcoat **9** davenport
Chesterton, G K (Gilbert Keith)
  author of: 20 The Man Who Was Thursday **24** The Napoleon of Notting Hill **25** The Innocence of Father Brown
chestnut 8 Castanea
  varieties: 4 Cape, Wild **5** Horse, Water **6** Guiana, Marron **7** Chinese, Spanish **8** American, Eurasian, European, Japanese, Red horse **10** Dwarf horse, Moreton Bay **11** Common horse **12** Chinese water **13** European horse, Japanese horse **15** California horse
chestnut-colored 6 auburn, russet, sienna **8** cinnamon, nut-brown **11** golden-brown, rust-colored **12** reddish-brown
chest of drawers 5 chest **6** bureau, lowboy **7** cabinet, commode, dresser, highboy, tallboy **10** chiffonier
cheval 5 horse
chevalier 4 lord **5** cadet, noble **6** knight **7** gallant **8** cavalier
Chevalier, Maurice

born: 5 Paris **6** France
roles: 4 Gigi **5** Fanny **6** Can-Can **13** The Love Parade, The Merry Widow **18** Love in the Afternoon

chew 4 gnaw **5** champ, crush, grind, munch **6** crunch, nibble **8** ruminate **9** masticate

Chew
character in: 21 The Master of Ballantrae
author: 9 Stevenson

chewing-out 6 rebuke **7** censure, chiding, reproof **8** reproach, scolding **9** reprimand **10** bawling-out, upbraiding **11** castigation, reprobation **12** dressing-down, remonstrance **13** tongue-lashing

chew noisily 4 gnaw **5** chomp, gnash, grind, munch **6** crunch

chew out 5 scold **6** berate, rail at, rebuke **7** bawl out, reprove, upbraid **8** reproach **9** castigate, reprimand **10** take to task, tongue-lash **14** read the riot act

chew the fat 3 gab, gas, jaw, rap, yak **4** blab, chat, chin, talk **5** prate **6** gossip, patter **7** blather, chatter, palaver, prattle, twaddle **8** chitchat, converse, talk idly **10** chew the rag **11** confabulate **14** chitterchatter

chew the rag 4 talk

Cheyenne
language family: 9 Algonkian **10** Algonquian
location: 6 Platte **7** Montana, Wyoming **8** Oklahoma, Red River **9** Minnesota **11** South Dakota
allied with: 7 Arapaho

Cheyenne
character: 6 Smitty **13** Cheyenne Bodie
cast: 7 L Q Jones **11** Clint Walker

chez 4 with **11** at the home of

Chiang Kai-shek
leader of: 5 China **6** Taiwan
ally: 9 Sun Yat-sen
party: 10 Kuomintang **11** Nationalist
defeated by: 10 Communists
wife: 12 Soong Mei-ling

Chibcha (Muisca)
location: 6 Bogota, Panama **8** Colombia **12** South America
associated with: 8 El Dorado

Chibchan
language family: 13 Macro-Chibchan
group: 4 Cuna, Paya, Rama **5** Lenca, Xinca **7** Chibcha

chic 4 tony **5** natty, ritzy, smart, swank **6** classy, modish, snazzy, swanky **7** elegant, stylish, voguish **11** fashionable

Chicago
author: 12 Carl Sandburg

Chicago
airport: 5 O'Hare **6** Midway
baseball team: 4 Cubs **8** White Sox

basketball team: 5 Bulls
downtown area: 4 Loop
football team: 5 Bears
fort: 8 Dearborn
hockey team: 10 Black Hawks
lake: 4 Wolf **7** Calumet **8** Michigan
landmark: 10 Meigs Field, Sears Tower **12** Board of Trade, Comiskey Park, Humboldt Park, Soldier Field, Wrigley Field **13** Shedd Aquarium **15** Lincoln Monument, Merchandise Mart, Newberry Library, Wrigley Building **16** Adler Planetarium **17** Holy Name Cathedral, John Hancock Center **18** Mercantile Exchange, Prudential Building **20** Midwest Stock Exchange **21** Art Institute of Chicago **23** Museum of Contemporary Art **26** Museum of Science and Industry **27** Field Museum of Natural History
mayor: 5 Byrne, Daley **10** Washington
nickname: 9 Windy City
river: 7 Chicago **10** Des Plaines
street: 11 Wacker Drive **13** Chicago Skyway **14** Lake Shore Drive
university: 6 DePaul, Loyola **9** Roosevelt **12** Northwestern **19** University of Chicago **29** Illinois Institute of Technology

chicanery 4 ruse, wile **5** craft, fraud, guile **6** deceit, duping **7** cunning, gulling, knavery, roguery **8** artifice, cozenage, trickery, villainy **9** deception, duplicity, rascality, sophistry **10** craftiness, hocus-pocus, humbuggery, subterfuge **11** hoodwinking **12** pettifoggery **13** double-dealing

chichi 4 arty **5** fussy, showy **6** flashy, frilly, garish, prissy, vulgar **7** finical, pompous, splashy **8** affected, gimcrack, overnice, precious, sissyish **9** arty-tarty, grandiose, nasty-nice **10** flamboyant **11** overrefined, pretentious **12** artsy-craftsy, ostentatious

chick
group of: 5 brood **6** clutch

Chickasaw
language family: 10 Muskhogean
location: 8 Oklahoma **9** Tennessee **11** Mississippi
related to: 7 Choctaw
member of: 19 Five Civilized Tribes

chicken, chickenhearted 3 hen **4** cock, fowl **5** layer, timid **6** afraid, coward, craven, pullet, scared, yellow **7** caitiff, dastard, fearful, gutless, rooster **8** cowardly, poltroon, timorous **9** flinching, fraidy-cat, shrinking **11** lily-livered, yellow-belly **12** fainthearted **13** pusillanimous, yellow-bellied **22** showing the white feather

chickenheartedness 8 timidity **9** cowardice **10** yellowness **11** fearfulness, poltroonery **12** timorousness **13** pusillanimity **16** faintheartedness

chide 5 scold **6** berate, rebuke **7** cen-

sure, chasten, reprove, upbraid **8** admonish, denounce, reproach **9** criticize, find fault, reprimand **10** take to task

chief 3 key **4** boss, head, lord, main **5** first, major, prime, ruler **6** leader, master, ruling **7** captain, highest, leading, monarch, primary, supreme **8** cardinal, chairman, crowning, director, dominant, foremost, greatest, overlord, overseer **9** chieftain, commander, governing, number-one, paramount, potentate, principal, sovereign, uppermost **10** prevailing, ringleader, supervisor **11** outstanding, predominant **12** preponderant **13** administrator

chief good
Latin: 11 summum bonum

chiefly 5 first **6** mainly, mostly **8** above all **9** expressly, in the main, most of all, primarily **10** especially **11** principally **12** particularly **13** predominantly

chieftan 4 boss, head **6** leader **7** captain, head man

chiffonier 6 bureau **7** dresser **8** cupboard **14** chest of drawers

chignon 3 bun **4** knot, roll **6** hairdo **9** hairpiece, hairstyle

child 3 boy, kid, lad, son, tad, tot **4** baby, girl, lass, tyke **5** youth **6** infant, moppet, rug rat **7** toddler **8** daughter, juvenile **9** little one, offspring, youngster

childbearing 5 birth **11** parturition

childbirth 8 delivery **11** confinement, parturition
French: 12 accouchement
goddess of: 4 Upis **5** Parca **6** Lucina, Matuta **7** Artemis **8** Ilithyia **10** Eileithyia

Childe Harold's Pilgrimage
author: 21 George Gordon Lord Byron

Childe Roland to the Dark Tower Came
author: 14 Robert Browning

childhood 5 youth **7** boyhood **8** girlhood **10** school days **11** adolescence, nursery days

childish 5 naive, silly **6** callow, simple **7** asinine, babyish, foolish, puerile **8** immature, juvenile **9** infantile **10** adolescent

childlike 8 childish, immature, innocent **9** ingenuous

child prodigy 7 quiz kid, whiz kid
German: 10 Wunderkind

children 4 boys, kids, sons, tads, tots **5** girls, issue, young **6** babies, result, youth **7** infants, product, progeny **9** daughters, juveniles **11** descendants

Children of God
author: 12 Vardis Fisher

Children of Paradise

director: 11 Marcel Carne
cast: 7 Arletty **11** Albert Remay **14** Pierre Brasseur **17** Jean-Louis Barrault

Child's Garden of Verses, A
author: 20 Robert Louis Stevenson

Chile
other name: 6 Tchile
name means: 21 deepest part of the Earth
capital/largest city: 8 Santiago
others: 4 Boco, Cuya, Lebu, Lota, Ocoa, Tome **5** Angol, Arica, Cobya, Talca **6** Arauco, Calama, Curico, Gatico, Osorno, Ovalle, Serena, Temuco, Vicuna, Yumbel, Yungay **7** Caldera, Chillan, Copiapo, Iquique, Valdiva **8** Coquimbo, Rancagua, Santiago, Vallenar **9** Cauquenes **10** Concepcion, Coquembana, Valparaiso, Vina del Mar **11** Antofagasta, Puerto Montt, Punta Arenas, San Bernardo
measure: 4 vara **5** legua, linea **6** cuadra, fanega
monetary unit: 4 peso **5** libra **6** condor, escudo
weight: 5 grano, libra **7** quintal
island: 3 Luz **4** Prat **5** Byron, Guafo, Hoste, Mocha, Nueva, Nunez, Vidal **6** Chiloe, Chonos, Dawson, Easter, Lennox, Piazzi, Picton, Quilan, Riesco, Stosch, Talcan **7** Angamos, Campana, Hanover, Hermite, Pajaros, Refugio, Tranqui **8** Chauques, Clarence, Huamblin, Nalcavec, Navarino, Traiguen **13** Juan Fernandez **14** Tierra del Fuego
lake: 5 Ranco **6** Yelcho **7** Puyehue, Rupanco **8** Cochrane **10** General Paz, Llanquihue **11** Buenos Aires
mountain: 4 Maca, Toro **5** Chato, Maipo, Maipu, Paine, Potro, Pular, Torre, Yogan **6** Apiwan, Burney, Conico, Jervis, Poquis, Rincon **7** Chaltel, Copiapo, Fitzroy, Palpana, Velluda **8** Cochrane, Tronador, Yanteles **9** Tupungato
highest point: 13 Ojos del Salado
river: 3 Loa **4** Laja, Yali **5** Alhue, Azapa, Bravo, Bueno, Elqui, Lauca, Lluta, Maipo, Maule, Puelo, Rahue, Rapel, Stata, Vitor **6** Biobio, Camina, Choapa, Choros, Cisnes, Colina, Huasco, Limari, Morado, Palena, Poscua, Tolten **7** Copiapo **8** Valdivia
sea: 7 Pacific
physical features:
  bay: 4 Cook, Eyre, Nena, Tarn **5** Lomas, Otway, Sarco **6** Darwin, Inutil, Moreno, Stokes, Tongoy **7** Dyneley, Inglesa, Skyring **8** Desolate
  cape: 4 Dyer, Horn **6** Choros, Falsos, Hornos, Quilan, Tablas **7** Deseado **10** Tres Montes
  channel: 5 Ancho, Cheap **6** Beagle **8** Cockburn, Moralcda
  desert: 7 Atacama

gulf: 5 Ancud, Guafo, Penas **6** Arauco
isthmus: 5 Ofqui
peninsula: 5 Hardy, Lacuy **6** Taitao, Tumbes
point: 4 Toro **5** Gallo, Liles, Lobos, Loros, Morro, Talca, Tetas, Vieja **6** Cachos, Galera, Molles **7** Angamos, Lavapie
strait: 6 Nelson **8** Magellan
volcano: 5 Lanin, Maipo **6** Antuco, Llaima, Oyahue, Tacora **7** Peteroa, Socomap
people: 3 Ona **4** Auca, Inca, Onan **6** Arauca, Chango, Yahgan **7** Mapuche, mestizo, Moluche, Pampean, Patagon, Puegian, Ranquel **8** Alikuluf, Picunche, Tsonecan
  author: 5 Bello **6** Donoso, Neruda **7** Mistral
  conqueror: 7 Valdiva
  explorer: 8 Magellan
  leader: 7 Allende **8** O'Higgins, Pinochet **9** San Martin **10** Alessandri
language: 7 Spanish
religion: 13 Roman Catholic
places:
  copper mine: 12 Chuquicamata
  resort: 8 Portillo **10** Vina del Mar
possession: 12 Easter Island **20** Juan Fernandez Islands
feature:
  cowboy: 5 huaso
  dance: 5 cueca **6** pequen **9** resbalosa
  shrub: 5 litre
  slum: 9 callempas
  tree: 5 rauli
  wind instrument: 4 sicu
food:
  drink: 5 pisco **6** chicha
  hot red pepper: 3 aji
  meat pie: 8 empanada
  soup: 7 cazuela **8** caldillo

chile peppers see **15** capsicum peppers

chill, chilly 3 icy, nip, raw **4** bite, cold, cool, keen **5** aloof, brisk, crisp, fever, harsh, nippy, sharp, stiff, stony **6** arctic, biting, bitter, frigid, frosty, frozen, wintry **7** callous, coolish, cutting, glacial, hostile, iciness, rawness, shivery **8** coolness, uncaring **9** crispness, frigidity, sharpness, unfeeling **10** forbidding, frostiness, unfriendly **11** indifferent, passionless, penetrating **12** unresponsive

chilled 4 cold, iced **6** cooled, frozen **7** frosted **8** hardened **10** dispirited **11** discouraged **12** refrigerated

chilling 3 icy, raw **5** nippy, on ice **6** frigid **7** bracing, cooling **10** unfriendly

Chillingworth, Roger
character in: 16 The Scarlet Letter
author: 9 Hawthorne

chime 4 gong, peal, ring, toll **5** knell, sound **6** jingle, tinkle **7** pealing, ring-

ing **8** carillon, ding-dong, tinkling, tollings **10** set of bells **14** tintinnabulate **16** tintinnabulation

Chimene
character in: 6 The Cid
author: 9 Corneille

chimera 5 dream, fancy **6** bubble, mirage **7** fantasy, monster, phantom **8** daydream, delusion, idle whim, illusion **9** pipe dream **10** self-deceit, shemonster **12** will-o'- the-wisp **13** castle in Spain, fool's paradise, hallucination, self-deception **14** castle in the air **24** figment of one's imagination

Chimera
form: 7 monster
father: 6 Typhon
mother: 7 Echidna
breathes: 4 fire

Chimera
author: 9 John Barth

chimerical 6 absurd, unreal **7** utopian **8** delusive, ethereal, fabulous, fanciful, illusory, mythical quixotic **9** fantastic, imaginary, visionary **10** impossible, phantasmal, **11** nonexistent

chimney 4 flue, tube, vent **5** cleft, gully, spout, stack **6** funnel, hearth **7** opening **9** stovepipe **10** smokestack

chimpanzee 3 ape **6** animal, baboon, monkey

chin 3 gab, jaw, rap **4** chat, talk **7** chatter, palaver **8** chitchat, converse **10** chew the fat, chew the rag **11** confabulate

china 6 dishes, plates **7** pottery **8** crockery **9** chinaware, porcelain, stoneware, tableware **11** ceramicware, earthenware **14** cups and saucers

China
other name: 3 PRC **13** Middle Kingdom **14** Flowery Kingdom **22** People's Republic of China
capital: 6 Peking **7** Beijing
largest city: 8 Shanghai
others: 3 Bai, Noh **4** Ahpa, Amoy, Fuyu, Guma, Hami, Huma, Ipin, Kian, Kisi, Lini, Loho, Luta, Moho, Moyu, Niya, Noho, Omin, Rima, Saka, Sian, Taku, Tali, Tayu, Wuhu, Yaan **5** Chiai, Fusin, Kirin, Koklu, Linyu, Macao, Penki, Shasi, Soche, Taian, Talai, Tihwa, Tuyun, Wuhan, Wusih, Yenan, Yenki, Yulin, Yumen **6** Anshan, Antung, Canton, Dairen, Fuchau, Fuchow, Fushun, Hankow, Harbin, Ilhasa, Kalgan, Loyang, Lushun, Mukden, Nanhai, Ningpo, Singan, Sining, Taipei, Tsinan, Yangku, Yunnan **7** Fuskhih, Hanyang, Kunming, Lanchow, Lioyang, Mengtze, Nanking, Nanning, Paoshan, Peiping, Soochow, Taiyuan, Tatshan, Urumchi, Urumsti, Waichow, Wuchang, Yenping **8** Chinchow, Fengkiek, Fengtien, Hangchow, Kingchow, Nanchang,

Shanghai, Shenyang, Siangtan, Tientsin, Tungchow, Wanchuan, Wanhsien **9** Chungking, Kiangling, Tsingyuan **10** Chiangling, Port Arthur
school: 5 Futan **6** Peking **7** Nanking **8** Hangchow **9** Sun Yat-sen **16** Cheng-tu Technical
division:
  province: 5 Honan, Hunan, Hupei, Kansu **6** Anhwei, Fukien, Shansi, Shensi, Yunnan **7** Kiangsi, Kiangsu **8** Chekiang, Kweichow, Shantung, Szechwan, Tientsin, Tsinghai **9** Kwangtung, Manchuria
measure: 3 cho, fan, fen, pau, tou, tun, yan, yin **4** chek, chih, fang, kish, papa, quei, shih, teke, tsan, tsun **5** catty, chang, ching, sheng, shing **6** chupak, gungli, kungho, kungmu, tching **7** kungfen, kungyin **8** kungchih, kungshih, **9** kungching
monetary unit: 4 cash, cent, fyng, mace, tael, tiao, yuan **5** sycee **12** jen nin piao pu
weight: 3 fan, fen, hao, kin, ssu, tan, yin **4** chee, chin, dong, shih, tael, tsin **5** catty, chien, picul, tchin, tsien **6** kungli **7** haikwan, kungfen, kungssu, kungtun **8** kungchin **9** candareen **10** kupingtael
island: 4 Amoy **5** Macao, Matsu, Namki, Taipa **6** Chusan, Hainan, Pratas, Quemoy, Taiwan, Tinian, Yuhwan **7** Coloane, Formosa, Hungtow, Tungsha **8** Ching Hai, Chouchan, Kulangsu
lake: 3 Tai **4** Chao, Na-mu **5** Kaoyu, Oling, Telli **6** Bamtso, Bornor, Ebinor, Erhhai, Khanka, Lopnor, Namtso, Poyang **7** Chaling, Hungtse, Karanor, Kokonor **8** Hulunnor, Montcalm, Taroktso, Tellinor, Tienchih, Tsinghai, Tungting
sea: 6 Yellow **9** East China **10** South China
physical features:
  bay: 7 Laichow **8** Hangchow
  cape: 7 Olwanpi
  channel: 5 Bashi
  desert: 4 Gobi **5** Ordos, Shamo **7** Alashan **10** Takla Makan
  dry lake: 6 Lopnor
  gulf: 5 Pohai **6** Chihli, Tonkin **7** Pechili **8** Liaotung
  peninsula: 6 Leichu **7** Luichow **8** Liaotung
  plateau: 5 Loess **7** Tibetan
  port: 4 Amoy, Wuhu **5** Aigun, Shasi **6** Antung, Canton, Chefoo, Dairen, Ichang, Ningpo, Pakhoi, Swatow, Wuchow **7** Foochow, Hunchun, Luichow, Nanking, Samshui, Santuao, Soochow, Wenchow, Yinkkow, Yungkia **8** Changsha, Hangchow, Kiukiang, Kongmoon, Shanghai, Tengyueh, Tientsin, Tsingtao, Wanhsien **9** Kwangchow, Weihaiwei **10** Tsing-

kiang
  strait: 6 Hainan, Taiwan **7** Formosa
people: 3 Han, Yis **4** Huis, Lolo, Miao, Pu-is **5** Hakka, Hoklo, Seres, Sinic **6** Cataia, Chuang, Johnny, Korean, Manchu, Mongol, Serian, Uighun **7** Sinaean, Tibetan
  leader: 9 Sun Yat-sen, Zhou Enlai **10** Kublai Khan, Mao Tse-tung **11** Genghis Khan **12** Deng Xiaoping **13** Chiang Kai-shek
  philosopher: 6 Lao-tzu **9** Confucius
language: 7 Chinese **8** Mandarin, Shanghai **9** Cantonese
religion: 5 Islam **6** Taoism **8** Buddhism **12** Christianity, Confucianism
place:
  palace: 6 Summer **8** Imperial **13** Forbidden City
  ruins: 9 Ming Tombs
  square: 9 Tiananmen
  wonder: 9 Great Wall
feature:
  boat: 4 junk
  conspirators: 10 Gang of Four
  dynasty: 3 Han, Sui **4** Chou, Ch'in, Ming, Sung, T'ang **5** Ch'ing, Shang **6** Manchu
  military academy: 7 whompoa
  watercolor: 8 shan shiu

China Syndrome, The
director: 12 James Bridges
cast: 9 Jane Fonda **10** Jack Lemmon, Scott Brady **14** Michael Douglas
setting: 17 nuclear power plant

Chinatown
director: 13 Roman Polanski
cast: 10 John Huston **11** Faye Dunaway **13** Jack Nicholson
Oscar for: 10 screenplay

chinaware 6 dishes, plates **7** pottery **8** crockery **9** porcelain, stoneware, tableware **11** ceramicware, earthenware **14** cups and saucers

chine 5 spine **6** dorsum **8** backbone

Chinese book of divination 6 I Ching

Chingachgook
character in: 13 The Pathfinder **20** The Last of the Mohicans
author: 6 Cooper

chink 3 cut, gap **4** gash, hole, rent, rift, ring, slit **5** break, clank, cleft, clink, crack, fault, split **6** breach, jangle, jingle, rattle, tinkle **7** crevice, fissure, opening **8** aperture

Chinook (Flathead)
language family: 9 Chinookan
location: 7 Pacific **10** Washington
ritual: 15 head deformation

Chinookan
tribe: 7 Chinook **8** Flathead

chintzy 5 cheap, close, dowdy, tacky, tatty, tight **6** frowzy, frumpy, shabby, sleazy, stingy **7** miserly **8** grudging, schlocky, stinting **9** niggardly, penuri-

ous **11** closefisted **12** parsimonious **13** penny-pinching

chip 3 bit, cut, hew **4** chop, gash, hack, nick **5** chunk, crumb, flake, scrap, shred, slice, split, wafer **6** chisel, morsel, paring, sliver **7** cutting, shaving, whittle **8** fragment, splinter

chipmunk 4 Chip, Dale **6** chippy, gopher, rodent **8** chipmuck, squirrel **14** ground squirrel **16** chipping squirrel

chipper 3 gay **4** pert, spry **5** alive, brisk, peppy **6** frisky, jaunty, lively **8** animated, carefree, cheerful, spirited **9** easygoing, energetic, sprightly, vivacious **12** high- spirited, light-hearted

Chippewa (Ojibwa, Ojibway)
language family: 9 Algonkian **10** Algonquian
tribe: 4 Cree **6** Ottawa **8** Chippewa **10** Missisauga
location: 6 Canada **9** Lake Huron **11** North Dakota **12** Lake Superior, Niagara Falls
leader: 7 Pontiac

CHiPS
character: 8 (Officer) Jon Baker **10** (Sgt) Joe Getraer **16** (Officer) Frank (Ponch) Poncherello
cast: 10 Robert Pine **11** Erik Estrada, Larry Wilcox

Chirico, Giorgio de
born: 5 Volos **6** Greece
artwork: 15 Enigma of the Hour **19** Enigma of an Afternoon **21** Enigma of an Autumn Night **22** Nostalgia of the Infinite **32** The Melancholy and Mystery of a Street

Chiron
also: 7 Cheiron
form: 7 centaur
father: 6 Cronos, Cronus, Kronos
mother: 7 Philyra
wife: 8 Chariclo
daughter: 6 Endeis
grandson: 6 Peleus
occupation: 7 teacher

chirp 4 peep, sing **5** cheep, chirr, tweet **7** chirrup, chitter, peeping, twitter **8** cheeping

chirrup 4 peep **5** cheep, chirp, tweet **7** chitter, twitter

chisel 3 cut, gyp **4** gull, hoax, rook, tool **5** blade, cheat, slice **6** incise
type: 4 cape, cold, wood **7** v-shaped

Chisel
constellation of: 6 Caelum

chiseler 4 fake **5** cheat, fraud, quack **7** cheater **8** swindler

Chislev 16 ninth Hebrew month

chit 3 IOU, tab **4** note **5** check **7** voucher

chitchat 3 gab **4** chat **5** prate **6** drivel, gossip **7** chatter, palaver, prattle **8** converse **9** small talk **10** chew the fat, chew the rag **11** confabulate **13** confabulation

Chitimacha
   language family: **6** Tunica
   location: **9** Louisiana
   noted for: **8** basketry

chitter 4 peep **5** cheep, chirp, tweet **7** chatter, chirrup, twitter

chitter-chatter 3 gab **4** blab **6** babble, drivel, gabble, jabber **7** blabber, prattle, twaddle **8** chitchat **9** jabbering **16** idle conversation

chivalrous 6 polite **7** courtly, gallant **8** mannerly

chivalry 8 courtesy **9** gallantry **10** knighthood, politeness **11** courtliness

Chivery, Young John
   character in: **12** Little Dorrit
   author: **7** Dickens

chivy 3 nag **4** hunt, race **5** annoy, chase, chevy, hound, trail, worry **6** badger, bother, harass, pursue **7** scamper, torment

Chlidanope
   form: **5** Naiad

Chloe
   epithet of: **7** Demeter
   means: **5** green

chloride 7 muriate **8** chemical, compound

chlorine
   chemical symbol: **2** Cl

chocolate 5 brown, candy, cacao, cocoa, drink **6** bon bon **10** confection

Choctaw
   language family: **10** Muskhogean
   location: **7** Alabama **11** Mississippi
   related to: **9** Chickasaw

Choephoroe
   author: **9** Aeschylus
   character: **6** Furies **7** Electra, Orestes, Pylades **9** Aegisthus **12** Clytemnestra

choice 3 say **4** A one, best, fine, pick, vote **5** array, elite, prime, prize, stock, store, voice **6** better, opting, option, select, supply, tip-top **7** display, special, variety **8** choosing, deciding, decision, superior **9** excellent, exclusive, first-rate, preferred, selection, top drawer **10** assemblage, assortment, collection, consummate, discretion, first-class, preferable, preference, well-chosen **11** alternative, appointment, exceptional, superlative **13** determination, extraordinary

choice food 5 treat **8** delicacy

choicest part
   French: **14** creme de la creme

choir 4 band **5** quire **6** angels, chorus **7** chorale, singers **10** choristers

Choirboys, The
   author: **14** Joseph Wambaugh

choke 3 dam, gag **4** clog, plug **5** block, check, dam up, stuff **6** arrest, bridle, hamper, hinder, impede, plug up, retard, stifle, stop up **7** congest, garrote, inhibit, repress, smother **8** blockade, hold back, obstruct, restrain, strangle,

suppress, throttle **9** constrain, constrict, suffocate **10** asphyxiate

choler 3 ire **4** fury, rage **5** anger, wrath **6** spleen, temper

choleric 3 mad **5** angry, irate, testy, vexed **6** cranky, grumpy, shirty, touchy **7** enraged, furious, grouchy, peevish, waspish **8** snappish, wrathful **9** dyspeptic, indignant, irritable, irascible, splenetic **10** infuriated, short-fused **11** contentious, hot-tempered, ill-tempered, thin-skinned **12** cantankerous, sour-tempered **13** quick-tempered, short-tempered

choose 3 opt **4** like, pick, take, wish **5** adopt, elect **6** decide, desire, intend, opt for, prefer, see fit, select **7** call out, embrace, espouse, extract, fix upon, pick out, resolve **8** decide on, settle on **9** determine, single out **10** be inclined **13** commit oneself **14** make up one's mind

choosy 5 fussy, picky **7** finicky **9** selective **10** fastidious, particular **14** discriminating

chop 3 cut, hew, hit, lop **4** blow, chip, crop, cube, dice, fell, gash, hack **5** cut up, mince, slash, slice, split, swipe, whack **6** cleave, cutlet, stroke, sunder **8** fragment, rib slice **9** cotelette, pulverize

Chopin, Frederic Francois
   born: **6** Poland **12** Zelazowawola
   companion: **10** George Sand
   composer of: **5** Etude **7** Ballade **8** Berceuse, Cat Valse, Dog Valse, Fantasie **9** Ecossaise **10** Barcarolle **11** Minute Valse **15** Andante Spianato, Heroic Polonaise (No 6), Raindrop Prelude, Winter Wind Etude **16** Shepherd Boy Etude **17** Impromptu Fantasie, Rondo a la Krakowiak **18** Revolutionary Etude **20** Butterfly's Wings Etude

choral ode
   Greek: **7** parodos **8** stasimon

chord 4 cord, line, note, tone **5** music, triad **6** accord, string, tendon **7** cadence, emotion, feeling, harmony **9** harmonize

chore 3 job **4** duty, task, work **5** stint **6** burden, errand, strain **8** farm task, small job **10** assignment **13** household task **14** responsibility

choreography 5 dance **12** stage dancing **16** dance composition

chorister 6 singer **7** changer **8** choirboy

chortle 5 laugh **7** chuckle

chorus 5 choir, unity **6** accord, unison **7** concert, concord, refrain **8** glee club, one voice, response **9** antiphony, consensus, unanimity **11** concordance **12** singing group

chosen 5 elite **6** picked, sorted **7** elected **8** selected **9** picked out

Chosen, The
   author: **10** Chaim Potok

Chosen see **5** Korea

Chouans, The
   author: **14** Honore de Balzac

chough
   group of: **10** chattering

Chowbok
   character in: **7** Erewhon
   author: **6** Butler

Christ, the see **5** Jesus

christen 3 dip, dub **4** name **6** launch **7** baptize, immerse **8** dedicate, sprinkle **9** designate

Christian
   character in: **16** Pilgrim's Progress
   author: **6** Bunyan

Christian, Fletcher
   character in: **17** Mutiny on the Bounty
   authors: **4** Hall **8** Nordhoff

Christian, Linda
   real name: **16** Blanca Rosa Welter
   husband: **11** Tyrone Power **12** Edmund Purdom
   born: **6** Mexico **7** Tampico
   roles: **6** Athena **15** Slaves of Babylon **18** Green Dolphin Street

Christiania
   capital of: **6** Norway
   now called: **4** Oslo

Christie, (Dame) Agatha
   author of: **7** Curtain **12** The Mousetrap **14** Death on the Nile **15** The Mirror Crack'd **16** Ten Little Indians **19** Murder at the Vicarage **20** And Then There Were None **22** What Mrs McGillicuddy Saw! **23** The Murder of Roger Ackroyd **24** Murder on the Orient Express, Witness for the Prosecution **27** The Mysterious Affair at Styles
   character: **6** Mr. Pine **10** Jane Marple **13** Hercule Poirot

Christie, Julie
   born: **5** Assam, India **6** Chukua
   roles: **7** Darling (Oscar), Shampoo **9** Billy Liar **11** Heat and Dust **13** Doctor Zhivago, Fahrenheit 451, Heaven Can Wait **18** McCabe and Mrs Miller **22** Far From the Madding Crowd

Christine
   author: **11** Stephen King

Christmas
   also: **4** Noel, Yule **8** Yuletide
   feature/symbol: **4** bell, star, tree **5** angel, gifts, holly **6** candle, carols, creche, manger, sleigh, wreath **7** Yule log **8** presents **9** evergreen, mistletoe, snowflake, stockings **10** Santa Claus

Christmas, Joe
   character in: **13** Light in August
   author: **8** Faulkner

Christmas Carol, A
   author: **14** Charles Dickens

character: 7 Tiny Tim **8** Fezziwig **11** Bob Cratchit **12** Marley's Ghost **15** Ebenezer Scrooge
  ghosts of: 13 Christmas Past **15** Christmas Future **16** Christmas Present
  director: 17 Brian Desmond Hurst
  cast: 10 Jack Warner **11** Alastair Sim (Ebenezer Scrooge), Mervyn Johns **14** Michael Hordern **16** Kathleen Harrison

Christopher Robin
  character in: 13 Winnie-the-Pooh
  author: 5 Milne

chromium
  chemical symbol: 2 Cr

chronic 7 abiding, lasting **8** constant, enduring, habitual, periodic **9** confirmed, continual, ingrained, perennial, recurrent, recurring **10** continuous, deep-rooted, deep-seated, inveterate, persistent, persisting **12** intermittent, longstanding

chronicle 3 log **4** epic, list, note, post, saga **5** diary, enter, story **6** annals, docket, record, relate, report **7** account, history, journal, narrate, recount, set down **8** archives **9** narrative **10** chronology

Chronicles of England, Scotland, and Ireland
  author: 16 Raphael Holinshed

chronological 5 dated **6** serial **7** ordered, sequent **10** sequential, succeeding, successive **11** consecutive, progressive, time-ordered **12** chronometric, chronoscopic **13** chronographic

chronology 6 annals, record **7** history **9** chronicle **13** order of events

chronometer 5 clock **8** horologe **9** timepiece

chrysanthemum
  varieties: 3 Max **4** Corn **5** Daisy, Tansy **6** Nippon **7** Garland **8** Florist's, Tricolor **10** Portuguese

chrysoberyl
  variety: 7 cat's-eye **11** alexandrite

chrysolite 4 iron, lava **5** beryl, green, stone **6** yellow **7** mineral, olivine, peridot **8** silicate **9** magnesium **10** aquamarine

chrysoprase
  species: 6 quartz
  color: 5 green

Chrysothemis
  father: 9 Agamemnon
  mother: 12 Clytemnestra
  brother: 7 Orestes
  sister: 7 Electra **9** Iphigenia
  daughter: 5 Rhoeo

Chthonian
  form: 5 deity **6** spirit
  habitat: 10 underworld

Chthonius
  member of: 6 Sparti

epithet of: 4 Zeus
  means: 15 of the underworld

Chuang-tzu, Chwang-tse
  author: 9 Chuang-tzu

chubby 3 fat **5** buxom, plump, podgy, pudgy, stout, tubby **6** chunky, flabby, fleshy, portly, rotund, stocky, zaftig **7** paunchy **8** heavyset, roly-poly, thickset **9** corpulent **10** overweight **15** pleasingly plump

chuck 3 pat, pet, tap **4** cast, toss **5** fling, heave, pitch, sling, throw **6** tickle

chuckle 5 cluck, laugh **6** clumsy **7** cackle, chortle, snicker

chum 3 pal **4** bait **5** buddy, crony **6** cohort, friend **7** comrade **8** intimate, playmate, sidekick **9** companion, confidant **10** bosom buddy, playfellow **11** close friend

chummy 5 close, palsy **7** devoted **8** familiar, friendly, intimate **9** congenial **10** buddy-buddy, palsy-walsy **12** affectionate

chump 4 dolt, dupe, fool, goof, goon, head **5** champ, munch **6** sucker **9** blockhead

chunk 3 gob, wad **4** clod, hunk, lump, mass **5** batch, block, piece **6** nugget, square

chunky 5 beefy, dumpy, lumpy, pudgy, squat, stout, thick **6** chubby, portly, stocky, stodgy, stubby **7** squabby **8** heavyset, thickset **11** thick-bodied

church 4 cult, sect **5** faith **6** belief, chapel, mosque, temple **7** service **8** basilica, religion **9** cathedral, devotions, synagogue **10** house of God, Lord's house, persuasion, tabernacle **11** affiliation **12** denomination **13** divine worship **14** house of worship

Church, Frederick Edwin
  born: 10 Hartford CT
  artwork: 14 Andes of Ecuador, Falls of Niagara (Niagara Falls) **18** The Heart of the Andes **19** Morning in the Tropics

Churchill, Frank
  character in: 4 Emma
  author: 6 Austen

Churchill, Sarah
  father: 19 Sir Winston Churchill
  born: 6 London **7** England
  roles: 12 Royal Wedding

Churchill, Winston Spencer
  born: 7 England **14** Blenheim Palace
  father: 8 Randolph
  mother: 12 Jennie Jerome
  wife: 16 Clementine Hosier
  daughter: 5 Sarah
  school: 6 Harrow **9** Sandhurst
  captured by: 5 Boers
  position: 13 prime minister
  author of: 11 Marlborough, My Early Life **14** The World Crisis **17** The Second World War **35** A History of the

English-Speaking Peoples
  won: 10 Nobel Prize

churchly 8 clerical, pastoral, priestly **9** parochial **11** ministerial **14** ecclesiastical

churchman 5 vicar **6** bishop, cleric, curate, deacon, parson, pastor, priest, rector **7** prelate **8** chaplain, minister, preacher **9** clergyman **12** ecclesiastic

church official 5 elder **6** beadle, deacon **9** presbyter

churchyard 8 cemetery **9** graveyard **12** burial ground **13** burying ground

churl 3 cad, oaf **4** boor, lout **7** bounder

churlish 4 rude, sour, tart **5** crude, surly, testy **6** crusty, sullen **7** bearish, bilious, boorish, brusque, crabbed, grouchy, ill-bred, uncivil, uncouth, waspish **8** arrogant, captious, choleric, impolite, impudent, insolent, petulant **9** dastardly, insulting, irascible, irritable, obnoxious, rancorous, splenetic **10** unmannerly **11** ill-mannered, ill-tempered, quarrelsome **12** contemptible, discourteous

churn 4 beat, foam, rage, roil, roll, toss, whip **5** heave, shake, swirl, whisk **6** stir up **7** agitate, disturb, pulsate, shake up, vibrate **8** convulse **9** palpitate

chute 5 rapid, slide, slope **7** incline, passage **9** parachute

chutzpa, chutzpah 4 gall **5** brass, cheek, nerve **8** audacity, boldness, temerity **9** brashness, impudence **10** brazenness, effrontery **11** forwardness, presumption

Chwatt, Aaron
  real name of: 10 Red Buttons

ciao 2 hi **5** hello **6** so long **7** goodbye **11** see you later

Cicero, Marcus Tullius
  lived in: 11 ancient Rome
  noted as: 6 author, lawyer, orator **9** statesman **11** philosopher **12** letter writer
  position: 6 aedile, consul **7** praetor
  author of: 9 De finibus, De oratore **10** De amicitia, De officiis **11** De republica, De senectute, In Catilinam **14** De natura deorum, Pro lege Manilia **23** Tusculanae Disputationes

cicerone 5 guide, pilot **8** conductor **9** explainer

cicisbeo 5 lover

Cid, The
  also: 11 Poema del Cid
  author: 7 unknown **15** Pierre Corneille
  character: 7 Chimene **8** Rodrigue
  Cid also called: 14 el Cid Campeador **18** Rodrigo Diaz de Bivar
  horse: 7 Babieca

ci-devant 6 former **7** retired **10** heretofore

cierge 3 dip, wax 5 light, taper 6 bougie, candle, tallow

cigar 4 toby 5 claro 6 corona, havana, maduro, stogie 7 cheroot 8 panatela, panetela, perfecto 9 cigarillo, panatella
  ingredient: 11 tobacco leaf
  part: 6 binder, filler 7 wrapper
  made in: 4 Cuba 6 Havana
  kept in: 7 humidor

cigarette, cigaret 3 cig, fag 4 biri, rett 5 smoke 6 gasper, grette, reefer 10 coffin nail
  ingredient: 3 tar 7 menthol, tobacco 8 nicotine

Cimabue
  real name: 11 Cenni di Pepi
  born: 5 Italy 8 Florence
  artwork attributed: 18 The S Trinita Madonna 29 Madonna Enthroned with St Francis 45 Madonna and Child Enthroned with Angels and Prophets

Cimarron
  author: 10 Edna Ferber
  director: 13 Wesley Ruggles
  cast: 10 Irene Dunne, Richard Dix 13 Estelle Taylor
  Oscar for: 7 picture 10 screenplay

Cimarron Strip
  character: 8 (US Marshal) Jim Crown 9 Mac Gregor 12 Francis Wilde 17 Dulcey Coopersmith
  cast: 10 Randy Boone 12 Jill Townsend, Percy Herbert 13 Stuart Whitman

Cimino, Michael
  director of: 11 Heaven's Gate 13 The Deer Hunter (Oscar)

Cimmerian
  mentioned by: 5 Homer
  form: 10 Westerners
  live in: 8 darkness

cinch 4 band, snap 5 girth 6 clinch, ensure, girdle, shoo-in 8 lead-pipe 9 pull tight, sure thing 11 piece of cake

Cincinnati
  baseball team: 4 Reds
  football team: 7 Bengals

cincture 4 band, belt, cord, sash 6 girdle

cinder 3 ash 4 slag 5 ashes, dross, ember 6 embers, scoria 8 clinkers, iron slag 10 burned coal, burned wood

Cinderella
  author: 7 unknown
  source: 8 Perrault
  character: 14 Fairy Godmother, Handsome Prince 15 Ugly Stepsisters 16 Wicked Stepmother
  coach: 7 pumpkin
  horses: 9 white mice
  footman: 4 frog
  loses: 12 glass slipper

cinema 5 films 6 flicks, movies 7 theater 14 motion pictures, moving pictures

cinnamon 5 spice
  botanical name: 20 Cinnamomum zeylanicum
  variety: 6 cassia, Ceylon 10 zeylanicum
  color: 4 buff 5 tawny 6 auburn 8 nut-brown 11 golden- brown, yellow-brown 12 reddish-brown 13 chestnut- brown 14 yellowish-brown
  origin: 5 China 7 Vietnam 9 Indonesia 10 East Indies

Cinyras
  king of: 6 Cyprus
  son: 5 Melus
  daughter: 6 Myrrha
  introduced worship of: 9 Aphrodite
  crime: 6 incest
  death by: 7 suicide

cipher 3 nil, zip 4 code, zero 5 aught 6 naught, nobody 7 anagram, nothing, nullity 8 acrostic, goose egg 9 nonentity, obscurity 10 cryptogram 11 cryptograph

Circe
  form: 11 enchantress
  father: 6 Helios
  mother: 5 Perse
  brother: 6 Aeetes
  son: 6 Agrius 7 Latinus 9 Telegonus
  home: 5 Aeaea
  turned men into: 4 pigs 5 swine

circle 3 orb, set 4 belt, curl, gird, girt, halo, hoop, knot, loop, reel, ring, turn 5 arena, bound, cabal, crowd, curve, cycle, field, girth, group, hem in, orbit, pivot, range, reach, realm, round, sweep, swing 6 border, bounds, clique, cordon, corona, course, domain, girdle, region, sphere 7 circlet, circuit, company, compass, coterie, enclose, envelop, hedge in, revolve, ringlet, society, theater 8 dominion, encircle, province, sequence, surround 9 bailiwick, encompass, territory, wind about 10 move around, revolution, ring around 11 curve around, progression 12 circumrotate, circumscribe 13 revolve around 14 circumnavigate

Circle 6 gilgal

circlet 4 band, halo, ring 5 tiara 6 diadem, fillet, wreath 7 chaplet, coronet, ringlet

circuit 3 lap, run 4 area, beat, edge, tour, trek, walk 5 jaunt, limit, round, route 6 border, bounds, course, margin, sphere 7 compass, confine, journey 8 circling, frontier, orbiting, pivoting 9 excursion, extremity, perimeter, revolving, territory 10 revolution 13 circumference 14 distance around

circuitous 7 devious, turning, winding 8 circular, indirect, rambling, tortuous, twisting 10 meandering, roundabout, serpentine 12 labyrinthine 14 circumlocutory

circular 4 bill 5 flier, round 6 curved, notice, rotary 7 coiling, curling, leaflet, rocking, rolling, rounded, turning, winding 8 bulletin, gyrating, handbill, pivoting, spinning, twirling 9 revolving, spiraling, swiveling, throwaway 10 circuitous, ring-shaped 12 announcement 13 advertisement

circulate 4 flow 5 issue, strew 6 circle, course, spread, travel 7 give out, go forth, journey, publish, radiate, scatter 8 announce, disperse, go around, put about 9 broadcast, get abroad, make known, move about, publicize 10 distribute, make public, move around, pass around, put forward 11 disseminate, pass through, visit around 13 make the rounds

circulation 4 flow 6 motion 7 flowing 8 circling, rotation 9 diffusion, radiation 10 dispersion 11 propagation 12 distribution, promulgation, transmission 13 dissemination

circulatory system
  part: 4 vein 5 heart 6 artery 9 capillary 15 lymphatic vessel
  carries: 6 plasma 9 platelets 13 red blood cells 15 white blood cells

circumcision
  Hebrew: 4 Bris, Brit 5 Berit, Brith 6 Berith
  performed by: 5 Mohel

circumference 3 rim 4 edge 5 girth 6 border, bounds, fringe, girdle, limits, margin 7 circuit, compass, outline 8 boundary 9 extremity, perimeter, periphery 14 distance around

circumlocution 8 rambling, verbiage 9 garrulity, verbosity, wordiness 10 digression, meandering 14 discursiveness, long-windedness, roundaboutness

circumlocutory 5 wordy 7 diffuse, verbose 8 rambling 9 wandering 10 digressive, discursive, maundering, roundabout

circumnavigate 5 skirt 6 bypass, circle 8 encircle, go around 10 circumvent

circumnavigation 8 circling, skirting 9 bypassing 11 going around 12 encirclement 13 circumvention

circumscribe 3 fix 4 curb 5 check, hem in, limit 6 bridle, circle, corset, define, impede 7 confine, enclose, outline 8 encircle, restrain, restrict, surround 9 constrain, delineate, encompass, proscribe

circumscribed 6 narrow 7 limited 10 restricted

circumscription 5 limit 7 outline 9 hemming in, restraint 10 constraint 11 confinement 12 encirclement 14 restrictedness

circumspect 4 sage, wary 5 alert 7 careful, guarded, prudent 8 cautious, discreet, vigilant, watchful 9 judicious, sagacious, wide-awake 10 deliberate, discerning, particular, thoughtful **13** contemplative, perspicacious **14** discriminating

circumspection 4 care, heed **7** caution **8** prudence **10** discretion, precaution, steadiness **11** carefulness, heedfulness, mindfulness **12** deliberation

circumstance 4 fact, item **5** event, point, thing **6** detail, factor, matter, ritual **7** element **8** ceremony, incident, splendor **9** condition, formality, happening, pageantry **10** brilliance, occurrence, particular, phenomenon **11** vicissitude **12** happenstance, magnificence, resplendence **14** state of affairs

circumstances 5 state **9** situation **11** environment **16** living conditions

circumstantial 4 full **6** minute **7** deduced, hearsay, implied, precise **8** accurate, complete, detailed, explicit, inferred, presumed, thorough **9** secondary **10** blow-by- blow, evidential, exhaustive, extraneous, incidental, particular, unabridged **11** conjectural, inferential, provisional **12** nonessential

circumvent 4 miss, shun **5** avoid, dodge, elude, evade, skirt **6** bypass, circle, escape, outwit, thwart **8** go around **9** frustrate **12** keep away from **14** circumnavigate

circumvention 7 dodging, ducking, eluding, evasion **9** avoidance, bypassing **11** frustration **12** sidestepping

circus 4 ring **5** arena **6** big top, circle, uproar **8** carnival, coliseum **9** spectacle **10** exhibition, hippodrome **11** ampitheater **12** intersection
  act: 5 clown, flyer **7** acrobat, juggler, trapeze **8** side show **9** lion tamer, menagerie **10** equestrian **13** flying trapeze
  famous: 6 Astley **12** Cirque d'Hiver **15** Barnum and Bailey **16** Ringling Brothers

Cist
  form: 9 sacred box
  used for: 8 utensils

cistern 3 box, tub, vat **4** tank, well **6** cavity, vessel **8** aqueduct **9** reservoir

citadel 4 fort **7** bastion, rampart **8** fortress **10** stronghold **13** fortification

citation 4 cite **5** award, honor, kudos, medal, quote **7** example, excerpt, extract, passage **8** instance **9** quotation **12** commendation, illustration **14** official praise

cite 4 name, note **5** honor, quote **6** praise **7** advance, commend, mention, present, refer to, specify **8** allude to, document, indicate **9** enumerate, exemplify **12** bring forward **13** give as example

Cithaeronian *see* **4** Zeus

citified 5 urban **6** urbane **12** cosmopolitan **13** sophisticated

citizen 6 native **7** denizen, subject **8** national, resident **10** inhabitant
  French: 7 citoyen

Citizen Kane
  director: 11 Orson Welles
  script: 11 Orson Welles **17** Herman J Mankiewicz
  cast: 11 Orson Welles **12** Joseph Cotten **13** Everett Sloane **14** Agnes Moorehead
  score: 15 Bernard Herrmann
  sled: 7 Rosebud

citizenry 4 folk **6** people, public **7** society **8** populace **9** community **10** population

citoyen 7 citizen

citrine
  species: 6 quartz
  color: 6 yellow

citron 3 rue **4** lime, rind **5** lemon **6** cedrat, orange, yellow **8** Rutaceae **9** tangerine **10** watermelon **12** citrus medica
  Jewish: 6 ethrog

city 4 burg, town **7** big town **8** denizens, township **9** residents **10** metropolis **11** inhabitants, megalopolis, townspeople **12** municipality **16** incorporated town, metropolitan area

city hall
  French: 12 hotel de ville

City Life
  author: 15 Donald Barthelme

City Lights
  director: 14 Charles Chaplin
  cast: 8 Hank Mann **10** Harry Myers **14** Charlie Chaplin **16** Virginia Cherrill

City of God, The (De Civitate Dei)
  author: 11 St Augustine

City of the Lion *see* **9** Singapore

city slicker 4 dude **8** urbanite **11** cosmopolite **12** sophisticate

City Without Walls and Other Poems
  author: 7 W H Auden

Ciudad Trujillo
  capital of: 17 Dominican Republic

Civ 17 second Hebrew month

civic 5 local **6** public **8** citizen's, communal **9** community

civil 3 lay **4** city **5** civic, state **6** genial, polite, public **7** affable, amiable, citizen, cordial, secular **8** citizen's, communal, decorous, gracious, mannerly, obliging **9** civilized, community, courteous, municipal **10** individual, neighborly, respectful **11** gentlemanly, nonmilitary **12** conciliatory, well-mannered

Civil Disobedience
  author: 17 Henry David Thoreau

civilian 9 lay person **14** private citizen **17** nonmilitary person **18** nonuniformed person

civility 4 tact **7** manners, respect **8**

courtesy **10** affability, amiability, cordiality, good temper, politeness **11** good manners **12** graciousness, pleasantness **13** agreeableness, courteousness **14** respectfulness

civilization 7 culture, society **10** refinement **11** cultivation, worldliness **13** enlightenment **14** sophistication

civilize 5 edify, teach, train **6** inform, polish, refine **7** culture, develop, educate, elevate **8** humanize, instruct **9** cultivate, enlighten **11** acculturate **12** sophisticate

civil law
  Latin: 9 jus civile

Civil War
  admirals: 6 DuPont, Semmes
  battles: 6 Shiloh **7** Bull Run **8** Antietam **9** Nashville, Vicksburg **10** Cold Harbor, Gettysburg **11** Chattanooga, Chickamauga **14** Fredericksburg
  coin: 10 copperhead
  Confederate commanders: 3 Lee **4** Hill, Hood **5** Bragg, Early, Ewell, Mosby, Smith **6** Stuart, Toombs **7** Buckner, Hampton, Jackson **10** Beauregard **12** Breckinridge
  Union commanders: 5 Banks, Buell, Grant, Logan **6** Butler, Custer, Hooker, Porter **7** Sherman, Hancock

clad 6 garbed **7** arrayed, attired, clothed, dressed **9** outfitted

Claggart
  character in: 9 Billy Budd
  author: 8 Melville

claim 3 ask **4** avow, call, plea, take **5** exact, right, title **6** access, affirm, allege, assert, avowal, charge, demand, pick up **7** call for, collect, command, declare, profess, request **8** exaction, insist on, maintain, proclaim **9** assertion, ownership, seek as due, statement **10** allegation, lay claim to, pretension, profession **11** affirmation, declaration, postulation, requirement **12** proclamation, protestation

claimant 6 suitor **9** applicant, pretender **10** petitioner

clairvoyant 7 psychic **8** divining, oracular **9** prescient, prophetic **10** telepathic **11** foreknowing, telekinetic **12** extrasensory, precognitive, psychometric **13** psychokinetic, second-sighted

clam 4 vise **5** clamp, clasp **6** dollar, marine **7** bivalve, mollusk
  kind: 5 pismo, razor **6** butter, quahog **7** geoduck, steamer **10** little neck **11** cherrystone
  part: 4 foot, palp **5** gills, shell, valve **6** mantle, siphon **7** sinuses **8** ligament
  habitat: 3 mud **4** sand
  relative: 6 mussel, oyster

clamber up 5 climb, mount, scale **10** scramble up, struggle up

clamminess 4 damp **7** wetness **8**

dampness, dankness **10** stickiness, sweatiness

clammy 3 wet **4** damp **5** pasty, slimy **6** sticky, sweaty **10** perspiring **11** cold and damp

clamor 3 cry, din **4** call, howl, yell **5** blast, chaos, noise, shout, storm **6** bedlam, bellow, cry out, hubbub, jangle, outcry, racket, rumpus, tumult, uproar **7** bluster, call out, clangor, thunder **8** brouhaha, shouting **9** commotion, hue and cry **10** hullabaloo, vociferate, wild chorus

clamorous 4 loud **5** noisy **10** boisterous, uproarious

clamp 4 clip, grip, vise **5** brace, clasp **6** clench, clinch, fasten, secure **7** bracket **8** fastener

clan 4 gang, knot, line, ring **5** breed, cabal, crowd, group, guild, house, party, stock **6** circle, league, strain **7** company, dynasty, lineage, society **8** alliance, pedigree **10** fraternity **11** affiliation, association, brotherhood, family group, lineal group **12** tribal family

clandestine 6 covert, hidden, masked, secret, veiled **7** cloaked, furtive, private **8** secluded, sneaking, stealthy **9** concealed, secretive, underhand **10** undercover, unrevealed **11** underground, underhanded, undisclosed **12** confidential **13** surreptitious

clang 3 din **4** bong, gong, peal, toll **5** chime, clank, clash, knell **6** jangle **7** clangor, resound, ringing, tolling **8** clashing **10** resounding, ring loudly

clangor 3 din **5** noise **6** clamor, hubbub, jangle, racket, uproar

clank 5 chink, clang, clash, clink **6** jangle, rattle **7** clangor, clatter **8** clashing

clannish 4 cold **5** aloof **6** narrow **7** distant, insular, cliquish, snobbish **9** exclusive, parochial, sectarian **10** provincial, restricted, unfriendly **11** unreceptive

Clan of the Cave Bear, The
author: **9** Jean M Auel

clap 3 bat, hit, rap, tap **4** bang, bump, cast, cuff, dash, hurl, peal, push, roar, rush, slam, slap, swat, toss **5** burst, clack, crack, drive, fling, force, pitch, shove, smack, smite, thump, whack **6** buffet, plunge, propel, strike, thrust, thwack, wallop **7** applaud, clatter **9** explosion **11** set suddenly

claptrap 3 rot **4** bosh, bull, bunk, sham, **5** bilge, hokum, hooey, stuff, trash, tripe **6** bunkum, drivel, hot air, humbug, tinsel **7** baloney, blarney, fustian, hogwash, spinach, twaddle **8** buncombe, nonsense, quackery, tommyrot **9** gaudiness, poppycock, staginess **10** applesauce, flapdoodle, tawdriness, tomfoolery **11** foolishness **15** pretentiousness **16** stuff and nonsense

claque 10 sycophants **15** cheering section

Clare, Ada
character in: **10** Bleak House
author: **7** Dickens

claret 3 red **5** blood **7** carmine, deep red, red wine **8** blood-red, Bordeaux, cardinal **11** purplish red, wine-colored

clarification 10 commentary **11** elucidation, explanation, explication **14** further comment
French: **15** eclaircissement

clarify 5 clear, purge, solve **6** purify, refine **7** clear up, explain, lay open, resolve **9** elucidate, explicate, make clear, make plain **10** illuminate **11** disentangle, shed light on **12** bring to light **18** make understandable

clarinet 4 wind **8** woodwind **11** transposing **13** licorice stick
mouthpiece: **4** reed
ancestor: **9** chalumeau
musician: **12** Benny Goodman

clarion 5 acute, clear, sharp **6** shrill **7** blaring, ringing **8** distinct, piercing, resonant, sonorous, stirring **10** commanding, compelling, imperative **11** high-pitched

Clarissa Harlowe
author: **16** Samuel Richardson
character: **8** Miss Howe **11** John Belford **14** Robert Lovelace **20** Colonel William Morden

clarity 6 purity **8** lucidity, radiance **9** clearness, exactness, plainness, precision **10** brightness, brilliance, directness, effulgence, glassiness, luminosity, simplicity **12** explicitness, translucence, transparency **15** intelligibility **17** comprehensibility

Clark, Mark W
served in: **3** WWI **4** WWII **9** Korean War
rank: **22** allied commander in Italy **24** commander of forces in Korea **30** chief of staff of army ground forces **42** commander of Allied occupation forces in Austria
president of: **7** Citadel

Clark, Walter Van Tilburg
author of: **16** The Ox-Bow Incident

Clarke, Arthur C
author of: **10** (2010) Odyssey Two **13** (2001) A Space Odyssey, Childhood's End **18** Rendezvous with Rama

clash 4 bang, boil, feud, fray, tiff **5** argue, clang, clank, crash, fight, set-to **6** battle, combat, fracas, jangle, rattle, tussle **7** clangor, clatter, contend, contest, discord, dispute, grapple, jarring, quarrel, wrangle **8** conflict, crashing, friction, skirmish, squabble, struggle **9** altercate, encounter, lock horns **10** antagonism, difference, disharmony, dissidence, opposition **11** cross

swords **12** disagreement **13** exchange blows

clash of arms 5 fight **6** battle, combat **8** conflict, skirmish, struggle **9** encounter **10** engagement

clash with 9 fight with **12** do battle with **14** contend against **15** cross swords with

clasp 3 hug **4** bolt, clip, grip, hasp, hold, hook, link, lock, snap **5** catch, clamp, grasp, latch, press **6** buckle, clinch, clutch, couple, fasten, secure **7** coupler, embrace, grapple, squeeze **8** fastener **9** fastening

clasp in the arms 3 hug **4** hold **6** enfold **7** embrace

class 3 set **4** form, kind, rank, rate, size, sort, type **5** brand, breed, caste, genre, genus, grade, group, index, label, order, state **6** circle, clique, codify, course, lesson, number, sphere, status **7** arrange, catalog, section, session, species, station, variety **8** category, classify, division, pedigree, position **9** condition, designate **10** categorize, pigeonhole, social rank **11** set of pupils **13** social stratum **14** classification **15** departmentalize, graduating group

classic, classical 4 epic **5** model **6** heroic **7** ageless, paragon **8** absolute, accepted, enduring, masterly **9** archetype, excellent, exemplary, first-rate, prototype **10** archetypal, consummate, definitive, first-class, Greco-Roman, prototypal **11** masterpiece, outstanding, traditional **12** ancient Greek, ancient Roman, standard work **13** authoritative, distinguished **14** distinguishing **17** first-class example

classification 4 kind, rank, sort, type **5** class, genus, group, order **6** family, series **7** section, species **8** category, classing, division, grouping, labeling, ordering, taxonomy **9** arranging, gradation **10** assortment, organizing **11** arrangement, designation, disposition **12** categorizing, codification, organization **14** categorization **15** systematization

classified 5 secret **6** sorted **7** classed **8** assorted **10** restricted **11** categorized **12** confidential

classify 3 tag **4** list, rank, rate, size, sort, type **5** brand, class, grade, group, index, label, order, range **6** assort, codify, number, ticket **7** arrange, catalog **8** organize **9** segregate **10** categorize, pigeonhole **11** distinguish

classy 4 chic, posh, tony **5** nifty, nobby, ritzy, smart, swank, swell **6** dressy, modish, spiffy, swanky **7** elegant, genteel, opulent, refined, stylish **8** cultured, polished, tasteful **9** highclass **10** ultrasmart **11** fashionable, in good taste **12** aristocratic, wellmannered

clatter 4 bang **5** clack, clang, clank, clash, clink, clump, crash **6** clamor, jangle, racket, rattle **7** chatter **8** crashing, rattling

clattering 3 din **6** clamor, hubbub, racket, uproar **7** clangor

Claude
real name: **12** Claude Gellee
also called: **14** Claude Lorraine
born: **6** France **9** Champagne
artwork: **7** The Mill **16** Hagar and the Angel **18** Ascanius and the Stag, The Enchanted Castle **27** The Rest on the Flight into Egypt **31** The Embarkation of the Queen of Sheba

Claudel, Paul
author of: **6** L'Otage **10** The Hostage **13** Partage de Midi **15** The Satin Slipper **20** Tidings Brought to Mary

Claudia Quinta
freed: **12** grounded ship
feat proved: **8** chastity

Claudio
character in: **17** Measure for Measure **19** Much Ado About Nothing
author: **11** Shakespeare

Claudius
character in: **6** Hamlet
author: **11** Shakespeare

Claudius the God
author: **12** Robert Graves
sequel to: **9** I Claudius

clause 4 term **7** article, proviso **8** covenant **9** condition, provision **11** proposition, stipulation **13** specification **14** simple sentence

claustrophobia
fear of: **12** closed spaces **14** confined spaces

Clavell, James
author of: **6** Shogun, Tai-Pan **7** King Rat **9** Whirlwind **10** Noble House

clavicle
bone of: **10** collarbone

claw 3 paw **4** foot, grip, maul, tear **5** seize, slash, talon **6** clutch, pincer, scrape **7** scratch **8** lacerate **10** animal nail

Clay, Cassius
former name of: **11** Muhammad Ali

Clayburgh, Jill
born: **9** New York NY
roles: **9** Semi-Tough **12** Starting Over **16** An Unmarried Woman, North Dallas Forty **21** I'm Dancing as Fast as I Can

Clayhanger Trilogy, The
author: **13** Arnold Bennett

clean 3 mop **4** dust, fine, neat, pure, tidy, trim, wash **5** bathe, clear, fresh, moral, order, scour, scrub, sweep **6** bathed, chaste, decent, neaten, tidy up, vacuum, washed **7** cleaned, cleanse, healthy, launder, orderly, perfect, scoured, shampoo, upright **8** cleansed, decorous, flawless, innocent,

sanitary, scrubbed, spotless, unsoiled, virtuous, well-made **9** exemplary, faultless, honorable, laundered, stainless, undefiled, unspotted, unstained, unsullied, untainted, wholesome **10** immaculate, uninfected, unpolluted **11** unblemished **13** unadulterated **14** uncontaminated

cleaner, cleanser 4 soap **5** borax **6** washer **7** ammonia, janitor **8** purifier, scrubber **9** detergent **14** scouring powder

cleaning 7 bathing, washing **8** scouring **9** cleansing, going-over, scrubbing, tidying up **10** laundering

cleanse 3 rid **4** free, wash **5** bathe, clean, clear, erase, flush, scour, scrub **7** absolve, deliver, expunge, launder, release, shampoo **8** sweep out, unburden **9** expurgate

clean-shaven 6 smooth **9** unbearded **11** unwhiskered **12** smooth-shaven

cleansing 7 bathing, healing, purging, washing **8** flushing, scouring **9** expunging, purifying, scrubbing **10** ablution

cleanup 4 gain **6** profit **8** windfall
baseball: **12** fourth batter

clear 3 rid **4** fair, free, keen, make, open **5** alert, clean, empty, gauzy, lucid, plain, sharp, sunny **6** acquit, bright, patent, remove, serene, unstop, wholly **7** absolve, audible, audibly, certain, clearly, evident, express, fly over, glowing, halcyon, hop over, lighten, obvious, plainly, radiant, unblock **8** apparent, brighten, clear-cut, dazzling, definite, distinct, entirely, explicit, gleaming, leap over, luminous, manifest, pass over, pellucid, positive, skip over, unhidden **9** all the way, bound over, brilliant, cloudless, exculpate, exonerate, sparkling, unblocked, unclouded, unimpeded, unmuddled, vindicate, wide-awake **10** articulate, become fair, completely, diaphanous, discerning, distinctly, glistening, pronounced, unconfused, undeniable, unobscured **11** crystalline, inescapable, self-evident, translucent, transparent, unambiguous, unconcealed, undisguised, unequivocal, unqualified **12** articulately, intelligible, recognizable, unencumbered, unmistakable, unobstructed **14** comprehensible **15** distinguishable, straightforward

clearance 4 room, sale **6** margin, permit **7** removal **8** clearing **10** offsetting **11** elimination **13** authorization, certification

clear as day 5 plain **7** obvious **8** apparent, clear-cut, manifest **11** self-evident

clear-cut 4 open **5** exact, lucid, plain **6** patent **7** evident, express, obvious, precise **8** definite, detailed, distinct,

explicit, manifest **10** clear as day, unconfused, undeniable **11** appreciable, conspicuous, self-evident, substantial, unambiguous, undisguised, unequivocal, well-defined **12** crystal-clear, unmistakable **14** comprehensible, understandable **15** straightforward

clearheaded 5 acute, alert, awake, aware, sharp **6** astute **8** rational, sensible **9** on the ball, practical, realistic, wide-awake **10** discerning, insightful, on one's toes, on the stick, perceptive **13** perspicacious

clearheadedness 7 insight **8** sagacity **9** alertness, sharpness **10** perception **11** discernment **12** perspicacity

clearing 5 glade

clearly 6 surely **7** plainly **8** markedly, palpably, patently **9** assuredly, certainly, decidedly, evidently, obviously **10** distinctly, manifestly, noticeably, observably, undeniably **11** beyond doubt, indubitably, perceptibly, undoubtedly **12** recognizably, unmistakably **13** unequivocally **14** beyond question, unquestionably

clearly expressed 8 coherent **10** articulate **11** unambiguous **12** intelligible

clearness 7 clarity **10** brightness, brilliance **12** explicitness **15** unmistakability

clear-sighted 4 sage, wise **5** acute, sharp **6** astute, shrewd **8** piercing **9** judicious, sagacious, sensitive **10** discerning, perceptive **11** intelligent, keen-sighted, penetrating **12** sharpsighted **13** perspicacious

clear up 6 settle **7** clarify, unsnarl **8** untangle **11** disentangle **12** uncomplicate **13** straighten out

Cleary, Beverly
author of: **6** Ramona **7** Fifteen **12** Henry Huggins **13** Jean and Johnny **15** Beezus and Ramona **16** Sister of the Bride

cleat 5 block, chock, spike, wedge **6** batten **7** bollard

cleavage 3 gap **4** rent, rift, slit **5** cleft, crack, notch, split **6** furrow, trench, trough **7** crevice, fissure, opening **8** crevasse

cleave 3 cut, hew **4** chop, fuse, hack, hold, open, part, plow, rend, rive, slit, tear **5** cling, crack, halve, sever, slash, slice, split, stick, unite **6** adhere, be true, bisect, cut off, detach, divide, furrow, sunder, uphold **7** abide by, chop off, disjoin, lay open, stand by **8** be joined, break off, hold fast, separate **9** disengage, dismember

cleaver 3 axe **4** tool **5** knife ridge

cleft 3 gap **4** rent, rift, slit **5** break, crack, notch, split **6** breach, cloven, cranny, divide, forked, furrow, trench, trough **7** crevice, divided, fissure, notched, opening, slotted **8** aperture, bisected, branched, cleavage, crevasse, division **10** separation **11** indentation

clemency 5 mercy **7** charity **8** humanity, kindness, leniency, mildness, softness, sympathy **9** tolerance **10** compassion, indulgence, moderation, temperance **11** benevolence, forbearance, magnanimity **12** mercifulness, pleasantness **13** forgivingness

clement 4 kind, mild, warm **5** balmy **6** benign, gentle, humane **7** lenient **8** merciful, tolerant **9** not severe, not strict **10** benevolent **13** compassionate

clench 3 set **4** grip **5** clasp, tense **6** clinch, clutch **7** stiffen, tighten **8** fasten on, hold fast **11** grasp firmly, strain tight **12** close tightly

Clennam, Arthur
character in: 12 Little Dorrit
author: 7 Dickens

Cleopatra
queen of: 5 Egypt
father: 7 Ptolemy
brother/husband: 7 Ptolemy
lover: 10 Mark Antony **12** Julius Caesar
son: 9 Caesarion **15** Alexander Helios **19** Ptolemy Philadelphos
daughter: 15 Cleopatra Selene
death by: 3 asp **7** suicide

Cleopatra
director:
1934 version: 13 Cecil B DeMille
1963 version: 17 Joseph L Mankiewicz
cast:
1934 version: 13 Henry Wilcoxon, Warren William **16** Claudette Colbert
1963 version: 11 Rex Harrison **13** Richard Burton, Roddy McDowall **15** Elizabeth Taylor

clergy 6 rabbis **7** clerics, pastors, priests **8** ministry, prelates, the cloth **9** churchmen, clergymen, clericals, ministers, pastorate, preachers, rabbinate, the church, the pulpit **10** priesthood **14** the first estate

clergyman 5 padre, rabbi **6** cleric, father, parson, pastor, priest **7** prelate **8** chaplain, minister, preacher, reverend, sky pilot **9** churchman **13** man of the cloth

cleric 6 parson, pastor **8** chaplain, preacher **9** churchman, clergyman **13** man of the cloth

clerical 6 cleric, filing, office, typing **7** clerkly **8** churchly, of clerks, pastoral, priestly **10** accounting, rabbinical **11** bookkeeping, ministerial **13** recordkeeping **14** ecclesiastical

clerical worker 5 clerk **6** typist **9** file clerk **10** bookkeeper, keypuncher **12** office worker **13** data processor

clerk 6 typist **8** salesman **9** file clerk **10** bookkeeper, salesclerk, sales-

woman **11** salesperson **12** office worker

Cleta
member of: 6 Graces
worshipped at: 6 Sparta

Cleveland
baseball team: 7 Indians
basketball team: 7 Rockers **9** Cavaliers
football team: 6 Browns

Cleveland, Grover
name at birth: 22 Stephen Grover Cleveland
nickname: 5 Grove
presidential rank: 12 twenty-fourth, twenty-second
party: 8 Democrat
state represented: 2 NY
defeated: 4 (Simon) Wing **6** (Benjamin Franklin) Butler, (James Baird) Weaver, (James Gillespie) Blaine, (John Pierce) St John **7** (John) Bidwell **8** (Belva Ann Bennett) Lockwood, (Benjamin) Harrison
vice president: 9 (Adlai Ewing) Stevenson, (Thomas Andrews) Hendricks
cabinet:
state: 5 (Richard) Olney **6** (Thomas Francis) Bayard **7** (Walter Quinton) Gresham
treasury: 7 (Daniel) Manning **8** (John Griffin) Carlisle **9** (Charles Stebbins) Fairchild
war: 6 (David Scott) Lamont **8** (William Crowninshield) Endicott
attorney general: 5 (Richard) Olney **6** (Judson) Harmon **7** (Augustus Hill) Garland
interior: 5 (Hoke) Smith, (Lucius Quintus Cincinnatus) Lamar, (William Freeman) Vilas **7** (David Rowland) Francis
born: 2 NJ **8** Caldwell
died/buried: 2 NJ **9** Princeton
education:
high school: 16 Liberal Institute
religion: 12 Presbyterian
interests: 7 fishing **8** shooting **13** gun collecting
political career:
mayor of: 7 Buffalo
governor of: 7 New York
civilian career: 6 lawyer
notable events of lifetime/term: 5 Panic (of 1893) **10** gold crisis (of 1895)
Act: 6 Tariff **14** Dawes Severalty **18** Interstate Commerce
strike: 7 Pullman
father: 13 Richard Falley
mother: 4 Anne (Neal)
siblings: 7 Ann Neal **9** Mary Allen **11** Susan Sophia, William Neal **12** Richard Cecil **13** Rose Elizabeth **14** Lewis Frederick **20** Margaret Louise Falley
wife: 7 Frances (Folsom)

children: 4 Ruth **6** Esther, Marion **13** Francis Grover, Richard Folsom

clever 4 able, cute, deft, keen **5** acute, quick, sharp, smart, witty **6** adroit, artful, astute, bright, crafty, expert, shrewd **8** creative, humorous, original **9** ingenious, inventive **11** imaginative, intelligent, quick-witted, resourceful

cleverly 6 deftly **7** sharply, smartly, wittily **8** adroitly, artfully, craftily, expertly **10** creatively, humorously **11** ingeniously, inventively **13** imaginatively, intelligently

cleverness 3 wit **6** acumen **8** ableness, deftness, keenness **9** expertise, ingenuity, quickness, sharpness, smartness **10** adroitness, artfulness, astuteness, brightness, craftiness **12** intelligence, skillfulness **13** inventiveness **15** imaginativeness, quick-wittedness

clew see **4** clue

Clew
thread in: 9 Labyrinth
showed way to: 7 Theseus
given by: 7 Ariadne

cliche 3 saw **6** old saw **7** bromide **8** banality, old story **9** platitude **10** stereotype **11** trite phrase

cliche-ridden 5 corny, stale, tired, trite, vapid **6** jejune **8** bromidic **9** hackneyed **10** unoriginal **13** platitudinous, unimaginative

click 3 tap **4** clap, snap **5** clack, clink, crack **6** rattle **7** crackle

client 5 buyer **6** patron **7** advisee, shopper **8** customer **9** purchaser **17** person represented

cliff 3 tor **4** crag **5** bluff, ledge **8** palisade **9** precipice **10** promontory

Cliff Dwellers see **6** Pueblo

Clift, Montgomery
real name: 21 Edward Montgomery Clift
nickname: 5 Monty
born: 7 Omaha NE
roles: 9 The Search **10** The Heiress, The Misfits **14** A Place in the Sun **18** From Here to Eternity, Suddenly Last Summer

climactic 7 crucial **8** critical, dramatic **11** sensational, suspenseful

climate 3 air **4** mood, tone **5** pulse **6** spirit, temper **7** quality, weather **8** ambience, attitude **9** character, condition **10** atmosphere **11** disposition, frame of mind, weather zone **12** usual weather **13** weather region **14** general feeling, weather pattern

climax 4 acme, apex, peak **5** crown **6** crisis, height, summit **8** best part, pinnacle **9** high point **10** denouement **11** culmination **12** highest point, turning point **13** critical point, crowning point, decisive point, supreme moment **18** moment of revelation

climb 4 go up, rise **5** mount, scale **6**

ascend, ascent, come up **8** climbing **9** clamber up **10** scramble up

climb down 6 go down **7** descend **8** back down, come down

clinch 3 cap, fix, win **4** bind, bolt, grip, nail **5** cinch, clamp, clasp, close, crown, grasp, screw **6** assure, clutch, couple, decide, fasten, obtain, secure, settle, verify, wind up **7** confirm, grapple **8** complete, conclude, make fast, make sure **9** culminate, establish, finish off **10** grab hold of, hold firmly **12** seize and hold **13** ensure victory

cling 3 hug **4** fuse, grip, hold **5** clasp, grasp, stick **6** adhere, be true, cleave, clutch **7** stand by **8** hang on to, hold fast, hold on to, maintain **9** stay close **10** be constant, be faithful, grab hold of

clinging 6 sticky **7** holding **8** adherent, adhering, adhesive, clasping, cleaving, grasping, gripping, sticking **9** hanging on, holding on **11** holding fast **12** grabbing hold

clinic 9 infirmary **10** polyclinic **13** medical center **15** outpatients' ward

clink 4 ting **5** clack, clank, click **6** jangle, jingle, rattle, tinkle **11** ring sharply

clinkers 4 duds, slag **5** dross, flops **6** cinder, scoria **8** failures

Clinton, William Jefferson
   original last name: 6 Blythe
   nickname: 4 Bill
   presidential rank: 11 forty-second
   party: 10 Democratic
   state represented: 2 AR **8** Arkansas
   defeated: 4 (George) Bush, (Bob) Dole
   vice president: 4 (Albert) Gore
   cabinet:
      state: 11 (Warren) Christopher
      treasury: 7 (Lloyd) Bentsen
      attorney general: 4 (Janet) Reno
      interior: 7 (Bruce) Babbitt
      labor: 5 (Robert) Reich
      HUD: 8 (Henry) Cisneros
   born: 2 AR **4** Hope
   education: 6 Oxford **7** Yale Law **10** Georgetown
      honor: 13 Rhodes Scholar
   political career:
      governor of: 7 Arkansas
      attorney general of: 7 Arkansas
   notable events of lifetime/term: 4 Waco **5** NAFTA **10** Whitewater **13** Anticrime Bill, Rhodes Scholar **15** Branch Davidians **17** Health Security Act
      Supreme Court appointments: 13 Stephen Breyer **17** Ruth Bader Ginsburg
   father: 13 William Blythe
   mother: 12 Virginia Cassidy Blythe
   stepfather: 12 Roger Clinton
   sibling: 12 Roger Clinton

   wife: 13 Hillary Rodham
   children: 7 Chelsea

Clio
   muse of: 7 history

clip 3 bob, cut, fix **4** crop, grip, hook, snip, trim **5** clamp, clasp, shear **6** attach, buckle, clinch, couple, cut off, cut out, fasten, paring, secure, staple **7** cutting, shorten **8** clipping, cropping, cut short, fastener, shearing, snipping

clipper 4 boat, ship **6** cutter, shears **8** aircraft, airplane, sailboat, scissors **9** racehorse

clipping 7 cutting, pruning, snippet **8** trimming

clique 3 set **4** clan, gang **5** crowd, group **6** circle **7** coterie, faction

cliquish 4 cold **5** aloof **7** distant **8** clannish, snobbish **9** exclusive **10** unfriendly **11** unreceptive

cloak 4 cape, hide, mask, robe, veil, wrap **5** cover, tunic **6** mantle, screen, shield, shroud **7** conceal, curtain, pelisse, secrete **8** burnoose, disguise **10** camouflage **11** concealment

cloaked 7 covered, muffled, wrapped **9** disguised

cloaking 7 masking, veiling **8** covering **9** obscuring **10** disguising

cloakroom 8 anteroom, coatroom

clobber 3 hit **4** beat, belt, drub, lick, maul, rout, slug, sock, trim, whip **5** clout, pound, punch, smash, smear, whack **6** batter, beat up, strike, subdue, thrash, wallop **7** conquer, shellac, trounce **8** beat up on, lambaste

clock 5 watch **8** horologe **9** timepiece **11** chronometer

Clockwork Orange, A
   author: 14 Anthony Burgess
   director: 14 Stanley Kubrick
   cast: 12 Patrick Magee **13** Adrienne Corri **15** Malcolm McDowell
   protagonist: 4 Alex

clod 3 oaf, wad **4** boor, dolt, dope, glob, hunk, lout, lump, rube **5** chunk, clown, clump, dummy, dunce, moron, yokel **7** bumpkin, fathead **8** imbecile, numskull **9** blockhead, ignoramus, simpleton

clodhopper 3 oaf **4** boot, clod, hick, lout, rube, slob **5** booby, clown, yokel **6** galoot, lubber, lummox, rustic **7** bumpkin, hayseed, peasant, plowboy, redneck **8** clodpole, lunkhead **9** heavy shoe, hillbilly **10** provincial

clog 4 stop **5** block, check, choke, close, dam up **6** stop up **7** barrier, congest **8** blockage, obstacle, obstruct, stoppage **9** restraint **10** impediment **11** obstruction

clogged 6 choked, halted, jammed **7** clotted, impeded **8** choked up, filled up, hampered, hindered, restrained **10** encumbered, obstructed, overloaded

cloister 4 stoa, walk **5** abbey, aisle **6** arcade, closet, coop up, friary, hole up, immure, shut up, wall up **7** conceal, confine, convent, embower, gallery, nunnery, passage, portico, seclude, walkway **8** shut away **9** colonnade, courtyard, monastery, promenade, sequester **10** ambulatory, passageway

cloistered 5 alone, aloof, apart **6** hidden **7** immured, recluse **8** closeted, confined, detached, isolated, secluded, secreted, separate, solitary **9** concealed, insulated, sheltered, withdrawn **11** dissociated, sequestered

clone 4 copy **5** robot **6** double **7** android, replica **9** automaton, duplicate, replicate **10** carbon copy **12** doppelganger **13** identical copy

close 3 end, hot, pen **4** akin, clog, fast, fill, firm, fuse, halt, join, keen, link, near, neat, nigh, plug, shut, stop, trim, warm **5** alert, block, cease, dense, fixed, humid, muggy, pen in, sharp, short, solid, stuff, tight, unite **6** allied, at hand, clog up, coop up, couple, ending, fill in, fill up, finale, finish, hard by, intent, jammed, loving, narrow, nearby, next to, plug up, recess, secure, shut in, shut up, smooth, stingy, stop up, stuffy, windup **7** adjourn, careful, close up, closing, compact, confine, connect, cramped, crowded, devoted, dismiss, enclose, intense, miserly, pinched, seal off, shut off, similar, stuffed, suspend, teeming **8** attached, blockade, break off, conclude, confined, familiar, friendly, grudging, imminent, intimate, leave off, obstruct, populous, shut down, squeezed, stagnant, stifling, stinting, swarming, thorough, vigilant, watchful **9** attentive, congested, impending, niggardly, penurious, scrimping, terminate **10** almost like, completion, compressed, conclusion, nearly even, nip-and-tuck, resembling, restricted, sweltering, ungenerous **11** almost alike, approaching, approximate, close-fisted, discontinue, forthcoming, impermeable, in proximity, inseparable, nearly equal, neighboring, suffocating, termination, tight-fisted, well-matched **12** bring to an end, impenetrable, parsimonious, unventilated **13** bring together, near to the skin, penny-pinching, uncomfortable **14** thick as thieves

closed 6 secret **7** private **9** exclusive

closed-minded 5 rigid **7** adamant, uptight **8** obdurate, stubborn **9** hidebound, obstinate, pig-headed, unbending **10** inflexible, unyielding **12** intransigent **14** uncompromising

Close Encounters of the Third Kind
   director: 15 Steven Spielberg

cast: 8 Teri Garr **13** Melinda Dillon **15** Richard Dreyfuss **16** Francois Truffaut

score: 12 John Williams

closefisted 4 mean **5** cheap, close, mingy, tight **6** stingy **7** miserly **8** grudging **9** niggardly, penurious **10** economical, ungenerous **11** close-handed, tightfisted **12** parsimonious **13** penny-pinching

close-fitting 4 snug **5** tight **9** skintight **11** constricted, form-fitting **12** constricting, tight-fitting **15** like a second skin

close friend 3 pal **4** chum, mate **5** buddy, crony **6** cohort **7** best pal **8** alter ego, intimate **9** companion, confidant **10** bosom buddy **17** intimate confidant

close loudly 4 bang, clap, slam

closely 6 keenly **7** alertly, sharply **8** intently **9** carefully, heedfully, intensely **10** diligently, vigilantly, vigorously, watchfully **11** attentively

close-mouthed 3 shy **4** cool **5** terse **7** bashful, distant **8** reserved, reticent, retiring, taciturn **9** diffident, secretive, withdrawn **11** tight-lipped **15** uncommunicative

closeness 8 meanness, nearness **10** stinginess **11** familiarity, miserliness **15** tightfistedness

close of day 3 eve **4** dusk, even **6** sunset **7** evening, sundown **8** eventide, gloaming, twilight **9** nightfall

closet 2 WC **4** eury, safe **5** ambry, cuddy **6** covert, hidden, locker pantry, secret, toilet **7** armoire, cabinet, private **8** coatroom, cupboard, imprison, secluded **9** cloakroom, storeroom, visionary **11** speculative, theoretical, unpractical, water closet

close tightly 3 set **4** seal, slam **5** latch **6** clench, secure **13** press together

close to 4 near **6** almost, around **9** just about **12** on the point of **13** approximately

closure 3 lid, tap **4** bung, cork, plug, stop **5** cover **6** ending, faucet, finish, spigot **7** barring, bolting, closing, cloture, locking, sealing, stopper **8** securing, shutting, stoppage **9** cessation **10** conclusion, stoppering **11** termination **14** discontinuance **15** discontinuation

clot 3 gob **4** lump, mass **7** congeal, thicken **8** embolism, solidify, thrombus **9** coagulate, occlusion **11** coagulation

Cloten
character in: **9** Cymbeline
author: **11** Shakespeare

cloth 5 goods **6** fabric **7** textile **8** dry goods, material **9** yard goods **10** piece goods

clothe 3 don **4** case, coat, deck, garb, robe, veil, wrap **5** array, cloak, cloud,

cover, drape, dress **6** attire, bedeck, encase, enwrap, outfit, rig out, screen, shroud **7** bedizen, costume, deck out, envelop, sheathe, swaddle **8** accouter

clothed 4 clad **5** robed **6** draped **7** cloaked, couched, covered, dressed, mantled, wearing **8** equipped, provided **9** expressed, furnished

clothes 4 duds, garb, rags, togs, wear **5** dress **6** attire, finery **7** apparel, costume, raiment, regalia **8** clothing, ensemble, garments, wardrobe **11** habiliments

clotheshorse 3 fop **4** dude **5** dandy, model **12** Beau Brummell, fashion plate, man of fashion, sharp dresser **14** woman of fashion

clothing see **7** clothes

Clotho
member of: **5** Fates
spinner of: **12** thread of life

cloud 3 dim, mar **4** blur, hide, veil **5** blind, cloak, cover, muddy, shade, sully, upset **6** darken, impair, muddle, screen, shadow, shroud **7** conceal, confuse, curtain, distort, disturb, eclipse, obscure, tarnish **8** overcast **9** discredit, make vague **10** overshadow **11** cast doubt on **14** call to question **19** place under suspicion

cloudburst 6 deluge **8** downpour, rainfall **9** rainstorm

clouded 3 dim **5** dusky, murky **7** blurred, obscure, sullied, tainted, unclear **8** confused, darkened, obscured **10** ill-defined, indistinct

cloudless 4 fair **5** clear, sunny **6** bright **7** halcyon **8** sunshiny **9** unclouded **10** unobscured

Clouds
goddess of: **3** Fri **5** Frigg, Frija **6** Frigga

Clouds, The (Nephelai)
author: **12** Aristophanes
character: **8** Just Plea, Socrates **10** Unjust Plea **11** Strepsiades **12** Pheidippides

cloudy 4 dark, gray, hazy **5** murky, vague **6** dreary, gloomy, leaden, veiled **7** clouded, obscure, sunless, unclear **8** confused, nebulous, overcast **9** confusing, undefined **10** indefinite, mysterious **11** overclouded

Clouet, Jean
born: **8** Flanders
artwork attributed: **13** Guillaume Bude **16** Madame de Canaples, Man with Gold Coins **17** The Count of Brissac, The Dauphin Francis **22** Man with a Book by Petrarch

clout 3 box, hit, jab **4** bash, belt, blow, pull, sock **5** crack, knock, punch, smack, thump, whack **6** wallop **9** influence **10** importance

clove
botanical name: **16** Eugenia aroma-

tica **18** Syzygium aromaticum
origin: **5** Pemba **7** Far East **8** Moluccas, Zanzibar **9** Mauritius **10** Madagascar
use: **3** ham **8** pickling, pomander **16** yellow vegetables

cloven 5 cleft, split **7** divided, notched, slotted **8** bisected

clover 9 Trifolium
varieties: **3** bur, elk, hop, low, pin, red **4** bush, holy, Kura, musk, owl's, tick **5** Alyce, Hubam, lucky, sweet, water, white **6** Alsike, cow hop, indoor, Korean, Ladino, yellow **7** Bukhara, crimson, Italian, mammoth, Mexican, Persian, prairie **8** four-leaf, Japanese, large hop, reversed, small hop, stinking **9** Hungarian **10** strawberry, toothed bur, white Dutch, white sweet **11** yellow sweet **12** silky prairie, subterranean, white prairie **13** European water **16** strawberry-headed

clown 3 wag, wit **4** card, fool, jest, joke, mime, zany **5** comic, cut up, joker **6** jester, madcap **7** buffoon **8** comedian, humorist **9** harlequin, kid around **10** comedienne, fool around **11** funny person, merry-andrew

Clown, The
author: **12** Heinrich Boll

clownishness 6 antics **10** buffoonery, tomfoolery **12** monkeyshines **14** playing the fool

Clowns of God, The
author: **11** Morris L West

cloy 3 gag **4** bore, glut, pall, sate, tire **5** choke, weary **6** benumb, overdo **7** exhaust, satiate, surfeit **8** nauseate, saturate

cloying 5 sweet **6** sugary **9** excessive, satiating **10** saccharine

club 3 bat, hit **4** bash, beat, flog, slug **5** billy, flail, group, guild, lay on, lodge, stick, union **6** batter, buffet, cudgel, league, pommel, pummel, strike **7** society **8** alliance, bludgeon, sorority **9** billyclub, clubhouse, truncheon **10** fraternity, shillelagh, sisterhood **11** affiliation, association, brotherhood, country club

clubhouse 4 club, hall **5** lodge **11** locker rooms **12** meeting house

clue 3 cue, key **4** clew, hint, mark, sign **5** guide, scent, trace **7** glimmer, inkling, pointer **8** evidence **9** indicator, inference **10** indication, intimation, suggestion **11** insinuation

clump 4 bulb, bump, knob, knot, lump, mass, plod, thud **5** batch, bunch, clomp, clunk, copse, group, grove, plunk, shock, stamp, stomp, thump, tramp **6** lumber **7** cluster, thicket **9** aggregate **10** assemblage, collection

clumsiness 9 gawkiness **10** ineptitude **11** awkwardness **12** carelessness, ungainliness **13** gracelessness, maladroitness

clumsy 5 bulky, crude, gawky, inept, rough **6** klutzy **7** awkward, unhandy **8** bungling, careless, ungainly, unwieldy **9** graceless, makeshift, maladroit, unskilled **10** blundering, cumbersome, ungraceful **11** heavy-handed **12** ill-contrived, unmanageable **14** butterfingered **21** like a bull in a china shop

cluster 4 band, bevy, heap, herd, knot, mass, pack, pile **5** amass, batch, block, bunch, clump, crowd, flock, group, sheaf, shock, swarm **6** gather, muster, throng **7** collect, company **8** assemble, converge **9** aggregate **10** accumulate, assemblage, collection, congregate **12** accumulation, congregation **13** agglomeration **14** conglomeration

cluster around 6 gather **7** collect **10** congregate **12** herd together **13** flock together

clutch 3 hug **4** grip, hold **5** clasp, grasp **6** clench **7** cling to, embrace, squeeze **8** hang on to

clutter 4 fill, heap, mess, pile **5** chaos, strew **6** jumble, litter, tangle **7** scatter **8** disarray, disorder **9** confusion **10** hodgepodge

cluttered 5 messy **7** chaotic, crowded, jumbled, muddled **8** confused, littered **9** scattered **10** disordered, disorderly

Clytemnestra
   father: 9 Tyndareus
   mother: 4 Leda
   brother: 6 Castor, Pollux
   sister: 5 Helen **8** Timandra
   cousin: 8 Perilaus
   husband: 9 Agamemnon
   son: 7 Orestes
   daughter: 7 Electra, Erigone **9** Iphigenia **12** Chrysothemis
   lover: 9 Aegisthus
   killed: 9 Agamemnon
   killed by: 7 Orestes

coach 3 bus **5** drill, guide, sedan, stage, teach, train, tutor **6** advise, direct, mentor **7** omnibus, trainer **8** carriage, instruct **9** limousine, preceptor **10** automobile, four-in-hand, motor coach, stagecoach **11** four-wheeler, second class **12** economy class **14** private teacher **16** athletic director

coachman 3 fly **4** jehu, whip **5** pilot **6** driver **10** charioteer

Coactrice 14 poisonous snake

coagulate 3 gel, set **4** clot, jell **6** curdle, harden **7** congeal, jellify, thicken **8** solidify

coagulation 3 gob **4** clot, mass **8** clotting, curdling, thrombus **10** thickening

coal 4 ash, bass, char, coke, coom, culm, dust, fuel, slag, smut, swad **5** ember **6** cannel, cinder **7** lignite, clinker **8** charcoal **10** fossil fuel **11** charred wood

box: 3 hod **7** scuttle
made from: 6 carbon
type: 4 hard, soft **7** lignite **10** anthracite, bituminous
mining method: 4 deep **8** opencast **10** strip auger **11** underground
mine: 5 drift, shaft, slope, strip
size: 3 egg, nut, pea **5** stove

coal-black 3 jet **4** dark, inky **5** black, ebony, raven, sable **9** pitch-dark

coalesce 3 mix **4** ally, form, fuse, join, meld **5** blend, merge, unify, unite **6** cohere **7** combine **9** become one, integrate **10** amalgamate, join forces **11** agglutinate, consolidate **12** band together, come together **14** form an alliance

coalition 5 union **6** fusion, league **7** society **8** alliance **9** syndicate **10** federation **11** affiliation, association, combination, confederacy, partnership **12** amalgamation **13** agglomeration, consolidation **14** conglomeration

Coal Miner's Daughter
   director: 12 Michael Apted
   cast: 9 Levon Helm **11** Sissy Spacek (Loretta Lynn) (Oscar) **13** Tommy Lee Jones **14** Beverly D'Angelo
   Oscar for: 7 actress (Spacek)
   screenplay: 10 Tom Rickman

Coaluitecan
   tribe: 6 Payaya

coarse 4 lewd, rude, vile **5** crass, crude, dirty, gross, harsh, rough **6** common, nubbly, odious, ribald, shaggy, sordid, vulgar **7** boorish, bristly, brutish, ill-bred, loutish, obscene, prickly, uncouth **8** impolite, improper, indecent, scratchy **9** bristling, inelegant, offensive, repulsive, revolting, sandpaper, unrefined **10** disgusting, indecorous, indelicate, lascivious, licentious, scurrilous, unladylike, unpolished **11** foul-mouthed, ill-mannered **12** lacking taste **13** rough-textured, ungentlemanly

coarse-grained 5 crude, harsh, nubby, rough **6** coarse, grainy, shaggy **7** bristly **8** scratchy **9** unrefined **13** rough- textured

coarseness 9 crudeness, grossness, roughness, vulgarity **10** indelicacy, inelegance **11** boorishness **16** lack of refinement

coast 4 skim, slip, waft **5** drift, float, glide, shore, slide, sweep **6** strand **7** seaside **8** glissade, littoral, seaboard, seacoast, seashore **9** shoreline

coaster 3 mat **4** ship, sled, tray **5** wagon **6** cradle, glider, slider **8** toboggan **9** tray stand **13** decanter stand, roller coaster

coat 3 fur **4** hair, hide, pelt, wrap **5** cover, glaze, layer, paint, smear **6** blazer, enamel, encase, jacket, spread **7** coating, encrust, envelop, lacquer, overlay, plaster, slicker, topcoat **8**

covering, laminate, mackinaw, overcoat, raincoat **9** whitewash **10** mackintosh, sports coat

coating 4 coat, film, skin **5** layer, sheet **6** veneer **7** overlay **8** covering, envelope

coat of arms 4 arms **5** crest **6** creast **8** insignia **9** blaconwry **10** escutcheon **14** heraldic emblem **16** armorial bearings

coat of mail 4 mail **5** armor **9** chain mail **11** suit of armor

Coat of Varnish, A
   author: 6 C P Snow

coax 6 cajole **7** wheedle **8** butter up, inveigle, soft-soap, talk into **9** sweet-talk

cobalt 4 blue **5** azure **7** element, sky blue **10** bright blue **12** greenish blue
   chemical symbol: 2 Co

Cobb, Lee J
   born: 9 New York NY
   roles: 10 Willy Loman **12** The Virginian **14** Twelve Angry Men **15** On the Waterfront **16** Death of a Salesman

Cobb, Ty (Tyrus Raymond)
   nickname: 12 Georgia Peach
   sport: 8 baseball
   position: 8 outfield
   team: 13 Detroit Tigers

cobbler 3 pie **9** bootmaker, shoemaker **12** shoe repairer **16** deepdish fruit pie

cobra
   also: 3 asp **5** mamba **11** hooded snake
   native to: 4 Asia **6** Africa
   kind: 4 king **6** hooded, Indian **8** Egyptian
   enemy: 8 mongoose

Coburn, Charles
   born: 10 Savannah GA
   roles: 9 Boss Tweed **17** The More the Merrier

Coburn, James
   born: 8 Laurel NE
   roles: 10 Hudson Hawk **11** In Like Flint, Our Man Flint **14** The Great Escape, The Muppet Movie **17** The Nutty Professor **19** The Magnificent Seven

Coca, Imogene
   partner: 9 Sid Caesar
   born: 14 Philadelphia PA
   roles: 15 Your Show of Shows

cock 3 tip **4** knob **5** raise, valve **6** faucet, handle, perk up **7** rooster, stand up **8** cockerel, male bird, set erect **9** bristle up **11** chanticleer **13** turn to one side **16** raise the hammer of **17** draw back the hammer

cockade 4 knot **5** badge **6** ribbon **7** rosette **8** ornament **10** party badge

Cockade State
   nickname of: 8 Maryland

cock-and-bull story 3 fib, lie **4** myth, yarn **5** fable **7** fiction, untruth, whopper **9** fairy tale, falsehood, fish story, invention, tall story **11** fabrication **13** prevarication

Cockcroft, John Douglas
  field: 7 physics
  nationality: 7 British
  developed: 24 Cockcroft-Walton generator
  worked with: 6 Walton
  awarded: 10 Nobel Prize

cockeyed 3 mad **4** awry, wild **5** askew, crazy, goofy, inane, nutty, weird **6** absurd, aslant, insane, tilted **7** crooked, foolish, twisted **8** lopsided, sideways **9** irregular, off-center, senseless **10** cockamamie, out of whack, ridiculous, unbalanced **11** nonsensical **12** asymmetrical, preposterous

Cockpit of Europe *see* **7** Belgium

cockscomb 4 comb **5** crest **7** celosia, coxcomb **8** amaranth, caruncle

cocksure 4 pert, smug, vain **5** brash, cocky, pushy **6** cheeky, snooty **8** arrogant, positive **9** assertive, audacious, bumptious, conceited **10** aggressive, swaggering **11** overbearing, self-assured, swell-headed **13** overconfident, self-confident

cocktail 5 drink, fruit, horse **6** shrimp **10** docked tail, semi-formal
  type: 4 grog **6** brandy, gibson, gimlet, mai tai, rob roy, zombie **7** Bellini, gin fizz, martini, negroni, sidecar, stinger **8** daiquiri, highball, hot toddy, pink lady **9** cuba libre, hurricane, gin rickey, manhattan, margarita, mint julep, rusty nail **10** bloody mary, tom collins **11** boilermaker, gin and tonic, grasshopper, screwdriver, sloe gin fizz **12** black russian, cosmopolitan, old-fashioned, tom and jerry, whiskey sour **13** planter's punch **15** brandy alexander
  mixer: 4 soda **5** tonic, water **7** bitters, seltzer **9** ginger ale
  garnish: 4 lime **5** lemon, olive, orange, twist **16** maraschino cherry
  stirrer: 7 muddler

cocktail lounge 3 bar **6** saloon, tavern **7** gin mill, taproom

cocky 5 brash, saucy **6** jaunty **8** arrogant, cocksure, impudent **9** conceited, egotistic **10** swaggering

Coco, James
  born: 9 New York NY
  roles: 11 Sancho Panza **13** Man of La Mancha **21** Last of the Red Hot Lovers

cocoa 5 brown, cacao **9** chocolate **12** hot chocolate

cocoon
  covering for: 5 larva
  stage: 5 pupal
  made of: 4 silk

Cocteau, Jean
  author of: 7 Orpheus **8** Antigone **12** Blood of a Poet **18** The Infernal Machine **19** Les Enfants Terribles, Les Parents Terribles **20** The Beauty and the Beast

Cocytus
  river in: 5 Hades

coddle 3 pat, pet **4** baby **5** humor, spoil **6** caress, cuddle, dote on, fondle, pamper **7** indulge **11** mollycoddle

code 4 laws **5** rules **6** cipher **7** statute **8** precepts **9** ordinance, standards **10** cryptogram, guidelines, principles **11** cryptograph, proprieties, regulations **13** secret writing **14** secret language

codger 5 crank, miser **6** geezer, oddity, old man **9** eccentric, odd person

codicil 5 rider **8** addendum, addition, appendix **9** extension, subscript **10** postscript, supplement **11** added clause

codify 4 rank, rate **5** grade, group, index, order **7** arrange, catalog **8** classify, organize, tabulate **9** methodize **10** categorize, coordinate, regularize **11** systematize

coelenterate 5 coral, hydra, polyp **6** Medusa **7** acaleph, radiate **8** acalephe **9** jellyfish **10** sea anemone
  habitat: 5 ocean **9** salt water

Coelophysis
  type: 8 dinosaur, therapod
  location: 7 Arizona
  period: 8 Triassic

coequal 5 equal **10** coordinate **16** equally important

coequality 6 parity **8** equality, evenness, sameness **10** uniformity **11** equivalency **14** correspondence

coerce 3 cow **4** make **5** bully, drive, force **6** compel, oblige **7** dragoon **8** browbeat, bulldoze, pressure, threaten **9** constrain, strong-arm **10** intimidate

coercer 5 bully **9** oppressor, tormenter, tormentor **10** browbeater **11** intimidator, petty tyrant

coercion 5 force **6** duress **7** threats **8** bullying, pressure **10** compulsion, constraint **11** browbeating **12** intimidation

coercive 8 enforced, forcible **10** compulsory, obligatory **11** threatening

coexist with 12 go hand in hand, go side by side, live together **13** go hand in glove

coffee 6 Coffea **13** Coffea arabica
  varieties: 4 Java, Kona, Wild **5** Irish, Mocha **6** Almond, Common **7** Arabian, Arabica, Robusta, Vanilla **8** Liberian, Liberica, Zanzibar **9** Colombian **11** French Roast, Wild robusta **13** Decaffeinated **20** Jamaican Blue Mountain
  beverage: 5 decaf, latte **6** kahlua **8** espresso **10** cafe au lait, cappuccino
  small cup: 9 demitasse

coffee (black)
  French: 8 cafe noir **10** cafe nature

coffee brandy 6 Kahlua **8** Tia Maria

coffee with milk 5 latte
  French: 10 cafe au lait

coffer 3 box **4** case **5** chest **9** strongbox **10** depository, repository **13** treasure chest

coffers 5 safes **6** vaults **8** treasury **9** cash boxes **11** money supply

coffin 3 box **4** pall **6** casket **10** catafalque **11** sarcophagus

cog 3 cam, lie **4** gear **5** cheat, cozen, tenon, tooth, wedge, wheel **8** small boat **10** projection

cogent 5 sound, valid **6** potent **7** weighty **8** forceful, powerful **9** effective, trenchant **10** compelling, convincing, persuasive, undeniable **11** meritorious, well-founded **12** well-grounded **16** incontrovertible

cogitate 5 study, think, weigh **6** ponder **7** reflect **8** meditate, mull over, ruminate **9** think over **10** deliberate, think about **11** contemplate, reflect upon **18** consider thoroughly

cogito ergo sum 18 I think therefore I am
  said by: 9 Descartes

cognac
  type: 6 brandy **7** liqueur
  origin: 6 France
  brand: 7 Bisquit, Martell **8** Hennessy **10** Remy Martin **11** Courvoisier
  label: 2 VO (very old), VS (very special), XO (extra old) **3** XXO (extra extra old) **4** VSOP (very superior old pale) **8** Napoleon (5 year premium)
  drink: 9 Andalusia
  with Cointreau: 10 Rolls Royce
  with Triple Sec: 7 Chicago **10** Rolls Royce
  with vodka: 7 Cossack

cognate 4 akin, like **5** alike, close **7** kindred, related, similar **8** familial, parallel, relative **9** affiliate **10** derivative **11** consanguine

cognition 7 knowing **9** awareness, knowledge **11** familiarity **13** comprehension, understanding

cognizance 4 heed, note **5** grasp **6** notice, regard **8** scrutiny **9** attention, awareness, cognition, knowledge **10** perception **11** familiarity, observation, recognition, sensibility **12** apprehension **13** comprehension, consciousness, understanding

cognizant 5 aware **6** posted **7** knowing, mindful **8** familiar, informed, versed in **9** conscious **10** acquainted, conversant, instructed **11** enlightened **13** knowledgeable, understanding

cognomen 4 name **6** handle **7** epithet, moniker, surname **11** appellation, designation

cognoscenti 6 judges **7** experts **8** insiders **11** authorities **12** connoisseurs **14** those in the know

cohere 3 fit, set 4 bind, fuse, glue, hold, jibe, join 5 agree, cling, match, stick, tally, unite 6 cement, concur, square 7 combine, conform, congeal 8 coalesce, coincide, dovetail, solidify 9 coagulate, harmonize 10 correspond 11 consolidate, synchronize 12 hold together 13 stick together

coherence 5 logic, unity 7 clarity, concord, harmony 8 cohesion 9 congruity 10 accordance, conformity, consonance 11 consistency, rationality 12 organization

coherent 5 clear, lucid 7 logical, orderly 8 cohesive, rational 9 congruous, connected, in keeping, organized 10 articulate, consistent, harmonious, meaningful, systematic 11 in agreement 12 intelligible 13 corresponding 14 comprehensible, understandable

cohesion 4 bond 5 union, unity 7 bonding 8 adhesion 10 attraction, solidarity

cohesive 3 set 5 solid 6 sticky 7 viscous 8 cemented, coherent, cohering, sticking 9 connected 11 indivisible, inseparable 12 consolidated 13 agglutinative

Cohn, Ferdinand Julius
field: 6 botany
nationality: 6 German
founded: 12 bacteriology

Cohn, Robert
character in: 15 The Sun Also Rises
author: 9 Hemingway

cohort 3 pal 4 chum 5 buddy, crony 6 fellow, friend 7 comrade 8 follower, myrmidon 9 associate, companion 10 accomplice

coif 3 cap 4 hood, veil 6 beggin, burlet, hairdo 8 biggonet, coiffure, skull cap 9 head-dress

coiffed 6 capped, styled 7 dressed 8 arranged

coiffeur 7 stylist 11 hairdresser 15 male hairdresser

coiffure 2 DA, GI 3 bob, bun 4 Afro, coif, perm, shag, trim, updo, wave 6 hairdo 7 beehive, blowcut, comb-out, flattop, haircut, pageboy, upsweep 8 cold wave, cornrows, ducktail 9 hairstyle, permanent, pompadour

coil 4 curl, loop, ring, roll, wind 5 braid, twine, twist 6 circle, spiral, writhe 7 entwine 8 encircle

coin 4 mint 5 hatch, money, piece 6 change, create, devise, invent, make up, silver, strike 7 concoct, dream up, think up 8 conceive 9 fabricate, originate

coin/currency
of **Afghanistan:** 3 pul 5 abaze, riyal, rupee 6 abbasi, amania 7 afghani
of **Albania:** 3 lek 5 franc 6 qintar 7 quintar
of **Algeria:** 5 dinar 7 centime
of **Andorra:** 5 franc 6 peseta
of **Angola:** 6 escudo, kwanza, macuta, macute 7 angolar, centavo
of **Argentina:** 4 peso 7 centavo 9 argentino
of **Armenia:** 5 ruble
of **Australia:** 4 dump, tray, zack 5 pound 6 dollar 8 shilling
of **Austria:** 4 lira 5 crown, ducat, krone 6 florin, gulden, heller, zehner 8 albertin, groschen, kreutzer 9 schilling
of **Azerbaijan:** 5 manat
of **Bahrain:** 5 dinar
of **Bangladesh:** 4 taka 5 paisa
of **Belarus:** 5 ruble
of **Belgium:** 5 belga, franc 7 brabant, centime, crocard
of **Benin:** 5 franc 7 centime
of **Bhutan:** 5 paisa, rupee 7 chetrum 8 ngultrum
of **Bolivia:** 4 peso 7 centavo 9 boliviano
of **Bosnia-Herzegovina:** 5 dinar
of **Botswana:** 4 pula, rand
of **Brazil:** 3 joe 4 reis 5 dobra 7 centara, halfjoe, milreis 8 cruzeiro
of **Bulgaria:** 3 lev 8 stotinki
of **Burkina Faso:** 5 franc 7 centime
of **Burundi:** 5 franc 7 centime
of **Cambodia:** 3 sen 4 quan, riel 6 puttan 7 piaster
of **Cameroon:** 5 franc 7 centime
of **Canada:** 6 loonie, toonie
of **Canary Islands:** 6 peseta
of **Cape Verde:** 6 escudo 7 centavo
of **Central African Republic:** 5 franc 7 centime
of **Chad:** 5 franc 7 centime
of **Chile:** 4 peso 5 libra 6 condor, escudo
of **China:** 4 cash, cent, fyng, mace, tael, tiao, yuan 5 sycee 12 jen nin piao pu
of **Colombia:** 4 peso, real 6 condor, peseta 7 centavo
of **Comoros:** 5 franc 7 centime
of **Congo:** 5 franc 7 centime
of **Costa Rica:** 5 colon 6 colone 7 centimo
of **Crete:** 7 drachma
of **Croatia:** 5 dinar
of **Cuba:** 4 peso 7 centavo 8 cuarenta
of **Cyprus** 4 para 5 pound
of **Czechoslovakia/ Czech Republic:** 5 crown, ducat 6 heller, koruna
of **Denmark:** 3 one, ora, ore 4 fyrk 5 krone 8 frederik, skilling 9 rigsdaler
of **Djibouti:** 5 franc 7 centime
of **Dominican Republic:** 3 oro 4 peso 6 franco
of **Ecuador:** 5 sucre 7 centavo
of **Egypt:** 4 fils, kees, para 5 asper, dinar, fodda, gersh, girsh, medin, pound, riyal 6 ahmadi, dirham, foddah, guinea, junayh, maidin, medine, medino 7 piaster, piastre, tallard 8 bedidlik, millieme
of **El Salvador:** 4 peso 5 colon 7 centavo
of **England:** 3 ora 4 rial 5 achey, crown, groat, noble, pence, penny, pound 6 bawbee, florin, guinea 7 angelet, hapenny 8 farthing, shilling, sixpence, tuppence, tuppenny 13 pound sterling
of **Equatorial Guinea:** 6 ekuele, peseta 7 centimo
of **Estonia:** 3 lat 4 sent 5 kroon 7 estmark
of **Ethiopia:** 4 besa, birr, harf 5 amole, girsh 6 dollar, kharaf, levant, pataca, talari 7 ashrafi, menelik, plaster, tallero 12 maria theresa
of **European Community:** 3 ecu
of **Fiji:** 6 dollar
of **Finland:** 4 mark 5 penni 6 markka 7 markkaa
of **France:** 5 franc 7 centime 8 napoleon
of **Gabon Republic:** 5 franc 7 centime
of **the Gambia:** 5 pound 6 butbut, dalasi
of **Georgia:** 5 ruble
of **Germany:** 4 mark 7 Ostmark, pfennig 12 Deutsche mark
of **Ghana:** 4 cedi, cidi 5 ackey
of **Greece:** 5 lepta 7 drachma
of **Greenland:** 3 ore 5 krone
of **Guatemala:** 4 peso 7 centavo, quetzal
of **Guinea:** 4 iliy, syli 5 franc 6 cauris
of **Guinea-Bissau:** 4 peso 6 escudo 7 centavo
of **Haiti:** 6 gourde 7 centime
of **Honduras:** 4 peso 7 centavo, lempira
of **Hungary:** 4 gara 5 balas, krone, pengo 6 filler, forint, gulden, korona, ongara, ungara
of **Iceland:** 5 aurar, eyrir, krona 6 kronur
of **India:** 3 lac, pie 4 anna, fels, lakh, pice, tara 5 abidi, crore, paisa, rupee
of **Indonesia:** 3 sen 6 rupiah
of **Iran:** 3 pul 4 asar, gran, lari, rial 5 bisti, daric, dinar, larin, shahi, toman 6 stater 7 ashrafi, kasbeke, pahlavi
of **Iraq:** 4 fils 5 dinar
of **Ireland:** 3 rap 4 real 5 pence, pound 6 turney 8 shilling
of **Israel:** 3 mil 5 agora, agura, pound, pruta 6 agorot, shekel
of **Italy:** 4 lira, lire, tara 5 grano, paoli, paolo, scudo, soldo 6 danaro, denaro, ducato, sequin 7 testone 8 zecchino 9 centesini
of **Ivory Coast:** 5 franc 7 centime
of **Jamaica:** 7 quattie
of **Japan:** 2 bu 3 mon, rin, rio, sen, shu, yen 4 cash, mibu, oban 5 koban, obang, tempo 6 cobang, ichebu, ichibu, itzebu, kogang 7 itzeboo, itziboo
of **Jordan:** 4 fils 5 dinar
of **Kazakhstan:** 5 ruble

of Kenya: 4 cent **5** pound **8** shilling
of Kiribati: 4 cent **6** dollar
of Korea: 3 woh, won **4** chun, hwan, kwan
of Kuwait: 4 fils **5** dinar
of Kyrgyzstan: 3 som
of Laos: 2 at **3** att, kip
of Latvia: 3 lat **4** latu **6** rublis, santim **7** kapeika, santima
of Lebanon: 5 livre, pound **7** piastre
of Lesotho: 4 cent, rand **6** maloti
of Liberia: 4 cent **6** dollar
of Libya: 5 dinar
of Liechtenstein: 5 franc **6** rappen **7** franken
of Lithuania: 3 lit **5** litas, marka **6** centas, fennig **7** ostmark, skatiku **8** auksinas, skatikas
of Luxembourg: 5 franc **7** centime
of Macao: 3 avo **6** pataca, pataco
of Macedonia: 5 denar
of Madagascar: 5 franc **7** centime
of Malawi: 6 kwacha **7** tambala
of Malaysia: 3 sen, tra **4** taro, trah **7** ringgit, tampang
of Maldives: 5 laree, rupee **7** rufiyaa
of Mali: 5 franc **7** centime
of Malta: 4 cent **5** grain, grano, pound
of Mauritania: 5 khoum **7** ouguiya
of Mauritius: 4 cent **5** rupee
of Mexico: 4 onza, peso **5** adobe, claco, tlaco **6** azteca, cuarto, dinero **7** centavo, piaster
of Moldova: 5 ruble
of Monaco: 5 franc **7** centime
of Mongolia: 5 mongo, mungo **6** tugrik **7** tughrik
of Montenegro: 4 para **6** florin **7** perpera
of Morocco: 4 flue, okia, rial **5** floos, franc, okich, ounce **6** dirham, miskal **8** mouzouna
of Mozambique: 6 escudo **7** centavo, metical
of Myanmar: 3 pya **4** kyat
of Namibia: 4 cent, rand
of Nauru: 4 cent **6** dollar
of Nepal: 4 anna, pice **5** mohar, rupee
of the Netherlands: 4 doit, oord, raps **5** crown, daler, rider, ryder **6** florin, gulden, stiver, suskin **7** daalder, ducaton, escalan, escalin, guilder, stooter, stuiver **8** albertin, ducatoon **9** dubbeltje **12** rijksdaalder **13** albertustaler
of New Guinea: 4 kina, toea
of New Zealand: 4 cent **6** dollar
of Nicaragua: 4 peso **7** centavo, cordoba
of Niger: 5 franc **7** centime
of Nigeria: 4 kobo **5** naira
of Norway: 3 ore **5** krone **6** kroner
of Oman: 3 gaj, gaz **4** rial **5** baiza, ghazi **7** mahmudi
of Pakistan: 4 anna, pice **5** paisa, rupee

of Panama: 4 cent **6** balboa **9** centesimo
of Paraguay: 4 peso **7** centimo, guarani
of Peru: 3 sol **5** libra **6** dinero, reseta **7** centavo
of the Philippines: 4 peso **6** conant, peseta **7** centavo
of Poland: 4 abia **5** dalar, ducat, grosz, marka, zloty **6** fening, groszy, gulden, halerz, korona **8** groschen
of Portugal: 3 avo, joe **4** peca, real **5** conto, crown, dobra, indio, justo, rupia **6** escudo, macuta, octave, pataca, testad, tostao, vintem **7** angalar, centavo, crusado, miereis, moidore, testone **8** equipaga, johannes
of Qatar: 5 riyal **6** dirham
of Rumania: 3 ban, lei, leu, lev, ley **4** bani **5** uncia **6** triens
of Russia: 5 altin, bisti, copec, genga, grosh, kopek, ruble, shaur **6** abassi, copeck, grivna, kopeck, piatak, rouble **7** poltina, valiuta **8** auksinas, deneshka, imperial, polushka **9** poltinnik **10** altininink, chervonets
of Rwanda: 5 franc **7** centime
of San Marino: 4 lira, lire **9** centesimi
of Samoa: 4 tala
of Sao Tome and Principe: 5 dobra **6** escudo **7** centavo
of Sardinia: 7 carline
of Saudi Arabia: 5 girsh, gursh, pound, riyal
of Scotland: 3 ecu **4** demy, doit, lion, mark, rial, ryal **5** bodle, broad, groat, plack, rider, turne **6** bawbee, folles **7** unicorn **8** atchison, hardhead **9** halfpenny **11** bonnetpiece
of Senegal: 5 franc **7** centime
of Sicily: 5 litra, oncia, uncia **6** carlin **7** carline, oncetta
of Sierra Leone: 4 cent **5** leone
of Singapore: 4 cent **6** dollar
of Slovakia: 6 koruna
of Slovenia: 5 tolar
of Solomon Islands: 4 cent **6** dollar
of Somalia: 4 besa **6** somalo **8** shilling **9** centesimi
of South Africa: 4 cent, pond, rand **5** pound **6** florin **7** daalder **9** krugerand
of Spain: 3 cob **4** duro, peso, real **5** dobla **6** cuarto, dinero, doblon, escudo, peseta **7** alfonso, centimo, pistole, realdor **8** doubloon
of Sri Lanka: 4 cent **5** rupee
of Sudan: 5 pound **7** piastre
of Suriname: 4 cent **7** guilder
of Swaziland: 4 rand **9** lilangeni
of Sweden: 3 ore **5** krona, krone **7** carolin **8** skilling **9** rigsdaler
of Switzerland: 5 franc, rappe **6** hallar, rappen **7** angster, centime, duplone **8** baetzner, blaffert
of Syria: 4 lira **5** pound **6** talent **7** piaster

of Taiwan: 4 yuan **6** dollar
of Tajikistan: 5 ruble
of Tanzania: 4 cent **8** shilling
of Thailand: 2 at **3** att **4** baht **5** cutty, fuang, tical **6** pynung, salung, satang **11** bullet money
of Tibet: 5 tanga
of Togo: 5 franc **7** centime
of Tonga: 6 paanga, seniti
of Trinidad and Tobago: 4 cent **6** dollar
of Tunisia: 5 dinar **6** dollar **7** millime
of Turkey: 4 lira, para **5** akcha, asper, attun, kurus, pound, rebia **6** akcheh, sequin, zequin **7** aetilik, beshlik, pataque, piaster **8** medjidie, zecchino
of Turkmenistan: 5 ruble
of Tuvalu: 4 cent **6** dollar
of Uganda: 4 cent **8** shilling
of Ukraine: 6 grivna **10** karbovanet
of United Arab Emirates: 3 fil **6** dirham
of Uruguay: 4 peso **9** centesimo, centisimo
of Uzbekistan: 5 ruble
of Vanuatu: 5 franc **6** dollar
of Venezuela: 4 peso, real **5** medio **6** fuerte **7** bolivar, centimo **8** morocota **10** venezolano
of Vietnam: 2 xu **4** dong **7** piaster
of Western Samoa: 4 sene, tala
of Yemen: 4 fils, rial **5** dinar, riyal
of Yugoslavia: 4 para **5** dinar
of Zaire: 5 zaire **6** makuta
of Zambia: 5 ngwee **6** kwacha
of Zimbabwe: 4 cent **6** dollar
coincide 3 fit **4** jibe, meet **5** agree, cross, match, tally **6** accord, concur, square **7** conform **8** converge, dovetail **9** harmonize **10** correspond **11** synchronize **12** be concurrent, come together **19** occur simultaneously
coincidence 4 fate, luck **6** chance **8** accident **11** concurrence, synchronism **12** happenstance **22** simultaneous occurrence
coincident 10 coexistent, concurrent **12** contemporary, simultaneous **15** contemporaneous
coincidental 6 chance **9** unplanned **10** accidental, contiguous, synchronal **11** concomitant, synchronous **12** happenstance, simultaneous
cointreau
  type: 7 liqueur
  variety: 7 curacao **9** triple sec
  origin: 6 France
  flavor: 6 orange
  drink: 8 Applecar
  with bourbon: 10 Temptation
  with brandy: 7 Sidecar
  with cognac: 10 Rolls Royce
  with gin: 7 Florida **9** White Lady **13** Sweet Patootie **14** Flying Dutchman
  with rum: 8 Acapulco **10** Casa Blanca **11** Beachcomber **12** Blue Hawaiian
  with rye: 10 Temptation

with tequila: 9 Margarita
with whiskey: 16 Canadian Cocktail
Colavito, Rocky (Rocco Domenico)
 sport: 8 baseball
 team: 16 Cleveland Indians
Colbert, Claudette
 real name: 22 Claudette Lily Chauchoin
 born: 5 Paris **6** France
 roles: 8 Tovarich **9** Cleopatra **14** Palm Beach Story **18** It Happened One Night (Oscar)
cold 3 icy, old **4** cool, dead, flat, hard **5** aloof, brisk, chill, crisp, cruel, faded, faint, gelid, harsh, nippy, polar, sharp, stale, stiff, stony **6** arctic, biting, bitter, chilly, cooled, frigid, frosty, frozen, inured, numbed, remote, severe, snappy, steely, wintry **7** callous, chilled, cutting, distant, frosted, glacial, haughty, nipping, passive, unmoved **8** chilling, coolness, detached, freezing, hardened, piercing, reserved, reticent, stinging, uncaring, unheated, unloving, unwarmed **9** apathetic, heartless, impassive, insensate, unfeeling, unstirred **10** disdainful, forbidding, impervious, insensible, phlegmatic, unfriendly **11** frozen stiff, indifferent, passionless, penetrating, unconcerned, unconscious, unemotional, unexcitable **12** antipathetic, bone-chilling, inaccessible, supercilious, uninterested, unresponsive **13** uninteresting, unsympathetic **14** marrow-chilling, unapproachable **15** teeth-chattering, uncommunicative, undemonstrative **16** chilled to the bone, unimpressionable **18** chilled to the marrow
cold-blooded 4 evil, hard **5** cruel, harsh, stiff, stony **6** brutal, flinty, formal, frigid, inured, savage, steely **7** callous, demonic, inhuman, passive, satanic, unmoved **8** detached, fiendish, hardened, inhumane, pitiless, reserved, ruthless, uncaring **9** barbarous, heartless, impassive, merciless, unfeeling, unpitying, unstirred **10** deliberate, diabolical, disdainful, impervious, implacable, unfriendly, unmerciful, villainous **11** calculating, hardhearted, indifferent, insensitive, passionless, unconcerned, unemotional, unexcitable **12** bloodthirsty, contemptuous, uninterested, unresponsive **13** disinterested, unimpassioned, unimpressible, unsympathetic **16** unimpressionable
cold-hearted 5 cruel **9** heartless, unfeeling **11** hard-hearted **13** unsympathetic
coldness 5 chill **7** iciness **9** aloofness **10** chilliness, frostiness **12** indifference **13** unfeelingness **14** unfriendliness **15** hardheartedness

Cole, Janet
 real name of: 9 Kim Hunter
Cole, Thomas
 born: 7 England **13** Bolton-le-Moors
 artwork: 8 The Ox-Bow **15** The Voyage of Life **17** The Course of Empire
coleoptera
 class: 8 hexopoda
 phylum: 10 arthropoda
 group: 8 beetle, weevil
Coleridge, Samuel Taylor
 author of: 9 Kubla Khan **10** Christabel **14** Dejection An Ode, Lyrical Ballads (with Wordsworth) **19** Biographia Literaria **26** The Rime of the Ancient Mariner
Colette (Sidonie)
 author of: 4 Gigi, Sido **5** Cheri **8** Claudine **11** La Vagabonde **14** The Evening Star
coliseum 4 bowl **5** arena **6** circus **7** stadium, theater **9** Colosseum **10** hippodrome **12** amphitheater **14** exhibition hall
collaborate 4 join **5** unite **6** assist, team up **7** collude **9** cooperate **10** join forces **12** work together **14** work side by side
collaborationist 6 puppet **7** traitor **8** quisling
collaborator 4 ally **6** puppet **7** traitor **8** co-worker, quisling, teammate **9** associate, colleague, co-partner **11** confederate
collapse 4 coma, fail, fall, flop, fold **5** faint, swoon **6** attack, buckle, cave-in, fizzle **7** break up, crack-up, crumple, failure, give way, seizure **8** be in vain, buckling, downfall, flounder, keel over, take sick **9** become ill, break down **10** be stricken, break apart, run aground **11** fall through **12** disintegrate, falling apart, fall helpless, fall to pieces **13** come to nothing, sudden illness **14** disintegration **17** become unconscious
collapsed 4 limp **7** caved in, compact **8** deflated, fallen in, folded up **13** disintegrated
Collapse of the Third Republic, The
 author: 14 William L Shirer
collapsible 7 folding **8** foldable **10** deflatable
collar 3 nab **4** eton, grab **5** catch, fichu, pinch, seize **6** arrest, bertha **7** capture **9** apprehend, neckpiece **12** take prisoner **15** take into custody
collate 5 order **6** bestow, verify **7** compare **8** assemble, organize **9** integrate **11** put together
collateral 4 bond **5** extra **6** pledge, surety **7** warrant **8** parallel, security, warranty **9** accessory, ancillary, auxiliary, guarantee, insurance, secondary **10** additional, incidental, supporting,

supportive **11** endorsement, subordinate **12** contributory **13** supplementary
collation 3 tea **4** meal **5** lunch **6** brunch, repast, sermon **7** address, reading **8** hotchpot, luncheon, treatise **10** comparison **11** description
colleague 4 mate **6** fellow **7** partner **8** confrere, co-worker, teammate **9** associate, co-partner **11** confederate **12** collaborator, fellow worker
collect 3 get **4** calm, meet **5** amass, raise, rally **6** gather, heap up, muster, obtain, pick up, pile up, summon **7** call for, compile, compose, control, convene, marshal, prepare, receive, solicit **8** assemble, gather up, scrape up **9** aggregate, get hold of **10** accumulate, congregate **11** concentrate, get together
collectanea 8 analects, treasury **9** anthology, gleanings **10** collection, miscellany, selections **11** miscellanea
collected 4 calm, cool **5** quiet **6** placid, poised, serene, steady **8** composed, peaceful, tranquil **9** confident, unruffled **10** cool-headed, restrained **11** level-headed, self-assured, undisturbed, unemotional, unflappable, unperturbed **12** even-tempered **13** self-possessed **14** self-controlled
collection 3 mob **4** bevy, body, gift, heap, mass, pack, pile **5** array, bunch, clump, crowd, drove, flock, group, hoard, store, swarm **6** corpus, jumble, muster, throng **7** cluster, clutter, variety **8** amassing, assembly, oblation, treasury **9** anthology, gathering, offertory, receiving **10** assemblage, assortment, hodgepodge, miscellany, soliciting **11** aggregation, compilation **12** accumulating, accumulation
Collection of Ten Thousand Leaves (Manyoshu)
 author: 7 unknown
collective 5 joint **6** common, mutual, united **7** unified **8** combined, gathered **9** aggregate, composite **10** cumulative, integrated **11** accumulated, cooperative
collector 6 grouper **7** dustman **8** antiquer, compiler, composer, gatherer, zamindar **9** assembler **10** garbageman **11** anthologist
Collector, The
 author: 10 John Fowles
college 7 academy **8** seminary **9** institute **10** university **11** institution
college-preparatory 4 prep **8** academic **11** liberal-arts **12** nontechnical **13** nonvocational
collegiate 8 academic **10** scholastic, university **11** educational
collide 3 hit **4** meet **5** clash, crash, smash **7** crack up, diverge, run into **8** bump into, conflict, disagree **9** knock

into **10** meet head on **11** beat against **13** hurtle against, strike against

Collier, Lucille Ann
  real name of: **9** Ann Miller

Collins, Mary Catherine
  real name of: **7** Bo Derek

Collins, Mr
  character in: **17** Pride and Prejudice
  author: **6** Austen

Collins, Wilkie
  author of: **6** No Name **12** The Moonstone **15** The Woman in White

collision 4 bump **5** clash, crash, fight, smash **6** battle, combat, impact **7** smash-up **8** accident, conflict, skirmish, struggle **9** encounter **10** engagement **11** clash of arms

colloquial 5 homey, plain **6** casual, chatty, common, folksy **8** everyday, familiar, homespun, informal, ordinary, workaday **9** idiomatic **10** vernacular **14** conversational **15** unsophisticated

colloquy 4 chat, talk **6** caucus, parley **7** council, palaver, seminar **8** commerce, congress, converse, dialogue **9** communion, discourse **10** conference, discussion, rap session **11** interchange, intercourse **12** conversation **13** confabulation

collude 4 plot **7** connive **8** conspire, intrigue **9** cooperate **11** collaborate

collusion 5 fraud **7** treason **8** intrigue **10** complicity, connivance, conspiracy **13** collaboration **15** secret agreement **17** guilty association

Colman, Ronald
  born: **7** England **8** Richmond
  roles: **9** Beau Geste **10** Arrowsmith **11** A Double Life (Oscar), Lost Horizon **16** A Tale of Two Cities

cologne 5 scent **7** essence, perfume **9** fragrance **11** toilet water

Colomba
  author: **14** Prosper Merimee

Colombia
  other name: **6** Darien **10** New Granada
  capital/largest city: **6** Bogota
  others: **3** Ten **4** Amza, Buga, Cali, Mitu, Muzo, Paez, Sipi, Tado, Tolu, Yari **5** Bello, Chinu, Guapi, Neiva, Pasto, Tulua, Tunja **6** Cucuta, Ibaque, Lorica, Quibdo, Sangil, Tumaco **7** Cartago, Ipiates, Leticia, Palmira, Pereira, Popayan **8** Girardot, Maganque, Medellin, Monteria **9** Cartagena, Manizales **10** Santa Marta **11** Bucaramanga **12** Barranquilla, Buenaventura
  school: **5** Andes, Valle **20** Instituto Caro y Cuervo **21** Industrial de Santander
  measure: **4** vara **7** azumbre, celemin
  monetary unit: **4** peso, real **6** condor, peseta **7** centavo
  weight: **3** bag **4** saco **5** libra **7** quintal

island: 4 Baru **5** Naipo **6** Fuerte **7** Gorgona, Malpelo **8** Cusachon **9** San Andres **11** Providencia

lake: 4 Tota

mountain: 5 Abibe, Andes, Baudo, Chita, Cocuy, Huila, Pasto **6** Ayapel, Perija, Purace, Tolima, Tunahi **7** Chamusa, del Ruiz **8** Oriengal **10** Santa Marta **17** Central Cordillera, Eastern Cordillera, Western Cordillera

highest point: 14 Cristobal Colon

river: 3 Uva **4** Bita, Meta, Muco, Sinu, Tomo, Yari **5** Cauca, Cesar, Isana, Mesai, Nechi, Pauto, Sucio **6** Amazon, Arauca, Ariari, Atrato, Atroto, Caguan, Pattia, Yapura **7** Apapois, Caqueta, Guainia, Inirida, Truando, Vichada **8** Casanare, Guaviara, Putumayo **9** Magdalena

sea: 7 Pacific **9** Caribbean

physical feature:
  cape: 4 Vela **5** Aguja, Marzo, Punta **7** Augusta **8** Gallinas
  falls: 10 Tequendama
  gulf: 5 Uraba **6** Cupica, Darien, Tibuga **8** Tortugas
  inlet: 6 Tumaco
  plains: 6 Ilanos
  point: 6 Cruces, Lacruz, Solano **8** Caribana, Gallinas

people: 4 Boro, Cuna, Duit, Hoka, Macu, Muso, Muzo, Paez, Tama, Tapa **5** Carib, Catio, Choco, Cofan, Cogui, Cubeo, Guane, Haida, Mocoa, Paeze, Pijao, Seona, Yagua **6** Arawak, Betoya, Calima, Colima, Ingano, Mirana, Saliva, Tahami, Ticunu, Tucano, Tunebo, Witoto, Yahuna **7** Achagua, Andaqui, Chibcha, Chimila, Churoya, Guahibo, Guajiro, Panches, Pumave, Purlulo, Quechua, Shuswap, Tairona, Telembi **8** Coconuco, Guarauno, mestizos, Motilone, Puinavis, Quimbaya, Sinsigas **9** Cocanucos, Coconucan, mulattoes, Panaquita **10** Bellacoola

leader: 7 Bolivar

language: 7 Spanish

religion: 13 Roman Catholic

place:
  museum: 4 Gold **8** Colonial
  palace: 11 Inquisition

feature:
  dance: 7 bambuco **8** merengue
  game: 4 tejo
  guitar: 5 tiple
  poncho: 5 ruana
  shoes: 10 alpargatas
  shoulder bag: 7 carriel
  tree: 8 arboloco
  woven hat: 5 jipas

Colombo
  capital of: **8** Sri Lanka

colon 4 coin **6** farmer, vitals **7** pioneer, planter, settler, viscera **9** hemistich,

intestine **15** plantation owner, punctuation mark

colonize 5 found, plant **6** gather, settle **7** migrate **8** establish **10** infiltrate

colonnade 3 row **4** stoa **5** porch **6** arcade, piazza **7** portico, terrace **8** cloister **9** peristyle

colony 3 set **4** band, body **5** flock, group, swarm **7** mandate **8** dominion, province **9** community, territory **10** dependency, possession, settlement **12** protectorate **14** satellite state

colophon 6 design, device, emblem **7** insigne **8** insignia **11** inscription

color 3 dye, hue **4** bias, burn, cast, glow, mood, tint, tone, warp, wash **5** bloom, blush, chalk, drift, flame, flush, force, paint, sense, shade, slant, stain, taint, tinge, twist **6** affect, aspect, crayon, effect, import, intent, redden, spirit, stress **7** distort, feeling, meaning, pervert, pigment, redness, skin hue **8** dyestuff, rosiness **9** go crimson, influence, intention, prejudice **10** intimation **11** connotation, implication, insinuation **12** become florid, pigmentation, significance **17** natural complexion

Colorado
  abbreviation: **2** CO **4** Colo
  nickname: **10** Centennial
  capital/largest city: **6** Denver
  others: **4** Vail **5** Aspen, Delta, Lamar, Ouray **6** Arvada, Aurora, Denver, Golden, Pueblo, Salida **7** Alamosa, Boulder, Durango, Greeley, Manassa, Manitou **8** Gunnison, Loveland, Trinidad **9** Purgatory, Silverton, Telluride **11** Central City **12** Cripple Creek **13** Grand Junction **15** Colorado Springs
  baseball team: **7** Rockies
  college: **5** Regis **6** Denver **7** Boulder **17** US Air Force Academy
  feature: **11** Four Corners **15** Garden of the Gods **17** Continental Divide
    national monument: **8** Dinosaur **14** Great Sand Dunes
    national park: **5** Estes **9** Mesa Verde **13** Rocky Mountain
  tribe: **3** Ute **7** Arapaho **8** Cheyenne
  people: **11** Jack Dempsey **12** Ralph Edwards **14** Scott Carpenter **18** Douglas Fairbanks Sr
  lake: **6** Frozen
  land rank: **6** eighth
  mountains: **5** Longs, Rocky **7** San Juan **9** Pikes Peak **14** Sangre de Cristo
    highest point: **6** Elbert
  physical feature:
    canyon: **5** Black
    gorge: **5** Royal
    plains: **5** Great
    wind: **7** Chinook
  river: **4** Gila **5** Yampa **6** Platte **7** Dolores **8** Apishapa, Arikaree, Arkansas, Gunnison **9** Rio Grande **10** Purgatoire

state admission: 12 thirty-eighth
state bird: 11 lark bunting
state flower: 22 Rocky Mountain columbine
state motto: 24 Nothing Without Providence
state song: 22 Where the Columbines Grow
state tree: 18 Colorado blue spruce

colored 4 dyed, hued **5** dusky **6** biased, shaded, tinged, tinted **7** blushed, excused, flushed, glossed, labeled, painted, stained **8** affected, labelled, reddened **9** chromatic, distorted, pigmented **10** influenced, prejudiced **12** complexioned **13** characterized **14** misrepresented

colorful 3 gay **4** loud **5** showy, vivid **6** bright, florid, unique **7** dynamic, graphic, unusual, vibrant, zestful **8** animated, forceful, spirited, vigorous **9** brilliant, full-toned, vivacious **10** compelling, variegated **11** distinctive, interesting, many-colored, picturesque **12** multicolored, particolored

coloring 3 dye **4** tint **5** color, shade, stain **10** coloration, complexion

colorless 3 wan **4** ashy, drab, dull, flat, pale **5** ashen, dingy, faded, pasty, vapid, white **6** anemic, boring, dreary, grayed, pallid, sallow, sickly, undyed **7** ghastly, ghostly, insipid, natural, neutral, prosaic **8** blanched, bleached, lifeless, ordinary, whitened **9** bloodless, washed out **10** cadaverous, lackluster, monotonous, spiritless, unanimated, unexciting, uninspired **11** commonplace **13** uninteresting

Color Purple, The
author: 11 Alice Walker
director: 15 Steven Spielberg
cast: 11 Danny Glover **12** Adolph Caesar, Oprah Winfrey **13** Margaret Avery **14** Whoopi Goldberg

colors 4 flag, jack **6** banner, ensign, pennon **7** pennant **8** standard

colossal 4 huge, vast **5** giant, grand, great **6** mighty **7** extreme, immense, mammoth, massive, titanic **8** enormous, gigantic, imposing **9** exceeding, excessive **10** incredible, inordinate, monumental, prodigious, tremendous **11** extravagant, spectacular **12** awe-inspiring, overwhelming

Colossus of Rhodes
statue of: 6 Apollo

colt 4 foal **5** horse **6** novice **8** equuleus, yearling **9** fledgling, youngster
constellation of: 8 Equuleus

columbium
chemical symbol: 2 Cb

Columbo
character: 9 Lt Columbo
cast: 9 Peter Falk

column 3 row **4** file, line, post **5** pylon, queue, shaft, train **6** parade, pillar, string **7** caravan, phalanx, sup-port, upright **8** pilaster **9** cavalcade, formation **10** procession **11** vertical row **12** vertical list

columnist 6 writer **7** analyst
famous: 7 Heloise **8** Dear Abby, Herb Caen **9** HL Mencken, Jack Smith **10** Ann Landers **11** Miss Manners **15** Abigail van Buren

coma 6 stupor, torpor **8** collapse **15** unconsciousness

Comanche
language family: 10 Shoshonean
location: 5 Texas **6** Kansas, Mexico **8** Oklahoma
noted as: 8 horsemen

comatose 3 lax **4** dull, idle, lazy **5** inert **6** leaden, torpid **7** drugged, languid, passive **8** inactive, indolent, lifeless, listless, slothful, sluggish **9** apathetic, catatonic, lethargic, stuporous **10** cataleptic, insensible, narcotized, phlegmatic, spiritless **11** indifferent, unconcerned, unconscious **12** unresponsive

comb 4 card, tuft **5** curry, dress, groom, plume, scour, style **6** search **7** arrange, explore, panache, ransack, topknot **8** head tuft, hunt over, untangle **9** cast about, cockscomb, currycomb **11** look through **14** rummage through

combat 5 clash, fight **6** action, attack, battle, oppose, resist **7** contest, go to war, wage war **8** conflict, fighting, skirmish, struggle **9** encounter **10** contention, engagement, war against **11** come to blows, grapple with, make warfare, work against **12** do battle with, march against **13** confrontation **14** military action

Combat
character: 4 Caje (Caddy Cadron) **5** Kirby **8** (Pvt) Braddock **9** Doc Walton, (Lt) Gil Hanley **12** (Sgt) Chip Saunders
cast: 9 Jack Hogan, Rick Jason, Vic Morrow **12** Shecky Greene, Steven Rogers **13** Pierre Jalbert

combatant 7 fighter, soldier, warrior **9** man-at-arms **10** serviceman **11** fighting man

combating 8 battling, clashing, fighting, opposing **9** waging war **10** contention, contesting, opposition, struggling **11** doing battle **13** grappling with **17** coming to blows with

combative 6 bantam **8** militant **9** agonistic, bellicose **10** aggressive, pugnacious **11** belligerent, contentious **12** antagonistic

combativeness 9 hostility, pugnacity **10** antagonism **12** belligerence **14** aggressiveness **15** contentiousness

combination 3 mix **5** alloy, blend, union **6** fusion, league, medley, merger, mixing **7** amalgam, joining, mixture, pooling, variety **8** alliance, blending, compound **9** coalition, composite, synthesis **10** assortment, coalescing, federation **11** association, composition, confederacy **12** amalgamation **13** confederation

combine 3 mix **4** fuse, join, pool **5** blend, merge, unify, unite **6** couple, league, mingle **8** compound **9** commingle **10** amalgamate, synthesize **11** consolidate, incorporate

combo 4 band **5** group **11** aggregation, combination

comb out 4 curl **5** dress **7** arrange, unsnarl **8** untangle

combustible 8 burnable **9** flammable, ignitable **10** combustive, incendiary **11** inflammable **13** conflagrative

combustion 6 firing **7** burning, flaming **8** ignition, kindling **12** incineration **13** conflagration

combustive 8 burnable **9** flammable, ignitable **11** combustible, inflammable **13** conflagrative

come 2 be, go **3** bud **4** fall, loom, rise **5** arise, issue, occur, range, reach **6** appear, arrive, be made, drop in, emerge, extend, follow, happen, impend, show up, spread, spring, turn up **7** advance, descend, emanate, stretch **8** approach, draw near, go toward, grow to be **9** be a native, germinate, take place **10** be imminent, move toward **11** be a resident, be in the wind, materialize, originate in, spring forth

come about 5 occur **6** chance, happen **7** turn out **10** come to pass

come afterward 5 ensue **6** derive, follow, result **7** succeed

come apart 6 detach **7** disjoin, unstick **8** separate

come back 5 rally **6** answer, retort, return **7** rebound **8** recovery

Come Back Little Sheba
director: 10 Daniel Mann
based on play by: 11 William Inge
cast: 10 Terry Moore **12** Shirley Booth **13** Burt Lancaster
Oscar for: 7 actress (Booth)

come clean 4 sing **5** own up **7** confess **14** unbosom oneself **18** make a clean breast of

come close to 7 verge on **8** approach, border on **11** approximate, nearly equal

comedian 3 wag **4** fool, zany **5** clown, comic, cutup, joker **6** jester, madcap **7** buffoon **8** humorist, jokester **9** prankster **10** comedienne, comic actor **14** practical joker

comedown 4 drop **8** lowering **10** anticlimax

come down 4 dive, drop, fall, sink **6** plunge, tumble **7** descend, plummet **8** decrease

come down a peg 5 deign, stoop **6**

unbend **7** descend **10** condescend **12** lower oneself **13** humble oneself

comedy 3 fun, wit **5** farce, humor **6** banter, joking, pranks, satire **7** foolery, jesting **8** drollery, raillery, travesty **9** burlesque, cutting up, horseplay, silliness **10** buffoonery, pleasantry, tomfoolery **13** fooling around

Comedy of Errors, The
author: **18** William Shakespeare
character: **6** Aegeon, Dromio **7** Adriana, Aemilia, Luciana, Solinus **10** Antipholus

come face to face with 4 meet **8** confront **9** encounter

come first 7 precede, predate **8** antecede, antedate, go before **10** anticipate

come into being 4 dawn, show **5** arise, begin, occur, set in, start **6** appear, be born, crop up, emerge, sprout **8** commence, spring up **9** germinate, originate **11** come to light

come into port 4 dock **5** berth

come into view 4 show **6** appear, come up, emerge, show up **7** surface **11** come to light **13** become visible

come loose 5 let go **6** detach, loosen **7** slip off **8** break off, separate, unfasten **9** break away **10** come undone, come untied, disconnect **11** come unglued, come unstuck

comely 4 fair, nice **5** bonny **6** pretty, proper, seemly, simple **7** correct, fitting, natural, sightly, winning, winsome **8** becoming, blooming, charming, decorous, engaging, fetching, pleasant, pleasing, suitable, tasteful **9** agreeable, appealing, wholesome **10** attractive, unaffected **11** well-favored

come near 4 loom, near **6** appear **8** approach **9** draw close **10** move toward

come-on 4 bait, hook, lure, trap **5** decoy, snare **6** magnet **9** seduction **10** allurement, attraction, bewitchery, enticement, inducement, seducement, temptation **12** inveiglement

comestibles 5 foods **7** edibles **8** victuals **10** foodstuffs, provisions

come to a decision 6 decide, settle **7** resolve **8** conclude **9** determine

come to an understanding 5 agree **6** settle **11** come to terms **12** agree to marry **16** reach an agreement

come to a standstill 4 halt, quit, stop **5** abate, cease **7** die away **8** quit cold

come to blows 5 fight **7** contest **8** do battle **9** square off **12** start to fight

come together 4 meet **5** flock, group, rally **6** gather **7** collect, convene **8** assemble **10** congregate **11** get together

come to light 4 dawn **5** arise **6** appear, crop up, emerge, evolve, show up, turn up, unfold **7** develop, surface, turn out

come to nothing 4 fail, flop, fold **6** fizzle **8** be in vain, collapse **9** break down **11** fall through **12** come to naught **17** fail to materialize

come to pass 5 ensue, occur **6** arrive, befall, follow, happen **9** take place

come to terms 5 agree, yield **6** give up, settle **7** succumb **8** contract, cry quits **9** make a deal, negotiate, surrender **10** capitulate, compromise **11** come to grips, meet halfway, sue for peace **13** resign oneself **14** strike a bargain **15** lay down one's arms **16** reach an agreement **17** acknowledge defeat, hoist the white flag **18** split the difference

come unglued 6 detach, loosen **8** separate **9** fall apart **11** come unstuck

come unstuck 4 lift **6** detach, loosen **8** break off, unfasten **9** break away, come apart, come loose, fall apart **11** come unglued

come up 4 rise **5** arise **7** quicken, sharpen **8** heighten, increase **9** intensify **10** accelerate, strengthen **12** be referred to

come upon 4 find, meet **7** learn of, run into **8** discover **9** encounter

comfit 5 candy, sweet **9** sweetmeat **10** confection, sugar candy **13** confectionery

comfort 4 calm, ease, help **5** cheer, peace, quiet **6** luxury, relief, solace, soothe, succor, warmth **7** cheer up, compose, console, hearten **8** coziness, opulence, pleasure, reassure, serenity, snugness **9** bolster up, comforter, composure, encourage, well-being **10** cheering up, relaxation **11** consolation, contentment, reassurance **12** satisfaction **13** encouragement, gratification **14** quiet one's fears **16** source of serenity **17** lighten one's burden **18** bolster one's spirits

Comfort, Alex
author of: **11** The Joy of Sex **12** More Joy of Sex

comfortable 4 cozy, easy **6** at ease, at home, serene **7** relaxed **8** adequate, pleasant, suitable **9** agreeable, congenial, contented **10** giving ease, gratifying, untroubled **11** pleasurable, undisturbed **12** satisfactory **16** free from distress

comforter 4 balm, puff **5** quilt, scarf **6** afghan, solace **7** anodyne, blanket, comfort, soother **8** coverlet **10** palliative

comic, comical 4 rich **5** droll, funny, merry, silly, witty **6** absurd, jocose, jovial **7** amusing, jocular, risible **8** farcical, humorous, mirthful **9** facetious, laughable, ludicrous, whimsical **10** ridiculous **11** nonsensical **12** nimble-witted

coming 4 next **6** advent, future, in view, to come **7** arrival, nearing **8** approach, arriving, imminent, on the way **9** advancing, emergence, imminence, impending, in the wind, proximity **10** appearance, occurrence, subsequent **11** approaching, forthcoming, prospective **12** on the horizon **13** materializing

Coming Home
director: **8** Hal Ashby
cast: **9** Bruce Dern, Jane Fonda, Jon Voight **15** Robert Carradine
Oscar for: **5** actor (Voight) **7** actress (Fonda) **10** screenplay

Coming into the Country
author: **10** John McPhee

Coming of Age, The
author: **16** Simone de Beauvoir

Coming of Age in Samoa
author: **12** Margaret Mead

Coming Race, The
author: **18** Edward Bulwer-Lytton

command 3 bid, get **4** boss, call, draw, fiat, grip, head, hold, lead, rule **5** edict, evoke, grasp, guide, order, power **6** adjure, behest, charge, compel, decree, demand, direct, elicit, enjoin, govern, incite, induce, kindle, manage, ordain, prompt, summon **7** call for, conduct, control, deserve, extract, inspire, mastery, provoke, receive, require, summons **8** call upon, instruct, motivate **9** authority, call forth, direction, directive, governing, knowledge, ordinance, supervise, ultimatum **10** administer, be master of, domination, injunction, leadership, management **11** familiarity, instruction, superintend, supervision **12** have charge of **13** comprehension, understanding **14** administration **17** have authority over

commandant 7 captain **9** commander **12** chief officer

commandeer 4 take **5** seize, usurp **8** shanghai **11** appropriate, expropriate

commander 4 boss, head **5** chief, ruler **6** leader **7** manager **8** director **9** conductor

commanding 4 head **5** chief, grand, lofty **6** ruling, senior, strong **7** dynamic, leading, ranking, stately **8** forceful, gripping, imposing, powerful, striking, towering **9** arresting, directing, governing, important, prominent **10** compelling, dominating, impressive **11** controlling, significant **13** authoritative, distinguished, overshadowing

commandment
Hebrew: **7** mitsvah, mitzvah

comme il faut 6 proper **7** fitting **12** as it should be

commemorate 4 hail, mark **5** extol, honor **6** hallow, revere, salute **7** acclaim, glorify, observe **8** venerate **9** celebrate, solemnize **11** acknowledge, memorialize, pay homage to **12** pay tribute to

commence 5 begin, start **8** get going, initiate **10** get started, inaugurate, originated

commencement 4 dawn **5** birth, onset, start **6** outset **7** genesis, morning **9** beginning, first step, inception **10** graduation, initiation **11** origination **12** inauguration **13** graduation day **20** graduation ceremonies

commend 2 OK **4** back, give, laud **5** extol **6** commit, confer, convey, praise **7** acclaim, approve, consign, endorse, entrust, stand by, support **8** delegate, give over, hand over, pass over, relegate, transfer **13** speak highly of

commendable 6 worthy **7** notable **8** laudable **9** admirable, deserving, estimable, exemplary, honorable **10** creditable **11** meritorious **12** praiseworthy

commendation 5 honor **6** praise **7** support **8** approval **10** acceptance **11** acclamation, approbation

commendatory 8 admiring, praising **9** laudatory, praiseful **10** plauditory **13** complimentary **14** congratulatory

commensurate, commensurable 4 even, meet **5** equal **6** square **7** fitting **8** balanced, in accord, parallel, relative, suitable **10** comparable, compatible, consistent, equivalent **11** appropriate, in agreement **13** corresponding, proportionate **14** on a proper scale

comment 4 note, word **6** remark **7** clarify, discuss, explain, expound **8** expand on **9** assertion, criticism, elucidate, shed light, statement, talk about, touch upon, utterance **10** annotation, expression, reflection **11** elucidation, explanation, explication, observation **13** clarification **15** exemplification

commentary 6 review **8** critique, scholium, treatise **9** criticism **10** exposition **11** explanation, explication **12** dissertation **14** interpretation **16** explanatory essay

commentator 6 critic, writer **7** speaker **8** panelist, reporter, reviewer **9** columnist, explainer **10** newscaster **11** interpreter, news analyst

comment upon 7 clarify, clear up, explain **8** spell out **9** delineate, elucidate, explicate, interpret, make plain **10** illuminate, illustrate **14** throw light upon

commerce 5 trade **6** barter **7** trading, traffic **8** business, exchange, industry **12** mercantilism **16** buying and selling **god of: 6** Hermes **7** Mercury

commercial 2 ad **5** sales, trade **8** business **10** mercantile, sales pitch **12** profit-making **13** advertisement **16** buying-and-selling

commingle 3 mix **4** fuse **5** blend,

merge, unify **7** combine **10** amalgamate

commiserate 7 feel for **8** show pity **10** grieve with, lament with **13** express sorrow **14** sympathize with **15** share one's sorrow **17** have compassion for

commiseration 4 pity **8** sympathy **10** compassion, tenderness **13** fellow feeling

commission 3 act, bid, cut, fee **4** duty, hire, name, rank, role, task **5** board, doing, order, piece, power, proxy, trust **6** agency, assign, charge, direct, employ, engage, office **7** appoint, certify, charter, conduct, council, empower, license, mandate, mission, portion, rake-off, stipend, warrant **8** capacity, contract, delegate, dividend, document, exercise, function, position **9** acting out, allotment, allowance, authority, authorize, committal, committee **10** assignment, commitment, committing, delegation, deputation, entrusting, percentage, performing **11** appointment, carrying out, certificate, performance, transacting **12** officer's rank, perpetration **13** authorization, written orders **14** give the go-ahead **15** representatives **16** piece of the action **17** appointment papers, grant officer's rank

commissioner 5 envoy, trier **7** officer, pristaw **8** delegate, official **9** authority, commissar

commissioning 10 assignment, delegation **11** appointment, designation, entrustment **13** authorization

commit 2 do **3** act, put **4** bind, pull **5** enact, place **6** assign, decide, effect, engage, intern, pursue **7** confine, consign, deliver, deposit, entrust, execute, perform, pull off, resolve **8** carry out, give over, obligate, practice, transact, transfer **9** determine **10** make liable, perpetrate **13** participate in **16** institutionalize

commitment 3 vow **4** bond, word **5** stand **6** pledge **7** promise **8** decision, delivery, transfer, warranty **9** assurance, detention, guarantee, liability, restraint **10** assignment, giving over, internment, obligation, resolution **11** confinement, consignment, dispatching **12** imprisonment **13** determination, incarceration **14** responsibility **18** institutionalizing

commit oneself 3 act **7** resolve **8** dedicate, obligate **9** determine

committed 6 active, liable **8** confined, detained, interned **9** concerned, delivered, entrusted, obligated **10** interested, responsive **11** responsible **17** institutionalized

committee 4 body, jury **5** bench, board, group, junta, table **6** bureau, soviet **7** cabinet, council **9** gathering,

syndicate **10** assemblage **12** organization

commode 6 bureau, toilet **7** cabinet, dresser **9** washstand **14** chest of drawers

commodious 5 ample, large, roomy **8** spacious **9** capacious, uncramped **11** unconfining

commodity 4 ware **5** asset, goods, stock **6** staple **7** chattel, holding, product **8** property **9** advantage, belonging **10** possession **11** convenience, merchandise **14** article of trade **17** article of commerce

common 3 bad, low **4** base, lewd, mean, rude, vile **5** brash, cheap, crass, crude, gross, joint, lowly, minor, plain, stock **6** brazen, brutal, coarse, lesser, normal, old-hat, public, ribald, shared, simple, smutty, tawdry, vulgar **7** average, boorish, callous, general, ignoble, ill-bred, loutish, low-bred, obscene, obscure, popular, prosaic, regular, routine, settled, uncouth, unknown, worn-out **8** communal, everyday, familiar, frequent, homespun, impolite, informal, mediocre, middling, nameless, ordinary, plebeian, shameful, standard, workaday, worn thin **9** bourgeois, customary, deficient, household, low-minded, moth-eaten, obnoxious, offensive, pervasive, shameless, tasteless, unexalted, universal, unnoticed, unrefined, well-known **10** collective, colloquial, despicable, dime-a-dozen, inglorious, threadbare, unblushing, uncultured, unpolished, widespread **11** disgraceful, established, ill-mannered, insensitive, middle-class, oft-repeated, subordinate, traditional, unimportant, widely known, without rank **12** contemptible, conventional, disagreeable **13** garden-variety, insignificant **15** undistinguished

commoners 5 plebs **6** masses **8** plebians

common law
Latin: **13** lex non scripta

commonly 5 often **6** widely **7** as a rule, usually **8** normally, of course **9** generally, in general, most often, popularly, regularly, routinely **10** by and large, familiarly, frequently, habitually, informally, ordinarily, repeatedly **11** customarily **13** traditionally **14** by force of habit, conventionally, for the most part **15** in most instances **17** generally speaking

common people 5 demos, plebs **6** masses **8** populace **9** hoi polloi, plebeians **11** bourgeoisie

commonplace 3 old **4** dull **5** adage, banal, stale, trite, usual **6** cliche, old-hat, truism **7** bromide, general, humdrum, regular, routine, worn-out **8** banality, everyday, familiar, ordinary, standard, worn thin **9** customary, hackneyed, moth-eaten, platitude **10** pedestrian, threadbare, un original, widespread **11** oft-repeated, stereotyped, traditional **12** received idea, run-of-the-mill **13** unimaginative, uninteresting

commonplace book 9 anthology, gleanings, scrapbook

Common Sense
author: **11** Thomas Paine

common-sense 5 sound **8** everyday, sensible **9** mother wit, practical, pragmatic, realistic **10** no-nonsense **11** down-to-earth, levelheaded, serviceable, utilitarian **12** matter-of-fact

commonwealth 5 state **6** nation **8** republic
Latin: **10** res publica

commotion 3 ado **4** fuss, stir, to-do **5** furor **6** bustle, racket, ruckus, tumult, uproar **7** clatter, turmoil **9** agitation **10** excitement, hullabaloo **11** disturbance **12** perturbation

communal 5 joint **6** common, mutual, public, shared **9** community **10** collective

commune 3 gab, rap, yak **4** chat, chin, farm, talk, town **5** visit **6** babble, confer, gossip, parley, powwow **7** chatter, palaver, prattle **8** converse, schmooze **9** chew the fat, chew the rag **11** communicate, confabulate **14** shoot the breeze

communicable 8 catching **10** contagious, infectious **12** transferable **13** transmissible, transmittable

communicate 3 say **4** give, show, talk, tell **5** state, write **6** advise, convey, impart, notify, pass on, relate, reveal **7** declare, divulge, exhibit, mention, publish, signify **8** announce, converse, disclose, inform of, proclaim, transmit **9** apprise of, bring word, broadcast, make known, publicize **10** correspond

communication 4 news, note, wire **5** cable **6** letter, missal, report **7** liaison, message, missive, notices, rapport, writing **8** bulletin, dispatch, document, speaking, telegram **9** broadcast, cablegram, directive, statement **10** communique **11** declaration, information **12** conversation, intelligence, proclamation, radio message **13** telephone call **14** correspondence

communicative 4 open **5** frank **6** candid, chatty **7** voluble **8** friendly, outgoing, sociable **9** revealing, talkative **10** expressive, forthright, freespoken, loquacious, revelatory, unreserved **11** informative

communion, Communion 6 accord **7** concord, harmony, rapport, sharing **8** affinity, sympathy **9** agreement **12** the Eucharist **13** communication, contemplation

communique 4 note, wire **5** aviso, cable, flash **6** report, letter, notice **7** epistle, message, missive, release, telegram **8** bulletin, dispatch **9** directive, statement **10** memorandum **12** announcement, intelligence, notification **13** communication

Communist 3 red **6** soviet **7** comrade, marxist **8** Leninist **9** bolshevik, socialist **10** bolshevist **12** totalitarian

Communist Manifesto
author: **8** Karl Marx **15** Friedrich Engels

community 4 area, folk, town **5** arena, field, group, range, realm, scope **6** locale, people, public, sphere, suburb **7** quarter, society **8** affinity, district, environs, likeness, populace, province, sameness, vicinity **9** agreement, citizenry **10** population, similarity **11** environment, social group **12** commonwealth, neighborhood, surroundings

commute 4 ride, trip **5** alter **6** adjust, change, redeem, soften, switch, travel **7** convert, journey, replace, reverse **8** diminish, exchange, mitigate **9** alleviate, supersede, transform, transmute, transpose **10** substitute **11** transfigure **12** metamorphose, transmogrify

comodo
music: **9** leisurely

Comoros
other name: **26** lost pearls of the Indian Ocean
capital/largest city: **6** Moroni
others: **6** Bambao **7** Fomboni **8** Dzaoudzi **9** Mutsamudu **11** Mitsamiouli
monetary unit: **5** franc **7** centime
island: **6** Moheli **7** Anjouan, Mayotte **12** Grande Comoro
highest point: **7** Kartala **8** Karthala
sea: **6** Indian
physical feature:
  channel: **10** Mozambique
people: **4** Arab **5** Bantu, Malay **7** African **8** Malagasy
language: **6** Arabic, French **7** Swahili **8** Malagasy
religion: **5** Islam **13** Roman Catholic

compact 4 bond, cram, deal, pack, pact, snug, tidy **5** close, dense, press, small, stuff **6** little, treaty **7** bargain, crammed, pressed, squeeze, stuffed **8** alliance, compress, contract, covenant **9** agreement, clustered, concordat **10** compressed **11** arrangement, pack closely **12** concentrated **13** tightly packed, understanding

compactness 7 density **8** snugness **9** smallness **10** littleness **11** compression **13** concentration

companion 3 pal **4** chum, mate **5** buddy, crony **6** escort, friend, helper **7** comrade **9** assistant, associate, attendant

companionable 6 social **7** amiable, cordial **8** friendly, sociable **9** agreeable, congenial, convivial

companionate 4 warm **6** genial **7** cordial **8** amicable, friendly, platonic, suitable **9** accordant, agreeable, consonant, easygoing, nonsexual, spiritual, unfleshly **10** compatible, concordant, harmonious **11** nonphysical, passionless, warm-hearted **12** affectionate **13** companionable

companionship 4 pals **5** chums **7** buddies, company, friends **8** comrades **10** associates, companions, fellowship, friendship **11** camaraderie, comradeship, familiarity, sociability **17** close acquaintance, friendly relations

company 3 mob **4** band, firm, gang **5** bunch, group, guest, party **6** guests, outfit, people, throng **7** callers, concern, friends, society, visitor **8** assembly, comrades, presence, visitors **9** gathering, multitude, syndicate **10** assemblage, companions, fellowship, friendship **11** camaraderie, comradeship, corporation, sociability **12** conglomerate, congregation **13** companionship, establishment **15** business concern

comparable 4 like, up to **5** close, equal **6** akin to **7** similar **8** as good as, parallel **9** a match for, analogous **10** equivalent, on a par with, tantamount **11** approaching, approximate **12** commensurate, in a class with **13** commensurable

comparative 4 near **8** relative **11** approximate

compare 5 equal, liken, match **6** be up to, equate, relate **7** vie with **8** approach, contrast **9** correlate **11** compete with **12** be on a par with **13** hold a candle to **14** be in a class with **20** draw a parallel between

compare notes 6 confer **7** consult **8** talk over **13** exchange views

comparison 7 analogy, kinship **8** contrast, equality, likeness, parallel, relation **10** connection, similarity **11** correlation, resemblance **13** comparability

compartment 3 box, pew **4** brig, cell, crib, hold, hole, nook, room **5** berth, booth, cabin, crypt, niche, stall, vault **6** alcove, bunker, closet **7** chamber, cubicle, section **8** anteroom, roomette **9** cubbyhole **10** pigeonhole **11** antechamber

compass 5 bound, range, reach, scope, sweep **6** domain, extent **8** boundary, province **13** circumference

Compass, Mariner's Compass
constellation of: **5** Pyxis

Compasses, Pair
constellation of: **8** Circinus

compassion 4 pity **5** heart **7** empathy, feeling **8** humanity, sympathy **10** ten-

derness **13** commiseration, fellow feeling **17** tender-heartedness
Latin: **12** misericordia

compassionate 4 kind **6** humane **7** pitying **8** merciful **10** benevolent, charitable **11** kindhearted, sympathetic **13** tender-hearted

compatibility 6 accord **7** concord, harmony, rapport **8** affinity **9** agreement, unanimity **12** congeniality **14** like- mindedness

compatible 3 apt, fit **6** seemly **7** fitting **8** in accord, suitable **9** congenial, in harmony, in keeping **10** likeminded **11** appropriate

compel 4 make **5** drive, force **6** oblige **7** require **11** necessitate

compelled 4 must **5** bound, urged **6** driven, forced **7** coerced, obliged, pressed **8** commanded, dragooned, enforced, impelled, obsessed, pressured, required **11** constrained, overpowered

compelling 7 driving, dynamic **8** forceful **10** commanding **12** overwhelming

compel obedience to 5 force **6** coerce **7** enforce **8** carry out, insist on **10** administer

compendium 4 list **5** brief **6** apercu, digest, precis, survey **7** abstract, capsule, catalog, epitome, summary **8** syllabus, synopsis **9** catalogue **11** abridgement, compilation **12** condensation

compensate 3 pay **5** cover, repay **6** make up, offset, redeem, square **7** balance, pay back, redress **9** indemnify, reimburse **10** make amends, recompense, remunerate **14** counterbalance **15** make restitution

compensation 3 fee, pay **4** gain **5** wages **6** income, profit, return, reward, salary **7** payment, redress **8** benefits, earnings, gratuity **9** indemnity, repayment **10** recompense, settlement **11** restitution **12** remuneration, satisfaction **13** consideration, reimbursement

compete 3 vie **5** fight **6** battle, combat, oppose **7** contend, contest **8** be rivals **9** lock horns, match wits

competence 5 skill **7** ability, knowhow, mastery **8** ableness **9** expertise **10** capability, competency, expertness **11** proficiency

competent 3 fit **6** expert, versed **7** skilled, trained **8** skillful **9** efficient, practiced, qualified **10** dependable, proficient **11** experienced, responsible, trustworthy

competition 4 game **5** event, match, rival **7** contest, rivalry, tourney **8** conflict, opponent, struggle **9** contender **10** contention, opposition, tournament

competitive 8 fighting, opposing,

striving **9** combative **10** aggressive, contending

competitor 5 rival **7** fighter **8** opponent **9** adversary, contender **10** contestant, opposition

compilation 4 body **5** group **9** collating, garnering, gathering, mustering **10** assemblage, assembling, assortment, collecting, collection, compendium, marshaling **11** aggregating, aggregation, marshalling **12** accumulating, accumulation

compile 5 amass **6** garner, gather, heap up, muster **7** collate, collect, marshal **8** assemble **10** accumulate

complacent 4 smug **6** at ease **7** content **9** contented **10** self-secure, unbothered, untroubled **13** self-satisfied

complain 3 nag **4** beef, carp, kick, moan, pick **5** cavil, gripe, whine **6** grouch, grouse, squawk **7** grumble **9** bellyache, criticize, find fault **15** state a grievance

complaint 4 beef, kick **5** gripe **6** malady, squawk, tirade **7** ailment, illness, protest **8** debility, disorder, sickness **9** criticism, grievance, infirmity, objection **10** impairment **12** faultfinding **15** dissatisfaction

complaisance 7 pliancy **8** docility **10** affability, amiability, compliance **12** acquiescence

complaisant 4 warm **7** affable, amiable, cordial **8** friendly, gracious, obliging, pleasant, pleasing **9** agreeable, compliant, congenial, easygoing **10** solicitous **11** good-humored, good-natured

Compleat Angler, The
author: **11** Izaak Walton

complement 3 cap **5** crown, match, total, whole **7** balance, perfect **8** ensemble, entirety, parallel, round out **9** aggregate, companion **10** completion, consummate, full amount, full number, supplement **11** counterpart, rounding-out **12** consummation **14** required number

complementary 7 matched **8** integral, opposite **9** companion **10** additional, compatible, completing **11** correlative **12** interrelated, supplemental **13** correspondent, corresponding

complete 3 cap, end **4** full **5** crown, total, utter, whole **6** entire, finish, intact, settle, wrap up **7** achieve, execute, fulfill, perfect, perform, plenary, settled **8** absolute, achieved, carry out, conclude, executed, round out, thorough, unbroken **9** discharge, make whole, performed, polish off, terminate, undivided **10** accomplish, carried out, complement, conclusive, consummate, unabridged **11** consummated **12** accomplished

completed 4 done **5** ended, whole **6** closed, entire, filled **7** matured,

through **8** achieved, finished, realized **9** concluded, executed, fulfilled, perfected **10** terminated, wrapped up **11** consummated **12** accomplished

completeness 8 fullness, richness **9** wholeness **10** perfection **12** thoroughness

completion 3 end **5** close **6** ending, finish, windup **7** closing **9** finishing **10** concluding, conclusion, expiration **11** fulfillment, terminating, termination **12** consummation

complex 4 maze **5** mixed **6** knotty, system **7** network, tangled **8** compound, involved, manifold, multiple, puzzling **9** aggregate, composite, difficult, enigmatic, fixed idea, intricate, obsession **10** perplexing, variegated **11** bewildering, complicated **12** conglomerate, labyrinthian, labyrinthine, multifarious **13** preoccupation

complexion 3 hue **4** look, tone **5** color, guise, image, slant **6** aspect **7** outlook **8** coloring **9** character **10** appearance, coloration, impression **11** countenance, skin texture **12** pigmentation, skin coloring

complexity 6 puzzle **9** intricacy, obscurity **10** bafflement, involution, perplexity **11** crabbedness, elaboration, involvement **12** complication, entanglement **15** inextricability **17** unintelligibility **19** incomprehensibility

compliance 6 assent **7** pliancy **8** docility, giving in, meekness, yielding **9** deference, obedience, passivity **10** conforming, conformity, submission **12** acquiescence, complaisance **13** nonresistance

compliant 8 flexible, yielding **9** agreeable **10** submissive

complicate 4 knot **5** ravel, snarl **6** muddle, tangle **7** confuse, involve **8** confound, entangle **11** make complex **13** make difficult, make intricate

complicated 7 complex **8** involved **9** elaborate, intricate

complication 4 snag **5** hitch **7** dilemma, problem **8** drawback, handicap, obstacle, quandary **9** hindrance **10** difficulty, impediment, perplexity **11** aggravation, obstruction, predicament **12** disadvantage **14** stumbling block

complicity 8 abetment, intrigue, plotting, schemery, scheming **9** collusion, finagling **10** connivance, conspiracy **11** confederacy, contrivance, implication, involvement **12** entanglement

compliment 5 honor, kudos **6** homage, praise **7** tribute **8** flattery **9** adulation, laudation **11** acclamation **12** commendation **14** congratulation

complimentary 4 free **6** gratis **8** admiring, praising **9** adulatory, extolling, laudatory, panegyric, praiseful **10** flattering, gratuitous, plauditory **12** ap-

preciative, commendatory **13** without charge **14** congratulatory

compliments 4 best, laud **5** exalt, extol, toast **6** homage, praise, salute **7** applaud, commend, regards **8** respects **9** greetings **10** best wishes, good wishes **11** salutations **13** felicitations **15** congratulations

comply 3 bow **4** bend, meet, mind, obey **5** defer, yield **6** accede, adhere, follow, give in, submit **7** abide by, conform, consent, fulfill, observe, satisfy **9** acquiesce, surrender

component 4 item, part **5** piece **6** detail, member, module **7** element, modular, segment **8** material **9** composing, elemental, essential, intrinsic **10** elementary, ingredient, particular **11** constituent, fundamental **13** component part

component part 4 item, part **5** piece **6** detail, member **7** element **10** ingredient, particular **11** constituent, fundamental

comport 3 act **4** bear **5** carry **6** acquit, behave, deport **7** conduct

comportment 7 bearing, conduct **8** attitude, behavior, carriage, demeanor, presence **9** acquittal **10** appearance, deportment

comport oneself 3 act **6** behave **13** acquit oneself **14** conduct oneself

compose 4 calm, form, lull, make **5** frame, quell, quiet, relax, shape, write **6** create, devise, make up, pacify, settle, soothe **7** collect, fashion, placate **8** be part of, belong to, comprise, conceive, modulate **9** formulate **10** constitute

composed 4 calm, cool **5** quiet **6** at ease, placid, poised, sedate, serene, steady **8** peaceful, tranquil **9** collected, quiescent, unexcited, unruffled **10** controlled, cool-headed, restrained, unagitated, untroubled **11** level-headed, undisturbed, unemotional, unflappable, unperturbed **12** even-tempered **13** dispassionate, imperturbable **15** undemonstrative

composer 4 bard, poet **6** author, writer **7** creator **8** musician, producer **10** compositor, typesetter

composite 6 mosaic **7** blended **8** combined, compound **10** compounded

composition 4 form, opus, work **5** essay, etude, piece **6** design, layout, make-up, making **7** forming, framing, product, shaping **8** creating, creation, devising, exercise **9** framework, structure **10** concoction, fashioning, organizing, production **11** arrangement, combination, compilation, formulation, preparation **12** constitution, organization **13** configuration

compos mentis 4 sane **13** mentally sound

composure 4 calm, cool, ease **5** poise

6 aplomb **7** control, dignity **8** calmness, coolness, patience, serenity **9** sang-froid **10** equanimity **11** self-control **13** self-assurance, self-restraint **14** cool-headedness, self-possession, unexcitability, unflappability **15** level-headedness **16** even-temperedness, imperturbability

compound 3 mix **4** fuse, make **5** add to, alloy, blend, boost, mixed, union, unite **6** devise, fusion, mingle **7** amalgam, amplify, augment, blended, combine, complex, concoct, enlarge, magnify, mixture, prepare **8** combined, heighten, increase **9** composite, fabricate, formulate, reinforce **10** synthesize **11** combination, complicated, composition, incorporate, put together **12** conglomerate **14** conglomeration

comprehend 3 dig, get **5** catch, grasp, savvy **6** absorb, digest, fathom **7** make out **8** conceive, perceive **9** penetrate **10** appreciate, assimilate, understand

comprehensible 5 clear, plain **7** evident **8** apparent **11** unambiguous **12** intelligible

comprehension 5 grasp **7** insight **9** awareness **10** conception, perception **11** realization **12** acquaintance, appreciation, apprehension **13** consciousness, understanding

comprehensive 4 full **5** broad **7** copious, general, overall **8** complete, sweeping, thorough **9** expansive, extensive, universal **10** exhaustive, widespread **11** compendious **12** all-embracing, all-inclusive

compress 4 cram, pack **5** press **6** reduce, shrink **7** abridge, bandage, compact, curtail, plaster, shorten, squeeze **8** condense, dressing **10** abbreviate

compressed 5 dense **6** jammed, packed **7** crowded **8** squashed, squeezed **9** compacted **12** concentrated

compressed form 6 digest **7** summary **8** cake form, synopsis **10** shortening **11** abridgment, contraction, curtailment **12** abbreviation, condensation

compression 9 narrowing, squeezing, stricture, tightness **10** compaction, constraint **12** constriction

compressor 4 pump **7** presser, reducer **8** squeezer **9** compactor, condenser

comprise 4 form **6** make up **7** compose, contain, include **8** be made of **9** consist of **10** constitute **12** be composed of

compromise 4 risk **5** agree, truce **6** settle **7** balance, compact, imperil **8** endanger, undercut **9** agreement, discredit, embarrass, implicate, make a deal, prejudice **10** adjustment, jeopardize, settlement **11** arrangement,

come to terms, happy medium, make suspect, meet halfway **12** conciliation **13** accommodation, rapprochement **14** make vulnerable, strike a bargain **16** mutual concession **18** split the difference **21** come to an understanding
German: 9 Ausgleich

compromising 7 risking **8** settling **9** adjusting **10** bargaining **11** give and take, making a deal **12** embarrassing, jeopardizing **13** accommodating, coming to terms **14** meeting halfway

Compsognathus
 type: 8 dinosaur, theropod
 characteristic: 8 smallest
 location: 6 Europe **7** Bavaria
 period: 8 Jurassic

Compson, Quentin
 character in: 14 Absalom Absalom **18** The Sound and the Fury
 author: 8 Faulkner

Compson family
 characters in: 18 The Sound and the Fury
 member: 5 Benjy, Caddy, Jason **7** Candace, Quentin **8** Benjamin
 author: 8 Faulkner

compte rendu 6 record, report, review **7** account **15** account rendered

comptroller 7 auditor **9** treasurer **10** accountant, bookkeeper, controller

compulsion 5 force **6** demand, duress, urging **8** coercion, pressure **9** necessity **10** obligation **11** domineering, requirement

compulsive 6 driven, hooked **7** driving, fanatic **8** addicted, habitual **9** compelled, obsessive **10** compelling **14** unable to resist, uncontrollable

compulsory 7 binding **8** coercive, demanded, enforced, forcible, required **9** mandatory, requisite **10** compulsive, imperative, obligatory **11** unavoidable **12** prescriptive

compunction 5 demur, qualm, shame **6** regret, unease **7** anxiety, concern, remorse, scruple **9** misgiving **10** contrition **16** pang of conscience

computation 5 tally, total **8** figuring **9** numbering, reckoning **10** numeration **11** calculation, enumeration

compute 3 add **5** add up, sum up, tally, total **6** figure, reckon **7** count up, work out **9** ascertain, calculate, figure out

computer 5 adder **9** processor **10** calculator
 language: 3 Ada, APL **4** Java, LISP, HTML, LOGO **5** ALGOL, BASIC, COBOL **6** Pascal **7** FORTRAN
 term: 2 PC **3** bit, bug, CAD, CAM, CPU, DOS, FAQ, RAM, ROM web, www **4** boot, byte, chip, file, hack, icon, spam, Unix **5** CD-Rom, crash, debug, drive, input, modem, mouse, pixel, queue, virus **6** analog, backup, cursor, glitch, hacker, laptop, mem-

ory, online, output, readme, window **7** digital, network, offline, program **8** database, hardware, lightpen, printout, software, terminal **9** hypertext interface, mainframe **10** binary code, floppy disk **11** application, interactive, spreadsheet **12** minicomputer, World Wide Web **13** microcomputer, word processor **14** microprocessor *17 desktop publishing*

comrade 3 pal **4** ally, chum **5** buddy, crony **6** friend **7** partner **8** confrere, co-worker, helpmate, intimate **9** associate, colleague, companion, confidant **10** bosom buddy **11** confederate **12** collaborator **13** boon companion **Russian: 8** tovarich

comradeship 8 alliance **10** fellowship, friendship **11** association, camaraderie **13** companionship

comte 5 count

Comte Ory, Le
  also: 8 Count Ory
  opera by: 7 Rossini
  character: 13 Countess Adele

Comus
  author: 10 John Milton
  subtitle: 7 A Masque

Comus
  origin: 5 Roman
  god of: 7 revelry **8** drinking

con 3 gyp **4** anti, bilk, coax, fool, gull, hoax, lure, rook **5** cheat, cozen, felon, trick **6** delude **7** against, beguile, convict, defraud, mislead, swindle **8** hoodwink, jailbird, prisoner, yardbird **9** bamboozle

Conakry
  capital of: 6 Guinea

concatenation 4 link **5** union **6** hookup **7** joining, linking, reunion **8** coupling, junction **10** bracketing, confluence, connection **11** conjunction **12** interlinking **15** interconnection **16** interassociation **18** intercommunication

concave 6 hollow, sunken **8** indented **9** depressed **13** curving inward

conceal 4 hide, mask **5** cloak, cover **6** screen, shield **7** cover up, obscure, secrete **8** disguise **10** camouflage, keep secret

concealed 5 blind, doggo **6** covert, hidden, latent, masked, perdue, secret, veiled **7** cloaked, covered, obscure, unknown, wrapped **8** abstruse, shrouded, ulterior **9** disguised, incognito **11** clandestine

concealment 5 cover **6** hiding **7** hideout, masking **8** covering, hideaway **9** screening, secreting, secretion **10** covering up, under cover

concede 3 own **4** cede **5** admit, agree, allow, grant, yield **6** accept, give up, resign, tender **7** abandon, confess, deliver **8** hand over **9** acquiesce, recognize, surrender, vouchsafe **10** relinquish **11** acknowledge, be persuaded

conceit 3 ego **5** pride **6** vanity **7** ego trip, egotism **8** bragging, self-love **9** vainglory **10** self- esteem **12** boastfulness **14** self-importance

conceited 4 smug, vain **7** stuck-up **8** arrogant, boasting, bragging, puffed up **9** bombastic, overproud, strutting **11** egotistical, swellheaded **12** vainglorious **13** self-important

conceivable 8 credible, knowable, possible **9** thinkable **10** believable, imaginable, supposable **11** perceivable

conceive 4 form **5** frame, hatch, start **6** create, ideate, invent **7** concoct, dream up, imagine, produce, think of, think up **8** consider, contrive, envisage, envision, initiate **9** originate **10** comprehend, understand

concentrate 4 mass **5** amass, bunch, focus, hem in **6** center, gather, heap up, reduce **7** close in, cluster, pay heed, thicken **8** assemble, attend to, condense, converge, fasten on **10** accumulate, congregate **11** bring to bear **12** direct toward

concentrated 5 dense **7** crowded, focused, thought **8** centered **10** compressed

concentration 4 mass **5** focus **7** cluster **9** diligence, gathering, reduction **10** absorption, assemblage, collection, intentness, thickening **11** aggregation, boiling down, convergence, deep thought, engrossment **12** accumulation **13** concentrating, consolidation **14** centralization

concept 4 idea, view **5** image **6** belief, notion, theory **7** opinion, surmise, thought **9** postulate **10** conviction, hypothesis, impression **11** supposition

conception 4 idea **5** birth, image, start **6** notion **7** forming, genesis, inkling, picture **8** creating, devising, hatching **9** beginning, formation, imagining, inception, invention, launching **10** conceiving, concocting, initiation, perception **11** envisioning, formulation, originating **12** apprehension **13** fertilization, understanding **16** becoming pregnant

conceptual 8 abstract **9** visionary **11** conjectural, ideological, speculative, theoretical **12** experimental, hypothetical **15** impressionistic

concern 3 job **4** care, duty, firm, heed **5** chore, house, store, touch, worry **6** affair, affect, charge, matter, occupy, regard **7** anxiety, apply to, company, disturb, involve, mission, trouble **8** bear upon, business, distress, interest, relate to **9** attention, pertain to **10** disconcert, enterprise, solicitude **11** appertain to, corporation, disturbance, involvement, undertaking **12** apprehension **13** consideration, establishment **14** thoughtfulness

concerned 5 upset **6** active, caring,

uneasy **7** alarmed, anxious, engaged, fearful, worried **8** involved, troubled **9** attentive, committed, disturbed **10** disquieted, distressed, interested, solicitous **12** apprehensive **13** participating

concerning 2 of, on, re **3** for **4** as to, over, upon **5** about, anent **7** apropos **8** engaging, touching, worrying **9** affecting, involving, mattering, regarding **10** relating to, respecting

concert 5 union, unity **6** accord, settle **7** concord, harmony **8** teamwork **9** agreement, congruity, unanimity **10** accordance, complicity **11** association, cooperation **13** collaboration **14** correspondence **18** musical performance

concerted 5 joint **6** united **7** planned **8** by assent **10** agreed upon **11** cooperative, prearranged **12** premeditated **13** predetermined

concert hall 5 odeum **6** lyceum **7** theater **9** music hall **10** auditorium **12** symphony hall

concession 5 lease **6** assent **8** giving in, yielding **9** admission, franchise, privilege **10** adjustment, compromise, indulgence **12** acquiescence, modification **14** acknowledgment

Conch
  form: 7 trumpet
  made of: 5 shell
  owned by: 7 Tritons

Conchobar
  origin: 5 Irish
  king of: 6 Ulster
  nephew: 10 Cuchulainn

concierge 7 janitor **9** custodian **10** doorkeeper

conciliate 6 pacify **7** appease, placate **9** make peace, reconcile **11** accommodate

conciliation 11 appeasement, peacemaking **12** propitiation **13** accommodation **14** reconciliation

conciliatory 8 friendly **9** appeasing, pacifying, placatory **10** mollifying, reassuring **11** peacemaking, reconciling **13** accommodative

concise 5 brief, pithy, short, terse **7** compact **8** succinct **9** condensed **10** to the point **11** abbreviated

conciseness 7 brevity **9** terseness **11** compactness **12** condensation, succinctness

conclave 6 parley, powwow **7** council, meeting, session **8** assembly **10** conference, convention **11** convocation **13** secret council

conclude 3 end **4** halt, stop **5** close, infer, judge **6** decide, deduce, effect, finish, gather, reason, settle **7** arrange, resolve, surmise **8** break off, carry out, complete **9** determine, terminate **10** accomplish **11** bring to pass, discontinue **12** draw to a close

concluded 5 bound, ended, guess **6** closed, judged **7** decided, deduced, expired, settled, wound up **9** completed **10** culminated, determined, restrained, terminated

conclusion 3 end **5** close **6** finale, finish, result, upshot, windup **7** finding, outcome **8** decision, judgment **9** agreement, deduction, final part, inference, summation **10** completion, denouement, resolution, settlement, working out **11** arrangement, presumption, termination **13** determination

conclusive 5 clear **6** patent **7** certain, obvious **8** absolute, decisive, definite, manifest, palpable **9** clinching **10** compelling, convincing, undeniable **11** categorical, determining, inescapable, irrefutable **12** demonstrable, unanswerable **13** incontestable, unimpeachable **14** unquestionable **16** incontrovertible

concoct 3 mix **4** brew **5** frame, hatch **6** cook up, create, devise, invent, make up **7** think up **8** compound, contrive **9** fabricate, formulate

concoction 4 brew **5** blend **6** jumble, medley **7** mixture **8** compound, creation **9** invention, potpourri **11** contrivance, fabrication **14** conglomeration

concomitant 7 related **9** accessory, attendant, connected, corollary, secondary **10** additional **12** accompanying, contributing, supplemental **13** complementary

concord 5 amity, peace **6** accord **7** harmony **8** goodwill **9** agreement **10** friendship **11** amicability, cooperation **16** cordial relations **19** mutual understanding

concordance 5 index **6** accord **7** concord **9** agreement, consensus, unanimity **17** meeting of the minds

concordant 6 unison **7** calming **8** agreeing, unifying **9** assenting, consonant **10** concurrent, harmonious

concordat 4 pact **8** covenant **9** agreement

Concorde 3 jet, SST **10** supersonic airline **9** Air France **14** British Airways

Concordia
origin: **5** Roman
goddess of: **5** peace **7** harmony

concourse 7 conflux, joining, linkage, meeting **8** junction **9** amassment **10** assembling, concursion, confluence **11** aggregation, association, convergence **12** congregation, focalization **13** concentration **14** conglomeration **15** flowing together **16** flocking together

concrete 4 real **5** solid **6** cement **7** express, factual, precise **8** definite, distinct, explicit, material, specific, tangible **10** particular **11** fused stones, substantial **12** alloyed rocks

concupiscence 4 itch, lust **6** desire **7** craving, lechery, longing, passion **8** appetite, hot pants, lewdness, satyrism **9** horniness, lubricity, prurience, randiness **10** wantonness **11** goatishness, libertinism, lustfulness **12** sexual desire **13** lecherousness **14** lasciviousness, libidinousness

concur 5 agree, match, tally **6** square **7** conform **8** coincide, hold with **9** be uniform **10** be in accord, correspond **11** go along with **12** go hand in hand

concur in 7 approve **9** agree with **11** go along with

concurrence, concurrency 6 accord **7** concord, consent, harmony **8** approval **9** agreement, consensus, unanimity **10** acceptance, conformity **11** affirmation, coexistence, coincidence, conjuncture, cooperation, synchronism **12** acquiescence **13** collaboration, mutual consent **14** correspondence **15** working together **17** meeting of the minds **22** simultaneous occurrence

concurrent 5 at one **6** allied **7** aligned **8** agreeing, matching **9** congenial, congruous, consonant **10** coexisting, coincident, coinciding, compatible, harmonious **11** in agreement, sympathetic, synchronous **12** commensurate, contemporary, in accordance, simultaneous **13** correspondent, of the same mind **15** contemporaneous

concurring 8 agreeing **10** consenting **11** affirmative, in agreement, synchronous **12** coincidental, simultaneous **13** corresponding

concussion 3 jar **4** blow, bump **5** clash, shock **6** buffet, impact **7** shaking **8** pounding **9** agitation, collision **11** brain injury

condemn 4 damn, doom **5** decry **6** rebuke **7** censure **8** denounce, sentence **9** criticize, proscribe, reprehend **10** disapprove

condemnation 6 rebuke **7** censure, reproof **8** judgment, reproach, sentence **9** criticism **10** conviction, punishment **11** disapproval **12** denunciation, reprehension **14** disapprobation **20** pronouncement of guilt

condensation 6 digest **9** reduction **10** abridgment **13** shortened form **16** condensed version

condense 3 cut **4** trim **6** digest, reduce **7** abridge, compact, liquefy, shorten, thicken **8** boil down, compress, contract, pare down **10** abbreviate, bluepencil **11** concentrate, consolidate, precipitate

condensed form 6 digest, precis **7** summary **8** synopsis **10** shortening **11** abridgement, compression, contraction, curtailment **12** abbreviation

condescend 5 deign, stoop **6** submit, unbend **7** descend, disdain **9** patronize **10** look down on, talk down to **12**

come down a peg, lower oneself **13** humble oneself

condescending 7 high-hat **8** superior **10** disdainful **11** overbearing, patronizing

condescension 4 airs **7** disdain, hauteur, modesty **8** humility **9** deference, loftiness **10** humbleness **11** haughtiness **12** graciousness **13** selfabasement **14** self-effacement **19** patronizing attitude **20** assumption of equality **21** high-and-mighty attitude

condign 3 due **4** fair, just, meet **5** right **6** earned, proper, worthy **7** fitting, merited **8** deserved, suitable **9** warranted **11** appropriate

condiment 4 herb **5** sauce, spice **8** dressing, flavorer, seasoner **9** seasoning
kind: **3** bay **4** dill, mace, mint, sage, salt **5** caper, clove, curry, onion, thyme **6** catsup, garlic, ginger, nutmeg, pepper, pickle, relish **7** caraway, chutney, ketchup, mustard, parsley, oregano, paprika, pimento, tabasco, vinegar **8** cardamon, marjoram, turmeric **9** pimpernel **10** hell pepper, mayonnaise

condition 3 fit **4** term **5** adapt, equip, ready, shape, state, train **6** demand, fettle, malady, status, tone up **7** ailment, prepare, problem, proviso **8** accustom, position, standing **9** agreement, complaint, provision, requisite, situation **10** limitation, make used to, put in shape **11** arrangement, contingency, malfunction, reservation, restriction, stipulation **12** prerequisite **13** circumstances, qualification, state of health **14** state of affairs **15** physical fitness

conditional 7 limited **9** dependent, qualified, tentative **10** contingent, restricted **11** provisional, stipulative **16** with reservations

condolence 4 pity **6** solace **7** comfort **8** sympathy **10** compassion **11** consolation **13** commiseration

Condon, Richard
author of: **11** Winter Kills **18** Death of a Politician **22** The Manchurian Candidate

condonation 11 forgiveness, overlooking **12** disregarding **13** putting up with

condone 6 excuse, forget, ignore, pardon, wink at **7** absolve, forgive, justify, let pass **8** overlook **9** disregard, put up with

conduce 3 aid **4** help, lead, tend **5** bring, favor, guide **6** effect **7** advance, forward, further, promote **10** contribute

conducive 7 helpful **8** salutary **9** favorable, promotive **10** beneficial **11** expeditious **12** contributive, contributory, instrumental **19** calculated to produce **22** helpful in bringing about

conduct 3 act **4** bear, lead, rule, ways **5** carry, chair, deeds, enact, guide, pilot, steer, usher **6** action, attend, behave, convey, convoy, direct, escort, govern, manage, manner **7** carry on, comport, control, execute, marshal, operate, perform **8** behavior, carry out, dispatch, guidance, regulate, transact **9** accompany, direction, discharge, look after, supervise **10** administer, deportment, government, leadership, management **11** comportment, generalship, preside over, superintend, supervision **14** administration

conduct oneself 3 act **6** behave **13** acquit oneself **14** comport oneself

conductor 3 cad **5** guide **6** carman, escort, leader **7** cathode, channel, maestro, manager **8** aqueduct, batonist, cicerone, conveyor, director, operator, stickman, trainman **9** collector, drum major **10** impresario, supervisor **11** choirmaster, transmitter **13** concert master

conduit 4 duct, main, pipe, tube **5** canal, drain, flume, sewer **6** gutter, trough **7** channel, passage **8** aqueduct **11** watercourse

cone 5 bevel, shape, spire **6** bobbin, conoid, funnel **7** pyramid, volcano **8** pyramid
kind: 3 fir **4** pine **5** larch **7** conifer, retinal **8** ice cream

confabulate 4 chat, talk **6** confer, patter **7** chatter, discuss **8** chitchat, converse, talk idly

confabulation 4 chat, talk **8** chitchat **10** conference, discussion **12** conversation

confection 3 jam **5** candy **6** pastry **7** dessert **8** conserve, delicacy **9** preserves, sweetmeat **10** sugar candy

confectionery 5 candy **6** sweets **7** goodies, pasties **10** sugar candy, sweetmeats

confederacy, Confederacy 3 CSA **4** band, bloc **5** guild, union **6** fusion, league **7** combine, society **8** alliance, the South **9** coalition, syndicate **10** federation **11** association **13** confederation **14** Southern states **18** secessionist states **26** Confederate States of America
capital: 8 Richmond
leader: 14 Jefferson Davis
flag: 12 Stars and Bars
See also **8** Civil War

confederate 4 ally **5** merge, unite **6** cohort, helper **7** abettor, comrade, partner **8** coalesce, coworker **9** accessory, affiliate, associate, colleague, companion **10** accomplice, cooperator, join forces **11** consolidate, helping

hand **12** band together, collaborator, right hand man **17** fellow conspirator

Confederates
author: 14 Thomas Keneally

confederation 4 band **5** guild, union **6** fusion, league **7** combine, society **8** alliance **9** coalition, syndicate **10** federation **11** association, confederacy

confer 4 give **5** award **6** accord, parley **7** consult, discuss, palaver **8** converse **9** present to **10** bestow upon **12** compare notes, talk together **15** hold a conference **18** deliberate together

conference 4 talk **6** parley **7** council, meeting, seminar **8** conclave **9** symposium **10** convention, discussion **12** consultation, deliberation

conferment 4 gift **5** award **8** bestowal **12** presentation

confess 3 own **4** avow, sing **5** admit, own up **6** expose, reveal **7** declare, divulge, lay bare **8** blurt out, disclose **9** come clean, make known **11** acknowledge **12** bring to light **14** unbosom oneself **18** make a clean breast of

confessed 6 avowed **8** admitted **9** professed **12** self-declared **14** self-proclaimed

confession 6 avowal, shrift **9** admission **10** disclosure, divulgence, revelation **11** declaration **12** confessional **14** acknowledgment

Confessions of an English Opium Eater
author: 15 Thomas DeQuincey

Confessions of Nat Turner, The
author: 13 William Styron

confidant, confidante 5 crony **6** friend **8** intimate **10** bosom buddy **15** trusty companion

confide 6 impart, reveal **7** confess, divulge, lay bare, let in on, let know **8** disclose **9** make known **12** tell secretly **13** tell privately **14** unbosom oneself

confidence 4 grit, guts **5** faith, nerve, pluck, spunk, trust **6** belief, daring, mettle, secret, spirit **7** courage **8** audacity, boldness, credence, intimacy, reliance **9** certainty, certitude **10** conviction **11** intrepidity **12** self-reliance **13** private matter, self-assurance **14** faith in oneself **17** inside information

confidence man 5 cheat **6** con man **8** swindler **9** charlatan, trickster **10** mountebank

confident 4 bold, sure **5** cocky **6** daring, secure **7** assured, certain **8** cocksure, intrepid, positive **9** convinced, dauntless, expectant **10** optimistic **11** self-assured, self-reliant **13** sure of oneself

confidential 5 privy **6** secret **7** private **8** hush-hush **9** top- secret **10** classi-

fied **11** undisclosed **12** off-the-record **16** not to be disclosed

confidentially 7 sub rosa **8** in secret, secretly **9** privately **16** between ourselves **17** behind closed doors
French: 9 entre nous

confiding 6 trusty **7** reliant **8** trustful, trusting **9** confident **11** trustworthy

configuration 4 form **6** design, makeup **11** arrangement, composition

confine 3 pen, tie **4** bind, cage, hold, jail, keep **5** limit **6** coop up, govern, keep in, lock up, shut in, shut up **7** fence in, impound **8** imprison, regulate, restrain, restrict **9** sequester **11** incarcerate **13** hold in custody

confined 4 pent **5** close, tight **6** jailed, narrow **7** cramped **8** locked up **10** imprisoned, restricted

confinement 7 custody, lying in **9** cooping up, detention, restraint **10** childbirth, constraint, limitation, shutting in **11** parturition, restriction **12** accouchement, imprisonment **13** incarceration **15** circumscription

confines 4 edge **6** border, bounds, limits **7** margins **8** precinct **10** boundaries **13** circumference

confirm 5 prove **6** accept, clinch, ratify, uphold, verify **7** agree to, approve, bear out, certify, sustain **8** make firm, validate **9** authorize, establish **11** acknowledge, corroborate, make binding, make certain **12** authenticate, substantiate

confirmation 5 proof **6** assent **8** approval, sanction **9** agreement **10** acceptance, validation **11** affirmation, endorsement **12** ratification, verification **13** corroboration **14** authentication, substantiation

confirmed 3 set **5** fixed **7** chronic **8** hardened, verified **9** ingrained, validated **10** deep-rooted, deep-seated, inveterate, proven true **11** established **12** corroborated **13** authenticated, dyed-in-the-wool, substantiated

confiscate 4 take **5** seize **7** impound, possess, preempt **8** take over **9** sequester **10** commandeer **11** appropriate, expropriate

confiscation 7 seizure **10** impounding, preemption **13** appropriation, commandeering, expropriation

conflagration 4 fire **5** blaze **7** bonfire, inferno **8** conflict, fighting, wildfire **9** brush fire, firestorm, holocaust **10** forest fire, raging fire, wall of fire **11** sea of flames **12** sheet of flame

conflagrative 8 burnable **9** flammable, ignitable **10** combustive, incendiary **11** combustible, inflammable

conflict 4 fray **5** clash, fight, melee, set-to **6** action, battle, combat, fracas, oppose, strife, tussle **7** collide, discord, dissent, scuffle, warfare **8** disa-

gree, division, friction, skirmish, struggle, variance **9** encounter, hostility **10** antagonism, be contrary, difference, dissension, engagement **12** disagreement **13** confrontation **14** be inharmonious **15** be contradictory
Spanish: 9 mano a mano

conflicting 7 warring **8** clashing, opposing **10** ambivalent **13** contradictory

confluence 5 union **7** conflux, joining, linkage, meeting **8** junction, juncture **9** concourse, gathering **10** assembling, concursion **11** association, convergence **13** concentration **14** coming together **15** flowing together

conform 3 fit **4** obey **5** adapt **6** adjust, follow **8** adhere to, jibe with, submit to **9** agree with, reconcile, tally with **10** be guided by, comply with, fall in with, square with **11** acquiesce in **12** correspond to

conformable 8 amenable **9** agreeable, malleable **10** submissive **12** in compliance

conformance 7 harmony **9** agreement **10** accordance, compliance, conformity **13** compatibility

conformation 4 form **5** build, shape **6** figure **7** anatomy **9** formation, framework, structure **11** arrangement **13** configuration

conformist 12 well-adjusted **13** unadventurous

conformity 6 accord, assent **7** harmony **8** likeness **9** agreement, obedience **10** compliance, observance, similarity, submission, uniformity **11** resemblance **12** acquiescence **14** correspondence **15** conventionality

confound 5 amaze, mix up **6** baffle, puzzle, rattle **7** astound, confuse, fluster, mystify, nonplus, perplex, startle **8** astonish, bewilder, dumfound, surprise, unsettle **10** disconcert **11** flabbergast **16** strike with wonder, throw off the scent

confounded 8 confused **10** bewildered, nonplussed **11** dumbfounded **12** disconcerted

confraternity 4 body **5** guild, union **7** society **8** sodality **9** confrairy **11** association, brotherhood

confrere 3 pal **4** ally, chum **5** buddy **6** friend **7** brother, comrade, partner **9** associate, colleague

confront 4 dare, defy, face, meet **5** brave **8** cope with, face up to **9** challenge, encounter, withstand

confrontation 5 clash, run-in, set-to **6** battle, combat, debate **7** contest, dispute, face-off **8** conflict, showdown, skirmish **9** encounter **10** engagement, opposition **11** controversy **17** face-to-face meeting
Spanish: 9 mano a mano

Confucius
    author of: 10 Book of Odes **11** The Analects

confuse 5 addle, befog, mix up, stump **6** baffle, muddle, puzzle, rattle **7** fluster, mistake, mystify, nonplus, perplex **8** befuddle, bewilder, confound, unsettle **10** discompose, disconcert **11** make unclear **12** make baffling **14** make perplexing **17** throw into disorder

confused 5 fazed **6** addled **7** abashed, baffled, chaotic, jumbled, mixed-up, muddled, tangled **8** rambling **9** befuddled, illogical, perplexed, unsettled **10** bewildered, disjointed, distracted, incoherent, nonplussed **11** dumbfounded **12** disconcerted, disorganized **13** disharmonious, heterogeneous

confusing 7 addling **8** baffling, blinding, blurring, dizzying, jumbling, mixing up, muddling **9** deranging, mistaking **10** befuddling, disorderly, flustering, mystifying, perplexing, stupefying **11** bewildering, confounding **13** disconcerting, unintelligible

confusion 4 mess, riot **5** chaos, snarl **6** bedlam, hubbub, jumble, muddle, tangle, tumult, uproar **7** clutter, ferment, turmoil **8** disarray, disorder, madhouse, shambles, upheaval **9** abashment, commotion **10** bafflement, hodgepodge, hullabaloo, perplexity, puzzlement, untidiness **11** disturbance, pandemonium **12** bewilderment, discomposure, stupefaction **13** mystification **14** disarrangement, disconcertment **15** disorganization
French: 14 bouleversement

confutation 6 denial **7** counter **8** negation, rebuttal **10** refutation **13** contradiction

confute 4 deny **5** rebut **6** impugn, oppose, refute **7** counter, gainsay **10** contradict, controvert **12** be contrary to

congeal 3 set **4** clot, jell **6** curdle, freeze, harden **7** stiffen, thicken **8** solidify **9** coagulate **10** gelatinize

congenial 4 like **6** genial, social **7** affable, cordial, kindred, related, similar **8** agreeing, amenable, gracious, pleasant, pleasing, sociable **9** agreeable, convivial **10** compatible, consistent, harmonious, well-suited **11** sympathetic **13** companionable, corresponding
French: 9 en rapport
German: 9 gemutlich

congeniality 7 harmony, rapport **8** affinity **11** sociability **12** conviviality, friendliness, pleasantness **13** compatibility **14** like-mindedness

congenital 6 inborn, inbred, innate, native **7** natural **8** inherent **9** ingrained, inherited, intrinsic **10** hereditary

congested 6 filled, gorged, jammed, packed **7** crowded **9** saturated **11** overcrowded

congestion 3 jam, mob **4** mass **5** snarl **6** pile-up **8** crowding **10** bottleneck **11** obstruction **12** overcrowding

conglomerate 4 heap, mass, pile **5** amass, blend, stack **7** mixture **8** assemble **9** aggregate **10** accumulate, assemblage **12** accumulation **16** large corporation

conglomeration 6 jumble, medley **7** mixture **8** mishmash **9** aggregate, potpourri **10** assortment, collection, hodgepodge **11** aggregation, combination **13** agglomeration

Congo
    other name: 10 Moyen Congo **11** Middle Congo
    capital/largest city: 11 Brazzaville
    others: 3 Ewo **4** Boko **5** Epena, Kayes, Kelle, Okoyo, Sembe **6** Dongou, Komono, Makoua, Matadi, M'Binda, M'Vouti, Ouesso, Sibiti, Zanaga **7** Cabinda, Dolisie, Etoumbi, Gamboma, Kinkala, Loubomo, Loudima, Madingo, Mossaka, Souanke **8** Djambala, Imptondo, Kibangou, Madingou, Mindouli **9** Mossendjo **11** Fort- Rousset, Pointe-Noire **17** Mayombe Escarpment
    school: 13 Marien Ngoubai
    monetary unit: 5 franc **7** centime
    lake: 5 Mweru, Tumba **6** Albert, Nyanza, Upemba **7** Leopold **11** Stanley Pool
    highest point: 6 Leketi
    river: 3 Dja **4** Uele **5** Alima, Congo, Kasal, Kwilu, Lulua, Ngoko, Niari, Sanga, Swilu, Wamba, Zahir, Zaire **6** Kwango, Kwenge, Loange, Lobaye, Lomami, Ogooue, Ubangi **7** Aruwima, Kouilou, Lualaba, Luapula, N'Gounie **8** Itimbiri, Likouala, Lubilash
    sea: 8 Atlantic
    physical feature:
        plateau: 6 Bateke
    people: 3 Rua **4** Akka, Susa, Teke, Vili **5** Amadi, Bantu, Figot, Kongo, Mantu, Pygmy, Sanga, Warua, Zambi **6** Ababua, Bafyot, Bateke, Mbochi, Nzambi, Wabuma **7** Bacongo, Bakongo, Bangala, Batetla, Manyema **10** Binga Pygmy
        discoverer: 3 Cam
    language: 4 Susu **5** Bantu, Fiote **6** French, Kituba **7** Bangala, Lingala
    religion: 5 Islam **7** animism **10** Protestant **13** Roman Catholic
    place:
        church: 9 Saint Anne
        stadium: 5 Eboue
    feature:
        tree: 5 limba

congratulate 4 hail **6** salute **10** compliment, felicitate, wish one joy **11** rejoice with **18** give one's best wishes

28 wish many happy returns of the day

congratulations 6 salute **8** mazeltov **9** blessings, greetings **10** best wishes, good wishes **11** well-wishing **13** felicitations **24** many happy returns of the day

congregate 4 mass **5** amass, flock, swarm **6** gather, throng **7** cluster, collect **8** assemble **12** come together **13** crowd together

congregation 5 crowd, flock, group, horde, laity **6** parish, throng **8** assembly, audience, brethren **9** gathering, multitude **12** parishioners **16** church membership **17** religious assembly

congress, Congress 4 diet **6** caucus **7** council **8** assembly **9** delegates, gathering **10** conference, convention, parliament **11** legislature **14** federal council **15** discussion group, legislative body, national council, representatives **17** chamber of deputies

Congreve, William
  author of: 11 Love for Love **15** The Double-Dealer **16** The Mourning Bride, The Way of the World

congruity 7 harmony **9** agreement, coherence **10** consonance **11** consistency **12** congeniality **13** compatibility **14** correspondence **15** appropriateness

congruous 4 meet **6** seemly **7** apropos **8** becoming, relevant, suitable **9** congenial, consonant, in keeping **10** harmonious **11** appropriate, in agreement **13** corresponding

conifer
  means: 11 cone bearing
  order: 11 coniferales
  class: 10 gymnosperm
  kind: 3 fir, yew **4** pine **5** cedar, larch, pinal **6** ginkgo, pinale, spruce, torrey **7** cypress, hemlock, juniper, redwood, sequoia **8** softwood **9** evergreen

Coningsby
  author: 16 Benjamin Disraeli

conjectural 7 reputed **8** abstract, academic, doubtful, putative, supposed, surmised **11** inferential, speculative, theoretical **12** hypothetical **13** suppositional **14** supposititious

conjecture 4 idea, view **5** fancy, guess, infer, judge, think **6** augury, notion, reckon, suppose, surmise **7** imagine, opinion, presume, suppose, surmise **8** estimate, forecast, judgment, theorize **9** calculate, deduction, guesswork, inference, speculate, suspicion **10** assumption, guestimate, hypothesis, presuppose **11** guesstimate, hypothesize, speculation, supposition **13** shot in the dark

conjoin 4 join, knit, link **5** touch, unite **7** combine, connect, overlap **8** together **9** associate

conjoined 6 joined, linked, united **7**

knitted, meeting **8** combined, touching **9** connected **10** associated **11** overlapping **14** joined together

conjugal 6 wedded **7** marital, married, nuptial, spousal **9** connubial **11** matrimonial

conjugate 4 join, pair, yoke **5** mated, unite, yoked **6** couple, joined, paired, united **7** connect, coupled, related **9** connected **10** paronymous

conjunction 3 and, but **5** union **7** joining, meeting **11** association, coincidence, combination, concurrence

conjuration 5 charm, spell, trick **11** incantation

conjure 5 allay, charm, raise **6** invoke, summon **7** bewitch, command, enchant **8** call away, call upon **9** call forth **10** cast a spell, make appear **13** make disappear **15** practice sorcery

conjurer 6 wizard **8** magician

conk 3 die, hit **4** bean, blow, fail, head **5** decay, faint, sleep, stall **6** fungus, strike **7** bracket **8** knock out **9** break down **10** straighten

Conn, Katherine
  real name of: 13 Kitty Carlisle

connect 3 tie **4** join **5** hinge, merge, unite **6** attach, couple, relate **7** combine, compare **9** associate, correlate **14** fasten together

connected 4 tied **6** joined, merged, united **7** coupled **8** abutting, adjacent, attached, combined, touching **9** bordering, proximate **10** connecting, contiguous, juxtaposed **12** conterminous **16** fastened together

connected group 5 cycle **6** series **8** sequence **11** progression

Connecticut
  abbreviation: 2 CT **4** Conn
  nickname: 6 Nutmeg **7** Blue Law **9** Freestone **12** Constitution **18** Land of Steady Habits
  capital/largest city: 8 Hartford
  others: 4 Avon **6** Bethel, Canaan, Cos Cob, Darien, Hamden, Mystic, Sharon, Storrs **7** Ansonia, Bristol, Danbury, Enfield, Madison, Meriden, Milford, Niantic, Norwalk, Norwich, Shelton, Tolland, Windsor **8** Guilford, New Haven, Simsbury, Stamford, Westport **9** Greenwich, Naugatuck, New London, Stratford, Waterbury **10** Bridgeport, Manchester, New Britain, Torrington **11** Wallingford
  college: 4 Yale **7** Trinity **8** Hartford, St Joseph, Wesleyan **9** Fairfield **10** Bridgeport, Quinnipiac **11** Connecticut, Sacred Heart **12** U S Coast Guard
  feature: 10 Charter Oak
    museum: 8 PT Barnum
    seaport: 6 Mystic
    theater: 27 American Shakespeare Festival

  tribe: 6 Pequot **7** Mohegan, Niantic **10** Quinnipiac
  people: 8 PT Barnum **9** John Brown **10** Nathan Hale **11** Noah Webster **12** Thomas Hooker **19** Harriet Beecher Stowe
  lake: 10 Candlewood
  land rank: 11 forty-eighth
  mountain: 4 Bear **7** Taconic
    hills: 10 Berkshires
    highest point: 8 Frissell
  physical feature: 15 Long Island Sound
  river: 6 Thames **9** Naugatuck **10** Housatonic **11** Connecticut
  state admission: 5 fifth
  state bird: 5 robin
  state flower: 14 mountain laurel
  state motto: 30 He Who Transplanted Still Sustains
  state song: 12 Yankee Doodle
  state tree: 8 white oak

Connecticut Yankee in King Arthur's Court, A
  author: 9 Mark Twain
  character: 5 Sandy **6** Merlin **8** Alisande, Clarence **11** Morgan le Fay **12** Hello-Central **18** Sir Kay the Seneschal

connection 3 kin, tie **4** bond, link **5** nexus **6** family, friend **7** contact, coupler, kinfolk, kinsman, linkage **8** affinity, alliance, coupling, junction, kinsfolk, relation, relative **9** associate, connector, fastening **10** attachment, kith and kin **11** association, correlation **12** acquaintance, relationship **13** flesh and blood, interrelation

Connelly, Marc
  author of: 16 The Green Pastures
    with Frank Elser: 19 The Farmer Takes a Wife
    with George S Kaufman: 5 Dulcy **11** To the Ladies **17** Beggar on Horseback, Merton of the Movies

Connery, Sean
  real name: 13 Thomas Connery
  born: 8 Scotland **9** Edinburgh
  roles: 6 Marnie **7** The Rock **10** Highlander **14** Robin and Marian **15** The Untouchables **16** The Molly Maguires **20** The Great Train Robbery, The Man Who Would Be King **28** Darby O'Gill and the Little People **29** Indiana Jones and the Last Crusade
    James Bond: 4 Dr No **10** Goldfinger **11** Thunderball **16** You Only Live Twice **18** Diamonds Are Forever, From Russia with Love, Never Say Never Again

connivance 4 plot **5** cabal **6** design, scheme **8** intrigue **9** collusion **10** complicity, conspiracy **11** machination

connive 3 aid **4** abet, plan, plot **5** allow **6** wink at **7** collude **8** conspire **10** be a party to **13** be accessory to, lend oneself to **14** shut one's eyes to

17 be in collusion with, cooperate secretly

conniving 4 wily **6** artful, crafty **7** cunning **8** plotting, scheming **9** designing **10** intriguing **11** calculating

connoisseur 5 judge, maven, mavin **6** expert **7** epicure, gourmet **9** authority **11** cognoscente **17** person of good taste

Connolly, Maureen
nickname: **8** Little Mo
sport: **6** tennis

Connor, Dale
creator/artist of: **9** Mary Worth

connotation 5 drift **6** import, spirit **8** coloring **9** evocation, undertone **10** intimation, suggestion **11** implication, insinuation **12** significance

connote 5 imply **6** hint at **7** suggest **8** intimate **9** insinuate **11** bring to mind

connubial 6 wedded **7** marital, married, nuptial **8** conjugal **11** matrimonial

conquer 4 beat, best, drub, lick, rout, rule, trim, whip **5** floor, quell **6** defeat, humble, master, occupy, subdue, thrash **7** possess, win over **8** overcome, surmount, vanquish **9** overpower, rise above, subjugate **11** prevail over, triumph over **14** get the better of

conqueror 6 victor, winner **7** subduer **8** champion **10** subjugator, vanquisher **12** conquistador

conquest 3 fan **4** sway **5** lover **6** adorer, defeat **7** captive, mastery, triumph, victory, winning **8** adherent, follower, whip hand **9** upper hand **10** ascendancy, conquering, domination, overcoming **11** acquisition, subjugation **12** vanquishment **17** captured territory

Conrad, Joseph
real name: **29** Josef Teodor Konrad Korzeniowski
author of: **6** Chance **7** Lord Jim, Typhoon, Victory **8** Nostromo **13** Almayer's Folly **14** The Secret Agent **15** Heart of Darkness **16** Under Western Eyes **21** An Outcast of the Islands **23** The Nigger of the Narcissus

consanguine 4 akin **7** cognate, kindred, related **8** relative

consanguineous 3 kin **4** akin **7** kindred, related **9** connected **21** having a common ancestor

conscience 8 scruples **10** moral sense, principles **15** ethical feelings **20** sense of right and wrong

conscience-stricken 6 guilty **7** ashamed **8** contrite, penitent **9** chastened, regretful, repentant **10** remorseful **13** guilt-stricken

conscientious 5 exact **6** honest **7** careful, dutiful, ethical, upright **10**

fastidious, meticulous, particular, scrupulous **11** painstaking, responsible, trustworthy **12** conscionable **14** high-principled

conscious 5 aware **7** alert to, alive to, awake to, studied **8** noticing, sensible, sentient **9** cognizant, in the know, observing **10** calculated, deliberate, discerning, perceiving **12** apperceptive, premeditated **13** knowledgeable

consciousness 4 mind **6** senses **8** feelings, thoughts **9** awareness **10** cognizance, perception **11** discernment, sensibility

conscript 3 PFC **4** boot, hire, levy **5** draft **6** call up, employ, engage, enlist, enroll, induct, muster, rookie, seaman, select, take on **7** draftee, impress, private, recruit **8** enlistee, inductee, mobilize, register, selectee, shanghai **9** conscribe **11** buck private

consecrate 5 bless **6** hallow **7** glorify **8** sanctify **10** make sacred **11** immortalize **13** declare sacred

consecrated 4 holy **7** blessed **8** hallowed **10** sanctified

consecutive 6 in turn, serial **8** unbroken **10** continuous, sequential, successive **11** progressive **13** uninterrupted **19** following one another

consensus 6 accord **7** concord **9** unanimity **11** concurrence **13** common consent **14** general opinion **15** majority opinion **16** general agreement

consent 5 agree, allow, yield **6** accede, accept, accord, assent, concur, permit, ratify, submit **7** approve, concede, concord, confirm, endorse **8** approval, sanction **9** acquiesce, agreement **10** acceptance, fall in with, permission **11** concurrence, endorsement, willingness **12** acquiescence, confirmation, ratification

Consenting Adults
author: **12** Peter DeVries

consent to 2 OK **4** okay **6** permit **7** approve **8** accede to **10** concur with **11** acquiesce to, go along with **14** give the go-ahead

consequence 3 end **4** note **5** avail, fruit, issue, value, worth **6** import, moment, result, sequel, upshot **7** account, gravity, outcome **9** aftermath, influence, magnitude, outgrowth **10** importance, notability, prominence, usefulness **11** development, distinction, seriousness **12** significance

consequent 7 ensuing **8** eventual **9** following, resulting

consequential 7 crucial, epochal **8** historic **9** important, momentous **10** meaningful **11** significant

consequently 2 so **4** ergo, then **5** and so, hence, later **9** as a result, therefore **11** accordingly **12** subsequently

conservation 4 care **6** upkeep **9** hus-

bandry **10** careful use, protection **11** maintenance, safekeeping **12** preservation

conservative 5 quiet **6** square **7** old-line **8** cautious, moderate, undaring **9** right-wing **10** nonliberal, unchanging **11** reactionary, right-winger, traditional **13** unprogressive **15** middle-of-the-road **16** opponent of change **17** middle-of-the-roader **22** champion of the status quo

conservatoire 11 music school **12** conservatory, music academy

conservatory 7 nursery **8** hothouse **9** arboretum **10** glasshouse, greenhouse **11** music school **12** music academy **13** conservatoire

conserve 4 save **5** guard **7** care for, cut back, husband, use less **8** maintain, not waste, preserve **9** safeguard **12** use sparingly

consider 4 deem, hold, note **5** gauge, honor, judge, opine, study, think, weigh **6** ponder, regard, review **7** believe, examine, pay heed, respect **8** appraise, envision, hold to be, mull over **9** be aware of, reflect on **10** bear in mind, cogitate on, think about **11** contemplate **12** deliberate on **17** make allowances for **18** turn over in one's mind

considerable 4 tidy **5** ample, great, large **6** goodly **7** notable, sizable **8** not small **9** estimable, important **10** impressive, noteworthy, noticeable, of some size, remarkable **11** a good deal of, significant, substantial

considerably 5 amply **7** greatly, largely, notably, sizably **9** estimably **10** abundantly, noticeably, remarkably **13** significantly, substantially

considerate 4 kind **6** kindly **7** mindful **8** obliging **9** attentive, concerned **10** solicitous, thoughtful

consideration 4 heed, tact **5** cause, honor, point, study **6** factor, ground, motive, notice, reason, regard, review **7** concern, respect, thought **8** interest, judgment **9** attention **10** advisement, cogitation, inducement, kindliness, meditation, reflection, solicitude **11** examination **12** deliberation **13** contemplation **14** thoughtfulness **15** considerateness

consider closely 7 pay heed **11** concentrate **12** pay attention **13** put one's mind to **21** give one's full attention

considered 5 mused **6** deemed, heeded, judged, mulled **7** advised, express, honored, noticed, studied, thought, weighed, willful **8** believed, esteemed, looked on, pondered, regarded, supposed **9** reflected, respected, ruminated **10** deliberate, looked upon, thought out **11** deliberated, entertained, intentional **12** contemplated, premeditated, thought about

consign 5 remit **6** assign, commit, convey, remand **7** deliver, entrust **8** delegate, hand over, relegate, transfer **9** commend to **11** deposit with

consignment 8 delivery, shipment, transfer **10** assignment, committing, consigning, delegation, depositing, entrusting, relegation **11** handing over **12** goods for sale, goods shipped **19** goods sent on approval

consist 3 lie **6** reside **7** contain, include **10** be made up of **11** to be found in **13** be comprised of **14** to be composed of

consistency, consistence 4 body **5** unity **6** makeup **7** density, harmony, texture **8** firmness **9** agreement, coherence, congruity, stiffness, structure, thickness, viscosity **10** accordance, conformity, connection, uniformity **11** compactness, composition, persistence **12** construction, faithfulness, steady effort **13** compatibility, steadfastness **14** correspondence **16** uniform standards **19** constant performance, undeviating behavior

consistent 4 meet **6** steady **7** regular, unified **8** agreeing, constant, of a piece, suitable **9** congenial, congruous, consonant **10** compatible, harmonious, persistent, unchanging **11** in agreement, undeviating **13** correspondent **16** conforming to type

consolation 4 help **5** cheer **6** relief, solace, succor **7** comfort, support **8** easement, soothing, sympathy **10** condolence **11** alleviation, assuagement **13** encouragement

Consolation of Philosophy (De Consolatione Philosophiae)
author: 31 Anicius Manlius Severinus Boethius

console 4 calm, ease **5** cheer **6** soothe, succor **7** comfort, support, sustain **10** lament with, sympathize **11** condole with **13** express sorrow **15** commiserate with **18** express sympathy for

consolidate 4 fuse, join **5** merge, unify, unite **6** league **7** combine, fortify **8** coalesce, compress, condense, federate, make firm, make sure, solidify **9** integrate, make solid **10** amalgamate, centralize, strengthen **11** concentrate, incorporate **12** band together **13** bring together

consolidation 5 union **6** fusion, merger **8** alliance **9** coalition **11** unification **12** amalgamation **13** agglomeration **14** conglomeration

consomme 4 soup **5** broth **9** madrilene

consonance 5 amity, unity **6** accord, unison **7** concord, harmony, oneness **9** agreement, coherence, congruity, unanimity **10** accordance, conformity,

congruence, consonancy **11** concordance, consistency, homogeneity **13** compatibility **14** correspondence, likemindedness

consonant 8 in accord **9** agreeable, congruous, in harmony **10** concordant, consistent **11** in agreement

consort 3 mix **4** club, mate, wife **6** mingle, spouse **7** hang out, husband, pair off, partner **8** go around, sidekick **9** accompany, associate, companion, other half, pal around, rub elbows **10** fraternize **11** keep company

conspicuous 5 clear, great, overt, plain **6** famous, patent **7** eminent, evident, glaring, notable, obvious **8** distinct, flagrant, glorious, manifest, renowned, splendid, striking **9** arresting, brilliant, memorable, notorious, prominent, well-known **10** celebrated, easily seen, remarkable **11** illustrious, outstanding, standing out **13** distinguished, easily noticed, highly visible

conspicuousness 9 celebrity, flagrance, notoriety **10** prominence, visibility **11** obviousness **13** noticeability

conspiracy 4 plot **7** treason **8** intrigue, sedition **9** collusion, treachery **10** connivance, secret plan **11** machination **12** criminal plan **14** treasonous plan

conspirator 7 plotter, schemer, traitor **8** conniver **9** intriguer **10** subversive

conspire 5 unite **6** concur, scheme **7** collude, combine, connive **8** intrigue **9** cooperate, machinate **11** plot treason **12** work together

Constable, John
born: 7 England **12** East Bergholt
artwork: 10 The Haywain **12** Cloud Studies **14** Hadleigh Castle **39** Salisbury Cathedral from the Bishop's Grounds

constancy 6 fealty **7** loyalty **8** devotion **9** fixedness, stability **10** allegiance, permanence **12** faithfulness, immutability **13** dependability, invariability, steadfastness **15** trustworthiness **16** unchangeableness

constant 4 even, true **5** fixed, loyal **6** stable, steady, trusty **7** abiding, devoted, endless, eternal, regular, staunch, uniform **8** diligent, enduring, faithful, resolute, stalwart, unbroken, unvaried **9** ceaseless, continual, immutable, incessant, permanent, perpetual, steadfast, sustained, unceasing, unfailing **10** dependable, invariable, persistent, unchanging, unflagging, unswerving, unwavering **11** everlasting, never-ending, trustworthy, unalterable, undeviating, unrelenting **12** interminable, tried-and-true **13** uninterrupted

Constant Nymph, The
director: 14 Edmund Goulding
cast: 11 Alexis Smith **12** Charles

Boyer, Joan Fontaine **14** Brenda Marshall

constellation 4 host **5** group, rally **6** circle, galaxy, nebula, spiral, throng **7** cluster, company, pattern **9** gathering **10** assemblage, collection **12** spiral nebula **13** configuration **14** island universe
name: 3 Ara, Leo **4** Apus, Crux, Grus, Lynx, Lyra, Pavo, Vela **5** Aries, Cetus, Draco, Hydra, Indus, Lepus, Libra, Lupus, Mensa, Musca, Norma, Orion, Pyxis, Virgo **6** Antlia, Aquila, Auriga, Bootes, Caelum, Cancer, Carina, Corvus, Crater, Cygnus, Dorado, Fornax, Gemini, Hydrus, Octans, Pictor, Pisces, Puppis, Scutum, Taurus, Tucana, Volans **7** Cepheus, Columba, Lacerta, Pegasus, Perseus, Phoenix, Sagitta, Serpens, Sextans **8** Aquarius, Circinus, Equuleus, Eridanus, Hercules, Leo Minor, Scorpius, Sculptor **9** Andromeda, Centaurus, Delphinus, Monoceros, Ophiuchus, Reticulum, Ursa Major, Ursa Minor, Vulpecula **10** Canis Major, Canis Minor, Cassiopeia, Chamaeleon, Horologium, Triangulum **11** Capricornus, Sagittarius, Telescopium **12** Microscopium **13** Canes Venatici, Coma Berenices **14** Camelopardalis, Corona Borealis **15** Corona Australis, Piscis Austrinus **18** Triangulum Australe

consternation 5 alarm, panic, shock **6** dismay, fright, horror, terror **11** trepidation **12** apprehension

constituent 4 atom, part **5** piece, voter **6** factor, member **7** elective, element, essence **8** electing, integral, making up **9** component, formative, principal, supporter **10** appointing, ingredient

constitute 4 form, make, name **5** found, set up **6** create, invest, make up **7** appoint, compose, empower, produce **8** compound, delegate **9** authorize, establish, institute **10** commission

constitution 6 figure, health, make-up, mettle **7** charter, stamina, texture **8** physique, strength, vitality **9** basic laws, formation, structure **10** figuration **11** composition **12** construction **13** configuration **16** governing charter **17** physical condition **21** fundamental principles

constitutional 4 turn, walk **5** basic **6** inborn, ramble, stroll, vested **7** natural, organic **8** inherent, internal, physical **9** chartered, intrinsic **10** congenital **11** fundamental

Constitution State
nickname of: 11 Connecticut

constrain 4 curb, urge **5** check, crush, drive, force, quash **6** coerce, compel, oblige, subdue **7** confine, enforce, put down, repress, squelch **8** hold back, pressure, restrain, restrict, suppress **9** fight down, necessity, strong-arm **14** put the screws on

constrained 3 shy **5** timid **6** forced **7** bashful **8** reserved, reticent **9** compelled, diffident **10** restricted **11** embarrassed

constraint 5 force **6** duress **7** reserve **8** coercion, pressure **9** restraint **10** compulsion, diffidence, inhibition, obligation **11** enforcement **13** necessitation

constrict 4 bind **5** choke, cramp, pinch **6** shrink **7** squeeze **8** compress, contract, strangle **11** strangulate

constriction 7 binding, choking **8** cramping, pinching **9** narrowing, shrinking, squeezing, stricture, tightness **10** constraint, strangling **11** compression, contraction

construct 4 form, make **5** build, erect, frame, set up, shape **6** create, design, devise **7** arrange, fashion **8** organize **9** fabricate, formulate

construction 4 form, make **5** build, style **6** format **7** edifice, raising, reading, rearing, version **8** building, creation, erecting **9** rendition, structure **10** fashioning, production **11** composition, elucidation, explanation, explication, fabrication, manufacture **12** conformation, constructing **13** configuration **14** interpretation **15** putting together

constructive 5 handy **6** useful **7** helpful **8** valuable **9** practical **10** beneficial, productive **12** advantageous

construe 4 read, take **7** explain, make out **8** decipher **9** elucidate, figure out, interpret, translate **10** comprehend, understand

Consuelo
author: **10** George Sand

consul 5 envoy **8** emissary, minister **14** foreign officer, representative **15** diplomatic agent

Consul, The
opera by: **7** Menotti
character: **10** Magda Sorel

consult 6 confer, parley, regard **7** refer to **8** consider, talk over **9** inquire of **11** ask advice of, have an eye to **12** compare notes **13** exchange views **15** discuss together, seek counsel from, take into account **16** seek the opinion of **18** deliberate together

consultant 6 expert **7** adviser, advisor, counsel **9** discusser

consultation 7 council, hearing, meeting, palaver **9** interview **10** conference, discussion **12** deliberation

consumable 6 edible **7** eatable **10** comestible

consume 3 eat **4** gulp **5** drain, eat up, spend, use up, waste **6** absorb, devour, expend, guzzle, ravage **7** de-

plete, destroy, drink up, engross, exhaust **8** demolish, lay waste, squander **9** devastate, dissipate, swallow up **10** annihilate

consumed 4 used **5** burnt, drank, drunk, eaten, spent **6** used up, wasted **7** drained, outworn **8** absorbed, burned up, expended, perished **9** destroyed, engrossed, exhausted, swallowed **10** squandered **11** annihilated

consume greedily 5 eat up, snarf **6** devour, inhale **7** stuff in **8** bolt down, gobble up, gulp down, wolf down **12** swallow whole **13** eat ravenously **14** eat voraciously

consumer 4 user **5** buyer, drain **6** client, patron, waster **7** spender **8** customer **9** purchaser **10** dissipater, squanderer

consummate 2 do **5** sheer, total, utter **6** effect, finish **7** achieve, execute, fulfill, perfect, perform, realize, supreme **8** absolute, carry out, complete, finished, thorough **9** faultless **10** accomplish, bring about, undisputed **11** unmitigated **12** accomplished, unquestioned **13** unconditional **17** through-and-through

consummation 3 end **5** close **6** finish **9** execution **10** attainment, completion, conclusion **11** achievement, culmination, fulfillment, realization **14** accomplishment

consumption 2 TB **3** use **7** using up **9** consuming, depletion **10** exhaustion **11** expenditure, utilization **12** exploitation, tuberculosis

Consus
origin: **5** Roman
god of: **11** good counsel, horse racing
protector of: **5** grain
corresponds to: **3** Ops

contact 4 join, meet **5** reach, touch, union **7** connect, meeting **8** abutment, junction, touching **9** adjacency, get hold of **10** connection **11** association **13** communication **14** get in touch with **15** communicate with

contagion 7 disease **8** epidemic, outbreak **9** infection, spreading **13** contamination

contagious 8 catching **9** spreading **10** infectious, spreadable **12** communicable **13** transmittable

contain 4 curb, hold **5** check **6** embody, hold in **7** control, embrace, enclose, include, inhibit, involve, repress **8** hold back, keep back, restrain, suppress **11** accommodate, incorporate **12** keep the lid on **16** keep within bounds

container 3 bag, box, can, jar, vat **4** pail **6** barrel, bottle, bucket, carton, holder, vessel **10** receptacle

containment 7 control **9** restraint, retention

contaminate 4 foul, soil **5** dirty, spoil,

taint **6** befoul, blight, debase, defile, infect, poison **7** corrupt, pollute **8** besmirch **10** adulterate, make impure

contamination 5 filth **7** fouling, soiling **8** dirtying, foulness, impurity, spoiling **9** dirtiness, poisoning, polluting, pollution, putridity **10** defilement **11** uncleanness **12** adulteration

Conte, Richard
real name: **18** Nicholas Peter Conte
born: **12** Jersey City NJ
roles: **8** Barabbas **13** A Bell for Adano **24** The Greatest Story Ever Told

contemplate 4 note, plan, scan **5** weigh **6** expect, gaze at, intend, ponder, regard, survey **7** examine, imagine, inspect, observe, project, stare at, think of **8** aspire to, envision, mull over, ruminate **9** muse about **10** anticipate, cogitate on, have in view, meditate on, think about **11** reflect upon **12** deliberate on **13** consider fully, look at fixedly, look forward to **14** speculate about **15** view attentively

contemplation 5 study **6** gazing, musing, seeing, survey **7** looking, reverie, thought, viewing **8** scanning, thinking **9** pondering **10** cogitation, inspection, meditation, reflection, rumination **11** examination, observation **12** deliberation **13** consideration

contemplative 6 musing **7** pensive **8** studious **9** engrossed **10** cogitative, meditative, reflective, ruminating, thoughtful **11** speculative **13** introspective, lost in thought

contemporaneous 6 coeval **10** coexistent, coincident, concurrent **11** synchronous **12** contemporary, simultaneous

contemporary 3 new **4** late **6** modern, recent, with-it **7** current **8** advanced, brand-new, up-to-date **10** coexistent, coincident, concurrent, newfangled, present-day **11** ultramodern **12** simultaneous **13** of the same time, up-to-the-minute **15** contemporaneous

contempt 4 hate **5** scorn, shame **6** hatred **7** disdain, disgust **8** aversion, derision, disfavor, disgrace, dishonor, distaste, ignominy, loathing, ridicule **9** antipathy, disregard, disrepute, revulsion **10** abhorrence, repugnance **11** detestation, humiliation

contemptible 3 low **4** base, mean, vile **5** cheap **6** abject, paltry, shabby **8** shameful, unworthy, wretched **9** miserable, repugnant, revolting **10** despicable, detestable, disgusting **11** ignominious

contemptuous 6 lordly **7** haughty, pompous **8** arrogant, derisive, insolent, scornful, snobbish **10** disdainful **12** supercilious **13** condescending, disrespectful

contemptuousness 5 scorn 7 disdain 8 contempt, rudeness 9 arrogance, insolence

contend 3 vie, war 4 aver, avow, hold, spar 5 argue, claim, clash, fight 6 allege, assert, battle, combat, debate, insist, jostle, strive, tussle 7 compete, contest, declare, dispute, grapple, quarrel, wrestle 8 be a rival, maintain, propound, skirmish, struggle 10 put forward

content 4 area, core, gist, load, size, text 5 cheer, happy, heart, ideas, peace 6 at ease, at rest, matter, please, serene, thesis, volume 7 appease, comfort, essence, gratify, insides, meaning, pleased, satisfy, suffice, unmoved 8 capacity, make easy, pleasure, serenity, thoughts 9 contented, gratified, happiness, satisfied, set at ease, substance 10 complacent, untroubled 11 comfortable, contentment, peace of mind, unconcerned 12 satisfaction 13 gratification

contented 5 happy 6 at ease, serene 7 at peace, content, pleased 9 gratified, satisfied 11 comfortable

contentedness 4 ease 5 peace 7 comfort, content 8 pleasure, serenity 9 happiness 11 contentment 12 satisfaction 13 gratification

contention 5 clash, fight 6 battle, combat, strife 7 contest, discord, dispute, rivalry 8 argument, conflict, disunity, fighting, friction, skirmish, struggle, variance 9 assertion, encounter, wrangling 10 dissension, quarreling 11 competition, discordance 12 disagreement 13 confrontation

contentious 5 angry, cross 7 bateful, scrappy 8 captious 9 bellicose 10 pugnacious 11 belligerent, competitive, quarrelsome 12 cantankerous, disputatious 13 argumentative, controversial

contentment 4 ease 5 peace 7 comfort, content 8 pleasure, serenity 9 happiness 12 satisfaction 13 contentedness, gratification

conterminous 8 abutting, adjacent, touching 9 bordering 11 right beside 14 contiguous with

contest 3 war 4 bout, game 5 fight, match 6 battle, combat, debate, oppose, vie for 7 dispute, rivalry, tourney 8 conflict, fight for, object to, struggle 9 battle for, challenge, combat for, encounter 10 compete for, contend for, controvert, engagement, tournament 11 competition, struggle for 12 argue against 14 call in question

contestant 5 rival 6 player 7 entrant, fighter 8 competer, prospect 9 combatant, contender 10 challenger, competitor

context 6 milieu 7 climate, meaning, setting 8 ambience 9 framework, precincts, situation 10 atmosphere, background, conditions, connection 11 environment 12 relationship, surroundings 13 circumstances 16 frame of reference

contiguous 5 close, handy 6 nearby 7 close-by, tangent 8 abutting, adjacent, next-door, touching 9 adjoining, bordering, in contact 10 juxtaposed 11 neighboring 12 conterminous

continence 6 purity 8 chastity, sobriety 10 abstinence, moderation, temperance 11 forbearance 13 self-restraint

continent 4 Asia, pure 6 Africa, chaste, Europe 7 Eurasia 8 celibate, land mass, mainland, virginal 9 abstinent, Australia, temperate 10 abstemious, Antarctica 12 North America, South America

contingency 7 urgency 8 accident 9 emergency, extremity 10 likelihood 11 possibility, predicament 15 unforeseen event

contingent 9 dependent, subject to 11 conditioned 12 controlled by

continual 7 endless, eternal 8 constant, frequent, habitual, unbroken, unending 9 ceaseless, incessant, perennial, perpetual, recurring, unceasing 10 continuous, persistent 11 everlasting, never-ending, oft-repeated, unremitting 12 interminable 13 uninterrupted

continually 3 aye 4 ever 6 always, steady 7 endless, eternal, forever, on and on 8 steadily 9 recurring 10 constantly, frequently, repeatedly

continuance 4 stay, term 6 extent, period 7 lasting 8 duration 9 extension 10 continuing, permanence 11 adjournment, persistence, protraction 12 continuation, perseverance, prolongation

continuation 6 sequel 8 addition, sequence 9 extension 10 continuing, supplement 11 continuance, protraction 12 prolongation

continue 4 go on, last, stay 5 abide 6 drag on, endure, extend, keep on, keep up, remain, resume, stay on 7 carry on, persist, proceed 9 persevere

continued 6 kept on, kept up, lasted, went on 7 endured 8 extended 9 carried on, persisted, proceeded, prolonged 10 persevered, protracted

continuing 6 steady 7 abiding, eternal, ongoing 8 constant, enduring, extended, unbroken, unending 9 ceaseless, incessant, perpetual, prolonged 10 dragged out, persistent, protracted 11 persevering, unremitting 12 interminable 13 uninterrupted

continuity 4 flow 5 chain 9 continuum 10 succession 11 continuance, progression 12 continuation

continuous 6 linked, steady 7 endless, eternal, lasting 8 constant, enduring, unbroken 9 ceaseless, connected, continual, extensive, incessant, perpetual, prolonged, unceasing 10 continuing, persistent, protracted, successive 11 consecutive, everlasting, persevering, progressive, unremitting 12 interminable 13 uninterrupted

continuum 4 flow 5 chain 8 sequence 10 continuity, succession 11 continuance, progression 12 continuation

contort 4 bend, warp 5 twist 6 deform 7 distort 11 be misshapen

contorted 4 bent 7 crooked, twisted 8 deformed 9 distorted

contortion 7 bending 8 twisting 10 distortion 11 crookedness

contour 4 form 5 lines, shape 6 figure 7 outline, profile 9 silhouette 11 physiognomy

contraband 11 bootlegging 13 smuggled goods 14 illegal exports, illegal imports 15 unlicensed goods 17 black-marketeering 18 prohibited articles 19 unlawful trafficking

contract 3 get 4 pact, take 5 agree, incur 6 absorb, assume, narrow, pledge, reduce, shrink, treaty 7 acquire, compact, develop, dwindle, promise, shorten, tighten 8 compress, condense, covenant, engender 9 constrict, enter into, negotiate, undertake 11 arrangement, come to terms 12 draw together, make a bargain 13 become smaller, legal document 15 sign an agreement 16 written agreement

contracted form 6 digest 7 summary 8 synopsis 9 short form 11 abridgement, compression 12 abbreviation, condensation

contraction 8 decrease 9 drawing in, lessening, narrowing, reduction, shrinkage 10 shortening, shriveling, tightening 11 compression 12 abbreviation, condensation, constriction

contradict 4 deny 5 belie, rebut 6 impugn, oppose, refute 7 confute, counter, dispute, gainsay 8 disprove 10 controvert 12 be contrary to, disagree with

contradiction 6 denial 7 counter 8 negation, rebuttal 10 refutation 11 confutation 12 disagreement

contradictory 8 contrary, opposing 10 discrepant, dissenting, refutatory 11 conflicting, disagreeing 12 antithetical, inconsistent 14 countervailing, irreconcilable

contradistinction 8 contrast 10 difference 13 dissimilarity

contraption 6 device, gadget 9 apparatus, invention 11 contrivance

contrariety 9 deviation 10 difference, divergence 13 contradiction

contrary 5 balky 6 ornery 7 adverse,

counter, froward, hostile, opposed, wayward, willful **8** converse, inimical, opposite, stubborn, untoward **9** disparate, obstinate, unfitting **10** at variance, discordant, headstrong, refractory, unsuitable **11** conflicting, disagreeing, intractable, unfavorable **12** antagonistic, antithetical, disagreeable, inauspicious, incompatible, recalcitrant, unpropitious **13** contradictory **15** at cross purposes, unaccommodating

contrast 6 depart, differ **7** deviate, diverge **8** variance **9** disparity **10** comparison, difference, divergence, unlikeness **11** distinction **12** disagree with **13** differentiate, dissimilarity **15** differentiation, set in opposition

contrasting 8 clashing, dividing, opposing **9** comparing, differing **10** discordant, juxtaposed **14** distinguishing **15** differentiating

contravene 4 deny **5** annul, fight, spurn **6** abjure, breach, combat, disown, negate, offend, oppose, reject, resist **7** disobey, exclude, gainsay, infract, nullify, violate **8** abrogate, disclaim, overstep **9** overreach, repudiate **10** act against, contradict, infringe on, transgress **12** encroach upon **15** trespass against

contretemps 4 spat **5** clash, set-to **7** dispute, quarrel **8** argument, squabble **10** difference, falling out **12** disagreement **18** embarrassing mishap

contribute 4 give **5** endow, grant **6** bestow, confer, donate, lead to **7** advance, forward, hand out, present **9** bear a part, influence **11** have a hand in **13** be conducive to **14** help bring about

contribution 4 alms, gift **5** grant **7** charity, subsidy **8** bestowal, donation, offering **9** endowment **11** benefaction **12** dispensation

contributive 8 valuable **9** favorable **10** beneficial

contributory 9 accessory, ancillary, auxiliary **13** supplementary

contrite 6 rueful **7** humbled **8** penitent **9** chastened, regretful, repentant, sorrowful **10** apologetic, remorseful **18** conscience-stricken

contrition 6 regret **7** penance, remorse **9** atonement, penitence **10** repentance **11** compunction **12** self-reproach **18** qualms of conscience

contrivance 4 plan, plot, tool **5** gizmo, trick **6** design, device, doodad, gadget **7** machine, measure **8** artifice, intrigue **9** apparatus, implement, invention, mechanism, stratagem **10** instrument **11** contraption, machination, thingamajig **12** Rube Goldberg

contrive 4 plan, plot **6** create, design, devise, invent, manage, scheme **7**

concoct **8** maneuver **9** improvise **11** devise a plan **17** effect by stratagem

contrived 7 labored, studied **8** mannered **9** unnatural **10** artificial

contriver 7 creator, deviser **8** designer, inventor **9** architect

control 4 curb, rule, sway **5** brake, steer **6** bridle, charge, govern, manage, master, subdue **7** command, contain, mastery, repress **8** dominate, dominion, regulate, restrain, restrict **9** authority, direction, reign over, restraint, supervise **10** domination, management, manipulate, regulation **11** superintend, supervision, suppressant **12** have charge of, jurisdiction

controlled 5 ruled **6** curbed, steady, swayed **7** checked, managed, powered, servile, subdued **8** directed, governed, held back, kept down, reserved, verified **9** commanded, contained, dominated, moderated, regulated, repressed **10** authorized, regimented, restrained, supervised **11** manipulated

controlling 6 ruling **8** dominant **9** governing **10** commanding **11** influencing, predominant **13** predominating

controversial 7 at issue **8** arguable **9** debatable, polemical **10** disputable **12** questionable **13** causing debate **15** widely discussed **16** open to discussion

controversy 6 debate **7** dispute, quarrel, wrangle **8** argument, squabble **10** contention, discussion, dissension **11** altercation **12** disagreement

controvert 4 deny **5** belie, rebut **6** negate, oppose, refute **7** confute, dispute, gainsay, protest **8** confound, disprove, question **9** challenge, disaffirm **10** contradict, contravene, invalidate **12** give the lie to

contumacious 6 unruly **7** froward **8** contrary, factious, insolent, mutinous, perverse **9** fractious, seditious **10** headstrong, rebellious, refractory **11** disobedient, intractable **12** ungovernable, unmanageable **13** disrespectful, insubordinate

contumely 5 abuse, insult, scorn **7** disdain, obloquy **8** contempt, diatribe, reproach, rudeness **9** arrogance, insolence, invective, pomposity **10** opprobrium, scurrility **11** brusqueness, haughtiness **12** billingsgate, vituperation **15** overbearingness

contusion 4 hurt, mark, sore **5** mouse **6** bruise, injury, shiner **7** blemish **8** abrasion, black eye **9** black mark **13** discoloration **16** black-and-blue mark

conundrum 6 poser, rebus **7** enigma, puzzle, riddle **7** arcanum, mystery, paradox, problem, puzzler, stopper, stumper **11** brain-teaser **13** Chinese puzzle

convalesce 4 mend **5** rally **6** revive **7** improve, recover, restore **8** progress **9** get better **10** recuperate

convalescence 7 recruit **8** recovery **11** restoration **12** recuperation **14** return to health

convene 6 gather, muster, summon **7** collect, convoke, round up **8** assemble **12** call together, come together, hold a session **13** bring together

convenience 3 use **4** ease **6** chance **7** benefit, comfort, service, utility **8** facility, pleasure **9** appliance, enjoyment, handiness, work saver **10** usefulness **11** opportunity **12** availability, satisfaction, suitable time **13** accessibility, accommodation

convenient 5 handy **6** at hand, nearby, suited, useful **7** adapted, helpful **8** suitable **9** easy to use **10** beneficial **11** serviceable **12** advantageous **16** easily accessible

convent 7 nunnery **8** cloister **13** society of nuns

convention 4 code **6** caucus, custom **7** meeting, precept **8** assembly, conclave, congress, practice, propriety, protocol, standard **9** formality, gathering **10** conference, social rule **11** convocation

conventional 5 usual **6** common, normal, proper **7** regular, routine **8** accepted, orthodox, standard **9** customary **11** traditional

converge 4 meet **5** focus **8** approach **11** concentrate **12** come together **13** bring together

convergence 6 accord **8** junction **9** congruity **10** confluence **12** meeting place **14** correspondence

conversant 4 up on **5** aware **6** au fait **7** erudite, privy to, skilled, tutored **8** familiar, informed, sensible, sentient **9** au courant, cognizant, practiced **10** acquainted, proficient **12** well-informed **13** knowledgeable

conversation 3 rap **4** chat, talk **7** gabfest, palaver **8** chit-chat, dialogue **9** discourse, tete-a-tete **11** bull session **13** confabulation
Italian: **13** conversazione

Conversation, The
director: **18** Francis Ford Coppola
cast: **10** John Cazale **11** Gene Hackman **13** Allen Garfield

conversational 6 casual, chatty **8** everyday, informal **9** idiomatic **10** colloquial, vernacular

conversazione 12 conversation

converse 3 gab, jaw, rap **4** chat, chin, talk **7** palaver, reverse **8** chitchat, contrary, opposite **10** antithesis, chew the fat, chew the rag **11** confabulate **13** speak together **14** shoot the breeze

conversely 12 contrariwise **14** antithetically, on the other hand

conversion 6 change 10 changeover 12 modification 13 change of heart, metamorphosis, transmutation 14 transformation 15 change in beliefs, transfiguration 16 change of religion

convert 4 turn 6 change, modify, novice 8 neophyte 9 proselyte, transform 11 proselytize

convex 7 bulging, rounded 11 protuberant 13 curved outward

convey 4 bear, cede, deed, give, move, tell, will 5 bring, carry, grant, leave 6 impart, relate, reveal 7 conduct, consign, deliver, divulge 8 bequeath, disclose, dispatch, transfer, transmit 9 confide to, make known, transport 11 communicate

conveyance 3 bus, car, rig, van 4 cart 5 buggy, truck, wagon 7 vehicle 8 carriage, carrying, movement, transfer 9 conveying, transport 12 transmission 14 transportation

convict 3 con 4 doom 5 felon 7 condemn 8 jailbird, prisoner, yardbird 10 find guilty 11 prove guilty 13 declare guilty

conviction 4 view, zeal 5 ardor, creed, dogma, faith, fever, tenet 6 belief, fervor 7 opinion 8 doctrine, judgment, position 9 assurance, certainty, certitude, intensity, principle, viewpoint 10 persuasion 11 earnestness 13 steadfastness

convince 4 sway 6 assure 7 satisfy, win over 8 persuade 9 influence 11 bring around, prevail upon

convincing 5 sound, valid 6 cogent, potent 7 evident 8 assuring, forceful, powerful 9 plausible 10 persuading, persuasive, satisfying

convivial 5 merry 6 genial, jovial 7 affable, festive 8 friendly, sociable 9 agreeable, fun-loving 10 gregarious 13 companionable

convocation 6 caucus, muster, roster 7 council, meeting, roundup 8 assembly, conclave, congress 9 gathering 10 conference, convention 11 ingathering

convoke 4 meet, open 6 gather, muster 8 assemble, converse 11 call to order 12 call together

convolute 4 coil, wave, wavy, wind 5 twirl, twist 6 coiled, rolled, spiral, tangle 7 contort, sinuous, twisted 8 involved, spiraled 9 intricate 11 complicated 12 turn and twist

convolution 4 coil, maze 5 twist 7 coiling, winding 8 twisting 9 labyrinth, sinuosity 10 contortion, undulation 11 sinuousness 12 tortuousness

convoy 5 fleet, usher 6 column, escort 7 conduct 9 accompany, formation, safeguard 10 armed guard, protection

convulse 4 rock, stir 5 laugh, shake, spasm, wring 6 excite 7 agitate, disturb, perturb, trouble 8 double up

convulsion 3 fit 5 spasm 6 tumult 7 seizure 8 outburst, paroxysm 9 agitation, commotion 10 contortion 11 disturbance

convulsive 6 fitful 7 hurtful, rending, shaking 8 exciting, stirring 9 agitating, epileptic, spasmodic, troubling 10 disturbing

Conway, Tim
  real name: 18 Thomas Daniel Conway
  born: 12 Willoughby OH
  roles: 11 McHale's Navy 16 Carol Burnett Show 17 The Steve Allen Show

coo 4 bill 6 babble, gurgle, murmur 20 whisper sweet nothings

Coogan, Jackie
  real name: 16 Jack Leslie Coogan
  wife: 11 Betty Grable
  born: 12 Los Angeles CA
  roles: 6 The Kid 9 Tom Sawyer 11 Oliver Twist, Peck's Bad Boy 15 Huckleberry Finn

cook 3 fix 4 chef, fire, heat, make 5 occur 6 cookie, doctor, happen, seethe 7 concoct, falsify, prepare, process 8 work well 9 improvise
  method: 3 fry 4 bake, boil, brew, sear, stew 5 baste, broil, grill, poach, roast, saute, scald, shirr, steam 6 braise, coddle, simmer 7 parboil, stir-fry 8 barbecue 9 fricassee

Cooke, Alistair
  author of: 14 One Man's America 18 A Generation on Trial 26 Around the World in Fifty Years
  TV host of: 18 Masterpiece Theatre

cooked sufficiently 4 done 5 ready 7 al dente 11 done to a turn

cookie 3 bar, gal, gul 4 cake, cook 5 wafer 6 person 7 biscuit, brownie 10 shortbread
  type: 4 oreo 5 sugar 7 oatmeal 8 macaroon, molasses 9 girl scout, tollhouse 10 gingersnap, lorna doone 12 peanut butter 13 chocolate chip

cooking, fine/gourmet
  French: 12 haute cuisine

cooking term 3 a la, cut, dot, fry 4 bake, beat, boil, chop, coat, cube, dice, dust, flan, fold, lard, roux, sear, snip, stew, toss, whip 5 aspic, au jus, baste, blend, bread, broil, brush, candy, cream, crepe, devil, dough, flake, glace, glaze, grate, grill, knead, plank, puree, roast, saute, scald, score, shirr, steep, stock, swear, torte 6 au lait, blanch, braise, coddle, devein, dredge, fillet, flambe, fondue, render, simmer, skewer, sliver 7 a la mode, compote, crouton, garnish, goulash, liquefy, parboil, precook, preheat, rissole, scallop, stir-fry 8 aperitif, au gratin, barbecue, conserve, consomme, julienne, marinate, pot roast 9 brochette, demitasse,

drippings, forcemeat, fricassee, lyonnaise, macedoine 10 caramelize, cracklings
  boneless strips of meat/ fish: 6 fillet
  clear soup: 8 bouillon, consomme
  cubed toasted bread: 7 crouton
  food cooked and served in foil or paper: 11 en papillote
  fruit preserve with nuts/raisins: 8 conserve
  fruits in syrup: 7 compote
  in the fashion: 7 a la mode
  remove veins: 6 devein
  skewered meat: 5 kebab 9 brochette
  small cup of black coffee: 9 demitasse
  thin strips: 6 sliver 8 julienne
  with cheese: 8 au gratin
  with ice cream: 7 a la mode
  with juice/with its own juices: 5 au jus
  with milk: 6 au lait

cook up 3 mix 4 brew 5 hatch 6 create, devise, invent, make up 7 concoct, think up 8 compound, contrive 9 fabricate, formulate

cool 3 icy 4 calm, cold 5 aloof, chill 6 chilly, frosty, offish, serene 7 distant, not warm 8 composed, lose heat, make cool, reserved 9 collected, impassive, uncordial, unexcited 10 become cool, cool-headed, deliberate, nonchalant, unfriendly, unsociable, untroubled 11 indifferent, standoffish, undisturbed, unemotional, unflappable 12 slightly cold, somewhat cold, unresponsive 13 dispassionate, imperturbable, self-possessed

cooler 3 ade, can, fan, jug 4 coop, icer, jail 5 drink, icer 6 calmer, icebox, lockup, prison 11 refrigerant 12 refrigerator 14 air conditioner

Cool Hand Luke
  director: 15 Stuart Rosenberg
  cast: 8 J D Cannon 10 Jo Van Fleet, Lou Antonio, Paul Newman 12 Anthony Zerbe, Dennis Hopper 13 George Kennedy 14 Strother Martin
  Oscar for: 15 supporting actor (Kennedy)

Coolidge, Calvin
  name at birth: 18 John Calvin Coolidge
  nickname: 9 Silent Cal
  presidential rank: 9 thirtieth
  party: 10 Republican
  state represented: 2 MA
  succeeded: 7 Harding
  defeated: 5 (Frank Thomas) Johns, (Herman P) Faris, (John William) Davis 6 (William Zebulon) Foster 7 (Gilbert O) Nations, (William James) Wallace 10 (Robert Marion) La Follette
  vice president: 4 none (first term) 5 (Charles Gates) Dawes
  cabinet:
    state: 6 (Charles Evans) Hughes 7

(Frank Billings) Kellogg
  treasury: 6 (Andrew William) Mellon
  war: 5 (Dwight Filley) Davis, (John Wingate) Weeks
  attorney general: 5 (Harlan Fiske) Stone **6** (Charles B) Warren **7** (John Garibaldi) Sargent **9** (Harry Micajah) Daugherty
  navy: 5 (Edwin) Denby **6** (Curtis Dwight) Wilbur
  postmaster general: 3 (Harry Stewart) New
  interior: 4 (Hubert) Work, (Roy Owen) West
  agriculture: 4 (Howard Mason) Gore **7** (Henry Cantwell) Wallace, (William Marion) Jardine
  commerce: 6 (Herbert Clark) Hoover **7** (William Fairfield) Whiting
  labor: 5 (James John) Davis
born: 2 VT **13** Plymouth Notch
died: 2 MA **10** Northampton
buried: 2 VT **8** Plymouth
education:
  College: 7 Amherst
  later studied: 3 law
religion: 17 Congregationalist
vacation spot: 10 Black Hills
author: 32 The Autobiography of Calvin Coolidge
political career: 13 vice president
  state senator/lieutenant governor/governor of: 2 Ma **13** Massachusetts
civilian career: 6 lawyer **17** bank vice president **18** newspaper columnist
notable events of lifetime/term: 22 Pennsylvania coal strike
  Act: 8 Volstead **10** Boulder Dam **11** Immigration **17** Japanese Exclusion
  bribery case: 8 Elks Hill
  conference: 11 Geneva Naval
  flight by: 16 Charles Lindbergh
  Lindbergh's plane: 15 Spirit of St Louis
  Pact: 13 Kellogg-Briand
  trial: 6 Scopes **12** Scopes monkey
quote: 35 (After all) the chief business of America is business **43** Spend less than you make and make more than you spend
father: 10 John Calvin
mother: 8 Victoria (Josephine Moor)
  stepmother: 8 Caroline (Brown)
sibling: 13 Abigail Gratia
wife: 5 Grace (Anna Goodhue)
children: 4 John **6** Calvin
coolness 5 chill **7** dislike, reserve **8** distance **9** aloofness, composure, sangfroid **10** chilliness, detachment, frostiness **11** impassivity **12** indifference **14** unfriendliness **15** emotionlessness, standoffishness **16** imperturbability, unresponsiveness
coop 3 mew, pen, sty **4** auto, cage,

cote **5** cramp, hutch, roost **6** encase, prison **7** confine **8** imprison **9** enclosure **11** cooperation, cooperative
Cooper, Gary
  real name: 16 Frank James Cooper
  born: 8 Helena MT
  roles: 8 High Noon (Oscar) **9** Beau Geste **12** Sergeant York (Oscar), The Virginian **15** A Farewell to Arms **17** Mr Deeds Goes to Town **19** For Whom the Bell Tolls, The Cowboy and the Lady **20** The Pride of the Yankees **22** North West Mounted Police
Cooper, James Fenimore
  author of: 6 The Spy **8** The Bravo, The Pilot **9** Wyandotte **10** The Prairie **11** The Pioneers, The Red Rover **13** The Deerslayer, The Pathfinder, The Water-Witch **20** Leatherstocking Tales, The Last of the Mohicans
  character: 4 Cora **5** Alice, Magua, Uncas **7** Hawkeye **11** Natty Bumppo **12** Chingachgook
cooperate 4 join **5** unite **7** go along, pitch in, share in **8** take part **9** join hands **10** act jointly, bear part in, join forces **11** collaborate, participate **12** pull together, work together **14** work side by side
cooperation 7 concert, detente **8** teamwork **9** agreement **10** accordance **11** concurrence, cooperating, give and take, joint action **13** collaboration, participation **15** pulling together, working together
coop up 3 pen **4** cage **5** pen in **6** closet, encage, shut in **7** confine, impound **8** restrain, restrict
coordinate 4 mesh **5** equal, match, order **6** relate **7** arrange, coequal **8** organize, parallel **9** correlate, harmonize **11** correlative, systematize **16** equally important
coordination 4 bond **5** skill **6** accord **7** harmony, liaison **10** adaptation, adjustment **12** equalization, organization **15** synchronization
cop 3 bag, nab, rob, win **4** bull, grab, take **5** bobby, catch, filch, pinch, snare, steal, swipe **6** peeler, pilfer, snatch **7** capture **8** flat foot, gendarme, purchase **9** policeman **11** acquisition, policewoman **13** police officer
cope 4 face, spar **6** handle, hurdle, manage, strive, tussle **7** contend, wrestle **8** struggle **11** hold one's own
copious 4 full **5** ample **6** lavish **7** liberal, profuse **8** abundant, generous **9** bountiful, extensive, plenteous, plentiful
copiousness 6 bounty, plenty, wealth **7** surfeit **8** fullness, plethora **9** abundance, ampleness, plenitude, profusion **10** lavishness, oversupply
Copland, Aaron

  born: 10 Brooklyn NY
  composer of: 5 Rodeo **9** Quiet City **10** Statements **11** Billy the Kid **12** Connotations **13** Dance Symphony, El Salon Mexico, The Tender Land **15** Outdoor Overture **17** Appalachian Spring **18** Music for a Great City, Music for the Theater
Copley, John Singleton
  born: 8 Boston MA
  artwork: 11 Samuel Adams **19** The Siege of Gibraltar **21** The Boy with the Squirrel **22** Brook Watson and the Shark, The Death of Major Pierson **26** The Death of the Earl of Chatham
copper
  chemical symbol: 2 Cu
copper-colored 5 henna **6** auburn, russet **11** golden-brown, rust-colored **12** reddish-brown
coppice 4 bosk, wood **5** bluff, copse, firth, grove **6** forest, growth **7** boscage, thicket
Coppola, Francis Ford
  director of: 12 The Godfather (Part I) (Part II, Oscar) **13** Apocalypse Now, The Cotton Club **15** The Conversation
copse 5 brush, clump, grove **6** forest **7** coppice, thicket **8** woodland
copy 3 ape **4** fake, sham, text **5** clone, mimic, story, Xerox **6** follow, mirror, parody, repeat **7** emulate, forgery, imitate, replica **8** likeness **9** duplicate, facsimile, imitation, photostat, reportage, reproduce **10** carbon copy, manuscript **11** counterfeit, make a copy of **12** reproduction **14** representation **15** written material
coquette 4 vamp **5** flirt, tease **12** heart-breaker
coquettish 3 coy **9** kittenish **11** flirtatious
coral 3 red **4** fire, pink, rose **5** horny, polyp, snake **6** orange, sea fan **8** acropora, hydrozoa, staghorn **9** gorgonian **10** sea feather **12** coelenterata
coram populo 8 publicly **15** before the public
corban 8 offering
Corbett, James (John)
  nickname: 12 Gentleman Jim
  sport: 6 boxing
  class: 11 heavyweight
cord 5 braid, twine **8** thin rope **11** heavy string
  abbreviation: 2 cd
Cordelia
  character in: 8 King Lear
  author: 11 Shakespeare
cordial 4 warm **6** genial, hearty **7** affable, amiable, sincere **8** friendly, gracious **9** heartfelt **11** good-natured **12** affectionate, wholehearted
cordiality 6 warmth **8** goodwill **9** af-

fection, geniality, sincerity **10** affability, amiability, heartiness **11** amicability, earnestness **12** friendliness,
graciousness, pleasantness **13** agreeableness

cordial relations 5 amity **6** accord **7**
concord, harmony **8** goodwill **9** agreement **10** friendship **11** amicability **15**
entente cordiale

cordon 4 cord, ring, rope **6** circle **8** encircle

cordon bleu 4 bird **5** finch **7** waxbill
10 red cheeked **11** estrildidae
school for: 5 chefs **7** cooking
where: 5 Paris **6** France
founded by: 13 Marthe Distell
means: 10 blue ribbon

core 3 nub, nut **4** crux, gist, guts,
meat, pith **5** heart **6** center, kernel **7**
essence, nucleus **9** substance **10** brass
tacks **11** central part, nitty-gritty **13**
essential part, innermost part **15** sum
and substance

Corelli, Arcangelo
born: 5 Imola, Italy
composer of: 7 La Folia (sonata No
12) **14** Concerti Grossi

coriander
botanical name: 17 Coriandrum sativum
origin: 13 Mediterranean
color: 5 brown, white **6** yellow
flavor: 4 sage **5** cumin **7** caraway **9**
lemon peel
candy: 6 comfit

Corinth, Lovis
born: 6 Tapiau **7** Prussia
artwork: 6 Salome **8** Ecce Homo **10**
Apocalypse **29** The Walchensee with
a Yellow Field

Coriolanus
author: 18 William Shakespeare
character: 8 Cominius, Virgilia,
Volumnia **12** Junius Brutus, Titus
Lartius **14** Tullus Aufidius **15**
Menenius Agrippa, Sicinius Velutus
22 Caius Marcius Coriolanus

cork 3 bob, oak **4** bark, bung, plug,
seal, stop **5** check, close, float **7** confine, filling stopper, stopple **8** restrain,
suppress **10** insulation

corker 3 ace **4** lulu, oner, whiz **7** stopper **8** clencher, striking, top notch **9**
excellent, humdinger **10** remarkable
11 astonishing

corkscrew 4 coil, curl **5** twist **6** spiral
7 winding **10** serpentine **12** bottle
opener

Corleone family
characters in: 12 The Godfather
author: 4 Puzo
member: 5 Fredo, Sonny **7** Don Vito,
Freddie, Michael

corn 4 cure **5** grain **6** callus **7** Zea
Mays **8** preserve, schmaltz **9** vegetable
varieties: 3 Pod **4** Crow, Dent, Rice,

Sand **5** Broom, Flint, Kafir, maize,
Sugar, Sweet **6** Indian, Turkey **8**
Egyptian, Squirrel
bread/cake: 4 pone **7** hoecake **8** tortilla **9** hushpuppy **10** johnnycake
beverage: 7 bourbon, whiskey

Corncracker State
nickname of: 8 Kentucky

Corneille, Pierre
author of: 5 Cinna, Le Cid, Medea,
Medee **6** Horace, The Cid **8** Ni-
comede **9** Polyeucte

Cornelius, Peter von (van)
born: 7 Germany **10** Dusseldorf
artwork: 12 Last Judgment **24** The
Wise and Foolish Virgins **30** The
Four Horsemen of the Apocalypse

Cornell, Katherine
nickname: 21 first lady of the theater
born: 6 Berlin **7** Germany
roles: 8 Dear Liar **9** Saint Joan **18**
Antony and Cleopatra **26** The Barretts of Wimpole Street

corner 3 fix, jam, nab **4** bend, grab,
hole, nail, nook, spot, trap **5** angle,
seize **6** collar, pickle, plight, scrape **7**
dead end, dilemma, impasse **10** blind
alley, pigeonhole **11** predicament

cornerstone 4 base **5** basis **9** principle
10 foundation **11** fundamental

cornet 4 cone, horn **7** trumpet **9**
cornopean

Cornhuskers, The
author: 12 Carl Sandburg

Cornhusker State
nickname of: 8 Nebraska

cornice 4 drip **5** ancon, crown **7** molding, valance **8** astragal

Cornwallis, Charles
also: 10 second Earl **13** first Marquess
nationality: 7 British
served in: 5 India **7** Ireland **18** American Revolution
battle: 8 Yorktown **10** Brandywine
captured: 10 Charleston **12** Philadelphia
surrendered at: 8 Yorktown

Cornwell, David
real name of: 11 John Le Carre

corny 5 banal, hokey, inane, stale,
tired, trite, vapid **6** jejune, square **7**
fatuous, insipid **8** bromidic, ordinary,
shopworn **9** hackneyed **10** threadbare,
unoriginal **11** commonplace, stereotyped **12** cliche-ridden, old-fashioned
13 platitudinous, unimaginative **15**
unsophisticated

corona 4 halo, ring **5** cigar **6** circle,
nimbus

coronet 5 tiara **6** diadem **7** chaplet,
circlet **10** small crown

Corot, Jean-Baptiste-Camille
born: 5 Paris **6** France
artwork: 9 Pastorale **11** Ville
d'Avray, Woman in Blue **15** Woman

with a Pearl **16** The Farnese Garden,
Woman in the Studio **21** Memory of
Mortefontaine **23** Souvenir de Morte-
fontaine

corporal 3 NCO **6** bodily **8** physical **9**
corporeal

corporation 7 combine, company **9**
syndicate **11** association **14** conglomeration

corporeal 6 bodily, mortal **7** worldly **8**
material, physical **11** perceptible **12**
nonspiritual

corps 4 band, crew, team **5** force,
party, squad, troop **6** outfit

corpse 4 body **5** stiff **7** cadaver,
remains **8** dead body

corpselike 4 pale **5** ashen **6** pallid **9**
bloodless, deathlike **10** cadaverous

corpulent 3 fat **5** dumpy, hefty, obese,
plump, pudgy, stout **6** chubby,
chunky, fleshy, portly, rotund **7** lumpish, well-fed **8** roly-poly **10** overweight, well-padded

corral 4 herd **5** pen in **6** shut in **7** enclose, fence in, round up

correct 3 fit, fix **4** true **5** alter, amend,
chide, emend, exact, right, scold **6** adjust, berate, change, modify, proper,
punish, rebuke, remedy, repair, revamp, revise, rework, seemly **7** censure, chasten, factual, fitting, improve,
lecture, perfect, precise, rectify, reprove **8** accurate, admonish, becoming, chastise, flawless, regulate, suitable, unerring **9** castigate, dress down,
faultless, make right, reprimand **10**
acceptable, discipline, take to task **11**
appropriate **12** conventional **16** haul
over the coals, read the riot act to

correction 6 change **8** revision **10** adjustment, alteration, discipline, emendation, punishment **11** castigation,
improvement, reformation **12** chastisement, modification **13** rectification

corrective 7 remedial **9** improving **10** palliative, rectifying **11** reformatory, restorative, therapeutic **12**
ameliorative, compensatory **13** counteractive **16** counterbalancing

correctness 8 accuracy **9** exactness,
precision, propriety, rightness **10** exactitude, seemliness **11** suitability **12**
becomingness, flawlessness **13** acceptability

Correggio
real name: 14 Antonio Allegri
born: 5 Italy **6** Emilia **9** Correggio
artwork: 5 Danae **12** Jupiter and Io
14 Leda and the Swan **17** The Rape
of Ganymede **21** The Madonna of St
Francis **23** Adoration of the Shepherds **28** Mystic Marriages of St
Catherine

correlate 7 compare, connect **8** parallel **10** correspond

correlation 8 parallel **10** comparison, connection **14** correspondence

correlative 4 akin **7** related **8** agreeing, parallel **9** analogous **10** comparable, connecting, equivalent **13** corresponding

correspond 3 fit **4** jibe, suit **5** agree, match, tally **6** accord, be like, concur, equate, square **7** conform **8** coincide, dovetail, parallel **9** harmonize **11** communicate, drop a line to, keep in touch

correspondence 4 mail **7** analogy, letters **8** epistles, missives, relation **9** bulletins **10** dispatches, similarity **11** association, communiques, resemblance

corresponding 4 akin **5** alike, equal **7** similar **8** agreeing, matching, tallying **9** according **10** equivalent **11** correlative **12** proportional

corridor 3 way **4** hall, road **5** aisle **6** artery **7** hallway, passage **8** approach **10** passageway

Corridors of Power
  author: **6** C P Snow

corroborate 4 back **5** prove **6** affirm, back up, uphold, verify **7** bear out, certify, confirm, endorse, support, sustain **8** validate **9** vindicate **12** authenticate, substantiate

corroborated 6 backed, proved, proven, upheld **7** factual **8** affirmed, backed up, borne out, verified **9** certified, confirmed, supported, sustained, validated **10** vindicated **11** well-founded **12** well-grounded **13** authenticated, substantiated

corroboration 5 proof **7** support **8** evidence **10** validation **11** affirmation, endorsement, vindication **12** confirmation, verification **13** certification, documentation **14** authentication, substantiation

corroborative 7 proving **9** affirming, backing up, upholding, verifying **10** bearing out, concurring, confirming, supporting, validating **11** affirmative **12** confirmative **14** substantiating

corrode 4 rust **7** oxidize **12** disintegrate

corrosive 4 acid **7** burning, caustic, erosive, mordant **8** abrasive **9** corroding **11** destructive

corrugated 6 fluted, ridged **7** creased, grooved, pleated **8** crinkled, furrowed, puckered, wrinkled **10** crenulated

corrupt 3 low **4** base, evil, mean **5** shady **6** debase, poison, seduce, sinful, wicked **7** crooked, debased, debauch, deprave, immoral, pervert, subvert **8** depraved **9** dishonest, unethical **10** fraudulent, iniquitous **11** contaminate **12** dishonorable, unprincipled, unscrupulous

corruption 4 vice **5** fraud, graft **7** bribery **8** iniquity **9** decadence, depravity, looseness, turpitude **10** debauchery, degeneracy, dishonesty, immorality, perversion, sinfulness, wickedness, wrongdoing **11** malfeasance

corsair 6 pirate, sea dog, Viking **7** brigand, sea wolf **8** marauder, picaroon, sea rover **9** buccaneer, plunderer, privateer, sea looter, sea robber **10** Blackbeard, freebooter **11** Captain Kidd **14** Long John Silver

corset 5 laces **6** girdle **8** corselet **17** foundation garment

Corsica 6 island
  located in: **16** Mediterranean Sea
  capital: **7** Ajaccio
  colony of: **4** Rome
  purchased by: **6** France
  birthplace of: **8** Napoleon
  industry: **7** tourism **10** wine making **12** sheep raising, cheese making

Corsican Brothers, The
  author: **14** Alexandre Dumas (pere)

Cortazar, Julio
  author of: **7** Rayuela **9** A Model Kit, Bestiario, Hopscotch **10** The Winners **12** Book of Manuel, End of the Game **15** All Fires the Fire **18** We Love Glenda So Much

cortege 4 line **5** court, staff, suite, train **6** column, escort, parade, string **7** caravan, company, retinue **9** cavalcade, entourage, following, motorcade **10** attendants, procession **17** funeral procession

corundum
  variety: **4** ruby **8** sapphire, star ruby **12** star sapphire

coruscate 4 beam **5** flash, gleam **7** glimmer, glitter, shimmer, sparkle

Corybant
  attendant of: **6** Cybele

Corythosaurus
  type: **8** dinosaur **10** ornithopod
  period: **10** Cretaceous
  characteristic: **10** duck-billed

Cosby, Bill
  born: **14** Philadelphia PA
  roles: **4** I Spy **8** Ghost Dad **12** The Cosby Show **19** Mother Juggs and Speed, Uptown Saturday Night
  nickname: **3** Cos

Cosby Show, The
  character: **4** Rudy, Theo **6** Denise, Sondra **7** Vanessa **13** Clair Huxtable, (Dr) Cliff (Heathcliff) Huxtable
  cast: **9** Bill Cosby, Lisa Bonet **14** Sabrina LeBeauf **15** Tempestt Bledsoe **18** Malcolm Jamal-Warner **19** Keshia Knight Pulliam, Phylicia Ayers-Rashad

Cosi fan tutte
  also: **11** So Do They All **16** Women Are Like That
  opera by: **6** Mozart
  character: **7** Despina **8** Ferrando **9** Dorabella, Guglielmo **10** Don Alfonso, Fiordiligi

cosmetic 5 blush, liner, paint, rouge **6** makeup, powder **7** mascara, surface **8** artifice, eyeliner, lipstick **9** cold cream, eye shadow **10** foundation, nail polish **11** beautifying **13** eyebrow pencil

cosmic 4 vast **7** immense **8** colossal, enormous, infinite **9** grandiose, universal **10** stupendous, widespread **12** interstellar **14** interplanetary **16** extra-terrestrial

cosmopolitan 5 suave **6** urbane **7** worldly **8** traveler **11** broad- minded, worldly-wise **12** globetrotter, sophisticate **13** international, sophisticated

cosmos 5 stars **8** universe **9** macrocosm **10** starry host **13** vault of heaven
  book by: **5** Sagan

Cossack 7 czarist, Russian, trooper **8** horseman **10** cavalry man

cosset 3 pet **6** caress, coddle, fondle, pamper

cost 3 fee, run, tab **4** bill, harm, hurt, loss, pain, take, toll **5** fetch, go for, price, value, worth **6** amount, burden, charge, come to, damage, injure, injury, outlay **7** bring in, expense, penalty, sell for, set back **8** amount to, distress **9** face value, sacrifice, suffering, valuation, weigh down **11** expenditure, market price

Costa-Gavras, Constantine
  director of: **7** Missing

Costard
  character in: **16** Love's Labour's Lost
  author: **11** Shakespeare

Costa Rica
  name means: **9** rich coast
  other name: **19** Land of Eternal Spring
  capital/largest city: **7** San Jose
  others: **5** Canas, Limon, Vesta **6** Boruca, Nicoya **7** Cartago, Golfito, Heredia, Liberia, Negrita **8** Alajuela, Colorado, Guapiles **9** Turrialba **10** Puntarenas
  measure: **4** vara **5** cafiz, cahiz **6** fanega, tercia **7** cajuela, cantaro, manzana **10** caballeria
  monetary unit: **5** colon **7** centimo
  weight: **3** bag **4** caja **5** libra
  island: **4** Cano, Coco
  lake: **6** Arenal
  mountain: **4** Poas **5** Barba, Irazu **6** Blanco **7** Central, Gongora **9** Talamanca, Turrialba **10** Guanacaste
  highest point: **14** Chirripo Grande
  river: **4** Poas **5** Irazu **6** Matina **7** San Juan, Sixaola, Tenoria **8** Tarcoles
  sea: **7** Pacific **9** Caribbean
  physical feature:
    bay: **7** Salinas **8** Coronada
    cape: **5** Velas **6** Blanco **8** Matapalo **10** Santa Elena

crater: 4 Poas
gulf: 5 Dulce **6** Nicoya **8** Pápagayo
hot springs spa: 12 Agua Caliente
peninsula: 3 Osa **6** Nicoya
point: 5 Judas **6** Blanca, Burica, Quepos **7** Cahuito, Galonos, Guionos, Llerena
valley: 8 Tarcoles **10** Reventazon
people: 4 Voto **6** Boruca, Bribri, Guaymi **7** Guatuso, mestizo, Spanish
explorer: 8 Columbus, Coronado
language: 7 Spanish
religion: 13 Roman Catholic
place:
  shrine: 18 Our Lady of the Angels
  theater: 14 Teatro Nacional
feature:
  barbecue: 5 asado
  dance: 6 torito **9** botijuela, zapateado **11** baile suelto **17** punto guanacasteco
  drum: 8 quijonga
  gourd: 4 caro
  outdoor concerts: 7 retreta
  plantation: 5 finca
  wind instrument: 8 chirimia
food:
  hearts of palm salad: 7 palmito
  pudding: 10 tamal asado

Costello, Lou
real name: 21 Louis Francis Cristillo
partner: 9 Bud Abbott
born: 10 Paterson NJ
roles: 11 Who's on First

costly 4 dear **5** steep, stiff **7** harmful **8** damaging, precious **9** expensive **10** disastrous, exorbitant, high-priced **11** deleterious, extravagant **12** catastrophic

Costner, Kevin
born: 2 CA **10** Los Angeles
films: 3 JFK **9** Silverado, Wyatt Earp **10** Bull Durham, The Postman, Waterworld **12** The Bodyguard **13** Field of Dreams, A Perfect World **15** The Untouchables **16** Dances With Wolves **24** Robin Hood: Prince of Thieves

costume 4 garb **5** dress **6** attire, livery, outfit **7** apparel, clothes, raiment, uniform **8** clothing, garments

costuming 8 disguise **10** masquerade

cot 3 bed, hut, pen **4** coop, crib **5** cover, stall **7** cottage

cotelette 3 cut **4** chop **5** slice **6** cutlet

coterie 3 set **4** band, camp, clan, club, crew, gang **5** crowd, group **6** circle, clique **7** faction

cottage 3 cot, hut **5** lodge, shack **6** chalet **8** bungalow

Cotten, Joseph
born: 12 Petersburg VA
roles: 8 Gaslight **11** Citizen Kane, The Third Man **12** Duel in the Sun **14** Shadow of a Doubt **15** Journey into Fear **16** Portrait of Jennie **23** The Magnificent Ambersons

cotton 9 Gossypium
varieties: 3 bog **4** tree, wild **6** kidney, levant, upland **8** lavender **9** sea island **11** Arizona wild
fabric: 4 duck, jean, lawn, pima **5** baize, chino, denim, drill, khaki, lisle, pique, scrim, terry, twill **6** burlap, calico, canvas, chintz, dimity, madras, muslin, nankin, oxford, poplin, sateen **7** batiste, buckram, cambric, flannel, fustian, gingham, holland, jaconet, oilskin, organdy, percale, ticking **8** chambray, cretonne, sheeting **9** crinoline, sailcloth **10** broadcloth, hopsacking, printcloth, seersucker, terrycloth **11** cheesecloth, dotted Swiss

Cotton Club, The
director: 18 Francis Ford Coppola
cast: 9 Diane Lane **11** Richard Gere **12** Gregory Hines

cotton gin
invented by: 7 Whitney

Cotton State
nickname of: 7 Alabama

cottonwood 7 Populus **16** Populus deltoides
varieties: 5 black, Jack's, swamp **7** Fremont **9** Rio Grande **10** Wislizenus **11** Great Plains

Cotyleus
epithet of: 9 Asclepius
means: 13 of the hip joint

couch 3 put **4** sofa, word **5** divan, draft, frame, state, utter, voice **6** daybed, draw up, lounge, phrase, settee **7** express **8** love seat, set forth **9** davenport **12** chesterfield

couch potato
activity: 7 viewing
loves: 10 television

cougar 3 cat **4** lion, puma **7** panther **9** catamount **12** mountain lion

cough 4 hack **6** tussis **9** pertussis

cough up 3 pay **5** eject, expel **7** deliver **8** disgorge, hand over **9** surrender **11** regurgitate

Coulomb, Charles Augustin de
field: 7 physics
nationality: 6 French
invented: 14 torsion balance
discovered: 16 inverse square law

council 5 board, panel, synod **7** cabinet, chamber **8** assembly, colloquy, conclave, congress, ministry **9** committee, gathering, sanhedrin **10** conference, convention **11** convocation **12** congregation **15** representatives

counsel 4 urge, warn **6** advice, advise, charge, lawyer, prompt **7** call for, caution, opinion, suggest **8** admonish, advocate, attorney, guidance, instruct **9** barrister, counselor, recommend, solicitor **10** advisement, suggestion **12** consultation **14** recommendation

counsel house
German: 7 Rathaus

Counsellor-at-Law
director: 12 William Wyler
based on play by: 9 Elmer Rice
cast: 11 Bebe Daniels, Doris Kenyon **12** Isabel Jewell **13** John Barrymore, Melvyn Douglas, Onslow Stevens

counselor, counsellor 5 tutor **6** lawyer, mentor **7** adviser **8** advocate, attorney, minister **9** barrister, solicitor **10** instructor

counselor-at-law 6 lawyer **8** advocate, attorney **9** barrister, solicitor **10** mouthpiece

count 4 deem, hold, lord, rate, tell **5** add up, judge, noble, tally, total **6** impute, look on, matter, number, reckon, regard **7** ascribe, include, tick off **8** consider, estimate, look upon, numerate **9** attribute, enumerate, numbering, reckoning **10** numeration **11** calculation, computation, enumeration
German: 4 Graf
French: 5 comte
Italian: 5 conte
famous: 7 Dracula **8** Almaviva **11** Monte Cristo

countenance 3 aid, air **4** back, face, help, look, mien **5** build, favor **6** aspect, permit, traits, uphold, visage **7** advance, approve, condone, endorse, forward, further, profile, promote, support, work for **8** advocacy, advocate, approval, auspices, champion, contours, features, presence, sanction **9** promotion **10** appearance, assistance, expression, silhouette **11** approbation, physiognomy **12** championship, moral support **13** encouragement

counter 3 bar, man **4** defy, disk **5** piece, stand, table **6** buffet, contra, offset, oppose, resist **7** against, get even, hit back, opposed, pay back, reverse **8** contrary, fountain, opposite **9** fight back, retaliate **11** conflicting **13** contradictory

counteract 4 curb, undo **5** check, fight **6** defeat, hinder, negate, offset, oppose, resist, thwart **7** assuage, nullify, repress **8** overcome, restrain **9** alleviate, frustrate, overpower **10** annihilate, contravene, neutralize

counteraction 8 negation **10** offsetting, opposition **13** contravention, nullification **14** neutralization

counteractive 7 adverse **8** inimical **10** corrective **11** unfavorable **12** antagonistic, neutralizing

counteractor 7 negator **9** nullifier, offsetter **11** neutralizer

counteragent 3 spy **4** mole **8** antidote **9** antitoxin **10** antipoison **11** double agent

counterbalance 5 amend, check **6** cancel, offset, redeem, set off **7** correct, rectify **8** atone for, equalize, make good, outweigh **9** make up for **10** balance out, neutralize, outbalance, recompense **12** compensation

counterfeit 4 copy, fake, sham **5** bogus, fraud, phony **6** ersatz, forged **7** feigned, forgery **8** spurious **9** facsimile, imitation, simulated **10** artificial, fraudulent, substitute **11** make-believe

Counterfeiters, The
author: **9** Andre Gide

countermand 4 void **5** annul, quash **6** cancel, recall, repeal, revoke **7** abolish, nullify, rescind, retract, reverse **8** abrogate, call back, disenact, override, overrule, set aside, withdraw, write off **12** disestablish

counterpart 4 copy, mate, twin **5** equal, match **6** double, fellow **8** parallel **9** duplicate **11** correlative **12** doppelganger **13** correspondent, spitting image

counterpoise 7 balance **9** stability **11** equilibrium

countersign 4 sign **7** certify, confirm, endorse **8** validate **9** authorize **11** corroborate **12** authenticate

countess
French: **8** comtesse
Italian: **8** contessa

countless 6 myriad, untold **7** endless **8** infinite **9** limitless, unlimited **10** numberless, unnumbered **11** innumerable, measureless **12** immeasurable, incalculable **13** multitudinous

Count of Monte Cristo, The
author: **14** Alexandre Dumas (pere)
character: **6** Albert, Haydee, Morrel **7** Fernand (Comte de Morcerf) **8** Danglars, Mercedes **9** Abbe Faria, Valentine, Villefort **10** Caderousse, Maximilian **12** Edmond Dantes
prison: **10** Chateau d'If

count on 6 expect **7** hope for **10** anticipate

countrified 5 rural **6** rustic **9** backwoods **15** unsophisticated

country 4 area, farm, land **5** realm, rural, state **6** nation, people, public, region, rustic, simple, sticks **7** boonies, farming, kingdom, natives, scenery, terrain **8** citizens, district, homeland, populace **9** backwoods, boondocks, community, landscape, territory **10** fatherland, native land, native soil, population, provincial, rural areas **11** farming area, hinterlands, inhabitants, nationality **12** commonwealth **15** unsophisticated

Country Cousin
author: **16** Louis Auchincloss

Country Girl, The
director: **12** George Seaton
based on play by: **13** Clifford Odets
cast: **10** Bing Crosby, Grace Kelly (Oscar) **11** Anthony Ross **13** William Holden
Oscar for: **7** actress (Kelly)

countryman 4 hick, rube **5** yokel **6** farmer, rustic **7** bumpkin, hayseed, peasant **8** landsman **10** clodhopper, compatriot, provincial

Country of the Pointed Firs, The
author: **15** Sarah Orne Jewett

country place 4 farm **5** manor **6** estate

countryside 6 sticks **7** boonies **9** backwater, backwoods, boondocks, rural area **10** hinterland

count up 3 add **5** tally, total **6** reckon **7** compute **9** calculate

count upon 6 expect **7** foresee **10** anticipate

coup 3 act **4** blow, deed, feat **6** stroke **12** master stroke

coup de grace 9 deathblow **11** mercy stroke **12** decisive blow **15** finishing stroke
literally: **11** blow of mercy

coup de main 14 surprise attack **17** sudden development
literally: **15** blow from the hand

coup d'etat 6 mutiny **8** uprising **9** overthrow, rebellion **10** revolution, subversion

coup de theatre 15 theatrical trick

coup d'oeil 11 quick glance
literally: **14** stroke of the eye

Couperin, Francois (Le Grand)
born: **5** Paris **6** France
composer of: **9** La Sultane, Les Fastes (de la grande et ancienne) **13** Concert Royaux **16** Apotheose de Lulli, Pieces de Clavecin **17** Lecons des Tenebres **20** Les Follies Francoises **31** Le Parnasse on l'Apotheose de Corelli

couple 3 duo, tie **4** bind, join, link, pair, yoke **5** hitch **6** fasten **7** connect, doublet, twosome **10** man and wife **11** man and woman **14** husband and wife

coupler 4 link, lock **5** clasp, hitch **6** buckle **8** fastener **9** fastening

Couples
author: **10** John Updike

coupling 5 clasp, hatch **6** hookup, yoking **7** joining, pairing **8** hitching **9** attaching, fastening **10** attachment, connecting, connection

courage 4 grit, guts, sand **5** nerve, pluck, spunk, valor **6** daring, mettle **7** bravery **8** boldness **9** derring-do, fortitude **11** intrepidity **12** fearlessness **13** dauntlessness **16** stout-heartedness

courageous 4 bold **5** brave, manly **6** dogged, heroic **7** dashing, doughty, gallant, valiant **8** fearless, intrepid, resolute, stalwart, unafraid, valorous **9** dauntless **10** chivalrous **11** indomitable **12** bold-spirited **13** stronghearted

Courbet, Jean Desire Gustave
born: **6** France, Ornans

artwork: **16** The Artist's Studio, The Stonebreakers **17** The Burial at Ornans **19** The Peasants of Flagey **25** Self-Portrait with a Black Dog

courier 4 mule **5** envoy **6** herald, legate, runner **7** Gabriel, mailman, Mercury, postman **8** emissary **9** go-between, harbinger, messenger, postrider **11** herald angel, internuncio

course 3 run, way **4** flow, gush, mode, path, pour, race, road **5** march, orbit, round, route, surge, track **6** action, circle, method, policy, stream **7** channel, circuit, classes, conduct, lessons, passage, subject **8** behavior, lectures, sequence **9** direction, procedure, unfolding **10** curriculum, racecourse, trajectory **11** development, progression

court 3 bar, woo **4** hall, quad, seek, suit, yard **5** bench, manor, plaza, staff, train **6** atrium, castle, homage, induce, invite, palace, pursue, wooing **7** address, attract, chateau, cortege, council, flatter, hearing, meeting, provoke, retinue, session **8** advisers, assembly, audience, blandish, fawn upon, pander to, respects, run after **9** entourage, following **10** attendants, quadrangle **13** solicitations

Courtenay, Tom
born: **4** Hull **7** England
roles: **9** Billy Liar **10** The Dresser **36** The Loneliness of the Long Distance Runner

courteous 4 kind, mild **5** civil **6** polite **7** refined, tactful **8** gracious, mannerly, well-bred **10** diplomatic, respectful, soft-spoken **11** considerate, well-behaved **12** well-mannered

courtesy 5 favor **7** manners, regards, respect **8** civility, kindness, respects **9** deference, gallantry, gentility **10** indulgence, politeness, refinement **11** cultivation **12** graciousness **13** consideration

courtier 4 beau **7** gallant **8** cavalier **9** attendant **18** gentleman-in-waiting

Courtier, The
author: **21** Baldassare Castiglione

Court Jester
director: **11** Melvin Frank **12** Norman Panama
cast: **9** Danny Kaye **11** Glynis Johns **13** Basil Rathbone **14** Angela Lansbury

courtly 5 suave **6** polite **7** elegant, gallant, genteel, refined, stately **8** debonair, decorous, highbred, ladylike, mannerly, polished **9** civilized, courteous, dignified **10** chivalrous **11** blue-blooded, gentlemanly **12** aristocratic **14** silk-stockinged

courtship 4 suit **6** wooing **14** keeping company

Courtship of Eddie's Father, The
character: **4** Tina **10** Tom Corbett **12** Eddie Corbett, Norman Tinker **13**

Mrs Livingston
cast: 9 Bill Bixby 11 Brandon Cruz, James Komack 12 Miyoshi Umeki 15 Kristina Holland

Courtship of Miles Standish, The
author: 24 Henry Wadsworth Longfellow
character: 9 John Alden, Priscilla

courtyard 4 area, quad 6 atrium 9 curtilage, enclosure 10 quadrangle

cousin 7 kinsman 8 relation, relative 9 kinswoman

Cousin Bette
author: 14 Honore de Balzac
character: 6 Crevel 7 Adeline 10 Baron Hulot 11 Mme Marneffe 13 Hortense Hulot, Marechal Hulot 14 Lisbeth Fischer 23 Count Wenceslas Steinbock

Cousin Pons
author: 14 Honore de Balzac

Cousy, Bob
nickname: 12 Mr Basketball
sport: 10 basketball
position: 5 guard
team: 13 Boston Celtics

couturier, couturiere 8 designer 9 midinette 10 dressmaker, seamstress

cove 3 bay 5 inlet 6 lagoon 7 estuary

covenant 3 vow 4 bond, oath, pact 6 pledge, treaty 7 bargain, promise 8 contract 9 agreement 15 solemn agreement
Hebrew: 4 Brit 5 Berit, Brith 6 Berith

Covenant, The
author: 13 James Michener

cover 3 cap, lid, top 4 case, hide, hood, mask, veil, wrap 5 cloak, cross, guard, lay on, put on, quilt 6 asylum, clothe, defend, embody, enwrap, jacket, refuge, report, screen, sheath, shield, shroud, take in, tell of 7 binding, blanket, conceal, contain, defense, embrace, envelop, include, involve, obscure, overlay, protect, put over, secrete, sheathe, shelter, wrapper, write up 8 comprise, deal with, describe, disguise, envelope, pass over, traverse 9 chronicle, comforter, eiderdown, encompass, sanctuary 10 camouflage, comprehend, encasement, protection 11 concealment, hiding place

coverage 7 payment 8 analysis 9 indemnity, reporting 10 protection, publishing 11 description 12 broadcasting 13 reimbursement

covered 4 clad 6 hidden 7 aimed at, cloaked, guarded, insured 8 included, overlaid, screened 9 blanketed, concealed, protected, sheltered, traversed 10 overspread

covering 6 casing, sheath 7 wrapper 8 envelope, wrapping 11 descriptive, explanatory 12 introductory

coverlet 5 quilt, throw 6 afghan, spread 7 blanket 9 bedspread, comforter

Coverly, Sir Roger de
character in: 12 The Spectator
authors: 6 Steele 7 Addison

covert 6 hidden, secret, veiled 7 sub rosa, unknown 9 concealed, disguised 11 clandestine 13 surreptitious

cover up 4 hide, mask, veil 6 hush up 7 conceal 8 disguise, keep back, suppress, withhold 9 gloss over, whitewash

cover-up 4 mask 5 blind 6 screen 8 disguise 9 whitewash 11 concealment

covet 4 want 5 crave, fancy 6 desire 7 long for

covetous 6 greedy 7 craving, envious, jealous, lustful, selfish 8 desirous, grasping, yearning 9 mercenary, rapacious 10 avaricious

covetousness 4 envy 5 greed 7 avarice 8 jealousy, rapacity 10 greediness 12 graspingness 13 mercenariness

covey 4 bevy 5 flock, group 6 family

cow 4 beef 5 abash, Bossy, bully, deter, Elsie, scare 6 bovine, cattle, dismay 7 terrify 8 browbeat, bulldoze, frighten, threaten 9 terrorize 10 discourage, dishearten, intimidate, make cringe
young: 4 calf 6 heifer

coward 3 cad 5 sissy 6 craven 7 caitiff, chicken, dastard, milksop 8 poltroon 11 Milquetoast, mollycoddle, yellow- belly

Coward, Sir Noel
author of: 8 Hay Fever 9 Cavalcade 10 Sigh No More 12 Blithe Spirit, Private Lives 14 In Which We Serve, Nude with Violin 15 Design for Living

cowardliness 8 timidity 10 yellowness 12 irresolution 13 pusillanimity, spinelessness 18 chicken-heartedness

cowardly 5 shaky, timid 6 afraid, craven, yellow 7 anxious, chicken, fearful, gutless, nervous 8 timorous 9 dastardly, tremulous 10 frightened 11 lily-livered 12 apprehensive, fainthearted, uncourageous 13 pusillanimous, yellow-bellied 14 chickenhearted

Cowardly Lion
character in: 13 The Wizard of Oz
author: 4 Baum
played by: 8 Bert Lahr

cowboy 6 drover, gaucho 7 vaquero 8 buckaroo 10 roughrider 12 broncobuster, cattle-herder

cowed 5 fazed 7 abashed, crushed, subdued 8 dismayed 11 intimidated 12 disconcerted 14 under one's thumb

cower 5 crawl, quail, toady 6 cringe, flinch, grovel, recoil, shrink 7 tremble, truckle 8 bootlick, draw back

cowl 4 cope, hood 5 cloak

Cowley, Malcolm
author of: 12 Exile's Return 16 A Second Flowering 27 And I Worked at the Writer's Trade 28 The Dream of the Golden Mountains

coworker 7 partner 8 teammate 9 associate, colleague 10 accomplice 11 confederate 12 collaborator

Cowper, William
author of: 7 The Task 11 The Cast-Away

Cowperwood, Frank
character in: 8 The Titan 12 The Financier
author: 7 Dreiser

coxcomb 3 fop 4 beau 5 dandy 8 popinjay

coy 3 shy 5 timid 6 demure, modest 7 bashful, prudish 8 blushing, sheepish, skittish, timorous 9 diffident, kittenish, shrinking 10 coquettish, overmodest

Coyote State
nickname of: 11 South Dakota

cozen 3 con, gyp 4 bilk, coax, dupe, gull, rook 5 cheat, trick 6 fleece 7 deceive, defraud, swindle, wheedle 9 bamboozle, victimize

cozener 4 fake 5 cheat, fraud, quack 6 con man 8 deceiver, swindler 9 charlatan, trickster 10 mountebank 13 confidence man

coziness 6 warmth 7 comfort 8 intimacy, snugness 11 contentment

cozy 4 easy, snug 5 comfy, homey 7 restful 8 homelike, relaxing 9 gemutlich, simpatico 11 comfortable 16 snug as a bug in a rug
French: 6 intime

Cozzens, James Gould
author of: 12 Guard of Honor 15 By Love Possessed

CPA 7 auditor 10 accountant, bookkeeper 25 certified public accountant

crab 4 carp 5 crank, gripe, grump 6 grouch, grouse 8 complain, sourball 9 shellfish 10 crustacean, curmudgeon
constellation of: 6 Cancer

Crabbe, Buster
real name: 20 Clarence Linden Crabbe
nickname: 16 King of the Serials
born: 9 Oakland CA
roles: 6 Tarzan 10 Buck Rogers 11 Flash Gordon 15 King of the Jungle

crabbed 4 mean, sour 6 cranky, morose 7 grouchy, peevish, pinched 8 churlish, spiteful 9 irascible, irritable, rancorous

crabby 5 cross, testy 6 cranky, touchy 7 grouchy, peevish 8 petulant, snappish 9 irritable 10 ill-humored, out of sorts 11 ill-tempered 12 cantankerous

crack 3 gag, jab, pop 4 chip, clap, gash, gibe, jest, joke, quip, rent, rift,

slit, snap **5** break, burst, cleft, split,
taunt **6** cleave, insult, report **7**
crackle, crevice, fissure, give way,
rupture, thunder **8** fracture, splinter **9**
break down, wisecrack, witticism **10**
go to pieces

cracked 3 mad **4** daft, nuts **5** crazy,
nutty **6** crazed, insane **8** demented,
deranged, unhinged **10** unbalanced **12**
mad as a hatter **13** off one's rocker,
out of one's head **14** off one's trolley
15 mad as a March hare

cracker 5 snack, wafer **7** biscuit, redneck **10** party favor **11** backsettler **12**
backwoodsman

crackerjack 2 A-1 **3** ace **4** a-one, fine
5 super **6** superb, tip-top **8** splendid,
terrific **9** excellent, fantastic, first-rate,
wonderful **10** first-class

Cracker State
  nickname of: 7 Georgia

crackle 4 snap **5** craze, crink **9** crepi-
tate

crackpot 3 nut, odd **4** fool, kook **5**
balmy, crank, flake, freak, kinky,
kooky, loony, nutty, wacko **6** freaky,
insane, looney, madman, maniac,
weirdo **7** dingbat, foolish, lunatic,
oddball **9** character, eccentric, screwball **11** impractical

cracksman 4 yegg **7** burglar **10** cat
burglar **14** second-story man

crackup 5 crash, smash, split, wreck **6**
mishap, pileup **7** breakup, debacle,
smashup **8** accident, calamity, collapse, disaster **9** breakdown, collision,
splitting **10** exhaustion, shellshock **11**
catastrophe, prostration **14** disintegration

cradle 3 hug **4** crib, font, rock **6** cuddle, enfold, origin, source, spring **7**
nursery, snuggle **8** bassinet, fountain
10 birthplace, wellspring **12** fountain
head

craft 3 art **4** boat, ruse, ship, wile **5**
guile, knack, plane, skill, trade **6** deceit, vessel **7** ability, calling, cunning,
know-how, mastery, perfidy, pursuit **8**
airplane, artifice, business, commerce,
deftness, fineness, industry, intrigue,
trickery, vocation **9** adeptness, chicanery, deception, duplicity, expertise,
technique **10** adroitness, artfulness,
competency, craftiness, employment,
expertness, handicraft, occupation **11**
proficiency

craftiness 4 ruse, wile **5** guile **7** cunning, slyness **8** artifice, foxiness,
scheming, trickery, wiliness **9** chicanery **10** artfulness **11** machination

craftsman 4 hand **5** smith **6** worker,
wright **7** artisan **8** mechanic

crafty 3 sly **4** foxy, wily **5** canny,
sharp **6** artful, astute, shifty, shrewd,
tricky **7** cunning, devious **8** guileful,
plotting, scheming **9** deceitful, deceptive, designing, dishonest, underhand,

unethical **10** intriguing, perfidious,
suspicious **11** calculating

crag 3 tor **4** rock **5** bluff, cliff **9** precipice

craggy 5 rocky, rough, sheer, steep,
stony **6** abrupt, jagged, ragged, rugged, snaggy **7** scraggy **8** bouldery **9**
rockbound **10** rock-ribbed **11** precipitous

Crain, Jeanne
  born: 9 Barstow CA
  roles: 5 Pinky **6** Margie **9** State Fair
    17 Cheaper by the Dozen **19** A Let-
    ter to Three Wives

cram 3 jam **4** fill, pack **5** crowd, force,
grind, press, stuff **7** congest, squeeze
8 compress **9** overcrowd, study hard

Cram, Ralph
  architect of: 17 US Military Academy
    (West Point) **29** Cathedral of Saint
    John the Divine (NYC)
  style: 13 Gothic Revival

crammed 4 full **6** filled, packed **7**
studied, stuffed **9** jam-packed **11**
overflowing, well-stocked

cramp 4 pang **5** block, check, crick,
limit, spasm **6** hamper, hinder, stitch,
stymie, thwart **7** prevent, seizure **8**
handicap, obstruct, restrain, restrict **9**
frustrate **12** charley horse

cramped 5 close, tight **6** narrow **7**
compact, pinched **8** confined **10** compressed, restrained, restricted

Cranach, Lucas (Lukas) (the Elder)
  born: 7 Kronach, Germany
  artwork: 6 Luther **10** Adam and Eve
    11 Crucifixion **14** Apollo and Diana
    15 Rest on the Flight **18** The Judg-
    ment of Paris **22** Duke and Duchess
    of Saxony

Cranaus
  king of: 6 Athens, Attica
  wife: 6 Pedias
  daughter: 6 Atthis, Cranae
  renamed Athens: 6 Attica

cranberry 9 Vaccinium **19** Vaccinium
vitis-idaea **20** Vaccinium macrocarpon
  varieties: 3 bog **4** rock, tree **5** large,
    small **8** American, European, high-
    bush, mountain **10** Australian

crane 4 bird, boom **5** davit, heron **7**
derrick **10** wading bird
  group of: 5 sedge, siege
  constellation of: 4 Grus

Crane, Bob
  born: 11 Waterbury CT
  roles: 12 Colonel Hogan, Hogan's He-
    roes

Crane, Hart
  author of: 9 The Bridge **14** White
    Buildings

Crane, Ichabod
  character in: 23 The Legend of Sleepy
    Hollow
  author: 6 Irving

Crane, Roy

creator/artist of: 9 Buz Sawyer,
    Wash Tubbs **11** Captain Easy

Crane, Stephen
  author of: 11 The Open Boat **20** The
    Red Badge of Courage **23** Maggie: A
    Girl of the Streets **24** The Bride Co-
    mes to Yellow Sky

Cranford
  author: 10 Mrs Gaskell

cranium 4 head **5** skull **6** noggin **8**
brain box, brainpan **9** brain case

crank 4 turn, whim **5** brace, winch
6 grouch, handle **7** fanatic **8** crotchet
9 eccentric

cranky 5 cross, testy **6** crabby, touchy
7 bearish, grouchy, peevish, waspish
8 captious, petulant **9** crotchety, irascible, splenetic **10** ill-humored, out of
sorts **11** ill-tempered **12** cantankerous

cranny 3 gap **4** nook, slit **5** break,
chink, cleft, crack, notch, split **7** crevice, fissure **8** cleavage

crash 3 din **4** bang, boom, bump, dash,
ruin **5** crack, slump, smash, wreck **6**
hurtle, invade, pileup, plunge, racket,
slip in, topple, tumble **7** bumping,
clangor, clatter, collide, crackup, decline, failure, hitting, intrude, setback,
shatter, smashup, sneak in **8** accident,
smashing, toppling, tumbling **9** collision, recession **10** bankruptcy, depression, shattering

crass 5 crude, cruel, gross **6** coarse,
oafish, vulgar **7** boorish **8** uncaring **9**
inelegant, unfeeling, unrefined **10** unpolished **11** hardhearted, insensitive
13 unsympathetic

crassness 9 crudeness, grossness, vulgarity **10** coarseness, inelegance, oafishness **11** boorishness **13** insensitivity

Cratchit, Bob
  character in: 15 A Christmas Carol
  author: 7 Dickens
  son: 7 Tiny Tim

crate 3 box, car **4** auto, case, pack **5**
plane **6** jalopy, pallet **8** airplane **9**
container

crater 3 pit **4** hole **6** cavity **10** depression

cravat 3 tie **5** ascot, scarf, stock **7**
necktie **11** neckerchief

crave 4 need, want **5** covet **6** desire **7**
hope for, long for, pine for, require,
sigh for, wish for **8** yearn for **9** hunger for, lust after, thirst for **11** hanker
after, have a yen for **13** have a fancy
for

craven 3 low **4** base **5** timid **6** scared,
yellow **7** fearful, lowdown **8** cowardly, timorous **9** dastardly **10** frightened **11** lily-livered **12** mean-spirited
13 pusillanimous **14** chicken-hearted

craving 3 yen **4** need **6** desire, hunger,
thirst **7** longing **9** hankering

Crawford, Broderick

real name: 24 William Broderick
Crawford
wife: 11 Jan Sterling
born: 14 Philadelphia PA
roles: 6 The Mob **10** The Interns **12**
Of Mice and Men **13** Born Yesterday,
Highway Patrol **14** All the King's
Men (Oscar)

Crawford, Henry
character in: 13 Mansfield Park
author: 6 Austen

Crawford, Joan
real name: 17 Lucille Fay Le Sueur
husband: 12 Franchot Tone **18** Douglas Fairbanks Jr
daughter: 6 Cheryl **9** Christina
born: 12 San Antonio TX
biography: 13 Mommie Dearest
roles: 8 The Women **10** Grand Hotel
13 Mildred Pierce (Oscar) **26** What
Ever Happened to Baby Jane

crawl 4 drag, inch, poke, worm **5**
creep, mosey **6** squirm, wiggle, writhe
7 slither, wriggle

Crawley, Rawdon
character in: 10 Vanity Fair
author: 9 Thackeray

crayon 5 chalk, draft **6** pastel, pencil,
sketch **7** drawing **8** charcoal

craze 3 fad **4** rage **5** furor, mania **6** de-
ment **7** derange, passion, unhinge **11**
infatuation

crazed 3 mad **6** insane **7** cracked, lunatic **8** demented, deranged

crazy 3 mad, odd **4** avid, daft, gaga,
keen, nuts, wild **5** nutty, rabid, silly,
weird **6** absurd, far-out, insane, stupid, unwise **7** berserk, bizarre,
cracked, excited, foolish, frantic, idiotic, strange, touched, unusual, zealous **8** demented, deranged, maniacal,
peculiar, uncommon, unhinged **9** fanatical, foolhardy, imprudent, laughable, senseless **10** hysterical, infatuated, outrageous, passionate,
ridiculous, unbalanced **11** smitten
with **12** enthusiastic, mad as a hatter
13 out of one's head **15** mad as a
March hare

creak 4 rasp **5** grate, grind **6** scrape,
screak, squeak **7** screech

Creakle
character in: 16 David Copperfield
author: 7 Dickens

cream 3 top **4** beat, best, drub **5** elite
6 choice, flower **7** the pick, trounce **8**
greatest, off-white **14** creme de la
creme

Cream, Arnold Raymond
real name of: 10 Joe Walcott

cream of the cream
French: 14 creme de la creme

Cream of the Jest, The
author: 17 James Branch Cabell

creamy 5 thick, foamy **6** smooth, yellow **8** emulsive

crease 4 fold **5** crimp, pleat, ridge **6**
furrow, pucker, ruffle, rumple **7** crimple, crinkle, wrinkle **9** corrugate **11**
corrugation

create 4 form, make, mold **5** cause,
erect, found, set up **6** design, devise,
invent **7** appoint, concoct, develop,
fashion **8** conceive, contrive, organize
9 construct, establish, fabricate, formulate, institute, originate

creation 5 world **6** making, nature **8**
building, devising, erection, founding
9 all things, formation, handiwork, invention **10** brainchild, conception,
concoction, fashioning, production **11**
development, fabrication, institution,
origination **12** construction **13** establishment

Creation
author: 9 Gore Vidal

creative 8 fanciful, original **9** ingenious, inventive **11** imaginative, resourceful

creator 5 maker **6** author, father,
framer **7** founder **8** begetter, designer,
inventor, producer **9** architect, generator, initiator **10** originator

creature 3 man **4** bird, fish **5** beast,
human **6** animal, insect, mammal,
mortal, person **7** critter, reptile **9**
earthling, quadruped **10** individual,
vertebrate **12** invertebrate

credence 5 faith, trust **6** belief, credit
8 reliance **9** certainty, certitude **10**
confi- dence **11** reliability **13** believa-
bility **14** acceptableness, dependable-
ness **15** trustworthiness

credentials 6 permit **7** diploma, license, voucher **9** reference **11** certificate, testimonial **13** authorization

credenza 5 shelf, table **6** buffet **8**
bookcase **9** sideboard

credible 6 likely **7** tenable **8** possible,
probable, reliable **9** plausible, thinkable **10** believable, dependable, imaginable, reasonable **11** conceivable,
trustworthy

credit 3 buy **4** time **5** glory, honor,
trust **6** accept, assign, esteem, rely on
7 acclaim, ascribe, believe, fall for,
swallow **9** allowance, attribute, recognize **10** prepayment **11** acknowledge,
recognition **12** commendation **14** acknowledgment

creditable 6 worthy **8** laudable **9** admirable, estimable, reputable **11** commendable, meritorious, respectable **12**
praiseworthy

credo 4 code, rule **5** maxim, motto,
tenet **8** doctrine **10** philosophy

credulous 5 naive **8** gullible, trusting
9 believing **12** overtrustful, unsuspecting, unsuspicious **13** unquestioning
15 unsophisticated

Cree
language family: 9 Algonkian **10** Al-

gonquian
tribe: 10 Plains Cree **13** Woodlands
Cree
location: 6 Canada **8** Manitoba
related to: 8 Chippewa

creed 5 dogma **6** belief, canons, gospel
8 doctrine

creek 3 run **4** rill **5** brook **6** branch,
spring, stream **7** freshet, rivulet **10**
millstream, small river

Creek
language family: 10 Muskhogean
location: 7 Alabama, Florida, Georgia
11 Mississippi
leader: 8 Red Eagle **15** William McIntosh **20** Alexander McGillivray

Creek Mary's Blood
author: 8 Dee Brown

creep 4 inch, worm **5** crawl, sneak,
steal **6** dawdle, squirm, writhe **7**
slither, wriggle

creeper 3 ivy **4** bird, iron, vine, worm
5 snake **7** climber, crawler, grapnel,
trailer

creepy 4 eery **5** eerie, scary **6** crawly,
spooky, uneasy **12** apprehensive

cremate 4 burn, char, fire, sear **5** roast
6 ignite, kindle, scorch **8** enkindle **10**
incinerate **11** conflagrate **17** consume
with flames

creme de banane
type: 7 liqueur
flavor: 6 banana
color: 6 yellow

creme de cacao
type: 6 brandy **7** liqueur
origin: 6 France
flavor: 9 chocolate
color: 5 brown, white
drink: 11 Fifth Avenue
with rum: 6 Panama
with tequila: 8 Toreador
with vodka: 9 Ninotchka **11** Russian
Bear **12** Velvet Hammer, White Russian

creme de cassis
type: 7 liqueur
origin: 6 France **8** Burgundy
flavor: 12 black currant
with gin: 8 Parisian

creme de fraise
type: 7 liqueur
flavor: 10 strawberry

creme de framboise
type: 7 liqueur
flavor: 9 raspberry

creme de la creme 3 top **4** best **5**
cream, elite **6** choice, flower **8** choicest, very best **12** choicest part **15**
cream of the cream

creme de menthe
type: 7 liqueur
flavor: 4 mint
color: 5 green, white
with brandy: 7 Stinger

with cream: 11 Grasshopper
with gin: 6 Caruso, Virgin
creme de noyau
  type: 7 liqueur
  flavor: 6 almond
creme de violette
  type: 7 liqueur
  flavor: 7 violets
  color: 8 lavender
creme Yvette
  type: 7 liqueur
  origin: 12 United States
  flavor: 7 violets
  with gin: 9 Union Jack
Crenna, Richard
  born: 12 Los Angeles CA
  roles: 9 Death Ship **13** Our Miss
  Brooks, The Real McCoys
Creole 6 patois **7** criollo, dialect, Haitian **10** West Indian
Creole State
  nickname of: 9 Louisiana
Creon
  king of: 6 Thebes **7** Corinth
  father: 9 Lycaethus, Menoeceus
  sister: 7 Jocasta
  daughter: 6 Creusa, Glauce
  nephew: 7 Oedipus **8** Eteocles **9** Polynices
  niece: 6 Ismene **8** Antigone
  defeated: 18 Seven against Thebes
crescendo
  music: 22 gradually getting louder
    abbreviation: 5 cresc
crescent 3 arc, bow **4** arch **5** curve **8** half-moon
crescit eundo 15 it grows as it goes
  motto of: 9 New Mexico
Cressida
  also: 8 Criseyde **9** Crisseyde
  based on characters of: 7 Bryseis **8** Chryseis
  setting: 9 Trojan War
  loved: 7 Troilus
  deserted Troilus for: 8 Diomedes
crest 3 tip, top **4** apex, arms, comb, peak, tuft **5** crown, plume **6** emblem, height, summit **7** topknot **8** pinnacle **10** coat of arms, escutcheon
crestfallen 8 dejected, downcast **9** depressed, woebegone **10** despondent, dispirited **11** discouraged, downhearted, low-spirited **12** disappointed, disheartened
Cretaceous period
  dinosaur from: 9 Euhelopus, Iguanodon **10** Allosaurus, Antrodemus **11** Anatosaurus, Ankylsaurus, Deinonychus, Gorgosaurus, Triceratops **12** Lambeosaurus, Ornithomimus **13** Albertosaurus, Corythosaurus, Hypselosaurus, Hypsilophodon, Palaeoscincus, Protoceratops, Struthiomimus, Styracosaurus, Tyrannosaurus **14** Psittacosaurus, Thescelosaurus **15** Parasaurolophus, Procheneosaurus

Cretan bull
  also: 15 Marathonian bull
  form: 4 bull
  son: 8 Minotaur
  captured on: 5 Crete
  captured by: 8 Hercules
  roamed: 8 Marathon
  recaptured by: 7 Theseus
Cretan Mythology
  goddess of fishermen/hunters/
  sailors: 11 Britomartis
    corresponds to Greek: 7 Artemis
  goddess of the sea: 8 Dictynna
  maze: 9 labyrinth
  monster: 8 Minotaur
Crete
  other name: 5 Kriti **6** Candia
  capital/largest city: 5 Canea **8** Iraklion
  others: 3 Hag **4** Lato **5** Khora, Sitia, Zakro **6** Anoyia, Candia, Khania, Lisamo, Mallia, Meleme, Retimo **7** Malerni **8** Kastelli, Nikolaos, Sphakion **9** Heraclion, Heraklion, Rethymnon, Tympakion **11** Palaiophora
  government: division of: 6 Greece
  monetary unit: 7 drachma
  mountain: 3 Ida **5** Dikte, Phino **6** Juktas **7** Lasithi, Madaras **8** Leuka Ori, Theodore, Thriphte **9** Psiloriti
  highest point: 3 Ida
  sea: 5 Crete **6** Aegean **13** Mediterranean
  physical feature:
    bay: 4 Suda **5** Kanca **6** Kisamo, Meaara
    cape: 4 Buza **5** Liano **6** Salome, Sidero, Spatha **7** Stavros **8** Lithinon, Sidheros
    gulf: 6 Khania **9** Merabello
  people: 7 Candiot, Cretans, Minoans **9** Caphtorim, Sphakiots **11** Philistines
    artist: 7 El Greco
    author: 11 Kazantzakis
    conqueror: 8 Metellus
    king: 5 Minos
  language: 5 Greek **6** Minoan **7** Linear A, Linear B
  religion: 14 Greek Orthodoxy
  place:
    ruins: 15 Palace at Knossos
Creusa
  also: 6 Glauce
  father: 5 Creon, Priam **8** Cychreus **10** Erechtheus
  mother: 6 Hecuba
  husband: 6 Aeneas **7** Telamon
  son: 3 Ion **8** Ascanius
  bride of: 5 Jason
  killed by: 5 magic, Medea
crevasse 3 gap **4** rift **5** abyss, break, chasm, cleft, gorge, gulch, gully, split **6** breach, divide **7** fissure
crevice 4 rent, rift, slit **5** chasm, cleft, crack, split **6** breach **7** fissure **8** crevasse, fracture
crew 3 men, mob **4** band, body, herd,

mass, pack, team **5** corps, force, group, hands, horde, party, squad, troop **6** seamen, throng **7** company, haircut, sailors **8** mariners **9** multitude, seafarers **10** assemblage, complement
crib 3 bed, bin, cot, hut, key **4** pony, trot **5** cheat, shack, stall, steal **6** creche, manger **7** purloin **8** bassinet **10** plagiarize
cribbage
  scorer: 3 peg
  score kept on: 5 board
  points/game: 8 sixty-one
  third hand: 4 crib
  jack: 7 his nobs
Crich, Gerald
  character in: 11 Women in Love
  author: 8 Lawrence
Crichton, Michael
  author of: 5 Congo **6** Sphere **8** Airframe **9** Rising Sun **10** Disclosure **12** Jurassic Park **14** The Terminal Man **15** Eaters of the Dead **18** The Andromeda Strain **20** The Great Train Robbery
cricket
  players/team: 6 eleven
  equipment: 3 bat **4** bail, ball **5** stump **6** wicket
  position: 5 gully, mid on, slops **6** bowler, long on, mid off **7** batsman, fine leg, long off **8** third man **9** mid wicket, square leg **10** cover point, extra cover, silly mid on **11** silly mid off **12** wicket keeper **13** deep mid wicket **16** backward short leg
  lines: 7 creases
  period of play: 4 over **7** innings
  championship game: 9 test match
  England/Australia match: 8 the Ashes
cricket
  variety: 4 bush, cave, fair, sand, tree **5** camel, field, house **6** ground **9** Jerusalem, pygmy mole
Cries and Whispers
  director: 12 Ingmar Bergman
  cast: 10 Liv Ullmann **12** Ingrid Thulin **16** Harriet Andersson
crime 3 sin **4** tort **5** wrong **6** felony **7** misdeed, offense, outrage **8** foul play, iniquity, villainy **10** misconduct, wrongdoing **11** abomination, lawbreaking, malfeasance, misdemeanor **13** transgression
Crime and Punishment
  author: 16 Fyodor Dostoevsky
  character: 5 Sonya **6** Dounia **7** Porfiry **9** Razumihin **11** Raskolnikov
criminal 4 hood **5** crook, felon, wrong **6** guilty, outlaw **7** crooked, culprit, illegal, illicit, lawless **8** culpable, offender, unlawful, wasteful **9** felonious, senseless, wrongdoer **10** abominable, delinquent, indictable, lawbreaker, malefactor, outrageous,

villainous **11** blameworthy, disgraceful, lawbreaking **12** transgressor

crimp 4 curl, fold, kink, wave **5** clamp, flute, frill, frizz **7** crinkle, frizzle, wrinkle **8** obstacle

crimple 4 curl **6** pucker **7** crinkle, crumple, wrinkle **9** corrugate

crimson 3 red **4** ruby **5** blush, flush **6** redden **7** carmine, scarlet

cringe 4 duck **5** cower, dodge, quail, toady **6** blench, flinch, grovel, recoil, shrink **7** truckle

cringing 6 abject **7** fawning, ignoble, servile, wincing **8** cowering, toadying **9** flinching, groveling, shrinking, sniveling

crinkle 5 crush **6** rumple, rustle **7** crumple, wrinkle

crinkly 4 wavy **5** curly, kinky **6** crimpy, frizzy **7** cockled, crimped, crimply, puckery, ruffled, rumpled, twisted, wrinkly **8** crimpled, frizzled, puckered, wrinkled **9** shriveled

crinoline 4 hoop **5** skirt **9** hoopskirt, petticoat **10** underskirt

cripple 4 gimp, halt, harm, maim, stop **6** damage, impair **7** disable **8** make lame, paralyze **9** hamstring **10** debilitate, inactivate **12** incapacitate

crisis 6 climax **9** emergency

crisp 5 brisk, fresh, nippy, sharp, terse, witty **6** candid, chilly, crispy, lively, snappy **7** bracing, brittle, crunchy, pointed **8** incisive **9** energetic, sparkling, vivacious **10** potato chip, refreshing **12** invigorating

crisscross 4 awry **5** cross **8** confused, traverse

Crisseyde see **8** Cressida

Cristillo, Louis Francis
real name of: **11** Lou Costello

criterion 3 law **4** norm, rule **5** gauge, model **7** example, measure **8** standard **9** guidepost, precedent, principle, yardstick **10** touchstone

critic 5 judge, mavin, scold **6** carper, censor, expert, rapper **7** analyst, arbiter, knocker, reviler **8** attacker, reviewer, vilifier, virtuoso **9** authority, backbiter, detractor, evaluator **10** antagonist, criticizer **11** cognoscente, commentator, connoisseur, faultfinder

critical 5 fussy, grave, hairy, picky, risky, vital **6** urgent **7** carping, crucial, finicky, judging, nagging, serious **8** caviling, decisive, perilous, pressing **9** dangerous, harrowing, hazardous, judicious, momentous, sensitive **10** analytical, censorious, derogatory, diagnostic, nitpicking, precarious **11** disparaging **12** disapproving, faultfinding

critical situation 3 jam **4** mess **6** crisis, pickle **7** straits, trouble **8** hot water **9** deep water **10** difficulty **11** predicament

critical stage 5 H-hour **6** climax, crisis **9** emergency

critical success
French: **13** succes d'estime

criticism 4 fire, flak, slam **5** blame, knock **6** review **7** censure, comment **8** analysis, critique, judgment **9** aspersion, stricture **10** commentary, evaluation **12** faultfinding

criticize 4 carp, fuss, pick **5** cavil, nag at **7** censure, nitpick, reprove **8** denounce, reproach **9** disparage

critique 6 review **8** analysis

Crna Gora see **10** Montenegro

croak 3 caw, die **4** kill, moan, roup **7** grumble, kick off **8** complain, harsh cry **13** kick the bucket

Croatia
capital/largest city: **5** Zagreb
others: **4** Knin **5** Split, Zadar **6** Osijek, Rijeka (Fiume) **7** Vukovar, Sibenik **8** Karlovac, Varazdin, Vinkovci **9** Dubrovnik **10** Kostajnica
head of state: **9** president
government: **9** democracy
monetary unit: **5** dinar
mountain: **10** Julian Alps **11** Styrian Alps
sea: **8** Adriatic
people: **5** Serbs **6** Croats **7** Muslims **9** Yugoslavs
language: **8** Croatian **10** Serbo Croat
religion: **17** Catholic Christian, Orthodox Christian

Crocetti, Dino Paul
real name of: **10** Dean Martin

crock 3 jar, pot **4** olla **9** container

crockery 5 china **6** dishes, plates **7** pottery **8** clayware **9** chinaware, tableware **11** ceramic ware, earthenware **14** cups and saucers

Crock of Gold
author: **13** James Stephens

crocodile 4 croc **6** cayman, gavial, lizard **7** reptile, asurian

crocus
varieties: **4** fall, wild **5** dutch **6** autumn, scotch **7** Chilean, saffron **8** tropical **9** celandine **12** iris-flowered

Crome Yellow
author: **12** Aldous Huxley

Crommyonian sow
also: **5** Phaea
killed by: **7** Theseus

Cromwell, Oliver
also: **13** Lord Protector
served in: **15** English Civil War
fought against: **8** Charles I **9** Cavaliers
fought for: **10** Parliament, Roundheads
regiment: **9** Ironsides
battle: **6** Naseby, Oxford **7** Preston **11** Marston Moor

crone 3 hag **5** witch **6** beldam **7** beldame, old wife

Cronus
also: **6** Cronos, Kronos
form: **5** Titan
father: **6** Uranus
mother: **4** Gaea
sister: **4** Rhea
wife: **4** Rhea
son: **4** Zeus **5** Hades **8** Poseidon
daughter: **4** Hera **6** Hestia **7** Demeter
corresponds to: **6** Saturn

crony 3 pal **4** ally, chum, mate **5** buddy **6** bunkie, cohort, friend **7** comrade **8** bunkmate, intimate, shipmate, sidekick **9** accessory, associate, companion, old friend **10** accomplice, bosom buddy **11** confederate **12** acquaintance, collaborator **13** coconspirator

Cronyn, Hume
wife: **12** Jessica Tandy
born: **6** London **7** Canada, Ontario
roles: **13** The Fourposter **17** Phantom of the Opera **19** Sunrise at Campobello

crook 3 arc, bow **4** bend, hook, thug, turn **5** angle, cheat, curve, knave, thief, twist **6** bandit, outlaw, robber **7** burglar **8** criminal, swindler **9** curvature, embezzler

crooked 4 awry, bent, wily **5** askew, bowed, shady **6** crafty, curved, hooked, shifty, sneaky, spiral, warped, zigzag **7** corrupt, sinuous, twisted, winding **8** criminal, deformed, tortuous, twisting, unlawful **9** deceitful, deceptive, dishonest, distorted, nefarious, unethical **10** fraudulent, meandering, perfidious, serpentine **11** underhanded **12** dishonorable, unscrupulous

crookedness 10 dishonesty **11** deviousness **13** deceitfulness, double-dealing

Crookes, William
nationality: **7** British
invented: **8** thallium **10** radiometer **11** Crookes tube

croon 3 hum **4** sing **6** murmur, warble

crop 3 bob, cut, lop **4** clip, snip, trim **5** prune, shear, yield **6** growth **7** harvest, reaping **8** cut short, gleaning **9** gathering **10** production

crop-raising 7 farming, tillage **11** agriculture **12** agribusiness, truck farming **15** market gardening

crop up 5 arise, ensue, occur **6** appear **7** develop, surface **11** come to light

croquet
equipment: **4** ball, hoop **6** mallet, wicket
variation: **5** roque
term: **5** rover
site: **4** lawn

Crosby, Bing
real name: **17** Harry Lillis Crosby
partner: **7** Bob Hope **10** Hedy Lamarr **13** Dorothy Lamour

nickname: 8 Der Bingle
wife: 8 Dixie Lee **12** Kathryn Grant
born: 8 Tacoma WA
roles: 10 Going My Way (Oscar), Holiday Inn **11** High Society **14** The Country Girl, White Christmas **17** The Bells of St Mary's **22** Christmas in Connecticut
   Road to: 3 Rio **4** Bali **7** Morocco **8** Hong Kong, Zanzibar **9** Singapore

cross 3 mad, mix, tau **4** crux, ford, meet, rood **5** angry, blend, erase, gruff, surly, testy, trial **6** burden, cancel, cranky, delete, go over, hybrid, ordeal, shirty, touchy **7** amalgam, annoyed, athwart, grouchy, oblique, peevish, trouble, waspish **8** captious, choleric, churlish, contrary, crucifix, distress, intermix, pass over, petulant, snappish, traverse **9** adversity, crotchety, half-breed, hybridize, intersect, irascible, irritable, querulous, splenetic, strike out, suffering **10** affliction, difficulty, ill-humored, interbreed, misfortune, obliterate, out of sorts, transverse **11** combination, ill-tempered, intractable, tribulation **12** cantankerous, disagreeable, intersecting

crossbar 3 bar **4** spar **5** sprit **6** stripe
crossbreed 3 mix **8** intermix **9** hybridize **10** interbreed
cross-fertilize 9 hybridize
crossing 4 pass **7** mixture, passage **8** blocking, opposing, traverse **9** thwarting **10** traversing **11** hybridizing, intersection **13** hybridization
cross over 4 span **5** cross **6** bridge **8** traverse
crosspiece 3 bar **4** spar **5** sprit
cross-pollinate 9 hybridize
crossroad 12 intersection, turning point
cross swords 5 clash, fight **6** battle, combat, tussle **7** contend, contest **8** skirmish
crossways 7 athwart **12** transversely
crosswise 6 across **7** athwart **8** sideways, traverse **10** transverse
crotchet 3 tat **4** bent, whim **5** habit, quirk, trait **6** foible, hang-up, oddity, vagary, whimsy **7** caprice **8** quiddity **9** mannerism **10** erraticism **11** peculiarity **12** eccentricity, idiosyncrasy, irregularity **14** characteristic
crotchety 3 odd **5** fussy **6** cranky **7** erratic, grouchy **8** contrary, peculiar **9** eccentric
crouch 4 bend, duck **5** cower, squat, stoop **6** cringe, recoil, shrink **9** hunch over **10** hunker down **11** scrooch down, scrunch down
crow 3 daw, jay, kae **4** blow, brag, rook **5** boast, crake, exult, gloat, raven, strut, vaunt **6** cackle, chough, corbie, magpie **7** corvine, jackdaw,

rejoice, swagger, triumph, trumpet **8** jubilate **14** cock-a-doodle-doo
group of: 6 murder
Crow
  constellation of: 6 Corvus
Crow
  language family: 6 Siouan
  tribe: 9 River Crow **12** Mountain Crow
  location: 7 Montana, Wyoming
  related to: 7 Hidatsa
crowbar 3 bar, pry **5** jimmy, lever
crowd 3 jam, mob, set **4** cram, gang, herd, host, mass, push **5** crush, flock, group, horde, press, shove, surge, swarm **6** circle, claque, clique, gather, huddle, legion, throng **7** cluster, coterie, elbow in, squeeze **8** assemble **9** gathering, multitude **10** assemblage, congregate **11** concentrate **12** congregation
Crowd, The
  director: 9 King Vidor
  cast: 9 Bert Roach **11** James Murray **15** Eleanor Boardman
crowded 4 full **6** filled, jammed, mobbed, packed **7** crammed, teeming **8** swarming, thronged **9** congested, jampacked **11** overflowing
crowd out 8 displace **9** overwhelm
crown 3 cap, top **4** acme, apex, head, pate, peak **5** crest, tiara **6** climax, diadem, noggin, noodle, summit, top off, wreath, zenith **7** chaplet, circlet, coronet, fulfill, garland, perfect, royalty **8** complete, monarchy, pinnacle, round out **11** sovereignty
Crowne, Lenina
  character in: 13 Brave New World
  author: 6 Huxley
crowning point 3 cap, tip **4** apex, peak **6** summit, vertex, zenith **8** pinnacle
crown of thorns 4 bane **5** cross **6** burden, ordeal **7** torment **8** vexation **10** affliction **11** tribulation
crow over 5 gloat **9** brag about **10** boast about
crucial 5 grave **6** knotty, urgent **7** serious, weighty **8** critical, decisive, pressing **9** essential, important, momentous **11** determining, significant
Crucible, The
  author: 12 Arthur Miller
crude 3 raw **5** crass, gross, rough **6** coarse, vulgar **7** obscene, sketchy, uncouth **9** imperfect, tasteless, unrefined **10** incomplete, unfinished, unpolished, unprepared **11** uncompleted, undeveloped, unprocessed
crudeness 7 rawness **8** bad taste **9** crassness, grossness, obscenity, vulgarity **10** coarseness, indelicacy **13** tastelessness
cruel 6 brutal, savage **7** inhuman, vicious **8** inhumane, pitiless, ruthless,

sadistic **9** heartless, merciless, unfeeling **10** unmerciful **11** cold-blooded, hardhearted, remorseless **15** uncompassionate
cruelty 6 sadism **8** ferocity, savagery **9** barbarity, brutality **10** bestiality, inhumanity **11** viciousness **12** ruthlessness **13** heartlessness
cruet 3 jar, jug **6** bottle **7** urceole **9** dispenser
cruise 4 sail, scud, skim **5** coast, drift, float, glide, sweep **6** stream, voyage **7** seafare **8** navigate
Cruise, Tom
  original name: 21 Thomas Cruise Mapother
  born: 10 Syracuse NY
  wife: 10 Mimi Rogers **12** Nicole Kidman
  films: 4 Taps **6** Top Gun **7** The Firm, Rain Man **8** Cocktail **10** Far and Away **11** Endless Love, A Few Good Men **12** Jerry Maguire, The Outsiders **13** Days of Thunder, Risky Business **15** The Color of Money **16** All the Right Moves **17** Mission Impossible **21** Born on the Fourth of July, Interview with a Vampire
crumb 3 bit, ort **5** grain, scrap, shred, speck **6** morsel, sliver **8** fragment, particle
crumble 5 crush, decay, grate, grind **6** powder **8** fragment, splinter **9** decompose, pulverize **12** disintegrate
crumbly 7 brittle, friable **9** breakable
Crummles, Vincent
  character in: 16 Nicholas Nickleby
  author: 7 Dickens
crummy 5 awful, lousy **6** rotten **8** terrible
crumple 4 fall **5** crush **6** cave in, crease, pucker, rumple **7** crimple, crinkle, wrinkle **8** collapse **9** corrugate
crunch 4 chew, gnaw **5** chomp, gnash, grind, munch **7** squeeze **8** showdown **9** masticate
Cruncher, Jerry
  character in: 16 A Tale of Two Cities
  author: 7 Dickens
crunchy 3 dry **5** crisp **6** crispy **7** crackly
crusade 5 drive, rally **8** campaign, movement
Crusader 6 knight, zealot **7** pilgrim, Templar **8** champion **11** Hospitaller
Crusades
  time: 10 Middle Ages
  cry: 8 deus vult
  foe: 4 turk **7** infidel, Saladin, saracen
  leader: 7 Tancred
  port: 4 Acre
crush 4 mash **5** break, press, quash, quell, smash **6** enfold, quench, squash, subdue **7** crumble, crumple, embrace, put down, shatter, squeeze, squelch **8** compress, overcome, sup-

press **9** granulate, overpower, overwhelm, pulverize **10** extinguish

crushed 3 sad **5** cowed **6** broken, mashed, woeful **7** abashed, doleful, forlorn, pressed, put down, quashed, quelled, smashed, subdued **8** crumbled, crumpled, dejected, desolate, overcame, overcome, quenched, squashed, squeezed, wretched **9** flattened, miserable, squelched, woebegone **10** compressed, despondent, pulverized, suppressed **11** overpowered, overwhelmed **12** disconsolate, extinguished, inconsolable **13** brokenhearted

crushing 7 mashing **8** decisive, quelling, smashing **10** shattering **11** humiliating, putting down, stamping out, suppression **12** obliterating, overwhelming **13** pulverization

crust 4 coat, gall, hull, rind, scab **5** brass, nerve, shell **6** harden **7** coating **8** chutzpah, covering, pie shell **9** impudence **11** pastry shell

crustacean 4 crab, flea **5** louse, prawn **6** isopod, shrimp **7** lobster **8** barnacle, crawfish, crayfish **9** shellfish, water flea

crusty 4 curt **5** blunt, gruff, rough, short, stern, surly, testy **6** abrupt, crabby, cranky, shirty, snippy, sullen **7** brusque, peevish, waspish **8** choleric, snappish, snippety **9** irascible, splenetic **10** ill-natured **11** illtempered **13** short-tempered

crux 3 nub **4** core, gist **5** basis, heart **7** essence **9** essential **10** brass tacks **11** nitty-gritty

cry 3 beg, sob, sue **4** bawl, call, hawk, howl, keen, moan, plea, roar, wail, weep, yell, yelp **5** blare, cheer, groan, mourn, plead, shout, utter, whoop **6** appeal, bellow, blazon, boohoo, clamor, hurrah, huzzah, lament, outcry, prayer, scream, shriek, snivel **7** blubber, call out, exclaim, implore, request, screech, trumpet, whimper **8** entreaty, petition, proclaim **9** advertise, importune **10** adjuration, promulgate **11** exclamation **12** solicitation, supplication

Cry, the Beloved Country
  author: 9 Alan Paton
  locale: 11 South Africa

cry out 4 bark, bawl, call, howl, roar, yell **5** shout **6** bellow, clamor, holler **7** exclaim **8** proclaim **9** ejaculate

cry over 5 mourn **6** bemoan, bewail, lament

crypt 4 tomb **5** vault **8** catacomb **9** mausoleum, sepulcher

cryptic 4 dark **5** vague **6** arcane, hidden, occult, secret **7** obscure, strange **8** esoteric, mystical, puzzling **9** ambiguous **10** cabalistic, mysterious, perplexing **11** enigmatical

cryptogram 4 code **6** cipher

cryptograph 4 code **6** cipher, encode

crystal 3 ice **5** clear, flake, glass, lucid **6** quartz **7** diamond **8** stemware **9** glassware, snowflake, watch part **10** rhinestone **11** transparent

crystallize 3 fix, gel **4** firm, jell **5** candy **6** harden **8** solidify **9** granulate

Csonka, Larry (Lawrence Richard)
  nickname: 9 Lawnmower
  sport: 8 football
  position: 8 fullback
  team: 13 Miami Dolphins, New York Giants

cub 3 boy, pup **4** bear, lion **5** scout, whelp **6** novice **8** reporter **9** youngling, youngster **10** apprentice

Cuba
  other name: 18 pearl of the Antilles
  capital/largest city: 6 Havana **8** Le Habana
  others: 5 Bauta, Colon, Duabi, Guane, Manes **6** Baines, Bayamo, Gibara, Guines, Mayari **7** Antilla, Baracoa, Fomento, Holguin, Holquin, Jiguani, Niquero, Palmira, Sanhuis **8** Artemisa, Camaguey, Cardenas, Guaimaro, Guayabal, Marianao, Matanzas, Nuevitas, Varadero, Yaguajay **9** Cabaiguan, Camajuani, Cienfuego **10** Cienfuegos, Guanabacoa, Guantanamo, Manzanillo, Santa Clara **11** Campechuela, Pinar del Rio, Puerto Padre **12** Ciego de Avila **13** Sagua de Tanamo **14** Sancti Spiritus, Santiago de Cuba **17** Aguada de Pasajeros, Consolacion del Sur
  measure: 4 vara **5** bocoy, cocoy, tarea **6** cordel, fanega **10** caballeria
  monetary unit: 4 peso **7** centavo **8** cuarenta
  weight: 5 libra **6** tercio
  island: 5 Pines, Pinos **6** Sabana **8** Camaguey, Juventud **9** Canarreos **17** Jardines de la Reina
    cay: 4 Coco **5** Largo **6** Romano **7** Guajaba, Rosareo, Sabinal **8** Cantiles **9** San Felipe **10** Santa Maria
  mountain: 6 Copper **7** Cristal, Maestra, Organos **8** Camaguey, Trinidad **9** Las Villas **11** Pinar del rio **12** Guaniguanico **14** Sancti-Spiritus
  highest point: 8 Turquino
  river: 4 Zaza **5** Cauto **8** San Pedro
  sea: 8 Atlantic **9** Caribbean
  physical feature:
    bay: 4 Nipe, Pigs **6** Jiguey **8** Cochinos **10** Buena Vista, Guantznamo
    cape: 4 Cruz **5** Maisi **8** Lucrecia **10** Corrientes, San Antonio
    channel: 8 Nicholas **9** Old Bahama
    falls: 3 Toa **7** Agabama, Caburni
    gulf: 6 Mexico **7** Cazones **8** Anamaria, Batabano **12** Guancanayabo
    inlet: 4 Broa **10** Corrientes
    peninsula: 6 Zapata
    point: 7 Guarico
    swamp: 6 Zapata

  people: 5 Carib, Negro, Taino, white **6** Arawak **7** Ciboney, mestizo **8** Ciboneye
    conqueror: 9 Velazquez
    explorer: 8 Columbus
    leader: 6 Castro **7** Batista **10** Che Guevara
  language: 7 Spanish
  religion: 13 Roman Catholic
    cult: 6 Chango, Yemaya
  places:
    castle: 5 Morro
    cathedral: 8 Santiago
  feature:
    dance: 5 conga, rumba **6** danzon, rhumba **8** guaracha, pachanga
    harvest: 5 zafra
    peasant: 7 guajiro
    tree: 5 jique, jiqui
    witch doctor: 7 nanigos
  food:
    dish: 6 paella
    drink: 4 pina

cubbyhole 4 nook **5** niche **6** cranny **10** pigeonhole **11** compartment

cube of deep-fried pork
  American Spanish: 10 cuchifrito

cubic centimeter
  abbreviation: 4 cu cm

cubic dekameter
  abbreviation: 5 cu dkm

cubic foot
  abbreviation: 4 cu ft

cubic inch
  abbreviation: 4 cu in

cubicle 3 bay **4** cell, nook **5** booth, niche **6** alcove, carrel, recess

cubic meter
  abbreviation: 3 cu m

cubic millimeter
  abbreviation: 4 cu mm

cubic yard
  abbreviation: 4 cu yd

cubit 15 Biblical measure

cuchifrito 19 cube of deep-fried pork

Cuchulainn
  origin: 5 Irish
  hero of: 6 Ulster
  uncle: 9 Conchobar
  guarded house of: 10 Smith Culan
  killed by: 6 Lugaid

cuckoo 3 ani **4** bats, bird, fool, gaga, nuts **5** balmy, batty, crazy, daffy, dotty, goofy, loony, nutty, silly, wacky **6** screwy **7** idiotic **9** screwball **12** crackbrained **13** off one's rocker **14** off one's trolley

cucumber 14 Cucumis sativus
  varieties: 3 bur **4** mock, star, wild **6** bitter, pickle **7** prickly, serpent **9** squirting **13** African horned

cuddle 3 hug, pet **5** clasp **6** caress, curl up, fondle, huddle, nestle, nuzzle **7** cling to, embrace, lie snug, snuggle

Cuddly Dudley
  nickname of: 11 Dudley Moore

cudgel 4 club 5 baton, staff, stick 8 bludgeon 9 billy club, blackjack, truncheon 10 shillelagh 12 quarterstaff

cue 3 key, tip 4 clue, hint, sign 6 signal 7 inkling 10 intimation, suggestion 11 insinuation

cuff 3 box, hit, rap 4 blow 5 clout, smack, thump, whack 6 thwack, wallop

cui bono 10 for what use, of what good 15 for whose benefit

cuisine 4 fare, food, menu 5 table 6 viands 7 cookery, cooking, edibles 8 victuals, vittles 11 comestibles

Cukor, George
  director of: 7 Camille 8 Adam's Rib, Gaslight, The Women 10 My Fair Lady (Oscar) 11 A Double Life, A Star Is Born, Little Women 13 Born Yesterday, Dinner at Eight 14 Romeo and Juliet 16 David Copperfield 18 A Bill of Divorcement 20 The Philadelphia Story

cul-de-sac 6 pocket 7 dead-end, impasse 10 blind alley

cull 4 junk, pick, sift, take 5 dross, glean, scrap, trash, waste 6 choose, divide, garner, gather, jetsam, reject, second, select, winnow 7 castoff, collect, discard, excerpt, extract, leaving 8 abstract, scouring, separate 9 segregate

culminate 3 cap, end, top 5 crown, end up 6 climax, finish, result, top off, wind up 8 complete, conclude 9 terminate 10 consummate

culmination 4 acme, apex, peak 6 apogee, climax, height, zenith 7 epitome 8 pinnacle 10 conclusion 11 fulfillment, realization 12 consummation

Culp, Robert
  born: 10 Berkeley CA
  roles: 4 I Spy 20 Greatest American Hero

culpability 4 onus 5 blame, fault, guilt 9 liability 14 accountability, responsibility

culpable 6 guilty, liable 7 at fault, to blame 8 blamable 10 censurable 11 blameworthy

culprit 5 felon 6 sinner 8 criminal, evildoer, offender 9 miscreant, wrongdoer 10 lawbreaker, malefactor 12 transgressor

cult 4 sect 7 faction, zealots 8 admirers, devotees, devotion 9 disciples, followers 10 admiration

cultivable 6 arable 7 fertile, friable 8 farmable, plowable, tillable

cultivate 3 dig, hoe, sow 4 farm, grow, plow, seek, till, weed 5 court, plant, spade 6 enrich, garden 7 acquire, advance, develop, elevate, enhance, improve

cultivated 3 dug 4 fine, grew, hoed 6 farmed, forked, sought, spaded, tilled, weeded 7 courted, planted 8 advanced, cultured, elevated, enhanced, enriched, finished, improved, polished 9 developed

cultivation 5 grace 6 polish, sowing 7 farming, manners, tilling 8 agronomy, planting 9 elevation, gardening, gentility, good taste, husbandry 10 refinement 11 agriculture

culture 3 art 5 music 7 the arts 8 learning 9 erudition, knowledge 10 enrichment, literature, refinement 12 civilization 13 enlightenment 15 accomplishments

Culture and Anarchy
  author: 13 Matthew Arnold

cultured 7 elegant, erudite, genteel, learned, refined 8 polished, well bred, well-read 11 enlightened 12 accomplished, well-educated 13 sophisticated

culture medium 4 agar 8 agar-agar

culvert 5 ditch, drain, sewer 6 trench 7 channel, conduit, fox-hole

cumbersome 5 bulky, hefty 6 clumsy 7 awkward 8 cumbrous, ungainly, unwieldy 9 ponderous 12 unmanageable

cum grano salis 15 not too seriously 16 with a grain of salt

cumin
  botanical name: 14 Cuminum cyminum
  other name: 6 comino, jiraka, kummel
  origin: 5 Egypt
  family: 7 parsley
  symbol of: 5 greed
  guards against straying: 7 pigeons 8 chickens, husbands
  use: 4 fish, meat, rice, soup, stew 5 bread, curry 6 cheese 7 pickles, sausage 8 potatoes 11 chili powder

cum laude 10 with praise

Cummings, E. E. (Edward Estlin)
  author of: 12 in just spring 15 The Enormous Room 17 Tulips and Chimneys 18 Chansons Innocentes

Cummings, Robert
  real name: 29 Clarence Robert Orville Cummings
  born: 8 Joplin MO
  roles: 8 King's Row 14 Dial M for Murder 18 The Bob Cummings Show

cumulate 5 amass 6 gather, heap up, pile up 10 accumulate

cumulative 7 amassed, piled up 8 additive, heaped up 9 aggregate 10 collective 12 accumulative, conglomerate

Cunegonde
  character in: 7 Candide
  author: 8 Voltaire

cunning 3 art, sly 4 foxy, wily 5 canny, craft, guile, knack, skill 6 artful, crafty, deceit, genius, shifty, shrewd, talent, tricky 7 ability, devious, finesse, slyness 8 aptitude, artifice, deftness, foxiness, guileful, subtlety, trickery, wiliness 9 chicanery, deceitful, deception, deceptive, dexterity, duplicity, ingenious, underhand 10 adroitness, artfulness, cleverness, craftiness, expertness, shrewdness 11 deviousness 13 Machiavellian
  god of: 6 Hermes

Cunning Little Vixen, The
  opera by: 7 Janacek

cup 3 cup 5 glass, grail, stein 6 beaker, goblet, vessel 7 chalice, tankard 8 half pint, schooner
  abbreviation: 1 c

Cup
  constellation of: 6 Crater

cupbearer of gods 8 Ganymede

cupboard 6 buffet, bureau, closet 7 armoire, cabinet 9 sideboard, storeroom 10 chiffonier 11 china closet 12 clothespress

Cupid 6 cherub
  also: 4 Amor
  origin: 5 Roman
  god of: 4 love
  mother: 5 Venus
  corresponds to: 4 Eros
  features: 3 bow 5 arrow, wings

cupidity 5 greed 7 avarice, avidity 8 rapacity 10 greediness 11 selfishness 12 covetousness, graspingness 13 concupiscence, insatiability, rapaciousness 14 avariciousness 15 acquisitiveness

cupola 4 dome, roof 5 tower, vault 6 belfry, turret 7 ceiling

cur 3 cad 4 mutt 5 rogue 6 rascal, varlet, wretch 7 mongrel, varmint, villain 9 scoundrel 10 blackguard

curacao
  type: 7 liqueur
  origin: 19 Netherlands Antilles
  flavor: 6 orange
  with gin: 8 Blue Moon, Napoleon 9 Blue Devil 14 Flying Dutchman
  with rum: 6 Mai-Tai 8 Blue Lady 12 Blue Hawaiian
  with vodka: 8 Aqueduct

curate 5 vicar 6 cleric, deacon, parson, pastor, priest, rector 8 minister, preacher 9 churchman, clergyman 12 ecclesiastic

curative 4 balm 7 healing 11 restorative

curator 5 doyen 6 keeper 7 steward 8 director, overseer 9 caretaker, custodian

curb 3 rim 4 edge, rein 5 brink, check, ledge, limit 6 border, bridle, halter, retard, slow up 7 control, harness, inhibit, repress, slacken 8 hold back, moderate, restrain, restrict, slow down, suppress 9 curbstone, hindrance, restraint 10 decelerate, limitation 11 restriction, retardation

curdle 3 rot 4 clot, curd, sour, turn 5 decay, go bad, go off, spoil 7 clabber, congeal, ferment, putrefy, thicken **8** putresce, solidify **9** coagulate **11** deteriorate

cure 3 dry **4** heal, salt **5** smoke **6** remedy **8** antidote, make well, preserve **10** corrective

cure-all 4 balm **6** elixir, remedy **7** panacea **10** catholicon

cured 5 dried **6** healed, mended, smoked **8** made well, remedied **9** preserved, recovered

Curie, Marie Sklodowska and Pierre
field: 7 physics **9** chemistry
discovered: 6 radium **8** polonium **13** radioactivity
awarded: 10 Nobel Prize
daughter: 5 Marie (Joliot-Curie, Nobelist)

curio 7 bibelot, trinket **9** bric-a-brac, objet d'art

curiosity 5 freak, sight **6** marvel, oddity, prying, rarity, wonder **7** novelty **8** interest, nosiness **10** phenomenon, rare object **11** questioning **15** inquisitiveness

curious 3 odd **4** nosy, rare **5** funny, novel, queer, weird **6** prying, quaint, unique **7** bizarre, strange, unusual **8** peculiar, singular, snooping, uncommon **9** inquiring, searching **11** inquisitive, questioning

curl 4 coil, lock, wave, wind **5** crimp, frizz, swirl, twirl, twist **6** spiral **7** frizzle, ringlet, scallop **8** curlicue **9** corkscrew

curled 3 set **5** kinky, waved, wound **6** coiled, frizzy, permed, spiral **7** crimped, frizzed, twisted **8** crinkled, scrolled **9** curlicued

curlicue 4 coil **5** twist **6** spiral **8** flourish

curly 4 wavy **5** kinky **6** frizzy **7** rippled **8** crinkled **9** ringleted

curmudgeon 4 crab **5** crank, grump **6** grouch **8** grumbler, sourball

currant 5 Ribes
varieties: 3 red **5** black, fetid, skunk, squaw, stink **6** alpine, cherry, common, garden, Indian, Sierra **7** Buffalo **8** Missouri, mountain, swamp red **9** chaparral, wild black **11** northern red **12** bristly black **13** American black, European black, northern black, white-flowered **15** California black

currency 4 cash, coin **5** bills, money, vogue **6** specie **7** coinage **9** bank notes **10** acceptance, popularity, prevalence **12** predominance, universality

current 3 now **4** flow, flux, mood, tide **5** draft, drift, trend **6** modern, spirit, stream, with-it **7** feeling, in style, in vogue, popular, present **8** existing, tendency, up-to-date **9** prevalent, zeitgeist **10** atmosphere, present-day, prevailing **11** inclination **12** contemporary, undercurrent

current of air 4 wind **5** draft **6** breeze, zephyr

curricle 3 gig **4** cart, trap **6** chaise **8** carriage

curry powder
origin: 5 India
ingredient: 5 cumin **6** cloves **8** capsicum, turmeric **9** coriander, fenugreek, red pepper **13** cayenne pepper
use: 5 kebab, kebob, kofta, malai **6** kormas **7** curries **8** meat loaf, vindaloo, zucchini **11** potato salad

curse 3 vex **4** bane, cuss, damn, oath **5** blast, cross, swear, trial **6** burden, ordeal, plague, whammy **7** afflict, condemn, evil eye, scourge, swear at, torment, trouble **8** anathema, denounce, execrate, swearing, vexation **9** annoyance, blasphemy, damnation, evil spell, expletive, obscenity, profanity **10** affliction, execration, misfortune **11** imprecation, malediction, tribulation **12** anathematize, denunciation

cursory 5 brief, hasty, quick, swift **6** casual, random **7** hurried, offhand, passing **8** careless **9** desultory, haphazard **11** inattentive, perfunctory, superficial

curt 4 rude **5** bluff, blunt, gruff, short, terse **6** abrupt, crusty, snappy **7** brusque, summary **8** petulant **10** peremptory

curtail 3 cut **4** clip, trim **6** reduce **7** abridge, shorten **8** condense, contract, cut short, decrease, diminish, pare down **10** abbreviate

curtailed 3 cut **7** checked, concise, cut back, reduced, slashed **8** abridged, cut short **9** shortened **10** retrenched

curtailment 7 cutback, cutting, halting, pruning **8** clipping, decrease, trimming **9** lessening, reduction, restraint **10** limitation, shortening **11** abridgement, contraction **12** abbreviation, condensation

curtain 3 end **4** mask, veil **5** blind, cover, drape, shade, sheet **6** screen, shroud **7** conceal, drapery, hanging **8** portiere

Curtis, Tony
real name: 15 Bernard Schwartz
wife: 10 Janet Leigh
daughter: 8 Jamie Lee
born: 9 New York NY
roles: 7 Houdini, Trapeze **12** The Great Race **13** Some Like It Hot **14** The Defiant Ones **16** The Great Imposter **18** The Boston Strangler **22** The Sweet Smell of Success

Curtius
also: 6 Marcus
volunteered as: 17 sacrificial victim

Curtiz, Michael
director of: 10 Casablanca (Oscar), The Sea Hawk **12** Captain Blood **13** Mildred Pierce **14** Life with Father **17** Yankee Doodle Dandy **24** The Adventures of Robin Hood (with William Keighley) **26** The Charge of the Light Brigade **34** The Private Lives of Elizabeth and Essex

curtsy, curtsey 3 bob, bow, dip **5** honor **6** homage **9** obeisance, reverence **11** bend the knee

curvature 3 arc **4** arch, bend **5** crook **6** bowing

curve 3 arc, bow, ess **4** arch, bend, coil, hook, loop, turn, wind **5** crook, twist **6** spiral, swerve

curved 4 bent **5** bowed **6** arched, looped, turned

curved span 3 bow **4** arch, dome **5** vault **6** bridge

Curve of Binding Energy, The
author: 10 John McPhee

curving 4 bent **5** bowed **6** arched **7** bending, looping, turning, winding **8** twisting

curving inward 6 hollow, sunken **7** concave **8** hollowed **9** depressed

curving outward 5 bowed **6** convex **7** bulging, rounded **8** bellying **11** protuberant

Cuscatlan see **10** El Salvador

Cush
father: 3 Ham
grandfather: 4 Noah
brother: 6 Canaan
son: 6 Nimrod
Hebrew for: 8 Ethiopia

cushion 3 mat, pad **4** damp **5** quiet **6** dampen, deaden, muffle, pillow, soften, stifle **7** bolster **8** suppress

Cushitic
language family: 11 Afro-Asiatic **13** Hamito-Semitic
branch: 6 Somali **8** Gallinya
spoken in: 7 Somalia **8** Ethiopia, Tanzania

cusp 4 apex, barb, horn, peak **5** angle, point, tooth **6** corner

custard 4 flan, fool **5** creme **6** junket **7** dessert, pudding **8** flummery **10** blanc-mange, zabaglione

Custer, George A
served in: 8 Civil War **10** Indian Wars
side: 5 Union
battle: 13 Little Big Horn
defeated: 11 Black Kettle
defeated by: 10 Crazy Horse

custodian 6 duenna, keeper, warden **7** janitor **8** chaperon, guardian, watchman **9** attendant, caretaker, chaperone, concierge **14** superintendent

custody 4 care **5** watch **6** charge **9** detention **10** possession, protection **11** confinement, safekeeping, trusteeship **12** conservation, guardianship, preservation

custom 4 form, mode **5** habit, usage **7** fashion **10** convention

customarily 7 as a rule, usually **8** commonly, normally **9** generally, regularly **10** frequently, habitually, ordinarily **13** traditionally

customary 5 usual **6** common, normal, wonted **7** general, regular, routine, typical **8** everyday, habitual, ordinary **10** accustomed **11** traditional **12** conventional

customer 5 buyer **6** client, patron **7** habitue, shopper **9** purchaser

customs 4 duty, levy, toll **6** excise, tariff **9** import tax **10** assessment

cut 3 mow, saw **4** chop, clip, crop, cube, dice, fall, gash, hack, move, nick, pare, part, rent, rive, slit, snip, snub, trim **5** carve, cross, lance, mince, piece, prune, sever, share, shave, shear, slash, slice, split, wound **6** bisect, course, delete, divide, furrow, hollow, ignore, incise, pierce, reduce, sunder, trench **7** abridge, channel, curtail, decline, dissect, opening, passage, portion, section, segment **8** condense, contract, decrease, diminish, incision, lacerate **9** abatement, intersect, lessening, reduction, shrinkage **10** abbreviate, diminution, excavation, shortening **11** contraction, curtailment, indentation

cut and run 4 bolt, flee, skip **6** escape **7** abscond, get away, make off, run away **8** slip away **9** break free **10** break loose, fly the coop **12** make a getaway

cut apart 7 dissect **9** anatomize

cutback 8 decrease, trimming **9** reduction **11** abridgement, curtailment

cut back 4 trim **5** prune **6** reduce **7** abridge, curtail **8** decrease

cut costs 4 save **5** skimp, stint **6** scrimp **7** husband **8** conserve, downsize **9** economize **15** tighten one's belt

cut down 4 kill, trim **5** limit **6** lessen, reduce **7** abridge, curtail, destroy, disable, remodel, shorten **8** condense, decrease, diminish, restrict **10** abbreviate

cut-down form 6 digest, precis **7** summary **8** synopsis, trimming **10** shortening **11** abridgement, contraction, curtailment **12** abbreviation, condensation

cut down to size 5 abase **6** humble **7** mortify **8** belittle, bring low, disgrace **9** humiliate **13** bring down a peg

cute 5 sweet **6** dainty, pretty **7** darling, lovable **8** adorable, handsome, precious **9** beautiful **10** attractive

cut expenses 4 save **5** skimp, stint **6** scrimp **8** conserve **9** economize **12** pinch pennies **15** tighten one's belt

cut in half 5 halve **6** bisect

cut in two 5 halve, sever **6** bisect

cutlet 3 cut **4** chop **5** slice **9** cotelette, croquette

cut off 4 dock, trim **5** apart, sever **6** detach, remove **7** chop off, divorce, isolate **8** amputate, divorced, isolated, separate **10** disconnect

cut out 2 go **4** blow, exit **5** be off, erase, leave, scram, split **6** beat it, delete, depart, escape, excise, go away, remove, set out **7** abolish **8** designed, get rid of, set forth **9** eliminate **10** do away with, hit the road, make tracks **11** exterminate, take a powder

cut short 4 clip, crop, dock, trim **7** abridge, shorten **8** truncate **10** abbreviate

cutter 4 boat **5** blade, hewer, knife **6** sledge, sleigh, tailor **11** cutting edge

cutthroat 5 cruel **6** outlaw **7** brigand, hoodlum, ruffian **8** ruthless **9** merciless

cutting 3 raw **4** acid, cold **5** harsh, nasty, sharp **6** biting, bitter **7** acerbic, caustic, nipping, pruning, searing **8** clipping, derisive, piercing, scathing, smarting, snubbing, stinging, trimming **9** reduction, sarcastic, stringent **11** abridgement, acrimonious, compression, contraction, curtailment, disparaging, penetrating **12** abbreviation, condensation

cutting edge 5 blade **8** vanguard **9** forefront

cutting off 8 severing **9** severance **10** detachment, separation **13** disconnection, disengagement

cutting remark 3 dig **4** gibe, jeer **5** taunt

Cuttle
　character in: **12** Dombey and Son
　author: **7** Dickens

cut up 4 chop, hack, maim, rend **5** caper, carve, halve, mince, slash, slice, split **6** cleave, deface, deform, divide **7** portion, quarter **8** dissever, mutilate **9** apportion, kid around **10** fool around **11** clown around, play the fool

Cuvier, Georges
　field: **7** geology, zoology
　nationality: **6** French
　founded: **12** paleontology **18** comparative anatomy

Cybele
　also: **9** Dindymene **10** Berecyntia, Magna Mater **11** Great Mother **12** Mater Turrita **17** Great Idaean Mother
　origin: **8** Phrygian **9** Asia Minor
　goddess of: **6** nature
　priest: **5** Galli **10** Corybantes
　corresponds to: **3** Ops **4** Rhea
　epithet: **6** Antaea

Cyclades 3 Dos, Zea **4** Keos, Nios, Sira, Syra **5** Delos, Melos, Naxos,

Paros, Siros, Syros, Tenos, Tinos **6** Andros **7** Amorgos, islands, Kythnos **13** Aegean islands

cycle 3 run **6** series **8** sequence **10** succession **11** progression **14** connected group

cyclone 4 gale, gust, wind **5** storm **7** tornado, twister, typhoon **9** whirlwind, windstorm
　Australian: **10** willy-nilly

Cyclone (Cy)
　nickname of: **15** Denton True Young

Cyclops, Cyclopes
　form: **5** giant
　number of eyes: **3** one
　father: **6** Uranus
　mother: **2** Ge
　blinded by: **8** Odysseus

Cycnus
　father: **4** Ares
　killed in: **4** duel
　killed by: **8** Hercules
　changed into: **4** swan

cylinder 3 can, tin **4** drum, pipe, roll, tube **5** spool **6** barrel, column, pillar, piston, platen, roller **13** piston chamber

cylindrical 5 round **6** tarete **7** tubular **8** columnar

Cymbeline
　author: **18** William Shakespeare
　character: **6** Cloten, Imogen **7** Iachimo, Pisanio **9** Bellarius **17** Leonatus Posthumus

Cymru see **5** Wales

cynic 7 scoffer, skeptic **9** pessimist **10** misogynist **11** faultfinder, misanthrope

cynical 8 derisive, sardonic, scoffing, scornful, sneering **9** misogynic, sarcastic, skeptical **12** misanthropic

cypress 8 Taxodium **9** Cupressus
　varieties: **3** toy **4** bald, berg, pond **5** false, Gowen, Modoc, Piute **6** Bhutan, Hinoki, Lawson, MacNab, Nootka, Sawara, summer, Tecate **7** African, Arizona, Italian, Mexican, Sargent **8** Cuyamaca, golf-ball, Monterey, mourning, Siskiyou, standing **9** Guadalupe, Mendocino, Montezuma, red summer, Santa Cruz **10** Portuguese, tennis-ball **12** Chinese swamp **18** rough-barked Arizona **19** smooth-barked Arizona

Cyprian see **9** Aphrodite

Cyprus
　biblical name: **6** Kittim
　capital/largest city: **7** Nicosia
　city: **6** Paphos **7** Kyrenia, Larnaca **8** Limassol **9** Famagusta
　monetary unit: **4** para **5** pound
　mountain: **7** Kyrenia, Troodos
　highest point: **7** Olympus
　river: **6** Pedias
　sea: **13** Mediterranean
　physical feature:
　　bay: **8** Episkopi
　　cape: **4** Gata **5** Greco **7** Andreas,

Arnauti **9** Kormakiti
peninsula: 6 Karpas
plain: 8 Mesaoria **9** Messaoria
people: 5 Greek, Turks **9** Cypriotes
ruler: 5 Turks **6** Greeks, Romans **7**
British **9** Egyptians, Lusignans,
Venetians **10** Byzantines **11** Phoenicians
language: 5 Greek **7** Turkish
religion: 5 Islam **6** Muslim **13** Greek
Orthodoxy **16** Eastern Orthodoxy

Cyrano de Bergerac
director: 13 Michael Gordon
author: 13 Edmond Rostand
cast: 10 Jose Ferrer (Cyrano), Mala
Powers **13** William Powers
character: 6 Roxane **22** Christian de
Neuvillette
setting: 5 Paris
Oscar for: 9 best actor (Ferrer)

Cyrano de Bergerac, Savinien
author of: 25 Voyages to the Moon
and the Sun
play based on his life by: 13 Edmond Rostand

cytology
study of: 5 cells

czar, tsar 4 king **5** ruler **6** caesar, despot, tyrant **7** emperor, monarch **8** dictator, overlord **9** potentate, sovereign

czarina 7 empress

czaristic 10 autocratic **11** all-powerful,
dictatorial, monarchical

Czechoslovakia/Czech Republic
see also **8** Slovakia
capital/largest city: 5 Praha **6** Prague
others: 2 As **4** Asch, Brno, Cheb,
Most **5** Brunn, Nitra, Opava, Plzen,
Tabor, **6** Aussig, Bilina, Kladno, Kosice, Pilsen, Presov, Sadowa, Trnava,
Vsetin **7** Budweis, Jihlava, Liberec,
Olomouc, Ostrava, Teplitz **8** Carlsbad, Jachymov, Karlsbad **9** Press-
burg **10** Austerlitz, Bratislava, Konig-
gratz **11** Reichenberg
university: 7 Charles
division: 7 Bohemia, Moravia, Silesia
8 Ruthenia, Slovakia
measure: 3 Lan **4** Mira **5** Korec, Liket, Stopa **6** Merice, Strych
monetary unit: 5 crown, ducat **6**
heller, Koruna
mountain: 3 Erz, Ore **5** Giant, Tatra
6 Sumava **7** Sudeten, Sudetes **8**
Krkonose **10** Carpathian
highest point: 7 Gerlach **11** Gerlachovka
river: 2 Uh, **3** Mze, Vag, Vah **4** Dyje,
Eger, Elbe, Gran, Hron, Ipel, Iser,
Labe, Nisa, Oder, Odra, Ohre, Olse,
Waag **5** Becva, Dunaj, March, Nitra,
Slana, Tisza **6** Danube, Moldau, Morava, Ondava, Sazava, Torysa, Vltava
7 Laborec, Luznice **8** Berounka

physical feature:
plateau: 8 Bohemian **11** Sudeten-
land
people: 4 Slav **5** Czech **6** Slovak **8**
Bohemian, Moravian
author: 5 Capek, Hasek, Havel **7**
Kundera, Seifert
composer: 6 Dvorak **7** Janacek,
Martinu, Smetana
director: 11 Milos Forman
philosopher/reformer: 8 Come-
nius, John Huss
language: 5 Czech **6** German, Magyar, Slovak **7** Russian **9** Hungarian
religion: 6 Uniate **8** Lutheran **9** Orthodoxy **13** Roman Catholic
place:
castle: 8 Hradcany
cathedral: 7 St Vitus **10** St Nicholas
resort/spa: 8 Carlsbad, Piestany **9**
Marienbad **10** Luhacovice **11** Kar-
lovy Vary **14** Marianske Lazne
square: 9 Wenceslas
feature:
dance: 5 polka **6** redowa, talian **7**
furiant
gymnastics festival: 11 spartakiada
song: 7 Ma Vlast
food:
beer: 6 pilsen
sausage: 5 parky **6** vursty

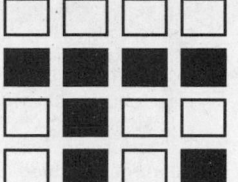
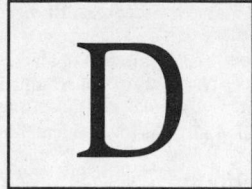
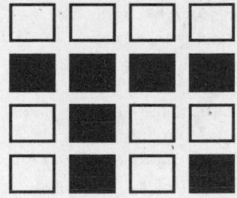

dab 3 bit, pat, tap **6** stroke **7** smidgen, soupçon

dabble 5 slosh **6** fiddle, putter, splash **7** spatter, toy with **8** sprinkle

dabbler 7 amateur, trifler **10** dilettante **12** experimenter **15** nonprofessional

da capo
 music: **22** repeat from the beginning
 abbreviation: **2** DC

Dacca
 capital of: **10** Bangladesh

d'accord 2 OK **6** agreed **7** granted

Dactyls
 also: **7** Daktyls
 dwellers of: **8** Mount Ida

dad 2 da, pa **3** pop **4** papa, pops, sire **5** daddy, pappy, pater **6** father, parent **11** the old man

Daedalus
 occupation: **9** architect
 father: **6** Metion
 son: **5** Iapyx **6** Icarus
 nephew: **5** Talos **6** Perdix
 killed: **5** Talos
 built: **9** labyrinth
  for: **5** Minos
 made: **5** wings

Daedalus, Stephen *see* **30** Portrait of the Artist as a Young Man

daffodil 9 Narcissus **24** Narcissus pseudonarcissus
 varieties: **3** sea **6** winter **8** Peruvian **9** petticoat **13** hoop-petticoat

daft 3 mad **4** loco **5** balmy, batty, crazy, daffy, dizzy, goofy, loony, nutty, silly, wacky **6** cuckoo, insane, screwy **7** foolish, lunatic, witless

Dagan
 origin: **12** Mesopotamian
 god of: **5** earth **11** agriculture
 corresponds to: **5** Dagon

dagger 4 dirk, snee **5** blade, knife **6** weapon **7** poniard **8** stiletto **11** snickersnee

Dagon
 origin: **10** Philistine, Phoenician
 god of: **5** earth **11** agriculture
 corresponds to: **5** Dagan

Daguerre, Louis J M
 nationality: **6** French
 inventor of: **11** photography **13** daguerreotype

Dagwood 8 sandwich
 see also **7** Blondie

dahlia

varieties: **3** sea **4** tree **6** common, garden **7** bedding **8** bell tree **10** candelabra

Dahomey, Republic of *see* **5** Benin

daily 7 diurnal, per diem **9** circadian, quotidian

Daimler, Gottlieb
 nationality: **6** German
 inventor of: **10** carburetor, motorcycle **14** gasoline engine **18** gasoline automobile **25** compression ignition engine

daimyo 4 lord **10** feudal lord

dainty 4 fine **5** fussy, tasty **6** choice, choosy, lovely, pretty, savory **7** choosey, elegant, refined **8** delicate, pleasing **9** beautiful, delicious, exquisite **10** attractive, fastidious, particular

Daira
 father: **7** Oceanus

dais 5 stage **6** podium **7** rostrum **8** platform

daisy 6 Bellis **23** Chrysanthemum frutescens **25** Chrysanthemum leucanthemum
 varieties: **4** blue, cape, high, lazy **5** crown, giant, globe, oxeye, Paris, veldt, white **6** butter, Easter, Nippon, shas- ta, sleepy, Tahoka **7** African, English, painted, seaside, turfing **8** Dahlberg, mountain, panamint **9** Barberton, Englemann, Swan River, Transvaal **10** Kingfisher, Michaelmas, Portuguese **11** Clanwilliam, Livingstone, Namaqualand **12** Boston yellow, double orange **15** blue-eyed African

Daisy Miller
 author: **10** Henry James
 character: **10** Giovanelli **12** Winterbourne

Dakar
 capital of: **7** Senegal

Dakota (Sioux)
 language family: **6** Siouan
 tribe: **5** Teton **6** Lakota, Nakota, Santee **7** Yankton **8** Sisseton, Wahpeton, Wiciyela **9** Wahpekute, Yanktonai **11** Mdewakanton
 location: **7** Montana **9** Minnesota **11** North Dakota, South Dakota
 leader: **4** Gall **10** Crazy Horse **11** Sitting Bull **13** Jashunca-Uiteo
 noted for: **15** military prowess
 deity: **10** Wakan Tanka

dale 4 dell, dene, glen, vale **6** dingle, hollow, valley

D'Alembert
 author of: **12** Encyclopedia

Dali, Salvador
 born: **5** Spain **7** Figuras
 artwork: **10** Last Supper **17** Atomic Leda and Swan **19** Persistence of Memory **22** Accommodations of Desire **24** Christ of St John of the Cross

Dalibor
 opera by: **7** Smetana
 character: **6** Milada

Dallas
 airport: **23** Dallas-Fort Worth Regional
 basketball team: **4** Mavs **9** Mavericks
 football team: **7** Cowboys
 landmark: **15** Turtle Creek Park **16** Museum of Fine Arts **19** Dallas Theater Center **25** Margo Jones Memorial Theater
 river: **7** Trinity
 stadium: **10** Cotton Bowl
 university: **3** SMU **13** Bishop College **17** Southern Methodist

Dallas
 character: **7** JR Ewing **9** Jack Ewing, Jenna Wade, Jock Ewing, Miss Ellie, Ray Krebbs **10** Bobby Ewing **11** Christopher, Cliff Barnes, Mandy Winger, Mark Graison **12** Digger Barnes **13** Clayton Farlow, John Ross Ewing, Sue Ellen Ewing **16** Donna Culver Krebs **17** Pamela Barnes Ewing **22** Eleanor Southworth Ewing
 cast: **8** John Beck **9** Dack Rambo, Linda Gray **10** Howard Keel **11** Larry Hagman, Steve Kanaly, Susan Howard **12** Ken Kercheval, Patrick Duffy **16** Barbara Bel Geddes, Priscilla Presley **17** Victoria Principal
 ranch: **9** Southfork
 business: **3** oil **8** Ewing Oil

dalliance 6 affair, toying **7** romance **8** fiddling, trifling **10** flirtation, lovemaking

dally 3 toy **4** play **5** flirt **6** dawdle, loiter, trifle

Dalmatia *see* **10** Yugoslavia

Dalmatian (dog) 5 spots **12** firehouse dog **13** black and white

Dalton, John
 field: **7** physics **9** chemistry
 nationality: **7** British
 formulated: **12** atomic theory

first: 18 atomic weights table
described: 14 color blindness

dam 3 bar, cow **4** clog, mare, plug, stop, wall **5** bitch, block, check **6** bridle, hinder, hold in, impede, plug up, stanch, stop up **7** barrier, block up, confine, congest, inhibit, repress, stopper, stuff up **8** blockade, hold back, obstruct, restrain **9** barricade, hindrance **11** obstruction

damage, damages 3 mar **4** cost, harm, hurt, loss **6** impair, injure, injury, ravage **10** impairment, reparation, settlement **11** destruction **12** compensation, despoliation

damaging 7 harmful, hurtful, ruinous **9** injurious **11** destructive, detrimental

Damascus
ancient kingdom: 8 Aramaean
Arabic: 7 Dimashq
capital of: 5 Syria
monastery: 22 Suleiman the Magnificent
mosque: 5 Great **7** Umayyad
mount: 6 Qasyun
museum: 8 National **9** Qasr al-Azm
river: 4 Awaj **6** Barada
rulers: 5 Arabs, Timur **6** Romans **7** Mongols, Saladin **8** Assyrian **9** Caliphate, Seleucids **12** Ottoman Turks **15** Byzantine Empire **17** Alexander the Great
tomb: 7 Saladin

Damastes *see* **10** Procrustes

Dame Pliant
character in: 12 The Alchemist
author: 6 Jonson

Damia
spirit of: 9 fertility

damn 4 doom **5** blast **6** rail at **7** censure, condemn **8** denounce **9** criticize, disparage

damned 4 lost **6** cursed, darned, doomed, fallen **7** doggone, dratted, godless **8** accursed, doggoned **9** condemned, execrated, reprobate **12** unregenerate

Damocles
of: 8 Syracuse
offended: 9 Dionysius
seated under: 14 suspended sword

Damon
friend: 7 Pythias

damp 3 wet **4** curb, dank, dash, dewy, dull, mist **5** check, foggy, humid, misty, moist, muggy, rainy, soggy, spoil **6** clammy, deaden, hamper, hinder, reduce, soaked, sodden **7** depress, drizzly, inhibit, sopping, wettish **8** dankness, diminish, dripping, humidity, moisture, restrain **9** mugginess, restraint **10** clamminess, discourage **14** discouragement

dampen 3 wet **4** mute **7** moisten, wet down

dampen one's spirits 5 daunt, un-

man **6** deject **7** depress **10** discourage, dishearten

damper 4 curb, mute **8** obstacle **9** hindrance, restraint **10** constraint, impediment, wet blanket **14** discouragement

damsel 4 girl, lass **6** maiden **9** young lady

damselfly
varieties: 8 forktail **10** civilbluet **11** black-winged, broad-winged **12** narrow-winged, spread-winged, violet dancer

dam up 4 clog, plug **5** block, choke **6** plug up, stop up **7** congest **8** obstruct

Dan
means: 5 judge
father: 5 Jacob
mother: 6 Bilhah
brother: 3 Gad **4** Levi **5** Asher, Judah **6** Joseph, Reuben, Simeon **7** Zebulun **8** Benjamin, Issachar, Naphtali
sister: 5 Dinah
descendant of: 6 Danite

Dana *see* **4** Danu

Dana, Richard Henry
author of: 21 Two Years Before the Mast

Danae
form: 6 maiden
father: 8 Acrisius
mother: 8 Eurydice
imprisoned by: 8 Acrisius
lover: 4 Zeus
son: 7 Perseus

Danai
members of: 6 Greeks **7** Argives

Danaides
daughters of: 6 Danaus
number of daughters: 5 fifty

Dan August
character: 9 (Sgt) Joe Rivera **14** (Sgt) Charles Wilentz **16** (Chief) George Untermeyer
cast: 9 Ned Romero **10** Norman Fell **12** Burt Reynolds **15** Richard Anderson

Danaus
ruler of: 5 Argos
father: 5 Belus
twin brother: 8 Aegyptus
daughters called: 8 Danaides
number of daughters: 5 fifty

dance 3 hop, jam **4** ball, jump, leap, prom, reel, skip **5** lindy, party, polka, twist **6** bounce, cavort, frolic, gambol, prance, square **7** fox-trot, perform **8** cakewalk **9** jitterbug **10** Charleston **11** Boston waltz **12** choreography, Virginia reel **15** hesitation waltz
Renaissance/17th century: 3 jig **5** galop, gigue **6** branle, pavane, redowa **7** bourree, gavotte, lancers, lavolta, mazurka **8** canaries, chaconne, courante, galliard, rigadoon, rigaudon, tourdion **9** allemande, passepied, polonaise, sarabande **10** danse basse, danse haute

18th century: 6 minuet **9** cotillion **11** contre danse **12** country dance
19th century: 5 waltz **9** quadrille
early 1900's: 7 foxtrot, one-step, two-step **8** bunny hug **10** turkey trot **11** grizzly bear
1920's: 5 tango **6** shimmy, toddle **10** Charleston **11** black bottom
1930's: 4 shag **5** conga, rumba, samba, Suzy-Q **7** pecking **8** big apple, lindy hop, trucking **9** jitterbug
1940's: 5 mambo **7** cha-cha
1950's and 1960's: 4 frug, go-go **5** twist **6** monkey **9** rock-'n'-roll
1970's: 5 disco
1980's: 7 lambada
1990's: 8 macarena
Argentine: 5 tango
Austrian: 13 schuhplattler
Balinese: 6 legong
Brazilian: 5 samba **6** maxixe **7** lambada
Cuban: 5 conga, rumba **6** cha-cha
Czech: 5 polka
Dominican: 8 marengue, merengue
folk: 6 Morris **7** maypole
French: 6 can-can **8** galliard **9** ecossaise
German: 11 schottische
Indian: 6 kathak **8** manipuri **9** kathakali **13** bharata nat yam
Japanese: 6 bugaku **7** dengaku **8** sarugaku
 dance/theater: 2 no **3** noh **6** kabuki
Mexican: 3 hat
Polish: 7 mazurka **9** krakoviak, polonaise **11** varsovienne
Scottish: 5 sword
Siamese: 10 wayang wong
Spanish: 4 jota **6** bolero **8** flamenco **9** sevillana **10** seguidilla
modern dancer/choreographer: 4 Juba **8** Ted Shawn **9** Eliot Feld, Gene Kelly, Ray Bolger **10** Alvin Ailey, Mary Wigman, Paul Draper, Twyla Tharp **11** Anna Sokolow, Antony Tudor, Eric Hawkins, Fred Astaire, Irene Castle, Ruth St Denis **12** Bill Robinson, Ginger Rogers, Martha Graham, Vernon Castle **13** Alwin Nikolais, Doris Humphrey, Isadora Duncan **14** Charles Weidman **15** Merce Cunningham
see also **6** ballet

dance of death
French: 12 danse macabre

Dandelion Wine
author: 11 Ray Bradbury

dander 3 ire **5** anger, Irish **6** temper

Dandie Dinmont terrier 24 soft-coated wheaten terrier, Staffordshire bull terrier, West Highland white terrier

dandy 3 fop **4** beau, dude, fine **5** beaut, great, super, swell **6** beauty, superb **7** coxcomb, peacock **8** terrific **9** excellent **12** clotheshorse

danger 4 risk **5** peril **6** hazard, menace, threat **8** jeopardy **12** endangerment

dangerous 5 hairy, risky **6** chancy, unsafe **8** menacing, perilous **9** hazardous **10** precarious **11** threatening, treacherous

danger signal 5 alarm, alert **7** red flag, warning

dangle 3 sag **4** drag, hang, sway **5** droop, swing, trail **6** depend **7** draggle, hang out, suspend **8** hang down, hang over **9** oscillate

Daniel
Babylonian name: 12 Belteshazzar
companion: 7 Meshach **8** Abednego, Shadrach

Daniel Boone
character: 5 Mingo **6** Yadkin **11** Cincinnatus, Israel Boone, Jemima Boone **12** Rebecca Boone
cast: 6 Ed Ames **10** Fess Parker **11** Albert Salmi, Dal McKennon, Darby Hinton **13** Patricia Blair **18** Veronica Cartwright

Danielovitch, Issur
real name of: 11 Kirk Douglas

dank 3 wet **4** cold, damp **5** humid, moist, muggy, soggy **6** chilly, clammy, sodden, sticky

danke 8 thank you

danke schon 16 thank you very much

dankness 4 damp **7** wetness **8** dampness, humidity **9** humidity, moistness, mugginess **10** clamminess

Danner, Blythe
born: 14 Philadelphia PA
roles: 8 Betrayal **15** The Great Santini **16** Man Woman and Child
daughter: 14 Gwyneth Paltrow

Danny Deever
story in: 18 Barrack-Room Ballads
author: 14 Rudyard Kipling

Danny Thomas Show, The
character: 6 Clancy **12** Uncle Tonoose **13** Danny Williams, Linda Williams, Rusty Williams, Terry Williams **16** Mrs Kathy Williams **18** Uncle Charley Halper
cast: 9 Sid Melton **10** Rusty Hamer **11** Hans Conried **12** Marjorie Lord, Penney Parker **13** Sherry Jackson **16** Angela Cartwright

danse macabre 12 dance of death

Dante (Alighieri)
author of: 9 Vita Nuova **15** The Divine Comedy
Divine Comedy Part I: 10 The Inferno
Divine Comedy Part II: 9 Purgatory **10** Purgatorio
Divine Comedy Part III: 8 Paradise, Paradiso
heroine: 8 Beatrice
guide: 6 Virgil

Dantes, Edmond

character in: 21 The Count of Monte Cristo
author: 5 Dumas (pere)

Danton, Ray
born: 9 New York NY
roles: 14 I'll Cry Tomorrow **18** The George Raft Story **27** The Rise and Fall of Legs Diamond

Danu
also: 4 Dana
origin: 5 Irish
mother of: 14 Tuatha De Danann

Danvers, Mrs
character in: 7 Rebecca
author: 9 Du Maurier
played by: 14 Judith Anderson

Daphnaea
epithet of: 7 Artemis
means: 11 of the laurel

Daphne
form: 5 nymph
father: 5 Ladon **6** Peneus
pursued by: 6 Apollo **9** Leucippus
changed into: 7 bay tree

Daphnis
occupation: 7 cowherd **8** shepherd
father: 6 Hermes
originated: 14 pastoral poetry
blinded by: 5 Nomia

Daphnis and Chloe
characters in: 12 Greek romance
author: 6 Longus

Daphnis et Chloe
ballet by: 5 Ravel
choreographer: 12 Michel Fokine

dapper 4 neat, trim **5** natty, smart **6** jaunty, modish, spiffy, sporty, spruce **7** stylish

dapple 3 dab, dot **4** spot **6** mottle

dappled 7 flecked, mottled, spotted **10** variegated

Darcy, Fitzwilliam
character in: 17 Pride and Prejudice
author: 6 Austen

Dardanus
father: 4 Zeus
mother: 7 Electra
twin brother: 6 Iasion
wife: 6 Myrina
son: 12 Erechthonius
ancestor of: 7 Trojans

dare 3 bet **4** defy **5** taunt **7** venture **9** challenge **11** provocation

daredevil 4 bold, rash **5** risky **8** heedless, reckless, stuntman **9** audacious, breakneck, risk-taker **11** adventurous, Evel Knievel **12** death-defying, devilmay-care **13** adventuresome

daredevilry 6 daring **8** rashness **9** derring-do **10** imprudence **12** carelessness, heedlessness, recklessness **13** foolhardiness

Dar es Salaam
former capital of: 8 Tanzania

Darien see **8** Colombia

daring 4 bold, game **5** brave **6** plucky

7 bravery, courage, gallant, valiant **8** audacity, boldness, intrepid **9** audacious, dauntless, undaunted **10** courageous **11** adventurous, venturesome **13** audaciousness **15** adventurousness

daring deed 4 feat **7** exploit **11** achievement

dark 3 dim **4** deep, evil, inky **5** angry, black, bleak, dingy, dusky, murky, night, shady **6** dismal, dreary, gloomy, hidden, opaque, secret, somber, sullen, wicked **7** evening, joyless, obscure, ominous, shadowy, sunless **8** eventide, frowning, hopeless, overcast, sinister, twilight **9** concealed, nightfall, nighttime, sorrowful **10** forbidding **11** threatening **12** discouraging **13** disheartening

darken 3 dim, dye **4** tint **5** cloud, color **6** sadden **7** blacken, obscure **8** dispirit

darkened 3 dim **5** dusky, unlit **6** cloudy, gloomy **7** clouded **9** blackened, tenebrous, unlighted **10** blacked out **13** unilluminated

darkening 7 eclipse, shading **8** clouding, lowering **9** obscuring, shadowing **10** blackening **12** clouding over

Dark Frontier, The
author: 10 Eric Ambler

dark-hued 5 black, dusky, ebony, raven **6** somber **7** swarthy

Dark Is Light Enough, The
author: 14 Christopher Fry

Dark Lady, The
author: 16 Louis Auchincloss

Dark Laughter
author: 16 Sherwood Anderson

darkness 4 dusk **5** night, shade **7** dimness, evening **8** eventide, twilight **9** blackness, nightfall, nighttime

Darkness at Noon
author: 14 Arthur Koestler

Darkness Visible
author: 14 William Golding

Dark Victory
director: 14 Edmund Goulding
cast: 10 Bette Davis **11** George Brent **12** Ronald Reagan **14** Humphrey Bogart **19** Geraldine Fitzgerald
remade as: 11 Stolen Hours

darling 4 cute, dear, love **5** loved, sweet **6** adored, lovely **7** beloved, dearest, lovable **8** adorable, charming, precious **9** cherished **10** attractive, enchanting, sweetheart **11** captivating

Darling
director: 15 John Schlesinger
cast: 11 Dirk Bogarde **13** Julie Christie **14** Laurence Harvey
Oscar for: 6 script **7** actress (Christie)

Darling, Wendy
character in: 8 Peter Pan
author: 6 Barrie

darn 4 damn, dang, dash, drat, mend **5** blast, patch, sew up **6** hang it, stitch

7 consarn, doggone, goldang **8** confound **10** confound it

Darnay, Charles
character in: **16** A Tale of Two Cities
author: **7** Dickens

darnel 12 Biblical weed

Darnell, Linda
real name: **20** Monetta Eloyse Darnell
born: **8** Dallas TX
roles: **12** Blood and Sand, Forever
Amber **14** The Mark of Zorro **17** Unfaithfully Yours

Darren, James
real name: **13** James Ercolani
born: **14** Philadelphia PA
roles: **6** Gidget **13** The Time Tunnel

dart 3 run **4** bolt, dash, flit, jump, leap,
race, rush, tear **5** bound, fling, hurry,
spear, spurt **6** hasten, spring, sprint **7**
javelin, missile **10** projectile

D'Artagnan
character in: **18** The Three Musketeers
author: **5** Dumas (pere)

Dartle, Rosa
character in: **16** David Copperfield
author: **7** Dickens

Darwin, Charles
author of: **15** The Descent of Man **18**
The Origin of Species **20** The Voyage
of the Beagle
studied: **16** Galapagos Islands
field: **6** nature **7** biology
nationality: **7** British
theory of: **9** evolution **16** natural selection
ship: **6** Beagle

dash 3 bit, run, zip **4** bolt, dart, drop,
elan, foil, hurl, race, ruin, rush, slam,
tear, zeal **5** bound, crash, flair, fling,
hurry, oomph, pinch, smash, speed,
spoil, throw, touch, verve, vigor **6**
dampen, energy, hasten, pizazz,
spirit, splash, sprint, thrust, thwart **7**
a little, panache, shatter, soupcon,
spatter **8** splatter, splinter, vivacity **9**
animation, frustrate **10** disappoint,
discourage

dashing 4 bold **5** brave **6** daring,
plucky **7** gallant **8** fearless, spirited,
unafraid **9** audacious, impetuous **10**
courageous **13** swashbuckling

dash one's hopes 5 daunt, unman **6**
deject **7** depress **8** dispirit **10** discourage, dishearten

Dashwood, Elinor and Marianne
characters in: **19** Sense and Sensibility
author: **6** Austen

Da Silva, Howard
real name: **17** Harold Silverblatt
born: **11** Cleveland OH
roles: **8** Oklahoma **12** Sergeant York
14 The Great Gatsby **20** Abe Lincoln
in Illinois

Dass, Secunda
character in: **21** The Master of

Ballantrae
author: **9** Stevenson

dastard 3 cad **6** coward, craven **7**
bounder, caitiff, chicken **8** poltroon
11 yellow-belly

dastardly 3 low **4** base, mean, vile **6**
sneaky **8** cowardly, shameful **9** atrocious **10** despicable

data 4 dope, info **5** facts, input **7** dossier, figures **8** evidence **9** documents
11 information

Datchery, Mr
character in: **22** The Mystery of Edwin Drood
author: **7** Dickens

date 3 age, era **5** court, epoch, stage **6**
escort, period **7** partner, take out **9**
companion, originate **10** engagement,
rendezvous **11** appointment

date 18 Phoenix dactylifera
varieties: **5** cliff **6** Ceylon **7** Chinese
9 Jerusalem **12** Canary Island

dated 5 passe **6** old hat **8** obsolete,
outmoded **9** out-of-date **10** antiquated
12 old-fashioned **13** unfashionable

daub 4 blot, coat, soil, spot **5** cover,
dirty, paint, smear, stain **6** blotch,
smirch, smudge **7** splotch

Daudet, Alphonse
author of: **6** Sappho **15** The Woman
of Arles **17** Letters from My Mill **18**
Tartarin of Tarascon

Daughter of the Regiment, The
opera by: **9** Donizetti

Daumier, Honore
born: **6** France **10** Marseilles
artwork: **7** Bathers **9** Gargantua **12**
Men of Justice **13** Bluestockings **14**
The Washerwoman **16** The Good
Bourgeois **18** The Legislative Body
19 Professors and Pupils **20** Stories
from Antiquity **21** The Third-Class
Carriage

daunt 3 cow **4** dash, faze **5** abash,
alarm, scare **6** deject, dismay, menace, subdue **7** depress, unnerve **8** affright, browbeat, frighten, threaten **10**
discourage, dishearten, intimidate

dauntless 4 bold **5** brave, gutsy **6** daring, heroic **7** gallant, valiant **8** fearless, resolute, unafraid, valorous **10**
courageous **12** stouthearted

dauntlessness 4 grit, guts, sand **5**
nerve, pluck, spunk, valor **6** daring,
mettle **7** bravery, courage, resolve **8**
boldness **9** fortitude **10** resolution **12**
fearlessness, resoluteness **16** stoutheartedness

Davers, Lady
character in: **6** Pamela
author: **9** Richardson

David 6 statue
by: **12** Michelangelo
site: **8** Florence
size: **6** heroic

David

king of: **6** Israel
father: **5** Jesse
wife: **6** Maacah, Michal **7** Abigail,
Ahinoam, Haggith **9** Bathsheba
son: **5** Amnon **7** Absalom, Chileab,
Solomon **8** Adonijah
daughter: **5** Tamar
brother: **5** Eliab **7** Shammah **8** Abinadab
sister: **7** Abigail
friend: **5** Abner **8** Jonathan
nephew: **5** Amasa
city of: **9** Bethlehem, Jerusalem
anointed by: **6** Samuel
killed: **7** Goliath
wrote: **6** Psalms
comforter: **7** Abishag
conspirators against: **4** Joab **8** Abiathar, Adonijah
pertaining to: **7** Davidic

David, Jacques-Louis
born: **5** Paris **6** France
artwork: **13** Mme de Verninac **15**
The Death of Marat **19** The Oath of
the Horatii **23** The Coronation of Napoleon **26** View of the Luxembourg
Gardens **31** The Intervention of the
Sabine Women

David Copperfield
author: **14** Charles Dickens
character: **3** Ham **6** Barkis, Mr Dick **7**
Creakle **8** Traddles **9** Mr Spenlow,
Uriah Heep **10** Aunt Betsey, Little
Em'ly, Mr Micawber, Rosa Dartle,
Steerforth **11** Dora Spenlow, Little
Emily, Mr Murdstone, Mr Wickfield,
Mrs Gummidge **13** Clara Peggotty **14**
Agnes Wickfield, Betsey Trotwood
director: **11** George Cukor
cast: **8** W C Fields **10** Madge Evans
11 Frank Lawton, Roland Young **13**
Basil Rathbone, Edna May Oliver **15**
Lionel Barrymore **16** Maureen
O'Sullivan **18** Freddie Bartholomew

David Harum
author: **19** Edward Noyes Westcott

Davies, Arthur Bowen
born: **7** Utica NY
artwork: **5** Dream **8** Unicorns **9** Crescendo **13** Every Saturday **15** Dancing Children, Sacramental Tree **17**
Along the Erie Canal **18** Leda and
the Dioscuri

Davies, Marion
real name: **19** Marion Cecilia Douras
lover: **21** William Randolph Hearst
born: **10** Brooklyn NY
roles: **12** Cain and Mable **13** Runaway Romany **15** Tillie the Toiler

Da Vinci, Leonardo
born: **5** Italy, Vinci
artwork: **8** Mona Lisa **10** La
Gioconda **13** The Last Supper **15**
The Annunciation **19** The Battle of
Anghiari **21** The Adoration of the
Magi

Davis, Bette

real name: 18 Ruth Elizabeth Davis
husband: 11 Gary Merrill
born: 8 Lowell MA
roles: 7 Jezebel (Oscar) **9** Dangerous (Oscar), The Letter **10** Now Voyager, The Old Maid **11** All About Eve, Dark Victory **14** Of Human Bondage, The Little Foxes **18** The Petrified Forest **22** Hush Hush Sweet Charlotte **26** What Ever Happened to Baby Jane?

Davis, H L
author of: 14 Honey in the Horn

Davis, Ossie
wife: 7 Ruby Dee
born: 9 Cogdell GA
author: 16 Purlie Victorious
roles/films: 7 Jamaica **15** A Raisin in the Sun **18** No Time for Sergeants **19** Cotton Comes to Harlem

Davis, Sammy Jr
wife: 8 May Britt
group: 14 Will Master Trio
born: 9 New York NY
autobiography: 7 Yes I Can
roles: 11 Mr Wonderful **12** Porgy and Bess **20** The Benny Goodman Story

Davis, Stuart
born: 14 Philadelphia PA
artwork: 4 Visa **9** Eggbeater **11** Lucky Strike, Ready to Wear **11** Owh! In Sao Pao **12** The Mellow Pad **14** Colonial Cubism **15** Cigarette Papers

Davy, Humphrey
field: 9 chemistry
nationality: 7 British
isolated: 5 boron **6** barium, sodium **7** calcium **8** chlorine **9** magnesium, potassium, strontium
invented: 8 Davy lamp **10** miner's lamp

dawdle 4 idle, loaf **5** dally, delay **6** loiter **10** dillydally **12** putter around **13** procrastinate

dawdler
French: 7 flaneur

dawdling
French: 8 flanerie

dawn 4 rise **5** begin, birth, occur, start, sunup **6** advent, appear, Aurora, emerge, origin, strike, unfold **7** develop, sunrise **8** commence, daybreak, daylight **9** beginning, emergence, inception, unfolding **12** commencement
god of: 8 Heimdall
goddess of: 3 Eos **6** Aurore, Matuta

dawning 5 sunup **7** morning, sunrise **8** daybreak, daylight

Dawn Patrol, The
director: 14 Edmund Goulding
cast: 10 David Niven, Errol Flynn **11** Donald Crisp **13** Basil Rathbone **14** Melville Cooper **15** Barry Fitzgerald

day 3 age, era **4** date, time **5** epoch **6** period

Day, Clarence (Jr)
author of: 14 God and My Father, Life with Father, Life with Mother

Day, Doris
real name: 18 Doris von Kappelhoff
born: 12 Cincinnati OH
autobiography: 19 Doris Day Her Own Story
roles: 10 Pillow Talk **12** Calamity Jane **13** The Pajama Game **15** Move Over Darling, The Doris Day Show **23** Please Don't Eat the Daisies

daybed 5 couch **6** lounge **12** chaise longue

day book 3 log **5** diary **6** agenda **7** journal **8** calendar, schedule

daybreak 4 dawn, morn **5** sunup **7** sunrise

daydream 4 muse **5** fancy **7** fantasy, imagine, reverie **9** fantasize **10** woolgather **14** castle in the air

Day for Night
director: 16 Francois Truffaut
cast: 15 Jean-Pierre Leaud **16** Francois Truffaut, Jacqueline Bisset, Jean-Pierre Aumont
Oscar for: 11 foreign film

daylight 4 dawn **5** sunup **7** morning, sunrise **8** full view, openness, sunlight, sunshine

Days and Nights
author: 17 Konstantin Simonov

day's end 3 een, eve **4** dusk, even **6** sunset **7** evening, sundown **8** gleaming, twilight **9** nightfall

Days of Heaven
director: 14 Terrence Malick
cast: 9 Linda Manz **10** Sam Shepard **11** Brooke Adams, Richard Gere
Oscar for: 14 cinematography

Days of Wine and Roses
director: 12 Blake Edwards
cast: 9 Lee Remick **10** Jack Lemmon **11** Jack Klugman **15** Charles Bickford
score: 12 Henry Mancini

daze 4 numb, stun **5** amaze, shock **6** benumb, dazzle, excite, muddle, stupor **7** astound, confuse, stagger, startle, stupefy **8** astonish, bewilder, surprise **9** disorient, electrify **11** flabbergast **12** astonishment, bewilderment, blow one's mind **14** discombobulate

dazed 5 woozy **6** groggy **7** confused, dazzled, stunned **9** befuddled, stupefied **10** bewildered, punch-drunk

dazzle 3 awe **4** blur, daze **5** blind **6** excite **7** confuse, overawe **9** electrify, overpower, overwhelm

dazzling 7 radiant **8** blinding **9** sparkling **10** impressive, staggering **11** coruscating **12** breathtaking, electrifying, overwhelming **14** flabbergasting

deacon 6 cleric **9** churchman, clergyman **12** ecclesiastic

deactivate 6 defuse **9** switch off **10** neutralize

Dead, The
author: 10 James Joyce

dead, the dead 4 beat, cold, dull, flat **5** depth, exact, midst, quiet, spent, tired, total, utter, vapid **6** entire, middle, unused **7** defunct, expired, extinct, insipid, precise, useless, utterly, worn-out **8** abruptly, absolute, complete, deceased, entirely, inactive, lifeless, obsolete, perished, stagnant, suddenly, thorough, unerring **9** exhausted, inanimate, inorganic **10** absolutely, completely, lackluster, unemployed, unexciting **11** ineffectual, inoperative **12** unproductive, unprofitable
Latin: 8 ad patres
god of: 6 Osiris **7** Vciovis

dead body 5 stiff **6** corpse **7** cadaver, remains

deaden 4 dope, drug, dull, mute, numb **5** abate, blunt **6** lessen, muffle, soothe, subdue, weaken **7** assuage, smother **8** diminish, mitigate, moderate **9** alleviate **11** anesthetize

deadened 5 muted **6** dulled, numbed **7** muffled, subdued

Dead Father, The
author: 15 Donald Barthelme

Dea Dia
origin: 5 Roman
goddess of: 11 agriculture
corresponds to: 13 Acca Laurentia

deadlock 7 impasse **8** standoff **9** stalemate **10** standstill

deadly 3 wan **4** dull **5** ashen, awful, fatal, fully, undue **6** boring, lethal, mortal, pallid **7** awfully, baneful, destroy, extreme, ghostly, tedious, totally **8** dreadful, untimely, horribly, terrible, terribly, tiresome **9** excessive, malignant, wearisome **10** cadaverous, completely, implacable, inordinate, relentless, thoroughly **11** destructive, unrelenting

deadpan 5 sober **8** detached **9** impassive **10** poker-faced **11** unemotional **13** straight-faced

dead ringer 4 copy, mate, twin **6** double **9** duplicate **11** counterpart **12** doppelganger **13** spitting image

Dead Souls
author: 12 Nikolai Gogol

dead to the world 6 asleep **7** out cold **9** konked out **10** fast asleep, slumbering **11** sound asleep

dead weight 7 ballast **9** inert mass

Dead Zone, The
author: 11 Stephen King

deal 3 act **4** give, hand **5** round, see to, trade, treat **6** behave, handle, market **7** bargain, concern, deliver, dole out, give out, mete out, oversee **8** consider, dispense **9** agreement, apportion **10** administer, distribute **11** arrangement **12** distribution **13** apportionment

dealer 5 agent **6** monger, trader, vendor **8** merchant **10** trafficker **11** distributor

dealing, dealings 5 trade **7** traffic **8** business, practice **9** relations, treatment **12** transactions

dealing out 8 dividing **9** allotting, bestowing **10** conferring, consigning, dispensing **12** apportioning, distributing

Dea Marica see **6** Marica

Dean, Dizzy (Jay Hanna)
 sport: **8** baseball
 position: **7** pitcher
 team: **16** St Louis Cardinals
 part of: **12** Gashouse Gang
 brother: **4** Paul

Dean, James (Jimmy)
 real name: **14** James Byron Dean
 born: **8** Marion IN
 roles: **5** Giant **10** East of Eden **18** Rebel Without a Cause

Deane, Seneca
 character in: **7** Babbitt
 author: **5** Lewis

Dean's December
 author: **10** Saul Bellow

dear 4 love **5** angel, loved **6** costly **7** beloved, darling **8** esteemed, favorite, precious **9** cherished, expensive, respected **10** sweetheart
 French: **5** cheri **6** cherie

Dear Antoine
 author: **11** Jean Anouilh

Dear Brutus
 author: **12** James M Barrie

dearest 7 beloved, darling

dearth 4 lack **7** paucity **8** scarcity, shortage **10** deficiency

death, Death 5 dying **6** demise **7** decease, passing **9** departure **10** expiration, grim reaper
 goddess of: **3** Hel **7** Berchta, Perchta **10** Ereshkigal

Death Be Not Proud
 author: **9** John Donne

death blow
 French: **11** coup de grace

Death Comes for the Archbishop
 author: **11** Willa Cather
 character: **7** Jacinto **9** Kit Carson **16** Bishop Jean Latour **20** Father Joseph Vaillant

death-dealing 5 fatal **6** lethal, mortal **7** killing **11** destructive

death-defying 4 bold, rash **5** risky **6** daring **8** reckless **9** audacious, breakneck, daredevil

Death in the Family, A
 author: **9** James Agee
 filmed as: **13** All the Way Home

Death in Venice
 director: **15** Luchino Visconti

author: **10** Thomas Mann
 cast: **9** Mark Burns **11** Dirk Bogarde **14** Marisa Berenson

deathless 7 eternal **8** immortal **9** perpetual **11** everlasting

deathlike 3 wan **4** pale **5** ashen **6** pallid **7** ghastly **9** bloodless **10** cadaverous, corpselike

deathly 4 very **7** extreme, intense **8** terrible **9** extremely **12** overwhelming **15** resembling death

Death of a Salesman
 director: **12** Laslo Benedek
 author: **12** Arthur Miller
 character: **4** Biff **5** Happy, Linda **7** Bernard, Charley **8** Uncle Ben **10** Willy Loman
 cast: **13** Frederic March, Kevin McCarthy **14** Mildred Dunnock **15** Cameron Mitchell

Death of Ivan Ilyich, The
 author: **10** Leo Tolstoy

Death of the Gods, The
 author: **17** Dmitri Merejkowski

Death of the Heart
 author: **14** Elizabeth Bowen

Death on the Nile
 author: **14** Agatha Christie

Death Takes a Holiday
 director: **14** Mitchell Leisen
 cast: **11** Guy Standing **13** Evelyn Venable, Frederic March (Death)

Death Valley Days
 host: **12** Robert Taylor, Ronald Reagan **13** Dale Robertson **14** Stanley Andrews

debacle 4 rout, ruin **5** havoc, wreck **8** collapse, disaster, downfall **9** breakdown, cataclysm, overthrow, ruination **10** bankruptcy **11** catastrophe, devastation, dissolution **12** vanquishment **14** disintegration

debar 3 ban **6** reject **7** exclude, keep out **8** preclude, prohibit **9** blackball, blacklist

debark 4 land

debarment 7 removal **8** omission **9** exception, exclusion, exemption, rejection **11** elimination, prohibition **12** nonadmission

debase 5 lower **6** befoul, defile **7** corrupt, degrade **8** disgrace, dishonor **9** desecrate **10** adulterate **11** deteriorate **16** impair the worth of **18** reduce the quality of

debased 4 vile **6** impure **7** corrupt, defiled, lowered **8** degraded, depraved **9** debauched, disgraced, dissolute, perverted **10** degenerate, dissipated **11** adulterated

debasement 9 decadence, depravity **10** corruption, debauchery, degeneracy, immorality, perversion **13** dissoluteness

debatable 4 iffy **6** unsure **7** dubious **8** arguable, doubtful **9** uncertain, unde-

cided **10** disputable **12** questionable **13** problematical

debate 5 argue **6** ponder **7** discuss, dispute, reflect **8** argument, cogitate, consider, hash over **10** cogitation, deliberate, discussion, meditation, reflection, think about **12** deliberation, meditate upon **13** consideration

debauch 4 orgy **5** revel, spree **6** debase **7** carouse, corrupt, deprave, revelry, subvert **8** carousal **9** bacchanal **10** lead astray, saturnalia

debauched 4 lewd **6** wanton **7** corrupt, debased, immoral **8** degraded, depraved, perverse, vitiated **9** abandoned, corrupted, dissolute, lecherous, led astray, pervert- ed, reprobate, shameless **10** degenerate, dissipated, lascivious, libidinous, licentious, profligate **12** disreputable

debauchery 6 excess **11** dissipation **12** immoderation, intemperance **14** self-indulgence

DeBeck, Billy
 creator/artist of: **12** Barney Google **20** Parlor Bedroom and Sink

debilitate 6 weaken **7** wear out **8** enervate **10** devitalize, make feeble **17** deprive of strength

debilitated 5 frail **6** feeble, infirm **7** worn out **8** delicate, weakened **9** enervated **11** devitalized

debilitation 8 handicap, weakness **9** infirmity **10** affliction, disability, impairment, inadequacy **11** disablement

debility 7 fatigue, frailty **8** asthenia, handicap, senility, weakness **9** infirmity, lassitude, weakening **10** affliction, enervation, exhaustion, feebleness, impairment, invalidism, sickliness **11** decrepitude, prostration

debit 4 debt **6** red ink **7** account, payable **9** liability **10** balance due, obligation **11** ledger entry, shortcoming

debonair 5 suave **6** dapper, jaunty, urbane **7** buoyant, elegant, genteel, refined **8** carefree, charming, gracious, well-bred **9** sprightly **11** free and easy **12** lighthearted **13** sophisticated

Deborah 11 Hebrew judge
 companion: **7** Rebekah
 summoned: **5** Barak

debouch 5 drain **6** emerge, let out **7** flow out **9** discharge

debris 4 crap, junk **5** dreck, dregs, dross, ruins, scrap, trash, waste **6** litter, rubble, shards **7** clutter, garbage, rubbish **8** detritus, wreckage **9** fragments

debt 4 bill **5** debit **7** arrears **9** liability **10** obligation **15** deferred payment, that which is owed

debunk 4 bare **5** strip **6** expose, send up, show up, unmask **7** deflate, lampoon, take off, uncloak, uncover

8 ridicule, satirize **9** burlesque, demystify, disparage **13** demythologize

Debussy, Claude Achille
  born: 6 France **15** St Germain-en-Laye
  composer of: 5 La Mer **6** Gigues, Iberia, Images **8** Estampes **9** Nocturnes, Printemps **11** Clair de Lune **13** En Blanc et Noir **15** Children's Corner, L'Enfant prodigue **16** La Demoiselle Elue, Suite Bergamasque **17** Rondes de Printemps, The Blessed Damozel **18** Pelleas et Melisande **24** The Girl with the Flaxen Hair **26** Prelude a l'apres-midi d'un faune **28** Prelude to the Afternoon of a Faun

debut 9 coming out **12** presentation

decadence 5 decay **7** decline **10** corruption, debasement, degeneracy, immorality **12** degeneration **13** deterioration

decadent 7 corrupt, debased, immoral **8** decaying, depraved, perverse **9** debauched, dissolute, perverted **10** degenerate
  French: 11 fin de siecle

Decalogue 15 Ten Commandments

Decameron, The
  author: 17 Giovanni Boccaccio

decamp 7 move off, run away, take off **8** march off, sneak off

decampment 6 escape, flight **7** getaway

decant 4 pour **7** draw off, pour out

decanter 6 bottle, carafe, vessel

decathlon winner 11 Bruce Jenner

Decatur, Stephen
  served in: 11 Algerine War, Barbary Wars **13** Tripolitan War **19** War of Eighteen Twelve
  commander of ship: 12 United States
  defeated ship: 10 Macedonian (British)
  saying: 22 "Our country right or wrong"

decay 3 rot **5** spoil **7** corrode, putrefy, rotting **8** spoiling **9** decompose **12** disintegrate, putrefaction **13** decomposition
  goddess of: 4 Hour **5** Horae

decayed 3 bad **6** putrid, rotted, rotten, ruined **7** corrupt, gone bad, spoiled **10** decomposed **12** deteriorated **13** disintegrated

deceased *see* **4** dead

deceit 5 fraud **8** cheating, trickery **9** duplicity **10** dishonesty, trickiness **11** fraudulence **13** double-dealing **15** underhandedness **17** misrepresentation

deceitful 5 false **6** crafty, sneaky, tricky **7** cunning **9** dishonest, insincere **11** duplicitous, treacherous, underhanded **12** hypocritical **13** double-dealing, untrustworthy

deceive 3 con **4** fool **5** cheat, put on, trick **6** delude **7** defraud, mislead, swindle

deceiver 4 fake **5** cheat, fraud, quack **6** con man **7** cozener **8** impostor, swindler **9** charlatan, trickster **10** mountebank **13** confidence man

decelerate 5 brake **8** slow down

deceleration 7 braking, slowing

December
  event: 11 Pearl Harbor (7), Winter solstice (21, 22)
  flower: 5 holly **9** narcissus
  French: 8 Decembre
  gem: 4 ruby **6** zircon **9** turquoise
  German: 8 Dezember
  holiday: 8 Hanukkah **9** Boxing Day (26), Christmas (25) **16** Saint Nicholas Day (6)
  Italian: 8 Dicembre
  number of days: 9 thirty-one
  origin of name: 5 decem (Latin meaning ten)
  place in year:
    Gregorian: 7 twelfth
    Roman: 5 tenth
    Julian: 7 twelfth
  Spanish: 9 Diciembre
  Zodiac sign: 9 Capricorn **11** Sagittarius

decency 7 decorum, modesty **9** propriety **14** respectability **15** appropriateness

decent 4 fair, nice **5** ample **6** proper, seemly **7** correct, fitting **8** adequate, gracious, obliging, passable, suitable **9** courteous **10** acceptable, sufficient **11** appropriate **12** satisfactory **13** accommodating

deception 3 con **4** scam **5** fraud, sting, trick **7** cunning, slyness **8** artifice, illusion, trickery **9** duplicity, falseness, hypocrisy, treachery **10** craftiness, dishonesty, uncleanness, trickiness **11** fraudulence, insincerity **13** deceitfulness, double-dealing **15** underhandedness **17** untrustworthiness

deceptive 5 phony **9** dishonest **10** fraudulent, misleading

decibel
  abbreviation: 2 dB

decide 4 rule **5** elect, judge **6** choose, decree, select, settle **7** resolve **9** determine

decided 4 firm **7** certain **8** clear-cut, definite, emphatic, resolute **9** assertive **10** deliberate, determined, unwavering **12** indisputable, strong-willed, unhesitating, unmistakable **14** unquestionable

decidedly 9 certainly **10** absolutely **11** indubitably, undoubtedly **12** indisputably, unmistakably **13** unequivocally **14** unquestionably

decidedness 7 purpose, resolve **10** resolution **12** resoluteness **13** determination **14** purposefulness

decide on 5 adopt, elect **6** choose, opt for, select, settle **7** appoint, arrange, embrace, espouse, pick out **8** settle on **9** deter- mine, establish, single out

decigram
  abbreviation: 2 dg

deciliter
  abbreviation: 2 dL

decimate 6 reduce **7** destroy **8** massacre **9** slaughter **13** greatly reduce

decimeter
  abbreviation: 2 dm

decipher 4 read **5** solve **6** decode, deduce, render **7** decrypt, dope out, explain, make out, unravel **8** construe, untangle **9** interpret, translate **12** cryptanalyze

decision 6 decree, ruling **7** finding, outcome, purpose, resolve, verdict **8** judgment **10** conclusion, resolution **12** resoluteness **13** determination **14** purposefulness

decisive 4 firm **5** final **8** absolute, definite, positive, resolute **10** conclusive, convincing, definitive, determined, undeniable **12** indisputable

decisive blow 9 deathblow **11** coup de grace

decisiveness 7 purpose, resolve **10** resolution **12** resoluteness **14** purposefulness

decisive point 3 nut **4** core, crux, gist **5** basis, heart **6** kernel **7** essence **9** essential

deck 4 garb, trim **5** adorn, array, dress, prank **6** clothe, doll up, enrich, outfit, tog out **7** apparel, bedizen, festoon, furbish, garnish, gussy up **8** accouter, beautify, ornament, spruce up **9** embellish

Decker, Mary
  sport: 7 running
  married name: 6 Slaney

deck out 5 adorn, array, dress **6** attire, clothe, fit out, outfit, rig out **7** costume

declaim 4 rail **5** orate **6** recite **7** inveigh **9** sermonize **11** pontificate

declaration 6 avowal, notice **8** document **9** assertion, statement, testimony **10** deposition **11** affirmation, attestation, publication **12** announcement, notification, proclamation **14** acknowledgment

declare 4 show **6** affirm, reveal **7** express **8** announce, proclaim **9** pronounce

declare null and void 6 cancel, repeal, revoke **7** abolish, rescind, retract **8** abrogate, set aside **9** repudiate **10** invalidate **11** countermand

declare untrue 4 deny **9** repudiate **10** contradict

decline 3 ebb **4** drop, fail, flag, sink, wane **5** decay, slump, spurn **6** balk at, eschew, lessen, refuse, reject, weaken, worsen **7** dwindle **8** decrease, diminish, downfall **9** downgrade, downswing **11** deteriorate **13** deterioration

Decline and Fall
author: **11** Evelyn Waugh

Decline and Fall of the Roman Empire, The
author: **12** Edward Gibbon

declivity 4 drop **5** slant, slope **6** plunge **7** descent

decompose 3 rot **5** decay, spoil **7** putrefy **8** separate **10** go to pieces **12** disintegrate

decomposed 6 putrid, rotted, rotten **7** decayed, spoiled **9** putrefied **13** disintegrated

decontaminate 6 purify **9** disinfect, sterilize

decor 13 ornamentation

decorate 4 trim **5** adorn, array, honor **7** festoon, garnish **8** beautify, ornament **9** embellish

decorated 5 fancy **6** decked, ornate **7** adorned, trimmed **8** bedecked **9** bemedaled, bedizened, garnished **10** ornamented **11** embellished

decoration 4 trim **5** award, badge, medal **6** emblem, ribbon **7** garnish **8** ornament, trimming **9** adornment **13** embellishment, ornamentation **14** beautification

decorous 3 fit **6** decent, polite, proper, seemly **7** correct **8** becoming, mannerly, suitable **9** dignified **10** respectful **11** appropriate

decorum 4 tact **5** taste **7** dignity **8** good form **9** gentility, propriety **10** politeness **14** respectability

decoy 4 bait, lure **5** plant, snare **6** allure, come-on, entice **10** enticement, inducement **11** smoke screen

decrease 4 drop, ease, loss **5** abate, taper **6** lessen, reduce **7** cutback, decline, dwindle, fall-off, slacken, subside **8** diminish **9** abatement, dwindling, lessening, reduction **10** de-escalate, diminution **12** de-escalation

decree 3 law **5** edict, order **6** dictum, ruling **7** command, mandate, statute **8** proclaim **9** authorize **12** proclamation

decrepit 7 rickety **8** battered **10** broken-down **11** dilapidated

decrescendo
music: **22** gradually getting softer
abbreviation: **4** decr

decry 7 censure, condemn **8** denounce **9** criticize, deprecate, disparage

Dedalus, Stephen
character in: **7** Ulysses **30** Portrait of the Artist as a Young Man
author: **5** Joyce

dedicate 6 commit, devote, launch, pledge **7** address, present **8** inscribe

dedication 8 devotion **10** commitment

11 devotedness **16** prefatory address **20** prefatory inscription

Dedlock, Sir Leicester and Lady
characters in: **10** Bleak House
author: **7** Dickens

deduce 5 infer **6** gather, reason **8** conclude **10** comprehend, understand

deduct 4 take **6** remove **8** subtract, take from, withdraw **10** decrease by

deduction 5 guess **6** belief, credit, rebate **7** removal **8** analysis, decrease, discount, judgment, markdown, rollback **9** abatement, allowance, exemption, gathering, inference, lessening, reasoning, reduction **10** assumption, concession, conclusion, diminuition, hypothesis, reflection, taking away, withdrawal **11** calculation, presumption, speculation, subtraction, supposition **13** comprehension, consideration, understanding **14** interpretation

Dee, Ruby
real name: **14** Ruby Ann Wallace
husband: **10** Ossie Davis
born: **11** Cleveland OH
roles: **15** A Raisin in the Sun **16** Purlie Victorious

Dee, Sandra
real name: **13** Alexandra Zuck
husband: **10** Bobby Darin
born: **9** Bayonne NJ
roles: **6** Gidget **12** A Summer Place **15** Tammy Tell Me True

deed 3 act **4** feat **5** title **6** action, effort **11** achievement **14** accomplishment

deeds are manly, words are womanish
Italian: **24** fatti maschii parole femine
motto of: **8** Maryland

deem 4 hold, view **5** judge, think **6** regard **7** believe **8** consider

de-emphasize 8 play down **9** underplay

deep 3 far, sea **4** dark, late, lost, rich, wise **5** far in, midst, ocean, vivid **6** astute, strong **7** extreme, intense, learned **8** absorbed, immersed, involved, profound, resonant, sonorous **9** engrossed, sagacious **10** discerning **11** intelligent **13** philosophical

Deep, The
author: **13** Peter Benchley

deeply 6 richly **7** acutely, gravely, greatly, vividly **8** entirely **9** intensely, seriously **10** completely, profoundly, resonantly, sonorously, thoroughly **12** passionately

deeply felt 6 ardent, fervid **7** earnest, fervent, intense, sincere, zealous **9** heartfelt **10** passionate **11** impassioned **12** wholehearted

deepness 10 profundity

deep-rooted 7 abiding, lasting **8** enduring **9** confirmed, ingrained

deep-seated 7 abiding, lasting **8** enduring **9** confirmed, ingrained

deep thought 10 absorption, brown study, intentness **11** engrossment **13** concentration

deep water 3 jam **4** mess **5** ocean **6** pickle **7** trouble **8** distress **10** difficulty **11** dire straits, predicament **12** over one's head

deer
young: **4** fawn
female: **3** doe
male: stag

Deer Hunter, The
director: **13** Michael Cimino
cast: **10** John Cazale, John Savage **11** Meryl Streep **12** Robert De Niro **17** Christopher Walken
Oscar for: **7** picture **8** director **15** supporting actor (Walken)

Deerslayer, The
author: **19** James Fenimore Cooper
first of: **20** Leatherstocking Tales
character: **4** Hist **5** Hetty **6** Judith **10** Hurry Harry **11** Natty Bumppo (Deerslayer) **12** Chingachgook, Thomas Hutter

de-escalate 5 limit **6** lessen, narrow **8** contract, minimize

deface 3 mar **4** mark, scar **5** spoil **6** bruise, damage, impair, injure **9** disfigure

de facto 4 real **6** actual, really **8** actually

defalcate 8 embezzle **14** misappropriate

defamation 5 libel **7** calumny, slander **12** vilification **13** disparagement

defamatory 8 libelous **9** vilifying **10** calumnious, derogatory, slanderous **11** disparaging

defame 5 libel **6** malign, vilify **7** degrade, slander **8** derogate **9** denigrate, discredit, disparage **10** calumniate

Defarge, Madame
character in: **16** A Tale of Two Cities
author: **7** Dickens

default 10 nonpayment

defeat 4 foil, loss, rout **5** cream, crush, elude, quell **6** baffle, thwart **7** conquer, setback, shellac, trounce **8** confound, overcome, vanquish **9** frustrate, overpower, overthrow, overwhelm, thwarting **11** frustration **14** disappointment

defeated 4 beat **5** upset **6** beaten, bested, licked, routed **7** outdone, whipped, worsted **8** overcame **9** conquered, overthrew, put to rout **10** frustrated, overthrown **11** overpowered, overwhelmed **12** hors de combat

defect 4 flaw, scar, spot **5** break, crack, fault, stain **6** blotch, foible **7** blemish, default, failing, frailty **8** omission, weakness **10** deficiency **11** shortcoming **12** imperfection **14** incompleteness

defective 6 broken, faulty, flawed

7 lacking, wanting **8** abnormal, impaired **9** deficient, imperfect, subnormal **10** inadequate, out of order **11** inoperative **12** insufficient

Defence of Poetry
   author: **18** Percy Bysshe Shelley

defend 5 guard **6** secure, shield, uphold **7** endorse, protect, shelter, stand by, support, sustain **8** advocate, champion, maintain, preserve **9** safeguard

defender 8 advocate, champion, guardian, upholder **9** protector, supporter

Defender of the Faith
   Latin: **13** Fidei Defensor
   title of: **17** English sovereigns

Defenders, The
   character: **10** Joan Miller **14** Helen Donaldson, Kenneth Preston **15** Lawrence Preston
   cast: **10** E G Marshall, Robert Reed **11** Joan Hackett, Polly Rowles

defense 4 care **5** guard **7** custody, support **8** advocacy, security **9** barricade, safeguard, upholding **10** protection, stronghold **11** maintenance, safekeeping **12** preservation **13** fortification, justification

defenseless 7 unarmed **8** helpless **10** on one's back, vulnerable, weaponless **11** unprotected, unresisting

defensible 3 fit **5** valid **6** proper **7** tenable **8** sensible, suitable **9** allowable, excusable **10** admissible, condonable, forgivable, pardonable, vindicable **11** justifiable, permissible, supportable, warrantable

defer 4 obey **5** delay, table, yield **6** accede, give in, put off, shelve, submit **7** respect, suspend **8** postpone **10** capitulate

deference 5 honor **6** esteem, regard **7** respect **9** obedience, reverence **12** capitulation **13** consideration

deferential 5 civil **6** polite **7** dutiful **8** obedient, reverent **9** courteous, regardful **10** respectful, submissive **11** acquiescent, considerate, reverential

deferment 4 stay **5** delay **9** extension **12** postponement

deferral 5 pause **6** hiatus, recess **8** abeyance **10** suspension **12** postponement **14** discontinuance

defiance 9 hostility, obstinacy, rebellion **12** disobedience **14** rebelliousness

defiant 4 bold **9** truculent **10** aggressive, rebellious **11** disobedient, provocative

Defiant Ones, The
   director: **13** Stanley Kramer
   cast: **10** Tony Curtis **11** Lon Chaney Jr **12** Cara Williams **13** Charles McGraw, Sidney Poitier, Theodore Bikel
   Oscar for: **10** screenplay

deficiency 4 flaw **6** defect **7** failing,

frailty **8** shortage, weakness **10** inadequacy **11** shortcoming **12** imperfection **13** insufficiency

deficient 4 weak **6** flawed **7** lacking, short on **8** inferior **9** defective **10** inadequate **11** substandard **12** insufficient **14** unsatisfactory

deficit 8 shortage **9** shortfall **10** deficiency

de fide 10 of the faith

defile 4 soil **5** dirty, smear, spoil, stain, taint **6** befoul, debase **7** degrade, profane, tarnish **8** besmirch, disgrace, dishonor **9** desecrate

defiled 5 dirty **6** fouled, impure, soiled **7** debased, dirtied, stained, sullied, tainted, unclean **8** befouled, polluted, ravished, smirched, violated **9** blackened, corrupted, tarnished **10** besmirched **12** contaminated

define 5 state **7** clarify, explain, specify **8** describe, spell out **9** delineate, designate

definite 3 set **4** sure **5** exact, fixed **7** certain, precise **8** clear-cut, positive

definitely 5 truly **6** indeed, surely **7** for sure, no doubt **9** assuredly, certainly, decidedly, doubtless, expressly **10** absolutely, decisively, explicitly, positively, undeniably **11** indubitably, inescapably, unavoidably, undoubtedly **12** unmistakably **13** categorically, unequivocally **14** unquestionably **16** incontrovertibly

definiteness 8 sureness **9** certainty, precision **10** exactitude **11** unambiguity

definition 6 limits **7** clarity, purpose **11** description **15** distinctiveness

definitive 5 exact **7** decided, perfect **8** complete, decisive, reliable **10** conclusive, consummate

deflate 6 reduce **7** flatten **8** contract **9** devaluate

deflect 6 divert, swerve

Defoe, Daniel
   author of: **6** Roxana **11** Colonel Jack **12** Moll Flanders **14** Robinson Crusoe **23** A Journal of the Plague Year

DeForest, Lee
   invented/worked on: **10** audion tube, television **13** sound pictures

deform 3 mar **4** maim **5** twist **6** mangle **7** blemish, contort, distort **9** disfigure

deformation 9 deformity **10** distortion **12** malformation **13** disfigurement

deformed 6 marred, warped **7** defaced, mangled, spoiled, twisted **8** crippled **9** misshapen, monstrous **10** disfigured

defraud 3 con **4** bilk, rook **5** cheat **6** fleece, rip off **7** swindle

defray 3 pay **5** cover **11** foot the bill

deft 3 apt **4** able, sure **5** quick **6** adroit, expert **8** skillful **9** dexterous

deftness 5 knack, skill **7** ability **8** facility **9** adeptness, dexterity, handiness **10** adroitness, competency **11** proficiency **12** skillfulness

defunct 4 dead **7** extinct

defy 5 spurn **6** oppose, resist **7** disdain **8** confront **9** challenge, disregard, withstand

degage 4 easy **8** detached **10** disengaged **13** unconstrained

Degas, (Hilaire Germain) Edgar
   born: **5** Paris **6** France
   artwork: **14** The Ballet Class, The Morning Bath **15** Ballet Rehearsal **16** The Millinery Shop **17** The Glass of Absinth **23** Woman with Chrysanthemums **30** The Little Fourteen-Year-Old Dancer

degeneracy 9 decadence, depravity **10** debasement, debauchery, immorality, perversion **11** dissolution

degenerate 3 rot **4** base, sink, vile **5** decay **6** revert, wanton, wicked, worsen **7** corrupt, debased, decline, go to pot, immoral, pervert, vicious **8** decadent, degraded, depraved **9** abandoned, backslide, debauched, dissolute, perverted **10** dissipated, go downhill, profligate, retrograde, retrogress **11** deteriorate, hit the skids **12** disintegrate

degeneration 7 decline **9** depravity **10** corruption, debasement, immorality, perversion **11** degradation, dissolution, viciousness **13** deterioration

degradation 8 disgrace **11** humiliation

Degradation of the Democratic Dogma, The
   author: **10** Henry Adams

degrade 5 lower, shame **6** debase, demote **7** corrupt **8** disgrace, dishonor

degraded 4 vile **6** wicked **7** corrupt, debased, lowered **8** depraved, shameful, unworthy **9** debauched, perverted, reprobate **10** degenerate **11** undignified **12** unregenerate

degrading 3 low **6** menial **8** shameful **11** humiliating

degree 4 mark, step, unit **5** grade, level, order, phase, point, stage **8** division, interval
   abbreviation: **3** deg

De Guiche, Lillian
   real name of: **11** Lillian Gish

de gustibus non est disputandum 29 there is no disputing about tastes

De Havilland, Joan de Beauvoir
   real name of: **12** Joan Fontaine

De Havilland, Olivia
   sister: **12** Joan Fontaine
   born: **5** Japan, Tokyo
   roles: **7** Melanie **10** The Heiress (Oscar) **11** The Snake Pit **12** Captain Blood, To Each His Own (Oscar) **14** Anthony Adverse, My Cousin Rachel **15** Gone With the Wind, Hold Back

the Dawn **16** Light in the Piazza **22** Hush Hush Sweet Charlotte **24** The Adventures of Robin Hood

dehydrate 3 dry **5** parch **6** dry out

dehydrated 3 dry **7** parched, thirsty **8** dried-out **9** shriveled **10** desiccated

deification 7 worship **8** idolatry **10** exaltation **13** glorification

deify 5 exalt **7** glorify, idolize, worship

Deighton, Len
    author of: 4 SS-GB **14** The Ipcress File **15** Funeral in Berlin **16** Catch a Falling Spy

deign 4 deem **5** stoop **6** see fit **7** consent **8** think fit **10** condescend

Dei gratia 15 by the grace of God

Deiphobus
    father: 5 Priam
    mother: 6 Hecuba
    brother: 6 Hector
    wife: 5 Helen
    killed by: 8 Menelaus

Deirdre
    origin: 5 Irish
    husband: 6 Naoise
    father-in-law: 6 Usnach
    uncle: 9 Conchobar

Deirdre of the Sorrows
    author: 19 John Millington Synge

deity, the Deity 3 god **4** idol **7** goddess, godhead, Jehovah **8** Almighty, divinity, immortal, Olympian

deja vu 11 already seen

dejected 3 low, sad **4** blue, down **7** doleful, unhappy **8** desolate **9** depressed, sorrowful **10** despondent, dispirited, spiritless **11** discouraged, downhearted, low-spirited **12** disconsolate, disheartened

dejection 5 gloom **7** sadness **10** depression, low spirits, melancholy **11** despondency **15** dispiritedness, downheartedness

dejeuner 5 lunch

de jure 7 by right **14** according to law

dekagram
    abbreviation: 3 dkg

dekaliter
    abbreviation: 3 dkL

dekameter, decameter
    abbreviation: 3 dkm

Dekker, Thomas
    author of: 11 Westward Ho! (with John Webster) **20** The Shoemaker's Holiday

de Kooning, Willem
    born: 9 Rotterdam **14** The Netherlands
    artwork: 5 Woman **8** Painting **15** Woman and Bicycle

Delacroix, Eugene
    born: 6 France **18** Charenton-St Maurice
    artwork: 8 Paganini **14** Women of Algiers **15** Massacre at Chios **16** The Barque of Dante **19** Chopin and George Sand **20** Dante and Virgil in Hell **22** Liberty at the Barricades, The Death of Sardanapalus

Delaroche, Paul
    born: 5 Paris **6** France
    artwork: 24 The Death of Queen Elizabeth, The Death of the Duke of Guise **26** The Execution of Lady Jane Grey **36** Children of Edward Imprisoned in the Tower

Delaunay, Robert
    born: 5 Paris **6** France
    artwork: 5 Disks **6** Cities, Rhythm **7** Runners, Windows **10** Cathedrals **11** City of Paris, Eiffel Tower **14** The Cardiff Team **19** Cosmic Circular Forms **28** Simultaneous Prismatic Windows

Delaware
    abbreviation: 2 DE **3** Del
    nickname: 5 First **7** Blue Hen, Diamond
    capital: 5 Dover
    largest city: 10 Wilmington
    others: 5 Acoma, Lewes **6** Easton, Newark, Smyrna **7** Briston, Elsmere, Milford **8** Claymont **9** New Castle **10** Georgetown
    college: 6 Wesley **10** Brandywine, Wilmington **12** Goldey Beacom
    feature: 10 Winterthur **15** Old Swedes Church **17** E I du Pont de Nemours
    tribe: 4 Leni **5** Lenni **6** Lenape, Munsee
    people: 10 Howard Pyle
    island: 7 Fenwick
    land rank: 10 forty-ninth
    physical feature:
        bay: 8 Delaware, Rehoboth
        sea: 8 Atlantic
    river: 8 Delaware **9** Christina, Nanticoke **10** Brandywine
    state admission: 5 first
    state bird: 14 blue hen chicken
    state flower: 12 peach blossom
    state motto: 22 Liberty and Independence
    state song: 11 Our Delaware
    state tree: 13 American holly

Delaware (Lenni-Lenape)
    language family: 9 Algonkian **10** Algonquian
    tribe: 5 Munsi, Unami **6** Munsee **11** Unalachtigo
    location: 7 New York **8** Delaware **9** Manhattan, New Jersey **10** Long Island **12** Pennsylvania, Staten Island
    leader: 7 Tamanen, Tammany
    deity: 11 Kitanitowet

delay 4 slow, stay **5** check, table, tarry **6** dawdle, detain, hamper, hinder, hold up, impede, linger, put off, retard, shelve **7** inhibit, slowing, suspend **8** dawdling, obstruct, postpone, reprieve, stoppage, tarrying **9** deferment, lingering, loitering **10** suspension **12** postponement, prolongation **13** procrastinate

delayed 4 late **6** put off, slowed **7** held up, stalled, tarried **8** arrested, deferred, detained, retarded **9** postponed, slackened **12** dillydallied **14** procrastinated **15** dragged one's feet

Delbruck, Max
    field: 7 biology **17** molecular genetics
    researched: 20 genetic recombination
    awarded: 10 Nobel Prize

delectable 5 tasty, yummy **8** pleasant **9** agreeable, delicious, enjoyable **10** delightful, gratifying **11** pleasurable

delegate 3 rep **4** give, name **5** agent, envoy, proxy **6** assign, charge, deputy **7** entrust **8** give over, transfer **9** authorize, designate **10** commission **14** representative

delegation 11 designation, entrustment **13** authorization, commissioning

delete 3 cut **4** omit **5** erase **6** cancel, remove

deleterious 7 harmful, hurtful, ruinous **9** dangerous, injurious **11** destructive, detrimental

Delia
    festival of: 6 Apollo

deliberate 4 easy, slow, wary **5** weigh **6** confer, debate **7** careful, discuss, examine, express, planned, prudent, willful **8** cautious, cogitate, consider, measured, meditate, mull over **9** leisurely, unhurried **10** calculated, considered, purposeful, thoughtful **11** circumspect, contemplate, intentional, prearranged **12** premeditated

deliberate together 6 confer **7** consult, discuss

deliberation 4 care **6** debate **10** conference, discussion, steadiness **11** calculation, carefulness, forethought **13** premeditation **14** circumspection

Delibes, C P (Clement Philibert) Leo
    born: 6 France **14** St Germain-du-Val
    composer of: 5 Lakme **6** Sylvia **8** Coppelia **10** Le Roi l'a dit

delicacy 4 tact **5** taste **7** frailty **8** accuracy, elegance, fineness, softness, weakness **9** fragility, frailness, lightness, precision **10** perfection, smoothness **11** savoir-faire, sensibility, sensitivity, unsoundness **13** consideration, exquisiteness, sensitiveness **14** discrimination

delicate 4 fine, soft **5** frail, muted **6** ailing, dainty, feeble, flimsy, infirm, minute, savory, sickly, touchy, unwell **7** careful, elegant, fragile, refined, subdued, tactful **8** detailed, luscious, tasteful, ticklish, weakened **9** breakable, delicious, difficult, exquisite, palatable, sensitive, toothsome **10** appetizing, diplomatic, fastidious, perishable, precarious, scrupulous **11** debilitated

Delicate Balance, A
author: 11 Edward Albee

delicious 5 tasty, yummy 6 joyful, savory 8 charming, luscious, pleasant 9 palatable 10 appetizing, delectable, delightful 11 pleasurable 13 mouthwatering

delight 3 joy 5 amuse, charm, cheer, revel 6 please 7 enchant, gratify, rapture 8 pleasure 9 enjoyment, fascinate, happiness 13 gratification

delighted 6 elated 7 pleased, psyched 8 ecstatic 9 enchanted 10 captivated, enraptured, enthralled 11 on cloud nine

delightful 6 peachy 7 amiable, amusing 8 charming, engaging, pleasing 9 agreeable, congenial, enjoyable 10 enchanting 11 pleasurable 12 entertaining

delight in 4 love 5 adore, eat up, enjoy, fancy, savor 6 dote on, relish 7 cherish 8 treasure 10 appreciate

Delilah
lover: 6 Samson
betrayed: 6 Samson

delineate 4 draw 5 draft 6 define, depict, design, lay out, sketch 7 outline, portray 8 describe 9 represent 12 characterize

delineation 9 depiction, portrayal 11 description 12 illustration 14 representation 16 characterization

delineavit 6 he drew (this) 7 she drew (this)

delinquency 7 misdeed 10 misconduct, negligence 11 dereliction, misbehavior 19 neglect of obligation

delinquent 3 due 4 late 6 remiss 7 hoodlum, misdoer, overdue 8 derelict 9 in arrears, miscreant, negligent, wrongdoer 10 neglectful

delirious 6 raving 7 excited, frantic 8 ecstatic, frenzied 10 incoherent 11 carried away 13 hallucinating

delirium 5 fever 6 frenzy, raving 7 madness, ranting 8 insanity 10 brain fever

Deliro
character in: 22 Every Man Out of His Humour
author: 6 Jonson

Delisle, Guillaume
field: 9 geography
nationality: 6 French
founder of: 15 modern geography

Delius, Frederick
born: 7 England 8 Bradford
composer of: 5 Paris 6 Koanga 7 Eventyr, Irmelin 8 Sea-Drift 9 Brigg Fair 10 Appalachia 11 A Mass of Life, Sur les Cimes 17 Fennimore and Gerda 20 North Country Sketches 22 A Village Romeo and Juliet, Over the Hills and Far Away

deliver 3 aim, say 4 bear, deal, free,

give, save 5 bring, carry, throw, utter 6 convey, direct, launch, rescue, strike 7 release, set free 8 give over, hand over, liberate, proclaim, turn over 9 surrender 10 emancipate

deliverance 6 rescue 7 release 9 salvation 10 liberation 12 emancipation

Deliverance
director: 11 John Boorman
author: 11 James Dickey
cast: 8 Ronny Cox 9 Jon Voight, Ned Beatty 12 Burt Reynolds
song: 13 Dueling Banjos

deliver up 4 cede, give 5 grant, yield 8 fork over, hand over, transfer 9 surrender 10 relinquish

delivery 8 transfer 11 transferral, transmittal 12 transmission

delivery service 3 DHL, UPS 4 USPS 5 FedEx 8 Airborne 11 Express mail

dell 4 dale, dene, glen, vale 5 glade 6 dingle, hollow, valley

Della Robbia, Luca
born: 5 Italy 8 Florence
artwork: 8 Cantoria (Singing Gallery) 12 The Ascension 13 Altman Madonna 15 Madonna and Child, The Resurrection

Dello Joio, Norman
born: 9 New York NY
composer of: 7 The Ruby 12 Psalm of David 15 New York Profiles, The Trial at Rouen, Triumph of St Joan 20 Proud Music of the Storm, The Lamentation of Saul

Delon, Alain
born: 6 France, Sceaux
roles: 10 Purple Noon, The Leopard 13 The Black Tulip 14 Is Paris Burning? 19 Rocco and His Brothers

Delphic
pertains to: 6 Apollo, Delphi

Delphic oracle
oracle of: 6 Apollo
located at: 6 Delphi
priestess: 6 Pythia

Delphinia
festival of: 6 Apollo

Del Rio, Dolores
real name: 21 Lolita Dolores Negrette
born: 6 Mexico 7 Durango
roles: 11 The Fugitive 13 Madame duBarry 15 Flying Down to Rio, Journey into Fear, Maria Candelaria

Delta Wedding
author: 11 Eudora Welty

delude 3 con 4 dupe, fool 5 put on, trick 7 deceive, mislead

deluge 4 bury, glut 5 drown, flood, spate, swamp 6 engulf 7 barrage, torrent 8 inundate, overflow, submerge 10 inundation

DeLuise, Dom
born: 10 Brooklyn NY
roles: 5 Fatso 6 The End 11 Silent Movie 14 Blazing Saddles

delusion 8 illusion 9 misbelief 10 aberration 11 derangement 13 hallucination, irrationality, misconception, self-deception

Delusions, Etc. of John Berryman
author: 12 John Berryman

deluxe 4 fine, posh 5 grand 6 choice, classy 7 elegant 8 splendid 9 luxurious

delve 5 probe 6 search 7 examine, explore 8 look into

demagogue 6 ranter 7 hothead, spouter 8 agitator, fomenter, inflamer 9 firebrand, haranguer 10 incendiary, malcontent, tub-thumper 12 rabble-rouser, troublemaker

demand 4 call, need, want 5 exact, order 7 command, require 11 requirement

demanding 4 hard 5 harsh, rigid 6 strict 8 exacting 9 difficult

demantoid
species: 6 garnet

demarche 4 gait, plan

demean 5 lower, shame 6 debase, humble 7 degrade 8 disgrace 9 humiliate

demeanor 4 mien 6 manner 7 bearing, conduct 8 behavior, presence 10 appearance, deportment 11 comportment

demented 3 mad 4 nuts 5 crazy 6 crazed, cuckoo, insane 7 lunatic 8 deranged

dementia praecox 13 schizophrenia

dementophobia
fear of: 8 insanity

demesne 4 land 5 realm 6 domain, estate 8 property

Demeter
origin: 5 Greek
goddess of: 5 earth 9 fertility
protectress of: 8 marriage 11 social order
father: 6 Cronus
mother: 4 Rhea
daughter: 10 Persephone
corresponds to: 5 Brimo, Ceres 8 Despoena
epithet: 5 Chloe, Lusia, Mysia 6 Antaea, Erinys, Stiria 7 Chamyne, Thesmia 8 Stiritis 9 Anesidora, Thermasia 11 Carpophorus 13 Thesimophorus

Demetrius
character in: 21 A Midsummer Night's Dream
author: 11 Shakespeare

De Mille, Agnes
choreographer of: 5 Rodeo 15 Fall River Legend

DeMille, Cecil B
director of: 9 Cleopatra 18 The Ten Commandments 22 The Greatest Show on Earth
niece: 5 Agnes (choreographer)

Demiphon
form: **4** king
sacrificed: **7** maidens
to prevent: **6** plague
demise 3 end **4** fall, ruin **5** death **7** decease, passing **8** collapse **10** expiration
demobilization 7 release **9** discharge **10** disbanding
demobilize 7 disband, release **9** discharge
Democoon
father: **5** Priam
birth: **12** illegitimate
killed by: **8** Odysseus
democracy 8 equality, fairness
Democracy
author: **10** Henry Adams
Democracy in America
author: **19** Alexis de Tocqueville
Democratic Party
symbol: **6** donkey
president belonging to: **4** Polk **6** Carter, Pierce, Truman, Wilson **7** Clinton, (Lyndon Baines) Johnson, Jackson, Kennedy **8** Buchanan, Van Buren **9** Cleveland, (Franklin D) Roosevelt
Democratic Republican Party
president belonging to: **5** (John Quincy) Adams **6** Monroe **7** Madison **9** Jefferson
demode 8 outmoded **13** unfashionable
demoiselle 4 girl
demolish 4 raze, ruin **5** level, total, wreck **7** destroy **9** devastate
demolition 6 razing **8** leveling, wrecking **11** destruction
demon 3 imp **4** jinn, ogre **5** afrit, devil, fiend, genie, harpy, jinni, lamia, satan, troll **6** afreet, dybbuk, goblin **7** incubus, monster, vampire, warlock **8** go-getter, succubus
demonic, demoniacal 6 hectic **7** frantic, hellish **8** devilish, fiendish, frenzied
demonstrable 7 evident **8** apparent, manifest, palpable **11** supportable
demonstrate 4 show **5** march, prove, teach **6** parade, picket, reveal **7** display, exhibit, explain **8** describe, manifest **9** establish **10** illustrate
demonstration 5 march, rally **6** parade **7** display **9** picketing **10** exhibition, exposition, expression **12** illustration, presentation **13** manifestation
demonstrative 7 gushing **8** effusive **12** affectionate
demonstrativeness 9 gushiness **12** effusiveness, emotionalism
demoralize 8 dispirit **9** undermine **10** disconcert, discourage, dishearten **11** disorganize
de mortuis nil nisi bonum 26 of the dead say nothing but good

demos 5 plebs **6** masses, people **7** commons **8** populace **9** commoners
demote 4 bust **5** abase **7** degrade
Dempsey, Jack (William Harrison)
nickname: **13** Manassa Mauler
sport: **6** boxing
class: **11** heavyweight
demur 5 qualm **6** object **7** protest, scruple **8** disagree **9** misgiving, objection **10** hesitation **11** compunction
demure 3 shy **4** prim **6** modest **7** bashful **8** reserved
demurrer 5 doubt, qualm **7** dissent, protest, scruple **8** objector, question, rebuttal **9** challenge, exception, misgiving, objection, protester, protestor, stricture **11** compunction **12** remonstrance
den 4 lair **5** haunt, study **6** hotbed **7** hangout, library, retreat, shelter **9** sanctuary
denial 7 refusal **9** disavowal, disowning, rejection **10** disclaimer
denigrate 4 soil **5** abuse, smear, sully **6** defame, dump on, malign, revile, vilify **7** asperse, blacken, degrade, run down, slander, traduce **8** backbite, badmouth, belittle, besmirch, tear down **9** call names, discredit, disparage, downgrade **10** calumniate, stigmatize
De Niro, Robert
born: **9** New York NY
roles: **4** Heat **6** Brazil **8** Cape Fear, Sleepers **10** A Bronx Tale, Angel Heart, Awakenings, Goodfellas, Raging Bull (Oscar), Taxi Driver **11** Mean Streets **13** The Deer Hunter **14** New York New York, The Godfather II **15** The King of Comedy, The Untouchables, True Confessions **17** Bang the Drum Slowly
denizen 7 dweller **8** resident **10** inhabitant
Denmark
other name: **17** Kongeriget Danmark
capital/largest city: **9** Kobenhavn **10** Copenhagen
others: **3** Hov **4** Hals, Koge, Nibe, Ribe, Soro **5** Arhus, Kosor, Vejle **6** Aarhus, Abenra, Alborg, Dorsor, Dragor, Nyberg, Odense, Skagen, Struer, Viborg **7** Aalborg, Esbjerg, Horsens, Kolding, Morsens, Randers **8** Ballerup, Elsinore, Gentofte, Glostrup, Hillerod, Naestred, Roskilde, Slagelse **9** Haderslev, Helsingor, Svendborg **10** Fredericia **13** Frederikshavn
school:
university institute of: **18** Theoretical Physics
folk high school: **14** folkehojskoler
continuation school: **11** efterskoler
division: **3** Fyn **7** Jutland, Lolland **9** Schleswig, Sjaelland
measure: **3** ell, fod, mil, pot **4** alen, favn, last, rode **5** album, anker,

kande, linje, paegl, tomme **6** achtel, paegel, skeppe **7** landmil, oltonde, ortonde, skieppe, viertel **8** fjerding **9** ottingkar **10** korntonmde
monetary unit: **3** one, ora, ore **4** fyrk **5** krone **8** frederik, skilling **9** rigsdaler
weight: **2** es **3** lod, ort, vog **4** last, mark, pund, unze **5** carat, kvint, pound, quint, tonde **6** toende **7** centner, lispund, quintin **8** lispound, skippund **9** skibslast, skippound **10** bismerpund
island: **2** Oe **3** Als, Fyn, Mon, Rum, Thy **4** Aaro, Aero, Fano, Fohr, Moen, Mors, Romo **5** Baago, Faero, Faroe, Funen, Laeso, Samso, Sando **6** Amager, Sandoy, Sejero, Sudero **7** Faeroes, Falster, Hesselo, Laaland, Lolland, Seeland, Zealand **8** Bornholm, Eysturoy, Sudhuroy **9** Greenland, Langeland, Sjaelland **10** Vendsyssel
lake: **6** Arreso
hill: **12** Ejer Bavnehoj **14** Himmelbjaerget
highest point: **12** Yding Skovhoj
river: **3** Asa **4** Holm, Omme, Stor **5** Skive, Susaa, Varde **6** Gelsaa, Gudena, Vorgod **7** Gudenaa, Lilleaa, Lonborg
sea: **5** North **6** Baltic **7** Oresund **8** Atlantic, Kattegat **9** Skagerrak
physical feature:
fjord: **3** Ise **4** Isse **5** Lamme
inlet: **3** Ise **5** Fjord, Vejle **6** Nissum, Odense **7** Horsens, Logstor **8** Limfjord, Mariager
peninsula: **7** Jutland
strait: **8** Otesund **8** Kattegat **9** Skagerrak
people: **4** Dane, Jute **5** Angle **6** Cimbri, Eskimo, German, Ostmen, Teuton, Viking **12** Scandinavian
astronomer: **10** Tycho Brahe
author: **11** Isak Dinesen **21** Hans Christian Andersen
founder: **4** Axel **7** Absalon
king: **4** Hans, Knud **6** Canute **8** Frederik **9** Christian **10** Gorm the Old **15** Harold Bluetooth
philosopher: **11** Kierkegaard
physicist: **9** Niels Bohr
queen: **9** Margrethe **12** Thyra Danebod
sculptor: **11** Thorvaldsen
teacher: **4** Kold
language: **4** Odan **6** Danish, German **8** Faeroese **11** Greenlander
religion: **19** Evangelical Lutheran
place:
airport: **7** Kastrup
castle: **7** Egeskov **8** Kronborg **13** Frederiksborg
museum: **6** Rebild **9** Glyptotek **11** Thorvaldsen **15** Rosenborg Castle
park: **10** Langelinie **13** Tivoli Gardens

royal palace: 11 Amalienborg
statue: 13 Little Mermaid
stock exchange: 5 Borse **6** Borsen
feature:
 dance: 6 sextur
 drink: 5 glogg **7** aquavit
 beer: 6 Tuborg **9** Carlsberg
food:
 cheese: 3 Ost **4** Blue, Tybo **5** Es-
 rom, Samso **6** Samsoe **7** Havarti,
 Mycella
 meat patty: 11 frikadeller
 pudding: 15 rodgrod med flode

Dennis, Patrick
 author of: 10 Auntie Mame
Dennis, Sandy
 real name: 16 Sandra Dale Dennis
 born: 10 Hastings NE
 roles: 12 Any Wednesday **15** A Thousand Clowns **18** Up the Down Staircase **25** Who's Afraid of Virginia
 Woolf?
Dennis the Hangman
 character in: 12 Barnaby Rudge
 author: 7 Dickens
Dennis the Menace
 creator: 11 Hank Ketcham
 character: 9 Mrs Elkins **10** John Wilson **12** Eloise Wilson, George Wilson, Joey McDonald, Martha Wilson
 13 Alice Mitchell, Henry Mitchell,
 Tommy Anderson **14** Dennis Mitchell
 dog: 4 Ruff
 cast: 8 Gil Smith, Jay North **10** Billy
 Booth, Gale Gordon, Sara Seeger **11**
 Gloria Henry, Irene Tedrow, Sylvia
 Field **12** Joseph Kearns **15** Herbert
 Anderson
denomination 4 name, sect, size **5**
 class, value **8** category, grouping **10**
 persuasion **11** designation
denotation 4 mark, name, sign **6**
 symbol **7** meaning **10** indication
denote 4 mark, mean, name **6** signal **7**
 signify **8** indicate
denouement 3 end **6** finale, upshot **7**
 outcome **8** solution **10** conclusion **11**
 termination
denounce 6 accuse, vilify **7** censure,
 condemn **9** criticize
denouncement 7 censure **12** condemnation, denunciation
de novo 4 anew **5** again **6** afresh **16**
 from the beginning
dense 4 dull, dumb, slow **5** close,
 heavy, thick **7** compact,
 crowded, intense **8** ignorant **9** dimwitted **10** compressed **11** thickheaded **12**
 concentrated, impenetrable
Densher, Merton
 character in: 17 The Wings of the
 Dove
 author: 5 James
density 4 mass **6** weight **7** opacity **8**
 dullness, solidity **9** stupidity, thickness **10** obtuseness, opaqueness **11**
 compactness

dent 3 pit **4** nick **6** hollow **10** depression **11** indentation
denude 4 bare **5** strip **6** divest **7** lay
 bare **8** unclothe
denuded 4 bare **5** naked **6** barren **8**
 stripped **9** unclothed, uncovered
denunciation 7 censure **12** condemnation, denouncement **13** attack
 against
Denver
 basketball team: 7 Nuggets
 football team: 4 Gold **7** Broncos
deny 6 refuse, refute **7** disavow **8** disallow, disclaim **9** disaffirm **10** contradict
deny oneself 5 avoid, forgo **6** eschew, give up, refuse **7** abstain, forbear **8** renounce **9** sacrifice
deny responsibility 7 disavow
Deo gratias 13 thanks be to God
Deo volente 10 God willing
DePalma, Brian
 director of: 6 Carrie **8** Scarface **11**
 Carlito's Way, Raising Cain **13**
 Dressed to Kill **15** The Untouchables
 17 Mission Impossible **20** Bonfire of
 the Vanities
depart 2 go **4** exit **5** leave **6** embark **7**
 deviate, digress, entrain
departed 4 dead, gone, late, left, past,
 went **6** at rest, bygone **7** gone off **8**
 gone away **10** passed away **11** gone
 to glory **12** late-lamented **20** gone the
 way of all flesh
depart for 8 leave for **9** adjourn to,
 set off for, set out for **10** head toward, move toward
depart hastily 3 fly **4** flee **5** elope **6**
 decamp, escape **7** abscond **9** skedaddle
department 4 unit **6** branch, bureau,
 sector **7** section **8** district, division,
 province
departure 4 exit **5** going **6** exodus **7**
 leaving **9** deviation **10** digression, divergence
depend 4 rely, rest **5** count, hinge **6**
 hang on
dependable 4 sure, true **5** loyal **6**
 steady, trusty **7** trusted **8** faithful, reliable **9** steadfast, unfailing **11** trustworthy
dependence 5 trust **8** reliance **10** confidence, dependency
dependency 10 dependence
dependent 7 reliant
depict 4 draw, limn **5** carve, chart,
 draft, paint **6** define, detail, map out,
 recite, record, relate, sculpt, sketch **7**
 diagram, narrate, picture, portray, recount **8** describe **9** chronicle, delineate, dramatize, represent, verbalize **10**
 illustrate **12** characterize
depiction 6 sketch **7** drawing, picture
 8 portrait **9** picturing, portrayal **11** de-

 lineation **12** illustration **14** representation **16** characterization
deplete 5 drain, use up **6** lessen, reduce **7** consume, exhaust **8** decrease
 10 impoverish
depleted 5 empty, spent, waste **6** barren, used up **7** drained, emptied, reduced, worn out **8** bankrupt, consumed, expended, lessened **9**
 exhausted, infertile **10** unfruitful
deplorable 5 awful **8** wretched **9** miserable **11** blameworthy **13** reprehensible **17** deserving reproach
deplore 5 mourn **6** bemoan, bewail,
 lament **7** censure, condemn **9** grieve
 for **12** disapprove of
deport 3 act **4** oust **5** carry, exile, expel **6** banish, behave **7** cast out **10**
 expatriate **14** conduct oneself
deported person 2 DP **5** exile **8** deportee **10** expatriate **14** banished person
deportment 7 conduct **8** behavior, demeanor **11** comportment
depose 4 oust **6** unseat **8** dethrone **16**
 remove from office
deposit 3 put **4** pile **5** place **7** put
 down, set down **8** sediment **10** accumulate **11** down payment, give in
 trust, installment **12** accumulation **14**
 partial payment
deposition 7 deposit **9** statement, testimony **11** declaration **12** accumulation
depository 4 bank, safe **5** vault **6** museum **7** library **8** archives **10** storehouse
depot 4 dump **7** station **8** terminal,
 terminus **10** bus station **15** railroad
 station **20** military storage place
depraved 4 vile **6** wicked **7** corrupt,
 debased **8** degraded **9** debauched,
 perverted **10** degenerate
depravity 8 vileness **9** decadence **10**
 corruption, debasement, debauchery,
 degeneracy, immorality, perversion,
 wickedness **11** degradation, dissolution
deprecate 6 insult **7** condemn, protest
 8 belittle, object to, play down **10** depreciate **15** take exception to
deprecated 7 defamed, put down **8**
 despised **9** belittled, derogated, disdained
deprecation 4 slur **5** abuse **7** protest,
 put-down **9** aspersion **10** aspersions,
 belittling, defamation, derogation **11**
 disapproval **12** condemnation **13** disparagement
deprecatory 8 critical **9** insulting, maligning, vilifying **10** belittling, defamatory, derogatory, slanderous **11** disparaging **12** disapproving
depreciate 5 scorn **7** run down **8** belittle, diminish **9** denigrate, disparage,

downgrade, lose value **13** reduce in value, lower the value

depreciation 5 scorn **7** disdain **8** contempt **9** criticism, deflation **10** belittling, disrespect **11** devaluation **13** disparagement

depredation 4 sack **6** rapine, ravage **7** looting, pillage, plunder, robbery, sacking **8** spoiling **9** marauding **10** brigandage, ravishment, spoliation **11** desecration, devastation, freebooting, laying waste

depress 5 lower **6** deject, lessen, reduce, sadden, weaken **7** cut back **8** diminish, dispirit **9** press down **10** dishearten **14** lower in spirits

depressed 3 sad **4** blue **7** unhappy **8** dejected, downcast **10** despondent, dispirited, melancholy **11** low-spirited **12** disconsolate, inconsolable

depressing 3 sad **6** gloomy **8** lowering **9** dejecting, saddening **10** oppressing **11** casting down, dispiriting, melancholic, pushing down **12** discouraging, pressing down, weighing down **14** causing sadness

depression 5 gloom **6** dimple, hollow **7** sadness **9** dejection, recession **10** desolation, melancholy **11** despondency, indentation, melancholia **14** discouragement **15** downheartedness, economic decline

deprive 5 strip **6** divest **8** take from **10** confiscate, dispossess

deprived 8 divested, stripped **11** handicapped **12** dispossessed, impoverished **13** disadvantaged **15** underprivileged

deprive of honor 5 abase, shame, sully **6** defame **7** blacken, tarnish **8** disgrace, dishonor **9** discredit **10** stigmatize

deprive of strength 6 hinder, weaken **7** disable, wear out **8** enervate, enfeeble, handicap **10** debilitate, devitalize

de profundis 13 from the depths

depth 6 timbre **8** deepness **10** profundity **19** downward measurement **24** perpendicular measurement

depths 4 deep **6** bowels **8** interior, recesses

deputation 9 committee **10** commission, delegation **15** representatives

deputize 6 assign **7** appoint **8** delegate **10** commission

deputy 4 aide **5** agent, envoy, proxy **6** second **8** delegate, emissary, minister **9** alternate, assistant, go-between, messenger, middleman, surrogate **10** ambassador, substitute **11** pinch hitter **12** spokesperson **14** representative **15** second-in-command

DeQuincey, Thomas
   author of: 19 The English Mail-Coach **31** On the Knocking at the Gate in

Macbeth **32** Confessions of an English Opium-Eater

derail 3 bar **4** balk, foil **5** block, check, spike **6** hinder, impede, thwart **7** inhibit, prevent **8** obstruct **14** throw off course

deranged 3 mad **5** crazy **6** insane **8** demented **10** irrational, unbalanced

derangement 6 lunacy **7** madness **8** insanity **9** craziness **11** peculiarity **13** irrationality, mental illness **14** mental disorder

Der Bingle
   nickname of: 10 Bing Crosby

Derby 4 race
   site: 5 Epsom **8** Kentucky **14** Churchill Downs

Derek, Bo
   husband: 4 John
   roles: 3 Ten (10) **6** Bolero, Tarzan

derelict 3 bum **4** hobo **5** tramp **6** remiss **7** outcast, vagrant **8** careless, deserted **9** abandoned, negligent **10** delinquent, neglectful

dereliction 7 failure, neglect **9** disregard **10** negligence **11** delinquency **13** noncompliance, nonobservance

De rerum natura
   author: 9 Lucretius

deride 4 mock **5** scoff, scorn **7** sneer at **8** ridicule

de rigueur 11 fashionable **16** strictly required

derision 5 scorn **7** disdain, mockery **8** ridicule, sneering

derivation 5 stock **6** origin, source **7** descent, getting, lineage **8** ancestry, deriving, heritage **9** acquiring, etymology, parentage **10** background, beginnings, extraction **21** historical development

derive 4 gain **5** arise, enjoy, glean **6** obtain **7** descend **8** stem from **9** originate

dermaptera
   class: 8 hexapoda
   phylum: 10 arthropoda
   group: 6 earwig

dermatitis 4 rash **6** eczema **9** psoriasis **12** inflammation

Dern, Bruce
   born: 9 Chicago IL
   roles: 6 Marnie, Tattoo **10** Coming Home, Family Plot **11** Black Sunday **13** The Wild Angels **14** The Great Gatsby **22** The King of Marvin Gardens

dernier 4 last **5** final **8** ultimate

dernier cri 9 latest cry **10** latest word **13** latest fashion

derogate 4 blot **5** taint **6** smirch **8** disgrace **9** disparage

derogation 4 blot **5** odium, stain **7** blemish **8** contempt, disfavor, disgrace, ignominy **9** disesteem, disre-

pute **10** disrespect **11** humiliation **13** disparagement

derogatory 9 injurious **10** belittling **11** disparaging, unfavorable **12** unflattering **15** uncomplimentary

derrick 3 rig **5** crane, hoist, tower **9** framework
   kind: 3 oil **6** sheers **7** gin-pole
   part: 3 gin, leg **4** boom, mast **6** pulley **7** guy line

derring-do 6 daring **8** audacity, boldness **11** daredevilry **12** daredeviltry, recklessness **15** venturesomeness

dervish 5 fakir **6** Muslim **7** ascetic

De Sapientia Veterum
   author: 12 Francis Bacon

Descartes, Rene
   author of: 17 Discourse on Method
   field: 11 mathemathics
   nationality: 6 French
   developed: 18 analytical geometry
   quote: 13 Cogito ergo sum **18** I think therefore I am
   pertaining to: 9 Cartesian

descend 3 dip **4** drop, pass **5** slant, slope, swoop **6** go down, invade **7** incline **8** come down, inherited **11** come in force **12** be handed down, move downward

descendant 5 issue, scion **7** progeny **9** offspring

descend upon 6 assail, attack, charge **7** assault, set upon **12** bear down upon

descent 4 drop, fall, raid **5** slant, slope **6** origin **7** assault, decline, lineage **8** ancestry **9** declivity, incursion **10** coming down **11** sneak attack, sudden visit

describe 4 draw **5** trace **6** depict, detail, recite, relate **7** explain, mark out, narrate, outline, portray, recount, speak of **9** delineate **10** illustrate **12** characterize

description 3 ilk **4** kind, sort, type **5** brand, class, genus **6** manner, nature **7** account, species, variety **9** depiction, narration, portrayal **12** illustration **16** characterization

descry 3 see **4** spot **6** behold, notice **7** discern, observe, pick out **8** discover **12** catch sight of

Desdemona
   character in: 7 Othello
   author: 11 Shakespeare

desecrate 6 defile **7** profane, violate **8** dishonor

desecration 8 dishonor **9** violation **10** defilement **11** profanation

desert 3 dry **4** arid, wild **5** leave, waste **6** barren **7** abandon, forsake **8** desolate, untilled **9** infertile, wasteland **10** arid region **11** run away from, uninhabited **12** uncultivated **16** barren wilderness
   world: 4 Gobi, Thar **6** Gibson, Lib-

yan, Mohave, Nubian, Sahara, Syrian **7** Arabian, Atacama, Kara Kum, Painted, Sonoran **8** Kalahari **9** Patagonia **10** Great Sandy **11** Death Valley
watering spot: 5 Oasis

deserted 4 AWOL, left **5** empty **6** lonely, vacant **7** cast off, forlorn, reneged **8** defected, desolate, forsaken, marooned **9** abandoned, absconded **12** quit one's post **14** left in the lurch

desertedness 9 emptiness **10** desolation **13** uncrowdedness

Deserted Village, The
author: 15 Oliver Goldsmith

desertion 8 quitting **9** forsaking **11** abandonment **14** relinquishment

desertlike 3 dry **4** arid, sere **5** sandy **6** barren **7** dried up, parched **9** waterless

deserts 3 due **5** worth **6** reward **7** payment

deserve 4 rate **5** merit **7** warrant **9** earn as due **10** be worthy of, qualify for **12** be entitled to **13** be deserving of

deserving 6 worthy **9** qualified

deserving reproach 8 blamable **10** deplorable, punishable, reprovable **11** blameworthy **12** reproachable **13** reprehensible

De Sica, Vittorio
director of: 15 The Bicycle Thief **27** The Garden of the Finzi-Continis

desiccate 5 dry up, parch **6** wither **7** shrivel **9** dehydrate

design 3 aim, end **4** draw, form, goal, plan, plot **5** draft, motif, set up **6** devise, intend, scheme, sketch, target **7** destine, diagram, drawing, fashion, outline, pattern, project, purpose **8** conceive, intrigue **9** blueprint, intention, objective **11** arrangement **14** draw up plans for

designate 4 call, name, term **5** elect, label **6** assign, choose, select **7** appoint, signify, specify **8** identify, indicate, nominate, pinpoint

designation 5 label **6** naming **10** delegation **11** appointment **13** specification **14** identification

designer 7 creator, deviser, planner **9** contriver **10** originator

designing 4 wily **6** artful, crafty **7** cunning **8** plotting, scheming **9** conniving

desirable 4 fine **8** in demand, pleasing **9** advisable **10** beneficial **11** worth having **12** advantageous

desire 3 yen **4** need, urge, want, wish **5** crave **6** ask for, hunger, thirst **7** craving, longing, long for, request **8** yearning, yearn for **9** hunger for, thirst for

Desire Under the Elms
author: 12 Eugene O'Neill

character: 4 Eben **5** Peter **6** Simeon **11** Abbie Putnam **12** Ephraim Cabot

desirous 4 avid, keen **5** eager **7** hopeful, longing, wishful **8** yearning

desist 4 stop **5** cease **6** lay off **7** suspend **8** leave off **11** discontinue, refrain from

Desk Set
director: 10 Walter Lang
cast: 8 Gig Young **11** Dina Merrill **12** Joan Blondell, Spencer Tracy **16** Katharine Hepburn

desolate 3 sad **4** bare, ruin **5** bleak, empty **6** barren, grieve, ravage, sadden **7** depress, destroy, forlorn **8** dejected, demolish, deserted, distress, downcast, forsaken, lay waste, wretched **9** abandoned, depressed, devastate, miserable, sorrowful **10** despondent, discourage, dishearten, melancholy **11** downhearted, uninhabited

desolating 6 tragic **7** ruinous **8** dreadful, grievous, terrible **10** calamitous, horrendous **11** devastating **12** catastrophic

desolation 4 ruin **6** misery, sorrow **7** sadness **8** bareness, distress, solitude **9** bleakness, dejection, emptiness, seclusion **10** barrenness, depression, dreariness, loneliness, melancholy, wilderness **11** destruction, devastation, unhappiness **12** solitariness

despair 5 gloom, trial **6** burden, ordeal **9** lose heart **10** depression, have no hope **11** despondency, lose faith in **12** hopelessness **14** discouragement

despair of 5 doubt **8** give up on **10** have no hope

desperado 4 thug **5** rowdy **6** bandit, gunman, outlaw **7** brigand, convict, hoodlum, ruffian **8** criminal, fugitive, hooligan **9** terrorist **10** lawbreaker

desperate 4 dire, rash, wild **5** grave, great **6** daring, urgent **7** extreme, frantic, serious **8** critical, hopeless, reckless, wretched **9** dangerous, incurable **10** beyond hope, despairing, despondent

Desperate Hours, The
director: 12 William Wyler
cast: 8 Gig Young **11** Dewey Martin, Martha Scott **13** Arthur Kennedy, Frederic March **14** Humphrey Bogart

Desperately Seeking Susan
director: 14 Susan Seidelman
cast: 7 Madonna **15** Rosanna Arquette

desperation 7 despair **12** hopelessness, recklessness

despicable 4 base, mean, vile **10** detestable, outrageous **11** disgraceful **12** contemptible **13** reprehensible

despise 5 abhor, scorn **6** detest, loathe **7** contemn, disdain, dislike **10** look down on

despoil 3 rob **4** loot **6** ravage **7** pillage, plunder

despoiler 6 looter, robber, vandal **7** brigand **8** pillager **9** plunderer

despondency 5 gloom **6** dismay **7** despair, sadness **9** dejection, pessimism **10** depression, desolation, low spirits, melancholy **11** melancholia **12** hopelessness **14** discouragement **15** downheartedness

despondent 3 low **4** blue, down **8** dejected, downcast, hopeless **9** depressed **11** discouraged, downhearted **12** disconsolate, disheartened

despot 4 czar, tsar **6** tyrant **8** autocrat, dictator **9** oppressor

despotic 9 imperious **10** autocratic, tyrannical **11** dictatorial **13** authoritarian

despotism 7 tyranny **9** autocracy **10** absolutism

dessert 3 pie **4** cake, nuts, tart **5** fruit, sweet, treat **6** pastry **7** cobbler **8** ice cream **11** final course

destination 3 aim, end **4** goal, plan **6** object, target **7** purpose **8** ambition **9** objective **11** journey's end

destiny 3 lot **4** fate **5** karma, moira **6** future, kismet **7** fortune **9** necessity
goddess of: 5 Fates, Morae, Parca **6** Moerae, Moirai, Parcae

destitute 4 poor **5** broke, needy **6** busted **8** indigent **9** penniless **15** poverty-stricken

destitution 4 lack, want **6** penury **7** beggary, poverty **9** indigence, privation **11** extreme want **13** pennilessness **14** impoverishment

destroy 4 ruin **5** waste, wreck **6** ravage **8** demolish **9** devastate

destroy completely 3 end **4** rase, raze **5** total **7** abolish, wipe out **8** lay waste **9** eradicate, extirpate, liquidate **10** annihilate, obliterate **11** exterminate

destroyer 4 bane **6** blight, killer **7** gunboat, warship **10** affliction **11** annihilator

destruct 3 gut **4** raze, ruin **5** wreck **7** despoil, destroy, wipe out **8** decimate, demolish, desolate, pull down, tear down **9** devastate **10** lay in ruins

destruction 4 ruin **5** havoc **8** wreckage, wrecking **10** demolition **11** devastation

destructive 7 harmful, hurtful, ruinous **8** damaging **9** injurious **11** detrimental, devastating **15** not constructive

Destry Rides Again
director: 14 George Marshall
based on a story by: 8 Max Brand
cast: 12 Brian Donlevy, James Stewart **15** Marlene Dietrich **16** Charles Winninger

song: **35** See What the Boys in the Back Room Will Have

desultory 4 idle **6** casual, chance, fitful, random **7** aimless, cursory **9** haphazard **10** without aim **11** unconnected

detach 5 sever **6** loosen **7** unhitch **8** separate, unfasten **9** disengage **10** disconnect **11** disentangle

detached 4 fair **5** aloof **7** distant, neutral, severed **8** reserved, unbiased **9** impartial, objective, separated, uncoupled, unhitched **10** disengaged, fairminded, unfastened **11** indifferent, unconnected **12** disconnected, unprejudiced **13** disinterested, dispassionate **French: 6** degage

detachment 4 unit **5** force **8** coolness, fairness, severing **9** aloofness, isolation, severance **10** cutting off, neutrality, separation **11** objectivity **12** impartiality, indifference **13** disconnection, disengagement, preoccupation **16** special task force

detail 4 fact, iota, item **6** aspect, relate **7** appoint, feature, itemize, recount, respect, specify **9** component, delineate, designate, enumerate **10** detachment, particular **11** special duty **13** assign to a task, particularize **14** special service **20** particular assignment

detailed 6 minute **8** itemized, thorough **10** item by item **12** point by point

detailed list 9 breakdown **11** itemization **14** categorization

detain 4 hold, slow, stop **5** delay **6** arrest, hinder, retard, slow up **7** confine **8** slow down **13** keep in custody

detainment 7 custody, holding **9** detention **11** confinement **12** imprisonment **13** incarceration

detect 3 see **4** espy, note, spot **5** catch **6** notice **7** observe, uncover **8** discover, perceive

detectable 10 noticeable **11** appreciable, discernible, perceivable, perceptible **13** ascertainable

detective 2 PI **3** tec **6** shamus, sleuth **7** gumshoe **10** private eye **12** investigator **19** special investigator

detectives 5 Kojak **7** Columbo, Matlock **8** Sam Spade, Magnum P.I. **9** James Bond, Nancy Drew, Hardy Boys **10** Bertha Cool, Goldfinger, Mike Hammer, Miss Marple, Perry Mason **11** Charlie Chan, Ellery Queen **13** Hercule Poirot, Father Dowling, Philip Marlowe **14** Sherlock Holmes **15** Jessica Fletcher

detention 7 custody, holding **9** keeping in **10** detainment **11** confinement, holding back **12** imprisonment **13** incarceration

deter 4 stop **5** daunt **6** divert, hinder,

impede **7** prevent **8** dissuade **10** discourage

deteriorate 3 ebb **4** fade, wane **5** decay, lapse **6** worsen **7** crumble, decline, fall off **10** degenerate **12** disintegrate

deteriorated 6 shabby **7** rickety **8** decaying, worsened **9** crumbling **10** broken-down, tumble-down **11** dilapidated, in disrepair **13** disintegrated

deterioration 5 decay, lapse **6** fading, waning **7** decline **9** crumbling, decadence, worsening **12** degeneration, dilapidation **14** disintegration

determination 4 grit **5** pluck, power, spunk **6** fixing **7** finding, resolve, verdict **8** boldness, decision, judgment, settling, solution, tenacity **9** reasoning, resolving **10** conclusion, resolution **11** determining, persistence **12** perseverance, resoluteness **13** act of deciding, steadfastness **16** stick-to-itiveness

determine 5 learn **6** affect, decide, detect, settle **7** control, find out, resolve **8** conclude, discover, regulate **9** ascertain, establish, figure out, influence **15** come to a decision, give direction to

determined 7 dead set, decided, settled **8** found out, obdurate, resolute, stubborn **9** obstinate, tenacious **10** figured out **11** ascertained, established **15** come to a decision

deterrent 4 curb **5** check **9** hindrance, restraint **14** discouragement

detest 4 hate **5** abhor **6** loathe **7** despise **10** recoil from **16** dislike intensely

detestable 4 vile **6** odious **7** hateful **9** abhorrent, loathsome, obnoxious, offensive, repulsive, revolting **10** disgusting, unpleasant **12** disagreeable

detestation 4 hate **6** hatred **7** disgust, dislike **8** aversion, distaste, loathing **9** antipathy, repulsion, revulsion **10** abhorrence, repugnance

dethrone 4 oust **6** depose, unseat

detonate 4 fire **5** blast, burst, erupt, go off, shoot **6** blow up, ignite, report, set off **7** explode **8** touch off **9** discharge, fulminate

detonation 5 blast, burst **6** report **9** discharge, explosion

detour 5 skirt **6** bypass, byroad, divert **7** digress **9** deviation, diversion **10** digression

detract 5 lower **6** lessen, reduce **8** diminish **12** subtract from, take away from

detraction 4 flaw **11** shortcoming **12** disadvantage

detractor 5 enemy **6** critic **8** opponent **9** adversary, belittler, slanderer **10** antagonist, bad mouther, disparager

detriment 4 harm, loss **6** damage, injury **10** impairment **12** disadvantage

detrimental 7 adverse, harmful **8** damaging **9** injurious **10** pernicious **11** deleterious, destructive, unfavorable **15** disadvantageous

Detroit
   baseball team: 6 Tigers
   basketball team: 5 Shock **7** Pistons
   football team: 5 Lions
   hockey team: 8 Redwings

de trop 7 too many, too much **8** in the way **9** not wanted

Deucalion
   father: 10 Prometheus
   mother: 7 Pronoia
   wife: 6 Pyrrha
   son: 6 Hellen
   founded: 9 human race
   after: 6 deluge

deus ex machina 15 god from a machine **18** improbable solution

Deus vobiscum 12 God be with you

Deus vult 8 God wills (it)
   cry of: 9 Crusaders

devaluate 6 lessen, reduce **7** deflate, degrade **10** depreciate

devaluation 4 drop **7** decline **12** depreciation

devalue 5 lower, taint **6** debase, defile, infect **7** cheapen, corrupt, degrade, pervert, pollute, revalue **8** mark down **9** devalu- ate, underrate, write down **10** adulterate, degenerate, demonetize, depreciate, remonetize **11** contaminate

devastate 4 ruin **5** level, spoil, waste, wreck **6** ravage **7** despoil, destroy **8** demolish, desolate, lay waste

devastating 7 ruinous **8** damaging **9** injurious **10** calamitous, disastrous **11** cataclysmic, destructive, detrimental **12** catastrophic

devastation 4 ruin **9** ruination **10** demolition **11** destruction

develop 4 grow **5** print, ripen **6** evolve, expand, finish, flower, mature, pick up, unfold **7** acquire, advance, amplify, augment, broaden, build up, convert, enlarge, improve, process, turn out **8** contract, energize **9** cultivate **10** come to have **11** come to light, elaborate on

development 5 event **6** growth, result **7** advance, history **8** progress **9** evolution

deviant 4 warp **5** shift **7** deviate, pervert **8** aberrant, abnormal **9** deflected, divergent

deviate 4 part, vary, veer **5** stray **6** depart, swerve, wander **8** go astray **9** sidetrack **10** come to have

deviation 6 change **7** veering **8** rambling, straying **9** wandering **10** aberration, digression, divergence **11** abnormality, fluctuation

device 4 plan, plot, ploy, ruse, wile

5 angle, trick **6** design, gadget, scheme **7** gimmick **8** artifice, strategy **9** apparatus, invention, mechanism, stratagem **11** contraption, contrivance

devil, the Devil 3 guy **5** rogue, Satan, thing **6** Azazel, fellow, wretch **7** hellion, Lucifer, ruffian, serpent, villain **8** creature **9** Archfiend, Beelzebub, scoundrel **11** unfortunate **12** spirit of evil **13** mischief-maker **16** prince of darkness

Devil and Daniel Webster, The
author: **19** Stephen Vincent Benet
director: **15** William Dieterle
character: **5** Devil **7** Webster **9** Mr Scratch
cast: **10** James Craig **11** Anne Shirley **12** Edward Arnold, Walter Huston
score: **15** Bernard Herrmann
Oscar for: **5** score
also titled: **18** All That Money Can Buy

devilish 4 evil **6** wicked **7** demonic, heinous, impious, satanic, vicious **8** demoniac, fiendish **9** nefarious **10** demoniacal, diabolical, villainous

devil-may-care 4 bold, rash, wild **5** risky **6** daring, rakish **8** heedless, reckless **9** audacious, daredevil

devil's advocate
Latin: **16** advocatus diaboli

Devil's Advocate
author: **14** Taylor Caldwell

Devil's Disciple, The
author: **17** George Bernard Shaw

Devine, Andy
real name: **16** Jeremiah Schwartz
born: **11** Flagstaff AZ
roles: **9** Jingles **9** Andy's Gang **14** Wild Bill Hickok

devious 3 sly **4** wily **6** sneaky, tricky **7** crooked **9** deceitful, dishonest **11** treacherous **12** dishonorable **13** double-dealing

devise 4 plot **5** forge, frame **6** design, invent, map out **7** concoct, prepare, think up **8** block out, conceive, contrive **9** construct, formulate

deviser 6 author, framer **7** creator, planner **8** inventor **9** architect, contriver **10** originator

devitalize 4 kill **6** deaden, weaken **8** enervate **10** debilitate

DeVito, Danny
born: **9** Neptune, NJ
wife: **11** Rhea Perlman
roles: **4** Taxi **5** Twins, Hoffa **6** Tin Men **7** Matilda **9** Get Shorty **11** Mars Attacks **13** Batman Returns, War of the Roses **14** Ruthless People **22** Throw Mamma From the Train

devoid 5 empty **6** barren **7** lacking, wanting, without **8** bereft of **9** destitute **11** unblest with

devote 5 apply **6** direct **7** address, utilize **8** dedicate **10** consecrate, give

over to **11** concentrate **15** give oneself up to **22** center one's attentions on

devoted 4 fond, true **5** loyal **6** ardent, loving **7** earnest, staunch, zealous **8** adhering, faithful **9** dedicated, steadfast **10** passionate, unwavering **17** strongly committed

devotedness 8 devotion **10** commitment, dedication **13** attentiveness **17** earnest attachment

devoted to luxury 9 epicurean, sybaritic **10** hedonistic, voluptuous

devotee 3 fan **6** rooter **7** booster, groupie **8** adherent, advocate, champion, disciple, follower **10** aficionado, enthusiast

devotion, devotions 4 love, zeal **5** ardor, piety **6** fealty, regard **7** loyalty **8** fondness, holiness **9** adherence, godliness, reverence **10** allegiance, commitment, concern for, dedication, devoutness, meditation **11** religiosity **12** faithfulness, spirituality **13** attentiveness, prayer service **15** religious fervor **17** earnest attachment **19** religious observance

De Voto, Bernard A
author of: **21** Across the Wide Missouri

devour 7 stuff in **8** bolt down, gobble up, gulp down, knock off, wolf down **9** go through **10** read widely **14** eat voraciously **15** absorb oneself in, consume greedily **16** read compulsively, take in ravenously **17** become engrossed in

devout 5 pious **6** ardent **7** earnest, fervent, intense, serious, zealous **8** orthodox, reverent **9** religious **10** passionate, worshipful

devoutness 5 piety **8** devotion, holiness **9** godliness, reverence **12** spirituality **15** religious fervor

DeVries, Hugo
field: **6** botany
nationality: **5** Dutch
researched: **8** heredity, mutation

DeVries, Peter
author of: **16** Consenting Adults **24** Slouching Toward Kalamazoo

dew 8 moisture **12** condensation **18** droplets of moisture

Dewar, James
field: **7** physics **9** chemistry
nationality: **8** Scottish
liquified: **8** hydrogen
solidified: **8** hydrogen
developed: **7** cordite **10** Dewar flask **12** liquid oxygen

Dewey, George
served in: **18** Spanish-American War
battle: **9** Manila Bay
destroyed: **12** Spanish fleet

Dewhurst, Colleen
husband: **12** George C Scott
born: **6** Canada **8** Montreal

roles: **12** The Nun's Story **18** Desire Under the Elms **22** A Moon for the Misbegotten

De Wilde, Brandon
born: **10** Brooklyn NY
roles: **3** Hud **5** Shane **11** All Fall Down

dewy 4 damp **5** moist **7** bedewed

dexterity 8 deftness, facility **9** handiness **10** adroitness, nimbleness **11** manual skill, proficiency

dexterous 4 able, deft **5** agile, quick **6** active, adroit, gifted, nimble **8** skillful **9** efficient, ingenious **11** resourceful

diabolic, diabolical 4 evil, foul **6** wicked **7** baleful, demonic, heinous, impious, satanic, vicious **8** devilish, fiendish **9** monstrous, nefarious **10** malevolent, villainous

diadem 4 halo **5** crown, tiara **7** circlet, coronet **8** headband

diagnosis 5 study **8** analysis, scrutiny **11** examination **13** investigation, medical report **16** scientific report **22** conclusion from symptoms, specification of illness

diagonal line 4 bias **5** angle, slant

diagram 3 map **4** plan **5** chart **6** sketch **7** drawing, outline **9** breakdown **11** line drawing **12** illustration **14** representation **15** rough projection

dialect 5 argot, idiom, lingo **6** accent, jargon, patois **8** localism **10** vernacular **11** regionalism **13** colloquialism, provincialism **15** language variety

Dial M for Murder
director: **15** Alfred Hitchcock
based on play by: **14** Frederick Knott
cast: **10** Grace Kelly, Ray Milland **14** Robert Cummings

dialogue, dialog 4 talk **5** lines **6** parley, speech **8** conclave **10** conference **12** conversation **14** verbal exchange **15** personal meeting **16** formal discussion

diamond
characteristic: **7** hardest
color: **4** blue, pink **9** blue-white **12** canary yellow
element: **6** carbon
famous: **4** Hope **6** Jonker **8** Cullinan, Idol's Eye, Koh-i-Noor **9** Excelsior **12** Star of Africa **13** Star of the East **17** Star of Sierra Leone
quality: **3** cut **4** fire **5** color **7** clarity **10** brilliance
source: **5** Congo, India **6** Africa, Borneo, Brazil, Guyana **8** Tanzania **9** Australia, Venezuela **11** South Africa, Soviet Union **12** South America **15** South West Africa
weight: **5** carat, point

Diamond State
nickname of: **8** Delaware

Diana
origin: **5** Roman

goddess of: 4 moon **6** slaves **7** hunting
protectress of: 5 women
corresponds to: 6 Phoebe **7** Artemis
epithet: 10 Nemorensis
 means: 10 of the grove

Diana of the Crossways
 author: 14 George Meredith
 character: 9 Mr Warwick **11** Diana Merion, Percy Dacier **12** Lady Dunstane **14** Thomas Redworth **15** Lord Dannisburgh

diaphanous 5 filmy, gauzy, lucid, sheer **6** flimsy, limpid **8** gossamer, pellucid **11** translucent, transparent

diary 3 log **7** daybook, journal **9** chronicle **12** daily journal **14** day-to-day record

Diary of Anne Frank, The
 author: 9 Anne Frank
 director: 13 George Stevens
 cast: 6 Ed Wynn **9** Lou Jacobi **10** Diane Baker **11** Millie Perkins, Richard Beymer **14** Shelley Winters (Mrs Van Daan) **17** Joseph Schildkraut (Father Frank)
 Oscar for: 17 supporting actress (Winters)

Diasia
 festival of: 4 Zeus

diatribe 6 tirade **9** contumely, invective **11** castigation **12** vituperation **13** stream of abuse **14** bitter harangue **18** accusatory language **19** violent denunciation

dice 4 chop, cube **5** bones, cubes, cut up, mince
 singular: 3 die

Dick, Mr
 character in: 16 David Copperfield
 author: 7 Dickens

Dickens, Charles
 author of: 9 Hard Times **10** Bleak House **11** Oliver Twist **12** Barnaby Rudge, Dombey and Son, Little Dorrit **14** Pickwick Papers **15** A Christmas Carol, Our Mutual Friend **16** A Tale of Two Cities, David Copperfield, Martin Chuzzlewit, Nicholas Nickleby **17** Great Expectations **19** The Old Curiosity Shop **22** The Mystery of Edwin Drood

dicker 4 deal **6** haggle, higgle, outbid **7** bargain, chaffer, quibble, wrangle **8** beat down, talk down, underbid **9** negotiate **17** drive a hard bargain

Dickey, James
 author of: 9 The Zodiac **11** Deliverance **16** Strength of Fields **17** Buckdancer's Choice

Dickinson, Angie
 real name: 13 Angeline Brown
 husband: 13 Burt Bacharach
 born: 6 Kulm ND
 roles: 8 Rio Bravo **11** Police Woman **13** Dressed to Kill **19** The Sins of Rachel Cade

Dick Tracy
 creator: 12 Chester Gould
 character: 8 BO Plenty, Moonmaid **12** Gravel Gertie **13** Sparkle Plenty **16** Jeremiah Truehart
 wife: 12 Tess Truehart
 daughter: 11 Bonny Braids
 assistant: 9 Pat Patton
 protege: 6 Junior
 villain: 5 Itchy **6** B-B Eyes **7** Flattop, Flyface, Measles, Mumbles, The Brow, The Mole **8** The Blank **9** Pruneface, The Midget, The Rodent
 equipment: 16 two-way wrist radio

Dick Van Dyke Show, The
 character: 9 Alan Brady, Rob Petrie **11** Jerry Helper, Laura Petrie, Sally Rogers **12** Buddy Sorrell, Melvin Cooley, Millie Helper **13** Ritchie Petrie
 cast: 9 Rose Marie **10** Carl Reiner, Jerry Paris **13** Larry Matthews, Richard Deacon **14** Mary Tyler Moore, Morey Amsterdam **17** Ann Morgan Guilbert

dictate 4 rule **5** edict, order **6** decree, dictum, direct, enjoin, impose, ordain, ruling, urging **7** bidding, counsel, lay down, mandate **8** set forth **9** determine, ordinance, prescribe, prompting, pronounce, stricture **11** exhortation, inclination, requirement

dictator 4 czar, duce, tsar **6** caesar, despot, fuhrer, kaiser, tyrant **7** emperor **8** autocrat **13** absolute ruler
 Argentinian: 5 Peron
 German: 6 Hitler
 Italian: 9 Mussolini
 Russian: 5 Lenin **6** Stalin
 Spanish: 6 Franco
 Ugandan: 7 Idi Amin

dictatorial 6 lordly **7** haughty, willful **8** absolute, arrogant, despotic **9** arbitrary, imperious, unlimited **10** autocratic, peremptory, tyrannical **11** categorical, domineering, magisterial, overbearing **12** supercilious, unrestricted **13** authoritative **17** inclined to command

diction 7 wording **8** delivery, rhetoric, verbiage **9** elocution **10** intonation, use of idiom, vocabulary **11** enunciation, phraseology, verbal style **12** articulation **13** choice of words, pronunciation **16** turn of expression **17** command of language **18** manner of expression

dictum 3 saw **4** fiat **5** adage, axiom, edict, maxim, order **6** decree, saying, truism **7** dictate, precept, proverb **11** commandment **13** pronouncement **15** dogmatic bidding **22** authoritative statement

Dictys
 occupation: 9 fisherman

found: 5 chest
 containing: 5 Danae **7** Perseus

didactic 7 donnish, preachy **8** academic, edifying, pedantic, tutorial **9** doctrinal, homiletic, pedagogic **10** expository, moralizing **11** educational, instructive, lecturelike, overbearing **12** prescriptive **17** inclined to lecture

didactics 8 teaching **9** education, teachings **10** pedagogics **11** instruction

Diderot, Denis
 author of: 12 Encyclopedia **13** Rameau's Nephew

Didion, Joan
 author of: 8 Salvador **10** White Album **14** Play It as It Lays **19** A Book of Common Prayer **24** Slouching Toward Bethlehem

Dido
 queen of: 8 Carthage
 father: 5 Mutto
 brother: 9 Pygmalion
 sister: 4 Anna
 husband: 8 Sychaeus
 lover: 6 Aeneas
 corresponds to: 6 Elissa

Dido and Aeneas
 opera by: 7 Purcell
 character: 4 Dido (Queen of Carthage) **6** Aeneas

die 3 ebb, rot **4** ache, fade, fail, long, pass, stop, wane **5** croak, yearn **6** depart, expire, go flat, pass on, perish, recede, run out, wither **7** be eager, decline, die away, go stale, run down, subside **8** fade away, melt away, pass away, pass over, wear away **9** be anxious, break down, lose force, lose power, meet death **10** degenerate, want keenly **11** come to an end, suffer death **12** wish ardently **13** come to one's end, desire greatly, go to one's glory, kick the bucket **14** leave this world, pine with desire, become inactive **15** slowly disappear **17** become inoperative
 plural: 4 dice

die away 4 fade **5** abate, cease **8** diminish

die down 5 abate **7** subside **8** diminish, slack off

die out 6 vanish **9** cease to be, disappear **13** become extinct

Diesel, Rudolf
 field: 11 engineering
 invented: 12 Diesel engine

diet 5 board, synod **7** edibles, nurture **8** congress, victuals **9** nutriment, nutrition **10** assemblage, convention, parliament, provisions, sustenance **11** comestibles, convocation, legislature, nourishment, subsistence **12** eating habits, eat sparingly **13** eating regimen, lawmaking body **14** eat judiciously **15** eat abstemiously, eat restrictedly, general assembly

16 limitation of fare, regulate one's food **17** bicameral assembly **18** nutritional regimen, representative body, restrict one's intake

Dietrich, Marlene
real name: **22** Maria Magdalene Dietrich
born: **7** Germany
roles: **8** Lola Lola **11** Blonde Venus **12** The Blue Angel **15** Rancho Notorious **16** Destry Rides Again, The Garden of Allah **17** The Scarlet Empress **24** Witness for the Prosecution

Dietrich von Bern
origin: **8** Germanic
king of: **10** Ostrogoths
Latin name: **9** Theodoric

Diety 3 Bel, God **4** Baal **6** Marduk, Molech, Moloch, Yahweh **7** Chemosh, Jehovah **10** Anammelech **11** Adrammelech

Dieu et mon droit 13 God and my right
motto of: **18** royal arms of England

differ 5 demur **7** dispute, dissent **8** be unlike, contrast, disagree **9** take issue **10** be distinct, depart from, stand apart **11** be disparate, deviate from, diverge from **12** be at variance, be dissimilar, stand opposed

difference 4 spat **5** clash, set-to **7** dispute, quarrel **8** argument, contrast, squabble **9** deviation, disparity, variation **10** divergence, falling out, unlikeness **11** contrariety, contretemps, discrepancy, distinction **12** disagreement **13** contradiction, dissimilarity, dissimilitude **17** contradistinction, lack of resemblance

different 4 rare **6** divers, sundry, unique, unlike **7** bizarre, diverse, foreign, several, strange, unusual, various **8** aberrant, atypical, distinct, manifold, not alike, peculiar, separate, singular, uncommon **9** anomalous, disparate, divergent, other than, unrelated **10** dissimilar, individual, variegated **11** contrasting, distinctive, diversified, not ordinary **12** not identical **13** miscellaneous **14** unconventional

differential 8 contrast **11** distinction

differentiate 6 set off **8** contrast, separate, set apart **11** distinguish, draw the line **12** discriminate **13** make different

differentiation 8 contrast **10** comparison, separation **11** discernment, distinction

differing 6 unlike **7** variant **8** distinct, opposing **9** deviating, disparate, dissident, divergent **10** dissenting, dissimilar **11** contrasting, disagreeing

difficult 4 grim, hard **5** hairy, rough, tough **6** knotty, thorny, trying, unruly, uphill **7** arduous, complex, forward, not easy, onerous, tedious, willful **8** critical, exacting, perverse, stubborn, ticklish, toilsome **9** demanding, enigmatic, fractious, Herculean, intricate, laborious, obstinate, Sisyphean, strenuous, wearisome **10** burdensome, exhausting, fastidious, formidable, inflexible, perplexing, unyielding **11** bewildering, complicated, hard to solve, intractable, troublesome **12** hard to manage, hard to please, obstreperous, rambunctious, recalcitrant, unmanageable **13** hard to satisfy, problematical, unpredictable **14** hard to deal with **15** unaccommodating

difficulty 3 jam, rub **4** mess, snag **5** trial **6** crisis, muddle, pickle, puzzle **7** barrier, dilemma, problem, straits, trouble **8** hot water, obstacle, quandary, tough job **9** deep water, hindrance, intricacy **10** impediment, perplexity, rough going, uphill work **11** arduousness, obstruction, predicament **12** hard sledding **13** laboriousness **14** stumbling block **15** troublesomeness **17** critical situation

diffidence 7 reserve, shyness **8** meekness, timidity **9** hesitancy, timidness **10** constraint, humbleness, insecurity, reluctance **11** bashfulness **12** introversion, sheepishness, timorousness **14** extreme modesty **15** unassertiveness **19** lack of self-assurance, retiring disposition

diffident 3 shy **6** modest **7** anxious, bashful **8** doubtful, hesitant, reserved, reticent, retiring **11** distrustful, unassertive **12** apprehensive

diffuse 5 wordy **7** verbose **8** rambling **9** desultory, dispersed, scattered, spread out, wandering **10** digressive, discursive, disjointed, long-winded, maundering, meandering, roundabout **14** circumlocutory, extended widely, unconcentrated, vaguely defined **15** not concentrated **18** lacking conciseness

diffuseness 8 rambling **9** prolixity, verbosity, wandering, wordiness **10** dispersion **11** indirection **14** circumlocution, long-windedness

diffusion 6 spread **8** rambling, verbiage **9** dispersal, prolixity, verbosity, wordiness **10** maundering, scattering **11** indirection, profuseness **14** circumlocution, discursiveness, disjointedness, roundaboutness

dig 3 jab **4** gibe, jeer, like, poke, prod, slur **5** aside, drive, gouge, punch, taunt **6** exhume, thrust **7** put-down, salvage, unearth **8** disinter, excavate, pinpoint, retrieve, scoop out **9** extricate, find among, hollow out **10** come up with, excavation, wry comment **11** bring to view **12** verbal thrust **13** cutting remark, search and find

digest 3 dig **5** grasp **6** absorb, fathom, precis, resume **7** realize, summary **8** abstract, dissolve, synopsis **10** abridgment, appreciate, assimilate, comprehend, understand **12** condensation, take in wholly **14** take in mentally

digestive system
component: **5** liver, mouth, teeth **6** tongue **7** stomach **8** appendix, pancreas **9** esophagus, intestine **11** gall bladder **13** salivary gland

dig in 3 eat **4** root **5** begin, embed, imbed, plant **6** anchor **7** pitch in **8** entrench, go to work **10** begin to eat **12** apply oneself

digit 3 one, six, two, toe **4** five, four, nine, unit, zero **5** light, seven, three **6** cipher, figure, finger, number **7** integer, numeral

dignified 5 proud **6** august, proper **7** upright **8** decorous, reserved **9** honorable **10** upstanding **11** circumspect **13** distinguished **14** self-respecting

dignify 5 raise **6** uplift **7** elevate, inflate, promote

dignitary 3 VIP **7** notable **8** luminary **9** personage **12** person of note

dignity 5 honor **7** decorum, majesty, station **9** loftiness, solemnity **10** augustness, importance **11** comportment, stateliness **12** high position, lofty bearing **13** proud demeanor **14** self possession

digress 5 stray **6** back up, wander **7** deviate **8** divagate **9** turn aside **15** go off on a tangent **17** depart from subject

digression 6 detour **8** straying **9** departure, deviation, diversion, wandering **10** divagation, divergence, side remark **12** obiter dictum

digressive 7 diffuse **9** wandering **10** disjointed, maundering, roundabout **11** off the point **14** circumlocutory

dig up 6 locate **7** find out, root out, uncover, unearth **8** discover **9** ferret out **12** bring to light

dike 4 bank **5** levee, ridge **10** embankment

Dike see **4** Dice

dikerion 11 candelabrum, candlestick **12** candleholder

dilapidated 4 shot **6** beat-up, ruined, shabby **7** rickety, run-down, worn-out **8** battered, decaying, decrepit **10** broken-down, ramshackle, tumble-down **11** in disrepair **12** deteriorated, falling apart **15** falling to pieces

dilate 5 swell, widen **6** expand, extend **7** broaden, distend, enlarge, inflate, puff out **9** make wider

dilation 8 swelling, widening **9** expansion **10** broadening, distension, distention

dilatory 4 lazy, slow **5** tardy **6** remiss **8** dawdling, indolent, slothful, sluggish **9** negligent, reluctant **10** phlegmatic **13** lackadaisical **15** inclined to delay, procrastinating

dilemma 4 bind 6 crunch, plight 7 impasse, problem 8 deadlock, quandary 9 stalemate 11 predicament 13 Hobson's choice 15 difficult choice

dilettante 7 amateur, dabbler, trifler 12 experimenter 16 cultured hobbyist

diligence 4 zeal 8 industry 10 commitment, dedication 11 persistence 12 perseverance

diligent 6 active 7 careful, earnest, patient, zealous 8 plodding, sedulous, studious, thorough, untiring 9 assiduous, concerted 10 persistent 11 hard-working, industrious, painstaking, persevering 12 pertinacious 15 well-intentioned

dill 4 anet
botanical name: 17 Anethum graveolens
origin: 9 Asia Minor 13 Mediterranean
family: 7 parsley
guards against: 7 Evil Eye 10 witchcraft
use: 6 sauces 7 pickles 10 vegetables

Dillon, Matt
roles: 3 Tex 10 Rumblefish 12 The Outsiders

dillydally 3 lag 4 idle, loaf 5 dally, delay 6 dawdle, loiter 8 kill time 9 waste time 10 fool around 13 procrastinate

Dilsey
character in: 18 The Sound and the Fury
author: 8 Faulkner

dilute 4 thin, weak 6 reduce, temper, watery, weaken 7 diffuse, diluted, thin out 8 decrease, diminish, make weak, mitigate, weakened 9 attenuate, liquidify, water down 10 add water to, adulterate, thinned out 11 adulterated, make thinner, watered down

diluted 4 weak 6 dilute, watery 8 weakened 10 thinned out 11 adulterated, watered down

dilution 8 thinning 9 weakening 12 watering down

dim 3 low 4 hazy, soft, weak 5 dusky, faint, foggy, murky, muted, vague 6 blurry, feeble, gloomy, remote 7 blurred, clouded, muffled, shadowy 8 darkened, nebulous, obscured 9 not bright, tenebrous 10 adumbrated, ill-defined, indefinite, indistinct, intangible 13 unilluminated

DiMaggio, Joe
nickname: 9 Joltin Joe
sport: 8 baseball
position: 8 outfield
team: 14 New York Yankees
wife: 13 Marilyn Monroe

dime-a-dozen 6 common 7 humdrum 8 ordinary, workaday 9 plentiful 10 ubiquitous 11 commonplace 12 easy to come by 13 garden-variety 15 undistinguished

dimension, dimensions 4 bulk, mass, size 5 range, scope, width 6 extent, height, length, volume, weight 7 measure 9 amplitude, greatness, magnitude, thickness 10 importance, proportion 11 massiveness 12 measurements 14 physical extent

diminish 3 ebb 4 wane 5 abate, lower 6 lessen, narrow, reduce, shrink 7 decline, dwindle, fall off, shorten, shrivel, subside 8 decrease, peter out 9 be reduced 11 make smaller 13 become smaller

diminuendo
music: 22 gradually getting softer
  abbreviation: 3 dim

diminution 6 ebbing, waning 7 decline 8 decrease, lowering 9 dwindling, lessening, reduction, shrinkage 10 falling off, shortening, shriveling, subsidence 11 petering out, slacking off

diminutive 3 wee 4 tiny 5 elfin, short, small, teeny 6 little, minute, petite, slight 7 pet name, stunted 8 dwarfish, half-pint, nickname 9 miniature, short form 10 pocket-size, undersized, vest-pocket 11 lilliputian, small-scale, unimportant 13 insignificant 14 inconsiderable

Dimmesdale, Arthur
character in: 16 The Scarlet Letter
author: 9 Hawthorne

dimness 4 dusk 5 gloom, shade 8 darkness 14 indistinctness

dimwit 4 fool 5 dummy, dunce, idiot, moron 6 cretin, nitwit 7 dingbat, dullard, dumbell, pinhead 8 dumbbell, dummkopf, imbecile, meathead, numskull 9 birdbrain, blockhead, ding-a-ling, lamebrain, numbskull, simpleton 11 chowderhead, knucklehead

dim-witted 4 dull, dumb 5 dense 6 stupid 7 foolish, idiotic, moronic, witless 8 retarded 9 cretinous, imbecilic

din 4 stir, to-do 5 bruit 6 babble, clamor, hubbub, racket, ruckus, tumult, uproar 7 clangor 9 commotion 10 clattering, hullabaloo

Dinah
father: 5 Jacob
mother: 4 Leah
brother: 3 Dan, Gad 4 Levi 5 Asher, Judah 6 Joseph, Reuben, Simeon 7 Zebulun 8 Benjamin, Issachar, Naphtali
violated by: 7 Shechem

dine 3 eat, sup 4 feed 5 feast, lunch 6 fall to, supper 7 banquet, partake 9 breakfast, eat dinner 10 break bread, gluttonize, have dinner 11 gourmandize 14 take sustenance

Dine see 6 Navajo

Dinesen, Isak
real name: 18 Karen Blixen-Finecke
author of: 9 Last Tales 11 Out of Af-rica 12 Winter's Tales 16 Seven Gothic Tales

dinghy 5 skiff 7 rowboat 8 sailboat 9 small boat

dingy 4 dull 5 dusty, grimy, murky, tacky 6 dismal, dreary, gloomy, shabby 12 dirty and drab

dining room
French: 12 salle a manger

dinner 4 food, meal 5 feast 6 repast, supper 7 banquet
French: 8 dejeuner 10 table d'hote

Dinner at Eight
director: 11 George Cukor
author: 10 Edna Ferber 14 George S Kaufman
cast: 8 Lee Tracy 10 Jean Harlow 11 Billie Burke 12 Wallace Beery 13 John Barrymore, Marie Dressler 15 Lionel Barrymore

dinosaur
means: 14 fearfully great, terrible lizard
subclass: 11 Archosauria
characteristic: 7 diapsid 14 teeth in sockets, two-arched skull 18 three-element pelvis
group: 11 Saurischian 13 Ornithischian
  flesh-eating biped: 8 therapod
  plant-eating quadruped: 8 sauropod
  plant-eating biped: 10 ornithopod
  armored: 10 ceratopsid
of Africa: 9 Iguanodon 13 Brachiosaurus 17 Heterodontosaurus
of Asia: 13 Hypselosaurus, Protoceratops
of Europe: 9 Iguanodon 12 Plateosaurus 13 Compsognathus, Hypselosaurus, Hypsilophodon
of North America: 10 Diplodocus, Edmontonia, Nodosaurus 11 Anatosaurus, Anchisaurus, Gorgosaurus, Monoclonius, Saurolophus, Scolosaurus, Stegosaurus, Triceratops 12 Ankylosaurus, Camarasaurus, Camptosaurus, Coelophysics, Lambeosaurus, Paleoscincus 13 Brachiosaurus, Styracosaurus, Tyrannosaurus 14 Thescelosaurus 15 Parasaurolophus, Procheneosaurus
of South America: 12 Pisanosaurus
fictional: 4 Puff 6 Barney 12 Jurassic Park

dint 4 push, will 5 drive, force, labor, might, power 6 charge, effort, energy, strain, stress 8 endeavor, exertion, strength, struggle 10 insistence 12 forcefulness 13 determination 14 relentlessness

diocese 3 see 7 eparchy 9 bishopric 14 church district
jurisdiction of: 6 bishop

Diomedes
king of: 6 Thrace
father: 4 Ares 6 Tydeus

mother: 6 Cyrene **7** Deipyle
member of: 7 Epigoni
kept: 9 wild mares
fed mares on: 10 human flesh
death planned by: 8 Hercules

Dione
consort of: 4 Zeus

Dionysia
festival of: 8 Dionysus

Dionysus *see* **7** Bacchus

Dioscuri *see* **15** Castor and Pollux

dip 4 bail, dish, dunk, sink, skim, soak **5** droop, ladle, scoop, slope, spoon **6** dabble, dish up, peruse, shovel **7** decline, descend, dish out, run over **8** drop down, glance at, submerge, turn down **13** study slightly **14** immerse briefly, lift by scooping, try tentatively **15** incline downward

dip into 4 scan, skim **5** ladle **6** browse, peruse **7** deplete **8** look over **13** glance through, make inroads in

Diplodocus
type: 8 dinosaur, sauropod
period: 8 Jurassic
location: 12 North America

diplomacy 4 tact **5** craft, skill **7** finesse **8** delicacy, prudence, subtlety **10** artfulness, discretion **11** maneuvering, savoir-faire **13** statesmanship **14** foreign affairs **16** artful management **18** foreign negotiation **21** international politics

diplomat 5 envoy **6** consul **7** attache **8** emissary, minister **9** statesman **10** ambassador, negotiator **12** interlocutor **13** tactful person
acceptable: 12 persona grata
unacceptable: 15 persona non grata

diplomatic 5 adept, suave **6** artful, urbane **7** attuned, politic, prudent, tactful **8** discreet **9** sensitive, strategic **13** ambassadorial **14** foreign-service **15** state department

Dipper
nickname of: 15 Wilt Chamberlain

Dipsas
form: 7 serpent

dipsomaniac 3 sot **4** lush, soak, wino **5** drunk, rummy, souse, toper **6** barfly, boozer **7** tippler **8** drunkard **9** alcoholic, inebriate

diptera
class: 8 hexapoda
phylum: 10 arthropoda
group: 7 true fly

Dirae *see* **6** Furies

dire 4 grim **5** awful, grave **6** dismal, urgent, woeful **7** crucial, extreme, fearful, ominous, ruinous **8** critical, dreadful, horrible, terrible **9** appalling, desperate, harrowing, ill-boding, ill-omened **10** calamitous, disastrous, portentous **11** apocalyptic, cataclysmic **12** catastrophic, inauspicious

direct 3 aim **4** head, lead, urge **5** blunt, clear, focus, frank, guide, order, pilot, usher **6** advise, candid, charge, enjoin, handle, head-on, honest, manage **7** address, command, conduct, control, earmark, forward, level at, oversee, pointed, sincere, train at **8** explicit, indicate, instruct, navigate, personal **9** conduct to, designate, firsthand, intend for, supervise **10** administer, face-to-face, forthright, point-blank, show the way, unmediated **11** plain-spoken, point the way, point toward, preside over, superintend **15** straightforward

direction 3 aim, ENE, ESE, NNE, NNW, SSE, SSW, way, WNW, WSW **4** bent, care, east, path, west **5** drift, north, order, route, south, track, trend **6** charge, course, recipe **7** bearing, command, control, current **8** guidance, headship, tendency **9** alignment **10** guidelines, leadership, management, regulation **11** inclination, instruction, line of march, supervision **12** line of action, prescription, surveillance **13** line of thought **14** administration, point of compass **15** superintendence

directive 5 ukase **8** bulletin **9** statement **10** communique **11** declaration **12** instructions, proclamation **13** communication

directly 4 soon **6** at once, openly **7** exactly, frankly **8** candidly, honestly, in person, promptly, straight **9** forthwith, precisely, presently, right away **10** face-to-face, in a beeline, personally **11** immediately, momentarily **12** in plain terms, not obliquely, unswervingly **13** unambiguously, unequivocally **14** as the crow flies **15** in a straight line **16** as soon as possible **17** on a straight course, straightforwardly

directness 6 candor **9** bluntness, frankness **10** candidness **14** forthrightness **19** straightforwardness

direct opposite 7 reverse **8** converse **10** antithesis

director 4 boss, head **5** chief **6** leader, master **7** curator, foreman, manager **8** chairman, governor, overseer **9** commander, conductor, organizer **10** controller, supervisor **13** administrator **14** superintendent

dirge 6 lament **7** requiem **8** threnody **9** death song **10** burial hymn, death march **11** funeral song **13** mournful sound **19** mournful composition

dirigo 7 I direct
motto of: 5 Maine

dirk 3 sny **4** snee, stab **5** knife, skean **6** dagger, skiver **7** poniard
origin: 8 Scotland

Dirks, Rudolph
creator/artist of: 12 Hans and Fritz **17** Captain and the Kids **19** The Katzenjammer Kids

dirt 3 mud **4** dust, loam, mire, muck, scum, slop, smut, soil, soot **5** dross, earth, filth, grime, humus, offal, rumor, slime, trash **6** gossip, ground, refuse, sludge, smudge **7** garbage, rubbish, scandal, slander **8** impurity, leavings, vileness **9** excrement, indecency, obscenity, profanity, sweepings **10** foul matter, moral filth, scurrility **11** pornography, scuttlebutt, squalidness **12** scabrousness **13** salaciousness **14** defamatory talk **15** filthy substance, unclean language **17** sensational expose

dirt-cheap 6 a steal **7** bargain **11** inexpensive **14** very reasonable **15** bargain-basement

dirty 4 base, foul, hard, lewd, mean, soil, spot, vile **5** grimy, messy, muddy, nasty, smear, stain, sully **6** coarse, filthy, grubby, mess up, muck up, risque, rotten, shabby, slop up, smudge, smudgy, smutty, soiled, sordid, untidy, vulgar **7** begrime, besmear, blacken, corrupt, crooked, devious, illegal, illicit, immoral, lowdown, muddied, obscene, pollute, squalid, sullied, tarnish, unclean **8** befouled, begrimed, indecent, off-color, polluted, prurient, scabrous, unwashed **9** besmeared, deceitful, difficult, dishonest, tarnished, unsterile **10** despicable, fraudulent, licentious, perfidious, unpleasant, villainous **11** distasteful, treacherous **12** contemptible, disagreeable, dishonorable, pornographic, unscrupulous **14** morally unclean

Dirty Dozen, The
director: 13 Robert Aldrich
cast: 8 Jim Brown **9** Lee Marvin **10** Robert Ryan, Trini Lopez **11** Clint Walker **13** George Kennedy **14** Charles Bronson, Ernest Borgnine, John Cassavetes, Richard Jaeckel **16** Donald Sutherland

Dis
also: 8 Dis Pater
means: 5 Hades
god of: 10 underworld
corresponds to: 5 Orcus, Pluto

dis 6 insult **9** disparage

disability 5 minus **6** defect **8** handicap, weakness **9** infirmity, unfitness **10** affliction, impairment, impediment, inadequacy **11** shortcoming **12** debilitation, disadvantage **16** disqualification

disable 6 damage, hinder, impair, weaken **7** cripple **8** handicap **12** incapacitate

disabled
French: 12 hors de combat

disabuse 8 set right **9** relieve of **10** disenchant **11** disillusion, set straight

disaccord 7 discord **10** disharmony **12** disagreement **15** incompatibility

disacknowledge 4 deny 6 disown 7 disavow 8 disallow, disclaim 9 repudiate

disadvantage 4 flaw 6 burden 7 trouble 8 drawback, handicap, hardship, nuisance, weakness 9 detriment, hindrance, in arrears, weak point 10 impediment 12 weak position 13 inconvenience 16 fly in the ointment

disadvantaged 8 deprived, emergent, emerging, troubled 10 struggling 11 handicapped 12 impoverished 14 underdeveloped 15 underprivileged

disadvantageous 7 harmful 9 injurious 11 detrimental, inadvisable, inexpedient, undesirable, unfavorable, unfortunate

disaffect 4 wean 8 alienate, estrange 10 drive apart

disaffected 5 upset 7 hostile 8 agitated, inimical 9 alienated, disturbed, estranged, withdrawn 10 unfriendly 11 belligerent, discomposed, disgruntled, quarrelsome 12 antipathetic, discontented, dissatisfied 14 irreconcilable

disaffection 7 dislike 8 aversion, distaste 9 antipathy 10 alienation, discontent, disloyalty 12 estrangement

disaffirm 4 deny 5 annul 6 disown 7 decline, disavow 8 abnegate, disclaim, forswear, renounce 9 repudiate 15 wash one's hands of

disaffirmation 6 denial 9 annulment, disavowal 10 abnegation, disclaimer 11 repudiation 12 renunciation 13 contradiction

disagree 4 vary 5 clash, upset 6 depart, differ 7 deviate, diverge, make ill 8 be unlike, conflict, distress 9 discomfit 10 disconcert, stand apart 11 be injurious, fail to agree, not coincide 12 be at variance, be discordant, be dissimilar 13 cause problems 14 be unreconciled 15 be at loggerheads, differ in opinion 16 oppose one another, think differently

disagreeable 5 cross, harsh, nasty, surly, testy 7 grating, grouchy, peevish 8 churlish, petulant 9 difficult, irascible, irritable, obnoxious, offensive, repellent, repugnant, repulsive, unamiable, unwelcome 10 disgusting, ill-natured, uninviting, unpleasant 11 acrimonious, bad-tempered, displeasing, distasteful, ill-tempered, uncongenial, unpalatable 13 uncomfortable

disagreeing 6 at odds 7 deviant, varying 8 clashing 9 deviating, differing, disputing 10 quarreling 11 conflicting 13 at loggerheads

disagreement 5 clash, fight 7 discord, dispute, quarrel 8 argument, squabble, variance 9 deviation, disaccord, disparity, diversity 10 difference, divergence, falling-out, unlikeness 11 discrepancy, incongruity 13 dissimilarity, dissimilitude, lack of harmony 15 incompatibility 16 misunderstanding

disallow 4 deny, veto 6 abjure, forbid, refuse, reject 8 prohibit 9 repudiate

disallowance 4 veto 6 denial 7 refusal 9 rejection 11 prohibition, repudiation

disallowed 6 vetoed 7 abjured, refused 8 rejected 9 forbidden 10 repudiated 12 inadmissible, unacceptable

disappear 2 go 3 end 4 exit, fade, flee 5 leave 6 be gone, depart, die out, retire, vanish 8 be no more, fade away, melt away, withdraw 9 evaporate 12 be lost to view, cease to exist, leave no trace 13 cease to appear, cease to be seen 14 become obscured, cease to be known, pass out of sight 15 vanish from sight

disappearance 9 vanishing 11 evanescence 16 passing from sight

disappoint 4 foil 6 hinder, sadden, thwart 7 chagrin, let down, mislead 9 frustrate 10 dishearten 11 disillusion

disappointing 11 frustrating 12 unfulfilling 13 dissatisfying 14 unsatisfactory

disappointment 3 dud 4 bomb, loss 6 defeat, fiasco, fizzle 7 failure, letdown, setback, washout 8 disaster 9 the knocks 11 frustration 13 unfulfillment, unrealization 15 disillusionment, dissatisfaction

disapprobation 7 censure 8 disfavor 9 criticism, disesteem, objection 11 disapproval, displeasure 12 condemnation 15 dissatisfaction

disapprove 4 veto 5 decry 6 refuse, reject 7 censure, condemn, deplore, dislike 8 denounce, disallow, object to, turn down 9 criticize, deprecate, disparage, frown upon 10 think ill of 13 look askance at, regard as wrong 14 discountenance, refuse assent to 15 take exception to 16 find unacceptable, view with disfavor

disapprove of 7 censure, condemn, deplore 8 object to

disarm 4 move, sway 5 charm 6 entice 7 attract, bewitch, enchant, win over 8 convince, persuade 9 captivate, fascinate, influence, prevail on

disarming 7 melting, winning, winsome 8 charming, magnetic 9 appealing, beguiling, ingenuous, seductive 10 bewitching, entrancing 11 captivating 12 ingratiating, irresistible

disarrange 5 mix up, upset 6 jumble, mess up, muddle, ruffle, rumple 7 confuse, scatter 8 disarray, dishevel, disorder, displace, put askew, scramble 11 disorganize 13 put out of order 14 turn topsy-turvy

disarranged 5 messy 6 mussed, sloppy, untidy 7 jumbled, ruffled, rumpled, tousled, unkempt 8 uncombed 9 cluttered 10 disarrayed, disheveled, disordered, disorderly, in disorder 11 in a shambles

disarrangement 4 mess 5 chaos, mix-up, upset 6 jumble, mixing, muddle 7 clutter 8 disarray, disorder, scramble, shambles 9 confusion, messiness, messing up 10 disharmony, disruption, sloppiness, untidiness 12 dishevelment 14 disorderliness 15 disorganization, heaping together

disarray 5 chaos, mix-up, upset 6 jumble 7 clutter 8 disorder, scramble, shambles 9 confusion, messiness 10 disharmony, sloppiness, untidiness 12 dishevelment 14 disarrangement 15 disorganization

disarrayed 5 messy 6 mussed, sloppy, untidy 7 chaotic, jumbled, mixed up 10 disheveled, disordered, disorderly, in disorder 11 disarranged

disarticulate 6 detach 7 unhinge 8 disjoint, disunite, separate 9 disengage, dislocate 10 disconnect 13 put out of joint

disarticulated 5 apart 7 divided 8 unhinged 9 disunited, separated 10 disengaged, disjointed, dislocated, unattached 11 unconnected 12 disconnected 13 helter-skelter

disassemble 7 disband, scatter 8 disperse 9 knock down, take apart

disassociate 7 divorce 8 separate 10 disconnect 9 disaffiliate

disassociation 5 break, split 6 schism 7 divorce 8 division 10 separation

disaster 4 harm 5 wreck 6 blight, fiasco 7 scourge, tragedy, trouble 8 accident, calamity 9 adversity, cataclysm, ruination 10 misfortune 11 catastrophe, great mishap 12 misadventure

disastrous 4 dire 5 fatal 6 tragic 7 adverse, hapless, harmful, ruinous 8 dreadful, grievous, ill-fated, terrible 9 harrowing 10 calamitous, desolating, horrendous, ill-starred 11 destructive, devastating, unfortunate 12 catastrophic, inauspicious

disavow 4 deny 6 abjure, disown, recant, reject 7 gainsay, retract 8 denounce 9 repudiate 10 contradict

disavowal 6 denial 8 demurrer 9 rejection 10 abjuration, disclaimer, refutation 11 repudiation 13 contradiction

disband 7 adjourn, dismiss, scatter 8 disperse, dissolve 11 disassemble

disbelief 5 doubt 7 dubiety 8 distrust, mistrust, unbelief 10 skepticism 11 incredulity 12 doubtfulness 14 lack of credence

disbelieve 5 doubt 6 refuse, reject 7 suspect 8 discount, distrust 9 discredit, unbelieve 10 misbelieve

disbeliever 7 atheist, skeptic 8 apostate

disbursable 7 payable 9 available, spendable 10 expendable

disburse 6 lay out, pay out 7 fork out 8 allocate, shell out 10 distribute

disbursement 6 outlay 7 payment 8 spending 9 paying out 10 dispensing 11 expenditure 12 dispensation, distribution

discard 4 drop, dump, junk, shed 5 scrap 6 remove, shelve 7 abandon, weed out 8 get rid of, jettison, throw out 9 cast aside, dispose of, eliminate, throw away 10 relinquish 11 thrust aside 12 dispense with, have done with 14 throw overboard

discarded 6 dumped, junked 7 cast off, dropped 8 deserted, forsaken, rejected, scrapped 9 abandoned, cast aside, tossed out 10 jettisoned, left behind, thrown away

discern 3 see 4 espy 6 behold, descry, detect, notice 7 make out, observe, pick out 8 perceive 9 ascertain 12 catch sight of

discernible 7 visible 8 apparent 10 detectable, noticeable 11 perceivable, perceptible

discerning 4 sage, wise 5 acute, sharp 6 astute, shrewd 8 piercing 9 judicious, sagacious, sensitive 10 perceptive 11 intelligent, keen-sighted, penetrating 12 clear-sighted, sharp-sighted 13 perspicacious 14 discriminating

discernment 6 acumen, senses 7 insight 8 feelings, sagacity, thoughts 10 cognizance, discretion, perception 11 distinction 13 consciousness, judiciousness 14 discrimination 15 differentiation

discharge 3 axe, can 4 emit, fire, flow, gush, ooze, oust, sack, shot 5 blast, burst, eject, expel, exude, issue, let go, shoot 6 bounce, firing, launch, lay off, let fly, propel, report, set off 7 cashier, dismiss, explode, fire off, project, release, seepage, set free, trigger 8 activate, detonate, drainage, emission, get rid of, liberate, throw off, touch off 9 allow to go, exploding, explosion, firing off, fusillade, give forth, pour forth, secretion, send forth, terminate 10 activating, detonating, detonation, triggering 11 send packing, suppuration 13 give the gate to, walking papers 14 demobilization 15 release document 16 remove from office

disciple 3 nut 5 freak, pupil 7 admirer, convert, devotee, pursuer, student 8 adherent, believer, follower, neophyte, partisan 9 proselyte, supporter 10 aficionado 11 afficionado

Disciple, The
   author: 11 Paul Bourget

Disciples see 8 Apostles

disciplinarian 8 martinet 13 authoritarian 16 stickler for rules, strict taskmaster

disciplinary 8 punitive 9 punishing 10 corrective 13 authoritarian

discipline 5 drill, prime, rigor, train 6 method, punish 7 break in, chasten, regimen 8 chastise, drilling, instruct, practice, training 9 schooling 11 preparation 14 indoctrination 15 prescribed habit, teach by exercise 16 course of exercise

disclaim 4 deny 6 disown 7 decline, disavow 8 abnegate, forswear, renounce 9 disaffirm, repudiate

disclaimer 6 denial 8 demurrer 9 disavowal 10 abnegation 11 repudiation 12 renunciation

disclose 4 bare, leak, show, tell 6 expose, impart, reveal, unveil 7 divulge, lay bare, publish, uncover 9 broadcast, make known 10 make public 11 communicate 12 bring to light 13 allow to be seen, bring into view, cause to appear

disco 4 club 5 agogo, dance 7 cabaret 9 dance club, nightclub

discolor 4 spot 5 stain, tinge 6 bleach, streak 7 tarnish

discoloration 4 blot, mark, spot 5 smear, stain 6 blotch, bruise, smudge 7 blemish 9 contusion

discolored 4 doty 5 dingy, dirty, faded, livid 6 soiled, tinged 7 bruised, stained 9 tarnished

discomfit 5 upset 6 thwart 7 chagrin 8 confound, distress 9 embarrass, frustrate 10 disconcert

discomfited 5 upset 6 uneasy 7 ashamed 8 thwarted 9 chagrined, ill at ease 10 distressed 11 embarrassed 12 disconcerted

discomfiture 7 anxiety 9 agitation, confusion 10 uneasiness 11 disquietude, distraction, nervousness 12 discomposure, perturbation 13 embarrassment

discomfort 3 try 4 ache, hurt, pain 5 trial 6 misery 7 malaise, trouble 8 disquiet, distress, hardship, nuisance, soreness, vexation 9 annoyance, discomfit, embarrass 10 affliction, discompose, irritation, make uneasy 11 disquietude

discompose 5 abash, upset 6 rattle 7 agitate, confuse, disturb, fluster, nonplus, perturb, trouble, unnerve 8 disquiet, distract, distress, unsettle 9 discomfit, embarrass 10 disconcert

discomposed 5 upset 6 jolted, rocked, shaken, uneasy 7 anxious, nervous, worried 8 agitated, confused, troubled 9 disturbed, flustered, perturbed 10 disquieted, distracted 11 discomfited, uncollected

discomposure 6 flurry 7 anxiety 8

disquiet 9 agitation, confusion 10 discomfort, uneasiness 11 awkwardness, disquietude, distraction, nervousness 12 discomfiture, perturbation 13 embarrassment 17 self-consciousness

disconcert 5 abash, annoy, upset 6 raffle, ruffle 7 agitate, confuse, disturb, nonplus, perturb, trouble 8 unsettle 10 discompose

disconcerted 5 fazed, upset 7 annoyed, rattled, ruffled 8 agitated, confused, troubled 9 disturbed, perturbed, thrown off, unsettled 10 distracted, nonplussed

disconcertment 8 rattling 9 abashment, agitation, confusion 11 disturbance 12 discomposure

disconnect 6 detach 8 separate, uncouple 9 disengage

disconnected 5 split 6 cut off 7 jumbled, mixed-up, severed 8 confused, detached, rambling 9 illogical, separated, uncoupled 10 disengaged, disjointed, incoherent, irrational, unattached, unfastened 12 disorganized

disconnection 8 severing 9 severance 10 cutting off, detachment, separation 13 disengagement

disconsolate 3 sad 4 blue, down 6 woeful 7 crushed, doleful, forlorn, unhappy 8 dejected, desolate, downcast, wretched 9 depressed, miserable, sorrowful, woebegone 10 despondent, dispirited, melancholy 11 discouraged, low spirited, pessimistic 12 heavyhearted, inconsolable 13 brokenhearted 14 down in the dumps, down in the mouth

discontent 9 displease 10 discomfort, disgruntle 11 displeasure, unhappiness 15 dissatisfaction

discontented 5 bored 7 fretful, unhappy 9 miserable, regretful 10 displeased, malcontent 11 disgruntled 12 dissatisfied

discontinuance 3 end 4 halt, stop 6 ending, recess 7 ceasing, halting 8 abeyance, giving up, quitting, stoppage, stopping, surcease 9 cessation, desisting 10 concluding, leaving off, suspension 11 abandonment, breaking off, termination

discontinue 3 end 4 drop, quit, stop 5 cease 6 desist, give up 7 abandon, abstain, suspend 8 break off, leave off 9 interrupt, terminate 10 put an end to

discontinuous 8 discrete, episodic, sporadic 9 segmented, spasmodic 10 occasional 11 interrupted 12 disconnected, intermittent

discord 6 strife 7 dispute 8 clashing, conflict, disunity, division, friction 9 cacophony, harshness, wrangling 10 contention, disharmony, dissension, dissonance, quarreling 11 being at odds, differences, discordance 12 disagreement, grating noise 13 lack of

concord **15** incompatibility **16** unpleasant sounds
goddess of: 4 Eris **9** Discordia

discordance 6 strife **7** discord, dispute **8** clashing, conflict, disunity, division, friction **9** wrangling **10** contention, disharmony, dissension, quarreling **12** disagreement **15** incompatibility

discordant 6 at odds **9** disparate, dissonant **10** at variance, discrepant **11** conflicting, disagreeing **12** unharmonious

Discordia
origin: 5 Roman
goddess of: 7 discord
corresponds to: 4 Eris

discount 3 cut **5** break **6** rebate **7** cut rate **9** abatement, allowance, deduction, exemption, reduction **10** concession **11** subtraction

discountenance 7 condemn, despise, disdain, dislike **8** object to **9** frown upon **10** disapprove, think ill of **12** look down upon **13** look askance at, regard as wrong **14** hold in contempt **15** take exception to

discourage 4 do in **5** daunt, deter, unman **6** deject, dismay **7** depress, unnerve **8** decimate, dispirit, dissuade, keep back, restrain **9** disparage, prostrate **10** dishearten, disincline, divert from **13** advise against, dash one's hopes **17** dampen one's spirits

discouraged 3 low **7** daunted **8** dejected, downcast, hopeless **9** depressed **10** despondent, dispirited **11** downhearted, pessimistic **12** disconsolate, disheartened

discouragement 4 curb **5** gloom, worry **6** damper, dismay **7** despair **8** obstacle **9** dejection, hindrance, pessimism, restraint **10** constraint, depression, impediment, low spirits, melancholy, moroseness **11** despondency **12** hopelessness, lack of spirit **13** consternation **15** downheartedness

discourse 3 gab **4** chat, talk **5** essay **6** confer, sermon, speech **7** address, discuss, lecture, oration **8** colloquy, converse, dialogue, diatribe, harangue, treatise **10** discussion **11** intercourse **12** conversation, dissertation, talk together **16** formal discussion

Discourse on Method
author: 13 Rene Descartes

discourteous 4 rude **5** fresh, surly **6** cheeky **7** boorish, ill-bred, uncivil, uncouth **8** impolite, impudent, insolent **9** uncourtly, ungallant **10** ill-behaved, ungracious, unladylike, unmannerly **11** ill-mannered, impertinent **13** disrespectful, ungentlemanly

discourtesy 8 rudeness **9** impudence, insolence **10** incivility **11** boorishness **12** impoliteness

discover 3 see **4** find, spot **5** dig up **6** detect, locate, notice **7** discern, find

out, learn of, realize, root out, uncover, unearth **8** come upon, perceive **9** ascertain, determine, ferret out, light upon, recognize **10** chance upon **11** gain sight of, stumble upon **12** bring to light

discredit 4 deny, slur **5** abuse, smear, sully, taint **6** debase, defame, demean, reject, smirch, vilify **7** degrade, dispute, tarnish, vitiate **8** disallow, disgrace, dishonor, disprove, question **9** challenge, disparage, undermine **10** prove false, stigmatize **16** shake one's faith in **17** drag through the mud

discreditable 8 shameful, shocking **9** appalling **10** outrageous, scandalous **11** disgraceful, ignominious **12** dishonorable, disreputable

discreet 6 polite **7** careful, politic, prudent, tactful **8** cautious **9** judicious, sensitive **10** diplomatic, thoughtful **11** circumspect

Discreet Charm of the Bourgeoisie, The
director: 10 Luis Bunuel
cast: 11 Fernando Rey **14** Delphine Seyrig, Stephane Audran
Oscar for: 11 foreign film

discrepancy 3 gap **8** variance **9** disparity **10** difference, divergence **11** discordance, incongruity **12** disagreement **13** dissimilarity, inconsistency

discrepant 6 at odds **8** contrary, opposing **9** disparate **10** at variance, discordant, dissimilar, refutatory **11** conflicting, contrasting, disagreeing **12** antithetical, inconsistent **13** contradictory **14** countervailing, irreconcilable

discrete 7 several, various **8** detached, distinct, separate **9** different **10** unattached **11** disjunctive, independent **12** disconnected, unassociated **13** discontinuous

discretion 4 tact **6** acumen, option **8** judgment, prudence, sagacity, volition **9** good sense **10** preference **11** discernment, inclination **12** good judgment, predilection **13** judiciousness, sound judgment **14** discrimination **15** power of choosing **16** individual choice

discretionary 8 optional **9** voluntary **10** nonbinding **11** nonrequired, unnecessary **12** nonrequisite, unimperative **13** nonobligatory

discriminate 7 disdain **8** separate **11** distinguish **12** disfranchise **13** differentiate

discriminating 5 acute **6** astute, biased, shrewd **7** bigoted, refined **9** judicious, sensitive **10** cultivated, discerning, fastidious **11** intelligent, prejudicial **13** perspicacious **15** differentiating

discrimination 4 bias **5** taste **6** acumen **7** bigotry **8** inequity, judgment, keenness, sagacity **9** prejudice **10** as-

tuteness, discretion, favoritism, refinement, shrewdness **11** discernment, distinction **12** perspicacity **21** differential treatment

discursive 7 diffuse **8** rambling **9** wandering **10** circuitous, digressive, longwinded, meandering, roundabout

discursiveness 8 rambling **10** digression, meandering **14** circumlocution

discuss 6 debate, parley, review **7** dissect, examine, speak of **8** consider, talk over **9** talk about **13** converse about, exchange views **14** discourse about

discussion 3 rap **4** talk **6** debate, parley, powwow, review **7** inquiry **8** analysis, argument, colloquy, dialogue, scrutiny **9** discourse **10** hashing-out **11** disputation **12** deliberation **13** consideration, investigation

disdain 4 snub **5** abhor, scorn, spurn **6** deride, detest, loathe **7** despise, dislike **8** contempt, distaste **9** frown upon **10** abhorrence, brush aside, disrespect **11** intolerance **12** icy aloofness, look down upon **14** deem unbecoming, discountenance

disdained 7 derided, scorned, spurned **8** abhorred, despised **10** deprecated, disparaged **14** held in contempt

disdainful 4 cold **5** aloof **7** haughty, high-hat **8** derisive, scornful, superior **11** overbearing, patronizing **12** contemptuous, supercilious **13** condescending

disease 6 malady **7** ailment, illness **8** sickness **9** ill health, infirmity **10** affliction **15** morbid condition **16** physical disorder

disembark 4 land **7** deplane, detrain, pile out **10** leave a ship **11** get off a ship

disenchant 6 put off **7** turn off **8** alienate, disabuse, turn away **9** undeceive **11** disenthrall, disillusion **12** open one's eyes **13** break the spell **15** burst one's bubble **16** bring down to earth

disencumber 3 rid **8** unburden **9** disburden, extricate **11** disentangle

disengage 4 sever **6** detach **7** disjoin **8** separate **9** extricate **10** disconnect

disengaged 7 unmoved **8** detached **9** apathetic, disjoined, separated **11** indifferent, uncommitted, unconcerned **12** disconnected, unresponsive
French: 6 degage

disengagement 6 apathy **8** severing **9** severance, unconcern **10** detachment, separation **12** indifference **13** disconnection **16** unresponsiveness

disentangle 4 free **6** detach, loosen, remove **7** unravel **9** extricate

disenthrall 9 undeceive **10** disenchant **11** disillusion **12** open one's eyes

13 break the spell **15** burst one's bubble **16** bring down to earth

disesteem 7 dislike **8** disfavor **9** disrepute **11** disapproval, displeasure **14** disapprobation

disfavor 5 odium **7** dislike, ill turn **8** disgrace, ignominy **9** disesteem, disregard **10** disrespect, disservice, harmful act **11** disapproval, discourtesy, displeasure **14** disapprobation **15** dissatisfaction **16** unacceptableness

disfigure 3 mar **4** maim, scar **5** cut up **6** damage, deface, deform, impair **7** blemish, scarify **8** make ugly, mutilate

disfigurement 4 blot, flaw, mark, scar, spot **6** blotch, defect **7** blemish **12** imperfection

disfranchise, disenfranchise 15 deprive of a right **19** discriminate against

disgorge 4 spew **5** eject, expel, spout, vomit **6** cast up, spew up **7** cough up, throw up **8** dislodge **9** discharge **10** vomit forth **11** regurgitate

disgrace 4 blot **5** abase, shame, stain, taint **6** debase, smirch **7** blemish, degrade, eyesore, scandal, tarnish **8** contempt, derogate, disfavor, dishonor, ill favor, reproach **9** discredit, disparage, disrepute, embarrass, humiliate **13** embarrassment, in the doghouse **14** bring shame upon

disgraceful 3 low **4** base, mean, vile **6** odious **8** infamous, shameful, shocking, unseemly, unworthy **9** appalling, degrading, obnoxious **10** despicable, detestable, inglorious, outrageous, scandalous, unbecoming **11** ignominious, opprobrious **12** dishonorable, disreputable **13** discreditable, reprehensible

disgruntled 5 sulky, testy, vexed **6** grumpy, shirty, sullen **7** grouchy, peevish **8** petulant **9** irritated **10** displeased, malcontent **12** discontented, dissatisfied

disguise 4 garb, hide, mask, pose, sham, veil **5** blind, cloak, cover, feign, getup, guise **6** facade, muffle, screen, shroud, veneer **7** conceal, cover-up, dress up, falsify **8** pretense, simulate **9** costuming, dissemble, gloss over **10** camouflage, false front, masquerade **11** concealment, counterfeit **12** misrepresent **13** false identity **15** false appearance

disguised 6 masked, veiled **7** cloaked **9** dressed up, incognito **10** undercover **11** camouflaged **14** unrecognizable

disgust 5 repel **6** appall, hatred, offend, put off, revolt, sicken **7** dislike **8** aversion, contempt, distaste, loathing, nauseate **9** antipathy, disrelish, repulsion, revulsion **10** abhorrence, repugnance **11** detestation, displeasure **12** disaffection **13** be repulsive to, cause aversion **15** turn one's stomach

disgusting 4 vile **5** hasty **6** horrid, odious **7** hateful **9** abhorrent, appalling, loathsome, offensive, repellent, repugnant, repulsive, revolting, sickening **10** abominable, despicable, nauseating **13** reprehensible

dish 4 dole, fare, food **5** ladle, place, plate, scoop, serve, spoon **6** recipe, saucer, vessel **7** bowlful, dishful, edibles, helping, platter, portion, serving **8** dispense, plateful, transfer, victuals **10** comestible **11** shallow bowl

dishabille 7 undress **8** bathrobe, disarray, disorder, informal, negligee **9** housecoat

disharmonious 7 chaotic **8** clashing, confused **9** dissonant, illogical **10** discordant, incoherent **11** conflicting, contentious **12** incompatible **13** heterogeneous

disharmony 5 chaos **6** strife **7** discord **8** clashing, conflict, disarray, disunity, division, friction **9** cacophony, confusion, disaccord, harshness **10** contention, dissension, dissonance **11** discordance **12** disagreement, grating noise **15** disorganization, incompatibility

dishearten 4 dash, faze **5** abash, crush, daunt **6** deject, dismay, sadden **7** depress **8** dispirit **10** discourage

disheartened 3 low **6** dismal **8** dejected, desolate, downcast **9** depressed **10** despondent, dispirited **11** discouraged **12** disconsolate

disheartening 4 dark **7** adverse **8** hopeless **11** dispiriting **12** discouraging, inauspicious

disheveled 5 messy **6** blowsy, frowzy, mussed, sloppy, untidy **7** ruffled, rumpled, tousled, unkempt **8** uncombed **10** bedraggled, disarrayed, disorderly, in disorder **11** disarranged

dishevelment 5 chaos, mix-up, upset **6** jumble **7** clutter **8** disarray, disorder, scramble, shambles **9** messiness **10** sloppiness, untidiness **14** disarrangement **15** disorganization

dishonest 5 false **7** corrupt, crooked **8** cheating, specious, spurious, two-faced **9** deceitful, deceptive, faithless, insincere, not honest **10** fraudulent, mendacious, misleading, perfidious, untruthful **11** underhanded **12** disingenuous, false-hearted, unprincipled, unscrupulous **13** untrustworthy

dishonesty 8 cheating **9** duplicity, falseness, mendacity **10** corruption **11** crookedness **12** speciousness **14** untruthfulness

dishonor 4 blot **5** abase, odium, shame, stain, sully **6** debase, defame, infamy, insult, slight, stigma **7** affront, blacken, blemish, degrade, offense, scandal, tarnish **8** disfavor, disgrace, ignominy **9** discredit, disparage, disre-

pute, humiliate, ill repute **10** derogation, stigmatize **11** discourtesy, humiliation **12** bring shame on **14** public disgrace

dishonorable 4 base **7** debased, ignoble **8** shameful **10** despicable **12** contemptible, disreputable **13** reprehensible

dishonorableness 4 blot **5** odium, shame, stain **6** stigma **7** blemish **8** disfavor, disgrace, ignominy **9** discredit, disrepute, ill repute **10** derogation **11** humiliation

dishonoring 8 disgrace **10** debasement **11** degradation, humiliation

dish up 3 dip **5** ladle, serve, spoon **7** dish out, serve up

disillusion 6 clue in **8** disabuse **9** undeceive **10** disenchant **11** disenthrall **13** break the spell, open the eyes of **14** burst the bubble **16** bring down to earth

disinclination 8 aversion **9** hesitancy **10** reluctance **13** indisposition, unwillingness

disincline 5 deter **8** dissuade, keep back, restrain **10** discourage, divert from **13** advise against **16** attempt to prevent

disinclined 5 loath **6** averse **8** hesitant **9** reluctant, unwilling **10** indisposed

disinfect 6 purify **7** cleanse **8** sanitize **9** kill germs, sterilize **13** decontaminate **15** destroy bacteria

disinfectant 9 germicide **10** antiseptic, germ killer **11** bactericide

disinherit 6 cut off, disown **15** deprive of rights

disintegrate 7 break up, crumble, shatter **8** splinter **9** fall apart **10** break apart, go to pieces

disintegration 4 ruin **5** decay **7** breakup, erosion **8** biolysis **9** crumbling **10** dispersion, dissolving, separation **11** decomposing **12** falling apart **13** decomposition, deterioration, pulverization

disinter 5 dig up **6** exhume **7** unearth

disinterest 6 apathy **9** disregard, unconcern **12** indifference

disinterested 7 neutral, outside **8** unbiased **9** impartial **10** impersonal, uninvolved **12** free from bias, unprejudiced **13** dispassionate

disinterment 9 digging up **10** exhumation, unearthing

disjecta membra 15 disjointed parts **16** scattered members

disjoin 4 part, undo **5** break, sever **6** detach, divide **8** disunite, separate **9** disengage

disjoint 6 detach **7** unhinge **8** disunite, separate **9** dislocate **10** disconnect **13** disarticulate

disjointed 5 apart, split **7** chaotic, divided, jumbled, mixed-up, tangled

8 confused, detached, rambling **9** illogical, spasmodic **10** incoherent, irrational, unattached **11** unconnected **12** disconnected, disorganized **13** discontinuous, disharmonious, helter-skelter, heterogeneous **14** disarticulated

disjointedness 8 rambling **11** indirection **14** discursiveness **16** disconnectedness

disjointed parts
Latin: **14** disjecta membra

disk, disc 3 cam **4** aten, coin, dial, face, plow, puck **5** plate, wafer, wheel **6** harrow, record, sequin **7** discuss **8** diskette **9** cultivate, videodisc **11** discotheque
type: **4** hard **5** fixed **6** floppy **8** magnetic **10** Winchester

dislike 4 hate **5** abhor, scorn **6** animus, detest, enmity, hatred, loathe, malice, rancor **7** despise, disdain, disgust, not like **8** aversion, distaste, loathing, object to **9** abominate, animosity, antipathy, hostility, repulsion, revulsion **10** abhorrence, antagonism, repugnance **11** abomination, detestation **12** disaffection

disliked 5 hated **7** loathed, unloved **8** abhorred, despised, detested **10** abominated

dislike intensely 4 hate **5** abhor **6** detest, loathe **7** despise **9** abominate **10** recoil from

dislocate 6 uproot **7** unhinge **8** disjoint, disunite, separate **9** disengage **10** disconnect **13** disarticulate, put out of joint

dislodge 4 oust **5** eject, expel **6** dig out, dispel, remove, uproot **7** disturb **8** displace, force out **9** extricate **11** disentangle

disloyal 6 untrue **8** recreant **9** faithless, seditious, undutiful **10** inconstant, perfidious, subversive, traitorous, unfaithful **11** treacherous, treasonable **12** dishonorable

disloyalty 7 falsity, perfidy, treason **8** apostasy, betrayal, sedition **9** falseness, rebellion, recreancy, treachery **10** infidelity, subversion **11** inconstancy **12** insurrection **13** breach of trust, deceitfulness, double-dealing, faithlessness **14** lack of fidelity, perfidiousness, unfaithfulness **15** betrayal of trust, breaking of faith **18** subversive activity

dismal 3 sad **4** drab, grim, poor **5** awful, bleak **6** dreary, gloomy, morbid, rueful, somber, woeful **7** abysmal, doleful, forlorn, joyless, unhappy, very bad, visaged **8** dejected, desolate, dolorous, downcast, dreadful, hopeless, horrible, mournful, terrible **9** cheerless, depressed, long-faced, sorrowful, woebegone **10** abominable, despondent, in the dumps, lugubrious, melancholy **11** pessimistic **12** discon-

solate, disheartened, heavy-hearted **13** unmentionable **14** down-in-the-mouth

dismantle 5 strip **6** denude, divest **9** take apart

dismay 3 cow **5** abash, alarm, daunt, dread, panic, scare **6** appall, fright, horror, put off, terror **7** anxiety, concern, horrify, unnerve **8** affright, distress, frighten **10** disappoint, discourage, dishearten, intimidate **11** disillusion, trepidation **12** apprehension, exasperation, intimidation, perturbation **13** consternation **14** disappointment, discouragement **15** disillusionment

dismayed 7 abashed, daunted **8** appalled **10** confounded, nonplussed **12** disconcerted

dismember 4 limb **6** hack up **8** disjoint **16** tear limb from limb

dismiss 3 can **4** fire, free, oust, sack **5** let go **6** bounce, excuse, reject **7** adjourn, cashier, disband, discard, release **8** disclaim, disperse, dissolve, lay aside, liberate, pink-slip, set aside **9** disregard, eliminate, repudiate, send forth, terminate **10** permit to go **11** send packing **12** allow to leave, put out of a job, put out of mind **14** give the heave-ho **17** remove from service, give walking papers **19** discharge from office

dismissal 6 firing **7** release **9** discharge, dispersal, disregard **10** disclaimer **11** adjournment, repudiation

Disney
theme parks **10** Disneyland, EuroDisney **15** Disneyland Paris, Tokyo Disneyland, Walt Disney World

Disney, Walt
creator/artist of: **5** Goofy, Pluto **10** Donald Duck **11** Mickey Mouse, Minnie Mouse

disobedience 8 defiance **9** rebellion **10** resistance **13** noncompliance, nonconformity **14** rebelliousness

disobedient 6 unruly **7** defiant, forward, haughty, wayward **8** contrary, mutinous, perverse, stubborn **9** fractious, insurgent, obstinate, seditious, undutiful **10** disorderly, rebellious, refractory, unyielding **11** intractable **12** noncompliant, recalcitrant, ungovernable, unmanageable, unsubmissive **13** insubordinate

disobey 4 defy **5** break **6** ignore, resist **7** violate **8** overstep **9** disregard **10** infringe on, transgress **11** go counter to **12** rebel against

disoblige 5 annoy **6** bother **7** trouble **13** inconvenience

disobliging 4 rude **8** churlish **9** unhelpful **13** inconsiderate

disorder 4 mess, riot **5** chaos **6** fracas, jumble, malady, muddle, ruckus, uproar **7** ailment, clutter, disease, illness, turmoil **8** disarray, sickness **9**

commotion, complaint, confusion **10** affliction, disruption, dissension **11** disturbance **13** indisposition, minor uprising **14** disarrangement **15** disorganization

disordered 7 jumbled **8** confused, messed up **9** haphazard **11** disarranged **12** disorganized

disorderliness 4 mess **5** chaos **6** muddle **8** disarray **9** confusion **10** disruption **14** disarrangement **15** disorganization

disorderly 3 bad **4** awry, wild **5** amiss, messy, noisy, rowdy **6** sloppy, unruly, untidy **7** chaotic, jumbled, lawless, riotous, unkempt, wayward **8** careless, confused, improper, pell-mell, rowdyish, slipshod, slovenly, unlawful, unsorted **10** boisterous, disheveled, disordered, disruptive, rebellious, straggling, topsy-turvy **11** disarranged **12** disorganized, disreputable, obstreperous, unrestrained, unsystematic **13** helter-skelter, undisciplined **14** rough-and-tumble, unsystematized

disorganization 4 mess **5** chaos, upset **6** jumble, muddle **7** clutter **8** disarray, disorder, shambles **9** confusion, messiness **10** disharmony, disruption, sloppiness, untidiness **12** dishevelment **14** disarrangement, disorderliness

disorganize 5 mix up, upset **6** jumble, mess up, muddle **7** confuse, scatter **8** disarray, disorder, put askew, scramble **10** disarrange **13** put out of order **14** turn topsy-turvy

disorganized 5 messy, upset **7** chaotic, jumbled, mixed-up, muddled **8** confused, rambling **9** haphazard, illogical **10** disordered, disorderly, incoherent, in disarray, irrational **12** unsystematic **16** at sixes and sevens

disoriented 7 mixed-up **8** confused, unstable **10** distracted, out of joint, out of touch **11** not adjusted

disown 4 deny **6** reject **7** cast off, disavow, forsake **8** denounce, disclaim, renounce **9** repudiate **10** disinherit **17** refuse to recognize **19** refuse to acknowledge

disparage 4 mock **6** demean, slight **7** put down, run down **8** belittle, derogate, ridicule **9** denigrate, discredit, underrate **10** depreciate, undervalue **11** detract from

disparagement 5 abuse, libel **7** slander **8** ridicule **9** criticism **10** belittling, defamation, derogation, detraction **11** denigration, putting down **12** vilification **17** defamatory remarks

disparaging 5 snide **10** belittling, derogatory **11** unfavorable **15** uncomplimentary

disparate 6 at odds, unlike **9** different **10** at variance, discordant, discrepant, dissimilar **11** contrasting

disparity 3 gap 8 contrast, imparity, variance 10 difference, divergence, inequality, unlikeness 11 discrepancy, incongruity 12 disagreement, dissemblance 13 contradiction, disproportion, dissimilarity, dissimilitude, inconsistency

dispassion 6 apathy 8 coolness 10 detachment 12 indifference

dispassionate 4 calm, cool, fair 6 serene 7 neutral, unmoved 8 composed, detached, unbiased 9 collected, impartial, unexcited, unruffled 10 impersonal, uninvolved 11 levelheaded, undisturbed, unemotional 12 unprejudiced 13 disinterested, imperturbable

dispatch 4 item, kill, post, slay 5 flash, haste, piece, speed, story 6 finish, letter, murder, report, settle, wind up 7 bump off, execute, forward, message, missive, send off 8 alacrity, bulletin, carry out, celerity, complete, conclude, expedite, massacre, rapidity 9 finish off, quickness, slaughter, swiftness 10 communique, expedition, promptness, put an end to, put to death 11 assassinate, news account 12 send on the way 14 execute quickly, summarily shoot, swift execution 15 make short work of, transmit rapidly 16 carry out speedily, dispose of rapidly 18 telegraphic message 21 official communication

Dia Pater see **Dia**

dispel 4 rout 5 allay, expel, repel 6 banish, remove 7 diffuse, dismiss, resolve, scatter 8 drive off 9 dissipate, drive away, eliminate 10 put an end to 11 disseminate 13 make disappear

dispensable 8 nonvital 9 accessory, extrinsic, secondary 10 disposable, expendable, extraneous 11 superfluous, unessential, unimportant, unnecessary 12 nonessential

dispensation 6 decree 8 approval, bestowal, division 9 allotment, diffusion, exemption, meting out 10 allocation, conferment, credential, dealing out, dispensing, permission, reparation 11 consignment, designation 12 apportioning, distribution, remuneration 13 authorization, dissemination

dispense 6 confer 7 dole out, mete out 8 allocate 9 apportion 10 administer, distribute

dispense with 4 drop, dump, junk, shed 5 scrap 6 shelve 7 abandon, discard 9 dispose of

dispensing 9 bestowing, doling out, meting out 10 allocating, conferring 12 distributing

dispersal 7 breakup, parting 9 dismissal 10 breaking up, scattering 12 distributing, distribution

disperse 4 rout 6 dispel 7 diffuse, disband, scatter, send off 8 drive off 9

dissipate 10 distribute 11 disseminate 13 send scurrying 16 spread throughout

dispersed 7 diffuse 9 scattered, spread out 10 dissipated 11 distributed 14 extended widely, unconcentrated

dispersion 9 dispersal 10 disbanding, scattering 11 dissipation 12 distribution

dispirit 5 cloud 6 darken, deject, sadden 7 depress 10 demoralize, dishearten

dispirited 3 sad 4 blue, down, glum 5 moody 6 morose 7 forlorn, unhappy 8 dejected, downcast, listless 9 cheerless, depressed 10 melancholy 11 crestfallen, demoralized, discouraged, downhearted, pessimistic 12 disconsolate, disheartened 14 down in the dumps, down in the mouth, unenthusiastic

dispiriting 4 cold, dark 6 chilly, dismal, gloomy 9 dampening 10 depressing 12 discouraging 13 disheartening

displace 4 bump, move, oust 5 shift 6 unseat 7 replace 8 crowd out, dislodge, force out, supplant 9 dislocate, supersede

displaced person 2 DP 5 exile 6 emigre 7 refugee 8 expellee 10 expatriate

display 4 show 6 reveal 7 exhibit 8 manifest 10 exhibition 11 demonstrate, make visible 12 presentation 13 bring into view, demonstration, manifestation 15 put in plain sight

display case 7 cabinet, vitrine 8 showcase

displease 3 irk 5 annoy, pique 6 offend 7 disturb, incense, provoke 8 irritate

displeasing 8 annoying 9 loathsome, offensive, repellent, repugnant 10 irritating 11 distasteful, distressing 12 disagreeable

displeasure 5 wrath 7 dislike 8 vexation 9 annoyance 10 irritation 11 disapproval, indignation 15 dissatisfaction

disport 3 act 4 play, romp 5 amuse, caper, sport 6 divert, frolic, gambol 7 display, pastime 9 amusement, entertain 10 recreation 13 entertainment

disposal 5 array, order, power 7 command, control, dumping, junking, pattern, ridding 8 grouping, riddance 9 authority, clearance, direction, placement 10 discarding, government, management, regulation, settlement 11 arrangement, destruction, disposition, supervision 12 distribution, organization, throwing away 13 authorization, configuration, juxtaposition 14 administration

dispose 4 rank 5 array, order, place 7 arrange, deal out, incline 8 classify,

get rid of, motivate, organize 9 be willing 10 distribute

dispose of 4 dump 5 scrap 6 unload 7 discard 8 get rid of, throw out 9 cast aside, throw away

disposition 6 nature, spirit 7 control 8 bestowal, grouping, tendency 9 placement 11 arrangement, inclination, temperament 12 distribution, organization 14 predisposition 15 final settlement

dispossess 4 oust 5 evict, expel 8 take away, take back 9 deprive of

disproportionate 7 unequal 9 disparate 10 dissimilar, unbalanced

disprove 6 refute 9 discredit 10 controvert

disputable 7 dubious 8 doubtful 9 debatable, uncertain 12 questionable 14 controvertible

disputant 5 rival 7 opposer 8 opponent 9 adversary 10 antagonist, competitor, contestant

disputation 6 debate, review 8 argument, dialogue 10 discussion

dispute 4 feud 5 argue, clash, doubt 6 debate, impugn 7 quarrel, wrangle 8 argument, question, squabble 9 bickering, challenge 10 contradict 11 altercation, controversy 12 disagreement

disputed 6 argued 8 wrangled 9 debatable, in dispute, quarreled 10 in question, unverified 12 questionable 13 controversial 15 unsubstantiated

disqualification 5 minus 8 handicap 10 disability 11 shortcoming 13 ineligibility

disqualify 7 disable 9 make unfit 17 declare ineligible, deny participation

disquiet, disquietude 3 awe 6 unease 7 anxiety 8 distress 9 agitation 10 uneasiness 11 fretfulness, trepidation 12 apprehension, discomposure, perturbation 13 consternation

disquieted 6 uneasy 7 anxious, worried 9 concerned 10 distressed 12 apprehensive

disquieting 6 vexing 8 annoying 9 troubling, upsetting 10 bothersome, disturbing, irritating, perturbing, unsettling 11 distressing 13 disconcerting

disquisition 8 tractate, treatise 9 discourse, monograph 12 dissertation

disregard 6 ignore 8 overlook 11 pay no heed to 13 lack of respect 14 take no notice of 15 lack of attention 16 willful oversight

disregardful 8 careless, heedless 9 unmindful 11 insensitive, thoughtless 13 inconsiderate

disreputable 5 shady 8 infamous, shameful, shocking 9 notorious 10 scandalous 11 disgraceful 12 dishonorable, unprincipled **14** not respectable, of bad character

disrespect 6 insult **8** contempt, dishonor, rudeness **9** disregard **11** discourtesy, irreverence **12** impoliteness

disrespectful 4 rude **8** impolite **11** impertinent **12** contemptuous, discourteous

disrobe 5 strip **7** undress **16** divest of clothing

disrupt 5 upset **9** interrupt **13** interfere with **17** throw into disorder

disruption 5 upset **8** disorder **9** confusion **11** disturbance **12** interference, interruption **14** disarrangement **15** disorganization

dissatisfaction 4 veto **7** protest **9** rejection **10** discontent **11** disapproval, displeasure, unhappiness

dissatisfied 7 unhappy **10** displeased **12** discontented

dissect 5 study **7** analyze, lay open **8** cut apart, separate **9** anatomize, break down

dissemble 4 hide, mask **5** feign **7** conceal **8** disguise **10** camouflage **11** dissimulate

disseminate 6 spread **7** diffuse, scatter **8** disperse **9** broadcast, circulate

dissemination 9 diffusion, dispersal, spreading **10** scattering **12** broadcasting, distribution

dissension 7 discord, dispute **8** conflict, disunity, division **9** rebellion **10** contention, disharmony, quarreling **11** discordance **12** disagreement **14** rebelliousness

dissent 6 object, oppose **7** discord, protest **8** disagree **10** difference, dissension, opposition **12** disagreement **14** withhold assent **16** withhold approval

dissenter 5 rebel **9** dissident, protester **13** nonconformist

dissenting 9 differing, dissident **11** disagreeing

dissertation 6 memoir, thesis **8** tractate, treatise **9** discourse, monograph **12** disquisition

disservice 4 harm, hurt **5** wrong **6** injury **7** bad turn **9** injustice

dissever 3 saw **4** hack, rend **5** carve, sever, slash, slice, split **6** cleave, divide **8** disunite, separate

dissident 5 rebel **8** agitator, opposing **9** differing, dissenter **10** dissenting **11** disagreeing

dissimilar 6 unlike **8** distinct **9** different, disparate

dissimilarity 8 contrast, variance **9** disparity **10** difference, dissonance, divergence, inequality, unlikeness **11** discrepancy **12** disagreement **13** inconsistency **17** lack of resemblance

dissimilitude 8 variance **9** disparity

10 difference, unlikeness **11** incongruity **12** disagreement **17** lack of resemblance

dissimulate 4 hide, mask **7** conceal **8** disguise **9** dissemble **10** camouflage

dissipate 5 waste **6** dispel **7** carouse, deplete, scatter **8** disperse, misspend, squander **11** fritter away, overindulge **13** be intemperate **14** spend foolishly

dissipated 6 wasted **8** misspent **9** abandoned, debauched, dispelled, dispersed, dissolute, scattered **10** squandered **11** intemperate **12** disreputable **13** frittered away

dissipater 5 waste **7** wastrel **8** prodigal **10** profligate, squanderer **11** spendthrift

dissipation 6 excess **7** wasting **9** dispersal **10** debauchery, dispelling, scattering **11** dissolution, loose living **12** immoderation, intemperance **14** disintegration, frittering away, self-indulgence

dissociate 8 separate **10** disconnect **12** break off with

dissociation 7 breakup **10** separation

dissolute 5 loose **7** corrupt, immoral **9** abandoned, debauched **10** dissipated **12** unrestrained

dissolution 9 annulment **10** separation **11** termination **14** disintegration

dissolve 3 end, run **4** fade, melt, thaw, void **5** annul, sever **6** finish, render, soften, vanish **7** break up, disband, liquefy, thaw out **8** abrogate, conclude, evanesce **9** disappear, dissipate, terminate **10** deliquesce **12** disintegrate **13** dematerialize

dissonance 5 clash **7** discord **9** cacophony, harshness **10** difference, disharmony **11** discordance **12** disagreement **13** dissimilarity

dissonant 5 harsh **7** grating, hostile, jarring, raucous, warring **8** clashing, jangling **10** discordant, discrepant **11** cacophonous, disagreeing, incongruent, incongruous, unmelodious **12** incompatible, inconsistent, inharmonious **13** contradictory **14** irreconcilable

dissuade 9 urge not to **10** discourage **13** advise against, persuade not to

distance 3 gap **4** span **7** reserve, stretch **8** coldness, coolness, interval **9** aloofness, formality, restraint, stiffness **11** reservation **16** intervening space

distant 3 far **4** cold, cool **5** aloof **6** far-off, remote **7** faraway **8** detached, reserved **10** far-removed, restrained, unfriendly **11** standoffish **17** not closely related

Distant Mirror, A
author: **15** Barbara W Tuchman

distaste 7 disgust, dislike **8** aversion **9** antipathy **10** repugnance **11** displeasure

distasteful 9 loathsome, repugnant **10** disgusting, unpleasant **11** displeasing **12** disagreeable

distastefulness 13 offensiveness **14** unpleasantness **16** disagreeableness

distasteful work 8 drudgery **11** menial labor

distend 5 bloat, bulge, swell **6** billow, expand **7** inflate, puff out **8** swell out

distended 4 full, taut **5** puffy, tumid **7** blown up, bloated, dilated, swelled, swollen **8** enlarged, expanded, extended, inflated, patulant **9** edematous, stretched

distill 7 draw out, extract **8** condense, vaporize **9** draw forth, evaporate

distillate 7 essence, extract **11** concentrate **13** concentration

distilled 9 condensed, extracted, vaporized **10** evaporated

distinct 5 clear, lucid, plain **7** diverse, supreme **8** clear-cut, definite, explicit, separate **9** different **10** dissimilar, individual **11** unmitigated, well-defined **12** not identical, unmistakable **13** extraordinary **14** unquestionable

distinction 6 renown **8** contrast, eminence **9** greatness **10** difference, excellence, importance, notability, prominence, separation **11** discernment, preeminence, superiority **12** differential **14** discrimination **15** differentiation

distinctive 6 unique **7** special **8** atypical, original, singular, uncommon **9** different **10** individual **13** extraordinary **14** characteristic

distinctiveness 7 clarity **9** character **10** definition, uniqueness **11** personality **13** individuality

distingue 13 distinguished

distinguish 6 decide, define **7** discern **8** set apart **9** single out **10** make famous **12** characterize, discriminate **13** differentiate, make prominent, make well known **14** make celebrated **15** make distinctive, note differences

distinguished 5 grand, great **6** famous, superb **7** elegant, eminent, notable, refined **8** renowned, splendid **9** acclaimed, dignified, distingue, prominent **10** celebrated **11** illustrious, magnificent
French: **9** distingue

distort 6 deform **7** contort **8** misshape **9** disfigure **11** misconstrue **12** misrepresent **15** twist out of shape, twist the meaning

distorted 4 awry **5** askew **6** belied, loaded, warped **7** altered, colored, crooked, twisted **8** cockeyed, deformed, wrenched **9** contorted, falsified, grotesque, irregular, misshapen, misstated, perverted **13** unsymmetrical **14** misrepresented **15** misproportioned

217 divine

distortion 7 skewing 8 twisting 10 aberration, caricature 11 crookedness, deformation 12 malformation 17 misrepresentation

distract 5 amuse, craze, worry 6 divert, madden 7 agitate, confuse, disturb, perplex, torment, trouble 8 bewilder, disorder 9 entertain

distracted 3 mad 4 wild 6 amused, crazed, insane, raving 7 frantic, pleased, puzzled 8 agitated, confused, deranged, diverted, frenzied, harassed, heedless, occupied 9 disturbed, stirred up 10 bewildered, distraught, irrational 11 entertained, turned aside

distraction 5 fazed, upset 6 frenzy 7 frantic, madness, pastime, rattled, ruffled 8 agitated, confused 9 amusement, diversion, unsettled 10 distraught, distressed, nonplussed, recreation 11 desperation 12 disconcerted 13 entertainment 14 mental distress

distractive 9 confusing 10 disturbing, unsettling 11 distressing, troublesome

distraught 3 mad 7 anxious, frantic 8 agitated, frenzied, seething 10 distracted, distressed 13 beside oneself

distress 4 need, pain, want 5 agony, upset 6 danger, grieve 7 anguish, disturb, torment, torture, trouble 14 acute suffering

distressed 5 upset 7 anxious, fearful, frantic, grieved, unhappy, worried 8 agitated, troubled 9 anguished, concerned, disturbed, tormented 10 distracted, distraught

distressing 5 acute 7 nagging, painful 8 grievous 9 agonizing, upsetting 10 disturbing, tormenting, unpleasant 11 displeasing, troublesome, unfortunate 13 uncomfortable

distribute 5 allot, class 6 divide, parcel 7 arrange, catalog, deliver, dole out, give out, scatter 8 classify, dispense, disperse, separate, tabulate 9 apportion, circulate, methodize, spread out 11 disseminate, systematize

distribution 7 sorting 8 division, grouping 9 allotment, spreading 10 allocation, dispersion, scattering 11 arrangement, circulation, disposition 12 organization 13 apportionment, dissemination

distribution center
French: 8 entrepot

district 4 area, ward 6 parish, region 8 precinct 12 neighborhood

distrust 5 doubt 7 suspect 8 question 9 misgiving, suspicion 11 lack of faith

distrustful 3 shy 4 wary 5 leery 7 dubious, jealous 8 cautious, doubtful, doubting 9 diffident 10 suspicious, untrusting 11 incredulous, mistrustful 12 disbelieving

disturb 5 annoy, upset, worry 6 bother 7 disrupt, perturb, trouble 8 distress, unsettle 9 dislocate, interrupt, intrude on 10 disarrange 11 disorganize

disturbance 5 upset, worry 6 bother, hubbub, ruckus, tumult, uproar 7 rioting, turmoil 8 disorder, distress, outbreak 9 annoyance 11 distraction 12 interruption, perturbation

disturbance of peace 4 riot 6 fracas, ruckus, uproar 7 turmoil 8 disorder 9 commotion 13 breach of order

disturbed 5 upset 6 uneasy 7 annoyed, anxious, nervous, rattled 8 agitated, confused, troubled 9 perturbed 10 disquieted 11 discomfited 12 disconcerted

disunion 7 divorce 8 division 9 secession 10 separation 14 disintegration

disunite 4 part 6 divide 7 divorce 8 separate 9 disengage 10 disconnect 12 disintegrate 13 disarticulate

disunited 6 parted 8 diverged, divorced, unallied 9 came apart, dispersed, separated 10 uncombined 13 disassociated

disunity 6 strife 7 discord 8 clashing, conflict, division, friction 9 wrangling 10 contention, dissension, separation 11 being at odds, discordance 12 disagreement 15 incompatibility

ditat Deus 11 God enriches
motto of: 7 Arizona

ditch 3 pit 4 junk 5 scrap 6 hollow, trench 7 abandon, discard 8 get rid of 10 excavation

dither 4 flap, fuss 5 tizzy, waver, whirl 6 bother, flurry, lather, quiver, shiver, thrill 7 fluster, tremble, twitter 8 hesitate, agitation, commotion, confusion, vacillate, vibration 10 excitement

Dithyrambus
epithet of: 8 Dionysus
means: 20 child of the double door

ditty 3 lay 4 song, tune 6 ballad 7 refrain

Dius Fidius
origin: 5 Roman
god of: 5 oaths 11 hospitality 20 international affairs
corresponds to: 6 Sancus 10 Semo Sancus

divagation 8 straying 9 wandering 10 digression, divergence

divan 4 book, hall, poem, room, salon, seat, sofa 5 couch, court 6 canape, daybed, leewan, lounge, settee 7 chamber, council, ottoman, davenport

dive 4 dash, fall, jump, leap 5 lunge 6 plunge 7 gin mill 9 honky-tonk, shabby bar 15 sleazy nightclub

Diver, Dick and Nicole
characters in: 16 Tender Is the Night
author: 10 Fitzgerald

diverge 6 differ, swerve 7 deflect,

deviate 8 be at odds, conflict, disagree, separate, split off

divergence 7 parting 8 conflict, rambling, straying, variance 9 deviation, disparity, wandering 10 difference, separation 11 discrepancy, incongruity 13 dissimilarity, inconsistency

divergent 8 separate 9 different 11 conflicting, disagreeing 12 drawing apart, splitting off

diverse 6 sundry, varied 8 eclectic, far-flung, opposite 9 different, differing, disparate 10 dissimilar 11 conflicting, of many kinds 13 contradictory

diversified 6 divers 7 various 8 manifold 9 different, unrelated 13 miscellaneous

diversify 4 vary 7 diffuse 8 divide up 9 spread out, variegate

diversion 5 hobby 7 pastime 9 amusement, avocation 10 deflection 11 distraction, drawing away 12 turning aside
French: 14 divertissement

diversity 7 variety 8 variance 10 assortment, difference 13 heterogeneity

divert 5 amuse 7 deflect 8 distract 9 entertain, sidetrack, turn aside

diverting 7 amusing 10 deflecting 11 distracting 12 entertaining, sidetracking

divertissement 9 diversion 13 entertainment

divest 3 rid 4 free 5 strip 7 deprive, disrobe, peel off, take off 8 get out of 10 dispossess 14 remove clothing

divest oneself of 6 give up 7 take off 8 get rid of, give over, hand over, put aside, strip off 9 surrender 10 relinquish

divide 4 part, sort 5 share, split 7 arrange, deal out, divvy up 8 allocate, classify, disunite, separate 9 apportion, partition 10 distribute, put in order

divide and rule
Latin: 14 divide et impera
maxim of: 11 Machiavelli

divided 5 apart, split 6 parted 8 meted out 9 disunited, separated 10 unattached 11 apportioned 12 disconnected, portioned out

divide et impera 13 divide and rule
maxim of: 11 Machiavelli

divide in two 5 halve, split 6 bisect 8 cut in two, separate 9 cut in half 10 break in two 11 split in half 18 split down the middle

dividing line 4 edge 5 brink, verge 6 border, margin 8 boundary 9 threshold

divination 5 guess 6 augury 8 prophecy 10 conjecture, foreboding, prediction, prescience 11 premonition, soothsaying 15 prognostication

divine 4 holy 5 guess 6 fathom, sacred

7 predict, surmise, suspect **8** forecast, foretell, heavenly, prophesy **9** admirable, celestial, excellent, marvelous, wonderful

divine being 3 god **5** deity **7** goddess **8** divinity **14** celestial being

Divine Comedy
author: 14 Dante Alighieri
part: 7 Inferno **8** Paradiso **10** Purgatorio
guide: 6 Virgil **8** Beatrice

diviner 4 seer **5** augur **10** soothsayer **14** prognosticator

Divine retribution
goddess of: 7 Nemesis **8** Adrastea

Divine Sarah
nickname of: 14 Sarah Bernhardt

divining rod 4 twig, wand **5** dowse **9** doodlebug

divinity 3 god **5** deity **7** goddess **8** holiness, religion, theology **9** theosophy **12** science of God **14** celestial being

division 4 part, unit, wing **5** split **6** branch **7** discord, divider, section **8** disunion, variance **9** partition **10** department, difference, divergence, separation **11** splitting up **12** disagreement

divorce 4 rift **5** split **6** breach, divide **7** rupture **8** disunite, separate **9** segregate **10** dissociate, separation

divulge 4 tell **6** impart, relate, reveal **8** disclose **9** make known **11** communicate

divulgence 7 telling **8** exposure **9** imparting **10** disclosure, giving away, laying open, revelation **13** communication **15** bringing to light **17** bring out in the open

divulge to 4 tell **6** advise, inform, notify, reveal **7** apprise **8** acquaint, disclose **9** enlighten, make aware **11** familiarize **13** spill the beans **20** let the cat out of the bag

Dix, Otto
born: 7 Germany **11** Unterhausen
artwork: 6 The War **7** The City **12** The Procuress **15** Sylvia von Harden **18** Parents of the Artist **39** Prague Street Dedicated to My Contemporaries

Dixie Dugan
creator: 8 J P McEvoy **13** John H Striebel

dizzy 5 fleet, giddy, quick, rapid, shaky, swift **6** whirly **7** confuse, reeling **8** bewilder, unsteady **9** make giddy **11** lightheaded, vertiginous **12** make unsteady

Djawa *see* **4** Java

Djebel al-Tarik *see* **9** Gibraltar

Djibouti
other name: 16 French Somaliland **39** The French Territory of the Afars and the Issas
capital/largest city: 8 Djibouti
others: 5 Obock **6** Dikhil **8** Tadjoura

9 Ali-Sabieh
monetary unit: 5 franc **7** centime
lake: 4 Abbe **5** Assal
mountain: 5 Gouda
highest point: 9 Moussa Ali
sea: 3 Red
physical feature:
gulf: 4 Aden **8** Tadjoura
strait: 11 Bab el-Mandeb
people: 4 Afar, Arab **5** Issas **6** French **8** European
language: 4 Afar **6** Arabic, French, Somali
religion: 5 Islam

do 3 act **4** fare **5** clean, cover, get on, serve, visit **6** behave, finish, look at, stop in **7** achieve, arrange, carry on, conduct, execute, fulfill, make out, perform, prepare, proceed, suffice **8** be enough, carry out, complete, conclude, organize **10** accomplish, administer, bring about, put in order **13** travel through **14** be satisfactory, comport oneself, conduct oneself

do a favor 4 help **6** assist, oblige **7** help out **11** accommodate, do a kindness

do away with 3 end **4** junk, kill, void **5** erase, quash **6** banish, cancel, cut out, give up, remove, repeal, revoke, rub out **7** abolish, blot out, nullify, rescind, weed out, wipe out **8** abrogate, stamp out, throw out **9** eliminate, eradicate, terminate **10** annihilate, put an end to **11** exterminate

Dobbin, Captain William
character in: 10 Vanity Fair
author: 9 Thackeray

Dobie Gillis, The Many Loves of
character: 11 Zelda Gilroy **13** Maynard G Krebs **14** Herbert T Gillis, Milton Armitage, Winifred (Winnie) Gillis **15** Thalia Menninger **19** Chatsworth Osborne Jr
cast: 9 Bob Denver **11** Frank Faylen, Sheila James, Tuesday Weld **12** Warren Beatty **13** Dwayne Hickman **14** Florida Friebus, Stephen Franken
Dobie imitated pose of: 7 Thinker

do business 4 deal **5** trade **10** buy and sell

docile 4 tame **7** willing **8** obedient, obliging **9** agreeable, compliant, tractable **10** manageable **11** complaisant

docility 7 pliancy **8** meekness **9** passivity **10** placidness **12** acquiescence, complaisance **13** nonresistance

dock 4 crop, join, pier, quay **5** berth, wharf **6** couple, cut off, deduct, hook up, link up **7** landing **8** cut short **10** waterfront **12** come into port **13** subject to loss **14** fasten together

dock 5 Rumux
varieties: 3 Bur **4** Sour **5** Green **6** Golden **7** Prairie, Spinach, Tanner's, Western **8** Patience **9** Purple-wen **10** Giant water

docket 4 bill, card, list **5** slate **6** agenda, lineup, roster **7** program **8** calendar, schedule **9** timetable **14** things to be done **15** order of business

doctor 2 GP, MD **3** PhD **5** alter, treat **6** change **7** dentist, falsify, surgeon **9** internist, osteopath, physician **10** podiatrist, tamper with **11** pathologist **12** gynecologist, obstetrician, pediatrician, psychiatrist, veterinarian **15** ophthalmologist **17** apply medication to **19** general practitioner, medical practitioner

Doctor Brodie's Report
author: 15 Jorge Luis Borges

Doctor Faustus
author: 10 Thomas Mann **18** Christopher Marlowe

Doctor Grimshaw's Secret
author: 18 Nathaniel Hawthorne

Doctor J
nickname of: 12 Julius Erving

Doctorow, E L
author of: 7 Ragtime **15** The Book of Daniel

Doctor's Dilemma, The
author: 17 George Bernard Shaw

Doctor Zhivago
director: 9 David Lean
author: 14 Boris Pasternak
cast: 10 Omar Sharif (Zhivago), Rod Steiger **12** Alec Guinness, Tom Courtenay **13** Julie Christie (Lara) **14** Rita Tushingham **15** Ralph Richardson **16** Geraldine Chaplin

doctrinaire 5 rigid **6** mulish **8** absolute, dogmatic, stubborn **9** arbitrary, imperious, pigheaded **10** bullheaded, inflexible, pontifical **11** dictatorial, opinionated, overbearing, stiff-necked **12** narrow-minded **13** authoritarian **14** disciplinarian

doctrinal 8 didactic, dogmatic, edifying, tutorial **11** educational, instructive **12** prescriptive

doctrine 5 dogma, tenet **6** belief, gospel **7** precept **8** teaching **9** principle **10** conviction, philosophy

document 6 back up, record, verify **7** certify, support **9** legal form **10** instrument **12** give weight to, substantiate **13** official paper

documentation 5 proof **7** support **8** evidence **12** verification **13** corroboration **14** substantiation

doddering 4 weak **6** feeble, senile **7** shaking **8** decrepit **9** tottering, trembling

dodge 4 duck, wile **5** avoid, elude, evade, hedge, trick **6** device, swerve **7** fend off **8** sidestep **9** jump aside, stratagem, turn aside **10** equivocate **11** machination

dodging 7 ducking, eluding, evading

8 shunning **12** sidestepping **13** circumventing

Dodgson, Charles Lutwidge
　real name of: **12** Lewis Carroll

Dodoma
　capital of: **8** Tanzania

Dodsworth
　director: **12** William Wyler
　author: **13** Sinclair Lewis
　character: **4** Fran **12** Arnold Israel **14** Edith Cortright, Renee de Penable **15** Samuel Dodsworth **16** Kurt von Obersdorf **17** Major Clyde Lockert
　cast: **9** Mary Astor, Paul Lukas **10** David Niven **12** Walter Huston **14** Ruth Chatterton

doer 6 dynamo **7** hustler **8** activist, go-getter **12** active person

doff 4 bare, drop, junk, shed **5** scrap, strip **6** put off, remove **7** abandon, cast off, discard, disrobe, take off, toss off, undress **8** throw off, throw out **9** eliminate, step out of **10** do away with

dog 3 cur, pup **4** heel, mutt **5** beast, puppy **6** canine **7** mongrel, villain **9** scoundrel **10** blackguard
　Alaskan: **5** husky **8** malamute, malemute
　anatomy: **3** hip, lip, pad, paw, toe **4** arch, back, hock, loin, rump, stop **5** cheek, crest, croup, flews, skull **6** carpus, dewlap, muzzle, stifle, tarsus **7** brisket, cushion, knuckle, occiput, pastern, withers **8** heelknob, shoulder **10** metacarpus, metatarsus
　Australian: **5** dingo **8** warragal
　barkless: **7** basenji
　breed:
　　herding group: **5** pulik **6** briard, collie **12** border collie **13** bearded collie **14** German shepherd **15** Belgian malinois, Belgian sheepdog, Belgian tervuren **16** Shetland sheepdog **18** Cardigan Welsh corgi, Old English sheepdog, Pembroke Welsh corgi **19** Australian cattle dog, Bouviers des Flandres
　　hound group: **6** beagle, borzoi, saluki **7** basenji, harrier, whippet **9** dachshund, greyhound **10** bloodhound, otter hound **11** Afghan hound, basset hound, Ibizan hound **12** pharaoh hound **14** Irish wolfhound **15** English foxhound **16** American foxhound **17** Norwegian elkhound, Scottish deerhound **18** Rhodesian ridgeback **20** black and tan coonhound
　　nonsporting group: **6** poodle **7** bulldog **8** chow chow, keeshond **9** dalmatian, lhasa apso **10** keeshonden, schipperke **11** Bichon frise **13** Boston terrier, French bulldog **14** Tibetan spaniel, Tibetan terrier
　　sporting group: **6** vizsla **7** pointer **8** Brittany **10** weimaraner **11** Irish setter **12** field spaniel, Gordon set-

ter **13** cocker spaniel, English setter, Sussex spaniel **14** Clumber spaniel **15** golden retriever **17** Irish water spaniel, Labrador retriever **19** flat-coated retriever **20** American water spaniel, curly-coated retriever, English cocker spaniel, Welsh springer spaniel **22** Chesapeake Bay retriever, English springer spaniel **23** German wirehaired pointer **24** German shorthaired pointer **25** wirehaired pointing griffon
　　terrier group: **10** fox terrier **11** bull terrier, Skye terrier **12** Cairn terrier, Irish terrier, Welsh terrier **13** border terrier **14** Norfolk terrier, Norwich terrier, wire fox terrier **15** Airedale terrier, Lakeland terrier, Scottish terrier, Sealyham terrier **16** Kerry blue terrier, smooth fox terrier **17** Australian terrier, Bedlington terrier, Manchester terrier **18** Jack Russell Terrier, miniature schnauzer **20** Dandie Dinmont terrier **24** soft-coated wheaten terrier, Staffordshire bull terrier, West Highland white terrier **28** American Staffordshire terrier
　　toy group: **3** pug **7** Maltese, shih tzu **8** papillon **9** chihuahua, pekingese, toy poodle **10** pomeranian **12** Japanese chin, silky terrier **13** affenpinscher **15** Brussels griffon **16** Italian greyhound, Yorkshire terrier **17** English toy spaniel, Manchester terrier, miniature pinscher **26** Cavalier King Charles Spaniel
　　working group: **5** akita, boxer **7** mastiff, samoyed **8** kuvaszok **9** great Dane, St Bernard **10** komondorok, rottweiler **11** bullmastiff **12** Newfoundland **13** great Pyrenees, Siberian husky **14** giant schnauzer **15** Alaskan malamute **16** doberman pinscher **17** standard schnauzer **18** Bernese mountain dog, Portuguese water dog

Buster Brown's: 4 Tige
Charles, Nick and Nora's: 4 Asta
Chinese: 7 shih tzu
coach: 9 dalmatian
combining form: 3 cyn **4** cani, cyno
constellation: 12 Canis Majoris
Dorothy's: 4 Toto
family: 7 Canidae
FDR's: 4 Fala **5** Falla
female: 3 dam, gip, gyp **4** slut **5** bitch, brach **7** brachet
genus: 5 Canis
group: 4 pack **5** leash **6** kennel
"His Master's Voice": 6 Nipper
Hungarian: 4 puli **6** kuvasz, vizsla
Indian: 5 dhole
Japanese: 5 akita
Little Orphan Annie's: 5 Sandy
male: 3 dog

movie/TV: 4 Asta, Lady **5** Benji, Tramp **6** Lassie **9** Old Yeller, Rin Tin Tin
mythical: 8 Cerberus
Nixon's: 8 Checkers
Punch and Judy's: 4 Toby
Russian: 6 borzoi **7** samoyed
star: 6 Sirius **8** Canicula
Thin Man movies, in: 4 Asta
Welsh: 5 corgi
wild: 5 adjag, dhole, dingo, guara, rabid **6** jackal **7** agouara **8** cimarron
young: 3 pup **5** puppy, whelp

Dogberry
　character in: **19** Much Ado About Nothing
　author: **11** Shakespeare

Dog Day Afternoon
　director: **11** Sidney Lumet
　cast: **8** Al Pacino **10** John Cazale **14** Charles Durning

dogged 8 stubborn **9** tenacious **10** determined, persistent **11** unremitting

dogie 4 calf **14** motherless calf

dogies 6 calves, cattle **16** motherless calves

dogma 5 credo, tenet **7** beliefs **8** doctrine **9** teachings **10** philosophy, principles **11** convictions

dogmatic 6 biased **8** stubborn **9** arbitrary, doctrinal, imperious, obstinate **10** prejudiced **11** dictatorial, domineering, opinionated

Dog Star
　constellation of:
　　Hunting Dogs: **13** Canes Venatici
　　Larger Dog: **10** Canis Major
　　Smaller Dog: **10** Canis Minor

dogwood 6 Cornus
　varieties: **5** Brown, Creek, False, Giant, Silky, Stiff **6** Pagoda, Poison **7** Chinese **8** American, Jamaican, Mountain, Panicled, Redosier, Siberian, Tatarian **9** Blood-twig, Flowering, Tartarian **10** Golden-twig, West Indian **11** Round-leaved **13** White Mountain

Doha, al-Dawha
　capital of: **5** Qatar

do in 4 kill **6** murder **7** destroy, exhaust, tire out

Doktor Faust
　opera by: **6** Busoni
　character: **5** Faust **14** Duchess of Parma **14** Mephistopheles

dolce
　music: **7** sweetly

dolce far niente 18 pleasing inactivity **20** it is sweet to do nothing

dolce vita 9 sweet life

Dol Common
　character in: **12** The Alchemist
　author: **6** Jonson

doldrums 5 blues, dumps, gloom **10** depression, melancholy

dole 4 deal, give **5** share **6** parcel

7 charity, handout, welfare **9** allotment **10** allocation **13** apportionment

doleful 3 sad **6** dismal, dreary, gloomy, woeful **7** joyless, unhappy **9** sorrowful

dolente
music: **9** sorrowful

dole out 4 give, mete **5** allot **6** parcel **7** portion **8** allocate, dispense **9** apportion **10** distribute

doling out 7 dealing **9** allotment, parceling **10** allocation, assignment **12** distribution **13** apportionment

doll 5 dolly, dummy, honey **6** beauty, puppet **7** darling, rag doll **8** baby doll, figurine, golliwog **9** teddy bear **10** marionette, sweetheart **11** pretty child

dollar 3 one **4** bean, bill, buck, coin, note, skin, yuan **5** money, tater, token **6** single **7** ironman, smacker **8** cartwheel, simolean

Dollar A Second
host: **9** Jan Murray

Dollar Bill
nickname of: **11** Bill Bradley

dollop 3 dab **4** blob, dash, lump **11** small amount

Doll's House, A
author: **11** Henrik Ibsen
character: **8** Krogstad **10** Nora Helmer **13** Torvald Helmer

dolly 3 toy **4** cart, doll **9** plaything **15** wheeled platform

dolor 5 grief **6** sorrow **7** anguish, sadness

dolorous 3 sad **6** rueful, woeful **7** doleful, tearful, unhappy **8** dejected, downcast, grievous, mournful, pathetic, pitiable, wretched **9** anguished, cheerless, harrowing, miserable, sorrowful, woebegone **10** calamitous, despondent, lamentable, melancholy **11** distressing **12** disconsolate, heavyhearted **13** grief-stricken

Dolphin
constellation of: **9** Delphinus

Dolphin, The
author: **12** Robert Lowell

dolt 4 clod, fool, jerk **5** idiot, moron **6** nitwit **7** half-wit, jackass **8** bonehead, imbecile, numskull **9** blockhead

doltish 4 dumb, slow **5** thick **6** simple, stupid **7** asinine, foolish, idiotic, moronic, witless **8** ignorant, retarded **9** brainless, imbecilic **10** half-witted, slow-witted **12** dunderheaded, muddleheaded, simple-minded **13** rattlebrained **14** featherbrained

domain 4 area, fief, land **5** field **6** empire, estate, region, sphere **7** kingdom **8** dominion, property, province **9** bailiwick, territory

Dombey and Son
author: **14** Charles Dickens
character: **4** Paul **5** Toots **6** Carker, Cuttle **8** Florence, Mr Dombey **9** Dr

Blimber, Walter Gay **11** Joe Bagstock, Susan Nipper **12** Cousin Feenix, Edith Granger, Solomon Gills

dome
Italian: **5** duomo

Domenichino
real name: **16** Domenico Zampieri
born: **5** Italy **7** Bologna
artwork: **11** Hunt of Diana **16** Monsignor Agucchi **18** The Four Evangelists, The Life of St Cecilia **23** Last Communion of St Jerome **30** Landscape with Tobias and the Angel

domestic 4 cook, maid, tame **6** au pair, butler, native **7** endemic, servant **8** homemade, houseboy **9** attendant, home-grown **10** indigenous, not foreign **11** housebroken, native-grown, not imported **12** domesticated, hearthloving **13** household help

domesticated 4 tame **11** housebroken

domicile 4 home **5** house **8** dwelling **9** residence **14** legal residence

dominance 4 edge **8** hegemony **9** advantage, authority, upper hand **10** precedence **11** preeminence, superiority

dominant 5 chief, major **6** ruling **8** superior **9** principal **10** commanding **11** controlling, outstanding **13** authoritative, most important, most prominent

dominate 4 rule **5** dwarf **6** direct, govern **7** command, control **8** domineer **9** tower over **11** preside over

dominating 6 lordly, ruling **7** topmost **8** dominant **9** directing, governing, principal, prominent **10** commanding **11** controlling, domineering, outstanding **12** advantageous **13** authoritative, most important **15** most outstanding

domination 4 rule **5** power **7** command, control, mastery **9** authority **11** superiority

domineer 7 control **8** dominate, lord over **9** dictate to, tyrannize

domineering 8 arrogant, despotic, dogmatic **9** imperious **10** commanding, oppressive, tyrannical **11** dictatorial, overbearing **13** authoritative

Dominican Republic
capital/largest city: **12** Santo Domingo **14** Ciudad Trujillo
others: **4** Azua, Bani, Moca, Pena, Polo **5** Bonao, Cotui, Nagua, Neiba, Nizao, Sosua **6** Higuey, La Vega, Oviedo **7** Sanchez **8** Barahona, Santiago **11** Puerto Plata **17** San Pedro de Macoris **21** San Francisco de Macoris
measure: **3** ona **5** tarea **6** fanega
monetary unit: **3** oro **4** peso **6** franco
island: **5** Beata, Saona **8** Altovelo, Catalina **10** Hispaniola
lake: **10** Enriquillo
mountain: **4** Tina **5** Gallo, Neiba **7** Baoruco, Central **8** Bahoruco, Oriental **13** Sententrional

highest point: **6** Duarte
river: **4** Yuna **5** Ozama **11** Yaque del Sur **13** Yaque del Norte
sea: **8** Atlantic **9** Caribbean
physical feature:
  bay: **4** Ocoa, Yuma **5** Neiba **6** Rincon, Samana **7** Isabela **8** Calderas, Escocesa
  cape: **5** Beata, Falso **6** Cabron, Engano **7** Caucedo, Isabela, Macoris
  valley: **4** Real **5** Neyba
people: **5** Negro, Taino **6** Indian **7** mulatto, Spanish **9** Caucasian
  discoverer: **8** Columbus
language: **6** French **7** English, Spanish
religion: **13** Roman Catholic
feature:
  dance: **8** merengue
  religious pilgrimage: **8** romerias
food:
  dessert: **8** pinonate
  fish/meat pastry: **10** pastelitos
  stew: **8** sancocho

dominion 4 land, rule **5** realm **6** domain, empire, region **7** command, mastery **9** authority, supremacy, territory **11** sovereignty **12** jurisdiction
Hindu: **3** raj

Dominus 3 God **4** Lord

Dominus vobiscum 16 the Lord be with you

don 4 wear **5** put on **6** pull on **7** dress in, get into

Don
origin: **5** Welsh
form: **7** goddess
son: **7** Gwydion
daughter: **8** Arianrod

dona 4 lady **5** madam

Dona Flor and Her Two Husbands
author: **10** Jorge Amado

Donalbain
father: **6** Duncan
brother: **7** Malcom

Donald Duck
creator: **10** Walt Disney
character:
  girlfriend: **5** Daisy
  nephew: **4** Huey **5** Dewey, Louie
  uncle: **7** Scrooge

Donar
origin: **8** Germanic
god of: **7** thunder

donate 4 give **6** bestow **7** present **8** bequeath **10** contribute **11** make a gift of

Donatello
real name: **15** Donato di Niccolo
born: **5** Italy **9** Florence
artwork: **5** David **6** St Mark **7** Zuccone **8** Jeremiah, St George **11** Gattamelata **12** Mary Magdalen **19** Judith and Holofernes, St John the Evangelist **22** Cavalcanti Annunciation

donation 4 gift 7 present 12 contribution

Don Careless
author: 8 Rex Beach

Don Carlos
author: 14 Johann Schiller
opera by: 5 Verdi
character: 7 Rodrigo 8 Philip II 9 Don Carlos 13 Princess Eboli 15 Grand Inquisitor 17 Elizabeth de Valois

Dondi
creator: 8 Gus Edson 10 Irwin Hasen
dog: 7 Queenie

done 5 ready 8 finished, prepared 9 completed 12 cooked enough 18 cooked sufficiently

done for 4 dead, gone, over, sunk 5 all up, ended, kaput, spent 6 beaten, doomed, ruined 7 all over, damaged, through 8 finished 9 exhausted

done in 4 beat 5 all in, slain, spent, tired, weary 6 bushed, killed, pooped 7 drained, wearied, worn out 8 dog tired, fatigued, murdered, tired out 9 bone weary, dead tired, played out 10 knocked off

Don Giovanni
also: 7 Don Juan 15 The Rake Punished
opera by: 6 Mozart
setting: 7 Seville
character: 7 Masetto, Zerlina 9 Donna Anna, Leporello 10 Don Ottavio 11 Donna Elvira 15 The Commendatore

Donizetti, Gaetano
born: 5 Italy 7 Bergamo
composer of: 10 Anna Bolena, La Favorita 11 Don Pasquale 12 Elixir of Love, Maria Stuarda 13 L'elisir d'amore, Marino Faliero, Torquato Tasso 14 Lucrezia Borgia 15 Roberto Devereux 16 Linda di Chamounix 17 Lucia di Lammermoor 21 Daughter of the Regiment

Don Juan 3 man 4 beau, wolf 5 Romeo, swain, wooer 6 fellow, squire, steady, suitor 7 admirer, courter, gallant, pursuer 8 Casanova, lothario, lover boy, paramour, young man 9 boyfriend, Lochinvar 10 lady-killer 15 gentleman caller

Don Juan
author: 21 George Gordon Lord Byron
character: 6 Haidee 9 Donna Inez 10 Donna Julia

donkey 3 ass 4 fool, mule 5 burro, idiot 7 jackass

Donlevy, Brian
wife: 12 Marjorie Lane
born: 7 Ireland 9 Portadown
roles: 9 Beau Geste 15 The Great McGinty 21 Two Years Before the Mast

Donn, Arabella

character in: 14 Jude the Obscure
author: 5 Hardy

donna 4 lady 5 madam

Donna Reed Show, The
character: 9 Jeff Stone, Mary Stone 10 Donna Stone 11 Dr Alex Stone, Midge Kelsey, Trisha Stone 12 Dr Dave Kelsey
cast: 8 Bob Crane, Carl Betz 9 Ann McCrea, Donna Reed 12 Paul Peterson 13 Patty Peterson 14 Shelley Fabares

Donne, John
author of: 7 Sermons 10 The Ecstasy, The Extasie 11 Holy Sonnets 15 Death Be Not Proud, Songs and Sonnets, The Canonization 20 Paradoxes and Problems 30 A Valediction Forbidding Mourning

donnish 7 preachy 8 academic, didactic, pedantic 9 pedagogic

Donnithorne, Arthur
character in: 8 Adam Bede
author: 5 Eliot

donnybrook 3 row 4 fray 5 brawl, fight, melee, set-to 6 affray, dustup, fracas, ruckus, rumpus 7 ruction, scuffle 8 skirmish 10 free-for-all 19 knock-down-and-drag-out

donor 5 giver 10 benefactor 11 contributor 12 humanitarian 14 philanthropist

do-nothing 5 idler 6 loafer 14 good-for-nothing

do not prosecute
Latin: 13 nolle prosequi

do not repeat
Latin: 12 non repetatur

Don Pasquale
opera by: 9 Donizetti
character: 6 Norina 7 Ernesto 11 Dr Malatesta

Don Quixote de la Mancha
also: 38 El ingenioso hidalgo Don Quijote de la Mancha
author: 17 Miguel de Cervantes (Saavedra)
character: 10 Pedro Perez 11 Sancho Panza 17 Dulcinea del Toboso
horse: 9 Rosinante
musical: 13 Man of La Mancha

doodad 5 gizmo 6 device, gadget 8 ornament 9 doohickey 10 decoration 11 contraption, contrivance, thingamabob, thingamajig 15 whatchamacallit

doohickey 5 gizmo, thing 6 device, dingus, gadget, object, widget 7 dojiggy, whatsis 8 dojigger 9 thingummy 11 thingamabob, thingamajig 14 thingamadoodle 15 whatchamacallit

Dooley, Thomas Anthony
founded: 6 MEDICO 31 Medical International Corporation
worked in: 13 Southeast Asia

doolie 4 USAF 8 freshman

Doolittle, Eliza

character in: 9 Pygmalion 10 My Fair Lady
author: 4 Shaw

doom 3 end, lot 4 fate, ruin 5 death, judge 7 condemn, convict, destiny, portion, verdict 8 judgment 10 Armageddon 11 destruction, Judgment Day 13 consign to ruin, end of the world, pronouncement 15 resurrection day, the Last Judgment 17 mark for demolition

doomed 5 fated 6 damned, ruined 8 ill-fated 9 condemned

doomsday 11 Judgment Day 13 Day of Judgment, end of the world 15 the Last Judgment

do one's best 3 try 6 strive 7 attempt 8 endeavor, go all out 9 take pains 12 make an effort 13 give all one has 15 knock oneself out

Doonesbury
creator: 12 Garry Trudeau
character: 2 B D 5 Honey, Rufus 6 Calvin, Zonker 7 Boopsie 9 Uncle Duke 12 Joanie Caucus 14 Mark Slackmeyer 18 Michael J Doonesbury

door 4 exit 5 entry 6 egress, portal 7 hallway, ingress 8 entrance 11 entranceway

doorway 5 entry 7 ingress, opening 8 entrance

Doorways
god of: 5 Janus

dope 3 pot, tip 4 dirt, drug, fool, jerk, junk, nerd, news 5 creep, drugs, dummy, klutz, scoop 6 heroin, sedate, uppers 7 downers, opiates 8 additive 9 narcotics, narcotize, substance 10 antiseptic, astringent, medication 11 anesthetize, preparation 12 disinfectant 17 inside information

dope fiend 4 head, user 5 doper, freak 6 addict, junkie 7 hophead 8 cokehead 10 dope addict, drug abuser, drug addict

do penance 5 atone 7 expiate 10 make amends

dopey 4 dumb 6 leaden, stupid, torpid 7 asinine, idiotic, witless 8 comatose, mindless, sluggish 9 brainless, lethargic 10 dull-witted, slow-witted, slumberous 11 block-headed, thickheaded 12 simple-minded

Doppelganger 6 double 13 ghostly double
literally: 12 double-walker

Doppler, Christian Johann
field: 7 physics
nationality: 8 Austrian
discovered: 13 Doppler Effect

Dorcas
also called: 7 Tabitha
revived by: 5 Peter
hometown: 5 Joppa

Doris
father: 7 Oceanus

mother: 6 Tethys
husband: 6 Nereus
mother of: 7 Nereids

dormancy 7 latency 8 inaction 10 inactivity, quiescence, somnolence 11 hibernation

dormant 4 idle 8 inactive, sleeping 9 quiescent, somnolent 11 hibernating

Dorothy
character in: 13 The Wizard of Oz
author: 4 Baum
dog: 4 Toto

Dorset, Bertha and George
characters in: 15 The House of Mirth
author: 7 Wharton

dorsum 5 chine, spine 8 backbone

dose 2 OD 3 cut, nip 4 dram, pill, shot, slug 5 quota, share, slice 6 amount, needle, ration, tablet 7 capsule, measure, portion, section, segment 8 division, overdose, quantity 9 allotment, allowance, daily dose, injection 10 percentage

Dos Passos, John
author of: 3 U S A 11 The Big Money 13 Three Soldiers 16 Nineteen Nineteen 17 Manhattan Transfer 22 The Forty-Second Parallel

dossier 4 file 5 brief 6 record 9 portfolio 14 detailed report

Dostoevsky, Fyodor Mikhailovich
author of: 8 The Idiot 9 The Double 10 The Gambler 12 The Possessed 18 Crime and Punishment 20 The Brothers Karamazov 23 Notes from the Underground

dot 3 dab 4 mark, spot 5 fleck, point, speck 6 dapple, period 7 stipple 9 small spot

dotage 8 senility 15 second childhood 16 feeblemindedness

dote 8 be senile, fuss over

dote on 5 adore, prize, spoil, value 6 pamper 7 cherish, indulge 8 fuss over, treasure 15 lavish affection

doting 4 fond 6 loving 9 indulgent, pampering 12 affectionate

double 4 dual, twin 5 clone 6 paired 7 replica, two-part 8 two-sided 9 ambiguous, duplicate 10 dead ringer 11 again as much, counterpart, meant for two, twice as much 12 twice as great 13 multiply by two, spitting image 15 increase twofold
German: 12 Doppelganger

Double, The
author: 16 Fyodor Dostoevsky

double-cross 5 rat on 6 betray, do dirt, tell on, turn in 7 abandon, deceive, let down, sell out, two-time 8 denounce, inform on, run out on, snitch on 9 play Judas 10 be disloyal 13 be treacherous, inform against, play false with 14 break faith with 16 blow the whistle on, sell down the river

double-crosser 5 cheat 7 traitor 8 betrayer, deceiver, informer

Double-Dealer, The
author: 15 William Congreve

double-dealing 5 false 6 deceit, sneaky, tricky 7 crooked, devious, perfidy 8 bad faith, betrayal, disloyal 9 deceitful, duplicity, falseness, treachery, two-timing 10 disloyalty, perfidious, sneakiness 11 crookedness, double-cross, duplicitous, treacherous 12 dishonorable 13 breach of faith, faithlessness

double entendre 12 off-color joke, risque remark 18 ambiguous statement

double entente 9 ambiguity

Double Indemnity
director: 11 Billy Wilder
cast: 13 Fred MacMurray 15 Barbara Stanwyck, Edward G Robinson
script: 9 James Cain 15 Raymond Chandler

Double Life, A
director: 11 George Cukor
cast: 10 Signe Hasso 12 Edmond O'Brien, Ronald Colman 14 Shelley Winters
Oscar for: 5 actor (Colman)
script: 10 Ruth Gordon 11 Garson Kanin

double meaning 9 ambiguity
French: 13 double entente 14 double entendre

doublet 4 pair 5 tunic 6 couple, jacket 10 two of a kind

double-talk 4 bunk, jazz 5 hokum 6 bunkum, drivel, gabble, jabber 7 baloney, blather, palaver, prattle, twaddle 8 flimflam, flummery, nonsense 9 gibberish 10 balderdash, hocus-pocus, mumbo jumbo 11 obfuscation 12 gobbledygook

double-walker
German: 12 Doppelganger

Double X
nickname of: 9 Jimmy Foxx

doubt 5 qualm 6 wonder 7 suspect 8 distrust, mistrust, question 9 misgiving, skeptical, suspicion 10 be doubtful, indecision 11 uncertainty 12 apprehension 13 feel uncertain 14 waver in opinion 15 have doubts about 16 lack confidence in, lack of conviction

Doubter see 6 Thomas

doubtful 5 vague 7 dubious, obscure, suspect, unclear 9 tentative, uncertain, undecided, unsettled 10 hesitating, irresolute, suspicious 11 unconvinced 12 inconclusive, questionable

doubtfulness 5 doubt 7 dubiety 8 distrust, mistrust, unbelief 9 disbelief, suspicion 10 skepticism 11 incredulity 14 lack of credence

Doubting see 6 Thomas

doucement
music: 6 gently

douceur 3 tip 5 bribe 8 gratuity 9 sweetness

dough 4 cash, duff, spud 5 bread, crust, money, paster 6 batter, change, leaven, noodle 8 doughboy 11 infantryman

doughnut 4 cake, tire 5 bagel, torus 6 cymbal, dunker, sinker 7 beignet, cruller, twister

doughty 4 bold 5 brave 6 strong 8 fearless, intrepid, unafraid 9 confident, dauntless 10 courageous, determined 12 stout-hearted

Douglas, Archibald
character in: 7 Marmion
author: 5 Scott

Douglas, Kirk
real name: 17 Issur Danielovitch
son: 7 Michael
born: 11 Amsterdam NY
roles: 8 Champion 9 Spartacus 10 The Vikings 11 Lust for Life 14 Detective Story, Seven Days in May 17 The Glass Menagerie, Young Man with a Horn 18 Letter to Three Wives 22 Mourning Becomes Electra

Douglas, Lloyd C
author of: 7 The Robe 23 The Magnificent Obsession

Douglas, Melvyn
real name: 23 Melvyn Edouard Hesselberg
wife: 12 Helen Gahagan
born: 7 Macon GA
roles: 3 Hud 9 Ninotchka 10 Being There

Douglas, Michael
father: 4 Kirk
roles: 4 Coma 7 The Game 10 Disclosure, Wall Street (Oscar) 11 Star Chamber 13 Basic Instinct 14 Jewel of the Nile 15 Fatal Attraction 16 The China Syndrome, The Perfect Murder 17 Romancing the Stone

dour 4 sour 6 gloomy, morose, solemn, sullen 9 cheerless 10 forbidding, unfriendly

Douras, Marion Cecilia
real name of: 12 Marion Davies

douse 4 soak 5 souse 6 drench 7 immerse 8 saturate, submerge 15 plunge into water

Dove, Noah's
constellation of: 7 Columba

Dover Beach
author: 13 Matthew Arnold

dovetail 4 jibe, join 5 match, tally, unite 8 coincide 9 harmonize 11 fit together 12 interlocking

dowager 5 widow 6 relict 7 elderly

dowdy 4 drab 5 tacky 6 frumpy, shabby, sloppy 8 slovenly 12 unattractive

dowel 3 peg, pin, rod 4 pole 5 stick 7 spindle

down 3 ill 4 blue, deck, drop, fell, gulp, sick 5 drink, floor 6 ailing 7 put away, swallow 8 dejected, downcast, feathers 9 depressed 10 dispirited 12 disheartened

down-and-out 4 sick 5 broke 9 penniless 12 impoverished, on one's uppers 13 incapacitated 15 under the weather

downcast 3 low, sad 4 blue 7 unhappy 8 dejected 9 cheerless, depressed 11 discouraged 12 disconsolate, disheartened

downfall 4 fall, ruin 6 shower 8 collapse, downpour 9 rainstorm, ruination 10 rain shower 11 destruction

downgrade 4 drop 5 lower 6 debase 7 decline, descent, way down 8 belittle, minimize 9 declivity, denigrate, devaluate 10 depreciate

downhearted 3 sad 7 unhappy 8 dejected, downcast 9 depressed, sorrowful 10 dispirited 11 discouraged 12 disheartened

downheartedness 5 gloom 6 dismay 7 despair, sadness 9 dejection, pessimism 10 depression, low spirits, melancholy 11 despondency 12 hopelessness 14 discouragement

down in the dumps 4 blue, glum 6 gloomy 7 in a funk 9 depressed 10 despondent 13 in the doldrums

down in the mouth 3 sad 6 dismal, woeful 7 joyless, unhappy 8 dejected, downcast 9 depressed, sorrowful, woebegone 10 lugubrious 12 disconsolate

downpayment 6 binder 7 advance, deposit 9 money down

downpour 6 shower 9 rainstorm 10 cloudburst, rain shower

downright 4 open 5 blunt, frank, total, utter 6 candid, direct, honest, really 7 in truth, plainly, sincere, utterly 8 absolute, actually, complete 9 out-and-out 10 aboveboard, completely, thoroughly 12 unmistakably 13 thoroughgoing, unequivocally 15 straightforward

Downright
character in: 19 Every Man in His Humour
author: 6 Jonson

downstairs 5 below 6 cellar 8 basement 10 first floor 11 ground floor

down the drain 4 gone, lost 9 up in smoke 12 out the window

down-to-earth 5 crass, plain, sober, solid 6 casual, coarse, earthy, simple 7 relaxed 8 informal, sensible 9 practical, pragmatic, realistic 10 hardheaded, hard-boiled, no-nonsense 11 plain-spoken, substantial 12 matter-of-fact, unidealistic 13 unsentimental

downtown 9 inner city, urban area 10 center city, metropolis 16 business district, metropolitan area

downtrodden 9 exploited, oppressed 10 tyrannized 11 subservient 12 harshly ruled

downturn 3 dip, sag 4 drop, fall, skid, slip 5 slide, slump 6 plunge, waning 7 decline, reverse, setback 8 decrease 9 downslide, downswing, downtrend, dwindling, recession 10 depression, diminution 12 degeneration 13 deterioration

Down Under see 9 Australia

down with
French: 4 a bas

downy 4 soft 5 fuzzy, nappy, plumy, quiet 6 fleecy, fluffy 7 cunning, knowing 8 feathery 9 featherbed

do wrong 3 err, sin 8 go astray 9 misbehave 10 transgress

Doyle, Sir Arthur Conan
see also 14 Holmes, Sherlock
author of: 13 The Sign of Four 15 A Study in Scarlet, The White Company 25 The Hound of the Baskervilles 26 Adventures of Sherlock Holmes
character: 10 Irene Adler 12 Dr John Watson 13 Mycroft Holmes 14 Sherlock Holmes 17 Inspector Lestrade, Professor Moriarty

doze 3 nap 6 catnap, siesta, snooze 10 forty winks, light sleep 12 sleep lightly

dozy 4 lazy 6 drowsy, sleepy 7 languid 9 lethargic, somnolent

D P 5 exile 6 emigre 7 outcast, refugee 8 deportee 10 expatriate 14 banished person, deported person 15 displaced person 16 political refugee

drab 4 dull, gray 5 dingy 6 dismal, dreary, gloomy, somber 9 cheerless, dull brown 10 lackluster

drabness 8 dullness 9 dinginess 10 dreariness, gloominess 13 colorlessness

Dracula
author: 10 Bram Stoker
character: 8 Dr Seward 10 Mina Murray 12 Count Dracula, Dr Van Helsing, Lucy Westenra 14 Arthur Holmwood, Jonathan Harker

draft 4 drag, gulp, haul, pull, wind 5 drink 6 breeze, induct, sketch 7 diagram, outline, swallow 9 conscript, induction 10 money order 11 postal order, rough sketch 12 conscription, current of air 15 military service 16 drawing from a cask 18 preliminary version 22 call for military service

drafty 6 breezy, chilly

drag 3 lug 4 bore, haul, pull 5 bring, crawl, trail 6 dredge 7 be drawn 9 inch along 10 creep along, move

slowly, spoilsport, wet blanket 11 party-pooper

Dragnet
character: 8 (Sgt) Ed Jacobs 9 (Sgt) Ben Romero, (Sgt) Joe Friday 10 (Officer) Bill Gannon, (Officer) Frank Smith
cast: 8 Jack Webb 9 Herb Ellis 11 Harry Morgan 12 Ben Alexander 14 Barney Phillips 16 Barton Yarborough
setting: 10 Los Angeles

Dragon 14 Leviathan
constellation of: 5 Draco

drag on 4 last 6 endure, keep on, keep up 7 persist 8 continue 9 persevere

drag one's feet 5 crawl, creep 6 dawdle 9 waste time 10 move slowly 13 procrastinate

dragonfly
varieties: 5 biddy 6 darner 7 skimmer 8 clubtail, grayback 9 amberwing 12 elisa skimmer

Dragon Seed
author: 10 Pearl S Buck

Dragon's teeth
sown by: 6 Cadmus
location: 6 Thebes
grew into: 8 warriors

dragoon 5 bully, force 6 coerce, compel 7 trooper 8 browbeat, bulldoze, cavalier, horseman, pressure 9 strongarm 10 cavalryman 12 horse soldier, horse trooper 14 mounted soldier

drag through the mud 5 smear, sully, taint 6 debase, defame, smirch, vilify 7 degrade, tarnish, vitiate 8 disgrace, dishonor 9 discredit, disparage 10 stigmatize

drain 3 sap 4 drag, pipe, tube 5 empty, sewer, use up 6 outlet, strain 7 channel, conduit, debouch, deplete, flow out, pump off 8 empty out 9 depletion, discharge, dissipate 10 impoverish

drainage 4 flow 9 discharge

drained 4 beat 5 all in, empty, spent, tired, weary 6 bushed, done in, pooped, used up 7 emptied, wearied, worn out 8 con- sumed, depleted, dog tired, expended, fatigued, finished, tired out 9 dead tired, enervated, exhausted, played out

Drake, Stan
creator/artist of: 21 The Heart of Juliet Jones

Drake, Temple
character in: 9 Sanctuary
author: 8 Faulkner

dram
abbreviation: 2 dr

drama 4 play 6 acting 8 the stage 9 direction, vividness 10 excitement, the theater 11 mise-en-scene 15 dramatic quality, intense interest, theatrical

piece
god of: 7 Bacchus

dramatic 8 striking **9** climactic, emotional **10** theatrical **11** sensational, suspenseful **12** melodramatic **13** for the theater

dramatics 6 acting **7** emoting **9** theatrics **10** dramaturgy, stagecraft **11** hamming it up, histrionics, thespianism

dramatis personae 4 cast **6** actors **7** players **10** performers **16** cast of characters, list of performers

dramaturgy 5 drama **7** theater **10** stagecraft **11** dramatic art

Drambuie
type: 7 liqueur
origin: 8 Scotland
flavor: 5 herbs, honey
with scotch: 9 Rusty Nail

drape 4 deck, garb, veil, wrap **5** adorn, array, cloak, cover, dress **6** attire, bedeck, enrobe, enwrap, shroud, swathe, wrap up **7** apparel, bedight, envelop, festoon, sheathe, swaddle **8** enshroud, enswathe

drastic 4 dire, rash **7** bizarre, extreme, radical **8** dreadful **9** dangerous **10** outlandish **11** deleterious

Dravidian
language group: 3 Kui **5** Ghond, Tamil **6** Teluga **8** Kanarese **9** Malayalam
spoken in: 5 India **6** Ceylon **8** Sri Lanka

draw 3 get, tie, tow **4** drag, etch, haul, limn, lure, pick, pull, take **5** charm, draft, drain, evoke, infer, write **6** allure, come-on, deduce, elicit, entice, extend, make up, siphon, sketch **7** attract, distort, draw out, extract, make out, pick out, pull out, pump out, stretch, suck dry, take out, wrinkle **8** contract, deadlock, elongate, protract **9** attenuate, pull along, stalemate **10** attraction, bring forth, enticement, inducement, make appear **14** make a picture of

draw away 2 go **5** leave **6** go back, shrink **7** retreat **8** withdraw

drawback 8 handicap, obstacle **9** detriment, hindrance **10** impediment **12** disadvantage **14** stumbling block

draw back 6 flinch, recoil **7** back off, retreat **8** move away, withdraw

draw close 3 hug **4** come, near **6** arrive, enfold **7** embrace **8** approach, come nigh, gain upon **10** move toward

drawers 5 pants **6** shorts **7** panties **8** bloomers, calzoons, trousers **9** pantalets, underwear **10** underpants

draw forth 5 evoke **6** elicit **7** distill, extract

drawing 5 study **6** sketch **7** lottery,

picture **9** depiction, selection **11** delineation **12** illustration

drawing apart 8 dividing **9** diverging **10** separating **12** splitting off

drawing out 9 expansion, extension **10** elongation, stretching **11** attenuation, lengthening, protraction **12** prolongation

drawing power 4 pull **6** allure, appeal **9** magnetism **10** attraction, enticement **11** fascination

drawing room 5 salon **6** parlor **10** living room **11** sitting room **13** reception room

drawn out 4 long **7** lengthy **8** extended **9** elongated, prolonged **10** lengthened, protracted

draw out 5 educe, evoke **6** elicit, expand, extend, extort **7** distill, enlarge, extract, prolong, spin out, stretch **8** elongate, lengthen, protract **9** attenuate, call forth **10** stretch out

draw the line 5 limit **8** contrast, separate **12** fix a boundary **13** differentiate

draw to a close 3 end **6** finish **8** conclude **11** come to an end

draw together 4 herd, mass, pack **5** bunch, crowd, flock, group **6** gather, huddle **7** cluster, collect, tighten **8** assemble, compress, contract **9** constrict **10** congregate

draw up 3 map **5** draft **6** make up, map out **7** charter, diagram, outline **9** blueprint

draw up plans 5 draft **6** design, sketch **7** outline

dray 4 cart **5** wagon **7** tipcart, tumbrel **8** dumpcart

dread 4 fear **5** awful **6** fright, terror **7** anguish, anxiety, cower at, fearful **8** alarming, cringe at **10** be afraid of, horrifying, shrink from, terrifying **11** fearfulness, frightening, trepidation **12** apprehension **20** anticipate with horror

dreaded object
French: 9 bete noire

dreadful 5 awful **6** tragic **7** fearful **8** alarming, horrible, shocking, terrible **9** frightful **11** distressing

dream 3 joy **4** goal, hope, muse, wish **5** think **6** desire, vision **7** delight, fantasy, hope for, incubus, reverie, think up **8** consider, pleasure, prospect **9** nightmare **11** expectation, have as a goal **13** look forward to, lost in thought

Dream Merchants, The
author: 13 Harold Robbins

Dream of the Golden Mountains, The
author: 13 Malcolm Cowley

Dreams
god of: 6 Icelus, Oniros **7** Oneiros **8** Morpheus **9** Phantasus

Dream Songs, The
author: 12 John Berryman

dream up 5 frame, hatch **6** create, invent **7** concoct **8** conceive, contrive

dreamy 4 airy **5** blank, empty, vague **6** absent, musing, unreal **8** ethereal, fanciful, illusory, soothing **9** fantastic, wonderful **10** delightful **11** preoccupied, unrealistic **13** unsubstantial **14** out of this world

dreariness 9 bleakness **10** desolation, dismalness, gloominess, melancholy **13** cheerlessness

dreary 3 sad **4** drab **5** bleak **6** dismal, gloomy **7** forlorn **8** mournful **9** cheerless **10** depressing, melancholy

dregs 6 rabble **7** deposit, grounds, residue **8** canaille, riffraff, sediment **9** settlings, worst part **11** lower depths

Dreiser, Theodore
author of: 8 The Titan **12** Sister Carrie, The Financier **17** An American Tragedy

drench 3 wet **4** soak **5** douse **8** saturate

dress 4 curl, deck, do up, garb, gown, robe, trim **5** adorn, frock, groom, treat **6** attire **7** apparel, arrange, bandage, cleanse, clothes, comb out, costume, garnish **8** clothing, decorate, ornament **9** disinfect, embellish **12** put on clothes **13** clothe oneself

Dressed to Kill
director: 12 Brian De Palma
cast: 10 Nancy Allen **11** Keith Gordon **12** Michael Caine **14** Angie Dickinson

dressed up 7 adorned, duded up **8** costumed, dolled up, tarted up **9** decorated, disguised, in costume **10** ornamented **11** embellished

dresser 6 bureau **7** cabinet, commode **8** cupboard **10** chiffonier **14** chest of drawers

dressing-down 6 rebuke **7** censure, chiding, reproof **8** reproach, scolding **9** reprimand **10** bawling-out, chewing-out, upbraiding **11** castigation, reprobation **12** remonstrance **13** tongue-lashing

dressing-gown
French: 13 robe-de-chambre

dressmaker 9 couturier, midinette **10** couturiere, seamstress

dress up 5 adorn **6** doll up **7** enhance, improve **8** beautify, ornament, spruce up **9** embellish, embroider, smarten up **10** exaggerate

Dreyfuss, Richard
born: 10 Brooklyn NY
roles: 4 Jaws **6** Tin Men **8** Stakeout **9** The Big Fix, Stand by Me **14** Mr. Holland's Opus, The Goodbye Girl (Oscar) **15** Moon Over Parador **16** American Graffiti **20** Postcards from the Edge **24** Down and Out in Bev-

erly Hills **29** Close Encounters of the Third Kind **31** The Apprenticeship of Duddy Kravitz

dribble 4 drip, kick **6** bounce **7** drizzle, trickle **11** fall in drops, run bit by bit

driblet 4 drip, drop, tear **7** droplet, globule

dried up 4 arid **7** drained, parched **9** prunelike, shriveled **10** dehydrated, desiccated

drift 3 aim **4** flow, gist, heap, mass, pile **5** amass, amble, sense **6** course, gather, object, pile up, ramble, stream, wander **7** current, meander, meaning, purpose, scatter **8** movement **9** direction, intention, objective **10** accumulate **11** implication, peregrinate **12** accumulation, be borne along

drifter 3 bum **4** hobo **5** idler, tramp **6** loafer **8** derelict, vagabond **16** ne'er-do-well

drill 4 bore **5** punch, train **6** pierce **8** exercise, practice, puncture, training, work with **10** boring tool, repetition **11** instruction **17** repeated exercises **type: 4** hand **5** twist **8** electric

drilling 4 rote **6** boring **8** practice, training **9** schooling **10** discipline **11** preparation

drink 3 sip **4** gulp, swig **5** booze, taste, toast **6** absorb, imbibe, ingest, salute, take in **7** alcohol, swallow **8** beverage, libation **9** partake of, the bottle **10** alcoholism **11** drunkenness **15** alcoholic liquor **17** liquid refreshment **type of: 3** cup, fix **4** fizz, flip, mull, puff, sour **5** daisy, julep, punch, shrub, sling, smash **6** cooler, frappe, rickey **7** cob- bler, stinger **8** highball

drinker 3 sot **4** lush, wino **5** dipso, drunk, rummy, souse **6** bibber, boozer, sponge **7** guzzler, imbiber, tippler, waterer **8** drunkard **9** alcoholic, inebriate

drink in 6 absorb, digest, soak up, take in **10** assimilate **14** immerse oneself

Drinking
god of: 5 Comus

drinking spree 4 orgy, toot **5** binge, drunk **6** bender **8** beer-bust, carousal **9** bacchanal

drink up 4 gulp **5** quaff **6** absorb, guzzle, soak up **7** consume, swallow

drip 3 ass **4** bore, jerk, nerd **5** creep, dummy, klutz **6** splash **7** dribble, driz- zle, trickle **8** sprinkle

dripping 3 wet **4** damp **5** soggy **6** soaked, sodden **10** soaking wet

drive 4 goad, lead, mean, move, prod, push, ride, rush, spur, urge **5** force, guide, impel, motor, press, steer, surge **6** co- erce, compel, incite, intend, outing **7** advance, conduct, go by car, impulse, operate, suggest **8** ambition, campaign, motivate **9** ex-

cursion, insinuate, trip by car, urge along **10** motivation

drive apart 8 alienate, estrange **9** disaffect

drive away 4 rout, shoo **5** chase, deter, repel **6** rebuff **7** repulse **8** alienate **11** put to flight, send packing

drive home 7 impress **8** hammer at

drivel 5 drool **6** babble, ramble, slaver **7** dribble, slobber **8** babbling, nonsense, rambling **9** gibberish **12** talk nonsense **13** senseless talk, talk foolishly

drive out 4 fire **5** chase, depel, eject, evict, exile, expel, force, roust **6** compel, remove **7** dismiss, repulse **8** discharge, exorcise

driver 6 cowboy, drover **8** herdsman **9** chauffeur

drizzle 3 fog **4** mist, rain **7** dribble **8** sprinkle

drizzly 3 wet **4** damp **5** foggy, misty, rainy

Dr Jekyll and Mr Hyde
author: 20 Robert Louis Stevenson
character: 5 Poole **10** Mr Utterson **13** Dr Henry Jekyll **14** Dr Hastie Lanyon

Dr Kildare
character: 14 Dr James Kildare **18** Dr Leonard Gillespie
cast: 13 Raymond Massey **18** Richard Chamberlain
hospital: 12 Blair General

Dr No
author: 10 Ian Fleming

droll 5 funny **7** offbeat, strange **8** humorous **9** eccentric, laughable, whimsical **12** oddly amusing

drollery 3 wit **5** humor **6** banter, comedy, whimsy **7** jesting

Dromio
character in: 17 The Comedy of Errors
author: 11 Shakespeare

drone 3 hum **4** buzz, whir **5** idler **6** loafer **7** vibrate **8** parasite **9** murmuring, vibration **10** lazy person

drool 6 drivel, slaver **7** dribble, slobber **8** salivate **15** water at the mouth

droop 3 dim, sag **4** flag, sink **5** lower **6** weaken, wither **8** diminish, hang down **9** lose vigor **14** hang listlessly **15** incline downward

droopy 4 bent, blue, down, limp **5** baggy, bowed, slack **6** dashed, pining **7** doleful, sagging, subdued **8** cast down, dangling, dejected, downcast **9** depressed **10** despairing, despondent, dispirited, spiritless, world-weary **11** downhearted, hanging down, languishing **14** down in the mouth

drop 3 can, dab **4** bead, dash, deck, dive, drip, fall, fell, fire, omit, sack, sink, tear **5** abyss, floor, leave, lower, pinch, slide, slope, smack, trace **6** give up, lessen, plunge **7** abandon,

decline, descend, descent, dismiss, dribble, driblet, dwindle, forsake, globule, plummet, slacken, smidgen, soupcon, trickle **8** decrease, diminish, leave out, lowering **9** declivity, discharge, knock down, precipice, terminate **10** sprinkling **12** bring to an end **13** fail to include **15** cease to consider, fail to pronounce

drop anchor 4 dock, moor **5** tie up

drop in 4 call, come **5** visit **6** appear, come by, look in, show up, stop by, turn up **7** stop off **9** pay a visit

droplet 4 bead, drip, tear **7** driblet, globule **8** spherule

droplets of moisture 3 dew, fog **4** mist **5** sweat **12** condensation

drop out 4 quit **5** leave **6** resign, retire

dross 4 scum, slag **5** waste **6** cinder, scoria **8** clinkers, impurity

drought, drouth 4 lack, need, want **6** dearth **7** aridity, paucity **8** scarcity, shortage **10** deficiency, dry weather, lack of rain **13** insufficiency

drover 6 cowboy, driver **7** cowpoke **8** herdsman, shepherd **10** cowpuncher

drown 4 soak **5** flood **6** deluge, drench, engulf **7** immerse **8** inundate, overcome, submerge **9** overpower, overwhelm, suffocate, swallow up **10** asphyxiate

drowse 3 nap, nod **4** doze, laze **5** dover, drone, sleep **6** snooze / slumber **8** languish **10** sleepiness

drowsy 4 dozy, lazy, slow **5** tired **6** sleepy **7** languid **8** hypnotic, listless, sluggish, soothing **9** lethargic, somnolent, soporific

Dr Strangelove or How I Learned to Stop Worrying and Love the Bomb
director: 14 Stanley Kubrick
cast: 9 Peter Bull **10** Keenan Wynn **11** Slim Pickens **12** George C Scott, Peter Sellers **14** James Earl Jones, Sterling Hayden

drub 3 hit **4** beat, cane, flog, whip **5** whale **6** thrash **9** bastinado

drubbing 6 caning **7** beating, licking, tanning **9** trouncing **11** shellacking

drudge 4 grub, hack, plod, toil **5** labor, slave **6** lackey, menial, toiler **7** grubber **8** inferior, struggle **9** underling **11** subordinate

drudgery 4 toil **5** grind **7** travail **8** hack work **11** menial labor **15** distasteful work

Druk-Yul *see* **6** Bhutan

drum 3 din, keg, rap, tap, tub **4** beat, cask, roar, roll **5** expel, force **6** barrel, harp on, rumble, tattoo **7** dismiss, tattoo **8** drive out, hammer at **9** discharge, drive home, reiterate **11** beat a tattoo, din in the ear, reverberate

Drums
author: 9 James Boyd

Drums Along the Mohawk
  author: **14** Walter D Edmonds
  character: **4** Lana **9** Blue Black, John Wolff **11** Joseph Brant, Mark Demooth **12** Mrs McKlennan **13** Gilbert Martin **20** Magdelena Borst Martin

drunk 3 sot **4** bust, lush, soak **5** binge, rummy, souse, tipsy, toper **6** barfly, bender, looped, sodden, soused, stewed, zapped, zonked **7** smashed **8** beer-bust, besotted, carousal **9** alcoholic, plastered **10** inebriated **11** dipsomaniac, intoxicated **13** drinking spree, under the influence

drunkard 3 sot **4** lush, soak, wino **5** rummy, souse, toper **6** barfly **9** alcoholic **11** dipsomaniac

drunkenness 10 alcoholism **11** inebriation **12** intoxication

Drury, Allen
  author of: **14** Capable of Honor, Return to Thebes **15** The Promise of Joy **16** Advise and Consent **19** Come Nineveh Come Tyre

Druse 5 Syria **6** Muslim **7** Lebanon

dry 4 arid, blot, dull, wipe **5** droll **6** boring, low-key **7** deadpan, parched, tedious, thirsty **8** rainless **9** dehydrate, desiccate, shrivel up, wearisome **10** dehydrated, monotonous **13** uninteresting

Dryad
  form: **5** deity, nymph
  location: **5** woods

dry as dust 4 arid, dull, sere **7** parched **8** pedantic, withered **9** shriveled **13** unimaginative

Dryden, John
  author of: **10** All for Love **11** Mac Flecknoe **14** Annus Mirabilis **15** Alexander's Feast, Marriage-a-la-Mode **20** Absalom and Achitophel, Essay on Dramatic Poesy, The Hind and the Panther **22** Fables Ancient and Modern

dry goods 5 cloth, goods **6** fabric **8** material **9** yard goods **10** piece goods

dryness 7 aridity, drought **8** aridness **11** dehydration

Dry Salvages
  author: **7** T S Eliot

dry up 6 wither **7** shrivel **9** dehydrate, desiccate, evaporate

Dr Zhivago
  author: **14** Boris Pasternak
  character: **4** Lara
  setting: **17** Russian Revolution

dual 6 double **7** twofold, two-part

dub 4 call, name **5** label **6** knight **7** baptize **8** christen, nickname **9** designate

Dubai
  part of: **3** UAE

dubiety 5 doubt **8** unbelief **9** disbelief **10** skepticism **11** incredulity **12** doubtfulness **14** lack of credence

Dubin's Lives
  author: **14** Bernard Malamud

dubious 5 shady **6** unsure **7** suspect **8** doubtful **9** skeptical, uncertain **10** suspicious, unreliable **11** unconvinced **12** questionable, undependable **13** untrustworthy

Dublin
  brewery: **8** Guinness
  capital of: **7** Ireland
  Irish: **8** Dubh Linn (black pool) **15** Baile Atha Cliath (town of the Hurdle Ford)
  landmark: **10** Four Courts **11** Custom House **12** Abbey Theater, Christ Church, Dublin Castle **13** Leinster House **18** Kilmainham **19** St Patrick's Cathedral
  mountain: **7** Wicklow
  museum: **8** National **10** James Joyce
  park: **7** Phoenix
  river: **6** Liffey
  rulers: **7** English, Vikings
  scene of: **12** Easter Rising (1916)
  university: **14** Trinity College

Dubliners
  author: **10** James Joyce

DuBois, Blanche
  character in: **21** A Streetcar Named Desire
  author: **8** Williams

Du Bois, W E B
  founded: **5** NAACP
  author of: **19** The Souls of Black Folk

Dubonnet
  type: **8** aperitif
  origin: **6** France
  ingredient: **7** quinine, red wine
  with gin: **3** BVD **8** Napoleon
  with rum: **10** Bushranger

duc 4 duke

Duccio di Buoninsegna
  born: **5** Italy **6** Sienna
  artwork: **6** Maesta **18** The Rucellai Madonna (attributed)

duce, il duce 6 despot, leader, tyrant **8** dictator **9** Mussolini

Duchamp, Marcel
  born: **6** France **8** Normandy **10** Blainville
  artwork: **5** LHOOQ **9** Given That **11** Etant Donnes **12** Bicycle Wheel **13** The Large Glass (The Bride Stripped Bare by Her Bachelors Even) **24** Nude Descending a Staircase **37** The King and Queen Surrounded by Swift Nudes

Duchess of Malfi, The
  author: **11** John Webster
  character: **6** Bosola **7** Antonio **8** Giovanna **9** Ferdinand **11** The Cardinal

duck 4 clee, coot, lory, smew, teal, veer **5** avoid, dodge, drake, eider, elude, evade, goose, ruddy, shirk, stoop **6** canard, canvas, crouch, gannet, Peking, scoter, swerve **7** gadwall,

mallard, Muscovy, pintail, pochard **8** baldpate, freckled, redshank, shelduck, shoveler, sidestep, submerge **9** merganser, whistling **10** bufflehead, canvasback **11** wood steamer **13** give the slip to
  male: **5** drake
  group of: **5** brace

Duck Soup
  director: **10** Leo McCarey
  cast: **5** Chico, Harpo, Zeppo **7** Groucho (Rufus T Firefly) **12** Louis Calhern, Raquel Torres **14** Margaret Dumont
  setting: **9** Freedonia

duct 4 pipe, tube **6** vessel **7** channel, conduit

ductile 6 docile, pliant, supple **7** elastic, plastic, pliable, tensile **8** amenable, bendable, flexible, formable, moldable, shapable, swayable **9** adaptable, compliant, malleable, tractable **10** extensible, manageable, submissive **11** complaisant, manipulable, stretchable, susceptible

dud 3 dog **4** bomb, bust, flop, hash **5** botch, lemon, loser **6** bummer, fiasco, fizzle **7** clinker, debacle, failure, washout **11** lead balloon, miscarriage **14** disappointment

dude 3 fop **4** beau **5** dandy **7** peacock **11** city dweller, city slicker **12** Beau Brummell

Dudevant, Aurore
  real name of: **10** George Sand

duds 4 togs **5** flops **6** attire **7** apparel, clothes, fizzles, threads **8** clothing, failures, garments

due 4 owed **5** ample, owing **6** enough, proper, unpaid **7** fitting, merited **8** adequate, becoming, deserved, expected, plenty of, rightful, suitable **9** in arrears, scheduled **10** sufficient **11** appropriate, outstanding

duel
  French: **15** affaire d'honneur

Duel, The
  author: **15** Alexander Kuprin

duenna 8 guardian **9** attendant, chaperone, custodian, protector

dues 4 fees **7** charges **10** assessment

Duessa
  character in: **15** The Faerie Queene
  author: **7** Spenser

duet 3 duo, two **4** pair **6** couple **7** twosome

Dufy, Raoul
  born: **6** France **7** Le Havre
  artwork: **7** The Palm **15** Riders in the Wood **16** Chateau and Horses **18** Deauville Racetrack, Posters at Trouville

dugout 3 den **4** cave **5** canoe **6** cavity, hollow **7** shelter

Duino Elegies
  author: **16** Rainer Maria Rilke

Dukas, Paul
born: **5** Paris **6** France
composer of: **6** La Peri **18** Ariane et Barbe-Bleue **19** Ariadne and Bluebeard **22** The Sorcerer's Apprentice

duke
French: **3** duc

Duke
nickname of: **9** John Wayne

Duke, Patty (Patty Duke Astin)
real name: **13** Anna Marie Duke
husband: **9** John Astin
born: **10** Elmhurst NY
roles: **11** Helen Keller **16** The Miracle Worker, The Patty Duke Show, Valley of the Dolls

Dukenfield, William Claude
real name of: **8** W C Fields

Duke Snider
nickname of: **11** Edwin Snider

dulcet 7 lyrical, musical, tuneful **8** pleasing, sonorous **9** melodious **11** mellifluous

Dulcinea del Toboso
character in: **10** Don Quixote
author: **9** Cervantes

dull 4 slow **5** blunt, dense, muted, quiet, thick, trite, vapid **6** boring, obtuse, stupid **7** muffled, not keen, prosaic, subdued, vacuous **8** deadened, inactive, not brisk, not sharp **9** dim-witted **10** indistinct, lackluster, uneventful **13** unimaginative, uninteresting

Dull
character in: **16** Love's Labour's Lost
author: **11** Shakespeare

dullard 4 dolt **5** dummy, dunce **6** nitwit **7** halfwit **8** dumbbell, imbecile

Dullea, Keir
born: **11** Cleveland OH
roles: **12** David and Lisa **18** Butterflies Are Free **27** Two Thousand One: A Space Odyssey

dullness 6 idiocy, tedium **8** dumbness, lethargy, monotony, slowness **9** bluntness, ignorance, stupidity, vapidness **10** boringness, imbecility, obtuseness **11** tediousness **13** dim-wittedness **15** thick-headedness

dull-witted 5 dazed, fuzzy **7** bemused, muddled, stunned **8** confused **9** stupefied

Dulong, Pierre-Louis
field: **7** physics **9** chemistry
nationality: **6** French
discovered: **19** nitrogen trichloride
studied: **4** heat **13** atomic weights

duly 6 on time **8** properly, suitably **9** correctly **10** deservedly, punctually, rightfully **13** appropriately **15** at the proper time

Dumaine
character in: **16** Love's Labour's Lost
author: **11** Shakespeare

Dumas, Alexandre (fils)
author of: **7** Camille **11** Le Demi-Monde **17** La Dame aux Camelias **21** The Lady of the Camellias
Camille inspired: **10** La Traviata
opera by: **5** Verdi

Dumas, Alexandre (pere)
author of: **17** The Queen's Necklace **18** The Three Musketeers **19** The Man in the Iron Mask **21** The Count of Monte Cristo **22** The Vicomte de Bragelonne

Du Maurier, Daphne
author of: **7** Rebecca **10** Jamaica Inn **11** Don't Look Now **14** My Cousin Rachel **15** Frenchman's Creek **19** The House on the Strand

Du Maurier, George
author of: **6** Trilby **10** The Martian **13** Peter Ibbetson

dumb 3 mum **4** dull, mute **5** dense, dopey **6** silent, stupid **7** foolish, aphasic **8** aphasiac **9** dim-witted **13** unintelligent **17** incapable of speech

dumbbell 3 ass, oaf **4** clod, dolt, dope, fool **5** booby, clown, dummy, dunce, idiot, moron, ninny **6** dimwit, nitwit **7** dullard, halfwit **8** dumb-dumb, dummkopf, imbecile, lunkhead, meathead, numskull **9** birdbrain, blockhead, ignoramus, lamebrain, numbskull, simpleton **10** noodlehead

dumbfound, dumfound 4 stun **5** amaze **7** startle **8** astonish **11** flabbergast

dumbfounded 5 agape **6** amazed **7** stunned **9** astounded, stupefied **10** astonished, speechless **11** openmouthed **13** flabbergasted

dumbness 6 idiocy **8** dullness **9** asininity, stupidity, thickness **10** imbecility **11** witlessness **12** wordlessness **14** speechlessness **15** thickheadedness

dumbstruck 5 agape **6** amazed, gaping **7** riveted **9** awestruck, stupefied **10** speechless **11** electrified, openmouthed **13** flabbergasted

dump 3 hut **4** hole, toss **5** empty, hovel, shack **6** shanty, unload **8** get rid of, junkyard **9** dispose of **10** refuse pile **11** rubbish heap

dumpy 5 squat **7** lumpish **13** short and stout

Dunaway, Faye
real name: **18** Dorothy Faye Dunaway
born: **8** Bascom FL
roles: **6** Barfly, Milady **7** Network (Oscar) **8** The Champ **9** Chinatown **13** Mommie Dearest **14** Bonnie and Clyde **15** Towering Inferno **17** The Four Musketeers **18** The Three Musketeers

Duncan
character in: **7** Macbeth
author: **11** Shakespeare

Duncan, Sandy
born: **11** Henderson TX

roles: **8** Peter Pan **9** Funny Face **12** The Boyfriend

dunce 4 fool **5** dummy, idiot, moron **6** dimwit, nitwit **8** imbecile, numskull **9** blockhead, numbskull, simpleton

Dunciad, The
author: **13** Alexander Pope

dune 4 bank **5** mound **8** sandbank, sandpile

dunk 3 dip, sop **4** duck, soak **5** bathe, douse, drown, slosh, souse, steep **6** deluge, drench, engulf, plunge **7** baptize, immerse **8** inundate, saturate, submerge

Dunne, John Gregory
author of: **11** Dutch Shea Jr **18** Quintana and Friends

Dunnock, Mildred
born: **11** Baltimore MD
roles: **8** Baby Doll **12** The Nun's Story **14** The Corn Is Green **16** Butterfield Eight, Cat on a Hot Tin Roof, Death of a Salesman

duo 4 pair **5** combo **6** couple **7** twosome **11** combination

duomo 4 dome **9** cathedral

dupe 4 fool, pawn **5** patsy, trick **6** humbug, sucker **7** cat's paw, deceive, fall guy, mislead **8** hoodwink **9** bamboozle

duplicate 4 copy **5** clone, match **6** repeat **7** replica **8** parallel **9** facsimile, imitation, make again, photocopy, photostat **10** carbon copy **12** reproduction

duplicity 5 fraud, guile **6** deceit **7** cunning **9** deception, falseness **10** dishonesty **13** deceitfulness

Du Pont Labs
founder: **17** E I du Pont de Nemours
inventor of: **5** nylon **6** Teflon **7** Gore-Tex

Duquesnoy, Francois
born: **8** Brussels, Flanders
nickname: **11** Il Fiammingo
artwork: **8** St Andrew **9** St Susanna

dur
musical term: **5** major **8** major key

durability 7 stamina **8** strength **9** endurance, toughness **10** sturdiness

durable 5 sound, tough **6** strong, sturdy **7** lasting **8** enduring **11** longwearing, substantial

Durand, Asher Brown
born: **18** Jefferson Village NJ
artwork: **14** Kindred Spirits

Durant, Will and Ariel
authors of: **20** The Story of Philosophy **21** Rousseau and Revolution **22** The Story of Civilization

Durante, Jimmy
real name: **19** James Francis Durante
nickname: **10** Schnozzola **15** Inka Dinka Doo Man
born: **9** New York NY

roles: 5 Jumbo 21 It's a Mad Mad Mad Mad World

duration 4 term 6 extent, period 11 continuance 12 continuation

Durdles
character in: 22 The Mystery of Edwin Drood
author: 7 Dickens

Durer, Albrecht
born: 7 Germany 9 Nuremberg
artwork: 10 Adam and Eve, Apocalypse, The Triumph 11 Wehlsch Pirg 12 Four Apostles, Large Passion, Melancholia I 13 Castle of Trent 15 Life of the Virgin 18 St Jerome in his Study 19 Virgin with the Siskin 21 Christ Among the Doctors 22 Knight Death and the Devil 24 Crowned Death on a Thin Horse 25 The Feast of the Rose Garlands 28 The Festival of the Rose Garlands

duress 5 force 6 threat 8 coercion, pressure 10 compulsion, constraint

Durgin, Francis Timothy
real name of: 11 Rory Calhoun

during litigation
Latin: 12 pendente lite

Durocher, Leo
nickname: 9 Leo the Lip
sport: 8 baseball
position: 7 manager
team: 11 Chicago Cubs 13 New York Giants 15 Brooklyn Dodgers
saying: 18 Nice guys finish last

Durrenmatt, Friedrich
author of: 5 Traps 8 The Visit 9 The Pledge, The Quarry 13 The Physicists 21 The Judge and His Hangman 27 The Marriage of the Mississippi

Durrie, James and Henry
character in: 21 The Master of Ballantrae
author: 9 Stevenson

dusk 6 sunset 7 sundown 8 twilight 9 nightfall

dusky 3 dim 4 dark 5 murky 6 cloudy, gloomy, veiled 7 swarthy 8 dark-hued

dust 4 dirt, lint 5 brush, motes 8 sprinkle

duster 3 rag 4 coat, robe 5 brush, cloth, whisk 9 housecoat 10 whisk broom

Dutch Guiana *see* 8 Suriname

Dutch Shea, Jr
author: 16 John Gregory Dunne

dutiful 5 loyal 8 diligent, faithful, obedient 9 compliant 13 conscientious

duty 3 tax 4 levy, onus, task 6 charge, excise, tariff 7 customs 8 business, function, province 10 assignment, obligation 14 responsibility

Duval, Armand
character in: 7 Camille
author: 5 Dumas (fils)

Duvall, Robert
born: 10 San Diego CA
roles: 4 MASH 10 The Apostle 11 Falling Down, Godfather II 12 Lonesome Dove, The Godfather 13 Apocalypse Now, Days of Thunder, Tender Mercies (Oscar) 15 The Great Santini, True Confessions 16 The Handmaid's Tale, The Scarlet Letter 18 To Kill a Mockingbird

Duvall, Shelley
born: 9 Houston TX
roles: 6 Popeye 9 Nashville 10 The Shining, Three Women 15 Brewster McCloud

Dvorak, Antonin
born: 11 Nelahozeves 14 Czechoslovakia
composer of: 5 Dumky 6 Hymnus, Te Deum 8 Carnival (overture) 10 St Ludmilla 11 Stabat Mater 15 American Quartet, From the New World (Symphony in E Minor) 16 The Specter's Bride 17 The Bells of Zlonice

dwarf 3 dim, elf, imp 4 baby, tiny 5 fairy, gnome, pixie, pygmy, small, troll 6 bantam, goblin, petite, sprite 8 diminish 9 miniature 10 diminutive, leprechaun, overshadow

dwarfish 3 wee 4 tiny 5 pygmy, short, small 6 bantam, little, midget 7 compact, squatty 10 diminutive, undersized 13 foreshortened

dweeb 4 fool, geek, nerd, wonk 5 grind

dwell 4 live 5 abide 6 harp on, reside 7 inhabit 10 linger over

dwelling 4 home 5 abode, house 8 domicile 9 residence 10 habitation

dwelling place 4 home 5 abode, house 7 habitat, lodging 8 domicile 9 residence 10 habitation 14 living quarters

dwell on 6 accent, stress 7 feature, iterate 9 emphasize, press home

dwindle 4 fade, wane 6 lessen, shrink 7 decline 8 decrease, diminish 13 become smaller

dye 4 tint 5 color, shade, stain 8 coloring 10 coloration

dyed-in-the-wool 9 confirmed, ingrained 10 deep-rooted, inveterate 11 established

dyestuff 14 coloring matter

dynamic 5 vital 6 active 7 driving 8 forceful, powerful, vigorous 9 energetic

dynamism 3 pep 4 life 5 verve, vigor 6 energy, spirit 8 vitality, vivacity 9 animation 10 liveliness

dynamite 4 raze, ruin 5 blast, trash, wreck 6 blow up, charge 7 destroy, shatter, wipe out 8 decimate, demolish 9 devastate, dismantle, eradicate, explosive 10 annihilate, extinguish, obliterate 11 exterminate

dynamo 4 doer 7 hustler 8 activist, go-getter 9 generator 12 active person 14 bundle of energy, mover and shaker

Dynasts, The
author: 11 Thomas Hardy
subject: 17 Napoleon Bonaparte

dynasty 4 line 5 crown, reign 6 regime 7 lineage, regency 8 dominion, hegemony, kingship, monarchy, regnancy 9 authority 10 government, suzerainty 11 ruling house 12 jurisdiction 14 administration

Dynasty
character: 9 Dex Dexter, Jeff Colby 12 Alexis (Morel Carrington Colby) Dexter 14 Adam Carrington 15 Blake Carrington 16 Amanda Carrington, Steven Carrington 17 Krystle Carrington 18 Dominique Devereaux, Krystina Carrington 21 Fallon Carrington Colby
cast: 9 John James 10 Linda Evans 11 Joan Collins 12 John Forsythe
setting: 6 Denver 8 Colorado
hotel: 8 La Mirage

dyspeptic 4 mean 6 crabby, grumpy, ornery, shirty, touchy 7 grouchy, waspish 8 choleric 9 crotchety, fractious, irascible, irritable 10 ill-humored, ill-natured 11 bad-tempered, contentious, hot-tempered 12 cantankerous, sour-tempered 13 short-tempered

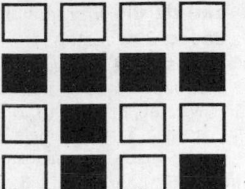

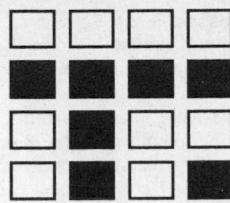

each 3 per 4 a pop 5 every 6 apiece 7 that one, this one 8 everyone, separate 12 respectively

Eagels, Jeanne
  born: 12 Kansas City MO
  roles: 4 Rain 8 Jealousy 9 The Letter 13 Sadie Thompson 14 Man Woman and Sin

eager 3 hot 4 agog, avid, keen 6 ardent, fervid, intent, raring 7 athirst, earnest, excited, fervent, intense, longing, zealous 8 desirous, diligent, resolute, spirited, yearning 9 ambitious, hungering, impatient, thirsting 10 aggressive, passionate 11 hardworking, impassioned, industrious, persevering 12 enterprising, enthusiastic

eagerly 6 avidly, keenly 8 ardently, desiring, fervidly, intently 9 anxiously, earnestly, fervently, zealously 16 enthusiastically

eagerness 4 zeal, zest 5 ardor 6 fervor 7 avidity 9 readiness 10 enthusiasm 11 willingness

eagle
  young: 6 eaglet

Eagle
  constellation of: 6 Aquila

Eakins, Thomas
  born: 14 Philadelphia PA
  artwork: 11 Agnew Clinic 13 Mrs Edith Mahon 14 The Gross Clinic 24 Max Schmitt in a Single Scull

ear
  section: 5 inner, outer 6 middle
  part: 4 drum 5 anvil, canal 6 hammer 7 cochlea, stirrup 8 hair cell 14 eustachian tube

earl 4 lord, peer 5 noble 8 nobleman
  wife: 8 countess

earlier 6 before, in time, sooner 9 before now, in advance 10 beforehand 11 ahead of time 13 before the fact

earliest 5 first 6 oldest, primal 7 ancient, initial, primary, soonest 8 original, primeval 9 beginning, primitive 10 aboriginal, indigenous 11 fundamental

Earl of Baltimore
  nickname of: 10 Earl Weaver

Earl the Pearl
  nickname of: 10 Earl Monroe

early 5 first 6 primal 7 ancient, archaic, betimes, initial, too soon, very old 8 primeval 9 in advance, premature, primitive 10 beforehand, in good time, primordial 11 ahead of time, prehistoric, prematurely

Early Autumn
  author: 14 Louis Bromfield

early man 6 Peking 9 Cro-Magnon, Steinheim 11 Neanderthal 18 Trobriand Islanders 24 Australopithecus robustus 25 Australopithecus africanus

earmark 3 tag 4 band, hold, sign 5 allot, label, stamp, token, trait 6 aspect, assign, dogear 7 feature, put away, quality, reserve 8 allocate, property, set aside 9 attribute, designate 11 peculiarity, singularity 14 characteristic

earn 3 get, net 4 draw, gain, make, rate, reap 5 clear, merit 6 attain, pick up, secure 7 achieve, collect, deserve, realize, receive, warrant 9 bring home 12 be entitled to

earn as due 4 rate 5 merit 7 deserve 10 be worthy of 12 be entitled to 13 be deserving of

earnest 4 firm 5 eager, fixed, grave, sober, staid 6 ardent, fervid, honest, intent, sedate, solemn, stable, steady, urgent 7 devoted, fervent, intense, serious, sincere, zealous 8 constant, diligent, resolute, spirited, vehement 9 ambitious, assiduous, heartfelt, insistent 10 deeply felt, determined, passionate, purposeful, thoughtful 11 hard-working, impassioned, industrious, persevering 12 enthusiastic, wholehearted

earnest request 4 plea 6 appeal 8 entreaty, petition 11 importunity 12 supplication

earnings 3 pay 5 wages 6 income, salary 7 payment, profits 8 proceeds, receipts, takehome 12 compensation

Earnshaw, Catherine
  character in: 16 Wuthering Heights
  author: 6 Bronte

ear-splitting 7 blaring 8 piercing 9 clamorous, deafening 10 thunderous

earth 3 sod 4 clay, dirt, dust, land, loam, soil, turf 5 terra 6 ground 7 topsoil
  god of: 3 Geb, Keb 5 Dagan, Dagon 10 Trophonius
  goddess of: 2 Ge 4 Gaea, Gaia 6 Hecate, Hekate, Tellus

earthen pot
  Spanish: 4 olla

earthenware 5 china 7 pottery 8 clayware, crockery 11 ceramic ware

earthly 6 bodily 7 mundane, secular, ungodly, worldly 8 feasible, material, physical, possible, temporal 9 corporeal, practical 10 imaginable 11 conceivable, terrestrial 12 nonspiritual 13 materialistic

earthquake 5 quake, seism, shock 6 tremor 8 temblor, upheaval 11 earth tremor

earth tremor 5 quake, seism, shock 6 tremor 8 temblor, upheaval 10 earthquake

earthy 5 bawdy, crude, dirty, funky, gross, lusty, rough 6 coarse, filthy, ribald, robust, smutty, vulgar 7 obscene, peasant, raunchy 8 indecent 9 primitive, unrefined 10 unblushing, uncultured 12 uncultivated

Earwicker family
  characters in: 13 Finnegans Wake
  author: 5 Joyce

earwig
  variety: 5 black 6 little 10 long horned

ease 4 calm, rest, slip 5 abate, allay, poise, quiet, slide, still 6 aplomb, lessen, luxury, pacify, plenty, relief, repose, solace, soothe 7 assuage, comfort, console, leisure, lighten, mollify, relieve 8 diminish, easement, cosiness, facility, maneuver, mitigate, palliate, security, serenity 9 abundance, affluence, alleviate, composure, disburden, readiness 10 confidence, prosperity, relaxation 11 assuagement, naturalness, peace of mind, restfulness 12 tranquillity, unconstraint 13 luxuriousness, move carefully, relaxed manner 14 effortlessness, handle with care, unaffectedness

easel 5 frame, stand 6 tripod

easement 4 ease 6 relief, solace, succor 7 comfort 8 soothing 10 right of way 11 assuagement

easily 5 by far 6 freely, surely 7 clearly, handily, lightly, plainly, readily 8 facilely, smoothly, with ease 9 certainly 10 far and away, undeniably 11 beyond doubt, undoubtedly 12 effortlessly, with facility 13 without a hitch 14 beyond question, without trouble 17 without difficulty 23 beyond the shadow of a doubt

easily embarrassed 3 shy 5 timid 7 bashful 8 blushing, skittish, timorous 9 diffident, shrinking 11 constrained, unconfident

easily noticed 5 clear, plain 6 patent 7 evident, glaring, obvious, visible 8 flagrant, striking 9 arresting, prominent 10 noticeable 11 conspicuous, outstanding

easily ruffled 9 emotional, excitable 11 hot-tempered 13 quick-tempered

easiness 4 ease 10 equanimity, simplicity 11 naturalness 12 indifference 13 impassiveness

East, the 4 Asia 9 the Orient 10 the Far East 11 the Near East 17 Eastern Hemisphere

East Bengal *see* 10 Bangladesh

East Berlin
former capital of: 11 East Germany

East Coker
author: 7 T S Eliot

Eastern Slavic
language family: 12 Indo-European
group: 11 Balto-Slavic
branch: 6 Slavic
language: 7 Russian 9 Ukrainian 12 White Russian

Easter Parade
director: 14 Charles Walters
based on musical by: 12 Irving Berlin
cast: 9 Ann Miller 11 Fred Astaire, Judy Garland 12 Peter Lawford

East Germany *see* 11 Germany, East

East Indies *see* 8 Malaysia 9 Indonesia

Eastman, George
nationality: 8 American
founder of: 14 Eastman Kodak Co
inventor of: 9 Kodak film 11 Kodak camera 20 transparent photo film

East of Eden
author: 13 John Steinbeck
director: 9 Elia Kazan
cast: 8 Burl Ives 9 James Dean 10 Jo Van Fleet 11 Julie Harris 13 Raymond Massey
Oscar for: 17 supporting actress (Van Fleet)
characters: 4 Abra, Adam, Aron 5 Caleb, Trask

East wind
associated with: 5 Eurus 9 Volturnus

Eastwood, Clint
born: 14 San Francisco CA
roles: 7 Firefox, Rawhide 10 Dirty Harry, Hang Em High, Unforgiven 11 Magnum Force, The Dead Pool 12 Coogan's Bluff, Kelly's Heroes, Sudden Impact 13 A Perfect World 14 Play Misty for Me 15 In The Line of Fire, Where Eagles Dare 17 A Fistful of Dollars, Any Which Way You Can, High Plains Drifter 18 Escape from Alcatraz, For a Few Dollars More 21 Two Mules for Sister Sara

23 The Good the Bad and the Ugly 25 The Bridges of Madison County
director of: 10 Unforgiven (Oscar) 12 Sudden Impact 13 Absolute Power, A Perfect World 14 Play Misty For Me 25 The Bridges of Madison County 32 Midnight in the Garden of Good and Evil
mayor of: 6 Carmel

easy 4 calm, mild, open, soft 5 cushy, frank, light, naive 6 benign, calmly, candid, docile, easily, gentle, secure, serene, simple 7 lenient, natural, not hard, relaxed, restful, wealthy 8 affluent, carefree, composed, friendly, gracious, gullible, informal, outgoing, painless, peaceful, pleasant, scarcely, serenely, tranquil, unforced, well-to-do, yielding 9 compliant, indulgent, leisurely, luxurious, tractable, unworried 10 effortless, peacefully, permissive, unaffected, untroubled 11 comfortable, comfortably 12 not difficult, unsuspicious 13 accommodating, unconstrained

easygoing 4 calm 6 casual 7 offhand, patient, relaxed 8 carefree, laidback 9 unruffled, unworried 10 insouciant, nonchalant 11 unconcerned, unexcitable 12 even-tempered, happy-go-lucky, mild-tempered

Easy Rider
director: 12 Dennis Hopper
cast: 10 Karen Black, Peter Fonda 11 Luana Anders 12 Dennis Hopper, Robert Walker 13 Jack Nicholson

easy to use 7 adapted, helpful 9 adaptable 10 convenient 11 serviceable 12 advantageous, user friendly

eat 3 sup 4 bolt, dine, feed, gulp, rust, take 5 feast, lunch 6 devour, gobble, ingest, nibble 7 consume, corrode 8 dispatch, dissolve, wear away, wolf down 9 breakfast, take a meal, waste away 10 break bread, gormandize 14 take sustenance 15 take nourishment

eatable 4 food 6 edible 8 fit to eat 10 comestible, consumable

eat away 4 rust 5 erode 7 corrode, oxidize

eating habits 4 diet 7 regimen

eat into 4 bite 5 erode 6 nibble 7 consume, corrode 8 wear away 9 swallow up

eat one's fill 5 feast, gorge 6 pig out 7 banquet 12 stuff oneself

eat rapidly 4 bolt, gulp, wolf 5 scarf 6 gobble 12 swallow whole

eat up 5 enjoy, savor 6 devour, relish 7 consume, swallow 9 delight in, rejoice in 13 be pleased with, get a kick out of 14 take pleasure in

eat voraciously 6 cram in, devour, gobble 7 stuff in 8 bolt down, gulp down, wolf down 10 gormandize 12 swallow whole

eau, eaux 5 water

eau de vie 6 brandy 11 water of life

eaves 8 overhang

eavesdrop 3 bug, pry, spy, tap 5 snoop 6 attend, harken 7 monitor, wiretap 8 listen in, overhear 9 bend an ear 11 cock one's ear 14 strain one's ears 15 prick up one's ears

ebb 5 abate, go out 6 go down, lessen, recede, shrink, weaken 7 decline, dwindle, retreat, slacken, subside 8 decrease, diminish, fade away, fall away, flow away, flow back, move back, withdraw 9 waste away 10 degenerate 11 deteriorate

ebony 3 jet 4 dark, inky 5 black, raven, sable 8 hardwood 9 coal-black 15 Diospyros Ebenum
varieties: 5 Green, Texas 8 Macassar, Mountain 10 East Indian, Queensland

Ebsen, Buddy
real name: 23 Christian Rudolph Ebsen Jr
born: 12 Belleville IL
roles: 12 Barnaby Jones, Davy Crockett 21 The Beverly Hillbillies

ebullience 3 zip 7 elation 8 buoyancy 9 animation 10 enthusiasm, exuberance, joyousness, liveliness 11 high spirits 12 exhilaration 13 effervescence

ebullient 6 elated, joyful, joyous 9 exuberant 11 exhilarated 12 effervescent, enthusiastic, high-spirited

ecce homo 12 behold the man
said by: 13 Pontius Pilate
spoken of: 6 Christ

eccentric 3 nut, odd 4 kook, rash, sick 5 curio, flake, funny, kooky, nutty, queer, weird 6 freaky, insane, quaint, unique, weirdo 7 bizarre, curious, erratic, oddball, offbeat, strange, unusual, weirdie 8 aberrant, abnormal, crackpot, freakish, peculiar, quixotic, singular, uncommon 9 character, irregular, odd person, off center, parabolic, psychotic, screwball, unnatural, whimsical 10 capricious, elliptical, outlandish, unorthodox 13 extraordinary 14 unconventional

eccentricity 6 oddity, whimsy 7 caprice 9 deviation, queerness 10 aberration 11 abnormality, peculiarity, strangeness 12 idiosyncrasy, irregularity

ecclesiastic, ecclesiastical 5 rabbi, vicar 6 cleric, curate, deacon, parson, pas- tor, priest, rector 7 prelate 8 chaplain, churchly, clerical, minister, pastoral, preacher 9 churchman, clergyman, episcopal, parochial, religious

echelon 4 file, line, rank, rung, tier 5 grade, level 6 office 8 position 9 authority, hierarchy

Echidna 8 anteater
feature: 5 snout

echinoderm 9 sea animal

characteristic: 10 spiny shell
form: 6 radial
kind: 6 cystid **7** crinoid **8** starfish **9** sea urchin **10** basket star **11** sea cucumber

echo 3 ape **4** copy, ring **5** match **6** follow, mirror, parrot, repeat **7** imitate, reflect, resound **8** parallel, simulate **9** duplicate, reproduce, take after **11** reverberate **13** reverberation
Echo
form: 5 nymph
location: 8 mountain
loved: 9 Narcissus
loved by: 3 Pan
changed into: 4 echo

eclair 6 pastry **7** dessert **9** creampuff
eclaircissement 11 explanation **13** clarification, (the) Enlightenment
eclat 4 fame, pomp **5** glory, honor **6** praise, renown, repute **7** acclaim, display, success
eclipse 3 dim **4** hide, loss, mask **5** cloak, cover, excel, outdo **6** darken, exceed **7** blot out, conceal, erasing, masking, obscure, surpass, veiling, wipe out **8** cloaking, clouding, covering, outrival, outshine **9** darkening, shadowing, transcend **10** obliterate, overshadow, tower above **11** blotting out, diminishing, eradicating, obscuration **12** annihilation, obliteration **13** overshadowing

eclogue 4 idyl, poem **5** idyll **7** bucolic **8** dialogue, pastoral
Eclogues
author: 6 Vergil, Virgil
ecole 6 school
economic 6 fiscal **8** material, monetary **9** budgetary, financial, pecuniary **10** productive **12** distributive
economical 5 chary, cheap **6** frugal, modest, saving **7** careful, prudent, sparing, spartan, thrifty **8** economic **9** low-priced, niggardly, penurious, scrimping **10** reasonable **11** close-fisted, tightfisted **12** parsimonious
economic decline 8 downturn **9** recession **10** depression
economics
term: 3 GNP **5** labor **7** capital, Marxism, surplus **8** property **9** commodity, Communism, inflation, Keynesian, recession **10** capitalism, monetarist, supply-side **11** bourgeoisie, central bank, competition, consumption, marketplace, proletariat, stagflation **12** distribution, econometrics, fiscal policy, interest rate, laissez-faire, mercantilism **14** federal deficit, macroeconomics, microeconomics, monetary policy **17** trickle-down theory **20** gross national product
economist
American: 6 George, Hansen, Sumner, Veblen **7** Commons **8** Friedman,

Laughlin **9** Greenspan **10** Schumpeter
British: 4 Mill **5** Smith **6** Keynes **7** Malthus, Ricardo **8** Marshall
French: 3 Say **7** Quesnay
German: 4 Marx **7** Schacht
Italian: 6 Pareto
Scottish: 5 Smith
economize 4 save **5** pinch, skimp, stint **6** scrimp **7** husband **8** be frugal, conserve, cut costs **9** be prudent **10** avoid waste **11** cut expenses **12** be economical, use sparingly **14** be parsimonious **15** practice economy, tighten one's belt
economizing 10 conserving **11** cutting down **13** penny-pinching **14** belt-tightening **15** pinching pennies **18** tightening one's belt
economy 6 thrift **8** prudence **9** frugality **10** providence **11** thriftiness **15** financial status, productive power
ecstasy 4 joy **5** bliss **6** frenzy, thrill, trance **7** delight, emotion, madness, rapture **8** delirium, gladness, pleasure **9** cloud nine, happiness, transport **10** enthusiasm, exultation
ecstatic 4 glad, rapt **5** happy **6** elated, joyful, joyous **7** exalted, excited **8** blissful **9** delighted, delirious, ebullient, entranced, overjoyed, rapturous **10** enraptured **11** transported **12** enthusiastic **13** beside oneself
Ecuador
name means: 7 equator
other name: 5 Quito
capital: 5 Quito
largest city: 9 Guayaquil
others: 4 Jama, Loja, Napo, Puyo, Tena **5** Guano, Manta, Pajan, Pinas, Piura, Pojan, Yaupi **6** Ambato, Cuenca, Ibarra, Tulcan, Zaruma **7** Azogues, Cayambe, Guamote, Guapulo, Machala, Pelileo, Pillaro, Salinas **8** Riobamba **10** Esmeraldas, Portoviejo
division: 5 Costa **6** Sierra **7** Oriente
measure: 5 libra **6** cuadra, fanega
monetary unit: 5 sucre **7** centavo
weight: 5 libra
island: 4 Puna, Wolf **5** Colon, Mocha, Pinta **6** Baltra, Chaves, Darwin, Pinzon, Rabida, Wenman **7** Isabela, La Plata, Sante Fe, Tortuga **8** Espanola, Floreana, Genovesa, Marchena, Santiago **9** Culpepper, Galapagos, Santa Cruz **10** Fernandina, Santa Maria **11** San Salvador **13** San Cristobal
mountain: 5 Andes **6** Condor, Sangay **7** Cayambe **8** Antisana, Cotopaxi **9** Cotacachi, Pichincha
highest point: 10 Chimborazo
river: 4 Coca, Mira, Napo **5** Cocoa, Daule, Paute, Pindo, Tigre **6** Blanco, Guayas, Tumbes, Zamora **7** Conambo, Curaray, Jubones, Pastaza, Puyango **8** Aguarico, Bobonaza, Cononaco, Naranjal, Putumayo **9** San

Miguel **10** Esmeraldas, Nangaritza **12** Guaillabamba
sea: 7 Pacific
physical feature:
bay: 5 Manta **7** Isabela **9** Elizabeth **11** Santa Elenas **15** Ancon de Sardinas
cape: 4 Rosa **6** Pasado **8** Marshall, Puntilla **10** San Lorenzo
channel: 7 Jambeli
gulf: 9 Guayaquil, Pichincha
peninsula: 10 Santa Elena
point: 4 Jama **5** Essex **6** Galera **9** Albemarle **10** Christobal
people: 4 Cara, Cixo, Inca **5** Ardan, Aucas, Macoa, Maina, Palta, Quitu, Yumbo **6** Canelo, Jibaro, Jivaro, Puruha **7** Cayapas, Jivaros, mestizo, mulatto **8** Barbacoa, Colorado, Montuvio, Serranos **9** Montubios
artist: 4 Egas **8** Santiago **9** Caspicara **10** Guayasamin
author: 6 Espejo **14** Carrera Andrade
conqueror: 7 Pizarro **10** Benalcazar **11** Huayna-Capac
god: 5 umina
leader: 6 Alfaro, Flores **10** Plaza Lasso, Rocafuerte **12** Garcia Moreno **13** Velasco Ibarra
language: 6 Jibaro **7** Quechua, Spanish
religion: 13 Roman Catholic
feature:
animal: 6 vicuna
dictator: 8 caudillo
estate: 8 hacienda
festival: 5 Yamor
hat: 6 Panama **8** jipijapa, toquilla
tree: 5 balsa
food:
baked guinea pig: 3 cuy
corn tamale: 6 humita
drink: 6 chicha
marinated raw shrimp/fish: 7 ceviche, seviche
potato/cheese patty: 11 llapingacho
potato soup: 5 locro
ecumenical 6 global **7** general **8** catholic **9** communist, planetary, universal, worldwide **10** heavenwide **11** communalist **12** all-embracing, all-including, all-inclusive, all-pervading, collectivist, cosmopolitan **13** communitarian, comprehensive, international
eczema 4 rash **8** eruption **10** dermatitis **12** inflammation
eddy 6 vortex **9** maelstrom, whirlpool **14** countercurrent
Eddy, Nelson
partner: 17 Jeanette MacDonald
born: 12 Providence RI
roles: 9 Rose Marie **15** Naughty Marietta **16** Northwest Outpost
Eden 8 Paradise
see also **4** Adam

Eden, Anthony 10 Earl of Avon 13 prime minister

Eden, Barbara
role: 7 Jeannie
TV: 15 I Dream of Jeannie
costar: 11 Larry Hagman

edentate 5 manis, sloth 7 antbear 8 aardvark, anteater 9 armadillo, toothless

Edgar Huntly
author: 20 Charles Brockden Brown

edge 3 hem, rim 4 bind, inch, line, side, trim 5 bound, brink, creep, limit, sidle, slink, sneak, steal, verge 6 border, fringe, margin 7 contour, outline 9 extremity, periphery, threshold 12 boundary line, dividing line, move sideways

Edgeworth, Maria
author of: 7 Belinda 11 The Absentee 14 Castle Rackrent

edging 3 hem 4 trim 5 limit 6 border, fringe, margin, ruffle 7 binding, curbing, salvage 8 boundary, fringing, trimming

edgy 5 sharp, testy 7 anxious, nervous 8 snappish 9 excitable, impatient, irascible, irritable 10 highstrung

edible 7 eatable 10 comestible, consumable, digestible 12 fit to be eaten, nonpoisonous 13 safe for eating

edict 3 law 4 bull, fiat 5 order, ukase 6 decree, dictum, ruling 7 command, dictate, mandate, statute 9 enactment, manifesto, ordinance, prescript 10 injunction, regulation 12 proclamation, public notice 13 pronouncement 14 pronunciamento

edification 8 guidance, teaching 9 direction, education, elevation, uplifting 11 advancement, information, instruction 13 enlightenment 14 indoctrination

edifice 8 building 9 structure 12 construction

edify 5 teach 6 inform 7 educate, improve 8 instruct 9 enlighten

edifying 8 didactic, tutorial 11 educational, instructive 12 enlightening

Edinburgh
bay: 12 Firth of Forth
capital of: 8 Scotland
Celtic: 11 Dune-eideann (Eidin's Fort)
church: 7 St Giles
landmark: 14 Holyrood Palace 15 Edinburgh Castle
port: 5 Leith
rocks: 10 Castle Rock 11 Arthur's Seat

Edison, Thomas Alva
nickname: 17 Wizard of Menlo Park
home: 11 Menlo Park, NJ
inventor of: 6 (wax cylinder) record 9 light bulb, (quadruplex) telegraph 10 phonograph 11 kinetoscope, stock ticker 14 movie projector 16 incan-

descent lamp 18 automatic telegraph (transmitter and receiver) 21 flexible celluloid film 22 alkaline storage battery

edit 5 adapt, emend 6 censor, polish, redact, revise 7 abridge, clean up, correct, expunge, rewrite, touch up 8 annotate, condense, copy-edit, rephrase 9 expurgate 10 blue-pencil, bowdlerize

edition 4 book, copy, kind 5 issue 6 number 7 imprint, version 8 printing 9 redaction

editor 2 ed 6 writer 7 newsman, reviser 8 compiler, redactor 10 journalist

Edmonds, Walter D
author of: 8 Rome Haul 19 Drums Along the Mohawk

Edmonton
hockey team: 6 Oilers

Edmontonia
type: 8 dinosaur 10 ornithopod
location: 12 North America

Edmund Campion
author: 11 Evelyn Waugh

Edom
name given: 4 Esau
descendants: 8 Edomites

Edson, Gus
creator/artist of: 5 Dondi 8 The Gumps

Ed Sullivan Show, The
regular cast: 17 June Taylor Dancers 23 Ray Bloch and His Orchestra
noted appearances: 7 Beatles, Bob Hope 9 Topo Gigio (mouse) 10 Walt Disney 11 Senor Wences 12 Elvis Presley 14 Martin and Lewis

educate 5 coach, edify, teach, train, tutor 6 inform, school 7 develop 8 civilize, instruct 9 enlighten

education 5 study 7 culture 8 learning, pedagogy, teaching, training, tutelage 9 didactics, erudition, knowledge, schooling 10 pedagogics 11 cultivation, edification, information, instruction, scholarship 13 enlightenment

Education of Henry Adams, The
author: 10 Henry Adams

educe 5 evoke 6 elicit, extort 7 draw out, extract 8 bring out 9 draw forth 12 bring to light

Edward II
author: 18 Christopher Marlowe

Edwards, Blake
director of: 3 SOB, Ten 14 The Pink Panther, Victor Victoria 18 Days of Wine and Roses 19 Breakfast at Tiffany's
wife: 12 Julie Andrews

Edwards, Vince
real name: 18 Vincent Edward Zoimo
roles: 8 Ben Casey 13 Devil's Brigade 14 The Desperadoes 15 Three Faces of Eve

Edwin Drood, The Mystery of
author: 14 Charles Dickens
character: 7 Durdles, Mr Tatar, Rosa Bud 8 Mr Sapsea 10 John Jasper, Mr Datchery 11 Mr Grewgious 12 Mr Crisparkle 13 Deputy Bazzard 14 Helena Landless, Miss Twinkleton, Mr Honeythunder 15 Neville Landless

eel 6 conger
young: 5 elver

eerie 3 odd 5 queer, weird 6 creepy, spooky, uneasy 7 bizarre, fearful, ghostly, ominous, strange, uncanny 10 mysterious, portentous 11 frightening 12 apprehensive

Eeyore 6 donkey
character in: 13 Winnie-the-Pooh
author: 5 Milne

efface 4 raze 5 erase 6 cancel, delete, excise, rub out 7 blot out, destroy, expunge, wipe out 9 eradicate, extirpate 10 annihilate, obliterate

effect, effects 4 fact, gist, make 5 cause, drift, force, goods, power, tenor, truth 6 action, assets, attain, create, impact, import, intent, result, sequel, things, upshot, weight 7 achieve, essence, execute, meaning, outcome, perform, produce, purport, reality, realize 8 carry out, chattels, efficacy, function, holdings, movables, validity 9 actuality, aftermath, execution, furniture, influence, intention, operation, outgrowth, trappings 10 accomplish, bring about, impression 11 commodities, consequence, development, enforcement, general idea, implication, possessions 12 significance 14 accomplishment

effective 4 real 6 active, actual, cogent, moving, potent, strong, useful 7 capable, current, dynamic, telling 8 a reality, eloquent, forceful, forcible, incisive, powerful, striking 9 activated, competent, effectual, efficient, operative 10 compelling, convincing, impressive, persuasive, productive, successful 11 efficacious, influential, in operation, serviceable

effectiveness 5 power 6 effect, impact 7 potency 8 efficacy, strength 9 influence 10 efficiency, usefulness 14 serviceability

effectual 6 acting, active, useful 7 working 9 adequate 9 effective, efficient, operative 11 efficacious, functioning

effectuate 6 effect 7 achieve, execute, realize 8 carry out, complete 9 discharge 10 accomplish, consummate, perpetrate 12 carry through 13 put into effect

effeminate 7 unmanly 8 sissyish, womanish 9 sissified

effervesce 4 fizz, foam 5 froth 6 bubble, fizzle 7 sparkle

effervescence 3 zip 4 dash, fizz, life 5 froth, vigor 6 fizzle, gaiety, spirit 7 foaming 8 bubbling, buoyancy, vitality, vivacity 9 animation, fizziness 10 bubbliness, bubbling up, ebullience, enthusiasm, liveliness

effervescent 3 gay 5 fizzy, merry 6 bubbly, lively 7 fizzing, foaming 8 animated, bubbling 9 ebullient, exuberant, sparkling, vivacious 13 irrepressible

effete 5 spent 6 barren, wasted 7 sterile, worn-out 8 decadent, depraved 9 enervated, exhausted 10 degenerate, unprolific 12 unproductive

efficacious 9 effective, effectual, efficient

efficacy 6 impact 10 efficiency 13 effectiveness

efficiency 5 skill 6 energy 8 efficacy, facility 9 apartment 10 competence 11 proficiency 13 effectiveness

efficient 3 apt 7 capable 8 skillful 9 competent, effective, effectual 10 productive, proficient, timesaving, unwasteful, work-saving 11 crackerjack, efficacious, workmanlike 12 businesslike

effigy 4 doll 5 dummy, image 6 puppet, statue 8 likeness, straw man 9 mannequin, scarecrow 10 marionette 14 representation

effluence 6 efflux 7 outflow, outpour 8 effluent 9 discharge

effluent 5 waste 6 efflux, sewage 7 outflow 9 effluence

effluvium 4 aura, odor, ooze, reek 5 vapor 6 efflux, flatus 8 outgoing

efflux 7 outflow 8 effluent, emission 9 discharge, effluence

effort 3 try 4 toil, work 5 force, labor, pains, power 6 energy, strain, stress 7 attempt, travail, trouble 8 endeavor, exertion, industry, struggle 11 elbow grease

effortless 4 easy 6 facile, simple, smooth 8 graceful, painless 12 not difficult 13 uncomplicated

effortlessness 4 ease 8 easiness, facility 9 readiness 12 painlessness

effrontery 4 gall 5 brass, cheek, nerve 8 audacity, temerity 9 arrogance, brashness, impudence, insolence 10 brazenness 11 presumption 12 impertinence 13 shamelessness
Yiddish: 7 chutzpa 8 chutzpah

effulgence 6 dazzle 8 radiance, splendor 10 brilliance 12 resplendence

effulgent 6 bright 7 radiant 8 dazzling, splendid 9 brilliant 11 resplendent

effusive 5 gushy 6 lavish 7 copious, gushing, profuse 9 ebullient, expansive, exuberant 10 unreserved 11 extravagant, free-flowing, overflowing 12 unrestrained

eft 4 newt 5 again 6 lizard 9 afterward

egalitarian 10 democratic 11 equal-rights 14 constitutional

egalite 8 equality

Egeria
  instructed: 4 Numa 5 nymph 7 advisor

egg 3 ova, roe 4 bomb, goad, mine, oval, ovum, seed, spur 6 embryo, fellow, incite, person 7 albumen 9 instigate, stimulate

Eggar, Samantha
  born: 6 London 7 England
  roles: 12 The Collector, Walking Stick 15 Doctor Doolittle, The Lady in the Car 16 The Molly Maguires

egghead 8 highbrow 13 intellectual

Eggleston, Edward
  author of: 15 The Circuit Rider 19 The Hoosier Schoolboy 22 The Hoosier Schoolmaster

egg on 4 abet, hack, goad, spur 6 exhort, incite 8 talk into 9 encourage

egg-shaped 4 oval 5 ovoid 7 oviform 10 elliptical

Egmont
  author: 12 Johann Goethe

egocentric 8 egoistic 11 egomaniacal, egotistical, on an ego trip, self-seeking, self-serving 12 narcissistic, self-absorbed, self-centered, self-involved, self-obsessed 13 self-concerned 14 megalomaniacal, stuck on oneself 18 wrapped up in oneself

egoism 6 vanity 8 self-love 10 narcissism 14 self-absorption, self-importance 16 overweening pride, self-centeredness

egoist 10 narcissist, selfish one 13 selfish person 18 self-centered person

Egoist, The
  author: 14 George Meredith

egoistic 7 selfish 12 narcissistic, self-centered

egotism 6 vanity 7 conceit 8 bragging, smugness 9 arrogance, immodesty, vainglory 10 self-praise 11 braggadocio 12 boastfulness

egotist 6 gascon 7 boaster, peacock 8 blowhard, braggart 9 swaggerer 11 braggadocio

egotistic 4 vain 10 egocentric 12 self-centered 13 self-important

egregious 5 gross 7 extreme, glaring, heinous 8 flagrant, grievous, shocking 9 monstrous, notorious 10 outrageous 11 intolerable 12 insufferable

egress 4 exit, vent 5 issue 6 escape, outlet, way out 7 leakage, outflow, seepage 8 aperture 9 departure, discharge 10 passage out, withdrawal

Egypt
  other name: 3 UAR 5 Kemet 6 Tomeri 11 The Two Lands 12 The Black Land
  capital/largest city: 5 Cairo

  others: 3 Tor 4 Edfu, Gaza, Giza, Idfu, Said, Suez 5 Altur, Aswan, Tanta 6 Boolak, Dumyat, Faiyum, Quseir, Safaga, Sallum 7 Alemein, Memphis, Raschid, Rosetta, Zagazig 8 Damietta, Hurghada, Ismailia, Mansurah 10 Alexandria
  school: 5 Cairo 7 Al-Azhar 8 American
  division: 5 Lower, Nubia, Upper
  measure: 3 apt, dra, hen, rob 4 arab, dira, draa, khet, nief, ocha, roub, theb, wudu 5 abdat, ardab, cubit, farde, fedan, keleh, kerat, kilah, sahme 6 artaba, aurure, baladi, kantar, keddah, robhah, schene 7 choryos, daribah, malouah, roubouh, toumnah 8 kassabah, kharouba 10 diramimari, diribaladi
  monetary unit: 4 fils, kees, para 5 asper, dinar, fodda, gersh, girsh, medin, pound, riyal 6 ahmadi, dirham, foddah, guinea, junayh, maidin, medine, medino 7 piaster, piastre, tallard 8 bedidlik, millieme
  weight: 3 kat, ket, oka, oke 4 dera, heml, khar, okia, rotl 5 artal, artel, deben, kerat, minae, minas, okieh, pound, ratel, uckia 6 hamlah, kantar 7 drachma, quintal
  island: 4 Roda 6 Philae 7 Shadwan 11 Elephantine
  lake: 4 Edku, Idku 5 Qarun 6 Maryut, Moeris, Nasser 7 Manzala 8 Burullus, Mareotis
  mountain: 5 Sinai, Uekia 6 Gharib 13 Shayib al-Banat
  highest point: 8 Katerina 9 Katherina
  river: 4 Bahr, Nile
  Nile branch: 7 Rosetta 8 Damietta
  sea: 3 Red 13 Mediterranean
  physical feature:
    cape: 4 Sudr 5 Banas 8 Rasbanas
    desert: 3 Tih 5 Dakla, Scete, Sinai, Skete 6 Libyan, Nubian, Sahara 7 Arabian
    gulf: 4 Suez 5 Aqaba
    isthmus: 4 Suez
    oasis: 4 Siwa 6 Dakhel, Dakhla, Kharga 7 Farafra, Khargeh 8 Bahariya 9 Bahariyeh 12 Wahel-Khargeh
    peninsula: 5 Sinai 6 Pharos
    plain: 7 Asaseff
    plateau: 3 Tih
  people: 3 Kem 4 Arab, Copt, Misr, Wafd 5 Gippy, Gyppy, Gypsy, Nilot 6 Ababda, Berber, Hyksos, Nubian, Tasian 7 Mizraim, Pharian 8 Badarian, Bisharin, Memphian
    leader: 5 Jawar, Sadat 6 Nasser 7 Mubarak, Saladin 10 King Farouk 11 Ismail Pasha, Mohammed Ali, Tawfiq Pasha
    pharaoh: 5 Khufu, Menes, Zoser 6 Khafre, Ptulol, Ramses 8 Horemheb, Menkaure 9 Akhenaten, Amenemhet, Amenhotep 10 Men-

tuhotep **11** Tutankhamen
queen: 9 Cleopatra, Nefertari, Nefertiti **10** Hatshepsut, Hetepheres
language: 6 Arabic, French **7** English
  for liturgy: 6 Coptic
religion: 5 Islam **18** Coptic Christianity
  ancient god: 2 Ra **3** Geb, Nut, Shu **4** Aton, Atum, Isis, Ptah, Seth **5** Horus, Thoth **6** Anubis, Hathor, Osiris, Tefnut **8** Nephthys
place:
  dam: 4 Sadd, Sudd **5** Aswan **6** Assuan
  mosque: 5 Rifai **9** Alabaster **11** Sultan Hasan
  palace: 6 Kubbeh
  pyramids: 4 Giza **5** Khufu **6** Cheops **7** Saqqara
  ruins: 5 Miroe **6** Abydos, Sphinx, Thebes **7** Memphis **8** Berenice **9** Abu Simbel **13** Valley of Kings, Valley of Tombs
  temple: 4 Idfu **5** Edoon, Luxor, Thoth **6** Abydos, Karnak, Osiris **7** Dendera
feature:
  dynasty: 5 Saite **7** Ayyubid, Fatimid **8** Mameluke **9** Ptolemaic
  long robe: 10 gallabiyea
  peasant: 6 fellah **8** fellahin **9** fellaheen
  sacred bird: 4 benu, ibis **5** bennu
  sailboat: 7 felucca
  statue: 6 Sphinx **15** Colossi of Memnon
food:
  bean: 5 lotus
  beer: 6 zythum
  bread: 6 herisa
  dish: 3 ful
  drink: 4 bosa, boza **5** bozah
Egyptian
  language family: 11 Afro-Asiatic **13** Hamito-Semitic
  later form: 6 Coptic
Egyptian cross 4 ankh
Egyptian Mythology
  deities: 6 Ennead
  eight gods: 3 Heh **6** Ogdoad
  goddess of evil: 7 Sekhmet
  goddess of fertility: 2 Io **4** Isis
  goddess of law/righteousness: 4 Maat
  goddess of love/joy/music/dance: 6 Hathor
  goddess of sky: 3 Nut
  goddess personifying sky: 6 Hathor
  god of bricks: 5 Kulla
  god of creation: 4 Ptah
  god of dead/Nile: 6 Osiris
  god of earth: 3 Geb, Keb
  god of ocean: 3 Nun **4** Nunu
  god of sun: 2 Ra, Re **5** Horus
    corresponds to Greek: 10 Harcorates
  god of tombs/embalming: 6 Anubis
  god of wisdom/magic/learning:

5 Thoth
  corresponds to Greek: 6 Hermes
immortal spirit: 2 Ka
judge of dead: 6 Osiris
king of dead: 6 Osiris
king of gods: 4 Amen, Amon **5** Ammon **6** Amen Ra, Amon Ra
  corresponds to Greek: 4 Zeus
  corresponds to Roman: 4 Jove **7** Jupiter
personification of femininity: 5 Neith
  corresponds to Greek: 6 Athena
ram god: 5 Khnum
vulture: 7 Nekhbet
Ehrlich, Paul
  field: 12 bacteriology
  nationality: 6 German
  studied: 6 toxins **8** immunity **10** antitoxins
  discovered: 9 salvarsan
  coined term: 12 chemotherapy
  awarded: 10 Nobel Prize
Eichmann in Jerusalem
  author: 12 Hannah Arendt
eiderdown 4 puff **5** cover, quilt **8** coverlet **9** comforter **10** featherbed
Eight and a Half, 8 1/2
  director: 15 Federico Fellini
  cast: 10 Anouk Aimee **16** Claudia Cardinale **19** Marcello Mastroianni
Eighteen Seventy-Six, 1876
  author: 9 Gore Vidal
Eijkman, Christiaan
  nationality: 5 Dutch
  discovered: 19 antineuritic vitamin
  researched: 8 beriberi
  awarded: 10 Nobel Prize
Einstein, Albert
  birthplace: 3 Ulm
  field: 7 physics
  theory of: 10 relativity **14** uranium fission
  awarded: 10 Nobel Prize
Eire see **7** Ireland
Eisenhower, Dwight David
  nickname: 3 Ike
    changed name from: 21 David Dwight Eisenhower
  presidential rank: 12 thirty-fourth
  party: 10 Republican
  state represented: 2 NY
  defeated: 4 (Eric) Hass, (Harry Flood) Byrd **5** (Farrell) Dobbs **6** (Darlington) Hoopes, (William Ezra) Jenner **7** (Stuart) Hamblen, (Thomas Coleman) Andrews **8** (Enoch Arden) Holtwick, (Vincent William) Hallinan **9** (Adlai Ewing) Stevenson
  vice president: 5 (Richard Milhous) Nixon
  cabinet:
    state: 6 (Christian Archibald) Herter, (John Foster) Dulles
    treasury: 8 (George Magoffin) Humphrey, (Robert Bernard) Anderson

  defense: 5 (Thomas Sovereign) Gates (Jr) **6** (Charles Erwin) Wilson **7** (Neil Hesler) McElroy
  attorney general: 6 (William Pierce) Rogers **8** (Herbert) Brownell (Jr)
  postmaster general: 11 (Arthur Ellsworth) Summerfield
  interior: 5 (Douglas) McKay **6** (Frederick Andrew) Seaton
  agriculture: 6 (Ezra Taft) Benson
  commerce: 5 (Sinclair) Weeks **7** (Frederick Henry) Mueller, (Lewis Lichtenstein) Strauss
  labor: 6 (Martin Patrick) Durkin **8** (James Paul) Mitchell
  HEW: 5 (Oveta Culp) Hobby **6** (Marion Bayard) Folsom **8** (Arthur Sherwood) Flemming
born: 9 Denison TX
died: 12 Washington DC
buried: 9 Abilene KS
education: 9 West Point **17** US Military Academy
religion: 12 Presbyterian
interest: 4 golf **6** flying **7** fishing, hunting **8** football, painting
vacation spot: 2 CA **11** Palm Springs
author: 11 Waging Peace **15** Crusade in Europe **16** Mandate for Change **27** At Ease: Stories I Tell to Friends
political career: 4 none (prior to presidency)
civilian career:
  president of: 18 Columbia University
military service: 7 general **9** World War I **10** World War II **16** Army Chief of Staff
  supreme commander of: 6 Allies **15** European Defense (NATO) **18** US occupation forces (Europe)
  head of: 18 Joint Chiefs of Staff
notable events of lifetime/term: 4 D-Day, NATO
  Acts: 11 Civil Rights
  battle of the: 5 Bulge
  conference: 7 Big Four **10** NATO Summit **11** Paris Summit
  Cuba taken over by: 11 Fidel Castro
  invasion: 8 Normandy
  trial/execution of: 14 Ethel Rosenberg **15** Julius Rosenberg
  USSR shot down: 9 U-Two plane
father: 10 David Jacob
mother: 3 Ida (Elizabeth Stover)
siblings: 3 Roy **4** Earl, Paul **5** Edgar **6** Arthur, Milton
wife: 5 Marie (Geneva Doud)
  nickname: 5 Mamie
children: 10 Doud Dwight **15** John Sheldon Doud
ejaculate 4 howl, yell, yelp **5** shout **6** bellow, cry out **7** exclaim **10** vociferate
ejaculation 3 cry **4** howl, yell, yelp **5** shout **6** bellow, outcry, shriek, squeal

7 screech **11** exclamation **12** vociferation

eject 4 emit, oust, spew **5** evict, exile, expel, exude, spout **6** banish, bounce, deport, remove **7** cast out, kick out, spit out, turn out **8** disgorge, drive out, force out, throw out **9** discharge **10** dispossess

ejection 4 gush **5** spurt **6** ouster **7** issuing, removal **8** emission, eruption, eviction **9** dismissal, expelling, expulsion **10** banishment **11** throwing out

Ekdal, Hjalmar
character in: **11** The Wild Duck
author: **5** Ibsen

eke 3 add **4** also **7** augment, enlarge, stretch **8** increase, lengthen, likewise, moreover **10** in addition, supplement

elaborate 5 fancy, gaudy, showy **6** expand, flashy, garish, ornate **7** clarify, complex, elegant, labored, specify **8** involved, overdone **9** embellish, intricate **10** add details **11** complicated, painstaking **12** ostentatious **13** particularize

elaborate on 6 expand **7** amplify, develop **9** embellish **10** supplement **11** expatiate on

elaboration 11 added detail, rounding out **12** augmentation **13** amplification, embellishment

Elaine
character in: **16** Arthurian romance
called: **8** lily maid
home: **7** Astolat
lover: **8** Lancelot
son: **7** Galahad
father: **6** Pelles

Elais
father: **5** Anius
mother: **7** Dorippe
changed things into: **3** oil

elan 4 dash, zeal **5** flair, verve, vigor **6** energy, spirit **8** vivacity **9** animation **10** enthusiasm

eland 3 elk **8** antelope **11** taurotragus

elapse 4 go by, pass **5** lapse **6** pass by, roll by, slip by **7** glide by, slide by **8** slip away **9** intervene

elastic 6 pliant, supple **7** pliable, rubbery, springy **8** flexible, tolerant, yielding **9** adaptable, recoiling, resilient **10** rebounding, responsive **11** complaisant, stretchable **12** recuperative **13** accommodating

elate 5 cheer, exalt **6** excite, lift up, please **7** animate, delight, elevate, enliven, gladden, gratify, inspire **10** exhilarate

elated 4 glad **5** happy, proud **6** joyful, joyous **7** exalted, excited, gleeful, pleased **8** animated, blissful, ecstatic, jubilant **9** overjoyed, rejoicing **10** delightful **11** exhilarated **13** in high spirits **18** flushed with success

elation 3 joy **4** glee **5** pride **7** triumph

8 gladness **9** happiness **10** excitement, exultation, jubilation **12** cheerfulness

elbow grease 4 work **5** force, labor **6** effort, energy, muscle **8** exertion, hard work **11** application

elbow in 4 push **5** force, press, shove **6** horn in **7** crowd in

El Cordobes (Manuel Benitez Perez)
sport: **12** bullfighting

elder 4 head **5** older **6** senior **8** old-timer **9** firstborn, patriarch, presbyter **14** church official **15** church dignitary
French: **4** aine

elder, elderberry 8 Sambucus
varieties: **3** Box **4** Blue **5** Dwarf, Sweet **6** Ground, Poison, Yellow **8** American, European, Stinking **10** Red-berried **11** American red, European red **15** Pacific Coast red

elderly 3 old **4** aged **9** venerable **11** over the hill **13** past one's prime

Eldorado
nickname of: **10** California

Eleanor and Franklin
author: **11** Joseph P Lash

Eleazar
father: **4** Dodo **5** Aaron, Elind, Mahli **6** Parosh **7** Phineas **8** Abinadab
mother: **8** Elisheba
brother: **5** Abihu, Nadab **7** Ithamar
succeeded: **5** Aaron

elect 4 pick **5** adopt **6** choose, opt for, select, take up **7** embrace, espouse, fix upon, pick out **8** decide on, settle on **9** single out

election 4 poll, vote **6** choice, option, voting **7** resolve **8** decision **9** balloting, selection **10** resolution **11** alternative **13** determination

electioneer 3 run **5** stump **8** campaign **11** whistle-stop **12** beat the drums, solicit votes

elective 8 optional **9** selective, voluntary **11** not required **12** open to choice, passed by vote **13** discretionary, not obligatory

Electra
author: **9** Euripides, Sophocles
character: **7** Orestes, Pylades **8** Dioscuri **9** Aegisthus **12** Clytemnestra
father: **9** Agamemnon
mother: **12** Clytemnestra
brother: **7** Orestes
sister: **9** Iphigenia **12** Chrysothemis
husband: **7** Pylades
son: **5** Medon **9** Strophius

electric 7 dynamic, rousing **8** exalting, exciting, spirited, stirring **9** inspiring, thrilling **10** full of fire **11** galvanizing, power-driven, stimulating **12** electrifying, soul-stirring

electric battery
invented by: **5** Volta

electricity measure 3 ohm **4** volt, watt **5** joule **6** ampere **10** horsepower

Electric Kool-Aid Acid Test, The
author: **8** Tom Wolfe

electrify 4 daze, stir, stun **5** amaze, rouse **6** dazzle, excite, fire up, thrill **7** animate, astound, quicken, startle **8** astonish, surprise **9** fascinate, galvanize, stimulate **18** take one's breath away

electrifying 8 dazzling, shocking, stunning **10** astounding, stupefying **11** astonishing

electromagnet
invented by: **8** Sturgeon

Electryon
king of: **7** Mycenae
father: **7** Perseus
mother: **9** Andromeda
brother: **6** Mestor **9** Sthenelus
wife: **5** Anaxo
son: **9** Licymnius
daughter: **7** Alcmene
grandson: **8** Hercules

eleemosynary 10 altruistic, beneficent, benevolent, charitable **13** philanthropic **15** non-profitmaking

elegance 5 class, grace, taste **6** purity **7** balance **8** delicacy, grandeur, richness, symmetry **10** refinement **12** gracefulness **13** exquisiteness, luxuriousness, sumptuousness

elegant 4 fine, rich **5** grand **6** classy, dapper, lovely, ornate, polite, urbane **7** classic, courtly, genteel, refined, stylish **8** artistic, charming, debonair, delicate, graceful, gracious, handsome, polished, tasteful, well-bred **9** beautiful, dignified, exquisite, luxurious, sumptuous **10** attractive, cultivated **11** fashionable, symmetrical **16** wellproportioned

elegiac 3 sad **8** funereal, mournful **10** melancholy

elegy 7 requiem, sad poem **11** funeral song **14** melancholy poem **16** lament for the dead **17** poem of lamentation, song of lamentation **22** melancholy piece of music

Elegy Written in a Country Churchyard
author: **10** Thomas Gray

Elektra *see* **7** Electra

element, elements 3 air **4** fire **5** earth, water **6** basics, member, milieu **7** essence, factors, origins **8** original **9** basic part, basic unit, component, rudiments **10** basic ideas, ingredient, principles, simple body **11** constituent, environment, foundations, native state, subdivision **13** building block, component part, natural medium **14** natural habitat

elemental 5 basal, basic **10** elementary **11** fundamental, rudimentary

elementary 4 easy **5** basal, basic,

crude, first, plain **6** simple **7** primary
8 original **9** elemental, primitive **11**
fundamental, rudimentary,
undeveloped **13** uncomplicated

elephant
group of: 4 herd
types: 5 Asian **7** African
features: 5 trunk, tusks
famous: 5 Babar, Dumbo
elephant boy: 4 Sabu **6** mahout
extinct: 7 mammoth **8** mastodon
produce: 5 ivory

elephantine 4 huge **7** immense, mammoth, titanic **8** colossal, enormous, gigantic **9** ponderous **10** gargantuan,
tremendous **14** Brobdingnagian

Elephant Man, The
director: 10 David Lynch
cast: 8 John Hurt **11** John Gielgud,
Wendy Hiller **12** Anne Bancroft **14**
Anthony Hopkins

Eleusinian mysteries
in memory of: 10 Persephone
in honor of: 7 Bacchus, Demeter
celebrated at: 6 Athens **7** Eleusis
founded by: 8 Eumolpus
god of: 7 Bacchus

elevate 4 lift **5** boost, cheer, elate,
heave, hoist, raise **6** better, excite, lift
up, move up, perk up, refine, uplift **7**
advance, animate, dignify, enhance,
ennoble, improve, inspire, promote,
upraise **8** heighten **9** place high **10**
exhilarate, raise aloft

elevated 4 high **5** lofty **6** raised **7** exalted **8** improved, uplifted **9** prominent **10** heightened

elevation 4 hill, lift, rise **5** boost **6** ascent, height **8** altitude, mountain **9**
acclivity, bettering, high place, promotion **10** prominence, refinement **11**
advancement, cultivation, improvement

elevator 4 cage, lift, silo, wing **5** hoist
7 granary **10** dumbwaiter
inventor: 4 Otis

elevator brake
invented by: 4 Otis

elf 4 puck **5** fairy, gnome, pixie, troll **6**
goblin, sprite **7** brownie, gremlin **9**
hobgoblin **10** leprechaun

elfin 3 fey, wee **4** tiny **7** pixyish **9**
fairylike **10** diminutive

Elgar, Sir Edward William
born: 7 England **10** Broadheath
composer of: 8 Falstaff **9** Cockaigne,
Froissart **10** Caractacus, The Kingdom **11** The Apostles **14** The Black
Knight, The Light of Life **16** Enigma
Variations **19** Pomp and Circumstance, The Banner of St George, The
Dream of Gerontius **30** Scenes from
the Bavarian Highlands

Eli
son: 6 Hophni **7** Phineas
home: 6 Shiloh **10** high priest
teacher of: 6 Samuel

Eli, Eli, Lama sabachthani
means: 31 My God My God why hast
thou forsaken me?

Elia *see* **11** Lamb, Charles

elicit 5 cause, educe, evoke, exact,
fetch, wrest **6** derive, extort **7** draw
out, extract **9** call forth, draw forth **10**
bring forth **12** bring to light

elide 4 omit, slur **5** annul **6** delete **7**
neglect **8** slur over, suppress **9** eliminate, strikeout **10** abbreviate

Eliezar
father: 5 Moses
mother: 8 Zipporah
brother: 7 Gershom

eligible 6 proper **7** fitting **8** suitable **9**
desirable, qualified **10** acceptable, applicable, authorized, worthwhile **11**
appropriate

Elihu
brother: 5 David
friend: 3 Job **6** Bildad, Zophar **7** Eliphaz

Elijah 7 prophet
opposed: 4 Ahab, Baal **7** Jezebel
successor: 6 Elisha

Elimelech
wife: 5 Naomi

eliminate 4 drop, omit, oust **5** eject,
erase, exile, expel **6** banish, cut out,
delete, except, reject, remove, rub out
7 abolish, cast out, dismiss, exclude,
weed out **8** get rid of, leave out,
stamp out, throw out **9** eradicate **10**
annihilate, do away with **11** exterminate

Eliot, George
real name: 13 Mary Anne Evans
author of: 6 Romola **8** Adam Bede
11 Middlemarch, Silas Marner **17**
The Mill on the Floss

Eliot, John
author of: 12 Bay Psalm Book

Eliot, T S
author of: 9 East Coker, Gerontion,
Hollow Men **11** Burnt Norton, Dry
Salvages **12** Ash Wednesday, Four
Quartets, The Waste Land **13** Little
Gidding, The Sacred Wood **16** The
Family Reunion **20** Murder in the
Cathedral **27** Sweeney Among the
Nightingales **28** The Love Song of J
Alfred Prufrock
inspiration for: 4 Cats

Eliphaz
father: 4 Adah, Esau
friend: 3 Job **5** Elihu **6** Bildad, Zophar

Elisabeth *see* **9** Elizabeth

Elisha 7 prophet
home: 11 Abelmeholah
succeeded: 6 Elijah

elite 3 top **4** best **5** cream **6** choice,
flower **7** bigwigs, society, the pick,
wealthy **8** big shots, notables **9** haut
monde **10** blue bloods, personages,

select body, upper class **11** aristocracy, celebrities, high society **14**
creme-de-la-creme

elixir 6 potion, remedy **7** essence, extract, panacea, spirits **8** tincture **11**
concentrate **17** alcoholic solution

Eliza
character in: 14 Uncle Tom's Cabin
author: 5 Stowe

Elizabeth
husband: 9 Zacharias, Zechariah
son: 14 John the Baptist

Elizabeth I
queen of: 7 England
father: 10 Henry Tudor **14** Henry the
Eighth
mother: 10 Anne Boleyn
sister: 4 Mary **10** Bloody Mary
brother: 14 Edward the Sixth
advisor: 5 Cecil **8** Burghley **10** Wal-
singham
suitor: 5 Essex **6** Dudley **9** Leicester
victory over: 13 Spanish Armada

Elizabeth II
father: 14 George the Sixth
mother: 9 Elizabeth
husband: 17 Philip Mountbatten
son: 6 Andrew, Edward **7** Charles
daughter: 4 Anne
daughter-in-law: 5 Diana, Sarah
(Fergie)

Elizabeth the Queen
author: 15 Maxwell Anderson

elk
group of: 4 gang

Ellas *see* **6** Greece

Ellerbee, Linda 6 writer **10** newscaster
book: 11 And So It Goes

Ellice Islands *see* **6** Tuvalu

Ellington, Duke
real name: 22 Edward Kennedy Ellington
born: 12 Washington DC
composer of: 10 Mood Indigo **14**
Creole Love Call, Creole Rhapsody,
Hot and Bothered **17** Concerto for
Cootie **18** Black and Tan Fantasy

Elliot family
characters in: 10 Persuasion
member: 4 Anne **7** William **9** Elizabeth, Sir Walter
author: 6 Austen

Ellison, Harlan
author of: 7 Paingod **10** Spider Kiss
13 A Boy and His Dog **16** Deathbird
Stories **19** Approaching Oblivion **20**
Alone Against Tomorrow

Ellison, Ralph
author of: 12 Invisible Man

elm 5 Ulmus
varieties: 3 red **4** bush, cork, rock,
vase, wych **5** cedar, Dutch, dwarf,
globe, wahoo, water, white **6** Exeter,
horned, Jersey, moline, Scotch, willow, winged **7** Belgian, Chinese, Cor-

nish, English, Holland **8** American, fern-leaf, Guernsey, Japanese, Siberian, slippery, tabletop, wheatley **9** September **10** camperdown, Chichester, Huntingdon, smooth-leaf **11** small-leaved **13** European white

Elmer Gantry
author: **13** Sinclair Lewis
director: **13** Richard Brooks
cast: **10** Dean Jagger **11** Jean Simmons **12** Shirley Jones **13** Arthur Kennedy, Burt Lancaster
Oscar for: **5** actor (Lancaster) **17** supporting actress (Jones)

elocution 6 speech **7** diction, oratory **10** intonation **11** enunciation **12** articulation **13** pronunciation **14** public speaking

Elohim 3 God

Eloisa to Abelard
author: **13** Alexander Pope

Elon 11 Hebrew judge

elongate 6 extend **7** draw out, prolong **8** lengthen, protract **10** stretch out

elongated 4 long **8** drawn out, extended **9** prolonged **10** attenuated, lengthened, protracted **12** stretched out

eloquence 5 force, grace **7** fluency, oratory **8** rhetoric **9** elocution, speakwell, vividness **10** expression **12** silver tongue
god of: **4** Ogma **6** Ogmios **7** Mercury

eloquent 5 vivid **6** moving, poetic **8** emphatic, forceful, spirited, stirring, striking **10** articulate, passionate, persuasive **11** impassioned

El Salvador
other name: **9** Cuscatlan
capital/largest city: **11** San Salvador
others: **6** Cutuco, Izalco **7** Corinto, Metapan **8** Acajutla, Libertad, Santa Ana, Usulutan **9** San Miguel, Sonsonate **10** San Vicente, Santa Tecla **11** Union-Cutuco **12** Chalatenango
school: **15** Jose Simeon Canas **16** Alberto Masferrer
measure: **4** vara **5** cafiz, cahiz **6** fanega **7** batella, botella, cantara, manzana
monetary unit: **4** peso **5** colon **7** centavo
weight: **3** bag **4** caja **5** libra
lake: **5** Guiha, Guija **8** Ilopango **10** Coatepeque
mountain: **6** Izalco
highest point: **8** Santa Ana
river: **5** Jiboa, Lempa, Lopaz **6** Torola **7** de la Paz **9** Goasoaran **17** Grande de San Miguel
sea: **7** Pacific
physical feature:
    bay: **10** Jiquilisco
    coast: **6** Balsam
    gulf: **7** Fonseca
    point: **7** Amapala **8** Remedios
    valley: **7** Hamacas

people: 5 Lenca, Pipil **6** Indian, Mangue **7** mestizo, Spanish **9** Matagalpa
    artist: **8** Salarrue **10** Mejia Vides
    author: **8** Salarrue **14** Antonio Gavidia
    conqueror: **8** Alvarado
    leader: **6** Osorio **8** Jose Arce **13** Matias Delgado **15** Manuel Rodriguez **17** Hernandez Martinez
    philosopher/journalist: **9** Masferrer
language: **7** Spanish
religion: **13** Roman Catholic
place:
    ruins: **7** Tazumal
feature:
    blouse: **9** volcanena
    dance: **7** pasillo **15** los historiantes
    drum: **8** huehuetl
    estate: **5** finca
    musical instrument: **7** caramba
food:
    bread: **10** quesadilla
    cheese pancake: **6** pupusa

Elscheimer, Adam
born: **7** Germany **15** Frankfurt am Main
artwork: **17** Tobias and the Angel **21** The Stoning of St Stephen **24** Rest on the Flight into Egypt

else 3 and, too **4** also, more **5** if not, other **7** besides, instead **9** different, otherwise **10** additional, contrarily, in addition

elsewhere 4 away **6** except **7** absence, not here

Elsinore
castle in: **6** Hamlet **7** Denmark
author: **11** Shakespeare

Elton, Mr
character in: **4** Emma
author: **6** Austen

elucidate 6 detail **7** clarify, clear up, explain, expound **8** describe, spell out **9** delineate, explicate, interpret, make plain **10** illuminate, illustrate **11** comment upon **14** throw light upon

elucidation 7 account **10** commentary **11** description, explanation, explication **13** clarification **14** interpretation **15** exemplification

elude 4 shun **5** avoid, dodge, evade **6** escape, slip by **10** circumvent, fight shy of **11** get away from, keep clear of

eluding 7 dodging, ducking, evading, evasion **8** avoiding **9** avoidance **12** escaping from, sidestepping **13** circumventing **15** getting away from

Elul 16 sixth Hebrew month

elusive 4 foxy, wily **6** crafty, shifty, tricky **7** evasive **8** baffling, puzzling, slippery **11** hard to catch, hard to grasp

elusory 4 wily **6** shifty **7** devious, dodging, elusive, evasive, hedging **8** slippery **9** ambiguous, deceitful,

deceptive, equivocal **10** misleading **12** equivocating

Elvsted, Thea
character in: **11** Hedda Gabler
author: **5** Ibsen

elysian 7 sublime **8** blissful, empyreal, empyrean, ethereal, heavenly **9** celestial, unearthly **12** otherworldly, paradisiacal

Elysium
also: **17** islands of the blest
afterworld of the: **7** blessed

Elytis, Odysseus
real name: **19** Odysseus Alepoudelis
author of: **10** Seemly It Is **20** Heroic and Elegiac Song

emaciated 4 lank, lean, thin **5** gaunt **6** sickly, skinny, wasted **7** haggard, scrawny, wizened **8** skeletal, starving, underfed **10** cadaverous **14** undernourished

emanate 4 flow, rise, stem, well **5** exude, issue **6** spring **7** give off, proceed **8** come from **9** come forth, originate, send forth

emanation 6 coming **7** arising, flowing, issuing **8** effusion **9** effluence, radiation, springing **10** exhalation **11** coming forth

emancipate 4 free **7** manumit, release, set free, unchain **8** liberate, unfetter **9** unshackle **12** set at liberty

emancipation 7 freedom, liberty **10** liberation **11** manumission **12** independence

emasculate 4 geld **5** alter **6** soften, weaken **8** castrate **9** undermine **10** devitalize

Emaux et Camees
author: **16** Theophile Gautier

Embalming
god of: **6** Anubis

embankment 4 bank, dike, wall **5** levee

embargo 3 ban **8** shutdown, stoppage **10** impediment, inhibition, injunction, quarantine, standstill **11** prohibition, restriction **12** interdiction, proscription **16** restraint of trade

embark 5 begin, board, start **6** launch, set out **7** enplane, entrain **8** commence, go aboard **9** board ship, enter upon

embark on 5 begin, start **8** approach, commence, initiate, set about **9** enter upon, undertake

embarras de richesses 13 overabundance **21** embarrassment of riches

embarrass 4 faze **5** abash, shame, upset **6** rattle **7** agitate, chagrin, confuse, fluster, mortify, nonplus **8** distress **9** discomfit **10** discompose, disconcert **13** make ill at ease **14** discountenance **17** make self-conscious

embarrassed 7 abashed **8** red-faced

9 chagrined, mortified **10** nonplussed **11** discomfited **13** self-conscious

embarrassing 7 awkward **8** confused, crushing **9** bothering **10** disturbing, mortifying, unpleasant **12** demoralizing, discomfiting **13** discomforting, disconcerting, uncomfortable

embarrassment 4 blot **5** stain **6** smirch **7** blemish, scandal, tarnish **8** disgrace **9** discredit **19** financial difficulty

embattled 8 fighting **9** embroiled, fortified **11** battle-ready, hard-pressed

embed 3 fix, set **4** bond **5** plant **6** fasten **8** ensconce **9** establish

embedded 3 set **5** fixed **6** bonded **7** engaged, planted **8** immersed, inserted **9** ensconced **11** established

embellish 4 gild **5** adorn, color **6** set off **7** dress up, enhance, fancy up, garnish, gussy up **8** beautify, decorate, ornament **9** elaborate, embroider **10** exaggerate

embellished 6 ornate **7** adorned, flowery **8** brocaded **9** decorated **10** beautified, elaborated, ornamented, rhetorical **11** embroidered

embellishment 5 frill **6** accent **7** garnish **8** furbelow, ornament, trimming **9** adornment **10** decoration, embroidery **11** elaboration **14** beautification **15** fuss and feathers

ember 3 ash **4** slag **6** cinder **7** clinker **8** live coal

embezzle 4 bilk, rook **5** cheat, filch **6** fleece **7** defraud, swindle **9** defalcate **14** misappropriate

embezzler 5 cheat, crook, thief **8** swindler

Embezzler, The
    author: **16** Louis Auchincloss

embitter 4 sour **6** rankle **7** envenom **10** make bitter **11** make cynical **13** make rancorous, make resentful **15** make pessimistic

Embla
    origin: **12** Scandinavian
    first: **5** woman
    made by: **4** gods
    made from: **4** tree

emblem 4 sign **5** badge **6** design, device, symbol **8** colophon, hallmark, insignia

emblematic 7 typical **8** symbolic **10** indicative **11** distinctive **14** characteristic, representative

embodiment 6 avatar **7** epitome, essence **14** representation **15** exemplification, personification

embody 4 fuse **5** blend, merge **6** typify **7** collect, contain, embrace, express, include, realize **8** manifest, organize **9** exemplify, personify, represent, symbolize **10** assimilate **11** consolidate, incorporate **12** substantiate

embolden 7 fortify, hearten, inspire **8** inspirit **9** encourage

emboldened 6 poised **7** assured, unfazed **9** confident, heartened, unabashed **10** courageous, encouraged, inspirited

embonpoint 9 plumpness, stoutness **15** in good condition

emboss 4 knob, knot, stud **5** adorn, chase **6** indent **7** engrave, exhaust **8** decorate

embossed 4 bold **6** raised **7** adorned, antique, knotted **8** engraved, indented **9** decorated, exhausted

embrace 3 hug **5** adopt, clasp, cover, grasp **6** accept, embody **7** contain, espouse, include, involve **8** comprise **9** encompass **10** comprehend **11** consolidate, incorporate

embroider 5 color **7** dress up **9** elaborate, embellish, fabricate **10** exaggerate **11** romanticize

embroidery 8 tapestry **9** adornment, gros point **10** crewelwork, decoration, needlework, petit point **11** imagination **12** exaggeration **13** ornamentation

embroil 4 trap **6** enmesh **7** ensnare, involve **8** entangle **10** complicate

embroiled 8 enmeshed **9** embattled, entangled **11** hard-pressed

embroilment 3 row **4** fray, tilt **5** brawl, brush, clash, melee **6** fracas, ruckus, rumpus, uproar **7** scuffle **8** conflict, disorder, struggle **9** confusion, imbroglio **10** contention **11** altercation **12** entanglement

embryo 3 bud, egg **4** germ **5** fetus, larva, ovule **6** budding, source **8** immature, rudiment **9** beginning **11** rudimentary, undeveloped

embryonic 5 rough **6** unborn **7** nascent **8** immature, inchoate **9** beginning, imperfect, incipient **10** incomplete, unfinished **11** rudimentary, undeveloped

emend 4 edit **6** change, revise **7** correct, improve, rectify

emendation 8 revision **10** alteration, correction **11** improvement

emerald
    species: **5** beryl
    source: **4** Muzo **5** Egypt, India **6** Chivor **8** Colombia, Rhodesia, Zimbabwe **11** South Africa, Soviet Union **13** Ural Mountains
    color: **5** green

Emerald City
    setting in: **13** The Wizard of Oz
    author: **4** Baum

Emerald Isle see **7** Ireland

emerge 3 run **4** dawn, emit, flow, gush, loom, pour, rise **5** arise, issue **6** appear, come up, crop up, escape, stream, turn up **7** develop, surface **9** come forth, discharge **11** come to

light **12** come into view **13** become visible **14** become apparent, become manifest

emergence 4 dawn **7** dawning **10** appearance **11** development **13** coming to light, manifestation **15** materialization

emergency 5 pinch **6** crisis **7** urgency **8** exigency **11** contingency, predicament **16** unforeseen danger

Emergency
    character: **8** (Dr) Joe Early, (Paramedic) John Gage **9** (Paramedic) Roy DeSoto **11** (Nurse) Dixie McCall **13** (Dr) Kelly Brackett
    cast: **10** Bobby Troup, Kevin Tighe **11** Julie London **12** Robert Fuller **16** Randolph Mantooth

Emerson, Ralph Waldo
    nickname: **13** Sage of Concord
    author of: **4** Fate **6** Brahma, Nature **10** Friendship, The Rhodora **12** Compensation, Self-Reliance **14** The Concord Hymn **18** The American Scholar
    philosophy: **17** Transcendentalism

emeute 4 riot

emigrant 6 emigre **8** wanderer, wayfarer **10** expatriate

Emigrants, The
    author: **10** Johan Bojer

emigrate 4 move, quit **5** leave **6** depart, remove **7** migrate

emigration 5 exile **6** exodus **12** expatriation

emigre 2 DP **5** alien, exile **7** evacuee, refugee **8** defector, emigrant, expellee, fugitive **9** immigrant **10** expatriate **15** displaced person **16** political refugee

Emile
    author: **19** Jean Jacques Rousseau
    treatise on: **9** education

Emilia
    character in: **7** Othello
    husband: **4** Iago
    author: **11** Shakespeare

eminence 4 fame, hill, note, peak, rise **5** bluff, cliff, glory, knoll, ridge **6** height, repute, summit, upland **7** hillock, hummock **8** mountain, standing **9** celebrity, elevation, greatness, high place, high point **10** excellence, importance, notability, prominence, promontory, reputation **11** distinction, preeminence **12** elevated rank, high position, public esteem **15** conspicuousness

eminence grise 15 unofficial power
    literally: **12** gray eminence

eminent 3 top **5** grand, great, noted **6** famous, signal, utmost **7** exalted, notable, unusual **8** elevated, esteemed, glorious, imposing, laureate, renowned **9** important, memorable, paramount, prominent, well-known **10** celebrated, noteworthy, preeminent, remarkable **11** high-ranking, illustrious, outstanding **13** distinguished, extraordinary

emir 4 amir, Arab, Turk **5** chief, emeer, ruler **6** leader, prince **9** chieftain, commander, dignitary

emissary 5 agent, envoy **6** deputy, herald, legate **7** courier **8** delegate **9** go-between, messenger **10** ambassador **14** representative

emission 5 fumes, smoke, waste **8** ejection, emitting, impurity, issuance, voidance **9** discharge, emanation, excretion, expulsion, extrusion, pollutant **10** sending out **11** throwing out **12** transmission

emit 4 beam, give, shed, vent **5** expel, issue **7** cast out, excrete, secrete, send out **8** dispatch, throw out, transmit **9** discharge, give forth, pour forth

Emma
author: **10** Jane Austen
character: **7** Mr Elton **9** Miss Bates, Mrs Weston **11** Jane Fairfax **12** Harriet Smith, Robert Martin **13** Emma Woodhouse **14** Frank Churchill **15** George Knightley

Emmanuel 7 Messiah **11** Jesus Christ
means: **9** God with us

emollient 3 oil **4** balm **5** balmy, cream, salve **6** lotion **7** calming, easeful, healing, unguent **8** allaying, lenitive, ointment, relaxing, soothing **9** assuasive, lubricant, relieving **10** palliative **11** alleviative, restorative

emolument 3 fee, pay **4** gain, wage **6** income, profit, salary **7** benefit, stipend **9** advantage **10** honorarium **12** compensation, remuneration

emotion 4 fear, hate, heat, love, zeal **5** anger, ardor, pride **6** fervor, sorrow, warmth **7** concern, despair, passion, sadness **8** jealousy **9** agitation, happiness, sentiment, vehemence **10** excitement **12** satisfaction

emotional 4 warm **5** fiery **6** ardent, moving **7** fervent, zealous **8** stirring, touching **9** excitable, impetuous, thrilling, wrought-up **10** high-strung, hysterical, passionate, responsive, vulnerable **11** impassioned, sentimental, tear-jerking **12** enthusiastic, heartwarming, heart-rending, soul-stirring **13** demonstrative, temperamental **14** hypersensitive

emotionalism 8 hysteria **9** gushiness, hysterics, melodrama, theatrics **11** mawkishness **13** melodramatics, show of emotion **14** sentimentality **17** demonstrativeness

emotionless 6 stolid **7** unmoved **9** apathetic, impassive, unfeeling **11** passionless, unemotional

emperor, empress 4 czar, king, shah **5** queen, ruler **6** caesar, kaiser, mikado, sultan **7** czarina, monarch, sultana **9** sovereign **14** dowager empress

Emperor Jones, The
author: **12** Eugene O'Neill
character: **4** Jeff **8** Smithers **11** Brutus Jones

Emperor's New Clothes, The
author: **21** Hans Christian Andersen

emphasis 6 accent, stress, weight **7** feature **10** focal point **12** accentuation, underscoring

emphasize 6 accent, stress **7** dwell on, feature, iterate, point up **9** press home, punctuate, underline **10** accentuate, underscore

emphatic 4 flat **6** marked, strong **7** certain, decided, express, telling **8** absolute, decisive, definite, distinct, forceful, striking, vigorous **9** assertive, insistent, momentous **10** pronounced, undeniable, unwavering, unyielding **11** categorical, conspicuous, significant, unequivocal, unqualified **12** unmistakable

empire 4 rule **5** realm **6** domain **8** dominion, imperium **11** sovereignty **12** commonwealth

Empire State
nickname of: **7** New York

Empire State of the South
nickname of: **7** Georgia

Empire Strikes Back, The
director: **13** Irvin Kershner
cast: **10** Kenny Baker, Mark Hamill (Luke Skywalker) **11** David Prowse, Peter Mayhew **12** Alec Guinness, Carrie Fisher (Princess Leia), Harrison Ford (Han Solo) **14** Anthony Daniels (C3PO) **16** Billy Dee Williams (Lando Calrissian)
sequel to: **8** Star Wars
sequel: **15** Return of the Jedi

empirical 9 firsthand, practical, pragmatic **12** experiential, experimental

employ 3 use **4** hire **5** apply **6** devote, engage, occupy, retain, take on **7** service, utilize **8** exercise, keep busy, put to use **9** make use of **10** commission, employment **12** retainership

employee 6 member, worker **8** hireling **9** job holder, underling **10** wage earner

employer 4 boss, firm **6** outfit **7** company **8** business **10** proprietor **12** organization **13** establishment

employment 3 job, use **4** line, task, work **5** chore, field, trade, using **6** employ **7** calling, pursuit, service **8** business, exercise, exertion, vocation **9** employing **10** engagement, occupation, profession **11** application, utilization **13** preoccupation

emporium 5 store **6** bazaar, market **9** warehouse **10** large store **12** general store **15** department store

empower 4 vest **5** allow, endow **6** enable, invest, permit **7** license **8** delegate, sanction **9** authorize **10** commission

empress 5 queen, ruler **7** czarina, monarch, sultana, tsarina **9** sovereign

emprise 7 venture **9** adventure **10** enterprise **11** undertaking

emptied 6 used up **7** drained, vacated **8** consumed, depleted, finished **9** evacuated, exhausted

emptiness 4 void **6** vacuum **7** vacancy **8** bareness **10** barrenness, desolation, hollowness

empty 4 bare, dump, flow, idle, void **5** banal, drain, inane **6** futile, hollow, vacant **7** aimless, debouch, insipid, pour out, shallow, trivial, vacuous **8** evacuate **9** discharge, frivolous, worthless **10** unoccupied **11** meaningless, purposeless, unfulfilled, uninhabited **13** insignificant

empty space 3 gap **4** void **5** blank **6** cavity, lacuna, vacuum **7** vacancy

empyrean 7 elysian, sublime **8** blissful, heavenly **9** celestial **12** paradisiacal

emu
also: **4** emeu
form: **4** bird
habitat: **9** Australia
characteristic: **9** nonflying, three toed

emulate 3 ape **4** copy **5** mimic, rival **6** follow **7** imitate

emulative 5 model **9** exemplary

enable 3 aid **5** allow **6** assist, permit **7** benefit, empower, qualify, support **8** make able **10** capacitate, facilitate **15** make possible for

enact 4 pass **6** decree, ratify **7** approve **8** proclaim, sanction **9** authorize, institute, legislate **11** pass into law **12** vote to accept

enactment 3 law **4** bill **5** canon, edict, ukase **6** decree **7** statute **9** ordinance, prescript **11** legislation **12** proclamation, ratification

enamel 4 coat **5** paint **7** coating **10** nail polish **12** glossy finish, tooth coating

enamor 5 charm **6** allure, attach, draw to, excite **7** bewitch, enchant **8** enthrall, entrance **9** captivate, enrapture, fascinate, infatuate **12** take a fancy to

enamored 6 in love **7** amorous **8** lovesick **10** infatuated

en arriere 8 backward

en avant 6 onward **7** forward

en bloc 8 as a whole

encage 3 pen **4** cage **5** pen in **6** coop up, lock up, shut in **7** confine **8** restrain **11** incarcerate

encamp 4 camp **7** bivouac **9** set up camp **10** pitch a tent

encampment 4 camp **5** tents **7** bivouac **8** tent city

encase 4 wrap **5** cover **6** enfold, enwrap **7** enclose, envelop, sheathe

enceinte 8 pregnant

Enceladus
form: **5** giant
hit by: **5** stone
stone flung by: **6** Athena
location: **6** Sicily
buried under: **9** Mount Etna

enchain 7 enslave, shackle **8** enthrall **11** put in chains **13** hold in bondage

enchant 3 hex **5** charm **7** bewitch, delight **8** enthrall, entrance **9** captivate, enrapture, fascinate, hypnotize, mesmerize, transport **14** cast a spell over **16** place under a spell

enchanted 7 charmed, pleased **9** bewitched, delighted, entranced **10** captivated, enraptured, enthralled, spellbound **11** under a spell

enchanting 8 charming, pleasant **9** agreeable, wonderful **10** bewitching, delightful, entrancing **11** captivating, enthralling, fascinating, hypnotizing **12** spellbinding **15** casting a spell on **17** casting a spell over

enchantment 5 spell **6** allure, appeal **9** magnetism **10** attraction **11** captivation, fascination

enchantress 4 vamp **5** siren, witch **7** charmer, vampire **9** sorceress, temptress **10** seductress **11** femme fatale

Enchiridion
author: **11** St Augustine

encircle 4 gird, ring, wall **5** fence, hem in **6** circle, girdle **7** enclose, wreathe **8** surround **9** encompass **12** circumscribe

enclose, inclose 4 ring **6** circle, girdle, insert, wall in **7** close in, fence in, include **8** encircle, surround **9** encompass, send along **12** circumscribe

enclosed area 4 quad **5** court, patio **6** atrium **9** courtyard **10** quadrangle

enclosure 3 sty **4** cage, coop, jail, wall **5** fence, hedge, stall **6** corral, kennel, pigsty **7** paddock, wrapper **8** envelope, stockade **9** cartridge, inclosure **10** receptacle

encomium 5 kudos, paean **6** eulogy **7** plaudit, tribute **8** citation **9** laudation, panegyric **11** acclamation

encompass 4 hold, ring **5** cover, hem in **6** circle, embody, girdle, take in, wall in **7** contain, embrace, enclose, fence in, include, involve, touch on **8** comprise, encircle, surround **11** incorporate **12** circumscribe

encounter 4 bout, face, meet **5** brush, clash, fight **6** affray, battle, combat, endure, fracas, suffer **7** run into, sustain, undergo **8** come upon, confront, meet with, skirmish **9** clash with **10** chance upon, engagement, experience **11** grapple with **12** do battle with, meet and fight, skirmish with **13** confrontation **14** contend against, engage in combat, hostile meeting **18** come face to face with

Encounters with the Archdruid
author: **10** John McPhee

encourage 3 aid **4** help, spur, sway **5** boost, cheer, egg on, favor, impel, rally **6** assist, exhort, foster, induce, prompt **7** advance, forward, further, hearten, inspire, promote **8** embolden, inspirit, reassure **10** give hope to

encouragement 4 lift **5** boost **6** praise **7** backing, support **11** approbation, encouraging, reassurance **12** shot in the arm **13** reinforcement

encroach 6 invade **7** impinge, intrude, overrun, violate **8** infringe, overstep, trespass **9** break into, interfere **10** transgress **11** make inroads

encumber 3 tax **4** lade, load **6** burden, hinder, impede, saddle **8** handicap, load down, obstruct, slow down **9** weigh down **13** inconvenience

encumbrance 4 load, onus **6** burden **9** hindrance **10** impediment **11** obstruction **13** inconvenience

Encyclopedia
author: **9** D'Alembert **12** Denis Diderot

encyclopedic 5 broad **7** erudite **9** scholarly, universal **10** exhaustive **11** wide-ranging **13** comprehensive **15** all-encompassing

end 3 aim **4** edge, goal, halt, kill, ruin, stop **5** cease, close, death, issue, limit, scrap **6** border, demise, design, effect, ending, finale, finish, object, result, run out, upshot, windup **7** destroy, outcome, purpose, remnant **8** boundary, conclude, fragment, leave off, leftover, terminus **9** cessation, eradicate, extremity, finish off, intention, objective, terminate **10** annihilate, completion, conclusion, denouement, expiration, extinction, extinguish, put an end to, settlement **11** consequence, culmination, destruction, exterminate, fulfillment, termination **12** annihilation, consummation, draw to a close **13** extermination **19** bring down the curtain

endanger 4 risk **6** expose, hazard **7** imperil **8** threaten **10** compromise, jeopardize **11** put in danger

endear 8 make dear **10** ingratiate **11** make beloved

endearment 7 pet name **9** sweet talk **10** loving word **12** sweet nothing **13** fond utterance

endeavor 3 aim, job, try **4** seek, work **5** essay, labor **6** aspire, career, effort, strive, work at **7** attempt **8** exertion, interest, striving, struggle, vocation **9** take pains, undertake **10** do one's best, enterprise, occupation **11** undertaking **12** make an effort **13** preoccupation

ended 4 done, over **6** ceased, closed, halted, runout **7** expired, stopped, wound up **8** finished, over with,

resulted **9** completed, concluded, destroyed **10** terminated **11** annihilated **12** discontinued, exterminated

Enderby
author: **14** Anthony Burgess

end from which
Latin: **12** terminus a quo

ending 3 end **5** close **6** finale, finish, windup **9** cessation **10** completion, conclusion, expiration **11** culmination, termination **12** consummation

ending point
Latin: **14** terminus ad quem

Ending Up
author: **12** Kingsley Amis

endless 7 eternal **8** constant, infinite, unbroken, unending **9** boundless, continual, perpetual, unlimited **10** continuous, persistent, without end **11** everlasting, measureless, never-ending **12** interminable **13** uninterrupted

endlessly 7 forever **10** constantly **11** ceaselessly, continually, perpetually **12** continuously
Latin: **11** ad infinitum

endocrine system
component: **5** ovary **6** testes, thymus **7** adrenal, thyroid **9** pituitary **11** parathyroid

endocuticle
consists of: **6** chitin

end of the century
French: **11** fin de siecle

End of the Road, The
author: **9** John Barth

end of the world 8 doomsday **10** Armageddon **11** Judgment Day **13** Day of Judgment **15** the Last Judgment

End of the World News, The
author: **14** Anthony Burgess

endorse, indorse 2 OK **4** back, sign **6** affirm, ratify, second **7** approve, certify, support **8** advocate, champion, sanction, validate, vouch for **9** authorize, recommend **11** countersign, stand behind, subscribe to **14** lend one's name to

endorsement 2 OK **7** support **8** approval **9** signature **10** acceptance **12** commendation, ratification **14** seal of approval **16** official sanction

endow 4 will **5** award, bless, equip, favor, grace, grant, leave **6** accord, bestow, confer, invest, supply **7** furnish, provide **8** bequeath, settle on

endowed 6 graced **7** blessed, favored **8** bestowed, enriched, provided **10** bequeathed

endowment 4 gift **5** award, flair, grant **6** legacy, talent **7** ability, bequest, faculty **8** aptitude, donation **9** attribute **10** capability **11** benefaction, natural gift

end to which
Latin: **14** terminus ad quem

endue 5 dress, endow, equip, indue,

put on **6** bestow, clothe, outfit, supply **7** furnish

endurable 8 bearable **9** tolerable **11** sustainable

endurance 7 stamina **8** strength, tenacity **9** fortitude, hardihood, stability **10** durability, permanence, resolution **11** durableness, persistence **12** immutability, perseverance, staying power **13** tenaciousness **14** changelessness **16** stick-to-itiveness

endure 4 bear, last, live **5** brave, brook, stand **6** live on, remain, suffer **7** persist, prevail, sustain, undergo, weather **8** continue, cope with, tolerate **9** go through, withstand **10** experience **11** bear up under, countenance

enduring 7 abiding, durable, eternal, lasting **8** constant, unending **9** immutable, permanent, steadfast **10** changeless, continuing, unchanging **11** everlasting, long-lasting **12** indissoluble

Endymion
  author: 9 John Keats
  form: 5 youth
  father: 8 Aethlios
  mother: 6 Calyce
  loved by: 4 Moon **6** Selene
  son: 5 Epeus, Paeon **7** Aetolus
  number of daughters: 5 fifty
  granddaughter: 7 Hyrmina

enemy 3 foe **5** rival **7** nemesis **8** armed foe, attacker, opponent **9** adversary, assailant, detractor **10** antagonist, competitor

Enemy of the People, An
  author: 11 Henrik Ibsen

energetic 5 alert, brisk, peppy, zippy **6** active, lively, robust **7** dynamic **8** animated, forceful, restless, spirited, vigorous **9** go-getting **11** hardworking, high-powered, industrious, quick-witted **12** enthusiastic

energize 7 animate, enliven, quicken **8** vitalize **9** galvanize, stimulate **10** invigorate, strengthen

energy 2 go **3** pep, vim, zip **4** elan, zeal, zest **5** drive, force, power, verve, vigor **6** hustle **8** dynamism, vitality, vivacity **9** animation **10** enterprise, liveliness

enervate 3 fag **4** bush, tire **5** weary **6** tucker, weaken **7** deplete, disable, exhaust, fatigue, wash out **8** enfeeble **9** prostrate **10** debilitate, devitalize **13** sap one's energy

enervated 5 spent **6** effete, wasted **7** languid, worn-out **8** fatigued, listless, sluggish, unmanned, unnerved, weakened **9** enfeebled, exhausted, lethargic, washed out **11** debilitated, devitalized, emasculated

enervation 7 fatigue **9** tiredness, weariness **10** exhaustion

en famille 11 in the family

Enfants Terribles, Les
  author: 11 Jean Cocteau

enfant terrible 16 indiscreet person **17** incorrigible child **19** irresponsible person

enfeeble 3 sap **6** impair, weaken **8** enervate **10** debilitate

enfin 7 finally **8** in the end **12** in conclusion

enfold 4 veil, wrap **5** cloak, cover **6** encase, enwrap, shroud **7** blanket, contain, embrace, enclose, envelop, sheathe **8** surround

enforce 5 apply, exact **6** defend, impose **7** execute, support **8** carry out, insist on **9** implement **10** administer

enforcement 5 force **6** duress **7** defense, support **8** coercion, pressure **9** execution **10** compulsion, constraint, imposition, obligation **11** carrying out **13** necessitation, strengthening **14** implementation

engage 4 hire **6** absorb, combat, employ, occupy, pledge, retain, secure, take on **7** betroth, engross, involve, partake, promise, war with **8** affiance, embark on, set about, take part **9** enter into, fight with, undertake **10** commission **11** busy oneself, participate **12** give battle to **15** take into service

engaged 5 hired, in use **6** active, took on **7** partook, pledged, secured **8** absorbed, employed, involved, occupied, promised, retained, took part **9** affianced, betrothed, engrossed, undertook **10** embarked on **11** entered into, particpated **15** took into service

engagement 3 gig, job **4** bout, date, duty, fray, post **5** banns, berth, brush, fight, troth **6** action, battle, billet, combat **7** contest, meeting, scuffle **8** conflict, position, skirmish **9** betrothal, encounter, situation **10** affiancing, commitment, employment, obligation **11** appointment, arrangement

engage pleasantly 5 amuse, charm **6** divert, please **7** beguile, delight **8** enthrall, interest **9** entertain

engaging 7 likable, lovable, winning, winsome **8** charming, fetching, pleasing **9** agreeable, appealing, disarming **10** attractive, enchanting **11** captivating **12** ingratiating

engender 5 beget, breed, cause **7** produce **8** generate, occasion **10** bring about, give rise to **11** precipitate

engine
  inventor:
    of compression ignition: 7 Daimler
    of electric ignition: 4 Benz
    of gas (compound): 10 Eickemeyer
    of gasoline: 7 Brayton, Daimler
    of piston steam: 4 Watt **8** Newcomen

engineer 5 pilot **6** driver, hogger **7** builder, hoghead, planner **8** maneu-

ver, motorman, operator **10** accomplish

England
  other name: 6 Albion **7** Britain **9** Britannia
  capital/largest city: 6 London
  others: 3 Ely **4** Bath, Deal, Hull, Ryde, Ware, York **5** Blyth, Brent, Derby, Dover, Erith, Flint, Leeds, Ripon, Truro, Wigan **6** Barnet, Bolton, Bootle, Camden, Durham, Ealing, Exeter, Henley, Jarrow, Leyton, Oldham, Oxford, Yeovil **7** Bristol, Bromley, Burnley, Chelsea, Croydon, Enfield, Grimsby, Halifax, Hornsey, Ipswich, Lambeth, Newport, Norwich, Preston, Salford, **8** Bradford, Brighton, Cornwall, Coventry, Dewsbury, Hastings, Plymouth **9** Cambridge, Greenwich, Liverpool, Newcastle, Sheffield **10** Birmingham, Manchester **15** Stratford-on-Avon
  school: 4 Eton **5** Leeds, Rugby **6** Harrow, London, Oxford **9** Cambridge, Sandhurst **23** London School of Economics
  division: 4 Avon, Kent **5** Devon, Essex, **6** Dorset, Durham, Surrey, Sussex **7** Norfolk, Suffolk **8** Cheshire, Cornwall, Somerset **9** Hampshire, Wiltshire, Yorkshire **10** Derbyshire, East Sussex, Humberside, Lancashire, Merseyside, Shropshire, West Sussex **11** Oxfordshire, Tyne and Wear **12** Bedfordshire, Lincolnshire, Warwickshire, West Midlands **13** Hertfordshire, Staffordshire, West Yorkshire **14** Cambridgeshire, Leicestershire, Northumberland, North Yorkshire, South Yorkshire **15** Buckinghamshire, Gloucestershire, Nottinghamshire **16** Northamptonshire **20** Hereford and Worcester
  head of state: 4 king **5** queen **7** monarch
  measure: 3 cut, lea, pin, rod, ton, tun, vat **4** acre, bind, butt, comb, coom, foot, gill, goad, hand, hank, heer, hide, inch, last, line, mile, nail, pace, palm, peck, pint, pipe, pole, pool, rood, rope, sack, seam, span, trug, typp, wist, yard, yoke **5** bodge, chain, coomb, cubit, digit, float, floor, fluid, hutch, jugum, minim, ounce, perch, point, prime, quart, skein, stack, truss **6** barrel, bovate, bushel, cranne, fathom, firkin, gallon, hobbet, hobbit, league, manent, oxgang, pottle, runlet, square, strike, sulung, thread, tierce **7** auchlet, furlong, kenning, quarter, rundlet, seamile, spindle, tertian, virgate **8** carucate, chaldron, hogshead, landyard, puncheon, quadrant, standard
  monetary unit: 3 ora **4** rial **5** ackey, crown, groat, noble, pence, penny, pound, sprat, unite **6** bawbee, florin, guinea, seskin **7** angelet, hapenny **8**

farthing, shilling, sixpence, tuppence

weight: 3 bag, kip, tod, ton 4 keel, last, mast, maun 5 barge, fagot, grain, pound, score, stone, truss 6 bushel, cental, fangot, fother, fotmal, pocket 7 quarter, sarpler

island: 3 Man 4 Holy 5 Farne, Lundy, Wight 6 Coquet, Mersea, Scilly, Thanet, Tresco, Walney 7 Bardsey, Channel, Hayling, Ireland, Sheppey 8 Anglesea, Anglesey, Foulness, Holyhead

lake: 8 Grasmere 9 Ennerdale, Ullswater, Wastwater 10 Buttermere, Windermere 12 Derwentwater 13 Coniston Water

mountain: 5 Black 7 Pennine, Snowdon 8 Cambrian, Cumbrian
  hill: 6 Formby, Lizard, Mendip 7 Brendon, Cemmaes, Trevose

highest point: 11 Scafell Pike

river: 3 Cam, Dee, Don, Esk, Exe, Lea, Nen, Ure, Wye 4 Aire, Avon, Eden, Lune, Nene, Nidd, Ouse, Penk, Tame, Tees, Till, Tyne, Wear, Yare 5 Anker, Colne, Deben, Stour, Swale, Tamar, Tawar, Trent, Tweed 6 Humber, Kennet, Mersey, Rother, Severn, Thames, Wharfe, Witham 7 Derwent, Parrett, Waveney, Welland 8 Torridge 9 Yorkshire 12 Wensum Ribble

sea: 5 Irish, North 6 Celtic 8 Atlantic

physical feature:
  bay: 3 Tor 4 Lyme, Wash 5 Start 6 Mounts 7 Bigbury 8 Bideford, Cardigan, Falmouth, Tremadoc, Weymouth
  chalk cliffs: 5 Dover
  channel: 6 Solent 7 Bristol, English 8 Spithead
  firth: 6 Solway
  forest: 5 Arden 6 Exmoor 8 Dartmoor, Sherwood
  point: 4 Naze 5 Lynas, Morte, Sales 6 Dodman, Lizard, Prawle 8 Hartland, Landsend
  region: 5 Weald 8 Midlands 10 West Riding 11 North Riding 12 Lake District
  valley: 4 Coom, Eden, Tees, Tyne 5 Combe, Coomb 6 Coquet

people: 4 Celt, Pict 5 Jutes, Norse, Saxon 6 Angles, Briton, Norman, Viking
  artist: 6 Romney, Turner 7 Hogarth 8 Reynolds, Rossetti 9 Constable 12 Gainsborough
  author: 3 Kyd 4 Bede, Hume, Pope, Shaw 5 Auden, Bacon, Blake, Burke, Byron, Defoe, Donne, Eliot, Hardy, Joyce, Keats, Scott, Swift, Waugh, Wilde, Woolf 6 Austen, Bronte, Bunyan, Conrad, Dryden, Gibbon, Jonson, Milton, Newton, Ruskin, Sterne, Thomas 7 Boswell, Chaucer, Dickens, Kipling, Marlowe, Shelley, Spenser, Walpole 8 Browning, Fielding, Lawrence, Sheridan, Smollett, Tennyson, Trollope 9 Churchill, Coleridge, Stevenson, Thackeray 10 Galsworthy, Richardson, Thomas More, Wordsworth 11 Shakespeare

king: 3 Hal 4 Cnut, John, Lear 5 Henry, James 6 Alfred, Arthur, Canute, Edmund, Edward, Egbert, George, Harold 7 Charles, Richard, Stephen, William 9 Cymbeline 18 Richard Coeur de Lion 19 Richard the Lionheart

leader: 4 Eden, Grey, Lamb, Peel, Pitt 5 Heath, Major 6 Attlee, Wilson 7 Baldwin, Balfour, Canning, Fitzroy, Spencer, Stanley, Walpole 8 Disraeli, Stanhope, Thatcher 9 Cavendish, Churchill, Gladstone, Grenville, MacDonald, Macmillan 10 Palmerston, Wellington 11 Chamberlain, Douglas-Home, Lloyd George

queen: 3 Mab 4 Anne, Bess, Jane, Mary 7 Eleanor 8 Boadicea, Victoria 9 Catherine, Charlotte, Elizabeth, Guinivere 10 Bloody Mary 11 Jane Seymour

language: 7 English

religion: 6 Jewish 8 Anglican 9 Methodist, Unitarian 13 Roman Catholic 15 Church of England

place:
  bridge: 5 Tower 6 London 11 Westminster
  cathedral: 4 York 6 Exeter 7 St Pauls 8 St Albans 9 Salisbury 10 Canterbury, Winchester 16 Westminster Abbey
  clock: 6 Big Ben
  fortification: 12 Hadrian's Wall
  museum: 4 Tate 7 British 9 Ashmolean 17 Madame Tussauds Wax
  palace: 7 St James, Windsor 10 Buckingham 12 Hampton Court
  racetrack: 5 Ascot
  ruins: 10 Stonehenge
  street: 4 Grub 5 Fleet 12 Threadneedle 16 Piccadilly Circus
  tower: 6 London

feature:
  dance: 6 morris

food:
  bacon: 6 gammon, rasher 7 streaky
  beer: 5 grout, stout
  cookie: 7 biscuit
  dessert: 6 trifle 11 plum pudding
  dish: 12 fish and chips 14 Cornish pasties 15 bubble and squeak 16 Yorkshire pudding
  drink: 3 ale, tea 6 squash

English, Julian
  character in: 20 Appointment in Samarra
  author: 5 O'Hara

English Mail-Coach, The
  author: 15 Thomas DeQuincey

engrave 3 cut 4 etch 5 carve, stamp 6 chisel 7 decorate, stipple

engraving 3 cut, die 5 print, stamp 7 etching, gravure 9 woodblock 11 copperplate, lithography 12 photogravure

engross 4 hold 6 absorb, arrest, engage, occupy, take up 7 immerse, involve 9 preoccupy

engrossed 4 busy, deep 6 intent 7 engaged 8 absorbed, immersed, involved, occupied 11 preoccupied

engrossing 8 engaging, exciting 9 absorbing, arresting, thrilling 10 intriguing 11 captivating, fascinating, interesting

engrossment 9 immersion 10 absorption, intentness 11 involvement 13 concentration, preoccupation

engulf 4 bury 5 swamp 6 deluge 7 envelop, immerse, overrun 8 inundate, submerge 9 swallow up

enhance 4 lift 5 add to, boost, raise 7 augment, elevate, magnify 8 heighten, redouble 9 embellish, intensify 10 complement

enhancement 11 heightening, improvement 15 intensification

Enid
  character in: 12 The Mabinogion 15 Idylls of the King 16 Arthurian romance
  husband: 7 Geraint
  known for: 9 constancy
  author: 8 Tennyson

enigma 6 puzzle, riddle, secret 7 mystery 8 question 9 conundrum 10 perplexity

enigmatic, enigmatical 7 cryptic, elusive 8 baffling, puzzling 9 ambiguous, equivocal, secretive 10 mysterious, perplexing 11 inscrutable, paradoxical 12 unfathomable 14 indecipherable

Eniwetok 5 atoll
  location: 15 Marshall Islands
  known for: 5 A bomb, H bomb (tests)

enjoin 3 ask, ban, bar, beg, bid 4 urge, warn 6 advise, charge, direct, forbid 7 command, counsel, entreat 8 admonish, call upon, instruct, prohibit, restrain, restrict 9 interdict, proscribe

enjoy 3 own 4 have, like 5 eat up, fancy, savor 6 admire, relish 7 possess 9 delight in, rejoice in 10 appreciate 11 think well of 13 be blessed with, be pleased with, get a kick out of 14 take pleasure in 16 have the benefit of

enjoyable 8 pleasant, pleasing 9 agreeable, fun-filled, rewarding 10 delightful, gratifying, satisfying 11 pleasurable

enjoyment 3 fun, joy 4 zest 5 gusto, right 6 relish 7 benefit, delight 8 blessing, exercise, good time, pleasure

9 advantage, amusement, diversion, happiness, privilege **10** possession, recreation **11** prerogative **12** satisfaction **13** entertainment, gratification

enlarge 4 grow **5** add to, swell, widen **6** expand, extend **7** amplify, augment, broaden, develop, expound, inflate, magnify **8** elongate, increase, lengthen, multiply **9** discourse, elaborate, expatiate

enlarged 7 swollen, widened **8** expanded, extended, inflated **9** amplified, broadened, distended, elongated, magnified

enlargement 6 growth **8** addition, increase, swelling, widening **9** expansion, extension, inflation **10** broadening, elongation **11** development, elaboration, expatiation, lengthening **12** augmentation **13** amplification, magnification **14** multiplication

enlighten 5 edify **6** advise, inform, wise up **7** apprise, clarify, educate **8** civilize, instruct **9** make aware **10** illuminate **12** sophisticate

enlightenment 8 learning **9** erudition, knowledge **11** edification, instruction
French: 15 Eclaircissement
German: 10 Aufklarung

enlist 4 join **6** engage, enroll, join up, obtain, secure, sign up **7** procure, recruit **8** register **9** volunteer **19** gain the assistance of

enlistment 9 signing up **10** admittance, enrollment, recruiting

enliven 4 fire **5** pep up, renew **6** excite, vivify, wake up **7** animate, cheer up, quicken **8** brighten, vitalize **10** make lively, rejuvenate

enlivened 7 revived **8** animated, vivified **9** refreshed **11** invigorated

en masse 7 in a body **8** as a group, as a whole, in a group, together **11** all together

enmesh 4 trap **5** catch, snare, snarl **6** tangle **7** embroil, ensnare, entwine, involve **8** entangle

enmity 6 animus, hatred, malice, rancor, strife **7** ill will **8** acrimony, bad blood **9** animosity, antipathy, hostility **10** bitterness

Ennead 7 dieties
origin: 8 Egyptian
number: 4 nine

ennoble 5 raise **6** refine **7** dignify, elevate

ennui 6 apathy, tedium **7** boredom, languor **9** lassitude, weariness **12** indifference, listlessness
Latin: 12 taedium vitae

Enoch
father: 4 Cain **5** Jared
son: 10 Methuselah
grandfather: 4 Adam

Enoch Arden
author: 18 Alfred Lord Tennyson

character: 8 Annie Lee **9** Philip Ray **10** Miriam Lane

enology see **8** oenology

enormity 8 baseness, evilness, hugeness, vastness, vileness, villainy **9** depravity, immensity, largeness, malignity **10** wickedness **11** heinousness, viciousness **12** enormousness **13** atrociousness, monstrousness, offensiveness **14** outrageousness

enormous 4 huge, vast **7** immense, mammoth, massive, titanic **8** colossal, gigantic **10** gargantuan, prodigious, tremendous **11** elephantine **14** Brobdingnagian

enormousness 8 enormity, hugeness, vastness **9** amplitude, immensity, largeness **11** massiveness

Enormous Room, The
author: 10 e e cummings

Enos
father: 4 Seth
grandfather: 4 Adam

enough 5 ample, amply **6** plenty **7** copious **8** abundant, adequate, passably **9** tolerably **10** abundantly, adequately, competence, plentitude, reasonably, sufficient **11** ample supply, full measure, sufficiency **12** sufficiently **14** satisfactorily

enounce 8 set forth **9** enunciate **10** articulate

en passant 8 by the way **9** chess term, in passing

enrage 5 anger **6** madden **7** incense, inflame **9** aggravate, infuriate **11** make furious **13** make one see red **14** throw into a rage **17** make one's blood boil

enraged 3 mad **5** angry, irate **7** angered, furious, violent **8** incensed, inflamed, maddened, provoked **9** irritated **10** aggravated, infuriated **11** exasperated

en rapport 8 in accord **9** congenial **10** in sympathy **11** in agreement

enrapture 5 charm **6** thrill **7** beguile, bewitch, delight, enchant **8** enthrall, entrance, hold rapt **9** captivate, transport

enraptured 4 rapt **8** beatific, blissful, ecstatic **9** delighted, enchanted **10** enthralled **11** transported

enravel 5 snare, snarl, twist **6** enmesh, tangle **7** ensnare, ensnarl, entwine **8** entangle **10** intertwine

enrich 5 adorn, endow **6** refine **7** elevate, enhance, fortify, improve, upgrade **8** make rich **9** embellish **10** ameliorate **11** make wealthy **15** feather one's nest

enroll 4 join **5** admit, enter **6** accept, engage, enlist, join up, sign up, take on **7** recruit **8** register

enrollment 6 roster **9** enrolling, signing up **10** admittance, enlistment, re-

cruiting **12** registration **13** matriculation

en route 8 on the way **9** in transit, on the road

ensconce 4 bury, hide, seat **5** lodge **6** settle **7** conceal, secrete, shelter **9** establish

ensemble 5 getup **6** attire, outfit, troupe **7** company, costume **8** assembly, entirety, grouping, totality **9** aggregate

ensign 4 flag, jack, mark, sign **5** badge **6** banner, colors, emblem, pennon, symbol **7** pennant **8** insignia, standard

enslave 6 addict, subdue **7** capture, control, enchain, shackle **8** dominate, enthrall **9** indenture, subjugate **13** hold in bondage, put in shackles

enslavement 4 yoke **6** chains, thrall **7** bondage, serfdom, slavery **9** captivity, servitude, thralldom, vassalage **11** subjugation

ensnare 4 trap **5** catch **6** enmesh, entrap, tangle **7** enravel **8** entangle

Ensor, James
born: 6 Ostend **7** Belgium
artwork: 8 Intrigue **19** Bourgeois Living Room **25** Entry of Christ into Brussels **26** The Tribulations of St Anthony **29** Self-Portrait Surrounded by Masks

enstatite
source: 5 Burma, Mogok

ensue 6 derive, follow, result **7** succeed **10** come to pass **13** come afterward

ensuing 8 eventual **9** following, resulting **10** consequent, succeeding

en suite 6 in a set **9** in a series **12** in succession

ensure, insure 5 guard **6** assure, clinch, secure **7** protect, warrant **8** be sure of, make safe, make sure **9** guarantee, safeguard **13** make certain of

entail 6 demand **7** call for, include, involve, require **8** occasion **11** incorporate, necessitate

entangle 4 trap **5** catch, mix up, snare, snarl **6** enmesh, foul up, muddle, tangle **7** confuse, embroil, enravel, ensnare, involve **8** encumber **9** embarrass, implicate **10** complicate, compromise, intertwine

entanglement 5 mixup, snarl **6** foul-up, muddle **7** problem **9** confusion, imbroglio **10** difficulty, entrapment **11** embroilment **12** complication

entente 4 pact **6** accord, treaty **7** compact **8** alliance, covenant **9** agreement, consensus, unanimity **10** consortium **12** conciliation **13** rapprochement, understanding **14** likemindedness

entente cordiale 21 friendly understanding

enter 4 go in, join, list, post **6** arrive,

come in, record **8** enlist in, enroll in, inscribe, pass into, set out on, trespass **9** penetrate, sign up for **10** embark upon, take part in

enterprise 4 push, task, zeal **5** drive, vigor **6** daring, effort, energy, spirit **7** attempt, program, project, venture **8** ambition, boldness, campaign, endeavor, industry **9** alertness, eagerness, ingenuity, operation **10** enthusiasm, initiative **11** undertaking, willingness **14** aggressiveness **15** adventurousness

enterprising 4 bold, keen **5** alert, eager **6** active **7** earnest, zealous **8** intrepid **9** ambitious, energetic, inventive, wide-awake **10** aggressive **11** hardworking, industrious, self-reliant, up-and-coming, venturesome **12** enthusiastic

entertain 4 heed **5** admit, amuse, charm **6** absorb, divert, foster, harbor, please, ponder, regale **7** beguile, delight, dwell on, engross, imagine, nurture, support **8** consider, enthrall, interest, muse over, play host **10** cogitate on, give a party, have guests, keep in mind, think about **11** contemplate **13** keep open house

entertainer 4 host **5** actor **6** amuser, artist, dancer, singer **7** hostess **8** magician, musician **9** performer

entertaining 3 fun **7** amusing, hosting **8** charming, pleasing **9** beguiling, diverting, enjoyable **10** delightful, hostessing **11** playing host **12** having guests **14** having people in

entertainment 3 fun **4** play **7** novelty, pastime **8** good time, pleasure **9** amusement, diversion, enjoyment **10** recreation **11** distraction **12** satisfaction
French: 14 divertissement

enter upon 5 begin **6** assume **9** undertake

enthrall, enthral 5 charm, rivet **6** seduce, thrill **7** beguile, bewitch, enchant, enslave **8** entrance, intrigue, transfix **9** captivate, enrapture, fascinate, hypnotize, overpower, spellbind, subjugate, transport **13** keep in bondage **14** put into slavery

enthralled 4 rapt **8** beguiled, enslaved **9** bewitched, enchanted, entranced, in bondage, intrigued **10** captivated, enraptured, fascinated, hypnotized, spellbound, subjugated

enthusiasm 4 love, rage, zeal, zest **5** ardor, craze, hobby, mania **6** fervor, relish **7** elation, passion **8** devotion, interest, keenness **9** diversion, eagerness **10** excitement, exuberance, hobbyhorse **11** distraction, pet activity **12** anticipation

enthusiast 3 bug, fan, nut **4** buff **5** freak **6** addict **7** devotee, fanatic **10** aficionado

enthusiastic 5 eager **6** ardent, fervid **7** fervent, zealous **8** spirited **9** exuberant **10** passionate, unstinting **11** unqualified **12** wholehearted

entice 4 coax, lure **5** tempt **6** allure, incite, induce, seduce **7** attract, beguile, wheedle **8** inveigle, persuade

enticement 4 bait, draw, lure **6** allure **9** seduction, siren song **10** attraction, temptation

entire 4 full **5** gross, total, whole **6** in toto, intact **8** absolute, complete, thorough, unbroken **9** undamaged **10** unimpaired **12** all-inclusive

entirely 5 fully **6** wholly **7** totally, utterly **10** absolutely, altogether, completely, thoroughly **12** unreservedly **13** unqualifiedly
French: 9 tout a fait

entitle 3 dub, tag **4** call, name **5** allow, label, style, title **6** enable, permit **7** qualify **9** authorize, designate **12** make eligible

entity 4 body **5** being, thing **6** matter, object **7** article **8** creature, presence, quantity **9** real thing, structure, substance **10** individual

entomb 4 bury **5** inter **7** confine

entombment 6 burial **9** interment **10** inhumation

Entommeures, Frere Jean des
character in: 22 Gargantua and Pantagruel
author: 8 Rabelais

entourage 5 court, staff, suite, train **6** convoy, escort **7** cortege, retinue **9** followers, following **10** associates, attendants, companions

entrails 4 guts **5** offal **6** bowels **7** innards, insides, viscera **10** intestines

entrance 4 door, gate **5** charm, entry, way in **6** access, entree, portal **7** beguile, bewitch, delight, doorway, gateway, gladden, ingress, opening **8** approach, coming in, enthrall **9** captivate, enrapture, fascinate, hypnotize, mesmerize, spellbind, transport **10** admittance, appearance, passageway **12** introduction

entranced 4 rapt **7** charmed **8** beguiled **9** entralled, rapturous **10** enraptured, fascinated, spellbound **11** carried away, transported

entranceway 5 entry, foyer, way in **7** doorway, ingress **8** entryway **9** front hall, vestibule

entrancing 6 lovely **8** adorable, charming **9** appealing, beautiful, beguiling, disarming **10** bewitching, delightful **11** captivating, fascinating **12** irresistible

entrap 3 bag, nab **4** hook, land, nail **5** catch, snare, tempt **6** allure, collar, drag in, draw in, entice, rope in, seduce, suck in **7** beguile, capture, ensnare **8** inveigle

entreat 3 beg **6** adjure, enjoin, exhort **7** beseech, implore, request **8** appeal to, petition **9** importune, plead with **10** supplicate

entreaty 4 plea **6** appeal, prayer **8** petition **11** importunity **12** supplication

entree 4 pull **5** entry **6** access **7** ingress **8** entrance, main dish **9** admission **10** acceptance, admittance, main course

entremets 8 side dish

entrench, intrench 3 fix, set **4** root **5** dig in, embed, plant **6** anchor **7** implant, ingrain, install, solidly **8** ensconce **12** establish

entrenched leaders 11 ruling class **12** powers that be **13** Establishment **14** power structure

entre nous 9 between us, privately **14** confidentially **15** between you and me **16** between me and thee, between ourselves **18** in strict confidence

entrepot 5 depot **9** warehouse **18** distribution center

entrepreneur 7 manager **8** director **9** organizer **10** impresario **11** coordinator

entrust, intrust 5 trust **6** assign, commit **7** consign **8** delegate, hand over, turn over **9** authorize **10** charge with

entrustment 10 delegation **13** authorization, commissioning

entry 3 way **4** door, gate, item, memo, note **5** foyer, way in **6** access, entree, minute, portal, record **7** account, doorway, gateway, ingress, jotting **8** approach, entrance **9** admission, vestibule **10** admittance, appearance, competitor, contestant, memorandum, passageway **11** entranceway **12** entrance hall, introduction, registration

entwine, intwine 4 fold, lace, wind **5** braid, plait, twine, twist, weave **9** interlace **10** interweave

enumerable 6 finite **7** limited **11** denumerable

enumerate 3 add **4** cite, list **5** add up, count, sum up, tally, total **6** detail, number, relate **7** count up, recount, specify, tick off **8** numerate, spell out, tabulate

enumeration 4 list **5** tally **7** account, listing **8** adding up, addition, citation, tallying, totaling **9** checklist, detailing, numbering, reckoning, summing up **10** counting up, recounting, tabulation, ticking off **11** spelling out

enunciate 5 sound, speak, voice **8** vocalize **10** articulate **15** utter distinctly **16** pronounce clearly

enunciation 6 accent, speech **7** diction **9** utterance **12** articulation **13** pronunciation

envelop 4 hide, veil, wrap **5** cloak, cover **6** encase, enfold, engulf, enwrap, shroud, swathe **7** blanket, conceal, contain, enclose, obscure, sheathe, swaddle **8** encircle, surround **9** encompass

envelope 5 cover **6** jacket **8** covering, wrapping

envenom 4 sour **6** rankle **8** embitter **13** make poisonous

enviable 5 lucky **8** salutary **9** agreeable, covetable, desirable, excellent, fortunate **10** beneficial **12** advantageous

envious 5 green **7** jealous **8** covetous, grudging, spiteful **9** jaundiced, resentful

enviousness 4 envy **8** jealousy **10** resentment **12** covetousness **13** resentfulness **19** the green-eyed monster

environment 5 scene **6** locale, medium, milieu **7** climate, element, habitat, setting **8** ambience **9** situation **10** atmosphere, background **12** surroundings **13** circumstances
French: 11 mise en scene

environs 6 exurbs **7** suburbs **8** vicinity **9** outskirts, precincts **11** outer limits **12** outlying area **15** surrounding area

envisage 5 fancy **7** dream of, dream up, imagine, picture **8** conceive, envision **9** conjure up, visualize **11** contemplate **13** conceptualize **14** have a picture of **16** picture to oneself

envoy 5 agent **6** deputy, legate **7** attache, courier **8** delegate, emissary, minister **9** messenger, middleman **10** ambassador **12** intermediary **14** representative

envy 5 greed, spite **6** resent **8** begrudge, grudging, jealousy **10** resentment **11** be jealous of, enviousness, malevolence **12** covetousness **13** resentfulness **16** be spiteful toward **19** the green-eyed monster

enwrap 6 absorb, engage, enrobe **7** engross, envelop **9** preoccupy

Enyo
origin: 5 Greek
goddess of: 3 war
companion of: 4 Ares
member of: 6 Graeae, Graiae
corresponds to: 7 Bellona

enzyme 7 protein **8** molecule **13** macromolecule
function: 8 catalyst
acts on: 9 substrate
kind: 5 amino, malic **6** lactic, lipase, pepsin, rennin, urease **7** amylase, glucose, trypsin **8** aldehyde, glutamic, glycolic, lipozyme, thrombin, xanthine **9** cellulase **12** ribonuclease

eon 3 age, era **8** eternity, long time **9** many years **15** one billion years

Eos
origin: 5 Greek
goddess of: 4 dawn
father: 8 Hyperion
mother: 5 Theia
brother: 6 Helios
sister: 6 Selene
husband: 8 Astraeus, Tithonus **10** Eosophorus
son: 6 Memnon **8** Phaethon, Zephyrus **10** Eosophorus
horse: 6 Lampos **8** Phaethon
mother of: 5 stars, winds
corresponds to: 6 Aurore **7** Hermera

Epha, Ephah, Epheh 15 Biblical measure

ephemeral 5 brief **7** passing **8** fleeting, flitting, fugitive, temporal **9** fugacious, momentary, temporary, transient **10** evanescent, fly-by-night, inconstant, nondurable, short-lived, transitory, unenduring **11** impermanent **21** here today gone tomorrow

ephemeroptera
class: 8 hexapoda
phylum: 10 arthropoda
group: 6 mayfly

Ephraim
father: 6 Joseph
mother: 7 Asenath
brother: 8 Manasseh
blessed by: 5 Jacob
descendant of: 10 Ephraimite

Ephraimi 16 Greek unical codex

epic 4 saga **5** drama, great, noble **6** fabled, heroic **7** exalted, storied **8** fabulous, imposing, majestic **9** legendary **10** heroic poem, superhuman **14** larger than life

Epicaste *see* **7** Jocasta

epicure 7 glutton, gourmet **8** gourmand, hedonist, sybarite **9** bon vivant **10** gastronome

epicurean 4 rich **6** lavish **7** gourmet, sensual **8** hedonist, Lucullan, sybarite **9** libertine, luxurious, sybaritic **10** hedonistic, sensualist, voluptuary, voluptuous **11** intemperate **13** self-indulgent

epidemic 4 rife **6** plague **7** rampant, scourge **8** catching, outbreak, pandemic **9** contagion, infection, pervasive, prevalent **10** infectious, pestilence, prevailing, widespread **11** far-reaching

Epigoni
sons of: 18 Seven against Thebes

epigram 4 quip **5** adage, maxim **6** bon mot **8** aphorism, apothegm **9** witticism

epilogue 4 coda **5** rider **7** codicil **8** addendum **9** afterword **10** supplement **12** final section

Epione
husband: 9 Asclepius

episcopal 8 churchly, diocesan, pastoral **12** ecclesiastic(al)

episode 4 part **5** event, scene **6** affair, period **7** chapter, passage, section **8** incident **9** adventure, happening,

milestone **10** experience, occurrence **11** installment

Episode of Sparrows, An
author: 11 Rumer Godden

episodic 7 halting **8** rambling **9** segmented, wandering **10** digressive, discursive, meandering **13** discontinuous

epistle 6 letter **7** message, missive **10** encyclical

Epistle to a Godson and Other Poems
author: 7 W H Auden

Epistle to Dr Arbuthnot
author: 13 Alexander Pope

Epithalamion
author: 13 Edmund Spenser

epithet 5 curse **6** insult **8** nickname **9** blasphemy, expletive, obscenity, sobriquet **10** ascription **11** appellation, designation

Epithet
of Aphrodite: 6 Acraea, Scotia **7** Doritis, Erycina, Limenia **8** Melaenis, Nymphaea, Pandemos **9** Migonitis **11** Aphrogeneia, Apostrophia
of Apollo: 6 Loxias **7** Acesius, Agraeus, Agyieus, Carneus, Phyteus, Spodius **8** Grynaeus **9** Parnopius, Smintheus **10** Alexicacus, Archegetes, Boedromius, Delphinius **11** Argyrotoxus, Epibaterius **12** Platanistius
of Ares: 8 Enyalius **14** Gynaecothoenas
of Argus: 8 Panoptes
of Artemis: 6 Orthia **7** Eurippa, Laphria, Limnaea, Pyronia **8** Aeginaea, Agrotera, Calliste, Caryatis, Daphnaea **9** Hemerasia, Lygodesma **10** Polymastus **11** Leucophryne
of Asclepius: 8 Cotyleus
of Athena: 4 Alea **5** Meter, Xenia **6** Ergane, Itonia, Polias **7** Agoraea, Cissaea, Paeonia, Pronaus, Pronoea **8** Anemotis, Poliates, Zosteria **9** Oxyderces, Parthenia, Poliuchus, Promachus **10** Axiopoenus, Chalinitis, Cyparissia **11** Promachorma
of Cybele: 6 Antaea
of Demeter: 5 Chloe, Lusia, Mysia **6** Antaea, Erinys, Stiria **7** Chamyne, Thesmia **8** Stiritis **9** Anesidora, Thermasia **11** Carpophorus **12** Thesmophorus
of Dionysus: 6 Lyaeus **7** Bromius, Cresius **8** Thyoneus, Triambus **9** Pyrigenes **11** Dithyrambus, Mitrephorus
of Hera: 6 Anthea, Bunaea **8** Henioche **9** Prodromia
of Hercules: 7 Charops **8** Buphagus **9** Ipoctonus
of Hermes: 6 Dolius **8** Agoraeus **9** Spelaites **10** Criophorus **11** Argiphontes **12** Argeiphontes, Psychopompus
of Icelus: 8 Phobetor

of Juno: 6 Moneta **7** Curitis, Pronuba, Sospita
of Jupiter: 5 Ultor **7** Elicius, Pluvius
of Mopsus: 9 Ampycides
of Nestor: 7 Nelides
of Odin: 7 Alfader, Alfadir
of Odysseus: 10 Laertiades
of Persephone: 11 Carpophorus
of Pheriphetes: 9 Corynetes
of Poseidon: 11 Ennosigaeus, Hippocurius **12** Prosclystius
of Rhea: 6 Antaea
of Sinis: 12 Pityocamptes
of Vulcan: 8 Mulciber
of Zeus: 5 Areus, Soter **6** Aqueus, Areius, Nemean, Philus **7** Alastor, Apemius, Ctesius, Lycaeus, Polieus, Stenius **8** Agoraeus, Aphesius, Apomyius, Cappotas, Cosmetas, Dodonian, Herceius, Leucaeus, Tropaean **9** Aegiochus, Chthonius, Coccygius, Hecaleius, Lecheates, Mechaneus **10** Cataebates, Catharsius, Coryphaeus, Homagyrius, Laphystius, Meilichius **11** Eleutherius **12** Panhellenius

epitome 4 peak **5** ideal, model **6** height **7** essence, summary **9** summation **10** embodiment **12** typification **14** representation **15** exemplification, sum and substance

e pluribus unum 12 out of many one
motto of: 12 United States

epoch 3 age, era **4** time **6** period **8** interval

epochal 7 weighty **8** historic **9** important, momentous **11** significant **13** consequential

Eppie
character in: **11** Silas Marner
author: **5** Eliot

Eppie
nickname of: **10** Ann Landers

Epstein, Sir Jacob
born: **9** New York NY
artwork: **4** Adam **7** Genesis **8** Ecce Homo, Einstein **9** Rock Drill **10** Visitation **11** Night and Day, Paul Robeson **12** Behold the Man, Joseph Conrad **13** Haile Selassie **14** Consummatum Est **19** Social Consciousness **20** Monument to Oscar Wilde, St Michael and his (the) Devil

equable 4 calm, even **5** sunny **6** placid, serene, stable, steady **7** regular, uniform **8** constant, pleasant, tranquil, unvaried **9** agreeable, easygoing, unruffled **10** consistent, dependable, unchanging **11** good-natured, predictable, unexcitable, unflappable **12** even-tempered **13** imperturbable

equably
Latin: **9** pari passu

equal 4 even, like, peer **5** match **7** matched, the same, uniform **8** balanced, be even to, equalize, jibe with, of a piece, parallel **9** agree with, identical, tally with **10** accord with, comparable, equate with, equivalent, square with, tantamount **11** balance with, be the same as, correlative, counterpart, symmetrical **12** commensurate, correspond to, proportional **13** be identical to, corresponding, evenly matched, one and the same

equality 6 parity **7** balance, justice **8** evenness, fair play, fairness, sameness **10** similarity, uniformity **11** equivalency **12** impartiality **13** fair treatment **14** correspondence
French: **7** egalite

Equality
author: **13** Edward Bellamy

Equality State
nickname of: **7** Wyoming

equalization 7 balance **9** stability **11** equilibrium **14** counterbalance
German: **9** Ausgleich

equalize 7 balance **9** make equal **11** make uniform **13** compensate for

equal to 3 fit **4** able, up to **5** adept **7** capable **8** adequate, master of **9** competent, qualified

equanimity 4 cool **5** poise **6** aplomb **8** calmness, coolness **9** composure, sangfroid **10** steadiness **11** self-control, tranquility **12** tranquillity **14** presence of mind, self-possession **16** imperturbability

equate 5 liken, match **7** average, balance, compare, even out **8** equalize, equal out **9** think of as **10** consider as **14** be commensurate, be equivalent to **17** be proportionate to

Equatorial
language family: **16** Andean-Equatorial
group: **8** Arawakan **11** Tupi-Guarani

Equatorial Guinea
other name: **13** Spanish Guinea
capital/largest city: **6** Malabo
others: **4** Bata **9** Rio Benito
division: **5** Bioko **7** Rio Muni
monetary unit: **6** ekuele, peseta **7** centimo
island: **5** Bioko **6** Pagalu **7** Corisco **11** Chico Elobey **12** Grande Elobey
mountain: **5** Mitra
highest point: **11** Santa Isabel
river: **5** Mbini
physical feature:
  gulf: **6** Guinea
people: **4** Bubi, Fang **5** Benge, Combe **6** Bujeba **10** Fernandino
  explorer: **2** Po
  leader: **12** Nguema Biyogo
language: **4** Bubi, Fang **7** Spanish **13** pidgin English
religion: **7** animism **10** Protestant **13** Roman Catholic

equilibrium 7 balance **8** symmetry **9** equipoise, stability **14** sense of balance

equip 3 rig **5** stock **6** fit out, outfit, supply **7** appoint, furnish, prepare, provide **8** accoutre **9** caparison, provision

equipage 4 gear **6** outfit **8** carriage **9** equipment **13** accoutrements

equipment 4 gear **5** stuff **6** tackle **8** equipage, material, materiel, supplies **9** apparatus **11** furnishings, outfittings **13** accoutrements, paraphernalia

equipoise 7 balance **9** stability **11** equilibrium

equitable 3 due **4** fair, just **6** proper **8** unbiased **9** impartial **10** evenhanded, reasonable **12** unprejudiced

equity 4 cash **5** value **6** assets, profit **7** justice **8** fairness, justness **9** cash value **10** investment **12** fair dealings, impartiality **14** evenhandedness, fair-mindedness, reasonableness

equivalency 6 parity **7** balance **8** equality **10** coequality, uniformity **14** correspondence

equivalent 4 even, peer **5** equal, match **8** of a piece, parallel **9** the same as **10** comparable, tantamount **11** correlative, counterpart, equal amount

equivocal 4 hazy **5** vague **7** dubious **8** doubtful **9** ambiguous, enigmatic, imprecise, qualified, uncertain, undecided **10** ambivalent, indefinite, suspicious **11** nonspecific **12** undetermined **13** indeterminate

equivocate 5 dodge, evade, fudge, hedge, stall **9** pussyfoot **10** mince words **11** be ambiguous, prevaricate **13** avoid the issue **16** straddle the fence **17** beat around the bush

equivocating 6 shifty **7** devious, dodging, elusive, elusory, evasive, hedging **8** stalling **9** ambiguous, deceptive, equivocal **10** misleading **11** dissembling

ERA
abbr. for: **16** earned run average (baseball) **20** equal rights amendment (failed)

era 3 age **4** time **5** epoch **6** period **8** interval

eradicate 5 erase **6** remove **7** abolish, blot out, destroy, expunge, wipe out **8** get rid of **9** eliminate, extirpate, liquidate **10** annihilate, do away with, extinguish, obliterate **11** exterminate

eradication 7 erasure, removal **9** abolition **11** blotting out, destruction, elimination **12** obliteration

erase 6 delete, remove, rub out **7** expunge, scratch **8** wipe away **9** eliminate, eradicate, strike out

Erasistratus
field: **10** physiology
nationality: **5** Greek
described: **5** brain, heart

Erasmus, Desiderius

author of: 14 Encomium Moriae **16** The Praise of Folly

Erato
muse of: **10** love poetry

Ercolani, James
real name of: **11** James Darren

erect 5 build, put up, raise, rigid, stiff **6** unbent **7** stand up, upright **8** straight, vertical **9** construct, unstooped **12** place upright

erection 7 raising **8** building **9** putting up **11** fabrication **12** construction

eremite 4 monk **6** essene, hermit **7** ascetic, recluse **9** anchorite, religious

Erewhon
author: **12** Samuel Butler
title spelled backwards, modified: **7** nowhere
character: **5** Higgs **6** Strong **7** Chowbok **8** Arowhena

erg
metric unit of: **4** work **6** energy

ergo 4 work **6** hence **7** because **9** therefore **11** accordingly

Eriboea
husband: **6** Aloeus

Ericson 4 Leif
son of: **10** Eric the Red
discovered: **7** Vinland
home: **6** Norway

Erie 4 lake, port **5** canal **9** Iroquoian

Erigone
father: **7** Icarius **9** Aegisthus
mother: **12** Clytemnestra
brother: **6** Aletes
death by: **7** suicide

Erin see **7** Ireland

Erin go bragh 14 Ireland forever

Erinys
also: **6** Furies
epithet of: **7** Demeter
means: **4** fury

Eris
origin: **5** Greek
goddess of: **7** discord
brother: **4** Ares
threw: **14** apple of discord
corresponds to: **9** Discordia

Eritrea
capital/largest city: **6** Asmara
others: **5** Assab, Keren **6** Ghinda **7** Massawa
formerly division of: **8** Ethiopia
river: **5** Mareb
highest point: **5** Soira
strait: **11** Bab el Mandeb
sea: **3** Red
language: **7** Amharic
religion: **5** Islam **6** Coptic, Muslim

Erlking
origin: **8** Germanic **12** Scandinavian
form: **6** spirit
personifies: **6** nature
works: **8** mischief
poem by: **6** Goethe
song by: **8** Schubert

ermine 3 fur **4** duty, rank **6** weasel **7** ermalin **8** position

Ernani
opera by: **5** Verdi
setting: **6** Aragon
character: **6** Ernani **11** Donna Elvira

Ernst, Max
born: **5** Bruhl **7** Germany
co-founder of: **7** Dadaism **10** Surrealism
artwork: **7** Moon Man **8** Lady Bird **11** A Little Calm, Femme Oiseau **12** The Whole City **13** The Table Is Set, Totem and Taboo **14** Lunar Asparagus

erode 3 eat **5** spoil, waste **6** ravage **7** corrode, despoil, eat away **8** wear away **12** disintegrate

Eros
origin: **5** Greek
god of: **4** love
mother: **9** Aphrodite
corresponds to: **4** Amor **5** Cupid

erosion 8 abrasion, ravaging **9** corrosion **10** eating away **11** wearing away, wearing down

erosive 7 burning, caustic **9** corrosive

erotic 3 hot **4** lewd, sexy **5** bawdy, lusty **6** ardent, carnal, impure, ribald, risque, sexual, wanton **7** amatory, amorous, obscene, raunchy **8** immodest, indecent, unchaste **9** salacious **10** lascivious, passionate, suggestive

err 3 sin **6** mess up, slip up **7** blunder, do wrong **8** go astray **9** be in error, misbehave **10** transgress **12** make a mistake, miscalculate **13** slip from grace

errand 4 duty, task **6** office **7** mission **10** assignment

errant 5 wrong **6** arrant, astray, erring, roving **7** erratic, wayward **8** mistaken, straying **9** incorrect, wandering, wayfaring **11** adventurous

errare humanum est 12 to err is human

erratic 3 odd **5** queer **6** fitful **7** strange, unusual, wayward **8** aberrant, abnormal, peculiar, shifting, unstable, variable **9** eccentric, unnatural **10** capricious, changeable **11** vacillating **12** inconsistent **13** unpredictable

erroneous 5 false, wrong **6** all wet, faulty, untrue **7** off base, unsound **8** mistaken, spurious **9** incorrect, unfounded **10** fallacious, inaccurate **12** full of hot air **13** unsupportable

error 4 flaw **5** boner, botch, fault **6** boo-boo, bungle, howler **7** blooper, fallacy, mistake **9** oversight **10** inaccuracy **13** misconception **14** miscalculation **15** misapprehension **16** misunderstanding **17** misinterpretation

ersatz 4 fake, sham **5** bogus, phony **9** imitation, pretended, synthetic **10** artificial, not genuine **11** counterfeit

Erse 4 Celt, Gael, Scot **5** Irish **6** Celtic, Gaelic **7** Ireland **8** Scottish **10** Highlander

erstwhile 2 ex **4** past **6** bygone, former **7** onetime **8** previous

eruct 4 burp **5** belch

eructation 4 burp **5** belch

erudite 4 wise **7** learned, sapient **8** cultured, literate, well-read **9** scholarly **10** cultivated, thoughtful, well-versed **11** intelligent **12** well-educated, well-informed, well-reasoned

erudition 5 skill **7** culture **8** learning, literacy **9** education, expertise, knowledge, schooling **10** refinement **11** cultivation, learnedness, scholarship **12** book learning **13** enlightenment

Erulus
king of: **5** Italy
mother: **7** Feronia
gift: **10** three lives

erupt 4 emit, gush, vent **5** eruct **6** blow up **7** explode **8** break out, throw off **9** be ejected, discharge, flow forth, pour forth **10** belch forth, burst forth

eruption 4 rash **6** eczema **7** flare-up, gushing, venting **8** ejection, emission, outbreak, outburst **9** blowing up, discharge, explosion, festering **10** dermatitis, outpouring **11** breaking out **12** flowing forth, inflammation, pouring forth **13** belching forth, bursting forth

Erving, Julius
nickname: **7** Doctor J
sport: **10** basketball
position: **7** forward
team: **11** New York Nets **15** Virginia Squires **25** Philadelphia Seventy-Sixers

Erymanthian boar
form: **4** boar
plagued: **7** Arcadia
captured by: **8** Hercules

erythrophobia
fear of: **8** blushing

Esau
also called: **4** Edom
father: **5** Isaac
mother: **7** Rebekah
twin brother: **5** Jacob
wife: **6** Judith **8** Makalath
son: **7** Eliphaz
birthright sold to: **5** Jacob

escadrille 6 armada **8** flotilla, squadron

escalate 4 rise **5** boost, mount, swell **6** ascend, expand, extend, step up **7** advance, amplify, broaden, elevate, enlarge, magnify **8** increase **9** intensify **10** accelerate, aggrandize

Escalus
character in: **17** Measure for Measure
author: **11** Shakespeare

escapade 4 lark **5** antic, caper, fling, prank, revel, spree, trick **7** caprice **8** mischief **9** adventure **11** high old time

escape 3 lam 4 bolt, exit, flee, flow, gush, leak, seep, shun, skip 5 avert, avoid, dodge, elude, issue, skirt 6 efflux, egress, emerge, eschew, exodus, flight, stream 7 abscond, emanate, getaway, leakage, make off, outflow, outpour, run away, seepage 8 breakout, emission, outburst, slip away, steal off 9 be emitted, break free, cut and run, discharge, diversion, effluence, pour forth 10 break loose, decampment, fly the coop 11 avoid danger, deliverance, distraction, extrication, safe getaway 12 make a getaway

escargot 5 snail

escarpment 4 bank, crag 5 bluff, cliff, ridge, slope 8 headland, palisade 9 precipice 10 promontory

eschew 4 shun 5 avoid, forgo 6 give up 7 forbear 9 keep shy of 11 abstain from 12 steer clear of

eschewal 7 refusal 8 forgoing, shunning 9 avoidance 10 abnegation, abstention, self-denial 11 forbearance 13 nonindulgence 16 nonparticipation

Escoffier, Auguste
nationality: 6 French
profession: 4 chef
worked in: 4 Ritz 6 London

escort 4 date, take 5 guard, guide, train, usher 6 squire 7 company, conduct, cortege, retinue 8 chaperon 9 companion, conductor, entourage 10 attendants, lead the way

escritoire 4 desk 5 table 9 secretary 10 secretaire 11 writing desk

escutcheon 4 arms 5 crest 6 shield 10 coat of arms 16 armorial bearings *see also* 8 Heraldry

Eskimo (Eskimantsic, Askkimey, Inuit, Yuit)
tribe: 5 Aleut
location: 6 Alaska, Arctic, Canada 9 Greenland
noted for: 7 fishing 9 mechanics

Eskimo-Aleut
language branch: 5 Aleut, Yupik
spoken in: 6 Alaska 7 Siberia 15 Aleutian Islands

Esmeralda
character in: 23 The Hunchback of Notre Dame
author: 4 Hugo

esoteric 6 arcane, covert, hidden, occult, secret, veiled 7 cloaked, cryptic, obscure, private 8 abstruse, mystical 9 concealed, enigmatic, recondite 10 inviolable, mysterious 11 inscrutable, undisclosed 12 confidential 16 incomprehensible

ESP 7 insight 9 foresight, intuition 10 sixth sense 11 premonition, second sight 12 clairvoyance 22 extrasensory perception

espanol 7 Spanish 13 Spanish person 15 Spanish language

especial *see* 7 special

especially 6 really 7 notably 9 expressly, intensely, primarily, unusually 10 singularly, uncommonly 11 exclusively, principally 12 particularly, specifically 13 exceptionally, outstandingly 15 extraordinarily

espiegle 7 playful, roguish

espieglerie 12 playful trick

esplanade 4 mall, path, walk 5 drive 9 boardwalk 10 quadrangle

espousal 7 backing, support, wedding 8 adoption, advocacy, marriage, taking up 9 betrothal, promotion 10 supporting 12 championship

espouse 3 wed 4 back, tout 5 adopt, boost, marry 6 take up 7 embrace, further, promote, support 8 advocate, champion, side with 10 stand up for

espressivo
music: 12 expressively
abbreviation: 4 espr

esprit de corps 10 fellowship, group pride, group unity, high morale, solidarity, team spirit 11 camaraderie

espy 3 see, spy 4 spot, view 6 behold, descry, detect, locate, notice 7 discern

essay 3 try 5 paper, theme, tract 6 effort, take on 7 article, attempt, venture 8 critique, endeavor, treatise 9 editorial, undertake 10 commentary, experiment 11 make a stab at, undertaking 12 dissertation, take a crack at, take a fling at 14 make an effort at 16 short composition

Essay on Criticism, An
author: 13 Alexander Pope

Essay on Man, An
author: 13 Alexander Pope

Essays
author: 12 Francis Bacon

Essays in Criticism
author: 13 Matthew Arnold

esse 5 being 9 existence

essence 4 core, germ, gist, pith, soul 5 heart, point, scent 6 elixir, nature, spirit 7 cologne, extract, meaning, perfume, spirits 8 tincture 9 fragrance, lifeblood, principle, substance 11 concentrate, toilet water 12 basic quality, quintessence, significance 15 sum and substance

essential, essentials 3 key 4 main 5 basic, vital 6 basics, needed 7 crucial, leading 8 cardinal, inherent 9 basic need, important, ingrained, intrinsic, necessary, necessity, principal, requisite, rudiments, vital part 10 key element, principles 11 fundamental, nitty-gritty 12 fundamentals 13 indispensable

essential ingredient 9 necessity 10 sine qua non 22 indispensable component

establish 3 fix 4 form, open, show 5 begin, found, prove, set up, start 6

create, settle, uphold, verify 7 confirm, implant, install, justify, situate, sustain, warrant 8 initiate, organize, validate 9 institute 10 bring about, inaugurate, make secure 11 corroborate, demonstrate 12 authenticate 16 win acceptance for 18 bring into existence

established 6 common 7 regular 8 accepted, familiar 9 customary 10 recognized

establishment, Establishment 4 firm 5 plant 6 office, outfit, system 7 company, concern, factory 8 building, business, creation, founding 9 formation, setting up 10 foundation 11 corporation, development, instituting, institution, ruling class 12 organization, powers that be 13 bringing about

estaminet 4 cafe 6 bistro

estate 4 rank, will 5 class, grade, manor, money, order, state 6 assets, legacy, status, wealth 7 bequest, fortune, station 8 compound, holdings, property 9 condition, situation 10 belongings, plantation 11 inheritance 12 country place

esteem 4 deem, hold 5 honor, judge, prize, think, value 6 admire, reckon, regard, revere 7 believe, cherish, respect 8 approval, consider, estimate, look up to, treasure, venerate 9 calculate, reverence 10 admiration, set store by, veneration 12 appreciation 13 think highly of 16 favorable opinion, hold in high regard 18 attach importance to

esteemed 5 great, noted 6 prized, valued, worthy 7 admired, eminent, honored, notable, revered 9 admirable, important, respected 10 looked up to, preeminent 11 illustrious 13 distinguished, well thought of 14 highly regarded

Estella
character in: 17 Great Expectations
author: 7 Dickens

Estevez, Ramon
real name of: 11 Martin Sheen

Esther
author: 10 Henry Adams

Esther
Persian name of: 8 Hadassah
father: 7 Abihail
grandfather: 6 Shimei
cousin: 8 Mordecai
husband: 9 Ahasuerus
displaced: 6 Vashti
enemy: 5 Haman
holiday: 5 Purim

Esther Waters
author: 11 George Moore

esthetic 7 refined 8 artistic 9 sensitive 10 cultivated, fastidious 12 aesthetic 14 discriminating

estimable 4 good 6 prized 7 admired, revered 8 laudable 9 admirable, honorable, important, reputable, respected, treasured **10** worthwhile **11** commendable **12** praiseworthy **14** highly regarded

estimate 4 view **5** assay, guess, judge, opine, think, value **6** assess, belief, fig- ure, reckon **7** believe, opinion, surmise **8** appraise, conclude, consider, evaluate, judgment, thinking **9** appraisal, calculate, reckoning **10** assessment, conjecture, evaluation **11** calculation

estimation 4 view **6** belief, esteem, regard **7** opinion, respect **8** approval, judgment **9** appraisal, reckoning **10** admiration, evaluation **13** consideration

estimator 7 analyst **8** assessor **9** appraiser, evaluator **10** calculator

Estonia
  capital/largest city: 7 Tallinn
  others: 5 Narva, Paide, Parnu, Tartu, Valga **6** Dorpat **7** Petseri **8** Paldiski **11** Kohtla-Jarve
  government: 8 republic
  measure: 3 tun **4** elle, liin, sund, toll, toop **5** verst **6** sagene, versta **7** kulimet **8** tonnland
  monetary unit: 3 lat **4** sent **5** kroon **7** estmark
  weight: 4 lood, nacl, puud
  island: 4 Dago, Muhu **5** Kihnu, Oesel, Saare **6** Sarema, Vormsi **7** Hiiumaa **8** Saaremaa
  lake: 5 Pskov **6** Peipus **9** Vortsjarv
  highest point: 8 Munamagi
  river: 3 Ema **5** Narva, Parnu
  sea: 6 Baltic
  physical feature:
    gulf: 4 Riga **5** Parnu **7** Finland
    strait: 4 Irbe
  people: 4 Esth, Finn **5** Aesti **6** Jewish **8** Estonian **9** Ukrainian **11** Belorussian
  language: 5 Tartu **10** Finno Ugric
  religion: 8 Lutheran

estop 3 bar **4** fill, plug, stop **7** prevent **8** obstruct

esto perpetua 17 may she live forever
  motto of: 5 Idaho

Estragon
  character in: 15 Waiting for Godot
  author: 8 Beckett
  French for: 8 tarragon

estrange 4 part **8** alienate **9** disaffect **10** antagonize, dissociate, drive apart

estranged 5 aloof **6** cut off **7** distant **8** detached, divorced **9** alienated, separated **10** unfriendly

estrangement 8 coolness **10** alienation **12** disaffection

estuary 5 firth, inlet **10** river mouth, tidal basin

eta 10 Greek vowel **22** estimated time of arrival

etagere 7 whatnot **11** open shelves

etc (&c) 4 et al **7** and so on, whatnot

8 et cetera, whatever **9** and others **10** and so forth, and the rest

etch 3 cut, fix **5** carve, stamp **7** corrode, engrave, impress, scratch

Eteocles
  father: 7 Oedipus
  mother: 7 Jocasta **10** Euryganeia
  uncle: 5 Creon
  brother: 9 Polynices
  sister: 6 Ismene **8** Antigone
  son: 8 Laodamas
  slain by: 9 Polynices

eternal 7 abiding, endless **8** constant, immortal, infinite, timeless, unending **9** ceaseless, continual, perpetual **10** persistent, relentless, without end **11** everlasting, never-ending **12** interminable **13** uninterrupted

eternity 4 Zion **6** Heaven **7** forever, nirvana **8** infinity, paradise **11** ages and ages, endlessness, eons and eons, immortality **12** New Jerusalem, the hereafter, the next world **13** the afterworld **14** the world to come, time without end **15** everlasting life

Ethan Frome
  author: 12 Edith Wharton
  character: 5 Zeena **7** Zenobia **12** Mattie Silver

Ethanim 18 seventh Hebrew month

ether 5 ester, ethyl, ozone, vapor **7** diethyl, solvent **10** anesthetic **11** refrigerant

ethereal 4 airy, rare **6** aerial **7** elusive, refined, sublime **8** delicate, rarefied **9** celestial, exquisite, unearthly, unworldly

ethical 4 fair, just **5** moral, right **6** decent, kosher, proper **7** correct, fitting, upright **8** virtuous **9** honorable **10** aboveboard, scrupulous **15** straightforward **17** open and aboveboard

ethical feelings 9 integrity **10** conscience, moral sense **16** incorruptibility

ethics, ethic 8 morality **9** integrity, moral code **10** conscience, principles **11** moral values, sense of duty **14** moral standards, rules of conduct

Ethics of Ambiguity
  author: 16 Simone de Beauvoir

Ethiopia
  Biblical name: 4 Cush
  other name: 9 Abyssinia
  capital/largest city: 10 Addis Ababa
  others: 3 Edd **4** Axum, Bako, Dori, Goba, Gore, Thio **5** Adola, Adowa, Aduwa, Aksum, Assab, Awash, Dimtu, Elfud, Harar, Jidda, Jimma, Kecha, Meroe, Mojjo **6** Antalo, Asmara, Dessye, Dunkur, Gondar, Harrar, Makale, Napata **7** Ankober, Gambela, Gardula, Magdala, Massawa, Nakamti **8** Dire Dawa, Lalibala, Mustahil
  school: 13 Haile Selassie
  division: 5 Tigre **6** Amhara, Ogaden

  former division: 7 Eritrea
  measure: 3 tat **4** cubi, kuba **5** derah, messe **6** cabaho, sinjer, sinzer, tanica **7** entelam, farsakh, farsang, ghebeta
  monetary unit: 4 besa, birr, harf **5** amole, girsh **6** dollar, kharaf, levant, pataca, talari **7** ashrafi, menelik, plaster, tallero **12** maria theresa
  weight: 3 pek **4** kasm, natr, oket, rotl **5** alada, artal, mocha, neter, ratel, wakea **6** wogiet **8** farasula **9** mutagalla
  island: 6 Dahlak
  lake: 3 Abe **4** Tana **5** Abaya, Shola, Tanna, Tsana, Tzana, Zeway **6** Dambea, Dembea **7** Rudolph **8** Stefanie **11** The Blue Nile
  mountain: 4 Amba, Batu, Guge, Guna, Talo **5** Ahmar, Choke **9** Rasdashan
  highest point: 9 Ras Deshen
  river: 3 Omo **4** Baro, Dawa, Gibe, Gila, Juba **5** Abbai, Akoho, Albai, Awash, Fafan, Mareb, Mofer, Rahad, Webbe **6** Tekeze **7** Tacazze, Takkaze **8** Gashgash, Shebante **11** The Blue Nile
  sea: 3 Red
  physical feature:
    desert: 17 Danakil Depression
    falls: 7 Tisisat **8** Blue Nile
    valley: 4 Rift
  people: 4 Afar, Agau, Beja, Doko, Kafa, Kala, Saho, Shoa **5** Afara, Agows, Galas, Galla, Negro, Tigre **6** Abigar, Amhara, Annuak, Gondar, Hamite, Harari, Sidama, Sidamo, Somali, Tigrai, Wolamo **7** Cushite, Danakil, Donakus, Falasha, Somalis **8** Assamite, Blemmyes **10** Abyssinian, Troglodyte
  leader: 7 Menelik **8** Mengistu **13** Haile Selassie
  language: 3 Giz **4** Afar, Agow, Geez, Saho **5** Geeze, Ghese, Smali, Tigre **6** Arabic, Harari **7** Amharic, English, Italian, Russian **8** Gallinya, Irob-Saho, Tigrinya
  religion: 5 Islam **7** Falasha, Judaism **18** Ethiopian Orthodoxy
  place:
    cathedral: 8 St George
    hall: 6 Africa
    palace: 7 Jubilee **9** Menelik II
    park: 4 Lion
  feature:
    flower: 7 brayera
    game: 5 dulla **8** shum-shir
    garment: 4 toga **5** kamis **6** barnos, chamma, netela, shamma
    tree: 4 koho, koso **5** cusso
  food:
    banana: 4 musa **6** ensete
    beer: 5 talla
    bread dish: 6 injera
    cereal: 4 teff

honey liquor: 3 tej
spicy sauce: 3 wat
ethnic 6 native, racial, unique **8** cultural, national, original **10** indigenous
ethnic group
of Afghanistan: 5 Aimak, Aymak, Kafir, Nuris **6** Baloch, Baluch, Chahar, Durani, Hasara, Hazara, Kaffir, Kirgiz, Pathan, Tajiks, Uzbeks **7** Beluchi, Belucki, Ghilzai, Pakhton, Pakhtun, Pashtun, Pukhtun, Pushtun, Sistani, Taimani, Taimuri, Taliban **8** Jamshidi, Siah Push **9** Firuzkuhi, Safed Push, Safid Push
of Albania: 3 Geg **4** Cham, Gheg, Gueg, Tost **6** Arnaut, Arnout **8** Illyrian, Skipetar
of Algeria: 4 Arab **6** Berber, Kabyle, Shawai, Tuareg **7** Haratin
of Andorra: 7 Catalan
of Angola: 5 Bantu, Kongo, Lundu **6** Chokwe, Herero, Mbundi, Ovambo **7** Bakongo, Kangela, Kikongo **8** Kimbundu, Kwangare **9** Ovinbundu **12** Nyaneka-Humbi
of Antigua and Barbuda: 7 African, British **8** Lebanese **10** Portuguese
of Argentina: 3 Api **4** Lule **5** Vejoz **6** Abipon, Vilela **7** Guarani, Puelche, Ranquel, Taluhet **8** Querandi, Querendy
of Armenia: 5 Armen, Ermyn, Gomer, Hadji
of Australia: 3 Abo **4** Koko, Mara, Wong **5** Anzac, Bieri, Binge, Maori, Myall **6** Aranda, Arunta, Aussie, Binghi, Digger, Kipper, Papuan **7** Arawong, Billjim, Ilpirra **8** Antipode, Barkinji, Euahlayi, Warragal, Warrigal **9** Aborigine **10** Austroloid, Melanesian, Sandgroper **12** Jindyworobak
of Austria: 4 Pole **5** Croat, Czech, Gypsy **6** German **7** Slovene **9** Hungarian
of Azerbaijan: 5 Azeri **11** Azerbaijani
of the Bahamas: 5 black **7** Haitian
of Bahrain: 4 Arab **6** Indian **7** Persian **8** European **9** Pakistani
of Bangladesh: 7 Bengali
of Barbados: 5 Bajan **9** Barbadian
of Belarus: 12 Byelorussian
of Belgium: 4 Remi **6** Nervii **7** Belgian, Fleming, Flemish, Walloon **9** Bellovaci
of Benin: 3 Fon, Pla **4** Adja, Aizo, Mina, Peul **5** Pedah, Peuhl, Somba **6** Bariba, Fulani, Yoruba **8** Pilapila **9** Dahomeyan
of Bhutan: 5 Monpa **6** Bhutia **7** Tibetan **8** Assamese, Nepalese
of Bolivia: 6 Aymara **7** mestizo, Quechua
of Borneo: 4 Iban **5** Bukat, Dajak, Dayak, Dusan, Malay, Punan **6** Illano **7** Bakatan, Chinese, Illanum
of Bosnia-Herzegovina: 4 Serb **5** Croat **8** Yugoslav
of Botswana: 5 Bantu **6** Tswana

7 Bakatla, Bakwena, Bushman **8** Bamalete, Baralong, Batawana, Batlokwa, Botswana **10** Bamangwato **11** Bangwaketse
of Brazil: 2 Ge **4** Anta **5** Acroa, Arara, Araua, Bravo, Carib, Guana, Negro **6** Arawak, Caraja **7** Carayan, Javahai, mulatto, Tariana **8** Botocudo, Chambioa, mameluco **9** Caucasian **10** Portuguese **11** Tupi-Guarani
of Bruneii: 4 Iban **5** Dayak, Malay **7** Chinese, Kadazan
of Bulgaria: 4 Slav, Turk **5** Gypsy, Pomak, Tatar **6** Bulgar, Slavic **7** Chuvash **9** Cheremiss **10** Macedonian
of Burkina Faso: 4 Bobo, Lobi, Samo **5** Bella, Bissa, Dyula, Fulbe, Hausa, Mande, Marka, Mossi, Puchl **6** Fulani, Senufo, Tuareg **7** Grunshi, Voltaic, Yatenga **8** Mandingo **9** Gourounsi **15** Bunsansi Gambaga
of Burundi: 3 Twa **4** Hutu **5** Bantu, Batwa, Pygmy, Tutsi **6** Bahutu, Watusi **7** Barundi
of Cambodia: 4 Cham, Thai **5** Khmer **7** Chinese **10** Vietnamese
of Cameroon: 3 Abo, Edo, Ibo **4** Beti, Bulu, Ekoi, Ijaw, Sara **5** Bantu, Bassa, Kirdi, Pygmy, Tikar **6** Bamoun, Donala, Ewondo, Fulani, Ibibio **7** Bakweri **8** Bamileke
of Canada: 6 Canuck, Eskimo, French, Innuit **7** English
of the Canary Islands: 7 Spanish
of Cape Verde: 6 Creole **7** African, mulatto **8** European **10** Portuguese
of Central African Republic: 4 Baya, Sara **5** Banda, Bwaki, Sango **6** Azande, Yakoma **7** Banziri, Mandjia, Nzakara
of Chad: 4 Arab, Daza, Maba, Sara, Teda, Tubu **5** Barma, Hakka, Kroda, Massa **6** Fulani, Kotoko, Toubou, Wadaii **7** Kamadja, Kanembu **8** Moundang
of Chile: 3 Ona **4** Auca, Inca, Onan **6** Arauca, Chango, Yahgan **7** Mapuche, mestizo, Moluche, Pampean, Patagon, Puegian, Ranquel **8** Alikuluf, Picunche, Tsonecan
of China: 3 Han, Yis **4** Huis, Lolo, Miao, Pu-is **5** Hakka, Hoklo, Seres, Sinic **6** Cataia, Chuang, Johnny, Korean, Manchu, Mongol, Serian, Uighun **7** Sinaean, Tibetan
of Colombia: 4 Boro, Cuna, Duit, Hoka, Macu, Muso, Muzo, Paez, Tama, Tapa **5** Carib, Catio, Choco, Cofan, Cogui, Cubeo, Guane, Haida, Mocoa, Paeze, Pijao, Seona, Yagua **6** Arawak, Betoya, Calima, Colima, Ingano, Mirana, Saliva, Tahami, Ticunu, Tucano, Tunebo, Witoto, Yahuna **7** Achagua, Andaqui, Chibcha, Chimila, Churoya, Guahibo, Guajiro, mestizo, mulatto, Panches,

Puinave, Puitoto, Quechua, Shuswap, Tairona, Telembi **8** Coconuco, Guarauno, Motilone, Puinavis, Quimbaya, Sinsigas **9** Cocanucos, Coconucan, Panaquita **10** Bellacoola
of Comoros: 4 Arab **5** Bantu, Malay **7** African **8** Malagasy
of the Congo: 3 Rua **4** Akka, Susa, Teke, Vili **5** Amadi, Bántu, Figot, Kongo, Mantu, Pygmy, Sanga, Warua, Zambi **6** Ababua, Bafyot, Bateke, Mbochi, Nzambi, Wabuma **7** Bacongo, Bakongo, Bangala, Batetla, Manyema **10** Binga Pygmy
of Costa Rica: 4 Voto **6** Boruca, Bribri, Guaymi **7** Guatuso, mestizo, Spanish
of Crete: 6 Cretan, Minoan **7** Candiot **8** Sphakiot **9** Caphtorim **10** Philistine
of Croatia: 4 Serb **5** Croat **8** Yugoslav
of Cuba: 5 Carib, Negro, Taino **6** Arawak **7** Ciboney, mestizo **8** Ciboneye **9** Caucasian
of Czechoslovakia/Czech Republic: 4 Slav **5** Czech **6** Slovak **8** Bohemian, Moravian
of Denmark: 4 Dane, Jute **5** Angle **6** Cimbri, Eskimo, German, Ostmen, Teuton, Viking **12** Scandinavian
of Djibouti: 4 Afar, Arab **5** Issas **6** French **8** European
of Dominican Republic: 5 Negro, Taino **6** Indian **7** mulatto, Spanish **9** Caucasian
of Ecuador: 4 Cara, Cixo, Inca **5** Ardan, Aucas, Macoa, Maina, Palta, Quitu, Yumbo **6** Canelo, Jibaro, Jivaro, Puruha **7** Cayapas, Jivaros, mestizo, mulatto **8** Barbacoa, Colorado, Montuvio, Serranos **10** Montubious
of Egypt: 3 Kem **4** Arab, Copt, Misr, Wafd **5** Gippy, Gyppy, Gypsy, Nilot **6** Ababda, Berber, Hyksos, Nubian, Tasian **7** Mizraim, Pharian **8** Badarian, Bisharin, Memphian
of El Salvador: 5 Lenca, Pipil **6** Indian, Mangue **7** mestizo, Spanish **9** Matagalpa
of England: 4 Celt, Jute, Pict **5** Norse, Saxon **6** Angles, Briton, Norman, Viking
of Equatorial Guinea: 4 Bubi, Fang **5** Benge, Combe **6** Bujeba **10** Fernandino
of Estonia: 4 Esth, Finn **5** Aesti **6** Jewish **8** Estonian **9** Ukrainian **11** Belorussian
of Ethiopia: 4 Afar, Agau, Beja, Doko, Kafa, Kala, Saho, Shoa **5** Afara, Agows, Galas, Galla, Negro, Tigre **6** Abigar, Amhara, Annuak, Gondar, Hamite, Harari, Sidama, Sidamo, Somali, Tigrai, Wolamo **7** Cushite, Danakil, Donakus, Falasha **8** Assamite, Blemmyes **10** Abyssinian, Troglodyte
of Fiji: 6 Fijian, Indian **7** Chinese

10 Melanesian, Polynesian **11** Micronesian
of Finland: 3 Jew, Vod, Vot, Yak **4** Avar, Finn, Hame, Lapp, Turk, Veps **5** Fioun, Gypsy, Ijore, Inger, Suomi, Vepse, Zyrin **6** Magyar, Ostiak, Ostyak, Tarast, Tavast, Ugrian **7** Lappish, Mordvin, Permiak, Samoyed, Uralian **8** Cheremis, Estonian, Karelian, Livonian, Swekoman **9** Tavastian **11** Karjalaiset, Suomalaiset
of France: 5 Frank
of the Gabon Republic: 4 Fang **6** Adouma, Bakota, Bateke, Echira, Okande, Omyene **7** Eshiras **8** Bandjabi, Bapounou
of The Gambia: 4 Fula, Jola **5** Foula, Wolof **6** Fulani **8** Mandingo, Serahuli **9** Seranuleh
of Georgia: 5 Azeri **7** Russian **8** Armenian, Georgian, Ossetian
of Germany: 3 Hun **4** Slav, Sorb, Wend **5** Saxon
of Ghana: 2 Ga **3** Ewe **4** Akan, Akim, Akra, Aksa **5** Ahafo, Brong, Inkra **7** Akwapim, Ashanti, Dagomba, Maprusi **11** Mole-Dagbani
of Gibraltar: 6 Jewish **7** British, Italian, Maltese, Spanish **10** Portuguese
of Greece: 5 Greek **6** Achean, Dorian, Ionian **7** Aeolian, Hellene
of Greenland: 3 Ita **6** Eskimo **8** European
of Grenada: 5 Negro **6** Indian
of Guatemala: 3 Mam **4** Chol, Itza, Ixil, Maya **5** Xinca **6** Caribe, Quiche **7** ladinos, mestizo, Pocomam **13** Guatemaltecos
of Guinea: 4 Koma, Loma, Nalu, Susu, Toma **5** Kissi, Manon **6** Fulani, Guerzi **7** Landoma, Malinke **8** Kouranke, Landuman **11** Kissi-Sherbo **12** Guerze- Kpelle
of Guinea-Bissau: 6 Fulani **7** Balanta, Balante, mulatto **8** Mandingo, Mandyako
of Guyana: 6 Akawai, Arawak, Creole, Taruma **7** African, Chinese, mulatto **10** Portuguese
of Haiti: 5 Taino **7** African, mulatto
of Honduras: 4 Maya, Paya, Sumo, Ulva **5** Carib, Lenoa, Pipil **6** Tauira **7** Jicaque, mestizo, Miskito **8** Mosquito
of Hong Kong: 5 Hakka, Haklo, Punti, Tanka **7** British, Chinese **8** American, Japanese **9** Cantonese **10** Portuguese
of Hungary: 3 Hun **4** Serb **5** Croat, Gypsy, Cigany, Magyar, Slovak, Ugrian
of Iceland: 6 Celtic, Viking **8** Norseman **9** Norwegian
of India: 2 Ao **3** Gor **4** Bhil **5** Aryan **6** Badaga, Pathan **7** Sherani **9** Dravidian **10** Andamanese
of Indonesia: 4 Dyak **5** Batak, Dayak, Malay **6** Battak, Papuan, Toraja **7** Chinese, Igorots **8** Acehnese, Achi-

nese, Balinese, Javanese, Madurese, Sudanese **11** Minang Kabau
of Iran: 3 Lur, Tat **4** Arab, Kurd, Turk **5** Medes **6** Galcha, Gilani, Jewish, Shugni **7** Baluchi, Persian **8** Armenian, Bactrian, Bartangi, Parthian, Scythian **9** Bakhtiari **11** Azerbaijani, Mazandarani
of Iraq: 4 Arab, Kurd **7** Bedouin
of Ireland: 4 Celt, Erse, Gael **5** Irish **6** Celtic **9** Hibernian
of Israel: 3 Jew **4** Arab **5** Druze **10** Circassian
of Italy: 5 Latin **6** Sabine **7** Italian, Lombard **8** Etruscan
of Ivory Coast: 3 Abe, Dan, Kru, Kwa **4** Akan, Bete, Dida, Guro, Koua, Lobi, Wobe **5** Abron, Abure, Attie, Baule, Guere, Mande, Mossi **6** Baoule, Lagoon, Senufo, Senufu **7** Kroumen, Malinke, Voltaic **8** Dan-Gouro **10** Anyi-Baoule **11** Lobi-Kulango **12** Agnis-Ashanti
of Jamaica: 7 African, Chinese **10** East Indian
of Japan: 3 Eta **6** Korean **8** Japanese, Okinawan **10** Buramkumin
of Java: 5 Krama, Kromo **6** Kalang **8** Javanese, Madurese, Sudanese
of Jordan: 4 Arab, Kurd **7** Bedouin, Checher **8** Armenian, Assyrian **10** Circassian **11** Palestinian
of Kazakhstan: 6 Kazakh
of Kenya: 7 Luo **4** Arab, Meru **5** Bantu, Elgey, Galla, Kamba, Kisii, Luhya, Masai, Nandi, Tugen **6** Kikuyu, Ogaden, Somali **7** Baluyha, Hamitic, Hilotic, Kipsigi, Swahili, Turkana **8** Kalenjin, Marakwet
of Kiribati: 8 Banabans **10** Polynesian **11** Micronesian
of Korea: 6 Korean
of Kuwait: 4 Arab **5** Iraqi, Saudi **6** Indian **7** Bedouin **8** Egyptian **9** Pakistani **11** Palestinian
of Kyrgyzstan: 5 Uzbek **6** Kyrgyz **7** Kirghiz
of Laos: 2 Lu **3** Kha, Lao, Man, Meo, Tai, Yao, Yun **4** Miao, Thai **5** Hmong **8** Lao Teung **10** Phoutheung
of Latvia: 3 Kur, Liv **4** Balt, Cour, Lett **7** Latgale, Latvian, Russian, Zemgale
of Lebanon: 4 Arab **9** Canaanite **10** Phoenician **11** Palestinian
of Lesotho: 4 Zulu **5** Bantu, Tembu **6** Basuto **7** Basotho
of Liberia: 2 Gi **3** Gio, Kra, Kru, Kwa, Vai, Vei **4** Gola, Kroo, Krou, Loma, Mano, Toma **5** Bassa, Gibbi, Gissi, Grebo **6** Gbande, Kpelle, Kpuesi, Krooby, Kruman **7** Krooboy, Krooman **8** Mandingo **15** Americo-Liberian
of Libya: 4 Arab, Tebu **6** Berber, Tuareg **7** Gaetuli **8** Getulans, Harratin
of Liechtenstein: 8 Alamanni, Ale-

manni
of Lithuania: 4 Balt, Lett, Pole **5** Zhmud **6** Jewish, Litvak **7** Aistian, Russian, Yatvyag **10** Lithuanian, Samogitian **11** Belorussian
of Luxembourg: 6 French, German **12** Luxembourger
of Macao: 6 Macaon **7** Chinese **10** Portuguese
of Macedonia: 4 Turk **8** Albanian **10** Macedonian
of Madagascar: 4 Arab, Bara, Hova **5** Malay **6** Merina, Tanala **7** African **8** Betsileo, Mahafaly, Malagasy, Sakalava **9** Antaimoro, Antaisaka, Antandroy, Tsimihety **10** Indonesian, Polynesian **13** Betsimisaraka
of Malawi: 3 Yao **4** Sena **5** Bantu, Lomwe, Ngoni **6** Cheiva, Maravi, Ngonde, Nyanja **7** Tumbuka
of Malaysia: 4 Iban **5** Dayak, Malay **6** Indian **7** Chinese, Kadazan **9** Pakistani, Sri Lankan **10** Bangladesh, Indonesian
of Maldives: 4 Arab **6** Indian **9** Sinhalese **10** Singhalese
of Mali: 3 Bwa **4** Fula, Kyan, Moor, Peul **5** Dogon, Dyula, Fulbe, Marka **6** Berber, Dognon, Fulani, Senufo, Tuareg **7** Bembara, Fellata, Malinke, Miniaka, Songhai, Soninke **8** Khasonke, Mandingo, Senoulfo
of Malta: 7 Maltese
of Mauritania: 4 Arab, Fula, Moor **5** Black, Fulbe, Wolof **6** Bafour, Berber, Fulani **7** African, Soninke, Tukulor **8** Sarakole **9** Sarakolle **10** Toucouleur **12** Halphoolaren
of Mauritius: 6 Creole, French, Indian **7** African, Chinese **8** European **13** Indo-Mauritian
of Mexico: 3 Ixe, Mam, Mie, Ser **4** Chol, Cora, Iova, Mege, Mixe, Pame, Pima, Roto, Seri, Teca, Teco, Texo, Xova **5** Aztec, Chizo, Chora, Mayan, Nahua, Opata, Otomi, Zoque **6** Eudeve, Indian, Mixtec, Pueblo, Toltec, Zotzil **7** Chincha, mestizo, Nahuatl, Nayarit, Spanish, Tehueco, Tepanec, Totonac, Zacatec, Zapotec **8** Lagunero, Mazateca, Tezcucan, Totonaco, Tzapotec, Yucateco, Zacateco, Zapoteca **9** Tlascalan **10** Coahuiltec, Cuitlateco, Tarahumara
of Moldova: 7 Gagauzi **8** Moldovan **9** Moldovian
of Monaco: 6 French **7** Italian **10** Monegasque
of Mongolia: 5 Oirat, Tungu **6** Buryat, Darbet, Khoton, Mongol **7** Kazakhs, Khalkha **8** Tuvinian **9** Dariganga
of Montenegro: 4 Serb, Slav **11** Montenegrin
of Morocco: 4 Arab, Moor **6** Berber, French **7** Spanish
of Mozambique: 3 Yao **5** Bantu, Chopi, Lomue, Lomwe, Macua,

Makua, Ngoni, Nguni, Shona **6** Maravi, Thouga **7** Maconde, Makonde **10** Portuguese

of Myanmar: 4 Shan **7** Burmese, Siamese

of Namibia: 4 Nama **5** Bantu **6** Damara, Herero, Ovambo, Tswara **7** Bushman, Colored **8** Okavango **9** Hottentot

of Nauru: 7 Chinese **10** Melanesian, Polynesian **11** Micronesian

of Nepal: 3 Rai **4** Aoul **5** Limbu, Magar, Murmi, Newar, Tharu **6** Gurkha, Gurung, Nepali, Sherpa, Tamang **7** Bhutias, Kiranti **8** Gorkhali, Nepalese

of the Netherlands: 5 Dutch **7** Frisian **9** Hollander **10** Surinamese **12** Netherlander **13** South Moluccan

of New Guinea: 5 Pygmy **6** Papuan **7** Negrito **10** Melanesian

of New Zealand: 3 Ati **5** Arawa, Dutch, Maori **7** British, Ringatu **10** Polynesian

of Nicaragua: 4 Mico, Mixe, Rama, Smoo, Ulva **5** Cukra, Diria, Lenca, Sambo, Toaca **6** Mangue **7** mestizo, Miskito **8** Mosquito **9** Matagalpa

of Niger: 4 Daza, Idjo, Idyo, Idzo, Peul, Teda **5** Hausa, Warri **6** Djerma, Fulani, Kanuri, Songha, Toubou, Tuareg **13** Djerma-Songhai

of Nigeria: 3 Abo, Aro, Djo, Ebo, Edo, Ibo, Ijo, Tiv, Vai **4** Beni, Bini, Eboe, Efik, Egba, Ejam, Ekoi, Idyo, Igbo, Ijaw, Nupe **5** Angas, Benin, Gwari, Hausa **6** Chamba, Fulani, Ibibio, Kanuri, Yoruba **11** Hausa-Fulani

of Norway: 4 Lapp **5** Samme **6** Nordic, Viking

of Oman: 4 Arab

of Pakistan: 5 Sindi, Wazir **6** Afridi, Bengal, Mahsud, Pathan, Puktun, Sindhi **7** Baluchi, Brahuis, Punjabi, Pushtun, Sherani **8** Khattack, Shinwari, Yusefazi **11** Mohammedzai

of Panama: 4 Cuna **5** Choco, **6** Guaymi **7** mestizo

of Qatar: 4 Arab **6** Pushtu, Yemeni **7** Baluchi, Iranian **9** Pakistani

of Romania: 6 Dacian **8** Romanian, Rumanian

of Russia: 4 Slav **5** Kulak **6** Jewish, Soviet, Velika **7** Chukchi, Latvian, Russian, Turkmen **8** Armenian, Estonian, Georgian, Siberian, Ukrainian **10** Lithuanian **11** Belorussian

of Rwanda: 3 Twa **4** Hutu **5** Batwa, Pygmy, Tutsi **6** Bahutu, Watusi **7** Batutsi

of Samoa: 6 Samoan **10** Polynesian

of San Marino: 7 Italian **11** San Marinese

of Sao Tome and Principe: 7 African **10** Portuguese **11** Cape Verdean

of Saudi Arabia: 4 Arab **7** Bedouin

of Scotland: 4 Gael, Pict, Scot **5** Norse

of Senegal: 4 Lebu, Peul, Soce **5** Diola, Dyola, Foula, Laobe, Peulh, Serer, Wolof **6** Fulani, Serere **7** Bambara, Malinke, Tukuler, Tukulor **8** Mandingo

of Seychelles: 5 Asian **6** Creole, French, Indian **7** African, Chinese

of Sicily: 5 Elymi, Sican, Sicel **6** Sicani, Siculi

of Sierra Leone: 3 Vai **4** Kono, Loko, Susu **5** Bulom, Kissi, Limba, Mande, Mendi, Temne **6** Creole, Fulani, Syrian **7** Gallina, Koranko, Kuranko, Sherbro, Yalunka **8** Lebanese, Mandingo

of Sikkim: 4 Rong **5** Bhote **6** Bhotia, Bhutia, Indian, Lepcha **7** Tibetan **8** Nepalese **9** Mongoloid

of Singapore: 5 Malay **6** Indian **7** Chinese **9** Malaysian, Pakistani, Sri Lankan

of Slovakia: 5 Czech **6** Slavic, Slovak **9** Hungarian

of Slovenia: 7 Slovene

of the Solomon Islands: 7 Chinese **8** European **10** Melanesian, Polynesian

of Somalia: 3 Sab **4** Asha **5** Galla **6** Hawiya, Isbaak, Somali **7** Danakil, Hamitic, Marehan, Samaale, Shuhali **8** Rahanwin

of South Africa: 4 Boer, Yosa, Zulu **5** Asian, Bantu, Namas, Nguni, Pondo, Sotho, Swazi, Tembu, Venda **6** Damara, Kaffir **7** African, British, Bushmen, English, Swahili **8** Bechuana, Coloured, Khoikhoi, San Xhosa **9** Afrikaner, Hottentot

of Spain: 4 Pict **5** Diego, Gente, Latin **6** Basque, Espana **7** Catalan, Espanol, Iberian **8** Galician, Gallegos, Maragato

of Sri Lanka: 5 Malay, Tamil, Vedda **6** Veddah, Weddah **7** Burgher, Mahinda, Malabar **8** Eurasian **9** Cingalese, Dravidian, Sinhalese **10** Ginghalese **12** Bandaranaike

of the Sudan: 3 Bor, Dor, Fur **4** Arab, Bari, Beri, Bobo, Daza, Egba, Fula, Golo, Nuba, Nuer, Poul, Sere **5** Anuak, Bongo, Dinka, Fulah, Hausa, Joluo, Junje, Mosgu, Mossi, Negro, Tibbu, Volta **6** Acholi, Azande, Gurusi, Hamite, Lotuho, Makari, Nilote, Nubian, Senufo, Surhai, Taureg **7** Balante, Baqqara, Gubayna, Jaaliin, Nilotes, Shilluk, Songhai, Songhay, Songhoi, Sourhai **8** Kababish, Mandingo, Menkiera **9** Sarakille **10** Gurmantshi, Shaiquiyya

of Suriname: 4 Boni, Bush, Trio **5** Djuka, Dutch **6** Creole, Wayana **7** African, Chinese **10** Amerindian, Boschneger, West Indian **11** Asian Indian

of Swaziland: 5 Asian, Bantu, Swazi **10** Eurafrican

of Sweden: 4 Lapp **5** Norse, Swede **6** Viking

of Switzerland: 5 Swiss, **6** Franks **8** Alamanni, Alemanni, Italians **12** Rhaeto-Romans

of Syria: 4 Arab, Kurd, Turk **5** Alawi, Aptal, Druse, Druze **6** Afshar, Aissor, Aushar, Avshar, Awshar **7** Amorite, Ansarie, Bedouin, Nosaris, Saracen, Shemite **8** Ansarieh, Armenian **9** Ansariyah **10** Circassian **12** Khachaturian

of Taiwan: 4 Yami **5** Hakka, Hoklo **7** Chinese, Malayan **9** Fukienese, Taiwanese **10** Indonesian, Polynesian **12** Kwangtungese

of Tajikistan: 5 Tajik, Uzbek **7** Tadzhik

of Tanzania: 2 Ha **4** Arab, Gogo, Goma, Haya, Hehe **5** Asian, Bantu, Masai **6** Arusha, Chagga, Sukuma, Wagogo, Wagoma **7** African, Makonde, Sambara, Sandawe, Shirazi, Swahili, Wabunga, Zongora **8** Nyakyusa, Nyamwezi

of Thailand: 3 Lao, Mon **4** Lawa, Shan, Thai **5** Malay **6** Indian, Khymer **7** Chinese, Siamese **9** Cambodian **10** Vietnamese

of Tibet: 5 Aslan, Balti, Bodpa, Drupa **6** Bhotia, Champa, Drokpa, Khamba, Khambu, Mongol, Panaka, Sherpa, Tangut **7** Bhotiya, Bhutani, Gyarung, Taghlik, Tibetan

of Togo: 3 Ana, Ewe, Twi **4** Mina **5** Hausa **6** Akposa, Kabrai **7** Bassari, Cabrais, Kabrais, Ouatchi **8** Konkomba, Kotokoli, Lotokoli

of Tongo: 10 Polynesian

of Trinidad and Tobago: 5 Irish **6** French, Indian, Syrian **7** African, Chinese, English, Spanish **8** European, Lebanese **10** East Indian, Portuguese, Venezuelan **11** Asian Indian **13** Latin American

of Tunisia: 4 Arab **6** Berber, Jewish

of Turkey: 4 Arab, Kurd, Turk **6** Seljuk

of Turkmenistan: 7 Turkmen **10** Turkmenian

of Tuvalu: 6 Samoan **10** Polynesian

of Uganda: 4 Alur, Gisu, Soga, Teso **5** Ateso, Bantu, Chiga, Ganda, Langi, Lango, Nkole, Pygmy **6** Acholi, Ankole, Bagisu, Bakega, Basoga, Batoro **7** Baganda, Banyoro, Bunyoro, Hamitic, Lugbara, Nilotic, Sudanic **9** Nyoro-Toro **10** Banyankole, Karamojong

of Ukraine: 7 Russian **9** Ukrainian

of United Arab Emirates: 4 Arab **6** Indian **7** African, Iranian **9** Pakistani **10** South Asian

of Uruguay: 4 Yaro **5** Swiss **6** Indian **7** Italian, mestizo, Russian, Spanish **8** Charruas

of Uzbekistan: 5 Uzbek

of Vanuatu: 8 European **10** Melanesian, Polynesian **11** Micronesian

of Venezuela: 4 Bare, Pume **5** Bello, Carib, pardo, zambo **6** Arawak,

Creole, Timote **7** Charoya, Guahibo, Kaliana, mestizo, mulatto, Otomaca, Timotex **8** Caquetio, Guarauno, Matilone **11** Maquiritare

of Vietnam: 3 Hoa, Man, Meo, Tai, Tay **4** Cham, Kinh, Nung, Thai **5** Khmer, Malay, Muong **7** Chinese **8** Annamese, Annamite **9** Cambodian **10** montagnard, Vietnamese

of Wales: 4 Celt, Kelt **5** Cymry, Kymry, Welsh **7** Brython, Silures, Taffies **8** Awabokal, Cambrian **9** Siluridan

of Western Sahara: 4 Arab **6** Berber

of Western Samoa: 6 Samoan **10** Melanesian, Polynesian

of Yemen: 4 Arab **5** Zaidi **6** Shafai, Yemeni **8** Yemenite

of Yugoslavia: 4 Serb, Slav **5** Croat **7** Bosnian, Slovene **8** Albanian, Croatian **9** Hungarian **10** Macedonian **11** Montenegrin **13** Herzegovinian

of Zaire: 4 Kuba, Luba, Yaka **5** Bantu, Bashi, Bemba, Kongo, Lulue, Lunda, Mongo, Pygmy **6** Azande, Baluba, Watusi **7** Bakongo, Nilotes, Tshokwe **8** European, Mangbetu, Sudanese

of Zambia: 4 Lozi **5** Bantu, Bemba, Ngoni, Tonga

of Zimbabwe: 3 Ila **4** Sena **5** Asian, Bantu, Bemba, Sotho, Tongo, white **6** Indian **7** Barotse, Chinese, English, Mashoma, Mashona, Ndebele **8** Coloured, Japanese, Matabele **9** Afrikaner **10** Bulakwakwa

etiquette 5 usage **7** decorum, manners **8** behavior, courtesy, good form, protocol **9** amenities, gentility, good taste **10** civilities, politeness **11** conventions, proprieties **15** rules of behavior

etoile 4 star **9** ballerina

Etruscan
　native of: (ancient) **7** Etruria
　location: **7** Tuscany
　king: **7** Tarquin **11** Lars Porsena

Ettarre
　character in: **16** Arthurian romance

ET The Extra-Terrestrial
　director: **15** Steven Spielberg
　cast: **10** Dee Wallace **11** Henry Thomas, Peter Coyote **13** Drew Barrymore **17** Robert MacNaughton

et tu, Brute 13 and thou Brutus
　spoken by: **12** Julius Caesar

etymology 7 history **10** derivation

Etzel
　origin: **8** Germanic
　mentioned in: **14** Nibelungenlied
　represents: **6** Attila
　wife: **9** Kriemhild

Eucharist 8 viaticum **9** Communion, sacrament **13** Holy Communion

euchre
　number of players: **3** two **4** four **5** three
　derived from: **8** triomphe

five tricks won: **5** march
jack of trump: **10** right bower
second highest trump: **9** left bower

Euclid
　field: **11** mathematics
　nationality: **5** Greek
　founder of: **8** geometry
　author of: **8** Elements

Eugene Onegin
　author: **16** Alexander Pushkin
　opera by: **11** Tchaikovsky
　character: **4** Olga **6** Lensky, Onegin **7** Tatyana **12** Prince Gremin, Tatyana Larin **14** Vladimir Lensky

Eugenie Grandet
　author: **14** Honore de Balzac
　character: **5** Nanon **7** Charles, Eugenie **11** Mme d'Aubrion

Euhelopus
　type: **8** dinosaur, sauropod
　period: **10** Cretaceous

Euler, Leonhard
　field: **7** physics **11** mathematics
　nationality: **5** Swiss
　first: **12** calculus book

eulogize 4 hail, laud, tout **5** boost, exalt, extol **7** acclaim, commend, glorify, magnify **9** celebrate **10** compliment, panegyrize **12** pay tribute to, praise highly

eulogy 5 paean **6** homage **7** hosanna, plaudit, tribute **8** citation, encomium **9** laudation, panegyric **10** high praise **11** acclamation

Eumenides
　author: **9** Aeschylus
　character: **6** Apollo, Athene, Furies **7** Orestes
　see **6** Furies

Eunice
　son: **7** Timothy

Eunomia
　member of: **5** Horae
　personifies: **5** order

Eunuch 6 Biztha, Careas, Zethar **7** Abagtha, Harbona, Mehuman **8** castrato

Eunuch, The
　author: **7** Terence

euphemism 11 prudishness, refined term **12** delicate term, overdelicacy **13** prudish phrase **14** mild expression, overrefinement

euphoria 7 ecstasy, elation, rapture **9** well-being

Euphrosyne
　member of: **6** Graces

Euphues
　character in: **20** Euphues and His England **22** Euphues The Anatomy of Wit
　author: **4** Lyly

Euripides
　author of: **3** Ion **5** Medea **6** Hecuba **7** Electra, Orestes **8** Alcestis, Heracles **10** Andromache, Heraclidae,

Hippolytus, Phoenissae, The Bacchae **13** The Suppliants **14** The Trojan Women **16** Iphigenia in Aulis **17** Iphigenia in Tauris **21** The Children of Heracles

Europa
　also: **6** Europe
　father: **6** Agenor
　mother: **10** Telephassa
　brother: **5** Cilix **6** Cadmus **7** Phoenix
　son: **5** Minos **8** Sarpedon **12** Rhadamanthus
　daughter: **5** Crete
　abducted by: **4** Zeus

Europe see **6** Europa

Europe
　country: **5** Italy, Malta, Spain, Wales **6** France, Greece, Latvia, Monaco, Norway, Poland, Russia, Sweden **7** Albania, Andorra, Armenia, Austria, Belarus, Belgium, Croatia, Denmark, England, Estonia, Georgia, Germany, Hungary, Iceland, Ireland, Romania, Ukraine **8** Bulgaria, Portugal, Scotland, Slovakia, Slovenia **9** Lithuania, Macedonia, San Marino **10** Azerbaijan, Luxembourg, Yugoslavia **11** Byelorussia, Netherlands, Switzerland, Vatican City **13** Czech Republic, Liechtenstein **14** Czechoslovakia **17** Bosnia Herzegovina
　city: **4** Bern, Bonn, Oslo, Rome **5** Paris, Sofia, Vaduz **6** Athens, Dublin, Lisbon, London, Madrid, Monaco, Moscow, Prague, Tirana, Vienna, Warsaw **7** Cardiff **8** Belgrade, Brussels, Budapest, Helsinki, Valletta **9** Amsterdam, Bucharest, Edinburgh, Reykjavik, San Marino, Stockholm **10** Bratislava, Copenhagen, Luxembourg **14** Andorra la Vella
　river: **3** Don **4** Ebro, Elbe, Oder **5** Loire, Neman, Rhine, Rhone, Seine, Tagus, Volga **6** Danube, Thames **7** Dnieper, Pechora, Vistula **8** Dniester
　island: **3** Man **4** Skye **5** Crete, Malta **6** Faeroe, Sicily **7** Corsica, Iceland, Ireland **8** Balearic, Sardinia **12** British Isles
　mountain/mountain range: **4** Alps **7** Balkans **8** Caucasus, Pyrenees **9** Apennines **11** Carpathians **12** Sierra Nevada
　highest point: **11** Mount Elbrus
　lowest point: **10** Caspian Sea
　sea: **4** Aral, Azov, Kara **5** Black, North, White **6** Aegean, Baltic **7** Caspian, Marmara **8** Adriatic **13** Mediterranean
　people: **3** Hun **4** Gael, Pict, Serb **5** Celts, Croat, Danes, Dutch, Jutes, Kymry, Marur, Poles, Scots, Slavs, Tatar, Welsh **6** Czechs, Franks **7** Basques, Britons, Gypsies, Iberian, Magyars, Slovaks, Slovene **9** Alamanni, Cossacks, Tyrolean, Walloons
　language: **5** Czech, Irish **6** Basque, Danish, French, Gaelic, German, Pol-

ish, Slovak **7** English, Italian, Romance, Russian, Spanish, Swedish **8** Germanic **9** Bulgarian, Portugese **11** Balto-slavic

religion: 5 Islam **6** Jewish, Muslim **8** Anglican, Lutheran **9** Methodist **10** Protestant **12** Presbyterian **13** Dutch Reformed, Greek Orthodox, Roman Catholic **15** Church of England, Eastern Orthodox

holiday: 11 Bastille Day, National Day **12** Guy Fawkes Day **13** Liberation Day, St Patricks Day **14** Queens Birthday **15** Independence Day **19** Heroes of the Republic

Eurus
origin: 5 Greek
personifies: 8 east wind **13** southeast wind

Euryale
member of: 7 Gorgons

Euryanthe
opera by: 5 Weber
character: 6 Adolar **7** Lysiart **9** Eglantine

Euryclea
nurse of: 10 Telemachus

Eurydamas
member of: 9 Argonauts

Eurydice
also: 7 Agriope
form: 5 dryad
husband: 7 Orpheus
daughter: 8 Themiste
pursued by: 9 Aristaeus

Eurynome
father: 7 Oceanus
mother: 6 Tethys
sister: 6 Thetis
daughters: 6 Graces

Eurysthenes
origin: 7 Spartan
father: 11 Aristodemus
twin brother: 7 Procles
shared: 6 throne
shared throne with: 7 Procles

Eurystheus
king of: 6 Tiryns **7** Mycenae
father: 9 Sthenelus
mother: 7 Nicippe
cousin: 8 Hercules
son: 9 Perimedes
imposed: 6 labors
   number of labors: 6 twelve
   imposed on: 8 Hercules

Euterpe
member of: 5 Muses
muse of: 5 music **11** lyric poetry

evacuate 4 quit **5** leave **6** desert, remove, vacate **7** abandon, forsake, move out, take out **8** order out **12** withdraw from

evade 4 duck, shun **5** avoid, dodge, elude, hedge, parry **6** escape, eschew **7** fend off **8** sidestep **10** circumvent, equivocate **12** steer clear of

evaluate 4 rate **5** assay, gauge, judge, value, weigh **6** assess, size up **8** appraise, estimate

evaluation 4 test **8** analysis, judgment **9** appraisal **10** assessment, estimation

evaluator 5 judge **6** critic, tester **7** analyst, arbiter **8** assessor, reviewer **9** appraiser, estimator

evanesce 6 vanish **8** fade away, pass away **9** disappear, dissipate, evaporate

evanescence 9 vanishing **10** fading away **12** ephemerality **13** disappearance **14** transitoriness

evanescent 8 fleeting **9** ephemeral, transient **10** short- lived, transitory

evangel 6 gospel

Evangeline
author: 24 Henry Wadsworth Longfellow
character: 17 Gabriel Lajeunesse **23** Evangeline Bellefontaine

evangelist 4 John, Luke, Mark **7** apostle, Matthew **8** disciple, minister, preacher, reformer **9** apostolic, missioner, soul-saver **10** missionary, revivalist **12** Bible Thumper, propagandist, proselytizer **17** religious crusader

Evan Harrington
author: 14 George Meredith
character: 6 Louisa **10** Jack Raikes **11** Rose Jocelyn **12** Tom Cogglesby **13** Count de Saldar, Juliana Bonner **14** Caroline Strike **15** Andrew Cogglesby, Ferdinand Laxley, Melville Jocelyn **16** Countess de Saldar, Harriet Cogglesby **21** Melchisedek Harrington

Evans, Dame Edith
born: 6 London **7** England
roles: 8 Tom Jones **11** A Doll's House **13** The Whisperers **14** The Chalk Garden **27** The Importance of Being Earnest

Evans, Mary Anne
real name of: 11 George Eliot

Evans, Maurice
born: 6 Dorset **7** England **10** Dorchester
roles: 9 Saint Joan **13** Rosemary's Baby **14** Man and Superman, Romeo and Juliet **15** Heartbreak House, Planet of the Apes **17** The Devil's Disciple **18** Gilbert and Sullivan **19** Androcles and the Lion

evaporate 5 dry up **6** dispel, vanish **7** scatter **8** dissolve, evanesce, fade away, melt away, vaporize **9** dehydrate, desiccate, disappear, dissipate

evasion 7 dodging, ducking, eluding **8** shunning **9** avoidance **12** sidestepping **13** circumventing, shrinking from **15** attempt to escape

evasive 6 shifty **7** devious, dodging, elusive, elusory, hedging **9** ambiguous, deceitful, deceptive, equivocal **10** misleading **11** dissembling **12** equivocating

Eva Trout
author: 14 Elizabeth Bowen

eve 4 dusk **6** female, sunset **7** evening, sunset **8** eventide **9** day before

Eve
husband: 4 Adam
son: 4 Abel, Cain, Seth
home: 4 Eden

Evelina
author: 11 Fanny Burney

even 4 calm, fair, flat, just, true **5** equal, flush, level, plane, plumb **6** placid, smooth, square, steady **7** balance, equable, flatten, regular, the same, uniform **8** balanced, constant, equalize, matching, parallel, straight, unbiased **9** equitable, identical, impartial, make flush, unruffled, unvarying **10** straighten, unwavering **11** make uniform, unexcitable **12** even-tempered, make parallel **13** dispassionate

evening 3 e'en, eve **4** dusk, even **6** sunset **7** day's end, sundown **8** eventide, gloaming, twilight **9** nightfall **10** close of day

evenly matched 5 equal **8** of a piece **9** identical **10** well suited **13** one and the same

evenness 7 balance **8** calmness, equality, fairness, flatness, sameness **9** placidity **10** regularity, smoothness, steadiness, uniformity **11** equivalency

event 4 bout, game **7** contest, episode **8** incident, occasion **9** happening, milestone **10** experience, occurrence, tournament **11** competition

even-tempered 4 calm **6** serene **7** equable, patient **11** good-natured, unflappable **12** mild-tempered, well-adjusted

eventful 7 crucial, epochal, fateful, notable, weighty **8** critical, exciting, historic **9** important, memorable, momentous, thrilling **10** noteworthy **11** significant **13** consequential, unforgettable

eventide 4 dusk **6** sunset **7** evening, sundown **8** gloaming, twilight **9** nightfall

eventual 5 final, later **6** coming, future **7** ensuing **8** imminent, ultimate, upcoming **9** following, impending, resulting **10** consequent, subsequent **11** prospective

eventually 6 one day **7** finally **8** in the end, sometime **10** ultimately **12** in the long run **13** sooner or later **17** in the course of time **20** when all is said and done

even up 3 tie **5** align **8** make even **10** straighten

Eve of St Agnes, The
author: 9 John Keats

ever 5 at all **6** always **7** forever **9** at any time, eternally, in any case **10** at all times, constantly **11** incessantly, perpetually **12** continuously

Everdene, Bathsheba
character in: **22** Far From the Madding Crowd
author: **5** Hardy

Everglade State
nickname of: **7** Florida

evergreen 3 fir, yew **4** pine **5** heath, holly **6** jujube, laurel, myrtle, needle, privet **7** arbutus, casiope, conifer, jasmine, juniper **8** camellia, hawthorn, oleander, rosemary **9** mistletoe, sugarbush **11** conebearing **12** rhododendrum

Evergreen State
nickname of: **10** Washington

everlasting 7 durable, endless, eternal, lasting, tedious, undying **8** constant, immortal, infinite, timeless, tiresome **9** ceaseless, continual, incessant, perpetual, unceasing, wearisome **10** continuous, ever-living **11** long-lasting, never-ending **12** imperishable, interminable **14** indestructible

evermore 6 always **7** forever **9** eternally **10** for all time **13** everlastingly

ever upward
Latin: **9** excelsior
motto of: **7** New York (state)

everybody
French: **11** tout le monde

everyday 4 dull **5** daily, stock, trite, usual **6** common, square **7** mundane, regular, routine **8** familiar, ordinary, workaday **9** customary, hackneyed, quotidian **11** commonplace, day after day, established, stereotyped **12** conventional, run-of-the-mill **13** unimaginative

Everyman
author: **7** unknown
character: **3** God **5** Death, Goods **6** Beauty **7** Kindred **8** Strength **9** Good Deeds, Knowledge, Messenger **10** Fellowship

every man for himself
French: **12** sauve qui peut

Every Man in His Humour
author: **9** Ben Jonson
character: **6** Kitely **7** Bridget **8** Bobadill, Wellbred **9** Brainworm, Downright **13** Edward Knowell **14** Justice Clement

Every Man out of His Humour
author: **9** Ben Jonson
character: **6** Deliro **7** Fungoso, Sordido **9** Macilente, Sogliardo **10** Puntarvolo **12** Carlo Buffone **15** Fastidious Brisk

everyone
French: **11** tout le monde

everywhere 7 all over **10** every place, far and near, far and wide, throughout **11** extensively, in all places, universally **12** the world over, ubiquitously **14** to the four winds

evict 4 oust **5** eject, expel **6** remove **7** kick out, turn out **8** dislodge, get rid of, throw out **10** dispossess

evidence 4 fact, sign **5** proof, token **7** exhibit, grounds **9** testimony **10** indication **11** affirmation **12** confirmation, illustration **13** corroboration, documentation, material proof **14** authentication, substantiation **15** exemplification

evident 5 clear, plain **6** patent **7** certain, obvious, visible **8** apparent, manifest, tangible **10** noticeable, undeniable **11** conspicuous, perceptible **12** demonstrable, unmistakable **14** unquestionable **24** plain as the nose on your face

evidently 7 clearly, plainly **9** assumedly, certainly, doubtless, obviously **10** apparently, undeniably **11** doubtlessly **12** unmistakably **14** unquestionably **16** to all appearances

evil 3 bad, sin **4** base, vice, vile **5** venal **6** sinful, wicked **7** heinous, immoral, vicious **8** baseness, iniquity, sinister **9** depravity, malicious, malignant, nefarious, turpitude **10** corruption, immorality, iniquitous, malevolent, pernicious, villainous, wickedness, wrongdoing **12** blackhearted, unprincipled, unscrupulous
goddess of: **7** Sekhmet

evildoer 6 sinner **7** culprit, villain **9** miscreant, wrongdoer **10** malefactor **12** transgressor

evil-minded 4 base **5** nasty **6** wicked **7** ignoble, immoral **8** depraved **10** despicable, iniquitous, villainous **12** dishonorable, unprincipled

evilness 6 malice **7** cruelty **8** villainy **9** barbarity, malignity **10** sinfulness, wickedness

evince 4 show **6** convey, reveal **7** display, exhibit, express **11** communicate, demonstrate **12** give evidence

Evius see **7** Bacchus

Evnissyen
origin: **5** Welsh
brother: **4** Bran **10** Manawyddan
sister: **7** Branwen
caused: **3** war
between: **5** Irish **7** British
killed: **6** nephew

evoke 4 stir **5** rouse, waken **6** arouse, awaken, call up, elicit, excite, induce, invite, invoke, summon **7** produce, provoke, suggest **9** call forth, conjure up, stimulate **10** bring forth

evolution 4 rise **6** change, growth **8** fruition, increase **9** expansion, unfolding **10** maturation **11** development, enlargement, progression **13** metamorphosis
founder of theory: **13** Charles Darwin

forerunner of theory: **12** Charles Lyell **18** Chevalier de Lamarck

evolve 4 grow **5** ripen **6** expand, mature, unfold, unroll **7** develop, enlarge **8** increase

Ewell, Tom
real name: **14** Yewell Tompkins
born: **11** Owensboro KY
roles: **8** Adam's Rib **9** State Fair **14** The Great Gatsby **16** Tender Is the Night, The Seven Year Itch

ewer 3 jug, urn **5** basin **6** vessel **7** pitcher

Ewing, Patrick
sport: **10** basketball
team: **13** New York Knicks **15** Georgetown Hoyas

exacerbate 3 irk **5** anger **6** deepen, worsen **7** inflame, magnify, provoke, sharpen **8** heighten, increase, irritate **9** aggravate, intensify **10** exaggerate **12** fan the flames **16** pour oil on the fire **17** add insult to injury **18** add fuel to the flames **19** rub salt into the wound

exact 4 take, true **5** claim, force, mulct, right, wrest **6** compel, demand, extort, strict **7** careful, correct, extract, literal, precise, require, squeeze **8** accurate, clear-cut, exacting, explicit, specific **9** on the head, on the nose **10** methodical, meticulous, scrupulous, systematic **11** painstaking, punctilious, to the letter, unequivocal

exacting 4 hard **5** harsh, rigid, stern, tough **6** severe, strict, trying **7** arduous **8** critical **9** demanding, difficult, hard-nosed, strenuous, unbending, unsparing **10** hard-headed, meticulous, no-nonsense

exactly 4 just **5** fully, quite, truly **6** indeed, just so, wholly **7** quite so **8** entirely, of course, strictly **9** assuredly, certainly, correctly, literally, precisely **10** absolutely, accurately, definitely, explicitly, that's right **12** specifically

exactness 8 accuracy **9** precision **10** exactitude **12** accurateness

exact satisfaction 6 avenge, punish **7** get back, get even, revenge **9** retaliate **14** get one's own back

exaggerate 5 boast **6** overdo **7** amplify, lay it on, magnify, stretch **9** embellish, embroider, enlarge on, overstate **11** hyperbolize

exaggerated 7 extreme, intense **10** inordinate, overstated **14** overemphasized

exalt 4 laud **5** cheer, elate, extol, honor **6** praise, uplift **7** acclaim, applaud, commend, elevate, ennoble, glorify, inspire, magnify, worship **8** venerate **9** celebrate, stimulate **10** exhilarate, make much of **12** pay tribute to

exaltation 4 high **5** bliss, glory, honor **6** praise **7** dignity, ecstasy, elation, rapture, tribute, worship **8** grandeur, nobility, praising **9** happiness, panegyric, transport **10** eulogizing, exultation, veneration **11** celebration, deification **12** exhilaration

exalted 2 up **5** grand, happy, lofty, noble **6** august, elated, lordly **7** excited, notable **8** blissful, ecstatic, elevated, glorious, inspired, uplifted **9** dignified, honorable, rapturous, venerable **10** heightened **11** high-ranking, illustrious, magnificent

exaltedness 5 bliss **6** height **7** ecstasy, elation, heights, rapture **8** highness, nobility **9** elevation, loftiness, transport

examination 4 exam, quiz, test **5** assay, audit, final, orals, probe, study **6** review, survey **7** midterm, perusal **8** analysis, scrutiny **10** inspection **11** looking over **13** investigation **15** physical checkup

examine 4 pump, quiz, scan, test, view **5** audit, grill, probe, query, study **6** peruse, ponder, review, survey **7** explore, inspect, observe **8** consider, look into, look over, question **10** scrutinize **11** inquire into, interrogate, investigate, take stock of

examiner 6 tester **8** inquirer, reviewer, surveyor **12** interrogator, investigator

example 5 ideal, model **6** sample **7** paragon, pattern **8** exemplar, specimen, standard **9** archetype, prototype **11** case in point **12** illustration **14** representation **15** exemplification

exasperate 3 bug, irk, vex **4** rile **5** anger, annoy, chafe, pique **6** bother, enrage, harass, madden, offend, rankle, ruffle **7** incense, provoke, turn off **8** irritate **9** aggravate, infuriate **15** try one's patience

exasperating 7 irksome **8** annoying **9** vexatious **10** irritating **11** infuriating

Excalibur 5 sword
  drawn from: 5 stone
    by: 6 Arthur
  given by: 5 Nimue **7** Viviane **13** Lady of the Lake

ex cathedra 12 from the chair **13** with authority **22** from the seat of authority

excavate 3 dig **4** mine **5** dig up, gouge **6** burrow, cut out, dig out, furrow, groove, quarry, tunnel **7** uncover, unearth **8** scoop out **9** hollow out **11** make a hole in

excavation 3 dig, pit **4** hole, mine, sump **5** ditch, grave, shaft, space **6** cavity, dugout, trench, trough **7** digging, opening

exceed 4 pass **5** excel **6** go over, outrun, overdo **7** outpace, outrank, surpass **8** go beyond, outreach, outrival, outstrip, surmount **9** come first, overshoot, transcend **10** be superior **11** predominate

exceedingly 4 very **6** vastly **7** greatly, notably **9** amazingly, eminently, extremely, supremely, unusually **10** enormously, especially, unwontedly, very highly **11** excessively **12** immeasurably, impressively, inordinately, preeminently, surpassingly **13** astonishingly, outstandingly, superlatively **15** extraordinarily

excel 5 outdo **6** exceed **7** prevail, surpass **8** outrival, outstrip **9** rank first **10** tower above **11** predominate, take the cake **20** walk off with the honors

excellence 5 merit **7** quality **8** eminence **9** greatness **10** perfection **11** distinction, high quality, preeminence, superiority **13** transcendence

excellent 4 aces, A-one, fine, tops **5** great, nifty, prime, super, swell **6** bang-up, choice, grade A, superb **7** capital, classic, notable **8** peerless, sterling, superior, terrific, top-notch **9** admirable, exemplary, first-rate, matchless, superfine, wonderful **10** first-class, preeminent, tremendous **11** exceptional, outstanding, superlative

excelsior 10 ever upward
  motto of: 7 New York (state)

Excelsior State
  nickname of: 7 New York

except 3 ban, bar, but **4** omit, save **6** enjoin, excuse, exempt, reject, remove, saving **7** barring, besides, exclude, shut out **8** count out, disallow, pass over **9** eliminate, excepting, excluding, other than **11** exclusive of

excepted 6 exempt **7** excused **8** excluded **11** not included

exception 6 oddity, rarity **7** anomaly, removal **8** omission **9** debarment, deviation, exclusion, exemption, isolation, rejection, seclusion **10** difference, leaving out, separation **11** elimination, peculiarity, repudiation, segregation, shutting out, special case **12** disallowment, irregularity, renunciation **13** inconsistency

exceptional 3 odd **4** rare **5** great, queer **6** unique **7** special, strange, unusual **8** aberrant, abnormal, atypical, freakish, peculiar, singular, superior, terrific, uncommon, unwonted **9** anomalous, excellent, irregular, marvelous, unheard of, unnatural, wonderful **10** first-class, inimitable, noteworthy, out-of-sight, phenomenal, remarkable **11** outstanding **12** incomparable **13** extraordinary, unprecedented **17** better than average

exception to the rule 7 anomaly **11** abnormality **12** irregularity

excerpt 4 part **5** piece **7** extract, portion, section **8** abstract, fragment **9** quotation, selection **13** quoted passage

excess 4 glut **5** extra, flood, spare **7** residue, surfeit, surplus, too much

8 fullness, overflow, plethora **9** avalanche, excessive, profusion, remainder, repletion **10** inundation, lavishness, oversupply **11** undue amount **13** overabundance **14** superabundance

excessive 5 undue **6** excess **7** extreme, profuse, too much **8** needless **9** senseless **10** immoderate, inordinate **11** exaggerated, extravagant, superfluous, unnecessary **12** overabundant, unreasonable **16** disproportionate

excessively 5 enorm **7** greatly **9** extremely, intensely **11** exceedingly, fanatically **12** boisterously, exorbitantly, inordinately **14** overabundantly

exchange 4 swap **5** trade **6** barter, switch **8** bandying, trade off **9** tit for tat **10** quid pro quo **11** convert into, give-and-take, interchange, reciprocate, reciprocity

exchange blows 3 box **5** clash, fight **6** battle, combat, tussle **7** contend, contest, grapple **8** skirmish **11** cross swords

exchange of viewpoints 6 debate, parley **8** dialogue **10** conference, discussion

exchange premium 4 agio

exchange views 6 confer, debate **7** consult, discuss **8** consider, talk over **12** compare notes

excise 3 tax **4** duty **6** cut off, cut out, impost, remove **7** extract **8** pluck out **9** eradicate, surcharge

excitable 4 edgy **5** jumpy **7** jittery, nervous **8** feverish, frenzied, skittish **9** flappable, hotheaded **10** highstrung, passionate **11** combustible, inflammable

excite 4 fire, move, whet **5** evoke, pique, rouse, waken **6** arouse, awaken, elicit, foment, incite, kindle, spur on, stir up, thrill **7** agitate, animate, inflame, provoke **8** energize **9** electrify, galvanize, instigate, stimulate, titillate **13** get a kick out of

excited 4 daft **5** afire, astir **6** ablaze **7** aroused **8** agitated, ecstatic, frenzied, inflamed, turned on **9** disturbed, stirred up **10** magnetized **11** electrified

excitement 3 ado **4** flap, stir, to-do **5** furor, kicks **6** action, flurry, frenzy, hoopla, thrill, tumult **7** elation, ferment, flutter, turmoil **8** activity, brouhaha, interest **9** adventure, agitation, animation, commotion, fireworks **10** enthusiasm **11** stimulation

exciting 5 spicy **6** moving, risque **7** rousing, zestful **8** dazzling, stirring **9** affecting, impelling, inspiring, thrilling **11** hair-raising, provocative, sensational, stimulating, titillating **12** breathtaking, electrifying **13** spine-tingling

exclaim 4 howl, yell **5** shout **6** bellow,

cry out **7** call out **8** proclaim **9** ejaculate **10** vociferate

exclamation 3 cry **4** howl, yell, yelp **5** shout **6** bellow, outcry, shriek, squeal **7** screech **9** expletive **11** ejaculation **12** interjection, vociferation

exclamation of:
approval: **3** ole, rah **5** bravo
despair: **4** alas **5** alack **7** woe is me
dicovery: **3** aha, oho
disdain: **3** duh, hah, tsk **4** bosh, bunk, pooh
disgust: **3** bah, ugh **4** damn, darn, drat, pfui, rats **5** shoot **6** humbug, phooey
joy: **3** yay **4** whee, yeah **6** hooray, hurrah, hurray **7** whoopie
pain: **4** ouch **5** yipes
relief: **4** phew, whew
other: **3** fie, hah, hey, tut, wow **4** oops, scat, shoo, ta-da **5** voila **6** hoopla
bacchanalian cry: **4** evoe

exclude 3 ban, bar **4** omit, oust **5** eject, evict, expel **6** banish, except, forbid, refuse, reject, remove **7** boycott, keep out, rule out, shut out **8** disallow, leave out, prohibit, set aside, throw out **9** blackball, repudiate **13** shut the door on

excluding 3 but **4** save **6** except, saving **7** banning, barring, besides **9** excepting, other than **10** keeping out

exclusion 6 ouster **7** barring, refusal, removal **8** ejection, eviction **9** debarment, dismissal, expelling, expulsion, rejection, restraint **10** banishment, keeping out, preclusion, prevention **11** prohibition, throwing out **12** nonadmission

exclusive 4 full, posh, sole **5** aloof, total **6** closed, entire, single **7** private **8** absolute, clannish, cliquish, complete, snobbish, unshared **9** undivided, selective **10** restricted **11** restrictive

exclusive of 3 but **4** save **6** except, saving **7** barring, besides **9** excepting, excluding, other than

excommunicate 3 ban **4** oust **5** eject, expel **6** banish, remove **8** unchurch **12** anathematize

excommunication 3 ban **6** ouster **8** anathema **10** banishment **12** proscription

excoriate 4 flay **5** curse **6** berate, revile **7** censure **8** denounce, execrate **9** skin alive

excrescence 4 bump, hump, knob, knot, lump **5** bulge, gnarl **6** nodule **8** swelling **10** protrusion **12** protuberance

excrete 4 void **5** expel **8** evacuate **9** discharge, eliminate

excruciating 5 acute **6** fierce, severe **7** cutting, extreme, intense, racking, violent **9** agonizing, exquisite, torturous

10 lacerating, tormenting, unbearable **11** unendurable **12** insufferable

exculpate 5 clear **6** acquit, excuse, pardon **7** absolve **9** exonerate, let one off, vindicate

excursion 4 hike, ride, tour, trek, trip, walk **5** drive, jaunt, sally, tramp **6** cruise, flight, junket, outing, ramble, sortie, stroll, voyage **10** expedition **12** pleasure trip

excusatory 9 defensive **10** apologetic **11** extenuatory, vindicatory **13** justificatory

excuse 4 free **5** alibi, clear, spare **6** acquit, defend, exempt, let off, pardon, reason **7** absolve, condone, defense, explain, forgive, indulge, justify, release **8** argument, bear with, mitigate, overlook, palliate, pass over **9** disregard, exculpate, exemption, exonerate, extenuate, gloss over, let one off, relieve of, vindicate, whitewash **10** absolution **11** exoneration, vindication **12** apologize for **13** justification **16** make allowance for **17** accept one's apology

execrable 4 vile **5** awful **8** dreadful, terrible **9** atrocious, revolting **10** abominable

execrate 4 hate **5** abhor **6** detest, loathe **7** despise **9** abominate, can't stand, excoriate **10** shrink from **11** can't stomach **12** be revolted by **13** be nauseated by, find repulsive **15** be disgusted with **20** regard with repugnance

execration 4 hate **6** hating **7** disgust **8** loathing **9** despising, repulsion, revulsion **10** repugnance **11** abomination, detestation

execute 2 do **3** act **4** kill, play, slay **5** enact **6** effect, murder, render **7** achieve, enforce, fulfill, perform, realize, sustain **8** carry out, complete, massacre **9** discharge **10** accomplish, administer, consummate, effectuate, perpetrate, put to death **11** assassinate **12** carry through **13** put into effect

execution 5 doing **7** killing, slaying **9** discharge, effecting, rendition **10** completion **11** achievement, carrying out, fulfillment, performance, realization, transaction **14** accomplishment, administration, implementation, interpretation, putting to death

executioner 6 hit man, killer, slayer **7** butcher, hangman **8** assassin, murderer

Executioner's Song, The
author: **12** Norman Mailer
subject: **11** Gary Gilmore

executive 3 CEO, CFO **4** suit **7** manager **8** chairman, director, overseer **9** president **10** leadership, managerial, supervisor **11** directorial, supervisory **13** administrator **14** administrative, superintendent

executives 5 suits **7** leaders **8** managers, officers **9** directors **13** governing body **14** administration

executor 4 doer **5** agent **9** performer **13** administrator

exegesis 10 exposition **11** explanation **14** interpretation **18** explication de texte

exemplar 5 ideal, model **7** example, pattern **8** original, specimen, standard **9** archetype, prototype

exemplary 5 ideal, model **6** sample **7** typical **8** laudable, sterling **9** admirable, emulative, estimable, nonpareil **10** noteworthy **11** commendable, meritorious **12** illustrative, praiseworthy **14** characteristic, representative

exemplification 7 epitome, essence, example **8** citation, evidence **10** embodiment **11** case in point **12** illustration **13** documentation **14** representation **15** personification

exemplify 6 depict, embody, typify **8** instance **9** epitomize, personify, represent **10** illustrate **11** demonstrate **12** characterize

exempli gratia 6 such as **10** for example **19** for the sake of example
abbreviation: **2** eg

exempt 4 free **5** clear, freed, spare **6** except, excuse, immune, pardon, spared **7** absolve, cleared, excused, release, relieve **8** absolved, excepted, relieved **9** not liable, privilege **10** privileged

exemption 6 excuse **7** expense, freedom, release **8** immunity **9** allowance, deduction, exception **10** absolution **12** dispensation

exercise 3 use **4** show **5** apply, drill, exert, teach, train, tutor, wield **6** employ, school, warm-up **7** break in, develop, display, execute, exhibit, perform, prepare, program, utilize, workout **8** accustom, aerobics, carry out, ceremony, movement, practice, training **9** discharge, inculcate, schooling **10** daily dozen, discipline, employment, gymnastics, isometrics **11** application, demonstrate, give lessons, performance, utilization **12** calisthenics **14** do calisthenics

exert 3 use **5** apply, wield **6** employ, expend **7** utilize **8** exercise, put forth, resort to **9** discharge, make use of **11** put in action, set in motion

exertion 4 toil, work **5** labor, pains **6** effort, energy **7** travail, trouble **8** activity, endeavor, industry, strength, struggle **11** application, elbow grease

ex facie 9 on the face **10** apparently **11** from the face

ex facto 8 actually **15** according to fact

exhalation 4 puff **6** breath, wheeze,

exhale whoosh **10** expiration **12** breathing out

exhale 4 huff, pant, puff **6** expire **7** breathe, respire **10** breathe out

exhaust 3 fag, tax **4** bush, poop, tire **5** drain, empty, spend, use up **6** expend, finish, strain, weaken **7** consume, deplete, disable, draw off, draw out, fatigue, wear out **8** enervate, overtire **9** dissipate **10** debilitate, devitalize, run through **13** sap one's energy

exhausted 4 beat, gone **5** all in, spent **6** bushed, done in, pooped, used up **7** drained, emptied, wearied, worn out **8** bankrupt, consumed, depleted, expended, fatigued, finished, tired out **9** dead tired, enervated, played out **11** devitalized **12** impoverished

exhausting 5 tough **6** tiring, uphill **7** arduous **8** toilsome **9** difficult, fatiguing, Herculean, laborious, Sisyphean, wearisome **10** burdensome

exhaustion 7 fatigue, using up **8** draining, spending **9** depletion, tiredness, weariness **10** enervation **11** consumption

exhaustive 6 all-out **7** in-depth **8** complete, profound, sweeping, thorough **9** intensive **12** all-embracing, all-inclusive **13** comprehensive

exhibit 3 air **4** show **6** flaunt, parade, reveal, unveil **7** display **8** brandish **9** put on view **10** exhibition, exposition, make public **11** demonstrate **12** bring to light **13** public showing

exhibition 4 show **5** array **7** display, exhibit, showing **9** unveiling **10** exposition **13** demonstration, public showing

exhibitionist 7 flasher, show-off **15** attention-seeker

exhilarate 4 lift **5** cheer, elate **6** excite, perk up **7** animate, delight, enliven, gladden, hearten, quicken **9** stimulate **10** invigorate

exhilaration 6 gaiety **7** delight, elation **8** gladness, vivacity **9** animation **10** exaltation, excitement, joyousness, liveliness **11** high spirits **16** lightheartedness

exhort 3 bid **4** goad, prod, spur, urge **5** egg on, press **6** advise, enjoin **7** beseech, implore **8** admonish, advocate, appeal to, persuade **9** encourage, plead with, recommend **14** give a pep talk to

exhortation 6 sermon, urging **7** bidding, lecture, pep talk **8** dictates, harangue, prodding **9** prompting

exhumation 9 digging up **12** disinterment **13** disentombment

exhume 5 dig up **8** disinter

exigency 3 fix, jam **5** needs, pinch **6** crisis, pickle, plight, scrape, strait **7** demands **8** hardship, quandary **9** emergency, extremity, urgencies **10** difficulty **11** constraints, contingency, necessities, predicament **12** circumstance, requirements

exigent 5 vital **6** urgent **8** critical, exacting, pressing **9** demanding, difficult, necessary

exile 2 DP **4** oust **5** eject, expel **6** banish, deport, emigre, pariah **7** outcast, refugee **8** drive out, expellee **9** expulsion **10** banishment, expatriate

Exile, The
author: **9** Pearl Buck

exiled person 5 exile **6** emigre **7** outcast **8** expellee **10** expatriate

Exile's Return
author: **13** Malcolm Cowley

exist 4 last, live, stay **5** abide, ensue, occur **6** endure, happen, obtain, remain **7** breathe, prevail, survive

existence 4 life **5** being **7** reality **8** presence, survival **9** actuality, animation, endurance **11** continuance, materiality, subsistence, tangibility

existent 4 real **5** alive **6** actual, extant, living **7** present **8** existing, tangible **9** surviving, to be found **11** in existence

existing 4 real **5** being **6** actual, extant, living **7** ongoing, present **9** existence, surviving, to be found **10** continuing, prevailing **11** established, in existence **12** accomplished

exit 4 blow **5** go out, leave, split **6** cut out, depart, egress, escape, exodus, way out **7** retreat **8** withdraw **9** departure **10** withdrawal **11** take a powder

ex libris 15 out of the books of **16** from the library of

ex nihilo nihil fit 25 out of nothing nothing is made **27** nothing is created from nothing

exocuticle
consists of: **9** sclerotin

exodus 4 exit **5** exile **6** flight, hegira **9** departure, migration **10** emigration, going forth

Exodus
author: **8** Leon Uris
story of founding of: **6** Israel

exonerate 4 free **5** clear **6** acquit **7** absolve, forgive **9** exculpate, vindicate **12** find innocent

exoneration 8 clearing **10** absolution **11** exculpation, vindication

exorbitant 4 dear **5** undue **6** costly **7** extreme **8** enormous **9** egregious, excessive, expensive, out-of-line **10** high-priced, inordinate, oppressive, outrageous, overpriced **11** extravagant **12** extortionate, preposterous, unreasonable

exorcise 5 expel **7** cast out **8** get rid of
Exorcist, The
author: **18** William Peter Blatty
director: **15** William Friedkin

cast: **8** Lee J Cobb **10** Linda Blair **11** Jason Miller, Max von Sydow **12** Ellen Burstyn
Oscar for: **10** screenplay

exoskeleton
of insect: **5** shell **8** body wall
part: **10** epicuticle, exocuticle **11** endocuticle

exoteric 4 open **6** public, simple **7** popular **8** exterior, external, outsider

exotic 5 alien **6** quaint, unique **7** foreign, strange, unusual **8** colorful, peculiar, striking **9** different, not native **10** from abroad, intriguing, outlandish, unfamiliar **11** exceptional **13** not indigenous

expand 4 grow, open **5** swell, widen **6** dilate, evolve, extend, fatten, spread, unfold, unfurl, unroll **7** amplify, augment, develop, distend, enlarge, inflate, magnify, stretch, unravel **8** heighten, increase, multiply **9** outspread, spread out **10** aggrandize

expanded 4 grew **5** grown **7** dilated, swelled, swollen, widened **8** enlarged, extended, unfolded, unfurled, unrolled **9** augmented, broadened, increased, outspread, spread out, stretched **10** heightened **11** aggrandized

expanse 4 area **5** field, range, reach, space, sweep **6** extent **7** breadth, compass, stretch **9** magnitude

expansion 6 growth **8** dilation, increase, swelling, widening **9** enlarging, extension, spreading **10** amplifying, distention, magnifying, stretching **11** development, enlargement, lengthening, multiplying **12** augmentation **13** amplification

expansive 4 free, open, vast, wide **5** broad **6** genial **7** affable, amiable, general, liberal **8** effusive, generous, outgoing **9** bounteous, bountiful, capacious, extensive, exuberant **10** voluminous **11** extroverted, far-reaching, uninhibited, unrepressed, wide-ranging **12** unrestrained **13** comprehensive

expatiate 6 expand **7** amplify, enlarge, expound **9** discourse, elaborate

expatriate 2 DP **5** exile **6** emigre, pariah **7** outcast, refugee **15** displaced person

expatriation 5 exile **9** expulsion **10** banishment

expect 5 guess, trust **6** assume, demand, plan on, reckon **7** believe, count on, foresee, hope for, imagine, look for, presume, require, suppose, surmise **8** envision, reckon on, rely upon **9** calculate **10** anticipate, bargain for, conjecture, reckon upon **11** contemplate **13** look forward to

expectancy 11 expectation **12** anticipation

expectant 4 agog **5** eager, ready **7** anxious, hopeful, waiting **9** expecting

10 looking for, optimistic **12** anticipating, apprehensive

expectation 4 hope **5** trust **6** belief, chance **8** prospect, reliance **9** assurance **10** confidence, expectancy, likelihood **11** presumption **12** anticipation **13** contemplation

expedient 4 help, wise **5** means **6** resort, tactic, useful **7** benefit, helpful, measure, politic, selfish, stopgap **9** advantage, advisable, conniving, desirable, effective, judicious, makeshift, opportune, practical, strategem **10** beneficial, instrument, profitable, worthwhile **11** calculating, self-seeking, self-serving **12** advantageous **14** self-interested

expedite 4 rush **5** hurry **6** hasten **7** advance, forward, further, promote, quicken, speed up **8** dispatch **10** accelerate, facilitate **11** precipitate, push through

expedition 4 trek **6** voyage **7** journey, mission **8** campaign, voyagers **9** explorers, travelers, wayfarers **10** enterprise **11** adventurers, exploration

expeditious 4 fast **5** alert, awake, hasty, quick, rapid, ready, swift **6** prompt, snappy, speedy **7** instant **8** punctual **9** effective, immediate **10** bright-eyed **11** efficacious

expel 4 fire, oust, sack, spew, void **5** eject, evict, exile **6** banish, bounce, remove **7** cashier, cast out, dismiss, drum out, excrete **8** dislodge, drive out, evacuate, force out, throw out **9** discharge, eliminate

expellee 2 DP **5** exile **14** banished person **15** displaced person

expend 3 pay **4** give **5** drain, empty, spend, use up **6** donate, lay out, pay out **7** consume, exhaust, fork out, wear out **8** disburse, dispense, shell out, squander **9** dissipate, go through **10** contribute

expendable 7 payable **9** available, forgoable, spendable **10** consumable, extraneous **11** disbursable, dispensable, replaceable, superfluous **12** nonessential **14** relinquishable

expended 5 spent **6** used up **7** drained, emptied, paid out **8** consumed **9** disbursed, exhausted **10** dissipated

expenditure 3 use **4** cost **5** price **6** charge, outlay, output **7** payment **8** exertion, expenses, spending **9** expending, paying out **10** employment, money spent **11** application, consumption **12** disbursement

expense 4 cost, rate **5** drain, price **6** amount, charge, figure, outlay **9** depletion, quotation

expensive 4 dear **6** costly **9** excessive **10** exorbitant, high-priced, immoderate, overpriced **11** extravagant **12** un-

economical, unreasonable **15** beyond one's means

experience 3 see **4** bear, feel, know, meet, view **5** doing, event, sense **6** affair, behold, endure, suffer **7** episode, observe, sustain, undergo **8** exposure, incident, perceive, practice, training **9** adventure, encounter, go through, happening, seasoning, withstand **10** occurrence **11** familiarity, live through, observation **17** personal knowledge **18** firsthand knowledge

experienced 4 able, wise **6** expert, master **7** capable, knowing, skilled, trained, veteran **8** seasoned **9** competent, efficient, practical, qualified **10** well-versed **11** worldly-wise **12** accomplished **13** sophisticated

experiential 9 empirical, firsthand, practical

experiment 4 test **5** assay, flier, trial **6** feeler, try out **7** analyze, examine, explore, venture **8** analysis, research **11** examination, investigate **12** seek proof for, verification **13** investigation **14** mess around with

experimental 3 new **4** test **5** fresh, rough, trial **7** radical **9** tentative **10** conceptual, first-draft **11** conjectural, speculative **13** developmental, trial-and-error

experimentation 7 testing **8** analysis, research **10** experiment **11** examination, exploration **13** investigation, trial and error

experimenter 6 tester **10** researcher **15** experimentalist

expert 3 ace, apt, pro, wiz **4** able, deft, whiz **5** adept, crack, doyen, maven, mavin, shark **6** adroit, artist, facile, master, wizard **7** artiste, capable, perfect, skilled, trained, veteran **8** masterly, skillful, virtuoso **9** authority, competent, masterful, practiced, qualified **10** first-class, past-master, proficient, specialist **11** connoisseur, crackerjack, experienced **12** accomplished, professional **13** knowledgeable French: **6** au fait

expertise 5 savvy, skill **7** know-how **10** expertness **12** special skill **14** specialization **15** professionalism

expertness 5 savvy, skill **7** ability, know how **8** training **9** expertise **10** capability, competence, experience **11** proficiency **12** special skill **13** qualification **14** accomplishment, specialization **15** professionalism

expiate 7 appease **8** atone for **13** make amends for **16** pay the penalty for

expiation 6 amends, shrift **7** penance **9** atonement **11** appeasement **16** paying the penalty

expiration 3 end **5** death, dying **6** demise, ending, finish **7** passing, closing

8 decrease, exhaling **10** conclusion **11** termination **12** breathing out

expire 3 die, end **5** cease, lapse **6** finish, perish, run out **7** decease, kick off, succumb **8** conclude, pass away **9** terminate **11** come to an end, discontinue **13** kick the bucket **14** give up the ghost

expired 4 dead, died **6** lapsed, ran out, run out **7** defunct, laspsed **8** deceased, lifeless, perished **10** passed away **11** came to an end, come to an end **14** gave up the ghost

explain 6 fathom **7** clarify, clear up, justify, resolve **8** describe, spell out **9** elucidate, explicate, interpret, make clear, make plain **10** account for, illuminate, illustrate **11** demonstrate, rationalize **14** give a reason for **20** give an explanation for

explainer 6 critic **7** analyst **8** reviewer **10** translator **11** commentator, interpreter

explanation
French: **15** eclaircissement

explicate 7 analyze, clarify, develop, explain **8** annotate **9** elucidate, interpret **10** elucidated, illuminate, illustrate

explication 8 analysis **10** commentary **11** elucidation, explanation **12** illumination **13** clarification **14** interpretation

explication de texte 8 exegesis **11** explanation **14** interpretation **17** literary criticism

explicit 5 blunt, clear, exact, frank, plain **6** candid, direct **7** certain, express, pointed, precise **8** absolute, definite, distinct, specific **9** outspoken **10** unreserved **11** categorical, unequivocal, unqualified **15** straightforward **16** clearly expressed

explicitness 7 clarity **9** clearness, precision **11** unambiguity

explode 5 belie, blast, burst, erupt, go off **6** blow up, expose, refute, set off **7** destroy **8** detonate, disprove **9** discredit, repudiate **10** invalidate, prove false, prove wrong **11** burst loudly **12** utter noisily **14** burst violently, express noisily **18** discharge violently **19** burst out emotionally

exploit 4 feat **5** abuse **6** misuse **7** utilize **8** profit by, put to use **9** adventure, brave deed, heroic act, make use of **10** daring deed **11** achievement **12** capitalize on **14** accomplishment, use to advantage **15** take advantage of **16** make selfish use of **21** take unfair advantage of **22** turn to practical account

exploited 6 abused **7** ill used, misused **11** downtrodden **15** took advantage of **16** taken advantage of

exploration 5 probe **7** inquiry **8** scrutiny **9** discovery **10** expedition, experiment **11** examination **12** scouting trip **13** investigation

explore 3 try **5** plumb, probe, scout **6** survey, try out **7** analyze, examine, feel out, pry into **8** look into, research, traverse **9** delve into, penetrate, range over **10** scrutinize, search into, travel over **11** inquire into, investigate, reconnoiter **14** experiment with

explorer
American: 4 Byrd, Pike **5** Boone, Clark, Lewis, Peary, Perry
Australian: 4 Hume **5** Sturt **6** Stuart **8** Mitchell
British: 4 Bell, Cook, Park **5** Baker, Bligh, Bruce, Cabot, Davis, Drake, Grant, Puget, Scott, Smith, Speke **6** Baffin, Burton, Hudson, Lander **7** Raleigh, Stanley **8** Franklin **9** Frobisher, MacKenzie, Vancouver **11** Livingstone
Danish: 6 Bering **7** Niebuhr
Dutch: 6 Tasman **7** Barents, Le Maire **8** Schouten **10** Linschoten
French: 6 Joliet **7** Cartier, Jolliet, La Salle **9** Champlain, Marquette **12** Bougainville
Italian: 8 Columbus **9** Marco Polo, Verrazano **15** Amerigo Vespucci
Moslem: 10 Ibn Battuta
Norwegian: 8 Amundsen
Portuguese: 3 Cam, Cao **4** Dias, Diaz **6** Cabral, Da Gama **7** Almeida **8** Covilhao, Magellan **11** Albuquerque **23** Prince Henry the Navigator
Russian: 10 Middendorf **11** Przhevalsky
Spanish: 6 Balboa, Cortes, De Soto **7** Pizarro **8** Coronado, Orellana, Valdivia **11** Ponce de Leon
Swedish: 12 Nordenskjold
Viking: 10 Eric the Red **11** Leif Ericson

explosion 3 fit **4** clap **5** blast, burst, crack **6** report **7** tantrum **8** eruption, outbreak, outburst, paroxysm **9** blowing up, discharge **10** detonation **11** fulmination

explosive 3 TNT **5** shaky, tense **6** touchy **7** cordite, keyed up **8** critical, dynamite, perilous, strained, ticklish, unstable, volatile **9** dangerous, emotional, gelignite **10** ammunition, precarious **12** pyrotechnics **13** nitroglycerin

exponent 6 backer **8** advocate, champion, defender, promoter **9** expounder, proponent, spokesman, supporter **12** propagandist

export 7 send out **8** dispatch **10** sell abroad **11** foreign sale **12** ship overseas

expose 4 bare, risk, show **5** brand, offer, strip **6** betray, denude, divest, hazard, let out, reveal, submit **7** display, divulge, exhibit, imperil, let slip,

subject, uncover, unearth **8** denounce, disclose, endanger **10** jeopardize, reveal to be **12** acquaint with, bring to light **16** leave unprotected

expose 6 baring **8** exposure **10** divulgence, revelation

exposed 4 open **5** bared **8** divulged, laid open, revealed, unmasked **9** denounced, disclosed, displayed, uncovered, unearthed **11** unprotected, unsheltered

exposition 4 expo, fair, mart, show **6** bazaar, market **7** account, display, exhibit, picture **8** exegesis **9** trade fair, trade show **10** commentary, exhibition, world's fair **11** description, elucidation, explanation, explication **12** illustration, presentation **13** clarification, demonstration **14** interpretation

expostulate 5 argue **6** enjoin, exhort, object, reason **7** caution, counsel, protest **8** forewarn **9** plead with **11** remonstrate **13** cry out against, reason against **14** inveigh against

exposure 4 view **5** vista **6** expose **7** outlook **8** frontage, prospect **9** divulging, unmasking **10** disclosure, divulgence, laying bare, laying open, revelation, subjection, submission, uncovering **11** perspective **12** public notice **15** bringing to light

expound 6 defend, uphold **7** explain **8** describe **9** elucidate, explicate, hold forth, make clear

express 3 say **4** fast, show, word **5** clear, couch, exact, lucid, plain, quick, rapid, speak, state, swift, utter, vivid, voice **6** convey, direct, evince, phrase, relate, reveal **7** certain, declare, divulge, exhibit, nonstop, precise **8** definite, describe, disclose, evidence, explicit, forceful, specific, vocalize **9** high-speed, make known, verbalize **10** articulate, particular **11** categorical, communicate, unequivocal **12** put into words

expression 4 look, mien, term, tone, word **5** idiom, style **6** airing, aspect, phrase, saying **7** emotion, meaning, stating, telling, venting, voicing, wording **8** language, locution, phrasing, relating, speaking, uttering **9** assertion, eloquence **10** appearance, modulation **11** countenance, declaration, enunciation, phraseology **12** articulation, setting forth, turn of phrase **13** communication

expressionless 5 blank, empty **6** vacant **7** deadpan **12** inexpressive

expressive 5 vivid **6** moving **7** telling **8** eloquent, forceful, poignant, powerful, striking **9** effective **10** compelling, indicative, meaningful, thoughtful **11** significant **14** characteristic

expressly 7 clearly, plainly **9** decidedly, pointedly, precisely, specially

10 definitely, distinctly, explicitly **12** particularly, specifically **13** categorically, unequivocally **18** in no uncertain terms

express sorrow 3 cry **4** weep **6** grieve, lament **7** condole, console **10** sympathize **11** commiserate

expropriate 4 take **5** seize **8** take over **10** commandeer, confiscate **11** appropriate

expropriation 7 seizure **10** arrogation, taking over **12** confiscation **13** commandeering

expulsion 5 exile **6** ouster **7** ousting, removal **8** ejection, eviction **9** debarment, discharge, dismissal, exclusion, expelling **10** banishment **11** elimination, prohibition, throwing out **12** proscription

expunge 5 erase **6** delete, efface, rub out **7** blot out, destroy, wipe out **9** eradicate, strike out **10** obliterate

expurgate 3 cut **4** blip, edit **5** bleep, purge **6** censor, cut out, delete, excise, remove **8** bleep out **10** blue-pencil, bowdlerize

exquisite 4 fine **5** dainty **6** choice, lovely, superb **7** elegant, perfect **8** delicate, flawless, peerless, precious, splendid **9** admirable, excellent, faultless, matchless **10** consummate, fastidious, impeccable, meticulous **11** superlative **12** incomparable **14** discriminating

exquisiteness 6 beauty **8** delicacy, elegance, fineness **10** loveliness, perfection **12** flawlessness

extant 6 living **7** present **8** existent, existing **9** surviving, to be found **11** in existence

Extasie, The
author: 9 John Donne

extemporaneous 5 ad-lib **7** offhand **9** extempore, impromptu **10** improvised, off the cuff, unprepared **11** extemporary, spontaneous, unrehearsed **12** without notes **13** without notice **14** unpremeditated **15** spur-of-the-moment **19** off the top of one's head

extemporary 5 ad-lib **9** extempore, impromptu **10** improvised, off the cuff, unprepared **14** extemporaneous **19** off the top of one's head

extempore 5 ad-lib **7** offhand **9** impromptu **10** improvised, off the cuff, unprepared **11** extemporary, unrehearsed **12** without notes **14** extemporaneous, unpremeditated **15** spur-of-the-moment **19** off the top of one's head

extemporize 5 ad-lib **6** make up **9** improvise **14** speak impromptu **15** speak off the cuff

extend 4 give **5** grant, offer, widen **6** bestow, expand, impart, put out, spread, submit **7** advance, amplify, augment, broaden, draw out, enlarge, hold out, proffer, prolong, stretch **8** continue, elongate, increase, lengthen, protract, reach out **10** make longer, stretch out **12** stretch forth

extended 4 long **7** widened **8** drawn out, enlarged, expanded, thorough, unfolded, unfurled **9** broadened, continued, extensive, prolonged, spread out **10** lengthened, protracted, widespread **12** stretched out **13** comprehensive

extending 8 full form **9** expansion **10** drawing out, elongation, proffering, stretching **11** enlargement, lengthening **12** putting forth

extension 3 arm, ell **4** wing **5** annex, delay **6** branch, length, outlay **7** adjunct **8** addition, appendix, increase **9** appendage, expansion, outgrowth **10** drawing out, proffering **11** enlargement, lengthening **12** continuation, postponement, prolongation

extensive 4 huge, long, vast, wide **5** broad, great, large **7** lengthy **8** enormous, extended, far-flung, thorough **9** capacious, universal **10** protracted, voluminous **12** all-inclusive, considerable **13** comprehensive

extensiveness 4 span **5** range, reach, scope **6** extent, spread **7** breadth, compass, expanse, stretch

extent 4 area, size, time **5** range, reach, scope, sweep **6** amount, degree, length **7** breadth, compass, expanse, stretch **8** duration **9** amplitude, magnitude **10** dimensions

extenuate 6 excuse, temper **7** explain, justify, qualify **8** mitigate, moderate

extenuating 9 lessening, tempering **10** mitigating, moderating, qualifying **11** attenuating, diminishing, explanatory, justifiable

exterior 4 face, skin **5** alien, outer, shell **6** exotic, facade, finish, manner **7** bearing, coating, foreign, outside, outward, surface **8** covering, demeanor, external **9** extrinsic, outer side, outermost **10** extraneous **11** superficial

exterminate 3 zap **4** kill **5** erase, waste **7** abolish, destroy, expunge, root out, wipe out **8** demolish, massacre **9** eliminate, eradicate, slaughter **10** annihilate, extinguish

external 5 alien, outer **7** foreign, outside, outward, surface **8** exterior **9** extrinsic, outermost **10** extraneous **11** superficial

extinct 4 dead, gone, lost **6** put out **7** defunct, died out, gone out **8** quenched, vanished **12** extinguished

extinction 5 death **7** eclipse **9** wiping out **11** destruction, eradication **13** disappearance

extinguish 3 end, zap **4** dash, do in, kill **5** crush, douse, quash **6** cancel,

dispel, put out, quench, stifle **7** abolish, blow out, destroy, smother, wipe out **8** demolish, snuff out **9** eliminate, eradicate, suffocate

extinguished 6 put out **7** gone out **8** quenched **15** no longer burning

extirpate 5 erase **7** abolish, destroy, extract, pull out, root out, wipe out **8** demolish **9** eradicate **10** annihilate, extinguish, obliterate **11** exterminate

extol 4 laud **6** praise **7** acclaim, applaud, commend, glorify **8** eulogize **9** celebrate **10** compliment **16** sing the praises of

extort 5 educe, exact **6** coerce, elicit **7** extract **9** shake down

extortion 5 force, graft **6** payola, ransom **7** threats, tribute **8** coercion **9** blackmail, hush money, shakedown **14** forced payments

extortionate 5 undue **7** extreme **9** excessive, out-of-line **10** exorbitant, inordinate **12** unreasonable

extra 4 more **5** spare **7** adjunct, further, surplus **9** accessory, auxiliary, redundant, unusually **10** additional, attachment, complement, especially, remarkably, uncommonly **11** superfluous, unnecessary **12** additionally, appurtenance, particularly, supplemental **13** exceptionally **15** extraordinarily

extract 3 get **4** cite, cull **5** educe, evoke, exact, glean, juice, quote, wrest **6** choose, deduce, derive, elicit, obtain, pry out, remove, select **7** copy out, distill, draw out, essence, excerpt, passage, pull out, root out, take out **8** abstract, bring out, citation, pluck out, press out, separate **9** extirpate, extricate, quotation, selection **10** distillate, squeeze out **11** concentrate

extraction 5 stock **7** descent, removal **8** ancestry **10** derivation, drawing out, pulling out

extraneous 5 alien **6** exotic **7** foreign, strange **9** extrinsic, unrelated **10** immaterial, incidental, irrelevant, not germane **11** superfluous **12** adventitious, inadmissible, nonessential, not pertinent **13** inappropriate

extraordinary 3 odd **4** rare **5** queer **6** unique **7** amazing, notable, strange, unusual **8** uncommon **9** fantastic, monstrous, unheard of **10** incredible, phenomenal, remarkable **11** exceptional **12** unbelievable **13** inconceivable

extraterrestrial 2 ET **3** Alf **6** cosmic **10** outer-space **12** interstellar, otherworldly **14** interplanetary

extravagance 5 folly, waste **6** excess **7** caprice **9** absurdity **10** profligacy **11** prodigality, squandering, unrestraint **12** immoderation, improvidence, overspending, recklessness, wastefulness **13** excessiveness **14** capriciousness **16** inordinate outlay, unreasonableness

extravagant 4 wild **6** absurd, costly, unreal **7** foolish **8** fabulous, lavishly, prodigal, spending, wasteful **9** excessive, expensive, fantastic, high-flown, imprudent **10** exorbitant, high-priced, immoderate, inordinate, openhanded, outlandish, outrageous, overpriced, profligate **11** improvident, spendthrift, squandering **12** overspending, preposterous, unreasonable, unrestrained

extravaganza 4 fair **5** opera **6** ballet **7** pageant **8** carnival, operetta **9** spectacle, stage show **10** exposition, vaudeville **11** opera bouffe, spectacular **12** Broadway show, opera comique, son et lumiere, wild west show **14** phantasmagoria **17** sound and light show

extreme 3 end **5** depth **6** excess, height, severe **7** intense, radical, unusual **8** advanced, boundary, farthest, uncommon **9** excessive, extremity, nth degree, outermost, very great **10** avant-garde, immoderate, inordinate, outrageous **11** exaggerated, extravagant, most distant **13** extraordinary

extremely 4 very **5** quite **7** awfully **8** terribly **9** curiously, intensely, unusually **10** abnormally, especially, freakishly, peculiarly, remarkably, singularly, uncommonly **11** exceedingly, excessively, unnaturally **12** immoderately, surprisingly **13** exceptionally **15** extraordinarily

extremely painful 7 racking **9** agonizing, torturous **10** tormenting, unbearable **11** intolerable, unendurable **12** excruciating, insufferable

extremity 3 arm, end, leg, tip, toe **4** edge, foot, hand, limb **5** bound, brink, limit, reach **6** border, finger, margin **7** confine, extreme **8** boundary, terminus **9** outer edge, periphery

extricate 4 free **5** loose **6** get out, rescue **7** deliver, release **8** liberate, untangle **9** disengage **11** disencumber, disentangle **12** wriggle out of

extrication 6 escape **7** loosing, release **10** liberation **11** deliverance **13** disengagement **15** disentanglement

extrinsic 5 alien **7** foreign **9** accessory **10** accidental, extraneous, incidental **11** dispensable **12** nonessential

extrovert 7 show-off **13** exhibitionist **14** life of the party **17** hail-fellow-well-met

extroverted 8 outgoing, sociable **9** expansive **10** gregarious **12** unrestrained

extrude 4 spew **5** eject, expel **7** project, push out **8** force out, protrude, stickout **9** thrust out

exuberance 3 zip **4** elan, life, zeal **5** vigor **6** energy, spirit **8** buoyancy, vitality, vivacity **9** animation, eagerness **10** enthusiasm, excitement, liveliness **13** effervescence, sprightliness

exuberant 4 lush, rich **5** eager

6 lavish, lively 7 copious, excited, profuse, zealous 8 abundant, animated, spirited, vigorous 9 bounteous, energetic, luxuriant, plenteous, plentiful, sprightly 12 enthusiastic 13 superabundant

exudation 3 sap, tar 4 ooze 5 pitch, sweat 7 leakage, seepage 8 bleeding, drainage 9 discharge, excretion

exude 4 drip, emit, ooze 5 sweat 7 secrete 9 discharge

exult 4 crow 5 gloat, glory 7 rejoice 8 be elated 10 be jubilant, jump for joy 11 be delighted 13 be exhilarated 15 be in high spirits

exultant 5 happy 6 elated, joyful 7 crowing 8 boasting, ecstatic, euphoric, gloating, jubilant 9 rapturous, rejoicing 10 triumphant

exultation 3 joy 7 elation, ovation, rapture, triumph 9 rejoicing 10 jubilation

Eyck, Jan van
  born: 8 Flanders, Maaseyck 10 Maastricht
  artwork: 9 Timotheos 15 Ghent Altarpiece 18 Adoration of the Lamb, The Man in a Red Turban, The Virgin in a Church 20 The Arnolfini Marriage 24 Arnolfini Wedding Portrait 29 The Madonna with Chancellor Rolin 30 The Madonna with Canon van der Paele

eye 3 orb 4 scan, view 5 sight, study, taste, watch 6 behold, gaze at, look at, peeper, regard, survey, take in, vision 7 inspect, observe, stare at 8 eyesight, glance at 10 perception, scrutinize 14 discrimination
  part: 4 iris, lens, rods 5 cones, nerve, pupil 6 cornea, muscle, retina 11 blood vessel

eyeful 4 doll 5 beaut, peach, Venus 6 beauty 7 stunner 8 knockout 10 good-looker 13 beautiful girl 14 beautiful woman

eyeglass, eyeglasses 4 lens 5 specs 6 eyecup, lenses 7 goggles, monocle 8 bifocals, cheaters, contacts, pincenez 9 lorgnette 10 spectacles

Eye of the Needle
  author: 10 Ken Follett

eyesight 4 eyes 5 sight 6 vision

eyewitness 5 gaper, gazer 6 gawker, viewer 7 witness 8 attester, attestor, beholder, informer, looker-on, observer, onlooker, passerby 9 bystander, spectator, testifier 10 rubberneck

eyre 4 lake, tour 7 circuit

Ezekiel
  father: 4 Buzi

Ezra
  father: 7 Seraiah

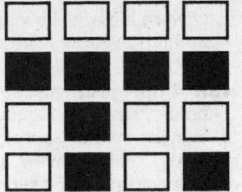  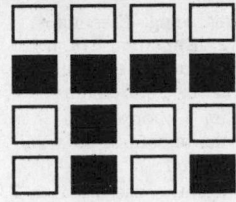

Fabares, Ruby Bernadette Nanette
  real name of: **13** Nanette Fabray
  aunt of: **14** Shelley Fabares
fable 3 fib, lie **4** hoax, myth, tale, yarn
  6 legend **7** fiction, leg-pull, parable,
  romance, untruth, whopper **8** allegory
  9 fairy tale, falsehood, invention, tall
  story **11** fabrication
fabled 6 unreal **7** storied **8** fabulous,
  fanciful, mythical **9** imaginary, legendary **10** fictitious **12** mythological
Fables
  author: **5** Aesop **16** Jean de La Fontaine
  ends with: **5** moral
  feature: **4** hare **8** tortoise **10** sour
  grapes
Fabray, Nanette
  real name: **28** Ruby Bernadette
  Nanette Fabares
  partner: **9** Sid Caesar
  born: **10** San Diego CA
  roles: **7** Baby Nan **12** The Band
  Wagon **13** Sid Caesar Hour **15** High
  Button Shoes, Our Gang comedies
fabric 5 cloth, frame, stuff **6** makeup **7**
  textile, texture **8** dry goods, material **9**
  framework, structure, substance, yard
  goods **10** foundation **12** organization,
  substructure **14** infrastructure, super-
  structure
  cotton: 4 duck **5** denim, drill, scrim,
  terry **6** burlap, calico, canvas, chintz,
  dimity, madras, muslin, oxford, poplin **7** batiste, buckram, flannel, gingham, organdy, percale, ticking **8**
  chambray **9** crinoline, sailcloth **10**
  broadcloth, printcloth, seersucker **11**
  cheesecloth, dotted Swiss
  linen: 6 canvas, damask **7** butcher,
  cambric **8** birds-eye **9** huckaback
  natural: 4 jute, silk, wool **5** linen **6**
  cotton **8** asbestos
  silk: 3 raw **4** tram **7** organza **8** organzie **9** organzine
  synthetic: 5 nylon, orlon, rayon **6**
  olefin **7** acetate, acrylic **9** polyester
  type: 4 felt, lace, lame **5** crepe,
  gauze, moire, serge, voile **6** damask,
  faille, jersey, melton, velour, velvet **7**
  brocade, chiffon, flannel, foulard,
  gingham, taffeta **8** chenille, cordu-
  roy, tapestry **9** gabardine, velveteen
  wool: 4 felt **5** crepe, serge, tweed,
  twill **6** boucle, covert, faille, melton,
  woolen **7** challis, doeskin, Donegal,
  worsted **8** homespun, Shetland **9** Astrakhan, gabardine, sharkskin **10**
  hopsacking **11** Harris tweed, herringbone
  from goats: 8 cashmere
  sheep: 5 Iraqi **6** Hirrik, merino,
  Romney, Somali **7** Lincoln **8** Cotswold, Tatarian **9** Hampshire,
  Southdown **10** Corriedale, Dorset
  Down, Dorset Horn, Shropshire,
  Sikkim Bera **13** Hampshire Down
  other wool-bearing animals:
  5 camel, llama **6** alpaca, vicuna
fabricate 4 fake, form, make **5** build,
  erect, feign, forge, frame, hatch, shape
  6 design, devise, invent, make up **7**
  compose, concoct, falsify, fashion,
  produce, trump up **8** assemble, contrive, simulate **9** construct, embroider,
  formulate **11** counterfeit, manufacture
fabrication 3 fib, lie **4** myth, yarn **5**
  fable **6** makeup **7** fiction, forgery, untruth **8** building, creation, erection **9**
  fairy tale, falsehood, invention **10** assemblage, concoction, fashioning, production **11** composition, manufacture
  12 constructing, construction **13** prevarication **16** cock-and-bull story
Fabritius, Carel
  real name: **13** Carel Pietersz
  born: **14** Midden-Beemster, The Netherlands
  artwork: **11** View of Delft **12** The
  Goldfinch **19** The Raising of Lazarus
fabulous 5 great **6** fabled, superb **7**
  amazing, storied **8** fanciful, invented,
  mythical, smashing **9** fantastic, imaginary, legendary, marvelous, wonderful
  10 apocryphal, astounding, fictitious,
  incredible, stupendous **11** astonishing,
  spectacular **12** mythological, unbelievable **13** extraordinary
facade 4 face, mask **6** veneer **8** frontage, pretense **9** front view **10** false
  front **13** building front
face 3 air, mug, pan **4** coat, gall, grit,
  look, pout, puss, sand **5** brass, cheek,
  cover, front, image, nerve, pluck,
  spunk **6** aspect, daring, facade, kisser,
  mettle, repute, visage **7** bravado, dignity, front on, grimace, obverse, overlay, surface **8** boldness, confront,
  features, forepart, frontage, good
  name, overlook, prestige **9** encounter,
  hardihood, impudence, semblance **10**
  appearance, confidence, effrontery, expression, give toward, look toward,
  reputation, turn toward **11** countenance, physiognomy, self-respect
Face
  character in: **12** The Alchemist
  author: **6** Jonson
facet 3 cut **4** part, side **5** angle, phase,
  plane **6** aspect **7** surface
facetious 5 comic, droll, funny, witty
  6 clever, jocose, joking, jovial **7**
  amusing, comical, jesting, jocular,
  playful **8** humorous **12** wisecracking
face-to-face 6 direct **8** one-on-one,
  personal **9** firsthand
facile 3 apt **4** glib **5** adept, handy,
  quick, slick **6** adroit, artful, casual,
  clever, fluent, smooth **7** cursory, shallow **8** careless, skillful **10** effortless,
  proficient **11** superficial
facilitate 3 aid **4** ease **6** foster, help
  in, smooth **7** advance, forward, further, lighten, promote, speed up **8** expedite, simplify **10** accelerate, make
  easier
facility 3 aid **4** bent, ease **5** knack,
  means, skill **7** aptness, fluency **8** deftness, easiness, resource **9** advantage,
  appliance, dexterity, readiness **10**
  adroitness, capability, competence, efficiency, expertness, smoothness **11**
  convenience, proficiency **14** effortlessness, practicability
facsimile 3 fax **4** copy **5** clone, xerox
  7 replica, reprint **8** likeness **9** duplicate, imitation, photostat **10** transcript
  12 reproduction
fact 3 act **4** deed **5** event, truth **6** verity **7** reality **8** incident, specific **9** actuality, certainty, happening, thing
  done **10** occurrence, particular **12** circumstance
faction 3 set **4** bloc, gang, ring, sect,
  side, unit **5** cabal, clash, group, split
  6 breach, circle, clique, schism, strife
  7 combine, coterie, discord, rupture,
  section **8** conflict, division, minority,
  sedition **9** rebellion **10** contention,
  disruption, dissension, dissidence, insurgency, quarreling **11** subdivision
  12 disagreement **13** splinter group **15**
  incompatibility
factious 7 warring **8** divisive, fighting,
  mutinous **9** alienated, bickering, combative, estranged **10** contending, rebellious **11** belligerent, contentious,

disaffected, disagreeing, dissentious, quarrelsome **12** disputatious **13** at loggerheads, insubordinate **15** insurrectionary **16** at sixes and sevens

factitious 4 sham **5** phony **9** pretended, synthetic, unnatural **10** artificial **12** manufactured

factor 4 part **5** agent, cause **6** reason **7** element **9** component, influence **11** constituent **12** circumstance **13** consideration

factory 4 mill, shop **5** plant, works **8** workshop **11** manufactory

factotum 4 aide **6** Figaro **8** handyman **9** gal Friday, guy Friday, man Friday **10** girl Friday **12** right-hand man **15** jack-of-all-trades

factual 4 real, true **5** exact, plain **6** actual **7** certain, correct, genuine, literal **8** accurate, concrete, definite, faithful **9** authentic, unadorned **10** scrupulous, verifiable

faculty, faculties 4 bent, gift, wits **5** flair, knack, power, skill **6** genius, reason, talent **7** quality **8** aptitude, capacity, function, penchant, teachers **9** adeptness, endowment **10** capability, professors **12** mental powers, skillfulness **13** teaching staff

fad 4 mode, rage, whim **5** craze, fancy, mania, vogue **6** whimsy **7** fashion **10** dernier cri, latest word **11** latest thing

faddish 2 in **6** trendy **10** innovative **11** fashionable

fade 3 die, dim, ebb **4** blur, dull, fail, flag, pale, wane **5** droop, taper **6** bleach, lessen, recede, whiten, wither **7** crumble, decline, dwindle, fall off, grow dim, shrivel **8** diminish, dissolve, evanesce, languish, make pale, melt away, pass away **9** disappear dissipate, evaporate, lose color

fade away 3 die, ebb **6** recede **7** subside **8** diminish

faded 4 drab, dull, pale **5** dingy **6** grayed **7** died out **8** bleached, dwindled, whitened, withered **9** colorless, shriveled, washed out

Faerie Queene, The
  author: 13 Edmund Spenser
  character: 3 Una **5** Guyon **6** Duessa **8** Artegall, Gloriana (the Faerie Queen) **9** Archimago, Britomart **12** Prince Arthur **14** Red Cross Knight

Fafnir
  origin: 12 Scandinavian
  form: 6 dragon
  father: 8 Hreidmar
  brother: 5 Otter, Regin
  killed: 8 Hreidmar
  killed by: 6 Sigurd

fag 4 bush, butt, poop, tire, weed **5** weary **6** tucker **7** exhaust **9** cigarette

Fagin
  character in: 11 Oliver Twist
  author: 7 Dickens

Fahrenheit
  abbreviation: 1 F

Fahrenheit 451
  author: 11 Ray Bradbury

Fahrenheit, Gabriel Daniel
  field: 7 physics
  nationality: 6 German
  invented: 16 thermometer scale **18** alcohol thermometer, mercury thermometer

fail 3 die, ebb **4** bomb, flag, flop, fold, wane **5** abort, crash, droop, flunk **6** desert, slip up **7** decline, dwindle, forsake, founder, give out, go under, let down, misfire **8** be in vain, collapse, fade away, languish, lay an egg, miscarry **9** disappear, fall short, fizzle out **10** end in smoke, go bankrupt, not succeed, run aground **11** be stillborn, come to grief, deteriorate, fall through, go up in smoke, miss the mark **12** come to naught, turn out badly **13** come to nothing **15** go out of business **16** meet one's Waterloo, meet with disaster

fail at 11 fall short of **12** be defeated in, not succeed at **16** be unsuccessful at

failed
  French: 6 manque

failing 4 weak **5** fault, shaky **6** defect, ebbing, foible, waning **7** folding, frailty **8** drooping, flagging, giving up, slipping, weakness **9** deficient, dwindling, giving out, weakening, weak point **10** deficiency, going under **11** shortcoming **12** unsuccessful **13** insufficiency

fail to include 4 drop, omit **5** elide **8** leave out, pass over

failure 3 dud **4** bomb, flop, mess, ruin **5** botch, crash, loser **6** fizzle, mishap, muddle, turkey **7** decline, default, failing, folding, misfire, washout **8** collapse, downfall **9** breakdown, ruination **10** bankruptcy, ne'er-do-well

Fainall, Mrs
  character in: 16 The Way of the World
  author: 8 Congreve

faint 3 dim, low **4** pale, soft, thin, weak **5** dizzy, faded, frail, giddy, muted, small, swoon, timid **6** dulcet, feeble, little, meager, remote, slight, subtle, torpid **7** fearful, fragile, languid, muffled, obscure, pass out, worn out **8** black out, collapse, cowardly, delicate, drooping, fatigued, timorous **9** exhausted, inaudible, lethargic, whispered **10** indistinct **11** lightheaded, lily-livered, vertiginous **13** inconspicuous **17** lose consciousness

fainthearted 4 weak **5** timid **6** feeble **8** cowardly **10** irresolute **11** half-hearted, indifferent, lily-livered

faintheartedness 9 cowardice **12**

cowardliness, yellow streak **13** pusillanimity, yellow feather **17** pusillanimousness **18** chickenheartedness

fair 4 fine, just, pale, so-so **5** blond, bonny, sunny **6** blonde, bright, comely, creamy, decent, honest, justly, kosher, lovely, medium, pretty, proper, square **7** average, cricket, legally, not dark, upright **8** adequate, candidly, carnival, honestly, mediocre, middling, moderate, ordinary, passable, pleasant, rainless, squarely, sunshiny, unbiased **9** beautiful, cloudless, equitable, ethically, honorable, honorably, impartial, justified, objective, tolerable, unclouded **10** aboveboard, attractive, evenhanded, exhibition, legitimate, pretty good, reasonable, truthfully **11** indifferent, respectable **12** forthrightly, light-colored, light-skinned, on the up-and-up, run-of-the-mill, satisfactory, unprejudiced **13** disinterested, dispassionate **19** according to the rules

Fair, A A
  pseudonym of: 18 Erle Stanley Gardner

Fairbanks, Douglas
  real name: 17 Douglas Elton Ulman
  wife: 12 Mary Pickford
  son: 18 Douglas Fairbanks Jr
  born: 8 Denver CO
  roles: 9 Robin Hood **11** The Iron Mask **14** The Black Pirate, The Mark of Zorro **16** The Thief of Bagdad **18** The Three Musketeers **23** The Private Life of Don Juan

Fairbanks, Douglas Jr
  father: 16 Douglas Fairbanks
  wife: 12 Joan Crawford
  born: 9 New York NY
  roles: 8 Gunga Din **12** Little Caesar **15** Sinbad the Sailor **16** That Lady in Ermine **17** Catherine the Great **18** The Prisoner of Zenda **19** The Corsican Brothers

fair dealing 7 honesty **8** fairness **15** trustworthiness

Fairfax, Gwendolen
  character in: 27 The Importance of Being Earnest
  author: 5 Wilde

Fairfax, Jane
  character in: 4 Emma
  author: 6 Austen

Fairfax, Mrs
  character in: 8 Jane Eyre
  author: 15 Charlotte Bronte

Fair Land, Fair Land
  author: 11 A B Guthrie Jr

fairly 5 fully **6** justly, rather, really **7** rightly **8** actually, honestly, passably, properly, somewhat, squarely **9** equitably, honorably, so to speak, tolerably **10** absolutely, completely, moderately, positively, reasonably **11** impartially, objectively **12** evenhand-

edly, legitimately **15** dispassionately **19** in a manner of speaking
Latin: 9 pari passu

fairness 7 balance, honesty, justice **8** equality, fair play **11** objectivity **12** impartiality **14** even-handedness **16** equal opportunity

fair play 7 cricket, justice **8** equality, fairness **12** impartiality **16** equal opportunity

fair-skinned 4 pale **5** blond, light **6** blonde **17** light-complexioned

fairy 3 elf **5** pixie **6** sprite **10** leprechaun

fairy tale 3 fib **4** myth **5** fable **6** legend **7** fantasy, fiction **8** tall tale **9** invention **11** fabrication **16** cock-and-bull story, Mother Goose story
German: 7 Marchen

fait accompli 16 accomplished fact, thing already done

faith 4 sect **5** creed, trust **6** belief, church, fealty **7** loyalty, promise **8** credence, fidelity, reliance, religion, security **9** assurance, certainty, certitude, constancy **10** confidence, conviction, obligation, persuasion

faithful 4 true **5** close, exact, loyal, tried **6** honest, strict, trusty **7** devoted, factual, precise, similar, staunch, upright **8** accurate, constant, lifelike, reliable, resolute, truthful **9** steadfast **10** dependable, scrupulous, true to life, unswerving, unwavering, verifiable **11** trustworthy **13** conscientious, incorruptible

faithfulness 6 fealty **7** loyalty **8** devotion, fidelity **9** constancy **10** allegiance **11** reliability **13** steadfastness

faithless 5 false **6** fickle **8** disloyal **10** inconstant, perfidious, unreliable **11** treacherous **13** untrustworthy

faithlessness 5 doubt **7** perfidy **9** disbelief, falseness, treachery **10** disloyalty, fickleness, infidelity, skepticism **11** inconstancy **13** unreliability **14** perfidiousness, unfaithfulness

fake 4 hoax, ruse, sham **5** bogus, dodge, dummy, faker, false, feign, forge, fraud, phony, put-on, quack, trick **6** deceit, forged, humbug, poseur, pseudo **7** falsify, forgery, not real, pretend, trump up **8** artifice, contrive, deceiver, delusion, imposter, invented, simulate, specious, spurious **9** charlatan, concocted, contrived, deception, dissemble, fabricate, imitation, imposture, pretender, simulated **10** artificial, fabricated, fictitious **11** contrivance, counterfeit, dissimulate, fabrication, make-believe

faker 5 fraud, phony **6** humbug **8** imposter **9** charlatan, pretender

fakir 5 Hindu **6** Muslim **7** ascetic, dervish

falcon 4 eyas **5** hobby, saker **6** desert,

lanner, merlin **7** goshawk, kestrel, prairie, shaheen, tiercel **8** caracara, falconet **9** gyrfalcon, peregrine
cover eyes: 4 seel

Falcon and the Snowman, The
author: 13 Robert Lindsey
director: 15 John Schlesinger
cast: 8 Sean Penn (Andrew Daulton Lee, the Snowman) **13** Timothy Hutton (Christopher John Boyce, the Falcon)

Falconer
author: 11 John Cheever

Falconet, Etienne-Maurice
born: 5 Paris **6** France
artwork: 9 The Bather **12** Bathing Nymph **13** Milo of Crotona, Peter the Great **19** Pygmalion and Galatea

falconry 7 hawking
equipment: 4 lure **5** cadge **6** jesses **7** creance

Falk, Lee
creator/artist of: 10 The Phantom **19** Mandrake the Magician

Falk, Peter
born: 9 New York NY
roles: 7 Columbo **9** Murder Inc **12** The Great Race **13** Murder by Death, Wings of Desire **17** The Cheap Detective **19** Pocketful of Miracles **21** It's a Mad Mad Mad Mad World, Robin and the Seven Hoods

fall, falls 3 die, ebb, err, sin **4** drop, plop, ruin, slip, wane **5** droop, lapse, occur, slope, slump, spill **6** autumn, crop up, defeat, happen, perish, plunge, topple, tumble **7** be slain, be taken, capture, cascade, cheapen, come off, crumple, decline, descend, descent, falling, plummet, sinking, succumb **8** cataract, collapse, come down, decrease, diminish, disgrace, downfall, drop down, dropping, go astray, hang down, lowering **9** crash down, overthrow, reduction, surrender, take place, waterfall **10** capitulate, come to pass, corruption, debasement, depreciate, diminution, subsidence, subversion, transgress **11** be destroyed, harvest time **12** capitulation, depreciation, Indian summer **15** loss of innocence

Fall, The
author: 11 Albert Camus

Falla, Manuel de
born: 5 Cadiz, Spain
composer of: 11 El Amor Brujo, La Atlantida, La Vida Breve, Life Is Short **14** Fantasia Betica **15** Love the Magician **19** The Three-Cornered Hat **21** El sombrero de tres picos **25** Nights in the Gardens of Spain

fallacious 5 false, wrong **6** faulty, flawed, untrue **8** delusive, mistaken **9** deceptive, erroneous, illogical, incorrect **10** inaccurate, misleading, untruthful

fallacy 4 flaw **5** catch, error, fault **7** mistake, pitfall **8** delusion, illusion **9** misbelief **10** faultiness **11** false belief, false notion **13** inconsistency, misconception **15** misapprehension

fall apart 5 decay **7** break up, crumble, shatter **8** fragment, splinter **10** go to pieces **11** fragmentize **12** disintegrate

fall away 4 fade, wane **5** abate **7** drop off, slacken, subside **8** mitigate, taper off

fall back 6 recede **7** back off, retreat

fallen 4 dead **5** loose, slain **6** ousted, ruined, sinful **7** debased, deposed, dropped, immoral, spilled, toppled, tumbled **8** sprawled **9** butchered, disgraced, massacred, turned out **10** discharged, overthrown **11** slaughtered

fallen short
French: 6 manque

fall for 7 believe, swallow

fall guy 4 dupe, pawn, tool **5** patsy **7** cat's-paw

fallible 5 frail, human **6** faulty, mortal, unsure **9** imperfect **10** unreliable

fall in drops 4 drip, rain **7** dribble, drizzle **8** sprinkle

falling apart 6 ruined, shabby **7** rickety, run-down **8** decaying, decrepit **9** crumbling **10** broken-down, collapsing, ramshackle, tumbledown **11** dilapidated **13** deteriorating

Falling in Place
author: 10 Ann Beattie

falling into decay 6 ruined, shabby **7** rotting, run-down **8** decrepit **9** crumbling, moldering **10** broken-down, tumbledown **11** dilapidated, in disrepair **13** deteriorating

falling off 3 ebb **4** fall, wane **7** decline **8** decrease **9** dwindling, lessening, reduction **10** diminution **13** deterioration

falling out 4 spat **7** dispute, quarrel **8** argument, squabble **10** difference **12** disagreement

fall in with 6 concur **7** conform **8** accede to **9** acquiesce **11** go along with

fall off 4 drop, wane **6** lessen, plunge, reduce, topple **7** decline, drop off, plummet, slacken, subside **8** decrease, diminish, moderate, peter out

Fall of the House of Usher, The
author: 13 Edgar Allan Poe
character: 8 Narrator **13** Madeline Usher, Roderick Usher

fallow 4 arid, idle **5** inert **6** barren, unused **7** dormant, unsowed, worn out **8** depleted, inactive, untilled **9** exhausted, unplanted **10** unfruitful **12** uncultivated, unproductive

fall short 6 be less, fail at, give up **9** be lacking, lag behind **10** have too few **11** fail to reach, miss the mark **12** be inadequate **14** be insufficient

fall to one's lot 4 fall **5** occur **6** befall, chance, happen **7** turn out **9** come about **10** come to pass

fall upon 5 fly at **6** assail, attack, dive at **7** embrace, lunge at, set upon **8** thrust at, tuck into

false 4 fake, sham **5** bogus, phony, wrong **6** ersatz, faulty, forged, pseudo, tricky, unreal, untrue **7** devious, feigned, inexact, invalid, unsound **8** delusive, disloyal, mistaken, spurious, two-faced **9** deceitful, deceiving, deceptive, dishonest, erroneous, faithless, imitation, incorrect, unfounded **10** apocryphal, artificial, factitious, fallacious, inaccurate, inconstant, misleading, not correct, perfidious, traitorous, unfaithful, untruthful **11** counterfeit, make-believe, treacherous **12** hypocritical **13** double-dealing

false front 4 mask, sham, show **6** facade, screen, veneer **8** pretense

false-hearted 8 two-faced **9** deceitful, deceiving, faithless **10** perfidious **13** double-dealing, untrustworthy

falsehood 3 fib, lie **5** lying, story **6** canard, deceit **7** fiction, figment, perfidy, perjury, untruth, whopper **8** bad faith, white lie **9** deception, duplicity, hypocrisy, invention, mendacity **10** dishonesty, distortion, inaccuracy **11** dissembling, fabrication, insincerity **12** misstatement, two-facedness **13** deceptiveness, dissimulation, double-dealing, falsification **17** misrepresentation

falseness 5 fraud **6** deceit **7** perfidy **9** duplicity, treachery **10** dishonesty **12** spuriousness **13** deceitfulness, double-dealing, faithlessness **14** untruthfulness

falsified 5 false, phony **6** forged, made-up **7** assumed **10** fictitious

falsify 4 fake **5** belie, rebut **6** doctor, misuse, refute **7** confute, distort, pervert **8** disprove **10** tamper with **12** misrepresent

Falstaff
   opera by: 5 Verdi
   character: 4 Anne **6** Fenton, Pistol **7** Dr Caius **8** Bardolph **11** Dame Quickly **12** Mistress Ford, Mistress Page **15** Mistress Quickly, Sir John Falstaff

Falstaff, Sir John
   character in: 12 Henry IV Part I **13** Henry IV Part II **22** The Merry Wives of Windsor
   author: 11 Shakespeare

falter 3 lag **4** halt, reel **5** demur, waver **6** dodder, mumble, shrink, teeter, totter **7** shamble, shuffle, stagger, stammer, stumble, stutter **8** hesitate **9** fluctuate, vacillate **10** dillydally **11** be undecided **12** be irresolute, show weakness **14** blow hot and cold

fame 4 note **5** eclat, glory **6** renown, repute **7** laurels **8** eminence, prestige **9** celebrity, notoriety **10** notability, popularity, prominence, reputation **11** distinction, preeminence **15** illustriousness

famed 5 noted **6** famous **7** notable **8** renowned **9** prominent, well-known **10** celebrated

familiar 3 pal **4** bold, chum, cozy, free, snug **5** buddy, close, crony, known, stock, usual **6** chummy, common, friend **7** forward, general **8** accepted, amicable, at home in, everyday, frequent, friendly, habitual, informal, intimate, ordinary, seasoned, versed in **9** abreast of, brotherly, confidant, customary, fraternal, gemutlich, intrusive, simpatico, skilled in, well-known **10** accessible, accustomed, acquainted, apprised of, conversant, proverbial, unreserved **11** cognizant of, commonplace, impertinent, traditional **12** confidential, conventional, hand and glove, no stranger to, proficient at **13** boon companion, companionable, disrespectful **15** taking liberties

familiarity 4 ease **5** amity, skill **7** know-how, mastery **8** coziness, intimacy **9** closeness, impudence, indecorum, knowledge, unreserve **10** casualness, chumminess, cognizance, disrespect, experience, fellowship, fraternity, friendship **11** association, brotherhood, conversance, forwardness, impropriety, informality, naturalness, presumption, proficiency **12** acquaintance, impertinence, unconstraint, undue liberty, unseemliness **13** brotherliness, comprehension, intrusiveness, understanding, undue intimacy **16** acquaintanceship

familiarize 5 edify, teach, tutor **6** inform, orient (oneself), school, season **7** educate **8** accustom, acquaint, instruct **9** enlighten, habituate, inculcate **11** acclimatize

family 3 kin, set **4** clan, kind, line, race, sept **5** blood, breed, brood, class, group, house, issue, order, stock, tribe **7** dynasty, kinfolk, kinsmen, lineage, progeny **8** ancestry, category, division, kinsfolk **9** forebears, genealogy, offspring, parentage, relations, relatives **10** extraction, kith and kin **11** forefathers **14** classification
   goddess of: 6 Cardea

Family Affair
   character: 4 Jody **5** Buffy, Cissy **8** Mr (Giles) French **9** Bill Davis
   cast: 10 Brian Keith **11** Anissa Jones, Kathy Garver **14** Sebastian Cabot **15** Johnnie Whitaker

family line 4 tree **7** lineage **8** ancestry **9** blood line, genealogy, parentage

Family Moskat, The
   author: 19 Isaac Bashevis Singer

Family Reunion, The
   author: 7 T S Eliot

Family Ties
   character: 4 Nick **5** Ellen **6** Skippy **10** Alex Keaton **11** Elyse Keaton **12** Andrew Keaton, Steven Keaton **13** Mallory Keaton **14** Jennifer Keaton
   cast: 9 Marc Price **11** Michael J Fox, Tina Yothers **12** Michael Gross **14** Justine Bateman **20** Meredith Baxter-Birney

family tree 7 lineage **8** ancestry, pedigree **9** blood line, genealogy

famine 4 lack, want **6** dearth, hunger **7** paucity, poverty **8** scarcity **9** depletion **10** deficiency, exhaustion, famishment, meagerness, scantiness, starvation **11** destitution, half rations, short supply **13** acute shortage, extreme hunger, insufficiency

famished 6 hungry **7** starved

famous 5 noted **7** eminent, notable **8** far-famed, renowned, well-known **9** notorious, prominent **10** celebrated **11** conspicuous, illustrious **13** distinguished

famous person 4 name, star **7** notable **8** luminary, somebody **9** celebrity, personage, superstar **11** personality

fan 3 bug, nut **4** buff **5** fiend, freak **6** addict, rooter, zealot **7** booster, fanatic **8** follower, partisan

fanatic 5 crazy **6** maniac, zealot **7** hothead, radical **8** activist, militant **9** extremist **10** enthusiast **24** member of the lunatic fringe

fanaticism 6 fervor **8** activism, zealotry **9** dogmatism, extremism, monomania, obsession **10** enthusiasm, radicalism **11** extreme zeal, militantism **12** intemperance **13** ruling passion **15** opinionatedness

fancied 5 liked **6** dreamt, took to, unreal **7** assumed, desired, dreamed, thought **8** imagined, supposed **9** conceived, imaginary, preferred

fanciful 3 odd **6** unreal **7** bizarre, curious, flighty, unusual **8** fabulous, humorous, illusory, mythical, quixotic, romantic **9** eccentric, fantastic, imaginary, invective, legendary, visionary, whimsical **10** apocryphal, capricious, chimerical, fictitious **11** imaginative

fanciful talk 7 blarney **9** hyperbole, tall tales **11** fish stories **12** exaggeration

fancy 3 yen **4** fine, idea, like, want **5** crave, dream, enjoy, favor, opine, showy, taste, think **6** assume, custom, deluxe, de-sire, florid, liking, notion, ornate, relish, rococo, take it, take to, vagary, vision, whimsy **7** baroque, caprice, conceit, dream of, elegant, fantasy, figment, gourmet, imagine, leaning, longing, long for, picture, presume, reverie, special, suppose, surmise, suspect, unusual **8** be fond of, crotchet, daydream, fondness, illusion, not plain, penchant, superior, weakness, yearn for **9** elaborate, epicurean, expensive, hankering, superfine **10** be bent upon, conceive of, conjecture, decorative, high-priced, ornamental, partiality **11** distinctive, exceptional, extravagant, gingerbread, hanker after, have a mind to, imagination, inclination **12** have an eye for, predilection **13** be pleased with, take a liking to

fancy house 4 stew **5** house **6** bagnio **7** brothel **8** bordello, cathouse **10** bawdy house, whorehouse **13** sporting house **14** house of ill fame **16** house of ill repute **19** house of prostitution

fang 4 claw, nail, root, take, tang, tusk **5** prong, seize, tooth **6** obtain **7** capture, procure **8** eyetooth **9** chelicera

fanny 3 bum **4** buns, rump, seat, tush **6** behind, bottom **8** backside, buttocks, derriere **9** fundament

Fanny
  author: **9** Erica Jong

Fanny
  character in: **13** Joseph Andrews
  author: **8** Fielding

fan out 7 scatter **8** disperse **9** spread out

fantasize 5 dream, fancy **7** imagine **8** daydream

fantastic 3 mad, odd **4** huge, wild **5** antic, crazy, great, queer, weird **6** absurd, superb, amazing, bizarre, extreme, strange **8** enormous, fabulous, fanciful, freakish, illusory, quixotic, romantic, terrific **9** grotesque, imaginary, marvelous, visionary, wonderful **10** chimerical, far-fetched, incredible, irrational, outlandish, ridiculous, tremendous **11** extravagant, implausible, sensational **12** preposterous, unbelievable

fantasy 4 mind **5** dream, fancy **6** mirage, notion, vision, whimsy **7** caprice, chimera, fiction, figment, phantom, reverie **8** daydream, illusion, phantasm **9** imagining, invention, nightmare, unreality **10** apparition **11** fabrication, imagination, make-believe, supposition **13** hallucination, realm of dreams, visionary idea

Fantasy Island
  character: **6** Tattoo **8** Mr Roarke
  cast: **16** Herve Villechaize, Ricardo Montalban

far 4 afar, much **6** deeply, remote, way-off, yonder **7** distant, greatly **11** beyond range, out-of-the-way **12** considerably, immeasurably, incomparably

Faraday, Michael
  field: **7** physics **9** chemistry
  worked in: **11** electricity
  developed: **9** generator **12** electrolysis
  liquified: **8** chlorine
  discovered: **6** carbon **7** benzene **24** electromagnetic induction
  named for him: **5** farad

far and near 10 every place, everywhere, far and wide **11** in all places

far and wide 10 every place, everywhere, far and near **11** in all places

Far Away and Long Ago
  author: **8** W H Hudson

farce 4 sham **6** parody **7** mockery **8** drollery, nonsense, pretense, travesty **9** absurdity, burlesque, horseplay, low comedy **10** buffoonery, tomfoolery **11** broad comedy, make-believe **12** harlequinade **14** ridiculousness

farceur 3 wag **5** joker

farcical 5 droll, funny, silly **6** absurd, stupid **7** asinine, comical, foolish **8** humorous **9** laughable, ludicrous, senseless **10** irrational, ridiculous

fare 2 do **3** fee **4** diet, food, menu **5** board, get on, rider, table **6** charge, client, manage **7** make out, perform, regimen, turn out **8** customer, get along, victuals **10** provisions **11** comestibles, ticket price **12** food and drink, passage money **15** paying passenger **20** cost of transportation

farewell 6 so long **7** good-bye, parting **8** Godspeed **9** departing, departure **11** leave-taking, parting wish, valediction **17** parting compliment
  French: **5** adieu **8** au revoir
  German: **14** auf Wiedersehen
  Hawaiian: **5** aloha
  Italian: **4** ciao **5** addio **11** arrivederci
  Japanese: **8** sayonara
  Latin: **4** vale
  Spanish: **5** adios

Farewell to Arms, A
  author: **15** Ernest Hemingway
  character: **13** Frederic Henry **16** Catherine Barkley

far-fetched 7 dubious **8** doubtful, strained, unlikely **10** cockamamie, improbable **11** implausible **12** preposterous, unconvincing

Far From the Madding Crowd
  author: **11** Thomas Hardy
  character: **10** Fanny Robin, Gabriel Oak **12** Sergeant Troy **14** Farmer Boldwood **17** Bathsheba Everdene
  setting: **6** Wessex

farina 4 meal, mush **5** flour **6** cereal, pollen, starch **8** semolina

farm 3 sow **4** plow, reap **5** plant, ranch, tract **6** grange, spread **7** harvest **9** cultivate **10** plantation **11** till the soil **12** country place

farmable 6 arable **7** friable **8** plowable, tillable **10** cultivable

farm animal 2 ox **3** cow, ewe, hen, hog, pig, ram, sow **4** bull, goat **5** beast, brute, horse, sheep **7** chicken, rooster

farm boundaries
  god of: **8** Silvanus, Sylvanus

farmer 6 grower, raiser, reaper **7** granger, planter, rancher **8** agrarian **9** harvester **10** agronomist, husbandman **12** sharecropper **13** agriculturist, truck gardener **15** tiller of the soil

farming
  god of: **4** Thor

far-off 6 remote **7** distant, far-away **11** unreachable **12** inaccessible **13** unforeseeable

farouche 3 shy **6** fierce, sullen **10** unsociable

far-out 3 mad **4** wild **5** crazy, weird **7** bizarre, strange **10** outlandish **14** fantastic

Far Pavilions, The
  author: **6** M M Kaye

Farragut, David
  served in: **8** Civil War **10** Mexican War **19** War of Eighteen Twelve
  captured: **9** Mobile Bay **10** New Orleans
  saying: **30** Damn the torpedoes full speed ahead

far-reaching 4 wide **5** broad **8** sweeping **9** expansive, extensive, universal, unlimited **11** wide-ranging

Farrell, James T
  author of: **11** Judgment Day **12** Studs Lonigan, Young Lonigan **29** The Young Manhood of Studs Lonigan

far-removed 6 far-off, remote **7** distant, faraway

farrow 6 barren **7** piglets, sterile **9** infertile **10** unpregnant

Farrow, Mia
  real name: **27** Maria de Lourdes Villier Farrow
  father: **10** John Farrow
  mother: **16** Maureen O'Sullivan
  husband: **11** Andre Previn **12** Frank Sinatra
  companion: **10** Woody Allen
  born: **12** Los Angeles CA
  roles: **5** Zelig **11** John and Mary, Peyton Place **12** The Hurricane **13** Rosemary's Baby **14** The Great Gatsby **16** Allison MacKenzie **19** Hannah and Her Sisters **20** The Purple Rose of Cairo

far side 4 back **7** reverse **8** back side

Far Side, The
  creator/artist: **10** Gary Larson

farsighted 4 wise **5** acute **6** shrewd **7** prudent **9** farseeing, hyperopic, judicious, prescient, provident **10** forehanded, foreseeing **11** clairvoyant, levelheaded

farther 6 beyond, deeper, longer **7** further, remoter **9** lengthier **10** more remote **11** more distant, more removed

farthermost 7 extreme 8 farthest, furthest 11 furthermost, most distant

farthest 3 end 4 most 7 extreme, longest 8 furthest, remotest, ultimate 9 uttermost 11 farthermost, furthermost

fascia 4 band, sash 5 board, strip 6 fillet, girdle, ribbon, tissue 7 bandage 8 membrane 9 dashboard

fascinate 5 charm, rivet 6 absorb, allure 7 beguile, bewitch, delight, enchant, engross 8 enravish, enthrall, entrance, transfix 9 captivate, enrapture, overpower, spellbind 14 hold spellbound

fascinating 8 alluring, charming, gripping, riveting 9 absorbing, beguiling 10 bewitching, delightful, enchanting, engrossing, entrancing 11 captivating, enthralling, interesting 12 overpowering, spellbinding

fascination 4 draw, lure 5 charm 6 allure 9 magnetism 10 attraction 11 captivation

fascism 6 Nazism 9 autocracy, oligarchy 10 plutocracy 11 corporatism, police state 13 corporativism 14 corporate state 15 totalitarianism 17 national socialism 21 right-wing dictatorship

fascist 8 dictator 9 Mussolini, right-wing 10 black shirt, brown shirt, repressive, tyrannical 11 dictatorial, doctrinaire 12 storm trooper

fashion 3 air, fad, hew, way 4 form, make, mode, mold, rage 5 carve, craze, forge, frame, habit, shape, style, tenor, trend, usage, vogue 6 create, custom, design, devise, manner 7 compose, pattern, produce 8 attitude, behavior, contrive, demeanor 9 construct, fabricate 10 convention 11 manufacture

fashionable 2 in 3 hip 4 chic 5 smart 6 modish, with-it 7 current, in style, in vogue, popular, stylish, voguish 9 in fashion 10 all the rage, prevailing
French: 9 de rigueur

fashionable world
French: 10 grand monde

fashion designer 4 (Christian) Dior 5 Kenzo, (Jean) Patou, Prada 6 Adolfo, (Georgio) Armani, Lanvin, Poiret, (Coco) Chanel 7 Galanos, (Gianni) Versace, Halston, Missoni, (Pierre) Balmain 8 Givenchy 9 Courreges, Mary Quant, Valentino 10 Balenciaga, Donna Karan, Mainbocher, Perry Ellis 11 Calvin Klein, Emilio Pucci, Ralph Lauren 12 Liz Claiborne, Lucien Lelong, Norman Norell, Pierre Cardin, Schiaparelli 13 Karl Lagerfeld, Rudi Gernreich 14 Pauline Trigere 15 Claire McCardell 16 Gloria Vanderbilt, Yves Saint-Laurent
Empress Eugenie's: 5 (Charles Frederick) Worth
Marie Antoinette's: 10 Rose Bertin

Empress Josephine's: 19 Louis Hippolyte Leroy

fashioned 4 made 5 built 6 formed, framed, molded, shaped, styled 7 adapted, crafted, created, devised, managed, modeled 9 contrived, patterned 11 constructed 12 accommodated

fashion plate 4 dude 5 dandy 12 Beau Brummell, clotheshorse, man of fashion, sharp dresser 14 woman of fashion

fast 4 firm, taut, true, wild 5 ahead, brisk, fleet, fully, hasty, loose, loyal, quick, rapid, rigid, swift, tight 6 famish, firmly, fly- ing, rakish, secure, speedy, stable, starve, steady, wanton, winged 7 abiding, devoted, durable, fasting, fast day, fixedly, hastily, hurried, immoral, lasting, lustful, quickly, rapidly, solidly, soundly, staunch, swiftly, tightly 8 constant, enduring, faithful, fastened, go hungry, immodest, reckless, resolute, securely, speedily, unfading 9 debauched, dissolute, hurriedly, immovable, immovably, in advance, permanent, resistant, steadfast 10 completely, dissipated, firmly tied, lascivious, licentious, profligate, starvation, stationary, unswerving, unwavering 11 accelerated, expeditious, extravagant, intemperate, pleasure-mad, tenaciously 12 hunger strike, ineradicable, lickety-split

Fast, Howard
author of: 9 Spartacus 11 Freedom Road 13 The Immigrants 15 Citizen Tom Paine

fasten 3 bar, fix, pin, tie, wed 4 bind, bolt, clip, fuse, hold, hook, join, lash, link, lock, moor, snap, weld, yoke 5 affix, clamp, clasp, dowel, focus, hitch, close, latch, rivet, screw, stick, truss, unite 6 adhere, anchor, attach, button, cement, couple, direct, pinion, secure, solder, tether 7 connect 8 dovetail 11 put together

fastener 3 peg, pin, tie 4 clip, glue, grip, hook, line, nail, snap, tack 5 catch, clamp, clasp, cleat, latch, screw, strap, truss 6 buckle, button, cement, staple, thread, zipper 7 bracket 8 barrette 9 fastening, safety pin, thumbtack 10 clothespin, connection, hook and eye

fastening 4 snap 5 clasp 8 coupling 9 attaching 10 attachment, connection

fasten together 3 tie 4 dock, join 6 couple, hook up, link up

fastidious 5 fussy, picky 6 choosy, dainty, proper, queasy 7 finicky 8 exacting, precious 9 difficult, squeamish 10 meticulous, particular 11 overprecise, overrefined, persnickety 12 hard to please, overdelicate 13 hypercritical

Fastidious Brisk
character in: 22 Every Man out of His Humour

author: 6 Jonson

fastidiousness 4 care 12 exactingness 14 discrimination 15 persnicketiness

fat 4 full, oily 5 beefy, fatty, flush, heavy, obese, palmy, plump, pudgy, stout, suety 6 chubby, fleshy, grease, greasy, portly, rotund 7 copious, fertile, lumpish, paunchy, replete, stuffed 8 abundant, blubbery, chockful, fruitful, thickset, unctuous 9 animal fat, corpulent, fortunate, lucrative, plenteous, plentiful, rewarding 10 overweight, potbellied, productive 11 well-stocked 12 remunerative

fatal 6 deadly, lethal, mortal 7 ruinous 8 terminal, virulent 10 calamitous, disastrous 11 destructive 12 catastrophic, causing death

fatalism 8 stoicism 11 resignation 12 acquiescence, helplessness 13 powerlessness 14 predestination

fatality 5 death 8 casualty 9 lethality, mortality 10 deadliness, malignancy 11 banefulness

fatal woman see 11 femme fatale

fate 3 lot 4 doom 5 karma, moira 6 effect, future, kismet, upshot 7 chances, destiny, fortune, outcome, portion 8 prospect 10 providence 11 consequence 12 will of heaven 14 predestination

fated 4 sure 5 bound, meant 6 doomed 7 certain 8 destined

fateful 5 fatal 7 crucial, ominous 8 critical, decisive 9 momentous 10 disastrous, portentous 11 significant

Fates
also: 5 Morae 6 Moerae, Moirai, Parcae
named: 6 Clotho 7 Atropos 8 Lachesis
goddesses of: 7 destiny
number of goddesses: 5 three
called: 12 weird sisters
parents: 4 Zeus 5 Night 6 Themis

father 3 dad, pop 4 abbe, cure, papa, sire 5 beget, begin, daddy, found, hatch, maker, padre, pater 6 author, create, design, old man, parson, pastor, priest 7 creator, founder 8 ancestor, begetter, designer, engender, forebear, inventor, preacher 9 architect, confessor, originate, procreate 10 forefather, male parent, originator, progenitor
French: 4 pere

Father 4 Abba

Father, The
author: 16 August Strindberg

Father Knows Best
character: 11 Jim Anderson 13 Betty Anderson (Princess), Kathy Anderson (Kitten) 15 James Anderson Jr (Bud) 16 Margaret Anderson
cast: 9 Billy Gray, Jane Wyatt 11 Ro-

bert Young **12** Lauren Chapin **13** Elinor Donahue

fatherland 6 Heimat, patria, patrie **8** homeland **10** birthplace, motherland, native land, native soil **13** mother country, native country

fatherly 6 benign, kindly, tender **8** parental, paternal **9** indulgent **10** beneficent, benevolent

father of his country
Latin: **12** Pater Patriae

father of stars/wind 8 Astraeus

Father of the Bride
director: **16** Vincente Minnelli
cast: **11** Billie Burke, Joan Bennett, Leo G Carroll **12** Spencer Tracy **15** Elizabeth Taylor
sequel: **21** Father's Little Dividend

father of the family
Latin: **13** paterfamilias

Father of the Rivers see **4** Nile

Fathers and Sons
author: **12** Ivan Turgenev
character: **5** Katya, Pavel **6** Arkady, Vasily **8** Bazaroff, Fenichka **9** Kirsanoff **15** Madame Odintzoff

fathom 5 probe **6** divine, follow **7** hunt out, root out, uncover, unravel **8** discover **9** ferret out, figure out, penetrate **10** comprehend, understand **16** get to the bottom of

fathom
abbreviation: **4** fath

fatigue 3 fag **4** bush, tire **5** drain, weary **6** tedium, tucker, weaken **7** exhaust, languor, wear out **8** enervate, overtire **9** heaviness, lassitude, tiredness, weariness **10** debilitate, drowsiness, enervation, exhaustion **12** debilitation, listlessness **13** overtiredness

fatigued 4 beat **5** all in, jaded, spent, tired, weary **6** bushed, done in, fagged, pooped **7** worn out **8** dogtired, weakened **9** dead tired, enervated, exhausted, overtaxed **10** overworked **11** debilitated, tuckered out

fatiguing 6 tiring **7** arduous, tedious **8** tiresome **9** wearisome **10** exhausting

Fatima
character in: **9** Bluebeard

fatti maschii, parole femine 29 deeds are manly words are womanish
motto of: **8** Maryland

fatty 4 oily **5** lardy, suety **6** greasy **7** buttery **8** blubbery **9** shortened

fatuous 5 inane, silly, vapid **6** obtuse, simple, stupid **7** asinine, foolish, idiotic, moronic, puerile, vacuous, witless **8** besotted, imbecile **9** brainless, senseless **10** ridiculous

faucet 3 tap **4** cock **5** spout, valve **6** nozzle, outlet, spigot **7** bibcock

Faulkland
character in: **9** The Rivals
author: **8** Sheridan

Faulkner, William

author of: **7** The Bear **8** Sartoris **9** Sanctuary, The Hamlet **10** The Reivers **11** As I Lay Dying **13** Light in August **15** Absalom Absalom! **17** Intruder in the Dust **18** The Sound and the Fury
fictional county: **13** Yoknapatawpha

fault 3 bug, sin **4** flaw, slip, snag **5** blame, crime, error, guilt, stain, taint, wrong **6** defect, foible, glitch, impugn **7** blemish, blunder, censure, failing, frailty, misdeed, mistake, offense, reprove **8** drawback, weakness **9** criticize, infirmity, oversight, weak point **10** deficiency, impediment, negligence, peccadillo, wrongdoing **11** culpability, dereliction, misdemeanor, shortcoming **12** imperfection, indiscretion **13** answerability, transgression **14** accountability, responsibility

faultfind 3 nag **4** beef, carp, kick **5** cavil, gripe, knock **6** deride, squawk **7** nitpick **8** complain **9** criticize

faultfinder 3 nag **4** bear, crab **5** crank **6** carper, censor, critic, grouch **7** caviler, grouser **8** quibbler, sorehead **9** derogator, detractor, Mrs Grundy, nitpicker **10** bellyacher, complainer, curmudgeon, fuddy-duddy, fussbudget

faultfinding 4 beef, kick **5** gripe **6** squawk **7** beefing, carping, griping, kicking, nagging **9** complaint, criticism, squawking **10** nitpicking **11** complaining, criticizing

faultless 5 ideal **7** correct, perfect **8** accurate, flawless **9** exemplary **10** immaculate, impeccable **11** unblemished **13** unimpeachable **14** irreproachable, without blemish

faulty 3 bad **4** awry **5** amiss, false, wrong **7** injured, unsound **8** impaired, inferior, mistaken **9** defective, deficient, erroneous, imperfect, incorrect **10** inadequate, out of order, unreliable **14** unsatisfactory

faun
form: **5** deity, satyr **7** goat-man
location: **5** rural

Fauna see **7** Bona Dea

Faunus
origin: **5** Roman
form: **5** deity
location: **5** woods
also called: **5** Inuus **6** Fatuus
king of: **6** Latium
father: **5** Picus
son: **7** Latinus
corresponds to: **3** Pan

Faure, Gabriel Urbain
born: **6** France **7** Pamiers
composer of: **5** Dolly **6** Pavane **7** Ballade, Mirages, Requiem, Shylock **8** Penelope **9** Fantaisie, Promethee **12** Le Jardin Clos **13** La Chanson d'Eve **14** La Bonne Chanson **18** L'Horizon Chimerique, Pelleas et

Melisande **21** Masques et Bergamasques

Faust
author: **12** Johann Goethe
character: **6** Wagner **8** Gretchen **10** Homunculus **11** Helen of Troy **14** Mephistopheles

Faust
opera by: **6** Gounod
character: **6** Siebel **8** Valentin **10** Marguerite **14** Mephistopheles

Faustulus
vocation: **8** herdsman, shepherd
raised: **5** Remus **7** Romulus

faute de mieux 24 for lack of something better

faux pas 4 goof **5** boner, error, gaffe, lapse **6** boo-boo, howler, slip-up **7** blooper, blunder, mistake **9** false step **11** impropriety **12** indiscretion

favela 4 slum **10** shanty town

Favell, Jack
character in: **7** Rebecca
author: **9** Du Maurier

Favonius
origin: **5** Roman
personifies: **8** west wind

favor 3 aid **4** abet, back, gift, help, like **5** be for, fancy, humor **6** assist, esteem, foster, oblige, pamper, prefer, succor, uphold **7** approve, commend, endorse, go in for, indulge, kind act, memento, present, service, support **8** advocacy, approval, courtesy, espousal, good deed, good turn, goodwill, largesse, look like, resemble, sanction, side with, souvenir **9** encourage, patronage, patronize, smile upon, take after, use gently **10** act of grace, use lightly **11** accommodate, approbation, be partial to, benefaction, countenance, good opinion **12** be the image of, championship, commendation, dispensation, kindly regard **13** accommodation, goodwill token

favorable 4 fair, good, kind **6** benign, timely **7** helpful, hopeful **8** amicable, friendly, salutary **9** approving, conducive, opportune, promising **10** auspicious, beneficial, convenient, propitious **11** predisposed, serviceable, sympathetic **12** advantageous, commendatory, well-disposed

favorable opinion 6 esteem, regard **7** respect **8** approval **10** admiration **12** appreciation

favorably disposed 7 willing **8** amenable, inclined, obliging **9** agreeable **11** sympathetic

favorite 3 pet **5** fancy, jewel **6** choice **7** darling, special **9** best-liked, preferred **11** front-runner, most popular **13** fair-haired one **14** apple of one's eye

favoritism 4 bias **10** partiality **12** onesidedness, partisanship

Fawley, Jude and Drusilla
  characters in: **14** Jude the Obscure
  author: **5** Hardy

fawn 5 toady **6** pander **7** flatter, truckle **8** pay court **9** be servile, seek favor **12** be obsequious, bow and scrape

fawning 7 servile **8** flattery, toadying **9** adulating, adulation, truckling **10** flattering, obsequious **11** sycophantic **12** ingratiating **14** obsequiousness

fax 4 send **8** transmit **9** facsimile

faze 4 fret **5** abash, daunt, upset, worry **6** bother, flurry, rattle **7** disturb, fluster, perturb **8** confound **9** discomfit, embarrass **10** discompose, disconcert

fazed 5 upset **7** abashed, ruffled **8** agitated, bothered, confused **9** chagrined, unsettled **10** confounded, distracted, nonplussed **11** embarrassed **12** disconcerted

FBI, The
  character: **10** Arthur Ward **21** Inspector Lewis Erskine
  cast: **12** Philip Abbott **16** Efrem Zimbalist Jr

fealty 7 loyalty **8** devotion, fidelity **9** adherence, constancy **10** allegiance, attachment **12** faithfulness

fear 3 awe **4** care **5** alarm, bogey, dread, panic, qualm, worry **6** dismay, esteem, fright, horror, phobia, revere, terror, threat, wonder **7** anxiety, bugaboo, bugbear, concern, quaking, specter **8** affright, venerate **9** cowardice, nightmare, reverence, shudder at, tremble at **10** be afraid of, be scared of, feel awe for, foreboding, take fright, veneration **11** trepidation **12** apprehension, perturbation **13** consternation **14** be frightened of

fearful 4 dire **5** awful, dread, eerie, lurid, timid **6** afraid, aghast, horrid, scared, uneasy **7** alarmed, anxious, ghastly, macabre, nervous, ominous, panicky, worried **8** alarming, dreadful, horrible, shocking, sinister, skittish, terrible, timorous **9** appalling, concerned, diffident, frightful, tremulous **10** formidable, frightened, portentous, terrifying **11** distressing, frightening, intimidated **12** apprehensive, fainthearted **13** panic-stricken **14** chickenhearted

fearfulness fear **5** alarm, dread, panic **6** fright, terror **7** anguish, anxiety **8** timidity **11** trepidation **12** apprehension

fearless 4 bold **5** brave **6** daring, gritty, heroic, plucky **7** doughty, gallant, valiant **8** intrepid, unafraid, valorous **9** audacious, confident, dauntless, unabashed, undaunted **10** courageous, undismayed **11** adventurous, indomitable, lionhearted, unflinching, unshrinking, venturesome, without fear **12** stout-hearted

fearlessness 4 grit **5** pluck, valor **7** bravery, courage **8** boldness **10** confidence **13** dauntlessness

Fear of Flying
  author: **9** Erica Jong

feasible 6 doable, viable **7** fitting, politic **8** possible, suitable, workable **9** advisable, desirable **10** achievable, attainable, reasonable **11** appropriate, conceivable, practicable

feast 4 dine, fete **5** festa, gorge **6** bounty **7** banquet, holiday, jubilee, surplus **8** feast day, festival **9** bacchanal, saint's day **10** gluttonize, gormandize, have a feast, rich supply **11** celebration, eat one's fill, elegant meal, wine and dine

feat 3 act **4** deed, task **6** action, stroke **7** exploit, triumph **8** maneuver **9** adventure **10** attainment, enterprise **11** achievement, performance, tour de force **14** accomplishment

feather 4 down, kind, sort **5** adorn, eider, pinna, plume, quill **7** bristle, plumage, variety **9** character, turn an oar

featherbrained 4 dumb **5** silly **6** simple, stupid **7** foolish, witless **9** brainless **12** muddleheaded, simple-minded **13** rattle-brained **14** scatterbrained

feather in one's cap 5 honor **6** credit **11** distinction

feather one's nest 6 enrich **15** fill one's pockets

feature, features 3 see **4** mark, star **5** fancy, trait **6** aspect, play up, visage **7** display, earmark, imagine, picture, present, quality **8** envision, hallmark, headline, main item, property **9** attribute, character, highlight, specialty, spotlight **10** conceive of, lineaments **14** characteristic

February
  event: **4** Lent **5** Purim **8** Leap year **9** Mardi Gras **12** Ash Wednesday, Groundhog Day (2)
  flower: **6** violet **8** primrose
  French: **7** Fevrier
  gem: **8** amethyst
  German: **7** Februar
  holiday: **9** Candlemas (2) **13** President's Day Valentine's Day (14) **14** Chinese New Year **16** Lincoln's Birthday (12) **19** Washington's Birthday (22)
  Italian: **8** Febbraio
  Latin: **6** Februa
  number of days: **10** twenty-nine (every 4 years) **11** twenty-eight
  origin of name: **7** Februus
    Roman god of: **12** purification
  place in year:
    Gregorian: **6** second
    Roman: **7** twelfth
  Spanish: **7** Febrero
  Zodiac signs: **6** Pisces **8** Aquarius

Fechner, Gustav Theodore

  nationality: **6** German
  founder of: **22** experimental psychology

fecit 6 he made (it) **7** she made (it)

feckless 3 lax **5** slack **6** remiss **8** careless, heedless **9** negligent, worthless **10** neglectful **11** thoughtless **13** irresponsible

Fecundity
  goddess of: **5** Freia, Freya

Fed
  Federal Reserve System: **6** the Fed
  FBI agent: **4** G-man **6** feebie, fibbie
  Treasury agent: **4** T-man
  head: **14** Alan Greenspan

Federalist Party
  president belonging to: **5** Adams **10** Washington

federate 5 unite **7** combine **12** join together

federation 5 union **6** league **7** combine **8** alliance **9** coalition, syndicate **10** sisterhood **11** association, brotherhood, confederacy **12** amalgamation **13** confederation

fee 4 fare, hire, toll, wage **5** price **6** charge, salary, tariff **7** payment, stipend **9** emolument **10** commission, honorarium **12** compensation, remuneration **13** consideration

feeble 4 flat, lame, poor, puny, tame, thin, weak **5** faint, frail, vapid **6** ailing, flabby, flimsy, infirm, meager, paltry, senile, sick-ly, slight **7** fragile, insipid **8** decrepit, delicate, disabled, impotent, weakened **9** colorless, declining, doddering, enervated, enfeebled, forceless, not strong, powerless **10** inadequate, spiritless, wishy-washy **11** debilitated, ineffective, ineffectual

feeble-minded 4 dull, dumb **6** senile, stupid **7** moronic **8** backward, childish, retarded **9** imbecilic, senseless, subnormal **10** half-witted, weakminded **12** mentally slow

feeble-mindedness 6 dotage, idiocy **8** dullness, senility, slowness **9** denseness, stupidity **11** retardation

feed 3 eat **4** fare, fuel, mash **5** cater, feast, graze **6** devour, fodder, forage, foster, viands **7** augment, bolster, consume, gratify, nourish, nurture, pasture, satisfy, support, sustain **8** maintain, take food, victuals **9** encourage, foodstuff, provender **10** minister to, provisions, strengthen **11** comestibles, nourishment, wine and dine

feeder 6 branch **7** channel **9** tributary

feel 3 paw, see **4** know **5** grope, press, probe, reach, sense, think, touch **6** finger, fumble, handle, makeup, notice **7** believe, discern, feeling, observe, palpate, texture **8** perceive **9** be aware of, be moved by, character, sensation **10** comprehend, experience, manipulate, suffer from, understand

11 be convinced, be stirred by, be touched by, composition

feel aversion toward 4 hate **5** abhor **6** detest **7** despise **9** abominate, can't abide, can't stand **11** can't stomach **12** be revolted by **13** find repugnant, find repulsive **14** view with horror

feeler 7 antenna **8** proposal, tentacle **10** experiment **12** trial balloon

feel indebted 10 appreciate, be beholden, be grateful **13** feel obligated

feeling 4 aura, pity, view, zeal **5** ardor, gusto, sense, verve **6** fervor, spirit, thrill, warmth **7** concern, emotion, opinion, passion **8** attitude, instinct, reaction, response, sympathy **9** affection, awareness, intuition, sensation, sentiment, vehemence **10** atmosphere, compassion, enthusiasm, impression **11** earnestness, inclination, point of view, sensibility, sensitivity

feeling life is wearisome
   Latin: 12 taedium vitae

feelings 3 ego **5** pride **8** emotions, passions **10** self- esteem **13** sensibilities, sensitivities **16** susceptibilities

feel pain 4 ache, hurt **5** smart **6** suffer **7** agonize **9** be in agony **11** be tormented **12** be in distress

Feenix, Cousin
   character in: 12 Dombey and Son
   author: 7 Dickens

feet 4 dogs, pads, paws **5** hoofs **6** hooves **8** gunboats, tootsies

feign 4 fake, sham **5** forge, put on **6** affect, assume, cook up, invent, make up **7** concoct, pretend **8** simulate **9** fabricate **11** counterfeit, make a show of, make believe

feigned 4 fake, sham **5** bogus, phony **6** ersatz **8** spurious **9** imitation, insincere, pretended, simulated **10** artificial **11** counterfeit, make-believe

feint 4 hoax, mask, move, pass, ploy, ruse, wile **5** blind, bluff, dodge, trick **6** gambit **7** pretext **8** artifice, maneuver, pretense **9** stratagem **10** subterfuge **13** feigned attack

Feldman, Marty
   born: 6 London **7** England
   roles: 11 Silent Movie **17** Young Frankenstein **24** The Last Remake of Beau Geste

feldspar
   varieties: 8 sunstone **9** amazonite, moonstone

felicitate 4 hail **6** salute **10** wish one joy **11** rejoice with **12** congratulate **18** give one's best wishes **28** wish many happy returns of the day

felicitations 3 joy **6** cheers **9** blessings, greetings **10** best wishes, good wishes **11** compliments, salutations **12** pat on the back **15** congratulations **24** many happy returns of the day

felicitous 3 apt **5** happy **6** joyful, joy-

ous **7** fitting, germane, well-put **8** inspired, pleasing, relevant, suitable, well-said **9** effective, fortunate, pertinent **10** propitious, well-chosen **11** appropriate

felicity 5 bliss, charm, grace, knack, skill **6** heaven, nicety **7** aptness, delight, ecstasy, fitness **8** paradise **9** beatitude, happiness **12** blissfulness **13** effectiveness **15** appropriateness

Felix the Cat
   creator: 11 Pat Sullivan

fell 4 raze **5** level **7** cut down, destroy, hew down **8** demolish **9** knock down, prostrate

Feller, Bob (Robert)
   nickname: 11 Rapid Robert
   sport: 8 baseball
   position: 7 pitcher
   team: 16 Cleveland Indians

Fellini, Federico
   director of: 8 Amarcord, Casanova, La Strada **11** La Dolce Vita **15** Nights of Cabiria **18** Juliet of the Spirits

fellow 3 boy, guy, mac, man, pal **4** chap, chum, dude, gent, mate, peer **5** equal **6** friend **7** comrade, consort **8** coworker **9** associate, colleague, companion **10** compatriot

fellow conspirator 4 ally **6** cohort **7** abettor **8** henchman **9** accessory **11** confederate **12** collaborator

fellow creature 5 human **6** mortal, person **10** individual

fellow feeling 6 regard **7** empathy, kinship **8** affinity, fondness **10** attraction, partiality

fellowship 5 amity **7** society **8** intimacy **10** affability, cordiality, fraternity, friendship **11** amicability, association, brotherhood, comradeship, familiarity, sociability **12** friendliness **13** companionship

felon 5 crook, cruel, thief **6** fierce, outlaw, wicked **7** convict, illegal, villain, whitlow **8** criminal, gangster, jailbird, murderer **10** law-breaker, malefactor **11** public enemy **12** inflammation

felony 5 arson, crime **6** murder **7** assault, misdeed, offense, robbery **8** burglary **9** blackmail **10** kidnapping, wrongdoing **12** capital offense

female 3 cow, dam, hen, sow **4** girl, mare **5** bitch, tabby, woman **6** heifer **7** distaff, womanly **8** feminine, ladylike **9** womanlike

feminine 4 soft **5** woman **6** dainty, female, gentle **7** distaff, girlish, womanly **8** delicate, ladylike **10** femalelike, like a woman **14** of the female sex

femininity 8 softness **10** femaleness, gentleness **11** girlishness, womanliness **12** feminineness **13** female quality

femme 4 wife **5** woman

femme de chambre 9 lady's maid **11** chambermaid

femme fatale 4 vamp **5** siren **7** charmer **10** fatal woman, seductress **11** enchantress

femur
   bone of: 5 thigh **8** upper leg

fen 3 bog **4** moor, sump **5** marsh, swale, swamp **6** bottom, morass, slough **7** lowland, wetland **8** quagmire

fence 3 pen **4** coop, duel, gird, rail **5** hedge, hem in **6** corral, secure, wall in **7** barrier, confine, palings **8** encircle, palisade, stockade, surround **9** barricade, encompass **11** cross swords

fencing
   equipment: 4 epée, foil, mask **5** saber, sword **8** plastron
   part of weapon: 5 blade, forte, guard **6** foible, handle, medium, pommel
   term: 3 hit **5** prime, sixte, touch **6** octave, quarte, quinte, tierce **7** en garde, on guard, seconde, septime
   deceptive move: 5 feint
   movement: 4 beat **5** lunge, parry **6** double, fleche, thrust **7** advance, cutover, recover, retreat, riposte **9** disengage **11** froissement

fend 2 do **5** avert, avoid, parry, repel, shift **6** manage **7** keep off, make out, provide, repulse, support, survive, ward off **8** push away

fender 3 pad **4** curb **5** guard **6** buffer, bumper, shield, sluice **7** cushion, railing **9** fireguard, protector **10** cowcatcher, fire screen, protection, wheel guard

fend off 5 avert, dodge, evade, parry, repel **6** escape **7** ward off **8** sidestep, stave off

fennel
   botanical name: 17 Foeniculum vulgare
   family: 7 parsley
   varieties: 3 dog **4** wild **5** giant **8** Florence **9** common dog **11** common giant
   mythical aid to: 9 fortifier **11** aphrodisiac, slenderizer **12** rejuvenation, stops hiccups **16** restores eyesight
   use: 4 duck, fish **5** bread, rolls **7** chicken **8** apple pie **16** seafood casserole

Fenrir
   also: 6 Fenris
   origin: 12 Scandinavian
   form: 4 wolf **7** monster
   father: 4 Loki
   mother: 9 Angerboda, Angrbodha, Anguboda
   sister: 3 Hel
   brother: 11 Iormungandr, Jormungandr **14** Midgard Serpent
   ate: 4 Odin **5** Othin
   killed by: 5 Vidar

Fenris *see* **6** Fenrir

Fenton
  character in: **22** The Merry Wives of Windsor
  author: **11** Shakespeare

feral 4 wild **6** brutal, deadly, ferine, fierce, savage **7** bestial, untamed, vicious **9** ferocious **12** uncultivated **14** undomesticated

Ferber, Edna
  author of: **5** Giant, So Big **8** Cimarron, Show Boat **9** Ice Palace, Stage Door (with George S Kaufman) **13** Dinner at Eight (with George S Kaufman), Saratoga Trunk **14** The Royal Family (with George S Kaufman)

Ferdinand
  king of: **5** Spain
  wife: **8** Isabella
  patron of: **8** Columbus

Ferdinand
  character in: **10** The Tempest
  author: **11** Shakespeare

Ferdinand
  character in: **16** Love's Labour's Lost
  author: **11** Shakespeare

Ferdinand the Bull
  author: **9** Munro Leaf
  disliked: **12** bullfighting

Ferd'nand
  creator: **3** Mik **13** Dahl Mikkelsen

Feria
  origin: **5** Roman
  form: **7** holiday

Fermat, Pierre de
  field: **11** mathematics
  nationality: **6** French
  discovered: **16** analytic geometry

ferment 4 foam, mold, sour, turn **5** froth, yeast **6** enzyme, fester, leaven, seethe, tumult, unrest, uproar **7** agitate, inflame, smolder, turmoil **8** bubble up, disquiet **9** agitation, commotion, leavening **10** disruption, effervesce, turbulence **11** be turbulent, fomentation

fermented 6 soured, worked **7** seethed **8** agitated

Fermi, Enrico
  field: **7** physics
  nationality: **7** Italian
  developed: **10** atomic bomb **20** uranium fission theory
  awarded: **10** Nobel Prize

fern
  varieties: **3** air, cup, lip, man, oak, saw **4** ball, blue, claw, deer, dish, felt, fire, gold, hand, iron, king, lace, lady, male, moss, nest, pine, sago, tara, tree, wall, wart, wood **5** beard, beech, chain, cloak, fancy, glade, glory, grape, grass, hedge, holly, marsh, plume, royal, strap, swamp, sweet, sword, table, water, whisk **6** adder's, bamboo, basket, Boston, button, carrot, coffee, cotton, cuplet, dagger, ladder, meadow, mother, ribbon, shield, silver, tongue, turnip, winter **7** bladder, boulder, brittle, bulblet, crested, emerald, feather, Fee's lip, fragile, Goldie's, hacksaw, Halberd, hammock, leather, New York, ostrich, parsley, peacock, rainbow, walking **8** bear-foot, bear's-paw, cinnamon, climbing, elk's-horn, fishtail, floating, florist's, fragrant, hairy lip, Hartford, licorice, mosquito, Nebraska, Savannah, snuffbox, soft tree, staghorn **9** asparagus, bird's-nest, black tree, blond tree, Christmas, common cup, deer's-foot, downy wood, flowering, glossy cup, hare's foot, long beech, sensitive, vegetable, Venus hair, viscid lip, wavy cloak, woolly lip **10** Alabama lip, Boott's wood, broad beech, deer-tongue, Duff's sword, erect sword, five-finger, hay-scented, lady ground, maidenhair, scented oak, shoestring, silver tree, silver-back, silver-lace, silver-leaf, slender lip, strawberry, upside-down, woolly tree **11** Braun's holly, coastal wood, Coville's lip, crested felt, crested wood, dwarf Boston, elephant-ear, Fendler's lip, hart's-tongue, interrupted, Jamaica gold, leatherleaf, leatherwood, narrow beech, netted chain, Northern oak, Parry's cloak, Pursh's holly, rabbit's-foot, rattlesnake, Sierra water, walking leaf **12** Adder's-tongue, American wall, berry bladder, Clinton's wood, Dudley's holly, Eaton's shield, English hedge, Hawaiian tree, Java staghorn, limestone oak, mountain wood, Northern lady, resurrection, Southern lady, squirrel-foot, toothed sword, Western holly, Western sword **13** California lip, Cleveland's lip, Dudley's shield, European chain, fan maidenhair, Fendler's cloak, Florida ribbon, leathery grape, Malay climbing, mountain holly, Northern holly, prickly shield, Prince-of-Wales, spinulose wood, Tasmanian tree, triangle water, Virginia chain, wild bird's nest **14** Anderson's holly, Australian tree, bulblet bladder, California gold, common staghorn, dissected grape, dwarf asparagus, hen-and-chickens, imbricate sword, silver-king tree, West Indian tree **15** American parsley, California cloak, California holly, Delta maidenhair, East Indian holly, European parsley, mountain bladder, mountain parsley **16** black-stemmed tree, daisy-leaved grape, Farley maidenhair, Tassel maidenhair, Tracy's maidenhair **17** Bermuda maidenhair, brittle maidenhair, climbing bird's nest, walking maidenhair **18** Aleutian maidenhair, American maidenhair, Barbados maidenhair, Northern maidenhair, Trailing maidenhair, Triangular staghorn **20** Australian maidenhair, California maidenhair

fernet-branca
  type: **8** aperitif
  origin: **5** Italy
  flavor: **4** herb

Fern Hill
  author: **11** Dylan Thomas

ferocious 6 brutal, deadly, fierce, savage **7** bestial, brutish, enraged, violent **8** fiendish, maddened, ravening, ruthless **9** atrocious, barbarous, merciless, murderous, predatory, rapacious **10** relentless **11** cold-blooded **12** bloodthirsty

ferocity 7 cruelty **8** savagery **9** barbarity, brutality, harshness **10** fierceness, inhumanity, savageness **11** brutishness, viciousness **12** ruthlessness

Ferrer, Jose
  real name: **33** Jose Vincente Ferrer de Otero y Cintron
  wife: **8** Uta Hagen **15** Rosemary Clooney
  son: **6** Miguel
  born: **8** Santurce **10** Puerto Rico
  roles: **7** I Accuse **9** Joan of Arc **11** Moulin Rouge, Ship of Fools **14** The Caine Mutiny **16** Cyrano de Bergerac (Oscar), Lawrence of Arabia **24** The Greatest Story Ever Told

ferret out 5 dig up **6** detect **7** find out, root out, uncover, unearth **8** discover **9** ascertain

fertile 4 rich **5** loamy **6** fecund **8** creative, fruitful, original, prolific **9** fructuous, ingenious, inventive, luxuriant, plenteous **10** fecundated, fertilized, fructified, generative, productive, vegetative **11** imaginative, resourceful **12** reproductive

Fertility
  god of: **7** Bacchus, Mutinus **8** Lupercus, Picumnus
  goddess of: **4** Isis **5** Fauna **6** Athena, Athene, Brigit, Libera, Pallas, Saitis, Tellus **7** Astarte, Berchta, Bona Dea, Demeter, Perchta **11** Tritogeneia **12** Pallas Athena **16** Alalcomean Athena

fertilize 6 enrich, manure **8** fructify **9** fecundate, pollinate **10** impregnate, inseminate

fertilizer 4 dung, muck **5** guano, niter **6** manure, potash **7** compost **8** bonemeal, dressing **10** enrichener **14** superphosphate

fervent 4 keen **5** eager, fiery **6** ardent, devout, fervid, fierce, hearty, heated **7** burning, earnest, intense, zealous **8** spirited, vehement **9** heartfelt **10** passionate **11** impassioned, warmhearted **12** enthusiastic, wholehearted

fervid 5 eager **6** ardent, raging **7** burning, earnest, fanatic, fervent, intense, zealous **8** spirited **10** passionate **11** impassioned **12** all-consuming

fervor 4 fire, zeal, zest **5** ardor, gusto,

piety, verve **6** warmth **7** passion **9** animation, eagerness, intensity, vehemence **10** devoutness, enthusiasm, heartiness **11** earnestness, seriousness **14** purposefulness

Feste
   clown in: **12** Twelfth Night
   author: **11** Shakespeare

Fester *see* **12** Addams Family

fester 3 rot, vex **4** fret, gall, grow, rile **5** chafe, pique **6** nettle, plague, rankle **7** blister, form pus, inflame, putrefy, smolder, torment **8** irritate, ulcerate **9** intensify, suppurate

festering 6 putrid **7** rotting **8** infected, inflamed, rankling **10** putrefying **11** suppurating

festina lente 15 make haste slowly

festival 4 fete, gala **5** feast **6** fiesta **7** gala day, holiday, jubilee **8** carnival, jamboree **11** celebration, festivities

Festival of
   Adonis: **6** Adonia
   Apollo: **5** Delia **8** Didymaea **9** Delphinia **12** Daphnephoria
   Athena: **6** Lenaea **8** Diipolia **9** Pyanepsia **11** Oschophoria
   Attica: **13** Rural Dionysia **14** Lesser Dionysia
   Bacchus: **11** Bacchanalia
   Boeotians: **7** Daedala **13** Little Doedala
   Demeter: **5** Haloa
   Dionysus: **5** Haloa **8** Dionysia
   flowers: **11** Anthesteria
   Greeks: **6** Heraea **9** Pyanepsia **11** Scirophoria, Skirophoria **13** Thesmorphoria
   Persephone: **5** Haloa
   Roman: **8** Floralia, Matralia **9** Lemuralia, Liberalia **10** Larentalia, Lupercalia, Matronalia, Parentalia, Saturnalia
   spring: **11** Anthesteria
   wine: **11** Anthesteria
   Zeus: **6** Diasia **8** Didymaea

festive 3 gay **4** gala **5** jolly, merry **6** festal, joyous **7** larkish, playful **8** sportive **9** convivial **10** frolicsome **11** celebratory **12** lighthearted

festivity 3 joy **4** fete, gala **5** feast, mirth **6** fiesta, gaiety, levity **7** fanfare, jollity, jubilee, revelry **8** festival, jamboree **9** merriment, rejoicing **11** celebration, merrymaking

festoon 3 lei **4** swag **5** chain, curve **6** wreath **7** garland, hanging **8** decorate

fetch 3 get **4** cost **5** bring, go for, yield **6** afford, obtain **7** procure, realize, sell for **8** amount to, retrieve

fetching 6 divine, lovely **8** adorable, becoming, charming, engaging, pleasing **9** appealing **10** attractive, delightful **11** captivating

fete 4 gala **5** feast, party, treat **6** regale **7** banquet, holiday **8** carnival, festival **9** bal masque **11** celebration, garden

party, wine and dine **13** fete champetre

fete champetre 11 garden party **15** outdoor festival

fetid 4 foul, gamy, rank **5** fusty, moldy, musty, nasty **6** putrid, rancid, rotten **7** noisome, stenchy, tainted **8** mephitic, stifling, stinking **9** stenchful **10** malodorous **11** ill-smelling, suffocating

fetish 4 idol, joss **5** charm, craze, image, mania, totem **6** amulet, scarab **7** passion **8** idee fixe, talisman **9** obsession **10** golden calf, phylactery **11** magic object **12** superstition **13** preoccupation

fetter 4 bind, bond, cage, curb, yoke **5** chain, tie up **6** duress, hamper, hinder, hobble, impede, shut in, tether **7** confine, durance, manacle, pin down, shackle, tie down, trammel, truss up **8** bracelet, encumber, handcuff, hold back, restrain **9** hindrance, restraint **13** put into bilbos **15** bind hand and foot

feud 3 row **4** fuss, spat, tiff **5** argue, brawl, clash, set-to **6** affray, bicker, breach, enmity, fracas, schism, strife **7** discord, dispute, faction, ill will, quarrel, rupture, wrangle **8** argument, bad blood, be at odds, clashing, conflict, disagree, squabble, vendetta **9** animosity, bickering, hostility **10** falling out **11** altercation, controversy **12** disagreement, hard feelings
   famous: **6** McCoys **9** Hatfields

Feud, The
   author: **12** Thomas Berger

feudal lord
   Japanese: **6** daimyo

Feuerbach, Anselm
   born: **6** Speyer **7** Germany
   artwork: **9** Iphigenia **15** Judgment of Paris, Plato's Symposium **18** The Fall of the Titans

fever 4 fire, heat **5** ardor, craze, flush, furor **6** desire, frenzy, warmth **7** ferment, illness, pyrexia **8** delirium, sickness **9** agitation **10** enthusiasm, excitement **11** temperature **12** restlessness

feverish 3 hot **5** fiery **6** ardent, red-hot **7** burning, excited, fanatic, febrile, fervent, fevered, flushed, parched, pyretic, zealous **8** frenzied, inflamed, restless **9** impatient, overeager, wrought-up **10** high-strung, passionate **11** impassioned

few 4 rare, some, thin **5** scant **6** meager, paltry, scanty, scarce, skimpy, sparse, unique **7** handful, limited, not many, several, unusual **8** exiguous, piddling, sporadic, uncommon **9** hardly any **10** infrequent, occasional **11** scarcely any, small number **13** infinitesimal, insignificant **14** inconsiderable

Fezziwig
   character in: **15** A Christmas Carol
   author: **7** Dickens

fiance, fiancee 6 future **7** engaged, pledge **8** intended, promised **9** affianced, betrothed, bride-to-be, groom-to-be **10** bride-elect, groom-elect

fiasco 4 bomb, flop **5** botch **6** fizzle **7** debacle, washout **8** disaster **10** non-success

fiat 3 act, law **4** rule **5** edict, order, ukase **6** decree, dictum, ruling **7** command, mandate **11** commandment

fiat lux 15 let there be light

fib 3 lie **5** hedge **7** fiction, untruth **8** white lie **9** half-truth, invention **10** equivocate **11** fabrication, harmless lie, prevaricate **13** falsification, prevarication, tell a white lie **15** stretch the truth **17** misrepresentation

fiber 4 hemp, jute, silk **5** fibre, linen, nylon, rayon, shred, sinew, sisal **6** cotton, dacron, manila, nature, strand, thread **7** quality, texture **8** filament **9** character, polyester, structure

fibrolite
   source: **5** Burma, Mogok

fibula
   bone of: **8** lower leg

fickle 5 giddy **6** fitful **7** erratic, flighty **8** shifting, unstable, unsteady, variable, volatile, wavering **9** frivolous, mercurial, spasmodic, whimsical **10** capricious, changeable, inconstant, irresolute, unreliable **11** fluctuating, light-headed, vacillating **12** inconsistent **13** feather-headed, unpredictable, untrustworthy **14** feather-brained

fiction 3 fib, lie **4** play, tale, yarn **5** fable, novel **7** fantasy, forgery, novella, romance, whopper **8** tall tale **9** falsehood, invention, narrative **10** concoction, short novel, short story **11** fabrication, imagination, made-up story **12** storytelling **13** prevarication **16** cock-and-bull story

fictional 6 made-up **8** invented, literary, mythical **9** storybook **10** fictitious **11** theoretical **12** hypothetical

fictitious 4 fake, sham **5** bogus, false, phony **6** forged, made-up, unreal, untrue **7** assumed, feigned **8** fanciful, invented, mythical, spurious **9** imaginary, legendary, simulated, trumped-up, unfounded **10** apocryphal, artificial, fabricated, fraudulent, not genuine **11** counterfeit **14** supposititious

fiddle 3 bow, saw, toy **4** fool **5** cheat, dally, fraud **6** dawdle, monkey, potter, putter, tamper, trifle, violin **7** falsify, finagle, fritter, swindle **9** deception **10** fool around, mess around **12** monkey around

Fidei Defensor 18 Defender of the Faith
   title of: **17** English sovereigns

Fidelio
  opera by: 9 Beethoven
  character: 5 Rocco **7** Leonora (Fidelio), Pizarro **8** Fernando **9** Florestan

fidelity 5 honor **6** fealty **7** honesty, loyalty, probity **8** accuracy, devotion **9** adherence, closeness, constancy, exactness, good faith, integrity, precision, sincerity **10** allegiance, exactitude **11** earnestness, reliability, staunchness **12** faithfulness, truthfulness **14** correspondency **15** trueheartedness, trustworthiness

Fides
  origin: 5 Roman
  personifies: 9 good faith

fidget 4 fret, fuss, jerk, stew, toss **5** chafe, worry **6** jiggle, squirm, twitch, wiggle, writhe **7** twiddle, wriggle

fidgety 5 antsy, fussy, jerky, jumpy **6** uneasy **7** jittery, nervous, restive, squirmy, twitchy, unquiet **8** restless **9** impatient, irritable, tremulous **12** apprehensive

fief 4 land **6** domain, estate **9** territory

field 3 lea **4** area, grab, lawn, line, mead, turf, yard **5** arena, catch, court, front, glove, green, heath, lists, orbit, range, reach, realm, scope, sward, sweep **6** circle, common, course, domain, extent, meadow, pick up, region, sphere **7** acreage, calling, diamond, expanse, pasture, run down, stretch **8** clearing, province, retrieve, spectrum **9** bailiwick, grassland, territory **10** department, occupation, profession **12** battleground

Field, Sally
  born: 10 Pasadena CA
  roles: 5 Sybil **6** Gidget **8** Norma Rae (Oscar) **9** Punchline, Surrender **12** The Flying Nun **14** Murphy's Romance **15** Absence of Malice **16** Places in the Heart (Oscar) **18** Smokey and the Bandit

Fielding, Cecil
  character in: 15 A Passage to India
  author: 7 Forster

Fielding, Henry
  author of: 6 Amelia **7** Shamela **8** Tom Jones, Tom Thumb **12** Jonathan Wild **13** Joseph Andrews

Field of Blood 8 Aceldama

Fields, W C
  real name: 23 William Claude Dukenfield
  born: 14 Philadelphia PA
  roles: 5 Poppy **8** Micawber **11** The Bank Dick **16** David Copperfield **17** My Little Chickadee **27** Never Give a Sucker an Even Break

Fields of Mourning
  location: 10 underworld
  inhabited by: 14 shades of lovers
  lovers who died by: 7 suicide

Fields of Visions, The
  author: 12 Wright Morris

fiend 5 beast, brute, demon, devil, Satan **6** dybbuk **7** incubus, monster, villain **8** succubus **9** barbarian, hellhound, scoundrel **10** evil spirit **12** wicked person **14** devil incarnate **16** prince of darkness

fiendish 4 evil, foul **5** cruel **6** wicked **7** demonic, heinous, impious, satanic, vicious **8** barbaric, demoniac, devilish **9** monstrous, nefarious **10** demoniacal, diabolical, villainous

fierce 4 fell, wild **5** cruel, feral, fiery **6** bru-tal, fervid, raging, savage, strong **7** enraged, extreme, fearful, fervent, furious, intense, leonine, untamed, violent **8** horrible, menacing, powerful, ravening, ravenous, terrible, tigerish, uncurbed, vehement **9** barbarous, bellicose, ferocious, impetuous, merciless, truculent, unbridled, voracious **10** immoderate, inordinate, passionate **11** threatening **12** bloodthirsty, overpowering, overwhelming, unrestrained
  French: 8 farouche

fierceness 4 zeal **7** passion **8** ferocity, wildness **9** pugnacity, vehemence **10** savageness

fiery 5 afire, angry, irate **6** ablaze, alight, ardent, fervid, fierce, red-hot, torrid **7** blazing, burning, febrile, fervent, fevered, flaming, glaring, glowing, peppery, pyretic, violent, zealous **8** choleric, feverish, flashing, headlong, inflamed, spirited, vehement, wrathful **9** excitable, hotheaded, impetuous, impulsive, irascible, irritable **10** full of fire, high-strung, mettlesome, passionate, sweltering **11** hot-tempered, impassioned, precipitate **12** enthusiastic

fiesta 4 fete, gala **5** feast, party **6** picnic **7** funfair **8** carnival, feast day, festival, jamboree **9** saint's day **10** block party, observance, street fair **11** celebration **13** com-memoration **15** festive occasion

fig 5 Ficus
  varieties: 3 keg, sea **4** bush, cape, Java, Zulu **5** cedar, clown, Congo, rusty **6** common, Devil's, exotic, golden, Indian, Kaffir, Mysore, sacred **7** Barbary, cluster, oak-leaf, spotted, weeping **8** climbing, creeping, Dracaena, mulberry, sycamore **9** Hottentot, mistletoe, strangler **10** East Indian, fiddle-leaf, glossy-leaf, little-leaf, Moreton Bay, Philippine **11** Port Jackson **16** West Indian laurel

Figaro
  character in: 18 The Barber of Seville **19** The Marriage of Figaro
  author: 12 Beaumarchais

fight 3 box, row, war **4** bout, duel, feud, fray, grit, spar, spat, tiff, tilt, wage **5** ar-gue, brawl, brush, clash, event, joust, match, melee, pluck, round, scrap, set-to **6** battle, bicker, combat, engage, fracas, mettle, oppose, resist, spirit, strife, tussle **7** carry on, conduct, contend, contest, discord, dispute, go to war, quarrel, repulse, scuffle, tourney, wage war, wrangle **8** confront, dogfight, gameness, skirmish, squabble, struggle **9** bickering, encounter, pugnacity, scrimmage, toughness, wrangling **10** contention, difference, dissension, prizefight, strive with, tournament **11** altercation, armed action, battle royal, bellicosity, clash of arms, controversy **12** belligerency, do battle with, rise up in arms, struggle with **13** armed conflict, combativeness, confrontation, exchange blows, pitched battle

fight back 7 counter, get even, hit back, pay back **9** retaliate **10** strike back **13** counterattack

fighter 5 boxer **7** soldier, sparrer, warrior **8** pugilist, scrapper **9** combatant **10** militarist **11** belligerent

fighting 3 war **4** fray **5** brawl, melee **6** action, battle, bicker, combat, rumpus, tumult, tussle **7** contest, dispute, quarrel, warfare **8** battling, brawling, conflict, skirmish, squabble **9** bickering, disputing **10** engagement, quarreling, squabbling **11** clash of arms, controversy, hostilities

Fighting Marine
  nickname of: 10 Gene Tunney

fighting men 4 army **6** legion, troops **7** legions, militia **8** military, soldiers, soldiery **13** military force **15** military machine

fighting spirit 9 animosity, hostility, pugnacity **10** antagonism **11** bellicosity **12** belligerence **14** aggressiveness

fight shy of 5 avoid, dodge, elude, evade, skirt **6** escape **8** sidestep

figment 5 fable, fancy, story **6** canard **7** fantasy, fiction, product **8** creation **9** falsehood, invention **10** concoction **11** fabrication

figuration 4 form **7** outline **9** formation, structure **12** constitution

figurative 6 florid, ironic, ornate **7** flowery **8** humorous, symbolic **9** satirical **10** not literal **11** allegorical **12** hyperbolical, metaphorical

figure, figures 3 cut, man, sum **4** body, cast, cost, foot, form, mark, plan, rate, sign, sums **5** add up, adorn, build, count, digit, force, frame, guess, judge, mo-tif, price, shape, think, total, tot up, value, woman **6** amount, appear, assess, cipher, design, device, emblem, factor, leader, number, person, reckon, schema, symbol **7** anatomy, believe, compute, contour, count up, diagram, drawing, imagine, notable, numeral, outline, pattern, presume, suppose **8** appraise, be placed, eminence, estimate, ornament, physique, presence **9** calculate, character, diversify, embellish, have a part, personage, play a part, quotation, variegate **10** arithmetic, conjecture, shine forth, silhouette **11** be mentioned, be prominent **12** calculations, computations, illustration

figurehead 4 tool **5** dummy, front, token **6** cipher, puppet **8** ornament **9** nonentity

figure out 6 reckon **7** compute, find out, work out **8** discover **9** ascertain, calculate, determine

figure roughly 5 guess **6** reckon **8** estimate **11** approximate, make a stab at

figure up 3 add **5** add up, total, tot up **6** reckon **7** compute, count up **9** calculate

figurine 7 bibelot **8** ornament **9** statuette

Fiji
  capital/largest city: 4 Suva
  others: 3 Mba **4** Mbua **5** Navua **6** Labasa **7** Lautoka, Nausori, Vaileka, Vunisea **8** Korolevu, Savusavu **9** Singatoka
  school: 12 South Pacific
  head of state: 14 British monarch **15** governor general
  monetary unit: 6 dollar
  island: 4 Ngau **6** Ovalau, Rotuma, Yasawa **7** Kandavu, Taveuni **8** Viti Levu **9** Vanua Levu
  highest point: 8 Victoria **9** Tomaniivi
  river: 4 Rewa **8** Ndreketi
  sea: 4 Koro **7** Pacific
  people: 6 Fijian, Indian **7** Chinese **10** Melanesian, Polynesian **11** Micronesian
  language: 5 Hindi **6** Fijian **7** English
  religion: 5 Hindu, Islam **9** Methodist **13** Roman Catholic
  feature:
    cluster houses: 5 mbure

filament 4 hair, line, wire **5** fiber, fibre **6** cilium, ribbon, strand, string, thread

filbert 7 Corylus
  varieties: 3 red **4** cork, Momi, plum **5** azure, China, giant, Greek, joint, Nikko, noble, white **6** alpine, balsam, Fraser, Korean, needle, Scotch, silver, summer **7** cascade, Douglas, lowland, Spanish **8** Algerian, Japanese, Sakhalin, Southern **9** Himalayan, Shasta Red **10** dwarf Nikko, Santa Lucia **11** bristle-cone **13** Pacific silver **14** Southern balsam

filch 3 cop, rob **4** copy, crib, hook, lift **5** boost, heist, steal, swipe **6** pilfer, pirate **7** purloin **8** arrogate **10** plagiarize **11** appropriate, expropriate

file 3 row **4** data, line, list, rank, tier **5** ap-ply, chain, index, put in, queue,

store **6** drawer, folder, record, stacks, string **7** catalog, dossier, put away, records, request **8** archives, classify, petition **9** catalogue, chronicle

type: 4 mill, nail, rasp, wood **5** round **9** half-round **13** three-cornered

filial 7 dutiful, sonlike **10** daughterly, respectful

fill 3 act **4** cram, glut, lade, load, meet, pack, puff, sate **5** crowd, gorge, lay by, lay in, serve, stock, store **6** answer, as-sign, blow up, charge, dilate, do duty, expand, infuse, make up, occupy, outfit, supply, take up **7** distend, execute, furnish, inflate, pervade, preside, provide, satiate, satisfy, suffuse, surfeit **8** carry out, function, permeate, saturate **9** discharge, provision, replenish **10** full amount, impregnate, overspread

filled in 7 stood in **9** completed, **11** substituted

filled out 6 marked **7** matured **9** completed

fillet 4 band **5** slice, strip **6** ribbon **7** bandeau, circlet

fillip 3 tap **4** flip, snap, toss **5** flick, tonic **6** buffet **8** stimulus

Fillmore, Millard
  presidential rank: 10 thirteenth
  party: 4 Whig
  state represented: 2 NY
  defeated: 5 no one
    succeeded upon death of: 6 Taylor
  vice president: 4 none
  cabinet:
    State: 7 (Daniel) Webster, (Edward) Everett
    Treasury: 6 (Thomas) Corwin
    War: 6 (Charles Magill) Conrad
    Attorney General: 10 (John Jordan) Crittenden
    Navy: 6 (William Alexander) Graham **7** (John Pendleton) Kennedy
    Postmaster General: 4 (Nathan Kelsey) Hall **7** (Samuel Dickinson) Hubbard
    Interior: 6 (Alexander Hugh Holmes) Stuart
  born: 7 Locke NY
  died/buried: 9 Buffalo NY
  education:
    college: 4 none
    studied: 3 law
  religion: 9 Unitarian
  interests: 5 civic
    first chancellor of University of: 7 Buffalo
    founder: 22 Buffalo General Hospital **24** Buffalo Historical Society
  author: 21 Millard Fillmore Papers
  political career: 13 state assembly, Vice President **24** US House of Representatives
  civilian career: 6 lawyer (New York Supreme Court) **7** teacher **10** wool

carder **12** cloth dresser
  notable events of lifetime/term: 25 Compromise of Eighteen-Fifty
  act: 13 Fugitive Slave
  father: 9 Nathaniel
  mother: 6 Phoebe (Millard)
  siblings: 5 Cyrus, Julia **11** Phoebe Maria **12** Almon Hopkins, Calvin Turner **13** Charles DeWitt **14** Darius Ingraham, Olive Armstrong
  wife: 7 Abigail (Powers) **8** Caroline (Carmichael McIntosh)
  children: 11 Mary Abigail **13** Millard Powers

fill with air 5 bloat **6** billow, blow up, expand **7** balloon, distend, inflate, puff out **8** swell out

fill with dread 5 alarm, panic **6** dismay **7** perturb, terrify, unnerve **8** disquiet, frighten

fill with gloom 6 darken, sadden **8** dispirit

fill with wonder 3 awe **5** amaze **7** astound **8** astonish **9** fascinate

film, films 4 cine, coat, haze, mist, skin, veil **5** cloud, flick, movie, sheet, shoot **6** cinema, flicks, movies, screen **7** coating **8** membrane

filmy 3 dim **4** fine, hazy, thin **5** gauzy, misty, sheer, wispy **8** cobwebby, finespun, gossamer **10** diaphanous, seethrough

fils 3 son

filter 4 leak, ooze, seep **5** drain, exude, sieve **6** effuse, purify, refine, screen, strain **7** clarify, cleanse, dribble, trickle, well out **8** filtrate, strainer

filth 3 mud **4** dirt, dung, mire, muck, porn, slop, smut **5** offal, slime, slush, trash **6** manure, ordure, refuse, sewage, sludge **7** carrion, excreta, garbage, squalor **8** impurity, lewdness, ribaldry, vileness **9** excrement, grossness, indecency, nastiness, obscenity, pollution **10** corruption, defilement, immorality, indelicacy, putridness **11** pornography, squalidness **13** contamination **14** suggestiveness

filthy 4 foul, vile **5** black, dirty, grimy, gross, messy, nasty **6** grubby, impure, odious, soiled **7** defiled, dirtied, obscene, smirchy, squalid, unclean **8** befouled, slovenly, unwashed **9** repulsive **10** besmirched, disgusting **12** contaminated

finagle 3 con, gyp **4** plot, rook **5** cheat, mulct, trick **6** chisel, fleece, scheme, wangle **7** defraud, swindle **8** engineer, intrigue, maneuver

final 4 last, rear **6** ending, latest **7** closing, extreme **8** complete, decisive, finished, hindmost, rearmost, terminal, thorough, ultimate **10** concluding, conclusive, definitive, exhaustive, hindmost **11** irrevocable, terminating **12** unappealable, unchangeable

13 determinative
French: **7** dernier

finale 3 end **5** close, finis **6** finish, windup **7** curtain **8** epilogue, last part, swan song **10** conclusion **11** culmination, termination

final limit
Latin: **14** terminus ad quem

finally 6 lastly **10** eventually, inexorably, ultimately **11** inescapably **12** conclusively, definitively, in conclusion **16** incontrovertibly
French: **5** enfin
Latin: **10** ad extremum

final section 4 coda **5** rider **6** ending **7** last act **8** addendum, epilogue **9** afterword **10** conclusion

final settlement 8 solution **11** disposition

finance 6 pay for **7** banking **8** accounts **9** economics **10** underwrite

financial backer 5 angel **6** patron **7** sponsor **9** supporter **10** benefactor

financial support 7 backing, subsidy **10** assistance **12** contribution

financier 5 angel **6** backer, banker, broker **7** rich man **10** capitalist **11** millionaire, underwriter

Financier, The
author: **15** Theodore Dreiser
character: **12** Aileen Butler, Edward Butler **15** Henry Cowperwood **16** Frank A Cowperwood **23** Lillian Semple Cowperwood

Finch, Peter
real name: **15** Peter Ingle-Finch
born: **6** London **7** England
roles: **7** Network (Oscar) **11** Lost Horizon **12** The Nun's Story **15** The Pumpkin Eater **18** Sunday Bloody Sunday

Finchley, Sondra
character in: **17** An American Tragedy
author: **7** Dreiser

find 3 get, see, win **4** earn, espy, gain, meet, rule, spot **5** award, catch, dig up, judge, learn **6** attain, come by, decide, decree, detect, expose, locate, regain **7** achieve, acquire, adjudge, bargain, bonanza, discern, get back, godsend, good buy, hit upon, procure, recover, uncover, unearth **8** bump into, come upon, discover, disinter, lucky hit, meet with, retrieve, windfall **9** ascertain, determine, discov-ery, encounter, pronounce, repossess **10** adjudicate **11** acquisition

fin de siecle 8 decadent **15** end of the century

find fault 3 nag **4** beef, carp **5** blame, cavil, gribe **6** grouse, squawk **7** nitpick **8** complain **9** bellyache, criticize, disparage **10** disapprove

find guilty 5 blame **6** indict **7** condemn, convict **8** sentence **9** implicate

finding 6 decree, ruling **7** verdict **8** decision

find innocent 5 clear **6** acquit **9** exonerate

find out 5 learn **6** detect, locate **7** uncover, unearth **8** discover **9** ascertain, determine, establish

find repulsive 4 hate **5** abhor **6** detest, loathe **7** despise **8** execrate, recoil at **9** abominate

fine 4 airy, chic, fair, keen, neat, nice, rare, thin **5** bonny, clear, dandy, gauzy, mulct, nifty, sharp, sheer, silky, small, smart, sunny, swell **6** assess, bonnie, bright, charge, choice, comely, dainty, flimsy, ground, lovely, minute, modish, pretty, silken, slight, spiffy, subtle, superb **7** damages, elegant, forfeit, fragile, penalty, perfect, powdery, precise, refined, slender, stylish, tenuous **8** cobwebby, delicate, ethereal, flawless, gossamer, handsome, penalize, pleasant, polished, powdered, rainless, skillful, splendid, superior, tasteful **9** admirable, beautiful, brilliant, cloudless, excellent, exquisite **10** assessment, attractive, consummate, diaphanous, fastidious, pulverized, swimmingly **11** excellently, exceptional, lightweight, magnificent, transparent, well-favored **12** accomplished **13** hairsplitting, unsubstantial
music: **3** end

fine clothes 8 glad rags **10** Sunday best **16** best bib and tucker

fine-looking 4 fair **5** bonny **6** bonnie, comely, lovely, pretty, seemly **8** gorgeous, handsome **9** beauteous, beautiful, exquisite, ravishing **10** attractive **11** resplendent **15** pulchritudinous

fineness 6 beauty **8** delicacy, elegance, thinness **10** perfection, smoothness **12** flawlessness **13** exquisiteness

fine points 3 art **7** finesse, nuances **8** niceties **10** subtleties **11** refinements **12** distinctions

finer 6 better **8** superior

finery 6 frills, tinsel **7** baubles, gaudery, gewgaws **8** frippery, spangles, trinkets **9** trappings, trimmings **13** paraphernalia

finesse 4 ruse, tact, wile **5** craft, dodge, guile, savvy **7** cunning **8** artifice, delicacy, intrigue, trickery **9** deception, stratagem **10** artfulness, discretion, subterfuge
French: **11** savoir-faire

fine workmanship 8 delicacy **9** precision **13** craftsmanship

finger 3 paw **4** feel, poke, ring **5** digit, index, punch, thumb, touch **6** caress, feeler, handle, middle, pinkie, pollex **7** pointer, squeeze, toy with, twiddle **8** identify, play with **10** manipulate

finicky 5 fussy, picky **6** choosy **8** niggling **10** fastidious, meticulous, nit-

picking, overprecise, particular, pernickety **11** persnickety **14** discriminating, overparticular

finish 3 end **4** coat, face, gild, goal, kill, last, seal, stop **5** cease, close, glaze, use up **6** clinch, defeat, devour, ending, finale, settle, veneer, wind up **7** achieve, coating, consume, curtain, destroy, fulfill, get done, lacquer, realize, surface, varnish **8** carry out, complete, conclude, dispatch, epilogue, exterior, get rid of, knock off, make good **9** discharge, eradicate, objective, polishing, terminate **10** accomplish, completion, conclusion, consummate, denouement **11** discontinue, exterminate, termination

finished 4 full **5** ended, final, ideal, whole **6** entire, urbane **7** classic, elegant, perfect, refined, shapely, skilled, trained, well-set **8** complete, flawless, polished, well-bred **9** beautiful, completed, concluded, exquisite, faultless **10** consummate, cultivated, impeccable **11** consummated **12** accomplished

finishing stroke 9 death blow
French: **11** coup de grace

finish off 4 kill, slay **7** destroy, execute, wipe out **8** complete, dispatch **9** eradicate, polish off **10** annihilate **11** exterminate

finite 7 bounded, limited **8** confined, temporal **9** countable **10** measurable, restricted, short-lived, terminable **13** circumscribed

Finland
other name: **5** Suomi **15** Suomen Tasavalta
capital/largest city: **8** Helsinki **11** Helsingfors
others: **3** Aba, Abo, Kem **4** Kemi, Ouli, Oulu, Ouou, Pori, Vasa **5** Enare, Espoo, Kotka, Lahti, Rauma, Turku, Vaasa **6** Imatra, Kuopio **7** Joensuu, Kajaani, Kokkola, Mikkeli, Tampere, Tapiola **9** Jyvaskyla, Mariehamn, Rovaniemi **12** Lappeenranta
measure: **5** kannu, verst **6** fathom, kannor **8** otlinger, skalpund, tunnland
monetary unit: **4** mark **5** penni **6** markka
island: **5** Aland, Karlo **6** Aaland **7** Hailuto **9** Vallgrund **10** Ahvenanmaa
lake: **3** Juo, Muo **4** Kemi, Kiui, Nasi, Oulu, Puru, Pyha, Simo **5** Enara, Enare, Hauki, Inari, Kalla, Lappa, Lesti, Puula, Saima **6** Ladoya, Lentua, Saimaa, Sounne, Syvari **7** Koitere, Nilakka, Pielien **9** Kallavesi, Pielavesi
mountain: **7** Laltiva **10** Saari Selka
highest point: **6** Haltia **11** Haldetsokka
river: **4** Kala, Kemi, Kymi, Oulu, Pats, Simo, Teno **5** Ivalo, Lotta, Ounas, Siika, Torne **6** Iijoki, Lapuan, Muonio, Pasvik, Tornoi, Vuoski **7** Kitinen **8** Kokemaki

sea: 6 Baltic **8** Atlantic
physical feature:
  gulf: 7 Bothnia, Finland
  isthmus: 7 Karelia
  peninsula: 13 Fennoscandian
people: 3 Jew, Vod, Vot, Yak **4** Avar, Finn, Hame, Lapp, Turk, Veps **5** Fioun, Gypsy, Ijore, Inger, Suomi, Vepse **6** Magyar, Ostiak, Ostyak, Tarast, Tavast, Ugrian, Zyrian **7** Lappish, Mordvin, Permiak, Samoyed, Uralian **8** Cheremis, Estonian, Karelian, Livonian, Swekoman **9** Tavastian **11** Karjalaiset, Suomalaiset
  athlete: 10 Paavo Nurmi
  composer: 8 Sibelius
  designer: 9 Marimekko
language: 4 Avar, Lapp **5** Karel, Ugric, Vogul **6** Magyar, Ostyak, Tarast **7** Finnish, Olonets, Samoyed, Swedish **8** Estonian **10** Olonetsian
religion: 19 Evangelical Lutheran
place:
  canal: 6 Saimaa
  castle: 10 Saint Olaf's **11** Olavinlinna
  fortress: 8 Sveaborg **11** Suomenlinna
  memorial: 8 Sibelius
  pine ridge: 10 Punkaharju
feature:
  game: 9 pesapallo
food:
  dish: 11 Karelian pie
  fruit: 16 yellow cloudberry
  liqueur: 9 Mesimarja

Finn
  also: 5 Fionn **13** Fionn MacCumal
  origin: 5 Irish
  king of: 4 gods **14** Tuatha De Danann
  son: 6 Ossian
  father: 5 Cumal **6** Comhal

Finnegans Wake
  author: 10 James Joyce
  family: 9 Earwicker

Finney, Albert
  wife: 10 Anouk Aimee
  born: 7 England, Salford
  roles: 5 Annie **7** Scrooge **8** Tom Jones **10** The Dresser **12** Shoot the Moon **13** Two for the Road **17** Under the Volcano **29** Saturday Night and Sunday Morning

Finnish Mythology *see* **21** Scandinavian Mythology

Finno-Ugric
  language family: 6 Uralic
  Finnic group: 4 Lapp **6** Votyak, Zyryan **7** Finnish, Mordvin, Permian **8** Estonian **9** Cheremiss
  Ugric group: 5 Vogul **6** Ostyak **7** Ob-Ugric **9** Hungarian

Fionn, Fionn MacCumal *see* **4** Finn
fiord, fjord 5 firth, inlet **7** estuary
  location: 6 Norway

fir 4 pine **5** cedar, larch **6** alpine, balsam, linden, spruce **7** conifer, cypress, douglas **9** evergreen

Firbolg
  origin: 5 Greek, Irish
  defeated by: 9 Fomorians
  ousted by: 4 gods **14** Tuatha De Danann

fire 3 can, vim **4** bake, boot, burn, cook, dash, dump, elan, hurl, oust, sack, stir **5** ardor, blaze, eject, flame, flare, flash, force, gusto, let go, light, power, punch, rouse, salvo, shell, shoot, spark, verve, vigor **6** arouse, bounce, depose, excite, fervor, foment, genius, ignite, incite, kindle, luster, spirit, stir up, vivify, volley **7** animate, bombard, bonfire, cashier, dismiss, inferno, inflame, inspire, project, quicken, sniping, trigger **8** enfilade, fervency, inspirit, radiance, splendor, vivacity **9** broadside, cannonade, discharge, eagerness, fusillade, galvanize, holocaust, instigate, intensity, stimulate, vehemence **10** brilliance, effulgence, enthusiasm **11** bombardment, earnestness, inspiration **13** conflagration, sharpshooting **15** imaginativeness
  god of: 4 Loki **5** Ishum **6** Vulcan **10** Hephaestus, Hephaistos
  goddess of: 6 Brigit

Fire and Ice
  author: 11 Robert Frost

firearm 3 gun, rod **5** piece, rifle **6** pistol **7** shotgun **8** revolver **10** machine gun **12** shooting iron **13** submachine gun **20** Saturday-night special

firefight 5 clash **6** battle, combat **8** skirmish

firefly 8 glowworm, lampyrid **9** candlefly **12** lightning bug

Fire Next Time, The
  author: 12 James Baldwin

fire off 5 eject, shoot **6** launch **8** detonate **9** discharge

Fireside Theatre
  host: 9 Jane Wyman **11** Frank Wisbar, Gene Raymond

Firestarter
  author: 11 Stephen King

fire up 4 fuel, rile **5** anger, light, rouse **6** arouse, excite, ignite, incite, kindle **7** animate, enthuse, inspire **8** activate, energize, irritate, vitalize **9** galvanize, stimulate

firm 4 bent, fast, grim, hard, taut **5** close, dense, fixed, house, rigid, rocky, solid, stiff, stony, tight, tough **6** dogged, flinty, intent, moored, rooted, secure, stable, steady, steely **7** compact, company, dead set, decided, earnest, serious, settled, staunch **8** anchored, business, constant, definite, fearless, obdurate, resolute, resolved, unshaken **9** confirmed, hard-nosed, immovable, obstinate, steadfast, tenacious, unbending **10** adamantine, compressed, determined, inexorable, inflexible, invincible, persistent, unwavering, unyielding **11** corporation, established, partnership, unalterable, unfaltering, unflinching **12** conglomerate, indissoluble, organization **13** establishment

firmament 3 air, sky **5** ether, space, vault **6** canopy, welkin **7** heavens, the blue, the void **10** outer space

firmness 8 tenacity **9** obstinacy **10** resolution **11** persistence, staunchness **12** resoluteness **13** determination, inflexibility, steadfastness

first 4 head, main **5** basic, prime, start, vital **6** before,eldest, maiden, outset, primal, rather, sooner **7** highest, leading, premier, primary, ranking, supreme **8** earliest, foremost, original, primeval, superior **9** beginning, essential, inception, initially, paramount, primitive, principal **10** aboriginal, elementary, preeminent, preferably, primordial **11** fundamental, rudimentary **12** commencement, introduction, introductory

first among equals
  Latin: 16 primus inter pares

first appearance 4 dawn **5** debut **9** beginning **12** introduction

firstborn 5 elder, older **6** eldest, oldest

Firstborn, The
  author: 14 Christopher Fry

First Circle
  author: 23 Aleksandr Solzhenitsyn Jr

first god *see* **8** god, first

firsthand 3 direct **8** personal **9** empirical **10** unmediated **12** experimental

First Lady of the Theater
  nickname of: 10 Helen Hayes **16** Katherine Cornell

first-line 4 main **5** chief **7** primary **8** foremost

first moving thing
  Latin: 12 primum mobile

first-rate 3 ace **4** A-one, best, fine, tops **5** crack, elite, great, prime **6** choice, finest, select **7** top-hole **8** splendid, superior, top-notch, very good **9** admirable, estimable, excellent, exclusive, nonpareil, top drawer, topflight, wonderful **10** noteworthy, stupendous **11** commendable, outstanding **12** above-average, incomparable **13** distinguished

First State
  nickname of: 8 Delaware

first step 5 start **9** beginning **12** commencement

firth 5 fjord, inlet **7** estuary

fiscal 8 economic, monetary **9** budgetary, financial, pecuniary

fish 3 net **4** cast, hook, hunt **5** angle, grope, seine, trawl, troll **6** ferret, search **7** rummage

fish

class: 7 Agnatha 12 Osteichthyes 14 Chondrichthyes

fin: 4 anal, tail 6 caudal, dorsal, median, paired, pelvic 7 adipose, ventral 8 pectoral

kind: 3 cod, eel, gar, ray 4 bass, carp, hake, opah, pike, tuna 5 brill, perch, shark, skate, sword, trout 6 bichir, blenny, marlin, minnow, mullet, salmon, tarpon 7 anchovy, catfish, dogfish, dolphin, hagfish, herring, lamprey, piranha, sunfish 8 bluefish, cavefish, crayfish, flounder, goldfish, lungfish, mackerel, menhaden, moray eel, pilchard, sea horse, squirrel, sturgeon 9 killifish, pygmy goby, swordfish 10 coelacanth, flying fish, paddlefish, rabbit fish, rocksucker, whale shark 11 anemonefish, electric eel, electric ray, lanternfish, longnose gar 13 butterflyfish 14 largemouth bass

part: 3 fin 4 gill 5 scale 6 cirrhi 10 gas bladder 11 swim bladder 12 rete mirabile

shellfish:
  crustacean: 4 crab 6 shrimp 7 lobster 8 blue crab, king crab, snow crab 9 langouste 11 langoustine 13 Dungeness crab, horseshoe crab
  mollusk: 4 clam 6 mussel, oyster, quahog 8 surf clam 9 horse clam, razor clam 11 geoduck clam

young: 3 fry 10 fingerling

Fisher, Bud
  creator/artist of: 11 Mutt and Jeff

Fisher, Carrie
  father: 11 Eddie Fisher
  mother: 13 Debbie Reynolds
  role: 12 Princess Leia
  films: 7 Shampoo 8 Star Wars 12 This Is My Life 16 The Blues Brothers 17 When Harry Met Sally 18 The Return of the Jedi 19 The Empire Strikes Back, Hannah and Her Sisters
  author: 20 Postcards from the Edge

Fisher, Ham
  creator/artist of: 10 Joe Palooka

Fisher, Vardis
  author of: 10 The Mothers 13 Children of God 17 The Testament of Man

fisherman 5 eeler 6 angler, caster, jacker, netter, seiner 7 trawler, troller 8 piscator 9 flycaster, Waltonian 17 the compleat angler

Fishermen
  goddess of: 11 Britomartis

Fishes
  constellation of: 6 Pisces

fish story 3 fib, lie 7 fiction, whopper 9 falsehood, tall story 16 cock-and-bull story

fishy 3 odd 4 dull 5 blank, queer, shady, weird 6 vacant 7 dubious,

strange, suspect 8 doubtful, peculiar, slippery 9 dishonest 10 farfetched, glassy-eyed, improbable, suspicious, unreliable 11 exaggerated, extravagant 12 questionable, unscrupulous 14 expressionless

fission 7 atomize 8 breaking, cleavage, scission 9 severance, splitting 10 breaking up, sunderance 12 disseverance, reproduction

fissure 3 gap 4 rift, slit 5 chink, cleft, crack, gully, split 6 breach, cranny, groove, hiatus 8 aperture, cleavage

fit 4 able, good, hale, meet, ripe, suit, well, whim 5 adapt, agree, alter, burst, equal, equip, hardy, match, ready, right, shape, sound, spasm, spell, train 6 access, accord, adjust, become, concur, enable, in trim, mature, primed, proper, robust, seemly, strong, timely, worthy 7 adapted, apropos, capable, caprice, conform, correct, empower, fashion, healthy, prepare, qualify, rectify, seizure, toned up, trained 8 apposite, becoming, coincide, crotchet, decorous, eligible, graduate, grand mal, outbreak, outburst, paroxysm, petit mal, prepared, relevant, suitable 9 calibrate, competent, consonant, deserving, efficient, explosion, harmonize, initiated, opportune, pertinent, qualified 10 acceptable, applicable, capacitate, convenient, convulsion, correspond, seasonable 11 appropriate, capacitated

fitful 4 weak 6 broken, random, uneven 7 erratic 8 listless, off-and-on, periodic, sporadic, unsteady, variable 9 irregular, spasmodic 10 capricious, changeable, convulsive 11 fluctuating 12 disconnected, intermittent

fitness
  Hebrew: 7 kashrut 8 kashruth

fit out 4 robe 5 array, dress, equip 6 attire, clothe, supply 7 appoint, deck out, prepare

fitting 3 apt 4 meet 6 proper, seemly 8 decorous, suitable 9 congruous 11 appropriate
  French: 11 comme il faut

fit to be eaten 6 edible 9 palatable 10 comestible, consumable, digestible

fit together 4 join 5 hinge, unite 6 hook up 7 connect 8 dovetail 9 interlock 10 articulate

Fitzgerald, Barry
  real name: 20 William Joseph Shields
  born: 6 Dublin 7 Ireland
  roles: 10 Going My Way 11 The Quiet Man 19 How Green Was My Valley

FitzGerald, Edward
  author of: 24 The Rubaiyat of Omar Khayyam (translation)

Fitzgerald, F Scott
  wife: 10 Zelda Sayre
  author of: 10 The Crack-Up 13 The

Last Tycoon 14 The Great Gatsby 16 Tender Is the Night 18 This Side of Paradise 24 The Beautiful and the Damned
  coined term: 7 Jazz Age

Fitzgerald, George Francis
  field: 7 physics
  nationality: 5 Irish
  theory of: 24 electromagnetic radiation

Fitzgerald, Geraldine
  born: 6 Dublin 7 Ireland
  roles: 11 Dark Victory 12 Ah Wilderness, Rachel Rachel 15 Watch on the Rhine 16 Wuthering Heights 24 Long Day's Journey into Night

Fitzsimmons, Bob (Robert Prometheus)
  sport: 6 boxing

Fitzsimmons, Maureen
  real name of: 12 Maureen O'Hara

Five, The
  group of: 16 Russian composers
  member: 3 Cui 7 Borodin 9 Balakirev 10 Mussorgsky 14 Rimsky-Korsakov

Five Easy Pieces
  director: 11 Bob Rafelson
  cast: 10 Karen Black 11 Fannie Flagg 12 Susan Anspach 13 Jack Nicholson 14 Billy Breen Bush, Sally Struthers

Five Men and Pompey
  author: 19 Stephen Vincent Benet

five-o'clock shadow 5 beard 7 stubble 8 bristles, whiskers

fix 3 jam, put, set 4 bind, make, mend, mess, moor, spot 5 place, rivet 6 adjust, anchor, attach, decide, fasten, harden, impose, muddle, pickle, plight, repair, scrape, secure, settle 7 congeal, connect, correct, dilemma, impasse, implant, patch up, prepare, rebuild 8 assemble, hot water, make fast, make firm, quandary, regulate, renovate, set right, solidify 9 establish, prescribe, retaliate, stabilize 10 difficulty 11 consolidate, involvement, predicament 12 entanglement

fixation 5 quirk 6 fetish 7 complex 8 crotchet, delusion 9 monomania, obsession 13 preoccupation

fixed 3 set 4 fast, firm 5 rigid, still 6 intent, rooted, stable, steady 8 constant, fastened, resolute, unpliant 9 immovable, unbending 10 determined, inflexible, motionless, persistent, stationary, unwavering

fixed idea 4 bias 5 slant 9 obsession 13 preconception
  French: 8 idee fixe

fixedness 8 firmness 9 constancy, stability 10 immobility 12 immutability 16 unchangeableness

fixed regard 7 staring 9 diligence 10 absorption, intentness 11 engrossment 13 concentration

Fixer, The
  author: **14** Bernard Malamud
fixing 6 repair **7** mending, mooring, placing, putting, setting **8** deciding, imposing, righting, riveting, settling, trimming **9** adjusting, anchoring, attaching, fastening, hardening, preparing, repairing **10** adjustment, assembling, congealing, connecting, correcting, implanting, rectifying, regulating, regulation **11** determining, prescribing, solidifying, stabilizing **12** establishing **13** consolidating
fixture 6 addict **7** devotee, habitue, regular **8** equipage **9** apparatus, appendage, appliance, equipment **10** attachment **11** appointment **12** appurtenance **13** paraphernalia
fix up 4 plan **6** design, devise **7** arrange, prepare **8** renovate, schedule
fix upon 4 pick **6** choose, opt for, select **7** call out, extract, pick out
fizz 4 foam **5** froth **7** bubbles **11** carbonation **13** effervescence
fizziness 9 foaminess **10** bubbliness, frothiness **13** effervescence
fizzing 6 bubbly **7** foaming **8** bubbling **9** sparkling **12** effervescent, effervescing
fizzle 3 dog, dud **4** bomb, fail, flop, hiss, mess **5** abort, botch **6** bubble, fiasco, gurgle, muddle, turkey **7** failure, founder, misfire, sputter, washout **8** collapse, disaster, miscarry
fizzy 6 bubbly **8** bubbling **9** sparkling **12** effervescent
flabbergast 4 stun **5** amaze, shock **6** puzzle **7** astound, stagger, stupefy **8** astonish, bewilder, bowl over, confound, overcome **9** dumbfound
flabbergasted 5 agape **6** amazed, gaping **9** awestruck, stupefied **10** astonished, dumbstruck, spellbound **11** dumbfounded **12** hornswoggled **13** thunderstruck
flabby 4 lame, limp, soft, weak **5** baggy, slack **6** doughy, effete, feeble, flimsy, floppy, spongy **7** flaccid **8** impotent, listless, yielding **9** enervated, inelastic **10** out of shape, spiritless **11** adulterated, emasculated
flag 3 ebb, sag **4** fade, fail, pall, sink, tire, wane, warn, wave, wilt **5** abate, faint, slump **6** banner, colors, dodder, emblem, ensign, signal, totter **7** decline, give way, pennant, subside, succumb **8** grow weak, languish, Old Glory, standard, streamer **9** grow weary, Union Jack **12** Stars and Bars **15** Stars and Stripes
flagellant 7 ascetic **8** penitent **13** self-mortifier
flagon 3 gun, jug, mug **4** ewer **5** flask, stein **6** bottle, carafe, vessel **7** canteen **8** schooner
flagrant 5 gross, sheer **6** arrant, brazen, crying **7** blatant, glaring, heinous, obvious **8** immodest **9** audacious, barefaced, flaunting, monstrous, notorious, shameless **10** outrageous, scandalous **11** conspicuous

Flaherty, Margaret (Pegeen)
  character in: **24** Playboy of the Western World
  author: **5** Synge
flail 4 beat, lash, whip **5** swing **6** thresh **7** scourge
flair 4 bent, dash, feel, gift **5** knack, style, taste, touch, verve **6** genius, talent **7** faculty, feeling, panache **8** aptitude, capacity **9** ingenuity **11** discernment
flake 3 bit **4** chip, peel **5** fleck, layer, patch, scale, sheet, strip **7** chip off, crumble, peel off, shaving **8** scale off
flaky 4 bats, gaga, nuts **5** balmy, batty, crisp, daffy, dotty, goofy, loony, nutty, scaly, short, wacky **6** scabby, screwy, scurfy **8** scabious, squamous **9** eccentric **10** flocculent
flamboyant 4 wild **5** gaudy, jazzy, showy **6** flashy, florid, garish, ornate, rococo **7** baroque, dashing **8** colorful, exciting **10** theatrical **11** sensational **12** ostentatious
flame 4 beau, fire, glow **5** ardor, blaze, blush, flare, flash, flush, glare, gleam, light, lover, spark, swain **6** fervor, ignite, kindle, redden, warmth **7** passion **8** fervency **9** affection, boyfriend, intensity **10** enthusiasm, excitement, girlfriend, sweetheart **13** conflagration
flaming 5 afire, fiery **6** ablaze, alight, ardent, bright, fervid, stormy **7** blazing, burning, fervent, glaring, glowing, igneous, intense, shining, violent **8** flagrant, vehement **9** brilliant, egregious **10** passionate, smoldering **11** conspicuous, inflammable
flammable 7 igneous **10** combustive, incendiary **11** combustible, inflammable
flan 3 pie **4** gust, puff, tart **6** expand, pastry **7** custard, dessert **12** creme caramel
flanerie 8 dawdling, idleness
flaneur 5 idler **6** loafer **7** dawdler
flank 3 hip **4** edge, line, loin, side, wing **5** cover, skirt **6** border, fringe, haunch, screen, shield
Flannagan, John Bernard
  born: **7** Fargo ND
  artwork: **6** New One, Not Yet **9** Beginning **11** Dragon Motif **15** Triumph of the Egg **16** Jonah and the Whale
flap 3 bat, fly, tab **4** bang, beat, flop **5** apron, shake, skirt **6** lappet **7** agitate, banging, flutter, vibrate **9** oscillate
flare 4 burn, glow **5** blaze, erupt, flame, flash, glare, gleam, taper, torch, widen **6** blow up, dilate, expand, ignite, signal, spread **7** bell out, broaden, distend, explode, stretch **8** boil over, break out **9** coruscate **10** incandesce
flash 4 glow, wink **5** blaze, blink, burst, flame, flare, glare, gleam, jiffy, shake, shine, spark, touch, trice **6** minute, moment, second, streak **7** flicker, glimmer, glisten, glitter, instant, sparkle **8** instance, outburst, radiance **9** coruscate **10** occurrence **11** coruscation, fulmination, scintillate **13** incandescence
Flash Gordon
  creator: **8** Dan Berry **11** Alex Raymond **12** Austin Briggs
  character: **11** Emperor Ming **12** Princess Aura
  companion: **4** Dale
  portrayed by: **12** Buster Crabbe
flashy 4 loud **5** gaudy, jazzy, showy, smart **6** garish, sporty, tawdry, tinsel, vulgar **7** raffish **8** dazzling **9** bedizened **10** flamboyant, tricked out **11** pretentious **12** ostentatious
flask 6 bottle **7** canteen **9** container
flat, flats 3 low **4** dead, dull **5** clear, equal, flush, level, marsh, plain, plane, prone, shoal, shoes, stale, total, vapid **6** direct, planar, smooth, supine **7** blowout, exact-ly, insipid, laid low, leveled, levelly, loafers, prairie, regular, shallow **8** absolute, complete, definite, lowlands, positive, puncture, thorough, unbroken **9** apartment, downright, precisely, prostrate, reclining, recumbent, tasteless **10** flavorless, horizontal, peremptory **11** unequivocal, unpalatable, unqualified **12** deflated tire, horizontally, unmistakable
flatfish 3 ray **4** sole **5** brill, fluke **6** turbot **7** halibut, sand dab, sunfish, teleost **8** flounder
Flathead *see* **5** Salis **7** Chinook
flatness 8 dullness **9** levelness, staleness **10** insipidity **13** tastelessness **14** flavorlessness
flatten 4 deck, even, fell **5** crush, floor, level, plane **6** defeat, ground, smooth **7** deflate **8** compress, overcome **9** overwhelm, prostrate
flatter 4 fool, laud **5** court, extol, honor, toady **6** become, cajole, delude **7** adulate, beguile, deceive, mislead, wheedle **8** blandish, bootlick, butter up, eulogize, soft-soap **9** brown-nose, sweet-talk, truckle to **10** compliment, overpraise, panegyrize
flatterer 5 toady **6** fawner, yes man **8** eulogist, truckler, wheedler **9** sycophant **10** bootlicker **11** lickspittle **13** apple-polisher
flattering 7 lauding **8** praising **9** extolling, favorable, laudatory **10** gratifying **13** complimentary
flattering attention 5 court **7** fawning

flattery 6 eulogy 7 blarney, fawning, snow job 8 cajolery, encomium, jollying, soft soap, toadying, toadyism 9 adulation, panegyric, servility, truckling, wheedling 10 sycophancy 12 blandishment 14 obsequiousness

Flaubert, Gustave
author of: 8 Salammbo 12 Madame Bovary 21 A Sentimental Education 24 The Temptation of St Anthony

flaunt 3 air 4 brag, wave 5 boast, sport, strut, vaunt 6 blazon, dangle, parade 7 exhibit, show off 8 brandish, flourish 9 advertise, broadcast

flavor 4 aura, lace, soul, tang, tone 5 gusto, imbue, savor, spice, style, tenor 6 aspect, infuse, lacing, relish, season, spirit 7 essence, instill 9 ambience, piquancy 9 attribute, seasoning

flavorful 4 rich 5 nutty, sapid, spicy, tangy, tasty, zesty 6 savory 7 peppery, piquant 8 aromatic 9 palatable, toothsome 10 appetizing

flavoring 4 herb, salt 5 spice 6 pepper 7 essence, extract, vanilla 8 additive, seasoner 9 chocolate, condiment, seasoning

flavorless 4 dull, flat, thin, weak 5 bland, stale, vapid 6 watery 7 insipid 9 tasteless

flaw 3 mar 4 blot, harm, spot, vice 5 error, fault, speck, stain 6 blotch, deface, defect, foible, impair, injure, injury, smudge, weaken 7 blemish, failing, fallacy, frailty, mistake 8 weak spot, weakness 9 deformity, disfigure 10 compromise, defacement 11 shortcoming 12 imperfection 13 disfigurement

flawed 6 faulty 8 impaired 9 defective, imperfect

flawless 5 sound 7 perfect 9 errorless, faultless 10 immaculate, impeccable

flawlessness 8 accuracy 10 perfection 11 correctness 14 immaculateness

flay 4 bark, pare, peel, skin 5 scalp, scold, strip 6 assail, fleece, punish, rebuke 7 plunder, upbraid 9 castigate, excoriate 11 decorticate

flea
varieties: 3 bat, dog, rat 5 mouse 6 rodent 9 carnivore 10 sticktight

fleck 3 dot, jot 4 drop, mark, mole, spot 5 flake, speck 6 bespot, dapple, mottle, streak, tittle 7 blemish, freckle, spatter, speckle, stipple 8 particle, small bit 9 bespeckle 10 besprinkle

Fledermaus, Die
also: 6 The Bat
operetta by: 7 (Johann) Strauss
character: 5 Adele, Falke, Frank 6 Alfred 9 Rosalinda 14 Prince Orlofsky 18 Baron von Eisenstein

fledgling 4 tyro 6 novice 8 beginner, freshman 9 greenhorn 10 apprentice, tenderfoot

flee 4 shun, skip 5 avoid, dodge, elude, evade, split 6 decamp, desert, vanish 7 abscond, fly away, make off 8 speed off 9 cut and run, disappear 10 fly the coop

fleece 3 gyp 4 bilk, dupe, gull, rook, wool 5 cheat, cozen, trick 7 deceive, defraud, swindle 9 bamboozle, victimize

fleet 3 run 4 band, fade, fast, flow, navy, skim, spry, swim, unit 5 agile, array, brief, creek, drift, float, hasty, inlet, light, quick, rapid, shift, ships, short, swift 6 abound, active, armada, nimble, number, speedy, sudden, vanish 7 caravan, cursory, hurried 8 flotilla, squadron 9 disappear, momentary, transient 10 evanescent, transitory 11 expeditious 13 instantaneous

fleeting 5 brief, quick 7 passing 8 flitting, fugitive, temporal 9 ephemeral, fugacious, momentary, temporary, transient 10 evanescent, perishable, transitory 11 impermanent, precarious, unenduring

Fleming, Alexander
field: 12 bacteriology
nationality: 7 British
discovered: 10 penicillin
awarded: 10 Nobel Prize

Fleming, Henry
character in: 20 The Red Badge of Courage
author: 5 Crane

Fleming, Ian
author of: 4 Dr No 9 Moonraker 10 Goldfinger 11 Thunderball 12 Casino Royale 13 Live and Let Die 15 For Your Eyes Only 16 The Spy Who Loved Me, You Only Live Twice 18 From Russia with Love 20 Chitty Chitty Bang Bang
character: 1 M, Q 6 Oddjob 7 Blofeld, SPECTRE (organization) 9 James Bond 14 Miss Moneypenny 15 Auric Goldfinger

Fleming, Victor
director of: 13 The Wizard of Oz 14 Treasure Island 16 Gone With the Wind (Oscar) 18 Captains Courageous

flesh 3 fat, man 4 body, meat, pulp 5 brawn, power, vigor 6 embody, fatten, people 7 fatness, fill out, mankind, realize 8 humanity, physique, strength 9 carnality, substance 10 sensuality 11 materiality 13 individualize, particularize

flesh and blood 3 kin 4 real 5 a body, child 6 family 7 kindred 8 children 9 corporeal, offspring, relations, relatives 10 kith and kin 11 substantial

flesh-eating 9 predatory 10 predaceous 11 carnivorous

fleshy 3 fat 5 beefy, obese, plump, stout, tubby 6 chubby, portly, rotund, stocky 7 paunchy 8 roly-poly, thickset 9 corpulent, succulent 10 overweight, potbellied

Fletcher, Louise
born: 12 Birmingham AL
roles: 17 The Cheap Detective 25 One Flew Over the Cuckoo's Nest (Oscar)

Fletcher, Susannah Yolande
real name of: 12 Susannah York

flex 4 bend 5 curve

flexible 4 mild, soft 5 lithe 6 docile, genial, gentle, limber, pliant, supple 7 amiable, ductile, elastic, plastic, pliable, springy 8 bendable, yielding 9 adaptable, compliant, malleable, resilient, tractable 10 changeable, extensible, manageable, responsive, submissive 11 complaisant

Flibbertigibbet
character in: 10 Kenilworth
author: 5 Scott

flick 4 film 5 brush, graze, movie, sweep, whisk

Flicka
nickname of: 17 Frederica Von Stade

Flicka 5 horse
in: 14 My Friend Flicka

flicker 4 flit, glow, sway 5 blaze, flame, flare, flash, gleam, glint, shake, spark, throb, trace, waver 6 quaver, quiver, waggle 7 flutter, glimmer, glisten, glitter, modicum, pulsate, shimmer, sparkle, tremble, vestige, vibrate, wriggle 8 undulate 9 coruscate, fluctuate, oscillate, scintilla, vacillate

Flickertail State
nickname of: 11 North Dakota

flicks 5 films 6 cinema, grazes, movies, sweeps, whisks 7 brushes

flier 4 bill 5 pilot 6 notice 7 aviator, leaflet, venture 8 brochure, bulletin, circular, handbill 10 experiment 12 announcement 13 advertisement

flight 4 rout, rush, wing 5 flock 6 escape, exodus, flying, hegira 7 fleeing, retreat, soaring, winging 8 squadron 10 withdrawal 11 aeronautics

flighty 5 dizzy, giddy 6 fickle 8 quixotic, reckless, unstable, volatile 9 frivolous, mercurial, whimsical 10 capricious, changeable, inconstant, indecisive, irresolute 11 harebrained, impractical, light-headed, thoughtless 13 irresponsible 14 scatterbrained

flimsy 4 poor, thin, weak 5 cheap, filmy, frail, gauzy, petty, sheer 6 feeble, shab-by, shoddy, sleazy, slight, trashy 7 foolish, fragile, ill-made, shallow, trivial 8 cobwebby, delicate, gossamer, trifling 9 frivolous, worthless 10 diaphanous, inadequate, jerry-built, ramshackle **11** dilapidated, superficial **13** unsubstantial

flinch 3 fly, shy **4** jerk **5** cower, quail, quake, start, wince **6** blench, cringe, falter, quaver, quiver, recoil, shiver, shrink **7** contort, grimace, retreat, shudder

fling 2 go **3** try **4** ball, bash, cast, dash, emit, hurl, lark, toss **5** eject, expel, heave, pitch, sling, spree, trial **6** let fly, propel **7** attempt **8** bit of fun **11** precipitate

Flintstones, The
character: **7** Pebbles **8** Bamm Bamm **11** Betty Rubble **12** Barney Rubble **14** Fred Flintstone **15** Dino the Dinosaur, Wilma Flintstone
voice: **8** Alan Reed, Mel Blanc **10** Don Messick **12** Bea Benaderet, Gerry Johnson **13** Jean Vander Pyl
city: **7** Bedrock
creator: **12** Hanna-Barbera

Flintwinch
character in: **12** Little Dorrit
author: **7** Dickens

flinty 4 cold, hard **5** cruel, harsh, stern, stony **6** inured, steely **7** callous **8** hardened **10** unyielding **11** hardhearted, insensitive

flip 3 tap **4** bold, pert, spin, toss, turn **5** brash, flick, fresh, throw, thumb **6** cheeky, fillip **8** impudent, insolent, turn over **9** unabashed

flippant 4 glib, pert, rude **5** brash, lippy, saucy **6** cheeky, nimble **7** voluble **8** impudent, insolent, trifling **9** bumptious, frivolous, talkative **11** impertinent **12** presumptuous **13** disrespectful

Flipper
character: **8** Bud Ricks **10** Sandy Ricks **11** Porter Ricks
cast: **10** Brian Kelly, Luke Halpin **11** Tommy Norden
Flipper played by: **4** Suzy

flirt 3 toy **4** play, vamp **5** dally, tease **6** trifle **8** coquette **12** heartbreaker

flit 4 dart, scud, skim, wing **5** speed **6** hasten, scurry **7** flicker, flutter

Flitch of Bacon, The
author: **16** William Ainsworth

Flite, Miss
character in: **10** Bleak House
author: **7** Dickens

flivver 3 car **4** auto, heap **5** motor **6** jalopy, wheels **7** machine, vehicle **8** motorcar **9** tin lizzie **10** automobile

float 3 bob **4** waft **5** drift, hover, slide **6** bear up, buoy up, hold up, launch **8** levitate

floating 4 free **5** awash, loose **6** adrift, afloat, errant **7** buoyant, wafting **8** drifting **9** fluctuant, wandering **10** unattached

flock 2 go **3** mob, run **4** band, bevy, gang, herd, mass, pack, rush **5** bunch,

crowd, crush, drove, group, surge, troop **6** clique, gather, huddle, muster, stream, throng **7** cluster, company, coterie **8** converge **9** gathering, multitude **10** assemblage, collection, congregate **11** aggregation **12** congregation
of fish: **6** school
of game birds: **5** covey
of geese: **6** gaggle
of insects: **5** swarm
of lions: **5** pride
of seals or whales: **3** pod
of young birds: **5** brood

flocks
god of: **3** Pan

flock together 6 gather, mingle **7** convene **8** assemble **9** associate **10** congregate

flog 4 beat, cane, club, cuff, drub, hide, lash, maul, whip **5** birch, flail, smite, strap **6** cudgel, paddle, strike, switch, thrash **7** scourge **8** lambaste **9** horsewhip **10** flagellate

flood 4 flow, glut, gush, tide **6** deluge, drench, shower, stream **7** cascade, current, torrent **8** downpour, flow over, inundate, overflow, saturate, submerge, wash over **9** overwhelm **10** cloudburst, inundation, outpouring, oversupply
period before: **12** antediluvian

Flood
author: **16** Robert Penn Warren

flooded 6 flowed, surged **7** deluged, glutted, overran, swamped **8** drenched, engulfed **9** inundated, outpoured, washed out **10** downpoured, overflowed

floor 2 KO **4** base, deck, fell, kayo, tier **5** level, stage, story **6** bottom, ground **7** minimum, parquet **8** base rate, flooring, pavement **9** prostrate

flop 4 bomb, bust, drop, fail, fold, plop **5** close **6** fiasco, fizzle, topple, tumble, turkey **7** failure, go under, shutter, washout **8** disaster, lay an egg **14** disappointment

Flora
origin: **5** Roman
goddess of: **7** flowers

floral 6 bloomy **7** verdant **8** blossomy **9** botanical **10** herbaceous

Floralia
origin: **5** Roman
form: **8** festival

Florence
artist: **6** Giotto **7** Cimabue **8** Ghiberti **9** Donatello **10** Michelozzi **11** della Robbia **12** Brunelleschi, Michelangelo
capital of: **7** Tuscany **15** Firenze province
cathedral/church: **10** San Lorenzo, San Miniato, Santa Croce **18** Santa Maria del Fiore
Italian: **7** Firenze

landmark: **5** David, Pieta **6** Uffizi **8** Bargello **11** Pitti Palace **12** Ponte Vecchio **13** Boboli Gardens **14** Loggia dei Lanzi, Palazzo Vecchio **19** Piazza della Signoria **22** Baptistry of San Giovanni, Ospedale degli Innocenti
mountain: **9** Apennines
religious reformer: **10** Savonarola
river: **4** Arno
ruler: **5** Goths **6** Medici, Romans **8** Lombards **9** Etruscans **15** Byzantine Empire
tomb of: **7** Galileo, Rossini **11** Machiavelli **12** Michelangelo **15** Lorenzo de Medici

florescence 5 bloom **9** flowerage **10** blossoming

florid 4 rosy **5** gaudy, ruddy, showy **6** blowsy, hectic, ornate, rococo **7** baroque, flowery, flushed, reddish **8** inflamed, red-faced, rubicund, sanguine **9** elaborate **10** flamboyant, ornamented **12** ostentatious **13** grandiloquent

Florida
abbreviation: **2** FL **3** Fla
nickname: **6** Flower **8** Sunshine **10** Peninsular
capital: **11** Tallahassee
largest city: **12** Jacksonville
others: **4** Tice **5** Cocoa, Miami, Ocala, Tampa **7** Hialeah, Orlando, Palatka, Sebring **8** Sarasota **9** Bradenton, Palm Beach, Pensacola **10** Clearwater **11** Brooksville, Coral Gables, Gainesville, St Augustine **12** Daytona Beach, Ft Lauderdale, St Petersburg
baseball team: **7** Marlins
college: **4** Nova **5** Barry, Miami, Tampa **6** Eckerd **7** Rollins, Stetson
explorer: **11** Ponce de Leon
feature:
amusement park: **5** Epcot **10** Marineland **11** Disney World
canal: **5** Miami **7** Tamiami
museum: **8** Ringling
national park: **10** Everglades
tribe: **3** Ais **5** Ocale, Utina **6** Calusa, Chatot, Potano **7** Timucua **8** Seminole
people: **5** conch **7** cracker, Osceola
island: **7** Bahamas, Sanibel **8** Biscayne
key: **4** Long, Vaca, West **5** Largo **7** Big Pine **8** Biscayne **9** Sugarloaf
lake: **4** Dora **6** Apopka, Harney, Jessup, Newnan **7** Ledwith **8** Arbuckle **9** Kissimmee **10** Okeechobee
land rank: **12** twenty-second
physical feature:
bay: **8** Biscayne **9** Apalachee **10** Waccasassa
cape: **5** Sable **7** Kennedy **9** Canaveral
gulf: **6** Mexico
sea: **8** Atlantic
springs: **6** Silver **7** Rainbow

swamp: 10 Everglades, Okefenokee
river: 6 Banana, Indian **7** Aucilla,
Manatee, Scambia, St Johns, Su-
wanee **9** Ochlawaha **12** Apalachicola
state admission: 13 twenty-seventh
state bird: 11 mockingbird
state fish: 16 Atlantic sailfish
state mammal: 7 dolphin
state flower: 13 orange blossom
state motto: 12 In God We Trust
state song: 11 Swanee River **14** Old
Folks at Home
state tree: 13 sabal palmetto **15** cabbage palmetto
florilegium 7 garland **8** chapbook,
treasury **9** anthology
Florizel
character in: 14 The Winter's Tale
author: 11 Shakespeare
floruit 12 he flourished **13** she flourished
flotilla 5 fleet **6** armada
Flotow, Friedrich von
born: 7 Germany **11** Mecklenburg
composer of: 6 Martha **11** Die
Matrosen **19** Alessandro Stradella
flotsam 4 junk **6** debris, refuse **7** garbage **8** castoffs
flounce 3 hem **4** edge, leap, skip, trim,
trip **5** bound, caper, frill, stamp,
stomp, storm, strut **6** bounce, edging,
fringe, gambol, prance, ruffle, sashay,
spring **7** valance **8** furbelow, ornament, skirting, trimming
flounder 4 fish, flop, halt, limp **5**
lurch, waver **6** falter, hobble, muddle,
totter, tumble, wallow, welter **7** blunder, shamble, stagger, stumble **8** flatfish, hesitate, struggle
Flounder, The
author: 11 Gunter Grass
flourish 4 curl, dash, grow, pomp,
rant, show, turn **5** bloom, bluff, get
on, shake, strut, sweep, swing, swish,
twirl, twist, wield **6** flaunt, flower, hot
air, parade, splash, thrive, waving **7**
blossom, bravado, burgeon, cadenza,
fanfare, fustian, glitter, prosper, shaking, succeed, swagger **8** boasting,
brandish, curlicue, fare well, get
ahead, swinging, vaunting, wielding **9**
agitation, grace note, thrashing **10**
decoration **11** braggadocio, brandishing, fanfaronade, ostentation **12** ap-
poggiatura **13** embellishment, magniloquence, swashbuckling **14**
grandiloquence
flourishing 8 swinging, swishing,
thriving, wielding **9** flaunting **10** prospering, successful **11** brandishing
flout 3 rag **4** defy, mock, twit **5** chaff,
scorn, spurn, taunt **6** gibe at, insult
flow 3 jet, run **4** flux, gush, pass, pour,
rush, seep, tide **5** drain, drift, float,
flood, glide, issue, spout, spurt, surge,
sweep, swirl, train **6** abound, course,
deluge, efflux, effuse, filter, plenty,

rapids, stream **7** cascade, current, debouch, torrent, well out **8** effusion,
millrace, plethora, sequence **9** abundance, discharge, effluence, emanation
10 outpouring, succession **11** de-
bouchment, progression
flower 3 bud **4** best, blow, open, pick,
posy **5** bloom, cream, elite, ripen **6**
mature **7** blossom, bouquet, burgeon,
develop, nosegay, prosper **8** flourish
11 aristocracy
flower arranging, art of
Japanese: 7 ikebana
Flower Fables
author: 15 Louisa May Alcott
flowering 4 peak **5** bloom **6** height,
heyday **8** blooming, maturing **10** blossoming, developing, prospering **11**
flourishing
Flowering Judas
author: 19 Katherine Anne Porter
flowers
goddess of: 5 Flora
Flowers of Evil
author: 17 Charles Baudelaire
French title: 14 Les Fleurs du Mal
Flower State
nickname of: 7 Florida
flowery 5 fancy **6** floral, florid, ornate
8 blooming **10** blossoming, burgeoning, euphuistic, figurative, florescent,
ornamental, rhetorical **11** embellished
12 efflorescent, magniloquent **13**
grandiloquent
Flowery Kingdom see **5** China
flowing 4 flux **5** fluid **6** ebbing, fluent,
smooth **7** current, copious, gliding,
running **8** abundant **9** liquefied, plentiful **10** continuity, pouring out, proceeding
fluctuate 4 sway, vary, veer **5** shift,
swing, waver **6** dawdle, falter, wobble
8 hesitate, undulate **9** alternate, oscillate, vacillate **10** dillydally
fluctuation 5 shift **6** change **7** veering
8 shifting, swinging **9** deviation, variation **11** alternation, oscillation, vacillation
flue 3 net **4** barb, down, pipe, tube,
vent **5** fluff, fluke, shaft **6** funnel **7**
channel, chimney, passage **9** smoke-
jack
fluent 4 glib **5** vocal **6** facile **7** voluble
8 effusive, eloquent **9** garrulous, talkative **10** articulate, effortless
fluff 3 err, nap **4** down, flub, fuzz, lint,
miss, puff, slip, soft **5** botch, floss,
froth, primp **6** forget **7** blunder **8**
feathers
fluffy 5 downy, fuzzy, nappy, wooly **6**
fleecy, woolly **8** feathery
fluid 6 liquid, watery **7** unfixed **8** flexible, floating, shifting, solution, unstable **9** adaptable, liquefied, unsettled
10 adjustable, changeable, indefinite

fluid ounce
abbreviation: 4 fl oz
fluke 3 hap **5** freak **6** chance **7** miracle
8 accident, windfall **9** mischance **11**
vicissitude **12** stroke of luck
flummery 7 dessert, pudding **9** gibberish **10** doubletalk, mumbo jumbo **11**
obfuscation
flunky 6 lackey, menial, minion **7** servant **9** attendant, underling
fluorine
chemical symbol: 1 F
flurry 3 ado **4** fuss, gust, heat, puff,
stir **5** alarm, fever, flush, haste, panic
6 breeze, bustle, pother, rattle,
shower, squall, tumult **7** agitate, confuse, disturb, fidgets, fluster, flutter,
perturb **8** confound, disquiet **9** agitation, commotion, confusion **10** discompose, disconcert, turbulence
11 disturbance, hurry-scurry, trepidation **12** discomposure, perturbation,
restlessness
flush 4 even, glow, swab, tint, wash **5**
bloom, blush, color, elate, flood, level,
rinse, scour, scrub, shock, spray **6** access, dampen, deluge, douche,
drench, excite, puff up, quiver, redden, sponge, thrill, tremor **7** animate,
flutter, glowing, impulse, moisten,
redness, wash out **8** rosiness, rosy
glow, squarely, strength **9** freshness,
make proud, ruddiness **10** exultation,
jubilation
flushed 3 hot, red **4** rosy, ruby **5**
aglow, **6** florid, torrid **7** crimson, excited, scarlet **8** blushing, feverish **10**
prosperous
flushed with success 5 proud **6**
elated
fluster 4 daze **5** shake, upset **6** dither,
flurry, hubbub, muddle, ruffle **7** agitate, confuse, disturb, flutter, perplex,
per-turb, startle, turmoil **8** befuddle,
bewilder **9** agitation, commotion, confusion, discomfit **10** discompose, disconcert **12** bewilderment, discomfiture, discomposure **14** discombobulate
flute 4 fife, fold, pipe, roll, tube, wind
5 crimp **6** furrow, groove **7** piccolo,
whistle **8** recorder **9** wine glass **14**
champagne glass
flutter 3 bob **4** flap, flit, soar, stir,
wave, wing **5** hurry, shake, throb **6**
flurry, quiver, ripple, thrill, tremor,
wobble **7** beating, flitter, fluster, pulsate, tremble, twitter **8** flapping, tingling **9** agitation, commotion, confusion, palpitate, sensation, vibration **12**
perturbation
fluvial 7 aquatic
fluviatile 7 aquatic
flux 4 flow, tide **5** flood **6** course, motion, stream, unrest **7** current **8** mutation, shifting **10** alteration, transition
11 fluctuation **12** modification **14**
transformation

fly 4 flap, flee, sail, skip, soar, wave, wing **5** coast, float, glide, hover, hurry, split, swoop **6** hasten, hustle **7** flutter, run away, take off, vibrate **8** take wing, undulate

fly
varieties: **3** bat, bot **4** blow, deer, dung, gnat, horn, moth, rust, sand **5** beach, black, crane, dance, drone, flesh, fruit, horse, house, march, marsh, midge, mydas, punky **6** bee fly, cactus, maggot, pomace, robber, stable, tsetse, warble, window **7** chalcid, seaweed, skipper, soldier, tachima **8** lousefly, mosquito, stiletto **9** leaf miner **10** flat-footed, fungus gnat, humpbacked **11** thickheaded **14** black scavenger

fly apart 5 burst **6** blow up **7** explode, shatter **8** detonate, fragment

fly at 6 assail, attack

fly-by-night 5 shady **6** shifty **7** crooked **8** unstable, untrusty **9** dishonest **10** unreliable **12** disreputable, undependable **13** irresponsible, untrustworthy

Flying Dutchman, The
opera by: **6** Wagner
character: **4** Erik **5** Senta **6** Daland **11** The Dutchman

Flying Fish
constellation of: **6** Volans

Flying Nun, The
character: **9** Sister Ana **11** Sister Sixto **13** Carlos Ramirez **14** Mother Superior **15** Sister Bertrille **16** Sister Jacqueline
cast: **10** Sally Field **12** Alejandro Rey, Linda Dangcil, Marge Redmond **14** Shelly Morrison **17** Madeleine Sherwood

fly in the ointment 5 hitch **7** problem, trouble **8** drawback, nuisance **9** hindrance **10** impediment **12** disadvantage

Flynn, Errol
real name: **17** Leslie Thomas Flynn
born: **6** Hobart **8** Tasmania **9** Australia
roles: **10** The Sea Hawk **12** Captain Blood **14** Too Much Too Soon **15** The Sun Also Rises **24** The Adventures of Robin Hood **26** The Charge of the Light Brigade

fly off the handle 6 see red

fly the coop 4 bolt, flee **6** escape, run off **7** abscond, get away, make off, run away, skip out, take off

foal 4 cade, colt **5** filly, young **9** fledgling

foam 4 fizz, head, scum, suds **5** froth, spume **6** lather **7** sparkle **8** bubbling **13** effervescence

foaming 5 sudsy **6** bubbly, frothy **7** lathery **8** bubbling, frothing

foamy 5 fizzy **6** frothy **7** lathery **8** bubbling **9** sparkling **12** effervescent

fob 5 chain, medal, strap **6** ribbon **8** ornament **9** medallion

focal 3 key **4** main **5** chief **7** central, pivotal **8** foremost **9** principal

Foch, Ferdinand
served in: **3** WWI
nationality: **6** French
rank: **7** marshal **16** commander-in-chief
battle: **5** Marne, Somme

Foch, Nina
real name: **20** Nina Consuelo Maud Fock
born: **6** Leyden **11** Netherlands
roles: **9** Spartacus **14** Executive Suite, Song to Remember **17** An American in Paris, My Name Is Julia Ross **18** The Ten Commandments

Fock, Nina Consuelo Maud
real name of: **8** Nina Foch

focus 3 aim, fix, hub **4** core **5** haunt, heart **6** adjust, center, direct, middle, resort **7** nucleus, retreat **8** converge **9** limelight, spotlight **10** rendezvous **11** concentrate **12** headquarters

focusing 6 aiming **9** adjusting, centering, directing **10** adjustment, converging **11** pinpointing **13** concentrating

fodder 4 feed, food **6** forage, silage **7** rations **9** provender

foe 5 enemy, rival **8** attacker, opponent **9** adversary, assailant, combatant, contender, disputant **10** antagonist, competitor

fog 3 dim **4** daze, haze, smog, soup **5** brume, cloud **6** darken, muddle, stupor, trance **7** confuse, obscure, pea soup, perplex **8** bewilder **9** murkiness **10** cloudiness **12** bewilderment

Fogg, Phileas
character in: **26** Around the World in Eighty Days
author: **10** Jules Verne
valet: **12** Passepartout

foggy 3 dim **4** dark, hazy **5** dusky, filmy, fuzzy, misty, murky, musty, soupy, vague **6** cloudy, smoggy, spacey **7** brumous, clouded, obscure, shadowy, unclear **8** confused, nebulous, overcast, vaporous **9** beclouded **10** indistinct

foible 4 kink **5** quirk **6** defect, whimsy **7** failing, frailty **8** crotchet, weak side, weakness **9** infirmity **10** deficiency **11** shortcoming **12** imperfection

Foible
character in: **16** The Way of the World
author: **8** Congreve

foil 3 nip **4** balk, film, leaf **5** check, flake, match, sheet, wafer **6** hinder, lamina, set off, thwart **7** enhance, prevent **8** backdrop, contrast **9** frustrate

10 antithesis, complement, supplement **11** correlative, counterpart

foist 6 impose, unload **7** palm off, pass off

fold 3 hug, lap, pen, sty **4** bend, curl, sect, tuck, wrap, yard **5** clasp, close, crimp, flock, group, layer, pleat **6** corral, crease, dog-ear, double, encase, enfold, fur-row, gather, parish, pucker, ruffle, rumple, wrap up **7** crinkle, crumple, embosom, embrace, entwine, envelop, flounce, overlap, wrinkle **8** barnyard, compound, doubling, stockade **9** community, corrugate, enclosure **12** congregation

folder 7 booklet, leaflet **8** brochure, circular, pamphlet **9** portfolio

foliage 6 leaves **7** leafage, verdure

folklore 5 myths **6** fables **7** legends **10** traditions

folks 3 kin **6** family, people **7** kinsmen, parents **8** everyone **9** relatives **10** kith and kin

folksy 6 casual, chatty **8** familiar, friendly, homespun, informal, sociable **10** neighborly **14** conversational **15** unsophisticated

folk tale
German: **7** Marchen

Follett, Ken
author of: **14** Eye of the Needle **15** On Wings of Eagles, The Key to Rebecca **22** The Man from St Petersburg

follow 3 dog **4** copy, heed, hunt, mind, note, obey, tail **5** aim at, chase, grasp, hound, stalk, trace, track, trail, watch **6** attend, notice, pursue, regard, shadow, take up **7** cherish, emulate, imitate, observe, replace, succeed **8** practice, supplant **9** accompany, cultivate, prosecute **10** comprehend, understand

follower 3 fan **4** tail **5** pupil, toady **6** chaser, hunter, shadow, stooge **7** admirer, apostle, convert, devotee, protege, pursuer, servant, stalker **8** adherent, advocate, disciple, hanger-on, henchman, parasite, partisan, retainer, servitor **9** accessory, attendant, dependent, proselyte, satellite, supporter, sycophant

following 4 next **5** below, suite, train **6** public **7** ensuing, retinue **8** audience **9** adherents, clientele, entourage, partisans, patronage **10** attendance, consequent, sequential, subsequent, succeeding, successive **11** consecutive

Follow the Fleet
director: **12** Mark Sandrich
cast: **11** Fred Astaire **12** Ginger Rogers **13** Randolph Scott **21** Harriet Hilliard Nelson
song: **11** We Saw the Sea **13** Let Yourself Go **24** Let's Face the Music and Dance

follow-up 7 ensuing 8 sequence 9 aftermath 10 subsequent

folly 6 idiocy, levity 7 inanity, mistake 8 nonsense, trifling 9 absurdity, asininity, frivolity, giddiness, silliness 10 imbecility, imprudence, tomfoolery 11 doltishness, fatuousness, foolishness 12 indiscretion 13 brainlessness, irrationality, senselessness

foment 4 goad, spur, urge 5 rouse 6 arouse, excite, foster, incite, kindle, stir up 7 agitate, inflame, promote, provoke, quicken 8 irritate 9 aggravate, galvanize, instigate, stimulate 10 exacerbate

fond 5 naive 6 ardent, doting, loving, tender 7 amorous, devoted 8 desirous, enamored, harbored, held dear 9 cherished, indulgent, preserved, sustained 10 infatuated, passionate 11 impassioned, sentimental 12 affectionate 16 overaffectionate

Fonda, Henry
  wife: 16 Margaret Sullavan
  son: 5 Peter
  daughter: 4 Jane
  born: 13 Grand Island NE
  roles: 7 Jezebel, Warlock 8 Fail Safe 10 Fort Apache, In Harm's Way, The Best Man, The Lady Eve 12 On Golden Pond (Oscar) 13 Mister Roberts, Ox-Bow Incident, The Longest Day 14 Twelve Angry Men, Young Mr Lincoln 16 Advise and Consent, Battle of the Bulge, How the West Was Won, The Grapes of Wrath 18 The Boston Strangler 19 My Darling Clementine, The Immortal Sergeant 21 Sometimes a Great Notion

Fonda, Jane
  father: 5 Henry
  brother: 5 Peter
  husband: 9 Ted Turner, Tom Hayden 10 Roger Vadim
  born: 9 New York NY
  roles: 5 Julia, Klute (Oscar) 10 Barbarella, Coming Home (Oscar) 11 A Doll's House 12 Any Wednesday, On Golden Pond 13 China Syndrome 17 Barefoot in the Park 23 They Shoot Horses Don't They?

Fonda, Peter
  father: 5 Henry
  sister: 4 Jane
  born: 9 New York NY
  roles: 7 The Trip 9 Easy Rider 13 The Wild Angels

fondle 3 hug, neck, pet 4 neck 5 spoon 6 caress, cuddle, nestle, nuzzle, smooch, stroke 7 embrace, make out 8 canoodle 10 bill and coo

fondness 4 bent, care, love 5 ardor, fancy 6 desire, liking 7 passion 8 devotion, penchant, weakness 9 affection 10 attachment, partiality, preference, propensity, tenderness 11

amorousness, inclination 12 predilection 14 susceptibility

fond utterance 9 sweet talk 10 endearment 12 sweet nothing

Fons
  origin: 5 Roman
  god of: 7 springs

fons et origo 15 source and origin

Fontaine, Joan
  real name: 25 Joan de Beauvoir de Havilland
  sister: 17 Olivia de Havilland
  husband: 11 Brian Aherne
  born: 5 Japan, Tokyo
  roles: 3 Ivy 7 Ivanhoe, Rebecca 8 Casanova, Gunga Din, Jane Eyre, The Women 9 Suspicion (Oscar) 12 The Devil's Own 15 Frenchman's Creek, September Affair 16 Tender Is the Night, The Constant Nymph

Fontanne, Lynn
  husband: 10 Alfred Lunt
  born: 6 London 7 England
  roles: 8 The Visit 9 Quadrille, The Pirate 10 The Sea Gull 13 O Mistress Mine 15 Design for Living 18 The Great Sebastians 19 The Taming of the Shrew

food 4 chow, feed, grub 5 board 6 fodder, forage, silage, viands 7 edibles, nurture, pasture, rations 8 eatables, victuals 9 nutrition, pasturage, provender 10 provisions, sustenance 11 comestibles, nourishment, subsistence

food, miraculous 5 manna

fool 3 ass, con, oaf 4 bilk, clod, dolt, dupe, gull, hoax, jest, joke 5 cheat, chump, clown, cozen, cut up, dummy, dunce, feign, goose, idiot, klutz, moron, nin-ny, tease, trick 6 diddle, fleece, frolic, hum-bug, jester, nitwit, rip off, stooge 7 beguile, buffoon, deceive, defraud, half-wit, Pierrot, pretend 8 bonehead, dummkopf, flimflam, hoodwink, imbecile, lunkhead, meathead, numskull 9 bamboozle, blockhead, harlequin, ignoramus, numbskull, simpleton 10 dunderhead, nincompoop, scaramouch 11 Punchinello

fool around 3 toy 4 idle 5 clown, dally 6 dawdle, loiter, trifle

foolhardy 4 rash 5 brash, hasty 6 madcap 8 careless, heedless, reckless 9 daredevil, hotheaded, impetuous, imprudent, impulsive 10 headstrong, incautious 11 harebrained, thoughtless

foolish 5 inane, silly 6 absurd, stupid, unwise 7 asinine, fatuous, idiotic, moronic, witless 9 brainless, imbecilic, imprudent, ludicrous, senseless 10 boneheaded, incautious, indiscreet, ridiculous 12 preposterous 13 irresponsible, unintelligent

foolishness 5 folly 6 idiocy, lunacy 8 unwisdom 9 absurdity, asininity, pu-

erility, silliness, stupidity 10 imbecility, imprudence 11 fatuousness, witlessness 12 childishness, extravagance, indiscretion 13 brainlessness, senselessness 14 ridiculousness 15 injudiciousness 16 irresponsibility, preposterousness

Fool of Quality, The
  author: 11 Henry Brooke

foot 3 dog, pad, paw 4 base, hoof 6 bottom, tootsy 7 trotter 8 infantry 10 foundation
  abbreviation: 2 ft

football
  term: 3 end 4 bomb, down, draw, flat, punt, sack 5 blitz, guard, zebra 6 center, fumble, option, pocket, safety, tackle 7 audible, bootleg, flanker, holding, kickoff, lateral, offside, platoon, reverse, rollout, shotgun 8 clipping, gridiron, halfback, turnover 9 crackback, field goal, nose guard, scrimmage, touchback 10 conversion, cornerback, linebacker, nose tackle 11 quarterback 12 encroachment

Hall of Fame:
  1963: 4 Bell (Bert), Carr (Joe), Hein (Mel), Mara (Tim) 5 Baugh (Sammy), Clark (Dutch), Halas (George) 6 Hutson (Don), Nevers (Ernie), Thorpe (Jim) 7 Hubbard (Cal), Lambeau (Curly), McNally (John Blood) 8 Nagurski (Bronko), Marshall (George P)
  1964: 5 Lyman (Link) 6 Healey (Ed), Hinkle (Clarke), Rooney (Art) 7 Trafton (George) 9 Conzelman (Jimmy), Michalske (Mike)
  1965: 6 Graham (Otto), Grange (Red) 7 Luckman (Sid) 8 Driscoll (Paddy), Fortmann (Daniel J), Van Buren (Steve) 10 Chamberlin (Guy), Waterfield (Bob)
  1966: 3 Ray (Hugh "Shorty") 5 Guyon (Joe), Owens (Steve) 6 Dudley (Bill), Herber (Arnie), McAfee (George) 7 Turner (Clyde "Bulldog") 8 Kiesling (Walt)
  1967: 5 Brown (Paul E), Layne (Bobby) 6 Reeves (Dan), Strong (Ken) 7 Bidwill (Charles W), Tunnell (Emlen) 8 Bednarik (Chuck), Stydahar (Joe)
  1968: 6 Hirsch (Elroy), Motley (Marion), Trippi (Charley) 7 Battles (Cliff), Donovan (Art), Millner (Wayne) 13 Wojciechowicz (Alex)
  1969: 5 Neale (Earle "Greasy"), Perry (Joe) 7 Edwards (Albert Glen "Turk") 8 Stautner (Ernie) 9 Nomellini (Leo)
  1970: 5 Fears (Tom), Pihos (Pete) 9 McElhenny (Hugh) 12 Christiansen (Jack)
  1971: 5 Brown (Jim) 6 Hewitt (Bill), Kinard (Frank "Bruiser"), Tittle (Y A) 8 Lombardi (Vince) 10 Robustelli

(Andy) **11** Van Brocklin (Norm)
1972: 4 Hunt (Lamar) **6** Matson (Ollie), Parker (Ace) **9** Marchetti (Gino)
1973: 5 Berry (Raymond) **6** Parker (Jim) **7** Schmidt (Joe)
1974: 4 Lane (Dick "Night Train") **5** Groza (Lou "The Toe") **6** George (Bill) **7** Canadeo (Tony)
1975: 5 Brown (Roosevelt), Moore (Lenny) **6** Connor (George) **7** Lavelli (Dante)
1976: 4 Ford (Len) **6** Taylor (Jim) **8** Flaherty (Ray)
1977: 5 Gregg (Forrest), Starr (Bart) **6** Sayers (Gale), Willis (Bill) **7** Gifford (Frank)
1978: 6 Ewbank (Weeb), Wilson (Larry) **7** Alworth (Lance), Leemans (Tuffy) **8** Nitschke (Ray)
1979: 3 Mix (Ron) **4** Lary (Yale) **6** Butkus (Dick), Unitas (Johnny)
1980: 4 Otto (Jim) **5** Jones (David "Deacon"), Lilly (Bob) **8** Adderley (Herb)
1981: 5 Davis (Willie), Ringo (Jim) **6** Badgro (Morris "Red"), Blanda (George)
1982: 4 Huff (Sam) **5** Musso (George), Olsen (Merlin) **6** Atkins (Doug)
1983: 4 Bell (Bobby) **6** Gilman (Sid) **8** Mitchell (Bobby), Warfield (Paul) **9** Jurgensen (Sonny)
1984: 5 Brown (Willie) **6** Taylor (Charley) **9** McCormack (Mike) **11** Weinmeister (Arnie)
1985: 6 Gatski (Frank), Namath (Joe) **7** Rozelle (Pete), Simpson (OJ) **8** Staubach (Roger)
1986: 6 Lanier (Willie), Walker (Doak) **7** Hornung (Paul), Houston (Ken) **9** Tarkenton (Fran)
1987: 6 Csonka (Larry), Dawson (Len), Greene (Joe), Langer (Jim), Upshaw (Gene) **7** Johnson (John Henry), Maynard (Don)
1988: 3 Ham (Jack) **4** Page (Alan) **5** Ditka (Mike) **11** Biletnikoff (Fred)
1989: 4 Wood (Willie) **5** Shell (Art) **6** Blount (Mel) **8** Bradshaw (Terry)
1990: 6 Griese (Bob), Harris (Franco), Landry (Tom) **7** Lambert (Jack), St Clair (Bob) **8** Buchanan (Buck) **9** Hendricks (Ted)
1991: 5 Jones (Stan) **6** Hannah (John) **7** Schramm (Tex) **8** Campbell (Earl), Stenerud (Jan)
1992: 5 Davis (Al) **6** Barney (Lem), Mackey (John) **7** Riggins (John)
1993: 4 Noll (Chuck) **5** Fouts (Dan), Walsh (Bill) **6** Little (Larry), Payton (Walter)
1994: 5 Grant (Bud), Kelly (Leroy), Smith (Jackie), White (Randy) **7** Dorsett (Tony), Johnson (Jimmy)
other player/coach: 8 Don Shula, Kyle Rote **9** Amos Stagg, Dan Marino, Earl Blaik, Jerry Rice, Lou Lit-

tle, **10** Bear Bryant, Bruce Smith, Bubba Smith, Joe Montana, Joe Paterno, Ken Stabler, Larry Brown, Troy Aikman, Walter Camp, Warren Moon **11** Ahmad Rashad, Craig Morton, Deion Sanders, Earl Morrall, Floyd Little, Jim Plunkett, Knute Rockne, Reggie White **12** Bud Wilkinson, Joe Thiesmann, Ozzie Newsome, Roman Gabriel, William Perry **13** Ara Parseghian, Eric Dickerson, **14** Lawrence Taylor, Lydell Mitchell

football bowl games 3 Sun **4** Rose **5** Aloha, Gator, Peach, Sugar, Super **6** Citrus, Copper, Cotton, Fiesta, Orange **7** Holiday, Liberty **10** Bluebonnet, California **12** Independence

football leagues
  National Football League (NFL): 11 New York Jets **12** Buffalo Bills, Chicago Bears, Detroit Lions **13** Dallas Cowboys, Denver Broncos, Miami Dolphins, New York Giants **14** Atlanta Falcons, Los Angeles Rams **15** Baltimore Ravens, Cleveland Browns, Green Bay Packers, Seattle Seahawks, Tennessee Oilers (formerly Houston) **16** Kansas City Chiefs, Minnesota Vikings, New Orleans Saints, Phoenix Cardinals (formerly St Louis), San Diego Chargers **17** Cincinnati Bengals, Indianapolis Colts (formerly Baltimore), Los Angeles Raiders (formerly Oakland) **18** New England Patriots, Philadelphia Eagles, Pittsburgh Steelers, Tampa Bay Buccaneers, Washington Redskins **23** San Francisco Forty-Niners
  United States Football League (USFL): 10 Denver Gold **12** Chicago Blitz **14** Baltimore Stars, Boston Breakers **15** Houston Gamblers, Oakland Invaders, Oklahoma Outlaws, Tampa Bay Bandits **16** Arizona Wranglers, Memphis Showboats, Michigan Panthers, Orlando Renegades, Portland Breakers **17** Jacksonville Bulls, Los Angeles Express, New Jersey Generals, Philadelphia Stars **18** Washington Federals **19** Birmingham Stallions **21** San Antonio Gunslingers

football team (NFC)
  Atlanta: 7 Falcons
    stadium: 11 Georgia Dome
  Chicago: 5 Bears
    stadium: 12 Soldier Field
  Dallas: 7 Cowboys
    stadium: 5 Texas
  Detroit: 5 Lions
    stadium: 17 Pontiac Silverdome
  Green Bay: 7 Packers
    stadium: 9 Milwaukee **12** Lambeau Field
  Los Angeles: 4 Rams
    stadium: 7 Anaheim
  Minnesota: 7 Vikings
    stadium: 9 Metrodome

  New Orleans: 6 Saints
    stadium: 18 Louisiana Superdome
  New York: 6 Giants
    stadium: 6 Giants
  Philadelphia: 6 Eagles
    stadium: 8 Veterans
  Phoenix: 9 Cardinals
    stadium: 8 Sun Devil
    formerly in: 7 St Louis
  San Francisco: 11 Forty-Niners
    stadium: 15 Candlestick Park
  Tampa Bay: 10 Buccaneers
    stadium: 5 Tampa
  Washington: 8 Redskins
    stadium: 14 Robert F Kennedy
football team (AFC)
  Buffalo: 5 Bills
    stadium: 4 Rich
  Cincinnati: 7 Bengals
    stadium: 10 Riverfront
  Cleveland: 6 Browns
    stadium: 9 Cleveland
  Denver: 7 Broncos
    stadium: 8 Mile High
  Houston: 6 Oilers
    stadium: 9 Astrodome
  Indianapolis: 5 Colts
    stadium: 11 Hoosier Dome
    formerly in: 9 Baltimore
  Kansas City: 6 Chiefs
    stadium: 9 Arrowhead
  Los Angeles: 7 Raiders
    stadium: 16 Memorial Coliseum
    formerly in: 7 Oakland
  Miami: 8 Dolphins
    stadium: 9 Joe Robbie
  New England: 8 Patriots
    stadium: 7 Foxboro
  New York: 4 Jets
    stadium: 6 Giants
  Pittsburgh: 8 Steelers
    stadium: 11 Three Rivers
  San Diego: 8 Chargers
    stadium: 8 San Diego
  Seattle: 8 Seahawks
    stadium: 8 Kingdome
footfall 3 pad **4** pace, step **5** tread **8** footstep
foothold 4 grip, hold **7** support **8** purchase
footloose 4 free **8** carefree **9** fancyfree **10** unattached **11** uncommitted **12** unencumbered
footnote 5 gloss **9** reference **10** annotation **11** explanation **12** afterthought
footnote abbreviations 2 ca, ms, nd, qv **3** mss **4** et al, ibid **5** et seq, infra, op cit, pseud, supra **6** loc cit
footpad 5 thief **6** bandit, mugger, outlaw, robber **10** highwayman
footpath 4 lane, ramp **5** jetty, trail **8** sidewalk
foot soldiers 8 infantry **10** fusilliers, musketeers
footstool 6 buffet **7** hassock, ottoman **8** footrest

footwear
   French: **9** chaussure

fop 4 beau, dude **5** dandy, swell **7** coxcomb **8** popinjay **9** prettyboy **11** Beau Brummel

foppish 4 vain **5** gaudy, showy **6** ornate **7** finical **8** affected, dandyish **9** dandified **12** ostentatious **13** overelaborate

forage 4 feed, food, hunt, raid, seek **6** fodder, ravage, search, silage **7** despoil, explore, pasture, plunder, rummage **8** scavenge, scrounge **9** pasturage, provender **10** provisions

foray 4 raid **5** sally **6** attack, inroad, invade, ravage, thrust **7** pillage, plunder, venture **8** invasion **9** incursion **10** expedition **11** depredation

forbear 4 quit, stop **5** cease, forgo **6** desist, endure, eschew, forego, give up, suffer **7** abstain, refrain **8** abnegate, renounce, tolerate

forbearance 4 pity **5** mercy **6** pardon **8** clemency, eschewal, leniency, meekness, mildness, patience **9** endurance, tolerance **10** abstention, abstinence, continence, indulgence, moderation, submission, temperance **11** longanimity, resignation **12** mercifulness

forbearing 6 denial **7** lenient, refusal **8** eschewal, tolerant **9** indulgent **10** abnegation, abstention, abstinence, permissive, refraining **13** nonindulgence **16** nonparticipation

forbid 3 ban, bar **4** veto **5** taboo **6** enjoin, hinder, impede, oppose, refuse, reject **7** exclude, gainsay, inhibit, obviate, prevent **8** disallow, obstruct, preclude, prohibit, restrain **9** interdict, proscribe

forbiddance 3 ban **4** no-no **5** taboo **7** barring, embargo **9** exclusion, interdict **11** prohibition **12** interdiction, proscription

forbidden 4 no-no, tabu **5** taboo **6** banned **8** debarred **10** prohibited, proscribed
   German: **8** verboten

forbidden fruit
   type: **6** brandy **7** liqueur
   origin: **7** America
   flavor: **5** honey **6** orange **10** grapefruit

forbidding 4 dour, grim, ugly **6** odious **7** hideous, ominous **8** horrible, sinister **9** abhorrent, offensive, repellent, repulsive **10** unfriendly, unpleasant **11** prohibitive, prohibitory, threatening **12** disagree-able, inhospitable **14** unapproachable

force 3 pry, vim **4** army, body, coax, crew, drag, gang, make, pull, push, team, unit, urge **5** break, clout, corps, drive, group, impel, might, power, press, squad, value, vigor, wrest **6** coerce, compel, duress, effect, elicit, energy, enjoin, extort, impact, import, impose, induce, oblige, propel, stress, thrust, weight, wrench **7** cogency, intrude, meaning, obtrude, potency, require, squeeze, stamina **8** charisma, coercion, division, efficacy, emphasis, momentum, persuade, pressure, squadron, strength, validity, violence, vitality **9** animation, battalion, constrain, magnetism, overpower, puissance **10** attraction, compulsion, constraint, detachment **11** necessitate, weightiness **12** significance **13** effectiveness
   Latin: **3** vis

forced 5 slave **7** binding, coerced, labored, obliged **8** affected, enslaved, grudging, mannered, required, strained **9** compelled, impressed, insincere, mandatory, unwilling **10** artificial, compulsory, obligatory **11** constrained, involuntary

forceful 5 pithy, valid, vivid **6** cogent, potent, robust, strong, virile **7** dynamic, intense **8** emphatic, powerful, puissant, vigorous **9** effective, energetic **10** impressive

forceless 4 weak **8** impotent

force measurement 4 dyne **6** newton **7** poundal

Force of Circumstance
   author: **16** Simone de Beauvoir

Force of Destiny, The
   also: **17** La Forza del Destino
   opera by: **5** Verdi
   character: **7** Leonora **8** Don Carlo **9** Don Alvaro

forcible 8 coercive **10** compulsory

ford 3 car **4** span, wade **5** cross, shoal **6** bridge, stream **7** passage **8** crossing, tin lizzy

Ford, Gerald Rudolph
   born: **17** Leslie Lynch King Jr
   adopted by/named after: **10** step father
   nickname: **5** Jerry **7** Mr Clean
   presidential rank: **12** thirty-eighth
   party: **10** Republican
   state represented: **2** MI
   defeated: **5** no one
   elected to neither: **10** presidency **14** vice presidency
   vice president: **11** (Nelson A) Rockefeller
   cabinet:
      state: **9** (Henry A) Kissinger
      treasury: **5** (William E) Simon
      defense: **8** (Donald H) Rumsfeld **11** (James) Schlesinger
      attorney general: **4** (Edward H) Levi **5** (William B) Saxbe
      interior: **6** (Rogers Clark Ballard) Morton, (Thomas S) Kleppe **8** (Stanley K) Hathaway
      agriculture: **4** (Earl Lauer) Butz **6** (John A) Knebel
      commerce: **4** (Frederick B) Dent **6** (Rogers Clark Ballard) Morton **10** (Elliot L) Richardson
      labor: **5** (W J) Usery (Jr) **6** (John T) Dunlop **7** (Peter J) Brennan
      HEW: **7** (F David) Mathews **10** (Caspar W) Weinberger
      HUD: **4** (James T) Lynn **5** (Carla Anderson) Hills
      transportation: **7** (William T) Coleman (Jr) **8** (Claude S) Brinegar
   born: **7** Omaha NE
   education:
      University: **8** Michigan
      Law School: **4** Yale
   religion: **12** Episcopalian
   interests: **4** golf **6** boxing, skiing **8** football, swimming
   vacation spot: **2** CO **4** Vail
   author: **21** Portrait of the Assassin (with John R Stiles) **27** A Time To Heal: An Autobiography
   political career: **13** vice president **19** House minority leader **24** US House of Representatives
   civilian career: **6** lawyer
      assistant football coach at: **4** Yale
   military service: **6** US Navy **10** lieutenant, World War II
   notable events of lifetime/term: **9** recession **12** Bicentennial
      assassination attempts on: **4** Ford
      clemency for: **12** draft dodgers, draft evaders
      kidnapping/trial/conviction of: **11** Patty Hearst
      scandal: **8** Lockheed **10** Hays Affair
      talks: **4** SALT
   quotes: **19** I am a Ford not a Lincoln **41** Indebted to no man{hp}---{hp}the president of all the people **50** Our long national nightmare is over Our constitution works
   father:
      natural: **15** Leslie Lynch King
      adoptive: **17** Gerald Rudolph Ford
   mother: **7** Dorothy (Gardner King Ford)
   siblings:
      half-brothers: **12** James Francis **13** Thomas Gardner **14** Richard Addison
   wife: **9** Elizabeth (Bloomer Warren)
      nickname: **5** Betty
   children: **4** John **5** Susan **6** Steven **7** Michael

Ford, Glenn
   real name: **11** Gwyllyn Ford
   wife: **13** Eleanor Powell
   born: **6** Canada, Quebec
   roles: **4** Rage **5** Gilda, Jubal **6** Santee **8** Cimarron **11** The Rounders **14** Is Paris Burning? **17** Interrupted Melody **18** Don't Go Near the Water **19** The Blackboard Jungle **23** Teahouse of the August Moon

Ford, Harrison
   born: **9** Chicago IL
   roles: **7** Frantic, Witness **8** Star Wars

11 Blade Runner **15** Return of the Jedi **16** American Graffiti **19** Raiders of the Lost Ark **20** The Empire Strikes Back **30** Indiana Jones and the Temple of Doom

Ford, John
author of: **13** Perkin Warbeck **17** 'Tis Pity She's a Whore **19** The Lover's Melancholy

Ford, John
director of: **10** Stagecoach **11** The Informer (Oscar), The Quiet Man (Oscar) **12** The Hurricane, The Searchers **13** Grapes of Wrath (Oscar), Mister Roberts (with Mervyn LeRoy), The Lost Patrol **17** The Long Voyage Home **19** How Green Was My Valley (Oscar), My Darling Clementine **27** The Man Who Shot Liberty Valence

Ford, Thelma Booth
real name of: **12** Shirley Booth

Ford and Mistress Ford
characters in: **22** The Merry Wives of Windsor
author: **11** Shakespeare

Ford automobiles 3 LTD **5** Edsel, Pinto, T-Bird **6** Model T, Taurus **7** Mustang **11** Thunderbird

fore 5 front **7** frontal **8** anterior, headmost

forearm 4 ulna **5** prime, ready **7** prepare

forebear 8 ancestor, begetter **10** antecedent, procreator, progenitor

foreboding 4 omen **5** dread **6** augury, boding **7** portent **9** intuition, misgiving **10** prescience, prognostic **11** premonition **12** apprehension, presentiment

forecast 5 augur **6** augury, divine, expect **7** outlook, portend, predict, presage, project **8** envisage, envision, prophesy **9** calculate, prevision, prognosis **10** anticipate, conjecture, prediction, prescience, projection **11** extrapolate **12** anticipation, precognition, presentiment **13** prognosticate **15** prognostication

forefather 6 author **8** ancestor, begetter **9** patriarch, precursor **10** antecedent, originator, procreator, progenitor **12** primogenitor

forefront 4 fame, head, lead **8** vanguard **9** celebrity

foreign 5 alien **6** exotic, remote **7** distant, strange, unknown, unusual **8** imported **9** barbarous, extrinsic, irregular, unrelated **10** extraneous, heathenish, introduced, irrelevant, outlandish, unfamiliar **11** incongruous, inconsonant, unconnected **12** antipathetic, inadmissible, inapplicable, incompatible, inconsistent **13** inappropriate **16** uncharacteristic

Foreign Correspondent
director: **15** Alfred Hitchcock
cast: **10** Joel McCrea, Laraine Day **13** George Sanders **14** Robert Benchley **15** Albert Basserman, Herbert Marshall

foreigner 5 alien, pagan **6** emigre **8** newcomer, outsider, stranger **9** barbarian, immigrant, nonnative, outlander
German: **9** Auslander

foreign officer 6 consul **8** diplomat, minister **10** ambassador **14** representative **15** charge d'affaires

foreknowledge 9 intuition, prevision **10** prescience **11** premonition **12** anticipation, apprehension, clairvoyance, precogni-tion, presentiment

foreman 4 boss **7** manager **8** chairman, overseer **9** president, spokesman **10** supervisor **11** coordinator **14** superintendent

foremost 4 head, main **5** chief, vital **7** capital, leading, supreme **8** cardinal **9** essential, paramount, principal **10** preeminent

forerunner 4 omen, sign **5** token **6** augury, herald **7** portent, presage **8** ancestor **9** harbinger, precursor, prototype **10** progenitor, prognostic **11** predecessor, premonition

foresee 5 augur **6** divine, expect **7** predict, presage **8** envision, prophesy **10** anticipate **13** prognosticate

foreshadow 5 augur **7** presage, promise **9** prefigure

foresight 6 wisdom **8** planning, prudence, sagacity **9** prevision **10** discretion, precaution, prescience, providence, shrewdness **12** anticipation, clairvoyance, perspicacity, precognition, preparedness **13** premeditation **14** farsightedness

forest 4 bush, wood **5** copse, grove, stand, woods **6** jungle **7** thicket **8** wildwood, woodland **10** timberland, wilderness

forestall 5 avert, avoid, block, deter **6** thwart **7** head off, obviate, prevent, ward off **8** preclude **10** anticipate, circumvent, counteract

Forester, C S (Cecil Scott)
author of: **6** The Gun **14** A Ship of the Line **15** Payment Deferred, The African Queen **24** Captain Horatio Hornblower

forests
god of: **3** Pan **7** Silenus, Virbius
pertaining to: **6** silvan, sylvan
nymph: **5** dryad

foretell 5 augur **6** divine **7** portend, predict, presage **8** prophesy, soothsay **9** apprehend **13** prognosticate

forethought 4 heed **7** caution **8** prudence, sagacity, wariness **10** discretion, precaution, providence, shrewdness **11** carefulness **12** anticipation, deliberation **13** consideration, premed-itation **14** circumspection, farsightedness

forever 6 always **9** eternally, undyingly **10** constantly **11** ceaselessly, continually, incessantly, perpetually, unceasingly **12** interminably **13** everlastingly, unremittingly
Latin: **11** in perpetuum

forewarn 4 bode **5** alert **6** advise, notify, signal, tip off **7** caution, portend, presage, prewarn **8** cry havoc

foreword 7 preface, prelude **8** preamble, prologue **12** introduction

Forewords and Afterwords
author: **7** W H Auden

for example
Latin: **2** eg **13** exempli gratia

forfeit 4 fine, miss **5** waive, waste, yield **6** waiver **7** damages, default, let slip, penalty **8** squander **9** surrender **10** assessment

Forfeit
author: **11** Dick Francis

forge 4 copy, form, make **5** clone, shape **6** devise, hearth, smithy **7** falsify, fashion, furnace, imitate, produce, turn out **8** contrive, simulate **9** fabricate, ironworks **11** counterfeit, manufacture

forgery 4 copy, fake, hoax, sham **5** clone, fraud **7** cloning **9** deception, imitation **11** counterfeit, fraudulence **13** falsification **14** counterfeiting **17** misrepresentation

forget 6 slight **7** neglect **8** overlook, pass over **9** disregard

forgetful 6 remiss **7** out of it **8** amnesiac, careless, heedless, mindless **9** negligent, oblivious, unmindful **10** neglectful **11** inattentive

forget-me-not 8 Myosotis
varieties: **5** white **6** alpine, garden **7** Chinese **8** creeping

forgive 5 clear **6** acquit, excuse, pardon **7** absolve, condone, release, set free **8** overlook, reprieve **9** discharge, exculpate, exonerate

forgiveness 6 pardon **7** amnesty **9** remission **10** absolution

forgiving 6 benign, kindly **8** excusing **9** benignant, pardoning **11** kindhearted

forgo 4 skip **5** waive, yield **6** eschew, give up **8** abnegate, renounce **9** sacrifice, surrender **10** relinquish

fork 4 bend, stab **5** angle, elbow, split **6** branch, crotch, divide, impale, pierce, ramify, skewer **7** diverge, trident **8** division **9** bifurcate, pitchfork **10** divergence, separation **11** bifurcation **12** intersection

forked 5 cleft, tined **6** horned, zigzag **7** angular, divided, pronged **8** branched **9** ambiguous, deceitful, equivocal **10** bifurcated

For Kicks
author: **11** Dick Francis

fork out 5 spend **6** expend **8** disburse, dispense

for lack of something better
French: **12** faute de mieux

forlorn 4 lone **6** abject, bereft, dismal, dreary, lonely **7** unhappy **8** bereaved, dejected, deserted, desolate, forsaken, helpless, hopeless, lonesome, pathetic, pitiable, solitary, wretched **9** abandoned, depressed, desperate, destitute, forgotten, miserable, woebegone **10** despairing, despondent, dispirited, friendless **11** comfortless **12** disconsolate, inconsolable **13** brokenhearted

form 3 cut, hew, way **4** body, cast, kind, make, mode, mold, plan, rite, rule, sort, trim, type **5** being, brand, build, carve, class, forge, found, frame, genre, genus, guise, habit, image, model, order, phase, set up, shape, stamp, style, usage **6** aspect, chisel, create, custom, design, devise, fettle, figure, manner, matrix, person, ritual, sculpt, system **7** acquire, anatomy, compose, conduct, contour, decorum, develop, fashion, fitness, harmony, liturgy, manners, outline, pattern, produce, species, variety **8** ceremony, comprise, contract, likeness, physique, practice, presence, rough-hew, symmetry **9** character, construct, establish, etiquette, fabricate, framework, propriety, sculpture, semblance, structure **10** appearance, constitute, deportment, figuration, proceeding, proportion, regularity **11** arrangement, description, incarnation, manufacture, orderliness, shapeliness **12** denomination **13** configuration, manifestation **15** conventionality

formal 4 cool, prim **5** aloof, fancy, fixed, grand, legal, rigid, smart, stiff **6** dressy, lawful, proper, solemn, strict **7** distant, outward, pompous, prudish, regular, settled, stilted, stylish **8** decorous, definite, expli-cit, external, official, positive, reserved, starched **9** customary **10** ceremonial, inflexible, prescribed **11** ceremonious, highfalutin, perfunctory, punctilious, ritualistic, standoffish, straitlaced **12** conventional **13** authoritative **14** uncompromising

formal discussion 6 debate, parley **8** dialogue **10** conference

formality 4 rite **6** custom, motion, ritual **7** decorum, reserve **8** ceremony, coolness **9** etiquette, propriety, punctilio **10** ceremonial, convention **15** conventionality

Forman, Milos
director of: **7** Amadeus (Oscar), Ragtime **25** One Flew Over the Cuckoo's Nest (Oscar)

formation 3 set **6** makeup **7** genesis **8** building, creation **9** structure **10** generation, production **11** arrangement, composition, development, fabrication, manufacture **12** organization **13** configuration, constellation, establishment

formative 7 plastic, shaping **9** sensitive **10** accessible **11** susceptible **13** determinative **14** impressionable

former 2 ex **4** gone, past **5** olden, prior **6** bygone, gone by, lapsed, of yore, whilom **7** ancient, earlier, elapsed, old-time, quondam **8** anterior, previous **9** aforesaid, erstwhile, preceding **10** antecedent, first-named **14** aforementioned
French: **8** ci-devant

formerly 4 once **5** of old **6** ere now, lately, of yore, whilom **7** long ago **8** hitherto **9** anciently **10** originally, previously

former student 6 alumna **7** alumnus, dropout **8** graduate

formidable 6 taxing **7** awesome, fearful, mammoth, onerous **8** alarming, dread-ful, imposing, menacing, terrific **9** dangerous, demanding, difficult **10** forbidding, impressive, portentous, terrifying **11** threatening **12** overpowering, overwhelming

formless 5 vague **9** amorphous, shapeless

Formosa *see* **6** Taiwan

formula 4 cant, plan, rule **5** chant **6** cliche, recipe, saying, slogan **7** precept **9** blueprint, guideline, platitude, principle, rigmarole **10** pleasantry **11** incantation **12** prescription

formulate 5 draft, frame, state **6** define, devise, invent **7** compose, itemize, specify **11** systematize **13** particularize

Fornax
origin: **5** Roman
goddess of: **6** baking

fornication 8 adultery

for one's country
Latin: **9** pro patria

Forrest, Nathan Bedford
served in: **8** Civil War
side: **11** Confederate
known for: **12** cavalry raids

forsake 4 deny, drop, flee, quit **5** leave, spurn, waive, yield **6** abjure, depart, desert, give up, reject, resign, vacate **7** abandon, cast off, disavow, discard, lay down **8** abdicate, disclaim, go back on, jettison, part with, renounce **9** repudiate, surrender **10** relinquish

forsaken 4 bare **5** empty **8** deserted, desolate, rejected **9** abandoned, discarded, neglected **11** uninhabited

Forsete *see* **7** Forseti

Forseti
also: **7** Forsete
origin: **12** Scandinavian
god of: **7** justice
father: **5** Baldr **6** Balder, Baldur
mother: **5** Nanna
dwelling place: **7** Glitnir

Forster, E M (Edward Morgan)
author of: **7** Maurice **10** Howards End **14** A Room with a View **15** A Passage to India **17** The Longest Journey **22** Where Angels Fear to Tread
member of: **15** Bloomsbury Group

forswear 4 deny **5** spurn **6** abjure, disown, eschew, give up, recant, reject, revoke **7** disavow, gainsay, retract **8** abdicate, disclaim, renounce, take back **9** disaffirm, repudiate **10** contravene

Forsyte Saga, The
author: **14** John Galsworthy
trilogy including: **5** To Let **10** In Chancery **16** The Man of Property
character: **3** Jon **4** June **5** Fleur **6** Dartie **7** Annette **8** Winifred **9** Old Jolyon **11** Young Jolyon **12** Irene Forsyte **13** Soames Forsyte **14** Philip Bosinney

Forsythe, John
real name: **17** John Lincoln Freund
born: **12** Penn's Grove NJ
roles: **5** Topaz **7** Dynasty, Madame X **11** In Cold Blood **14** Bachelor Father, Charlie's Angels **15** Blake Carrington **16** And Justice for All **19** The Trouble with Harry **23** Teahouse of the August Moon

fort 4 base, camp **6** castle **7** bastion, bulwark, citadel, station **8** fastness, garrison **10** stronghold

forte 4 bent **5** knack, skill **6** talent **8** strength **9** specialty **11** proficiency
music: **4** loud
abbreviation: **1** f

forth 5 ahead **6** onward **7** outward

forthcoming 5 handy, on tap **6** at hand **7** helpful **8** imminent **9** available, impending **10** accessible, obtainable, openhanded **11** approaching, cooperative, prospective

for the greater glory of God
Latin: **19** ad majorem Dei gloriam

for the public good
Latin: **14** pro bono publico

for the time being
Latin: **10** pro tempore

For the Time Being
author: **7** W H Auden

for this purpose only
Latin: **5** ad hoc

forthright 4 open **5** blunt, frank **6** candid, direct, openly **7** bluntly, frankly, up-front **8** candidly, directly, straight **9** outspoken **10** truthfully **11** outspokenly, plain-spoken **15** straightforward **17** straightforwardly

forthrightness 6 candor **7** honesty **8**

openness **9** frankness, sincerity **19** straightforwardness

forthwith 4 ASAP, stat **6** at once, pronto **7** quickly **8** directly, in a jiffy, promptly, right off **9** instantly **11** immediately **12** straightaway

fortification 5 tower **7** bastion, bulwark, citadel, rampart **8** fortress, garrison **9** earthwork **10** breastwork, stronghold

fortify 4 lace **5** boost, brace, cheer **6** buoy up, enrich, harden, secure, shield, urge on **7** build up, bulwark, hearten, protect, shore up, stiffen, support, sustain **8** buttress, embolden, garrison, reassure **9** encourage, reinforce, stimulate **10** invigorate, strengthen

fortissimo
music: **8** very loud
abbreviation: **2** ff

fortitude 4 dash, grit, guts, sand **5** nerve, pluck, spunk, valor **6** daring, mettle, spirit **7** bravery, courage, heroism, prowess **8** backbone, boldness, firmness, tenacity **9** endurance, hardihood **10** resolution **11** intrepidity **12** fearlessness, resoluteness **13** dauntlessness, determination

Fortitude
author: **11** Hugh Walpole

Fort-Lamy
former name of: **8** N'Djamena
capital of: **4** Chad

fortress 7 bastion, bulwark, citadel, rampart **8** buttress **9** acropolis **10** stronghold

Fortress, The
author: **11** Hugh Walpole

fortuitous 5 happy, lucky, stray **6** casual, chance, random **9** haphazard, hit-or-miss **10** accidental, incidental, undesigned, unexpected, unintended, unpurposed **11** inadvertent **12** adventitious **13** serendipitous, unintentional **14** unpremeditated

fortuity 6 chance **8** accident **12** happenstance

Fortuna
origin: **5** Roman
goddess of: **7** fortune
corresponds to: **5** Tyche

fortunate 4 fair, rich, rosy **5** happy, lucky, palmy **6** benign, bright, timely **7** blessed, booming, favored, halcyon, well-off **8** well-to-do **9** favorable, opportune, promising **10** auspicious, convenient, felicitous, profitable, propitious, prosperous, successful **11** encouraging, flourishing **12** advantageous, providential

Fortunate Isles see **13** Canary Islands

Fortunato
character in: **20** The Cask of Amontillado
author: **3** Poe

fortune, fortunes 3 lot **4** doom, fate, luck, mint, pile, star **5** karma, means **6** chance, es-tate, income, kismet, riches, wealth **7** bonanza, capital, destiny, godsend, portion, revenue **8** accident, fatality, gold mine, good luck, lady luck, opulence, property, treasure, windfall **9** affluence, haphazard, substance **10** prosperity, providence **11** dame fortune **12** circumstance **13** circumstances
goddess of: **5** Tyche **7** Fortuna

Fortunes of Nigel, The
author: **14** Sir Walter Scott

fortuneteller 4 seer **5** augur, Gypsy, sibyl **6** medium, oracle **7** palmist, prophet **8** magician **10** soothsayer **11** chiromancer, clairvoyant **12** crystal gazer

for two
French: **5** a deux

Forty Days of Musa Dagh, The
author: **11** Franz Werfel

42nd Parallel, The
author: **13** John Dos Passos

Forty-Second Street
director: **10** Lloyd Bacon
cast: **9** Guy Kibbee, Una Merkel **10** Dick Powell, Ruby Keeler **11** Bebe Daniels, George Brent **12** Ginger Rogers, Warner Baxter
choreographer: **13** Busby Berkeley
song: **15** Young and Healthy **17** Forty-second Street **19** Shuffle Off to Buffalo **20** You're Getting to Be a Habit with Me

Forty Thieves, The
story in: **13** Arabian Nights
character: **7** Ali Baba
code word: **10** Open Sesame

forty winks 3 nap **4** doze **6** catnap, snooze

forum 6 medium, outlet **7** rostrum, seminar **8** platform **9** symposium **10** colloquium

forward, forwards 3 out **4** back, bold **5** ahead, brash, fresh, relay, sassy **6** assist, brazen, cheeky, hasten, onward, pass on, send on, spread **7** advance, frontal, further, go-ahead, promote, quicken, re-route **8** anterior, champion, immodest, impudent, insolent, up-to-date **9** advancing, barefaced, intrusive, offensive, presuming, readdress, shameless **10** accelerate, unmannerly **11** impertinent, progressive **12** enterprising, presumptuous **13** overconfident
French: **7** en avant

forwardness 4 gall **5** brass, cheek **8** audacity, boldness **10** brazenness, effrontery **11** presumption **13** bumptiousness, obtrusiveness

for what use
Latin: **7** cui bono

For Whom the Bell Tolls
author: **15** Ernest Hemingway

director: **7** Sam Wood
character: **5** Maria, Pablo, Pilar **6** Andres, Rafael **7** Anselmo, El Sordo **8** Augustin, Fernando **12** Robert Jordan
cast: **10** Gary Cooper **12** Akim Tamiroff **13** Ingrid Bergman, Joseph Calleia, Katina Paxinou **15** Arturo de Cordova
score: **11** Victor Young
Oscar for: **17** supporting actress (Paxinou)

for whose benefit
Latin: **7** cui bono

For Your Eyes Only
author: **10** Ian Fleming

Forza del Destino, La see **17** Force of Destiny, The

Fosse, Bob
director of: **5** Lenny **7** Cabaret (Oscar) **11** All That Jazz

fossil 4 fogy, rock **5** fogey, oldie, relic, stone **7** imprint, antique **9** remainder **13** petrification

foster 3 aid **4** back, feed, rear, tend **5** favor, nurse, raise **6** foment, harbor, mother, rear up, take in **7** advance, bring up, care for, cherish, forward, further, nourish, nurture, promote, protect, support, sustain **8** advocate, befriend, hold dear, sanction, side with, treasure **9** encourage, patronize, stimulate **11** accommodate, countenance

Foster, Alicia Christian
real name of: **11** Jodie Foster

Foster, Harold
creator/artist of: **6** Tarzan **13** Prince Valiant

Foster, Jodie
real name: **21** Alicia Christian Foster
born: **7** Bronx NY
roles: **7** Contact **8** Maverick **9** Tom Sawyer **10** Taxi Driver, The Accused (Oscar) **11** Bugsy Malone **13** Little Man Tate **20** The Silence of the Lambs (Oscar)

Foster, Stephen Collins
born: **15** Lawrenceville PA
composer of: **11** Swanee River **13** Camptown Races **16** Beautiful Dreamer **17** My Old Kentucky Home, The Old Folks at Home **27** Jeanie with the Light Brown Hair

Foucault, Jean Bernard Leon
field: **7** physics
nationality: **6** French
proved: **19** Earth spins on its axis
measured: **15** velocity of light
named for him: **8** pendulum **16** Foucault currents

Foucault's Pendulum
author: **10** Umberto Eco

foul 3 wet **4** base, clog, evil, lewd, soil, vile **5** dirty, foggy, grimy, gross, gusty, misty, muddy, murky, nasty, rainy, sully, taint **6** choked, cloudy, coarse, defile, filthy, grubby, odious, putrid, risque, scurvy, smelly, smutty, soiled, sordid, stormy, tangle, turbid, vulgar, wicked **7** abusive, begrime, drizzly, ensnare, hateful, heinous, impeded, obscene, pollute, profane, smeared, squalid, squally, stained, sullied, tangled, unclean **8** begrimed, besmirch, blustery, ensnared, entangle, immodest, indecent, infamous, stinking, unseemly **9** atrocious, besmeared, entangled, insulting, loathsome, monstrous, nefarious, notorious, obnoxious, repulsive, revolting **10** abominable, bedraggled, detestable, disgusting, encumbered, flagitious, indelicate, malodorous, putrescent, scurrilous, villainous **11** blasphemous, disgraceful **12** contemptible

foul-mouthed 4 lewd, rude, vile **5** dirty, gross **6** coarse, filthy, vulgar **7** abusive, obscene, profane **9** offensive **10** indelicate

foul play 5 crime **6** murder **8** violence **9** treachery

foul-smelling 4 rank **5** acrid, fetid, musty **6** putrid, smelly **7** noisome, reeking **8** stinking **10** malodorous

foul up 3 mar **4** goof, muff, ruin **5** botch, mix up, spoil **6** bungle, mess up, muddle **7** blunder, butcher, confuse, louse up, screw up **9** mismanage

found 4 base, rear, rest **5** build, erect, raise, set up, start **6** create, ground, locate, settle **7** develop, sustain **8** colonize, organize **9** construct, establish, institute, originate

foundation 3 bed **4** base, foot, fund, rock, root **5** basis, cause **6** bottom, cellar, ground, motive, origin, reason, source **7** charity, premise, purpose, support **8** basement, creation, pedestal **9** endowment, rationale **10** assumption, groundwork, settlement **11** benefaction, institution **12** commencement, installation, philanthropy, substructure, underpinning **13** establishment, justification **14** infrastructure, understructure

foundational 3 key **4** base, core **5** basic, prime **7** primary **9** essential **10** elementary

foundation garment 6 corset, girdle **8** corselet

founder 4 fall, limp, reel, sink, trip **5** abort, drown, lurch, swamp **6** author, father, go down, go lame, hobble, perish, plunge, sprawl, topple, tumble **7** break up, builder, capsize, creator, go under, planner, stagger, stumble, succumb **8** collapse, miscarry **9** architect, organizer, shipwreck **10** originator, strategist **12** disintegrate

foundered 4 sank **6** failed **7** beached, swamped **8** capsized, went down **9** collapsed

founding 5 birth **8** creation, settling **9** beginning **11** institution, origination **12** introduction, organization **13** establishment

found on 6 base on **7** model on **8** stem from **10** derive from **11** establish on

fountain 3 jet **4** flow, gush, well **5** birth, cause, spout **6** cradle, feeder, origin, reason, source, spring **7** genesis **8** purveyor, supplier **9** beginning, reservoir, upswelling **10** derivation, wellspring

fountainhead 4 font **6** origin, source, spring **9** beginning **10** wellspring

Fountainhead, The
author: 7 Ayn Rand
character: 11 Howard Roark
profession: 9 architect

fourgon 3 van **7** tumbril

Four Horsemen of the Apocalypse, The
author: 19 Vicente Blasco Ibanez
based on: 10 Revelation

400 Blows, The
director: 16 Francois Truffaut
cast: 10 Albert Remy **13** Claire Maurier **14** Patrick Auffray **15** Jean-Pierre Leaud

Four Quartets
author: 7 T S Eliot

Four-Season Recreation State
nickname of: 7 Vermont

fourth class mail 10 parcel post

fourth dimension 4 time

fourth estate 5 press **10** journalism

fowl 3 hen **4** cock, duck, game **5** banty, capon, chick, goose, quail **6** bantam, grouse, pigeon, turkey **7** chicken, cornish, leghorn, poultry **8** duckling

Fowles, John
author of: 8 Mantissa, The Magus **10** The Aristos **12** Daniel Martin, The Collector **13** The Ebony Tower **25** The French Lieutenant's Woman

fox 9 scavenger
young: 3 kit, pup
group of: 5 leash, skulk

Fox (Mesquakie, Red Earth People)
language family: 9 Algonkian **10** Algonquian
location: 4 Iowa **9** Wisconsin
allied with: 4 Sauk **8** Kickapoo

Fox, Fontaine
creator/artist of: 16 Toonerville Folks **18** Toonerville Trolley

foxglove 9 digitalis
varieties: 5 false, rusty **6** common, yellow **7** Grecian, Mexican **10** downy false **12** willow-leaved

foxiness 5 guile **7** cunning, slyness **8** artifice, trickery, wiliness **10** craftiness, shrewdness

fox-trot 5 dance **13** ballroom dance

Foxx, Jimmy (James Emory)
nickname: 7 Double X
sport: 8 baseball
team: 12 Boston Red Sox **21** Philadelphia Athletics

Foxx, Redd
real name: 16 John Elroy Sanford
born: 9 St Louis MO
roles: 13 Sanford and Son **19** Cotton Comes to Harlem

foxy 3 sly **4** wily **5** canny, sharp, slick **6** artful, astute, clever, crafty, shifty, shrewd, sneaky, tricky **7** cunning, devious, oblique **8** guileful, scheming, stealthy **9** conniving, deceitful, deceptive, designing, insidious, underhand **10** intriguing

foyer 4 hall **5** lobby **6** loggia **8** anteroom **9** vestibule **11** antechamber

fracas 3 row **4** fray, to-do **5** brawl, broil, clash, fight, melee, scrap **6** battle, ruckus, rumpus, strife, uproar **7** scuffle **9** imbroglio **10** donnybrook, free-for-all **11** altercation, embroilment

fraction 3 bit, few **4** chip **5** crumb, piece, ratio, scrap **6** morsel, trifle **7** cutting, portion, section, segment, shaving **8** fragment, particle, quotient **10** proportion **11** subdivision

fractious 5 cross, huffy **6** shirty, touchy, unruly **7** fretful, grouchy, peevish, pettish, waspish, wayward, willful **8** contrary, perverse, petulant, shrewish, snappish **9** irascible, irritable, querulous **10** rebellious, refractory **11** quarrelsome **12** disputatious, recalcitrant, unmanageable

fracture 4 rend, rift **5** break, crack, fault, sever, split **6** breach, cleave **7** disrupt, rupture, shatter **8** cleavage, division **9** severance **10** separation

Fra Diavolo, ou L'Hotellerie de Terracine
also: 31 Brother Devil or The Inn at Terracina
comic opera by: 5 Auber
character: 7 Lorenzo, Zerlina **11** Lady Allcash, Lord Allcash **17** Marquis di San Marco

fragile 4 soft, weak **5** crisp, frail **6** dainty, feeble, flimsy, infirm, sleazy, slight, tender **7** brittle, crumbly, friable, rickety, shivery **8** decrepit, delicate **9** breakable, ephemeral, frangible, splintery **10** evanescent, tumbledown **11** dilapidated **13** unsubstantial

fragility 7 frailty **8** delicacy, weakness **9** frailness **10** feebleness **11** brittleness **12** frangibility

fragment 3 bit **4** chip, snip **5** crumb, cut up, piece, scrap, shard, shred, trace **6** chop up, divide, morsel **7** break up, crumble, portion, remnant, section, segment, shatter, vestige **8** disunite, fraction, separate, splinter, survival **12** disintegrate

fragmentary 6 broken, choppy **7** scrappy **8** detached **9** piecemeal, scattered, segmented **10** disjointed, fractional, incomplete, unfinished **12** disconnected

Fragonard, Jean-Honore
 born: 6 France, Grasse
 artwork: 8 The Swing **10** Stolen Kiss, The Bathers, The Warrior **12** Le Billet Doux **14** Progress of Love **16** La Chemise Enlevee **18** Storming the Citadel **40** Coresus Sacrificing Himself to Save Callirhoe

fragrance 4 aura, balm **5** aroma, scent **7** bouquet, incense, perfume **9** redolence, sweetness

fragrant 5 balmy, spicy **7** odorous **8** aromatic, perfumed, redolent **11** odoriferous

Fragrant Harbor *see* **8** Hong Kong

frail 4 puny, weak **6** feeble, flimsy, infirm, sleazy, slight, weakly **7** brittle, crumbly, fragile, rickety, shivery **8** decrepit, delicate, fallible **9** breakable, frangible, splintery **10** perishable, vulnerable **11** dilapidated **13** unsubstantial

frailness 8 delicacy, weakness **9** fragility **11** unsoundness

frailty 3 sin **4** flaw, vice **5** fault **6** defect, foible **7** blemish, failing **11** fallihility **12** imperfection **14** susceptibility

Fra Lippo Lippi
 author: 14 Robert Browning

frame 3 rim, set **4** body, case, cast, form, make, mold, mood, plan **5** build, draft, hatch, humor, set up, shape, state **6** border, casing, design, devise, edging, figure, indite, invent, map out, nature, scheme, sketch, system, temper **7** anatomy, backing, chassis, concoct, contour, housing, outline, setting **8** attitude, conceive, contrive, mounting, organize, physique, skeleton **9** formulate, structure **11** disposition, scaffolding, systematize, temperament **12** constitution, construction

frame of mind 4 mood **7** climate **8** attitude **10** atmosphere **11** disposition

framer 6 author, shaper **7** creator, planner **10** formulator

framework 5 shell, truss **7** carcass **8** skeleton, template **9** structure **10** foundation **11** scaffolding **14** infrastructure

Framley Parsonage
 author: 15 Anthony Trollope

France
 other name: 4 Gaul
 anthem: 14 La Marseillaise
 capital/largest city: 5 Paris
 others: 4 Nice, St.-Lo **5** Brest, Lille, Lyons, Rouen, Vichy **6** Amiens, Calais, Cannes, Carnac, Cognac, Dieppe, Grasse, Nantes, Prades, Rheims **7** Antibes, Avignon, Bayonne, Dunkirk,

Le Havre, Les Baux **8** Bordeaux, Boulogne, Chartres, Grenoble, Poitiers, Toulouse **9** Cherbourg, Roquefort **10** La Rochelle, Marseilles, Saint-Denis, Strasbourg **12** Saint-Nazaire **13** Aix-en- Provence, Fontainebleau
 school: 8 Grenoble, Saint Cyr, Sorbonne **10** Montpelier
 division: 5 Anjou, Bearn, Berry, Maine, Savoy **6** Alsace, Artois, Marche, Poitou **7** Gascony, Guienne, Picardy **8** Auvergne, Bordeaux, Brittany, Burgundy, Dauphine, Flanders, Lorraine, Lyonnais, Normandy, Provence, Touraine **9** Aquitaine, Champagne, Languedoc **11** Ile de France **12** Bourbonnaise, Franche-Comte
 measure: 3 pot, sac **4** aune, mine, muid, pied, velt **5** arpen, carat, ligne, minot, pinte, point, pouce, velte **6** arpent, hemine, league, quarte, setier
 monetary unit: 5 franc **7** centime
 weight: 3 sol **4** gros, kilo, once **5** carat, livre, pound, tonne **6** gramme **7** tonneau **8** esterlin **9** esterling
 island: 2 Re **3** Yeu **4** Cite **5** Groix, Hyere **6** Comoro, Oleron, Tahiti, Ushant **7** Corsica, Leeward, Reunion **8** Windward **10** Guadeloupe, Martinique **12** New Caledonia
 lake: 6 Annecy, Cazaux, Geneva
 mountain: 4 Jura **5** Pelat **6** Vosges **8** Ardennes, Pyrenees **10** French Alps **11** Pic Montcalm
 highest point: 5 Blanc **9** Mont Blanc
 river: 3 Lys **4** Oise, Yser **5** Aisne, Eiser, Isere, Loire, Meuse, Rhine, Rhone, Saone, Seine **7** Garonne, Gironde
 sea: 5 North **8** Atlantic **13** Mediterranean
 physical feature:
  bay: 6 Biscay **7** Arachon
  beach: 4 Utah **5** Omaha
  cape: 5 Hague, Talma
  channel: 7 English **8** La Manche
  gulf: 4 Lion
 people: 6 Franks
  artist: 5 Corot, David, Degas, Manet, Monet **6** Braque, Ingres, Millet, Renoir, Seurat **7** Cezanne, Daumier, Gauguin, Matisse, Utrillo **8** Pissarro **9** Delacroix, Fragonard, Gericault
  author: 4 Gide, Hugo, Zola **5** Camus, Dumas **6** France, Proust, Racine, Sartre, Villon **7** Moliere **8** Rabelais, Rousseau, Voltaire **9** Corneille, Descartes, Giraudoux, Montaigne **10** Baudelaire
  composer: 5 Bizet, Ravel, Satie **6** Franck, Gounod **7** Berlioz, Debussy, Poulenc
  king: 5 Henri, Louis **6** Clovis, Philip **7** Charles **9** Hugh Capet **11** Charlemagne **13** Louis Philippe **14** Henry of Navarre

  leader: 6 Danton, Petain **7** Colbert, Mazarin **8** de Gaulle, D'Estaing, Pompidou **9** Joan of Arc, Richelieu **10** Mitterrand **11** Robespierre **17** Napoleon Bonaparte
  queen: 7 Eugenie **9** Josephine **13** Marie de Medici **15** Marie Antoinette
 language: 6 French
 expressions: 6 deja vu **7** apropos, detente, en masse, faux pas, vis-a-vis **8** de riguer **9** bete noire, c'est la vie, coup d'etat **10** bon appetit **11** coup de grace, joie de vivre, raison d'etre, savoir faire, tour de force **12** carte blanche, cause celebre, je ne sais quoi, nouveau riche, fait accompli **14** creme de la creme, noblesse oblige
 religion: 5 Islam **7** Judaism **8** Huguenot **10** Protestant **13** Roman Catholic
 place:
  cathedral: 6 Rheims **8** Chartres **9** Madeleine, Notre Dame **10** Sacre-Coeur **14** Sainte-Chapelle **15** Mont-Saint-Michel
  chapel: 8 Ronchamp
  gardens: 9 Tuileries
  hall of mirrors: 16 Galerie des Glaces
  museum: 6 Louvre
  palace: 6 Elysee **10** Luxembourg, Versailles **12** Grand Trianon, Petit Trianon, **13** Fontainebleau
  prison: 8 Bastille
  racetrack: 6 Le Mans **7** Auteuil **10** Longchamps
  resort: 3 Pau **5** Vichy **6** Cannes, Menton **7** Antibes, Mentone, Riviera **8** Biarritz, Chamonix, Grenoble **9** Cote d'Azur **11** Aix-les-Bains
  section of Paris: 8 Left Bank **9** Right Bank **10** Montmartre, Rive Droite, Rive Gauche **12** Latin Quarter
  street: 13 Champs-Elysees **17** Place de la Concorde
  woods: 14 Bois de Boulogne **15** Bois de Vincennes
 possession: 12 French Guiana
  island: 6 Futuna, Hoorne, Wallis **7** Reunion **8** Miquelon **10** Guadeloupe, Martinique **11** Saint Pierre **12** New Caledonia **15** French Polynesia
 feature:
  airport: 4 Orly **9** Le Bourget **15** Charles de Gaulle
  bicycle race: 12 Tour de France
  dance: 5 gavot **6** branle, canary, cancan **7** boutade, gavotte
  fortification: 11 Maginot Line
  holiday: 11 Bastille Day
  monument: 13 Arc de Triomphe **14** Tomb of Napoleon
  national theater: 16 Comedie Francaise
  sightseeing boat: 12 bateau mou-

che
tower: 6 Eiffel
food:
  cheese: 4 bleu, Brie **6** bonbel **7** boursin **8** Muenster **9** camembert, marcillat, port-salut, Roquefort **11** coulommiers
  dessert: 6 mousse
  dish: 4 pate **5** crepe **6** canape, quiche **7** souffle **8** escargot, piperade, pot au feu **9** cassoulet, tournedos **14** pate de foie gras
  drink: 6 cognac **8** bordeaux, burgundy **9** champagne
  french fries: 12 pommes frites
  pastry: 7 brioche **8** napoleon **9** croissant
  soup: 8 a l'oignon **13** bouillabaisse
  steak: 7 bifteck

France, Anatole
  real name: 30 Jacques Anatole Francois Thibault
  author of: 5 Thais **12** Golden Verses **13** My Friend's Book, Penguin Island **17** The Gods Are Athirst **20** The Revolt of the Angels **25** Le Crime de Sylvestre Bonnard **27** At the Sign of the Reine Pedauque

franchise 5 grant, right **6** ballot **7** charter, freedom, license **8** immunity, suffrage **9** privilege **10** permission **11** prerogative **13** authorization

Franciosa, Anthony
  real name: 14 Anthony Papales
  born: 9 New York NY
  wife: 14 Shelley Winters
  roles: 12 The Naked Maja **13** A Hatful of Rain, Long Hot Summer, Name of the Game, Wild Is the Wind **15** Assault on a Queen

Francis, Dick
  author of: 4 Bolt, Risk **5** Nerve, Proof **6** Banker, Reflex **7** Break In, Enquiry, Forfeit, Rat Race **8** Dead Cert, For Kicks, Slayride, Trial Run, Twice Shy, Whip Hand **9** Bonecrack, The Danger, Knockdown **10** Blood Sport, High Stakes, In the Frame **11** Smokescreen **12** Flying Finish

Franck, Cesar
  born: 5 Liege **7** Belgium
  composer of: 4 Ruth **5** Hulda **6** Psyche **7** Rebecca **8** Ghiselle **9** Les Djinns **10** Les Eolides, Redemption **13** La Tour de Babel, Les Beatitudes, The Beatitudes **16** Le Chasseur Maudit **17** The Accursed Hunter

Franco, Francisco
  dictator of: 5 Spain
  title: 10 el caudillo
  party: 7 falange, fascist
  followers: 11 fifth column

frank 4 bold, free, open **5** clear, plain, round **6** candid, direct, honest, patent **7** artless, evident, genuine, natural, sincere, up-front **8** apparent, distinct, explicit, manifest **9** downright, ingen-uous, outspoken **10** aboveboard, forthright, unreserved **11** plain-spoken, transparent, unambiguous, undisguised, unequivocal **12** unmistakable **15** straightforward

Frank, Anne
  author of: 19 The Diary of Anne Frank

Frankenstein
  author: 17 Mary Godwin Shelley
  character: 7 Clerval, Justine, William **9** Elizabeth **10** The Monster **12** Robert Walton **18** Victor Frankenstein

Franklin, Benjamin
  author of: 20 Poor Richard's Almanack
  inventor of: 12 lightning rod **13** bifocal lenses, Franklin stove

frankness 6 candor **7** honesty **8** openness **9** bluntness, sincerity **10** directness **11** artlessness **13** guilelessness **14** forthrightness **19** straightforwardness

frantic 3 mad **4** wild **5** crazy, rabid **6** hectic, insane, raging, raving **7** berserk, excited, furious, nervous, violent **8** agitated, deranged, frenetic, frenzied **9** delirious **10** distracted, distraught, infuriated **11** impassioned, overwrought **12** ungovernable

Frasier
  network: 3 NBC
  cast: 5 Eddie (dog) **10** Peri Gilpin (Roz), Jane Leeves (Daphne) **11** John Mahoney (Martin) **13** Kelsey Grammer (Frasier) **15** David Hyde Pierce (Niles)
  characters: 5 Eddie **8** Roz Doyle **10** Niles Crane, Daphne Moon **11** Martin Crane **12** Frasier Crane
  spinoff of: 6 Cheers

fraternal 6 hearty, loving, social **7** devoted, kindred, related **8** amicable, friendly **9** brotherly **11** warmhearted **12** affectionate **14** consanguineous

fraternity 4 clan, club **5** Greek, union **6** circle, clique, league **7** company, coterie, kinship, society **8** alliance **9** coalition **10** federation **11** association, brotherhood, confederacy, propinquity **13** brotherliness, consanguinity, interrelation

Fraternity
  author: 14 John Galsworthy

fraternize 3 mix **5** unite **6** concur, hobnob, mingle **7** combine, consort **8** coalesce **9** associate, cooperate, harmonize, pal around, socialize **10** sympathize **11** confederate

Fratres Arvales see **5** Arval

frau 4 lady, wife **12** married woman

fraud 4 fake, hoax, hype, ruse, sham **5** cheat, craft, guile, knave, quack, rogue, trick **6** deceit, humbug, rascal **7** swindle **8** artifice, cheating, cozenage, impostor, swindler, trickery **9** charlatan, chicanery, con artist, decep-tion, duplicity, impos-ture, pretender, stratagem, swindling, treachery **10** dishonesty, mountebank, subterfuge **11** counterfeit, four-flusher, machination **13** dissimulation

fraudulence 6 deceit **8** trickery **9** deception **13** deceitfulness, deceptiveness **17** misrepresentation

fraudulent 4 sham, wily **5** bogus, false **6** crafty, tricky **7** crooked, cunning, knavish **8** cheating, guileful, spurious **9** deceitful, deceptive, dishonest **11** counterfeit, treacherous, underhanded **12** dishonorable, unprincipled

fraught 4 full **5** heavy, laden **6** filled, loaded **7** charged, replete, teeming **8** attended, pregnant **9** abounding

fraulein 4 miss **9** young lady **14** unmarried woman

fray 3 rub **4** fret, fuss, riot, spat, tiff **5** brawl, chafe, fight, melee, ravel, set-to **6** bat-tle, combat, fracas, rumble, rumpus, strain, tatter, tumult, tussle **7** contest, dispute, frazzle, quarrel, scuffle, warfare, wear out, wrangle **8** conflict, skirmish, squabble **9** bickering, commotion **10** contention, dissension, engagement **11** altercation, controversy **12** disagreement

Frazer, Sir James G
  author of: 14 The Golden Bough

freak 3 fad, odd **4** kink, turn, whim **5** craze, fancy, humor, queer, quirk, sport, twist **6** marvel, oddity, vagary, whimsy, wonder **7** anomaly, bizarre, caprice, erratic, monster, strange, unusual **8** crotchet, mutation, peculiar **9** curiosity, deviation **10** aberration **11** abnormality, monstrosity **12** irregularity

freakish 3 odd **5** queer, weird **7** bizarre, strange, unusual **8** peculiar, singular, uncommon **9** eccentric, fantastic **10** outlandish **13** extraordinary

Frederick
  character in: 11 As You Like It
  author: 11 Shakespeare

Frederick I
  nickname: 10 Barbarossa
  position: 16 Holy Roman Emperor
  dynasty: 12 Hohenstaufen
  wife: 7 Beatrix
  battle: 7 Legnano

Frederick the Great
  nickname: 8 Old Fritz
  position: 13 King of Prussia
  invaded: 7 Silesia
  war: 13 Seven Years' War **18** Austrian Succession

free 3 big, lax **4** able, bold, easy, idle, idly, open, save **5** clear, extra, let go, loose, rid of, spare **6** daring, devoid, exempt, giving, gratis, lavish, parole, ransom, redeem, unbond, uncage, wanton **7** allowed, assured, forward, liberal, loosely, manumit, release, unchain, unleash **8** at no cost, careless, costless, devoid of, familiar, fearless, generous, handsome, immune to, informal, let loose, liberate, prodigal, released, unfasten **9** abandoned, audacious, available, boundless, bounteous, bountiful, confident, delivered, discharge, disengage, dissolute, expansive, extricate, footloose, lacking in, leisurely, liberated, permitted, unblocked, unbridled, unchained, unclogged, unimpeded, unmuzzled, unshackle **10** autonomous, bighearted, carelessly, chargeless, emancipate, gratuitous, licentious, manumitted, munificent, openhanded, unattached, unconfined, unfettered, unhampered, unoccupied, unreserved, unshackled **11** emancipated, enfranchise, independent, uncluttered, uncommitted, uninhibited, unrepressed **12** enfranchised, overfamiliar, uncontrolled, unencumbered, unobstructed, unrestrained **13** complimentary, unceremonious, unconstrained

free-and-easy 6 breezy, casual, jaunty **7** buoyant, relaxed **8** debonair, informal **12** lighthearted, presumptuous, unrestrained **13** unconstrained

freed 6 exempt, loosed, spared **7** cleared, excused **8** absolved, let loose, released, relieved **11** emancipated

freedom 4 play **5** range, scope, sweep, swing **6** candor, margin **7** abandon, license, release **8** autonomy, boldness, latitude, openness, rudeness **9** bluntness, frankness, impudence, indecorum **10** directness, disrespect, liberation **11** abandonment, forwardness, impropriety, inormality, manumission, naturalness, sovereignty, unrestraint **12** emancipation, impertinence, unconstraint **13** downrightness **14** unreservedness **15** enfranchisement

Freedom of the Poet, The
author: **12** John Berryman

free-flowing 7 copious, gushing, profuse **8** effusive

free-for-all 3 row **4** fray **5** brawl, fight, melee, scrap **6** affray, fracas, ruckus, tussle **7** rhubarb, ruction, wrangle **9** brannigan **10** donnybrook

free from bias 7 neutral **9** impartial, unbigoted **12** unprejudiced **13** disinterested

free from moisture 3 dry **4** arid, sere **5** parch **6** dry out **7** parched **8** dried out, rainless **9** dehydrate **10** dehydrated, desertlike, desiccated

free hand 12 carte blanche, open sanc-tion **13** full authority

free rein 12 carte blanche, open sanction **13** full authority

free-spoken 6 chatty **7** voluble **9** talkative **10** loquacious, unreserved **13** communicative

Free State
nickname of: **8** Maryland

Freestone State
nickname of: **11** Connecticut

Free to Choose
author: **14** Milton Friedman (with Rose Friedman)

Freetown
capital of: **11** Sierra Leone

freeze 3 nip **4** bite, cool, halt, stop **5** chill, frost, sting **6** arrest, benumb, harden, pierce **7** ceiling, congeal, terrify **8** glaci-ate, solidify **11** anesthetize, refrigerate, restriction

freezing 3 icy **6** arctic, frigid **7** glacial

Frege, Gottlieb
field: **11** mathematics
nationality: **6** German
founded: **13** symbolic logic

Frela see **5** Freya

freight 4 haul, lade, load, ship **5** cargo, carry, goods **6** burden, charge, convey, lading **7** baggage, cartage, luggage, portage **8** transmit, truckage **9** transport **10** conveyance **13** transshipment

Freischutz, Der
also: **11** The Marksman
opera by: **5** Weber
character: **3** Max **6** Agathe, Caspar, Samiel

Freki
origin: **12** Scandinavian
form: **4** wolf
owner: **4** Odin **5** Othin
received: **4** food
exception: **4** meat
fellow wolf: **4** Geri

French, Daniel Chester
born: **8** Exeter NH
artwork: **7** (seated) Lincoln (at Lincoln Memorial) **21** The Minute Man of Concord

French-American
French: **9** Franglais

French civil code 12 Code Napoleon

French Connection, The
director: **15** William Friedkin
cast: **11** Fernando Rey, Gene Hackman (Popeye Doyle), Roy Scheider
Oscar for: **5** actor (Hackman) **7** editing, picture **8** director **10** screenplay
sequel: **21** The French Connection II

French-English
French: **9** Franglais

French Guinea see **6** Guinea

French Indonesia see **7** Vietnam

French is spoken here
French: **18** ici on parle francais

French Lieutenant's Woman, The
director: **10** Karel Reisz
author: **10** John Fowles
cast: **9** Leo McKern **11** Hilton McRae, Jeremy Irons, Meryl Streep
script: **12** Harold Pinter

French national anthem 12 Marseillaise

French national theater 16 Comedie Francaise

French parliament
formal sessions: **12** lit de justice

French Somaliland see **8** Djibouti

French Sudan, Soudan see **4** Mali

French Togoland see **4** Togo

frenzied 3 mad **4** wild **7** excited, frantic, furious **8** agitated, ecstatic **9** delirious

frenzy 3 fit **4** fury **5** craze, furor, mania, state **6** access **7** mad rush, madness, seizure, turmoil **8** delirium, hysteria, outburst **9** obsession, transport **11** distraction

Frenzy
director: **15** Alfred Hitchcock
cast: **8** Jon Finch **10** Anna Massey **11** Barry Foster **16** Barbara Leigh-Hunt

frequency 9 iteration **10** recurrence, regularity, repetition **11** persistence, reiteration

frequent 5 daily, haunt, usual **6** common, wonted **7** regular **8** constant, everyday, familiar, habitual, numerous, ordinary, resort to **9** continual, customary, incessant, perpetual, recurrent **10** accustomed **11** reiterative

frequently 5 often **7** usually **8** ofttimes **9** generally **10** constantly, habitually, ordinarily, repeatedly **11** continually, customarily, incessantly, perpetually, recurrently

frere 4 monk **5** friar **7** brother

Frescobaldi, Girolamo
born: **5** Italy **7** Ferrara
composer of: **13** Fiori Musicali **14** Musical Flowers

fresh 3 fit, hot, new **4** bold, cool, fair, keen, late, pert, pure, rare, rosy, rude **5** alert, brisk, chill, clear, green, nervy, novel, ready, ruddy, sassy, saucy, stiff, sweet **6** active, biting, brassy, brazen, bright, cheeky, lively, modern, recent, rested, snotty, unique, unused, unworn **7** bracing, cutting, forward, glowing, just out, nipping, strange, uncured, undried, unfaded, untried, unusual **8** assuming, blooming, brand-new, creative, flippant, gleaming, impudent, insolent, original, stinging, unabated, undimmed, unsalted, unsmoked, unwilted, up-to-date **9** energetic, inventive, obtrusive, refreshed, sparkling, undecayed, unpickled, unspoiled, unwearied, wholesome **10** meddlesome, new-fangled, refreshing, unfamiliar, unimpaired, unwithered **11** flourishing, invigorated, modernistic, smartalecky, untarnished **12** presumptuous, unaccustomed

freshen 4 wash **5** brace, calve, clean, groom, renew **6** air out, breeze, desalt, revive **7** cool off, sweeten **8** renovate, spruce up **9** deodorize

freshet 5 crest, flood **11** overflowing

Freshman, The
director: 9 Sam Taylor **12** Fred Newmeyer
cast: 11 Harold Lloyd **13** Jobyna Ralston **14** Brooks Benedict

Fresnel, Augustin Jean
field: 7 physics
nationality: 6 French
worked in: 6 optics

fret 3 eat, rub, vex **4** fray, fume, gall, gnaw, mope, pine, pout, stew, sulk **5** brood, chafe, erode, sulks, worry **6** abrade, lament, ruffle, tatter **7** agonize, corrode, fidgets **8** disquiet, distress, irritate, vexation, wear away **9** annoyance, excoriate **10** irritation **11** displeasure, peevishness **12** discomposure

fretful 5 cross, huffy, sulky, tense **6** cranky, shirty, touchy **7** grouchy, nervous, peevish, pettish, waspish **8** contrary, petulant, snappish **9** crotchety, irritable, querulous **11** complaining **12** cantankerous

fretfulness 5 worry **6** unease **7** anxiety **10** crankiness **11** peevishness **12** irritability

Freud, Sigmund
lived in: 6 Vienna
collaborator: 6 Breuer
disciple: 4 Jung **5** Adler
daughter: 4 Anna
method: 15 free association **19** dream interpretation
coined: 2 id **8** superego **14** psychoanalysis
author of: 13 Totem and Taboo **22** Interpretation of Dreams **37** Group Psychology and the Analysis of the Ego, Jokes and Their Relation to the Unconscious

Freund, John Lincoln
real name of: 12 John Forsythe

Frey
also: 5 Freyr
origin: 12 Scandinavian
god of: 5 peace **8** marriage **10** prosperity
race: 5 Vanir
father: 5 Niord, Njord
home: 7 Alfheim

Freya
also: 5 Freia
origin: 8 Teutonic
goddess of: 4 love **6** beauty **9** fecundity
race: 5 Vanir
leader of: 9 Valkyries
father: 5 Niord, Njord

Fri see **5** Frigg

friable 7 crumbly **9** breakable, frangible

friar
French: 5 frere

Friar Lawrence
character in: 14 Romeo and Juliet
author: 11 Shakespeare

Friar Tuck
character in: 9 Robin Hood

friary 5 abbey **6** priory **8** cloister **9** hermitage, monastery

friction 6 strife **7** chafing, discord, grating, quarrel, rubbing **8** abrasion, bad blood, conflict, fretting **9** animosity, attrition, hostility **10** antagonism, contention, dissension, dissidence, opposition, resentment, resistance **12** disagreement **13** counteraction

Friday
character in: 14 Robinson Crusoe
author: 5 Defoe

Friday
from: 5 Freya, Frigg
heavenly body: 5 Venus
French: 8 vendredi
Italian: 7 venerdi
Spanish: 7 viernes
German: 7 freitag

Friedan, Betty
author of: 19 The Feminine Mystique
co-founder of: 3 NOW **28** National Organization for Women

Friedkin, William
director of: 11 The Exorcist **19** The French Connection (Oscar)

Friedman, Milton
author of: 12 Free to Choose (with Rose Friedman) **20** Capitalism and Freedom

Friedrich, Caspar David
born: 7 Germany **10** Greifswald
artwork: 22 The Cross on the Mountains **26** Man and Woman Gazing at the Moon, The Ruined Monastery of Eldena, Two Men Contemplating the Moon

friend 3 pal **4** ally, beau, chum, date, mate **5** amigo, buddy, crony, lover **6** backer, cohort, escort, fellow, intime, minion, patron **7** brother, comrade, consort, partner **8** adherent, advocate, confrere, co-worker, defender, favorite, follower, henchman, intimate, mistress, myrmidon, paramour, partisan, playmate, retainer, sidekick, soul mate **9** associate, bedfellow, colleague, companion, confidant, copartner, supporter **10** benefactor, encourager, playfellow, well-wisher **12** acquaintance
French: 3 ami **4** amie **9** bonne amie
Spanish: 5 amiga, amigo

friendliness 5 amity **8** bonhomie, good will **9** geniality **10** affability, amiability, cordiality, fraternity **11** amicability, camaraderie, sociability **14** neighborliness **16** companionability

friendly 4 kind **6** allied, ardent, benign, chummy, clubby, genial, kindly, loving, social **7** affable, amiable, cordial, devoted, helpful **8** amicable, familiar, generous, gracious, intimate, salutary **9** brotherly, convivial, favorable, fortunate, fraternal, opportune **10** accessible, auspicious, beneficial, hospitable, neighborly, not hostile, propitious **11** kindhearted, sympathetic, warmhearted **12** advantageous, affectionate **13** companionable

Friendly, Fred W
president of: 7 CBS News
collaborator: 13 Edward R. Murrow
show: 8 See It Now

Friendly Fire
author: 8 C D B Bryan

Friendly Islands see **5** Tonga

friendly understanding
French: 15 entente cordiale

friend of the court
Latin: 12 amicus curiae

Friends
network: 3 NBC
cast: 10 Lisa Kudrow **11** Matt LeBlanc **12** Courteney Cox, Matthew Perry **14** David Schwimmer **15** Jennifer Aniston
characters: 10 Ross Geller **11** Rachel Green **12** Chandler Bing, Phoebe Buffay, Monica Geller **13** Joey Tribbiani

friendship 5 amity **6** accord, comity **7** concord, harmony **8** close tie, goodwill, intimacy, sympathy **10** consonance, cordiality, fellowship, fraternity **11** brotherhood, comradeship, familiarity **12** amicableness **13** companionship, understanding **14** neighborliness **16** acquaintanceship

Frigg
also: 3 Fri **5** Frija **6** Frigga
origin: 8 Teutonic
goddess of: 3 sky **6** clouds **8** marriage
husband: 4 Odin **5** Othin
race: 4 Asar **5** Aesir

Frigga see **5** Frigg

fright 4 fear, funk **5** alarm, dread, panic, scare **6** dismay, horror, terror, tremor **7** anxiety, concern, flutter, quaking **8** cold feet **9** misgiving, quivering, the creeps **10** the jitters, the willies **11** disquietude, palpitation, trepidation **12** apprehension, intimidation, perturbation **13** consternation

frighten 5 alarm, daunt, scare, shock **6** affray, excite **7** agitate, horrify, petrify, startle, terrify **8** disquiet **9** terrorize **10** intimidate

frightened 6 afraid, scared **7** alarmed, panicky **9** horrified, petrified, terrified **10** terrorized

frightening 5 awful, dread **7** fearful **8** alarming, dreadful **10** horrifying, terrifying **11** hair-raising

frightful 5 awful, lurid, nasty **6** grisly, horrid **7** baleful, extreme, fearful, ghastly, hideous, macabre, ogreish **8** alarming, dreadful, fearsome, freakish, gruesome, horrible, horrific, shocking, sinister, terrible, terrific **9** appalling, loathsome, monstrous, offensive, repellent, repulsive, revolting **10** abominable, detestable, disgusting, horrendous **12** insufferable

frigid 3 icy, raw **4** cold, cool, prim **5** aloof, bleak, gelid, stiff **6** biting, bitter, chilly, formal, frosty **7** austere, cutting, distant, glacial, nipping **8** freezing, piercing **10** forbidding **11** straitlaced **12** unresponsive

frigidity 7 iciness **8** coldness **9** aloofness **10** frostiness **16** unresponsiveness

Frija see **5** Frigg

frill 3 air **5** extra **6** edging, fringe, ruffle **7** flounce **8** falderal, frippery, furbelow, ornament **9** gathering, mannerism **10** decoration **11** affectation, superfluity **13** embellishment

fringe 3 hem, rim **4** edge, mane **5** limit, skirt **6** border, edging, margin, tassel **7** enclose, outline, selvage **8** decorate, frontier, skirting, surround, trimming **9** embellish, periphery

frisk 3 hop **4** jump, lark, leap, romp, skip, trip **5** bound, caper, cut up, dance, sport **6** bounce, cavort, frolic, gambol, prance, search, spring **7** disport, examine, inspect, ransack **8** look over

frisky 4 spry **5** agile, peppy **6** active, lively, nimble **7** jocular, playful, waggish **8** animated, mirthful, prankish, spirited, sportive **9** vivacious **10** frolicsome, rollicking

fritter 4 blow **5** use up, waste **7** deplete, pancake **8** fool away, idle away, squander **9** dissipate

fritter away 4 blow **5** waste **6** misuse **8** misspend, squander **9** dissipate

fritter away time 4 idle **6** dawdle **10** dillydally

Fritzi Ritz
  aunt to: 5 Nancy
  creator: 15 Ernie Bushmiller **16** Larry Whittington
  character: 4 Phil **5** Nancy, Rollo **6** Sluggo

frivolity 3 fun **4** jest, play **5** folly, sport **6** levity, whimsy **7** abandon **8** airiness, dallying, frippery **9** emptiness, flippancy, giddiness, lightness **10** fickleness, triviality, wantonness **11** flightiness **15** thoughtlessness

frivolous 4 airy, vain **5** barmy, dizzy, emp- ty, inane, light, minor, petty, silly **6** flimsy, frothy, paltry, slight, stupid **7** fatuous, flighty, foolish, trivial, witless **8** careless, flippant, heedless, niggling, piddling, trifling **9** brainless, imprudent, pointless, senseless, unserious, worthless **10** insouciant **11** extravagant, harebrained, impractical, improvident, nonsensical,

superficial, unimportant **13** insignificant, rattlebrained **14** shallowbrained

frizzle 4 curl **5** crimp

frock 4 coat, gown, robe, suit **5** cloak, dress, smock **6** blouse **7** cassock, soutane **8** chasuble, surplice, vestment **9** clericals **10** canonicals

frog 3 pad, pod **4** knot, wood **5** frosh, hitch, track **6** holder, peeper, toggle **7** crawler, croaker, cushion, leopard, tadpole **8** bullfrog, fastener, pickerel, pollywog **9** amphibian, plow frame **12** flower holder

Frogs, The
  author: 12 Aristophanes
  character: 5 Pluto **6** Charon **7** Bacchus **8** Dionysus, Hercules, Xanthias **9** Aeschylus, Euripides

Froissart, Jean
  author of: 8 Meliador **10** Chronicles

frolic 3 fun **4** lark, play, romp, skip **5** act up, antic, caper, frisk, mirth, prank, sport, spree **6** cavort, gaiety, gambol **7** disport, jollity, make hay **8** escapade **9** amusement, festivity, joviality, merriment **10** buffoonery, pleasantry, recreation, skylarking, tomfoolery **11** merrymaking **13** entertainment

frolicsome 5 antic, jolly, merry **6** cheery, jaunty, lively **7** playful **8** cheerful, mirthful, prankish **9** sprightly **12** lighthearted

Frollo, Claude
  character in: 23 The Hunchback of Notre Dame
  author: 4 Hugo

from 2 de, ex, of **3** for, fro **5** off of, out of **7** against **8** starting **9** beginning

from abroad 5 alien **6** exotic **7** foreign **8** imported

fromage 6 cheese

from behind
  Latin: 6 a tergo

From Here to Eternity
  director: 13 Fred Zinnemann
  author: 10 James Jones
  cast: 9 Donna Reed **11** Deborah Kerr **12** Frank Sinatra, George Reeves **13** Burt Lancaster **14** Ernest Borgnine **15** Montgomery Clift
  setting: 11 Pearl Harbor
  Oscar for: 7 picture **8** director **12** screenwriter **15** supporting actor (Sinatra) **17** supporting actress (Reed)

from inside
  Latin: 7 ab intra

from outside
  Latin: 7 ab extra

From Russia With Love
  author: 10 Ian Fleming

from scratch 4 anew **14** from ground zero **16** from the beginning **20** from fresh ingredients

from side to side 4 over, sway **5**

cross **7** athwart, swaying, zigzag **12** back and forth

from the beginning
  Latin: 5 ab ovo **6** de novo **8** ab initio

from the chair
  Latin: 10 ex cathedra

from the depths
  Latin: 11 de profundis

from the face
  Latin: 7 ex facie

from the fact
  Latin: 7 de facto

from the founding of the city
  Latin: 13 ab urbe condita

from the library of
  Latin: 8 ex libris

from the seat of authority
  Latin: 10 ex cathedra

front 3 air, top **4** face, fore, head, lead, mask, mien **5** first **6** facade, give on, regard **7** bearing, initial, look out **8** anterior, carriage, demeanor, presence, pretense, trenches, vanguard **9** beginning, semblance

Front, The
  director: 10 Martin Ritt
  cast: 10 Lloyd Gough, Woody Allen, Zero Mostel **13** Joshua Shelley, Michael Murphy **16** Herschel Bernardi

frontage 7 outlook **8** exposure, prospect

frontier 4 edge **5** march, verge **6** border, limits **7** extreme, marches **8** boundary, confines, outposts **9** backlands, backwoods, outskirts, perimeter **10** hinterland **11** territories

front matter 8 foreword **9** title page **12** introduction **15** table of contents **20** introductory material

Front Page, The
  author: 8 Ben Hecht **16** Charles MacArthur
  director: 11 Billy Wilder **14** Lewis Milestone
  actor: 9 Mae Clarke, Mary Brian, Pat O'Brien **10** Jack Lemmon, David Wayne **12** George E Stone, Carol Burnett **13** Adolphe Menjou, Allen Garfield, Susan Sarandon, Walter Catlett, Walter Matthau **14** Charles Durning **15** Andrew Pendleton, Vincent Gardenia **19** Edward Everett Horton
  character: 4 Earl **5** Burns, Grant, Hildy, Peggy **6** Walter **7** Hartman, Johnson **8** Williams

frost 4 rime **5** chill **7** iciness **8** coolness, distance **9** aloofness, cold spell, frigidity **10** chilliness, glaciality **13** inhospitality **14** unfriendliness

Frost, Robert
  author of: 7 Birches **10** Fire and Ice, Home Burial **11** Mending Wall **13** Brown's Descent **15** The Road Not Taken **17** After Apple-Picking **21** The

Death of the Hired Man **30** Stopping by Woods on a Snowy Evening

frostiness 3 nip **4** bite **5** chill **7** iciness **8** coldness, coolness **9** crispness, frigidity, hoariness, sharpness **10** chilliness, wintriness

frosting 3 mat **4** trim **5** glass, icing **7** cooling, topping **8** chilling, divinity, freezing, trimming **13** embellishment, ornamentation

frosty 3 icy **4** cold, cool **5** bleak, chill, hoary **6** frigid, wintry **8** freezing

froth 4 bosh, fizz, foam, fume, head, scum, suds, surf **5** spume, trash, yeast **6** lather, trivia **7** bubbles, rubbish **8** flummery, frippery, nonsense, trumpery, whitecap **9** frivolity **10** balderdash, triviality **12** fiddle-faddle

frothy 5 fizzy, foamy, light **6** bubbly **7** trivial **9** frivolous **15** inconsequential

froward 5 balky **6** unruly **7** wayward, willful **8** contrary, perverse, stubborn **9** difficult, fractious, obstinate **10** headstrong, refractory **11** disagreeing, intractable **12** recalcitrant **13** contradictory **15** unaccommodating

frown 4 fret, mope, muse, pout, sulk **5** glare, scowl **6** glower, ponder **14** discountenance

frowning 4 dark **5** angry **6** gloomy, somber, sullen **8** scowling **9** glowering

frown upon 7 condemn, dislike **8** object to **14** discountenance

frowsy, frowzy 5 fusty, musty, stale **6** sloppy, untidy **7** tousled, unkempt **8** slovenly

frozen 3 icy **4** cold, iced, numb **5** chill, gelid, polar **6** arctic, chilly, cooled, wintry **7** chilled, clogged, glacial, stymied **8** benumbed, hibernal, icebound **10** obstructed, stalemated **11** frostbitten, immobilized **12** refrigerated

fructify 5 bloom **6** sprout, thrive **7** blossom, prosper, succeed **8** flourish

frugal 4 slim **5** scant, tight **6** skimpy, stingy **7** ascetic, sparing, thrifty **9** niggardly, penny-wise **10** abstemious, economical, unwasteful **12** parsimonious

frugality 6 thrift **7** economy **8** prudence, stinting **9** parsimony **10** scantiness, stinginess **11** thriftiness **12** cheeseparing **13** niggardliness, penny-pinching **16** parsimoniousness

fruit 4 crop **5** award, issue, yield, young **6** effect, profit, result, return, reward, upshot **7** benefit, harvest, outcome, produce, product, progeny, revenue **8** earnings **9** advantage, emolument, offspring, outgrowth **10** production **11** consequence **12** remuneration

fruitful 6 fecund **7** fertile **8** blooming, prolific, yielding **9** effective **10** productive, profitable, successful **11** efficacious **12** advantageous, fructiferous

fruition 8 maturity, ripeness **10** attainment **11** achievement, fulfillment, realization **12** consummation, satisfaction **13** actualization, gratification **15** materialization

fruitless 4 arid, vain **5** empty, inept **6** barren, futile, hollow **7** sterile, useless **8** abortive, bootless, nugatory **9** infertile, pointless, worthless **10** profitless, unavailing, unprolific **11** incompetent, ineffective, ineffectual, inoperative, purposeless, unrewarding **12** unproductive, unprofitable, unsuccessful **13** inefficacious

fruit trees
goddess of: **6** Pomona

frumpy 4 drab **5** dowdy **8** slovenly **10** slatternly **12** unattractive

frustrate 3 bar **4** balk, foil **5** block, check, upset **6** baffle, cancel, defeat, hinder, impede, thwart **7** counter, cripple, fluster, inhibit, nullify, prevent **8** dispirit, obstruct, prohibit, suppress **9** forestall, hamstring, undermine **10** circumvent, disappoint, disconcert, discourage, dishearten

frustration 6 defeat **7** balking, chagrin, failure, foiling, letdown **8** futility **9** hindrance, thwarting **10** bafflement, inhibition, nonsuccess **11** obstruction **12** discomfiture, interference **13** contravention, counteraction **14** disappointment, nonfulfillment **15** dissatisfaction

fry 4 cook **5** brown, grill, saute **7** frizzle **9** fricassee

fry 4 fish **5** child, young **8** children, small fry

Fry, Christopher
author of: **9** Yard of Sun **12** The Firstborn **13** Venus Observed **20** The Dark Is Light Enough **21** The Lady's Not for Burning

frying pan 3 wok **6** frypan **7** browner, griddle, skillet

fuchsia
varieties: **4** cape, tree **5** hardy **10** California **11** honeysuckle

fuddled 5 bosky, dopey, drunk, tipsy **6** boozed, groggy **7** maudlin, muddled, sozzled, tippled **8** confused **9** stupefied **10** inebriated **11** intoxicated

fudge 3 lie **4** bosh, fake **5** candy, cheat, evade, hedge, hunch, patch, welch **7** falsify, penuche **8** divinity

fuel 3 fan, gas, oil **4** coal, feed, fire, wood **5** light, means, stoke **6** charge, fill up, fodder, ignite, incite, kindle **7** impetus, inflame, sustain **8** activate, energize, gasoline, material, recharge, stimulus **9** petroleum, stimulate **10** ammunition, motivation, sustenance **11** inspiration, wherewithal

fugitive 4 hobo **5** brief, exile, hasty,

nomad, rover, short, tramp **6** errant, fading, flying, loafer, outlaw **7** cursory, elusive, erratic, escaped, escapee, fleeing, hurried, passing, refugee, runaway, summary, vagrant **8** apostate, deserter, escaping, fleeting, flitting, renegade, shifting, unstable, vagabond, volatile, wanderer **9** ephemeral, fugacious, itinerant, momentary, straggler, temporary, transient, uncertain **10** evanescent, expatriate, short-lived, transitory **11** impermanent

Fugitive, The
character: **9** Donna Taft **11** Fred Johnson (one-armed man) **12** (Lt) Philip Gerard **13** (Dr) Richard Kimble
cast: **10** Barry Morse, Bill Raisch **12** David Janssen **15** Jacqueline Scott

fuhrer, Fuhrer, der fuhrer 4 Nazi **6** Hitler, leader, tyrant **8** dictator **11** Adolf Hitler

fulfill 2 do **4** heed, keep, meet, obey, suit **6** answer, effect, follow, redeem **7** achieve, execute, observe, perfect, perform, realize, satisfy **9** discharge, establish, implement **10** accomplish, consummate, effectuate

fulfillment, fulfilment 7 delight **8** crowning, pinnacle, pleasure **9** execution, happiness **10** attainment, completion **11** achievement, contentment, culmination, realization **12** effectuation, satisfaction **13** contentedness, establishment, gratification **14** accomplishment, implementation

Fulks, Sarah Jane
real name of: **9** Jane Wyman

full 3 big **4** rich, very, wide **5** ample, broad, flush, laden, large, plump, quite, round, sated, total, whole **6** entire, gorged, in- tact, loaded, mature, packed, rotund **7** brimful, crammed, exactly, fraught, glutted, heaping, maximum, perfect, plenary, replete, shapely, stuffed, teeming **8** brimming, bursting, complete, resonant, swarming, thorough **9** abounding, capacious, perfectly, precisely, saturated, surfeited **10** unabridged, voluminous

full amount 3 all, sum **5** total, whole **8** entirety, totality **9** aggregate **10** complement

full-bodied 3 fat **4** rich **5** ample, lofty **6** hearty, mature, robust **9** flavorful **10** meaningful

Fuller, R Buckminster
architect of: **10** US Pavilion (Expo '67 Montreal) **13** Dymaxion House
form: **12** geodesic dome

full-fledged 5 adept **6** expert, mature **7** skilled, trained **8** complete, masterly, schooled **9** qualified, topflight **10** proficient **11** experienced **13** authoritative

full form 9 extension **10** elongation **11**

enlargement 12 augmentation **13** amplification

full-grown 4 ripe **5** adult, manly, of age, matured, womanly **9** developed

full measure 6 enough, plenty **9** abundance, plenitude **10** competence **11** sufficiency

Full Moon
　author: **11** P G Wodehouse

fullness 7 satiety **8** richness **9** amplitude, roundness, satiation **12** completeness **14** voluminousness

full of fire 7 rousing **8** electric, exciting, spirited **9** thrilling **11** galvanizing, stimulating **12** electrifying, soulstirring

full of life 5 vital **8** animated, spirited, vigorous **9** ebullient, energetic, exuberant, vivacious

full of pep 5 vital **6** lively **8** animated

full of vim and vigor 5 peppy **6** lively **11** invigorated

full view 7 the open **8** daylight, openness

fully 5 amply, quite **6** richly, wholly **7** totally, utterly **8** entirely **9** copiously, perfectly **10** abundantly, altogether, completely, positively, throughout **11** plentifully **12** sufficiently **13** substantially

fully realized 7 perfect **8** achieved, complete, executed, finished **9** completed, perfected, performed **11** consummated **12** accomplished

fulminate 4 boil, rage, rant **7** explode **8** denounce

fulminate against 5 roast **6** berate **7** scourge **8** call down, chastise **9** castigate

fulmination 7 violent **8** bursting, eruption **9** discharge, explosion

fulsome 3 fat **4** foul **5** suave **6** lavish, odious **7** cloying, lustful, noisome, ob scene **8** overdone, unctuous **9** excessive, obnoxious, offensive, repulsive, tasteless **10** disgusting, obsequious

Fulton, Robert
　nationality: **8** American
　inventor of: **9** steamboat (Clermont), submarine **12** Fulton's folly **13** marine torpedo

fumble 3 err, mar **4** blow, muff **5** grope, spoil **6** bobble, boggle, bollix, bungle, goof up, mess up, muddle **7** butcher, louse up, screw up **9** mishandle

fume 3 gas **4** boil, burn, emit, foam, haze, puff, rage, rant, rave, reek, waft **5** exude, scent, smell, smoke, stink, vapor **6** bil-low, exhale, miasma, seethe, stench **7** carry on, explode, flame up, flare up, smolder **10** exhalation

fun 3 gas **4** ball, game, jest, lark, play, romp, trip **5** antic, blast, cheer, mirth, prank, sport, spree **6** frolic, gaiety,

joking **7** jollity, revelry, whoopee **8** escapade, good time, pleasure **9** amusement, diversion, enjoyment, horseplay, joviality, merriment **10** buffoonery, recreation, relaxation, skylarking, tomfoolery **11** distraction, playfulness, waggishness **13** entertainment

Funafuti
　capital of: **6** Tuvalu

function 3 act, job **4** duty, fete, gala, help, role, task, work **5** feast, field, niche, party, place, power, range, scope, serve **6** affair, behave, do duty, office, soiree, sphere **7** banquet, benefit, concern, faculty, operate, perform, purpose **8** activity, business, capacity, ceremony, occasion, province **9** festivity, objective, operation, reception **13** entertainment

functional 6 useful **7** working **8** operable **9** operative, practical **11** serviceable, utilitarian

functionary 8 employee, official **10** bureaucrat **13** administrator

functioning 5 in use **6** active, at work, usable **7** working **9** effectual, operating, operative

fund 3 pot **4** bank, foot, lode, mine, pool, vein, well **5** endow, float, fount, hoard, kitty, stock, store **6** pay for, spring, supply **7** finance, nest egg, reserve, savings, support **8** treasure **9** endowment, patronize, reservoir **10** foundation, investment, repository, storehouse, underwrite **12** accumulation

fundament 3 can **4** buns, rump, seat **5** fanny **6** behind, bottom **8** backside, buttocks, haunches **9** posterior **12** hindquarters

fundamental 3 key **4** ABC's, base, main **5** axiom, basic, basis, chief, first, major, vital **7** central, crucial, element, primary **8** cardinal, integral **9** component, essential, necessary, principal, principle, requisite **10** elementary, foundation, groundwork, underlying **11** cornerstone **13** indispensable

funds 4 cash, jack, pelf **5** bread, dough, lucre, means, money, moola **6** assets, income, wampum, wealth **7** capital, scratch **8** finances, property **9** resources **11** wherewithal

funeral 4 wake **5** rites **6** burial **7** requiem **9** cremation, interment, obsequies **10** entombment, inhumation

funeral song 5 dirge, elegy **6** lament **7** requiem **8** threnody **11** lamentation

funereal 3 sad **4** grim **5** weepy **6** dismal, dreary, gloomy, solemn, somber, woeful **7** doleful **8** desolate, dirgeful, grieving, mournful **9** cheerless, woebegone **10** depressing, lachrymose, lugubrious **13** brokenhearted

fun-filled 5 happy **6** joyful, joyous **8**

pleasant, pleasing **9** enjoyable **10** delightful **11** pleasurable

Fungoso
　character in: **22** Every Man Out of His Humour
　author: **6** Jonson

fungus, fungi 4 mold, myco, rust, smut **5** ergot, yeast **6** mildew **7** truffle **8** mushroom **9** toadstool **11** thallophyte

fun-loving 5 jolly, merry **6** genial, jovial **7** affable **8** sociable **9** convivial **10** gregarious

funnel 4 cone, duct, flue, pipe, pour **5** focus, shaft **6** direct, filter, siphon **7** channel, chimney, conduit **9** stovepipe **10** smokestack, ventilator **11** concentrate

funny 3 odd **5** antic, comic, droll, merry, queer, weird, witty **6** absurd, jocose **7** amusing, bizarre, comical, curious, jesting, jocular, offbeat, strange, unusual, waggish **8** farcical, humorous, mirthful, peculiar, sporting, uncommon **9** diverting, facetious, hilarious, laughable, ludicrous **10** outlandish, ridiculous

Funny Girl
　director: **12** William Wyler
　cast: **8** Lee Allen **10** Kay Medford, Omar Sharif **11** Anne Francis **13** Walter Pidgeon **15** Barbra Streisand (Fanny Brice)
　score: **9** Jule Styne **10** Bob Merrill
　sequel: **9** Funny Lady
　song: **6** People **18** Don't Rain on My Parade

funnyman 3 wag, wit **4** card, fool, mime, zany **5** clown, comic, joker **6** jester, madcap **7** buffoon **8** comedian, humorist, jokester **9** harlequin

fuoco, con
　music: **8** with fire

fur 3 fox **4** down, hair, lamb, mink, pelt, seal **5** coney, lapin, otter, sable **6** beaver, fleece, jaguar, kit fox, nutria, rabbit, red fox **7** blue fox, cheetah, leopard, muskrat, opossum, raccoon **8** black fox, cross fox, squirrel, white fox **9** silver fox **10** animal skin, chinchilla **11** karakul lamb, Persian lamb **13** broadtail lamb **14** mouton-dyed lamb

furbelow 5 frill **6** fringe **7** falbala, flounce **8** trimming

furbish 4 buff **5** renew, shine **6** polish **7** burnish **8** renovate

Furiae see **6** Furies

Furies
　5 Dirae **6** Erinys, Furiae, Semnai **7** Alecto, Erinyes, Megaera **9** Eumenides, Tisiphone
　form: **7** spirits
　sex: **6** female
　mother: **4** Gaea
　father: **6** Uranus
　born of the blood of: **6** Uranus

Greek name: 6 Erinys **7** Erinyes **9** Eumenides
Roman name: 5 Dirae **6** Furiae

furious 3 mad **4** wild **5** angry, fiery, irate, rabid **6** enrage, fierce, fuming, raging, savage, stormy **7** intense, rampant, violent **8** frenetic, frenzied, heedless, maddened, provoked, reckless, up in arms, vehement, wrathful **9** fanatical, irascible, turbulent **10** infuriated, passionate, tumultuous, unbalanced **11** tempestuous **12** ungovernable, unrestrained

furl 4 coil, curl, fold, roll, wrap **5** truss **6** curl up, fold up, furdle, roll up, spiral

furlong
abbreviation: 3 fur

furnace 4 kiln, oven **5** forge, stove **6** boiler, heater **11** incinerator

Furnace
constellation of: 6 Fornax

furnish 3 arm, rig **4** gird, give, vest **5** array, dress, endow, equip, favor, fit up, grant, stock **6** fit out, outfit, purvey, render, supply **7** appoint, indulge, prepare, provide **8** accoutre, bestow on, decorate **9** provision **11** accommodate

furnishings 5 decor **9** equipment **11** accessories **12** haberdashery

furnish room for 5 lodge, put up **6** billet **7** shelter **11** accommodate

furniture 7 effects **8** chattels, movables, property **11** possessions **12** appointments

furor 3 fad **4** flap, rage, to-do, word **5** craze, mania, noise, thing, vogue **6** fervor, frenzy, hoopla, lunacy, raving, uproar **7** fashion, madness, passion **8** brouhaha, insanity, reaction **9** agitation, commotion, obsession, transport **10** dernier cri, enthusiasm, excitement, fanaticism

furrow 3 cut, dig, rut **4** knit, line, plow, rift, seam **5** cleft, crack, ditch, ridge, track **6** crease, groove, pucker, trench, trough **7** channel, crevice, fissure, wrinkle **10** depression **11** corrugation

furry 4 soft **5** downy, hairy, scary **6** cuddly, fleecy, pelted, shaggy **8** fearsome, horrible **11** hair-raising

further 3 aid, new, too, yet **4** also, back, help, more **5** again, extra, favor, fresh, other, spare, speed **6** abroad, assist, back up, beyond, foster, hasten, oblige, to boot, yonder **7** advance, afar off, besides, farther, forward, promote, quicken, stand by, work for **8** champion, expedite, likewise, moreover **9** accessory, ancillary, auxiliary, encourage, propagate **10** accelerate, additional, strengthen **11** accommodate **12** additionally, contributory, supplemental **13** supplementary

furtherance 3 aid **4** help, lift **5** favor **6** succor **7** advance, defense, support **8** advocacy, interest **9** patronage, promotion **10** assistance **11** advancement, cooperation, countenance **12** championship

furthering 3 aid **6** aiding, growth **8** abetting, advocacy, espousal **9** assisting, fostering, promoting, promotion **10** assistance, supporting **11** advancement, encouraging, propagating, propagation **12** accelerating, acceleration, encouragement **13** strengthening

furthermore 3 too **4** also **6** as well, to boot **7** besides **8** likewise, moreover **10** in addition **12** additionally

furthermost 7 extreme **8** farthest **11** farthermost

furtive 3 sly **4** wily **5** shady **6** covert, crafty, hidden, masked, secret, shifty, sneaky, unseen, veiled **7** cloaked, elusive, evasive, private **8** secluded, shrouded, skulking, sneaking, stealthy **9** collusive, secre-tive, underhand **10** mysterious, undercover, unrevealed **11** clandestine **12** confidential **13** surreptitious **14** conspiratorial

fury 3 fit, hag, ire, pet **4** gall, huff, rage, snit **5** force, might, shrew, vixen, wrath **6** attack, choler, frenzy, spleen, virago **7** assault, bluster, dudgeon, hellcat, tantrum **8** acerbity, acrimony, ferocity, outburst, severity, she-devil, spitfire, violence **9** intensity, termagant, vehemence, virulence **10** excitement, fierceness, turbulence **11** impetuosity

fuse 4 join, link, meld, melt, weld, wick **5** blend, merge, smelt, torch **6** league, mingle, solder **7** combine **8** coalesce, federate, ignition, solidify **9** associate, detonator **10** amalgamate, assimilate **11** confederate, consolidate, incorporate, intermingler

fusillade 4 hail, rain **5** salvo, spray **6** volley **7** barrage, battery **8** drumfire, enfilade **9** broadside, cannonade **11** bombardment

fusion 5 blend, union **6** league **7** combine, melding, melting, merging **8** alliance, blending, compound, smelting **9** coalition, synthesis **10** commixture, dissolving, federation **11** association, coalescence, combination, commingling, confederacy, unification **12** amalgamation, intermix-ture, liquefaction **13** agglomeration, confederation

fuss 3 ado, nag **4** carp, fool, fret, fume, pomp, spat, stew, stir, tiff, to-do **5** annoy, cavil, labor, set-to, worry **6** bother, bustle, excite, fidget, flurry, hubbub, hustle, niggle, pester, pother, potter, putter, rattle, scurry, tinker **7** agitate, confuse, dispute, fluster, flutter, nitpick, quarrel, quibble, perturb, trouble, turmoil **8** ceremony **9** agitation, commotion, confusion **10** disconcert, hurly-burly, turbulence **11** disturbance, superfluity **12** perturbation **15** ceremoniousness
Yiddish: 7 tzimmes

fuss over 6 dote on

fussy 4 busy **6** ornate **7** finical, finicky, nervous **8** bustling, critical, exacting **9** assiduous, cluttered, crotchety, demanding, squeamish **10** compulsive, fastidious, meticulous, nitpicking, oldmaidish, particular, scrupulous **11** painstaking, persnickety

fusty 5 moldy, musty, stale **6** foisty, rancid, stuffy **8** obsolete **9** out of date **10** malodorous **12** old fashioned

Futabatei, Shimei
author of: 16 The Drifting (Floating) Cloud

futile 4 idle, vain **5** empty, petty **7** trivial, useless **8** abortive, bootless, nugatory, trifling **9** frivolous, fruitless, valueless, worthless **10** profitless, unavailing **11** ineffective, ineffectual, unimportant **12** unprofitable, unsuccessful **13** insignificant

future 4 hope **5** after, later **6** coming, lat-ter, morrow, offing, to come **7** by-and-by, ensuing, outlook **8** eventual, prospect, tomorrow, ultimate **9** following, hereafter, impending, projected **10** in prospect, subsequent, succeeding **11** anticipated, expectation, opportunity, prospective **12** anticipating
Spanish: 6 manana

Future Shock
author: 12 Alvin Toffler

fuzz 4 down, lint **5** fluff **6** police

fuzzy 3 dim **4** hazy **5** downy, foggy, linty, misty, murky, vague, wooly **6** fluffy, frizzy, woolly **7** blurred, obscure, shadowy, unclear **8** confused **9** pubescent **10** indefinite, indistinct

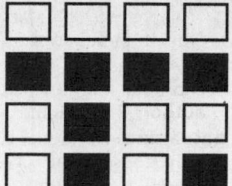  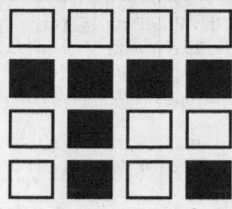

gab 3 jaw, rap, yak **4** blab, chat **5** prate **6** babble, gibber, gossip, jabber, patter **7** baloney, blarney, blather, chatter, prattle **8** chitchat, idle talk, talk idly **10** balderdash **12** conversation

gabble 3 rap **4** blab **5** prate **6** babble, drivel, gossip, jabber **7** blather, chatter, prattle, twaddle **8** babbling, chitchat, idle talk **9** gibbering, jabbering **10** blathering, chattering **14** chitterchatter

gabfest 3 rap **4** chat, talk **7** palaver **8** chitchat **10** discussion **12** conversation **13** confabulation

gable 4 edge, peak, roof, wall **6** detail, dormer, pinion **7** aileron **8** pediment, triangle

Gable, Clark
    real name: 17 William Clark Gable
    wife: 13 Carole Lombard
    nickname: 7 The King
    born: 7 Cadiz OH
    roles: 7 Red Dust **8** Saratoga **10** The Misfits **11** Rhett Butler **15** Gone With the Wind **18** It Happened One Night (Oscar)

Gabo, Naum
    real name: 17 Naum Neemia Pevsner
    born: 6 Russia **7** Brainsk
    founder: 14 Constructivism
    artwork: 6 Column **11** Spiral Theme **16** Sculptural Models **19** Kinetic Construction **24** Variations of Spheric Theme

Gabon Republic
    capital/largest city: 10 Libreville
    others: 4 Oyem **5** Bongo, Kango **6** Mitzic, Moanda, Mouila, Omvane **7** Makokou, Mounana **9** Lambarene **10** Port-Gentil **11** Franceville
    monetary unit: 5 franc **7** centime
    lake: 7 Anengue, Azinguo
    mountain: 5 Mpele **7** Chaillu, Cristal, Mikongo **8** Balaquri, Birougou
    highest point: 8 Iboundji
    river: 4 Como **6** Abanga, Ivindo, Ogooue **7** Ngounie
    sea: 8 Atlantic
    physical feature:
        cape: 5 Lopez
    people: 4 Fang **6** Adouma, Bakota, Bateke, Echira, Okande, Omyene **7** Eshiras **8** Bandjabi, Bapounou
        leader: 3 Mba **5** Bongo
        philanthropist: 16 Albert

Schweitzer
    language: 6 French
    religion: 5 Islam **7** animism **10** Protestant **13** Roman Catholic
    feature:
        tree: 6 okoume
    food: 6 manioc **9** Dika bread

Gabor, Eva
    mother: 5 Jolie
    sister: 5 Magda **6** Zsa Zsa
    born: 7 Hungary **8** Budapest
    roles: 4 Gigi **10** Green Acres **12** My Man Godfrey **13** A Royal Scandal, Forced Landing **15** Youngblood Hawke **18** The Truth About Women **20** The Last Time I Saw Paris

Gabor, Zsa Zsa
    real name: 9 Sari Gabor
    mother: 5 Jolie
    sister: 3 Eva **5** Magda
    husband: 10 Nick Hilton **13** George Sanders
    born: 7 Hungary **8** Budapest
    roles: 4 Lili **11** Moulin Rouge **14** Lovely To Look At **20** The Story of Three Loves

Gaborone, Gaberones
    capital of: 8 Botswana

Gabriel 9 archangel
    means: 8 man of God **11** God is strong
    spoke to: 4 Mary **9** Zacharias, Zechariah

Gad
    father: 5 Jacob
    mother: 6 Zilpah
    brother: 3 Dan **4** Levi **5** Asher, Judah **6** Joseph, Reuben, Simeon **7** Zebulun **8** Benjamin, Issachar, Naphtali
    sister: 5 Dinah
    descendant of: 6 Gadite

gadget 4 tool **6** device, doodad, jigger **7** gimmick, novelty **9** accessory, doohickey **10** attachment **11** contraption, contrivance, thingamabob, thingamajig

Gaea
    also: 2 Ge **4** Gaia
    origin: 5 Greek
    goddess of: 5 earth
    husband: 6 Uranus
    children: 6 Pontus, Titans, Uranus **7** Cyclops, Erinyes **9** mountains **13** Hecatonchires
    son: 6 Nereus **7** Iapetus, Oceanus
    daughter: 4 Rhea **5** Theia **6** Phoebe,

Tethys, Themis **9** Mnemosyne
    corresponds to: 6 Tellus

Gaelic
    language family: 12 Indo-European
    branch: 4 Erse **6** Celtic
    subgroup: 4 Manx **5** Irish **8** Scottish

gaffe 4 goof **5** boner **6** boo-boo **7** blunder **11** impropriety **12** indiscretion
    French: 7 faux pas **9** gaucherie

gag 4 hoax, hush, jest, joke, stop **5** block, choke, heave, retch **6** muffle, muzzle, stifle **7** cloture, foolery, silence, smother **8** stoppage, suppress **9** horseplay, restraint **13** facetiousness

Gaia *see* **4** Gaea

gaiety, gayety 3 fun **4** show **5** mirth **6** frolic, tinsel **7** elation, glitter, jollity, spirits **8** airiness, frippery, trumpery, vivacity **9** amusement, animation, brummagem, gaudiness, merriment, showiness **10** brightness, brilliance, garishness, jauntiness, joyousness, liveliness **11** celebration, merrymaking **12** cheerfulness, colorfulness, exhilaration, sportiveness **13** effervescence, sprightliness

gain, gains 3 add, bag, get, hit, net, win **4** jump, leap, plus, reap **5** bloom, bonus, fetch, glean, put on, reach, wages, yield **6** attain, come to, gather, income, obtain, pick up, profit, return, salary, secure, thrive **7** achieve, acquire, blossom, capture, collect, improve, procure, produce, prosper, recover, revenue **8** addition, arrive at, black ink, dividend, earnings, flourish, increase, overtake, proceeds, winnings **9** accretion, advantage, increment **10** attainment **11** improvement **12** accumulation, compensation, remuneration

Gaines, Ernest J
    author of: 33 The Autobiography of Miss Jane Pittman

gainful 4 rich **6** paying **9** lucrative **10** productive, profitable **12** remunerative

gainfully 8 usefully **10** profitably **11** lucratively **12** productively **14** remuneratively

gain recognition 9 establish

gainsay 4 deny **6** abjure, oppose, refute **7** disavow, dispute **9** repudiate **10** contradict, controvert

Gainsborough, Thomas
    born: 7 England, Sudbury

artwork: 10 The Blue Boy **14** The Morning Walk **15** Mr and Mrs Andrews, The Hon Mrs Graham **16** Viscount Ligonier **26** Peasant Girl Gathering Sticks

gait 4 pace, step, walk **5** tread **6** stride **7** bearing **8** carriage **10** deportment **French: 8** demarche

gaiter 4 boot, shoe, spat, vamp **5** chaps, strad **6** gaskin, hugger, puttee **7** legging **8** cuttikin, overshoe

gala 3 gay **5** grand, party **7** benefit, festive, opulent **8** festival, majestic, splendid **9** festivity, glamorous, sumptuous **10** ceremonial, fancy-dress, glittering **11** celebration, celebratory, magnificent, spectacular, star-studded **French: 4** fete

Galahad
character in: 16 Arthurian romance
father: 8 Lancelot
mother: 6 Elaine
quest: 9 Holy Grail
symbol of: 6 purity **8** nobility

Galatea
form: 6 maiden, statue **8** sea nymph
father: 6 Nereus
mother: 5 Doris
courted by: 10 Polyphemus
lover: 4 Acis
killed: 4 Acis
statue carved by: 9 Pygmalion
brought to life by: 9 Aphrodite
son: 6 Paphos

gale 3 fit **4** blow, gust, stir **6** flurry, squall, tumult, uproar **7** cyclone, tempest **8** eruption; outbreak, outburst **9** agitation, commotion, windstorm

Galileo Galilei
nationality: 7 Italian
birthplace: 4 Pisa
inventor of: 6 sector **11** thermometer
studied: 6 motion **8** pendulum
discovered: 18 Jupiter's satellites
constructed: 9 telescope
formulated: 18 law of falling bodies
author of: 8 Dialogue **10** Discourses **18** The Starry Messenger
condemned for: 6 heresy

gall 3 bug, irk, vex **4** bile, flay, fret, miff, rile **5** anger, annoy, brass, chafe, cheek, gripe, nerve, score, sting, venom **6** abrade, bruise, enrage, harass, injure, nettle, offend, rancor, ruffle, spleen **7** affront, incense, provoke, rub sore **8** acrimony, audacity, boldness, irritate, rudeness, temerity **9** animosity, assurance, displease, excoriate, impudence, insolence, malignity, sauciness, virulence **10** bitterness, brazenness, effrontery, exacerbate, exasperate **11** presumption

gallant 3 fop **4** bold, dude, game, stud **5** blood, brave, dandy, gutsy, noble, suave, swell **6** daring, heroic, kindly, plucky, polite, urbane **7** courtly, dashing, valiant **8** cavalier, fearless, gay

blade, intrepid, mannerly, obliging, resolute, stalwart, valorous, well-bred **9** attentive, courteous, dauntless **10** chivalrous, courageous, thoughtful **11** considerate, gentlemanly, lionhearted **12** stouthearted

gallantries 10 attentions **11** compliments **12** pleasantries

gallantry 4 grit, sand **5** nerve, pluck, valor **6** daring, mettle, spirit **7** bravery, courage, dashing, heroism, prowess, suavity **8** chivalry, courtesy, urbanity **9** derring-do, fortitude, gentility **10** politeness **11** courtliness, intrepidity **12** fearlessness, resoluteness **13** attentiveness, dauntlessness, determination **14** courageousness

gallery 4 stoa **5** salon **6** arcade, loggia, piazza **7** balcony, passage, portico **8** cloister, corridor **9** bleachers, colonnade, mezzanine, triforium **10** ambulatory, grandstand, passageway

Gallia Belgica *see* **7** Belgium

galliano
type: 7 liqueur
origin: 5 Italy
flavor: 5 herbs, spice
color: 6 yellow
with creme de cacao: 14 Golden Cadillac
with rum: 9 Bossa Nova
with vodka: 16 Harvey Wallbanger

gallinule 3 hen **4** coot, fowl, rail, sora **7** moorhen **8** dabchick, hyacinth, rallidae, ricebird, swamphen

Gallipoli
director: 9 Peter Weir
cast: 7 Mark Lee **8** Bill Kerr **9** Mel Gibson **11** Robert Grubb

gallivant, galavant 3 gad **4** kite, roam, rove **5** jaunt, range, stray **6** ramble, travel, wander **7** gallant, meander, traipse, **8** gad about **9** philander

gallon
abbreviation: 3 gal

gallop 3 fly, hie, jog, run **4** bolt, dart, dash, flit, race, rush, scud, skim, trot, whiz **5** bound, hurry, scoot, shoot, speed, whisk **6** hasten, scurry, spring, sprint **7** mad dash, scamper, scuttle, tear off **8** fast clip, fast gait **9** skedaddle

Galloping Ghost
nickname of: 9 Red Grange

gallows 4 rope **5** noose **6** gibbet, halter **8** scaffold

galore 7 aplenty, to spare

galosh, galoche 4 boot, clog, shoe **6** arctic, patten, rubber **8** overshoe

Galsworthy, John
author of: 5 To Let **6** Strife **7** Justice **9** Loyalties **10** In Chancery **11** The Skin Game **13** A Modern Comedy **14** The Forsyte Saga **15** End of the

Chapter **16** The Man of Property **22** Indian Summer of a Forsyte

Galt, John
character in: 13 Atlas Shrugged
author: 7 Ayn Rand

galvanize 4 fire, move, stir, wake **5** rally, rouse, treat **6** arouse, awaken, charge, excite, foment, spur on, thrill **7** inspire, provoke, quicken **8** activate, energize, vitalize **9** electrify, stimulate

galvanizing 7 rousing **8** electric, exciting, spirited **9** inspiring, thrilling **11** stimulating **12** electrifying, soul-stirring

Galveston Giant
nickname of: 11 Jack Johnson

Gamaliel
father: 6 Simeon **8** Pedahzur
grandfather: 6 Hillel
taught: 4 Paul

Gambia
capital/largest city: 6 Banjul **8** Bathurst
others: 5 Bakau, Basse, Mansa **7** Bintang, Brikama, Kuntaur **10** Georgetown
monetary unit: 5 butut, pound **6** dalasi
island: 7 Ft James, St Mary's **8** Elephant
river: 3 Bao **6** Gambia **7** Bintang, Nianija **9** Sandougou
sea: 8 Atlantic
people: 4 Fula, Jola **5** Foula, Wolof **6** Fulani **8** Mandingo, Serahuli **9** Seranuleh
language: 4 Fula **5** Wolof **6** Fulani **7** English, Malinke **8** Mandingo
religion: 5 Islam **10** Protestant **13** Roman Catholic

gambit 4 ploy, ruse **5** feint, trick **6** scheme **8** artifice, maneuver **9** stratagem

gamble 3 bet **4** back, risk **5** flyer, wager **6** chance, hazard, toss-up **7** trust in, venture **9** speculate **11** speculation, uncertainty

gambler 5 dicer, shark, sharp, sport **6** banker, bettor, bookie, dealer, player **7** hustler **8** gamester, hazarder **10** speculator

Gambler, The
author: 16 Fyodor Dostoevsky
character: 6 Astley, Polina **10** The General **11** Mlle Blanche **15** Marquis de Grieux **16** Alexey Ivanovitch **22** Antonida Tarasyevitchev

gambol 3 hop **4** leap **5** bound, caper, frisk, sport, vault **6** bounce, cavort, frolic, prance, spring **7** disport, rollick

game 3 bad, fun **4** golf, halt, lame, lark, play, polo, pool, prey, romp **5** antic, brave, cocky, darts, gimpy, jacks, match, rugby, sport, spree **6** boccie, boxing, daring, frolic, gaiety, gambol, heroic, plucky, quarry, soccer, spunky, squash, tennis **7** archery, bowling, contest, crooked, croquet, curling, fencing, frisbee, gallant, hawking, hunting, hurling, jai alai, limping, pastime, tourney, valiant, willing **8** baseball, crippled, deformed, disabled, fearless, football, handball, hobbling, intrepid, lacrosse, ping pong, resolute, skittles, spirited, valorous, wild fowl **9** amusement, badminton, billiards, dauntless, diversion, festivity, merriment, wrestling **10** basketball, courageous, determined, horseshoes, ice-skating, lawn tennis, recreation, tournament, volleyball **11** competition, distraction, merrymaking, racquetball, table tennis, unflinching **12** shuffleboard **13** entertainment, incapacitated, roller-skating

board game: 4 Clue, Life, ludo **5** chess **7** Othello **8** checkers, cribbage, dominoes, draughts, fanorona, Monopoly, Scrabble **10** backgammon **14** Trivial Pursuit

 Chinese: 6 Ma-jong, wei ch'i **7** mahjong **8** Mah-jongg
 Egyptian: 5 Senat
 Indian: 7 pachisi **8** parchesi, shatranj **9** ashtapada, parcheesi **10** shaturanga
 Japanese: 2 Go **3** I-go **5** Sho-gi
 Korean: 5 Nyout, Pa-tok
 Swedish: 6 tablut

card game: 3 loo, war **4** brag, fish, skat, vint **5** ombre, poker, rummy, tarot, whist **6** boston, bridge, casino, chemmy, écarté, euchre, go fish, hearts, memory, piquet, pocher **7** bezique, canasta, concan, old maid, plafond, primero **8** baccarat, conquian, cribbage, gin rummy, napoleon, patience, pinochle, slapjack **9** blackjack, pelmanism, solitaire, spoil five, twenty-one **11** chemin de fer, crazy eights **13** concentration **14** contract bridge **16** beggar-my-neighbor, trente et quarante

gamete 3 egg **4** ovum **5** sperm **6** oocyte, zygote **8** germ cell, oosphere **12** spermatozoan, spermatozoon

Gamow, George
 field: 7 physics **9** cosmology
 proponent of: 13 big bang theory
 deciphered: 11 genetic code
 proposed: 13 quantum theory
 established: 17 Gamow-Teller theory

Gamp, Sarah
 character in: 16 Martin Chuzzlewit
 author: 7 Dickens

gamut 3 ken **5** reach, scope, sweep **6** extent **7** compass, purview

Gandhi
 director: 19 Richard Attenborough
 cast: 11 Ben Kingsley **13** Candice Bergen
 Oscar for: 5 actor (Kingsley) **7** picture

gang 3 mob **4** band, body, crew, pack, pals, ring, team **5** chums, crowd,

flock, group, party, relay, shift, squad, troop **6** clique, outfit **7** buddies, company, coterie, cronies, friends, phalanx **8** comrades **9** coworkers, neighbors **10** associates, classmates, companions, contingent, detachment **11** schoolmates

gangster 4 goon, hood, thug **5** crook, felon, tough **6** bandit, gunman **7** hoodlum, mafioso, mobster, ruffian **8** criminal, hooligan **9** racketeer

Gant, Eugene
 character in: 17 Look Homeward Angel, Of Time and the River
 author: 5 Wolfe

Ganymede
 also: 9 Catamitus
 cupbearer of: 4 gods

gap 3 cut **4** gash, hole, rent, rift, slit, slot, void **5** abyss, break, chasm, chink, cleft, crack, gulch, gully, notch, pause **6** breach, canyon, cavity, divide, hiatus, lacuna, ravine, recess, vacuum, valley **7** crevice, fissure, interim, opening **8** aperture, crevasse, fracture, interval, puncture **9** disparity, interlude **10** difference, divergence **12** intermission, interruption

gape 4 gasp, gawk, gaze, ogle, part, peer, yawn **5** split, stare **6** cleave, expand **7** fly open **8** wide open, separate **10** rubberneck

gaping 6 astare **7** gawking, staring, yawning **13** rubbernecking

garb 3 rig **4** gear, gown, robe, suit, togs **5** dress, getup, habit **6** attire, finery, livery, outfit **7** apparel, clothes, costume, raiment, uniform, vesture **8** clothing, garments, vestment, wardrobe **9** trappings **11** habiliments

garbage 4 dirt, junk **5** offal, swill, trash, waste **6** debris, litter, refuse **7** carrion, rubbish **9** sweepings

garbage in, garbage out 4 GIGO
 term in: 9 computers

garble 5 mix up **6** jumble **7** confuse, distort **8** fragment

Garbo, Greta
 real name: 21 Greta Louisa Gustaffson
 born: 6 Sweden **9** Stockholm
 roles: 4 Love **7** Camille **8** Conquest, Mata Hari **9** Ninotchka **10** Grand Hotel **12** Anna Christie, Anna Karenina **13** Queen Cristina, Two-Faced Woman **14** The Painted Veil **16** Flesh and the Devil

Garcia Lorca, Federico
 author of: 5 Yerma **12** Blood Wedding, Gypsy Ballads **19** House of Bernarda Alba

Garcia Marquez, Gabriel
 author of: 9 Leaf Storm **23** The Autumn of the Patriarch **25** One Hundred Years of Solitude

garcon 3 boy **6** waiter **7** servant

garden 4 Eden, lawn, plot, yard **7** Arcadia **8** paradise **10** Gethsemane
 type: 4 herb, rock, rose **5** truck **6** flower, formal **7** kitchen **9** botanical, vegetable

gardenia
 varieties: 5 crape **9** butterfly

Garden of the Finzi Continis, The
 director: 14 Vittorio De Sica
 author: 14 Giorgio Bassani
 cast: 10 Fabio Testi **11** Romolo Valli **12** Helmut Berger **14** Dominique Sanda **15** Lino Capolicchio
 Oscar: 11 foreign film

Garden of the West
 nickname of: 6 Kansas

garden party
 French: 13 fete champetre

gardens
 god of: 9 Vertumnus
 goddess of: 5 Venus

Garden State
 nickname of: 9 New Jersey

garden variety 5 plain **6** common, simple **7** regular **8** everyday, familiar, ordinary **11** commonplace

Gardner, Ava
 husband: 9 Artie Shaw **12** Frank Sinatra, Mickey Rooney
 born: 12 Smithfield NC
 roles: 7 Mogambo **8** Show Boat **9** Mayerling, Naked Maja **10** On the Beach **15** The Sun Also Rises **18** Snows of Kilimanjaro **19** The Barefoot Contessa, The Night of the Iguana

Gardner, Erle Stanley
 character: 9 Paul Drake **10** Perry Mason **11** Della Street **14** Hamilton Burger
 also wrote as: 6 A A Fair

Gardner, John
 author of: 7 Grendel **12** October Light **14** Nickel Mountain, The Art of Living, The King's Indian **17** Michelsson's Ghosts **20** The Sunlight Dialogues, The Wreckage of Agathon

Gareth
 character in: 16 Arthurian romance

Garfield, James Abram
 presidential rank: 9 twentieth
 party: 10 Republican
 state represented: 2 OH
 defeated: 3 (Neal) Dow **6** (James Baird) Weaver, (John Wolcott) Phelps **7** (Winfield Scott) Hancock
 vice president: 6 (Chester Alan) Arthur
 cabinet:
  state: 6 (James Gillespie) Blaine
  treasury: 6 (William) Windom
  war: 7 (Robert Todd) Lincoln
  attorney general: 8 (Isaac Wayne) MacVeagh
  navy: 4 (William Henry) Hunt
  postmaster general: 5 (Thomas Lemuel) James

interior: 8 (Samuel Jordan) Kirkwood
born: 2 OH **6** Orange **8** log cabin
died: 9 Elberon NJ
died by: 13 assassination
buried: 11 Cleveland OH
education:
seminary: **6** Geauga
college: **5** Hiram (Eclectic Institute) **8** Williams
studied: **3** law
religion: 17 Disciples of Christ
political career: 8 US Senate (declined seat) **11** state Senate **24** US House of Representatives
civilian career: 6 lawyer **7** teacher **11** lay preacher
military service: 6 US Army **8** Civil War **12** major general
notable events of lifetime/term:
exposure of: **15** Star Route frauds
father: 7 Abraham
mother: 5 Eliza (Ballou)
siblings: 4 Mary **5** James **6** Thomas **9** Mehitabel
wife: 8 Lucretia (Rudolph)
nickname: **5** Crete
children: 4 Mary **5** Abram, Eliza **6** Edward **12** James Rudolph **13** Harry Augustus, Irvin McDowell

Garfield, John
real name: 15 Julius Garfinkle
born: 9 New York NY
roles: 6 Juarez **10** Humoresque **11** Body and Soul **26** The Postman Always Rings Twice

Gargamelle
character in: 22 Gargantua and Pantagruel
author: 8 Rabelais

Gargantua and Pantagruel
author: 16 Francois Rabelais
character: 7 Panurge **10** Gargamelle, Grangosier, Picrochole **23** Frere Jean des Entommeures

gargantuan 4 huge, vast **5** great **7** hulking, immense, mammoth, massive, titanic **8** colossal, enormous, gigantic, lubberly, towering **9** herculean, monstrous, overgrown **10** prodigious, stupendous, tremendous **11** elephantine **13** amplitudinous

Gargery, Joe
character in: 17 Great Expectations
author: 7 Dickens

garish 4 loud **5** cheap, gaudy, showy **6** brassy, bright, flashy, tawdry, tinsel, vulgar **7** blatant, glaring **9** flaunting, obtrusive **11** pretentious **12** ostentatious **13** overelaborate

garland 3 bay, lei **4** halo **5** crown **6** corona, diadem, fillet, laurel, wreath **7** chaplet, circlet, coronet, festoon **8** chapbook, headband, treasury **9** anthology **10** collection **11** florilegium

Garland, Hamlin

author of: 18 Main-Travelled Roads **20** Rose of Dutcher's Coolly

Garland, Judy
real name: 11 Frances Gumm
husband: 7 Sid Luft **16** Vincente Minnelli
daughter: 9 Lorna Luft **12** Liza Minnelli
costar: 12 Mickey Rooney
born: 13 Grand Rapids MN
roles: 7 Dorothy **11** A Star Is Born, Babes in Arms **12** Easter Parade **13** The Wizard of Oz **14** The Harvey Girls **15** A Child Is Waiting, Meet Me in St Louis

garlic
botanical name: 13 Allium sativum
origin: 4 Asia **13** Mediterranean
charm against: 7 poverty, witches **13** whooping cough
use: 4 fish, fowl, meat **5** salad **10** vegetables **13** Italian dishes, salad dressing
varieties: 4 crow, hog's, wild **5** bear's, false, field, giant, grace, mouse, stag's, sweet **6** levant **7** serpent, society, Spanish, striped **8** daffodil, oriental **11** great-headed, round-headed **16** fragrant-flowered

Garm
origin: 12 Scandinavian
form: 8 watchdog
watches over: 3 Hel
location: 8 Niflheim

garment, garments 4 garb, gear, togs **5** dress, habit **6** attire, outfit **7** apparel, clothes, costume, raiment **8** clothing, vestment **10** habiliment

garner 4 reap **5** amass, hoard **6** gather, heap up **7** acquire, collect **8** assemble **10** accumulate

Garner, James
real name: 15 James Baumgarner
born: 8 Norman OK
roles: 8 Maverick, Sayonara **11** Jim Rockford **12** Bret Maverick, Hour of the Gun **13** Darby's Rangers, Rockford Files **14** Murphy's Romance, Victor Victoria **23** Support Your Local Sheriff **25** The Americanization of Emily

garnet
varieties: 6 syrope **9** almandite, demantoid, hessonite, rhodolite **12** grossularite
month: 7 January

garnish 4 deck, gild, trim **5** adorn, array **6** bedeck, doll up, set off **7** festoon, furbish, smarten **8** beautify, decorate, emblazon, ornament, spruce up, trimming **9** adornment, embellish, embroider **10** decoration **13** embellishment

garret 4 loft **5** attic

garrison 4 fort **5** guard **6** patrol, secure **7** battery, bivouac, brigade, platoon, station **8** division, regiment,

squadron **10** detachment, escadrille **13** fortification

garrulity 8 verbiage **9** loquacity, prosiness, verbosity, wordiness **13** talkativeness

garrulous 5 gabby, windy, wordy **6** chatty **7** gossipy, prating, verbose, voluble **8** babbling, chattery, effusive **9** prattling, talkative **10** loquacious

Garry Moore Show, The
cast: 9 Allen Funt, Denise Lor, John Byner, Ken Carson **11** Chuck McCann, Marion Lorne **12** Carol Burnett, Durward Kirby, Jackie Vernon, Pete Barbutti **13** Dorothy Loudon

Garson, Greer
born: 7 Ireland **10** County Down
roles: 10 Mrs Miniver (Oscar) **11** Madame Curie **12** Her Twelve Men **13** Mrs Parkington, Random Harvest **14** Goodbye Mr Chips **16** That Forsyte Woman **17** Pride and Prejudice **19** Sunrise at Campobello

gas 4 fuel, fume **5** vapor **6** petrol **7** essence

gascon 7 boaster, bragger, egotist **8** blowhard, braggart **9** swaggerer **11** braggadocio

gasconade 4 brag, crow **5** boast **7** bravado **8** boasting **11** braggadocio

gash 4 hack, rend, rent, slit, tear **5** carve, cleft, crack, lance, slash, slice, split, wound **6** cleave, incise, pierce **7** dissect, fissure, quarter **8** incision, lacerate

Gaskell, Elizabeth
author of: 4 Ruth **8** Cranford **10** Mary Barton **13** North and South **24** The Life of Charlotte Bronte

Gaslight
director: 11 George Cukor
cast: 10 Terry Moore **12** Charles Boyer **13** Dame May Whitty, Ingrid Bergman **14** Angela Lansbury **15** Halliwell Hobbes

Gasoline Alley
creator: 9 Bill Perry, Frank King **10** Dick Moores
character: 3 Eve **4** Adam, Hope **6** Clovia, Gideon, Nubbin **7** Chipper, Gabriel **10** Walt Wallet
wife: 14 Phyllis Blossom
children: 4 Judy **5** Corky **7** Skeezix
daughter-in-law: 9 Nina Clock
dog: 5 Punky

gasp 4 gulp, pant, puff **5** blurt **6** suck in, wheeze **10** vociferate

gastronome 7 epicure, gourmet **9** bon vivant

gastronomy 9 epicurism

gastropod, gasteropod 4 slug **5** cowry, snail, whelk **6** cowrie, limpet, nerite **7** abalone, mollusk **8** univalve

gate 3 tap **5** crowd, house, valve **6** por- tal, sluice, spigot **7** doorway

8 audience, hatchway **9** turnstile **10** attendance

gateau 4 cake **7** dessert

gatekeeper 5 guard **6** porter **7** St. Peter **8** watchman

Gates, Horatio
    served in: **16** Revolutionary War **18** French and Indian War
    battle: **6** Camden **8** Saratoga
    defeated: **8** Burgoyne
    defeated by: **10** Cornwallis

gateway 4 adit **5** entry **6** access, portal **7** doorway, opening **8** entrance, entryway **10** passageway

Gath 14 Philistine city

gather 4 fold, mass **5** amass, group, infer, learn, pleat, shirr, stack **6** assume, deduce, heap up, muster, pile up, pucker, ruffle **7** cluster, collect, convene, marshal, observe **8** assemble, conclude **9** stockpile **10** accumulate, congregate, understand **11** concentrate

gathering 3 mob **4** gang, pack **5** bunch, crowd, crush, drove, flock, horde, party, press **6** throng **7** company, meeting, roundup, turnout **8** assembly, conclave **9** concourse, multitude **10** assemblage, collection, conference, convention **11** aggregation, convergence, convocation **12** accumulation, congregation **13** concentration

gather together 4 herd **5** amass, hoard, rally **6** muster **7** collate, collect, compile, marshal, round up, sweep up **8** assemble, shepherd **9** aggregate, stockpile **10** accumulate, congregate

Gatling, Richard Jordan
    nationality: **8** American
    inventor of: **10** machine gun **16** steam-powered plow

gatophobia
    fear of: **4** cats

gauche 5 inept **6** clumsy, oafish **7** awkward, boorish, ill-bred, uncouth **8** bungling, tactless **9** inelegant, maladroit, tasteless, unrefined **10** blundering, uncultured, ungraceful, unmannerly, unpolished **11** proletarian **13** ungentlemanly

gaucherie 5 gaffe **7** blunder, faux pas **11** impropriety **12** indiscretion

Gaudeamus igitur 22 Let us therefore be joyful

gaudy 4 loud, sham **5** cheap, showy, vivid **6** flashy, flimsy, garish, tawdry, tinsel, vulgar **7** glaring, intense **8** colorful, dazzling, lustrous, striking **9** brilliant, sparkling, tasteless, worthless **10** bespangled, glittering **11** pretentious **12** ostentatious

gauge, gage 4 rate, size **5** guess, judge, meter **6** assess **7** adjudge, measure **8** appraise, estimate, evalu-

ate, standard **9** ascertain, calculate, criterion, yardstick **11** measurement
    type: **4** ring **5** bevel

Gauguin, Paul Eugene Henri
    born: **5** Paris **6** France
    artwork: **9** Nevermore **12** The Tahitians **13** The White Horse **15** The Yellow Christ **18** Horsemen on the Beach **23** The Vision after the Sermon (Jacob Wrestling with the Angel) **25** Be in Love and You Will Be Happy **26** The Spirit of the Dead Watching **36** Where Do We Come From? Who Are We? Where Do We Go?
    book: **6** Noa Noa

Gaul see **6** France

gaunt 4 bony, grim, lank, lean, slim, thin **5** bleak, lanky, spare **6** barren, meager, skinny, wasted **7** haggard, pinched, scraggy, scrawny, slender, spindly, starved **8** deserted, desolate, forsaken, raw-boned, skeletal, withered **9** emaciated, shriveled **10** cadaverous, forbidding **14** spindle-shanked

Gauss, Carl Friedrich
    field: **7** physics **9** astronomy **11** mathematics
    nationality: **6** German
    worked in: **9** magnetism **11** electricity **12** number theory
    named for him: **9** Gauss's Law

Gautier, Marguerite
    character in: **7** Camille
    author: **5** Dumas (fils)

Gautier, Theophile
    author of: **6** La Peri **7** Giselle **8** Albertus **11** Young France **13** Emaux et Camees **16** Enamels and Cameos **20** Mademoiselle de Maupin, The Romance of the Mummy
    doctrine: **14** Art for art's sake

gauzy 5 filmy, sheer **6** flimsy, sleazy **10** diaphanous **11** translucent, transparent

gave up 4 quit **5** ceded **7** dropped, forsook, yielded **8** forswore, resigned **9** abandoned, abdicated, forfeited, renounced **11** surrendered **12** discontinued, relinquished

Gawain
    character in: **16** Arthurian romance
    opponent: **11** Green Knight

gawk 4 gape, gaze, peer **10** rubberneck

gawky 6 clumsy, klutzy **7** awkward, lumpish **8** bungling, fumbling, lubberly, ungainly, unwieldy **9** all thumbs, graceless, ham-fisted, ham-handed, maladroit **10** blundering, ungraceful

gay 3 fun **4** airy, glad **5** happy, jolly, merry, showy, sunny, vivid **6** blithe, bright, cheery, elated, frisky, genial, jaunty, jocose, jovial, joyful, joyous, lively, social **7** buoyant, chipper, coltish, dashing, festive, gleeful, glowing, intense, jocular, playful, smiling, wag-

gish **8** animated, cheerful, colorful, exultant, gladsome, humorous, jubilant, lustrous, skittish, spirited, splendid, sportive, volatile **9** brilliant, convivial, frivolous, hilarious, rejoicing, sparkling, sprightly, sumptuous, vivacious **10** flamboyant, frolicsome, glittering, homosexual, insouciant, theatrical, variegated **12** effervescent, lighthearted, multicolored

Gay, John
    author of dialogue/lyrics for: **15** The Beggar's Opera

Gay, Walter
    character in: **12** Dombey and Son
    author: **7** Dickens

gay blade 3 fop **4** beau **5** blade, dandy **7** playboy **8** cavalier **9** ladies' man **12** boulevardier, man-about-town

Gay Divorcee, The
    director: **12** Mark Sandrich
    cast: **10** Alice Brady, Erik Rhodes **11** Betty Grable, Fred Astaire **12** Ginger Rogers **19** Edward Everett Horton
    song: **11** Continental, Night and Day

Gay-Lussac, Joseph
    field: **7** physics **9** chemistry
    nationality: **6** French
    discovered: **24** law of combining gas volumes
    invented: **10** hydrometer

Gaynor, Mitzi
    real name: **20** Franceska Mitzi Gerber
    husband: **8** Jack Bean
    born: **9** Chicago IL
    roles: **8** Les Girls **10** Golden Girl **12** Anything Goes, South Pacific **14** The Joker Is Wild **32** There's No Business Like Show Business

gaze 3 eye **4** gape, ogle, peek, peer, scan **5** glare, lower, stare, study, watch **6** behold, glance, glower, peruse, regard, survey **7** examine, inspect, observe, witness **8** look long, pore over, scrutiny **10** rubberneck, scrutinize **11** contemplate

gaze at 4 view **5** watch **6** behold, look at **7** stare at **8** look upon **11** contemplate

gazpacho 4 soup
    ingredients: **6** onions **7** peppers **8** tomatoes **9** cucumbers

Gazza Ladra, La
    also: **17** The Thieving Magpie
    opera by: **7** Rossini

Ge see **4** Gaea

gear 3 cam, rig **4** duds, garb, togs **5** dress, tools **6** attire, outfit, tackle, things **7** apparel, clothes, rigging **8** clothing, cogwheel, flywheel, garments, material, property **9** apparatus, equipment, trappings **10** belongings, implements **11** accessories, instruments **12** contrivances **13** accoutrements, paraphernalia

Geb
    also: **3** Keb

origin: 8 Egyptian
god of: 5 earth
daughter: 4 Isis
son: 6 Osiris
sister: 3 Nut

Geer, Will
born: 11 Frankfort IN
roles: 7 Grandpa **10** The Waltons **11** In Cold Blood

Gehenna 4 hell

Gehrig, Lou (Henry Louis)
nickname: 9 Iron Horse
sport: 8 baseball
position: 9 first base
team: 14 New York Yankees

Geist 4 mind **6** spirit

gelatin 4 agar, glue **5** aspic, gelee, jelly **6** glutin, pectin **7** protein, sericin

gelatinize 3 set **4** jell **7** congeal, stiffen, thicken **9** coagulate

gelatinous 7 colloid, viscous **8** muculent **9** jelly-like

geld 5 alter **8** castrate **10** emasculate

gelid 3 icy **6** frigid, frozen **8** freezing

gem 4 dear, doll, rock **5** beaut, bijou, jewel, peach, prize **6** marvel, wonder **8** treasure
type: 4 jade, opal, ruby, sard **5** agate, amber, beryl, coral, pearl, topaz **6** garnet, pyrope, quartz, spinel, zircon **7** apatite, cat's-eye, citrine, diamond, emerald, jadeite, kunzite, olivine, peridot **8** amethyst, corundum, feldspar, hematite, lazurite, nephrite, sapphire, steatite, sunstone **9** almandite, amazonite, carnelian, demantoid, enstatite, fibrolite, malachite, moonstone, morganite, rhodolite, scapolite, spodumene, tiger's-eye, turquoise **10** aquamarine, bloodstone, chalcedony, hessionite, rose quartz, tourmaline **11** alexandrite, chrysoberyl, chrysocolla, chrysoprase, lapis lazuli, rock crystal, topaz quartz **12** grossularite

Gemini
symbol: 5 twins
planet: 7 Mercury
rules: 14 communications
born: 3 May **4** June
twins: 6 Castor, Pollux

Gemini Contenders, The
author: 12 Robert Ludlum

Gem State
nickname of: 5 Idaho

gemutlich 4 easy **9** agreeable, congenial, simpatico **11** comfortable

gendarme 9 policeman

gender 3 sex **4** kind, male, sort, type **5** class **6** female, neuter **8** feminine **9** masculine

genealogy 4 line **5** birth, house, stock **7** lineage **8** ancestry, pedigree **9** parentage **10** derivation, extraction

Gene Autry Show, The
cast: 10 Pat Buttram

horse: 8 Champion
theme song: 20 Back in the Saddle Again

general 5 basic, broad, usual, vague **6** common, normal, public, wonted **7** blanket, current, generic, inexact, natural, overall, popular, regular, typical **8** everyday, frequent, habitual, ordinary, pandemic, sweeping **9** customary, extensive, imprecise, panoramic, prevalent, universal, worldwide **10** accustomed, collective, ecumenical, prevailing, widespread **11** unspecified **12** conventional, nonexclusive, nontechnical **13** comprehensive, miscellaneous

General Electric Theater
host: 12 Ronald Reagan

general idea 4 gist **5** drift, tenor **6** effect, import **7** purport **10** impression **11** implication

generality 6 cliche, truism **9** platitude **12** universality **14** collectiveness **17** miscellaneousness **18** indiscriminateness

generalization 3 law **5** axion **7** bromide **9** inference, statement

generalize 5 infer, judge **8** conclude

generally 5 often **6** always, mainly, mostly **7** as a rule, chiefly, largely, usually **9** currently, typically **10** frequently, habitually, ordinarily, repeatedly **11** extensively, principally, universally

general/military leader
American:
Revolutionary War: 3 (Light Horse Harry) Lee **5** Allen, Barry, Gates, Jones, Wayne **6** Arnold, Greene, Marion, Morgan **10** Washington
War of 1812: 4 Hull **5** Perry, Scott **7** Decatur
Mexican War: 5 Scott **6** Kearny
Civil War: 3 Lee **5** Early, Grant, Meade **6** Thomas, (JEB) Stuart **7** Forrest, Pickett, Sherman, (Stonewall) Jackson **8** Farragut, Sheridan **9** McClellan **10** Beauregard, Longstreet
Indian Wars: 6 Custer **7** Houston **10** Crazy Horse
WWI: 4 Sims **8** Mitchell, Pershing
WWII: 4 King **5** Clark **6** Arnold, Halsey, Nimitz, Patton **7** Bradley, Merrill **8** Marshall, Stilwell **9** Chennault, Doolittle, MacArthur **10** Eisenhower, Wainwright
Korean War: 5 Clark **9** MacArthur
Vietnam War: 6 Abrams **12** Westmoreland
Gulf War: 6 Powell **11** Schwarzkopf
British: 4 Byng, Haig, Howe, Slim **5** Wolfe **6** French, Gordon, Harris, Nelson, Wavell **7** Allenby, Clinton, Dowding, Wingate **8** Braddock, Burgoyne, Cromwell, Jellicoe, Lawrence

9 Alexander, Kitchener **10** Cornwallis, Montgomery, Wellington **11** Marlborough, Mountbatten
Carthagenian: 8 Hannibal **13** Hamilcar Barca
French: 3 Ney **4** Foch **5** Murat **6** Giraud, Joffre, Petain, Roland **7** Nivelle **8** De Gaulle, Montcalm, Napoleon **9** Lafayette **10** Bernadotte
German: 5 Kluck **6** Moltke, Paulus, Rommel, Scheer **7** Blucher, Goering, Tirpitz **8** Bismarck, Goebbels, Guderian **9** Rundstedt **10** Falkenhayn, Hindenburg, Kesselring, Ludendorff, Schlieffen **17** Frederick the Great
Israeli: 5 Dayan
Japanese: 10 Tojo Hideki **15** Yamamoto Isoroku
Macedonian: 7 Ptolemy **8** Philip II **9** Alexander (the Great)
Norman: 7 William (the Conqueror)
Roman: 5 Sulla **6** Brutus, Pompey, Seneca, Trajan **7** Crassus, Hadrian, Lepidus **8** Gracchus, Octavian (Caesar Augustus), Tiberius **9** Vespasian **10** Flamininus, Mark Antony **11** Gaius Marius **12** Julius Caesar **15** Cassius Longinus, Scipio Africanus **18** Tarquinius Superbus
Russian: 6 Zhukov **7** Kutuzov, Voronov **8** Brusilov, Kerensky, Kornilov, Samsonov **9** Bagration **10** Timoshenko, Vasilevsky

generate 4 bear, coin, form, make, sire **5** beget, breed, cause, frame, spawn, yield **6** create, evolve, father, induce, invent **7** develop, fashion, produce **8** contrive, engender, fructify, occasion **9** construct, fabricate, fecundate, fertilize, institute, originate, procreate, propagate, reproduce **10** effectuate, impregnate **11** proliferate

generation 3 kin **4** clan, line, race **5** breed, house, issue, stock, tribe **6** family, growth, strain **7** genesis, lineage, progeny **8** breeding, creation **9** begetting, causation, evolution, formation, offspring **10** production **11** development, engendering, origination, procreation, propagation **12** impregnation, reproduction **13** fertilization, proliferation

generic 6 common **7** general **8** sweeping **9** universal **10** collective **11** generalized, unspecified **12** nonexclusive **13** comprehensive **14** nonrestrictive

generosity 6 bounty **7** charity **8** altruism, courtesy, kindness, largesse **9** abundance, nobleness **10** liberality **11** benevolence, hospitality, magnanimity

generous 5 ample, large, lofty, noble **6** humane, lavish **7** copious, liberal **8** abundant, effusive, obliging, princely, prodigal **9** bounteous, bountiful, honorable, plenteous, plentiful, plethoric, unselfish, unstinted **10** altruistic, beneficent, benevolent, bighearted, charitable, freehanded, free-giving, high-minded, hospitable, munificent, open-handed, ungrudging, unstinting **11** considerate, extravagant, magnanimous, overflowing **12** humanitarian, largehearted, unrestricted **13** accommodating, philanthropic

genesis 4 rise, root **5** birth **6** origin **8** creation **9** begetting, beginning, inception **10** generation **11** engendering **12** commencement

geneticist
American: **5** Temin **6** Morgan, Muller

genetics
science of: **8** heredity
researcher: **6** Mendel

Genghis Khan
also: **11** Jenghiz Khan
name means: **14** universal ruler
position: **13** Mongol emperor
defeated: **6** Russia **10** Chin empire
occupied: **6** Peking

genial 3 gay **4** glad, kind, warm **5** civil, happy, jolly, merry, sunny **6** bright, cheery, hearty, jaunty, jocund, jovial, joyful, joyous, kindly, lively, social **7** affable, amiable, chipper, cordial, festive **8** cheerful, friendly, gracious, mirthful, pleasant, sociable **9** agreeable, congenial, convivial, courteous, expansive, sparkling, vivacious **10** neighborly **12** lighthearted **13** companionable

geniality 10 affability, cordiality **11** sociability **12** conviviality, friendliness **13** expansiveness

genius 3 ace, wit **4** bent, gift, mind, whiz **5** brain, flair, knack **6** expert, master, wisdom **7** faculty, insight, prodigy **8** aptitude, judgment, penchant, sagacity, wizardry **9** ingenuity, intuition, invention **10** mastermind, perception, proclivity, propensity **11** imagination, percipience **12** intelligence, predilection **13** understanding

Genius, The
author: **15** Theodore Dreiser

genius loci 16 guardian of a place

genre 4 kind, sort, type **5** breed, class, genus, group, order, style **6** school **7** fashion, species, variety **8** category, division **11** description **14** classification

genteel 4 tony **5** civil, elite, ritzy, swank, swell **6** modish, poised, polite, urbane **7** courtly, elegant, high-hat, refined, stylish **8** cultured, decorous, ladylike, mannerly, polished, wellbred **9** courteous, high-class, hightoned, patrician **10** cultivated, wellspoken **11** fashionable, gentlemanly, highfalutin, over-refined, pretentious **12** aristocratic, silk-stocking, thoroughbred

gentian 8 Gentiana
varieties: **5** blind, green, horse **6** alpine, bottle, closed, Sierra, yellow

7 crested, fringed, prairie, spurred **8** Catesby's, soapwort, stemless **9** Mendocino **10** pine barren

gentil 4 kind **5** noble **6** gentle

gentile
Yiddish: **3** goy
man: **7** shegetz
woman: **6** shiksa

gentility 6 polish **7** decorum, suavity **8** breeding, chivalry, civility, courtesy, urbanity **9** gallantry, propriety, punctilio **10** refinement **11** cultivation, savoir-faire **12** mannerliness

gentle 3 low **4** calm, easy, kind, meek, mild, soft, tame **5** balmy, bland, light, quiet **6** benign, broken, docile, kindly, placid, serene, slight, smooth, tender **7** lenient, pacific, subdued **8** harmless, merciful, moderate, peaceful, tolerant, tranquil **9** indulgent, temperate, tractable **10** manageable, thoughtful, untroubled **11** considerate, sympathetic **12** domesticated **13** compassionate, tenderhearted
French: **6** gentil

gentleman 3 don, guy, man, one **4** chap, gent **5** swell **6** fellow, person, squire **7** esquire, hidalgo **8** cavalier **9** caballero, chevalier, patrician **10** aristocrat, individual

Gentleman Jim
nickname of: **12** James Corbett

gentlemanly 6 polite **7** courtly, gallant, refined **8** cultured, decorous, mannerly, polished, well-bred **9** courteous, dignified **10** cultivated

Gentleman's Agreement
director: **9** Elia Kazan
based on novel by: **12** Laura Z Hobson
cast: **10** Anne Revere **11** Celeste Holm, Gregory Peck **12** John Garfield **14** Dorothy McGuire
Oscar for: **7** picture **17** supporting actress (Holm)

Gentlemen Prefer Blondes
author: **9** Anita Loos

gentleness 8 calmness, docility, mildness, serenity, tameness **10** compassion, tenderness **12** mercifulness, peacefulness, tractability

gentle wind 4 waft **6** breath, breeze, zephyr

gently 6 easily, kindly, meekly, mildly, softly, tamely **7** amiably, lightly **8** benignly, placidly, smoothly, tenderly **9** gradually **10** delicately, moderately, pleasantly, soothingly **15** compassionately, sympathetically

gentry 5 elite **7** society **8** nobility **10** blue bloods, gentlefolk **11** aristocracy, aristocrats

genuflect 4 bend **6** kowtow

genuine 4 open, pure, real, true **5** frank, naive, plain, solid **6** actual, candid, hon- est, proven, simple **7** art-

less, earnest, natural, sincere **8** bona fide, sterling, true-blue **9** authentic, guileless, heartfelt, ingenuous, simon-pure, unalloyed, veritable **10** legitimate, unaffected **13** unadulterated **15** straightforward, unsophisticated

genuineness 7 honesty **9** frankness, sincerity **10** candidness, simplicity **11** artlessness **13** guilelessness **14** unaffectedness **19** straightforwardness

genus 4 kind, sort, type **5** class, group **7** variety **8** category, division **14** classification

geologist
British: **4** Hall
German: **6** Werner
Scottish: **6** Hutton

geoponics 7 tillage **8** agronomy **9** husbandry **10** agronomics **11** agriculture, cultivation

George Burns and Gracie Allen Show, The
character: **9** Mr Beasley (Mailman) **11** Harry Morton **13** Blanche Morton
theme song: **8** Love Nest

Georgetown
capital of: **6** Guyana

Georgia (former Soviet Union)
capital/largest city: **7** Tbilisi
others: **6** Batumi **7** Kutaisi, Rustavi, Sukhumi
division: **7** Ossetia **8** Abkhazia, Adzharia
head of state: **9** president
government: **8** republic
monetary unit: **5** ruble
mountain: **8** Caucasus
river: **4** Kura **5** Rioni
sea: **5** Black
people: **5** Azeri **7** Russian **8** Armenian, Georgian, Ossetian **9** Abkhazian
language: **8** Georgian
religion: **14** Georgian Church **15** Russian Orthodox

Georgia (US)
abbreviation: **2** GA
nickname: **5** Peach **7** Cracker **21** Empire State of the South
capital/largest city: **7** Atlanta
others: **4** Rome **5** Jesup, Macon **6** Albany, Athens, Dalton, Plains, Sparta **7** Augusta, Conyers, Cordele, Decatur, Griffen, Vidalia **8** Columbus, LaGrange, Marietta, Moultrie, Savannah, Valdosta, Waycross **9** Brunswick **11** College Park, Gainesville, Thomasville **13** Andersonville
college: **4** Tift **5** Clark, Emory, Paine **6** Mercer **7** Atlanta, Spelman **8** Wesleyan **9** Morehouse **10** Agnes Scott **11** Georgia Tech
explorer: **15** James Oglethorpe
feature: **16** Little White House
amusement park: **19** Six Flags Over Georgia
national cemetery: **13** Anderson-

ville

national monument: 8 Ocmulgee **11** Fort Pulaski **13** Fort Frederica

tribe: 5 Creek, Guale, Yuchi **6** Chiaha, Oconee, Uchean **7** Yamasee **8** Hitchiti

people: 6 Ty Cobb **7** cracker **10** Bobby Jones **11** Juliette Low **15** Erskine Caldwell **16** Margaret Mitchell **18** Joel Chandler Harris

island: 3 Sea **6** Jekyll, Sapelo **7** Ossabaw **10** Cumberland

lake: 6 Lanier, Martin **7** Harding, Nottely **8** Bankhead, Hartwell, Sinclair

land rank: 11 twenty-first

mountain: 5 Stone **7** Lookout **8** Kennesaw **9** Blue Ridge **11** Alleghenies **13** High Point Peak

highest point: 17 Brasstown Bald Peak

physical feature:

sea: 8 Atlantic

springs: 4 Warm

swamp: 10 Okefenokee

president: 11 Jimmy Carter

river: 3 Pea **5** Flint **6** Etowah, Oconee, Pigeon **7** Conecuh, Satilla, St Mary's, Tugaloo **8** Altamaha, Ocmulgee, Ogeechee, Savannah, Suwannee **9** Chattooga **13** Chattahoochie

state admission: 6 fourth

state bird: 13 brown thrasher

state fish: 14 largemouth bass

state flower: 12 Cherokee rose

state motto: 6 Wisdom **20** Justice and Moderation

state song: 7 Georgia

state tree: 7 live oak

Georgia Peach

nickname of: 6 Ty Cobb

Georgics, The

author: 6 Vergil, Virgil

Geraint

character in: 16 Arthurian romance

wife: 4 Enid

geranium 11 Pelargonium

varieties: 3 ivy **4** fish, lime, mint, pine, rock, rose, show, wild **5** apple, fancy, house, lemon, regal, zonal **6** almond, alpine, cactus, jungle, nutmeg, orange **7** apricot, bedding, coconut, feather, hanging, knotted, polecat **8** crowfoot, fern-leaf, horsehoe **9** beefsteak, oak-leaved **10** California, gooseberry, peppermint, strawberry, sweetheart, village-oak **11** grape-leaved, herb-scented, maple-leaved, rose-scented **12** silver-leaved, southernwood, sweet-scented **13** black-flowered, pansy-flowered, pheasant's-foot **14** Lady Washington, little-leaf rose **15** mint-scented rose **16** Martha Washington **17** English finger-bowl

Gerber, Franceska Mitzi

real name of: 11 Mitzi Gaynor

Gerd, Gerda

origin: 12 Scandinavian

husband: 4 Frey **5** Freyr

Gere, Richard

roles: 5 Yanks **10** Breathless, Cotton Club **11** Pretty Woman **12** Days of Heaven **14** American Gigolo **19** Looking for Mr Goodbar **22** An Officer and a Gentleman

former wife: 13 Cindy Crawford

cause 5 Tibet

germ 3 bud, bug, egg **4** ovum, root, seed **5** ovule, spark, spore, virus **6** embryo, origin, source, sprout **7** microbe, nucleus, seed bud **8** bacillus, offshoot, rudiment **9** bacterium, beginning **12** fountainhead **13** microorganism

German 3 Hun **4** balt, Goth **5** boche, heine, jerry, kraut, Saxon **6** Teuton **7** tedesco **8** Prussian, Teutonic **9** deutscher

article: 3 das, dem, den, der, des, die, ein **4** eine, eins

empire: 5 reich

pronoun: 3 ich, mir, sie, uns

man: 4 herr

storm and stress: 13 sturm und drang

thank you: 5 danke **10** danke schon

toast: 6 prosit **10** gesundheit

woman: 4 frau **8** fraulein

German-Dutch

language family: 12 Indo-European

branch: 8 Germanic

group: 15 Western Germanic

language: 9 Low German **10** High German

germane 3 apt, fit **6** native, proper **7** apropos, fitting, related **8** material, relative, relevant, suitable **9** connected, intrinsic, pertinent **10** applicable **11** appropriate **12** appertaining

germaneness 9 relevance **10** pertinence **13** applicability **15** appropriateness

Germanic

language family: 12 Indo-European

group: 6 Gothic **15** Western Germanic

Germanic Mythology

chief of gods: 5 Wotan

corresponds to Scandinavian: 4 Odin

dwarf: 15 Rumpelstiltskin

dwarves: 8 Niblungs **9** Nibelungs

emperor: 15 Dietrich von Bern

epic: 14 Nibelungenlied

goddess of clouds/sky/marriage: 3 Fri **5** Frigg, Frija **6** Frigga

goddess of death/fertility: 7 Berchta, Perchta

goddess of love/ beauty/fecundity: 5 Freya

goddess of moon/ witch: 5 Holle

god of thunder: 5 Donar

god of winter sports: 4 Ullr **5** Uller

hero: 6 Sigurd **9** Siegfried

heroine: 6 Gudrun, Kudrun **7** Guthrun **8** Brunhild **9** Kriemhild

king: 7 Siggeir

king of dwarves: 8 Alberich

knight of the holy grail: 9 Lohengrin

magic cloak: 9 Tarnkappe

maidens: 9 Valkyries

nature spirit: 7 Eriking

nymph: 7 Lorelei, Lurelei

water spirit: 3 Nix

German is spoken here

German: 25 hier wird Deutsch gesprochen

German literary movement (18th cent) 13 sturm und drang

Germany (see also *Germany, East* and *Germany, West*)

capital: 6 Berlin

government leader: 10 chancellor, Helmut Kohl

monetary unit: 12 Deutsche mark

people: 3 Hun **4** Slav, Sorb, Wend **5** Saxon

artist: 4 Marc **5** Durer **7** Barlach, Cranach, Gropius, Holbein **9** Grunewald **14** Mies van der Rohe

author: 4 Mann, Marx **5** Grass **6** Brecht, Elsner, Goethe **7** Johnson, Lessing **8** Hochhuth

composer: 4 Bach **5** Weill **6** Brahms, Handel, Wagner **7** Strauss **8** Schumann **9** Beethoven, Hindemith **11** Mendelssohn

conductor: 5 Henze **6** Walter **9** Klemperer **11** Furtwangler, Stockhausen

historical leader: 6 Hitler, Kaiser **8** Bismarck **10** Barbarossa

Prussian noble: 6 Junker

religious leader: 6 Luther

language: 6 German **10** High German **11** Hochdeutsch

religion: 8 Lutheran **10** Protestant **13** Roman Catholic **17** Evangelical Church

food:

bread: 12 pumpernickel

dish: 9 lebkuchen

dumpling: 6 knodel

frankfurter: 15 wiener wurstchen

fruit bread: 7 stollen

ham: 11 Westphalian

potato salad: 14 kartoffelsalat

pot roast: 11 sauerbraten

sausage: 5 wurst **9** blutwurst, bratwurst **10** brockwurst, knackwurst, leberwurst

sole: 8 seezunge

Germany, East (former) (see also *Germany*)

capital/largest city: 10 East Berlin

others: 4 Jena **5** Halle, Waren **6** Erfurt, Weimar **7** Cottbus, Dresden, Leipzig, Meissen, Potsdam, Rostock, Schwedt, Wannsee, Zwickau **9** Frankfurt, Magdeburg **10** Angermunde, Warnemunde, Wittenberg **11** Neustrelitz **13** Karl-Marx-Stadt

(Chemnitz)
school: 8 Humboldt
division: 6 Saxony **9** Thuringia **11** Brandenburg, Mecklenburg **12** Saxony-Anhalt
government: 11 Volkskammer (Peoples' Chamber)
monetary unit: 4 mark **7** Ostmark, pfennig
lake: 6 Muritz
mountain: 3 Ore **4** Harz **10** Erzgebirge
highest point: 11 Fichtelberg
river: 4 Elbe, Oder **5** Havel, Saale, Spree **6** Neisse, Warnow
sea: 6 Baltic
physical feature:
  forest: 10 Thuringian
place: 10 Berlin Wall **17** Checkpoint Charlie
  castle: 9 Sans Souci
  church: 8 St Thomas **12** Thomaskirche
  city center: 13 Karl Marx Platz **14** Alexanderplatz, Neubrandenberg
  comic opera: 12 Komische Oper
  gate: 11 Brandenburg
  museum: 7 Zwinger **8** Pergamon **10** Goethe Haus
  opera house: 18 Deutsche Staatsoper
feature:
  china: 7 Dresden
  fair: 7 Leipzig
  theater company: 16 Berliner Ensemble

Germany, West (former) (see also *Germany*)
capital: 4 Bonn
largest city: 10 West Berlin
others: 4 Kiel **5** Essen, Mainz, Trier **6** Aachen, Bochum, Bremen, Kassel, Lubeck, Minden, Munden, Munich **7** Cologne, Hamburg, Hanover, Krefeld, Munster **8** Augsburg, Biberach, Dortmund, Duisburg, Duisburg, Freiburg, Mannheim, Solingen **9** Darmstadt, Karlsruhe, Nuremberg, Oldenburg, Stuttgart, Wiesbaden, Wuppertal **10** Dusseldorf, Heidelberg, Steingaden **11** Saarbrucken **12** Oberammergau **13** Gelsenkirchen **15** Frankfurt am Main **16** Mulheim an der Ruhr
school: 4 Bonn **7** Hamburg **10** Heidelberg **16** Ludwig-Maximilian
division: 4 Saar **5** Baden, Hesse **6** Bremen **7** Bavaria **9** Rhineland **10** Palatinate, Westphalia **11** Lower Saxony, Wurttemberg **17** Schleswig-Holstein
head of government: 10 chancellor
monetary unit: 4 mark **7** pfennig **12** Deutsche mark
island: 11 East Frisian **12** North Frisian
lake: 9 Constance **11** Inner Alster, Outer Alster
mountain: 4 Harz **8** Feldberg

11 Black Forest **12** Bavarian Alps
highest point: 9 Zugspitze
river: 3 Ems **4** Elbe, Main, Nahe, Ruhr, Saar, Wese **5** Donau, Rhine, Weser **6** Danube, Neckar **7** Moselle, Pegnitz
sea: 5 North **6** Baltic
physical feature:
  canal: 4 Kiel **10** Mittelland
  forest: 5 Black **7** Bohemia **9** Teu Toburg
  place: 17 Checkpoint Charlie
  botanical garden: 18 Pflantzen und Blumen
  boulevard: 14 Kurfurstendamm
  church: 12 Frauenkirche (Cathedral of Our Lady) **13** Kaiser Wilhelm **16** Gadachtniskirche
  city center: 11 Marienplatz
  fortress: 9 Marksburg
  fountain: 14 Schoner Brunnen
  garden: 10 Englischer
  hall: 9 Beethoven
  museum: 8 Residenz **9** Durer Haus **12** Schatzkammer **14** Alte Pinakothek
  opera house: 18 Deutsches Opern Haus
  park/zoo: 18 Hagenbecks Tierpark
  residential district: 11 Hansa Vierte **12** Hanse Viertel
  resort (on Baltic): 10 Travemunde
  theater: 9 Cuvillies
feature:
  beer cellar: 11 bierkellern
  beer garden: 10 biergarten
  beer hall: 10 bierhallen
  beer room: 10 bierstuben
  cars: 3 BMW **4** Opel **7** Porsche **10** Volkswagen **12** Mercedes-Benz
  children: 6 kinder
  city hall: 5 Romer **7** Rathaus
  festival: 11 Oktoberfest
  folk songs: 11 volkslieder
  kitchen: 5 kuche
  old city: 8 Altstadt
  pre-Lent carnival: 8 Fasching
  secondary school: 9 gymnasium
  states: 6 lander
  wine street: 11 Weinstrasse

germicide 11 bactericide **12** disinfectant
Germinal
  author: 9 Emile Zola
germinate 3 bud **4** blow, open **5** bloom, shoot **6** flower, push up, sprout **7** blos- som, burgeon, develop **8** generate, spring up, vegetate
germination 9 sprouting **11** propagation
Gershom
  father: 5 Moses
  mother: 8 Zipporah
  brother: 12 Eliezar
Gershwin, George
  born: 10 Brooklyn NY
  partner/lyricist: 11 Ira Gershwin
  composer of: 9 Funny Face **11** Of

Thee I Sing **12** Porgy and Bess **13** Cuban Overture **14** Rhapsody in Blue **15** Strike Up the Band **17** An American in Paris
Gertrude
  character in: 6 Hamlet
  author: 11 Shakespeare
  husband: 8 Claudius
  widow of: 6 Hamlet
Gervin, George
  nickname: 6 Iceman
  sport: 10 basketball
  team: 15 San Antonio Spurs
Gesta Romanorum
  author: 7 unknown
gestation 9 evolution, pregnancy **10** epigenesis, generation, incubation, maturation **11** development, propagation
gesticulate 3 nod **4** wink **5** nudge, shrug **6** beckon, motion, signal **8** indicate **9** pantomime
gesture 3 nod **4** sign, wave, wink **5** nudge, shrug, touch **6** beckon, motion, signal **8** courtesy, dumb show, flourish, high sign **9** formality, pantomime **13** demonstration
get 3 bag, fix, net, wax, win **4** beat, coax, earn, gain, grab, grip, grow, have, hear, move, reap, sway, take, turn **5** annoy, catch, fetch, glean, grasp, learn, reach, seize, sense, upset **6** arrive, attain, baffle, become, collar, come by, come to, enlist, entrap, fathom, follow, induce, obtain, pick up, pocket, prompt, puzzle, secure, snatch, suborn, take in, turn to **7** achieve, acquire, capture, confuse, contact, dispose, ensnare, go after, incline, inherit, mystify, perplex, prepare, procure, realize, receive, wheedle, win over **8** bewilder, confound, contract, irritate, perceive, persuade **9** influence, transport **10** comprehend, disconcert, predispose, understand
get a kick out of 4 like **5** eat up, enjoy, fancy, savor **6** relish **10** appreciate
getaway 6 escape, exodus, flight **10** decampment
get done 2 do **6** finish **8** complete **10** accomplish
get even 6 avenge **7** counter, hit back, pay back, revenge **9** retaliate
Gethsemane 6 garden
get into 3 don **5** enter, put on
get in touch with 5 reach **7** contact
get lost 4 scat, shoo **5** be off, leave, scram **6** beat it, begone, depart, go away **7** vamoose
get one's dander up 4 gall, rile **5** anger **6** enrage, madden, nettle, ruffle **7** incense, inflame, outrage **9** infuriate
get out of bed 4 rise **5** arise **12** rise and shine
get rid of 4 drop, dump, junk, shed **5**

get rid of 4 drop, dump, junk, shed **5** ditch, scrap **6** banish, cut out, delete, remove, unload **7** abolish, discard, weed out **8** jettison, stamp out, throw out **9** eliminate, eradicate **10** annihilate **11** exterminate

Get Smart
  character: 5 Hymie (CONTROL robot) **7** Agent 99, Carlson, Starker **8** Larrabee, The Chief (Thaddeus) **12** Maxwell Smart (Agent 86) **15** Conrad Siegfried
  cast: 8 Don Adams **9** King Moody **10** Stacy Keach **11** Dave Ketchum, Dick Gautier, Edward Platt **12** Bernie Kopell **13** Barbara Feldon **14** Robert Karvelas
  Max worked for: 7 CONTROL
  foe: 4 KAOS

get the better of 4 foil, rout **5** crush, quell **6** baffle, defeat, thwart **7** conquer **8** confound, overcome **9** frustrate, overthrow

get the upper hand of 5 quell **6** master **7** conquer **8** dominate, overcome, surmount

get the worst of 4 fail, fall, lose

Getting Even
  author: 10 Woody Allen

get to 5 reach **8** approach

get-together 2 do **3** bee **4** meet **5** agree, party, visit **6** affair, gather, hobnob **7** meeting **8** assemble, assembly **9** gathering

getup 3 rig **6** attire, outfit **7** costume **8** disguise, ensemble

get up 4 find, rise **5** arise, rouse, stand **8** assemble

get used to 5 adapt, inure **6** adjust **8** accustom **9** acclimate, habituate

gewgaws 7 baubles, doodads, trifles **8** trinkets **9** bric-a-brac, gimcracks, kickshaws, ornaments **11** knickknacks

Ghana
  other name: 9 Gold Coast
  capital/largest city: 5 Accra, Akkra
  others: 3 Oda **4** Axim, Fian, Keta, Tala, Tema **5** Bawku, Enchi, Lawra, Legon, Sampa, Yapei **6** Dunkwa, Karaga, Kpandu, Kumasi, Nsawam, Obuasi, Swedru, Tamale, Tarkwa, Wasipe **7** Antubia, Damongo, Mampong, Prestea, Sekondi, Sunyani, Winneba **8** Akosombo, Kintampo, Takoradi **9** Cape Coast **15** Sekondi-Takoradi
  school: 6 Kumasi **9** Cape Coast
  monetary unit: 4 cedi **5** ackey
  lake: 5 Volta **8** Bosumtwi
  mountain: 12 Akwapim Hills
  highest point: 8 Afadjato
  river: 3 Oti, Pra **4** Daka, Tano **5** Afram, Volta **7** Ankobra, Kulpawn **10** Black Volta, White Volta
  sea: 8 Atlantic
  physical feature:
    gulf: 6 Guinea
  people: 2 Ga **3** Ewe **4** Akan, Akim, Akra, Aksa **5** Ahafo, Brong, Inkra **7** Akwapim, Ashanti, Dagomba **8** Mamprusi **11** Mole-Dagbani
  language: 2 Ga **3** Ewe, Gur, Kwa, Twi **5** Fanti, Hausa **7** Dagomba, English
  religion: 5 Islam **7** animism **13** Roman Catholic
  feature:
    castle: 14 Christiansborg
    dam: 8 Akosombo
    national dress: 5 kente

ghastly 3 wan **4** grim, ugly **5** ashen, pasty, weird **6** dismal, glassy, grisly, horrid, odious, pallid **7** fearful, ghostly, haggard, hideous, uncanny **8** blanched, dreadful, gruesome, horrible, shocking, spectral, terrible **9** appalling, colorless, deathlike, frightful, ghostlike, loathsome, repellent, repulsive, revolting **10** cadaverous, corpselike, forbidding, horrendous, lackluster, terrifying

Ghiberti, Lorenzo
  born: 5 Italy **8** Florence
  artwork: 9 St Matthew, St Stephen **15** Gates of Paradise (baptistry doors) **16** St John the Baptist **19** The Sacrifice of Isaac

ghost 4 hint **5** demon, shade, spook, trace **6** goblin, shadow, sprite, wraith **7** banshee, chimera, phantom, specter **8** phantasm **9** hobgoblin, phantasma, semblance **10** apparition, suggestion **12** Doppelganger **13** manifestation **15** materialization

Ghost and Mrs Muir, The
  character: 11 Candice Muir, Martha Grant **12** Jonathan Muir **13** Claymore Gregg **14** Mrs Carolyn Muir **18** Captain Daniel Gregg
  TV cast: 8 Reta Shaw **9** Hope Lange **13** Edward Mulhare **14** Harlen Carraher, Kellie Flanagan **19** Charles Nelson Reilly
  setting: 11 Gull Cottage
  director: 17 Joseph L Mankiewicz
  movie cast: 8 Edna Best **11** Gene Tierney, Rex Harrison **13** George Sanders

Ghostbusters
  director: 11 Ivan Reitman
  screenplay: 10 Dan Aykroyd **11** Harold Ramis
  cast: 10 Bill Murray, Dan Aykroyd **11** Harold Ramis **15** Sigourney Weaver

ghostly 4 pale **5** eerie, weird **6** spooky, unreal **7** ghastly, phantom, shadowy, uncanny **8** illusive, spectral **9** unearthly **10** phantasmal, wraithlike **11** phantomlike **12** supernatural

ghostly double
  German: 12 Doppelganger

Ghosts
  author: 11 Henrik Ibsen
  character: 7 Manders **12** Oswald

Alving **14** Jacob Engstrand, Mrs Helen Alving **15** Regina Engstrand

ghoulish 5 eerie, scary, weird **7** demonic, hellish, macabre, ogreish, satanic **8** diabolic, fiendish, gruesome, infernal, sinister **9** monstrous **10** horrifying, zombielike **11** hair-raising, necrophilic

Giacometti, Alberto
  born: 11 Switzerland **12** Stampa-Tessin
  artwork: 3 Dog **7** The Cage **8** Caroline **10** City Square **11** Head of Diego, Man Pointing **14** Reclining Woman **17** The Palace at Four Am **19** Hands Holding the Void

Gianni Schicchi
  opera by: 7 Puccini
  character: 11 Buoso Donati

giant 3 big **4** huge **5** titan **7** Goliath, spanker, thumper, whopper **8** behemoth, colossus, strapper **9** Gargantua **14** Brobdingnagian

Giant
  director: 13 George Stevens
  author: 10 Edna Ferber
  cast: 9 James Dean **10** Chill Wills, Rock Hudson **11** Jane Withers **12** Carroll Baker **15** Elizabeth Taylor
  setting: 5 Texas
  Oscar for: 8 director

Giant *see* **8** Gigantes

giant people 6 Anakim

Giants in the Earth
  author: 9 O E Rolvaag
  character: 3 Ole **5** Beret **8** Per Hanea **9** Anna Marie **12** Hans Kristian **15** Peder Victorious

gibber 3 gab **4** blab **5** prate **6** babble, gabble, jabber **7** blabber, blather, chatter, prattle **8** chitchat

gibberish 4 blab, bosh **6** babble, drivel, gabble **7** blather, twaddle **8** nonsense **10** balderdash, double-talk, flapdoodle, hocus-pocus, mumbo-jumbo **12** gobbledegook

Gibbon, Edward
  author of: 33 The (History of the) Decline and Fall of the Roman Empire

gibbous 6 convex, curved, humped **7** bulging, rounded, swollen **8** swelling **10** humpbacked, protuberant

Gibbs family
  characters in: 7 Our Town
  member: 6 George **7** Rebecca
  author: 6 Wilder

gibe, jibe 3 rag **4** jeer, mock, quip, razz, twit **5** chaff, flout, knock, toast, scoff, sneer, taunt **6** deride, needle, rail at **7** mockery, poke fun, sarcasm **8** brickbat, derision, ridicule, taunting **9** criticism, wisecrack

Gibraltar
  other name: 11 rock of Tarik **13** Djebel al-Tarik **15** rock of Gibraltar

largest city: 9 Gibraltar
government: 18 British crown colony
head of government: 15 governor general
mountain: 6 Misery
sea: 13 Mediterranean
physical feature:
  bay: 5 Ceuta, Rosia, Sandy **6** Catlan **9** Algeciras
  cliffs: 17 Pillars of Hercules
  people: 6 Jewish **7** British, Maltese, Spanish **8** Italians **10** Portuguese
  language: 7 English, Spanish
  feature: 12 King's Bastion
    gardens: 7 Alameda **11** Barbary apes

Gibson, Mel
  roles: 6 Mad Max **9** Gallipoli, The Bounty **10** Braveheart **12** Lethal Weapon **14** The Road Warrior **26** The Year of Living Dangerously

Giddens, Regina
  character in: 14 The Little Foxes
  author: 7 Hellman

giddy 5 dizzy, faint, silly **6** fickle, fitful **7** awesome, erratic, flighty, muddled, reeling **8** careless, dizzying, fainting, fanciful, reckless, swimming, unsteady, volatile, whirling **9** befuddled, frivolous, impulsive, mercurial, whimsical **10** capricious, changeable, inconstant **11** hare-brained, harum-scarum, lightheaded, thoughtless, vacillating, vertiginous **12** inconsistent, overpowering **13** irresponsible, rattlebrained

Gide, Andre
  author of: 13 The Immoralist **15** Strait Is the Gate **17** The Counterfeiters **18** Lafcadio's Adventure (The Vatican Swindle) **19** The Pastoral Symphony

Gideon 11 Hebrew judge
  father: 5 Joash, Ophra
  son: 9 Abimelech
  also called: 9 Jerubbaal

Gidget
  character: 5 Larue **10** Anne Cooper, John Cooper **16** Francine (Gidget) Lawrence **21** Professor Russ Lawrence
  cast: 9 Don Porter **10** Peter Deuel, Sally Field **11** Betty Conner **13** Lynette Winter
  film role: 9 Sandra Dee

Gielgud, Sir John
  born: 6 London **7** England
  roles: 6 Arthur, Becket, Hamlet **7** Macbeth **9** Saint Joan **26** The Barretts of Wimpole Street **27** The Importance of Being Earnest

gift 3 aid, dot, fee, sop, tip **4** alms, bent, boon, dole, help, turn **5** award, bonus, bribe, craft, dower, dowry, favor, flair, forte, graft, grant, knack, power, prize, skill **6** genius, legacy, talent, virtue **7** aptness, bequest, faculty, handout, largess, premium, present, quality, tribute **8** aptitude, capacity, donation, facility, gratuity, offering, property **9** attribute, endowment, expertise, ingenuity **10** adroitness, capability, competency **11** benefaction, proficiency **12** contribution **13** consideration, qualification

gifted 4 able, deft **5** adept, crack, handy, quick, slick **6** adroit, bright, clever, expert, facile, master, wizard **7** capable, skilled **8** finished, masterly, polished, superior, talented **9** brilliant, ingenious, inventive, practiced, qualified **10** proficient **11** crackerjack, experienced, resourceful **12** accomplished

Gift From the Sea, The
  author: 19 Anne Morrow Lindbergh

gig 3 job **4** trap **5** stint **6** chaise **7** dogcart **8** carriage, curricle **10** engagement

Gigantes
  single member: 5 giant
  father: 6 Uranus
  mother: 4 Gaea
  heads of: 3 men
  bodies of: 8 serpents
  attacked: 4 gods

gigantic 4 huge, vast **5** bulky, jumbo **6** mighty **7** hulking, immense, lumpish, mammoth, massive, titanic **8** colossal, enormous, lubberly, towering, unwieldy **9** herculean, monstrous, ponderous, strapping **10** gargantuan, prodigious, stupendous, tremendous, voluminous **11** elephantine

giggle 6 cackle, hee-hee, simper, tee-hee, titter **7** chuckle, snicker, snigger, twitter

Gigi
  director: 16 Vincente Minnelli
  based on story by: 7 Colette
  cast: 8 Eva Gabor **11** Leslie Caron **12** Louis Jourdan **15** Hermione Gingold, Jacques Bergerac **16** Maurice Chevalier
  score: 14 Lerner and Loewe
  Oscar for: 7 picture **8** director
  song: 4 Gigi **15** I Remember It Well **25** Thank Heaven for Little Girls **29** The Night They Invented Champagne

Gilbert, Cass
  architect of: 14 US Customs House (NYC) **17** Woolworth Building (NYC) **20** Supreme Court Building (Washington DC) **21** Minnesota State Capitol (St Paul) **22** George Washington Bridge

Gilbert, John
  real name: 11 John Pringle
  wife: 9 Ina Claire **11** Leatrice Joy **13** Virginia Bruce
  born: 7 Logan UT
  roles: 4 Love **12** The Big Parade **13** The Merry Widow **15** A Woman of Affairs **16** Flesh and the Devil

Gilbert, William
  field: 7 physics
  nationality: 7 British
  father of: 11 electricity
  named for him: 27 CGS unit of magnetomotive force

Gilbert, W S, and Sullivan, Arthur Seymour
  composers of: 7 Ivanhoe **8** Iolanthe, Patience **9** Ruddigore, The Mikado **11** H M S Pinafore, Princess Ida, The Sorcerer, Trial by Jury **12** The Grand Duke **13** The Gondoliers, Utopia Limited **19** The Yeoman of the Guard **20** The Pirates of Penzance **24** Thespis or The Gods Grown Old
  produced by: 10 D'Oyly Carte
  devotees: 9 Savoyards

Gilbert Islands *see* **8** Kiribati

Gil Blas (of Santillane)
  author: 11 Alain LeSage
  character: 6 Scipio **11** Don Alphonso

Gilbreth, Frank B, Jr
  author of: 17 Cheaper by the Dozen (with Ernestine Gilbreth Carey)

gild 4 bend **5** slant, twist **7** cover up, stretch, touch up **10** exaggerate

Gilded Age, The
  authors: 9 Mark Twain **19** Charles Dudley Warner

gilded youth
  French: 13 jeunesse doree

Gileadite password 10 Shibboleth

Giles Goat-Boy
  author: 9 John Barth

Gilgal 5 wheel **6** circle

Gilgamesh
  origin: 8 Sumerian
  king of: 4 Uruk **5** Erech
  servant: 6 Enkidu
  event: 5 flood

gill
  abbreviation: 2 gi

Gilligan's Island
  character: 7 Skipper (Jonas Grumby) **8** Gilligan **9** Mrs Howell (Lovey), Professor (Roy Hinkley) **11** Ginger Grant **14** Mary Ann Summers **17** Thurston Howell III
  cast: 9 Bob Denver, Dawn Wells, Jim Backus **10** Alan Hale Jr, Tina Louise **14** Natalie Schafer, Russell Johnson
  ship: 6 Minnow

Gills, Solomon
  character in: 12 Dombey and Son
  author: 7 Dickens

gimcrack 5 bijou, curio **6** bauble, gewgaw, trifle **7** trinket, whatnot **8** kickshaw, ornament **9** bagatelle, plaything **10** knickknack **11** contrivance, thingamabob, thingamajig

gimmick 4 plan, ploy, ruse, wile **5** angle, dodge, stunt **6** design, device, gadget, scheme **7** wrinkle **9** stratagem **10** subterfuge **11** contrivance

gin
  origin: 11 Netherlands

ingredient: 4 sloe **6** grains **12** juniper berry
type: 6 Geneva **8** Plymouth **9** London dry
drink: 5 Allen **6** Gibson, gimlet **7** Belmont, Bennett, gin Fizz, swizzle **8** Pink Lady **9** Gin Rickey **10** Tom Collins **11** Alabama Fizz, gin and tonic **12** Grand Passion **14** Casino Cocktail
with anisette: 8 Snowball **11** Bachio Punch
with apricot brandy: 14 Boston Cocktail
with brandy: 15 Bermuda Highball
with Chartreuse: 5 Bijou **9** Green Lady
with cherry brandy: 14 Singapore Sling
with Cointreau: 7 Florida **9** White Lady **13** Sweet Patootie **14** Flying Dutchman
with creme de cacao: 9 Alexander
with creme de cassis: 8 Parisian
with creme de menthe: 6 Caruso, Virgin
with creme Yvette: 9 Union Jack
with Curacao: 8 Blue Moon, Napoleon **9** Blue Devil **14** Flying Dutchman
with Dubonnet: 3 BVD **8** Napoleon
with Grand Marnier: 7 Red Lion
with grapefruit juice: 8 Salty Dog
with kirsch, kirschwasser: 7 Florida **10** Lady Finger
with onions: 6 Gibson
with orange juice: 5 Abbey **13** Orange Blossom
with Pernod: 7 Dubarry
with rum: 3 BVD
with scotch: 12 Barbary Coast
with sherry: 11 Renaissance
with strawberries: 10 Bloodhound
with Swedish Punch: 5 Biffy
with vermouth: 5 Bijou, Bronx, Tango **6** Caruso **7** Bermuda, Cabaret, Martini **10** Bloodhound
with vodka: 15 Russian Cocktail

ginger 3 pep, tan **5** brown, spice **6** energy
varieties: 3 red **4** wild **5** crape, crepe, shell, torch, white **6** canton, common, Kahili, orchid, spiral, yellow **9** butterfly **10** small shell, variegated
botanical name: 8 Zingiber **12** Z officinales
Sanskrit: 9 singabera
origin: 4 Asia **5** China, India **7** Jamaica
use: 6 tongue **7** vinegar **9** beef stock **11** baked dishes, gingerbread **12** chicken stock

gingerly 6 warily **7** charily, timidly **8** daintily **9** carefully, finically, guardedly, heedfully, mincingly, prudently **10** cautiously, delicately, discreetly, hesitantly, vigilantly, watchfully **11** squeamishly **12** fastidiously, suspiciously **13** circumspectly

gingham 5 cloth **6** cotton, fabric, striped **8** chambray **9** checkered

gin mill 3 bar **4** dive **6** saloon, tavern **9** honky-tonk, roadhouse

Ginnungagap
origin: 12 Scandinavian
void filled with: 4 mist
between: 9 Nifelheim **10** Muspelheim

Ginsberg, Allen
author of: 4 Howl **7** Kaddish **10** Planet News **11** Mind Breaths **16** The Fall of America **20** Reality and Sandwiches

Giordano, Umberto
born: 5 Italy **6** Foggia
composer of: 6 Fedora **8** Mala Vita **13** Andrea Chenier **14** Madame Sans-Gene

Giorgione da Castelfranco
born: 5 Italy **12** Castelfranco
artwork: 10 The Tempest **13** Ordeal of Moses, Sleeping Venus **17** Judgment of Solomon **19** The Concert Champetre (disputed) **20** The Three Philosophers **23** Adoration of the Shepherds

Giotto di Bondone
born: 5 Italy **8** (near) Florence
artwork attributed: 17 Ognissanti Madonna **31** Presentation of Christ in the Temple **32** St Francis Surrounded by his Brothers

Giovanelli
character in: 11 Daisy Miller
author: 5 James

Giovanni's Room
author: 12 James Baldwin

giraffe
constellation of: 14 Cameolopardalis
kin: 5 okapi
other name: 10 cameolopard

girandole 11 candelabrum, candlestick **12** candleholder

Girardon, Francois
born: 6 France, Troyes
artwork: 13 Bathing Nymphs **14** Galley of Apollo, Virgin of Troyes **16** Rape of Persephone **17** (tomb for) Cardinal Richelieu **23** Apollo Tended by the Nymphs

Giraudoux, Jean
author of: 5 Bella **6** Judith, Ondine, Racine **7** Electra **12** Amphitryon 38 **15** Tiger at the Gates **18** Madwoman of Chaillot **20** My Friend from Limousin

gird 3 pen, tie **4** belt, girt, loop, ring **5** brace, hem in, hitch, steel, strap, truss **6** circle, fasten, girdle, harden, secure, wall in **7** besiege, confine, enclose, fortify, hedge in, prepare, stiffen, sustain, tighten **8** blockade, buttress, encircle, lay siege, surround **9** encompass **10** strengthen **12** circumscribe

girder 4 beam **5** brace, truss **6** binder, rafter **7** support, tie-beam

girdle 3 hem **4** band, belt, ring, sash **5** girth, hedge, stays **6** bodice, circle, corset **7** baldric, circlet, contour **8** boundary, cincture, corselet **9** surcingle, waistband **10** cummerbund **12** waist cincher **17** foundation garment

girl 4 bird, cook, help, lass, maid, minx, miss **5** angel, chick, nymph, wench **6** damsel, kitten, lassie, maiden, pigeon, virgin **7** baggage, colleen, darling, fiancee, ingenue, nymphet **8** daughter, domestic, handmaid, lady love, mistress, scullion **9** affianced, betrothed, inamorata, lady's maid, soubrette **10** sweetheart **11** maidservant
French: 10 demoiselle, jeune fille

girl Friday 4 aide **6** helper **9** assistant, secretary **10** amanuensis **12** office worker **23** administrative assistant

girlfriend 6 steady **7** beloved, sweetie **8** best girl **10** one and only, sweetheart

Girl in a Swing
author: 12 Richard Adams

girlish 8 girl-like, maidenly, youthful **10** maidenlike

Girl of the Golden West, The
opera by: 7 Puccini
setting: 8 Gold Rush **10** California
character: 6 Minnie **7** Johnson, Sheriff

Girl Scouts
founded by: 11 Juliette Low
abbr: 5 GSUSA
rank: 7 brownie **10** tenderfoot

girt 4 belt, bind, gird, ring **5** bound, girth **6** belted, circle, girdle, ringed **7** circled, girdled **9** encircled

girth 5 cinch **9** perimeter **10** saddle band **13** circumference

Giselle
ballet by: 4 (Adolphe Charles) Adam

Gish, Lillian
real name: 12 Lillian Gishi **15** Lillian de Guiche
born: 13 Springfield OH
roles: 8 La Boheme **10** Enoch Arden **11** Annie Laurie, Intolerance, Way Down East **12** Duel in the Sun **13** Scarlet Letter **14** Broken Blossoms **16** Portrait of Jennie **17** Orphans of the Storm, The Birth of a Nation

Gissing, George
author of: 5 Demos **13** New Grub Street **14** The Nether World

gist 3 nut **4** core, crux, meat, pith **5** drift, force, heart, sense, tenor, theme **6** burden, center, effect, import, kernel, marrow, spirit **7** essence, purport **8** main idea **9** main point, substance **11** implication **12** significance

give 3 buy, pay, tip **4** bend, ease, emit, hire, lend, show, sink **5** admit, allot, allow, apply, award, bribe, deign, endow, grant, issue, leave, offer, relax, utter, voice, yield **6** accord, addict, afford, assign, attach, bestow, bounce, commit, confer, convey, devote, donate, enable, enrich, hand to, impart, loosen, notify, open on, permit, recede, relent, render, shrink, supply, tender, unbend, vest in **7** concede, consign, deliver, entrust, fork out, furnish, hand out, let know, present, proffer, provide, requite, retreat, slacken **8** announce, bequeath, collapse, dispense, exchange, fork over, hand over, lead on to, make over, move back, put forth, shell out **9** apportion, break down, dispose of, equip with, favor with, look out on, present to, pronounce, subscribe, surrender, vouchsafe **10** articulate, become soft, compensate, contribute, deliquesce, distribute, recompense, remunerate, resilience, supply with **11** communicate, flexibility, provide with, springiness

give aid to 4 help **6** assist, succor **7** help out **8** befriend **9** look after **10** minister to

give a leg up 3 aid **4** help, lift **5** boost, hoist, raise **6** assist **7** elevate

give and take 8 exchange **10** compromise **11** interchange, reciprocity

give a pep talk to 4 goad, prod, spur **5** press **6** exhort **9** encourage

give a reason for 7 clarify, clear up, explain, justify **9** elucidate **10** account for

give as security 4 pawn **6** pledge **7** deposit, pay down, put down

give away 6 bestow, betray, donate, reveal **7** hand out

give birth 4 bear **5** hatch **6** create, invent **7** deliver, develop **9** originate **10** bring forth

give confidence to 7 inspire **8** embolden, inspirit **9** encourage

give courage 5 brace **6** buck up **7** hearten **8** inspirit, motivate

give energy to 7 animate, enliven **8** activate, energize, vitalize **9** stimulate **10** invigorate

give enjoyment 5 amuse, charm **6** divert, please **7** beguile, delight **8** enthrall **9** entertain

give forth 4 emit, gush **5** exude, issue **7** send out **8** throw off, transmit **9** discharge

give full attention 7 pay heed **8** fasten on **11** concentrate

give in 5 defer, yield **6** accede, cave in, submit **7** succumb **9** surrender **10** capitulate **12** knuckle under

give in to 7 yield to **9** indulge in, partake of **16** abandon oneself to

give leave 3 let **5** allow **6** permit **8** sanction **9** authorize **14** give permission

give moral support to 3 aid **4** abet,

back, help **6** assist, uphold **7** support, sustain **8** sanction **9** encourage

given 3 apt **4** wont **5** prone **6** likely, wonted **7** awarded, donated, granted, offered **8** accorded, bestowed **9** committed, conferred, entrusted, presented **10** accustomed, handed over, in the habit **11** contributed **13** furnished with, made a donation, presented with **17** made a contribution

give new life to 3 fan **4** fire **6** awaken, revive **8** revivify **10** rejuvenate **11** reincarnate

give oneself to 8 dedicate **10** buckle down, consecrate

give one's word 3 vow **5** swear **6** assure, pledge **7** certify, promise, warrant **9** guarantee

give one walking papers 3 axe, can **4** fire, oust, sack **5** let go **6** bounce, lay off **7** cashier, dismiss, release **8** get rid of **9** discharge, terminate **11** give the gate, send packing

give out 4 quit, tell, tire **6** assign, inform, reveal, run out **7** divulge, dole out, mete out **8** allocate, announce, disclose, dispense, proclaim **9** apportion, broadcast, parcel out **10** distribute, make public, portion out **11** disseminate

give over 4 cede **5** yield **9** surrender **10** relinquish

give permission 3 let **5** allow **6** accede, permit **7** approve **8** sanction **9** acquiesce, authorize, give leave

give rise to 4 sire **5** breed, cause **6** lead to **7** produce **8** engender, generate, occasion **9** call forth **10** bring about

give support to 3 aid **4** abet **5** serve **6** defend, prop up, second **7** bolster, comfort, sustain **8** buttress, champion **10** contribute, minister to, provide for, stick up for

give the go-ahead 4 okay **5** order **6** direct **7** appoint, charter, empower **8** contract **9** authorize **10** commission

give the lie to 5 belie **8** disprove **9** repudiate **10** contradict, controvert

give the raspberry 3 boo, pan **4** razz **6** deride, hoot at **11** ridicule **11** give the bird **17** give the Bronx cheer

give the right to 5 allow **6** permit **7** entitle, qualify **9** authorize

give the slip 4 duck **5** avoid, dodge, elude, evade

give up 4 cede, drop, lose, quit, skip **5** forgo, let go, waive, yield **6** eschew, resign **7** abandon, forfeit, forsake **8** abdicate, forswear, renounce **9** sacrifice, surrender **10** relinquish **11** discontinue

give up the ghost 3 die **6** expire, pass on, perish **7** decease **8** pass away **15** breathe one's last

give vent 4 free **5** let go **7** release **8** let loose, liberate **12** give free rein

give way 4 fall **6** buckle, cave in **7** crumple **8** collapse **10** break apart

giving birth 7 bearing **8** creating, creation, delivery, hatching **9** inventing, invention **10** childbirth, delivering **11** originating, origination, parturition

giving up 7 refusal **8** dropping, quitting, yielding **9** resigning **10** abandoning, abdicating, abdication, abstinence, continence, forbearing, forfeiting, forfeiture, self-denial **11** abandonment, forswearing, resignation **12** renunciation, surrendering **14** relinquishment

gizmo 4 tool **6** device, doodad, gadget **7** whatsis **9** apparatus, implement, invention, mechanism **10** instrument **11** contraption, contrivance, thingamabob, thingamajig

glacial 3 icy, raw **4** cold **5** chill, gelid, polar **6** arctic, biting, bitter, frigid, frosty, frozen, wintry **7** hostile **8** freezing, inimical, piercing **9** congealed **10** disdainful, unfriendly **12** antagonistic, bone-chilling, contemptuous

Glackens, William James
born: 14 Philadelphia PA
artwork: 9 Promenade **11** Chez Mouquin **15** Nude with an Apple **16** Washington Square (A Holiday in the Park) **17** Luxembourg Gardens

glad 5 happy **6** elated, joyful, joyous **7** elating, gleeful, pleased, tickled **8** blissful, cheerful, cheering, pleasing, rejoiced **9** contented, delighted, joygiving **10** delightful, entrancing, gratifying **11** exhilarated, tickled pink **12** exhilarating

gladden 5 cheer, elate **6** please **7** animate, cheer up, delight, enliven, gratify, hearten, rejoice **8** inspirit, pleasure **9** make happy **10** exhilarate

gladdened 5 happy **6** joyful, joyous **8** cheerful

glade 4 dell, glen, lawn, vale, wood **5** grove, marsh, vista **6** canada, hollow, valley **7** opening **8** clearing

gladness 3 joy **4** glee **5** bliss, cheer, mirth **7** delight, gaiety, jollity **8** pleasure **9** happiness **10** joyfulness **11** contentment **12** cheerfulness

glad rags 5 array **6** attire, finery **10** Sunday best

Gladsheim
origin: 12 Scandinavian
palace of: 4 Odin **5** Othin
location: 8 Valhalla

gladsome 3 gay **5** happy, merry **6** cheery, joyful, joyous **8** cheerful **12** lighthearted

glamor, glamour 5 charm, magic **6** allure **7** glitter, romance **8** illusion **9** adventure, challenge, magnetism **10**

excitement **11** enchantment, fascination **14** attractiveness

glamorous, glamourous 8 alluring, charming, dazzling, exciting, magnetic **10** attractive, bewitching, enchanting **11** captivating, charismatic, fascinating

glance 4 kiss, peek, peep, scan, skim, slip **5** brush, graze, shave, touch **6** bounce, careen, squint **7** glimpse, rebound **8** ricochet **9** brief look, quick look, quick view
French: **6** apercu

glance through 4 scan, skim **6** browse, peruse **7** dip into **8** look over **9** check over

gland
part of: **15** endocrine system
type: **4** duct **8** ductless
kind: **3** oil **5** sweat **7** adrenal, thyroid **8** pancreas **9** pituitary **11** parathyroid
ductless gland secretes: **8** hormones

glare 4 glow **5** blaze, flame, flare, flash, gleam, glint, gloss, lower, scowl, sheen **6** dazzle, glower **7** flicker, glimmer, glisten, glitter, radiate, shimmer, sparkle, twinkle **8** radiance **9** angry look, black look, dirty look **10** brightness, harsh light, luminosity **12** resplendence

glaring 4 rank **5** gross, harsh, vivid **6** arrant, bright, strong **7** blatant, flaring, intense, obvious **8** blinding, dazzling, flagrant, piercing **9** audacious, brilliant, egregious **10** glittering, outrageous, shimmering **11** conspicuous, penetrating, resplendent, unconcealed, undisguised **12** unmistakable

Glasgow, Ellen
author of: **10** Vein of Iron **12** Barren Ground **13** In this Our Life, Sheltered Life **18** They Stooped to Folly **20** The Romantic Comedians

glass 6 beaker, goblet **7** chalice, tumbler **10** tumblerful
type of: **4** fizz, sour **5** flute, tulip **6** jigger, sherry **7** balloon, collins, cordial, red wine, snifter **8** cocktail, highball **9** champagne, white wine **10** hollow-stem, pousse cafe **12** old-fashioned

glasshouse 7 nursery **8** hothouse **10** greenhouse **12** conservatory

glassiness 7 clarity **8** dullness, flatness **9** shininess **10** brilliance, luminosity **12** lifelessness, transparency

Glass Key, The
author: **15** Dashiell Hammett
character: **9** Shad O'Rory **10** Janet Henry, Opal Madvig, Paul Madvig **11** Ned Beaumont **12** Senator Henry **13** Bernie Despain

Glass Menagerie, The
director: **12** Irving Rapper
author: **17** Tennessee Williams
character: **5** Laura **6** Amanda **12** Tom

Wingfield
cast: **9** Jane Wyman **11** Kirk Douglas **13** Arthur Kennedy **16** Gertrude Lawrence

glassware 5 agata **6** aurene **7** crystal, favrile, steuben, vitrics **8** amerina, stemware
worker: **7** glazier

glassy 4 dull **5** clear, shiny **6** glazed, smooth **8** lifeless **10** glittering **11** transparent

Glauber, Johann Rudolf
field: **9** chemistry
nationality: **6** German
prepared: **12** tartar emetic **13** sodium sulfate (Glauber's salt) **16** hydrochloric acid

Glaucus
god of: **3** sea
father: **5** Minos
ally of: **7** Trojans
loved by: **5** Circe **6** Scylla **10** Amphitrite

glaze 4 blur **5** gloss **6** enamel, finish **7** grow dim, varnish **8** film over **9** glass over

glazed 4 iced **5** filmy **6** coated, glassy, shined, smooth **7** glossed, sugared **8** enameled, lustrous, polished **9** burnished, varnished

Glazunoff, Alex K (Glazunov, Alexander Konstantinovich)
born: **6** Russia **12** St Petersburg
composer of: **10** Chopiniana, The Seasons **11** Stenka Razin **13** Hymn to Pushkin **15** Memorial Cantata

gleam 3 bit, jot, ray **4** beam, drop, glow, hint, iota **5** blink, flare, flash, glare, glint, gloss, grain, sheen, shine, spark, speck, trace **6** luster, streak **7** flicker, glimmer, glimpse, glisten, glitter, inkling, shimmer, sparkle, tiny bit, twinkle **8** least bit, radiance **9** coruscate **10** brightness, brilliance, effulgence **11** coruscation, scintillation

gleaming 5 clear, shiny **6** bright, flashy, glossy **7** shining, radiant **8** dazzling, glinting, luminous, lustrous, polished, splendid **9** brilliant, burnished, sparkling **10** glistening

glean 4 cull **5** amass **6** gather, pick up **7** harvest **10** accumulate **13** piece together **14** scrape together

gleanings 8 analects, extracts **10** miscellany, selections **11** collectanea, miscellanea **15** commonplace book

Gleason, Jackie
real name: **18** Herbert John Gleason
nickname: **15** Mr Saturday Night
born: **10** Brooklyn NY
roles: **5** Gigot **6** The Toy **10** The Hustler **11** Life of Riley, The Poor Soul **12** Ralph Kramden **15** Joe the Bartender, The Honeymooners **17** Don't Drink the Water, Jackie Gleason Show, The Time of Your Life **22**

Requiem for a Heavyweight **24** Reggie Van Gleason the Third

glebe 3 sod **4** clod, land, plot, soil **5** earth, field **6** termon **8** kirktown **10** church land

glee 3 joy **5** mirth, verve **6** gaiety **7** delight, ecstasy, jollity, rapture **8** gladness, hilarity, laughter **9** joviality, merriment **10** exultation, jocularity, joyfulness, joyousness, liveliness **11** playfulness **12** cheerfulness, exhilaration, sportiveness **13** jollification, sprightliness

glee club 6 chorus **12** singing group **13** choral society

gleeful 3 gay **4** glad **5** happy, jolly, merry **6** elated, jocund, jovial, joyful, joyous, lively **7** festive **8** blissful, cheerful, exultant, mirthful **9** delighted **11** exhilarated **12** lighthearted

Gleipnir
origin: **12** Scandinavian
chain that bound: **6** Fenrir, Fenris

glen 4 dale, dell, vale **6** bottom, hollow

Glencaire Cycle
author: **12** Eugene O'Neill

glib 4 oily **5** gabby, quick, ready, suave **6** facile, fluent, smooth **7** devious, voluble **8** flippant, slippery, unctuous **9** insincere, talkative

glide 3 run **4** flow, roll, sail, skim, slip, soar **5** coast, drift, float, issue, skate, slide, steal **6** elapse, stream **7** proceed **8** glissade

glider 5 swing **7** aviator **9** sailplane **10** hydroplane

glimmer 3 bit, ray **4** beam, drop, glow, hint **5** blink, flare, flash, glare, gleam, grain, shine, speck, trace **7** flicker, glimpse, glisten, glitter, shimmer, sparkle, twinkle **9** coruscate, scintilla **10** flickering, intimation **11** scintillate

glimpse 3 see, spy **4** espy, peek, peep, spot **6** glance, peek at, peep at, squint **9** brief look, quick look, quick view **12** catch sight of, fleeting look
French: **6** apercu

Glinka, Mikhail Ivanovich
born: **6** Russia **8** Smolensk
composer of: **12** Ivan Sussanin, Karaminskaya **13** Jota Aragonesa **18** Russlan and Ludmilla

glint 4 gaze, look, peep **5** flash, gleam, sheen, shine, stare **6** glance **7** appear, glimmer, glimpse, glisten, glitter, shim- mer, sparkle, twinkle **9** coruscate **11** scintillate

glissade 5 coast, glide, slide

glissando
music: **7** sliding

glisten 4 glow **5** flash, gleam, glint, shine **7** flicker, glimmer, glister, glitter, radiate, shimmer, sparkle, twinkle **9** coruscate **11** scintillate

glitter 4 fire, glow, pomp, show **5**

flare, flash, gleam, glint, sheen, shine **6** luster, thrill, tinsel **7** beaming, display, glamour, glimmer, glisten, radiate, sparkle, twinkle **8** grandeur, radiance, splendor **9** pageantry, showiness **10** brilliance, excitement, refulgence **11** electricity

glittering 6 bright **7** radiant, shining **8** luminous, lustrous **9** brilliant, sparkling **11** coruscating

gloaming 4 dusk **7** evening **8** twilight

gloat 4 bask, brag **5** exult, strut, vaunt **7** revel in, swagger, triumph **8** crow over **9** glory over

global 5 world **6** all-out **7** general **9** planetary, unbounded, universal, unlimited, worldwide **10** widespread **13** comprehensive, international **16** intercontinental

globe 3 orb **4** ball **5** Earth, world **6** planet, sphere **7** globule **8** spheroid, spherule **9** biosphere

globule 4 ball, bead, bleb, blob, drop **5** globe **6** bubble, pellet, sphere **7** blister, droplet **8** particle, spheroid

glogg
type: 5 punch
origin: 6 Sweden

gloom 3 woe **4** dark, dusk, murk **5** blues, dolor, grief, shade **6** misery, sorrow **7** despair, dimness, sadness, shadows **8** darkness, distress, doldrums **9** blackness, dejection, dinginess, duskiness, murkiness, obscurity **10** cloudiness, depression, gloominess, low spirits, melancholy, mopishness, moroseness, oppression **11** despondency, forlornness, unhappiness **12** hopelessness **13** cheerlessness **16** disconsolateness, heavy-heartedness

gloomy 3 dim, sad **4** dark, dour, down, dull, glum, grim, mopy, sour **5** dusky, moody, mopey, murky, shady **6** cloudy, dismal, dreary, morbid, morose, shaded, somber **7** doleful, forlorn, shadowy, sunless, unhappy **8** dejected, desolate, downcast, frowning, funereal, overcast **9** cheerless, depressed, heartsick, miserable, sorrowful, woebegone **10** chapfallen, despondent, dispirited, ill-humored, melancholy **11** comfortless, crestfallen, discouraged, downhearted, low-spirited, pessimistic **12** disconsolate, disheartened, heavy-hearted **13** in the doldrums **14** down in the dumps, down in the mouth

Gloria in Excelsis Deo 22 Glory in the highest to God

Gloriana
character in: 15 The Faerie Queene
author: 7 Spenser

Gloriana
opera by: 7 Britten
character: 10 Elizabeth I **11** Earl of Essex

glorification 7 worship **8** devotion **9**

adoration, adulation **10** exaltation, veneration **13** magnification

glorify 4 laud **5** adore, deify, exalt, extol, honor **6** praise, revere **7** beatify, dignify, elevate, ennoble, idolize, worship **8** canonize, enshrine, sanctify, venerate **9** celebrate, glamorize **10** consecrate **11** apotheosize, immortalize, romanticize

glorious 4 fine **5** grand, great, noble, noted **6** august, divine, famous, superb **7** eminent, glowing, honored, notable, radiant, shining, stately, sublime, supreme **8** dazzling, gorgeous, imposing, lustrous, majestic, renowned, splendid **9** beautiful, brilliant, dignified, excellent, marvelous, sparkling, wonderful **10** celebrated, delightful, impressive, preeminent **11** illustrious, magnificent, resplendent **12** praiseworthy **13** distinguished

glory 4 fame, mark, name **5** boast, honor, revel, vaunt **6** esteem, homage, praise, renown, repute **7** dignity, majesty, worship **8** blessing, eminence, grandeur, nobility, prestige, splendor **9** adoration, celebrity, gratitude, solemnity, sublimity **10** admiration, excellence, notability, veneration **11** benediction, distinction, preeminence, stateliness **12** magnificence, resplendence, thanksgiving **14** impressiveness **15** illustriousness

Glory in the highest to God
Latin: **19** Gloria in Excelsis Deo

gloss 4 glow, mask, veil **5** cloak, color, glaze, gleam, japan, sheen, shine **6** enamel, excuse, luster, polish, veneer **7** cover up, lacquer, shimmer, varnish **8** annotate, disguise, mitigate, radiance **9** whitewash **10** annotation, brightness, brilliance, commentary, smooth over **11** explain away, explanation, rationalize **12** luminousness, treat lightly **14** interpretation

gloss over 4 hide, mask, veil **7** conceal, cover up **9** dissemble, whitewash **12** misrepresent

glossy 5 photo, shiny, showy, silky, sleek, slick **6** bright, satiny, smooth **7** picture, shining **8** gleaming, lustrous, magazine, polished **9** burnished

glove 3 kid **4** cuff, mitt **5** catch, thumb **6** gusset, mitten, muffle **7** chevron **8** gauntlet

glow 4 fill, heat **5** ardor, bloom, blush, color, flush, gleam, gusto, shine **6** fervor, thrill, tingle, warmth **7** flicker, glimmer, glisten, glitter, radiate, shimmer, smolder, twinkle **8** radiance **9** eagerness, intensity, radiation, reddening, vividness **10** brightness, enthusiasm **11** earnestness

glower 4 pout, sulk **5** frown, glare, lower, scowl, stare

glowing 3 hot, red **4** rave **5** ruddy, vivid **6** ardent, bright, florid, raving **7**

fervent, flaming, flushed **8** ecstatic, exciting **9** rhapsodic, thrilling **10** passionate **11** luminescent, sensational, stimulating **12** enthusiastic

Glubbdubdrib
fictional land in: 16 Gulliver's Travels
author: 5 Swift

Gluck, Christoph Willibald (von)
born: 7 Bavaria **8** Neumarkt
composer of: 5 Orfeo **6** Armide **7** Alceste **13** Paride ed Elena **14** Echo et Narcisse **17** Iphigenie en Aulide **18** Iphigenie en Tauride

glue 3 fix, gum **5** affix, epoxy, paste, putty, stick **6** adhere, cement, fasten, mortar **7** plaster, stickum **8** adherent, adhesive, concrete, fixative, mucilage **11** agglutinate

gluey 5 gooey, gummy, mucid, ropey, slimy, tacky, thick, **6** sticky, viscid **7** stringy, viscous **8** adhesive **12** mucilaginous

glum 6 gloomy, morose **8** dejected **9** cheerless **10** melancholy **14** down in the mouth

glut 4 bolt, clog, cram, drug, fill, gulp, jade, load, sate **5** choke, flood, gorge, stuff **6** burden, deluge, devour, excess, gobble **7** congest, overeat, satiate, surfeit, surplus **8** gobble up, obstruct, overdose, overfeed, overload, plethora, saturate **10** gormandize, oversupply, saturation **11** obstruction, superfluity **13** overabundance, super saturate **14** superabundance **15** supersaturation

glutinous 5 gluey, gummy, mucid, ropey, slimy, tacky, thick **6** sticky, viscid **7** viscous **8** adhesive **10** gelatinous **12** mucilaginous

glutton 3 hog, pig **6** gorger **7** stuffer **8** gourmand **9** chowhound, overeater **10** belly-slave **11** gormandizer, trencherman

gluttonous 6 greedy **7** hoggish, piggish, swinish **8** edacious, grasping, ravening, ravenous **9** excessive, voracious **10** insatiable, omnivorous **11** intemperate

gluttony 8 rapacity, voracity **10** overeating **11** gourmandism, hoggishness, piggishness **12** gormandizing, intemperance, ravenousness **13** voraciousness

gnarled 6 knotty, rugged, snaggy **7** crooked, knotted, nodular, twisted **8** leathery, wrinkled **9** contorted, distorted **11** full of knots **13** weatherbeaten

gnash 4 gnaw **5** chomp

gnat 7 no-see-um
group of: 5 cloud, horde

gnaw 4 bite, chew, fret, gall **5** chafe, chomp, eat at, grate, graze, munch, worry **6** browse, crunch, harrow, nibble, rankle **7** torment, trouble **8**

distress, nibble at, ruminate **9** eat away at, masticate

gnome 3 elf **4** pixy **5** dwarf, troll **6** goblin, sprite **10** leprechaun

gnostic 4 sage, wise **6** clever, shrewd **7** knowing **8** mandaean, simonian **10** insightful

gnothi seauton 11 know thyself

gnu 7 brindle **8** antelope **10** wildebeest
type: 5 C gnou **9** C taurinus **12** Connochaetes

go 3 act, end, fit, fly, pep, run, try, vim **4** blow, dash, elan, fare, flee, flow, jibe, lead, life, pass, quit, stir, turn, wend, work **5** agree, begin, be off, blend, drive, force, get on, lapse, leave, reach, scram, slide, split, steam, tally, trial, verve, vigor, whirl **6** accord, beat it, be used, belong, chance, decamp, depart, effort, elapse, energy, expire, extend, mettle, pass by, repair, result, retire, spirit **7** advance, attempt, be given, be known, comport, fall out, glide by, move out, operate, perform, proceed, slip off, take off, turn out, vamoose, work out **8** ambition, endeavor, function, move away, progress, slip away, sneak off, spread to, start for, steal off, vitality, vivacity, withdraw **9** animation, harmonize, terminate, transpire **10** enterprise, experiment, initiative

goad 4 move, prod, push, spur, urge, whet **5** drive, egg on, impel, press, prick, set on **6** arouse, exhort, fillip, incite, motive, propel, stir up **8** pressure, stimulus **9** constrain, incentive, stimulant, stimulate **10** cattle prod, inducement, motivation **11** instigation

goal 3 aim, end **4** home, mark, wire **5** point, score, tally **6** design, intent, object, target **7** end line, purpose **8** ambition, goal line, terminus **9** intention, objective **10** finish line

go along with 5 usher **6** assent, convoy, escort **8** accede to, shepherd **9** accompany, agree with, chaperone, consent to **10** comply with

go ashore 4 land **6** debark **9** disembark

go astray 3 err, sin **6** wander **7** deviate, do wrong **9** misbehave **10** transgress **13** fall from grace

goat 3 kid **4** buck, butt **5** billy, nanny **6** victim **7** fall guy **9** scapegoat **11** whipping boy **13** laughingstock
breed: 6 Angora, Chamal, Nubian, Saanen **7** Granada **8** La Mancha **10** Toggenburg **11** Anglo-Nubian **12** French Alpine **13** British Alpine
combining form: 4 aego **5** capri
family: 7 Bovidae
female: 3 doe **5** capra, nanny **7** doeling
genus: 5 Capra
goat-boy: 5 Giles
goat-milk cheese: 7 chevret

goat-man: 5 satyr
god: 3 Pan **5** satyr **7** Aegipan
group of: 4 herd **5** tribe
hair: 5 kasha, tibet
hair of Angora goat: 6 mohair
male: 4 buck **5** billy
meat: 7 cabrito
star: 7 capella
young: 3 kid

Goat, Horned Goat
constellation of: 11 Capricornus

goat god 3 Pan **5** satyr

go away 3 ebb **4** fade, scat, wane **5** abate, leave, scram **6** depart, lessen, retire **8** withdraw **9** disappear

gob 3 dab, tar **4** clot, glob, lump, mass **6** sailor **7** Jack Tar

go back 6 return **7** retreat

gobble 3 caw **4** bolt, gulp, wolf **5** raven, stuff **6** cackle, devour, gabble, gaggle **8** bolt down, cram down, gulp down

gobbledygook 4 bosh, bunk, cant, tosh **6** jargon **7** rubbish, twaddle **8** buncombe, nonsense, tommyrot **9** gibberish, moonshine **10** balderdash, double-talk, hocus-pocus, mumbo jumbo **11** foolishness **12** fiddle-faddle

gobble up 6 devour **8** bolt down, gulp down, wolf down

go before 7 precede, predate **8** antecede, antedate **9** come first, go ahead of **10** anticipate

go-between 5 agent, envoy, fixer, proxy **6** deputy, second **7** arbiter **8** delegate, emissary, mediator **9** messenger, middleman, moderator **10** arbitrator, interceder, negotiator **12** intermediary **13** intermediator **14** representative

goblet 3 cup **5** glass **6** vessel **7** chalice

goblin 4 ogre **5** bogey, demon, troll **7** gremlin **8** bogeyman

Gobseck
author: 14 Honore de Balzac

go by 4 pass **6** elapse, pass by, roll by, rush by, slip by **7** glide by, slide by **8** slip away

go by car 4 ride **5** drive, motor

go-cart 4 cart **5** buggy **6** barrow **8** carriage, handcart, pushcart, stroller **11** wheelbarrow

go crimson 4 burn, glow **5** blush, color, flame, flush **6** redden

God, god 4 Lord **5** Allah, deity **6** Elohim, Jahveh, Yahweh **7** Holy One, Jehovah, Skaddai **8** divinity, the Deity **9** Our Father **10** the Creator, the Godhead **11** divine being, God Almighty, the Almighty **13** the Omnipotent, the Omniscient **14** the All-Merciful, the Man Upstairs **15** the Supreme Being
Hebrew: 6 Adonai
Latin: 7 Dominus

god, first

origin: 12 Scandinavian
known as: 7 Forsete, Forseti

God and Man at Yale
author: 17 William F Buckley Jr

God and my right
French: 14 Dieu et mon droit
motto of: 18 royal arms of England

God be with us
German: 10 Gott mit uns

God be with you
Latin: 12 Deus vobiscum

Godbole, Professor
character in: 15 A Passage to India
author: 7 Forster

Goddard, Jean-Luc
director of: 10 Breathless

Goddard, Paulette
real name: 10 Marion Levy
husband: 14 Charlie Chaplin **15** Burgess Meredith **18** Erich Maria Remarque
born: 11 Great Neck NY
roles: 11 Modern Times, Unconquered **15** So Proudly We Hail **16** Standing Room Only, The Great Dictator **19** Diary of a Chambermaid

Goddard, Robert Hutchings
nationality: 8 American
inventor of: 12 rocket engine **22** liquid propellant rocket

Godden, Rumer
author of: 8 The River **14** Black Narcissus, Kitchen Madonna **16** The Peacock Spring **18** In This House of Brede, The Greengage Summer **19** An Episode of Sparrows **23** The Battle of Villa Fiorita

God enriches
Latin: 9 ditat Deus
motto of: 7 Arizona

Godfather, The
author: 9 Mario Puzo
family: 8 Corleone
director: 18 Francis Ford Coppola
cast: 8 Al Pacino (Michael) **9** James Caan (Sonny) **10** John Cazale (Fredo), John Marley, Talia Shire **11** Diane Keaton **12** Marlon Brando (Don Vito Corleone), Richard Conte, Robert Duvall **14** Sterling Hayden **17** Richard Castellano
Oscar for: 5 actor (Brando) **7** picture **10** screenplay
sequel: 18 The Godfather Part II

Godfather, The, Part II
director: 18 Francis Ford Coppola
cast: 8 Al Pacino **10** John Cazale, Talia Shire **11** Diane Keaton **12** Lee Strasberg, Robert DeNiro, Robert Duvall
Oscar for: 7 picture **10** screenplay **15** supporting actor (DeNiro)
sequel to: 12 The Godfather

godforsaken 5 bleak **6** lonely, remote **8** deserted, desolate, wretched **9** abandoned, neglected

god from a machine
  Latin: **13** deux ex machina
God is with us
  German: **10** Gott mit uns
godless 4 evil **6** wicked **7** heathen, impious, profane, ungodly **8** agnostic, depraved **9** atheistic **10** unhallowed **11** blasphemous, irreligious, unrepentant, unrighteous **12** sacrilegious, unsanctified
godlessness 7 atheism **8** apostasy, unbelief **9** disbelief **10** irreligion
godlike 4 holy **5** godly, pious **6** deific, divine, sacred **8** immortal, olympian
godliness 5 piety **8** devotion, holiness **9** reverence **10** devoutness **12** spirituality
godly 4 good, holy **5** moral, pious **6** devout, divine, sacred **7** devoted, saintly **8** faithful, hallowed, reverent **9** believing, God-loving, pietistic, religious, righteous, spiritual **10** God-fearing, sanctified **11** consecrated, pure in heart, reverential
go down 3 ebb **4** drop, fade, wane **5** abate, lower, slide **6** lessen, plunge, reduce, weaken **7** descend, plummet, slacken, subside **8** decrease, diminish, moderate
God Save the Queen
  author: **17** William F Buckley Jr
God's Grace
  author: **14** Bernard Malamud
God's Little Acre
  author: **15** Erskine Caldwell
Godthaab
  capital of: **9** Greenland
God willing
  Latin: **10** Deo volente
God wills it
  Latin: **8** Deus vult
  cry of: **9** Crusaders
Goes, Hugo van der
  born: **5** Ghent **8** Flanders
  artwork: **7** The Fall **14** The Lamentation **19** The Death of the Virgin **21** The Adoration of the Magi **22** The Adoration of the Child **26** The Adoration of the Shepherds
Goethe, Johann
  author of: **5** Faust **6** Egmont **24** The Sorrows of Young Werther **29** Wilhelm Meister's Apprenticeship
go-getter 4 doer **7** hustler **8** achiever, live wire
go-getting 7 driving, dynamic **8** forceful, hustling **9** ambitious, assertive, energetic **10** aggressive **11** hard-driving, hard-working, industrious
Gogol, Nikolai
  author of: **7** The Nose **9** Dead Souls **10** Taras Bulba **11** The Overcoat **19** The Inspector-General
go hand in hand 5 match, tally **6** concur, square **7** coexist **9** accompany

go hungry 4 fast **6** famish, starve **7** abstain
Going My Way
  director: **10** Leo McCarey
  cast: **10** Bing Crosby (Father O'Malley) **12** Gene Lockhart **15** Barry Fitzgerald
  Oscar for: **4** song **5** actor (Crosby) **7** picture **8** director **15** supporting actor (Fitzgerald)
  song: **15** Swinging on a Star
gold 3 bar **4** gilt **5** aurum, ingot **6** beauty, nugget, purity, yellow **7** bullion **8** goodness, goodwill, humanity, kindness **11** beneficence
  chemical symbol: **2** Au
gold and silver
  Spanish: **9** oro y plata
  motto of: **7** Montana
Gold Bug, The
  author: **13** Edgar Allan Poe
Gold Coast see **5** Ghana **11** Sierra Leone
golden 4 best, gilt, rosy **5** blest, blond, great, happy, palmy **6** bright, gilded, joyous, timely **7** aureate, halcyon, richest, shining **8** beatific, glorious, happiest, splendid **9** favorable, opportune, priceless, promising **10** auspicious, delightful, propitious, seasonable **11** exceptional, flourishing, resplendent **12** advantageous, bright-yellow **13** extraordinary
Golden Age
  first age of: **3** man
  world ruled by: **6** Cronus, Saturn
Golden Ass, The
  author: **14** Lucius Apuleius
  character: **4** Milo **5** Fotis **6** Lucius **8** Charites, Pamphile **9** Lepolemus **10** Thrasillus
Goldenberg, Emmanuel
  real name of: **15** Edward G Robinson
Golden Bough, The
  branch of: **9** mistletoe
  sacred to: **10** Proserpina
  used by: **6** Aeneas
  at shrine of: **5** Diana **7** Virbius
  author: **15** Sir James G Frazer
Golden Bowl, The
  author: **10** Henry James
  character: **8** Mr Verver **12** Maggie Verver, Mrs Assingham **13** Prince Amerigo **14** Charlotte Stant
Golden Boy
  nickname of: **11** Paul Hornung
golden brown 3 tan **5** tawny, toast **6** sienna **7** tobacco **8** chestnut
Golden Cockerel, The
  also: **8** Le Coq d'Or **15** Zolotoy Petushok
  opera by: **14** Rimsky-Korsakov
  character: **9** King Dodon **14** Queen of Shemaka
golden egg-layer

  form: **5** goose
  made of: **4** gold
Golden Fleece
  made of: **4** gold
  kept at: **7** Colchis
  kept by: **10** King Aeetes
  stolen by: **5** Jason **9** Argonauts
  accomplice: **5** Medea
Golden Legend
  author: **13** William Caxton
goldenrod 8 Solidago
  varieties: **5** sweet, white **6** Wreath **7** seaside **8** blue- stem, European **10** California
Golden State
  nickname of: **10** California
golden youth
  French: **13** jeunesse doree
goldfinch
  group of: **5** charm
Goldfinger
  director: **11** Guy Hamilton
  author: **10** Ian Fleming
  cast: **9** Gert Frobe (Auric Goldfinger) **10** Bernard Lee (M) **11** Lois Maxwell (Miss Moneypenny) **12** Harold Sakata (Oddjob), Shirley Eaton **13** Honor Blackman (Pussy Galore), Sean Connery (James Bond, 007)
Golding, William
  author of: **8** Free Fall **13** A Moving Target **14** Lord of the Flies, Rites of Passage **15** Darkness Visible
gold mine 7 bonanza **10** mother lode
Gold Rush, The
  director: **14** Charlie Chaplin
  cast: **9** Mack Swain, Tom Murray **11** Georgia Hale **14** Charlie Chaplin (Little Tramp)
  setting: **5** Yukon
Goldsmith, Oliver
  author of: **18** She Stoops to Conquer, The Deserted Village **19** The Vicar of Wakefield
goldwasser
  form: **7** liquor
  origin: **6** France **7** Germany
  flavor: **4** herb **5** spice **7** caraway
  flecked with: **8** gold leaf
golf
  average number strokes to reach a hole: **3** par
  ball in another's path: **6** stymie
  championship: **6** US Open **9** Grand Slam **11** British Open **17** Masters' Tournament
  club: **4** iron, wood **6** driver, putter **7** brassie **8** long iron **9** sand wedge, short iron **10** middle iron **13** pitching wedge
  club carrier: **6** caddie
  course also called: **5** links
  golf ball formerly called: **6** guttie **8** feathery
  hole scored in one stroke: **3** ace **9** hole-in-one
  one stroke less than par: **6** birdie

one stroke more than par: 5 bogey
part of the course: 3 cup, tee **4** hole **5** apron, green, rough **6** bunker, hazard **7** fairway **8** sand trap
position: 3 lie
stance: 4 open **6** closed, square **7** address
two strokes less than par: 5 eagle
type of competition: 5 match, skins **6** stroke
uprooted turf: 5 divot
warning cry: 4 fore

golfer 8 Ben Hogan, Ernie Els, Lee Elder, Sam Snead **9** Carol Mann, Hale Irwin, Patty Berg, Tom Watson **10** Betsy Rawls, Bobby Jones, Deane Beman, Gary Player, Hubie Green, Jim Demaret, Judy Rankin, Lee Trevino, Nancy Lopez, Tiger Woods **11** Ben Crenshaw, Billy Casper, Byron Nelson, Calvin Peete, Donna Caponi, Gene Sarazen, Julius Boros, Tom Weiskopf, Walter Hagen **12** Arnold Palmer, Jack Nicklaus, Joanne Carner, Johnny Miller, Mickey Wright, Sandra Haynie **14** Cary Middlecoff, Kathy Whitworth **16** Roberto DeVicenzo **19** Susie Maxwell Berning **20** Severiano Ballesteros **21** Babe Didrikson Zaharias

Golgotha 7 Calvary
means: 10 skull place

Goliath 5 giant
home: 4 Gath **9** Philistia
slain by: 5 David
weapon: 9 slingshot

golliwogg 3 toy **4** doll **9** plaything

Gomer Pyle USMC
character: 5 Bunny **7** Frankie **9** Corp Boyle **11** Duke Slayter, (Sgt) Vince Carter
cast: 9 Jim Nabors, Roy Stuart **10** Ted Bessell **11** Frank Sutton **12** Ronnie Schell **13** Barbara Stuart

Gomorrah
destroyed with: 5 Sodom **6** Zeboim **10** Admah

Gondoliers, The
operetta by: 18 Gilbert and Sullivan
character: 4 Luiz **5** Tessa **7** Casilda **8** Gianetta **9** Marco Palmieri **15** Duke of Plaza-Toro **16** Giuseppe Palmieri

gone 3 ago, out **4** away, dead, left, lost, past **6** absent, ruined, used up **7** defunct, died out, extinct, missing **8** departed, finished, hopeless, vanished **11** disappeared

Goneril
character in: 8 King Lear
author: 11 Shakespeare

Gone With the Wind
author: 16 Margaret Mitchell
character: 5 Mammy **6** Big Sam, Prissy **7** Dr Meade **10** Ellen (Robillard) O'Hara **11** Gerald O'Hara, Honey Wilkes, India Wilkes **12** Ashley Wilkes, Aunt Pittypat, Belle Watling **13** Scarlett O'Hara, Tarleton twins **15** Mrs Merriweather **21** Melanie Hamilton Wilkes
Scarlett's husband: 11 Rhett Butler **12** Frank Kennedy **15** Charles Hamilton
Scarlett's children: 4 Emma, Wade **6** Bonnie
Scarlett's sister: 7 Carreen, Suellen
director: 13 Victor Fleming
cast: 9 Ona Munson **10** Clark Gable (Rhett Butler) **11** Evelyn Keyes, Vivien Leigh (Scarlett O'Hara) **12** Leslie Howard (Ashley Wilkes) **13** Ann Rutherford **14** Hattie McDaniel (Mammy), Thomas Mitchell (Gerald O'Hara) **16** Butterfly McQueen (Prissy) **17** Olivia de Havilland (Melanie Hamilton Wilkes)
score: 10 Max Steiner
Oscar for: 7 actress (Leigh), picture **8** director **12** screenwriter **17** supporting actress (McDaniel)
producer: 14 David O Selznick

good 3 ace, fit, new **4** best, boon, fine, full, gain, kind, pure, real **5** ample, crack, favor, great, large, merit, moral, pious, prize, right, solid, sound, sunny, valid, value, worth **6** adroit, choice, devout, entire, genial, honest, humane, kindly, lively, newest, profit, proper, seemly, select, tiptop, useful, virtue, wealth, worthy **7** adapted, benefit, capable, capital, dutiful, fitting, genuine, godsend, healthy, orderly, service, sizable, skilled, success, upright, welfare **8** adequate, becoming, blessing, bonafide, cheerful, complete, decorous, gracious, innocent, interest, kindness, obedient, obliging, pleasant, precious, reliable, salutary, skillful, smartest, sociable, splendid, suitable, thorough, topnotch, valuable, virtuous, windfall **9** admirable, advantage, agreeable, authentic, convivial, deserving, efficient, enjoyable, enjoyment, excellent, exemplary, expensive, favorable, first-rate, happiness, healthful, honorable, priceless, qualified, religious, righteous, unsullied, untainted, wholesome, wonderful **10** altruistic, beneficent, beneficial, benevolent, excellence, first-class, legitimate, proficient, prosperity, sufficient, worthwhile **11** appropriate, commendable, considerate, improvement, kindhearted, substantial, sympathetic, well-behaved **12** advantageous, considerable, praiseworthy, satisfactory **13** companionable, conscientious, righteousness
French: 3 bon **4** bien
Spanish: 5 bueno
German: 3 gut

Good as Gold
author: 12 Joseph Heller

Good Book 5 Bible

good breeding 5 grace **6** polish **7** manners **9** gentility **10** refinement **11** cultivation

good buy 4 deal **5** steal **7** bargain

goodby, goodbye 3 bye **6** bye-bye, bye now, so long **7** parting, send-off **8** farewell, Godspeed **9** departure **10** separation **11** be seeing you, leave-taking, see you later **12** God be with you **15** till we meet again
French: 5 adieu **8** au revoir
German: 14 auf Wiedersehen
Hawaiian: 5 aloha
Italian: 4 ciao **5** addio **11** arrivederci
Japanese: 8 sayonara
Latin: 4 vale
Spanish: 5 adios **12** hasta la vista

Goodbye, Mr Chips
director: 7 Sam Wood
author: 11 James Hilton
cast: 11 Greer Garson, Paul Henreid (von Henreid), Robert Donat
Oscar for: 5 actor (Donat)
character: 7 Mr Chips **10** Mrs Wickett **12** Kathy Bridges
school: 10 Brookfield

Goodbye Girl, The
director: 11 Herbert Ross
based on play by: 9 Neil Simon
cast: 11 Marsha Mason **13** Quinn Cummings **15** Richard Dreyfuss
Oscar for: 5 actor (Dreyfuss)

Good Companions, The
author: 11 J B Priestley

good counsel
god of: 6 Consus

good day
French: 7 bonjour
German: 8 guten tag
Spanish: 10 buenos dias
Italian: 10 buon giorno

good deal 3 buy **5** steal **7** bargain

good deed 8 kindness **11** benefaction **12** philanthropy
Hebrew: 7 mitsvah, mitzvah

Good Earth, The
author: 10 Pearl S Buck
character: 4 O-Lan **6** Nung En **7** Nung Wen, The Fool **8** Wang Lung **11** Pear Blossom **12** Lotus Blossom
director: 14 Sidney Franklin
cast: 8 Keye Luke, Paul Muni **10** Tilly Losch **11** Jessie Ralph, Luise Rainer **14** Walter Connolly **15** Charley Grapewin
Oscar for: 7 actress (Rainer)

good feelings 3 era **8** good will **11** benevolence **12** friendliness

good form 9 etiquette, good taste **10** politeness **11** good manners

good-for-nothing 5 idler **6** loafer **7** useless **9** no-account, shiftless, worthless

good fortune 4 luck **7** bonanza **8** fortuity, lady luck, windfall **9** blessings **10** lucky break

good friend
French: **6** bon ami **9** bonne amie

good health 5 vigor **7** fitness **8** vitality **10** robustness

Goodhue, Bertram Grosvenor
architect of: **13** St Bartholomew (NYC) **14** St Thomas Church (NYC) **25** Chapel at US Military Academy (West Point), National Academy of Sciences (Washington DC) **28** Nebraska State Capitol Building (Lincoln)
style: **13** Gothic Revival **15** Spanish Colonial

good humor 10 affability, amiability, cheeriness, kindliness, mellowness **12** cheerfulness, complaisance, pleasantness **15** kindheartedness

good-humored 4 mild, warm **6** cheery, genial, gentle, kindly, mellow **7** affable, amiable **8** cheerful, pleasant **9** congenial, easygoing **11** complaisant

good-looker 3 fox **4** doll, hunk **5** beaut, Venus **6** Adonis, beauty, eyeful **7** stunner **8** knockout **11** handsome Dan

good-looking 4 fair, foxy, sexy **5** bonny **6** comely, lovely, pretty **8** alluring, clean-cut, gorgeous, handsome, stunning **9** beauteous, beautiful, exquisite, ravishing **10** attractive, bewitching, enchanting **11** captivating, eye-catching, well favored **15** pulchritudinous

good looks 6 beauty **10** comeliness, loveliness **11** pulchritude **12** handsomeness **14** attractiveness

good luck
Yiddish: **8** mazel tov

goodly 4 tidy **5** ample, large **7** sizable **11** substantial **12** considerable

good manners 8 courtesy **9** amenities, etiquette, gentility **10** politeness, refinement

good name 4 face **5** image **10** reputation **11** self-respect

good nature 6 warmth **9** geniality, good humor **10** affability, amiability, cordiality, likability **12** complaisance, pleasantness **13** agreeableness

good-natured 4 warm **5** sunny **6** genial, kindly **7** affable, amiable **8** cheerful, friendly, obliging, pleasant **9** agreeable, congenial, easygoing **11** complaisant, good-humored, warmhearted **13** accommodating

goodness 3 boy, gee, hey, say, wow **5** favor, honor, mercy, merit, piety, value, worth, wowee **6** profit, purity, virtue **7** benefit, decorum, gee whiz, heavens, honesty, probity, service **8** boy-oh-boy, devotion, gracious, kindness, morality **9** advantage, innocence, integrity, land alive, landsakes, nutrition, propriety, rectitude **10** generosity, kindliness, sakes alive, usefulness **11** benevolence, nourishment

12 virtuousness **13** righteousness, wholesomeness **14** heavens to Betsy

good night
French: **7** bon soir **9** bonne nuit
German: **9** gute nacht
Spanish: **12** buenas noches
Italian: **10** buona notte

good opinion 6 esteem, regard **7** respect **8** approval **10** admiration

good person 4 dear, love **5** angel **7** darling **10** sweetheart

goods 4 gear **5** cloth, stock, wares **6** fabric, things **7** effects, fabrics **8** chattels, material, movables, property, textiles **9** inventory, trappings **11** commodities, furnishings, merchandise, possessions **13** appurtenances, paraphernalia

good sense 6 brains, wisdom **8** judgment **12** intelligence

good taste 10 refinement **11** cultivation, discernment **14** discrimination

good-tempered 5 sunny **7** amiable, smiling **8** cheerful **12** sweet-natured

good time 3 fun **9** amusement, diversion, enjoyment **13** entertainment

good times 4 boom **8** fat years

good turn 5 favor **7** service **8** good deed

goodwill 5 amity **8** kindness **9** benignity **10** cordiality, kindliness **11** amicability, benevolence **12** friendliness **15** kindheartedness

good wishes 4 best **5** favor **6** regard **7** consent, regards **8** approval, blessing, respects, sanction **11** compliments

Goodwood, Caspar
character in: **18** The Portrait of a Lady
author: **5** James

good word 6 praise **10** compliment **11** approbation **12** commendation **14** congratulation

Goodyear, Charles
nationality: **8** American
developed: **16** vulcanized rubber

goof 3 err **4** boob, flub, fool, mess **5** botch, error, gum up **6** bollix, booboo, bungle, fumble, slip up **7** blunder, mistake **9** oversight

Goolagong Cawley, Evonne
sport: **6** tennis
heritage: **19** Australian Aborigine

go on all fours 5 crawl, creep

goose
young: **7** gosling
group of: **5** flock, skein **6** gaggle

goose egg 3 nil, zip **4** zero **5** aught **6** cipher, naught **7** nothing **11** horse collar

go over 5 audit, check **6** review **7** examine, inspect **10** scrutinize **11** investigate

Gopher State
nickname of: **9** Minnesota

Gorbachev, Mikhail Sergeyevich
party: **9** Communist
country: **4** USSR **6** Russia **31** Union of Soviet Socialist Republics
born: **9** Stavropol **10** Privolnoye **16** Krasnogvardeisky
education: **21** Moscow State University
political career: **9** Politburo **16** General Secretary **20** Agriculture Secretary **23** Stavropol Communist Party **35** Deputy Supreme Soviet Central Committee
policy: **8** glasnost **11** perestroika
distinguishing characteristic: **19** strawberry birthmark (head)
wife: **15** Raisa Maksimovna
    occupation: **7** teacher
daughter: **5** Irisa
    occupation: **6** doctor **9** physician
grandchild: **6** Oksana

Gorcey, Leo
born: **9** New York NY
roles: **4** Spit **10** Bowery Boys **11** Dead End Kids

Gordimer, Nadine
author of: **11** July's People **12** The Lying Days **13** A Guest of Honor **15** Burger's Daughter **16** A Soldier's Embrace **21** The Late Bourgeois World
award: **10** Nobel Prize

Gordon, Ruth
real name: **15** Ruth Gordon Jones
husband: **11** Garson Kanin
born: **11** Wollaston MA
roles: **11** Where's Poppa? **13** Rosemary's Baby **14** Harold and Maude **17** Inside Daisy Clover **20** Abe Lincoln in Illinois

gore 5 blood **7** carnage **8** butchery **9** bloodshed, slaughter

Gore, Albert
born: **10** Washington (DC)
wife: **6** Tipper **13** Mary Elizabeth
children: **5** Sarah **6** Albert **7** Karenna, Kristin
education: **7** Harvard **10** Vanderbilt
profession: **10** journalist
author of: **17** Earth in the Balance
political career: **6** Senate **13** vice president **22** House of Representatives

Gorgas, William Crawford
field: **8** medicine
position: **18** army surgeon general
conquered: **7** malaria **11** yellow fever
location: **11** Panama Canal

gorge 3 gap, ire **4** bolt, cram, craw, dale, dell, fill, glen, glut, gulp, pass, sate, vale **5** abyss, anger, blood, chasm, cleft, gulch, gully, mouth, stuff, wrath **6** canyon, defile, devour, gobble, gullet, hatred, hollow, muzzle, nausea, ravine, throat **7** disgust, indulge, overeat, satiate **8** crevasse **9** animosity, esophagus, repulsion, revulsion **10** gluttonize, gormandize, repugnance **11** overindulge

gorgeous 4 fine, rich **5** grand **6** bright, costly, lovely **7** elegant, opulent, shining **8** dazzling, glorious, imposing, splendid, stunning **9** beautiful, brilliant, exquisite, luxurious, ravishing, sumptuous **10** attractive, glittering, impressive **11** good-looking, magnificent, resplendent, splendorous **13** splendiferous

Gorgons
  form: 7 maidens **8** monsters
  names: 6 Medusa, Stheno **7** Euryale, Sthenno
  father: 7 Phorcys
  mother: 4 Ceto
  protectress: 6 Graeae, Graiae
  hair of: 6 snakes
  hands of: 5 brass
  turned viewers to: 5 stone

Gorgosaurus
  type: 8 dinosaur, theropod
  location: 7 Alberta **12** North America
  period: 10 Cretaceous

gorilla
  group of: 4 band
  studied by: 10 Dian Fossey

Gorky, Arshile
  real name: 21 Vosdanig Manoog Adokian
  born: 7 Armenia **11** Khorkomvari
  artwork: 5 Agony **15** Diary of a Seducer **17** Making the Calendar **21** The Artist and his Mother, Water of the Flowery Hill **22** The Liver is the Cock's Comb

Gorky, Maxim (Maksim)
  real name: 25 Alekseimaksimovich Peshkov
  author of: 7 V I Lenin **11** My Childhood **14** The Lower Depths **18** The Small Town Okurov **20** City of the Yellow Devil, Twenty-six Men and a Girl **27** The Life of Matthew Kozhemyakin

gormandize 5 feast, raven **6** devour

gory 5 scary **6** bloody, creepy **9** murderous **10** horrifying, sanguinary, terrifying **11** bloodsoaked, ensanguined, frightening **12** bloodstained, bloodthirsty **13** bloodcurdling

gospel, Gospel 5 credo, creed **8** doctrine **11** the good news, the last word **12** the final word **13** the whole truth, ultimate truth
  the first four books of the New Testament: 4 Luke, John, Mark **7** Matthew

Gospel writers 4 John, Luke, Mark **7** Matthew **9** synoptist

gospodin (Russian) 2 Mr **6** Mister

gossamer 5 filmy, gauzy, sheer **8** cobwebby **10** diaphanous **13** insubstantial

gossip 4 news **6** babble, report, tattle **7** comment, hearsay, prattle, scandal, twaddle **8** idle talk **10** backbiting **12** tittle-tattle **13** newsmongering

gossiper 3 pry **4** blab **5** prate, snoop, yenta **6** gabble, magpie, meddle, tattle **7** babbler, meddler, prattle, snooper, tattler **8** busybody **9** chatterer **10** chatterbox, newsmonger, talebearer, tattletale **11** rumormonger **12** blabbermouth, gossipmonger **13** scandalmonger

Go Tell It on the Mountain
  author: 12 James Baldwin

Gothic
  language family: 12 Indo-European

go through 4 bear **6** endure, suffer **7** sustain, undergo **9** encounter, withstand **10** experience

go to 3 see **5** visit **6** attend **8** appear at, frequent

go to bed 6 retire, turn in **7** lie down, sack out **8** flake out **9** hit the hay **10** call it a day, hit the sack **11** catch some z's

go to pieces 5 break, crack **7** break up, crack up, crumble, give way, shatter **8** splinter **9** break down, fall apart **11** lose control **12** disintegrate

go to work on 6 attack, tackle **8** set about **9** undertake

go to wrack and ruin 5 decay **7** crumble **9** fall apart **12** disintegrate

Gotterdammerung 17 Twilight of the Gods
  see: 8 Ragnarok

Gott mit uns 11 God be with us, God is with us

gouge 5 carve, drill, scoop **6** chisel, extort **10** overcharge

gouge out 5 drill **6** hollow **8** carve out, scoop out **9** chisel out, hollow out **10** whittle out

Gould, Chester
  creator/artist of: 9 Dick Tracy

Gould, Elliott
  real name: 16 Elliott Goldstein
  wife: 15 Barbra Streisand
  born: 10 Brooklyn NY
  roles: 4 MASH **13** Little Murders **14** The Long Goodbye **15** California Split, Getting Straight **19** Bob & Carol & Ted & Alice

Goulding, Edmund
  director of: 10 Grand Hotel **11** Dark Victory **13** The Dawn Patrol

go under 4 fail, fall, sink **9** go belly up **10** go bankrupt

Gounod, Charles Francois
  born: 5 Paris **6** France
  composer of: 5 Faust **6** Gallia, Sappho, Te Deum **8** Cinq-Mars, Mireille **9** La Colombe, Polyeucte **10** Mors et Vita **11** Marie Stuart, Stabat Mater **13** La Reine de Saba **14** Romeo and Juliet **16** La Nonne Sanglante, Phile-

mon et Baucis **17** La Tribute de Zamora **18** Le Medecin Malgre Lui

gourd 4 pepo **9** Cucurbita
  varieties: 3 ash, ivy, rag, wax **4** club **5** snake, white **6** bitter, bottle, dipper, sponge, teasel, viper's **7** fig-leaf, Malabar, serpent, trumpet **8** calabash, hedgehog, Missouri **9** dishcloth **10** goareberry, gooseberry, knobkerrie, silver-seed **11** sugar- trough **12** Hercules'-club **14** scarlet-fruited

gourmand 7 glutton **8** big eater **9** bon vivant, chowhound **11** gormandizer, trencherman

gourmet 7 epicure **9** bon vivant **10** gastronome **11** connoisseur; gastronomer **12** gastronomist

gourmet cooking
  French: 12 haute cuisine

gout 5 style, taste **10** preference

govern 3 run **4** boss, curb, form, head, lead, rule, sway, tame **5** check, guide, pilot, steer **6** bridle, direct, manage **7** command, control, incline, inhibit, oversee **8** dominate, restrain **9** influence, supervise **10** administer, discipline, hold in hand **11** hold in check, superintend **13** be at the helm of **14** pull the strings **16** keep under control **17** exercise authority **18** be in the driver's seat

governed 3 led **5** ruled **6** guided **7** steered, subject **8** directed **9** dependent **10** controlled, supervised **12** administered **13** superintended

governing 6 ruling **7** curbing, guiding, heading, leading, swaying **8** bridling, checking, managing, piloting, reigning, steering **9** directing, inclining **10** inhibiting, management, overseeing **11** controlling, influencing, restraining, supervision **13** administering **14** administrating, administration, superintending

governing body 10 government, management, parliament **12** powers that be **14** administration **16** board of directors, board of governors **18** executive committee

government 3 law **4** rule **5** state **6** regime **7** command, control **8** dominion, guidance **9** authority, direction **10** domination, management, regulation **11** supervision **13** governing body, statesmanship **14** administration
  absence of: 7 anarchy
  absolute: 7 czarism, tsarism, tyranny **9** autocracy, despotism
  by the best: 11 aristocracy
  by church: 9 theocracy
  by elders: 12 gerontocracy
  by technologists: 11 technocracy
  by few: 9 oligarchy
  by mob: 10 ochlocracy
  by people: 9 democracy
  by rich: 10 plutocracy
  by three: 8 triarchy **11** triumvirate

by two: 7 biarchy 10 duumvirate
by women: 8 gynarchy 10 matriarchy

governor
Turkish: 3 bey
Barbary States: 3 dey

Gowan
character in: 12 Little Dorrit
author: 7 Dickens

go with 6 convey, convoy, escort 7 conduct 9 accompany

gown 4 robe 5 dress, frock 10 nightdress

goy 6 non-Jew 7 Gentile

Goya (y Lucientes, Francisco Jose de)
born: 5 Spain 13 Fuente de todos
artwork: 8 Proverbs 10 Disparates 11 Tauromaquia 12 Los Caprichos, The Naked Maja 15 Majas on a Balcony 17 The Disasters of War 21 Charles IV and his Family

grab 3 bag, nab 4 grip, hold, pass 5 catch, clasp, grasp, lunge, pluck, seize 6 clutch, collar, snatch 7 capture

grace 4 deck, love, tact, trim 5 adorn, charm, endow, exalt, favor, honor, mercy, merit, piety, skill, taste 6 beauty, bedeck, enrich, pardon, polish, set off, virtue 7 charity, culture, decorum, dignify, dress up, elevate, enhance, garnish, glorify, manners, smarten, suavity 8 beautify, clemency, decorate, elegance, felicity, fluidity, God's love, holiness, lenience, ornament, reprieve, sanctity, spruce up, urbanity 9 embellish, endowment, etiquette, exemption, extra time, God's favor, good looks, propriety 10 aggrandize, comeliness, devoutness, excellence, indulgence, refinement 11 cultivation, forgiveness, lissomeness, pulchritude, saintliness, willowiness 12 dispensation, gracefulness, mannerliness 14 accomplishment, divine goodness
French: 11 savoir faire

graceful 5 lithe 6 comely, limber, lovely 7 elegant, lissome, shapely, sinuous, willowy 8 delicate 9 beautiful, lithesome, sylphlike 10 attractive 11 light-footed

gracefulness 8 delicacy, fluidity 10 suppleness 11 lissomeness

graceless 5 gawky, inept 6 clumsy 7 awkward 10 ungraceful 11 heavy-handed

Graces
also: 7 Gratiae 9 Charities
goddesses of: 6 beauty
father: 4 Zeus
mother: 8 Eurynome
names: 4 Auxo 5 Cleta 6 Aglaia, Thalia 7 Phaenna 8 Hegemone 10 Euphrosyne

gracious 2 my 3 boy, gee, wow 4 kind 5 civil, mercy, oh boy 6 benign, humane, kindly, polite, tender, ye gods 7 affable, amiable, clement, cordial, courtly, gee whiz, lenient, my stars 8 friendly, goodness, merciful, obliging, pleasant 9 benignant, courteous, landsakes 10 benevolent, charitable, chivalrous, hospitable 11 good heavens, good natured, kindhearted 13 compassionate 14 heavens to Betsy

gradation 4 step 5 stage 6 degree 7 shading 8 grouping, ordering 9 arranging 11 arrangement 12 organization 14 classification

grade 4 bank, even, hill, mark, ramp, rank, rate, sort, step 5 brand, caste, class, level, order, pitch, place, slope, stage, value 6 degree, estate, rating, smooth, sphere, status 7 flatten, incline, quality, station 8 classify, gradient, position, standing 9 acclivity, condition, declivity, intensity

grade-A 2 A-1 4 aces, a-one, fine, tops 5 grade, great, prime, super 6 choice, superb, tip-top 7 capital 8 peerless, sterling, superior, top-notch 9 excellent, first-rate, matchless, superfine 10 first-class, preeminent, tremendous 11 outstanding, superlative

Gradgrind, Thomas and Louisa
characters in: 9 Hard Times
author: 7 Dickens

gradient 4 ramp, tilt 5 pitch, slant, slope 6 ascent 7 incline, leaning 9 steepness 11 inclination

gradual 4 slow 6 gentle, steady 7 regular 8 measured 9 graduated, piecemeal 10 continuous, deliberate, drop-by-drop, inch-by-inch, step-by-step, successive 11 incremental, progressive 13 imperceptible, slow-but-steady 14 little-by-little

graduate 5 grade 6 alumna 7 alumnus, mark off 9 calibrate 10 measure out 14 grant a degree to, receive a degree

Graduate, The
director: 11 Mike Nichols
cast: 12 Anne Bancroft (Mrs Robinson) 13 Dustin Hoffman, Katharine Ross 14 Murray Hamilton, William Daniels
score: 17 Simon and Garfunkel
Oscar for: 8 director

Graeae
also: 6 Graiae
goddesses of: 3 sea
number: 5 three
names: 4 Enyo 5 Deino 9 Pemphredo
father: 7 Phorcys
mother: 4 Ceto
sisters: 7 Gorgons
protectresses of: 7 Gorgons
personified: 6 old age
three shared: 6 one eye 8 one tooth
eye stolen by: 7 Perseus
corresponds to: 4 Enyo

Graeme, Alison
character in: 21 The Master of Ballantrae
author: 9 Stevenson

Graf 5 count

graffito, graffiti 4 name 6 slogan 7 drawing, scratch 8 scribble 10 defacement

graft 3 bud 4 join, last, slip, swag 5 booty, infix, inset, plant, scion 6 bribes, payola, splice, spoils, sprout 7 bribery, implant, ingraft, payoffs, plunder, rake-off 8 kickback 9 hush money 10 corruption, transplant 12 implantation 13 inserted shoot

Graham, Bruce
architect of: 17 John Hancock Center (Chicago)

Grahame, Kenneth
author of: 19 The Wind in the Willows

Graiae see 6 Graeae

grain 3 bit, dot, jot, rye 4 atom, corn, dash, iota, mite, oats, seed, whit 5 crumb, grist, maize, ovule, pinch, spark, speck, touch, trace, wheat 6 barley, cereal, kernel, millet, morsel, pellet, little, trifle 7 granule, modicum 8 fragment, molecule, particle 9 scintilla
abbreviation: 2 gr
god of: 7 Robigus
goddess of: 6 Ribigo

Grain Coast see 11 Sierra Leone

Grainger, Percy Aldridge
born: 9 Australia, Melbourne
composer of: 14 Country Gardens 17 Handel in the Strand 19 Rosenkavaller Ramble

gram
abbreviation of: 1 g

Gram
origin: 12 Scandinavian
mentioned in: 8 Volsunga
form: 5 sword
owned by: 7 Sigmund
used by: 6 Sigurd
killed: 6 Fafnir

grand 2 A-1 3 big 4 fine, full, good, head, huge, keen, main 5 chief, fancy, great, large, lofty, noble, regal, royal, showy, super, swell 6 august, choice, groovy, kingly, lordly, superb 7 dashing, elegant, exalted, haughty, mammoth, opulent, pompous, queenly, stately, sublime, supreme 8 arrogant, complete, elevated, fabulous, glorious, imperial, imposing, majestic, palatial, princely, real cool, real gone, smashing, splendid, striking, terrific 9 admirable, dignified, excellent, first-rate, grandiose, luxurious, marvelous, principal, sumptuous, wonderful 10 impressive, monumental, out-of-sight 11 highfalutin, magnificent, pretentious, sensational 12 ostentatious 13 comprehensive, distinguished

Grand Canyon State
  nickname of: **7** Arizona
grande dame 9 great lady
grandee 5 noble **8** nobleman **9** blue blood **10** aristocrat
Grandees
  author: **17** Stephen Birmingham
grandeur 4 fame, pomp **5** glory, state **6** luster **7** dignity, majesty **8** eminence, nobility, splendor **9** celebrity, loftiness, solemnity, sublimity **10** augustness, excellence, importance **11** distinction, stateliness **12** magnificence, resplendence **14** impressiveness
Grand Hotel
  author: **9** Vicki Baum
  character: **9** Miss Flamm **12** Baron Gaigern **14** Dr Otternschlag, Otto Kringelein **27** Herr Generaldirektor Preysing **32** Elisaveta Alexandrovna Grusinskaya
  director: **14** Edmund Goulding
  cast: **10** Greta Garbo **12** Joan Crawford, Wallace Beery **13** John Barrymore **15** Lionel Barrymore
  setting: **6** Berlin
Grand Illusion
  director: **10** Jean Renoir
  cast: **5** Dalio **7** Carette **9** Dita Parlo, Jean Gabin **13** Pierre Fresnay **16** Erich von Stroheim
grandiloquent 5 lofty **6** florid, turgid **7** flowery, pompous, stilted, swollen **8** inflated **9** bombastic, grandiose, highflown **10** rhetorical **11** highfalutin, pretentious **12** high-sounding, magniloquent
grandiose 5 grand **7** pompous, splashy **8** affected **9** high-flown **10** flamboyant, theatrical **11** extravagant, highfalutin, pretentious
Grand Marnier
  type: **6** brandy, cognac **7** liqueur
  origin: **6** France
  flavor: **6** orange
  with gin: **7** Red Lion
grand monde 10 great world **11** best society **16** fashionable world
grand prix 10 grand prize
grand prize
  French: **9** grand prix
Grange, Red (Harold)
  nickname: **14** Galloping Ghost
  sport: **8** football
  team: **11** U of Illinois **12** Chicago Bears
Granger, Edith
  character in: **12** Dombey and Son
  author: **7** Dickens
Grangosier
  character in: **22** Gargantua and Pantagruel
  author: **8** Rabelais
Granite State
  nickname of: **12** New Hampshire

grant 4 boon, cede, gift, give **5** admit, allot, allow, award, endow, favor, yield **6** accord, assign, bestow, confer, donate, permit **7** agree to, bequest, concede, consent, deal out, largess, present, subsidy, tribute **8** accede to, allocate, bestowal, dispense, donation, gratuity, offering **9** allotment, allowance, apportion, consent to, endowment, vouchsafe **10** assignment, concession, indulgence **11** benefaction **12** contribution, presentation **13** appropriation
Grant, Cary
  real name: **23** Archibald Alexander Leach
  wife: **10** Dyan Cannon **13** Barbara Hutton
  born: **7** England **8** Bristol
  roles: **6** Topper **9** Dream Wife, Houseboat **10** Indiscreet **11** Blonde Venus, Father Goose **13** To Catch a Thief **14** Bringing Up Baby, Monkey Business, The Bishop's Wife **15** She Done Him Wrong **16** North by Northwest **17** Arsenic and Old Lace, I Was a Male War Bride **18** Operation Petticoat **20** The Philadelphia Story **21** None But the Lonely Heart
Grant, Lee
  real name: **21** Lyova Haskell Rosenthal
  born: **9** New York NY
  roles: **7** Shampoo **10** Plaza Suite **11** Peyton Place, The Landlord **14** Detective Story **19** In the Heat of the Night **20** Divorce American Style
Grant, Ulysses Simpson
  real name: **17** Hiram Ulysses Grant
  nickname: **3** Sam **4** Lyss **27** Unconditional Surrender Grant
  presidential rank: **10** eighteenth
  party: **10** Republican
  state represented: **2** IL
  defeated: **5** (David) Davis, (James) Black **6** (Charles) O'Conor **7** (Horace) Greeley, (Horatio) Seymour **9** (William Slocomb) Groesbeck
  vice president: **5** (Thomas W) Ferry (acting) **6** (Henry) Wilson (died in office 1875), (Schuyler) Colfax
  cabinet:
    state: **4** (Hamilton) Fish **9** (Elihu Benjamin) Washburne
    treasury: **7** (Alexander Turney) Stewart, (Benjamin Helm) Bristow, (Lot Myrick) Morrill **8** (George Sewall) Boutwell **10** (William Adams) Richardson
    war: **4** (Alphonso) Taft **7** (James Donald) Cameron, (John Aaron) Rawlins, (William Worth) Belknap
    attorney general: **4** (Alphonso) Taft, (Ebenezer Rockwood) Hoar **7** (Amos Tappan) Akerman **8** (George Henry) Williams **10** (Edwards) Pierrepont
    navy: **5** (Adolph Edward) Borie **7**

(George Maxwell) Robeson
    postmaster general: **5** (James Noble) Tyner **6** (Marshall) Jewell **8** (James William) Marshall, (John Angel James) Creswell
    interior: **3** (Jacob Dolson) Cox **6** (Columbus) Delano **8** (Zachariah) Chandler
  born: **15** Point Pleasant OH
  died: **15** Mount McGregor NY
  buried: **9** New York NY
  education: **9** West Point **17** US Military Academy
  religion: **9** Methodist
  author: **24** Personal Memoirs of US Grant **30** Around the World with General Grant
  political career:
    secretary of: **3** War (interim appointment)
  civilian career: **6** farmer
  military service: **6** US Army **8** Civil War **10** Mexican War **18** Illinois Volunteers **20** Commander of Union Army
  notable events of lifetime/career: **5** Panic (of 1873) **11** Black Friday (gold panic) **16** Custer's Last Stand
    Act: **10** Salary Grab
    conspiracy: **11** Whiskey Ring
    scandal: **14** Credit Mobilier
  quote: **60** "No terms except unconditional and immediate surrender can be accepted"
  father: **9** Jesse Root
  mother: **6** Hannah (Simpson)
  siblings: **5** Clare **10** Orvil Lynch **11** Mary Frances **13** Samuel Simpson, Virginia Paine
  wife: **5** Julia (Boggs Dent)
  children: **5** Ellen **9** Jesse Root **13** Frederick Dent **14** Ulysses Simpson
granted
  French: **7** d'accord
grantee 8 receiver **9** recipient **11** beneficiary
grant immunity to 4 free **5** clear, spare **6** except, excuse, exempt **7** absolve, release, relieve **9** privilege
grantor 5 giver **8** bestower **10** benefactor
granulate 5 crush **6** powder **9** pulverize **11** crystallize
granulated 6 ground **7** crushed **8** powdered **10** pulverized **12** crystallized
granule 5 grain **7** crystal **8** particle
grape 5 Vitis **13** Vitis vinifera
  varieties: **3** cat, red, sea **4** amur, blue, bush, cape, rock, sand, tail **5** bear's, bunch, frost, Javan, sugar, veldt **6** canyon, Damson, Miller, Oregon, pigeon, possum, summer, winter **7** African, Bullace, catbird, chicken, Concord, Spanish **8** European, mountain **9** evergreen, panhandle, river-bank **10** silver-leaf **11**

southern fox **13** sweet mountain

wine: 5 Gamay **6** Cayuga, Duriff, Merlot, Muscat, Shiraz **7** Barbera, Catawba **8** Baco Noir, Dolcetto, Labrusca, Nebbiolo, Verduzzo **9** Aglianico, Fume Blanc, Huxelrebe, Pinot Noir, Primitivo, Trebbiano, Zinfandel **10** Chardonnay, Sangiovese **11** Chenin Blanc, Petite Sirah, Pinot Bianco, Seyval Blanc **13** Cabernet Franc, Montepulciano **14** Sauvignon Blanc **15** Gewurztraminer **17** Cabernet Sauvignon **20** Johannisberg Riesling

Grapes of Wrath, The
author: 13 John Steinbeck
character: 4 Noah **6** Connie, Ma Joad, Pa Joad **7** Jim Casy, Tom Joad **12** Rose of Sharon
director: 8 John Ford
cast: 10 Henry Fonda **11** Jane Darwell **12** Dorris Bowden **13** John Carradine **15** Charley Grapewin
Oscar for: 17 supporting actress (Darwell)

graphic 4 seen **5** clear, drawn, lucid, vivid **6** visual **7** painted, printed, visible, written **8** distinct, explicit, forcible, lifelike, pictured, striking **9** pictorial, realistic, trenchant **10** expressive **11** descriptive, picturesque **12** illustrative

grappa
type: 6 brandy **7** liqueur
origin: 5 Italy
made from: 9 grape pulp

grapple 4 face, grip, hold, meet **5** catch, clasp, fight, grasp, seize **6** breast, clutch, combat, engage, fasten, tackle, take on **7** contend, grapnel, wrestle **8** confront, deal with, do battle, make fast, struggle **9** encounter, large hook, lay hold of **11** hold tightly

grasp 3 get, ken **4** grab, grip, hold, sway, take **5** catch, clasp, infer, power, range, reach, savvy, scope, seize, sense, skill, sweep **6** clinch, clutch, deduce, fathom, follow, master, snatch, take in, talent **7** catch at, compass, control, embrace, grapple, mastery, seizing, seizure **8** clutches, gripping, perceive **9** handclasp, knowledge, seize upon **10** comprehend, perception, understand **13** comprehension, understanding

grasping 5 venal **6** greedy **7** hoggish, miserly, selfish, wolfish **8** covetous **9** mercenary, predatory, rapacious **10** avaricious **11** acquisitive

graspingness 5 greed **7** avarice **8** rapacity, venality **10** greediness **12** covetousness

grass
varieties: 3 cup, cut, dog, eel, elk, mat, nut, oat, oil, pin, rib, rye, Uva **4** barn, bear, bent, blue, chee, cord, crab, deer, fish, hair, lace, love, Lyme, moor, Nard, palm, Para, rice, rush, silk, star, tape, worm, yard **5** arrow, Bahia, beach, beard, Brome, Carib, China, cloud, curly, Ditch, fever, goose, lemon, Means, Melic, Mondo, natal, quack, sedge, shave, shore, Smilo, spike, squaw, Sudan, sword, Vasey, wheat, white, witch, zebra **6** Aleppo, alkali, basket, Bengal, Buffel, Canary, carpet, Dallis, Dudder, finger, gallow, Guinea, Indian, Korean, Manila, Napier, orange, orchid, Pampas, Rescue, Rhodes, ribbon, ripple, scurvy, signal, starry, switch, Tobosa, velvet, vernal, viper's, Zoysia **7** Bermuda, Brahman, Bristle, Buffalo, Esparto, Harding, Johnson, Kleberg, Pangola, poverty, pudding, quaking, Ravenna, sea lyme, serpent, tall oat, Wallaby, Widgeon **8** Angleton, blue-eyed, blue love, Boer love, elephant, fountain, hairy cup, lazy- man's, molasses, Ree wheat, sand love, scorpion, tuber oat **9** blue conch, centipede, common rye, hairy crab, hare's-tail, Hungarian, Malojilla, Mascarene, Oregon rye, rancheria, tall wheat, water star, yellow nut **10** Amur silver, beavertail, big quaking, blue finger, citronella, English rye, false wheat, golden-eyed, Indian rice, Italian rye, Korean lawn, Kuma bamboo, purple-eyed, rabbit foot, rabbit-tail, reed canary, tufted hair, Washington, western rye, yellow-eyed **11** annual beard, branched cup, desert wheat, domestic rye, dwarf meadow, feather love, giant finger, green needle, Lehmann love, Nepal silver, Pentz finger, prairie cord, ringed beard, St Augustine, sweet vernal, Texas needle, Texas winter, weeping love **12** Common carpet, crested wheat, crinkled hair, European dune, Indian basket, Japanese lawn, Japanese love, Korean velvet, perennial rye, slender wheat, squirreltail, western wheat **13** American beach, Australian rye, billion-dollar, European beach, Himalaya fairy, Japanese sedge, little quaking, Paraguay Bahia, plains bristle, Siberian wheat **14** African Bermuda, bluebunch wheat, Japanese carpet, Pensacola Bahia, perennial veldt, pubescent wheat, Saint Augustine, stiff-hair wheat **15** European feather, Wilmington Bahia **16** creeping windmill, Pacey's English rye **17** Australian feather, intermediate wheat, Mediterranean salt, Transvaal dog-tooth **18** Australian windmill, California blue-eyed, Mexican everlasting **19** Fairway crested wheat **20** standard crested wheat

Grass, Gunter
author of: 6 Floods **8** Dog Years **10** The Tin Drum **11** Cat and Mouse, The Flounder **16** Local Anaesthetic **18** The Meeting at Telgte **20** From the Diary of a Snail **33** Headbirths or The Germans Are Dying Out

grasshopper
variety: 5 pygmy **6** meadow, monkey **7** katydid **10** band winged, cone headed, long-horned, slant-faced **11** bush katydid, leaf-rolling, short-horned **12** shield-backed, spur-throated

grassland 3 lea **4** farm, vale, veld **5** field, pampa, plain, range, veldt **6** meadow **7** pasture, prairie, savanna **8** farmland, flatland, savannah **10** plantation

grate 3 irk, jar, rub, vex **4** bars, burr, buzz, gall, rasp **5** annoy, chafe, clack, grill, grind, mince, shred **6** abrade, gnaw at, hearth, jangle, rankle, scrape, scream, screen **7** firebed, firebox, grating, lattice, scratch, screech **8** irritate **9** fireplace, pulverize **10** exasperate, firebasket **11** latticework

grateful 7 obliged **8** beholden, indebted, thankful **9** gratified, obligated **12** appreciative

gratefulness 6 thanks **9** gratitude **12** appreciation, thankfulness

Gratiae see **6** Graces

Gratiano
character in: 19 The Merchant of Venice
author: 11 Shakespeare

gratification 3 joy **4** glee, kick **5** bliss **6** relish, solace, thrill **7** comfort, delight, ecstasy, elation, rapture **8** gladness, humoring, pleasing, pleasure, soothing **9** enjoyment, happiness, transport **10** indulgence, jubilation, satisfying **11** contentment, enchantment **12** exhilaration, satisfaction

gratified 5 happy **7** content, pleased **9** satisfied **11** comfortable

gratify 4 suit **5** amuse, favor, humor **6** coddle, divert, pamper, please, regale, soothe, thrill, tickle **7** appease, delight, enchant, flatter, gladden, indulge, refresh, satisfy **8** enthrall, entrance, interest, recreate **9** enrapture, entertain, transport **10** compliment, exhilarate

gratifying 8 humoring, pleasant, pleasing, soothing **9** agreeable, enjoyable, indulging, pampering, rewarding **10** delightful, satisfying **11** pleasurable

grating 4 bars, fret, grid **5** grate, harsh, raspy **6** creaky, grille, shrill **7** jarring, lattice, rasping, raucous, squeaky, tracery, trellis **8** abrasive, annoying, filigree, fretwork, gridiron, jangling, piercing, scraping, strident **9** offensive, vexatious **10** discordant, gate of bard, irritating, unpleasant **11** cacophonous, displeasing, high-pitched **12** disagreeable, exacerbating, exasperating

grating noise 7 discord, rasping 8 grinding 9 cacophony, harshness 10 disharmony, dissonance

gratis 4 free 10 gratuitous, on the house 13 complimentary, without charge

gratitude 6 thanks 10 obligation 11 recognition 12 appreciation, beholdenness, gratefulness, thankfulness, thanksgiving 14 acknowledgment

gratuitous 4 free 6 gratis, wanton 7 donated, willing 8 baseless, unproven 9 unfounded, voluntary 10 free of cost, groundless, irrelevant, unasked for, unprovoked 11 conjectural, impertinent, presumptive, spontaneous, uncalled for, unjustified, unwarranted 13 complimentary, unrecompensed

gratuity 3 tip 4 gift 8 donation
French: 7 douceur 9 pourboire

Graustark
author: 20 George Barr McCutcheon

grave 4 dour, sage, tomb 5 acute, crypt, mound, quiet, sober, staid, vault, vital 6 gloomy, sedate, solemn, somber, urgent 7 crucial, earnest, ossuary, serious, subdued, weighty 8 catacomb, cenotaph, critical, frowning, pressing 9 dignified, important, long-faced, mausoleum, momentous, sepulcher 10 thoughtful 11 burial ground, grim visaged, significant 13 consequential, philosophical 16 last resting place, place of interment
music: 6 solemn 7 serious

Graves, Robert
author of: 9 I Claudius, King Jesus 14 Claudius the God 15 The White Goddess 16 Goodbye to All That

graveyard 7 charnel, ossuary 8 boneyard, boot hill, cemetery 10 churchyard, necropolis 12 memorial park, potter's field 13 burying ground

gravitate 4 fall, head, move, sink, tend 6 settle 7 be drawn, descend, incline 8 converge, zero in on 9 be prone to 10 lean toward

gravity 4 pull 6 danger, import, moment 7 concern, dignity, urgency 8 calmness, enormity, grimness, serenity, sobriety 9 emergency, magnitude, solemnity, staidness 10 attraction, gloominess, importance, sedateness, solemnness, somberness 11 consequence, earnestness, gravitation, seriousness 12 significance, tranquillity 13 consideration, crucial nature 14 critical nature, pull of the earth, thoughtfulness 16 mutual attraction

gray, grey 3 dun 4 ashy, dark, drab, pale 5 ashen, foggy, hoary, misty, murky, slate 6 cloudy, dismal, gloomy, silver, somber 7 clouded, grayish, grizzly, neutral, silvery, sunless 8 overcast 9 cheerless, pearl-gray 10 depressing, gray-haired, grayheaded 11 dove-colored, hoary-headed 12 mouse-colored, silverhaired 13 salt and pepper

Gray, Harold
creator/artist of: 17 Little Orphan Annie

Gray, Thomas
author of: 32 Elegy Written in a Country Churchyard

grayness 4 murk 6 pallor 8 drabness 9 bleakness 10 somberness

Grayson, Kathryn
real name: 19 Zelma Kathryn Hedrick
born: 14 Winston-Salem NC
roles: 8 Show Boat 10 Kiss Me Kate 13 Anchors Aweigh, The Desert Song 15 The Vagabond King

graze 3 rub 4 crop, rasp, skim, skin 5 brush, grind, swipe 6 abrade, browse, bruise, glance, scrape 7 pasture, scratch 8 abrasion, eat grass 16 turn out to pasture

grease 3 fat, oil 4 balm, lard 5 salve 6 anoint, tallow 7 unguent 8 ointment 9 drippings, lubricant, lubricate

grease the palm 3 tip 5 bribe 6 buy off, pay off

greasy 3 fat 4 oily, waxy 5 fatty, lardy, slick 7 buttery 8 slippery, slithery 10 lardaceous, oleaginous

great 3 apt, big 4 able, a-one, cool, fine, good, high, huge, kind, many, phat, vast, well 5 chief, crack, grand, grave, gross, heavy, large, noble, noted, super, swell 6 adroit, choice, expert, famous, groovy, humane, loving, strong, superb 7 awesome, crucial, decided, eminent, extreme, grandly, immense, leading, mammoth, notable, serious, titanic, weighty 8 abundant, colossal, critical, enormous, esteemed, fabulous, generous, gigantic, glorious, gracious, manifold, renowned, skillful, smashing, splendid, superbly, superior, terrific, very well 9 boundless, countless, cyclopean, excellent, fantastic, first-rate, important, marvelous, momentous, monstrous, prominent, unlimited, wonderful 10 altruistic, celebrated, gargantuan, high-minded, inordinate, out-of-sight, prodigious, proficient, pronounced, remarkable, splendidly, stupendous, tremendous, voluminous 11 crackerjack, excellently, extravagant, illustrious, magnanimous, magnificent, outstanding, sensational, significant, superlative, wonderfully 12 considerable 13 consequential, distinguished, inexhaustible, magnificently, multitudinous 14 out of this world

Great Ajax
origin: 5 Greek
hero of: 9 Trojan War

greater 4 more 5 finer 6 better, bigger, larger 8 superior

Great Escape, The
director: 11 John Sturges
cast: 11 James Coburn, James Garner 12 Steve McQueen 13 David McCallum 14 Charles Bronson 15 Donald Pleasance 19 Richard Attenborough
setting: 7 Germany, POW camp

greatest 4 best, most 5 ultra 6 picked, select, utmost 7 extreme, highest, maximal, maximum, noblest, supreme 8 champion 9 first-rate 11 superlative, unsurpassed

Greatest Show on Earth, The
director: 13 Cecil B DeMille
cast: 11 Betty Hutton, Cornel Wilde 12 James Stewart 13 Dorothy Lamour, Gloria Grahame 14 Charlton Heston
Oscar for: 7 picture

Great Expectations
author: 14 Charles Dickens
character: 3 Pip 7 Estella 9 Compeyson, Mr Jaggers 10 Joe Gargery 12 Abel Magwitch, Miss Havisham 13 Herbert Pocket
director: 9 David Lean
cast: 9 John Mills 11 Martita Hunt 12 Alec Guinness, Bernard Mills 13 Valerie Hobson 16 Francis L Sullivan

Great Gatsby, The
author: 16 F Scott Fitzgerald
character: 9 Jay Gatsby 11 Tom Buchanan 12 Myrtle Wilson, Nick Carraway 13 Daisy Buchanan

Great God Brown, The
author: 12 Eugene O'Neill

great lady
French: 10 grande dame

Great Lake 4 Erie 5 Huron 7 Ontario 8 Michigan, Superior

Great Land
nickname of: 6 Alaska

greatly 6 vastly 7 largely, notably 8 markedly, mightily, very much 9 immensely 10 abundantly, enormously, infinitely, powerfully, remarkably 12 considerably, immeasurably, tremendously

great mishap 5 wreck 6 blight, fiasco 7 tragedy 8 calamity, disaster 9 cataclysm, ruination 11 catastrophe

greatness 8 eminence, nobility 9 loftiness 10 excellence, importance, notability, prominence 11 preeminence, superiority 12 magnificence 15 illustriousness

Great Profile
nickname of: 13 John Barrymore

Great Railway Bazaar, The
author: 11 Paul Theroux

great world
French: 10 grand monde

Great Ziegfeld, The
director: 14 Robert Z Leonard
cast: 8 Myrna Loy 10 Fanny Brice 11 Frank Morgan, Luise Rainer (Anna Held) 13 Virginia Bruce, William

Powell
Oscar for: 7 actress (Rainer), picture
grebe 4 bird, fowl, loon **5** diver **6** dipper **7** henbill **8** dabchick **9** hell-diver **10** water witch
Grecco, Al
  character in: 20 Appointment in Samarra
  author: 5 O'Hara
Greco, El Greco
  real name: 23 Domenikos Theotokopoulos
  born: 5 Crete **6** Candia
  artwork: 7 Espolio (Disrobing of Christ), Laocoon **12** View of Toledo **19** Cleaning of the Temple **20** Healing of the Blind Man **21** Burial of the Count Orgaz **27** Christ Stripped of his Garments **28** San Ildefonso at his Writing Desk **29** Cardinal Fernando Nino de Guevara **42** Christ Driving the Money-Changers from the Temple
Greece
  other name: 5 Ellas **16** Hellenic Republic
  capital/largest city: 6 Athens
  others: 4 Enor **5** Canea, Corfu, Pylos, Volos **6** Delphi, Patras, Sparta **7** Chalcis, Corinth, Olympia, Piraeus **8** Salonika, Thessaly **9** Epidaurus, Gallipoli **10** Herakleion **11** Hermoupolis
  school: 5 Crete **6** Athens, Patras, Thrace **8** Ioannina, Salonika
  division: 6 Attica, Epirus, Thrace **7** Boeotia **8** Thessaly **9** Macedonia
  measure: 3 pik **4** bema, piki, pous **5** baril, chous, cubit, diote, doron, maris, pekhe, podos, pygon, xylon **6** acaena, bacile, barile, cotula, dichas, gramme, hemina, koilon, lichas, milion, orgyia, palame, pechys, schene, xestes **7** amphora, bacvhel, chenica, choenix, cyathos, diaulos, metreta, stadium, stremma **8** condylos, daktylos, dekapode, dolichos, medimnos, medimnus, metretes, palaiste, plethron, plethrum, stathmos **9** hemiekton, oxybaphon
  monetary unit: 5 lepta **7** drachma
  weight: 3 mna, oke **4** mina, obol **5** livre, pound **6** diobol, kantar, obolos, obolus, talent **7** chalcon, drachma **8** diobolon
  island: 3 Ios **5** Chios, Corfu, Crete, Delos, Melos, Naxos, Paros, Samos, Syros, Tenos, Thera, Zante **6** Andros, Euboea, Ionian, Ithaca, Lemnos, Lesbos, Patmos, Rhodes, Skyros, Thasos **7** Mykonos **8** Cyclades, Mytilene, Skiathos, Skopelos **9** Alonnisos **10** Cephalonia, Dodecanese, Samothrace **16** Northern Sporades
  lake: 5 Karla, Volve **6** Copais, Kopais, Prespa, Voweis **8** Ioannina, Koroneia, Vistonis **9** Trichonis, Vegoritis
  mountain: 3 Ida **4** Idhi, Oeta, Oite,

Ossa **5** Athos **6** Ithome, Peleon, Pelion, Pindus **7** Grammos, Helicon, Rhodope **8** Hymettos, Smolikas, Taygetos, Taygetus **9** Parnassus **10** Hagion Oros, Lycabettus, Pentelicus
  highest point: 7 Olympus
  river: 4 Arta **6** Peneus, Struma, Vardar **7** Hellada, Maritsa **8** Achelous, Aliakmon
  sea: 5 Crete **6** Aegean, Ionian **7** Mirtoon **13** Mediterranean
  physical feature:
    gulf: 7 Corinth, Saronic
    peninsula: 6 Balkan **10** Chalcidice **12** Peloponnesus
    plain: 7 Boeotia **8** Thessaly
    plateau: 7 Arcadia
    valley: 5 Nemea
  people: 5 Greek **6** Achean, Dorian, Ionian **7** Aeolian, Hellene
    artist: 7 El Greco
    author: 5 Homer **6** Hesiod, Pindar **8** Menander **9** Aeschylus, Euripides, Sophocles **11** Kazantzakis **12** Aristophanes
    god: 4 Ares, Hera, Leto, Zeus **5** Cupid **6** Apollo, Cronus, Hermes, Hestia **7** Artemis, Demeter **8** Dionysus, Poseidon **9** Aphrodite **10** Hephaestus, Persephone **12** Pallas Athena **13** Phoebus Apollo
    historian: 9 Herodotus **10** Thucydides
    king: 11 Constantine
    lawmaker: 5 Draco, Solon **8** Lycurgus, Pericles
    leader: 10 Papandreou
    mathematician: 6 Euclid **10** Archimedes, Pythagoras
    mythological: 5 Atlas, Helen, Jason, Medea, Paris **6** Hector, Medusa **7** Ariadne, Chimera, Pandora, Pegasus, Perseus, Theseus **8** Achilles, Heracles, Minotaur, Odysseus **9** Agamemnon, Andromeda, Iphigenia, King Minos **10** Prometheus **11** Bellerophon
    orator: 11 Demosthenes
    philosopher: 5 Plato **8** Socrates **9** Aristotle
    physician: 11 Hippocrates
    sculptor: 5 Myron **7** Phidias **10** Praxiteles
    tycoon: 7 Onassis
  language: 5 Greek
  religion: 14 Greek Orthodoxy
  place:
    ruins: 5 Delos, Pella, Pylos, Samos **6** Delphi, Sparta, Thebes, Tiryns **7** Corinth, Eleusis, Elevsis, Knossos, Mycenae, Olympia **9** Acropolis, Epidaurus, Parthenon **13** Palace of Minos
  feature:
    coffeeshop: 7 kaphene
    marketplace: 5 agora
    port 7 Piraeus
    presidential guard: 7 Evzones

    village square: 7 plateia
  food:
    dish: 4 gyro **7** baklava, mousaka **8** moussaka, souvlaki, dolmades **10** shish kabob
    liquor: 4 ouzo
    wine: 7 retsina
greed 7 avarice, avidity, craving **8** cupidity, rapacity **11** itching palm, money-hunger, piggishness, selfishness **12** covetousness **13** rapaciousness **14** avariciousness
greediness 7 avarice **8** gluttony, rapacity, voracity **12** covetousness, graspingness **15** acquisitiveness
greedy 4 avid **5** eager **6** ardent, hungry **7** anxious, burning, craving, fervent, hoggish, piggish, selfish, swinish, wolfish **8** covetous, famished, grasping, ravenous **9** devouring, impatient, mercenary, predatory, rapacious, thirsting, voracious **10** avaricious, gluttonous, insatiable **11** acquisitive, money-hungry **12** gormandizing
Greek
  language family: 12 Indo-European
  ancient branch: 5 Attic, Doric, Ionic **6** Aeolic
Greek alphabet 5 alpha **4** beta **5** gamma **5** delta **7** epsilon **4** zeta **3** eta **5** theta **4** iota **5** kappa **6** lambda **2** mu **2** nu **2** xi **7** omicron **2** pi **3** rho **5** sigma **3** tau **7** upsilon **3** phi **3** chi **3** psi **5** omega
Greek Anthology, The
  author: 8 Cephalas, Meleager
Greek measure 4 mina **5** cubit **6** obolos, talent **7** drachma, stadion
Greek Mythology
  afterworld of the blessed: 7 Elysium
  amber islands: 10 Electrides
  architect of labyrinth: 8 Daedalus
  blood-sucking monster: 5 Lamia
  cupbearer to the gods: 8 Ganymede **9** Catamitus
  dragon: 8 basilisk
  drink of the gods: 6 nectar
  eagle/lion monster: 7 griffin, griffon, gryphon
  enchantress: 5 Circe
  female warrior: 6 Amazon
  fire-breathing monster: 7 Chimera
  first man: 12 Alalcomeneus
  food/drink/perfume of the gods: 8 ambrosia
  the Furies: 5 Dirae **6** Erinys, Furiae, Semnai **7** Erinyes **9** Eumenides
    names: 7 Allecto, Megaera **9** Tisiphone
  goat god: 7 Aegipan
  goddess of beauty: 6 Graces **7** Gratiae **9** Charities
    names: 4 Auxo **5** Cleta **6** Aglaia, Thalia **7** Phaenna **8** Hegemone **10** Euphrosyne
  goddess of childbirth: 8 Ilithyia **10** Eileithyia

corresponds to Roman: 6 Lucina
goddess of the dawn: 3 Eos
corresponds to Roman: 6 Aurora
goddesses of destiny: 5 Fates, Morae
6 Moerae, Moirai
names: 5 Moira **6** Clotho **8** Lachesis
corresponds to Roman: 6 Parcae
goddess of discord: 4 Eris
corresponds to Roman: 9 Discordia
goddess of divine punishment/recklessness: 3 Ate
goddess of divine retribution: 8 Adrastea
goddess of the earth: 2 Ge **4** Gaea, Gaia
corresponds to Roman: 6 Tellus
goddess of earth/fertility: 7 Demeter
corresponds to Roman: 5 Ceres
goddess of earth/Hades: 5 Brimo **6** Hecate, Hekate
goddess of fortune: 5 Tyche
corresponds to Roman: 7 Fortuna
goddess of healing: 4 Iaso
goddess of health: 6 Hygeia
corresponds to Roman: 5 Salus
goddess of the hearth: 6 Hestia
corresponds to Roman: 5 Vesta
goddess of justice: 4 Dice, Dike **6** Astrea **7** Astraea
goddesses of literature/the arts: 5 Muses **7** the Nine **8** Pierides **10** Castalides
names: 4 Clio **5** Aoede, Erato, Mneme **6** Melete, Thalia, Urania **7** Euterpe **8** Calliope **9** Melpomene **10** Polyhymnia **11** Terpsichore
corresponds to Roman: 7 Camenae
muse of astronomy: 6 Urania
muse of dancing/choral song: 11 Terpsichore
muse of history: 4 Clio
muse of idyllic poetry/comedy: 6 Thalia
muse of love poetry: 5 Erato
muse of meditation: 6 Melete
muse of memory: 5 Mneme
muse of music/lyric poetry: 7 Euterpe
muse of poetry/epic: 8 Calliope
muse of sacred music/dance: 10 Polyhymnia
muse of song: 5 Aoede
muse of tragedy: 9 Melpomene
goddess of love/beauty: 6 Urania **7** Cyprian, Paphian **8** Cytherea **9** Aphrodite **10** Anadyomene
corresponds to Roman: 5 Venus
goddess of memory: 9 Mnemosyne
goddess of the night: 3 Nyx
goddess of peace: 5 Irene
corresponds to Roman: 3 Pax
goddess of the rainbow: 4 Iris
goddess of sailors: 5 Brizo
goddess of the sea: 10 Amphitrite
goddesses of the sea: 6 Graeae,

Graiae
names: 4 Enyo **5** Deino **9** Pemphredo
goddesses of seasons/growth/decay/social order: 4 Hour **5** Horae
names: 4 Dice, Dike **5** Carpo, Irene **6** Thallo **7** Eunomia
goddess of spring flowers: 6 Thallo
goddess of summer fruit: 5 Carpo
goddess of victory: 4 Nike
corresponds to Roman: 6 Athena **8** Victoria
goddess of war: 4 Enyo
corresponds to Roman: 7 Bellona
goddess of wisdom/fertility/arts/warfare: 6 Athena, Athene, Pallas, Saitis **11** Tritogeneia **12** Pallas Athena **18** Alalcomenean Athena
corresponds to Roman: 7 Minerva
goddess of youth/spring: 4 Hebe
god of beekeeping/winemaking/husbandry: 9 Aristaeus
god of censure/ridicule: 5 Momos, Momus
god of dreams: 6 Icelus, Oniros **7** Oneiros **8** Morpheus
god of earth: 10 Trophonius
god of Eleusinian mysteries: 7 Bacchus
god of erotic desire: 7 Himeros
god of fire/metalworking/handicrafts: 10 Hephaestus, Hephaistos
corresponds to Roman: 6 Vulcan
god of the heavens: 4 Zeus
corresponds to Roman: 4 Jove **7** Jupiter
corresponds to Egyptian: 4 Amen, Amon **5** Ammon **6** Amen Ra, Amon Ra
god of light/healing/music/poetry/prophecy/beauty: 6 Apollo
god of love: 4 Eros
corresponds to Roman: 4 Amor **5** Cupid
god of male power/procreation: 7 Priapus
corresponds to Roman: 7 Mutinus
god of marriage: 5 Hymen **9** Hymenaeus
corresponds to Roman: 8 Talassio
god of medicine/healing: 9 Asclepius
corresponds to Roman: 11 Aesculapius
god of oaths: 6 Horcus
god of recovery from illness: 11 Telesphorus
god of sea/caused earthquakes: 8 Poseidon
corresponds to Roman: 7 Neptune
god of shepherds/flocks/pastures/forests: 3 Pan **7** Sinoeis
god of sleep: 6 Hypnos, Hypnus
corresponds to Roman: 6 Somnus
god of the sun: 6 Helios **8** Hyperion
corresponds to Roman: 3 Sol
god of the underworld: 6 Infiri

god of war: 4 Ares **8** Theritas
corresponds to Roman: 4 Mars
god of wine/fertility/drama: 5 Evius **7** Bacchus **8** Dionysus
Gorgon monster: 6 Medusa
hundred-headed monster: 5 Ladon **8** Typhoeus
islands of the blessed: 10 Hesperides
man/horse monster: 7 centaur
messenger of gods/god of roads/commerce/invention/cunning/thieves: 6 Hermes
corresponds to Roman: 7 Mercury
monster that asked riddles: 6 Sphinx
monsters that turn people to stone: 7 Gorgons
moon goddess/huntress/virgin: 6 Phoebe, Selene **7** Artemis
corresponds to Roman: 5 Diana
corresponds to Cretan: 11 Britomartis
nine-headed water serpent: 5 Hydra
nymph: 7 Calypso
one-eyed giant: 7 Cyclops
oracle of Apollo: 13 Delphic oracle
personification of death: 4 Mors **8** Thanatos
personification of punishment/revenge: 5 Poena, Poine
personification of soul: 6 Psyche
physician to gods of Olympia: 5 Paeon
prophetess: 9 Alexandra, Cassandra
queen of heaven: 4 Hera, Here
corresponds to Roman: 4 Juno
race of gods: 6 Titans
names: 4 Rhea, Thia **5** Coeus, Crius **6** Cronus, Phoebe, Tethys, Themis **7** Iapetus, Oceanus **8** Hyperion **9** Mnemosyne
river god: 6 Asopus, Peneus, Simois **7** Inachus, Pelegon **8** Achelous
river in Hades: 4 Styx **5** Lethe **7** Acheron, Cocytus
ferryman: 6 Charon
river of forgetfulness: 5 Lethe
ruler of the winds: 6 Aeolus
satyr/god of the forest: 7 Silenus
sea god: 6 Nereus, Triton **7** Glaucus, Phorcys, Proteus
sea monster: 6 Scylla
seer: 6 Mopsus **8** Tiresias
serpent: 6 dipsas
serpent of darkness: 5 Apepi **7** Apophis
seven against Thebes: 6 Tydeus **8** Adrastus, Capaneus **9** Polynices **10** Amphiaraus, Hippomedon **13** Parthenopaeus
seven sisters: 8 Pleiades
names: 4 Maia **6** Merope **7** Alcyone, Celaeno, Electra, Sterope, Taygete
sorceress: 5 Medea
spirits of disease/evil/old age/death: 5 Keres
three-headed dog that guards un-

derworld: 8 Cerberus
twins: 8 Dioscuri **15** Castor and Pollux
two-headed serpent: 11 Amphisbaena
underworld: 5 Hades,
   corresponds to Roman: 3 Dis **5** Orcus, Pluto **8** Dis Pater
underworld darkness: 6 Erebus
underworld spirit: 9 Chthonian
virgin huntress: 8 Atalanta, Atalante
whirlpool: 9 Charybdis
winged horse: 5 Arion **7** Pegasus
woman/beast monster: 6 Python **8** Delphyne
woman/bird monster: 5 Harpy
woman/serpent monster: 7 Echidna
wood nymph: 5 dryad

Greek uncial codex 4 Syri **6** Regius **8** Ephraemi **9** Laudianus, Vaticanus **10** Sinaiticus **11** Basiliensis **12** Alexandrinus, Sangallensis **13** Koridethianus

green 3 raw **4** jade, lawn, lime, turf **5** crude, heath, olive, rough, sward, young **6** callow, campus, common, tender, unripe **7** awkward, emerald, verdant, verdure **8** greenish, gullible, ignorant, immature, inexpert, not cured, not dried, pea-green, sea-green, unsmoked, untanned, unversed **9** blue-green, credulous, grassplot, lime-green, unfledged, unskilled, untrained **10** aquamarine, chartreuse, golf course, grass-green, greensward, kelly-green, olive green, uninformed, unmellowed, unpolished, unseasoned **11** cobalt green, forest green, undeveloped, yellow-green **12** easily fooled, green-colored, not fully aged, putting green, village green **13** inexperienced, undisciplined **14** underdeveloped **15** unsophisticated

Green Acres
  character: 7 Mr Haney **8** Eb Dawson **10** Fred Ziffel, Sam Drucker **11** Doris Ziffel, Hank Kimball, Lisa Douglas **20** Oliver Wendell Douglas
  cast: 8 Eva Gabor, Fran Ryan **9** Alvy Moore, Frank Cady, Tom Lester **10** Pat Buttram **11** Eddie Albert **13** Barbara Pepper, Hank Patterson
  pig: 6 Arnold
  town: 11 Hooterville

green at the gills 6 queasy, sickly **7** bilious **8** nauseous **9** nauseated, sickening

greenback 4 bill **8** banknote **12** treasury note **15** legal-tender note **17** silver certificate

Green Bay
  football team: 7 Packers

Green Bay Tree, The
  author: 14 Louis Bromfield

Greene, Graham
  author of: 11 The Third Man **12** Brighton Rock, Ways of Escape **14** The Human Factor **16** Monsignor

Quixote **17** The End of the Affair, The Ministry of Fear, Travels with My Aunt **19** The Heart of the Matter, The Power and the Glory

Greene, Joe
  nickname: 7 Mean Joe
  sport: 8 football
  position: 7 lineman
  team: 18 Pittsburgh Steelers

Greene, Lorne
  born: 6 Canada, Ottawa **7** Ontario
  roles: 5 Adama **7** Bonanza **11** Peyton Place **12** Autumn Leaves, The Buccaneer **13** Ben Cartwright **16** The Silver Chalice **19** Battlestar Galactica

Greene, Nathanael
  served in: 16 Revolutionary War
  rank: 16 brigadier general **20** quartermaster general
  battle: 7 Cowpens, Trenton **12** Eutaw Springs, Hobkirk's Hill **18** Guilford Court House

green-eyed monster 4 envy **8** jealousy **12** covetousness

Green for Danger
  director: 13 Sidney Gilliat
  cast: 7 Leo Genn **9** Sally Gray **11** Alastair Sim **12** Rosamund John, Trevor Howard

greenhorn 4 rube, tyro **6** novice, rookie **7** learner **8** beginner, neophyte, newcomer **9** fledgling **10** apprentice, tenderfoot **14** babe in the woods

Green Hornet, The
  character: 4 Kato **9** Britt Reid (The Green Hornet)
  cast: 8 Bruce Lee **11** Van Williams
  car: 11 Black Beauty
  creator: 11 Bert Whitman
  sidekick: 4 Kato

Green House, The
  author: 16 Mario Vargas Llosa

Greening of America, The
  author: 12 Charles Reich

greenish 6 sickly **7** bilious

Greenland
  alternate name: 14 Kalaalit Nunaat
  capital/largest city: 3 Nuk **8** Godthaab, The Point
  others: 4 Etah, Nord **5** Thule **6** Ivigut, Umanak **7** Godhavn, Ivigtut **10** Nanortalik **11** Julianehaab **12** Angmagssalik, Sukkertoppen **14** Christianshaab
  government: 20 home rule under Denmark
  monetary unit: 3 ore **5** krone
  island: 5 Disko
  mountain: 5 Forel, Payer **7** Khardyu **8** Peterman **15** Petermannsbjerg
  highest point: 9 Gunnbjorn **16** Gunnbjornsfjaeld
  sea: 6 Arctic **9** Greenland
  physical feature: 9 Inland Ice
   bay: 5 Disko **6** Baffin **8** Melville
   cape: 4 Jaal **6** Grivel, Walker **8** Bismarck, Brewster, Farewell, Lowen-

orn **11** Morris Jesup
   glacier: 10 Jacobshavn
   strait: 5 Davis **7** Denmark
  people: 3 Ita **6** Eskimo **8** European
   explorer: 10 Eric the Red
  language: 6 Danish, Eskimo **11** Greenlandic
  religion: 19 Evangelical Lutheran
  feature:
   airbase: 4 Etah **5** Thule
   animal: 7 caribou

Green Mansions
  author: 8 W H Hudson
  character: 4 Rima **5** Nuflo **6** Mr Abel

Greenmantle
  author: 10 John Buchan

Green Mountain State
  nickname of: 7 Vermont

Greenough, Horatio
  born: 8 Boston MA
  artwork: 16 George Washington **18** The Chanting Cherubs

Green Pastures, The
  author: 12 Marc Connelly

Greenstreet, Sydney
  born: 7 England **8** Sandwich
  roles: 9 The Fat Man **10** Casablanca **16** The Maltese Falcon **19** Passage to Marseilles

green with envy 7 envious, jealous **8** covetous

greet 4 hail, meet **5** admit **6** accept, accost, salute **7** receive, speak to, welcome **9** smile upon, recognize **10** bid welcome

greeting 6 salute **7** welcome **8** saluting **9** reception, welcoming **10** salutation **12** introduction, presentation

greetings 4 best **5** hello **7** regards **8** respects **10** best wishes, good wishes, salutation **11** compliments, remembrance, well-wishing **13** felicitations
  Latin: 5 salve

gregarious 6 genial, lively, social **7** affable **8** friendly, outgoing, sociable **9** convivial, talkative, vivacious **11** extroverted **13** companionable

gremlin 3 imp **5** demon, gnome **6** goblin

Grenada
  other name: 11 Isle of Spice
  capital/largest city: 9 St Georges
  others: 8 Sauteurs
  head of state: 14 British monarch **15** governor general
  island: 8 Windward **9** Carriacou **10** Grenadines
  lake: 10 Grand Etang
  highest point: 11 St Catherine
  sea: 9 Caribbean
  physical feature:
   bay: 9 St Georges'
  people: 5 Black, Negro **6** Indian
   discoverer: 8 Columbus
  language: 7 English
  religion: 8 Anglican **10** Protestant **13** Roman Catholic

food:
    spice: 4 mace **6** nutmeg
grenade 7 missile **9** pineapple
Grendel
    character in: 7 Beowulf
    author: 11 John Gardner
Grewgious, Mr
    character in: 22 The Mystery of Edwin Drood
    author: 7 Dickens
Grey, Joel
    real name: 8 Joel Katz
    born: 13 Cleveland Ohio
    roles: 7 Cabaret, George M **13** Come September **23** The Seven Percent Solution
Grey, Zane
    author of: 18 Valley of Wild Horses **20** The Spirit of the Border **21** Riders of the Purple Sage, The Last of the Plainsmen
greyhound
    group of: 5 leash
Greystoke, Lord
    real identity of: 6 Tarzan
griddle cake 6 blintz, waffle **7** crumpet, hot cake, pancake **8** corncake, flapcake, flapjack **10** battercake **11** flannel cake **13** buckwheat cake
    French: 5 crepe **12** crepe suzette
    German: 11 pfannkuchen
    Hungarian: 10 palacsinta
    Indian: 8 chapatty
Gride, Arthur
    character in: 16 Nicholas Nickleby
    author: 7 Dickens
grief 3 woe **4** care **5** agony, worry **6** burden, misery, ordeal, sorrow **7** anguish, anxiety, concern, despair, remorse, sadness, trouble **8** distress, grieving, hardship, nuisance, vexation **9** grievance, heartache, suffering **10** affliction, desolation, discomfort, heartbreak **11** despondency, tribulation **12** wretchedness **13** inconvenience
griefstricken 7 joyless, unhappy **8** saddened, wretched **9** sorrowful **13** brokenhearted
Grieg, Edvard Hagerup
    born: 6 Bergen, Norway
    composer of: 5 I Host **8** Bergljot, In Autumn, Peer Gynt **11** Lyric Pieces **12** Landjaenning **14** Fra Holbergs Tid, Lyriske Stykker **15** Sigurd Jorsalfar **16** From Holberg's Time **17** Recognition of Land **18** Foran Sydens Kloster **22** At a Southern Convent Gate
grievance 4 beef, hurt **5** wrong **6** injury **7** outrage **8** hardship, iniquity **9** complaint, injustice **10** affliction, bone to pick, disservice
grieve 3 cry, rue, sob **4** moan, pain, wail, weep **5** be sad, mourn **6** bemoan, deject, harass, lament, sadden, sorrow **7** afflict, agonize, depress, op-

press, torture **8** disquiet, distress **10** discomfort **11** be anguished
grieve over 5 mourn **6** bemoan, bewail, lament **7** cry over **8** moan over, weep over
grievous 3 sad **5** acute, grave, harsh, heavy **6** severe, tragic, woeful **7** crucial, glaring, harmful, heinous, painful, serious, very bad **8** critical, shameful, shocking **9** agonizing, appalling, atrocious, monstrous, nefarious, sorrowful **10** burdensome, calamitous, deplorable, iniquitous, lamentable, outrageous, unbearable **11** destructive, distressing, intolerable, significant **12** insufferable **13** heartbreaking
griffin
    also: 7 griffon, gryphon
    form: 7 monster
    head of: 5 eagle
    wings of: 5 eagle
    body of: 4 lion
    guards of: 4 gold
    location: 7 Scythia
Griffith, Andy
    real name: 20 Andrew Samuel Griffith
    born: 8 Mt Airy NC
    roles: 7 Matlock **13** Will Stockdale **15** A Face in the Crowd, Angel in My Pocket **18** No Time for Sergeants **19** The Andy Griffith Show
Griffith, D W
    director of: 11 Intolerance **14** Broken Blossoms **17** Orphans of the Storm, The Birth of a Nation
Griffith, Hugh
    born: 5 Wales **8** Anglesey **10** Marian Glas
    roles: 6 Ben-Hur **8** Lucky Jim, Tom Jones
griffon see **7** griffin
grill 3 fry **4** cook, grid, pump, quiz, sear **5** broil, query **7** broiler, grating, griddle **8** gridiron, question **9** crossbars **11** interrogate **12** cross-examine
grim 4 foul, hard, ugly **5** cruel, harsh, lurid, stern, sulky **6** brutal, fierce, gloomy, grisly, grumpy, horrid, morose, odious, severe, somber, sullen **7** austere, ghastly, hideous, inhuman, macabre, squalid, vicious **8** dreadful, fiendish, gruesome, horrible, resolute, scowling, shocking, sinister **9** appalling, ferocious, frightful, heartless, loathsome, merciless, obstinate, repellent, repugnant, repulsive, revolting **10** determined, forbidding, implacable, inexorable, relentless, unyielding
grimace 4 face **5** scowl, smirk, sneer **6** glower **7** wry face
    French: 4 moue
grime 4 dirt, dust, smut, soil, soot **5** filth **6** smudge
Grimhild
    origin: 12 Scandinavian

    mentioned in: 8 Volsunga
    form: 9 sorceress
    husband: 5 Giuki, Gjuki
    daughter: 6 Gudrun, Kudrun **7** Guthrun
    son: 6 Gunnar
    tricked Sigurd to marry: 6 Gudrun, Kudrun **7** Guthrun
Grimm Brothers (Jakob and Wilhelm)
    editors of: 15 Hansel and Gretel **16** Grimm's Fairy Tales
grim reaper 5 death **12** angel of death
grim-visaged 8 frowning, scowling **9** long-faced **10** stern-faced
grin 4 beam **5** smile, smirk **6** rictus, simper **11** crack a smile
grind 4 file, grit, mill, rasp, whet **5** chore, crush, gnash, grate **6** abrade, drudge, polish, powder, scrape **7** crammer, hard job, plodder, sharpen, slavery **8** bookworm, drudgery **9** granulate, pulverize, triturate
Gringoire
    character in: 23 The Hunchback of Notre Dame
    author: 4 Hugo
grip 3 bag **4** grab, hilt, hold **5** clasp, grasp, rivet, seize **6** clench, clutch, handle, retain, snatch, valise **7** attract, control, impress, mastery, satchel **8** clutches, hold fast, suitcase **9** gladstone, handclasp, handshake, retention, spellbind **10** domination, perception
gripe, gripes 4 beef, carp, fret, kick, pain, pang, rail **5** cavil, colic, spasm, whine **6** cramps, grouch, grouse, kvetch, mutter, squawk, twinge, twitch **7** grumble, protest, whining **8** complain, distress, grousing, bellyache, complaint, find fault, grievance, grumbling **10** affliction
Grisham, John
    author of: 7 The Firm **9** The Client **10** The Chamber, The Partner **11** A Time to Kill **12** The Rainmaker **14** The Runaway Jury **15** The Pelican Brief, The Street Lawyer
    movie: 7 The Firm
        actors: 9 Tom Cruise **11** Gene Hackman
    movie: 9 The Client
        actors: 13 Tommy Lee Jones, Susan Sarandon **17** Jeanne Tripplehorn
    movie: 15 The Pelican Brief
        actors: 12 Julia Roberts **16** Denzel Washington
grisly 4 foul, gory, grim **5** lurid **6** horrid, odious **7** ghastly, hideous, macabre **8** dreadful, gruesome, horrible, shocking, sinister **9** abhorrent, appalling, frightful, loathsome, repellent, repugnant, repulsive, revolting **10** abominable, forbidding, horrendous
grit 3 rub **4** dirt, dust, guts, muck,

rasp, sand, soot **5** filth, gnash, grate, nerve, pluck, spunk **6** crunch, mettle, scrape **7** courage, stamina **8** backbone, tenacity **9** fortitude **10** doggedness, resolution **12** perseverance **13** determination, grind together

Grizzly Bear State 10 California

groan 4 howl, moan, roar, wail **5** bleat, crack, creak, whine **6** bellow, bemoan, lament, murmur, squeak **7** grumble, screech, whimper **8** complain

grocery store
   Spanish: 6 bodega

groggy 5 dazed, dizzy, dopey, shaky, woozy **6** addled, punchy **7** muddled, reeling, stunned **8** confused, sluggish, unsteady **9** befuddled, lethargic, perplexed, stupefied **10** bewildered, punch-drunk, staggering

groom 4 comb, wash **5** boots, brush, curry, dress, drill, preen, prime, primp, train, valet **6** flunky, lackey, spouse **7** clean up, consort, develop, educate, footman, freshen, hostler, husband, prepare, refresh, rub down, servant **8** exercise, initiate, make neat, make tidy, practice, spruce up **9** currycomb, make ready, stableboy **10** bridegroom, manservant **12** indoctrinate **13** livery servant

groove 3 cut, rut, use **4** rule **5** flute, habit, score, usage **6** custom, furrow, gutter, hollow, trench **7** channel, cutting, scoring **8** practice **9** procedure **10** beaten path, convention **11** corrugation **12** fixed routine, second nature

grope 3 paw **5** probe **6** finger, fumble **7** fish for, venture **9** feel about **11** feel one's way, move blindly, try one's luck **13** search blindly

Gropius, Walter
   architect of: 5 Fagus (factory) **7** Bauhaus (Dessau) **13** Pan Am Building (NYC) **31** Harvard University Graduate Center

gross 3 bag, big, fat **4** bulk, earn, huge, lewd, mass, rank, reap, vast **5** bulky, crude, great, heavy, large, obese, plain, sheer, total, utter, whole **6** carnal, coarse, earthy, entire, pick up, ribald, smutty, sordid, take in, vulgar **7** glaring, heinous, immense, lump sum, massive, obscene, obvious, titanic, uncouth **8** colossal, complete, enormous, flagrant, gigantic, improper, indecent, manifest, unseemly, unwieldy **9** aggregate, downright, egregious, lecherous, monstrous, offensive, unrefined **10** gargantuan, indelicate, lascivious, licentious, outrageous, overweight, prodigious, stupendous **11** unequivocal, unmitigated, unqualified

grossness 7 obesity **8** hugeness, lewdness, ribaldry **9** crudeness, heaviness, indecency, obscenity, roughness, vul-

garity **10** coarseness, indelicacy, inelegance **14** lasciviousness

grossularite
   species: 6 garnet

grotesque 3 odd **4** wild **5** antic, weird **6** absurd, exotic, far-out, rococo, way-out **7** baroque, bizarre, strange **8** deformed, fanciful, peculiar **9** contorted, distorted, eccentric, fantastic, misshapen, odd-shaped, unnatural **10** outlandish **11** extravagant, incongruous **12** preposterous

grotto 4 cave **6** burrow, cavern, hollow, recess, tunnel **8** catacomb

grouch 3 cry **4** beef, carp, crab, fret, kick, mope, pout, rail, sulk **5** cavil, crank, gripe, growl, moper, whine **6** grouse, mutter, pouter **7** grumble, killjoy, protest **8** complain, grumbler **9** bellyache, find fault **10** complainer, curmudgeon, spoilsport, wet blanket

grouchy 5 cross, testy **6** crabby, cranky, grumpy, touchy **8** snappish **10** ill-humored, out of sorts **11** ill-tempered **12** cantankerous **13** shorttempered

ground, grounds 3 set, sod **4** area, base, call, dirt, farm, land, loam, soil, turf, yard **5** acres, basis, beach, cause, dregs, drill, earth, field, found, lawns, realm, teach, train **6** campus, domain, estate, excuse, inform, motive, object, reason, region, secure, settle, sphere, strand **7** account, confirm, deposit, dry land, educate, founder, gardens, habitat, prepare, purpose, support, terrain **8** district, exercise, firm land, initiate, instruct, occasion, organize, practice, premises, property, province, sediment, the earth **9** arguments, bailiwick, establish, fix firmly, institute, principle, rationale, settlings, territory **10** discipline, inducement, real estate, terra firma **11** pros and cons **12** indoctrinate **14** considerations

grounded 5 based **6** kept in, taught **7** aground, beached, bounded, drilled, founded, secured, trained **8** informed, prepared, stranded **9** foundered, initiated **10** kept at home, instructed, restricted **11** disciplined, established **12** washed ashore **13** indoctrinated

grounding 8 training **9** education **10** background, experience **11** preparation **14** indoctrination **15** familiarization

groundless 4 idle **5** empty, false **6** faulty, flimsy, unreal, untrue **8** baseless, needless, unproved **9** erroneous, illogical, imaginary, unfounded **10** chimerical, fallacious, gratuitous **11** uncalled for, unjustified, unsupported, unwarranted **13** unjustifiable, without reason

groundwork 4 base, root **5** basis **6** cradle, ground, origin, source, spring **7** bedrock, footing, grounds, taproot **8**

keystone, learning, planning, practice, training **9** spadework **10** foundation **11** cornerstone, fundamental, preparation **12** fundamentals, underpinning **14** apprenticeship, indoctrination

group 3 set **4** band, clan, file, gang, herd, pack, sift, size, sort **5** align, bunch, class, crowd, flock, grade, hoard, index, party, place, range, swarm, tribe, troop **6** as- sign, branch, circle, clique, family, hobnob, league, line up, mingle, throng **7** arrange, catalog, cluster, combine, company, consort, coterie, faction, marshal, section, species, variety **8** classify, division, graduate, organize, register **9** associate, gathering **10** assemblage, collection, coordinate, detachment, fraternity, fraternize **11** aggregation, alphabetize, association, brotherhood, subdivision **12** congregation **14** classification, representation

Group, The
   author: 12 Mary McCarthy

grouping 7 sorting **8** arraying, ordering **10** assemblage, assortment **11** arrangement, disposition **12** distribution, organization

group of performers 6 troupe **7** company **8** ensemble

Group Portrait of a Lady
   author: 12 Heinrich Boll

grouse 4 beef, crab, fret, fume, fuss, kick **5** gripe **6** grouch, mutter, squawk, take on **7** carry on, grumble **8** complain, gamebird **9** bellyache

grove 4 bosk **5** brake, copse **6** forest, pinery, timber **7** coppice, orchard, thicket, wood lot **8** wildwood, woodland **9** shrubbery **10** plantation

grovel 4 fawn **5** cower, crawl, stoop, toady **6** cringe, kowtow, snivel **7** flatter, truckle **12** bow and scrape **13** demean oneself, humble oneself **14** lick the boots of

groveling 6 abject **7** fawning, servile **8** cowering, crawling, cringing, toadying **9** kowtowing, truckling **11** bootlicking **17** bowing and scraping

grow 3 bud, sow, wax **4** boom, farm, rise, till **5** bloom, breed, plant, raise, ripen, surge, swell, widen **6** become, expand, extend, flower, garden, mature, spread, sprout, thrive **7** advance, amplify, blossom, develop, enlarge, fill out, get to be, improve, magnify, produce, prosper, shoot up, stretch, succeed **8** come to be, flourish, fructify, increase, mushroom, progress, spring up, vegetate **9** cultivate, germinate, propagate, skyrocket **10** aggrandize

Growing Up in New Guinea
   author: 12 Margaret Mead

growl 4 fret, snap **5** croak, grind, gripe, groan, grunt, snarl, whine **6**

grouse, murmur, mutter, rumble **7** grumble **8** complain, talk back

grown-up 3 big, man **4** lady, ripe **5** adult, of age, woman **6** mature, senior **7** worldly **8** full-blown, full-grown, gentleman **11** full-fledged **13** sophisticated

growth 4 crop, hump, lump, rise **5** gnarl, prime, surge, swell, tumor **6** sowing, spread **7** advance, harvest, produce, success **8** increase, maturity, planting, progress **9** expansion, extension, flowering, increment **10** burgeoning, matureness, production, prospering **11** advancement, cultivation, development, enlargement, excrescence, flourishing, improvement, propagation **12** augmentation, mass of tissue **13** amplification
  goddess of: 4 Hour **5** Horae

Groza, Lou
  nickname: 6 The Toe
  sport: 8 football
  team: 15 Cleveland Browns

grub 3 bum, dig **4** food, toil, worm **5** cadge, dig up, larva, mooch, slave **6** drudge, sponge **7** rummage

grubber 5 slave **6** drudge, toiler **7** laborer

grubby 4 foul **5** dirty, grimy, messy, muddy, nasty, seedy, tacky **6** beat-up, filthy, frowzy, frumpy, shabby, shoddy, sloppy, smudgy, soiled, sordid **7** squalid, unclean, unkempt **8** begrimed, slovenly, unwashed **9** besmeared **10** bedraggled

grudge 4 envy **5** pique, spite **6** animus, hatred, malice, rancor, resent **7** dislike, ill will **8** aversion, begrudge **9** animosity **10** resentment **11** malevolence **12** hard feelings

grudging 7 envious **8** hesitant, spiteful **9** reluctant, resentful, unwilling **10** ungenerous **13** penny-pinching

grueling 4 hard **6** brutal, tiring **7** racking **9** fatiguing, punishing, torturous **10** exhausting

gruesome 4 gory, grim **5** awful **6** grisly, horrid **7** fearful, ghastly, hideous, macabre **8** horrible, shocking, terrible **9** frightful, loathsome, repellent, repulsive, revolting **10** forbidding, horrendous, horrifying **13** blood-curdling, spine-chilling

gruff 4 curt, rude, sour, tart **5** bluff, blunt, harsh, husky, raspy, rough, sharp, short, stern, sulky, surly **6** abrupt, croaky, crusty, grumpy, hoarse, ragged, sullen **7** bearish, brusque, caustic, crabbed, cracked, grouchy, peevish, throaty, uncivil, waspish **8** churlish, guttural, impolite, snarling, strident **9** bristling, insulting **10** ill-humored, ill-natured, ungracious **11** ill-tempered **12** discourteous

grumble 4 fret **5** chafe, gripe, growl **6**

grouch, grouse, mutter **8** complain **9** find-fault

grump 4 crab **5** crank **6** grouch **8** grumbler, sourball **10** curmudgeon

grumpy 4 sour **5** moody, sulky, surly, testy **6** crabby, cranky, crusty, sullen **7** grouchy, peevish, pettish **8** churlish **9** irritable, splenetic **10** ill-humored, out of humor, out of sorts **11** disgruntled, ill-disposed, ill-tempered **12** cantankerous

grunt 3 cry **4** bark, call, gasp, howl **5** burro, croak, groan, snort, utter **6** bellow, grouch, mumble, murmur, mutter, shriek **7** howling, whisper **8** complain **9** ululation **11** foot soldier, infantryman

Grunwald, Matthais (Grunewald, Mathis)
  real name: 23 Mathis Gothardt Neithardt
  born: 7 Germany **8** Wurzburg
  artwork: 14 The Crucifixion **15** The Resurrection **20** Altarpiece at Isenheim

Grushenka
  character in: 20 The Brothers Karamazov
  author: 11 Dostoyevsky

Gryce, Percy
  character in: 15 The House of Mirth
  author: 7 Wharton

gryphon *see* **7** griffin

Guam
  capital: 5 Agana
  largest city: 8 Tamuning
  others: 4 Agat, Apra, Toto, Yigo **5** Magua **6** Dededo, Merizo **8** Inarajan, Mangilao, Mongmong, Sinajana, Talofofo, Tamuning **9** Barrigada, Finegayan, Santa Rita
  member of: 7 Mariana (islands)
  mountain: 5 Tenjo
  highest point: 6 Lamlam
  sea: 7 Pacific **10** Philippine
  people: 7 Spanish **8** American, Chamorro, Filipino **11** Micronesian
    explorer: 8 Magellan
    ruler: 5 Japan, Spain **12** United States
  language: 7 English **8** Chamorro
  religion: 16 Roman Catholicism
  feature: 7 typhoon **9** coral reef
  Air Force base: 8 Andersen
  product: 5 copra **6** banana, papaya

guarantee, guaranty 4 avow, bail, bond, pawn, word **5** swear **6** affirm, allege, assure, attest, avowal, insure, pledge, surety **7** deposit, endorse, promise, sponsor, testify, voucher, warrant **8** contract, covenant, security, vouch for, warranty **9** agreement, answer for, assurance, insurance, testimony **10** collateral, underwrite **11** affirmation, endorsement, word of honor **12** give one's word

guard 4 mind, save, tend **5** watch **6** at-

tend, convoy, defend, escort, patrol, picket, screen, secure, sentry, shield, warder **7** conduct, defense, protect, shelter **8** defender, garrison, guardian, keep safe, preserve, security, sentinel, watchdog, watchman **9** bodyguard, concierge, custodian, guardsman, protector, safeguard, watch over **10** doorkeeper, gatekeeper, protection **12** preservation **13** keep watch over

guard against 6 beware **10** look out for **11** take warning, watch out for

guarded 4 wary **5** cagey, chary, leery **7** careful, heedful, mindful, prudent **8** cautious, discreet, hesitant **9** in custody, protected, tentative **10** restrained, suspicious, under guard **11** circumspect, on one's guard

guardian 5 guard **6** convoy, escort, keeper, patrol, patron, picket, sentry, warden, warder **7** curator, trustee **8** advocate, champion, defender, sentinel, shepherd, wardsman, watchdog **9** attendant, bodyguard, caretaker, conductor, custodian, preserver, protector, safeguard, vigilante **10** benefactor **11** conservator **13** friend at court, guardian angel **14** legal custodian

guardian of a place
  Latin: 10 genius loci

guardianship 4 care **6** charge **7** custody, keeping **10** protection **11** safekeeping, supervision, trusteeship

Guatemala
  capital/largest city: 13 Guatemala City
  others: 4 Ocos **5** Coban, Vieja **6** Chahal, Chisec, Cuilco, Flores, Iztapa, Jalapa, Salama, Solola, Tacana, Tecpan, Yaloch, Zacapa **7** Antigua, Cuilapa, Jutiapa, San Jose **8** Progreso **9** Escuintla, Tiquisate **10** Livingston **11** Totonicapan **13** Puerto Barrios, Quezaltenango **14** San Pedro Carcha **16** Chichicastenango
  school: 9 San Carlos
  measure: 4 vara **6** cuarta, tercia **7** cajuela, manzana **10** caballeria
  monetary unit: 4 peso **7** centavo, quetzal
  weight: 4 caja **5** libra
  lake: 5 Dulce, Guija, Peten **6** Izabal **7** Atitlan **9** Amatitlan, Peten Itza
  mountain: 4 Agua, Mico **5** Fuego, Madre **6** Pacaya, Tacana **7** Atitlan, Toliman **8** La Candon, Las Minas **10** Acatenango, Santa Maria **12** Cuchumatanes
  highest point: 8 Tajumuko **9** Tajamulco
  river: 4 Azul **5** Bravo, Dulce, Lapaz **6** Belize, Chixoy, Negino, Pasion, Samala **7** Chiapas, Motagua, Sarstun, Sastoon **8** Polochic, Rio Dulce, Sarstoon **10** Usumacinta
  sea: 7 Pacific **8** Atlantic **9** Caribbean
  physical feature:
    bay: 8 Amatique

gulf: 8 Honduras
people: 3 Mam **4** Chol, Itza, Ixil, Maya **5** Xinca **6** Caribe, Quiche **7** ladinos, mestizo, Pocomam **13** Guatemaltecos
language: 6 Quiche **7** Spanish
religion: 13 Roman Catholic
place:
  church: 10 Santo Tomas
  ruins: 5 Mayan, Tikal **8** Uaxactun
feature:
  bird: 7 quetzal
  clarinet: 8 chirimta
  dance: 5 elson **8** guarimba
  flute: 3 xul
  military dictator: 8 Caudillo
food:
  dish: 6 pepian **10** enchiladas **13** gallo en chicha
  fruit: 4 anay
guava 7 Psidium **16** Psidium guineense
  varieties: 5 apple **6** common, purple, yellow **7** Cattley, Chilean **9** pineapple **10** Costa Rican, strawberry **13** yellow cattley **16** purple strawberry, yellow strawberry
Gudrun
  also: 6 Kudrun **7** Guthrun
  origin: 12 Scandinavian
  mentioned in: 8 Volsunga
  father: 5 Giuki, Gjuki **6** Hertel
  mother: 8 Grimhild
  brother: 6 Gunnar
  husband: 4 Atli **6** Herwig, Sigurd
  killed: 4 Atli
  corresponds to: 9 Kriemhild
guess 4 deem, view **5** fancy, judge, opine, think **6** assume, belief, deduce, divine, gather, reckon, regard, theory **7** believe, daresay, feeling, imagine, opinion, predict, suppose, surmise, suspect, venture **8** conclude, estimate, theorize **9** postulate, speculate, suspicion **10** assumption, conjecture, divination, hypothesis, prediction **11** hypothesize, make a stab at, postulation, presumption, speculation, supposition
guesswork 7 surmise **10** conjecture, hypothesis **11** supposition **13** shot in the dark
guest 5 diner **6** caller, client, friend, inmate, lodger, patron, roomer **7** boarder, company, habitue, invitee, patient, visitor **8** customer **9** sojourner **10** frequenter **14** paying customer
Guest, Edgar A
  author of: 12 A Heap of Livin'
Guest, Judith
  author of: 14 Ordinary People
Guevara 3 Che **7** Ernesto
  born: 9 Argentina
  active in: 15 Cuban Revolution
  friend: 6 Castro
  role in: 5 Evita
  killed in: 7 Bolivia
guffaw 4 howl **6** scream **10** belly laugh, horse laugh

guidance 3 tip **4** clue, help, hint, lead **6** advice, escort **7** conduct, counsel, pointer **8** auspices **9** direction **10** leadership, management, protection, suggestion **11** information, instruction, supervision **12** intelligence **13** enlightenment
guide 4 lead, rule **5** model, pilot, steer, usher **6** beacon, convoy, direct, escort, govern, handle, leader, manage, marker, master, mentor **7** adviser, command, conduct, control, example, marshal, monitor, oversee, pattern, steerer, teacher **8** chaperon, cicerone, director, engineer, helmsman, landmark, lodestar, maneuver, polestar, regulate, shepherd, signpost **9** accompany, attendant, conductor, counselor **10** manipulate
guidebook 5 bible **6** manual **8** Baedeker, handbook **13** reference book
Guidry, Ron (Ronald Ames)
  nickname: 18 Louisiana Lightning
  sport: 8 baseball
  position: 7 pitcher
  team: 14 New York Yankees
guild 5 hansa, hanse, order, union **6** league **7** company, society **8** alliance **9** coalition **10** craft union, federation, fraternity, labor union, sisterhood, trade union **11** association, brotherhood, confederacy, corporation
Guildenstern
  character in: 6 Hamlet
  author: 11 Shakespeare
guile 5 craft, fraud **6** deceit, tricks **7** cunning, slyness **8** artifice, strategy, trickery, wiliness **9** chicanery, deception, duplicity, treachery **10** artfulness, craftiness, dishonesty, hankypanky, stratagems, trickiness **11** fraudulence **13** sharp practice
guileless 4 open **5** frank, naive **6** candid, honest, simple **7** artless, natural, sincere **8** harmless, innocent, truthful **9** ingenuous, innocuous **10** above board, unaffected **11** undesigning, unoffending **15** straightforward, unselfconscious, unsophisticated
guilelessness 6 candor **9** innocence, sincerity **10** candidness, directness **11** artlessness **13** ingenuousness
guilt 3 sin **4** blot, vice **5** shame, wrong **6** infamy, stigma **7** misdeed **8** disgrace, dishonor, misdoing, trespass **9** black mark, turpitude **10** guiltiness, misconduct, sinfulness, wrongdoing **11** criminality, culpability, degradation, delinquency, dereliction, humiliation, misbehavior, self-disgust **13** transgression
guiltless 4 good, pure **5** clean **6** chaste **7** angelic, sinless **8** innocent, unfallen, virtuous **9** blameless, childlike, faultless **10** immaculate, inculpable, unblamable **11** uncorrupted
  French: 12 sans reproche

guilt-stricken 7 ashamed **18** conscience-stricken
guilty 5 sorry, wrong **6** erring, sinful **7** ashamed, corrupt, hangdog, immoral **8** blamable, contrite, criminal, culpable, penitent, sheepish **9** offensive, regretful, repentant **11** blameworthy **18** conscience-stricken
Guinea
  other name: 12 French Guinea **13** Rivieres du Sud
  capital/largest city: 7 Conakry
  others: 4 Boke, Fria, Labe **5** Beyla **6** Dabola, Kankan, Kindia **7** Dubreka, Siguiri **8** Kerouane **9** Kouroussa, Nzerekore
  measure: 7 jacktan
  monetary unit: 4 iliy, syli **5** franc **6** cauris
  weight: 4 akey, piso, uzan **5** benda, seron **6** quinto **8** aguirage
  island: 3 Los **5** Tombo **7** Tristao
  mountain: 4 Loma **6** Tamgue **11** Fouta Djalon
  highest point: 5 Nimba
  river: 4 Milo **5** Kogon, Niger **6** Bafing, Faleme, Gambia **7** Kolente, Senegal **8** Konkoure, Tinkisso **13** Great Scarcies
  sea: 8 Atlantic
  physical feature:
    cape: 5 Verga
  people: 4 Koma, Loma, Nalu, Susu, Toma **5** Kissi, Manon **6** Fulani, Guerzi **7** Landoma, Malinke **8** Kouranke, Landuman **11** Kissi-Sherbo **12** Guerze-Kpelle
  language: 5 Fulbe, Mande **6** Arabic, French, Fulani **7** English
  religion: 5 Islam **7** animism
  feature:
    plant: 11 globeflower
    tree: 4 akee **5** dalli
Guinea-Bissau
  other name: 16 Portuguese Guinea
  capital/largest city: 6 Bissau
  others: 4 Buba **5** Catio, Farim **6** Bafata, Bolama, Cacheu, Cacine, Dandum, Mansoa **7** Bissora, Bubaque, San Joav **9** Fulacunda **10** Nova Lamego **11** Madina do Boe, Madine do Boe, Sao Domingos
  monetary unit: 4 peso **6** escudo **8** centavos
  island: 4 Roxa **6** Orango **7** Bijagos, Formosa
  river: 4 Geba **6** Cacheu, Mansoa **7** Corubal
  sea: 8 Atlantic
  people: 6 Fulani **7** Balanta, Balante, mulatto **8** Mandingo, Mandyako
  language: 5 Fulah **7** Balante, Crioulo **8** Mandingo **10** Portuguese **21** Cape Verde-Guinea Creole
  religion: 5 Islam **7** animism **12** Christianity
Guinevere
  character in: 16 Arthurian romance

husband: 6 Arthur
lover: 8 Lancelot

Guinness, Sir Alec
  born: 6 London **7** England
  roles: 8 Star Wars **11** Oliver Twist **13**
  Doctor Zhivago **14** Our Man in Havana, The Ladykillers **15** A Passage to India, Ben Obi Wan Kenobi, Lavender Hill Mob **16** Lawrence of Arabia **17** Great Expectations **21** Kind Hearts and Coronets **22** Tinker Tailor Soldier Spy **23** The Bridge on the River Kwai (Oscar)
  guise 4 garb, mode **5** dress, habit **6** attire **7** apparel, clothes, costume, fashion **8** clothing, disguise, pretense **10** masquerade

Gulag Archipelago, The
  author: 23 Aleksandr Solzhenitsyn Jr
  gulch 3 gap **4** rift **5** abyss, chasm, cleft, crack, gorge, gully, split **6** arroyo, breach, divide, ravine **8** crevasse

gulf 4 cove, rent, rift **5** abyss, chasm, cleft, firth, fjord, gully, inlet, split **6** canyon, lagoon **7** estuary, opening **8** crevasse **10** separation

gull 3 gyp **4** dupe, rook **5** cozen, trick **7** deceive, defraud, sea gull, sea bird, swindle **9** bamboozle, victimize

gullet 3 maw **4** craw, crop **5** belly, gorge, tummy **6** dewlap, throat **7** abdomen, channel, stomach, weasand **9** beer belly, esophagus

gullible 5 green, naive **6** simple **8** innocent, trustful, trusting **9** credulous **11** easily duped **12** easily fooled, overtrusting, unsuspicious **13** easily cheated, inexperienced **14** easily deceived **15** unsophisticated

Gulliver's Travels
  author: 13 Jonathan Swift
  character: 14 Lemuel Gulliver
  visited: 6 Laputa, Yahoos **8** Blefuscu, Lilliput, Luggnagg **9** Balnibari **10** Houyhnhnms **11** Brobdingnag **12** Glubbdubdrib

gully 3 gap **5** ditch, gorge, gulch **6** defile, furrow, gutter, ravine, trench **7** channel **11** small canyon, small valley, watercourse **13** drainage ditch

gulp 4 bolt, swig, wolf **5** quaff, swill **6** devour, guzzle **7** swallow, toss off **8** mouthful

gulp down 4 bolt **6** devour, gobble **7** swallow **8** gobble up, wolf down

gum 3 wax **5** latex, resin **6** chicle **8** mucilage **10** Eucalyptus
  varieties: 3 cup, red **4** blue, cape, gray, rose, snow, sour **5** apple, black, cider, coral, giant, gully, Karri, Manna, sug- ar, swamp, sweet **6** cotton, Deane's, desert, gimlet, salmon, snappy, Tupelo **7** Barbary, cabbage, Fuchsia, maiden's, Morocco, scarlet, spotted **8** Formosan, Lehmann's, mountain, scribbly, spinning **9** forest

red, Murray red, steedman's **10** Australian, candle-bark, red-spotted, Sydney blue, Timor white, tumble-down, urn-fruited **11** Blakely's red, blue weeping, salmon white, small-leaved, strickland's **12** lemon-scented, red-flowering, silver-dollar **13** American sweet, Oriental sweet, Tasmanian blue, Tasmanian snow **14** yellow-flowered **15** Omeo round-leaved, round-leaved snow **16** rough-barked manna, scarlet-flowering **17** heart-leaved silver **20** silver-leaved mountain

gummed 5 glued, gummy, stuck **6** sticky **8** adhering, adhesive

Gummidge, Mrs
  character in: 16 David Copperfield
  author: 7 Dickens

gummy 5 gluey, gooey, gunky **6** gloppy, sticky, viscid **7** rubbery, viscous **8** adhesive **10** gelatinous **12** muciIaginous

gumption 3 zip **4** dash, push **5** drive, spunk, verve **6** energy, hustle, pizazz, spirit **7** courage **10** enterprise, get-up-and-go, initiative **12** forcefulness **14** aggressiveness **15** resourcefulness

gumshoe 3 tec **4** dick **6** shamus **9** detective **10** private eye **12** investigator

gun 3 aim, gat, rod, try **4** Colt, hunt, iron **5** piece, rifle, shoot **6** cannon, Magnum, mortar, musket, pistol **7** attempt, carbine, firearm, Gatling, go after, Long Tom, shotgun **8** howitzer, ordnance, revolver **9** automatic, Big Bertha, derringer, equalizer, flintlock, forty-five, twenty-two, Remington **10** fieldpiece, machine gun, six-shooter, three-fifty, Walther PPK, Winchester **11** blunderbuss, thirty-eight, trusty-rusty **12** fowling piece, muzzle loader, shooting iron **13** Kentucky rifle **14** artillery piece, Smith and Wesson
  invented by:
    breechloader: 8 Thornton
    magazine: 9 IIotchkiss
    silencer: 5 Maxim

Gunga Din
  story in: 18 Barrack-Room Ballads
  author: 14 Rudyard Kipling
  director: 13 George Stevens
  cast: 8 Sam Jaffe **9** Cary Grant **12** Joan Fontaine **14** Victor McLaglen **18** Douglas Fairbanks Jr
  setting: 5 India
  remade as: 13 Soldiers Three **14** Sergeants Three

gunman 6 bandit, outlaw, robber, sniper **7** hoodlum **9** assailant, desperado, holdup man

Gunn, Ben
  character in: 14 Treasure Island
  author: 9 Stevenson

Gunnar
  origin: 12 Scandinavian
  father: 5 Giuki, Gjuki

  mother: 8 Grimhild
  sister: 6 Gudrun, Kudrun **7** Guthrun
  wife: 8 Brynhild
  Brynhild won by: 6 Sigurd

Gunsmoke
  character: 3 Sam (the bartender) **8** Doc (Dr Galen) Adams **10** Quint Asper **11** Newly O'Brien **12** Chester Goode, Festus Haggen, Kitty Russell (Miss Kitty) **18** Marshall Matt Dillon **24** Clayton Thaddeus (Thad) Greenwood
  cast: 9 Ken Curtis **10** Buck Taylor, Roger Ewing **11** Amanda Blake, James Arness **12** Burt Reynolds, Dennis Weaver, Glenn Strange, Milburn Stone
  setting: 9 Dodge City
  saloon: 10 Longbranch

Guns of August, The
  author: 15 Barbara W Tuchman

Guns of Navarone, The
  director: 12 J Lee Thompson
  based on novel by: 15 Alistair MacLean
  cast: 10 David Niven **11** Gregory Peck, James Darren **12** Anthony Quinn, Stanley Baker **13** Anthony Quayle

Gunther
  origin: 8 Germanic
  mentioned in: 14 Nibelungenlied
  king of: 8 Burgundy
  wife: 8 Brunhild
  sister: 9 Kriemhild
  killed by: 9 Kriemhild

Guppy
  character in: 10 Bleak House
  author: 7 Dickens

gurgle 5 plash **6** babble, bubble, burble, murmur, ripple **7** sputter **8** bubbling, gurgling

guru 5 guide **6** leader, master **7** teacher **9** preceptor **10** instructor

gush 3 gab, gas, jet, run **4** blab, bull, rush, well **5** issue, prate, spout, spurt **6** bab- ble, burble, drivel, hot air, splash, squirt, stream **7** baloney, blabber, blather, chatter, pour out, prattle, rubbish, torrent, twaddle **8** nonsense, outburst, rattle on **10** outpouring **11** mawkishness **12** emotionalism **14** sentimentalism, talk effusively **16** run off at the mouth

gushiness 12 effusiveness, emotionalism **17** demonstrativeness

gushing 6 lavish **7** pouring, profuse **8** effusive, spurting **10** flattering **11** free-flowing **12** demonstative, unrestrained **16** overenthusiastic

gushy 8 effusive **12** unrestrained **13** demonstrative **16** overenthusiastic

gussy up 5 adorn **7** dress up, enhance **8** beautify, decorate, ornament **9** embellish

gust 3 fit **4** blow, puff, wind **5** blast, burst, draft **6** breeze, flurry, squall,

zephyr **8** outbreak, outburst, paroxysm **9** explosion

Guster
character in: **10** Bleak House
author: **7** Dickens

gusto 3 joy **4** zeal, zest **5** savor **6** fervor, relish **7** delight **8** appetite, pleasure **10** enthusiasm **12** appreciation,
exhilaration, satisfaction

gusto, con
music: **9** with style, with taste

gusty 5 blowy, windy **6** breezy **7**
squally **8** blustery

gut 4 raze **5** belly, clean, level, tummy
6 bowels, paunch, ravage **7** abdomen,
consume, midriff, stomach, viscera **8**
entrails, lay waste **9** bay window,
beer belly, spare tire **10** disembowel,
eviscerate, intestines, midsection **11**
breadbasket

guten abend 11 good evening

Gutenberg
nationality: **6** German
inventor of: **11** movable type
printer of: **14** Gutenberg Bible

guten morgen 11 good morning

guten tag 7 good day

Guthrie, A B Jr
author of: **6** Arfive **9** The Big Sky **10**
The Way West **13** The Last Valley
16 Fair Land Fair Land, The Blue
Hen's Chick, The Thousand Hills

Guthrun see **6** Gudrun

Gutman, Casper
character in: **16** The Maltese Falcon
author: **7** Hammett

guts 4 dash, grit **5** nerve, pluck, spunk
6 bowels, daring, mettle, spirit, vitals
7 bravado, bravery, courage, gizzard,
innards, insides, viscera **8** audacity,
backbone, boldness **9** fortitude **10**
intestines **11** intrepidity

gutsy 4 game **5** brave **6** heroic, plucky
7 doughty, valiant **8** fearless, intrepid,
stalwart, unafraid, valorous **9** dauntless, undaunted **10** courageous
11 lionhearted, unflinching **12** stouthearted

guttural 3 low **4** deep **5** gruff, harsh,
husky, raspy, thick **6** hoarse **7** throaty
8 croaking **12** inarticulate

guy 3 boy, joe, kid, man **4** body, chap,
dude, gent, rope **5** bloke, human,
joker **6** fellow, hombre, person **8**
blighter, up-holder **9** supporter **10** individual

Guyana
name means: **12** land of waters
other name: **13** British Guiana
capital/largest city: **10** Georgetown
others: **7** Charity **8** Hyde Park, Ro-
signol **9** Jonestown, Mackenzie
island: **6** Leguan **8** Wakenaam
mountain: **5** Amuku, Ariwa, Kamoa
6 Akarai, Kanuku **7** Caburai **9** Pacaraima
highest point: **7** Roraima
river: **5** Waini **6** Barama **7** Amakura,
Baruima, Berbice **8** Demerara, Ma-
zaruni, Rupununi **9** Essequibo **10**
Burro-Burro
ocean: **8** Atlantic
physical feature:
falls: **5** Great, Tiger **7** Kamaria **8**
Kaieteur **9** Serikoeng **10** Surwak-
wima **15** Fredrik Willem IV
people: **6** Akawai, Arawak, Creole,
Taruma **7** African, Chinese, mulatto
10 Portuguese
language: **5** Hindi **7** English
religion: **5** Hindu, Islam **8** Anglican
13 Roman Catholic

Guy Fawkes
author: **16** William Ainsworth

Guy Mannering
author: **14** Sir Walter Scott

Guyon
character in: **15** The Faerie Queene
author: **7** Spenser

Guys and Dolls
director: **17** Joseph L Mankiewicz
based on story by: **11** Damon Runyon
cast: **10** Stubby Kaye **11** Jean Simmons **12** Frank Sinatra, Marlon
Brando, Vivian Blaine
setting: **11** New York City
score: **12** Frank Loesser
song: **11** Luck Be a Lady **12** Guys
and Dolls **26** Sit Down You're Rocking the Boat

guzzle 4 bolt, swig **5** quaff, swill **6** devour, imbibe, tipple **7** toss off **8** gulp
down

guzzler 5 drunk **6** boozer **7** imbiber,
tippler **8** devourer, drunkard **9** alcoholic

Gwawl
origin: **5** Welsh
mentioned in: **10** Mabinogion
rival of: **5** Pwyll
sought hand of: **8** Rhiannon

Gwydion
origin: **5** Welsh
son: **14** Llew Llaw Gyffes
sister: **9** Arianhrod
lover: **9** Arianhrod

Gwyn
origin: **7** British
god of: **7** rebirth **9** afterlife

Gyas
companion of: **6** Aeneas

Gyes see **5** Gyges

Gygaea, Gyge
form: **5** nymph
location: **4** lake

Gyges
also: **4** Gyes
member of: **13** Hecatonchires

gymnasium 5 arena **6** circus **7** stadium **10** hippodrome

gymnast 10 Olga Korbut **13** Mary Lou
Retton, Nadia Comaneci

gymnastics 9 exercises **10** acrobatics
11 contortions **16** physical training

Gynaecothoenas
epithet of: **4** Ares
means: **17** feasted by the women

gynophobia
fear of: **5** women

gyp 3 con **4** bilk, burn, fake, hoax,
rook, scam, soak **5** cheat, cozen,
fraud, phony, trick **6** diddle, fleece,
humbug, ripoff **7** con game, defraud,
swindle **8** flimflam, hoodwink **9** bamboozle, deception

gypsy
Italian: **7** zingara, zingaro

gyrate 5 swirl, twirl, wheel, whirl **6**
circle, rotate, spiral **7** revolve **9** pirouette **10** spin around

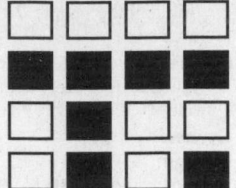

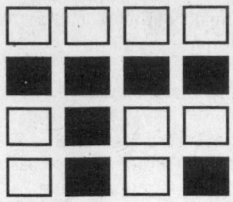

habeas corpus 11 have the body **23** produce the person in court
legal writ guards against: 19 illegal imprisonment

habiliments 4 garb, wear **5** dress **6** attire, outfit **7** clothes, costume, raiment, regalia **8** clothing, wardrobe **9** vestments

habit 3 rut, way **4** garb, gear, robe, rule, wont **5** dress, trait, usage **6** attire, custom, groove, livery, manner, outfit **7** apparel, clothes, costume, garment, leaning, raiment, routine, uniform, vesture **8** clothing, fondness, habitude, nun's wear, practice **9** mannerism, trappings **10** beaten path, convention, observance, partiality, proclivity, propensity **11** habiliments, inclination, peculiarity **12** predilection, second nature **13** accoutrements, fixed practice **14** matter of course, predisposition **15** behavior pattern

habitat 3 pad **4** digs, home, spot, zone **5** abode, haunt, place, range, realm, roost **6** domain, locale, milieu, region **7** housing, lodging, setting, terrain **8** domicile, dwelling, home base, lodgment, precinct, quarters **9** territory **10** habitation **11** environment, natural home **12** place of abode **13** dwelling place **14** stamping ground **15** natural locality **17** native environment

habitation 3 pad **4** digs, home **5** abode, haunt, house, roost **6** colony **7** habitat, housing, lodging, shelter, tenancy **8** domicile, dwelling, lodgment, quarters **9** community, occupancy, residence **10** occupation, settlement **12** place of abode **13** dwelling place, temporary stay **16** place of residence

Habit of Being, The
author: 15 Flannery O'Connor

habitual 5 fixed, usual **6** common, normal, wonted **7** chronic, natural, regular, routine, typical **8** addicted, constant, expected, familiar, frequent, periodic, repeated **9** confirmed, continual, customary, incessant, ingrained, perpetual, recurrent **10** accustomed, deep-rooted, deep-seated, inveterate, methodical, systematic **11** established, traditional **12** conventional, second nature **14** by force of habit

habitual practice 4 wont **5** habit **6** custom

habituate 5 adapt, drill, imbue, inure, train **6** harden, school, season **7** break in, instill **8** accustom, initiate **9** inculcate **10** discipline, make used to **12** indoctrinate

habitue 7 regular **10** frequenter **13** regular patron **15** frequent visitor **16** constant customer

hacek 13 inverted caret **15** diacritical mark

hack 3 cab, cut, hew, nag **4** bark, chip, chop, gash, plug, rasp, slit, taxi **5** coach, cut up, notch, slash, slice, whack **6** cleave, mangle **7** hackney, taxicab **8** lacerate, mutilate **9** cart horse, dray horse, scribbler, workhorse **10** cough drily, cut roughly, draft horse, hired horse, shaft horse **11** common horse, penny-a-liner **12** hackney coach, worn-out horse **13** carriage horse **16** grubstreet writer **18** horse-drawn carriage

hackle 3 peg **4** card, comb, hack, hook, ruff **5** curry, plume, quill **6** heckle, mangle **7** bristle, feather, plumage

Hackman, Gene
born: 15 San Bernardino CA
roles: 8 Superman **9** Popeye Doyle **14** Bonnie and Clyde **15** The Conversation **19** The French Connection (Oscar) **20** The Poseidon Adventure

hackneyed 4 dull, worn **5** banal, inane, stale, stock, trite, vapid **6** common, jejune **7** cliched, humdrum, insipid, routine, worn-out **8** bromidic, ordinary, shopworn, well-worn **9** moth-eaten **10** pedestrian, threadbare, uninspired **11** commonplace, stereotyped **12** conventional **13** platitudinous, unimaginative

Hadassah 6 Esther

Hades 4 hell
also: 3 Dis **5** Pluto **10** lower world, Underworld
corresponds to: 5 Orcus
god of: 5 Orcus, Pluto
goddess of: 6 Hecate, Hekate

Haenigsen, Harry
creator/artist of: 5 Penny **7** Our Bill

hafnium
chemical symbol: 2 Hf

hag 3 bat, nag **4** drab, fury **5** biddy, crone, frump, harpy, shrew, vixen, witch **6** beldam, gorgon, ogress, vi-

rago **7** hellcat **8** battle-ax, harridan **9** termagant

Hagar
servant of: 5 Sarah
husband: 7 Abraham
son: 7 Ishmael

Hagar the Horrible
creator: 9 Dik Browne

Hagen
origin: 8 Germanic
mentioned in: 14 Nibelungenlied
killed by: 9 Kriemhild
killed: 9 Siegfried

Haggadah 7 parable **8** anecdote
source: 6 Talmud
read at: 5 seder **8** Passover

haggard 4 beat, wild, worn **5** gaunt, spent, tired, upset, weary **6** bushed, fagged, pooped, raging, wasted **7** ranting **8** careworn, drooping, fatigued, flagging, frenzied, harassed, harrowed, overcome, toilworn, wild-eyed **9** exhausted, woebegone **10** hollow-eyed **11** debilitated, overwearied, overwrought, tuckered out, wild-looking **12** tired-looking

Haggard, H Rider
author of: 3 She **17** King Solomon's Mines
noted phrase: 18 She who must be obeyed

haggle 6 barter, bicker, dicker, higgle **7** bargain, dispute, quarrel, quibble, wrangle **8** beat down, squabble

Hagiographa
Hebrew: 7 Ketubim

hagiographer 19 writer of saints' lives

Hagman, Larry
mother: 10 Mary Martin
born: 13 Weatherford TX
roles: 6 Dallas **7** J R Ewing **15** I Dream of Jeannie

Hahn, Otto
field: 9 chemistry
nationality: 6 German
discovered: 13 protoactinium **14** nuclear isomers
awarded: 10 Nobel Prize

Haida
language family: 6 Masset, Na-Dene **10** Skidegatta
tribe: 7 Kaigani
location: 6 Alaska **15** British Columbia **21** Queen Charlotte Islands

related to: 7 Tlingit **9** Tsimshian
associated with: 9 totem pole **13**
wood sculpture
hail 3 ave **4** call **5** cheer, exalt, extol,
greet, hello, honor, shout **6** accost,
call to, esteem, salute **7** acclaim, address, applaud, commend, glorify, receive, shout at, usher in, welcome **8**
cry out to, eulogize, greeting **9** accost-
ing **10** calling out, compliment, panegyrize, salutation **11** make welcome
German: 4 heil
Latin: 3 ave **5** salve
Hailey, Arthur
author of: 5 Hotel **6** Wheels **7** Airport **12** In High Places **14** Final Diagnosis **16** The Moneychangers
hail-fellow-well-met 8 familiar,
friendly, intimate, outgoing, sociable **9**
extrovert **10** gregarious
Hail Mary
Latin: 8 Ave Maria **12** rosary prayer
Hail the Conquering Hero
director: 14 Preston Sturges
cast: 10 Ella Raines **12** Eddie Bracken
14 Raymond Walburn **15** William
Demarest **16** Franklin Pangborn
hail to victory
German: 8 sieg heil
Hair
writers: 9 James Rado **11** Gerome
Ragni
composer: 13 Galt MacDermot
character: 3 Hud **4** Woof **6** Berger,
Claude, Crissy, Dionne, Jeanie,
Sheila
songs: 4 3500 **8** Aquarius **9** Ain't Got
No **12** Colored Spade **17** Manchester
England
hair 3 fur, mop **4** coat, down, iota,
mane, pelt, wool **5** bangs, curls, locks
6 fleece **7** tresses **8** ringlets **12** narrow
margin
loss: 8 alopecia, baldness
haircut, hairdo 3 bob, bun, cut **4**
Afro, clip, crop, fade, perm, shag,
trim, updo **5** bangs, braid, butch,
swirl **6** boogie, mohawk **7** beehive,
buzzcut, chignon, cornrow, crewcut,
flattop, fuzz cut, natural, pachuco,
page boy, pigtail, shingle, tonsure, upsweep **8** bouffant, brushcut, coiffure,
ducktail, ponytail, razorcut **9** barber-
ing, hairstyle, permanent, pompadour
10 feathercut, french knot
haircutter 6 barber **11** hairdresser,
hair stylist
hairdresser 8 coiffeur **9** coiffeuse **10**
beautician, haircutter **11** beauty salon
12 beauty parlor
French: 8 coiffeur
hair-raising 5 eerie **7** bristle **8** exciting
9 thrilling **10** terrifying **11** astonishing
12 breathtaking, electrifying **13** hor-
ripilation, spine-tingling
hairsplitting 4 fine **6** minute, subtle **7**
carping **8** caviling, delicate, hairline,

niggling **9** minuscule, quibbling **10**
nitpicking, unapparent **12** faultfinding,
overcritical **13** imperceptible, inappreciable, infinitesimal **15** inconsequential
hairy 5 bushy, furry, wooly **6** fleecy,
pilose, shaggy, woolly **7** hirsute
Hairy Ape, The
author: 12 Eugene O'Neill
Haiti
name means: 15 mountainous land
other name: 12 Santo Domingo
capital/largest city: 12 Port-au-Prince
others: 5 Aquin, Furcy, Limbe **6** Hin-
che, Jacmel, St Marc **7** Jeremie, Leo-
gane, Saltrou **8** Gonaives, Kenscoff,
Les Cayes **10** Cap-Haitien
monetary unit: 6 gourde **8** centimes
island: 5 Vache **6** Gonave, Tortue **7**
Navassa, Tortuga **8** Caymites **10** Hispaniola **14** Grande Cayemite **15**
Greater Antilles
lake: 8 Saumatre
mountain: 4 Nord **5** Cahos **6** Macaya, Noires **7** Lahotte **8** Troudeau
highest point: 7 La Selle, Laselle
river: 9 Guayamoul **10** Artibonite
sea: 8 Atlantic **9** Caribbean
physical feature:
gulf: 6 Gonave
passage: 8 Windward
people: 5 Taino **7** African, mulatto
discoverer: 8 Columbus
liberator: 19 Toussaint Louverture
ruler: 7 Papa Doc **8** Duvalier
language: 6 Creole, French, patois
religion: 6 voodoo **13** Roman Catholic
feature:
dance: 5 mambo
festival: 9 Mardi Gras
fortress: 10 La Ferriere **24** Citadelle
du Roi Christophe
security force: 8 bogeymen **15**
Tontons Macoutes
food:
sweet potato: 6 batata
Hakenkreuz 11 hooked cross **12** Nazi
swastika
HAL
character in: 14 Two Thousand One
(2001)
author: 6 Clarke
Halas, George
nickname: 8 Papa Bear
sport: 8 football
position: 5 coach
team: 12 Chicago Bears
halcyon 4 calm, fair **5** happy, quiet,
sunny **6** blithe, golden, hushed, joyous, placid, serene **7** pacific **8** carefree, cheerful, peaceful, tranquil **9**
cloudless, contented, reposeful, unclouded, unruffled **10** unagitated, untroubled
hale 3 fit **4** well **5** hardy, sound **6**
hearty, robust, rugged, sturdy **7**

healthy, in shape **8** vigorous **9** energetic, in the pink, strapping **10** able-
bodied, robustious **12** in fine fettle
Hale, Edward Everett
author of: 21 The Man Without a
Country
hero: 11 Phillip Nolan
Hale, George Ellery
field: 9 astronomy
initiated: 20 Mt Palomar Observatory
invented: 17 spectroheliograph
Hale, Nathan, 7 patriot
hanged as a: 3 spy
Hale-Bopp 5 comet
Haley, Alex
author of: 5 Roots **26** The Autobiography of Malcolm X
Haley, Jack
born: 8 Boston MA
roles: 6 Tin Man **13** The Wizard of
Oz
half 4 part, some **6** all but, barely,
fairly, feebly, halved, in part, meager,
partly, rather, scanty, skimpy, slight,
weakly **7** divided, faintly, limited, partial, portion, section **8** fraction, middling, moderate, passable, passably,
slightly **9** deficient, imperfect, partially, tolerable, tolerably **10** fractional, inadequate, incomplete, moderately, relatively **12** fifty percent,
inadequately, insufficient, pretty
nearly **13** after a fashion, comparatively **14** insufficiently
half-asleep 6 drowsy, groggy, unwary
7 out-of-it, unaware **8** sluggish **9** not-
with-it, oblivious
half-hearted 4 cold, cool, tame **5**
blase, faint **7** languid, passive **8** listless, lukewarm **9** apathetic, lethargic
10 ambivalent, irresolute, lackluster,
phlegmatic, spiritless, unappling **11**
indifferent, perfunctory **13** lackadaisical **14** unenthusiastic
half homer 15 Biblical measure
half-moon 3 arc, bow **4** arch **5** curve
8 crescent
Half Moon 4 ship
of: 11 Henry Hudson
halfway 6 almost, in part, medial, medium, middle, midway, nearly, partly,
rather **7** midmost **8** somewhat **9** partially, to a degree **10** middlemost,
moderately **11** equidistant, in the middle **12** intermediate, pretty nearly, to
some extent **13** in some measure **18**
between two extremes
half-wit 4 dolt, dope, fool **5** dummy,
dunce, idiot, moron, ninny **6** dimwit,
nitwit **7** dullard **8** dumb-dumb, imbecile, numskull **9** blockhead, numbskull, simpleton **10** nincompoop **15**
mental defective, mental deficient
half-witted 4 dumb **5** silly **6** stupid **7**
asinine, foolish, idiotic, moronic **9**
dimwitted, imbecilic, senseless

11 lamebrained 12 feeble-minded, simple-minded

hall 5 entry, foyer, lobby 6 arcade 7 chamber, gallery, hallway, passage 8 anteroom, club room, corridor, entrance 9 vestibule 10 auditorium, dining hall, passageway 11 antechamber, banquet hall, concert hall, waiting room 12 amphitheater, assembly room, meeting place 13 reception room

Hall, Diane
real name of: 11 Diane Keaton

Hall, James
field: 7 geology 9 chemistry
nationality: 7 British
founded: 12 geochemistry 19 experimental geology

Hall, James Norman
author of: 17 Mutiny on the Bounty
co-author: 15 Charles Nordhoff

Hallel 6 praise 16 liturgical prayer

Haller, Albrecht von
field: 7 biology
nationality: 5 Swiss
founded: 15 modern neurology

Haller, Harry
character in: 11 Steppenwolf
author: 5 Hesse

Halley, Edmund
field: 9 astronomy
nationality: 7 British
discovered: 12 Halley's Comet

hallmark 4 sign 5 badge, stamp 6 device, emblem, symbol 14 characteristic

halloo 3 cry 4 call, hail, yell 5 shout 6 cry out, holler

hallow 5 bless 7 respect 8 dedicate, sanctify, venerate 10 consecrate

hallowed 4 holy 6 sacred 7 blessed, honored 9 beatified, dedicated 10 sacrosanct, sanctified 11 consecrated

Halloween
date: 7 October (31)
also called: 13 All Hallows Eve
symbol: 7 pumpkin 12 jack-o-lantern
saying: 12 trick or treat

hallucination 5 dream 6 mirage, vision 7 chimera, fantasy, figment 8 delusion, illusion 9 nightmare 10 aberration, apparition 14 phantasmagoria

hallway 4 hall 5 entry, foyer 7 passage 8 corridor, entryway 10 passageway

halo 6 aurora, corona, luster, nimbus 7 aureole, dignity, majesty 8 grandeur, holiness, radiance, sanctity, splendor 9 solemnity, sublimity 11 ring of light 12 chromosphere, luminousness, magnificence, resplendence 13 spiritual aura 15 illustriousness

Hals, Franz
born: 7 Antwerp, Holland
artwork: 9 Gypsy Girl 10 Hille Bobbe (The Witch of Haarlem) 13 The Jolly Toper 14 Jacobus Zaffius 15 The

Merry Company 19 The Laughing Cavalier 22 Portrait of a Standing Man 24 The Regents of the Almshouse 26 Yonker Ramp and his Sweetheart 28 The Regentesses of the Almshouse 33 The Banquet of the St George Civic Guard

Halsey, William F
served in: 3 WWI 4 WWII
rank: 12 fleet admiral
battle: 9 Leyte Gulf 11 Philippines 14 Solomon Islands

halt 3 end 4 balk, curb, foil, quit, rest, rout, stay, stem, stop, wait, whoa 5 abate, block, brake, break, cease, check, close, crush, delay, pause, quash, quell, stall, tarry 6 bridle, cut off, defeat, draw up, hamper, hinder, impede, linger, pull up, recess, rein in, scotch, subdue, thwart, wind up 7 heave to, inhibit, prevent, put down, repress, respite, squelch, suspend, time out 8 break off, breather, choke off, don't move, hang fire, interval, knock off, leave off, overturn, prohibit, restrain, restrict, shut down, suppress, vanquish 9 cessation, frustrate, interlude, interrupt, overthrow, terminate 10 call it a day, extinguish, shut up shop, standstill, suspension 11 come to a halt, come to a stop, discontinue, hold in check, termination 12 intermission, interruption, throttle down 13 spike one's guns 14 breathing spell, discontinuance

halting 6 ending 7 curbing 8 episodic, hesitant, stopping 9 faltering, stumbling 10 calling off, discursive, suspending 11 restraining, terminating 13 discontinuous 14 calling a halt to, putting a stop to

halting place
Spanish: 6 posada

halutz 7 pioneer 26 person who emigrates to Israel

halve 6 bisect 9 cut in half 10 split in two 13 divide equally

ham, 6 emoter 9 overactor 20 amateur radio operator

Ham
character in: 16 David Copperfield
author: 7 Dickens

Ham
father: 4 Noah
brother: 4 Shem 7 Japheth
son: 3 Put 4 Cush 6 Canaan 7 Misraim
descendant of: 6 Hamite

Hamadryad
form: 5 dryad
spirit of: 4 tree

Haman
served: 9 Ahasuerus also see 6 Esther

Hamill, Mark
born: 9 Oakland CA
roles: 8 Star Wars 13 Luke Skywalker

15 Return of the Jedi 20 The Empire Strikes Back

Hamilton
capital of: 7 Bermuda

Hamilton, Alexander
1st Secretary:, 8 Treasury
slain by: 9 Aaron Burr
in: 4 duel

Hamilton, Charles
character in: 15 Gone With the Wind
author: 8 Mitchell

Hamilton, Iain
composer of: 6 Aurora 7 Alastor 8 Sinfonia 9 Pharsalia 11 The Bermudas 18 Threnos In Time of War 20 The Royal Hunt of the Sun 21 The Catiline Conspiracy

Hamilton, Margaret
real name: 23 Margaret Hamilton Meserve
born: 11 Cleveland OH
roles: 4 Cora 13 The Wizard of Oz 23 The Wicked Witch of the West

Hamito-Semitic
language also known as: 11 Afro-Asiatic
branch: 6 Berber, Chadic 7 Semitic 8 Cushitic, Egyptian

hamlet 4 burg 7 village 8 hick town, tank town 10 crossroads 11 whistle stop 12 one-horse town, small village 13 jerkwater town

Hamlet
author: 18 William Shakespeare
character: 7 Horatio, Laertes, Ophelia 8 Claudius, Gertrude, Polonius, The Ghost 11 Rosencrantz 12 Guildenstern
soliloquy: 13 To be or not to be
skull: 6 Yorick
castle: 8 Elsinore
setting: 7 Denmark
director: 15 Laurence Olivier
cast: 11 Basil Sydney, Felix Aylmer, Jean Simmons 12 Eileen Herlie 15 Laurence Olivier
Oscar for: 5 actor (Olivier) 7 picture

Hamlet, The
author: 15 William Faulkner
character: 4 Eula, Jody 6 Labove 8 Ab Snopes 9 V K Ratliff 10 Flem Snopes, Mink Snopes, Will Varner 11 Isaac Snopes 12 Henry Armstid

Hamlin, Vincent T
creator/artist of: 8 Alley Oop

Hammarskjold, Dag 7 Swedish 13 United Nations 16 secretary-general

hammer 3 hit, tap 4 bang, form, make, nail 5 drive, forge, knock, pound, punch, shape, whack 6 pummel, rammer, strike 7 beat out, fashion
type: 4 claw, jack, tack 5 gavel, steam 6 mallet, sledge 8 ballpeen 10 pile driver 12 upholsterers

Hammer, Mike

detective created by: 14 Mickey Spillane
hammered 5 drunk **6** banged, beaten, shaped **7** knocked, pounded, whipped, wrought **8** battered, repeated **10** terrorized
Hammett, Dashiell
  author of: 10 Red Harvest, The Thin Man **11** The Glass Key **12** The Dain Curse **16** The Maltese Falcon
  character: 4 Asta (dog) **8** Sam Spade **11** Miles Archer, Nick Charles, Nora Charles **13** Continental Op
hamper 3 gag **4** balk, curb, stem **5** block, check, stall **6** fetter, hinder, hog-tie, hold up, impede, muzzle, retard, thwart **7** inhibit, prevent, shackle **8** encumber, handicap, obstruct, restrain, restrict **9** frustrate **13** interfere with
Hampton, Hope
  nickname: 22 The Duchess of Park Avenue
  born: 14 Philadelphia PA
  roles: 8 Star Dust **13** Lawful Larceny, The Road to Reno **16** The Price of a Party
hamstring 6 impair, muscle, tendon **7** cripple, disable **8** handicap **10** debilitate
Hamsun, Knut
  author of: 3 Pan **6** August, Hunger **8** Victoria **9** Mysteries, Vagabonds **16** Children of the Age **18** The Growth of the Soil
Hananiah see **8** Shadrach
hand, hands 3 aid, man, paw **4** care, fist, give, help, hold, lift, mitt, palm, pass **5** guide, power, reach **6** assist, charge, convey, helper, menial, script, worker **7** command, control, custody, deliver, keeping, laborer, ovation, present, support, workman **8** auspices, dominion, employee, guidance, handyman, hired man, longhand, meat-hook **9** assistant, associate, authority, hired hand **10** assistance, domination, management, minister to, penmanship, possession, turn over to, workingman **11** calligraphy, furnish with, handwriting, supervision **12** jurisdiction **13** member of a crew **15** burst of applause, manual extremity, round of applause
handbag 3 bag **4** grip **5** purse **6** clutch, valise **7** satchel **8** moneybag, reticule **10** pocketbook, portmanteau
handbill 5 flier, tract **6** notice **7** leaflet **8** bulletin, circular **12** announcement **13** advertisement
handbook 5 bible **6** manual **8** baedeker **9** guidebook, vade mecum **13** reference book
handcart 4 cart **6** barrow **8** pushcart **10** handbarrow **11** wheelbarrow
handcuffs 5 cuffs, irons **6** chains **7** fetters **8** manacles, shackles **9** bracelets
hand down 4 will **5** leave **6** hand on, pass on **8** bequeath
Handel, George Frederick (Georg Friedrich)
  born: 5 Halle **7** Germany
  lived in: 7 England
  composer of: 4 Nero, Saul **5** Serse, Silla, Siroe, Teseo **6** Admeto, Alcina, Almira, Esther, Flavio, Jeptha, Joseph, Ottone, Samson, Semele, Xerxes **7** Amadigi, Athalia, Deborah, Lotario, Messiah, Rinaldo, Rodrigo, Solomon, Tolomeo **8** Atalanta, Berenice, Hercules, Scipione, Theodora **9** Agrippina, Radamisto, Rodelinda, Tamerlano **10** Alessandro, Belshazzar, Floridante, Water Music **12** Giulio Cesare, Il Pastor Fido, Muzio Scevola **13** Israel in Egypt, Riccardo Primo **14** Acis and Galatea, Fireworks Music **15** Alexander's Feast, Judas Maccabaeus **16** Hornpipe Concerto **19** Julius Caesar in Egypt, Ode for St Cecilia's Day **22** The Royal Fireworks Music **23** Hallelujah Organ Concerto, The Harmonious Blacksmith **24** The Triumph of Time and Truth
handful 7 minimum, modicum **10** scattering, smattering, sprinkling, thimbleful, tiny amount **11** scant amount, small number **13** small quantity
handgun 3 rod **5** piece, rifle **6** pistol, weapon **7** firearm, shotgun **8** revolver **9** automatic, twenty-two **12** shooting iron **20** Saturday night special
handicap 4 curb **5** limit **6** burden, defect, hamper, hinder, impede, retard, thwart **7** barrier, inhibit, repress, shackle **8** deafness, drawback, encumber, hold back, lameness, obstacle, restrain, restrict, suppress **9** blindness, detriment **10** difficulty, impediment, inhibition, limitation **11** encumbrance, restriction, shortcoming **12** disadvantage **13** inconvenience **14** stumbling block
handicapped 7 limited **8** burdened, disabled, held back, hindered, impaired, retarded **10** encumbered, restrained, restricted **13** disadvantaged
handicrafts
  god of: 10 Hephaestus, Hephaistos
handicraftsman 7 artisan **10** handworker **12** handicrafter
handiness 7 utility **8** deftness **9** dexterity **10** adroitness, usefulness **11** convenience **12** availability **13** accessibility
hand in glove 5 as one **10** side by side **13** close together
handle 3 paw, ply, run, tag, use **4** feel, grip, hilt, hold, knob, name, poke, pull, sell, work **5** carry, grasp, guide, knead, pilot, pinch, shaft, shank, steer, swing, touch, treat **6** caress, CB name, deal in, employ, finger, fondle, manage, market, pick up, stroke **7** care for, command, conduct, control, massage, moniker, operate, paw over, trade in, utilize **8** cognomen, deal with, maneuver **9** traffic in **10** manipulate, take care of **11** appellation, merchandise **12** offer for sale **13** bring into play
handout 4 alms, dole **7** freebie **19** something for nothing
hand out 4 deal, give **5** grant **6** bestow, confer, donate **7** dole out, mete out, present **8** dispense **9** apportion **10** contribute, distribute
hand over 4 cede **5** grant, yield **6** give up, tender **7** abandon, release **8** transfer **9** deliver up, surrender **10** relinquish
handsome 4 fair **5** ample, bonny, noble **6** benign, comely, lovely, pretty **7** elegant, liberal, sightly, sizable, stately **8** abundant, generous, gracious, imposing, merciful, princely, splendid, stunning, tasteful **9** beauteous, beautiful, bountiful, exquisite, unselfish **10** attractive, benevolent, big-hearted, impressive, sufficient, well-formed **11** fine-looking, good-looking, magnanimous **12** considerable, easy to look at, humanitarian **13** compassionate, easy on the eyes **16** well-proportioned
hand to hand
  Spanish: 9 mano a mano
handy 4 deft, near, nigh **5** adept, on tap **6** adroit, at hand, clever, expert, on call, on hand, useful, wieldy **7** capable, helpful, skilled **8** skillful **9** available, competent, dexterous, easy to use, efficient, practical **10** accessible, convenient, manageable, obtainable, proficient **11** at one's elbow, close at hand, in readiness, ready to hand, serviceable **12** accomplished **14** nimble-fingered **15** within easy reach **16** easily accessible **17** at one's beck and call
hang 3 bow, sag **4** drop, gist, rest **5** affix, hinge, knack, lie in, lower, lynch, point, trail **6** append, attach, dangle, depend **7** incline, meaning, suspend, thought **8** lean over, let droop, repose in, string up, turn upon **9** be pendant, be pendent **11** be dependent, be subject to, bend forward, swing freely **12** be contingent, bend downward **13** revolve around **15** die on the gallows, fasten from above **16** execute by hanging, send to the gallows
hangdog 6 abject **7** ashamed **8** defeated, degraded, hopeless, resigned, wretched **9** miserable **10** browbeaten, chapfallen, humiliated, shamefaced **11** crestfallen, embarrassed, intimidated **13** guilty-looking

hang down 3 sag **5** droop
hanger-on 7 admirer, groupie **8** follower .9 sycophant
hanging object
Japanese: **8** kakemono
hang loosely 3 bag, sag **5** droop
hangout 3 den **5** haunt
hang out 3 mix **4** live **5** dwell **6** hobnob, loiter, mingle, reside **7** consort **9** associate, be friends, pal around, run around **10** fraternize, hang around **11** keep company
hanker after 4 want **5** covet, crave, fancy **6** desire **7** long for, pine for **8** aspire to, yearn for **9** lust after **11** have a yen for, have an eye on, hunger after, thirst after
hankering 3 yen **4** itch, urge **6** aching, desire, hunger, pining, thirst **7** craving, longing **8** yearning
Hanna-Barbera
creators of: **6** Top Cat **7** Jetsons **8** Yogi Bear **11** Tom and Jerry **15** Quickdraw McGraw **16** Huckleberry Hound **14** The Flintstones
Hannah
husband: **7** Elkanah
son: **6** Samuel
Hanoi
capital of: **7** Vietnam **12** North Vietnam
river: **3** Red **4** Yuan **7** Song Koi
delta: **6** Tonkin
airport: **6** Gia Lam
Hans Brinker
author: **5** (Mary Elizabeth Mapes) Dodge
character: **4** Raff **5** Gleck, Hilda **6** Gretel **7** Boekman, Mevrouw
feature: **12** silver skates
Hansel and Gretel
author: **13** Grimm Brothers (Jakob and Wilhelm)
opera by: **11** Humperdinck
character: **5** Witch
feature **4** oven **16** gingerbread house
Hans Kristian
character in: **16** Giants of the Earth
author: **7** Rolvaag
Hanson, Howard
born: **7** Wahoo NE
composer of: **5** Sacra (symphony No 5) **6** Nordic (symphony No 1) **7** Requiem (symphony No 4) **8** Romantic (symphony No 2) **10** Merry-Mount
haphazard 6 casual, chance, fitful, random **7** aimless, chaotic **8** careless, on-and-off, slapdash, sporadic **9** arbitrary, hit-or-miss **10** accidental, disordered, disorderly, fortuitous, undesigned, undirected, unthinking **11** purposeless, unorganized **12** disorganized, unmethodical, unsystematic **14** indiscriminate, unpremeditated **15** catch-as-catch-can
hapless 6 cursed, jinxed, no-good, rot-

ten, woeful **7** forlorn, unhappy, unlucky **8** accursed, hopeless, ill-fated, luckless, wretched **9** miserable **10** ill-starred **11** star-crossed, unfortunate
happen 5 arise, ensue, occur **6** appear, befall, betide, crop up, result **7** turn out **8** become of, spring up **9** be borne by, be the case, come about, eventuate, take place, transpire **10** be one's fate, come to pass **11** be endured by **12** be suffered by **13** be one's fortune, fall to one's lot, present itself
happening 4 case **5** event **6** advent, affair, matter **7** episode **8** accident, incident, occasion **9** adventure, incidence **10** experience, occurrence, proceeding **11** vicissitude **12** circumstance, happenstance **20** just one of those things
happenstance 4 luck **6** chance **8** accident, fortuity
happiness 3 joy **4** glee **5** bliss, cheer, mirth **6** gaiety **7** comfort, content, delight, ecstasy, elation, jollity, rapture **8** blessing, felicity, gladness, pleasure **9** beatitude, enjoyment, merriment, rejoicing, transport **10** cheeriness, exuberance, exultation, jubilation **11** blessedness, contentment, high spirits **12** cheerfulness, satisfaction **13** gratification **16** lightheartedness, sense of well-being
happy 3 fit, gay **4** glad, meet **5** lucky **6** elated, joyful, joyous, timely **7** content, fitting, gleeful, pleased, tickled **8** blissful, cheerful, cheering, ecstatic, exultant, jubilant, pleasant, pleasing **9** agreeable, contented, delighted, exuberant, favorable, fortunate, gratified, opportune, overjoyed, rapturous, rhapsodic **10** auspicious, convenient, delightful, felicitous, gratifying, propitious, seasonable **11** exhilarated, tickled pink, transported **12** advantageous **13** in high spirits **15** in seventh heaven
Happy Days
character: **6** Arnold, Fonzie **10** Ralph Malph **11** Potsie Weber **12** Chachi Arcola **14** Pinky Tuscadero **15** Chuck Cunningham **16** Alfred Delvecchio, Arthur Fonzarelli, Howard Cunningham, Joanie Cunningham, Leather Tuscadero, Marion Cunningham, Richie Cunningham
cast: **8** Roz Kelly **9** Donny Most, Erin Moran, Pat Morita, Ron Howard, Scott Baio, Tom Bosley **10** Al Molinaro, Marion Ross, Suzi Quatro **12** Henry Winkler **13** Anson Williams, Gavan O'Herlihy **15** Randolph Roberts
happy-go-lucky 6 blithe **7** buoyant, flighty, relaxed **8** carefree, careless, feckless, heedless, skittish **9** easygoing, unworried **10** insouciant, noncha-

lant, optimistic, untroubled **11** free-and-easy, unconcerned **12** devil-may-care, light-hearted **13** irresponsible **14** scatterbrained **23** without a worry in the world
harangue 6 speech, tirade **7** lecture, oration **8** diatribe, scolding **9** contumely, sermonize **12** denunciation, vituperation
Harare
capital of: **8** Zimbabwe
harass 3 cow, irk, vex **4** bait, ride **5** annoy, beset, bully, harry, hound, tease, worry **6** attack, badger, bother, heckle, hector, pester, plague **7** assault, bedevil, besiege, disturb, torment **8** browbeat, distress, irritate **9** persecute **10** discommode, exasperate, intimidate **14** raid frequently
harbinger 4 clue, omen **5** token **6** herald, symbol **7** portent **8** signaler **9** announcer, first sign, precursor **10** forerunner, indication, proclaimer
Harbonna 6 eunuch
harbor 3 bay **4** cove, dock, feel, goal, hide, hold, keep, pier, port, quay **5** basin, haven, house, inlet, lodge, wharf **6** asylum, billet, foster, lagoon, refuge, retain, shield, take in **7** care for, cling to, conceal, nurture, protect, quarter, retreat, shelter **8** hideaway, keep safe, maintain, muse over, terminus **9** brood over, sanctuary **11** concealment, destination, hiding place **12** give refuge to **13** bear in the mind, terminal point **18** protected anchorage
Harcorates see **5** Horus
hard 3 sad **4** cold, firm, mean, ugly **5** cruel, eager, harsh, heavy, rigid, rough, solid, stern, stiff, stony, tight, tough **6** bitter, brutal, fierce, firmly, keenly, knotty, severe, steely, strict, strong, sullen, thorny, unkind **7** angrily, arduous, callous, closely, complex, cryptic, eagerly, earnest, harmful, heavily, hostile, hurtful, inhuman, intense, onerous, sharply, solidly, tightly, to heart, vicious, violent, willing, zealous **8** animated, baffling, critical, diligent, exacting, fiercely, forceful, forcibly, hardened, intently, involved, pitiless, powerful, puzzling, rocklike, ruthless, severely, spirited, spiteful, steadily, strongly, stubborn, untiring, venomous, vigorous **9** arduously, assiduous, bellicose, confusing, difficult, earnestly, energetic, furiously, Herculean, insulting, intensely, intricate, laborious, malicious, merciless, painfully, rancorous, seriously, strenuous, stringent, unbending, unpliable, unsparing, violently, wearisome **10** burdensome, diligently, forcefully, formidable, impervious, implacable, inexorable, inflexible, lamentable, melancholy, oppressive, perplexing, persistent, powerfully,

relentless, resolutely, rigorously, tormenting, unbearable, unflagging, unfriendly, unpleasant, untiringly, unyielding, vigorously, vindictive **11** acrimonious, agonizingly, assiduously, belligerent, bewildering, complicated, distressing, emotionally, hardhearted, industrious, insensitive, intolerable, laboriously, persevering, troublesome, unceasingly, unmalleable, unrelenting, unremitting, unsparingly **12** antagonistic, cantankerous, determinedly, disagreeable, enterprising, impenetrable, persistently, relentlessly, thick-skinned, unfathomable, unflaggingly **13** conscientious, disheartening, distressfully, energetically, indefatigable, industriously, with much anger **14** uncompromising, with much sorrow **15** conscientiously **16** with all one's might **18** with strong feelings

hard-and-fast 3 set **6** strict **7** binding **8** exacting, rigorous **9** mandatory, unbending **10** compelling, compulsory, inflexible, obligatory, undeniable, unyielding **11** irrevocable, unalterable, unremitting **12** indisputable **13** incontestable **14** uncompromising

Hardcastle family
  characters in: 18 She Stoops to Conquer
  author: 9 Goldsmith

hard drinker 3 sot **4** lush, soak, wino **5** drunk, rummy, souse, toper **6** barfly, boozer **7** guzzler, imbiber, tippler **8** drunkard **9** alcoholic **11** dipsomaniac **14** problem drinker **16** two-fisted drinker

harden 3 dry, gel, set **4** cake, fire, firm **5** adapt, adjust, blunt, enure, inure, steel **6** anneal, freeze, season, temper **7** calcify, callous, congeal, fortify, petrify, stiffen, thicken, toughen **8** accustom, solidify **9** fossilize, make tough, reinforce **10** discipline, invigorate, strengthen **11** crystallize, turn to stone **12** restrengthen **13** make unfeeling

hard feelings 5 anger **6** grudge, hatred, rancor **7** ill will **8** acrimony **9** animosity, hostility **10** antagonism, bitterness **12** spitefulness

hardheaded 4 cool **5** balky **6** astute, mulish, poised, shrewd **7** willful **8** contrary, sensible, stubborn **9** immovable, objective, obstinate, pigheaded, practical, pragmatic, realistic, unbending, unfeeling **10** coolheaded, impersonal, inflexible, refractory, self-willed, unyielding **11** down-to-earth, intractable, tough-minded, unemotional, unflappable **14** self-controlled

hardhearted 4 cold, hard, mean **5** cruel, stony **6** brutal, Hannah **7** callous, inhuman **8** pitiless, ruthless, uncaring **9** heartless, merciless, unfeeling, unpitying, unsparing **11**

coldblooded, indifferent, insensitive, remorseless, unforgiving **12** cruelhearted, thick-skinned **13** unsympathetic

hardihood 4 grit **5** pluck, spunk **6** mettle **7** courage **8** strength **9** endurance, fortitude **10** resolution **12** resoluteness

Harding, Warren Gamaliel
  presidential rank: 11 twenty-ninth
  party: 10 Republican
  state represented: 2 OH
  defeated: 3 (James Middleton) Cox, (William Wesley) Cox **4** (Eugene Victor) Debs **7** (Aaron Sherman) Watkins **8** (Robert Charles) Macauley **11** (Parley Parker) Christensen
  vice president: 8 (Calvin) Coolidge
  cabinet:
    state: 6 (Charles Evans) Hughes
    treasury: 6 (Andrew William) Mellon
    war: 5 (John Wingate) Weeks
    attorney general: 9 (Harry Micajah) Daugherty
    navy: 5 (Edwin) Denby
    postmaster general: 3 (Harry Stewart) New **4** (Hubert) Work, (William Harrison) Hays
    interior: 4 (Albert Bacon) Fall, (Hubert) Work
    agriculture: 7 (Henry Cantwell) Wallace
    commerce: 6 (Herbert Clark) Hoover
    labor: 5 (James John) Davis
  born: 9 Corsica OH (now Blooming Grove)
  died: 2 CA (while in office) **12** San Francisco
  buried: 8 Marion OH
  education:
    College: 11 Ohio Central
  religion: 7 Baptist
  interests: 5 poker
    played musical instrument: 6 cornet **7** helicon
  political career: 8 US Senate **15** Ohio State Senate
    lieutenant governor of: 4 Ohio
  civilian career: 9 publisher **13** schoolteacher **15** newspaper editor **17** insurance salesman
  notable events of lifetime/term:
    Act: 21 Fordney-McCumber Tariff
    peace treaty with: 7 Austria, Germany, Hungary
    scandal: 10 Teapot Dome (oil)
    Treaty: 9 Five-Power, Nine-Power **16** Four-Power Pacific
  father: 11 George Tryon
  mother: 6 Phoebe (Elizabeth Dickerson)
    stepmother: 4 Mary (Alice Severns) **6** Eudora (Kelley Luvisi)
  siblings: 11 George Tryon **12** Mary Clarissa **14** Charity Malvina, Phoebe Caroline **15** Abigail Victoria **16**

Charles Alexander, Eleanor Priscilla
  wife: 8 Florence (Kling DeWolfe)
  children:
    illegitimate daughter: 21 Elizabeth Ann Christian (by mistress Nan Britton)

hardly 4 just, only **6** barely, rarely **7** faintly, in no way **8** not often, not quite, scarcely **9** almost not, by no means **10** in no manner, uncommonly **12** certainly not, infrequently **13** not by any means **15** not by a great deal

hardnosed 4 hard **5** harsh, rigid, stern, tough **6** severe, shrewd, strict **8** critical, hard-line, exacting, stubborn **9** demanding, unbending, unsparing **10** hardheaded, inflexible, nononsense, unyielding **11** calculating, intractable **12** unsentimental **14** uncompromising

Hardouin-Mansart, Jules
  architect of: 8 Orangery (Versailles) **12** Chateau du Val (St Germain-en-Laye), Grand Trianon (Versailles), Place Vendome (Paris) **15** Chateau de Clagny (Versailles) **16** Galerie des Glaces (Hall of Mirrors at Versailles), Les Invalides (Church of the Dome, Paris)

hard-pressed 7 harried, put-upon **9** embattled **10** overworked

hardship 3 woe **4** load **5** agony, grief **6** burden, misery, ordeal, sorrow **7** problem, travail, trouble **8** handicap **9** adversity, privation, suffering **10** affliction, difficulty, misfortune **11** cross to bear, encumbrance, tribulation, unhappiness **12** wretchedness

hard sledding 8 tough job **10** difficulty, tough going, uphill work **11** arduousness **13** laboriousness

hard times 4 bust **5** slump **8** bad times **9** recession **10** depression

Hard Times
  author: 11 Studs Terkel

Hard Times
  author: 14 Charles Dickens
  character: 9 Sissy Jupe **10** Mrs Sparsit **11** Mr Bounderby **12** Tom Gradgrind **14** James Harthouse **15** Louisa Gradgrind, Thomas Gradgrind **16** Stephen Blackpool

hard to catch 3 sly **4** foxy, wily **6** crafty, shifty, tricky **7** elusive, evasive **8** slippery

hard to grasp 6 arcane **7** complex, elusive **8** abstruse, baffling, puzzling, slippery **9** difficult, enigmatic **10** perplexing **16** incomprehensible

hard to manage 6 unruly **7** froward, willful **8** perverse, stubborn **9** difficult, fractious, obstinate **10** inflexible, refractory, unyielding **11** intractable **12** obstreperous, unmanageable

hard to please 5 fussy, picky **7** exigent, finicky **8** critical **10** fastidious, meticulous, particular

Hardwick, Elizabeth
  author of: **11** Simple Truth **12** A
    View of My Own **15** Sleepless Nights
    20 Seduction and Betrayal
Hardwicke, Sir Cedric
  born: **3** Lye **7** England
  roles: **14** On Borrowed Time **21** Liv-
    ingstone and Stanley **36** A Connecti-
    cut Yankee in King Arthur's Court
hardwood 4 wood **8** leadwood
  kind: **3** ash, elm, oak **4** teak **5** beech,
    birch, maple **6** cherry, linden, wal-
    nut **7** hickory **8** mahogany, rose-
    wood, sycamore
hardworking 8 diligent, sedulous **9**
    assiduous **11** industrious, persevering
    12 enterprising **13** conscientious
hardy 3 fit **4** hale **5** tough **6** hearty,
    mighty, robust, rugged, strong, sturdy
    7 healthy **8** stalwart, vigorous **9** strap-
    ping **10** able-bodied **12** in fine fettle
    13 physically fit **15** in good condition
Hardy, Oliver
  partner: **10** Stan Laurel
  born: **8** Harlem GA
  roles: **8** Pardon Us **9** Saps at Sea **10**
    Way Out West
Hardy, Thomas
  author of: **10** The Dynasts **14** Jude
    the Obscure **20** The Return of the
    Native **21** Tess of the D'Urbervilles
    22 Far from the Madding Crowd,
    The Mayor of Casterbridge
  mythical county: **6** Wessex
  represents: **11** Dorsetshire
hare
  constellation of: **5** Lepus
  group of: **4** down, husk
harebrained 5 silly, wacko, wacky **7**
    asinine, flighty, foolish **8** skittish **9**
    dimwitted, senseless **10** half-witted **11**
    empty-headed **12** simple-minded **13**
    rattlebrained **14** featherbrained, scat-
    terbrained
Haredale, Reuben
  character in: **12** Barnaby Rudge
  author: **7** Dickens
harem 5 serai, wives **6** purdah, serail,
    senana, zenana **8** love nest, seraglio
    10 concubines
  room: **3** oda
  guard **6** eunuch
Hargreaves, James
  nationality: **7** English
  inventor of: **13** spinning jenny
Harker, Jonathan
  character in: **7** Dracula
  author: **6** Stoker
harlot 3 pro **4** bawd, doxy, jade, pros,
    slut, tart **5** whore **6** chippy, wanton **7**
    jezebel, trollop **8** call girl, mistress,
    strumpet **9** courtesan, kept woman **10**
    prostitute **11** fallen woman **12** painted
    woman, scarlet woman, streetwalker
Harlow, Jean
  real name: **16** Harlean Carpenter
  nickname: **15** Blonde Bombshell

born: 12 Kansas City MO
  roles: **7** Red Dust **8** Riffraff, Saratoga
    9 Bombshell, China Seas **11** Hell's
    Angels, Libeled Lady **13** Dinner at
    Eight
harm 3 ill, mar, sin **4** evil, hurt, maim,
    pain, ruin, vice **5** abuse, agony,
    havoc, spoil, wound, wrong **6** dam-
    age, debase, deface, ill-use, impair, in-
    jure, injury, malice, misuse, trauma **7**
    blemish, cripple, degrade, scourge **8**
    aggrieve, calamity, hardship, iniquity,
    maltreat, mischief, villainy **9** adver-
    sity, detriment, disfigure, suffering,
    undermine **10** defacement, immoral-
    ity, impairment, misfortune, sinful-
    ness, wickedness **11** destruction, dev-
    astation, malevolence **12** do violence
    to **13** deterioration, maliciousness
harmful 3 bad **7** adverse, baneful,
    hurtful, ruinous **8** damaging **9** danger-
    ous, injurious, unhealthy **10** perni-
    cious **11** deleterious, destructive, det-
    rimental, unhealthful, unwholesome
    17 counterproductive
harmless 4 mild, safe **6** benign, gentle
    7 sinless **8** innocent, nontoxic **9**
    blameless, guiltless, incorrupt, innocu-
    ous, peaceable **10** not hurtful **11** inof-
    fensive **12** not dangerous **15** unobjec-
    tionable
harmlessness 6 safety **9** innocence **10**
    gentleness **11** nontoxicity **12** nonviru-
    lence **13** innocuousness **15** inoffen-
    siveness
Harmon, Young John
  character in: **15** Our Mutual Friend
  author: **7** Dickens
Harmonia
  father: **4** Ares
  mother: **9** Aphrodite
  husband: **6** Cadmus
  daughter: **3** Ino
harmonious 5 sweet **6** dulcet **7** amia-
    ble, cordial, unified **8** amicable,
    friendly, in accord, matching **9** agree-
    able, congenial, in harmony, melodi-
    ous **10** compatible, consistent, eupho-
    nious, likeminded **11** coordinated,
    harmonizing, in agreement, melliflu-
    ous, sympathetic **12** synchronized **13**
    sweet-sounding **17** agreeably com-
    bined
harmonium 9 reed organ
harmonize 3 fit **4** jibe, mesh **5** agree,
    blend, chime, tally **6** accord, adjust,
    attune **7** conform **8** be in tune **9** rec-
    oncile **10** complement, correspond, go
    together **13** sing in harmony
harmony 5 amity, order, peace, unity
    6 accord **7** balance, concord **8** match-
    ing, symmetry, sympathy **9** agree-
    ment, unanimity **10** conformity, fel-
    lowship, friendship, proportion **11**
    amicability, cooperation, correlation,
    parallelism **12** congeniality, coordina-
    tion, mutual regard **13** compatibility,

    mutual fitness **14** like-mindedness **15**
    organic totality **17** good understand-
    ing **19** harmonious relations, pleasing
    consistency **21** concurrence in opin-
    ions
Harmony
  goddess of: **9** Concordia
harness 4 curb, rein, tugs, yoke **5**
    lines, reins, rig up **6** bridle, collar,
    employ, halter, muzzle, straps, tackle,
    traces **7** exploit, hitch up, utilize **8** re-
    strain **9** caparison, trappings **12** put in
    harness, render useful **13** control and
    use, turn to account **14** make produc-
    tive **22** direct to a useful purpose
Harper, Joe
  character in: **9** Tom Sawyer
  author: **5** Twain
harp on 7 dwell on **9** reiterate **18** re-
    peat persistently
Harpy
  form: **7** monster
  head of: **5** woman
  body of: **4** bird
  father: **7** Thaumas
  mother: **7** Electra
  names: **5** Aello **7** Celaeno, Ocypete,
    Podarge
harridan 3 hag **5** crone, shrew, witch
    6 virago **8** battle-ax, old crone **12**
    mean old woman
harried 5 upset **7** worried **8** harassed,
    troubled **10** distraught
Harris, Joel Chandler
  author of: **10** Uncle Remus (His
    Songs and Sayings)
  character: **7** Brer Fox, tar baby **8** Brer
    Bear **10** Brer Rabbit
Harris, Julie
  real name: **14** Julia Ann Harris
  born: **18** Grosse Pointe Park MI
  roles: **6** Harper **10** East of Eden, I Am
    a Camera **11** The Haunting **14** A
    Shot in the Dark, The Hiding Place
    19 The Last of Mrs Lincoln **21** The
    Member of the Wedding **22** Requiem
    for a Heavyweight **27** And Miss Re-
    ardon Drinks a Little
Harris, Richard
  born: **7** Ireland **8** Limerick
  roles: **7** Camelot **8** Cromwell **15** A
    Man Called Horse **16** The Molly
    Maguires, This Sporting Life **17** Mu-
    tiny on the Bounty, The Guns of
    Navarone **20** The Cassandra Crossing
    26 The Return of a Man Called
    Horse
Harris, Roy
  composer of: **16** Folksong Symphony
    17 American Portraits **27** When
    Johnny Comes Marching Home
    (overture)
Harrison, Benjamin
  nickname: **3** Ben **9** Little Ben
  presidential rank: **11** twenty-third
  party: **10** Republican
  state represented: **2** IN

defeated: 4 (Clinton Bowen) Fisk **6** (James Langdon) Curtis **7** (Robert Hall) Cowdrey **8** (Albert) Redstone, (Alson Jenness) Streeter, (Belva Ann Bennett) Lockwood **9** (Grover) Cleveland
vice president: 6 (Levi Parsons) Morton
cabinet:
  state: 6 (James Gillespie) Blaine, (John Watson) Foster
  treasury: 6 (Charles) Foster, (William) Windom
  war: 6 (Stephen Benton) Elkins **7** (Redfield) Proctor
  attorney general: 6 (William Henry Harrison) Miller
  navy: 5 (Benjamin Franklin) Tracy
  postmaster general: 9 (John) Wanamaker
  interior: 5 (John Willock) Noble
  agriculture: 4 (Jeremiah McLain) Rusk
born: 11 North Bend OH
died/buried: 14 Indianapolis IN
education:
  prep school: 14 Farmer's College
  University: 21 Miami University of Ohio
  later studied: 3 law
religion: 12 Presbyterian
interests: 7 fishing, hunting **8** swimming
author: 17 This Country of Ours **20** Views of An Ex- President
political career: 8 US Senate
  city attorney: 12 Indianapolis
  reporter of: 19 Indiana supreme court
  secretary of: 31 Republican state central committee
civilian career: 6 lawyer **12** law professor
military service: 8 Civil War **16** brigadier general
notable events of lifetime/term:
  Act: 16 Dependent Pension, Sherman Anti-Trust **21** Sherman Silver Purchase
  Tariff: 8 McKinley
father: 9 John Scott
mother: 9 Elizabeth (Ramsey Irwin)
siblings: 8 Mary Jane **9** John Irwin, John Scott **10** Anna Symmes, James Irwin **12** James Findlay **13** Carter Bassett **14** Archibald Irwin
  half sisters: 9 Elizabeth **13** Sarah Lucretia
wife: 4 Mary (Scott Lord Dimmick) **8** Caroline (Lavinia Scott)
children: 9 Elizabeth, Mary Scott **15** Russell Benjamin

Harrison, Lou
  born: 10 Portland OR
  composer of: 8 Rapunzel, Solstice **13** Changing World **15** Four Strict Songs, Johnny Appleseed **17** The Perilous Chapel **19** Almanac of the

Seasons **22** At the Tomb of Charles Ives
Harrison, Peter
  architect of: 11 Brick Market (Newport RI), King's Chapel (Boston) **14** Redwood Library (Newport RI), Touro Synagogue (Newport RI)
Harrison, Rex
  real name: 21 Reginald Carey Harrison
  nickname: 8 Sexy Rexy
  wife: 10 Kay Kendall **11** Lilli Palmer **13** Rachel Roberts
  born: 6 Huyton **7** England
  roles: 9 Cleopatra **10** My Fair Lady (Oscar) **12** Blithe Spirit, Henry Higgins **14** Doctor Dolittle **16** The Foxes of Harrow **17** Unfaithfully Yours **18** The Ghost and Mrs Muir **20** Anna and the King of Siam
Harrison, Wallace K
  architect of: 13 Lincoln Center (NYC) **14** Socony Building (NYC) **17** Rockefeller Center (NYC) **22** Metropolitan Opera House (NYC) **25** United Nations Headquarters (NYC) **34** Nelson A Rockefeller Empire State Plaza (Albany NY), ALCOA Building (Pittsburgh, with Max Abramovitz)
Harrison, William Henry
  nickname: 6 Old Tip **22** The Washington of the West
  presidential rank: 5 ninth
  party: 4 Whig
  state represented: 2 OH
  defeated: 6 (James G) Birney **8** (Martin) Van Buren
  vice president: 5 (John) Tyler
  cabinet:
    state: 7 (Daniel) Webster
    treasury: 5 (Thomas) Ewing
    war: 4 (John) Bell
    attorney general: 10 (John Jordan) Crittenden
    navy: 6 (George Edmund) Badger
    postmaster general: 7 (Francis) Granger
  born: 2 VA **17** Charles City County **18** Berkeley plantation
  died: 12 Washington DC
  buried: 11 North Bend OH
  education: 16 privately tutored (at home)
    College: 13 Hampden-Sydney (did not graduate)
    later studied: 8 medicine
  religion: 12 Episcopalian
  political career: 8 US Senate **11** state Senate **24** US House of Representatives
    governor of: 16 Indiana Territory
    minister: 8 Columbia
  civilian career: 6 farmer **7** soldier
  military service: 6 US Army **12** major general **19** War of Eighteen Twelve
    battle: 6 (the) Thames **8** Lake Erie **10** Tippecanoe
  notable events of lifetime/term: 24

Land Act of Eighteen Hundred
  campaign slogan: 21 Tippecanoe and Tyler too
  treaty of: 10 Greenville
father: 8 Benjamin
mother: 9 Elizabeth (Bassett)
siblings: 3 Ann **4** Lucy **5** Sarah **8** Benjamin **9** Elizabeth **13** Carter Bassett
wife: 4 Anna (Tuthill Symmes)
children: 8 Benjamin **9** John Scott **10** Mary Symmes **11** Anna Tuthill **12** James Findlay, William Henry **13** Carter Bassett, Lucy Singleton **16** Elizabeth Bassett, John Cleves Symmes
Harrow 10 prep school
  rival: 4 Eton
harrowing 7 fearful, painful **8** alarming, chilling **9** traumatic, upsetting **10** disturbing, terrifying, tormenting **11** distressing, frightening **13** bloodcurdling
harry 3 irk, vex **4** bait, gall, raid, ride, sack **5** annoy, beset, bully, haunt, hound, tease, worry **6** badger, bother, harass, heckle, hector, pester, plague **7** disturb, pillage, plunder, torment, trouble **8** distract, distress, irritate **9** terrorize **10** exasperate, intimidate **16** attack repeatedly
harsh 4 hard, mean **5** cruel, raspy, rough, sharp, stern **6** bitter, brutal, hoarse, severe, shrill, unkind **7** abusive, caustic, glaring, grating, jarring, rasping, raucous, squawky **8** piercing, pitiless, ruthless, scratchy, strident, ungentle **9** Draconian, heartless, merciless, too bright, unmusical, unsparing **10** discordant, overbright, unpleasant, vindictive **11** cacophonous, hardhearted **12** uncharitable, unharmonious
harshness 5 rigor **7** cruelty, discord **9** brutality, cacophony, raspiness, roughness, sternness, stridency **10** dissonance, shrillness, unkindness **12** ungentleness **13** heartlessness **14** unpleasantness **15** hardheartedness
Hart, Johnny
  creator/artist of: 2 B C **13** The Wizard of Id
Hart, Moss
  author of: 15 Once in a Lifetime **20** You Can't Take It with You (with George S Kaufman) **21** The Man Who Came to Dinner (with George S Kaufman)
Harte, Bret
  author of: 20 The Luck of Roaring Camp **22** The Outcasts of Poker Flat
Hartford
  hockey team: 7 Whalers
Harthouse, James
  character in: 9 Hard Times
  author: 7 Dickens

Hartley, Vivian Mary
real name of: **11** Vivien Leigh

harum-scarum 5 giddy **6** wildly **7** erratic, flighty, foolish **8** careless, confused **9** aimlessly, haphazard, impetuous, impulsive, unplanned, unsettled **10** bewildered, recklessly, unreliable **11** haphazardly, harebrained, impulsively **12** absent-minded, capriciously, disorganized, inconsistent, undependable **13** rattlebrained **14** featherbrained, scatterbrained

Harun ar-Rashid 6 caliph **7** Baghdad **13** Arabian Nights

harvest 3 cut, mow **4** crop, gain, pick, reap **5** amass, fruit, pluck, yield **6** gather, haying, mowing, output, result, return, reward **7** benefit, collect, cutting, picking, produce, product, reaping **8** fruition, gleaning, proceeds **9** aftermath, amassment, gathering, outgrowth **10** accumulate, collection, harvesting **12** accumulation **13** season's growth

harvest time 4 fall **6** autumn **8** maturity **12** Indian summer

Harvey
director: **11** Henry Koster
based on play by: **9** Mary Chase
cast: **6** rabbit **8** Peggy Dow **12** James Stewart (Elwood P Dowd) **13** Cecil Kellaway, Josephine Hull
Oscar for: **17** supporting actress (Hull)

Harvey, Laurence
real name: **19** Larushka Misch Skikne
wife: **16** Margaret Leighton
born: **9** Lithuania, Yomishkis
roles: **7** Darling **12** Life at the Top, Room at the Top **14** Of Human Bondage, Summer and Smoke **16** Butterfield Eight **17** Walk on the Wild Side

Harvey, William
field: **7** anatomy
nationality: **7** British
discovered: **18** circulation of blood

Hasen, Irwin
creator/artist of: **5** Dondi **9** Goldbergs **11** Wonder Woman **12** Green Lantern

hash out 6 review **7** discuss **8** consider, talk over

hasp 4 lock **5** catch, clasp, latch **7** closure **8** fastener

Hassam, (Frederick) Childe
born: **12** Dorchester MA
artwork: **13** Southwest Wind **14** Summer Sunlight, Washington Arch **15** Against the Light **23** Boston Commons at Twilight

hassle 3 bug, row, vex **5** annoy, fight, harry, hound, scrap, set-to **6** badger, battle, bother, harass, tussle **7** contest, dispute, quarrel **8** argument, conflict, squabble, struggle **9** persecute

hassock 4 boss, pess, seat, tuft, weed **5** bunch, chair, group, trush **6** buffet, plants, tuffet **7** ottoman, tussock **9** footstool, vegetable

hasta la vista 6 good-by, so long **7** goodbye **12** until I see you **16** until we meet again

hasta manana 13 until tomorrow **14** see you tomorrow

haste 4 rush **5** hurry, speed **8** celerity, dispatch, rapidity, rashness **9** fleetness, quickness, swiftness **10** expedition, speediness, undue speed **11** hurriedness **12** recklessness **13** careless hurry, impetuousness, impulsiveness, precipitation

hasten 3 fly, run **4** bolt, dart, dash, flit, jump, race, rush **5** egg on, hurry, impel, speed, whisk **6** hustle, incite, scurry, sprint, urge on **7** advance, drive on, hurry on, hurry up, promote, quicken, scamper, scuttle, speed up **8** expedite, make time **10** accelerate, lose no time **11** go full blast, precipitate, push forward **12** step on the gas **13** go on the double **14** step right along **15** go like lightning, make short work of, work against time **20** go hell-bent for leather

hastily 4 fast **5** apace **6** pronto, rashly **7** quickly **8** promptly, speedily **9** hurriedly, like a shot, posthaste, summarily **10** carelessly, heedlessly, recklessly, too quickly **11** impetuously, impulsively, on the double **12** lickety-split, straightaway **13** precipitately, thoughtlessly **18** hell-bent for leather **20** like greased lightning, on the spur of the moment

Hastings, Thomas see **17** Carrere, John Merven

hasty 4 fast, rash **5** brief, fleet, quick, rapid, swift **6** abrupt, prompt, rushed, speedy **7** cursory, hurried, passing **8** fleeting, headlong, heedless, reckless **9** impetuous, impulsive, momentary **10** breathless **11** precipitate, superficial, unduly quick **12** quick as a wink **19** without deliberation

hat
French: **7** chapeau

hatch 4 plan, plot **5** frame **6** cook up, create, design, devise, evolve, invent, make up **7** concoct, dream up, fashion, produce, think up **8** conceive, contrive **9** construct, fabricate, formulate, improvise, originate **10** bring forth **11** give birth to, manufacture

hatchlings 5 brood, young **6** chicks **9** offspring

hate 5 abhor, dread, venom **6** animus, detest, enmity, hatred, loathe, malice, rancor **7** be sorry, despise, dislike, wince at **8** acrimony, aversion, be sick of, distaste, execrate, loathing **9** abominate, animosity, antipathy, be tired of, disliking, hostility, not care to **10** abhorrence, be averse to, feel sick at, recoil from, repugnance, resentment, shrink from **11** abomination, be hostile to, be reluctant, be unwilling, detestation, malevolence, wish to avoid **12** be repelled by **14** have no taste for, hold in contempt, revengefulness, vindictiveness **16** bear malice toward, have no stomach for **17** feel disinclined to, not have the heart to **19** regard as distasteful

hateful 4 evil, foul, mean, ugly, vile **5** nasty **6** odious, sinful, wicked **7** heinous **8** infamous, scornful **9** abhorrent, atrocious, loathsome, monstrous, obnoxious, offensive, repellent, repugnant, revolting, sickening **10** abominable, deplorable, despicable, detestable, disdainful, disgusting, forbidding, full of hate, irritating, unbearable, unpleasant, villainous **11** distasteful, intolerable, unendurable **12** contemptible, contemptuous, insufferable **13** objectionable

Hathaway, Anne
husband: **11** Shakespeare

Hathor
origin: **8** Egyptian
goddess of: **3** joy **4** love
symbol: **4** ears, head **5** horns
patron of: **5** dance, music
personifies: **3** sky

Hat on the Bed, The
author: **9** John O'Hara

hatred 4 hate **5** venom **6** animus, enmity, malice, rancor **7** disgust, dislike, ill will **8** acrimony, aversion, bad blood, distaste, loathing **9** animosity, antipathy, hostility, revulsion **10** abhorrence, antagonism, bitterness, repugnance, resentment **11** abomination, detestation, malevolence **14** revengefulness, vindictiveness

haughtiness 4 airs **5** pride **7** conceit, hauteur **8** snobbery **9** arrogance **10** snootiness **13** condescension **14** disdainfulness, high-handedness **16** superciliousness

haughty 5 aloof **6** lordly, snooty, uppish, uppity **7** high-hat, stuck-up **8** arrogant, scornful, snobbish **9** conceited, officious **10** disdainful, high-handed, hoity-toity **11** highfalutin, overbearing, overly proud, patronizing, swell-headed **12** contemptuous **13** condescending, high and mighty

haul 3 bag, lug, tow, tug **4** cart, drag, draw, gain, jerk, move, pull, swag, take, tote, yank **5** booty, bring, carry, catch, fetch, heave, truck, yield **6** convey, profit, remove, reward, spoils, wrench **7** capture, takings **9** transport

haunches 4 buns, rear, rump, seat **5** nates **7** rear end **8** buttocks **9** fundament, posterior **12** hindquarters

haunt 3 vex **5** beset, worry **6** live in, obsess, plague, prey on **7** disturb, terrify, torment, trouble, weigh on **8** distress, frequent, frighten **9** hang out at, preoccupy, terrorize **10** hang around, hover about, loiter near, visit often **11** beat a path to **12** linger around

haunts 3 den **4** cave, hole, lair, nest **6** burrow **7** hangout **8** hideaway **9** waterhole **10** rendezvous **12** meeting place **14** gathering place **15** stamping grounds

Hauptmann, Gerhart
  author of: **10** Before Dawn, The Weavers

haute couture 11 high fashion

haute cuisine 11 fine cooking **14** gourmet cooking

hauteur 5 swank **7** conceit, disdain **8** snobbery **9** arrogance, loftiness **10** snootiness **11** haughtiness **12** affectedness, snobbishness **13** condescension **14** disdainfulness, high-handedness **16** superciliousness **19** patronizing attitude

haut monde 5 elite **10** blue bloods, upper class, upper crust **11** aristocracy, high society **14** creme de la creme

Havana
  capital of: **4** Cuba
  gulf: **6** Mexico
  landmark: **15** Cabaret Parisien **16** Castillo del Morro **17** Castillo de la Punta, Jose Marti Monument **18** Castillo de la Atares, Castillo de la Fuerza, Garcia Lorca Theater **19** Maximo Gomez Monument **21** Latinamericano Stadium **22** Academy of Science of Cuba
  river: **10** (Rio) Almendares
  Spanish: **8** La Habana

Havasupai, Supai
  location: **7** Arizona **11** Grand Canyon
  related to: **7** Yavapai **8** Hualapai

have 3 buy, eat, get, own, use **4** bear, fool, gain, gull, hold, host, keep, make, must **5** beget, carry, cheat, drink, enjoy, force, grasp, ought, smoke, trick **6** accept, affirm, compel, harbor, obtain, outwit, permit, retain, suffer **7** achieve, acquire, defraud, exhibit, possess, realize, receive, swindle **8** comprise, maintain, manifest, outsmart, perceive, tolerate **9** encompass, encounter, partake of, recognize, victimize **10** comprehend, experience, understand

have a go at 3 try **6** hazard, tackle **7** attempt **8** give a try **9** undertake **10** give a whirl **12** take a crack at, take a whack at

have a good opinion of 5 favor **6** admire, revere **7** approve, respect **9** believe in **10** appreciate

have a hand in 7 advance, forward **9** influence **10** take part in **12** contribute to **13** be conducive to, participate in **14** help bring about

have an eye on 4 want **5** covet,

crave, fancy **6** desire **7** long for, pine for **8** aspire to, yearn for **9** lust after **11** have a yen for

have a yen for 4 want **5** covet, crave **6** desire **7** long for, wish for **8** yearn for **9** lust after **11** hanker after **13** have a fancy for

have bearing on 5 apply, refer **6** relate **7** concern, pertain **9** appertain, touch upon **13** be pertinent to, have respect to

have done with 4 drop, junk, shed **7** abandon, discard **9** dispose of **10** relinquish **12** dispense with

have faith in 5 trust **6** rely on **9** believe in **16** have confidence in

have guests 8 play host **9** entertain **10** give a party **13** keep open house **16** offer hospitality

Have Gun Will Travel
  character: **6** Hey Boy **7** Hey Girl, Paladin
  cast: **6** Lisa Lu **7** Kam Tong **12** Richard Boone
  setting: **12** San Francisco **13** Hotel Carleton

have in mind 4 mean, want, wish **6** desire, intend **10** think about

haven 4 port **5** cover **6** asylum, harbor, refuge **7** hideout, retreat, shelter **8** hideaway **9** sanctuary

have no hope 6 give up **7** despair **11** be desperate

have plenty 6 abound, be rich **8** flourish, overflow **10** be numerous, have enough **11** be plentiful **14** be well supplied **18** have more than enough

have the body
  Latin: **12** habeas corpus
  legal writ guards against: **19** illegal imprisonment

have too few 4 lack, want **7** be scant **9** fall short **13** be deficient in, have a dearth of **14** have a paucity of **15** be in short supply, have a scarcity of, not have enough of

having life 5 alive, vital **6** living, viable **7** animate

having the means 3 fit **4** able **6** fitted **7** capable, equal to **8** adequate **9** qualified **12** being solvent **20** having the wherewithal

Havisham, Miss
  character in: **17** Great Expectations
  author: **7** Dickens

havoc 4 ruin **5** chaos **8** calamity, disaster, disorder, upheaval **9** cataclysm, ruination **11** catastrophe, destruction, devastation **12** wrack and ruin **16** widespread damage

Havoc, June, **7** actress
  sister: **12** Gypsy Rose Lee
  dramatized as: **5** Gypsy
  billed as: **8** Baby June

Hawaii

  abbreviation: **2** HI
  nickname: **5** Aloha **15** Sandwich Islands **20** Paradise of the Pacific
  capital/largest city: **8** Honolulu
  others: **3** Ewa **4** Aiea, Hana, Hilo, Laie, Paia **5** Kapaa, Kapaa, Lihue, Maili **6** Kailua, Kekaha **7** Kahului, Kaneohe, Lanikae, Wahiawa, Waianae, Wailuku
  college: **9** Chaminade, Hawaii Loa **12** Brigham Young **13** Hawaii Pacific
  dance: **4** hula
  explorer: **4** Cook **7** Gaetano
  feature:
    district: **7** Lahaina
    national park: **9** Haleakala **15** Hawaii Volcanoes
  festivity: **4** luau
  food: **3** poi **4** taro
  foreigner: **5** haole
  gift: **3** lei
  greeting: **5** aloha
  goddess: **4** Pele
  king: **10** Kamehameha
  medicine man: **6** Kahuna
  musical instrument: **3** uke **7** ukulele, ukelele
  native woman: **6** wahine
  people: **5** Don Ho **9** Hiram Fong **10** Polynesian **11** Sanford Dole, Bette Midler **12** Daniel Inouye, Father Damien
  porch: **5** lanai
  queen **12** Liliuokalani
  island name: **4** Kure **9** Kahoolawe
    big isle: **6** Hawaii
    friendly isle: **7** Molokai
    garden isle: **5** Kauai
    gathering place: **4** Oahu
    house of the sun: **9** Haleakala
    mystery isle: **6** Niihau
    pineapple isle: **5** Lanai
    valley isle: **4** Maui
  lake: **5** Waiau
  land rank: **12** forty-seventh
  mountain: **3** Kea, Loa **5** Kaala **6** Kohala, Kohala, Koolau **7** Kamakou, Waianae **8** Maunaloa **9** Lanaihale
    highest point: **8** Maunakea
  physical feature:
    bay: **5** Pohue **6** Halawa, Kiholo, Mamala **7** Kamohio, Kaneohe, Waiagua **8** Kawaihae, Maunalua
    beach: **7** Waikiki
    canyon: **6** Waimea
    channel: **3** Aua **5** Kaiwi **6** Kalohi **7** Pailolo
    crater: **7** Kilauea **9** Punchbowl
    desert: **3** Kau
    harbor: **5** Pearl
    promontory: **11** Diamond Head
    valley: **3** Iao **5** Manoa
    volcano: **7** Kilauea **8** Maunakea, Maunaloa **9** Haleakala
  state admission: **8** Fiftieth
  state bird: **4** nene **13** Hawaiian goose
  state flower: **5** lehua **11** red hibiscus **15** scarlet hibiscus

state motto: 44 The Life of the Land is Perpetuated in Righteousness
state song: 11 Hawaii Ponoi **12** Our Own Hawaii
state tree: 5 kukui **9** candlenut

Hawaii
author: 13 James Michener

Hawaiian swimmer 14 Duke Kahanamoku

Hawaii Five-O
character: 4 Kono **5** Wo Fat **8** Ben Kokua **11** Chin Ho Kelly **13** Danny Williams **14** Steve McGarrett
cast: 4 Zulu **7** Kam Fong **8** Jack Lord **11** Khigh Dhiegh **12** Al Harrington **14** James MacArthur

hawk 4 bird, sell, vend **6** falcon, peddle **8** militant **9** accipiter, warmonger
young: 4 eyas
group of: 4 cast

Hawk, Sir Mulberry
character in: 16 Nicholas Nickleby
author: 7 Dickens

Hawkes, John
author of: 10 Second Skin **11** The Cannibal, The Lime Twig **12** The Beetle Leg **15** The Blood Oranges

Hawkeye 11 Natty Bumppo
author: 6 Cooper

Hawkeye Pierce 4 Mash **8** Alan Alda

Hawkeye State
nickname of: 4 Iowa

Hawkins, Jim
character in: 14 Treasure Island
author: 9 Stevenson

Hawkline Monster, The
author: 16 Richard Brautigan

Hawks, Howard
director of: 8 Red River, Rio Bravo, Scarface **11** The Big Sleep **12** Sergeant York **13** His Girl Friday **14** Bringing Up Baby **16** To Have and Have Not, Twentieth Century

Hawn, Goldie
husband: 12 Gus Trinkonis
born: 12 Washington DC
roles: 7 Laugh-In, Shampoo **8** Foul Play **12** Cactus Flower **15** Private Benjamin **18** Butterflies Are Free

hawser 4 line, rope **5** cable **7** mooring

hawthorn 9 Crataegus
varieties: 5 water, yeddo **6** Indian **7** English

Hawthorne, Nathaniel
author of: 13 The Marble Faun **14** Twice-told Tales **16** The Scarlet Letter **20** Mosses from an Old Manse **24** The House of the Seven Gables

Haydee
character in: 21 The Count of Monte Cristo
author: 5 Dumas (pere)

Haydn, Franz Joseph
born: 6 Rohrau **7** Austria
called: 9 Papa Haydn
composer of: 7 The Bird, The Joke

10 Gypsy Rondo, The Seasons **11** The Creation **12** Emperor's Hymn, Wild Band Mass **13** The Apothecary **14** Lord Nelson Mass, Theresienmesse **15** Mass in Time of War **16** Il Mondo della Luna, Mariazellermesse **17** The World of the Moon **38** The Seven Last Words of Our Savior on the Cross
quartet: 3 Sun **4** Bird, Frog, Lark, Tost **5** Dream, Razor, Witch **6** Fifths, Maiden **7** Emperor, Erdoedy, Russian, Sunrise, The Bell, The Hunt **8** Farmyard, Horseman, The Jokes **9** The Donkey **14** The House on Fire, The Row in Vienna
symphony: 4 Fire **5** Paris **6** Le Midi, Le Soir, Loudon, Merkur, Oxford, The Hen **7** Evening, Le Matin, Mercury, Morning, Salomon, The Bear, The Hunt **8** Abschied, Alleluia, Drum Roll, Farewell, Military, Mourning, Surprise, The Clock, The Queen, The Storm **9** Children's, Christmas **10** La Passione, La Tempesta, The Miracle, The Passion **11** The Imperial **12** Der Philosoph, Maria Theresa, The Afternoon **13** Auf dem Anstand **14** The Philosopher **15** The Schoolmaster, Trauersymphonie, With the Horn Call **17** At the Hunting Place **18** Mit dem Hornersignal

Hayes, Elvin
nickname: 4 Big E
sport: 10 basketball
team: 8 San Diego **14** Houston Rockets

Hayes, Helen
real name: 15 Helen Hayes Brown
nickname: 29 First Lady of the American Theater
son: 14 James MacArthur
roles: 7 Airport **9** Anastasia **22** The Sin of Madelon Claudet (Oscar)

Hayes, Rutherford B (Birchard)
nickname: 8 Rud Hayes
presidential rank: 10 nineteenth
party: 10 Republican
state represented: 2 OH
defeated: 5 (Green Clay) Smith **6** (James B) Walker, (Peter) Cooper, (Samuel Jones) Tilden
vice president: 7 (William Almon) Wheeler
cabinet:
state: 6 (William Maxwell) Evarts
treasury: 7 (John) Sherman
war: 6 (Alexander) Ramsey **7** (George Washington) McCrary
attorney general: 6 (Charles) Devens
navy: 4 (Nathan) Goff (Jr) **8** (Richard Wigginton) Thompson
postmaster general: 3 (David McKendree) Key **7** (Horace) Maynard
interior: 6 (Carl) Schurz

born: 10 Delaware OH
died/buried: 9 Fremont OH
education:
preparatory school: 4 Webb
College: 6 Kenyon
Law School: 7 Harvard
religion: 9 Methodist
political career: 24 US House of Representatives
city solicitor of: 10 Cincinnati
governor of: 4 Ohio
civilian career: 6 farmer, lawyer
military service: 6 US Army **8** Civil War **12** Ohio infantry **18** brevet major general
notable events of lifetime/term: 10 Depression (of 1873) **15** railroad strikes (of 1877) **18** civil service reform **24** specie payments resumption
Act: 26 Bland-Allison Silver Purchase
father: 10 Rutherford
mother: 6 Sophia (Birchard)
siblings: 7 Lorenzo **11** Sarah Sophia **13** Fanny Arabella
wife: 4 Lucy (Ware Webb)
children: 5 Fanny **9** James Webb (renamed Webb Cook) **11** George Crook **12** Manning Force, Scott Russell **14** Joseph Thompson, Sardis Birchard (renamed Birchard Austin) **15** Rutherford Platt

hayseed 4 hick, rube **5** yokel **6** rustic **7** bumpkin, peasant **10** clodhopper

Hayward, Susan
real name: 14 Edythe Marrener
husband: 10 Jess Barker
born: 10 Brooklyn NY
roles: 11 I Want to Live (Oscar) **14** I'll Cry Tomorrow, My Foolish Heart **18** With a Song in My Heart **23** Smash Up The Story of a Woman

Hayworth, Rita
real name: 22 Margarita Carmen Cansino
husband: 7 Aly Khan **10** Dick Haymes **11** Orson Welles
born: 10 Brooklyn NY
roles: 5 Gilda **9** Cover Girl **14** Separate Tables **17** Miss Sadie Thompson, You'll Never Get Rich

hazan 18 cantor of a synagogue

hazard 3 bet **4** dare, luck, risk **5** fluke, guess, offer, peril, stake, wager **6** chance, danger, expose, gamble, menace, mishap, submit, threat **7** advance, daresay, imperil, pitfall, presume, proffer, suppose, venture **8** accident, chance it, endanger, jeopardy, theorize, threaten, throw out **9** mischance, speculate, tempt fate, volunteer **10** conjecture, jeopardize, misfortune **11** coincidence, hypothesize, imperilment, take a chance, trust to luck **12** endangerment, happenstance, stroke of luck

Hazard of New Fortunes, A
author: 18 William Dean Howells

hazardous 4 iffy 5 risky, shaky 6 chancy, unsafe, unsure 7 dubious, unsound 8 doubtful, insecure, perilous, unstable 9 dangerous, uncertain 10 precarious, unreliable 11 speculative, threatening 13 untrustworthy

haze 3 fog 4 daze, film, mist, pall, veil 5 cloak, cloud, smoke, vapor 6 mantle, muddle, screen 9 fogginess 12 befuddlement, bewilderment 16 state of confusion

hazel 3 nut 4 tree 5 brown, shrub, tawny 8 brownish 14 yellowish-brown

varieties: 4 tree 5 Chile, witch 6 winter 7 Chinese, Turkish 8 American, European, Japanese 11 spike winter 12 Chinese witch 13 Japanese witch 15 buttercup winter

Hazel

character: 12 George Baxter, Harold Baxter 13 Dorothy Baxter

cast: 9 Don DeFore 12 Shirley Booth, Whitney Blake 13 Bobby Buntrock

creator: 6 Ted Key

hazelnut 7 Corylus

varieties: 6 beaked 7 Chinese, Turkish 8 American, European, Japanese

Hazlitt, William

author of: 6 essays 17 The Spirit of the Age 32 The Characters of Shakespeare's Plays

hazy 3 dim 5 dusky, faint, filmy, foggy, misty, murky, smoky, vague 6 bleary, blurry, cloudy, smoggy, veiled 7 bleared, general, muddled, obscure, unclear 8 confused, nebulous, overcast 9 ambiguous, uncertain 10 ill-defined, indefinite

head 2 go, IQ 3 aim, CEO, end, hie, tip, top 4 acme, apex, bent, boss, czar, duce, font, fore, gift, jefe, king, lead, main, mind, peak, rise, rule, tsar, turn, well 5 begin, brain, chief, crest, crown, drive, first, front, guide, pilot, prime, queen, ruler, start, steer 6 climax, crisis, direct, genius, govern, honcho, launch, leader, manage, origin, ruling, source, spring, summit, talent, vertex, zenith 7 ability, admiral, captain, command, conduct, control, foreman, general, go first, highest, leading, make for, manager, marshal, monarch, precede, premier, primary, proceed, ranking, supreme, topmost 8 aptitude, be head of, big wheel, capacity, chairman, dictator, director, dominant, foremost, fountain, fruition, headmost, initiate, judgment, managing, pinnacle, start off, superior, suzerain, upper end 9 acuteness, beginning, commander, commodore, extremity, forefront, front rank, governing, intellect, introduce, mentality, paramount, potentate, president, principal, sovereign, supervise, uppermost 10 administer, be master of,

birthplace, cleverness, commandant, commanding, conclusion, first place, gray matter, inaugurate, lead the way, move toward, perception, preeminent, supervisor, wellspring 11 be at the helm, controlling, culmination, discernment, forward part, highest rank, officiate at, preside over, superintend, take the lead, termination 12 apprehension, field marshal, fountainhead, guiding light, place of honor, take charge of, take the reins, turning point, utmost extent 13 administrator, go at the head of, most prominent, prime minister, understanding 14 chief executive, highest ranking, superintendent 15 be in the vanguard, make a beeline for, quickness of mind 16 commander-in-chief, direct one's course, inevitable result 17 commanding general, have authority over 18 be in the driver's seat, chairman of the board, go in the direction of 21 chief executive officer

head

contains: 4 eyes 5 brain, mouth, skull 9 braincase 10 optic nerve 12 ocular muscle 13 cranial cavity, lacrimal organ, orbital cavity 14 buccaval cavity

headache 5 trial 6 strain, stress 7 problem, trouble 8 migraine, nuisance 10 affliction, difficulty 13 inconvenience, pain in the neck

headdress 3 cap, hat 6 bonnet 7 chapeau 12 headcovering

headgear 3 cap, fez, hat, tam 4 cowl, hood, kepi, topi, veil 5 beret, busby, crown, derby, miter, mitre, opera, shako, shawl, snood, straw, terai, tiara, topee, toque 6 beanie, boater, bonnet, bowler, cloche, fedora, helmet, mobcap, panama, sailor, trilby, turban 7 bicorne, biretta, chapeau, hardhat, homberg, pillbox, porkpie, stetson, 8 babushka, kerchief, mantilla, nightcap, skullcap, snap-brim, sombrero, tarboosh, tricorne, yarmulke 9 stovepipe, sunbonnet, tengallon 10 pith helmet 11 deerstalker, dolly varden

headland 4 bank, crag 5 bluff, cliff 8 palisade 9 precipice 10 promontory

headlong 6 abrupt 8 abruptly, heedless, pell-mell, reckless 9 headfirst, impetuous 10 heedlessly, recklessly 11 impetuously, precipitate, precipitous 13 head over heels, precipitously

headman 5 chief 6 leader 7 foreman 8 alderman, princeps 9 commander 10 councilman, supervisor 14 public official, superintendent

head-on 6 direct 7 frontal 10 face-to-face

headshrinker 6 shrink 7 analyst 12 psychiatrist 13 psychoanalyst

headstrong 4 rash 6 dogged, mulish,

unruly 7 defiant, froward, willful 8 contrary, obdurate, reckless, stubborn 9 hotheaded, imprudent, impulsive, obstinate, pigheaded 10 bullheaded, incautious, refractory 11 intractable 12 incorrigible, recalcitrant, ungovernable, unmanageable 14 uncontrollable 22 bent on having one's own way

heady 4 hard 6 potent, strong 8 alluring, exciting, inviting, stirring, tempting 9 seductive, thrilling 10 high-octane 11 high-voltage, tantalizing 12 exhilarating, intoxicating

heal 4 cure, knit, mend 5 right, salve, treat 6 heal up, remedy, settle, soothe 7 compose, get well, improve, recover, rectify, relieve 8 heal over, make well 9 alleviate, make whole, reconcile 10 conciliate, convalesce, recuperate 11 set to rights 14 make harmonious, return to health 20 restore good relations

healed 4 knit 5 cured 6 mended 7 got well 8 relieved

healing 6 curing 7 mending 8 knitting, soothing 9 emollient, improving, restoring 10 making well 11 restorative 13 strengthening

god of: 6 Apollo 7 Phoebus, Pythius 9 Asclepius, Musagetes 11 Aesculapius

goddess of: 4 Iaso

health 5 vigor 7 fitness, stamina 8 strength, vitality 9 hardihood, hardiness, well being 10 robustness 16 general condition 17 physical condition

goddess of: 6 Hygeia

healthful 7 healthy 8 hygienic, salutary 9 wholesome 10 beneficial, nourishing, nutritious, salubrious 12 healthgiving, invigorating

healthiness 6 health 9 good shape, soundness 10 good health, robustness 12 salutariness 13 good condition, healthfulness, wholesomeness 14 salubriousness

healthy 3 fit 4 hale 5 hardy, sound 6 hearty, robust, strong, sturdy 8 vigorous 9 in the pink 10 able-bodied 12 in fine fettle 18 sound of mind and limb

heap 3 gob, lot 4 fill, gobs, hunk, load, lots, lump, mass, mess, pack, pile, slew 5 amass, award, batch, bunch, flood, group, mound, ocean, slews, stack, store, world 6 accord, assign, bundle, deluge, engulf, gather, jumble, load up, oceans, oodles, pile up, plenty, worlds 7 barrels, cluster, collect, mete out, present 8 good deal, inundate, pour upon 9 abundance, gathering, great deal, multitude, profusion 10 assemblage, collection, shower upon 11 aggregation, concentrate 12 accumulation 13 agglomeration

heap up 5 amass **6** pile up **7** stack up **10** accumulate

hear 4 heed **5** admit, favor, grant, judge, learn **6** attend, be told, gather, look on **7** approve, concede, examine, find out, receive, witness **8** accede to, appear at, discover, hear tell, hold with, listen to **9** acquiesce, ascertain, hearken to **10** understand **11** acknowledge

hear!
French: **4** oyez
cry used by: **10** court crier
precedes: **5** trial **12** proclamation

hearing 5 probe, sound **6** review **7** council, earshot, inquiry **8** audience **9** interview **10** conference **11** examination, questioning **12** consultation **13** interrogation, investigation

hearken to 4 heed, mark, mind **6** attend **8** listen to **11** take to heart **14** pay attention to

Hearns, Thomas
nickname: **6** Hitman
sport: **6** boxing
class: **12** middleweight, welterweight

hearsay 4 talk **5** rumor **6** gossip, report **8** idle talk **9** grapevine **11** scuttlebutt

heart 3 hub, nub **4** base, core, crux, guts, love, meat, mood, pith, root, soul **5** humor, pluck, spunk, valor **6** center, daring, desire, kernel, middle, nature, source, spirit **7** bravery, charity, courage, emotion, essence, nucleus, stomach **8** audacity, backbone, boldness, clemency, feelings, firmness, fondness, gameness, interior, main part, sympathy **9** affection, fortitude, gallantry, inner part, rudiments, sentiment, tolerance **10** brass tacks, compassion, enthusiasm, essentials, foundation, gentleness, indulgence, manfulness, principles, resolution, tenderness, true nature **11** busiest part, central part, disposition, forgiveness, nitty-gritty, temperament **12** fearlessness, fundamentals, quintessence, resoluteness **13** audaciousness
part: **5** aorta, valve **6** atrium **7** chamber **9** ventricle
pumps: **5** blood

heartache 3 woe **4** pain **5** grief **6** misery, sorrow **7** anguish, sadness, torment, trouble **8** distress **9** suffering **11** tribulation, unhappiness

heartbreaker 4 vamp **5** flirt, tease **8** coquette

Heartbreak House
author: **17** George Bernard Shaw

hearten 4 abet **5** cheer **6** assure, solace **7** animate, cheer up, comfort, console, enliven, gladden **8** brighten, embolden, energize, inspirit, reassure **9** encourage **10** invigorate

heartening 7 hopeful **9** favorable **10** auspicious, reassuring **11** encouraging

heartfelt 4 deep, full **5** total **6** ardent, devout, entire, honest **7** earnest, fervent, genuine, intense, sincere **8** complete, profound, thorough **10** keenly felt **12** all-inclusive, wholehearted

hearth 4 home **5** abode, house **8** fireside **9** fireplace, household **10** family life **12** family circle **13** chimney corner
goddess of: **4** Caca **5** Salus, Vesta **6** Hestia

Heart Is a Lonely Hunter, The
author: **15** Carson McCullers
character: **8** Mr Singer **9** Mick Kelly **10** Dr Copeland, Jake Blount **11** Biff Brannon

heartless 4 cold, mean **5** cruel **6** brutal, savage, unkind **7** callous, inhuman, unmoved **8** pitiless, ruthless, uncaring **9** unfeeling, unpitying, unstirred **10** unmerciful **11** coldhearted, cold-blooded, hardhearted, insensitive **12** cruelhearted, unresponsive **13** unsympathetic

Heart of Darkness
author: **12** Joseph Conrad
character: **5** Kurtz **7** Marlowe

Heart of Dixie
nickname of: **7** Alabama

Heart of Juliet Jones, The
creator: **9** Stan Drake
character: **3** Eve

Heart of Midlothian, The
author: **14** Sir Walter Scott

Heart of the Matter, The
author: **12** Graham Greene
character: **5** Yusef **6** Wilson **7** Mrs Rolt **9** Mrs Scobie **11** Major Scobie

heart-stopper 5 belle **6** beauty **7** charmer, stunner **8** knockout **10** good-looker **13** beautiful girl **14** beautiful woman

hearty 4 hale, warm, well **5** ample, hardy, sound **6** lively, robust, strong **7** cordial, genuine, healthy, profuse, sincere, zestful **8** complete, effusive, generous, thorough, vigorous **9** heartfelt, unbounded **10** unreserved **12** enthusiastic, unrestrained, wholehearted **13** physically fit

hearty appetite
French: **10** bon appetit

Heaslop, Ronald
character in: **15** A Passage to India
author: **7** Forster

heat 3 fry **4** bake, boil, cook, sear, stew, warm, zeal **5** ardor, broil, roast, steam **6** braise, climax, fervor, height, simmer, stress, thrill, warmth, warm up **7** hotness, make hot, passion, rapture, swelter **8** fervency, hot spell, warmness **9** eagerness, intensity, transport **10** enthusiasm, excitement **12** bring to a boil

heated 3 hot **5** angry, fiery, irate **6** bitter, fierce, raging, stormy **7** excited, fervent, furious, intense, violent **8** frenzied, inflamed, vehement **9** emotional **10** infuriated, passionate **11** impassioned, tempestuous

heated discussion 7 dispute **8** argument **10** war of words **11** controversy **12** disagreement

heath 5 Erica
varieties: **4** Tree **5** Berry, Besom, Irish, Otago, Spike **6** Dorset, Scotch, Spring **7** Cornish, Fringed, Spanish, Twisted **9** Cranberry **11** Cross-leaved

Heathcliff
character in: **16** Wuthering Heights
loved: Cathy
author: **6** Bronte

heathen 4 goy **4** boor **5** pagan **6** savage **7** atheist, gentile, infidel **8** agnostic, idolator **9** barbarian, ignoramus **10** polytheist, troglodyte, unbeliever **11** non-believer **17** uncivilized native

heather 7 Calluna
varieties: **3** Bog, Red **4** Bell, Snow **5** Beach, False, White **6** French, Golden, Scotch **8** Corsican, Mountain **9** Christmas **11** White winter **13** Mediterranean **18** Everblooming French

heat up 3 fan, zap **4** goad, nuke, warm, whet **6** arouse **7** enhance, sharpen **8** increase **9** aggravate, intensify **10** strengthen

heave 3 peg, pry, sob **4** arch, blow, cast, emit, fire, hurl, lift, moan, pant, puff, puke, toss **5** boost, bulge, chuck, eject, fling, groan, hoist, lever, pitch, raise, retch, sling, surge, swell, throw, vomit **6** dilate, drag up, draw up, exhale, expand, haul up, launch, let fly, propel, pull up, tilt up, yank up **7** elevate **8** thrust up **9** discharge, palpitate **11** regurgitate

heaven, Heaven, the Heavens 3 wow **4** Zion **5** bliss, glory, mercy, space **6** my oh my, utopia **7** delight, ecstasy, Elysium, my stars, nirvana, Olympus, rapture **8** boy oh boy, goodness, land sake, paradise, Valhalla **9** afterlife, dreamland, next world, Shangri-la **10** afterworld, Beulah Land, life beyond, outer space, perfection, sheer bliss **11** enchantment, the Holy City, world beyond, world to come **12** eternal bliss, good gracious, New Jerusalem, the City of God, the firmament **13** Abraham's bosom, Elysian fields, seventh heaven **14** heavens to Betsy, our eternal home **15** life everlasting, our Father's house, the heavenly city **16** goodness gracious, Isle of the Blessed, supreme happiness, the abode of saints, the Celestial City, the vault of heaven **17** complete happiness, the wild blue yonder **18** Island of the Blessed, the celestial sphere, the heavenly kingdom, the kingdom of Heaven **19** the celestial expanse **21** the happy hunting ground

god of: 2 An **3** Anu **4** Jove, Zeus **7** Jupiter

Heaven Can Wait (1943)
director: **13** Ernst Lubitsch
cast: **9** Don Ameche **11** Gene Tierney **12** Marjorie Main **13** Charles Coburn

Heaven Can Wait (1978)
director: **9** Buck Henry **12** Warren Beatty
cast: **10** Dyan Cannon, Jack Warden **12** Warren Beatty **13** Julie Christie
remake of: **17** Here Comes Mr Jordan

heavenly 6 divine **7** angelic, blessed, saintly, sublime **8** beatific, blissful

Heavens and Earth
author: **19** Stephen Vincent Benet

Heaven's My Destination
author: **14** Thornton Wilder

heavy 3 big, fat, sad **4** deep, dull, full, hard, lazy, slow **5** broad, bulky, dense, grave, gross, harsh, hefty, large, obese, plump, rough, stout, thick **6** clumsy, coarse, deadly, dreary, fierce, gloomy, leaden, pained, portly, raging, rugged, savage, solemn, strong, sturdy, torpid, woeful **7** awesome, complex, copious, doleful, forlorn, furious, intense, joyless, languid, lumpish, massive, notable, onerous, profuse, roaring, ruinous, serious, tearful, tedious, violent, weighty **8** abundant, agonized, burdened, crushing, cumbrous, damaging, dejected, desolate, downcast, forceful, grieving, grievous, imposing, lifeless, listless, mournful, pedantic, profound, seething, sluggish, stricken, tiresome, unwieldy **9** apathetic, cheerless, corpulent, depressed, difficult, excessive, extensive, harrowing, important, injurious, laborious, lethargic, lumbering, miserable, momentous, ponderous, rampaging, sorrow- ful, turbulent, wearisome **10** burden- some, calamitous, cumbersome, dis- tressed, full of care, immoderate, impressive, inordinate, melancholy, monotonous, noteworthy, oppressive, overweight, pernicious, phlegmatic, unbearable, unstinting **11** crestfallen, deleterious, destructive, detrimental, distressing, extravagant, intemperate, intolerable, significant, tempestuous, unendurable, unrelenting, unremitting **12** considerable, disconsolate, hard to endure, overwhelming, unrestrained **13** consequential, grief- stricken, of great import **16** laden with sorrows **18** of great consequence

heavy-handed 5 harsh **6** clumsy **7** awkward **8** bungling **9** graceless, maladroit **10** blundering, oppressive, ungraceful

heavyhearted 3 sad **4** glum **6** dismal, gloomy, morose **7** doleful, forlorn, joyless, unhappy **8** dejected, downcast **9** cheerless, depressed, sorrowful **10** despondent, melancholy **11** downhearted **14** down in the dumps, down in the mouth

Hebe
goddess of: **5** youth **6** spring
father: **4** Zeus
mother: **4** Hera
brother: **4** Ares
husband: **8** Hercules
handmaiden to: **4** gods
corresponds to: **8** Juventas

Hebrew alphabet
or: **5** aleph
b/v: **4** beth
g: **5** gimel
d: **6** daleth
h: **2** he **5** cheth
v/w: **3** vav
z: **5** zayin
y/j/i: **3** yod
k/kh: **4** kaph
l: **5** lamed
m: **3** mem
n: **3** nun
': **4** ayin
p/f: **2** pe
k: **4** koph
r: **4** resh
sh/s: **4** shin
s: **3** sin **4** sadi **6** samekh
t: **3** tav **4** teth

Hebrew Judge 4 Ehud, Elon, Jair, Tola **5** Ahdon, Ibzan **6** Gideon, Samson, Samuel **7** Deborah, Othniel, Shamgar **8** Jephthah

Hebrew months
first: **4** Abib, Nisn **6** Ehanim, Tishri
second: **3** Bul, Civ **4** Iyar **7** Heshvan
third: **5** Sivan **6** Kislev
fourth: **5** Tebet **6** Tammuz, Tebeth
fifth: **2** Ab **7** Shebat
sixth: **4** Adar, Elul **6** Veadar
seventh: **4** Abib **5** Nisan **6** Tishri **7** Ethanim
eighth: **3** Zif **4** Iyer **11** Marcheshvan
ninth: **5** Sivan **7** Chislev
tenth: **6** Tabeth, Tammuz
eleventh: **2** Ab **6** Shebat
twelfth: **4** Adar, Elul

he carved it
Latin: **8** sculpsit

Hecate
also: **6** Hekate
goddess of: **5** earth, Hades
associated with: **6** hounds **7** sorcery **10** crossroads
corresponds to: **5** Brimo

heckle 3 boo **4** bait, hiss, hoot, mock, razz, ride, twit **5** annoy, bully, chivy, harry, hound, taunt **6** badger, harass, harrow, hector, jeer at, molest, needle **7** provoke **9** shout down

Heckle and Jeckle 7 magpies **8** cartoons

hectare
abbreviation of: **2** ha

hectic 3 mad **4** wild **6** stormy **7** cha-

otic, frantic, furious **8** feverish, frenetic, frenzied, headlong **9** breakneck, turbulent **10** tumultuous

hectoliter
abbreviation of: **2** hl

hectometer
abbreviation of: **2** hm

hector 4 bait, ride **5** bully, harry, hound, tease, worry **6** badger, harass, needle, plague **7** torment, swagger **8** browbeat

Hector
father: **5** Priam
mother: **6** Hecuba
brother: **5** Paris
sister: **9** Cassandra
wife: **10** Andromache
son: **8** Astyanax
hero of: **9** Trojan War
killed by: **8** Achilles

Hecuba
also: **5** Maera **6** Hecabe
father: **5** Atlas
husband: **5** Priam **8** Tegeates
son: **5** Paris **6** Hector **7** Helenus, Polites, Troilus **9** Deiphobus, Polydorus
daughter: **6** Creusa **7** Laodice **8** Polyxena **9** Cassandra
changed into: **3** dog **5** bitch
hound of: **7** Icarius

Hecuba
author: **9** Euripides
character: **8** Odysseus, Polyxena **9** Agamemnon, Polydorus **10** Polymestor

Hedda Gabler
author: **11** Henrik Ibsen
character: **10** Judge Brack **11** Hedda Tesman, Thea Elvsted **12** George Tesman **13** Eilert Lovborg **17** Miss Juliana Tesman

heder 12 Jewish school

hedge 3 hem **4** duck, edge, ring, wall **5** bound, dodge, evade, fence, guard, hem in, limit **6** border, margin, shut in, waffle **7** barrier, enclose, mark off, outline **8** encircle, hedgerow, surround **9** be evasive, delineate, demarcate, insurance, pussyfoot, temporize **10** equivocate, protection **11** delineation, row of bushes **12** compensation **13** circumference, fence of shrubs **14** beg the question, counterbalance **17** beat around the bush

he died
Latin: **5** obiit

he does not pursue
Latin: **14** non prosequitur

hedonist 8 Sybarite **9** debauchee, libertine **10** dissipater, profligate, sensualist, voluptuary **14** pleasure seeker

hedonistic 7 sensual **9** epicurean, libertine, sybaritic **10** voluptuous **11** intemperate **13** self-indulgent **15** pleasure-seeking

he drew this
Latin: **10** delineavit

heed 4 care, mind, obey 5 bow to, pains, study 6 concur, follow, hold to, notice, regard 7 defer to, observe, perusal, respect, yield to 8 accede to, consider, listen to, prudence, scrutiny, submit to 9 attention, be ruled by, give ear to 10 bear in mind comply with, precaution, take note of 11 carefulness, examination, heedfulness, mindfulness, observation, take to heart 12 take notice of 13 attentiveness 14 fastidiousness, meticulousness, pay attention to, scrupulousness 17 conscientiousness

heedful 4 wary 5 alert, aware, cagey, chary 7 alive to, careful, mindful, prudent 8 cautious, discreet, vigilant, watchful 9 attentive, concerned, conscious

heedless 3 lax 4 rash 5 slack 6 remiss, unwary 7 foolish, unaware, witless 8 careless, mindless, reckless, uncaring 9 foolhardy, frivolous, impetuous, imprudent, negligent, oblivious, unheeding, unmindful 10 incautious, neglectful, unthinking, unwatchful 11 harebrained, improvident, inattentive, thoughtless, unconcerned, unobservant, unobserving 12 happy-go-lucky 14 scatterbrained

heedlessly 5 blind 6 rashly 8 headlong 9 foolishly, witlessly 10 carelessly, mindlessly, recklessly 11 frivolously, impetuously, impulsively, negligently, unmindfully 12 neglectfully, unthinkingly 13 inattentively, thoughtlessly, unconcernedly 15 inconsiderately, uncooperatively

heedlessness 8 rashness 9 unconcern 10 negligence 11 inattention, unawareness 12 carelessness, indiscretion, mindlessness, recklessness 13 unmindfulness 15 thoughtlessness 16 irresponsibility

heel 3 cad, cur, end, rat 4 list, rind, tilt 5 churl, crust, louse 6 rotter 7 bounder, caitiff, dastard

he engraved it
    Latin: 8 sculpsit
Heep, Uriah
    character in: 16 David Copperfield
    author: 7 Dickens
he flourished
    Latin: 7 floruit
hefty 3 big 5 beefy, bulky, burly, heavy, husky, large, stout 6 brawny, hearty, mighty, robust, rugged, strong, sturdy 7 hulking, massive, sizable, weighty, well-fed 8 muscular, powerful, stalwart, thickset 9 corpulent, strapping 11 substantial

hegemony 7 control 9 authority, dominance, influence, supremacy
Heggen, Thomas
    author of: 9 Mr Roberts
hegira 6 exodus, flight 7 journey

he himself said it
    Latin: 9 ipse dixit
Heidi 4 girl
    location: 9 Swiss Alps
    author 12 Johanna Spyri
    friend: 5 Peter
Heifetz, Jascha
    born: 6 Russia
    instrument: 6 violin
height 4 acme, apex, hill, peak, rise 5 bluff, cliff, crest, knoll, limit, mound, tower 6 apogee, heyday, summit, zenith 7 hilltop, maximum, plateau 8 altitude, eminence, highland, highness, mountain, palisade, pinnacle, tallness, ultimate 9 elevation, extremity, flowering, high point, loftiness, supremacy 10 perfection, promontory 11 culmination 12 consummation, upward extent, utmost degree, vantage point
heighten 5 raise 7 elevate 8 increase 9 aggravate, intensify
heil 4 hail
Heimberger, Eddie Albert
    real name of: 11 Eddie Albert
Heine, Heinrich
    author of: 9 Atta Troll 11 Book of Songs 19 Germany A Winter's Tale
Heinlein, Robert
    author of: 10 Double Star 16 Starship Troopers 20 The Green Hills of Earth 22 Stranger in a Strange Land 23 The Moon Is a Harsh Mistress
heinous 4 evil, foul, vile 5 gross, nasty 6 grisly, horrid, odious, sinful, wicked 7 beastly, ghastly, hideous, inhuman, vicious 8 infamous, shocking, terrible 9 abhorrent, atrocious, loathsome, monstrous, nefarious, offensive, repugnant, repulsive, revolting, sickening 10 abominable, deplorable, despicable, detestable, disgusting, iniquitous, outrageous, scandalous, villainous 11 disgraceful, distasteful 12 contemptible 13 objectionable, reprehensible
heinousness 4 evil 7 outrage 8 atrocity, baseness, enormity, foulness, savagery, vileness, villainy 9 barbarity, depravity, malignity 10 inhumanity 13 loathsomeness, monstrousness 14 outrageousness
heir, heiress 7 legatee 9 inheritor 10 inheritrix 11 beneficiary, inheritress 12 heir apparent 15 heir presumptive
Heiress, The
    director: 12 William Wyler
    based on novel by: 10 Henry James
        film title: 16 Washington Square
    cast: 13 Miriam Hopkins 15 Montgomery Clift, Ralph Richardson 17 Olivia de Havilland
    score: 12 Aaron Copland
    Oscar for: 7 actress (de Havilland)
Hekate see 6 Hecate
Hel
    origin: 12 Scandinavian

    goddess of: 5 death
    rules: 8 Niflheim 10 underworld
    father: 4 Loki
    mother: 9 Angerboda, Angrbodha, Angurboda
    brother: 6 Fenrir, Fenris 11 Iormungandr, Jormungandr 14 Midgard Serpent
    color of body: 4 blue 5 flesh
    home of: 4 dead
Helen
    father: 4 Zeus
    mother: 4 Leda
    brother: 6 Castor, Pollux
    sister: 8 Timandra 12 Clytemnestra
    husband: 8 Menelaus
    abducted by: 5 Paris
    carried off to: 4 Troy
    abduction caused: 9 Trojan War
    quote: 33 the face that launched a thousand ships
Helena
    character in: 20 All's Well That Ends Well 21 A Midsummer Night's Dream
    author: 11 Shakespeare
helicopter
    invented by: 8 Sikorsky
    also: 8 autogyro 9 eggbeater
Helios
    origin: 5 Greek
    god of: 3 sun
    father: 8 Hyperion
    mother: 4 Thia
    children: 5 Circe 6 Aeetes 8 Phaethon
    corresponds to: 3 Sol
heliotrope 12 Heliotropium
    varieties: 6 garden, winter, yellow 7 seaside
helium
    chemical symbol: 2 He
hell, Hell 5 agony, grief, Hades 6 misery, the pit 7 Abaddon, anguish, despair, Gehenna, inferno, remorse, torment 8 Appolyons, hell fire, the abyss 9 martyrdom, perdition, suffering 10 lake of fire 12 hopelessness, wretchedness 13 bottomless pit, Satan's kingdom, the lower world, the underworld 14 place of the lost, the Devil's house, the nether world, the shades below 15 everlasting fire, home of lost souls, infernal regions 16 abode of the damned
Hellen
    king of: 8 Thessaly
    father: 9 Deucalion
    mother: 6 Pyrrha
    wife: 6 Orseis
    son: 5 Dorus 6 Aeolus, Xuthus
    ancestor of: 8 Hellenes
Hellenic Republic see 6 Greece
Heller, Joseph
    author of: 7 Catch-22 10 Good as Gold 17 Something Happened
hellion 5 devil, rogue, scamp 9 scoundrel 13 mischief-maker

hellish 4 foul, vile **5** awful **6** brutal **7** hateful **8** accursed, damnable, dreadful, horrible, infernal **9** atrocious, revolting **10** abominable, disgusting

Hellman, Lillian
author of: **5** Maybe **10** Pentimento **13** Scoundrel Time **14** The Little Foxes, Toys in the Attic **15** Watch on the Rhine **16** The Children's Hour **17** An Unfinished Woman **22** Another Part of the Forest

hello
French: **7** bonjour
German: **8** guten tag
Spanish: **10** buenos dias
Hebrew **6** shalom
Italian: **4** ciao **10** buon giorno
Latin: **3** ave

Hello-Central
character in: **36** A Connecticut Yankee in King Arthur's Court
author: **5** Twain

help 3 aid **4** back, balm, calm, care, crew, cure, ease, gift, lift, save **5** allay, emend, force, guide, hands, salve, serve, staff **6** advice, advise, assist, give to, menial, relief, remedy, rescue, soothe, succor, uphold **7** advance, backing, console, correct, endorse, further, helpers, improve, nurture, promote, rectify, relieve, servant, service, stand by, support, welfare, workers, workmen **8** advocate, befriend, champion, domestic, factotum, farmhand, guidance, laborers, maintain, mitigate, retainer, retrieve, side with **9** alleviate, chip in for, employees, encourage, extricate, lend a hand, make whole, promotion, put at ease, underling, workhands, work force **10** ameliorate, apprentice, assistance, assistants, bring round, corrective, friendship, go to bat for, hired hands, kind regard, minister to, preventive, protection, stick up for **11** advancement, benevolence, cooperation, endorsement, furtherance, good offices, helping hand, make healthy, restorative **12** bring through, contribute to, contribution, hired helpers, intercede for **13** collaboration, cooperate with, encouragement, take the part of

helper 3 aid **4** aide **5** angel **6** backer, deputy, patron, second **7** adjunct, partner, servant **8** adjutant, advocate, champion, confrere, co-worker, employee, retainer **9** assistant, associate, auxiliary, colleague, man Friday, right hand, supporter **10** accomplice, aide-de-camp, apprentice, benefactor, girl Friday **11** confederate, helping hand, subordinate **12** collaborator, right-hand man **13** good samaritan **14** fairy godmother

helpful 4 fine, good, kind, nice **6** usable, useful **8** obliging, splendid, valuable **9** excellent, favorable, practical **10** beneficial, profitable, supportive

11 considerate, cooperative, serviceable **12** advantageous, constructive **13** accommodating

helping hand 3 aid **4** aide, hand **5** boost **6** assist, hand up, helper, succor **7** abettor, support **9** assistant **10** assistance

helplessness 8 weakness **9** impotence, inability, infirmity **10** dependence, feebleness, ineptitude **12** incapability, incompetence, inefficiency **13** powerlessness, vulnerability

Helsinki
capital of: **7** Finland

hem 3 box, rim **4** bind, brim, edge, welt **5** bound, brink, skirt, verge **6** border, edging, fringe, impede, margin, turn up **7** confine, enclose, stammer, stutter, turning **8** compress, encircle, restrain, surround

he made it
Latin: **5** fecit

hem in 4 best **5** fence **7** besiege, confine, enclose **8** encircle, surround

Hemingway, Ernest
author of: **9** In Our Time **14** A Moveable Feast **15** A Farewell to Arms, The Sun Also Rises **16** To Have and Have Not **18** Islands in the Stream, The Old Man and the Sea **19** For Whom the Bell Tolls **21** The Snows of Kilimanjaro **34** The Short Happy Life of Francis Macomber

hemlock 5 Tsuga **15** Conium maculatum
varieties: **5** Dwarf, Water **6** Canada, Ground, Poison **7** Siebold, Spotted, Western **8** Carolina, Japanese, Mountain

hemp 14 Cannabis sativa
varieties: **3** Bog **5** Cuban, Sisal **6** Deccan, Indian, Manila **7** African **8** Deckaner **9** Bowstring, Mauritius **10** New Zealand **13** Colorado River **15** Ceylon bowstring, Indian bowstring **16** African bowstring

hen
young: **6** pullet **7** lobster

Henchard, Michael
character in: **22** The Mayor of Casterbridge
author: **5** Hardy

henchman 4 goon, thug **6** flunky, lackey, minion, stooge, yes-man **7** gorilla **8** hanger-on, hireling, retainer **9** attendant, bodyguard **10** hatchet man, lieutenant **12** right-hand man, strong-arm man

Henderson, Marge
creator/artist of: **10** Little Lulu

henna 3 dye **5** rinse **6** auburn, russet **8** cinnamon **11** rust-colored **12** reddish-brown **13** copper-colored

henpecked 4 meek **5** timid **6** docile **8** obedient **10** browbeaten, submissive, wife-ridden **11** unassertive

Henry, Frederic
character in: **15** A Farewell to Arms
author: **9** Hemingway

Henry Esmond
author: **16** William Thackeray
character: **5** Frank **7** Beatrix **9** Lord Mohun **10** Father Holt **11** James Stuart **12** Rachel Esmond **13** Francis Esmond

Henry IV
author: **18** William Shakespeare
character: **7** Hotspur **11** Prince Henry, Thomas Percy **14** Edmund Mortimer, Sir Walter Blunt **15** John of Lancaster, Mistress Quickly, Sir John Falstaff **18** Earl of Westmoreland, King Henry the Fourth

Henry V
author: **18** William Shakespeare
character: **7** Dauphin, Montjoy **15** Charles the Sixth (King of France) **17** Princess Katharine
director: **15** Laurence Olivier
cast: **11** Leslie Banks **12** Robert Newton **13** Renee Asherson **15** Laurence Olivier

Henry VI
author: **18** William Shakespeare
character: **6** Edward (Prince of Wales) **7** Charles (Dauphin of France), Eleanor, Louis XI (King of France) **8** Lady Bona, Lady Grey **9** Joan of Arc **10** Lord Talbot **11** Bolingbroke **12** John Beaufort, Lord Clifford, Lord Hastings **13** Henry Beaufort, Joan La Pucelle **15** Margaret of Anjou, Margery Jourdain **16** Bastard of Orleans, Cardinal Beaufort
duke: **4** York (Richard Plantagenet) **7** Bedford, Suffolk **8** Somerset **10** Gloucester
earl: **7** Suffolk, Warwick **9** Salisbury
Richard Plantagenet's son: **6** Edmund, Edward, George **7** Richard

Henry VIII
author: **18** William Shakespeare
character: **7** Cranmer **8** Gardiner **10** Anne Boleyn **12** Thomas Wolsey **14** Queen Katharine, Thomas Cromwell **16** Cardinal Campeius
duke: **7** Norfolk, Suffolk **10** Buckingham

Henze, Hans Werner
born: **7** Germany **10** Westphalia
composer of: **6** Ariosi, Ondine **8** King Stag **10** El Cimarron **11** Konig Hirsch **12** The Bassarids, The Young Lord **14** Being Beauteous **15** The Runaway Slave **17** Boulevard Solitude **18** Der Prinz von Homburg, The Raft of the Medusa **19** Elegy for Young Lovers **48** The Long and Weary Journey to the Flat of Natasha Ungeheur

Heorot
great hall in: **7** Beowulf

he painted it
 Latin: **6** pinxit
Hepburn, Audrey
 real name: **19** Audrey Hepburn-Ruston
 husband: **9** Mel Ferrer
 born: **7** Belgium **8** Brussels
 roles: **6** Ondine **7** Charade, Sabrina **9** Bloodline, Funny Face **10** My Fair Lady **11** War and Peace **12** Roman Holiday (Oscar), The Nun's Story **13** Green Mansions, Wait Until Dark **18** Love in the Afternoon **19** Breakfast at Tiffany's
Hepburn, Katharine
 co-star: **12** Spencer Tracy
 born: **10** Hartford CT
 roles: **7** Desk Set, Holiday **8** Adam's Rib **10** Alice Adams, Pat and Mike, Summertime **12** Morning Glory (Oscar), On Golden Pond (Oscar), The Rainmaker **14** Woman of the Year **15** The African Queen, The Lion in Winter (Oscar) **18** Suddenly Last Summer **20** The Philadelphia Story **23** Guess Who's Coming to Dinner (Oscar) **24** Long Day's Journey into Night
Hephaestus
 also: **10** Hephaistos
 father: **4** Zeus
 mother: **4** Hera
 god of: **4** fire **11** handicrafts **12** metalworking
 vocation: **5** smith
 wife: **9** Aphrodite
 corresponds to: **6** Vulcan
Hephzibah
 husband: **8** Hezekiah
 son: **8** Manasseh
Hepzibah *see* **9** Hephzibah
Hera
 also: **4** Here
 origin: **5** Greek
 queen of: **6** Heaven
 father: **6** Cronos, Cronus, Kronos
 mother: **4** Rhea
 brother: **4** Zeus
 husband: **4** Zeus
 son: **4** Ares
 daughter: **9** Eilithyia **10** Hephaestus
 birthplace: **5** Samos
 festival: **7** Daedala
 counterfeit: **7** Nephele
 corresponds to: **4** Juno
 epithet: **6** Anthea, Bunaea **8** Henioche **9** Prodromia
Heracles *see* **8** Hercules
Heracles, Children of
 author: **9** Euripides
 character: **6** Hyllus, Iolaus **7** Alcmene, Macaria **8** Demophon **10** Eurystheus
Heracles, Madness of
 author: **9** Euripides
 character: **4** Hera **5** Lycus **6** Megara **7** Theseus **8** Heracles **10** Amphitryon

Herakles *see* **8** Hercules
herald 4 clue, omen, sign **5** crier, envoy, token, usher **6** augury, inform, report, reveal, symbol **7** courier, divulge, portent, presage, publish, usher in, warning **8** announce, forecast, foregoer, foretell, proclaim **9** advertise, harbinger, indicator, make known, messenger, precursor, prefigure, publicize **10** forerunner, indication, proclaimer **11** bruit abroad, communicate, give voice to, predecessor **13** give tidings of
heraldic emblem 4 arms **5** crest **8** blazonry, insignia **10** coat of arms
heraldry
 also called: **4** arms **10** coat of arms
 band: **3** bar **4** bend, fess, orle
 black: **5** sable
 blue: **5** azure
 border: **4** orle
 bottom: **4** base
 center: **5** fesse
 coat of arms of cities/countries/colleges: **14** impersonal arms
 coat of arms on shield/crest/helmet/motto: **19** armorial achievement
 colors: **8** tincture
 concerns family's: **8** heritage **9** genealogy
 described as: **9** blazoning
 divided diagonally: **7** per bend
 divided vertically and horizontally: **9** quartered
 expert: **8** armorist
 for holding shield: **10** supporters
 fur: **4** vair **6** ermine
 gold/yellow: **2** or
 green: **4** vert
 helmet top: **5** crest
 horizontal band: **4** fess
 illegitimacy mark: **5** baton **6** baston **11** bar sinister **12** bend sinister
 intrafamily distinctions: **12** differencing
  daughter: **7** lozenge
  eldest son: **5** label
  younger son: **7** cadency
 left part: **8** sinister
 main figure: **6** charge **8** ordinary **14** heraldic device
 metal: **2** or **6** argent
 motto in: **6** scroll
 orange: **5** tenne
 placed on lord's: **6** banner, shield **8** garments **14** horse trappings
 portrayed as: **6** emblem, symbol
 position: **7** courant, dormant, passant, rampant, salient **8** couchant, trippant
 purple: **7** purpure
 red: **5** gules
 red-purple: **8** sanguine
 right part: **6** dexter
 shield: **10** escutcheon
 sunshade: **8** mantling
  held by: **6** wreath
  made of: **4** silk

 surface/background: **5** field
 top: **5** chief
 two or more colors: **16** lines of partition
 vertical band: **4** pale
 wavy: **4** ente, onde, unde
 when worn by followers: **5** badge **6** livery
 white/silver: **6** argent
herb 4 drug **5** plant, spice **6** annual, physic **7** herbage, perfume **8** aromatic, biennial, medicine **9** flavoring, perennial, seasoning, succulent
 kind: **3** bay, rue **4** corn, dill, hemp, mint, rose, sage **5** anise, basil, curry, chili, grass, onion, peony, thyme, wheat **6** catnip, celery, chives, clover, fennel, garlic, pepper, sesame **7** boneset, caraway, ginseng, lavender, mustard, oregano, parsley **8** camomile, licorice, rosemary, tarragon **9** buttercup, marijuana, spearmint **10** peppermint **11** wintergreen
Herbert, George
 author of: **9** The Temple
Herbert, Victor
 born: **6** Dublin **7** Ireland
 composer of: **14** Babes in Toyland, Hero and Leander **15** Naughty Marietta
herbivorous 10 vegetarian **11** planteating **14** noncarnivorous
Herceius
 epithet of: **4** Zeus
 means: **14** of the courtyard
herculean, Herculean 4 hard **5** burly, hefty, tough **6** brawny, mighty, robust, rugged, strong, sturdy **7** arduous, onerous **8** muscular, powerful, toilsome, wearying **9** difficult, fatiguing, laborious, strapping, strenuous **10** burdensome, exhausting, formidable, prodigious **12** backbreaking
Hercules
 also: **7** Alcides **8** Heracles, Herakles **9** Carnopian
 father: **4** Zeus
 mother: **7** Alcmene
 cousin: **10** Eurystheus
 wife: **4** Hebe **6** Megara **8** Deianira
 son: **6** Lamus **6** Hyllus **8** Telephus **11** Therimachus
 daughter: **7** Macaria
 teacher: **6** Chiron
 gift: **8** strength
 performed: **6** labors
 number of labors: **6** twelve
 epithet: **7** Charops **8** Buphagus **9** Ipoctonus
 corresponds to: **6** Sancus **10** Semo Sancus
Hercyna
 form: **5** nymph
 location: **8** fountain
 playmate: **10** Persephone
herd 3 lot, mob **4** army, band, body, gang, goad, host, lead, mass, pack,

spur **5** array, bunch, crowd, drive, drove, flock, force, group, guide, horde, party, press, rally, swarm, tribe, troop **6** gather, huddle, legion, muster, number, throng **7** cluster, collect, company, convene, round up **8** assemble, assembly, conclave **9** gathering, multitude **10** assemblage, collection **11** convocation **12** congregation

Herds
  god of: **8** Silvanus, Sylvanus

herdsman 6 cowboy, driver, drover **7** cowpoke **8** shepherd

Herdsman
  constellation of: **6** Bootes

herd together 5 flock, group **6** gather **7** cluster, collect **10** congregate **12** band together

hereafter 5 limbo **6** heaven **8** paradise **9** afterlife, from now on, next world, Purgatory **10** afterworld, future life, henceforth, life beyond, ultimately **11** in the future, world to come **12** at a later date, at a later time, henceforward, subsequently **14** life after death **15** heavenly kingdom

here and there 6 around **11** at intervals **18** in this place and that
  Latin: **6** passim

Here Comes Mr Jordan
  director: **13** Alexander Hall
  cast: **11** Claude Rains, Evelyn Keyes, Rita Johnson **16** Robert Montgomery
  remade as: **13** Heaven Can Wait

hereditary 6 inborn, inbred **7** genetic **9** ancestral, heritable, inherited **10** congenital, handed-down **11** established, inheritable, traditional

here lies
  Latin: **8** hic jacet

heresy 7 dissent, fallacy **8** apostasy **10** dissension, heterodoxy, iconoclasm, irreligion **11** unorthodoxy **13** nonconformity **15** unsound doctrine

heretic 7 skeptic **8** apostate, recreant, recusant, renegade **9** dissenter **10** backslider **11** freethinker, misbeliever **12** deviationist **13** nonconformist

heretical 7 radical **9** dissident **10** unorthodox **12** iconoclastic **13** nonconforming, nonconformist **14** unconventional

heretofore
  French: **8** ci-devant

Hereward the Wake
  author: **15** Charles Kingsley

Hergesheimer, Joseph
  author of: **8** Java Head **19** The Three Black Pennys

heritage 6 estate, legacy **7** portion **9** patrimony, tradition **10** birthright **11** inheritance **16** family possession

Hermaphroditus
  father: **6** Hermes
  mother: **9** Aphrodite

loved by: 8 Salmacis
joined with: 8 Salmacis
became: 8 bisexual

Hermes
  origin: **5** Greek
  occupation: **6** herald
  messenger of: **4** gods
  father: **4** Zeus
  mother: **4** Maia
  son: **3** Pan **6** Prylis **7** Abderus, Daphnis **14** Hermaphroditus
  birthplace: **7** Arcadia
  god of: **4** luck **5** roads, sleep **6** dreams, wealth **7** cunning, thieves **8** commerce **9** fertility, invention, merchants
  invented: **4** lyre
  sandals had: **5** wings
  epithet: **6** Dolius **8** Agoraeus **9** Spelaites **10** Criophorus **11** Argiphontes **12** Argeiphontes, Psychopompus
  corresponds to: **5** Thoth **7** Mercury

hermetic 6 mystic, occult **7** obscure **8** abstruse, airtight, esoteric, mystical **9** recondite

Hermia
  character in: **21** A Midsummer Night's Dream
  author: **11** Shakespeare

hermine, L'
  author: **11** Jean Anouilh

Hermione
  character in: **14** The Winter's Tale
  author: **11** Shakespeare

Hermione
  father: **8** Menelaus
  mother: **5** Helen
  husband: **7** Orestes
  son: **9** Tisamenus

hermit 7 eremite, recluse **8** cenobite, monastic, solitary **9** anchorite **11** desert saint **14** solitudinarian **16** religious recluse

hermitage 5 abbey **6** friary, priory **7** convent, retreat **8** cloister **9** monastery

hero, heroine 4 idol, star **7** gallant **8** brave man, champion, great man, male lead, male star, noble man **9** daredevil, daring man, main actor **10** adventurer, leading man **11** protagonist, valorous man **12** man of courage, man of the hour **13** chivalrous man, popular figure **15** fearless fighter, idealized person, intrepid warrior, legendary person

Hero
  character in: **19** Much Ado About Nothing
  author: **11** Shakespeare

Hero
  vocation: **9** priestess
  priestess of: **9** Aphrodite
  lover: **7** Leander
  death by: **7** suicide **8** drowning

Herod Antipas
  father: **13** Herod the great

mother: 8 Malthace
grandfather: 9 Antipater
wife: 8 Herodias
half brother: 6 Philip
beheaded: 14 John the Baptist

Herodias
  husband: **6** Philip **12** Herod Antipas
  daughter: **6** Salome

Herodotus
  called: **15** Father of History
  wrote history of: **11** Persian Wars

Herod Philip
  daughter: **6** Salome

heroic 4 bold, epic **5** brave, grand, noble **6** daring **7** classic, exalted, gallant, Homeric, valiant **8** elevated, fearless, highbrow, inflated, intrepid, mythical, resolute, valorous **9** bombastic, dauntless, dignified, grandiose, high-flown, legendary, undaunted **10** chivalrous, courageous **11** exaggerated, extravagant, lionhearted, pretentious, unflinching **12** mythological, ostentatious, stouthearted

heroic act 4 feat **7** exploit **9** brave deed

heroism 5 valor **6** daring **7** bravery, courage, prowess **8** boldness, chivalry, nobility **9** fortitude, gallantry **11** intrepidity **12** fearlessness **13** dauntlessness **14** courageousness **15** lionheartedness

Herophilus
  field: **7** anatomy
  nationality: **5** Greek
  experimented with: **15** post-mortem exams

Heros
  author: **8** Menander

herpetophobia
  fear of: **8** reptiles

Herrenvolk 10 master race

Herrick, Robert
  author of: **10** Hesperides **20** Corinna's Going A Maying **26** Gather ye rosebuds while ye may

Herriman, George
  creator/artist of: **8** Krazy Kat

Herschel, William
  field: **9** astronomy
  nationality: **7** British
  discovered: **6** Uranus

Hersey, John
  author of: **7** The Wall **9** Hiroshima **13** A Bell for Adano, The Conspiracy **22** My Petition for More Space

Hertz, Heinrich
  field: **7** physics
  nationality: **6** German
  discovered: **13** electric waves **18** wireless telegraphy
  named for him: **13** hertzian waves
  unit of: **9** frequency

Herzog
  author: **10** Saul Bellow

he sculptured it
Latin: **8** sculpsit

Hesiod
author of: **8** Theogony **12** Works and Days

hesitancy 10 indecision, reluctance, unsureness **11** uncertainty, vacillation **12** irresolution

hesitant 5 loath **6** unsure **7** halting **8** doubtful, wavering **9** diffident, faltering, reluctant, tentative, uncertain, undecided **10** hesitating, indecisive, irresolute **11** half- hearted, hanging back, vacillating **15** shilly-shallying **17** lacking confidence, sitting on the fence

hesitate 4 balk, halt **5** delay, pause, shy at, waver **6** falter **7** scruple, stick at **8** be unsure, hang back **9** stickle at, vacillate **10** dillydally, shrink from, think twice **11** be reluctant, be uncertain, be undecided, be unwilling, stop briefly **12** be irresolute, shilly-shally **16** straddle the fence

hesitating 8 doubtful, hesitant **10** indecisive, irresolute, on the fence

he speaks
Latin: **8** loquitur

Hesperia
also: **5** Italy **16** Iberian Peninsula

Hesperides
author: **13** Robert Herrick

Hesperides
form: **6** nymphs
guarded: **12** golden apples
guarded with: **5** Ladon **6** dragon
names: **5** Aegle **6** Hestia **7** Erythea, Hespera **8** Arethusa **9** Hespereia, Hesperusa
islands of the: **7** blessed
form of: **6** heaven

Hess, Victor Francis
field: **7** physics
discovered: **10** cosmic rays
awarded: **10** Nobel Prize

Hesse, Hermann
author of: **6** Demian **9** Rosshalde **10** Siddhartha **11** Steppenwolf **12** Magister Ludi **14** Peter Camenzind **15** Beneath the Wheel **16** Death and the Lover, Journey to the East, The Glass Bead Game

Hesselberg, Melvyn Edouard
real name of: **13** Melvyn Douglas

Hessian
native of: **5** Hesse **7** Germany
soldier: **9** mercenary
aided: **7** British
in: **16** Revolutionary War

Hestia
origin: **5** Greek
goddess of the: **6** hearth
father: **6** Cronos, Cronus, Kronos
mother: **4** Rhea
corresponds to: **5** Vesta

Heston, Charlton

real name: **13** Charles Carter
born: **10** Evanston IL
roles: **5** El Cid, Moses **6** Ben-Hur (Oscar) **15** Planet of the Apes **18** The Ten Commandments **21** The Agony and the Ecstasy **22** The Greatest Show on Earth

heterogeneous 5 mixed **6** motley, unlike, varied **7** diverse, jumbled **8** assorted **9** composite, disparate, divergent, unrelated **10** dissimilar, variegated **11** diversified **13** miscellaneous

hew 2 ax **3** cut, lop **4** chop, form, hack, mold **5** carve, model, prune, sever, shape **6** chisel, cut out, devise **7** cut down, fashion, whittle **8** chop down **9** sculpture

He Who Gets Slapped
author: **14** Leonid Andreyev

he wrote it
Latin: **8** scripsit

hex 4 harm, jinx, sign **5** curse, spell, witch **6** hoodoo, voodoo, whammy **7** bewitch, enchant, evil eye, ill wind, possess **8** sorcerer **9** sorceress **11** malediction

Hexateuch 27 first six books of Old Testament
see also **7** Books of **12** Old Testament

heyday 4 acme **5** bloom, crest, flush, prime, vigor **6** zenith **9** flowering, salad days

Heyerdahl, Thor
author of: **7** Kon-Tiki **16** The Ra Expeditions

Hi and Lois
creator: **9** Dik Browne **10** Mort Walker
character:
brother: **12** Beetle Bailey
children: **3** Dot **4** Chip **5** Ditto **6** Trixie
dog: **4** Dawg
friend: **7** Thirsty

hiatus 3 gap **4** void **5** blank, break, lapse, space **6** lacuna, vacuum **7** interim **8** interval **10** disruption **12** interruption

Hiawatha, The Song of
author: **24** Henry Wadsworth Longfellow
character: **5** Nahma **7** Kwasind, Nokomis, Wenonah **8** Mondamin **9** Chibiabos, Minnehaha **11** Mudjekeewis **12** Pau-Puk-Keewis, Pearl-Feather

hibernate 5 sleep **6** retire **8** withdraw **13** become dormant

hibernating 6 asleep **7** dormant **8** inactive, sleeping **9** quiescent

Hibernia see **7** Ireland

hibiscus
varieties: **7** Chinese **8** Hawaiian, Japanese

hic jacet 8 here lies

hick 4 boor, rube **5** yokel **6** rustic **7** hayseed

Hickock, James B 5 scout **7** marshal
called: **8** Wild Bill

hickory 5 Carya
varieties: **4** Pale, Sand **5** Broom, Swamp, Water **6** Pignut **7** Chinese **8** Mountain, Shagbark **9** Mockernut, Shellbark **10** White-heart **12** Small-fruited

Hicks, Edward
born: **11** Attleboro PA
artwork: **19** The Peaceable Kingdom

hidden away 6 buried, cached **7** stashed **8** closeted, pocketed, secluded, secreted **9** concealed **10** out of sight **11** stashed away **12** inaccessible, undiscovered

hidden meaning 6 enigma, puzzle, riddle, secret **7** mystery

hidden motive
French: **13** arriere pensee

hide 4 mask, pelt, skin, veil **5** cache, cloak, cloud, cover **6** lie low, screen, shroud **7** conceal, curtain, leather, obscure, repress, seclude, secrete **8** disguise, suppress

hideaway 7 hideout, retreat **11** hiding place, secret place

hideous 4 grim, ugly, vile **5** awful **6** horrid, odious **7** ghastly, macabre **8** dreadful, gruesome, horrible, shocking **9** abhorrent, appalling, frightful, grotesque, loathsome, monstrous, repellent, repugnant, repulsive, revolting, sickening **10** abominable, detestable, disgusting, horrendous

hiding place 5 cache **8** hideaway **9** hidey hole **10** repository **11** secret place

Hieronimo
character in: **17** The Spanish Tragedy
author: **3** Kyd

hier wird Deutsch gesprochen 18 German is spoken here

Higgins, Henry
character in: **9** Pygmalion **10** My Fair Lady
author: **4** Shaw

Higgs
character in: **7** Erewhon
author: **6** Butler

high 3 gay, top **4** main, tall **5** aloft, chief, far up, grand, great, jolly, lofty, merry, noble, prime, sharp, undue, way up **6** alpine, august, elated, jovial, joyful, joyous, shrill **7** capital, eminent, exalted, excited, extreme, gleeful, leading, notable, playful, primary, serious, soaring, soprano **8** cheerful, elevated, exultant, foremost, imposing, jubilant, mirthful, peerless, piercing, strident, superior, towering, uncurbed **9** ascendant, excellent, excessive, exuberant, important, overjoyed, principal, prominent, unbridled, uppermost **10** exorbitant, immoderate, inordinate, preeminent **11** cloud-capped, exaggerated, exhilarated, extravagant, high-pitched, illustrious, intemperate, predominant, significant, sky- scraping **12** earsplitting, high-reaching, lighthearted, unreasonable, unrestrained **13** consequential, distinguished

high-and-mighty 5 lofty **6** lordly **7** haughty **8** arrogant **9** imperious **11** overbearing

highborn 5 noble **8** highbred, well-born **9** patrician **10** of high rank, upper-class **12** aristocratic, of high degree, silk-stocking **13** of gentle blood

highbred 5 noble, regal **6** lordly **7** refined **8** highborn, wellborn **9** patrician **11** aristocracy, blue-blooded

highbrow 4 snob **5** brain **7** bookish, Brahmin, egghead, elitist, erudite, scholar, thinker **8** cultured, mandarin, snobbish **9** scholarly **10** cultivated, double-dome, mastermind **12** intellectual **13** knowledgeable

highest good
Latin: **11** summum bonum

highest point
Latin: **11** ne plus ultra

high fashion
French: **12** haute couture

high-flown 4 wild **5** lofty, proud **6** absurd, florid, lordly, turgid, unreal **7** flowery, orotund, pompous **8** elevated, fabulous, inflated **9** bombastic, excessive, fantastic, grandiose **10** flamboyant, immoderate, inordinate, outrageous **11** exaggerated, extravagant, highfalutin, pretentious, sententious **12** magniloquent, preposterous, presumptuous, unreasonable, unrestrained **13** grandiloquent, self important

High German
language family: **12** Indo-European
branch: **8** Germanic
group: **15** Western Germanic
subgroup: **11** German-Dutch
division: **6** German **7** Yiddish

high-hat 5 aloof **6** formal, la-di-da, snooty **7** haughty **8** snobbish **12** supercilious

highjinks, hijinks 6 antics, capers, pranks, stunts **11** shenanigans **12** monkeyshines

highland, Highlands 4 rise **7** heights, plateau, uplands **8** headland **9** tableland **10** promontory **11** hill country **17** mountainous region
refers especially to: **8** Scotland
dance: **5** fling

highlight 4 peak **6** accent, climax, stress **7** feature, point up **9** emphasize, high point, underline **10** accentuate, focal point, make bright

highly qualified 3 fit **4** able **7** trained **8** eligible, prepared, skillful **9** practiced **10** proficient **11** experienced **12** accomplished

highly regarded 6 prized **7** admired, revered **8** esteemed **9** respected, treasured **13** well thought of

highly valued 4 dear **5** loved **6** adored **7** beloved, revered **8** esteemed, precious **9** cherished, treasured

highly visible 7 glaring, obvious **8** distinct **9** prominent **11** conspicuous, outstanding

high-minded 4 fair, just **5** lofty, moral, noble **6** honest, worthy **7** ethical, sincere, upright **8** truthful, virtuous **9** exemplary, honorable, reputable, righteous, uncorrupt **10** chivalrous, idealistic, principled, scrupulous **13** conscientious, square-dealing

High Noon
director: **13** Fred Zinnemann
cast: **10** Gary Cooper (Will Kane), Grace Kelly **12** Lloyd Bridges **14** Thomas Mitchell
score: **14** Dimitri Tiomkin
Oscar for: **5** actor (Cooper)

high old time 4 ball, lark **5** fling, revel, spree **8** escapade

high-pitched 5 acute, sharp **6** shrill **7** clarion, squeaky **8** piercing

high place 3 tor **4** hill, peak, rise **5** acrie, bluff, cliff, knoll, ridge **6** height, summit, upland **7** hillock, hummock, plateau **8** eminence, mountain **9** elevation **10** prominence, promontory

high point, highest point 3 cap, top **4** acme, apex, peak **5** crest, crown **6** apogee, climax, height, heyday, summit, tiptop, vertex, zenith **8** eminence, pinnacle **9** flowering **10** prominence **11** culmination

high position 4 note **8** eminence, high rank, standing **9** supremacy **10** ascendancy, importance, notability, prominence **11** distinction, preeminence

high-powered 7 driving, dynamic **8** forceful **9** ambitious, assertive, energetic, go-getting **10** aggressive **11** hard- driving

high praise 5 kudos, paean **6** eulogy **7** hosanna, plaudit **8** encomium **9** laudation, panegyric **11** acclamation

high-priced 4 dear, high **6** costly, pricey **9** expensive **10** exorbitant, overpriced **11** extravagant

high-principled 5 moral, noble **6** chaste, honest, worthy **7** ethical, upright **9** honorable, reputable **10** idealistic **11** responsible, trustworthy **13** conscientious

high quality 5 merit **7** quality **9** greatness **10** excellence, perfection **11** distinction, superiority

high-ranking 3 top **5** grand, great, lofty, regal, royal **6** august **7** eminent, exalted, supreme **8** elevated, es-

teemed, imposing **9** important, paramount, venerable **10** preeminent **11** illustrious **13** distinguished

High Sierra
director: **10** Raoul Walsh
cast: **9** Ida Lupino **10** Alan Curtis, Joan Leslie **13** Arthur Kennedy **14** Humphrey Bogart (Mad Dog Earle)
remade as: **17** Colorado Territory **19** I Died a Thousand Times

high society 5 elite **6** jet set **9** haut monde, top drawer **11** aristocracy **14** creme de la creme
French: **9** haut monde

High Society
director: **14** Charles Walters
cast: **10** Bing Crosby, Grace Kelly **11** Celeste Holm **12** Frank Sinatra, Louis Calhern **14** Louis Armstrong
score: **10** Cole Porter
remake of: **20** The Philadelphia Story
song: **8** True Love **10** Did You Evah? **16** You're Sensational

high-speed 4 fast **5** quick, rapid, swift **6** speedy **7** express

high-spirited 5 vital **6** lively **8** animated **9** exuberant, vivacious **12** effervescent, enthusiastic

high spirits 5 vigor **6** gaiety **7** delight, elation **8** gladness, vitality, vivacity **9** animation **10** enthusiasm, exaltation, excitement, joyousness, liveliness **12** exhilaration **16** lightheartedness

high-strung 4 edgy **5** jumpy, moody, tense **6** uneasy **7** jittery, nervous, uptight **8** neurotic, restless, skittish **9** emotional, excitable, impatient, wrought-up **10** hysterical **13** oversensitive, temperamental **14** easily agitated, hypersensitive

High Tor
author: **15** Maxwell Anderson

highway 7 freeway, parkway, thruway **8** hard road, highroad, main road, speedway, turnpike **9** paved road **10** expressway, interstate, main artery **12** four-lane road, thoroughfare
British: **9** coach road, royal road **12** King's highway **13** Queen's highway

highwayman 5 crook, thief **6** bandit, outlaw, robber **7** brigand, footpad

hike 4 rise, roam, rove, trek, walk **5** leg it, march, raise, tramp **6** draw up, hoof it, jerk up, pull up, ramble, trudge, wander **7** hitch up, raise up **8** addition, increase **9** expansion **10** escalation **12** augmentation **13** journey on foot **14** go by shank's mare

hilarious 3 gay **5** jolly, merry, noisy **6** jocund, jovial, joyful, joyous, lively **7** comical, gleeful, riotous **8** jubilant, mirthful **9** exuberant, laughable, very funny **10** boisterous, hysterical, rollicking, uproarious, vociferous **11** exhilarated **12** high-spirited **13** highly amusing **14** laugh- provoking

hilarity 3 fun, gig, joy **4** glee, riot **5**

laugh, mirth, noisy **6** comedy, gaiety, giggle, levity **7** chortle, chuckle, jollity **8** hysteria, laughter **9** amusement, funniness, joviality, jubilance, merriment **10** exuberance **12** exhilaration, humorousness **14** uproariousness

Hilbert, David
field: **8** geometry **11** mathematics
nationality: **6** German
formulated: **12** modern axioms

Hilda Lessways
author: **13** Arnold Bennett

hill 4 bank, dune, heap, pile, ramp, rise **5** bluff, butte, cliff, climb, grade, knoll, mound, mount, slope **6** height **7** hillock, hilltop, hummock, incline, upgrade **8** eminence, foothill, highland, hillside **9** acclivity, declivity, downgrade, elevation **10** prominence, promontory

Hill, Arthur
born: **6** Canada **7** Melfort **12** Saskatchewan
roles: **13** All the Way Home **15** The Ugly American **17** Look Homeward Angel **25** Who's Afraid of Virginia Woolf?

Hill, George Roy
director of: **8** The Sting (Oscar) **23** The World According to Garp **29** Butch Cassidy and the Sundance Kid

Hillary, Edmund
born: **10** New Zealand
climbed: **9** Mt. Everest
explored: **9** South Pole

Hiller, Arthur
director of: **25** The Americanization of Emily

hillock 4 hill, rise **5** knoll, mound **7** hummock **8** eminence

Hill Street Blues
character: **5** LaRue, Renko **9** Bobby Hill, Jablonski, Joe Coffey, Lucy Bates **10** Fay Furillo, Mick Belker, Washington **11** (Lt) Norman Buntz **12** Howard Hunter, (Captain) Frank Furillo **13** Henry Goldblum **14** Joyce Davenport
cast: **8** Joe Spano **10** Bruce Weitz, Ed Marinaro, Kiel Martin **11** Betty Thomas, Charles Haid, Dennis Franz **12** Robert Prosky **13** James B Sikking, Michael Warren, Veronica Hamel **14** Taurean Blacque **15** Daniel J Travanti

Hilton, James
author of: **11** Lost Horizon **14** Good-Bye Mr Chips

Himalayas 9 mountains
countries **5** India, Nepal, Tibet, **6** Bhutan **8** Pakistan
peak: **7** Everest **9** Annapurna
native: **6** sherpa
Climber: **7** Hillary **13** Tenzing Norkay
legendary creature: **4** yeti **17** Abominable Snowman

Hind see **5** India

Hind and the Panther, The
author: **10** John Dryden

Hindemith, Paul
born: **5** Hanau **7** Germany
composer of: **8** The Demon **9** Cardillac **10** Heriodiade **12** Ludus Tonalis, Neues vom Tage, News of the Day **13** Sancta Susanna **14** Cupid and Psyche, Mathis Der Maler **15** In Praise of Music **17** Murder Hope of Women **18** Die Harmonie der Welt, Nobilissima Visione **19** The Four Temperaments **23** Morder Hoffnung der Frauen

hinder 3 bar **4** curb, foil, stay, stop **5** block, check, delay, deter, spike, stall **6** arrest, detain, fetter, hamper, hobble, hog-tie, hold up, impede, retard, stifle, stymie, thwart **7** inhibit **8** encumber, handicap, hold back, obstruct, restrain, slow down **9** frustrate, hamstring **13** interfere with

Hindi
language family: **12** Indo-European
branch: **11** Indo-Iranian
group: **5** Indic
official language of: **5** India

hindmost 4 last, rear **7** tail end **12** farthest back

hindpart 4 tail **6** far end **7** rear end **8** backside, buttocks, haunches **9** afterpart, posterior

hindquarters 4 rear, rump **7** rear end, tail end **8** back legs, backside, buttocks, haunches **9** posterior

hindrance 3 bar **4** clog, curb, snag **5** catch **6** fetter **7** barrier, shackle **8** blockade, blockage, handicap, obstacle **9** barricade, restraint, retardant **10** constraint, difficulty, impediment, limitation **11** encumbrance, obstruction, restriction **12** interference **14** stumbling block

hinge 4 hang, rest, turn **5** pivot, swing **6** depend **7** be due to **9** arise from **10** result from **11** be subject to, emanate from **13** revolve around

hint 3 bit, jot, tip **4** clue, idea, iota **5** grain, imply, pinch, tinge, touch, trace, whiff **6** little, notion, tip off **7** inkling, pointer, signify, soupcon, suggest, whisper **8** allusion, indicate, innuendo, intimate **9** insinuate, suspicion **10** impression, indication, intimation, smattering, suggestion **11** implication, indirection, insinuation **12** flea in the ear, slight amount **13** word to the wise

hinted 7 implied, oblique **8** implicit, indirect **9** suggested

hinterland 6 sticks **7** boonies, country **8** interior, midlands **9** backwater, backwoods, boondocks, rural area **11** countryside

Hippalectryon
form: **7** monster

head and forelegs of: **5** horse
legs, tail and body of: **4** cock

Hippocampus
form: **7** monster
body of: **5** horse
tail of: **4** fish

Hippocrene
form: **6** spring
location: **12** Mount Helicon

hippodrome 5 arena **6** circus **7** stadium **8** coliseum

Hippogriff
form: **7** monster
combined: **5** horse **7** griffin

Hippolyte
also: **7** Antiope **9** Hippolyta
queen of: **7** Amazons
husband: **7** Theseus
son: **10** Hippolytus
Hercules stole her: **6** girdle

Hippolytus
author: **9** Euripides
character: **7** Artemis, Phaedra, Theseus **9** Aphrodite

Hippolytus
father: **7** Theseus
mother: **9** Hippolyta
stepmother: **7** Phaedra
loved by: **7** Phaedra
killed by: **8** Poseidon

hire 3 fee, get, let, pay **4** cost, gain, rent **5** lease, wages **6** charge, employ, engage, income, obtain, profit, retain, reward, salary, secure, take on **7** appoint, charter, payment, procure, stipend **8** earnings, receipts **9** emolument **10** recompense **12** compensation, remuneration

hireling 4 goon, thug **6** flunky, lackey, menial, minion, stooge **7** gorilla **8** henchman, retainer **9** strong-arm **10** hatchet man

Hiroshima
author: **10** John Hersey

hirsute 5 bushy, downy, hairy, nappy, wooly **6** shaggy, woolly **7** bearded, bristly, prickly, unshorn **8** bristled, unshaven **9** whiskered **11** bewhiskered

His Girl Friday
director: **11** Howard Hawks
cast: **9** Cary Grant **12** Gene Lockhart, Ralph Bellamy **15** Rosalind Russell
remake of: **12** The Front Page

Hispania see **5** Spain

hiss 3 boo **4** mock, razz **6** deride, heckle, hoot at, jeer at, revile **7** catcall, scoff at, sneer at **9** shout down **10** Bronx cheer **16** give the raspberry

histology
study of: **6** tissue

historian
American: **4** Webb **5** Adams **6** Brooks, De Voto, Durant, Fisher, Miller, Nevins, Sparks, Turner **7** Morison, Parkman, Taussig, Tuch-

man **8** Bancroft, Channing, Prescott, Robinson **10** Hofstadter

British: 4 Bede (the Venerable) **6** Gibbon, Turner **7** Toynbee **8** Macaulay **9** Trevelyan

Chinese: 10 Ssu-ma Ch'ien, Ssu-Ma Kuang

French: 5 Bayle, Blanc, Bloch, Taine **7** Braudel **8** Mabillon, Michelet, Voltaire **11** Tocqueville

German: 5 Ranke **7** Mommsen **8** Spengler **10** Burckhardt, Treitschke

Greek: 8 Polybius **9** Herodotus **10** Thucydides

Islamic: 8 al Tabari **10** Ibn Khaldun

Italian: 4 Polo, Vico **5** Croce **11** Machiavelli **12** Guicciardini

Latin: 4 Livy **7** Sallust, Tacitus

Scottish: 7 Carlyle

historic 5 famed **7** notable **8** renowned **9** memorable, well-known **10** celebrated **11** outstanding

historical 4 past, real, true **6** actual, bygone, former **7** ancient, factual **8** attested, recorded **9** authentic **10** chronicled, documented

historical period 3 age, era **4** date, time **5** epoch, stage

history 4 epic, saga, tale **5** story **6** annals, change, growth, record, resume, review **7** account, the past **8** old times **9** chronicle, days of old, narration, narrative, portrayal, tradition, yesterday **10** bygone days, days of yore, olden times, the old days, yesteryear **11** bygone times, development, former times, local events, major events, world events **12** actual events **13** an unusual past, human progress **14** military action, national events, recapitulation **15** political change

History of Colonel Jacque, The
  author: 11 Daniel Defoe

History of Henry VII
  author: 12 Francis Bacon

History of Mr Polly, The
  author: 7 H G Wells
  character: 6 Miriam **8** Uncle Jim **13** The Plump Woman

History of the English-Speaking Peoples, A
  author: 17 Winston S Churchill

His Toy, His Dream, His Rest
  author: 12 John Berryman

histrionics 4 fuss **6** acting, tirade **7** bluster, bombast **8** outburst **9** dramatics, hamminess, staginess, theatrics **10** dramaturgy, playacting **11** performance, rodomontade **13** melodramatics, temper tantrum, theatricality **16** ranting and raving

hit 3 bat, jab, lob, rap, tap **4** bang, bash, beat, belt, blow, boon, bump, butt, clip, club, coup, cuff, damn, drub, find, flog, hurt, move, pelt, poke, slam, slap, slug, sock, stir, swat **5** abash, baste, clout, crack, crush, flail, knock, paste, pound, punch, reach, rouse, smack, smash, smite, thump, touch, upset, whack **6** affect, arouse, assail, attack, attain, batter, cudgel, effect, impact, incite, pommel, revile, strike, thrash, thwack, wallop, winner **7** achieve, assault, censure, clobber, condemn, execute, godsend, impress, inflame, provoke, quicken, realize, shatter, success, triumph, trounce, victory **8** arrive at, bang into, blessing, bring off, denounce, lambaste, overcome, reproach **9** criticize, deal a blow, devastate, lash out at, overwhelm, sensation, smash into **11** collide with, connect with, deal a stroke, strike out at **12** go straight to **13** make a bull's-eye, send to the mark **14** popular success, strike together **16** mount an offensive

hit back 7 counter, get even, pay back **9** fight back, retaliate **10** strike back

hitch 3 tie, tug **4** curb, draw, halt, haul, hike, jerk, knot, loop, pull, snag, stop, yank, yoke **5** catch, check, clamp, delay, raise, tying **6** attach, couple, fasten, mishap, secure, tether **7** bracket, connect, harness, joining, mistake, problem, trouble **8** coupling, handicap, make fast, obstacle **9** attaching, fastening, hindrance, mischance, restraint **10** connection, difficulty, impediment, limitation **11** restriction **12** complication, interruption, loop together, put in harness **14** stumbling block

Hitchcock, Alfred
  director of: 6 Frenzy, Marnie, Psycho **7** Rebecca, Vertigo **8** Lifeboat, The Birds **9** Notorious, Suspicion **10** Family Plot, Rear Window, Spellbound **13** To Catch a Thief **14** Dial M for Murder, Shadow of a Doubt **15** The Lady Vanishes **16** North by Northwest **17** Strangers on a Train **18** The Thirty-Nine Steps **19** The Trouble with Harry **20** Foreign Correspondent

hither 2 on **4** here, near **5** close **6** closer, nearby, nearer, onward **7** close by, forward **8** over here **11** to this place **12** to the speaker

hitherto 6 ere now, hereto **7** thus far, till now, up to now **8** until now **10** before this, heretofore

Hitler, Adolf
  author of: 9 Mein Kampf

hit man 6 killer, slayer **8** assassin, hired gun, murderer **11** executioner **12** exterminator

Hitman
  nickname of: 12 Thomas Hearns

hit-or-miss 3 lax **6** casual, fitful **7** aimless, cursory **8** slapdash **9** haphazard **10** incomplete **11** purposeless, superficial, unorganized **12** unsystematic **15** catch-as-catch-can

hive 3 hub **5** heart **6** center, colony **7** cluster **9** busy place **11** swarm of bees

H M S Pinafore
  subtitle: 23 The Lass That Loved a Sailor
  operetta by: 18 Gilbert and Sullivan
  character: 11 Dick Deadeye **14** Ralph Rackstraw **15** Captain Corcoran, Little Buttercup, Sir Joseph Porter **17** Josephine Corcoran

Hoagland, Edward
  author of: 15 African Calliope **17** The Tugman's Passage

hoar 3 old **4** aged, rime **5** frost, moldy, mushy, passe, stale, white **6** old hat **7** ancient, antique, elderly, grayish **8** grizzled **9** out of date

hoard 4 fund, heap, mass, pile **5** amass, buy up, cache, lay up, store **6** save up, supply **7** acquire, collect, lay away, reserve **8** quantity **9** amassment, gathering, stockpile, store away **10** accumulate, collection **12** accumulation

hoarse 5 gruff, harsh, husky, raspy, rough **6** croaky **7** cracked, rasping, raucous, throaty **8** gravelly, guttural, scratchy

hoary 3 old **4** aged, gray, hoar **5** dated, passe, white **6** grayed, old hat **7** ancient, antique, grizzly **8** grizzled, whitened **9** out-of-date **11** gray with age **12** white with age

hoax 3 gyp **4** bilk, dupe, fake, fool, gull, yarn **5** bluff, cheat, cozen, fraud, prank, spoof, trick **6** canard, delude, humbug, take in **7** deceive, defraud, fiction, mislead, swindle **8** hoodwink **9** bamboozle, chicanery, deception, fish story, victimize **10** hocus-pocus

Hoban, James
  architect of: 13 The White House, Great Hotel (Washington, DC)

Hobbes, Thomas
  author of: 9 Leviathan

Hobbit, The
  prelude to: 14 Lord of the Rings
  author: 10 J R R Tolkien
  character: 5 Bilbo **7** Baggins
  wizard:: 7 Gandalf

hobble 4 bind, gimp, halt, limp **5** block, check, cramp **6** fetter, hamper, hinder, hog-tie, impede, lumber, stymie, thwart, toddle **7** inhibit, manacle, shackle, shamble, shuffle, stagger, stumble **8** encumber, handicap, hold back, lame gait, obstruct, restrain, restrict **9** constrain, frustrate, hamstring **10** uneven gait, walk lamely **13** interfere with

hobby 7 pastime, pursuit **8** sideline **9** amusement, avocation, diversion **10** relaxation **13** entertainment **14** divertissement

hobbyhorse 5 hobby 7 pastime 8 interest, toy horse 9 diversion 10 enthusiasm 11 distraction 12 rocking horse

hobgoblin 3 imp 4 ogre 5 bogey 6 goblin 7 bugaboo, bugbear 9 betenoire

hobnob 3 mix 4 club 6 mingle 7 consort, hang out 9 associate, rub elbows 10 fraternize

hobo 3 beg, bum 5 stiff, tramp 6 beggar, cadger, loafer 7 drifter, migrant, moocher, vagrant 8 derelict, vagabond, wanderer 9 scrounger 11 beachcomber

hoc est 6 this is

Ho Chi Minh City
  formerly: 6 Saigon
  river: 6 Saigon
  delta: 6 Mekong
  former capital of: 9 Indochina 11 Cochin China 12 South Vietnam

hockey
  athlete: 8 Bobby Orr, Brad Park 9 Bobby Hull, Ken Dryden, Mike Bossy 10 Doug Harvey, Eddie Shore, Ed Giacomin, Gordie Howe, Guy Lafleur, Ray Bourque, Rod Gilbert, Stan Mikita 11 Bobby Clarke, Brian Leetch, Denis Potvin, Eric Lindros, Jean Ratelle, Mark Messier 12 Emile Francis, Jean Beliveau, Marcel Dionne, Mario Lemieux, Phil Esposito, Wayne Gretzky 13 Bernard Parent, Jacques Plante, Larry Robinson, Pat La Fontaine 14 Alex Delvecchio, Maurice Richard 15 Bernie Geoffrion 18 Yvan Serge Courneyer

hockey team
  Anaheim: 11 Mighty Ducks
  Atlanta: 9 Thrashers
  Boston: 6 Bruins
  Buffalo: 6 Sabres
  Calgary: 6 Flames
  Carolina: 10 Hurricanes
  Chicago: 10 Black Hawks
  Columbus: 11 Blue Jackets
  Dallas: 5 Stars
  Detroit: 8 Red Wings
  Edmonton: 6 Oilers
  Florida: 8 Panthers
  Hartford: 7 Whalers
  Los Angeles: 5 Kings
  Montreal: 9 Canadiens
  New Jersey: 6 Devils
  New York: 7 Rangers 9 Islanders
  Ottawa: 8 Senators
  Philadelphia: 6 Flyers
  Phoenix: 7 Coyotes
  Pittsburgh: 8 Penguins
  Quebec: 9 Nordiques
  St Louis: 5 Blues
  San Jose: 6 Sharks
  Tampa Bay: 9 Lightning
  Toronto: 10 Maple Leafs
  Vancouver: 7 Canucks
  Washington: 8 Capitals
  Winnipeg: 4 Jets

hocus-pocus 4 bosh, bull, hoax, sham 5 chant, charm, cheat, magic, spell 6 bunkum, deceit, fakery, humbug 7 con game, hogwash, rubbish, swindle 8 delusion, flimflam, tommyrot, trickery 9 deception, moonshine, poppycock 10 dishonesty, flapdoodle, hanky-panky, magic spell, magic words, mumbo jumbo, subterfuge 11 bewitchment, incantation, legerdemain, magic tricks 12 fiddle-faddle, magic formula 13 sleight of hand

Hoder
  also: 5 Hodur
  origin: 12 Scandinavian
  brother: 5 Baldr 6 Balder, Baldur
  father: 4 Odin 5 Othin
  killed: 5 Baldr 6 Balder, Baldur

hodgepodge, hotchpotch 3 mix 4 hash, mess, olio 6 jumble, medley, muddle 7 melange, mixture 8 mishmash 9 composite, confusion, patchwork, potpourri 10 miscellany

Hoff, Jacobus Hendricus van't
  field: 9 chemistry
  nationality: 5 Dutch
  researched: 7 gas laws 10 carbon atom 14 thermodynamics
  awarded: 10 Nobel Prize

Hoffman, Dustin
  born: 12 Los Angeles CA
  roles: 5 Lenny 6 Ishtar 7 Tootsie 8 Papillon 10 Ratso Rizzo 11 The Graduate 12 Little Big Man 14 Kramer vs Kramer (Oscar), Midnight Cowboy 19 All the President's Men

Hofmann, Hans
  born: 7 Germany 11 Weissenberg
  artwork: 6 Spring 7 The Gate 13 Effervescence 14 Fantasia in Blue, Magenta and Blue 16 Sanctum Sanctorum

Hofstadter, Richard
  author of: 14 The Age of Reform

hog 3 pig, sow 4 arch, boar, trim 5 broom, sheep, swine 6 gorger, porker 7 baconer, glutton, take all 9 razorback 10 locomotive

Hogan, Paul
  country: 9 Australia
  roles: 10 Mick Dundee 15 Crocodile Dundee

Hogan's Heroes
  character: 7 (Peter) Newkirk 8 Lt Carter 10 Sgt (Hans) Schultz 11 Louis LeBeau 14 Col Robert Hogan 15 Col Wilhelm Klink
  cast: 8 Bob Crane 10 John Banner, Larry Hovis 11 Robert Clary 13 Richard Dawson 15 Werner Klemperer

Hogarth, William
  born: 6 London 7 England
  artwork: 12 Captain Coram 14 A Rake's Progress 15 Marriage a la Mode, The Beggar's Opera 16 A Harlot's Progress 19 Garrick as Richard III

hogshead 3 keg, tun, vat 4 butt, cask, drum 6 barrel

hogwash 3 rot 4 bull, bunk 5 hokum, hooey, stuff 6 bunkum, drivel, hot air, humbug 7 baloney, blather, spinach, twaddle 8 claptrap, nonsense, tommyrot 9 poppycock 10 applesauce 11 foolishness 13 horsefeathers 16 stuff and nonsense

hoi polloi 6 rabble, the mob 7 the herd 8 canaille, populace, riffraff, the crowd, the plebs 9 the masses, the proles, the vulgar 10 commonalty 12 the multitude 14 the lower orders, the proletariat, the rank and file 15 the common people, the lower classes, the working class

hoist 4 lift 5 heave, raise, run up 6 bear up, pull up, take up, uplift 7 elevate, raise up, upraise 9 bear aloft

Hokusai, Katsushika
  born: 3 Edo 5 Japan, Tokyo
  artwork: 5 Crabs, Manga 10 Waterfalls 11 Chushingura 25 Thirty-six Views of Mount Fuji

Holabird, William
  partner: 11 Martin Roche
  architect of: 12 Gage Building 13 Cable Building, Crerar Library (City Hall, Chicago) 14 Tacoma Building 15 McClurg Building 17 Marquette Building

Holbein, Hans (the Elder)
  born: 7 Germany 8 Augsburg
  son: 11 Hans Holbein (the Younger)
  artwork: 11 St Sebastian 14 Fountain of Life 18 Kaisheim Altarpiece 31 Presentation of Christ in the Temple

Holbein, Hans (the Younger)
  born: 7 Germany 8 Augsburg
  father: 11 Hans Holbein (the Elder)
  artwork: 7 Erasmus 9 Henry VIII 11 Jane Seymour 12 Dance of Death 13 The Dead Christ

hold 4 bear, bind, bond, curb, deem, grip, halt, have, hilt, keep, knob, lock, prop, rule, stay, sway, take, urge 5 block, brace, carry, check, clasp, cling, count, defer, grasp, guard, limit, offer, power, shaft, shore, stall, stand, stick, strap, think, unite, watch 6 adhere, affirm, assert, assume, cleave, clinch, clutch, deduct, detain, direct, enfold, handle, hinder, hold up, join in, manage, occupy, reckon, regard, retain, submit, take in, tender, thwart, uphold 7 advance, believe, carry on, command, conduct, confine, contain, control, declare, embrace, enclose, enforce, execute, hold off, include, inhibit, mastery, possess, present, presume, prevent, profess, propose, protect, repress, reserve, support, suppose, surmise, suspend, toehold, venture 8 advocate, conceive, conclude, consider, engage in, foothold, handhold, hold back, hold down, leverage, maintain, obligate, postpone, purchase, put forth, restrain, restrict, set aside, suppress, withhold **9** advantage, anchorage, authority, be in force, dominance, forestall, frustrate, influence, keep valid, ownership, stay fixed, stick fast **10** ascendancy, attachment, desist from, domination, possession, put forward, understand **11** accommodate, preside over

hold a candle to 5 equal, match **6** be up to **7** compare **8** approach **10** be as good as **11** come close to, compete with **12** be comparable **14** bear comparison

hold against 6 resent **8** begrudge

hold back 3 lag **4** curb, deny, keep, slow **5** check, dally, limit, stall **6** arrest, bridle, falter, refuse **7** contain, inhibit, keep out, reserve, retrain **8** hesitate, keep back, maintain, restrain, withhold **9** constrain

hold close 3 hug **5** clasp **6** cuddle, harbor **7** cherish, embrace, snuggle

Holden, William
  real name: 23 William Franklin Beedle Jr
  nickname: 4 Bill
  born: 9 O'Fallon IL
  roles: 6 Picnic **7** Network, Sabrina **9** Golden Boy **13** Born Yesterday **14** The Country Girl **15** Stalag Seventeen (Oscar), Sunset Boulevard **23** The Bridge on the River Kwai

hold fast 4 fuse, hold **5** cling, stick **6** adhere

hold firmly 4 grip **5** clasp, grasp **6** clench, clinch, clutch **10** grab hold of

hold forth 5 orate **7** expound **9** discourse, expatiate, speechify

hold in abeyance 5 table **6** recess, shelve **7** suspend **8** lay aside, postpone

hold in bondage 7 control, enchain, enslave, entrall **8** dominate **9** subjugate **12** make a slave of

holdings 6 assets **8** property **10** securities **11** commodities

hold in high regard 5 honor, prize, value **6** admire, esteem, revere **7** cherish, respect **8** look up to, treasure, venerate **10** rate highly, set store by **13** think highly of **18** attach importance to

hold one's own 4 cope **6** manage **7** contend **11** be a match for **20** maintain one's position **22** keep one's head above water

hold rapt 5 charm **7** beguile, bewitch, enchant **8** enthrall, entrance **9** captivate, enrapture, fascinate, spellbind, transport

hold to 4 bind **8** obligate

hold together 4 bind, fuse, glue, hold, join **5** cling, stick, unite **6** cement, cohere **7** combine **11** consolidate

holdup 3 rob **4** bear, halt, stay, stop **5** delay, heist, steal, theft **6** hijack, retain, uphold **7** robbery, stickup, support, sustain **8** stoppage **9** hindrance **12** interruption

hold up 4 prop, slow **5** block, brace, check, delay **6** bear up, detain, endure, hinder, impede, manage **7** bolster, present, stand up, support, sustain **8** keep back, obstruct **13** rob at gunpoint

hold up under 4 bear **6** endure, manage **8** tolerate

hold warmly 3 hug **5** clasp **6** cuddle **7** embrace, snuggle

hole 3 den, gap, pit **4** brig, cage, cave, flaw, keep, lair, rent, slit, slot **5** break, crack, fault, shaft **6** breach, burrow, cavern, cavity, crater, defect, dugout, lockup, pocket, prison, tunnel **7** dungeon, fallacy, opening, orifice, slammer **8** aperture, dark cell, puncture **9** concavity, open space **10** depression, excavation **11** discrepancy, hollow place, indentation, perforation **13** inconsistency

Holgrave, Mr
  character in: 24 The House of the Seven Gables
  author: 9 Hawthorne

holiday 3 gay **4** fete, gala **5** feria **6** cheery, fiesta, joyful, joyous, junket, outing **7** festive, holy day, jubilee **8** cheerful, feast day, festival, vacation **11** celebrating, celebration, merrymaking
  American: 6 Easter **8** Arbor Day, Labor Day **9** Christmas (Dec 25), Halloween (Oct 31) **10** Father's Day, Good Friday, Mother's Day **11** Columbus Day, Election Day, Memorial Day, New Year's Day (Jan 1), Veterans' Day (Nov 11) **12** Children's Day, Thanksgiving **15** Independence Day (July 4), St Valentine's Day (Feb 14) **23** National Grandparents' Day
    birthday: 8 Lincoln's **11** Robert E Lee's (Jan 19), Washington's **17** Martin Luther King's (Jan 15)
    Hawaiian: 13 Kamehameha Day (June 11)
  British: 8 Hogmanay (Dec 31) **9** Boxing Day (Dec 26) **11** Harvest Home **12** Guy Fawkes Day (Nov 5), Twelfth Night (Jan 5) **14** Queen's Birthday (June) **15** Commonwealth Day (May 24), Mothering Sunday **19** Feast of Saint Swithin (July 15)
  Canadian: 11 Victoria Day **14** Queen's Birthday, Remembrance Day
  Chinese: 7 New Year **15** Lantern Festival **17** Confucius' Birthday (Sept 28) **18** Dragon Boat Festival
  French: 11 Bastille Day (May 14)
  German: 11 Oktoberfest

  Greek: 7 Genesia **11** Feast of Pots
  Indian: 4 Holi **6** Basant, Diwali (New Year) **17** Hindu fire festival **22** Mahatma Gandhi's Birthday (Oct 2)
  Irish: 16 Saint Patrick's Day (March 17)
  Italian: 13 Liberation Day (April 25)
  Japanese: 11 Hina-Matsuri **12** Children's Day (May 5), Feast of Dolls (March 3) **15** Constitution Day (May 3) **17** Girls' Doll Festival
  Jewish: 5 Purim **6** Sukkot **7** Shavuot, Sukkoth **8** Hanukkah, Passover **9** Yom Kippur **12** Rosh Hashanah **20** Hamishah Assar B'Shevat, The New Year of the Trees **21** Feast of the Tabernacles
  Korean: 6 Ch'usok
  Latin American: 12 Day of the Race
  Moslem: 7 Mouloud **8** Id-al-Adha, Id-al-Fitr **12** Maulid-an-Nabi **14** month of Ramadan
  religious: 6 Advent **7** Lady Day (Mar 25) **8** Epiphany, Shabuoth **9** Candlemas, Mardi Gras, Martinmas (Nov 11), Pentecost **10** Whitsunday **11** All Souls' Day (Nov 2) **12** Ascension Day, Ash Wednesday, Feast of Weeks **13** Shrove Tuesday, Trinity Sunday **15** Annunciation Day (Mar 25) **16** Feast of All Saints **20** Feast of Corpus Christi **23** Day of Our Lady of Guadalupe (Dec 12) **27** Purification of the Virgin Mary **30** Feast of the Immaculate Conception (Dec 8)
  Roman: 7 Feralia **10** Saturnalia
  Scottish: 8 Hogmanay **12** Candlemas Day **19** Festival of the Virgin
  South American: 21 Simon Bolivar's Birthday (July 24)
  Sri Lankan: 5 Wesak
  Soviet Union: 6 May Day (May 1) **14** Lenin's Birthday (April 22) **39** Day of the Great October Socialist Revolution (Nov 7)
  Swedish: 13 Santa Lucia Day (Dec 13)
  Thai: 11 Visakha Puja
  Vietnamese: 3 Tet

holiness 8 sanctity **9** godliness **10** sacredness **11** blessedness, saintliness

Holland see **11** Netherlands

holler 4 bark, roar, yell **5** gripe, shout **6** bellow, cry out, grouse **8** complain **9** hue and cry

Holliday, Judy
  real name: 11 Judith Tuvim
  born: 9 New York NY
  roles: 8 Adam's Rib **13** Born Yesterday (Oscar) **15** Bells Are Ringing

Hollinshed, Raphael
  author of: 37 Chronicles of England Scotland and Ireland

hollow 3 dip, low, rut **4** cave, dale, deep, dell, dent, dull, glen, hole, sink, vain, vale, void **5** ditch, empty, false, muted **6** cavern, cavity, crater, dig out, dimple, furrow, futile, groove, pocket, sunken, vacant, vacuum, valley **7** channel, concave, useless **8** crevasse, empty out, excavate, gouge out, indented, not solid, nugatory, rumbling, scoop out, specious, unfilled **9** cavernous, concavity, deceptive, depressed, fruitless, pointless, valueless, worthless **10** depression, profitless, sepulchral, unavailing, unresonant **11** indentation, meaningless, nonresonant **12** unprofitable **13** curving inward, disappointing, reverberating **14** expressionless, unsatisfactory **15** inconsequential

Holloway, Stanley
  born: **6** London **7** England
  roles: **10** My Fair Lady **15** Alfred Doolittle **18** The Lavender Hill Mob

Hollow Men
  author: **7** T S Eliot

hollowness 4 void **6** vacuum **7** vacancy **9** emptiness

hollow out 4 bore **5** drill **6** dig out **8** carve out, gouge out, scoop out **9** chisel out **13** tunnel through

holly 4 Ilex
  varieties: **3** box, sea **4** dune **5** Cuban, Dutch, dwarf, false, Furin, Kashi, swamp, Tsuru **6** desert, horned, Oregon, Sarvis, Soyogo, summer **7** African, Chinese, English, Georgia, Madeira **8** American, European, hedgehog, Japanese, Kurogane, mountain **9** box- leaved, Highclere, miniature, moonlight, porcupine, Singapore **10** Costa Rican, luster-leaf, West Indian **11** large-leaved, Puerto Rican, screw-leaved **12** Canary Island, gold hedgehog, myrtle-leaved, smooth-leaved **14** silver hedgehog

hollyhock 6 mallow **7** Antwerp, figleaf **8** biennial **9** ficifolia, Malvaceae **10** alcea rosea

Hollywood's Mermaid
  nickname of: **14** Esther Williams

Hollywood Squares
  host: **9** Jon Bauman **12** John Davidson **13** Peter Marshall
  regular: **8** Wally Cox **10** Joan Rivers **13** Cliff Arquette (Charley Weaver), Shadoe Stevens

Holmes, Oliver Wendell
  author of: **12** Old Ironsides **30** The Autocrat of the Breakfast Table

Holmes, Sherlock
  address: **11** (221B) Baker Street
  appears in: **13** The Sign of Four **14** The Naval Treaty **15** A Study in Scarlet, The Speckled Band **16** Scandal in Bohemia, The Blue Carbuncle, The Copper Beeches **18** The Red-Headed League, The Solitary Cyclist **22** Hound of the Baskervilles
  assistants: **21** Baker Street Irregulars
  author: **16** (Sir) Arthur Conan Doyle
  brother: **7** Mycroft
  femme fatale **10** Irene Adler

  foe: **17** Professor Moriarty
  hat: **11** deerstalker
  hobby: **6** violin
  housekeeper/landlady: **9** Mrs Hudson
  keeps tobacco in: **7** slipper **14** Turkish slipper
  police: **17** Inspector Lestrade
  sidekick: **12** Dr John Watson

Holmwood, Arthur
  character in: **7** Dracula
  author: **6** Stoker

holocaust 4 ruin **5** havoc **6** ravage **7** bonfire, carnage, inferno, killing **8** butchery, genocide, massacre **10** deadly fire, mass murder **11** devastation **12** annihilation **13** conflagration

Holofernes
  character in: **16** Love's Labour's Lost
  author: **11** Shakespeare

Holofernes
  general of: **14** Nebuchadnezzar
  killed by: **6** Judith

Holst, Gustav Theodore
  born: **7** England **10** Cheltenham
  composer of: **7** Savitri **10** Egdon Heath, Ode to Death, The Planets **11** Hammersmith **12** St Paul's Suite **13** Fugal Concerto **14** The Hymn of Jesus, The Perfect Fool **16** Somerset Rhapsody **17** The Cloud Messenger **19** Hymns from the Rig-Veda

holy 4 pure **5** godly, moral, pious **6** adored, devout, divine, sacred, solemn **7** angelic, blessed, from God, revered, saintly, sinless **8** faithful, hallowed, heavenly, reverent, virtuous **9** from above, guileless, religious, righteous, spiritual, undefiled, unspotted, unstained, unworldly, venerated, worshiped **10** heaven-sent, immaculate, inviolable, sacrosanct, sanctified, worshipped **11** consecrated, pure in heart, uncorrupted
  Latin: **7** sanctus

Holy Ark
  Hebrew: **10** Aron Kodesh

holy of holies
  Latin: **16** sanctum sanctorum

Holy one *see* **5** Jesus

Holy Spirit, Holy Ghost 9 Paraclete **13** presence of God **23** third person of the Trinity
  Latin: **15** Spiritus Sanctus
  Greek: **12** Hagion Pneuma

holy war
  Arabic: **5** jehad, jihad

Holy Willie's Prayer
  author: **11** Robert Burns

Homadus
  form: **7** centaur
  killed by: **8** Hercules

homage 5 honor **6** esteem, praise, regard **7** respect, tribute, worship **8** devotion **9** adoration, adulation, deference, obeisance, reverence **10** exaltation, veneration **13** glorification

Homagyrius
  epithet of: **4** Zeus
  means: **9** assembler

hombre 3 man

home 5 abode, haunt, haven, house **6** asylum, cradle, refuge **7** habitat, hangout **8** domicile, dwelling, hospital **9** orphanage, poorhouse, residence **10** habitation, native land, sanatorium **11** institution **12** fountainhead **13** dwelling place, home sweet home **14** stamping ground **16** place of residence **18** natural environment **25** place where one hangs one's hat

Home Burial
  author: **11** Robert Frost

homegrown 5 local **6** native **8** domestic **10** indigenous

Home Is the Sailor
  author: **10** Jorge Amado

homelike 4 cozy **5** comfy, homey **6** simple **8** cheerful, domestic, familiar, informal, inviting **11** comfortable

homely 4 cozy, drab, snug **5** comfy, homey, plain **6** modest, rustic, simple **7** artless, natural **8** everyday, familiar, homelike, homespun, ordinary, uncomely **9** graceless **10** ill-favored, provincial, unaffected, unassuming, ungraceful, unhandsome **11** comfortable **12** plain-looking, unattractive **13** unpretentious

Homer
  author of: **5** Iliad **7** Odyssey

Homer, Winslow
  born: **8** Boston MA
  painter of: **9** seascapes
  artwork: **9** High Cliff **10** Breezing Up, Eight Bells **11** Marine Coast, Northeaster, The Life Line **13** The Fog Warning, The Gulf Stream **21** Inside the Bar Tynemouth, Prisoners from the Front

home rule 8 autonomy **11** sovereignty **12** independence **14** self-government

homespun 5 plain **6** folksy, homely, modest, native, simple **7** artless, natural **8** down-home, homemade **9** handwoven **10** hand-loomed, unaffected **11** hand-crafted, hand-wrought **13** unpretentious

homey 4 cozy **6** casual, folksy **8** down-home, homelike, homespun, informal **15** unsophisticated

homicide 6 killer, murder, slayer **7** slaying **8** foul play, murderer, regicide, vaticide **9** bloodshed, man killer, manslayer, matricide, parricide, patricide, uxoricide **10** fratricide **11** infanticide **12** manslaughter

homiletic 7 preachy **8** didactic **10** moralizing

homily 6 sermon **7** lecture **10** preachment **11** exhortation

homogeneous 4 akin, pure **7** kindred, similar, uniform, unmixed **8** all alike, constant, of a piece **9** identical, unvarying **10** consistent **13** of the same kind, unadulterated

homology 7 analogy **8** likeness, relation **10** similarity **12** relationship **14** correspondence

Honduras
name means: 6 depths
capital/largest city: 11 Tegucigalpa
others: 4 Tela, Yoro **5** Copan, Danli, Lapaz **6** Roatan **7** Gracias, La Ceiba **8** Trujillo, Yuscaran **9** Choluteca, Juticalpa **10** El Progreso **11** Comayaguela **12** Puerto Cortes, San Pedro Sula
measure: 4 vara **5** milla **6** mecate **7** cajuela
monetary unit: 4 peso **7** centavo, lempira
island: 3 Bay **5** Bahia, Utila **6** Roatan **7** Bonacca, Guanaja
lake: 5 Criba, Yojoa **6** Brewer
mountain: 4 Pija **6** Agalta **7** Celaque **9** Esperanza
highest point: 8 Las Minas
river: 4 Coco, Sico, Ulua **5** Aguan, Lempra, Negro, Tinto, Wanks **6** Patuca, Sulaco **7** Olancho, Paulaya, Segovia **8** Guiavope, Santiago **9** Choluteca **10** Chamelecon
sea: 7 Pacific **8** Atlantic **9** Caribbean
physical feature:
  coast: 5 North **8** Mosquito **10** Costa Norte
  gulf: 7 Fonseca **8** Honduras
  port: 7 Laceiba **8** Trujillo
people: 4 Maya, Paya, Sumo, Ulva **5** Carib, Lenca, Pipil **6** Tauira **7** Jicaque, mestizo, Miskito **8** Mosquito
  discoverer: 8 Columbus
  farmer: 9 campesino
language: 7 English, Spanish
religion: 13 Roman Catholic
place:
  ruins: 5 Copan **8** Tenampua
feature:
  bird: 9 zenzontle
  dance: 5 sique **7** mascaro
  estate: 10 latifundia
  farm: 6 milpas **10** minifundia
  musical instrument: 7 caramba, marimba
  tree: 8 cockspur
food:
  beans: 8 frijoles
  beef dish: 6 tapado
  corn: 5 maize
  stuffed corn cake: 10 naca tamale
  tripe stew: 8 mondongo
hone 4 long, moan, pine, tool, whet **5** stroke, strope, whine, yearn **6** hanker, grumble, mutter, sharpen **9** whetstone

Honegger, Arthur
born: 5 Havre **6** France
nationality: 5 Swiss
member of: 6 Les Six, The Six
composer of: 5 Rugby **6** Judith **7** L'Aiglon **8** Antigone **9** The Eaglet

10 Le Roi David **13** Pastorale d'ete **18** Jeanne d'Arc au Bucher, Liturgical Symphony **19** Pacific Two-Thirty-One

honest 4 fair, just, open, real, true **5** blunt, frank, legal, plain, solid, valid **6** candid, decent, lawful, proper, square **7** artless, ethical, genuine, sincere, upright **8** bona fide, clear-cut, faithful, innocent, reliable, straight, true-blue, truthful, virtuous **9** authentic, blameless, guileless, honorable, ingenuous, reputable, righteous **10** aboveboard, dependable, forthright, law-abiding, legitimate, on the level, principled, reasonable, scrupulous, unaffected, unreserved **11** plainspoken, trustworthy, undisguised **12** on the up-and-up, tried and true **13** conscientious, fair and square **15** straightforward, unsophisticated **16** as good as one's word, straight-shooting **17** open and aboveboard
honest man: 10 Abe Lincoln
Searcher: 8 Diogenes

honesty 4 word **5** honor **7** probity **8** fairness, good name, morality, scruples, veracity **9** innocence, integrity, rectitude, sincerity **10** principles **11** just dealing, uprightness **12** faithfulness, reputability, truthfulness **13** guillessness, square dealing **15** trustworthiness **16** incorruptibility, straight shooting

honeybee
classification: 6 social
live in: 4 hive **6** colony
headed by: 5 queen
male: 5 drone
laborer: 6 worker
food-gatherer: 7 forager
gather: 6 nectar, pollen
produce: 5 honey
queen's food: 10 royal jelly
pertaining to: 5 apian
keeper: 8 apiarist
honeyed 4 kind **5** sweet **6** sugary **7** cloying, fawning **10** flattering, saccharine **12** ingratiating **13** complimentary
honeyed words 4 line **7** blarney **8** cajolery, flattery, soft soap **9** sweet talk

Honey in the Horn
author: 7 H L Davis
Honeymooners, The
character: 8 Ed Norton **12** Alice Kramden, Ralph Kramden, Trixie Norton
cast: 8 Jane Kean **9** Art Carney **12** Sheila MacRae **13** Audrey Meadows, Jackie Gleason, Joyce Randolph
Ralph's job: 9 bus driver
Ed's job: 5 sewer
lodge: 8 Raccoons
Saying: 16 You're the greatest **38** One of these days Alice, pow, right in the kisser

honeysuckle 8 Lonicera **19** Aquilegia canadensis, Justicia californica **24** Rhododendron prinophyllum
varieties: 3 fly **4** bush, cape **5** coral, giant, grape, hairy, swamp **6** desert, French, purple, yellow **7** Arizona, Jamaica, trumpet **8** Himalaya, Japanese, swamp fly, Tatarian **9** chaparral, Tartarian **10** yellow cape **11** European fly **12** giant Burmese, longflowered, South African **13** Hall's Japanese

Honeythunder, Mr
character in: 22 The Mystery of Edwin Drood
author: 7 Dickens

Hong Kong
name means: 13 incense harbor **14** fragrant harbor
capital: 8 Victoria
largest city:
  section: 7 Kowloon **8** Hong Kong, Victoria
others: 4 Tai O **5** Tai Po **8** Aberdeen, Pingshan, Yuenlong **9** Shataukok **10** Sheungshui
division: 7 Kowloon **8** Hong Kong **14** New Territories
government: 18 British crown colony
head of state: 14 British monarch **15** governor general
island: 5 Lamma **6** Lan Tao, Lantau, Middle, Poi Toi **8** Hong Kong **9** Ap Lei Chau **11** Stonecutter
mountain: 6 Castle **8** Victoria
highest point: 9 Tai Mo Shan
river: 5 Pearl **6** Canton **8** Sham Chun
sea: 10 South China
physical feature:
  bay: 4 Mirs **6** Quarry **7** Kowloon, Repulse **9** Deep Water
  harbor: 4 Tolo **8** Aberdeen, Hong Kong, Victoria
  peak: 8 Victoria
  peninsula: 7 Kowloon
people: 5 Hakka, Haklo, Punti, Tanka **7** British, Chinese **8** American, Japanese **9** Cantonese **10** Portuguese
language: 7 Chinese, English **9** Cantonese
religion: 5 Hindu, Islam **6** Taoism **8** Buddhism **12** Christianity
feature:
  airport: 6 Kai Tak
  clothing: 6 samfoo **9** cheongsam
  houseboat: 6 sampan
  rock: 5 Amahs **6** Sha Tin
  temple: 18 Ten Thousand Buddhas
Honiara
capital of: 14 Solomon Islands
honi soit qui mal y pense 31 shamed be the one who thinks evil of it
motto of: 16 Order of the Garter
honk 4 toot **5** blare, blast **7** trumpet
honky-tonk 4 dive **7** gin mill **9** road house, nightclub

honor 3 pay **4** cash, fame, laud, note, take **5** adore, exalt, extol, favor, glory, grant, leave, power, right, truth, value **6** accept, admire, credit, esteem, homage, praise, redeem, regard, renown, repute, revere, virtue **7** acclaim, commend, decency, dignify, glorify, honesty, liberty, probity, respect, tribute, worship **8** eminence, fairness, good name, goodness, justness, look up to, make good, pleasure, prestige, sanction, venerate, veracity **9** adoration, celebrity, constancy, deference, greatness, integrity, principle, privilege, rectitude, reverence, sincerity **10** admiration, compliment, exaltation, good report, importance, notability, permission, prominence, veneration **11** acknowledge, approbation, distinction, pay homage to, recognition, think much of, uprightness **12** commendation, faithfulness, high standing, pay tribute to, truthfulness **13** authorization, have regard for, honorableness, make payment on **14** high-mindedness, scrupulousness **15** illustriousness, trustworthiness **17** a feather in one's cap, conscientiousness

honorable 4 good **5** noble, title **6** decent, honest, lordly, square **7** upright **9** elevated, reputable, respected **10** creditable **11** distinctive, illustrious, respectable, trustworthy **12** considerable **13** distinguished

hood 4 cowl, lout, punk **5** bully, rowdy, scarf, tough **6** vandal **7** hoodlum, ruffian **8** hooligan **9** barbarian, roughneck **10** delinquent **12** headcovering, neighborhood

Hood, Raymond
  architect of: 11 RCA Building (Rockefeller Center) **17** Daily News Building (NYC) **18** McGraw-Hill Building (NYC) **22** Chicago Tribune Building **24** American Radiator Building
  style: 13 International

hoodlum 4 hood, punk, thug **5** crook, rowdy, tough **6** gunman **7** bruiser, gorilla, mobster, ruffian **8** criminal, gangster, hooligan, plug-ugly **9** desperado, strong arm **10** delinquent

hoodwink 3 gyp **4** dupe, fool, gull, hoax, rook **5** cheat, cozen, trick **7** deceive, defraud, mislead, swindle **8** inveigle **9** bamboozle, victimize

hook 3 arc, bag, bow, nab, net **4** arch, bend, bill, curl, gaff, grab, loop, take, trap, wind **5** angle, catch, crook, curve, elbow, fluke, hitch, latch, seize, snare **6** buckle, collar, fasten, peavey, secure **7** capture, crampon, ensnare, grapnel, grapple, pothook **8** crescent, make fast **9** horseshoe

Hooke, Robert
  field: 7 physics **9** astronomy
  nationality: 7 British

discovered: 9 Orion star **15** Jupiter rotation **20** moon's center of gravity **21** earth's center of gravity
  invented: 10 microscope
  named for him: 15 law of elasticity

hooked 8 addicted **9** compelled, obsessive **10** compulsive, habituated **14** uncontrollable

hooked cross
  German: 10 Hakenkreuz

hook up 4 ally, dock, join **5** hinge **6** couple, link up **7** connect **8** assemble **10** articulate **11** fit together **14** fasten together

hooligan 4 hood, lout, punk **5** bully, rowdy, tough **6** vandal **7** hoodlum, ruffian **9** barbarian, roughneck **10** delinquent

hoopla 4 hype **8** ballyhoo **9** promotion, publicity **10** hullabaloo, propaganda **11** advertising **15** public relations

Hoosier Schoolmaster, The
  author: 15 Edward Eggleston

Hoosier State
  nickname of: 7 Indiana

hoot 3 boo, din **4** bawl, blow, hiss, honk, howl, jeer, moan, mock, razz, roar, wail, yelp, yowl **5** shout, sneer, taunt, whoop **6** bellow, chorus, cry out, deride, outcry, racket, scream, shriek, shrill, tumult, uproar **7** catcall, cry down, scoff at, screech, sing out, sneer at, snicker, ululate, wailing, whistle **8** proclaim, shouting **9** caterwaul, commotion, raspberry, screaming, snicker at **10** Bronx cheer, screeching

Hoover, Herbert Clark
  nickname: 13 Great Engineer **14** Great Secretary **17** Great Humanitarian **18** Great Public Servant
  presidential rank: 11 thirty-first
  party: 10 Republican
  state represented: 2 CA
  defeated: 5 (Alfred Emanuel) Smith **6** (George William) Norris, (Norman) Thomas, (William Frederick) Varney, (William Zebulon) Foster **8** (Verne L) Reynolds
  vice president: 6 (Charles) Curtis
  cabinet:
    state: 7 (Henry Lewis) Stimson
    treasury: 5 (Ogden Livingston) Mills **6** (Andrew William) Mellon
    war: 4 (James William) Good **6** (Patrick Jay) Hurley
    attorney general: 8 (William DeWitt) Mitchell
    navy: 5 (Charles Francis) Adams
    postmaster general: 5 (Walter Folger) Brown
    interior: 6 (Ray Lyman) Wilbur
    agriculture: 4 (Arthur Mastick) Hyde
    commerce: 6 (Robert Patterson) Lamont, (Roy Dikeman) Chapin

    labor: 4 (William Nuckles) Doak **5** (James John) Davis
  born: 12 West Branch IA
  died: 13 New York City NY
  buried: 12 West Branch IA
  education:
    University: 8 Stanford
  religion: 5 Quaker **16** Society of Friends
  interests: 7 fishing
  vacation spot: 10 Camp Hoover **11** Rapidan Camp **22** Shenandoah National Park
  author: 7 Memoirs **11** On Growing Up **14** An American Epic **16** Years of Adventure **18** Principles of Mining, The Great Depression **20** America's First Crusade **21** American Individualism, The Challenge to Liberty **24** The Ordeal of Woodrow Wilson **25** The Problems of Lasting Peace **26** The Cabinet and the Presidency **28** Addresses Upon the American Road **51** The State Papers and Other Public Writings of Herbert Hoover
  political career: 19 US Food Administrator
    head of: 23 American Relief Committee **28** Commission for Relief in Belgium
    director: 38 General Relief and Reconstruction of Europe
    member/chairman: 22 Supreme Economic Council
    secretary of: 8 Commerce
    chairman of: 17 Hoover Commissions
  civilian career: 6 author **14** mining engineer **18** consulting engineer
  notable events of lifetime/term: 15 Great Depression
    conference: 11 London Naval
    crash of: 11 stock market
    independence for: 11 Philippines
    Tariff: 11 Hawley-Smoot
  named for him: 11 Hoover apron, Hoover plate (clean plate), Hooverville (shantytown)
  father: 10 Jesse Clark
  mother: 6 Huldah (Randall Minthorn)
  siblings: 3 May **13** Theodore Jesse
  wife: 3 Lou (Henry)
  children: 10 Allan Henry **12** Herbert Clark
  first lady:
    vice president of: 10 Girl Scouts

hop 3 bob **4** ball, jump, leap, prom, romp, skip, step, trip **5** bound, caper, dance, frisk, mixer, vault **6** bounce, gambol, prance, soiree, spring **7** Humulus
  varieties: 4 Wild **5** False **6** Common **8** European, Japanese

hope 3 yen **4** help, wish **5** crave, dream, faith, fancy, trust **6** aspire, belief, chance, desire, expect, hunger, rescue, yen for **7** believe, count on, craving, dream of, longing, long for **8**

ambition, daydream, feel sure, optimism, prospect, reckon on, reliance, yearn for, yearning **9** assurance, hankering, have faith, hunger for, salvation, take heart **10** anticipate, aspiration, assumption, be bent upon, confidence, conviction, expectancy **11** be confident, contemplate, expectation, have an eye to, possibility, presumption, reassurance, saving grace **12** anticipation, be optimistic, heart's desire **13** encouragement, have a fancy for, look forward to **14** have a hankering **17** great expectations **18** have one's heart set on **19** look on the bright side

Hope, Anthony
real name: **21** Sir Anthony Hope Hawkins
author of: **15** Rupert of Hentzau **18** The Prisoner of Zenda

Hope, Bob
real name: **16** Leslie Townes Hope
co-star: **10** Bing Crosby **13** Dorothy Lamour
born: **6** Eltham **7** England
roles:
Road to: **3** Rio **4** Bali **6** Utopia **7** Morocco **8** Hong Kong, Zanzibar **9** Singapore
performed for: **3** USO

hopeful 7 assured, in hopes **8** cheering, sanguine, trusting **9** confident, expectant, favorable, fortunate, promising **10** auspicious, heartening, of good omen, optimistic, propitious, reassuring **11** encouraging **12** anticipative

hopeless 3 sad **4** lost, vain **6** abject, futile **7** forlorn, useless **8** dejected, downcast **9** depressed, incurable, pointless **10** beyond help, despairing, despondent, impossible, melancholy, past remedy **11** downhearted, heartbroken, irreparable, irrevocable, pessimistic, sick at heart **12** beyond recall, disconsolate, heavyhearted, irredeemable, irreversible **13** grief-stricken, irretrievable **14** down in the mouth, sorrow-stricken

hopelessness 7 despair **8** futility **9** pessimism **11** uselessness

Hopi (Hopitu, Moki)
language family: **10** Shoshonean
location: **7** Arizona
adapted culture of: **6** Pueblo
ceremony: **10** snake dance

Hopkins, Anthony
born: **5** Wales **10** Port Talbot
roles: **10** Audrey Rose **11** A Doll's House **12** Young Winston **14** The Elephant Man **15** The Lion in Winter

Hopper, Edward
born: **7** Nyack NY
artwork: **10** Nighthawks **18** Early Sunday Morning, House by the Railroad **19** Second Story Sunlight **20** Sunlight in a Cafeteria **21** Lighthouse at Two Lights

Horae
also: **5** Hours
goddesses of: **5** decay **6** growth **7** seasons **11** social order
names: **4** Dice, Dike **5** Irene **7** Eunomia

Horatio
character in: **6** Hamlet
author: **11** Shakespeare

Horatio
character in: **17** The Spanish Tragedy
author: **3** Kyd

Horatius
origin: **5** Roman
defended: **6** bridge
over: **5** Tiber
against: **9** Etruscans

horde 3 mob **4** band, gang, host, pack **5** bunch, crowd, crush, drove, party, swarm, tribe, troop **6** legion, throng **7** company **8** assembly **9** gathering, multitude **10** assemblage **12** congregation

Horgan, Paul
author of: **10** Whitewater **13** Lamy of Santa Fe **18** The Thin Mountain Air

horizon 4 area **5** field, range, realm, scope, vista, world **6** bounds, domain, sphere **7** compass, expanse, outlook, purview, stretch **8** frontier, prospect **11** perspective

horizontal 4 even, flat **5** flush, level, plane, plumb, prone **6** supine **8** parallel (to something) **9** lying down, prostrate, reclining, recumbent **14** flat on one's back

horizontal support 3 tie **4** beam **5** brace, joist **6** girder, header, lintel **8** crossbar

hormone 4 ACTH **5** auxin **6** cortin **7** estrone, insulin, steroid **8** endocrin, estrogen, galactin, lactogen, secretin **9** adrenalin, cortisone **12** progesterone, testosterone

horn 4 tusk **5** cornu, point, spike **6** antler **11** excrescence
brass instrument: **4** oboe, tuba **5** bugle **6** cornet **7** bassoon, trumpet **8** alto horn, baritone, clarinet, trombone **9** euphonium, saxophone **10** French horn, mellophone, sousaphone **11** English horn

Horn of Africa see **7** Somalia

Hornung, Paul
nickname: **9** Golden Boy
sport: **8** football
position: **6** runner **11** placekicker
team: **15** Green Bay Packers

horny 4 hard **5** tough **7** callous, lustful **8** callused, hardened **12** thick-skinned **14** pachydermatous

horologe 5 clock **9** timepiece **11** chronometer

horoscope see **9** astrology

horrendous 4 gory **5** awful **6** horrid **7** ghastly, hideous **8** dreadful, horrible, shocking, terrible **9** appalling, frightful, repellent, repulsive, revolting **10** horrifying

horrible 3 bad **4** foul, rank, vile **5** awful, nasty **6** grisly, horrid, odious **7** ghastly, hideous **8** dreadful, gruesome, shocking, terrible, unsavory **9** abhorrent, appalling, atrocious, frightful, harrowing, loathsome, monstrous, obnoxious, repellent, repulsive, revolting, sickening **10** abominable, despicable, detestable, disgusting, forbidding, nauseating, unbearable, unpleasant **11** disquieting, distasteful, unspeakable **12** disagreeable, insufferable

horrid 3 bad **4** foul, grim, ugly **5** awful, nasty, rough **6** bratty, horror, shaggy, wicked **7** fearful, hideous **8** dreadful, gruesome, horrible, shocking, terrible **9** bristling, frightful, offensive, revolting, vexatious **10** abominable, detestable, unpleasant **11** troublesome **12** disagreeable

horrific 4 dire **5** awful **7** fearful, ghastly **8** dreadful, horrible, shocking, terrible **9** appalling

horrified 6 aghast **8** appalled **9** petrified, terrified **10** frightened **13** thunderstruck **14** terror-stricken

horrify 5 daunt, repel, shock **6** appall, dismay, revolt, sicken **7** disgust, petrify, terrify **8** affright, disquiet, frighten, nauseate **10** disconcert, dishearten **11** make one sick **15** make one turn pale **18** make one's flesh creep **22** make one's hair stand on end

horrifying 5 awful, dread **8** alarming, dreadful **10** terrifying **11** frightening, hair-raising

horror 3 woe **4** fear **5** alarm, crime, dread, panic **6** dismay, hatred, misery, terror **7** anguish, cruelty, disgust, dislike, outrage, torment **8** atrocity, aversion, distaste, distress, hardship, loathing **9** antipathy, awfulness, privation, repulsion, revulsion, suffering **10** abhorrence, affliction, discomfort, inhumanity, repugnance **11** abomination, detestation, hideousness, trepidation **12** apprehension, terribleness, wretchedness

horror-struck 6 aghast **7** fearful **8** appalled **9** horrified, terrified **10** frightened **13** scared to death

hors de combat 8 disabled **13** out of the fight

hors d'oeuvre 3 dip **6** canape, relish, tidbit **9** antipasto, appetizer **10** finger food

horse 4 colt, foal, hack, jade, mare, plug, pony, sire, stud **5** bronc, filly, mount, pacer, pinto, steed **6** bronco, dobbin, equine, nellie **7** cavalry,

charger, cow pony, gelding, hackney, hussars, lancers, mustang, palfrey, trotter **8** cossacks, dragoons, galloper, stallion, troopers, yearling **9** broodmare, racehorse **10** cavalrymen, draft horse **12** horse cavalry, horse marines, quarter horse, thoroughbred **13** horse soldiers, mounted troops **15** mounted troopers, mounted warriors
Achilles': 7 Xanthus
Alexander the Great's: 10 Bucephalus
anatomy: 4 hock, hoof, loin, mane, tail **5** croup, flank, shank **6** cannon, gaskin, haunch, stifle **7** coronet, crupper, fetlock, gambrel, nostril, pastern, withers **11** throatlatch
Australian: 5 myall **8** warragal, warrigal, yarraman
breed: 6 Morgan, Nubian, Tarpan **7** Arabian, Belgian, mustang **8** Galloway, Shetland **9** Appaloosa, Percheron **10** Clydesdale, Lippizaner **12** Narragansett, Standardbred, Thoroughbred **15** Tennessee Walker
Bellerophon's: 7 Pegasus
Caligula's: 9 Incitatus (made a senator)
castrated: 7 gelding
color: 3 bay, dun **4** gray, pied, roan, zain **5** morel, pinto **6** calico, dapple, sorrel **7** piebald **8** chestnut, palomino, schimmel (gray)
combining form: 4 eque, equi **5** hippo
Dick Turpin's: 9 Black Bess
Don Quixote's: 9 Rosinante
family: 7 Equidae **9** Miohippus, Orohippus
female: 3 dam **4** mare **5** filly
French: 6 cheval
gear: 3 bit **4** rein, tack **6** saddle **7** blinder, harness, snaffle **9** surcingle **11** saddlecloth
Gen Custer's: 8 Comanche
Gen Grant's: 10 Cincinnati
Gen Robert E Lee's: 9 Traveller
Gen Sherman's: 6 Rienzi
genus: 5 equus
Gulliver's Travels: 9 Houyhnhnm
kind: 3 cob **4** race **6** bronco, hunter, jumper **7** charger, mustang, palfrey, quarter, trotter **8** destrier
legendary: 6 Trojan
Lone Ranger's: 6 Silver
male: 4 colt **8** stallion
measure: 4 hand
Mohammed's: 7 Alborak
movie/story: 6 Flicka **8** Champion **11** Black Beauty **14** National Velvet **16** The Black Stallion
Napoleon's: 7 Marengo
Odin's: 8 Sleipnir
Orlando's: 9 Vegliantino
pace: 4 lope, trot **5** amble **6** canter, gallop
pair of: 4 span, team **6** tandem
race: 5 derby, plate **6** exacta **7** pick

six **8** claiming, handicap **9** allowance **11** daily double, sweepstakes **12** steeplechase, weight-for-age
   Triple Crown: 7 Belmont **9** Preakness **13** Kentucky Derby
riding show: 8 gymkhana
riding sport: 4 polo
Rinaldo's: 6 Bayard
Roy Rogers': 7 Trigger
Siegfried's: 5 Grani
small: 4 pony
Stonewall Jackson's: 12 Little Sorrel
Tom Mix's: 4 Tony
Tonto's: 5 Scout
television: 4 Mr. Ed
three: 6 random, troika **7** unicorn
Wellington's (at Waterloo): 10 Copenhagen
wild: 5 fuzzy **6** bramby, kumrah, outlaw, tarpan **7** jughead **8** bangtail, fuzztail, warragal, warrigal
Will Rogers': 8 Soapsuds **10** Bootlegger
winged: 7 Pegasus
young: 4 colt, foal **5** filly **8** yearling
horseback riding
athlete: 11 Frank Chapot **17** William Steinkraus
horse collar 3 zip **4** zero **5** aught, zilch **6** cipher, naught **8** goose egg
Horse Knows the Way, The
   author: 9 John O'Hara
horseman 5 groom, rider **6** hussar, jockey, lancer, ostler **7** cossack, dragoon, hostler, trainer, trooper **9** postilion, stableboy, stableman **10** cavalryman, equestrian, roughrider **11** horse marine, stable owner **12** equestrienne, horse breeder, horse soldier, stable keeper **14** cavalry soldier, horseback rider, mounted trooper
horseplay 6 pranks **7** foolery **9** cutting up **10** buffoonery, tomfoolery **13** fooling around, horsing around
horse racing
   jockey: 8 Del Insko **11** Bill Hartack, Eddie Arcaro **12** Angel Cordero, Bill Haughton, Laffit Pincay, Steve Cauthen **13** Johnny Longden, Stanley Dancer **15** Willie Shoemaker
   god of: 6 Consus
Horseshoe Robinson
   author: 12 John P Kennedy
horse soldier 6 hussar, lancer **7** dragoon, trooper **8** cavalier, horseman **10** cavalryman
horse trooper 6 hussar, lancer **7** dragoon, Mountie **8** cavalier, horseman **10** cavalryman **12** horse soldier **14** mounted soldier **16** mounted policeman
Horton, Edward Everett
   sidekick of: 11 Fred Astaire
   born: 10 Brooklyn NY
   roles: 15 Cinderella Jones, Her Primitive Man **18** Springtime for Henry
Horus

   origin: 8 Egyptian
   god of: 3 sun
   Greek name: 10 Harcorates
   symbol: 6 falcon
   mother: 4 Isis
   father: 6 Osiris
   enemy: 3 Set **4** Seth
hosannas 4 yeas **5** kudos **6** bravos, cheers, paeans **7** acclaim, hurrahs, huzzahs, yippees **8** applause **10** hallelujas **11** halleluiahs
hose, hosiery 5 socks **6** nylons, tights **7** anklets, argyles, hosiery **9** knee-highs, pantyhose, stockings **10** bobbysocks
Hosea
   father: 5 Beeri
hospitable 4 open, warm **6** genial **7** cordial **8** amenable, amicable, friendly, gracious, sociable, tolerant **9** agreeable, convivial, receptive, welcoming **10** accessible, gregarious, neighborly, openhanded, open-minded, responsive **12** approachable
hospital 4 home **6** asylum, clinic **7** sick bay **8** pavilion, rest home **9** infirmary **10** polyclinic, sanatorium **11** nursing home **13** medical center
   French: 9 hotel Dieu
hospital, private
   French: 13 maison de sante
hospitality 5 cheer **6** warmth **7** welcome **8** openness **9** geniality **10** cordiality, heartiness, kindliness **11** amicability, sociability **12** congeniality, conviviality, friendliness **13** Gemutlichkeit **14** hospitableness, neighborliness **15** warmheartedness
   god of: 6 Sancus **10** Dius Fidius, Semo Sancus
host, hostess 3 lot, mob **4** army, band, body, crew, gang, mess **5** array, crowd, drove, emcee, group, horde, party, swarm, troop **6** legion, throng **7** company, maitre d', meeting **8** conclave, congress, hosteler, hotelier, landlord, welcomer **9** gathering, innkeeper, multitude **10** confluence, convention, headwaiter, party giver, proprietor **11** convocation, hotel keeper **12** congregation, head waitress, hotel manager, proprietress, receptionist **17** restaurant manager **18** master of ceremonies **20** mistress of ceremonies
hostage 6 pledge **7** captive **8** prisoner
Hostage, The
   author: 12 Brendan Behan
hostel 3 inn **4** hall **5** hotel, lodge **7** hospice, lodging, shelter **8** hospital, hostelry
hostile 3 icy **4** cold, mean, ugly **5** angry, at war, enemy, testy **6** at odds, at outs, bitter, chilly, cranky, malign, touchy, unkind **7** opposed, vicious, warring **8** battling, clashing, contrary, fighting, opposing, snappish, spiteful, venomous **9** bellicose, bristling, dissi-

dent, malicious, malignant, truculent **10** contending, ill-natured, malevolent, on bad terms, unfriendly **11** belligerent, contentious, disagreeing, ill-disposed, quarrelsome **12** antagonistic, cantankerous, disagreeable, disputatious, incompatible **13** argumentative, at loggerheads, unsympathetic

hostile act 4 raid **6** strike, threat **7** assault, offense **8** act of war, invasion **9** hostility, incursion **10** aggression

hostile nation 3 foe **5** enemy **7** invader

hostility 3 war **4** duel, feud, fray, hate **5** anger, clash, fight, venom **6** battle, combat, enmity, fracas, hatred, malice, rancor, spleen **7** contest, dispute, ill will, scuffle, warfare, warring **8** act of war, argument, battling, conflict, fighting **9** animosity, antipathy, bickering **10** antagonism, bitterness, contention, dissidence, opposition, state of war **11** altercation, malevolence, viciousness **12** belligerence, contrariness, disagreement **14** unfriendliness, vindictiveness

hot 3 new, top **4** good, late, live, near, warm **5** fiery, fresh, nippy, sharp **6** ardent, baking, biting, fervid, fierce, heated, hectic, latest, molten, raging, recent, red-hot, stormy, sultry, torrid **7** boiling, burning, earnest, excited, furious, intense, melting, peppery, piquant, popular, pungent, searing, violent **8** agitated, animated, broiling, feverish, frenzied, roasting, scalding, sizzling, steaming, vehement, very warm **9** emotional, excellent, scorching, simmering, very close, wrought-up **10** attractive, blistering, passionate, smoldering, successful, sweltering **11** electrified, fast-selling, most popular, radioactive, sought after, tempestuous **12** incandescent **14** fast and furious, highly seasoned, in close pursuit

hot air 7 bombast **8** rhetoric **9** hyperbole **12** exaggeration **13** overstatement

hotel de ville 9 a city hall
literally: **16** mansion of the city

hotel Dieu 9 a hospital **12** mansion of God

Hotel New Hampshire, The
author: **10** John Irving

hothouse 6 tender **7** fragile, nursery **8** delicate **10** glasshouse, greenhouse **12** conservatory **13** over-protected

hot temper 4 fire **5** anger **6** pepper **8** acrimony **9** short fuse

hot-tempered 7 peppery **9** emotional, excitable **13** easily ruffled, quick-tempered

hot water 3 jam **4** mess **6** pickle **7** trouble **10** difficulty **11** predicament

Houghston, Walter
real name of: **12** Walter Huston

hound 3 dog, fan, nag, nut, pup **4** bait, buff, hunt, mutt, tail **5** annoy, chase, doggy, freak, harry, lover, pooch, puppy, stalk, track, trail, whelp, worry **6** addict, badger, canine, follow, harass, hector, keep at, needle, pester, pursue **7** bedevil, poochie **9** keep after **10** aficionado, hunting dog **11** afficionado
dog breed: **6** beagle, borzoi, saluki **7** basenji, harrier, whippet **9** dachshund, greyhound **10** bloodhound, otter hound **11** Afghan hound, basset hound, Ibizan hound **12** pharaoh hound **14** Irish wolfhound **15** English foxhound **16** American foxhound **17** Norwegian elkhound, Scottish deerhound **18** Rhodesian ridgeback **20** black and tan coonhound
group of: **3** cry **4** mute, pack

Hound of the Baskervilles, The
author: **19** Sir Arthur Conan Doyle
character: **8** Dr Watson **14** Sherlock Holmes **19** Sir Henry Baskerville

hour 3 day **4** span, time **5** space **6** period **8** interval
abbreviation: **2** hr

Hour see **5** Horae

house, House 4 clan, firm, hall, home, keep, line, shop **5** abode, board, lodge, put up, store **6** billet, church, family, garage, harbor, strain, temple **7** Commons, company, concern, contain, council, descent, dynasty, lineage, quarter, shelter, theater **8** ancestry, assembly, audience, building, business, congress, domicile, dwelling **9** ancestors, household, residence **10** auditorium, family tree, habitation, hippodrome, opera house, spectators **11** accommodate, concert hall, corporation, legislature, noble family, partnership, royal family **12** business firm, lower chamber, meeting place, organization **13** dwelling place, establishment
god of: **8** Silvanus, Sylvanus

housebreaker 5 thief **6** robber **7** burglar **8** pilferer **9** purloiner **10** cat burglar **14** second-story man

housebreaking 5 theft **7** break-in, robbery **8** burglary, stealing **12** burglarizing **19** breaking and entering

House Divided, A
author: **9** Pearl Buck

House for Mr Biswas, A
author: **9** V S Naipaul

household 4 home **5** house **6** family, hearth, menage **8** of a house **9** for a house **10** for a family, for home use **12** family circle
goddess of: **6** Brigit

household gods 5 lares, Roman **7** penates

household help 4 cook, maid **7** foot-

man, steward **8** domestic, gardener, handyman, houseboy **9** charwoman, chauffeur, domestics, majordomo, nursemaid **11** housekeeper

household of three
French: **12** menage a trois

House of Atreus, The
author: **9** Aeschylus
character: **7** Electra, Orestes **9** Aegisthus, Agamemnon, Cassandra **12** Clytemnestra

house of health
French: **13** maison de sante

House of Mirth, The
author: **12** Edith Wharton
character: **8** Lily Bart, Mr Selden **9** Gus Trenor **10** Judy Trenor, Mr Rosedale, Percy Gryce **12** Bertha Dorset, George Dorset

House of the Seven Gables, The
author: **18** Nathaniel Hawthorne
character: **10** Mr Holgrave **14** Phoebe Pyncheon **16** Clifford Pyncheon **20** Judge Jaffrey Pyncheon, Miss Hepzibah Pyncheon

house of worship 6 chapel, church, mosque, temple **8** basilica **9** cathedral, synagogue **10** house of God, Lord's house, tabernacle

housewife 4 wife **8** hausfrau **9** homemaker **11** housekeeper

housing 4 case, home **5** abode, house **6** casing, jacket, sheath, shield **7** lodging, shelter **8** covering, domicile, dwelling, envelope, lodgment, quarters **9** enclosure, residence **10** habitation **14** accommodations

Housman, A E
author of: **14** A Shropshire Lad

Houston
baseball team: **6** Astros
basketball team: **6** Comets **7** Rockets
canal: **11** Houston Ship
channel: **12** Buffalo Bayou
football team: **6** Oilers **8** Gamblers
landmark: **4** NASA **12** Alley Theater **14** Jesse Jones Hall **22** Manned Spacecraft Center **29** San Jacinto Battlefield Monument
battleship: **5** Texas
named after: **10** Sam Houston
planned by: **7** A C Allen, J K Allen
stadium: **9** Astrodome
street: **15** Old Spanish Trail
university: **4** Rice **12** Texas Medical **13** Texas Southern

Houston, Sam
position: **9** US Senator
governor of: **5** Texas **9** Tennessee
president of: **15** Republic of Texas
served in: **9** Creek Wars **15** Texas Revolution
battle: **10** San Jacinto
defeated: **9** Santa Anna

Houyhnhnms
race of horses in: **16** Gulliver's

Travels
author: **5** Swift

hovel 3 hut **4** dump, hole **5** cabin, shack **6** shanty

hover 4 flit, hang **5** float, haunt, pause, poise, waver **6** attend, falter, seesaw **7** flitter, flutter **9** fluctuate, hang about, vacillate

Hovhaness, Alan
born: **12** Somerville MA
composer of: **10** Magnificat

how
Latin: **7** quo modo

Howard, Catherine
husband: **9** Henry VIII
number: **5** fifth
fate: **8** beheaded

Howard, Ron
born: **2** OK **6** Duncan
roles: **4** Opie **9** Happy Days **16** American Graffiti, Richie Cunningham **19** The Andy Griffith Show
director of: **6** Cocoon, Gung Ho, Splash, Willow

Howard, Sidney
author of: **13** The Silver Cord **22** They Knew What They Wanted

Howard, Trevor
born: **7** England **12** Cliftonville
roles: **6** The Key **13** Ryan's Daughter, Sons and Lovers **14** Brief Encounter **23** The Invincible Mr Disraeli

Howards End
author: **9** E M Forster
character: **9** Jacky Bast **10** Paul Wilcox, Ruth Wilcox **11** Henry Wilcox, Leonard Bast **13** Charles Wilcox, Helen Schlegel **16** Margaret Schlegel, Theobald Schlegel

how are you
German: **8** wie geht's **9** wie geht es

Howe, Elias
nationality: **8** American
invented: **13** sewing machine

Howells, William Dean
author of: **12** Indian Summer **15** A Modern Instance **20** A Hazard of New Fortunes, The Rise of Silas Lapham

How Green Was My Valley
author: **16** Richard Llewellyn
director: **8** John Ford
character: **6** Marged **7** Bronwen **10** Beth Morgan **11** Iestyn Evans **12** Gwilym Morgan
  Morgan children: **4** Davy, Huur, Ivor, Owen **5** Ianto **6** Gwilym **8** Angharad
cast: **7** Anna Lee **9** John Loder **11** Donald Crisp **12** Maureen O'Hara **13** Roddy McDowall, Walter Pidgeon
Oscar for: **7** picture **8** director **15** supporting actor (Crisp)

howl 3 bay, cry **4** bark, hoot, roar, wail, yell, yelp, yowl **5** groan, shout, whine **6** bellow, clamor, cry out, outcry, scream, shriek, uproar **7** ululate

howler 4 goof **5** error **6** boo-boo **7** blooper, blunder, mistake

How To Win Friends and Influence People
author: **12** Dale Carnegie

hoyden 3 imp **4** brat, chit **6** tomboy

Hoyle, Edmund 9 authority, (card games)

Hoyle, Fred
field: **9** astronomy
nationality: **7** British
developed: **17** steady-state theory

Hoyt, Rosemary
character in: **16** Tender Is the Night
author: **10** Fitzgerald

Hsitsang *see* **5** Tibet

Hualapai
language family: **5** Yuman
location: **7** Arizona
related to: **7** Yavapai **9** Havasupai

hub 3 nub **4** axis, core **5** focus, heart, pivot **6** center, middle **10** focal point

Hubble, Edwin Powell
field: **9** astronomy
studied: **15** galactic nebulae
named for him: **14** Hubble constant, space telescope

hubbub 3 din **4** fuss, stir, to-do **5** noise **6** babble, bedlam, bustle, clamor, pother, racket, ruckus, tumult, uproar **7** ferment, turmoil **8** disorder **9** agitation, commotion, confusion, hue and cry **10** hullabaloo, hurlyburly **11** disturbance, pandemonium **12** perturbation

Hubert
creator: **11** Dick Wingert

huckleberry 9 Vaccinium **11** Gaylussacia
varieties: **2** He **3** Box, Red **4** Blue, Shot **5** Black, Dwarf, Hairy, Squaw, Sugar **6** Garden **8** Thin-leaf **9** Evergreen **10** California, Little-leaf

Huckleberry Finn (The Adventures of)
author: **9** Mark Twain
character: **3** Jim **9** Tom Sawyer **12** Widow Douglas **13** Judge Thatcher

huckster 5 adman **6** badger, hawker, kidder, seller, vendor **7** haggler, peddler

Hud
director: **10** Martin Ritt
cast: **10** John Ashley, Paul Newman **12** Patricia Neal **13** Melvyn Douglas **14** Brandon de Wilde
Oscar for: **7** actress (Neal) **15** supporting actor (Douglas)

huddle 4 heap, herd, mass, mess **5** bunch, crowd, group **6** cuddle, curl up, jumble, medley, muddle, nestle, throng **7** cluster, collect, meeting, snuggle **8** converge, disarray, disorder **9** confusion, gathering **10** conference, discussion, hodge-podge **12** think session

Hudibras
author: **12** Samuel Butler
character: **6** Ralpho **8** Crowders **9** Sidrophel

Hudson, Rock
real name: **12** Roy Scherer Jr
co-star: **8** Doris Day
born: **10** Winnetka IL
roles: **5** Giant **10** Pillow Talk **15** A Farewell to Arms, McMillan and Wife **20** Magnificent Obsession

Hudson, W H
author of: **13** Green Mansions, The Purple Land **17** Far Away and Long Ago
bird-girl: **4** Rima

hue 4 cast, tint, tone **5** color, shade, tinge **8** tincture **10** coloration

hue and cry 4 call, howl, roar, yell, yowl **5** alarm, alert, shout, storm **6** bellow, clamor, hubbub, outcry, shriek, uproar **7** thunder **10** cry of alarm, hullabaloo

huff 3 pet **4** fury, rage, snit **7** bad mood, dudgeon, outrage **8** ill humor, vexation **9** annoyance, petulance **10** fit of anger, fit of pique, resentment

huffy 4 curt, hurt **5** angry, cross, irate, moody, sulky, surly, testy **6** cranky, grumpy, moping, morose, shirty, sullen, touchy **7** in a snit, peevish, waspish, wounded **8** churlish, offended, petulant, snappish **9** glowering, in a lather, in a pucker, irritable, querulous, rancorous, resentful, sensitive **10** ill-humored, out of sorts **11** disgruntled, quarrelsome, thin-skinned **12** discontented **14** easily offended, hard to live with, hypersensitive

hug 4 hold **5** clasp **6** clutch, cuddle, nestle **7** cling to, embrace, snuggle, squeeze **9** hold close, hover near **11** keep close to **13** cling together, follow closely **15** parallel closely, press to the bosom

huge 4 vast **5** giant, great, jumbo **6** mighty **7** immense, mammoth, massive, titanic **8** colossal, enormous, gigantic, imposing **9** cyclopean, extensive, herculean, leviathan, monstrous **10** gargantuan, monumental, prodigious, staggering, stupendous **11** elephantine, extravagant, spectacular **12** overwhelming **14** Brobdingnagian

hugeness 4 bulk **8** enormity, vastness **9** great size, immensity, largeness, magnitude **11** massiveness

Huggins, Charles Brenton
field: **10** physiology
researched: **6** cancer **12** chemotherapy
awarded: **10** Nobel Prize

Hughes, Langston
author of: **9** The Big Sea **12** One-Way Ticket **13** The Weary Blues **19** Shakespeare in Harlem **20** The Panther and the Lash

Hughes, Richard
  author of: **18** A High Wind in Jamaica
Hughes, Thomas
  author of: **19** Tom Brown's Schooldays
Hugh the Drover
  opera by: **15** Vaughan Williams
  character: **4** Mary **12** The Constable **14** John the Butcher
Hugin
  origin: **12** Scandinavian
  form: **5** raven
  owned by: **4** Odin **5** Othin
  personifies: **7** thought
  duty: **10** newsbearer
  other raven: **5** Munin
Hugo, Victor
  author of: **7** Ruy Blas **13** Les Miserables **16** Notre Dame de Paris **23** The Hunchback of Notre Dame
  character: **6** Javert **9** Esmeralda, Quasimodo **15** Jean Valjean
hulk 4 ship **5** giant, wreck **8** behemoth
hulking 3 big **5** bulky, heavy, husky **7** massive **8** powerful, unwieldy **9** oversized, ponderous **10** cumbersome
hull 3 pod **4** case, husk, peel, rind, skin **5** shell, shuck **7** coating **8** carapace **9** epidermis, tegmentum **10** integument
Hull, Isaac
  served in: **19** War of Eighteen-Twelve
  sunk ship: **9** Guerriere (British)
  commander of ship: **12** Constitution
hullabaloo 3 din **4** stir **5** babel **6** bedlam, clamor, hubbub, ruckus, tumult, uproar **9** confusion **11** pandemonium **Yiddish: 7** tzimmes
hum 4 buzz, purr, whir **5** croon, drone, thrum **6** be busy, bustle, intone, murmur, thrive **7** buzzing, droning, purring, vibrate **8** be active, whirring **9** vibration **10** faint sound **13** be in full swing
human 3 man **5** of man, of men **6** gentle, humane, kindly, mortal, person **7** hominid, like man, manlike **8** merciful, personal **10** anthropoid, individual **11** Homo sapiens, sympathetic
Human Comedy, The
  author: **14** Honore de Balzac, William Saroyan
Human Condition, The
  author: **12** Hannah Arendt
humane 4 kind **5** human **6** kindly, tender **7** pitying **8** merciful **9** unselfish **10** benevolent, bighearted, charitable, goodwilled **11** magnanimous, sympathetic, warmhearted **12** humanitarian **13** compassionate, philanthropic
Human Factor, The
  author: **12** Graham Greene
humanitarian 4 kind **6** humane **8**

generous **10** altruistic, benevolent, charitable **11** kind-hearted **12** large-hearted **13** compassionate, philanthropic **14** philanthropist
humanity 3 man **4** love **5** mercy **6** people **7** charity, mankind, mortals **8** goodwill, kindness, sympathy **9** humankind, humanness, mortality **10** compassion, gentleness, humaneness, kindliness, tenderness **11** benevolence, Homo sapiens, human beings, human nature, magnanimity **12** the human race **13** brotherly love, fellow feeling **15** warmheartedness **16** fraternal feeling
humanum est errare 12 to err is human
Humbert Humbert
  character in: **6** Lolita
  author: **7** Nabokov
humble 3 low **4** meek, poor **5** abase, abash, crush, lower, lowly, plain, shame **6** common, debase, demean, demure, gentle, modest, shabby, simple, subdue **7** chasten, conquer, degrade, mortify, obscure, put down **8** bring low, derogate, disgrace, dishonor, inferior, ordinary, plebeian, pull down, wretched **9** bring down, embarrass, humiliate, make lowly, miserable **10** inglorious, low ranking, make humble, obsequious, put to shame, respectful, unassuming **11** deferential, subservient, unimportant, unpresuming **12** self-effacing, take down a peg **13** insignificant, unpretentious **14** unostentatious **15** inconsequential, undistinguished
humbled 5 cowed **7** abashed, debased, subdued **9** conquered, disgraced **10** brought low, humiliated
Humboldt, Alexander von
  nationality: **6** German
  originator of: **7** ecology **10** geophysics
Humboldt's Gift
  author: **10** Saul Bellow
humbug 3 fib, gyp, lie **4** bull, bunk, dupe, fake, fool, gull, hoax, liar, lies, sham **5** cheat, cozen, dodge, faker, fraud, hokum, lying, quack, spoof, trick **6** bunkum, con man, deceit, fibber, phooey, take in **7** beguile, blather, cheater, deceive, falsify, fiction, forgery, mislead, rubbish, sharper, swindle **8** artifice, claptrap, flimflam, flummery, hoodwink, impostor, nonsense, perjurer, pretense, swindler, trickery **9** bamboozle, charlatan, deception, fabricate, falsehood, hypocrisy, hypocrite, imposture, mendacity, poppycock, trickster **10** balderdash, hocus-pocus, mountebank, pretension **11** counterfeit, make-believe **12** equivocation, misrepresent **13** confidence man, double-dealing, falsification **15** pretentiousness

humdinger 4 lulu, oner **5** dandy, doozy **6** beauty, hummer, marvel **8** Jim dandy, superior **10** ripsnorter **12** lollapalooza **13** extraordinary
humdrum 4 blah, dull, dumb, flat **5** banal, trite **6** boring, common, dreary **7** insipid, mundane, routine, tedious, trivial **8** everyday, lifeless, mediocre, ordinary, tiresome, wearying **9** hackneyed, unvarying, wearisome **10** monotonous, pedestrian, uneventful, unexciting, uninspired **11** commonplace, indifferent, uninspiring **12** conventional, run-of-the-mill **13** unexceptional, uninteresting
humerus
  bone of: **8** upper arm
humid 4 damp, dank **5** moist, muggy, soppy **6** clammy, steamy, sticky, sultry
humidity 4 smog **8** dampness, moisture **9** mugginess **10** stickiness
humiliate 5 abash, crush, shame **6** debase, humble, subdue **7** chagrin, chasten, degrade, mortify, put down **8** belittle, bring low, disgrace, dishonor **9** discomfit, embarrass **11** make ashamed **13** bring down a peg
humiliated 7 abashed, crushed, debased, humbled **8** degraded **9** chagrined, disgraced, mortified
humiliation 5 shame **7** chagrin **8** disgrace, dishonor **9** abasement **10** debasement **11** degradation **12** discomfiture **13** embarrassment, mortification
humility 7 modesty, shyness **8** meekness, timidity **9** lowliness **10** demureness, diffidence, humbleness **11** bashfulness **13** self-abasement **17** unpretentiousness
hummock 4 hill, rise **5** knoll, mound **7** hillock, tussock
Humologumena 17 New Testament books
humor 3 wit **4** baby, gags, mood, puns **5** farce, jests, jokes, spoil **6** cajole, comedy, joking, pamper, parody, satire, soothe, suffer, temper, whimsy **7** appease, flatter, foolery, fooling, indulge, jesting, mollify, placate, spirits, waggery **8** drollery, give in to, jocosity, low humor, nonsense, raillery, ridicule, tolerate, travesty, wordplay **9** burlesque, funniness, low comedy, put up with, slapstick, wittiness **10** buffoonery, caricature, comicality, comply with, high comedy, jocoseness, jocularity, tomfoolery, wisecracks, witticisms **11** broad comedy, disposition, foolishness, frame of mind, go along with **12** monkeyshines **13** ludicrousness **14** ridiculousness
humorist 3 wag, wit **4** card **5** comic **8** comedian
humorous 5 comic, droll, funny, witty **6** jocose **7** amusing, comical, jocular, waggish **8** farcical, mirthful, sportive

9 facetious, laughable, ludicrous, satirical, whimsical **10** ridiculous **11** nonsensical, rib-tickling **13** sidesplitting

hump 4 arch, bend, bump, knob, lift, lump, rise **5** bulge, hunch, knurl, mound, put up, tense **8** swelling **9** convexity **10** projection, prominence **11** excrescence

Humperdinck, Engelbert
  born: 4 Bonn **7** Germany
  composer of: 10 The Miracle **15** Hansel and Gretel

Humphry Clinker
  author: 19 Tobias George Smollet
  character: 10 Mr Dennison **12** Jerry Melford, Lydia Melford **14** George Dennison, Matthew Bramble **15** Winifred Jenkins **18** Miss Tabitha Bramble **26** Lieutenant Obadiah Lismahago

Humpty Dumpty
  character in: 12 nursery rhyme **22** Through the Looking Glass
  author: 7 Carroll

hunch 4 arch, bend, clue, hump, idea **5** tense **7** feeling, glimmer, inkling **8** good idea **9** intuition, suspicion **10** foreboding **11** premonition **12** presentiment

Hunchback of Notre Dame, The
  author: 10 Victor Hugo
  character: 9 Esmeralda, Gringoire, Quasimodo **12** Claude Frollo **20** Phoebus de Chateaupers

hunched 4 bent **7** crooked, slumped, stooped **9** contorted

hundredweight
  abbreviation: 3 cwt

Hungary
  capital/largest city: 8 Budapest
  others: 4 Gyor, Pecs **5** Harta **6** Mohacs, Sopron, Szeged **7** Komarom, Miskolc, Szentes **8** Dubrecen, Kaposuar, Szegedin **9** Kecskemet **10** Albertirsa **11** Nagykanizsa, Szombathely
  measure: 3 ako **4** hold, yoke **5** itcze, marok, metze **7** huvelyk
  monetary unit: 4 gara **5** balas, krone, pengo **6** filler, forint, gulden, korona, ongara, ungara
  weight: 7 vamfont **8** vammazsa
  island: 8 Margaret
  lake: 5 Ferto **7** Balaton, Velence **9** Blatensee **10** Neusiedler, Plattensee
  mountain: 4 Alps, Bukk **5** Matra, Tatra **6** Bakony, Mecsek, Vertes **7** Cserhat, Gerecse **8** Borzsony, Zempleni **9** Korishegy **10** Carpathian
  highest point: 5 Kekes
  river: 3 Mur, Sio **4** Duna, Raab, Raba, Sajo, Zala **5** Bodva, Drava, Drave, Ipoly, Kapos, Koros, Maros, Tarna, Tisza **6** Danube, Henrad, Poprad, Szamos, Theiss, Zagyva **7** Vistula **8** Berretyo
  physical feature:
    canal: 3 Sio **6** Sarviz

  forest: 6 Bakony
  plain: 6 Puszta
  port: 5 Fiume
  people: 3 Hun **4** Serb **5** Croat, Gypsy **6** Cigany, Magyar, Slovak, Ugrian
    composer: 5 Lehar, Liszt **6** Bartok, Kodaly
    national hero: 5 Arpad
    playwright: 6 Molnar
  language: 6 German, Magyar, Slovak **8** Croatian **9** Hungarian **10** Finno-Ugric
  religion: 8 Lutheran **9** Calvinism **13** Roman Catholic **16** Eastern Orthodoxy
  place:
    church: 32 Gothic Coronation Church of Matthias
    ruins: 8 Aquincum
    square: 6 Heroes
    tomb: 14 Turbe of Gul Baba **16** Father of the Roses
  feature:
    dance: 3 kos **7** czardas **10** varsoviana
    dog: 4 puli
    musical instrument: 8 taragata **9** czimbalom
  food:
    dish: 6 gulyas **7** goulash **15** chicken paprikas
    pastry: 4 rete **5** torte
    wine: 5 Tokay **10** Bulls Blood

hunger 3 yen **4** itch, love, lust, want, wish **5** crave, greed **6** desire, famine, hanker, liking, relish, thirst **7** burn for, craving, itch for, long for, pant for **8** appetite, fondness, voracity, yearn for, yearning **9** hankering, lust after **10** greediness, starvation **11** have a yen for, thirst after **12** malnutrition, ravenousness

hungry 5 eager **6** greedy **7** starved **8** ravenous, starving **9** voracious

hunk 3 gob, wad **4** clod, glob, lump, mass **5** block, chunk, piece **6** gobbet **7** portion **8** quantity

hunt 4 seek **5** chase, probe, shoot, stalk, trace, track, trail **6** course, follow, pursue **7** explore, go after, look for **8** coursing, drive out **9** ferret out, search for, try to find **11** go in quest of, inquire into **14** riding to hounds **20** leave no stone unturned

Hunt, Richard Morris
  architect of: 8 Biltmore (Asheville NC) **11** Marble House (Newport RI), The Breakers (Newport RI) **12** Lenox Library (NYC) **14** Studio Building (NYC) **19** National Observatory (Washington DC) **22** William Vanderbilt House (NYC) **23** Metropolitan Museum of Art (NYC)

hunter
  constellation of: 5 Orion
  French: 8 chasseur

Hunter, Jim

  nickname: 7 Catfish
  sport: 8 baseball
  position: 7 pitcher
  team: 14 New York Yankees **16** Oakland Athletics

Hunter, Kim
  real name: 8 Jane Cole
  born: 9 Detroit MI
  roles: 16 Stairway to Heaven, The Seventh Victim **21** A Streetcar Named Desire

Hunting
  god of: 7 Verbius
  goddess of: 5 Diana **7** Artemis

Hunting Dogs
  constellation of: 13 Canes Venatici

hurdle 4 jump, leap, snag, wall **5** bound, clear, fence, hedge, vault **6** hazard **7** barrier **8** obstacle, surmount **9** hindrance, roadblock **10** difficulty, impediment, spring over **11** obstruction **12** interference **14** stumbling block

hurl 4 cast, toss **5** chuck, fling, heave, pitch, sling, throw **6** launch, let fly, propel **7** fire off, project **9** discharge

hurly-burly 4 stir **5** furor **6** action, bustle, hubbub, hustle, uproar **8** activity **9** commotion **10** hullabaloo

hurrah, hurray 4 fine, good **5** bravo, cheer, great, huzza **6** huzzah, salute **7** acclaim, hosanna **9** excellent, halleluia, wonderful **10** exaltation, hallelujah

hurricane 7 cyclone, monsoon, tempest, typhoon **9** windstorm

Hurricane, The
  director: 8 John Ford
  cast: 7 Jon Hall **9** Mary Astor **12** C Aubrey Smith **13** Dorothy Lamour, Raymond Massey
  setting: 9 Manikoora

hurried 4 fast **5** hasty **6** hectic, rushed, speedy **7** cursory, frantic **8** careless, feverish, frenetic, headlong, slapdash, slipshod **9** breakneck, haphazard, impulsive **11** precipitate, superficial

hurry 3 ado, zip **4** bolt, dart, dash, fuss, goad, prod, rush, stew, whiz **5** egg on, haste, speed **6** flurry, hasten, hustle, push on, scurry, tumult, urge on **7** drive on, flutter, press on, scuttle, speed up, turmoil **8** make time, move fast, pressure, scramble, step on it **9** commotion, go quickly, make haste, step along **10** accelerate, get a move on, get hopping, lose no time, make tracks **11** come quickly, get cracking, go like a shot, go like sixty **12** step on the gas **13** go like the wind **14** cover the ground **15** hustle and bustle

hurt 3 cut, mar **4** ache, balk, burn, foil, harm, lame, maim, mark, maul, pain, pang, scar **5** agony, block, check, grief, limit, lower, pique, smart, spike, sting, stung **6** aching, bruise, damage, deface, dismay, grieve, hamper, hinder, impair, impede, injure, lessen, mangle, marked, miffed, misery, morose, narrow, offend, oppose, pained, piqued, reduce, retard, thwart, weaken **7** agonize, bruised, chagrin, cripple, crushed, damaged, disable, exclude, inhibit, injured, mangled, painful, scarred, scratch, torment, torture, trouble, wounded **8** aggrieve, crippled, decrease, dejected, diminish, disabled, dismayed, distress, encumber, hold back, minimize, mutilate, obstruct, offended, preclude, restrain, smarting, soreness, wretched **9** aggrieved, annoyance, chagrined, dejection, disfigure, forestall, frustrate, heartsick, indignant, miserable, mortified, mutilated, resentful, scratched, suffering **10** discomfort, distressed, heartbreak, melancholy, resentment **11** aggravation, crestfallen, heartbroken **12** disheartened, wretchedness **13** embarrassment, mortification

Hurt, John
born: **7** England **22** Chesterfield Derbyshire
roles: **5** Alien **8** Partners **9** I Claudius (TV: Caligula) **14** The Elephant Man **15** Midnight Express

Hurt, William
roles: **8** Body Heat **9** Gorky Park **10** Eyewitness **11** The Big Chill **13** Broadcast News **20** Kiss of the Spider Woman, Children of a Lesser God

hurtful 5 cruel **6** deadly **7** abusive, baleful, harmful **8** crushing, improper, stinging, wounding **9** injurious

hurtle 3 fly, hie, run, zip **4** bolt, dart, dash, race, rush, tear, whiz **5** bound, lunge, scoot, shoot, speed, spurt, whisk **6** charge, gallop, plunge, scurry **7** scamper, scuttle **11** go like a shot **13** go like the wind **14** go lickety-split

husband 3 man **4** keep, mate, save **5** amass, groom, hoard, hubby, store **6** old man, retain, save up, spouse **7** consort **8** conserve, maintain, preserve, set aside **10** accumulate, bridegroom, married man

husbandry 7 farming **9** geoponics **11** agriculture, crop- raising **12** conservation
god of: **9** Aristaeus

hush 4 calm **5** quell, quiet, shush, still **6** shut up, soothe **7** be quiet, be still, keep mum, mollify, silence **8** be silent, pipe down, quietude **9** quiet down, quietness, stillness **10** knock it off **11** tranquility **12** peacefulness, tranquillity

hushed 4 calm **5** quiet, still **6** calmed, gentle, lulled, silent **7** allayed, quieted, soothed, stifled **8** pacified, silenced, tranquil **12** tranquilized **13** tranquillized

hush money 5 bribe **6** payoff, payola **7** tribute **9** blackmail, extortion

huskiness 5 brawn **9** beefiness **10** hoarseness, robustness, ruggedness, sturdiness **11** muscularity

husky 3 big **5** beefy, burly, gruff, harsh, hefty, plump, rough, solid, stout, thick **6** brawny, coarse, hoarse, robust, stocky, strong, sturdy **7** cracked, grating, rasping, raucous, throaty **8** athletic, croaking, guttural, muscular, powerful, thickset **9** strapping **10** overweight **12** strong as an ox **15** broad-shouldered

husky, 8 Siberian
work: **7** sled dog

hussar 8 cavalier, horseman **10** cavalryman **12** horse soldier, horse trooper **14** mounted soldier

hussy 4 bawd, jade, minx, slut, tart **5** wench, whore **6** harlot, wanton **7** baggage, trollop **8** strumpet **9** brash girl, lewd woman, saucy miss **10** adulteress, loose woman, prostitute **11** brazen woman, fallen woman **12** scarlet woman **17** woman of easy virtue

hustle 3 ado, fly **4** bolt, dart, dash, fuss, prod, push, rush, stir, toss **5** elbow, hurry, nudge, scoot, shove, throw **6** bounce, bustle, flurry, hasten, hubbub, jostle, scurry, tumult **7** flutter, scuttle, speed up, turmoil **8** make time, scramble, shoulder, step on it **9** commotion, make haste, step along **10** lose no time **11** hurry-scurry, move quickly **12** be aggressive

hustler 4 doer **6** con man, dynamo, hooker **8** go-getter, live-wire, swindler **10** prostitute **12** streetwalker

Hustler, The
director: **12** Robert Rossen
cast: **10** Paul Newman **11** Piper Laurie **12** George C Scott **13** Jackie Gleason (Minnesota Fats)

Huston, John
director of: **8** Key Largo **10** The Misfits **11** Moulin Rouge **12** Prizzi's Honor **13** Asphalt Jungle **15** The African Queen **16** The Maltese Falcon **19** The Night of the Iguana **27** The Treasure of the Sierra Madre (Oscar)
father: **12** Walter Huston
wife: **11** Evelyn Keyes
born: **8** Nevada MO
daughter: **8** Anjelica
roles: **9** Chinatown **11** Winter Kills

Huston, Walter
real name: **15** Walter Houghston
son: **10** John Huston
born: **6** Canada **7** Toronto
roles: **9** Dodsworth **18** All That Money Can Buy **27** The Treasure of the Sierra Madre

hut 4 shed **5** cabin, hutch, shack **6** lean-to, shanty **7** cottage, shelter

hutch 3 pen, sty **4** cage, coop, cote, crib, shed **5** stall **9** enclosure

Hutchinson, A S M
author of: **13** If Winter Comes

Hutton, Betty
real name: **18** Betty June Thornburg
born: **13** Battle Creek MI
roles: **15** Annie Get Your Gun **19** Greatest Show on Earth

Hutton, James
field: **7** geology
nationality: **8** Scottish
founder of: **7** geology

Hutton, Timothy
father: **9** Jim Hutton
roles: **4** Taps **6** Daniel **14** Ordinary People **22** The Falcon and the Snowman

Huxley, Aldous
author of: **11** Crome Yellow **13** Brave New World **17** Point Counter Point
brother: **6** Julian

Huxley, Julian
field: **7** biology
nationality: **7** British
promoted theory of: **9** evolution

Huygens, Christiaan
nationality: **5** Dutch
invented: **13** pendulum clock
discovered: **12** Saturn's rings
formulated: **17** wave theory of light

hyacinth 10 Hyacinthus **20** Hyacinthus orientalis
varieties: **4** musk, pine, star, wild, wood **5** Dutch, grape, Roman, water **6** common, garden, meadow, nutmeg, starry, summer, Tassel **7** feather, peacock **11** common grape

Hyacinthus
father: **7** Amyclas
daughter: **7** Orthaea
loved by: **6** Apollo **8** Zephyrus
killed by: **5** quoit **6** discus
from his blood sprang: **6** flower
petals marked: **4** AI-AI
means: **4** alas

Hyades
also: **5** Hyads **10** Palilicium
form: **6** nymphs
father: **5** Atlas **7** Oceanus
mother: **6** Tethys **7** Pleione
sisters: **8** Pleiades
nurtured: **8** Dionysus
placed among: **5** stars

hybrid 5 cross **7** amalgam, mixture **9** composite, half- breed **10** crossbreed

hybridize 5 cross **14** cross-fertilize, cross-pollinate

Hydra
form: **12** water serpent
number of heads: **4** nine
killed by: **8** Hercules

hydrangea
varieties: **4** Wild **6** French, Peegee **8** Climbing

hydrogen
  chemical symbol: **1** H
hydrophobia 6 rabies
  fear of: **5** water
Hygeia
  father: **9** Asclepius
  goddess of: **6** health
  corresponds to: **5** Salus
hygienic 4 pure **5** clean **7** aseptic,
  healthy, sterile **8** germ- free, harmless,
  salutary, sanitary **9** healthful, wholesome **10** salubrious, unpolluted **11**
  disease-free, disinfected, uninjurious
  12 prophylactic **14** uncontaminated
Hylaeus
  form: **7** centaur
  born on: **5** cloud
Hymen
  also: **9** Hymenaeus
  god of: **8** marriage
  holds: **5** torch
  corresponds to: **8** Talassio
hymenoptera
  class: **8** hexapoda
  phylum: **10** arthropoda
  group: **3** ant, bee **4** wasp **6** chacid,
  sawfly **12** ichneumon fly
hymn 5 paean, psalm **6** anthem **12**
  song of praise **14** devotional song **17**
  song in praise of God
Hymn to Proserpine
  author: **24** Algernon Charles Swinburne
Hypatia
  author: **15** Charles Kingsley
hyper 7 keyed-up **10** high-strung, over-
  active
hyperbole 8 metaphor **11** enlargement
  12 exaggeration **13** magnification,
  overstatement **14** figure of speech
hyperbolize 6 overdo **7** amplify, magnify, stretch **9** embroider, overstate **10**
  exaggerate
hyperborean 6 arctic **8** freezing,
  northern **13** septentrional

Hyperborean
  inhabitant of: **8** Paradise
Hyperion
  also: **6** Helios
  form: **5** Titan
  father: **6** Uranus
  mother: **4** Gaea
  sister: **5** Theia
  son: **6** Helios
  daughter: **3** Eos **6** Selene
  corresponds to: **6** Apollo
Hyperion
  author: **9** John Keats **24** Henry Wadsworth Longfellow
hypersensitive 6 touchy **9** emotional
  13 temperamental
Hypnos
  also: **6** Hypnus
  god of: **5** sleep
  father: **6** Erebus
  mother: **3** Nyx
  brother: **8** Thanatos
  corresponds to: **6** Somnus
hypnotic 9 soporific **11** mesmerizing
  12 spellbinding
hypnotize 7 control **9** mesmerize,
  spellbind
hypocrisy 6 deceit, fakery **7** falsity **9**
  duplicity, mendacity, phoniness **10**
  dishonesty **11** dissembling, insincerity
  12 two-facedness
hypocrite 5 phony **8** deceiver **9** pretender **10** dissembler
Hypocrite 15 whited sepulcher
hypocritical 5 false, phony **7** feigned
  8 feigning, two- faced **9** deceitful, deceptive, dishonest, insincere, truthless
  11 counterfeit
hyporchema
  form: **9** choral ode
  origin: **5** Greek
  honored: **6** Apollo **8** Dionysus
hypothalamus
  regulates: **15** body temperature
  located in: **5** brain

hypothesis 6 theory, thesis **7** premise,
  theorem **8** proposal **9** assertion, postulate **10** assumption, conclusion,
  conjecture **11** explanation, guesstimate, presumption, proposition, speculation, supposition
hypothesize 5 infer **6** assume **7** imagine, presume, suppose **8** theorize **9**
  postulate, speculate **10** conjecture
hypothetical 7 assumed, dubious **8**
  possible, supposed **9** imaginary, uncertain **10** contingent, postulated **11**
  conditional, conjectural, presumptive,
  speculative, theoretical **12** questionable **13** suppositional
Hypselosaurus
  type: **8** dinosaur, sauropod
  location: **6** France **8** Mongolia
  period: **10** Cretaceous
Hypsilophodon
  type: **8** dinosaur **10** ornithopod
  location: **7** England
  period: **10** Cretaceous
Hyrie
  transformed into: **4** swan
hyssop 8 Hyssopus **18** Hyssopus offi-
  cialis
  varieties: **5** anise, giant, water **9** blue
  giant **10** nettle-leaf **11** fennel giant,
  purple giant, yellow giant **12** Mexican giant **13** fragrant giant, wrinkled
  giant
Hyssop 13 Biblical plant
hysteria 3 fit **5** panic **6** frenzy **8** delirium
hysterical 5 crazy, droll **6** absurd,
  crazed, raving **7** amusing, comical **8**
  farcical, frenzied, worked-up **9** laughable, ludicrous, wrought-up **10** distracted, distraught, ridiculous, uproarious **11** carried away, overwrought,
  wildly funny **13** beside oneself, out of
  one's wits **14** uncontrollable
hysterics 3 fit **12** emotionalism

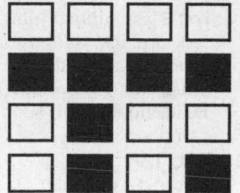

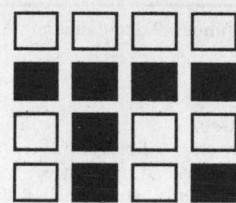

I, Claudius
  author: **12** Robert Graves
  story of: **36** Tiberius Claudius Drusus
    Nero Germanicus (Emperor of Rome)
    (on Masterpiece Theater) actors: **8**
    John Hurt **11** Derek Jacobi, Sheila
    White **12** Brian Blessed, Sian Phillips
    14 Patrick Stewart, Margaret Tyzack

I, the Jury
  author: **14** Mickey Spillane
  hero: **10** Mike Hammer

**I Am a Fugitive from a Chain
Gang**
  director: **11** Mervyn LeRoy
  cast: **8** Paul Muni **11** Helen Vinson
    13 Glenda Farrell, Preston Foster

I am unwilling to contend
  Latin: **14** nolo contendere

Ibanez, Vicente Blasco
  author of: **30** The Four Horsemen
    of the Apocalypse

Iberian Peninsula
  also: **8** Hesperia
  comprising: **5** Spain **8** Portugal

Ibsen, Henrik
  author of: **6** Ghosts **8** Peer Gynt **11**
    A Doll's House, Hedda Gabler,
    Rosmersholm, The Wild Duck **16**
    The Master Builder **18** An Enemy of
    the People, John Gabriel Borkman

I came, I saw, I conquered
  Latin: **12** veni vidi vici
  author: **12** Julius Caesar

Icarus
  father: **8** Daedalus
  built: **5** wings
  flew too near: **3** sun
  death by: **8** drowning

ICC 28 Interstate Commerce Commission

ice 3 gem **4** berg, floe, gems, rime **5**
  chill, frost, glace **6** freeze, icicle,
  jewels **7** crystal, dessert, glacier, jewelry, sherbet **8** diamonds **11** refrigerant, refrigerate

ice-cold 3 icy **4** cold **5** gelid, polar **6**
  arctic, bitter, frigid, frosty, wintry **7**
  chilled, frosted, glacial, subzero **8**
  chilling, freezing, Siberian, unheated,
  unwarmed **9** stone-cold, supercold **11**
  hyperborean, supercooled **12** bone-
  chilling

ice cream 7 dessert, sherbet **4** soda **5**
  glace **6** frappe, sundae **7** dessert, parfait, sherbet, spumoni, tortoni

Iceland
  other name: **15** Lydveldid Island
  capital/largest city: **9** Reykjavik
  others: **3** Hof **6** Geysir **7** Akranes,
    Husavik **8** Akureyri, Keflavik, Ko-
    pasker **9** Kopavogur **10** Hveragerdi,
    Isafjordur **12** Siglufjordur **13** Hafnar-
    fjordur, Neskaupstadur, Seydisfjordur
  government:
    general assembly: **7** Althing
  measure: **3** set **4** alin **5** almud **6** al-
    menn, ferfet, pattur **7** fathmur, fer-
    mila, oltunna
  monetary unit: **5** aurar, eyrir, krona
  weight: **4** pund **5** pound, tunna **6**
    smjors
  island: **7** Heimaey, Surtsey, Westman
  lake: **6** Myvatn **10** Thorisvatn
    14 Thingvallavatn
  mountain: **5** Jokul **10** Orafajokul
    volcano: **4** Laki **5** Askja, Hekla,
      Katla **7** Surtsey
  highest point: **17** Hvannadalshjukur
  river: **5** Hvita **7** Fnjoska, Thjorsa **15**
    Jokulsa a Fjollum
  sea: **9** Greenland **13** North Atlantic
  physical feature:
    fjord: **4** Eyja
    geyser: **5** gryla **6** geysir **11** Great
      Gusher
    glacier: **6** Jokull **11** Orafajokull,
      Vatnajokull
    plain: **15** Skeidharasandur
    waterfall: **8** Godafoss, Gullfoss **9**
      Dettifoss
  people: **6** Celtic, Viking **8** Norseman
    9 Norwegian
    first settler: **8** Arnarson
    hero: **4** Bele, Eric, Leif **10** Sigurds-
      son
  language: **5** Norse **9** Icelandic
  religion: **19** Evangelical Lutheran
  place:
    national shrine: **11** Thingvellir
  feature:
    airport: **9** Kopavogur
    bird: **4** gull **6** falcon **9** gyrfalcon
    literary genre: **4** saga
    wrestling: **5** glima
  food:
    dish: **4** skyr, svio **7** bloomor **8**
      harofisk

Iceman
  nickname of: **12** George Gervin

Iceman Cometh, The
  author: **12** Eugene O'Neill
  role: **6** Hickey

Ice Palace
  author: **10** Edna Ferber

ice skating
  athlete: **9** Janet Lynn, John Curry **10**
    Carol Heiss, Dick Button, Eric Hei-
    den, Sonja Henie **11** Sheila Young
    12 Peggy Fleming, Tara Lipinski **13**
    Dorothy Hamill, Scott Hamilton **14**
    Linda Fratianne

ich dien 6 I serve
  motto of: **13** Prince of Wales

I Ching 30 ancient Chinese book of
  divination

ichor
  form: **5** fluid
  in veins of: **4** gods

Ichthyocentaur
  form: **8** creature
  location: **3** sea
  head/torso: **5** human
  legs: **5** horse
  tail: **4** fish

iciness 4 cold **5** chill **9** frigidity **10**
  chilliness, frostiness, wintriness **12**
  slipperiness

ici on parle francais 18 French is
  spoken here **19** here one speaks
  French

icky 5 gluey, gooey, gross, gucky,
  gummy, mushy, nasty, tacky, weepy
  6 sticky, syrupy, viscid **7** maudlin,
  viscous **8** bathetic **9** glutinous, offensive, repulsive, revolting **10** disgusting
  12 mucilaginous

icon, ikon 4 idol **5** image **6** effigy, figure, statue **7** picture **8** likeness **11** sacred image

iconoclast 5 rebel **7** radical, upstart **9**
  dissenter **13** nonconformist, revolutionary

icy 3 raw **4** cold, cool **5** aloof, gelid **6**
  arctic, chilly, frigid, frosty, frozen,
  glazed, sleety, wintry **7** distant, glacial, haughty, hostile **8** chilling, freezing, slippery **9** impassive **10** forbidding, unfriendly **11** coldhearted,
  unemotional

Ida
  form: **5** nymph
  watched over: **4** Zeus
  mount: **5** Crete **7** Phrygia

Idaea
  form: **5** nymph
  domain: **8** Mount Ida

husband: 7 Phineus **9** Scamander
son: 6 Teucer

Idaho
 abbreviation: 2 ID **3** Ida
 nickname: 3 Gem
 capital/largest city: 5 Boise
 others: 4 Buhl **5** Malad, Nampa **6** Moscow **7** Orofino, Rexburg **8** Caldwell, Lewiston **9** Pocatello, Twin Falls **10** Idaho Falls **11** Coeur d'Alene
 college: 17 Northwest Nazarene
 explorer: 13 Lewis and Clark
 feature: 9 Sun Valley **17** Continental Divide
   dam: 5 Oxbow **8** Brownlee
   national monument: 16 Craters of the Moon
 tribe: 5 Banak, Shake **6** Cayuse, Paiute, Spokan **7** Bannock, Kutenai, Spokane **8** Kalispel, Nez Perce, Sahaptin, Shoshone, Shoshoni **9** Shoshonee **11** Coeur d'Alene
 people: 9 Ezra Pound, Sacagawea **11** Chief Joseph **17** William Edgar Borah
 lake: 4 Bear **5** Grey's **6** Priest **11** Coeur d'Alene, Pend Oreille **22** American Falls Reservoir
 land rank: 10 thirteenth
 mountain: 4 Ryan **5** Rocky **6** Rhodes, Taylor, Tetons **7** Cabinet **8** Bannocks, Big Baldy, Bluenose, Sawtooth **9** Wasatches **10** Clearwater **11** Beaverheads, Bitterroots **13** Selkirk Ranges
   highest point: 5 Borah
 physical feature:
   falls: 5 Moyie **8** Shoshone **9** Upper Mesa
   springs: 4 Soda **6** Hooper **7** Lavahot
 river: 4 Bear **5** Boise, Snake, St Joè **6** Locksa, Salmon **7** Payette, Spokane **8** Kootenai **11** Coeur d'Alene, Pend Oreille
 state admission: 10 forty-third
 state bird: 16 mountain bluebird
 state flower: 7 syringa
 state motto: 13 It Is Perpetual **16** Let It Be Perpetual
 state song: 15 Here We Have Idaho
 state tree: 16 western white pine

Idas
 father: 8 Aphareus
 mother: 5 Arene
 brother: 7 Lynceus
 wife: 8 Marpessa
 daughter: 9 Cleopatra

idea 4 clue, hint, view **6** belief, notion **7** concept, feeling, inkling, insight, opinion, outlook, thought **8** approach, proposal, solution **9** sentiment **10** conception, conclusion, conviction, impression, indication, intimation, suggestion **12** apperception, appreciation **13** approximation, mental picture, understanding **14** interpretation, recommendation

ideal 3 aim **4** hero, idol **5** dream, model **7** epitome, optimal, pattern, perfect **8** exemplar, last word, paradigm, standard, ultimate **9** archetype, criterion, excellent, exemplary, faultless, matchless, objective **10** impeccable **11** inspiration

idealism 8 optimism **9** meliorism **10** utopianism **11** romanticism

idealist 7 dreamer, utopian **8** romantic **9** Pollyanna, stargazer, visionary **11** romanticist **13** perfectionist

idealized 6 dreamy **7** utopian, wishful **8** fanciful, illusory, romantic **10** optimistic **11** pie-in-the-sky, unrealistic **13** insubstantial

idea man 7 advisor **8** inventor **9** innovator **10** consultant **12** entrepreneur

idee fixe 9 fixed idea
 music: 14 recurring motif

idem 24 the same as previously given **28** the same as previously mentioned

identical 4 twin **7** uniform **8** self-same, very same **9** duplicate **15** interchangeable **17** indistinguishable

identification 2 ID **5** badge, label **6** dogtag **7** license **8** passport **9** detection **10** connection, revelation **11** affiliation, association, credentials, pinpointing, recognition **12** confirmation, verification **13** ascertainment

identify 4 know **5** place **6** finger, verify **7** combine, pick out, specify **9** associate, designate, determine, recognize, single out **11** distinguish

identifying device 4 logo, mark, sign **5** badge **6** emblem, ensign, symbol **8** insignia, logotype

identity 4 name, self **6** accord **7** harmony, oneness, rapport **9** unanimity **11** delineation, duplication, personality **13** individuality **15** differentiation, distinctiveness

ideology 5 dogma, ethos **6** ideals, theory **7** program **8** doctrine **9** rationale **10** principles

Ides of March, The
 author: 14 Thornton Wilder

id est 6 that is
 abbreviation: 2 ie

idiocy 5 folly **6** lunacy **7** fatuity, inanity, madness, suicide **8** insanity **9** absurdity, asininity, cretinism, mongolism, stupidity **11** foolishness **13** foolhardiness, senselessness

idiom 5 argot, lingo, slang **6** brogue, jargon, patois, phrase, speech **7** dialect **8** language, localism, parlance **10** vernacular **13** colloquialism

idiomatic 6 common **8** informal, ordinary **10** vernacular **14** conversational

idiosyncrasy 3 tic **5** quirk **6** oddity **7** anomaly **9** mannerism **11** distinction, peculiarity **12** eccentricity

idiot 3 ass **4** boob, dolt, dope, fool, jerk **5** cluck, dummy, dunce, moron, ninny **6** cretin, dimwit, nitwit **7** halfwit **8** dumbbell, numskull **9** blockhead, numbskull, simpleton **10** nincompoop

Idiot, The
 author: 16 Fyodor Dostoevsky
 character: 7 Myshkin **11** Mme Epanchin **14** Aglaya Epanchin, Parfen Rogozhin **16** Natasya Filipovna **19** Ganya Ardalionovitch **22** Prince Lef Nicolaievitch

idiotic 5 crazy, dopey, nutty **6** absurd, addled, stupid **7** asinine, doltish, foolish, moronic **9** foolhardy, imbecilic, senseless **10** half-witted, irrational, ridiculous **12** feebleminded **13** rattlebrained

I direct
 Latin: 6 dirigo
 motto of: 5 Maine

idle 4 laze, lazy, loaf, vain **5** empty, inert, petty, vapid, waste, while **6** drowsy, fallow, futile, otiose, putter, torpid, unused **7** aimless, fritter, jobless, languid, trivial, useless, wait out **8** baseless, bootless, fool away, inactive, indolent, listless, slothful, sluggish, trifling **9** at leisure, enervated, fruitless, lethargic, out of work, pointless, somnolent, valueless, worthless **10** not working, unemployed, unoccupied **11** unimportant **12** unproductive **15** unsubstantiated

idleness 5 sloth **7** inertia **8** laziness, lethargy **9** indolence **10** inactivity **11** joblessness, languidness **12** sluggishness, unemployment
 French: 8 flanerie

idler 3 bum **6** loafer **7** drifter, vagrant **10** ne'er-do-well
 French: 7 flaneur

idol 4 hero, icon **5** relic **6** effigy, statue **7** darling **8** artifact **9** superstar **10** simulacrum, golden calf **11** graven image, inspiration

idolatry 5 mania **7** madness, passion, worship **8** devotion **9** adoration, obsession **10** veneration **11** idolization, infatuation **12** image worship **13** preoccupation

idolization 7 worship **9** adulation, reverence **10** exaltation, veneration

idolize 5 adore, deify, honor, prize **6** admire, revere **7** worship **8** treasure, venerate **9** reverence **11** apotheosize

Idomeneo, re di Creta
 also: 20 Idomeneus King of Crete
 opera by: 6 Mozart
 character: 4 Ilia **7** Electra **8** Idamante, Poseidon

Idomeneus
 king of: 5 Crete
 father: 9 Deucalion

I don't know what
 French: 12 je ne sais quoi

I Dream of Jeannie
character: 7 Jeannie **9** Dr Bellows **10** (Captain) Tony Nelson **11** Gen Peterson, (Captain) Roger Healey **13** Amanda Bellows
cast: 9 Bill Daily **11** Barbara Eden, Hayden Rorke, Larry Hagman **13** Barton MacLane, Emmaline Henry
Tony's job: 9 astronaut

idyllic 6 rustic, sylvan **7** bucolic **8** arcadian, pastoral, peaceful, romantic **9** unspoiled

Idylls of the King, The
author: 18 Alfred Lord Tennyson
based on story of: 10 King Arthur

if 2 an **6** though **7** whether **8** although, provided **9** condition, supposing **10** even though **11** stipulation, supposition

iffy 4 moot **5** risky **6** chancy, unsure **7** dubious, erratic **8** arguable, doubtful **9** debatable, uncertain, undecided, unsettled, whimsical **10** capricious, disputable, unresolved **11** conjectural, speculative **12** questionable **13** problematical, unpredictable

If Winter Comes
author: 13 A S M Hutchinson

if you please
French: 12 s'il vous plait

ignitable 8 burnable **9** flammable **10** combustive, incendiary **11** combustible, inflammable **13** conflagrative

ignite 4 burn, fire **5** blaze, flame, light **6** blow up, kindle **7** explode, inflame **8** take fire, touch off **9** catch fire, set fire to, set on fire **11** catch on fire

ignoble 3 low **4** base, foul, mean, vile **6** craven **7** debased, heinous **8** cowardly, degraded, depraved, indecent, infamous, inferior, shameful, unworthy **9** dastardly, nefarious **10** degenerate, despicable **11** disgraceful **12** contemptible, dishonorable **13** discreditable, pusillanimous **14** unconscionable

ignominious 3 low **5** sorry **6** abject **8** grievous, shameful, wretched **9** degrading **10** despicable, inglorious, unbearable **11** disgraceful, humiliating **12** dishonorable, disreputable **13** discreditable

ignominy 5 shame **6** infamy **8** contempt, disgrace, dishonor **11** degradation, humiliation

ignoramus 4 fool **5** dunce **6** nitwit **7** low-brow **8** numskull **9** numbskull, simpleton **10** illiterate **11** know-nothing

ignorance 9 confusion **10** illiteracy **11** unawareness **12** backwardness **13** obliviousness, unfamiliarity **15** unenlightenment

ignorant 4 dumb **5** naive **6** stupid **7** asinine, blind to, fatuous, shallow, unaware **8** innocent, untaught **9** in the dark, unknowing, unlearned, un-

trained, untutored, unworldly **10** illiterate, uneducated, uninformed, unlettered, unschooled **11** insensitive, uncognizant **12** unperceptive **13** irresponsible, unenlightened, unintelligent **15** unknowledgeable

ignore 4 omit, skip, snub **5** scorn **6** eschew, slight **7** neglect **8** overlook, pass over **9** disregard

Igraine
character in: 16 Arthurian romance
son: 6 Arthur
by: 14 Uther Pendragon

Iguanodon
type: 8 dinosaur **10** ornithopod
means: 11 iguana tooth
found by: 13 Gideon Mantell
location: 6 Africa, Europe, Sussex **7** Belgium, England
period: 10 Cretaceous
characteristic: 10 duck-billed

ikebana
Japanese: 21 art of arranging flowers

Ile de France *see* **9** Mauritius

Ilha Formosa *see* **6** Taiwan

Iliad, The
author: 5 Homer
character: 5 Paris, Priam **6** Hector **8** Achilles, Menelaus **9** Agamemnon, Patroclus **11** Helen of Troy
subject: 9 Trojan War

Iliniwek *see* **8** Illinois

Ilion
Greek name for: 11 ancient Troy

Ilium
Latin name for: 11 ancient Troy

ill, ills 3 woe **4** evil, foul, harm, sick, vile **5** abuse, cross, no way, surly, trial **6** ailing, damage, hardly, injury, laid up, malady, malice, nowise, plague, poorly, sickly, sorrow, unkind, unwell, wicked **7** ailment, cruelty, disease, failing, harmful, invalid, not well, ominous, outrage, peevish, trouble, unlucky, unsound **8** diseased, mischief, scarcely, sinister, vengeful **9** afflicted, complaint, infirmity, malicious, unhealthy **10** affliction, disturbing, foreboding, indisposed, misfortune, wickedness **11** abomination, acrimonious, malefaction, threatening, unfavorable **12** inauspicious, unpropitious **15** under the weather

ill-advised 4 dumb, rash **5** hasty, silly **6** myopic, stupid, unwise **7** foolish **9** foolhardy, ill-judged, impolitic, imprudent, misguided, senseless **10** indiscreet, unthinking **11** injudicious **12** shortsighted **13** ill-considered, irresponsible

ill-at-ease 3 shy **4** edgy **6** on edge, uneasy **7** abashed, fidgety, nervous **8** bothered, troubled **9** disturbed, nonplused, perturbed **10** disquieted, nonplussed **11** discomfited, discomposed, embarrassed **12** disconcerted **13** self-

conscious, uncomfortable **15** discountenanced

ill-boding 4 dire **7** ominous **9** ill-omened **11** apocalyptic **12** inauspicious

ill-bred 4 rude **5** crude **7** boorish, uncivil, uncouth **8** churlish, impolite **10** unmannerly **11** ill-mannered **12** discourteous

ill-defined 3 dim **4** hazy **5** faint, murky **6** blurry **7** blurred, clouded, shadowy **8** nebulous, obscured **10** indistinct

illegal 5 wrong **6** banned **7** illicit **8** criminal, not legal, outlawed, unlawful **9** felonious, forbidden **10** actionable, prohibited, proscribed **12** illegitimate, unauthorized, unsanctioned **13** against the law

illegible 7 unclear **8** obscured **9** scribbled **10** unreadable **14** indecipherable, undecipherable, unintelligible

illegitimate 7 bastard, illegal, illicit, lawless, natural **8** baseborn, improper, unlawful **10** prohibited **11** misbegotten, unwarranted **12** unauthorized, unsanctioned

ill-fated 6 doomed, jinxed **7** hapless, unlucky **8** blighted, luckless **9** ill-omened **10** ill-starred

ill-favored 4 ugly **5** plain **6** homely **8** unlovely **9** repulsive, unsightly **12** disagreeable, unattractive

ill-fortune 6 mishap **7** bad luck **8** calamity, disaster, hardship **9** adversity **10** misfortune **11** catastrophe

ill health 6 malady **7** ailment, disease, illness **8** sickness **9** infirmity

ill-humored 5 sulky, testy **6** crabby, grumpy, sullen **7** grouchy **10** in a bad mood, unfriendly, unsociable

illiberal 5 petty, small **6** biased, narrow **7** bigoted **9** hidebound **10** brassbound, intolerant, prejudiced, ungenerous **11** opinionated, small-minded **12** narrow-minded, short-sighted

illicit 7 illegal, lawless **8** criminal, improper, not legal, unlawful **9** felonious **10** prohibited **11** black-market, clandestine **12** illegitimate, not permitted, unauthorized **13** against the law, impermissible **15** under-the-counter

Illinois
abbreviation: 2 IL **3** Ill
nickname: 4 Tall **6** Sucker **7** Prairie **13** Land of Lincoln
capital: 11 Springfield
largest city: 7 Chicago
others: 4 Pana **5** Alton, Cairo, Elgin, Flora, Olney, Pekin **6** Albion, Berwyn, Canton, Herrin, Joliet, Peoria, Skokie **7** Batavia, Decatur, Genesco, Mendota, Nokomis **8** Evanston, Rockford, Waukegan **9** Centralia **10** Barrington **11** Bloomington
college: 4 Knox **5** Barat **6** Aurora, DePaul, Eureka, Loyola, Olivet,

Quincy, Shimer **7** Bradley, Chicago, Wheaton **8** Millikin **9** Augustana **12** Northwestern **16** Illinois Wesleyan **23** Illinois Institute of Tech
explorer: 6 Joliet **7** Jolliet **9** Marquette
feature: 10 stockyards
  airport: 5 O'Hare
  museum: 18 Science and Industry
  seaway: 10 St Lawrence
  trail: 7 Lincoln
tribe: 3 Fox **4** Sauk **9** Kaskaskia
people: 9 Black Hawk, Jack Benny **10** Jane Addams, Walt Disney **12** Carl Sandburg **15** Ernest Hemingway **18** Engineer Casey Jones **20** William Jennings Bryan
lake: 3 Fox **5** Grass **7** Calumet **8** Michigan, Pistakee
land rank: 12 twenty-fourth
mountain: 6 Ozarks
  highest point: 12 Charles Mound
physical feature:
  hills: 7 Shawnee
president: 14 Abraham Lincoln
river: 4 Ohio, Rock **5** Spoon **6** Wabash **7** Chicago, Elkhorn **8** Big Muddy, Illinois, Mackinaw, Sangamon **9** Kaskaskia **10** Des Plaines **11** Mississippi
state admission: 11 twenty-first
state bird: 8 cardinal
state flower: 6 violet
state motto: 29 State Sovereignty, National Union
state song: 8 Illinois
state tree: 7 burl oak **8** white oak

Illinois (Iliniwek)
language family: 9 Algonkian **10** Algonquian
tribe: 6 Peoria **7** Cahokia, Tamaroa **9** Kaskaskia, Moingwena **10** Michigamea
location: 4 Iowa, Ohio **7** Indiana **8** Illinois, Michigan, Missouri **9** Wisconsin
built: 12 Cahokia Mound
murdered: 7 Pontiac
related to: 5 Miami **6** Ojibwa **7** Ojibway

illiterate 7 witless **8** childish, ignorant, unversed **9** unlearned, untutored **10** amateurish, incoherent, uneducated, uninformed, unlettered, unreliable, unschooled **11** not educated, uninitiated, unscholarly **12** uninstructed **13** unenlightened, ungrammatical **15** unknowledgeable

ill-made 6 shoddy **7** awkward **8** deformed, inferior **9** makeshift, malformed **10** jerry-built, jury-rigged **15** misproportioned

ill-mannered 4 rude **5** crude **6** coarse **7** boorish, ill-bred, loutish, uncivil **8** impolite **9** offensive, ungallant **10** ill-behaved, ungracious **12** discourteous **13** disrespectful

ill-natured 4 sour **5** cross, nasty, surly **6** bitter, cranky, malign **7** caustic, grouchy, peevish **8** captious, churlish, spiteful, venomous **9** crotchety, irascible, irritable, malignant, rancorous, splenetic **10** ill-humored, unfriendly **11** acrimonious, contentious, quarrelsome **12** antagonistic, cantankerous

illness 6 malady **7** ailment, disease **8** disorder, sickness **9** complaint, ill health, infirmity **10** affliction, disability, poor health **11** malfunction **13** indisposition

illogical 4 wild **5** crazy, dopey, nutty, silly, wacky **6** absurd, far-out, screwy **7** asinine, offbeat, unsound **9** erroneous, senseless **10** fallacious, irrational, off-the-wall, ridiculous **11** incongruent, incongruous, nonsensical, unreasoning **12** inconsistent, preposterous, unreasonable **13** contradictory

ill-omened 4 dire **7** adverse, ominous **9** ill-boding **11** apocalyptic, unfavorable **12** inauspicious, unpropitious

ill-smelling 4 foul, high, olid, rank **5** fetid, fusty **6** putrid, rancid, smelly, stinky, strong **7** reeking **8** stinking **10** malodorous

ill-starred 4 dire **5** fatal **6** tragic **7** adverse **8** ill-fated **10** calamitous, disastrous **11** unfortunate **12** catastrophic, inauspicious

ill-suited 5 inapt **8** mismated, unsuited **9** misjoined, unfitting **10** ill-adapted, ill-matched, malapropos, mismatched, unbecoming, unsuitable **11** incongruous, unbefitting, uncongenial **12** incompatible, inconsistent **13** inappropriate

ill-tempered 4 mean, rude, sour **5** angry, cross, harsh, nasty, testy **6** bitter, cranky, shirty **7** acerbic, furious, grouchy, peevish, waspish **8** choleric, churlish, petulant **9** crotchety, irascible, irritable **10** bad-natured, ill-humored, ill-natured, in a bad mood, unpleasant **11** acrimonious **12** cantankerous

ill-treatment 4 harm **5** abuse **6** ill-use, injury, misuse **7** cruelty **13** mortification

illuminate 5 edify, light **7** clarify, enhance, explain, light up **8** brighten, illumine, instruct, spell out **9** elucidate, enlighten, exemplify, irradiate, make clear **12** throw light on **13** cast light upon

illuminated 3 lit **5** lit up **6** bright **7** lighted **9** clarified, decorated, illumined **10** brightened, elucidated, irradiated

illumination 6 lights, wisdom **7** insight **8** lighting **9** education, knowledge **10** illuming, lighting up, perception, revelation **11** edification, information, instruction, irradiation **13** comprehension, enlightenment

Illuminations, Les
author: 13 Arthur Rimbaud
illumined 3 lit **7** lighted **8** luminous **11** illuminated

ill-use 4 harm, hurt **5** abuse **6** injure, misuse **7** assault, cruelty, harming **8** maltreat, mistreat **10** bodily harm **12** maltreatment, mistreatment

illusion 5 error, fancy **6** mirage, vagary, vision **7** caprice, chimera, fallacy **8** delusion, phantasm **9** deception, false idea, misbelief, semblance, unreality **10** apparition, false image, hocus-pocus, humbuggery, impression **11** false belief, fata morgana **13** hallucination, misconception, misimpression **15** misapprehension

illusive 5 false **6** unreal **7** phantom, seeming **8** apparent, chimeric, fanciful, fantastic, illusory **9** deceptive **10** ostensible **11** illusionary

illusory 4 sham **5** false **6** unreal **7** seeming **8** apparent, delusive, fanciful, illusive, spurious **9** deceptive, erroneous, imaginary **10** fallacious, misleading, ostensible **11** counterfeit, unrealistic **13** hallucinatory

illustrate 4 show **6** define **7** clarify, explain, picture, point up, portray **8** decorate, ornament **9** bring home, delineate, elucidate, emphasize, make clear, represent **10** illuminate **11** demonstrate **12** pictorialize, throw light on **16** make intelligible

illustration 5 image, plate **6** figure **7** drawing, example, picture **8** instance, specimen **9** portrayal **10** photograph **14** representation **15** exemplification

illustrious 5 famed, great, noted **6** famous **7** eminent, honored, notable **8** glorious, lustrous, peerless, renowned, splendid **9** acclaimed, brilliant, exemplary, matchless, prominent **10** celebrated **11** magnificent **13** distinguished

illustriousness 8 grandeur **9** greatness **11** distinction **12** magnificence

ill will 4 gall **5** anger, spite **6** animus, enmity, hatred, malice, rancor, spleen **7** dislike **8** acrimony, aversion, bad blood, loathing **9** animosity, antipathy, hostility **10** abhorrence, antagonism, bitterness, contention **11** malevolence **12** hard feelings, spitefulness

ill wind 7 bad luck **8** bad break, hard luck **9** adversity, mischance **10** misfortune

Illyrius
father: 6 Cadmus
Ilmarinen
origin: 7 Finnish
form: 10 blacksmith
hero in: 8 Kalevala
forged: 5 Sampo
Sampo's owner: 5 Louhi
I Love Lucy
character: 9 Fred Mertz **10** Ethel

Mertz **11** Little Ricky, Lucy Ricardo **12** Ricky Ricardo
cast: 9 Desi Arnaz **11** Lucille Ball, Vivian Vance **14** William Frawley
Ricky's club: 7 Babaloo **9** Tropicana

Il Penseroso
author: 10 John Milton
companion piece: 8 L'Allegro

image 4 copy, icon, idea, idol **6** double, effigy, fetish, figure, memory, simile, statue, symbol, visage **7** concept, picture, replica **8** likeness, metaphor, portrait **9** depiction, duplicate, facsimile, mirroring, semblance **10** photograph, reflection, simulacrum **11** countenance, delineation, incarnation **12** recollection, reproduction **13** mental picture **14** figure of speech, representation

imaginable 8 feasible **9** thinkable **11** conceivable

imaginary 4 sham **5** fancy, phony **6** made-up, unreal **7** fancied, fiction, figment **8** delusion, fabulous, fanciful, illusion, illusory, invented, mythical, romantic **9** fantastic, figmental, legendary **10** factitious, fictitious **11** counterfeit, make-believe

imagination 5 fancy **7** cunning, thought **9** ingenuity, invention **10** astuteness, creativity, enterprise **12** creativeness **13** inventiveness **14** thoughtfulness **15** creative thought, resourcefulness

imaginative 6 clever **7** unusual **8** creative, inspired, original **9** ingenious, inventive **10** innovative **11** resourceful **12** enterprising **16** off the beaten path, out of the ordinary

imagine 5 fancy, guess, infer, judge **6** assume, gather **7** believe, dream up, picture, presume, pretend, project, suppose, surmise, suspect **8** conceive, envisage, envision, fantasize, visualize **10** conjecture

imbecile 3 ass **4** dolt, dope, fool, jerk **5** dummy, dunce, idiot, moron, ninny **6** nitwit **7** dingbat **8** dumbbell **9** blockhead, simpleton **10** nincompoop

imbecilic 4 dumb **5** inane, silly **6** absurd, stupid **7** asinine, foolish **8** careless, mindless **11** thoughtless

imbecility 6 idiocy **8** dullness, dumbness **9** asininity, stupidity, thickness **16** simplemindedness

imbibe 4 swig, tope **5** drink, quaff **6** guzzle, ingest, tipple **7** consume, partake, swallow **8** chugalug, toss down, wash down

imbiber 3 sot **4** wino **5** drunk, toper **7** drinker, tippler **8** consumer, drunkard, ingester

imbroglio 3 row **4** fray **5** brawl, broil, clash, fight, melee, scrap **6** fracas, ruckus, rumpus, uproar **7** scuffle **8** argument **9** confusion **11** altercation,

embroilment **12** entanglement **13** embarrassment

imbue 4 fill, fire, tint **5** bathe, color, endow, steep, tinge **6** arouse, infuse **7** animate, impress, ingrain, inspire, instill, pervade, suffuse **8** permeate, tincture **9** inculcate

Imhotep
father: 4 Ptah
mother: 7 Sekhmet
position: 6 scribe, vizier, writer **9** architect, physician
architect of pyramid: 8 Sakkarah

imitate 3 ape **4** copy, mime **5** mimic **6** mirror, parody, parrot **7** emulate, pass for **8** look like, simulate **9** duplicate, represent **10** caricature **11** counterfeit, impersonate

imitation 4 fake, mock, sham **5** aping, phony **6** ersatz, parody **7** man-made, mimicry, takeoff **8** travesty **9** burlesque, facsimile, semblance, simulated, synthetic **10** adaptation, artificial, caricature, impression, similarity, simulation **11** counterfeit, duplication, make-believe **12** reproduction **13** impersonation **14** representation

Imitation of Christ, The
author: 13 Thomas a Kempis

immaculate 4 pure **5** clean, ideal **6** chaste, intact, virgin **7** perfect, saintly, sinless **8** flawless, innocent, spotless, unsoiled, virginal, virtuous **9** faultless, guiltless, shipshape, stainless, unstained, unsullied **11** spic and span, untarnished **13** above reproach, unimpeachable **14** irreproachable **15** unexceptionable

immanent 6 inborn, inbred, innate **7** natural **8** inherent **9** ingrained, intrinsic **10** congenital, deep-rooted, deepseated, indigenous, indwelling **11** instinctive, instinctual

Immanuel 7 Messiah **11** Jesus Christ
means: 9 God with us

immaterial 7 ghostly, shadowy, trivial **8** bodiless, ethereal, mystical, noumenal, spectral, trifling, unbodied **9** spiritual, unearthly **10** evanescent, extraneous, impalpable, intangible, irrelevant, of no moment **11** disembodied, incorporeal, not relevant, unimportant **12** extramundane, extrasensory **13** insignificant, insubstantial, unsubstantial **14** of no importance **15** inconsequential, of little account

immature 5 green, young **6** callow, unripe **7** babyish, kiddish, puerile **8** childish, juvenile, unformed, youthful **9** embryonic, half-grown, infantile, not mature, pubescent **10** unfinished, unmellowed **11** out of season, rudimentary, undeveloped **16** wet behind the ears

immeasurable 7 endless, immense **8** infinite **9** boundless, limitless, unbounded, unlimited **10** fathomless **11**

illimitable, inestimable, measureless, never-ending **12** incalculable, interminable, unfathomable **13** inexhaustible

immediate 4 near, next, nigh **5** close, hasty, local, swift **6** abrupt, nearby, prompt, recent, speedy, sudden **7** express, instant, nearest **8** adjacent, punctual **9** proximate, undelayed **10** contiguous **13** instantaneous

immediately 3 now **4** ASAP, stat **9** instantly, right away **10** this minute **12** without delay
French: 11 tout de suite

immemorial 5 olden **7** ageless, ancient **8** dateless, hallowed, timeless **9** ancestral, legendary, venerable **11** time-honored **12** long-standing, mythological **15** long-established

immense 4 huge, vast **5** great **7** mammoth, massive **8** colossal, enormous, gigantic **9** extensive, monstrous **10** prodigious, stupendous, tremendous **11** measureless **14** Brobdingnagian

immensity 8 enormity, hugeness, vastness **9** largeness **12** enormousness

immerse 3 dip **4** duck, dunk, sink, soak **5** bathe, douse, lower, steep **6** absorb, drench, engage, occupy, plunge **7** engross **8** submerge

immerse briefly 3 dip **4** dunk

immersion 7 bathing, dunking **8** drowning **10** absorption, submersion **11** engrossment, involvement, submergence **13** concentration, preoccupation

immigrant 5 alien **7** migrant, settler **8** colonist, newcomer **9** foreigner, nonnative

immigrate 6 move to, settle **7** migrate **8** colonize

imminent 4 near **7** looming **8** menacing, perilous **9** immediate, impending **10** near at hand **11** approaching, close at hand, threatening

immobile 4 fast **5** fixed, quiet, rigid, stiff, still **6** at rest, laid up, rooted, secure, stable, static **7** riveted **9** immovable, not moving, quiescent, steadfast **10** motionless, stationary, stock-still **11** unbudgeable **13** incapacitated

immobilize 3 fix, set **4** stud **6** disarm, freeze, splint **7** disable **8** paralyze, transfix **12** incapacitate

immoderate 5 undue **7** extreme **8** whopping **9** excessive, unbridled **10** exorbitant, gargantuan, inordinate, prodigious **11** extravagant, intemperate, uncalled-for **12** unreasonable, unrestrained **14** unconscionable

immoderation 6 excess **10** debauchery **11** dissipation, prodigality, unrestraint **12** extravagance, intemperance, recklessness **13** excessiveness **14** prodigiousness

immodest 4 lewd, vain **5** gross, loose **6** brazen, coarse, risque, wanton **7**

pompous 8 boastful, braggart, indecent, inflated, unchaste **9** bombastic, conceited, shameless **10** indecorous, indelicate, peacockish, suggestive **11** exaggerated, pretentious **12** self-centered

immoral 4 evil, lewd **5** dirty, wrong **6** sinful, wicked **7** corrupt, heinous, obscene, raunchy, vicious **8** depraved, indecent, infamous, prurient **9** debauched, dissolute, nefarious, salacious, unethical **10** dissipated, iniquitous, licentious, profligate **12** pornographic, unprincipled

Immoralist, The
author: 9 Andre Gide

immorality 3 sin **4** evil **9** decadence, depravity, indecency, obscenity, prurience **10** corruption, debasement, degeneracy, sinfulness **13** salaciousness

immortal 3 god **6** divine **7** abiding, eternal, undying **8** enduring **9** deathless **11** everlasting **12** imperishable

Immortals 6 giants, greats, titans **7** the gods **8** demigods **13** all-time greats
Greek/Roman: 8 pantheon

immovable 3 icy, set **4** cold, fast **5** fixed **6** dogged, secure, steely, stolid **7** adamant, settled **8** detached, fastened, immobile, obdurate, resolute, stubborn **9** heartless, impassive, unfeeling **10** inexorable, inflexible, stationary, unbendable **11** coldhearted, unbudgeable **12** unchangeable **13** unimpressible, unsympathetic **16** unimpressionable

immune 4 free, safe **5** clear **6** exempt **9** protected, resistant **12** invulnerable **13** unsusceptible

immunity 7 freedom **9** exemption **10** resistance **16** unsusceptibility

immure 3 hem, pen **4** cage, coop, jail, wall **6** entomb, intern, wall in, wall up **7** confine, enclose, seclude **8** cloister, imprison **11** incarcerate

immutability 9 endurance, stability **14** changelessness

immutable 4 firm **5** fixed, solid **6** stable **7** lasting **8** constant, enduring **9** permanent, unaltered, unvarying **10** changeless, inflexible, unchanging **11** unalterable **12** unchangeable, unmodifiable **14** intransmutable **16** incontrovertible

Imogen
character in: 9 Cymbeline
author: 11 Shakespeare

imp 3 elf **4** brat **5** demon, devil, gnome, pixie, scamp **6** goblin, hoyden, rascal, sprite, urchin **7** upstart **9** hobgoblin **10** evil spirit, leprechaun

impact 4 jolt **5** brunt, crash, force, shock, smash **6** burden, effect, thrust **7** contact **9** collision, influence **10** concussion **11** implication **12** repercussion

impair 3 mar **4** harm, hurt **6** damage, hinder, injure, lessen, reduce, weaken, worsen **7** cripple, subvert, vitiate **8** decrease, enervate, enfeeble, undercut **10** debilitate **11** detract from

impaired 6 broken, faulty, flawed **7** damaged **9** defective, deficient, imperfect

impairment 4 flaw, harm **5** fault **6** damage, defect, injury, malady **7** ailment, illness **8** debility, disorder, handicap, sickness, weakness **9** detriment, hindrance, infirmity **10** disability, impediment, inadequacy **12** debilitation

impale 3 fix, pin **4** gore, stab, tack **5** affix, stick **8** transfix **10** run through

impart 4 give, lend, tell **5** grant, offer, share **6** accord, afford, pass on, relate, render, report, reveal **7** confide, consign, deliver, divulge, mention **8** bestow on, confer on, disclose, dispense **9** make known **10** contribute **11** communicate

impartial 4 fair, just **7** neutral **8** detached, unbiased **9** equitable, objective **10** evenhanded, fair-minded, open-minded **11** nonpartisan **12** unprejudiced **13** disinterested, dispassionate

impartiality 7 justice **8** equality, fair play, fairness **10** detachment, neutrality **11** objectivity

impasse 4 snag **7** dead end, dilemma **8** cul-de-sac, deadlock, quandary, standoff **9** stalemate **10** blind alley, bottleneck, standstill **11** predicament

impassioned 5 eager, fiery **6** ardent, heated **7** earnest, excited, fervent, intense, rousing, zealous **8** animated, forceful, inspired, stirring

impassive 4 calm, cool **5** aloof, stony **6** sedate, stolid **7** stoical, unmoved **8** reserved **9** apathetic, untouched **10** impervious, insensible, phlegmatic **11** emotionless, indifferent, inscrutable, unemotional, unperturbed **13** dispassionate, imperturbable, unimpressible **16** unimpressionable

impassiveness 8 coldness **9** aloofness, stolidity **12** indifference **15** emotionlessness

impassivity 6 apathy **8** coolness, stoicism **9** aloofness, stolidity **10** dispassion **15** emotionlessness **16** imperturbability

impatient 4 edgy **5** fussy, hasty, itchy, rabid, tense, testy **6** ardent, touchy **7** annoyed, anxious, brusque, hurried, nervous, peevish, restive **8** agitated, feverish, restless **9** excitable, irascible, irritable, irritated **10** high-strung, intolerant, passionate **12** enthusiastic

impeach 4 slur **6** accuse, assail, attack, charge, impugn, indict **7** arraign, slander **8** badmouth, belittle, question **9** challenge, discredit, disparage, incul-

pate 11 incriminate **16** call into question

impeccable 7 perfect **8** flawless **9** blameless, excellent, faultless **10** immaculate **11** unblemished **12** irreprovable, unassailable **13** unimpeachable **14** irreproachable **15** unexceptionable

impecunious 4 poor **5** broke, needy **6** hard-up **7** pinched **8** bankrupt, indigent **9** destitute, insolvent, penniless **10** down-and-out, straitened **12** impoverished **15** poverty-stricken

impede 5 block, check, delay, deter, stall **6** arrest, halter, hamper, hinder, retard, stymie, thwart **7** disrupt, inhibit **8** hold back, obstruct, slow down **9** frustrate, interrupt, sidetrack **13** interfere with

impediment 4 flaw **5** block, delay **6** defect **7** barrier **8** blockage, drawback, handicap, obstacle **9** deformity, hindrance **10** detraction **11** obstruction **12** interference **14** stumbling block

impedimenta 4 gear **7** baggage **9** equipment **13** accoutrements, paraphernalia

impel 4 goad, prod, push, spur, urge **5** drive, force **6** compel, incite, induce, prompt **7** require **8** motivate **9** constrain, stimulate **11** necessitate

impend 4 brew, hang, loom **5** hover, lower **6** menace **8** approach, draw near, overhang, threaten

impending 4 near **6** coming **7** brewing, looming **8** imminent, menacing, oncoming **9** immediate **11** approaching, forthcoming, threatening

impenetrable 5 dense, solid, thick **6** sealed **7** elusive, obscure **8** puzzling **9** insoluble **10** impassable, impervious, insensible, intangible, inviolable, mysterious, unpalpable **11** inscrutable, unenterable **12** inaccessible, inexplicable, invulnerable, unfathomable **16** incomprehensible

impenitent 4 lost **6** inured **7** callous, defiant **8** hardened, obdurate **9** unashamed **10** uncontrite **11** remorseless, unrepentant, unrepenting **12** incorrigible, unapologetic **13** irreclaimable

imperative 6 urgent **7** crucial, needful **8** critical, pressing **9** essential, mandatory, necessary, requisite **10** compulsory, obligatory **11** unavoidable

imperceptible 5 minor, scant, small **7** hidden, minute, slight, subtle **7** minimal **8** academic **10** indistinct **12** undetectable, unnoticeable **13** infinitesimal, insignificant, unappreciable, unperceivable **14** inconsiderable

imperceptive 5 blind **9** unfeeling **11** insensitive, unobservant **12** inpercipient, unperceptive **13** unsympathetic

imperfect 6 faulty, flawed **8** deformed, fallible, impaired **9** blemished, defective

imperfection 4 flaw **5** fault **6** defect **7** blemish **8** weakness **9** deformity **10** faultiness, impairment, inadequacy **11** fallibility, shortcoming **13** insufficiency **14** incompleteness

imperial 5 bossy **6** feudal, lordly **8** despotic **9** arbitrary, imperious **10** autocratic, high-handed, peremptory, repressive, tyrannical **11** dictatorial, domineering, magisterial, overbearing **13** authoritarian

Imperial Presidency, The
author: **20** Arthur M Schlesinger Jr

imperil 4 risk **6** chance, expose, gamble, hazard **8** endanger **10** compromise, jeopardize **13** put in jeopardy

imperious 5 bossy, lofty **6** lordly **7** haughty **8** arrogant, despotic, imperial **10** autocratic, commanding, peremptory, tyrannical **11** dictatorial, domineering, overbearing **13** high-and-mighty

imperiousness 9 arrogance, loftiness **11** haughtiness

imperishable 6 stable **7** durable, lasting **14** indestructible

imperium 4 rule **5** realm **6** domain, empire **8** dominion **11** sovereignty

impermanent 7 passing **8** fleeting, fugitive, not fixed, unstable **9** ephemeral, temporary, transient **10** evanescent, transitory, unenduring

impermeable 5 dense, solid, tight **6** opaque **9** nonporous **10** impervious, waterproof

impersonal 4 dead **6** remote **7** general, inhuman, neutral **8** detached, lifeless, soulless **9** impartial, impassive, inanimate, inorganic, objective **10** spiritless **11** perfunctory **13** disinterested, dispassionate

impersonate 3 ape **4** copy, mime **5** mimic **6** pose as **7** imitate, portray **9** personify, represent **11** pretend to be **12** masquerade as

impertinence 4 sass **5** cheek, sauce **7** affront **8** audacity, boldness, rudeness **9** freshness, impudence, insolence, sauciness **10** cheekiness, disrespect, effrontery, incivility **11** irrelevance **17** disrespectfulness, inappropriateness

impertinent 4 rude **5** fresh, surly **6** brassy, brazen, smarty **7** uncivil **8** arrogant, impudent, insolent **9** extrinsic, insulting, unrelated **10** extraneous, immaterial, irrelevant, not germane, peremptory, unmannerly **11** unimportant **12** discourteous, presumptuous **13** disrespectful, inappropriate **14** beside the point

imperturbability 5 poise **6** aplomb **8** calmness, coolness **9** composure, sangfroid **10** equanimity, steadiness **11** self-control, tranquility **12** tranquillity **14** presence of mind, self-possession

imperturbable 4 calm, cool **6** sedate, serene **8** composed **9** collected, impassive, unanxious, unfazable, unruffled **10** impervious **11** levelheaded, undisturbed, unexcitable, unflappable, unflustered **13** dispassionate, unsusceptible

impervious 6 closed **8** immune to **11** impermeable **12** impenetrable, inaccessible, invulnerable **14** unapproachable

impetuosity 8 rashness **11** spontaneity, unrestraint **12** recklessness **13** impulsiveness **14** capriciousness

impetuous 4 rash **5** hasty **6** abrupt, stormy **7** rampant, violent **8** forcible, headlong, vehement **9** impulsive **10** capricious, inexorable, relentless, unexpected **11** precipitate **14** unpremeditated

impetus 4 prod, push, spur **5** boost, drive, force, start **6** motive **7** impulse **8** momentum, stimulus, impulsion, incentive **10** motivation, propulsion **11** moving force, stimulation

impiety 9 blasphemy, sacrilege **10** disrespect, irreligion **11** irreverence, ungodliness

impinge 7 intrude, obtrude, violate **8** encroach, infringe, trespass **10** transgress

impious 7 godless, immoral, profane, ungodly **8** apostate, renegade **9** perverted **10** iniquitous, irreverent **11** blasphemous, irreligious **12** iconoclastic, sacrilegious **13** disrespectful

impiousness 7 impiety **9** blasphemy, sacrilege **10** disrespect **11** irreverence, ungodliness

impish 5 elfin **7** implike, puckish, roguish **8** prankish, rascally, sportive **11** mischievous

implacable 10 inexorable, inflexible, relentless, unamenable **11** intractable, unrelenting **12** unappeasable, unpacifiable **14** irreconcilable, uncompromising

implant 3 fix, set, sow **4** root **5** embed, graft, imbed, inlay, teach **6** infuse, insert **7** impress, instill **8** entrench **9** establish, inculcate **10** impregnate

implausible 8 doubtful, unlikely **9** illogical, senseless **10** far-fetched, improbable, incredible, outrageous, ridiculous **12** preposterous, unbelievable, unreasonable **13** inconceivable

implement 4 tool **5** begin, enact, piece, start **6** device **7** achieve, article, fulfill, realize, utensil **8** activate, carry out **9** apparatus, appliance, equipment, materials **10** accomplish, bring about, instrument **11** set in motion **13** put into effect

implicate 7 connect, embroil, ensnare, involve **8** entangle **9** associate, inculpate **11** incriminate

implication 6 effect **7** outcome **8** innuendo, overtone **9** inference **10** connection, intimation, suggestion **11** association, connotation, consequence, insinuation, involvement **12** entanglement, ramification, significance

implicit 5 total **6** hinted, innate **7** certain, implied, staunch **8** absolute, complete, inferred, inherent, profound, resolute **9** deducible, steadfast, suggested **10** understood, unreserved, unshakable **13** unquestioning

implied 5 tacit **7** oblique **8** indirect **9** implicity, indicated

implode 11 burst inward **17** compress violently

implore 3 beg **4** urge **6** obtest **7** beseech, entreat **9** importune, plead with **10** supplicate

imply 4 hint, mean **6** denote **7** bespeak, betoken, connote, presume, signify, suggest **8** evidence, indicate, intimate **9** insinuate **10** presuppose

impolite 4 rude **7** ill-bred, uncivil **9** impolitic, unfitting, ungenteel, unrefined **10** undecorous, unmannerly **12** discourteous **13** disrespectful, inconsiderate

impoliteness 8 rudeness **10** bad manners, incivility **11** boorishness, discourtesy

import 6 burden, moment, thrust **7** meaning **9** overtones **10** importance **11** connotation, implication **12** ramification, significance

importance 4 rank **5** value, worth **6** esteem, import, moment, repute, weight **7** stature **8** eminence, position **9** influence, relevance **11** consequence, seriousness, weightiness **12** significance **13** essentialness, momentousness

Importance of Being Earnest, The
author: **10** Oscar Wilde
character: **12** Cecily Cardew, Jack Worthing, Letitia Prism **16** Gwendolen Fairfax **17** Algernon Moncrieff (Algy) **20** Lady Augusta Bracknell **21** Reverend Canon Chasuble

important 5 great, major **7** leading, notable, seminal, serious, weighty **8** creative, esteemed, foremost, original **9** momentous, prominent **10** imperative, meaningful, preeminent, remarkable **11** distinctive, influential, significant **13** consequential

imported 5 alien **6** exotic **7** foreign **9** not native

importunate 7 begging **8** pleading **9** imploring **10** entreating, persistent **11** troublesome **12** supplicating

importune 3 beg, sue **4** pray **5** plead **6** adjure, exhort **7** beseech, entreat, implore **8** appeal to, petition **10** supplicate

importunity 4 plea 6 appeal 7 request 8 entreaty, petition 12 supplication

impose 3 set 4 levy 5 apply, enact, foist, force, lay on 6 peddle, slap on 7 command, dictate, inflict, palm off, place on 9 establish, institute, introduce, prescribe 10 thrust upon

impose upon 5 annoy 6 bother, ill-use 8 ill-treat, maltreat, mistreat 15 take advantage of

imposing 5 grand, lofty 7 massive, stately 8 majestic, striking, towering 10 commanding, impressive, monumental 11 outstanding 12 awe-inspiring

imposition 5 abuse 6 burden, ill use 8 foisting 10 obligation 15 taking advantage

impossible 8 stubborn 9 insoluble 10 unbearable, unsolvable, unyielding 11 intolerable, intractable, not possible 12 insufferable, intransigent, unachievable, unanswerable, unattainable, unimaginable, unmanageable 13 inconceivable 16 out of the question

impost 3 fee, tax 4 duty, fine, toll 6 charge, excise, tariff 10 assessment

impostor 4 sham 5 cheat, duper, fraud, phony, quack 6 con man 7 bluffer, shammer 8 deceiver 9 charlatan, defrauder, pretender, trickster 10 dissembler, mountebank 11 counterfeit, flimflam man, masquerader, pettifogger 12 impersonator

imposture 4 fake, hoax, play, ruse, sham 5 cheat, fraud, trick 6 deceit, humbug 7 forgery, swindle 8 artifice, delusion, pretense, quackery 9 deception, falsehood, imitation 10 pretension 11 charlatanry, counterfeit, fraudulence 12 charlatanism 13 impersonation, mountebankery

impotence 8 weakness 9 paralysis 10 disability, incapacity, inefficacy 12 helplessness 13 powerlessness 14 ineffectuality 15 ineffectiveness

impotent 4 weak 5 frail 6 feeble 7 hapless 8 disabled, feckless, helpless 9 paralyzed, powerless 11 ineffective

impound 3 pen 4 cage 5 pen in, seize 6 coop up, encage, lock up, shut in 7 confine 13 hold in custody

impoverish 4 bust, ruin 5 break, drain 6 beggar, pauper, reduce 7 deplete, exhaust 8 bankrupt, make poor 9 pauperize 18 send to the poorhouse

impoverished 4 poor 6 abject, barren, bereft, effete, used up 7 drained, sterile, wanting, worn out 8 depleted, indigent, wiped out 9 destitute, exhausted 10 down-and-out, pauperized 11 impecunious 12 unproductive, without means

impractical 6 sloppy, unwise 8 careless, quixotic, romantic 10 loose-ended, starry-eyed 11 unrealistic 12

disorganized 13 helter-skelter, unintelligent

imprecation 5 curse 8 anathema 11 malediction

impregnable 6 mighty, potent, strong, sturdy 8 powerful 10 invincible 12 invulnerable, unassailable, unattackable 13 unconquerable

impregnate 3 wet 4 soak 5 steep 6 dampen, drench, imbrue, infuse 7 moisten, suffuse 8 fructify, inundate, permeate, saturate 9 fecundate, fertilize 10 inseminate

impresario 7 manager, sponsor 8 director 9 conductor, organizer 12 entrepreneur

impress 4 grab, move, stir, sway 5 reach, touch 6 affect, excite, sink in, strike 8 bedazzle 9 electrify, influence, overpower, overwhelm

impression 4 idea, mark, mold, view 5 hunch, stamp, trace, track 6 belief, effect, impact, notion 7 contour, feeling, impress, imprint, opinion, outline, surmise 9 influence, reception, sensation 10 conviction 11 indentation 13 understanding

impressionable 8 gullible, passible, sentient 9 affective, receptive 10 vulnerable 11 suggestible

impressive 5 grand 6 august, moving 8 exciting, imposing, majestic, striking 9 memorable, thrilling 11 magnificent, outstanding 12 awe-inspiring, overpowering, soul-stirring 13 unforgettable

imprimis 15 in the first place

imprint 3 fix 4 etch, mark, sign 5 infix, press, stamp, title 6 indent 7 engrave, impress 8 inscribe 9 engraving 10 depression, impression 11 indentation

imprison 3 pen 4 jail 6 coop up, engage, entomb, immure, lock up 7 confine, fence in, impound, shackle 8 restrain 9 constrain 11 hold captive, incarcerate

improbable 8 doubtful, unlikely 9 illogical 11 implausible 12 unreasonable 13 unforeseeable

improbable solution in a play's plot
Latin: 13 deus ex machina

impromptu 6 sudden 7 offhand 9 impulsive, makeshift, on the spot 10 improvised, off the cuff, unexpected, unprepared 11 spontaneous, unrehearsed 14 extemporaneous, unpremeditated, without warning 15 spur-of-the-moment 16 extemporaneously, on a moment's notice 19 off the top of one's head

improper 4 lewd 5 inapt, unfit 8 indecent, off-color, unseemly 9 ill-suited, irregular 10 indecorous, malapropos, out of place, suggestive, unbecoming,

unsuitable 12 inharmonious 13 inappropriate, unconformable
French: 5 outre

impropriety 5 gaffe 7 blunder, faux pas 9 gaucherie, indecorum, vulgarity 10 bad manners 11 boorishness 12 impoliteness, indiscretion

improve 4 help 5 rally 6 better, enrich, repair 7 correct, develop, enhance 9 cultivate 10 ameliorate, recuperate

improvement 4 gain 6 reform, repair 7 advance, upswing 8 additive, progress 9 amendment 10 betterment, emendation, refinement 11 advancement, enhancement, reclamation 12 amelioration 14 reconstruction

improvidence 10 imprudence 11 prodigality 12 extravagance, wastefulness 13 shiftlessness 16 shortsightedness

improvident 6 lavish 8 prodigal, reckless, wasteful 9 imprudent, negligent, unthrifty 10 thriftless 11 extravagant, spendthrift 12 shortsighted 14 unparsimonious

improvise 5 ad-lib 6 make up, wing it 11 extemporize

improvised 5 ad-lib 7 devised, offhand 8 invented 9 concocted, contrived, dreamed-up, extempore, hatched-up, impromptu, makeshift 10 off-the-cuff, originated, unprepared 11 extemporary, spontaneous, unrehearsed 12 extemporized 14 extemporaneous, unpremeditated 15 improvisational, spur-of-the- moment

imprudent 4 rash 5 crazy, dopey 6 unwise 7 foolish 8 heedless, mindless, untoward 9 foolhardy 10 ill-advised, incautious, indiscreet, unthinking 11 inadvisable, injudicious, thoughtless 13 ill-considered

impudence
Yiddish: 7 chutzpa 8 chutzpah

impudent 4 bold, rude 5 brash, fresh, nervy, saucy 6 brazen, cheeky 7 forward, upstart 8 impolite, insolent 9 bumptious, shameless 11 impertinent, smart-alecky, wiseacreish 12 discourteous 13 disrespectful

impugn 4 deny 5 knock, libel 6 assail, attack, berate, negate, oppose 7 asperse, slander 8 denounce, question 9 challenge, criticize 10 contradict 14 call in question, cast aspersions 16 call into question

impugnment 7 slander 10 aspersions

impulse 4 bent, goad, push, spur, urge, whim 5 drive, fancy, force 6 desire, motive, notion, thrust, whimsy 7 caprice, impetus, whimsey 8 instinct, momentum, movement, stimulus, stirring 9 incentive 10 incitement, motivation 11 inclination, inspiration, instigation

impulsive 4 rash 7 driving, offhand 8

forceful, forcible, notional **9** impelling, impetuous, impromptu, unplanned, whimsical **10** capricious, incautious, propellant, propelling **11** involuntary, spontaneous **12** devil-may-care **13** unpredictable **14** extemporaneous, unpremeditated **15** spur-of-themoment

impulsiveness 8 rashness **11** impetuosity, spontaneity, unrestraint **12** recklessness, whimsicality **14** capriciousness

impunity 8 immunity **9** clearance, exemption, privilege **10** absolution **11** prerogative **12** dispensation

impure 4 foul, lewd **5** dirty **6** coarse, filthy, smutty **7** debased, defiled, immoral, lustful, noisome, noxious, obscene, sullied, tainted, unclean **8** degraded, devalued, immodest, improper, indecent, polluted, prurient, unchaste, vitiated **9** lecherous, salacious, unrefined **10** indecorous, indelicate, libidinous, licentious **11** adulterated, depreciated, unwholesome **12** contaminated

impurity 5 alloy, dross, filth, taint **8** foulness **9** dirtiness, pollutant, pollution **10** adulterant, corruption, defilement **11** contaminant, taintedness, uncleanness **12** adulteration **13** contamination, foreign matter **15** unwholesomeness

imputation 6 charge **10** accusation, allegation, ascription **11** attribution

impute 5 refer **6** assign, charge, credit, relate **7** ascribe **9** attribute

inability 10 inaptitude, incapacity, ineptitude **12** helplessness, incapability, incompetence **13** maladroitness, powerlessness

in absence
Latin: **10** in absentia

in absentia 9 in absence

inaccessible 9 not at hand **11** unreachable **12** unattainable, unobtainable **14** unapproachable

in accord 9 agreeable, approving, in harmony, of one mind **10** concurring, consenting **11** in agreement
French: **9** en rapport

inaccuracy 4 goof, slip **5** error, fault, wrong **6** boo-boo **7** blunder, erratum, fallacy, mistake **9** unclarity **10** faultiness **11** imprecision, inexactness **13** incorrectness, unreliability **14** fallaciousness

inaccurate 3 off **5** false, wrong **6** faulty **7** inexact **8** mistaken **9** erroneous, imprecise, incorrect, off target **10** fallacious, unreliable **11** not on target, off the track **13** wide of the mark

inaction 8 abeyance, deferral, dormancy, dullness, idleness **9** cessation, indolence **10** inactivity, quiescence, somnolence, suspension **11** complacency

inactive 4 dull, idle, lazy **5** inert, quiet, still **6** low-key, otiose, static, torpid, unused **7** dormant, languid **8** indolent, slothful, sluggish **9** do-nothing, easygoing, leisurely, sedentary, somnolent **10** on the shelf **11** inoperative **12** out of service

inactivity 4 rest **5** quiet **6** disuse **7** inertia **8** dormancy, idleness, inaction **9** stillness **10** quiescence

in actuality
Latin: **6** in esse

in addition 3 and, too **4** also, more, plus, then **5** above, added, again, extra **6** as well, beyond **7** besides, further **8** moreover **10** additional **12** additionally, supplemental

inadequacy 4 lack **7** failing **10** deficiency, impairment **11** shortcoming **13** insufficiency

inadequate 5 inept, short, unfit **6** meager, scanty, too raw **7** lacking, not up to, wanting **8** below par, unfitted **9** deficient, imperfect, incapable **11** incompetent, unqualified **12** insufficient

inadmissible 10 disallowed, extraneous **11** intolerable **12** not permitted, unacceptable **14** nonpermissible

in advance 6 before, in time, sooner **7** earlier **9** before now **10** beforehand **11** ahead of time **13** before the fact

inadvertent 7 unmeant **10** accidental, fortuitous, unintended, unthinking **11** involuntary **13** unintentional **14** unpremeditated

inadvisable 5 risky **6** chancy, unwise **9** impolitic, imprudent **10** ill-advised **11** inexpedient, injudicious, inopportune

in aeternum 7 forever

in agreement
French: **9** en rapport

inalienable 6 sacred **8** absolute, defended, inherent **9** protected **10** inviolable, sacrosanct **12** unassailable **13** unforfeitable, unimpeachable

in all
Latin: **6** in toto

in all places 10 every place, everywhere, far and near, far and wide

in a low voice
Latin: **9** sotto voce

inamorata 4 lady, love **5** lover **7** beloved, darling **8** ladylove, mistress, paramour, truelove **10** sweetheart

inane 4 dumb **5** dopey, empty, silly, vapid **6** absurd, jejune, stupid **7** asinine, fatuous, foolish, idiotic, insipid, shallow, vacuous **9** pointless, senseless **10** ridiculous, unthinking **11** meaningless, nonsensical **13** unintelligent

inanimate 4 cold, dead, dull **5** inert **6** asleep, stolid **8** lifeless, soulless **9** inorganic, insensate, nonliving, sense-

less, unfeeling **10** insensible, insentient **11** unconscious

inanity 6 drivel **7** hogwash, vacuity **8** nonsense, vapidity **9** absurdity, asininity, silliness **11** foolishness **13** pointlessness, senselessness **14** ridiculousness

Inanna
origin: **8** Sumerian
goddess of: **3** war **4** love
sister: **10** Ereshkigal
realm: **6** heaven
corresponds to: **6** Ishtar **7** Astarte, Mylitta **9** Ashtoreth

in any case 6 anyhow, anyway **9** at any rate **10** in any event

inapplicable 5 unfit **6** not apt **8** unsuited **10** inapposite, irrelevant, not germane, unsuitable **12** incompatible, not pertinent **13** inappropriate

inappropriate 5 inapt **8** ill-timed, improper, unsuited **9** unfitting **10** indecorous, in bad taste, out of place, unbecoming, unsuitable **11** incongruous **12** incompatible, infelicitous
French: **10** mal a propos

inapt 8 improper, unseemly, unsuited **9** ill-suited, incorrect, unfitting **11** incongruous **13** inappropriate

inaptness 9 inability, ineptness **10** clumsiness, inaptitude, ineptitude **12** incompetence **13** maladroitness **14** unskillfulness

in arrears 4 late **7** overdue **10** delinquent

inarticulate 4 dumb, mute **7** babbled, blurred, garbled, mumbled **8** confused, wordless **9** paralyzed **10** incoherent, indistinct, speechless, tongue-tied **12** inexpressive **14** unintelligible **15** uncommunicative

inartistic 9 graceless, inelegant, tasteless **10** ungraceful **11** unaesthetic **12** unattractive

in a series
French: **7** en suite

in a set
French: **7** en suite

in attendance 4 here **7** present, serving **9** appearing, caring for, on the spot, waiting on **12** accompanying, looking after, taking care of

inattention 6 apathy **10** negligence **12** carelessness **14** lack of interest **16** absentmindedness, unresponsiveness

inattentive 7 unaware **8** careless, heedless **9** forgetful, negligent, unmindful **10** distracted **11** daydreaming, thoughtless, unobservant **12** absentminded

inaugurate 5 set up, start **6** induct, launch **7** instate, kick off, usher in **8** initiate **9** institute, undertake **10** embark upon **11** set in action

inauguration 5 start **9** beginning, induction **10** dedication **11** origination **12** commencement

inaugurator 6 author, father **7** creator, founder, starter **9** initiator, organizer **10** originator, prime mover

inauspicious 7 unlucky **9** ill-chosen, ill-omened **10** badly timed, disastrous **11** unfavorable, unfortunate, unpromising **12** infelicitous, unpropitious

in a vacuum
Latin: **7** in vacuo

in bad faith
Latin: **8** mala fide

in being
Latin: **6** in esse

inborn 5 basic **6** inbred, innate, native **7** natural **8** inherent **9** inherited, intrinsic, intuitive **10** congenital **11** fundamental, instinctive **14** constitutional

inbred 6 inborn, innate, primal **7** natural **8** inherent **9** ingrained, inherited, intrinsic, intuitive **10** congenital, deep-rooted, deep-seated, hereditary, indwelling **11** instinctive, instinctual **12** deeply rooted **14** constitutional

Inca
language family: **7** Quechua
location: **4** Peru **5** Chili **7** Bolivia, Ecuador **9** Argentina **12** South America
leader: **7** Huascar **8** Topa Inca **9** Atahualpa, Pachacuti **10** Manco Capac **11** Huayna Capac
conquered by: **7** Pizarro
ruins: **11** Machu Picchu, Sacsahuaman, Tambo Machay

incalculable 7 dubious **8** infinite **9** countless, uncertain **11** inestimable, innumerable, measureless, uncountable **12** immeasurable, incomputable **13** unforeseeable, unpredictable

incandesce 4 burn, glow **5** flare, flash

incandescent 7 dynamic, glowing, radiant **8** electric, galvanic, magnetic, white-hot **9** brilliant **11** high-powered **12** electrifying **13** scintillating

Incantation 3 hex **4** jinx **5** chant, charm, magic, spell **6** voodoo **7** sorcery **8** wizardry **10** black magic, hocus-pocus, invocation, mumbo-jumbo, necromancy, witchcraft **11** abracadabra, conjuration

incapable 5 inept, unfit **6** unable **8** helpless, impotent, inferior **9** powerless, unskilled, untrained **10** inadequate **11** incompetent, ineffective, inefficient, unqualified

incapacitate 4 maim, undo **5** lay up **7** cripple, disable **8** enfeeble, handicap, paralyze, sideline **9** make unfit **10** disqualify **13** make powerless **14** put out of action **15** render incapable

incapacitated 6 laid up **8** crippled, disabled, disarmed, helpless, stricken **9** hamstrung, paralyzed, sidelined **10** on the shelf, prostrated **11** immobi-

lized, out of action **12** hors de combat **14** flat on one's back

incapacity 7 illness **8** sickness **9** crippling **10** deficiency, disability **12** incapability

incarcerate 3 pen **4** jail **6** commit, coop up, immure, intern, lock up **7** confine, impound **8** imprison, restrain

incarceration 9 detention **10** commitment, internment **11** confinement, durance vile **12** imprisonment **18** institutionalizing

incarnate 8 embodied, manifest **9** personify **10** actualized, in the flesh **11** objectified, personified

Incarnations
author: **16** Robert Penn Warren

incautious 4 rash **5** brash **6** unwary **8** careless, heedless, reckless **9** hotheaded, impetuous, imprudent, impulsive, overhasty **10** headstrong, indiscreet, unthinking **11** injudicious, thoughtless

incendiary 8 agitator, arsonist **12** inflammatory

incense 3 ire **5** anger **6** burn up, enrage, madden **7** inflame, provoke **9** infuriate, make angry **13** make indignant
spice: **6** stacte

incensed 3 mad **5** angry, irate **6** fuming, raging **7** enraged, furious **8** burned up, inflamed, outraged, provoked **9** affronted, indignant **10** infuriated

incentive 4 lure, spur **6** come-on, motive **8** stimulus **10** enticement, inducement, motivation **11** inspiration **13** encouragement

inception 5 birth, debut, onset, start **6** origin, outset **7** arrival **9** beginning **12** commencement, inauguration

incessant 8 constant, unbroken, unending **9** ceaseless, continual, perpetual, unceasing **10** continuous, persistent **11** everlasting, unrelenting, unremitting **12** interminable **13** uninterrupted

inch
abbreviation: **2** in

In Chancery
author: **14** John Galsworthy
part of trilogy: **11** Forsyte Saga

inchoate 7 budding, nascent **8** formless, unformed, unshaped **9** amorphous, beginning, embryonic, incipient, shapeless **10** commencing, disjointed, uncohesive **11** unorganized **12** disconnected

incidence 4 rate **5** range, scope **6** extent **8** occasion **9** frequency, happening **10** commonness, occurrence, phenomenon **11** routineness

incident 5 clash, event, scene **6** affair **7** episode, related **8** occasion **9** hap-

pening **10** incidental, occurrence **11** contretemps, disturbance

incidental 5 minor **9** accessory, secondary **10** extraneous, unexpected **11** subordinate, unlooked-for

incidentally 7 apropos, by the by **8** by the way **9** in passing **14** speaking of that **15** parenthetically **21** while we're on the subject

incidentals 6 extras **8** minutiae **10** minor items **11** accessories, odds and ends **13** appurtenances

incinerate 4 burn **7** consume, cremate **9** carbonize **13** reduce to ashes

incineration 6 firing **7** burning, flaming **8** ignition, kindling **9** cremation **10** combustion **13** carbonization

incinerator 4 oven **6** burner **7** furnace

incipient 7 budding, nascent **8** inchoate **9** beginning, embryonic, fledgling, promising **10** developing, half-formed **11** rudimentary

in circulation 4 rife **6** abroad, around **7** at large **9** all around **11** going around **12** spread around **14** around and about **15** making the rounds

incise 4 etch **5** carve **7** cut into, engrave

incision 3 cut **4** scar, gash, nick, slit **5** cleft, notch, score, slash, slice, wound **6** furrow

incisive 4 curt, keen **5** acute, brisk, crisp, sharp **6** biting, shrewd **7** cutting, express, mordant, precise, probing, summary **8** analytic, piercing **9** trenchant, well-aimed **10** perceptive **11** intelligent, penetrating

incite 4 goad, prod, stir **5** drive, egg on, impel, rouse **6** arouse, excite, fire up, foment, induce, prompt, stir up, urge on **7** actuate, agitate, inflame, provoke **8** activate **9** instigate, stimulate

incitement 6 urging **7** arousal, driving, goading **8** egging on, exciting, firing up, stirring **9** agitating, fomenting, inflaming, prompting, provoking **10** activation, stirring up **11** provocation, stimulation

incivility 8 rudeness **9** barbarism, impudence, indecorum, surliness, vulgarity **10** bad manners, coarseness, disrespect **12** boorishness, discourtesy, misbehavior, uncouthness **12** impoliteness, tactlessness **14** unpleasantness

inclement 3 raw **4** foul **5** harsh, nasty, rough **6** bitter, severe, stormy **7** violent **11** tempestuous

inclination 3 bow, dip, nod **4** bend, bent, hill, rake, rise **5** grade, pitch, slant, slope **6** liking **7** bending, leaning, sloping **8** fondness, lowering, penchant, tendency **9** acclivity, inclining, proneness **10** preference, proclivity, propensity **11** disposition **12** predilection **14** predisposition

incline 3 bow **4** bend, cant, hill, lean, like, rake, seem, tend, tilt, wont **5** be apt, enjoy, pitch, slant, slope **6** prefer **7** decline **8** be likely, gradient **9** acclivity **10** lean toward **11** bend forward, have a mind to

inclined 3 apt **5** prove **6** liable, likely **7** given to **10** disposed to **11** predisposed

incline downward 3 dip, sag **4** sink **5** droop, slant, slope

inclined to delay 4 slow **5** tardy **6** remiss **8** dawdling, dilatory, sluggish **9** reluctant **12** foot-dragging **13** dillydallying **15** procrastinating

include 5 cover **6** enfold, entail, take in **7** contain, embrace, involve, subsume **8** comprise **9** encompass **10** comprehend **11** incorporate

inclusive 7 general, overall **8** sweeping, taking in **9** embracing, including **10** comprising, encircling **11** surrounding **12** encyclopedic **13** comprehending, comprehensive, incorporating **15** all-encompassing

incognito 7 unknown, unnamed **8** nameless **9** concealed, disguised, protected **10** in disguise, uncredited, undercover, unrevealed **11** undisclosed **12** unidentified **14** unacknowledged, unrecognizable

incognizant 6 obtuse **7** unaware **8** ignorant, unseeing **9** unknowing **13** unconscious of **15** uncomprehending

incoherent 7 muddled, unclear **8** confused, rambling **9** illogical **10** disjointed, irrational **11** bewildering, nonsensical **12** inconsistent **14** unintelligible

In Cold Blood
   author: 12 Truman Capote
   director: 13 Richard Brooks
   cast: 11 Paul Stewart, Robert Blake, Scott Wilson **12** John Forsythe

income 5 means, wages **6** salary **7** revenue **8** earnings **9** emolument **10** livelihood

income, annual
   French: 5 rente

incomparable 8 peerless **9** matchless, unequaled, unrivaled **10** inimitable **11** ne plus ultra, superlative **12** transcendent **13** beyond compare **14** unapproachable

incompatibility 6 strife **7** discord **8** friction, variance **9** disaccord, wrangling **10** antagonism **11** being at odds, discordance **13** lack of harmony

incompatible 6 at odds **7** jarring **8** clashing, contrary, unsuited **10** at variance, discordant, mismatched **11** disagreeing, incongruous, uncongenial **12** antagonistic, inconsistent, inharmonious **13** contradictory, inappropriate

incompetency 9 inability, unfitness **10** ineptitude **11** lack of skill **12** inefficiency **15** ineffectiveness

incompetent 5 inept, unfit **8** inexpert **9** incapable, unskilled, untrained **11** ineffective, ineffectual, inefficient, unqualified **14** lacking ability

incomplete 6 broken **7** partial, wanting **9** defective, deficient **10** unfinished **11** fragmentary

incompleteness 8 omission **10** deficiency **11** shortcoming **15** unfinished state

incomprehensible 7 obscure **8** abstruse, baffling **9** confusing **10** befuddling **11** bewildering, inscrutable, ungraspable **12** impenetrable, unfathomable **14** unintelligible **19** beyond comprehension, beyond understanding

incomprehension 10 bafflement, puzzlement **12** bewilderment **19** failure to understand

inconceivable 7 strange **8** unlikely **10** improbable, incredible **11** unthinkable **12** beyond belief, unbelievable, unimaginable **14** highly unlikely

in conclusion
   French: 5 enfin

inconclusive 4 open **9** unsettled **10** indecisive, indefinite, unresolved, up in the air **11** not definite **12** unconvincing, undetermined **13** indeterminate

incongruity 8 variance **9** disparity **10** aberration, disharmony, divergence **11** abnormality, discrepancy **13** dissimilarity, inconsistency, unsuitability **17** inappropriateness

incongruous 3 odd **6** far-out **8** contrary **10** at variance, discrepant, out of place, outlandish, unsuitable **11** conflicting, disagreeing **12** incompatible, inconsistent, out of keeping **13** contradictory, inappropriate **14** irreconcilable

inconsequential 5 petty **6** slight **7** trivial **8** nugatory, picayune, piddling, trifling **9** valueless **10** negligible, of no moment **11** meaningless, unimportant **13** insignificant **15** of no consequence

inconsiderable 5 light, minor, petty, small **6** little, modest, paltry, slight **7** minimal, trivial **8** picayune, trifling **9** no big deal **10** negligible **11** unimportant **13** insignificant, no great shakes **15** inconsequential

inconsiderate 4 rash, rude **6** remiss, unkind **7** uncivil **8** careless, impolite, tactless, uncaring **9** negligent **10** ungracious, unthinking **11** insensitive, thoughtless **12** disregardful, uncharitable

inconsistency 8 variance **9** disparity **10** difference, divergence **11** discrep-

ancy, incongruity **12** disagreement **13** dissimilarity

inconsistent 6 fickle **7** erratic, wayward **8** contrary, notional, unstable, variable **9** changeful, dissonant **10** changeable, discrepant, inconstant, irresolute **11** inaccordant, incongruous, inconsonant, vacillating **12** incompatible, inharmonious **13** contradictory, unpredictable **14** irreconcilable

inconsolable 7 crushed **8** dejected, desolate, wretched **9** miserable **10** despondent **12** disconsolate **13** brokenhearted

inconsonant 10 discordant **12** out of keeping, unharmonious

inconspicuous 3 dim **5** faint, muted **6** modest **9** unnoticed **10** unapparent, unassuming **11** unobtrusive **12** not egregious, unnoticeable **14** unostentatious

inconstancy 10 fickleness, infidelity **11** instability **14** capriciousness, changeableness, unfaithfulness

inconstant 6 fickle, untrue **7** erratic **8** cavalier, disloyal, unstable **9** mercurial **10** capricious, changeable, unfaithful **11** interrupted, uncommitted, undedicated, unsteadfast

incontinence 8 rashness **12** recklessness **13** lack of control **16** irresponsibility

incontinent 8 unchaste **12** unrestrained

incontrovertibility 8 sureness **9** certainty **12** absoluteness, definiteness **13** undeniability **14** irrefutability, conclusiveness **15** indisputability **16** incontestability **17** unquestionability

incontrovertible 9 apodictic **10** unarguable, undeniable **11** established, irrefutable **12** indisputable **14** beyond question, unquestionable

inconvenience 6 bother, put out **7** trouble **8** hardship, headache, nuisance **9** annoyance, disoblige, put one out **10** discomfort **13** be a nuisance to, pain in the neck

inconvenient 7 awkward, unhandy **8** annoying, tiresome, untimely **10** bothersome, burdensome **11** distressing, inopportune, troublesome

Incoronazione di Poppea, L'
   also: 22 The Coronation of Poppaea
   opera by: 10 Monteverdi
   character: 4 Nero **6** Ottone **7** Ottavia

incorporate 4 fuse **6** embody, work in **7** include **10** amalgamate, assimilate **11** consolidate

incorporated 6 united **8** embodied, included **11** amalgamated, assimilated **12** consolidated

incorporeal 6 occult, unreal **7** ghostly, phantom **8** bodiless **9** spiritual, unearthly, unfleshly, unworldly **10** immaterial, intangible **11** disembodied **12** supernatural **13** insubstantial

incorrect 5 false, wrong **6** untrue **7** inexact **8** mistaken **9** erroneous **10** fallacious, inaccurate

incorrectness 5 error **9** wrongness **10** inaccuracy **12** carelessness, slovenliness

incorrigible 6 unruly **8** hardened, hard-core, hopeless **10** beyond help, delinquent **11** intractable **12** beyond saving, past changing, unmanageable **14** uncontrollable

incorrigible child
French: **14** enfant terrible

incorruptible 4 pure **6** honest **7** upright **8** reliable **9** faultless, righteous **10** unbribable **11** trustworthy **14** irreproachable

increase 3 wax **4** grow **5** add to, swell **6** enrich, expand **7** advance, augment, burgeon, enhance, enlarge **8** multiply **12** become larger

increasing 7 growing **9** enlarging, expansion, extending, extension **10** drawing out **11** enlargement **12** augmentation

incredible 6 absurd **7** amazing, awesome **10** astounding, farfetched, remarkable **11** astonishing **12** preposterous, unbelievable, unimaginable **13** extraordinary, inconceivable

Incredible Hulk, The
character: **9** Jack McGee **11** David Banner
cast: **9** Bill Bixby **10** Jack Colvin **11** Lou Ferrigno

incredulous 7 dubious **8** doubtful **9** skeptical **10** suspicious **11** distrustful **12** disbelieving

increment 4 gain, rise **5** raise **6** growth, profit **7** benefit **8** addition, increase **9** accretion **10** supplement **11** enlargement **12** accumulation, appreciation, augmentation **13** proliferation

incriminate 5 blame **6** accuse, charge, indict

incrimination 5 blame **7** charges **10** accusation, indictment

incubate 3 set, sit **4** plot **5** breed, brood, clock, cover, hatch **6** scheme **7** develop, gestate, sit upon **8** generate

incubus 5 demon **8** bad dream **9** nightmare

inculcate 5 drill, imbue, infix, teach, train **6** impart, infuse **7** implant, impress, instill **8** instruct **9** brainwash, condition, enlighten **12** indoctrinate

inculpable 5 clear **8** innocent **9** blameless, guiltless, not guilty **10** not at fault, unblamable **14** not responsible

incur 6 arouse, assume, incite, stir up **7** acquire, bring on, involve, provoke **8** bring out, contract, fall into

incurable 8 cureless, hopeless **9** cease-

less **10** beyond cure, inveterate, relentless, unflagging **12** incorrigible, irremediable **13** dyed-in-the-wool, uncorrectable

incursion 4 push, raid **5** foray **6** attack, inroad, sortie **7** assault **8** invasion **11** advance into, impingement **12** encroachment, infiltration

indebted 5 bound **7** bounden **8** beholden, grateful, thankful **9** obligated **10** chargeable **11** accountable **15** under obligation

indebtedness 4 debt **5** debit **7** arrears **9** liability **10** balance due, obligation **11** liabilities

indecency 10 immorality **12** unseemliness **13** offensiveness, salaciousness **14** indecorousness

indecent 4 blue, lewd, rude **5** bawdy, dirty **6** filthy, smutty, vulgar **7** ignoble, ill-bred, immoral, obscene, uncivil **8** immodest, improper, prurient, unseemly **9** offensive, salacious **10** in bad taste, indecorous, indiscreet, licentious, unbecoming **11** unwholesome **12** pornographic

Indecent Obsession, An
author: **17** Colleen McCullough

indecipherable 7 cryptic **9** enigmatic, illegible **10** unreadable **11** inscrutable

indecision 5 doubt **6** acrisy **7** dilemma, swither **8** wavering **10** hesitation **11** fluctuation, vacillating, vacillation, uncertainty **12** irresolution

indecisive 4 weak **7** dubious, unclear **8** doubtful, hesitant, wavering **9** confusing, debatable, mercurial, uncertain, unsettled **10** disputable, hesitating, irresolute, wishy-washy **11** halfhearted, vacillating **12** inconclusive **13** indeterminate **17** blowing hot and cold

indecorous 5 gross **6** sinful, wicked **7** ill-bred **8** immodest, improper, low-class, unseemly **9** unfitting **10** unbecoming, unsuitable **11** blameworthy **13** inappropriate, reprehensible

indecorum 8 bad taste **9** immodesty, indecency, vulgarity **11** impropriety **12** impoliteness, unseemliness

indeed 5 truly **6** in fact, really **7** for sure, in truth **8** actually, to be sure **9** certainly, in reality, veritably **10** positively, to be honest, undeniably **11** joking apart **13** in point of fact, with certainty **14** to tell the truth **15** as a matter of fact, without question **16** strictly speaking

indefatigable 6 dogged **7** staunch **8** diligent, sedulous, tireless, untiring **9** energetic **10** persistent, unflagging, unwearying **11** persevering, unfaltering **13** inexhaustible

indefensible 8 improper, vincible **9** pregnable, untenable **10** vulnerable **11** defenseless, inexcusable, unpro-

tected, unspeakable **12** open to attack, unpardonable **13** unjustifiable

indefinite 3 dim **5** vague **6** unsure **7** inexact, obscure, unknown **8** doubtful **9** ambiguous, amorphous, limitless, tentative, uncertain, unsettled **10** ill-defined, indecisive, indistinct, inexplicit **11** illimitable, measureless, unspecified **12** undetermined **13** indeterminate

indefiniteness 6 vagary **9** ambiguity, vagueness **10** indecision **11** uncertainty **12** equivocation

indelible 4 fast **5** fixed, vivid **7** lasting **8** deep-dyed **9** ingrained, memorable, permanent **10** unerasable **11** unremovable **12** ineradicable **13** unforgettable

indelicate 4 lewd, rude **5** broad, crude, gross **6** clumsy, coarse, risque, vulgar **7** awkward, obscene **8** immodest, improper, indecent, off-color, unseemly **9** offensive, unrefined **10** indecorous, indiscreet, suggestive, unbecoming

in demand 7 popular **9** desirable **11** sought after

indemnification 7 payment **10** recompense, reparation **12** compensation

indemnify 3 pay **5** atone, cover, repay **6** insure, secure **7** pay back, protect, rectify, requite, satisfy **8** make good **9** make right, make up for, reimburse **10** compensate, make amends, recompense, remunerate **15** make restitution

indemnity 7 redress **8** coverage, security **9** insurance, repayment **10** protection **11** restitution **12** compensation **15** indemnification

indent 5 notch, set in **6** recess **7** set back

indentation 3 bay, cut, pit **4** dent, nick **5** gouge, inset, niche, notch, score **6** cavity, furrow, pocket, recess **8** incision **9** concavity **10** depression

indented 6 hollow, sunken, zigzag **7** concave, notched **9** depressed

indenture 4 bind **8** contract **10** apprentice

indentured 5 bound **10** contracted **11** apprenticed

independence 7 freedom, liberty **8** autonomy **10** liberation **11** sovereignty **12** emancipation, self-reliance **14** self-government **17** self-determination

independent 4 free **7** solvent, well-off **8** affluent, separate, unallied, well-to-do **9** apart from, exclusive, on one's own, sovereign, uncoerced, well-fixed **10** autonomous, well-heeled **11** self-reliant, unconnected **12** unassociated, uncontrolled **13** self-directing, self-governing, unconstrained **15** individualistic, self-determining

indescribable 9 ineffable **11** beyond words, indefinable, unutterable **12** overwhelming **13** inexpressible **17** beyond description **20** beggaring description

indestructible 8 enduring **9** permanent **11** everlasting, infrangible, unbreakable **12** imperishable

indeterminate 5 vague **7** obscure, unclear **8** not clear **9** ambiguous, uncertain, undefined **10** indefinite, perplexing, unresolved **11** problematic, unspecified **12** undetermined, unstipulated

index 4 clue, mark, sign **5** proof, token **7** catalog, symptom **8** evidence, glossary, register **9** catalogue, indicator **10** indication **13** manifestation **16** alphabetical list

Index Librorum Prohibitorum 22 index of prohibited books

index of prohibited books
  Latin: 25 Index Librorum Prohibitorum

India
  other name: 4 Hind **6** Bharat **12** Bharat Varsha
  capital: 8 New Delhi
  largest city: 8 Calcutta
  others: 4 Agra, Gaya, Pune **5** Dacca, Poona, Surat **6** Bombay, Jaipur, Kanpur, Lahore, Madras, Madura, Mysore, Nagpur **7** Banaras **8** Kolhapur, Mandalay, Mirzapur, Shahpura, Srinagar **9** Ahmedabad, Bangalore, Hyderabad **10** Darjeeling
  division: 3 Goa **5** Assam, Bihar, Jammu **6** Kerala, Orissa, Punjab, Sikkim **7** Gujarat, Haryana, Kashmir, Manipur, Tripura **8** Nagaland **9** Karnataka, Meghalaya, Rajasthan, Tamil Nadu **10** West Bengal **11** Daman and Diu, Maharashtra, Pondicherry **12** Uttar Pradesh **13** Andhra Pradesh, Madhya Pradesh **15** Himachal Pradesh
  measure: 3 ady, gaz, gez, jow, lan **4** byee, coss, depa, doph, hath, koss, kunk, raik, rati, seit, taun, tola **5** bigha, covid, crosa, denda, depoh, drona, erosa, garce, hasta, krosa, parah, ratti, salay, yojan **6** adhaka, amunam, covido, cudava, dumbha, geerah, moolum, mushti, ouroub, palgat, parran, prasha, ropani, tipree, unglee, yojana **7** dhanush, gavyuti, khahoon, niranga, prastha **8** okthabah
  monetary unit: 3 lac, pie **4** lakh, pice **5** abidi, rupee
  weight: 3 mod, pai, vis **4** drum, hoen, kona, pala, pank, pice, ruay, tael, tali, tola, wang, yava **5** adpad, candy, hubba, maund, tical **6** karsha **8** mangelin
  island: 6 Agatti, Chilka **7** Andaman, Minicoy, Nicobar **8** Amindivi **9** Laccadive **11** Lakshadweep

lake: 5 Jheel, Lonar, Wular **6** Chilka, Colair, Dhebar, Kolair **7** Kolleru, Pulicat, Pushkar, Sambahr
mountain: 8 Aravalli **9** Broad Peak, Distaghil, Himalayas, Karakoram, Nanda Devi, Rakaposhi **10** Gasherbrum, Masherbrum **11** Nanga Parbat **12** Eastern Ghats, Kanchenjunga, Western Ghats
  hills: 4 Chin, Naga **5** Khasi **6** Lushai **7** Nilgiri
highest point: 12 Godwin Austen
river: 3 Son **4** Beas, Kosi, Tapi **5** Gogra, Indus, Jumna, Tapti **6** Gandak, Ganges, Jhelum, Kaveri, Kistna, Sutlej, Yamuna **7** Cauveri, Cauvery, Chambal, Damodar, Hooghly, Krishna, Narbada, Narmada **8** Godavari, Mahanadi **10** Bhagirathi **11** Brahmaputra
sea: 6 Indian **7** Arabian
physical feature:
  bay: 6 Bengal
  cape: 7 Comorin
  desert: 4 Thar **9** Rajasthan
  forest: 3 Gir
  gulf: 5 Kutch **6** Cambay, Mannar
  pass: 9 Karakoram
  plain: 12 Indo-Gangetic
  plateau: 6 Deccan **7** Shillon **11** Chota Nagpur
  rains: 7 monsoon
  strait: 4 Palk
  swamp: 9 Sunderban **11** Rann of Kutch
  valley: 13 Vale of Kashmir
people: 2 Ao **3** Gor **4** Bhil **5** Aryan **6** Badaga, Pathan **7** Sherani **9** Dravidian **10** Andamanese
  caste: 3 Jat **5** Sudra **6** Rajput, Shudra **7** Brahman, Brahmin, Harijan, Maratha, Vaishya **9** Kshatriya **11** Untouchable
  dynasty: 5 Gupta, Mogul **6** Maurya, Rajput **8** Marathas **14** Delhi Sultanate
  god: 4 Kali, Rama, Siva **5** Durga, Laxmi, Shiva **6** Brahma, Kumara, Vishnu **7** Ganesha, Hanuman, Krishna, Lakshmi **9** Kartikeya **10** Subramanya
  ruler: 5 Akbar, Asoka, Babur, Timur **7** Humayun **8** Hyder Ali, Jahangir **9** Aurangzeb, Shah Jahan **11** Rajiv Gandhi, Tippu Sultan **12** Indira Gandhi **13** Queen Victoria **15** Jawaharlal Nehru, Mohandas K (Mahatma) Gandhi **18** Chandragupta Maurya
language: 4 Urdu **5** Hindi, Oriya, Tamil **6** Sindhi, Telugu **7** Bengali, English, Kannada, Malayam, Marathi, Punjabi **8** Assamese, Gujarati, Kashmiri, Sanskrit **9** Malayalam
religion: 4 Sikh **5** Hindu, Islam, Parsi **7** Jainist, Judaism **8** Buddhism **11** Zoroastrian **12** Christianity
place:

  cathedral: 10 Saint Thome
  fortress: 3 Red **11** Saint George
  mausoleum: 8 Taj Mahal
  minaret: 9 Qutb Minar
  mosque: 10 Jama Masjid
  park: 6 Maidan
  president's residence: 17 Rashtrapati Bhavan
  railway station: 8 Victoria
  shrine: 7 Raj Ghat
  street: 7 Raj Path **11** Chowringhee, Marine Drive **12** Chandni Chauk **14** Connaught Place
  temple: 5 Birla **6** Ellora, Golden **7** Kailasa **10** Ajanta Cave
feature:
  dance: 6 nautch **7** cantico
  religious text: 7 Rig Veda
  shrine: 5 stupa
food:
  beer: 5 apong
  bread: 7 chapati
  liquor: 4 soma, sura **5** shrab
  tea: 5 assam

Indian
  constellation: 5 Indus

Indiana
  abbreviation: 2 IN **3** Ind
  nickname: 7 Hoosier
  capital/largest city: 12 Indianapolis
  others: 4 Gary, Peru **6** Brazil, Goshen, Hobart, Jasper, Kokomo, Marion, Muncie, Wabash **7** Elkhart, Ft Wayne, Hammond, LaPorte, Whiting **8** Columbus, Richmond **9** Lafayette, Mishawaka, South Bend, Vincennes **10** Evansville, Huntington, Logansport, Terre Haute **11** Bloomington, East Chicago **12** Connorsville, Michigan City
  college: 4 Ball **6** Bethel, Butler, DePauw, Goshen, Marion, Purdue, Wabash **9** Notre Dame **10** Evansville, Valparaiso
  explorer: 7 La Salle
  feature: 10 New Harmony **12** Indian mounds
    national memorial: 14 Lincoln boyhood
  tribe: 3 Wea **5** Miami **7** Shawnee
  people: 7 Hoosier **10** Cole Porter, Eugene Debs, Gus Grissom, Red Skelton **12** Wilbur Wright **15** Booth Tarkington, Theodore Dreiser **18** James Whitcomb Riley
  lake: 5 Clear, James **6** Monroe **7** Manitou, Wawasee **8** Michigan **9** Mansfield **11** Maxinkuckee
  land rank: 12 thirty-eighth
  mountain: 13 Greensfort Top
  physical feature:
    cave: 9 Wyandotte
  river: 4 Ohio **5** White **6** Maumee, Wabash **8** Kankakee **10** Tippecanoe, Whitewater
  state admission: 10 nineteenth
  state bird: 8 cardinal
  state flower: 5 peony **6** zinnia

state motto: 19 Crossroads of America

state song: 28 On the Banks of the Wabash Far Away

state tree: 5 tulip **11** tulip poplar

Indiana
basketball team: 6 Pacers

Indiana
author: 10 George Sand
character: 4 Noun **7** Delmare **13** Rodolphe Brown **15** Raymon de Ramiere

Indianapolis
football team: 5 Colts

Indic
language family: 12 Indo-European
branch: 11 Indo-Iranian
subgroup: 5 Hindi, Oriya **6** Nepali, Sindhi **7** Bengali, Marathi, Pakrits, Panjabi **8** Assamese, Gujarati, Kashmiri **9** Sinhalese

indicate 4 mean, show, tell **5** imply **6** denote, evince, record, reveal **7** bespeak, point to, signify, specify, suggest **8** point out, register, stand for **9** be a sign of, designate, establish, make known, represent, symbolize

indication 4 clue, hint, mark, omen, sign **5** token **6** augury, boding, signal **7** gesture, mention, portent, presage, showing, symptom, telling, warning **8** evidence, pointing **9** foretoken **10** foreboding, indicating, intimation, signifying, suggestion **11** designation, premonition **13** demonstration, manifestation

indicative 8 symbolic **10** denotative, emblematic, evidential, expressive, indicatory, suggestive **11** connotative, designative, significant, symptomatic **13** symptomatical **14** characteristic, representative

indicator 4 clue **5** guide **7** pointer **10** indication

indict 4 cite **6** accuse, charge, have up, impute, pull up **7** arraign, bring up, impeach **9** criminate, inculpate, prosecute **11** incriminate **13** prefer charges

indifference 6 apathy **7** disdain, neglect **8** coldness, no import **9** aloofness, unconcern **10** negligence, paltriness, triviality **11** disinterest, impassivity, inattention, insouciance, nonchalance **12** carelessness, unimportance **13** impassiveness, insensibility, insensitivity **14** insignificance, lack of interest

indifferent 4 cool, fair, rote, so-so **5** aloof **6** medium, modest **7** average, unmoved **8** detached, mediocre, middling, moderate, ordinary, passable **9** apathetic, impassive, not caring, unmindful **10** impervious, insensible, insouciant, nonchalant, second-rate, uninspired **11** commonplace, perfunctory, unconcerned **12** uninterested **13** insusceptible **15** undistin-

guished **17** betwixt and between, neither good nor bad

indigence 4 need, want **6** penury **7** begarry, poverty **9** pauperism, privation **11** destitution, dire straits **13** pennilessness

indigenous 6 native **7** endemic **8** domestic, homebred **9** home-grown **10** aboriginal **13** autochthonous, originating in

indigent 4 poor **5** needy **6** hard-up, in need, in want **7** pinched **8** badly off **9** destitute, moneyless, penniless **12** impoverished **15** poverty-stricken

indiges
title in: 4 Rome
suggests: 11 deification
for service to: 7 country

indigestible 4 rich **13** unassimilable

indignant 3 mad **4** sore **5** angry, huffy, irate, riled **6** fuming, miffed, peeved, piqued, put off, put out **8** incensed, offended, provoked, steaming, worked up, wrathful **9** resentful, wrought up **10** displeased, infuriated **15** on one's high horse

indignation 3 ire **4** fury, huff, rage **5** pique, wrath **6** animus, choler, dismay, uproar **7** umbrage **8** vexation **9** annoyance **10** irritation, resentment **11** displeasure

indignity 4 slur **5** abuse **6** insult, slight **7** affront, offense, outrage **8** dishonor, rudeness **9** injustice **11** discourtesy, humiliation **12** mistreatment **13** slap in the face

indigo 3 dye **4** blue **8** dark blue, deep blue, navy blue **10** Indigofera
varieties: 4 wild **5** false **7** bastard **8** wild blue **9** blue false **10** plains wild, white false **12** prairie false **13** fragrant false

indirect 5 vague **6** remote, zigzag **7** crooked, devious, distant, evasive, hedging, oblique, winding **8** rambling, tortuous **9** ancillary, secondary **10** circuitous, derivative, digressive, discursive, incidental, meandering, roundabout, unintended **13** unintentional

indirection 8 rambling **10** digression, meandering, zigzagging **14** circuitousness, circumlocution, roundaboutness

indiscernible 6 hidden **9** invisible **10** indistinct **12** undetectable, unnoticeable **13** imperceptible

indiscreet 6 unwise **7** foolish **8** careless, tactless, unseemly **9** foolhardy, ill-judged, impolitic, imprudent, tasteless, untactful **10** incautious **11** improvident, injudicious, thoughtless, unbefitting, uncalled-for **12** undiplomatic **13** inconsiderate, uncircumspect

indiscretion 8 rashness **10** imprudence **12** carelessness, heedlessness, recklessness, tactlessness **13** foolhardiness, insensitivity **15** thoughtlessness **16** irresponsibility

indiscriminate 6 motley, random **7** aimless, chaotic, jumbled, mongrel **8** confused, slapdash, unchoosy **9** haphazard, hit-or-miss **10** hodgepodge **11** promiscuous, unselective **12** disorganized, unsystematic **16** higgledy-piggledy, undistinguishing

in disorder 5 messy **6** blowsy, frowsy, mussed, sloppy, untidy **7** ruffled, rumpled, tousled, unkempt **8** uncombed **10** disarrayed, disheveled, disordered, disorderly **11** disarranged

indispensable 5 basic, vital **6** needed **7** crucial, needful **8** required **9** essential, mandatory, necessary, requisite **10** compulsory, imperative, obligatory **11** fundamental

indispensable condition
Latin: 10 sine qua non

indispensable element 9 basic need, essential, necessity, requisite **10** sine qua non **11** requirement

indisposed 3 ill **5** loath **6** ailing, averse, laid up, sickly, unwell **7** opposed **8** hesitant, taken ill **9** bedridden, reluctant, unwilling **10** not oneself **11** disinclined **15** under the weather

indisposition 5 upset **6** malady **7** ailment, illness **8** sickness **9** complaint, ill health

indisputable 4 sure **7** assured, certain, decided, evident, obvious **8** absolute, apparent, clear-cut, definite, positive **10** conclusive, unarguable, undeniable **11** indubitable, irrefutable **12** unassailable, unmistakable **13** incontestable **14** unquestionable **16** incontrovertible **20** beyond a shadow of doubt

indissoluble 5 fixed **7** abiding, lasting **8** constant, enduring **9** immutable, indelible, permanent, perpetual **11** everlasting **12** imperishable, ineradicable

indistinct 3 dim **4** weak **5** faint, muddy, murky, vague **6** cloudy, hidden **7** blurred, clouded, muffled, obscure, shadowy, unclear **8** confused, nebulous, puzzling **9** ambiguous, enigmatic, illegible, inaudible, uncertain **10** ill-defined, incoherent, indefinite, mysterious, out of focus **11** not distinct **13** indeterminate **14** indecipherable, unintelligible **16** incomprehensible

indistinguishable 7 obscure, unclear **9** invisible **10** indistinct, unapparent **12** unnoticeable, unobservable **13** a carbon copy of, identical with, imperceptible, inconspicuous, indiscernible

individual 6 person, unique **7** one's own, private, special, unusual **8** distinct, especial, original, personal, separate, singular, somebody, specific, uncommon **9** different, exclusive **10** particular **11** distinctive, independent

12 personalized **14** characteristic, unconventional

individuality 6 cachet **10** uniqueness **11** distinction, singularity, specialness **13** particularity **15** distinctiveness

individually 4 each **5** apart **6** apiece, singly **8** a la carte, uniquely **10** one at a time, peculiarly, personally, separately **12** respectively **13** distinctively **18** characteristically

Indochina 9 peninsula
　includes: 4 Laos **6** Malaya **7** Myanmar, Vietnam **8** Cambodia, Thailand

indoctrinate 5 brief, drill, teach, train, tutor **6** infuse, school **7** educate, implant, instill **8** initiate **9** brainwash, inculcate **12** propagandize

indoctrination 5 drill **8** drilling, teaching, training **9** education, schooling **10** initiation, instilling **11** inculcation, instruction

Indo-European
　language branch: 5 Greek **6** Celtic, Italic **7** Romance **8** Albanian, Armenian, Germanic **9** Anatolian, Tocharian **11** Balto-Slavic, Indo-Iranian

Indo-Iranian
　language family: 12 Indo-European
　ancient: 7 Avestan **8** Sanskrit **10** Old Persian
　modern Iranian: 5 Indic, Tajik **6** Pashto **7** Baluchi, Kurdish, Persian
　modern Indic: 4 Pali **5** Hindi, Oriya **6** Nepali, Sindhi **7** Bengali, Marathi, Panjabi **8** Assamese, Gujarati, Kashmiri **9** Sinhalese

indolence 5 sloth **7** inertia, languor, laxness **8** idleness, laziness **10** inactivity

indolent 4 lazy **5** inert, slack **7** lumpish **8** dawdling, dilatory, inactive, listless, slothful, sluggish **9** do-nothing, easygoing, lethargic, shiftless **13** lackadaisical

indomitable 6 dogged **7** doughty, staunch, valiant **8** cast-iron, fearless, intrepid, resolute, stalwart, stubborn **9** dauntless, steadfast, undaunted **10** courageous, formidable, invincible, unwavering, unyielding **11** insuperable, persevering, unflinching, unshrinking **12** invulnerable, unassailable **13** indefatigable, irrepressible, unconquerable

Indonesia
　other name: 9 Nusantara **12** Tanah Airkita **21** Netherlands East Indies
　capital/largest city: 7 Jakarta **8** Djakarta
　others: 5 Bogor, Medan **6** Malang, Manado **7** Bandung **8** Macassar, Semarang, Surabaya **9** Hollandia, Palembang, Surakarta **10** Jogjakarta, Yogyakarta **11** Banjarmasin
　measure: 5 depah, depoh
　monetary unit: 3 sen **6** rupiah
　weight: 5 catty, ounce, thail **6** soekoe

island: 3 Aru **4** Bali, Buru, Java **5** Ambon, Ceram, Seram, Spice, Sumba, Timor **6** Bangka, Borneo, Flores, Lombok, Madura, Tidore **7** Belawan, Celebes, Morotai, Sumatra, Sumbawa, Ternate **8** Belitung, Moluccas, Sulawesi **9** Halmahera, New Guinea **10** Kalimantan **11** Lesser Sunda **12** Greater Sunda

lake: 4 Toba **5** Ranau **6** Towuti

river: 4 Hari, Musi, Solo **5** Rokan **6** Asahan, Barito, Kampar **7** Brantas, Kaptuas **9** Indrogiri, Mamberamo, Martapura

sea: 4 Java, Savu **5** Banda, Ceram, Timor **6** Flores, Indian **7** Arafura, Celebes, Molucca, Pacific **10** Philippine, South China

physical feature:
　strait: 5 Sunda **7** Makasar, Malacca **8** Makassar
　volcano: 6 Slamet **8** Krakatoa

people: 5 Batak, Dayak, Dyaks, Malay **6** Papuan, Toraja **7** Battaks, Chinese, Igorots **8** Acehnese, Achinese, Balinese, Javanese, Madurese, Sudanese **11** Minang Kabau
　leader: 7 Suharto, Sukarno

language: 5 Tetum **6** Bahasa, Igorot **7** English, Gyarung, Malayan **8** Balinese, Chamorro, Javanese, Madurese, Sudanese **10** Indonesian, Polynesian

religion: 5 Hindu, Islam **7** animism **8** Buddhism **12** Christianity, Confucianism

place:
　palace: 6 Kraton
　pyramid: 5 Stupa **9** Borobudur
　shrine: 6 Dagoba, Kraton

feature:
　cap: 5 pitji
　cloth: 5 batik
　jacket: 6 kebaja
　lizard: 12 Komodo dragon
　scarf: 9 selendang
　shadow play: 6 wajang, wayang
　skirt: 4 kain **6** sarong
　tree: 4 supa

food:
　ceremonial dinner: 9 selamatan

indoors 6 at home, inside, shut in, shut up, within **10** in the house **11** sequestered

Indo-Pacific
　language subgroup: 4 Kate **5** Kiwai **7** Andaman, Merauke **8** Highland, Tasmania **9** Ekari-Moni, Hollandia, Timor-Alor **10** New Britain **12** Astrolabe Bay, Bougainville **14** Vogelkop-Kamoro **16** Eastern New Guinea, Northern Salomons **17** Northern Halmahera

indorse see **7** endorse

In Dubious Battle
　author: 13 John Steinbeck

indubitable 4 sure **7** certain **9** undoubted **10** conclusive **11** irrefutable,

unequivocal **12** indisputable, unmistakable **14** unquestionable **16** incontrovertible

indubitably 6 surely **7** for sure **8** of course **9** certainly, doubtless **10** for certain **11** undoubtedly **12** without doubt **14** unquestionably, with no question

induce 3 get **4** coax, spur, sway **5** cause, impel **6** arouse, effect, incite, lead to, prompt **7** actuate, bring on, dispose, incline, inspire, produce, provoke, win over **8** activate, motivate, occasion, persuade **9** encourage, influence, instigate, prevail on **10** bring about, bring round, give rise to **11** prevail upon, set in motion

inducement 4 bait, goad, spur **5** cause **6** ground, motive, reason **8** stimulus **9** incentive **10** allurement, attraction, enticement, incitement, persuasion, temptation **11** inspiration, instigation, provocation

induct 5 crown, draft, frock **6** enlist, invest, lead in, ordain, sign up **7** bring in, install, instate, usher in **8** enthrone, initiate, register **9** conscript, establish, introduce **10** consecrate, inaugurate

in due course 4 then **6** thence **10** eventually **11** accordingly **15** at the proper time **19** in the fullness of time

indulge 4 baby **5** favor, humor, serve, spoil, treat **6** coddle, cosset, oblige **7** appease, cater to, gratify, yield to **8** pander to **9** give way to **11** accommodate, go along with, mollycoddle

indulgence 6 excess, luxury **8** kindness, lenience, patience **9** allowance, benignity, tolerance **10** compassion, debauchery, profligacy, sufferance **11** dissipation, forbearance, forgiveness **12** extravagance, graciousness, immoderation, intemperance **13** understanding **14** permissiveness

indulgent 4 kind **6** benign, tender **7** clement, lenient, patient, sparing **8** humoring, obliging, tolerant, yielding **9** easygoing, forgiving, pampering **10** forbearing, permissive **11** complaisant, forebearing **12** conciliatory **13** understanding

Indus
　constellation near: 4 Grus, Pavo
　river in: 4 Asia **5** India, Tibet **8** Pakistan
　into: 10 Arabian Sea

industrious 4 busy **6** active **7** zealous **8** diligent, occupied, sedulous, tireless **9** assiduous, energetic **10** productive, purposeful, unflagging **11** hardworking, painstaking, persevering, unremitting **12** businesslike, enterprising **13** indefatigable

industry 2 go **4** toil, zeal **5** field, labor, trade **6** bustle, energy, hustle **8** activity, business, commerce, hard work **9** assiduity, diligence **10** enterprise **11** application, manufacture **12** perseverance, sedulousness **13** assiduousness **15** industriousness **16** indefatigability

inebriate 3 sot **4** lush, soak, wino **5** drunk, rummy, souse, toper **6** barfly, boozer **7** tippler **8** drunkard **9** alcoholic **11** dipsomaniac

inebriated 4 high **5** drunk, oiled, tight, tipsy **6** bombed, loaded, potted, stoned, tanked, zonked **7** drunken, smashed, sozzled, wrecked **8** besotted **9** befuddled, plastered **10** in one's cups **11** intoxicated **12** drunk as a lord **17** under the influence **20** three sheets to the wind

ineffable 5 ideal **6** divine, sacred **9** spiritual **10** indefinite, untellable **11** indefinable, unspeakable, unutterable **12** transcendent **13** indescribable, inexpressible **14** incommunicable, transcendental

in effect 6 active **8** a reality **9** activated, effective, operative **11** in operation

ineffective 4 vain, weak **6** futile **7** useless **8** impotent **9** fruitless, incapable, powerless, worthless **10** inadequate **11** inefficient, inoperative, not much good, of little use **12** unproductive

ineffectual 4 lame, vain, weak **5** inept **6** feeble, futile **7** hapless, useless **8** impotent **10** inadequate, not up to par, profitless, unavailing **11** incompetent, ineffective, inefficient **12** unproductive, unprofitable, unsuccessful **13** inefficacious **14** unsatisfactory

inefficient 5 inept, slack **6** futile **8** slipshod **9** pointless, unskilled **10** inadequate **11** incompetent, indifferent, ineffective, ineffectual **12** not efficient, unproductive **13** inefficacious **14** good-for-nothing

inelegance 9 crudeness, grossness, roughness, vulgarity **10** coarseness **13** tastelessness

inelegant 4 ugly **6** coarse, common **8** inferior **9** tasteless, unrefined **10** ungraceful

ineligible 5 unfit **10** unentitled, unsuitable **11** not eligible, unqualified **12** disqualified, unacceptable

ineluctable 4 sure **5** fated **7** certain **10** ineludible, inevasible, inevitable, inexorable, sure as fate, unevadable **11** inescapable, irrevocable, unavoidable, unstoppable **13** unpreventable

inept 5 empty, inane, silly, unapt **6** clumsy **7** asinine, awkward, fatuous, foolish **8** bungling **9** maladroit, pointless, senseless, unfitting, unskilled, untrained **10** out of place, unsuitable **11** incompetent, ineffective, ineffectual, inefficient, nonsensical, unqualified **13** inappropriate, inefficacious

ineptitude 9 inability **10** clumsiness, inadequacy **11** awkwardness **12** incompetence **14** ineffectuality **15** ineffectiveness

inequality 8 imparity, inequity **9** disparity, diversity, prejudice **10** difference, divergence, favoritism, unfairness, unlikeness **11** inconstancy, unequalness **12** irregularity, variableness **13** disproportion, dissimilarity, dissimilitude

inequity 4 bias **9** injustice, prejudice **10** favoritism, inequality, unfairness **14** discrimination

ineradicable 7 lasting **9** indelible, permanent **10** inerasable **12** ineffaceable **14** indestructible

inert 4 dull, numb **5** slack, still **6** leaden, static, supine, torpid **7** languid, passive **8** immobile, inactive, listless, sluggish **9** impassive, inanimate, quiescent **10** motionless, phlegmatic, stationary

inertia 6 apathy, stupor, torpor **7** languor **8** dullness, inaction, laziness, lethargy **9** indolence, inertness, lassitude, passivity, torpidity, weariness **10** inactivity, supineness **11** passiveness **12** listlessness, sluggishness

inertness 6 apathy **8** lethargy **9** passivity **10** quiescence **12** sluggishness **14** motionlessness

inescapable 4 sure **7** certain, evident **8** manifest, positive **10** inevitable **11** ineluctable, predestined, unavoidable

in esse 7 in being **11** in actuality **16** actually existing

inestimable 7 sumless **8** precious **9** priceless **10** invaluable **11** beyond price, measureless **12** immeasurable, incalculable, unmeasurable

inevitable 4 sure **5** fated **7** certain **8** destined **10** ineludible **11** ineluctable, inescapable, predestined, unavoidable **13** predetermined, unpreventable

inexact 3 off **6** faulty, sloppy **8** careless, slovenly **9** defective, imperfect, imprecise **10** inaccurate, unspecific **11** approximate

in exactly the same words
Latin: **19** verbatim et literatim

inexcusable 10 unbearable **11** intolerable, unallowable **12** indefensible, unforgivable, unpardonable **13** unjustifiable

inexhaustible 7 endless **8** infinite, tireless, unending **9** boundless **13** indefatigable **15** measurelessness

in existence 5 alive **6** extant, living **8** existent, existing **9** surviving, to be found

inexorable 4 firm **5** cruel, stiff **6** dogged **7** adamant **8** obdurate, pitiless, ruthless **9** immovable, merciless, unbending **10** adamantive, determined, inflexible, relentless, unyield-

ing **11** inescapable, intractable **12** irresistible **14** uncompromising

inexpedient 6 futile, unwise **7** useless **11** detrimental, impractical, inadvisable, injudicious, undesirable **13** not worthwhile **15** disadvantageous

inexpensive 5 cheap **8** moderate **9** low-priced **10** economical, reasonable **13** nominal-priced, popular-priced

inexpensive table wine
French: **12** vin ordinaire

inexperienced 5 fresh, green, naive **6** callow **7** untried **8** inexpert, unversed **9** unfledged, unskilled, untrained, untutored **10** unfamiliar, unschooled, unseasoned **11** uninitiated, unpracticed **12** unaccustomed, unacquainted, unconversant **15** unsophisticated

inexpert 5 inept **6** clumsy, gauche **7** awkward **8** bungling **9** incapable, maladroit **10** amateurish, unpolished, unskillful **11** incompetent, ineffective, inefficient, unqualified **14** unaccomplished

inexplicable 8 abstruse, baffling, puzzling **9** insoluble **10** insolvable, mysterious, mystifying, perplexing **11** enigmatical, inscrutable **12** unfathomable **13** unaccountable, unexplainable **14** undecipherable **16** incomprehensible

inexpressive 5 blank, empty **6** vacant **14** expressionless

in extenso 12 at full length

in extremis 9 near death **11** in extremity **15** on the outer edges **19** at the uttermost limit

in extremity
Latin: **10** in extremis

in fact
Latin: **7** de facto

infallible 4 sure **7** assured, certain, perfect **8** flawless, inerrant, positive, reliable, surefire, unerring **9** apodictic, faultless, foolproof, unfailing **10** dependable, impeccable **11** irrefutable **13** unimpeachable **16** incontrovertible

infamous 3 low **4** base, evil, foul, vile **6** odious, sinful, sordid, wicked **7** corrupt, heinous, ignoble, immoral, knavish **8** damnable, recreant, shameful **9** abhorrent, monstrous, nefarious, notorious **10** abominable, detestable, iniquitous, of evil fame, outrageous, perfidious, profligate, scandalous, scurrilous, villainous **11** disgraceful, of ill repute, opprobrious, treacherous **12** dishonorable, disreputable

infamy 4 evil **5** odium, shame **7** scandal **8** contempt, disgrace, dishonor, ignominy, villainy **9** discredit, disesteem, disrepute, notoriety **10** corruption, opprobrium, wickedness **11** abomination **13** despicability, notoriousness

infancy 6 cradle, nonage **8** babyhood,

minority 9 beginning, childhood, inception **10** immaturity

infant 3 kid **4** babe, baby **5** child **7** neonate, newborn, preemie, toddler **8** nursling, suckling

infantile 7 babyish **8** childish, juvenile **9** childlike, infantine **10** infantlike, sophomoric

infantryman 6 Zouave **7** dogface, dragoon **8** chasseur, doughboy, sorefoot **11** foot soldier

infatuated 7 charmed, smitten **8** beguiled, enamored, inflamed, obsessed **9** bewitched, enchanted, entranced **10** captivated, enraptured, enthralled, spellbound **11** carried away, intoxicated **12** having a crush

infatuation 4 rave **5** craze, crush, folly, mania **6** desire **7** passion **9** obsession, puppy love **10** enthusiasm **11** fascination, foolishness **12** passing fancy

infect 4 ruin **5** spoil, taint, touch **6** blight, damage, poison **7** afflict, corrupt **9** indispose, influence **11** contaminate

infected 6 impure, morbid, septic **7** corrupt, tainted **8** cankered, diseased, poisoned **12** contaminated

infection 6 blight **7** disease **9** contagion, virulence **11** suppuration

infectious 8 catching, epidemic, virulent **9** catchable, infective, spreading **10** compelling, contagious, inoculable **11** captivating **12** communicable, irresistible

infecund 6 barren, farrow **7** sterile **9** infertile **12** unproductive

infer 4 deem **5** glean, guess, judge, opine **6** deduce, gather, reason, reckon **7** presume, suppose, surmise **8** conclude **9** speculate **10** conjecture

inference 4 clue **10** intimation, suggestion **11** insinuation

inferior 4 poor **6** junior **8** low-grade, mediocre **9** secondary **10** low-quality, second-rate, subsidiary **11** indifferent, subordinate, subservient, substandard **12** not up to snuff

infernal 4 vile **5** awful, black, lower **6** cursed, Hadean, nether **7** heinous, hellish, Stygian, vicious **8** accursed, damnable, devilish, fiendish, horrible, terrible **9** atrocious, execrable, malicious, monstrous, nefarious, Plutonian **10** abominable, demoniacal, diabolical, flagitious, horrendous, iniquitous **also: 9** Tartarean **refers to: 10** underworld

inferno 4 hell, oven **5** abyss, Hades **6** hotbox, the pit, Tophet **7** furnace, roaster, sizzler **8** hellfire, hellhole, scorcher **9** perdition **10** lower world, underworld **11** netherworld **12** fiery furnace **13** nether regions **15** infernal

regions **16** fire and brimstone, the bottomless pit

Inferno
part I of: 12 Divine Comedy
author: 14 Dante Alighieri

infertile 4 arid, bare **6** barren, effete, fallow **7** drained, sterile **8** depleted, desolate, impotent, infecund **9** exhausted, fruitless **10** unfruitful, unprolific **12** unproductive **13** nonproductive

infest 4 team **5** beset, crawl, creep, swarm **6** abound, infect, plague, ravage **7** overrun, torment **9** crawl with, swarm with

infestation 6 plague, ravage **9** lousiness, pervasion **11** overrunning **12** overswarming

in few words
Latin: 12 paucis verbis

infidel 5 pagan **6** savage **7** atheist, heathen, heretic, skeptic **8** agnostic, apostate, idolater **9** barbarian **10** unbeliever **11** nonbeliever

infidelity 6 breach **7** falsity, perfidy **8** adultery, betrayal **9** disregard, violation **10** disloyalty, infraction **12** nonadherence **13** nonobservance, transgression **14** unfaithfulness

infiltrate 4 leak, seep **5** imbue, steep **6** absorb, seep in **7** pervade **8** colonize, permeate **9** insinuate, penetrate

infinite 4 vast **5** great **7** endless, immense **8** enormous **9** boundless, limitless, unbounded, unlimited **10** tremendous, without end **11** illimitable, measureless **12** immeasurable, incalculable, interminable **13** inexhaustible **15** uncircumscribed

infinitesimal 3 wee **4** puny, tiny **6** minute **10** diminutive, negligible **11** microscopic **13** imperceptible, inappreciable, insignificant, undiscernible **14** extremely small, inconsiderable

infinity 7 forever **8** eternity **10** infinitude, perpetuity **11** endlessness, eternal time **12** sempiternity **13** boundlessness, limitlessness **14** illimitability **15** everlastingness, immeasurability, incalculability, measurelessness **16** inexhaustibility **19** incomprehensibility

Infiri
gods of: 10 underworld

infirm 3 ill **4** weak, worn **5** anile, frail, shaky **6** ailing, feeble, poorly, sickly **7** failing, fragile, unsound **8** decrepit, disabled, helpless, unstable, weakened **9** doddering, emaciated, enervated, enfeebled, powerless **11** debilitated **12** strengthless

infirmary 6 clinic **7** sick bay **8** hospital

infirmity 4 flaw **5** fault **6** defect, malady **7** ailment, failing, frailty, illness **8** debility, disorder, handicap, sickness **9** fragility, frailness **10** deficiency, dis-

ability, infirmness **11** instability **12** debilitation, imperfection, unstableness **13** indisposition, vulnerability

in flagrante delicto 8 in the act **9** red-handed

inflame 4 fire, rile **5** craze, rouse **6** arouse, enrage, excite, heat up, ignite, incite, kindle, madden, stir up, work up **7** agitate, incense, provoke **8** enkindle **9** electrify, stimulate **10** intoxicate

inflamed 3 mad **5** angry, irate, riled **6** crazed, fuming, roused **7** aroused, enraged, excited, fired up, furious, incited **8** agitated, incensed, provoked, reddened **9** steamed up, stirred up **10** infuriated **11** intensified

inflame with love 6 enamor **9** enrapture, impassion, infatuate

Inflammable 5 fiery **8** choleric, volatile **9** excitable, flammable, ignitable, impetuous, overhasty, sensitive **10** high-strung, incendiary **11** combustible, precipitate **12** inflammatory

inflammation 4 acne, fire, gout, sore **6** canker, firing **7** arousal, chafing **8** bursitis, ignition, kindling, soreness, sore spot, swelling **9** agitation **10** incitement, irritation **13** conflagration, rabblerousing **suffix: 4** itis

inflammatory 5 fiery, rabid **8** arousing, enraging, inciting, mutinous, volcanic **9** demagogic, explosive, insurgent **10** incendiary, rebellious **11** combustible, fulminating, inflammable, intemperate, provocative **13** rabble-rousing, revolutionary

inflate 5 bloat, swell **6** blow up, dilate, expand, fill up, pump up **7** distend, improve, puff out **10** appreciate **11** rise in value

inflated 5 blown, gassy, tumid, wordy **6** blew up, turgid **7** bloated, blown up, dilated, flowery, pompous, swollen, verbose **8** boastful, enlarged, expanded **9** bombastic, distended, overblown, swelled up **10** rhetorical, swelled out **11** exaggerated, pretentious

inflection 4 tone **5** tenor **6** accent **10** modulation **11** enunciation, tone of voice **12** articulation **13** pronunciation

inflexible 4 firm, hard, taut **5** fixed, rigid, solid, stiff **6** dogged, mulish **7** adamant **8** obdurate, resolute, stubborn **9** hidebound, immovable, immutable, ironbound, obstinate, pigheaded, stringent, tenacious, unbending, unplastic **10** adamantine, determined, headstrong, impervious, implacable, inexorable, unwavering, unyielding **11** hard and fast, intractable, not flexible, unmalleable **12** unchangeable **14** uncompromising

inflict 4 dump **5** lay on, wreak **6** impose, unload **7** put upon **9** visit upon

10 administer, perpetrate **11** bring to bear

inflorescence 5 bloom **6** flower **7** blossom, cluster **8** blooming **9** flowering **10** blossoming
type: 4 cyme **5** spike, umbel **6** corymb, raceme, spadix **7** panicle **9** capitulum **14** verticillaster

influence 4 hold, move, pull, stir, sway **5** clout, guide, impel, power **6** arouse, effect, incite, induce, prompt, weight **7** act upon, actuate, control, dispose, incline, inspire, mastery, potency, provoke **8** dominion, leverage, persuade, pressure, prestige **9** advantage, authority **10** ascendancy, domination, predispose

influential 6 moving, potent, strong **7** leading, weighty **8** forceful, powerful, puissant **9** effective, effectual, important, inspiring, momentous **10** activating **11** efficacious, significant **12** instrumental **13** consequential

influx 5 entry **6** inflow **7** arrival, indraft, ingress **9** flowing in, incursion, inpouring **10** converging, inundation **12** infiltration

in force 6 extant **7** en masse **8** in

inform 3 rat **4** fink, tell **5** edify **6** advise, clue in, notify, snitch, squeal, tattle, tell on, tip off **7** apprise, let know **8** acquaint, denounce, forewarn, report to **9** declare to, enlighten **11** communicate, familiarize, serve notice **14** blow the whistle

inform against 5 rat on **6** betray, fink on, tell on **7** sell out **8** denounce, squeal on **11** double-cross **16** blow the whistle on

informal 4 easy **6** casual, simple **7** natural, offhand **8** familiar **9** easygoing, not formal **10** unofficial **11** spontaneous **12** come-as-you-are **13** unceremonious, unconstrained **14** unconventional

informal preliminary conference
French: **10** pourparler

informant 6 source **7** adviser, tipster **8** appriser, informer, notifier, reporter **9** announcer, spokesman **10** respondent **11** enlightener, horse's mouth, spokeswoman

information 4 data, news **5** facts, notes **6** notice, papers, report **7** account, tidings **8** briefing, bulletin, evidence, material **9** documents, knowledge, materials **10** communique **11** fact-finding **12** announcement, intelligence, notification **13** enlightenment

informed 4 told, up on, wise **5** aware, posted, talked, taught, warned **7** abreast, advised, knowing, learned, tattled **8** apprised, betrayed, educated, notified, reported, snitched, up to date **9** au courant, permeated **10** acquainted, instructed **11** enlightened, intelligent **13** knowledgeable

informer 3 rat **4** fink **5** Judas **6** canary **7** blabber, stoolie, tattler, traitor **8** betrayer, mouchard, snitcher, squealer **11** stool pigeon

Informer, The
author: **13** Liam O'Flaherty
director: **8** John Ford
cast: **10** Una O'Connor **11** Wallace Ford **12** Heather Angel **13** Margot Grahame, Preston Foster **14** Victor McLaglen
score: **10** Max Steiner
remade as: **7** Up Tight

infraction 6 breach **8** trespass **9** violation **10** peccadillo **11** lawbreaking **12** disobedience, encroachment, infringement, unobservance **13** nonobservance, transgression

infrastructure 4 base, root **5** basis **6** bottom, fabric, ground **7** bedrock, footing, support **9** framework, substrate **10** foundation, groundwork, substratum **12** substructure, underpinning **14** understructure

infrequent 3 few **4** rare **6** fitful, seldom, unique **7** unusual **8** sporadic, uncommon **9** spasmodic **10** occasional **16** few and far between

infringe 5 break **6** butt in, invade **7** disobey, impinge, infract, intrude, violate **8** encroach, overstep, trespass **10** contravene, transgress

in front 5 ahead, first **6** before **7** forward

in full possession of one's faculties
Latin: **12** compos mentis

infuriate 3 vex **4** gall, rile **5** anger, chafe **6** enrage, madden, offend **7** incense, inflame, outrage, provoke **8** irritate **9** aggravate, burn one up, make angry **10** exasperate **15** raise one's dander

infuriating 7 irksome **8** annoying, enraging **9** maddening, provoking **10** irritating **11** aggravating **12** exasperating, inflammatory

infuse 5 imbue **7** fortify, implant, inspire, instill **8** impart to, pour into **9** inculcate, insinuate, introject

in futuro 11 in the future

Inge, William
author of: **6** Picnic **7** Bus Stop **19** Come Back Little Sheba **26** The Dark at the Top of the Stairs

in general 7 as a rule, usually **10** by and large, on the whole

ingenious 4 deft **6** adroit, artful, clever, crafty, expert, shrewd **7** cunning **8** masterly, original, skillful, stunning **9** brilliant, dexterous, inventive, masterful **11** resourceful

ingenuity 5 flair, skill **7** cunning, know-how, mastery **8** aptitude, deftness, facility **9** adeptness, dexterity, expertise, sharpness **10** adroitness, as-

tuteness, brilliance, cleverness, shrewdness **11** imagination **12** good thinking, skillfulness **13** ingeniousness, inventiveness **15** imaginativeness, quick-wittedness, resourcefulness

ingenuous 4 open **5** frank, naive **6** direct, honest **7** artless, genuine, natural, up front **8** trusting **9** guileless **10** unaffected **11** openhearted **13** simplehearted **15** straightforward, unsophisticated **16** straight-shooting

ingenuousness 7 naivete **8** openness **9** frankness **11** artlessness

ingest 3 eat **4** gulp, take **5** drink **6** absorb, devour, imbibe, take in **7** consume, swallow **8** gulp down

inglorious 3 low **4** base, evil, mean, vile **6** odious **7** corrupt, heinous, ignoble **8** depraved, flagrant, infamous, shameful, shocking **9** atrocious, degrading, nefarious **10** despicable, detestable, outrageous, scandalous **11** disgraceful, ignominious, opprobrious **12** contemptible, dishonorable

in good condition
French: **10** embonpoint

in good health 2 OK **4** fine, hale, well **6** hearty, robust, tiptop **7** healthy **8** all right, blooming, vigorous **9** full of pep, in the pink **17** full of vim and vigor

in good time 5 early **7** betimes **11** ahead of time

ingot 3 bar **5** block

ingrained 4 deep, firm **5** fixed **6** inborn, inbred, innate, rooted **8** inherent, thorough **9** confirmed, implanted, indelible, intrinsic **10** deep-rooted, deep-seated, inveterate **14** constitutional

Ingram, Blanche
character in: **8** Jane Eyre
author: **6** Bronte

ingratiating 4 oily **5** sweet **6** genial, smarmy **7** affable, amiable, cordial, fulsome, gushing, likable, lovable, winning, winsome **8** charming, engaging, friendly, gracious, magnetic, pleasing, unctuous **9** appealing, congenial **10** attractive, enchanting, obsequious, oleaginous, personable, persuasive **11** captivating, good-humored, self-serving **12** presumptuous

ingratiation 7 blarney **8** flattery **9** sweet talk **12** inveiglement **13** blandishments

ingratitude 14 ungratefulness **18** lack of appreciation

ingredient 4 part **6** aspect, factor **7** element, feature **9** component, essential, principle **11** constituent, contributor **12** integral part

Ingres, Jean-Auguste-Dominique
born: **6** France **9** Montauban
artwork: **9** Odalisque, The Source **13**

Mme Moitessier **14** The Turkish Bath **15** Valpincon Bather **16** Roger and Angelica **17** The Vow of Louis XIII **21** Comtesse d'Haussonville **25** The Ambassadors of Agamemnon **26** The Vow of Louis the Thirteenth

ingress 5 entry, way in **6** access **8** entrance

inhabit 5 lodge **6** live in, occupy, people, settle, tenant **7** dwell in **8** populate, reside in

inhabitant 6 inmate, lessee, lodger, native, renter, tenant **7** boarder, citizen, denizen, dweller, settler **8** occupant, occupier, resident, villager **9** inhabiter

inhalation 4 gasp **5** sniff **6** breath **11** breathing in

inhale 5 sniff, snuff **6** suck in **7** inspire, respire **9** breathe in, inbreathe

inherent 6 inborn, inbred, innate, native **7** natural **9** essential, ingrained, intrinsic **10** deep-rooted, hereditary, inveterate **11** inalienable, inseparable **14** constitutional

inherit 3 get **6** be left, come by **7** acquire **8** come into **9** come in for **10** fall heir to

inheritance 6 devise, estate, legacy **7** bequest **8** bestowal, heritage **9** endowment, patrimony **10** bequeathal, birthright

inherited 8 came into, heirloom, unearned **10** handed down

inheritor 4 heir **7** legatee **11** beneficiary

Inherit the Wind
   director: 13 Stanley Kramer
   based on play by: 10 Robert E Lee **14** Jerome Lawrence
   cast: 8 Dick York **9** Gene Kelly **10** Elliot Reid **11** Harry Morgan **12** Spencer Tracy (Clarence Darrow) **13** Frederic March (William Jennings Bryan) **16** Florence Eldridge

inhibit 3 bar, gag **4** curb, stop **5** block, check **6** arrest, enjoin, forbid, hinder, impede, muzzle **7** control, harness, prevent, repress, smother **8** hold back, obstruct, prohibit, restrain, restrict, suppress **9** constrain **11** hold in leash

inhibited 4 cold **6** barred, curbed, frigid **7** bridled, checked, guarded **8** hindered, reserved **9** repressed **10** controlled, obstructed, restrained **11** constrained, discouraged, held in check **12** unresponsive **14** under restraint

inhibition, inhibitions 5 check **7** reserve **8** blockage **9** misgiving, restraint, stricture **10** constraint, impediment **11** guardedness, mental block, obstruction, restriction **12** constriction **17** self-consciousness

in high spirits 2 up **3** gay **5** happy,

merry **6** elated, jaunty, joyful, joyous **7** buoyant **8** carefree, ecstatic, exultant, jubilant **9** overjoyed **11** exhilarated, on cloud nine **13** up in the clouds **15** on top of the world

in hoc signo vinces 26 in this sign shalt thou conquer
   motto of: 19 Constantine the Great
   from vision of: 5 cross

inhospitable 4 cold, cool, rude **5** aloof **6** unkind **7** distant, hostile **8** impolite **10** unfriendly, ungracious, unobliging, unsociable **11** standoffish, uncongenial, unreceptive, unwelcoming **12** discourteous, unneighborly **13** inconsiderate **14** unapproachable **15** unaccommodating

inhuman 5 cruel **6** brutal, savage **7** brutish, satanic, vicious **8** barbaric, demoniac, fiendish, pitiless, ruthless, venomous **9** barbarous, heartless, malignant, merciless, monstrous, unfeeling **10** diabolical, malevolent **11** coldhearted, cold-blooded, hardhearted

inhumane 6 brutal, savage **7** inhuman **8** fiendish, pitiless, ruthless **9** barbarous, heartless, merciless, unfeeling, unpitying **10** unmerciful **11** cold-blooded, hardhearted **12** bloodthirsty **13** unsympathetic

inhumanity 6 sadism **7** cruelty **8** atrocity, savagery **9** barbarism, barbarity, brutality **11** brutishness, heinousness, malevolence, viciousness **12** fiendishness, ruthlessness **13** heartlessness, mercilessness **15** cold-bloodedness **16** bloodthirstiness

inhumation 6 burial **9** interment **10** entombment

inimical 5 toxic **6** at odds **7** harmful, hateful, hostile, hurtful, ruinous **8** venomous, virulent **9** dangerous, ill-willed, injurious, on the outs, poisonous, rancorous **10** unfriendly **11** acrimonious, deleterious, destructive, detrimental, ill-disposed **12** antagonistic, antipathetic, disputatious **13** at loggerheads, at sword's point

inimitable 4 rare **6** unique **7** supreme **8** peerless **9** matchless, nonpareil, unequaled, unmatched, unrivaled **10** consummate, preeminent, unexcelled **11** superlative, unsurpassed **12** incomparable, unparalleled **13** beyond compare

iniquitous 4 base, evil, vile **6** sinful, wicked **7** corrupt, debased, immoral, vicious **8** depraved, infamous **9** nefarious **10** evil-minded **12** blackhearted **13** reprehensible

iniquity 3 sin **4** evil, vice **5** wrong **6** infamy **7** knavery, outrage, roguery **8** inequity, villainy **9** depravity, evildoing, flagrancy, turpitude **10** corruption, dishonesty, immorality, miscreancy, profligacy, sinfulness, unfairness, unjustness, wickedness,

wrongdoing **11** abomination **13** transgression **14** gross injustice **15** unrighteousness

in isolation
   Latin: 7 in vacuo

initial 5 first **6** maiden, primal **7** opening, primary **8** germinal, original, starting **9** beginning, inaugural, incipient **10** commencing, initiatory **12** introductory

initiate 4 haze, open **5** begin, found, set up, start **6** induct, invest, launch, take in **7** bring in, install, kick off, receive, usher in **8** be opened, commence, get going, set afoot, set going **9** enter upon, establish, institute, introduce, originate **10** inaugurate, lead the way **11** break ground, get under way, take the lead **12** acquaint with **13** blaze the trail **15** familiarize with **16** lay the first stone, lay the foundation **19** start the ball rolling

initiation 5 onset, start **6** outset **7** genesis, opening **8** entrance, guidance, outbreak, starting **9** beginning, inception, induction **10** admittance, initiating, ushering in **11** inculcation **12** commencement, inauguration, introduction **14** indoctrination **15** formal admission

initiative 4 lead **8** dynamism **9** first move, first step **10** creativity, enterprise, get-up-and-go, leadership **11** originality **12** forcefulness **14** aggressiveness

in its original place
   Latin: 6 in situ

inject 3 put **4** pump **5** force, imbue, infix **6** infuse, insert **7** instill, throw in **8** intromit **9** interject, introduce **11** interpolate

injection 4 hypo, shot **7** booster, vaccine **9** antitoxin, insertion **10** hypodermic **11** inoculation, vaccination **12** shot in the arm

injudicious 4 dumb, wild **5** crazy **6** stupid, unwise **7** foolish, unsound **8** heedless, reckless **9** audacious, foolhardy, hotheaded, imprudent, senseless **10** self-willed, unsuitable **11** inadvisable

injunction 4 writ **5** edict, order **7** command **10** admonition, court order

Injun Joe
   character in: 9 Tom Sawyer
   author: 9 Mark Twain

injure 3 mar **4** harm, hurt, lame, maim **5** abuse, spoil, stain, sting, sully, wound, wrong **6** bruise, damage, debase, deface, deform, impair, malign, mangle, misuse, offend, scathe **7** afflict, affront, blemish, violate, vitiate **8** do harm to, ill-treat, lacerate, maltreat, mutilate **9** disfigure

injured 4 hurt, lame **6** abused, harmed, maimed, marred, piqued **7** bruised, damaged, defaced, grieved, scathed, wounded, wronged **8** crippled, deformed, impaired, insulted, offended **9** afflicted, affronted, aggrieved **10** disfigured

injurious 7 abusive, adverse, harmful, hurtful, noxious, ruinous **8** damaging, inimical **9** corrosive **10** calamitous, disastrous, pernicious **11** deleterious, destructive, detrimental

injury 3 cut **4** blow, gash, harm, hurt, stab **5** abuse, wound **6** bruise, damage, lesion **7** affront, outrage, scratch **9** aspersion, contusion, indignity, injustice **10** affliction, defamation, detraction, disservice, impairment, laceration, mutilation **12** vilification

injustice 3 sin **4** bias, evil **5** wrong **6** injury **7** bigotry, offense, tyranny **8** foul play, inequity, iniquity **9** prejudice, unjust act **10** disservice, favoritism, inequality, infraction, partiality, unfairness, unjustness, wrongdoing **11** malpractice, persecution **12** encroachment, infringement, partisanship **13** transgression

in keeping 6 normal **7** natural **8** becoming **9** congruous, consonant **10** consistent **11** appropriate, in agreement **12** in compliance, in conformity

inkling 3 cue, tip **4** clue, hint, idea **6** notion **7** glimmer, whisper **8** innuendo **9** suspicion, vague idea **10** conception, glimmering, indication, intimation, suggestion **11** insinuation, supposition

inky 3 jet **4** dark **5** black, raven, sable **7** stygian **9** coal-black

inlet 3 bay **4** cove, gulf **5** bight, fiord, firth, fjord **6** harbor, strait **7** estuary, narrows **8** waterway

in line 4 even **6** in a row **7** aligned, in order **8** queued up, straight **12** under control

in loco 7 in place **16** in the proper place

in loco parentis 16 replacing a parent **19** in the place of a parent

inmate 3 con **5** felon **6** lodger, tenant **7** convict, denizen **8** prisoner, resident **10** inhabitant

in medias res 19 in the middle of things **21** in the middle of the story

in memoriam 10 in memory of **13** as a memorial to, to the memory of

In Memoriam A H H
  author: **18** Alfred Lord Tennyson
in memory of
  Latin: **10** in memoriam
In Memory of W B Yeats
  author: **7** W H Auden
inmost 5 inner **6** inside **7** central **8** interior **9** innermost

in motion 5 afoot, astir **6** active, moving **7** on the go, working **8** under way **9** on the move, operating, operative **10** responsive

In My Father's Court
  author: **19** Isaac Bashevis Singer
inn 5 hotel, lodge, motel, serai **6** hostel, imaret, tavern **7** hospice, pension **8** hostelry **9** roadhouse **11** caravansary, public house
  French: **7** auberge
  Spanish: **6** posada
innards 4 guts **6** bowels, vitals **7** gizzard, insides, viscera **10** intestines **14** liver and lights

innate 6 inborn, inbred, native **7** natural **8** inherent **9** essential, ingrained, inherited, intrinsic, intuitive **10** congenital, hereditary, indigenous **11** instinctive **14** constitutional

inner 6 hidden, inside, inward, mental, middle **7** central, private, psychic **8** esoteric, interior, internal, personal **9** concealed, emotional, spiritual, unobvious **10** more secret **12** more intimate **13** psychological

inner circle 4 core **5** bosom, cadre, heart **6** center **7** nucleus

inner city 8 core city, downtown **9** urban area **10** city limits, metropolis **11** central city **16** metropolitan area

Inner Mongolia
  other name: **9** Neimenggu, Neimengku
  capital: **6** Hohhot **7** Huhehot
  desert: **4** Gobi
  tent: **4** yurt

innermost 6 inmost, secret **7** deepest **10** deep-rooted, deep-seated **11** most private **12** most intimate, most personal

innermost part 4 core, crux, pith, soul **6** center, kernel **7** essence, nucleus

Inness, George
  born: **10** Newburgh NY
  artwork: **7** The Monk **14** Home of the Heron, Peace and Plenty **16** Delaware Water Gap **17** The Delaware Valley **19** The Lackawanna Valley

Innisfail *see* **7** Ireland

innkeeper 4 host, oste **6** tapper, venter **7** padrone **8** boniface, hosteler, hotelier, landlord, publican **10** proprietor **12** maitre d'hotel, restaurateur

innocence 6 purity **7** naivete **8** chastity **9** freshness **10** clean hands, simplicity **11** artlessness, sinlessness **12** incorruption, spotlessness **13** blamelessness, guilelessness, guiltlessness, impeccability, inculpability, ingenuousness, stainlessness **14** immaculateness

innocent 3 tot **4** baby, naif, open, pure, tyro **5** clean, naive **6** chaste, honest, novice, simple **7** artless, ingenue, sinless, upright **8** harmless, pristine, spotless, virginal, virtuous **9** blameless, childlike, faultless, greenhorn, guileless, guiltless, ingenuous, innocuous, little one, stainless, uncor-

rupt, undefiled, unstained, unsullied, unworldly, well-meant **10** artless one, immaculate, impeccable, inculpable, tenderfoot, young child **11** inoffensive, unblemished, uncorrupted, unmalicious, unoffending **12** unsuspicious **13** meaning no harm, unimpeachable **14** above suspicion, irreproachable **15** unsophisticated
  Latin: **12** integer vitae

Innocents, The
  director: **11** Jack Clayton
  based on story by: **10** Henry James (The Turn of the Screw)
  cast: **11** Deborah Kerr, Megs Jenkins **13** Peter Wyngarde **15** Michael Redgrave
  script: **12** Truman Capote **16** William Archibald

Innocents Abroad, The
  author: **9** Mark Twain (Samuel Clemens)

innocuous 4 dull, mild **5** banal, empty, trite, vapid **6** barren **7** insipid **8** harmless, innocent, painless **9** pointless **11** commonplace, inoffensive, meaningless

innocuousness 6 safety **9** blandness, innocence **12** harmlessness **15** inoffensiveness

in no uncertain terms 7 clearly, plainly **9** expressly **10** definitely, distinctly **13** categorically, unequivocally

innovation 5 shift **7** novelty **8** updating **10** alteration, dernier cri, new measure, remodeling, renovation **11** institution, latest thing **12** commencement, inauguration, introduction, streamlining **13** modernization

innovator 7 deviser, planner **9** contriver **10** instigator, originator **11** inaugurator

Inns of Court 8 Gray's Inn **11** Inner Temple, Lincoln's Inn **12** Middle Temple **14** legal societies
  in: **6** London
  member: **9** barrister

innuendo 4 hint **7** whisper **8** overtone **9** inference **10** imputation, intimation **11** implication, insinuation

innumerable 6 myriad **8** numerous **9** countless **10** numberless, unnumbered **12** incalculable **13** multitudinous

Ino
  also: **9** Leucothea
  goddess of: **3** sea
  father: **6** Cadmus
  mother: **8** Harmonia
  sister: **5** Hgave **6** Semele **7** Autonoe
  husband: **7** Athamas
  son: **8** Learchus **10** Melicertes
  stepson: **7** Phrixus
  stepdaughter: **5** Helle
  saved: **8** Odysseus
  cared for infant: **8** Dionysus
  changed into: **10** sea goddess

inoculate 5 imbue, shoot **6** infuse, inject, insert **7** implant, instill **8** immunize **9** inculcate, vaccinate

inoculation 4 shot **6** needle **7** booster **9** injection **10** hypodermic **11** vaccination **12** immunization

inoffensive 4 mild, safe **5** bland **7** neutral **8** harmless, innocent **9** endurable, innocuous, tolerable **10** sufferable **11** unoffending **15** unobjectionable

inoffensiveness 6 safety **9** innocence **10** neutrality **12** harmlessness **13** innocuousness

in one's debt 7 obliged **8** beholden, indebted **9** obligated **15** under obligation

in one's own person
Latin: **16** in propria persona

in one's own place
Latin: **7** suo loco

in one's own right
Latin: **7** suo jure

in one's rightful place
Latin: **7** suo loco

inoperable 6 broken **10** broken down, unworkable **11** ineffective

in operation 5 in use **7** in force, working **8** in effect **9** operating, operative

inoperative 4 dead, down **8** inactive **10** not working, out of order

inopportune 7 awkward **8** ill-timed, untimely **10** badly timed, ill-advised, unsuitable **11** troublesome, undesirable, unfavorable, unfortunate **12** inauspicious, incommodious, inconvenient, unpropitious, unseasonable **13** inappropriate **15** disadvantageous

in order 2 OK **4** neat, tidy **6** proper **7** correct, perfect **8** all right

inordinate 5 undue **6** lavish, wanton **7** extreme, profuse, surplus **8** needless, overmuch, shocking **9** excessive **10** deplorable, exorbitant, immoderate, irrational, outrageous, scandalous **11** disgraceful, extravagant, intemperate, overflowing, superfluous, uncalled-for, unnecessary **12** unreasonable, unrestrained **13** superabundant **14** super-saturated, unconscionable **16** disproportionate

inordinately 6 overly, unduly **9** extremely **11** excessively **12** immoderately, outrageously, prodigiously **13** extravagantly, intemperately, superfluously, unnecessarily

inorganic 4 dead **7** mineral **8** lifeless **9** inanimate, nonliving **10** artificial

in passing
French: **9** en passant

in perpetuum 7 forever

in petto 11 in the breast **12** not disclosed

in pieces 6 broken **7** asunder, smashed **8** in shreds, sundered **9** torn apart **13** in smithereens

in place
Latin: **6** in loco, in situ

in plain sight 7 exposed, obvious **10** in full view, noticeable **12** out in the open **17** in front of one's nose

in posse 11 potentially **13** in possibility

in possibility
Latin: **7** in posse

In Praise of Darkness
author: **15** Jorge Luis Borges

in propria persona 15 in one's own person

inquest 5 probe **7** autopsy, delving, hearing, inquiry, probing **8** necropsy **10** postmortem **11** inquisition **13** investigation

inquire 3 ask **5** probe, query, study **6** search **7** examine, explore, inspect **8** check out, look into, look over, question **9** track down **10** look deeper, scrutinize **11** investigate

inquirer 5 asker, snoop **6** seeker **7** auditor, querier, quizzer, student **8** pollster, searcher **9** catechist **10** inquisitor, questioner **12** interlocutor, interrogator, investigator

inquiry, enquiry 4 hunt, quiz **5** probe, query, quest, study **6** search, survey **7** inquest **8** analysis, question, research, scrutiny **9** interview **10** inspection **11** examination, exploration, inquisition, questioning **13** interrogation, investigation

inquisitive 4 nosy **6** prying, snoopy **8** meddling, snooping **9** inquiring, intrusive, searching **10** meddlesome, too curious **11** interfering, overcurious, questioning

in re 13 in the matter of

in reality
Latin: **7** de facto

in rem 15 against the thing
of a legal proceeding: **18** against the property

in rerum natura 19 in the nature of things

in retreat 10 backing off, retreating **11** withdrawing, backing away

in reverse 8 backward **9** backing up **22** in the opposite direction

insalubrious 7 harmful, noisome, noxious **8** inimical, virulent **9** injurious, unhealthy **10** pernicious **11** deleterious, detrimental, unhealthful, unwholesome

insane 3 mad **4** bats, daft, dumb, loco, nuts, wild, zany **5** balmy, batty, crazy, loony, manic, nutty, potty **6** absurd, crazed, raving **7** berserk, bizarre, bonkers, cracked, foolish, idiotic, lunatic, tetched, touched, unsound **8** demented, frenzied, maniacal, unhinged **9** eccentric, imbecilic, imprudent, insensate, paranoiac, psychotic, senseless **10** ridiculous, un-

balanced **11** injudicious **12** mad as a hatter, off one's chump, round the bend, unreasonable **13** off one's rocker, out of one's head, out of one's mind, out of one's wits, schizophrenic **15** bats in the belfry, mad as a March hare, stark staring mad **17** nutty as a fruitcake

insanity 5 folly, mania **6** idiocy, lunacy, raving **7** madness **8** dementia, paranoia **9** aberrance, absurdity, craziness, monomania, psychosis, stupidity **10** aberration **11** derangement, foolishness, unsoundness **12** loss of reason **13** hallucination, mental illness, schizophrenia, senselessness

insatiable 8 ravenous **9** insatiate, limitless, voracious **10** bottomless, gluttonous, implacable, omnivorous **12** unappeasable, unquenchable

inscribe 3 pen **4** etch, mark, seal, sign **5** blaze, brand, carve, write **6** chisel, incise, letter, scrawl **7** engrave, impress, imprint **8** scribble **9** autograph

inscription 5 motto, title **6** legend, rubric **7** address, caption, epigram, epitaph, heading, titulus, writing **8** colophon, epigraph, graffiti **9** engraving, lettering **10** dedication

inscrutable 6 arcane, hidden, masked, veiled **7** deadpan, elusive **8** baffling, puzzling **9** concealed, enigmatic **10** mysterious, mystifying, perplexing, poker-faced, unknowable, unreadable, unrevealed **12** inexplicable, unfathomable, unsearchable **14** indecipherable, unintelligible **16** incomprehensible

In Search of Identity
author: **12** Anwar el-Sadat

insect 3 ant, bee, bug, fly **4** flea, gnat, moth, pest, wasp **5** aphid, imago **6** bedbug, beetle, cicada, earwig, hornet, mantis, mayfly, vermin **7** chigger, cricket, firefly, katydid, ladybug, termite **8** horsefly, housefly, lacewing, mosquito **9** arthropod, butterfly, cockroach, dragonfly **10** silverfish **11** grasshopper

study of: **10** entomology

young: **4** grub, pupa **5** larva, nymph **6** larvae, maggot **9** chrysalis **11** caterpillar

anatomy: **4** palp **5** cerci, notum **6** cercus, feeler, labium, labrum, ocelli, thorax **7** antenna, maxilla, ocellus **8** antennae, mandible, maxillae **9** proboscis, spiracles **10** ovipositor **11** exoskeleton

insectivore 4 mole **5** shrew **6** desman, tenrec **7** moon rat **8** alamiqui, anteater, hedgehog **9** solenodon

insecure 4 weak **5** frail, risky, shaky **6** infirm, unsafe, unsure, wobbly **7** dubious, exposed, not firm, not sure, rickety, unsound **8** critical, doubtful, in danger, perilous, unstable, unsteady **9** dangerous, diffident, hazardous, in a bad way, tottering, unassured, uncertain, under fire **10** endangered, precarious, ramshackle, unreliable, unshielded, vulnerable **11** defenseless, dilapidated, unprotected, unsheltered

insecurities 4 risk **5** peril **6** danger, hazard **7** pitfall **8** jeopardy **11** contingency

insecurity 5 doubt **9** self-doubt, shakiness **10** diffidence, unsafeness **11** dubiousness, incertitude, instability, uncertainty **12** doubtfulness, endangerment, insecureness, unsteadiness **13** vulnerability **14** precariousness **15** defenselessness, lack of assurance **16** apprehensiveness

insensate 4 cold **5** cruel **6** brutal **8** inhumane **9** heartless, unfeeling **11** unconscious

insensibility 4 coma **5** swoon **6** apathy, torpor, trance **8** blackout, dullness, lethargy, numbness, obduracy, oblivion, stoicism **9** analgesia, catalepsy **10** anesthesia, obtuseness **12** incognizance, indifference, mindlessness **13** insensitivity, unfeelingness **15** unconsciousness

insensible 4 cold **9** insensate, senseless **11** unconscious

insensitive 4 cold, dead, numb **5** blase **7** callous **8** hardened **9** apathetic, impassive, insensate, unaware of, unfeeling **10** impervious, insensible **11** indifferent, unconcerned **12** thick-skinned **15** uncompassionate

insensitiveness 8 rudeness **10** coarseness, indelicacy **12** tactlessness **13** insensibility, insensitivity **17** inconsiderateness

inseparable 8 attached **11** indivisible, unseverable **12** indissoluble

insert 3 add **5** embed, enter, imbed, infix, inlay, inset, pop in, put in, set in **6** infuse, inject, push in, tuck in **7** drive in, implant, intrude, place in, press in, slide in, stick in, stuff in, wedge in **8** thrust in **9** interject, interlard, interpose, introduce **10** put between **11** interpolate, intersperse

insertion 2 ad **5** entry, graft, inlay, inset **7** implant **11** insinuation, parenthesis **12** interjection **13** advertisement

inset 4 gore **5** embed, godet, imbed, inlay, panel **6** insert **9** insertion

in seventh heaven 6 elated, joyful, joyous **8** ecstatic, euphoric **9** exuberant, rapturous **11** on cloud nine **13** up in the clouds

inside 2 in **5** inner **6** inmost, inward, secret **7** private **8** cliquish, esoteric, interior, internal, intimate **9** inner part, inner side, innermost **12** confidential

inside information 3 tip **10** inside dope

inside out 9 backwards **10** in disorder, topsy turvy **11** wrong side to

insides 4 guts **6** bowels, vitals **7** gizzard, innards, viscera **10** intestines

insidious 3 sly **4** foxy, wily **5** shady **6** artful, covert, crafty, sneaky, subtle, tricky **7** crooked, cunning, devious, furtive **8** guileful, slippery, sneaking, stealthy **9** concealed, deceitful, designing, disguised, secretive, underhand **10** contriving, perfidious, pernicious, undercover, undetected **11** clandestine, deleterious, treacherous, underhanded **12** disingenuous, falsehearted **13** Machiavellian, surreptitious

insight 6 acumen **9** intuition **10** perception **11** discernment, penetration **12** apprehension, perceptivity, perspicacity **13** comprehension, intuitiveness **14** perceptiveness
French: 6 apercu

insignia 3 bar **4** mark, sign, star **5** badge, medal, patch **6** emblem, stripe, symbol **7** chevron, epaulet, oak leaf **10** decoration **13** badge of office

insignificance 8 puniness **9** pettiness, smallness **10** meagerness, triviality **11** irrelevance **12** unimportance

insignificant 4 puny **5** petty, small **6** flimsy, meager, minute, paltry **7** trivial **8** niggling, not vital, nugatory, picayune, piddling, trifling **9** minuscule, worthless **10** immaterial, irrelevant, negligible, of no moment, second-rate **11** indifferent, meaningless, unimportant **12** nonessential **13** small potatoes **14** inconsiderable **15** inconsequential, of little account, of no consequence **18** not worth mentioning

insincere 5 false, lying **6** untrue **7** devious, evasive **8** guileful, two-faced, uncandid **9** deceitful, dishonest, equivocal **10** fraudulent, perfidious, untruthful **11** dissembling **12** disingenuous, hypocritical, mealymouthed **13** dissimulating, double-dealing

insincerity 4 sham **6** deceit **8** pretense, uncandor **9** deception, falseness, hypocrisy, mendacity **11** affectation, shallowness, unfrankness **12** uncandidness **13** artificiality **16** disingenuousness

insinuate 5 imply **6** inject, insert **7** asperse, let fall, suggest, wheedle, whisper **8** intimate **10** ingratiate **11** worm one's way

insinuation 4 hint **8** allusion, infusion, innuendo **9** aspersion, insertion, intrusion **10** allegation, imputation, intimation, suggestion **11** implication, penetration **12** ingratiation, interjection

insipid 4 arid, blah, drab, dull, flat, lean **5** banal, bland, empty, inane, stale, trite, vapid **6** barren, boring, jejune, stupid **7** prosaic **8** lifeless, zestless **9** pointless, savorless, tasteless,

wearisome **10** monotonous, namby-pamby, wishy-washy **11** commonplace **12** unappetizing **13** characterless, uninteresting

insist 4 aver, hold, urge, warn **5** claim, vouch **6** assert, demand, exhort, repeat, stress **7** caution, command, contend, persist, protest, require **8** admonish, maintain **9** reiterate **10** asseverate **13** lay down the law **14** take a firm stand **15** stand one's ground

insistence 6 demand, urging **7** urgency **8** exigency, pressure **9** clamoring **11** persistence **12** perseverance **14** imperativeness

insistent 4 firm **7** adamant **8** emphatic, repeated, stubborn **9** assertive, demanding **10** determined, unyielding **11** unrelenting

in situ 7 in place **18** in its original place

insolence 4 gall **7** disdain, hauteur **8** audacity **9** arrogance, impudence **10** brazenness, disrespect, effrontery, incivility, lordliness **11** haughtiness, presumption **12** disobedience, impertinence, impoliteness **13** bumptiousness, imperiousness **14** unmannerliness **16** superciliousness

insolent 4 rude **5** fresh, nervy **6** brazen, cheeky **7** defiant, galling, haughty **8** arrogant, impolite, impudent **9** audacious, bumptious, insulting **10** disdainful, outrageous, unmannerly **11** impertinent, overbearing **12** contemptuous, discourteous, presumptuous, supercilious **13** disrespectful

insoluble 12 inexplicable, unanswerable **13** undissolvable, unexplainable **14** undecipherable **16** incomprehensible

insolvent 5 broke **6** ruined **8** bankrupt, wiped out **9** destitute, moneyless, penniless **10** down-and-out, out of money **11** impecunious **12** impoverished, overextended

insomnia 11 nuit blanche, pervigilium, wakefulness **12** insomnolence **13** sleeplessness

insouciant 4 airy **5** perky **6** breezy, casual, jaunty **7** buoyant, offhand **8** carefree, debonair, flippant **9** easygoing, mercurial, unruffled, sans souci, whimsical **10** capricious, nonchalant, untroubled **11** free and easy, indifferent, unconcerned **12** devil-may-care, happy-go-lucky, lighthearted

inspect 3 eye **4** scan **5** probe, study **6** peer at, peruse, review, survey **7** examine, explore, observe **8** pore over **10** scrutinize **11** contemplate, investigate, reconnoiter

inspection 4 scan **5** audit, check, probe, study **6** review, survey **7** perusal **8** checking, scrutiny **9** appraisal, oversight **11** examination

inspector 7 analyst, auditor **8** analyzer, examiner, overseer, reviewer **9** appraiser, detective **11** scrutinizer **12** investigator
famous: 3 Fix, Fox **4** Japp **5** Queen **6** Alleyn, Bucket, Gerard, Gideon, Javert **7** Maigret **8** Clouseau, Lestrade **9** Dalgliesh

Inspector-General, The
author: 12 Nikolai Gogol
character: 4 Anna, Osip **5** Maria **26** Ivan Alexandrovich Hlestakov **35** Anton Antonovich Skvoznik-Dmukhanovsky

inspiration 4 idea, spur **5** fancy, flash **6** motive **7** impulse **8** afflatus, stimulus **9** incentive, influence, prompting **10** compulsion, incitement, motivation, revelation **13** encouragement

inspire 4 fire, stir **5** cause, exalt, impel, rouse **6** arouse, excite, induce, prompt, vivify **7** animate, enliven, hearten, produce, promote, provoke, quicken **8** embolden, engender, enkindle, illumine, inspirit, motivate, occasion **9** encourage, galvanize, influence, stimulate **10** give rise to, illuminate

inspired 3 apt **5** fired, moved **6** elated **7** elegant, exalted, excited, incited, touched, well-put **8** creative, original, prompted **9** impressed, ingenious, inventive, motivated **10** encouraged, felicitous, influenced, stimulated, well-chosen **11** exhilarated, imaginative **13** well-expressed

inspiring 5 grand **6** moving **7** awesome **8** eloquent, stirring **9** affecting, brilliant **10** impressive **11** encouraging, magnificent, stimulating

inspirit 5 boost, cheer, rouse **6** buoy up, uplift **7** animate, comfort, enliven, hearten, inspire **9** encourage, give a lift

in spite of himself
French: 9 malgre lui

instability 8 wavering, weakness **9** hesitancy **10** fitfulness, hesitation, indecision, insecurity **11** flightiness, fluctuation, inconstancy, vacillation **12** irresolution, unstableness, unsteadiness **13** changeability, inconsistency, mercurialness, vulnerability **14** capriciousness, changeableness

install, instal 3 lay **4** seat **5** crown, embed, imbed, lodge, plant **6** induct, invest, locate, move in, ordain **7** arrange, emplace, instate, receive, situate, station, usher in **8** coronate, initiate, position **9** establish **10** inaugurate, set in place

installation 5 plant **6** agency **8** facility **9** formation, induction **10** foundation, initiation, ordination **11** appointment, institution, investiture **12** inauguration, military base, organization **13** establishment

installment 4 part, unit **5** issue **6** laying **7** chapter, payment, section, segment **8** division, fragment, locating

instance 4 case, time **6** sample **7** example **8** occasion, specimen **9** precedent, prototype **10** antecedent **11** case in point **12** circumstance, illustration

instant 5 flash, jiffy, quick, trice **6** abrupt, minute, moment, prompt, second, sudden **8** premixed **9** immediate, on the spot, precooked, twinkling **10** ready-to-use **11** split second **12** unhesitating

instantaneous 5 rapid, swift **6** abrupt, direct, prompt, speedy, sudden **9** immediate **13** quick as a flash

instantaneously 6 at once **7** quickly, rapidly **8** in a flash, in no time, instanter, right now **9** on the spot, right away **11** immediately **21** in the twinkling of an eye

instantly 6 at once **7** quickly **8** directly, in a flash, promptly, right now **9** instanter, on the spot **10** here and now **11** immediately **12** quick as a wink, without delay **15** instantaneously **17** without hesitation

instar
insect period between: 5 molts **7** molting

in statu quo 17 in the state in which (something is or was)

Instauratio Magna
author: 12 Francis Bacon

instead 6 in lieu, rather **10** in its place

instigate 4 goad, spur, urge **5** begin, rouse, start **6** foment, incite, kindle, prompt, stir up **7** provoke **8** initiate **9** stimulate **10** bring about **11** set in motion

instigator 6 shaper **7** inciter **9** architect, innovator **10** prime mover, ringleader

instill, instil 4 pour **5** mix in, teach **6** impart, induce **7** implant, inspire **8** engender **9** inculcate

instinct 4 gift **5** knack **6** genius, nature **7** faculty **8** aptitude, capacity, tendency **9** intuition, mother wit **10** proclivity

instinctive 6 inborn, inbred, innate, native **7** natural **8** inherent, inspired **9** automatic, impulsive, intuitive, unlearned **10** deep-seated, unacquired **11** instinctual, involuntary, spontaneous

institute 4 pass **5** begin, enact, found, set up, start **6** ordain, school **7** academy, college, society **8** commence, get going, initiate, organize **9** establish, introduce, originate, prescribe, undertake **10** constitute, foundation, inaugurate **11** association, get under way **13** put into effect **14** bring into being

institution 4 rite **5** habit, usage **6** custom, prison, ritual, school **7** academy,

college, company, fixture **8** bughouse, madhouse, nuthouse, seminary **9** institute **10** convention, crazy house, foundation, university **11** association **12** organization **13** establishment

institutionalize 6 commit, detain **7** confine, put away **8** imprison **11** incarcerate

in strict confidence 7 sub rosa **9** between us, entre nous, privately **14** confidentially **15** between you and me **16** between me and thee, between ourselves

instruct 3 bid **5** brief, coach, drill, guide, order, teach, train, tutor **6** advise, direct, inform, notify, school **7** apprise, command, educate **8** acquaint **9** catechize, enlighten **12** indoctrinate

instruction 8 coaching, guidance, pedagogy, teaching, training, tutelage, tutoring **9** education **11** instructing **14** indoctrination

instructions 4 rule **5** maxim, moral, motto **6** advice, homily, lesson **7** precept **9** direction, guideline **11** explanation, information **12** prescription **13** specification **14** recommendation

instructive 8 didactic, edifying **11** educational **12** enlightening

instructor 3 don **4** guru **5** coach, guide, tutor **6** mentor **7** counsel, maestro, teacher, trainer **8** educator, lecturer **9** governess, pedagogue, preceptor, professor **10** schoolmarm **12** schoolmaster **13** schoolteacher **14** schoolmistress

instrument 4 deed, tool **5** agent, grant, means, paper **6** agency, device, gadget, medium **7** charter, machine, utensil, vehicle **8** contract **9** apparatus, appliance, equipment, expedient, implement, mechanism **11** contrivance

Instrument, The
author: 9 John O'Hara

instrumental 5 vital **6** active, useful **7** crucial, helpful **8** a means to, decisive, valuable **9** assisting, conducive, effective, effectual, essential **10** functional **12** contributory

instrumentality 5 force, means **6** agency, charge **9** influence, mediation **12** intervention

insubordinate 6 unruly **7** defiant **8** insolent, mutinous **9** fractious **10** disorderly, rebellious, refractory **11** disobedient, intractable, uncompliant **12** recalcitrant, ungovernable, unsubmissive

insubordination 6 mutiny, revolt **7** anarchy **8** sedition **9** rebellion **10** dissention, insurgence, unruliness **12** disobedience, insurrection **13** noncompliance **14** refractoriness

insubstantial 4 airy, weak **5** frail, shaky, small **6** flimsy, modest, paltry, slight, unreal **7** fragile, trivial, un-

sound 8 baseless, bodiless, delicate, ethereal, gossamer, piddling, trifling, unstable **9** imaginary, visionary **10** groundless, immaterial, impalpable, intangible **12** apparitional **14** inconsiderable

in succession
French: **7** en suite

insufferable 7 hateful **8** dreadful **10** abominable, detestable, disgusting, outrageous, unbearable **11** intolerable, unendurable, unspeakable **13** insupportable

insufficiency 4 lack, need, want **6** dearth **7** drought, paucity **8** scarcity, shortage **10** deficiency, inadequacy, meagerness, scantiness **11** undersupply

insufficient 6 scanty, skimpy, sparse **7** lacking, wanting **8** impotent **9** deficient, not enough **10** inadequate **11** incompetent **14** unsatisfactory

insular 5 petty **6** biased, narrow **7** bigoted, limited **8** isolated **9** illiberal, insulated, parochial **10** intolerant, prejudiced, provincial **12** narrow-minded

insulate 5 cover **6** cut off, detach, enisle, shield **7** cushion, isolate, protect, seclude **8** separate **9** segregate, sequester **10** disconnect

insult 3 cut **4** slap **5** abuse, cheek, scorn **6** deride, offend, slight **7** affront, offense, outrage **8** be rude to, belittle, rudeness **9** disparage, impudence, indignity **11** discourtesy, lese majesty

insulting 4 rude **5** nasty **7** abusive, uncivil, vicious **8** impolite, insolent **9** invidious, offensive **10** defamatory, derogatory **11** disparaging **12** discourteous **13** disrespectful

insuperable 8 crushing **9** defeating **10** impassable, impossible, invincible, unbeatable, unyielding **12** inexpugnable, overpowering, overwhelming **13** overmastering, unconquerable **14** insurmountable

insurance 6 policy **8** coverage, security, warranty **9** assurance, guarantee, indemnity

insure 6 secure **10** underwrite

insurgent 5 rebel **7** lawless **8** mutineer, mutinous, partisan, renegade, resister, revolter **9** breakaway, dissident, guerrilla **10** disorderly, rebellious **11** disobedient **13** insubordinate, revolutionary, revolutionist **15** insurrectionist

insurmountable 8 hopeless, too great **10** unbeatable **11** beyond reach, insuperable **13** unconquerable

insurrection 4 riot **6** mutiny, revolt, rising **8** outbreak, uprising **9** rebellion **10** insurgence, revolution

intact 4 safe **5** sound, whole **6** unhurt **7** perfect **8** complete, integral, unbro-

ken, unharmed **9** undamaged, uninjured, untouched **10** in one piece, unimpaired **11** in good shape **15** without a scratch

intangible 5 vague **7** elusive, shadowy **8** abstract, ethereal, fleeting, fugitive **9** transient **10** accidental, evanescent, immaterial, impalpable **11** abstraction, untouchable **12** imponderable **13** imperceptible, insubstantial

integer 5 digit, whole **6** entity, figure, number **7** numeral **11** whole number

integer vitae 8 innocent **15** blameless in life

integral 4 full **5** basic, total, whole **6** entire, intact **7** perfect, rounded **8** complete, finished, inherent **9** component, essential, fulfilled, necessary, requisite **10** fulfilling **11** constituent, well-rounded **13** indispensable

integrate 3 mix **4** fuse **5** blend, merge, unify, unite **6** mingle **7** combine **8** intermix **10** amalgamate **11** desegregate **13** bring together

integrated 6 entire, joined, linked, united **7** blended, merged, unified, unitary **8** combined **9** composite, undivided **10** harmonized, reconciled **11** coordinated, synthesized **12** desegregated, unsegregated

integration 5 union **6** fusion, mixing **8** blending **9** combining, synthesis **11** combination **12** assimilation **13** desegregation

integrity 5 unity **6** purity, virtue **7** decency, honesty, probity **8** cohesion, morality, strength **9** character, coherence, principle, rectitude, wholeness **11** reliability, self-respect, uprightness **12** completeness

integument 4 coat, hide, husk, rind, skin **5** shell, **7** coating, cuticle, epiderm, exoderm **8** covering, envelope, membrane

integumentary system
component: **4** hair, skin **5** nails

intellect 3 wit **4** mind **5** brain, sense **6** brains, wisdom **7** thinker **9** cognition, mentality **10** perception **11** mental power, rationality **12** intellectual, intelligence **13** consciousness, understanding

intellectual 4 sage **5** brain **6** brainy, mental, pundit, savant **7** bookish, egghead, scholar, thinker **8** abstract, academic, cerebral, highbrow, longhair, mandarin, rational, studious **9** intellect, of the mind, reasoning, scholarly **10** thoughtful **11** intelligent
French: **9** bel-esprit

intelligence 4 dope, news **6** acumen, advice, brains, notice, report, wisdom **7** tidings **8** sagacity **9** intellect, knowledge **10** advisement, shrewdness **11** information **12** notification, perspicacity **13** comprehension, understanding

intelligent 4 keen, sage, wise **5** alert,

canny, quick, sharp, smart **6** astute, brainy, bright, clever, shrewd **7** knowing, prudent **8** informed, sensible, thinking **9** brilliant, sagacious **10** perceptive, thoughtful **11** clearheaded, quick-witted, sharp-witted **12** well-informed **13** perspicacious

intelligentsia 5 mensa **7** academe **8** thinkers **10** ivory tower **13** intellectuals

intelligible 5 clear, lucid **7** evident, obvious **8** apparent, clear-cut, coherent, definite, distinct **11** unambiguous, well-defined **12** unmistakable **14** comprehensible, understandable

intemperance 10 alcoholism, insobriety **11** dissipation, drunkenness, inebriation **12** immoderation, recklessness **13** excessiveness **16** irresponsibility

intemperate 5 harsh **6** brutal, rugged, severe **7** extreme, violent **8** bibulous, uncurbed **9** dissolute, excessive, inclement **10** dissipated, gluttonous, immoderate, inordinate **11** extravagant, inabstinent, incontinent **12** unrestrained **13** overindulgent

intend 3 aim **4** mean, plan, wish **6** aspire, design, expect **7** project, propose, resolve **9** calculate, determine **10** have in mind **11** contemplate

intended 5 meant **6** fiance, future **7** engaged, fiancee, implied, willful **8** proposed, purposed **9** affianced, betrothed, bride-to-be, groom-to-be, voluntary **10** calculated, deliberate **11** intentional

intense 4 deep, keen **5** acute, sharp **6** ardent, potent, strong **7** burning, earnest, extreme, fervent, violent **8** emphatic, forceful, forcible, powerful, vehement **10** passionate **12** concentrated, considerable

intensely 4 very **5** hotly **6** deeply, keenly **7** acutely, eagerly, vividly **8** ardently, heatedly, terribly **9** extremely, fervently, seriously, violently, zealously **10** forcefully, powerfully, profoundly, vehemently, vigorously **11** excessively, exquisitely, strenuously **12** considerably, passionately **13** energetically

intensify 5 boost **6** deepen, worsen **7** magnify, quicken, sharpen **8** escalate, heighten, increase, redouble **9** aggravate, reinforce **10** accelerate, strengthen

intensifying 9 worsening **10** increasing, magnifying, redoubling, sharpening **11** aggravating, heightening, reinforcing **12** exacerbating **13** strengthening

intensity 4 zeal **5** ardor, depth, force, power, vigor **6** energy, fervor **7** emotion, passion, potency **8** severity, strength **9** magnitude, vehemence **11** earnestness **12** forcefulness

intensive 6 all-out **7** growing, radical **8** complete, sweeping, thorough **10** exhaustive, increasing **11** comprehensive **12** concentrated **13** thoroughgoing

intent 3 aim, end, set **4** bent, gist, plan **5** drift, fixed **6** burden, design, import, steady **7** earnest, intense, meaning, purport, purpose **8** absorbed, piercing, resolved **9** engrossed, insistent, intention, steadfast, substance, tenacious, unbending **10** determined, unwavering **11** preoccupied **12** concentrated, significance, undistracted **13** determination, premeditation

intention 3 aim, end **4** goal, plan **6** design, intent, object, target **7** purpose, resolve **9** objective **10** resolution **13** determination

intentional 6 willed **7** planned **8** designed, intended **9** voluntary **10** calculated, deliberate, purposeful **12** contemplated, premeditated **13** done on purpose

intently 6 deeply, raptly **9** fervently, zealously **10** absorbedly **11** attentively **12** passionately **18** without distraction **22** with undivided attention

intentness 10 absorption **11** engrossment **13** concentration

inter 4 bury, inurn **6** entomb, inhume **7** inearth, lay away **9** lay to rest **11** ensepulcher

interact 4 join, mesh **5** coact, unite **6** engage **7** combine, conjoin **8** dovetail **9** cooperate, interlace, intermesh, interplay, interwork **10** coordinate, interreact

inter alia 16 among other things
inter alios 17 among other persons

interbreed 3 mix **5** cross **8** intermix **10** crossbreed

intercede 5 plead **6** step in **7** mediate, speak up **9** arbitrate, interpose, intervene, offer help **12** offer support **14** put in a good word **16** lend a helping hand

intercept 3 nab **4** grab, stay, stop, take **5** catch, seize **6** ambush, arrest, cut off, detain **7** deflect, reroute

intercessor 5 agent **6** bishop, broker **8** advocate, mediator **9** go-between, middleman **12** intermediary, spokesperson

interchange 5 shift **6** switch **7** trading **8** exchange, junction, swapping, transfer **9** alternate, crossover **10** substitute **11** give and take, reciprocity

interchangeable 8 parallel, tradable **9** analogous **10** equivalent, switchable, synonymous **12** exchangeable, transposable **13** corresponding

interconnected 8 adjacent **10** contiguous, juxtaposed **12** conterminous, labyrinthine

intercourse 4 talk **5** trade **6** coitus,

parley **7** pairing, traffic **8** colloquy, commerce, congress, coupling, dealings, exchange **9** communion, discourse, relations **10** connection, copulation **12** conversation **14** communications, correspondence

interdict 3 ban, bar **5** taboo **6** enjoin, forbid **7** barring, censure **8** prohibit, restrain, restrict **9** proscribe **11** forbiddance, prohibition **12** proscription

interdiction 3 ban **7** barring **11** forbiddance, prohibition **12** proscription

interest, interests 4 gain, good, part, weal **5** bonus, hobby, share, stake, touch, yield **6** absorb, affect, behalf, divert, engage, notice, profit, regard **7** attract, benefit, concern, holding, involve, pastime, portion, pursuit, service **8** dividend **9** advantage, attention, avocation, curiosity, preoccupy, suspicion **10** absorption, investment **11** engrossment **13** preoccupation

interested 6 active **7** engaged **8** diverted **9** committed, concerned **10** fascinated, responsive

interesting 7 curious **8** engaging, magnetic, pleasing, riveting, striking **9** absorbing, appealing, arresting **10** attractive, suspicious **11** fascinating, stimulating **12** entertaining

interfere 3 jar, mix **6** butt in, horn in, meddle, rush in, step in **7** counter, intrude **8** conflict **9** frustrate, intercede, interpose, intervene **11** get in the way **14** be a hindrance to, be an obstacle to, be inconsistent, stick in one's oar

interference 3 bar **6** static **8** clashing, conflict, friction, invasion, meddling **9** collision, hindrance, intrusion **12** interception, interruption, intervention

interfere with 6 hinder, impede, thwart **7** disrupt **9** interrupt

interim 7 stopgap **8** interval, meantime, temporal **9** interlude, temporary, tentative **10** pro tempore **11** provisional

interior 4 bush **5** inner **6** inmost, inside, inward **8** internal **9** backwoods, heartland, innermost, upcountry **10** hinterland

Interiors
director: **10** Woody Allen
cast: **10** E G Marshall **11** Diane Keaton **12** Marybeth Hurt **13** Geraldine Page **15** Kristin Griffith **16** Maureen Stapleton
screenplay: **10** Woody Allen

interject 5 put in **6** inject, insert, slip in **7** force in, sneak in, throw in **9** interpose, introduce **11** interpolate

interjection 2 ah, er, lo, oh, ow, um **3** aha, cry, fie, hey, huh, ugh, wow **4** ahem, alas, darn, dear, drat, egad, gosh, heck, jeez, oops, ouch, phew, rats **5** aside, golly, zowie **6** eureka, hooray, hurrah, hurray **7** gee-whiz, jeepers **9** insertion **11** ejaculation, ex-

clamation **13** interpolation, interposition

interlace 3 mix **4** knit, link **5** braid, plait, twine, twist, weave **7** wreathe **9** alternate **10** intertwine, interweave **11** intersperse

interlaced 5 woven **6** linked, twined **7** braided, knitted, plaited, twisted **8** entwined, latticed, wreathed **9** interknit **10** interwoven **11** intertwined **12** interspersed

interlocutor 8 minstrel **9** converser, dialogist **12** interrogator **14** man in the middle

interlope 6 invade, meddle **7** intrude, obtrude **8** encroach, infringe, trespass **9** interfere

interloper 7 invader, meddler **8** intruder, outsider **10** interferer, trespasser **11** gatecrasher **15** persona non grata

interlude 5 break, event, letup, pause **6** recess **7** episode, respite **8** incident, interval **12** intermission **14** breathing spell

intermediary 6 midway, umpire **7** referee **8** bridging, mediator **9** go-between, in-between, mediating, middleman **10** arbitrator **11** adjudicator, arbitrating

intermediate 3 mid **4** fair, mean, so-so **6** median, medium, middle, midway **7** average, halfway, mediate, midmost **8** mediocre, middling, moderate **11** intervening

interment 6 burial **7** funeral **10** entombment, inhumation

Intermezzo
director: **13** Gregory Ratoff
cast: **8** Edna Best **12** Leslie Howard **13** Cecil Kellaway, Ingrid Bergman

interminable 6 prolix **7** endless **8** infinite, unending **9** boundless, ceaseless, incessant, limitless, perpetual, unlimited **10** continuous, long-winded **11** illimitable **12** long-drawn-out

intermingle 3 mix **4** fuse **5** blend, merge, mix up, unite **6** commix **7** combine **8** emulsify, intermix **9** commingle, interfuse, interlace **10** amalgamate, homogenize, interblend **12** conglomerate

intermission 3 gap **4** halt, rest, stop **5** break, pause **6** hiatus, recess **7** interim **8** interval, stoppage **9** interlude **10** suspension

intermittent 6 fitful **8** on and off, periodic, sporadic **9** irregular, recurrent, spasmodic **10** occasional **13** discontinuous **15** on-again-off-again

intermix 3 mix **5** blend, cross, mix in **6** mingle **10** crossbreed, interbreed **11** intermingle, intersperse

intern 6 commit, detain **7** confine, impound **8** imprison, restrain

internal 5 inner, state **6** inmost **8** domestic, interior **9** executive, political, sovereign **12** governmental **14** administrative

international 9 worldwide **12** cosmopolitan

international affairs
  god of: 6 Sancus **10** Dius Fidius, Semo Sancus

Internet
  terms: 3 AOL, FAQ, FTP, net, URL, web, WWW **4** chat, host, link, post **5** cyber, flame, Lycos, Yahoo, e-mail, TCP/IP **6** dial-up, Gopher, online, server, Usenet, Excite **7** browser, Web site **8** firewall, Username **9** hypertext, newsgroup, webmaster, AltaVista **11** interactive **12** search engine, World Wide Web
  based on: 7 ARPAnet

internment 9 detention **10** commitment, impounding **11** confinement **12** imprisonment

inter nos 16 between ourselves

interpolate 3 add **5** put in **6** inject, insert, work in **7** implant, intrude, stick in, throw in, wedge in **8** sandwich **9** insinuate, interject, interlard, interline, intervene, introduce **11** intercalate, intersperse

interpose 6 butt in, impose, inject, insert, meddle, step in **7** intrude, mediate, obtrude **9** arbitrate, insinuate, intercede, interfere, interject, interrupt, intervene, negotiate **11** come between, interpolate

interpret 3 see **4** read, take **6** accept, define, render, reword **7** clarify, explain, make out, restate, unravel **8** construe, decipher **9** elucidate, explicate, figure out, make clear, puzzle out, translate **10** account for, paraphrase, understand

interpretation 7 reading, version **8** analysis **9** rendition **10** commentary **11** explanation **12** construction

interpreter 7 analyst **9** explainer **10** translator **11** commentator

interrelated 9 companion, connected **10** compatible, correlated **13** complementary, correspondent, corresponding

interrelation 10 connection **11** association, correlation **12** relationship

interrogate 3 ask **4** test **5** grill, probe, query **7** examine **8** question **9** catechize **11** investigate **12** cross-examine **18** give the third degree

interrogation 4 quiz **5** probe, query **7** inquiry **8** grilling, querying, question, quizzing **9** catechism, inquiring **11** examination, inquisition, questioning

interrupt 4 stop **5** sever **7** cut in on, disjoin, disturb **8** break off **9** break in on, intersect, punctuate **10** disconnect **11** discontinue **13** interfere with

interrupted 6 broken, cut off, halted **7** checked, stalled, stopped **8** arrested, broke off, deferred **9** broken off, disturbed, suspended **11** broke in upon, intercepted **12** discontinued

interruption 3 gap **4** halt, rift, stop **5** break, pause **6** hiatus, lacuna **9** hindrance, interlude **11** obstruction **12** interference, intermission **13** disconnection, discontinuity

inter se 15 among themselves **17** between themselves

intersect 4 meet **5** cross **6** bisect, divide **7** overlap **8** crosscut, transect, traverse **9** cut across **10** crisscross

intersection 6 corner **8** crossing, junction **10** crossroads **11** interchange

intersperse 3 dot, mix **5** strew **6** mingle, pepper **7** bestrew, scatter, wedge in **8** disperse, intermix, sprinkle **9** broadcast, interfuse, interject, interlard, interpose **11** intercalate, interpolate

interstice 4 slit, slot **5** crack, space **7** opening, orifice **8** aperture, interval

intertwine 4 lace **5** braid, plait, twine, twist, weave **7** entwine **8** entangle **9** interlace

interval 3 gap **4** gulf, rest, rift **5** break, cleft, pause, space, spell **6** breach, hiatus, recess, season **7** interim, opening **9** interlude **10** interspace, separation **12** intermission, interruption

intervene 4 pass **6** befall, butt in, step in **7** break in, intrude, mediate **9** arbitrate, intercede, interfere, interpose, interrupt, take place **10** come to pass **11** come between

intervention 9 butting in, intrusion, mediation **10** breaking in, stepping in **11** arbitration **12** intercession, interference **13** interposition **14** intermediation

interview 4 chat, talk **6** parley **7** meeting **8** audience **10** conference, evaluation, round table **11** questioning **12** consultation, conversation

interweave 3 mix **4** fuse, join, knit, lace, link **5** blend, braid, plait, twine, twist **6** splice **7** wreathe **9** interlace, interknit **10** intertwine **11** intersperse

intestinal 5 inner **7** enteric **8** internal, visceral

intestines 4 guts **6** bowels **7** insides, viscera **8** entrails

in the air 2 up **5** above, aloft **7** skyward **8** all about, in the sky, overhead **10** everywhere **11** in the clouds

in the doghouse 9 in bad odor **10** in disfavor, in disgrace, in ill favor **11** in disrepute

in the end 6 one day **7** finally **8** sometime **10** eventually, ultimately **13** sooner or later **17** in the course of time
  French: 5 enfin

in the family
  French: 9 en famille

in the first place
  Latin: 8 imprimis

in the future
  Latin: 8 in futuro
  Spanish: 6 manana

In the Heat of the Night
  director: 13 Norman Jewison
  cast: 8 Lee Grant **10** Rod Steiger **11** Warren Oates **13** Sidney Poitier (Virgil Tibbs)
  score: 11 Quincy Jones
  Oscar for: 5 actor (Steiger) **7** picture **10** screenplay

in the know 9 cognizant **11** on the inside **13** fully informed, knowledgeable **23** having inside information

in the manner of
  French: 3 a la

in the matter of
  Latin: 4 in re

in the meantime
  Latin: 9 ad interim

in the middle of things
  Latin: 11 in medias res

in the midst of 5 among **7** amongst **12** surrounded by **13** in the middle of

in the nature of things
  Latin: 13 in rerum natura

in the neighborhood of 6 almost, around, nearly **7** close to **9** generally, just about **10** more or less, not far from **13** approximately **15** in the vicinity of

in the place cited
  Latin: 6 loc cit **10** loco citato

in the place of a parent
  Latin: 14 in loco parentis

in the same manner that
  Latin: 7 quo modo

in the same place
  Latin: 4 ibid **6** ibidem

in the state in which
  Latin: 10 in statu quo

in the style of
  French: 7 a la mode

in the very act of committing the crime
  Latin: 18 in flagrante delicto

in the vicinity of 4 near **6** almost, around, nearly **7** close to **9** just about **10** more or less, not far from **13** approximately **19** in the neighborhood of

in the way
  French: 6 de trop

in the whole
  Latin: 6 in toto

in the work cited
  Latin: 5 op cit **11** opere citato

in the year of the reign
  Latin: 9 anno regni

in the year of the world
  Latin: 9 anno mundi

In This House of Brede
　author: **11** Rumer Godden
in this sign shalt thou conquer
　Latin: **16** in hoc signo vinces
　motto of: **19** Constantine the Great
　from vision of: **5** cross
intimacy 5 amity **6** caring, warmth **8** dearness, fondness **9** affection, closeness **10** chumminess, endearment, fraternity, lovemaking, tenderness **11** brotherhood, camaraderie, familiarity **12** friendliness
intimate 3 pal **4** chum, dear, deep, hint **5** bosom, buddy, close, crony, imply, rumor **6** allude, direct **7** guarded, private, special, suggest **8** detailed, familiar, indicate, personal, profound, thorough **9** cherished, confidant, first-hand, innermost, insinuate **12** confidential
　French: **6** intime
intimately 7 closely **8** secretly, very well **9** privately **10** familiarly, personally **11** essentially **13** intrinsically **14** confidentially
intimation 4 clue, hint, sign **5** rumor **7** inkling, portent **8** allusion, innuendo **10** indication, suggestion **11** insinuation **13** veiled comment
Intimations of Immortality
　author: **17** William Wordsworth
intime 4 cozy **8** intimate
in time 6 before, sooner **7** earlier **9** before now, in advance **10** beforehand, eventually **11** ahead of time **13** before the fact, sooner or later
intimidate 3 cow **5** alarm, bully, daunt, scare **6** coerce, menace, subdue **7** buffalo, terrify **8** browbeat, frighten **9** terrorize
intimidated 5 cowed, fazed **6** scared **7** crushed, daunted, subdued **10** browbeaten, frightened, terrorized
intimidation 7 tyranny **8** bullying, coercion **9** despotism **11** browbeating, terrorizing, tyrannizing **12** scare tactics
intimidator 5 bully **6** despot **7** coercer **9** oppressor, tormenter, tormentor **10** browbeater
into 2 in, to **5** among **6** inside, toward, within **7** against
intolerable 7 hateful, racking **9** abhorrent, agonizing, excessive, loathsome, torturous **10** abominable, outrageous, unbearable **11** unendurable **12** excruciating, insufferable, unreasonable **13** insupportable
intolerance 4 bias **6** racism **7** bigotry **8** weak spot **9** no stomach, prejudice **10** chauvinism, xenophobia **12** low tolerance **16** hypersensitivity, narrow-mindedness
Intolerance
　director: **10** D W Griffith
　cast: **8** Mae Marsh **11** Lillian Gish

12 Robert Harron **17** Constance Talmadge
intolerant 7 bigoted, hostile, jealous **9** fanatical, parochial, resentful, sectarian **10** prejudiced, xenophobic **11** mistrustful **12** chauvinistic, closed-minded, narrow-minded
intonation 4 tone **5** pitch **6** accent **8** chanting **10** modulation, inflection
intone 3 hum, say **4** song **5** chant, croon, drawl, mouth, speak, utter, voice **6** murmur, recite **8** intonate, modulate, singsong, vocalize **9** enunciate, pronounce **10** articulate
in toto 5 in all, uncut **6** entire, wholly **7** totally **8** as a whole, entirely, outright **10** completely, in the whole, unabridged **11** all together, uncondensed
intoxicant 3 gin, rum **4** beer, grog, wine **5** booze, drink **6** liquor, tipple, whisky **7** alcohol, spirits, whiskey **8** cocktail, highball **9** inebriant
intoxicated 4 high, rapt **5** drunk, oiled, tight, tipsy **6** bombed, elated, loaded, stewed, stinko, stoned, zonked **7** drunken, exalted, smashed, wrecked **9** delighted, enchanted, entranced, plastered **10** enthralled, inebriated, infatuated, in one's cups **11** exhilarated, transported
intoxicating 4 hard **5** heady **6** potent **7** elating **9** alcoholic, spiritous **11** inebriating **12** exhilarating
intoxication 3 joy **5** bliss **7** elation, rapture **8** euphoria **9** poisoning, tipsiness **10** excitement, insobriety **11** drunkenness, inebriation **12** befuddlement, stupefaction
intractable 6 mulish, ornery, unruly **7** froward, willful **8** obdurate, perverse, stubborn **9** fractious, obstinate **10** headstrong, inflexible, refractory **11** unmalleable **12** contumacious, incorrigible, ungovernable, unmanageable **14** hard to cope with, uncontrollable
intransigent 7 diehard **8** obdurate, stubborn **9** steadfast, unmovable **10** inflexible, iron-willed, unyielding **11** intractable, unbudgeable **14** uncompromising
intrepid 4 bold **5** brave **6** daring, heroic **7** doughty, valiant **8** fearless, resolute, valorous **9** audacious, dauntless **10** courageous, undismayed **11** adventurous
intrepidity 4 guts **5** spunk, valor **6** mettle **7** bravery, courage **8** backbone **9** fortitude, sangfroid **12** fearlessness **13** dauntlessness
intricacy 10 complexity **11** involvement **12** complication, entanglement **15** complicatedness
intricate 6 knotty, tricky **7** complex, devious, tangled **8** involved **9** entangled **11** complicated
intrigue 3 spy **4** fire, plot **5** amour **6**

absorb, arrest, scheme **7** attract, collude, knavery, romance **8** conspire, enthrall, scheming **9** fascinate, machinate, titillate **10** conspiracy, love affair **11** machination **13** double-dealing **15** interest greatly, tickle one's fancy
intriguer 7 cheater, plotter, schemer **8** conniver, finagler **9** trickster **10** machinator, wirepuller **11** conspirator, Machiavelli, manipulator
intriguing 8 engaging, exciting **9** absorbing, beguiling **11** captivating, enthralling, fascinating, interesting
intrinsic 5 basic, per se **6** inborn, inbred, innate, native **7** natural **8** inherent **9** essential, ingrained **10** indigenous, underlying **11** fundamental
introduce 3 add **4** show, urge **5** begin, offer, put in, start **6** create, expose, import, inform, infuse, insert **7** advance, bring in, kick off, lead off, present, propose, sponsor, throw in **8** acquaint, initiate, lead into **9** establish, institute, interject, interpose, make known, originate, recommend **10** put forward **11** familiarize, interpolate
introduction 6 change **7** novelty, opening, preface, prelude **8** foreword, preamble, prologue **9** insertion, precursor **10** bringing in, conducting, innovation, ushering in **11** instituting, institution
introductory 7 initial **9** beginning, prefatory **10** initiatory, precursory **11** acquainting, preliminary **13** get-acquainted
introspection 8 brooding **10** meditation, reflection, rumination **12** deliberation, self-analysis, self-scrutiny **13** contemplation, soul-searching **15** self-examination, self-observation, self-questioning
introspective 7 pensive **10** reflective **13** contemplative, lost in thought
introversion 7 reserve **8** brooding **10** constraint, diffidence, withdrawal **13** introspection
introvert 5 loner **7** brooder, thinker **13** contemplative, private person
introverted 3 shy **5** stiff **8** reserved **9** inhibited, repressed, withdrawn **10** antisocial, restrained **13** inner-directed, introspective
intrude 4 push **6** butt in, impose, meddle, thrust **7** obtrude **8** encroach, trespass **9** interfere, interlope, interpose, intervene
intruder 10 encroacher, interferer, interloper, intervener, trespasser **11** gate-crasher
Intruder in the Dust
　author: **15** William Faulkner
intrusive 4 nosy **5** pushy **6** prying, snoopy **8** in the way, invasive **9** hindering, obtrusive, officious, unwel-

come **10** meddlesome **11** impertinent, interfering, interruptive

intuition 5 flash, hunch **7** insight, surmise **8** instinct **9** guesswork, telepathy **10** sixth sense **11** second sight **12** clairvoyance, precognition

intuitive 6 inborn, inbred, innate, native **7** natural, psychic **10** telepathic **11** clairvoyant, instinctive, intuitional, nonrational **12** extrasensory

Inuit *see* **6** Eskimo

inundate 4 glut **5** drown, flood, swamp **6** deluge, drench, engulf **8** load down, overcome, overflow, saturate, submerge **9** overwhelm **10** overburden, overspread

inundation 4 glut **5** flood **6** deluge **9** avalanche

in unison 5 as one **8** in chorus **9** all at once **11** all together

inure 5 adapt, steel, train **6** adjust, custom, harden, season, temper **7** toughen **8** accustom **9** acclimate, get used to, habituate **10** discipline, naturalize, strengthen **11** acclimatize, desensitize, familiarize **12** become used to **15** learn to live with **16** become hardened to

in use 8 employed **9** operating **11** functioning, operational

in vacuo 9 in a vacuum **11** in isolation

invade 5 flood, limit **6** assail, attack, engulf, infect, infest **7** assault, overrun, violate **8** permeate, restrict, strike at, trespass **9** intrude on, march into, penetrate

invader 6 raider **8** attacker, intruder, marauder **9** aggressor, assailant **10** trespasser

invalid 4 null, sick, void, weak **5** false **6** ailing, infirm, sickly, unwell **7** amputee, cripple, unsound, useless **8** disabled, not valid, nugatory, weakened **9** enfeebled, forceless, illogical, paralytic, powerless, worthless **10** dead letter, fallacious, paraplegic **11** debilitated, ineffective, inoperative, unsupported **12** unconvincing **13** incapacitated, unsupportable **14** good-fornothing, valetudinarian

invalidate 5 annul **6** cancel, refute, repeal, weaken **7** nullify, vitiate **8** abrogate, make void, undercut **9** discredit, undermine **11** countermand

invalidation 7 voiding **9** annulment **10** abrogation **12** cancellation **13** nullification

invaluable 4 rare **6** choice **9** priceless **11** beyond price, inestimable

invariable 7 uniform **8** constant **9** immutable, unfailing, unvarying **10** changeless, consistent, unchanging, unwavering **11** unalterable, undeviating **12** unchangeable

invariably 4 ever **6** always **7** forever **9** every time, uniformly **10** all the time,

constantly **11** perpetually, universally **15** in every instance **16** without exception

invasion 4 raid **5** foray **6** attack, breach, inroad, sortie **7** assault **8** trespass **9** incursion, intrusion, onslaught **10** aggression, juggernaut, usurpation **11** penetration **12** encroachment, infiltration, infringement, overstepping

Invasion of the Body Snatchers
director:
    1956 version: **9** Don Siegel
    1978 version: **13** Philip Kaufman
cast:
    1956 version: **10** Dana Wynter, Larry Gates **11** King Donovan **13** Kevin McCarthy
    1978 version: **11** Brooke Adams **12** Jeff Goldblum, Leonard Nimoy **16** Donald Sutherland

invective 4 rant **5** venom **6** insult **7** censure, railing, sarcasm **8** diatribe **9** contumely **10** execration, harsh words, revilement **11** verbal abuse **12** billingsgate, denunciation, vilification, vituperation

inveigh 4 rail, slam **5** abuse, knock, scold **6** rebuke, revile **7** censure, put down, run down, upbraid **8** belittle, denounce, harangue, reproach **9** castigate, criticize, dress down **10** vituperate

inveigh against 5 abuse **6** defame, rail at, revile **7** protest **8** denounce **9** castigate

inveigle 4 coax, lure **5** tempt, trick **6** allure, cajole, entice, rope in, seduce, suck in **7** beguile, ensnare, flatter, mislead, wheedle **8** persuade, softsoap **9** bamboozle, sweet-talk

inveiglement 7 coaxing **8** cajolery, flattery **9** wheedling **10** enticement, persuasion **11** blandishments

invent 4 coin **6** cook up, create, devise, make up **7** concoct, develop, fashion, think up, trump up **8** conceive, contrive **9** conjure up, fabricate, formulate, originate **10** come up with **11** put together

invented 6 fabled, made up **8** fabulous, fanciful, mythical **9** fantastic, imaginary, legendary **10** apocryphal, fictitious

Inventing America
author: **10** Garry Wills

invention 3 lie **4** fake, sham **6** design, device, gadget **7** fiction, forgery, machine **8** creation, trumpery **9** apparatus, discovery, fertility, implement, ingenuity, inventing **10** concoction, creativity, production **11** contraption, contrivance, development, fabrication, imagination, originality, origination **13** dissimulation, inventiveness, prevarication **15** resourcefulness

invention
god of: **6** Hermes

inventive 6 bright, clever **9** ingenious **11** resourceful

inventiveness 9 ingenuity **10** cleverness, creativity **11** imagination, originality **15** imaginativeness

inventor 5 maker **6** author **7** creator, deviser **8** engineer, producer, tinkerer **9** architect, generator, innovator **10** discoverer, originator
of air brake: **12** Westinghouse
of automobile: **7** Daimler
of barometer: **10** Torricelli
of camera: **7** Eastman
of cotton gin: **7** Whitney
of cylinder lock: **4** Yale
of dynamite: **5** Nobel
of elevator: **4** Otis
of gyrocompass: **6** Sperry
of helicopter: **8** Sikorsky
of linotype: **12** Mergenthaler
of machine gun: **7** Gatling
of movable type: **9** Gutenberg
of phonograph, incandescent lamp, mimeograph, dictating machine, fluoroscope: **6** Edison
of photography: **6** Niepce, Talbot **8** Daguerre
of Polaroid: **4** Land
of quick-freezing: **8** Birdseye
of reaper: **9** McCormick
of radio: **7** Marconi
of revolver: **4** Colt
of rocket engine: **7** Goddard
of sewing machine: **4** Howe
of sleeping car: **7** Pullman
of steamboat: **6** Fulton
of steam engine: **4** Watt
of steam locomotive: **10** Stephenson
of telegraph: **5** Morse
of telephone: **4** Bell
of wireless telegraph: **7** Marconi
of vulcanized rubber: **8** Goodyear

inventory 4 roll **5** goods, index, stock **6** roster, supply **7** catalog **8** register, schedule **9** stock list **10** accounting **11** merchandise, stock-taking

inverse 8 backward, contrary, converse, indirect, inverted, opposite, reversed **11** back to front, bottom-totop, right-to-left

inversion 7 turning **8** reversal **9** ectropion, turnabout **10** transposal **12** resupination **13** transposition

inverted 7 inverse **8** bottom up **10** upside-down

invest 4 fill, garb, give **5** adorn, allot, array, color, cover, dress, endow, imbue **6** clothe, devote, enable, enrich, infuse, supply **7** appoint, license **8** set aside **9** apportion

investigate 4 sift **5** probe, query, study **6** survey **7** analyze, dissect, explore, inspect **8** ask about, look into, pore over, question, research **9** anatomize, delve into **10** scrutinize

investigation 5 probe, study **6** review, search, survey **7** anatomy, inquiry **8** analysis, research, scrutiny **10** dissection, inspection **11** fact-finding

investigator 6 shamus **7** analyst, gumshoe **8** examiner, inquirer, observer **9** detective **10** private eye, researcher

investment 4 ante, risk **5** share, stake **7** venture **8** offering

inveterate 6 inured **7** adamant, chronic, diehard **8** constant, habitual, hardened **9** confirmed, incurable, ingrained, recurrent, steadfast **10** continuous, deep-rooted, deep-seated **11** established **12** long-standing, unregenerate **15** unreconstructed

invidious 7 vicious **8** spiteful **9** insulting, malicious, offensive, rancorous, resentful, slighting **10** malevolent

invigorate 4 stir **5** brace, cheer, liven, pep up, renew, rouse, zip up **6** jazz up, vivify **7** animate, enliven, fortify, refresh, restore **8** energize, vitalize **9** stimulate **10** exhilarate, rejuvenate, strengthen

invigorated 6 braced **7** revived **8** animated, restored, vivified **9** energized, full of pep, quickened, refreshed **10** stimulated **11** rejuvenated **12** strengthened **17** full of vim and vigor

invigorating 7 bracing **9** animating, healthful **10** energizing, enlivening, quickening, refreshing, vitalizing **11** restorative, stimulating **12** rejuvenating **13** strengthening

invincible 10 unbeatable **11** impregnable, indomitable, insuperable **12** invulnerable, undefeatable **13** irrepressible, unconquerable **14** insurmountable

in vino veritas 18 in wine there is truth

inviolable 4 holy, pure **6** chaste, divine, sacred, secret **7** blessed **8** hallowed **9** dedicated, inviolate, undefiled **10** sacrosanct **11** consecrated, impregnable, trustworthy **12** impenetrable, invulnerable, unassailable **13** incorruptible

inviolate 4 pure **6** intact, sacred, secret **8** hallowed **9** unaltered, unchanged, undefiled, unstained **10** inviolable, sacrosanct

invisible 6 covert, hidden, unseen, veiled **7** obscure **9** concealed, unseeable **10** unapparent **13** imperceptible, undiscernible

Invisible Man
    author: **12** Ralph Ellison

Invisible Man, The
    author: **7** H G Wells
    character: **4** Hall **6** Dr Kemp, Marvel **7** Griffin **11** Colonel Ayde

invitation 3 bid **4** call, lure **5** offer **7** bidding, summons **8** open door **9** challenge **10** allurement, enticement, inducement, temptation **12** solicitation

invite 3 bid **4** call, lure, urge **5** tempt **6** entice, induce **7** attract, solicit, welcome **9** encourage

inviting 4 warm **8** alluring, charming, engaging, enticing, magnetic, tempting **9** appealing, welcoming **10** attractive, intriguing

invocation 4 plea **6** appeal, orison, prayer **8** petition **9** summoning **12** supplication

in vogue 2 in **6** modish **7** a la mode, current, in style, stylish **9** in fashion **11** fashionable **12** le dernier cri

invoke 3 beg, use **5** apply **6** ask for, employ **7** beseech, conjure, entreat, implore, pray for **8** call upon, petition, resort to **9** appeal for, call forth, implement, importune, introduce **10** supplicate

involuntary 6 forced, reflex **7** coerced **8** unchosen, unwilled **9** automatic, reluctant, unwilling **10** compulsory **11** inadvertent, instinctive, spontaneous, unconscious **13** unintentional **15** against one's will

involve 5 imply, mix up **6** commit, engage, entail, wrap up **7** contain, embroil, include **8** comprise, depend on, entangle **9** implicate, preoccupy

involved 7 complex, engaged, mixed up, wound up **8** absorbed, immersed **9** committed, elaborate, embroiled, engrossed, entangled, intricate, wrapped up **10** implicated **11** complicated, preoccupied

involve deeply 5 mix up **6** absorb, commit, wrap up **7** embroil, engross, immerse **8** entangle **9** implicate, preoccupy

invulnerable 10 formidable, invincible, unbeatable **11** impregnable, indomitable, insuperable **12** imperishable, inexpugnable, unassailable, undefeatable **13** unconquerable, undestroyable

inward, inwards 5 inner **6** mental, toward **7** going in, ingoing, private **8** incoming, interior, inwardly, personal **9** spiritual, the inside **10** interiorly

in what way
    Latin: **7** quo modo

in which case 4 then, when **6** thence **9** whereupon **11** accordingly **12** at which point

In Which We Serve
    director: **9** David Lean **10** Noel Coward
    script: **10** Noel Coward
    cast: **9** John Mills **10** Noel Coward **12** Bernard Miles, Celia Johnson

in wine there is truth
    Latin: **13** in vino veritas

Io
    father: **7** Inachus
    husband: **9** Telegonus
    loved by: **4** Zeus
    son: **7** Epaphus
    changed into: **6** heifer
    color of heifer: **5** white
    guarded by: **5** Argus
    pursecuted by: **6** gadfly
    sent by: **4** Hera
    corresponds to: **4** Isis

iodine
    chemical symbol: **1** I

Iolanthe
    author: **9** W S Gilbert

Iole
    father: **7** Eurytus
    loved by: **8** Heracles
    captive of: **8** Heracles, Hercules

Ion
    author: **9** Euripides
    character: **6** Apollo, Athene, Crensa, Xuthus

ion 15 charged particle
    part of: **8** molecule
    charge: **8** negative, positive
    loses or gains: **8** electron
    called: **5** anion **6** cation **12** dissociation

Ionesco, Eugene
    born: **7** Romania, Slatina
    author of: **9** The Lesson, The Chairs **10** Rhinoceros **14** The Bald Soprano

iota 3 bit, jot **4** atom, spot, whit **5** shred, spark, speck **7** smidgin **8** particle **9** scintilla **11** faint degree, small amount **15** tiniest quantity

IOU 4 chit, debt, note **6** marker **10** obligation **12** promise to pay **14** promissory note

Iowa
    abbreviation: **2** IA
    nickname: **7** Hawkeye
    capital/largest city: **9** Des Moines
    others: **4** Ames **5** Amana, Mason, Perry **6** Algona, Keokuk, Le Mars, Marion, Newton **7** Anamosa, Clinton, Dubuque, Ft Dodge, Ottumwa **8** Waterloo **9** Davenport, Ft Madison, Marquette, Mason City, Sioux City **10** Burlington, Cedar Falls, West Branch **11** Cedar Rapids **12** Marshalltown **13** Council Bluffs
    college: **3** Coe **5** Corot, Drake, Loras **7** Cornell, Parsons **8** Grinnell, Wartburg **12** Iowa Wesleyan
    explorer: **6** Joliet **7** Jolliet **9** Marquette **13** Lewis and Clark
    feature: **13** Amana Colonies **17** first apple orchard
        church: **11** Little Brown
        national historical site: **13** Herbert Hoover
        national monument: **12** Effigy Mounds
        state fair: **4** Iowa
    tribe: **3** Fox **4** Sauc **5** Ioway, Omaha **9** Muscoutin, Winnebago
    people: **7** Hawkeye **9** Grant Wood **10** John L Lewis **11** Billy Sunday **15** Buffalo Bill Cody, Charles Ringling
    lake: **5** Clear, Storm **6** Spirit **7** Rath-

bun **11** East Okoboji, West Okoboji
land rank: 11 twenty-fifth
president: 13 Herbert Hoover
river: 4 Iowa **5** Cedar, Floyd, Skunk **8** Big Sioux, Missouri **9** Des Moines **11** Mississippi, Nishnabotna **12** Wapsipinicon
state admission: 11 twenty-ninth
state bird: 16 eastern goldfinch
state flower: 8 wild rose
state motto: 45 Our Liberties We Prize and Our Rights We Will Maintain
state song: 13 The Song of Iowa
state tree: 3 oak

Iowa, Ioway
language family: 6 Siouan
location: 4 Iowa
related to: 3 Oto **8** Missouri

Iphigenia
father: 9 Agamemnon
mother: 12 Clytemnestra
brother: 7 Orestes
sister: 7 Electra **12** Chrysothemis
saved by: 7 Artemis

Iphigenia in Aulis
author: 9 Euripides
character: 8 Achilles, Menelaus **9** Agamemnon **12** Clytemnestra

Iphigenia in Tauris
author: 9 Euripides
character: 5 Thoas **6** Athena **7** Orestes, Pylades

Iphigenie en Aulide
also: 16 Iphigenia in Aulis
opera by: 5 Gluck
character: 7 Artemis, Calchas **8** Achilles **9** Agamemnon **12** Clytemnestra

Iphigenie en Tauride
also: 17 Iphigenia in Tauris
opera by: 5 Gluck
character: 5 Diana, Thoas (King of Scythia) **7** Orestes, Pylades **9** the Furies

ipse dixit 15 he himself said it **21** assertion without proof
ipsissima verba 8 verbatim **12** the very words
ipso facto 15 by the fact itself **24** by the very nature of the deed
ipso jure 14 by the law itself **16** by operation of law
IRA 19 Irish Republican Army **27** Individual Retirement Account

Iraklion
capital of: 5 Crete

Iran
name means: 15 land of the Aryans
earlier name: 5 Media **6** Persia
capital/largest city: 6 Tehran **7** Teheran
others: 3 Qum **4** Shah **5** Ahwaz, Urmia **6** Abadan, Bandar, Kashan, Meshed, Shiraz, Tabriz **7** Birjand, Hamadan, Isfahan, Mashhad, Zahidan **11** Bandar Abbas
supreme head of state: 5 faghi **17** religious guardian
measure: 3 gaz, zar, zer **4** cane **5** gareh, kafiz, makuk, qasab **6** charac, chebel, ghalva **7** capicha, chenica, farsakh, mansion, mishara **8** parasang, piamaneh, stathmos
monetary unit: 3 pul **4** asar, gran, rial **5** bisti, daric, dinar, larin, shahi, toman **6** stater **7** ashrafi, pahlavi
weight: 3 ser **4** dung, rotl, seer **5** abbas, artel, pinar, ratel **6** batman, dirhem, kárwar, miscal, nimman **7** abbassi **8** tcheirek
lake: 5 Niris, Tasht, Tuzlu, Urmia **6** Sahweh, Sistan **7** Maharlu **8** Nemekser, Urumiyeh
mountain: 6 Elburz, Zagros
highest point: 8 Demavend
river: 4 Aras **5** Araks, Atrak, Atrek, Karun, Safid, Sefid **6** Gargan
sea: 7 Arabian, Caspian
physical feature:
  desert: 9 Dasht-i-Lut **11** Dasht-i-Kavir
  gulf: 4 Oman **7** Persian
  strait: 6 Hormuz
people: 3 Lur, Tat **4** Arab, Kurd, Turk **5** Medes **6** Galcha, Gilani, Jewish, Shugni **7** Baluchi, Persian **8** Armenian, Bactrian, Bartangi, Parthian, Scythian **9** Bakhtiari **11** Azerbaijani, Mazandarani
  mister: 4 agha
  dynasty: 5 Qajar **7** Arsacid, Pahlavi, Safavid **8** Parthian, Seleucid **9** Sassanian **10** Achaemenid
  statesman, mathematician, poet: 11 Omar Khayyam
  ruler: 5 Abbas, Cyrus **6** Darius, Xerxes **10** Rafsanjani **23** Shah Mohammed Reza (Riza) Pahlavi **25** Ayatollah Ruhollah Khomeini
language: 4 Luri, Zend **5** Farsi, Turki **6** Arabic, Baluchi, Kurdish, Persian **8** Armenian **11** Azerbaijani
religion: 5 Baha'i, Islam **7** Judaism **9** Shia Islam **11** Zoroastrian **12** Christianity
place:
  dam: 5 Karaj
  mosque: 4 Shad **5** Royal **12** Masjidi-i-Shah **18** Madreseh Chahar Bagh
  ruins: 4 Susa **10** Persepolis
feature: 13 Peacock Throne
  head cloth: 6 chador **7** chawdar
  parliament: 6 majlis
  underground water channel: 5 qanat
food: 5 kabob
  soured milk: 4 mast
  stuffed vegetables/leaves: 5 dolma **6** dolmeh

Iraq
capital/largest city: 7 Baghdad
others: 2 Ur **3** Kut **5** Al Faw, Amara, Ashur, Basra, Erbil, Mosul, Najaf, Qurna **6** Hillah, Kirkuk, Tikrit **7** Karbala, Mandali, Samarra, Umm Qasr **8** Al Zubair
division:
  ancient: 5 Akkad, Sumer **7** Assyria **9** Babylonia **11** Mesopotamia
monetary unit: 4 fils **5** dinar
lake: 6 al-Milh **7** Sanniya **8** al-Hammar
mountain: 6 Qalate, Zagros **7** Qaarade **9** Kurdistan
highest point: 7 Halgurd
river: 6 Diyala, Hawran, Tigris **8** Great Zab **9** al-Ubayyid, Euphrates, Little Zab **11** Shatt-al-Arab
physical feature:
  desert: 6 Syrian **8** al-Hajava
  gulf: 7 Persian
people: 4 Arab, Kurd **7** Bedouin
  leader: 6 Faisal, Sargon **7** Abbasid, Hussein, Ottoman **9** Hammurabi **13** Harun al-Rashid, Saddam Hussein **14** Nebuchadnezzar **16** Abbasid Caliphate
language: 5 Farsi **6** Arabic **7** Kurdish, Persian, Turkish
religion: 5 Islam **12** Christianity
place:
  ancient: 14 Hanging Gardens
  arch: 9 Ctesiphon
  mosque: 5 Great **9** Kadhimain
  ruins: 2 Ur **7** Babylon, Nineveh, Samarra
  Sumerian temple tower: 8 Ziggurat
feature:
  marketplace: 4 souk
  war: 4 Gulf **11** Desert Storm **12** Desert Shield

irascibility 8 acerbity **9** bad temper, crossness, testiness **10** crabbiness, crankiness **11** peevishness, waspishness **12** irritability **16** cantankerousness
irascible 5 cross, testy **6** cranky, grumpy, ornery, touchy **7** grouchy, peevish, waspish **8** choleric **9** irritable, splenetic **10** ill-humored **11** badtempered, hot-tempered, intractable **12** cantankerous
irate 3 mad **5** angry, livid, rabid, riled, vexed **6** galled **7** angered, annoyed, enraged, furious **8** burned up **9** indignant, irritated **10** infuriated
ire 4 fury, rage **5** anger, wrath **6** choler **7** outrage, umbrage **8** vexation **10** resentment **11** indignation

Ireland
other name: 4 Eire, Erin **5** Ierne **8** Hibernia **9** Innisfail **11** Emerald Isle
capital/largest city: 6 Dublin
others: 4 Cobh, Cork, Erne, Suir, Tara **5** Adare, Ennis, Sligo **6** Bangor, Galway, Lurgan, Mallow, Tralee, Ulster **7** Athlone, Belfast, Donegal, Dundalk, Kildare, Wexford **8** Drogheda, Kilkenny, Limerick **9** Craigavon, Tipperary, Waterford **10** Queenstown **11** Londonderry

school: 7 Trinity
division: 4 Cork, Down, Mayo **5** Clare, Kerry, Meath **6** Antrim, Armagh, Galway, Tyrone, Ulster **7** Donegal, Kildare, Wexford, Wicklow **8** Kilkenny, Limerick **9** Fermanagh, Killarney, Tipperary, Waterford **11** Londonderry
 ancient: 6 Ulster **7** Munster **8** Connacht, Leinster
head of government: 9 taoiseach (prime minister)
measure: 4 mile **6** bandle **8** crannock
monetary unit: 3 rap **4** real **5** pence, pound **6** turney **8** shilling
island: 3 Man **4** Aran, Bear, Holy, Tory **5** Clare, Clear, Magee **6** Achill, Saltee, Whiddy **7** Blasket, Gorumna, Rathlin **8** Aranmore, Inisheer **9** Inishmore **10** Inishbofin
lake: 3 Doo, Key, Ree, Tay **4** Conn, Derg, Erne, Mask **5** Allen, Barra, Capra, Gowna, Leane, Lough, Neagh **6** Boderg, Cooter, Corrib, Ennell **7** Dromore, Gougane, Oughter, Sheelin **9** Killarney
mountain: 5 Galty **6** Croagh, Mourne **7** Errigal, Muckish, Patrick, Wicklow **8** Comeragh **10** Benna Beola, Twelve Bens, Twelve Pins **13** Knockmealdown **19** Macgillycuddy's Reeks
highest point: 13 Carrantuohill
river: 3 Lee, May **4** Bann, Deel, Erne, Nore, Suir **5** Boyne, Clare, Feale, Flesk, Foyle, Laune **6** Bandon, Barrow, Corrib, Liffey, Slaney **7** Kenmare, Munster, Shannon **10** Blackwater
sea: 5 Irish **8** Atlantic
physical feature:
 bay: 4 Clew **5** Sligo **6** Bantry, Dingle, Galway, Tralee **7** Donegal, Dundalk
 cape: 5 Clear
 channel: 5 North **9** St George's
 cliffs: 5 Moher
 point: 6 Cahore **8** Carnsore
people: 4 Celt, Erse, Gael **6** Celtic **9** Hibernian
 author: 4 Shaw **5** Behan, Burke, Joyce, Swift, Synge, Wilde, Yeats **6** O'Casey, Steele **7** Beckett, O'Connor **8** O'Faolain, Sheridan, Stephens **9** Goldsmith, O'Flaherty **13** St John Gogarty
 leader: 4 Tone **6** Devlin, Valera **7** Grattan, Parnell, Redmond **8** O'Connell **9** Brian Boru **12** Saint Patrick
 legend: 9 Cuchulain **11** Finn MacCool
language: 4 Erse **5** Irish **6** Gaelic **7** English
religion: 8 Anglican **13** Roman Catholic
feature:
 airport: 7 Shannon
 castle: 4 Tara **7** Blarney

crystal: 9 Waterford
dance: 3 jig **4** reel
game: 7 hurling
lottery: 16 Irish Sweepstakes
manuscript: 11 Book of Kells
museum: 10 James Joyce
political movement: 8 Sinn Fein
race: 10 Irish Derby
relic: 13 Ardagh Chalice
revolutionary society: 6 Fenian
stone: 7 Blarney
street: 8 O'Connell
theater: 5 Abbey
food:
 beer: 5 stout
Ireland forever
 Gaelic: 11 Erin go bragh
I Remember Mama
 director: 13 George Stevens
 based on play by: 13 John Van Druten
 cast: 10 Ellen Corby, Irene Dunne, Philip Dorn **12** Oscar Homolka **16** Barbara Bel Geddes
 setting: 12 San Francisco
Irene
 member of: 5 Horae, Hours
 personifies: 5 peace
 corresponds to: 3 Pax
iridescence 7 glitter **11** opalescence, pearliness **12** nacreousness, play of colors
iridescent 5 shiny **7** glowing **8** colorful, nacreous **9** prismatic **10** changeable, opalescent **11** rainbowlike
Iris
 varieties: 3 fan, red **4** roof, wall, wild **5** Dutch, dwarf, house **6** copper, German, orchid, Sierra, Spuria, violet, yellow **7** African, bearded, crested, English, Evansia, Lamance, peacock, Persian, Prairie, Spanish, walking **8** Japanese, mourning, Siberian, stinking **9** beachhead, beardless, butterfly, Palestine **10** snake's head
Iris
 goddess of: 7 rainbow
 messenger of: 4 gods
 father: 7 Thaumas
 mother: 7 Electra
 sisters: 7 Harpies
 husband: 8 Zephyrus
Irish 4 Erse **4** Celtic, dander, Gaelic, temper
 accent: 6 brogue
 death spirit: 7 banshee
 flower: 8 shamrock
 girl: 7 colleen
 king: 9 Brian Boru
 legislature: 4 Dail
 saint: 7 Patrick
 society: 8 Sinn Fein
 theater: 5 Abbey
Irish gods 14 Tuatha De Danann
Irishman 4 Celt, Gael, Kelt, Mick **5**

Paddy **7** Irisher **9** Hibernian, orangeman **10** bogtrotter
Irish Mythology
 cats: 8 Kilkenny
 fairies: 4 Side
 god of love/beauty/youth: 7 Angus Og
 god of poetry/eloquence: 4 Ogma
 god of sea: 8 Manannan
 gods: 14 Tuatha De Danann
 hero: 10 Cuchulainn
 invaders/ancestors: 9 Milesians
 king: 4 Bres **5** Ronan **9** Conchobar **10** Matholwych
 king of gods: 4 Finn **5** Fionn
 pirate/demon: 8 Fomorian
 sea goddess: 3 Ler, Lir
 spirit: 4 Puca **5** Pooka
 corresponds to British: 4 Puck
irk 3 bug, vex **4** gall **5** annoy **6** bother, pester, ruffle **7** provoke **8** irritate
irksome 5 pesky **6** plaguy, vexing **7** plaguey, tedious **8** annoying, tiresome, wearying **9** difficult, provoking, vexatious, wearisome **10** bothersome, irritating, nettlesome **11** troublesome
iron
 chemical symbol: 2 Fe
Iron Age
 period of: 4 time
 followed age of: 6 Bronze
ironclad 5 fixed **6** strict **9** immutable, permanent **10** inexorable, inflexible, rigoristic, unchanging **11** irrevocable, unalterable **12** irreversible, unchangeable, unmodifiable
Iron Horse
 nickname of: 9 Lou Gehrig
ironic, ironical 3 odd **5** funny, weird **6** biting **7** abusive, caustic, curious, cutting, mocking, strange **8** derisive, sardonic, sneering, stinging **9** facetious, insincere, pretended, sarcastic **10** surprising, unexpected **11** implausible, incongruous **12** inconsistent **13** contradictory
irons 5 bonds **6** chains **7** fetters, presses, smooths **8** manacles, shackles **9** golf clubs, handcuffs **10** restraints
Ironside
 character: 7 (Det Sgt) Ed Brown **10** Mark Sanger **11** Fran Belding **12** Eve Whitfield **14** Robert Ironside
 cast: 11 Don Galloway, Don Mitchell, Raymond Burr **13** Elizabeth Baur **15** Barbara Anderson
irony 7 mockery, sarcasm **9** absurdity **11** incongruity, indirection **12** contrariness **13** facetiousness **14** implausibility
Iroquoian
 tribe: 6 Cayuga, Mohawk, Oneida, Seneca **8** Cherokee, Iroquois, Onandaga **9** Tuscarora **12** Kaniengehaga
Iroquois
 language family: 9 Iroquoian
 tribe: 6 Cayuga, Mohawk, Oneida,

Seneca **8** Onondaga **9** Tuscarora
location: 6 Canada **7** New York **11**
Connecticut **13** Massachusetts
leader: 11 Cornplanter, Joseph Brant
formed: 10 Six Nations **19** League of
the Iroquois
supernatural force: 6 Orenda
prophet: 10 Ganiodaiyo

irrational 6 absurd **7** foolish, unsound
8 baseless **9** illogical, unfounded **10**
ill-advised, unthinking **11** nonsensical,
unreasoning **12** unreasonable

irreclaimable 4 lost **6** wicked **7** corrupt, debased **9** abandoned, reprobate
12 disreputable, irredeemable, irreformable **16** beyond redemption

irreconcilable 7 opposed **12** incompatible, inconsistent, intransigent, un-
adjustable, unappeasable, unbridge-
able

irreformable 6 wicked **7** corrupt **9**
abandoned, reprobate, shameless
11 unrepentant **12** disreputable **13** irreclaimable

irrefutable 10 undeniable **12** indisputable, not refutable **13** proof positive
14 unquestionable **16** incontrovertible

irrefutably 6 surely **10** definitely, positively, undeniably **12** conclusively,
indisputably **13** incontestably **14** unquestionably **16** incontrovertibly

irregular 3 odd **5** bumpy, queer, rough
6 broken, uneven **7** crooked, unusual
8 aberrant, abnormal, improper, peculiar, singular **9** anomalous, desultory,
eccentric, haphazard, not smooth, out
of line, unaligned, unfitting **10** indecorous, unexpected, unsuitable **12** asymmetrical, unmethodical, unsystematic
13 inappropriate, nonconforming **14**
unconventional **16** uncharacteristic

irregularity 7 anomaly **9** asymmetry,
deviation **10** aberration, divergence,
unevenness **11** abnormality, peculiarity **12** constipation, eccentricity

irrelevant 5 inapt **7** foreign, off base **9**
unfitting, unrelated **10** extraneous, immaterial, malapropos, not apropos,
not germane **11** impertinent, unconnected **12** nonpertinent **14** beside the
point

irreligion 7 atheism **8** apostasy, unbelief **9** disbelief **11** godlessness

irreligious 6 unholy **7** godless, impious, profane, ungodly **8** agnostic **9**
atheistic **10** irreverent **11** unbelieving
12 not religious, sacrilegious

irremediable 8 hopeless **9** incurable
11 irreparable **12** beyond remedy

irreparable 9 unfixable **10** remediless
12 irremediable, irreversible **13** beyond redress, uncompensable, uncorrectable

irreplaceable 6 unique **9** essential **13**
indispensable

irrepressible 7 vibrant **8** bubbling,

galvanic, undamped **9** ebullient **10**
boisterous, full of life **11** tempestuous
12 unquenchable **13** unsquelchable
14 uncontrollable, unrestrainable

irreproachable 8 flawless **9** blameless, faultless, stainless, unspotted **10**
impeccable, inculpable **11** unblemished **12** above reproof, without fault
13 unimpeachable

irresistible 8 alluring, enticing **9** beck-
oning, seductive **10** enchanting, superhuman **11** tantalizing **12** overpowering, overwhelming

irresolute 4 weak **6** fickle, unsure **8**
doubtful, hesitant, unsteady, wavering
9 faltering, uncertain, undecided, unsettled **10** changeable, hesitating, indecisive, unresolved **11** vacillating

irresolution 5 doubt **9** hesitancy **10**
hesitation, indecision

irresponsibility 8 rashness **10** immaturity, imprudence **11** foolishness
12 carelessness, heedlessness, indifference, indiscretion, recklessness **13** unreliability **15** thoughtlessness, unde-
pendability **17** untrustworthiness

irresponsible 4 rash **7** foolish **8** careless, immature, reckless **9** imprudent,
overhasty **10** capricious, incautious,
unreliable **11** harebrained, indifferent,
injudicious, thoughtless **12** undependable **13** ill-considered, untrustworthy
14 not responsible, scatterbrained

irresponsible person
French: 14 enfant terrible

irreverence 7 impiety **9** blasphemy,
sacrilege **10** irreligion

irreverent 5 saucy **6** brazen **7** impious, profane **8** critical, impudent,
sneering **9** debunking, shameless,
skeptical, slighting **11** blasphemous,
disparaging, irreligious **12** nose-
thumbing **13** disrespectful

irrevocable 5 final **10** conclusive **11**
unalterable **12** irreversible, unchangeable

irritability 6 spleen **8** acerbity, edginess **9** crossness, huffiness, petulance,
testiness **10** crabbiness, crankiness,
impatience **11** fretfulness, peevishness, short temper, waspishness **12**
irascibility

irritable 5 testy **6** grumpy, touchy **7**
fretful, grouchy, peevish, pettish,
waspish **8** snappish **9** impatient, irascible **10** ill-humored **11** easily vexed,
ill-tempered

irritate 3 irk, vex **5** anger, annoy,
chafe, peeve **6** nettle, worsen **7** inflame, provoke **8** make sore **9** aggravate, make angry **10** exasperate

irritated 3 mad, raw **4** sore **5** cross,
irked, irate, testy, vexed **6** chafed,
crabby, galled, miffed, peeved,
piqued, put out **7** annoyed, burning,
nettled, peevish **8** burned up, choleric, incensed, inflamed, provoked **9**

impatient, irascible **10** aggravated **11**
exasperated

irritating 5 acrid, harsh, rough **7** caustic, chafing, galling, irksome, rasping
8 abrasive, annoying **9** provoking,
vexatious **10** bothersome **11** infuriating, troublesome **12** exasperating

irritation 6 bother **7** chafing **8** distress, vexation **9** annoyance **10** discomfort **11** irksomeness

irruption 4 raid **5** break, foray **6** inroad **7** upsurge **8** bursting, invasion
9 incursion, intrusion

Irving, John
author of: 16 A Widow for One Year
18 The Cider-House Rules **19** A
Prayer for Owen Meany **20** The Hotel New Hampshire **23** The World
According to Garp

Irving, Washington
author of: 10 Salmagundi **12** Rip Van
Winkle **13** The Sketch Book **23** The
Legend of Sleepy Hollow

Isaac
father: 7 Abraham
mother: 5 Sarah
brother: 7 Ishmael
wife: 7 Rebekah
son: 4 Esau **5** Jacob
birthplace: 5 Gerar
burial place: 9 Machpelah
blessed: 5 Jacob
sacrificed at: 6 Moriah

Isaac of York
character in: 7 Ivanhoe
author: 5 Scott

Isabella
character in: 17 Measure for Measure
author: 11 Shakespeare

Isaiah
means: 12 Jehovah saves
father: 4 Amoz
son: 11 Shearzashub **18** Maharshalal-
hashbaz

Iscariot *see* **5** Judas

Isenstein
origin: 12 Scandinavian
home of: 8 Brunhild
location: 8 Isenland

I serve
German: 7 ich dien
motto of: 13 Prince of Wales

Iseult, Isolde, Isolt
character in: 16 Arthurian romance
lover: 7 Tristan **8** Tristram
betrothed to: 8 King Mark

I shall rise again
Latin: 8 resurgam

Isherwood, Christopher
author of: 10 I Am a Camera **13** Berlin Stories **17** Down There on a Visit
character: 11 Sally Bowles

Ishmael
narrator in: 8 Moby Dick
author: 8 Melville

Ishmael

father: 7 Abraham
mother: 5 Hagar
means: 11 God will hear
brother: 5 Isaac
son: 5 Kedar **7** Kedemah
descendant of: 10 Ishmaelite

Ishtar
also: 7 Mylitta
origin: 8 Assyrian **10** Babylonian
goddess of: 3 war **4** love
queen of: 6 heaven
corresponds to: 6 Inanna **7** Astarte
9 Ashtoreth

Isis
origin: 8 Egyptian
goddess of: 9 fertility
hieroglyphic symbol: 6 throne
husband: 6 Osiris
brother: 6 Osiris
son: 5 Horus
father: 3 Geb, Keb
mother: 3 Nut
horns of: 3 cow
headdress: 9 solar disk
corresponds to: 2 Io

Islam
adherent: 4 Sufi **5** Shiah **6** Moslem,
Muslim, Shiite, Wahabi **7** Sunnite **8**
Islamite **9** Mussulman **10** Mohammedan
crusade: 5 Jahad, Jihad
deity: 5 Allah
flight from Mecca: 6 hegira
founder/prophet: 8 Mohammed, Muhammad
holy city: 5 Mecca **6** Medina
other names: 9 Moslemism **13** Mo-
hammedanism
pilgrimage to Mecca: 4 hadj
priest: 4 imam
scripture: 5 Koran

Islamabad
capital of: 8 Pakistan
Islamic 6 Moslem, Muslim **10** Mohammedan
Island 4 isle **5** atoll, haven, islet, oasis
6 refuge **7** enclave, retreat, shelter **9**
sanctuary
Islands of the Blessed *see* **10** Hesperides
isle, islet 3 ait, cay, key **4** holm **5** atoll, islet **6** island
Isle of Cloves *see* **8** Tanzania
Isle of Spice *see* **7** Grenada
Isleta (Tuei)
language family: 6 Pueblo, Tanoan
location: 9 New Mexico, Rio Grande
isn't that so?
French: 9 n'est-ce pas?
German: 9 nicht wahr?
isolate 6 banish, detach, enisle **7** seclude **8** insulate, separate, set apart **9**
segregate, sequester **10** disconnect,
place apart, quarantine
isolated 4 lone, solo **5** alone, apart **6**
cut off, lonely, remote, unique **7** insular, removed **8** detached, secluded, set

apart, solitary **9** separated, unrelated
10 segregated **11** out-of-the-way,
quarantined, sequestered
isolation 7 privacy **8** solitude **9** aloneness, apartness, hermitism, seclusion
10 desolation, detachment, insularity,
insulation, quarantine, separation **11**
confinement, segregation **12** separate-
ness

isoptera
class: 8 hexapoda
phylum: 10 arthropoda
group: 7 termite **8** white ant

Ispahan
also: 7 Isfahan **8** Aspadana
location: 4 Iran
capital of: 6 Persia
river: 8 Zayandeh

I Spy
character: 13 Kelly Robinson **14** Alexander Scott
cast: 9 Bill Cosby **10** Robert Culp
Kelly's cover: 9 tennis bum

Israel
former name: 5 Jacob
means: 12 soldier of God
wrestled with: 5 angel

Israel
other name: 4 Zion **6** Canaan,
Yishuv **9** Palestine **12** Promised
Land
capital: 9 Jerusalem
largest city: 12 Tel Aviv-Jaffa
others: 4 Acre, Elat, Gaza **5** Eilat,
Elath, Haifa, Holon, Jaffa, Jenin **6**
Ashdod, Bat Yam, Dimona, Hebron,
Nablus **7** Netanya, Rehovot, Tel Aviv
8 Nazareth, Ramallah, Ramat Gan **9**
Beersheba, Bene Beraq, Bethlehem
school: 6 Hebrew **14** Technion-Israel
26 Weizmann Institute of Science
division: 5 Judea, Negev, Sinai **7** Galilee **8** West Bank **9** Gaza Strip **12**
Golan Heights
government:
  legislature: 7 Knesset
  political parties: 5 Labor, Likud,
  Mapam
measure: 3 cab, car, hin, kab, kor **4**
bath, ezba, omer, reed **5** cubit,
donum, dunam, ephah, ganeh, homer, kaneh
monetary unit: 3 mil **5** agora, agura,
pound, pruta **6** agorot, shekel
lake: 5 Huleh **7** Dead Sea **8** Kinneret,
Tiberias **12** Sea of Galilee
mountain: 4 Nafh, Sagi **5** Harif, Ramon, Tabor **6** Atzmon, Carmel, Hatira
highest point: 5 Meron **6** Meiron
river: 4 Qarn **5** Faria, Malik, Sareq **6**
Hadera, Jordan, Kishon, Qishon,
Sarida, Yarkon, Yarmuk **7** Lakhish
sea: 3 Red **4** Dead **7** Galilee **13** Mediterranean
airline: 4 El Al
physical feature:
  bay: 5 Haifa

desert: 5 Negev, Sinai
gulf: 5 Aqaba
plain: 5 Judea **6** Sharon **7** Zebulun
9 Esdraelon
people: 3 Jew **4** Arab **5** Druze **10**
Circassian
  ancient: 6 Hebrew
  immigrant: 4 olim
  Jew born in Israel: 5 sabra
  leader: 4 Eban, Meir **5** Begin, Dayan, Herzl, Peres, Rabin **6** Ben-
  Zvi, Eshkol **7** Sharett **8** Weizmann
  9 Ben- Gurion
language: 6 Arabic, French, Hebrew
7 English, Yiddish
religion: 5 Baha'i, Islam **7** Judaism
12 Christianity
place:
  church: 13 Holy Sepulcher
  gates to Old Jerusalem: 3 New **4**
  Dung, Zion **5** Jaffa **6** Herod's
  8 Damascus **10** St Stephen's
  mosque: 13 Dome of the Rock
  mount: 4 Zion **6** Olives, Scopus
  shrine: 3 Bab **4** Book **11** Wailing
  Wall, Western Wall **18** Garden of
  Gethsemane
  tomb: 9 Sanhedrin **10** King David's
  way of sorrows: 11 Via Dolorosa
feature: 14 Dead Sea Scrolls
  collective village: 7 kibbutz **9** kib-
  butzim
  cooperative village: 6 moshav **8**
  moshavim
  dance: 4 hora
  movement: 7 Zionism
  Palestinian uprising: 8 intifada
  peace agreement: 16 Camp David
  Accords
  tree: 5 judas
  wave of immigration: 5 aliya **6**
  aliyot
food:
  dish: 4 pita **6** hummus **7** falafel
Israel, tribes of 3 Dan, Gad **4** Levi **5**
Asher, Judah **6** Joseph, Reuben, Simeon **7** Zebulun **8** Benjamin, Issachar,
Naphtali
Israel-born
Hebrew: 5 sabra
Israelite 3 Jew **6** Hebrew, Jewish,
Semite **7** Judaist **8** Hebraist
descended from: 5 Jacob
king: 4 Ahab, Elah, Jehu, Omri, Saul
5 David, Hosea, Nadab, Zimri
Issachar
father: 5 Jacob
mother: 4 Leah
brother: 3 Dan, Gad **4** Levi **5** Asher,
Judah **6** Joseph, Reuben, Simeon **7**
Zebulun **8** Benjamin, Naphtali
sister: 5 Dinah
descendant: 11 Issacharite
Is Sex Necessary?
author: 7 E B White **12** James Thurber
issuance 8 emission **9** allotment, dis-

charge, emanation **12** dispensation, distribution

issue 4 gush, rise, stem **5** allot, arise, ensue, erupt, go out, heirs, spout, yield **6** emerge, follow, number, result, spring **7** dispute, emanate, flow out, give out, outcome, outflow, pass out, problem, proceed, product, progeny **8** children, dispense, drainage, eruption, granting, heritors, issuance, question **9** circulate, discharge, effluence, grow out of, offspring, posterity, pour forth **10** distribute, outpouring **11** consequence, descendants, publication **12** dispensation, distributing

Istanbul
 area: 7 Beyoglu **8** Stamboul
 capital of: 6 Turkey
 formerly: 9 Byzantium **14** Constantinople
 landmark: 10 Hippodrome **11** Hagia Sophia **12** Galata Bridge **14** Bosporus Bridge **26** Palais de la Culture d'Istanbul
 mosque: 3 New **8** Mihrimah **9** Yeni Camii **11** Suleymaniye
 museum: 13 Topkapi Palace **14** Archaeological **20** Turkish and Islamic Art
 rulers: 4 Rome **6** Athens, Darius, Rhodes, Sparta **8** Persians, Suleiman **9** Macedonia **11** Latin Empire **12** Ottoman Turks **15** Byzantine Empire, Turkish Republic **19** Constantine the Great
 sea: 5 Black **7** Marmara **8** Bosporus **10** Golden Horn

isthmus 4 neck, spit **5** point, strip **6** narrow, strait, tongue **7** narrows
 name: 4 Suez **6** Panama **7** Corinth

I sustain the wings
 Latin: 12 sustineo alas
 motto of: 10 US Air Force

Italic
 language family: 12 Indo-European
 branch: 5 Latin, Oscan **7** Umbrian

italics 11 slanted type

Italy
 also: 8 Hesperia
 capital/largest city: 4 Roma, Rome
 others: 4 Pisa **5** Genoa, Milan, Padua, Turin, Udine **6** Amalfi, Ancona, Assisi, Naples, Rimini, Savona, Venice, Verona **7** Bologna, Bolzano, Brescia, Catania, Messina, Palermo, Ravenna, Taranto, Trieste **8** Florence
 division: 6 Apulia, Latium, Marche, Molise, Umbria, Veneto **7** Abruzzi, Liguria, Tuscany **8** Calabria, Campania, Lombardy, Piedmont **10** Basilicata **12** Valle d'Agosta **13** Emilia-Romagna **17** Trentino-Alto Adige **19** Friuli-Venezia Giulia
  independent enclave: 9 San Marino **11** Vatican City
 measure: 3 pie **4** orna **5** palma, palmo, punto, salma, stero **6** barile,

miglie, moggio, rubbio, tomolo **7** braccio, secchio **8** giornata, quadrato
 monetary unit: 4 lira, lire, tara **5** grano, paolo, soldo **6** danaro, denaro, ducato **7** testone **8** zecchino **9** centesini
 weight: 5 carat, libra, oncia, pound **6** denaro, libbra
 island: 4 Elba **5** Capri, Egadi, Eolie **6** Ischia, Istria, Linosa, Lipari, Sicily, Ustica **7** Aeolian, Trieste, Vulcano **8** Lampione, Sardinia **9** Borromean, Lampedusa, Stromboli **10** Isola Bella **11** Pantelleria
 lake: 4 Como, Iseo, Nemi **5** Garda **6** Albano, Lesina, Lugano, Varano **7** Bolsena, Perugia **8** Maggiore **9** Bracciano, Trasimeno
 mountain: 4 Alps, Etna, Visa **5** Amaro, Blanc, Corno, Somma **6** Cimone, Ortles **9** Apennines, Dolomites, Maritimes **11** Gennargentu **12** Gran Paradiso **16** Abruzzi Apennines
  Alps: 6 Apuane, Carnic, Julian, Otztal **7** Bernina **8** Ligurian **9** Lepontine
  volcano: 4 Etna **7** Vulcano **8** Vesuvius **9** Stromboli
 highest point: 4 Rosa
 river: 2 Po **4** Adda, Agri, Arno, Liri, Nera, Reno, Sele, Taro **5** Adige, Crati, Mannu, Oglio, Parma, Piave, Salso, Stura, Tiber, Tirso **6** Aniene, Belice, Isonzo, Mincio, Ofanto, Panaro, Rapido, Sangro, Simeto, Tanaro, Tevere, Ticino **7** Biferno, Bradano, Chienti, Metauro, Montone, Ombrone, Pescara, Rubicon, Secchia, Trebbia **8** Volturno
 sea: 6 Ionian **8** Adriatic, Ligurian **10** Tyrrhenian **13** Mediterranean
 physical feature:
  bay: 6 Naples
  channel: 5 Malta
  grotto: 4 Blue
  gulf: 5 Gaeta, Genoa **6** Venice **7** Salerno, Taranto **11** Manfredonia
  hills of Rome: 7 Caelian, Viminal **8** Aventine, Palatine, Quirinal **9** Esquiline **10** Capitoline
  lagoon: 6 Venice
  pass: 5 Resia **6** Maloja **7** Bernina, Brenner, Simplon **9** Mont Cenis **13** Saint Gotthard **17** Great Saint Bernard
  resort: 14 Italian Riviera
  strait: 6 Sicily **7** Messina, Otranto **9** Bonifacio
 people: 7 Italian
  ancient: 5 Latin, Remus **6** Sabine **7** Lombard, plebian, Romulus **8** Etruscan **9** patrician
  architect: 5 Nervi, Ponti, Salvi **6** Vasari **7** Alberti, Guarini, Juvarra, Vignola **8** Ammanati, Bramante, Palladio **9** Borromini, De Sanctis **12** Brunelleschi, Michelangelo
  artist: 5 Balla, Carra **6** Batoni,

Gaulli, Guardi, Titian **7** Bellini, Chirico, Cimabue, Cortona, Da Vinci, Raphael, Tiepolo, Uccello **8** Carracci, Mantegna, Masaccio, Severini **9** Benvenuti, Canoletto, Giorgione **10** Botticelli, Caravaggio, Modigliani, Tintoretto **11** Buoninsegna, Fra Angelico **12** Michelangelo **13** Giotto Bondone **14** della Francesca
  composer: 5 Verdi **7** Bellini, Cavalli, Corelli, Puccini, Rossini, Vivaldi **8** Mascagni, Piccinni **9** Donizetti, Scarlatti **10** Monteverdi, Palestrina **11** Leoncavallo
  emperor: 4 Nero, Otho **5** Galba, Nerva, Titus **6** Trajan **7** Hadrian **8** Caligula, Claudius, Commodus, Domitian, Octavian, Tiberius **9** Caracalla, Vespasian, Vitellius **10** Diocletian **11** Constantine **13** Antoninus Dius **14** Caesar Augustus, Marcus Aurelius
  film director: 6 de Sica **7** Fellini **8** Visconti **9** Antonioni **10** Bertolucci, Rossellini, Wertmuller, Zeffirelli
  god: 4 Juno, Mars **5** Ceres, Diana, Janus, Lares, Venus **6** Apollo, Vulcan **7** Bacchus, Jupiter, Minerva, Neptune, Penates **8** Quirinus
  Italian author: 3 Eco **4** Levi **5** Bembo, Bruno, Pulci, Tasso **6** Artino, Vasari **7** Ariosto, Bassani, Deledda, Moravia **8** Bandello, Petrarch **9** Boccaccio, D'Annunzio, Sannazaro **10** Cavalcanti, Guinicelli, Metastasio, Pirandello, Straparola **11** Castiglione, Machiavelli **12** Guicciardini, Michelangelo **14** Dante Alighieri
  Latin author: 4 Cato, Livy, Ovid **5** Pliny, Varro **6** Cicero, Gallus, Horace, Seneca, Vergil, Virgil **7** Donatus, Juvenal, Martial, Plautus, Sallust, Tacitus, Terence **8** Boethius, Catullus, Lucilius, St Jerome **9** St Ambrose, Suetonius **11** St Augustine
  ruler: 4 Moro **6** Cavour, Enrico **7** Mazzini **9** Mussolini **10** Berlinguer **14** Victor Emmanuel **15** Alcide de Gasperi
  ruler/military leader: 5 Sulla **6** Brutus, Pompey, Seneca **7** Crassus, Lepidus **8** Gracchus **10** Mark Antony **12** Gaius Marious, Julius Caesar **15** Cassius Longinus, Scipio Africanus **18** Tarquinius Superbus
  old ruling family: 4 Este **6** Borgia, Medici, Sforza **8** Visconti
  sculptor: 6 Canova, Marini, Pisano **7** Bernini, Bologna, Cellini **8** Antelami, Boccioni, Ghiberti **9** Donatello, Sansovino **10** Giacometti, Pollaiuolo, Verrocchio **11** Della Robbia **12** Michelangelo

wife: 7 Poppaea **9** Agrippina, Messalina **13** Livia Drusilla
language: 5 Ladin, Latin **6** French, German **7** Italian, Slovene **8** Friulian **9** Sardinian
expressions: 4 ciao **5** bella **10** primadonna
religion: 13 Roman Catholic
place:
  arch: 11 Constantine
  baths: 9 Caracalla
  bridge: 5 Sighs **12** Ponte Vecchio
  cathedral/church: 5 Siena **7** St Mark's, Vatican **8** San Marco, St Peter's **13** Sistine Chapel
  fountain: 5 Trevi
  museum: 5 Duomo **6** Uffizi **8** Bargello, National **10** Capitoline **11** Pitti Palace, Villa Giulia **16** Gallerio Borghese
  opera house: 7 La Scala
  palace: 5 Doges
  road: 9 Appian Way
  ruins: 5 Forum **7** Capitol, Pompeii **8** Pantheon **9** Catacombs, Colosseum **11** Herculaneum **13** Circus Maximus
  steps: 7 Spanish
  tower: 18 Leaning Tower of Pisa
feature:
  unification movement: 12 Risorgimento
food:
  cheese: 6 romano **7** fontina, ricotta **8** parmesan
  dish: 5 pizza **6** scampi **7** gnocchi, lasagna, lasagne, polenta, ravioli, risotto **9** antipasti, antipasto **17** chicken cacciatora, cacciatore
  ice cream: 6 gelato **7** spumoni
  meat: 6 salami **9** pepperoni **10** mortadella, prosciutto
  soup: 8 caciucco **10** minestrone
  wine: 7 Chianti

itch 3 yen **4** ache, long, pine **5** crave, crawl, creep, yearn **6** desire, hanker, hunger, thirst, tickle **7** craving, prickle **8** appetite, have a yen, pruritis, tingling, yearning **9** hankering

it does not follow
  Latin: 11 non sequitur

item 4 unit **5** entry, piece, point, story, thing **6** detail, matter, notice, report **7** account, article, feature, subject **8** dispatch, notation **9** paragraph **10** particular **11** news article

itemization 4 list **7** listing **11** enumeration

itemize 6 detail **7** specify **8** spell out **9** enumerate

items of business 4 list **6** agenda, docket **7** program **8** schedule

iterate 6 repeat **7** restate **9** reiterate

It Girl
  nickname of: 8 Clara Bow

it grows as it goes

Latin: 12 crescit eundo
motto of: 9 New Mexico

Ithaca
  ancient home of: 8 Odysseus, Penelope
  modern home of: 7 Cornell (University)

It Happened One Night
  director: 10 Frank Capra
  cast: 8 Alan Hale, Ward Bond **10** Clark Gable **11** Roscoe Karns **14** Walter Connolly **16** Claudette Colbert
  Oscar for: 5 actor (Gable) **7** actress (Colbert), picture **8** director
  remade as: 16 Eve Knew Her Apples **20** You Can't Run Away from It

I think therefore I am
  Latin: 13 cogito ergo sum
  said by: 9 Descartes

itinerant 5 nomad, rover **6** roamer, roving **7** migrant, nomadic, roaming, vagrant **8** vagabond, wanderer, wayfarer **9** footloose, transient, traveling, wandering, wayfaring **11** peripatetic

itinerary 3 log **5** diary, route **6** course **7** account, circuit, day book, journal **8** schedule **9** timetable **10** travel plan

it is not clear; it is not evident
  Latin: 9 non liquet

it is not lawful; it is not permitted
  Latin: 8 non licet

it is sweet to do nothing
  Italian: 14 dolce far niente

It's a Gift
  director: 13 Norman Z McLeod
  cast: 8 W C Fields **9** Baby LeRoy, Tommy Bupp **10** T Roy Barnes **13** Charles Sellon, Morgan Wallace **14** Kathleen Howard
  remake of: 17 It's the Old Army Game

It's a Wonderful Life
  director: 10 Frank Capra
  cast: 9 Donna Reed **11** Beulah Bondi **12** Henry Travers, James Stewart **13** Gloria Grahame **15** Lionel Barrymore
  remade as: 22 It Happened One Christmas

itsy-bitsy 3 wee **4** tiny **5** dwarf, pygmy, small, teeny **6** bantam, little, minute, petite **9** miniature, miniscule **10** diminutive, teeny-weeny **11** microscopic, pocket-sized

It Takes a Thief
  character: 8 Noah Bain **12** Alister Mundy, Wallie Powers **14** Alexander Mundy
  cast: 11 Edward Binns, Fred Astaire **12** Robert Wagner **13** Malachi Throne

Itza
  language family: 6 Toltec
  location: 6 Mexico **7** Chichen, Yucatan **14** Central America

Iulus see **8** Ascanius

Ivan 4 czar, tsar **8** the Great **11** the Terrible **18** grand duke of Muscovy
  English equivalent: 4 John
  personifies: 6 Russia

Ivanhoe
  author: 14 Sir Walter Scott
  character: 7 Rebecca **8** Guilbert **9** Robin Hood **10** Lady Rowena **11** Isaac of York **12** King Richard I **14** Cedric the Saxon, Sir Brian de Bois **16** Wilfred of Ivanhoe **19** King Richard the First

Ivanhoe, Burle Icle
  real name of: 8 Burl Ives

I've Got a Secret
  host: 10 Bill Cullen, Garry Moore, Steve Allen

Ives, Burl
  real name: 16 Burle Icle Ivanhoe
  nickname: 17 Wayfaring Stranger
  born: 6 Hunt IL
  roles: 8 Big Daddy **10** East of Eden **13** The Big Country **14** Our Man in Havana **16** Cat on a Hot Tin Roof **18** Desire Under the Elms

Ives, Charles
  born: 9 Danbury CT
  composer of: 11 Putnam's Camp **13** Concord Sonata **19** Washington's Birthday **20** Central Park in the Dark **21** The Unanswered Question **23** Three Places in New England

ivory 4 tusk **6** dentin
  source: 6 walrus **8** elephant
  used for: 4 dice **9** piano keys **13** billiard balls
  color: 5 cream **8** off-white

Ivory Coast
  capital/largest city: 7 Abidjan
    new capital: 12 Yamoussoukro
  others: 3 Man **4** Divo **5** Daloa, Tabou **6** Adzobe, Bonoua, Bouake, Danane, Gagnoa **7** Korhogo, Odienne, Seguela **8** Dimbokro **9** Agboville, Bondoukou, Sassandra **10** Abengourou **11** Grand Bassam **14** Ferkessedougou
  monetary unit: 5 franc **7** centime
  highest point: 5 Nimba
  river: 3 Bia **5** Comoe, Komoe **7** Bandama, Cavally **9** Sassandra
  ocean: 8 Atlantic
  physical feature:
    cape: 6 Palmas
    gulf: 6 Guinea
    lagoon: 3 Aby **5** Ebrie
    wind: 9 harmattan
  people: 3 Abe, Dan, Kru, Kwa **4** Akan, Bete, Dida, Guro, Koua, Lobi, Wobe **5** Abron, Abure, Attie, Baule, Guere, Mande, Mossi **6** Baoule, Lagoon, Senufo, Senufu **7** Dan Guro, Kroumen, Malinke, Voltaic **10** Anyi-Baoule **11** Lobi-Kulango **12** Agnis-Ashanti
  language: 4 Akan **6** Dioula, French
  religion: 5 Islam **7** animism **13** Roman Catholic

place:
  canal: 5 Vridi
  dam: 7 Bandama
  game reserve: 9 Sassandra
  feature: 7 kola nut
Ivory Coast *see* **11** Sierra Leone
ivory-towered 6 remote **8** academic, romantic **11** conjectural, impractical, theoretical, unrealistic **12** hypothetical
ivy 6 Cissus, Hedera **15** Kalmia latifolia
  varieties: 3 fan, red **4** baby, tree **5** grape, Irish, Nepal, water **6** aralia, Baltic, Boston, canary, devil's, German, ground, marine, parlor, poison, spider, switch **7** colchis, English, Italian, Madeira, Mexican, parsley, Persian, Swedish **8** Algerian, American, coliseum, fragrant, Japanese, red-flame **9** bird's-foot, ghost-tree, heart-leaf **10** five-leaved, Kenilworth, variegated **12** Hagenburger's **13** Solomon Island **14** miniature grape **15** Gloire-de-Marengo

Ivy League colleges 4 Yale **5** Brown **7** Cornell, Harvard **8** Columbia **9** Dartmouth, Princeton **12** Pennsylvania (Penn)

I Want to Live!
  director: 10 Robert Wise
  cast: 12 Simon Oakland, Susan Hayward (Barbara Graham) **13** Theodore Bikel **15** Virginia Vincent
  score: 12 Johnny Mandel
  Oscar for: 7 actress (Hayward)

I will defend
  Latin: 6 tuebor

IWW 8 Wobblies **10** labor union **27** Industrial Workers of the World
  leader: 4 Debs **6** DeLeon **7** Haywood

members: 6 miners **9** lumbermen **16** migratory workers

Ixion
  king of: 8 Lapithae
  wife: 3 Dia
  son: 9 Pirithous
  children: 8 centaurs
  loved: 4 Hera
  punished by: 4 Zeus
  bound to: 5 wheel

Iyar 17 second Hebrew month

Iynx
  father: 3 Pan
  mother: 4 Echo

Izmir
  formerly: 6 Smyrna
  location: 6 Turkey **9** Aegean Sea **11** Gulf of Izmir
  settle by: 7 Ionians **8** Aeolians
  ruled by: 13 Ottoman Empire

izzard 3 zed, zee

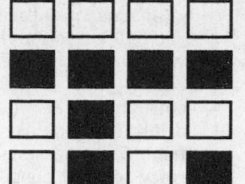
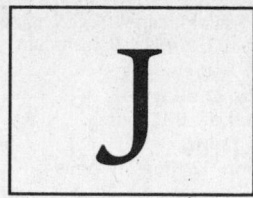
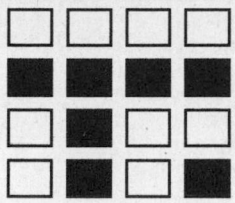

ja 3 yes

jab 3 cut, dig, hit, rap, tap **4** belt, blow, bump, clip, goad, lick, pelt, plug, poke, poke, prod, sock, stab, swat **5** elbow, nudge, paste, swing **6** strike, stroke

jabber 3 gab, gas **4** blab **5** clack, prate **6** babble, cackle, drivel, gibber, gossip, hot air, patter, ramble, rattle, raving **7** blabber, blather, chatter, gushing, maunder, palaver, prating, prattle, ranting, twaddle, twattle **8** chitchat, idle talk, nonsense, talk idly **9** gibberish **10** maundering **14** chitterchatter

jack 4 flag **5** knave, money **6** ensign, sailor

jackass 3 ass **4** fool, mule **5** burro, dummy, idiot **6** donkey

Jack Benny Show, The
  cast: **8** Mel Blanc **9** Dennis Day, Don Wilson **11** Frank Nelson **13** Artie Auerbach, Eddie (Rochester) Anderson **14** Mary Livingston
  Jack's car: **7** Maxwell
  Jack played: **6** violin

jacket 4 case, coat **5** cover **6** blazer, casing, folder, sheath **7** wrapper **8** envelope, mackinaw, wrapping **9** container, enclosure, short coat, sport coat **10** dinner coat **11** windbreaker

Jackson, Andrew
  nickname: **10** Old Hickory
  presidential rank: **7** seventh
  party: **10** Democratic
  state represented: **2** TN **9** Tennessee
  defeated: **4** (Henry) Clay **5** (John Quincy) Adams
  vice president: **7** (John Caldwell) Calhoun **8** (Martin) Van Buren
  cabinet:
    state: **6** (Louis) McLane **7** (John) Forsyth **8** (Martin) Van Buren **10** (Edward) Livingston
    treasury: **5** (William John) Duane **6** (Louis) McLane, (Samuel Dulucenna) Ingham **8** (Levi) Woodbury
    war: **4** (Lewis) Cass **5** (John Henry) Eaton
    attorney general: **5** (Roger Brooke) Taney, (Benjamin Franklin) Butler **7** (John McPherson) Berrien
    navy: **6** (John) Branch **8** (Levi) Woodbury **9** (Mahlon) Dickerson
    postmaster general: **5** (William Taylor) Barry **7** (Amos) Kendall

  born: **8** Waxhaw SC
  died/buried: **11** Nashville TN
  education:
    college: **4** none
    studied: **3** law
    admitted to: **3** bar
  religion: **12** Presbyterian
  political career: **8** US Senate **24** US House of Representatives
    judge: **22** Tennessee Superior Court
  civilian career: **6** lawyer
  military service: **12** major general **16** brigadier general
    defeated: **6** Creeks **9** Cherokees
    captured: **9** Pensacola
    military governor of: **7** Florida
  notable events of lifetime/term:
    battle: **5** Alamo **10** New Orleans
    fought: **5** duels
    scandal/wife suspected of: **6** bigamy
    war: **8** Creek War **13** Revolutionary **16** First Seminole War **19** War of Eighteen Twelve
  father: **6** Andrew
  mother: **9** Elizabeth (Hutchinson)
  siblings: **4** Hugh **6** Robert
  wife: **6** Rachel (Donelson Robards)
  children:
    adopted: **11** wife's nephew **15** Andrew Jackson Jr

Jackson, Anne
  husband: **10** Eli Wallach
  born: **10** Millvale PA
  roles: **3** Luv **10** The Typists

Jackson, Charles
  author of: **14** The Lost Weekend

Jackson 5 4 Tito **6** Jackie, Marlon **7** Michael **8** Jermaine
  songs: **3** ABC **10** I'll Be There **12** I Want You Back **14** The Love You Save

Jackson, Glenda
  born: **7** England **10** Birkenhead
  roles: **10** Elizabeth R **11** Women in Love (Oscar) **13** A Touch of Class (Oscar) **14** The Music Lovers **16** Mary Queen of Scots **18** Sunday Bloody Sunday
  politics: **11** Labour Party **18** Member of Parliament

Jackson, Jesse Louis
  title: **8** Reverend
  party: **10** Democratic
  born: **12** Greenville SC
  education: **20** University of Illinois

26 Chicago Theological Seminary **49** North Carolina Agricultural and Technical State College
  religion: **7** Baptist
  political career: **17** Democratic primary
  civilian career: **4** SCLC **9** PUSH Excel **13** Operation PUSH **20** Operation Breadbasket **24** National Rainbow Coalition **37** Southern Christian Leadership Conference

Jackson, Michael
  born: **2** IN **4** Gary
  father: **6** Joseph
  mother: **9** Katherine
  siblings: **4** Tito **5** Janet, Randy **6** Jackie, La Toya, Marlon **7** Maureen **8** Jermaine
  wife: **16** Lisa Marie Presley
  trademark: **5** glove
  recordings: **3** Bad **7** Triumph, Victory **8** Thriller **9** Dangerous **10** Off the Wall
  film: **6** The Wiz
  group: **8** Jacksons **11** Jackson Five

Jackson, Reggie
  nickname: **13** Mister October
  sport: **8** baseball
  position: **8** outfield
  known for: **7** hitting
  team: **9** Oakland A's **14** New York Yankees **16** California Angels

Jackson, Shirley
  author of: **10** The Lottery **28** We Have Always Lived in the Castle

Jackson, Stonewall (Thomas)
  served in: **8** Civil War **10** Mexican War
  side: **11** Confederate
  battle: **7** Bull Run **8** Antietam, Richmond **9** Seven Days **14** Fredericksburg **16** Chancellorsville, Shenandoah Valley

Jacksonville
  football team: **5** Bulls **7** Jaguars

Jacob
  father: **5** Isaac
  mother: **7** Rebekah
  brother: **4** Esau
  wives: **4** Leah **6** Rachel
  concubines: **5** Bilah **6** Zilpah
  son: **3** Dan, Gad **4** Levi **5** Asher, Judah **6** Joseph, Reuben, Simeon **7** Zebulun **8** Benjamin, Issachar, Naphtali
  daughter: **5** Dinah

dream of: 6 ladder
wrestled with: 5 angel
name changed to: 6 Israel
burial place: 9 Machpelah

Jacob, Francois
   field: 7 biology
   nationality: 6 French
   discovered: 3 RNA
   awarded: 10 Nobel Prize

jacuzzi 4 bath **9** whirlpool

jade
   species: 7 jadeite **8** nephrite
   source: 5 Burma, China **6** Mexico **7**
     Mogaung **10** New Zealand **12** United
     States

jaded 5 blase, bored, sated, spent,
stale, tired, weary **6** cloyed, dulled,
fagged **7** glutted, satiate, spoiled, wearied, worn-out **8** dog-tired, fatigued,
overused, satiated, shopworn, tired
out **9** exhausted, played out, surfeited
11 overwearied **12** overindulged

jadeite
   variety: 4 jade

jagged 5 jaggy, rough, spiny **6** barbed,
broken, craggy, nicked, ridged, rugged, snaggy, spiked, thorny, uneven,
zigzag **7** angular, bristly, cragged,
notched, pointed, spinous, studded **8**
indented, serrated **9** irregular, knife-
like **10** crenulated, saw-toothed **12**
sharp-toothed

Jagger, Mick
   born: 12 Dartford, Kent (UK)
   musician for: 13 Rolling Stones
   songs: 8 Star, Star, Lady Jane **9** Start
     Me Up **10** Brown Sugar, The Citadel,
     She's So Cold, Wild Horses **11** Ruby
     Tuesday **12** Paint It Black **13** Get Off
     My Cloud **14** Honky Tonk Woman
     15 Jumpin' Jack Flash
   body feature: 4 lips
   wife: 6 Bianca
   companion: 9 Jerri Hall

Jaggers, Mr
   character in: 17 Great Expectations
   author: 7 Dickens

jaguar 3 cat **5** tiger **6** feline **7** panther
8 uturuncu

jail 3 bag, can, jug, nab, pen **4** book,
brig, bust, cell, keep, stir **5** clink,
pinch, pound, run in, seize **6** arrest,
collar, cooler, lockup, prison, take in
7 arraign, bring in, capture, confine,
dungeon, slammer **8** bastille, big
house, hoosegow, imprison, stockade
9 apprehend, black hole, calaboose,
guardroom, workhouse **10** guardhouse
11 incarcerate, reformatory **12** halfway house, penitentiary, reform
school, station house **13** hold in custody, police station **14** detention
house **16** penal institution **17** house
of correction

jailbird 3 con **5** felon, lifer **7** convict **8**
prisoner

jailer 5 guard, screw **6** gaoler, keeper,
warden **7** turnkey **9** custodian

Jair 11 Hebrew judge

Jakarta, Djakarta
   capital of: 9 Indonesia

Jake's Thing
   author: 12 Kingsley Amis

jalopy 3 car **4** auto, heap **5** motor **6**
wheels **7** flivver, machine, vehicle **8**
motorcar **9** tin lizzie **10** automobile

jam 3 fix, mob, ram, sea **4** army, cram,
herd, host, mess, pack, push, stop **5**
block, cease, crowd, crush, drove,
flock, horde, pinch, press, shove,
stall, stick, stuff, swarm, tie-up,
wedge **6** arrest, edge in, pickle, plight,
scrape, strait, throng, thrust, work in,
worm in **7** congest, dilemma, foist in,
force in, squeeze, suspend, trouble **8**
hot water, obstruct, quandary, sandwich **9** interrupt, multitude, overcrowd **11** malfunction, predicament
13 agglomeration

Jamaica
   name means: 18 land of wood and
     water
   capital/largest city: 8 Kingston
   others: 6 May Pen **8** Ocho Rios **9**
     Morant Bay, Port Maria, Port Royal
     10 Mandeville, Montego Bay **11** Port
     Antonio, Spanish Town **12** Saint
     Ann's Bay, Savanna-la-Mar
   head of state: 14 British monarch **15**
     governor general
   monetary unit: 7 quattie
   island: 4 Navy **15** Greater Antilles
   mountain: 8 Sir John's
   highest point: 4 Blue
   river: 5 Black, Cobre, Great, Minho,
     White **9** Rio Grande
   sea: 8 Atlantic **9** Caribbean
   physical feature: 13 Portland Bight
     area: 14 Cockpit Country
     bay: 4 Buff, Hope, Long **6** Morant
       9 Discovery **10** Black River, Blue-
       field's, Old Harbour
     point: 6 Galina **8** Portland **9** North
       East, North West, South East **11**
       North Negril, South Negril
   people: 7 African, Chinese **10** East
     Indian
     ancient: 6 Arawak **7** Ciboney
     discoverer: 8 Columbus
     leader: 5 Seaga **6** Garvey, Manley
       10 Bustamente
   language: 6 Creole **7** English
   religion: 7 Baptist **8** Anglican **9** Meth-
     odist **11** Church of God, Rastafarian
     13 Roman Catholic
   place:
     beach: 11 Doctor's Cave
     botanical garden: 4 Hope
     racetrack: 12 Caymanas Park
   feature:
     evil spirits: 7 duppies
     guerrilla fighters: 7 Maroons
     tree: 4 poui **5** cedar, ceiba, mahoe,
       saman **6** cassia, guango **7** logwood

     8 mahogany **9** casuarina, poinci-
       ana **10** silkcotton **11** lignum vitae
   witch doctor: 8 obeah man
   food:
     coffee: 12 Blue Mountain
     drink: 3 rum **4** jake **8** tia maria
     fruit: 5 guava, mango **6** pawpaw
     spicy soup: 9 pepper pot

jamboree 2 do **4** bash, gala **5** party,
revel, spree **6** fiesta, frolic **7** blowout,
jubilee, shindig **8** carnival, carousal,
festival **9** festivity **11** celebration
   French: 4 fete **13** fete champetre

James 7 apostle
   also called: 12 James the Less
   father: 7 Zebedee **8** Alphaeus
   brother: 4 John, Levi **5** Judas
   disciple of: 5 Jesus
   killed by: 12 Herod Agrippa
   with John called: 13 sons of thunder

James, Henry
   author of: 11 Daisy Miller, The
     American **13** The Bostonians, The
     Golden Bowl **14** Roderick Hudson,
     The Ambassadors **15** The Aspern
     Papers **16** Washington Square **17**
     The Turn of the Screw, The Wings of
     the Dove **18** The Portrait of a Lady
     19 Princess Casamassima

James, P D
   author of: 12 Cover Her Face **13** In-
     nocent Blood **15** Unnatural Causes
     17 Devices and Desires **21** Shroud
     for a Nightingale **22** Death of an Ex-
     pert Witness
   character: 13 Adam Dalgliesh

James the Less *see* **5** James

jammed 4 full **5** stuck **6** filled, loaded,
massed, packed, rammed, wedged **7**
blocked, crammed, crowded, crushed,
pressed, stuffed **8** overfull, squeezed
10 obstructed, sandwiched **11** overcrowded

Janacek, Leos
   born: 8 Hukvaldy **14** Czechoslovakia
   composer of: 5 Mladi, Youth **6** Je-
     nufa **9** In the Mist **10** Taras Bulba
     13 Katya Kabanova **14** Glagolitic
     Mass **17** On an Overgrown Path **18**
     The Makropoulus Case **21** From the
     House of the Dead, The Cunning Lit-
     tle Vixen **24** The Diary of One Who
     Vanished, The Excursions of Mr
     Broucek

Jane
   character in: 6 Tarzan
   author: 9 Burroughs

Jane Eyre
   author: 15 Charlotte Bronte
   character: 5 Mason **7** Mrs Reed **10**
     Grace Poole, Mary Rivers, Mrs Fair-
     fax **11** Adele Varens, Bertha Mason,
     Diana Rivers **12** Bessie Leaven, St
     John Rivers **13** Blanche Ingram **15**
     Edward Rochester
   school: 6 Lowood
   house: 10 Thornfield

director: 15 Robert Stevenson
cast: 11 Orson Welles **12** Joan Fontaine **14** Margaret O'Brien

jangle 3 din, jar **4** ring **5** annoy, chime, clang, clank, clash, crash, upset **6** jingle, racket, rattle **7** clangor, clatter, grate on **8** irritate **9** cacophony **11** reverberate **13** reverberation **14** tintinnabulate

janitor 5 super **6** porter **8** handyman **9** caretaker, custodian, janitress **11** cleaning man **12** cleaning lady **13** cleaning woman **14** maintenance man, superintendent

Janssen, David
  real name: 16 David Harold Meyer
  born: 9 Naponee NE
  roles: 6 Harry O **11** The Fugitive **14** Richard Diamond **15** Dr Richard Kimble

January
  event: 15 Inauguration Day (every 4 years)
  flower: 8 snowdrop **9** carnation
  French: 7 Janvier
  gem: 6 garnet
  German: 6 Januar
  holiday: 8 Epiphany (6) **11** New Year's Day (1) **12** Twelfth Night (5)
  Italian: 7 Gennaio
  number of days: 9 thirty-one
  origin of name: 5 Janus
    Roman god of: 5 doors **8** doorways **10** beginnings
  place in year:
    Gregorian: 5 first
    Julian/Roman: 8 eleventh
  Spanish: 5 Enero
  Zodiac sign: 8 Aquarius **9** Capricorn

Janus
  origin: 5 Roman
  god of: 8 doorways **9** rising sun **10** beginnings, setting sun

Japan
  other name: 5 Nihon **6** Nippon
  name means: 18 Land of the Rising Sun
  capital/largest city: 3 Edo **5** Tokyo
  others: 4 Kobe, Naha **5** Kyoto, Osaka **6** Nagoya, Sendai **7** Fukuoka, Niigata, Sapporo **8** Kanazawa, Kawasaki, Nagasaki, Yokohama **9** Hiroshima, Kagoshima **10** Kitakyushu
  school: 4 Chuo, Keio **5** Hosei, Kyoto, Nihon, Tokyo **6** Sophia, Waseda **7** Fukuoka **8** Doshisha
  head of state: 7 emperor
  measure: 2 go **3** boo, cho, djo, fun, inc, ken, kin, kon, rin, shi, sho, sun, tan **4** hiro, isse, kati, koku, niyo, shoo **5** carat, catty, issho, ittan, momme, picul, shaku **6** kwamme **8** hiyak-kin **9** hiyak-hiro **11** komma-ichida, kujira-shaku
  monetary unit: 2 bu **3** mon, rin, rio, sen, shu, yen **4** cash, mibu, oban **5** kohan, obang, tempo **6** cobang, ichebu, ichibu, itzebu, kobang **7** itze-boo, itziboo

weight: 2 mo **3** fun, kon, rin **4** kati, kwan **5** carat, catty, momme **8** hiyakkin

island: 3 Iki, Izu, Oki, Tsu **4** Oita, Sado, Yaku **5** Amami, Awaji, Bonin, Hondo, Kuril, Rebun, Sikok **6** Honshu, Kiushu, Kyushu, Loochu, Marcus, Riukiu, Tanega, Tyukyu **7** Cipango, Hachijo, Iwo Jima, Okinawa, Rishiri, Shikoko, Shikoku, Volcano **8** Hokkaido, Miyajima, Okigunto, Okushiri, Tsushima, Yakujima

lake: 4 Biwa, Suwa, Toya **6** Towada **8** Kutchawa, Shikotsu

mountain: 3 Uso, Zao **5** Asahi, Asama, Hondo, Yesso **6** Asosan, Enasan, Hiuchi, Kiusiu, Yariga **7** Hakusan, Kujusan, Tokachi **8** Fujiyama **9** Japan Alps

highest point: 4 Fuji **7** Fujisan

river: 4 Tone, Yalu **8** Ishikari, Tonegawa **11** Shinano- gawa

sea: 3 Suo **5** Japan **6** Inland **7** Amakusa, Okhotsk, Pacific **8** Tsushima

physical feature:
  bay: 3 Ise **4** Miku, Tosa, Yedo **5** Amort, Mutsu, Osaka, Otaru, Tokyo **6** Ariake, Atsumi, Sendai, Suruga, Toyama, Wakasa **7** Uchiura
  cape: 3 Iro, Oki, Oma, Toi **4** Daio, Esan, Jizo, Mela, Mino, Noma, Nomo, Sada, Sawa, Shio, Suzu **5** Erimo, Kyoga, Rurui **6** Todoga **7** Shiriya **8** Ashizuri, Shakotan **12** Muroto Nojima
  channel: 3 Kii **5** Bungo
  current: 5 Japan **7** Okhotsk **8** Kuro Shio
  divine wind: 8 kamikaze
  gulf: 6 Sagami
  plain: 4 Nobi **5** Kanto
  strait: 4 Soya **5** Korea, Osumi **6** Nemuro, Tanega, Tokara **7** Tsugaru **8** Tsushima **9** La Perouse
  people: 3 Eta **6** Korean **8** Japanese, Okinawan **10** Buramkumin
  ancient: 4 Ainu **5** Jomon, Yayoi
  artist: 4 Okyo **5** Buson, Jocho, Korin, Taiga, Unkei **6** Buncho, Eitoku, Kenzan, Koetsu, Reisai, Sesshu, Sesson, Shubun **7** Baiitsu, Choshun, Foujita, Gyokudo, Hokusai, Josetsu, Sanraku, Sharaku, Sotatsu, Utamaro **8** Harunobu, Kiyonaga, Motonobu **9** Hiroshige, Mitsunobu
  author: 5 Basho **7** Abe Kobo **8** Mori Ogai **11** Ueda Akinari **12** Ihara Saikaku, Mishima Yukio, Sakyo Komatsu **13** Natsume Soseki, Zeami Motokiyo **14** Shimazaki Toson, Tsubouchi Shoyo **15** Motoori Norinaga, Murasaki Shikibu **16** Fujiwara Nokisaki, Kawabata Yasunari **17** Tanizaki Junichiro **19** Chikamatsu Monzaemon

dynasty: 5 Meiji, Taira **6** Yamato **8** Fujiwara, Minamoto
leader: 4 Hojo **5** Kammu, Meiji **6** Go-Toba, Ieyasu **7** Akihito, Go-Daigo **8** Hirohito, Nobunaga, Yoritomo **9** Hideyoshi, Yoshimasa **10** Tojo Hideki, Yoshimitsu **11** Hara Takashi, Ito Hirobumi **12** Tanaka Kakuei **13** Konoe Fumimaro, Shotoku Taishi **14** Yoshida Shigeru **15** Ashikaga Takauji **18** Matsukata Mayayoshi
legendary ruler: 5 Jimmu, Jingo **7** Izanagi
shogunate: 8 Ashikaga, Kamakura, Tokugawa
language: 8 Japanese
  alphabet/characters: 4 kana **5** kanji **8** hiragana, katakana
  dialect: 5 Kanto
religion: 6 Tendai **7** Shingon **8** Buddhism **9** Shintoism **12** Confucianism
place:
  castle: 4 Nijo
  hall: 5 Hoodo **7** Phoenix **12** Golden Buddha
  mausoleum: 4 Ojin **7** Nintoku
  palace: 7 Akasaka, Katsura
  shrine: 5 Heian **11** Itsukushima **16** Grand Shrine of Ise
  temple: 6 Kotoku **7** Byodoin, Horyuji, Ryoanji, Senso-ji, Todaiji **8** Enkakuji, Kenchoji, Kofukuji **9** Kinkakuji **13** Asakusa Kannon
feature:
  abacus: 7 soroban
  bed: 5 futon
  clothing: 6 kimono
  festival: 13 Cherry Blossom
  firm: 4 Sony **5** Honda **6** Mitoui, Nissan, Toyota, Yasuda **7** Iwasaki **8** Sumitomo **10** Mitsubishi
  flower arranging: 7 ikebana
  painting style: 4 kano, tosa **5** nanga, nisee, onnae, rarae, rimpa, shijo **6** chinso, otokoe, sesshu, ukiyoe **7** konpeki, nihonga, yamatoe
  paper folding art: 7 origami
  poem: 4 waka **5** haiku, tanka
  puppet theater: 7 bunraku
  rush floor covering: 6 tatami
  sport: 4 judo **6** karate **13** sumo wrestling
  statue: 8 Daibutsu **11** Great Buddha
  tea ceremony: 7 chanoyu
  theater: 2 no **3** noh **6** kabuki
  the way of the warrior/code of honor: 7 bushido
  tree: 6 bonsai
  wood block print: 6 ukiyoe
food:
  beverage: 4 sake **8** green tea
  dish: 5 sushi **7** sashimi, tempura **8** sukiyaki, teriyaki, yakitori
  noodle: 4 soba

Japanese

independent language of: 5 Japan **13** Ryukyu Islands

jape 4 gibe, joke **5** antic, caper, prank **7** mockery

Japheth
father: 4 Noah
brother: 3 Ham **4** Shem

Jaques
character in: 11 As You Like It
author: 11 Shakespeare

jar 3 din, jug, pot, urn **4** bong, bray, buzz, daze, faze, jolt, rock, stir, stun **5** blare, blast, brawl, clang, clank, crash, crock, flask, floor, quake, shake, shock, throw, upset **6** beaker, bottle, impact, jangle, jiggle, joggle, racket, rattle, vessel **7** agitate, astound, clangor, clatter, confuse, disturb, fluster, perturb, shake up, startle, stupefy, trouble, upheave, vibrate **8** befuddle, bewilder, bleating, canister, clashing, convulse, decanter, demijohn, disquiet, distract, unsettle **9** agitation, cacophony, container **10** concussion, discompose, disconcert, receptacle **11** discordance
Spanish: 4 olla

jargon 4 bosh, bull, bunk, cant **5** argot, fudge, hooey, idiom, lingo, prate, usage **6** babble, brogue, drivel, patois, pidgin, piffle **7** baloney, blabber, blather, dialect, fustian, hogwash, prattle, rubbish, twaddle **8** folderol, malarkey, nonsense, parlance, tommyrot, verbiage **9** gibberish, moonshine, poppycock, rigmarole **10** balderdash, flapdoodle, hocus-pocus, rigamarole, vernacular, vocabulary **11** abracadabra, jabberwocky, phraseology, shibboleths **12** gobbledygook, lingua franca **14** grandiloquence

Jarley, Mrs
character in: 19 The Old Curiosity Shop
author: 7 Dickens

Jarndyce, John
character in: 10 Bleak House
author: 7 Dickens

jarring 4 rude **5** harsh, rough **6** jangly **7** grating, jolting, rasping, shaking **8** clashing, grinding, jangling, rattling, strident **9** dissonant, wrenching **10** discordant **12** nerve- racking **13** nerve-wracking

Jarry, Alfred
author of: 7 King Ubu **11** Ubu in Chains **13** Ubu the Cuckold

jasmine 8 Jasminum
varieties: 4 blue, cape, rock, star **5** crape, night, royal **6** orange, yellow **7** Arabian, Chilean, Italian, Spanish **8** Carolina, cinnamon, Japanese, Paraguay, pinwheel, primrose, windmill **9** angel-wing **10** Catalonian, Madagascar **11** Confederate

Jason
leader of: 9 Argonauts

father: 5 Aeson
mother: 8 Alcimede, Polymede
half-brother: 6 Pelias
son: 5 Thoas **6** Euneus, Pheres **7** Medeius **8** Mermerus, Tisander **9** Alcimenes, Thessalus
daughter: 7 Eriopis
teacher: 6 Chiron **7** centaur, Cheiron
retrieved: 12 Golden Fleece
ship: 4 Argo
loved by: 5 Medea
loved: 6 Glauce

Jasper, John
character in: 22 The Mystery of Edwin Drood
author: 7 Dickens

jaundiced 5 blase, bored **6** bitter **7** cynical, envious, hostile, jealous **8** covetous, doubting, satiated **9** green-eyed, resentful, skeptical **10** embittered, suspicious **11** mistrustful

jaunt 4 spin, tour, trip **6** airing, flight, junket, outing, ramble, stroll **9** adventure, excursion, promenade, short trip **10** expedition

jaunty 4 airy, neat, trim **5** natty, perky **6** blithe, bouncy, breezy, dapper, lively, sporty, spruce **7** buoyant **8** carefree, debonair **9** sprightly, vivacious **12** lighthearted, high-stepping, high-spirited

Java
other name: 5 Djawa
capital/largest city: 7 Jakarta **8** Djakarta
others: 5 Bogor, Dessa **6** Kediri, Malang **7** Bandung, Batavia **8** Semarang, Surabaja, Surabaya **9** Surakarta **11** Djokjakarta **13** Pelabuhanratu
government: 17 island of Indonesia
measure: 3 kan **4** paal, rand **5** palen
weight: 4 amat, pond, tali **5** pound **6** soekel
island: 4 Bali **5** Sunda **6** Lombok, Madura
mountain: 4 Amat, Gede **5** Lawoe, Murjo, Prahu **6** Raoeng, Slamet **8** Soembing
highest point: 6 Semuru **7** Semeroe
river: 4 Solo **7** Brantas
sea: 4 Java **6** Indian **7** Pacific
physical feature:
plateau: 4 Ijen
strait: 5 Sunda
people: 5 Krama, Kromo **6** Kalang **8** Javanese, Madurese **9** Sundanese
dynasty: 7 Mataram **9** Majapahit, Srivijaya
language: 4 Kavi, Kawi **5** Malay **6** Sassak **8** Balinese, Madurese, Sudanese **16** Bahasa Indonesian
religion: 5 Hindu, Islam **7** animism **8** Buddhism
place:
temple: 6 Chandi, Thandi **9** Borobudur, Prambanan
feature:
cloth: 3 kat **5** batik, kapok

dance: 7 seri mpi
dancer: 6 bedoyo
fishing boat: 4 prau
ornamental dagger: 4 kris
puppet play: 6 wajang, wayang
food:
fruit: 6 durian, lomboy, nangca **7** gondang

javelin 4 dart **5** lance, shaft, spear **10** projectile

jaw 3 gab, rap **4** chat, chin, talk **7** jawbone, palaver **8** chitchat, converse, mandible **10** chew the fat, chew the rag **11** confabulate

Jaws
author: 13 Peter Benchley
director: 15 Steven Spielberg
cast: 10 Robert Shaw **11** Roy Scheider **12** Lorraine Gary **15** Richard Dreyfuss
score: 12 John Williams
Oscar for: 5 score

Jayhawker State
nickname of: 6 Kansas

jazz musician 8 Art Tatum **9** Bud Powell **10** Miles Davis **11** Lester Young **12** Benny Goodman, John Coltrane **13** Charles Mingus, Charlie Parker, Duke Ellington, Thelonius Monk **14** Dizzy Gillespie, Louis Armstrong, Ornette Coleman, Wynton Marsalis

jealous 4 wary **7** anxious, envious, mindful **8** covetous, grudging, watchful **9** concerned, green-eyed, regardful, resentful **10** possessive, protective, suspicious **11** mistrustful, mistrusting **12** apprehensive

jealousy 4 envy **8** distrust, jaundice, mistrust **9** suspicion **10** resentment **12** covetousness **14** possessiveness **16** green-eyed monster
color: 5 green

Jebus
city captured by: 5 David
renamed: 9 Jerusalem
inhabitant: 8 Jebusite

jeer 3 boo, bug, dig, rap **4** barb, hiss, hoot, mock, razz, slam, slur **5** abuse, flout, hound, knock, scoff, scorn, sneer, taunt, whoop **6** deride, harass, heckle, hector, insult, revile **7** catcall, laugh at, mockery, obloquy **8** derision, ridicule, scoffing **9** aspersion, contumely, poke fun at, whistle at

Jeffers, Robinson
author of: 5 Medea, Tamar **6** Cawdor **8** Solstice **9** Dear Judas **12** Roan Stallion **14** Thurso's Landing **18** The Women at Point Sur **21** The Tower Beyond Tragedy

Jefferson, Thomas
nickname: 16 Sage of Monticello
presidential rank: 5 third
party: 20 Democratic-Republican
state represented: 2 VA
defeated: 5 (John) Adams **8** (Charles

Cotesworth) Pinckney
vice president: 4 (Aaron) Burr **7** (George) Clinton
cabinet:
  state: 7 (James) Madison
  treasury: 6 (Samuel) Dexter **8** (Albert) Gallatin
  war: 8 (Henry) Dearborn
  attorney general: 6 (Caesar Augustus) Rodney **7** (Levi) Lincoln **12** (John) Breckenridge
  navy: 5 (Robert) Smith
born: 2 VA **14** Shadwell estate **15** Goochland (Albemarle) County
died/buried: 10 Monticello
education: 14 William and Mary
interests: 6 violin **7** writing **11** agriculture **12** architecture
favorite foods: 10 French food **11** French wines
vacation: 12 Poplar Forest
author: 25 Declaration of Independence, Notes on the State of Virginia **39** A Summary View of the Rights of British America
political career: 8 governor **16** House of Burgesses **19** Virginia legislature **25** Declaration of Independence, Second Continental Congress
  secretary of: 5 state
  minister to: 6 France
civilian career: 6 farmer, lawyer
notable events of lifetime/term:
  expedition: 13 Lewis and Clark
  prohibition of: 19 importation of slaves
  purchase: 9 Louisiana
father: 5 Peter
mother: 4 Jane (Randolph)
siblings: 4 Jane, Lucy, Mary **6** Martha **8** Randolph **9** Anna Scott, Elizabeth **10** Peter Field
wife: 6 Martha (Wayles Skelton)
children: 4 Mary **6** Martha
Jeffersons, The
character: 8 Florence **9** Tom Willis **11** Helen Willis **12** Harry Bentley **15** George Jefferson, Lionel Jefferson, Louise Jefferson, Ralph the Doorman **20** Jenny Willis Jefferson
cast: 9 Mike Evans **10** Damon Evans, Marla Gibbs, Roxie Roker **11** Ned Wertimer **12** Paul Benedict **13** Franklin Cover, Isabel Sanford **14** Sherman Hemsley **15** Berlinda Tolbert
George's business: 11 dry cleaning
spinoff from: 14 All in the Family
Jeffreys, Harold
field: 7 physics **9** astronomy
nationality: 7 British
explained: 7 weather
studied: 10 Earth's core **11** solar system
Jeffries, James Jackson
nickname: 14 The Boilermaker
sport: 6 boxing
class: 11 heavyweight

jehad, jihad 6 strife **7** holy war **8** struggle
Jehioada
father: 7 Paseach
son: 7 Benaiah
means: 12 Jehovah knows
Jehoshaphat
father: 3 Asa **6** Ahitub, Nimshi, Parnah
mother: 8 Jehorani
means: 13 Jehovah judges
Jehovah 3 god **4** YHWH **5** diety
Jehu
father: 6 Hanani **11** Jehoshaphat **14** reckless driver
jejune 4 dull **5** banal, inane, stale, trite, vapid **7** humdrum, insipid, puerile **8** ordinary **9** hackneyed **10** pedestrian, unexciting, unoriginal, wishy-washy **11** commonplace **12** conventional **13** uninteresting
jell 3 gel, jam, set **4** clot, firm **5** jelly **7** congeal, thicken **9** coagulate **10** gelatinize
Jellyby, Mrs
character in: 10 Bleak House
author: 7 Dickens
jellyfish 5 hydra, polyp, softy **6** coward, medusa, nettle **8** sunfish **9** sunfish **8** weakling **10** ctenophore, pantywaist **11** milquetoast, mollycoddle **12** coelenterate, invertebrate, siphonophore **18** Portuguese man-of-war
je ne sais quoi 12 I don't know what **18** indefinable quality
Jenner, Bruce
sport: 13 track and field
known for: 9 decathlon
won: 8 Olympics
Jenner, Edward
nationality: 7 British
discovered: 11 vaccination **19** smallpox inoculation
Jenney, William Le Baron
architect of: 21 Home Insurance Building (Chicago)
jeopardize 4 risk **6** expose, hazard **7** imperil **8** endanger **10** compromise **11** put into danger
jeopardy 4 risk **5** peril **6** danger, hazard **8** exposure, unsafety **9** liability **10** insecurity **11** imperilment **12** endangerment **13** vulnerability **14** precariousness
Jephthah 11 Hebrew judge
father: 6 Gilead
Jeremiah
father: 7 Hilkiah **10** Habazaniah
daughter: 7 Mamutal
grandson: 7 Jehohaz
friend, scribe: 6 Baruch
jerk 3 ass, tic, tug **4** dope, dupe, fool, pull, snap, yank **5** dummy, dunce, idiot, klutz, pluck, shake, spasm, start, twist **6** quiver, reflex, thrust, twitch,

wrench **7** tremble **8** convulse **9** trembling
jerky 4 beef, meat **5** jolty, jumpy **6** choppy, elboic, jouncy **7** biltong, charqui, fidgety, twitchy **9** dried beef, spasmodic, twitching
Jeroboam
father: 5 Joash, Nebat
successor: 9 Zachariah
Jerry
(British): 6 German
jerry-built 4 weak **5** frail, run-up, shaky, tacky **6** faulty, flimsy, shoddy, sleazy **7** rickety, unsound **8** gimcrack, slipshod, thrown-up, unstable **9** cheap-jack, defective **10** ramshackle **13** unsubstantial **14** thrown-together
jersey 3 cow **5** maillot, shirt **6** tricot **7** sweater **8** camisole, guernsey, pullover **10** undershirt
Jersey Joe
nickname of: 10 Joe Walcott
Jerusalem
author: 12 William Blake
Jerusalem
former name: 5 Jebus
pool of: 6 Siloam **8** Bethesda
Jerusalem
Arabic: 14 Bayt al-Muqaddas
capital of: 6 Israel
Hebrew: 12 Yerushalayim
hills: 7 Judaean
landmark: 6 al-Aqsa **11** Wailing Wall, Western Wall **12** Israel Museum **13** Dome of the Rock **14** Dead Sea Scrolls **15** Shrine of the Book **17** Rockefeller Museum **24** Church of the Holy Sepulcher
mount: 6 Olives, Scopus
river: 6 Kidron
ruler: 5 Arabs, David, Herod **6** Persia, Romans **7** British, Saladin, Seljuks, Solumon **8** Ayyubids, Fatimids, Ptolemy I **9** Crusaders, Maccabees, Mamelukes **10** Canaanites **12** Antiochus III **13** Pontius Pilate **15** Byzantine Empire **17** Alexander the Great, Antiochus the Third
street: 12 Via Dolorosa
Jerusalem Delivered
author: 13 Torquato Tasso
Jervis, Mrs
character in: 6 Pamela
author: 10 Richardson
jessamine 8 Jasminum
varieties: 3 day **5** night, poet's **6** orange, yellow **12** willow-leaved **13** night-blooming **14** Carolina yellow
Jesse
father: 4 Obed
grandfather: 4 Boaz
grandmother: 4 Ruth
great-grandfather: 5 Rahab
son: 5 David, Eliab **7** Shammah **8** Abinadab
jest 3 gag, pun **4** fool, game, gibe, jape, joke, josh, quip **5** act up, crack,

laugh, prank, tease, trick **6** banter, bon mot **9** wisecrack, witticism **10** crack jokes, pleasantry **11** horse around

jester 3 wag, wit **4** card, fool, mime, zany **5** clown, comic, joker, mimer, mimic **6** madcap, mummer **7** buffoon **8** comedian, funnyman, humorist, quipster **9** harlequin **10** motley fool **11** merry-andrew, pantomimist, punchinello

jesting 6 joking **7** teasing **8** sportive **9** bantering, unserious **12** wisecracking

Jesus
also called: 7 Holy One, Messiah **8** Nazarene, Son of God **9** the Christ **12** Man of Sorrows **13** Prince of Peace **14** Savior Anointed
mother: 4 Mary
stepfather: 6 Joseph
birthplace: 9 Bethlehem
lived in: 8 Nazareth
death place: 9 Jerusalem
buried by: 17 Joseph of Arimathea
disciples: 4 John, Jude **5** James, Peter, Simon **6** Andrew, Philip, Thomas **7** Matthew **12** James the Less **13** Judas Iscariot **20** Bartholomew Nathanael
secret follower: 9 Nicodemus
famous discourse: 16 Sermon on the Mount

jet 4 gush **5** flush, issue, shoot, spout, spray, spurt, surge, swash **6** effuse, nozzle, rush up, squirt, stream **7** sparger, sprayer, Spritze, syringe **8** atomizer, fountain, shoot out, Spritzer **9** discharge, sprinkler

Jethro
daughter: 8 Zipporah
son-in-law: 5 Moses

Jetsons, The
character: 5 Astro **10** Jane Jetson, Judy Jetson **11** Elroy Jetson **12** George Jetson **13** Cosmo G Spacely
voices: 8 Mel Blanc **10** Daws Butler, Don Messick, Janet Waldo **13** George O'Hanlon **14** Penny Singleton

jettison 4 dump **5** eject, scrap **6** unload **7** cast off, discard **8** throw out **9** discharge, eliminate, pitch over, throw over **13** toss overboard

jetty 4 dike, dock, mole, pier, quay, slip **5** black, ebony, groin, levee, raven, sable, wharf **6** bridge **7** sea wall **8** buttress **10** breakwater

jeu de mots 3 pun **11** play on words

jeu d'esprit 9 witticism **17** witty literary work
literally: 12 play of spirit

jeune fille 4 girl **9** young girl **13** unmarried girl

jeunesse doree 11 gilded youth, golden youth

Jew 6 Essene, Hebrew, Judean, Semite **7** Edomite, Judaist, Moabite **8** Hebraist, Sephardi **9** Israelite

jewel 3 ace, gem, pip **4** bead, dear, find, ring, whiz **5** honey, pearl, prize, stone, tiara **6** bangle, bauble, brooch, locket, winner **7** earring, pendant, trinket **8** bracelet, knockout, necklace, ornament, pure gold, treasure **9** humdinger, lavaliere **10** topnotcher **11** crackerjack, masterpiece

jewelry 4 gems, gold **6** silver **7** bangles, gewgaws, regalia **8** trinkets **10** adornments **14** precious stones

Jewett, Sarah Orne
author of: 26 The Country of the Pointed Firs

Jewish 6 Hebrew, Judaic **7** Hebraic, Semitic
bread: 5 matzo **6** matzoh **7** challah
candelabrum: 7 menorah
ceremonial robe: 5 kitel
color: 5 white
coming of age: 10 bar mitzvah, bat mitzvah
dietary laws: 7 kashrut **8** kashruth
fit to eat: 6 kosher
not fit to eat: 4 tref
group: 8 Hadassah **9** B'nai B'rith
holy day/festival: 5 Purim, seder **6** Sukkot **7** Shavuot **8** Chanukah, Hanukkah, Passover **9** Yom Kippur **12** Rosh Hashanah
law/scripture: 5 Torah **6** Gemara, Talmud, Tanach **7** Mishnah
liturgical prayer: 6 Yigdal **8** Kol Nidre
recited on eve of: 9 Yom Kippur
marriage canopy: 6 chupah
months:
1st: 6 Tishri
2nd: 7 Heshvan
3rd: 6 Kislev
4th: 5 Tevet
5th: 6 Shevat
6th: 4 Adar
7th: 5 Nisan
8th: 4 Iyar
9th: 5 Sivan
10th: 6 Tammuz
11th: 2 Av
12th: 4 Elul
prayerbook: 6 mahzor, siddur **7** machzor
quarter: 6 ghetto, mellah
school: 5 heder **6** cheder
skullcap: 5 kipah **8** yarmulka
service to commemorate the dead: 6 Yizkor
synagogue: 4 shul **5** schul
toast: 8 mazel tov

Jewkes, Mrs
character in: 6 Pamela
author: 10 Richardson

Jew of Malta, The
author: 18 Christopher Marlowe
character: 7 Abigail, Barabas **8** Ithamore **15** Governor of Malta

Jezebel
director: 12 William Wyler
cast: 10 Bette Davis, Fay Bainter,

Henry Fonda **11** Donald Crisp, George Brent **15** Margaret Lindsay
Oscar for: 7 actress (Davis) **17** supporting actress (Bainter)

Jezebel
father: 7 Ethbaal
husband: 8 King Ahab
daughter: 8 Athaliah
opposed: 6 Elijah
killed: 6 Naboth
father-in-law: 4 Omri

jib 3 arm, shy **4** balk, boom, sail, tack **5** demur, gigue, stick **6** recoil **7** scruple

jibe 2 go **3** fit **4** mesh, tack **5** agree, fit in, match, shift, tally **6** accord, concur, square **7** conform **8** coincide, dovetail **9** harmonize **10** correspond, go together **11** fit together

jiffy 3 sec **4** jiff **5** flash, shake, trice **6** minute, moment, second **7** half a mo, instant **9** twinkling **10** nanosecond **11** microsecond, millisecond, split second

jigger 4 dram, shot **5** glass **6** device, doodad, gadget, object **7** bicycle, gimmick, measure **9** doohickey, shot glass **10** boneshaker **11** contraption, thingumabob

jiggle 4 jerk **5** shake **6** bounce, fidget, joggle, jostle, twitch, wiggle **7** agitate, wriggle

jihad *see* **5** jehad

jilt 5 leave **6** betray, desert **7** forsake, let down **12** break off with **17** break an engagement

Jim
character in: 15 (The Adventures of) Huckleberry Finn
author: 5 Twain

jimmy 3 bar, pry **5** force, lever **7** crowbar

jingle 4 ring **5** clang, clank, clink, ditty **6** jangle, tinkle **7** clatter, ringing **8** doggerel, facetiae, limerick **10** catchy poem, catchy song **12** product theme **13** reverberation **14** commercial tune **16** tintinnabulation

Jingle, Alfred
character in: 14 Pickwick Papers
author: 7 Dickens

jingoism 10 chauvinism, flag-waving, patriotics **11** nationalism **14** overpatriotism, spread-eagleism **15** superpatriotism **16** ultranationalism

jinn 3 imp **5** afrit, demon, genie, jinni **6** afreet, spirit **8** jinniyeh

jinx 3 hex **5** curse **6** plague, whammy **7** bugaboo, bugbear, evil eye, ill wind, nemesis **9** evil spell
French: 9 bete noire

jitney 3 bus, cab

jitterbug 5 dance, lindy **8** lindy hop **12** boogie-woogie

jitters 6 shakes **7** anxiety, fidgets, jim-jams, shivers, willies **9** jumpiness, quivering, shakiness, tenseness, the creeps, whim-whams **10** uneasiness **11** butterflies, fidgetiness, nervousness **12** skittishness **13** heebie- jeebies **16** screaming-meemies

jittery 5 jumpy **6** uneasy **7** anxious, nervous

Jivaro, Shuara, Jibaro
tribe: **6** Achual, Antipa **8** Aguaruna, Huambiza
location: **4** Peru **7** Ecuador **12** South America
noted for: **7** tsantsa (shrunken heads)

Joab
mother: **7** Zeruiah
brother: **6** Asahel **7** Abishai
commanded: **10** David's army
killed: **5** Abner, Amasa **7** Absalom
killed by: **7** Benaiah
conspired to overthrow: **5** David

Joad family
characters in: **16** The Grapes of Wrath
members: **2** Ma, Pa **3** Tom **4** Noah **6** Connie **12** Rose of Sharon
author: **9** Steinbeck

job 3 lot **4** care, duty, part, role, spot, task, work **5** chore, craft, field, place, quota, share, stint, trade, trust **6** affair, career, charge, errand, living, metier, office, output **7** calling, concern, mission, opening, portion, product, pursuit **8** activity, business, capacity, contract, exercise, function, position, province, vocation **9** allotment, piecework, situation **10** assignment, commission, engagement, enterprise, livelihood, occupation, profession **11** achievement, appointment, performance, undertaking **14** accomplishment, responsibility

Job 8 sufferer
father: **8** Issachar
friend: **5** Elihu **6** Bildad, Zophar **7** Eliphaz

job holder 6 worker **8** employee, hireling

job seeker 7 hopeful **8** aspirant **9** applicant, candidate

Jocasta
also: **8** Epicaste
queen of: **6** Thebes
father: **9** Menoeceus
brother: **5** Creon
husband: **5** Laius **7** Oedipus
son: **7** Oedipus **8** Eteocles **9** Polynices
daughter: **6** Ismene **8** Antigone
death by: **7** hanging, suicide

Jochebed
father: **4** Levi
husband: **5** Amram
nephew: **5** Amram
son: **5** Aaron, Moses

jockey 5 Baeza, Krone **6** Arcaro, Pincay **7** Cauthen, Cordero, Cruguet, Hartack **8** McCarron, McHargue, Turcotte **9** Shoemaker, Velasquez

jocose 3 fun **4** arch **5** comic, droll, funny, jolly, merry, witty **6** joking, jovial **7** amusing, comical, jesting, jocular, playful, roguish, teasing, waggish **8** humorous, mirthful, prankish, sportive **9** facetious

jocular 3 gay **5** droll, funny, jolly, merry, witty **6** jocose, jocund, joking, jovial **7** amusing, jesting, playful, roguish, rompish, waggish **8** humorous, mirthful, prankish, sportive **9** facetious **10** frolicsome **12** entertaining, lighthearted

jocund 5 jolly, merry **6** breezy, cheery, elated, jovial, lively **8** cheerful, debonair, pleasant **9** easygoing **10** untroubled **12** happy-go-lucky, lighthearted

Joel
means: **12** Jehovah is God
father: **4** Nebo **6** Samuel **7** Azariah, Pedaiah, Pethuel
brother: **6** Nathan

Joe Palooka
creator: **9** Ham Fisher **11** Tony Di-Preta
character:
children: **3** Joe **5** Buddy **7** Joannie
friend: **9** Little Max **10** Jerry Leemy
manager: **11** Knobby Walsh
valet: **6** Smokey
wife: **8** Anne Howe
profession: **5** boxer

jog 3 bob, jar, tug **4** jerk, pull, rock, stir, trot, yank **5** nudge, shake, twist **6** bounce, jiggle, jostle, jounce, prompt, twitch, wrench **7** actuate, animate **8** activate, energize **9** stimulate

jogger 4 memo **6** layboy, runner **7** trotter **8** reminder **10** memorandum

Johannesburg
airport: **8** Jan Smuts
area: **4** Rand **9** Transvaal
capital of: **11** South Africa
landmark: **13** Carlton Centre **14** Africana Museum **16** Union Observatory **17** Zoological Gardens **20** Melrose Bird Sanctuary
township: **6** Soweto **7** Lenasia **10** Nancefield
university: **13** Rand Afrikaans, Witwatersrand

John
father: **7** Zebedee
brother: **5** James
son: **5** Peter
called, with brother: **9** Boanerges **13** sons of thunder
pertaining to John or his writings: **9** Johannine

John Barleycorn
personification of: **6** liquor **7** whiskey

John Brown's Body
author: **19** Stephen Vincent Benet

John Bull
personification of: **7** England **10** Englishman

John Gabriel Borkman
author: **11** Henrik Ibsen

John Mark see **4** Mark

Johnny Belinda
director: **13** Jean Negulesco
cast: **8** Lew Ayres **9** Jane Wyman **15** Charles Bickford
Oscar for: **7** actress (Wyman)

Johnny Cash Show, The
cast: **9** Jim Varney **10** Howard Mann **11** Carl Perkins, Steve Martin **14** June Carter Cash, Tennessee Three **15** Statler Brothers **32** Mother Maybelle and the Carter Family

Johnny-come-lately 8 newcomer **9** latecomer **10** new arrival **11** late arrival

Johnny U
nickname of: **12** Johnny Unitas

Johns, Glynis
born: **8** Pretoria **11** South Africa
roles: **11** Mary Poppins **13** The Sundowners **17** A Little Night Music **26** Around the World in Eighty Days

Johns, Jasper
born: **9** Augusta GA
artwork: **4** Flag **6** Studio, Target **8** Watchman **10** Fool's House **12** Device Circle **13** Painted Bronze (Beer Cans) **14** The Barber's Tree **19** Target with Four Faces **22** Target with Plaster Casts

Johnson, Andrew
presidential rank: **11** seventeenth
party: **8** Democrat
state represented: **2** TN
defeated: **5** no one
succeeded upon death of: **7** Lincoln
vice president: **4** none
cabinet:
state: **6** (William Henry) Seward
treasury: **9** (Hugh) McCulloch
war: **7** (Edwin McMasters) Stanton **9** (John McAllister) Schofield
attorney general: **5** (James) Speed **6** (William Maxwell) Evarts **8** (Henry) Stanbery
navy: **6** (Gideon) Welles
postmaster general: **7** (Alexander Williams) Randall **8** (William) Dennison
interior: **5** (John Palmer) Usher **6** (James) Harlan **8** (Orville Hickman) Browning
born: **9** Raleigh NC
died: **16** Carter's Station TN
buried: **13** Greeneville TN
education: **9** no college **12** self-educated
political career: **8** US Senate **13** vice president **22** House of Representatives
only president to be: **9** impeached (1868)
found: **9** not guilty
mayor of: **11** Greeneville (TN)

governor of: 9 Tennessee
civilian career: 6 tailor
military service: 8 Civil War **12** US Volunteers **16** brigadier general
  military governor of: 9 Tennessee
notable events of lifetime/term: 14 Reconstruction
  Purchase: 6 Alaska
father: 5 Jacob
mother: 4 Mary (McDonough)
  stepfather: 15 Turner Dougherty
sibling: 7 William
wife: 5 Eliza (McCardle)
children: 4 Mary **6** Andrew, Martha, Robert **7** Charles

Johnson, Don
born: 10 Flatt Creek (MO)
roles: 7 Melanie **8** Dead-Bang, Paradise **9** Miami Vice, Cease Fire **11** Guilty as Sin **16** In Pursuit of Honor, The Long Hot Summer
wife: 15 Melanie Griffith

Johnson, Earvin
nickname: 5 Magic
sport: 10 basketball
position: 5 guard
team: 16 Los Angeles Lakers

Johnson, Jack (John Arthur)
nickname: 11 Little Artha **14** Galveston Giant
sport: 6 boxing
class: 11 heavyweight

Johnson, Lyndon Baines
nickname: 3 LBJ **15** Landslide Lyndon
presidential rank: 11 thirty-sixth
party: 10 Democratic
state represented: 2 TX
succeeded upon death of: 7 Kennedy
defeated: 4 (Earle Harold) Munn, (Eric) Hass **6** (John) Kasper **7** (Clifton) DeBerry **9** (Barry Morris) Goldwater
vice president: 4 none (first term) **8** (Hubert Horatio) Humphrey
cabinet:
  state: 4 (David Dean) Rusk
  treasury: 4 (Joseph William) Barr **6** (Clarence Douglas) Dillon, (Henry Hamill) Fowler
  defense: 8 (Clark McAdams) Clifford, (Robert Strange) McNamara
  attorney general: 5 (William Ramsey) Clark **7** (Robert Francis) Kennedy **10** (Nicholas deBelleville) Katzenbach
  postmaster general: 6 (Lawrence Francis) O'Brien, (William Marvin) Watson **9** (John Austin) Gronouski
  interior: 5 (Stewart Lee) Udall
  agriculture: 7 (Orville Lothrop) Freeman
  commerce: 5 (Cyrus Rowlett) Smith **6** (John Thomas) Connor, (Luther Hartwell) Hodges **10** (Alexander Buel) Trowbridge
  labor: 5 (William Willard) Wirtz

HEW: 5 (Wilbur Joseph) Cohen **7** (John William) Gardner **10** (Anthony Joseph) Celebrezze
HUD: 4 (Robert Colwell) Wood **6** (Robert Clifton) Weaver
  transportation: 4 (Alan Stevenson) Boyd
born: 11 (near) Stonewall TX
died/buried: 13 (near) Johnson City TX
education:
  teachers' college: 19 Southwest Texas State
  law school: 10 Georgetown
religion: 17 Disciples of Christ
vacation spot: 8 LBJ Ranch
author: 15 The Vantage Point
political career: 8 US Senate **13** vice president **24** US House of Representatives
civilian career: 7 teacher
military service: 6 US Navy **10** World War II **11** World War Two
notable events of lifetime/term: 9 race riots **12** Great Society
  act: 11 Civil Rights **12** Voting Rights **19** Economic Opportunity
  assassination of: 14 Robert F Kennedy **18** Martin Luther King Jr
  capture of: 6 Pueblo
  Pueblo captured by: 10 North Korea
  treaty: 23 Nuclear Non-Proliferation
  war: 7 Vietnam **11** Arab-Israeli
father: 7 Sam Ealy
mother: 7 Rebekah (Baines)
siblings: 10 Sam Houston **12** Lucia Huffman **13** Josefa Hermine, Rebekah Luruth
wife: 7 Claudia (Alta Taylor)
  nickname: 8 Lady Bird
children: 9 Lynda Bird **10** Luci Baines
First Lady:
  responsible for: 24 Highway Beautification Act
  author: 16 A White House Diary

Johnson, Philip Cortelyou
architect of: 10 Glass House (New Canaan CT), Wiley House (New Canaan CT) **12** Hodgson House (New Canaan CT) **13** Pennzoil Place (Houston TX) **14** Bolssonas House (New Canaan CT) **16** Amon Carter Museum (Ft Worth TX) **17** Sheldon Art Gallery (Lincoln NE) **18** A T and T Headquarters (NYC), Kline Science Center (Yale) **19** New York State Theater (Lincoln Center)

Johnson, Samuel
author of: 8 Rasselas, The Idler **18** The Lives of the Poets **22** The Vanity of Human Wishes **30** Dictionary of the English Language

Johnson, Walter
nickname: 8 Big Train
sport: 8 baseball

position: 7 pitcher
team: 18 Washington Senators

John the Baptist
father: 9 Zechariah
mother: 9 Elizabeth
descendant of: 5 Aaron
precurser of: 5 Jesus **10** the Messiah

joie de vivre 11 joy of living **19** delight in being alive

join 3 hug, mix **4** abut, ally, band, bind, fuse, glue, link, meet, pool **5** affix, brush, chain, enter, graze, marry, merge, paste, reach, skirt, stick, touch, unify, unite **6** adjoin, attach, bridge, cement, cohere, couple, fasten, scrape, solder, splice **7** combine, connect, verge on **8** border on, enlist in, enroll in, federate, hold fast **9** associate, cooperate, syndicate **10** amalgamate, fraternize **11** confederate, consolidate **12** conglomerate

joined 3 met, wed **4** tied **5** bound, fused, glued, mated, yoked **6** allied, bonded, linked, merged, paired, seamed, united, welded **7** coupled, married, related, spliced **8** attached, cemented, combined, enlisted, fastened **9** bracketed, connected **10** associated, hand-in- hand, integrated **11** hand-in-glove

join forces 4 ally **5** merge, unite **6** league, team up **7** combine **8** coalesce **9** affiliate, cooperate **11** consolidate **12** band together

joint 4 hock, knee, knot, link **5** elbow, hinge, nexus **6** allied, common, mutual, shared, united **7** knuckle, unified **8** combined, communal, coupling, junction, juncture **9** associate, community, conjoined, corporate, unanimous **10** associated, collective, connection, hand-in- hand, like-minded **11** coalitional, conjunctive, cooperative **12** articulation, consolidated **13** collaborative
  kind:
    ball and socket: 3 hip **8** shoulder
    fused: 5 skull **11** base of spine
    hinged: 4 knee **5** elbow
    unfused: 3 hip, jaw **4** knee **5** elbow **8** shoulder

joint action 7 concert **8** teamwork **11** cooperating, cooperation, give-and-take **13** collaboration, participation

joint effort 7 concert **8** teamwork **11** cooperation **13** collaboration

jointly 8 arm in arm, in common, in unison, mutually, together, unitedly **10** conjointly, hand-in-hand, side by side **12** collectively **13** in association, in conjunction

join together 3 wed **4** fuse, weld **5** marry, unify, unite **6** solder **9** integrate **10** amalgamate **11** consolidate, incorporate

join up 6 enlist, enroll, sign up **9** volunteer

joist 4 beam **5** brace **6** timber **7** support

joke 3 gag, pun, wit **4** butt, dupe, fool, gibe, goof, gull, jape, jest, josh, lark, mock, quip **5** antic, caper, cinch, clown, farce, prank, put-on, roast, tease, trick **6** banter, bon mot, deride, frolic, gambol, gibe at, jeer at, parody, satire, take in, target, trifle, whimsy **7** buffoon, bumpkin, chortle, lampoon, laugh at, nothing, scoff at, smile at, snicker **8** anecdote, badinage, poohpooh, pushover, repartee, ridicule, town fool, travesty **9** burlesque, diversion, horseplay, simpleton, wisecrack, witticism **10** pleasantry **11** horse around, monkeyshine **13** facetiousness, laughingstock

joker 3 wag, wit **4** snag, trap, zany **5** catch, clown, hitch, mimic, rider, snare, trick **6** jester, madcap **7** codicil, pitfall, punster **8** addendum, comedian, funnyman, humorist **10** subterfuge, supplement **11** wisecracker **French: 7** farceur

jokester 3 wag **5** comic, cutup, joker **8** comedian **9** prankster

Joliba *see* **5** Niger

Joliot-Curie, Frederic
  field: 9 chemistry
  nationality: 6 French
  discovered: 23 artificial radioisotopes
  awarded: 10 Nobel Prize
  wife: 16 Irene Joliot-Curie

Joliot-Curie, Irene
  field: 7 physics
  nationality: 6 French
  discovered: 23 artificial radioisotopes
  awarded: 10 Nobel Prize
  husband: 14 Frederic Joliot
  father: 11 Pierre Curie
  mother: 10 Marie Curie

joility 3 fun **4** glee, play, romp **5** cheer, mirth, revel, sport **6** frolic, gaiety **7** revelry, whoopee **8** hilarity **9** amusement, festivity, jocundity, joviality, merriment, pleasure **10** jocularity **11** merrymaking **12** conviviality

jolly 3 gay **5** droll, funny, happy, merry **6** jocund, jovial **7** gleeful, jocular, playful **8** cheerful, mirthful, sportive **9** fun-loving **10** delightful, rollicking **12** high-spirited

Jolly Roger 11 pirate's flag **18** skull and crossbones

jolt 3 bob, jar, jog **4** bump, jerk, jump, stun **5** lurch, quake, shake, shock, start, throw, upset **6** bobble, bounce, jiggle, joggle, jostle, jounce, quiver, trauma, twitch **7** disturb, perturb, setback, shake up, shaking, startle **8** convulse, reversal **9** agitation, take aback **11** thunderbolt

Joltin' Joe
  nickname of: 11 Joe DiMaggio

Jonah
  father: 7 Amittai

swallowed by: 9 large fish
  preached in: 7 Nineveh
  hometown: 10 Gaththepher

Jonathan
  means: 11 Jehovah gave
  father: 4 Jada, Saul **6** Joiada, Kereah **8** Abiathar
  friend: 5 David
  son: 9 Meribbaal **12** Mephibosheth

Jonathan Livingston Seagull
  author: 11 Richard Bach

Jonathan Wild
  author: 13 Henry Fielding

Jones, Carolyn
  born: 10 Amarillo TX
  roles: 8 Morticia **15** The Addams Family

Jones, Inigo
  architect of: 11 Queen's House (Greenwich) **14** Banqueting Hall (Whitehall Palace, London)
  restoration: 16 St Paul's Cathedral

Jones, James
  author of: 7 Whistle **14** The Thin Red Line **15** Some Came Running **18** From Here to Eternity

Jones, James Earl
  born: 11 Arkabutla MS
  roles: 6 The Man **7** Othello **8** Star Wars **15** The Emperor Jones **17** The Great White Hope
  voice of: 10 Darth Vader

Jones, John Paul
  served in: 11 Russian navy **16** Revolutionary War **21** British merchant marine
  commander of ship: 6 Ranger **10** Providence **15** Bonhomme Richard
  defeated ship: 7 Serapis
  saying: 23 "I have not yet begun to fight"

Jones, Shirley
  husband: 11 Jack Cassidy, Marty Ingels
  born: 10 Smithton PA
  roles: 8 Carousel, Oklahoma **11** Elmer Gantry, The Music Man **18** The Partridge Family

Jones, Tom
  born: 5 Wales **10** Pontypridd
  songs: 7 Delilah **9** She's a Lady **11** Thunderball **13** Love Me Tonight **15** Letter to Lucille **16** What's New Pussycat **21** Green Green Grass of Home

Jong, Erica
  author of: 5 Fanny **12** Fear of Flying **18** At the Edge of the Body **20** How to Save Your Own Life

jonquil 4 bulb, lily **8** daffodil **9** narcissus

Jonson, Ben
  author of: 6 The Fox **7** Sejanus, Volpone **11** A Tale of a Tub **12** The Alchemist **15** Bartholomew Fair **18** Every Man in His Humo(u)r **21**

Every Man out of His Humo(u)r **23** Epicene or the Silent Woman

Jordan
  other name: 24 Hashemite Kingdom of Jordan
  capital/largest city: 5 Amman
    ancient name: 12 Philadelphia
  others: 4 Krak, Ma'an, Salt **5** Aqaba, Ariha, Irbid, Jenin, Karak, Kerak, Sarga, Zarga, Zerke **6** Bethel, Hebron, Jarash, Jerash, Madaba, Nablus, Ramtha **7** Al-Aqaba, Bethany, El-Kerak, El Zerga, Jericho, Kirmoab, Nabulus, Samaria **8** Al-Khalil, Ram Allah **9** Bethlehem, Jerusalem
  school: 7 yarmouk
  division: 8 East Bank, West Bank **11** Transjordan
  ancient state: 4 Edom, Moab **5** Ammon, Judah **6** Gilead
  head of state: 11 King Hussein
    wife: 4 Noor (nee Lisa Walaby)
  monetary unit: 4 fils **5** dinar
  mountain: 3 Hor **4** Nebo **5** Bukka, Dabab **6** Ataiba, Gilead, Mubrak
  highest point: 9 Jabal Ramm, Jebel Ramm
  river: 6 Jordan, Yarmuk **11** Nahr-az-Zarga
  sea: 3 Red **4** Dead **7** Galilee **13** Mediterranean
  physical feature:
    desert: 6 Syria
    gulf: 5 Aqaba
    plateau: 11 Transjordan
    valley: 4 Ghor **9** Great Rift
    wind: 7 Khamsin
  people: 4 Arab, Kurd **7** Bedouin, Checher **8** Armenian, Assyrian **10** Circassian **11** Palestinian
    ancient: 8 Armonite **9** Nabataean
    ruler: 5 Talal **6** Faisal, Greeks, Romans **7** Hussein **8** Abdullah, Selucidas **9** Crusaders **10** Ibn Hussein, Nabataeans **12** Ottoman Turks **18** Abdullah Ibn Hussein
    tribe: 5 Qaysi **6** Yamani
  language: 6 Arabic
  religion: 5 Islam **13** Greek Orthodox
  place:
    canal: 8 East Gher
    ruins: 5 Ajlun, Petra **6** Jarash **7** Al Karak
  feature:
    headdress: 8 kaffiyeh
    village headman: 7 mukhtar
    village square: 5 sahah
  food:
    dessert: 7 baklava
    pastry: 7 katayif

Jordan, Robert
  character in: 19 For Whom the Bell Tolls
  author: 9 Hemingway

Jormungandr
  also: 10 Jormungand **11** Iormungandr **14** Midgard Serpent
  origin: 12 Scandinavian

form: 7 serpent
father: 4 Loki
mother: 9 Angerboda, Angrbodha, Angurboda
brother: 6 Fenrir, Fenris
sister: 3 Hel
wrapped around: 5 world
killed by: 4 Thor
death place: 6 Vigrid
killed: 4 Thor

Jo's Boys
author: 15 Louisa May Alcott
sequel to: 11 Little Women

Joseph
father: 4 Bani 5 Aseph, Jacob 10 Mattathias
mother: 6 Rachel
brother: 3 Dan, Gad 4 Levi 5 Asher, Judah 6 Reuben, Simeon 7 Zebulun 8 Benjamin, Issachar, Naphtali
wife: 4 Mary 7 Asenath
stepson: 5 Jesus
also called: 20 Barsabbas of Arimathea 21 Barsabbas of Arimathaea
buried: 5 Jesus
slave of: 8 Potiphar

Joseph Andrews
author: 13 Henry Fielding
character: 5 Fanny 9 Lady Booby 11 Mrs Slipslop, Parson Adams, Peter Pounce 13 Pamela Andrews

josh 3 guy, kid, rag, rib 4 dish, haze, jape, jest, jive, joke, quiz, razz, ride, twit 5 chaff, jolly, put on, roast, tease 6 banter, needle 8 ridicule

Joshua
means: 18 Jehovah is salvation
father: 3 Nun
succeeded: 5 Moses
captured: 7 Jericho, Lachish
hid spies: 5 Rahab

jostle 3 jab 4 bump, butt, poke, prod, push 5 crowd, elbow, shove 7 collide 8 shoulder 10 hit against, run against 12 knock against

jot 3 bit, dot 4 iota, list, mite, note, snip, whit 5 enter, speck, trace 6 record, trifle 7 modicum, one iota, put down, set down, smidgen, snippet 8 flyspeck, register, scribble, take down 9 scintilla

Jo the crossing sweeper
character in: 10 Bleak House
author: 7 Dickens

jotting 4 memo, note 6 doodle 8 scribble 10 memorandum, scribbling

Jotun
origin: 12 Scandinavian
form: 5 giant
conflicts with: 4 gods
enemy: 4 Asar 5 Aesir

Joule, James Prescott
field: 7 physics
nationality: 7 British
established law of: 20 conservation of energy
named for him: 10 unit of work

jounce 3 bob 6 bounce 7 rebound 8 ricochet

Jourdain, Monsieur
character in: 21 The Bourgeois Gentleman 22 Le Bourgeois Gentilhomme
author: 7 Moliere

Jourdan, Louis
real name: 11 Louis Gendre
born: 6 France 9 Marseille
roles: 4 Gigi 6 Can Can 9 Octopussy 15 The Paradine Case 23 Three Coins in the Fountain 24 Letter from an Unknown Woman

journal 3 log 5 album, daily, diary, paper, sheet 6 annual, ledger, memoir, record, weekly 7 almanac, daybook, gazette, history, logbook, monthly, tabloid 8 calendar, magazine, notebook, register, yearbook 9 chronicle, newspaper, quarterly, scrapbook 10 chronology, confession, memorandum, memory book, periodical, record book 11 account book, daily record, publication 13 autobiography

journalism 15 the fourth estate

journalist 6 author, editor, writer 7 byliner, diarist, newsman 8 reporter 9 columnist, newswoman 12 newspaperman 13 correspondent 14 newspaperwoman

Journal of the Plague Year, A
author: 11 Daniel Defoe

journey 3 fly, way 4 roam, rove, sail, tour, trek, trip, wend 5 jaunt, quest, route, tramp 6 course, cruise, flight, junket, outing, ramble, roving, travel, voyage, wander 7 circuit, meander, odyssey, passage, transit 8 divagate, navigate, sightsee, vagabond 9 excursion, itinerary, take a trip, wandering 10 divagation, expedition, pilgrimage 11 peregrinate 13 peregrination

Journey Into Fear
author: 10 Eric Ambler

journey's end 4 goal 9 objective 11 destination

joust 4 tilt 5 combat, jostle 7 contend, contest, tourney 8 run a tilt 10 contention, tournament

Jove *see* 7 Jupiter

jovial 3 gay 5 jolly, merry, sunny 6 blithe, cheery, hearty, jocose, jocund 7 buoyant, gleeful, jocular, playful, zestful 8 cheerful, humorous, laughing, mirthful, sportive 9 convivial, fun-loving, hilarious 10 delightful, frolicsome, rollicking

joviality 3 fun 4 glee 5 cheer, gaity, mirth 7 delight, jollity, revelry 8 buoyancy 9 jocundity, merriment 10 joyfulness, liveliness 11 high spirits

jowl 3 jaw 5 cheek, chops 6 muzzle 8 mandible

joy 3 gem 4 glee 5 jewel, pride, prize 6 gaiety 7 delight, ecstasy, elation, rap-

ture 8 gladness, pleasure, treasure 9 enjoyment, happiness 10 excitement, exultation, jubilation 11 contentment, delectation 12 cheerfulness, exhilaration, satisfaction
goddess of: 6 Hathor

Joyce, James
author of: 7 Ulysses 9 Dubliners 13 Finnegans Wake 31 A Portrait of the Artist as a Young Man

joyful 4 glad, rosy 5 happy 6 bright, elated 7 blessed, pleased 8 cheerful, ecstatic, exultant, gladsome, jubilant, pleasing 9 delighted, full of joy, overjoyed 10 delightful, enraptured, gratifying, heartening 11 pleasurable, transported 12 heartwarming

joyless 3 sad 4 glum, grim 5 black 6 dismal, gloomy, morbid, woeful 7 doleful, forlorn, unhappy 8 dejected, desolate, dolorous, downcast, mournful 9 cheerless, depressed, sorrowful, woebegone 10 despondent, in the dumps, lugubrious, melancholy 11 downhearted, pessimistic 12 disconsolate, heavyhearted 14 down in the mouth

joy of living
French: 11 joie de vivre

Joy of Sex, The
author: 11 Alex Comfort

joyous 3 gay 4 glad 5 happy, merry 7 festive, gleeful 8 cheerful, gladsome, mirthful 9 rapturous, wonderful 10 delightful, gratifying, heartening 11 pleasurable 12 heartwarming, lighthearted

joyousness 4 glee 8 gladness 9 happiness, merriment 10 blitheness, exuberance 11 high spirits 16 lightheartedness

jubilant 3 gay 4 glad 5 happy, jolly, merry 6 blithe, cheery, elated, enrapt, joyful, joyous 7 buoyant, charmed, gleeful, pleased, radiant, smiling 8 cheerful, ecstatic, exultant, gladsome, laughing, mirthful 9 delighted, delirious, exuberant, gladdened, gratified, overjoyed, rapturous, rejoicing, rhapsodic 10 blithesome, captivated, enraptured 11 exhilarated, intoxicated, tickled pink 12 happy as a lark, lighthearted 13 in high spirits

jubilation 5 bliss 9 rejoicing 11 celebration 12 exhilaration

jubilee 2 do 4 bash, fete, gala 5 blast, party 6 frolic, revels 7 blowout, holiday, revelry, shindig 8 festival, wingding 9 festivity 10 jubilation, observance 11 anniversary, celebration, merrymaking 12 conviviality 13 commemoration

Judah
father: 5 Jacob
mother: 4 Leah
brother: 3 Dan, Gad 4 Levi 5 Asher, Judah 6 Joseph, Reuben, Simeon 8

Benjamin, Issachar, Naphtali
sister: 5 Dinah
wife: 5 Shuah
son: 2 Er **4** Onan **5** Perez, Zerah **6** Baruch, Shelah
daughter-in-law: 5 Tamar
last king of: 8 Zedekiah
descendant of: 8 Judahite
Judah, tribes of see **14** Israel, tribes of
Judas
brother: 5 James
also called: 8 Thaddeus
disciple of: 5 Jesus
Judas Iscariot 8 betrayer
disciple of: 5 Jesus
betrayed: 5 Jesus
replaced by: 8 Matthias
Jude 7 apostle
brother: 5 James
Jude the Obscure
author: 11 Thomas Hardy
character: 10 Jude Fawley **12** Arabella Donn, Sue Bridehead **14** Drusilla Fawley **16** Little Father Time **17** Richard Phillotson
judge 3 try **4** deem, find, hear, rank, rate **5** fancy, gauge, guess, infer, juror, value, weigh **6** assess, assume, censor, critic, decide, deduce, expert, reckon, regard, review, rule on, settle, size up, umpire **7** adjudge, analyze, arbiter, believe, conduct, discern, imagine, justice, referee, resolve, suppose, surmise **8** appraise, assessor, conclude, consider, estimate, official, reviewer **9** appraiser, arbitrate, ascertain, authority, determine, evaluator, moderator **10** adjudicate, arbitrator, conjecture, magistrate **11** adjudicator, connoisseur, distinguish **12** pass sentence
judgment, judgement 4 view **5** sense, taste **6** acumen, belief, decree, ruling **7** finding, opinion, verdict **8** decision, estimate, sentence **9** appraisal, deduction, valuation **10** assessment, conclusion, conviction, discretion, perception, persuasion, shrewdness **11** arbitration, discernment, percipience **14** discrimination, perceptiveness
Judgment at Nuremberg
director: 13 Stanley Kramer
cast: 11 Judy Garland **12** Spencer Tracy **13** Burt Lancaster **14** Richard Widmark, William Shatner **15** Marlene Dietrich, Montgomery Clift **16** Maximilian Schell (Oscar)
Judgment Day 8 doomsday **13** end of the world **14** day of reckoning **15** the Last Judgment
Judgment Day
author: 13 James T Farrell
Judgment of Paris see **5** Paris
judicial 5 legal **8** imposing, juristic,

majestic, official **9** magistral **11** magisterial **13** distinguished
judiciary 5 bench, court **11** court system
judicious 4 just, sage, wise **5** acute, sober, sound **6** astute, shrewd **7** knowing, politic, prudent, tactful **8** sensible **9** sagacious **10** diplomatic, discerning, percipient, reasonable, reflective, thoughtful **11** levelheaded **13** perspicacious **14** discriminating
judiciousness 4 tact **6** acumen, wisdom **8** prudence, sagacity **9** good sense **10** discretion **11** discernment, percipience **12** perspicacity **14** discrimination
Judique, Mrs Tanis
character in: 7 Babbitt
author: 5 Lewis
Judith
husband: 4 Esau
killed: 10 Holofernes
Judith Paris
author: 11 Hugh Walpole
jug 3 jar, urn **4** ewer **5** crock, stein **6** bottle, carafe, flagon, vessel **7** pitcher, tankard **8** decanter, demijohn **9** container
juggle 4 redo **5** alter **6** modify **7** falsify **8** disguise, fool with **9** keep aloft **10** manipulate, meddle with, reorganize, tamper with, tinker with **12** misrepresent
juggler 5 cheat **6** jester **8** conjuror, deceiver, jongleur, magician, shuffler **15** prestidigitator
Juice
nickname of: 9 O J Simpson
juicy 3 wet **4** lush, racy **5** fluid, lurid, moist, pulpy, runny, sappy, spicy, vivid **6** fluent, liquid, risque, watery **7** flowing, graphic **8** colorful, dripping, exciting, luscious **9** succulent, thrilling **10** intriguing **11** captivating, fascinating, picturesque, provocative, sensational, tantalizing
Jules and Jim
director: 16 Francois Truffaut
cast: 10 Henri Serre **11** Marie Dubois, Oskar Werner **12** Jeanne Moreau
Julia
character in: 20 Two Gentlemen of Verona
author: 11 Shakespeare
Julia
character: 10 Corey Baker, Eddie Edson, Julia Baker **11** Hannah Yarby **14** Earl J Waggedorn, Marie Waggedorn **15** Dr Morton Chegley
cast: 10 Lloyd Nolan, Marc Copage **11** Betty Beaird, Michael Link **12** Eddie Quillan, Lurene Tuttle, Paul Winfield **14** Diahann Carroll
Julia
director: 13 Fred Zinnemann
based on story by: 14 Lillian

Hellman (Pentimento)
cast: 9 Jane Fonda (Lillian Hellman) **11** Hal Holbrook **12** Jason Robards (Dashiell Hammett) **15** Vanessa Redgrave (Julia) **16** Maximilian Schell
Oscar for: 12 screenwriter **15** supporting actor (Robards) **17** supporting actress (Redgrave)
Julius Caesar
author: 18 William Shakespeare
character: 6 Brutus (Marcus Brutus), Portia **7** Cassius (Gaius Cassius) **9** Calpurnia **10** Mark Antony (Marcus Antonius)
director: 17 Joseph L Mankiewicz
cast: 10 James Mason **11** Deborah Kerr, Greer Garson, John Gielgud **12** Edmond O'Brien, Louis Calhern, Marlon Brando
July
flower: 8 larkspur **9** water lily
French: 7 Juillet
holiday: 11 Bastille Day (14), Dominion Day (1) **15** Independence Day (4) **16** Saint Swithin's Day (15)
gem: 4 ruby
German: 4 Juli
Italian: 6 Luglio
number of days: 9 thirty-one
origin of name: 12 Julius Caesar
place in year:
Gregorian: 7 seventh
Roman: 5 fifth
Spanish: 5 Julio
Zodiac sign: 3 Leo **6** Cancer
jumble 3 mix **4** heap, mess, olio, stew **5** bunch, chaos, mix up, pitch, snarl **6** ball up, medley, muddle, pile up, tangle, tumble **7** clutter, farrago, melange, mixture, scatter **8** disarray, mishmash **9** aggregate, confusion, patchwork, potpourri **10** hodgepodge, miscellany, salmagundi **11** gallimaufry **12** accumulation **14** conglomeration
jumbled 5 messy **7** chaotic, mixed up, snarled, tangled **8** confused **9** cluttered, illogical **10** disjointed, incoherent **11** disarranged **12** disconnected, disorganized
jumbo 4 huge, vast **5** giant **6** mighty **7** immense, mammoth, titanic **8** colossal, enormous, gigantic, towering **9** cyclopean, monstrous, oversized **10** monumental, stupendous **11** elephantine, mountainous
jump 3 hop **4** buck, leap, pass, skip **5** boost, bound, pitch, start, surge, vault, wince **6** ambush, attack, blench, bounce, flinch, gambol, go over, hurdle, prance, recoil, spring, switch, upturn, zoom up **7** advance, barrier, digress, maunder, overrun, upsurge **8** fall upon, obstacle **9** barricade, increment, skyrocket **10** impediment **11** obstruction **12** augmentation
jumper 4 frog, sled, toad **5** dress, horse, shirt, smock **6** blouse, hopper,

jacket, leaper **7** overall **8** coverall, kangaroo

jump for joy 5 exult **7** rejoice

jumpy 5 nervy, shaky **6** goosey, uneasy **7** alarmed, anxious, fidgety, fretful, jittery, nervous, panicky, twitchy, uptight **8** aflutter, agitated, fluttery, skittish **9** trembling, twitching **10** frightened **12** apprehensive

junction 6 linkup **7** conflux, joining **10** confluence, crossroads **11** concurrence, convergence, interchange **12** intersection

juncture 4 pass, seam **5** joint **6** crisis, linkup, moment **7** closure, joining, meeting **8** interval, occasion **10** confluence, connection **11** convergence, point in time **12** intersection **13** critical point

June
  characteristic: **8** weddings
  event: **12** Midsummer Day (24), Midsummer Eve (23) **14** summer solstice (21)
  flower: **4** rose
  French: **4** Juin
  gem: **5** pearl **9** moonstone **11** alexandrite
  German: **4** Juni
  holiday: **7** Flag Day (14) **10** Father's Day (third Sunday) **13** Kamehameha Day (11) **22** Jefferson Davis' birthday (3)
  Italian: **6** Giugno
  number of days: **6** thirty
  origin of name: **4** Juno (Roman goddess) **6** Junius (Roman clan) **8** juniores (youths)
  place in year:
    Gregorian: **5** sixth
    Roman: **6** fourth
  saying: **24** What is so rare as a day in June
  Spanish: **5** Junio
  Zodiac sign: **6** Cancer, Gemini

jungle 4 bush, wild **5** woods **10** rain forest, wilderness **11** undergrowth **12** swampy forest, virgin forest

Jungle, The
  author: **13** Upton Sinclair
  character: **3** Ona **5** Jonas **6** Marija **8** Elzbieta **12** Jurgis Rudkus **13** Antanas Rudkus
  criticism of: **19** meat-packing industry

Jungle Books, The
  author: **14** Rudyard Kipling
  character: **3** Kaa **5** Akela, Baloo, Hathi **6** Buldeo, Messau, Mowgli **8** Bagheera **9** Shere Khan **11** Gray Brother

Jungle Jim
  creator: **11** Alex Raymond
  character: **4** Joan, Kolu

junior 5 later, lower, minor, newer **6** lesser **7** younger **8** inferior **9** secondary **11** subordinate

juniper 9 Juniperus

varieties: **4** ashe, plum **5** Greek, Irish, shore **6** common, ground, needle, Polish, Sierra, Syrian **7** African, incense, prickly, Sargent **8** creeping, drooping, mountain, red-berry, Waukegan **9** alligator, blue-spire, Himalayan, prostrate **10** California **11** cherrystone **12** Canary Island, sweetfruited **13** Rocky Mountain

junk 4 dump **5** scrap, trash, waste **6** debris, litter, refuse **7** clutter, discard, garbage, rubbish, rummage **8** castoffs, oddments, throw out **9** dispose of, throw away **11** odds and ends

junket 4 tour, trip **7** journey **9** excursion

Juno
  origin: **5** Roman
  queen of: **6** heaven
  father: **6** Saturn
  brother: **7** Jupiter
  husband: **7** Jupiter
  son: **4** Mars
  protectress of: **5** women **8** marriage
  epithet: **6** Lucina, Moneta **7** Curitis, Pronuba, Sospita
  festival: **10** Matronalia
  corresponds to: **4** Hera, Here

Juno and the Paycock
  author: **10** Sean O'Casey

junta 5 cabal **7** council **9** committee **18** military government

Jupe, Sissy
  character in: **9** Hard Times
  author: **7** Dickens

Jupiter
  also: **4** Jove
  god of: **5** light **7** heavens, weather **9** lightning **11** thunderbolt
  epithet: **5** Ultor **7** Elicius, Pluvius
  corresponds to: **4** Zeus

Jupiter
  position: **5** fifth
  satellite: **2** Io **6** Europa **8** Amalthea, Callisto, Ganymede
  characteristic: **7** red spot

Jura 11 Swiss canton **13** mountain range

Jurassic period
  dinosaur from: **10** Diplodocus **11** Apatosaurus, Stegosaurus **12** Brontosaurus, Camarasaurus, Camptosaurus, Ceratosaurus, Megalosaurus **13** Brachiosaurus, Compsognathus, Ornitholestes

Jurgen
  author: **17** James Branch Cabell

Jurgens, Curt
  also: **11** Curd Jurgens
  born: **6** Munich **7** Germany
  roles: **12** The Blue Angel **16** The Spy Who Loved Me

jurisdiction 4 say **4** area, beat, rule, sway, zone **5** field, range, reach, scope **6** bounds, domain, sphere **7** circuit, command, compass, control, quarter **8** district, dominion, hegem-

ony, latitude, precinct, province **9** authority, bailiwick **10** legal right **11** prerogative

jurist 5 judge **6** lawyer **7** counsel, justice **8** advocate, attorney **9** barrister, counselor, solicitor **10** magistrate **12** legal adviser **13** attorney-at-law

jury 5 panel, peers **6** assize, twelve **9** committee, makeshift, veniremen

jury-rigged 9 improvised, makeshift, temporary

jus 3 law **5** right

jus civile 8 civil law

jus gentium 12 law of nations

jus naturale 11 law of nature

jus sanguinis 12 right of blood
  (law) citizenship of child is same as: **7** parents

jus soli 11 right of land, right of soil
  (law) citizenship of child based on place of: **5** birth

just 3 but, due **4** fair, firm, good, only, sane **5** fully, moral, quite, solid, sound **6** at most, barely, decent, hardly, honest, lately, merely, proper, simply, strong, worthy **7** condign, ethical, exactly, fitting, logical, merited, only now, upright **8** adequate, balanced, deserved, entirely, narrowly, recently, scarcely, sensible, suitable, unbiased **9** befitting, blameless, equitable, honorable, impartial, justified, objective, perfectly, precisely, reputable, righteous, unbigoted, uncorrupt **10** aboveboard, absolutely, acceptable, completely, evenhanded, fair-minded, high-minded, no more than, nothing but, not long ago, principled, reasonable, scrupulous, upstanding **11** appropriate, justifiable, trustworthy, well-founded **12** conscionable, open to reason, unprejudiced, well-grounded **13** conscientious, disinterested, dispassionate

just about 6 almost, around, barely, nearly **7** close to **10** not far from **12** on the point of **13** approximately

Just Above My Head
  author: **12** James Baldwin

just a moment ago
  French: **11** tout a l'heure

justice 5 honor, right, truth **6** amends, equity, the law, virtue **7** honesty, payment, penalty, probity, redress **8** fair play, fairness, goodness, legality **9** atonement, integrity, rightness **10** correction, lawfulness, legitimacy, reparation **11** just desserts, proper cause, uprightness **12** chastisement, compensation, equitability, remuneration, satisfaction **13** due punishment, equitableness, justification, righteousness **17** constitutionality
  god of: **7** Forsete, Forseti
  goddess of: **4** Dice, Dike **6** Astrea **7** Astraea

Justice
author: **14** John Galsworthy
Justice Clement
character in: **19** Every Man in His Humour
author: **6** Jonson
justice to all
Latin: **15** justitia omnibus
motto of: **18** District of Columbia
justifiable 9 excusable **10** defensible **11** explanatory, extenuating, support able
justification 5 alibi **6** excuse **7** apology, defense, pretext, support **8** sanction **10** accounting, adjustment, validation **11** explanation, vindication **12** confirmation **13** rectification **14** reconciliation

justification for existence
French: **11** raison d'etre
justify 6 back up, defend, excuse, uphold **7** bear out, confirm, explain, support, sustain, warrant **8** sanction, validate **9** vindicate **10** account for, prove right
justitia omnibus 12 justice to all
motto of: **18** District of Columbia
just now
French: **11** tout a l'heure
just the same 6 anyhow, anyway **12** nevertheless
just the thing 7 apropos **8** suitable **11** appropriate **12** exactly right
Justus *see* **5** Titus
jut 5 bulge **6** beetle, extend **7** poke out, project **8** overhang, protrude, shoot

out, stand out, stick out **13** thrust forward
jute 19 Corchorus capsularis
varieties: **5** Bimli, China, Tossa, white **7** bastard **10** Bimlipatum
juvenile 5 child, minor, young, youth **6** boyish, callow, infant, junior **7** girlish **8** childish, immature, teenager, youthful **9** childlike, pubescent, stripling, youngster **10** adolescent, sophomoric **15** unsophisticated
juxtaposed 6 next to **8** adjacent, touching **9** proximate **10** contiguous, side by side **12** conterminous
juxtaposition 5 touch **7** balance, contact **8** contrast, nearness **9** adjacency, proximity **10** apposition, contiguity

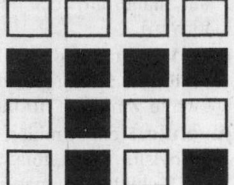
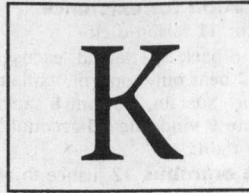
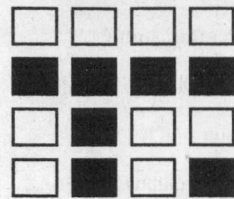

K
  character in: **9** The Castle
  author: **5** Kafka

Ka
  origin: **8** Egyptian
  form: **6** spirit
  trait: **11** immortality

kabob 5 cabab, cabob, kabab, kebab, kebob **7** shaslik **8** shashlik **9** shashlick

Kabul
  capital of: **11** Afghanistan

Kafka, Franz
  author of: **7** Amerika **8** The Trial **9** The Castle **16** The Metamorphosis

kahlua
  type: **6** brandy
  origin: **6** Mexico
  flavor: **6** coffee
  with rum: **10** Black Maria
  with tequila: **9** Brave Bull
  with vodka: **12** Black Russian

Kahn, Albert
  architect of: **15** River Rouge Plant **17** Highland Park Plant **20** Athletic Club Building (Detroit) **21** General Motors Building (Detroit)

Kahn, Louis Isadore
  architect of: **16** Kimbell Art Museum (Ft Worth TX) **23** Yale Center for British Art **24** Yale University Art Gallery **28** Phillips Exeter Academy Library (NH) **31** Richards Medical Research Building (U of PA) **33** Salk Institute for Biological Studies (La Jolla CA)

Kahn, Madeline
  born: **8** Boston MA
  roles: **5** Cosby **9** Paper Moon **10** What's Up Doc? **14** Blazing Saddles **17** Young Frankenstein

kaiser 5 ruler **7** emperor, Wilhelm **8** autocrat

kakemono 6 scroll **13** hanging object

kale 16 Brassica oleracea (Acephala Group)
  varieties: **3** sea **4** Ruvo, tall, tree **6** Indian, Scotch **7** cabbage, Chinese, Italian, kitchen **8** Siberian **9** flowering, Tronchuda **10** decorative, ornamental, Portuguese **13** dwarf Siberian **16** ornamental-leaved

kaleidoscopic 6 mobile, motley **7** protean **8** shifting, unstable, variable **9** checkered **10** changeable, variegated **11** fluctuating, many colored, rainbowlike, vacillating **12** ever-changing

Kaleva 8 folk hero
  origin: **7** Finnish **8** Estonian

Kali
  also: **3** Uma **5** Durga **7** Parvati
  husband: **4** Siva **5** Shiva
  festival: **6** dewali
  goddess of: **5** death **7** disease

Kalimantan see **6** Borneo

Kalki
  author: **9** Gore Vidal

Kampala
  capital of: **6** Uganda

Kampuchea see **8** Cambodia

Kandinsky, Wassily (Vasily)
  born: **6** Moscow, Russia
  artwork: **7** Striped **8** Twilight **10** Black Lines **11** Impressions **12** Blue Mountain (no 84), Compositions, Violet Orange **13** Black Relation **14** Improvisations **15** Capricious Forms **17** Bavarian Mountains, The Street in Murnau **23** Painting with White Border

Kanga
  character in: **13** Winnie the Pooh
  author: **5** Milne
  child: **3** Roo

kangaroo
  young: **4** joey
  group of: **3** mob **5** troop

Kaniengehaga see **6** Mohawk

Kansas
  abbreviation: **2** KS **4** Kans
  nickname: **5** Wheat **9** Jayhawker, Sunflower **15** Garden of the West
  capital: **6** Topeka
  largest city: **7** Wichita
  others: **4** Hays, Iola **5** Colby, Dodge **6** Salina **7** Abilene, Chanute, Emporia, Liberal **8** Atchison, Lawrence **9** Great Bend **10** Belleville, Hutchinson, Kansas City **11** Coffeeville, Leavenworth **12** Junction City
  college: **5** Baker, Tabor **7** Bethany **8** Sterling, Washburn
  explorer: **8** Coronado
  feature: **16** Eisenhower Center
    fort: **5** Riley, Scott
    Indian training school: **16** Haskell Institute
    penitentiary: **11** Leavenworth
    reservoir: **11** Tuttle Creek
  tribe: **3** Kaw **4** Pani **5** Kansa, Kiowa, Osage **6** Pawnee **7** Arapaho, Wichita **8** Cheyenne, Comanche, Kickapoo
  people: **7** Jayhawk **11** Damon Runyon **13** Amelia Earhart, Karl Menninger **14** Walter Chrysler **15** Edgar Lee Masters
  lake: **6** Cheney, Kerwin, Neosho **7** Milford
  land rank: **10** fourteenth
  mountain:
    highest point: **9** Sunflower
  physical feature:
    plains: **5** Great, Osage
  president: **17** Dwight D Eisenhower
  river: **3** Kaw **6** Kansas **8** Arkansas, Cimarron, Missouri **9** Smoky Hill **10** Republican
  state admission: **12** thirty-fourth
  state bird: **17** western meadowlark
  state flower: **9** sunflower
  state motto: **29** To the Stars Through Difficulties
  state song: **14** Home on the Range
  state tree: **10** cottonwood

Kansas City
  baseball team: **6** Royals
  football team: **6** Chiefs
  landmark: **12** Union Station **22** Nelson-Atkins Art Gallery
  river: **6** Kansas **8** Missouri

Kant, Immanuel
  author of: **20** Critique of Pure Reason

Kantor, MacKinlay
  author of: **13** Andersonville

Karloff, Boris
  real name: **17** William Henry Pratt
  born: **7** Dulwich, England
  roles: **12** Frankenstein

karma 3 act **4** aura, deed, duty, fate, rite **5** force, power **6** action, kismet, spirit **7** destiny **9** vibration

Kasdan, Lawrence
  director of: **11** The Big Chill

Kashmiri
  language family: **12** Indo-European
  branch: **11** Indo-Iranian
  group: **5** Indic
  spoken in: **5** (northern) India

kashruth, kashrut 7 fitness **17** Jewish dietary laws

Katharina
  character in: **19** The Taming of the Shrew
  author: **11** Shakespeare

Katmandu, Kathmandu
  capital of: **5** Nepal

Katzenjammer Kids
also: 17 Captain and the Kids
creator: 12 Rudolph Dirks
character: 4 Hans **5** Fritz, Momma **10** der Captain **12** der Inspector

Kaufman, George S
author of:
with Edna Ferber: 9 Stage Door **13** Dinner at Eight **14** The Royal Family
with Moss Hart: 15 Once in a Lifetime **20** You Can't Take It with You **21** The Man Who Came to Dinner

Kay (Sir Kay)
character in: 16 Arthurian romance
foster brother: 6 Arthur

Kaye, Danny
real name: 19 David Daniel Kaminski
born: 10 Brooklyn NY
wife: 10 Sylvia Fine
roles: 14 The Court Jester **19** The Inspector General **21** Hans Christian Andersen **26** The Secret Life of Walter Mitty

Kaye, M M
author of: 9 Trade Wind **12** Death in Kenya **15** Death in Zanzibar, Shadow of the Moon, The Far Pavilions

Kazakhstan
capital/largest city: 7 Alma-Ata
others: 9 Karaganda **13** Petropavlovsk, Semipalatinsk
head of state: 9 president
government: 8 republic
monetary unit: 5 ruble
sea: 4 Aral **7** Caspian
physical feature: 7 steppes **12** Lake Balkhash
people: 6 Kazakh
language: 6 Kazakh

Kazan, Elia
director of: 10 East of Eden, Viva Zapata **15** On the Waterfront (Oscar) **18** Splendor in the Grass **19** Gentleman's Agreement (Oscar) **20** A Tree Grows in Brooklyn **21** A Streetcar Named Desire

Kazantzakis, Nikos
author of: 13 Zorba the Greek **14** Freedom or Death, The Greek Passion **25** The Last Temptation of Christ

kazoo 5 bazoo, zarah **6** hewgag **11** eunuch flute
French: 8 mirliton

Keach, Stacy
real name: 18 Walter Stacy Keach Jr
born: 10 Savannah GA
brother: 5 James
roles: 3 Doc **6** Luther **10** Mike Hammer **24** Twinkle Twinkle Killer Kane

Kearny, Stephen Watts
served in: 10 California, Mexican War
commander of: 13 Army of the West

occupied: 9 New Mexico
battle: 10 San Gabriel, San Pasqual

Keaton, Buster
real name: 19 Joseph Francis Keaton
born: 7 Piqua KS
roles: 6 Go West **7** College **10** The General **12** The Cameraman

Keaton, Diane
real name: 9 Diane Hall
born: 12 Los Angeles CA
roles: 4 Reds **7** Sleeper **8** Baby Boom **9** Annie Hall (Oscar) **12** Shoot the Moon, The Godfather **13** The Good Mother **14** Play It Again Sam **19** Looking for Mr Goodbar **20** The Little Drummer Girl

Keats, John
author of: 5 Lamia **8** Endymion, Hyperion, Isabella **11** Ode to Autumn, Ode to Psyche **14** Ode on Indolence **15** Ode on Melancholy, The Eve of St Agnes **16** Ode on a Grecian Urn **17** Ode to a Nightingale **20** La Belle Dame Sans Merci **31** On First Looking into Chapman's Homer

Kedemah
also called: 5 Kedar
father: 7 Ishmael
mother: 5 Hagar
descendant of: 8 Kedarite

Keel (of Argo)
constellation of: 6 Carina

Keel, Howard
real name: 17 Harry Clifford Leek
costar: 14 Kathryn Grayson
born: 11 Gillespie IL
roles: 6 Dallas, Kismet **8** Show Boat **10** Kiss Me Kate **13** Clayton Farlow **15** Annie Get Your Gun **27** Seven Brides for Seven Brothers

Keeler, Ruby
husband: 8 Al Jolson
costar: 10 Dick Powell
born: 6 Canada **7** Halifax
roles: 15 Footlight Parade **17** Forty-Second Street **32** Gold Diggers of Nineteen Thirty Three

keel over 5 faint, swoon, upset **7** capsize, tip over **8** collapse, fall down, fall flat, flip over, overturn, turn over **10** turn turtle

keen 4 avid, fine **5** acute, alert, eager, sharp **6** ardent, astute, clever, fervid, fierce, shrewd **7** earnest, excited, fervent, intense, zealous **8** incisive **9** impatient, paper thin, razorlike **10** discerning **11** finely honed, impassioned, penetrating, quick-witted **12** enthusiastic **13** perspicacious **14** discriminating

Keene, Carolyn
created: 18 Nancy Drew mysteries
father 17 Edward Stratemeyer

keen-eyed 5 alert **8** vigilant, watchful **9** attentive, eagle- eyed, observant, sharp-eyed, wide awake

keen-minded 5 acute, sharp, smart **6**

astute, clever, shrewd **10** perceptive **11** penetrating

keenness 4 zeal, zest **5** ardor **6** acumen, fervor **7** passion **9** acuteness, eagerness, sharpness **10** astuteness, cleverness, enthusiasm, excitement, shrewdness **11** discernment **12** anticipation, intelligence, perspicacity

keen-sighted 4 sage, wise **5** acute, sharp **6** astute, shrewd **8** piercing **9** eagle-eyed, judicious, sagacious, sharp-eyed **10** discerning **11** intelligent, penetrating **12** clear-sighted, sharp-sighted **13** perspicacious

keep 3 bar **4** clog, fort, have, heap, hold, mind, pile, stay **5** abide, block, carry, cramp, delay, deter, guard, honor, lay in, place, stack, stall, stand, stick, stock, store, tie up, tower **6** arrest, castle, detain, donjon, endure, hamper, hinder, hobble, hold up, impede, living, pay for, remain, retain, retard **7** care for, carry on, citadel, deposit, furnish, inhibit, observe, possess, prevent, shackle, support, sustain **8** conserve, continue, encumber, fortress, hang on to, hold back, maintain, obstruct, preserve, restrain **9** celebrate, constrain, hamstring, persevere, persist in, ritualize, safeguard, solemnize, watch over **10** accumulate, daily bread, livelihood, provide for, stronghold, sustenance **11** commemorate, maintenance, memorialize, subsistence **12** room and board **13** fortification

keep an eye on 5 watch **7** oversee **9** chaperone, look after, watch over

keep apart 7 isolate **8** separate **9** segregate

keep at bay 7 beat off, fend off, ward off **8** stave off

keep back 5 check, delay **6** detain, hold up, retain **8** withhold

keep busy 3 use **6** employ, engage, occupy **7** utilize

keep clear of 4 shun **5** avoid, dodge, elude, evade, skirt **6** escape

keep company 4 date **5** court **7** consort, hang out **8** go around, go steady **9** accompany, associate **10** fraternize, go together

keeper 5 guard, nurse **6** duenna, escort, jailer, sentry, warden **7** curator **8** chaperon, guardian, retainer, sentinel, wet nurse **9** attendant, bodyguard, caretaker, chaperone, custodian, governess, nursemaid, protecter, protector **11** conservator, nurserymaid **13** guardian angel

keep in mind 8 consider, remember **10** think about

keep mum 13 button one's lip

keep off 7 fend off, stay off, ward off **8** stave off

keep one's counsel 12 remain silent **13** button one's lip

keep open 8 hold open **16** leave unscheduled

keep out 6 reject **8** prohibit **9** blackball, blacklist

keep out of sight 4 hide **5** cover **6** lay low, lie low **7** conceal, cover up, secrete **10** camouflage

keep private 4 hide **7** conceal, reserve **8** withhold

keepsake 5 relic, token **6** emblem, memory, symbol **7** memento **8** memorial, reminder, souvenir **11** remembrance **18** token of remembrance

keep secret 4 hide **6** hush up **7** conceal, cover up **8** suppress, withhold

keep silent 10 remain dumb **15** not breathe a word

keep steady 5 poise **7** balance **9** stabilize

keep to 5 cling, stick **6** adhere, be true, cleave, hold to **7** be loyal, stand by **8** maintain

keg 3 tub, tun, vat **4** butt, cask, drum, tank **6** barrel **7** rundlet **8** hogshead, puncheon **9** container, kilderkin

Keller, Helen
born: **4** deaf **5** blind
teacher: **12** Anne Sullivan
play and film: **16** The Miracle Worker
author: **13** William Gibson
actors: **9** Patty Duke **12** Anne Bancroft
both won: **6** Oscars

Kellerman, Sally
born: **11** Long Beach CA
roles: **4** MASH **15** Hot Lips Houlihan

Kelly, Gene
real name: **17** Eugene Curran Kelly
born: **12** Pittsburgh PA
roles: **7** Pal Joey **9** Brigadoon, On the Town **13** Anchors Aweigh **15** Singin' in the Rain **17** An American in Paris **18** The Three Musketeers

Kelly, Grace
husband: **21** Prince Rainier Grimaldi
nickname: **11** Ice Princess
born: **14** Philadelphia PA
princess of: **6** Monaco
roles: **7** Mogambo **8** High Noon **10** Rear Window **11** High Society **13** To Catch a Thief **14** Dial M for Murder, The Country Girl (Oscar)

Kelly, Walt
creator/artist of: **4** Pogo

kelp 3 ash **4** agar, alga, leag **5** varec, varic, wrack **7** seaweed
source of: **4** soda **6** iodine **9** potassium

Kelpie
origin: **8** Scottish
form: **5** horse **6** spirit
habitat: **4** lake **5** river

causes: **8** drowning
warns of: **8** drowning

Kelvin
abbreviation: **1** K

Kelvin, William Thomson
field: **7** physics **11** mathematics
nationality: **7** British
worked on: **4** heat **11** electricity
invented: **12** electrometer, galvanometer **13** tide predictor
named for him: **22** Kelvin temperature scale

Kempis, Thomas a
author of: **20** The Imitation of Christ

Keneally, Thomas
author of: **12** Confederates **14** Schindler's List

Kenilworth
author: **14** Sir Walter Scott
character: **6** Alasco, Dudley (Earl of Leicester) **10** Amy Robsart **12** Wayland Smith **13** Richard Varney **14** Queen Elizabeth **15** Flibbertigibbet **16** Edmund Tressilian

Kennedy, Arthur
real name: **17** John Arthur Kennedy
born: **11** Worcester MA
roles: **6** Becket **9** All My Sons **11** Peyton Place **12** Blind Victory **16** Death of a Salesman

Kennedy, Frank
character in: **15** Gone With the Wind
author: **8** Mitchell

Kennedy, John Fitzgerald
nickname: **3** JFK **4** Jack
presidential rank: **11** thirty-fifth
party: **10** Democratic
state represented: **2** MA
defeated: **5** (Richard Milhous) Nixon
vice president: **7** (Lyndon Baines) Johnson
cabinet:
state: **4** (David Dean) Rusk
treasury: **6** (Clarence Douglas) Dillon
defense: **8** (Robert Strange) McNamara
attorney general: **7** (Robert Francis) Kennedy
postmaster general: **3** (James Edward) Day **9** (John Austin) Gronouski
interior: **5** (Stewart Lee) Udall
agriculture: **7** (Orville Lothrop) Freeman
commerce: **6** (Luther Hartwell) Hodges
labor: **5** (William Willard) Wirtz **8** (Arthur J) Goldberg
HEW: **8** (Abraham Alexander) Ribicoff **10** (Anthony Joseph) Celebrezze
born: **11** Brookline MA
died: **8** Dallas TX
died by: **13** assassination
assassinated by: **6** (Lee Harvey) Oswald

buried: **25** Arlington National Cemetery
education:
prep school: **6** Choate
University: **7** Harvard **9** Princeton **23** London School of Economics
religion: **13** Roman Catholic
interests: **7** sailing **8** football **13** touch football
vacation spot: **9** Cape Cod MA **13** Hyannis Port MA
author: **15** Strategy of Peace, Why England Slept **17** Profiles in Courage (Pulitzer Prize)
political career: **9** US Senator **24** US House of Representatives
civilian career: **17** newspaper reporter
military service: **6** US Navy **10** lieutenant **11** World War Two
commander of: **6** PT boat
notable events of lifetime/term: **9** Bay of Pigs **10** Berlin Wall, Peace Corps **18** Cuban missile crisis
march: **11** Civil Rights
treaty: **14** Nuclear Test-Ban
quote: **17** Ich bin ein Berliner (I am a Berliner) **35** We stand today on the edge of a New Frontier **61** Ask not what your country can do for you ask what you can do for your country
father: **13** Joseph Patrick
mother: **4** Rose (Fitzgerald)
siblings: **4** Jean **6** Eunice, Joseph **8** Kathleen, Patricia, Rosemary **11** Edward Moore **13** Robert Francis
wife: **10** Jacqueline (Lee Bouvier)
nickname: **6** Jackie
second marriage to: **7** Onassis
children: **14** John Fitzgerald (John-John, JFK Jr.), Patrick Bouvier (died in infancy) **15** Caroline Bouvier

Kennicott, Dr Will and Carol
characters in: **10** Main Street
author: **5** Lewis

Kentucky
abbreviation: **2** KY
nickname: **9** Bluegrass **11** Corncracker
capital: **9** Frankfort
largest city: **10** Louisville
others: **5** Berea **6** Corbin, Hazard **7** Ashland, Glasgow, Newport, Paducah, Shively **8** Danville **9** Covington, Henderson, Lexington, Owensboro **12** Bowling Green, Hopkinsville, Madisonville
college: **5** Berea **6** Centre **7** Ashbury, Brescia **8** Ursuline **12** Transylvania
explorer: **11** Daniel Boone
feature: **7** Obelisk
birthplace: **14** Abraham Lincoln
fort: **4** Knox
national park: **11** Mammoth Cave
race: **13** Kentucky Derby
racetrack: **14** Churchill Downs
trail: **10** Wilderness
tribe: **7** Shawnee **8** Cherokee,

Iroquois
people: 11 corncracker, John M Harlan **13** Louis Brandeis **16** Frederick M Vinson, Robert Penn Warren
lake: 8 Kentucky **10** Cumberland
land rank: 13 thirty-seventh
mountain: 4 Pine **10** Cumberland
  highest point: 5 Black **8** Big Black
physical feature:
  basin: 9 Bluegrass
  cave: 7 Mammoth
  gap: 10 Cumberland
  plain: 7 Coastal
  plateau: 10 Cumberland
president: 14 Abraham Lincoln
  Confederate president: 14 Jefferson Davis
river: 3 Dix **4** Ohio, Salt **5** Green **6** Barren **7** Licking **8** Big Sandy, Kentucky **9** Tennessee **10** Cumberland **11** Mississippi
state admission: 9 fifteenth
state bird: 8 cardinal
state flower: 9 goldenrod
state motto: 26 United We Stand Divided We Fall
state song: 17 My Old Kentucky Home
state tree: 10 coffee tree **11** tulip poplar **12** yellow poplar

Kenya
capital/largest city: 7 Nairobi
others: 5 Nyeri, Thika, Wajir **6** Kisumu, Kitale, Lodwar, Moyale, Nakuru, Wehuye **7** Eldoret, Kericho, Malindi, Mandera, Mombasa, Nanyuki **9** Lokitaung
measure: 4 wari
monetary unit: 4 cent **5** pound **8** shilling
island: 5 Manda, Patta
lake: 6 Magadi, Nakuru, Natron, Rudolf **7** Turkana **8** Naivasha, Victoria
mountain: 5 Elgon, Kulai, Nyira, Nyiru **6** Matian **7** Logonot **8** Aberdare
highest point: 5 Kenya **6** Kinyaa **9** Kirinyaga
river: 3 Lak **4** Athi, Dawa, Kuja, Tana **5** Nzoia **6** Galana **8** Turkwell
sea: 6 Indian
physical feature:
  bay: 7 Formosa
  desert: 6 Chalbi
  escarpment: 3 Mau
  gulf: 9 Kavirondo
  highlands: 5 Kenya, Kisii, Luyla **7** Kericho
  plain: 4 Kano
  plateau: 5 Nandi, Yatta **6** Elgeyo
  valley: 9 Great Rift
people: 3 Luo **4** Arab, Meru **5** Bantu, Elgey, Galla, Kamba, Kisii, Luhya, Masai, Nandi, Tugen **6** Kikuyu, Ogaden, Somali **7** Baluhya, Hamitic, Hilotic, Kipsigi, Swahili, Turkana **8** Kalenjin, Marakwet
  god: 4 Ngai
  leader: 5 Mboya **12** Jomo Kenyatta

13 Daniel Arap Moi
language: 3 Luo **5** Bantu, Luhya, Masai **6** Kikuyu **7** English, Swahili **8** Guyerati **10** Hindustani
religion: 5 Islam **7** animism **8** Anglican **13** Roman Catholic
place:
  archeological excavation: 11 Gamble's Cave
  mosque: 5 Khoja
  museum: 9 Fort Jesus
  national park/wildlife preserve: 4 Meru **5** Nyeri, Tsavo **6** Arusha **7** Manyara, Nairobi, Samburu **8** Aberdare, Amboseli **10** Lake Nakuru, Mount Kenya, Rift Valley
  ruins: 4 Gedi
feature:
  garment: 5 kanga **7** kitenge
  round house: 6 shamba
  secret organization: 6 Mau Mau
  tree: 6 ayieke, baobab
food:
  fish: 7 tilapia
  wine: 5 tembo

Kepler, Johannes
nationality: 6 German
invented: 14 convex eyepiece **21** astronomical telescope
formulated:
  three laws of planetary motion (Kepler's Laws): 10 law of areas **11** harmonic law **24** elliptical orbit of planets
author of: 14 Astronomia nova, Harmonice mundi **16** Rudolphine Tables **23** Mysterium cosmographicum **30** Epitome astronomiae Copernicanae

kerchief 5 cloth, scarf **7** muffler **8** babushka, bandanna, kaffiyah, neckwear **9** headpiece, neckcloth **11** neckerchief **12** handkerchief

Keres
origin: 5 Greek
spirits of: 4 evil **5** death **6** old age **7** disease

Keres-Siouan
language branch: 5 Keres **7** Caddoan **9** Iroquoian **11** Siouan-Yuchi

kernel 3 nub, nut, pip, pit **4** core, germ, gist, pith, seed **5** grain, stone **6** center, marrow **7** nucleus **12** quintessence

Kerouac, Jack
author of: 6 Big Sur **9** On the Road **13** The Dharma Bums **16** Lonesome Traveler

Kerr, Deborah
real name: 22 Deborah Jane Kerr-Trimmer
born: 8 Scotland **11** Helensburgh
roles: 11 Edward My Son, The King and I **12** The Hucksters **13** The Sundowners **14** Separate Tables, The Chalk Garden **18** From Here to Eternity **19** The Night of the Iguana **20** Heaven Knows Mr Allison

Kesey, Ken
author of: 21 Sometimes a Great Notion **25** One Flew Over the Cuckoo's Nest

Ketcham, Hank
creator/artist of: 15 Dennis the Menace

kettle 3 pan, pot, tub, vat **6** boiler, teapot, tureen **8** cauldron, crucible, saucepan

Ketubim 8 writings **11** Hagiographa

Keturah
husband: 7 Abraham

kewpie 4 doll
originator: 9 Rose O'Neil **13** carnival prize

key 3 cue, fit **4** clue, gear, mode, suit **5** adapt, light, point, scale **6** adjust, answer, direct, opener **7** address, finding, meaning, pointer **8** indicant, solution, tonality **9** indicator **10** exposition, indication, resolution **11** elucidation, explanation, explication, translation **14** interpretation

Key, Ted
creator/artist of: 5 Hazel

keyboard instrument 5 organ, piano **6** spinet **8** psaltery, virginal **9** harmonium **10** clavichord, pianoforte **11** harpsichord

keyed up 5 tense **7** excited, nervous **8** volatile **9** emotional, explosive

key element 9 essential, vital part **18** primary constituent **20** indispensable element

Key Largo
director: 10 John Huston
based on story by: 15 Maxwell Anderson
cast: 12 Claire Trevor, Lauren Bacall **14** Humphrey Bogart **15** Edward G Robinson, Lionel Barrymore
Oscar for: 17 supporting actress (Trevor)

Keynes, John Maynard
author of: 44 The General Theory of Employment Interest and Money

keynote 3 nub **4** core, gist, pith **5** heart, theme **6** marrow **7** essence, nucleus, pattern **8** main idea, quiddity **9** substance **11** nitty-gritty, salient idea **12** central point

keystone 4 base, crux, root **5** basis **8** gravamen, linchpin **9** principle **10** foundation, mainspring

Keystone State
nickname of: 12 Pennsylvania

Key to Rebecca, The
author: 10 Ken Follett

KGB 4 USSR **14** security police **18** intelligence agency

Khachaturian, Aram Ilich
born: 6 Tiflis **7** (Soviet) Georgia
composer of: 6 Gayane **9** Spartacus **12** Song of Stalin

khaki 5 cloth **6** fabric **7** uniform **9** olive-drab **14** yellowish- brown

khan, kahn 3 inn **4** lord **5** chief, ruler **6** prince **7** emperor **9** chieftain, sovereign **11** caravansary
   famous: 3 Aga, Ali **4** Yuan **6** Kublai **7** Genghis **8** Ghenghis

Khartoum
   capital of: 5 Sudan

Khayyam, Omar
   born: 6 Persia
   famous as: 4 poet **9** statesman **13** mathematician
   name means: 9 tentmaker
   author of: 11 The Rubaiyat

Khoisan
   language spoken by: 3 San **7** Bushmen **9** Khoikhoin **10** Hottentots
   includes: 5 Hatsa **7** Sandawe
   distinguishing sound: 5 click

Khomeini, Ruholla
   title: 9 ayatollah
   ruled: 4 Iran

Khruschev, Nikita
   premier of: 4 USSR
   followed: 8 Bulganin
   preceded: 7 Kosygin

Khyber Pass
   between: 8 Pakistan and **11** Afghanistan
   range: 9 Hindu Kush

kibbutz 10 collective **11** Israeli Farm

kibitzer 3 pry **5** prier, snoop **6** butt-in **7** advisor, meddler, snooper, watcher **8** busybody, onlooker **9** buttinsky

kick 3 fun, hit, out, pep, vim **4** beef, boot, dash, fret, fume, fuss, life, punt, snap, tang, zest **5** eject, force, gripe, growl, power, punch, verve, vigor **6** flavor, grouch, grouse, object, recoil, remove, return, strike, stroke, thrill **7** boot out, cast out, grumble, fly back, protest, rebound, sparkle, turn out **8** backlash, complain, jump back, piquancy, pleasure, pungency, reaction, throw out, vitality **9** amusement, animation, complaint, enjoyment, find fault, grievance, intensity, make a fuss, objection **10** excitement, spring back **11** give the gate, remonstrate, send packing, show the door **12** protestation **13** gratification, remonstration

Kickapoo
   language family: 9 Algonkian **10** Algonquian
   location: 5 Texas **6** Kansas, Mexico **9** Chihuahua, Wisconsin
   related to: 3 Fox, Sac **4** Sauk

kickback 3 cut **5** bribe, graft, share **6** boodle, payoff, payola **9** hush money **10** commission, percentage, protection, recompense **12** compensation, remuneration **15** protection money

kick downstairs 4 bust **6** demote **7** degrade

kickoff 5 start **7** opening **9** beginning, inception, launching **12** inauguration

kick out 4 oust **5** eject, evict, expel **8** throw out **9** discharge

kicks 3 fun **7** thrills **8** pleasure **10** excitement **11** stimulation

kick upstairs 5 boost **7** advance, elevate, promote

kid 3 rag, rib, tot **4** baby, fool, gull, jest, joke, josh, mock, ride, tyke **5** bluff, child, cozen, harry, put on, tease, trick, youth **6** delude, infant, moppet, plague, shaver, squirt **7** beguile, deceive, laugh at, mislead **8** goat hide, goatskin, hoodwink, juvenile, ridicule, teenager, yearling **9** bamboozle, billy goat, little one, make fun of, nanny goat, offspring, young goat, youngster **10** adolescent **11** goat leather, young person **12** little shaver

Kid, The
   nickname of: 11 Ted Williams **13** William Bonney (Billy)

kid around 5 clown, cut up **10** fool around, play around **11** clown around

Kidd, William 13 pirate captain
   born: 8 Scotland
   end: 6 hanged

Kidder, Margot
   born: 6 Canada **11** Yellow Knife
   roles: 7 Sisters **8** Lois Lane, Superman **14** Some Kind of Hero **19** The Amityville Horror

Kiddush 6 prayer **8** blessing **14** sanctification

kidnap 5 seize, steal **6** abduct, hijack, snatch **7** bear off, capture, impress, skyjack **8** bear away, carry off, shanghai **10** run off with **11** make off with **13** hold for ransom

Kidnapped
   author: 20 Robert Louis Stevenson
   character: 9 Alan Breck **10** Rankeillor **12** David Balfour **15** Ebenezer Balfour

Kigali
   capital of: 6 Rwanda

Kiley, Richard
   born: 9 Chicago IL
   roles: 7 Redhead **13** Man of La Mancha **16** Advise and Consent

Kilimanjaro, Mount
   in 6 Africa **8** Tanzania
   feature: 15 highest in Africa
   see also **9** Hemingway

Kilkenny Cats
   origin: 5 Irish
   form: 4 cats
   number: 3 two
   left after fight: 5 tails

kill 4 beat, do in, halt, hang, ruin, slay, stay **5** break, check, drown, erase, lynch, quell, shoot, waste **6** behead, defeat, murder, poison, rub out, stifle **7** bump off, butcher, cut down, destroy, execute, garrote, silence, smother, squelch, wipe out **8** blow away, dispatch, get rid of, knock off, massacre, strangle, string up **9** dismember, finish off, shoot down, slaughter, suffocate **10** asphyxiate, decapitate, disembowel, extinguish, guillotine, put a stop to, put an end to, put to death **11** assassinate, burn to death, electrocute, exterminate **13** mortally wound

killer 6 hit man, slayer **7** butcher **8** assassin, murderer **11** executioner **12** exterminator

Killers, The
   director: 13 Robert Siodmak
   based on story by: 15 Ernest Hemingway
   cast: 10 Ava Gardner **12** Edmond O'Brien **13** Burt Lancaster

killer whale 4 orca **7** grampus **11** Orcinus orca

killing 4 coup **5** fatal **6** big hit, deadly, lethal, mortal, murder **7** bonanza, cleanup, deathly, hanging, slaying, success, suicide **8** butchery, fatality, homicide, lynching, massacre, regicide, shooting, smash hit, stabbing, windfall **9** bloodshed, execution, garroting, martyrdom, matricide, murderous, patricide, poisoning, slaughter, uxoricide **10** cleaning up, decimation, fratricide, immolation, impalement, sororicide, strangling **11** crucifixion, devastating, elimination, infanticide **12** annihilation, death-dealing, decapitation, excruciating, guillotining, manslaughter, master stroke, stroke of luck, violent death **13** electrocution, extermination, strangulation **17** capital punishment

Killing Fields
   director: 11 Roland Joffe
   based on article by: 15 Sydney Schanberg (The Death and Life of Dith Pran)
   cast: 10 Haing S Ngor **12** Sam Waterston
   setting: 8 Cambodia
   Oscar for: 15 supporting actor (Ngor)

Killing Time
   author: 12 Thomas Berger

killjoy 6 grouch **8** grumbler, sourball, sourpuss **9** Cassandra, gloomy Gus, worrywart **10** complainer, malcontent, spoilsport, wet blanket **11** crapehanger, party-pooper

kill time 4 idle **6** dawdle **9** waste time **10** fool around

Kilmer, Joyce
   author of: 5 Trees

kiln 3 ost **4** bake, burn, fire, oast, oven **5** drier, glaze, stove, tiler **7** furnace **8** calciner, limekiln **9** oasthouse

kiloliter
   abbreviation: 2 kL

kilometer
   abbreviation: 2 km

Kim
  author: **14** Rudyard Kipling
  character: **9** Mahbub Ali **11** Tibetan Lama **12** Kimball O'Hara **16** Colonel Creighton **22** Hurree Chunder Mookerjee

kimono 4 gown, robe
  traditional costume of: **5** Japan
  sash: **3** obi
  ornament: **7** netsuke

kin 4 akin, clan, kith, race **5** folks, tribe **6** family, people **7** kinfolk, kinsmen, related **8** clansmen, kinfolks **9** next of kin, relations, relatives, tribesmen **10** kith and kin **11** connections, consanguine, distaff side, spindle side **13** flesh and blood **14** kissing cousins

kind 3 ilk **4** cast, make, mold, sort, type **5** brand, breed, caste, civil, class, genre, genus, style **6** benign, gentle, kidney, kindly, nature, polite, strain, tender **7** amiable, cordial, variety **8** amicable, friendly, generous, gracious, merciful, obliging **9** courteous **10** bighearted, charitable, neighborly, thoughtful **11** considerate, description, designation, good-hearted, good-humored, good-natured, softhearted, sympathetic, warmhearted, well-meaning **12** affectionate, well-disposed **13** accommodating, compassionate, tenderhearted, understanding
  French: **6** gentil

kindhearted 4 good, warm **6** benign, gentle, humane, kindly, loving **7** helpful **8** amicable, generous, gracious, merciful **10** altruistic, charitable, thoughtful **11** considerate, good-hearted, good-natured, softhearted, sympathetic, warmhearted, well-meaning **12** affectionate, humanitarian **13** accommodating, compassionate, philanthropic, tenderhearted, understanding

kindheartedness 5 mercy **8** altruism, goodness, goodwill, humanity, sympathy **10** compassion, humaneness, tenderness **11** benefaction, benevolence, magnanimity **12** graciousness, philanthropy **13** consideration, understanding, unselfishness **14** charitableness **15** humanitarianism

kindle 4 fire, goad, prod, stir, urge, whet **5** awake, light, rouse, waken **6** arouse, excite, foment, ignite, incite, induce, stir up **7** agitate, animate, inflame, inspire, provoke, quicken, sharpen **8** enkindle **9** call forth, intensify, set fire to, set on fire, stimulate **10** invigorate

kindling 4 fuel **5** brush, paper, twigs **6** firing, tinder **7** burning, flaming **8** firewood, igniting, ignition, lighting, shavings **9** brushwood **10** combustion, enkindling

kindly 4 good, warm **6** benign, gentle, gently, humane, tender, warmly **7**

amiable, amiably, civilly, cordial, devoted, patient **8** amicable, amicably, benignly, friendly, generous, gracious, humanely, merciful, tenderly **9** cordially, courteous **10** benevolent, bighearted, charitable, charitably, generously, graciously, mercifully, neighborly **11** considerate, good-humored, good-natured, magnanimous, softhearted, sympathetic, warmhearted, well-meaning **12** affectionate, benevolently, bigheartedly, humanitarian **13** compassionate, considerately, good-humoredly, good-naturedly, magnanimously, philanthropic, softheartedly, tenderhearted, understanding, warmheartedly, well-meaningly **14** affectionately, well-manneredly **15** compassionately, sympathetically, tenderheartedly, understandingly **17** philanthropically

kindness 3 aid **4** gift, help **5** favor, grace, mercy **6** bounty **7** charity **8** good deed, good turn, goodness, goodwill, humanity, patience, sympathy **9** tolerance **10** act of grace, assistance, compassion, generosity, humaneness, kind office, toleration **11** benefaction, beneficence, benevolence, magnanimity **12** act of charity, graciousness, philanthropy **13** consideration, understanding, unselfishness **14** charitableness **15** humanitarianism

Kind of Anger, A
  author: **10** Eric Ambler

kindred 4 akin, like **5** alike **6** allied, united **7** related, similar **8** agreeing, familial, matching **9** accordant, analogous, congenial, simpatico **10** harmonious, resembling **11** consanguine, sympathetic **13** corresponding

kine 4 cows, oxen **6** cattle **9** livestock

kinfolk 3 kin **6** family **7** kinsmen **8** clansmen **9** relations, relatives **10** kith and kin

king 3 HRH **5** liege, ruler **7** monarch **8** suzerain **9** potentate, protector, sovereign **10** His Majesty **11** crowned head, royal person, the anointed **18** defender of the faith
  Latin: **3** rex

king/emperor/dynasty
  of Afghanistan: **8** Barakzai
  of Albania: **3** Zog **9** Ahmet Zogu
  of Algeria: **3** bey, dey **6** disawa **8** Jugurtha **9** bevlerbay, Masinissa
  of Austria: **7** Charles, Francis **9** Ferdinand, Habsburgs **10** Franz Josef
  of Bahrain: **7** al-Khalifa
  of Belgium: **7** Leopold **8** Baudouin
  of China: **3** Han, Sui **4** Chou, Ch'in, Ming, Sung, T'ang **5** Ch'ing, Shang **6** Manchu
  of Crete: **5** Minos
  of Denmark: **4** Hans, Knud **6** Canute **8** Frederik **9** Christian **10** Gorm the Old **15** Harold Bluetooth

  of Egypt: **5** Khufu, Menes, Zoser **6** Farouk, Khafre, Ptulol, Ramses **7** Saladin **8** Horemheb, Menkaure **9** Akhenaten, Amenemhet, Amenhotep **10** Mentuhotep **11** Tutankhamen
  of England: **3** Hal **4** Cnut, John, Lear **5** Henry, James **6** Alfred, Arthur, Canute, Edmund, Edward, Egbert, George, Harold **7** Charles, Richard, Stephen, William **9** Cymbeline **18** Richard Coeur de Lion **19** Richard the Lionheart **21** Richard the Lion-hearted
  of France: **5** Henri, Louis **6** Clovis, Philip **7** Charles **8** Napoleon **9** Hugh Capet **11** Charlemagne **21** Richard the Lionhearted **13** Louis Philippe **14** Henry of Navarre
  of Germany: **6** Kaiser **7** Wilhelm **9** Frederick **10** Barbarossa
  of Greece: **5** Creon **6** Atreus **7** Theseus **8** Menelaus **10** Agammemnon **11** Constantine
  of India: **5** Akbar, Asoka, Babur, Gupta, Mogul, Timur **6** Maurya, Rajput **7** Humayun **8** Hyder Ali, Jahangir, Marathas **9** Aurangzeb, Shah Jahan **11** Tippu Sultan **14** Delhi Sultanate **18** Chandragupta Maurya
  of Iran: **5** Abbas, Cyrus, Qajar **6** Darius, Xerxes **7** Arsacid, Pahlavi, Safavid **8** Parthian, Seleucid **9** Sassanian **10** Achaemenid **15** Shah Reza Pahlavi
  of Iraq: **6** Faisal, Sargon **7** Hussein **9** Hammurabi **13** Harun al-Rashid **14** Nebuchadnezzar
  of Ireland: **9** Brian Boru
  of Italy/Rome: **4** Nero, Otho **5** Galba, Nerva, Titus **6** Trajan **7** Hadrian **8** Caligula, Claudius, Commodus, Domitian, Octavian, Tiberius **9** Caracalla, Vespasian, Vitellius **10** Diocletian **11** Constantine **13** Antoninus Dius **14** Caesar Augustus, Marcus Aurelius, Victor Emmanuel
  of Japan: **5** Jimmu, Jingo, Meiji, Taira **6** Yamato **7** Akihito, Izanagi **8** Ashikaga, Fujiwara, Hirohito, Kamakura, Minamoto, Tokugawa
  of Java: **7** Mataram **9** Majapahit, Srivijaya
  of Jordan: **5** Talal **6** Faisal **7** Hussein **8** Abdullah, Selucidas **10** Ibn Hussein, Nabataeans
  of Korea: **2** Yi **4** Choe **5** Ki-tse, Koryo **6** Chi-tsi, Chi-tzu, Tangun
  of Kuwait: **5** Ahmad, Sabah, Salem **7** Mubarak **12** Jaber al-Ahmed, Sabah al-Salim **15** Abdullah al-Salim
  of Liechtenstein: **7** Florian **13** Francis Joseph **16** von Liechtenstein
  of Luxembourg: **8** Sigefroi, Wencelas **12** Jean l'Aveugle **21** House of Nassau-Weilburg
  of Madagascar: **6** Merina
  of Malawi: **6** Maravi
  of Maldives: **4** Didi

of Mexico: 10 Maximilian
of Monaco: 5 Louis **6** Albert, Honore **7** Antoine, Charles, Rainier **9** Florestan
of Mongolia: 8 Jahangir, Jehangir **10** Kublai Khan, Tsendenbal **11** Genghis Khan
of Morocco: 7 Alawite, Almohad **9** Almoravid
of Nepal: 8 Mahendra **9** Tribhuwan **10** Birenda Bir **12** Bikram Sha Dev **17** Prithwi Narayan Sha
of the Netherlands: 7 William
of Nigeria: 3 Ife, Nok, Oyo **5** Benin **6** Fulani **10** Kanem- Borno
of Norway: 4 Olaf, Olav **5** Olave, Oscar **6** Haakon, Harold, Magnus, Sverre
of Peru: 7 Huascar **9** Atahualpa **10** Manco Capac
of Poland: 5 Piast **7** Casimir, Jagello' **8** Augustus
of Portugal: 6 Manuel, Philip, Sancho **7** Alfonso **9** Ferdinand, Sebastian **23** Prince Henry the Navigator
of Qatar: 18 Ahmad bin Ali al-Thani **22** Khalifa bin Hamad al-Thani
of Rumania: 5 Carol **7** Michael
of Russia: 4 Ivan, Paul **5** Peter **6** Alexis **7** Michael **8** Nicholas **9** Alexander **12** Boris Godunov
of Sardinia: 12 Charles Felix **13** Charles Albert **14** Victor Emmanuel
of Saudi Arabia: 4 Fahd, Saud **6** Faisal, Khalid **7** Ibn Saud **9** Abdul Aziz
of Scotland: 5 David, James **6** Duncan **7** Kenneth, Macbeth, Malcolm, Stuarts, William **9** Alexander **14** Robert the Bruce **19** Bonnie Prince Charlie
of Sicily: 4 Eryx **5** Bomba, Henry, Peter, Roger **7** Charles, Cocalus, Leontes **9** Ferdinand, Frederick
of Spain: 6 Pelayo, Philip, Ramiro, Sancho, Witiza **7** Alfonso, Almohad, Charles, Umayyad **8** al-Mansur, Reccared, Roderick **9** Almoravid, Ferdinand, Leovigild **10** Juan Carlos **11** Abd al-Rahman, Reccosvinth
of Swaziland: 3 Kbe **5** Nyama **6** Mswati, Sozisa **7** Sobhuza
of Sweden: 4 Vosa, Wasa **5** Oscar **6** Gustav **8** Gustavus **10** Carl Gustav **12** Gustav Adolph **13** Charles Gustav **22** Jean Baptiste Bernadotte
of Syria: 5 Rezin **6** Faisal, Hazael **8** Benhadad **9** Antiochus
of Thailand: 4 Rama **7** Chakkri, Mongkut **10** Chao Phraya **12** Prahjadhipok **13** Chulalongkorn **17** Bhumibol Adulyadej
of Tongo: 11 George Tupou **14** Taufaahau Tupou
of Tunisia: 6 Hafsid **7** Fatimid **8** Aghlabid, Almohade **10** Husseinite
of Turkey: 8 Mausolus
of Uganda: 6 Mutesa, Mwanga **8** Kabarega

of Upper Volta: 4 Naba **5** Mogho
of Zimbabwe: 9 Lobengula, Mzilikaze

King, Frank
creator/artist of: **13** Gasoline Alley

King, Martin Luther
born: 7 Atlanta, Georgia
died: 7 Memphis **9** Tennessee
wife: 12 Coretta Scott
career: 8 minister (Southern Baptist), activist
notable moments: 17 "I Have A Dream" speech **26** march from Selma to Montgomery

King, Stephen
author of: 2 It **4** Cujo **6** Carrie, Misery **9** Christine, Salem's Lot, The Stand **10** Night Shift, The Shining **11** Firestarter, Pet Sematary, The Dead Zone **12** Skeleton Crew, The Dark Tower **16** Different Seasons, The Tommyknockers

King and I, The
director: 10 Walter Lang
cast: 10 Rita Moreno, Yul Brynner **11** Deborah Kerr **12** Martin Benson
score: 21 Rodgers and Hammerstein
from the book: 20 Anna and the King of Siam
song: 12 Shall We Dance? **16** Getting to Know You, Hello Young Lovers **18** Something Wonderful

King Arthur
opera by: 7 Purcell
character: 6 Merlin, Osmond, Oswald **8** Emmeline, Philadel **14** Duke of Cornwall

kingdom 4 land **5** duchy, field, realm, state **6** domain, empire, nation, sphere **7** country, dukedom **8** dominion, monarchy **9** territory **12** principality

King John
author: 18 William Shakespeare
character: 6 Elinor **9** Constance **11** Prince Henry **13** Hubert de Burgh **15** Blanch of Castile, Lewis the Dauphin **16** Arthur of Bretagne Cardinal Pandulph, William Longsword, William Mareshall **19** Philip Faulconbridge, Robert Faulconbridge

King Kong
director: 13 Merian C Cooper **17** Ernest B Schoedsack
cast: 7 Fay Wray **10** Bruce Cabot **11** James Flavin **12** Noble Johnson **15** Robert Armstrong
setting (final scene): 19 Empire State Building
score: 10 Max Steiner

King Lear
author: 18 William Shakespeare
character: 5 Edgar, Regan **6** Edmund **7** Goneril **8** Cordelia **10** Earl of Kent **12** Duke of Albany, King of France **14** Duke of Cornwall **16** Earl of Gloucester

kingly 5 grand, noble, regal, royal **6**

august, lordly, mighty **7** queenly, stately **8** absolute, despotic, glorious, kinglike, imperial, majestic, princely, splendid **9** imperious, monarchal, patrician, sovereign **10** autocratic, commanding, tyrannical **11** magnificent **12** awe- inspiring

Kingman, Dave
nickname: 4 Kong
sport: 8 baseball
position: 8 outfield **9** first base
team: 11 Chicago Cubs, New York Mets **14** New York Yankees, San Diego Padres **16** California Angels **18** San Francisco Giants

king of gods 4 Amen, Amon, Finn, Zeus **5** Ammon, Enlil, Fionn, Wotan **6** Marduk **7** Jupiter **8** Merodach **12** Baal Merodach **13** Fionn MacCumal

King of Hearts
character in: 28 Alice's Adventures in Wonderland
author: 7 Carroll

King of Righteousness 11 Melchizedek

Kingsley, Ben
roles: 6 Gandhi (Oscar) **8** Betrayal **14** Schindler's List

Kingsley, Charles
author of: 7 Hypatia **10** Alton Locke **11** Westward Ho! **14** The Water Babies **15** Hereward the Wake

King Solomon's Mines
author: 13 H Rider Haggard
character: 5 Twala **6** Gagool, Umbopa **14** Sir Henry Curtis **15** Allan Quatermain, Captain John Good

King's Row
author: 14 Henry Bellamann
director: 7 Sam Wood
cast: 10 Betty Field **11** Ann Sheridan, Claude Rains **12** Ronald Reagan **13** Charles Coburn **14** Judith Anderson, Robert Cummings
score: 21 Erich Wolfgard Korngold
character: 11 Drake McHugh, Elise Sandor **13** Randy Monaghan **14** Cassandra Tower, Parris Mitchell

Kingston
capital of: 7 Jamaica

kink 4 coil, flaw, knot, pang **5** cramp, crick, crimp, frizz, gnarl, hitch, quirk, snarl, spasm, twist **6** defect, foible, glitch, oddity, tangle, twinge, vagary **7** crinkle, frizzle **8** crotchet **9** queerness, stiffness, weirdness **10** difficulty **11** peculiarity, singularity **12** charley horse, complication, eccentricity, freakishness, idiosyncrasy, imperfection

kinky 3 odd **4** sick, wiry **5** kooky, queer **6** frizzy, matted, quirky, twisty **7** bizarre, deviant, frizzly, knotted, strange, tangled, twisted, unusual **8** aberrant, abnormal, crinkled, freakish, frizzled, peculiar, perverse **9** eccen-

tric, unnatural **10** unorthodox **13** idiosyncratic

Kinshasa
  capital of: 5 Zaire

kinsman 3 sib, son **4** aunt, heir **5**
  child, uncle **6** cousin, father, mother,
  parent, sister **7** brother **8** daughter,
  landsman, relation, relative **9** offspring **10** countryman **11** grandfather,
  grandmother **13** blood relation, blood
  relative

Kiowa
  language family: 6 Tanoan
  location: 6 Plains **7** Montana **8** Colo-
    rado, Oklahoma
  allied with: 7 Arapaho **8** Comanche
    11 Kiowa Apache
  deity: 5 Taime

Kiowa Apache
  language family: 12 Shapwailutan
  location: 6 Plains

Kipling, Rudyard
  author of: 3 Kim **8** Gunga Din, Man-
    dalay **11** Danny Deaver **12** The
    Seven Seas **13** Just So Stories, The
    Jungle Book **18** Barrack-Room Bal-
    lads, Captains Courageous

Kipps
  author: 7 H G Wells

Kirchhoff, Gustav Robert
  field: 7 physics
  nationality: 6 German
  discovered: 6 cesium **8** rubidium
  developed: 12 spectroscope
  named for him: 19 electric circuit
    laws

Kirchner, Ernst Ludwig
  born: 7 Germany **13** Aschaffenburg
  artwork: 11 Street Scene **12** Street
    Berlin **13** Moonlit Winter **21** Self-
    portrait with Model

Kirghiz see **10** Kyrgyzstan

Kiribati
  other name: 14 Gilbert Islands
  capital/largest city: 6 Tarawa
  others: 5 Betio **7** Bairiki, Bonriki **9**
    Bikenibeu
  school: 12 South Pacific
  monetary unit: 4 cent **6** dollar
  island: 5 Flint, Ocean **6** Banaba, Can-
    ton, Malden, Tarawa **7** Abemama,
    Fanning, Gilbert, Marakei, Nonouti,
    Phoenix, Vostock **8** Caroline, Star-
    buck **9** Christmas, Enderbury, Tabit-
    euea **10** Butaritari, Equatorial, Wash-
    ington **12** Northern Line, Southern
    Line
  sea: 7 Pacific
  people: 8 Banabans **10** Polynesian **11**
    Micronesian
  language: 6 Samoan **7** English **10**
    Gilbertese
  religion: 5 Baha'i **8** Anglican **9** Meth-
    odist **11** Church of God **13** Roman
    Catholic **19** Seventh Day Adventist

kirsch, kirschwasser
  type: 6 brandy **7** liqueur

origin: 6 France **7** Germany **11** Switz-
    erland
  flavor: 6 cherry
  with gin: 7 Florida **10** Lady Finger
  with vodka: 12 Volga Boatman

kismet 3 end, lot **4** doom, fate **5**
  karma, moira **7** destiny, fortune, portion **8** God's will **10** Providence **11**
  will of Allah **12** circumstance **13** inevitability **14** predestination

kiss 4 buss, neck **6** smooch, salute **8**
  osculate

Kiss for Cinderella, A
  author: 12 James M Barrie

Kissinger, Henry
  born: 6 Fuerth **7** Germany
  career: 9 statesman **11** businessman
    16 Secretary of State
  won: 10 Nobel Prize

kit 3 rig **4** gear **5** tools **6** outfit, tackle,
  things **7** devices **8** supplies, utensils **9**
  equipment, trappings **10** implements,
  provisions **11** furnishings,
  impediments, instruments, necessaries
  13 accoutrements, paraphernalia

Kitasato, Shibasaburo
  field: 12 bacteriology
  nationality: 8 Japanese
  isolated: 7 anthrax, tetanus **9** dysen-
    tery **13** bubonic plague
  developed: 19 diphtheria antitoxin

kitchen 6 bakery, cocina, galley **7** cuisine **8** cookroom, scullery **9** bake-
  house, cookhouse

Kitchener, Horatio Herbert
  also: 18 first Earl Kitchener
  nationality: 7 British
  served in: 7 Boer War **15** South Afri-
    can War
  battle: 8 Khartoum, Omdurman
  governor of: 8 the Sudan
  commander in chief of: 5 India **12**
    Egyptian army
  consul general of: 5 Egypt

kitel 20 Jewish ceremonial robe
  color: 5 white

Kitely
  character in: 19 Every Man in His
    Humour
  author: 6 Jonson

kittenish 3 coy **7** playful **10** coquettish

Klamath
  language family: 8 Penutian
  location: 6 Oregon **10** California
  related to: 5 Modoc **6** Cayuse, Mo-
    lala

Klee, Paul
  born: 11 Switzerland **14** Munchen-
    buchsee
  artwork: 9 Locksmith **11** Ad Parnas-
    sum **18** Barbarian Sacrifice, Demon
    above the Ships **20** The Twittering
    Machine **22** Revolution of the Via-
    duct **23** Dance-Play of the Red Skirts
    24 Dance Monster to my Soft Song
    35 The Vocal Fabric of the Singer
    Rosa Silber

Kleist, Heinrich von
  author of: 11 Penthesilea **14** The
    Marquise of O **16** The Broken
    Pitcher **18** The Prince of Homburg

Kline, Kevin
  roles: 4 Dave **8** In and Out **11** The
    Big Chill **13** Sophie's Choice **16** A
    Fish Called Wanda **17** Pirates of Pen-
    zance

Klugman, Jack
  born: 14 Philadelphia PA
  roles: 6 Quincy **12** Oscar Madison,
    The Odd Couple

klutz 5 dummy **9** blockhead **11** satchel-
  foot **13** fumblefingers

klutzy 4 dumb **6** clumsy, stupid **7**
  awkward **9** graceless

knack 4 bent, gift, turn **5** flair, forte,
  skill **6** genius, talent **7** ability, faculty,
  finesse **8** aptitude, capacity, facility **9**
  dexterity, expertise, ingenuity, quickness, readiness **10** adroitness, capability, cleverness, competence, efficiency,
  propensity **11** inclination, proficiency
  13 dexterousness

knave 3 cad, cur, dog, rat **4** jack
  (cards) **5** phony, rogue, scamp **6** con
  man, rascal, rotter, varlet, wretch **7**
  bounder, culprit **8** scalawag, swindler
  9 charlatan, con artist, reprobate,
  scoundrel **10** blackguard **11** rapscallion **14** good for nothing

knee breeches 8 breeches, jodhpurs,
  knickers **9** plus fours **14** knickerbockers

kneel 3 bow **6** curtsy, kowtow, salaam
  7 bow down **9** genuflect **13** make
  obeisance **16** prostrate oneself

knell 4 peal, ring, toll **5** chime, sound
  6 stroke **7** pealing, ringing, tolling

Knickerbocker Holiday
  author: 15 Maxwell Anderson

knickknack, nicknack 3 toy **6** bauble,
  gewgaw, trifle **7** bibelot, trinket **8**
  frippery, gimcrack **9** bagatelle, bric-a-
  brac, plaything **11** thingamajig

knife 3 cut **4** dirk, shiv, stab **5** blade,
  slash, wound **6** cutter, pierce **7** cut
  down, cutlery **8** cut apart, lacerate,
  mutilate
  type: 3 pen **4** jack **5** bowie, bread,
    putty, table **6** dagger, paring, pocket
    7 butcher, carving, hunting, ma-
    chete, palette, pruning, scalpel **8**
    skinning, stiletto, surgical **11** switch-
    blade

knight 4 hero **7** fighter, gallant, paladin, soldier, Templar, warrior **8** cavalier, champion, defender, guardian,
  horseman, Lancelot **9** gentleman,
  man-at-arms, protecter, protector **10**
  equestrian, vindicator

Knight
  character in: 18 The Canterbury Tales
  author: 7 Chaucer

Knightley, George

character in: 4 Emma
author: 6 Austen

Knights, The
author: 12 Aristophanes
character: 5 Demus **6** Nicias **11** Demosthenes **20** Cleon the Paphlagonian

knit 3 tat **4** ally, bind, draw, join, knot, link **5** braid, plait, twist, unify, unite, weave **6** attach, crease, fasten, furrow, stitch **7** connect, crochet, wrinkle **10** intertwine, interweave **12** draw together

knob 3 nub **4** bulb, bump, grip, hold, hump, knot, knur, lump, node, snag **5** bulge, gnarl, knurl, latch, lever, swell **6** handle, nubbin **8** handhold, swelling, tubercle **9** convexity **10** projection, prominence, protrusion **12** protuberance, protuberancy

knock 3 bat, hit, pat, rap, tap **4** bang, beat, belt, blow, bomb, bump, clip, cuff, dash, kick, lick, push, slam, slap, sock, swat, thud **5** abuse, cavil, clout, crack, crash, decry, pound, punch, smack, smash, smite, thump, whack **6** batter, carp at, defeat, hammer, jostle, murder, peck at, pummel, strike, stroke, thwack, wallop **7** censure, condemn, failure, setback **8** belittle, lambaste **9** criticism, criticize, deprecate, disparage, reprehend **12** condemnation, faultfinding, reprehension

knock down 4 deck, down, drop, fell **5** floor **7** flatten **8** bowl over, discount **9** take apart **11** disassemble

knock off balance 6 rattle **7** shake up **8** unsettle **9** take aback **11** disorganize

knockout 2 KO **4** doll **5** beaut, Venus **6** beauty, eyeful **7** stunner

knock out of shape 4 maul **5** crush **6** batter, beat up, mangle

knoll 4 hill, rise **5** mound

knot 3 bun **4** bump, frog, heap, hump, loop, lump, mass, pack, pile, star, tuft **5** braid, bunch, clump, group, hitch, knurl, plait, twist **6** bundle, circle **7** cat's-paw, chignon, cluster, epaulet, rosette **8** ornament **9** gathering **10** assemblage, collection, intertwist **13** interlacement
type: 3 bow, top **4** flat, slip **5** slide **6** double, single, square **7** running **8** hangman's, overhand, shoulder, surgeon's **9** half-hitch **11** figure-eight, midshipman's

Knots Landing
character: 9 Abby Ewing, Gary Ewing **10** Greg Sumner **11** Valene Ewing **12** Mac Mackenzie **14** Karen Mackenzie, Paige Forrester
cast: 10 Donna Mills, Joan Van Ark **11** Julie Harris, Kevin Dobson, Michelle Lee **13** William Devane **14** Douglas Sheehan, Ted Shackelford **17** Nicolette Sheridan

knotty 4 hard **5** bumpy, rough, tough **6** coarse, flawed, knobby, knurly, rugged, snaggy, thorny, tricky, uneven **7** complex, gnarled, knurled, nodular **8** baffling, involved, puzzling, ticklish, unsmooth **9** blemished, difficult, intricate **10** perplexing **11** complicated, troublesome **12** rough-grained **13** coarse-grained, problematical

know 3 see **6** be sure, be wise, notice **7** be smart, discern, make out, realize **8** identify, perceive **9** apprehend, be assured, be aware of, be certain, be close to, get wise to, recognize **10** be informed, be positive, understand **11** be confident, be sagacious, be thick with, distinguish, feel certain, have down pat, have no doubt **12** discriminate, have down cold, have the ear of **13** be cognizant of, be intelligent, have knowledge, rub elbows with **14** be familiar with

knowable 9 thinkable **11** conceivable, discernible, perceivable **14** understandable

Knowell, Edward
character in: 19 Every Man in His Humour
author: 6 Jonson

know for sure 9 be certain **10** be positive

know-how 3 art **4** bent, gift **5** craft, flair, knack, savvy, skill **6** talent **7** ability, mastery **8** aptitude, capacity, deftness **9** adeptness, expertise, knowledge, technique **10** adroitness, capability, competence, experience, expertness **11** proficiency **12** skillfulness **15** professionalism
French: 11 savoir-faire

knowing 4 deep, wise **5** aware, canny, sharp, smart, sound **6** astute, brainy, bright, clever, shrewd **7** erudite, fraught, learned, sapient **8** academic, educated, eloquent, highbrow, literary, profound, schooled, sensible **9** conscious, judicious, revealing, sagacious **10** discerning, expressive, meaningful, perceptive, percipient, scholastic, widely read **11** enlightened, intelligent, significant **12** intellectual, well-informed **13** comprehending, knowledgeable, perspicacious, philosophical, sophisticated, understanding

knowing how to live
French: 11 savoir-vivre

knowing just what to do
French: 11 savoir-faire

know-it-all 5 brash **13** overconfident

knowledge 3 ken, tip **4** data, hint, lore, news **5** sense **6** memory, notice, report, wisdom **7** inkling, mention, tidings **8** learning **9** awareness, education, erudition, schooling, statement **10** cognizance, intimation, perception **11** cultivation, declaration, familiarity, information, realization, recognition,

revelation, scholarship **12** announcement, book learning, intelligence, notification **13** communication, comprehension, consciousness, enlightenment, pronouncement
god of: 4 Odin **5** Othin

knowledgeable 3 hip **4** up on **8** at home in, versed in **12** familiar with, well-informed **14** acquainted with, conversant with
French: 9 au courant

knowledge of the world
French: 11 savoir-vivre

known 5 noted, plain **6** common, famous, patent **7** evident, obvious, popular **8** apparent, definite, distinct, familiar, manifest, palpable **9** notorious, prominent **10** celebrated, recognized **11** self-evident

know thyself
Greek: 13 gnothi seauton

knuckle under 5 yield **6** give in, submit **7** bow down **9** surrender **10** capitulate

knurled 5 bumpy, lumpy **6** gnarly, knobby, knotty, knurly, nubbly, ridged **7** bulging, gnarled, knotted, nodular

koala
family: 9 marsupial
habitat: 9 Australia
food: 10 eucalyptus
resembles: 9 small bear
kin of: 6 wombat

Koch, Robert
field: 12 bacteriology
nationality: 6 German
isolated: 2 TB **12** tuberculosis
awarded: 10 Nobel Prize

Kodaly, Zoltan
born: 7 Hungary **9** Kecskemet
composer of: 9 Hary Janos **11** Czinka Panna, Missa Brevis, Szekely Fono **14** Budavari Te Deum **15** Dances of Galanta **17** Dances of Marosszek, Peacock Variations, Psalmus Hungaricus **28** The Spinning Room of the Szekelys

Koestler, Arthur
author of: 14 Darkness at Noon **15** The Sleepwalkers

Kohinoor, Koh-i-noor 7 diamond **6** (106) carats
from: 5 India
part of: 18 British Crown Jewels

kohoutek 5 comet
named for: 15 Czech astronomer

Kojak
character: 5 (Det) Rizzo **7** (Det) Stavros **9** (Lt) Theo Kojak **10** (Det) Saperstein **11** Frank McNeil **12** (Lt) Bobby Crocker
cast: 9 Dan Frazer **10** Vince Conti **11** Kevin Dobson, Mark Russell **12** Telly Savalas **13** George Savalas (Demosthenes)

trademark: 8 lollipop
phrase: 14 Who loves ya baby?
Kollwitz, Kathe
　real name: 12 Kathe Schmidt
　born: 10 Konigsberg **11** East Prussia
　artwork: 3 War **5** Death, Pieta **11**
　　Proletariat **13** Weavers' Revolt
　　(Weaver's Rebellion) **14** Mother and
　　Child, The Peasants' War **18** Death
　　Seizing a Woman
Kol Nidre 4 vows **8** promises **22** Jewish liturgical prayer
　recited on eve of: 9 Yom Kippur
Kong
　nickname of: 11 Dave Kingman
Kon-Tiki
　author: 13 Thor Heyerdahl
　name of: 4 raft
kook 3 nut **5** crazy, flake, loony,
　wacko **6** cuckoo, weirdo **7** dingbat **8**
　crackpot **9** ding-a-ling, eccentric, fruit-
　cake, harebrain, screwball **10** crack-
　brain
Koran 5 Islam, Quran **9** Word of God
　10 Sacred book
　revelations to: 8 Mohammed
　division: 4 sura
　dictated by: 7 Gabriel **9** archangel
Korea
　other name: 6 Chosen **17** land of
　　morning calm
　capital:
　　North Korea: 9 Pyongyang
　　South Korea: 5 Seoul
　largest city: 5 Seoul
　others: 5 Masan, Mokpo, Pusan,
　　Sinpo, Suwon, Taegu, Wonju **6**
　　Chonju, Inchon, Kangso, Kunsan,
　　Taejon, Wonsan **7** Hanyang, Hung-
　　nam, Kaesong, Kangson, Kwangju **8**
　　Chongjin, Chunchon, Kimchaek
　school: 5 Busan **6** Yonsei **7** Hanyang
　　8 Kim Chaek, Kyung Hee **9** Kim Il
　　Sung
　division:
　　ancient: 5 Silla **6** Chosen **7** Ko-
　　　guryo, Paekche
　monetary unit: 3 woh, won **4** chun,
　　hwan, kwan
　weight: 3 won
　island: 4 Chin, Koje **5** Cheju, Sinmi **6**
　　Anmyon, Huksan, Namhae **7** Tok-
　　chok **8** Quelpart **10** Paengnyong
　mountain: 4 Wang **5** Chiri, Halla **6**
　　Kwanmo, Sobaek **7** Diamond, Kye-
　　bang, Nangnim, Taebaek **8** Chang-
　　pai, Hamgyong, Myohyang **9** Paektu-
　　san **10** Kumgang-san
　highest point: 6 Paektu **9** Paektu-san
　river: 3 Han, Kin, Kum, Kun, Nam **4**
　　Lobk, Yalu **5** Amnok, Imjin, Tumen
　　6 Namhan, Pukhan, Somjin, Soyang,
　　Yesong **7** Naktong, Taedong **8**
　　Changjin, Youngsan **9** Chongchon
　sea: 5 Japan **6** Yellow **9** East China
　physical feature:
　　bay: 5 Korea **6** Yongil **7** Kanghwa,

　　Kyonggi **9** Tongjoson
　cape: 4 Musu
　point: 7 Changgi **8** Changsan
　strait: 5 Korea
　valley: 7 Naktong
　people: 6 Korean
　artist: 8 Chong Son **10** Kimtlong-do
　dynasty: 2 Yi **4** Choe **5** Koryo
　leader: 6 Sejong **8** Yi Sung-gy **9**
　　Kim Il Sung **11** Chun Doo Hwan,
　　Syngman Rhee **12** Park Chung Hee
　legendary leader: 5 Ki-tse **6** Chi-
　　tse, Chi-tzu, Tangun
　poet: 10 Hwang Chini
Unification Church Leader 12 Sun
　Myung Moon
language: 6 Korean
　alphabet: 6 hangul
religion: 6 Taoism **7** animism **8** Bud-
　dhism **9** Chondogyo **12** Christianity,
　Confucianism
place:
　palace: 8 Kyongbok
　temple: 7 Haein-sa **17** Hall of Eter-
　　nal Life
　tomb: 14 Dancing Figures
feature:
　clothing: 5 chima
　game: 3 yut **5** akoan **6** ho-hpai **7**
　　kol-ye-si **9** ryong-hpai, sang-ryouk
　　10 ke-pouk-hpai, sin-syo-tyen **12**
　　tjak-ma- tchi-ki **15** kko-ri-pouk-
　　tchi-ki
　martial art: 9 tae-kwon-do
　musical instrument: 6 chaing **7**
　　kayagum, komungo
　porcelain: 7 Celadon
　porch: 4 maru
　pottery: 8 pun-chong
food:
　bean curd: 4 tubu
　hot pickle: 6 kimchi
　meat filled dumpling: 5 mandu
　noodle: 5 kuksu
Korman, Harvey
　born: 9 Chicago IL
　roles: 11 High Anxiety **13** Danny
　　Kaye Show **14** Blazing Saddles **16**
　　Carol Burnett Show
Kornberg, Arthur
　field: 12 biochemistry
　sythesized: 3 DNA, RNA **15** ribonu-
　　cleic acid **20** deoxyribonucleic acid
　awarded: 10 Nobel Prize
kosher 5 right **6** proper **7** ethical **8** fit
　to eat **10** aboveboard **12** on the up
　and up
Kosinski, Jerzy
　author of: 5 Steps **7** Cockpit **9** Blind
　　Date **10** Being There **11** Passion Play
　　12 The Devil Tree **14** The Painted
　　Bird
Kowalski, Stanley
　character in: 21 A Streetcar Named
　　Desire
　wife: 6 Stella
　sister-in-law: 7 Blanche
　author: 8 Williams

kowtow 4 bend, fawn **5** cower, stoop,
　toady **6** bow low, cringe, curtsy,
　grovel, salaam **7** truckle **8** bootlick,
　butter up, softsoap **9** genuflect **11** ap-
　ple-polish **12** bow and scrape **16**
　prostrate oneself
kowtowing 7 fawning, servile **8** toad-
　ying **9** groveling **10** obsequious
Kraken
　origin: 9 Norwegian
　form: 7 monster
　habitat: 3 sea
　caused: 10 whirlpools
Kramer, Stanley
　director of: 10 On the Beach **11** Ship
　　of Fools **14** Inherit the Wind, The
　　Defiant Ones **19** Judgment at Nurem-
　　berg
Kramer vs Kramer
　director: 12 Robert Benton
　based on novel by: 11 Avery Cor-
　　man
　cast: 10 Howard Duff **11** Justin
　　Henry, Meryl Streep **13** Dustin Hoff-
　　man, Jane Alexander
　Oscar for: 5 actor (Hoffman) **7** pic-
　　ture **8** director **10** screenplay **17** sup-
　　porting actress (Streep)
Krantz, Judith
　author of: 8 Scruples **13** Princess
　　Daisy **16** I'll Take Manhattan, Mis-
　　tral's Daughter
Krazy Kat
　creator: 14 George Herriman
　character:
　　cop: 12 Offissa B Pupp
　　mouse: 6 Ignatz
　prop: 5 brick
　place: 4 jail **14** Coconino County **24**
　　Kelly's Exclusive Brick Yard
Krebs, Hans Adolf
　field: 9 chemistry
　nationality: 6 German
　discovered: 15 citric acid cycle
　awarded: 10 Nobel Prize
Kreisler, Fritz
　born: 6 Vienna **7** Austria
　composer of: 7 Allegro **10** Pr-
　　aeludium **15** Caprice Viennois **16**
　　Tambourin Chinois
Kreutzer, Rodolphe
　born: 6 France **10** Versailles
　composer of: 16 Etudes ou Caprices
Kreutzer Sonata, The
　author: 10 Leo Tolstoy
　character: 13 Mme Pozdnishef,
　　Trukhashevsky **16** Vasyla Pozdnishef
Krieg 3 war
Kriemhild
　origin: 8 Germanic
　mentioned in: 14 Nibelungenlied
　brother: 7 Gunther
　husband: 9 Siegfried
　slew: 5 Hagan **7** Gunther
　avenged: 6 murder **9** Siegfried
　corresponds to: 6 Gudrun, Kudrun **7**
　　Guthrun

Kristin Lavransdatter
author: **12** Sigrid Undset

Kronos *see* **6** Cronus

Krook
character in: **10** Bleak House
author: **7** Dickens

Kropp, Albert
character in: **25** All Quiet on the Western Front
author: **8** Remarque

krypton
chemical symbol: **2** Kr

Kuala Lumpur
capital of: **8** Malaysia

Kubla Khan
author: **15** Samuel Coleridge
city: **6** Xanadu
river: **4** Alph

Kubrick, Stanley
director of: **6** Lolita **9** Spartacus **11** Barry Lyndon **12** Paths of Glory **13** Dr Strangelove (or How I Learned to Stop Worrying and Love the Bomb) **16** A Clockwork Orange **30** Two Thousand and One A Space Odyssey

kudos 4 fame **5** award, glory, honor, prize **6** esteem, praise, renown, repute **7** acclaim, plaudit **8** citation, prestige **9** celebrity, laudation **10** admiration, decoration **12** commendation **14** celebratedness

Kudrun *see* **6** Gudrun

Kukla, Fran & Ollie
hostess: **11** Fran Allison
puppet: **5** Kukla, Ollie (Oliver J Dragon) **8** Mercedes **9** Cecil Bill **10** Col Crackie **11** Beulah Witch **12** Olivia Dragon **13** Delores Dragon **14** Fletcher Rabbit **18** Mme Ophelia Oglepuss

kummel
origin: **7** Germany
flavor: **7** caraway

kumquat 10 Fortunella
varieties: **4** oval **5** round **6** Marumi, Nagami **16** Australian desert

Kung Fu
character: **8** Master Po **9** Master Kan **14** Kwai Chang Caine
cast: **8** Keye Luke **9** Philip Ahn **11** Radames Pera **14** David Carradine
Caine raised in: **13** Shaolin Temple

kunzite
species: **9** spodumene

Kupka, Frank (Frantisek)
born: **6** Opocno **7** Bohemia **14** Czechoslovakia
artwork: **12** Black Accents, The Cathedral **16** Etude pour la Fugue **17** Fugue in Red and Blue **23** Fugue in Two Colors Amorpha **25** Philosophical Architecture

Kuprin, Aleksandr
author of: **7** The Duel **10** Yama the Pit

Kurosawa, Akira
director of: **3** Ran **8** Rashomon **12** Seven Samurai

Kurtz
character in: **15** Heart of Darkness
author: **6** Conrad

Kuwait
name means: **9** small fort
capital/largest city: **10** Kuwait City
others: **6** Ahmadi **7** Hawalli **8** Abdullah, al-Jahrah, Fahaheel, Shuwaykh **9** al-Shuayba **12** Mena al- Ahmadi, Mina Abd Allah, Mina al-Ahmadi
head of state: **4** emir
monetary unit: **4** fils **5** dinar
island: **5** Warba **7** Bubiyan, Failaka
physical feature:
bay: **6** Kuwait **12** Khor Abdullah
duststorm: **4** kaus
gulf: **7** Persian
oasis: **6** Jahrah
people: **4** Arab **5** Iraqi, Saudi **6** Indian **7** Bedouin **8** Egyptian **9** Pakistani **11** Palestinian
ruling family: **5** Sabah
sheikh (Sabah family): **5** Ahmad, Salem **7** Mubarak **12** Jaber al-Ahmed, Sabah al-Salim **15** Abdullah al-Salim
religion: **5** Islam
war: **4** Gulf **11** Desert Storm, Persian Gulf **12** Desert Shield
enemy: **4** Iraq **13** Saddam Hussein

Kwa
language family: **16** Niger-Kordofanian
group: **10** Niger-Congo
includes: **3** Ewe, Ibo, Twi **4** Bini, Nupe, Togo **6** Yoruba **7** Dahomey

Kwakiutl
language family: **8** Wakashan
location: **6** Canada **15** British Columbia, Vancouver Island **20** Queen Charlotte Island
related to: **6** Nootka **10** Bellabella
noted for: **10** totem poles **15** Cannibal Society, wooden sculpture
called: **14** potlatch people

Kwanza, Kwanzaa 15 harvest festival
celebrated by: **16** African-Americans

Kyd, Thomas
author of: **17** The Spanish Tragedy

Kyrgyzstan
formerly: **10** Kirghiz SSR
capital/largest city: **6** Frunze **7** Bishkek
head of state: **9** president
government: **8** republic
monetary unit: **3** som
mountain: **8** Tian Shan
people: **5** Uzbek **6** Kyrgyz **7** Kirghiz, Russian
language: **6** Turkic **7** Kirghiz, Russian
religion: **6** Muslim **10** Sunni Islam

Kyrie eleison 13 Lord have mercy

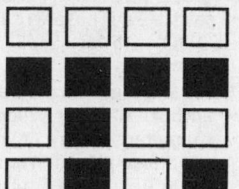 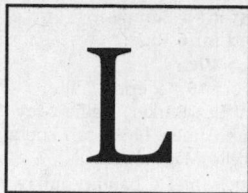 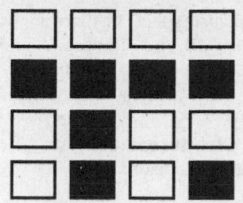

Laban
father: 7 Bethuel
grandfather: 5 Nahor
daughter: 4 Leah 6 Rachel
sister: 7 Rebekah
son-in-law: 5 Jacob

label 3 tag 4 mark, name, note, seal, sign, slip 5 brand, stamp, tally, title 6 define, docket, ticket 7 earmark, mark off, sticker 8 classify, describe 9 designate 10 denominate, put a mark on 11 appellation, designation, inscription 12 characterize 13 specification 14 classification, identification 16 characterization

labor, labour 4 plod, toil, work 5 slave, sweat 6 drudge, effort, suffer 7 agonize, travail, workers, workmen 8 drudgery, exertion, laborers, manpower, plodding, plug away, struggle 9 employees, grind away, work force 10 birth pangs, childbirth, menial work, smart under 11 birth throes, manual labor, parturition 12 accouchement, be affected by, be burdened by, be troubled by 13 be the victim of 14 employ one's time, work like a slave

labored 5 heavy, stiff 6 clumsy, forced, wooden 7 awkward, cramped, halting, studied 8 drawnout, overdone, strained 9 contrived, difficult, laborious, maladroit, ponderous, unnatural 13 self-conscious, unspontaneous

laborer 4 esne, hand, peon, serf 6 coolie, drudge, menial, toiler, worker 7 plodder, workman 8 handyman, hired man, hireling, workhand 9 hired hand 10 roustabout, wage earner, workingman 11 proletarian 12 manual worker 16 blue-collar worker

laborious 4 hard 6 brutal, severe, uphill 7 arduous, irksome, labored, onerous, wearing 8 rigorous, tiresome, toilsome, wearying 9 demanding, difficult, effortful, fa-tiguing, herculean, strenuous, wearisome 10 burdensome, oppressive, struggling 11 troublesome

laboriously 4 hard 9 arduously 14 with difficulty 15 with great effort

laboriousness 5 trial 8 tough job 10 difficulty, rough going, uphill work 11 arduousness 12 hard sledding 15 troublesomeness

labor omnia vincit 15 work conquers all
motto of: 8 Oklahoma

Labors of Hercules *see* 8 Hercules

labyrinth 3 web 4 knot, maze 5 snarl 6 jungle, morass, riddle, tangle 7 complex, network 9 intricacy, mare's nest 10 complexity, perplexity, wilderness 11 convolution

Labyrinth
form: 4 maze
location: 5 Crete
built by: 8 Daedalus
for: 9 King Minos
challenged by: 7 Theseus
he was aided by: 7 Ariadne
with: 6 thread
housed: 8 Minotaur

Lacaille, Nicholas Louis de
field: 9 astronomy
nationality: 6 French
mapped: 14 constellations

lace 3 tie 4 beat, bind, cane, dope, lash, whip 5 braid, cinch, close, flail, spank, spike, strap, tie up, truss 6 dope up, fasten, flavor, infuse, punish, secure, switch, tether, thrash 7 fortify, spice up, suffuse, tighten 8 chastise, make fast, make taut 10 strengthen 11 add liquor to 12 add spirits to, draw together, give a beating

Lacedaemon
founder of: 6 Sparta
father: 4 Zeus
mother: 8 Taygete
wife: 6 Sparta
son: 7 Amyclas
daughter: 8 Eurydice
descendants: 5 Helen 6 Castor, Pollux 8 Dioscuri 9 Hippocoon, Tyndarius 12 Clytemnestra

lacerate 3 cut, rip 4 gash, hurt, pain, scar, stab, tear 5 lance, sever, slash, slice, wound 6 deface 7 agonize, scratch, torment, torture 8 distress, give pain, puncture 10 excruciate 11 inflict pain

lacerating 5 acute 6 fierce, severe 7 cutting, extreme, intense, violent 12 excruciating

laceration 3 cut, rip 4 tear 5 wound 10 mutilation

Lachaise, Gaston
born: 5 Paris 6 France
artwork: 12 Standing Nude 13 Standing Woman 14 Floating Figure

Lachesis
form: 4 Fate
holds: 12 thread of life
determines: 6 length 7 destiny

lachrymose 3 sad 5 teary, weepy 6 crying 7 maudlin, tearful, weeping 8 mournful 10 melancholy

lack 4 miss, need, want 6 dearth 7 absence 8 omission, scarcity, shortage 9 be missing, be short of, depletion, neediness, privation, scantness 10 deficiency, exhaustion 11 deprivation, fall short of 12 be inadequate 13 be caught short, be deficient in 14 be found wanting, be insufficient

lackadaisical 4 idle 7 languid, loafing 8 lifeless, listless, mindless 9 apathetic, lethargic, unexcited 10 inanimated, phlegmatic, spiritless, unaspiring, uninspired 11 indifferent, languishing, unambitious, unconcerned, unexcitable, unmotivated 12 uninterested 13 dillydallying

lackey 4 page 5 slave, toady, usher, valet 6 butler, flunky, helper, menial, minion, squire, waiter 7 servant, steward 8 employee, follower, hanger-on, hireling, inferior, retainer 9 assistant, attendant, cupbearer, mercenary, underling

lacking 7 needing, wanting 9 deficient 10 inadequate 12 falling short, insufficient
French: 6 manque

lackluster 4 blah, dead, drab, dull 5 bland, muted 6 boring, dreary, leaden, pallid, somber 7 humdrum, nothing, prosaic, subdued 8 lifeless, mediocre, ordinary 9 colorless 10 lusterless 11 commonplace 12 run-of-the-mill 13 uninteresting

lack of conviction 5 doubt 8 question 9 misgiving 10 hesitation, indecision 11 uncertainty
trait of: 14 Doubting Thomas

lack of faith 5 doubt 7 atheism 8 distrust, mistrust 9 disbelief, suspicion

lack of feeling 6 apathy 8 coldness, numbness 11 impassivity 15 emotionlessness, hardheartedness, passionlessness

lack of interest 5 ennui 6 apathy 7 boredom 9 unconcern 12 indifference

lack of respect 8 contempt, rudeness

9 disregard **10** disrespect **11** discourtesy, irreverence **12** impoliteness

lack of skill 9 inability **10** clumsiness, ineptitude **11** awkwardness **12** incompetency

Laclos, Pierre Choderlos de
author of: **22** Les Liaisons Dangereuses

Lacombe, Lucien
director: **10** Louis Malle
cast: **12** Pierre Blaise **13** Aurore Clement **16** Holger Lowenadler

laconic 4 curt **5** blunt, brief, pithy, short, terse **7** compact, concise, pointed, spartan, summary **8** succinct **9** condensed **10** to the point **12** concentrated **14** sparing of words

lacquer 4 coat **5** glaze **7** coating, shellac, varnish

lacrimoso
music: **7** tearful

lacrosse
Indian name: **9** bagataway
circle around goal: **6** crease
played with: **6** crosse **14** pouched racquet
players/team: **3** ten
position: **6** goalie **9** attackman **10** defenseman, midfielder
term: **6** riding **8** clearing

lacuna 3 gap, pit **4** gulf, hole, void **5** blank, break, crack, ditch, pause, space **6** breach, cavity, hiatus **7** caesura, fissure, interim, opening, vacancy **8** interval, omission **10** interstice, suspension **12** interruption **13** discontinuity

lacustrine 7 aquatic **8** riparian **11** lake-growing **12** lake-dwelling

lacy 4 fine **5** filmy, gauzy, meshy, netty, sheer, webby **6** barred, frilly, netted, porous, webbed **7** gridded, netlike **8** cobwebby, delicate, filigree, gossamer, lacelike, retiform **9** filigreed **10** diaphanous, reticulate **11** latticelike, transparent

lad 3 boy, kid **5** sprig, youth **6** shaver, sprout **8** juvenile, young man **9** schoolboy, stripling, young chap, youngster **11** young fellow

Ladd, Alan
son: **5** David **6** Alan Jr
co-star: **12** Veronica Lake
born: **12** Hot Springs AR
roles: **5** Shane **13** The Blue Dahlia **14** The Great Gatsby, This Gun for Hire

ladies' man 4 beau, stud **5** spark **6** escort, gigolo **7** playboy **8** cavalier, gay blade

Ladino
also: **7** Judezmo **12** Judeo-Spanish
spoken by: **9** Sephardim
based on: **10** Old Spanish
script: **6** Hebrew **7** mestizo

Ladoga, Lake

largest in: **6** Europe
located in: **6** Russia

La Dolce Vita
director: **15** Federico Fellini
cast: **9** Lex Barker, Nadia Gray **10** Anouk Aimee **11** Anita Ekberg **19** Marcello Mastroianni

ladrone 5 thief **6** bandit, outlaw

lady 4 wife **5** woman **6** female, matron, spouse **7** duchess, peeress **8** baroness, countess **10** aristocrat, noblewoman **11** gentlewoman, marchioness, viscountess, woman of rank **13** well-bred woman
German: **4** frau
Italian: **5** donna
Spanish/Portuguese: **4** dona

Lady Chatterley's Lover
author: **10** D H Lawrence
character: **7** Mellors **19** Constance Chatterley

Lady Eve, The
director: **14** Preston Sturges
cast: **10** Henry Fonda **13** Charles Coburn **14** Eugene Pallette **15** Barbara Stanwyck, William Demarest

Lady for a Day
director: **10** Frank Capra
based on story by: **11** Damon Runyon
cast: **9** Guy Kibbee, May Robson **13** Warren William
remade as: **19** Pocketful of Miracles

Lady from Dubuque, The
author: **11** Edward Albee

Lady from the Sea, The
author: **11** Henrik Ibsen

Lady in Chair
constellation of: **10** Cassiopeia

ladylike 5 civil **6** modest, polite, proper **7** courtly, elegant, genteel, refined **8** cultured, decorous, mannerly, polished, well-bred **9** courteous, dignified **10** cultivated **11** respectable **12** well mannered **13** well brought up

Lady of the Camellias, The *see* **7** Camille

Lady of the Lake, The
author: **14** Sir Walter Scott
character: **9** Allan Bane **11** Roderick Dhu **12** Ellen Douglas **13** Malcolm Graeme **14** James Fitz-James, James of Douglas

Lady Oracle
author: **14** Margaret Atwood

lady's maid
French: **14** femme de chambre

Lady's Not for Burning, The
author: **14** Christopher Fry

lady's-slipper, lady-slipper
varieties: **4** pink **5** showy **6** orchid **8** mountain, ram's-head **9** two-leaved **10** small white **11** large yellow, small yellow

Lady Vanishes, The
director: **15** Alfred Hitchcock

cast: **9** Paul Lukas **13** Dame May Whitty **15** Michael Redgrave **16** Margaret Lockwood

Lady Windermere's Fan
author: **10** Oscar Wilde
character: **10** Mrs Erlynne **14** Lord Darlington, Lord Windermere **18** Lord Augustus Lorton

Laertes
son: **8** Odysseus

Laertes
character in: **6** Hamlet
sister: **7** Ophelia
father: **8** Polonius
author: **11** Shakespeare

La Farge, John
born: **9** New York NY
artwork: **14** Maua Our Boatman **17** The Muse of Painting **18** Red and White Peonies

La Fayette, Comtesse de
author of: **19** La Princesse de Cleves

Lafayette, Marquis de
also: **38** Marie Joseph Paul Yves Roch Gilbert du Motier
nationality: **6** French
served in: **14** July Revolution **16** French Revolution **18** American Revolution
battle: **8** Yorktown **10** Brandywine

Lafcadio's Adventures (The Vatican Swindle)
author: **9** Andre Gide

La Fontaine, Jean de
author of: **6** Fables

lag 4 drag, halt, inch, limp, snag **5** dally, delay, hitch, tarry, trail **6** be idle, be late, be slow, dawdle, falter, hold up, linger, loiter, trudge **7** be tardy, setback, slacken, stagger **8** be behind, hang back, slowdown **9** be overdue, inch along **10** drag behind, slackening **11** slowing down **12** bide one's time, take one's time **13** falling behind, procrastinate

laggard 4 mope, poke, slow, slug **5** idler, snail, tardy **6** loafer, remiss **7** dallier, dawdler, lounger, putterer, slowfoot, slowpoke, sluggard, sluggish **9** donothing, straggler **12** dilly-dallier **13** stick-in-the-mud

lagniappe, lagnappe 3 tip **4** gift, perk **5** bonus, favor, prize **7** largess, memento, present **8** gratuity, largesse **9** pourboire

Lagos
former capital of: **7** Nigeria

Lahr, Bert
real name: **14** Irving Lahrheim
born: **9** New York NY
roles: **12** Cowardly Lion **13** The Wizard of Oz

laic 3 lay **5** civil **6** laical **7** amateur, popular, profane, secular, worldly **8** temporal **11** nonclerical, nonpastoral

12 secularistic **13** inexperienced **15** nonprofessional **17** nonecclesiastical

lair 3 den, lie, mew **4** hole, nest **5** cover, haunt **6** burrow, cavern, covert **7** hideout, retreat **8** hideaway **9** sanctuary **12** resting place

laissez-faire, laisser-faire 8 hands off **9** let them be, unconcern **12** indifference **14** let-alone policy, live and let live **15** noninterference, nonintervention

laissez-passer 4 pass **6** permit **11** allow to pass

Laius
  king of: **6** Thebes
  father: **8** Labdacus
  great-grandfather: **6** Cadmus
  wife: **7** Jocasta
  son: **7** Oedipus
  killed by: **7** Oedipus

Lajeunesse, Gabriel
  character in: **10** Evangeline
  author: **10** Longfellow

lake
  of Afghanistan: 7 Helmand **13** Hamud-i-Helmand
  of Albania: 4 Ulze **5** Matia, Ohrid **6** Prespa **7** Ochrida, Scutari, Shkoder **8** Ohridsko
  of Algeria: 5 Hodna **6** Sabkha **7** Cherqui, Fedjadj, Meirhir **10** Azzel Matti, Meherrhane
  of Andorra: 11 Engolasters
  of Argentina: 6 Viedma **7** Cardiel, Fagnano, Musters **11** Buenos Aires, Mar Chiquita, Nahuel Huapi
  of Armenia: 3 Van **5** Sevan, Urmia **8** Urumiyah
  of Australia: 4 Eyre **5** Carey, Cowan, Frome, Moore, Wells **6** Austin, Barlee, Bulloo, Dundas, Harris, Mackay **7** Amadeus, Blanche, Everard, Torrens **8** Carnegie, Gairdner **9** MacDonald **10** Yammayamma **14** Disappointment
  of Austria: 6 Almsee **7** Fertoto, Mondsee **8** Bodensee, Traunsee **9** Constance **10** Neusiedler
  of Benin: 5 Aheme **6** Nokoue
  of Bolivia: 5 Poopo **7** Allagas, Coipasa, Rogagua **8** Titicaca **10** Desaguader
  of Botswana: 3 Dow, Xau **5** Ngami
  of Brazil: 4 Aima, Feia **5** Mirim **13** Logo dos Platos
  of Burundi: 7 Rugwero **8** Tshohoha **10** Tanganyika
  of Cambodia/Kampuchea: 8 Tonle Sap
  of Cameroon: 4 Chad
  of Canada: 4 Cree, Erie, Gras, Seul **5** Garry, Huron, Rainy **6** Louise, St John **7** Abitibi, Dubawnt, Nipigon, Ontario, Testlin **8** Kootenay, Manitoba, Okanagan, Reindeer, Superior, Winnipeg **9** Athabaska, Great Bear, Nipissing **10** Great Slave, Mistassini **12** Winnipegosis

  of Central African Republic: 4 Assa
  of Chad: 4 Chad
  of Chile: 5 Ranco **6** Yelcho **7** Puyehue, Rupanco **8** Cochrane **10** General Paz, Llanquihue **11** Buenos Aires
  of China: 3 Tai **4** Chao, Na-mu **5** Kaoyu, Oling, Telli **6** Bamtso, Bornor, Ebinor, Erhhai, Khanka, Lopnor, Namtso, Poyang **7** Chaling, Hungtse, Karanor, Kokonor **8** Hulunnor, Montcalm, Taroktso, Tellinor, Tienchih, Tsinghai, Tungting
  of Colombia: 4 Tota
  of the Congo: 5 Mweru, Tumba **6** Albert, Nyanza, Upemba **7** Leopold **11** Stanley Pool
  of Costa Rica: 6 Arenal
  of Denmark 6 Arreso
  of Djibouti: 4 Abbe **5** Assal
  of Dominican Republic: 10 Enriquillo
  of Egypt: 4 Edku, Idku **5** Qarun **6** Maryut, Moeris, Nasser **7** Manzala **8** Burullus, Mareotis
  of El Salvador: 5 Guiha, Guija **8** Ilopango **10** Coatepeque
  of England: 8 Grasmere **9** Ennerdale, Ullswater, Wastwater **10** Buttermere, Windermere **12** Derwentwater **13** Coniston Water
  of Estonia: 5 Pskov **6** Peipus **9** Vortsjarv
  of Ethiopia: 3 Abe **4** Tana **5** Abaya, Shola, Tanna, Tsana, Tzana, Zeway **6** Dambea, Dembea, Rudolf **8** Blue Nile, Stefanie
  of Finland: 3 Juo, Muo **4** Kemi, Kiui, Nasi, Oulu, Puru, Pyha, Simo **5** Enara, Enare, Hauki, Inari, Kalla, Lappa, Lesti, Puula, Saima **6** Ladoya, Lentua, Saimaa, Soume, Syvari **7** Koitere, Nilakka **8** Pielinen **9** Kallavesi, Pielavesi
  of France: 6 Annecy, Cazaux, Geneva
  of Gabon Republic: 7 Anengue, Azinguo
  of Germany, East: 6 Muritz
  of Germany, West: 9 Constance **11** Inner Alster, Outer Alster
  of Ghana: 5 Volta **8** Bosumtwi
  of Greece: 5 Karla, Volve **6** Copais, Kopais, Prespa, Voweis **8** Ioannina, Koroneia, Vistonis **9** Trichonis, Vegoritis
  of Grenada: 10 Grand Etang
  of Guatemala: 5 Dulce, Guija, Peten **6** Izabal **7** Atitlan **9** Amatitlan, Peten Itza
  of Haiti: 8 Saumatre
  of Honduras: 5 Criba, Yojoa **6** Brewer
  of Hungary: 5 Ferto **7** Balaton, Velence **9** Blatensee **10** Neusiedler, Plattensee
  of Iceland: 6 Myvatn **10** Thorisvatn **14** Thingvallavatn
  of India: 5 Jheel, Lonar, Wular **6** Chilka, Colair, Dhebar, Kolair **7** Kol-

  leru, Pulicat, Pushkar, Sambahr
  of Indonesia: 4 Toba **5** Ranau **6** Towuti
  of Iran: 5 Niris, Tasht, Tuzlu, Urmia **6** Sahweh, Sistan **7** Maharlu **8** Nemekser, Urumiyeh
  of Iraq: 6 al-Milh **7** Sanniya **8** al-Hammar
  of Ireland: 3 Doo, Key, Ree, Tay **4** Conn, Derg, Erne, Mask **5** Allen, Barra, Carra, Gowna, Leane, Lough, Neagh **6** Boderg, Cooter, Corrib, Ennell **7** Dromore, Gougane, Oughter, Sheelin **9** Killarney
  of Israel: 5 Huleh **7** Dead Sea **8** Kinneret, Tiberias **12** Sea of Galilee
  of Italy: 4 Como, Iseo, Nemi **5** Garda **6** Albano, Lesina, Lugano, Varano **7** Bolsena, Perugia **8** Maggiore **9** Bracciano, Trasimeno
  of Japan: 4 Biwa, Suwa, Toya **6** Towada **8** Kutchawa, Shikotsu
  of Kazakhstan: 8 Balkhash
  of Kenya: 6 Magadi, Nakuru, Natron, Rudolf **7** Turkana **8** Naivasha, Victoria
  of Lebanon: 5 Quran **6** Qirawn
  of Lithuania: 5 Dysna
  of Luxembourg: 8 Haut Sure
  of Macedonia: 5 Ohrid **6** Prespa **7** Ochrida
  of Madagascar: 5 Itasy **7** Alaotra, Kinkony
  of Malawi: 5 Nyasa **6** Chilwa, Malawi
  of Mali: 2 Do **4** Debo **5** Garou **7** Korarou **9** Faguibine
  of Mexico: 7 Chapala, Texcoco **9** Patzcuaro
  of Mongolia: 3 Uvs **5** Har Us **6** Bor Nor **7** Ghirgis, Ubsa Nor **8** Airik Nor, Durga Nor, Hobsogol, Khara Usu **9** Khubsugul, Khukhu-Nur **10** Khirgis Nur
  of Montenegro: 7 Scutari, Shkoder
  of Mozambique: 5 Nyasa **6** Chuali, Nyassa **8** Nhavarre
  of Myanmar: 4 Inle
  of Nauru: 11 Buada Lagoon
  of the Netherlands: 7 Haarlem **10** Ijsselmeer **11** Grevelingen, Hazinguliet
  of New Zealand: 3 Ada **4** Gunn, Ohau **5** Hawea, Taupo **6** Pukaki, Pupuke, Te Anau, Tekapo, Wanaka **7** Brunner, Diamond, Kanieri, Okareka, Rotorua **8** Okataina, Paradise, Rotoaira, Wakatipi **9** Manapouri
  of Nicaragua: 7 Managua **9** Nicaragua
  of Niger: 4 Chad
  of Nigeria: 4 Chad
  of the Nile: 4 Tana **5** Kyoga, Tsana **6** Albert, Edward, Nasser **8** Victoria
  of Norway: 4 Alte **5** Ister, Mjosa, Snasa **6** Femund **7** Rostavn, Tunnsjo
  of Panama: 5 Gatun
  of Paraguay: 4 Vera, Ypoa **8** Ypa-

carai
of Peru: 8 Titicaca
of Poland: 5 Goplo, Mamry **8** Niegocin, Sniardwy **13** Stettin Lagoon
of Puerto Rico: 5 Loiza **6** Carite **8** Dos Bocas **9** Caonillas, Guatajaca
of Romania: 5 Sinoe **6** Snagov
of Russia: 3 Seg **4** Azov, Kola, Neva **5** Byelo, Chany, Elton, Erara, Ilmen, Lacha, Onega, Vozhe **6** Baikal, Ladoga **10** Caspian Sea
of Rwanda: 4 Kivu **5** Ihema **6** Bufera, Bulera, Mohasi **7** Rugwero, Ruhnodo **8** Mugesera, Tshohoha
of Sardinia: 6 Omodeo
of Scotland: 3 Awe, Dee, Lin, Tay **4** Earn, Fyne, Gair, Gare, Linn, Ness, Oich, Ryan, Sloy **5** Duich, Leven, Lochy, Lough, Morar, Maree, Nevis **6** Laggan, Linnhe, Lomond **7** Katrine, Rannoch, St Marys
of Senegal: 6 Guiers
of Sicily: 7 Pergusa **8** Camarina
of Slovenia: 4 Bled
of Spain: 4 Lago **9** Albrifera
of the Sudan: 2 No **4** Chad, Toad **6** Nasser
of Sweden: 4 Ster **5** Asnen, Malar, Silja, Vaner **6** Vanern, Vatter, Wennen **7** Hielmar, Malaren, Vattern **8** Dalalven **9** Hjalmaren
of Switzerland: 3 Uri, Zug **4** Biel, Thon, Thun **5** Ageri, Leman, Morat **6** Bienne, Brienz, Geneva, Lugano, Sarnen, Wallen, Zurich **7** Hallwil, Lucerne, Lungern **8** Maggiore, Vierwald **9** Bielersee, Constance, Neuchatel, Sarnersee, Thunersee
of Syria: 5 Merom **7** Djeboid **8** Tiberias
of Tanzania: 5 Eyasi, Nyasa, Rukwa **6** Malawi, Natron, Nyassa **7** Manyara **8** Victoria **10** Tanganyika
of Thailand: 9 Nong Lahan
of Tibet: 3 Aru, Bam, Bum, Nam **4** Mema, Tosu **5** Jagok, Tabia **6** Dagtse, Garhur, Kashun, Nam Iso, Seling, Tangra, Yamdok **7** Kyaring, Terinam, Tsaring, Zilling **8** Jiggitai **9** Tengrinor **11** Manasarowar
of Tunisia: 6 Achkel, Djerid **7** Bizerte
of Turkey: 3 Tuz, Van **7** Egridir **8** Beysehir
of Uganda: 5 Kioga, Kyoga **6** Albert, Edward, George **8** Victoria
of the United States: 4 Erie, Mead **5** Huron, Tahoe **6** Cayuga, Finger, George, Itasca, Oneida, Seneca **7** Iliamma, Ontario **8** Michigan, Superior **9** Champlain, Great Salt, Salton Sea, Teshekpuk, Winnebago **10** Okeechobee **11** Yellowstone **13** Pontchartrain, Wallenpaupack, Winnipesaukee **14** Lake of the Woods
of Uruguay: 5 Merin, Mirim **18** Embalse del Rio Negro
of Venezuela: 9 Maracaibo, Tacarigua

of Wales: 4 Bala **6** Vyrnwy
of Yugoslavia: 4 Bled **5** Ohrid **6** Prespa **7** Ochrida, Scutari
of Zaire: 4 Kivu **5** Mweru, Tumba **6** Albert, Edward, Upemba **9** Mai-Ndombe **10** Tanganyika
of Zambia: 5 Mweru **6** Kariba **9** Bangweulu **10** Tanganyika
of Zimbabwe: 4 Kyle **6** Kariba
Lake, Veronica
  real name: 29 Constance Frances Marie Ockelman
  co-star: 8 Alan Ladd
  born: 10 Brooklyn NY
  roles: 13 The Blue Dahlia **14** I Married a Witch, This Gun for Hire **16** Sullivan's Travels
Lake Isle of Innisfree, The
  author: 7 W B Yeats
L'Allegro
  author: 10 John Milton
  companion piece: 11 Il Penseroso
Lalo, (Victor Antoine) Edouard
  born: 5 Lille **6** France
  composer of: 7 Namouna **8** Le Roi d'Ys **11** The King of Ys **15** Spanish Symphony **18** Symphonie Espagnole
lama 4 monk **6** priest
  in: 7 Lamaism
  high priest: 9 Dalai Lama
  locale: 5 Tibet
Lamar, Ruby
  character in: 9 Sanctuary
  author: 8 Faulkner
Lamarck, Jean B
  field: 7 biology
  forerunner of theory of: 9 evolution
  author of: 21 Philosophie Zoologique
La Mare, Walter de
  author of: 16 Memoirs of a Midget
Lamarr, Hedy
  real name: 21 Hedwig Eva Maria Kiesler
  born: 6 Vienna **7** Austria
  roles: 7 Ecstasy **16** Samson and Delilah
Lamas, Fernando
  wife: 10 Arlene Dahl **14** Esther Williams
  son: 7 Lorenzo
  born: 9 Argentina **11** Buenos Aires
  roles: 13 The Merry Widow **16** Dangerous When Wet **23** The Girl Who Had Everything
Lamb, Charles
  author of: 12 Essays of Elia **13** Dream Children **20** Tales From Shakespeare **25** A Dissertation upon Roast Pig **31** Specimens of English Dramatic Poets
  pseudonym: 4 Elia
  sister: 4 Mary
lambaste 4 beat, drub, lick, pelt, whip **5** scold, smear **6** berate, defeat, pummel, rebuke, subdue, thrash, wallop **7** bawl out, censure, chew out, clobber, cuss out, shellac, trounce **8** bludgeon,

denounce, vanquish **9** castigate, dress down, light into, overwhelm, reprimand
lambent 6 bright **7** radiant, shining **8** luminous, lustrous **10** flickering, shimmering
Lambert, Constant
  born: 6 London **7** England
  composer of: 9 Horoscope, Rio Grande **14** Romeo and Juliet **17** Music for Orchestra **27** Summer's Last Will and Testament
lame 4 game, halt, weak **5** sorry **6** clumsy, feeble, flimsy, infirm, maimed; uncool **7** failing, halting, hobbled, limping, unsound, wanting **8** crippled, deformed, disabled **9** deficient, faltering **10** inadequate **11** ineffectual **12** insufficient, unconvincing, unpersuasive **14** unsatisfactory
lamebrain 3 ass, sap **4** fool **5** booby, dunce, idiot, moron, ninny **6** dimwit, nitwit **7** fathead, half-wit **8** bonehead, dumb-dumb, imbecile, lunkhead, numskull **9** blockhead, numbskull **10** dunderhead, nincompoop **11** chowderhead
lamebrained 4 dumb **6** stupid **7** asinine, foolish, idiotic, moronic **8** crackpot **9** dimwitted, imbecilic **10** halfwitted **12** feeble-minded, simpleminded
Lamech
  father: 9 Methusael **10** Methuselah
  wives: 4 Adah **6** Zillah
  son: 5 Jabal, Jubal **9** Tubalcain
  daughter: 6 Naamah
lament 3 cry, sob **4** moan, wail, weep **5** dirge, mourn **6** bewail, outcry, plaint, regret **7** deplore, keening, requiem, whimper **8** mourning **9** death song **11** condole with, lamentation **12** funeral music **13** complain about **14** express pity for, show concern for, sympathize with **15** commiserate with
lamentable 4 dire **6** woeful **7** piteous **8** dreadful, grievous, pathetic, pitiable, shameful, terrible, wretched **9** miserable **10** deplorable **11** distressing, regret- table, unfortunate **13** disheartening, heart- breaking
Lamia
  author: 9 John Keats
Lamia
  form: 7 monster
  characteristic: 12 blood-sucking
La Motta, Jake (Jacob)
  nickname: 9 Bronx Bull
  sport: 6 boxing
  class: 12 middleweight
  movie biography: 10 Raging Bull
Lamour, Dorothy
  real name: 23 Mary Leta Dorothy Kau- meyer
  trademark: 6 sarong
  co-star: 7 Bob Hope **10** Bing Crosby
  born: 12 New Orleans LA

roles:
  Road to: **3** Rio **4** Bali **6** Utopia **7** Morocco **8** Hong Kong, Zanzibar **9** Singapore

L'Amour, Louis
  author of: **5** Hondo, Lando **7** Sackett, Shalako **8** Conagher **10** Key-Lock Man, Rivers West **14** The Californios, The Daybreakers **15** Westward the Tide **16** How the West Was Won, Over on the Dry Side **21** The Man from Broken Hills, To the Far Blue Mountains

lamp 4 bulb **5** light, torch **6** beacon **7** blinker, lantern **9** headlight, spotlight **10** chandelier, floodlight, Klieg light, night light **11** searchlight **12** ceiling light, reading light **14** ceiling fixture
  invented by:
    arc: **6** Staite
    incandescent: **6** Edison
    incandescent frosted: **6** Pipkin
    incandescent gas: **8** Langmuir
    Klieg: **7** Kleigel
    mercury vapor: **6** Hewitt
    miner's safety: **4** Davy
    neon: **6** Claude

Lampedusa, Giuseppe di
  author of: **10** The Leopard

lampoon 5 farce, put-on, spoof, squib **6** parody, satire, send up **7** mockery, takeoff **8** diatribe, ridicule, satirize, travesty **9** broadside, burlesque **10** caricature, pasquinade **11** make light of

Lamus
  father: **8** Hercules
  mother: **7** Omphale
  attacked: **5** ships

Lamy of Santa Fe
  author: **10** Paul Horgan

lanai 4 deck **5** porch **7** terrace, veranda

Lancaster 17 English royal house
  faction in: **13** War of the Roses
  founder: **11** John of Gaunt
  symbol: **7** red rose

Lancaster, Burt
  real name: **22** Burton Stephen Lancaster
  born: **9** New York NY
  roles: **5** Moses **9** All My Sons, Local Hero **11** Elmer Gantry (Oscar) **12** Atlantic City, The Rainmaker **13** The Rose Tattoo **14** Seven Days in May **16** Sorry Wrong Number **17** Birdman of Alcatraz **18** From Here to Eternity **19** Come Back Little Sheba, Sweet Smell of Success

lance 4 gaff, pike **5** shaft, spear **7** assegai, halberd, harpoon, javelin

Lancelot, Launcelot
  character in: **16** Arthurian romance
  also called: **13** Lancelot du Lac
  father: **3** Ban
  son: **7** Galahad
  lover: **6** Elaine **9** Guinevere
  home: **10** Joyous Gard

lancer 8 cavalier, horseman **10** cavalryman **12** horse soldier, horse trooper **14** mounted soldier

Lanchester, Elsa
  real name: **17** Elizabeth Sullivan
  husband: **15** Charles Laughton
  born: **7** England **8** Lewisham
  roles: **15** Come to the Stable **22** The Bride of Frankenstein **24** Witness for the Prosecution **25** The Private Life of Henry VIII **31** The Private Life of Henry the Eighth

land 3 get, lea, nab, net **4** area, dirt, dock, gain, grab, lawn, loam, moor, park, soil, take, ward, zone **5** acres, catch, earth, grass, green, humus, light, put in, realm, seize, shire, snare, state, tie up, tract **6** alight, anchor, canton, clinch, colony, county, debark, domain, empire, fields, ground, meadow, nation, parish, realty, region, secure **7** acreage, capture, country, descend, dry land, grounds, kingdom, pasture, section, set down, subsoil, terrain, win over **8** come down, district, dominion, farmland, homeland, location, mainland, make land, make port, precinct, property, province, republic, vicinity **9** cornfield, disembark, grassland, lay anchor, lay hold of, lead one to, reach land, territory **10** bring one to, carry one to, come to land, drop anchor, fatherland, motherland, native land, native soil, real estate, settle down, settlement, terra firma, wheat field **11** countryside, put into port **12** commonwealth, put into shore, real property, village green **13** the old country

Landau, Lev Davidovich
  field: **7** physics
  nationality: **7** Russian
  discovered: **12** liquid helium **14** ferromagnetism
  awarded: **10** Nobel Prize

landed property 5 manor **6** estate **8** compound **12** countryplace

land force 4 army **6** legion, troops **7** legions **8** infantry, soldiers, soldiery **9** artillery

Landless, Neville and Helena
  characters in: **22** The Mystery of Edwin Drood
  author: **7** Dickens

landlord 5 owner **6** holder, squire **8** landlady **9** landowner, possessor **10** freeholder, landholder, proprietor **13** property owner **14** lord of the manor

landmark 8 keystone, monument, signpost **9** benchmark, guidepost, highlight, high point, milestone, watershed **11** cornerstone **12** turning point **16** historic building

Landmarks
  god of: **8** Terminus

Land of Enchantment
  nickname of: **9** New Mexico

Land of Lincoln
  nickname of: **8** Illinois

Land of Opportunity
  nickname of: **8** Arkansas

Land of Sky-blue Waters
  nickname of: **9** Minnesota

Land of Steady Habits
  nickname of: **11** Connecticut

Land of Ten Thousand Lakes
  nickname of: **9** Minnesota

Land of the Dakotas
  nickname of: **11** North Dakota

Land of the Midnight Sun
  nickname of: **6** Alaska

Landon, Michael
  real name: **20** Eugene Maurice Orowitz
  born: **13** Forest Hills NY
  roles: **7** Bonanza **15** Highway to Heaven **19** Little Joe Cartwright **20** I Was a Teenage Werewolf **23** Little House on the Prairie

landscape 4 view **5** scene, sight, vista **6** aspect **7** scenery **8** panorama, prospect **9** spectacle **10** rural scene, scenic view **14** natural scenery

landscape architect 7 Le Notre, Olmsted

landsman 10 countryman **13** fellow citizen

Landsteiner, Karl
  field: **8** medicine **9** pathology
  distinguished: **10** blood types
  identified: **8** RH factor
  awarded: **10** Nobel Prize

lane 3 way **4** pass, path, road **5** alley, byway, drive, route, track, trail **6** access, avenue, bypath, course **7** passage, roadway **8** alleyway, approach, footpath **10** passageway

Lang, Walter
  director of: **7** Desk Set **11** The King and I

Lange, Jessica
  born: **9** Cloquet MN
  roles: **7** Country, Frances, Tootsie **8** Cape Fear, King Kong **11** All That Jazz **16** Crimes of the Heart **26** The Postman Always Rings Twice

Langella, Frank
  born: **9** Bayonne NJ
  roles: **7** Dracula **23** The Diary of a Mad Housewife

Langland, William
  author of: **12** Piers Plowman

Langmuir, Irving
  field: **9** chemistry
  invented: **15** atomic blowtorch **17** gas-tungsten lights
  awarded: **10** Nobel Prize

language 4 cant, jive **5** argot, idiom, lingo, prose, slang, words **6** jargon, patois, speech, tongue **7** cursing, cussing, dialect, diction, wording **8** parlance, rhetoric, swearing, verbiage **9** discourse, elocution, profanity **10** expression, use of words, vernacular, vocabulary **11** imprecation, phraseology, profane talk **12** mother tongue, native tongue **13** colloquialism **14** public speaking, self-expression **16** manner of speaking, mode of expression **17** oral communication, reading and writing, verbal intercourse

of Afghanistan: 4 Dari **5** Farsi **6** Afghan, Pashto, Pushtu **7** Balochi, Baluchi, Persian

of Albania: 3 Geg **4** Cham, Gheg, Hish, Tosk **5** Greek **8** Albanian

of Algeria: 6 Arabic, Berber, French, Zenata **7** Senhaja

of Andorra: 6 French **7** Catalan, Spanish

of Angola: 5 Bantu **8** Kimbundu, Oumbundu **9** Ovimbundu **10** Portuguese

of Antigua and Barbuda: 7 English

of Argentina: 7 Spanish

of Armenia: 7 Russian **8** Armenian

of Australia: 6 Yabber **7** English **9** aborigine (dialects)

of Austria: 5 Czech **6** German, Magyar **8** Croatian **9** Slovenian

of Azerbaijan: 6 Turkic

of the Bahamas: 6 Creole **7** English

of Bahrain: 4 Urdu **5** Farsi **6** Arabic **7** English, Persian

of Bangladesh: 6 Bihari **7** Bengali, English

of Barbados: 7 English

of Belgium: 5 Dutch **6** French, German **7** Flemish

of Benin: 3 Fon **5** Dendi **6** Bariba, French, Fulani, Yoruba

of Bermuda: 7 English

of Bhutan: 5 Hindi, Lhoke **7** Tibetan **8** Dzongkha, Nepalese

of Bolivia: 6 Aymara **7** Quechua, Spanish

of Borneo: 5 Malay **7** Chinese, English

of Bosnia-Herzegovina: 13 Serbo Croatian

of Botswana: 5 Bantu, Click **6** Tswana **7** English, Khoisan **8** Setswana

of Brazil: 10 Portuguese

of Brunei: 4 Iban **5** Malay **7** Chinese, English

of Bulgaria: 9 Bulgarian

of Burkina Faso: 4 Bobo, Lobi, More, Samo **5** Dyula, Mande, Mossi **6** French

of Burundi: 6 French **7** Kirundi, Swahili

of Cambodia/Kampuchea: 5 Khmer **6** French

of Cameroon: 4 Bulu **5** Bantu, Bassa, Hausa **6** Douala, Ewondo, French, Fulani **7** English **8** Bamileke, Fulfulde

of Canada: 6 Eskimo, French **7** English

of Canary Islands: 7 Spanish

of Cape Verde: 7 Crioulo **10** Portuguese **13** Verdean Creole

of Central African Republic: 5 Sango, Zande **6** French

of Chad: 4 Sara **5** Turku **6** Arabic, French

of Chile: 7 Spanish

of China: 7 Chinese **8** Mandarin, Shanghai **9** Cantonese

of Colombia: 7 Spanish

of Comoros: 6 Arabic, French **7** Swahili **8** Malagasy

of Congo: 4 Susu **5** Bantu, Fiote **6** French, Kituba **7** Bangala, Lingala

of Costa Rica: 7 Spanish

of Crete: 5 Greek **6** Minoan **7** Linear A, Linear B

of Croatia: 8 Croatian **10** Serbo Croat

of Cuba: 7 Spanish

of Cyprus: 5 Greek **7** Turkish **8** Armenian

of Czechoslovakia/Czech Republic: 5 Czech **6** German, Magyar, Slovak **7** Russian **9** Hungarian

of Denmark: 4 Odan **6** Danish **8** Faeroese **11** Greenlander

of Djibouti: 4 Afar **6** Arabic, French, Somali

of Dominican Republic: 6 French **7** English, Spanish

of Ecuador: 6 Jibaro **7** Quechua, Spanish

of Egypt: 6 Arabic, Coptic, French **7** English

of El Salvador: 7 Spanish

of England: 7 English

of Equatorial Guinea: 4 Bubi, Fang **6** pidgin **7** Spanish

of Eritrea: 7 Amharic

of Estonia: 5 Tartu **10** Finno-Ugric

of Ethiopia: 3 Giz **4** Afar, Agow, Geez, Saho **5** Geeze, Ghese, Smali, Tigre **6** Arabic, Harari **7** Amharic, English, Italian, Russian **8** Gallinya, Irob-Saho, Tigrinya

of Fiji: 5 Hindi **6** Fijian **7** English

of Finland: 4 Avar, Lapp **5** Karen, Ugric, Vogul **6** Magyar, Ostyak, Tarast **7** Finnish, Olonets, Samoyed, Swedish **8** Estonian **10** Olenetsian

of France: 6 French

of Gabon Republic: 6 French

of The Gambia: 4 Fula **5** Wolof **6** Fulani **7** English, Malinke **8** Mandingo

of Georgia: 8 Georgian

of Germany: 6 German **10** High German **11** Hochdeutsch

of Ghana: 2 Ga **3** Ewe, Gur, Kwa, Twi **5** Fanti, Hausa **7** Dagomba, English

of Gibraltar: 7 English, Spanish

of Greece: 5 Greek

of Greenland: 6 Danish, Eskimo **11** Greenlandic

of Grenada: 7 English

of Guatemala: 6 Quiche **7** Spanish

of Guinea: 5 Fulbe, Mande **6** Arabic, French, Fulani **7** English

of Guinea-Bissau: 5 Fulah **7** Balante, Crioulo **8** Mandingo **10** Portuguese **21** Cape Verde--Guinea Creole

of Guyana: 5 Hindi **7** English

of Haiti: 6 Creole, French, patois

of Honduras: 7 English, Spanish

of Hong Kong: 7 Chinese, English **9** Cantonese

of Hungary: 6 German, Magyar, Slovak **8** Croatian **9** Hungarian **10** Finno-Ugric

of Iceland: 5 Norse **9** Icelandic

of India: 4 Urdu **5** Hindi, Oriya, Tamil **6** Sindhi, Telugu **7** Bengali, English, Kannada, Malayam, Marathi, Punjabi **8** Assamese, Gujarati, Kashmiri, Sanskrit **9** Malayalam

of Indonesia: 5 Tetum **6** Bahasa, Igorot **7** English, Gyarung, Malayan **8** Balinese, Chamorro, Javanese, Madurese, Sudanese **10** Indonesian, Polynesian

of Iran: 4 Luri, Zend **5** Farsi, Turki **6** Arabic **7** Baluchi, Kurdish, Persian **8** Armenian **11** Azerbaijani

of Iraq: 5 Farsi **6** Arabic **7** Kurdish, Persian, Turkish

of Ireland: 4 Erse **5** Irish **6** Gaelic **7** English

of Israel: 6 Arabic, French, Hebrew **7** English

of Italy: 5 Ladin, Latin **6** French, German **7** Italian, Slovene **8** Friulian **9** Sardinian

of Ivory Coast: 4 Akan **6** Dioula, French

of Jamaica: 6 Creole **7** English

of Japan: 5 Kanto **8** Japanese

of Java: 4 Kavi, Kawi **5** Malay **6** Sassak **8** Balinese, Madurese, Sudanese **16** Bahasa Indonesian

of Jordan: 6 Arabic

of Kazakhstan: 6 Kazakh

of Kenya: 3 Luo **5** Bantu, Luhya, Masai **6** Kikuyu **7** English, Swahili **8** Buyerati **10** Hindustani

of Kiribati: 6 Samoan **7** English **10** Gilbertese

of Korea: 6 Korean

of Kuwait: 6 Arabic

of Kyrgyzstan: 6 Turkic **7** Kirghiz

of Laos: 3 Lao, Man, Meo **6** French **7** English

of Latvia: 7 Lettish

of Lebanon: 6 Arabic, French, Syriac **7** English, Turkish **8** Armenian

of Lesotho: 5 Sotho **7** English, Sesotho

of Liberia: 3 Kru, Kwa **5** Mande **7** English

of Libya: 6 Arabic, Berber **7** English, Italian

of Liechtenstein: 6 German **10** Alemannish

of Lithuania: 5 Zmudz **6** Baltic **10** Lithuanian

of Luxembourg: 6 French, German **7** English **13** Letzeburgesch

of Macao: 7 Chinese, English **9** Cantonese **10** Portuguese
of Macedonia: 10 Macedonian
of Madagascar/Malagasy Republic: 6 French **8** Malagasy, Malgache
of Malawi: 3 Yao **4** Cewa **5** Bantu, Ngoni, Tonga **6** Nyanja **7** English, Tumbuka **8** Chichewa **10** Chitumbuka
of Malaysia: 4 Bugi, Dyak **5** Malay, Tamil **6** Battok, Rejang **7** Chinese, English, Lampong, Niasese **8** Achinese, Javanese, Makassar **14** Bahasa Malaysia
of Maldives: 6 Arabic, Divehi
of Mali: 5 Dogon, Dyula, Feulh, Mande, Marka **6** Berber, French, Fulani **7** Bambara, Malinke, Senoufo, Songhai
of Malta: 7 English, Italian, Maltese
of Mauritania: 4 Fula **5** Wolof **6** Arabic, French **7** Phoolor, Tukulor **8** Fulfulde, Mandingo **9** Sarakolle **10** Hassaniyya
of Mauritius: 4 Urdu **5** Hindi, Tamil **6** Creole, French **7** English
of Mexico: 5 Mayan, Otomi **6** Mixtec **7** Mazahua, Mazatec, Nahuatl, Spanish, Totonac, Zapotec **8** Tarascan
of Moldova: 8 Romanian **9** Moldovian
of Monaco: 6 French **7** English, Italian **10** Monegasque
of Mongolia: 6 Kazakh **16** Khalkha Mongolian
of Montenegro: 13 Serbo-Croatian
of Morocco: 6 Arabic, Berber, French **7** Spanish
of Mozambique: 3 Yao **5** Makua **6** Nyanji, Thonga **7** Swahili **10** Portuguese
of Myanmar: 3 Lai **4** Chin, Kuki, Pegu, Shan **5** Karen **6** Kachin **7** Burmese
of Namibia: 5 Bantu **6** German **7** English, Khoisan **9** Afrikaans
of Nauru: 7 English, Nauruan
of Nepal: 6 Nepali, Newari **7** English
of the Netherlands: 5 Dutch **7** English, Frisian
of New Guinea: 4 Motu **7** English **16** Melanesian Pidgin
of New Zealand: 5 Maori **7** English
of Nicaragua: 7 English, Spanish
of Niger: 5 Hausa, Mande **6** Djerma, French, Fulani, Tuareg **8** Mandingo, Tamashek
of Nigeria: 3 Ibo **4** Efik, Igbo **5** Hausa **6** Yoruba **7** English
of Norway: 4 Lapp **5** Norse **6** Bokmal **7** Nynorsk, Riksmal **8** Landsmal, Samnorsk **9** Landsmaal, Norwegian
of Oman: 4 Urdu **5** Hindi **6** Arabic **7** Baluchi
of Pakistan: 4 Urdu **6** Pushtu, Sindhi **7** Baluchi, Bengali, English, Punjabi
of Panama: 7 English, Spanish
of Paraguay: 6 German **7** Guarani, Spanish
of Peru: 6 Aymara **7** English, Quechua, Spanish
of the Philippines: 4 Moro **5** Bicol, Bikol **6** Ibanag **7** Cebuano, English, Ilocano, Spanish, Tagalog, Visayan **8** Filipino **9** Pampangan, Philipino **10** Samar-Leyte **13** Bamboo-English **14** Panay-Hiligayon
of Poland: 6 Kaszub, Polish **10** Pomeranian
of Polynesia: 4 Niue, Uvea **5** Maori **6** Samoan, Tongan **7** Austral, Tagalog, Tokelau **8** Hawaiian, Tahitian **9** Marquesan, Tuamatuan **10** Mangarevan
of Portugal: 10 Portuguese
of Qatar: 6 Arabic
of Romania: 6 French, Magyar **7** Russian **8** Romanian, Rumanian **9** Hungarian
of Russia: 5 Evenk **6** Buriat, Kalmyk **7** Finnish, Russian **8** Ossetian
of Rwanda: 6 French **7** Swahili **11** Kinyarwanda
of Samoa: 6 Samoan **7** English
of San Marino: 7 Italian
of Sao Tome and Principe: 10 Portuguese
of Sardinia: 7 Italian
of Saudi Arabia: 6 Arabic
of Scotland: 4 Erse **6** Celtic, Gaelic, Keltic, Lallan **7** English, Lalland
of Senegal: 5 Wolof **6** French
of the Seychelles: 6 Creole, French **7** English
of Sierra Leone: 4 Krio **5** Limba, Mende, Mendi, Temne **6** Creole **7** English
of Singapore: 5 Malay, Tamil **7** Chinese, English **8** Mandarin
of Slovakia: 6 Slovik Slovak
of Slovenia: 7 Slovene
of the Solomon Islands: 7 English **13** Pidgin English **16** Melanesian Pidgin
of Somalia: 6 Arabic, Somali **7** English, Italian
of South Africa: 4 Taal, Zulu **5** Bantu, Hindi, Nguni, Sotho, Swazi, Tamil, Venda, Xhosa **6** Telegu, Thonga **7** English, Khoisan, Ndebele, Sesotho **8** Bujarati, Fanakalo **9** Afrikaans **13** Kitchen-Kaffir
of Spain: 6 Basque **7** Catalan, Spanish **8** Balearic, Galician **9** Castilian, Valencian
of Sri Lanka: 4 Pali **5** Tamil **7** English **9** Sinhalese
of Sudan: 2 Ga **3** Efe, Ewe, Ibo, Kru, Vak, Vei **4** Efik, Mole, Tshi **6** Arabic, Nubian, Yoruba **7** English **8** Mandango, Mandingo **9** Ta Bedawie
of Suriname: 5 Carib, Dutch, Hindi **6** Arawak **7** English **8** Javanese, Taki-Taki **10** Hindustani **11** Sranan Tongo **12** Sranang Tongo
of Swaziland: 5 Ngumi **7** English, Siswati **9** Afrikaans **10** Portuguese
of Sweden: 4 Lapp **7** Swedish
of Switzerland: 5 Ladin **6** French, German **7** Italian **8** Romansch **14** Switzerdeutsch
of Syria: 6 Arabic, French, Syriac **7** Aramaic, English, Kurdish, Turkish **8** Armenian
of Taiwan: 4 Amon, Amoy **5** Hakka, Kuo Yu **6** Minnan **9** Taiwanese **15** Mandarin Chinese
of Tajikistan: 5 Tajik **7** Tadzhik
of Tanzania: 5 Bantu **6** Arabic **7** English, Khoisan, Nilotic, Swahili **8** Cushitic, Gujarati
of Thailand: 3 Lao, Tai **4** Ahom, Shan, Thai **5** Kadai **7** Bangkok, English **9** Krung Thep **12** Chinese Malay
of Tibet: 5 Balti **6** Ladkhi **7** Bhutani, Bodskad **8** Sanskrit **9** Bhutanese
of Togo: 3 Ana, Ewe, Twi **4** Mina **5** Hausa **6** French, Kabrai, Kabrie **7** Bassari, Dagomba, Quatchi **8** Kotokoli, Lotocoli
of Tonga: 6 Tongan **7** English
of Trinidad and Tobago: 6 French **7** Chinese, English, Spanish **10** Portuguese **12** French Patois
of Tunisia: 6 Arabic, Berber, French
of Turkey: 6 Arabic **7** Kurdish, Turkish
of Turkmenistan: 6 Turkic **10** West Turkic
of Tuvalu: 6 Samoan **7** English **8** Tuvaluan **10** Polynesian
of Uganda: 5 Ateso, Ganda **7** English, Luganda, Swahili
of Ukraine: 9 Ukrainian
of United Arab Emirates: 5 Farsi **6** Arabic **7** English, Persian
of Uruguay: 7 Italian, Spanish
of Uzbekistan: 5 Uzbek
of Vanuatu: 6 French **7** Bislama, English **16** Melanesian Pidgin
of Venezuela: 4 Pume **7** Spanish
of Vietnam: 3 Yue **4** Cham **5** Khmer, Rhade **6** French **7** Chinese, English **9** Cantonese **10** Vietnamese
of Wales: 5 Welsh **6** Celtic, Cymric, Keltic, Kymric **7** Cymraeg, English
of Western Sahara: 16 Hassaniyya Arabic
of Western Samoa: 6 Samoan **7** English
of Yemen: 6 Arabic
of Yugoslavia: 7 Bosnian, Slovene **8** Albanian, Croatian **9** Hungarian, Slovenian **10** Macedonian **11** Montenegrin **13** Herzegovinian, Serbo-Croatian
of Zaire: 5 Bantu **6** French **7** Chiluba, Kikongo, Lingala, Swahili **8** Sudanese, Tshiluba
of Zambia: 4 Lozi **5** Bemba, Lunda, Tonga **6** Luvale, Nyanja **7** English **9** Afrikaans
of Zimbabwe: 3 Ila **5** Bantu, Shona **7** English, Ndebele

language, artificial
of James Cooke Brown: 6 Loglan

of Hans Freudenthal: 6 Lincos **13** Lingua Cosmica
of Alexander Gode: 11 Interlingua
of C K Ogden: 12 Basic English
of J M Schleyer: 7 Volapuk
of Jean Francois Sudre: 8 Solresol
of L L Zamehof: 9 Esperanto

language, extinct 6 Dacian, Hattic, Lycian, Lydian, Palaic **7** Cornish, Elamite, Hittite, Hurrian **8** Etruscan, Illyrian, Phrygian, Sumerian, Thracian, Urartian **9** Dalmatian **15** Cuneiform Luwian **18** Hieroglyphic Luwian

languid 4 dull, slow, weak **5** faint, heavy, inert, shaky, spent, weary **6** feeble, infirm, leaden, sickly, supine, torpid **7** rickety, unsound, worn-out **8** drooping, fatigued, inactive, lifeless, listless, sluggish, unstable **9** apathetic, declining, doddering, enervated, exhausted, inanimate, lethargic, trembling, unhealthy **10** indisposed, spiritless **11** debilitated **12** on the decline **13** lackadaisical

languidness 6 apathy, torpor **7** inertia **8** lethargy **12** listlessness, sluggishness **13** indisposition

languish 3 ebb **4** fade, fail, flag, wane, wilt **5** covet, droop, faint **6** desire, hunger, sicken, thirst, wither **7** dwindle, long for, pine for, sigh for **8** diminish, give away, take sick, yearn for **9** become ill, break down, hanker for, hunger for, thirst for, waste away **10** go downhill **11** deteriorate, have a yen for, hunger after **12** be desirous of **13** go into decline

Languish, Lydia
character in: 9 The Rivals
author: 8 Sheridan

languor 5 ennui **6** torpor **7** inertia **8** dullness, hebetude, lethargy **9** indolence, lassitude, torpidity, weariness **10** dispassion, dreaminess **11** languidness, leisureness **12** lifelessness, listlessness, sluggishness

lank 4 bony, lean, limp, thin **5** gaunt, spare **6** skinny, slight **7** angular, scrawny **8** straight

lanky 4 bony, lean **5** gaunt, gawky, rangy, spare, weedy **6** skinny **7** angular, scrawny **8** gangling, rawboned **11** tall and thin

La Nouvelle Heloise
author: 10 J J Rousseau

Lansbury, Angela
born: 6 London **7** England
roles: 4 Mame **8** Gaslight **10** JB Fletcher **11** Sweeney Todd **14** Murder She Wrote **15** Jessica Fletcher **22** The Manchurian Candidate

Laocoon
vocation: 6 priest
father: 5 Priam
mother: 6 Hecuba
sons: 3 two (unnamed)
warned: 7 Trojans

warned of: 11 Trojan horse
killed by: 11 sea serpents

Laomedon
king of: 4 Troy
father: 4 Ilus
wife: 6 Strymo
son: 5 Priam **6** Lampus **7** Clytius **8** Hicetaon, Tithonus
daughter: 7 Hesione **8** Themiste

Laos
other name: 7 Lan Xang **23** land of a million elephants
capital/largest city: 9 Viengchan, Vientiane
others: 4 Nape **5** Pakse, Xieng **6** Paklay **7** Thakhek **11** Savannakhet, Xiang Khoang **12** Luang Prabang **14** Louangphrabang
school: 12 Sisavangvong
measure: 3 bak
monetary unit: 2 at **3** att, kip
mountain: 3 Lai, Loi, San **4** Copi, Khat **5** Atwat **6** Khoung, Tiubia **15** Annam Cordillera
highest point: 3 Bia **7** Phou Bia
river: 3 Noi **4** Done **5** Khong **6** Mekong, Sebang
physical feature:
　plain: 4 Jars
　plateau: 8 Bolovens
people: 2 Lu **3** Kha, Lao, Man, Meo, Tai, Yao, Yun **4** Miao, Thai **5** Hmong **8** Lao Teung **10** Phoutheung
　leader: 7 Fa Ngoun **13** Souphanouvong **14** Souligna Vongsa, Souvanna Phouma
language: 3 Lao, Man, Meo **6** French **7** English
religion: 7 animism **8** Buddhism **17** Theravada Buddhism
feature:
　Buddhist priest: 5 bonze
　Communist guerrilla group: 9 Pathet Lao
　musical instrument: 5 khene
　temple: 3 wat
　trail: 9 Ho Chi Minh

Laothoe
concubine of: 5 Priam
son: 6 Lycaon **9** Polydorus

Lao-tzu, Lao-tze, Lao-Tse, Lao-tsze
author of: 10 Tao Te Ching
founder of: 6 Taoism

lap 3 sip **4** lick, wash **5** awash, drink, plash, slosh **6** babble, bubble, gurgle, lick up, murmur, ripple, splash, tongue

La Paz
administrative capital of: 7 Bolivia

Laphria
epithet of: 7 Artemis

Laphystius
epithet of: 4 Zeus

lapidary 11 stonecutter
expert in: 4 gems

lapis lazuli 9 azure-blue **17** semiprecious stone

species: 8 lazurite
source: 10 Badakhshan **11** Afghanistan

Laplace, Pierre S
field: 7 physics **9** astronomy
nationality: 6 French
hypothesis of: 18 nebular solar system

Lapland
region of: 6 Norway, Sweden **7** Finland
peninsula: 4 Kola
native: 4 Lapp
herders of: 8 reindeer

lapse 3 gap, sag **4** drop, fall, flaw, go by, loss, sink, slip, stop, wane **5** boner, break, cease, droop, error, fault, pause, slump **6** breach, elapse, expire, hiatus, laxity, pass by, period, recede, recess, run out, slip by, wither, worsen **7** blunder, decline, descent, failing, failure, faux pas, interim, passage, relapse, respite, subside **8** collapse, downfall, elapsing, interval, omission, slip away **9** backslide, disregard, interlude, oversight, slump down, terminate **10** degenerate, falling off, forfeiture, infraction, negligence, peccadillo, regression **11** backsliding, delinquency, dereliction, deteriorate, shortcoming **12** degeneration, intermission, interruption, lose validity **13** deterioration, process of time, slight mistake **14** become obsolete, fall into disuse

lapsus linguae 16 a slip of the tongue

Laputa 12 Flying Island
inhabitants: 11 visionaries
in: Gulliver's Travels

lar *see* **5** lares

Lara
character in: 9 Dr Zhivago
author: 9 Pasternak

larboard 8 left side
same as: 4 port

larceny 5 fraud, theft **7** bilking, forgery, looting, robbery, sacking **8** burglary, cheating, fleecing, stealing **9** extortion, pilferage, pilfering, swindling **10** absconding, peculation, plagiarism, purloining **11** defalcation, depredation **12** embezzlement, grand larceny, petit larceny, petty larceny, safecracking **13** appropriation, housebreaking **16** misappropriation

larder 5 cuddy **6** pantry, spence **7** buttery **8** food room **9** stillroom, storeroom **10** supply room **11** storage room

Lardner, Ring
author of: 11 The Love Nest, You Know Me Al **12** Treat Em Rough **16** Gullible's Travels

Larentalia
origin: 5 Roman
event: 8 festival

lares

form: 7 spirits
watched over: 5 house **6** hearth **9** community **10** crossroads
single member: 3 lar
companions: 7 penates
correspond to: 8 Dioscuri

large 3 big, fat **4** high, huge, vast, wide **5** ample, broad, grand, great, heavy, hulky, obese, plump, roomy **6** goodly, mighty, portly, rotund **7** copious, immense, liber- al, massive, sizable **8** colossal, enormous, gigantic, imposing, man-sized, outsized, spacious, sweeping, towering **9** boundless, capacious, expansive, extensive, giantlike, kingsized, limitless, monstrous, overgrown, ponderous, strapping, unlimited, unstinted **10** exorbitant, gargantuan, stupendous **11** extravagant, far- reaching, magnificent, substantial **12** considerable **13** comprehensive **14** Brobdingnagian

large-hearted 8 generous **10** altruistic, benevolent, charitable **12** humanitarian **13** philanthropic

largely 6 mainly, mostly, widely **7** chiefly, greatly **9** generally, primarily **10** on the whole **11** extensively, principally **12** considerably **13** predominantly, substantially **14** for the most part, to a great extent

large-scale 3 big **4** epic, huge, vast, wide **5** broad, great **6** all-out, heroic, mighty **8** colossal, far-flung, gigantic **9** extensive, monstrous **10** gargantuan, stupendous, tremendous **11** far-reaching, wide-ranging **15** allencompassing

largess, largesse 3 aid **4** boon, gift, help **5** favor, mercy **6** bounty, reward **7** charity, payment **8** bestowal, donation, gratuity, kindness, offering **9** benignity **10** assistance, generosity **11** benefaction, benevolence **12** philanthropy, remuneration

large store 8 emporium **11** supermarket **15** department store

largo
music: 4 slow **14** dignified tempo

lark 3 gag **4** game, jape, romp, whim **5** antic, caper, fling, prank, spree, trick **6** frolic, gambol **7** caprice **8** escapade **11** high old time **12** sportiveness
group of: 10 exaltation

larkspur 9 Consolida **10** Delphinium
varieties: 4 Tall **5** Dwarf **6** Rocket

La Rochefoucauld, Francois
author of: 6 Maxims **7** Maximes

larva
insect stage after: 3 egg
insect stage before: 4 pupa
legless: 6 maggot

lascivious 4 foul, lewd **5** bawdy, dirty, gross, lurid **6** coarse, filthy, impure, rib- ald, sordid, vulgar, wanton **7** immoral, lustful, obscene, ruttish, squalid **8** depraved, immodest, im-

proper, indecent, prurient **9** lecherous, salacious, shameless **10** indelicate, licentious, unblushing **11** dirty-minded, unwholesome

lash 3 fix, hit, tie **4** beat, bind, blow, flog, moor, rope, whip **5** brace, curse, flail, hitch, knock, leash, pound, scold, smack, strap, thong, tie up, truss **6** attach, be- rate, buffet, fasten, hammer, pinion, revile, secure, strike, stroke, tether, thrash, whip up **7** lecture, scourge, upbraid **8** lambaste, make fast **9** castigate, horsewhip **10** take to task, tongue-lash **11** rail against **13** cat-o'- nine-tails

Lash, Joseph P
author of: 18 Eleanor and Franklin

lashed together 4 tied **5** bound **6** tied up **7** secured, trussed **8** fastened

lash out at 5 fly at **6** assail, attack, strike **8** fall upon

Las Palmas
capital of: 13 Canary Islands

lass 4 girl, maid, miss **5** wench **6** damsel, female, lassie, lovely, maiden, pretty, virgin **7** colleen **10** schoolgirl, young woman

Lasser, Louise
father: 8 S J Lasser
husband: 10 Woody Allen
born: 9 New York NY
roles: 22 Mary Hartman Mary Hartman

lassie 4 girl, lass, maid **6** maiden **7** colleen **10** young woman

Lassie
character: 5 Timmy **9** Doc Weaver **10** Jeff Miller, Paul Martin, Ruth Martin **11** Corey Stuart, Ellen Miller **12** Gramps Miller **17** Sylvester (Porky) Brockway
cast: 10 Jan Clayton, Jon Provost, Jon Shepodd, Robert Bray **11** Arthur Space, Tommy Rettig **12** Donald Keeler, June Lockhart **14** Cloris Leachman, George Chandler **15** George Cleveland
type of dog: 6 collie

lassitude 5 ennui **6** apathy, torpor **7** boredom, fatigue, inertia, languor, malaise **8** debility, doldrums, dullness, lethargy, weakness **9** faintness, indolence, tiredness, torpidity, weariness **10** droopiness, drowsiness, enervation, exhaustion, feebleness, supineness **11** languidness, prostration **12** indifference, lack of energy, listlessness, sluggishness

lasso 4 lash, rope **5** catch, noose, reata, riata, thong **6** lariat

last 3 end **4** go on, keep, live, stay, wear **5** abide, after, exist, final, stand **6** behind, ending, endure, extend, finale, finish, hold on, hold up, remain, utmost **7** carry on, closing, extreme, finally, hold out, outlive, outwear, persist, stand up, subsist, survive, tail-

ing **8** at the end, continue, doomsday, farthest, final one, furthest, hindmost, hold good, in back of, maintain, rearmost, terminal, terminus, trailing, ultimate **9** in the rear, persevere **10** Armageddon, concluding, conclusion, conclusive, eventually, terminally, ultimately **11** crack of doom, crucial time **12** in conclusion, tagging along **13** Day of Judgment
French: 7 dernier

Last Analysis, The
author: 10 Saul Bellow

Last Days of Pompeii, The
author: 18 Edward Bulwer-Lytton
character: 4 Ione **5** Nydia **7** Arbaces, Glaucus **9** Apaecides

Last Frontier
nickname of: 6 Alaska

lasting 4 firm **5** fixed, solid **7** abiding, chronic, durable, eternal **8** constant, enduring, immortal, lifelong, longterm **9** incessant, lingering, long-lived, permanent, perpetual, steadfast, unceasing **10** continuing, deep-rooted, deep-seated, perdurable, persistent, protracted **11** established, neverending **12** indissoluble **14** indestructible, of long duration **17** firmly established

Last Lion, The
author: 17 William Manchester

lastly 6 at last **7** finally, to sum up **8** after all, in the end **10** on the whole **12** in conclusion **19** all things considered **33** taking everything into consideration

Last of the Barons, The
author: 18 Edward Bulwer-Lytton

Last of the Mohicans, The
author: 19 James Fenimore Cooper
character: 5 Magua, Uncas **9** Cora Munro **10** Alice Munro **11** Natty Bumppo **12** Chingachgook **18** Major Duncan Heyward

last part 3 end **6** ending, finale, finish **8** third act **10** denouement **12** final chapter

Last Picture Show, The
director: 16 Peter Bogdanovich
based on story by: 13 Larry McMurtry
cast: 10 Ben Johnson **11** Jeff Bridges **12** Ellen Burstyn **13** Eileen Brennan **14** Cloris Leachman, Cybill Shepherd, Timothy Bottoms
Oscar for: 15 supporting actor (Johnson) **17** supporting actress (Leachman)

Last Puritan, The
author: 15 George Santayana

La Strada
director: 15 Federico Fellini
cast: 11 Aldo Silvana **12** Anthony Quinn **15** Giulietta Masina, Richard Basehart

score: 8 Nino Rota
Oscar for: 11 foreign film
last resort
  French: 8 pis aller
Last Tango in Paris
  director: 18 Bernardo Bertolucci
  cast: 12 Marlon Brando **14** Maria Schneider
Last Things
  author: 6 C P Snow
Last Valley, The
  author: 11 A B Guthrie Jr
Last Waltz, The
  director: 14 Martin Scorsese
  cast: 7 The Band **8** Bob Dylan **9** Neil Young **10** The Staples **11** Eric Clapton, Muddy Waters, Neil Diamond, Van Morrison **12** Joni Mitchell **13** Emmylou Harris
last word
  French: 10 dernier cri
latch 3 bar **4** bolt, clip, hasp, hook, lock, loop, shut, snap **5** catch, clamp, close **6** buckle, button, clinch, fasten, secure **8** make fast **9** fastening
late 3 new **4** dead, gone, slow **5** fresh, tardy **6** held up, put off, recent **7** delayed, newborn, overdue, tardily **8** departed, detained, dilatory, passed on **9** after time, postponed **10** behindhand, behind time, dilatorily, unpunctual **16** recently deceased
late arrival 7 laggard **8** lateness, newcomer **9** immigrant, latecomer, tardiness **16** Johnny-come-lately
Late George Apley, The
  author: 10 J P Marquand
lately 6 of late **7** just now **8** latterly, recently, right now **9** currently, presently, yesterday **10** not long ago **13** a short time ago
Late Mattia Pascal, The
  author: 15 Luigi Pirandello
latency 8 abeyance, deferral, dormancy, inaction **10** quiescence, suspension
Late Night with David Letterman
  feature: 11 Ask Mr Melman **15** Stupid Pet Tricks **18** Brush with Greatness, Stupid People Tricks
  bandleader: 10 Paul Shafer
  city: 7 New York
latent 6 covert, hidden **7** abeyant, dormant, lurking, passive **8** inactive, sleeping **9** concealed, potential, quiescent, suspended, unaroused, unexposed **10** in abeyance, intangible, unapparent, unrealized **11** not manifest, undeveloped, unexpressed **13** inconspicuous
later 4 next **5** since **6** behind, in time, mature **7** ensuing, tardily **8** in a while, in sequel **9** afterward, following, presently, thereupon **10** consequent, more re- cent, most recent, subsequent, succeeding, successive,

thereafter **11** after a while, consecutive **12** subsequently, successively, toward the end
lateral 4 side **5** sided **7** flanked, oblique, sloping **8** edgeways, edgewise, flank- ing, sidelong, sideward, sideways, sidewise, skirting, slanting
latest fashion
  French: 10 dernier cri
lather 4 foam, head, scum, soap, suds **5** froth, spume, sweat **6** soap up **8** make foam, soapsuds **9** make froth **11** shaving foam
Latin
  language family: 12 Indo-European
  branch: 6 Italic
  group: 7 Romance
  subgroup: 6 French **7** Catalan, Italian, Romansh, Spanish **8** Romanian **9** Provencal **10** Portuguese **13** Rhaeto- Romanic
Latino, Latina 8 Hispanic **13** Latin American
Latinus
  king of: 6 Latium
  father: 6 Faunus
  mother: 6 Marica
  wife: 5 Amata
  daughter: 7 Lavinia
latitude 5 range, scope, sweep **6** leeway, margin **7** license **8** free play **9** amplitude, elbowroom, full swing **10** indulgence, liberality **11** opportunity, unrestraint **12** independence **15** freedom of action, freedom of choice **16** unrestrictedness
Latona *see* **4** Leto
La Tour, Georges de
  born: 3 Vic **6** France **8** Lorraine
  artwork: 7 Peasant **10** The New Born **12** Peasant's Wife, The Card Cheat **15** St Peter Penitent **16** The Fortune Teller **18** The Denial of St Peter **23** The Education of the Virgin **31** St Sebastian Tended by the Holy Women
Latrobe, Benjamin Henry
  architect of: 9 US Capitol **15** Sedgeley Mansion (PA) **18** Baltimore Cathedral **22** Philadelphia Waterworks
  style: 12 Greek Revival, Neoclassical **13** Gothic Revival
latter 3 end **4** last **5** final, later **6** ending, latest, modern **7** ensuing **8** terminal **10** most recent, subsequent, succeeding, successive **13** last-mentioned **15** second-mentioned
lattice 4 fret, grid **5** frame, grate **6** grille, screen **7** framing, grating, network, trellis, webwork **8** fretwork, openwork **9** framework, reticulum **11** trelliswork **12** reticulation
Latvia
  former name: 30 Latvian Soviet Socialist Republic
  capital/largest city: 4 Riga
  others: 5 Cesis, Libau **6** Dvinsk, Li-

bava, Tukums **7** Jelgava, Jurmala, Liepaja, Rezekne **8** Dunaberg, Dunaburg, Valmiera **9** Ventspils **10** Daugavpils
  government: 8 republic
  measure: 3 let **4** stof **5** stoff, verst **6** arshin, kulmet **7** verchoc, verchok **8** krouchka, pourvete **9** deciatine, lofstelle, pourvette **10** tonnseteel
  monetary unit: 3 lat **4** latu **6** rublis, santim **7** kapeika, santima
  weight: 9 liespfund
  lake: 7 Aluksne
  river: 4 Ogre **5** Gauja, Venta **6** Salaca **7** Daugava, Lielupe **12** Western Dvina
  sea: 6 Baltic
  physical feature:
    cape: 8 Domesnes
    gulf: 4 Riga
    strait: 4 Irbe
  people: 3 Kur, Liv **4** Balt, Cour, Lett **7** Latgale, Latvian, Russian, Zemgale
    former ruler: 15 Teutonic Knights
  language: 7 Lettish
  religion: 8 Lutheran **13** Roman Catholic
laud 5 extol, honor **6** praise **7** acclaim, commend, glorify
laudable 5 model, noble **8** sterling **9** admirable, estimable, excellent, exemplary **10** creditable **11** commendable, meritorious **12** praiseworthy **13** unimpeachable **17** deserving of esteem **18** worthy of admiration
laudation 6 praise **7** acclaim **8** applause, approval **11** approbation **12** commendation
laudatory 8 admiring, honoring, praising **9** adulatory, approving, extolling, favorable **10** eulogistic, eulogizing, flattering, glorifying **11** acclamatory, approbatory, celebratory, encomiastic, panegyrical **12** commendatory **13** complimentary
laugh 4 glee, ha-ha, ho-ho, howl, roar **5** mirth **6** cackle, giggle, guffaw, titter **7** break up, chortle, chuckle, snicker, snigger **10** bellylaugh, horselaugh **12** express mirth **14** roll in the aisle, split one's sides
laughable 5 comic, dopey, droll, funny, inane, merry, silly, witty **6** absurd, stupid **7** amusing, asinine, comical, foolish, risible **8** farcical, tickling **9** diverting, grotesque, hilarious, ludicrous **10** outlandish, outrageous, ridiculous **11** rib-tickling **12** preposterous **13** sidesplitting
Laugh-In, Rowan & Martin's
  regular: 8 Dan Rowan **9** Gary Owens, Judy Carne, Ruth Buzzi **10** Dick Martin, Goldie Hawn, Larry Hovis, Lily Tomlin **11** Arte Johnson, Henry Gibson **12** Jo Anne Worley **13** Eileen Brennan
  saying: 10 Sock it to me **15** Here

come de judge, You bet your bippy **24** Beautiful downtown Burbank **31** Look that up in your Funk and Wagnalls

laughingstock 3 ass **4** butt, dupe, fool, joke **8** fair game **11** figure of fun

laugh off 6 deride **7** dismiss, put down **8** belittle, ridicule **9** disparage

laughter 3 joy **4** glee **5** mirth **6** gaiety **7** jollity, revelry **8** hilarity **9** joviality, merriment **11** merrymaking **12** conviviality, exhilaration

Laughton, Charles
  wife: 14 Elsa Lanchester
  born: 7 England **11** Scarborough
  roles: 9 Rembrandt **10** Jamaica Inn **13** Les Miserables **15** Ruggles of Red Gap, The Paradine Case **16** Advise and Consent **17** Mutiny on the Bounty **23** Barretts of Wimpole Street, The Hunchback of Notre Dame **24** Witness for the Prosecution **25** The Private Life of Henry VIII (Oscar)

launch 4 fire, hurl **5** begin, eject, float, found, impel, shoot, start, throw **6** let fly, propel, unveil **7** fire off, project, send off **8** catapult, initiate, premiere, put to sea **9** cast forth, discharge, establish, institute, introduce, set afloat **10** embark upon, inaugurate, set forth on **11** set in mo- tion, venture upon **13** thrust forward **15** set into the water

launder 4 soak, wash **5** clean, rinse, scour, scrub **7** cleanse, wash out **11** wash and iron

Launfal
  knight of: 10 round table

Laura
  director: 13 Otto Preminger
  cast: 11 Clifton Webb, Dana Andrews, Gene Tierney **12** Vincent Price **14** Judith Anderson

laurel 6 Kalmia, Laurus **13** Laurus nobilis **14** Ficus benjamina **15** Cordia alliodora
  varieties: 3 bog, pig **4** pale **5** black, dwarf, great, sheep **6** Alpine, cherry, ground, Indian, purple, Sierra, spurge, tropic **7** Chinese, English, red-twig, weeping, western **8** American, drooping, Himalaya, Japanese, mountain, Portugal **9** Tasmanian **10** Australian, California, variegated **11** Alexandrian

Laurel, Stan
  real name: 22 Arthur Stanley Jefferson
  partner: 11 Oliver Hardy
  born: 7 England **9** Ulverston
  roles: 8 Pardon Us **9** Saps at Sea **10** Way Out West

laurels 4 fame **5** award, glory, honor, kudos, prize **6** credit, praise, renown, reward **7** acclaim, tribute **8** accolade, applause, citation **9** celebrity **10** deco-

ration, popularity **11** acclamation, distinction, recognition **12** commendation **15** illustriousness

Laurie
  also: 16 Theodore Laurence
  character in: 11 Little Women
  author: 6 Alcott

laus Deo 11 praise to God **13** praise be to God

lavation 7 bathing, washing **8** ablution, cleaning **9** cleansing

lavender 4 herb, mint **5** aspic, behen, lilac, spick, spike **6** purple **7** inkroot **8** amethyst, stichado **9** lavendula
  represents: 6 purity
  uses: 6 sachet **7** perfume **8** medicine **9** cosmetics

laver 11 footed basin

Laverne and Shirley
  character: 12 Frank De Fazio **13** Carmine Ragusa, Lenny Kolowski, Mrs Edna Babish, Shirley Feeney **14** Laverne De Fazio **15** Andrew (Squiggy) Squiggman
  cast: 10 Eddie Mekka, Phil Foster **12** Betty Garrett, David L Lander **13** Cindy Williams, Michael McKean, Penny Marshall
  girls worked in: 12 Shotz Brewery
  theme song: 23 Making Our Dreams Come True
  spinoff from: 9 Happy Days

Lavinia
  father: 7 Latinus
  mother: 5 Amata
  husband: 6 Aeneas

lavish 4 free, lush, wild **5** plush, waste **6** shower **7** copious, opulent, pour out, profuse **8** abundant, effusive, generous, prodigal, squander **9** bounteous, bountiful, dissipate, excessive, exuberant, impetuous, luxuriant, plenteous, plentiful, sumptuous, unsparing **10** immoderate, munificent, profligate, unstinting **11** extravagant, fritter away, intemperate, overindulge, overliberal, spend freely **12** give overmuch, greathearted, overwhelming, unrestrained, without limit

lavishness 6 bounty **8** lushness, opulence **9** profusion **10** luxuriance **11** munificence, prodigality **12** extravagance, immoderation **13** bountifulness, plenteousness, sumptuousness

Lavoisier, Antoine
  field: 9 chemistry
  nationality: 6 French
  founder: 15 modern chemistry
  named: 6 oxygen **8** hydrogen

law 3 act **4** bill, code, fuzz, rule, writ **5** axiom, bylaw, canon, dogma, edict, model, truth **6** decree, police **7** justice, mandate, precept, statute, theorem **8** absolute, legality, standard **9** criterion, enactment, gendarmes, legal form, ordinance, postulate, principle **10** civil peace, convention, due proc-

ess, invariable, regulation **11** commandment, formulation, fundamental, orderliness, working rule **13** jurisprudence, standing order **14** generalization, rules of conduct **15** legal profession
  Latin: 3 jus
  goddess of: 4 Maat

law-abiding 6 honest **7** upright **9** honorable **10** aboveboard, principled

lawbreaker 3 con **4** hood, thug **5** crook, felon **6** outlaw **7** convict, culprit **8** criminal, jailbird, offender, scofflaw **9** miscreant, wrongdoer **10** delinquent, malefactor, recidivist **11** perpetrator **12** transgressor

lawful 3 due **5** legal, licit **6** proper, titled **7** allowed, granted **8** rightful **9** legalized, statutory, warranted **10** authorized, legitimate, prescribed **11** legitimized, permissible **15** legally entitled **16** legally permitted

lawless 6 unruly, wanton **7** chaotic, defiant, illegal, riotous, wayward **8** anarchic, mutinous, unlawful, wide open **9** insurgent, out of hand, unbridled **10** disorderly, licentious, rebellious, refractory, ungoverned **11** disobedient, lawbreaking, terroristic **12** disorganized, freewheeling, illegitimate, noncompliant, unrestrained **13** insubordinate, transgressive **14** uncontrollable

lawlessness 5 chaos **7** anarchy **8** disorder

lawn 4 park, turf, yard **5** glade, grass, sward **7** grounds, terrace **10** grassy plot, green field, greensward, meadowland **12** grassy ground

law of a place
  Latin: 7 lex loci

Law of Moses 5 Torah **10** Pentateuch **15** Ten Commandments

law of nations
  Latin: 10 jus gentium

law of nature
  Latin: 11 jus naturale

Lawrence, Carol
  real name: 16 Carol Maria Laraia
  husband: 12 Robert Goulet
  born: 13 Melrose Park IL
  roles: 5 Maria **13** West Side Story

Lawrence, D H
  author of: 10 The Rainbow **11** Women in Love **13** Sons and Lovers **20** Lady Chatterley's Lover

Lawrence, Ernest Orlando
  field: 7 physics
  invented: 9 cyclotron
  awarded: 10 Nobel Prize

Lawrence, Gertrude
  real name: 29 Alexandra Dagmar Lawrence Klasen
  born: 6 London **7** England
  roles: 9 Pygmalion **11** The King and I **17** The Glass Menagerie

Lawrence, T E
also: 16 Lawrence of Arabia
served in: 3 WWI **10** Arab Revolt
advisor to: 6 Faisal **12** Husayn Ibn Ali
fought against: 5 Turks **8** Ottomans
author of: 20 Seven Pillars of Wisdom

Lawrence of Arabia
director: 9 David Lean
cast: 10 Jose Ferrer, Omar Sharif **11** Claude Rains, Jack Hawkins, Peter O'Toole (T E Lawrence) **12** Alec Guin- ness, Anthony Quinn **13** Anthony Quayle
Oscar for: 7 picture **8** director **14** cinematography

Lawrence Welk Show, The
champagne lady: 8 Alice Lon **11** Norma Zimmer
cast: 7 Aladdin **11** Larry Hooper, Myron Floren **12** Bobby Burgess **13** Barbara Boylan, Lennon Sisters
Welk played: 9 accordion

lawyer 6 jurist, legist **7** counsel, shyster **8** advocate, attorney **9** barrister, counselor, solicitor **10** mouthpiece, prosecutor **11** pettifogger **12** legal advisor **14** special pleader **15** ambulance chaser

lax 4 hazy, limp, weak **5** agape, loose, slack, vague **6** casual, flabby, floppy, remiss **7** cryptic, flaccid, inexact, lenient, not firm, relaxed **8** careless, derelict, droop- ing, heedless, nebulous, slipshod, uncaring, yielding **9** confusing, imprecise, negligent, oblivious, undutiful, unheeding, unmindful **10** ill-defined, incoherent, neglectful, permissive **11** hanging open, indifferent, thoughtless, unconcerned **12** loosemuscled, unstructured **13** irresponsible **15** unconscientious

laxness 7 neglect **9** looseness, slackness **10** negligence **11** imprecision **12** carelessness, indifference

Laxness, Halldor Kiljan
author of: 12 Iceland's Bell **14** The Atom Station **17** Independent People **25** The Great Weaver from Kashmir
won: 10 Nobel Prize

lay 3 air, bet, put, set **4** bear, fell, fine, form, give, laic, lend, levy, make, plan, poem, raze, rest, seat, song, tune **5** align, allot, apply, ditty, exact, floor, hatch, level, offer, place, stage, wager **6** assess, assign, ballad, charge, demand, depict, devise, gamble, ground, hazard, impose, impute, laical, layout, locate, melody, repose, strain **7** amateur, arrange, concoct, contour, deposit, dispose, forward, present, produce, profane, proffer, refrain, secular, set down, situate, station **8** allocate, assemble, beat down, give odds, inexpert, organize, oviposit, position **9** attribute, elucidate, enunci-

ate, formulate, knock down, knock over, prostrate, roundelay, situation **10** cause to lie, topography **11** arrangement, disposition, nonclerical, orientation, put together **12** conformation **13** configuration, inexperienced, nonspecialist **14** partly informed, unprofessional **15** nonprofessional **17** nonecclesiastical

lay at the door of 6 assign **7** ascribe **8** charge to **9** attribute

lay bare 4 bare, show **6** expose, reveal, unmask, unveil, unwrap **7** divulge, exhibit, publish, uncover **8** disclose **9** broadcast, make known **10** make public **11** communicate

lay down arms 5 yield **6** give up **7** succumb **8** cry quits **9** surrender **10** capitulate **11** come to terms, sue for peace **13** declare a truce **17** acknowledge defeat

layer 3 bed, lap, ply **4** coat, fold, leaf, seam, slab, tier, zone **5** level, plate, scale, sheet, stage, story **6** lamina **7** stratum **9** thickness

layman 4 laic **6** sister **7** amateur, brother **8** outsider **9** churchman **10** catechumen **11** churchwoman, communicant, parishioner **15** nonprofessional **16** member of the flock

layoff 4 fire **6** firing, idling, ouster, the axe **7** dismiss, release, sacking, the boot, the gate, the sack **8** pink slip, shutdown **9** closedown, discharge, dismissal, hard times, the bounce **10** cashiering, depression, the heave-ho **11** furloughing, termination **12** unemployment **13** disemployment, walking papers **20** discharge temporarily

lay off 7 dismiss, forfeit, release, set free **8** get rid of, liberate **9** discharge, terminate **11** give the gate, send packing

Lay of the Last Minstrel, The
author: 14 Sir Walter Scott
character: 8 Margaret, The Dwarf **13** Lady Buccleuch, Lord Cranstoun **17** Master of Buccleuch **19** Ghost of Michael Scott **21** Sir William of Deloraine

lay on 6 bestow, confer, supply **7** present, provide

lay open 4 open **6** expose, open up **7** clarify **9** make plain **18** make understandable

layout 4 form, plan **5** chart, draft, dummy, model, motif, spend **6** design, expend, pay out, sketch, spread **7** diagram, drawing, fork out, outline, pattern **8** disburse, shell out **9** blueprint, delineate, placement, spread out, structure **11** arrangement, composition

lay waste 4 ruin **5** level, wreck **6** ravage **7** despoil, destroy, wipe out **8** demolish, desolate **9** devastate, eradicate **10** annihilate, obliterate

Lazarus 6 beggar
means: 8 God helps
sister: 4 Mary **6** Martha
hometown: 7 Bethany
resurrected by: 5 Jesus

Lazarus
author: 14 Leonid Andreyev

Lazarus, Mell
creator/artist: 5 Momma **9** Miss Peach

lazurite
variety: 11 lapis lazuli

lazy 3 lax **4** idle, slow **5** inert, slack **6** drowsy, sleepy, torpid **7** laggard, languid **8** inactive, indolent, listless, slothful, sluggish **9** apathetic, easygoing, lethargic, shiftless **10** languorous, slow-moving **13** unindustrious **15** unwilling to work

lazy person 5 drone, idler **6** loafer **14** good-for-nothing

l'chaim, l'chayim 5 toast **6** Hebrew, to life

Leachman, Cloris
born: 11 Des Moines IA
roles: 7 Phyllis **11** High Anxiety **12** Kiss Me Deadly **17** Young Frankenstein **18** Mary Tyler Moore Show, The Last Picture Show

lead 2 go **3** aim, top **4** clue, draw, edge, have, head, hero, hint, live, lure, pass **5** charm, excel, guide, model, outdo, pilot, steer, tempt **6** allure, convey, direct, en- tice, extend, induce, manage, margin, pursue, seduce **7** advance, attract, bring on, command, conduct, control, example, go first, incline, issue in, marshal, pioneer, precede, proceed, produce, stretch, surpass, undergo **8** domineer, go before, guidance, moderate, outstrip, persuade, priority, result in, shepherd, star part **9** advantage, come first, direction, go through, headliner, influence, plurality, rank first **10** branch into, experience, first place, indication, precedence, precedency, set the pace, show the way, tend toward **11** antecedence, be in advance, leading role, preside over, protagonist

lead
chemical symbol: 2 Pb
mineral: 10 fiedlerite
ore: 6 galena, pyrite

lead astray 4 dupe, lure **6** delude **7** beguile, deceive, ensnare, mislead **19** lead up the garden path

leaden 4 dark, dull, glum, gray **5** inert, murky **6** dreary, gloomy, numbed, somber, torpid **7** grayish, languid **8** burdened, careworn, darkened, deadened, listless, sluggish, unwieldy **9** depressed, inanimate **10** cumbersome, hard to move

leader 4 boss, guru, head **5** chief, guide, mogul **6** bigwig, honcho, master, mentor, tycoon **7** captain, foreman, kingpin, magnate, manager, pioneer, prophet **8** director, superior **9** chieftain, commander, conductor, godfather, pacemaker, patriarch **10** forerunner, pacesetter, pathfinder, supervisor **11** frontrunner, torchbearer, trailblazer

leadership 4 helm, lead, sway **5** reins, wheel **7** command, primacy **8** charisma, guidance, headship, hegemony **9** captaincy, supremacy **10** domination, mastership **11** managership, preeminence, stewardship **12** directorship, governorship, guardianship, self-reliance **13** ability to lead, self-assurance **14** administration **15** managerial skill, superintendency **17** authoritativeness

leading 3 top **4** head, main **5** basic, chief, first, great, prime **6** ruling **7** advance, guiding, initial, leadoff, notable, primary, ranking, stellar, supreme, topmost **8** advanced, dominant, foremost **9** directing, essential, governing, nonpareil, paramount, principal, prominent, sovereign, unrivaled **10** motivating, preeminent, underlying **11** controlling, outstanding, pacesetting **12** unchallenged, unparalleled **13** most important **14** quintessential **15** most influential, most significant

lead on 4 goad **5** egg on **6** entice **7** mislead, support **9** encourage **19** lead up the garden path

lead the way 4 lead, show, take **5** guide **6** escort **7** conduct

leaf 4 flip, foil, page, skim **5** blade, bract, folio, frond, green, inset, petal, sheet, thumb **6** browse, glance, insert, needle **7** foliole, lamella, leaflet **9** cotyledon, extension, turn green **10** lamination **12** sheet of metal
edge: **5** cross **7** crenate, dentate
angle: **4** axil
aperture: **5** stoma
kind: **5** calyx, petal, sepal **7** corolla

leaflet 2 ad **4** bill **5** flier, flyer, tract **6** folder, notice **7** booklet, handout **8** brochure, bulletin, circular, handbill, pamphlet **9** broadside, throwaway **10** broadsheet **12** announcement **13** advertisement

league 4 ally, band **5** cabal, group, guild, merge, union **6** cartel **7** combine, compact, company, network, society **8** alliance **9** coalition **10** conspiracy, federation, frater- nity, join forces **11** association, confederacy, confederate, consolidate, cooperative, partnership **13** collaboration, confederation, confraternity

Leah
means: **7** wild cow
father: **5** Laban
husband: **5** Jacob
sister: **6** Rachel

slave: **6** Zilpah
son: **4** Levi **5** Judah **6** Reuben, Simeon **7** Zebulun **8** Issachar
daughter: **5** Dinah
burial place: **9** Machpelah

leak 3 ebb, rip **4** blab, gash, hole, ooze, rent, rift, seep, vent **5** break, chink, cleft, crack, drain, exude, fault, spill **6** breach, efflux, escape, filter, let out, reveal, take in **7** confide, crevice, divulge, dribble, fissure, let slip, opening, outflow, rupture, seepage **8** aperture, disclose, draining, give away, puncture **9** discharge, percolate **10** interstice, make public **11** be permeable, perforation **12** admit leakage **16** let enter or escape

leakage 5 issue **7** outflow, seepage **9** discharge

Leakey, Louis S Bazett
field: **12** anthropology
discovered: **8** early man
worked at: **8** Tanzania **12** Olduvai Gorge
wife: **4** Mary
son: **7** Richard

lean 3 aim, bow, tip **4** bend, cant, lank, list, poor, rely, rest, slim, tend, thin, tilt **5** gaunt, lanky, lurch, scant, slant, slope, small, spare, weedy **6** barren, depend, meager, modest, nonfat, prefer, scanty, skinny, sparse, svelte **7** angular, count on, incline, recline, scraggy, scrawny, slender, spindly, trust in, willowy **8** exiguous, rawboned, resort to, skeletal **9** emaciated **10** inadequate, set store by **11** be partial to, have faith in, prop oneself **12** insufficient, seek solace in **14** rest one's weight, support oneself

Lean, David
director of: **10** Summertime **11** Oliver Twist **13** Doctor Zhivago, Ryan's Daughter **15** A Passage to India **16** Lawrence of Arabia (Oscar) **17** Great Expectations **23** The Bridge on the River Kwai (Oscar)

Leander
loved: **4** Hero
swam nightly: **10** Hellespont
death by: **8** drowning

leaning 4 bent, turn **5** slant **7** relying **8** affinity, tendency **9** proneness **10** dependence, partiality, preference, proclivity, propensity **11** inclination **14** predisposition

leap 3 hop **4** jete, jump, romp, rush, skip **5** bound, caper, frisk, vault **6** bounce, cavort, frolic, gambol, hasten, hurtle, prance, spring **7** hop over **8** jump over **9** bound over, saltation **10** hurtle over, jump across, spring over

Lear, Norman
TV producer of: **5** Maude **13** The Jeffersons **14** All in the Family

Learchus
father: **7** Athamas

mother: **3** Ino
killed by: **7** Athamas

learn 3 con **4** hear **6** detect, master, pick up **7** find out, uncover, unearth **8** discover, memorize **9** ascertain, determine, ferret out **10** become able **12** find out about

learned 4 deep, wise **7** erudite **8** cultured, educated, informed, lettered, literate, profound, schooled, well-read **9** scholarly **10** cultivated **12** accomplished, intellectual, well-educated **13** knowledgeable

Learned, Michael
roles: **5** Nurse **10** The Waltons

learner 4 tyro **5** pupil, tutee **6** novice, rookie **7** draftee, recruit, scholar, student, trainee **8** beginner, disciple, enlistee, follower, freshman, neophyte **9** fledgling, greenhorn, novitiate, proselyte, schoolboy **10** apprentice, schoolgirl, tenderfoot **11** schoolchild

learning 4 lore **5** study **6** wisdom **7** culture **8** teaching **9** education, erudition, knowledge, schooling **11** cultivation, edification, information, instruction, scholarship **13** comprehension, enlightenment, understanding

Learning
god of: **5** Thoth

Leary, Timothy
phrase: **19** Tune in, turn on, drop out

leash 4 curb, lead, line, rein, ruin **5** strap, thong **6** bridle, choker, fasten, hold in, stifle, string, tether **7** contain, control, harness **8** restrain, suppress

leatherneck 6 gyrene, marine

Leather-Stocking Tales
author: **19** James Fenimore Cooper
includes: **10** The Prairie **11** The Pioneers **13** The Deerslayer, The Pathfinder **20** The Last of the Mohicans
hero of: **7** Hawkeye **10** Pathfinder, The Trapper **11** Natty Bumppo **13** The Deerslayer **15** Leather-stocking **16** Le Longue Carabine

leave 2 go **3** fly **4** cede, exit, flee, jilt, keep, quit, will **5** allot, be off, cause, endow, forgo, going, split, waive, yield **6** assign, bug out, commit, decamp, depart, desert, eschew, forego, give up, legate, move on, recess, resign, retain, set out **7** abandon, abscond, bequest, consent, consign, deposit, entrust, forsake, holiday, let stay, liberty, parting, produce, push off, release, respite, retreat, sustain, take off, time off **8** approval, bequeath, farewell, furlough, generate, give over, maintain, result in, sanction, shove off, vacation **9** allowance, apportion, departure, hotfoot it, let remain, surrender, tolerance **10** concession, depart from, embark from, go away from, indulgence, permission, relinquish, retire from, sabbatical, sufferance, withdrawal **11** bid farewell, endorsement **13** absent oneself, understanding

leave a ship 4 land **6** debark **8** go ashore **9** disembark **11** abandon ship

leave behind 4 jilt **6** desert, vacate **7** abandon, discard, forsake **8** evacuate **9** cast aside **10** relinquish **11** outdistance

leave cold 4 bore **12** leave unmoved **15** leave unaffected

Leave It To Beaver
character: **11** June Cleaver, Ward Cleaver **12** Eddie Haskell, Wally Cleaver **13** Beaver (Theodore) Cleaver
cast: **7** Tony Dow **9** Ken Osmond **12** Hugh Beaumont, Jerry Mathers **18** Barbara Billingsley

leave off 3 end **4** halt, quit, stop **5** cease **6** desist, finish **7** suspend **8** conclude **11** discontinue, refrain from

leave out 4 drop, omit **6** except, reject **7** exclude

Leaves of Grass
author: **11** Walt Whitman

leave suddenly 3 fly **4** flee **6** cut out, decamp, run off **7** abscond, make off, run away, rush off, take off **11** take a powder **15** be off and running

leave-taking 4 exit **5** adieu **7** goodbye, leaving, parting, send-off **8** au revoir, farewell **9** departure **10** withdrawal

leave undone 4 quit **6** give up **7** abandon, forsake, neglect **8** give up on

Lebanon
ancient name: **9** Phoenicia
capital/largest city: **6** Beirut **8** Beyrouth
others: **3** Sur **4** Arca, Tyre **5** Ehden, Halba, Hamat, Sahle, Saida, Sayda, Sidon, Sofar, Zahla, Zahle **6** Byblos, Ghazir, Juniye, Tibnin **7** Baalbek, Batroun, Bsherri, Rachaya, Tripoli, Zgharta **8** Djezzine, El Hermel, Hasbaiya, Merjuyun **9** Broummana, Marjayoun **10** Beited Dine, Heliopolis
  ancient city: **8** Carthage
school: **4** Arab **8** American, Lebanese **11** Saint Joseph
division:
  ancient: **4** Tyre **5** Arwad, Sidon **6** Byblos, Jubayl
monetary unit: **5** livre, pound **7** piastre
lake: **5** Quran **6** Qirawn
mountain: **4** Mzar **5** Aruba **6** Hermon **7** Lebanon, Sannine **8** Kadischa, Kenisseh **9** Kennisseh **10** al- Mukammal **11** Anti-Lebanon
highest point: **7** es Sauda **13** Qurnat al-Sawda
river: **3** Dog, Joz **5** Barid, Kebir, Lycos **6** Auwali, Barada, Damour, Litani **7** Hasbani, Leontes, Orontes **8** Kasemieh

sea: **13** Mediterranean
physical feature:
  cape: **10** Pigeon Rock **11** Ras esh Shiqa **12** Qadisha Gorge
  plain: **4** Bika **5** Bekaa
  valley: **5** Beqaa **6** al-Biqa **9** Great Rift
  wind: **7** khamsin
people: **4** Arab **11** Palestinian
  ancient: **9** Canaanite **10** Phoenician
  leader: **6** Bashir, Sarkis **7** Chamoun **8** Franjieh **9** al-Din Maan **11** Amin Gemayel **13** Bashir Gemayel
  poet: **11** Kahlil Gibran
  rulers: **5** Arabs **6** French, Greeks, Romans **8** Hittites, Ottomans, Persians **9** Assyrians, Crusaders, Egyptians, Mamelukes **11** Babylonians
language: **6** Arabic, French, Syriac **7** English, Turkish **8** Armenian
religion: **5** Druse, Druze, Islam **8** Maronite, Melchite **10** Protestant **11** Monophysite **12** Christianity **13** Greek Catholic **14** Greek Orthodoxy **17** Armenian Orthodoxy
place:
  dam: **5** Qarun
  ruins: **7** Baalbek **15** Temple of Bacchus, Temple of Jupiter
feature:
  Christian group: **10** Phalangist
  dance: **6** dabkeh, dabkey
  tree: **5** cedar
food:
  dish: **6** kibbeh **8** tabouleh
  drink: **4** arak **6** arrack

Le Bel, Joseph Achille
field: **9** chemistry
nationality: **6** French
founded: **15** stereochemistry

Le Bourgeois Gentilhomme
author: **7** Moliere
character: **7** Cleonte, Dorante **9** M Jourdain **16** Monsieur Jourdain

Le Carre, John
real name: **13** David Cornwell
author of: **11** A Perfect Spy **13** Smiley's People **18** The Looking Glass War **19** A Small Town in Germany **20** The Little Drummer Girl **21** The Honorable Schoolboy **22** Tinker Tailor Soldier Spy **26** The Spy Who Came in from the Cold

lechayim, lehayim 6 to life

lecherous 4 lewd **5** randy **6** carnal **7** goatish, lustful, ruttish **8** prurient **9** sala- cious, satyrlike **10** lascivious, libidinous, licentious, lubricious

lechery 4 lust **8** lewdness **9** carnality, prurience **10** satyriasis **11** lustfulness, nym- phomania **13** salaciousness **14** lasciv- iousness

Le Cid
author: **9** Corneille
composer: **21** Leconte Dehisle, Charles **13** Jules Massenet

Leconte de Lisle, Charles
author of: **14** Poemes Antiques, Poemes Barbares

Le Corbusier
real name: **23** Charles Edouard Jeanneret
architect of: **10** La Tourette (monastery) **15** Notre Dame du Haut (Ronchamp France) **16** Unite d'Habitation (Marseilles)
planned city of: **10** Chandi garh (capital of the Punjab)
style: **6** Purism **12** New Brutalism

lecture 4 talk **5** chide, scold, speak **6** homily, preach, rail at, rebuke, sermon, speech **7** address, censure, chiding, expound, oration, reading, re proof, reprove, upbraid, warning **8** admonish, call down, harangue, moralize, reproach **9** discourse, hold forth, reprimand, sermonize, talking-to **10** preachment, take to task **12** chastisement, disquisition, remonstrance

lecture hall 9 classroom **10** auditorium **12** amphitheater, assembly hall

lecturelike 7 donnish, preachy **8** academic, didactic, pedantic **9** homiletic **10** moralizing

LED 18 light emitting diode **19** alphanumeric display

Leda
father: **8** Thestius
husband: **9** Tyndareus
lover: **4** swan, Zeus
son: **6** Castor, Pollux **8** Dioscuri **10** Polydeuces
daughter: **5** Helen **6** Phoebe **8** Philonoe, Timandra **12** Clytemnestra

Leda and the Swan
author: **7** W B Yeats

ledge 4 sill, step **5** ridge, shelf **6** mantel, offset **8** foothold, shoulder **10** projection **11** mantelpiece, mantelshelf, outcropping

Lee, Bruce
born: **12** San Francisco
son: **7** Brandon
roles: **7** Marlowe **11** Fists of Fury, Game of Death **14** The Green Hornet, Enter the Dragon **17** Return of the Dragon, Chinese Connection **24** Bruce Lee: Curse of the Dragon

Lee, Christopher
born: **6** London
roles: **5** Jocks **6** Albino, Serial **7** The Girl **8** Caravans **9** Shaka Zulu, The Keeper, The Gorgon **10** Dark Places **11** Eye for an Eye, Horror Hotel, Moulin Rouge, Killer Force **12** Count Dracula, The Wicker Man, The Oblong Box, Scream of Fear **13** The Death Train **14** Treasure Island **15** Journey of Horror **16** Castle of Fu Manchu, The Creeping Flesh, A Tale of Two Cities **17** The Four Musketeers **23** Return from Witch Mountain

25 The Hound of the Baskervilles **30** The Private Life of Sherlock Holmes

Lee, Gypsy Rose
born: **7** Seattle
author of: **5** Gypsy **8** Doll Face **15** Lady of Burlesque
roles: **11** The Stripper, My Lucky Star **13** Screaming Mimi

Lee, Harper
author of: **18** To Kill a Mockingbird

Lee, Johnny
born: **8** Alta Loma (TX)
roles: **11** Urban Cowboy **12** School Spirit

Lee, Henry
nickname: **15** Light Horse Harry
served in: **16** Revolutionary War
member of: **10** US Congress **19** Continental Congress
governor of: **8** Virginia
suppressed: **16** Whiskey Rebellion
son: **7** Robert E

Lee, Peggy
born: **9** Jamestown (ND)
roles: **7** Mr. Music **13** The Jazz Singer **15** Pete Kelly's Blues **18** Ladies Sing the Blues

Lee, Robert E
father: **5** Henry **15** Light Horse Harry
born: **11** Stratford VA **18** Westmoreland County
wife: **21** Mary Ann Randolph Custis
served in: **8** Civil War **10** Mexican War
commander of: **22** Army of Northern Virginia
suppressed raid: **9** John Brown **12** Harper's Ferry
battle: **7** Bull Run **8** Antie tam **10** Gettysburg **14** Fredericksburg **16** Chancellorsville, Seven Days' Battles
surrendered at: **20** Appomattox Court House
president of: **17** Washington College

Lee, Spike
original name: **17** Sheldon Jackson Lee
born: **2** GA **7** Atlanta
wife: **17** Tonya Linette Lewis
films: **8** Malcolm X **10** School Daze **11** Jungle Fever **15** Do the Right Thing, She's Gotta Have It
company: **18** Forty Acres and A Mule
ads for: **4** Nike

Lee, Stan 10 cartoonist
of: **9** Spider-Man

leek 18 Allium ampeloprasum
emblem of: **5** Wales
varieties: **4** lily, rose, sand, wild **5** lady's **6** meadow

leer 4 ogle **5** fleer, smirk **6** goggle

leery 4 wary **5** cagey, chary **6** unsure **7** guarded, doubtful, hesitant **9** skeptical, undecided **10** suspicious **11** circumspect, distrustful, mistrustful

Leeuwenhoek, Anton van

field: **10** microscopy
father of: **12** microbiology
discovered: **13** red blood cells

leeway 4 play **5** scope, slack **6** margin **7** cushion, headway, reserve **8** headroom, latitude **9** allowance, clearance, elbow room, extra time, tolerance **11** flexibility **13** room for choice **14** margin for error **15** maneuverability

left behind 7 vacated **8** deserted, forsaken, forsook **9** abandoned, discarded, evacuated **12** relinquished

leftover 6 excess, legacy, unused **7** overage, residue, surplus, uneaten **8** leavings, oddments, residual, survivor **9** carry-over, remainder, remaining

left-wing 7 leftist, liberal, radical **9** socialist **11** progressive

left-winger 7 leftist, liberal, radical **9** socialist **11** progressive

Lefty
nickname of: **5** Gomez **12** Steve Carlton

leg 3 gam, lap, pin **4** limb, part, post, prop **5** brace, femur, shank, stage, stump, tibia **6** column, fibula, member, pillar **7** portion, section, segment, stretch, support, upright

legacy 4 gift **6** devise, estate **7** bequest, vestige **8** heirloom, heritage, leftover, survivor **9** carry-over, throwback, tradition **10** birthright, hand medown **11** inheritance

legal 4 fair **5** licit, of law, valid **6** kosher, lawful **7** cricket **8** forensic, judicial, juristic, rightful **9** courtroom, juridical **10** legiti- mate, sanctioned **11** permissible

legal advisor 6 lawyer **7** counsel **8** advocate, attorney **9** barrister, counselor, solicitor **13** attorney-at-law **14** counselor-at-law

legal form 4 writ **8** document **10** instrument

legality 8 validity **9** licitness **10** lawfulness, legitimacy **17** constitutionality

legalization 8 sanction **9** enactment **10** permission, validation **13** authorization **14** legitimization

legalize 5 enact **6** permit **8** sanction, validate **9** authorize **10** legitimize

legal residence 4 home **8** domicile, dwelling

legal tender 4 cash **5** money **8** currency

legate 5 agent, envoy **6** deputy **8** emissary **14** representative

legatee 4 heir **7** heiress **9** inheritor **11** beneficiary

legation 7 embassy, mission **8** ministry **9** consulate **10** delegation **11** chancellery

legend 3 key **4** edda, lore, myth, saga, tale **5** fable, motto, story, title **7** caption, fiction, proverb **8** folklore **11** inscription

legendary 5 famed **6** fabled, famous, mythic **7** storied **8** fabulous, fanciful, mythical **9** imaginary **10** apocryphal, celebrated, fictitious, proverbial

Legend of Good Women, The
author: **15** Geoffrey Chaucer
character: **4** Dido **5** Medea **6** Thisbe **7** Alceste, Ariadne, Lucrece, Phyllis **9** Cleopatra, Hypsipyle, Philomela **12** Hypermnestra

Legend of Sleepy Hollow, The
author: **16** Washington Irving
character: **12** Brom Van Brunt (Brom Bones), Ichabod Crane **16** headless horseman, Katrina Van Tassel

Leger, Fernand
born: **6** France **8** Argentan
artwork: **8** Bargeman **10** Adam and Eve, The Wedding, Three Women **11** The Builders, The Cyclists, The Mechanic, The Stairway **14** The Great Parade **15** Le Grand Dejeuner **16** Contrasting Forms, Nudes in the Forest **21** Butterflies and Flowers

legerdemain 7 cunning **8** deftness, jugglery, juggling, trickery **9** deception **10** adroitness, artfulness **11** maneuvering **13** sleight of hand **16** prestidigitation

legible 4 neat **5** clear, plain **7** visible **8** clear-cut, distinct, readable **12** decipherable **14** comprehensible, understandable

legion 3 mob, sea **4** army, host, mass **5** corps, drove, horde, spate, swarm **6** myriad, throng, troops **7** brigade **8** division **9** multitude

leg irons 5 bonds, irons **6** chains **7** fetters **8** shackles

legislation 3 act **4** bill **6** ruling **7** measure, statute **9** amendment, enactment, law making, ordinance

legislator 7 senator **8** alder man, delegate, lawgiver, lawmaker **10** councilman **11** assemblyman, congressman **13** congresswoman **14** representative **15** parliamentarian

legislature 4 diet **5** house **6** senate **7** chamber, council **8** assembly, congress **10** parliament

legitimacy 8 legality, validity **10** lawfulness **11** correctness, genuineness **12** authenticity, rightfulness **15** appropriateness

legitimate 4 fair, just, true **5** legal, licit, sound, valid **6** lawful, proper **7** correct, genuine, logical, tenable **8** rightful **9** authentic, justified, plausible **10** believable, reasonable **11** appropriate, well-founded

leg-pull 4 hoax **9** deception **13** practical joke

Legree, Simon 13 cruel overseer
character in: **14** Uncle Tom's Cabin
author: **5** Stowe

LeGuin, Ursula K

author of: 13 Lathe of Heaven **14** Rocannon's World **15** The Dispossessed **16** Always Coming Home **21** The Left Hand of Darkness

Lehar, Franz (Ferencz)
born: 7 Komarno (then Hungary, now Czechoslovakia)
composer of: 9 Gipsy Love **13** The Merry Widow **20** The Count of Luxembourg

Lehmbruck, Wilhelm
born: 7 Germany **9** Meiderich
artwork: 11 Rising Youth **12** Man Flung Down, Praying Woman, Seating Youth **13** Kneeling Woman, Standing Woman, Standing Youth

Leigh, Janet
husband: 10 Tony Curtis
daughter: 14 Jamie Lee Curtis
born: 8 Merced CA
roles: 6 Psycho, The Fog **10** The Vikings **11** Little Women, Touch of Evil

Leigh, Vivien
real name: 17 Vivian Mary Hartley
husband: 15 Laurence Olivier
born: 5 India **10** Darjeeling
roles: 11 Ship of Fools **12** Anna Karenina **13** Blanche du Bois, Scarlett O'Hara **14** Waterloo Bridge **15** Gone With the Wind (Oscar) **17** That Hamilton Woman **21** A Streetcar Named Desire (Oscar), Roman Spring of Mrs Stone

Leighton, Margaret
husband: 12 Max Reinhardt **14** Laurence Harvey, Michael Wilding
born: 7 England **10** Barnt Green **14** Worcestershire
roles: 12 The Go-Between **13** The Winslow Boy **14** Separate Tables **19** The Night of the Iguana

leisure 4 ease, rest **6** recess, repose **7** holiday, respite, time off **8** free time, vacation **9** diversion, idle hours, spare time **10** recreation, relaxation

leisurely 4 idle, slow **6** casual, slowly **7** languid, relaxed, restful **9** unhurried **10** slow-moving **11** lingeringly, unhurriedly **12** without haste **13** lackadaisical

Lemmon, Jack
real name: 18 Jack Uhler Lemmon III
wife: 11 Felicia Farr
born: 8 Boston MA
roles: 7 Missing **10** April Fools **12** Grumpy Old Men, Save the Tiger (Oscar), The Apartment, The Great Race, The Odd Couple **13** China Syndrome, Mister Roberts, Some Like It Hot **18** Days of Wine and Roses, Under the Yum-Yum Tree **19** How to Murder Your Wife

lemon 11 Citrus limon
varieties: 4 wild **5** dwarf, giant, Meyer, water **6** garden, wonder **9** wild water **12** Chinese dwarf

14 American wonder
slang for: 3 dud **9** defective

lemures
form: 6 ghosts
characteristic: 10 maleficent **11** troublesome

lend 4 give, loan **6** impart, in vest, supply **7** advance, furnish **10** contribute

lend a hand 3 aid **6** assist **7** help out

lend assistance 3 aid **4** abet, help **6** succor **7** relieve **16** give a helping hand

lend one's name to 7 endorse, support **9** recommend

length 3 run **4** span, term, time **5** piece, range, reach **6** extent, period **7** com- pass, measure, portion, section, segment, stretch **8** distance, duration, end to end **9** longitude, magnitude **11** elapsed time, measurement

lengthen 3 pad **5** add to **6** expand, extend, let out, pad out **7** augment, drag out, draw out, fill out, prolong, spin out, stretch **8** elongate, flesh out, increase, protract **9** attenuate, string out

lengthening 8 full form **9** extending, extension **10** elongation, stretching **11** extenuation, protraction **12** prolongation

lengthy 5 windy, wordy **6** padded, prolix **7** endless **8** drawn out, extended, over- long, rambling **9** elongated, extensive, garrulous, long-drawn, prolonged **10** digressive, discursive, long- winded, protracted **12** interminable

leniency 5 mercy **7** charity **8** clemency **9** tolerance **10** compassion **11** forbearance, magnanimity **12** mercifulness **13** forgivingness

lenient 4 kind, mild, soft **6** gentle **7** clement, liberal, patient, sparing **8** merciful, moderate, tolerant **9** easygoing, forgiving, indulgent **10** benevolent, charitable, forbearing, permissive **11** kindhearted, soft-hearted, sympathetic **13** compassionate, tenderhearted

Lenin, Vladimir Illyich
surname: 7 Ulyanov
also called: 7 Nikolai
founder of: 10 Bolshevism
leader of: 17 Russian Revolution
premier of: 4 USSR

Lenni-Lenape *see* **8** Delaware

Lennon, John
born: 9 Liverpool (UK)
songs: 5 Woman **6** Mother **9** Stand By Me **10** Jealous Guy
see also **7** Beatles

Lenny
director: 8 Bob Fosse
cast: 8 Jan Miner **11** Stanley Beck **13**

Dustin Hoffman (Lenny Bruce) **14** Valerie Perrine (Honey Harlowe)

Leno, Jay
host of: 14 The Tonight Show
author of: 9 Headlines (Books I-IV) **17** Leading with My Chin

Le Notre, Andre
landscape architect of: 6 Clagny **9** Tuileries **10** Ver sailles **12** Saint Germain **13** Fontainebleau **22** Chateau de Vaux-le-Vicomte

lens
invented by:
  achromatic: 7 Dollond
  bifocal: 8 Franklin
  fused bifocal: 6 Borsch

Lenya, Lotte
real name: 16 Karoline Blamauer
husband: 9 Kurt Weill
born: 7 Austria, Hitzing
roles: 5 Jenny **18** From Russia with Love, The Seven Deadly Sins, The Three-penny Opera

Leo
symbol: 4 lion
planet: 3 Sun
rules: 7 romance **10** creativity
born: 4 July **6** August

Leonard, Elmore
author of: 4 Swag **5** Glitz, Stick **6** Hombre **7** La Brava **9** Cat Chaser, Gold Coast, Gunsights, The Hunted **10** Mr Majestyk **12** The Big Bounce **14** Fifty-Two Pick-Up, Valdez Is Coming **16** Double Dutch Treat, The Bounty Hunters **18** Forty Lashes Less One

Leonato
character in: 19 Much Ado About Nothing
author: 11 Shakespeare

Leoncavallo, Ruggiero
born: 5 Italy **6** Naples
composer of: 8 Serafita **10** I Pagliacci

Leontes
character in: 14 The Winter's Tale
author: 11 Shakespeare

Leonteus
leader of: 6 Greeks
leader at: 4 Troy
suitor of: 5 Helen

leopard 3 cat **7** panther **10** spotted cat
group of: 4 leap

Leo the Lip
nickname of: 11 Leo Durocher

lepidoptera
class: 8 hexapoda
phylum: 10 arthropoda
group: 4 moth **9** butterfly

leprechaun 3 elf, imp **5** dwarf, gnome **6** sprite **12** little person

Ler
also: 3 Lir
origin: 5 Irish
personifies: 3 sea

son: **8** Manannan
corresponds to: **4** Llyr
Lerner, Alan J.
born: **7** New York
author of: **4** Gigi **7** Camelot **9** Brigadoon **10** My Fair Lady **17** An American in Paris
composer of: **7** Tribute **15** The Little Prince
producer of: **14** Paint Your Wagon
Lesage, Le Sage, Alain
author of: **7** Gil Blas **8** Turcaret
Lesbos
island in: **6** Aegean
home of: **6** Sappho
Lescaze, William
architect of: **18** Borg-Warner Building (Chicago) **38** Philadelphia Savings Fund Society Building
Lescot, Pierre
architect of: **10** Cour Carree **20** Fontaine des Innocents
rebuilding of: **6** Louvre
lese-majeste, lese majesty 5 crime **7** treason
against: **12** king's dignity
Lesotho
other name: **10** Basutoland
capital/largest city: **6** Maseru
others: **4** Roma **5** Joels **6** Leribe, Morija **7** Quthing, Sekakes **8** Mafeteng, Matsieng **9** Marakabei, Qachas Nek, Semonkong **10** Butha Buthe, Mokhotlong, Thaba Bosiu **11** Mohales Hoek **12** Sehlabathebe, Teyateyaneng
head of state: **4** king
monetary unit: **4** cent, rand
mountain: **5** Maloti, Maluti **7** Central **8** Injasuti, Machache **10** Ben Macdhui **11** Drakensberg, Thaba Putnoa
highest point: **16** Thabana Ntlenyana
river: **5** Senqu **6** Orange, Tugela **7** Caledon **9** Makhaleng
physical feature:
gorge: **5** Oxbow
people: **4** Zulu **5** Bantu, Tembu **6** Basuto **7** Basotho
leader: **7** Moshesh **9** Mosheshwe **10** Moshoeshoe **14** Leabua Jonathan
language: **5** Sotho **7** English, Sesotho
religion: **7** animism **13** Roman Catholic **18** Lesotho Evangelical
feature:
blanket: **4** kobo
house: **4** rondavel
water project: **11** Malibamatso
less 5 fewer **6** barely, little **7** smaller **8** meagerly, slighter **10** not as great **11** more limited
lessen 3 ebb **4** ease, sink, thin, wane **5** abate, lower **6** dilute, reduce, shrink **7** abridge, decline, dwindle, lighten, slacken, subside **8** contract, decrease, diminish, mitigate, wind down **9** alleviate **10** depreciate

lessening 6 waning **8** decrease, dilution **9** abatement, deduction, dwindling, reduction, shrinkage **10** diminution, lightening, mitigation, shortening, slackening **11** abridgement, alleviation, contraction, diminishing, slacking off **12** abbreviation, condensation, depreciation
Lesseps, Ferdinand 8 engineer **9** Suez Canal
lesser 4 less **5** minor **7** humbler, smaller **8** inferior, slighter **9** secondary **11** sec- ondarily
Lessing, Doris
author of: **8** Shikasta **16** The Four-Gated City **17** The Golden Notebook **20** The Sirian Experiments **21** The Children of Violence **37** Marriages Between Zones Three Four and Five **42** The Making of the Representative for Planet Eight
lesson 5 class, drill, guide, model, moral, study **6** caveat, notice, rebuke **7** cau- tion, example, message, reading, segment, warning **8** exemplar, exercise, homework **9** deterrent **10** admonition, advisement, assignment, punishment, recitation, Scriptures **11** instruction **12** remonstrance
Lestrade, Inspector
character in: **14** (The Adventures of) Sherlock Holmes
author: **10** Conan Doyle
let 4 make, rent **5** admit, allow, cause, grant, lease, leave **6** enable, permit, sublet, suffer **7** approve, charter, concede, empower, endorse, hire out, license, warrant **8** sanction, sublease, tolerate **9** authorize
let
term in: **6** tennis
serve touches: **3** net
let down 4 drop **5** lower **6** betray **8** push down **10** disappoint **11** disillusion
letdown 3 rue **4** balk, blow **6** fizzle, regret **7** chagrin, set back **8** comedown **10** anticlimax, bafflement, bitter pill, dashed hope, discontent **11** frustration **12** blighted hope, discomfiture **13** mortification **14** disappointment, disenchantment, disgruntlement **15** disillusionment, dissatisfaction
let fall 4 drop **5** let go **7** release
let fly 4 cast, hurl **5** eject, fling, heave, sling, throw **6** launch, propel
let go 3 axe, can **4** fire, free, lose, oust, sack **6** bounce, give up
lethal 5 fatal, toxic **6** deadly, mortal **7** baneful, killing **8** venomous, virulent **9** dan gerous, malignant, poisonous **11** destructive **13** mortally toxic
lethargic 4 dull, idle, lazy **5** inert **6** drowsy, sleepy, torpid **7** languid, passive **8** comatose, indolent, listless, slothful, sluggish **9** apathetic, enervated, somnolent, soporific **10** dispir-

ited, lackluster, unspirited **11** debilitated, indifferent
lethargy 5 sloth **6** apathy, stupor, torpor **7** inertia, languor **8** dullness, laziness **9** indolence, lassitude, torpidity **10** drowsiness, inactivity **12** indifference, listlessness, slothfulness, sluggishness
Lethe
form: **5** river
location: **5** Hades
caused: **13** forgetfulness
let in 5 admit **7** receive **12** allow to enter
let loose 4 free **5** let go **6** let fly **7** release, set free, unleash **8** give vent, liberate **12** give free rein
Leto
also: **6** Latona
father: **6** Coeus
mother: **6** Phoebe
son: **6** Apollo
consort: **4** Zeus
daughter: **5** Diana **7** Artemis
let off 5 let go **6** acquit, excuse, exempt **7** release, set free **8** liberate **9** discharge
let slip 6 betray, expose, reveal **7** divulge, uncover **8** blurt out, disclose, give away
Let's Make a Deal
host: **9** Monty Hall
announcer: **10** Jay Stewart
letter 4 note **7** epistle, message, missive **8** dispatch, document **9** substance **10** billet-doux
Letter, The
director: **12** William Wyler
based on story by: **15** Somerset Maugham
cast: **10** Bette Davis **14** Frieda Inca cort **15** Gale Sondergaard, Herbert Marshall, James Stephenson
setting: **6** Malaya
Letterman, David
Host of: **26** Late Show with David Letterman
letter ordering imprisonment
French: **14** lettre de cachet
carried seal of: **4** king **9** sovereign
letters 8 learning **9** erudition **10** literature **13** belles lettres
Letters from the Underground
author: **16** Fyodor Dostoevsky
Letter to Three Wives, A
director: **17** Joseph L Mankiewicz
cast: **10** Ann Sothern **11** Jeanne Crain, Jeffrey Lynn, Kirk Douglas, Paul Douglas **12** Linda Darnell, Thelma Ritter
Oscar for: **6** script **8** director
let the buyer beware
Latin: **12** caveat emptor
let the people rule
Latin: **13** regnat populus
motto of: **8** Arkansas

let there be light
Latin: **7** fiat lux

lettre de cachet 26 letter ordering imprisonment **28** letter under the sovereign's seal

lettuce 7 Lactuca
varieties: **3** cos **5** chalk, frog's, lamb's, water **6** Boston, garden, miner's **7** iceberg, prickly, romaine **8** escarole **9** asparagus **11** common lamb's

letup 4 lull **5** pause **6** relief **7** respite **8** decrease, interval, slowdown, stopping, surcease, vacation **9** abatement, cessation, interlude, lessening, remission **10** slackening **11** retardation

Let Us Now Praise Famous Men
author: **9** James Agee

Let us therefore be joyful
Latin: **15** Gaudeamus igitur

Le Vau, Louis
architect of: **6** Louvre **10** Versailles **12** Hotel Lambert **22** Chateau de Vaux-le-Vicomte **24** College des Quatres Nations

levee 3 dam **4** bank, dike, pier, quay, wall **5** ditch, jetty, ridge, wharf **6** durbar **9** reception **10** embankment

level 3 aim, bed **4** even, flat, rank, raze, tied, vein, zone **5** align, floor, flush, grade, layer, plane, point, stage, story, wreck **6** direct, height, lay low, reduce, smooth, topple **7** aligned, even out, flatten, landing, on a line, station, stratum, uniform **8** equalize, make even, position, tear down, together **9** devastate, elevation, knock down **10** consistent, horizontal, on a par with, unwrinkled **11** achievement, neck and neck **12** on an even keel

level-headed 4 sage **5** sound **6** poised, stable, steady **7** prudent **8** balanced, cautious, composed, sensible **9** collected, judicious, practical, unruffled **10** cool-headed, dependable, thoughtful **11** circumspect **12** eventempered **13** dispassionate **14** selfcontrolled

levelheadedness 6 aplomb **9** good sense, soundness, stability **10** equanimity **11** common sense **13** judiciousness

Levene, Sam
real name: **12** Samuel Levine
born: **6** Russia
roles: **12** Guys and Dolls **13** Nathan Detroit **15** The Sunshine Boys

lever 3 bar, pry **5** jimmy, raise **7** crowbar

Lever, Charles
author of: **14** Charles O'Malley

Leverrier, Urbain Jean Joseph
field: **9** astronomy
nationality: **6** French
co-discovered: **7** Neptune
worked with: **14** John Couch Adams

Levi
father: **5** Jacob **6** Melchi, Symeon
mother: **4** Leah
son: **6** Kohath, Merari **7** Gershom
brother: **3** Dan, Gad **5** Asher, Judah **6** Joseph, Reuben, Simeon **7** Zebulun **8** Benjamin, Issachar, Naphtali
sister: **5** Dinah
violated: **5** Dinah
also called: **7** Matthew
descendant of: **6** Levite

Leviathan 6 dragon **10** sea monster
means: **13** spirally bound
represents: **14** terrible powers

Leviathan
author: **12** Thomas Hobbes

Levin, Ira
author of: **6** Sliver **13** Rosemary's Baby **16** The Stepford Wives

Levin, Konstantin
character in: **12** Anna Karenina
author: **7** Tolstoy

Levi-Strauss, Claude
method: **13** structuralism
author of: **13** Mythologiques, The Savage Mind **16** Tristes Tropiques **22** Structural Anthropology **29** Elementary Structures of Kinship

Levitch, Joseph
real name of: **10** Jerry Lewis

levity 3 fun **5** mirth **6** joking, whimsy **8** hilarity, trifling **9** flippancy, frivolity, lightness, silliness **10** jocularity, pleasantry, triviality **11** flightiness, foolishness **16** lightheartedness

levy 3 fee, tax **4** duty, make, toll, wage **5** draft, exact, start **6** assess, call up, charge, demand, enlist, excise, impose, muster, pursue, tariff **7** carry on, collect **9** calling up, conscript, prosecute **10** assess ment, imposition **12** conscription

Levy, Marion
real name of: **15** Paulette Goddard

Lew Archer, Private Detective
author: **13** Ross MacDonald

lewd 5 bawdy **6** ribald, risque, vulgar, wanton **7** goatish, immoral, lustful, obscene **8** indecent, prurient **9** lecherous, libertine, salacious **10** lascivious, libidinous, licentious, lubricious **11** Rabelaisian **12** pornographic

Lewis, C S
author of: **10** Perelandra **13** Prince Caspian, The Last Battle **14** Surprised by Joy, The Silver Chair, Til We Have Faces **17** The Horse and His Boy **18** The Magician's Nephew **19** The Screwtape Letters **20** Out of the Silent Planet **21** The Chronicles of Narnia **25** The Voyage of the Dawn Treader **29** The Lion the Witch and the Wardrobe

Lewis, Jerry
real name: **13** Joseph Levitch
partner: **10** Dean Martin
born: **8** Newark NJ

roles: **8** The Caddy **10** The Bellboy, The Sad Sack **11** Cinderfella **12** The Geisha Boy **16** Artists and Models **17** The Nutty Professor **20** The Disorderly Orderly

Lewis, Sinclair
author of: **7** Babbitt **9** Dodsworth **10** Arrowsmith, Main Street **11** Elmer Gantry **14** Cass Timberlane

lexicon 5 gloss, index **8** code book, glossary, synonymy, wordbook, wordlist **9** thesaurus, wordstock **10** dictionary, vocabulary **11** concordance, onomasticon

lex loci 11 law of a place

lex non scripta 9 common law **12** unwritten law

lex scripta 10 statute law, written law

Leyden, Lucas (Lukas) van
born: **6** Leiden, Leyden **14** The Netherlands
artwork: **12** Last Judgment **14** The Card Players, The Game of Chess **26** Mohammed and the Murdered Monk

Lhasa
capital of: **5** Tibet

liability 4 debt, drag, duty, onus **5** debit, minus **6** arrear, burden **8** drawback, handicap, obstacle **9** hindrance **10** impediment, obligation **11** encumbrance, shortcoming **12** disadvantage, indebtedness **13** inconvenience **14** responsibility, stumbling block

liable 3 apt **4** open **5** prone **6** likely **7** exposed, ripe for, subject **8** disposed, inclined **9** obligated, sensitive **10** answerable, chargeable, vulnerable **11** accountable, responsible, susceptible

liaison 4 bond, link **5** amour, union **7** contact **8** alliance, intrigue, mediator **9** ad- venture, dalliance, go-between **10** connection, flirtation, love affair **11** association, cooperation, interchange **12** coordination, entanglement **13** communication

liar 6 fibber **8** perjurer **9** falsifier **10** fabricator **11** story teller **12** prevaricator

libation 4 wine **5** drink, water **6** liquid **8** ambrosia, beverage, offering, potation **9** sacrifice

libel 4 slur **5** smear **6** defame, malign, revile, vilify **7** asperse, blacken, calumny, obloquy, slander **8** derogate **9** aspersion, discredit, disparage **10** calumniate, defamation **12** vilification

Libeled Lady
director: **10** Jack Conway
cast: **8** Myrna Loy **10** Jean Harlow **12** Spencer Tracy **13** William Powell **14** Walter Connolly
remade as: **9** Easy to Wed

Libera
origin: **7** Italian
goddess of: **4** wine **9** fertility, vineyards

husband: 5 Liber
corresponds to: 10 Persephone
liberal 5 ample, broad **6** casual, lavish **7** leftist, lenient **8** abundant, advanced, flexible, generous, handsome, left-wing, prodigal, reformer, tolerant, unbiased **9** bounteous, bountiful, impartial, not strict, plenteous, reformist, unbigoted, unspar- ing **10** fairminded, forbearing, left-winger, munificent, not literal, openhanded, open-minded, unrigorous, unstinting **11** broad-minded, enlightened, extravagant, libertarian, magnanimous, progressive **12** freethinking, humanitarian, open to reason, unprejudiced **14** latitudinarian
liberal arts
  7 trivium: 5 logic **7** grammar **8** rhetoric
  10 quadrivium: 5 music **8** geometry **9** astronomy **10** arithmetic
liberality 10 generosity **11** benevolence, munificence **12** philanthropy **13** bountifulness **14** openhandedness
liberate 5 let go **6** let out, redeem, rescue, spring **7** absolve, deliver, manumit, release, set free **8** let loose **9** discharge, disengage, extricate, unshackle **10** emancipate **11** disencumber
liberated 5 freed, let go **7** rescued, set free **8** let loose, released **10** discharged, extricated **11** emancipated
liberation 6 escape, rescue **7** freedom, freeing, release **8** delivery **9** letting go, releasing **11** manumission **12** emancipation
Liberia
  capital/largest city: 8 Monrovia
  others: 4 Sino **5** Gribo, Rebbo **6** Bopora, Ghanga, Harper, Kakata **7** Bgarnga, Kolahun, Nanakru, Tappita, Voinjama **8** Buchanan, Garraway, Marshall, Nanakaru, Sass Town **9** Grand Cess, River Cess, Roysville **10** Careysburg, Green ville, Sanoquelli **11** Robertsport **12** Sanniquellie
  school: 7 Liberia **10** Cuttington **15** Our Lady of Fatima **16** Booker Washington
    religious school/secret society: 4 poro **5** sande
  measure: 4 kuba
  monetary unit: 4 cent **6** dollar
  mountain: 3 Uni **4** Bong, Putu **5** Niete, Nimba **9** Bomi Hills
  highest point: 6 Wutivi
  river: 4 Cess, Lofa, Mano **5** Duobe, Lotta, Manna, Morro, Sinoe **6** Cestos, Douobe **7** Cavalla, Cavally **8** San Pedro **9** Saint John, Saint Paul, Sehnkwehn
  sea: 8 Atlantic
  physical feature:
    wind: 9 harmattan
  people: 2 Gi **3** Gio, Kra, Kru, Kwa, Vai, Vei **4** Gola, Kroo, Krou, Loma, Mano, Toma **5** Bassa, Gibbi, Gissi, Grebo **6** Gbande, Kpelle, Kpuesi, Krooby, Kruman **7** Krooboy, Krooman **8** Mandingo **15** Americo-Liberian
    leader: 3 Doe **6** Tubman **7** Roberts, Tolbert
  language: 3 Kru, Kwa **5** Mande **7** English
  religion: 5 Islam **7** animism **10** Protestant **12** Christianity
  feature:
    clothing: 5 lappa
    rubber plantation: 9 Firestone
Libertas
  origin: 5 Roman
  personifies: 7 liberty
liberte egalite fraternite 25 liberty equality fraternity
  motto of: 16 French Revolution
liberties 6 misuse **7** license **9** violation **10** distortion **11** familiarity, impropriety **13** falsification
libertine 4 goat, lewd, rake, roue **5** loose, satyr **6** lecher, wanton **7** immoral, lustful, seducer **8** unchaste **9** debauchee, dissolute, lecherous, reprobate, womanizer **10** immoralist, lascivious, libidinous, licentious, profligate, sensualist, voluptuary
liberty 5 leave, right **7** freedom, license **8** autonomy, delivery, free time, furlough, sanction, vacation **9** privilege **10** liberation, permission, shore leave **11** citizenship, manumission **12** carte blanche, dispensation, emancipation, independence **15** enfranchisement **17** self- determination
liberty equality fraternity
  French: 24 liberte egalite fraternite
  motto of: 16 French Revolution
Libra
  symbol: 6 scales **7** balance
  planet: 5 Venus
  rules: 8 marriage
  born: 7 October **9** September
Libreville
  capital of: 13 Gabon Republic
Libya
  capital/largest city: 7 Tripoli
    summer capital: 8 Benghazi
  others: 4 Homs, Marj, Surt **5** Beida, Darna, Derna, Khums, Kufra, Sebha, Sidri, Zawia **6** Garian, Murzuq, Tobruk **7** Es Sidar, Gharyan, Misrata **8** Ajdabiya, Misurata, Rashanuf **12** Marsa el Brega
  school: 7 Alfateh **9** Garyounis
  division: 6 Fezzan **9** Cyrenaica **12** Tripolitania
  measure: 3 dra, pik, saa **4** kele **5** bozze, donum, jabia, teman, uckia **6** barile, gorraf, misura **7** mattaro, termino **8** kharouba
  weight: 4 kele **6** gorraf **8** kharouba
  monetary unit: 5 dinar
  mountain: 5 Green **13** Jabal al Akhdar, Tibesti Massif
  highest point: 9 Bette Peak
  sea: 13 Mediterranean
  physical feature:
    desert: 6 Libyan, Sahara **9** Calanscio
    gulf: 5 Bomba, Sidra, Sirte
    oasis: 4 Ghat **5** Kufra, Sebha **7** Tazerbo **8** Al-Kufrah, Ghudamis
    plain: 6 al Marj, Gefara **7** Jaffara
    plateau: 12 Gebel Nefuisa, Jabal Nafusah
    wind: 6 ghibli
  people: 4 Arab, Tebu **6** Berber, Tuareg **7** Gaetuli **8** Getu lans, Harratin
    leader: 6 Battus **7** Jalloud, Qadhafi **8** Aegyptus **9** al- Qaddafi, Karamanli **13** Idris al-Senusi
    religious leader: 8 al-Senusi
    ruler: 4 Rome **5** Italy **6** Greece **9** Phoenicia **12** Ottoman Turks
  language: 6 Arabic, Berber **7** English, Italian
    alphabet: 8 tifinagh
  religion: 5 Islam
  feature: 14 Tropic of Cancer
    clothing: 5 lanaf **9** barracano
    festival: 3 Mez **7** Fantasi
    Islamic law: 6 sharia
    leader: 6 sheikh
    ruins: 11 Leptis Magna
  food:
    dish: 5 bazin **8** couscous
    red pepper: 6 filfil
license 3 let **4** pass, visa **5** allow, grant, leave, right **6** enable, laxity, permit **7** anarchy, approve, certify, charter, empower, endorse, freedom, liberty, warrant **8** accredit, audacity, disorder, latitude, passport, sanction, temerity **9** admission, allowance, authorize, franchise, looseness, privilege, slackness **10** brazenness, commission, debauchery, unruliness **11** certificate, free passage, lawlessness, libertinism, presumption, safe- conduct **12** carte blanche, dispensation, recklessness
licentious 4 lewd **5** dirty, loose **6** amoral, sleazy, wanton **7** brutish, goatish, immoral, lawless, lustful, raunchy, ruttish **8** depraved, prodigal **9** abandoned, debauched, dissolute, excessive, lecherous, libertine, salacious **10** dissipated, lascivious, libidinous, lubricious, profligate, ungoverned **11** promiscuous **12** unprincipled, unrestrained, unscrupulous **13** irresponsible, unconstrained
licentiousness 7 abandon **8** lewdness **10** immorality, wantonness
licit 5 legal, legit, valid **6** kosher, lawful **9** allowable, statutory **10** acceptable, admissible, authorized, legitimate, sanctioned **11** permissible **12** authorizable, sanctionable **14** constitutional
lick 3 bit, dab, hit, jot, lap **4** beat, blow, drub, fire, hint, iota, rout, slap, snip, sock, suck, whip **5** crack,

punch, sally, shred, spank, speck, taste, touch, trace **6** defeat, ignite, kindle, master, sample, stroke, subdue, thrash, tongue, wallop **7** clobber, conquer, modicum, smidgen, trounce **8** outmatch, overcome, particle, vanquish **9** overpower, overthrow, scintilla, subjugate **10** smattering **12** denunciation

lid 3 cap, top **4** cork, curb, plug **5** cover, limit **7** ceiling, maximum, stopper, stopple **9** operculum, restraint

lie 3 fib **4** loll, rest, stay **5** abide, exist, range, story **6** belong, deceit, extend, inhere, lounge, obtain, remain, repose, sprawl **7** falsify, fiction, perjury, recline, romance, untruth **8** misstate, tall tale **9** deception, embellish, embroider, fabricate, falsehood, invention **10** equivocate **11** fabrication, prevaricate **12** equivocation **13** falsification, prevarication **17** misrepresentation

Liechtenstein
capital/largest city: 5 Vaduz
others: 4 Haag **6** Balzer, Eschen, Iradug, Schaan **7** Balzers, Bendern, Nendeln, Planken, Triesen **12** Schellenberg
division:
ancient province: 6 Rhaeti **7** Rhaetia
government:
legislature: 7 Landtag
monetary unit: 6 rappen **7** franken
mountain: 4 Alps **8** Naafkopf, Rhatikon **12** Three Sisters
highest point: 15 Vorder-Grauspitz
river: 5 Rhine
physical feature:
valley: 6 Lavena, Samina
people: 8 Alemanni
leader: 7 Florian **15** Francis Joseph II **16** von Liechtenstein
language: 6 German **10** Alemannish
religion: 13 Roman Catholic
place:
castle: 9 Gutemburg, Gutenberg
feature:
legendary dwarf: 10 wildmannli
wine: 7 Vaduzer

lie down 6 retire **7** go to bed, recline **8** take a nap **11** take a snooze **15** catch forty winks

life 4 path, soul, zest **5** being, human, plant, story, verve, vigor **6** animal, career, course, energy, memoir, person, spirit **8** creature, duration, life span, lifetime, lifework, organism, survival, vitality, vivacity **9** animation, biography, existence, life story, longevity **11** subsistence **13** autobiography
French: 3 vie

Life Before Man
author: 14 Margaret Atwood

Lifeboat
director: 15 Alfred Hitchcock
cast: 10 John Hodiak **12** Mary Ander-

son **13** William Bendix **16** Tallulah Bankhead

life-giving 5 vital **9** vivifying **12** invigorating

life jacket 7 Mae West

lifeless 4 dead, dull, flat, late **5** inert, stiff, vapid **6** boring, hollow, static, torpid, wooden **7** defunct **8** deceased, departed, inactive, lifeless, sluggish **9** colorless, inanimate **10** lackluster, spiritless

lifelessness 5 death **7** inertia **8** dullness, limpness, vapidity **9** blandness **10** flaccidity, inactivity **13** colorlessness

Life Magazine
founder: 9 Henry Luce

Life of Dante
author: 17 Giovanni Boccaccio

Life of Emile Zola
director: 15 William Dieterle
cast: 8 Paul Muni **11** Donald Crisp **12** Cloria Holden **15** Gale Sondergaard **17** Joseph Schildkraut (Dreyfus)
Oscar for: 7 picture

Life of Man, The
author: 14 Leonid Andreyev

Life of Riley, The
character: 4 Babs **6** Dangle, Junior **8** Peg Riley **9** Jim Gillis **10** Cunningham, Digby (Digger) O'Dell **11** Waldo Binney **13** Chester A Riley **14** Honeybee Gillis
cast: 9 John Brown, Lanny Rees, Sid Tomack **10** Tom D'Andrea **12** Emory Parnell, Wesley Morgan **13** Gloria Winters, Jackie Gleason, Lugene Sanders, Robert Sweeney, William Bendix **14** Gloria Blondell, Rosemary DeCamp **16** Douglas Dumbrille, Marjorie Reynolds, Sterling Holloway

Life of Samuel Johnson, The
author: 12 James Boswell

life of the party 7 show-off **9** extrovert **13** exhibitionist **17** hail-fellow-well-met

Life on the Mississippi
author: 9 Mark Twain

life span 4 life **8** lifetime **14** life expectancy

Life Studies
author: 12 Robert Lowell

Life With Father
author: 13 Clarence Day Jr
director: 13 Michael Curtiz
cast: 9 ZaSu Pitts **10** Irene Dunne **11** Edmund Gwenn **13** William Powell **15** Elizabeth Taylor
setting: 11 New York City

lifework 6 career **7** calling **8** vocation **10** livelihood, occupation, profession

lift 4 high, palm, pick, rear, rise, soar, take **5** boost, climb, exalt, filch, heave, hoist, pinch, raise, steal, swipe **6** ascend, ascent, banish, cancel, pilfer, pirate, pock- et, remove, revoke,

snatch, thieve, uplift, vanish **7** elation, elevate, purloin, raise up, raising, rescind, scatter, upraise **8** disperse **9** disappear, dissipate, float away **10** ascendance, move upward, plagiarize, put an end to **11** appropriate, countermand, inspiration, make off with, reassurance **12** give a boost to, shot in the arm **13** encouragement, enheartenment

ligament
holds: 5 bones

Ligeia
author: 13 Edgar Allan Poe
character: 19 Lady Rowena Trevanion

light 3 gay **4** airy, beam, easy, fair, fall, find, fire, glow, lamp, land, pale, puny, side, soft, stop **5** aglow, angle, blaze, blond, faint, flame, funny, glare, guide, happy, jolly, match, model, perch, petty, put on, roost, shine, slant, small, spare, spark, sunny, torch **6** alight, aspect, beacon, blithe, bright, candle, chance, frugal, gentle, get off, ignite, jaunty, kindle, luster, meager, paltry, scanty, settle, simple, slight, turn on **7** amusing, buoyant, chipper, clarify, come off, descend, get down, gleeful, insight, lantern, lighten, lighter, lucifer, not dark, not rich, paragon, radiant, radiate, sparkle, sunbeam, trivial **8** approach, attitude, bleached, blondish, brighten, carefree, cheerful, come upon, discover, dismount, ethereal, exemplar, gossamer, graceful, illumine, jubilant, luminous, meet with, moderate, moonbeam, not heavy, paradigm, radiance, sportive, step down, switch on, trifling, untaxing **9** brilliant, catch fire, direction, encounter, frivolous, irradiate, light-hued, set fire to, sprightly, stumble on, sylphlike, viewpoint **10** abstemious, brightness, brilliance, burdenless, come across, come to rest, effortless, effulgence, floodlight, happen upon, illuminate, light-toned, luminosity, manageable, restricted, set burning, weightless **11** conflagrate, elucidation, illuminated, information, make radiant, superficial, undemanding, underweight **15** inconsequential
god of: 6 Apollo **7** Mithras, Phoebus, Pythius **8** Heimdall **9** Musagetes
Latin: 3 lux
measurement: 7 candela **11** candle-power

light-colored 4 pale **5** beige, blond **6** blonde, flaxen, pastel **7** neutral, whitish **9** yellowish

light-complexioned 4 fair, pale **12** white-skinned

lighten 4 buoy, ease, lift **5** abate, allay, blaze, elate, flare, flash, gleam, shine **6** buoy up, lessen, reduce, revive, temper, unload, uplift **7** assuage, enliven, gladden, inspire, light up, re-

lieve 8 brighten, mitigate, moderate, **unburden 9** alleviate, coruscate, disburden, irradiate **10** illuminate, make bright **11** become light, disencumber, make lighter, scintillate

light-filled 5 sunny **6** bright **7** well-lit **11** illuminated

lighthearted 3 gay **4** airy, glad **5** jolly, merry, sunny **6** blithe, cheery, joyful, joyous, lively **7** buoyant, cheered, chipper **8** carefree, cheerful, sanguine **9** sprightly **10** insouciant, untroubled **11** free and easy **12** effervescent

lightheartedness 3 joy **4** glee **5** mirth **8** gladness **9** happiness, merriment **10** blitheness, exuberance, joyfulness, joyous ness **11** high spirits

Light in August
author: **15** William Faulkner
character: **8** Doc Hines, Joe Brown **9** Lena Grove, McEachern **10** Byron Bunch **12** Joanna Burden, Joe Christmas

lightless 4 dark **5** black, murky **7** stygian **9** unlighted **13** unilluminated

lightly 6 airily, easily, gently, nimbly, softly, thinly, weakly **7** blandly, faintly, quickly, readily, swiftly, timidly **8** blithely, fac- ilely, gingerly, meagerly, slightly, sparsely **9** buoyantly, sparingly **10** carelessly, flippantly, hesitantly, moderately **11** frivolously, slightingly **13** indifferently, thoughtlessly, unconcernedly, without effort **14** without concern

lightness 8 airiness, radiance **10** brightness, fluffiness, luminosity **12** illumination, luminousness

lightning rod
invented by: **8** Franklin

light of day 8 daylight, sunlight, sunshine

light sleep 3 nap **4** doze **6** catnap, snooze **10** forty winks

light wind 4 waft **6** breeze, zephyr **10** gentle wind **11** breath of air

Lightwood, Mortimer
character in: **15** Our Mutual Friend
author: **7** Dickens

lignum vitae 10 wood of life
tree species: **8** Guaiacum

likable, likeable 4 nice **6** genial **7** amiable, lovable, winsome **8** charming, engaging, loveable, pleasant, pleasing **9** agreeable, appealing, simpatico **10** attractive **11** complaisant, sympathetic

like 4 akin, care, dote, same, wish **5** enjoy, equal, fancy, favor, savor **6** admire, allied, choose, esteem, relish **7** approve, cognate, endorse, matched, related, similar, support, uniform **8** be fond of, parallel, selfsame, think fit **9** analogous, congru- ent, have a mind, identical **10** comparable, equivalent,

homologous, resembling **11** be partial to, much the same **12** feel in clined, have a crush on, take a shine to **13** cor- responding, find agreeable **14** take plea- sure in

Like a Bulwark
author: **13** Marianne Moore

likelihood 8 prospect **10** good chance **11** possibility, probability **12** potentiality

likely 3 apt, fit **4** able **6** liable, proper **8** credible, destined, inclined, probable, probably, rational, reliable, suitable **9** befitting, plausible, promising, qualified **10** believable, presumably, reasonable **11** appropriate, verisimilar **16** in all probability

like-mindedness 6 accord **7** concord, harmony, rapport **8** affinity **9** agreement **12** congeniality **13** compatibility

likeness 5 image, model, study **6** effigy **7** analogy, picture, replica **8** affinity, portrait **9** agreement, depiction, facsimile, portrayal, rendition, semblance **10** similarity, similitude **11** delineation, resemblance **14** correspondence, representation

likes 9 favorites **10** prejudices **11** preferences **12** inclinations, partialities

likewise 3 and, eke, too **4** also **5** ditto **6** as well **7** be sides, equally, the same **8** moreover **9** similarity **10** in addition

liking 4 bent **5** fancy, taste **7** leaning **8** affinity, appetite, fondness, penchant, soft spot, weakness **9** affection **10** partiality, preference, proclivity, propensity **11** inclination **12** predilection

Li'l Abner
creator: **6** Al Capp
character: **5** Pappy **7** Salomey (pig), Wolf Gal **10** Joe Btfsplk, Mammy Yokum, Marryin' Sam **11** Adam Lazonga, Hairless Joe **12** Lena the Hyena, Tobacco Rhoda **13** Joanie Phoanie **14** Daisy Mae Scragg, Evil-Eye Flee gle, Stupefyin' Jones **15** Fearless Fosdick, Henry Cabbage Cod, Lonesome Polecat, Moonbeam McSwine **16** General Bullmoose, Sir Cecil Cesspool **17** Sen Jack S Phogbound **18** J Roaringham Fatback **21** Appassionata von Climax
brewery: **23** Big Barnsmell's Skonk Works
event: **15** Sadie Hawkins Day
juice: **16** Kickapoo Joy Juice
kingdom: **14** Lower Slobbovia
mountain: **11** Onnecessary
animal: **6** Schmoo
people: **7** kygmies
place: **8** Dogpatch
railroad: **11** West Po'k Chop
ruler: **14** King Nogoodnick

lilac 7 Syringa
varieties: **4** late, vine, wild **6** common, Indian, summer **7** Chinese, cut-

leaf, Persian **9** Himalayan, Hungarian **12** Japanese tree **16** Catalina mountain

Lili
director: **14** Charles Walters
cast: **9** Mel Ferrer **11** Leslie Caron, Zsa Zsa Gabor **16** Jean-Pierre Aumont

Lilies of the Field
director: **11** Ralph Nelson
cast: **8** Lisa Mann **10** Lilia Skala **13** Sidney Poitier
Oscar for: **5** actor (Poitier)

Liliom
author: **12** Ferenc Molnar
source for: **8** Carousel

lillet
type: **8** aperitif
origin: **6** France
flavor: **6** orange
color: **3** red **5** white

Lilliput
fictional land in: **16** Gulliver's Travels
inhabitants: **10** tiny people
author: **5** Swift

lilliputian 3 wee **4** tiny **5** dwarf, short, small, teeny, weeny **6** little, midget, minute, petite **9** miniature **10** diminutive, teeny-weeny **11** pocket-sized

Lilongwe
capital of: **6** Malawi

lily 6 Lilium
varieties: **3** Alp, cow, day, pig **4** Arum, bell, boat, corn, fawn, fire, flax, herb, palm, pine, pond, rain, roan, rock, sand, Sego, star, toad, wood **5** adobe, Aztec, blood, bugle, calla, coast, cobra, crane, Cuban, fairy, globe, glory, Cray'o, Ifafa, lemon, magic, natal, queen, regal, royal, showy, snake, spear, swamp, sword, tiger, torch, trout, water, wheel **6** Alpine, Amazon, Canada, Crinum, desert, Easter, eureka, ginger, hidden, Kaffir, Marhan, meadow, one-day, orange, Oregon, shasta, Sierra, spider, sunset, tartar, turban, voodoo, yellow, Zephyr **7** African, Bermuda, chamise, checker, garland, leopard, madonna, Nankeen, panther, redwood, thimble, toad-cup, triplet, trumpet, western **8** Atamasco, Barbados, bluebead, Carolina, climbing, Columbia, flamingo, gloriosa, Guernsey, Humboldt, Jacobean, Japanese, long's red, Mariposa, Martagon, Michigan, mountain, paradise, Peruvian, plan tain, Siberian, Solomon's, St Bruno's, St James's, turk's cap **9** alligator, avalanche, butterfly, caucasian, celestial, chaparral, checkered, Eucharist, Kamchatka, naked-lady, orange-cup, pineapple, pinewoods, pot-of-gold, red ginger, red spider, St Joseph's **10** belladonna, blackberry, blue funnel,

fairy water, giant water, globe spear, gold-banded, Josephine's, orange-bell, pink Easter, pygmy water, royal water, small tiger, St Bernard's, Washington, white water, wild yellow, yellow-bell, yellow pond **11** African corn, Amazon water, blue African, candlestick, dwarf ginger, golden-rayed, milk-and-wine, Palmer spear, Scarborough, southern red, yellow water **12** African blood, Chinese white, golden spider, prickly water, resurrection, speckled wood, white trumpet **13** Bermuda Easter, cape blue water, Chinese sacred, Egyptian water, fragrant water, India red water, lavender globe, magnolia water, minor Turk's-cap, per fumed fairy, pink porcelain, scarlet ginger, showy Japanese, tuberous water, wild orange-red **14** Chinese-lantern, lesser Turk's cap, little Turk's-cap, Santa Cruz water, yellow Turk's-cap **15** Australian water, backhouse hybrid, golden hurricane, scarlet Turk's-cap **16** American Turk's cap, Bellingham hybrid, Cape Cod pink water, fragrant plantain, Japanese Turk's-cap, western orange-cup **17** midsummer plantain **18** European white water, seer sucker plantain **20** narrow-leaved plantain

lily-livered 6 afraid, craven, scared, yellow **7** chicken, fearful, gutless **8** cowardly **9** dastardly **12** fainthearted **13** pusillanimous, yellow-bellied **14** chicken-hearted, chicken-livered **22** showing the white feather

lily-white 4 good, pure **6** biased, decent, proper, racist **7** bigoted, upright **8** all-white, innocent, virtuous **9** blameless, exclusive, exemplary, faultless, guiltless, honorable, righteous **10** impeccable, inculpable, prejudiced, segregated, upstanding **11** uncorrupted **12** unintegrated **13** unimpeachable **14** discriminatory, irreproachable

Lima
capital of: 4 Peru
foothills of: 5 Andes
founder: 7 Pizarro
nickname: 11 city of kings
ocean: 7 Pacific
port: 6 Callao
river: 5 Rimac
square: 13 Plaza de Armas

limb 3 arm, gam, leg, pin **4** part, spur, twig, wing **5** bough, shoot, sprig **6** branch, member **9** appendage, extension, outgrowth **10** projection, prosthesis

limber 5 agile, lithe, relax **6** loosen, pliant, supple **7** bending, elastic, lissome, pliable **8** flexible **9** lithesome, malleable

lime 18 Citrus aurantifolia
varieties: 3 key **4** wild **7** Mexican,

Persian, Rangpur, Spanish **8** Mandarin **10** West Indian **14** Australian wild **15** Australian round **16** Australian desert, Australian finger

Limenia
epithet of: 9 Aphrodite
means: 11 of the harbor

Limerick
county in: 7 Ireland
gave name to: 12 nonsense poem
rhyme scheme: 5 aabba
popularized by: 10 Edward Lear

limit 3 end **4** curb **8** boundary, end point, restrain, ultimate **13** breaking point

limitation 4 curb **5** quota **8** boundary, decrease **9** lessening, reduction, restraint **10** shortening **11** abridgement, restriction, shortcoming **13** qualification, specification

limited 5 fixed **6** finite, narrow **7** bounded, cramped, defined, minimal, special **8** confined **9** delimited, specified **10** controlled, restrained, restricted **13** circumscribed

limitless 7 endless, eternal, unbound **8** infinite, unending **9** boundless, unlimited **11** measureless **12** immeasurable

limits 3 rim, top **4** curb, edge **5** bound, check, quota **6** border, define, fringe, margin, narrow **7** ceiling, confine, delimit, inhibit, maximum, qualify **8** confines, frontier, restrain, restrict **9** perimeter, periphery, prescribe, restraint **10** boundaries **11** limitations **12** restrictions

limn 4 draw **6** sketch **7** picture **9** delineate

Limnaea
epithet of: 7 Artemis
means: 9 of the lake

limp 3 lax **4** gimp, halt, soft, weak **5** crawl, loose, skulk, slack **6** droopy, falter, flabby, floppy, hobble **7** flaccid **8** drooping, lameness, yielding **9** dead tired, enervated, exhausted

limpid 4 pure **5** clear, lucid **8** clear-cut, pellucid, vitreous **11** crystalline, perspicuous, translucent, transparent, unambiguous **15** straightforward

Lincoln, Abraham
nickname: 9 Honest Abe **20** Illinois Rail Splitter
presidential rank: 9 sixteenth
party: 4 Whig **10** Republican
state represented: 2 IL
defeated: 4 (John) Bell **7** (John Charles) Fremont, (Stephen Arnold) Douglas **9** (George Brinton) McClellan **12** (John Cabell) Breckinridge
vice president: 6 (Hannibal) Hamlin **7** (Andrew) Johnson
cabinet:
  state: 6 (William Henry) Seward
  treasury: 5 (Salmon Portland) Chase **9** (Hugh) McCulloch, (William Pitt) Fessenden

  war: 7 (Edwin McMasters) Stanton, (Simon) Cameron
  attorney general: 5 (Edward) Bates, (James) Speed
  navy: 6 (Gideon) Welles
  postmaster general: 5 (Montgomery) Blair **8** (William) Dennison
  interior: 5 (Caleb Blood) Smith, (John Palmer) Usher
born: 2 KY **8** log cabin **11** Larue County **17** Sinking Spring farm
died: 12 Washington DC, Fords Theater
  died by: 13 assassination
  assassinated by: 15 John Wilkes Booth
buried: 13 Springfield IL
education:
  educated by: 4 self
  studied: 3 law
interests: 7 theater
  received patent for: 25 adjustable buoyant chambers (for lifting boats)
political career: 16 state legislature **24** US House of Representatives
civilian career: 6 lawyer **8** surveyor **10** postmaster
military service:
  War: 9 Black Hawk
  US Army: 7 private
  captain of company of: 10 volunteers
notable events of lifetime/term: 8 Civil War **24** Emanci pation Proclamation
  Act: 9 Homestead, Income Tax, Judiciary **12** Conscription
  debates: 14 Lincoln-Douglas
  speech: 17 Gettysburg Address
father: 6 Thomas
mother: 5 Nancy (Hanks)
  stepmother: 5 Sarah (Bush Johnston)
siblings: 5 Sarah **6** Thomas
  stepbrother: 4 John
  stepsister: 7 Matilda **9** Elizabeth
wife: 4 Mary (Ann Todd)
children: 6 Thomas **10** Robert Todd **11** Edward Baker **14** William Wallace

Lind, James
field: 8 medicine
nationality: 8 Scottish
eliminated: 6 scurvy

Lindbergh, Anne Morrow
author of: 14 Gift from the Sea **15** Bring Me a Unicorn **16** North to the Orient **19** War Within and Without

linden 5 Tilia
varieties: 6 Indoor **7** Crimean **8** American, Japanese **9** Mongolian **10** Manchurian **11** Large-leaved **13** Pendent silver **19** Small-leaved European

lindy 5 dance **8** lindy hop **9** jitterbug
nickname for: 16 Charles Lindbergh

line, lines 4 card, cord, dash, draw,

file, idea, mark, note, part, race, rank, rope, rule, tier, word **5** align, array, breed, cable, craft, front, house, model, queue, range, score, slash, stock, trade **6** belief, border, column, crease, family, furrow, letter, method, metier, policy, report, scheme, series, stance, strain, strand, streak, stripe, system, thread **7** calling, circuit, conduit, contour, cordage, example, lineage, marshal, outline, pattern, purpose, pursuit, queue up, routine, towline, wrinkle **8** ancestry, business, dialogue, doctrine, fishline, ideology, inscribe, position, postcard, trenches, vanguard, vocation **9** conductor, crow's foot, direction, frontline, genealogy, intention, principle **10** barricades, convention, firing line, livelihood, long stroke, occupation, procession, profession, underscore **11** demarcation

lineage 4 line **5** blood, stock **7** descent **8** ancestry, heredity, pedigree **9** genealogy, parentage **10** derivation, extraction

linen
 fabric: **6** canvas, damask **7** butcher, cambric **8** birds-eye **9** huckaback
 plant: **4** flax
 finest from: **7** Belgium, Ireland
 processing term: **6** shives, sliver **7** carding, hackled, retting **8** beetling, breaking, rippling, spinning **9** scutching

line of march 4 path **5** route, track **11** parade route

line of reasoning 4 case **7** premise **8** argument **10** hypothesis

line up 4 book **5** align **6** engage, even up **7** arrange, procure, program, queue up **8** schedule **9** form a line, put in a row **10** arrange for

line-up 5 slate **6** roster **8** schedule

linger 3 lag **4** idle, last, stay, wait **5** dally, delay, tarry, trail **6** dawdle, hang on, loiter, remain **7** persist, survive **9** die slowly **10** dillydally, hang around

lingering 4 slow **7** abiding, chronic, delayed, lagging, lasting, staying, waiting **8** dawdling, delaying, dragging, drawn out, dwelling, enduring, hovering, tarrying **9** loitering, remaining **10** protracted, sauntering **15** procrastinating

lingo 4 cant, talk **5** argot, idiom, slang **6** jargon, patois, tongue **7** dialect **8** language, parlance **10** vernacular

linguist 8 polyglot **10** grammarian, translator **11** etymologist, interpreter, philologist, phonetician, phonologist, semanticist **12** morphologist **13** lexicographer

liniment 4 balm **5** salve **7** unguent **8** ointment **9** emollient

link 3 tie **4** bind, bond, fuse, loop, ring **5** group, joint, tie in, unite **6** couple, relate, splice **7** bracket, combine, conjoin, connect, involve, liaison **8** junction, relation **9** associate, implicate **10** connection, connective **11** association **12** interconnect, relationship

linkage 3 tie **4** bond **6** hookup **10** connection **11** affiliation, association, correlation

link up 4 dock, join **6** couple, hook up **7** connect **9** affiliate **14** fasten together

Linnaeus, Carolus
 field: **6** botany
 nationality: **7** Swedish
 developed: **8** taxonomy **18** nomenclature system

linotype
 invented by: **12** Mergenthaler

Linton, Edgar
 character in: **16** Wuthering Heights
 author: **6** Bronte

Linus
 vocation: **4** poet **8** musician
 father: **6** Apollo
 mother: **8** Psamathe
 inventor of: **6** melody, rhythm
 identified with: **5** crops **9** withering **10** harvesting
 student: **8** Hercules
 killed by: **8** Hercules

lion 3 cat **6** cougar **7** wildcat **9** celebrity **12** man of the hour **15** king of the jungle
 group of: **5** pride
 constellation of: **3** Leo

lionhearted 4 bold **5** brave **6** heroic **7** valiant **8** fearless, intrepid, stalwart, unafraid, valorous **9** audacious, dauntless **10** courageous **11** indomitable **12** stouthearted
 see **8** Richard I

Lion in Winter, The
 director: **13** Anthony Harvey
 cast: **10** Jane Merrow **11** Peter O'Toole (Henry II) **13** Timothy Dalton **14** Anthony Hopkins **16** Katharine Hepburn (Eleanor of Aquitaine)
 Oscar for: **7** actress (Hepburn)

lionize 5 exalt **6** admire, praise, revere **7** acclaim, adulate, ennoble, flatter, glorify **8** enshrine, eulogize **9** celebrate, glamorize **10** aggrandize **11** immortalize

lion's share 4 bulk, most **8** majority **9** major part **11** greater part **13** preponderance

lip 3 lap, rim **4** brim, edge, kiss, lick, wash **5** apron, mouth, spout, utter **6** labial, labium, margin **8** backtalk, labellum **9** insincere **10** embouchure, mouthpiece **11** superficial

Lipchitz, Jacques
 real name: **17** Chaim Yakob Lipchiz
 born: **9** Lithuania **11** Druskieniki **12** Druskininkai
 artwork: **4** Head **6** Bather, Figure **7** Harpist **9** Sacrifice **10** Prometheus **11** Benediction, Joie de Vivre **12** Peace on Earth **14** Man with a Guitar **15** Acrobats on a Ball, Man with Mandolin, Song of the Vowels **17** Notre Dame de Liesse, Sailor with a Guitar **19** Pierrot with Clarinet, Return of the Prodigal **24** Virgin of the Inverted Heart

Lipizzaner 11 stocky horse
 bred in: **7** Austria
 color: **5** white
 used in: **8** dressage **18** jumping exhibitions

Lipmann, Fritz Albert
 field: **12** biochemistry
 discovered: **9** Coenzyme A
 awarded: **10** Nobel Prize

Lippi, Filippino
 born: **5** Italy, Prato
 father: **15** Fra Filippo Lippi
 artwork: **20** The Vision of St Bernard **24** The Life of St Thomas Aquinas **26** The Lives of Sts Philip and John

Lippi, Fra Filippo
 born: **5** Italy **8** Florence
 son: **9** Filippino
 artwork: **15** Madonna and Child, The Feast of Herod **19** The Tarquinia Madonna **21** Coronation of the Virgin **25** The Madonna Adoring Her Child

liqueur 5 booze, drink, hooch **7** alcohol, potable, spirits **8** beverage, potation **9** aqua vitae, drinkable, inebriant, moonshine **10** intoxicant
 almond: **8** amaretto
 anise: **8** absinthe
 apple: **8** calvados
 apricot: **10** abricotine
 caraway: **6** kummel **7** aquavit
 chocolate: **12** crème de cacao
 citrus: **10** goldwasser, liquor d'or
 coffee: **6** Kahlua
 grape: **6** Metaxa
 herb: **6** pernod **7** raspail **10** vielle cure **11** fiori alpini
 honey: **8** Drambuie
 medicinal: **11** Benedictine
 mint: **13** creme de menthe
 orange: **6** strega **7** curacao **9** cointreau **12** Grand Marnier
 raspberry: **9** framboise

liquid 5 drink, fluid **6** melted, molten, thawed **7** potable **8** beverage, solution

liquidate 3 hit, pay **4** kill **5** clear, erase, waste **6** cancel, murder, pay off, rub out, settle, wind up **7** abolish, break up, destroy, wipe out **8** close out, conclude, demolish **9** discharge, dispose of, eradicate, put to rest, terminate **10** account for, do away with **11** assassinate

liquor 3 gin, rum, rye **5** booze, broth, hooch, juice, sauce, vodka **6** brandy, liquid, redeye, rotgut, Scotch **7** bourbon, extract, spirits, whiskey **9** drippings, moonshine **10** inebriants

11 intoxicants
measure: 4 pint, pony, shot **5** fifth, quart **6** jigger, magnum
symbol: 14 John Barleycorn

Lir *see* **3** Ler

Lisbon
capital of: 8 Portugal
landmark:
  castle: 11 Saint George
  monastery: 9 Jeronimos
  square: 10 Black Horse
  tower: 5 Belem
Moorish name: 7 Lixbuna
ocean: 8 Atlantic
Portuguese: 6 Lisboa
river: 5 Tagus
Roman name: 14 Felicitas Julia
rulers: 5 Moors **6** French, Romans **7** British, Germans, Spanish **11** Phoenicians

lissome 5 agile, lithe, quick **6** limber, lively, nimble, pliant, supple **7** slender **8** flexible, graceful **9** lithesome, sprightly **11** light-footed

list 3 tip **4** bend, heel, lean, roll, tilt **5** index, slant, slate, slope, table **6** careen, muster, record, roster **7** catalog, in cline, leaning **8** register, schedule, tabulate **9** catalogue, inventory

listen 4 hark, hear, heed, list **6** attend **7** give ear, hearken **8** give heed, listen in, overhear **9** be all ears, bend an ear, eavesdrop **10** take notice **12** pay attention

listener 3 ear **6** hearer **7** auditor **10** overhearer **12** eavesdropper

Lister, Joseph
field: 7 surgeon **8** medicine
nationality: 7 British
pioneer of: 17 antiseptic surgery

listless 4 down, dull, lazy **6** dreamy, drowsy, leaden, mopish, torpid **7** languid **8** in active, indolent, lifeless, sluggish **9** apathetic, enervated, lethargic, soporific **10** phlegmatic, spiritless **11** indifferent, unconcerned **12** uninterested **13** lackadaisical

Liston, Charles
nickname: 5 Sonny
sport: 6 boxing
class: 11 heavyweight

Liszt, Franz (Ferencz)
born: 7 Hungary, Raiding
teacher: 6 Czerny
daughter: 6 Cosima
son-in-law: 6 Wagner
composer of: 5 Dante (symphony), Faust (symphony) **8** Christus **9** Psalm XIII **10** Nuages gris **13** Psalm Thirteen **17** Years of Pilgrimage **18** Annees de Pelerinage **19** Hungarian Rhapsodies **22** The Legend of St Elizabeth

litany 4 list **7** account, catalog, recital **9** catalogue, narration, rendition **10** recitation, repetition **11** description, enumeration

literacy 7 culture **8** learning **9** erudition **11** edification, eruditeness, learnedness, scholarship **12** intelligence **13** enlightenment

literal 4 real, true **5** exact **6** actual, direct, honest, strict **7** correct, factual, precise, prosaic **8** accurate, faithful, reliable, truthful, verbatim **9** authentic **10** adlitteram, dependable, meticulous, scrupulous, un-disputed **11** trustworthy, undeviating, word-for-word **12** matter-of-fact **13** authoritative, conscientious, unimaginative, unimpeachable

literary 6 poetic **7** bookish, of books **8** artistic, lettered, literate **12** intellectual

literate 7 learned **8** cultured, educated, lettered, literary, schooled, well-read **12** well-informed **13** knowledgeable

literati 9 highbrows **12** connoisseurs **13** intellectuals **14** intelligentsia

literature 4 lore **5** books, works **6** papers, theses **7** letters **8** classics, writings **9** treatises **11** scholarship **12** publications **13** belles lettres, dissertations

lithe 5 agile **6** limber, nimble, pliant, supple **7** lissome, pliable **8** bendable, flexible, graceful

Lithgow, John
roles: 9 Footloose **17** Terms of Endearment **19** Third Rock From the Sun **21** Harry and the Hendersons **23** The World According to Garp **29** The Adventures of Buckaroo Banzai

lithium
chemical symbol: 2 Li

Lithuania
other/former name: 5 Litva **7** Lietuva **33** Lithuanian Soviet Socialist Republic
capital/largest city: 5 Vilna **6** Kaunas **7** Vilnius
others: 4 Balt, Lett **5** Aesti, Kouno, Memel **6** Kovnac **7** Jel gava, Palanga, Telsiai **8** Ignalina, Kapsukas, Klaipeda, Siauliai **9** Panevezys **10** Elektrenai
government: 8 republic
monetary unit: 3 lit **5** marka **6** centas **7** ostmark, skatiku **8** auksinas
lake: 5 Dysna
mountain: 15 Samogitian Hills
highest point: 9 Juozapine
river: 5 Neman, Neris, Rusne **6** Dubysa, Nieman, Viliya **7** Nemunas, Nevezis, Nevezys **8** Pregolya
sea: 6 Baltic
physical feature:
  lagoon: 8 Courland, Kuronian
people: 4 Balt, Lett **5** Zhmud **6** Jewish, Litvak, Polish **7** Aistian, Russian, Yatvyag **10** Lithuanian, Samogitian **11** Belorussian
language: 5 Zmudz **6** Baltic **10** Lithuanian

religion: 8 Lutheran **13** Roman Catholic

litigation 4 suit **7** contest, dispute, lawsuit **10** contention, day in court **11** controversy, disputation, legal action, prosecution

litter 3 bed **4** heap, junk, lair, mess, nest, pile **5** issue, strew, trash, young **6** de- bris, jumble, pallet, refuse **7** bedding, clutter, kittens, progeny, puppies, rubbish, scatter **8** leavings **9** offspring, stretcher

little 3 bit, dot, jot, wee **4** dash, drop, hint, iota, mean, mild, tiny, whit **5** brief, crumb, elfin, faint, fleet, hasty, never, petty, pinch, pygmy, quick, scant, short, small, speck, trace **6** bantam, hardly, meager, minute, narrow, paltry, petite, rarely, seldom, skimpy, slight, trifle **7** minimum, modicum, not much, passing, stunted, trivial **8** dwarfish, fragment, inferior, mediocre, not at all, not often, particle, piddling, pittance, scarcely, slightly, some what, trifling, unworthy **9** by no means, deficient, hardly any, itsy- bitsy, itty-bitty, miniature, momentary, pint-sized, third- rate, worthless **10** diminutive, inflexible, negligible, short-lived, suggestion, undersized **11** commonplace, Lilliputian, microscopic, of no account, opinionated, pocket-sized, scarcely any, small amount, unimportant **12** insufficient, run-of-the-mill, short-sighted **13** infinitesimal, insignificant, next to nothing

Little America
on: 10 Antarctica **12** Ross Ice Shelf
bases established by: 11 Admiral Byrd

Little Annie Rooney
creator: 14 Darrell McClure

Little Artha
nickname of: 11 Jack Johnson

Little Bighorn 5 river **7** Wyoming
battle site of: 5 Sioux **6** Custer, Dakota **8** Cheyenne
called: 16 Custer's last stand
see also **13** Custer, George A.

Little Big Man
author: 12 Thomas Berger
director: 10 Arthur Penn
cast: 11 Faye Dunaway **12** Martin Balsam **13** Dustin Hoffman (Jack Crabb) **14** Chief Dan George **15** Richard Mulligan

little by little
French: 7 peu a peu
Spanish: 9 poco a poco

Little Caesar
director: 11 Mervyn LeRoy
cast: 13 Glenda Farrell **15** Edward G Robinson (Rico) (Caesar Enrico Bandello) **18** Douglas Fairbanks Jr

Little Corporal 8 Napoleon

Little Dipper 11 star cluster
  in: 9 Ursa Minor 10 Little Bear
Little Dorrit
  author: 14 Charles Dickens
  character: 3 Amy (Little Dorrit), Tip
  4 Rugg 5 Casby, Fanny, Flora,
  Gowan 6 Affery, Merdle, Pancks, Rigaud (Blandois) 7 Meagles 8 Mr F's
  Aunt 9 Mrs Merdle 10 Flintwinch 13
  Arthur Clennam, William Dorrit 16
  Monsieur Blandois, Young John
  Chivery
Little Drummer Girl, The
  author: 11 John Le Carre
Little Emily, Little Em'ly
  character in: 16 David Copperfield
  author: 7 Dickens
Little Fox
  constellation of: 9 Vulpecula
Little Foxes, The
  author: 14 Lillian Hellman
  character: 13 Regina Giddens
  director: 12 William Wyler
  cast: 10 Bette Davis (Regina) 12 Teresa Wright 14 Richard Carlson 15
  Herbert Marshall
  prequel: 22 Another Part of the Forest
Little Gidding
  author: 7 T S Eliot
Little House on the Prairie
  author: 18 Laura Ingalls Wilder
  character: 6 Albert 7 Dr Baker 8 Rev
  Alden 9 Mr Edwards 10 Andy Garvey, Lars Hanson, Nels Oleson 11
  Adam Kendall, Alice Garvey, Mary
  Ingalls 12 Grace Ingalls, Laura Ingalls, Nellie Oleson, Willie Oleson 13
  Carrie Ingalls, Harriet Oleson 14
  Charles Ingalls, Eva Beadle Simms,
  Jonathan Garvey 15 Caroline Ingalls
  cast: 10 Dabbs Greer, Kevin Hagen
  11 Karl Swenson, Merlin Olsen,
  Richard Bull 12 Hersha Parady, Ka-
  ren Grassle, Victor French 13 Alison
  Arngrim, Linwood Boomer, Michael
  Landon 14 Melissa Gilbert 15
  Jonathon Gilbert, Sidney Greenbush,
  Wendy Turnbeaugh 16 Brenda Turn-
  beaugh, Charlotte Gilbert, Lindsay
  Greenbush 17 Katherine McGregor,
  Matthew Laborteaux, Patrick La-
  borteaux 18 Melissa Sue Anderson
  setting: 6 Winoka 9 Minnesota, Plum
  Creek 11 Walnut Grove
Little John
  character in: 9 Robin Hood
Little King, The
  creator: 10 Otto Soglow
  technique: 9 pantomine
little-known 6 unsung 7 obscure, un-
  noted 10 unrenowned
Little Learning, A
  author: 11 Evelyn Waugh
Little Lord Fauntleroy
  author: 15 Frances H Burnett

Little Lulu
  creator: 14 Marge Henderson
Little Match Girl, The
  author: 21 Hans Christian Andersen
Little Men
  author: 15 Louisa May Alcott
Little Mermaid, The
  author: 21 Hans Christian Andersen
Little Minister, The
  author: 12 James M Barrie
Little Mo
  nickname of: 15 Maureen Connolly
Little Nemo in Slumberland
  creator: 11 Winsor McCay
  character: 6 Dr Pill 8 cannibal, princess
    clown: 4 Flip
    dog: 6 Blutch
little one 3 tot 4 babe, baby, tyke 5
  child 6 infant, wee one 7 toddler
Little Orphan Annie
  creator: 10 Harold Gray
  character:
    foster father: 13 Daddy Warbucks
    dog: 5 Sandy
    saying: 13 Leapin' Lizards
little people 5 elves 6 dwarfs 7 fairies, midgets 11 leprechauns
Little Prince, The
  author: 21 Antoine de Saint-Exupery
Little Rhody
  nickname of: 11 Rhode Island
Little Rock see 8 Arkansas
Little Tramp
  nickname of: 14 Charlie Chaplin
Little Women
  author: 15 Louisa May Alcott
  character: 6 Laurie (Theodore Laurence), Marmee 10 John Brooke 14
  Professor Bhaer
    March sisters: 2 Jo 3 Amy, Meg 4
    Beth
  director:
    1933 version: 11 George Cukor
    1949 version: 11 Mervyn LeRoy
  cast (1933): 9 Paul Lukas 10 Frances
  Dee, Jean Parker 11 Joan Bennett 16
  Katharine Hepburn (Jo)
  cast (1949): 9 Mary Astor 10 Janet
  Leigh 11 June Allyson 12 Peter Lawford 14 Margaret O'Brien 15 Elizabeth Taylor
liturgical 6 ritual 10 ceremonial 11
  ceremonious, sacramental
liturgy 4 mass, rite 6 ritual 7 service,
  worship 8 ceremony, services 9 communion, sacrament
lituus
  form: 5 staff
  shape: 7 crooked
Lityerses
  father: 9 King Midas
  held: 15 reaping contests
  killed: 6 losers
livable, liveable 4 cozy, snug 5
  comfy, homey 8 bearable, passable,

pleasant, suitable 9 agreeable, endurable, enjoyable, habitable, tolerable 10
acceptable, convenient, gratifying, satisfying, worthwhile 11 comfortable
live 2 be 3 hot 4 bunk, feed, stay 5
  abide, afire, aglow, alive, exist,
  fiery, lodge, quick, stand, vital 6
  ablaze, active, aflame, alight, at hand,
  billet, bodily, endure, hold on, living,
  obtain, occupy, red-hot, remain, reside, settle, thrive 7 animate, at issue,
  be alive, blazing, breathe, burning,
  current, flaming, fleshly, going on, ignited, persist, prevail, subsist, survive
  8 existent, flourish, get ahead, get
  along, have life, increase, multiply,
  physical, pressing, take root, up to-
  date, white-hot 9 breathing, corporeal
  10 draw breath
live and keep well
  Latin: 11 vive valeque
Live and Let Die
  author: 10 Ian Fleming
live dissolutely 7 carouse, debauch 9
  dissipate 11 overindulge
livelihood 3 job 5 trade 6 career, living, metier 7 calling, support, venture
  8 business, position, vocation 9 situation 10 enterprise, line of work, occupation, profession, sustenance 11
  maintenance, subsistence, undertaking
liveliness 3 pep, zip 4 brio, elan 6
  vigor 7 agility 8 alacrity, vitality, vivacity 9 animation, briskness, eagerness 10 ebullience, nimbleness 13
  sprightliness
lively 5 alert, brisk, eager, peppy,
  perky, vivid 6 active, ardent, bouncy
  7 buoyant, excited, fervent, intense 8
  animated, spirited, vigorous 9 energetic, excitable, sprightly, vivacious
  12 enthusiastic
liven 4 buoy 5 cheer, elate, pep up 6
  perk up, vivify 7 animate, delight, enliven, fortify, gladden, hearten, punch
  up, quicken 8 brighten, embolden, energize, inspirit 10 exhilarate, invigorate, strengthen
liver
  stores: 8 glycogen
  color: 3 red 5 brown
  produces: 4 bile 10 blood cells
Livermore Larruper
  nickname of: 7 Max Baer
livery 4 garb, suit 5 dress 6 attire 7
  costume, raiment, regalia, uniform 8
  clothing 9 vestments
Lives of a Bengal Lancer
  director: 13 Henry Hathaway
  cast: 10 Gary Cooper 12 Franchot
  Tone 14 Sir Guy Standing 15 Richard Cromwell
Lives of the Poets, The
  author: 13 Samuel Johnson
live through 4 know 7 survive, undergo 9 go through 10 experience

livid 3 mad 4 pale 5 angry, irate, riled, vexed 6 fuming, galled, purple, raging 7 bruised, enraged, furious 8 contused, incensed, inflamed, outraged, provoked, wrathful 9 indignant, steamed up, ticked off 10 discolored, infuriated 11 exasperated 12 black-and-blue

living 3 job 4 life, live, work 5 alive, being, quick, trade 6 active, bodily, career, extant, income 7 animate, calling, fleshly, going on, organic, venture 8 business, embodied, enduring, existent, existing, material, up-to-date, vocation 9 animation, breathing, corporeal, existence, incarnate, life-style, operative, permanent, remaining, surviving, way of life 10 employment, enterprise, having life, in the flesh, line of work, livelihood, occupation, persisting, prevailing, profession, subsisting, sustenance 11 maintenance, subsistence 13 drawing breath

living being 8 creature, organism

living conditions 10 atmosphere 11 environment 13 circumstances

living picture
　French: 13 tableau vivant

living quarters 4 home 5 abode, house 6 billet 7 housing, lodging, shelter 8 domicile, dwelling, quarters 9 apartment, residence 10 habitation 13 dwelling place

Livy
　also: 11 Titus Livius
　author of: 13 Ab urbe condita 26 From the Foundation of the City

lizard 3 dab, eft, uma 4 adda, gila, newt, seps, tegu, uran 5 agama, anole, anoli, gecko, idler, shrink 6 aguana, dragon, iguana, komodo, moloch 7 lounger, monitor, reptile, saurian 8 dinosaur, lacerata, scorpion 9 alligator, blind worm, chameleon, crocodile, galliwasp 10 chuckwalla, glass snake, horned toad, salamander 11 gila monster 12 Komodo dragon
　characteristic: 6 scales 7 molting 9 oviparous 11 cold-blooded 12 regeneration
　constellation of: 7 Lacerta

llama 6 alpaca, kechua, mammal, vicuna 7 guanaco 8 ungulate 13 Peruvian sheep

llano 11 grassy plain
　in: 12 South America

Llewellyn, Richard
　author of: 19 How Green Was My Valley

Llew Llaw Gyffes
　origin: 5 Welsh
　father: 7 Gwydion
　mother: 9 Arianhrod
　wife: 10 Blodenwedd
　curses bestowed by: 9 Arianhrod

Lloyd
　origin: 5 Welsh

　form: 8 magician
　cast spells upon: 7 Pryderi

Lloyd, Harold
　born: 10 Burchard NE
　roles: 9 Feet First 10 Safety Last 11 The Freshman 13 The Kid Brother

Lloyd Webber, Andrew
　born: 6 London
　Composer of: 4 Cats 5 Evita 6 Jeeves 12 Song and Dance 13 Aspects of Love 15 Tell Me on a Sunday 16 Starlight Express 20 Jesus Christ Superstar, The Phantom of the Opera 39 Joseph and the Amazing Technicolor Dreamcoat

Llud
　also: 4 Ludd, Nudd
　origin: 5 Welsh
　king of: 7 Britain
　rid kingdom of: 6 plague
　famous for: 10 generosity

Llyr
　origin: 5 Welsh
　son: 10 Manawyddan
　corresponds to: 3 Ler, Lir

load 3 try, vex 4 care, fill, haul, heap, lade, pack, pile 5 cargo, crush, stack, stuff, worry 6 burden, hamper, hinder, lad- ing, misery, strain, weight 7 afflict, carload, freight, oppress, trouble 8 capacity, contents, encumber, handicap, pressure, shipload; shipment 9 overwhelm, plane load, truckload, wagonload, weigh down 10 affliction, deadweight, depression, misfortune, oppression 11 encumbrance

loads 4 lots, much 5 heaps, piles, scads 6 oodles, plenty 14 more than enough

loaf 4 idle, loll 5 dally 6 be lazy 7 goof off 8 kill time, malinger 9 do nothing, gold brick, laze about, waste time 10 take it easy 12 lounge around

loafer 3 bum 4 shoe 5 idler 6 no-good 7 laggard, shirker, sponger, wastrel 8 deadbeat, loiterer, sluggard 9 goldbrick, lazybones 10 lazy person, malingerer, ne'er-do- well 11 couch potato 12 lounge lizard 15 drugstore cowboy
　French: 7 flaneur

loan 4 lend 5 allow 6 credit 7 advance, lending 8 mortgage 9 advancing

loath 4 loth 6 averse 7 against, counter, hostile, opposed 8 inimical 9 reluctant, resisting, unwilling 10 indisposed, set against 11 disinclined

loathe 4 hate 5 abhor, scorn 6 detest, eschew 7 deplore, despise, disdain, dislike 9 abominate 10 blench from, flinch from, recoil from, shrink from 11 keep clear of, shy away from 12 draw back from 14 be unable to bear, find disgusting, view with horror 16 have no stomach for

loathing 4 hate 5 odium 6 hatred 7

disgust, dislike 8 aversion, distaste 9 antipathy, repulsion, revulsion 10 abhorrence, repugnance 11 abomination, detestation

loathsome 4 foul, mean, rank, vile 5 nasty 6 odious 7 hateful 9 abhorrent, invidious, obnoxious, offensive, repugnant, re- pulsive, revolting, sickening 10 abominable, despicable, detestable, disgusting, nauseating, unbearable 11 distasteful

lobby 5 foyer 8 anteroom, politick 9 vestibule 11 antechamber, pull strings, waiting room 12 entrance hall

lobscouse 4 meat 8 hardtack 10 vegetables 11 sailor's stew

local 6 narrow, native, nearby 7 insular, limited 8 citywide, confined, regional 9 adjoining, homegrown, parochial, sectional 10 provincial 11 territorial 12 neighborhood 13 circumscribed

locale 4 area, site, spot, zone 6 region 7 quarter, section, setting 8 locality, location, precinct, province, vicinity 12 neighborhood

locality 4 area, site, spot, zone 5 place 6 locale, region 7 quarter, section 8 district, location, precinct, province, vicinity 9 territory 12 neighborhood

locate 3 fix, put 4 find, live, post, seat, stay 5 dwell, place 6 detect, move to, reside, settle 7 deposit, discern, hit upon, set down, situate, station, uncover, unearth 8 come upon, meet with, pinpoint 9 establish, ferret out, light upon, search out, stumble on, track down 10 settle down 12 put down roots

location 4 site, spot 5 place 6 locale 8 district, position 9 situation 11 whereabouts 12 neighborhood

Lochinvar
　character in: 7 Marmion
　bride: 5 Ellen
　author: 5 Scott

Loch Ness
　in: 8 Scotland
　home of: 6 Nessie 7 monster

lock 3 bar, dam, pen 4 bang, bolt, cage, coil, curl, grab, grip, hank, hold, hook, jail, join, link, tuft 5 catch, clamp, clasp, grasp, latch, seize, skein, tress, unite 6 clinch, coop up, fasten, lock up, secure, shut in 7 confine, embrace, entwine, grapple, impound, padlock, ringlet 8 dock gate, imprison 9 canal gate, fastening, floodgate, interlink 10 intertwine, sluice gate 11 incarcerate

lock, cylinder
　invented by: 4 Yale

Lockhart, Gene
　daughter: 12 June Lockhart
　granddaughter: 11 Ann Lockhart
　born: 6 Canada, London 7 Ontario
　roles: 12 Madame Bovary 16 Death

of a Salesman **19** The Inspector General **20** Abe Lincoln in Illinois

lock horns 4 feud, tiff **5** argue, brawl, clash, fight **7** dispute, quarrel, wrangle **8** squabble **9** altercate

Lockit 4 Lucy
  character in: **12** Beggar's Opera
  author: **3** Gay

lockup 3 jug, pen **4** jail, stir **5** clink, pokey **6** cooler, prison **7** slammer **8** big house, hoosegow **11** reformatory **12** penitentiary

lock up 3 pen **4** cage, jail **6** coop up, secure **7** confine, impound **8** imprison, restrain, restrict **11** incarcerate

Lockyer, Joseph Norman
  field: **9** astronomy
  nationality: **7** British
  discovered: **6** helium

loco citato 15 in the place cited
  abbreviation: **6** loc cit

locomotive
  invented by:
    electric: **4** Vail
    experimental: **6** Fenton, Hedley **10** Stephenson, Trevithick
    first US: **6** Cooper
    practical: **10** Stephenson

locust 7 Robinia
  varieties: **4** moss **5** black, honey, mossy, swamp, sweet, water **6** clammy, yellow **7** African, bristly **8** ship-mast **10** West Indian **13** Allegheny moss, South American

locution 4 term **5** idiom, trope, usage **6** phrase, saying **7** wording **8** idiolect, phrasing **9** set phrase, utterance, verbalism **10** expression **11** phraseology, regionalism **12** turn of phrase **14** figure of speech

lode 3 bed **4** seam **7** deposit

lodge 3 bed, hut **4** camp, file, room, stay **5** cabin, catch, hotel, house, motel, put up **6** billet, harbor, resort, submit **7** cottage, quarter, shelter, sojourn **8** register

lodging 4 room **8** quarters **13** accommodation

Loewe, Frederick
  born: **6** Vienna
  Composer of: **4** Gigi **7** Camelot **8** Galateya **9** Brigadoon **10** My Fair Lady **14** Paint Your Wagon **15** The Little Prince

loft 3 lob **5** attic, pop up **6** belfry, garret **7** balcony, gallery, hit high, mansard **8** top floor **9** attic room, throw high **10** clerestory

loftiness 5 pride **9** arrogance **11** haughtiness **13** imperiousness **16** superciliousness

Lofting, Hugh
  author of: **10** Dr Dolittle

lofty 4 cold, high, tall **5** aloof, grand, great, noble, proud **6** lordly, mighty, remote, snooty **7** distant, eminent, exalted, haughty, leading, soaring, stately, stuck-up, sublime **8** arrogant, eleva- ted, glorious, imposing, insolent, majestic, puffed-up, scornful, snobbish, superior, towering **9** conceited, dignified, imperi- ous, important **10** disdainful, hoity-toity, preeminent **11** high ranking, illustrious, patronizing **12** high-reaching **13** condescending, distinguished, high-and-mighty, self-important

lofty bearing 7 dignity, majesty **10** augustness **11** stateliness

log 5 block, diary, stump **6** docket, lumber, record, timber **7** account, daybook, journal, logbook **8** calendar, schedule

Logan, Mount
  in: **5** Yukon **12** St. Elias range
  highest mt. in: **6** Canada

loges 5 boxes **7** balcony **9** mezzanine

loggia 5 lanai, porch **6** arcade, piazza **7** balcony, gallery

logic 5 sense **6** reason **7** cogency **8** analysis, argument **9** coherence, deduction, good sense, induction **10** dialectics

logical 5 clear, sound, valid **6** cogent, likely **7** germane **8** coherent, rational, relevant, sensible **9** deducible, pertinent, plausible **10** analytical, consistent, most likely, reasonable **11** enlightened, intelligent **13** well-organized

logos 4 word **5** ratio **6** saying, speech **7** thought **9** discourse, reckoning **10** proportion

logy 4 dull **5** inert, tired, weary **6** drowsy, groggy, sleepy, torpid **8** comatose, life- less, listless, sluggish **9** enervated, inanimate, lethargic **10** phlegmatic **12** hebetudinous

Lohengrin
  opera by: **6** Wagner
  character: **4** Elsa **6** Ortrud **9** Gottfried (Duke of Brabant) **25** Count Frederick of Telramund

Lohengrin
  origin: **8** Germanic
  knight of: **9** Holy Grail
  father: **8** Parsifal, Parzival

loiter 4 idle, laze, loaf, loll, lurk **5** dally, skulk, slink, tarry **6** dawdle **10** dillydally, hang around **11** hover around **12** shilly-shally

Loki
  origin: **12** Scandinavian
  mentioned in: **9** Lokasenna
  god of: **4** fire
  son: **6** Fenrir, Fenris
  daughter: **3** Hel
  fathered: **10** Jormungand **11** lormungandr, Jormungandr **14** Midgard Serpent
  mother of his children: **9** Angerboda, Angrbodha, Angurboda
  caused death of: **5** Baldr **6** Balder, Baldur
  form: **5** giant
  extorted treasure from: **7** Andvari
  function: **4** evil **6** strife **7** discord **8** mischief

Lolita
  author: **15** Vladimir Nabokov
  character: **6** Lolita **14** Humbert Humbert
  director: **14** Stanley Kubrick
  based on novel by: **15** Vladimir Nabokov
  cast: **7** Sue Lyon (Lolita) **10** James Mason (Humbert Humbert) **12** Peter Sellers **14** Shelley Winters

loll 3 sag **4** drag, drop, flap, flop, idle, lean, loaf **5** droop, relax, slump **6** dangle, dawdle, lounge, repose, slouch, sprawl **7** goof off, recline **8** flop over, languish

Lollobrigida, Gina
  born: **5** Italy **7** Subiaco
  roles: **7** Trapeze **14** Anne of Brooklyn, The Wayward Wife **15** Solomon and Sheba **20** Buona Sera Mrs Campbell **27** The World's Most Beautiful Woman

Loman, Willy
  character in: **16** Death of a Salesman
  author: **6** Miller
  epitome of: **8** salesman

Lombard, Carole
  real name: **15** Jane Alice Peters
  husband: **10** Clark Gable
  born: **11** Fort Wayne IN
  roles: **12** My Man Godfrey **13** Nothing Sacred, To Be Or Not To Be **16** Twentieth Century

Lome
  capital of: **4** Togo

London
  airport: **7** Gatwick **8** Heathrow, Stansted
  architect: **4** Wren
  area: **4** Soho **6** Camden **7** Brixton, Chelsea, Holborn, Pimlico **8** Vauxhall **9** Bayswater, Belgravia, Islington, Southwark **10** Bloomsbury, Kensington, Paddington, Shoreditch **11** Notting Hill, St John's Wood **13** Knightsbridge
  capital of: **7** England **12** Great Britain **13** United Kingdom
  landmark: **6** Big Ben **8** Hyde Park **9** Whitehall, Wimbledon **11** Regent's Park, Saint James's, Tate Gallery, Tower Bridge **12** Covent Garden, London Bridge **13** British Museum, Tower of London **14** British Library, Speaker's Corner **15** National Gallery, Trafalgar Square **16** Buckingham Palace, Piccadilly Circus, Westminster Abbey **17** Kensington Gardens, Royal Festival Hall, Westminster Palace **18** Houses of Parliament **19** Saint Paul's Cathedral **23** Victoria and Albert Museum

police: **7** bobbies
  established by: **13** Sir Robert Peel
prime minister's residence: **16** Ten Downing Street
river: **6** Thames
Roman name: **9** Londinium
subway: **11** Underground

London, Jack
author of: **9** White Fang **10** The Sea Wolf **16** The Call of the Wild

lone 4 only, sole **5** alone **6** single, unique **8** isolated, singular, solitary, unpaired **9** unabetted **10** individual, unattended, unescorted **13** companionless, unaccompanied

loneliness 9 isolation, seclusion **12** lonesomeness, solitariness **14** friendlessness

Loneliness of the Long Distance Runner, The
author: **12** Alan Sillitoe
director: **14** Tony Richardson
cast: **11** Avis Bunnage, Peter Madden **12** Tom Courtenay **15** Michael Redgrave

lonely 6 remote **7** forlorn **8** deserted, desolate, forsaken, hermitic, isolated, lonesome, secluded, solitary, unsocial **9** by oneself, reclusive, withdrawn **10** friendless, unattended **11** uninhabited, unpopulated **12** unfrequented **13** companionless, unaccompanied

Lone Ranger, The
character: **5** Tonto
cast: **8** John Hart **12** Clayton Moore **14** Jay Silverheels
horse: **5** Scout **6** Silver
saying: **8** kemo sabe
Lone Ranger used: **13** silver bullets
theme: **19** William Tell Overture

lonesome 5 alone, aloof **6** lonely **7** forlorn, insular **8** desolate, detached, forsaken **9** alienated, withdrawn **10** friendless, unfriended **13** companionless

Lone Star State
nickname of: **5** Texas

long 4 hope, lust, pine, sigh, want, wish **5** covet, crave, yearn **6** aspire, hanker, hunger, thirst **7** lengthy, spun out **8** drawn-out, extended, have a yen, in length, unending **9** elongated, extensive, prolonged **10** be bent on, protracted **11** far-reaching, have a desire **12** from end to end, interminable, outstretched

Long, Crawford Williamson
field: **8** medicine
first used: **5** ether

Longaville
character in: **16** Love's Labour's Lost
author: **11** Shakespeare

Long Day's Journey into Night
author: **12** Eugene O'Neill
director: **11** Sidney Lumet
cast: **13** Dean Stockwell **14** Jason Ro-

bards Jr **15** Ralph Richardson **16** Katharine Hepburn

Longest Day, The
director: **10** Ken Annakin **12** Andrew Marton, Bernard Wicki
cast: **9** John Wayne, Mel Ferrer **10** Henry Fonda, Red Buttons, Robert Ryan, Rod Steiger **12** Peter Lawford
setting: **4** D-Day **8** Normandy (Allied invasion)

long-faced 4 glum **6** dismal, gloomy **7** doleful, unhappy **8** dejected, mournful **10** lugubrious **14** down in the mouth

Longfellow, Henry Wadsworth
author of: **8** Hyperion, (The Song of) Hiawatha **10** Evangeline **15** Paul Revere's Ride **18** Tales of a Wayside Inn **21** The Wreck of the Hesperus **27** The Courtship of Miles Standish

longing 3 yen **4** wish **6** ardent, pining, thirst **7** craving, wishful **8** desirous, yearning **9** hankering, hungering **10** aspiration **11** languishing

long-lasting 7 chronic, lengthy, tedious **8** enduring, extended **9** prolonged **10** continuing, protracted

long live
French: **4** vive

long past 3 old **5** olden **6** gone by, of yore **7** ancient, long ago **8** long gone

long-standing 4 long **5** hardy, hoary **6** rooted **7** abiding, ancient, chronic, durable, lasting **8** enduring, habitual, hallowed, unfading **9** confirmed, continual, long-lived, perennial, perpetual, venerable **10** continuous, deep-rooted, deep-seated, inveterate, persistent, persisting **11** long-lasting, time-honored **15** long-established

Longstreet, James
served in: **8** Civil War
side: **11** Confederate
battle: **7** Bull Run **10** Gettysburg **11** Chickamauga **14** Fredericksburg **18** Wilderness Campaign
after war joined: **11** Republicans
US minister to: **6** Turkey

Long Voyage Home, The
director: **8** John Ford
based on play by: **12** Eugene O'Neill
cast: **9** Ian Hunter, John Wayne **13** Wilfrid Lawson **14** Thomas Mitchell **15** Barry Fitzgerald

long-wearing 5 tough **6** strong, sturdy **7** durable, lasting **8** enduring **11** substantial

long-winded 5 wordy **6** prolix **7** lengthy, tedious, verbose **8** rambling **9** garrulous **10** digressive, discursive

long-windedness 8 rambling **9** garrulity, prolixity, verbosity, wordiness **14** discursiveness

look 3 air, see **4** cast, face, gape, gaze, mien, ogle, peek, peep, scan, seem, show, view **5** front, glare, guise, sight, stare, study, watch **6** appear, behold, glance, regard, survey **7** bear-

ing, examine, exhibit, glimpse **8** demeanor, manifest, once-over, presence, scrutiny **10** appearance, be directed, cut a figure, expression, scrutinize **11** contemplate, countenance, observation

look after 4 help **6** assist, defend **7** help out, protect **10** minister to **11** watch out for **17** take under one's wing

look askance at 7 condemn **8** object to **9** frown upon **10** disapprove **14** discountenance **15** take exception to **16** find unacceptable, view with disfavor

look at 3 see **4** view **6** behold, notice, regard **7** examine, inspect, witness **10** scrutinize

Look Back in Anger
director: **14** Tony Richardson
based on play by: **11** John Osborne
cast: **7** Mary Ure **10** Edith Evans **11** Claire Bloom **13** Richard Burton **15** Donald Pleasance

look down on 7 despise, disdain **9** frown upon, patronize **10** condescend **13** put on airs with **14** hold in contempt

looker-on 6 viewer **7** watcher, witness **8** beholder, observer, onlooker **9** bystander, spectator

look for 4 seek **5** await **6** expect, pursue **7** hunt for **9** search for **10** anticipate

look for the woman
French: **15** cherchez la femme

look forward to 5 await **6** expect **7** long for, wait for **9** pin hope on **10** anticipate **17** count the days until

Look Homeward, Angel
author: **11** Thomas Wolfe
character: **7** Ben Gant **9** Eliza Gant **10** Eugene Gant, Laura James, Oliver Gant **15** Margaret Leonard

look in the eye 4 defy, face **5** brave **8** confront **9** challenge

look into 5 probe **7** examine, explore **10** scrutinize **11** inquire into, investigate

lookout 4 heed **5** guard, scout, vigil **6** patrol, sentry **7** spotter **8** observer, sentinel, watchdog, watchman **9** alertness, attention, awareness, readiness, vigilance **10** precaution **11** guardedness, mindfulness, watchkeeper **12** surveillance, watchfulness

look out 4 mind **6** beware **8** take care, watch out **9** be careful, be on guard **11** take warning **12** be on the alert

look over 4 scan, skim **5** judge **6** assess, peruse, survey **7** dip into **8** appraise, evaluate **13** browse through, glance through

look through 4 scan, skim **6** browse, peruse **7** dip into **8** look over **9** check over **13** glance through

look toward 7 count on 10 anticipate 13 look forward to

look upon 3 see 4 view 6 be hold, gaze at, look at 7 observe, stare at

look upon as 4 deem, hold 5 count, judge, think 6 regard, view as 7 account, believe 8 consider, take to be

look up to 5 honor 6 admire, esteem, revere 7 respect 8 venerate

loom 4 hulk, rise, soar 5 tower 6 appear, ascend, emerge 8 stand out 9 take shape

loom, power
  invented by: 10 Cartwright

loop 3 eye 4 bend, coil, curl, furl, ring, roll, turn 5 braid, curve, noose, plait, twirl, twist, whorl 6 circle, eyelet, spiral 7 opening, ringlet 8 aperture, encircle, loophole 10 wind around 11 convolution, curve around

Loos, Anita
  author of: 22 Gentlemen Prefer Blondes

loose 4 fast, free, lewd, undo, wild 5 freed, let go, slack, untie, vague 6 freely, loosen, unbind, undone, untied, wanton 7 immoral, inexact, loosely, release, set free, slacken, unbound, uncaged, unchain, unleash, unloose, unyoked 8 careless, heedless, liberate, not tight, rakehell, unbridle, unchaste, unfasten, unjoined, untether 9 abandoned, debauched, dissolute, imprecise, liberated, libertine, unbridled, unchained, unleashed, unmanacle, un shackle 10 dissipated, inaccurate, licentious, not binding, profligate, unattached, unexacting, unfastened, unfettered, unhandcuff, untethered 11 not fastened, unconnected 12 unimprisoned 13 unconstrained

loose-fitting 4 limp 5 baggy, loose, slack 6 draped, droopy 7 sagging 9 overlarge, oversized

loosely connected 5 jerky 6 fitful 8 episodic, rambling 9 spasmodic, wandering 10 digressive, discursive, meandering

loosen 3 lax 4 ease, free, undo 5 break, relax, untie 6 limber, unbend, unbind 7 release, relieve, slacken, unchain, unscrew 8 liberate, unbuckle, unfasten, work free 10 emancipate

looseness 8 fastness, lewdness, wildness 9 slackness, vagueness 10 debauch- ery, immorality, inaccuracy, profligacy, wantonness 11 dissipation, dissolution, imprecision 12 carelessness, heedlessness, inexactitude 14 licentiousness

loot 3 rob 4 haul, raid, sack, swag, take 5 booty, prize, strip 6 boodle, fleece, pilfer, ravage, spoils 7 pillage, plunder, ransack 11 stolen goods

looter 5 thief 6 robber, vandal 7 brigand 8 pillager 9 despoiler, plunderer

lop 3 cut 4 chip, chop, crop, dock, flop, sned, snip, trim 5 droop, prune, sever 6 cut off, deduct, detach, remove, slouch 7 cut back 8 amputate, truncate

Lopez, Nancy
  sport: 4 golf
  husband: 9 Ray Knight
    plays: 8 baseball

lopsided 4 awry 5 askew 6 aslant, tipped, uneven 7 crooked, leaning, listing, slanted, tilting, unequal 8 cockeyed, inclined, slanting 9 irregular 10 asymmetric, off- balance, unbalanced 15 disproportional 16 disproportionate

loquacious 5 gabby, talky, windy, wordy 6 blabby, chatty, prolix 7 prating, verbose, voluble 8 babbling, chattery 9 garrulous, prattling, talkative 10 chattering, long-winded

loquitur 8 he speaks 9 she speaks

lord 4 king 5 chief, crown, ruler 6 leader, master 7 monarch 8 overlord, seign- ior, superior 9 commander, landowner, sovereign 10 landholder, proprietor
  Japanese: 6 daimyo
  Turkish: 3 beg, bey

Lord
  Latin: 7 Dominus

Lord be with you, the
  Latin: 15 Dominus vobiscum

Lord have mercy
  Greek: 12 Kyrie eleison

Lord Jim
  author: 12 Joseph Conrad
  character: 5 Stein 6 Marlow 9 Dain Waris 14 Gentleman Brown

lordliness 7 disdain 8 contempt 9 arrogance, insolence, loftiness 11 haughtiness 13 imperiousness 16 superciliousness

lordly 4 cold 5 aloof, bossy, grand, lofty, noble, proud, regal 6 august, remote, snooty 7 distant, elegant, eminent, exalted, haughty, stately, stuck-up 8 arrogant, despotic, imposing, majestic, princely, puffed-up, scornful, snobbish 9 conceited, dignified, imperious, sumptuous 10 disdainful, hoity-toity, tyrannical 11 dictatorial, domineering, magisterial, magnificent, patronizing 13 condescending, high-and-mighty, self- important

Lord of the Flies
  author: 14 William Golding

Lord of the Rings, The
  author: 10 J R R Tolkien
  creatures: 3 elf, ent, orc 5 dwarf 6 hobbit

Lord Weary's Castle
  author: 12 Robert Lowell

lore 7 beliefs, legends 10 traditions

Lorelei

  also: 7 Lurelei
  origin: 8 Germanic
  form: 5 nymph
  dwelling place: 5 cliff, Rhine
  lured: 7 boatmen
  caused shipwrecks by: 7 singing

Lorelei Lee
  role in: 22 Gentlemen Prefer Blondes
  played by: 6 Monroe 8 Channing
  song: 27 Diamonds Are a Girl's Best Friend

Loren, Sophia
  real name: 14 Sofia Scicolone
  husband: 10 Carlo Ponti
  born: 4 Rome 5 Italy
  roles: 5 El Cid 8 Two Women (Oscar) 9 Arabesque, Houseboat 13 Man of La Mancha 14 The Black Orchid 18 Desire Under the Elms 20 Marriage Italian Style 21 A Countess from Hong Kong, The Pride and the Passion

Lorentz, Hendrik Anton
  field: 7 physics
  nationality: 5 Dutch
  discovered: 17 special relativity
  named for him: 21 Lorentz transformation 34 Lorentz- Fitzgerald Length Contraction
  awarded: 10 Nobel Prize

Loring, Eugene
  choreographer of: 11 Billy the Kid

Lorna Doone
  author: 11 R D Blackmore
  character: 8 John Ridd 9 Tom Faggus 11 Carver Doone 13 Sir Ensor Doone 14 Jeremy Stickles 15 Reuben Huckaback

Lorre, Peter
  real name: 16 Laszlo Lowenstein
  born: 7 Hungary 9 Rosenberg
  roles: 1 M 6 Mr. Moto 7 Mad Love 9 Joel Cairo 10 Casablanca, The Verdict 12 The Big Circus 14 Three Strangers 16 The Maltese Falcon 18 Crime and Punishment, The Mask of Dimitrios

Lorry, Jarvis
  character in: 16 A Tale of Two Cities
  author: 7 Dickens

Los Angeles
  airport: 3 LAX 7 Burbank 23 Los Angeles International
  area: 5 Watts 6 Bel Air, Downey, Venice 7 Anaheim, Compton, Norwalk 8 Mar Vista, Pasadena, Torrance, Westwood 9 Brentwood, Hollywood, Inglewood, Long Beach 10 Culver City 11 Century City, Garden Grove, Palos Verdes, Santa Monica 12 Beverly Hills, Marina del Rey 16 Pacific Palisades
    San Fernando Valley: 6 Encino 7 Tarzana, Van Nuys, Ventura 10 Northridge 11 Sherman Oaks
  baseball team: 7 Dodgers
  basketball team: 6 Lakers, Sparks

8 Clippers
football team: 4 Rams **7** Express, Raiders
hockey team: 5 Kings
landmark: 5 Forum **10** Disneyland **11** Civic Center, Getty Museum, Watts Towers **12** Griffith Park **13** Farmers' Market, Hollywood Bowl, Hollywood Park, La Brea Tar Pits, Magic Mountain **15** Knott's Berry Farm **16** Bonaventure Hotel **17** Norton Simon Museum **22** Grauman's Chinese Theater **23** Griffith Park Observatory
mountains: 10 San Gabriel **11** Santa Monica
nickname: 15 City of the Angels
street: 4 Vine **10** Rodeo Drive **12** Olvera Street **15** Mulholland Drive **16** Van Nuys Boulevard **17** Wilshire Boulevard **18** Hollywood Boulevard **20** Santa Monica Boulevard
university: 3 USC **4** UCLA **7** Caltech **10** Pepperdine **17** Occidental College **31** California Institute of Technology

lose 4 fail, miss **6** forget, ignore, mislay **7** confuse, forfeit **8** misplace **9** fail to win, stray from **10** be the loser, fail to heed **11** be thrown off **12** be defeated in, be deprived of, suffer loss of, take a licking

lose control 5 break, crack **7** crack up **9** fall apart **10** go to pieces **15** go off the deep end

lose faith 6 give up **7** despair **9** lose heart **10** have no hope **18** become disenchanted

lose force 3 die **7** run down **9** lose power

lose heart 6 give up **7** de spair **17** become discouraged

lose one's cool 12 fly into a rage **13** become enraged, throw a tantrum **14** lose one's temper **15** fly off the handle

loser 4 flop **7** failure **8** defeated **9** conquered **10** vanquished

lose track of 4 lose **9** let escape **11** lose sight of

lose vigor 4 flag **5** droop **6** sicken, weaken, wither **7** decline

Losing Battles
author: **11** Eudora Welty

loss 4 ruin **5** wreck **6** defeat, losing **7** licking, removal, undoing **8** overturn, riddance, wrecking **9** abolition, mislaying, privation **10** amount lost, demolition, extinction, forfeiture, misplacing, number lost **11** bereavement, deprivation, destruction, dissolution, eradication, expenditure, extirpation

loss of life 5 death **8** fatality **9** mortality

lost 5 stray **6** absent, astray, killed, ruined, wasted **7** lacking, mislaid, missing, misused, strayed, wrecked **8** absorbed, murdered, perished, vanished, wiped out **9** abolished, destroyed, en-grossed, misplaced, off- course **10** demolished, eradicated, extirpated, gone astray, misapplied, squandered **11** annihilated, misdirected, obliterated, preoccupied **12** exterminated

Lost Honor of Katharina Blum, The
author: **12** Heinrich Boll

Lost Horizon
author: **11** James Hilton
character: **10** Hugh Conway, Rutherford **12** Henry Barnard, Miss Brinklow **14** Father Perrault **20** Captain Mallison Chang
director: **10** Frank Capra
cast: **5** Margo **8** H B Warner, Sam Jaffe **9** Jane Wyatt **10** John Howard **12** Isa- bel Jewell, Ronald Colman **14** Thomas Mitchell **19** Edward Everett Horton
setting: **5** Tibet

Lost Illusions
author: **14** Honore de Balzac

Lost in America
director: **12** Albert Brooks
cast: **12** Albert Brooks, Julie Hagerty

Lost in Space
character: **5** Robot **7** Don West **12** Judy Robinson, Wlll Robinson **13** Pen- ny Robinson **14** Dr Zachary Smith **15** Maureen Robinson **16** Prof John Rob- inson
cast: **9** Billy Mumy **11** Guy Williams, Mark Goddard **12** June Lockhart, Marta Kristen **14** Jonathan Harris **16** Angela Cartwright
ship: **9** Jupiter II

Lost in the Funhouse
author: **9** John Barth

Lost in the Stars
author: **15** Maxwell Anderson

lost in thought 7 pensive **8** absorbed **9** engrossed, wrapped up **13** contemplative, in a brown study, introspective

Lost Lady, A
author: **11** Willa Cather

Lost Ones, The
author: **13** Samuel Beckett

Lost Patrol, The
director: **8** John Ford
cast: **8** Alan Hale **11** Wallace Ford **12** Boris Karloff **14** Victor McLaglen
score: **10** Max Steiner

Lost Weekend, The
author: **14** Charles Jackson
director: **11** Billy Wilder
cast: **9** Jane Wyman, Mary Young **10** Frank Falen, Ray Milland **11** Philip Terry **12** Doris Dowling **13** Howard da Silva
Oscar for: **5** actor (Milland) **7** picture **8** director **10** screenplay

lot 4 fate, lots, many, much, plot **5** field, patch, quota, share, straw, tract **6** oceans, oodles, ration **7** counter,

measure **8** beaucoup, property **9** allotment, allowance, great deal

Lot
grandfather: **5** Terah
father: **5** Haran
uncle: **7** Abraham
son: **5** Ammon
hometown: **5** Sodom
rescued by: **6** angels
fled to: **4** Zoar

lothario 3 rip **4** rake, roue, wolf **5** lover, Romeo, sheik **6** lecher **7** Don Juan, seducer, swinger **8** Casanova, lover- boy **9** debauchee, debaucher, libertine, womanizer **10** lady-killer, profligate, sensualist **11** philanderer, skirt-chaser

Lothario
character in: **15** The Fair Penitent
author: **4** Rowe

Loti, Pierre
author of: **18** An Iceland Fisherman
pseudonym of: **5** Viaud

lotion 4 balm, wash **5** salve **6** liquid **7** unction, unguent **8** cosmetic, liniment, ointment, solution **9** demulcent, emollient, freshener, skin cream **10** after-shave, astringent **11** conditioner, embrocation, moisturizer

Lotis
form: **5** nymph
changed into: **4** tree **5** lotus

lotophagi
means: **11** lotus-eaters

lots 4 much **5** heaps, loads, plots, scads **10** quantities

lotus 7 Nelumbo **13** Nymphaea lotus
varieties: **4** blue **5** water, white **6** sacred **8** American, Egyptian **10** East Indian

lotus-eaters 9 lotophagi
appear in: **7** Odyssey

loud 5 gaudy, noisy, showy, vivid **6** bright, flashy, garish **7** blatant, booming, intense, splashy **8** colorful, sonorous **9** clam- orous, deafening **10** resounding, stentorian, thundering, vociferous **11** ear-piercing, loud-mouthed **12** earsplitting, ostentatious

loud sound 4 bang, boom, clap, honk, howl, peal, roar, slam, toot **5** blare, blast, burst, crash **6** bellow, report, scream, shriek **7** clatter, thunder **9** explosion **10** detonation

Lou Grant
character: **6** Animal **8** Joe Rossi **10** Art Donovan **11** Charlie Hume **12** Billie Newman **15** Margaret Pynchon
cast: **10** Jack Bannon, Mason Adams **11** Edward Asner, Linda Kelsey **12** Robert Walden **13** Nancy Marchand **14** Darryl Anderson
paper: **17** Los Angeles Tribune
spinoff of: **18** Mary Tyler Moore Show

Louis, Joe
real name: **14** Joe Louis Barrow

nickname: 11 Brown Bomber
sport: 6 boxing
class: 11 heavyweight
Louis, Morris
  born: 11 Baltimore MD
  artwork: 4 Veil **5** Signa **7** Stripes **8** Unfurled **15** Mountains and Sea
Louise
  opera by: 11 Charpentier
  character: 6 Julian
Louisiana
  abbreviation: 2 LA
  nickname: 5 Bayou, Sugar **6** Creole **7** Pelican
  capital: 10 Baton Rouge
  largest city: 10 New Orleans
  others: 5 Houma **6** Bunkie, Gretna, Kenner, Minden, Monroe, Ruston **7** Bastrop **8** Bogalusa **9** Lafayette, Opelousas **10** Alexandria, Shreveport **11** Lake Charles
  college: 3 LSU **6** Loyola, Tulane **7** Dillard, Newcomb **9** Grambling
  explorer: 7 La Salle **9** Iberville **13** Pierre Lemoyne
  feature:
    area: 5 bayou **13** French Quarter
    festival: 9 Mardi Gras
    music: 4 jazz
    stadium: 9 Sugar Bowl
    street: 7 Bourbon
  tribe: 4 Adai, Ioni, Rees, Waco **5** Caddo, Haini, Washa **6** Eyeish, Pawnee **7** Andarko, Arikara, Atakapa **8** Ovachita **9** Bayogoula, Nachitoch
  people: 5 Cajun **6** Creole **7** Acadian, pelican **8** Huey Long **14** Lillian Hellman, Louis Armstrong
  island: 5 Avery
  lake: 3 Iat **4** Iatt **5** Caddo, Clear, Cross, Larto, White **6** Borgne, Saline **8** Darbonne, Maurepan **9** Bistineau, Calcasieu, Catahoula **10** False River **13** Pontchartrain
  land rank: 11 thirty-first
  mountain:
    highest point: 8 Driskill
  physical feature: 15 Head of the Passes **17** coastal marshlands
    delta: 11 Mississippi
    gulf: 6 Mexico
    salt domes: 11 Five Islands
  river: 3 Red **5** Amite, Bayou, Pearl **6** Tensas **8** Ouachita **11** Mississippi
  state admission: 10 eighteenth
  state bird: 19 eastern brown pelican
  state flower: 8 magnolia
  state motto: 5 Union **7** Justice **10** Confidence
  state song: 15 Give Me Louisiana **16** You Are My Sunshine
  state tree: 11 bald cypress
Louisiana Lightning
  nickname of: 9 Ron Guidry
lounge 4 flop, idle, laze, loaf, loll, rest, sofa **5** couch, dally, divan, lobby, relax, sleep, slump **6** dawdle, daybed, repose, slouch, sprawl **7** recline,

slumber **8** kill time, languish **9** davenport, do nothing, lie around, vestibule **10** dillydally, stretch out, take it easy **12** chaise longue
lourd
  music: 5 heavy
Lourenco Marques
  capital of: 10 Mozambique
louse 3 cad, rat **4** heel **5** churl, knave **6** rascal, rotter, vermin **8** parasite **9** scoundrel
louse up 3 mar **4** goof, muff, ruin **5** botch, spoil **6** bungle, foul up, mess up **7** butcher, do badly, screw up **9** mismanage **11** make a mess of
lousy 3 bad **4** mean **5** awful, nasty **6** crummy, rotten, shabby, unkind **7** hateful, vicious **8** dreadful, inferior, infested, terrible **9** unethical, worthless **10** pediculous, second-rate, unpleasant **12** contemptible
lout 3 ape, oaf **4** boor, clod **5** booby, churl, clown, dummy, dunce, klutz, yokel **6** lummox, rustic **7** bumpkin, dullard
loutish 4 rude **5** crude **6** coarse, gauche, oafish, vulgar **7** boorish, uncouth **9** unrefined **10** unpolished **11** peasantlike
lovable, loveable 4 cute **5** sweet **6** cuddly, lovely, taking **7** darling, winning, winsome **8** adorable, charming, engaging, fetching **9** endearing **10** enchanting **11** captivating
Lovberg, Eilert
  character in: 11 Hedda Gabler
  author: 5 Ibsen
love 3 man **4** beau, bent, dear, girl, mind, turn **5** adore, amity, amour, angel, ardor, enjoy, fancy, flame, honey, lover, savor, taste, woman **6** admire, bask in, choice, esteem, fellow, relish **7** beloved, charity, cherish, concord, darling, dearest, emotion, leaning, passion, rapture, revel in, sweetie **8** affinity, be fond of, devotion, fondness, goodwill, hold dear, loved one, mistress, paramour, penchant, precious, sympathy, treasure, truelove, weakness **9** adoration, affection, boyfriend, delight in, inamorata, rejoice in, sentiment **10** admiration, appreciate, attachment, cordiality, friendship, girlfriend, partiality, proclivity, solicitude, sweetheart, sweetie pie, tenderness **11** amorousness, benevolence, brotherhood, inclination, infatuation **12** be enamored of, congeniality, predilection
  god of: 4 Amor, Eros **5** Cupid **7** Angus Og
  goddess of: 5 Freia, Freya, Venus **6** Hathor, Inanna, Ishtar **7** Astarte, Mylitta **9** Aphrodite
Love, the Magician
  also: 11 El Amor Brujo
  ballet by: 5 Falla

love affair 5 amour **7** liaison, romance **14** affaire de coeur
Love Boat, The
  character: 3 Ace **10** (Cruise Director) Julie McCoy **11** (Dr) Adam Bricker, (Purser Burl) Gopher Smith **14** (Captain) Merrill Stubing **15** (Bartender) Isaac Washington
  cast: 8 Ted Lange **10** Fred Grandy **11** Lauren Tewes **12** Bernie Kopell, Gavin MacLeod
  ship: 15 Pacific Princess
love child 7 bastard **12** natural child **17** illegitimate child
love conquers all
  Latin: 15 omnia vincit amor
loved one 4 love, wife **5** lover **6** fiance, spouse **7** be loved, dearest, fiancee, husband **9** boyfriend **10** girlfriend, sweetheart **12** family member
Love for Three Oranges, The
  opera by: 9 Prokofiev
Love in the Afternoon
  director: 11 Billy Wilder
  cast: 10 Gary Cooper **13** Audrey Hepburn **16** Maurice Chevalier
  setting: 5 Paris
Lovelace, Richard
  author of: 18 To Althea from Prison **23** To Lucasta Going to the Wars
loveliness 6 beauty **9** good looks **11** pulchritude **14** attractiveness
lovely 4 cute, fine, good **5** sweet **6** comely **7** elegant, lovable, winning, winsome **8** adorable, alluring, charming, engaging, fetching, handsome, pleasant, pleasing **9** agreeable, beautiful, endearing, enjoy- able, exquisite **10** attractive, delightful, en- chanting **11** captivating, fascinating **12** irresistible
Love Machine, The
  author: 16 Jacqueline Susann
Love Me Tonight
  director: 15 Rouben Mamoulian
  cast: 8 Myrna Loy **14** Charlie Ruggles **16** Maurice Chevalier **17** Jeanette MacDonald
  score: 14 Rodgers and Hart
  song: 4 Mimi **5** Lover **14** Isn't It Romantic
love of country
  Latin: 11 amor patriae
Love of One's Neighbor
  author: 14 Leonid Andreyev
lover 3 fan, man, nut **4** beau, buff, dear, girl, love **5** flame, freak, honey, Romeo, swain, woman, wooer **6** fellow, suitor **7** admirer, beloved, darling, devotee, Don Juan, fanatic, sweetie **8** Casanova, follower, Lothario, loved one, lover boy, mistress, paramour, truelove **9** boyfriend, inamorata **10** aficionado, enthusiast, girlfriend, sweetheart **11** afficionado
  French: 6 bon ami **9** bonne amie
  Italian: 8 cicisbeo

Lovers and Other Strangers
director: **8** Cy Howard
cast: **8** Gig Young **9** Anne Meara, Bea Arthur **11** Anne Jackson **13** Bonnie Bedelia, Harry Guardino **14** Cloris Leachman, Michael Brandon **17** Richard Castellano

love seat 4 sofa **5** couch **6** settee **13** courting chair

lovesick 7 amorous **8** yearning **10** moonstruck

Love's Labour's Lost
author: **18** William Shakespeare
character: **4** Dull **5** Maria **7** Berowne, Costard, Dumaine **8** Rosaline **9** Ferdinand, Katherine **10** Holofernes, Jaquenetta, Longaville **16** Princess of France **18** Don Adriano de Armado

Love Song of J Alfred Prufrock, The
author: **7** T S Eliot

Love Story
author: **10** Erich Segal

Love-wit
character in: **12** The Alchemist
author: **6** Jonson

loving 4 fond, kind, warm **6** ardent, caring, doting, erotic, tender **7** amatory, amorous, devoted **8** enamored, friendly **10** benevolent, passionate, solicitous **11** sympathetic, warm hearted **12** affectionate

loving word 9 sweet talk **10** endearment **12** sweet nothing

low 4 base, blue, deep, down, evil, glum, mean, soft, vile **5** awful, cruel, dirty, dumpy, faint, gross, lower, lowly, muted, prone, quiet, short, small, squat **6** brutal, coarse, common, cruddy, crummy, fee- ble, gentle, gloomy, humble, hushed, little, paltry, scurvy, softly, sordid, stubby, stumpy, sunken, vulgar, wicked **7** coastal, concave, corrupt, doleful, heinous, muffled, obscene, quietly, snubbed, squalid, subdued, unhappy **8** cowardly, degraded, dejected, depraved, downcast, inferior, low-lying, low-slung, mediocre, murmured, sawed-off, soothing, terrible, trifling, undersea, unworthy **9** dastardly, depressed, lethargic, nefarious, prostrate, repugnant, repulsive, submarine, submerged, truncated, unethical, whispered **10** abominable, despicable, despondent, dispirited, melancholy, outrageous, scandalous **11** ignominious, scoundrelly, underground, unimportant **12** contemptible, disheartened, dishonorable **14** down in the mouth

Low, Juliette
founder of: **10** Girl Scouts

lowbred 4 non-u **6** coarse, common, vulgar **7** lowbrow, peasant **10** lower-class, uncultured

low-down 4 base, mean **5** dirty **10** despicable **12** contemptible **13** reprehensible

Lowell, James Russell
author of: **12** The Cathedral **15** The Biglow Papers **16** A Fable for Critics **21** The Vision of Sir Launfal

Lowell, Robert
author of: **8** Day by Day **9** Skunk Hour **10** The Dolphin **11** Life Studies **15** For the Union Dead **16** Lord Weary's Castle

lower 3 cut, dim **4** damp, drop, duck, mute, pare, sink, sulk **5** frown, glare, pared, prune, scowl **6** deduct, glower, lop off, muffle, reduce, soften, subdue **7** curtail, depress, immerse, let down, put down, reduced, repress, shorten **8** decrease, diminish, grow dark, lessened, make less, pare down, pull down, submerge, take down, tone down **9** curtailed, decreased, make lower, pared down **10** abbreviate, diminished

lower-case letter 9 minuscule **11** small letter

lower-class 4 poor **6** common **7** lowbred, lowbrow, peasant **9** unrefined **10** blue-collar **12** working-class

lower classes 6 proles, rabble **8** canaille, riffraff **9** hoi polloi, peasantry **11** proletariat **13** the common herd, working people **16** the great unwashed

lower depths 4 pits, scum **5** dregs **6** rabble **8** canaille, riffraff **14** scum of the earth

Lower Depths, The
also called: **11** At the Bottom **14** A Night's Lodging
author: **10** Maxim Gorky

lower in rank 4 bust **6** demote **7** degrade

lower in spirits 6 deject, sadden **7** depress **8** dispirit **10** dishearten

low-key 4 soft **5** loose, muted **6** gentle, subtle **7** muffled, relaxed, subdued **8** laid-back, softened, soft-sell **9** modulated, toned-down **10** low-pitched, restrained **11** low- pressure, understated, unobtrusive **14** unostentatious

lowliness 8 baseness **9** obscurity **10** humbleness

lowly 3 low **6** humble, modest, simple, softly **7** ignoble, low born, lowbred, obscure **8** baseborn, plebeian **10** unassuming **11** proletarian **13** unpretentious

low-minded 4 lewd, vile **5** crude, gross **6** coarse, smutty, vulgar **7** obscene, uncouth **9** obnoxious, offensive **11** disgraceful **12** contemptible

low point, lowest point 4 base, foot, zero **5** depth, nadir, worst **6** bottom **7** perigee **10** rock bottom

low-priced 5 cheap, token **6** budget,

modest **7** bargain, cut-rate, low-cost, nominal, reduced **8** closeout, moderate **9** dirt-cheap **10** discounted, economical, marked-down, reasonable **11** inexpensive **15** bargain-basement

low-ranking 5 minor, petty **11** subordinate, unimportant

low-spirited 3 low, sad **4** blue, down, glum **6** gloomy, morose, woeful **7** doleful, forlorn, unhappy **8** dejected, desolate, downcast **9** depressed, heart sore, sorrowful, woebegone **10** despondent, dispirited, melancholy **11** crestfallen, discouraged, downhearted **12** disconsolate, disheartened **14** down-in-the-mouth

low spirits 4 funk **5** gloom **6** dismay, sorrow **7** despair **8** dejected **9** pessimism **10** depression, desolation, melancholy, moroseness **11** despondency **12** hopelessness **14** discouragement **15** downheartedness

Loy, Myrna
real name: **13** Myrna Williams
co-star: **13** William Powell
born: **13** Raidersburg MT
roles: **10** The Thin Man **11** Nora Charles **17** Cheaper by the Dozen **22** The Best Years of Our Lives

loyal 4 firm, true **6** trusty **7** devoted, dutiful, staunch **8** constant, faithful, reliable, resolute, true-blue **9** steadfast **10** dependable, scrupulous, unswerving, unwavering **11** trustworthy **12** tried and true

loyalist 4 tory **12** conservative

Loyalties
author: **14** John Galsworthy

loyalty 6 fealty **8** devotion, fidelity, firmness **9** adherence, constancy **10** allegiance **11** reliability, staunchness **12** faithfulness **13** dependability, steadfastness **15** trustworthiness

lozenge 4 drop, pill **6** tablet, troche **8** pastille **9** cough drop

Luanda
capital of: **6** Angola

Lubitsch, Ernst
director of: **9** Ninotchka **13** Heaven Can Wait, To Be or Not To Be

Lucas, Charlotte
character in: **17** Pride and Prejudice
author: **6** Austen

Lucas, George
director of: **8** Star Wars **16** American Graffiti

Lucentio
character in: **19** The Taming of the Shrew
author: **11** Shakespeare

Lucerne
German: **6** Luzern
river: **5** Reuss
landmark: **9** Hofkirche **11** Am Rhyn House **15** Mariahilf Church

Lucia di Lammermoor

opera by: 9 Donizetti
based on novel by: 14 Sir Walter
Scott
   called: 20 The Bride of Lammermoor

Luciana
character in: 17 The Comedy of Errors
author: 11 Shakespeare

Luciani, Albino 13 Pope John Paul I
20 Pope John Paul the First

lucid 5 clear **6** bright, direct, normal **7**
certain, precise, radiant, shining **8** accurate, apposite, dazzling, luminous,
lustrous, pellucid, positive, rational,
specific **9** brilliant, sparkling **10** articulate, perceptive, responsive, to the
point **11** clearheaded, crystalline, illuminated, resplendent, transparent **12**
crystal clear, intelligible **13** clear
thinking, scintillating, well-organized
14 comprehensible, understandable
15 straightforward

Lucifer
means: 5 Satan **11** fallen angel, light
bearer **13** friction match

Lucina
origin: 5 Roman
goddess of: 10 childbirth
corresponds to: 4 Juno **8** Ilithyia **10**
Eileithyia

Lucio
character in: 17 Measure for Measure
author: 11 Shakespeare

luck 3 lot **4** fate **5** karma **6** chance, kismet **7** destiny, fortune, success, tri-
umph, victory **8** accident, fortuity,
good luck, Lady Luck **11** good fortune, piece of luck **12** happenstance
god of: 12 Bonus Eventus

lucky 4 good **5** happy **6** in luck, timely
7 blessed, favored **9** favorable, fortunate, opportune, promising **10** auspicious, beneficial, felicitous, of good
omen, propitious **12** providential

Lucky Jim
author: 12 Kingsley Amis

lucky piece 4 tiki **5** charm **6** amulet,
grigri **8** shamrock, talisman **10** lucky
charm **11** rabbit's foot

lucrative 7 gainful **8** fruitful **10** beneficial, high-income, high-paying, profita-
ble **11** moneymaking **12** remunerative

Lucretia
husband: 26 Lucius Tarquinius Col-
latinus
raped by: 16 Sextus Tarquinius
death by: 7 suicide

Lucretius
author of: 13 De rerum natura **19** On
the nature of things

Lucullan 4 rich **6** lavish **7** gourmet **9**
epicurean, luxurious

Lucy Show, The
also: 9 Here's Lucy
character: 9 Kim Carter **10** Lucy

Carter **11** Craig Carter **12** Harry Con-
ners, Vivian Bagley **13** Mary Jane
Lewis, Sherman Bagley **14** Lucy Carmichael **15** Chris Carmichael, Harrison Cheever, Jerry Carmichael, Theodore J Mooney **18** Harrison Otis
Carter
cast: 9 Ralph Hart **10** Candy Moore,
Dick Martin, Gale Gordon, Lucie Arnaz, Roy Roberts **11** Desi Arnaz Jr,
Lucille Ball, Vivian Vance **12** Jimmy
Garrett **13** Mary Jane Croft

ludicrous 4 wild **5** comic, crazy, funny
6 absurd, far-out **7** amusing, comical
8 farcical **9** laughable **10** outlandish,
ridiculous **11** nonsensical **12** preposterous

Ludlum, Robert
author of: 15 The Matlock Paper **17**
The Bourne Identity, The Parsifal
Mosaic, The Road to Gandolfo **18**
The Osterman Weekend **19** The
Gemini Contenders **20** The Rhine-
mann Exchange **23** The Chancellor
Manuscript, The Scarlatti Inheritance

Luftwaffe 9 air weapon **18** German
Nazi air force

lug 3 tow, tug **4** bear, drag, draw, haul,
pull, tote **5** carry, heave **9** transport

luggage 4 bags, gear **6** trunks **7** baggage, effects, valises **9** suitcases **13**
accouterments

Luggnagg
fictional land in: 16 Gulliver's
Travels
author: 5 Swift

Lugnasad
origin: 5 Irish
feast date: 11 August first

Lugosi, Bela
real name: 10 Bela Blasko
born: 5 Lugos **7** Hungary
roles: 7 Dracula **21** Murders in the
Rue Morgue

lugubrious 4 dour, glum **6** gloomy,
morose, rueful, somber, woeful **7**
doleful, elegiac **8** dolorous, downcast,
funereal, mournful **9** miserable, sorrowful, woebegone **10** depressing,
melancholy

Luke
birthplace: 7 Antioch
companion: 4 Paul
occupation: 9 physician
wrote: 6 Gospel

lukewarm 4 cool, mild, warm **5** aloof,
tepid **8** detached, uncaring **9** apathetic, temp- erate **11** halfhearted, indifferent, per- functory, unconcerned
12 uninterested **13** lackadaisical **14**
unenthusiastic **15** body-temperature,
room- temperature

lull 3 gap **4** calm, ease, halt, hush **5**
break, pause, quell, quiet, still **6** hiatus, la- cuna, pacify, recess, soothe,
subdue **7** assuage, caesura, compose,

mollify, respite **8** breather, calmness **9**
interlude **12** brief silence, interruption

Lully, Jean-Baptiste
born: 5 Italy **8** Florence
composer of: 4 Atys, Isis **6** Persee,
Psyche, Roland, Thesee **7** Alceste,
Phaeton **10** Le Sicilien, Proserpine
11 Bellerophon **13** Acis et Galatee,
Amadis de Gaule, L'Amour medecin
14 Acis and Galatea, Armide et Re-
naud, Le mariage force **16** Cadmus
et Hermione **17** Achille et Polyxene,
Cadmus and Hermione **19** Achilles
and Polyxene **20** Les Amants magni-
fiques **22** Le Bourgeois Gentilhomme, Monsieur de Pourceaugnac

lulu 3 pip **4** oner **5** dandy, doozy **8** Jim
Dandy **9** allowance, humdinger, won-
derful **10** remarkable

lumber 3 log **4** plod, wood **5** barge,
clump, stamp **6** boards, planks,
trudge, waddle **7** shamble, shuffle **8**
flounder **9** fell trees

Lumber State
nickname of: 5 Maine

Lumet, Sidney
director of: 7 Network, Serpico **13**
The Pawnbroker **14** Twelve Angry
Men **15** Dog Day Afternoon **24** Long
Day's Journey Into Night

luminary 3 VIP **5** light, wheel **6** bigwig **7** big shot, notable **8** somebody **9**
celebrity, dignitary, personage **10** luminosity **11** illuminator

luminescent 5 aglow **7** glowing **8**
gleaming, luminous **9** twinkling **10**
flickering, glimmering, glistening,
shimmering **11** fluorescent **14** phosphorescent

luminosity 4 glow **5** gleam, sheen,
shine **6** luster **8** radiance **10** brightness, brilliance

luminous 6 bright **7** glowing, radiant,
shining **8** lustrous **9** brilliant **10** irradiated **11** illuminated, luminescent **15**
reflecting light

lump 3 gob, mix **4** bump, cake, clod,
fuse, heap, hunk, knob, knot, mass,
node, pile, pool **5** amass, batch,
blend, bunch, chunk, clump, group,
knurl, merge, tumor, unite **6** gather,
growth, nodule **7** collect, combine,
compile **8** assemble, swelling **9** aggregate **10** protrusion, tumescence **11** excrescence **12** protuberance

lumpish 4 dull, slow **5** bulky, dumpy,
heavy, lumpy **6** clumsy **7** awkward **8**
clod dish, ungainly, unwieldy **9** corpulent **10** cumbersome, overweight

Lumpkin, Tony
character in: 18 She Stoops to Conquer
author: 9 Goldsmith

lump together 4 fuse, pool **7** combine **10** amalgamate **11** consolidate,
incorporate

Luna

personifies: 4 moon
Greek: 6 Selene

lunacy 5 folly, mania **6** idiocy **7** madness **8** dementia, insanity **9** absurdity, asininity, craziness, silliness, stupidity **10** imbecility, imprudence, insaneness **11** foolishness **13** foolhardiness, senselessness

lunatic 3 mad, nut **4** daft, loco **5** batty, crazy, loony, nutty, potty **6** cuckoo, in- sane, madman, maniac, screwy **7** bonkers, cracked, touched **8** crackers, demented, demo niac, deranged, maniacal, unhinged **9** psychotic, senseless **10** irrational, psychopath, reasonless, unbalanced **11** crazy person, mentally ill, not all there **12** crackbrained, insane person, psychopathic, round the bend **13** off one's rocker, of unsound mind, out of one's mind

lunch
French: 8 dejeuner

luncheonette 4 cafe **5** diner **7** beanery **8** snack bar **9** hash house, lunchroom **10** coffee shop **11** eating house **12** lunch counter, sandwich shop

lunchroom 4 cafe **5** diner, grill **8** snack bar **9** cafeteria **12** luncheonette

lunge 3 cut, jab **4** dash, dive, pass, rush, stab **5** hit at, lurch, swing, swipe **6** attack, charge, plunge, pounce, thrust **7** set upon **8** fall upon, strike at **9** make a pass

lunkhead 3 ass **4** dope, fool **5** booby, dunce, idiot, moron, ninny **6** dimwit, nitwit **7** fat head, halfwit **8** bonehead, dumb-dumb, imbecile, numskull **9** blockhead, lamebrain, numbskull **10** dunderhead, nincompoop **11** chowderhead

Lunt, Alfred
wife: 12 Lynn Fontanne
born: 11 Milwaukee WI
roles: 12 The Guardsman **13** The Ragged Edge

Lupercalia
origin: 5 Roman
event: 8 festival
honoring: 6 Faunus **8** Lupercus
to procure: 9 fertility

Lupercus
origin: 5 Roman
god of: 9 fertility
corresponds to: 3 Pan **6** Faunus

Lupino, Ida 7 actress **8** director
husband: 10 Howard Duff **12** Collier Young, Louis Hayward
born: 6 London **7** England
roles: 8 Devotion **10** The Hard Way **12** Junior Bonner, Women's Prison **13** Escape Me Never **15** Strange Intruder **17** On Dangerous Ground **18** The Light That Failed, While the City Sleeps

lurch 4 cant, keel, list, reel, roll, sway, tilt, toss **5** lunge, pitch, slant **6** careen, plunge, swerve, teeter, totter **7** incline, stagger, stumble

Lurch 6 butler
on: 15 The Addams Family

lure 4 bait, coax, trap **5** bribe, decoy, snare, tempt **6** allure, cajole, come-on, entice, induce, seduce **7** attract, beguile **8** cajolery, persuade **9** fascinate, tantalize **10** allurement, attraction, enticement, inducement, temptation **11** drawing card **12** blandishment

Lurelei see **7** Lorelei

lurid 4 gory, grim **5** eerie, fiery, vivid **6** bloody **7** carmine, flaming, ghastly, glaring, glowing, graphic, scarlet, shining **8** dramatic, rubicund, sanguine, shocking **9** appalling, bright-red **11** sensational **12** melodramatic **13** bloodcurdling

lurk 4 hide **5** prowl, skulk, slink, sneak **9** lie in wait

Lusaka
capital of: 6 Zambia

luscious 5 tasty **6** savory **7** scented **8** aromatic, fragrant, perfumed **9** delicious, flavorful, succulent, toothsome **10** appetizing, delectable **13** mouthwatering

lush 4 posh, rich **5** dense, fancy, grand **6** ornate **7** elegant, profuse **8** abundant, pro lific, splendid **9** elaborate, luxuriant, lux- urious, sumptuous **11** flourishing, magnificent

lust 5 covet, crave **6** be lewd **7** craving, lechery, passion **8** lewdness **9** carnality, hunger for, sexuality **10** satyriasis **14** lasciviousness, libidinousness

lust after 4 want **5** covet, crave **6** desire **11** have a yen for, have an eye on, hunger after, thirst after

luster 4 fame, glow **5** gleam, glory, gloss, honor, merit, sheen, shine **6** dazzle **7** burnish, glimmer, glitter, sparkle **8** prestige, radiance **9** radiation **10** brightness, brilliance, luminosity, notability, refulgence **11** distinction **12** luminousness, resplendence **15** illustriousness

lusterless 3 dim, wan **4** dead, drab, dull, flat **5** faded, matte, muted **7** prosaic **9** colorless, tarnished

Lust for Life
author: 11 Irving Stone
director: 16 Vincente Minnelli
based on story by: 11 Irving Stone
cast: 11 James Donald, Kirk Douglas (Vincent Van Gogh), Pamela Brown **12** Anthony Quinn (Gaugin)
Oscar for: 15 supporting actor (Quinn)

lustful 4 lewd **6** carnal **8** prurient **9** lecherous, salacious **10** lascivious, libidinous

lustrous 6 bright, glossy **7** glowing, radiant, shining **8** dazzling, gleaming,

luminous, polished **9** burnished, effulgent **10** glistening **11** coruscating, illuminated **12** incandescent

lusty 4 hale **5** husky, sound **6** brawny, hearty, robust, rugged, sturdy, virile **7** healthy **8** vigorous **9** exuberant, strapping **10** full of life **11** uninhibited **12** unrestrained, wholehearted **13** irrepressible

Lutetia
Latin: 5 Paris

Luther, Martin
born: 7 Germany **8** Eisleben
author: 16 Ninety-Five Theses **27** On the Freedom of a Christian Man **46** Address to the Christian Nobility of the German Nation **51** A Prelude Concerning the Babylonian Captivity of the Church
excommunicated by: 8 Pope Leo X **15** Pope Leo the Tenth
summoned before: 11 Diet of Worms
founded: 11 Lutheranism, Reformation **13** Protestantism

lux 5 light

Luxembourg
other name: 9 Luxemburg **13** Lucilinburhuc
name means: 10 little fort
capital/largest city: 10 Luxembourg
others: 4 Hamm **5** Roodt, Wiltz **6** Mersch, Remich **7** Kopstal, Lintgen, Petange, Redange, Vianden **8** Capellen, Clervaux, Diekirch, Frisange **9** Dudelange **10** Echternach, Ettel bruck, Hesperange, Larochette **11** Differdange, Wormeldange **12** Grevenmacher, Troisvierges, Wasserbillig **14** Esch-sur-Alzette
division: 6 Esleck **7** Bon Pays, Gutland, Oesling
measure: 5 fuder
monetary unit: 5 franc **7** centime
lake: 8 Haut Sure
mountain: 8 Ardennes
highest point: 9 Huldange **9** Burgplatz **11** Wemperhardt
river: 3 Our **4** Sure, Syre **5** Alert, Clerf, Eisch, Mosel, Sauer, Wiltz **6** Chiers **7** Alzette, Moselle **8** Petrusse **11** Ernz Blanche
physical feature:
plateau: 4 Bock **8** Ardennes, Lorraine
valley: 7 Moselle
people: 6 French, German **12** Luxembourger
ruler: 8 Sigefroi, Wencelas **12** Jean l'Aveugle **21** House of Nassau-Weilburg
saint: 10 Willibrord
language: 6 French, German **7** English **13** Letzeburgesch
religion: 13 Roman Catholic
food:
pastry: 20 les pensees brouillees

luxuriant 4 lush, rank **5** dense, fancy, grand **6** florid, ornate **7** elegant, flowery, profuse, teeming **8** abundant, splendid **9** elaborate, exuberant, luxurious, overgrown, sumptuous **10** flamboyant **11** extravagant, flourishing, magnificent

luxuriate 4 bask **6** relish **7** delight **8** wallow in **9** indulge in

luxurious 4 rich **5** grand **6** costly, effete **7** elegant, wealthy **8** decadent, pampered **9** enjoyable, expensive, indulgent, sumptuous **10** gratifying **11** comfortable, pleasurable

luxuriousness 4 ease **6** luxury comfort **8** richness **10** costliness **11** sumptuousness

luxury 5 bliss **6** heaven, riches, wealth **7** delight **8** paradise, pleasure **9** enjoyment **10** high living, indulgence **12** extravagance, nonessential, nonnecessity, satisfaction **13** gratification

LXX *see* **15** Septuagint

Lycaon
   king of: 7 Arcadia
   father: 8 Pelasgus
   son: 8 Maenalus, Tegeates
   tested: 4 Zeus
   turned into: 4 wolf

Lycidas
   author: 10 John Milton
   elegy for: 10 Edward King

Lycus
   king of: 6 Thebes **7** Cilicia

.ather: 7 Pandion **9** Chthonius
mother: 5 Pylia
brother: 7 Nycteus
wife: 5 Dirce
niece: 7 Antiope
son: 5 Lycus
succeeded: 8 Sarpedon
killed by: 6 Zethus **7** Amphion **12** Antiope's sons

Lydia
   kingdom in: 9 Asia Minor
   king: 7 Croesus
   queen: 7 Omphale
   capital: 6 Sardis
   conquered by: 8 Persians

lying down 5 in bed, prone **6** supine **7** napping, resting **8** snoozing **9** reclining, recumbent **10** taking a nap **13** taking a snooze

Lyle, Albert Walter
   nickname: 6 Sparky
   sport: 8 baseball
   position: 7 pitcher
   team: 12 Boston Red Sox **14** New York Yankees
   author of: 11 The Bronx Zoo

Lyly, John
   author of: 20 Euphues and His England **22** Euphues the Anatomy of Wit

lynch 4 hang **6** gibbet **8** string up

Lynde, Paul

born: 13 Mount Vernon OH
roles: 12 Bye Bye Birdie **16** Hollywood Squares **17** Beach Blanket Bingo **18** Under the Yum-Yum Tree

lynx 3 cat **6** bobcat **7** wildcat

Lyonnesse
   place: 12 near Cornwall **16** Arthurian romance
   birthplace of: 8 Tristram
   fate: 11 sunk into sea

Lyre
   constellation of: 4 Harp, Lyra
   star: 4 Vega

lyric, lyrical 6 poetic **7** lilting, melodic, musical, singing, tuneful **8** songlike **9** melodious **10** euphonious **11** mellifluent, mellifluous **13** sweetsounding

Lyrical Ballads
   author: 17 William Wordsworth **21** Samuel Taylor Coleridge

lyrics 4 poem **5** words

Lysander
   character in: 21 A Midsummer Night's Dream
   author: 11 Shakespeare

Lysistrata
   author: 12 Aristophanes
   character: 7 Lampito **8** Cinesias, Cleonice, Myrrhine **10** Magistrate **14** Old Men of Athens (Chorus)

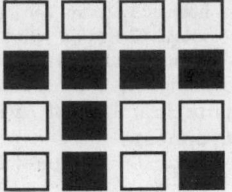

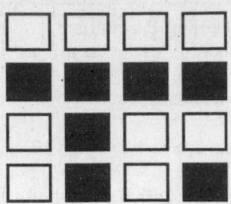

M
  director: **9** Fritz Lang
  cast: **10** Peter Lorre **11** Inge Landgut
  12 Ellen Widmann **15** Gustav Grundgens
  setting: **6** Berlin
Mabinogian
  origin: **5** Welsh
  tales of: **7** romance
macabre 4 grim **5** eerie, weird **6** grisly, horrid **7** ghastly, ghostly **8** dreadful, gruesome, horrible, horrific **9** frightful, ghostlike, unearthly **11** frightening
Macao
  other name: **5** Ao-men, Macau
  territory of: **8** Portugal
  monetary unit: **3** avo **6** pataca, pataco
  island: **5** Taipa **7** Coloane
  highest point: **5** Hag-Sa
  river: **5** Pearl **6** Canton
  sea: **10** South China
  people: **7** Chinese, Macaoan **10** Portuguese
  language: **7** Chinese, English **9** Cantonese **10** Portuguese
  religion: **6** Taoism **8** Buddhism **13** Roman Catholic
  place:
    street: **11** Praia Grande
  feature:
    houseboat: **6** sampan
Macareus
  father: **6** Aeolus
  mother: **7** Encrete
  sister: **6** Canace
MacArthur, Douglas
  served in: **3** WWI **4** WWII **9** Korean War, World War I **10** World War II **11** World War One, World War Two
  commander of: **15** Rainbow (42nd) Division **19** United Nations forces **24** US Army forces in the Pacific
  rank: **15** five-star general **16** army chief of staff
  battle: **5** Luzon, Pusan **6** Inchon **9** New Guinea **11** Leyte Island, Philippines **14** Bismark Islands, Solomon Islands **16** Bataan Peninsula **18** Admiralty Islands, Corregidor Island
  accepted surrender of: **5** Japan
    surrender occurred aboard: **8** Missouri
  chairman of: **13** Remington Rand
  author of: **13** Reminiscences

smoked: **11** corncob pipe
saying: **12** "I shall return"
Macbeth
  author: **18** William Shakespeare
  character: **6** Banquo, Duncan (King of Scotland) **7** MacDuff, Malcolm **11** Lady Macbeth **12** Three Witches
  title: **5** thane
  domain: **6** Glamis
  director: **13** Roman Polanski
  cast: **8** Jon Finch **10** Martin Shaw **13** Nicholas Selby **14** Francesca Annis
Maccabees
  title of: **5** Judas
  patriarch: **10** Mattathias
  means: **8** hammerer
  holiday: **8** Hanukkah
MacDonald, John D
  author of: **11** Condominium
  character: **11** Travis McGee
MacDonald, Ross
  real name: **13** Kenneth Millar
  author of: **8** The Chill **10** Black Money **13** The Blue Hammer **14** The Goodbye Look
  character: **9** Lew Archer
MacDowell, Edward Alexander
  born: **9** New York NY
  composer of: **9** Sea Pieces **11** To a Wild Rose **13** Fireside Tales **15** Poems after Heine **16** Hamlet and Ophelia, New England Idylls, Woodland Sketches **17** Idylls after Goethe
MacDuff
  character in: **7** Macbeth
  author: **11** Shakespeare
mace
  origin: **9** Indonesia
  from same tree as: **6** nutmeg
  tree: **17** Myristica fragrans
  use: **4** fish **7** seafood **9** cherry pie, pound cake **16** chicken fricassee
Macedonia
  capital/largest city: **6** Skopje
  head of state: **9** president
  government: **8** republic
  monetary unit: **5** denar
  river: **6** Struma, Vardar
  people: **4** Turk **9** Albanian **10** Macedonian
  language: **10** Macedonian
  religion: **27** Macedonian Orthodox Christian
macerate 4 fade, mash, pulp, soak **5** souse, steep **6** shrink, soften, squash, wither **7** decline, liquefy, shrivel

8 dissolve, emaciate, fluidize, permeate, saturate **9** liquidize, waste away **10** lose weight
MacGraw, Ali
  real name: **12** Alice MacGraw
  husband: **8** Bob Evans **12** Steve McQueen
  born: **12** Pound Ridge NY
  roles: **7** Dynasty **9** Love Story **10** The Getaway **13** The Winds of War **15** Goodbye Columbus
Macheath, Captain
  character in: **12** Beggar's Opera
  author: **3** Gay
  see Threepenny Opera
ma chere 6 my dear
Machiavelli, Niccolo
  author of: **9** The Prince **11** The Art of War **16** Discourses on Livy
  home: **8** Florence
  The "Prince": **12** Cesare Borgia
Machiavellian 6 amoral, crafty **7** cunning, devious **8** scheming **9** deceitful, designing **10** perfidious **11** self-serving, treacherous, underhanded **12** falsehearted, unscrupulous
machination 4 plot, rule, ruse **5** dodge **6** design, device, scheme **8** artifice, intrigue, maneuver **9** stratagem **10** conspiracy **11** contrivance
machine 3 set **4** army, body, camp, club, gang, pool, ring **5** corps, crowd, force, group, setup, trust, union **6** device, system **7** combine, coterie, faction, society **9** apparatus, appliance, machinery, mechanism, structure **11** association **12** organization **13** establishment
machine gun
  invented by: **7** Gatling
  improved by: **5** Maxim **9** Hotchkiss
machinery 4 gear **5** setup, tools **6** agency, makeup, system, tackle, wheels **9** apparatus, mechanism, resources, structure **12** contrivances, organization
macho 5 he-man, manly **6** strong, virile
Machpelah
  location: **6** Hebron
  burial place of: **4** Leah **5** Isaac, Jacob, Sarah **7** Abraham, Rebekah
Machu Picchu 5 ruins
  of: **5** Incas
  in: **4** Peru

Macilente
  character in: 22 Every Man out of His
  Humour
  author: 6 Jonson
MacInnes, Helen
  author of: 13 North from Rome 14
  Above Suspicion 16 Decision at Delphi 17 The Venetian Affair 21 The
  Salzburg Connection
macintosh, mackintosh 7 slicker 8
  raincoat 10 waterproof
Mack, Connie
  real name: 30 Cornelius Alexander
  McGillicuddy
  sport: 8 baseball
  position: 7 manager
  team: 21 Philadelphia Athletics
MacKellar
  character in: 21 The Master of Ballantrae
  author: 9 Stevenson
mackerel
  young: 5 spike 6 tinker 7 blinker
mackinaw 4 coat 6 jacket 8 overcoat
Mack the Knife *see* 15 Three Penny
  Opera
MacLaine, Shirley
  real name: 19 Shirley MacLean Beaty
  brother: 12 Warren Beatty
  born: 10 Richmond VA
  roles: 6 Can Can 10 Being There 11
  Irma La Douce 12 Sweet Charity,
  The Apartment 15 Some Came Running, The Turning Point, Two for the
  Seesaw 16 The Children's Hour 17
  Terms of Endearment (Oscar) 19 The
  Trouble with Harry 20 The Bliss of
  Mrs Blossom
MacMurray, Fred
  wife: 9 June Haver
  born: 10 Kankakee IL
  roles: 11 My Three Sons 12 The
  Apartment 14 Above Suspicion, The
  Caine Mutiny 15 Double Indemnity
  20 The Miracle of the Bells
macrocosm 6 cosmos, nature 7
  heavens 8 creation, universe 9 firmament
mad 4 avid, daft, loco, nuts, wild 5 angry, balmy, crazy, irate, nutty 6 ardent, crazed, cuckoo, fuming, insane,
  miffed, screwy, ticked 7 cracked, enraged, excited, fanatic, furious, in a
  huff, lunatic, riled up, teed off,
  touched 8 crackers, demented, deranged, frenzied, incensed, maniacal,
  provoked, unhinged, up in arms,
  worked up, wrathful 9 devoted to,
  non compos, seeing red, ticked off,
  wrought up 10 distracted, distraught,
  infatuated, infuriated, in love with, irrational, unbalanced 11 boiling over,
  exasperated, impassioned, not all
  there 12 enthusiastic, round the bend
  13 beside oneself, in high dudgeon,
  not quite right, off one's rocker, out
  of one's mind

Madagascar
  other name: 16 Malagasy Republic
  capital/largest city: 10 Tananarive 12
  Antananarivo
  others: 6 Tulear 7 Majanga, Nossibe,
  Toliary 8 Manakara, Tamatave 9
  Faradofay, Mananjory, Toamasina 10
  Antisirabe 11 Antsiranana, Diego-
  Suarez, Fort Dauphin
  measure: 7 gantang
  monetary unit: 5 franc 7 centime
  island: 6 Barren, Radama 7 Nossi-Be
  11 Sainte-Marie 12 Chesterfield
  lake: 5 Itasy 7 Alaotra, Kinkony
  mountain: 4 Boby 9 Ankaratra 12
  High Plateaus, Tsiafajavona 17
  Tsaratanana Massif
  highest point: 11 Maromokotro
  river: 5 Ikopa, Mania, Sofia 7 Man-
  goky, Mangoro, Onilahy 8 Ivoloina,
  Manambao, Mananara 9 Betsiboka,
  Manambolo 10 Manarandra 11 Tsiri-
  bihina
  ocean: 6 Indian
  physical feature:
    bay: 6 Radama 8 Antongil 9 Maha-
    jamba 10 Sahamalaza
    cape: 5 Amber 10 Saint-Andre 11
    Sainte-Marie 14 Saint-Sebastien
    channel: 10 Mozambique
    lagoon: 9 pangalane
    plateau: 9 Ankaizina
  people: 4 Arab, Bara, Hova 5 Malay
    6 Merina, Tanala 7 African 8 Bet-
    sileo, Mahafaly, Malagasy, Sakalava
    9 Antaimoro, Antaisaka, Antandroy,
    Tsimi-hety 10 Indonesian, Polynesian
    13 Betsimisaraka
    dynasty: 6 Merina
    leader: 9 Ratsiraka, Tsiranana 11
    Ranamantsoa
  language: 6 French 8 Malagasy, Malgache
  religion: 5 Islam 7 animism 10 Protestant 13 Roman Catholic
  place:
    market: 4 Zoma
    royal estate: 4 Rova
  feature:
    animal: 4 zebu 5 lemur 6 foussa
    musical instrument: 11 jego
    vaotavo
    proverb: 8 hainteny
    shawl: 5 lamba
  food:
    vegetable: 7 brettes
madam, madame 3 Mrs 4 dame,
  lady 6 matron 7 dowager 8 mistress
  German: 4 Frau
  Spanish: 6 senora
  Italian: 5 donna 7 signora
  Spanish/Portuguese: 4 dona
Madame Bovary
  author: 15 Gustave Flaubert
  character: 10 Emma Bovary, Leon
  Dupuis 13 Charles Bovary 17 Rodolphe Boulanger
Madame Butterfly

  also: 15 Madama Butterfly
  opera by: 7 Puccini
  character: 5 Bonze 6 Suzuki 9 Cho-
  Cho-San, Cio-Cio-San, Sharpless 14
  Prince Yamadori 19 Lieutenant Pinkerton
  aria: 7 Un beldi
mad as a hatter 3 mad 4 daft, nuts 5
  crazy, nutty 6 insane 7 cracked,
  touched 8 demented, deranged, unhinged 10 unbalanced 13 off one's
  rocker, out of one's head 14 off one's
  trolley 15 mad as a March hare 17
  nutty as a fruitcake
mad as a March hare 3 mad 4 daft,
  nuts 5 crazy, nutty 6 insane 7
  cracked, touched 8 demented, deranged, unhinged 10 unbalanced 12
  mad as a hatter 13 out of one's head
  14 off one's trolley 17 nutty as a
  fruitcake
madcap 4 rash, wild, zany 5 brash,
  clown, giddy, joker 6 unruly 7 erratic,
  flighty, foolish 8 reckless 9 hotheaded, impetuous, impulsive, senseless 10 incautious 11 impractical,
  thoughtless 12 unconsidered 13 inconsiderate, undisciplined
madden 3 vex 4 gall 5 anger, craze,
  pique, upset 6 enrage, frenzy 7 derange, incense, inflame, outrage, provoke, torment, unhinge 9 aggravate,
  infuriate, unbalance 10 exasperate
made 5 built 6 formed 7 created 8
  composed, produced 9 assembled, developed 10 fabricated 11 constructed
  12 manufactured
madeira
  type: 4 wine 6 brandy 7 liqueur 8
  aperitif
  origin: 7 Madeira
Madeira Islands
  capital: 7 Funchal
  city: 5 Monte
  island: 6 Grande 7 Dezerte, Madeira
  8 Desertas 9 Selvagens 10 Porto
  Santo
  ocean: 8 Atlantic
  owned by: 8 Portugal
  stone aqueduct: 7 levadas
  wine: 4 Bual 5 Tinta, Tinto 6 Canary,
  Gomera 7 Malmsey, Marsala, Sercial
  8 Verdelho
made-up 5 false 7 assumed, created 8
  fanciful, invented 9 fictional, imaginary, pretended, thought-up 10 fictitious 11 make-believe, theoretical 12
  hypothetical
Mad Hatter
  character in: 28 Alice's Adventures in
  Wonderland
  author: 7 Carroll
madhouse 6 asylum, bedlam, uproar
  7 turmoil 8 loony bin, nuthouse
Madison, James
  nickname: 23 Father of the Constitution

presidential rank: 6 fourth
party: 20 Democratic-Republican
state represented: 2 VA
defeated: 7 (DeWitt) Clinton **8** (Charles Cotesworth) Pinckney
vice president: 5 (Elbridge) Gerry **7** (George) Clinton
cabinet:
  state: 5 (Robert) Smith **6** (James) Monroe
  treasury: 6 (Alexander James) Dallas **8** (Abraham Alfonse Albert) Gallatin, (George Washington) Campbell, (William Harris) Crawford
  war: 6 (James) Monroe, (William) Eustis **8** (William Harris) Crawford **9** (John) Armstrong
  attorney general: 4 (Richard) Rush **6** (Caesar Augustus) Rodney **7** (William) Pinkney
  navy: 6 (William) Jones **8** (Paul) Hamilton **13** (Benjamin Williams) Crowninshield
born: 12 Port Conway VA **16** King George County
died/buried: 2 VA **12** Orange County **16** Montpelier estate
education:
  tutored at home by: 15 Rev. Thomas Martin
  school: 15 Donald Robertson
  college of: 9 New Jersey (now Princeton University)
religion: 12 Episcopalian
interests: 3 law **11** agriculture **14** natural history
author: 16 Federalist Papers (with Hamilton and Jay) **24** Memorial and Remonstrances **29** Journal of the Federal Convention
political career: 24 US House of Representatives **25** Second Continental Congress
  secretary of: 5 state
  signed: 12 Constitution
civilian career: 6 farmer **7** planter
military service:
  colonel of: 19 Orange County militia
notable events of lifetime/term: 19 War of Eighteen Twelve
  battle of: 10 New Orleans
  treaty of: 5 Ghent
  Washington DC burned by: 7 British
father: 5 James
mother: 7 Eleanor (Rose Conway)
siblings: 5 Sarah **6** Reuben **7** Ambrose, Catlett, Francis, William **9** Elizabeth **11** Nelly Conway **13** Frances Taylor
wife: 8 Dorothea (Payne Todd)
  nickname: 6 Dolley
first lady:
  saved: 11 state papers **25** George Washington's portrait
madman 3 nut **5** loony **6** maniac

7 lunatic **8** demoniac **9** psychotic **10** psychopath

Mad Max
  director: 12 George Miller
  cast: 9 Mel Gibson
  sequel: 14 The Road Warrior **17** Beyond Thunderdome (with Tina Turner)

madness 6 lunacy, oddity **8** delusion, dementia, illusion, insanity **9** craziness **11** derangement

Madonna
  nickname: 15 The Material Girl
  husband: 8 Sean Penn
  recordings: 7 Madonna **8** True Blue **11** Like A Prayer, Like A Virgin
  films: 9 Dick Tracy **11** Truth or Dare **12** Who's That Girl **14** Body of Evidence **16** Shanghai Surprise **17** A League of Their Own **23** Desperately Seeking Susan
  tour: 6 Girlie **13** Blond Ambition
  books: 3 Sex

Madrid
  area: 9 Salamanca **19** Ciudad Universitaria
  capital of: 5 Spain
  landmark: 14 National Palace **18** Biblioteca Nacional
    bull ring: 22 Plaza de Toros Monumental
    museum: 5 Prado
  mountain: 18 Sierra de Guadaramma
  river: 10 Manzanares
  square: 10 Plaza Mayor **11** Plaza del Sol **13** Plaza de Espana
  street: 13 Paseo del Prado

Madwoman of Chaillot
  author: 13 Jean Giraudoux

maelstrom 4 eddy **5** shoot, swirl **6** bedlam, rapids, tumult, uproar, vortex **7** riptide, torrent **8** disorder, madhouse, undertow, upheaval **9** confusion, whirlpool **10** white water **11** pandemonium
  location: 6 Norway

maenad, menad 5 lenae **7** bacchae, bassara **8** clodones, thyiades **9** bacchante **10** mimallones
  companion of: 7 Bacchus **8** Dionysus

Maeterlinck, Maurice
  author of: 8 The Blind **11** The Blue Bird, The Intruder **19** Pelleas and Melisande

ma foi 6 my word, really **7** my faith

magazine 6 weekly **7** arsenal, journal, monthly **9** quarterly **10** periodical, powder room **13** military depot, munitions room

Magdalene see **4** Mary

magenta 6 maroon **7** carmine, crimson, fuchsia **9** vermilion **12** purplish rose **13** reddish purple

Maggie: A Girl of the Streets
  author: 12 Stephen Crane

maggot 4 grub, worm **5** larva **8** mealworm

Magi
  also called: 7 wise men **11** astrologers
  followed: 15 Star of Bethlehem
  visited: 5 Jesus
  gifts: 4 gold **5** myrrh **12** frankincense
  singular: 5 magus

magic 4 lure **5** charm, spell **6** hoodoo, voodoo **7** sorcery **8** charisma, jugglery, witchery, wizardry **9** occultism, voodooism **10** allurement, black magic, demonology, divination, hocuspocus, witchcraft **11** captivation, conjuration, enchantment, fascination, legerdemain, the black art **12** entrancement **13** sleight of hand **16** prestidigitation
  god of: 5 Thoth

Magic
  nickname of: 13 Earvin Johnson

Magic Flute, The
  also: 14 Die Zauberflote
  opera: 6 Mozart
  character: 6 Pamina, Tamino **8** Papagena, Papageno, Sarastro **10** Monostatos **12** Queen of Night

magician 5 magus **6** shaman, wizard **7** juggler, warlock **8** conjurer, sorcerer **9** alchemist **11** illusionist, medicine man, necromancer, witch doctor **12** escape artist **15** prestidigitator

Magic Mountain, The
  author: 10 Thomas Mann
  character: 6 Naphta **7** Clavdia **11** Hans Castorp, Settembrini **15** Joachim Ziemssen

magisterial 9 imperious **10** autocratic, peremptory **11** dictatorial, domineering, overbearing **13** condescending

Magister Ludi: The Glass Bead Game
  author: 12 Hermann Hesse

magistrate 2 JP **5** judge **7** prefect **17** justice of the peace

Magna Carta 7 charter
  forced by: 6 barons
  upon: 8 King John
  at: 9 Runnymede
  guaranteeing: 14 civil liberties

magna cum laude 15 with great praise

Magna Graecia 27 ancient Greek colonies in Italy

Magna Mater 3 Ops **4** Rhea **6** Cybele

Magnani, Anna
  nickname: 10 Nannerella
  roles: 8 Open City **13** The Rose Tattoo (Oscar) **15** The Fugitive Kind **21** Secret of Santa Vittoria

magnanimous 7 liberal **8** generous, princely **9** forgiving, unselfish **10** altruistic, beneficent, charitable **12** largehearted **13** philanthropic

magnate 3 VIP **5** giant, mogul, nabob **6** big gun, bigwig, leader, tycoon **7** big shot, notable **8** big wheel, great man **9** celebrity **13** empire builder, industrialist

magnesium
chemical symbol: **2** Mg

magnetic 8 alluring, charming, inviting **9** of a magnet, seductive **10** attractive, enchanting, entrancing, persuasive **11** captivating, charismatic, fascinating **12** irresistible

magnetism 4 lure **5** charm **6** allure **8** charisma **9** mesmerism, seduction **10** allurement, attraction, enticement **11** captivation, enchantment, fascination

magnification 5 honor **7** worship **9** adoration, blowing up, expansion, inflation, reverence **11** acclamation, enlargement, idolization **12** exaggeration **13** amplification, glorification, overstatement

magnificence 4 pomp **5** glory, state **6** luxury **7** glitter, majesty, royalty **8** grandeur, richness, splendor **10** brilliance **13** sumptuousness

magnificent 4 fine **5** grand, noble **6** august, superb **7** elegant, exalted, stately, sublime **8** glorious, imposing, majestic, splendid **9** brilliant, exquisite, wonderful **10** commanding, impressive **11** resplendent **12** transcendent **13** extraordinary

Magnificent Ambersons, The
director: **11** Orson Welles
based on novel by: **15** Booth Tarkington
cast: **7** Tim Holt **10** Anne Baxter **12** Joseph Cotten **14** Agnes Moorehead **15** Dolores Costello

Magnificent Obsession, The
author: **13** Lloyd C Douglas

Magnificent Seven, The
director: **11** John Sturges
cast: **10** Brad Dexter, Eli Wallach, Yul Brynner **11** James Coburn **12** Robert Vaughn, Steve McQueen **13** Horst Buchholz **14** Charles Bronson
setting: **6** Mexico
score: **14** Elmer Bernstein
remake of: **12** Seven Samurai
sequel: **16** Return of the Seven **20** Magnificent Seven Ride

magnify 4 laud **5** adore, boost, exalt, extol **6** blow up, double, expand, praise, puff up, revere **7** acclaim, amplify, enlarge, glorify, greaten, inflate, stretch, worship **8** heighten, maximize, overrate **9** embroider, overstate, reverence **10** exaggerate

magniloquence 7 bombast, fustian **8** euphuism, tumidity **9** pomposity, turgidity **10** orotundity **11** fanfaronade, grandiosity **14** grandiloquence **15** pretentiousness

magniloquent 5 tumid, windy, wordy **6** turgid **7** pompous, verbose **8** inflated **9** bombastic **13** grandiloquent

magnitude 4 bulk, fame, mass, size **6** extent, renown, repute, volume **7** bigness, expanse, measure **8** eminence, enormity, hugeness, vastness

magnolia
varieties: **4** ashe, star **6** saucer **7** Chinese **8** southern, umbrella **11** great-leaved

Magnum, P. I.
character: **2** TC **4** Rick **7** Higgins **12** Thomas Magnum
cast: **10** Tom Selleck **12** Roger E Mosley **13** John Hillerman
setting: **6** Hawaii

Magog
father: **7** Japheth

Magritte, Rene Francois Ghislain
born: **7** Belgium **8** Lessines
artwork: **14** La Belle Captive, The False Mirror, The Key of Dreams **15** Memory of a Voyage **18** L'Empire des Lumieres (The Empire of Light), The Menaced Assassin

Magua
character in: **20** The Last of the Mohicans
author: **6** Cooper

Magus see **4** Magi

Magwitch, Abel
character in: **17** Great Expectations
author: **7** Dickens

Magyar 9 Hungarian

Mahican see **7** Mohican

mah-jongg 4 game
origin: **7** Chinese
play piece: **4** tile
suit: **3** bam, dot **5** crack, winds
dragon: **3** red **5** white
term: **4** kong, pung **6** flower

Mahler, Gustav
born: **7** Austria, Bohemia
composer of: **12** Resurrection (symphony No 2) **15** Das Klagendelied **16** Songs of a Wayfarer **17** Das Lied von der Erde, Kindertotenlieder, The Song of the Earth **19** Des Knaben Wunderhorn **28** Lieder eines fahrenden Gesellen

mahogany 4 tree, wood **5** brown **8** hardwood **9** Swietenia **12** reddish-brown
varieties: **3** red **5** swamp, white **7** African, big-leaf, Florida, Senegal, Spanish **8** Honduras, mountain **9** Nyasaland, Venezulan **10** West Indian

Mahon, Christopher
character in: **27** The Playboy of the Western World
author: **5** Synge

mahzor, machzor 16 Jewish prayer book

Maia
member of: **8** Pleiades
place in group: **6** eldest
father: **5** Atlas
mother: **7** Pleione
son: **6** Hermes

maid 6 tweeny **7** servant **8** domestic **9** hired girl, housemaid, lady's maid, nursemaid **10** parlor maid **11** maid-servant **12** upstairs maid **13** female servant
French: **6** au pair

maiden, maidenly 4 girl, lass, maid, miss **5** chick, first **6** chaste, damsel, lassie, virgin **7** colleen, girlish, ingenue, initial, untried **8** original, virginal, youthful **9** inaugural, soubrette, unmarried **10** demoiselle, initiatory **12** introductory

Maid Marian
beloved of: **9** Robin Hood

maidservant 4 amah, ayah, char, lass, maid **5** bonne **6** au pair, tweeny **7** abigail **8** charlady, domestic **9** hired girl, lady's maid, tirewoman **10** handmaiden, parlormaid

Maidu
language family: **8** Penutian
location: **10** California
noted for: **8** basketry

mail 4 arms, post **5** armor **6** get out **7** airmail, harness, letters, panoply **8** dispatch, packages **9** postcards **10** send by mail, send by post, suit of mail **11** surface mail **12** mail delivery, put in the mail **13** postal service **14** defensive armor, drop in a mailbox **17** post-office service

Mailer, Norman
author of: **15** An American Dream **16** Armies of the Night **18** The Naked and the Dead **19** The Executioner's Song

Maillol, Aristide
born: **6** France **13** Banyuls sur mer
artwork: **5** Night, Torso **7** Le Desir (Desire) **11** Ile de France **12** Young Cyclist **14** Action in Chains, The Three Nymphs **16** The Mediterranean (Seated Woman) **17** Monument to Cezanne, Monument to Debussy **18** Venus with a Necklace

maim 3 cut, rip **4** gash, lame, maul, rend, tear **5** slash, wound **6** deface, hobble, injure, mangle, savage **7** cripple, disable **8** lacerate, mutilate **9** disfigure, dismember, hamstring **12** incapacitate

main 4 head **5** chief, prime, vital **6** urgent **7** capital, central, crucial, leading, primary, special, supreme **8** critical, foremost, pressing **9** essential, important, necessary, paramount, principal, requisite **10** particular, preeminent **11** outstanding, predominant **13** consequential, indispensable

Main, Marjorie
real name: **13** Mary Tomlinson
partner: **12** Wallace Beery **13** Percy Kilbride
born: **7** Acton IN
roles: **7** Dead End **8** Ma Kettle

Maine

abbreviation: 2 ME
nickname: 6 Lumber **8** Pine Tree **10** Wonderland
capital: 7 Augusta
largest city: 8 Portland
others: 4 Bath, Saco **5** Hiram, Orono **6** Auburn, Bangor **7** Kittery **8** Boothbay, Lewiston, Ogunquit **9** Bar Harbor, Biddeford, Brunswick, Skowhegan **10** Waterville **11** Millinocket, Presque Isle
college: 5 Bates, Colby **7** Bowdoin
explorer: 6 Cabots **8** Norsemen
feature: 8 lobsters **19** West Quoddy Headlight
  beach: 10 Old Orchard
  national park: 6 Acadia
  waterway: 18 Allagash Wilderness
tribe: 6 Abnaki **7** Wewenoc
people: 10 downeaster **11** Dorothea Dix **19** Edna St Vincent Millay **24** Henry Wadsworth Longfellow
island: 4 Orrs **8** Mt Desert **10** Campobello
lake: 5 Sebec, Wyman **6** Sebago **8** Rangeley, Schoodic **9** Flagstaff, Moosehead **10** Chesuncook
land rank: 11 thirty-ninth
mountain: 5 Kineo, White **7** Bigelow **8** Cadillac
  highest point: 8 Katahdin
physical feature:
  bay: 5 Casco **9** Penobscot **12** Merrymeeting **13** Passamaquoddy
  sand dunes: 13 Desert of Maine
river: 4 Saco **6** St John **7** St Croix **8** Allagash, Kennebec **9** Aroostook, Kennebago, Penobscot **12** Androscoggin
state admission: 11 twenty-third
state bird: 9 chickadee
state fish: 16 land-locked salmon
state flower: 7 thistle **8** pine cone **22** white pine cone and tassel
state motto: 7 I Direct
state song: 16 State of Maine Song
state tree: 16 eastern white pine

mainly 6 mostly **7** chiefly **8** above all **9** in the main, most of all, primarily **10** on the whole **11** principally **13** predominantly **14** for the most part, in great measure **16** first and foremost

main point 3 nut **4** core, crux, gist, meat **5** basis, heart, theme **6** kernel **7** essence **10** brass tacks **11** nitty-gritty **15** sum and substance

mainspring 5 agent, cause **6** motive **9** incentive **10** motivation

mainstay 4 prop **6** anchor, pillar **7** bulwark **8** backbone, buttress **16** pillar of strength

Main Street
  author: 13 Sinclair Lewis
  character: 14 Carol Kennicott **15** Dr Will Kennicott

maintain 4 aver, avow, hold, keep **5** claim, state, swear **6** affirm, allege, assert, defend, insist, keep up, uphold **7** care for, contend, declare, finance, profess, stand by, support, sustain **8** conserve, continue, preserve **9** keep alive, keep going **10** provide for, take care of

maintenance 4 keep **6** living, repair, upkeep **7** keeping, support **10** livelihood, protection, sustenance **11** safekeeping, subsistence, sustainment **12** conservation, preservation, safeguarding

maison de sante 10 sanitarium **13** house of health

maize 4 corn, milo **5** grain **6** cereal, silage, yellow **7** zea mays **10** Indian corn

majestic, majestical 5 grand, lofty, noble, regal, royal **6** august, famous, superb **7** elegant, eminent, stately, sublime **8** esteemed, glorious, imperial, imposing, princely, renowned, splendid **10** impressive **11** illustrious, magnificent **13** distinguished

majesty 4 pomp **5** glory **6** luster **7** dignity **8** elegance, eminence, grandeur, mobility, splendor **9** elevation, loftiness, solemnity, sublimity **10** augustness **11** distinction, stateliness **12** gloriousness, magnificence **14** impressiveness

major 4 main **5** chief, prime, vital **6** larger, urgent **7** capital, crucial, greater, leading, primary, ranking, serious, supreme **8** critical, foremost, pressing **9** essential, important, necessary, paramount, principal, requisite **10** preeminent **11** outstanding, predominant, significant **13** consequential, indispensable

Major Barbara
  director: 13 Gabriel Pascal
  based on play by: 17 George Bernard Shaw
  cast: 11 Deborah Kerr, Rex Harrison, Wendy Hiller **12** Robert Morley, Robert Newton **14** Sybil Thorndike

majority 4 bulk, mass **8** best part, legal age, maturity **9** adulthood, seniority, womanhood **10** lion's share **13** preponderance

major key (in music)
  German: 3 dur

Major prophets *see* **8** prophets

majuscule 7 capital **11** large letter **13** capital letter **15** upper-case letter

make 3 fix **4** form, kind, mark, meet, pass **5** beget, brand, build, catch, cause, enact, erect, force, frame, impel, press, reach, shape, speak, utter **6** attain, compel, create, devise, draw up, effect, foment, makeup, oblige, render **7** appoint, compose, deliver, dragoon, fashion, produce, require **8** arrive at, assemble, engender **9** cause to be, constrain, construct, establish, fabricate, formation, legislate, pronounce, structure **10** bring about, fashioning **11** composition, manufacture

make a bet 3 bet **4** risk **5** stake, wager **6** chance, gamble, hazard, plunge **7** venture

make a clean breast of 7 confess, lay bare, own up to **8** blurt out **14** come clean about

make a dash 3 fly, run **4** flee **6** escape **7** get away **8** make a run **10** make a break, take flight **12** make a getaway

make a deal 5 agree **6** settle **10** compromise **11** come to terms, meet halfway **14** strike a bargain

make advances 8 approach, come on to, sound out **11** proposition **13** make overtures, put the moves on

make a fuss over 6 dote on **7** protest **8** crow over

make again 4 copy **6** remake, repeat **9** duplicate **11** reconstruct

make a getaway 4 bolt, flee, skip **6** escape **7** get away, make off, run away **8** make a run, slip away **9** break free, cut and run, make a dash **10** break loose, fly the coop, take flight

make a gift of 4 give **6** donate **7** present **8** bequeath **10** contribute

make allowance for 6 excuse, pardon **7** forgive, indulge **8** bear with, pass over

make amends 5 atone **6** make up, square **7** expiate **9** do penance **10** compensate

make a mess of 3 mar **4** goof, muff, ruin **5** botch, spoil **6** bungle, foul up, mess up **7** butcher, do badly, louse up, screw up **9** mismanage

make a mistake 3 err **4** goof **6** mess up, slip up **12** miscalculate

make an effort 3 try **5** essay **6** strive, work at **7** attempt **8** endeavor

make appear 5 evoke **6** elicit **7** produce **9** conjure up **10** bring forth

make a racket 3 cry **4** howl, yell **5** shout **6** bellow, clamor, holler, scream **7** bluster **8** make a din **10** vociferate **12** raise a rumpus

make a stab at 3 try **5** essay, guess **6** reckon, take on **7** attempt, surmise, venture **8** estimate, give a try **9** undertake **10** conjecture **11** approximate **12** take a crack at, take a fling at

make a stand 9 stand fast **13** refuse to yield **17** fight to the last man

make a statement 6 remark **7** clarify, comment, discuss, explain, expound **9** elucidate, talk about

make aware 4 tell **5** edify **6** advise, inform, notify, reveal **7** apprise **8** acquaint, disclose **9** divulge to, enlighten, introduce **11** familiarize **16** bring to (one's) attention

make away with 3 eat **4** kill, take

5 spend, steal **6** kidnap, murder **7** abolish, consume, destroy **8** carry off, embezzle, get rid of **9** dissipate

make-believe 4 fake, sham **5** false, phony **6** made-up, make-up, unreal **7** assumed, charade, fantasy, feigned, fiction **8** creation, imagined, invented, pretense, spurious **9** fantastic, imaginary, invention, pretended, simulated **10** artificial, fictitious **11** counterfeit, fabrication **13** falsification

make certain of 6 assure, clinch, ensure **8** be sure of **10** make sure of

make damp 5 bedew **6** dampen **7** moisten **8** sprinkle

make dark 3 dim **6** darken **7** blacken, obscure

make different 4 vary **5** alter, amend **6** change, modify, mutate **7** convert, remodel **9** transform, transmute **12** metamorphose

make distinctive 8 set apart **9** single out **11** distinguish **12** characterize **13** differentiate

make easy 4 ease **6** smooth **7** explain, lighten **8** simplify **10** clear a path, facilitate

make eligible 5 allow **6** permit **7** entitle, qualify **9** authorize

make evident 4 show **5** prove **6** reveal **7** exhibit **8** manifest **9** establish, make clear, make plain **11** demonstrate

make fast 3 fix **4** moor **5** affix, tie up **6** attach, fasten, secure **7** connect

make feeble 6 weaken **7** wear out **8** enervate **10** debilitate, devitalize

make furious 5 anger **6** enrage, madden **7** incense, inflame **9** infuriate

make giddy 5 dizzy **12** make unsteady **15** make lightheaded

make good 5 repay **6** arrive, make it **7** fulfill, succeed **11** reach the top **15** make restitution

make happy 5 amuse, cheer, elate **6** please **7** delight, gratify **9** entertain

make haste slowly
    Latin: **12** festina lente

make hostile 5 repel **6** offend **7** provoke **8** alienate **10** antagonize

make ill 5 repel **6** infect, revolt, sicken **7** afflict, disgust, repulse **8** disagree, distress, make sick, nauseate **9** discomfit **14** turn the stomach

make ill at ease 5 upset **6** rattle **7** fluster **8** distress **9** discomfit, embarrass **10** disconcert

make impure 4 foul, soil **5** dirty, spoil, taint **6** befoul, blight, defile, infect, poison **7** corrupt, pollute **10** adulterate **11** contaminate

make inroads 6 invade **7** impinge, intrude **8** encroach, infringe, trespass **9** penetrate

make known 4 tell **6** advise, impart, inform, notify, report, reveal, unveil **7** apprise, divulge, lay bare, publish, uncover **8** disclose **9** broadcast **10** give notice, make public **11** communicate

make less forceful 6 soften, weaken **9** undermine **10** devitalize, emasculate

make light of 8 belittle, minimize, pooh-pooh, sneeze at **9** deprecate, disparage, underrate **10** depreciate, undervalue **13** underestimate

make merry 5 revel **7** carouse, roister **9** celebrate, have a ball **15** paint the town red

make much of 5 honor **6** praise **7** acclaim, applaud, commend, flatter **8** fuss over

make nervous 5 annoy, upset **7** agitate, disturb, perturb, trouble, unnerve **10** disconcert

make off with 4 lift **5** boost, steal, swipe **6** abduct, kidnap, snatch **7** bear off **8** carry off **10** run off with **11** get away with

make one's blood boil 5 anger **6** enrage, madden **7** incense, inflame **9** infuriate

make one's eyes pop 4 stun **5** amaze, shock **6** dazzle **7** stagger, startle **8** astonish **9** electrify **11** flabbergast

make out 3 see **4** espy **6** behold, descry, detect, fill in, notice **7** discern, observe, pick out **8** get along, perceive, write out **12** catch sight of

make plain 7 clarify, clear up, explain, lay open **9** elucidate, explicate, make clear **10** illuminate **11** disentangle, shed light on **12** bring to light

make possible for 5 allow **6** enable, permit **7** empower, qualify **10** capacitate

make public 3 air **4** tell, vent **5** print, utter, voice **6** expose, inform, reveal, spread **7** declare, display, divulge, exhibit, express, give out, publish **8** announce, disclose, proclaim, televise **9** broadcast, circulate, publicize

maker, Maker 3 god **4** poet **5** smith **6** author, forger **7** builder, creator, founder **8** declarer, inventor, producer **9** architect, generator **10** originator **12** manufacturer

make ready 5 prime **7** arrange, forearm, prepare

make reparation for 5 atone, repay **6** pay for **10** compensate, recompense, remunerate

make restitution 5 repay **7** pay back **9** reimburse **10** compensate, recompense

make right 3 fix **5** amend, emend **6** remedy, repair **7** correct, improve, rectify

make self-conscious 5 abash **6** rattle **7** chagrin, fluster **9** discomfit, embarrass **10** disconcert

makeshift 6 make-do **7** standby, stopgap **8** slapdash **9** alternate, expedient, temporary, tentative **10** substitute **11** provisional

make sick 6 revolt **7** disgust **8** nauseate

make smaller 6 lessen, reduce, shrink, take in **8** decrease, diminish

make sure 5 cinch **6** assure, clinch, decide, ensure, secure, settle **9** ascertain **11** double-check

make thinner 4 thin **6** dilute **9** water down **10** adulterate

make tracks 2 go **4** scat, shoo **5** be off, leave, scram **6** beat it, cut out, depart, go away **8** withdraw **10** hit the road

make uncomfortable 3 try **7** agitate, perturb **8** disquiet, distress **9** discomfit, embarrass **10** discompose

make uneasy 6 rattle **7** disturb, perturb, trouble, unnerve **8** disquiet, distress **9** discomfit, embarrass **10** discomfort, discompose, disconcert

make uniform 4 even **5** equal **6** smooth **7** balance **8** equalize **10** straighten

makeup 5 frame **9** character, cosmetics, framework, structure **11** composition, personality **12** constitution, organization

make up 4 form **5** cover **6** invent / arrange, concoct **8** assemble **9** improvise, reconcile **10** compensate, constitute **11** put together

make up for 5 atone **7** expiate **8** make good **10** make amends **13** compensate for

make up one's mind 6 decide **7** resolve **9** determine

make use of 3 use **5** apply **6** employ, engage, occupy **7** exploit, utilize **8** keep busy, put to use **13** turn to account

make weary 4 do in, poop, tire **7** exhaust, wear out **8** enervate

makeweight 6 weight **7** ballast

make well 4 cure, heal

make wider 5 widen **6** dilate, expand **7** broaden, stretch **9** spread out

make worse 6 worsen **8** heighten, increase **9** aggravate, intensify **10** exacerbate

making excuses 8 alibiing **9** defending **10** justifying **11** apologizing

Making of the President, The (series)
    author: **14** Theodore H White

making the rounds 5 about **6** abroad **11** circulating, going around **13** going the route

Malachi
    means: **11** my messenger
    identified with: **4** Ezra **8** Mordecai, Nehemiah **10** Zerubbabel

maladroit 5 inept **6** clumsy, gauche **7** awkward, unhandy **8** bumbling, bungling, tactless **9** impolitic, unskilled **10** blundering, left-handed, ungraceful

maladroitness 9 gaucherie, inability **10** clumsiness, ineptitude **11** awkwardness, unhandiness **12** incompetence

malady 7 ailment, disease, illness **8** disorder, sickness **9** affection, complaint, infirmity **10** affliction, disability

mala fide 10 in bad faith, not genuine

malaise 4 pang **5** throb **6** twinge **7** anxiety **8** disquiet **9** lassitude **10** uneasiness, discomfort **11** nervousness

Malamud, Bernard
  author of: 8 The Fixer **9** God's Grace **10** The Natural, The Tenants **11** Dubin's Lives **12** The Assistant

Malaprop, Mrs
  character in: 9 The Rivals
  author: 8 Sheridan

Malawi
  other name: 9 Nyasaland
  capital: 8 Lilongwe
  largest city: 8 Blantyre
  others: 4 Bana **5** Dedza, Limbe, Mzuzu, Zomba **6** Kasese, Mzimba, Salima **7** Chipoka, Chiromo, Deep Bay, Karonga, Katumbi **8** Chikwawa, Chilumbe, Kota Kota, Nkata Bay **9** Monkey Bay **10** Port Herald **12** Fort Johnston, Livingstonia
  monetary unit: 6 kwacha **7** tambala
  lake: 5 Nyasa **6** Chilwa, Malawi
  mountain: 11 Livingstone
  highest point: 6 Mlanje **7** Mulanje
  river: 3 Bua **5** Shire **7** Dwangwa **11** South Rukuru
  physical feature:
    highlands: 5 Shire
    plateau: 5 Nyika
    valley: 5 Shire **9** Great Rift
  people: 3 Yao **4** Sena **5** Bantu, Lomwe, Ngoni **6** Cheiva, Maravi, Ngonde, Nyanja **7** Tumbuka
    dynasty: 6 Maravi
    explorer: 16 David Livingstone
    leader: 5 Banda
  language: 3 Yao **4** Cewa **5** Bantu, Ngoni, Tonga **6** Nyanja **7** English, Tumbuka **8** Chichewa **10** Chitumbuka
  religion: 5 Islam **7** animism **10** Protestant **12** Presbyterian **13** Roman Catholic
  feature:
    village: 5 mudzi

Malaysia
  capital/largest city: 11 Kuala Lumpur
  others: 4 Ipoh, Sibu **5** Anson, Davao, Telok **6** Iloilo, Johore, Kupang, Manado, Penang, Pinang **7** Bintulu, Kuantan, Kuching, Melalap **8** Port Weld, Sandakan **10** Georgetown, Kota Baharu **11** Johor Baharu, Port Dickson **12** Kota Kinabulu **14** Port Swettenham

division: 5 Sabah **6** Malaya **7** Malacca, Sarawak

head of state:
  supreme head of state: 18 yang di-pertuan agong

measure: 3 pau, tun **4** para, pipe, tael, wang **5** parah **6** chupak, parrah **7** gantang

monetary unit: 3 sen, tra **4** taro, trah **7** ringgit, tampang

weight: 4 chee, mace, tael, wang **7** tampang

island: 6 Banggi, Borneo, Labuan, Penang, Pinang, Tioman **7** Pangkor, Sebatik **8** Langkawi **10** Perhentian **11** Balambangan

mountain: 4 Bulu, Hose, Iban, Iran, Main, Mulu, Niut, Raja **5** Murjo, Niapa, Ophir **6** Blumut, Kapuas, Leuser, Slamet **7** Binaija, Brassey, Crocker **8** Rindjani **11** Gunong Korbu, Gunong Tahan

highest point: 8 Kinabalu

river: 5 Klang, Kutai, Perak **6** Barito, Pahang, Rajang, Rejang **7** Sarawak **12** Kinabatangan

sea: 4 Sulu **7** Celebes **10** South China

physical feature:
  bay: 5 Labuk
  cape: 5 Sirik
  highlands: 7 Cameron
  passage: 6 Sibutu
  peninsula: 5 Malay
  point: 13 Tanjong Gelang
  strait: 6 Johore **7** Balabac, Malacca

people: 4 Iban **5** Dayak, Malay **6** Indian **7** Chinese, Kadazan **9** Pakistani, Sri Lankan **10** Bangladesh, Indonesian

language: 4 Bugi, Dyak **5** Malay, Tamil **6** Battok, Rejang **7** Chinese, English, Lampong, Niasese **8** Achinese, Javanese, Makassar **14** Bahasa Malaysia
  alphabet: 5 tagal

religion: 5 Hindu, Islam **6** Taoism **7** animism **8** Buddhism **12** Christianity, Confucianism

place:
  mosque: 8 National

feature:
  cap: 7 songkok
  cloth: 4 tapa **5** batik
  clothing: 4 baju, malo, sari **5** badju, pareu **6** cabaya, kebaya, sam-foo, sarong **9** cheongsam
  dance: 4 haka, hula **5** joget
  game: 9 sepakraga
  hamlet: 7 kampong
  parish: 5 mukim
  rice paddy: 4 padi
  scarf: 9 selendang
  self-defense: 5 silat
  shadow play: 6 menora
  spirit: 5 hantu

food:
  drink: 4 kava
  fruit: 6 durian **8** rambutan **10** mangosteen

Malcolm
  character in: 7 Macbeth
  author: 11 Shakespeare

Malcolm X
  original name: 13 Malcolm Little
  born: 7 Omaha NE
  religion: 5 Islam **11** Black Muslim **13** Nation of Islam
  assassinated in: 6 Harlem **11** New York City
  book about: 26 The Autobiography of Malcolm X
    author: 9 Alex Haley
  film about: 8 Malcolm X
    director: 8 Spike Lee

malcontent 4 glum, sour **5** rebel **6** grouch, grumpy, morose, sullen, uneasy **7** grouchy, growler, repiner, restive **8** dejected, downcast, grumbler, restless **9** insurgent, irritable **10** complainer, despondent **11** faultfinder **12** discontented, dissatisfied, faultfinding, hard to please

mal de mer 11 seasickness

Malden, Karl
  real name: 16 Mladen Sekulovich
  born: 6 Gary IL
  roles: 6 Patton **8** Baby Doll **15** On the Waterfront **21** A Streetcar Named Desire **24** The Streets of San Francisco

Maldives
  capital/largest city: 4 Male
  government:
    legislature: 6 Majlis
  monetary unit: 5 laree, rupee
  island: 3 Ari, Gan **4** Addu, Male **5** Rasdu **6** Felidu, Hulele, Mulaku **7** Malcolm, Minicoy, Nilandu **8** Maldives, Suvadiva **9** Fadiffolu, Wilingili **10** Haddummati, Kolumadulu **11** Tiladummati **13** Ihavandiffulu, Miladummadulu **16** North Malosmadulu, South Malosmadulu
  sea: 6 Indian **7** Arabian **9** Laccadive
  physical feature:
    channel: 4 Wadu **7** Kardiva **8** Veimandu **10** Equatorial **11** Eight Degree **17** One and a Half Degree
  people: 4 Arab **6** Indian **9** Sinhalese **10** Singhalese
    ruling family/sultans: 4 Didi
  language: 6 Arabic, Divehi
  religion: 5 Islam
  feature:
    coconut fiber: 4 coir
    dried coconut: 5 copra

male 3 boy, man, ram, tom **4** bull **5** manly, youth **6** tomcat **7** manlike, rooster **8** stallion **9** billy goat, masculine

Male
  capital of: 8 Maldives

male bird 4 cock **5** drake **6** gander **7** rooster

maledict 4 damn **5** curse **8** denounce **9** proscribe **12** anathematize

malediction 5 curse **8** anathema, diatribe **9** damnation, evil spell **10** execration **11** fulmination, imprecation **12** denunciation, proscription

malefactor 5 felon, knave, rogue **6** sinner **7** culprit **8** criminal, evil-doer, offender **9** miscreant, scoundrel, wrongdoer **10** malfeasant

male hairdresser
   French: **8** coiffeur

malentendu 7 mistake **16** misunderstanding

male power
   god of: **7** Priapus

Malevich, Kasimir Severinovich
   born: **4** Kiev **6** Russia
   artwork: **11** Black Square **15** The Knife Grinder **18** Eight Red Rectangles **19** Woman with Water Pails **34** Suprematist Composition White on White

malevolence 4 evil, hate **5** spite **6** enmity, grudge, hatred, malice, rancor, spleen **7** despite, ill will **9** hostility, malignity **10** antagonism, malignance, malignancy **12** spitefulness **13** maliciousness

malevolent 5 surly **6** malign, sullen **7** baleful, vicious **8** sinister, spiteful, venomous **9** invidious, malicious, malignant, rancorous, resentful **10** ill-natured, pernicious, revengeful **11** acrimonious, ill-disposed **14** ill-intentioned

malfeasance 5 crime **8** misdeeds **10** misconduct, wrongdoing

malformation 9 deformity **10** aberration, distortion **11** abnormality, monstrosity, peculiarity **12** grotesquerie, irregularity **13** disfigurement

malformed 7 twisted **8** deformed **9** contorted, distorted, grotesque, irregular, misshapen

malfunction 6 glitch, malady **7** problem **9** complaint

malgre lui 16 in spite of himself

Mali
   other name: **11** French Sudan **12** French Soudan **16** Sudanese Republic
   capital/largest city: **6** Bamako
   others: **3** Gao **5** Kayes, Mopti, Segou **6** Djenne **7** Sikasso **8** Taoudeni, Timbuktu **10** Tombouctou
   division: **5** Sahel **7** Azaouad
   monetary unit: **5** franc **7** centime
   lake: **2** Do **4** Debo **5** Garou **7** Korarou **9** Faguibine
   mountain: **4** Mina **6** Iforas **7** Manding
   highest point: **12** Hombori Tondo
   river: **4** Bani **5** Bagoe, Bakoy, Diaka,

Niger **6** Bafing, Bakoye, Baoule, Faleme **7** Azaouak, Senegal
   physical feature:
     desert: **6** Sahara **8** Chech Erg **10** Sekkane Erg **13** Haricha Hamada
     plateau: **14** Adrar des Iforas
     valley: **5** Niger **7** Tilemsi
   people: **3** Bwa **4** Fula, Kyan, Moor, Peul **5** Dogon, Dyula, Fulbe, Marka **6** Berber, Dognon, Fulani, Senufo, Tuareg **7** Bambara, Fellata, Malinke, Miniaka, Songhai, Soninke **8** Khasonke, Mandingo, Senoulfo
     leader: **4** Umar **5** Keita **6** Traore **9** Mansa Musa
   language: **5** Dogon, Dyula, Feulh, Mande, Marka **6** Berber, French, Fulani **7** Bambara, Malinke, Senoufo, Songhai
   religion: **5** Islam **7** animism
   place:
     ruins: **8** Terhazza
   feature:
     empire: **4** Mali **5** Ghana **7** Bambara, Songhai

malice 4 hate **5** spite, venom **6** enmity, grudge, hatred, rancor **7** ill will **8** acrimony **9** animosity, malignity **10** antagonism, bitterness, evil intent, resentment **11** malevolence **12** spitefulness

malice aforethought
   legal term: **51** planning to commit a crime without just cause or provocation

malicious 7 baleful, harmful, hateful, vicious **8** spiteful **9** invidious, malignant, rancorous, resentful **10** malevolent, revengeful, vindictive **11** acrimonious, ill-disposed

malign 3 bad **4** evil **5** abuse, black **6** defame, revile, vilify **7** baneful, harmful, hateful, noxious, ominous, put down, run down, slander **8** backbite, bad mouth, belittle, derogate, menacing, sinister **9** denigrate, deprecate, disparage, injurious, malicious, malignant **10** malevolent, pernicious, speak ill of **11** deleterious, detrimental, threatening **14** inveigh against

malignancy 5 spite, tumor **6** cancer, malice, rancor **7** ill will, sarcoma **8** acrimony, neoplasm, toxicity **9** carcinoma, hostility, virulence **10** bitterness **11** malevolence, viciousness **12** hard feelings, spitefulness, vengefulness **13** poisonousness

malignant 4 evil **5** fatal, toxic **6** bitter, deadly **7** hateful, hostile, vicious **8** fiendish, spiteful, venomous, virulent **9** invidious, malicious, poisonous, rancorous, resentful **10** diabolical, evil-minded, malevolent, pernicious, revengeful, vindictive **11** acrimonious, ill-disposed

malignant spirit 3 imp **5** demon, devil **7** gremlin

malignity 4 evil **5** spite, venom **6** animus, rancor, spleen **7** ill will **8** acrimony **9** animosity **12** hard feelings, spitefulness, venomousness

malinger 4 loaf **5** dodge, evade, shirk, slack **7** goof off **9** goldbrick

mall 4 yard **5** court, plaza **6** arcade, circus, piazza, square **8** cloister **9** colonnade, esplanade, promenade **10** quadrangle **12** parade ground

Mallarme, Stephane
   author of: **8** Herodias **18** L'Apres Midi d'un faune **19** The Afternoon of a Faun

Malle, Louis
   director of: **10** Pretty Baby **12** Atlantic City **13** Lacombe Lucien **16** Murmur of the Heart
   wife: **13** Candice Bergen

malleable 6 docile, pliant **7** ductile, plastic, pliable **8** flexible, moldable, workable **9** adaptable, compliant, teachable, tractable **10** governable, manageable **12** easily shaped **13** easily wrought **14** impressionable

mallet
   type: **6** rubber, wooden **12** plastic-faced

malnutrition 10 emaciation, starvation **16** undernourishment

malodorous 4 rank **5** acrid, fetid, musty **6** putrid, smelly **7** noisome, reeking **8** stinking **12** foul-smelling

Malone, Dorothy
   real name: **20** Dorothy Eloise Maloney
   husband: **15** Jacques Bergerac
   born: **9** Chicago IL
   roles: **11** Peyton Place **14** Too Much Too Soon **16** Written on the Wind

Malory, Sir Thomas
   author of: **14** Le Morte d'Arthur

Malpighi, Marcello
   field: **10** physiology
   nationality: **7** Italian
   founded: **18** microscopic anatomy

malpractice 10 negligence

Malraux, Andre
   author of: **8** Man's Fate **11** Anti-Memoirs, Days of Wrath, The Royal Way **13** The Conquerors **18** The Voices of Silence

Malta
   capital: **8** Valletta
   largest city: **6** Sliema
   others: **5** Marfa, Mdina, Mgarr, Mosta, Nadut, Paola **6** Zejtun **7** Senglea, Zeibrun **8** Cospicua, Floriana, Mellieha, Victoria **10** Birkirkara, Birzebbuga, Vittoriosa
   measure: **4** rotl **5** artal, canna, parto, ratel, salma **6** kantar **7** caffiso
   monetary unit: **4** cent **5** grain, grano, pound
   island: **4** Gozo **5** Malta **6** Comino, Filfla **7** Filfola **9** Cominotto **10** Cominotto

highest point: 12 Dingli Cliffs
sea: 13 Mediterranean
physical feature:
  bay: 7 St Paul's **8** Mellieha **10** Marsaxlokk
  channel: 11 North Comino, South Comino
  harbor: 5 Grand **10** Marsamxett
people: 7 Maltese
  leader: 7 Mintoff **9** Buttigieo **18** Parisot de La Valette
  ruler: 5 Arabs **6** Romans **7** British **8** Napoleon **10** Byzantines **11** Hospitalers, Phoenicians **13** Carthaginians **15** Holy Roman Empire, Knights of St John
language: 7 English, Italian, Maltese
religion: 13 Roman Catholic
feature:
  gondola boat: 7 dghaisa
Maltese Falcon, The
  author: 15 Dashiell Hammett
  director: 10 John Huston
  cast: 9 Mary Astor (Brigid O'Shaughnessy) **10** Peter Lorre (Joel Cairo) **12** Elisha Cook Jr (Wilmer), Gladys George **14** Humphrey Bogart (Sam Spade) **17** Sydney Greenstreet (the Fat Man)
  character: 6 Wilmer **8** Sam Spade **9** Joel Cairo **11** Miles Archer **12** Casper Gutman, Floyd Thursby **18** Brigid O'Shaughnessy
  remade as: 13 Satan Met a Lady
malt liquor 3 ale **4** beer, bock, brew **5** stout **6** porter
maltreat 4 harm, hurt **5** abuse **6** ill-use, injure **8** mistreat
maltreatment 5 abuse **6** ill-use, injury **7** assault, cruelty **10** bodily harm, oppression **11** manhandling, molestation, persecution **12** mistreatment
Malvolio
  character in: 12 Twelfth Night
  author: 11 Shakespeare
Mama
  character: 4 Nels **6** Dagmar, Katrin, TR Ryan **9** Aunt Jenny **10** (Papa) Lars Hansen **11** (Mama) Marta Hansen
  cast: 8 Iris Mann **9** Peggy Wood, Ruth Gates **11** Judson Laire, Robin Morgan **12** Rosemary Rice **13** Dick Van Patten, Kevin Coughlin
  dog: 6 Willie
  based on book: 16 Mama's Bank Account
  author: 13 Kathryn Forbes
  setting: 12 San Francisco
  theme: 12 Holverg Suite **13** The Last Spring
mamma, mama 2 ma **3** mam, mom, mum **4** wife **5** madre, mammy, mater, mommy, mummy, mumsy, woman **6** mother, parent
mammal

bat (chiroptera): 4 tomb **5** fruit, naked, smoky **7** mastiff, vampire **9** fisherman, horseshoe, leaf-nosed, sac-winged, slit-faced, thumbless **10** disk-winged, free-tailed, moustached **11** funnel-eared, hollow-faced, mouse-tailed **12** false vampire, sheath-tailed, sucker-footed, yellow-winged **14** vespertilionid **21** New Zealand short-tailed
carnivore: 3 cat, dog, fox **4** bear, lion, lynx, mink, puma, wolf **5** civet, dingo, fossa, hyena, otter, panda, skunk, tayra, tiger **6** badger, bobcat, coyote, ferret, grison, hyaena, jackal, jaguar, marten, olingo, weasel **7** polecat, raccoon **8** aardwolf, kinkajou, mongoose, suricate **9** wolverine **10** cacomistle, coatimundi
cetacea: 4 gray **5** pilot, right, whale **6** beluga, killer **7** dolphin, rorqual **8** humpback, narwhale, porpoise **10** sperm whale **11** beaked whale **16** bottle-nosed whale
edentata: 5 sloth **8** anteater **9** armadillo, tree sloth
egg-laying: 7 echidna **13** spiny anteater **18** duck-billed platypus
even-toed ungulate: 2 ox **3** elk, hog, pig **4** deer, goat, oxen **5** bison, camel, llama, moose, okapi, sheep **6** alpaca, cattle, duiker, vicuna **7** buffalo, caribou, gazelle, giraffe, guanaco, muntjak, peccary **8** antelope **9** mouse deer **10** chevrotain **12** hippopotamus
hyracoidea: 5 hyrax
insect-eating: 4 mole **5** shrew **8** desman, tenrec **7** gymnure, moon rat **8** hedgehog **9** shrew-mole, solenodon **10** golden mole, otter shrew, water shrew **13** elephant shrew
lagomorpha: 4 hare, pika **6** rabbit
marsupials/pouched: 5 koala **6** cuscus, numbat, possum, wombat **7** opossum, wallaby **8** kangaroo **9** bandicoot, phalanger **14** Tasmanian devil
odd-toed ungulate: 3 ass **5** horse, kiang, tapir, zebra **6** onager, quagga **10** rhinoceros
pinnipedia: 4 seal **6** walrus **7** sea lion
primate: 5 lemur, loris, potto **6** avahis, aye-aye, baboon, galago, gibbon, indris, monkey, people **7** gorilla, tamarin, tamant **8** marmoset, simpoona **9** orangutan, tree shrew **10** chimpanzee
proboscidea: 8 elephant
rodent: 4 cavy, vole **5** coypu, gundi, hutia, mouse **6** agouti, beaver, coruro, gerbil, gopher, jerboa, nutria **7** blesmol, cane rat, hamster, lemming, mole-rat, rock rat **8** capybara, chipmunk, dormouse, sewellel, spiny rat, squirrel, tucu-tuco, viscacha **9** chozchori, false paca, pacaranas,

porcupine, woodchuck **10** chinchilla, prairie dog, springhare **11** kangaroo rat, pocket mouse, viscacha rat **13** kangaroo mouse **16** Speke's pectinator
sirenia: 6 dugong, sea cow **7** manatee
tubulidentata: 8 aardvark
mammon, Mammon 4 gain, gold **5** money **6** profit, riches, wealth **9** affluence **11** possessions **13** material goods, the god of money
Mammon, Sir Epicure
  character in: 12 The Alchemist
  author: 6 Jonson
mammoth 4 huge **5** great **6** mighty **7** immense, massive **8** colossal, enormous, gigantic, whopping **9** cyclopean, herculean, monstrous, ponderous, very large **10** gargantuan, monumental, prodigious, stupendous, tremendous **11** elephantine, mountainous
Mammy
  character in: 15 Gone With the Wind
  author: 8 Mitchell
Mamoulian, Rouben
  director of: 13 Love Me Tonight, Silk Stockings **14** Queen Christina, The Mark of Zorro
man 3 boy, guy, one **4** chap, gent, hand, male, soul **5** equip, hubby, human, staff **6** anyone, attend, butler, fellow, fit out, helper, outfit, people, person, spouse, waiter, worker **7** footman, husband, laborer, mankind, someone, subject, workman **8** employee, garrison, handyman, henchman, humanity, liegeman, somebody **9** assistant, gentleman, hired hand, humankind **11** Homo sapiens
  Spanish: 6 hombre
Man, first 4 Adam **12** Alalcomeneus
  Nordic: 3 Ask
Man, Isle of
  capital: 7 Douglas
  location: 8 Irish Sea
  native: 4 Manx **7** Manxman
  Manx cat lacks: 4 tail
Man, Woman and Child
  author: 10 Erich Segal
man about town 5 blade **7** playboy **8** cavalier, gay blade **12** boulevardier
manacle, manacles 3 ply, run, use **4** cope, fare, head, rule, work **5** bonds, get on, guide, irons, order, pilot, shift, steer, wield **6** chains, direct, fetter, govern, handle, make go **7** command, conduct, control, operate, oversee, shackle, succeed, survive, work out **8** cope with, deal with, dominate, get along, handcuff, maneuver, shackles **9** bracelets, handcuffs, look after, supervise, watch over **10** accomplish, administer, bring about, manipulate, put in irons, take care of **11** be at the helm, hand-fetters, preside over, put

in chains, superintend **12** have charge of, hold the reins

manage 4 care, rule **6** bosses, charge, wheels **7** bigwigs, command, conduct, control, dealing, running, tactics **8** big shots, guidance, handling, ordering, planning, strategy, top brass **9** direction, directors, operation **10** conducting, executives, overseeing, regulation **11** generalship, negotiation, supervision, supervisors, transaction **12** manipulation, organization **14** administration, administrators **15** superintendence

manageable 4 easy **6** docile, pliant, wieldy **8** amenable, flexible **9** compliant, tractable **10** governable, submissive **12** controllable

management 4 boss, head **5** agent, chief **7** foreman, planner **8** overseer **9** budgeteer, majordomo, organizer, tactician **10** impresario, negotiator, supervisor **11** manipulator **13** administrator **14** superintendent

manager 4 boss, head **5** agent, chief **7** foreman, planner **8** overseer **9** budgeteer, majordomo, organizer, tactician **10** impresario, negotiator, supervisor **11** manipulator **13** administrator **14** superintendent

managerial 9 executive **10** management **11** supervisory **14** administrative, organizational

Managua
  capital of: **9** Nicaragua
Manala see **7** Tuonela
Manama
  capital of: **7** Bahrain
manana 6 future **8** tomorrow **11** in the future
Man and Superman
  author: **17** George Bernard Shaw
Manassa Mauler
  nickname of: **11** Jack Dempsey
Manasseh
  father: **6** Joseph
  mother: **7** Asenath
  great uncle: **4** Esau
  grandfather: **5** Jacob
  descendant of: **9** Manassite
man-at-arms 7 fighter, soldier, warrior **9** combatant **10** cavalryman
Manchester, William
  author of: **11** The Last Lion **14** American Caesar **15** Goodbye Darkness
Manchuria
  also: **7** Manchow
  city: **5** Aigun, Hulan, Kirin, Peian, Penki **6** Anshan, Antung, Dairen, Fu-Shun, Hailar, Harbin, Hokang, Mukden, Penchi, Yenchi **7** Hulutao, Ikuliho, Ssuping, Tantung **8** Chinchao, Paicheng, Shenyang **9** Changchun, Chiamussu, Manchouli, Miuchwang **10** Port Arthur

11 Chichihaerh, Mutanchiang
  peninsula: **8** Liaotung
  province: **5** Jehol, Jilin, Kirin **8** Liaoning **12** Heilongjiang, Heilungkiang
  river: **4** Amur, Liao, Yalu **5** Argun, Mutan, Nonni, Tumen **6** Ussuri **7** Sungari
  tribe: **5** Tungu **6** Manchu, Mongol
Mandalay
  found in: **18** Barrack-Room Ballads
  author: **14** Rudyard Kipling
mandamus
  legal term: **48** writ from a superior court commanding that a thing be done
  literally: **9** we command
Mandan
  language family: **6** Siouan
  location: **11** North Dakota
  ceremony: **5** Okipa
Mandarins, The
  author: **16** Simone de Beauvoir
mandate 5 edict, order **6** behest, charge, decree **7** bidding, command, dictate **8** approval, sanction **9** authority, direction, directive **10** commission, dependency **11** instruction, requisition **12** protectorate **13** authorization
mandatory 7 binding, exigent, needful **8** required **9** called for, essential, necessary, requisite **10** compulsory, imperative, obligatory, peremptory
Mandelbaum Gate, The
  author: **11** Muriel Spark
Manderley
  house in: **7** Rebecca
  author: **9** Du Maurier
mandible 3 jaw **4** beak, bill, jowl **7** maxilla **8** lower jaw
  part: **4** mala **5** angle, molar, ramus **6** corpus
Mandrake the Magician
  creator: **7** Lee Falk **9** Phil Davis
  character: **5** Narda **6** Lothar
Manes
  spirits or souls of: **4** dead
Manet, Edouard
  born: **5** Paris **6** France
  artwork: **7** Olympia **8** The Fifer **9** Emile Zola **10** Argenteuil **12** The Guitarist **19** Le Dejeuner sur l'Herbe (Luncheon on the Grass) **25** The Bar at the Folies- Bergeres **31** Execution of the Emperor Maximilian
Manette, Dr and Lucie
  characters in: **16** A Tale of Two Cities
  author: **7** Dickens
maneuver 4 move, plot, ploy **5** dodge, guide, pilot, steer, trick **6** deploy, device, gambit, scheme, tactic **7** finagle **8** arti- fice, contrive, intrigue **9** stratagem **10** manipulate **11** contrivance, machination, pull strings
Man for All Seasons, A

  director: **13** Fred Zinnemann
  based on play by: **10** Robert Bolt
  cast: **9** Leo McKern **10** Robert Shaw **11** Orson Welles, Wendy Hiller **12** Paul Scofield (Sir Thomas More), Susannah York **14** Nigel Davenport **15** Vanessa Redgrave
  Oscar for: **5** actor (Scofield) **7** picture **8** director
man Friday 4 aide **8** adjutant, employee **9** assistant **10** aide de camp **12** right-hand man
  source: **14** Robinson Crusoe
Man from St Petersburg, The
  author: **10** Ken Follett
Man from UNCLE, The
  character: **9** Mr Waverly **12** Napoleon Solo **13** Illya Kuryakin
  cast: **11** Leo G Carroll **12** Robert Vaughn **13** David McCallum
  foe: **6** THRUSH
manful 5 brave **8** resolute **10** courageous
manganese
  chemical symbol: **2** Mn
mangle 3 cut **4** harm, hurt, lame, maim, maul, ruin, tear **5** crush, press, slash **6** damage, impair, injure **7** flatten **8** lacerate, mutilate **9** disfigure
manhandle 4 maul **5** abuse **6** batter **7** rough up **8** maltreat, mistreat **9** pull about, push about **10** knock about, slap around
Manhattan
  director: **10** Woody Allen
  cast: **9** Anne Byrne **10** Woody Allen **11** Diane Keaton, Meryl Streep **13** Michael Murphy **15** Mariel Hemingway
Manhattan Transfer
  author: **13** John Dos Passos
manhood 5 prime **8** legal age, machismo, majority, maleness, maturity, virility **9** adulthood, manliness, mature age **10** manfulness **11** masculinity
mania 4 rage **5** craze **6** frenzy, lunacy, raving **7** craving, madness, passion **8** delirium, delusion, dementia, fixation, hysteria, insanity **9** monomania, obsession **10** aberration, compulsion, enthusiasm, fanaticism **11** fascination, infatuation
maniac 3 ass, nut **4** fool **5** loony **6** cuckoo, madman, nitwit **7** half-wit, lunatic **9** psychotic, screwball, simpleton **10** crackbrain, psychopath
manic 2 up **4** high **7** excited, frantic, hyped up **8** agitated, frenzied, worked up **9** wrought up **10** freaked out, switched on **11** hyperactive
manifest 4 bare, open, show **5** clear, frank, plain **6** candid, evince, expose, patent, reveal, unveil **7** display, divulge, evident, exhibit, express, obvious, uncover, visible **8** apparent, disclose, evidence, indicate, palpable

9 make known **10** noticeable **11** demonstrate, make visible, self-evident, transparent, unconcealed, undisguised

manifestation 4 show **7** display, example, symptom **8** evidence, instance **10** exhibition, expression, indication, revelation **12** illustration, presentation, proclamation, public notice **13** demonstration

manifesto 4 bull **5** edict, ukase **6** notice **9** broadside, statement **10** communique, encyclical **11** declaration **12** announcement, annunciation, notification, proclamation, public notice **13** position paper, pronouncement **14** pronunciamento ·

manifold 4 many **6** myriad, varied **7** complex, diverse **8** multiple, numerous **9** many-sided, multiform **10** variegated **11** diversified, innumerable **12** multifarious **13** multitudinous

Manila
    capital of: 11 Philippines
    former name: 8 Maynilad
    island: 5 Luzon
    landmark: 9 Rizal Park **16** San Agustin Church
    river: 5 Pasig
    section: 10 Quezon City
    university: 10 Santo Tomas

Man in the Gray Flannel Suit, The
    author: 11 Sloan Wilson

manipulate 3 pat, ply, use **4** feel, work **5** drive, pinch, wield **6** employ, finger, handle, manage, stroke **7** control, deceive, defraud, massage, operate, squeeze

Manitoba
    bay: 6 Hudson
    capital: 8 Winnipeg
    city: 6 Carman, The Pas **7** Brandon, Caribou, Dauphin, Selkirk **8** Flin Flon, Lynn Lake, Wabowden, Winnipeg **9** Churchill, Killarney, Sherridon, Swan River **10** St Boniface **11** Norway House, York Factory **16** Portage La Prairie
    flower: 11 windflower **13** prairie crocus
    Indian tribe: 4 Cree **6** Eskimo, Ojibwa **8** Chippewa **10** Assiniboin
    lake: 4 God's, Swan **5** Cedar, Moose **6** Island **7** Dauphin, Red Deer **8** Manitoba, Reindeer, St Martin, Waterhen, Winnipeg **9** Granville
    mountain: 4 Hart **5** Baldy
    name means: 16 lake of the prairies **18** Great Spirit's strait **19** Great Spirit's narrows
    nickname: 15 Prairie Province **16** Keystone Province
    province of: 6 Canada
    river: 3 Red **4** Seal, Swan **5** Hayes **6** Nelson, Roseau, Souris **7** Pembina **8** Winnipeg **9** Churchill **11** Assiniboine **12** Saskatchewan
    university: 7 Brandon **10** St Boniface

Mankiewicz, Joseph L
    director of: 6 Sleuth **9** Cleopatra **11** All About Eve (Oscar) **12** Guys and Dolls, Julius Caesar **18** The Ghost and Mrs Muir **19** A Letter to Three Wives (Oscar)

mankind 3 man **6** people **7** mortals, persons, society **8** humanity **9** humankind **11** Homo sapiens

manlike 5 macho, manly **6** virile **8** hominoid **9** masculine

manly 4 bold, male **5** brave, hardy, husky, noble **6** brawny, daring, heroic, manful, plucky, robust, strong, sturdy, virile **7** gallant, staunch, valiant **8** athletic, fearless, malelike, muscular, powerful, resolute, stalwart, vigorous **9** masculine, strapping **10** chivalrous, courageous **11** gentlemanly, indomitable, self-reliant **12** stouthearted
    Spanish: 5 macho

man-made 4 mock, sham **6** formed **7** crafted, created **8** produced **9** fashioned, ready-made, simulated, synthetic **10** artificial, fabricated, factitious, originated **11** constructed, handcrafted **12** manufactured

Mann, Delbert
    director of: 5 Marty (Oscar) **14** Separate Tables

Mann, Thomas
    author of: 12 Buddenbrooks **13** Death in Venice, Doctor Faustus **16** The Magic Mountain

manna 4 boon **5** award **6** reward **7** bonanza **16** divine sustenance

mannequin 4 form **5** dummy, model **6** figure

manner 3 air, way **4** form, kind, make, mode, mold, race, rank, sort, type **5** brand, breed, caste, genre, grade, guise, habit, stamp, style **6** aspect, custom, method, strain **7** bearing, conduct, fashion, species, variety **8** behavior, carriage, category, demeanor, practice, presence **9** character **10** appearance, deportment **14** classification

mannered 6 formal **7** stilted, studied **8** affected **9** contrived, unnatural **10** artificial **11** ceremonious

mannerism 4 airs, pose **5** habit **8** pretense **10** pretension **11** affectation, singularity **12** eccentricity, idiosyncrasy

mannerly 5 civil **6** polite **7** courtly, gallant, genteel, refined **8** well-bred **9** courteous **10** chivalrous **11** gentlemanly, well-behaved

manner of living
    Latin: 12 modus vivendi

manner of looking at the world
    German: 14 Weltanschauung

manner of speaking 7 diction **9** elocution **10** intonation **13** pronunciation

manners 6 polish **7** decorum **8** behavior, breeding, courtesy **9** amenities, deference, etiquette, gallantry, gentility, politesse, propriety **10** deportment, politeness, refinement **11** courtliness

Mannix
    character: 9 Joe Mannix, Peggy Fair **10** (Lt) Adam Tobias **13** Lou Wickersham
    cast: 10 Gail Fisher, Robert Reed **11** Mike Connors **16** Joseph Campanella

Mannon family
    members: 4 Ezra, Orin **7** Lavinia **9** Christine
    characters in: 22 Mourning Becomes Electra
    author: 6 O'Neill

Manoah
    son: 6 Samson

mano a mano 5 alone **8** conflict **13** confrontation, in a small group
    literally: 10 hand to hand

Man of a Thousand Faces
    nickname of: 9 Lon Chaney

Man of Nazareth
    author: 14 Anthony Burgess

Man of Property, The
    author: 14 John Galsworthy

Man of Sorrows *see* **5** Jesus

Manolin
    character in: 18 The Old Man and the Sea
    author: 9 Hemingway

Manon Lescaut
    author: 11 Abbe Prevost

Manor, The
    author: 19 Isaac Bashevis Singer

manor house 6 estate, manoir **7** chateau, mansion **11** stately home

manpower 4 help **5** brawn, labor **9** work force, employees

manque 6 failed, missed **7** lacking **11** fallen short, unfulfilled

Mansart, Francois
    architect of: 14 Chateau de Berny **18** Hotel de la Vrilliere **33** Church of Sainte Marie de la Visitation
    feature: 11 mansard roof

manservant 5 groom, valet **6** butler **7** footman **8** factotum **9** chauffeur

Man's Fate
    author: 12 Andre Malraux

Mansfield, Jayne
    real name: 14 Vera Jane Palmer
    husband: 14 Mickey Hargitay
    born: 10 Bryn Mawr PA
    roles: 15 Hell on Frisco Bay **26** Will Success Spoil Rock Hunter

Mansfield, Katherine
    author of: 5 Bliss **12** The Dove's Nest **14** The Garden Party

Mansfield Park
    author: 10 Jane Austen
    character: 5 Yates **8** Mrs Grant **9** Mrs Norris, Rushworth **10** Fanny Price

11 Lady Bertram **12** Mary Crawford **13** Henry Crawford **16** Sir Thomas Bertram
  Bertram children: 3 Tom **5** Julia, Maria **6** Edmund

mansion 5 manor, villa **6** castle, estate, palace **7** chateau **10** manor house

manslaughter 6 murder **7** killing **8** homicide

manta 3 ray **4** cape **5** cloak, shawl **9** devilfish

Mantegna, Andrea
  born: 5 Italy **14** Isola di Carturo
  artwork: 9 Parnassus **16** Camera degli Sposi (Bridal Chamber) **18** The Triumph of Caesar, The Triumph of Virtue **20** Madonna della Vittoria

Man That Corrupted Hadleyburg, The
  author: 9 Mark Twain

Mantius
  father: 8 Melampus
  son: 6 Clitus

mantle 4 cape, film, mask, pall, veil **5** cloak, cloud, cover, scarf, tunic **6** canopy, screen, shroud **7** blanket, curtain, wrapper **8** covering, envelope, mantilla

Mantle, Mickey (Charles)
  sport: 8 baseball
  position: 8 outfield
  team: 11 New York Yankees

manual 6 primer **8** handbook, physical, textbook, workbook **9** guidebook **10** done by hand **12** hand-operated, nonautomatic **15** instruction book

manual skill 8 deftness **9** dexterity, handiness **10** adroitness **12** coordination

manufacture 4 form, make, mold **5** build, frame **6** cook up, create, devise, invent, make up **7** concoct, fashion, produce, think up, trump up **8** assemble **9** construct, fabricate **11** mass-produce, put together

manufacturing 8 devising **9** inventing, producing **10** industrial **11** fabricating, nonagrarian

manumission 7 freeing **10** liberation **11** setting free **12** emancipation

manumit 4 free **7** set free **8** liberate **10** emancipate

manure 4 dung **5** feces **6** ordure **7** compost, excreta **8** dressing **10** fertilizer

manuscript 6 script **10** typescript **14** shooting script **15** written document

Manvah
  son: 6 Samson

Man Who Came to Dinner, The
  director: 15 William Keighley
  based on play by: 8 Moss Hart **14** George S Kaufman
  cast: 10 Bette Davis **11** Ann Sheridan,

Billie Burke **12** Monty Woolley **13** Richard Travis

Man Who Fell to Earth, The
  director: 12 Nicholas Roeg
  cast: 7 Rip Torn **9** Buck Henry **10** Candy Clark, David Bowie

Man Who Shot Liberty Valence, The
  director: 8 John Ford
  cast: 9 John Wayne, Lee Marvin, Vera Miles **12** Edmund O'Brien, James Stewart

Man Who Was Thursday, The
  author: 12 G K Chesterton

Man Without a Country, The
  author: 17 Edward Everett Hale
  character: 11 Philip Nolan

Manx 3 cat **8** Goidelic
  spoken on: 10 Isle of Man
  manx cat lacks: 4 tail

many 4 a lot, lots **5** a heap, heaps, piles **6** divers, dozens, myriad, scores, sundry **7** numbers, several, various **8** numerous **9** countless **10** a profusion, numberless **11** an abundance, innumerable **13** multitudinous

manzanita 14 Arctostaphylos
  varieties: 4 dune, Ione, Otay **5** hairy, hoary, Morro, Parry, Pecho **6** island, Sonoma, woolly **7** Mexican, Pajarro, pine-mat **8** big-berry, Del Norte, Eastwood, Mariposa, Monterey, shagbark, Stanford **9** Fort Bragg, greenleaf, heart-leaf, little Sur, white-leaf **10** serpentine, silver-leaf **11** brittleleaf, pink-bracted

Maori
  native of: 10 New Zealand

Mao Tse-Tung
  also: 8 Mao Zedong
  born: 5 China
  leader of: 10 communists
  title: 8 Chairman
  led: 9 Long March
  book: 16 The Little Red Book

map 4 plan, plot **5** chart, graph, ready **6** design, devise, lay out **7** arrange, diagram, prepare, project **8** contrive, organize **9** elevation **10** make a map of, projection **14** representation **18** topographical chart

maple 4 Acer
  varieties: 3 red **4** Amur, hard, rock, soft, vine **5** black, chalk, field, hedge, Nikko, river, sugar, swamp, white **6** Balkan, canyon, Norway, Oregon, parlor, sierra, silver, Triden **7** big-leaf, Florida, Persian, scarlet, striped **8** big-tooth, Drummond, fullmoon, Hawthorn, Hornbeam, Japanese, mountain, Shantung, Sycamore, Tatarian **9** ash-leaved, eagleclaw, flowering, paperbark, Schwedler, Tartarian **11** Montpellier **12** Pennsylvania **13** Rocky Mountain, Southern sugar **18** Rocky Mountain sugar

map out 3 map **5** chart, draft **6** devise, lay out **7** diagram, outline **8** block out **9** delineate, formulate

Maputo
  capital of: 10 Mozambique

mar 4 hurt, maim, mark, nick, ruin, scar **5** botch, spoil, stain, taint **6** blight, damage, deface, defile, impair **7** blemish, destroy, scratch **8** diminish, mutilate **9** disfigure

Marabar Caves
  setting in: 15 A Passage to India
  author: 7 Forster

Maranatha
  means: 9 O Lord come

maraschino
  type: 7 liqueur
  origin: 5 Italy
  flavor: 6 cherry
  color: 3 red **5** white

Marathi
  language family: 12 Indo-European
  branch: 11 Indo-Iranian
  group: 5 Indic
  spoken in: 5 (northern) India

Marathonian bull see **10** Cretan bull

marauder 6 looter, pirate, ranger **7** corsair, ravager, spoiler **8** pillager **9** buccaneer, despoiler, guerrilla, plunderer, privateer **10** depradator, freebooter

marble 3 jet **4** vein **5** agate **6** basalt, blotch, mottle, streak **7** calcite **8** dolomite **9** limestone **10** serpentine, travertine **12** anthraconite
  quarry: 7 Carrara

Marble Faun, The
  author: 18 Nathaniel Hawthorne
  character: 5 Hilda **6** Kenyon, Miriam **9** Donatello

marbles
  type: 3 mib, taw **4** aggy, duck, immy, migg **5** agate, monny, scrap **6** commie, glassy, hoodle, marine **7** cat's eye, rainbow, shooter **9** carnelian **16** peppermint stripe
  term: 3 hit **4** shot **6** edgers, ringer **7** bowling, for fair, histing, lagging, lag line, lofting **8** circling, for keeps, hunching **9** pitch line **10** roundsters **11** knuckle down **13** knuckling down

Marc, Franz
  born: 6 Munich **7** Germany
  artwork: 10 Blue Horses **12** Yellow Horses **13** Fighting Forms

Marceline
  character in: 19 The Marriage of Figaro
  author: 12 Beaumarchais

march 2 go **4** hike, rise, step, trek, walk **5** tramp **6** file by, growth, parade **7** advance, proceed **8** progress **9** group walk **10** go directly, procession, walk in step **11** advancement, development, progression **12** martial music

March

event: 9 Mardi Gras **11** Ides of March (15) **12** Ash Wednesday **13** vernal equinox (21)
flower: 7 jonquil **8** daffodil
French: 4 Mars
gem: 10 aquamarine, bloodstone
German: 4 Marz
holiday: 12 St Joseph's Day (19) **13** St Patrick's Day (17)
Italian: 5 Marzo
number of days: 9 thirty-one
origin of name: 4 Mars
　Roman god of: 3 war
place in year:
　Gregorian: 5 third
　Roman: 5 first
saying: 20 Beware the Ides of March **40** March comes in like a lion and goes out like a lamb
Spanish: 6 Marcha
Zodiac sign: 5 Aries **6** Pisces

March, Fredric
real name: 29 Ernest Frederick McIntyre Bickel
born: 8 Racine WI
roles: 11 A Star Is Born **12** Anna Karenina, The Buccaneer **13** Les Miserables **14** Anthony Adverse, Inherit the Wind, Mary of Scotland, Seven Days in May **16** Death of a Salesman **17** Alexander the Great, Dr Jekyll and Mr Hyde (Oscar), The Desperate Hours **18** Death Takes a Holiday **19** The Affairs of Cellini **22** The Best Years of Our Lives (Oscar) **23** Barretts of Wimpole Street

Marchen 8 folk tale **9** fairy tale

March family
members: 2 Jo **3** Amy, Meg **4** Beth **6** Marmee
characters in: 11 Little Women
author: 6 Alcott

March Hare
character in: 28 Alice's Adventures in Wonderland
author: 7 Carroll

Marchmain family
characters in: 19 Brideshead Revisited
author: 5 Waugh

Marciano, Rocky
real name: 23 Rocco Francis Marchegiano
nickname: 19 Brockton Blockbuster
sport: 6 boxing
class: 11 heavyweight

Marconi, Guglielmo
nationality: 7 Italian
nickname: 16 father of wireless
invented/discovered: 5 radio **12** radio signals **16** magnetic detector **30** wireless high frequency telegraph
shared (1919): 20 Nobel Prize for physics

Marcus Welby MD
character: 11 (Dr) Steven Kiley **13** Consuelo Lopez
cast: 11 James Brolin, Robert Young **12** Elena Verdugo

Mardi (and a Voyage Thither)
author: 14 Herman Melville
character: 4 Alma, Jarl, Mohi, Taji **5** Media, Samoa, Yoomy **6** Yillah **7** Annatoo **10** Babbalanja, Braidbeard **11** Queen Hautia

Mardi Gras 7 holiday **8** carnival, festival, jamboree **10** fat Tuesday **13** Shrove Tuesday
king: 3 rex
social club: 5 krewe

Marduk
also: 8 Merodach **12** Baal Merodach
origin: 10 Babylonian
chief of: 4 gods

mare 3 sea **9** brood-mare **11** female horse

mare nostrum 6 our sea
ancient Roman name for: 13 Mediterranean

margin 3 hem, rim **4** edge, side **5** bound, skirt, verge **6** border, fringe, leeway **7** confine **8** boundary **9** allowance, extra room, safeguard

marginal 9 on the edge **11** in the margin **12** barely useful

mariage de convenance 21 marriage of convenience

marigold 7 Tagetes
varieties: 3 big, bur, fig, pot **4** cape, corn, wild **5** Aztec, fetid, field, marsh, water **6** desert, French, signet **7** African **12** sweet-scented

marijuana, marihuana 3 boo, kif, pot, tea **4** hash, hemp, herb, weed **5** bhang, blunt, dagga, ganja, grass, joint **6** buddha, moocah, reefer **7** chronic, hashish **8** cannabis, locoweed, mary jane

Marin, John Cheri (3rd)
born: 12 Rutherford NJ
artwork: 8 Sea Piece **12** Maine Islands **13** Tunk Mountains **16** Beach Flint Island **19** Movement Fifth Avenue **21** Seaside Interpretation **26** Camden Mountain across the Bay

marine 3 sea **5** naval **6** gyrene **7** aquatic, oceanic, of ships, pelagic **8** maritime, nautical, of the sea, seagoing **9** salt-water, seafaring **10** oceangoing **11** leatherneck **13** oceanographic

mariner 3 gob, tar **4** salt **5** pilot **6** sailor, sea dog, seaman **7** boatman **8** deck hand, helmsman, seafarer **9** navigator, yachtsman **10** bluejacket **12** seafaring man **16** able-bodied seaman

Marion, Francis
nickname: 8 Swamp Fox
served in: 16 Revolutionary War
type of warfare: 9 guerrilla
area fought in: 13 South Carolina
battle: 12 Eutaw Springs

marionette 6 puppet **10** fantoccino

famous: 4 Judy **5** Punch **9** Pinocchio
dummy: 13 Mortimer Snerd **15** Charlie McCarthy
maker: 4 Sarg

marital 6 wedded, wifely **7** married, nuptial, spousal **8** conjugal **9** connubial, husbandly **10** of marriage **11** matrimonial

maritime 5 naval **6** marine **7** aquatic, coastal, oceanic, of ships **8** nautical, of the sea, seagoing **9** seafaring

marjoram
botanical name: 8 Majorana, O vulgare, Origanum **16** M hortensis moench
origin: 4 Asia **13** Mediterranean
family: 4 mint
symbol of: 5 honor **9** happiness
charm against: 10 witchcraft
used as: 12 air sweetener
use: 4 eggs, fish, meat **5** salad **8** stuffing **9** vegetable

Marjorie Morningstar
author: 10 Herman Wouk

mark 3 cut, mar, pit **4** dent, goal, harm, heed, line, mind, nick, note, pock, rate, scar, show, sign, spot **5** badge, brand, grade, judge, label, notch, point, proof, score, stain, stamp, token, track **6** attend, bruise, deface, denote, emblem, evince, injure, intent, rating, regard, reveal, streak, symbol, target, typify **7** betoken, blemish, correct, imprint, measure, scratch, signify, suggest, symptom, write in, write on **8** bull's-eye, colophon, disclose, evidence, hallmark, indicate, manifest, point out, standard, stand for **9** be a sign of, criterion, designate, disfigure, objective, symbolize, yardstick **10** impression, indication, touchstone **11** distinguish **12** characterize **13** differentiate

Mark
also: 8 John Mark
mother: 4 Mary
cousin: 8 Barnabas
wrote: 11 Gospel

Mark (King Mark)
character in: 16 Arthurian romance

Mark Antony
also: 14 Marcus Antonius
character in: 12 Julius Caesar
author: 11 Shakespeare

mark down 4 note **5** enter, lower **6** record, reduce **7** put down **9** write down

marked 5 clear, great, noted, plain **6** dotted, scored, severe, showed, spotty, tabbed, tagged, traced **7** branded, labeled, pointed, specked, spotted, stained, tracked **8** destined, speckled, striking, targeted **9** indicated, prominent **10** emphasized, identified, made note of, noticeable, remarkable, singled out **11** conspicu-

ous, distinctive, outstanding **12** considerable **13** distinguished

marker 3 IOU, peg, run, tab **4** chip, flag, sign **5** score **6** etcher, scorer, tablet, ticket **7** counter **8** bookmark, memorial, monument, recorder

market 4 hawk, sell, vend **5** stand **6** bourse, peddle, retail **7** grocery **9** dispose of **10** curb market, meat market **11** butcher shop, grocer's shop, marketplace

marketplace 4 mart **5** agora, arena, plaza **6** bazaar, market, square **8** exchange

Mark of Zorro, The
   director: 15 Rouben Mamoulian
   cast: 11 Tyrone Power **12** Linda Darnell **13** Basil Rathbone **15** Gale Sondergaard
   score: 12 Alfred Newman

mark out 8 describe **9** delineate

marksman 8 dead shot, good shot, sure shot **9** crack shot **12** sharpshooter

marksmanship 3 aim **5** skill **8** accuracy **13** sharpshooting

Marley's Ghost
   character in: 15 A Christmas Carol
   author: 7 Dickens

Marlow
   character in: 7 Lord Jim
   author: 6 Conrad

Marlowe
   character in: 15 Heart of Darkness
   author: 6 Conrad

Marlowe, Christopher
   author of: 8 Edward II **13** Doctor Faustus, The Jew of Malta **14** Hero and Leander **15** Edward the Second **19** Tamburlaine the Great

Marmee
   character in: 11 Little Women
   author: 6 Alcott

Marmion
   author: 14 Sir Walter Scott
   character: 11 Lord Marmion **13** Ralph de Wilton **14** Clare Fitz-Clare **16** Archibald Douglas **19** Constance de Beverley

Marnie
   director: 15 Alfred Hitchcock
   cast: 10 Diane Baker **11** Sean Connery, Tippi Hedren

maroon 4 plum, wine **6** desert, strand **7** abandon, forsake, magenta **8** cast away, jettison **9** put ashore **10** cast ashore, terra cotta **11** brownish-red, leave behind **15** leave high and dry

Marple, Miss Jane
   detective created by: 14 Agatha Christie

Marquand, J P
   author of: 13 Wickford Point **18** The Late George Apley
   character: 6 Mr Moto

marquee 4 tent **6** awning, canopy **8** marquise

marred 6 ruined **7** damaged, injured, spoiled **8** impaired **9** blemished, destroyed **10** disfigured

marriage 7 wedding, wedlock **8** nuptials **9** matrimony
   god of: 4 Frey **5** Freyr, Hymen **9** Hymenaeus
   goddess of: 3 Fri **5** Frigg, Frija **6** Frigga, Tellus

marriage broker
   Yiddish: 8 shadchan **9** schatchen

marriage of convenience
   French: 19 mariage de convenance

Marriage of Figaro, The
   also: 15 Le Nozze di Figaro
   opera: 6 Mozart
   character: 7 Susanna **8** Countess **9** Cherubino, Dr Bartolo **10** Marcellina **13** Count Almaviva

Marriage of Figaro, The
   author: 12 Beaumarchais
   character: 6 Figaro **7** Suzanne **8** Cherubin **9** Marceline **10** Dr Bartholo **13** Count Almaviva **16** Countess Almaviva

Marriages Between Zones Three, Four and Five
   author: 12 Doris Lessing

married 3 wed **5** mated **6** joined, united, wedded **7** hitched, marital **8** combined, espoused **9** connubial **11** matrimonial, tied the knot

married woman
   German: 4 frau

marry 3 wed **7** espouse, make one **10** get spliced, tie the knot **13** join in wedlock **14** join in marriage, lead to the altar, take in marriage

Marryat, Frederick
   author of: 11 Peter Simple **16** Mr Midshipman Easy

Mars
   also: 6 Mamers, Mavors
   origin: 5 Roman
   god of: 3 war
   mother: 4 Juno
   wife: 5 Nerio
   epithet: 5 Ultor **8** Gradivus
   corresponds to: 4 Ares

Mars
   position: 6 fourth
   nickname: 9 Red Planet
   satellite: 6 Deimos, Phobos

Marseillaise 20 French national anthem

marsh 3 bog, fen **5** swamp **6** morass, slough **7** bottoms, wetland **8** quagmire **9** everglade, marshland, quicksand

Marsh, Dame Ngaio
   author of: 9 Dead Water **12** Final Curtain **13** Death at the Bar **14** Enter a Murderer **19** Singing in the Shrouds

character: 10 Troy Alleyn **14** Roderick Alleyn

Marsh, Reginald
   born: 5 Paris **6** France
   artwork: 9 The Bowery **10** Pip and Flip **14** Why Not Use the El? **16** Tattoo and Haircut **17** Twenty-Cent Haircut

marshal 5 align, array, chief, group, order **6** deploy, draw up, gather, leader, line up, muster **7** arrange, collect, manager, sheriff **8** assemble, director, marechal, mobilize, organize **9** fire chief **10** law officer, supervisor **11** police chief **12** chief officer, field marshal **13** generalissimo

Marshall, George C
   served in: 3 WWI **4** WWII **9** Korean War, World War I **10** World War II **11** World War One, World War Two
   rank: 12 chief of staff **16** general of the army
   author of: 12 Marshall Plan
   secretary of: 5 state **7** defense
   winner of: 15 Nobel Peace Prize (1953)

Marshall, Penny
   husband: 9 Rob Reiner
   born: 7 Bronx NY
   roles: 5 Myrna **12** The Odd Couple **14** Laverne DeFazio **17** Laverne and Shirley
   director: 3 Big

marshy 3 wet **4** miry **5** boggy, fenny, muddy **6** swampy **7** paludal, paludic **11** waterlogged

marsupial 5 koala **6** numbat, possum, wombat **7** cuscuse, opossum, wallaby **8** kangaroo **9** bandicoot, phalanger **14** Tasmanian devil

mart 4 show **6** market **8** exchange **9** trade fair, trade show **10** exposition

Martha
   sister: 4 Mary
   brother: 7 Lazarus
   home: 7 Bethany

martial 7 hostile, Spartan, warlike **8** military **9** bellicose, combative, soldierly **10** pugnacious **11** belligerent, contentious

Martian Chronicles, The
   author: 11 Ray Bradbury

Martin, Dean
   real name: 16 Dino Paul Crocetti
   partner: 10 Jerry Lewis
   born: 14 Steubenville OH
   roles: 8 Matt Helm, Rio Bravo, The Caddy **9** The Stooge **10** Living It Up **12** Four for Texas, Sailor Beware **14** Toys in the Attic **15** Some Came Running **16** Artists and Models

Martin, Mary
   son: 11 Larry Hagman
   born: 13 Weatherford TX
   roles: 6 I Do I Do **8** Peter Pan **12** Sound of Music, South Pacific

Martin, Steve

born: 6 Waco TX

roles: 7 The Jerk **17** Pennies From Heaven, Saturday Night Live **19** The Man with Two Brains **20** Dead Men Don't Wear Plaid **26** Planes Trains and Automobiles

Martin Chuzzlewit

author: 14 Charles Dickens

character: 5 Mercy **7** Charity **8** Tom Pinch **9** Pecksniff, Ruth Pinch, Sarah Gamp **10** Mark Tapley, Mary Graham **15** Jonas Chuzzlewit **17** Anthony Chuzzlewit

martinet 6 despot, tyrant **8** dictator **10** hard master, taskmaster **11** drillmaster, Simon Legree **12** little Caesar **13** authoritarian, drill-sergeant

Marty

director: 11 Delbert Mann

cast: 10 Betsy Blair **11** Joe De Santis **14** Ernest Borgnine **15** Esther Minciotti

Oscar for: 5 actor (Borgnine) **7** picture

script: 14 Paddy Chayefsky

martyr 5 saint **8** sufferer

martyrdom 5 agony **6** ordeal **7** anguish, torment, torture **9** bitter cup, suffering **10** affliction **11** cup of sorrow **13** crown of thorns

marvel 4 gape **6** be awed, rarity, wonder **7** miracle **8** be amazed **9** spectacle **10** phenomenon

Marvell, Andrew

author of: 9 The Garden **16** To His Coy Mistress

marvelous, marvellous 4 A-one, fine **5** grand, great, super **6** divine, lovely, superb **7** amazing **8** colossal, fabulous, heavenly, smashing, splendid **9** fantastic, first-rate, wonderful **10** phenomenal, remarkable, stupendous **11** astonishing, magnificent, outstanding, sensational **13** extraordinary

marvelous to relate

Latin: 13 mirabile dictu

Marwood, Mrs

character in: 16 The Way of the World

author: 8 Congreve

Marx, Bernard

character in: 13 Brave New World

author: 6 Huxley

Marx, Karl

author of: 10 Das Kapital **18** Communist Manifesto (with Friedrich Engels)

Marx Brothers 5 Chico (Leonard), Gummo (Milton), Harpo (Adolph, Arthur) Zeppo (Herbert) **7** Groucho (Julius)

costar: 14 Margaret Dumont

born: 9 New York NY

roles: 8 Coconuts, Duck Soup **11** The Big Store **13** Horse Feathers **14** A Day at the Races, Animal Crackers, Monkey Business **16** A Night at the Opera

Groucho's TV show: 14 You Bet Your Life

Mary 6 Virgin **7** Madonna **8** Holy Mary **9** Magdalene, of Cleopas **10** Virgin Mary **11** Mother of God, Regina Coeli **13** Queen of Heaven **15** Mother of Sorrows **17** Mother of the Church

mother: 4 Anna, Anne

husband: 6 Joseph **7** Alpheus, Cleopas

son: 4 Jude, Mark **5** Jesus, Moses, Simon **12** James the Less

sister: 6 Martha

brother: 7 Lazarus **8** Barnabas

cousin: 9 Elizabeth

home: 8 Nazareth

visitor: 7 Gabriel

flower: 4 lily **8** marigold

Mary

author: 10 Sholem Asch

Maryland

abbreviation: 2 MD

nickname: 4 Free **7** Cockade **12** Old Line State

capital: 9 Annapolis

largest city: 9 Baltimore

others: 5 Essex **6** Easton, Laurel, Towson **8** Aberdeen, Bethesda, Pocomoke **9** Frederick, Ocean City, Rockville **10** Cumberland, Hagerstown, Pikesville **11** Catonsville, College Park

college: 4 Hood **7** Goucher, St John's **10** Washington **11** Towson State **12** Johns Hopkins **21** Annapolis Naval Academy

feature:

fort: 7 McHenry

national battlesite: 8 Antietam

presidential retreat: 9 Camp David

race: 9 Preakness **12** Steeplechase

racetrack: 5 Bowie **6** Butler, Laurel **7** Pimlico

tribe: 5 Conoy **9** Nanticoke

people: 6 Wesort **8** Terrapin **10** Spiro Agnew **11** crawthumper **14** Sargent Shriver **15** Francis Scott Key

explorer: 7 Calvert

lake: 8 Patapsco **9** Deep Creek, Loch Raven, Pretty Boy **10** Rocky Gorge **11** Triadelphia

land rank: 11 forty second

mountain: 4 Dans **8** Piedmont **9** Blue Ridge **11** Appalachian

highest point: 8 Backbone

physical feature:

bay: 10 Chesapeake

sea: 8 Atlantic

swamp: 7 Pocoson

valley: 5 Great **10** Hagerstown

river: 3 Elk **7** Chester, Potomac **8** Choptank, Patapsco, Patuxent, Pocomoke **11** Susquehanna

state admission: 7 seventh

state bird: 15 Baltimore oriole

state fish: 11 striped bass

state flower: 14 black-eyed Susan

state motto: 22 Manly Deeds Womanly Words **43** Thou Hast Crowned Us With the Shield of Thy Good Will

state song: 18 Maryland My Maryland

state tree: 8 white oak

Mary Poppins

director: 15 Robert Stevenson

based on story by: 9 P L Travers

cast: 6 Ed Wynn **11** Dick Van Dyke (Bert), Glynis Johns **12** Julie Andrews **14** David Tomlinson **16** Hermione Baddeley

score: 13 Robert Sherman **14** Richard Sherman

Oscar for: 4 song **5** score **7** actress (Andrews) **13** visual effects

song: 14 Chim-chim-cheree

Mary Queen of Scots

director: 14 Charles Jarrott

cast: 12 Trevor Howard **13** Glenda Jackson (Elizabeth I), Timothy Dalton **14** Nigel Davenport **15** Patrick McGoohan, Vanessa Redgrave (Mary of Scotland)

Mary Tyler Moore Show, The

character: 8 Lou Grant **9** Ted Baxter **12** Gordon (Gordy) Howard, Mary Richards, Sue Ann Nivens **13** Bess Lindstrom **14** Marie Slaughter **15** Murray Slaughter **16** Phyllis Lindstrom, Rhoda Morgenstern **23** Georgette Franklin Baxter

cast: 8 John Amos **9** Ted Knight **10** Betty White **11** Edward Asner **12** Gavin MacLeod, Georgia Engel **13** Joyce Bulifant, Lisa Gerritsen, Valerie Harper **14** Cloris Leachman

setting: 11 Minneapolis

Mary Worth

creator: 8 Carey Orr **9** Dale Allen **10** Dale Connor **13** Allen Saunders

character: 4 Bill, Slim

Masaccio

real name: 26 Tommaso di Ser Giovanni di Mone

born: 5 Italy **27** Castel San Giovanni di Valdarno

artwork: 14 The Holy Trinity **15** The Tribute Money **24** The Expulsion from Paradise

Mascagni, Pietro

born: 5 Italy **7** Leghorn

composer of: 4 Iris **6** Nerone **7** Isabeau **10** Le Maschere **11** L'Amico Fritz **14** Il Piccolo Marat **19** Cavalleria Rusticana

masculine 4 bold, male **5** brave, hardy, husky, macho, manly **6** brawny, daring, manful, plucky, robust, strong, sturdy, virile **7** staunch, valiant **8** athletic, fearless, forceful, intrepid, muscular, powerful, resolute, vigorous **9** strapping **10** courageous **11** indomitable, self-reliant **12** stouthearted

Masefield, John

author of: 7 Cargoes **8** Sea Fever **16** Salt Water Ballads

Maseru
  capital of: 7 Lesotho

mash 4 mush **5** crush, paste, puree, smash **6** squash **8** mishmash **9** pulverize

M*A*S*H (TV Series)
  character: 10 (Capt) BJ Hunnicut, (Lt Col) Henry Blake, (Maj) Frank Burns **12** (Corp) Radar O'Reilly **13** Father (John) Mulcahy, (Capt Benjamin Franklin) Hawkeye Pierce, (Col) Sherman Potter **14** (Corp) Maxwell Klinger **15** (Maj Margaret) Hot Lips Houlihan **19** (Capt) Trapper John McIntyre **24** (Maj) Charles Emerson Winchester
  cast: 8 Alan Alda **9** Jamie Farr **11** Harry Morgan, Loretta Swit, Mike Farrell, Wayne Rogers **12** Gary Burghoff **13** Larry Linville **15** McLean Stevenson **16** David Ogden Stiers **18** William Christopher
  war: 6 Korean
  MASH stands for: 26 Mobile Army Surgical Hospital
  tent: 5 Swamp
  theme: 17 Suicide Is Painless

M*A*S*H (Film)
  director: 12 Robert Altman
  cast: 10 Jo Ann Pflug **11** Elliot Gould (Trapper John McIntyre), Tom Skerritt (BJ Hunnicut) **12** Gary Burghoff (Radar O'Reilly), Robert Duvall (Frank Burns) **14** Sally Kellerman (Margaret Hot Lips Houlihan) **16** Donald Sutherland (Hawkeye Pierce)

masjid 6 mosque

mask 4 hide, veil **5** blind, cloak, cover **6** domino, screen, shroud **7** conceal, cover-up, curtain, obscure **8** disguise **9** face guard, false face **10** camouflage, keep secret

Mask
  director: 16 Peter Bogdanovich
  cast: 4 Cher **10** Eric Stoltz (Rocky Dennis), Sam Elliott

masked 9 concealed, covered up, disguised **10** in disguise, masquerade

Masked Ball, A
  also: 17 Un Ballo in Maschera
  opera by: 5 Verdi
  character:
    first version: 9 Count Horn **10** King Gustav **12** Count Ribbing **second version: 3** Sam, Tom **13** Count Riccardo

masking 6 hiding **7** veiling **8** covering **9** eclipsing, obscuring **10** concealing, covering up

Mason, Bertha
  character in: 8 Jane Eyre
  author: 6 Bronte

Mason, James
  wife: 6 Pamela
  born: 7 England **12** Huddersfield

roles: 6 Lolita **7** Lord Jim **9** Bloodline **10** Georgy Girl **13** Heaven Can Wait **14** Humbert Humbert, Murder by Decree, The Seventh Veil **15** Prisoner of Zenda **16** North by Northwest **17** The Boys from Brazil

Mason, Marsha
  husband: 9 Neil Simon
  born: 9 St Louis MO
  roles: 10 Chapter Two **11** Blume in Love **14** The Goodbye Girl **15** Max Dugan Returns **17** Cinderella Liberty

Masque of the Red Death, The
  author: 13 Edgar Allan Poe

masquerade 4 mask, ruse, veil **5** cloak, cover, guise, trick **6** masque, pose as, screen, shroud **7** cover-up, pretext **8** artifice, pretense **9** bal masque **10** camouflage, masked ball, subterfuge **11** impersonate **12** harlequinade

Masquerade Party
  host: 9 Bert Parks **10** Bud Collier **11** Peter Donald **12** Eddie Bracken, Robert Q Lewis **14** Douglas Edwards

mass, Mass 3 jam, lot, mob **4** body, bulk, cake, clot, heap, host, hunk, knot, lump, pack, pile **5** amass, batch, block, bunch, chunk, clump, corps, crowd, crush, group, horde, press, stack, troop **6** bundle, gather, matter, throng, weight **7** collect, pyramid **8** assemble, best part, main body, majority, material **9** aggregate, Eucharist, gathering, plurality **10** accumulate, assemblage, assortment, collection, concretion, congregate, cumulation, lion's share **11** aggregation, consolidate, greater part **12** accumulation, congregation **13** Holy Communion, holy sacrament, preponderance **14** conglomeration

Massachusetts
  abbreviation: 2 MA **4** Mass
  nickname: 3 Bay **7** Puritan **9** Baked Bean, Old Colony
  capital/largest city: 6 Boston
  others: 4 Ayer, Lynn, Otis **5** Athol, Barre, Lenox, Salem **6** Agawam, Dedham, Groton, Nahant, Natick, Revere, Saugus, Woburn **7** Belmont, Beverly, Concord, Danvers, Everett, Holyoke, Ipswich, Medford, Peabody, Taunton, Waltham **8** Brockton, Chicopee, Cohasset, Plymouth, Scituate, Yarmouth **9** Arlington, Attleboro, Braintree, Brookline, Cambridge, Lexbridge, Lexington, Worcester **10** Gloucester, New Bedford, Pittsfield **11** Springfield **12** Provincetown, Williamstown
  college: 3 MIT **5** Clark, Curry, Smith, Tufts **6** Babson **7** Amherst, Harvard, Simmons, Wheaton **8** Brandeis, Williams **9** Hampshire, Holy Cross, Merrimack, Radcliffe, Wellesley **11** Springfield **12** Mount Holyoke, Northeastern **13** Boston College

feature: 10 Walden Pond **12** Plymouth Rock
    national seashore: 7 Cape Cod
    village: 13 Old Sturbridge
  tribe: 6 Nauset **8** Pocomtuc **10** Wampanoags
  people: 8 Pilgrims **9** Amy Lowell, Elias Howe **10** Cyrus Field, Eli Whitney **11** Clara Barton, John Hancock, Samuel Adams, Samuel Morse **12** Henry Thoreau, Robert Lowell, Winslow Homer **13** James Whistler, Joseph Kennedy, Robert Kennedy **14** Emily Dickinson **15** Henry Cabot Lodge **16** Benjamin Franklin, Edward "Ted" Kennedy **17** Ralph Waldo Emerson **18** Bartholomew Gosnold, James Russell Lowell, Nathanial Hawthorne **19** Oliver Wendell Holmes, William Cullen Bryant **21** John Greenleaf Whittier
    explorer: 8 Norsemen
  island: 5 Duke's **9** Nantucket **13** Chappaquidick **15** Martha's Vineyard
  lake: 5 Onota **7** Quabbin, Rohunta, Webster **8** Long Pond **11** Watuppa Pond **16** Assawompsett Pond **17** Chaubunagungamaug
  land rank: 10 forty-fifth
  mountain: 3 Tom **6** Brodie, Potter **7** Alander, Everett, Taconic **10** Berkshires
    highest point: 8 Greylock
  physical feature:
    bay: 8 Buzzard's
    cape: 3 Ann, Cod
    sea: 8 Atlantic
  president: 9 John Adams **14** Calvin Coolidge **15** John Quincy Adams **21** John Fitzgerald Kennedy
  river: 6 Nashua **7** Charles, Concord, Quaboag, Taunton **8** Chicopee **9** Deerfield, Merrimack **10** Blackstone, Housatonic **11** Connecticut
  state admission: 5 sixth
  state bird: 9 chickadee
  state flower: 9 mayflower **15** trailing arbutus
  state motto: 37 With the Sword She Seeks Peace Under Liberty **45** By the Sword We Seek Peace But Peace Only Under Liberty
  state song: 22 All Hail to Massachusetts
  state tree: 11 American elm

massacre 7 butcher, carnage **8** butchery, decimate **9** bloodbath, slaughter **10** mass murder **12** bloodletting

massage 3 rub **4** flex **5** chafe, knead **6** finger, handle, stroke **7** rubbing, rub down, stretch **8** kneading, stroking **10** manipulate **12** manipulation

Massasoit *see* **10** Wampanoags

Massenet, Jules Emile Frederic
  born: 6 France **9** St Etienne
  composer of: 5 Le Cid, Manon, Thais **7** Werther **9** Herodiade **11** David Rizzio **12** Don Quichotte **13** Le Roi

de Lahore **21** Le Jongleur de Notre-Dame

masses 6 plebes, proles, rabble, the mob **7** the many **8** the crowd **9** hoi polloi, plebeians **11** the populace, the riffraff **12** the multitude **13** the common herd **14** the proletariat, the rank and file **15** the common people, the lower classes, the working class **16** the great unwashed

massive 4 huge, vast **5** ample, bulky, great, heavy, hefty, massy, solid **7** hulking, immense, mammoth, titanic, weighty **8** colossal, enormous, gigantic, imposing, towering, whopping **9** cyclopean, extensive, monstrous, ponderous **10** gargantuan, impressive, monumental, stupendous **11** elephantine, substantial

massiveness 4 bulk, size **6** volume, weight **7** bigness **8** enormity, hugeness, vastness **9** amplitude, bulkiness, greatness, immensity, largeness, magnitude

mast 4 main, nuts, pole, post, spar **5** spirit, staff, stick, stuff **6** acorns, pillar **9** beechnuts, chestnuts
type: 4 fore, main **6** jigger, mizzen
support: 4 bibb

master 3 ace **4** able, A-one, best, boss, curb, deft, head, lord, main, tame, whiz **5** check, chief, crack, grasp, owner, prime, ruler **6** bridle, choice, expert, genius, gifted, govern, leader, manage, subdue, wizard **7** conquer, control, excel at, head man, manager, primary, skilled, skipper, supreme **8** director, dominate, finished, governor, masterly, overcome, overlord, overseer, regulate, suppress, talented, virtuoso **9** authority, conqueror, craftsman, first-rate, paramount, practiced, principal **10** controller, proficient, supervisor **12** get the hang of, ship's captain

Master Builder, The
author: **11** Henrik Ibsen
character: **5** Hilda **7** Solness

master craftsman 7 artisan **12** masterworker **13** skilled worker

masterful 4 able, deft **5** bossy **6** expert, superb **7** dynamic, skilled **8** finished, forceful, masterly, resolute, skillful, virtuoso **9** excellent **10** commanding **11** domineering, self-reliant **12** accomplished, strong-willed **13** authoritarian, self-confident

masterfulness 6 genius **10** capability, competence, excellence **11** proficiency

Master Melvin
nickname of: **6** Mel Ott

mastermind 4 plan, sage **6** direct, expert, genius, master, pundit, wizard **7** old hand, planner **8** conceive, director, engineer, organize, virtuoso **9** authority, initiator, organizer **10** specialist **11** moving force

Master of Ballantrae, The
author: **20** Robert Louis Stevenson
character: **4** Chew **5** Teach **9** MacKellar **11** Henry Durrie, James Durrie **12** Alison Graeme, Francis Burke, Secundra Dass

master of ceremonies 4 host **5** emcee **11** toastmaster

master of the family
Latin: **13** paterfamilias

masterpiece 5 jewel, prize **7** classic, paragon **8** monument, treasure **9** nonpareil **10** brainchild **11** chef d'oeuvre, ne plus ultra, prizewinner

Masterpiece Theater
host: **13** Alistair Cooke

master race
German: **10** Herrenvolk

Masters, Edgar Lee
author of: **19** Spoon River Anthology

Mastersingers of Nuremberg, The
also: **27** Die Meistersinger von Nurnberg
opera by: **6** Wagner
character: **9** Eva Pogner, Hans Sachs **10** Beckmesser **18** Walther von Stolzing

mastery 4 rule, sway **5** grasp **7** ability, command, control **8** deftness, whip hand **9** dominance, supremacy, upper hand **10** adroitness, attainment, domination, leadership **11** achievement, acquirement, proficiency, superiority **14** accomplishment

masticate 4 chew, gnaw **5** chomp, munch **6** nibble

Mastroianni, Marcello
born: **5** Italy **11** Fontana Liri
roles: **13** Eight and a Half **7** La Notte **11** La Dolce Vita, The Stranger, White Nights **19** Divorce Italian Style

mat 3 dim, pad, rug **4** dead, dull, flat **5** doily, muted **6** carpet, matrix, tangle **7** bedding, bolster, coaster, cushion, support **8** entangle **10** lackluster, lusterless
Japanese: **6** tatami

Mata Hari
real name: **21** Gertrud Margarete Zelle
worked as: **3** spy **6** dancer
worked for: **7** Germans
executed by: **6** French

match 3 fit **4** game, join, mate, meet, pair, peer, suit, twin, yoke **5** adapt, agree, equal, event, unite **6** couple, double, oppose **7** be alike, be equal, combine, connect, contend, contest, vie with **8** parallel **9** companion, duplicate, harmonize **10** correspond, equivalent, tournament **11** competition, counterpart

matched 5 equal **8** of a piece **9** identical **11** coordinated

matching 4 twin **5** equal **6** paired

10 equivalent **11** harmonizing **13** corresponding

matchless 4 rare **7** supreme **8** crowning, foremost, peerless, sterling, superior **9** exemplary, first rate, priceless, paramount, unequaled, unmatched, unrivaled **10** invaluable, preeminent, unbeatable, unexcelled **11** inestimable, superlative, unsurpassed **12** incomparable, unparalleled

matchmaker
Yiddish: **8** shadchan **9** schatchen

mate 3 pal **4** chum, twin, wife **5** buddy, crony, hubby, match **6** couple, friend, spouse **7** cohabit, comrade, consort, husband, pair off, partner **8** copulate, coworker, sidekick **9** associate, colleague, companion, duplicate **10** better half, equivalent **11** confederate, counterpart **12** fellow worker, ship's officer

materfamilias 15 mother of a family

material 5 stuff **6** matter **8** elements **9** substance **12** constituents

materialism 5 greed **12** covetousness **15** acquisitiveness

materialistic 6 greedy **8** covetous, grasping **11** acquisitive, unspiritual

materiality 9 existence **11** tangibility

materialization 5 ghost, shade **6** coming, wraith **7** phantom, specter **9** emergence **10** apparition, appearance **13** manifestation

materialize 4 loom, rise, show **5** bob up, issue, pop up **6** appear, crop up, emerge, turn up **9** come forth **10** burst forth **11** come to light, spring forth **12** come into view

materially 7 vitally **8** palpably, tangibly **9** in the main, seriously **10** monetarily **11** corporeally, essentially, financially, in substance **12** considerably, emphatically **13** significantly, substantially **14** for the most part

material possessions 6 assets, estate, wealth **7** fortune **8** property **10** belongings **12** worldly goods

material proof 8 evidence **13** documentation

materials 4 data **5** cloth, facts, notes, tools **6** stocks, stores, timber **7** fabrics, figures **8** concrete, dry goods, supplies, textiles **9** citations, equipment, machinery, yard goods **10** essentials, piece goods, quotations, references **11** impressions **12** observations **15** bricks and mortar

materiel 4 gear **6** stores **8** supplies **9** equipment, materials **10** provisions **16** military supplies

Mater Matuta *see* **6** Matuta

maternal 4 fond **6** doting **8** motherly **9** of a mother, shielding **10** motherlike, protective, sheltering

maternity 5 labor **8** delivery

9 pregnancy **10** childbirth, motherhood **11** parturition **12** accouchement, childbearing

mathematical, mathematic 5 exact, rigid **6** strict **7** precise **8** accurate, rigorous, unerring **10** meticulous, scientific, scrupulous **11** punctilious, well-defined **13** computational

mathematician
  American: 5 Aiken **6** Wiener
  British: 6 Newton **7** Babbage
  French: 6 Fermat **9** D'Alembert, Descartes
  German: 5 Frege, Gauss **6** Bessel **7** Hilbert
  Greek: 6 Euclid, Thales **11** Anaximander
  Norwegian: 4 Abel
  Swiss: 5 Euler **9** Bernoulli

Mathewson, Christy
  nickname: 5 Matty **6** Big Six
  sport: 8 baseball
  position: 7 pitcher
  team: 13 New York Giants

Matholwych
  king of: 7 Ireland
  wife: 7 Branwen

matinee 9 early show **16** early performance **20** afternoon performance

Mating Season, The
  author: 11 P G Wodehouse

Matisse, Henri Emile Benoit
  born: 6 France **16** Chateau Cambresis (Le Cateau)
  artwork: 5 Dance, Music **8** The Slave **10** Odalisques **11** Joie de Vivre **12** Harmony in Red, La Serpentine **13** Head with Tiara, The Open Window **15** Bathers by a River, Memory of Oceania, Woman with the Hat **16** Heads of Jeannette **19** Torso with Arms Raised **20** Goldfish and Sculpture

matriarch 7 dowager **10** female head, grande dame **11** female ruler **12** female leader **13** materfamilias

matriculate 4 join **5** enter **6** enlist, enroll, sign up **7** check in **8** register

matriculation 9 signing up **10** enrollment **12** registration

matrimonial 6 bridal, wedded, wifely **7** marital, married, nuptial, spousal **8** conjugal, hymeneal **9** affianced, connubial, husbandly **11** epithalamic

matrimony 7 wedlock **8** marriage **11** holy wedlock

matrix 3 die **4** cast, form, mold **5** frame, punch, stamp

matron 4 dame **5** madam **7** dowager **8** forelady, mistress, overseer **9** forewoman **10** directress **11** housekeeper **12** married woman **14** superintendent

matter 3 fix **4** gist, snag, text **5** count, drift, event, sense, stuff, theme, thing, topic **6** affair, crisis, import, moment, object, scrape, strait, thesis **7** content,

dilemma, episode, essence, purport, signify, subject, trouble **8** argument, business, elements, exigency, material, obstacle, quandary **9** adventure, emergency, happening, situation, substance **10** difference, difficulty, experience, impediment, importance, occurrence, perplexity, proceeding **11** carry weight, consequence, predicament, transaction **12** circumstance, significance

matter-of-course 5 usual **6** common **7** routine **8** everyday, ordinary, standard **9** customary **11** commonplace, established

matter-of-fact 4 real **5** blunt, frank **6** candid, direct **7** factual, literal, mundane, natural, prosaic **8** ordinary, sensible **9** outspoken, practical, pragmatic, realistic **10** hardheaded, nononsense, unaffected, uninspired, unromantic **11** commonplace, common-sense, down-to- earth, straight out **13** unimaginative, unsentimental **15** straightforward

matter-of-factness 10 detachment **11** impassivity **12** practicality **13** impassiveness **17** unimaginativeness

Matter of Time, A
  author: 12 Jessamyn West

Matthau, Walter
  real name: 13 Walter Matthow **23** Walter Matuschanskavasky
  born: 9 New York NY
  roles: 5 Kotch **8** A New Leaf **10** Plaza Suite **11** Pete n Tillie **12** Bad News Bears, Ensign Pulver, Grumpy Old Men, Oscar Madison, The Front Page, The Odd Couple **15** California Suite, The Sunshine Boys **16** The Fortune Cookie **22** A Guide for the Married Man

Matthew 7 apostle
  father: 7 Alpheus
  also called: 4 Levi
  wrote: 6 Gospel

Matthiessen, Peter
  author of: 10 Sand Rivers **14** The Snow Leopard

maturation 6 growth **8** fruition, ripening **9** growing up

mature 4 ripe **5** adult, bloom, grown, manly, of age, ready, ripen **6** flower, grow up, mellow, nubile, virile **7** blossom, develop, grown-up, matured, womanly **8** finished, maturate, seasoned **9** come of age, completed, full-blown, full-grown, perfected, practiced **10** middle- aged **11** become adult, experienced, full-fledged, in one's prime **12** marriageable

Mature, Victor
  born: 12 Louisville KY
  roles: 7 The Robe **11** After the Fox, Kiss of Death **12** Cry of the City, One Million BC **16** Samson and Delilah **19** Androcles and the Lion

matured 3 big **4** aged, ripe **5** adult, grown **6** formed **7** ripened **8** flowered, mellowed, seasoned **9** blossomed, developed, full-blown, full-grown **11** full-fledged

maturity 7 manhood **8** legal age, majority, practice, ripeness **9** adulthood, composure, full bloom, readiness, seasoning, womanhood **10** completion, experience, full growth, maturation, matureness, perfection **11** culmination, fulfillment **12** age of consent

Matuta
  origin: 5 Roman
  goddess of: 3 sea **4** dawn **7** harbors **10** childbirth
  called: 11 Mater Matuta

Maud
  author: 18 Alfred Lord Tennyson

Maude
  character: 5 Carol **7** Phillip **10** Henry Evans **12** Florida Evans, Maude Findlay, Mrs Naugatuck **13** Walter Findlay **14** Dr Arthur Harmon **20** Vivian Cavender Harmon
  cast: 8 Bill Macy, John Amos **10** Conrad Bain **11** Esther Rolle **13** Brian Morrison, Rue McClanahan **14** Beatrice Arthur, Kraig Metzinger **15** Adrienne Barbeau **16** Hermione Baddeley
  spinoff from: 14 All in the Family
  spinoff: 9 Good Times

maudlin 5 gushy, mushy, teary **6** slushy **7** gushing, mawkish, tearful **8** bathetic **9** emotional **10** lachrymose **11** sentimental **13** overemotional

maudlinism 6 bathos **11** mawkishness **14** sentimentalism, sentimentality

Maugham, W Somerset
  author of: 9 The Circle **10** Our Betters **11** Cakes and Ale **12** Miss Thompson **13** The Razor's Edge **14** Of Human Bondage **15** The Constant Wife **18** The Moon and Sixpence **21** Lady Frederick Ashenden

maul 4 beat **5** stomp **6** batter, beat up, bruise, mangle, pummel, thrash **7** rough up **9** manhandle **10** knock about

Mauldin, Bill
  creator/artist of: 7 Up Front **12** Willie and Joe

Mau Mau 13 secret society
  of: 6 Kikuyu
  in: 5 Kenya

maunder 4 loaf **5** drift, run on, stray **6** babble, dawdle, gabble, gibber, ramble, wander **7** blather, meander, prattle, saunter **8** flounder, ramble on, straggle **9** go on and on, hem and haw **10** dillydally

maundering 7 diffuse **8** rambling **9** wandering **10** digressive, disjointed, roundabout **14** drift, run on, stray **6** babble, dawdle, gabble, gibber, ramble, wander **7** blather, meander, prattle, saunter **8** flounder, ramble on, straggle **9** go on and on, hem and haw **10** dillydally

Maupassant, Guy de
  author of: 6 Belami **9** Ball of Fat, Mont-Oriol **11** A Woman's Life, The Necklace **12** Ball of Tallow **16** Mademoiselle Fifi

Mauriac, Francois
  author of: 8 Genitrix **10** The Egoists **12** Viper's Tangle **15** A Kiss to the Leper, The Desert of Love **20** A Woman of the Pharisees

Mauritania
  capital/largest city: 10 Nouakchott
  others: 4 Atar **5** Kaedi, Rosso **6** Fderik **7** Akjoujt **10** Nouadhibou
  division: 5 Sahel **7** Chemama
  monetary unit: 5 khoum **7** ouguiya
  highest point: 11 Kediat Idjil
  river: 7 Senegal
  sea: 8 Atlantic
  physical feature:
    desert: 6 Sahara
    valley: 7 Chemama **12** Senegal River
  people: 4 Arab, Fula, Moor **5** Black, Fulbe, Wolof **6** Bafour, Berber, Fulani **7** African, Soninke, Tukulor **8** Sarakole **9** Sarakolle **10** Toucouleur **12** Halphoolaren
    leader: 4 Luly **5** Salek **6** Daddah **8** Haidalla
    ruler: 6 France **9** Almoravid **14** Kingdom of Ghana
  language: 4 Fula **5** Wolof **6** Arabic, French **7** Phoolor, Tukulor **8** Fulfulde, Mandingo **9** Sarakolle, Hassaniya
  religion: 5 Islam
  place:
    mosque: 5 Grand
  feature:
    beehive hut: 4 ruga
    priest-teacher: 8 marabout
    waterskin: 6 guerba
  food:
    dish: 7 meshuri
    tea: 5 attay

Mauritius
  other name: 11 Ile de France
  capital/largest city: 9 Port Louis
  others: 6 Reduit **8** Curepipe **9** Mahebourg **13** Quartre Bornes **19** Grande Riviere Sud-Est
  head of state: 14 British monarch **15** governor general
  monetary unit: 4 cent **5** rupee
  island: 3 Est **4** Flat **5** Ambre, Cerf's, Morne, Round **7** Agalega, Serpent **9** Mauritius, Rodrigues, Rodriguez, St Brandon **12** Gunner's Quoin **15** Cargados Carajos
  highest point: 27 Piton de la Petite Riviere Noire
  sea: 6 Indian
  people: 6 Creole, French, Indian **7** African, Chinese **8** European

13 Indo-Mauritian
    leader: 8 Jugnauth **9** Ramgoolam
    ruler: 5 Dutch **6** French **7** English
  language: 4 Urdu **5** Hindi, Tamil **6** Creole, French

mausoleum 10 family tomb **11** stately tomb **18** sepulchral monument

mauve 4 plum, puce **5** lilac **6** violet **8** lavender **11** light purple **12** bluish purple

maverick 5 loner **8** yearling **9** dissenter, dissident, eccentric **11** independent **13** individualist, noncomformist

Maverick
  character: 12 Bart Maverick, Bret Maverick **13** Brent Maverick **16** Samantha Crawford **24** Cousin Beauregard Maverick
  cast: 9 Jack Kelly **10** Roger Moore **11** James Garner **13** Diane Brewster, Robert Colbert

maw 4 craw, crop, jaws **5** mouth **6** gullet, muzzle, throat

mawkish 5 gushy, mushy, teary **7** maudlin, tearful **9** emotional, nostalgic, schmaltzy **10** lachrymose **11** sentimental **15** oversentimental

mawkishness 4 mush **5** slush **6** bathos **9** mushiness, soppiness **10** maudlinism, slushiness **14** sentimentalism, sentimentality

maxim 3 saw **4** rule **5** adage, axiom, motto **6** old saw, saying, truism **7** proverb **8** aphorism, apothegm **9** platitude

Maximes
  author: 23 Francois La Rochefoucauld

Maxims of the Law
  author: 12 Francis Bacon

maximum 3 top **4** most **6** utmost **7** highest, largest, maximal, optimum, supreme **8** foremost, greatest **9** paramount **11** unsurpassed

Maxwell, Elsa 6 author **7** hostess **9** socialite **10** party-giver **23** "The hostess with the mostes'"

May
  characteristic: 7 Maypole **13** queen of the May
  flower: 8 hawthorn **15** lily of the valley
  French: 3 Mai
  gem: 7 emerald
  German: 3 Mai
  holiday: 6 May Day (1) **10** Mother's Day (2nd Sunday) **11** Memorial Day (last Monday) **14** Armed Forces Day (3rd Saturday)
  Italian: 6 Maggio
  number of days: 9 thirty-one
  origin of name: 4 Maia
    Roman goddess of: 6 spring
  place in year:
    Gregorian: 5 fifth
    Roman: 5 third
  saying: 27 April showers bring May

flowers
  Spanish: 4 Mayo
  Zodiac sign: 6 Gemini, Taurus

May, Elaine
  real name: 12 Elaine Berlin
  partner: 11 Mike Nichols
  born: 14 Philadelphia PA
  roles: 8 A New Leaf **15** California Suite
  director of: 16 The Heartbreak Kid
  writer/director of: 8 A New Leaf

Maya
  city: 4 Coba **5** Tulum, Uxmal **6** Akumal, Cuello, Izamal **8** Calakmul, Palenque **11** Chichen Itza
  conqueror: 8 Alvarado
  day: 5 uayeb
  language family: 5 Mayan **10** Maya-Quiche
  location: 5 Tikal **6** Belize, Mexico **7** Chiapas, Mayapan, Tabasco, Yucatan **8** Honduras **9** Guatemala **11** Chichen Itza **14** Central America
  month: 5 uinal **6** uninal
  noted for: 9 astronomy **12** architecture **19** hieroglyphic writing
  rain god: 4 Chac **5** Chaac **7** Chac Mol **8** Chac Mool
  ruins: 9 Yaxchilan **20** Temple of Inscriptions
  underworld: 7 Xibalba
  year: 4 haab

maybe 6 mayhap **7** perhaps **8** feasibly, possibly **9** perchance **10** God willing, imaginably **11** conceivably **12** peradventure

Maybe
  author: 14 Lillian Hellman

Mayberry RFD
  character: 5 Alice **7** Aunt Bee **8** Sam Jones **9** Mike Jones **10** Goober Pyle **11** Emmett Clark **13** Howard Sprague, Millie Swanson
  cast: 8 Ken Berry **10** Jack Dodson **11** Buddy Foster, Paul Hartman **13** Alice Ghostley, Arlene Golonka, Frances Bavier, George Lindsey

mayfly
  varieties: 5 small **6** stream **9** burrowing

mayhem 4 maim **6** felony **7** battery, cripple **8** mutilate, violence **9** crippling, dismember **10** mutilation **13** disfigurement

may he rest in peace
  Latin: 16 requiescat in pace

may it do good
  Latin: 6 prosit

Maylie, Mrs and Rose
  characters in: 11 Oliver Twist
  author: 7 Dickens

Mayo, Virginia
  real name: 13 Virginia Jones
  husband: 12 Michael O'Shea
  born: 9 St Louis MO
  roles: 17 The West Point Story

22 The Best Years of Our Lives **26** The Secret Life of Walter Mitty

Mayor of Casterbridge, The
 author: **11** Thomas Hardy
 character: **13** Donald Farfrae, Richard Newson **14** Lucetta Le Sueur **15** Michael Henchard **19** Elizabeth Jane Newson, Susan Henchard-Newson

Mays, Willie
 nickname: **9** Say Hey Kid
 sport: **8** baseball
 position: **11** center field
 team: **11** New York Mets **13** New York Giants **18** San Francisco Giants

may she live forever
 Latin: **12** esto perpetua
 motto of: **5** Idaho

may she rest in peace
 Latin: **16** requiescat in pace

maze 5 snarl **6** jungle, tangle **7** complex, meander, network **9** labyrinth **11** convolution

mazel tov 8 good luck

Mbabane
 capital of: **9** Swaziland

McBeal, Ally see **10** Ally McBeal

McCambridge, Mercedes
 real name: **32** Carlotta Mercedes Agnes McCambridge
 born: **8** Joliet IL
 roles: **5** Giant **8** Cimarron **11** Touch of Evil **14** All the King's Men **15** A Farewell to Arms **18** Suddenly Last Summer

McCarey, Leo
 director of: **8** Duck Soup **10** Going My Way (Oscar) **13** The Awful Truth (Oscar) **15** Ruggles of Red Gap **17** The Bells of St Mary's

McCarthy, Mary
 author of: **8** The Group
 sister of: **5** Kevin

McCay, Winsor
 creator/artist of: **23** Little Nemo in Slumberland

McClellan, George B
 nickname: **25** Little Mac the Young Napoleon
 served in: **8** Civil War **10** Mexican War
 side: **5** Union
 commander of: **16** Army of the Potomac
 battle: **8** Antietam **18** Peninsular campaign
 governor of: **9** New Jersey

McCloud
 character: **10** Sam McCloud **13** Chris Coughlin, (Sgt) Joe Broadhurst **14** Peter B Clifford
 cast: **8** JD Cannon **11** Terry Carter **12** Dennis Weaver, Diana Muldaur

McClure, Darrell
 creator/artist of: **17** Little Annie Rooney

McCrea, Joel
 wife: **10** Frances Dee
 born: **12** Los Angeles CA
 roles: **11** Buffalo Bill **14** Palm Beach Story **16** Sullivan's Travels, The Great Man's Lady **17** Reaching for the Sun, The More the Merrier **20** Foreign Correspondent

McCreary, Fainy (Mac)
 character in: **3** USA
 author: **9** Dos Passos

McCullers, Carson
 author of: **17** The Mortgaged Heart **18** Member of the Wedding **21** The Ballad of the Sad Cafe **23** Reflections in a Golden Eye, The Heart Is a Lonely Hunter

McCullough, Colleen
 author of: **13** The Thornbirds **19** An Indecent Obsession

McCutcheon, George Barr
 author of: **9** Graustark

McEvoy, JP
 creator/artist of: **10** Dixie Dugan

McFee, William
 author of: **15** Casuals of the Sea

McGinley, Phyllis
 author of: **12** Three Decades **15** A Pocketful of Wry **24** The Horse Who Lived Upstairs

McHale's Navy
 character: **7** Christy **9** Willy Moss **11** Fuji Kobiaji, Happy Haines **12** Harrison (Tinker) Bell, Lester Gruber **13** Virgil Farrell, (Ensign) Charles Parker, (Lt Cdr) Quinton McHale **14** (Lt) Elroy Carpenter **18** (Capt) Wallace B Binghamton
 cast: **8** Joe Flynn **9** Tim Conway **10** Billy Sands, Gary Vinson, John Wright, Yoshio Yoda **11** Bob Hastings, Edson Stroll **12** Gavin Mac Leod **14** Carl Ballantine, Ernest Borgnine

McKenna, Siobhan
 born: **7** Belfast, Ireland
 roles: **11** King of Kings **13** Doctor Zhivago **14** Of Human Bondage **24** Playboy of the Western World

McKim, Charles M
 architect of: **27** Lutheran Church of the Redeemer (Houston)

McKim, Mead, and White
 partners: **13** Stanford White **18** Charles Follen McKim **21** William Rutherford Mead
 architects of: **11** Century Club **14** University Club, Washington Arch **17** Vanderbilt Mansion **18** Columbia University (NYC) **19** Boston Public Library, Pennsylvania Station (NYC), (first) Madison Square Garden (NYC) **21** New York Herald Building, Pierpont Morgan Library (NYC) **31** Madison Square Presbyterian Church
 style: **7** Shingle **18** Italian Renaissance

McKinley, William
 nickname: **13** Major McKinley
 presidential rank: **11** twenty-fifth
 party: **10** Republican
 state represented: **2** OH
 defeated: **4** (Eugene Victor) Debs **5** (Seth Hockett) Ellis, (William Jennings) Bryan **6** (John McCauley) Palmer, (Wharton) Barker **7** (Charles Eugene) Bentley, (John Granville) Woolley, (Jonah Fitz Randolph) Leonard **8** (Charles Horatio) Matchett, (Joseph Francis) Malloney, (Joshua) Levering
 vice president: **6** (Garret Augustus) Hobart **9** (Theodore) Roosevelt
 cabinet:
  state: **3** (John Milton) Hay, (William Rufus) Day **7** (John) Sherman
  treasury: **4** (Lyman Judson) Gage
  war: **4** (Elihu) Root **5** (Russell Alexander) Alger
  attorney general: **4** (Philander Chase) Knox **6** (John William) Griggs **7** (Joseph) McKenna
  navy: **4** (John Davis) Long
  postmaster general: **4** (James Albert) Gary **5** (Charles Emory) Smith
  interior: **5** (Cornelius Newton) Bliss **9** (Ethan Allen) Hitchcock
  agriculture: **6** (James) Wilson
 born: **7** Niles OH
 died: **9** Buffalo NY
 died by: **13** assassination
 buried: **8** Canton OH
 education:
  college: **10** Allegheny
  law school: **6** Albany
 religion: **9** Methodist
 author: **37** The Tariff in the Days of Henry Clay and Since
 political career: **24** US House of Representatives
  governor of: **4** Ohio
 civilian career: **6** lawyer
 military service: **7** captain **8** Civil War **11** brevet major
 notable events of lifetime/term:
  Act: **13** Dingley Tariff
  Peace Conference: **5** Hague
  Treaty of: **5** Paris
  war with: **5** Spain
 father: **7** William
 mother: **5** Nancy (Campbell Allison)
 siblings: **4** Anna, Mary **5** Abner, Helen, James **10** Abbie Celia **12** David Allison **14** Sarah Elizabeth
 wife: **3** Ida (Saxton)
 children: **3** Ida **9** Katherine

McManus, George
 creator/artist of: **12** The Newlyweds **16** Bringing Up Father

McMillan, Edwin Mattison
 field: **7** physics **9** chemistry
 developed: **16** synchrocyclotron
 awarded: **10** Nobel Prize

McMillan and Wife
 character: **7** Mildred **13** Sally McMil-

McMurtry, Larry (cont.)
lan **14** (Sgt) Charles Enright **15** (Commissioner) Stewart McMillan
cast: **10** John Schuck, Rock Hudson **11** Nancy Walker **15** Susan Saint James

McMurtry, Larry
author of: **10** Texasville **12** Lonesome Dove **14** Horseman Pass By **18** The Last Picture Show

McPhee, John
author of: **16** In Suspect Terrain **20** Coming into the Country **23** The Curve of Binding Energy **26** Encounters with the Archdruid

McQueen, Steve
real name: **21** Terrence Steven McQueen
wife: **10** Ali MacGraw
born: **8** Slater MO **14** Indianapolis IN
roles: **7** Bullitt, The Blob **8** Papillon **14** The Great Escape, The Sand Pebbles **16** The Cincinnati Kid **17** Thomas Crown Affair, Wanted Dead or Alive **19** The Magnificent Seven

McTeague
author: **11** Frank Norris

mea culpa 7 my fault **14** through my fault

Mead, Margaret
author of: **14** My Earlier Years **16** Blackberry Winter **18** Coming of Age in Samoa **42** Growing Up in New Guinea **42** Sex and Temperament in Three Primitive Societies
husband: **14** Gregory Bateson

Meade, Dr and Mrs
characters in: **15** Gone With the Wind
author: **8** Mitchell

Meade, George Gordon
served in: **8** Civil War **10** Mexican War
side: **5** Union
battle: **7** Bull Run **8** Antietam **10** Gettysburg **13** South Mountain **14** Fredericksburg **16** Chancellorsville **18** Peninsular campaign
commander of: **16** Army of the Potomac

meadow 3 lea **4** mead, park **5** field, green **6** forage **7** herbage, pasture, savanna **9** grassland, pasturage

meager 4 bare, lean, slim, thin **5** scant, short, spare, token **6** little, paltry, scanty, scarce, skimpy, slight, sparse **7** scrimpy, slender, stinted, wanting **9** deficient **10** inadequate **12** insufficient **13** insubstantial

meagerness 8 sparsity **9** smallness **10** inadequacy, measliness, scantiness, skimpiness, sparseness **13** insufficiency **14** insignificance

Meagles
character in: **12** Little Dorrit
author: **7** Dickens

meal 4 bran, chow, diet, eats, fare, food, grub, menu **5** feast, flour, grits **6** farina, groats, repast, spread **7** banquet, cooking, cuisine, oatmeal **8** cornmeal, victuals **10** bill of fare **11** nourishment, refreshment

mealymouthed 6 unsure **7** devious **8** hesitant **9** deceptive, insincere

mean 3 low, par, say **4** base, evil, norm, plan, poor, rude, rule, vile, want, wish **5** aim at, cheap, close, cruel, imply, nasty, petty, small, tight, venal **6** denote, flimsy, greedy, hint at, intend, malign, medium, menial, normal, paltry, sleazy, sordid, stingy, tell off, trashy, unfair **7** average, balance, betoken, dream of, drive at, express, hoggish, inhuman, miserly, point to, propose, purpose, regular, resolve, selfish, signify, squalid, suggest, think of, trivial, vicious **8** aspire to, gimcrack, grasping, indicate, inferior, inhumane, intimate, low-grade, picayune, piddling, pitiless, rubbishy, say truly, shameful, standard, stand for, trifling, uncaring, wretched **9** illiberal, low-paying, malicious, mercenary, merciless, miserable, niggardly, penurious, symbolize, unfeeling **10** avaricious, compromise, despicable, have in mind, have in view, jerry-built, low-ranking, malevolent, pinchpenny, second-rate, ungenerous, villainous **11** closefisted, commonplace, disgraceful, happy medium, hard-hearted, self-seeking, small-minded, tightfisted, unimportant **12** contemptible, disagreeable, dishonorable **13** insignificant, unsympathetic **15** inconsequential

meander 4 loop, rove, wind **5** snake, stray, twist **6** circle, ramble, spiral, wander, zigzag **8** undulate **9** convolute, corkscrew

meandering 7 devious, sinuous, turning, winding **8** indirect, rambling, tortuous, twisting **9** wandering **10** circuitous, roundabout, serpentine

meaning 3 aim, end **4** gist, goal, hint, meat, pith, plan, view **5** drift, force, point, sense, value, worth **6** burden, design, intent, object, scheme, thrust, upshot **7** content, essence, pointer, purport, purpose **9** intention, substance **10** denotation, indication, intimation, suggestion **11** implication **12** significance **15** sum and substance

meaningful 4 deep **5** meaty, pithy **6** useful **7** pointed, serious **8** eloquent, explicit, pregnant **9** designing, important **10** expressive, gratifying, portentous, purposeful, suggestive, worthwhile **11** significant, substantial **13** consequential

meaningless 5 trite **6** absurd, paltry, stupid **7** aimless, fatuous, foolish, idiotic, shallow, trivial, useless **8** baffling, piddling, puzzling **9** enigmatic, facetious, frivolous, illegible, senseless, valueless, worthless **10** incoherent, mystifying, perplexing **11** bewildering, inscrutable, nonsensical, purposeless, unessential, unimportant **12** impenetrable, inexplicable, inexpressive, preposterous **13** insignificant, unsubstantial **14** undecipherable

Mean Joe
nickname of: **9** Joe Greene

means 3 way **4** jack, mode **5** bread, dough, funds, money **6** avenue, course, income, method, resort, riches, wealth **7** capital, dollars, measure, process, revenue **8** property **9** affluence, long green, resources, substance **11** alternative, wherewithal

mean-spirited 3 low **4** base, poor, vile **5** cheap, nasty, petty, small, snide, sorry, tight, venal **6** abject, measly, paltry, scurvy, shabby, sordid, stingy **7** ignoble, miserly, selfish, vicious **8** tightwad, wretched **9** miserable, penurious **10** ungenerous **12** parsimonious

Mean Streets
director: **14** Martin Scorsese
cast: **11** Amy Robinson, David Proval **12** Harvey Keitel, Robert DeNiro

meantime 7 interim **8** interval **9** meanwhile

meanwhile 8 meantime **12** concurrently, in the interim **13** at the same time **14** simultaneously

measurable 10 assessable, computable, mensurable, reckonable **11** appraisable **12** determinable

measure 3 act, law **4** bill, plan, rule, size, step, time **5** bound, clock, gauge, judge, limit, means, plumb, quota, range, scale, scope, share, sound, value **6** amount, assess, course, degree, design, extent, method, resort, scheme, survey **7** portion, project **8** appraise, evaluate, proposal, quantity **9** allotment, allowance, enactment, procedure, restraint, yardstick **10** limitation, moderation, proceeding, temperance

measure, unit of
of Afghanistan: **3** paw, sir **5** jerib, karoh **6** khurds **7** kharwar
of Algeria: **3** pik **5** rebis, tarri **6** termin
of Argentina: **4** sino **5** legua **6** cuadra, lastre **7** manzana
of Australia: **4** arna, naut, saum
of Austria: **4** fass, fuss, joch, mass, muth, yoke **5** halbe, linie, meile, metze, pfiff, punkt **6** achtel, becher, leipoa, seidel **7** klafter, viertel **8** dreiling **12** futtermassel
of Belgium: **3** vat **4** aune, pied **5** carat **6** perche **8** boisseau
of Bolivia: **6** league **7** celemin
of Borneo: **7** gantang
of Brazil: **2** pe **4** moio, sack, vara **5** braca, legoa, milha, tonel **6** canada,

cuarto, quarto, tarefa **7** garrafa **8** alqueire
of Bulgaria: 3 oka, oke **5** krine, lekhe, likhe
of Canada: 3 ton **5** minot, perch, point **6** arpent **7** chainon
of the Canary Islands: 8 fanegada
of Chile: 4 vara **5** legua, linea **6** cuadra **7** fanega
of China: 3 cho, fan, fen, pau, tou, tun, yan, yin **4** chek, chih, fang, kish, papa, quei, shih, teke, tsan, tsun **5** catty, chang, ching, sheng, shing **6** chupak, gungli, kungho, kungmu, tching **7** kungfen, kungyin **8** kungchih, kungshih **9** kungching
of Colombia: 4 vara **7** azumbre, celemin
of Costa Rica: 4 vara **5** cafiz, cahiz **6** fanega, tercia **7** cajuela, cantaro, manzana **10** caballeria
of Cuba: 4 vara **5** bocoy, cocoy, tarea **6** cordel, fanega **10** caballeria
of former Czechoslovakia: 3 lan **4** mira **5** korec, liket, stopa **6** merice, strych
of Denmark: 3 ell, fod, mil, pot **4** alen **5** album, anker, kande, linje, paegl **7** landmil, oltonde, ortonde, skieppe, viertel **8** fjerding **9** ottingkar **10** korntonde
of the Dominican Republic: 3 ona **5** tarea **6** fanega
of Ecuador: 5 libra **6** cuadra, fanega
of Egypt: 3 apt, dra, hen, rob **4** arab, dira, draa, khet, nief, ocha, roub, theb, wudu **5** abdat, ardab, cubit, farde, fedan, keleh, kerat, kilah, sahme **6** artaba, aurure, baladi, kantar, keddah, robhah, schene **7** choryos, daribah, malouah, roubouh, toumnah **8** kassabah, kharouba **10** diramimari, diribaladi
of El Salvador: 4 vara **5** cafiz, cahiz **6** fanega **7** batella, botella, cantara, manzana
of England: 3 cut, ell, lea, pin, rod, ton, tun, vat **4** acre, bind, butt, comb, coom, cran, foot, gill, goad, hand, hank, heer, hide, inch, last, line, mile, nail, pace, palm, peck, pint, pipe, pole, pool, rood, rope, sack, seam, span, trug, typp, wist, yard, yoke **5** bodge, chain, cubit, digit, float, floor, fluid, hutch, jugum, minim, ounce, perch, point, prime, quart, skein, stack, truss **6** barrel, bovate, bushel, cranne, fathom, firkin, gallon, hobbet, hobbit, league, manent, oxgang, pottle, runlet, square, strike, sulung, thread, tierce **7** auchlet, furlong, kenning, quarter, rundlet, seamile, spindle, tertian, virgate **8** carucate, chaldron, hogshead, landyard, puncheon, quadrant, standard
of Estonia: 3 tun **4** elle, liin, sund, toll, toop **5** verst **6** sagene, versta

7 kulimet **8** tonnland
of Ethiopia: 3 tat **4** cubi, kuba **5** derah, messe **6** cabaho, sinjer, sinzer, tanica **7** entelam, farsakh, farsang, ghebeta
of Finland: 5 kannu, verst **6** fathom, kannor **8** ottinger, skalpund, tunnland
of France: 3 pot, sac **4** aune, mine, pied, velt **5** arpen, carat, ligne, minot, pinte, point, pouce, velte **6** arpent, hemine, league, quarte, setier
of Greece: 3 pik **4** bema, piki, pous **5** baril, chous, cubit, diote, doron, maris, pekhe, podos, pygon, xylon **6** acaena, bacile, barile, cotula, dichas, gramme, hemina, koilon, lichas, milion, orgyia, palame, pechys, schene, xestes **7** bacvhel, chenica, choenix, cyathos, diaulos, metreta, stadium, stremma **8** condylos, daktylos, dekapode, dolichos, medimnos, medimnys, metretes, palaiste, plethron, plethrum, stathmos **9** hemiekton, oxybaphon
of Guatemala: 4 vara **6** cuarta, tercia **7** cajuela, manzana **10** caballeria
of Guinea: 7 jacktan
of Honduras: 4 vara **5** milla **6** mecate **7** cajuela
of Hungary: 3 ako **4** hold, yoke **5** itcze, marok, metze **7** huvelyk
of Iceland: 3 sel **4** alin **5** almud **6** almenn, ferfet, pottur **7** fathmur, fermila, oltunna
of India: 3 ady, gaz, gez, jow, lan **4** byee, coss, depa, doph, hath, koss, kunk, raik, rati, seit, taun, tola **5** bigha, covid, crosa, danda, depoh, drona, erosa, garce, hasta, krosa, parah, ratti, salay, yojan **6** adhaka, amunam, covido, cudava, cumblia, geerah, moolum, mushti, ouroub, palgat, parran, prasha, ropani, tipree, unglee, yojana **7** dhanush, gavyuti, khahoon, niranga, prastha **8** okthabah
of Indonesia: 5 depah, depoh
of Iran: 3 gaz, zar, zer **4** cane **5** gareh, kafiz, makuk, qasab **6** charac, chebel, ghalva **7** capicha, chenica, farsakh, mansion, mishara **8** parasang, piamaneh, stathmos
of Ireland: 4 mile **6** bandle **8** crannock
of Israel: 3 cab, car, hin, kab, kor **4** bath, ezba, omer, reed **5** cubit, donum, dunam, ephah, ganeh, homer, kaneh
of Italy: 3 pie **4** orna **5** palma, palmo, punto, salma, stero **6** barile, miglie, moggio, rubbio, tomolo **7** braccio, secchio **8** giornata, quadrato
of Japan: 2 go **3** boo, cho, djo, fun, inc, ken, kin, kon, rin, shi, sho, sun, tan **4** hiro, isse, kati, koku, niyo, shoo **5** carat, catty, issho, ittan, momme, picul, shaku **6** kwamme

8 hiyak-kin **9** hiyak-hiro **11** komma-ichida, kujira-shaku
of Java: 3 kan **4** paal, rand **5** palen
of Kenya: 4 wari
of Laos: 3 bak
of Latvia: 3 let **4** stof **5** stoff, verst **6** arshin, kulmet **7** verchoc, verchok **8** krouchka, pourvete **9** deciatine, lofstelle, pourvette **10** tonnseteel
of Liberia: 4 kuba
of Libya: 3 dra, pik, saa **4** kele **5** bozze, donum, jabia, teman, uckia **6** barile, gorrah, misura **7** mattaro, termino **8** kharouba
of Luxembourg: 5 fuder
of Madagascar: 7 gantang
of Malaysia: 3 pau, tun **4** para, pipe, tael, wang **5** parah **6** chupak, parrah **7** gantang
of Malta: 4 rotl **5** artal, canna, parto, ratel, salma **6** kantar **7** caffiso
of Mexico: 3 bag, pie **4** alma, onza, vara **5** almud, baril, carga, jarra, labor, legua, libra, linea, marco, sitio **6** adarme, almude, arroba, carega, fanega, ochaua, terceo **7** pulgada, quintal **9** cuarteron, cuartillo **10** caballeria
of Morocco: 4 kala, muhd, rotl, saah, sahh, ueba **5** artal, cadee, gerbe, ratel **6** covado, dirhem, fanega, izenbi, kintar, tangin, tomini **8** quintral
of Myanmar: 2 ly **3** dha, gon, mau, sao, tao, tat **4** byee, phan, seit, taun, that **5** shita, thuoc **6** lamany, palgat **7** chaivai **8** okthabah
of the Netherlands: 2 el **3** aam, ahm, ell, kan, vat **4** duim, mijl, rood, rope **5** anker, roede, wisse **6** hunder, legger, maatje, mutsje, streep **7** schepel **8** mimgelen, steekkan
of Nicaragua: 4 vara **5** cahiz **6** suerte **7** cajuela, manzana **10** cabelleria
of Norway: 3 fot, mal **4** alen **5** kande **6** fathom **7** skieppe **9** korntonde
of Panama: 7 celemin
of Paraguay: 3 pie **4** lino, lira, lire, vara **5** legua **6** cuadra, fanega
of Peru: 4 topo **5** galon **7** celemin **8** fanegada
of the Philippines: 4 loan **5** braza, catty, cavan, chupa, fardo, ganta, picul, punto **6** apatan, balita, lachsa, quinon **7** quilate **8** chinanta
of Poland: 3 cal **4** mila, pret **5** morga, sazen, vloka, wloka **6** cwierc, cwierk, kwarta, lokiec **7** garniec **9** kwarterka
of Portugal: 2 pe **4** bota, moio, vara **5** almud, fanga, geira, linha, milha **6** almude, covado **7** alquier, ferrado, selamin **8** alqueire
of Puerto Rico: 6 cuerda **10** cabelleria
of Rumania: 7 faitche
of Russia: 3 fut, lof **4** duim, fass, loof, pood, quar, stof **5** duime, foute,

korec, korek, ligne, osmin, pajak, st-off, stoof, vedro, verst **6** charka, liniya, osmina, paletz, sagene, stekar, tchast, tsarki, versta, verste **7** archine, arsheen, botchka, chkalik, garnetz, verchoc, verchok **8** boutylka, chetvert, krouchka, kroushka **9** chetverik **10** dessiatine **11** polugarnetz

of Scotland: 3 cop **4** boll, cran, fall, mile, peck, pint, rood, rope, span **5** crane, lippy **6** audlet, davach, firlot, lippie, noggin **7** chalder, choppin **8** mutchkin, stimpart, stimpert **9** particate, shaftment, shathmont

of Sicily: 5 salma **7** caffiso

of Sierra Leone: 4 load **6** kettle

of Somalia: 3 top **4** caba **5** chela, darat, tabla **6** cubito **8** parsalah

of South Africa: 4 vara

of Spain: 3 pie **4** codo, dedo, paso, vara **5** braza, cahiz, carga, legua, medio, palmo, sesma **6** cordel, cuarta, fanega, racion, yugada **7** azumbre, celemin, estadel, pulgada **8** fanegada

of Sri Lanka: 4 para, seer **5** parah **6** amunam, parrah

of Sudan: 2 ud

of Suriname: 7 ketting

of Sweden: 3 aln, fot, ref, tum **4** alar, amar, famn, kapp, last, stop **5** carat, foder, kanna, linje, nymil, spann **6** fathom, jumfru **7** oxhuvud, tunland **8** fjarding, koltunna, tunnland

of Switzerland: 3 imi, pot **4** aune, fuss, muid, pied, zoll **5** lieue, linie, maass, pouce, staab, toise **6** perche, strich **7** klafter, viertel **9** quarteron **10** holzlafter **11** holzklafter

of Syria: 5 makuk **6** garava

of Thailand: 2 wa **3** can, ken, niv, rai, sat, sok, wah **4** cohi, keup, niou, tang **5** kwien, leeng, sesti, vouah **6** kabiet, kanahn **7** chaimeu **8** changawn **9** anukabiet

of Tunisia: 3 saa **4** saah **5** cafiz **6** mettar **8** milerole

of Turkey: 3 dra, oka, pik **4** draa, khat, kile, zira **5** berri, kileh, zirai **6** arshin, chinik, fortin, halebi **7** nocktat

of Uruguay: 4 vara **6** cuadra, suerte

of Venezuela: 5 galon, milla **6** fanega **7** estadel

of Vietnam: 4 gang, phan, thon

of Wales: 5 cover **7** cantred, crannoc, listred

of Yugoslavia: 3 oka, rif **4** akov, ralo **5** donum, khvat, lanaz, plaze, stopa **6** motyka, ralico **9** danoranja

measured 5 equal, exact **6** steady **7** precise, regular, studied, uniform **8** verified **10** calculated, deliberate **11** cold-blooded, intentional, well-planned **12** premeditated **13** predetermined

Measure for Measure

author: 18 William Shakespeare
character: 5 Lucio **6** Angelo, Juliet **7** Claudio, Escalus, Mariana **8** Isabella **9** Vincentio

measureless 7 endless **8** infinite **9** boundless, unlimited **12** immeasurable

measurement 4 area, mass, size **5** depth, width **6** extent, height, length, volume, weight **7** breadth, content, gauging **8** capacity, plumbing, sounding **9** amplitude, appraisal, dimension, magnitude, measuring, reckoning, surveying **10** assessment, estimation, evaluation **11** mensuration

Biblical: 4 omer **5** cubit, ephah **6** shekel

champagne: 6 magnum **8** jeroboam, rehoboam **9** balthazar **10** methuselah, salmanazar **14** Nebuchadnezzar

cloth: 4 bolt

cotton: 4 bale

electricity: 3 ohm **4** volt, watt **5** joule **6** ampere **10** horsepower

energy: 3 BTU **5** joule **7** calorie **11** kilocalorie **18** British thermal unit

firewood: 4 cord

force: 4 dyne **6** newton **7** poundal

gold/jewelry: 5 carat, karat, point

Greek: 4 mina **5** cubit **6** obolos, talent **7** drachma, stadion

gun: 5 gauge **6** caliber

light: 7 candela **11** candlepower

liquor/spirits: 4 pint, pony, shot **5** fifth, quart **6** jigger, magnum

metric system: 5 liter, meter **9** deciliter, decimeter, dekaliter, dekameter, kiloliter, kilometer, nanometer **10** centiliter, centimeter, cubic meter, hectoliter, hectometer, milliliter, millimeter **11** square meter **14** cubic dekameter **15** cubic centimeter, cubic millimeter, square decimeter, square dekameter, square kilometer **16** square centimeter, square hectometer, square millimeter

metric weight: 3 ton **4** gram **5** tonne **7** quintal **8** dekagram, kilogram **9** centigram, hectogram, microgram, milligram

paper: 4 ream **5** quire

pressure: 6 pascal **10** atmosphere

Roman: 2 as **5** cubit, libra **6** pondus **7** stadium

sound: 7 decibel

temperature: 6 degree, Kelvin **7** Celsius **10** Fahrenheit

time: 3 day **4** hour, week, year **5** month, score **6** decade, minute, second **7** century **10** millennium, nanosecond **11** microsecond, millisecond

typography: 2 em, en **4** pica **5** point

unit: 3 cup, rod **4** acre, dram, foot, gill, inch, link, mile, peck, pint, yard **5** chain, minim, ounce, quart **6** barrel, bushel, circle, degree, fathom, gallon **7** furlong, hectare **8** angstrom, hogshead, teaspoon **9** cubic foot, cubic inch, cubic yard, square rod

10 fluid ounce, right angle, square foot, square inch, square mile, square yard, tablespoon **25** international nautical mile

weight: 3 ton **4** dram **5** grain, ounce, pound **7** scruple **8** short ton **9** ounce troy, pound troy **11** pennyweight **13** hundredweight

measure out 6 ration **7** dole out, mete out **9** apportion

meat 3 nut **4** core, fare, food, gist, grub **5** heart, point **6** kernel **7** edibles, essence, nucleus **8** victuals **9** provender, substance **10** provisions, sustenance **11** comestibles, nourishment

mechanic 6 joiner **7** artisan **9** automatic, craftsman, machinist **11** uninspired **12** grease monkey

mechanical 6 cold **7** routine **9** automatic, unfeeling **10** impersonal, self-acting, unthinking **11** instinctive, involuntary, machinelike, perfunctory, unconscious **13** machine-driven

mechanism 4 tool **5** motor, works **7** machine, utensil **9** apparatus, appliance, implement, machinery **10** instrument **11** contrivance

medal 5 award, honor, prize **6** laurel, reward, ribbon, trophy **8** citation **9** medallion **10** decoration

Medawar, Peter Brian
field: 7 biology
nationality: 7 British
discovered: 23 acquired immune tolerance
awarded: 10 Nobel Prize

meddle 5 mix in **6** butt in, horn in, kibitz **7** intrude, pry into **9** interfere, interlope, intervene **10** tamper with

meddler 3 pry **5** snoop **7** Paul Pry **8** busybody **10** interferer, Nosy Parker

meddlesome 4 nosy **5** pushy **6** prying, snoopy **7** pushing **8** meddling, snooping **9** intrusive, obtrusive, officious **11** impertinent, interfering **12** presumptuous

Medea
author: 9 Euripides
character: 5 Creon, Jason **6** Aegeus, Glauce

Medea
form: 9 sorceress
father: 6 Aeetes
mother: 5 Idyia
aunt: 5 Circe
brother: 8 Apsyrtus
sister: 9 Chalciope
lover: 5 Jason
son: 6 Medeus, Pheres **8** Mermerus, Tisander **9** Alcimenes, Thessalus
killed: 7 her sons
escaped to: 6 Athens

Medeus
father: 6 Aegeus
mother: 5 Medea

Media 14 ancient kingdom
present day: 4 Iran

capital: 8 Ecbatana
King: 6 Darius, Xerxes **9** Ahasueras
inhabitant: 4 Mede **5** Aryan **7** Persian **8** Parthian
media 5 press, radio **9** magazines **10** billboards, journalism, newspapers, television **11** journalists
singular: 6 medium
medial 4 mean **6** median **7** average
median 3 mid, par **4** mean, norm **5** mesne **6** center, medial, medium, middle **7** average, central, halfway **8** middling, midpoint, moderate **12** intermediate
mediate 6 pacify, step in, umpire **7** referee **8** moderate **9** arbitrate, intercede, interpose, intervene, negotiate, reconcile **10** conciliate, propitiate
mediation 6 parley **10** adjustment, com- promise, discussion **11** arbitration, give- and-take, negotiation, peacemaking **12** conciliation, intercession, intervention, pacification **14** reconciliation
mediator 6 umpire **7** referee **9** go-between, moderator **10** arbitrator, negotiator, peacemaker, reconciler **12** intermediary
medical 7 healing **8** curative, remedial, salutary, sanative **9** medicinal **10** medicative **11** restorative, therapeutic
medical abbreviation
  a c: 11 before meals
  ad lib: 8 as needed **9** as desired
  agit: 5 shake
  aq: 5 water
  b i d: 9 twice a day
  cap: 4 take **7** capsule
  coch: 8 spoonful
  dil: 6 dilute **8** dissolve
  fldxt: 12 fluid extract
  ft: 4 make
  ft mist: 12 make a mixture
  ft pulv: 11 make a powder
  gr: 5 grain
  gt: 4 drop
  gtt: 5 drops
  h s: 9 at bedtime
  in d: 5 daily
  lot: 6 lotion
  mod praesc: 21 in the manner prescribed
  O: 4 pint
  O D: 8 right eye
  O S: 7 left eye
  O U: 9 in each eye
  ol: 3 oil
  p c: 9 after food **10** after meals
  p o: 7 by mouth
  p r n: 25 as circumstances may require
  pil: 3 pill
  pulv: 6 powder
  q i d: 14 four times daily
  rep: 6 repeat
  s o s: 11 if necessary
  ss: 7 one half
  tab: 6 tablet
  t i d: 15 three times daily
  ut dict: 10 as directed
Medical Center
  character: 9 (Dr) Joe Gannon **11** Nurse Wilcox, (Dr) Paul Lochner **13** Nurse Chambers **14** Nurse Courtland, (Dr) Jeanne Bartlett
  cast: 9 James Daly **11** Chad Everett, Chris Hutson **12** Audrey Totter, Jayne Meadows **14** Corinne Camacho
medical practitioner 6 doctor, medico **9** physician
medication 4 balm **5** tonic **6** elixir, remedy **7** nostrum, panacea **8** medicine **10** medicament, palliative **11** restorative
Medici, Giovanni de' 8 Pope Leo X **15** Pope Leo the Tenth
Medici, Giulio 14 Pope Clement VII **21** Pope Clement the Seventh
medicine 4 balm, drug, pill **5** salve, tonic **6** remedy **7** nostrum **10** healing art, medication **11** restorative **12** therapeutics **13** materia medica
  god of: 9 Asclepius **11** Aesculapius
medieval 8 Dark Ages **10** antiquated, Middle Ages **12** old-fashioned **14** pre-Renaissance
mediocre 4 so-so **5** petty **6** common, meager, medium, normal, paltry, slight **7** average **8** inferior, ordinary, passable, trifling **9** tolerable **10** negligible, pedestrian, second-rate **11** commonplace, indifferent, unimportant **12** run-of-the-mill **13** inappreciable, insignificant **14** fair- to-middling, inconsiderable **15** inconsequential, undistinguished
mediocrity 8 poorness **9** pettiness **10** low-quality, meagerness, paltriness, triviality **11** inferiority **12** indifference, ordinariness, unimportance **14** insignificance **15** commonplaceness
meditate 4 muse, plan **5** aim at, study, think **6** devise, ponder **7** concoct, dream of, propose, reflect **8** cogitate, consider, contrive, mull over, ruminate **9** dwell upon **10** deliberate **11** contemplate
meditation 4 yoga **5** study **6** musing, poring **7** mulling, reverie, thought **8** brooding **9** discourse, pondering **10** cogitation, reflection, rumination **12** deliberation **13** consideration, contemplation
Mediterranean
  called by ancient Romans: 11 mare nostrum
  coast: 7 Riviera
  gulf: 5 Lions, Sidra, Tunis **7** Antalya, Catania, Taranto **8** Hammamet **9** Iskenderon
  island: 4 Elba **5** Capri, Corfu, Crete, Ibiza, Malta **6** Cyprus, Euboea, Lesbos, Rhodes, Sicily **7** Corsica, Majorca, Minorca **8** Balearic, Sardinia
  resort: 4 Nice **5** Capri **6** Cannes **7** Riviera **9** Cote d'Azur **10** Costa Brava
  river into: 2 Po **4** Ebro, Nile **5** Rhone
  sea: 5 Black **6** Aegean, Ionian **8** Adriatic, Ligurian **10** Tyrrhenian
  strait: 8 Bosporus **9** Bosphorus, Gibraltar **11** Dardanelles
  wind: 7 mistral, sirocco
medium 3 way **4** form, mean, mode, tool **5** means, organ **6** agency, avenue, common, milieu, normal **7** average, balance, channel, diviner, psychic, setting, vehicle **8** middling, moderate, ordinary **9** go-between, middle way, mid-course **10** atmosphere, compromise, golden mean, instrument, moderation **11** clairvoyant, environment, happy medium **12** crystal-gazer, intermediary, intermediate, middle ground, spiritualist, surroundings **13** fortuneteller **15** instrumentality
The Medium
  composer: 7 Menotti **5** opera
medley 4 hash, mess, olio **6** jumble, mosaic **7** farrago, melange, mixture **8** mishmash, pastiche **9** patchwork, potpourri **10** assortment, hodgepodge, miscellany **11** gallimaufry
Medon
  mentioned in: 5 Iliad **7** Odyssey
  father: 6 Oileus
  mother: 5 Rhene
  position: 6 herald
  friend of: 8 Penelope
  killed by: 6 Aeneas
medulla
  part of: 5 brain
  controls: 6 glands / muscles
Medusa
  form: 6 Gorgon
  father: 7 Phorcys
  mother: 4 Ceto
  sisters: 6 Graiae
  loved by: 8 Poseidon
  children: 7 Pegasus **8** Chrysaor
  sight of her caused people to turn to: 5 stone
  killed by: 7 Perseus
meek 4 mild **6** docile, gentle, humble, modest **8** lamblike, retiring, tolerant, yielding **9** compliant, spineless, tractable, weak-kneed **10** spiritless, submissive, unas- suming **11** acquiescent, complaisant, deferential, unassertive, unresisting **13** long-suffering, tenderhearted, unpretentious
meekness 7 pliancy, shyness **8** docility, humility **9** passivity **10** diffidence, humbleness **11** bashfulness **13** nonresistance **14** self-effacement
meet 3 apt, fit **4** abut, face, good, heed, obey **5** cross, equal, greet, match, rally, right **6** adjoin, answer, border, follow, gather, muster, proper, seemly **7** abide by, collect, convene,

execute, fitting, fulfill, observe, perform, respect, run into, satisfy, welcome **8** assemble, becoming, bump into, confront, converge, decorous, opposite, relevant, suitable **9** agreeable, allowable, befitting, congruous, discharge, encounter, intersect, permitted, pertinent **10** admissable, comply with, congregate, felicitous **11** acknowledge, appropriate, permissible **12** come together

meet eye to eye 4 face **8** confront, face up to **11** meet vis- a-vis

meet halfway 6 settle **9** make a deal **10** compromise **11** come to terms **14** strike a bargain **18** split the difference

meet head on 4 face **5** crash **6** oppose **7** collide, crack up **8** confront, face up to **9** challenge, encounter

meeting 4 date **5** group, tryst **6** caucus **7** council **8** assembly, conclave, congress **9** encounter, gathering **10** conference, convention, engagement, rendezvous **11** assignation, convocation, get-together **12** introduction, presentation **13** confrontation

Meeting at Telgte
   author: **11** Gunter Grass

meeting of the minds 7 concert, concord, harmony **9** agreement **11** concordance **13** understanding

meeting place 5 mecca **10** focal point, rendezvous

Meet Me in St Louis
   director: **16** Vincente Minnelli
   cast: **8** Leon Ames, Tom Drake **9** Mary Astor **11** Judy Garland **12** June Lockhart, Marjorie Main **13** Lucille Bremer **14** Margaret O'Brien
   song: **11** Trolley Song **14** The Boy Next Door **33** Have Yourself a Merry Little Christmas

Meet the Press
   moderator: **9** Ned Brooks **10** Bill Monroe **11** Edwin Newman **14** Lawrence Spivak, Martha Rountree

meet with 4 meet **6** endure **7** undergo **8** come upon **9** encounter **10** come across, experience

Mefitis
   also: **8** Mephitis
   prevented: **5** winds
   kind of winds: **7** harmful

Megaera
   member of: **6** Furies

Megamede
   husband: **12** King Thespius
   number of daughters: **5** fifty

Megara
   father: **5** Creon
   husband: **8** Hercules
   son: **11** Therimachus

Mehuman 6 eunuch

Mein Kampf
   author: **11** Adolf Hitler
   means: **7** my fight **8** my battle

Meitner, Lise
   field: **7** physics
   nationality: **8** Austrian
   collaborator: **8** Otto Hahn
   contributed to: **21** atomic bomb development
   discovered: **12** protactinium **16** fission of uranium

Melaenis
   epithet of: **9** Aphrodite
   means: **5** black

melancholia 7 despair **10** depression, desolation, melancholy **11** despondency

melancholy 4 blue, glum **5** blues, dumps, gloom, moody **6** dismal, dreary, gloomy, mopish, morose, somber **7** despair, doleful, forlorn, joyless, unhappy **8** dejected, desolate, doldrums, dolorous, downcast, funereal, mournful **9** cheerless, dejection, depressed, heartsick, moodiness, plaintive **10** calamitous, depressing, depression, despondent, dispirited, gloominess, low spirits **11** despondency, discouraged, downhearted, forlornness, languishing, melancholia, sick at heart, unfortunate **12** disconsolate, heavyhearted **14** down in the dumps, down in the mouth **16** disconsolateness
   French: **6** triste **9** tristesse

melange 3 mix **4** olio **6** jumble, medley **7** mixture **8** compound, mishmash, pastiche **9** pasticcio, patchwork, potpourri **10** assemblage, assortment, hodgepodge, miscellany **11** gallimaufry

Melanippe
   form: **4** foal
   foal born to: **6** Euippe
   transformed into: **4** Arne, girl
   father: **4** Ares
   queen of: **7** Amazons

Melanosaurus
   type: **8** dinosaur
   period: **8** Triassic

Melba, Nellie
   title: **4** dame
   born: **9** Australia
   voice: **7** soprano
   named for her: **10** Melba toast, Peach melba

Melbourne
   bay: **7** Hobson's **11** Port Phillip
   landmark: **20** Flemington Racecourse
   river: **5** Yarra **6** Plenty **9** Mary Creek, Patterson **11** Maribyrnong **12** Diamond Creek **13** Kororoit Creek **14** Dandenong Creek, Gardiner's Creek **16** Moonee Ponds Creek
   state: **8** Victoria
   university: **6** Monash **7** La Trobe

Melchizedek
   means: **19** king of righteousness
   hometown: **5** Salem
   contemporary: **7** Abraham

meld 3 mix **4** fuse, join **5** blend, merge, unite **6** jumble, mingle **7** combine **8** coalesce, intermix, scramble **9** commingle **10** amalgamate, intertwine, interweave **11** consolidate, incorporate, intermingle

Meleager
   father: **4** Ares **6** Oeneus
   mother: **7** Althaea
   uncle: **9** Plexippus
   slew: **14** Calydonian boar
   loved: **8** Atalanta
   killed: **15** mother's brothers
   sisters: **11** Meleagrides

melee 3 row **4** fray, riot **5** brawl, scrap, set-to **6** fracas, rumpus, tussle **7** scuffle **8** disorder, dogfight **9** commotion, fistfight **10** free-for-all **11** altercation, pandemonium

Meliad
   form: **5** nymph
   nymph of: **6** flocks **10** fruit trees

mellifluous 4 soft **5** sweet **6** dulcet, mellow, smooth **7** musical **8** resonant **9** full-toned, melodious **10** euphonious, harmonious, sweet-toned **13** sweet-sounding

Mellors
   character in: **20** Lady Chatterley's Lover
   author: **8** Lawrence

mellow 4 rich, ripe, soft **5** drunk, sweet **6** mature, season, soften **7** matured, relaxed **8** luscious, tolerant **9** delicious **10** full-bodied **11** sympathetic **12** full-flavored **13** compassionate, understanding

mellowness 8 full body, fullness, maturity, richness, ripeness, softness **9** tolerance **10** compassion, smoothness **12** lusciousness, pleasantness

melodic 5 lyric **7** tuneful

melodious 4 rich, soft **5** clear, lyric, sweet **6** dulcet, mellow, smooth **7** melodic, musical, ringing, tuneful **8** resonant **9** full-toned **10** euphonious, sweet-toned **11** mellifluent, mellifluous

melodrama 9 theatrics **12** emotionalism **13** theatricality

melodramatic 5 corny, hammy, hokey, stagy **7** maudlin, mawkish **8** cornball, frenzied **10** flamboyant, histrionic **11** exaggerated, overwrought, sensational, sentimental, spectacular **13** overemotional

melody 3 air **4** aria, song, tune **5** ditty, theme **6** ballad, strain, timbre **7** concord, euphony **10** musicality **11** tunefulness **12** mellifluence **13** melodiousness **14** harmoniousness **15** mellifluousness

melon
   varieties: **4** pear **5** mango, snake, stink **6** casaba, citron, Dudaim, netted, nutmeg, orange, winter **7** Persian, serpent **8** honeydew

Melpomene
  member of: **5** Muses
  personifies: **7** tragedy

melt 4 fade, fuse, pass, thaw **5** blend, merge, shade, touch **6** affect, disarm, dispel, soften, vanish **7** appease, dwindle, liquefy, mollify, scatter **8** dissolve **9** disappear, dissipate, evaporate, waste away **10** arouse pity, conciliate, propitiate

melt away 5 dry up **8** vaporize **9** evaporate

Melville, Herman
  author of: **4** Omoo **5** Mardi, Typee **7** Redburn **8** Moby Dick **9** Billy Budd **12** Benito Cereno **16** The Confidence Man **20** Bartleby the Scrivener

Melville, Julia
  character in: **9** The Rivals
  author: **8** Sheridan

Melvin and Howard
  director: **13** Jonathan Demme
  cast: **9** Paul LeMat **12** Jason Robards **15** Mary Steenburgen
  Oscar for: **6** script **17** supporting actress (Steenburgen)

member 3 arm, leg, toe **4** foot, hand, limb, part, tail, wing **5** bough, digit, organ, piece, shoot **6** branch, finger, pinion **7** element, portion, section, segment **8** fragment **9** appendage, component, extremity **10** ingredient **11** constituent

member
  of the bar: **4** beak **7** counsel **8** advocate, attorney **9** barrister, counselor **10** mouthpiece **12** legal advisor **13** attorney-at-law
  of a crew: **4** hand, mate **6** ensign, ganger, gunner, purser, yeoman **7** bowsman, oarsman, steward, swabbie **8** cabin boy, coxswain, deckhand, helmsman **9** first mate, navigator
  of faculty: **3** don, PhD **4** prof **5** tutor **6** doctor, master **7** teacher **8** lecturer **9** professor **10** instructor
  of family: **3** son **4** aunt **5** niece, uncle **6** cousin, father, mother, nephew, sister **7** brother **8** daughter, grandson **11** grandfather, grandmother **13** granddaughter
  of legislature: **4** whip **6** deputy **7** senator, speaker **8** delegate, lawmaker **10** legislator, politician **11** congressman **12** congresswoman **14** representative
  of religious order: **3** nun **4** dame, monk **5** Clare, friar, priest **6** father, hermit, Jesuit, sister **7** Alexian, ascetic, brother, Cluniac, Templar **8** Capuchin, cenobite, minister, Trappist **9** Carmelite, Dominican **10** Carthusian, Cistercian, Franciscan **11** Augustinian, Benedictine **14** mother superior

Member of the Wedding, The
  author: **15** Carson McCullers
  character: **6** Jarvis **11** Janice Evans **13** Frankie Addams, John Henry West **16** Honey Camden Brown **18** Berenice Sadie Brown

membership 4 club **6** league, roster **7** company, society **9** community, personnel **10** connection, fellowship, fraternity **11** affiliation, association, brotherhood

membrane 3 web **4** film, skin **6** lining, sheath **7** coating **8** envelope, pellicle **9** thin sheet **10** integument

memento 5 favor, relic, token **6** record, trophy **8** keepsake, memorial, reminder, souvenir **11** memorabilia, remembrance **12** remembrancer **13** commemoration

memento mori 23 remember that thou must die **31** object serving as a reminder of death

Memnon
  origin: **8** Oriental **9** Ethiopian
  father: **8** Tithonus
  mother: **3** Eos **4** Dawn
  brother: **8** Emathion
  companions: **10** Memnonides
  fought with: **7** Trojans
  killed by: **8** Achilles
  made immortal by: **4** Zeus
  commemorated with: **11** giant statue at: **6** Thebes

Memnonides see **6** Memnon

memo
  French: **11** aide memoire

memoir 4 life **5** diary **7** journal **9** biography, life story **10** adventures **11** confessions, experiences, reflections **13** autobiography, recollections, reminiscences

Memoirs of a Dutiful Daughter
  author: **16** Simone de Beauvoir

memorabilia 6 papers **7** records **8** archives **9** documents

memorable 6 famous **7** eminent, notable, salient **8** historic, stirring, striking **9** important, momentous, prominent, red-letter **10** celebrated, impressive, noteworthy, remarkable **11** illustrious, outstanding, significant **13** distinguished, extraordinary, unforgettable

memorandum 4 memo, note **5** brief **6** agenda, minute, record **7** jotting **8** reminder **11** brief report, list of items

memorial 6 homage **7** tribute **8** monument **10** monumental **11** testimonial **13** commemorative

memorialization 11 celebration **13** commemoration

memorialize 4 mark **5** honor

9 celebrate **11** commemorate, pay homage to **12** pay tribute to

memory 4 fame, mark, name, note **5** glory, honor, token **6** esteem, recall, regard, renown, repute **7** memento, respect **8** eminence, keepsake, memorial, prestige, reminder, souvenir **10** estimation, reputa- tion **11** distinction, remembering, remembrance, testimonial **12** recollection, remembrancer, reminiscence **13** commemoration
  goddess of: **9** Mnemosyne

Memphis
  football team: **9** Showboats

menace 3 cow **4** risk **5** bully, daunt, peril **6** danger, hazard, threat **7** imperil, pitfall, portend, presage, terrify **8** browbeat, endanger, forebode, jeopardy, threaten **9** terrorize **10** intimidate, jeopardize **11** be a hazard to, imperilment **12** endangerment

menacing 7 hostile **9** dangerous **11** belligerent, threatening, treacherous **12** antagonistic

menage a trois 9 threesome **16** household of three

Menander
  author of: **5** Heros **13** Perikeiromene **14** The Arbitration, The Misanthrope **16** The Rape of the Lock

Men at Arms
  author: **11** Evelyn Waugh

Mencken, H L
  author of: **10** Prejudices **19** The American Language
  editor of: **10** The Mercury **11** The Smart Set
  coined word: **9** booboisie, eclysiast

mend 3 fix **4** cure, darn, heal, knit **5** amend, emend, patch **6** better, reform, remedy, repair, revise **7** correct, improve, rectify, restore, retouch, touch up **8** overhaul, renovate **9** meliorate **10** ameliorate **11** recondition

mendacious 5 false, lying **8** spurious **9** deceptive **10** misleading, untruthful

mendacity 5 fraud, lying **6** deceit **7** falsity, perfidy **9** chicanery, deception, duplicity, falsehood, hypocrisy **10** dishonesty **11** insincerity **13** double-dealing, falsification, prevarication **14** untruthfulness **17** misrepresentation

Mendel, Gregor Johann
  field: **6** botany
  nationality: **8** Austrian
  discovered: **14** laws of heredity
  founded: **8** genetics

Mendeleyev (Mendeleev), Dimitri Ivanovich
  field: **9** chemistry
  nationality: **7** Russian
  devised: **11** periodic law **13** periodic table

Mendelssohn, (Jakob Ludwig) Felix
  born: **7** Germany, Hamburg
  composer of: **6** Elijah, St Paul

7 Athalie, Italian (symphony No 4), Lorelei, Ruy Blas **8** Antigone, Scottish (symphony No 3) **11** Reformation (symphony No 5), The Hebrides **12** Hymn of Praise (symphony No 2) **17** Songs without Words **21** A Midsummer Night's Dream

mendicant 6 beggar **10** alms-seeker, panhandler

Mending Wall
   author: **11** Robert Frost

Menelaus
   king of: **6** Sparta
   father: **6** Atreus
   mother: **6** Aerope
   brother: **9** Agamemnon
   wife: **5** Helen
   son: **11** Megapenthes, Nicostratus
   daughter: **8** Hermione

mene mene tekel upharsin 20 handwriting on the wall **30** numbered numbered weighed divided
   foretells destruction of: **10** Belshazzar
   from Biblical book of: **6** Daniel

menhaden 4 pogy **5** pogie **6** bunker **7** alewife, bugfish, ellfish, fatback, herring, oldwife, sardine **8** bonyfish, hardhead, ladyfish **10** mossbunker

menial 3 low **4** mean **5** drone, lowly, slave, toady **6** abject, drudge, flunky, helper, humble, lackey **7** fawning, ignoble, servant, servile, slavish **8** cringing, employee **9** degrading, groveling, sycophant, truckling, underling **10** apprentice, obsequious **11** bootlicking, subordinate, subservient, sycophantic

menial labor 4 toil **5** grind **8** drudgery

Menjou, Adolphe
   born: **12** Pittsburgh PA
   roles: **9** Golden Boy, Pollyanna **11** A Star Is Born **12** The Front Page **13** A Woman of Paris **15** A Farewell to Arms, State of the Union **16** Little Miss Marker **18** A Bill of Divorcement

Mennonite 4 sect
   oppose: **15** military service
   favor: **10** plain dress
   kin to: **5** Amish

meno
   music: **4** less

Menominee, Menomini, Menomonie
   language family: **9** Algonkian **10** Algonquian
   location: **4** Ohio **7** Indiana **8** Illinois, Michigan **9** Wisconsin

menorah 11 candelabrum, candlestick **12** candleholder
   number of candles: **5** seven

Menotti, Gian-Carlo
   born: **5** Italy **10** Cadigliano
   composer of: **9** The Consul, The Medium **12** The Island God, The Tele-

phone **19** Amelia Goes to the Ball **24** Amahl and the Night Visitors

mens sana in corpore sano 22 a sound mind in a sound body

mental 5 crazy, nutty **6** insane, psycho **7** cracked, lunatic, psychic **8** abstract, cerebral, neurotic, rational **9** disturbed, in the mind, of the mind, psychotic **10** disordered, subjective, unbalanced **11** intelligent, mentally ill **12** intellectual, metaphysical **13** psychological

mental application 9 diligence **10** absorption, intentness **11** deep thought, engrossment, fixed regard **13** concentration **14** close attention

mental disorder 5 quirk **6** lunacy, oddity **7** madness **8** delusion, insanity, neurosis **9** craziness, psychosis **10** aberration **11** abnormality, derangement, mental lapse, peculiarity, strangeness **12** eccentricity, idiosyncrasy **13** schizophrenia **15** manic depression

mental hospital 6 asylum **8** madhouse **11** institution

mental institution 6 asylum **8** madhouse **9** funny farm **12** insane asylum

mentality 4 mind **6** acumen, brains, wisdom **8** judgment, sagacity **9** intellect **10** gray matter, perception **11** discernment **12** intelligence, perspicacity

mental lapse 5 quirk **6** lunacy, oddity **7** madness **8** rambling, straying **9** wandering **10** aberration **11** derangement, peculiarity **12** eccentricity **13** forgetfulness

mentally incapable
   Latin: **15** non compos mentis

mentally sound
   Latin: **12** compos mentis

mention 3 say **4** cite, hint, name, tell **5** imply, state **6** hint at, notice, remark, report, tell of **7** comment, divulge, inkling, narrate, observe, recount, refer to, specify **8** allude to, allusion, disclose, intimate **9** insinuate, make known, reference, statement, touch upon, utterance **10** advisement, indication, suggestion **11** designation, insinuation, observation **12** acquaintance, announcement, notification **13** communication, enlightenment, specification

mentor 4 guru **5** guide, tutor **6** master **7** adviser, monitor, proctor, teacher **9** counselor, preceptor, professor **10** instructor

Mentor
   advisor of: **8** Odysseus
   educated: **10** Telemachus

Mephibosheth
   father: **8** Jonathan
   also called: **9** Meribbaal
   grandfather: **4** Saul
   son: **5** Micha

Mephistopheles
   character in: **5** Faust
   author: **6** Goethe

Mephitis *see* **7** Mefitis

mer 3 sea

Merab
   father: **4** Saul
   sister: **6** Michal
   brother-in-law: **5** David

mercantile 5 trade **8** business **10** commercial **16** buying-and-selling

mercantilism 5 trade **8** business, commerce, exchange **13** commercialism

Mercedes
   character in: **21** The Count of Monte Cristo
   author: **5** Dumas (pere)

mercenary 5 venal **6** for pay, greedy **7** for gain, selfish **8** covetous, grasping, hireling, monetary **10** avaricious **11** acquisitive, paid soldier **12** hired soldier

merchandise 4 sell **5** goods, stock, trade, wares **6** deal in, market **7** effects, staples **8** huckster **9** advertise, publicize, traffic in **10** belongings, buy and sell, distribute **11** commodities **12** stock in trade

merchant 6 broker, dealer, hawker, jobber, monger, trader, vendor **7** peddler **8** chandler, retailer, salesman **9** purchaser, tradesman **10** saleswoman, shopkeeper, wholesaler **11** storekeeper, tradeswoman

Merchant of Venice, The
   author: **18** William Shakespeare
   character: **6** Portia **7** Antonio, Jessica, Lorenzo, Nerissa, Shylock **8** Bassanio, Gratiano

merci 8 thank you

merci beaucoup 16 thank you very much

merciful 4 kind **6** benign, humane, tender **7** clement, feeling, lenient, pitying, sparing **8** gracious **9** forgiving **10** beneficent **11** kindhearted, softhearted, sympathetic **13** compassionate, understanding

merciless 4 fell **5** cruel, harsh **6** fierce, severe **7** callous, inhuman **8** inhumane, pitiless, ruthless **9** ferocious, heartless, unpitying, unsparing **10** relentless, unmerciful **11** cold-blooded, hardhearted, remorseless, unrelenting

Mercouri, Melina
   husband: **11** Jules Dassin
   born: **6** Athens, Greece
   roles: **7** Topkapi **10** Gaily Gaily **13** Never on Sunday **15** Once Is Not Enough

mercurial 6 fickle, lively, mobile **7** erratic, flighty, kinetic, protean **8** electric, spirited, unstable, variable, volatile **9** impetuous, impulsive **10** capricious, changeable, inconstant

11 fluctuating **13** irrepressible, unpredictable

mercury
chemical symbol: **2** Hg

Mercury
origin: **5** Roman
messenger of: **4** gods
god of: **7** science, thieves **8** commerce **9** eloquence
corresponds to: **6** Hermes, Ogmios

Mercutio
character in: **14** Romeo and Juliet
author: **11** Shakespeare

mercy 4 pity **5** grace **6** lenity **7** charity **8** blessing, clemency, humanity, kindness, lenience, leniency, sympathy **9** good thing, tolerance **10** compassion, humaneness, lucky break **11** benevolence, forbearance, forgiveness, piece of luck **13** commiseration, fellow feeling **15** softheartedness **17** tenderheartedness
Latin: **12** misericordia

Mercy seat see **16** Ark of the Covenant

Merdle
character in: **12** Little Dorrit
author: **7** Dickens

mere 4 bald, bare, sole **5** plain, scant, sheer, utter **6** common, paltry **7** mundane **8** nugatory, ordinary, trifling **10** negligible, uneventful **11** commonplace, unmitigated **13** insignificant, unappreciable **14** inconsiderable

mere 6 mother

Meredith, Burgess
wife: **15** Paulette Goddard
born: **11** Cleveland OH
roles: **5** Magic, Rocky **6** Batman (the Penguin) **7** Madame X **8** Foul Play **12** Hurry Sundown, Of Mice and Men **15** Magnificent Doll, Such Good Friends **16** Advise and Consent

Meredith, George
author of: **9** The Egoist **10** Modern Love **14** Evan Harrington **16** Beauchamp's Career **19** Diana of the Crossways **25** The Ordeal of Richard Feverel

merely 3 but **4** just, only **5** quite **6** barely, in part, purely, simply, solely **7** utterly **8** scarcely, wholly **10** absolutely

meretricious 4 mock, sham **5** bogus, false, phony **6** pseudo, shoddy, tawdry **8** delusive, specious, spurious **9** deceptive, fraudulent, misleading **11** counterfeit

merge 4 fuse, join, weld **5** blend, unify, unite **6** link up **7** combine **8** coalesce, converge, intermix **9** associate, become one, integrate, interfuse, interlock **10** amalgamate, synthesize **11** confederate, consolidate **12** band together, interconnect

mergence 3 mix **5** blend **7** merging,

mixture **8** mingling **10** concoction **11** combination

Mergenthaler, Ottmar
nationality: **8** American
invented: **8** linotype

merger 5 union **7** wedding **8** marriage **9** coalition **12** amalgamation **13** confederation, consolidation

meridian 3 tip, top **4** acme, apex, brow, peak **5** crest, crown, point, ridge **6** apogee, climax, summit, vertex, zenith **7** heights **8** pinnacle **11** culmination

Merimee, Prosper
author of: **6** Carmen **7** Colomba

merit 4 earn, rate **5** value, worth **6** credit, desert, invite, prompt, talent, virtue **7** ability, benefit, deserve, quality, stature, warrant **8** efficacy **9** advantage **10** be worthy of, excellence, worthiness **11** distinction **12** be entitled to, have a right to **13** justification

merited 3 due **5** rated **6** earned **8** deserved, rightful

meritorious 4 fine **6** worthy **8** laudable **9** admirable, estimable, excellent, exemplary **10** creditable, noteworthy **11** commendable, exceptional **12** praiseworthy

Mermaid Tycoon
nickname of: **14** Esther Williams

Merman, Ethel
real name: **20** Ethel Agnes Zimmermann
husband: **14** Ernest Borgnine
born: **9** Astoria NY
autobiography: **6** Merman
roles: **11** Call Me Madam **12** Anything Goes, Panama Hattie **15** Annie Get Your Gun **16** Stage Door Canteen **21** Alexander's Ragtime Band

Mermerus
father: **5** Jason
mother: **5** Medea

Merope
member of: **8** Pleiades
father: **5** Atlas **8** Oenopion
husband: **7** Polybus **8** Sisyphus **11** Cresphontes, Polyphontes
son: **7** Aepytus
raped by: **5** Orion
raised: **7** Oedipus

merrily 5 gaily **6** gladly **7** briskly, happily, lightly, lustick, quickly **8** blithely, jocundly, jovially, joyfully, joyously **9** festively, gleefully **10** cheerfully, laughingly, mirthfully **11** hilariously, vivaciously **14** lightheartedly

Merrimac see **9** Pennacook

merriment 3 fun **4** glee **5** cheer, mirth **6** frolic, gaiety, hoopla, levity **7** good fun, jollity, revelry, whoopee **8** hilarity, laughter **9** amusement, festivity, good humor, jocundity, joviality **10** jocularity, jubilation, liveliness, skylarking **11** celebration, gleefulness,

good spirits, merrymaking **12** conviviality, exhilaration, sportiveness **16** lightheartedness

Merriweather, Mrs
character in: **15** Gone With the Wind
author: **8** Mitchell

merry 3 gay **5** happy, jolly **6** blithe, cheery, jocund, jovial, joyous, lively **7** festive, gleeful, jocular **8** animated, carefree, cheerful, gladsome, laughing, mirthful, partying, reveling, sportive **9** convivial, fun-loving, sprightly, vivacious **10** frolicsome, rollicking, skylarking **12** high-spirited, lighthearted

merrymaking 5 sport **6** frolic, gaiety, hoopla, revels **7** jollity, revelry, whoopee **8** carousal **9** festivity, funmaking, high jinks, merriment, rejoicing, whoop-de-do **10** saturnalia **11** bacchanalia, celebration, festivities **12** conviviality

Merry Wives of Windsor, The
author: **18** William Shakespeare
character: **4** Ford, Page **5** Caius **6** Doctor, Fenton **7** Slender **8** Anne Page **12** Mistress Ford, Mistress Page **15** Mistress Quickly, Sir John Falstaff

mesa 4 hill, peak **5** bench, butte, table **7** plateau, terrace **9** cartouche, tableland

Mescalero
language family: **6** Apache
location: **6** Mexico **9** New Mexico
related to: **5** Lipan **10** Chiricahua

mesh 3 fib, net, web **4** grid, jibe **5** agree, sieve, tally **6** engage, enmesh, grille, plexus, screen **7** connect, engaged, netting, network, webbing, webwork **8** dovetail, interact, lacework, meshwork, openwork **9** grillwork, interlock, inter-mesh **10** coordinate, correspond, interweave, wickerwork **11** fit together, latticework **12** reticulation

Meshach
former name: **7** Mishael
companion: **6** Daniel
friend: **8** Abednego, Shadrach

Mesmer, Franz (Friedrich) Anton
nationality: **6** German
developed: **8** hypnosis

mesmerize 5 charm **7** bewitch **8** enthrall, entrance **9** fascinate, hypnotize, magnetize, spellbind, transport

Mesopotamian mythology
god of agriculture/earth: **5** Dagan
corresponds to Phoenician: **5** Dagon

Mesquakie see **3** Fox

mess 3 fix **4** hash, stew **5** mix-up, pinch **6** crisis, jumble, litter, muddle, pickle, plight, scrape, strait **7** clutter, dilemma, trouble **8** disarray, disorder, hot water, mess hall, mishmash, quandary **9** cafeteria, confusion, imbroglio, refectory, situation **10** commissary, difficulty, dining hall, dining room, hodgepodge **11** predicament **14** conglomeration

message 4 news, note, word **5** moral, point, theme **6** letter, notice, report **7** meaning, missive, purport, tidings **8** bulletin, dispatch **9** statement **10** communique, memorandum **12** intelligence **13** communication

mess around with 4 test **6** try out **8** fool with, play with **10** tinker with **14** experiment with

messenger 5 envoy **6** bearer, runner **7** carrier, courier **8** delegate, emissary **9** deliverer, go-between **11** delivery boy, delivery man **12** intermediary

messenger of gods 4 Iris **6** Hermes **7** Mercury

Messiaen, Olivier Eugene Prosper Charles
   born: 6 France **7** Avignon
   composer of: 11 Exotic Birds, Turangalila **13** Chronochromie **20** Le Nativite du Seigneur **22** Quartet for the End of Time **27** Vingt Regards sur l'Enfant Jesus **33** Et exspecto resurrectionem mortuorum **41** Transfiguration de Notre Seigneur Jesus Christ

Messiah
   means: 11 anointed one
   see also **10** Jesus

Messick, Dale
   creator/artist of: 19 Brenda Starr Reporter

messiness 5 chaos, mix-up, upset **6** jumble **7** clutter **8** disarray, disorder, scramble, shambles **9** confusion **10** disharmony, sloppiness, untidiness **12** dishevelment **14** disarrangement **15** disorganization

mess up 3 mar **4** goof, muff, ruin **5** botch, spoil **6** bungle, foul up, jumble **7** blunder, butcher, disturb, do badly, louse up, screw up **9** mismanage **10** disarrange **11** disorganize, make a mess of, make an error **12** make a mistake

messy 4 ugly **6** blowsy, frowsy, grubby, sloppy, tricky, untidy **7** awkward, chaotic, jumbled, tangled, unkempt **8** confused, littered **9** cluttered, difficult **10** bedraggled, disheveled, disordered, slatternly, topsy-turvy, unenviable, unpleasant **11** disarranged **12** embarrassing, inextricable **13** uncomfortable

mesto
   music: 8 mournful

metal
   alloy: 5 brass, monel **6** bronze, nickel, niello, pewter, solder
   bar: 3 gad **4** risp **5** ingot
   bolt: 5 rivet
   box: 8 canister
   casting: 3 peg
   classification: 5 light, noble **6** alkali, common **7** coinage **8** platinum, precious **9** rare earth **10** low-melting,

refractory, transition **11** high-melting **14** semiconductors
   clippings: 7 scissel
   coarse: 5 matte
   corrosion: 4 rust
   crude: 3 ore **4** slug
   cymbals: 3 tal
   deposit: 4 lode, vein
   design: 7 chasing
   disk or plate: 4 shim **5** medal, paten **6** platen, sequin
   eyelet: 7 grommet
   filings: 5 lemel
   god of: 6 Vulcan **10** Hephaestus
   heaviest: 6 osmium
   kind: 3 tin **4** gold, iron, lead, zinc **6** barium, cerium, cesium, copper, erbium, nickel, osmium, radium, silver, sodium **7** arsenic, bismuth, calcium, holmium, iridium, lithium, rhodium, silicon, terbium, thulium **8** actinium, aluminum, antimony, europium, lutetium, platinum, rubidium, samarium, selenium, titanium, tungsten **9** beryllium, magnesium, palladium, potassium, ruthenium, strontium **10** molybdenum, phosphorus
   layer: 7 plating
   leaf: 4 foil
   lightest: 7 lithium
   liquid: 7 mercury
   mass: 3 pid **5** ingot **7** bullion
   piece: 4 jack, slug
   refuse: 4 slag **5** dross
   shaper: 5 swage
   suit: 4 mail **5** armor **6** armour
   thread: 4 lame, wire
   trademark: 5 monel
   ware: 4 tole **6** Revere
   worker: 5 smith **6** forger, welder **7** armorer, riveter **8** armourer **9** goldsmith, ironsmith **10** blacksmith **11** coppersmith, silversmith **12** metallurgist

Metalious, Grace
   author of: 11 Peyton Place

metalworking
   god of: 6 Vulcan **10** Hephaestus, Hephaistos

metamorphose 6 change, mutate **7** convert **9** transform **11** transfigure

Metamorphoses
   author: 4 Ovid

metamorphosis 8 mutation **10** alteration, conversion **11** permutation **12** change of form, modification **13** radical change, transmutation **14** transformation **15** series of changes, startling change, transfiguration **18** transmogrification

Metamorphosis, The
   author: 10 Franz Kafka

metaphor 5 image, trope **6** simile **7** analogy **8** metonymy, parallel **11** equivalence **14** figure of speech, representation

metaphysical 5 basic, lofty, vague

6 far-out **7** eternal **8** abstract, abstruse, esoteric, mystical, ultimate **9** essential, high-flown, recondite, universal **10** impalpable, intangible, jesuitical, oversubtle **11** existential, fundamental, ontological, speculative **12** cosmological, intellectual, unanswerable **13** philosophical **15** epistemological

Metaphysics
   author: 9 Aristotle

metaxa
   type: 6 brandy **7** liqueur
   origin: 6 Greece

mete, mete out 5 allot **6** assign, divide **7** deal out, dole out **8** allocate, disburse, dispense **9** apportion, parcel out **10** administer, distribute, measure out

meteoric 4 fast **5** fiery, rapid, swift **6** speedy, sudden **7** blazing, flaming, instant **8** flashing, unabated **10** inexorable **11** ineluctable, unstoppable

meter
   abbreviation: 1 m

method 3 way **4** form, mode, plan, tack **5** means, order, style, usage **6** course, design, manner, scheme, system **7** fashion, formula, process, program, purpose, routine **8** approach, efficacy **9** procedure, technique, viability **13** modus operandi

methodical, methodic 4 neat, tidy **5** exact **7** careful, logical, orderly, precise, regular, uniform **10** analytical, deliberate, meticulous, systematic **12** businesslike **13** well-regulated

methodization 5 order **11** arrangement **12** organization **14** categorization, classification **15** systematization

methodize 5 order **7** arrange **8** classify, organize **11** systematize

Methuselah
   father: 5 Enoch
   son: 6 Lamech
   years lived: 23 nine hundred and sixty-nine
   known as: 9 oldest man

meticulous 4 nice **5** exact, fussy **7** finical, finicky, precise **8** exacting, sedulous **10** fastidious, particular, scrupulous **11** painstaking, punctilious **13** conscientious, perfectionist

meticulousness 4 care **5** pains **12** sedulousness, thoroughness **14** fastidiousness, scrupulousness **17** conscientiousness

metier 3 job **4** area, line, work **5** craft, field, forte, trade **7** calling, pursuit **8** activity, business, lifework, province, vocation **9** specialty **10** employment, livelihood, occupation, profession

meting out 8 alloting **9** bestowing, doling out **10** allocating, conferring, consigning, dealing out, dispensing **11** designating **12** apportioning, distributing, measuring out

Metis
  member of: **6** Titans
  father: **7** Oceanus
  mother: **6** Tethys
  consort of: **4** Zeus
  daughter: **6** Athena
Metropolis
  director: **9** Fritz Lang
  cast: **10** Alfred Abel **12** Brigitte Helm
metropolitan area 4 city **8** core city, downtown, environs **9** inner city, precincts, urban area **10** city limits, metropolis **11** central city **16** business district
mettle 3 vim **4** grit, guts **5** nerve, pluck, spunk, valor, vigor **6** spirit **7** bravery, courage, heroism **8** audacity, backbone, boldness, gameness, temerity **9** derring-do, fortitude, gallantry, manliness **10** enthusiasm, resolution **11** intrepidity **12** fearlessness **13** determination
mettlesome 4 bold, edgy **5** brave, fiery **6** ardent, plucky, spunky **7** gingery, peppery **8** restless, skittish, spirited **9** excitable, impatient **10** courageous, high-strung **12** high-spirited
Mexica *see* **5** Aztec
Mexico
  other name: **8** New Spain
  capital/largest city: **10** Mexico City
  others: **4** Leon **5** La Paz, Taxco **6** Cancun, Celaya, Merida, Oaxaca, Puebla, Toluca **7** Durango, Guaymas, Tampico, Tijuana, Torreon **8** Acapulco, Culiacan, Ensenada, Irapuato, Mazatlan, Mexicali, Saltillo, Veracruz **9** Chihuahua, Matamoras, Monterrey, Queretaro, Salamanca, Zacatecas **10** Hermosillo **11** Guadalajara, Nuevo Laredo **12** Ciudad Juarez, Villahermosa **13** Coatzacoalcos, Piedras Negras, San Luis Potosi **14** Puerto Vallarta **15** Netzahualcoyotl
  ancient city: **4** Tula **7** Texcoco **8** Tlacopan **10** Monte Alban **11** Teotihuacan **12** Tenochtitlan **13** Tula de Allende
  division: **6** Colima, Oaxaca, Puebla, Sonora **7** Chiapas, Durango, Hidalgo, Jalisco, Sinaloa, Tabasco, Yucatan **8** Campeche, Coahuila, Tlaxcala, Veracruz **9** Chihuahua, Michoacan, Nuevo Leon, Zacatecas **13** San Luis Potosi **14** Baja California
  measure: **3** bag, pie **4** alma, onza, vara **5** almud, baril, carga, jarra, labor, legua, libra, linea, marco, sitio **6** adarme, almude, arroba, carega, fanega, ochaua, terceo **7** pulgada, quintal **9** cuarteron, cuartillo **10** caballeria
  monetary unit: **4** onza, peso **5** adobe, claco, tlaco **6** azteca, cuarto, dinero **7** centavo, piaster
  weight: **3** bag **4** onza **5** libra, marco **6** arroba, tercio **7** quintal
  island: **6** Carmen, Cedros **7** San Jose, Tiburon **8** Cerralvo **10** Tres Marias **13** Espiritu Santo **14** Santa Magdelena, Santa Margarita **15** Angel de la Guarda
  lake: **7** Chapala, Texcoco **9** Patzcuaro
  mountain: **6** Colima, Tacana, Toluca **9** Paricutin **11** Ixtacihuatl, Sierra Madre **12** Popocatepetl **14** Sierra Zacateca **16** Chiapas Highlands **24** Transverse Volcanic Sierra
  highest point: **7** Orizaba **12** Citlaltepetl
  river: **4** Mayo **5** Yaqui **6** Balsas, Fuerte, Grande, Panuco **8** Colorado, Grijalva **10** Papaloapan, Usumacinta **13** Bravo del Norte, Coatzacoalcos, Lerma-Santiago
  sea: **7** Pacific **8** Atlantic **9** Caribbean
  physical feature:
    bay: **8** Campeche **9** Olas Atlas
    cape: **10** Corrientes
    desert: **6** Sonora
    gulf: **6** Mexico **8** Campeche **10** California **11** Tehuantepec
    isthmus: **11** Tehuantepec
    peninsula: **7** Yucatan **14** Baja California
    plain: **7** Tabasco
    plateau: **7** Mexican
    valley: **7** Chiapas
  people: **6** Indian **7** Mestizo, Spanish
    architect: **7** O'Gorman
    artist: **6** Orozco, Rivera, Tamayo **9** Siqueiros
    composer: **6** Chavez
    emperor: **10** Maximilian
    explorer: **6** Cortes, Cortez **7** Cordoba **8** Alvarado, Grijalva
    god: **6** Tlaloc **12** Quetzalcoatl **14** Huitzilopochtl
    leader: **3** Gil **4** Diaz **5** Lopez, Rubio, Villa **6** Calles, Huerta, Juarez, Madero, Valdes, Zapata **7** Obregon **8** Carranza, Iturbide, Portillo, Santa Ana **9** Diaz Ordaz, Montezuma, Rodriguez **13** Madrid Hurtado **16** Salinas de Gortari
    revolutionary/priest: **13** Morelos y Pavon **16** Hidalgo y Costilla
    soldier/explorer: **12** conquistador
    viceroy: **7** Mendoza
    writer: **3** Paz **5** Nervo, Reyes, Yanez **6** Azuela, Guzman, Najera **7** Fuentes
  language: **5** Mayan, Otomi **6** Mixtec **7** Mazahua, Mazatec, Nahuatl, Spanish, Totonac, Zapotec **8** Tarascan
  religion: **13** Roman Catholic
  place:
    cathedral: **10** Assumption
    center of Mexico City: **6** Zocalo **21** Plaza de la Constitucion
    floating gardens: **10** Xochimilco
    museum: **28** Shrine of the Virgin of Guadalupe
    park: **7** Alameda **11** Chapultepec
    ruins: **5** Mitla, Uxmal **8** Palenque **10** Monte Alban **11** Chichen Itza, Teotihuacan **20** Temple of Quetzalcoatl
    street: **13** Avenida Juarez **16** Paseo de la Reforma
    temple/pyramid: **7** Cholula **8** Castillo
  feature:
    agreement: **5** NAFTA
    Christmas tradition: **6** pinata
    coffee plantation: **5** finca
    empire: **4** Maya **5** Aztec, Olmec **6** Mixtec, Toltec **7** Zapotec
    large estate: **8** hacienda
    musician: **8** mariachi
    small farm/commune: **6** ejidos
    sport: **7** jai alai **12** bullfighting
    tree: **9** sapodilla **11** chicozapote
  food:
    corn cake: **8** tortilla
    dish: **4** mole, taco **5** huevo, pollo **6** tamale **7** burrito, chorizo, taquito, tostada **8** empanada **9** enchilada, guacamole, sopadilla **10** chili verde, quesadilla **11** chimichanga **12** chili relleno
    drink: **6** pulque **7** tequila
Mexico City
  Aztec name: **12** Tenochtitlan
  capital of: **6** Mexico
  landmark: **13** Mercado Merced **15** Chapultepec Park **19** Basilica of Guadalupe
    bull ring: **11** Plaza Mexico
    floating gardens: **10** Xochimilco
    pyramids: **11** Teotihuacan
    square: **6** Zocalo **22** Plaza de las Tres Culturas
    street: **16** Paseo de la Reforma
Meyerbeer, Giacomo
  real name: **17** Jacob Liebmann Beer
  born: **6** Berlin **7** Germany
  composer of: **7** Dinorah **10** Le Prophete, The African, The Prophet **12** Les Huguenots, The Huguenots, The North Star **14** Robert le Diable, Robert the Devil
mezza voce
  music: **9** half voice **10** half volume
mezzo
  music: **4** half
Miami
  bay: **8** Biscayne
  county: **4** Dade
  developer: **7** Flagler
  football team: **8** Dolphins
  museum: **4** Lowe **12** Villa Viscaya
  ocean: **8** Atlantic
  people: **5** Cuban **8** Hispanic
  section: **7** Hialeah **10** Bal Harbour **11** Coral Gables
  stadium: **10** Orange Bowl
  tropical garden: **9** Fairchild
  university: **5** Barry **8** St Thomas
  zoo: **11** Crandon Park
Miami (Twightwee)
  language family: **9** Algonkian **10** Algonquian
  tribe: **3** Wea **5** Miami **10** Piankashaw

location: 4 Ohio **7** Indiana **8** Illinois, Michigan **9** Wisconsin
leader: 12 Little Turtle
allied with: 6 Peoria
Miami Vice
 character: 4 Gina **5** Trudy **8** (Capt) Castillo **13** Riccardo Tubbs, Sonny Crockett
 cast: 10 Don Johnson **11** Olivia Brown **15** Saundra Santiago **16** Edward James Olmos **20** Phillip Michael Thomas
Micah Clarke
 author: 19 Sir Arthur Conan Doyle
Micawber, Mr
 character in: 16 David Copperfield
 author: 7 Dickens
Michael
 author: 17 William Wordsworth
Michael
 means: 12 Who is like God
 father: 8 Izrahiah **11** Jehoshaphat
 son: 4 Omri **8** Zabadiah
 also: 9 archangel
Michel
 father: 4 Saul
 husband: 5 David, Palti
 sister: 5 Merab
Michelangelo Buonarotti (Simoni)
 architect of: 11 Campidoglio (Capitoline Hill) **12** Medici Chapel (Florence) **13** Farnese Palace **21** Palazzo Medici-Riccardi (Florence) **22** Palazzo dei Conservatori (Capitoline Hill) **24** Convent of San Marco Library
 born: 5 Italy **7** Caprese
 patron: 12 Pope Julius II **14** Lorenzo d'Medici **19** Pope Julius the Second **21** Lorenzo the Magnificent
 artwork: 5 David, Moses, Pieta **6** Brutus, Slaves **7** Bacchus **9** The Victor **10** Holy Family **12** Madonna Pitti **15** The Last Judgment **18** Conversion of St Paul **20** Madonna Seated on a Step, Sistine Chapel Ceiling **21** The Flight of the Lapites, The Martyrdom of St Peter
Michelozzo
 architect of: 21 Palazzo Medici-Riccardi (Florence) **24** Convent of San Marco Library
Michelson, Albert A
 field: 7 physics
 established: 12 speed of light **15** velocity of Earth
 awarded: 10 Nobel Prize
Michener, James A
 author of: 5 Space **6** Alaska, Hawaii, Iberia, Legacy, Poland **8** Caravans, Sayonara **9** The Source **10** Centennial, Chesapeake **11** The Covenant, The Drifters **16** The Fires of Spring **18** The Bridges at Toko-ri **22** Tales of the South Pacific
Michigan
 abbreviation: 2 MI **4** Mich

nickname: 4 Lake **9** Wolverine **10** Automobile **15** Water Wonderland **16** Winter Wonderland
capital: 7 Lansing
largest city: 7 Detroit
others: 4 Caro, Troy **5** Flint, Niles, Wayne **6** Adrien, Alpena, Bad Axe, Monroe, Owosso, Warren, Wassar **7** Bay City, Holland, Jackson, Livonia, Midland, Pontiac, Saginaw, Trenton, Wyoming **8** Ann Arbor, Cadillac, Dearborn, Escanaba, Ironwood, Manistee, Muskegon, Petoskey, Royal Oak **9** Cheboygan, Hillsdale, Kalamazoo, Marquette, Port Huron, Roseville, Wyandotte **10** Birmingham, River Rouge **11** Battle Creek, Grand Rapids **12** Benton Harbor, Traverse City **13** Sault Ste Marie, St Clair Shores
college: 4 Alma, Hope **5** Wayne **6** Adrian, Albion, Calvin, Olivet, Owosso **7** Detroit, Oakland **9** Hillsdale, Kalamazoo, Marygrove
feature:
 bridge: 8 Mackinac
 canal: 3 Soo **12** Sault St Marie
 festival: 12 Holland Tulip
 national park: 10 Isle Royale
 village: 10 Greenfield
tribe: 6 Ojibwa, Ottawa **8** Chippewa **10** Potawatomi
people: 9 Henry Ford, wolverine **11** Bruce Catton, Edgar A Guest, Julie Harris, Ralph Bunche, Ring Lardner **16** Charles Lindbergh
 explorer: 6 Joliet **7** La Salle, Nicolet **9** Marquette **12** Etienne Brule, Sault St Marie
island: 8 Mackinaw
lake: 4 Burt, Erie **5** Clear, Huron, Round, Torch **6** Austin, Devils, Moline **7** Bawbees, St Clair **8** Houghton, Michigan, Superior
land rank: 11 twenty-third
mountain: 6 Copper **7** Gogebic **9** Menominee, Porcupine
 highest point: 12 Mount Curwood
physical feature:
 bay: 7 Saginaw, Thunder **8** Keweenaw, Sturgeon
 straits: 8 Mackinac
president: 10 Gerald Ford
river: 4 Cass **5** Grand, Huron **6** Raisin **7** Detroit, Saginaw, St Clair, St Mary's **8** Escanaba, Muskegon **9** Menominee
state admission: 11 twenty-sixth
state bird: 5 robin
state fish: 5 trout
state flower: 12 apple blossom
state motto: 11 I Will Defend **39** If You Seek a Pleasant Peninsula Look About You
state song: 18 Michigan My Michigan
state tree: 16 eastern white pine
Mickey Mouse
 creator: 10 Walt Disney

character: 5 Morty **6** Ferdie **11** Minnie Mouse
cow: 10 Clarabelle
Micklewhite, Maurice Joseph
 real name of: 12 Michael Caine
Micmac
 language family: 9 Algonkian **10** Algonquian
 location: 6 Canada **10** Nova Scotia **12** Newfoundland, New Brunswick **14** Gaspe Peninsula **16** Cape Breton Island **18** Prince Edward Island
microbe 4 germ **5** virus **6** gamete, zygote **8** bacillus, parasite **9** bacterium **10** spirochete **13** microorganism, streptococcus **14** staphylococcus
microbiologist
 American: 7 Waksman **9** Baltimore
 Dutch: 11 (van) Leeuwenhoek
Micronesia
 part of: 7 Oceania
 island: 3 Nui **4** Guam, Rota, Truk, Wake **5** Makin, Nauru, Wotho **6** Bikini, Ellice, Majuro, Ponape **7** Gilbert, Mariana **8** Caroline, Kiribati, Marshall
microorganism 3 bug **4** germ **5** virus **7** microbe **8** bacillus, pathogen **9** bacterium
microphobia
 fear of: 12 small objects
microscope
 invented by:
  compound: 7 Janssen
  electronic: 5 Knoll, Ruska
  field ion: 7 Mueller
 single lens model improved by: 11 (van) Leeuwenhoek
  first observed: 8 protozoa **13** red blood cells **19** single-celled animals
microscopic, microscopical 4 tiny **5** teeny **6** atomic, minute **9** invisible **10** diminutive, very little **13** imperceptible, infinitesimal
microscopy
 founder: 11 Robert Hooke **13** Jan Swammerdam **16** Marcello Malpighi **19** Anton van Leeuwenhoek
Midas
 king of: 7 Phrygia
 father: 7 Gordius
 gift: 11 golden touch
 gift from: 7 Silenus
 ears changed to those of: 3 ass
 changed by: 6 Apollo
midday 4 noon **7** noonday **8** meridian, noontide, noontime
middle 3 act, gut, hub, mid **4** core, main **5** belly, heart, midst, waist **6** center, course, medial, median, midway, throes **7** central, halfway, midmost, midriff, nucleus, process, stomach **8** midpoint **9** heartland **10** midsection **12** intermediate
Middle Ages
 French: 8 moyen age

middle-class 4 mass **8** ordinary **9** bourgeois **10** mainstream, middlebrow

middle Europe
German: **12** Mitteleuropa

middle ground 4 mean **7** balance **8** midpoint **11** equilibrium **12** common ground

Middle Kingdom *see* **5** China

middleman 5 agent **6** broker, dealer, jobber **7** liaison **8** mediator **9** go-between **10** wholesaler **11** distributor, intercessor **12** entrepreneur, intermediary

Middlemarch
author: **11** George Eliot
character: **5** Celia **12** Will Ladislaw **13** Rosamond Viney **14** Dorothea Brooke, Edward Casaubon, Tertius Lydgate **15** Sir James Chettam

middlemost 4 mean **5** inner **6** inmost, median **7** central, midmost **8** interior

middle-of-the-road 8 moderate **10** mainstream

middle-of-the-roader 8 moderate **12** mainstreamer

middle way
Latin: **8** via media

middling 4 fair, so-so **6** medium **7** average, fairish, minimal **8** mediocre, moderate, ordinary, passable **9** tolerable **10** pretty good, second-rate **11** indifferent **12** run of the mill, unremarkable

Midgard
also: **10** Mithgarthr
origin: **12** Scandinavian
means: **10** abode of man
located between: **8** Niflheim **10** Muspelheim
connected to Asgard by: **7** bifrost **13** rainbow bridge
formed from brow of: **4** Ymir

midget 4 doll, runt **5** dwarf, pygmy **6** peewee, puppet, shrimp, squirt **7** manikin **8** half-pint, munchkin, small fry, Tom Thumb **9** pipsqueak **10** fingerling, homunculus **11** hop-o'-my-thumb, lilliputian

Midi 5 skirt **16** the south of France

midlands 8 interior **10** hinterland **13** central region

midmost 5 inner **6** inmost, middle **7** central, pivotal **8** interior **10** middlemost

Midnight Cowboy
director: **15** John Schlesinger
cast: **9** Jon Voight **11** John McGiver, Sylvia Miles **13** Brenda Vaccaro, Dustin Hoffman (Ratso Rizzo)
Oscar for: **7** picture

Midnight Express
director: **10** Alan Parker
cast: **8** John Hurt **9** Bo Hopkins, Brad Davis (Billy Hayes) **10** Randy Quaid **12** Irene Miracle
setting: **13** Turkish prison

score: **14** Giorgio Moroder
Oscar for: **5** score **6** script

midori
type: **7** liqueur
origin: **5** Japan
flavor: **5** melon

midpoint 4 core, mean **5** focus **6** center, middle **15** point of no return

midriff 3 gut **4** guts **5** belly, tummy **6** paunch **7** abdomen, stomach **9** diaphragm **10** midsection **11** breadbasket

midst 3 eye, hub **4** core **5** bosom, heart, thick **6** center, depths, middle **7** nucleus **8** interior

Midsummer Night's Dream, A
author: **18** William Shakespeare
character: **4** Puck (Robin Goodfellow) **6** Bottom, Helena, Hermia, Oberon **7** Theseus, Titania **8** Lysander **9** Demetrius, Hippolyta

midterm 4 exam, test **6** review **11** examination

midwife
French: **11** accoucheuse

mien 3 air **4** look **5** guise, style **6** aspect, manner, visage **7** bearing, feature **8** attitude, behavior, carriage, demeanor, presence **9** semblance **10** appearance, deportment, expression **11** countenance

Mies van der Rohe, Ludwig
architect of: **14** German Pavilion (1929 International Exposition, Barcelona), Lake Shore Drive (apartment towers, Chicago), Tugendhat House (Brno Czechoslovakia) **15** National Gallery (West Berlin), Seagram Building (NYC)
style: **13** International
principle: **10** less is more

miff 3 irk, vex **4** rile **5** anger, annoy, chafe, pique **6** nettle, offend, rankle **7** affront, provoke **8** irritate **9** put one off **10** exasperate **11** make one sore **14** rub the wrong way **15** raise one's dander

Mifune, Toshiro
born: **5** China **8** Tsingtao
roles: **6** Midway, Shogun **8** Rashomon **12** Seven Samurai **13** Throne of Blood

Miggs, Miss
character in: **12** Barnaby Rudge
author: **7** Dickens

might 3 may **5** brawn, clout, force, power, vigor **6** energy, muscle **7** potency, prowess **8** strength **9** influence, lustihood, puissance, toughness **10** capability, competence, durability, robustness, sturdiness **11** capableness **12** forcefulness

mighty 4 able, bold, huge, vast, very **5** brave, hardy, husky, lusty, stout, truly **6** brawny, manful, potent, really, robust, strong, sturdy **7** immense, massive, titanic, valiant **8** colossal, enormous, forceful, gigantic, imposing,

majestic, powerful, puissant, stalwart, towering, valorous, vigorous **9** monstrous, strapping **10** courageous, gargantuan, invincible, monolithic, monumental, prodigious, stupendous **11** elephantine, exceedingly, indomitable, of great size **12** overpowering, particularly **13** exceptionally **14** Brobdingnagian

migrate 4 move, trek **6** travel **7** journey **8** emigrate, relocate, resettle **9** immigrate

migration 4 trek **6** exodus, flight, moving **7** passage **8** diaspora, movement

mikado 5 ruler **7** emperor, monarch **9** sovereign **10** locomotive **15** Japanese emperor

Mikado, The
subtitle: **15** The Town of Titipu
operetta by: **18** Gilbert and Sullivan
character: **4** Ko-Ko **6** Mikado, Peep-Bo, Yum-Yum **7** Katisha, Pooh-Bah **8** Nanki-Poo, Pish-Tush **9** Pitti-Sing

Mikkelsen, Dahl
also: **3** Mik
creator/artist of: **8** Ferd'nand

mikrophobia
fear of: **5** germs

mikvah 16 public ritual bath
used by: **12** Orthodox Jews

mild 4 calm, easy, soft, warm **5** balmy, bland **6** docile, gentle, placid, serene, smooth **7** pacific, summery **8** delicate, moderate, not sharp, pleasant, soothing, tranquil **9** easygoing, emollient, not severe, not strong, temperate **10** forbearing, not extreme, springlike **11** complaisant, uninjurious **12** good-tempered

mildew 4 mold **6** blight, fungus

mildewed 5 fusty, moldy **10** discolored

mildness 8 calmness, delicacy, serenity, softness **9** placidity **10** gentleness, good temper

Mildred Pierce
director: **13** Michael Curtiz
based on novel by: **10** James M Cain
cast: **8** Ann Blyth, Eve Arden **10** Jack Carson **12** Bruce Bennett, Joan Crawford, Zachary Scott
Oscar for: **7** actress (Crawford)

mild-tempered 7 equable, patient **9** easygoing **11** good-natured, unflappable

mile
abbreviation: **2** mi

Miles, Sarah
brother: **11** Christopher
husband: **10** Robert Bolt
born: **7** England **11** Ingatestone
roles: **6** Blow-Up **10** The Servant **11** The Hireling **13** Ryan's Daughter **16** Lady Caroline Lamb

miles gloriosus 15 boastful soldier
Miles Gloriosus
  author: 7 Plautus
Milesian
  origin: 5 Irish
  invaders from: 5 Spain
  invaded: 7 Ireland
  defeated: 14 Tuatha De Danann
  ancestors of: 5 Irish
milestone 7 jubilee 8 milepost, sign-post 10 road marker 11 anniversary 12 red-letter day, turning point
Milestone, Lewis
  director of: 12 Of Mice and Men, The Front Page 13 A Walk in the Sun 17 Mutiny on the Bounty 25 All Quiet on the Western Front (Oscar)
Milestones
  author: 13 Arnold Bennett
milieu 5 scene 7 culture, element, setting 8 ambience, backdrop 10 background 11 environment, mise-en-scene 12 surroundings
militant 7 defiant, extreme, martial, warlike, warring 8 fighting, military 9 assertive, bellicose, combatant, combative 10 aggressive, pugnacious 11 belligerent, contentious 12 disputatious, paramilitary, warmongering 14 uncompromising
military 4 army 5 armed, crisp 6 strict, troops 7 martial, militia, Spartan, warlike 8 generals, soldiers 9 combative, defensive, regulated, soldierly, warmaking 10 regimented 11 armed forces, belligerent, soldierlike
military force 4 army, navy 6 legion, troops 7 legions, militia 8 military, regiment, soldiers, soldiery 9 battalion 11 fighting men 13 fighting force
military machine 4 army 6 legion, troops 11 armed forces 13 fighting force
military rank abbreviation
  admiral: 3 adm
  brigadier general: 2 bg 7 brig gen
  captain: 3 cpt 4 capt
  chief petty officer: 3 CPO
  colonel: 3 col
  commander: 5 comdr
  corporal: 3 cpl
  ensign: 3 ens
  general: 3 gen
  lieutenant: 2 lt 5 lieut
  lieutenant colonel: 3 ltc 5 lt col
  lieutenant general: 5 lt gen 8 lieut gen
  major: 3 maj
  master sergeant: 4 msgt
  non-commissioned officer: 3 nco
  private: 3 pvt
  private first class: 3 pfc
  sergeant: 3 sgt
  sergeant first class: 3 sfc
  sergeant major: 4 smaj 6 sgt maj
  specialist: 4 spec
  staff sergeant: 4 ssgt

military storehouse 6 armory 7 arsenal 8 magazine 9 arms depot 13 ordnance depot 14 ammunition dump
military stores 7 arsenal, weapons 8 ordnance 9 munitions 10 ammunition
military unit 4 army, crew, unit 5 corps, force, squad 6 legion, outfit 7 brigade, company 8 regiment, squadron 9 battalion, task force 10 contingent, detachment
milksop 4 baby, wimp 5 mouse, pansy, sissy, softy 6 coward 7 crybaby, nebbish 8 mama's boy, poltroon, weakling 9 fraidy-cat 10 namby-pamby, pantywaist, scaredy-cat, weak sister 11 milquetoast, mollycoddle
mill 4 roam, teem 5 crush, grind, shape, swarm, works 6 finish, groove 7 factory, meander 8 converge 9 granulate, pulverize
Mill, John Stuart
  author of: 9 On Liberty 14 Utilitarianism 20 The Subjection of Women 28 Principles of Political Economy
Millais, Sir John Everett
  born: 7 England 12 Southampton
  artwork: 7 Bubbles 9 Blind Girl 12 Autumn Leaves, Chill October 13 My First Sermon 18 Lorenzo and Isabella 25 Christ in the Carpenter's Shop 36 Young Men of Benjamin Seizing Their Brides
Millament, Mrs
  character in: 16 The Way of the World
  author: 8 Congreve
Milland, Ray
  real name: 21 Reginald Truscott-Jones
  born: 5 Neath, Wales
  roles: 9 Beau Geste 11 Blonde Crazy 14 Dial M for Murder, The Lost Weekend (Oscar) 22 Bulldog Drummond Escapes
Millay, Edna St Vincent
  author of: 11 Second April 13 The Harp Weaver 19 Make Bright the Arrows 20 A Few Figs from Thistles
millennium 13 thousand years 9 age of gold 21 one-thousandth anniversary
Miller
  character in: 18 The Canterbury Tales
  author: 7 Chaucer
Miller, Ann
  real name: 17 Lucille Ann Collier
  autobiography: 15 Miller's High Life
  born: 9 Chireno TX
  roles: 9 On the Town, Stage Door 10 Hit the Deck, Kiss Me Kate 11 Sugar Babies 16 The Kissing Bandit
Miller, Arthur
  wife: 13 Marilyn Monroe
  author of: 8 The Price 11 The Crucible 12 After the Fall 16 Death of a Salesman 18 A View from the Bridge

Miller, Henry
  author of: 5 Nexus, Sexus 6 Plexus 14 Tropic of Cancer 17 Tropic of Capricorn 18 The Rosy Crucifixion 21 The Colossus of Maroussi
Milles, Carl
  real name: 23 Wilhelm Carl Emil Andersen
  born: 5 Lagga 6 Sweden
  artwork: 5 Diana, Jonah 6 Europa 12 Man and Nature, Playing Bears 13 Peace Monument 15 Orpheus Fountain 18 Meeting of the Waters, Saltsjobaden Church (bronze doors)
millet 16 Panicum miliaceum
  varieties: 3 hog 5 pearl, Sanwa 6 finger, Indian 7 African, foxtail, Italian 8 barnyard, browntop, Japanese 16 Japanese barnyard
Millet, Jean-Francois
  born: 6 France, Gruchy
  artwork: 5 Sower 7 Angelus 11 The Gleaners, The Winnower 14 Potato Planters, The Man with a Hoe 23 Oedipus Taken from the Tree
Millett, Kate
  author of: 6 Flying 14 Sexual Politics
milligram
  abbreviation: 2 mg
milliliter
  abbreviation: 2 mL
millimeter
  abbreviation: 2 mm
Millionaire, The
  character: 14 Michael Anthony
  cast: 12 Marvin Miller
Mill on the Floss, The
  author: 11 George Eliot
  character: 8 Bob Jakin, Mrs Glegg 9 Lucy Deane, Mrs Pullet 11 Philip Wakem, Tom Tulliver 12 Stephen Guest 14 Maggie Tulliver
Mills, Hayley
  real name: 15 Rose Vivian Mills
  father: 4 John
  sister: 6 Juliet
  husband: 11 Ray Boulting
  born: 6 London 7 England
  roles: 8 Tiger Bay 9 Pollyanna 11 Summer Magic 13 The Parent Trap 14 The Chalk Garden 15 The Moon-Spinners 19 In Search of Castaways 20 The Trouble with Angels
Mills, John
  daughter: 6 Hayley, Juliet
  born: 7 England 10 Felixstowe
  roles: 12 Tunes of Glory 13 Ryan's Daughter 14 The Chalk Garden 17 Great Expectations 19 Swiss Family Robinson
Mills, Robert
  architect of: 10 Post Office (Washington DC) 12 Patent Office (Washington DC) 14 Circular Church (Charleston) 15 Unitarian Church (Philadelphia) 16 Treasury Building (Washington DC) 18 Washington

Monument 25 Sansom Street Baptist Church (Philadelphia) **29** Egyptian Revival Monument Church (Richmond VA)
  style: 12 Greek Revival
millstream 3 run **4** race **5** brook, canal, creek, river **6** branch
Milne, A A
  author of: 13 Winnie-the-Pooh **20** The House at Pooh Corner
  character: 3 Roo **4** Pooh **5** Kanga **6** Eeyore, Piglet, Tigger **16** Christopher Robin
Milo, Milos
  island of: 6 Greece **8** Cyclades **9** Aegean Sea
  found: 5 Venus **6** statue
  missing: 4 arms
Milosz, Czeslaw
  author of: 11 Native Realm, The Usurpers **13** Bells in Winter **14** Seizure of Power, The Captive Mind
milquetoast 4 wimp **7** milksop, nebbish **11** mollycoddle
Milton
  author: 12 William Blake
Milton, George
  character in: 12 Of Mice and Men
  author: 9 Steinbeck
Milton, John
  author of: 7 Lycidas **8** L'Allegro **11** Il Penseroso **12** Areopagitica, Paradise Lost **15** Samson Agonistes **16** Paradise Regained **29** On the Morning of Christ's Nativity
Milton Berle Show, The
  host: 11 Milton Berle
  regulars: 10 Fatso Marco **11** Arnold Stang, Jack Collins, Milton Frome, Ruth Gilbert **13** Irving Benson **13** Bobby Sherwood
  announcer: 8 Sid Stone **11** Jimmy Nelson **13** Jack Lescoulie
  orchestra: 8 Alan Roth, Billy May **11** Victor Young
  theme: 7 Near You
  Milton Berle's nickname: 12 Mr Television
  sponsor: 5 Buick **6** Texaco
Milwaukee
  baseball team: 7 Brewers
  basketball team: 5 Bucks
  Indian name: 16 Mahn-a-waukee Seepe
  lake: 8 Michigan
  river: 9 Milwaukee, Menomonee, **12** Kinnickinnic
  university: 9 Marquette
mimic 3 ape **4** aper, copy, echo, mime **6** mirror, parrot **7** copycat, copyist, feigner, imitate, take off **8** imitator, simulate **9** reproduce **10** burlesquer **11** counterfeit, impersonate **13** impressionist
Mimir
  origin: 12 Scandinavian
  god of: 3 sea

decapitated by: 5 Vanir
  head sent to: 4 Odin **5** Othin
  oracle for: 4 Asar **5** Aesir
mimosa 14 Acacia dealbata **18** Albizia Julibrissin
  varieties: 5 Texas **6** golden **7** prairie **8** Egyptian
  cocktail contains: 9 champagne **10** orange juice
mince 4 dice, pose **5** grate, shred **6** refine, soften **7** posture, qualify **8** chop fine, hold back, mitigate, moderate, palliate **9** gloss over, put on airs, whitewash **12** attitudinize **14** affect delicacy, affect primness **15** give oneself airs **16** affect daintiness, soften one's speech **18** cut into small pieces **19** be mealymouthed about **20** cut into tiny particles
mince words 5 dodge, hedge, stall **10** equivocate **11** be ambiguous **13** avoid the issue **17** beat around the bush
mind 4 hate, heed, note, obey, tend, will, wits **5** abhor, bow to, brain, focus, sense, watch **6** brains, choice, detest, eschew, follow, intent, liking, memory, notice, notion, reason, recall, regard, resent, sanity **7** dislike, marbles, observe, opinion, outlook, thought **8** adhere to, attend to, be wary of, judgment, object to, reaction, response, submit to, take care, thinking **9** attention, awareness, be careful, cognition, faculties, intellect, intention, look after, sentiment **10** be cautious, comply with, conception, conclusion, gray matter, impression, perception, propensity, recoil from, reflection, shrink from, take care of **11** acquiesce to, be wary about, inclination, percipience, point of view, rationality, remembrance **12** apprehension, disapprove of, intelligence, recollection, reminiscence, take charge of, take notice of **13** be conscious of, comprehension, concentration, consciousness, consideration, contemplation, look askance at, preoccupation, ratiocination, retrospection, understanding **14** pay attention to
  German: 5 Geist
mindful 4 wary **5** aware **7** alert to, alive to, careful, heedful **8** cautious, sensible, watchful **9** cognizant, conscious, observant, regardful **10** absorbed in, open-eyed to, thoughtful **11** attentive to, engrossed in, taken up with **12** occupied with **15** preoccupied with
mindfulness 9 alertness, awareness **10** perception **12** acquaintance **13** attentiveness, consciousness, understanding
mindless 6 insane, obtuse, stupid **7** asinine, doltish, idiotic, unaware, witless **8** careless, heedless **9** apathetic, cretinous, imbecilic, oblivious, unat-

tuned, unheeding **10** neglectful, regardless, sophomoric, unthinking **11** inattentive, indifferent, nonsensical, thoughtless, unobservant, unreasoning **12** disregardful, simple-minded **13** inconsiderate, unintelligent **14** indiscriminate
mine 3 pit **4** fund **5** cache, hoard, shaft, stock, store **6** dig for, quarry, supply, tunnel, wealth **7** extract, reserve **8** dig under, excavate, treasure **9** abundance, booby-trap **10** excavation **12** accumulation
Mineo, Sal
  real name: 14 Salvatore Mineo
  born: 7 Bronx NY
  roles: 5 Giant, Tonka **6** Exodus **18** Rebel Without a Cause, Who Killed Teddy Bear?
mineral 3 jet, ore **4** coal, gold, iron, mica, opal, spar, talc **5** beryl, topaz **6** augite, barite, blende, cerine, copper, galena, garnet, iolite, pinite, rutile, sandix, silver, sphene, spinel, sulfur **7** amesite, apatite, azurite, biotite, bornite, calcite, citrine, coesite, crystal, cuprite, cyanite, element, gahnite, helvite, jadeite, kernite, kunzite, niobite, olivine, prasine, zeolite, zircon **8** asbestos, borocite, chlorite, cinnabar, corundum, dolomite, epsomite, fayalite, feldspar, fluorite, graphite, hematite, lazulite, siderite, sodalite, stibnite, triplite, wellsite **9** aragonite, argentite, carnelian, celestite, cerussite, danburite, fosterite, kaolinite, lawsonite, magnetite, malachite, muscovite, petroleum, phenakite, scapolite, tridymite, turquoise, wulfenite **10** calaverite, chalcedony, orthoclase, pyrrhotite, sphalerite, tourmaline, wolfachite **11** alexandrite, chrysoberyl, melanterite **12** brazilianite, chalcopyrite, fincalconite, fluorapatite **13** rhodochrosite
Minerva
  origin: 5 Roman
  goddess of: 3 war **4** arts **6** wisdom **11** handicrafts
  corresponds to: 6 Athena
mingle 3 mix **4** fuse, join **5** blend, merge, unite **6** hobnob **7** combine, consort **8** coalesce, intermix **9** associate, circulate, commingle, interfuse, interlard, socialize **10** amalgamate, fraternize, intertwine, interweave **11** intermingle, intersperse **12** rub shoulders
miniature 3 wee **4** tiny **5** elfin, pygmy **6** bantam, little, petite **9** minuscule **10** diminutive, pocket-size, small-scale **11** lilliputian, microcosmic, microscopic
minim
  abbreviation: 3 min
minimal 5 token **7** minimum, nominal **13** least possible, unappreciable
minimize 5 dwarf **6** reduce, shrink

8 belittle, mitigate **9** underrate **10** depreciate, undervalue

minimum 4 base **5** basic, least **7** modicum **8** smallest

minister 4 abbe, tend **5** padre, rabbi, serve, vicar **6** answer, cleric, father, oblige, parson, pastor, priest **7** care for, cater to **8** attend to, chaplain, pander to, preacher, reverend **9** clergyman, secretary **10** evangelist, revivalist, take care of **11** accommodate **12** ecclesiastic **13** cabinet member

ministerial 6 cleric **8** churchly, clerical, pastoral, priestly **14** ecclesiastical

ministration 3 aid **4** care **6** charge **7** comfort **9** attention **10** protection **11** supervision

Ministry of Fear, The
  author: **12** Graham Greene

Minnehaha
  character in: **8** Hiawatha
  author: **10** Longfellow

Minnelli, Liza
  father: **8** Vincente
  mother: **11** Judy Garland
  born: **12** Los Angeles CA
  roles: **6** Arthur **7** Cabaret (Oscar) **14** New York New York **16** The Sterile Cuckoo **17** Flora the Red Menace

Minnelli, Vincente
  director of: **4** Gigi (Oscar) **9** Brigadoon **11** Lust for Life **15** Bells Are Ringing, Meet Me in St Louis **16** Father of the Bride **17** An American in Paris

Minnesota
  abbreviation: **2** MN **4** Minn
  nickname: **6** Gopher **9** North Star **19** Land of Sky-blue Waters **22** Land of Ten Thousand Lakes
  capital: **6** St Paul
  largest city: **11** Minneapolis
  others: **3** Ada, Ely **4** Mora **5** Edina **6** Austin, Duluth, Newulm, Winona **7** Babbitt, Bemidji, Fosston, Hibbing, Mankato, Red Wing, St Cloud **8** Brainerd, Moorhead **9** Albertlea, Blue Earth, Richfield, Rochester, Roseville **10** Minnetonka, Robinsdale **11** Bloomington, St Louis Park **14** Brooklyn Center **18** International Falls
  college: **6** Bethel, St Olaf, Winona **7** Bemidji, Hamline **8** Adolphus, Augsburg, Carleton, St Thomas **10** Macalester
  feature:
    monument: **10** Paul Bunyan
    national monument: **9** Pipestone **12** Grand Portage
    national park: **9** Voyageurs'
    Norse artifact: **19** Kensington Rune Stone
  tribe: **5** Sioux **6** Dakota, Ojibwa, Santee **8** Chippewa **9** Menominee
  people: **11** Judy Garland **12** Mayo brothers **13** Harold Stassen, Lauris Norstad, Sinclair Lewis **16** F Scott Fitzgerald
  explorer: **8** Hennepin, Norsemen, Radisson **9** Greysolon **12** Groseilliers **19** Sieur Duluth of du Lhut
  lakes: **3** Red **5** Leech, Rainy **6** Itasca **7** Bemidji **8** Superior **9** Mille Lacs **10** Minnewaska **14** Lake of the Woods, Winnibigoshish
  land rank: **7** twelfth
  mountain: **6** Cuyuna, Mesabi **7** Misquah **9** Vermilion
    highest point: **5** Eagle
  physical feature: **6** Big Bog **14** Northwest Angle
    falls: **9** Minnehaha
  river: **3** Red **5** Rainy **6** Pigeon **7** St Croix, St Louis **9** Des Moines, Minnesota **10** St Lawrence **11** Mississippi
  state admission: **12** thirty-second
  state bird: **10** common loon
  state fish: **7** walleye
  state flower: **14** moccasin flower **24** pink and white lady's slipper
  state motto: **17** The Star of the North
  state song: **13** Hail Minnesota
  state tree: **13** Norway red pine
  baseball team: **5** Twins
  football team: **7** Vikings
  hockey team: **10** North Stars

Minni *see* **7** Armenia

minor 5 child, light, petty, small, youth **6** infant, lesser, paltry, slight **7** trivial **8** nugatory, picayune, piddling, teenager, trifling **9** secondary, youngster **10** adolescent **11** subordinate, unimportant **13** insignificant **14** inconsiderable **15** inconsequential

minority 4 less **5** youth **6** lesser, nonage **7** boyhood, infancy **8** girlhood **9** childhood, juniority **10** immaturity **11** adolescence

minor-league 4 punk **5** dinky, seedy, tacky **6** cheesy, common, lesser, shabby **8** inferior, small-fry **9** secondary, small-time **10** bush-league, second-rate **13** insignificant

Minos
  king of: **5** Crete
  father: **4** Zeus
  mother: **6** Europa
  brother: **8** Sarpedon **12** Rhadamanthys
  wife: **8** Pasiphae
  daughter: **7** Ariadne, Phaedra
  ordered: **9** Labyrinth
  became: **5** judge
    in: **5** Hades

Minotaur
  form: **7** monster
  combined: **3** man **4** bull
  father: **10** Cretan bull
  mother: **8** Pasiphae
  home: **9** Labyrinth
  ate flesh of: **6** humans
  killed by: **7** Theseus

minstrel 4 bard, poet **6** dancer, end man, lyrist, player, singer **8** comedian, songster **9** blackface, poetaster, serenader, versifier **10** troubadour **11** entertainer **12** interlocutor, vaudevillian **15** song-and-dance man

mint
  varieties: **3** dog, red **4** wood **5** apple, field, lemon, stone, water **6** coyote, dotted, orange, Scotch **7** Meehan's **8** bergamot, Corsican, creeping, Japanese, mountain **9** pineapple
  flavor: **7** menthol **9** spearmint **10** peppermint
  liqueur: **13** creme de menthe
  botanical name: **6** Mentha **8** Labiatae, M spicata **9** M piperita
  origin: **13** Mediterranean
  related herb: **7** oregano **8** marjoram, rosemary
  symbol of: **11** hospitality
  mythical nymph: **6** Mintha
    beloved of: **5** Pluto
    Mintha trod underfoot by: **10** Persephone
  cure for: **7** hiccups
  antidote for: **16** sea serpent stings
  use: **4** lamb **5** salad **6** fruits

Minthe
  form: **5** nymph
  changed into: **9** mint plant
  changed by: **10** Persephone

minuscule 3 wee **4** tiny **5** small **6** minute **10** teeny-weeny **11** small letter **13** infinitesimal **15** lower-case letter

minute 3 wee **4** fine, puny, tiny, wink **5** close, exact, flash, jiffy, petty, scant, shake, teeny, trice **6** breath, little, moment, petite, second, slight, strict **7** careful, instant, minikin, precise **8** detailed, itemized, trifling **9** miniature, twinkling **10** a short time, diminutive, exhaustive, meticulous, negligible, scrupulous **11** lilliputian, microscopic **12** sixty seconds **13** conscientious, imperceptible, inappreciable, infinitesimal, insignificant **14** extremely small, inconsiderable
  abbreviation: **3** min

minute portion 3 bit, sip **4** bite **5** crumb, grain, scrap, shred, speck **6** morsel, sliver **7** swallow **8** fragment, mouthful, particle

minutiae 6 trivia **7** trifles **8** niceties **10** bagatelles, pedantries, subtleties **11** odds and ends, particulars **12** minor details, trivialities **15** particularities

minx 4 jade, slut **5** hussy, huzzy, wench **7** baggage **10** prostitute

Minyades
  daughters of: **6** Minyas

Miolnir
  hammer of: **4** Thor

mir 5 peace, world **21** Russian village commune

mirabile dictu 12 strange to say **17** marvelous to relate

miracle 4 omen, sign **6** marvel, wonder **7** mystery, portent, prodigy **9** divine act, sensation, spectacle **10** phenomenon **11** masterpiece

Miracle of Morgan's Creek, The
director: **14** Preston Sturges
cast: **9** Diana Lynn **11** Betty Hutton **12** Brian Donlevy, Eddie Bracken **15** William Demarest

Miracle on 34th Street
director: **12** George Seaton
based on story by: **15** Valentine Davies
cast: **9** John Payne **11** Edmund Gwenn (Kris Kringle), Natalie Wood **12** Gene Lockhart, Maureen O'Hara, Thelma Ritter
Oscar for: **12** screenwriter **15** supporting actor (Gwenn)

Miracle Worker, The
director: **10** Arthur Penn
cast: **9** Patty Duke (Helen Keller) **10** Victor Jory **11** Inga Swenson **12** Anne Bancroft (Anne Sullivan)
Oscar for: **7** actress (Bancroft) **17** supporting actress (Duke)

miraculous 6 divine **7** amazing, magical **9** marvelous, visionary, wonderful **10** incredible, mysterious, phenomenal, prodigious, remarkable **11** astonishing, astounding, exceptional, spectacular, supernormal **13** extraordinary, preternatural, wonderworking **14** thaumaturgical

miraculous food 5 manna

Miraculous writing
also: **4** mene **5** perez, tekel **8** upharsin
means: **7** divided, weighed **8** numbered
interpreted by: **6** Daniel

mirage 5 fancy **7** fantasy **8** delusion, illusion, phantasm **9** unreality **12** will-o'-the-wisp **13** hallucinations, misconception **14** castle in the air **15** optical illusion

Miranda
character in: **10** The Tempest
author: **11** Shakespeare

Miranda, Carmen
real name: **26** Maria do Carmo Miranda da Cunha
nickname: **18** Brazilian Bombshell
born: **8** Portugal **16** Marco de Canavezes
roles: **10** Copacabana **14** That Night in Rio **15** Weekend in Havana **16** Down Argentine Way **22** Springtime in the Rockies

mire 3 bog, fen, mud **4** cake, muck, ooze, soil **5** marsh, muddy, slime, slush, smear **6** enmesh, sludge **7** begrime, bog down, ensnare, spatter **8** besmirch, entangle, quagmire

Miriam
father: **5** Amram

mother: **8** Jochebed
brother: **5** Aaron, Moses

Miro, Joan
born: **5** Spain **8** Montroig **9** Barcelona
artwork: **9** Help Spain, The Reaper **13** Dutch Interior **14** Constellations **16** Catalan Landscape **19** Dog Barking at the Moon **20** Still Life with Old Shoe **26** Woman and Bird in the Moonlight

mirror 4 copy, show **5** glass, image, model **7** epitome, example, paragon, reflect **8** exemplar, manifest, paradigm, standard **10** reflection **11** cheval glass **12** looking glass

mirth 4 glee **6** gaiety, levity **7** jollity **8** drollery, hilarity, laughter **9** amusement, festivity, happiness, jocundity, joviality, merriment **10** jocularity **11** good spirits, merrymaking, playfulness **12** cheerfulness

mirthful 3 gay **4** glad **5** happy, jolly, merry **6** blithe, jocose, jovial, joyful, joyous **7** gleeful, jocular, risible

mirthless 3 sad **4** dour, glum **6** gloomy, morose **7** joyless, unhappy **8** dejected **9** cheerless, sorrowful **10** in the dumps, melancholy **14** down in the mouth

miry 3 wet **4** oozy **5** boggy, mucky, muddy, slimy, slushy, soggy **6** claggy, swampy **7** sloughy

misadventure 3 ill **4** slip **6** mishap **7** debacle, failure, reverse, setback **8** bad break, calamity, casualty, disaster **9** adversity, mischance **10** infelicity, misfortune **11** catastrophe, contretemps

misanthrope 5 cynic **7** skeptic **9** pessimist **10** misogynist

Misanthrope, Le
author: **7** Moliere
character: **7** Alceste, Arsinoe, Eliante **8** Celimene, Philinte

misanthropic 4 cold **5** surly **6** morose **7** cynical, distant **10** antisocial, unfriendly, unsociable **11** distrustful **12** discourteous, inhospitable, unneighborly, unpersonable, unresponsive **14** unapproachable **15** unaccommodating

misapply 5 abuse **6** misuse **9** misemploy **13** use improperly

misapprehension 5 mixup **7** mistake **11** misjudgment **13** misconception **14** miscalculation **15** false impression, misconstruction **16** misunderstanding **17** misinterpretation

misappropriate 4 bilk **5** abuse, cheat, mulct, steal **6** misuse **7** defraud, purloin, swindle **8** embezzle, misapply, peculate **9** defalcate, misemploy

misappropriation 6 misuse, taking **11** defalcation **12** embezzlement

misbehave 5 act up **7** disobey, do wrong **10** transgress **15** get into mischief

misbehavior 5 lapse **7** misdeed, offense **8** acting up, trespass **9** impudence **10** bad conduct, bad manners, disrespect, misconduct **11** delinquency, dereliction, impropriety, misdemeanor **12** indiscretion **13** transgression **16** obstreperousness, unmanageableness

miscalculate 3 err **8** misjudge **10** guess wrong **11** misestimate

miscalculation 5 error **10** inaccuracy **13** misestimation

miscarriage 4 slip **5** botch **6** fizzle **7** default, failing, failure, misfire, undoing, washout **8** casualty, collapse

miscarry 4 fail **5** abort, botch **6** fizzle, go awry **9** terminate **12** come to naught

miscellanea 8 analects **9** anthology, gleanings, scrapbook **10** collection, miscellany, selections **11** collectanea

miscellaneous 5 mixed **6** divers, motley, sundry, varied **7** diverse, mingled, various **8** assorted, manifold **9** different **11** diversified **13** heterogeneous

miscellaneous collection
Latin/pseudo Latin: **14** omniumgatherum

miscellany 5 blend **6** jumble, medley **7** melange, mixture, variety **8** analects, extracts, mishmash, pastiche **9** anthology, gleanings, potpourri **10** assortment, collection, hodgepodge, salmagundi, selections **11** collectanea, compilation, gallimaufry, miscellanea **14** conglomeration, omnium-gatherum

mischance 6 ill lot, mishap **7** bad luck, ill luck, ill wind **8** accident **9** adversity **10** infelicity, misfortune **12** misadventure

mischief 4 evil **5** wrong **6** injury, malice **7** devilry, knavery, roguery **8** deviltry, foul play, plotting, scheming, villainy **9** depravity, devilment, rascality **10** orneriness, wrongdoing **11** naughtiness, playfulness, roguishness, shenanigans, willfulness **12** prankishness, sportiveness **14** capriciousness

mischief-maker 3 imp **5** demon, devil, scamp **7** gremlin, hellion **9** scoundrel **10** hell-raiser

mischievous 3 sly **5** elfin **6** elfish, impish, malign, vexing, wicked **7** harmful, naughty, noxious, playful, roguish, teasing, vicious, waggish **8** annoying, devilish, prankish, spiteful, sportive **9** injurious, malicious, malignant, uninvited **10** frolicsome, gratuitous, pernicious **11** deleterious, destructive, detrimental, uncalled for **12** exacerbating

misconceive 3 err **4** lose, miss **8** misjudge **12** misinterpret **13** misunderstand

misconception 5 error **8** delusion **11** misjudgment **13** erroneous idea **14** mis- information **15** misapprehension, mis- construction **16** misunderstanding **17** misinterpretation, misrepresentation

misconduct 7 misdeed, misstep **10** mis- prision, peccadillo, wrongdoing **11** delinquency, dereliction, impropriety, malefaction, malfeasance, misbehavior, misdemeanor **13** transgression

misconstrue 7 distort, mistake **8** misjudge **9** misreckon, misrender **12** misapprehend, miscalculate, misinterpret, mistranslate **13** misunderstand

miscreant 3 bum **4** heel **5** knave, scamp **6** bad egg, rascal, sinner, wretch **7** villain **8** evildoer, lost soul, scalawag **9** reprobate, scoundrel **10** blackguard, black sheep, malefactor

misdeed 3 sin **4** slip **5** crime, lapse, wrong **6** felony **7** faux pas, offense, outrage **8** atrocity, trespass **9** violation **10** misconduct, peccadillo **11** malfeasance, misbehavior, misdemeanor **12** indiscretion, infringement **13** transgression

misdemeanor 3 sin **5** crime, fault **7** offense, misdeed **8** disorder **10** peccadillo **11** misbehavior **13** transgression

misdoer 5 crook **8** criminal **9** miscreant, wrongdoer **10** delinquent

mise en scene 6 milieu **7** setting **8** ambience **10** atmosphere, background **11** environment **12** stage setting, surroundings

miser 5 piker **7** hoarder, niggard, Scrooge, skimper **8** tightwad **9** skinflint **10** cheapskate, pinchpenny **12** pennypincher, stingy person

Miser, The
also: 6 L'Avare
author: 7 Moliere
character: 5 Elise **6** Valere **7** Anselme, Cleante, Mariane **8** Harpagon

miserable 3 sad **4** mean **5** inept, needy, sorry **6** abject, scurvy, shabby, sordid, woeful **7** abysmal, crushed, doleful, forlorn, grieved, hapless, unhappy **8** beggarly, degraded, dejected, desolate, dolorous, feckless, inferior, mournful, pathetic, pitiable, rubbishy, very poor, wretched **9** appalling, atrocious, cheerless, depressed, desperate, heartsick, sorrowful, woebegone **10** chapfallen, deplorable, despicable, despondent, heavy- laden, lamentable, second-rate, unbearable **11** crestfallen, heartbroken, unfortunate **12** contemptible, disconsolate, impoverished **13** brokenhearted **14** down in the mouth

Miserables, Les
author: 10 Victor Hugo
character: 6 Javert **7** Cosette, Fantine **10** Thenardier **11** Jean Valjean **15** Father Madeleine, Marius Pontmercy **17** Eponine Thenardier

misericordia 5 mercy **10** compassion

miserliness 6 penury **9** frugality, par-

simony **10** stinginess **13** niggardliness, penny-pinching **15** tight-fistedness

miserly 4 mean, near **5** cheap, tight **6** frugal, greedy, meager, stingy **7** selfish **8** grasping, grudging, pinching **9** illiberal, niggardly, penurious, scrimping **10** avaricious, ungenerous **11** closefisted, closehanded, tight-fisted **12** parsimonious **13** penny-pinching

misery 3 woe **4** blow **5** agony, curse, grief, trial **6** ordeal, regret, sorrow **7** anguish, bad deal, bad news, chagrin, despair, sadness, torment, trouble **8** bad scene, calamity, disaster, distress, exaction, hardship **9** dejection, heartache, privation, suffering **10** affliction, bitter pill, depression, desolation, melancholy, misfortune **11** catastrophe, despondency, tribulation **12** wretchedness

Misfits, The
director: 10 John Huston
based on story by: 12 Arthur Miller
cast: 10 Clark Gable, Eli Wallach **12** Thelma Ritter **13** Marilyn Monroe **15** Montgomery Clift

misfortune 4 blow, loss **6** misery, mishap **7** bad luck, reverse, setback, tragedy, trouble **8** calamity, casualty, disaster, downfall, hard luck, hardship **9** adversity, hard times, ruination **10** affliction, ill fortune **11** catastrophe, tribulation **12** misadventure

misgiving, misgivings 4 fear **5** alarm, doubt, dread, qualm, worry **7** anxiety, dubiety **8** disquiet, mistrust **9** suspicion **10** foreboding, skepticism **11** dubiousness, uncertainty **12** apprehension, doubtfulness, presentiment, reservations **14** second thoughts

misguided 5 at sea **6** adrift, faulty, misled, unwise **7** in error **8** mistaken **9** erroneous, imprudent, led astray, off course **10** ill-advised, indiscreet, misadvised **11** injudicious, misdirected, misinformed

mishap 4 slip, snag **5** botch **6** fiasco, slipup **7** reverse, setback **8** casualty, disaster **9** mischance **10** difficulty, misfortune **11** miscarriage **12** misadventure

mishmash 3 mix **4** hash, stew **5** salad **6** jumble, medley, muddle **7** melange **8** mixed bag, pastiche, scramble **9** patchwork **10** assemblage, crazy quilt, hodgepodge, miscellany, salmagundi **14** conglomeration, omnium-gatherum

misinform 7 deceive, mislead **8** misguide **9** misdirect **10** lead astray **12** misrepresent

misinterpret 11 misconstrue **12** misapprehend **13** misunderstand

misinterpretation 13 misconception **16** misunderstanding **17** misrepresentation

misjudge 3 err **7** mistake **10** exaggerate, understate **11** misconceive, mis-

construe **12** misapprehend, miscalculate, misinterpret, overestimate **13** misunderstand, underestimate

mislay 4 lose, miss **8** displace, misplace

mislead 4 dupe, fool, gull **6** betray, delude, entice, seduce, take in **7** beguile, deceive **8** hoodwink, inveigle, misguide **9** bamboozle, misdirect, misinform, play false, victimize **10** lead astray **11** double-cross, string along

misleading 6 luring **8** deluding **9** deceiving **10** misguiding **11** hoodwinking

mismanage 3 mar **4** flub, muff, ruin **5** botch, spoil **6** bollix, bungle, foul up, mess up **7** louse up, screw up **9** mishandle **11** make a hash of, make a mess of

misnomer 8 misusage, solecism **9** barbarism, misnaming **11** malapropism

misogynic 7 cynical **11** woman-hating **12** misanthropic

misogynist 5 cynic **10** woman-hater **11** misanthrope

misplace 4 lose **5** abuse **6** mislay **11** lose track of

misreckon 8 misjudge **10** guess wrong, miscompute **11** misestimate **12** miscalculate

misrepresent 7 falsify, mislead **8** disguise

misrepresentation 7 mockery **8** altering, travesty, twisting **9** burlesque, doctoring **10** caricature, distortion, falsifying **12** adulteration, exaggeration, misstatement **13** falsification

miss 4 blow, girl, lack, lady, lass, lose, loss, maid, muff, skip, slip, want **5** avert, avoid, error, forgo, let go, woman **6** bypass, damsel, escape, forego, lassie, maiden, miscue, pass by **7** blunder, colleen, default, failure, fly wide, let pass, let slip, long for, mistake, neglect, old maid, overrun, pine for **8** leave out, omission, overlook, pass over, senorita, slip up on, spinster, yearn for **9** disregard, fall short, false step, gloss over, go without, overshoot, oversight, surrender, young lady **10** demoiselle, schoolgirl **12** be absent from **13** feel the loss of, mademoiselle

missal 10 prayer book

missed
French: 6 manque

misshapen 7 twisted **8** deformed **9** contorted, distorted

missile 4 ball, dart **5** arrow, lance, shaft, shell, spear, stone **6** bullet, rocket **7** harpoon, javelin **10** projectile

missing 4 AWOL, gone, lost **6** absent **7** lacking, left out, not here **8** avoiding, skipping **10** longing for, not present **11** overlooking, yearning for **12** disregarding

Missing
   director: **22** Constantine Costa-Gavras
   cast: **8** John Shea **10** Jack Lemmon
   11 Sissy Spacek **13** Melanie Mayron
Missing Persons and Other Essays
   author: **12** Heinrich Boll
mission 3 end, job **4** task **5** quest **6**
   charge **7** calling, mandate, pursuit **8**
   legation, ministry **9** objective **10** assignment, commission, delegation, enterprise **11** raison d'etre, undertaking
Mission
   tribe: **7** Chumash, Juaneno, Luiseno
   8 Diegueno **9** Costanoan **10** Gabri-
   elino **11** Fernandario
   location: **10** California
Mission: Impossible
   character: **5** Casey, Paris **10** Rollin
   Hand **11** Dana Lambert, James
   Phelps **12** Daniel Briggs **13** Barney
   Collier **14** Cinnamon Carter, Willie
   Armitage
   cast: **10** Greg Morris, Peter Lupus,
   Steven Hill **11** Barbara Bain, Peter
   Graves **12** Leonard Nimoy, Martin
   Landau **14** Lynda Day George **15**
   Lesley Ann Warren
Mississippi
   abbreviation: **2** MS **4** Miss
   nickname: **5** Bayou **6** Mudcat **8** Magnolia
   capital/largest city: **7** Jackson
   others: **6** Biloxi, Helena, Laurel, Tupelo, Winona **7** Belzoni, Corinth,
   Grenada, Natchez **8** Bogalusa, Columbus, Gulfport, Meridian **9** Kosciusko, Vicksburg **10** Clarksdale, Pascagoula **11** Hattiesburg **13** Pass
   Christian
   college: **4** Rust **6** Alcorn **7** Jackson **8**
   Belhaven, Millsaps, Tougaloo **11**
   Mississippi **12** Blue Mountain, William Carey
   feature: **12** Natchez Trace
      national military park: **9** Vicksburg
      national seashore: **11** Gulf Islands
   tribe: **3** Sac **5** Tious **6** Biloxi, Mandan, Tunica **7** Choctaw, Natchez,
   Tonikan **8** Chicksaw
   people: **11** Eudora Welty **15** William
   Faulkner **17** Tennessee Williams
      explorer: **6** DeSoto, Joliet **9** Iber-
      ville, Marquette
   island: **3** Cat **4** Horn, Ship **9** Petit
   Bois
   lake: **4** Enid **6** Sardis **7** Barnett, Grenada **8** Pickwick **9** Arkabutla, Oka-
   tibbee
   land rank: **12** thirty-second
   highest point: **7** Woodall
   physical feature:
      delta: **10** Yazoo Basin
      hills: **8** Fall Line **9** Tennessee **11**
      Loess Bluffs
      prairie: **5** Black **7** Jackson
      sound: **11** Mississippi
   river: **4** Leaf **5** Pearl, Yazoo **8** Big
   Black **9** Tombigbee, Yalobusha

   10 Homochitto, Pascagoula **11** Mississippi **12** Tallahatchie
   state admission: **9** twentieth
   state bird: **11** mockingbird
   state flower: **8** magnolia
   state motto: **14** By Valor and Arms
   state song: **13** Go Mississippi
   state tree: **8** magnolia
missive 4 note **6** billet, letter **7** epistle,
   message **13** communication **14** correspondence
Miss Julie
   author: **16** August Strindberg
Miss Lonelyhearts
   author: **13** Nathanael West
Missouri
   abbreviation: **2** MO
   nickname: **5** Ozark **6** Show-Me **7** Bullion **15** Mother of the West
   capital: **13** Jefferson City
   largest city: **7** St Louis
   others: **5** Eldon, Hayti, Lamar, Macon, Rolla **6** Butler, Joplin, Mexico **7**
   Bethany, Bolivar, Cameron, Clayton,
   Lebanon, Moberly, Sedalia **8** Berkeley, Columbia, Hannibal, Kirkwood,
   Sikeston, St Joseph **10** Bonne Terre,
   Kansas City **11** Springfield, Warrens-
   burg **12** Independence **13** Cape Gi-
   rardeau, Webster Groves
   college: **5** Avila, Drury **6** Tarkio **7**
   Lincoln, St Louis, Webster **8** Stephens **10** Washington **11** Westminster
   feature:
      dam: **5** Osage
   tribe: **3** Fox, Sac **4** Sauk **5** Osage **7**
   Shawnee **8** Cherokee, Missouri
   people: **7** TS Eliot **9** Mark Twain **10**
   Jesse James **11** Omar Bradley **12**
   Helen Traubel, Sara Teasdale **13**
   John J Pershing, Marianne Moore,
   Samuel Clemens **15** Reinhold Niebuhr **22** George Washington Carver
      explorer: **6** Joliet **7** La Salle **9** Mar-
      quette
   lake: **7** Norfolk **9** Tablerock, Taney-
   como **10** Bull Shoals **14** Kaysinger
   Bluff **15** Lake of the Ozarks
   land rank: **10** nineteenth
   mountain: **6** Ozarks **10** St Francois
      highest point: **8** Taumsauk
   physical feature: **8** Bootheel **9** Big
   Spring
      plains: **4** Till **5** Osage
      plateau: **5** Ozark
   president: **12** Harry S Truman
   river: **4** Salt **5** Grand, Osage, White **6**
   Platte **7** Current, Meramec **8** Big
   Muddy, Chariton, Missouri **9** Des
   Moines, Gasconade, St Francis **11**
   Mississippi
   state admission: **12** twenty-fourth
   state bird: **8** bluebird
   state flower: **8** hawthorn
   state motto: **41** The Welfare of the
   People Shall Be the Supreme Law

   state song: **13** Missouri Waltz
   state tree: **7** dogwood
Miss Peach
   creator: **11** Mell Lazarus
   character: **3** Ira **6** Arthur, Lester,
   Marcia **8** Francine
   place: **9** Kamp Kelly **11** Kelly School
misspend 5 waste **8** squander **9** dissipate, throw away **11** fritter away
misspent 6 wasted **8** depraved **9** debauched, dissolute, idled away **10**
   misapplied, profitless, squandered,
   thrown away
misstate 5 alter **6** bollix, garble **7** confuse, distort, falsify, pervert **8** mis-
   quote **9** misreport **12** misrepresent
misstatement 3 fib, lie **4** tale **5** error
   7 falsity, untruth **9** falsehood **13** prevarication **17** misrepresentation
misstep 3 sin **4** goof, slip, vice **5**
   boner, error, fault, gaffe, lapse **6** boo-
   boo, defect, foul-up **7** blooper, faux
   pas, offense, screw-up **11** delinquency, dereliction, shortcoming **12**
   indiscretion **13** transgression
miss the mark 4 fail **9** fall short **11**
   come up short
miss the point 7 mistake **11** fail to
   catch, misconceive **12** misapprehend
   13 misunderstand
mist 3 fog **4** haze, murk, smog **5**
   steam, vapor **7** drizzle
mistake 4 slip **5** boner, error, gaffe,
   mix-up **6** slipup **7** blooper, blunder,
   confuse, faux pas, misstep **8** confound, misjudge **9** misreckon, oversight **11** misconstrue, misidentify **12**
   misapprehend, miscalculate, misinterpret **13** misunderstand **14** miscalculation
   French. 10 malentendu
mistaken 5 at sea, false, wrong **6**
   faulty, untrue **7** at fault, in error, unsound **8** deceived **9** erroneous, illogical, incorrect, off course, unfounded
   10 fallacious, groundless, inaccurate,
   ungrounded **11** unjustified
Mister 3 aga, dom, don, pan, reb, sir **4**
   agha, babu, herr **5** sahib, senor **6** senhor, signor **7** mynheer **8** monsieur
Mister Roberts
   author: **12** Thomas Heggen
   director: **8** John Ford **11** Mervyn Le-
   Roy
   cast: **8** Ward Bond **10** Henry Fonda,
   Jack Lemmon (Ensign Pulver) **11**
   Betsy Palmer, James Cagney **13** William Powell
   Oscar for: **15** supporting actor (Lemmon)
Mister Saturday Night
   nickname of: **13** Jackie Gleason
mistreat 4 harm **5** abuse, bully,
   hound, wrong **6** harass, ill-use, injure,
   misuse, molest **7** assault, oppress,
   outrage, pervert, torment, violate

8 ill-treat, maltreat **9** brutalize, manhandle, mishandle, persecute

mistreatment 5 abuse **6** ill-use, injury **7** assault, cruelty, harming **10** bodily harm, oppression **11** manhandling, molestation, persecution **12** maltreatment

mistress 3 Mrs **4** doxy, lady, Miss **5** lover, Madam **6** matron **8** ladylove, paramour **9** concubine, headwoman, housewife, inamorata, kept woman **10** chatelaine, girlfriend, sweetheart

mistrust 5 doubt, qualm **7** anxiety, dubiety, suspect **8** distrust, question, wariness **9** challenge, chariness, leeriness, misgiving, suspicion **10** disbelieve, skepticism

misty 4 dewy, hazy **5** filmy, foggy, murky **6** cloudy, opaque, steamy **8** nebulous, overcast, vaporous **10** indistinct

misunderstand 7 confuse, misread, mistake **8** misjudge **9** misreckon **11** misconceive, misconstrue **12** misapprehend, miscalculate, misinterpret, miss the point

misunderstanding 4 rift, spat **5** set-to **7** discord, dispute, quarrel, wrangle **8** conflict, squabble **10** difference, dissension, misreading **11** altercation, contretemps, misjudgment **12** disagreement **13** misconception **15** false impression, misapprehension **16** miscomprehension **17** misinterpretation
French: 10 malentendu

misuse 4 harm, hurt **5** abuse, waste, wrong **6** debase, injure **7** corrupt, exploit, outrage, pervert, profane **8** illtreat, maltreat, misapply, mistreat, wrong use **9** misemploy **10** corruption, perversion, prostitute **11** desecration, profanation, squandering **12** ill treatment, maltreatment, mistreatment, prostitution **13** misemployment **14** misapplication **15** take advantage of

Mitchell, Billy (William Lendrum)
advocate of: **8** air power
court-martialed for: **15** insubordination
served in: **3** WWI
rank: **16** brigadier general
commander of: **15** US army air forces

Mitchell, Margaret
author of: **15** Gone With the Wind

Mitchell, Silas Weir
author of: **9** Hugh Wynne (Free Quaker) **11** Roland Blake

Mitchell, Thomas
born: **11** Elizabeth NJ
roles: **7** Our Town **8** Doc Boone **9** The Outlaw **10** Stagecoach **11** Gerald O'Hara, Lost Horizon **15** Gone With the Wind **19** Only Angels Have Wings

Mitchum, Robert
born: **12** Bridgeport CT
roles: **6** Midway **10** Winds of War **11** Thunder Road **13** Ryan's Daughter, The Longest Day, The Sundowners **15** The Story of G I Joe **16** Farewell My Lovely **20** Heaven Knows Mr Allison

mite 3 bit, jot **4** atom, iota, whit **5** scrap, speck **6** spider **7** smidgen **8** arachnid, particle

Mitford, Jessica
author of: **21** The American Way of Death **22** Kind and Usual Punishment

Mitford, Nancy
author of: **14** Noblesse Oblige **16** The Pursuit of Love **18** Love in a Cold Climate
coined term: **1** U **4** non-U

Mithgarthr *see* **7** Midgard

Mithras
origin: **7** Persian
god of: **5** light, truth
corresponds to: **3** Sol

mitigate 4 ease **5** allay, blunt **6** lessen, reduce, soften, soothe, temper, weaken **7** assuage, lighten, mollify, placate, relieve **8** diminish, moderate, palliate **9** alleviate, extenuate **10** ameliorate

mitigating 6 easing **8** allaying, blunting, reducing **9** assuaging, lessening, relieving, softening, tempering **10** lightening, moderating, palliating, palliative **11** diminishing, extenuating **12** ameliorating

Mitteleuropa 12 middle Europe

mitzvah, mitsvah 8 good deed **11** commandment

mix 3 add **4** beat, club, fold, fuse, join, stir, whip **5** admix, alloy, blend, merge, put in, unite **6** commix, fusion, hobnob, mingle **7** combine, consort, include, mixture **8** assembly, coalesce, compound, intermix, mingling **9** associate, commingle, interfuse, interlard, introduce, socialize **10** amalgamate, fraternize, intertwine, interweave **11** incorporate, intermingle, intersperse, put together

mixed 4 coed **5** fused **6** hybrid, motley **7** alloyed, blended, inmixed, mingled, mongrel, not pure **8** combined **9** composite, uncertain **10** ambivalent, indecisive, interwoven, variegated **11** adulterated, diversified, half and half, put together **12** conglomerate, inconclusive **13** heterogeneous, male-and-female, miscellaneous

mixed-up 6 addled **7** chaotic, jumbled, muddled, tangled **8** confused, rambling **9** befuddled, illogical, nonplused, perplexed **10** bewildered, disjointed, incoherent, irrational, nonplussed **12** disconnected, disorganized **13** disharmonious, heterogeneous

Mixtec
tribe: **7** Zapotec

mixture 3 mix **4** hash, stew **5** alloy, blend, union **6** fusion, jumble, medley **7** amalgam, melange **8** compound, mishmash, pastiche **9** admixture, composite, potpourri **10** commixture, hodgepodge, salmagundi **11** association, combination **12** adulteration, amalgamation, intermixture

mixup 4 mess, riot **5** fight, melee, snafu **6** fracas, muddle, tangle **7** mistake **8** disorder **9** confusion, imbroglio **11** misjudgment **14** miscalculation **16** miscomprehension, misunderstanding

mix up 5 addle **6** mess up, muddle **7** confuse, nonplus, perplex **8** befuddle, bewilder **10** disarrange

Mneme
member of: **5** Muses
personifies: **6** memory

Mnemosyne
origin: **5** Greek
member of: **6** Titans
goddess of: **6** memory
father: **6** Uranus
mother: **4** Gaea
daughters: **5** Muses

Moab
son of: **3** Lot
land near: **7** Dead Sea
home of: **4** Ruth **5** Naomi

Moabite god 7 Chemosh

moan 3 sob **4** keen, wail **5** groan **6** bemoan, bewail, lament, plaint **7** grumble **11** lamentation

moan over 5 mourn **6** bemoan, bewail, lament **7** cry over **8** weep over **10** grieve over

moat 4 foss **5** ditch, fosse, graff **6** gutter, rundel, trench

mob 4 gang, herd **5** crowd, crush, horde, Mafia, swarm **6** masses, rabble, throng **7** flock to **8** assembly, populace, surround **9** gathering, hoi polloi, multitude, plebeians, syndicate **10** converge on **11** proletariat, rank and file **14** organized crime

mobile 6 active, motile **7** kinetic, movable, nomadic **8** portable, rootless **9** footloose, traveling, wandering **10** ambulatory, locomotive

mobilize 6 call up, muster, summon **7** marshal **8** activate, organize **10** call to arms **11** put in motion

mobster 4 hood **6** hitman **7** hoodlum, Mafioso **8** gangster **10** gang member

Moby Dick
author of: **14** Herman Melville
character: **4** Ahab **5** Stubb **7** Ishmael **8** Fedallah, Queequeg, Starbuck

mock 3 ape **4** copy **5** belie, mimic, scorn, spurn, taunt **6** deride, insult, jeer at, parody, revile, show up **7** imitate, laugh at, let down, profane, scoff at, sneer at **8** ridicule **9** burlesque, frustrate, make fun of, poke fun at **10** caricature, disappoint, make game of **11** make sport of

mockery 4 joke, sham **5** farce, scorn **7** jeering, mimicry, sarcasm **8** derision, raillery, ridicule, scoffing, travesty **9** burlesque, contumely **10** disrespect, ridiculing **13** laughingstock

Mock Turtle
    character in: **28** Alice's Adventures in Wonderland
    author: **7** Carroll

mode 3 cut, fad, way **4** form, rage, rule **5** craze, means, style, taste, trend, vogue **6** course, custom, manner, method, system **7** fashion, process **8** approach, practice **9** condition, procedure, technique **10** appearance

model 4 cast, copy, form, mold, show, type **5** build, dummy, ideal, shape, sport, style **6** design, mirror, mock-up **7** display, example, fashion, outline, paragon, pattern, perfect, replica, subject, variety, version **8** exemplar, paradigm, peerless, standard **9** archetype, criterion, exemplary, facsimile, mannequin, prototype, simulated **10** simulacrum **14** representation, representative

model on 6 base on **7** found on **10** derive from

mode of operating
    Latin: **2** mo **13** modus operandi

moderate 4 calm, cool, curb, fair, hush, mild, tame **5** abate, chair, sober **6** direct, gentle, lessen, manage, medium, modest, soften, subdue, temper **7** average, careful, conduct, control, oversee **8** diminish, measured, mediocre, middling, ordinary, passable, rational, regulate, restrain, tone down **9** judicious, peaceable, temperate, unruffled **10** not violent, reasonable **11** inexpensive, preside over **12** mainstreamer, medium-priced

moderation 7 abating, economy **8** allaying **9** abatement, frugality, lessening, remission, restraint **10** continence, diminution, mitigation, palliation, relaxation, temperance **11** alleviation, forbearance, self-control **12** moderateness **13** temperateness **14** abstemiousness **19** avoidance of extremes

moderator 8 chairman, mediator **10** chairwoman, negotiator

modern 3 new **6** modish, recent **7** current, in vogue **8** up-to-date **10** present-day **11** fashionable, streamlined **12** contemporary **15** contemporaneous **16** twentieth-century

Modern Comedy, A
    author: **14** John Galsworthy

modernistic 3 neo **6** modern **7** moderne **10** new-fangled **12** contemporary

modernity 5 vogue **7** fashion, new

look, novelty, the rage **8** last word **14** newfangledness **15** contemporaneity **16** new fashionedness

modernize 4 redo **5** renew **6** do over, revamp, update **7** restore **8** redesign, renovate **9** refurbish **10** regenerate, rejuvenate, streamline **11** recondition **13** bring up to date **16** move with the times

modern times 5 today **8** nowadays **10** the present **13** the here and now

Modern Times
    director: **14** Charles Chaplin
    cast: **12** Henry Bergman **14** Charlie Chaplin, Chester Conklin **15** Paulette Goddard **19** Stanley "Tiny" Sandford

modest 3 coy, shy **4** meek, prim **5** plain, quiet, timid **6** demure, humble, proper, simple **7** bashful, limited, nominal, prudish, unshowy **8** blushing, discreet, moderate, reserved, timorous **9** diffident, shrinking **10** unassuming **11** circumspect, constrained, inexpensive, puritanical, straitlaced, unassertive, unobtrusive **12** medium-priced, not excessive, self-effacing, unpretending **13** unpretentious **14** unostentatious

modesty 7 coyness, prudery, reserve, shyness **8** humility, plainness, timidity **9** propriety, restraint, reticence **10** constraint, demureness, diffidence, humbleness, simplicity **11** bashfulness, naturalness **12** timorousness **14** reasonableness, self-effacement **15** inexpensiveness

modicum 3 bit, dab, jot **4** atom, dash, drop, inch, iota, mite, whit **5** crumb, grain, pinch, scrap, speck, tinge, touch **6** morsel, sliver, snatch, trifle **7** handful, minimum, smidgen **8** fraction, fragment, particle **9** little bit **10** sprinkling **11** small amount **13** small quantity

modification 6 change **8** revision **9** variation **10** adjustment, alteration, conversion, emendation, regulation **14** transformation **15** differentiation

modify 4 redo, vary **5** adapt, alter, limit, lower, remit **6** adjust, change, narrow, reduce, remold, revise, rework, soften, temper **7** control, convert, qualify, remodel, reshape **8** moderate, modulate, restrain, restrict, tone down **9** condition, refashion, transform, transmute **10** reorganize **12** transmogrify

Modigliani, Amedeo
    born: **5** Italy **7** Leghorn, Livorno
    artwork: **10** Seated Nude **13** Reclining Nude, Yellow Sweater **15** Jeanne Hebuterne

modish 2 in **3** now **4** chic **5** natty, nifty, sharp, smart, today **6** dapper, snazzy, spiffy, trendy, with it **7** a la mode, current, faddish, in style, in

vogue, stylish, voguish **9** high-style **11** fashionable **13** up-to-the-minute

Modoc
    language family: **12** Shapwailutan
    division: **10** Lutuamnian
    location: **6** Oregon **10** California
    leader: **14** Chief Kintpuash (Captain Jack)
    related to: **7** Klamath

Modred
    character in: **16** Arthurian romance

Mod Squad, The
    character: **9** Linc Hayes, (Capt) Adam Greer **11** Julie Barnes, Pete Cochran
    cast: **11** Michael Cole, Peggy Lipton, Tige Andrews **19** Clarence Williams III

modulate 4 pass **5** lower **6** accord, attune, change, reduce, soften, temper **8** moderate, progress, regulate, tone down, turn down **9** harmonize

modulation 4 tone **5** pitch **6** accent **9** reduction **10** expression, regulation, transition

modus operandi 15 mode of operating
    abbreviation: **2** mo

modus vivendi 14 manner of living

Mogadishu, Mogadiscio
    capital of: **7** Somalia

mogul 3 VIP **4** czar, lord **5** baron, power, wheel **6** bigwig, tycoon **7** big shot, magnate, notable **8** big wheel **9** personage, potentate

Mohammed
    also: **7** Mahomet, Prophet **8** Muhammad
    born: **5** Mecca
    clan: **6** Hashim
    daughter: **6** Fatima
    deity: **5** Allah
    died: **6** Medina
    father: **8** Abdallah, Abdullah
    father-in-law: **7** Abu Bakr, Abubekr
    flight: **4** hadj **6** hegira, hejira
    follower: **6** Moslem, Muslim, Wahbi **10** Mohammedan
    grandfather: **13** Abd al-Muttalib
    horse: **5** Buraq **7** Alborrak
    mother: **5** Amina
    religion: **5** Islam
    shrine: **5** Kaaba
    son: **7** Ibrahim
       adopted: **3** Ali
    successor: **4** imam **5** calif **6** caliph **7** Abu Bakr
    tribe: **7** Koreish, Quraysh
    uncle: **5** Abbas **8** Abu Talib
    wife: **5** Aisha **6** Ayesha, Safiya **7** Khadija **8** Khadidja, Kadijah

Mohammedan 4 Sufi **6** Moslem, Muslim, Shiite **7** Islamic, Moorish, Sunnite **10** Mahometan, Muhammadan, Muhammedan

Mohave, Mojave
    language family: **5** Yuman
    location: **7** Arizona **10** California

Mohawk (Kaniengehaga)
language family: 9 Iroquoian
location: 6 Canada, Quebec 7 New
  York 11 Lake Ontario
leader: 8 Hiawatha 11 Joseph Brant
member of: 19 League of the Iroquois

Mohegan, Mohican, Mahican
language family: 9 Algonkian 10 Algonquian
location: 7 New York 9 Wisconsin 11
  Connecticut 12 Hudson Valley
leader: 5 Occom, Uncas 12 Chingachgook
allied with: 6 Pequot
with Delaware: 11 Loup Indians,
  Wolf Indians
subject of novel: 20 The Last of the
  Mohicans
    author: 19 James Fenimore Cooper

Moira
personifies: 4 fate

moist 3 wet 4 damp, dank, dewy 5
  humid, misty, muggy, rainy 6
  clammy, drippy, watery 7 aqueous,
  drizzly, tearful, wettish, wet-eyed 8
  dripping, vaporous 10 lachrymose

moisten 3 dew, wet 4 damp, hose,
  mist, soak 5 spray, water 6 dampen,
  douche, splash, sponge 8 humidify, irrigate, saturate, vaporize 10 moistur-
  ize

moisture 3 dew, wet 4 damp, mist 5
  sweat, vapor 7 drizzle, exudate, wetness 8 dampness, dankness, humidity
  9 moistness, mugginess 10 wateriness
  11 evaporation 12 perspiration

Mojave see 6 Mohave

Moki see 4 Hopi

mold 3 cut, die, ilk 4 cast, form, kind,
  line, make, rust, sort, turn, type 5
  brand, frame, knead, model, shape,
  stamp, train 6 blight, create, figure,
  fungus, kidney, lichen, matrix, mildew, render, sculpt, shaper 7 contour,
  convert, develop, fashion, outline, pattern, quality, remodel 9 character,
  construct, formation, structure, transform

molding 4 cyma, dado, gula, ogee 5
  ovolo

Moldova
other name: 8 Moldavia
capital/largest city: 8 Chisinau, Kishinev
head of state: 9 president
government: 8 republic
monetary unit: 5 ruble
river: 8 Dniester
people: 7 Gagauzi 8 Moldovan 9
  Moldavian
language: 8 Romanian 9 Moldavian
religion: 15 Russian Orthodox

moldy 5 fusty, hoary, musty, stale 7
  spoiled 8 mildewed

molest 3 irk, vex 4 fret, harm, hurt 5
  abuse, annoy, beset, harry, worry

6 attack, bother, harass, hector, injure, pester, plague 7 assault, disturb,
  torment, trouble 8 maltreat

Moliere (Jean-Baptiste Poquelin)
author of: 6 Scapin 8 Tartuffe, The
  Miser 10 Amphitryon 13 Le Misanthrope 17 The School for Wives 19
  The Imaginary Invalid 20 The School
  for Husbands 22 Le Bourgeois Gentilhomme

Moll Flanders
author: 11 Daniel Defoe
character: 5 Robin 6 Jemmy E 10 Sea
  Captain

mollification 8 soothing 9 placation
  11 appeasement, assuagement 12 conciliation

mollify 4 calm, curb, dull, ease, lull 5
  abate, allay, blunt, check, quell, quiet,
  still 6 lessen, pacify, reduce, soften,
  soothe, temper 7 appease, assuage,
  lighten, placate 8 decrease, mitigate,
  moderate, palliate, tone down

mollusk 4 clam, slug 5 conch, cowry,
  murex, snail, squid, whelk 6 chiton,
  cockle, cowrie, limpet, mussel, oyster,
  teredo, triton 7 abalone, bivalve, geoduck, octopus, scallop 8 argonaut,
  nautilus, shipworm 9 shellfish 10 cuttlefish, nudibranch, peri- winkle

mollycoddle 3 pet 4 baby, wimp 5
  sissy, spoil 6 cosset, coward, pamper
  7 cater to, crybaby, indulge, milksop
  8 give in to, mama's boy, weakling 9
  cream puff 11 milquetoast, overindulge

Molnar, Ferenc
author of: 6 Liliom 7 The Swan 12
  The Guardsman

Moloch 3 god 5 diety
also: 6 Molech
worshiped by: 9 Ammonites

molt 4 cast, shed, slip 6 change,
  slough 7 castoff, discard, ecdysis 8
  exuviate

molten 6 melted, red-hot 7 fusible, igneous, smelted 8 magmatic 9 liquefied

molto
music: 4 very

Moly
form: 4 herb
given to: 8 Odysseus
given by: 6 Hermes
to counteract spells of: 5 Circe

Momaday, N Scott
author of: 18 The House Made of
  Dawn 21 The Way to Rainy Mountain

moment 5 flash, jiffy, trice, value,
  worth 6 import, minute, second,
  weight 7 concern, gravity, instant 8
  interest, juncture 9 twinkling 10 importance 11 consequence, weightiness
  12 significance

momentary 5 brief, hasty, quick,

short 6 sudden 7 instant, passing 8
  flashing, fleeting, fugitive, imminent 9
  ephemeral, immediate, temporary,
  transient 10 short-lived, transitory 13
  instantaneous

momentous 5 grave 7 crucial, fateful,
  salient, serious, weighty 8 critical, decisive, eventful 9 essential, important,
  ponderous 11 far-reaching, influential,
  significant, substantial 12 earthshak-
  ing 13 consequential

momentous occurrence 5 event 8
  occasion 9 milestone 12 red-letter
  day, turning point

momentum 2 go 4 dash, push 5
  drive, force, speed, vigor 6 energy,
  moment, thrust 7 headway, impetus,
  impulse 8 velocity 10 propulsion

Mommsen, Theodor
author of: 16 The History of Rome

Momus
also: 5 Momos
god of: 7 censure 8 ridicule

Monaco
capital: 11 Monaco-Ville
largest city: 10 Monte Carlo
others: 9 Fontville
division: 9 Fontville 10 Monte Carlo
  11 La Condamine, Monaco-Ville
head of government: 15 minister of
  state
head of state: 6 prince
monetary unit: 5 franc 7 centime
river: 7 Vesubie
sea: 13 Mediterranean
physical feature: 9 Cote d'Azur
people: 6 French 7 Italian 10 Monegasque
  oceanographer: 15 Jacques Cous-
    teau
  prince: 5 Louis 6 Albert, Honore 7
    Antoine, Charles, Rainier 9 Flore-
    stan
  princess: 10 Grace Kelly
  ruler: 4 Rome 5 Genoa 6 Greece 8
    Grimaldi, Saracens 9 Phoenicia
language: 6 French 7 English, Italian
  10 Monegasque
religion: 13 Roman Catholic
place:
  beach: 8 Larvotto
  casino: 10 Monte Carlo
  gardens: 6 Exotic
  museum: 12 Oceanography
  park: 18 Princess Antoinette
feature:
  auto race: 15 Monaco Grand Prix

Monaco-Ville
capital of: 6 Monaco

Mona Lisa
also called: 10 La Gioconda
artist: 15 Leonardo da Vinci
noted for: 5 smile
museum: 6 Louvre

monarch 3 HRH 4 czar, doge, emir,
  khan, king, rani, shah, tsar 5 rajah,
  ruler, queen 6 caesar, kaiser, prince

7 czarina, emperor, empress, majesty, pharaoh **8** kaiserin, princess **9** chieftain, potentate

monarchical 9 czaristic **10** autocratic **11** dictatorial

monastery 5 abbey **6** friary, priory **7** convent, nunnery, retreat **8** cloister

monastic 7 ascetic, monkish, recluse **8** celibate, hermitic, secluded, solitary **9** cloistral, reclusive, unworldly **10** cloistered, hermitlike **11** sequestered **13** contemplative

mon cher 6 my dear

Moncrieff, Algernon (Algy)
  character in: **27** The Importance of Being Earnest
  author: **5** Wilde

Mond, Mustapha
  character in: **13** Brave New World
  author: **6** Huxley

Monday
  French: **5** lundi
  German: **6** montag
  heavenly body: **4** moon
  Italian: **6** lunedi
  means: **12** day of the moon
  Spanish: **5** lunes

Mondrian, Piet
  real name: **23** Pieter Cornelis Mondriaan
  born: **10** Amersfoort **14** The Netherlands
  artwork: **5** Trees **10** The Red Tree **12** Ocean and Pier **17** Evening Landscapes **18** Landscape with a Mill **20** Broadway Boogie-Woogie **29** Composition in Red Yellow and Blue

Monet, Claude Oscar
  born: **5** Paris **6** France
  artwork: **7** Poplars **9** Haystacks, The Thames **11** Water Lilies **14** Rouen Cathedral **16** Women in the Garden **17** Impression Sunrise **18** Mornings on the Seine **21** The Bridge at Argenteuil

monetary 6 fiscal **9** budgetary, financial, pecuniary, sumptuary

money 4 cash, coin **5** bread, bucks, dough, funds **6** assets, riches, specie, wealth **7** capital, coinage, payment, revenue, scratch **8** currency, hard cash, proceeds **9** affluence, long green **10** collateral, greenbacks **11** wherewithal

money-carrier
  French: **12** porte-monnaie

moneyed, monied 4 rich **5** flush, swell **6** flashy, loaded **7** elegant, opulent, solvent, wealthy **8** affluent **10** prosperous

money-grubbing 5 venal **6** greedy **8** covetous, grasping **9** mercenary **10** avaricious

money lender 6 banker, lender, usurer **7** lombard, shylock **9** loanshark **10** pawnbroker

money saved 7 nest egg, savings **10** investment

money spent 6 outlay **7** payment **8** expenses **11** expenditure

Mongolia
  other name: **13** Outer Mongolia
  capital/largest city: **9** Ulan Bator
  others: **5** Kobdo **6** Darhan **10** Choibalsan, Sukhe Bator, Tsetserlik, Uliassutai
    ancient capital: **9** Karakoram
  government:
    legislature: **17** People's Great Hural **18** People's Great Khural
  monetary unit: **5** mongo, mungo **6** tugrik **7** tughrik
  weight: **3** lan
  lake: **3** Uvs **5** Har Us **6** Bor Nor **7** Ghirgis, Ubsa Nor **8** Airik Nor, Durga Nor, Hobsogol, Khara Usu **9** Khubsugul, Khukhu-Nur **10** Khirgis Nor
  mountain: **4** Cast, Orog **5** Altai **6** Kentei, Sevrej **7** Ich Ovoo, Khangai, Khentei **8** Tannu-Ola **9** Edrengijn **10** Cagaan Bogd **11** Munky Sardyk **14** Hangayn-Hentiyn, Monch Chajrchan
  highest point: **10** Tabun Bogdo
  river: **3** Tes **4** Egin, Onon, Tuul, Uldz **5** Kobdo, Tesin **6** Orkhon **7** Kerulen, Selenga, Selenge **8** Dzabkhan, Dzavchan
  physical feature:
    desert: **4** Gobi **5** Ordos, Shamo
    plateau: **8** Mongolia
    region: **10** Great Lakes
  people: **5** Oirat, Tungu **6** Buryat, Darbet, Khoton, Mongol **7** Kazakhs, Khalkha **8** Tuvinian **9** Dariganga
    leader: **8** Jahangir, Jehangir **10** Kublai Khan, Tsendenbal **11** Genghis Khan
    ruler: **4** Huns **5** Ching **6** Manchu **7** Kirghiz, Uighurs **8** Hsiung nu
    spiritual/secular ruler: **12** Living Buddha **21** Jebtsun Damba Khutu Khtu
  language: **6** Kazakh **16** Khalkha Mongolian
  religion: **7** Lamaism **9** Shamanism **15** Tibetan Buddhism
  place:
    monastery: **6** Gandun
  feature:
    felt tent: **4** yurt
    nomadic herder: **4** arat
  food:
    fermented mare's milk: **5** airag

Mongolian
  language family: **6** Altaic
  group: **6** Buryat **7** Khalkha

Mongoose, The
  nickname of: **11** Archie Moore

mongrel 3 cur **4** mutt **5** mixed **6** hybrid **7** bastard **8** offshoot **9** anomalous, crossbred **10** crossbreed

moniker 3 tag **4** name **5** label, title **6** eponym, handle **7** epithet, surname **8** cognomen, nickname, taxonomy

9 sobriquet **11** appellation, designation **12** denomination

monitor 2 TV **4** tend **5** guide, teach **6** censor, direct, pickup, police, screen, sensor **7** oversee, proctor, scanner **8** overseer, watchdog **9** supervise **14** disciplinarian

Monkees, The
  cast/musician: **9** Davy Jones, Peter Tork **10** David Jones **11** Micky Dolenz, Mike Nesmith

monkey 3 ape, ass, toy **4** butt, dupe, fool, jerk **5** clown, jimmy **6** baboon, fiddle, meddle, simian, tamper, tinker, trifle **7** buffoon, primate **13** laughingstock
  group of: **5** troop
  god: **7** Hanuman
  kind: **3** owl **4** saki, titi **5** aotus, lemur, titis **6** baboon, guenon, howler, langur, rhesus, spider **7** colobus, Goeldi's, guereza, macaque, tamarin, tarsier, uakaris **8** capuchin, mandrill, marmoset, squirrel, talapoin **11** douroucouli

monkey business 6 capers **9** highjinks **11** shenanigans

monkeyshines 6 antics, capers, pranks **7** hijinks **10** buffoonery, tomfoolery **11** foolishness

Monks (Edward Leeford)
  character in: **11** Oliver Twist
  author: **7** Dickens

monocle 4 quiz **5** glass **7** lorgnon **8** eyeglass

Monoclonius
  type: **8** dinosaur **10** ceratopsid
  location: **12** North America
  characteristic: **6** horned

Monod, Jacques
  field: **7** biology
  nationality: **6** French
  researched: **3** RNA **8** genetics
  awarded: **10** Nobel Prize

monograph 8 tractate, treatise **9** discourse **12** disquisition, dissertation

monolith 5 stone **6** column, menhir, pillar, statue **7** obelisk **8** memorial, monument

monologue, monolog 6 screed, sermon, speech **7** address, lecture, oration **9** discourse, soliloquy **11** expatiation **12** disquisition

monopolize 3 own **6** absorb, corner, manage, take up **7** consume, control, preempt **8** arrogate, dominate, regulate, take over **9** cartelize **11** appropriate

monopoly 4 bloc **5** trust **6** cartel, corner **7** combine, control **8** dominion **9** copyright, ownership, syndicate **10** consortium, domination **11** sovereignty **12** jurisdiction **14** proprietorship

Monopoly 9 board game
  invented by: **6** Darrow

places: 2 go, RR **4** jail **6** chance **9** Boardwalk, Park Place
piece: 5 hotel, house
monotonous 3 dry **4** dull, flat **5** banal **6** boring, dreary, jejune, stodgy, torpid **7** droning, humdrum, insipid, mundane, prosaic, routine, tedious **8** plodding, singsong, tiresome, toneless, unvaried **9** colorless, soporific, wearisome **10** pedestrian **11** repetitious, somniferous **13** uninteresting
monotony 3 rut **5** ennui **6** tedium **7** boredom, humdrum **8** dullness, flatness, prosaism, sameness **9** iteration **10** dreariness, redundancy, uniformity **11** reiteration, tediousness **13** wearisomeness **14** predictability

Monroe, Earl
nickname: 12 Earl the Pearl
sport: 10 basketball
position: 6 guard
team: 16 Baltimore Bullets **21** New York Knickerbockers

Monroe, James
presidential rank: 5 fifth
party: 20 Democratic-Republican
state represented: 2 VA
defeated: 4 (Rufus) King **5** (John Quincy) Adams
vice president: 8 (Daniel D) Tompkins
cabinet:
  state: 5 (John Quincy) Adams
  treasury: 8 (William Harris) Crawford
  war: 7 (John Caldwell) Calhoun
  attorney general: 4 (Richard) Rush, (William) Wirt
  navy: 8 (Samuel Lewis) Southard, (Smith) Thompson **13** (Benjamin Williams) Crowninshield
born: 2 VA **18** Westmoreland County
died: 13 New York City NY
buried: 10 Richmond VA
education: 14 William and Mary (did not graduate)
religion: 12 Episcopalian
author: 67 A View of the Conduct of the Executive in the Foreign Affairs of the United States
political career: 8 US Senate
  governor of: 8 Virginia
  minister: 5 Spain **6** France **12** Great Britain
  secretary of: 3 war **5** state
civilian career: 6 lawyer
military service: 5 major **7** captain **10** lieutenant **16** Revolutionary War **17** lieutenant colonel
  wounded in Battle of: 7 Trenton
notable events of lifetime/term: 5 Panic (of 1819) **14** Monroe Doctrine
  Agreement: 9 Rush-Bagot
  Compromise: 8 Missouri
  war: 8 Seminole
father: 6 Spence
mother: 9 Elizabeth (Jones)
siblings: 6 Andrew, Spence

9 Elizabeth **11** Joseph Jones
wife: 9 Elizabeth (Kortright)
  nickname: 5 Eliza
children: 11 Maria Hester **14** Eliza Kortright

Monroe, Marilyn
real name: 23 Norma Jean Mortenson Baker
husband: 11 Joe DiMaggio **12** Arthur Miller
born: 12 Los Angeles CA
roles: 7 Bus Stop, Niagara **10** The Misfits **13** Some Like It Hot **16** The Seven-Year Itch **22** Gentlemen Prefer Blondes, How To Marry a Millionaire **23** The Prince and the Showgirl

Monrovia
capital of: 7 Liberia
monseigneur 6 my lord
monsieur 2 Mr **3** sir **6** mister, my lord

Monsieur Beaucaire
author: 15 Booth Tarkington

Monsignor Quixote
author: 12 Graham Greene

monster 4 Fury, gila, ogre, yeti **5** argus, beast, brute, demon, devil, fiend, freak, ghoul, giant, golem, harpy, hydra, lamia, satyr, titan **6** dragon, gorgon, marvel, oddity, savage, threat, wonder, wretch, zombie **7** anomaly, caitiff, centaur, chimera, deviant, grendel, incubus, mammoth, mermaid, vampire, variant, villain **8** bogeyman, colossus, gargoyle, Loch Ness, succubus, werewolf **9** barbarian, curiosity, cutthroat, scoundrel **10** blackguard, phenomenon **11** abnormality, miscreation **12** Frankenstein, lusus naturae
monstrous 4 bald, evil, huge **5** cruel, giant **6** grisly, mighty, odious **7** ghastly, harried, heinous, hideous, hulking, immense, mammoth, obscene, obvious, satanic, titanic, vicious **8** colossal, enormous, fiendish, flagrant, gigantic, gruesome, horrible, outright, shocking **9** atrocious, egregious, nefarious, revolting **10** diabolical, gargantuan, outrageous, prodigious, scandalous, stupendous, tremendous, villainous **14** Brobdingnagian
monstrousness 8 baseness, enormity, evilness, vileness, villainy **9** barbarity, depravity, malignity **10** inhumanity, wickedness **11** heinousness, viciousness **13** atrociousness, offensiveness **14** outrageousness

Montague family
characters in: 14 Romeo and Juliet
author: 11 Shakespeare
member: 5 Romeo

Montaigne, Michel de
author of: 6 Essais, Essays

Montalban, Ricardo
born: 6 Mexico **10** Mexico City
roles: 4 Khan **8** Mr Roarke **9** The

Colbys **13** Fantasy Island **24** Star Trek II The Wrath of Khan

Montalvo, Garcia de
author of: 12 Amadis of Gaul

Montana
abbreviation: 2 MT **4** Mont
nickname: 6 Big Sky **7** Bonanza, Stubtoe **8** Mountain, Treasure
capital: 6 Helena
largest city: 8 Billings
others: 4 Kipp **5** Butte, Havre, Malta **6** Hardin **7** Bozeman, Chinook, Choteau, Forsyth, Glasgow, Roundup **8** Anaconda, Missoula **9** Kalispell **10** Great Falls
college: 7 Carroll **10** Great Falls **13** Rocky Mountain
feature: 17 Continental Divide
  cemetery: 6 Custer
  national park: 7 Glacier **11** Yellowstone
tribe: 4 Cree, Crow, Hohe **5** Sioux **6** Atsima, Atsina, Salish **7** Arapaho, Bannock, Kutenai, Siksika **8** Cheyenne, Chippewa, Flatfoot, Flathead, Shoshone **9** Blackfeet **11** Assiniboine
people: 8 Myrna Loy **9** Will James **10** Gary Cooper **14** Charles Russell **15** Jeannette Rankin
  explorer: 13 Lewis and Clark **16** Pierre Jean de Smet
lake: 5 Tiber **6** Hebgen **8** Flathead, Fort Peck, Medicine **10** Yellowtail **11** Canyon Ferry, Hungry Horse
land rank: 6 fourth
mountain: 4 Ajax **5** Baldy, Cowan, Crazy, Lewis **6** Sphinx, Torrey **7** Bighorn, Big Belt, Hilgard, Purcell, Rockies, Trapper **8** Absaroka, Gallatin, Pentagon, Snowshoe
  highest point: 11 Granite Peak
physical feature: 10 Great Falls
river: 3 Sun **4** Milk **5** Clark, Teton **6** Marias, Powder, Tongue, Willow **7** Madison, Shields **8** Columbia, Kootenai, Missouri **9** Blackfoot **10** Bitterroot **11** Musselshell, Yellowstone
state admission: 14 forty-first
state bird: 17 western meadowlark
state fish: 26 black-spotted cutthroat trout
state flower: 10 bitterroot
state motto: 13 Gold and Silver
state song: 7 Montana
state tree: 13 Ponderosa pine

Montana, Bob
creator/artist of: 6 Archie

Montand, Yves
real name: 7 Ivo Livi
wife: 14 Simone Signoret
born: 5 Italy **14** Monsummano Alto
roles: 1 Z **12** Let's Make Love **14** Is Paris Burning?

montani semper liberi 28 mountaineers are always free men
motto of: 12 West Virginia

Montcalm, Louis Joseph
also: 17 Marquis de Montcalm

nationality: 6 French
served in: 18 French and Indian War
battle: 6 Oswego, Quebec (siege) **8** Carillon **11** Ticonderoga **16** Fort William Henry
killed in battle at: 6 Quebec **15** Plains of Abraham

mont-de-piete 10 pawnbroker
literally: 10 bank of pity

Montenegro
name means: 13 black mountain
other name: 4 Zeta **8** Crna Gora
capital: 7 Cetinje **8** Titograd **9** Podgorica
cities: 3 Bar **5** Kotor, Tivat **6** Niksic, Ulcinj **8** Antivari, Dulcigno, Ivangrad, Pljevlja **10** Hercegnovi **11** Sveti Stefan
division:
  Roman province: 7 Illyria
governed by: 10 Yugoslavia
monetary unit: 4 para **6** florin **7** perpera
lake: 7 Scutari, Shkoder
mountain: 8 Durmitor **11** Dinaric Alps
river: 3 Lim **4** Piva, Tara, Zeta **6** Moraca **7** Ceotina
sea: 8 Adriatic
physical feature:
  gulf: 5 Kotor
people: 4 Serb, Slav **11** Montenegrin
  former ruler (Orthodox bishop): 7 vladike **8** vladlika
language: 13 Serbo-Croatian
religion: 16 Serbian Orthodoxy

Monteverdi, Claudio
born: 5 Italy **7** Cremona
composer of: 5 Adone, Orfeo **7** Arianna **14** La Favola d'Orfeo **17** The Fable of Orpheus **21** The Coronation of Poppea **22** L'Incoronazione di Poppea **24** Il Ritorno d'Ulisse in patria **34** Il Combattimento di Tancredi e Clorinda

Montevideo
capital of: 7 Uruguay

Montezuma
emperor of: 6 Aztecs
in: 6 Mexico
conquered by: 6 Cortez

Montgomery, Bernard Law
also: 27 (first) Viscount Montgomery of Alamein
author of: 7 Memoirs **17** A History of Warfare
battle: 9 El Alamein
chief: 19 British general staff
commander of: 17 British Eighth Army **32** British occupation forces in Germany
commando raid: 6 Dieppe
deputy supreme commander: 4 NATO
Eighth Army called: 10 Desert Rats
evacuation of: 7 Dunkirk
fought against: 6 Rommel **11** Africa Corps, Afrika Korps

invasion: 6 Sicily **8** Normandy
member: 12 House of Lords
nationality: 7 British
nickname: 5 Monty
served in: 3 WWI **4** WWII

Montgomery, Robert
real name: 17 Henry Montgomery Jr
daughter: 9 Elizabeth
born: 8 Beacon NY
roles: 11 The Big House **13** Night Must Fall **17** Here Comes Mr Jordan

month
1st day: 7 calends
13th or 15th: 4 ides
9th before ides: 5 nones
half: 9 fortnight
next: 7 proximo
preceding: 3 ult(imo)
present: 4 inst(ant)

Month in the Country, A
author: 12 Ivan Turgenev

Mont-Oriol
author: 15 Guy de Maupassant

Montreal
airport: 6 Dorval **8** St Hubert **12** Cartierville
baseball team: 5 Expos
founder: 11 Maisonneuve
hill: 10 Mount Royal
hockey team: 9 Canadiens
island: 5 Jesus **6** Bizard, Perrot **8** Montreal **9** des Soeurs **14** de Boucherville
lake: 7 St Louis
landmark: 12 Place des Arts **13** Molson Stadium **16** Chateau de Ramezay **17** Church of Notre Dame, St Sulpice Seminary **21** Man and His World Exhibit
original name: 10 Ville-Marie
province: 6 Quebec
river: 6 Ottawa **10** St Lawrence **11** des Prairies **14** des Milles Isles
subway: 5 Metro
university: 6 McGill

Montresor
character in: 20 The Cask of Amontillado
author: 3 Poe

Mont Saint Michel and Chartres
author: 10 Henry Adams

Monty
nickname of: 15 Montgomery Clift **17** (General) Bernard Montgomery

monument 4 slab **5** token **6** shrine **7** memento, obelisk, witness **8** cenotaph, memorial, monolith, reminder **9** testament, tombstone **10** gravestone **11** remembrance, testimonial **13** commemoration

monumental 4 huge **5** fatal, heavy **7** awesome, classic, epochal, immense, lasting, massive **8** colossal, decisive, enduring, gigantic, historic, immortal, statuary **9** cyclopean, egregious, memorable **10** horrendous, monolithic,

shattering, stupendous **11** inestimable **12** catastrophic **13** unprecedented

mooch 3 beg, bum **5** cadge **6** hustle, sponge **7** solicit **8** freeload

mood 5 blues, dumps, humor **6** spirit, temper **7** feeling **8** doldrums, vexation **9** condition **10** depression, gloominess, melancholy **11** disposition, melancholia, temperament **14** predisposition **16** hypersensitivity

moody 4 mean **5** sulky, surly, testy **6** crabby, dismal, fickle, gloomy, mopish, morbid, morose, sullen **7** erratic, flighty, peevish, unhappy **8** brooding, dejected, notional, variable, volatile **9** impetuous, impulsive, irascible, irritable, mercurial, saturnine, whimsical **10** capricious, changeable, despondent, inconstant, lugubrious, melancholy **11** pessimistic **12** inconsistent **13** temperamental, unpredictable

Mookerjee, Hurree Chunder
character in: 3 Kim
author: 7 Kipling

moon 4 gape, lamp, luna, roam **5** dream, month, stare **6** dawdle, wander **8** daydream **9** satellite
god of: 3 Sin **5** Nanna **6** Mextli
goddess of: 4 Luna **5** Diana, Holle, Tanit **6** Hecate, Hekate, Phoebe, Selena, Selene, Tanith **7** Artemis, Astarte, Cynthia
full: 9 plenilune
new: 5 prime
waning: 7 waiand

Moon and Sixpence, The
author: 16 W Somerset Maugham

moonless 4 dark **5** black, murky **7** stygian **9** lightless, unlighted **13** unilluminated

Moonlighting
character: 11 Maddie Hayes **12** Agnes Dipesto, David Addison
cast: 11 Bruce Willis **13** Allyce Beasley **14** Cybill Shepherd
detective agency: 8 Blue Moon

Moon Mullins
creator: 12 Frank Willard
character: 4 Kayo **5** Mamie **9** Mushmouth **11** Uncle Willie **15** Lady Plushbottom, Lord Plushbottom **16** Moonshine Mullins

Moon of the Caribbees, The
author: 12 Eugene O'Neill

moonshine 5 hokum **6** bunkum, humbug **7** bootleg **8** clockade, homebrew, malarky, nonsense **10** balderdash, bathtub gin **11** mountain dew

moonstone
species: 8 feldspar
source: 5 Burma, Mogok

Moonstone, The
author: 13 Wilkie Collins
character: 7 Dr Candy **12** Lady Verinder, Sergeant Cuff **13** Franklin Blake **14** John Herncastle, Rachel

Verinder **15** Rosanna Spearman **16** Godfrey Ablewhite

moor 3 fen **4** dock, down, fell, lash, wold **5** affix, berth, heath, marsh, tie up **6** anchor, attach, fasten, secure, steppe, tether, tundra, upland **7** savanna, tie down **8** make fast **9** wasteland

Moore, Archie
nickname: **11** The Mongoose
real name: **18** Archibald Lee Wright
sport: **6** boxing
class: **16** light-heavyweight

Moore, Clement C
author of: **23** A Visit from Saint Nicholas

Moore, Dick
creator/artist of: **13** Gasoline Alley

Moore, Dudley
nickname: **12** Cuddly Dudley
wife: **11** Suzy Kendall, Tuesday Weld
born: **5** Essex **7** England **8** Dagenham
roles: **3** Ten **6** Arthur **8** Lovesick, Six Weeks **9** Bedazzled **13** Micki and Maude **16** Arthur on the Rocks **17** Like Father Like Son
plays: **5** piano

Moore, George
author of: **12** Esther Waters **15** Hail and Farewell

Moore, Henry
born: **7** England **10** Castleford
artwork: **4** Mask **8** Two Forms **9** North Wind **10** Bird Basket **11** Family Group, Head of a Girl **12** Locking Piece **13** Nuclear Energy **15** Reclining Figure **20** Four-Piece Composition

Moore, Marianne
author of: **12** Like a Bulwark, Nevertheless, O To Be a Dragon, Tell Me Tell Me

Moore, Mary Tyler
husband: **11** Grant Tinker
born: **10** Brooklyn NY
roles: **4** Mary **12** Mary Richards **14** Ordinary People **18** The Dick Van Dyke Show **21** The Mary Tyler Moore Show

Moore, Mrs
character in: **15** A Passage to India
author: **7** Forster

Moore, Roger
born: **6** London **7** England
roles: **8** The Saint **12** Simon Templar
as James Bond: **9** Moonraker, Octopussy **13** Live and Let Die **16** The Spy Who Loved Me **22** The Man with the Golden Gun

Moorehead, Agnes
born: **9** Clinton MA
roles: **6** Endora **9** Bewitched **11** Citizen Kane **13** Johnny Belinda **15** Dear Dead Delilah **20** Magnificent Obsession **23** The Magnificent Ambersons

mooring 4 hook, line, rope **5** cable, chain **6** anchor, hawser

moot 4 open **7** eristic **8** arguable, disputed **9** debatable, undecided, unsettled **10** disputable, unresolved **11** conjectural **12** questionable **13** controversial, problematical **14** controvertible

mope 4 fret, pine, pout, sulk **5** brood, worry **6** grieve, grouse, lament, repine **7** grumble **8** languish

Mopsus
occupation: **4** seer
mother: **5** Manto
grandfather: **8** Tiresias
member of: **9** Argonauts
founded: **6** oracle
location: **6** Mallus **7** Cilicia
cofounder: **11** Amphilochus
epithet: **9** Ampycides

moral 3 tag **4** fair, just, pure **5** adage, maxim, motto, noble, right **6** honest, lesson, proper, saying **7** epigram, ethical, message, proverb, saintly **8** aphorism, didactic, personal, virtuous **9** estimable, homiletic, honorable, preaching **10** aboveboard, high-minded, principled **11** meritorious, sermonizing, tendentious **12** conscionable

moral code 5 ethos **6** ethics **9** integrity, standards **10** principles

morale 4 mood **6** spirit, temper **10** confidence, resolution **11** disposition
French: **13** esprit de corps

morality 5 honor **6** ethics, habits, tastes, virtue **7** modesty, probity **8** fairness, goodness **9** integrity, rectitude **10** chasteness **11** uprightness **13** righteousness

moralize 6 preach **7** lecture

moralizing 7 preachy **8** didactic **9** homiletic

morally corrupt 6 effete **8** decadent, depraved **10** degenerate

moral sense 9 integrity **10** conscience

morass 3 bog, fen **4** mire **5** marsh, swamp **6** slough **8** quagmire, wetlands **9** quicksand

morbid 3 sad **4** dour, glum, grim **5** moody **6** gloomy, morose, somber **8** brooding **9** depressed, saturnine **10** despondent, lugubrious **11** melancholic, pessimistic, unwholesome

morbid condition 6 malady **7** ailment, disease, illness **8** sickness **9** infirmity

Morcerf, Comte de (Fernand)
character in: **21** The Count of Monte Cristo
author: **5** Dumas (pere)

mordant 6 biting, bitter **7** acerbic, caustic, cutting, waspish **8** incisive, piercing, scathing, scornful, stinging, venomous, virulent **9** acidulous, mali-

cious, sarcastic, trenchant **11** acrimonious

Mordecai
cousin: **6** Esther
served: **15** Ahasuerus Xerxes
enemy: **5** Haman

more 5 added, extra, other, spare **6** longer **7** further, reserve **10** additional **12** additionally, supplemental **13** supplementary

More, Thomas
author of: **6** Utopia

Moreau, Frederic
character in: **21** A Sentimental Education
author: **8** Flaubert

Moreau, Gustave
born: **5** Paris **6** France
artwork: **7** Orpheus **13** Dance of Salome (Salome Dancing), The Apparition **16** Hesiod and the Muse **18** The Poet and the Siren **19** Oedipus and the Sphinx **27** Diomedes Devoured by His Horses

Morehouse, J Ward
character in: **3** USA
author: **9** Dos Passos

Morel, Paul
character in: **13** Sons and Lovers
author: **8** Lawrence

Moreno, Rita
real name: **20** Rosita Dolores Alverio
born: **7** Humacao **10** Puerto Rico
roles: **13** Pagan Love Song, The Deerslayer, West Side Story **15** Singin' in the Rain

more or less 5 about **6** around **8** somewhat **9** generally, just about **13** approximately

moreover 3 too **4** also **7** besides, further **11** furthermore **12** more than that

mores 4 code **5** ethos, forms, rules **6** usages **7** customs, rituals **9** etiquette, practices, standards **10** traditions **11** conventions, observances, proprieties

more than enough 5 ample **6** excess, plenty **7** copious, profuse **8** plethora **9** abundance, amplitude, bountiful, excessive, profusion **10** oversupply

Morgan, Daniel
served in: **16** Revolutionary War
commander of: **8** riflemen **13** sharpshooters
battle: **7** Cowpens **8** Saratoga **12** Bemis Heights, Freeman's Farm
helped suppress: **16** Whiskey Rebellion

Morgan, Thomas Hunt
founder of: **8** genetics
awarded: **10** Nobel Prize

Morgan family
characters in: **19** How Green Was My Valley
members: **4** Beth, Davy, Huur, Ivor,

Owen **5** Ianto **6** Gwilym **8** Angharad
author: **9** Llewellyn

morganite
color: **4** pink **5** peach

Morgan le Fay
character in: **16** Arthurian romance

Moriarty, Professor
villain in: **14** (The Adventures of)
Sherlock Holmes
author: **10** Conan Doyle

moribund 5 dying **6** doomed, waning
10 stagnating

Morier, James
author of: **18** Hajji Baba of Ispahan

morituri te salutamus 28 we who
are about to die salute thee
said by: **15** Roman gladiators
said to: **13** Roman emperors

Mork & Mindy
character: **4** Mork **6** Eugene **10** Cora
Hudson **13** Mindy McConnel **17**
Frederick McConnel
cast: **9** Pam Dawber **11** Conrad Janis
13 Elizabeth Kerr, Robin Williams **14**
Jeffrey Jacquet
Mork's planet: **3** Ork
phrase: **8** nanu nanu
spinoff from: **9** Happy Days

Morland, Catherine
character in: **15** Northanger Abbey
author: **6** Austen

Morley, Robert
born: **6** Semley **7** England
roles: **5** Melba **10** Oscar Wilde **11**
Beau Brummel, Edward My Son **12**
Major Barbara **15** Marie Antoinette,
The African Queen **21** The Man Who
Came to Dinner

Mormon State
nickname of: **4** Utah

morning 4 dawn **5** early, sunup **7**
sunrise **8** daybreak, daylight, forenoon
9 matutinal

morning-glory 7 Ipomoea **10**
Calystegia **11** Convolvulus
varieties: **3** red **4** wild **5** beach,
dwarf **6** Ceylon, common, silver,
woolly, yellow **9** Brazilian **16** Imperial Japanese

Morocco
other name: **7** Barbary **8** Maroquin **9**
Al Maghrib **13** Maghrib el Aksa **19**
Mauretania Tingitana
capital: **5** Rabat **6** Rabbat
largest city: **10** Casablanca
others: **3** Fes, Fez, Sla **4** Ifni, Safi,
Sale, Sali, Taza **5** Ceuta, Oujda,
Porte, Saffi **6** Agadir, Meknes, Se-
mara, Tetuan **7** Elarish, Kenitra, Lar-
ache, Mazagan, Mililla, Mogador,
Tangier, Tetouan **8** Kouribga,
Tinerhir **9** Marrakech, Marrakesh **10**
Youssoufia **11** Port-Lyautey
division:
disputed territory: **13** Western Sahara
head of state: **4** king

measure: **4** kala, muhd, rotl, saah,
sahh, ueba **5** artal, cadee, gerbe, ratel **6** covado, dirhem, fanega, izenbi,
kintar, tangin, tomini **8** quintral
monetary unit: **4** flue, okia, rial **5**
floos, franc, okieh, ounce **6** dirham,
miskal **8** mouzouna
weight: **4** rotl **5** artel, ratel **6** dirhem,
kintar **7** quintal
island: **7** Madeira
mountain: **3** Rif **4** Bani **5** Abyla, Atlas, Sarro **8** Tidiguin **9** Anti-Atlas,
High Atlas, Jebel-Musa **11** Middle
Atlas
highest point: **12** Jebel Toubkal **13**
Djebel Toubkal
river: **3** Dra, Ziz **4** Sous **5** Sebou **6**
Gheris **7** Tensift **8** Moulouya **9** Oum
er Rbia
sea: **8** Atlantic **13** Mediterranean
physical feature:
cape: **3** Nun, Sim **4** Juby, Noun,
Rhir **6** Cantin
desert: **6** Sahara
oasis: **8** Tafilelt
plain: **5** Rharb
strait: **9** Gibraltar
valley: **7** Ouergha
wind: **5** leste **7** charqui
people: **4** Arab, Moor **6** Berber,
French **7** Spanish
dynasty: **7** Alawite, Almohad **9** Almoravid
leader: **5** Idris **7** Lyautey **8** Hassan
II **9** Abd el-Krim
philosopher: **8** Averroes
language: **6** Arabic, Berber, French **7**
Spanish
religion: **5** Islam
place:
ruins: **9** Volubilis
feature:
clothing: **4** haik **7** jellaba
hat: **3** fez
Islamic holy war: **5** jehad, jihad
shanty town: **10** bidonville
food:
dish: **8** couscous

moron 3 ass, nut, oaf, sap **4** boob,
dolt, dope, fool **5** dummy, dunce, idiot, loony, ninny **6** dimwit, nitwit **7**
half-wit, jackass **8** bonehead, dumbbell, dumbhead, imbecile, numskull **9**
blockhead, numbskull, simpleton **10**
muttonhead, nincompoop

Moroni
capital of: **7** Comoros

Moros
mother: **3** Nyx
personifies: **4** fate

morose 3 low, sad **4** blue, dour, glum,
sour **5** cross, moody, sulky, surly,
testy **6** cranky, gloomy, grumpy, mopish, solemn, sullen **7** waspish **8** churlish, downcast, mournful **9** depressed,
irascible, saturnine **10** despondent,
melancholy **11** crestfallen

moroseness 5 gloom **8** glumness

9 pessimism, sulkiness, surliness **10**
sullenness

Morpheus
god of: **6** dreams
father: **6** Hypnos

morphology
study of: **9** structure

Morris, Dinah
character in: **8** Adam Bede
author: **5** Eliot

Morris, Willie
author of: **5** Yazoo **10** Good Old Boy
15 North Toward Home

Morris, Wright
author of: **8** Will's Boy **10** Plain's
Song **13** Field of Vision, My Uncle
Dudley

Morrison, Toni
real name: **19** Chloe Anthony Wofford
author of: **4** Sula, Jazz **7** Beloved,
Tar Baby **12** The Bluest Eye **13** Song
of Solomon
honor: **10** Nobel Prize **13** Pulitzer
Prize

Morrow, Vic
born: **7** Bronx NY
roles: **6** Combat **8** Cimarron **14** God's
Little Acre **15** The Twilight Zone **18**
Portrait of a Mobster **19** The Blackboard Jungle
daughter: **18** Jennifer Jason Leigh

Morse, Samuel F B
nationality: **8** American
invented: **9** Morse code **17** electric
telegraph **24** electromagnetic telegraph

morsel 3 bit, nip, sip **4** bite, drop, iota,
whit **5** crumb, grain, piece, scrap,
snack, speck, taste, touch, trace **6** dollop, nibble, sliver, tidbit **7** modicum,
segment, swallow **8** fraction, fragment, mouthful, particle **9** scintilla

mortal 4 deep, type **5** fatal, grave, human **6** deadly, lethal, living, person,
severe **7** earthly, extreme, intense,
mundane **8** creature, enormous, fleeting, temporal **9** character, corporeal,
ephemeral **10** individual, transitory **12**
unimaginable

mortality 7 carnage **8** fatality **9** bloodshed, ephemeral, slaughter **10** transience **11** evanescence **12** impermanence **13** extermination **14**
transitoriness

mortar 6 cannon, cement, vessel **7**
plaster **8** adhesive

Morte d'Arthur, Le
author: **12** Thomas Malory

Mortgaged Heart, The
author: **15** Carson McCullers

mortification 3 rot **5** decay, shame **7**
chagrin, penance **8** ignominy **11** humiliation **12** putrefaction **13** embarrassment

mortified 6 rotted **7** abashed,

ashamed, debased **8** dismayed, festered, tortured **9** chagrined, putrefied **11** discomfited, embarrassed

mortify 3 rot **4** deny, fast **5** abash, decay, shame **6** appall, fester **7** chagrin, horrify, putrefy **9** discomfit, embarrass **10** discipline, disconcert

Mosaic law 10 Pentateuch **15** Ten Commandments

Moscow
airport: **12** Sheremetyevo
canal: **11** Moscow-Volga
capital of: **4** USSR **6** Russia **11** Soviet Union
hills: **5** Lenin
landmark: **7** Kremlin **9** Gorky Park, Red Square **12** Lenin Library **13** Izmailovo Park, Sokolniki Park **14** Bolshoi Theater **16** Moscow Art Theater **21** Luzhniki Sports Complex
museum: **6** Armory **7** Pushkin **10** Historical **16** Tretyakov Gallery **28** Central Museum of the Soviet Army
river: **5** Setun, Volga, Yauza **6** Moscow
Russian: **6** Moskva

Moses
father: **5** Amram
mother: **8** Jochebed
sister: **6** Miriam
brother: **5** Aaron
wife: **8** Zipporah
son: **7** Eliezar, Gershom
father-in-law: **6** Jethro
received: **15** Ten Commandments
patriarch of: **10** Israelites
saw: **11** burning bush
successor: **6** Joshua
pertaining to: **6** Mosaic

Moses, Grandma
real name: **17** Anna Mary Robertson, Mary Anne Robertson
born: **11** Greenwich NY
artwork: **23** Out for the Christmas Trees

mosey 4 poke **5** amble **6** stroll **7** saunter, shuffle

Moslem 4 Moor **5** Islam, Sunni **6** Muslim, Shiite **7** Islamic **10** Mohammadan, Muhammadan

mosque 6 temple
Arabic: **6** masjid, musjid

Mosquito Coast, The
author: **11** Paul Theroux
director: **9** Peter Weir
cast: **11** Helen Mirren **12** Harrison Ford, River Phoenix

Mosquito State
nickname of: **9** New Jersey

moss
varieties: **4** ball, club, gold, rose **5** broom, bunch, coral, ditch, fairy, Irish, spike, water **6** Scotch, spring **7** cushion, haircap, peacock, Spanish **8** floating, fountain, Japanese, mat spike **9** dwarf club, flowering **10** little club, pincushion **11** basket spike,

meadow spike, shining club **12** treelet spike **13** Douglas's spike

Mossbauer, Rudolph Ludwig
field: **7** physics
nationality: **6** German
discovered: **15** Mossbauer effect **28** recoil-free gamma ray absorption
awarded: **10** Nobel Prize

Mosses from an Old Manse
author: **18** Nathaniel Hawthorne

most 4 best, very **6** degree **7** maximum **9** extremely

most distant point 5 limit, reach **8** boundary **9** extremity **11** ultima Thule

Mostel, Zero
real name: **16** Samuel Joel Mostel
born: **10** Brooklyn NY
roles: **8** The Front **10** Rhinoceros **11** The Enforcer **12** The Producers **15** Du Barry Was a Lady **16** Fiddler on the Roof **17** Panic in the Streets

most important 3 key, top **4** head, main **5** chief **7** central, highest, leading **8** cardinal, dominant, foremost, greatest **9** paramount, principal, uppermost **10** preeminent **11** outstanding, predominant

mostly 6 mainly **7** as a rule, chiefly, greatly, largely **8** above all **9** generally, primarily, specially **10** especially **11** principally **12** particularly **13** predominantly

most prominent 7 leading **8** dominant **10** preeminent **11** outstanding

most successful 6 banner, record **7** winning **10** triumphant **11** outstanding

mote 3 dot **4** iota **5** speck **8** particle **9** scintilla

moth
varieties: **4** hawk, luna, tent **5** ghost, gypsy, plume, royal, swift, yucca **6** hornet, lappet, miller, urania **7** clothes, emperor, flannel, hook tip, leopard, tussock **8** army worm, forester, imperial, polka dot **9** carpenter, clearwing **10** forest tent **11** pseudosphex **12** African peach **13** American tiger, giant Hercules **14** tropical sphinx **15** Chinese silkworm, glover's silkworm **20** striped morning sphinx

moth-eaten 5 holey **6** old-hat **7** wornout **8** outmoded **10** antiquated, threadbare **11** dilapidated

mother 3 mom, mum **4** bear, mama, mind, mums, rear, tend **5** beget, breed, mammy, mater, momma, mommy, mummy, nurse, raise **6** origin, source **7** care for, indulge, nurture, old lady, produce, protect **8** conceive, stimulus **10** wellspring **11** inspiration
French: **4** mere **5** maman
Spanish: **5** madre
Italian: **5** mamma
of wind: **3** Eos

of stars: **3** Eos
of gods: **5** Nammu

mother country 8 homeland **10** fatherland, native land, native soil, old country **13** native country

Mother Goose in Prose
author: **14** Lyman Frank Baum

motherly 4 kind **6** gentle, loving, tender **7** devoted **8** maternal, parental **9** indulgent **10** protective, sheltering

mother of a family
Latin: **13** materfamilias

Mother of the West
nickname of: **8** Missouri

mother's helper
French: **6** au pair

motif 4 form, idea **5** shape, style, theme, topic **6** design, figure, thread **7** pattern, refrain, subject **9** treatment

motion 3 cue, nod **4** flow, flux, move, sign, stir **5** drift **6** action, beckon, signal, stream **7** gesture, kinesis, passage, request **8** mobility, movement, progress **10** indication, suggestion **11** gesticulate, proposition **13** gesticulation **14** recommendation

motionless 4 calm, dead, idle **5** fixed, inert, still **6** at rest, frozen, stable, static **8** immobile, inactive, lifeless, tranquil, unmoving **9** immovable, quiescent **10** stationary, transfixed **11** immobilized **12** unresponsive

motion picture 3 pic **4** cine, film, show **5** flick, movie **6** cinema, talkie **8** flickers **10** photodrama **11** picture show **13** moving picture

motivate 4 goad, move, stir **5** egg on, impel **6** arouse, induce, prompt, stir up, turn on **7** actuate, provoke **8** activate, persuade **9** influence, stimulate

motivation 5 cause **6** reason **7** impetus, impulse **9** causation, impulsion **11** provocation

motive 3 aim, end **4** goal, spur **5** cause **6** design, object, reason **7** grounds, purpose **8** occasion, stimulus, thinking **9** incentive, intention, prompting, rationale **10** enticement, incitement, inducement **11** inspiration, instigation, provocation

motley 4 pied **5** mixed, tabby **6** hybrid, sundry, unlike, varied **7** dappled, piebald, watered **8** assorted, brindled, speckled **9** checkered, composite, different, disparate, divergent, harlequin, patchwork **10** dissimilar, iridescent, polychrome, variegated **11** diversified, incongruous, varicolored **12** multicolored **13** heterogeneous, kaleidoscopic, miscellaneous

motor 3 car **4** auto, ride, tour **5** drive, pilot, wheel **6** engine, turbine **7** machine **8** efferent **10** automobile

motorcar 4 auto, heap **6** jalopy, wheels **7** flivver, machine, vehicle **9** tin lizzie **10** automobile

motor vehicle 3 bus, cab, car, van **4** auto, heap, jeep, limo, taxi **5** motor, sedan, truck, wagon **6** jalopy, jitney, pickup, wheels **7** flivver, hardtop, machine, omnibus, town car, vehicle **9** limousine, tin lizzie **10** automobile **11** convertible

mottled 4 pied **5** tabby **7** blotchy, flecked, piebald, specked **8** brindled, speckled, stippled **10** iridescent, multicolor, variegated **11** varicolored **12** parti-colored **13** kaleidoscopic, polychromatic

motto 3 saw **4** rule **5** adage, axiom, maxim **6** byword, dictum, saying, slogan, truism **7** epigram, precept, proverb **8** aphorism **9** catchword, principle, watchword

moue 4 pout **7** grimace

Moulin Rouge
   director: **10** John Huston
   cast: **10** Jose Ferrer (Toulouse-Lautrec) **11** Suzanne Flon, Zsa Zsa Gabor **12** Eric Pohlmann
   setting: **5** Paris **10** Montmartre

mound 4 bump, dune, heap, hill, pile, rick **5** knoll, mogul, ridge, stack **7** bulwark, hillock, hummock, rampart **9** earthwork **10** embankment **12** entrenchment

Mound Builders
   location: **15** Ohio River Valley **22** Mississippi River Valley
   known for: **13** earthen mounds

mount 3 fit, fix, rig, set, wax **4** go up, grow, pony, rise, soar **5** affix, camel, climb, equip, frame, horse, scale, steed, surge, swell **6** ascend, fit out, outfit, set off **7** augment, charger, climb up, get over, get upon, install, set into **8** elephant, increase, multiply, straddle **9** intensify

mountain 3 alp **4** peak **5** bluff, butte, range, ridge **6** height, massif **7** volcano **8** eminence, highland **9** elevation
   of Afghanistan: **3** Koh **5** Safeo **6** Chagai, Pamirs **7** Nowshak **8** Koh-i-Baba, Safed Koh, Sulaiman **9** Himalayas, Hindu Kush, Istoro Nal **11** Khwaja Amran, Paropamisus
   of Albania: **5** Shala **6** Pindus **8** Koritnjk **10** Mount Korab **12** Albanian Alps
   of Algeria: **5** Aissa, Atlas, Aures, Dahra, Tahat **6** Chelia **7** Ahaggar, Kabylia, Mouydir **8** Djurjura **9** Djurdjura, Tell Atlas **12** Saharan Atlas
   of Andorra: **6** d'Etats **8** l'Estanyo **8** Pyrenees **10** Cataperdis **11** Como Pedrosa
   of Angola: **4** Moco **5** Chela **6** Loviti **16** Humpata Highlands
   of Antigua and Barbuda: **9** Boggy Peak
   of Argentina: **4** Toro **5** Andes, Chato, Laudo, Potro **6** Conico, Pissis, Rin-

con **8** Famatina, Murallon, Olivares, Tronador, Zapaleri **9** Aconcagua, Tupungato **10** Cordillera **13** Ojos del Salado **15** Cerro Mercedario, Sierra de Cordoba
   of Armenia: **6** Ararat, Taurus **8** Karabekh **7** Aladagh **12** Mount Aragats
   of Australia: **3** Ise **4** Blue, Olga, Ossa, Zeil **5** Bruce, Snowy **6** Cradle, Doreen, Garnet, Gawler, Magnet, Morgan **7** Bongong, Gregory **8** Augustus, Brockman, Cuthbert, Herbert, Jusgrave, Mulligan, Surprise **9** Murchison, Kosciusko, Woodroffe **14** Australian Alps **15** New England Range **18** Great Dividing Range
   of Austria: **4** Alps **6** Tirols, Tyrols, Stubai **8** Eisenerz, Rhatikon **9** Dolomites, Kitzbuhel **10** Hohe Tauern **13** Grossglockner **14** Silvretta Group
   of Azerbaijan: **8** Caucasus
   of Bangladesh: **10** Keokradong **15** Chittagong Hills
   of Barbados: **6** Chalky **7** Hillaby
   of Belgium: **8** Ardennes **16** Signal de Botrange
   of Benin: **7** Atakora
   of Bhutan: **5** Black **9** Himalayas **10** Chomo Lhari, Kula Kangri
   of Bolivia: **4** Jara **5** Andes, Cusco, Cuzco **6** Sajama, Sorata, Sunsas **7** Illampu **8** Ancohuma, Illimani, Mururata, Sansimon, Santiago, Zapaleri **12** Eastern Range, Western Range **18** Cordillera Oriental **20** Cordillera Occidental
   of Borneo: **4** Iran, Raja **5** Saran **6** Kapuas, Muller, Nijaan, Tebang **8** Kinabalu, Kinibalu, Schwaner
   of Bosnia-Herzegovina: **11** Dinaric Alps
   of Brazil: **3** Mar **5** Geral, Organ, Piaui **6** Acarai, Gurupi, Parima, Urucum **7** Amambai, Carajas, Gradaus, Neblina, Oragaos, Roraima **8** Bandeira, Itatiaia, Roncador, Tombador **9** Pacaraima, Sugar Loaf **10** Tumuc-Humac
   of Brunei: **6** Teraja **9** Ulu Tutong **10** Pagon Priok
   of Bulgaria: **3** Kom **5** Botev, Pirin, Sapka **6** Balkan, Musala, Sredna **7** Vikhren **8** Musallah **11** Rila-Rhodope
   of Burkina Faso: **4** Tema **8** Nakourou **10** Tenakourou, Tenekourou
   of Burundi: **8** Nyarwana **9** Nyamisana
   of Cambodia: **3** Pan **7** Dangrek, Dong Rek **8** Cardamom, Elephant **10** Phnom Aoral, Phnom Aural
   of Cameroon: **5** Mbabo **7** Bambuto, Kapsiki, Mandara **8** Batandji, Cameroon **9** Atlantika
   of Canada: **4** Coast, Logan, Royal **6** Robson, Skeena **7** Cariboo, Cascade, Purcell, Rockies, Selkirk, Stelias, St Elias **8** Columbia, Hazelton, Monashee **9** Mackenzie, Notre

Dame, Tremblant **10** Laurentian, Richardson, Shickshock **14** Jacques Cartier
   of Canary Islands: **5** Teide, Teyde **6** La Cruz **8** El Cumbre, Tenerife
   of Cape Verde: **4** Cano, Fogo **10** Pico de Cano
   of Central African Republic: **5** Karre, Tinga **6** Mongos **9** Dar Challa **11** Kayagangiri
   of Chad: **7** Tibesti, Touside **9** Emi Koussi
   of Chile: **4** Maca, Toro **5** Chato, Maipo, Maipu, Paine, Potro, Pular, Torre, Yogan **6** Apiwan, Burney, Conico, Jervis, Poquis, Rincon **7** Chaltel, Copiapo, Fitzroy, Palpana, Velluda **8** Cochrane, Tronador, Yanteles **9** Tupungato **13** Ojos del Salado
   of Colombia: **5** Abibe, Andes, Baudo, Chita, Cocuy, Huila, Pasto **6** Ayapel, Perija, Purace, Tolima, Tunahi **7** Chamusa, del Ruiz **8** Oriengal **10** Santa Marta **14** Cristobal Colon **17** Central Cordillera, Eastern Cordillera, Western Cordillera
   of Costa Rica: **4** Poas **5** Barba, Irazu **6** Blanco **7** Central, Gongora **9** Talamanca, Turrialba **10** Guanacaste **14** Chirripo Grande
   of Crete: **3** Ida **5** Dikte, Phino **6** Juktao **7** Lasidhi, Madaras **8** Leuka Ori, Theodore, Thriphte **9** Psiloriti
   of Croatia: **10** Julian Alps **11** Styrian Alps
   of Cuba: **6** Copper **7** Cristal, Maestra, Organos **8** Camaguey, Trinidad, Turquino **9** Las Villas **11** Pinar del rio **12** Guaniguanico **14** Sancti-Spiritus
   of Czechoslovakia: **3** Ore **5** Grant, Tatra **6** Sumava **7** Gerlach, Sudeten **8** Krkonose **9** High Tatra **10** Carpathian **11** Gerlachovka
   of Denmark: **12** Ejer Bavnehoj, Yding Skovhoj **14** Himmelbjaerget
   of Djibouti: **5** Gouda **9** Moussa Ali
   of Dominican Republic: **4** Tina **5** Gallo, Neiba **6** Duarte **7** Baoruco, Central **8** Bahoruco, Oriental **13** Septentrional
   of Ecuador: **5** Andes **6** Condor, Sangay **7** Cayambe **8** Antisana, Cotopaxi **9** Cotacachi, Pichincha **10** Chimborazo
   of Egypt: **5** Sinai, Uekia **6** Gharib **8** Katerina **9** Katherina **13** Shayib al-Banat
   of El Salvador: **6** Izalco **8** Santa Ana
   of England: **5** Black **7** Pennine, Snowdon **8** Cambrian, Cumbrian **11** Scafell Pike
   of Equatorial Guinea: **5** Mitra **11** Santa Isabel
   of Ethiopia: **4** Amba, Batu, Guge, Guna, Talo **5** Ahmar, Choke **9** Rasdashan, Ras Deshen
   of Finland: **6** Haltia **7** Laltiva

10 Saari Selka **11** Haldetsokka

of France: 4 Alps, Jura **5** Blanc, Pelat **6** Vosges **8** Ardennes, Pyrenees **9** Mont Blanc **10** French Alps **11** Pic Montcalm

of Gabon Republic: 5 Mpele **7** Chaillu, Cristal, Mikongo **8** Balaquri, Birougou, Iboundji

of Georgia: 8 Caucasus

of Germany: 3 Ore **4** Harz **8** Feldberg **9** Zugspitze **10** Erzgebirge **11** Black Forest, Fichtelberg **12** Bavarian Alps

of Ghana: 8 Afadjato **12** Akwapim Hills

of Gibraltar: 6 Misery

of Greece: 3 Ida **4** Idhi, Oeta, Oite, Ossa **5** Athos **6** Ithome, Peleon, Pelion, Pindus **7** Grammos, Helicon, Olympus, Rhodope **8** Hymettos, Smolikas, Targetos, Taygetus **9** Parnassus **10** Hagion Oros, Lycabettus, Pentelicus

of Greenland: 5 Forel, Payer **7** Khardyu **8** Peterman **9** Gunnbjorn **15** Petermannsbjerg **16** Gunnbjornsfjaeld

of Guatemala: 4 Agua, Mico **5** Fuego, Madre **6** Pacaya, Tacana **7** Atitlan, Toliman **8** La Candon, Las Minas, Tajumuko **9** Tajamulco **10** Acatenango, Santa Maria **12** Cuchumatanes

of Guinea: 4 Loma **5** Nimba **6** Tamgue **11** Fouta Djalon

of Guyana: 5 Amuku, Ariwa, Kamoa **6** Akarai, Kanuku **7** Caburai **9** Pacaraima

of Haiti: 4 Nord **5** Cahos **6** Macaya, Noires **7** Lahotte, Laselle **8** Troudeau

of Honduras: 4 Pija **6** Agalta **7** Celaque **8** Las Minas **9** Esperanza **25** Central American Cordillera

of Hong Kong: 6 Castle **8** Victoria **9** Tai Mo Shan

of Hungary: 4 Alps, Bukk **5** Kekes, Matra, Tatra, Vetes **6** Bakony, Mecsek **7** Cserhat, Gerecse **8** Borzsony, Zempleni **9** Korishegy **10** Carpathian

of Iceland: 4 Laki **5** Askja, Hekla, Jokul, Katla **7** Surtsey **10** Orafajokul **16** Hvannadalshnukur

of India: 8 Aravalli **9** Broad Peak, Distaghil, Himalayas, Karakoram, Nanda Devi, Rakaposhi **10** Gasherbrum, Masherbrum **11** Nanga Parbat **12** Eastern Ghats, Godwin Austen, Kanchenjunga, Western Ghats

of Iran: 6 Elburz, Zagros **8** Demavend

of Iraq: 6 Qalate, Zagros **7** Halgurd, Qaarade **9** Kurdistan

of Ireland: 5 Galty **6** Croagh, Mourne **7** Errigal, Muckish, Patrick, Wicklow **8** Comeragh **10** Benna Beola, Twelve Bens, Twelve Pins **13** Carrantuohill, Knockmealdown **19** Macgillycuddy's Reeks

of Israel: 4 Nafh, Sagi **5** Harif, Meron, Ramon, Tabor **6** Atzmon,

Carmel, Hatira, Meiron

of Italy: 4 Alps, Etna, Rosa, Viso **5** Amaro, Blanc, Corno, Somma **6** Cimone, Ortles **7** Vulcano **8** Vesuvius **9** Apennines, Dolomites, Maritimes, Stromboli **10** Apuane Alps, Carnic Alps, Julian Alps, Otztal Alps **11** Bernina Alps, Gennargentu **12** Gran Paradiso, Ligurian Alps **13** Lepontine Alps **16** Abruzzi Apennines

of Jamaica: 4 Blue **8** Sir Johns

of Japan: 3 Uso, Zao **4** Fuji **5** Asahi, Asama, Hondo, Yesso **6** Asosan, Enasan, Hiuchi, Kiusiu, Yariga **7** Fujisan, Hakusan, Kujusan, Tokachi **8** Fujiyama **9** Japan Alps

of Java: 4 Amat, Gede **5** Lawoe, Murjo, Prahu **6** Raoeng, Semuru, Slamet **7** Semeroe **8** Soembing

of Jordan: 9 Jabal Ramm, Jebel Ramm

of Kenya: 5 Elgon, Kenya, Kulai, Nyira, Nyiru **6** Kinyaa, Matian **7** Logonot **8** Aberdare **9** Kirinyaga

of Korea: 4 Wang **5** Chiri, Halla **6** Kwanmo, Paektu, Sobaek **7** Diamond, Kyebang, Nangnim, Taebaek **8** Chang-pai, Hamgyong, Myohyang **9** Paektu-san **10** Kumgang-san

of Kyrgyzstan: 8 Tian Shan

of Laos: 3 Bia, Lai, Loi, San **4** Copi, Khat **5** Atwat **6** Khoung, Tiubia **7** Phou Bia **15** Annam Cordillera

of Lebanon: 4 Mzar **5** Aruba **6** Hermon **7** es Sauda, Lebanon, Sannine **8** Kadischa, Kenisseh **9** Kennisseh **10** al-Mukammal **11** Anti-Lebanon **13** Qurnat al-Sawda

of Lesotho: 6 Maloti, Maluti **7** Central **8** Injasuti, Machache **10** Ben Macdhui **11** Drakensberg, Thaba Putsoa **16** Thabana Ntlenyana

of Liberia: 3 Uni **4** Bong, Putu **5** Niete, Nimba **6** Wutivi **9** Bomi Hills

of Libya: 5 Green **9** Bette Peak **13** Jabal al Akhdar, Tibesti Massif

of Liechtenstein: 4 Alps **8** Naafkopf, Rhatikon **12** Three Sisters **15** Vorder-Grauspitz

of Lithuania: 9 Juozapine **15** Samogitian Hills

of Luxembourg: 8 Ardennes, Huldange **9** Burgplatz **11** Wemperhardt

of Madagascar: 4 Boby **9** Ankaratra **11** Maromokotro **12** High Plateaus, Tsiafajavona **17** Tsaratanana Massif

of Malawi: 6 Mlanje **7** Mulanje **11** Livingstone

of Malaysia: 4 Bulu, Hose, Iban, Iran, Main, Mulu, Niut, Raja **5** Murjo, Niapa, Ophir **6** Blumut, Kapuas, Leuser, Slamet **7** Binaija, Brassey, Crocker **8** Kinabalu, Rindjani **11** Gunong Korbu, Gunong Tahan

of Mali: 4 Mina **6** Iforas **7** Manding **12** Hombori Tondo

of Mexico: 6 Colima, Tacana, Toluca **7** Orizaba **9** Paricutin **11** Ixtacihuatl,

Sierra Madre **12** Citlaltepetl, Popocatepetl **14** Sierra Zacateca **16** Chiapas Highlands **24** Transverse Volcanic Sierra

of Mongolia: 4 Cast, Orog **5** Altai **6** Kentei, Sevrej **7** Ich Ovoo, Khangai, Khentei **8** Tannu-Ola **9** Edrengijn **10** Cagaan Bogd, Tabun Bogdo **11** Munky Sardyk **14** Hangayn-Hentiyn, Monch Chajrchan

of Montenegro: 8 Durmitor **11** Dinaric Alps

of Morocco: 3 Rif **4** Bani **5** Abyla, Atlas, Sarro **8** Tidiguin **9** Anti-Atlas, High Atlas, Jebel-Musa **11** Middle Atlas **12** Jebel Toubkal **13** Djebel Toubkal

of Mozambique: 5 Binga **7** Lebombo

of Myanmar: 4 Chin, Naga, Pegu, Popa **5** Dawna **6** Arakan, Kachin, Lushai, Patkai **7** Karenni **8** Nattaung, Peguyoma, Saramati, Victoria **10** Tenasserim **11** Hkakabo Razi, Manipur Hill **12** Tanen Taunggi

of Namibia: 9 Brandberg **14** Khomas Highland, Koakoveld Hills

of Nepal: 6 Cho Oyu, Churia, Makalu **7** Everest, Lhotse I, Manaslu, Siwalik **8** Lhotse II **9** Annapurna, Himalayas **10** Dhaulagiri, Gosainthan, Himalchuli **11** Ganesh Himal **12** Kanchenjunga **14** Mahabharat Lekh

of New Guinea: 4 Snow **6** Orange **7** Bismark, Wilhelm **8** Victoria **9** Carstensz **10** Puncak Jaya **11** Owen Stanley **12** Albert Edward

of New Zealand: 4 Cook, Eden, Flat, Owen **5** Allen, Chope, Lyall, Mitre, Ohope, Otari, Young **6** Egmont, Stokes, Tasman **7** Aorangi, Cameron, Coronet, Ernslaw, Huiarau, Pihanga, Ruahine, Ruapehu, Tauhera, Tutamee, Tyndall **8** Aspiring, Richmond, Tauranga **9** Messenger, Murchison, Ngauruhoe, Raukumara, Tongariro **11** Remarkables **12** Southern Alps

of Nicaragua: 4 Leon **5** Negro, Viejo **6** Madera, Telica **7** Managua, Mogoton, Saslaya **9** Momotombo

of Niger: 7 Bagzane, Greboun **9** Air Massif

of Norway: 5 Sogne **6** Kjolen **7** Numedal **8** Blodfjel, Snohetta, Telemark, Ustetind **9** Harteigen, Jotunheim, Langfjell, Ramnanosi **10** Dovrefjell, Galdhoepig, Glitretind, Vibmesnosi **11** Myrdalfjell **12** Galdhopiggen **13** Glittertinden **14** Aardangerjokul, Hallingskarvet, Skagastolstind

of Oman: 4 Qara **5** Green, Hafit, Harim, Nakhl, Tayin **6** al-Sham **8** el-Akhdar **11** Jabal Akhdar **13** Green Mountain

of Pakistan: 3 Pab, Pub **4** Salt **6** Makran **7** Kirthar **8** Himalaya, Safed Koh, Sulaiman **9** Hindu Kush,

Karakoram, Tirich Mir **11** Makran Coast **12** Godwin Austin **13** Central Makran **14** Takht-i-Sulaiman

of Panama: 4 Baru, Maje **5** Chico, Gandi **6** Darien **7** Columan, San Blas, Veragua **8** Chiriqui, Santiago, Tabasara **10** Costa Rican **14** Serrania de Sapo **15** Aspave Highlands **17** Cordillera Central

of Peru: 5 Andes **7** El Misti, Huamina **8** Coropuna **9** Huascaran

of Philippines: 3 Apo, Iba **4** Mayo, Taal **5** Albay, Askja, Hibok, Mayon, Pulog **6** Pagsan **7** Banahao, Canlaon

of Poland: 4 Rysy **5** Tatra **6** Beskid **7** Pieniny, Sudeten **9** Beshchady, High Tatra, Holy Cross **10** Carpathian

of Portugal: 4 Acor, Lapa **5** Gerez, Marao, Mousa **6** Bornes, Peneda **7** Larouco **8** Caramulo **9** Caldeirao, Monchique **11** Pico da Serra **14** Serra da Estrela

of Puerto Rico: 4 Toro **5** Cayey, Punta **6** Yunque **8** Guilarte, Luquilla **10** Torrecilla **17** Cordillera Central

of Romania: 5 Banat, Bihor, Negoi **6** Codrul, Rodnei **7** Apuseni, Balkans, Caliman, Fagaras **8** Pietrosu **9** Moldavian **10** Carpathian, Moldoveanu **17** Transylvanian Alps

of Russia: 5 Altai, Lenin, Sayan, Urals **6** Anadyr, Elbrus, Koryak, Pamirs, Pobedy **7** Belukha, Crimean, Khibiny, Stanovi, Zhiguli **8** Caucasus, Dzhughur, Stanavoi, Tien Shan **9** Kopet Dagh, Narodnaya, Pamir-Alai, Yablonovy **11** Sikhote-Alin, Verkhoyansk

of Rwanda: 7 Mitumba, Virunga **8** Muhavura **9** Karisimbi

of Samoa: 4 Fito, Vaea **5** Alava **6** Savaii **7** Matafao **8** Silinili **9** Rahnnaker

of San Marino: 6 Titano **9** Apennines

of Sardinia: 4 Rasu **5** Ferry, Linas **7** Gallura, Limbara **8** Marghine, Serpeddi, Vittoria **11** Gennargentu

of Saudi Arabia: 5 Razih **6** Tuwayq **10** Jebal Sawda

of Scotland: 5 Attow, Ochil **6** Sidlaw **7** Cheviot **8** Ben Nevis, Grampian **9** Ben Lomond, Highlands, Trossachs

of Senegal: 6 Gounou **12** Fouta Djallon

of Sicily: 4 Erei, Etna, Moro, Sori **5** Aetna, Atlas, Erici, Hybla, Iblei, Ibrei **7** Nebrodi, Vulcano **9** Apennines, Le Madonie, Stromboli **10** Peloritani

of Sierra Leone: 4 Loma **9** Bintimani **10** Tingi Hills

of Sikkim: 7 Dongkya, Donkhya **9** Himalayas, Singalili **10** Darjeeling **12** Kanchenjunga

of Singapore: 6 Mandai **7** Panjang **10** Bukit Timah

of Slovakia: 7 Sudetes **8** Low Tatra **9** High Tatra, Slovak Ore **10** Carpathian, Nizke Tatry **11** Visoke Tatry **15** White Carpathian

of the Solomon Islands: 5 Balbi **11** Popomanasiu

of Somalia: 5 Guban **7** Surud Ad **11** Migiurtinia, Ogo Highland

of South Africa: 3 Aux, Kop **5** Table **7** Kathkin **8** Injasuti **9** Stormberg **10** Devil's Peak, Sneeuwberg **11** Drakensberg **12** Giant's Castle **13** Witwatersrand **14** Mont-aux-Sources **15** Great Escarpment

of Spain: 4 Gata **5** Aneto, Rouch, Teide **6** Cuenca, Estats, Europa, Gredos, Magina, Morena, Nethou, Nevada, Teleno, Toledo **7** Alcaraz, Banuelo, Catalan, Cerredo, Demanda, Iberian, La Sagra, Moncayo, Perdido **8** Almanzor, Asturias, Galician, Maladeta, Monegros, Montseny, Mulhacen, Penalara, Pyrenees **10** Albarracin, Cantabrian, Guadarrama, Torrecilla

of Sri Lanka: 5 Pedro **7** Sri Pada **9** Adams Peak **14** Pidurutalagala

of Sudan: 4 Nuba **6** Red Sea **7** Imatong, Kinyeti **9** Dongotona **10** Jabal Marra, Jebel Marra **18** Ethiopian Highlands

of Surinam: 4 Emma **6** Kayser, Oranje **10** Julianatop, Tumuc-Humac, Wilhelmina **13** Eilert's Il Haan, Van Ach Van Wyck **15** Guiana Highlands

of Swaziland: 7 Emlembe **8** Highveld **11** Drakensberg

of Sweden: 4 Sarv **5** Ammar, Kebne **6** Helags, Kjolen, Ovniks, Sarjek **7** Kjollen **10** Kebnekaise

of Switzerland: 3 Dom **4** Alps, Jura, Rigi, Rosa, Todi **5** Adula, Blanc, Cenis, Eiger, Genis, Karpf, Righi **6** Linard, Pizela, Sentis **7** Bernina, Beverin, Grimsel, Pilatus, Rotondo **8** Balmhorn, Jungfrau **9** Weisshorn **10** Diablerets, Matterhorn, St Gotthard, Wetterhorn **11** Burgenstock **12** Dufourspitze **13** Rheinwaldhorn **14** Finsteraarhorn

of Syria: 6 Carmel, Hermon **7** Alawite, Libanus **10** Nusairiyya **11** Anti-Lebanon

of Taiwan: 5 Tatun **6** Tzukao, Yu Shan **7** Taitung **8** Morrison **10** Sinkao Shan **11** Hsin-Kao Shan **15** Chungyang Shanmo

of Tajikistan: 13 Communism Peak

of Tanzania: 4 Kibo, Mero **8** Usambara **11** Kilimanjaro

of Thailand: 5 Dawna, Khieo **6** Phanom **8** Dang Raek, Inthanon, Kao Prawa, Maelamun **9** Khao Luang **11** Bilauktaung, Doi Inthanon

of Tibet: 5 Kamet, Sajum **6** Kailas, Kunlun **7** Bandala, Everest **9** Himalayas, Karakoram

of Togo: 4 Togo **7** Atakora, Baumann, Koronga

of Tunisia: 5 Atlas **6** Chambi, Mrhila **7** Tebessa **8** High Tell, Zaghouan

12 Northern Tell **18** Dorsale Tunnisienne

of Turkey: 2 Ak **3** Ala **4** Alai, Dagh, Kara **5** Hasan, Hinis, Honaz, Murat, Murit **6** Ala Dag, Ararat, Bingol, Bolgar, Pontic, Suphan, Taurus **7** Aladagh, Erciyas **8** Karacali **10** Kackar Dagi

of Uganda: 4 Oboa **5** Elgon **7** Virunga **9** Mufumbiro, Ruwenzori **10** Margherita **18** Mountains of the Moon

of Ukraine: 7 Crimean **10** Carpathian

of United States: 4 Hood **5** Coast, Green, Kenai, Ozark, Rocky, White **6** Alaska, Brooks, DeLong, Elbert, Helena, Mesabi, Pocono, Shasta **7** Cascade, Chugach, Foraker, Harvard, Kilauea, Massive, Olympic, Olympus, Rainier, St Elias, Whitney **8** Catskill, Davidson, Endicott, Katahdin, Mauna Loa, McKinley, Mitchell, Ouachita, St Helens, Wrangell **9** Allegheny, Blue Ridge, Kuskokwim, North Peak, Pike's Peak **10** Black Hills, Blanca Peak, Grand Teton, Washington, Williamson **11** Appalachian, Santa Monica **12** Sierra Nevada **14** Berkshire Hills

of Uruguay: 6 Animas **10** Grand Hills **14** Cuchilla Grande **15** Mirador Nacional

of Vanuatu: 6 Lopevi **11** Tabwemasana

of Venezuela: 3 Pao **4** Pava, Yair **5** Andes, Duida, Icutu **6** Concha, Cuneva, Merida, Parima, Sierra, Yumari **7** Bolivar, Imutaca, Masaiti, Roraima **8** Gurupira **9** Pacaraima **10** Auyan Tepul **11** Turimiquire **18** Cordillera del Norte

of Vietnam: 6 Badinh, Badink **7** Nindhoa, Ninhhoa **8** Fansipan, Knontran, Ngoklinh, Ngoklink, Tchepone, Tclepore **18** Annamese Cordillera

of Wales: 6 Berwyn **7** Snowdon **8** Cambrian **9** Prescelly **13** Brecon Beacons

of Western Samoa: 4 Fito, Vaea **13** Mauga Silisili

of Yemen: 6 Shuayb, Thamir **7** Djehaff

of Yugoslavia: 5 Karst **6** Balkan **7** Rhodope, Triglav **8** Crna Gora, Durmitor **9** Sar-Pindus **10** Carnic Alps, Julian Alps, Karawanken **11** Dinaric Alps **13** Slovenian Alps **20** Northern Albanian Alps

of Zaire: 7 Crystal, Mitumba, Virunga **9** Ruwenzori **10** Margherita, Nyaragongo **18** Mountains of the Moon

of Zambia: 8 Muchinga **12** Mafinga Hills

of Zimbabwe: 5 Vumba **6** Manica **7** Inyanga **9** Inyangani **11** Chimanimani, Matopo Hills

Mountain
constellation of: **5** Mensa

mountaineers are always free men
Latin: **19** montani semper liberi
motto of: **12** West Virginia

Mountain State
nickname of: **7** Montana **12** West Virginia

Mountbatten, Louis
also: **27** first Earl Mountbatten of Burma
nationality: **7** British
position: **12** first sea lord
supreme allied commander of: **13** Southeast Asia
chief of: **25** British combined operations
viceroy of: **5** India
served in: **3** WWI **4** WWII
directed invasion of: **10** Madagascar
recaptured: **5** Burma

mountebank 5 cheat, fraud, phony, quack **6** con man, humbug **7** hustler, sharper **8** huckster, operator, swindler **9** charlatan, con artist **11** quacksalver

mounted soldier 6 hussar, lancer **7** dragoon **8** cavalier, horseman **10** cavalryman

mourn 3 cry, rue, sob **4** keen, pine, wail, weep **6** bemoan, bewail, grieve, lament, regret, sorrow **7** deplore, despair **8** languish, weep over

mournful 3 sad **5** black, sorry, weepy **6** dismal, rueful, somber, triste, woeful **7** doleful, joyless, unhappy **8** dejected, dirgeful, dolorous, funereal, grievous, saddened **9** depressed, plaintive, sorrowful **10** depressing, dispirited, lamentable, lugubrious, melancholy **11** distressing, melancholic **12** heavy hearted

mourning 3 woe **5** black, crape, dolor, grief, weeds **6** sorrow **7** anguish, despair **8** grieving **9** lamenting, sorrowing **11** bereavement, lamentation

Mourning Becomes Electra
author: **12** Eugene O'Neill
character: **4** Seth **10** Hazel Niles, Peter Niles **16** Captain Adam Brant
Mannon family: **4** Ezra, Orin **7** Lavinia **9** Christine

mourning period
Hebrew: **6** shibah, shivah

mouser 3 cat **4** puss **5** kitty, pussy **6** feline **8** pussycat

Mousetrap, The
author: **14** Agatha Christie

mousseline 6 muslin

mousy 3 shy **4** drab, dull **5** timid, wimpy **7** bashful, fearful **8** timorous **9** colorless, unnoticed, withdrawn **11** unobtrusive **13** inconspicuous

mouth 3 bay, say **4** bell, jaws, lips **5** inlet, speak, voice **6** outlet, portal **7** declare, estuary, opening **8** aperture, propound **9** pronounce

mouthful 3 dab **4** bite **5** taste **6** morsel, nibble

mouthpiece 4 reed **6** lawyer **7** counsel **8** advocate, attorney **9** counselor

mouth-watering 8 inviting, tempting **9** appealing **10** appetizing **11** tantalizing

movable, moveable 4 free **5** loose **6** mobile, motile, moving **8** portable **10** changeable

movables 4 gear **5** goods **7** baggage, effects, luggage **9** equipment **10** belongings **11** impedimenta, possessions **13** accoutrements, paraphernalia

move 2 go **3** act, ask, get **4** bear, deed, fire, lead, pass, ploy, step, stir, sway, turn, urge **5** begin, budge, carry, cause, drive, impel, plead, rouse, shift, touch **6** action, affect, arouse, attack, convey, excite, exhort, incite, induce, motion, prompt, strike, stroke, switch **7** advance, budging, gesture, go ahead, impress, inspire, measure, operate, proceed, propose, provoke, request, suggest **8** function, interest, locomote, maneuver, motivate, persuade, relocate, start off, stirring, transfer, transmit **9** impassion, influence, recommend, stimulate, transport, transpose **10** transplant **11** opportunity

move downward 3 dip **4** dive, drop, fall, sink **6** plunge, tumble **7** decline, descend, plummet **8** decrease

movement 4 part **5** drive, steps, works **6** action, effort, motion **7** crusade, measure, program, section **8** activity, division, gestures, maneuver, progress, stirring **9** agitation, execution, mechanism, operation **10** locomotion **11** undertaking

move out 5 leave **6** depart, vacate **8** evacuate

move quickly 3 fly, run **4** bolt, dash, race, rush, tear **5** hurry **6** hasten, sprint

move sideways 4 edge **5** sidle **8** sidestep

move slyly 4 edge, lurk **5** sidle, skulk, slink, sneak, steal

move up 5 boost, climb, heave, hoist, raise, scale **6** ascend, uplift **7** advance, elevate, promote, upraise

move upward 4 rise, soar **5** climb, mount **6** ascend **7** take off

movie 4 film, show **5** flick **6** cinema **7** feature, picture, showing **9** screening
invented by:
machine: **7** Jenkins
panoramic: **6** Waller
projector: **6** Edison
talking: **14** Warner Brothers

moving 5 motor **6** mobile, motile **8** exciting, poignant, spurring, stirring, touching **9** affecting, inspiring **10** impressive, locomotive, motivating **11** interacting, stimulating

moving about 5 astir **6** active **7** on the go

Moving Target, A
author: **14** William Golding

Mowgli
character in: **14** The Jungle Books
author: **7** Kipling

moxie 4 grit, guts, sand **5** nerve, pluck, spunk **6** mettle, spirit **7** courage, stamina **8** audacity, backbone **9** hardihood, toughness **10** pluckiness **13** dauntlessness

moyen age 10 Middle Ages

Mozambique
capital/largest city: **6** Maputo **15** Lourenco Marques
others: **4** Tete **5** Beira, Pemba, Zumbo **6** Chemba, Nacala, Pafuri, Sofala **7** Nampula **8** Mutarara **9** Inhambane, Quelimane **11** Porto Amelia
school: **15** Eduardo Mondlane
monetary unit: **6** escudo **7** centavo, metical
island: **6** Inhaca **7** Angoche **8** Bazanuto **9** Benguerua
lake: **5** Nyasa **6** Chuali, Nyassa **8** Nhavarre
mountain: **7** Lebombo
highlands: **6** Namuli **9** Gorongosa
highest point: **5** Binga
river: **4** Buzi, Save **5** Lurio, Msalu **6** Rovuma, Ruvuma **7** Ligonha, Limpopo, Lugenda, Messaio, Zambezi **8** Changane
ocean: **6** Indian
physical feature:
cape: **7** Delgado
channel: **10** Mozambique
people: **3** Yao **5** Bantu, Chopi, Lomue, Lomwe, Macua, Makua, Ngoni, Nguni, Shona **6** Maravi, Thouga **7** Maconde, Makonde **10** Portuguese
explorer: **11** Vasco de Gama
leader: **8** Chissano **9** Dos Santos **12** Samora Machel **15** Eduardo Mondlane
language: **3** Yao **5** Makua **6** Nyanji, Thonga **7** Swahili **10** Portuguese
religion: **5** Islam **7** animism **13** Roman Catholic
place:
game reserve: **8** Marromeu **9** Gorongosa, Gorongoza **18** Maputo Elephant Park
reservoir: **11** Cabora Bassa
feature:
bride price: **6** lobolo

Mozart, Wolfgang Amadeus
born: **7** Austria **8** Salzburg
cataloguer: **6** Kochel
composer of: **4** Linz (symphony No 36) **5** Paris (symphony No 31)

6 Prague (symphony No 38) **7** Don Juan, Haffner (symphony No 35), Jupiter (symphony No 41), Requiem, Turkish (concerto) **8** Idomeneo **9** Credo Mass, Mitridate **10** Lucio Silla **11** Don Giovanni, Hunt Quartet, Il Re Pastore, Sparrow Mass **12** A Musical Joke, Cosi Fan Tutte (So Do They All or Women Are Like That), Haydn Quartet, Spatzenmesse **13** The Magic Flute, Trumpet Sonata, Turkish Sonata **14** Coronation Mass, Stadler Quintet, Die Zauberflote **15** Haffner Serenade, La Finta Semplice, Prussian Quartet **16** Dissonant Quartet, La Clemenza di Tito, Posthorn Serenade, Serenata Notturna **17** A Little Night Music **18** Jeunehomme Concerto, La Finta Giardiniera, The Clemency of Titus **19** Bastien und Bastienne, The Marriage of Figaro **20** Eine Kleine Nachtmusik, The Pretender Gardener **21** Der Schauspieldirektor, Ein Musikalischer Spass **22** The Pretending Simpleton **25** Die Entfuhrung aus dem Serail **27** The Abduction from the Seraglio

Mr, Mister
　Russian: **8** gospodin
　French: **8** monsieur
　Yiddish: **3** Reb

Mr B
　character in: **6** Pamela
　author: **10** Richardson

Mr Basketball
　nickname of: **8** Bob Cousy

Mr Britling Sees It Through
　author: **7** H G Wells

Mr Cub
　nickname of: **10** Ernie Banks

Mr Deeds Goes to Town
　director: **10** Frank Capra
　cast: **10** Gary Cooper (Longfellow Deeds), Jean Arthur **14** George Bancroft

Mr Ed
　character: **9** Carol Post **10** Kay Addison, Wilbur Post **12** Roger Addison **14** Gordon Kirkwood, Winnie Kirkwood
　cast: **8** Leon Ames **9** Alan Young **11** Connie Hines, Edna Skinner **12** Larry Keating **18** Florence MacMichael
　Mr Ed was: **12** talking horse

Mr Flood's Party
　author: **22** Edwin Arlington Robinson

Mr Midnight
　nickname of: **10** Steve Allen

Mr Peepers
　character: **9** Mrs Gurney **11** Marge Weskit, Mr Remington **12** Harvey Weskit **14** Nancy Remington **15** Robinson Peepers **20** Superintendent Bascom
　cast: **8** Wally Cox **9** Gage Clark **11** Ernest Truex, Marion Lorne, Tony Randall **14** Patricia Benoit **16** Geor-

giann Johnson
　Mr Peepers taught: **7** science
　school: **13** Jefferson High

Mr Sammler's Planet
　author: **10** Saul Bellow

Mrs Dalloway
　author: **13** Virginia Woolf
　character: **10** Miss Kilman, Peter Walsh, Sally Seton **15** Richard Dalloway **16** Clarissa Dalloway **17** Elizabeth Dalloway

Mrs Miniver
　director: **12** William Wyler
　cast: **11** Greer Garson **12** Teresa Wright **13** Dame May Whitty, Walter Pidgeon
　Oscar for: **7** actress (Garson), picture **8** director **17** supporting actress (Wright)

Mr Smith Goes to Washington
　director: **10** Frank Capra
　cast: **9** Guy Kibbee **10** Jean Arthur **11** Claude Rains **12** Edward Arnold, James Stewart **14** Thomas Mitchell

Mrs Parkington
　author: **14** Louis Bromfield

Mrs Stevens Hears the Mermaids Singing
　author: **9** May Sarton

Mrs Warren's Profession
　author: **17** George Bernard Shaw

Mr Television
　nickname of: **11** Milton Berle

much **3** far **4** a lot, lots **5** about, ample, heaps, loads, often **6** almost, indeed, nearly, overly, rather, scores **7** copious, greatly **8** abundant, good deal, plenty of, quantity, somewhat, striking **9** decidedly, important, plenteous, plentiful, regularly **10** frequently, impressive, noteworthy, oftentimes, satisfying, sufficient, worthwhile **11** appreciable, exceedingly, excessively, sufficiency **12** considerable **13** approximately, consequential

Much Ado About Nothing
　author: **18** William Shakespeare
　character: **4** Hero **7** Claudio, Don John, Leonato **8** Beatrice, Benedick, Dogberry, Don Pedro

much in little
　Latin: **13** multum in parvo

much loved **4** dear **7** beloved, darling, dearest **8** precious **9** cherished, treasured

mucilage **3** gum **4** glue **5** paste **6** cement **8** adhesive

mucilaginous **5** gluey, gummy, gunky **6** gloppy, sticky **8** adhesive

muck **3** mud **4** dirt, dung, gunk, mire, ooze, slop **5** filth, slime **6** sewage, sludge **7** compost, garbage

muck up **4** soil **5** dirty, muddy **7** pollute

mud **4** dirt, muck, soil, wire

Mudcat State
　nickname of: **11** Mississippi

muddied **5** dirty, grimy **6** grubby, soiled **7** stained **8** begrimed, confused

muddle **3** fog **4** blow, daze, haze, mess, muff, ruin **5** botch, chaos, mix up, spoil, throw **6** boggle, bungle, fumble, goof up, jumble, mess up, pother, rattle **7** blunder, clutter, confuse, nonplus, stupefy **8** bewilder, confound, disarray, disorder **13** disconcertion **14** disarrangement

muddlebrained **5** inept **7** witless **8** confused **11** lamebrained

muddled **5** fuzzy **7** bemused **8** confused **10** bewildered

muddy **4** dull **5** dirty, grimy, vague **6** filthy, grubby **7** obscure **8** begrimed, confused

muff **5** botch, spoil **6** bungle **10** handwarmer

muffle **3** gag **4** dull, hush, mask, mute, veil, wrap **5** cloak, cover, quell, quiet, still **6** dampen, deaden, shroud, soften, stifle, swathe **7** conceal, enclose, envelop, silence, swaddle

muffled **3** low **4** dull, soft **5** faint, muted **6** dulled, feeble, hushed, veiled **7** cloaked, covered, quelled, quieted, stilled, subdued, swathed, wrapped **8** deadened, shrouded, silenced, softened, swaddled **9** concealed, enveloped, inaudible **10** indistinct, suppressed

mug **3** cup **4** face, puss, toby **5** stein, stoup **6** beaker, flagon, goblet, kisser, visage **7** chalice, tankard, toby jug, tumbler **11** countenance

mugger **8** assailer, attacker **9** assailant, assaulter

mugginess **4** damp **8** dampness, dankness, humidity **9** humidness **10** sultriness **14** oppressiveness

muggy **5** close, humid **6** clammy, steamy, sticky, stuffy, sultry, sweaty **8** steaming, vaporous **10** oppressive, sweltering

mulberry **5** Morus
　varieties: **3** red **4** Aino **5** black, paper, white **6** French, Indian **7** Russian **8** American, silkworm

mulct **4** bilk **6** extort **7** defraud, swindle

mule **3** ass **5** burro **6** donkey **7** jackass
　group of: **4** span

mulish **5** balky **6** ornery **8** perverse, stubborn **9** fractious, obstinate **10** refractory **11** intractable **12** recalcitrant

mull, mull over **5** study, weigh **6** ponder **8** consider, meditate, pore over, ruminate **10** deliberate

Muller
　character in: **25** All Quiet on the Western Front
　author: **8** Remarque

Muller, Hermann Joseph

field: 8 genetics
researched: 5 X-rays 8 mutation
awarded: 10 Nobel Prize

Muller, Paul
field: 9 chemistry
nationality: 5 Swiss
established: 16 DDT as insecticide
awarded: 10 Nobel Prize

Mulligan, Buck
character in: 7 Ulysses
author: 5 Joyce

multicolored 10 variegated

multifarious 4 many 5 mixed 6 divers, motley, sundry, varied 7 diverse, protean, several, various 8 manifold, numerous 9 different, multiplex 10 variegated 11 diversified 13 heterogeneous, miscellaneous

multiple 4 many 7 various 8 manifold

multiply 5 add to, beget, breed, raise 6 extend, spread 7 augment, enhance, enlarge, magnify 8 generate, heighten, increase 9 intensify, procreate, propagate, reproduce 11 proliferate

multitude 3 mob 4 army, herd, host, mass, pack, slew 5 array, crowd, crush, drove, flock, flood, horde, troop 6 legion, myriad, scores, throng 7 conflux

multum in parvo 12 much in little 23 a great deal in a small space

mum 4 mute 5 quiet, still, tacit 6 silent 8 taciturn, wordless 9 secretive 12 closemouthed 15 uncommunicative

mumble 5 growl, grunt, mouth 6 murmur, mutter, rumble 7 stammer 9 hem and haw

mumbo jumbo 3 rot 4 blah, bosh, cant, tosh 5 bilge, hokum, hooey, tripe 6 hot air, humbug 7 baloney 8 flummery 9 gibberish, sophistry 10 double talk, hocus pocus 11 doublespeak, jabberwocky, obfuscation 12 fiddle-faddle, gobbledygook, obscurantism

Mummy, The
director: 10 Karl Freund
cast: 10 Zita Johann 12 Boris Karloff, David Manners 16 Bramwell Fletcher

munch 4 chew, gnaw 5 champ, chomp, crush, grind 9 masticate

Munch, Edvard
born: 5 Loten 6 Norway 10 Hedemarken
artwork: 6 The Cry 7 Puberty, The Kiss 9 The Scream 11 Dance of Life 12 Frieze of Life 21 Death in the Sick Chamber

Munchausen, Baron 4 liar 7 solider 10 adventurer 11 exaggerator

Munchkins
characters in: 13 The Wizard of Oz
author: 4 Baum

mundane 5 petty 7 earthly, humdrum, prosaic, routine, worldly 8 day-to-day, everyday, ordinary 9 practical 10 pedestrian 11 commonplace, down-to-earth, terrestrial

Muni, Paul
real name: 16 Muni Weisenfreund
born: 7 Austria, Lemberg (now Lvov Ukraine)
roles: 6 Juarez 8 Scarface 10 The Valiant 12 The Good Earth 14 Clarence Darrow, Inherit the Wind 15 The Last Angry Man 18 The Life of Emile Zola 22 The Story of Louis Pasteur (Oscar) 26 I Am a Fugitive from a Chain Gang

municipal 4 city 5 civic 6 public 9 community 14 administrative

municipality 4 city, town 6 parish 7 village 8 township 9 bailiwick

munificence 6 bounty 7 charity 8 largesse 9 patronage 10 generosity, liberality 11 benefaction, beneficence, benevolence 12 philanthropy 13 bounteousness, bountifulness 14 charitableness 15 humanitarianism

munificent 4 free 6 kindly, lavish 7 liberal, profuse 8 generous, princely 9 bounteous, bountiful 10 altruistic, beneficent, benevolent, charitable, freehanded, open-handed 11 extravagant, magnanimous 12 eleemosynary, humanitarian 13 philanthropic

Munin
origin: 12 Scandinavian
form: 5 raven
owned by: 4 Odin 5 Othin
personifies: 6 memory
duty: 10 newsbearer
other raven: 5 Hugin

Munsters, The
character: 11 Lily Munster 12 Eddie (Edward Wolfgang) Munster 13 Herman Munster 14 Grandpa Munster, Marilyn Munster
cast: 7 Al Lewis 9 Pat Priest 10 Fred Gwynne 11 Beverly Owen 12 Butch Patrick 13 Yvonne DeCarlo

Muppet Show, The
character: 4 Rolf 5 Gonzo 6 Animal, Beaker 7 Scooter 9 Miss Piggy 10 Fozzie Bear 13 Kermit the Frog (Kermie)

Murasaki, Lady
author of: 14 The Tale of Genji

murder 4 kill, slay 5 abuse, waste 6 mangle, misuse 7 butcher, corrupt, cut down, killing 8 homicide, knock off 9 agonizing, slaughter 10 bastardize, formidable, impossible, oppressive, unbearable 11 assassinate, intolerable 12 manslaughter 13 assassination, very difficult 14 commit homicide, use incorrectly

Murder, She Wrote
character: 15 Jessica (JB) Fletcher
cast: 14 Angela Lansbury
setting: 9 Cabot Cove

murderer 4 Cain 6 killer, slayer 7 butcher 8 assassin, Barabbas, homicide 9 cutthroat

Murder in the Cathedral
author: 7 T S Eliot

Murder of Roger Ackroyd, The
author: 14 Agatha Christie

Murder on the Orient Express
author: 14 Agatha Christie
detective: 13 Hercule Poirot

murderous 4 gory 5 cruel, rough 6 bloody, brutal, deadly, savage, trying 7 killing 9 dangerous, difficult, ferocious 11 devastating 12 bloodthirsty, disagreeable

Murdoch, Iris
author of: 7 The Bell 11 Under the Net 12 A Severed Head, The Sea the Sea 14 The Black Prince 15 Nuns and Soldiers 17 The Good Apprentice, The Nice and the Good 20 The Philosopher's Pupil 24 The Book and The Brotherhood 30 The Sacred and Profane Love Machine

Murdstone, Mr
character in: 16 David Copperfield
author: 7 Dickens

Murillo, Bartolome (Bartolomeo) Esteban
born: 5 Spain 7 Seville
artwork: 13 Angels' Kitchen 14 Death of St Clare 15 The Two Trinities 17 Vision of St Anthony 23 The Immaculate Conception 24 Dream of the Roman Patrician

murk 3 fog 4 haze, mist 5 gloom 6 miasma 7 pea soup 8 darkness

murky 3 dim 4 dark, gray, hazy 5 dusky, foggy, misty 6 cloudy, dismal, dreary, gloomy, somber 7 obscure, sunless 8 lowering, overcast, vaporous 9 cheerless

murmur 3 hum 4 buzz, purl, purr, sigh 5 drone, sough, swish 6 lament, mumble, mutter, rumble, rustle 7 grumble, lapping, whimper, whisper 8 low sound, susurrus 9 complaint, undertone

murophobia
fear of: 4 mice

Murphy, Eddie
roles: 3 Raw 13 Trading Places 14 The Golden Child 15 Coming to America, Forty-Eight Hours 16 Beverly Hills Cop 17 Saturday Night Live, The Nutty Professor 19 Beverly Hills Cop Two

Murray, Bill
roles: 7 Stripes 9 Meatballs 10 Caddyshack 12 Ghostbusters, Groundhog Day 13 The Razor's Edge 17 Saturday Night Live 27 Not Ready for Prime Time Players

Murray, Don
wife: 9 Hope Lange
born: 11 Hollywood CA
roles: 7 Bus Stop 13 A Hatful of Rain

16 The Bachelor Party, The Hoodlum Priest

Murray, Jeanne
real name of: 13 Jean Stapleton
Murray, Mina
character in: 7 Dracula
author: 6 Stoker
Musaeus
occupation: 4 poet, seer
Musagetes see 6 Apollo
Muscat, Masqat
capital of: 4 Oman
muscle 4 grit, thew 5 bicep, brawn, force, might, power, sinew, vigor 6 energy, flexor, tendon 7 potency, prowess, stamina 8 virility 9 puissance 10 sturdiness 16 muscular strength
  kind: 4 limb 5 axial 6 smooth 7 dynamic, flexors, special, striped 8 postural, striated 9 abductors, extensors, voluntary 11 involuntary
  fuel: 4 food
  action: 4 pull
  specific: 6 rectus 7 deltoid, oblique 8 omohyoid 9 abdominal, abdominis, sartorius 10 pectoralis 11 intercostal, sternohyoid 13 biceps brachii, rectus femoris 14 vastus medialis 15 brachioradialis, vastus lateralis 16 serratus anterior, tensor fascia lata 17 quadriceps femoris 18 transverse thoracic 19 sternocleidomastoid 20 transversus abdominis
  supplementary structure: 6 sheath 10 deep fascia, retinacula 14 synovial bursae, synovial sheath
muscular 3 fit 5 burly, husky, tough 6 brawny, sinewy, strong 8 athletic, powerful 9 strapping
muscular contraction 3 tic 5 cramp, crick, spasm 6 stitch 12 charley horse
musculoskeletal system
  component: 4 bone 6 muscle, tendon 8 ligament
muse 4 mull 6 ponder, review 7 reflect 8 cogitate, consider, meditate, ruminate 9 speculate 10 deliberate 11 contemplate
Musee des Beaux Arts
author: 7 W H Auden
Muses
  also: 7 the Nine 8 Pierides 10 Castalides
  form: 9 goddesses
  names: 4 Clio (history) 5 Erato (love poetry) 6 Thalia (comedy), Urania (astronomy) 7 Euterpe (music, lyric poetry) 8 Calliope (epic poetry) 9 Melpomene (tragedy) 10 Polyhymnia (sacred poetry) 11 Terpsichore (dance)
  father: 4 Zeus
  mother: 9 Mnemosyne
  corresponds to: 7 Camenae
Musgrave, Thea
  born: 8 Scotland 9 Edinburgh

composer of: 11 The Decision 16 The Five Ages of Man 17 Beauty and the Beast, The Voice of Ariadne
mush 5 slush 6 drivel 8 porridge 14 sentimentalism, sentimentality
mushiness 5 slush 6 bathos 10 sponginess 11 mawkishness 14 sentimentalism, sentimentality
mushroom 4 grow 5 burst, fungi 6 blow up, expand, fungus, spread, sprout 7 burgeon, explode, shoot up 8 flourish, increase, spring up 9 toadstool 11 proliferate
  part: 3 cap 4 veil 5 gills, stalk, tubes, volva 6 button, hyphae, spores 7 annulus, basidia 10 rhizomorph
  non-poisonous: 5 field, honey, morel, table 6 oyster 7 inky cap, parasol 8 puffball, shiitake 9 fairy-ring, morchella, shaggy cap, stinkhorn 10 champignon 11 chanterelle 12 edible bolete, slippery jack 16 old man of the woods
  poisonous: 7 amanita 8 death cap, sickener 9 fly agaric 12 jack-o-lantern 13 devil's boletus 15 destroying angel
  study of: 8 mycology
mushy 4 soft 5 foggy, misty, pappy, pulpy, vague 6 cloudy, quaggy, spongy 7 maudlin, mawkish, squashy, squishy 8 effusive, romantic, squelchy 10 lovey-dovey 11 sentimental, tearjerking 12 affectionate
Musial, Stan
  nickname: 10 Stan the Man
  sport: 8 baseball
  team: 16 St Louis Cardinals
music 4 song, tune 5 score 6 melody 7 euphony, harmony 8 lyricism 10 minstrelsy 11 tunefulness 13 melodiousness
  god of: 5 Brage, Bragi 6 Apollo 7 Phoebus, Pythius 9 Musagetes
musical 5 lyric, sweet 6 dulcet 7 lilting, lyrical, melodic, tuneful 9 melodious 10 euphonious, harmonious 11 mellifluent
musical instrument 3 lur, sax, saz 4 bass, bell, drum, fife, gong, harp, horn, lute, lyre, oboe, outi, pipe, tuba, viol 5 argul, banjo, bugle, cello, cobza, flute, kazoo, organ, piano, guena, rabob, sansa, shawm, sheng, sitar, viola 6 bagana, chimes, cornet, cymbal, fiddle, guitar, spinet, treble, violin, zither 7 bagpipe, bassoon, cittern, clavier, kithara, marimba, panpipe, pibcorn, piccolo, samisen, strings, tambura, theorbo, timpani, trumpet, ukulele 8 autoharp, bass drum, calliope, clarinet, dulcimer, Jew's harp, mandolin, psaltery, recorder, talharpa, triangle, trombone, virginal 9 accordion, balalaika, castanets, harmonica, harmonium, krummhorn, rommelpot, saxophone, snare

drum, xylophone 10 bongo drums, clavichord, concertina, flugelhorn, French horn, kettledrum, sousaphone, tambourine, vibraphone 11 English horn, harpsichord 12 jouhikantele
  classification: 4 horn, reed, wind 5 brass 6 string 8 keyboard, woodwind 10 electronic, percussion
musical terms
  agitated: 7 agitato
  all players/singers together: 5 tutti
  becoming quicker: 11 accelerando
  continue without a break: 5 segue
  disconnected/each note separate: 8 staccato
  end: 4 fine
  expressively: 10 espressivo
    abbreviation: 4 espr
  fast: 6 veloce 7 allegro
  gentle: 5 soave
  gently: 9 doucement
  getting slower: 10 allargando
  getting weaker and slower: 7 calando
  gradually getting louder: 9 crescendo
    abbreviation: 5 cresc
  gradually getting softer: 10 diminuendo 11 decrescendo
    abbreviation: 3 dim 4 decr
  gradually slowing: 11 rallentando
    abbreviation: 4 rall
  half: 5 mezzo
  half voice/half volume: 9 mezza voce
  heavy: 5 lourd
  in an undertone/in a low voice: 9 sotto voce
  leisurely: 6 comodo
  less: 4 meno
  light: 8 leggiero
  little: 4 poco
  lively: 3 vif
  loud: 5 forte
    abbreviation: 1 f
  moderately slow and even: 7 andante
  more: 3 piu
  mournful: 5 mesto
  not too much: 9 non troppo
  plucked instead of bowed: 9 pizzicato
    abbreviation: 4 pizz
  quick/vivacious: 6 vivace
  repeat from beginning: 6 da capo
    abbreviation: 2 D C
  shaking and quavering/rapid alternation of notes: 5 trill
  silent: 4 tace
  singing/songlike/flowing: 9 cantabile
  sliding: 9 glissando
  slow: 5 lento 6 adagio
  slow dignified tempo: 5 largo
  slow down: 5 cedez
  smooth/connected: 6 legato
  soft: 5 piano
    abbreviation: 1 p
  solemn/serious: 5 grave

sorrowful: 7 dolente
strict time: 10 tempo gusto
sudden accent: 9 sforzando
   abbreviation: 2 sf
sweetly: 5 dolce
tearful: 9 lacrimoso
tenderly: 10 affettuoso
trembling vibrating effect/rapid reiteration of a single pitch: 7 tremolo
very: 5 molto
very loud: 10 fortissimo
   abbreviation: 2 ff
very soft: 10 pianissimo
   abbreviation: 2 pp
with fire: 8 con fuoco
with spirit/vigor: 7 con brio
with style/taste: 8 con gusto
with the mute: 10 con sordino
musician 4 bard **5** piper **6** artist, player, singer, violer **7** bandman, cellist, drummer, pianist, twanger **8** minstrel, organist, virtuoso **9** performer, trumpeter, violinist **11** saxophonist

Music Man, The
   director: 13 Morton Da Costa
   cast: 12 Buddy Hackett, Shirley Jones (Marian the librarian) **13** Robert Preston (Professor Harold Hill) **15** Hermione Gingold
   setting: 9 River City
   score: 15 Meredith Willson
   song: 15 Till There Was You **19** Seventy-six Trombones
music school 12 conservatory
   French: 13 conservatoire
musing 6 absent, dreamy **7** mulling **8** absorbed **9** pondering **10** meditating, meditative, reflecting, reflective
musjid 6 mosque
Muskogean, Muskhogean
   tribe: 4 Cree **7** Alabama, Alibamu, Choctaw, Natchez **8** Seminole **9** Chickasaw
Muslim see **6** Moslem
muslin
   French: 10 mousseline
muss 4 mess **6** foul up, jumble, ruffle, rumple, tangle, tousle **7** crumple, disturb **8** dishevel, disorder **9** bedraggle **10** disarrange
mussed 5 messy **6** frowzy, untidy **7** ruffled, rumpled, tousled, unkempt **8** uncombed **10** disarrayed, disheveled, disordered, disorderly **11** disarranged
Mussorgsky (Moussorgsky), Modest Petrovich
   born: 5 Pskov **6** Russia
   member of: 7 The Five
   composer of: 7 Sunless **10** The Nursery **12** Boris Godunov **13** Khovanshchina **19** Night on Bald Mountain **21** Songs and Dances of Death **22** Pictures at an Exhibition
mustard
   botanical name: 5 B alba **6** B hirta, B nigra **7** B juncea **8** Brassica

also called: 7 sinapis
   origin: 4 Asia **5** China
   use: 6 hotdog, sauces **7** egg roll **9** hamburger **13** salad dressing
muster 4 call **5** amass, raise, rally **6** gather, line up, summon **7** collect, company, convene, convoke, marshal, meeting, round up, turnout **8** assemble, assembly, mobilize **9** convocate, gathering **10** assemblage, confluence, congregate, inspection **11** aggregation **12** accumulation **13** agglomeration
musty 3 old **4** damp, dank, worn **5** banal, dirty, dusty, moldy, stale, tired, trite **6** frousy, frouzy, frowsy, frowzy, old hat, stuffy **7** worn-out **8** familiar, mildewed **9** hackneyed **10** antiquated, threadbare **11** commonplace
mutable 6 fickle **7** pliable **8** flexible, variable **9** adaptable, alterable, mercurial, versatile **10** adjustable, changeable, inconstant, modifiable, permutable **11** convertible, metamorphic **13** transformable
mutate 4 turn **5** alter **6** change **7** convert **9** transform
mutation 6 change **7** anomaly **9** deviation, variation **10** alteration **12** modification **13** metamorphosis **14** transformation **15** transfiguration **18** transmogrification
mutatis mutandis 30 necessary changes having been made
mute 3 mum **4** dumb **5** quiet, tacit **6** silent **8** aphasiac, nonvocal, reserved, reticent **9** unsounded, unuttered, voiceless **10** speechless **12** inarticulate, noncommittal, unpronounced **13** unarticulated **15** uncommunicative
muted 3 dim, low **4** dull, soft, weak **5** quiet **6** dulled, feeble **7** muffled **8** deadened, softened **10** indistinct, lackluster
mutilate 4 lame, maim **6** cut off, deform, excise, mangle **7** butcher, cripple **8** amputate, lacerate, truncate **9** disfigure, dismember
mutineer 5 rebel **9** dissident, insurgent **10** malcontent **15** insurrectionist
mutinous 6 unruly **10** dissenting, rebellious **13** revolutionary
Mutinus
   origin: 5 Roman **7** Italian
   god of: 9 fertility
   fertility in: 8 marriage
   corresponds to: 7 Priapus
mutiny 4 coup **5** rebel **6** revolt, rise up **8** takeover, upheaval, uprising **9** overthrow, rebellion **10** insurgency **12** insurrection
Mutiny on the Bounty
   author: 15 Charles Nordhoff, James Norman Hall
   character: 6 Tehani **9** Roger Byam **12** William Bligh (Captain Bligh) **13** George Stewart **17** Fletcher Christian
   director: 10 Frank Lloyd

   cast: 10 Clark Gable (Fletcher Christian) **12** Eddie Quillan, Franchot Tone **13** Herbert Mundin **15** Charles Laughton (Captain Bligh)
   Oscar for: 7 picture
mutt 3 cur, dog, pup **5** puppy **7** mongrel
Mutt and Jeff
   creator: 7 Al Smith **9** Bud Fisher
   character: 5 A Mutt **6** Cicero **7** Mrs Mutt
mutter 4 carp **5** gripe, growl, grunt **6** grouch, grouse, kvetch, mumble, murmur, rumble **7** grumble, whisper **8** complain
mutual 5 joint **6** common, shared **7** related **8** communal, returned **10** coincident, reciprocal **11** correlative, interactive
mutual understanding 6 accord **9** agreement
muzzle 3 gag **4** bind, curb **5** check, quiet, still **6** bridle, rein in, stifle **7** harness, silence **8** strangle, suppress, throttle
Myanmar
   former name: 5 Burma
   other name: 16 Land of the Pagodas
   capital: 6 Yangon **7** Rangoon
      ancient capital: 3 Ava **4** Pegu **8** Mandalay
   largest city: 7 Rangoon
   others: 2 Ye **3** Ava **4** Pegu **5** Akyab, Bhamo, Katha, Minbu, Namtu, Papun, Prome, Tavoy **6** Hsenwi, Hsipaw, Lashio, Maymyo, Monywa, Shwebo **7** Bassein, Henzada, Pakokku, Toungoo **8** Moulmein, Myingyan
   measure: 2 ly **3** dha, gon, mau, sao, tao, tat **4** byee, phan, seit, taun, that **5** shita, thuoc **6** lamany, palgat **7** chaivai **8** okthabah
   monetary unit: 3 pya **4** kyat
   weight: 2 ta **3** can, pai, vis **4** binh, kyat, ruay, viss **5** behar, candy, ticul **6** abucco **7** peiktha
   lake: 4 Inle
   mountain: 4 Chin, Naga, Pegu, Popa **5** Davna **6** Arakan, Kachin, Lushai, Patkai **7** Karenni **8** Nattaung, Peguyoma, Saramati, Victoria **10** Tenasserim **11** Manipur Hill **12** Tanen Taunggi
   highest point: 11 Hkakabo Razi
   river: 3 Hka **6** Salwin, Sutang **7** Irawadi, Kaladan, Myitnge, Salween, Schweli, Sittang **8** Chindwin, Indawgyi **9** Irrawaddy
   sea: 7 Andaman
   physical feature:
      bay: 4 Siam **6** Bengal, Hunter **7** Heanzay **8** Thailand
      gulf: 8 Martaban
      plateau: 4 Shan
      port: 5 Akyab **7** Bassein, Henzada **8** Moulmein
   people: 2 Ao, Vu, Wa **3** Kaw, Lai,

Lao, Mon, Pyu, Tai, Was **4** Akha, Chin, Juki, Kadu, Laos, Lolo, Miao, Naga, Sema, Shan, Thai, Tsin **5** Karen, Lhota **6** Birman, Burman, Kachin, Peguan, Rengma **7** Akhlame, Burmese, Kakhyen, Palauna, Palaung, Siamese **8** Mon-Khmer **9** Arakanese **12** Tibeto-Berman
language: 3 Lai **4** Chin, Kuki, Pegu, Shan **5** Karen **6** Kachin **7** Burmese, English
religion: 5 Hindu, Islam **8** Buddhism **12** Christianity
place:
  mines: 6 Mawchi **7** Bawdwin
  pagoda: 9 Shwe Dagon
  road: 4 Ledo **5** Burma **9** Stillwell
feature:
  ball game: 7 chin-lon
  festival: 5 Water **6** Lights **10** Thadin-gyut
  silk head band: 10 gaungbaung
  skirt: 6 longyi
  traveling theatrical group: 4 Pwes
My Antonia
  author: 11 Willa Cather
  character: 9 Jim Burden **15** Antonia Shimerda
My Darling Clementine
  director: 8 John Ford
  cast: 7 Tim Holt **8** Ward Bond **10** Henry Fonda (Wyatt Earp) **12** Linda Darnell, Victor Mature (Doc Holliday) **13** Walter Brennan
my dear
  French: 7 ma chere, mon cher
My Fair Lady
  director: 11 George Cukor
  based on play by: 17 George Bernard Shaw (Pygmalion)
  cast: 11 Rex Harrison (Professor Henry Higgins) **13** Audrey Hepburn (Eliza Doolittle) **15** Stanley Holloway **16** Wilfrid Hyde-White
  score: 14 Lerner and Loewe
  Oscar for: 7 picture
  song: 14 The Rain in Spain **24** I Could Have Danced All Night
my faith
  French: 5 ma foi
my fault
  Latin: 8 mea culpa
My Favorite Martian
  character: 8 Tim O'Hara **11** Uncle Martin **15** Mrs Lorelei Brown
  cast: 9 Bill Bixby **10** Ray Walston **13** Pamela Britton
Myles
  king of: 7 Laconia
  invented: 9 grain mill
My Little Margie

character: 7 Charlie **9** Mrs Odetts **11** Mr Honeywell **13** Freddie Wilson **14** Margie Albright, Vernon Albright **15** Roberta Townsend
  cast: 9 Don Hayden, Gale Storm **10** Willie Best **12** Clarence Kolb **13** Hillary Brooke **14** Charles Farrell **15** Gertrude Hoffman
my lord
  French: 8 monsieur **11** monseigneur
  Italian: 9 monsignor **10** monsignore
My Man Godfrey
  director: 13 Gregory La Cava
  cast: 10 Alice Brady, Mischa Auer **11** Gail Patrick **13** Carole Lombard, William Powell
myriad 6 untold **7** endless **8** infinite, manifold **9** boundless, countless, limitless, uncounted **11** innumerable, measureless **12** immeasurable, incalculable **13** multitudinous
Myrina
  husband: 8 Dardanus
myrmidon 6 cohort **8** follower, henchman
Myrmidons
  people of: 6 Aegina **8** Thessaly
  created by: 4 Zeus
  created from: 4 ants
  characteristic: 7 warlike
  leader: 6 Peleus **8** Achilles
Myrrha
  also: 6 Smyrna
  father: 11 King Cinyras
  loved: 7 Cinyras
  crime: 6 incest
  son: 6 Adonis
  changed into: 6 myrtle **9** myrrh tree
Myrtilus
  charioteer of: 8 Oenomaus
myrtle 6 Myrtus **10** Vinca minor **14** Myrtus communis **18** Cyrilla racemiflora **23** Umbellularia californica
  varieties: 3 bog, gum, sea, wax **4** cape, Jew's, sand **5** crape, crepe, downy, dwarf, Greek, honey, scent **6** German, Oregon, Polish, willow **7** box sand, classic, running, Swedish **10** Western tea **11** candleberry, Queen's crape, sandverbena **13** Allegheny sand, bracelet honey, California wax **16** Australian willow
Mysia
  epithet of: 7 Demeter
mysophobia
  fear of: 4 dirt
Mysteries of Paris, The
  author: 9 Eugene Sue
Mysteries of Udolpho, The
  author: 15 Mrs Ann Radcliffe

mysterious 4 dark **6** cloudy, covert, hidden, secret **7** cryptic, obscure, strange, unknown **8** baffling, puzzling **9** enigmatic, secretive **10** perplexing, sphinxlike, undercover **11** clandestine, inscrutable **12** impenetrable, inexplicable, supernatural, unfathomable **13** surreptitious **14** undecipherable
Mysterious Stranger, The
  author: 9 Mark Twain
mystery 6 enigma, occult, puzzle, riddle, secret **7** problem, secrecy **9** conundrum, obscurity, symbolism, vagueness **11** ambivalence, elusiveness **12** ineffability, quizzicality **13** ineffableness, mystification
Mystery of Edwin Drood, The *see* **10** Edwin Drood
mystical, mystic 5 inner **6** hidden, occult **7** cryptic, obscure **8** abstruse, esoteric, ethereal, symbolic **9** enigmatic, secretive **10** cabalistic, symbolical, unknowable **11** inscrutable, nonrational **12** metaphysical, otherworldly **14** transcendental
mystification 9 confusion **10** bafflement, perplexity, puzzlement **12** bewilderment
mystify 4 fool **5** elude **6** baffle, puzzle **7** confuse, deceive, mislead, perplex **8** bewilder, confound **9** bamboozle
myth 3 fib, lie **4** tale, yarn **5** error, fable, story **6** canard, legend **7** fantasy, fiction, hearsay, parable **8** allegory, delusion, illusion, tall tale **9** fairy tale, falsehood **10** shibboleth **13** prevarication
mythical, mythic 6 fabled, unreal **8** illusory **9** imaginary, legendary, pretended **10** conjured-up, fabricated, fantasized, fictitious **13** unsubstantial
mythological, mythologic 6 unreal **8** fabulous, illusory, imagined **9** fantastic, imaginary, legendary, unfactual **10** fictitious
My Three Sons
  character: 11 Chip Douglas, Mike Douglas **12** Steve Douglas **13** Robbie Douglas **18** Katie Miller Douglas, Uncle Charley O'Casey **20** Ernie Thompson Douglas, Michael Francis (Bub) O'Casey
  cast: 8 Don Grady, Tina Cole **12** Tim Considine **13** Fred MacMurray **14** William Frawley **15** Barry Livingston, William Demarest **17** Stanley Livingston
  dog: 5 Tramp
my word
  French: 5 ma foi

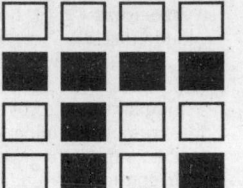

N

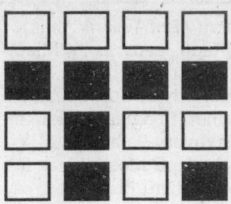

nab 4 bust, grab, nail, snag **5** catch, pinch, seize, snare **6** arrest, collar, detain, haul in, pick up, pull in, snatch **7** capture **9** apprehend

nabob 3 VIP **4** lord **5** mogul, nawab **6** deputy, tycoon **7** magnate **8** governor **9** plutocrat **10** capitalist **11** billionaire, millionaire

Nabokov, Vladimir
  author of: 3 Ada **4** Mary, Pnin **6** Lolita **8** Pale Fire

nadir 4 base, zero **5** floor **6** apogee, bottom **7** nothing **8** low point **10** rock bottom **11** lowest point

Nadja
  author: 11 Andre Breton

nag 4 fury, goad, harp **5** annoy, devil, harpy, scold, shrew, vixen **6** badger, bicker, harass, hassle, heckle, hector, nettle, peck at, pester, pick at, pick on, plague, rail at, tartar, virago **7** bedevil, upbraid **8** battle-ax, irritate **9** importune, termagant, Xanthippe

Nahua *see* Aztec

Nahuatl *see* Uto-Aztecan

Naiad
  form: 5 nymph
  location: 5 water

nail 3 fix, pin **4** brad, claw, spad **5** talon **6** fasten, hammer, secure
  part: 3 bed **4** root

Naipaul, V S
  author of: 10 Guerrillas **15** A Bend in the River **17** A House for Mr Biswas **19** The Return of Eva Peron, The Suffrage of Elvira

Nairobi
  capital of: 5 Kenya

naive 4 open **5** green, plain **6** candid, simple, unwary, unwise **7** artless, foolish, natural, unjaded **8** gullible, immature, innocent **9** childlike, credulous, guileless, ingenuous, unspoiled, unworldly **10** unaffected, unassuming **11** susceptible **12** unsuspecting, unsuspicious **15** unsophisticated

naivete, naïveté 6 candor **7** modesty **8** openness **9** credulity, frankness, greenness, innocence, sincerity **10** callowness, simplicity **11** artlessness, foolishness, naturalness **12** childishness, inexperience **13** ingenuousness **14** unaffectedness **16** simplemindedness

naked 4 bald, bare, nude, pure **5** bared, frank, plain, sheer **6** patent, simple, unclad **7** blatant, exposed **8** disrobed, laid bare, manifest, palpable, undraped, wide- open **9** in the buff, unclothed, uncovered, undressed **11** perceptible, unappareled, unqualified, unvarnished **15** in the altogether

Naked and the Dead, The
  author: 12 Norman Mailer

Naked City
  character: 5 Libby **9** (Det) Adam Flint **10** (Det Lt) Dan Muldoon, (Lt) Mike Parker **11** (Det) Jim Halloran, (Sgt) Frank Arcaro **13** Janet Halloran
  cast: 9 Paul Burke **11** Nancy Malone **12** John McIntire **13** Harry Bellaver, Horace McMahon, Suzanne Storrs **15** James Franciscus
  setting: 11 New York City
  theme: 19 Somewhere in the Night

Namath, Joe (Joseph William)
  nickname: 11 Broadway Joe
  sport: 8 football
  position: 11 quarterback
  team: 11 New York Jets

namby-pamby 3 coy **4** dull, prim, weak **5** banal, inane, vapid **6** prissy **7** insipid, mincing, sapless **9** colorless, innocuous, simpering **10** indecisive, wishy-washy **13** characterless

name 3 dub, tag **4** call, term **5** label, title **6** choose, ordain, select **7** appoint, baptize, epithet, specify **8** christen, cognomen, delegate, deputize, nominate, taxonomy **9** authorize, designate, signature, sobriquet **10** commission **11** appellation, designation **12** denomination, nomenclature

nameless 5 minor **7** obscure, unknown, unnamed, untitled **9** anonymous, unheard-of, unhonored **12** undesignated

namely
  Latin: 3 viz **9** videlicet

Name of the Game
  character: 8 Andy Hill **9** Joe Sample, Ross Craig **10** Dan Farrell, Jeff Dillon **11** Glenn Howard **12** Peggy Maxwell
  cast: 9 Ben Murphy, Gene Barry **10** Mark Miller **11** Cliff Potter, Robert Stack **13** Tony Franciosa **15** Susan Saint James
  business: 8 magazine **10** publishing

Name of the Rose, The
  author: 10 Umberto Eco

Name That Tune
  host: 9 Red Benson **10** Bill Cullen **12** George de Witt
  orchestra: 11 Harry Salter

Namibia
  other name: 15 South West Africa
  capital/largest city: 8 Windhoek
  others: 6 Tsumeb **8** Luderitz **9** Walvis Bay **10** Oranjemund, Swakopmund **12** Keetmanshoop
  monetary unit: 4 cent, rand
  mountain: 14 Khomas Highland, Koakoveld Hills
  highest point: 9 Brandberg
  river: 4 Fish **6** Cunene, Orange **7** Zambezi **8** Okavango
  sea: 8 Atlantic
  physical feature:
    bay: 6 Walvis
    desert: 5 Namib **8** Kalahari
    region: 12 Caprivi Strip
  people: 4 Nama **5** Bantu **6** Damara, Herero, Ovambo, Tswara **7** Bushman, colored **8** Okavango **9** Hottentot
  language: 5 Bantu **6** German **7** English, Khoisan **9** Afrikaans
  religion: 7 animism **8** Lutheran
  feature:
    homeland: 9 bantustan

Nammu
  origin: 8 Sumerian
  mother of: 4 gods
  personifies: 3 sea

Namtar
  origin: 8 Akkadian, Sumerian
  form: 5 demon
  personifies: 5 death

Nana
  author: 9 Emile Zola

Nana (Nurse) (dog)
  character in: 8 Peter Pan
  author: 6 Barrie

Nancy
  character in: 11 Oliver Twist
  author: 7 Dickens

Nancy
  creator: 15 Ernie Bushmiller
  character: 5 Rollo **6** Sluggo **10** Aunt Fritzi

Nanna
  origin: 12 Scandinavian
  husband: 5 Baldr **6** Balder, Baldur
  habitat: 4 moon

Nannerella
  nickname of: 11 Anna Magnani

nanometer
   abbreviation: **2** nm
Naoise
   origin: **5** Irish
   wife: **7** Deirdre
   uncle: **9** Conchobar
   killed by: **9** Conchobar
   father: **6** Usnach, Usnech
Naomi
   husband: **9** Elimelech
   daughter-in-law: **4** Ruth
   son: **6** Mahlon **7** Chilion
nap 3 nod **4** doze, rest **6** cat nap,
   drowse, siesta, snooze **7** doze off,
   drop off, goof off, shut-eye, slumber **8**
   drift off **10** forty winks
napery 5 doily **6** linens, napkin **10** ta-
   blecloth
Naphtali
   father: **5** Jacob
   mother: **6** Bilkah
   brother: **3** Dan, Gad **4** Levi **5** Asher,
      Judah **6** Joseph, Reuben, Simeon **7**
      Zebulun **8** Benjamin, Issachar
   sister: **5** Dinah
   descendant of: **10** Naphtalite
Napoleon Bonaparte
   also: **9** Napoleon I **18** Emperor of the
      French
   battle: **3** Ulm **5** Eylau **6** Lutzen, Mos-
      cow, Toulon (siege), Wagram **7** Bau-
      tzen, Dresden, Leipzig, Marengo,
      Mondovi **8** Borodino, Waterloo **9**
      Friedland **10** Austerlitz **13** Aspern-
      Essling, Jena-Auerstadt, Peninsular
      War **22** War of the Fifth Coalition
   born: **7** Corsica
   exile to: **4** Elba **11** Saint Helena
   fought against: **7** Kutuzov **10** von
      Blucher, Wellington **14** Barclay de
      Tolly
   French fleet destroyed at: **9** Trafal-
      gar
      destroyed by: **6** Nelson
   laws: **14** Napoleonic Code
   marshal/general under: **3** Ney **5** Mu-
      rat **7** Massena **10** Bernadotte
   position: **7** emperor **11** first consul
      13 consul for life
   tomb: **5** Paris **9** Invalides
   wife: **9** Josephine **20** Marie-Louise of
      Austria
Napoleon of Notting Hill, The
   author: **12** G K Chesterton
narcissism 6 egoism, vanity **7** conceit
   8 self-love **11** egocentrism **16** selfcen-
   teredness
narcissist 6 egoist **7** egotist **11** egocen-
   trist **12** self- absorbed, self-admiring
narcissistic 4 smug, vain **6** vanity **7**
   conceit, selfish **8** egotistic, puffed-up
   9 conceited **10** egocentric, egoistical
   11 egomaniacal, egotistical
narcissus
   varieties: **5** poet's **6** poetaz **7** leedsii,
      trumpet **10** paper-white, polyanthus
      16 primrose peerless

Narcissus
   father: **8** Cephisus
   mother: **8** Leiriope
   loved: **7** himself
   loved by: **4** Echo
   punished by: **9** Aphrodite
   changed into: **6** flower
narcotic 4 drug, morphine **5** opium **6**
   herion, opiate **8** medicine, sedative **9**
   soporific **10** medicament, medication,
   painkiller **12** tranquilizer **14** pharma-
   ceutical
Narragansett
   language family: **9** Algonkian **10** Al-
      gonquian
   location: **11** Connecticut, Rhode Is-
      land
   related to: **7** Niantic
   involved in: **9** Pequot War **14** King
      Philip's War **15** Great Swamp Fight
narrate 6 detail, recite, relate, render,
   repeat, retell **7** portray, recount **8** describe, set forth **9** chronicle **10** tell a
   story **15** give an account of
narration 7 recital, telling **8** relating,
   speaking **9** voice-over **10** recitation,
   recounting **11** chronicling, description
   12 storytelling
narrative 4 tale **5** story **6** report **7** account, recital **8** dialogue, episodic **9**
   anecdotal, chronicle, statement **10** historical **12** storytelling
**Narrative of Arthur Gordon Pym,
The**
   author: **13** Edgar Allan Poe
narrow 3 set **4** fine, slim **5** close,
   scant, small, tight **6** biased, scanty **7**
   bigoted, cramped, pinched, shallow,
   slender, tapered **8** confined, dogmatic,
   isolated, squeezed **9** hidebound, illiberal, parochial **10** attenuated, com
   pressed, intolerant, provincial, restricted **11** constricted, incapacious,
   opinionated, reactionary **12** conservative
narrowing 5 taper **8** tapering **9**
   squeezing **11** compressing **12** constricting
narrow-minded 5 petty **7** bigoted,
   prudish **8** one-sided **9** hidebound, parochial, unworldly **10** provincial **11**
   opinionated, reactionary, straitlaced
   12 conservative **15** unsophisticated
narrow-mindedness 4 bias **7** bigotry
   9 prejudice **10** unfairness **11** intolerance
narrows 4 neck, pass **5** canal **6** ravine,
   strait **7** channel, isthmus, passage
Nasca *see* **5** Nazca
Nascimento, Edson Arantes do
   real name of: **4** Pele
Nash, Ogden
   author of: **6** Versus **9** Hard Lines **20**
      The Private Dining Room **21** I'm a
      Stranger Here Myself
Nashville

   director: **12** Robert Altman
   cast: **10** Karen Black, Lily Tomlin **11**
      Henry Gibson **12** Ronee Blakley **13**
      Barbara Harris, Michael Murphy **14**
      Keith Carradine **16** Geraldine Chaplin
   Oscar for: **4** song
   song: **6** I'm Easy
Nassau
   capital of: **7** Bahamas
Nasser, Gamal Abdel
   president of: **5** Egypt **18** United Arab
      Republic
nasty 4 foul, mean, vile **5** awful **6** odious **7** beastly, hateful, vicious **8** horrible **9** repellent, revolting **10** abominable, disgusting, nauseating, unpleasant
   11 distasteful **12** disagreeable
Natchez
   language family: **10** Muskhogean
   tribe: **6** Avoyel, Taensa
   location: **11** Mississippi **13** South Car-
      olina
   allied with: **7** Choctaw
   practiced: **14** head flattening
nates 4 buns, rear, rump, seat **7** rear
   end **8** buttocks, haunches **9** fundament, posterior **12** hindquarters
Nathan
   father: **5** Attai
   served: **5** David **7** Solomon
Nathanael, Nathaniel *see* **5** Jesus **8**
   Apostles **11** Bartholomew
nation 4 host, race **5** realm, state, tribe
   6 empire, people **7** country, kingdom
   8 republic **9** community **11** sovereignty **12** commonwealth
national park
   Alaska: **13** Mount McKinley
   Arizona: **11** Grand Canyon **15** Petri-
      fied Forest
   Arkansas: **10** Hot Springs
   California: **7** Redwood, Sequoia **8** Yo-
      semite **11** Kings Canyon **14** Channel
      Islands, Lassen Volcanic
   Canada: **4** Yoho **5** Banff, Fundy **6**
      Jasper, Kluane **8** Kootenay **9** Auyuit-
      tuq **13** Waterton Lakes
   Colorado: **5** Estes **9** Mesa Verde **13**
      Rocky Mountain
   Florida: **10** Everglades
   Hawaii: **9** Haleakala **15** Hawaii Volca-
      noes
   Kentucky: **11** Mammoth Cave
   Maine: **6** Acadia
   Michigan: **10** Isle Royale
   Minnesota: **9** Voyageurs
   Montana: **7** Glacier **11** Yellowstone
   New Mexico: **15** Carlsbad Caverns
   North Carolina: **19** Great Smoky
      Mountains (with Tennessee)
   North Dakota: **17** Theodore Roose-
      velt
   Oklahoma: **6** Platte
   Oregon: **10** Crater Lake
   South Dakota: **8** Badlands, Wind
      Cave
   Tennessee: **6** Shiloh **13** Cumberland

Gap **19** Great Smoky Mountains (with North Carolina)
Texas: 7 Big Bend **18** Guadalupe Mountains
Utah: 4 Zion **6** Arches **11** Bryce Canyon, Canyonlands, Capital Reef
Virginia: 10 Shenandoah **26** Colonial National Historical
Washington: 7 Olympic **12** Mount Rainier **13** North Cascades
Wyoming: 10 Grand Teton **11** Yellowstone

National Velvet
director: 13 Clarence Brown
cast: 10 Anne Revere **11** Donald Crisp **12** Mickey Rooney **14** Angela Lansbury **15** Elizabeth Taylor
horse: 6 The Pie
Oscar for: 17 supporting actress (Revere)
sequel: 19 International Velvet

native 4 home **5** basic, local, natal **6** inborn, inbred, innate, savage **7** citizen, endemic, natural **8** domestic, inherent, national, paternal **9** aborigine, elemental, homegrown, ingrained, inherited, intrinsic, primitive **10** congenital, countryman, hereditary, indigenous **11** instinctive **12** countrywoman **13** autochthonous

Native Americans
Registered tribes and/or nations, by state:
AL: **11** Poorch Creek
AK: **5** Aleut, Haida **6** Eskimo **7** Tlingit **10** Athabascan, Tsimpshian
AZ: **4** Hopi, Pima **6** Navajo, Apache, Papago **7** Yavapai
CA: **5** Hoopa, Yurok, Karok **6** Paiute **8** Cherokee
CO: **3** Ute
CT: **18** Mashantucket Pequot
FL: **8** Seminole, Cherokee **10** Miccosukee
ID: **7** Bannock **8** Shoshone, Nez Perce
IA: **9** Sac and Fox
KS: **4** Iowa **8** Kickapoo **10** Potawatomi
LA: **9** Coushatta **10** Chitimacha **12** Tunica-Biloxi
ME: **8** Maliseet **9** Penobscot **13** Passamaquoddy
MA: **9** Wampanoag
MI: **6** Ottawa **8** Cherokee, Chippewa **10** Potawatomi
MN: **5** Sioux **8** Chippewa
MS: **7** Choctaw
MO: **4** Crow **5** Sioux **8** Cheyenne **9** Blackfoot **11** Assiniboine
NE: **5** Omaha **9** Winnebago **11** Santee Sioux
NV: **6** Paiute, Washoe **8** Shoshone
NM: **6** Apache, Navajo, Pueblo
NY: **6** Mohawk, Seneca, Oneida **8** Onondaga
NC: **6** Lumbee **8** Cherokee
ND: **5** Sioux **6** Mandan **7** Arikara,

Hidatsa **8** Chippewa
OK: **5** Creek, Kiowa, Osage **7** Choctaw **8** Cherokee, Cheyenne, Comanche, Arapahoe, Chicasaw
OR: **5** Wasco **6** Siletz, Paiute **11** Warm Springs
RI: **12** Narragansett
SC: **7** Catawba
SD: **5** Sioux
TX: **4** Tiwa **8** Kickapoo **16** Alabama-Coushatta
UT: **3** Ute **6** Navajo **7** Goshute **14** Southern Paiute
WA: **5** Lummi **6** Yakama **8** Quinault
WI **6** Oneida **8** Chippewa **9** Winnebago
WY: **8** Shoshone, Arapahoe
see also Individual Entries

native country 7 country **8** homeland **10** fatherland **13** mother country

native-grown 5 local **8** domestic **9** homegrown **10** indigenous

native land 8 homeland **10** birthplace, fatherland, native soil **13** mother country, native country

native of Israel
Hebrew: 5 sabra

native soil 8 homeland **10** fatherland, native land **13** mother country, native country

Native Son
author: 13 Richard Wright

NATO
members: 5 Italy, Spain **6** Canada, France, Greece, Norway, Turkey **7** Belgium, Denmark, Germany, Iceland **8** Portugal **10** Luxembourg **11** Netherlands **12** United States **13** United Kingdom
proposed: 6 Poland **7** Hungary **13** Czech Republic

natty 4 chic, neat, posh, tidy, trim **5** smart **6** dapper, jaunty, snappy, spruce **7** dashing, modish, stylish **11** fashionable

Natty Bumppo
also: 7 Hawkeye **10** Pathfinder, The Trapper **13** The Deerslayer **15** Leatherstocking **16** Le Longue Carabine
character in: 23 The Leatherstocking Tales
friend: 5 Uncas **12** Chingachgook
author: 6 Cooper

natural 5 plain **6** inborn, native, normal **7** earthly, genuine, regular **8** God-given, inherent **9** essential, intuitive, unstudied **10** unaffected, unmannered **11** instinctive, spontaneous, terrestrial **13** unpretentious **14** characteristic **15** straightforward
in craps: 5 seven **6** eleven

Natural, The
director: 13 Barry Levinson
based on story by: 14 Bernard Malamud
character: 7 Roy Hobbs

cast: 10 Glenn Close **12** Robert Duvall **13** Robert Redford

natural child 7 bastard **9** love child **17** illegitimate child

natural gift 5 flair **6** talent **7** ability, faculty **8** aptitude **9** attribute, endowment

natural habitat 5 range **6** domain, milieu **7** element **9** territory **11** environment

naturalize 5 adapt, adopt **6** adjust **8** accustom **9** acclimate **11** domesticate, familiarize

naturalness 4 ease **9** sincerity **10** simplicity **11** artlessness, genuineness **12** unconstraint **14** unaffectedness

nature 4 bent, kind, mood, sort, type **5** birth, earth, globe, humor, stamp, style, trait **6** cosmos, spirit **7** essence, feature, variety **8** category, creation, instinct, property, universe **9** character **11** disposition, peculiarity **12** constitution **13** particularity **14** characteristic
goddess of: 6 Cybele **9** Dindymene **10** Berecyntia

Nature
author: 17 Ralph Waldo Emerson

naught 3 nil **4** zero **5** nihil, zilch **6** cipher **7** nothing, useless **9** worthless

naughty 3 bad **4** blue **5** bawdy, dirty **6** ribald, risque, vulgar **7** wayward, willful **8** devilish, off-color, perverse **9** fractious, obstinate **11** disobedient, misbehaving, mischievous **12** pornographic, recalcitrant, unmanageable **13** disrespectful

Nauru
other name: 14 Pleasant Island
capital: 13 Yaren District
cities: 3 Boe, Ewa **4** Aiwo, Ijuw **5** Baiti, Buada, Nibok, Uaboe, Yaren **6** Anabar, Anetan, Meneng **7** Anibare **10** Denigomodu
monetary unit: 4 cent **6** dollar
lake: 11 Buada Lagoon
sea: 7 Pacific
physical feature:
bay: 7 Anibare
lagoon: 5 Buada
point: 4 Anna **6** Meneng
people: 7 Chinese **9** Melanesian, Polynesian **11** Micronesian
explorer: 9 John Fearn
language: 7 English, Nauruan
religion: 10 Protestant **13** Roman Catholic
feature: 9 phosphate

nausea 7 disgust, heaving **8** contempt, loathing, retching, sickness, vomiting **9** repulsion, revulsion **10** queasiness **11** airsickness, biliousness, car sickness, seasickness **12** upset stomach **14** motion sickness, travel sickness

Nausea, Nausee
author: 14 Jean-Paul Sartre

nauseate 5 repel, upset **6** offend,

revolt, sicken **7** disgust, repulse **8** make sick **15** turn one's stomach

nauseated 3 ill **4** sick **5** upset **6** queasy **8** repelled, revolted **9** disgusted

nauseating 9 offensive, repellent, repulsive, revolting, sickening **10** disgusting

nauseous 4 sick **5** upset **6** queasy **9** abhorrent, nauseated, offensive, repellent, repulsive, revolting, sickening, upsetting **10** disgusting, nauseating **12** unappetizing

Nausicaa
  father: **8** Alcinous
  position: **8** princess
  aided: **8** Odysseus

Nausithous
  father: **8** Poseidon
  mother: **8** Periboea
  occupation: **8** helmsman
  employer: **7** Theseus
  became: **4** king
  realm: **8** Phaeacia

nautical 5 naval **6** marine **7** aquatic, boating, oceanic **8** maritime, of the sea, seagoing, yachting

nautical mile
  abbreviation: **3** nmi

Nautilus
  submarine in: **32** Twenty Thousand Leagues Under the Sea
  skipper: **11** Captain Nemo
  author: **5** Verne

Navajo, Navaho (Dine)
  language family: **10** Athapascan, Athapaskan
  location: **4** Utah **7** Arizona **9** New Mexico
  noted for: **7** weaving **14** silversmithing
  dwelling: **5** hogan

navigate 3 fly **4** ride, sail, ship **5** cross, steer **6** cruise, voyage **8** maneuver, sail over **11** plot a course **12** chart a course

navigation 7 boating, sailing **8** cruising, piloting, voyaging **9** traveling **10** seamanship
  god of: **5** Niord, Njord

Navigators Islands *see* **12** Western Samoa

navy 5 fleet **6** armada, convoy **8** flotilla, warships

navy-blue 6 indigo **8** dark blue, deep blue

nay 4 also, deny, vote **5** never **6** denial, refuse **7** against, but also, refusal **8** negative

Nazarene *see* **5** Jesus

Nazarene, The
  author: **10** Sholem Asch

Nazca, Nasca
  location: **4** Peru **12** South America
  noted for: **8** ceramics, textiles **10** Nazca lines (sketches on plain)

Nazi 7 facost
  air force: **9** Luftwaffe
  swastika: **10** Hakenkreuz
  collaborator: **8** quisling
  elite guard: **13** schutzstaffel
  leader: **4** Hess **6** Hitler **7** Himmler **8** Goebbels
  police: **7** gestapo
  trials: Nuremberg

N'Djamena
  capital of: **4** Chad

Neal, Patricia
  husband: **9** Roald Dahl
  born: **9** Packard KY
  roles: **3** Hud (Oscar) **15** A Face in the Crowd, The Fountainhead **18** The Subject Was Roses

near 4 nigh **5** about, close **6** all but, almost **7** close by, close to, looming **8** approach, come up to, imminent, next door **9** alongside, close with, impending **10** hereabouts **11** approaching, practically, proximately, threatening **13** approximately

nearby 5 close, handy **6** at hand **7** close by **8** next door **9** adjoining **10** accessible, hereabouts

near death
  Latin: **10** in extremis

near home 5 close **7** close by **10** hereabouts

nearly 4 nigh **5** about **6** all but, almost **7** close to, roughly **11** practically **13** approximately

nearly equal 5 close **7** similar **10** nip-and-tuck **11** approaching

nearly even 5 close **10** head to head, nip-and-tuck **11** neck and neck

nearness 8 intimacy, vicinity **9** adjacency, closeness, handiness, immediacy, proximity **10** contiguity **11** propinquity **12** availability, neighborhood **13** accessibility, approximation

nearsighted 6 myopic
  opposite: **9** hyperopic **10** presbyopic

neat 4 tidy **5** clean, great **6** groovy **7** concise, correct, orderly **8** accurate, exciting, original, straight, striking, succinct **9** competent, dexterous, efficient, ingenious, organized, purposive, shipshape **10** controlled, immaculate, methodical, systematic **11** imaginative, intelligent, uncluttered

neatness 5 order **8** tidiness **11** orderliness **12** organization

Nebraska
  abbreviation: **2** NE **4** Nebr
  nickname: **4** Beef **8** Antelope **10** Blackwater, Cornhusker **12** Treeplanter's
  capital: **7** Lincoln
  largest city: **5** Omaha
  others: **5** Cozad **6** Gering **7** Kearney **8** Beatrice, Hastings **9** Broken Bow **11** Grand Island, North Platte, Scottsbluff
  college: **4** Dana **5** Doane **8** Duchesne,

Hastings **9** Creighton **15** Midland Lutheran
  feature: **8** Boys' Town
    national monument: **11** Scott's Bluff **15** Agate Fossil Beds
  tribe: **3** Oto **4** Otoe **5** Kiowa, Omaha, Ponca, Sioux **6** Pawnee
  people: **10** Henry Fonda **11** Fred Astaire, Roscoe Pound
  lake: **7** Merritt, Sherman, Swanson **10** McConaughy **13** Lewis and Clark
  land rank: **9** fifteenth
  physical feature: **8** Badlands
    hills: **4** Sand **5** Drift, Loess
    plains: **5** Great
  river: **4** Loup **5** Logan **6** Dismal, Nemaha, Platte **7** Big Blue, Elkhorn **8** Missouri, Niobrara **10** Little Blue, Republican **12** Harlan County
  state admission: **13** thirty-seventh
  state bird: **17** western meadowlark
  state flower: **9** goldenrod
  state motto: **20** Equality Before the Law
  state song: **17** Beautiful Nebraska
  state tree: **3** elm **10** cottonwood

nebris
  skin of: **4** fawn

Nebrophonus *see* **5** Thoon

Nebuchadnezzar
  father: **12** Nabopolassar
  son: **10** Belshazzar **12** Evilmerodach
  same as: **7** Nabucco **14** Nebuchadrezzar
  king of: **7** Babylon
  conquered: **9** Jerusalem
  destroyed: **6** temple
  deported: **4** Jews
  into: **7** slavery
  general: **11** Holophernes

nebula 4 Crab, Ring, Veil **5** Great **6** Lagoon **7** Rosette **9** Horsehead

nebulous 3 dim **4** dark, hazy **5** murky, vague **6** cloudy **7** obscure, unclear **8** confused **9** ambiguous, uncertain **10** impalpable, indefinite, indistinct, intangible **13** indeterminate

necessarily 8 perforce **9** naturally **10** inevitably, inexorably **11** accordingly **12** compulsorily **13** automatically, axiomatically, unqualifiedly **16** incontrovertibly

necessary 6 needed, urgent, wanted **7** crucial, desired, exigent, fitting, needful **8** required **9** called for, essential, requisite **10** compulsory, imperative, obligatory **13** indispensable

necessary changes having been made
  Latin: **15** mutatis mutandis

necessitate 5 cause, force, impel **6** compel, demand, oblige **7** call for, enforce, require **9** constrain, prescribe

necessitation 5 cause, force **6** demand, duress **8** coercion, pressure **10** compulsion, constraint, obligation **11** enforcement, requirement

necessity, necessities 4 must, need **6** demand, needed **7** urgency **8** exigency, pressure **9** essential, requisite **10** sine qua non **11** requirement **13** indispensable
Latin: 10 sine qua non

neck 3 pet **4** kiss, nape, pass **6** caress, cervix, cuddle, fondle, smooth, strait **7** channel, isthmus, make out **9** narrowing

neckerchief 5 scarf **8** bandanna, kerchief

necklace 3 tie **5** beads, chain, noose **6** choker, collar, locket, pearls, string **7** jewelry, pendant **8** ornament **9** lavaliere

necktie 3 bow **4** band **5** ascot, black, scarf **6** cravat, string **7** Windsor **10** four in hand **11** half Windsor **12** hangman's rope

necromancer 5 hexer, magus, witch **6** wizard **7** charmer, warlock **8** conjurer, exorcist, magician, sorcerer **9** enchanter, occultist, voodooist **10** soothsayer **13** black magician, thaumaturgist

necromancy 5 magic, spell **7** sorcery **8** black art **10** witchcraft **11** enchantment, foretelling

necrophobia
fear of: 5 death **10** dead bodies

necropolis 8 cemetery **9** graveyard **12** burial ground **13** burying ground

nectar
drink of: 4 gods
gives: 4 life

nee 4 born **11** maiden-named

need 4 lack, want, wish **5** crave, exact **6** demand, penury **7** call for, longing, poverty, require, straits **8** distress, exigency, yearn for **9** essential, extremity, indigence, necessity, requisite **10** bankruptcy, insolvency **11** desideratum, destitution, necessitate, requirement **13** impecuniosity, pennilessness

needed 5 vital **7** crucial **9** essential, necessary, requisite **13** indispensable

needful 7 wishful **8** required **9** essential, necessary, requisite **10** imperative **13** indispensable

needle 3 vex **4** josh, leaf, ride, twit **5** annoy, chaff, harry, taunt, tease **6** badger, harass, hector **7** torment **9** indicator
prefix: 3 acu

needle-shaped 5 sharp **6** peaked, spiked **7** pointed **8** piercing **10** bodkin-like

needless 7 useless **9** excessive, pointless, redundant **10** gratuitous, pleonastic, unavailing **11** dispensable, purposeless, superfluous, uncalled-for, unessential, unnecessary **12** overabundant

needlework 6 sewing **7** basting, brocade, darning, tacking, tatting **8** appli-

que, knitting, quilting **9** stitching **10** embroidery **11** cross stitch, needle point

needy 4 poor **5** broke **6** hard-up, in want **8** indigent, strapped **9** destitute, money less, penniless **10** down-and-out **12** impoverished **15** poverty-stricken

ne'er-do-well 3 bum **5** idler, loser **6** loafer, no-good **7** goof-off, sad sack, wastrel **8** layabout **9** do-nothing, no-account **10** black sheep **14** good-for-nothing

nefarious 3 bad, low **4** base, evil, foul, vile **6** odious, wicked **7** beastly, ghastly, heinous, hellish, ungodly, vicious **8** depraved, devilish, infamous, infernal, shameful **9** atrocious, execrable **10** abominable, despicable, detestable, iniquitous, scandalous, villainous **11** disgraceful, opprobrious, unspeakable **12** dishonorable **13** unmentionable

Nefertem
origin: 8 Egyptian
personifies: 5 lotus
true identity: 4 Ptah

Nefertiti
queen: 5 Egypt
husband: 8 Ikhnaton **9** Amenhotep
nephew: 11 Tutankhamen

negate 4 deny, veto, void **5** quash, quell, rebut **6** defeat, disown, refute, repeal, revoke, squash **7** blot out, destroy, disavow, gainsay, nullify, retract, reverse, squelch, wipe out **8** abrogate, disallow, disclaim, set aside, vanquish **9** overthrow, overwhelm, repudiate **10** contradict, invalidate

negating 7 denying, voiding **8** refuting, revoking **9** reversing **10** cancelling, nullifying **11** disallowing **12** invalidating, setting aside **13** contradicting

negation 6 denial **7** counter **8** reversal **9** rejection **10** abrogation, disclaimer, refutation **11** confutation, repudiation **12** invalidation **13** contradiction, nullification

negative 4 blue, dark **5** bleak **6** at odds, gloomy **7** dubious, opposed **8** contrary, doubtful, downbeat, inimical, opposing, refusing **9** declining, demurring, dissident, jaundiced, objecting, rejecting, reluctant, skeptical, unwilling **10** dissenting, fatalistic **11** disagreeing, pessimistic **12** antagonistic, disapproving **13** uncooperative **14** unenthusiastic

neglect 4 fail, omit **5** let go, shirk **6** forget, ignore, laxity, pass by, pass up, slight **7** abandon, default, laxness, let pass, let ride, let slip **8** be remiss, idleness, let slide, omission, overlook, pass over, shake off **9** disregard, oversight, passivity, slackness **10** inaccuracy, negligence, remissness **11** dere-

liction, inattention, inexactness **12** carelessness, fecklessness, indifference, slovenliness **13** noncompliance, unfulfillment **14** nonpreparation **16** underachievement

neglected 7 dropped, ignored, omitted, shirked, unkempt **8** forsaken, untended **9** abandoned, cast aside, forgotten **10** overlooked, uncared for **11** disregarded

neglectful 4 lazy **5** slack **6** remiss, untrue **8** careless, derelict, heedless **9** forgetful, negligent, oblivious, unheeding, unmindful **10** inconstant, thriftless, unfaithful, unthinking, unwatchful **11** improvident, inattentive, indifferent, respectless, thoughtless, unobservant **12** devil-may-care, disregardant, disregardful, happy-go-lucky **15** procrastinating

negligee, neglige 4 robe **6** kimono **7** wrapper **8** bathrobe, peignoir **9** housecoat **12** dressing gown

negligence 6 laxity **7** neglect **11** disregarded **12** carelessness

negligent 3 lax **5** slack **6** remiss, untidy **8** careless, heedless, slovenly **9** forgetful, unheeding, unmindful **10** neglectful, unthinking, unwatchful **11** inattentive, indifferent, thoughtless, unobservant **13** inconsiderate

negligible 5 minor, petty, small **6** minute, paltry, slight **7** trivial **8** piddling, trifling **11** unimportant **13** insignificant **15** inconsequential

negotiate 4 cash, make, pass **6** barter, cash in, convey, dicker, haggle, handle, manage, redeem, settle **7** arrange, consign, deliver, discuss, get over **8** contract, cope with, deal with, hand over, make over, pass over, sign over, transact, transfer, transmit, turn over **10** bargain for **11** come to terms, meet halfway

negotiation 4 deal **6** treaty **8** argument, haggling **9** dickering **10** bargaining **11** arbitration, arrangement **12** compromising

negotiator 7 arbiter **8** mediator **9** go-between **10** arbitrator **12** intermediary

Nehemiah
father: 5 Azbuk **14** Hachaliah

neigh 5 hinny **6** nicker, whinny

neighbor 4 abut, meet **5** touch **6** adjoin, be near, border, friend **7** conjoin **8** borderer, border on **9** associate **12** acquaintance

neighborhood 4 area, part, side, ward **5** place, range **6** locale, parish, region, sphere **7** quarter, section **8** confines, district, environs, precinct, purlieus, vicinity **9** community

neighboring 4 near, next **5** close **6** at hand, nearby **7** close by **8** abutting, adjacent **9** adjoining, bordering **10** contiguous **11** surrounding **12** circumjacent

neighborly 4 kind **5** civil **6** chummy, kindly, polite **7** affable, amiable, cordial, helpful **8** amicable, friendly, gracious, obliging **9** courteous **10** hospitable **11** considerate, warmhearted **12** well-disposed

Neighbors
author: **12** Thomas Berger

Neith
origin: **8** Egyptian
personifies: **10** femininity
son: **2** Ra
corresponds to: **6** Athena

Nekhbet
origin: **8** Egyptian
form: **7** vulture
guardian of: **5** Egypt **10** Upper Egypt

Nelson, Harriet Hilliard
real name: **14** Peggy Lou Snyder
husband: **5** Ozzie
son: **4** Rick **5** David
born: **11** Des Moines IA
roles: **30** The Adventures of Ozzie and Harriet

Nelson, Horatio
also: **14** Viscount Nelson
nationality: **7** British
battle: **9** Trafalgar **11** Bay of Abukir **15** Battle of the Nile **16** Cape Saint Vincent **18** Battle of Copenhagen
defeated: **5** Danes **6** French **7** Spanish
flagship: **7** Victory
killed at: **9** Trafalgar
lover: **16** Emma Lady Hamilton

Nelson, Ozzie
real name: **18** Oswald George Nelson
wife: **15** Harriet Hilliard
son: **4** Rick **5** David
born: **12** Jersey City NJ
roles: **30** The Adventures of Ozzie and Harriet

Nemean
epithet of: **4** Zeus **5** games
precursor of: **8** Olympics

Nemean lion
strangled by: **8** Hercules

nemesis 4 ruin **5** match, **6** rival **7** avenger, goddess, justice, revenge, undoing **8** downfall, punisher, Waterloo **9** overthrow, vengeance **10** punishment **11** destruction, retaliation, retribution **16** instrument of fate

nemine contradicente 11 unanimously **18** no one contradicting

nemine dissentiente 11 unanimously **15** no one dissenting

Nemo
character in: **10** Bleak House
author: **7** Dickens

Nemo, Captain
character in: **32** Twenty Thousand Leagues Under the Sea
author: **5** Verne
submarine: **8** Nautilus

nene 13 Hawaiian goose

neologism, neology 7 coinage **9** nonce word

neon
chemical symbol: **2** Ne

neonate 4 baby **6** infant **7** newborn

neophyte 4 tyro **5** pupil **6** novice, rookie **7** amateur, convert, entrant, learner, recruit, student, trainee **8** beginner, disciple, newcomer **9** greenhorn, novitiate, proselyte **10** apprentice, tenderfoot **11** probationer

neoplasm 5 tumor **6** cancer, growth **7** sarcoma **9** carcinoma **10** malignancy **14** carcinosarcoma

Nepal
other name: **9** Shangri-La
capital/largest city: **8** Katmandu **9** Kathmandu
others: **5** Patan, Patna **6** Gurkha **7** Birganj **8** Bhadgaon, Lalitpur **9** Bhaktapur **10** Biratnagar
university: **9** Tribhuvan
division: **5** Terai **13** High Himalayas
monetary unit: **4** anna, pice **5** mohar, paisa, rupee
mountain: **6** Cho Oyu, Churia, Lhotse, Makalu **7** Manaslu, Siwalik **9** Annapurna, Himalayas **10** Dhaulagiri, Gosainthan, Himalchuli **11** Ganesh Himal **12** Kanchenjunga **14** Mahabharat hekh
highest point: **9** Mt Everest
river: **4** Kali, Kosi, Mugu, Seti **5** Babai, Bheri, Rapti, Sarda, Tamur **6** Gandak **7** Karnali **8** Narayani
physical feature:
  plain: **5** Terai
  valley: **5** Nepal **8** Katmandu
people: **3** Rai **4** Aoul **5** Bhote, Limbu, Magar, Murmi, Newar, Tharu **6** Bhutia, Gurkha, Gurung, Nepali, Sherpa, Tamang **7** Kiranti, Tibetan **8** Corkhali, Nepalese
  birthplace of: **6** Buddha **13** Gautama Buddha **17** Siddhartha Gautama
king: **8** Mahendra **9** Tribhuwan **18** Prithwi Narayan Shah **23** Birenda Bir Bikram Shah Dev
ruler: **4** Rana **5** Malla **6** Rajput
language: **6** Nepali, Newari
religion: **8** Buddhism, Hinduism
place:
  dam: **6** Gandak
  shrine: **9** Swayambhu **10** Gorakhnath
feature:
  animal: **3** dzo, yak **7** dzopkyo
  arch: **6** Juddha
  god/goddess: **5** Indra **6** Kumari
  legend: **4** Yeti **17** abominable snowman
  soldiers: **6** Gurkha

Nepali
language family: **12** Indo-European
branch: **11** Indo-Iranian
group: **5** Indic
spoken in: **5** Nepal

nepenthe 4 drug **5** drink, opium **6** heroin, opiate **7** hashish **8** narcotic

nephrite
variety: **4** jade

ne plus ultra 4 acme **6** finest **8** ultimate **12** highest point

nepotism 10 favoritism
patron of: **9** relatives

Neptune
origin: **5** Roman
god of: **3** sea
corresponds to: **8** Poseidon

Neptune
position: **6** eighth
satellite: **6** Nereid, Triton
color: **4** blue
studied by: **7** Voyager (2)

Nereid
form: **5** nymph
location: **3** sea
father: **6** Nereus

Nereus
god of: **3** sea
father: **6** Pontus
mother: **4** Gaea
father of: **7** Nereids
number of Nereids: **5** fifty
son: **7** Nerites

Nerissa
character in: **19** The Merchant of Venice
author: **11** Shakespeare

neritic 7 aquatic, coastal **8** offshore

Nero
name: **18** Nero Claudius Caesar
emperor of: **4** Rome
mother: **9** Agrippina
father: **19** Domitius Ahenobarbus
stepfather: **8** Claudius
tutor: **6** Seneca
son: **11** Britannicus
wife: **7** Octavia **13** Poppaea Sabina
successor: **5** Galba

nerve 4 dash, gall, grit, guts, sass **5** brass, cheek, crust, pluck, spunk, valor **6** mettle, spirit **7** bravery, courage **8** backbone, boldness, coolness, gameness, strength, tenacity **9** arrogance, assurance, derring-do, endurance, flippancy, fortitude, gallantry, hardihood, hardiness, impudence, insolence, sauciness **10** assumption, brazenness, confidence, effrontery, steadiness **11** intrepidity, presumption **12** fearlessness, impertinence, resoluteness **13** determination **16** stoutheartedness

nerveless 4 calm, dead, weak **5** brave, frail, inert **6** feeble, flabby **7** flaccid **8** cowardly **9** powerless **10** courageous **12** fainthearted

nervous 4 wild **5** jumpy, shaky, tense **6** touchy, uneasy **7** alarmed, anxious, excited, fearful, fidgety, jittery, peevish, ruffled **8** feverish, neurotic, skittish, startled, timorous, unstrung **9** delirious, disturbed, excitable, impatient, irritable, sensitive, trembling, tremulous, unsettled **10** high-strung, hysterical **12** apprehensive

nervousness 6 tremor **7** anxiety, flutter, shaking, tension **8** hysteria, timidity **9** agitation, quivering, the creeps, the shakes, trembling, twitching **10** the fidgets, touchiness **11** disturbance, fidgetiness, stage fright **12** apprehension, excitability, irascibility, irritability, perturbation, timorousness **16** hypersensitivity

nervous system
  component: **3** CNS **4** ears, eyes **5** brain, taste, touch **7** ganglia **8** nerve end **10** nerve fiber, spinal cord

nervy 4 bold, firm, rude **5** brash, gutty, gutsy, sassy **6** brassy, brazen, cheeky, gritty, plucky, strong **7** assured, nervous **10** courageous, determined **12** stouthearted

Nesbitt, Cathleen
  born: **7** England **8** Cheshire
  roles: **10** My Fair Lady **18** Upstairs Downstairs **23** Three Coins in the Fountain

Nessus
  form: **7** centaur
  shot by: **8** Hercules
  caused death of: **8** Hercules

n'est-ce pas? 10 isn't that so?

nestle 3 lie, pet **4** live, snug, stay **5** clasp, dwell, lodge **6** bundle, caress, coddle, cosset, cuddle, enfold, fondle, huddle, nuzzle, occupy, remain, settle **7** embrace, inhabit, lie snug, snuggle **8** lie close **10** settle down

Nestor
  origin: **5** Greek
  attributes: **6** oldest, wisest
  father: **6** Neleus
  son: **10** Thasymedes **11** Pisistratus
  epithet: **7** Nelides

net 3 web **4** earn, gain, grab, grid, grip, mesh, snag, take, trap **5** catch, clasp, grate, seize, snare **6** clutch, enmesh, gather, grille, obtain, pick up, screen, snap up, take in **7** acquire, bring in, capture, collect, ensnare, grating, lattice **8** entangle, gather in, gridiron, Internet, meshwork **9** apprehend, grillwork, lay hold of, screening **10** accumulate **11** latticework
  constellation of: **9** Reticulum

nether 5 basal, below, lower, under **6** bottom, lowest **8** downward, inferior **9** subjacent **10** bottommost

Netherlands
  other name: **7** Holland **12** Low Countries
  capital/largest city: **9** Amsterdam
  others: **3** Urk **5** Delft, Lisse **6** Almelo, Arnhem, Leiden, Velsen **7** Haarlem, Helmond, Hengelo, Limburg, Tilberg, Tilburg, Utrecht **8** Aalsmeer, Enschede, Ijmuiden, Nijmegen, The Hague **9** Apeldoorn, Dordrecht, Eind-

hoven, Groningen, Rotterdam **12** Scheveningen
  division: **6** Twente **7** Drenthe, Limburg, Utrecht, Zeeland **9** Friesland, Groningen **10** Gelderland, Overijssel **12** North Brabant, North Holland, South Holland **19** Netherlands Antilles
  government:
    legislature: **4** Raad **11** Eerste Kamer, Tweede Kamer
  head of state: **5** queen
  measure: **2** el **3** aam, ahm, ell, kan, vat **4** duim, mijl, rood, rope **5** anker, roede, wisse **6** bunder, legger, maatje, mutsje, streep **7** schepel **8** mimgelen, steekkan
  monetary unit: **4** doit, oord, raps **5** crown, daler, rider, ryder **6** florin, gulden, stiver, suskin **7** daalder, ducaton, escalan, escalin, guilder, stooter, stuiver **8** albertin, ducatoon **9** dubbeltje **12** rijksdaalder **13** albertustaler
  weight: **3** ons **4** last, pond **5** bahar **6** korrel **7** wichtje
  island: **5** Texel **7** Ameland, Frisian **8** Antilles, Vlieland
  lake: **7** Haarlem **10** Ijsselmeer **11** Grevelingen, Havingvliet
  highest point: **11** Vaalserberg
  river: **3** Eem, Lek **4** Leck, Maas, Waal, Ysel **5** Donge, Hunse, Meuse, Rhine, Schie, Yssel **6** Dintel, Dommel, Ijssel, Kromme **7** Scheldt
  sea: **5** North
  physical feature:
    canal: **6** Oranje **7** Juliana, Merwede **8** Drentsch, North Sea **10** Wilhelmina **11** New Waterway
    former bay: **9** Zuider Zee
    port: **9** Europoort
  people: **5** Dutch **7** Frisian **9** Hollander **10** Surinamese **12** Netherlander **13** South Moluccan
    artist: **4** Eyck, Hals **5** Appel, Bosch **7** Van Gogh, Vermeer **8** Mondrian, Ruisdael **9** Rembrandt
    author: **6** Vondel **7** Erasmus, Grotius, Spinoza **8** Vestdijk **9** Anne Frank
    explorer: **6** Tasman
    king: **7** William
    queen: **7** Beatrix, Juliana **10** Wilhelmina
    ruler: **5** Spain **13** House of Orange **15** Holy Roman Empire
    scientist: **7** Huygens **11** Leeuwenhoek
  language: **5** Dutch **7** English, Frisian
  religion: **13** Dutch Reformed, Protestantism **16** Roman Catholicism
  place:
    airport: **8** Schiphol
    bird sanctuary: **9** Waddenzee
    miniature town: **9** Madurodam
    museum: **9** Frans Hals, Stedelijk **11** Mauritshuis, Rijksmuseum

14 Vincent Van Gogh **19** Boymans-van Beuningen
    seat of government: **7** Den Haag **8** The Hague **11** 'sGravenhage
    tower: **14** Schreierstoren
  feature:
    cheese market: **9** kaasmarkt
    earth mounds: **6** terpen
    flower: **5** tulip
    flower parade: **12** Bloemencorso
    pottery: **5** Delft
    reclaimed land: **6** polder
    wooden shoes: **7** klompen
  food:
    cheese: **4** Edam **5** Gouda **6** Leyden **7** cottage
    dish: **10** nasi goreng, rijsttafel
    drink: **3** gin **8** anisette, schnapps
    pea soup: **10** erwtensoep

Netherlands East Indies see **9** Indonesia

netherworld 4 hell **5** Hades **10** underworld **14** infernal region

nettle 3 vex **4** bait, gall, miff, rile **5** annoy, beset, chafe, harry, pique, sting **6** bother, harass, ruffle **7** perturb, prickle, provoke **8** irritate **9** displease **10** exasperate

nettle 6 Urtica
  varieties: **4** dead, dumb, hemp, rock **5** false, flame, hedge, horse, Roman **6** spurge **7** painted **8** stinging **9** white dead **11** spotted dead **12** western horse

network 3 web **4** grid, mesh, trap **5** grate, group, snare **6** grille, scheme, system **7** complex, netting, station

Network
  director: **11** Sidney Lumet
  based on story by: **14** Paddy Chayefsky
  cast: **9** Ned Beatty **10** Peter Finch, Wesley Addy **11** Faye Dunaway **12** Robert Duvall **13** William Holden **16** Beatrice Straight
  Oscar for: **5** actor (Finch) **7** actress (Dunaway) **17** supporting actress (Straight)

networks see **18** Television Networks

neuroptera
  class: **8** hexapoda
  phylum: **10** arthropoda
  group: **7** ant lion, fishfly **8** alderfly, lacewing, snakefly

neurotic 4 sick **7** anxious, intense, nervous **8** abnormal, unstable **9** disturbed, obsessive, unhealthy **10** distraught, immoderate **11** overwrought

neuter 5 fixed **6** barren, fallow, gelded, spayed **7** asexual, sexless, sterile **8** impotent **9** infertile

Neutra, Richard J
  architect of: **15** Mathematics Park (Princeton) **16** Lovell Heath House (Los Angeles CA) **17** von Sternberg House (Northridge CA) **22** Orange County Courthouse (Santa Ana CA)

neutral 4 mean **5** aloof **6** medium, middle, normal, remote **7** average **8** pacifist, peaceful, unbiased **9** impartial, in-between, peaceable, withdrawn **10** achromatic, indefinite, of two minds, unaffected, uninvolved **11** half-and-half, indifferent, nonpartisan, unconcerned **12** fence sitting, intermediate, noncombatant **13** disinterested, dispassionate **14** nonbelligerent, noninterfering **16** nonparticipating **18** noninterventionist

neutralize 4 halt, stop **5** annul, block, check **6** cancel, defeat, impede, negate, offset, stymie **7** balance, disable, nullify, prevent **8** overcome, suppress **9** frustrate, overpower **10** counteract **12** counterpoise, incapacitate **14** counterbalance

neutralizer 7 blocker **9** nullifier **12** counteractor, counteragent **15** counterbalancer

Neuvillette, Christian de
   character in: **16** Cyrano de Bergerac
   author: **7** Rostand

Nevada
   abbreviation: **2** NV **3** Nev
   nickname: **6** Silver **9** Sagebrush
   capital: **10** Carson City
   largest city: **8** Las Vegas
   others: **3** Ely, Nyc **4** Elko, Reno **6** Fallon, Nellis, Sparks, Storey, Washoe **7** Boulder, Gerlach **9** Hawthorne, Henderson **11** Weed Heights **12** Virginia City
   explorer: **7** Fremont **13** Jedediah Smith
   feature: **12** Comstock Lode
      dam: **5** Davis **6** Hoover
      hot springs: **4** Tule **9** Punch Bowl, Steam Boat
      national monument: **11** Death Valley
   tribe: **5** Modoc, Washo **6** Digger, Mohave, Paiute **7** Klamath **8** Acho mawi, Atsugewi, Shoshone
   lake: **4** Mead, Ruby **5** Tahoe, Weber **6** Mohave, Walker **7** Pyramid **8** Lahontan, Rye Patch **9** Wild Horse
   land rank: **7** seventh
   mountain: **4** East, Pine, Ruby **5** White **7** Rockies, Toiyabe, Wasatch **13** Sierra Nevadas
      highest point: **12** Boundary Peak
   physical feature: **7** geysers **10** hot springs
      basin: **5** Great
      cave: **6** Gypsum
      desert: **7** Sonoran
      plateau: **8** Columbia
   river: **5** Reese **6** Carson, Walker **7** Truckee **8** Colorado, Humboldt
   state admission: **11** thirty-sixth
   state bird: **7** sagehen **16** mountain bluebird
   state flower: **9** sagebrush
   state motto: **16** All for Our Country
   state song: **15** Home Means Nevada

state tree: **9** pinon pine **15** single-leaf pinon

never 4 ne'er **7** not ever **8** at no time, not at all

never-ending 6 steady **7** abiding, eternal, lasting, nonstop **8** constant, enduring, immortal, infinite, repeated, unbroken **9** ceaseless, continual, incessant, perennial, perpetual, recurring, unceasing **10** continuous, persistent, relentless **11** everlasting, unremitting **12** interminable, undiminished **13** uninterrupted

never-failing 4 firm, sure **6** proven, trusty **7** abiding **8** enduring, reliable **9** steadfast **10** dependable **11** trustworthy, undeviating, unfaltering **12** unhesitating, tried-and-true

nevermore 6 no more **10** never again

Never on Sunday
   director: **11** Jules Dassin
   cast: **11** Jules Dassin, Titos Vandis **14** Georges Foundas, Melina Mercouri
   setting: **6** Greece

nevertheless 3 but, yet **6** anyhow, anyway, even so, though **7** however **8** after all, although **10** contrarily, in any event, regardless **12** contrariwise **15** notwithstanding

Neville, Constance
   character in: **18** She Stoops to Conquer
   author: **9** Goldsmith

new 4 late **5** fixed, fresh, green, novel **6** modern, reborn, recent, remote, unused **7** altered, changed, current, just out, rebuilt, resumed, untried **8** original, reopened, repaired, restored, up-to-date **9** recreated, refreshed, remodeled, renovated, uncharted, unessayed, untouched **10** revivified, unexplored, unfamiliar, ungathered, unseasoned, unventured **11** regenerated, uncollected, unexercised **12** unaccustomed **13** reconstructed, reinvigorated

New Atlantis
   author: **12** Francis Bacon

New Brunswick
   abbreviation: **2** NB
   bay: **5** Fundy, Maces **7** Shepody **9** Chignecto, Miramichi **13** Passamaquoddy
   channel: **5** Minas **10** Grand Manan
   city: **7** Moncton **8** Bathurst **9** Riverview **10** Edmundston, Saint John **11** Fredericton
   island: **4** Deer **6** Miscou **7** Machias **10** Campobello, Grand Manan
   known as: **16** Atlantic province, maritime province
   lake: **5** Grand **8** Oromocto **12** Magagudavic **14** Chiputneticook
   people: **5** Irish **6** French **7** Acadian, English **8** American, Scottish **9** Algonkian **10** Anglo Saxon
   religion: **6** Canaan **7** Baptist **8** Angli-

can **10** Protestant **12** Presbyterian, United Church **13** Roman Catholic
   river: **5** Cains, Green **6** Renous, Salmon **7** Tobique **8** Kedgwick, Nashwak, Oromocto **9** Miramichi, Patapedia, Saint John **10** Nepisiguit, Richibucto, Saint Croix **11** Petitcodiac, Restigouche, Upsalguitch **12** Kennebecasis

New Centurions, The
   author: **14** Joseph Wambaugh

newcomer 4 tyro **5** alien **6** novice **7** entrant **8** intruder, neophyte, outsider, stranger **9** foreigner, immigrant, outlander **10** interloper, trespasser

New Deal Agency 3 AAA, CCC, CWA, FCA, FHA, FSA, NRA, NYA, PWA, REA, SEC, SSB, TVA, WPA **4** FCIC, FDIC, FERA, HOLC, NLRD, USHA

New Delhi
   capital of: **5** India
   designed by: **7** Lutyens
   earlier city: **5** Dilli **8** Dhillika, Din Panah, Kilookai **9** Firozabad **11** Tughlukabad **12** Indraprastha **13** Shah Jahanabad
   invader: **5** Timur **6** Abdali **7** British, Rohilas **8** Marathas **9** Nadir Shah
   landmark: **7** Red Fort **9** India Gate, Qutb Minar **10** Iron Pillar, Jama Masjid **13** Humayun's Tomb **14** Connaught Place **15** Rajghat Memorial **17** Rashtrapati Bhavan (Presidential Palace) **23** Jantar Mantar Observatory **30** Gandhi National Museum and Library
   river: **6** Yamuna
   street: **7** Raj Path (Kingsway)
   university: **15** Jawaharlal Nehru

New England
   capital: **6** Boston **7** Augusta, Concord **8** Hartford **10** Montpelier, Providence
   city: **4** Lynn **5** Barre **6** Bangor, Lowell, Nashua **7** Hyannis, Rutland, Warwick **8** Brockton, Cranston, Lawrence, Lewiston, New Haven, Portland, Stamford **9** Cambridge, Fall River, New London, Pawtucket, Waterbury, Worcester **10** Bridgeport, Burlington, Manchester, Pittsfield, Portsmouth, Woonsocket **11** Brattleboro, Springfield
   football team: **8** Patriots
   Indians: **6** Abnaki, Pequot **7** Mahican, Mohegan, Niantic, Nipmuck, Wangunk **8** Algonkin, Iroquois **9** Algonquin, Pennacook **10** Quinnipiac **12** Narragansett
   lake: **6** Sebago, Tiogue **7** Sunapee **9** Champlain, Moosehead **10** Candlewood **11** Pemaduncook **13** Winnipesaukee
   mountain: **5** Green, White **8** Greylock, Katahdin **9** Berkshire, Mansfield **10** Washington **11** Appalachian
   river: **5** Otter **6** Thames **7** Charles **8** Kennebec, Pawtucket, Winooski

9 Merrimack, Missiquoi, Naugatuck, Pawcatuck, Penobscot, Saint John **10** Housatonic, Providence, Quinnipiac **11** Connecticut **12** Androscoggin
state: **5** Maine **7** Vermont **11** Connecticut, Rhode Island **12** New Hampshire **13** Massachusetts

newfangled 5 novel **6** modern, modish **7** stylish

new-fashioned 6 modern, modish **7** stylish **8** up-to-date

Newfoundland
abbreviation: **4** Nfld
capital: **10** Saint Johns
city: **19** Happy Valley Goose Bay
lake: **7** Jeddore, Melville **8** Meelpaeg **10** Michikamau
mountain: **9** Long Range
river: **5** Eagle **6** Fraser, Gander **8** Exploits, Naskaupi **9** Churchill
section: **8** Labrador

New Granada see **8** Colombia

New Guinea
other name: **14** Papua New Guinea
capital/largest city: **11** Port Moresby
others: **3** Lae, Wau **4** Daru **5** Soron, Wewak **6** Aitape, Kikori, Medang, Rabaul **7** Gorolka, Kitbadi
division:
  eastern half of island: **9** Indonesia, Irian Jaya
  western half of island: **14** Papua New Guinea
government: **22** constitutional monarchy
head of state: **14** British monarch **15** governor-general
monetary unit: **4** kina, toea
island: **3** Aru **4** Aroe, Buka **5** Arroe, Ceram, Japen, Jobie, Manus **6** Cretin, Mussau, Ninigo, Waigeu **7** Sainson, Solomon **8** Bismarck, Kiriwina, Schouten, Woodlark **9** Admiralty, Trobriant **10** Louisiande, New Britain, New Ireland **12** Bougainville **14** D'Entrecasteaux
mountain: **4** Snow **6** Orange **8** Bismarck, Victoria **9** Carstensz **11** Owen Stanley **12** Albert Edward
highest point:
  Irian Jaya: **9** Carstensz **10** Puncak Jaya
  Papua New Guinea: **7** Wilhelm
river: **3** Fly **4** Hamu, Hany, Ramu **5** Degul, Sepik **6** Kikori, Purari **7** Amberno, Markham
sea: **5** Ceram, Coral, Sepik **6** Indian **7** Arafura, Pacific, Solomon **8** Bismarck
physical feature:
  bay: **3** Oro **5** Milne **8** Geelvink
  gulf: **4** Huon **5** Papua
  strait: **6** Torres, Vitiaz
people: **5** Pygmy **6** Papuan **7** Negrito **10** Melanesian
  explorer: **15** Jorge de Menesses
  ruler: **7** Germany **9** Australia **12** Great Britain
language: **4** Motu **7** English **16** Mela-

nesian Pidjin
religion: **7** animism **10** Protestant **13** Roman Catholic
feature:
  bird: **7** mudlark **9** cassowary
food:
  dried coconut meat: **5** copra

New Hampshire
abbreviation: **2** NH
nickname: **7** Granite
capital: **7** Concord
largest city: **10** Manchester
others: **5** Dover, Keene **6** Berlin, Durham, Exeter, Nashua **7** Hanover, Laconia **8** Sandwich **9** Claremont, Rochester **10** Portsmouth **12** Bretton Woods
college: **5** Keene **6** Rivier **9** Dartmouth, St Anselms **10** New England
feature: **14** Great Stone Face
  notch: **7** Kinsman, Pinkham **8** Crawford **9** Franconia
  tribe: **6** Abnaki **9** Pennacook
people: **11** Robert Frost **12** Daniel French **13** Daniel Webster, Horace Greeley, Mary Baker Eddy
  explorer: **9** Champlain **16** Captain John Smith
island: **4** Star **5** White **6** Shoals **7** Lunging
lake: **5** Squam **7** Ossipee, Sunapee, Umbagog **8** Newfound **10** Winnisquam **13** Winnipesaukee
land rank: **11** forty-fourth
mountain: **5** Flume, White **6** Moriah, Paugus **7** Waumbek **8** Chocorua, Sandwich **9** Franconia, Monadnock **11** Profile Peak **12** Presidential
  highest point: **10** Washington
physical feature:
  bay: **5** Great
president: **14** Franklin Pierce
river: **4** Saco **6** Israel **7** Bellamy **8** Souhegan **9** Merrimack **10** Piscataqua **11** Connecticut, Salmon Falls **12** Androscoggin
state admission: **5** ninth
state bird: **11** purple finch
state flower: **11** purple lilac
state motto: **13** Live Free Or Die
state song: **15** Old New Hampshire **26** New Hampshire My New Hampshire
state tree: **10** paper birch, white birch

Newhart
character: **4** Dick **6** Joanna **7** Michael **9** Stephanie
cast: **9** Mary Frann **10** Bob Newhart, Julia Duffy **12** Peter Scolari

Newhart, Bob
born: **9** Chicago IL
roles: **3** Bob **7** Newhart **10** Cold Turkey **12** George and Leo **17** The Bob Newhart Show
films: **7** catch-22 **8** In and out

New Hebrides see **7** Vanuatu

New Jersey

abbreviation: **2** NJ
nickname: **6** Garden **8** Mosquito
capital: **7** Trenton
largest city: **6** Newark
others: **4** Lodi **5** Ewing, Ft Lee **6** Camden, Dumont, Haddon, Kearny, Linden, Nutley, Orange, Rahway, Totowa **7** Bayonne, Cape May, Clifton, Hoboken, Hohokus, Keyport, Madison, Matawan, Netcong, Oradell, Paramus, Passaic, Raritan, Teaneck, Tenafly, Wyckoff **8** Carteret, Cranford, Freehold, Garfield, Hillside, Metuchen, Paterson, Secaucus, Watchung **9** Bridgeton, Elizabeth, Engle wood, Hawthorne, Irvington, Maplewood, Montclair, Ocean City, Princeton **10** Asbury Park, Belleville, Ft Monmouth, Hackensack, Jersey City, Livingston, Long Branch, Morristown, Perth Amboy **11** Bergenfield **12** Atlantic City, Collingswood, New Brunswick
colleges: **4** Drew **6** Upsala **7** Rutgers **8** Caldwell, Monmouth, St Peter's **9** Princeton, Seton Hall **10** Bloomfield **18** Fairleigh-Dickinson
feature: **9** Boardwalk **16** Delaware Water Gap
tribe: **8** Delaware **11** Lenni-Lanape
people: **9** Aaron Burr **11** Joyce Kilmer, Paul Robeson **12** Stephen Crane, Thomas Edison **13** James Lawrence **19** James Fenimore Cooper **21** William Carlos Williams
  explorer: **6** Hudson **9** Verrazano
lake: **6** Mohawk **9** Greenwood, Hopatcong
land rank: **10** forty-sixth
mountain: **8** Piedmont **10** Kittatinny **13** First Watchung **14** Second Watchung
  highest point: **9** High Point
physical feature: **9** Palisades, Sandy Hook
  bay: **8** Delaware
  cape: **3** May
  ocean: **8** Atlantic
president: **15** Grover Cleveland
river: **4** Toms **6** Dennis, Haynes, Hudson, Mantua, Ramapo **7** Mullica, Passaic, Raritan **8** Cohansey, Delaware, Tuckahoe **10** Hackensack
state admission: **5** third
state bird: **16** eastern goldfinch
state flower: **6** violet
state motto: **20** Liberty and Prosperity
state tree: **6** red oak
basketball team: **4** Nets
football team: **8** Generals
hockey team: **6** Devils

Newley, Anthony
wife: **11** Joan Collins
born: **6** London **7** England
roles: **11** Oliver Twist **25** Stop the World I Want to Get Off

41 The Roar of the Greasepaint The Smell of the Crowd

newly 4 anew **6** afresh, lately, of late **7** freshly, just now **8** recently

newly rich person
French: **12** nouveau riche

Newlywed Game, The
host: **10** Bob Eubanks
executive producer: **11** Chuck Barris

Newlyweds, The
creator: **13** George McManus
character: **12** Baby Snookums

Newman, Barnett
born: **9** New York NY
artwork: **7** Abraham, The Wild **8** Onement I **18** Stations of the Cross **19** Vir Heroicus Sublimis

Newman, Christopher
character in: **11** The American
author: **5** James

Newman, John Henry (Cardinal)
author of: **18** Apologia pro Vita Sua

Newman, Paul
wife: **14** Joanne Woodward
born: **11** Cleveland OH
company: **10** Newman's own
roles: **3** Hud **6** Harper, Picnic **8** The Sting, Twilight **10** The Hustler, The Verdict **11** Nobody's Fool **12** Cool Hand Luke **15** Absence of Malice, The Color of Money **16** Cat on a Hot Tin Roof, The Left Handed Gun, The Long Hot Summer, The Silver Chalice **17** The Hudsucker Proxy **29** Butch Cassidy and the Sundance Kid

New Mexico
abbreviation: **2** NM **4** N Mex
nickname: **8** Sunshine **17** Land of Enchantment
capital: **7** Santa Fe
largest city: **11** Albuquerque
others: **3** Jal **4** Taos **5** Aztec, Belen, Hobbs, Raton **6** Clovis, Deming, Gallup, Grants **7** Artesia, Bananea, Roswell, Socorro, Torreon **8** Carlsbad **9** Las Cruces, Los Alamos **10** Alamogordo **13** Piedras Negras
college: **7** Sante Fe **11** Albuquerque
feature: **11** Four Corners
dam: **5** Butte **8** Elephant
labs: **6** Sandia **17** Los Alamos National
national monument: **10** Aztec Ruins, White Sands **11** Chaco Canyon **17** Gila Cliff Dwelling
national park: **15** Carlsbad Caverns
observatory: **14** Sacramento Peak
tribe: **3** Sia **4** Hano, Piro, Tano, Taos, Tewa, Tiwa, Zuni **5** Acoma, Jemez, Kares, Manso, Pecos, Tiqua, Tonoa **6** Apache, Isleta, Laguna, Navaho, Navajo, Pueblo **7** Anasazi, Picuris **8** Santa Ana **9** Mescalero **12** Santo Domingo
people: **9** Kit Carson, Peter Hurd **11** Bill Mauldin
explorer: **5** Onate **6** de Niza, de

Vaca **8** Coronado
lake: **6** El Vado, Navajo, Sumner **7** Conchas **8** McMillan **10** Alamogordo **13** Elephant Butte
land rank: **5** fifth
mountain: **5** Jemez **6** Sandia **7** Manzano, Mimbres, Rockies, Truchas **8** Mogollon **9** Guadalupe, San Andres **10** Nacimiento, Sacramento **11** Mount Taylor **15** Sangre de Christo
highest point: **11** Wheeler Peak
physical feature:
basin: **8** Tularosa
desert: **15** Jornada de Muerto
plains: **5** Great
river: **3** Ute **4** Gila **5** Pecos **7** San Jose, San Juan **8** Canadian **9** Rio Grande
state admission: **12** forty-seventh
state bird: **10** roadrunner
state fish: **14** cutthroat trout
state flower: **5** yucca
state motto: **15** It Grows as It Goes
state song: **14** O Fair New Mexico **16** Asi es Nuevo Mexico
state tree: **5** pinon **8** tarantah **15** velvet ash pinyon

New Orleans
basketball team: Jazz
event: **9** Mardi Gras, Sugar Bowl **25** International Jazz Festival
football team: **6** Saints
landmark: **7** Cabildo **9** Old Square, Superdome **10** Vieux Carre **12** Pirate's Alley **13** French Quarter
noted for: **4** jazz
people: **5** Cajun **6** Creole **7** Acadian
river: **11** Mississippi
street: **5** Royal **7** Bourbon
university: **6** Loyola, Tulane

news 4 dirt, dope, talk, word **5** flash, libel, piece, rumor, story **6** babble, expose, gossip, report **7** account, article, chatter, hearsay, lowdown, mention, message, release, scandal, slander, tidings **8** bulletin, dispatch, exposure **9** statement **10** communique, disclosure, divulgence, revelation **11** information **12** announcement, intelligence

news account 4 item **5** story **6** report **7** release **8** bulletin, dispatch **10** communique

newsmonger 6 gossip **8** busybody, reporter

News of the Day
also: **12** Neues vom Tage
opera by: **9** Hindemith
character: **5** Laura **7** Eduoard

Newsome, Chadwick
character in: **14** The Ambassadors
author: **5** James

New Spain see **6** Mexico

newspaper 3 rag **5** daily, paper, sheet **6** herald, weekly **7** courant, gazette, journal, tabloid, tribune **10** periodical **11** publication

New Testament

books of: **4** Acts, John, Jude, Luke, Mark **5** James, Peter, Titus **6** Romans **7** Hebrews, Matthew, Timothy **8** Philemon **9** Ephesians, Galatians **10** Colossians, Revelation **11** Corinthians, Philippians **13** Thessalonians
books: **12** Humologumena

Newton, Isaac
field: **11** mathematics
nationality: **7** English
discovered laws of: **6** motion **7** gravity **8** calculus
discovered: **13** color spectrum **15** binomial theorem **16** method of fluxions
invented: **21** infinitesimal calculus

New York
abbreviation: **2** NY
nickname: **6** Empire **9** Excelsior
capital: **6** Albany
largest city: **7** New York
others: **3** Rye **4** Rome, Troy **5** Ilion, Islip, Nyack, Olean, Owego, Utica **6** Attica, Auburn, Cohoes, Elmira, Goshen, Ithaca, Oneida, Oswego, Tappan **7** Ardsley, Babylon, Batavia, Buffalo, Congers, Endwell, Geneseo, Hewlett, Mahopac, Merrick, Messena, Mineola, Montauk, Oneonta, Pennyan, Suffern, Syosset, Wantagh, Yaphank, Yonkers **8** Bethpage, Catskill, Endicott, Herkimer, Kingston, Ossining, Pottsdam, Saratoga, Tuckahoe **9** Rochester, Scarsdale **10** Binghamton, Bronxville, Mamaroneck **11** Cooperstown, New Rochelle, Schenectady, White Plains **12** Poughkeepsie
college: **4** Bard, CUNY, Iona, Pace, SUNY **5** Finch, Keuka **6** Hobart, Hunter, Vassar **7** Adelphi, Barnard, Colgate, Cornell, Fordham, St John's **8** Columbia, Skidmore, Syracuse **9** Juilliard, Rochester, West Point **13** Sarah Lawrence **30** Rensselaer Polytechnic Institute
feature:
prison: **6** Attica **8** SingSing
tribe: **4** Erie **6** Cayuga, Mohawk, Oneida, Seneca **7** Mohican, Montauk **8** Iroquois, Onondaga **9** Manhattan
people: **7** John Jay **8** Walloons **9** Jonas Salk **10** Henry James **11** Rockefeller, Walt Whitman **12** Eugene O'Neill **13** DeWitt Clinton, John Burroughs **14** Herman Melville **15** Peter Stuyvesant **16** Eleanor Roosevelt, Washington Irving **17** Fiorello La Guardia
explorer: **6** Hudson **9** Champlain, Verrazano **16** Dutch West India Co
island: **4** Fire, Long **5** Ellis **6** Staten **7** Bedloe's, Fisher's, Liberty, Shelter, Welfare **8** Thousand **9** Governors, Manhattan
lake: **4** Erie **6** Cayuga, Finger, George, Oneida, Otisco, Otsego, Owasco, Placid, Seneca **7** Conesus, Ontario,

Saranac, Schroon **8** Saratoga **9** Champlain
land rank: 9 thirtieth
mountain: 4 Bear **5** Slide **7** Taconic **9** Catskills **11** Adirondacks
  highest point: 5 Marcy
physical feature:
  bay: 7 Jamaica, Peconic **8** Moriches
  canal: 4 Erie **7** Gowanus
  falls: 7 Niagara
  valley: 6 Mohawk
president: 14 Martin Van Buren **14** Teddy Roosevelt **15** Millard Fillmore **17** Theodore Roosevelt **23** Franklin Delano Roosevelt
river: 4 East **5** Black, Tioga **6** Harlem, Hoosic, Hudson, Mohawk, Oswego **7** Ausable, Genesee, Niagara **10** St Lawrence **11** Susquehanna
state bird: 8 bluebird
state fish: 10 brook trout
state flower: 4 rose
state motto: 9 Excelsior (Ever upward, Still higher)
state tree: 10 sugar maple

New York City
nickname: 6 Gotham **8** Big Apple
airport: 3 JFK **6** Newark **9** La Guardia **12** John F Kennedy
area: 4 Soho **6** Harlem **7** Chelsea, Midtown, Tribeca **8** Broadway **9** Chinatown, Manhattan **10** Stuyvesant **11** Bensonhurst, Brownsville, Little Italy **12** Hell's kitchen **13** Spanish Harlem **16** Greenwich Village **17** Bedford-Stuyvesant
baseball team: 4 Mets **7** Yankees
basketball team: 6 Knicks **7** Liberty **14** Knickerbockers
borough: 5 Bronx **6** Queens **8** Brooklyn, Richmond **9** Manhattan **12** Staten Island
early governor: 10 Stuyvesant
feature:
  building: 11 Empire State
  hall of fame: 8 baseball
  park: 7 Central
  square: 5 Times, Union **6** Herald
  statue: 7 Liberty
  street/avenue: 4 Park, Wall **5** Fifth **7** Madison **8** Broadway
  tomb: 6 Grant's
football team: 4 Jets **6** Giants
former name: 12 New Amsterdam
hockey team: 7 Rangers **9** Islanders
island: 4 City, Long **5** Ellis, Ward's **6** Riker's, Staten **7** Liberty **8** Randall's **9** Governor's, Manhattan, Roosevelt
landmark: 5 Macy's **8** Aqueduct, Bronx Zoo **9** Unisphere **10** Jones Beach **11** Battery Park, Central Park, Coney Island, Penn Station, Shea Stadium, Times Square **12** Carnegie Hall **13** Gracie Mansion, Lincoln Center, Port Authority, Rockaway Beach, Trinity Church, United Nations, Yankee Stadium **14** Waldorf-Astoria **15** NY Public Library, NY

Stock Exchange, Seagram Building, Statue of Liberty **16** Chrysler Building, World Trade Center **17** Arthur Ashe Stadium, Hayden Planetarium, Rockefeller Center, Woolworth Building **18** Astoria Film Studios, Radio City Music Hall **19** Empire State Building, Grand Central Station, Madison Square Garden, St Patrick's Cathedral **22** Metropolitan Opera House **29** Cathedral of Saint John the Divine
mayor: 4 Koch **6** Walker **9** La Guardia
museum: 6 Jewish **7** Whitney **9** Cloisters **10** Guggenheim **12** Cooper-Hewitt, Metropolitan **15** Frick Collection **17** Museum of Modern Art (MoMA) **30** American Museum of Natural History
river: 4 East **6** Harlem, Hudson
street: 6 Bowery **8** Broadway **9** Lexington **10** Park Avenue, Wall Street **11** Central Park, Fifth Avenue, Sutton Place **13** Madison Avenue **17** Forty-Second Street
university: 3 NYU **6** Queens **7** Barnard, Fordham, Yeshiva **8** Brooklyn, Columbia **13** Hunter College **22** Juilliard School of Music **23** City University of New York

New Zealand
native's nickname: 4 Kiwi
other name: 8 Aotearoa **12** Nieuw Zeeland **23** Land of the Long White Cloud
capital: 10 Wellington
largest city: 8 Auckland
others: 5 Leuin, Oreti, Otaki, Taupo **6** Clutha, Foxton, Oamaru, Picton, Timaru **7** Dunedin, Manu Kau, Raetihi, Rotorua **8** Hamilton, Kawakawa, Touranga **9** Lyttelton **10** Queenstown **12** Christchurch, Invercargill, Port Chalmers **13** Port Nicholson **14** Napier-Hastings **15** Palmerston North
school: 5 Otago **6** Massey **7** Waikato **8** Auckland, Victoria **10** Canterbury
division: 11 North Island, South Island
head of state: 14 British monarch **15** governor general
monetary unit: 4 cent **6** dollar
island: 4 Cook, Niue, Otea **5** North, South **6** Bounty, Chatam, Snares **7** Stewart, Tokelau **8** Auckland, Campbell, Kermadec, Puketutu **9** Antipodes **10** Resolution, Three Kings **12** Great Barrier
lake: 3 Ada **4** Gunn, Ohau **5** Hawea, Taupo **6** Pukaki, Pupuke, Te Anau, Tekapo, Wanaka **7** Brunner, Diamond, Kanieri, Okareka, Rotorua **8** Okataina, Paradise, Rotoaira, Wakatipu **9** Manapouri
mountain: 4 Eden, Flat, Owen **5** Allen, Chope, Lyall, Mitre, Ohope, Otari, Young **6** Egmont, Stokes, Tas-

man **7** Cameron, Coronet, Ernslaw, Huiarau, Pihanga, Ruahine, Ruapehu, Tauhera, Tutamoe, Tyndall **8** Aspiring, Richmond, Tauranga **9** Messenger, Murchison, Ngauruhoe, Raukumara, Tongariro **11** Remarkables **12** Southern Alps
highest point: 4 Cook **7** Aorangi
river: 4 Avon **5** Mokau, Waipa **6** Clutha, Rakaia, Tamaki, Waihou, Wairau, Wairoa **7** Waikato, Waitaki **8** Clarence, Manawatu, Wanganui **10** Rangitikei
sea: 6 Tasman **12** South Pacific
physical feature:
  bay: 4 Ohua **5** Evans, Hawke, Lyall **6** Awarua, Cloudy, Golden, Plenty, Tasman **7** Fitzroy, Pegasus, Poverty **8** Halfmoon, Rangaunu
  bight: 7 Karamea **10** Canterbury **13** North Taranaki, South Taranaki
  cape: 4 East, West **5** North **6** Egmont **8** Farewell, Foulwind, Paliser **9** Southwest
  channel: 8 Colville
  falls: 10 Sutherland
  glacier: 3 Fox **6** Tasman **11** Franz Joseph
  gulf: 7 Hauraki
  harbor: 7 Kaipara, Manukau **9** Waitemata
  peninsula: 5 Mahia, Otago
  plains: 10 Canterbury
  sound: 8 Doubtful
  strait: 4 Cook **7** Foveaux
people: 3 Ati **5** Arawa, Dutch, Maori **7** British, Ringatu **10** Polynesian
  author: 5 Frame **9** Mansfield **10** Ngaio Marsh **12** Ashton-Warner
  explorer: 4 Cook **6** Tasman
  mountain climber: 7 Hillary
language: 5 Maori **7** English
religion: 8 Anglican **9** Methodist **10** Protestant **12** Presbyterian **13** Roman Catholic
place:
  national park: 9 Fiordland, Fjordland, Tongariro
feature:
  animal: 7 tuatara
  bird: 3 kea, tui **4** kiwi, weka **6** takahe **7** apteryx **8** bellbird
  tree: 4 rimu, tawa **5** kauri, matai **6** totara
food:
  fish: 4 mako
  fruit: 4 kiwi **9** tamarillo **17** Chinese gooseberry

next-door 8 adjacent **9** adjoining **10** connecting, contiguous, juxtaposed, side-by-side, **12** conterminous
next to 6 beside **8** abutting, adjacent **9** adjoining **10** contiguous, bordering **11** juxtaposed **12** conterminous
next world, the 6 Heaven **8** eternity, paradise **12** the hereafter **14** the world to come
Nez Perce (Numipu)

language family: **10** Shahaptian
location: **5** Idaho **6** Oregon **10** Washington
leader: **11** Chief Joseph
Niamey
capital of: **5** Niger
nib 3 end, tip, top **4** apex, peak **5** point **6** height, tiptop, vertex **7** extreme **8** pinnacle **9** extremity
nibble 3 nip **4** bite, chew, gnaw, peck **5** crumb, munch, speck, taste **6** crunch, morsel, peck at, tidbit **8** fragment, particle
Nibelung, ring of
origin: **8** Germanic
mentioned in: **14** Nibelungenlied
stolen by: **8** Alberich
Nibelungenlied
origin: **8** Germanic
form: **4** epic
date written: **17** thirteenth century
related to: **8** Volsunga
author: **7** unknown
character: **5** Etzel (Attila), Hagen **6** Gernot **7** Gunther **8** Brunhild, Dankwart, Giselher **9** Kriemhild, Siegfried
inspired: **6** Wagner
Nibelungs, Niblungs
origin: **8** Germanic, Teutonic
followers of: **9** Siegfried
race: **6** dwarfs
possessed: **8** treasure
captured by: **9** Siegfried
family of: **7** Gunther
Nicaragua
capital/largest city: **7** Managua
others: **4** Leon, Rama **6** Masaya **7** Corinto, Granada **8** Jinotega **9** Matagalpa **10** Bluefields, Chinandega
division: **13** Mosquito Coast
measure: **4** vara **5** cahiz **6** suerte **7** cajuela, manzana **10** cabelleria
monetary unit: **4** peso **7** centavo, cordoba
weight: **3** bag **4** caha, caja **8** tonelada
island: **7** Ometepe
lake: **7** Managua **9** Nicaragua
mountain: **4** Leon **5** Negro, Viejo **6** Madera, Telica **7** Managua, Saslaya **9** Momotombo
highest point: **7** Mogoton
river: **4** Coco, Tuma **5** Wanks **6** Grande, Poteca **7** San Juan **8** Tipitapa **9** Escondido
sea: **7** Pacific **9** Caribbean
physical feature:
    gulf: **7** Fonseca
people: **4** Mico, Mixe, Rama, Smoo, Ulva **5** Cukra, Diria, Lenca, Sambo, Toaca **6** Mangue **7** mestizo, Miskito **8** Mosquito **9** Matagalpa
    author: **5** Dario
    explorer: **6** Davila **7** Cordoba **8** Columbus
    group: **6** Contra **10** Sandinista
    leader: **6** Somoza, Walker, Zelaya

7 Nicardo **8** Chamorro
language: **7** English, Spanish
religion: **13** Roman Catholic
place:
    cathedral: **12** Metropolitan
feature:
    dance: **5** sones **10** zapateados, zarabandas
food:
    beans: **8** frijoles
    dish: **10** naca tamale
    drink: **5** tiste **9** pinolillo
    fruit: **6** zapote
nice 4 deft, fine, good, kind **5** dandy, exact, fussy, great, swell **6** divine, genial, lovely, proper, seemly, strict, subtle **7** amiable, amusing, careful, cordial, correct, finicky, genteel, likable, precise, refined, winning **8** accurate, charming, cheerful, delicate, friendly, gracious, jim-dandy, ladylike, pleasant, pleasing, rigorous, skillful, unerring, virtuous, well-bred **9** agreeable, congenial, excellent, fantastic, marvelous, sensitive, wonderful **10** attractive, delightful, enchanting, entrancing, fastidious, methodical, meticulous, scrupulous **11** interesting, painstaking, pleasurable, punctilious, respectable, sympathetic, warmhearted **13** compassionate, understanding, well brought up **17** overconscientious
Nice and the Good, The
author: **11** Iris Murdoch
nicely 6 neatly **7** exactly, fussily, happily **9** carefully, precisely **10** accurately, critically, pleasantly, unerringly **11** faultlessly, fortunately, opportunely **12** attractively, fastidiously
nicety 4 care, tact **5** flair, grace **6** acumen, polish **7** culture, finesse, insight **8** accuracy, delicacy, elegance, subtlety **9** attention, exactness, precision **10** refinement **11** cultivation, penetration, preciseness, sensitivity **12** perspicacity, subtle detail, tastefulness **13** elaborateness, particularity **14** discrimination, fastidiousness, meticulousness
niche 4 cove, nook, slot **5** berth, trade **6** alcove, cavity, corner, cranny, dugout, hollow, metier, recess **7** calling **8** position, vocation **9** cubby hole **10** depression, pigeon hole **11** proper place **13** hole in the wall
Nicholas Nickleby
author: **14** Charles Dickens
character: **5** Smike **11** Arthur Gride, Newman Noggs **12** Kate Nickleby, Madeline Bray **13** Lord Verisopht, Ralph Nickleby **14** Frank Cheeryble **15** Sir Mulberry Hawk, Vincent Crummles, Wackford Squeers **17** Cheeryble Brothers
Nichols, Mike
Wife: **11** Diane Sawyer

director of: **7** Catch-22 **11** The Birdcage, The Graduate (Oscar) **15** Carnal Knowledge **25** Who's Afraid of Virginia Woolf?
Nicholson, Ben
born: **6** Denham **7** England
artwork: **9** Fireworks **11** White Relief **12** Tuscan Relief **13** Painted Relief **14** At the Chat Botte
Nicholson, Jack
born: **9** Neptune NJ
roles: **4** Wolf **5** Hoffa **6** Batman **8** Ironweed **9** Chinatown, Easy Rider **10** The Shining **11** A Few Good Men, Mars Attacks, The Two Jakes **12** Prizzi's Honor, The Passenger **13** The Last Detail **14** As Good As It Gets (Oscar), Five Easy Pieces **15** Carnal Knowledge **17** Terms of Endearment **20** The Witches of Eastwick **22** The King of Marvin Gardens **25** One Flew Over the Cuckoo's Nest (Oscar) **26** The Postman Always Rings Twice
nicht wahr? 10 isn't that so?
nick 3 cut, jag, mar **4** chip, dent, gash, mark, scar **5** cleft, gouge, notch, score, wound **6** damage, deface, indent, injure, injury **7** marking, scarify, scoring, scratch **8** incision, lacerate **10** depression **11** indentation
nickel
chemical symbol: **2** Ni
Nickel Mountain
author: **11** John Gardner
nickname 6 handle **7** agnomen, epithet, moniker, pet name **8** baby name, cognomen **9** pseudonym, sobriquet **10** diminutive **11** appellation, designation
Nicomachean Ethics
author: **9** Aristotle
Nidhogg
origin: **12** Scandinavian
form: **7** serpent
domain: **8** Niflheim
gnaws on lowest root of: **9** Iggdrasil, Yggdrasil
niello 5 alloy
of: **6** sulfur
with: **4** lead **6** copper, silver
used as: **5** inlay
Nielsen, Carl August
born: **6** Odense **7** Denmark
composer of: **9** Maskarade **12** Saul and David **16** Inextinguishable (symphony No 4)
Nietzsche, Friedrich
author of: **14** The Will to Power **17** Beyond Good and Evil, The Birth of Tragedy **20** Thus Spake Zarathustra
Niflheim
origin: **12** Scandinavian
ruler of: **3** Hel
purpose: **10** punish dead
climate: **3** fog **4** cold **8** darkness
nifty 4 chic, fine, neat, posh **5** natty, smart **6** clever, dapper **7** dashing,

stylish **8** splendid **10** attractive **11** fashionable

Niger
other name: 6 Joliba, Kworra, Ramtil
capital/largest city: 6 Niamey
others: 5 Goure **6** Agadex, Agadez, Maradi, Tahoua, Zinder
division:
  region: 3 Air **5** Arlit, Sahel
monetary unit: 5 franc **7** centime
lake: 4 Chad
mountain: 7 Bagzane **9** Air Massif
highest point: 7 Greboun
river: 5 Niger **6** Dillia
physical feature:
  desert: 6 Sahara
  oasis: 6 Kaouar
  plateau: 5 Djado **6** Tegama **7** Tchigai **8** Mengueni **11** Adar Doutchi, Djerma Ganda
people: 4 Daza, Idjo, Idyo, Idzo, Peul, Teda **5** Hausa, Warri **6** Djerma, Fulani, Kanuri, Songha, Toubou, Tuareg **13** Djerma-Songhai
  conqueror: 13 Usman Dan Fodio
  leader: 5 Diori **6** Saibou **7** Ousmane **8** Kountche
language: 5 Hausa, Mande **6** Djerma, French, Fulani, Tuareg **8** Mandingo, Tamashek
religion: 5 Islam **7** animism **12** Christianity
place:
  ruins: 6 Agadez
  feature:
  cavalry: 5 Dosso
  empire: 4 Mali **6** Fulani **7** Songhai **10** Kanem-Borno
  tree: 6 acacia, baobab

Nigeria
capital: 5 Abuja
largest city: 5 Lagos
new capital: 5 Abuja
others: 3 Aba, Ado, Ede, Isa, Iwo, Jos, Oyo **4** Bida, Bidi, Buea, Kano, Offa, Yola **5** Benin, Bonny, Enugu, Warri, Zaria **6** Burutu, Ibadan, Ilesha, Ilorin, Kachia, Kaduna, Kadune, Kokoto, Mushin, Takoba **7** Calabar, Onitsha, Oshogbo **8** Abeokuta **9** Maiduguri, Ogbomosho **12** Port Harcourt
division: 3 Air, Isa, Oyo **4** Kano, Nupe, Ondo **5** Asben, Benin, Bornu, Ijebu, Ogoja, Warri **6** Biafra, Degema, Owerri, Sokoto **7** Adamawa
monetary unit: 4 kobo **5** naira
lake: 4 Chad
highest point: 7 Dimlang
river: 3 Oli **4** Gana, Yobe **5** Benin, Benue, Cross, Niger **6** Kaduna, Sokoto **7** Calabar, Gongola **8** Komadugu **9** Sambreiro
sea: 8 Atlantic
physical feature:
  bight: 5 Benin, Bonny **6** Biafra
  delta: 5 Niger
  gulf: 6 Guinea
  plains: 5 Bornu **9** Hausaland

  plateau: 3 Jos, Udi **6** Bauchi
  port: 5 Lagos **7** Calabar **8** Harcourt
people: 3 Abo, Aro, Djo, Ebo, Edo, Ibo, Ijo, Tiv, Vai **4** Beni, Bini, Eboe, Efik, Egba, Ejam, Ekoi, Idyo, Igbo, Ijaw, Nupe **5** Angas, Benin, Gwari, Hausa **6** Chamba, Fulani, Ibibio, Kanuri, Yoruba **11** Hausa-Fulani
  author: 6 Achebe
  British colonial ruler: 6 Goldie, Lugard
  kingdom: 3 Ife, Nok, Oyo **5** Benin **6** Fulani **10** Kanem-Borno
  leader: 5 Gowon **6** Balewa, Ojukwu, Schick **7** Awolowo, Azikine, Azikiwe, Shagari **8** Obasanjo **9** Babangida **13** Usman dan Fodio
  language: 3 Ibo **4** Efik, Igbo **5** Hausa **6** Yoruba **7** English
  religion: 5 Islam **7** animism **12** Christianity
place:
  dam: 6 Kainji
  mosque/walled city: 4 Kano
  feature:
  dress: 4 riga **7** agbados
  tree: 5 abura, afara **6** obeche **10** terminalia
  war: 7 Biafran

niggard 4 mean **5** cheap, miser, tight **6** stingy **7** miserly **8** scrimper **9** skinflint **10** ungenerous **12** parsimonious

niggardliness 6 penury **8** meanness **9** closeness, parsimony **10** stinginess **11** miserliness **13** penny-pinching **15** tight-fistedness

niggardly 4 mean, poor **5** cheap, close, sorry, tight **6** flimsy, frugal, meager, measly, paltry, saving, scanty, shabby, stingy, tawdry **7** miserly, scrubby, sparing, thrifty **8** beggarly, grubbing, grudging, stinting, wretched **9** illiberal, mercenary, miserable, penurious **10** hardfisted, second-rate, ungenerous **11** closefisted **12** contemptible, insufficient, parsimonious

niggling 5 fussy, minor, petty, small **7** finicky **8** caviling, nugatory, picayune, piddling, trifling **9** quibbling **10** negligible, nit-picking **12** pettifogging **13** insignificant **15** inconsequential

nigh 4 near **5** close, handy **6** almost, at hand, nearly **7** close by **8** adjacent **9** bordering **11** neighboring, practically

night 4 dark, dusk **7** bedtime, evening, sundown **8** darkness, eventide **9** murkiness, obscurity **13** tenebrousness
  goddess of: 3 Nox

nightclub
  French: 5 boite **11** boite de nuit

nightfall 4 dark, dusk **6** sunset **7** evening, sundown **8** darkness, eventide, gloaming, moonrise, twilight
  French: 10 crepuscule

Night Gallery
  host: 10 Rod Serling
Nightingale, Florence
  birthplace: 7 England
  worked in: 10 Crimean War
  founded: 13 modern nursing
  nickname: 18 The Lady with the Lamp
  first woman to receive: 12 Order of Merit
nightingale
  group of: 5 watch
Nightline
  host: 9 Ted Koppel
nightly 4 dark **7** evening, obscure **9** nocturnal **11** nocturnally
nightmare 7 incubus **8** bad dream, succubus **13** hallucination
Night of the Iguana, The
  director: 10 John Huston
  based on play by: 17 Tennessee Williams
  cast: 7 Sue Lyon **8** Skip Ward **10** Ava Gardner **11** Deborah Kerr **13** Richard Burton
  setting: 6 Mexico
nightshade 16 Solanum dulcamara
  varieties: 4 ball **5** black **6** common, deadly, sticky **7** Malabar **8** stinking **9** melon-leaf, poisonous, soda-apple **10** enchanter's
Nights of Cabiria
  director: 15 Federico Fellini
  cast: 13 Amedeo Nazzari **14** Francois Perier **15** Giulietta Masina
  remade as: 12 Sweet Charity
nightstick 3 rod **4** mace, wand **5** baton, staff **6** cudgel **7** scepter **8** bludgeon **9** billy club, truncheon **10** shillelagh
nighttime 4 late **5** night **9** late-night, nighttide, nocturnal
Night to Remember, A
  director: 8 Roy Baker
  based on story by: 10 Walter Lord
  cast: 9 Jill Dixon **11** Kenneth More **13** David McCallum **16** Laurence Naismith
  setting: 7 Titanic
nihil 7 nothing
nihilism 5 chaos **6** anomie **7** license **9** amorality, anarchism, emptiness, terrorism **10** alienation, iconoclasm, radicalism, skepticism **11** agnosticism, lawlessness, nothingness **12** nonexistence **16** irresponsibility
nihilist 5 rebel **9** anarchist, terrorist **13** revolutionary
Nihon *see* **5** Japan
Nike
  origin: 5 Greek
  goddess of: 7 victory
  father: 11 Titan Pallas
  mother: 4 Styx
  brother: 5 Zelos
  corresponds to: 6 Athena **8** Victoria

nil 4 none, null, zero **6** cipher, naught **7** nothing, nullity **11** nonexistent

Nile
  boat: 5 baris **6** cangia, nuggar, sandal **7** felucca, gaiassa **8** dahabeah
  cities: 3 Qus **4** Abri, Argo, Idfu, Isna, Juba, Qina **5** Aswan, Asyut, Cairo, Kokka, Kusti, Luxor, Meroe, Minya, Rejaf, Saite, Tanis, Tanta **6** Atbara, Faiyum **7** Malakel, Mansura, Rosetta **8** Khartoum, Omdurman, Rusayris **9** Was Madani **10** Alexandria
  dam: 6 Sannar **9** Aswan High, White Nile
  desert bordering: 6 Libyan, Nubian **7** Arabian
  falls: 5 Ripon **8** Kabalega **9** Murchison
  feature: 6 Sphinx
    pyramid: 4 Giza
    temple: 8 Ramses II **9** Abu Simbel **11** Deir el-Bahri, Medinet Habu
  flows into: 13 Mediterranean
  flows through: 5 Egypt, Kenya, Sudan, Zaire **6** Rwanda, Uganda **7** Burundi **8** Ethiopia, Tanzania
  island: 4 Roda **6** Philae
  lake: 4 Tana **5** Kyoga, Tsana **6** Albert, Edward, Nasser **8** Victoria
  other name: 4 Hapi **20** The Father of the Rivers
  people: 3 Jur, Luo, Lwo, Nuo, Suk **4** Bari, Beja, Golo, Luoh, Madi **5** Nilot **7** Shilluk
  plain: 6 Gezira
  plant: 4 sudd **5** lotus
  starting point: 5 Tsana **8** Victoria
  swamp: 4 Sudd
  tributary: 4 Arab **5** Rahad, Sobat **6** Atbara, Ghazai, Kagera **7** Rosetta **8** Blue Nile, Damietta **9** Bahr Jebel, White Nile

Niles, Hazel and Peter
  characters in: 22 Mourning Becomes Electra
  author: 6 O'Neill

nil nisi bonum 21 nothing unless it is good

nil sine numine 27 nothing without the divine will
  motto of: 8 Colorado

nimble 4 deft, spry **5** agile, fleet, light, quick, rapid, ready, swift **6** active, expert, lively, prompt, speedy, supple **8** animated, skillful, spirited **9** dexterous, mercurial, sprightly **10** proficient

nimbleness 7 agility **8** alacrity, spryness **9** dexterity, quickness **10** limberness, suppleness

nimble-witted 5 droll, witty **6** clever **11** resourceful

nimbus 4 aura, disk, halo **5** cloud, vapor **7** aureole **8** radiance

Nimitz, Chester
  served in: 3 WWI **4** WWII
  commander of: 12 Pacific fleet
  rank: 12 fleet (five-star) admiral

22 chief of naval operations
  battle: 6 Midway **9** Leyte Gulf **13** Philippine Sea

Nimoy, Leonard
  born: 8 Boston MA
  films: 7 Mr Spock **8** Star Trek **14** Funny About Love **16** Three men and a Baby **17** Mission: Impossible **21** Star Trek: The Voyage Home **22** Star Trek: The Wrath of Khan **24** Star Trek: The Final Frontier **25** Star Trek: The Search for Spock

Nimrod
  father: 4 Cush
  grandfather: 3 Ham
  great grandfather: 4 Noah
  founded: 5 Accad, Calah, Resen **7** Nineveh **8** Rehoboth
  famed as: 6 hunter

nincompoop 4 boob, dolt, dope, fool, jerk **5** dummy, dunce, idiot, klutz, moron, ninny **6** dimwit, lummox, nitwit **7** half wit, jackass **8** bonehead, dummkopf, imbecile, lunkhead, numskull **9** blockhead, dumb bunny, harebrain, numbskull, simpleton **10** dunderhead, dunderpate, muddlehead, noodlehead **11** knucklehead, rattlebrain **12** featherbrain, scatterbrain

Nine, the *see* **5** Muses

Nineteen Eighty-Four
  author: 12 George Orwell
  character: 4 Syme **5** Julia **6** O'Brien **11** Charrington **12** Winston Smith

1919
  author: 13 John Dos Passos

Ninety-Five Theses
  author: 12 Martin Luther

Nineveh
  founder: 6 Nimrod

Nine worthies
  mentioned in: 16 medieval romances
  three each of: 4 Jews **6** Pagans **10** Christians
  names: 5 David **6** Arthur, Hector, Joshua **11** Charlemagne **12** Julius Caesar **15** Judas Maccabaeus **17** Alexander the Great **18** Godefroy de Bouillon

ninny 3 ass, sap **4** fool, simp **5** booby, dunce, idiot, moron **6** dimwit, nitwit **7** fathead, half-wit **8** bonehead, dumb-dumb, imbecile, lunkhead, numskull **9** blockhead, dumb bunny, lamebrain, numbskull **10** dunderhead, nincompoop **11** chowderhead

Ninotchka
  director: 13 Ernst Lubitsch
  cast: 9 Ina Claire **10** Bela Lugosi, Greta Garbo **13** Melvyn Douglas
  setting: 5 Paris
  remade as: 13 Silk Stockings

Ninurta
  also: 5 Ninib
  origin: 8 Sumerian **10** Babylonian
  type of god: 4 hero
  personifies: 4 wind **9** south wind

father: 5 Enlil
  avenger of: 5 Enlil

Ninus
  wife: 9 Semiramis
  founder of: 7 Nineveh

Niobe
  father: 8 Tantalus
  mother: 5 Dione
  brother: 6 Pelops
  husband: 7 Amphion
  children: 9 seven sons **14** seven daughters
  children called: 6 Niobid
  taunted: 4 Leto
  children killed by: 6 Apollo **7** Artemis
  changed into: 5 stone
  changed by: 4 Zeus

Niord
  also: 5 Njord
  origin: 12 Scandinavian
  god of: 4 wind **10** navigation, prosperity
  king of: 5 Vanir
  son: 4 Frey **5** Freyr
  daughter: 5 Freia, Freya

nip 3 cut, lop **4** bite, clip, crop, dock, grab, grip, ruin, snag, snap, snip **5** blast, check, chill, clamp, clasp, crack, crush, frost, grasp, pinch, quash, seize, sever, shear, snarc, tweak **6** benumb, clutch, cut off, freeze, pierce, snatch, sunder, thwart **7** curtail, destroy, shorten, squeeze **8** compress, cut short, demolish **9** frustrate **10** abbreviate

nip-and-tuck 5 close

nip in the bud 7 prevent **8** preclude **9** forestall, frustrate

Nipper, Susan
  character in: 12 Dombey and Son
  author: 7 Dickens

Nippon *see* **5** Japan

nippy 3 raw **5** brisk, chill, crisp, sharp **6** biting, chilly **7** cutting

nit-pick 4 carp, pick **5** cavil **9** criticize

nitrate 4 salt **5** ester **6** sodium **9** potassium **10** fertilizer

nitrogen
  chemical symbol: 1 N

nitty-gritty 4 core, crux, gist, meat, pith **5** heart **7** essence **9** substance

nitwit 3 ass **4** clod, dolt, fool **5** booby, dummy, dunce, idiot, klutz, moron, ninny **7** fathead, pinhead **8** bonehead, dumb-dumb, imbecile, lunkhead, meathead, numskull, peabrain **9** birdbrain, blockhead, lamebrain, numbskull **10** dunderhead, nincompoop, noodlehead **11** chowderhead

Niven, David
  real name: 21 James David Graham Niven
  autobiography: 16 The Moon's a Balloon **21** Bring on the Empty Horses
  born: 8 Scotland **10** Kirriemuir

roles: 11 Phileas Fogg **12** Casino Royale, My Man Godfrey **14** The Pink Panther, Separate Tables (Oscar) **16** Stairway to Heaven, Wuthering Heights **18** The Prisoner of Zenda **26** Around the World in Eighty Days

Nix, nixie
  origin: 8 Germanic
  form: 6 spirit
  habitat: 5 water

Nixon, Richard Milhous
  presidential rank: 13 thirty-seventh
  party: 10 Republican
  state represented: 2 CA
  defeated: 7 (George Corley) Wallace **8** (Hubert Horatio) Humphrey
  vice president: 4 (Gerald Rudolph) Ford **5** (Spiro Theodore) Agnew
  cabinet:
    state: 6 (William Pierce) Rogers **9** (Henry A) Kissinger
    treasury: 5 (William E) Simon **6** (George P) Shultz **7** (David Matthew) Kennedy **8** (John Bowden) Connally
    defense: 5 (Melvin Robert) Laird **10** (Elliot L) Richardson **11** (James R) Schlesinger
    attorney general: 5 (William B) Saxbe **8** (John Newton) Mitchell **10** (Elliot L) Richardson **11** (Richard G) Kleindienst
    postmaster general: 6 (Winton Malcolm) Blount
    interior: 6 (Rogers Clark Ballard) Morton, (Walter Joseph) Hinkel
    agriculture: 4 (Earl Lauer) Butz **6** (Clifford Morris) Hardin
    commerce: 4 (Frederick B) Dent **5** (Maurice Hubert) Stans
    labor: 6 (George Pratt) Shultz **7** (James Day) Hodgson, (Peter J) Brennan
    HEW: 5 (Robert Hutchinson) Finch **10** (Caspar W) Weinberger, (Elliot Lee) Richardson
    HUD: 4 (James T) Lynn **6** (George Wilcken) Romney
    transportation: 5 (John Anthony) Volpe **8** (Claude S) Brinegar
  born: 2 CA **10** Yorba Linda
  died: 7 New York **11** New York City
  education:
    college: 8 Whittier
    law school: 14 Duke University
  religion: 6 Quaker **16** Society of Friends
  interests: 8 football
  vacation spot: 11 Key Biscayne (FL), San Clemente (CA)
  dog: 8 Checkers **11** King Timahoe
  author: 9 Six Crises **10** The Real War **11** Beyond Peace **27** RN: The Memoirs of Richard Nixon
  political career: 8 US Senate **13** Vice President **24** US House of Representatives
  civilian career: 6 lawyer

  military service: 6 US Navy **10** lieutenant, World War II
  notable events of lifetime/term:
    Calley court martialed for: 13 Mylai Massacre
    court martial of: 6 Calley
    creation of: 10 Bangladesh
    crisis: 3 oil **6** energy
    embargo on: 3 oil
    first men on: 4 moon
    incident: 11 Wounded Knee
    pardon of Nixon by: 4 Ford
    publication of: 14 Pentagon Papers
    resignation of: 5 Agnew, Nixon
    scandal: 9 Watergate
    student deaths at: 9 Kent State
    treaty: 10 Seabed Arms **32** Nonproliferation of Nuclear Weapons
    trip to: 5 China
    war: 7 Vietnam **10** Middle East **12** East Pakistan
  quotes: 31 A respectable Republican cloth coat **35** You won't have Nixon to kick around any more
  father: 14 Francis Anthony
  mother: 6 Hannah (Milhous)
  siblings: 11 Arthur Burdg **12** Harold Samuel **13** Edward Calvert, Francis Donald
  wife: 8 (Thelma Catherine) Patricia (Ryan)
    nickname: 3 Pat
  children: 5 Julie **8** Patricia
    Julie married: 15 David Eisenhower
    Patricia married: 9 Edward Cox
    Patricia's nickname: 6 Tricia

Njord *see* **5** Niord

no 3 nay, nix, not **4** none, veto
  French: 3 non
  German: 4 nein
  Spanish: 2 no
  Italian: 2 no
  Russian: 4 nyet

Noah
  father: 6 Lamech
  grandfather: 10 Methuselah
  son: 3 Ham **4** Shem **7** Japheth
  grandson: 3 Put **4** Cush **6** Canaan **7** Misraim
  great grandson: 6 Nimrod
  built: 3 ark
  collected: 5 pairs **7** animals
  survived: 5 flood
  pertaining to: 8 Noachian

Noah's Ark
  made of: 10 gopherwood
  landfall: 6 Ararat

nob 4 peer, toff **5** swell **9** patrician **10** aristocrat

Nobel, Alfred
  nationality: 7 Swedish
  invented: 8 dynamite
  originated: 10 Nobel Prize

Nobel Prizes
  Literature:
    1901: 20 Rene F A

Sully-Prudhomme
1902: 14 Theodor Mommsen
1903: 20 Bjornstjerne Bjornson
1904: 13 Jose Echegaray **15** Frederic Mistral
1905: 17 Henryk Sienkiewicz
1906: 14 Giosue Carducci
1907: 14 Rudyard Kipling
1908: 13 Rudolf C Eucken
1909: 13 Selma Lagerlof
1910: 12 Paul von Heyse
1911: 18 Maurice Maeterlinck
1912: 16 Gerhart Hauptmann
1913: 21 Sir Rabindranath Tagore
1915: 13 Romain Rolland
1916: 19 Verner von Heidenstam
1917: 11 K A Gjellerup **17** Henrik Pontoppidan
1919: 15 Carl F G Spitteler
1920: 10 Knut Hamsun
1921: 13 Anatole France
1922: 25 Jacinto Benavente y Martinez
1923: 18 William Butler Yeats
1924: 17 Wladyslaw S Reymont
1925: 17 George Bernard Shaw
1926: 13 Grazia Deledda
1927: 12 Henri Bergson
1928: 12 Sigrid Undset
1929: 10 Thomas Mann
1930: 13 Sinclair Lewis
1931: 14 Erik A Karlfeldt
1932: 14 John Galsworthy
1933: 10 Ivan A Bunin
1934: 15 Luigi Pirandello
1936: 12 Eugene O'Neill
1937: 17 Roger Martin du Gard
1938: 10 Pearl S Buck
1939: 15 Frans E Sillanpaa
1944: 15 Johannes V Jensen
1945: 15 Gabriela Mistral
1946: 12 Hermann Hesse
1947: 9 Andre Gide
1948: 7 T S Eliot
1949: 15 William Faulkner
1950: 15 Bertrand Russell (Earl Russell)
1951: 14 Par F Lagerkvist
1952: 15 Francois Mauriac
1953: 21 Sir Winston L S Churchill
1954: 15 Ernest Hemingway
1955: 15 Halldor K Laxness
1956: 16 Juan Ramon Jimenez
1957: 11 Albert Camus
1958: 15 Boris L Pasternak
1959: 18 Salvatore Quasimodo
1960: 14 Saint-John Perse
1961: 9 Ivo Andric
1962: 13 John Steinbeck
1963: 13 George Seferis
1964: 14 Jean Paul Sartre
1965: 17 Mikhail A Sholokhov
1966: 10 Nelly Sachs **17** Samuel Joseph (Shmuel Y) Agnon
1967: 19 Miguel Angel Asturias
1968: 16 Yasunari Kawabata
1969: 13 Samuel Beckett
1970: 22 Aleksandr I Solzhenitsyn

1971: **11** Pablo Neruda
1972: **12** Heinrich Boll
1973: **12** Patrick White
1974: **13** Eyvind Johnson **14** Harry Martinson
1975: **14** Eugenio Montale
1976: **10** Saul Bellow
1977: **17** Vicente Aleixandre
1978: **19** Isaac Bashevis Singer
1979: **14** Odysseus Elytis
1980: **13** Czeslaw Milosz
1981: **12** Elias Canetti
1982: **20** Gabriel Garcia Marquez
1983: **14** William Golding
1984: **15** Jaroslav Seifert
1985: **11** Claude Simon
1986: **11** Wole Soyinka
1987: **13** Joseph Brodsky
1988: **13** Naguib Mahfouz
1989: **10** Camilo Cela
1990: **10** Octavio Paz
1991: **14** Nadine Gordimer
1992: **12** Derek Walcott
1993: **12** Toni Morrison
1994: **11** Kenzaburo Oe
1995: **12** Seamus Heaney
1996: **17** Wislawa Szymborska
1997: **7** Dario Fo

Physiology/Medicine:
1901: **15** Emil A von Behring
1902: **13** Sir Ronald Ross
1903: **12** Niels R Finsen
1904: **11** Ivan P Pavlov
1905: **10** Robert Koch
1906: **12** Camillo Golgi **19** Santiago Ramon y Cajal
1907: **16** Charles L A Laveran
1908: **11** Paul Ehrlich **15** Elie Metchnikoff
1909: **11** Emil T Kocher
1910: **14** Albrecht Kossel
1911: **16** Allvar Gullstrand
1912: **12** Alexis Carrel
1913: **14** Charles R Richet
1914: **12** Robert Barany
1919: **11** Jules Bordet
1920: **12** Shack A S Krogh
1922: **12** Otto Meyerhof **14** Archibald V Hill
1923: **13** John J R Macleod **20** Sir Frederick G Banting
1924: **15** Willem Einthoven
1926: **15** Johannes Fibiger
1927: **19** Julius Wagner-Jauregg
1928: **16** Charles J H Nicolle
1929: **17** Christiaan Eijkman **20** Sir Frederick G Hopkins
1930: **15** Karl Landsteiner
1931: **12** Otto H Warburg
1932: **12** Edgar D Adrian **21** Sir Charles Sherrington
1933: **13** Thomas H Morgan
1934: **12** George R Minot **14** George H Whipple, William P Murphy
1935: **11** Hans Spemann
1936: **9** Otto Loewi **13** Sir Henry H Dale

1937: **31** Albert Szent-Gyorgyi von Nagyrapolt
1938: **16** Corneille Heymans
1939: **13** Gerhard Domagk
1943: **9** Henrik Dam **12** Edward A Doisy
1944: **14** Herbert S Gasser, Joseph Erlanger
1945: **11** Ernst B Chain **16** Sir Howard W Florey **19** Sir Alexander Fleming
1946: **14** Hermann J Muller
1947: **9** Carl F Cori **10** Gerty T Cori **16** Bernardo A Houssay
1948: **11** Paul H Muller
1949: **11** Walter R Hess **21** Antonio C de A F Egas Moniz
1950: **12** Philip S Hench **14** Edward C Kendall **16** Tadeus Reichstein
1951: **10** Max Theiler
1952: **14** Selman A Waksman
1953: **13** Fritz A Lipmann, Sir Hans A Krebs
1954: **11** John F Enders **13** Thomas H Weller **17** Frederick C Robbins
1955: **14** Axel H T Theorell
1956: **13** Andre Cournand **15** Werner Forssmann **20** Dickenson W Richards Jr
1957: **11** Daniel Bovet
1958: **12** Edward L Tatum **13** George W Beadle **15** Joshua Lederberg
1959: **11** Severo Ochoa **14** Arthur Kornberg
1960: **13** Peter B Medawar **15** Sir Frank M Burnet
1961: **14** Georg von Bekesy
1962: **12** James D Watson **14** Francis H C Crick **16** Maurice H F Wilkins
1963: **16** Alan Lloyd Hodgkin **18** Sir John Carew Eccles **20** Andrew Fielding Huxley
1964: **11** Feodor Lynen **12** Konrad E Bloch
1965: **10** Andre Lwoff **12** Jacques Monod **13** Francois Jacob
1966: **17** Francis Peyton Rous **21** Charles Brenton Huggins
1967: **10** George Wald **12** Ragnar Granit **20** Haldan Keffer Hartline
1968: **13** Robert W Holley **14** H Gobind Khorana **18** Marshall W Nirenberg
1969: **11** Max Delbruck **14** Alfred D Hershey, Salvador E Luria
1970: **11** Ulf von Euler **13** Julius Axelrod **14** Sir Bernard Katz
1971: **17** Earl W Sutherland Jr
1972: **12** Rodney R Porter **14** Gerald M Edelman
1973: **12** Konrad Lorenz **13** Karl von Frisch **17** Nikolaas Tinbergen
1974: **12** Albert Claude **15** Christian de Duve **16** George Emil-Palade
1975: **12** Howard M Temin **14** Da-

vid Baltimore, Renato Dulbecco
1976: **15** Baruch S Blumberg **22** Daniel Carleton Gajdusek
1977: **13** Andrew Schally, Rosalyn S Yalow **14** Roger Guillemin
1978: **11** Werner Arber **13** Daniel Nathans, Hamilton Smith
1979: **13** Allan M Cormack **17** Godfrey Hounsfield
1980: **11** Jean Dausset **12** George D Snell **15** Baruj Benacerraf
1981: **11** David H Hubel **12** Roger W Sperry **14** Torsten N Wiesel
1982: **9** John R Vane **15** Bengt Samuelsson **17** Sune Karl Bergstrom
1983: **17** Barbara McClintock
1984: **11** Niels K Jerne **13** Cesar Milstein **16** Georges J F Koehler
1985: **13** Michael S Brown **16** Joseph L Goldstein
1986: **12** Stanley Cohen **18** Rita Levi-Montalcini
1987: **14** Susumu Tonegawa
1988: **10** James Black **14** Gertrube B Elion **16** George H Hitchings
1989: **12** Harold Varmas **14** J Michael Bishop
1990: **12** Joseph Murray **14** E Donnall Thomas
1991: **10** Edwin Neher **11** Bert Sakmann
1992: **10** Edwin Krebs **12** Edmond Fisher
1993: **12** Phillip Sharp **14** Richard Roberts
1994: **12** Alfred Gilman **13** Martin Rodbell
1995: **12** Edward B Lewis **14** Eric F Wieschaus
1996: **13** Peter C Doherty **16** Rolf M Ziwkernagel
1997: **16** Stanley B Prusiner

Chemistry:
1901: **16** Jacobus H van't Hoff
1902: **11** Emil Fischer
1903: **16** Svante A Arrhenius
1904: **16** Sir William Ramsay
1905: **17** J F W Adolf von Baeyer
1906: **12** Henri Moissan
1907: **13** Eduard Buchner
1908: **19** Sir Ernest Rutherford
1909: **14** Wilhelm Ostwald
1910: **11** Otto Wallach
1911: **11** Marie S Curie
1912: **12** Paul Sabatier **14** Victor Grignard
1913: **12** Alfred Werner
1914: **17** Theodore W Richards
1915: **18** Richard Willstatter
1918: **10** Fritz Haber
1920: **13** Walther Nernst
1921: **14** Frederick Soddy
1922: **13** Francis W Aston
1923: **10** Fritz Pregl
1925: **16** Richard Zsigmondy
1926: **15** Theodor Svedberg
1927: **15** Heinrich Wieland

1928: 12 Adolf Windaus
1929: 15 Sir Arthur Harden **19** Hans von Euler-Chelpin
1930: 11 Hans Fischer
1931: 9 Carl Bosch **16** Friedrich Bergius
1932: 14 Irving Langmuir
1934: 11 Harold C Urey
1935: 16 Irene Joliot-Curie **19** Frederic Joliot-Curie
1936: 12 Peter J W Debye
1937: 10 Paul Karrer **17** Sir Walter N Haworth
1938: 11 Richard Kuhn
1939: 14 Adolf Butenandt, Leopold Ruzicka
1943: 14 Georg von Hevesy
1944: 8 Otto Hahn
1945: 16 Artturi I Virtanen
1946: 12 James B Sumner **13** John H Northrop **15** Wendell M Stanley
1947: 17 Sir Robert Robinson
1948: 12 Arne Tiselius
1949: 15 William F Giauque
1950: 9 Kurt Alder, Otto Diels
1951: 13 Glenn T Seaborg **14** Edwin M McMillan
1952: 14 Archer J P Martin, Richard L M Synge
1953: 17 Hermann Staudinger
1954: 13 Linus C Pauling
1955: 17 Vincent du Vigneaud
1956: 15 Nikolai N Semenov **20** Sir Cyril N Hinshelwood
1957: 17 Sir Alexander R Todd (Baron Todd)
1958: 15 Frederick Sanger
1959: 17 Jaroslav Heyrovsky
1960: 13 Willard F Libby
1961: 12 Melvin Calvin
1962: 10 Max F Perutz **12** John C Kendrew
1963: 11 Giulio Natta, Karl Ziegler
1964: 26 Dorothy Mary Crowfoot Hodgkin
1965: 19 Robert Burns Woodward
1966: 15 Robert S Mulliken
1967: 12 Manfred Eigen **15** Sir George Porter **27** Ronald George Wreyford Norrish
1968: 11 Lars Onsager
1969: 9 Odd Hassel **13** Derek H R Barton
1970: 18 Luis Federico Leloir
1971: 15 Gerhard Herzberg
1972: 13 Stanford Moore **18** Christian B Anfinsen, William Howard Stein
1973: 16 Ernst Otto Fischer **17** Geoffrey Wilkinson
1974: 10 Paul J Flory
1975: 14 John W Cornforth, Vladimir Prelog
1976: 16 William N Lipscomb
1977: 13 Ilya Prigogine
1978: 13 Peter Mitchell
1979: 11 Georg Wittig **13** Herbert C Brown

1980: 8 Paul Berg **13** Walter Gilbert **15** Frederick Sanger
1981: 12 Kenichi Fukui **13** Roald Hoffmann
1982: 9 Aaron Klug
1983: 10 Henry Taube
1984: 21 Robert Bruce Merrifield
1985: 11 Jerome Karle **16** Herbert A Hauptman
1986: 8 Yuan T Lee **12** John C Polanyi **16** Dudley Herschbach
1987: 11 Donald J Cram **16** Charles J Pederson
1988: 11 Robert Huber **13** Hartmut Michel **17** Johann Deisenhofer
1989: 10 Thomas Cich **12** Sidney Altman
1990: 10 Elias Corey
1991: 12 Richard Ernst
1992: 13 Rudolph Marcus
1993: 10 Kary Mullis **12** Michael Smith
1994: 10 George Olah
1995: 11 Paul Crutzen, Mario Molina **16** F Sherwood Rowland
1996: 11 Robert F Curl **15** Richard E Smalley, Sir Harold W Kroto
1997: 9 Jens C Skou **10** Paul D Boyer **11** John E Walker
Physics:
1901: 16 Wilhelm K Roentgen
1902: 12 Pieter Zeeman **15** Hendrik A Lorentz
1903: 11 Marie S Curie, Pierre Curie **15** A Henri Becquerel
1904: 11 John W Strutt (Lord Rayleigh)
1905: 13 Philipp Lenard
1906: 16 Sir Joseph Thomson
1907: 16 Albert A Michelson
1908: 15 Gabriel Lippmann
1909: 10 Karl F Braun **16** Guglielmo Marconi
1910: 20 Johannes D van der Waals
1911: 11 Wilhelm Wien
1912: 10 Nils G Dalen
1913: 20 Heike Kamerlingh Onnes
1914: 10 Max von Laue
1915: 16 Sir William H Bragg, Sir William L Bragg
1917: 14 Charles B Barkla
1918: 9 Max Planck
1919: 13 Johannes Stark
1920: 17 Charles E Guillaume
1921: 14 Albert Einstein
1922: 10 Nils H D Bohr
1923: 15 Robert A Millikan
1924: 14 Karl M G Siegbahn
1925: 11 Gustav Hertz, James Franck
1926: 11 Jean B Perrin
1927: 14 Arthur H Compton **15** Charles T R Wilson
1928: 18 Sir Owen W Richardson
1929: 15 Louis V de Broglie
1930: 23 Sir Chandrasekhara V Raman

1932: 16 Werner Heisenberg
1933: 11 Paul A M Dirac **16** Erwin Schrodinger
1935: 16 Sir James Chadwick
1936: 11 Victor F Hess **13** Carl D Anderson
1937: 16 Clinton J Davisson **17** Sir George P Thomson
1938: 11 Enrico Fermi
1939: 15 Ernest O Lawrence
1943: 9 Otto Stern
1944: 11 Isidor I Rabi
1945: 13 Wolfgang Pauli
1946: 14 Percy W Bridgman
1947: 18 Sir Edward V Appleton
1948: 17 Patrick M S Blackett
1949: 12 Hideki Yukawa
1950: 12 Cecil F Powell
1951: 14 Ernest T S Walton **17** Sir John D Cockcroft
1952: 10 Felix Bloch **14** Edward M Purcell
1953: 12 Frits Zernike
1954: 7 Max Born **12** Walther Bothe
1955: 13 Polykarp Kusch, Willis E Lamb Jr
1956: 11 John Bardeen **15** Walter H Brattain **16** William B Shockley
1957: 11 Tsung Dao Lee **12** Chen Ning Yang
1958: 9 Igor Y Tamm **10** Ilya M Frank **15** Pavel A Cherenkov
1959: 11 Emilio Segre **15** Owen Chamberlain
1960: 13 Donald A Glaser
1961: 16 Robert Hofstadter, Rudolf L Mossbauer
1962: 10 Lev D Landau
1963: 11 J Hans Jensen **16** Eugene Paul Wigner **18** Maria Goeppert Mayer
1964: 17 Charles Hard Townes **25** Nikolai Gennadiyevich Basov **30** Aleksandr Mikhailovich Prokhorov
1965: 18 Shinichiro Tomonaga **22** Julian Seymour Schwinger, Richard Phillips Feynman
1966: 13 Alfred Kastler
1967: 17 Hans Albrecht Bethe
1968: 12 Luis W Alvarez
1969: 14 Murray Gell-Mann
1970: 12 Hannes Alfven **15** Louis Eugene Neel
1971: 11 Dennis Gabor
1972: 11 John Bardeen, Leon N Cooper **20** John Robert Schreiffer
1973: 8 Leo Esaki **11** Ivar Giaever **15** Brian D Josephson
1974: 12 Antony Hewish **13** Sir Martin Ryle
1975: 8 Aage Bohr **13** Ben R Mottelson **15** L James Rainwater
1976: 12 Samuel C C Ting **13** Burton Richter
1977: 13 John H Van Vleck, Sir Nevill Mott **15** Philip W Anderson
1978: 12 Arno A Penzias, Peter

Kapitza (Pyotr Kapitsa) **13** Robert W Wilson

1979: 10 Abdus Salam **14** Sheldon Glashow, Steven Weinberg

1980: 9 Val L Fitch **12** James W Cronin

1981: 12 Kai M Siegbahn **14** Arthur Schawlow **19** Nicolaas Bloembergen

1982: 14 Kenneth G Wilson

1983: 14 William A Fowler **25** Subrahmanyan Chandrasekhar

1984: 11 Carlo Rubbia **15** Simon van der Meer

1985: 16 Klaus von Klitzing

1986: 10 Ernst Ruska, Gerd Binner **14** Heinrich Rohrer

1987: 12 K Alex Mueller **13** J Georg Bednorz

1988: 13 Leon M Lederman **14** Melvin Schwartz **15** Jack Steinberger

1989: 11 Hans Dehmelt **12** Norman Ramsey, Wolfgang Paul

1990: 12 Henry Kendall **13** Richard Taylor **14** Jerome Friedman

1991: 12 Pierre Gennes

1992: 13 George Charpak

1993: 12 Joseph Taylor, Russell Hulse

1994: 13 Clifford Shull **17** Bertram Brockhouse

1995: 11 Martin I Perl **15** Frederick Reines

1996: 9 David M Lee **16** Douglas D Osheroff **17** Robert C Richardson

1997: 9 Steven Chu **16** William D Phillips **20** Claude Cohen-Tannoudji

Peace:

1901: 13 Frederic Passy **15** Jean Henri Dunant

1902: 12 Elie Ducommun **18** Charles Albert Gobat

1903: 17 Sir William R Cremer

1904: 27 Institute of International Law

1905: 24 Baroness Bertha von Suttner

1906: 17 Theodore Roosevelt

1907: 12 Louis Renault **14** Ernesto T Moneta

1908: 12 Fredrik Bajer **14** Klas P Arnoldson

1909: 16 Auguste Beernaert **35** Paul H Balluat d'Estournelles de Constant

1910: 24 International Peace Bureau

1911: 12 Alfred H Fried **13** Tobias M C Asser

1912: 9 Elihu Root

1913: 15 Henri La Fontaine

1917: 30 International Red Cross Committee

1919: 13 Woodrow Wilson

1920: 13 Leon Bourgeois

1921: 15 Christian L Lange **19** Karl Hjalmar Branting

1922: 14 Fridtjof Nansen

1925: 13 Charles G Dawes **26** Sir Joseph Austen Chamberlain

1926: 14 Aristide Briand **16** Gustav Stresemann

1927: 12 Ludwig Quidde **17** Ferdinand E Buisson

1929: 13 Frank B Kellogg

1930: 15 (Lars Olof Jonathan) Nathan Soderblom

1931: 10 Jane Addams **20** Nicholas Murray Butler

1933: 15 Sir Norman Angell

1934: 15 Arthur Henderson

1935: 16 Carl von Ossietzky

1936: 19 Carlos Saavedra Lamas

1937: 13 E A Robert Cecil (Viscount Cecil)

1938: 36 Nansen International Office for Refugees

1944: 30 International Red Cross Committee

1945: 11 Cordell Hull

1946: 9 John R Mott **11** Emily G Balch

1947: 21 Friends Service Council **31** American Friends Service Committee

1949: 11 John Boyd Orr (Baron Orr)

1950: 12 Ralph J Bunche

1951: 11 Leon Jouhaux

1952: 16 Albert Schweitzer

1953: 15 George C Marshall

1954: 51 Office of the United Nations High Commissioner for Refugees

1957: 14 Lester B Pearson

1958: 28 Rev Dominique Georges Henri Pire

1959: 16 Philip J Noel-Baker

1960: 14 Albert J Luthuli

1961: 15 Dag Hammarskjold

1962: 13 Linus C Pauling

1963: 25 League of Red Cross Societies **30** International Red Cross Committee

1964: 18 Martin Luther King Jr

1965: 26 United Nations Children's Fund (UNICEF)

1968: 10 Rene Cassin

1969: 30 International Labor Organization (ILO)

1970: 14 Norman E Borlaug

1971: 11 Willy Brandt

1973: 8 Le Duc Tho **15** Henry A Kissinger

1974: 11 Eisaku Sato **12** Sean MacBride

1975: 15 Andrei D Sakharov

1976: 13 Betty Williams **15** Mairead Corrigan

1977: 20 Amnesty International

1978: 10 Anwar Sadat **13** Menachem Begin

1979: 12 Mother Teresa

1980: 19 Adolfo Perez Esquivel

1981: 51 Office of the United Na-

tions High Commissioner for Refugees

1982: 10 Alva Myrdal **19** Alfonso Garcia Robles

1983: 10 Lech Walesa

1984: 17 Bishop Desmond Tutu

1985: 51 International Physicians for the Prevention of Nuclear War

1986: 10 Elie Wiesel

1987: 17 Oscar Arias Sanchez

1988: 31 United Nations peacekeeping troops

1989: 9 Dalai Lama

1990: 16 Mikhail Gorbachev

1991: 13 Aung San Suu Kyi

1992: 15 Rigoberta Menchu

1993: 9 F W de Klerk **13** Nelson Mandela

1994: 11 Yasir Arafat, Shimon Peres **12** Yitzhak Rabin

1995: 13 Joseph Rotblat

1996: 14 Jose Ramos Horta **23** Carlos Filepe, Ximenes Belo

1997: 12 Jody Williams

Economics:

1969: 12 Jan Tinbergen, Ragnar Frisch

1970: 14 Paul A Samuelson

1971: 13 Simon S Kuznets

1972: 13 Kenneth J Arrow, Sir John R Hicks

1973: 15 Wassily Leontief

1974: 12 Gunnar Myrdal **18** Friedrich A von Hayek

1975: 17 Tjalling C Koopmans **18** Leonid V Kantorovich

1976: 14 Milton Friedman

1977: 11 Bertil Ohlin, James E Meade

1978: 13 Herbert A Simon

1979: 14 Sir Arthur Lewis **15** Theodore Schultz

1980: 14 Lawrence R Klein

1981: 10 James Tobin

1982: 14 George J Stigler

1983: 12 Gerard Debreu

1984: 15 Sir Richard Stone

1985: 16 Franco Modigliani

1986: 19 James McGill Buchanan

1987: 12 Robert M Solow

1988: 13 Maurice Allais

1989: 12 Trygve Haavelmo

1990: 12 Merton Miller **13** William Sharpe **14** Harry Markowitz

1991: 11 Ronald Coase

1992: 10 Gary Becker

1993: 11 Robert Fogel **12** Douglas North

1994: 8 John Nash **12** John Harsanyi **14** Reinhard Selten

1995: 14 Robert E Lucas Jr.

1996: 14 James A Mirrlees **15** William S Vickrey

1997: 13 Myron S Scholes, Robert C Merton

nobility 5 elite, lords **7** dignity, majesty, peerage, primacy, royalty **8** breeding, eminence, grandeur, high rank, prestige, splendor **9** gentility, grandness, greatness, loftiness, sublimity, supremacy **10** blue bloods, mightiness, patricians, patriciate, upper crust **11** aristocracy, distinction, exaltedness, preeminence, stateliness, superiority **12** magnificence

nobility obliges
French: **14** noblesse oblige

noble 3 don **4** high, just, lord, peer **5** famed, grand, great, lofty, moral, regal, royal **6** famous, gentle, honest, knight, lordly, squire, superb, worthy **7** awesome, courtly, eminent, ethical, exalted, grandee, stately, sublime, supreme, upright **8** baronial, cavalier, elevated, glorious, handsome, highborn, imperial, imposing, lordlike, majestic, princely, renowned, selfless, splendid, superior, virtuous **9** chevalier, dignified, estimable, excellent, exemplary, gentleman, honorable, patrician, personage, reputable **10** aristocrat, impressive, preeminent **11** magnanimous, magnificent, meritorious, pureblooded, trustworthy **12** aristocratic, thoroughbred **13** distinguished, incorruptible
French: **6** gentil

Noble House
author: **12** James Clavell

nobleman 4 lord, peer **7** grandee **9** patrician **10** aristocrat

noblesse oblige 15 nobility obliges

noblewoman 4 dame, lady, rani **5** begum, queen **6** milady **7** czarina, duchess, empress, peeress, sultana **8** baroness, contessa, countess, maharani, princess **11** marchioness

Nobody Knows My Name
author: **12** James Baldwin

nock 5 notch
in: **5** arrow

nocturnal 4 dark **5** night **7** nightly, obscure **8** darkling **9** nighttime

nod 3 bob **4** doze, hail, show, sign **5** agree, greet, lapse, let up **6** assent, beckon, concur, drowse, motion, reveal, salute, signal **7** consent, drop off, fall off, gesture, signify **9** recognize

node 3 bud **4** bump, burl, hump, knob, knot, lump **5** bulge, joint **6** button **8** swelling **10** prominence, tumescence **11** excrescence **12** protuberance

nodule 3 sac, wen **4** bump, cyst, knob, knot, lump, stud **5** bulge **6** growth **8** swelling **9** outgrowth **10** projection, prominence, protrusion, tumescence **11** excrescence **12** protuberance

noel, Noel 4 yule **5** carol **8** yuletide **9** Christmas **13** Christmastide

No Exit
author: **14** Jean-Paul Sartre

noggin 3 cup, mug **4** bean, head, pate **5** gourd **6** noodle

Noggs, Newman
character in: **16** Nicholas Nickleby
author: **7** Dickens

Noguchi, Hideyo
field: **12** bacteriology
nationality: **8** Japanese
isolated: **8** syphilis

noise 3 ado, din **4** bang, blab, boom, echo, pass, roar, stir, wail **5** babel, blare, blast, bruit, rumor, sound, voice **6** bedlam, clamor, hubbub, racket, repeat, report, rumble, tumult, uproar **7** barrage, bluster, clatter, thunder **8** brawling, gabbling, rumbling, shouting **9** cacophony, cannonade, circulate, commotion, discharge **10** dissonance, hullabaloo **11** pandemonium **12** caterwauling, vociferation **13** reverberation

noiseless 5 quiet, still, tacit **6** hushed, silent **9** soundless, voiceless

noisemaker 4 bell, horn **5** siren **6** rattle **7** clacker, clapper, snapper, whistle

noisome 4 foul, rank **5** acrid, fetid, toxic **6** putrid, rotten, smelly **7** baneful, harmful, hurtful, noxious, reeking **8** mephitic, stinking **9** injurious, offensive, poisonous, unhealthy **10** malodorous, nauseating, pernicious **11** deleterious, detrimental **12** evil-smelling

noisy 4 loud **5** alive **6** lively, raging, shrill, stormy **7** blaring, blatant, furious, grating, jarring, rackety **8** animated, piercing, strident **9** clamorous, deafening, dissonant, turbulent **10** boisterous, clangorous, discordant, rampageous, resounding, thundering, thunderous, tumultuous, uproarious **11** cacophonous, tempestuous **12** ear-splitting

Nolan, Lloyd
born: **14** San Francisco CA
roles: **22** Lieutenant Colonel Queeg **26** The Caine Mutiny Court Martial

Nolde, Emil
real name: **10** Emil Hansen
born: **5** Nolde **7** Germany
artwork: **7** Prophet **10** Papua Youth **11** Tropical Sun **12** The Magicians, The Pentecost **13** The Last Supper, Three Russians **14** Doubting Thomas **20** Life of Maria Aegyptica **22** Christ Among the Children, Christ and the Adulteress

nolens volens 10 willy-nilly **19** whether willing or not

noli me tangere 10 touch me not

nolle prosequi 14 do not prosecute **19** be unwilling to pursue

nolo contendere 21 I am unwilling to contend

no longer able to fight
French: **12** hors de combat

no longer in existence 4 dead, gone, lost **7** defunct, died out, extinct **8** vanished

Nolte, Nick
born: **7** Omaha NE
roles: **5** U-Turn, Weeds **7** The Deep, Cape Fear **10** Cannery Row **11** Lorenzo's Oil, Mother Night **12** I Love Trouble **13** Prince of Tides **14** Rich Man Poor Man **15** Forty-Eight Hours **16** North Dallas Forty

nomad 4 arab, hobo, okie **5** gypsy, mover, rover, stray, tramp **6** roamer **7** migrant, rambler, refugee, runaway, strayer, tuareg, vagrant **8** bohemian, emigrant, migrator, renegade, traveler, vagabond, wanderer **9** immigrant, itinerant, straggler

nomadic 6 roving **7** migrant, roaming, vagrant **8** drifting, vagabond **9** footloose, itinerant, migratory, strolling, traveling, wandering

nom de guerre 5 alias **7** war name **9** pseudonym **11** assumed name

nom de plume 5 alias **7** pen name **9** false name, pseudonym **11** assumed name, writing name

nomenclature 5 lingo, terms **6** jargon, naming **8** glossary, language, taxonomy **10** nomination, vocabulary

nominal 3 low **5** cheap, small **6** puppet **7** minimum, titular, trivial **8** baseless, moderate, official, so-called, trifling **9** pretended, professed, purported, suggested **10** groundless, ostensible, reasonable

nominate 3 tag **4** call, name, pick, term **5** elect, label, style **6** choose, invest, select **7** elevate, install, propose, suggest **9** authorize, recommend

nomination 8 election **9** accession, selection **10** suggestion

nominee 7 hopeful **8** aspirant, eligible **9** applicant, candidate **10** competitor, contestant

nonadjustable 5 fixed, rigid **9** immovable **10** inflexible

nonalcoholic 4 soft **15** nonintoxicating

nonattendance 3 cut **7** absence, truancy **11** absenteeism

nonbeliever 5 cynic, pagan **7** atheist, doubter, heathen, infidel, skeptic **8** agnostic, apostate **10** backslider, empiricist, questioner, unbeliever **11** disbeliever, freethinker **14** doubting Thomas

nonbinding 8 optional **9** voluntary **12** unimperative **13** discretionary

nonce 6 pro tem **7** present **9** time being

nonchalance 9 composure, unconcern **13** offhandedness
French: **11** insouciance

nonchalant 3 lax **4** cool, idle, lazy **5** blase, slack **6** casual **7** languid, offhand, unmoved **8** careless, heedless, indolent, listless **9** apathetic, collected, easygoing, lethargic, unexcited, unheeding, unmindful, unruffled, unstirred, withdrawn **10** insensible, insouciant, phlegmatic, unaffected

noncombatant 7 neutral **8** civilian

noncommittal 3 mum **4** cool, mute, safe, wary **5** vague **7** careful, evasive, guarded, neutral, politic, prudent **8** cautious, discreet, reserved **9** ambiguous, equivocal, tentative **10** indecisive, indefinite, unspeaking **11** circumspect, temporizing

noncompliance 6 breach **7** failure, neglect **9** disregard **10** resistance **11** dereliction

noncompliant 6 unruly **7** defiant, froward, naughty, wayward **8** contrary, mutinous, perverse, stubborn **9** differing, dissident, fractious, objecting, obstinate, resistant, resistive, undutiful **10** disorderly, dissenting, rebellious, refractory, unorthodox, unyielding

non compos mentis 14 not of sound mind **17** mentally incapable

nonconfirming 7 denying **8** negating, refuting **9** rejecting **10** disavowing **11** disclaiming, repudiating

nonconformist 3 nut **4** beat, card **5** freak, hippy, loner, rebel **6** oddity, weirdo **7** heretic, oddball, radical **8** bohemian, crackpot, deserter, maverick, original, reformer, renegade, vagabond **9** character, dissenter, dissident, eccentric, exception, insurgent, protester, screwball **10** dissenting, iconoclast, rebellious, schismatic **13** individualist, revolutionary

nonconformity 5 quirk **6** oddity **7** anomaly **9** deviation, rebellion **10** aberration, divergence, resistance

noncongenial 6 unlike **8** opposite **9** different, disparate, ill-suited, unrelated **10** dissimilar **11** disagreeing **12** disagreeable, incompatible **13** unsympathetic

nondescript 5 usual, vague **8** ordinary **9** amorphous, colorless **11** stereotyped **12** unimpressive **13** characterless, undistinctive, unexceptional **15** undistinguished

nonentity 4 zero **6** cipher, nobody **7** nothing, no-count, nullity **8** small-fry, unperson **10** mediocrity

nonessential 5 frill **6** luxury, trivia **7** trivial **9** extrinsic, secondary, trimmings **10** accidental, extraneous, incidental, irrelevant, peripheral, subsidiary

nonexclusive 4 open **6** public, shared **7** divided **12** unrestricted

nonexistence 4 lack, void **7** absence **8** oblivion **11** nothingness

nonexistent 4 gone **5** short **6** absent **7** lacking, missing, wanting **11** unavailable **12** insufficient

nonindulgence 7 refusal **8** eschewal, forgoing **9** avoidance, eschewing **10** abstaining, abstention, refraining **11** forbearance **16** nonparticipation

nonirritating 4 calm **5** bland **6** benign **7** calming **8** soothing, tranquil **9** temperate

non licet 13 it is not lawful **16** it is not permitted

non liquet 12 it is not clear **14** it is not evident

nonmaterialistic 9 spiritual **10** idealistic **12** intellectual

nonmember 5 guest **7** outcast, visitor **8** outsider

nonnatural 7 manmade **9** synthetic **10** artificial, fabricated, factitious **12** manufactured

nonobservance 6 breach **7** failure, neglect **9** disregard **11** dereliction **13** noncompliance

non obstante 15 notwithstanding

no-nonsense 4 grim, hard **5** grave, harsh, rigid, sober, stern **6** ardent, intent, severe, solemn, strict **7** earnest, serious **8** critical, diligent, exacting, resolute **9** committed, dedicated, demanding, hardnosed, practical, pragmatic, unbending, unsparing **10** determined, hardheaded, purposeful, sobersided **12** businesslike

nonpareil 5 elite, ideal, model, super **6** symbol, unique **7** epitome, paragon, pattern, supreme **8** exemplar **9** unequaled, unmatched, unrivaled **10** apotheosis **11** exceptional, unsurpassed **13** extraordinary **14** representative
French: 11 ne plus ultra **14** creme de la creme

nonparticipation 7 refusal **8** eschewal, forgoing **9** avoidance, eschewing **10** abstaining, abstention, refraining, sitting out **11** forbearance

nonpartisan 4 fair, just **8** unbiased, unswayed **9** equitable, impartial, objective, unbigoted **10** impersonal, uninvolved **12** freethinking, unaffiliated, unimplicated, uninfluenced, unprejudiced **13** disinterested

nonpermissible 9 forbidden **10** disallowed **11** intolerable **12** inadmissible, unacceptable

nonplus 4 balk, faze, foil, halt, stop **5** abash, stump, upset **6** baffle, bother, dismay, muddle, puzzle, stymie **7** astound, confuse, disturb, mystify, perplex **8** astonish, bewilder, confound, deadlock **9** dumbfound, embarrass **10** disconcert **11** flabbergast **14** discountenance

nonplussed, nonplused 5 at sea, fazed **7** at a loss, baffled, floored, mixed-up, muddled, puzzled, stumped **8** confused **9** befuddled, mystified, unsettled **10** bewildered, confounded **12** disconcerted

nonpoisonous 4 safe **8** nontoxic **11** nonvenomous, nonvirulent

non possumus 8 we cannot

nonpresence 3 cut **7** absence, truancy **11** absenteeism

nonprofessional 3 lay **4** laic **7** dabbler
French: 7 amateur **10** dilettante

non prosequitur 15 he does not pursue

non repetatur 11 do not repeat

nonresident 7 tourist, visitor **9** transient **11** out-of-towner

nonresistance 6 assent **7** pliancy **8** docility, giving in, meekness, yielding **9** deference, obedience, passivity **10** compliance, conforming, conformity, pliability, submission **12** acquiescence, complaisance

nonresistant 4 meek **6** docile, pliant **7** passive, pliable **8** deferent, obedient, yielding **9** compliant **10** conforming, submissive **11** acquiescent, complaisant, deferential

nonscholarly 8 untaught **9** unlearned **10** uneducated, unlettered, unpedantic, unschooled

nonsectarian 10 ecumenical **11** interchurch **16** undenominational **17** nondenominational **19** interdenominational

nonsense 3 rot **4** bosh, bunk **5** folly, trash **6** antics, babble, drivel, joking, piffle **7** baloney, blather, bombast, chatter, fooling, garbage, hogwash, inanity, prattle, rubbish, trifles, twaddle **8** claptrap, flummery **9** absurdity, frivolity, gibberish, high jinks, horseplay, moonshine, silliness, stupidity **10** balderdash, flapdoodle, tomfoolery, triviality **11** foolishness, shenanigans **12** childishness, extravagance **13** facetiousness, ludicrousness, senselessness **14** ridiculousness **15** meaninglessness

nonsensical 4 wild **5** crazy, funny, inane, silly **6** absurd, stupid **7** asinine, comical, foolish **8** farcical **9** facetious, laughable, ludicrous **10** irrational, ridiculous

non sequitur 15 it does not follow

nonspecialized 11 generalized

nonspecific 4 hazy **5** vague **7** general, inexact **9** imprecise, uncertain **10** indefinite, undetailed **11** approximate, generalized

nonspiritual 7 earthly, profane, secular, worldly **8** material, temporal **13** materialistic

nonstop 7 endless, express **8** constant, unbroken **9** incessant **10** continuous, unrelieved **11** unremitting **12** interminable

nonstudious 9 unlearned **10** uneducated, unlettered, unpedantic, unschooled

nontaxable 9 sheltered **10** deductible

nontechnical 6 simple 8 academic 13 uncomplicated

nontypical 7 unusual 8 abnormal, uncommon 9 anomalous, irregular 16 unrepresentative

non-U *see* 12 Mitford, Nancy

nonuniform 5 mixed 6 unlike 7 altered, changed, erratic, unalike 8 changing, variable 9 deviating, different, irregular, multiform 10 dissimilar 11 fluctuating, nonstandard 12 inconsistent

nonvital 9 accessory, extrinsic 10 disposable, expendable, incidental 11 dispensable, superfluous, unessential, unimportant, unnecessary

nonvocational 8 academic

nonvolitional 6 reflex 8 unwilled 9 automatic 11 instinctive, involuntary, spontaneous 12 uncontrolled

noodle 4 bean, head, pate 5 gourd, pasta 6 noggin 8 practice 9 improvise

nook 3 den 4 cove, lair 5 haven, niche 6 alcove, cavity, corner, cranny, dugout, recess, refuge 7 retreat, shelter 8 hideaway 9 cubbyhole 10 depression 11 hiding place

noon 6 midday, zenith 8 high noon, meridian

no one contradicting
 Latin: 19 nemine contradicente

no one dissenting
 Latin: 18 nemine dissentiente

noose 3 tie 4 bond, hang, loop 5 catch, hitch, lasso, snare 6 choker, entrap, halter, lariat, tether

Nootka
 language family: 8 Wakashan
 tribe: 5 Makah 6 Hoiath, Ozette 7 Ahosath, Nitinat 8 Machlath, Otsosath, Tokwaath 9 Ihatisath, Mowachath, Nochalath, Qayokwath, Tsishaath, Yoloilath 10 Hishkwiath, Hochoqtlis, Manohisath, Tlaokwiath 11 Chiqtlisath, Hopachasath, Qiltsamaath
 location: 10 Washington 15 Vancouver Island
 leader: 8 Maquinna 10 Wikaninish
 related to: 5 Makah
 noted for: 7 whaling

Nordhoff, Charles
 author of: 17 Mutiny on the Bounty (with James Norman Hall)

Nordic Mythology *see* 21 Scandinavian Mythology

Norge *see* 6 Norway

noria 10 water wheel

norm 3 par 4 rule, type 5 gauge, model 7 average, measure, pattern 8 standard 9 barometer, criterion, yardstick 12 measuring rod

normal 3 fit, par 4 sane 5 sound, usual 6 steady 7 average, healthy, natural, regular, typical, uniform 8 constant, expected, mediocre, middling, ordinary, rational, reliable, standard 9 incessant, steadfast, unceasing 10 conforming, consistent, continuous, dependable, reasonable, unchanging 11 conformable, rightminded, unremitting 12 conventional 13 uninterrupted 14 representative

Normandy, Normandie
 beach: 4 Gold, Juno, Utah 5 Omaha, Sword
 borders: 7 Picardy 8 Brittany 14 English Channel
 church/shrine: 12 Saint Etienne 15 Mont Saint Michel
 city: 4 Caen, St. Lo 5 Rouen 7 Le Havre 9 Cherbourg
 event: 4 D Day 17 Operation Overlord
 region of: 6 France
 river: 5 Seine

Norma Rae
 director: 10 Martin Ritt
 cast: 9 Pat Hingle 10 Ron Liebman, Sally Field 11 Beau Bridges
 Oscar for: 4 song 7 actress (Field)
 song: 16 It Goes Like It Goes

Norn
 origin: 12 Scandinavian
 form: 6 virgin 7 goddess
 personifies: 4 fate
 original Norn: 5 Urdar
 the three: 3 Urd 5 Skuld 8 Verdandi
 known as: 12 weird sisters

Norris, Frank
 author of: 6 The Pit 8 McTeague 10 The Octopus

Norse Mythology
 abode of man: 7 Midgard 10 Mithgarthr
 afterworld: 6 Manala 7 Tuonela
 began race of giants: 4 Ymir
 blacksmith/hero: 9 Ilmarinen
 boar: 10 Saehrimnir
 bridge of gods: 7 Bifrost
 dragon: 6 Fafnir
 dwarf: 5 Skuld 7 Andvari
 earth is made from: 4 Ymir
 elf: 4 Norn 8 Verdandi
 epic: 8 Kaleva
 final battle: 15 Gotterdammerung 17 Twilight of the Gods
 first god: 4 Buri 7 Forsete, Forseti
 first man: 3 Ask
 first woman: 5 Embla
 folk hero: 8 Kalevala
 giant: 4 Loki 5 Jotun, Thrym 6 Thiazi, Thjazi 7 Skrymir
 giantess: 3 Urd 5 Thokk 9 Angerboda, Angrbodha, Angurboda
 giant's realm: 9 Jotunheim
 goat: 7 Heidrun
 goddesses: 7 Asynjur
 goddess of death: 3 Hel
 goddess of forbidden marriages: 4 Lofn
 goddess of marriage: 4 Frey 5 Freyr
 goddess of peace: 4 Frey 5 Freyr
 goddess of prosperity: 4 Frey

 5 Freyr
 goddess of spring: 4 Idun 5 Iduna, Ithun 6 Ithunn
 goddess of the sea: 3 Ran
 god of beauty/radiance: 5 Baldr 6 Balder, Baldur
 god of dawn: 8 Heimdall
 god of farming: 4 Thor
 god of fire: 4 Loki
 god of knowledge: 4 Odin 5 Othin
  corresponds to Germanic: 5 Wotan
 god of justice: 7 Forseti
 god of light: 8 Heimdall
 god of music: 5 Bragi
 god of navigation: 5 Niord, Njord
 god of poetry: 4 Odin 5 Bragi, Othin
  corresponds to Germanic: 5 Wotan
 god of prosperity: 5 Niord, Njord
 god of rain: 4 Thor
 god of sea: 5 Aegir, Mimir
 god of thunder: 4 Thor
 god of underworld: 8 Niflheim
 god of victory: 3 Tyr
 god of war: 4 Odin 5 Othin
  corresponds to Germanic: 5 Wotan
 god of wind: 5 Niord, Njord
 god of wisdom: 4 Odin 5 Othin
  corresponds to Germanic: 5 Wotan
 hero: 11 Vainamoinen 12 Lemminkainen
 home of dead: 3 Hel
 king: 5 Gjuki
 magician: 11 Joukahainen
 magic necklace: 11 Brisingamen
 misty void: 11 Ginnungagap
 mountain: 11 Hindarfjall
 nature spirit: 7 Eriking
 oak tree: 9 Barnstock, Branstock
 Odin's court/hall: 8 Valhalla
 Odin's father: 3 Bor
 Odin's horse: 8 Sleipnir
 Odin's magic ring: 8 Draupnir
 Odin's palace: 9 Gladsheim
 Odin's raven: 5 Hugin, Munin
 Odin's spear: 6 Gungni
 Odin's throne: 10 Hlidskjalf
 Odin's wolf: 4 Geri 5 Freki
 race of gods: 5 Vanir
 saga: 8 Vulsunga
 sea monster: 6 Kraken
 serpent: 7 Nidhogg 11 Jormungandr
 Sigmund's sword: 4 Gram
 slave: 8 Kullervo
 sorceress: 5 Louhi 8 Grimhild
 Thor's hammer: 7 Miolnir
 Thor's servant: 7 Thialfi
 tree with three roots: 9 Iggdrasil, Yggdrasil
 Valkyrie: 8 Brynhild 9 Brunhilde, Sigrdrifa 11 Brunnehilde
 virgin goddess: 3 Urd 4 Norn 5 Skuld, Urdar 8 Verdandi
 warrior: 8 Baresark 9 Berserker

watchdog: 4 Garm
wolf monster: 6 Fenrir, Fenris
north 5 polar, upper **6** arctic
North America
  nation: 4 Cuba **5** Haiti **6** Belize, Canada, Mexico, Panama **7** Bahamas, Jamaica **8** Barbados, Honduras **9** Costa Rica, Guatemala, Nicaragua **10** El Salvador, Puerto Rico, Saint Lucia **12** Saint Vincent, United States **17** Dominican Republic, Trinidad and Tobago **28** Saint Vincent and the Grenadines
  desert: 6 Mojave **7** Painted, Sonoran **11** Death Valley
  island: 4 Long **6** Baffin, Cayman, Kodiak **7** Antigua, Bermuda, Iceland **8** Aleutian, Catalina, Thousand **9** Antilles, Greenland, Nantucket, Vancouver **10** Cape Breton **12** Newfoundland, Prince Edward **14** Queen Charlotte
  ocean/sea/bay: 6 Arctic, Baffin, Bering, Hudson, Mexico **7** Chukchi, Lincoln, Pacific **8** Amundsen, Atlantic, Beaufort, Labrador **9** Caribbean, Greenland **10** California, Chesapeake, St Lawrence
  river: 3 Red **4** Ohio **5** Peace, Snake, Yukon **6** Hudson **8** Arkansas, Colorado, Columbia, Missouri **9** Churchill, Mackenzie, Rio Grande **10** St Lawrence **11** Mississippi **12** Saskatchewan
  lake: 4 Erie **5** Huron **7** Ontario **8** Michigan, Superior, Winnipeg **9** Great Bear, Nicaragua **10** Great Lakes, Great Slave
  mountain range: 5 Ozark, Rocky **6** Alaska **7** Cascade **9** Blue Ridge **10** Laurentian **11** Appalachian, Sierra Madre **12** Sierra Nevada
  highest point: 13 Mount McKinley
  lowest point: 11 Death Valley
  city: 4 Nome **5** Miami **6** Boston, Dallas, Denver, Havana, Ottawa, Quebec **7** Atlanta, Calgary, Chicago, Detroit, Houston, Memphis, New York, Phoenix, Seattle, Toronto **8** Montreal, Portland, San Diego **9** Anchorage, Milwaukee, Reykjavik, Vancouver **10** Kansas City, Los Angeles, Mexico City, New Orleans, Washington **11** Philadelphia, San Antonio, San Francisco
  mineral: 3 oil, tin **4** coal, gold, lead, salt, zinc **6** cobalt, copper, nickel, quartz, silver **7** iron ore, mercury, sulphur, uranium **8** aluminum, antimony, asbestos, chromium, platinum, titanium, tungsten **9** magnesium, manganese, petroleum **10** molybdenum, natural gas
Northanger Abbey
  author: 10 Jane Austen
  character: 8 Mrs Allen **10** John Thorpe **12** James Morland **14** Isabella Thorpe **16** Catherine Morland

Tilney family: 5 Henry **7** Captain, Eleanor, General
North by Northwest
  director: 15 Alfred Hitchcock
  cast: 9 Cary Grant **10** James Mason **11** Leo G Carroll **12** Martin Landau **13** Eva Marie Saint **17** Jessie Royce Landis
  setting (climax): 13 Mount Rushmore
  score: 15 Bernard Herrmann
North Carolina
  abbreviation: 2 NC **4** N Car
  nickname: 7 Tar Heel **8** Old North **10** Turpentine
  capital: 7 Raleigh
  largest city: 9 Charlotte
  others: 4 Bath **6** Durham, Lenoir, Shelby, Wilson **7** Edenton, Hickory, Kinston, New Bern, Roxboro, Tarboro **8** Gastonia **9** Albemarle, Asheville, Goldsboro, Henderson, Kitty Hawk, Lumberton **10** Chapel Hill, Greensboro, Greenville, Kannapolis, Wilmington **11** Statesville, Thomasville, Williamston **12** Fayetteville, Jacksonville, Winston-Salem
  college: 4 Duke, Elon **7** Catawba **8** Davidson **10** Wake Forest
  feature:
    battle site: 18 Guilford Courthouse
    national park: 19 Great Smoky Mountains (with Tennessee)
    national seashore: 11 Cape Lookout **12** Cape Hatteras
  tribe: 3 Eno **5** Coree **6** Cheraw **7** Buffalo, Moratok, Pamlico **8** Chowanoc, Hatteras **9** Tuscarora
  people: 6 O Henry (William Sidney Porter) **7** tarheel **11** Billy Graham, Thomas Wolfe **13** Dolley (Dolly) Madison, Edward R Murrow **14** Richard Gatling
    explorer: 6 de Soto **8** de Ayllon **9** Verrazano
  island: 7 Roanoke
  lake: 6 Norman, Phelps **7** Fontana **8** Waccamaw **12** Mattamuskeet
  land rank: 12 twenty-eighth
  mountain: 5 Black, Unaka **6** Harris **9** Blue Ridge **10** Great Smoky **13** Clingman's Dome
    highest point: 8 Mitchell
  physical feature: 10 Outer Banks **11** French Broad **15** Little Tennessee
    cape: 4 Fear **7** Lookout **8** Hatteras
    plateau: 8 Piedmont
    sea: 8 Atlantic
    sound: 4 Core **5** Bogue **7** Croatan, Pamlico
    swamp: 6 Dismal
  president: 9 James Polk **13** Andrew Johnson
  river: 3 Haw, Tar **4** Fear **5** Neuse **6** Chowan, Lumber, Peedee, Yadkin **7** Roanoke, Wateree
  state admission: 7 twelfth
  state bird: 8 cardinal
  state fish: 11 channel bass

state flower: 7 dogwood **9** goldenrod
state motto: 20 To Be Rather Than To Seem
state song: 16 The Old North State
state tree: 4 pine
state dance: 4 shag
North Dakota
  abbreviation: 2 ND **4** N Dak
  nickname: 5 Sioux **11** Flickertail **16** Land of the Dakotas
  capital: 8 Bismarck
  largest city: 5 Fargo
  others: 5 Minot **9** Bottineau, Jamestown, Williston **10** Grand Forks
  college: 4 Mary **9** Jamestown
  feature:
    dam: 4 Oahe **8** Garrison
    garden: 18 International Peace
    national park: 17 Theodore Roosevelt
  tribe: 5 Sioux **6** Mandan **7** Arikara, Hidatsa **8** Chippewa
  people: 12 Eric Sevareid
    explorer: 6 Carver **8** Thompson, Varennes **13** Lewis and Clark
  lake: 5 Stump **6** Devils **9** Sakakawea
  land rank: 11 seventeenth
  mountain: 6 Turtle **8** Killdeer **10** Black Butte
    highest point: 10 White Butte
  physical feature:
    basin: 9 Williston
    plain: 8 The Slope
    valley: 8 Red River
  river: 3 Red **4** Park, Rush **5** Cedar, Goose, Heart, James, Knife, Mouse **6** Souris **7** Deslacs, Pembina **8** Missouri, Cheyenne, Wild Rice **9** Otter Tail **10** Cannonball **11** Yellowstone **12** Boise de Sioux **14** Little Missouri **18** Red River of the North
  state admission: 8 fortieth **11** thirty-ninth (with South Dakota)
  state bird: 17 western meadowlark
  state fish: 12 northern pike
  state flower: 15 wild prairie rose
  state motto: 45 Liberty and Union Now and Forever One and Inseparable
  state song: 15 North Dakota Hymn
  state tree: 11 American elm
North Dallas Forty
  director: 11 Ted Kotcheff
  based on story by: 9 Peter Gent
  cast: 8 Mac Davis **9** Nick Nolte **11** Dayle Haddon **14** Charles Durning
Northern Crown
  constellation of: 14 Corona Borealis
Northern Rhodesia *see* **6** Zambia
North Korea *see* **5** Korea
North Star State
  nickname of: 9 Minnesota
North Vietnam *see* **7** Vietnam
Northwest Passage
  director: 9 King Vidor
  author: 14 Kenneth Roberts
  cast: 10 Ruth Hussey **11** Robert

Young **12** Spencer Tracy **13** Walter Brennan

Northwest Territories
abbreviation: 3 NWT
borders: 7 Alberta **8** Manitoba **9** Baffin Bay, Hudson Bay **11** Arctic Ocean, Beaufort Sea, Labrador Sea **12** Saskatchewan **15** British Columbia
city: 6 Inuvik **8** Hay River **9** Fort Smith **11** Yellowknife **12** Frobisher Bay
country: 6 Canada
Inuit land: 7 Nunavut
island: 5 Banks, Devon **6** Baffin **7** Melville **8** Bathurst, Somerset, Victoria **9** Ellesmere **11** King William **13** Prince of Wales, Prince Patrick **14** Queen Elizabeth
mineral: 3 oil **4** gold, lead, zinc **6** silver **8** tungsten **9** petroleum
mountain: 21 Mount Sir James MacBrien
native: 5 Inuit **6** Eskimo
territory: 8 Franklin, Keewatin **9** Mackenzie

North wind
associated with: 6 Boreas

Norway
other name: 5 Norge **20** Land of the Midnight Sun
capital: 4 Oslo **11** Christiania
largest city: 4 Oslo
others: 3 Gol, Nes **4** Bodo, Moss, Odda, Rena, Voss **5** Bjort, Floro, Hamar, Molde, Skien, Skjak, Vadso **6** Bergen, Horton, Larvik, Narvik, Tromso **7** Alesund, Arendal, Drammen, Harstad, Sandnes **8** Aalesund, Kirkenes **9** Stavanger, Trondheim **10** Hammerfest **12** Kristiansand
division: 3 Amt **4** Oslo **5** Fylke, Troms **6** Bergen, Opland, Tromso **7** Finmark, Hedmark, Ostfold **8** Letemark, Nordland, Rogaland, Vestfold **9** Ostlandet
　former: 11 Kalmar Union
　province called: 6 fylker
government:
　legislature: 8 Storting
head of state: 4 king
measure: 3 fot, mal **4** alen **5** kande **6** fathom **7** skieppe **9** korntonde
monetary unit: 3 ore **5** krone
weight: 3 lod **4** mark, pund **10** bismerpund
island: 4 Vega **5** Bomlo, Donna, Froya, Hitra, Hopen, Senja, Smola, Soroy **6** Alsten, Averoy, Bouvet, Hinnoy, Karmoy, Kvaloy, Solund, Vannoy **7** Gurskoy, Lofoten, Mageroy, Seiland **8** Jan Mayen, Svalbard
lake: 4 Alte **5** Ister, Mjosa, Snasa **6** Femund **7** Rostavn, Tunnsjo
mountain: 5 Sogne **6** Kjolen **7** Numedal **8** Blodfjel, Snohetta, Telemark, Ustetind **9** Harteigen, Jotunheim, Langfjell, Ramnanosi **10** Dovrefjell, Galdhoepig, Glitretind, Vibmesnosi **11** Myrdalfjell **14** Aardangerjokul, Hallingskarvet, Skagastolstind
highest point: 12 Galdhopiggen **13** Glittertinden
river: 3 Ena **4** Alta, Klar, Otra, Rana, Tana, Teno **5** Bardu, Begna, Glama, Lagen, Orkla, Otter, Rauma, Reisa **6** Glomma, Lougen, Namsen, Pasvik
sea: 5 North **6** Arctic **7** Barents **8** Atlantic **9** Norwegian, Skagerrak
physical feature:
　cape: 4 Naze **7** Nordkyn **8** Nordkapp **9** Lindesnes
　fjord: 4 Oslo **5** Sogne
　glacier: 12 Jostedalsbre
　inlet: 2 Is **3** Kob, Ran **4** Alst, Ands, Bokn, Nord, Ofot, Salt, Sunn, Tyri, Vest **5** fiord, fjord, Folda, Lakse, Sogne **6** Bjorna, Hadsel **7** Hortens **9** Trondheim
　plateau: 5 Doure, Dovre, Fjeld **9** Hardanger
people: 4 Lapp **5** Samme **6** Nordic, Viking
　artist: 5 Munch
　author: 5 Ibsen **6** Hamsun, Undset **7** Holberg **8** Bjornson **9** Wergeland
　composer: 5 Grieg **7** Sinding **8** Svendsen
　explorer: 4 Eric, Leif, Mohn, Sars **6** Nansen **8** Amundsen
　explorer/statesman: 6 Nansen **8** Amundsen **8** Heyerdahl
　king: 4 Olaf, Olav **5** Olave, Oscar **6** Haakon, Harold, Magnus, Sverre
　mathematics: 4 Abel
　Nazi collaborator: 8 Quisling
　Norse god/goddess: 3 Sif, Tyr **4** Frey, Idun, Loki, Odin, Thor **5** Bragi, Freya, Hoder, Woden **6** Balder, Eostre, Frigga, Hermod
　sculptor: 8 Vigeland
language: 4 Lapp **5** Norse **6** Bokmal **7** Nynorsk, Riksmal **8** Landsmal, Samnorsk **9** Landsmaal, Norwegian
religion: 19 Evangelical Lutheran **22** National Church of Norway
place:
　castle: 8 Akershus
　cathedral: 7 Nidaras
　museum: 7 Kon Tiki **10** Viking Ship **15** Polar Expedition
　park: 7 Frogner
former colony: 7 Vinland
feature:
　dance: 6 gangar **7** halling **8** springar **9** spingleik
　literature form: 4 edda, saga
food:
　bread: 8 flat brod
　cheese: 3 Ost **7** gjetost **9** gammelost, Jarlsberg
　drink: 7 aquavit

Norwegian Mythology see **21** Scandinavian Mythology

nose
sense of: 5 smell
part: 7 nostril **14** olfactory patch
nosegay 4 posy **7** bouquet **10** tussymussy
nosiness 6 prying **9** curiosity **15** inquisitiveness
nostalgia 6 pining, regret **7** longing **11** remembrance **12** homesickness **13** regretfulness
Nostradamus
　name: 7 Michael **17** Michelde Notredame
　occupation: 7 prophet **9** physician **10** astrologer **13** metaphysicist
　wrote: 9 Centuries
Nostromo
　author: 12 Joseph Conrad
nostrum 4 balm, cure, dose, drug **5** draft **6** elixir, physic, potion, remedy **7** cure-all, formula, panacea **8** medicine **9** treatment **10** medicament **12** prescription
nosy, nosey 6 prying, snoopy **7** all ears, curious **8** snooping **9** intrusive **11** inquisitive, overcurious **13** eavesdropping
nota bene 8 note well **10** take notice
notability 4 fame **6** import, moment, renown **8** eminence **9** celebrity **10** importance, prominence **11** consequence, distinction, preeminence **12** significance
notable 3 VIP **4** name **5** famed, wheel **6** biggie, bigwig, famous, marked **7** eminent, salient **8** luminary, renowned, striking **9** celebrity, dignitary, personage, prominent, reputable **10** celebrated, pronounced, remarkable **11** conspicuous, outstanding, personality **13** distinguished
notably 7 visibly **8** markedly **10** distinctly, strikingly **11** prominently **12** unmistakably **13** conspicuously, outstandingly
not alike 8 distinct **9** different, differing, disparate, divergent **10** dissimilar **11** contrasting
notation 5 entry **10** memorandum
not bright 3 dim **4** dark, dull **5** dense, dusky, murky **6** cloudy, stupid **7** clouded **8** obscured **13** unilluminated
notch 3 cut **4** dent, mark, nick, nock **5** grade, level, score **6** degree **7** scoring, scratch **11** indentation
not disclosed
　Italian: 7 in petto
note 4 bill, fame, line, mark **5** bread, draft, enter, green, money, write **6** regard, renown **7** epistle, jot down, lettuce, message, missive, put down, scratch, set down, voucher **8** currency, dispatch, eminence, mark down, perceive **9** bank draft, celebrity, greenback **10** communique, importance, memorandum, prominence,

reputation **11** certificate, consequence, distinction

notebook 3 log **5** diary **6** record **7** journal **9** looseleaf
French: 6 cahier

noted 6 famous **7** eminent **8** renowned **9** prominent, reputable **10** celebrated, remarkable **11** illustrious, outstanding **13** distinguished

Notes from the Underground
author: 16 Fyodor Dostoevsky

note well
Latin: 8 nota bene

noteworthy 7 unusual **8** singular **9** important **10** remarkable **11** outstanding, significant, substantial **12** considerable **13** distinguished, exceptional

not far from 4 near **6** all but, almost, nearly **7** close to **8** not quite **13** approximately

not genuine 4 fake, sham **5** bogus, false, phony **6** ersatz, unreal **7** feigned **8** spurious **9** imitation, insincere, pretended, synthetic **10** artificial, fraudulent **11** counterfeit **12** hypocritical
Latin: 8 mala fide

not germane 9 extrinsic, unrelated **10** extraneous, immaterial, irrelevant **11** incongruous, inconsonant, unconnected **12** incompatible, nonessential **13** inappropriate

not guilty 3 clear **8** innocent **9** blameless **10** inculpable, unblamable

nothing 3 air, nix, zip **4** none, zero **5** stuff, trash, zilch **6** bauble, bubble, cipher, gewgaw, naught, trifle, trivia **7** duck egg, nullity, rubbish, trinket **8** goose egg **9** bagatelle, obscurity **14** insignificance **16** inconsequentials
Latin: 5 nihil

nothing is created from nothing
Latin: 16 ex nihilo nihil fit

nothingness 4 void **5** death **8** oblivion **9** emptiness **10** triviality **12** nonexistence **14** insignificance

Nothing Sacred
director: 14 William Wellman
cast: 13 Carole Lombard, Frederic March **14** Walter Connolly
score: 11 Oscar Levant
remade as: 10 Living It Up
script: 8 Ben Hecht

nothing unless it is good
Latin: 12 nil nisi bonum

nothing without the divine will
Latin: 13 nil sine numine
motto of: 8 Colorado

notice 3 eye, see **4** dope, heed, info, mark **5** goods **6** poster, rating, regard, review, take in **7** leaflet, mention, observe, warning **8** brochure, circular, critique, handbill, pamphlet **9** appraisal, attention, knowledge, statement **10** advisement, cognizance, disclosure **11** declaration, information

12 announcement, intelligence **13** advertisement, communication, specification

noticeable 5 clear, plain **7** evident, obvious **8** definite, distinct, manifest, palpable, striking **10** observable **11** appreciable, conspicuous, perceivable, perceptible **12** unmistakable

notification 4 news, word **6** advice, report **7** message, release **8** bulletin, dispatch **9** statement **10** communique **11** information **12** announcement, intelligence **13** communication

notify 4 tell, warn **6** advise, inform **7** apprise, let know **8** acquaint, send word **9** enlighten

not indigenous 5 alien **6** exotic **7** foreign **8** imported **9** nonnative **10** extraneous **11** naturalized

notion 4 idea, view, whim **5** fancy, humor, quirk **6** belief, vagary, whimsy **7** caprice, conceit, concept, opinion **8** crotchet **9** suspicion **10** conception, intimation **12** eccentricity

not native 5 alien **6** exotic **7** foreign **8** imported **10** extraneous **11** naturalized

not of sound mind
Latin: 15 non compos mentis

not ordinary 4 rare **6** exotic, unique **7** bizarre, foreign, strange, unusual **8** peculiar, singular, uncommon **9** anomalous, different, fantastic **11** distinctive, outstanding **14** unconventional

notoriety 4 blot **5** shame, stain **6** infamy, stigma **7** scandal **8** disgrace, dishonor, ignominy **9** discredit, disrepute **11** degradation

notorious 6 arrant **7** blatant, glaring **8** infamous, renowned **9** egregious **10** celebrated, outrageous **11** outstanding

Notorious
director: 15 Alfred Hitchcock
cast: 9 Cary Grant **11** Claude Rains **12** Louis Calhern **13** Ingrid Bergman

not pertinent 9 unrelated **10** extraneous, immaterial, irrelevant **11** incongruous, unconnected **13** inappropriate

not quite 6 all but, almost, nearly

Notre Dame 9 cathedral
style: 6 Gothic
location: 5 Paris
setting for: 20 Hunchback of Notre Dame
feature: 7 statues **9** gargoyles

not required 8 elective, optional **9** voluntary

not too seriously
Latin: 13 cum grano salis

Notus
origin: 5 Greek
personifies: 9 south wind

not wanted
French: 6 de trop

notwithstanding
Latin: 11 non obstante

not working 4 dead **8** inactive **10** unemployed **11** inoperative **12** unresponsive

Nouakchott
capital of: 10 Mauritania

Noumea
capital of: 12 New Caledonia

nourish 4 feed **5** nurse **6** suckle **7** nurture, sustain

nourishing 4 rich **6** hearty **7** healthy **9** fostering, nurturing, wholesome **10** nutritious, sustaining **11** maintaining **12** invigorating **13** strengthening

nourishment 4 chow, eats, food, grub, meat **5** bread **6** viands **8** victuals **9** nutriment, nutrition **10** sustenance **11** comestibles

nouveau riche 9 newly rich (person)

Novak, Kim
real name: 19 Marilyn Pauline Novak
born: 9 Chicago IL
roles: 6 Picnic **7** Pal Joey, Vertigo **14** Of Human Bondage **17** Bell Book and Candle **20** The Jeanne Eagels Story **22** The Man with the Golden Arm **31** Amorous Adventures of Moll Flanders

Nova Scotia
borders: 10 Bay of Fundy **12** New Brunswick **13** Atlantic Ocean **16** Gulf of St Lawrence **20** Northumberland Strait
city: 5 Truro **6** Sydney **7** Amherst, Halifax **8** Glace Bay, Yarmouth **9** Dartmouth **10** New Glasgow
country: 6 Canada
island: 10 Cape Breton
means: 11 New Scotland
mineral: 3 oil **4** lead, salt, sand, zinc **6** barite, gravel, gypsum, silver **9** celestite, petroleum **10** natural gas
mountain: 5 North **8** Cobequid
part of: 6 Acadia **12** Appalachians **17** Maritime Provinces **18** Atlantic Provinces
river: 4 Avon **5** Clyde **6** LaHave, Medway, Mersey **7** St Mary's **12** Shubenacadie

novel 3 new **6** unique **7** unusual **8** original, singular, uncommon **9** different **10** innovative, unorthodox **14** unconventional
French: 5 roman

novelty 5 token **6** bauble, change, gewgaw **7** memento, newness, trinket **8** gimcrack, souvenir, surprise **9** bagatelle, variation **10** innovation, knickknack, uniqueness **11** originality

November
event: 11 Election Day
flower: 13 chrysanthemum
French: 8 Novembre
gem: 5 topaz
German: 8 November
holiday: 11 All Souls' Day (2),

Veterans Day (11) **12** All Saints' Day (1), Guy Fawkes Day (5), Thanksgiving (4th Thursday)
Italian: 8 Novembre
number of days: 6 thirty
origin of name: 5 novem (Latin meaning nine)
place in year:
  Gregorian: 8 eleventh
  Roman: 5 ninth
Spanish: 9 Noviembre
Zodiac sign: 7 Scorpio **11** Sagittarius
novice 4 tyro **5** pupil **7** amateur, learner, student **8** beginner, disciple, newcomer **9** greenhorn **10** apprentice, tenderfoot

Novum Organum
  author: 12 Francis Bacon
novus ordo seclorum 24 a new order of the ages is born
  author: 6 Vergil, Virgil
  work: 8 Eclogues
  motto of: 11 US Great Seal

Now, Voyager
  director: 12 Irving Rapper
  cast: 10 Bette Davis **11** Claude Rains, Janis Wilson, Paul Henreid **12** Gladys Cooper
  score: 10 Max Steiner

now and then 8 on-and-off, periodic, sometime, sporadic **9** irregular, sometimes, temporary **10** infrequent, occasional **11** irregularly **12** infrequently, occasionally, periodically, sporadically

Nox, Nyx
  goddess of: 5 night
noxious 4 foul **6** deadly, lethal, putrid **7** baneful, beastly, harmful, hurtful, noisome **8** damaging, virulent **9** injurious, loathsome, poisonous, revolting **10** abominable, disgusting, pernicious, putrescent **11** deleterious **12** foul-smelling

nth degree 5 limit **6** utmost **7** extreme

nuance 5 shade, touch **6** nicety **7** finesse **8** delicacy, fineness, keenness, subtlety **9** sharpness, variation **10** modulation, refinement **11** discernment

nub 4 core, crux, gist, hump, knob, knot, lump, node **5** bulge, heart **6** kernel **7** essence **8** swelling **10** projection, prominence, tumescence **11** nitty-gritty **12** protuberance

nubbin 3 ear **4** corn, lump, stub **5** bulge, fruit, piece, stump **10** diminutive

Nubbles, Kit
  character in: 19 The Old Curiosity Shop
  author: 7 Dickens
nubbly 5 lumpy, rough **6** coarse, knobby, pebbly
nucleus 3 nub **4** core, pith, seed **5** heart **6** center, kernel

nude 3 raw **4** bare **5** bared, naked **6** unclad **7** exposed **8** in the raw, stripped **9** unadorned, unarrayed, unclothed, uncovered, undressed
  French: 9 au naturel
nudge 3 jab, jog, nod **4** bump, jolt, poke, prod, push **5** elbow, press, punch, shove, touch **6** jostle, motion, signal **8** indicate
nugatory 4 idle **5** empty **6** hollow, otiose, paltry **7** trivial, useless **8** piddling, trifling **9** meritless, valueless, worthless **10** profitless **11** ineffectual **12** functionless **15** inconsequential
nugget 4 hunk, lump **5** chunk, piece
nuisance 4 bore, fret, hurt, pain, pest **5** curse, thorn, worry **6** blight, bother, burden, plague **7** scourge, torment, trouble **8** handicap, vexation **9** annoyance, grievance **10** affliction, irritation, misfortune, pestilence **11** aggravation, botheration **13** inconvenience

Nuk
  capital of: 9 Greenland

Nukualofa
  capital of: 5 Tonga

null 2 NG **4** void **6** no good **7** invalid **9** valueless, worthless **10** immaterial **11** inoperative, nonexistent, unimportant **13** insignificant
nullification 6 repeal **7** voiding **8** recision **9** abolition, annulment **10** abrogation, rescinding **11** abolishment **12** cancellation, invalidation
nullify 4 veto, void **5** annul **6** cancel, repeal, revoke **7** abolish, rescind, retract **8** abrogate, make void, override, set aside **10** invalidate
nullity 6 cipher, naught **7** nothing **9** nonentity
numb 4 dead **6** frozen **8** deadened **9** insensate, unfeeling **10** insensible, narcotized **12** anesthetized
number 3 mob, sum, tot **4** army, bevy, book, herd, host, mass, part **5** array, bunch, count, crowd, digit, group, issue, swarm, tally, total **6** amount, cipher, figure, reckon, scores, symbol **7** chapter, company, compute, edition, foliate, integer, numeral, passage, section **8** division, estimate, magazine, numerate, paginate, quantity **9** abundance, aggregate, calculate, character, enumerate, multitude, paragraph, quarterly **10** assemblage, quantities **13** preponderance

numbered numbered weighed divided
  Aramaic: 21 mene mene tekel upharsin
  called: 16 writing on the wall
  foretells destruction of: 10 Belshazzar
  Biblical book of: 6 Daniel
numberless 6 myriad **7** copious, umpteen **8** unending, zillions **9** countless, plenteous, unbounded, uncounted

11 illimitable, uncountable **12** immeasurable **13** multitudinous
numbness 8 deadness **11** insentience
numeral 5 digit **6** cipher, figure, letter, number, symbol **7** integer **9** character
numerate 3 add **5** count, tally, total **6** number, reckon **7** compute, tick off **9** calculate
numerophobia
  fear of: 7 numbers
numerous 4 many **6** myriad **7** copious, profuse **8** abundant **9** plentiful **13** multitudinous
Numidia see **7** Algeria
Numipu see **8** Nez Perce
Numitor
  king of: 9 Alba Longa
  father: 5 Proca
  brother: 7 Amulius
  daughter: 10 Rhea Silvia
  grandson: 5 Remus **7** Romulus
numskull, numbskull 3 sap **4** dolt, dope, fool, jerk **5** dummy, dunce, idiot, klutz, ninny **6** dimwit, nitwit **7** dullard, half-wit **8** bonehead, dummkopf, imbecile, lunkhead, silly ass **9** blockhead, simpleton **10** dunderhead, muttonhead, nincompoop, noodlehead **11** chowderhead, knucklehead **12** scatterbrain
Nun see **4** Nunu
nuncio 5 envoy **6** legate **8** diplomat, minister **9** messenger **10** ambassador **11** papallegate **14** representative
nunnery 5 abbey, order **6** priory **7** cenacle, convent **8** cloister **9** hermitage, monastery **10** sisterhood
Nun's Story, The
  director: 12 Fred Zinneman
  based on story by: 12 Kathryn Hulme
  cast: 10 Dean Jagger, Edith Evans, Peter Finch **13** Audrey Hepburn, Peggy Ashcroft **15** Colleen Dewhurst
Nunu
  also: 3 Nun
  origin: 8 Egyptian
  god of: 5 ocean
  personifies: 5 chaos
nuptial 7 marital **8** conjugal, hymeneal **9** connubial **11** matrimonial
nuptials 7 wedding **8** marriage **9** espousals, hymeneals **12** matrimonials
Nurmi, Paavo
  nickname: 13 The Flying Finn
  sport: 5 track
  won: 8 Olympics
nurse 4 feed **5** nanny, treat **6** attend, doctor, foster, harbor, remedy, sister, succor, suckle **7** care for, nourish, nurture, promote **8** attend to, guardian **9** attendant, cultivate, encourage, governess
  Hindi/Indian: 4 ayah
  Orient: 4 amah

famous: 11 Edith Cavell, Sister Kenny **19** Florence Nightingale

nursery 6 hotbed **9** incubator, preschool **10** greenhouse, schoolroom **12** conservatory, kindergarten

nursery rhyme character 3 Tom **4** Jack, Jill, Mary **5** Peter, Polly **6** Bo-Peep **8** King Cole **9** Jack Sprat **10** Jack Horner, Miss Muffet **11** Mother Goose **12** Humpty Dumpty **13** Little Boy Blue, Mother Hubbard

nurture 4 feed, mess, rear, tend **5** breed, raise, teach, train, tutor **6** foster, school **7** bring up, develop, educate, nourish, prepare, sustain, victual **8** instruct, maintain **9** cultivate, provision **10** discipline, strengthen

Nusantara *see* **9** Indonesia

nut 3 fan, pit **4** buff, seed **5** freak, idiot, loony, stone **6** madman, maniac, zealot **7** devotee, fanatic, lunatic, oddball **8** crackpot **9** eccentric, screwball **10** aficionado, enthusiast, psychopath **11** afficionado

Nut
  origin: 8 Egyptian
  goddess of: 3 sky

nut-brown 5 tawny **6** auburn, brunet **8** brunette, cinnamon

Nutcracker, The
  also: 13 Shchelkunchik
  ballet by: 11 Tchaikovsky
  based on fairy tale by: 11 ETA Hoffmann
  contains: 17 Waltz of the Flowers **24** Dance of the Sugarplum Fairy
  characters: 4 mice **5** Clara, Fritz **6** prince **10** nutcracker **11** toy soldiers **12** Drosselmeyer **14** Sugarplum Fairy

nutmeg
  botanical name: 17 Myristica fragrans
  from same plant as: 4 mace
  origin: 9 Indonesia
  use: 5 punch **6** eggnog **8** desserts **10** vegetables **11** baked dishes

Nutmeg State
  nickname of: 11 Connecticut

nutriment 4 chow, eats, fare, feed, food, meat, mess **5** board **6** fodder, forage **7** aliment, edibles **8** eatables, victuals **9** foodstuff, groceries, provender **10** provisions, sustenance **11** nourishment, subsistence

nutrition 4 chow, feed, food, grub **6** fodder, forage, silage **7** edibles, rations **8** eatables **9** groceries, pasturage, provender **10** foodstuffs, provisions, sustenance **11** nourishment, subsistence

nutritious 9 wholesome **10** nourishing, sustaining

nuts 3 mad **4** bats, daft **5** balmy, crazy, dotty, loony, potty, wacko, wacky **6** insane **7** bananas, bonkers, cracked, touched **8** demented, deranged, unhinged **10** unbalanced

nutty 3 mad **4** daft **5** balmy, crazy, dippy, dotty, goofy, inane, loony, silly, wacko, wacky **6** cuckoo, insane, screwy, weirdo **7** bonkers, cracked, foolish, lunatic, meshuga, touched **8** bughouse, demented **9** senseless **10** addlepated, squirrelly **11** harebrained **12** crackbrained

nuzzle 3 pat, pet **4** buss, kiss **5** smack **6** caress, coddle, cosset, cuddle, fondle, nestle **7** embrace, snuggle

Nyasaland *see* **6** Malawi

nyctophobia
  fear of: 8 darkness **14** the dark of night

nyet
  Russian: 2 no

nymph 5 belle, dryad, houri, naiad, nixie, oread, sylph **6** beauty, daphne, kelpie, maenad, nereid, ondine, sprite, undine **7** charmer, galatea **8** Eurydice **9** hamadryad

Nymphaea
  epithet of: 9 Aphrodite
  means: 6 bridal

Nyx, Nox
  form: 7 goddess
  personifies: 5 night
  originated from: 5 Chaos
  children: 3 Ker **4** Eris **5** Fates, Geras, Momus, Moros, Oiayo **6** Aether, Hemera, Hypnos, Somnus **7** Nemesis, Oneiroi **8** Thanatos

  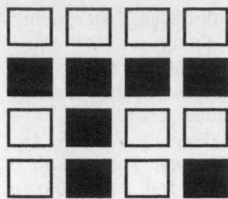

O

oaf 3 sap **4** boob, boor, clod, dolt, dope, fool, jerk, lout **5** booby, dummy, dunce, idiot, klutz, moron, ninny **6** lummox, nitwit **7** dullard, half-wit **8** bonehead, imbecile, numskull **9** blockhead, ignoramus, numbskull, simpleton **10** dunderhead, nincompoop

oafish 4 rude **5** crude **6** coarse, gauche, vulgar **7** boorish, doltish, loutish, uncouth **9** unrefined **10** unpolished

oak 7 Quercus

   varieties: 3 bur, cow, pin, red, she **4** bear, blue, cork, deer, Holm, jack, live, maul, post, silk **5** black, Emory, holly, scrub, ubame, water, white **6** basket, Belote, canyon, Ceylon, Daimyo, gambel, gander, Havard, Indian, island, Kermes, Konara, laurel, Oregon, poison, possum, Turkey, Turner, valley, willow, yellow **7** Ballota, Bartram, Belloot, Catesby, Durmast, English, Georgia, Italian, Kellogg, leather, Lebanon, overcup, scarlet, shingle, Spanish, tanbark, truffle, western **8** Arkansas, bluejack, chestnut, McDonald, mossy-cup, shinnery, Texas red **9** blackjack, Engelmann, flowering, Jerusalem, Mongolian, pubescent, swamp post **10** Chinquapin, Darlington, ring-cupped, Spanish red, swamp white **11** huckleberry, Japanese red, northern pin, northern red, Shumard's red **12** interior live, laurel-leaved, rock chestnut, southern live, yellow-barked **13** dwarf chestnut, oriental white, swamp chestnut **14** Austrian turkey, California live, yellow chestnut **15** California black, California field, California scrub, California white **16** high- ground willow **17** Japanese evergreen **18** Rocky Mountain scrub

   venerated by: 6 Druids

Oak, Gabriel

   character in: 22 Far From the Madding Crowd

   author: 5 Hardy

Oakie, Jack

   real name: 19 Lewis Delaney Offield

   born: 9 Sedalia (Sadalia) MO

   roles: 16 The Great Dictator **17** Alice in Wonderland

Oakland

baseball team: 2 A's **9** Athletics

football team: 8 Invaders

oar 3 row **4** pole **5** blade, rower, scull **6** paddle, propel **9** propeller

   blade: 4 palm, peel

   fulcrum: 5 thole **7** oarlock, rowlock

   part: 4 loom **5** shaft **6** collar

oarsman 5 pilot, rower **6** bowman **7** mariner, sculler **8** helmsman **9** gondolier, propeller

oasis 5 haven **6** asylum, harbor, refuge **7** retreat, sanctum, shelter **9** green spot, sanctuary, water hole **11** fertile area **13** watering place

oast 4 kiln, oven

oat, oats 5 Avena **11** Avena sativa

   varieties: 3 sea **4** wild **6** potato **8** animated **9** Tartarian **11** slender wild

Oates, Joyce Carol

   author of: 4 Them **9** Childwold **10** Bellefleur, Wonderland **11** Unholy Loves, Wheel of Love **15** Son of the Morning **18** A Bloodsmoor Romance **19** Do With Me What You Will

oath 3 vow **5** curse **6** avowal, pledge **8** cuss word, swearing **9** affidavit, blasphemy, expletive, obscenity, profanity **10** adjuration, deposition **11** affirmation, attestation, declaration, imprecation, malediction

oaths

   god of: 6 Horcus, Sancus **10** Dius Fidius, Semo Sancus

oatmeal 6 cereal **7** pottage **8** drammock, porridge

Obadiah 4 Obad **7** prophet **12** minor prophet

   father: 4 Azel **6** Jehiel **8** Izrahiah, Shemaiah

   son: 8 Ishmaiah

   predicted fall of: 4 Edom

Obata, Gyo

   architect of: 20 Dallas--Ft Worth Airport **25** National Air and Space Museum (Smithsonian Institution)

obdurate 5 cruel, harsh **6** mulish **7** adamant, callous, unmoved, willful **8** hardened, pitiless, stubborn, uncaring **9** immovable, merciless, obstinate, pigheaded, unfeeling, unpitying, unsparing, untouched **10** bullheaded, headstrong, inflexible, unmerciful, unyielding **11** cold-blooded, hardhearted, intractable **12** ungovernable, unmanageable **13** unsympathetic **14** uncontrollable **15** uncompassionate

obeah 5 charm, magic **6** fetish, voodoo **7** sorcery **10** witchcraft

   practiced in: 6 Guiana **10** West Indies

obedience 8 docility, yielding **9** deference, ductility, obeisance **10** accordance, allegiance, compliance, subjection, submission **11** conformance, dutifulness, willingness **12** acquiescence, subservience, tractability **14** conformability, submissiveness

obedient 5 loyal **6** docile **7** devoted, dutiful **8** amenable, faithful, obeisant, yielding **9** compliant, tractable **10** governable, law-abiding, respectful, submissive **11** acquiescent, deferential, subservient

obeisance 3 bow **5** honor **6** curtsy, esteem, fealty, homage, regard **7** loyalty, respect **8** courtesy, fidelity, humility, kneeling **9** deference, obedience, reverence **10** allegiance, humbleness, subjection, submission, veneration **11** prostration **12** genuflection **13** self-abasement

obelisk 5 pylon, shaft, tower **6** column, dagger, needle, pillar **8** memorial, monolith, monument

Oberon

   character in: 21 A Midsummer Night's Dream

   author: 11 Shakespeare

   consort: 7 Titania

Oberon

   opera by: 5 Weber

   character: 5 Reiza

   setting: 18 court of Charlemagne **21** court of Haroun al Rashid

Oberon, Merle

   real name: 26 Estelle Merle O'Brien Thompson

   husband: 14 Alexander Korda

   born: 8 Tasmania

   roles: 5 Hotel **7** Desiree **15** A Song to Remember **16** Wuthering Heights **19** The Scarlet Pimpernel **25** The Private Life of Henry VIII **30** The Private Life of Henry the Eighth

obese 3 fat **5** gross, heavy, plump, porky, pudgy, stout, tubby **6** chubby, fleshy, portly, rotund **7** paunchy **9** corpulent **10** overweight, potbellied

obesity 3 fat **7** fatness, liposis **8** adiposis, enormity **9** heaviness, plumpness, stoutness **10** corpulence, overweight

obey 4 heed, mind 5 bow to, serve 6 assent, concur 7 abide by, observe, respect, yield to 8 accede to, submit to 9 acquiesce, conform to, succumb to 10 comply with, toe the line 12 follow orders

obfuscate 4 blur 5 befog 6 garble, mess up, muddle 7 becloud, confuse, distort, fluster, obscure, stupefy 8 confound, scramble 10 complicate

obfuscation 8 flummery 9 confusion 10 doubletalk, mumbo jumbo

obi 4 sash 5 obeah 6 girdle

obiit 6 he died 7 she died

obiter dictum 9 diversion 10 digression, divagation, side remark

object 3 aim, end, use 4 body, butt, dupe, form, gist, goal, pith, prey 5 abhor, basis, cause, knock, point, sense, thing 6 balk at, carp at, design, device, dingus, gadget, intent, loathe, motive, oppose, quarry, reason, target, victim 7 article, cavil at, condemn, dislike, essence, frown on, meaning, mission, protest, purpose, subject 8 be averse, cynosure, denounce 9 abominate, criticize, doohickey, incentive, intention, objective, principle, recipient, substance 10 inducement, phenomenon 11 contrivance, explanation, thingamabob, thingamajig 12 be at odds with, disapprove of, significance 13 find fault with, take exception 18 remonstrate against

objection 4 beef, kick 5 cavil 7 protest 8 demurral, rebuttal 9 challenge, complaint, criticism, exception 10 dissension, opposition 11 disapproval, reservation 12 disagreement 13 contradiction 14 disapprobation, opposing reason 15 counter argument

objectionable 4 foul, vile 5 nasty 6 odious 8 unseemly 9 abhorrent, loathsome, obnoxious, offensive, revolting 10 abominable, despicable, disgusting, unbearable, unpleasant 11 displeasing, distasteful, intolerable, unendurable 12 disagreeable, unacceptable 13 inappropriate

objective 3 aim, end 4 fair, goal, just, mark, real 6 actual, design, intent, target 7 mission, purpose 8 detached, unbiased, unswayed 9 impartial, intention, uncolored 10 impersonal, open-minded 11 destination 12 uninfluenced, unprejudiced 13 disinterested, dispassionate

objectivity 8 fairness 10 detachment, neutrality 12 impartiality

object to 7 condemn, dislike 9 frown upon 12 disapprove of 14 discountenance 15 take exception to 16 find unacceptable

objet d'art 5 bijou, curio 7 bibelot, trinket 9 art object

oblation 4 gift 8 offering 9 offertory 10 collection

obligated 5 bound 6 forced, liable 7 pledged 8 beholden, indebted 9 committed 11 constrained

obligation 4 bond, care, debt, duty, oath, onus, word 6 charge, pledge 7 compact, promise 8 contract, guaranty, warranty 9 agreement, guarantee, liability 10 a favor owed, commitment, constraint 12 indebtedness 13 answerability, understanding 14 accountability, responsibility

obligatory 7 binding 8 coercive, enforced, required 9 mandatory, necessary, requisite 10 compulsory, imperative, peremptory 11 unavoidable

oblige 3 aid 4 bind, help, make 5 favor, force, impel, serve 6 assist, coerce, compel 7 require, support 8 obligate 9 constrain 11 accommodate, do a favor for, necessitate 13 do a service for, to be duty bound

obliged 5 bound 7 favored, pleased 8 assisted, beholden, indebted, required, thankful 9 compelled 12 accommodated

obliging 4 kind 6 polite 7 amiable, helpful 8 cheerful, friendly, gracious 9 agreeable, courteous 10 solicitous 11 complaisant, considerate, cooperative, good-natured, sympathetic 12 well-disposed 13 accommodating

oblique 3 sly 4 awry 5 askew 6 aslant, covert, hinted, masked, tilted, veiled 7 cloaked, devious, furtive, implied, slanted, sloping 8 allusive, diagonal, inclined, indirect, slanting, sneaking 9 suggested, underhand

obliterate 4 raze 5 erase, level 6 cancel, delete, efface, remove, rub out 7 abolish, blot out, destroy, expunge, wipe out 9 eradicate, write over 10 annihilate, strike over

obliteration 8 deletion 9 abolition, expunging, wiping out 11 blotting out, destruction, eradication 12 annihilation

oblivion 5 limbo 7 the void 9 blankness, disregard, obscurity, unconcern 11 blotting out, nothingness 12 nonexistence 13 forgetfulness, insensibility, obliviousness 14 insignificance 15 unconsciousness

oblivious 8 careless 9 forgetful, unaware of, unmindful 10 heedless of, insensible 11 inattentive, unconcerned, unobservant 12 disregardful, undiscerning 13 unconscious of

Oblonsky, Prince Stepan
character in: 12 Anna Karenina
author: 7 Tolstoy

obloquy 5 abuse, odium, shame 6 infamy, rebuke 7 calumny, censure, railing 8 contempt, disfavor, disgrace, ignominy, reviling 9 discredit, invective 10 defamation, opprobrium, scurrility 11 degradation, humiliation, verbal abuse 12 billingsgate, condemnation, denunciation, dressing-down, vilification

obnoxious 4 foul, vile 5 nasty 6 odious 7 hateful 8 unseemly 9 abhorrent, loathsome, offensive, repellent, repugnant, revolting 10 abominable, despicable, detestable, disgusting, nauseating, unbearable, unpleasant 11 displeasing, intolerable, unendurable 12 disagreeable, insufferable 13 inappropriate, objectionable

oboe family
instruments: 5 shawm 6 curtal, pommer, racket 7 bassoon, bombard, curtall, hautboy 8 crumhorn, schalmey, tenoroon 10 Cor Anglais, oboe d'Amore 11 English horn, heckelphone, sarusophone 12 oboe da caccia, sarrusophone 13 contra bassoon, double bassoon

O'Brian, Hugh
real name: 11 Hugh J Krampe
born: 11 Rochester NY
roles: 9 Wyatt Earp 27 The Life and Legend of Wyatt Earp

O'Brien, Edna
author of: 5 Night 11 A Pagan Place 13 The Lonely Girl 14 The Country Girl 20 August Is a Wicked Month 24 Girls in Their Married Bliss

O'Brien, Margaret
real name: 18 Angela Maxine O'Brien
born: 12 Los Angeles CA
roles: 8 Jane Eyre 11 Little Women 15 Meet Me in St Louis 24 Our Vines Have Tender Grapes

O'Brien, Pat
real name: 26 William Joseph Patrick O'Brien
born: 11 Milwaukee WI
roles: 12 Hildy Johnson, The Front Page 13 Some Like It Hot, The Last Hurrah 20 Angels with Dirty Faces 22 Knute Rockne All American
autobiography: 12 Wind on My Back

obscene 4 blue, foul, lewd 5 bawdy, dirty 6 filthy, smutty, vulgar, x-rated 8 indecent, prurient 9 salacious 10 lascivious, lubricious 12 pornographic, scatological 16 morally offensive

obscenity 8 cuss word, lewdness 9 dirtiness, indecency, profanity, prurience, swear word, taboo word, vulgarity 10 filthiness, smuttiness 11 pornography 13 salaciousness 14 four-letter word, lasciviousness

obscuration 7 eclipse, masking, veiling 8 cloaking, clouding, covering 9 darkening, shadowing 10 concealing 11 concealment

obscure 3 dim, fog 4 blur, dark, hide, mask, veil 5 bedim, befog, block, cloak, cloud, cover, dingy, dusky, faint, murky, vague 6 cloudy, darken, hidden, muddle, screen, shadow, shroud, somber, unsung 7 becloud, conceal, confuse, cryptic, curtain, eclipse, shadowy, unclear, unknown, unnoted **8** befuddle, confused, disguise, nameless, puzzling **9** confusing, enigmatic, forgotten, lightless, obfuscate, uncertain, unheard of, unlighted **10** indefinite, indistinct, overshadow, perplexing, unrenowned **11** indefinable, inscrutable, little known, out-of-the-way, unimportant **12** unfathomable **13** inconspicuous, insignificant, unilluminated **15** inconsequential

obscurity 3 fog **4** mist **5** cloud, shade **6** shadow **7** dimness, mystery, opacity, privacy **8** darkness **9** ambiguity, seclusion, vagueness **10** cloudiness

obsequies 5 rites **6** burial **7** funeral **15** memorial service

obsequious 6 menial **7** fawning, servile, slavish **8** cowering, cringing, toadying **9** kowtowing, truckling **11** bootlicking, deferential, subservient, sycophantic **12** ingratiating, mealy-mouthed **14** apple-polishing

observance 4 rite **6** custom, regard, ritual **7** heeding, keeping, obeying **8** ceremony, practice **9** adherence, attending, attention, following, formality, solemnity **10** ceremonial, compliance **11** celebration, observation **13** commemoration **15** memorialization

observant 5 alert, awake, aware **7** careful, heedful, mindful **8** vigilant, watchful **9** attentive, conscious, regardful, wide-awake **10** perceptive **12** on the lookout

observation 4 heed, idea, view **5** probe **6** eyeing, notice, remark, search, seeing, survey, theory **7** comment, finding, opinion, viewing **8** interest, judgment, scrutiny, spotting, watching **9** assertion, attention, beholding, detection, diagnosis, discovery, glimpsing, observing, statement **10** cognizance, commentary, inspection, reflection **11** description, examination, heedfulness **12** surveillance, watchfulness **13** pronouncement **20** firsthand information

observatory 5 tower **7** lookout **9** satellite **11** planetarium
name: **4** Hale, Lick **6** Yerkes **7** Palomar, Whipple **8** Kitt Peak, Mt Wilson **11** Las Campanas, Mount Wilson **12** Big Bear Solar **14** Royal Greenwich

observe 3 eye, say, see **4** espy, heed, keep, mark, note, obey, ogle, spot, view **5** honor, opine, state, watch **6** assert, behold, detect, follow, notice, peer at, regard, remark, size up, survey **7** abide by, comment, declare, defer to, execute, fulfill, glimpse, inspect, make out, mention, perform, reflect, respect, stare at **8** adhere to, announce, carry out, discover, perceive, sanctify, theorize **9** celebrate, recognize, solemnize **10** be guided by,

comply with, consecrate **11** acknowledge, acquiesce to, commemorate, take stock of **12** catch sight of **14** pay attention to

observer 6 viewer **7** watcher **8** onlooker **12** investigator

obsessed 5 beset **7** haunted **8** hung up on, maniacal **9** dominated, possessed **10** controlled **15** having a fixation

obsession 5 craze, mania, quirk **6** phobia **8** fixation **9** fixed idea, monomania **11** infatuation **13** preoccupation **16** overwhelming fear **18** neurotic conviction

obsolescent 8 dying out **9** declining **11** on the way out **12** disappearing **16** becoming obsolete **17** becoming out-of-date

obsolete 3 out **5** dated, passe **6** bygone **7** antique, archaic, extinct **8** outdated, out of use, outmoded **9** out-of-date **10** antiquated **12** old-fashioned, out of fashion

obstacle 3 bar **4** curb, snag **5** block, catch, check **6** hurdle **7** barrier, problem **8** blockade, stoppage **9** barricade, hindrance, roadblock **10** difficulty, impediment, limitation **11** obstruction, restriction **12** interference **14** stumbling block

obstetrician
French: **10** accoucheur

obstinacy 8 rigidity **10** mulishness, resistance **11** willfulness **12** stubbornness **13** inflexibility, intransigence, pigheadedness

obstinate 6 dogged, mulish **7** staunch, willful **8** obdurate, resolute, stubborn **9** pigheaded, steadfast, tenacious, unbending **10** headstrong, inflexible, refractory, self-willed, unyielding **11** intractable **12** recalcitrant, ungovernable, unmanageable **14** uncontrollable **20** unreasonably stubborn

obstreperous 4 loud **5** noisy **6** unruly **8** perverse **9** clamorous, rampaging **10** boisterous, disorderly, refractory, roistering, uproarious, vociferous **11** disobedient **12** uncontrolled, ungovernable, unmanageable, unrestrained **14** uncontrollable

obstruct 3 bar **4** curb, halt, hide, mask, stop **5** block, check, cloak, close, cover, dam up, debar, delay, limit, stall **6** arrest, hinder, hobble, impede, plug up, retard, shroud, stifle, thwart **7** eclipse, inhibit, shut off **8** blockade, choke off, close off, restrict, suppress, throttle **9** barricade, frustrate **18** bring to a standstill

obstruction 3 bar **4** curb, snag, stop **5** block, check, hitch **6** hurdle **7** barrier **8** blockade, obstacle, stoppage **9** barricade, hindrance **10** bottleneck, impediment **11** encumbrance

obtain 3 get **4** earn, gain, hold, take

5 exist, glean, stand **6** attain, come by, gather, pick up, secure **7** achieve, acquire, prevail, procure, receive **9** get hold of **14** get one's hands on **16** gain possession of

obtainment 11 achievement, acquirement, acquisition, procurement

obtrude 5 eject, expel, force **6** butt in, impose, meddle, thrust **7** presume, project **9** interfere

obtrusive 4 nosy **5** brash **6** prying, snoopy **7** bulging, forward, salient **8** familiar, meddling **9** intruding, intrusive, prominent **10** aggressive, jutting out, meddlesome, projecting, protruding **11** conspicuous, impertinent, interfering, outstanding, protuberant, sticking out, trespassing **12** interrupting, presumptuous

obtuse 4 dull, slow **5** blunt, dense, thick **6** simple, stupid **7** blunted **8** ignorant, not sharp **9** unpointed **10** insensible, not pointed, slow-witted **11** insensitive, unsharpened **12** imperceptive, thick skinned **15** uncomprehending

obtuseness 8 dullness **9** denseness, ignorance, stupidity **13** insensitivity **14** slow-wittedness **15** thick-headedness **16** lack of perception, simplemindedness **19** lack of comprehension

obverse 4 face **5** front **10** complement **11** counterpart
of coin: **4** head

obviate 5 avert, avoid, parry **6** divert, remove **7** fend off, prevent, ward off **8** preclude, stave off **9** forestall, sidetrack, turn aside **10** circumvent, do away with **11** nip in the bud

obvious 5 clear, plain **6** patent **7** evident, glaring, visible **8** apparent, distinct, man- ifest, palpable, striking, unhidden, unmasked, unveiled **10** undeniable **11** conspicuous, discernible, perceptible, self-evident, unconcealed, undisguised **12** in plain sight, unmistakable **24** plain as the nose on your face

ocarina 11 sweet potato **14** wind instrument

O'Casey, Sean
author of: **10** Purple Dust **12** The Green Crow **17** Juno and the Paycock **18** The Shadow of a Gunman **20** The Plough and the Stars

occasion 4 base, time **5** basis, cause, event **6** advent, affair, chance, elicit, ground, lead to, motive, prompt, reason **7** episode, grounds, inspire, opening, provoke, venture **8** incident, instance **9** adventure, happening, rationale, situation **10** bring about, experience, motivation, occurrence **11** celebration, explanation, opportunity, provocation **12** circumstance, special event, suitable time **13** justification,

opportune time
14 convenient time, important event, particular time

occasional 4 rare **6** fitful, random **8** sporadic, uncommon **9** irregular, recurring, scattered, spasmodic, uncertain **10** incidental, infrequent, now and then, unreliable **12** intermittent

occasionally 6 rarely, seldom **7** at times **8** fitfully **9** sometimes **10** now and then **11** irregularly **12** infrequently, once in a while, periodically, sporadically **14** from time to time, intermittently **15** every now and then, once in a blue moon

occidental 7 Western **8** American, European **9** Hesperian, Westerner

occlude 4 clog, plug **5** block, choke, close **6** shut up, stop up **7** congest, shut off, stopper **8** choke off, obstruct **9** barricade, constrict **11** strangulate

occult 4 dark **5** magic **6** arcane, hidden, mystic, secret, veiled **7** obscure, private **8** esoteric, mystical, shrouded **9** concealed **10** cabalistic, mysterious, unrevealed **11** undisclosed **12** supernatural

occupancy 3 use **6** tenure **7** tenancy **8** lodgment **9** enjoyment, habitancy **10** engagement, habitation, occupation, possession **11** inhabitancy

occupant 5 owner **6** lessee, lodger, native, renter, roomer, tenant **7** dweller, settler **8** colonist, occupier, resident **9** addressee **10** inhabitant **11** householder

occupation 3 job **4** line, work **5** craft, forte, trade **6** career, living, metier, sphere **7** calling, control, pursuit, seizure **8** activity, business, capacity, conquest, lifework, vocation **9** specialty **10** employment, line of work, livelihood, possession, profession, subjection **11** foreign rule, subjugation **14** specialization **15** military control **18** military occupation

occupied 5 in use **6** amused, took up, used up **7** dwelt in, engaged, lived in, overran, overrun, taken up **8** absorbed, tenanted **9** concerned, conquered, inhabited, resided in **12** had control of, held in thrall **13** was situated in **16** took possession of

occupy 3 use **4** be in, be on, busy, fill, hold **5** amuse, sit in **6** absorb, employ, engage, fill up, room in, take up **7** concern, conquer, dwell in, engross, enslave, inhabit, lodge in, overrun, pervade, possess **8** permeate, reside in, saturate **9** entertain, subjugate **10** monopolize **11** have control **12** be situated in, hold in thrall **14** be the tenants of **16** take possession of

occur 3 hit **4** rise **5** arise, ensue **6** appear, befall, crop up, emerge, happen, result, strike, turn up **7** be found, come off, develop **8** spring up **9** come

about, eventuate, take place, transpire **10** come to pass **11** materialize **13** cross one's mind, enter one's mind

occurrence 5 event **6** affair **7** episode, venture **8** business, incident, instance, occasion **9** adventure, emergence, happening, situation, unfolding **10** appearance, experience, proceeding **11** development, transaction **12** circumstance **13** manifestation **15** materialization

ocean 3 sea **4** deep, main, pond **5** flood, water **7** big pond, high sea **9** briny deep
   god of: 3 Nun **4** Nanu **7** Neptune, Oceanus **8** Poseidon

Oceania, Oceanica 9 Melanesia, Polynesia **10** Micronesia **11** Australia
   ocean: 12 South Pacific
   island: 4 Cook, Guam, Fiji, Maui, Niue, Wake **5** Aunuu, Bonin, Kauai, Lanai, Tonga **6** Bikini, Futuna, Hawaii, Marcus, Midway, Rurutu, Tahiti, Tubuai, Tuvalu, Wallis **7** Gambier, Gilbert, Iwo Jima, Leeward, Mariana, Molokai, Phoenix, Solomon, Tokelau, Tuamotu, Tutuila, Vanuatu, Volcano **8** Aitu taki, Bismarck, Bora-Bora, Johnston, Kiribati, Marshall, Pitcairn, Windward **9** Australia, Christmas, Marquesas, Trobriand **10** New Zealand **12** New Caledonia, Western Samoa **14** Papua New Guinea **15** French Polynesia

oceanic 6 marine **7** aquatic, pelagic **8** seagoing **9** thalassic

Oceanid
   form: 5 nymph
   location: 3 sea
   father: 7 Oceanus
   mother: 6 Tethys

Oceanus
   member of: 6 Titans
   father: 6 Uranus
   mother: 4 Gaea
   consort of: 6 Tethys
   father of: 8 Oceanids **9** river gods
   son: 7 Proteus
   daughter: 5 Doris, Persa **7** Philyra
   form: 6 stream

ocelot 3 cat **7** wildcat

ochlophobia
   fear of: 6 crowds

Ochoa, Severo
   born: 5 Spain
   profession: 10 biochemist

Ockelman, Constance Frances Marie
   real name of: 12 Veronica Lake

O'Connor, Carroll
   born: 7 Bronx NY
   roles: 12 Archie Bunker, Archie's Place **14** All in the Family
   restaurant: 12 The Ginger Man

O'Connor, Donald
   born: 9 Chicago IL
   roles: 9 Beau Geste **15** Singin' in the

Rain **18** Tom Sawyer Detective **21** Francis the Talking Mule

O'Connor, Flannery
   author of: 9 Wise Blood **15** The Habit of Being **17** Mystery and Manners **20** A Good Man Is Hard to Find, The Violent Bear It Away

Octavia
   brother: 8 Augustus
   husband: 4 Nero **10** Mark Antony
   grandson: 8 Caligula

October
   flower: 6 cosmos **9** calendula
   French: 7 Octobre
   gem: 4 opal **10** tourmaline
   German: 7 Oktober
   holiday: 9 Halloween (31) **11** Columbus Day (12) **16** United Nations Day (24)
   Italian: 7 Ottobre
   number of days: 9 thirty-one
   origin of name: 4 octo (Latin meaning eight)
   place in year:
     Gregorian: 5 tenth
     Roman: 6 eighth
   Spanish: 7 Octubre
   Zodiac sign: 5 Libra **7** Scorpio

October Light
   author: 11 John Gardner

Octopus, The
   author: 11 Frank Norris

odd 4 rare **5** extra, funny, queer, spare, weird **6** casual, far-out, quaint, single, sundry, unique **7** bizarre, curious, not even, strange, surplus, unusual, various **8** freakish, left over, peculiar, periodic, singular, sporadic, uncommon **9** irregular, remaining, spasmodic, unmatched **10** occasional, outlandish **13** miscellaneous **15** being one of a pair **16** out of the ordinary **17** not divisible by two

oddball 3 nut **4** kook **5** freak **6** weirdo **8** crackpot, original **9** character, eccentric, screwball **10** one-of-a-kind

Odd Couple, The
   character: 3 Roy **5** Myrna, Roger, Speed **6** Miriam, Murray, Vinnie **10** Felix Unger **11** Gloria Unger **12** Cecily Pigeon, Oscar Madison **14** Blanche Madison **15** Gwendolyn Pigeon, (Dr) Nancy Cunningham
   cast: 10 Al Molinaro, Archie Hahn **11** Brett Somers, Carol Shelly, Jack Klugman, Larry Gelman, Monica Evans, Tony Randall **12** Garry Walberg, Janice Hansen, Ryan McDonald **13** Elinor Donahue, Joan Hotchkiss, Penny Marshall
   setting: 11 New York City
   Felix's job: 12 photographer
   Oscar's job: 12 sportswriter
   based on play by: 9 Neil Simon

Odd Couple, The
   director: 8 Gene Saks
   based on play by: 9 Neil Simon

cast: 10 Jack Lemmon (Felix Unger) **11** Herb Edelman, John Fiedler **13** Walter Matthau (Oscar Madison)

oddity 5 freak, sight **6** marvel, rarity, wonder **9** curiosity, queerness **10** phenomenon, uniqueness **11** abnormality, bizarreness, peculiarity, singularity, strangeness, unusualness **12** eccentricity, freakishness **13** individuality, unnaturalness **14** outlandishness
Latin: 8 rara avis

oddly amusing 5 droll, kooky **9** laughable, whimsical **10** ridiculous

odd person 3 nut **4** kook **5** flake, freak **6** looney, weirdo **7** oddball **8** crackpot **9** character, eccentric, screwball

odds and ends 4 olio **6** scraps **8** remnants **9** leftovers **10** hodgepodge, miscellany **11** this and that **13** bits and pieces **18** miscellaneous items

ode 4 epic, hymn, poem **5** lyric, paean, psalm, verse **6** ballad **8** canticle
type: 8 Horatian, Pindaric

Ode on a Grecian Urn
author: 9 John Keats

Ode on Indolence
author: 9 John Keats

Ode on Melancholy
author: 9 John Keats

Ode to a Nightingale
author: 9 John Keats

Ode to Autumn
author: 9 John Keats

Ode to Duty
author: 17 William Wordsworth

Ode to Psyche
author: 9 John Keats

Ode to the West Wind
author: 18 Percy Bysshe Shelley

Odets, Clifford
author of: 9 Golden Boy **12** Awake and Sing **14** The Country Girl **15** Waiting for Lefty **17** The Flowering Peach

Odin
also: 5 Othin
brother: 2 Ve **4** Vili
children: 4 Hodr, Thor **5** Baldr **6** Balder, Baldur
counterpart: 5 Woden, Wotan
court: 8 Valhalla
father: 3 Bor
god of: 3 war **6** poetry, wisdom **9** knowledge
grandson: 7 Volsung
home: 9 Gladsheim
horse: 8 Sleipnir
magic ring: 8 Draupnir
Norse myth: 10 chief deity
origin: 12 Scandinavian
raven: 5 Hugin, Munin
remaining eye: 3 sun
ruler of: 5 Aexir
spear: 7 Gungnir
throne: 10 Hlidskjalf

wife: 3 Fri **5** Frigg, Frija **6** Frigga
wolf: 4 Geri **5** Freki

odious 4 evil, foul, vile **5** hated, nasty **6** rotten **7** hateful, heinous, hideous **8** infamous **9** invidious, loathsome, monstrous, obnoxious, offensive, repugnant, repulsive, revolting, sickening **10** abominable, despicable, detestable, disgusting, nauseating, unbearable **11** intolerable, unendurable **12** contemptible **13** objectionable

odium 5 shame **6** hatred, infamy **7** disgust **8** contempt, disfavor, disgrace, dishonor, ignominy **9** antipathy, discredit, disesteem, disrepute **10** abhorrence, disrespect, opprobrium, repugnance **11** detestation, disapproval **14** disapprobation

odonata
class: 8 hexapoda
phylum: 10 arthropoda
group: 9 damselfly, dragonfly

odor 4 aura **5** aroma, scent, smell, stink **6** flavor, stench **7** bouquet, essence, perfume **9** effluvium, fragrance **10** atmosphere

odoriferous 4 rank **5** acrid, fetid **6** putrid, smelly **7** noisome, odorous, pungent, reeking, scented **8** aromatic, fragrant, perfumed, stinking **10** malodorous

odorous 4 rank **5** acrid, fetid **6** smelly **7** noisome, pungent, reeking, scented **8** aromatic, fragrant, perfumed, stinking

Odysseus
also: 7 Ulysses
king of: 6 Ithaca
father: 7 Laertes
mother: 8 Anticlea
hero of: 5 Iliad **7** Odyssey
wife: 8 Penelope **9** Callidice
son: 9 Telegonus **10** Polypoetes, Telemachus **11** Polyporthis
seduced by: 5 Circe
killed by: 9 Telegonus
epithet: 10 Laertiades

Odyssey
author: 5 Homer
character: 4 Zeus **5** Arete, Circe, Helen **6** Athene, Nestor, Scylla, Sirens **7** Calypso, Cyclops **8** Alcinous, Menelaus, Nausicaa, Odysseus, Penelope, Poseidon, Tiresias **9** Charybdis **10** Telemachus **11** Lotus-eaters

Oedipus
king of: 6 Thebes
father: 5 Laius
mother: 7 Jocasta
foster father: 7 Polybus
foster mother: 6 Merope **8** Periboea
wife: 7 Jocasta
son: 8 Eteocles **9** Polynices
daughter: 6 Ismene **8** Antigone
killed: 5 Laius
defeated: 6 Sphinx

Oedipus at Colonus

author: 9 Sophocles
character: 5 Creon **6** Elders, Ismene **7** Theseus **8** Antigone **9** Polynices

Oedipus Rex (Oedipus Tyrannus)
author: 9 Sophocles
character: 5 Creon, Laius **7** Jocasta **8** Tiresias

oeil-de-boeuf 16 small round window
literally: 8 bull's eye

Oeneus
king of: 7 Calydon
wife: 7 Althaea
son: 8 Meleager

oenology
science of: 5 wines **10** winemaking

Oenone
form: 5 nymph
father: 6 Cebren
husband: 5 Paris

Oersted, Hans Christian
field: 7 physics
nationality: 6 Danish
founded: 16 electromagnetism
isolated: 16 metallic aluminum
named for him: 11 oersted unit

oeuvre 4 work **5** works **13** artist's output

O'Faolain, Sean
author of: 15 The Heat of the Sun **17** A Nest of Simple Folk **22** Midsummer Night's Madness

of a piece 5 alike, equal **7** matched, the same **8** all in one **9** analogous, identical **10** equivalent, homogenous, synonymous **13** evenly matched, one and the same

of bad character 5 shady **8** unsavory **11** of ill repute **12** disreputable, unprincipled

off 2 by **3** bad, far, ill, odd **4** afar, away, down, from, kill, poor, stop **5** amiss, apart, aside, crazy, wrong **6** absent, begone, lessen, remote **7** distant, further, in error, stopped, tainted **8** abnormal, canceled, inferior, mistaken **9** imperfect

offal 4 junk, slag **5** dregs, trash, waste **6** debris, refuse **7** carcass, carrion, garbage, grounds, remains, residue, rubbish **8** leavings

off base 5 amiss, wrong **8** improper, mistaken **10** out of order, unsuitable **13** inappropriate

offbeat 3 odd **7** strange **8** peculiar **9** different, eccentric **14** unconventional

off-center 6 askew **7** strange **9** eccentric **10** imbalanced, nonaligned, unbalanced **12** unreasonable **14** unconventional

off-color 4 blue, lewd, racy, sexy **5** bawdy, dirty, salty, spicy **6** earthy, risque, smutty, wicked **7** naughty, obscene, raunchy **8** improper, indecent, scabrous **9** offensive **10** indelicate, indiscreet, suggestive

off duty 8 inactive 9 at leisure 10 unoccupied 13 on one's own time

Offenbach, Jacques
born: 7 Cologne, Germany
composer of: 13 La Belle Helene 15 Tales of Hoffmann, La Vie Parisienne 22 Orpheus in the Underworld

offend 3 err, sin, vex 4 fret, gall, miff, rile 5 anger, annoy, chafe, lapse, pique, wound 6 insult, madden, nettle, rankle 7 affront, disgust, incense, inflame 8 irritate 9 aggravate, displease, misbehave 10 antagonize, disgruntle, exasperate, transgress 13 fall from grace

offender 5 crook, felon 6 sinner 7 culprit 8 criminal, violator 9 wrongdoer 10 malefactor, trespasser

offense 3 sin 4 gibe, harm, slap, slip, snub, twit 5 abuse, crime, felony, insult 7 affront, assault, misdeed, outrage, umbrage 8 atrocity, enormity, evil deed, rudeness 9 impudence, indignity, insolence, offensive, violation 10 aggression, disrespect, infraction, peccadillo, wickedness 11 delinquency, humiliation, malfeasance, misdemeanor, shortcoming 13 embarrassment, transgression 15 breach of conduct

offensive 4 foul, rank, rude, ugly 5 nasty, onset 6 attack, horrid 7 abusive, assault, hideous, offense, uncivil 8 charging, impudent, insolent, storming 9 abhorrent, assailing, attacking, insulting, loathsome, obnoxious, onslaught, repugnant, repulsive, revolting, sickening, ungallant 10 abominable, aggression, aggressive, assaulting, bombarding, detestable, disgusting, nauseating, unmannerly, unpleasant 11 belligerent, distasteful, intolerable 12 disagreeable, embarrassing, insufferable 13 disrespectful, objectionable

offensiveness 8 rudeness 9 impudence, insolence, nastiness 10 disrespect, horridness, incivility 13 repulsiveness 14 unpleasantness 15 distastefulness

offer 3 bid 5 put up 6 bestow, extend, render, submit, tender 7 advance, hold out, present, proffer, propose, suggest 8 bestow on, offering, overture, proposal, propound, put forth 9 be willing, volunteer 10 invitation, put forward, submission, suggestion 11 make a motion, proposition 12 bring forward 14 put on the market 19 place at one's disposal

offer hospitality 4 host 7 welcome 8 play host 9 entertain 10 give a party, have guests 13 keep open house

offering 3 bid 4 alms, gift 5 goods, wares 6 course 7 charity, present, tribute 8 anathema, bestowal, donation, oblation 9 sacrifice 11 benefi-

cence 12 contribution
to God: 6 corban 7 deodate
to household deities: 4 bali

offertory 4 gift 8 oblation, offering 10 collection

offhand, offhanded 5 ad-lib, hasty 6 casual, chance, random 7 relaxed 8 careless, cavalier, heedless 9 facetious, haphazard, impromptu, unplanned, unstudied 10 improvised, nonchalant, off-the-cuff, unprepared 11 spontaneous, thoughtless, unconcerned, unrehearsed 12 off-the-record 14 extemporaneous, unpremeditated

office 3 job 4 post, role 8 capacity, function, position 10 commission, occupation 11 appointment

officer 3 cop 4 head 7 manager 8 director, gendarme, governor 9 constable, detective, executive, patrolman, policeman, president, secretary, treasurer 10 bureaucrat 12 commissioner 13 administrator, vice president

officers 8 managers 10 executives, management 14 administration

Officers and Gentlemen
author: 11 Evelyn Waugh

offices 4 duty, help, task 5 favor, trust 6 charge 7 service 8 function, province 10 assistance

office seeker 7 hopeful, nominee 8 aspirant 9 candidate

office worker 5 clerk, steno 6 typist 9 file clerk, secretary 10 bookkeeper, keypuncher 13 data processor 14 clerical worker

official 5 agent 6 formal, vested 7 manager, officer 8 approved, chairman, director, licensed 9 authentic, certified, dignitary, executive, warranted 10 accredited, authorized, sanctioned, supervisor 11 functionary 13 administrator, authoritative 14 administrative 18 administrative head

official communication 5 edict, order, ukase 6 report 7 release 8 bulletin 10 communique 12 proclamation

officialdom 10 government 11 authorities, bureaucracy 14 administration

official paper 4 writ 5 order 8 document 10 instrument

officiate 3 run 4 head, lead 5 chair, emcee 6 direct, handle, manage 7 oversee, preside 8 moderate, regulate 9 supervise 10 administer 11 superintend 12 be in charge of

officious 6 prying 7 pompous 8 meddling 9 intrusive, kibitzing, obtrusive 10 high-handed, meddlesome 11 domineering, interfering, overbearing, patronizing 13 high and mighty, self-assertive, self-important 16 poking one's nose in

Offield, Lewis Delaney
real name of: 9 Jack Oakie

offset 6 redeem 7 balance, nullify 8

equalize, knock out 9 cancel out, make up for 10 counteract, neutralize 11 countervail 13 compensate for, counterweight 14 counterbalance

offshoot 4 limb 5 scion, shoot 6 branch 7 adjunct 9 aftermath, byproduct, outgrowth 10 descendant

offspring 3 fry 4 heir, seed 5 brood, child, issue, scion, spawn, young 6 family, litter 7 progeny 8 children, increase 9 posterity 10 descendant, succession 11 descendants

off the mark 5 amiss 6 afield, astray 9 off target 16 off the right track

off-the-record 5 privy 6 secret 7 private 11 undisclosed 12 confidential 16 not to be disclosed 17 not for publication

off the top of one's head 5 ad-lib 7 offhand 9 extempore, impromptu 10 improvised, unprepared 11 extemporary, unrehearsed 14 extemporaneous, unpremeditated

of good quality 4 good 6 worthy 8 superior 9 excellent 10 creditable

of high rank 5 noble, regal, royal 6 lordly, titled 7 courtly 11 blueblooded 12 aristocratic

Of Human Bondage
author: 16 W Somerset Maugham
director: 12 John Cromwell
character: 5 Weeks 7 Hayward 11 Louisa Carey, Philip Carey 12 Sally Athelny, William Carey 13 Mildred Rogers, Miss Wilkinson, Thorpe Athelny
cast: 10 Bette Davis, Frances Dee, Kay Johnson 12 Leslie Howard

of its own kind
Latin: 10 sui generis

Of Mice and Men
author: 13 John Steinbeck
director: 14 Lewis Milestone
character: 4 Slim 5 Candy 6 Crooks, Curley 11 Lennie Small 12 George Milton
cast: 10 Betty Field 11 Lon Chaney Jr (Lenny) 15 Burgess Meredith, Charles Bickford
score: 12 Aaron Copland

of one's own right
Latin: 8 sui juris

of poor quality 5 junky 6 flimsy, shoddy, sleazy, trashy 8 inferior 11 substandard

of secondary importance 8 nonvital 9 accessory, extrinsic 10 incidental 11 dispensable, unnecessary 12 nonessential

often 3 oft 4 much 7 usually 8 commonly, ofttimes 9 generally, regularly 10 constantly, frequently, habitually, oftentimes, repeatedly 11 continually, customarily, over and over, recurrently 12 periodically, time and again

of the dead say nothing but good
Latin: **21** de mortuis nil nisi bonum
of the faith
Latin: **6** de fide
of their own kind
Latin: **10** sui generis
of the old school 5 passe **8** outdated, outmoded **9** out-of-date **12** conservative, old-fashioned **18** establishmentarian
Of Time and the River
author: **11** Thomas Wolfe
character: **10** Eugene Gant
oft-repeated 5 trite **7** popular **8** constant, familiar, frequent, habitual, well-worn **9** continual, recurring, well-known **10** persistent **11** widely known
of what good
Latin: **7** cui bono
Ogdoad
also: **3** Heh
origin: **8** Egyptian
number of gods: **5** eight
ogle 3 eye **6** gape at, gawk at, goggle, leer at **7** stare at **8** goggle at **10** give the eye, scrutinize **15** give the once-over, stare at greedily **16** cast sheep's eyes at, gaze at with desire
Ogma
origin: **5** Irish
god of: **6** poetry **9** eloquence
inventor of: **12** Ogham letters
Ogmios
origin: **6** Gaelic
god of: **9** eloquence
corresponds to: **7** Mercury
ogre, ogress 5 brute, demon, fiend, ghoul, harpy **6** despot, tyrant **7** bugbear, monster **8** bogeyman, dictator, martinet **11** slave driver
Ogygia
island of: **7** Calypso
Ogygus
king of: **7** Boeotia
father: **8** Poseidon
O'Hara, John
author of: **7** Pal Joey **11** A Rage to Live **13** The Instrument **14** From the Terrace, The Hat on the Bed **16** Butterfield Eight **17** Ten North Frederick **19** The Horse Knows the Way **20** Appointment in Samarra
O'Hara, Maureen
real name: **18** Maureen Fitzsimmons
nickname: **18** Queen of Technicolor
born: **7** Ireland **8** Milltown
roles: **10** Lady Godiva **11** The Quiet Man **13** North to Alaska, The Parent Trap **16** The Foxes of Harrow **19** How Green Was My Valley **20** Hunchback of Notre Dame **27** Miracle on Thirty-fourth Street
O'Hara, Scarlett
character in: **15** Gone With the Wind

family: **6** Gerald **7** Carreen, Suellen
author: **8** Mitchell
O Henry
real name: **19** William Sidney Porter
author of: **11** The Last Leaf **16** Cabbages and Kings, The Gift of the Magi **18** The Cop and the Anthem **19** The Ransom of Red Chief
Ohio
abbreviation: **2** OH
nickname: **7** Buckeye
capital: **8** Columbus
largest city: **9** Cleveland
others: **3** Ada **4** Kent, Lima **5** Akron, Berea, Cadiz, Niles, Parma, Piqua, Xenia **6** Athens, Canton, Dayton, Elyria, Lorain, Marion, Newark, Tiffin, Toledo, Warren **7** Ashland, Findlay, Fremont, Norwood, Wooster **8** Alliance, Bluffton, Fostoria, Lakewood, Marietta, Sandusky **9** Ashtabula, Kettering, Lancaster, Massillon, Struthers, Vermilion, Willowick **10** Cincinnati, Huntington, Portsmouth, Rocky River, Willoughby, Youngstown, Zanesville **11** Painesville, Springfield **12** Steubenville
college: **4** Kent **5** Akron, Hiram, Miami **6** Dayton, Kenyon, Xavier **7** Antioch, Oberlin, Wooster **8** Defiance, Dennison, Marietta, Ursuline **10** Wittenberg **11** Case Western **12** Bowling Green, Ohio Wesleyan
feature:
hall of fame: **11** Pro Football
race: **12** Soap Box Derby
tribe: **4** Erie **7** Wyandot **13** Mound Builders
people: **7** buckeye, Cy Young **8** Zane Grey **10** Clark Gable, T Hart Crane **11** Annie Oakley, Lillian Gish **12** James Thurber, Lowell Thomas, Norman Thomas **13** Neil Armstrong, Orville Wright, Thomas A Edison **14** Barney Old field, Clarence Darrow **15** William T Sherman **16** Sherwood Anderson **18** Norman Vincent Peale
explorer: **7** La Salle
lake: **4** Erie **5** Grand **6** Berlin, Dillon, Hoover, Indian **8** Delaware **13** Mosquito Creek
land rank: **35** thirty-fifth
mountain:
highest point: **12** Campbell Hill
physical feature:
caverns: **4** Ohio, Zane **6** Seneca
spring: **8** Blue Hole
president: **13** Ulysses S Grant **14** James A Garfield, Warren G Harding **15** William McKinley **16** Rutherford B Hayes **17** William Howard Taft **20** William Henry Harrison
river: **5** Grand, Miami **6** Maumee, Scioto, Wabash **7** Hocking **8** Cuyahoga, Sandusky **9** Muskingum, Tennessee **10** Cumberland **11** Monongahela
state admission: **11** seventeenth
state bird: **8** cardinal

state flower: **16** scarlet carnation
state motto: **27** With God All Things Are Possible
state song: **13** Beautiful Ohio
state tree: **7** buckeye
Ohm, Georg Simon
field: **7** physics
nationality: **6** German
discovered: **20** electrical resistance
named for him: **7** ohm unit
oil 4 balm, lard **5** cream, salve **6** anoint, grease, pomade **7** unguent **8** liniment, ointment **9** lubricant, lubricate, melted fat, petroleum **12** melted grease
type: **4** corn, fuel, hair **5** crude, motor, olive, whale **6** canola **7** cooking, mineral **9** safflower, vegetable
oily 5 fatty, lardy, slick **6** greasy, smarmy **7** buttery, fawning, servile **8** slippery, slithery, toadying, unctuous **9** groveling, sebaceous **10** lubricious, oleaginous **11** bootlicking, subservient **12** ingratiating
ointment 4 balm **5** salve **6** lotion, pomade **7** pomatum, unguent **8** liniment **9** emollient, spikenard
Ojibwa, Ojibway see **8** Chippawa
OK 4 fine, good **7** approve, endorse **8** all right, approval **9** authorize **11** endorsement **13** authorization
French: **7** d'accord
O'Keeffe, Georgia
born: **12** Sun Prairie WI
artwork: **7** Stables **9** Black Iris **14** Patio with Cloud **15** Lake George Barns **22** Light Coming on the Plains **26** Black Flower and Blue Larkspur
husband: **15** Alfred Stieglitz
Oklahoma
abbreviation: **2** OK **4** Okla
nickname: **6** Boomer, Sooner
capital/largest city: **12** Oklahoma City
others: **3** Ada **4** Alva, Enid, Hugo **5** Altus, Miami, Ponca, Tulsa **6** Duncan, El Reno, Guymon, Idabel, Lawton **7** Ardmore, Guthrie, Sapulpa, Shawnee **8** Anadarko, Fort Sill, Muskogee **9** Blackwell, Claremore, McAlester **10** Stillwater **12** Bartlesville
college: **5** Tulsa **6** Norman **7** Cameron **8** Langston, Phillips **10** Stillwater **11** Oral Roberts **12** Oklahoma City **15** Bethany Nazarene **17** American Christian
feature:
hall of fame: **14** American Indian
national park: **6** Platte
tribe: **3** Kaw, Oto **4** Iowa, Loup, Otoe, Waco **5** Caddo, Kansa, Osage, Ponca **6** Apache, Ottawa, Pawnee, Quapaw **7** Shawnee, Wichita **8** Arapahoe, Tawakoni
Five Civilized Tribes: **5** Creek **7** Choctaw **8** Cherokee, Seminole **9** Chickasaw

people: 4 Okie 6 Sooner 9 Jim Thorpe 10 Will Rogers 12 Mickey Mantle 14 Maria Tallchief
  explorer: 8 Coronado
lake: 5 Atoka, Grand, Hulah 6 Texoma, Wister 7 Eufaula, Heyburn, Oologah 8 Keystone 9 Pensacola, Tenkiller 10 Fort Gibson 11 Thunderbird 12 Markham Ferry 17 Lake O' The Cherokees
land rank: 10 eighteenth
mountain: 6 Ozarks 8 Ouachita
  highest point: 9 Black Mesa
physical feature: 9 Panhandle
  plains: 5 Great
river: 3 Red 5 Grand 6 Little, Neosho 7 Washita 8 Arkansas, Canadian, Cimarron 9 Verdigris 15 Muddy Boggy Creek
state admission: 10 forty-sixth
state bird: 23 scissor-tailed flycatcher
state fish: 9 white bass
state flower: 9 mistletoe
state motto: 22 Labor Conquers All Things
state song: 8 Oklahoma
state tree: 6 redbud

Oklahoma!
director: 13 Fred Zinnemann
cast: 10 Rod Steiger 11 Eddie Albert 12 Gordon MacRae, Shirley Jones 13 Gloria Grahame, James Whitmore 18 Charlotte Greenwood
score: 21 Rodgers and Hammerstein
choreographer: 12 Agnes de Mille
song: 23 People Will Say We're in Love 24 Surrey with the Fringe on Top

Olbers, Heinrich Wilhelm Matthaus
field: 9 astronomy
nationality: 6 German
discovered: 5 Vesta 6 comets, Pallas 9 asteroids

old 4 aged, used 5 hoary, of age 6 beat-up, bygone, of yore 7 ancient, antique, archaic, elderly, outworn, rundown, vintage, wornout 8 battered, decrepit, familiar, grizzled, much-used, obsolete, outdated, timeworn 9 crumbling, hackneyed, out-of-date, venerable, weathered 10 antiquated, broken-down, gray-headed, ramshackle, tumbledown 11 dilapidated, from the past, gray with age, obsolescent, time-honored, traditional 12 deteriorated, old-fashioned, white with age 13 weather-beaten 14 of long standing 15 long established

Old Aches and Pains
nickname of: 11 Luke Appling
old age 6 dotage 7 ripe age 8 maturity, senility 11 advanced age 15 second childhood

Old and the Young, The
author: 15 Luigi Pirandello

Old Bay State
nickname of: 13 Massachusetts
Old Bulgarian
also: 15 Old Church Slavic
language family: 12 Indo-European
group: 11 Balto-Slavic
status: 7 archaic
used in: 14 Orthodox church
Old Chinook
nickname of: 10 Washington
Old Colony State
nickname of: 13 Massachusetts
Old Curiosity Shop, The
author: 14 Charles Dickens
character: 5 Quilp 9 Fred Trent, Mrs Jarley 10 Kit Nubbles, Sally Brass 11 Grandfather 12 Sampson Brass 13 Dick Swiveller 15 Little Nell Trent 18 The Single Gentleman
Old Dominion
nickname of: 8 Virginia
olden 4 past 6 bygone, former, of yore 7 ancient, long-ago 8 departed
Oldest Man 10 Methuselah
old-fashioned 5 corny, dated, passe 7 antique, archaic 8 obsolete, outdated, outmoded 9 out-of-date 10 antiquated, out of style 11 obsolescent, traditional 12 long-standing, out of fashion 13 unfashionable 14 behind the times
Old-Fashioned Girl, An
author: 15 Louisa May Alcott
Old Franklin State
nickname of: 9 Tennessee
old hand 3 pro 6 expert, master 8 virtuoso 9 authority 12 professional
old hat 5 passe, stale 6 demode 7 archaic, outworn 8 obsolete, outdated, outmoded 9 out-of-date 10 antiquated, superseded 11 obsolescent 12 old-fashioned 13 unfashionable 14 behind the times
old-line 11 established, traditional 12 conservative
Old Line State
nickname of: 8 Maryland
Old Love
author: 19 Isaac Bashevis Singer
Old Maid, The
author: 12 Edith Wharton
Old Man and the Sea, The
author: 15 Ernest Hemingway
character: 7 Manolin 8 Santiago
Old Mortality
author: 14 Sir Walter Scott
character: 5 Edith 11 Henry Morton 12 Basil Olifant, Lord Evandale 19 John Balfour of Burley 21 Lady Margaret Bellenden 27 Colonel Grahame of Claverhouse
Old Mortality
author: 19 Katherine Anne Porter
Old North
nickname of: 13 North Carolina

Old Patagonian Express, The
author: 11 Paul Theroux
old saw 5 adage, maxim 6 cliche, saying, truism 7 bromide, proverb 9 old saying 10 expression 11 old chestnut
oldster 5 elder 6 codger, old man 7 ancient 8 old woman 13 senior citizen
Old Testament
first five books: 10 Pentateuch
first six books: 9 Hexateuch
first seven books: 10 Heptateuch
books of: 3 Job 4 Amos, Ezra, Joel, Ruth 5 Hosea, Jonah, Kings, Micah, Na- hum, Songs, Tobit 6 Baruch, Daniel, Esther, Exodus, Haggai, Isaiah, Joshua, Judges, Judith, Psalms, Samuel, Sirach, Wisdom 7 Ezekiel, Genesis, Malachi, Numbers, Obadiah 8 Habakkuk, Jeremiah, Macabees, Nehemiah, Proverbs 9 Leviticus, Zechariah, Zephaniah 10 Chronicles 11 Deuteronomy 12 Ecclesiastes 13 Song of Solomon 14 Ecclesiasticus
Oldtown Folks
author: 19 Harriet Beecher Stowe
Old Wives' Tale, The
author: 13 Arnold Bennett
old-world 6 formal 7 courtly, gallant, old-line 8 European, orthodox 10 ceremonial, chivalrous, prescribed 11 ceremonious, continental, established, traditional 12 conservative, conventional, old-fashioned
Ole
character in: 16 Giants of the Earth
author: 7 Rolvaag
Olenska, Ellen
character in: 17 The Age of Innocence
author: 7 Wharton
oleoresin 3 gum 5 anime, apiol, elemi 6 balsam 7 solvent 10 turpentine
olio 4 stew 6 jumble, medley 7 melange, mixture 8 mishmash 9 potpourri 10 assortment, collection, hodgepodge, hotchpotch, miscellany
olive 12 Olea europaea
varieties: 3 tea 4 wild 5 black, false, holly, sweet 6 common, desert, spurge 7 Russian 8 American, fragrant 11 Californian
olive-drab 5 khaki 13 greenish-brown
Oliver
character in: 11 As You Like It
author: 11 Shakespeare
Oliver!
director: 9 Carol Reed
based on story by: 14 Charles Dickens (Oliver Twist)
cast: 8 Jack Wild, Ron Moody (Fagin) 10 Mark Lester (Oliver), Oliver Reed 11 Shani Wallis
Oscar for: 7 picture 8 director
remake of: 11 Oliver Twist
song: 16 Consider Yourself, Food Glo-

rious Food **17** As Long As He Needs Me

Oliver Twist
author: **14** Charles Dickens
character: **5** Fagin, Monks (Edward Leeford), Nancy **6** Bumble **9** Bill Sikes, Mrs Maylie **10** Mr Brownlow, Rose Maylie
director: **9** David Lean
cast: **8** Kay Walsh **12** Alec Guinness (Fagin), Robert Newton **13** Anthony Newley (Artful Dodger) **16** Francis L Sullivan, John Howard Davies
remade as: **7** Oliver!

Olivia
character in: **12** Twelfth Night
author: **11** Shakespeare

Olivier, Sir Laurence
born: **7** Dorking, England
wife: **11** Vivien Leigh **13** Joan Plowright
roles: **6** Becket, Hamlet (Oscar), Henry V, Sleuth **7** Rebecca **11** Marathon Man **16** Wuthering Heights **17** Pride and Prejudice, The Boys from Brazil, The Devil's Disciple **19** Shoes of the Fisherman **23** The Prince and the Showgirl

olivine
variety: **7** peridot

olla **3** jar, pot **10** earthen pot

Olmsted, Frederick Law
landscape architect of: **11** Central Park (NYC, with Calvert Vaux) **12** Prospect Park (Brooklyn NY) **13** Fairmount Park (Philadelphia) **14** Biltmore Estate (Asheville NC), Mount Royal Park (Montreal)

Olsen, Merlin (Jay)
sport: **8** football
team: **14** Los Angeles Rams
TV roles: **12** Father Murphy **15** Highway to Heaven **23** Little House on the Prairie

O Lucky Man
director: **15** Lindsay Anderson
cast: **9** Alan Price **13** Rachel Roberts **15** Malcolm McDowell, Ralph Richardson
score: **9** Alan Price

Olwen
origin: **5** Welsh
form: **8** princess
father: **16** Yspadaden Penkawr

Olympic Games
site:
1896: 6 Athens
1900: 5 Paris
1904: 7 St Louis
1906: 6 Athens
1908: 6 London
1912: 9 Stockholm
1920: 7 Antwerp
1924: 5 Paris **8** Chamonix
1928: 8 St Moritz **9** Amsterdam
1932: 10 Lake Placid, Los Angeles
1936: 6 Berlin **21** Garmisch-

Partenkirchen
1948: 6 London **8** St Moritz
1952: 4 Oslo **8** Helsinki
1956: 9 Melbourne **15** Cortina d'Ampezzo
1960: 4 Rome **11** Squaw Valley
1968: 8 Grenoble **10** Mexico City
1972: 6 Munich **7** Sapporo
1976: 8 Montreal **9** Innsbruck
1980: 6 Moscow **10** Lake Placid
1984: 8 Sarajevo **10** Los Angeles
1988: 5 Seoul **7** Calgary
1992: 9 Barcelona **11** Albertville
1994: 11 Lillehammer
1996: 7 Atlanta
1998: 6 Nagano
2000: 6 Sydney

Omaha
language family: **6** Siouan **7** Dhegiha
location: **4** Iowa **8** Nebraska, Oklahoma

Oman
other name: **13** Muscat and Oman
capital: **6** Masqat, Muscat
largest city: **5** Matra **6** Matrah
others: **3** Sur **4** Fida **5** Dubai, Nazwa, Nigwa, Sohar, Wazit **6** Khasab, Marbat, Murbat, Suwaih, Tinouf **7** Khabura, Salalah **8** Ashkhara
government: **9** Sultanate
head of state/government: **6** sultan
monetary unit: **3** gaj, gaz **4** rial **5** baiza, ghazi **7** mahmudi
island: **6** Masera, Masira **7** Masirah **10** Kuria Muria
mountain: **4** Qara **5** Hafit, Harim, Nakhl, Tayin **8** el-Akhdar **11** Jabal Akhdar **13** Green Mountain
highest point: **8** al-Sham
sea: **6** Indian **7** Arabian
physical feature:
  cape: **7** Madraka **9** Ras Al Hadd **13** Ras Dharbat 'Ali
  gulf: **4** Oman
  peninsula: **7** Arabian **8** Musandam
  plain: **6** Dhofar **7** Batinah
  strait: **6** Hormuz
people: **4** Arab
ruler: **12** Qabus Bin Said **13** Said Bin Taimur
language: **4** Urdu **5** Hindi **6** Arabic **7** Baluchi
religion: **5** Islam
war: **4** Gulf **11** Desert Storm

omega **3** end **4** last **5** final **6** ending **8** terminus
opposite: **5** alpha

omen **4** sign **5** token **6** augury, herald **7** auspice, portent, presage, warning **9** foretaste, harbinger, precursor **10** foreboding, indication

ominous **7** unlucky **8** menacing, minatory, monitory, sinister **9** dismaying, ill-omened **10** foreboding, ill-starred, portentous

omission **3** gap **4** hole **7** neglect **9** exception, exclusion, oversight **10** leaving out, negligence **11** delinquency,

elimination **12** noninclusion **13** neglected item **16** something omitted

omit **3** cut **4** drop, fail, jump, miss, shun, skip **5** avoid, elide **6** bypass, delete, except, forget, ignore, slight **7** excerpt, exclude, let slip, neglect **8** leave out, overlook, pass over, preclude, set aside **11** forget about

omnia vincit amor **15** love conquers all

Omnibus
host: **13** Alistair Cooke

omnipotent **6** mighty **7** supreme **8** almighty, powerful, puissant **11** all-powerful

omniscient **7** all-wise, supreme **8** infinite **9** all-seeing **10** all-knowing, preeminent

omnium gatherum **23** miscellaneous collection

omnivorous **7** hoggish **8** edacious, ravenous **9** crapulous, rapacious, voracious **10** gluttonous, polyphagic, predacious **12** pantophagous

Omoo
author: **14** Herman Melville
character: **10** Captain Bob **15** Doctor Long Ghost

Omphale
queen of: **5** Lydia
father: **8** Iardanus
husband: **6** Tmolus
son: **5** Lamus
served by: **8** Hercules

Omri
father: **6** Becher **7** Michael
son: **4** Ahab
daughter-in-law: **7** Jezebel

on **2** at **4** atop, near, over, upon **5** about, above, ahead, along, anent **7** against, forward, planned **8** abutting, adjacent, attached, intended, touching **9** occurring **10** concerning, juxtaposed

on-and-off **6** spotty **8** episodic **9** irregular, spasmodic, temporary **10** now-and-then, occasional

On Beginning and Perishing
author: **9** Aristotle

once **7** ages ago, long ago, one time **8** formerly, hitherto, years ago **9** at one time **10** heretofore, previously **11** a single time, for the nonce, in times past, some time ago **12** in the old days, some time back **13** once upon a time, on one occasion

once-in-a-lifetime **6** unique **7** special **8** singular **11** one-time-only

once more **4** anew **5** again **9** once again, over again **11** one more time

on cloud nine **6** elated, joyful, joyous **8** ecstatic, euphoric **9** exuberant, rapturous **15** in seventh heaven

oncoming **5** close **7** looming, nearing **8** imminent **9** advancing, impending, onrushing **11** approaching, bearing down

on course 8 on target 15 on the right track

Ondine
   author: 13 Jean Giraudoux

one 2 an 3 you 4 a man, lone, only, sole 5 a body, a soul, whole 6 a thing, entire, single, unique 7 a person, someone 8 complete, singular, solitary, somebody 10 individual, unrepeated

One, Two, Three
   director: 11 Billy Wilder
   cast: 11 James Cagney 12 Pamela Tiffin 13 Arlene Francis, Horst Buchholz
   setting: 10 West Berlin
   score: 11 Andre Previn

O'Neal, Ryan
   real name: 16 Patrick Ryan O'Neal
   born: 12 Los Angeles CA
   daughter: 10 Tatum O'Neal
   roles: 9 Love Story, Paper Moon 10 What's Up Doc 11 Barry Lyndon, Peyton Place 16 Rodney Harrington

O'Neal, Tatum
   born: 12 Los Angeles CA
   father: 9 Ryan O'Neal
   roles: 9 Paper Moon 12 Bad News Bears 14 Little Darlings 19 International Velvet
   husband: 11 John McEnroe

one and the same 5 equal 7 matched 9 identical

one by one 6 singly 10 one at a time, separately, single file 12 individually

One Day at a Time
   character: 9 Ann Romano 11 Julie Cooper 13 Barbara Cooper 15 Dwayne Schneider
   cast: 14 Bonnie Franklin 15 Pat Harrington Jr 17 Mackenzie Phillips, Valerie Bertinelli

One Day in the Life of Ivan Denisovich
   author: 23 Aleksandr Solzhenitsyn Jr

One Flew Over the Cuckoo's Nest
   director: 11 Milos Forman
   based on story by: 8 Ken Kesey
   cast: 13 Jack Nicholson 14 Louise Fletcher, Michael Beryman 15 William Redfield
   Oscar for: 5 actor (Nicholson) 7 actress (Fletcher), picture 8 director 10 screenplay

One Hour with You
   director: 11 George Cukor 13 Ernst Lubitsch
   cast: 14 Genevieve Tobin 16 Maurice Chevalier 17 Jeanette MacDonald
   remake of: 17 The Marriage Circle
   song: 14 What Would You Do

one-hundred percent 5 sheer, total, utter, whole 7 supreme 8 absolute, complete 10 consummate 17 through-and-through

O'Neill, Eugene
   author of: 8 The Straw 11 The Hairy Ape 12 Ah Wilderness, Anna Christie 13 Marco Millions 14 Glencairn Cycle 15 The Emperor Jones, The Iceman Cometh 16 Beyond the Horizon, Strange Interlude, The Great God Brown 18 Desire Under the Elms 20 The Moon of the Caribees 22 A Moon for the Misbegotten, All God's Chillun Got Wings, Mourning Becomes Electra 24 Long Day's Journey into Night
   daughter: 4 Oona
   son-in-law: 7 Chaplin

Oneiros
   also: 6 Oniros
   origin: 5 Greek
   god of: 6 dreams

oneness 5 union, unity 7 concord, harmony 8 entirety, identity, sameness, totality 9 agreement, aloneness, integrity, wholeness 10 uniformity, uniqueness 11 singularity 12 completeness 13 individuality

one-of-a-kind 4 rare 6 unique 7 strange, unusual 8 original 9 eccentric

oneology
   science of: 5 wines 10 winemaking

onerous 5 heavy 6 taxing 7 arduous, painful, weighty 8 crushing, grievous 9 demanding, wearisome 10 burdensome, exhausting, oppressive 11 distressing 12 hard to endure

one thing in return for another
   Latin: 10 quid pro quo

one-time 3 old 4 past 5 early, prior 6 former, recent 7 earlier, quondam 8 previous 9 erstwhile
   French: 8 ci-devant

one voice 4 solo 6 unison 7 concert

one who has a fixed income
   French: 7 rentier

On First Looking Into Chapman's Homer
   author: 9 John Keats

on foot
   French: 5 a pied

ongoing 7 endless, lasting 8 enduring, unbroken, unending 10 continuing, proceeding 11 never-ending, unremitting 13 uninterrupted

On Golden Pond
   director: 10 Mark Rydell
   based on play by: 14 Ernest Thompson
   cast: 9 Jane Fonda 10 Doug McKeon, Henry Fonda (Norman Thayer Jr) 16 Katharine Hepburn
   setting: 5 Maine
   Oscar for: 5 actor (Fonda) 7 actress (Hepburn)

on guard 4 wary 5 alert 7 careful, heedful 8 cautious, vigilant, watchful

on hand 5 handy, on tap 6 at hand 9 available 10 accessible, convenient 14 at one's disposal

on horseback
   French: 7 a cheval

onion 6 Allium 10 Allium cepa
   varieties: 3 red, sea, top 4 leek, tree, wild 5 green, gypsy, pearl, swamp, Welsh, white 6 German, potato, yellow 7 Bermuda, Danvers, nodding, prairie, shallot, Spanish 8 climbing, Egyptian, false sea, scallion, Valencia 9 Catawissa, ever-ready, flowering, two-bladed 10 multiplier, red-skinned 16 Japanese bunching
   origin: 9 Asia Minor
   called by Robert Louis Stevenson: 14 rose among roots

Onion Field, The
   author: 14 Joseph Wambaugh

Oniros see 7 Oneiros

On Liberty
   author: 14 John Stuart Mill

onlooker 5 gazer, ogler 6 viewer 7 watcher, witness 8 beholder, kibitzer, observer 9 bystander, spectator 10 eyewitness, rubberneck

only 4 just, lone, sole 5 alone 6 barely, merely, purely, simply, single, singly, solely, unique 7 at least 8 by itself, singular, solitary 9 by oneself, exclusive, unmatched 10 individual, no more than, nothing but, one and only, unrepeated 11 exclusively 12 individually, unparalleled

on one's uppers 5 broke 9 destitute 10 down and out

On Plants
   author: 9 Aristotle

On Revolution
   author: 12 Hannah Arendt

onrush 4 flow, flux, gush, tide, wave 5 flood, onset, storm, surge 6 attack, charge, deluge, spring, stream 7 assault, cascade, current, torrent 9 avalanche

onset 4 push, raid 5 birth, sally, start 6 attack, charge, onrush, outset, thrust 7 assault, genesis, infancy, offense 8 founding, invasion, outbreak, storming 9 beginning, inception, incursion, offensive, onslaught 10 incipience, initiation 12 commencement, inauguration

onslaught 4 coup, push, raid 5 blitz, foray, onset, sally 6 attack, charge, putsch, thrust 7 assault, offense 8 invasion 9 incursion, offensive 10 aggression, blitzkrieg

on tap 5 handy 6 at hand, on hand 9 available 10 accessible, convenient

Ontario
   bay: 6 Hudson
   canal: 5 Trent 6 Rideau
   capital: 7 Toronto
   city: 3 Emo 4 Galt 6 London, Ottawa 7 Windsor 8 Hamilton, Kingston 9 Kitchener
   explored by: 5 French 6 British
   industry: 6 mining 11 agriculture 13

manufacturing
lake: 6 Simcoe
province of: 6 Canada
river: 6 Ottawa, Thames **7** Niagara **10** St Lawrence
settled by: 9 Loyalists
university: 4 York **5** Brock, Trent **8** McMaster

on the alert 4 wary **7** careful, mindful, on guard **8** cautious, watchful **9** wide awake **12** on the lookout

On the Beach
author: 10 Nevil Shute
director: 13 Stanley Kramer
cast: 10 Ava Gardner **11** Fred Astaire, Gregory Peck **13** Donna Anderson **14** Anthony Perkins

on the contrary
French: 11 au contraire

on the dot 7 exactly **8** promptly **9** on the nose, precisely **10** punctually

on the face
Latin: 7 ex facie

on the go 4 busy **6** active, mobile **8** in motion **9** energetic, on the move **13** indefatigable

On the Heavens
author: 9 Aristotle

On the Morning of Christ's Nativity
author: 10 John Milton

on the move 5 astir **6** active, mobile **7** on the go **8** in motion

on the nose 5 exact **7** exactly, precise **8** accurate, on target **9** precisely **10** accurately, on the money

on the outer edges
Latin: 10 in extremis

on the right track 8 on course, on target

On the Soul
author: 9 Aristotle

On the Town
director: 9 Gene Kelly **12** Stanley Donen
cast: 9 Ann Miller, Gene Kelly, Vera-Ellen **12** Betty Garrett, Frank Sinatra
setting: 11 New York City
score: 11 Adolph Green, Betty Comden **16** Leonard Bernstein
song: 14 New York New York

On the Waterfront
director: 9 Elia Kazan
cast: 8 Lee J Cobb **10** Karl Malden, Pat Henning, Rod Steiger **12** Leif Erickson, Marlon Brando **13** Eva Marie Saint
Oscar for: 5 actor (Brando) **7** picture **8** director **10** screenplay **17** supporting actress (Saint)

on the whole 9 in general **10** by and large **27** considering the circumstances

onto 4 atop, upon **5** aware, privy **6** aboard

onus 4 duty, load **5** cross **6** burden, strain, weight **9** liability **10** obligation **11** encumbrance **13** burden of proof **14** responsibility

onus probandi 13 burden of proof

onward, onwards 5 ahead, along **7** forward, ongoing **9** advancing, frontward **11** moving ahead, progressive
French: 7 en avant, en route

On Wings of Eagles
author: 10 Ken Follett

oodles 4 gobs, lots, many **5** heaps, loads, scads **6** plenty

ooze 4 drip, leak, mire, muck, seep, silt **5** bleed, drain, exude, slime, sweat **6** filter, sludge **7** dribble, leakage, seepage, soft mud, trickle **8** alluvium **9** discharge, exudation, percolate, secretion, transpire

oozing 5 leaky, weepy **6** sweaty **7** exuding, seepage, seeping **8** bleeding, sweating

opal
color: 3 red **5** black, white **6** orange **11** transparent
source: 6 Mexico **9** Australia **14** Lightning Ridge
variety: 8 fire opal

opalescent 5 milky **6** pearly **8** irisated, luminous **10** iridescent

opaque 4 dark, dull, hazy **5** muddy, murky **7** clouded, muddied, obscure, unclear **8** abstruse **9** difficult **12** impenetrable, unfathomable **14** nontranslucent, nontransparent, unintelligible **16** incomprehensible

opaqueness 7 opacity **8** dullness **9** denseness, muddiness, murkiness, obscurity **10** cloudiness **11** unclearness **15** impenetrability **17** unintelligibility **19** incomprehensibility

open 4 ajar, fair, just, wide **5** agape, begin, clear, crack, found, frank, plain, unbar **6** candid, create, direct, expand, gaping, honest, launch, unfold, unlock, unseal, unshut **7** artless, exposed, lay open, natural, not shut, sincere, unblock, unclose, yawning **8** commence, extended, outgoing, unbiased, unclosed, unfasten, unfenced, unfolded, unlocked, unsealed **9** available, coverless, establish, expansive, impartial, institute, not closed, objective, originate, receptive, unbigoted, unbounded, uncovered, uncrowded, undertake, welcoming **10** accessible, forthright, impersonal, inaugurate, responsive, unenclosed, unfastened **11** extroverted, uncluttered, uninhabited **12** permit access, unobstructed, unprejudiced **13** disinterested, doing business **15** straightforward

open-air 7 outdoor, outside **10** unconfined
Italian: 8 al fresco

open and aboveboard 6 candid, honest **7** ethical **10** forthright **12** on the up and up **15** straightforward

Open Boat, The
author: 12 Stephen Crane

Open City
director: 17 Roberto Rossellini
cast: 11 Aldo Fabrizi, Anna Magnani **16** Marcello Pagliero
setting: 4 Rome

open-eyed 5 alert, awake, aware **7** heedful, mindful **8** vigilant, watchful, wide-eyed **9** attentive, wide-awake

open-handed 6 lavish **7** liberal **8** generous, prodigal **9** bounteous, bountiful **10** altruistic, beneficent, benevolent, ungrudging, unstinting **11** magnanimous

openhandedness 10 generosity, liberality **11** benevolence, generousity, munificence **12** extravagance

openhearted 7 artless, sincere **8** trusting **9** ingenuous

opening 3 gap, job **4** gash, hole, rent, rift, slit, slot, spot, tear, vent **5** break, chink, cleft, crack, place, space, start **6** breach, chance **7** fissure, kickoff, preface, prelude, send-off, vacancy **8** aperture, occasion, overture, position **9** be ginning, first part, launching, situation **10** initiation **11** opportunity, possibility **12** commencement, inauguration, installation, introduction

openly 6 freely **7** frankly **8** directly, honestly, publicly **9** obviously

open-minded 4 fair **7** liberal **8** amenable, flexible, tolerant, unbiased **9** adaptable, impartial, objective, receptive **10** responsive, undogmatic **11** broad-minded **12** unprejudiced **13** disinterested, nonjudgmental

openmouthed 4 agog, awed **5** agape **6** aghast, amazed **8** wide-eyed **9** awestruck, bewitched, marveling, staggered, stupefied, surprised **10** astonished, confounded **10** dumbstruck, enthralled, spellbound **11** dumbfounded **12** wonderstruck **13** flabbergasted, thunderstruck

openness 6 candor **7** honesty **8** daylight **9** frankness, sincerity **11** artlessness **13** guilelessness **14** forthrightness **19** straightforwardness

open sanction 8 free hand, free rein **13** full authority
French: 12 catre blanche

open the eyes of 8 disabuse **11** set straight

open to choice 8 elective, optional **9** voluntary

openwork 3 net **4** lace **6** eyelet **7** lattice, Madeira, tracery **8** filigree

opera 5 score **7** musical **8** libretto **11** composition
by Bellini: 5 Norma
by Bizet: 6 Carmen
by Delibes: 5 Lakme
by Donizetti: 10 La Favorita **11** Don

Pasquale **12** Maria Stuarda **13** L'Elisir d'Amore **17** Lucia di Lammermoor **19** La Figlia di Regimente
by Gounod: 5 Faust
by Leoncavallo: 10 I Pagliacci
by Mozart: 8 Idomeneo **10** Magic Flute **11** Don Giovanni **12** Cosi fan tutte **16** Marriage of Figaro
by Offenbach: 15 Tales of Hoffmann
by Ponchielli: 10 La Gioconda
by Puccini: 5 Tosca **8** La Boheme **12** Manon Lescaut **15** Madame Butterfly
by Rossini: 8 Tancredi **11** William Tell **15** The Barber of Seville
by Smetana: 13 The Bartered Bride
by Strauss: 6 Salome **7** Elektra **15** Ariadne auf Naxos **16** Der Rosenkavalier
by Tchaikovsky: 12 Eugene Onegin
by Verdi: 4 Aida **6** Otello **8** Falstaff **9** Rigoletto **10** La Traviata **11** Il Trovatore
by Wagner: 8 Parsifal **9** Lohengrin **10** Tannhauser **16** Tristan and Isolde **17** The Flying Dutchman **21** The Ring of the Nibelungs
comic: 5 buffa **7** comique
glass: 9 lorgnette
hat: 5 crush, gibus
house: 3 Met **6** Sydney **7** La Scala **12** Covent Garden, Metropolitan
singer: 4 bass, diva **5** basso, buffa, buffo, tenor **7** soprano **8** baritone **9** contralto **10** coloratura, prima donna **12** mezzo soprano
singular: 4 opus
solo: 4 aria
text: 8 libretto
operate 2 go **3** run **4** go in, work **6** behave, manage, open up **7** oversee, perform **8** function **11** superintend **14** perform surgery **18** perform an operation
operating 6 active **7** working **8** in motion **9** operative **10** responsive
operation 5 force **6** action, agency, effect **7** conduct, pursuit, running, surgery, working **8** activity, exertion **9** influence, procedure **10** management, overseeing **11** exploratory, performance, supervision **15** instrumentality, superintendence
operative 3 spy **4** dick **5** agent, in use **6** acting, active, shamus, worker **7** in force, working **8** in effect, in motion, workable **9** activated, detective, effective, effectual, operating **10** functional, private eye, responsive **11** efficacious, secret agent
operator 4 doer, user **5** agent, pilot **6** driver, worker **7** manager **9** performer
opere citato 14 in the work cited
abbreviation: 5 op cit
Ophelia
character in: 6 Hamlet
author: 11 Shakespeare

ophidiophobia
fear of: 6 snakes
Ophion
form: 7 serpent
created from: 9 north wind
created by: 8 Eurynome
Ophir
father: 6 Joktan
source of: 4 gold
opiate 4 dope **6** downer **7** anodyne **8** hypnotic, narcotic, nepenthe, sedative **9** analgesic, calmative, soporific, stupefier **10** depressant, painkiller, palliative **12** somnifacient, stupefacient, tranquilizer
opine 3 say **4** deem **5** allow, guess, offer, state, think **6** assume, reckon **7** believe, imagine, presume, suggest, surmise **8** conclude, consider, estimate **9** speculate, volunteer **10** conjecture, have a hunch
opinion 4 idea, view **6** belief, notion, theory **7** surmise **8** estimate, judgment, thinking **9** sentiment, suspicion **10** assessment, assumption, conception, conclusion, conjecture, conviction, estimation, evaluation, impression, persuasion **11** speculation
opinionated 8 dogmatic, obdurate, stubborn **9** obstinate, pigheaded, unbending **10** bullheaded, headstrong, inflexible, unyielding **12** closedminded **14** uncompromising
O Pioneers!
author: 11 Willa Cather
Opis
companion of: 7 Artemis
Opobalsammum 12 Biblical tree
Oppenheimer, Julius Robert
field: 7 physics
directed development of: 10 atomic bomb
  location: 9 Los Alamos, New Mexico
chaired: 3 AEC **22** Atomic Energy Commission
Opper, Frederick
creator/artist of: 13 Happy Hooligan **17** Alphonse and Gaston, And Her Name Was Maud
opponent 3 foe **5** enemy, rival **8** resister **9** adversary, assailant, contender, disputant **10** antagonist, challenger, competitor, opposition
opportune 3 apt **5** happy, lucky **6** proper, timely **7** fitting **8** suitable **9** expedient, favorable, fortunate, welltimed **10** auspicious, convenient, felicitous, profitable, propitious, seasonable **11** appropriate **12** advantageous
opportunity 4 time, turn **5** means **6** chance, moment **7** opening **8** occasion **9** situation **10** good chance **11** contingency
oppose 4 buck, defy **5** fight **6** battle, combat, resist, thwart **7** contest **8** ob-

struct **9** withstand **12** be set against, speak against
opposed 3 con **4** anti **6** averse, pitted **7** adverse, against, counter, hostile **8** contrary, disputed, objected, resisted **9** contested, countered **10** confronted, contrasted, reciprocal **12** contradicted
opposer 5 rival **8** opponent **9** adversary **10** antagonist, competitor
opposite 5 other **6** facing **7** adverse, counter, reverse **8** contrary, converse, opposing **9** differing **11** conflicting **12** antagonistic, antithetical **13** contradictory, counteractive
opposite number 5 equal **8** parallel **10** equivalent **11** correlative, counterpart
opposition 3 foe **5** enemy, rival **6** enmity **8** aversion, defiance, opponent **9** adversary, contender, hostility, other side, rejection **10** antagonism, antagonist, competitor, negativism, resistance **11** contrariety, disapproval **12** disagreement
oppress 3 tax, try, vex **4** pain **5** abuse, worry **6** burden, deject, grieve, sadden, sorrow **7** depress, trouble **8** cast down, dispirit, maltreat **9** despotize, persecute, tyrannize, weigh down **10** discourage, dishearten
oppressed 7 crushed **9** exploited **10** tyrannized **11** downtrodden, subservient
oppressive 5 cruel, harsh **6** brutal, severe, trying, vexing **7** onerous, painful, wearing **8** despotic, grievous, pressing **9** worrisome **10** burdensome, depressing, repressive, tyrannical, unbearable **11** distressing, hardhearted, troublesome **12** discouraging **13** uncomfortable
oppressor 6 despot, tyrant **8** autocrat, dictator
opprobrious 4 base **6** wicked **7** abusive, corrupt, damning **8** infamous, reviling, shameful, shocking **9** malicious, maligning, nefarious, vilifying, vitriolic **10** censorious, deplorable, despicable, malevolent, outrageous, scandalous, scurrilous, unbecoming **11** acrimonious, disgraceful, fulminating **12** condemnatory, denunciatory, dishonorable, disreputable, faultfinding **13** hypercritical, objectionable, reprehensible
opprobrium 5 shame **6** infamy **8** disgrace, dishonor **9** disrepute **12** denunciation
Ops
origin: 5 Roman
goddess of: 6 plenty
husband: 6 Saturn
son: 7 Jupiter
called: 10 Magna Mater
corresponds to: 4 Rhea **6** Cybele **9** Dindymene **10** Berecyntia
opt for 4 pick, take **5** adopt **6** choose,

select, take up **7** embrace, espouse, fix upon, pick out **8** decide on, settle on

optimism 10 confidence **11** hopefulness **12** cheerfulness, sanguineness **13** bright outlook, encouragement

optimistic 6 bright **7** hopeful, roseate **8** buoyed up, cheerful, sanguine **9** confident, favorable, heartened, promising **10** auspicious, encouraged, heartening, propitious **11** encouraging, rose-colored **12** enthusiastic

Optimist's Daughter, The
  author: 11 Eudora Welty

optimum 4 acme, A-one, best, peak **5** crest, ideal, prime **6** choice, height, select, zenith **7** capital, perfect, supreme **8** flawless **9** faultless, first-rate **10** perfection, unexcelled **11** superlative **12** quintessence

option 4 will **5** voice **6** choice, liking **8** decision, election, free will, pleasure **9** franchise, privilege, selection **10** discretion, partiality, preference **11** alternative **12** predilection

optional 4 open **8** elective, unforced **9** allowable, open- ended, voluntary **10** volitional **11** not required **12** discretional **13** discretionary, nonobligatory

opulence 6 bounty, plenty, riches, wealth **7** fortune **8** elegance, luxuries, richness **9** abundance, affluence, amplitude, profusion **10** cornucopia, lavishness, plentitude, prosperity **11** copiousness, great wealth **13** sumptuousness

opus 4 work **5** piece **6** effort **7** attempt, product **8** creation **9** handiwork, invention **10** brainchild, production **11** composition

oracle, Oracle 4 sage, seer **5** augur, sibyl **6** wizard **7** adviser, diviner, prophet **9** predictor, Scripture **10** forecaster, soothsayer **11** clairvoyant

oral 5 vocal **6** spoken, verbal, voiced **7** uttered **8** ingested **9** swallowed **10** of the mouth, verbalized **11** articulated, using speech
  Latin: 8 viva voce

orange
  varieties: 4 king, mock, sour, wild **5** blood, hardy, natal, navel, Osage, sweet **6** bitter, common, Panama, Temple **7** Florida, Mexican, Satsuma, Seville, Spanish **8** Bergamot, Mandarin, Otaheite, Valencia **9** Tachibana, vegetable **10** Chinese box, trifoliate **13** African cherry, Mediterranean **15** Jamaica mandarin **17** house-blooming mock
  liqueur: 7 Curacao

orangutan, orang-outang 3 ape **4** mias **5** satyr **6** primate **10** anthropoid
  characteristic: 8 arboreal **11** herbivorous
  native land: 6 Borneo **7** Sumatra
  species: 13 Pongo pygmaeus

ora pro nobis 9 pray for us

orate 6 recite, speak **7** declaim **11** make a speech

oration 4 talk **5** spiel **6** eulogy, sermon, speech **7** address, lecture, recital **9** discourse, monologue, panegyric **10** peroration **11** declamation **12** disquisition, formal speech

orator 6 talker **7** speaker **8** lecturer, preacher **9** declaimer **10** sermonizer **11** rhetorician, speechmaker, spellbinder **12** elocutionist **13** public speaker

oratory 6 speech **7** bombast **8** delivery, rhetoric **9** elocution, eloquence, preaching **11** declamation **12** speechifying, speechmaking **14** grandiloquence

orb 4 ball, moon **5** globe **6** sphere **7** globule **8** spheroid

orbit 3 way **4** path **5** cycle, route, track **6** circle, course **7** channel, circuit, pathway **10** trajectory **13** revolve around **14** circumnavigate

orchards
  god of: 9 Vertumnus

orchestra 3 pit **4** band **6** stalls **7** parquet **8** ensemble, parterre **12** Philharmonic

orchestrate 5 adapt, score **7** arrange, compose

orchestration 5 score **10** adaptation **11** arrangement **12** organization

orchid
  varieties: 3 bat, bee, fen, fly, nun, nut **4** baby, blue, dove, moth, nun's, rein, swan **5** black, chain, cigar, cobra, coral, giant, jewel, pansy, Salep, showy, snowy, spice, tiger, water, widow **6** bamboo, bottle, cradle, dollar, Easter, helmet, mirror, monkey, pigeon, ragged, sawfly, shower, spider, stream, virgin **7** Alaskan, cowhorn, fringed, hooker's, jumping, peacock, rainbow, rosebud, scarlet, soldier **8** bee-swarm, Cooktown, cranefly, fried-egg, gold-lace, greenfly, hyacinth, nun's-hood, poorman's, Savannah, scorpion, white nun, windmill, woodland **9** bluntleaf, butterfly, chocolate, Christmas, clam-shell, green rein, green swan, white rein **10** buttonhole, five-leaved, golden swan, hay-scented, late spider, leafy white, Sierra rein, slender bog **11** cockle-shell, crested rein, dancing-doll, dancing-lady, early spider, golden chain, green-winged, one-leaf rein, pink slipper, purple-spire, rattlesnake, round-leaved **12** green fringed, pink scorpion, purple-hooded, Southern rein, tall white bog, white fringed **13** crested yellow, golden fringed, green woodland, Northern green, ragged fringed, yellow fringed **14** crested fringed, large butterfly, little club-

spur, white butterfly **15** lesser butterfly, lily-of-the-valley **16** downy rattlesnake, Florida butterfly, Northern small bog, purple fringeless, small round-leaved, white-flowered bog **18** large purple fringed, leafy Northern green, small purple fringed, Southern small white **19** lesser purple fringed **20** greater purple fringed

Orcus
  god of: 10 underworld
  punishes: 7 perjury
  corresponds to: 3 Dis **5** Hades, Pluto **8** Dis Pater

ordain 4 name, rule, will **5** elect, enact, frock **6** decree, invest **7** adjudge, appoint, command, dictate **8** delegate, deputize, instruct **9** determine, legislate, prescribe, pronounce **10** commission, consecrate

ordeal 4 care, pain **5** agony, grief, trial, worry **6** burden, misery, sorrow, strain, stress **7** anguish, concern, torment, tragedy, trouble **8** calamity, distress, pressure, vexation **9** heartache, nightmare, suffering **10** affliction, oppression **11** tribulation, unhappiness **12** wretchedness **16** trying experience

order 3 bid, law **4** body, book, calm, club, fiat, form, kind, rank, rule, sort, type **5** breed, caste, class, grade, group, guild, house, lodge, quiet, ukase **6** adjure, ask for, charge, decree, degree, demand, dictum, direct, engage, enjoin, family, status, stripe, system **7** agree to, bidding, caliber, call for, command, company, control, dictate, harmony, pattern, quality, request, reserve, silence, society, species, station **8** alliance, category, division, grouping, instruct, neatness, position, purchase, sorority, standing, tidiness **9** framework, structure, ultimatum **10** discipline, federation, fraternity, imperative, sisterhood, tabulation **11** arrangement, association, brotherhood, commandment, confederacy, designation, instruction, tranquility **12** codification, organization, peacefulness, tranquillity **13** pronouncement **14** categorization, classification

ordered 4 bade, neat, trim **7** regular, uniform **8** arranged **9** shipshape **10** systematic

orderliness 8 neatness, tidiness **10** discipline **12** organization

orderly 4 neat, tidy **5** civil, quiet **6** proper, spruce **8** peaceful **9** organized, peaceable, shipshape, tractable **10** classified, controlled, methodical, restrained, system atic **11** disciplined, uncluttered, well-behaved

ordinance 3 act, law **4** bull, fiat, rule, writ **5** canon, edict, order **6** decree, dictum, ruling **7** command, mandate, statute **9** enactment **10** regulation **11** commandment

ordinarily 7 as a rule, usually **8** commonly, normally **9** generally, regularly, routinely **10** habitually **11** customarily **12** on the average **14** conventionally

ordinary 4 dull, so-so **5** usual **6** common, normal **7** average, humdrum, routine, trivial, typical **8** everyday, familiar, habitual, mediocre, standard **9** customary **10** pedestrian, uninspired **11** commonplace, indifferent, stereotyped, traditional, unimportant **12** conventional, run-of-the-mill, unimpressive **13** insignificant, unexceptional, unimaginative, uninteresting **15** inconsequential, undistinguished

Ordinary People
director: **13** Robert Redford
author: **11** Judith Guest
cast: **10** Judd Hirsch **13** Timothy Hutton **14** Mary Tyler Moore **16** Donald Sutherland
Oscar for: **7** picture **8** director **12** screenwriter **15** supporting actor (Hutton)

ordinary wine
French: **12** vin ordinaire

ordnance 4 arms **6** cannon **9** armaments, artillery, munitions

ordnance depot 6 armory **7** arsenal **18** military storehouse

ore 3 tin **4** gold, iron, lead, paco, rock, zinc **5** metal **6** bronze, copper, galena, sulfur **7** halvans, mineral **8** aluminum, cinnabar, hematite **9** melachite
byproduct: **6** gangue
deposit: **3** bed **4** lode, mine, vein **7** bonanza
layer: **4** seam **5** stope
trough: **6** strake
worthless: **4** slag **5** dross, matte

Oread
form: **5** nymph
location: **8** mountain
companion of: **7** Artemis

oregano
name means: **16** joy of the mountain
botanical name: **8** O vulgare, Origanum
also: **6** organy, origan **8** marjoram **9** pizza herb **11** Mexican sage, winter sweet
origin: **13** Mediterranean
family: **4** mint
cure for: **11** indigestion **14** loss of appetite
first aid for: **12** spider stings **14** scorpion stings
use: **5** pizza **6** broths **8** stuffing **12** tomato dishes **13** Italian dishes

Oregon
abbreviation: **2** OR **4** Oreg
nickname: **6** Beaver, Sunset **7** Webfoot **13** Sawdust Empire

capital: **5** Salem
largest city: **8** Portland
others: **5** Nyssa **6** Albany, Eugene **7** Ashland, Astoria, Medford **8** Portland, Roseburg **9** Corvallis, Pendleton **10** Grant's Pass, Willamette **12** Klamath Falls
college: **4** Reed **7** Pacific **8** Linfield, Portland **10** Willamette **13** Lewis and Clark
feature:
  fort: **5** Boise **6** Casper **7** Kearney, Laramie
  national park: **10** Crater Lake
tribe: **4** Coos **5** Alsea, Kusan, Modoc, Wasco, Yanan, Yunca **6** Cayuse, Chetco, Chinoo, Kuitsh, Molala, Siletz, Tenino, Umpqua **7** Bannock, Clatsop, Klamath, Sastean, Shastan, Takelma, Walpapi, Yaquina **8** Clackama, Klikitat, Nez Perce, Sahaptin, Umatilla **9** Kalapuyan, Tillamook **10** Kalapooian, Wallawalla
people: **10** Wayne Morse **12** Linus Pauling **15** Phyllis McGinley
  explorer: **13** Lewis and Clark
lake: **5** Abert, Waldo **6** Harney, McNary **7** John Day, Klamath, Malheur
  deepest in US: **6** Crater
land rank: **5** tenth
mountain: **6** Mazama, Tacoma, Walker, Wilson **7** Elkhorn, Grizzly, Jackson, Rainier, Tidbits, Wallowa **8** Cascades **9** Blue Coast, Marys Peak **10** Strawberry
  highest point: **4** Hood
physical feature:
  bay: **4** Coos
  caves: **11** Marble Halls
  wind: **7** Chinook
river: **5** Rogue, Snake **6** Imnaha, Owyhee, Powder, Umpqua **7** Blitzen, John Day, Klamath, Silvie's **8** Columbia **9** Deschutes **10** Willamette
state admission: **11** thirty-third
state bird: **17** western meadowlark
state fish: **13** Chinook salmon
state flower: **7** mahonia **11** Oregon grape
state motto: **8** The Union
state song: **14** Oregon My Oregon
state tree: **10** Douglas fir

Oregon Trail, The
author: **14** Francis Parkman

Oresteia
author: **9** Aeschylus
trilogy includes: **9** Agamemnon, Eumenides **10** Choephoroe

Orestes
author: **9** Euripides
character: **5** Helen **6** Apollo, Furies **7** Electra, Pylades **8** Menelaus

Orestes
father: **9** Agamemnon
mother: **12** Clytemnestra
sister: **7** Electra **9** Iphigenia
wife: **8** Hermione

son: **9** Tisamenus
killed: **9** Aegisthus **12** Clytemnestra
pursued by: **6** Furies

Orfeo, L'
also: **17** The Story of Orpheus
opera by: **10** Monteverdi

Orfeo ed Euridice
also: **18** Orpheus and Eurydice
opera by: **5** Gluck
character: **4** Amor, Zeus **6** Furies

Orff, Carl
born: **6** Munich **7** Germany
composer of: **7** Der Mond, The Moon **8** Antigone, Die Kluge **9** Schulwerk **10** Prometheus **13** Carmina Burana, The Clever Girl **14** Catulli Carmina **16** Oedipus der Tyrann, Oedipus the Tyrant

organ 6 agency **7** journal, vehicle **9** harmonium **10** hurdy-gurdy, instrument **11** publication

organic 5 alive, quick **6** living **7** animate, natural, ordered, planned, unified **8** designed, physical **9** patterned **10** anatomical, harmonious, methodical, systematic **12** nonsynthetic **13** physiological **14** constitutional

organism 4 cell **5** plant, whole **6** animal, entity, system **7** complex, network, society **8** creature **9** bacterium **10** federation **11** association, corporation, institution, living thing **13** microorganism

organization 4 club, firm, sect **5** corps, group, order, party, union **6** design, league, making, outfit **7** company, forming, harmony, pattern, society **8** alliance, assembly, business, grouping, ordering **9** arranging, formation **10** federation, fellowship, fraternity **11** arrangement, association, composition, corporation, formulation, structuring **12** constitution, coordination **13** establishment, incorporation

organizational 10 managerial **13** developmental **14** administrative

organize 4 file, form, tidy **5** found, group, index, order, set up **6** codify, create, neaten, tidy up **7** arrange, catalog, develop **8** classify, tabulate **9** establish, formulate, originate **10** categorize, coordinate **11** make orderly, systematize

organized 4 neat, tidy **7** logical, orderly **8** coherent **10** methodical, systematic

orgiastic 4 wild **6** wanton **7** drunken, riotous **9** abandoned, debauched, Dionysian, dissolute, libertine **10** dissipated, licentious **12** bacchanalian, unrestrained **13** overindulgent, undisciplined

orgy 7 debauch, wassail **8** carousal **9** bacchanal **10** saturnalia **11** bacchanalia

orient, the Orient 3 fix, set **4** Asia, find **6** locate, relate, square **7** situate

8 accustom **9** acclimate, reconcile **10** the Far East **11** Eastern Asia, familiarize

oriental 4 Arab, fine, Thai, Turk **5** Asian **6** bright, Indian, Korean **7** Asiatic, Chinese, Eastern, Iranian, shining **8** Japanese, lustrous, precious, superior **10** Vietnamese
   animal: 4 zebu **5** rasse
   building: 6 pagoda
   dish: 5 pilau, pilaw **6** pilaff
   drum: 6 tomtom
   food fish: 3 tai
   garment: 3 aba **6** sarong
   inn: 4 Khan **5** serai **6** imaret **11** caravansary
   laborer: 6 coolie
   market: 3 suk, sug **4** souk **6** bazaar
   nurse: 4 amah, ayah
   prince: 4 amir, haja
   sail: 6 lateen
   sash: 3 obi
   shrub: 3 tea **5** henna **8** oleander
   wagon: 5 araba
   weight: 2 mo **4** rotl, tael **5** catty, liang **6** cantar

orientation 8 location **9** alignment, direction, situation **10** adjustment **11** acclimation **15** acclimatization, familiarization

orifice 3 gap, pit **4** hole, slit, slot, vent **5** cleft, inlet, mouth **6** cavity, cranny, hollow, lacuna, pocket, socket **7** crevice, fissure, opening, passage **8** alveolus, aperture, entrance

origami
   Japanese art of: 12 paper folding

origin 4 base, line, race, rise, root **5** agent, basis, birth, breed, cause, house, stock **6** author, family, father, ground, growth, mother, reason, source, spring, strain **7** creator, descent, genesis, lineage, taproot **8** ancestry, nativity, producer **9** beginning, emergence, evolution, generator, inception, parentage, principle **10** derivation, extraction, foundation **12** commencement, fountainhead

Origin, The
   author: 11 Irving Stone

original 3 new **4** bold **5** basic, basis, first, fresh, novel **6** daring, primal, unique **7** example, initial, pattern, primary, seminal, strange, unusual **8** atypical, creative, ear- liest, germinal, primeval, singular, uncommon **9** different, essential, first copy, formative, inaugural, ingenious, inventive, prototype **10** aboriginal, newfangled, primordial, underlying, unfamiliar, unorthodox **11** fundamental, imaginative **12** introductory **13** extraordinary **14** unconventional

Original Amateur Hour, The
   host: 7 Ted Mack

originality 6 daring **7** newness, novelty **8** boldness **9** freshness, ingenuity **10** cleverness, creativity, uniqueness **11** imagination, singularity, unorthodoxy **13** individuality, inventiveness **17** unconventionality

originally 7 at first, by birth **8** uniquely **9** initially, unusually **10** creatively **11** differently, inventively **13** imaginatively

originate 4 come, flow, rise, stem **5** arise, begin, draft, found, issue, start **6** create, crop up, derive, design, devise, emerge, evolve, father, invent, sprout **7** develop, emanate, proceed **8** commence, conceive, envision, initiate, organize, spring up **9** establish, fabricate, formulate, germinate **10** inaugurate

origination 5 birth **7** genesis **9** inception, invention **10** conception, initiation **11** germination **12** commencement **13** establishment

Origin of Species, The
   author: 13 Charles Darwin

Origins of Totalitarianism, The
   author: 12 Hannah Arendt

Orion
   form: 5 giant
   vocation: 6 hunter
   pursued: 8 Pleiades
   killed by: 7 Artemis
   became: 13 constellation

Oriya
   language family: 12 Indo-European
   branch: 11 Indo-Iranian
   group: 5 Indic
   spoken in: 5 (northern) India

Orkney Islands
   county seat: 8 Kirkwall
   country: 8 Scotland
   firth: 8 Pentland
   island: 3 Hay **6** Rousay, Sanday **7** Westray **8** Stronsay **14** South Ronaldsay
   largest city: 6 Pomona

Orlando
   author: 13 Virginia Woolf
   character: 5 Sasha **14** Nicholas Greene **28** Archduchess Harriet of Roumania, Marmaduke Bonthrop Shelmerdine

Orlando
   character in: 11 As You Like It
   author: 11 Shakespeare

Orlando Furioso
   author: 7 Ariosto
   character: 6 Rogero **7** Rinaldo **8** Agramant, Angelica, Rodomont **9** Bradamant **11** Charlemagne

Ormazd 10 Ahura Mazda **12** supreme deity
   religion: 14 Zoroastrianism

ormolu 5 alloy, brass, paste **6** bronze **7** gilding **8** ornament
   imitation of: 4 gold
   used to decorate: 5 clock **9** furniture

ornament 4 deck, gild, trim **5** adorn **6** bedeck, enrich, finery, frills **7** festoon, furbish, garnish **8** beautify, decorate, furbelow, trick out, trimming **9** accessory, adornment, embellish **10** decoration, enrich ment **11** elaboration **13** embellishment **14** beautification

ornamental 4 gilt **5** fancy **6** chichi, rococo **10** decorative
   ball: 4 bead **6** pompom
   button: 4 stud
   grass: 4 neti
   loop: 5 picot
   metal: 5 niello

ornamentation 7 garnish **8** trimming **9** adornment **10** decoration **13** embellishment

ornate 5 fancy, showy **6** flashy, florid, lavish, rococo **7** adorned, baroque, flowery **9** decorated, elaborate, sumptuous **10** flamboyant **11** embellished, pretentious **12** ostentatious

ornery 4 curt, mean **5** surly, testy **6** crabby, grumpy, shirty **7** grouchy, peevish, waspish **8** snappish **9** dyspeptic, irascible, irritable **10** illnatured **11** ill-tempered, quarrelsome **12** cantankerous

ornithophobia
   fear of: 5 birds

ornithopod
   type of: 8 dinosaur
   member: 9 Iguanodon **10** Edmontonia, Nodosaurus **11** Anatosaurus, Polacanthus, Saurolophus, Scolosaurus, Stegosaurus **12** Ankylosaurus, Camptosaurus, Lambeosaurus, Pisanosaurus **13** Acanthopholis, Corythosaurus, Hypsilophodon, Palaeoscincus **14** Thescelosaurus **15** Parasaurolophus, Procheneosaurus **17** Heterodontosaurus

orotund 4 full, rich **5** clear **6** strong **7** pompous, ringing, vibrant **8** resonant, sonorous **9** bombastic **10** resounding, rhetorical, stentorian
   Latin: 10 ore rotundo

oro y plata 13 gold and silver
   motto of: 7 Montana

Orozco, Jose Clemente
   born: 6 Mexico **7** Jalisco (Zapotlan) **12** Ciudad Guzman
   artwork: 5 Grief **9** Catharsis **11** Omniscience **12** House of Tears **16** National Allegory, Social Revolution **18** Hidalgo and Castillo

Orphans of the Storm
   director: 10 D W Griffith
   cast: 11 Dorothy Gish, Lillian Gish **17** Joseph Schildkraut

Orpheus
   vocation: 4 poet **8** musician
   mother: 8 Calliope
   wife: 8 Eurydice
   member of: 9 Argonauts
   went into: 5 Hades
   killed by: 7 Maenads

Orpheus in the Underworld

also: 15 Orphee aux Enfers
operetta by: 9 Offenbach

Orsino
  character in: 12 Twelfth Night
  author: 11 Shakespeare

ort 3 bit **5** crumb, dregs, scrap **6** morsel, refuse, trifle **7** remnant **8** leavings, leftover

orthodox 5 fixed, pious, usual **6** devout, narrow **7** limited, regular, routine **8** accepted, approved, official, ordinary, standard **9** customary, religious **11** commonplace, conformable, established, traditional **12** conventional **13** authoritative, circumscribed

orthoptera
  class: 8 hexapoda
  phylum: 10 arthropoda
  group: 4 leaf **5** stick **6** locust, mantid **7** cricket **9** cockroach **11** grasshopper

Orwell, George
  real name: 15 Eric Arthur Blair
  author of: 4 1984 **10** Animal Farm **18** Nineteen Eighty- Four **29** Politics and the English Language

oryx 5 beisa **6** pickax **7** gazelle, gemsbok **8** antelope, leucoryx

Osage (Wazhazhe)
  language family: 6 Siouan
  location: 6 Kansas **8** Arkansas, Missouri, Oklahoma

Oscan
  language family: 12 Indo-European
  branch: 6 Italic

Oschophoria
  origin: 8 Athenian
  event: 8 festival
  honoring: 7 vintage **8** Dionysus

oscillate 4 vary, **5** pulse, swing, waver **6** change, seesaw **7** librate, pulsate, vibrate **8** hesitate **9** alternate, come and go, fluctuate, hem and haw, vacillate **10** ebb and flow, equivocate **12** shilly-shally **16** move back and forth

O'Shaughnessy, Brigid
  character in: 16 The Maltese Falcon
  author: 7 Hammett

osier 3 rod **4** wand **5** salix, withe **6** willow **7** dogwood, wilgers **9** twigwithy
  species: 14 Salix viminalis
  use: 6 wicker **8** basketry

Osiris
  origin: 8 Egyptian
  god of: 4 dead, Nile
  judge of: 4 dead
  king of: 4 dead
  wife: 4 Isis
  sister: 4 Isis
  son: 5 Horus
  brother: 3 Set **4** Seth **5** Horus
  killed by: 3 Set **4** Seth

Oskar Matzerath
  character in: 7 Tin Drum
  author: 5 Grass

Oslo
  capital of: 6 Norway
  former name: 11 Christiania
  landmark: 8 Storting (Parliament) **11** Royal Palace
  mountain: 12 Holmenkollen
  park: 7 Frogner
  peninsula: 8 Akershus
  street: 14 Karl Johansgate

Osmond, Gilbert
  character in: 18 The Portrait of a Lady
  author: 5 James

Osslan
  character in: 12 Gaelic poetry

ossify 6 harden **7** stiffen **9** fossilize

ossuary 8 boneyard **10** depository, receptacle

ostensible 6 avowed **7** alleged, assumed, feigned, implied, nominal, outward, seeming, surface, titular, visible **8** apparent, declared, illusory, manifest, specious **9** pretended, professed **10** presumable **11** perceivable

ostentation 4 airs, dash, fuss, pomp, ritz, show **5** glitz, gloss, swank **6** splash **7** display, glitter **8** flourish, pretense **9** pageantry, pomposity, showiness, spectacle
  French: 7 etalage

ostentatious 4 loud **5** gaudy, showy **6** flashy, florid, garish **7** pompous **8** affected, immodest, overdone **9** grandiose, obtrusive **10** flamboyant, showing off **11** conspicuous, exaggerated, pretentious **15** flaunting wealth

Osterreich see **7** Austria

ostracize 3 cut **4** oust, shun, snub **5** avoid, expel **6** banish, disown, reject **7** exclude, shutout **9** blackball, blacklist

Ostwald, Wilhelm
  field: 9 chemistry
  nationality: 6 German
  founded: 17 physical chemistry

O'Sullivan, Maureen
  born: 5 Boyle **7** Ireland **15** County Roscommon
  daughter: 9 Mia Farrow
  roles: 4 Jane (Tarzan movies) **16** David Copperfield **17** Pride and Prejudice **19** Hannah and Her Sisters

Otello
  also: 7 Othello
  opera by: 5 Verdi **7** Rossini

O tempora! O mores! 14 O times! O customs!
  said by: 6 Cicero

Othello
  director: 11 Stuart Burge
  author: 18 William Shakespeare
  character: 4 Iago **6** Cassio, Emilia **9** Desdemona
  cast: 11 Frank Finlay, Joyce Redman, Maggie Smith **15** Laurence Olivier

other 4 more **5** added, extra, spare **6** unlike **7** further, reverse **8** contrary, opposite **9** alternate, auxiliary, different, remaining **10** additional, contrasted, dissimilar **11** contrasting **13** contradictory, supplementary **14** differentiated

Other Gods
  author: 9 Pearl Buck

Other Side of Midnight, The
  author: 13 Sidney Sheldon

other than 3 but **4** save **6** except, saving **7** barring, besides **9** excepting, excluding

otherwise 5 if not **6** or else **9** inversely **10** contrarily **11** differently **12** contrariwise

otherworldly 7 sublime **8** heavenly **9** celestial **14** transcendental

O times! O customs!
  Latin: 14 O tempora! O mores!

Otionia
  father: 10 Erechtheus
  sister: 10 Protogonia
  death by: 9 sacrifice
    for victory of: 9 Athenians
    over: 11 Eleusinians

otiose 4 idle, lazy **6** futile **7** laggard, resting, useless, worn-out **8** abortive, impotent, inactive, indolent, listless, slothful, sluggish **9** fruitless, lethargic, powerless, somnolent **10** unavailing **11** incompetent, ineffective, inoperative, unrewarding **12** unproductive

Otomi
  tribe: 7 Capotec

O'Toole, Peter
  born: 7 Ireland **9** Connemara
  roles: 6 Becket **7** Creator, Lord Jim **13** Man of La Mancha **14** Goodbye Mr Chips, My Favorite Year, The Last Emperor **15** The Lion in Winter **16** Lawrence of Arabia, What's New Pussycat **18** How to Steal a Million

O'Trigger, Sir Lucius
  character in: 9 The Rivals
  author: 8 Sheridan

Ott, Mel
  nickname: 9 Boy Wonder **12** Master Melvin
  sport: 8 baseball
  position: 8 outfield
  team: 13 New York Giants

Ottawa
  capital of: 6 Canada
  early name: 6 Bytown
  falls: 6 Rideau **9** Chaudiere
  landmark: 18 National Arts Centre **19** Dominion Observatory, Parliament Buildings
  river: 6 Ottawa, Rideau **8** Gatineau
  university: 8 Carleton

Ottawa
  language family: 9 Algonkian **10** Algonquian
  location: 4 Ohio **6** Canada, Kansas **7** Ontario **12** Lake Michigan
  leader: 7 Pontiac

Otter
  origin: **12** Scandinavian
  mentioned in: **8** Volsunga
  form: **5** otter
  father: **8** Hreidmar
  killed by: **4** Loki
ottoman, Ottoman 4 seat, Turk **5**
  couch, divan, stool **7** sultane, Turkish
  9 footstool
  color: **3** red **9** vermilion
  governor: **3** bey, dey **5** pasha
  ruler: **5** Osman **8** Suleiman
  standard: **4** ale
Ouagadougou
  capital of: **10** Upper Volta **11** Burkina
  Faso
oui 3 yes
ounce
  abbreviation of: **2** oz
ounce troy
  abbreviation of: **3** oz t
Our Bill
  creator: **14** Harry Haenigsen
  character: **6** Walter
Our Crowd
  author: **17** Stephen Birmingham
Our Miss Brooks
  character: **8** Mrs Davis **12** Connie
  Brooks, Walter Denton **13** Osgood
  Conklin, Philip Boynton **14** Harriet
  Conklin
  cast: **8** Eve Arden **10** Dick Crenna,
  Gale Gordon, Jane Morgan **14** Gloria
  McMillan, Robert Rockwell
  Miss Brooks taught: **7** English
  school: **11** Madison High
Our Mutual Friend
  author: **14** Charles Dickens
  character: **4** Wegg **5** Venus **6** Boffin
  11 Bella Wilfer **17** Mortimer Lightwood, Young John Harmon (Hand-
  ford, Rokesmith)
our sea
  Latin: **11** mare nostrum
  ancient Roman name for: **13** Mediterranean
Our Town
  author: **14** Thornton Wilder
  character: **5** Simon Stimson
  Gibbs family: **2** Dr **3** Mrs **6** George
  7 Rebecca
  Webb family: **2** Mr **3** Mrs **5** Emily,
  Wally
  director: **7** Sam Wood
  cast: **10** Fay Bainter **11** Martha Scott
  13 William Holden
oust 4 fire, sack **5** eject, evict, expel **6**
  banish, bounce, put out, remove, un-
  seat **7** boot out, cashier, cast out, dismiss, kick out **8** throw out **9** discharge, give the ax **11** give the gate,
  send packing
ouster 6 firing **7** removal, sacking **8**
  bouncing, ejection, eviction **9** discharge, dismissal, expelling, expulsion, overthrow **10** banishment, cash-

iering **11** dislodgment, drumming out,
  throwing out **13** dispossession
out 2 ex **4** away **5** aloud, eject, forth,
  not in, passe **6** absent, begone, excuse, public **7** outside **8** exterior, external, revealed **9** in society, in the
  open, published **10** extinguish
out-and-out 4 pure, sure **5** sheer, total, utter **6** arrant **7** perfect **8** absolute, complete, hardened, outright,
  positive, thorough **9** confirmed, downright, unlimited **10** inveterate **11**
  straight out, unequivocal, unmitigated,
  unqualified **12** unregenerate, unrestricted **13** dyed-in-the-wool, thoroughgoing, unadulterated, unconditional
  14 unquestionable
outbrazen 4 dare, defy, face **8** confront **9** challenge, stand up to
outbreak 5 burst **7** display **8** epidemic, eruption, invasion, outburst **9**
  explosion **10** outpouring **13** demonstration
outbuilding 4 barn, shed **5** privy **6**
  garage, stable **7** latrine **8** outhouse,
  woodshed
outburst 5 blast, burst **7** display, thunder **8** eruption, outbreak **9** explosion
  10 outpouring **11** fulmination **13**
  demonstration
outcast 5 exile, rover **6** ousted, outlaw, pariah, roamer **7** refugee, runaway **8** banished, castaway, deportee,
  derelict, expelled, fugitive, rejected,
  vagabond **9** discarded **10** expatriate
Outcast of the Islands, The
  author: **12** Joseph Conrad
Outcault, R F
  creator/artist of: **11** Buster Brown **12**
  The Yellow Kid
outcome 3 end **5** fruit, issue **6** effect,
  payoff, result, upshot **9** aftermath,
  outgrowth **11** aftereffect, consequence
outcry 3 cry **4** howl, roar, yell, yelp,
  yowl **5** noise, shout, whoop **6** bellow,
  clamor, hubbub, scream, shriek, uproar **7** clangor, protest, screech **9**
  commotion, complaint, crying out,
  hue and cry, objection **10** cry of
  alarm, hullabaloo **12** caterwauling, remonstrance
outdated 5 passe **7** antique **8** outmoded **9** out-of-date **10** antiquated **12**
  old-fashioned
outdo 3 top **4** beat, best **5** excel, worst
  6 better, defeat, exceed, outfox, outwit **7** eclipse, outplay, outrank, surpass **8** outclass, outshine, outstrip **9**
  overcome **9** transcend
outdoor festival
  French: **13** fete champetre
outdoor market 5 agora **6** bazaar **10**
  flea market **11** marketplace
outer 6 distal, remote **7** extreme, farther, outside, outward, without **8** ex-

terior, external, outlying **9** outermost
  10 farther out, peripheral
outer edge 3 lip, rim, tip **5** bound **6**
  margin **8** boundary **9** extremity
Outer Mongolia
  also: **24** Mongolian People's Republic
  border: **5** China **6** Russia **11** Soviet
  Union
  capital: **4** Urga **5** Kulun **9** Ulan Bator
  currency: **5** mongo **6** tugrik
  desert: **4** Gobi **5** Shamo
  language: **7** Khalka
  mountain range: **5** Altai, Altay **7**
  Khangai
outermost 5 outer **6** utmost **7** extreme, outside, outward, surface **8** exterior, external **11** farthest out, most
  distant, superficial
outfit 3 fit, rig **4** gear **5** array, dress,
  equip, getup, habit, rig up **6** clothe,
  supply **7** appoint, costume, furnish **8**
  accouter, ensemble, wardrobe **9**
  equipment, provision, trappings **13**
  accoutrements, paraphernalia
outflow 5 issue **7** leakage, seepage **8**
  drainage **9** discharge
outgo 4 beat, cost, exit, pass **5** excel,
  issue, outdo **6** efflux, egress, outlay,
  outlet **7** outflow, surpass **8** outstrip **9**
  departure **11** expenditure
outgoing 4 warm **6** genial, social **7**
  amiable, cordial, exiting, leaving **8**
  friendly, going out, outbound, sociable
  9 convivial, departing **10** gregarious
  11 extroverted, sympathetic, warmhearted
outgoing person 9 extrovert **17** hail-
  fellow-well-met
outgrowth 3 end **4** knob, knot, node
  5 bulge, fruit, issue, shoot **6** result,
  sequel, sprout, upshot **7** product **8**
  offshoot **9** aftermath **10** conclusion,
  projection **11** aftereffect, consequence,
  culmination, excrescence, outcropping
  12 protuberance
outing 4 hike, ride, spin, tour, trip,
  walk **5** drive, jaunt, tramp **6** airing,
  junket, ramble **7** holiday **9** excursion
  10 expedition
outlander 5 alien, exile **6** emigre **7** invader, settler **8** intruder, newcomer,
  stranger, wanderer **9** Auslander, barbarian, foreigner, immigrant **10** tra-
  montane **12** ultramontane
outlandish 3 odd **5** kooky, queer,
  weird **6** far-out **7** bizarre, curious,
  strange, unusual **8** freakish, peculiar **9**
  eccentric, fantastic, grotesque, unheard-of **10** incredible, outrageous, ridiculous **12** preposterous, unbelievable, unimaginable, unparalleled **13**
  inconceivable **14** unconventional
outlast 6 endure, hold on, keep on, remain, stay on **7** carry on, hold out,
  outstay, outwear, perdure, persist,
  prevail, survive **8** continue
outlaw 3 ban, bar **4** deny, stop **5** felon

6 bandit, forbid, pariah **7** exclude, outcast **8** criminal, disallow, fugitive, prohibit, suppress **9** desperado, interdict, miscreant, proscribe **10** highwayman

outlay 3 fee **4** cost **5** outgo, price **6** charge **7** expense, payment **8** spending **11** amount spent, expenditure **12** disbursement

outlet 3 way **4** door, duct, exit, gate, path, vent **5** means **6** avenue, egress, escape, portal **7** channel, conduit, gateway, opening, passage

outline 4 plot **5** brief, trace **6** digest, limits, resume, review **7** contour, diagram, profile, summary, tracing **8** abstract, synopsis **9** blueprint, delineate, lineation, perimeter, periphery, sketch out **10** abridgment, silhouette **11** delineation **12** condensation
French: **6** apercu

outlook 4 view **5** scene, sight, vista **6** aspect, chance **7** picture, promise **8** attitude, forecast, panorama, prospect **9** spectacle, viewpoint **10** assumption **11** expectation, frame of mind, perspective, point of view, presumption, probability **12** anticipation

outlying 5 outer, rural **6** far-off, remote **7** distant, exurban **8** exterior, suburban **10** peripheral

outmoded 5 corny, dated, passe, tired **6** demode, old hat **7** antique, archaic, vintage **8** obsolete, old-timey, outdated **9** out-of-date **10** antiquated **12** old-fashioned, out-of-fashion **14** behind the times
French: **6** demode

Out of Africa
director: **13** Sydney Pollack
cast: **11** Meryl Streep (Baroness Karen Blixen, Isak Dinesen) **13** Robert Redford (Denys Finch Hatton) **19** Klaus Maria Brandauer (Baron Bror von Blixen)

out of bed 2 up **5** astir **9** up and at 'em **10** on one's feet, up and about **12** rise and shine

out-of-date 5 dated, passe **8** outmoded **10** antiquated **12** old-fashioned
French: **6** demode

out of doors 3 out **5** forth **6** abroad **7** outside **8** alfresco **12** in the open air

out-of-fashion 5 passe **8** obsolete, outmoded **9** out-of-date **12** old-fashioned
French: **6** demode

out of hand 4 wild **5** rowdy **6** unruly **10** disorderly **12** obstreperous, out of control, unmanageable, unrestrained **14** uncontrollable

out of keeping 8 atypical, peculiar, unseemly **9** anomalous, irregular **11** incongruous **12** inconsistent **13** inappropriate

out of kilter 4 awry **5** askew **6** uneven **7** crooked, oblique

out of line 6 unruly **9** excessive **10** exorbitant **12** presumptuous, unreasonable

out of many one
Latin: **13** e pluribus unum
motto of: **12** United States

out of one's head 3 mad **4** daft, nuts **5** crazy, nutty **6** insane **7** cracked, touched **8** demented, deranged, unhinged **10** unbalanced **12** mad as a hatter, off his rocker **15** mad as a March hare **17** nutty as a fruitcake

out of operation 4 dead, down **8** inactive **10** not working, out of order **11** inoperative

out of order 5 amiss **6** faulty **10** not working **11** inoperative, uncalled-for **13** inappropriate

out of place 3 odd **8** unseemly **10** unsuitable **11** incongruous, inconsonant **13** inappropriate

out of shape 4 bent **5** unfit **6** flabby, warped **7** crooked **8** deformed **9** distorted, untrained

out of sorts 5 cross, huffy, testy **6** crabby, cranky, touchy **7** bearish, grouchy, peevish **8** petulant, snappish **9** crotchety, irritable **10** ill-humored **11** ill-tempered **12** cantankerous **13** short-tempered

out of the books of
Latin: **8** ex libris

out of the fight
French: **12** hors de combat

out of the ordinary 4 rare **6** unique **7** notable, unusual **8** singular, uncommon **10** phenomenal, remarkable **11** exceptional **13** extraordinary

Out of the Past
director: **15** Jacques Tourneur
based on novel by: **13** Geoffrey Homes (Daniel Mainwaring) (Build My Gallows High)
cast: **9** Jane Greer **11** Kirk Douglas, Richard Webb **13** Rhonda Fleming, Robert Mitchum

out of touch 7 mixed-up **8** unstable **11** disoriented **12** out of contact **13** incommunicado

out-of-towner 7 tourist, visitor **9** sojourner, transient **11** nonresident

outpace 4 pass **5** outdo **6** exceed, outrun **8** outstrip

outpouring 6 deluge **7** barrage, gushing, outflow **8** effusion

output 4 crop, gain, take **5** yield **6** profit **7** harvest, produce, product, reaping, turnout **8** gleaning, proceeds **9** gathering **10** production **11** achievement **12** productivity **14** accomplishment

outrage 4 evil, gall, rile **5** anger, shock, wrong **6** arouse, enrage, insult, madden, offend, ruffle **7** affront, incense, provoke, steam up **8** atrocity, disquiet, enormity, iniquity **9** barbarity, indignity, infuriate **10** discompose, disrespect, exasperate, gross crime, scandalize **11** desecration, monstrosity, profanation **13** barbarousness, get one's back up, make one see red, slap in the face, transgression **17** make one's blood boil

outraged 3 mad **5** angry, irate, riled **6** fuming, raging **7** enraged, furious **8** incensed, inflamed, offended **9** affronted, indignant **10** displeased, infuriated

outrageous 4 base, foul, rank, rude, vile **5** gross **6** brutal, odious, wicked **7** abusive, extreme, galling, heinous, immense, inhuman **8** enormous, flagrant, inhumane, insolent, scornful, shocking **9** atrocious, barbarous, excessive, insulting, maddening, monstrous, nefarious, offensive, shameless **10** despicable, exorbitant, horrifying, immoderate, iniquitous, scandalous **11** disgraceful, infuriating, unspeakable, unwarranted **12** contemptible, contemptuous, exasperating, preposterous, unreasonable **13** disrespectful, reprehensible **14** unconscionable

outrageousness 8 enormity **9** immensity **10** wickedness **13** atrociousness, monstrousness offensiveness **16** preposterousness

outre 8 improper

outreach 6 exceed **7** surpass

outright 4 full **5** sheer, total, utter **6** at once, entire, openly **7** utterly, visibly **8** absolute, complete, entirely, patently, promptly, thorough **9** downright, forthwith, instantly, on the spot, out-and-out **10** absolutely, altogether, completely, manifestly, thoroughly, unreserved **11** immediately, unmitigated, unqualified **12** demonstrably, undiminished **13** thoroughgoing, unconditional

outrival 3 dim **5** excel, outdo **6** exceed **7** eclipse, surpass **8** outshine **9** transcend **10** overshadow, tower above

outrush 4 gust **8** overflow

outset 4 dawn **5** birth, start **7** dawning **9** beginning, departure, threshold **12** commencement

outshine 3 dim **5** excel, outdo **6** exceed **7** eclipse, surpass **9** transcend **10** overshadow

outside 4 case, face, skin **5** alien, faint, outer **6** facade, remote, sheath, slight **7** coating, distant, foreign, obscure, outdoor, outward, strange, surface **8** covering, exterior, external, outdoors **9** nonnative, outer side, outermost **10** extraneous, out-of-doors, unfamiliar

outsider 5 alien **7** outcast **8** onlooker, stranger **9** bystander, foreigner, nonmember **14** nonparticipant

outskirts 3 rim 4 edge 6 limits, verges 7 borders, fringes, margins, suburbs 8 environs 9 periphery, precincts 10 perimeters 11 extremities

outspoken 5 blunt, frank 6 candid, direct, honest 7 artless 9 guileless, ingenuous, unsparing 10 forthright, unreserved 11 opinionated, plainspoken 13 undissembling 15 straightforward, undissimulating

outspread 5 broad 6 opened, spread 7 laid out 8 expanded, extended, unfolded, unfurled, unrolled 9 spread out, stretched 12 outstretched

outstanding 3 due 5 famed, great, owing 6 famous, unpaid 7 eminent, notable, payable 8 foremost, renowned, striking 9 best known, exemplary, in arrears, marvelous, memorable, prominent, unsettled 10 celebrated, noteworthy, phenomenal, remarkable 11 exceptional, magnificent, uncollected 13 distinguished, extraordinary, unforgettable

outstrip 4 pass 6 exceed, outrun 7 outpace, surpass 11 leave behind

outward 5 outer 7 evident, outside, surface, visible 8 apparent, exterior, external, manifest 10 observable, ostensible 11 perceivable, perceptible, superficial

outward appearance 4 mien 6 aspect, facade, manner 7 bearing 8 demeanor, exterior

Outward Bound
  author: 10 Sutton Vane

outwardly 7 clearly, visibly 9 evidently, seemingly 10 apparently, manifestly, ostensibly 13 on the face of it 16 to all appearances

outwards 3 out 4 away

outweigh 6 exceed 7 eclipse, surpass 8 override 9 rise above 10 overshadow 11 predominate, prevail over 13 be heavier than, weigh more than

outwit 4 dupe, foil, fool, trap 5 trick 6 baffle, outfox, take in, thwart 7 ensnare 8 outsmart 9 get around 10 circumvent 11 outmaneuver

outworn 5 dated, passe 6 bygone 7 defunct, disused, extinct 8 obsolete, rejected 9 abandoned, discarded, forgotten, out-of-date 10 antiquated, superseded 12 old-fashioned 13 unfashionable

ouzo
  type: 7 liqueur
  origin: 6 Greece
  flavor: 5 anise
  substitute for: 8 absinthe

oval 5 ovate, ovoid 6 curved, ovular 7 obovate, oviform, rounded 9 egg-shaped 10 elliptical 11 ellipsoidal

ovation 6 cheers, homage, hurrah, hurray, huzzah 7 acclaim, fanfare, tribute 8 applause, cheering 9 adulation 11 acclamation

oven 3 umu 4 kiln, oast 5 baker, range, stove 6 hearth 7 broiler, chamber, kitchen, roaster
  clay: 7 tandoor
  fork: 7 fruggan, fruggin
  mop: 6 scovel

over 3 too 4 also, anew, done, else, gone, past 5 above, again, ended, extra, often 6 afresh, bygone, lapsed, no more, to boot 7 at an end, elapsed, expired, settled, surplus 8 finished, in excess, once more, too great 9 completed, concluded, excessive, remaining 10 additional, all through, in addition, passed away, repeatedly, terminated 11 a second time, superfluous

overabundance 4 glut 6 excess 7 surfeit, surplus 8 plethora 9 abundance, profusion 10 oversupply 11 superfluity 14 superabundance 15 supersaturation 21 embarrassment of riches
  French: 19 embarras de richesses

over again 4 anew 5 again 7 all over 8 once more 9 once again

overall 5 total 6 entire 7 general 8 complete, long-term, sweeping 9 extensive, long-range, panoramic 10 exhaustive, widespread 12 all-embracing, all-inclusive 13 comprehensive, thoroughgoing

over-and-above 5 added, extra 7 added on, besides 10 additional, in addition 13 supplementary

overawe 6 dazzle 9 overpower, overwhelm 10 intimidate

overbalance 5 upset 6 topple 8 outweigh

overbearing 5 cocky 6 lordly, snooty 7 haughty, high-hat, pompous, stuck-up 8 arrogant, despotic, egoistic 9 conceited, imperious, know-it-all 10 autocratic, disdainful, egotistical, high-handed, tyrannical 11 dictatorial, domineering, egotistical 13 high-and-mighty, self-assertive, self-important

overburden 3 tax 4 load, task, tire 5 whelm 7 exhaust, wear out 8 encumber, overwork, surcharge 9 overwhelm

overcast 4 dark, dull, gray, hazy 5 foggy, misty, murky 6 cloudy, dreary, gloomy, leaden 7 sunless 8 lowering 11 overclouded, threatening

overcharge 3 gyp, pad 4 rook, skin, soak 5 bleed, cheat, gouge, stick, sting, usury 6 extort, fleece 7 exploit 10 exaggerate

overcoat 3 mac 5 parka 6 duster, poncho, raglan, tabard, ulster 7 oilskin, paletot, topcoat 8 burberry, mackinaw 9 greatcoat, inverness, pea jacket 10 mackintosh, trenchcoat 12 chesterfield, Prince Albert

Overcoat, The
  author: 12 Nikolai Gogol
  character: 9 Petrovich 26 A Certain Important Personage 28 Akakii Akakiievich Bashmachkin

overcome 4 beat, best, lick 5 crush, quell 6 defeat, master, subdue 7 conquer, put down, survive, win over 8 suppress, surmount, vanquish 9 overpower, overthrow, overwhelm, transcend 11 prevail over, triumph over 14 get the better of

overconfident 5 brash 6 cheeky 8 arrogant, cocksure, egoistic, immodest, impudent 9 conceited 10 egoistical 11 egotistical, self-assured 12 presumptuous

overcrowd 3 jam 4 cram, fill, pack 5 stuff 7 congest

overcrowded 6 filled, jammed, packed 7 crammed, stuffed 9 congested, jampacked

overdecorated 5 gaudy, showy 6 flashy, garish 9 unsightly 12 ostentatious

overdelicacy 11 genteelness, prudishness 12 priggishness 14 overrefinement

overdo 4 gild 6 expand 7 amplify, ham it up, magnify, overact 8 overplay 9 embroider, overstate 10 do to excess, exaggerate 11 carry too far, hyperbolize 12 lay it on thick 13 stretch a point

overdue 4 late, slow 5 tardy 7 belated, delayed, past due 8 dilatory 10 behindhand, behind time, unpunctual 11 long delayed

overdue debt 7 arrears 10 balance due 18 balance outstanding

overflow 4 glut 5 flood 6 excess 7 run over, surplus 8 flow over, inundate, plethora, slop over 9 overspill, profusion 10 overspread, oversupply 11 copiousness, superfluity 13 overabundance 14 superabundance

overflowing 4 full 5 flush 7 replete, swamped 8 abundant, flooding 9 abounding, inundated 11 running over

overgarment 4 cape, coat, robe 5 cloak, habit, parka, shawl, smock 6 blazer, blouse, duster, jacket, kimono, mantle, poncho 7 sweater, topcoat, wrapper 8 cardigan, raincoat 9 gaberdine, housecoat

overgrown 4 rank 5 giant 7 blown-up 8 colossal, enlarged, forested, gigantic 9 luxuriant, oversized

overhang 3 jut 4 eave 5 bulge, drape, eaves, jetty 6 beetle, impend, sadden, shelve 7 project, suspend 8 protrude, threaten 9 projection

overhaul 4 beat, pass 5 catch 6 revamp 7 rebuild, remodel, restore, service 8 overtake, renovate 11 catch up with, recondition, reconstruct

overhead 3 nut **4** atop, roof **5** above, aloft, on top, upper **6** upward **7** ceiling, topmost, up above **8** superior **9** overlying, uppermost **11** overhanging

overindulge 4 baby **5** spoil, stuff **6** overdo, pamper, pig out **7** carouse, overeat **9** dissipate **11** mollycoddle

overjoyed 6 elated, joyous **8** ecstatic, euphoric, exultant, jubilant, thrilled **9** delighted, enchanted, exuberant, gratified **10** enraptured, enthralled **11** carried away, tickled pink, transported **12** happy as a lark

overlay 4 coat **5** cover, layer **6** carpet, veneer **7** blanket, coating **8** covering **11** superimpose

overload 3 tax **4** glut **5** flood, whelm **6** deluge, excess **7** burnout, surfeit **8** encumber **9** innundate, surcharge

overlook 4 miss, omit, skip **6** excuse, forget, give on, ignore, pass up, slight, survey, wink at **7** blink at, command, forgive, let ride, neglect **8** leave out, look over, pass over, shrug off **9** disregard, look out on **10** tower above **11** forget about, have a view of, leave undone

overlord 4 czar, tsar **7** emperor, monarch **8** autocrat **12** supreme ruler **13** absolute ruler

overly 3 too **4** very **6** highly, unduly **7** acutely, too much **8** overmuch, severely, to a fault, unfairly **9** extremely, intensely **10** needlessly **11** exceedingly, excessively **12** exorbitantly, immoderately, inordinately, unreasonably **18** disproportionately

overly trusting 5 naive **8** gullible **9** credulous **12** unsuspicious

overmodest 3 coy **4** prim **7** prudish **8** priggish **11** puritanical

overmuch 3 too **6** excess **7** surplus **8** plethora **9** profusion

overpass 4 span **6** bridge **9** crossover

overpower 4 beat, best, move, sway **5** crush, quell, worst **6** defeat, master, subdue **7** conquer **8** overcome, vanquish **9** influence, overwhelm

overpowering 6 mighty, strong **8** crushing **10** astounding **12** overwhelming

overpraise 4 line **7** blarney, fawning **8** flattery **11** fulsomeness

overpriced 6 costly **7** too high **9** expensive **10** exorbitant

overproud 4 vain **8** arrogant, egoistic **9** conceited **10** egoistical **11** egotistical, swell-headed **13** self-important

overrate 9 overprize, overvalue **10** overesteem, overpraise **12** overestimate **13** make too much of

overrefined 7 genteel, prudish **8** priggish **12** overdelicate

override 5 crush, quash **7** reverse **8** set aside **10** commission **11** countermand

overrule 4 deny, veto **5** annul, eject, repel, waive **6** cancel, refuse, reject, revoke **7** dismiss, nullify, outvote **8** disallow, outweigh, override, overturn, preclude, set aside, throw out **9** repudiate **10** invalidate **11** countermand

overrun 4 loot, raid, sack **5** choke **6** deluge, engulf, infest, invade **7** despoil, pillage, plunder, surplus **8** inundate, overgrow, pour in on, rove over **9** overwhelm, surge over, swarm over

overseas, oversea 5 alien **6** abroad, exotic **7** foreign **8** external **11** ultramarine **12** transoceanic **14** in foreign lands

oversee 3 run **4** boss, rule **5** guide, pilot, see to, steer, watch **6** direct, govern, handle, manage **7** carry on, command **8** attend to, overlook, regulate **9** supervise **10** administer **11** keep an eye on, preside over, superintend **12** have charge of

overseeing 7 bossing, guiding, running **8** guidance, handling, managing **10** leadership, management **11** attending to, supervising, supervision **13** administering **14** administrating, administration, superintending **15** superintendence

overseer 4 boss, head **5** chief **7** captain, foreman, manager **8** director, governor **10** supervisor, taskmaster **11** slave driver **13** administrator **14** superintendent

overshadow 3 fog **4** hide, mask, veil **5** cover, dwarf, shade **6** darken, screen, shroud **7** conceal, eclipse, obscure **8** outshine **9** tower over

overshadowing 7 eclipse, masking, shading, veiling **8** cloaking **9** darkening, eclipsing, obscuring **10** concealing, surpassing **11** concealment, obscuration **12** towering over

overshoe 3 gum **4** boot **6** arctic, gaiter, galosh, patten, rubber **7** galoshe

overshoot 4 pass **6** exceed, go over **8** go beyond

oversight 6 laxity, slight **7** blunder, mistake, neglect **8** omission **9** disregard **10** negligence **11** inattention **12** carelessness, heedlessness, inadvertence **13** careless error **14** neglectfulness **15** thoughtlessness

oversized 4 huge, vast **7** immense, mammoth **8** colossal, enormous, gigantic **10** monumental **14** Brobdingnagian

overspending 12 extravagance, throwing away

overspread 3 fog **4** coat, fill, pave **5** bathe, cloud, cover, paint, plate, smear **6** clothe, infest **7** blanket, diffuse, overlay, overrun, pervade, suffuse **8** disperse **9** whitewash

overstate 6 overdo, play up **7** enlarge,

inflate, lay it on, magnify, stretch, touch up **8** increase, overdraw, oversell **9** embellish, embroider, enlarge on, overpaint **10** exaggerate, overstress **15** spread it on thick

overstep 6 exceed **7** violate **10** transgress

oversupply 4 glut **6** excess **7** surfeit, surplus, too much **8** plethora **11** undue amount **13** overabundance **14** superabundance

overt 4 open **5** plain **6** public **7** evident, obvious, visible **8** apparent, manifest, palpable, revealed **10** easily seen, noticeable, observable, ostensible **11** perceivable, perceptible, unconcealed, undisguised

overtake 4 go by, pass **5** catch, reach **6** befall, gain on **7** run down **8** approach, overhaul **11** catch up with

overtax 4 tire **5** abuse, hoist **6** burden, exceed, strain, stress **7** exhaust **8** overload, overwork **9** misemploy **10** overburden

over the hill 3 old **4** aged **5** aging **7** elderly **11** past the peak **13** past one's prime

overthrow 4 undo **5** crush **6** defeat, mutiny, topple **7** abolish, undoing **8** downfall, overcome, overturn, toppling **9** abolition, bring down, overpower, rebellion **10** do away with, revolution

overtire 3 fag **4** bush, do in, poop **5** drain **7** exhaust, fatigue, wear out **8** enervate

overtone 3 hue **4** hint **5** drift **8** coloring, innuendo **10** intimation, suggestion **11** connotation, implication, insinuation

overtrustful 8 gullible **9** credulous **12** unsuspecting, unsuspicious **13** unquestioning

overture 3 bid **6** motion, signal, tender **7** advance, gesture, preface, prelude **8** approach, foreword, offering, preamble, prologue, proposal **9** beginning **10** invitation, suggestion **11** opening move, proposition **12** introduction

overturn 4 beat, oust **5** crush, upend, upset **6** defeat, depose, thrash, topple **7** capsize, conquer, turn out **8** overcome, push over, vanquish **9** knock down, knock over, overpower, overthrow, overwhelm **14** turn topsy-turvy, turn upside down

overturning
French: **14** bouleversement

overweening 5 bossy, cocky, pushy **6** brassy **7** haughty, pompous **8** arrogant, egoistic **9** bigheaded, imperious **10** disdainful, egoistical, high-handed, immoderate **11** domineering, egotistical, overbearing, patronizing **12** presumptuous **13** high-and-mighty, overconfident, self-important

overweight 3 fat 5 dumpy, fatty, gross, hefty, obese, piggy, plump, pudgy, stout, tubby 6 chubby, chunky, fleshy, portly, rotund 7 fattish, well-fed 8 roly-poly 9 corpulent 10 potbellied, well-padded 11 beerbellied, overstuffed 15 wellupholstered

overwhelm 4 beat, bury 5 crush, quash, quell, swamp 6 defeat, engulf 7 conquer, overrun, stagger 8 bowl over, confound, inundate, overcome, vanquish 9 devastate, overpower, overthrow, subjugate

overwhelming 8 crushing 10 staggering 11 astonishing, devastating 12 overpowering

overwork 3 tax 4 task, tire, toil 5 labor 6 burden, strain 7 exhaust, overtax, wear out 9 misemploy 10 overburden

overwrought 4 wild 5 riled 6 touchy, uneasy 7 excited, nervous, ruffled 8 agitated, frenzied, inflamed, wildeyed, worked up 9 perturbed, wrought up 10 distracted, high-strung 11 carried away, overexcited

Ovid
  author of: 6 Amores 7 Tristia 8 Heroides 11 Ars Amatoria 12 The Art of Love 13 Metamorphoses

ovule 3 egg, nit 4 germ, ovum 6 embryo 7 seedlet

ovum 3 egg 4 cell, germ, seed 5 spore 6 gamete 8 oosphere

owe 8 be in debt 11 be obligated 12 be beholden to, be indebted to

owed 3 due 5 owing 6 unpaid 9 in arrears 11 outstanding

Owen Marshall, Counselor at Law
  character: 11 Jess Brandon 12 Frieda Krause 15 Melissa Marshall

  cast: 9 Lee Majors 10 Arthur Hill 11 Joan Darling 17 Christine Matchett

owing 3 due 4 owed 6 unpaid 9 in arrears 11 outstanding

own 4 avow, have, hold, keep, tell 5 admit, allow, grant, yield 6 assent, concur, retain 7 concede, possess, private 8 disclose, maintain, personal 9 acquiesce, confess to, consent to, recognize 10 individual, particular 11 acknowledge

owner 6 holder, master 7 partner 8 landlady, landlord, mistress 9 copartner, landowner, possessor 10 landholder, proprietor 11 householder, titleholder 12 proprietress

own up to 5 admit 6 accept 7 confess 8 blurt out 9 recognize 11 acknowledge 14 come clean about

ox 3 oaf 4 bull, clod, musk, urus, zebu 5 aiver, beast, bison, gayal, steer 6 auroch, bantin, bovine 7 banteng, buffalo 10 clodhopper
  Cambodian: 7 Kouprey, Kouproh
  Celebesian: 3 goa, noa 4 anoa
  extinct: 4 urus 7 aurochs
  family: 7 bovidae
  genus: 3 bos
  horned: 4 reem
  hornless: 4 moil
  Indian: 4 gaur
  Paul Bunyan's: 4 Babe
    color: 4 blue
  stall: 4 crib
  team: 4 yoke
  Tibetan: 3 yak
  wild: 3 ure 4 anoa
  young: 4 stot 5 stirk

Ox-Bow Incident, The
  author: 21 Walter Van Tilburg Clark
  character: 5 Canby, Croft 6 Davies, Gerald, Martin, Tetley 9 Gil Carter
  director: 14 William Wellman
  cast: 10 Henry Fonda 11 Dana Andrews 12 Anthony Quinn 13 William Blythe 14 Mary Beth Hughes

oxen
  group of: 4 yoke

oxide 8 compound
  afterburn: 4 calx
  calcium: 4 calx, lime
  cobalt: 6 zaffer, zaffre
  element: 6 oxygen
  iron: 4 rust 8 hematite, limonite 9 colcothar, magnetite
  make by heat: 7 calcine
  sodium: 4 soda
  zinc: 6 cadmia

oxidize 4 burn, char, rust 7 corrode

Oxyderces
  epithet of: 6 Athena
  means: 10 bright-eyed

oxygen
  chemical symbol: 1 O

Oxylus
  origin: 8 Aetolian
  punishment: 5 exile
  chosen leader of: 10 Heraclidae
  led invasion of: 12 Peloponnesus

oyez 4 hear 6 attend
  cry used by: 10 court crier
  preceded: 12 proclamation

Oz see Wizard of Oz

Ozark Jubilee
  host: 8 Red Foley 10 Webb Pierce
  theme: 12 Sugarfoot Rag

Ozark State
  nickname of: 8 Missouri

Ozick, Cynthia
  author of: 10 Levitation 17 The Cannibal Galaxy 21 The Messiah of Stockholm

Ozzie and Harriet, The Adventures of
  cast: 11 David Nelson, Ozzie Nelson, Ricky (Eric) Nelson 13 Harriet Nelson

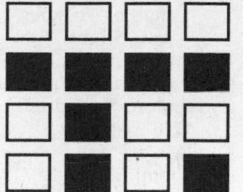
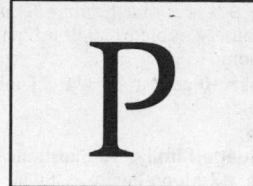
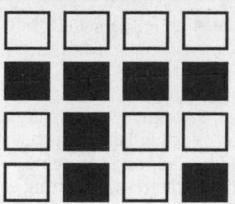

pa **3** dad, paw, pop **4** papa **5** daddy, pater **6** father
  mate: 2 ma

pace **4** clip, flow, gait, rate, step, walk **5** amble, speed, tread **6** motion, stride, stroll **7** saunter **8** momentum, slow gait, velocity

Pacelli, Eugenio Maria Giuseppe Giovanni **11** Pope Pius XII

pachyderm **5** hippo, rhino **8** elephant, ungulate **10** rhinoceros **12** hippopotamus
  characteristic: 4 tusk **5** ivory, trunk **12** thick-skinned
  prehistoric: 7 mammoth **8** mastodon

pachydermatous **4** hard **5** horny, tough **7** callous **8** callused, hardened, leathery **12** thick-skinned **13** elephant-hided

pacific **4** calm **5** quiet, still **6** gentle, placid, serene, smooth **7** halcyon, restful **8** dovelike, peaceful, tranquil **9** pacifying, peaceable, reposeful, unruffled **10** harmonious, untroubled **11** inoffensive, undisturbed **12** conciliatory

pacification **8** soothing **11** appeasement, peacemaking **12** conciliation, nonagression **14** reconciliation

Pacific island **3** Aru, Yap **4** Bali, Fiji, Guam, Maui, Oahu, Rapa, Truk, Wake **5** Nauru, Papua, Samoa **6** Hawaii, Kodiak, Midway, Ryukyu, Tahiti, Taiwan **7** Okinawa **8** Borabora, Eniwetok, Pitcairn, Tasmania **9** New Guinea **12** Bougainville

pacify **4** calm **5** allay, quiet **6** soothe **7** appease, assuage, compose, mollify, placate **9** reconcile **10** conciliate, propitiate

Pacino, Al
  real name: 13 Alberto Pacino
  born: 9 New York NY
  roles: 7 Serpico **8** Scarface **12** Author Author, Donnie Brasco, The Godfather **13** Scent of a Woman (Oscar) **15** Dog Day Afternoon **16** And Justice for All **17** Glengary Glen Ross **22** Does a Tiger wear a Necktie (Tony)

pack **3** box, jam, kit, lot, mob, set, tie **4** bevy, bind, cram, fill, heap, herd, load, mass **5** batch, bunch, clump, covey, crowd, drove, flock, group, horde, stuff, swarm, truss **6** bundle, gaggle, gather, packet, parcel, passel, throng **7** cluster, package **8** assemble **9** container, multitude **10** assortment, collection, miscellany **12** accumulation

package **3** box, kit **4** case, pack, wrap **6** bundle, carton, encase, packet, parcel, wrap up **9** container, wrappings

pack closely **4** cram, pack **5** press, stuff **7** compact **8** compress

packed **4** full **6** filled, jammed, loaded, massed, rammed, wedged **7** crammed, crowded, crushed, pressed, stuffed **8** overfull, squeezed **10** sandwiched **11** overcrowded

packet **3** bag, box **4** bale, pack, roll **5** pouch, sheaf **6** bundle, parcel, quiver **7** package

pact **4** bond **6** treaty **7** compact **8** alliance, contract, covenant **9** agreement, concordat **10** convention **11** concordance **13** understanding

pad **3** mat **4** fill **5** stuff **6** blow up, fat ten, tablet **7** bolster, cushion, inflate, protect, puff out **8** mattress, notebook **9** upholster **10** cushioning, stretch out

padding **6** filler, lining **7** filling, packing, surfeit, surplus, wadding **8** stuffing, verbiage, wrapping **9** prolixity, verbosity, wordiness **10** redundancy **11** verboseness **12** extravagance **14** superabundance

Paderewski, Ignace (Ignacy Jan)
  born: 6 Poland **9** Kurilowka
  composer of: 5 Manru **9** Minuet in G

pad out **5** add to **6** expand, extend **7** amplify, augment, enlarge, stretch **8** elongate, increase, lengthen

padre **6** cleric, father, priest **8** chaplain **9** clergyman

paean **6** anthem, eulogy **7** hosanna **9** laudation, panegyric **10** hallelujah **11** acclamation **12** hymn of praise
  form: 4 hymn, song
  characteristic: 6 joyful **12** thanksgiving

Paeon
  form: 3 god
  position: 9 physician
  served gods of: 7 Olympia
  corresponds to: 6 Apollo

Paezan
  language family: 13 Macro-Chibchan
  group: 4 Paez **5** Choco **6** Warrau **8** Colorado

pagan **7** atheist, heathen, infidel **8** idolator **9** barbarian **10** heathenish, idolatrous, polytheist, unbeliever **11** nonbeliever **12** polytheistic

Paganini, Niccolo
  born: 5 Genoa, Italy
  played: 6 violin
  composer of: 19 The Carnival of Venice

page **3** boy, lad **4** beep, call, girl, leaf **5** folio, groom, sheet, youth **6** knight, number, summon **7** callboy, contact **8** announce **9** attendant, messenger **10** apprentice, manservant
  blank: 7 flyleaf
  left-hand: 5 verso
  right-hand: 5 recto

Page, Geraldine
  born: 12 Kirksville MO
  husband: 7 Rip Torn
  roles: 5 Hondo **9** Interiors **11** Pete-n-Tillie **14** Summer and Smoke **16** A Trip to Bountiful (Oscar), Sweet Bird of Youth

Page and Mistress Page
  characters in: 22 The Merry Wives of Windsor
  author: 11 Shakespeare

pageant **4** pomp, rite, show **6** parade, ritual **7** display **8** ceremony **9** spectacle **10** exhibition, procession **12** extravaganza

pageantry **4** pomp, rite, show **5** drama, flair **6** ritual, splash **7** display, glitter, pageant **8** ceremony, grandeur, splendor **9** showiness, spectacle, theatrics **10** flashiness **11** ostentation **12** extravagance, magnificence

Paget, James
  field: 7 surgery **8** medicine
  nationality: 7 British
  founder of: 9 pathology

Pagliacci, I
  also: 9 The Clowns
  opera by: 11 Leoncavallo
  character: 5 Canio, Nedda, Tonio **6** Silvio

Pagnol, Marcel
  author of: 5 Cesar, Fanny **6** Marius, Topaze

Pago Pago
  capital of: 13 American Samoa

Pahlavi see Iran

Paige, Leroy
  nickname: 7 Satchel
  sport: 8 baseball
  position: 7 pitcher

pain 3 vex, woe 4 ache, gall, hell, hurt, pang, rile 5 agony, annoy, chafe, grief, pinch, pique, smart, sting, throb, worry 6 aching, grieve, harass, misery, ordeal, sadden, sorrow, stitch, twinge 7 agonize, anguish, disturb, hurting, malaise, sadness, torment, torture, trouble 8 distress, smarting, soreness 9 displease, heartache, suffering 10 affliction, discomfort, exasperate, heartbreak 11 unhappiness 12 wretchedness

Paine, Thomas
author of: 9 The Crisis 11 Common Sense 14 The Rights of Man

painful 3 sad 4 dire 5 sharp 6 aching, dismal, dreary, trying 7 arduous, hurtful, racking 8 grievous, grueling, pathetic, piercing, smarting, stinging, very sore 9 agonizing, difficult, sorrowful, throbbing, torturous 10 afflictive, disturbing, lamentable, unpleasant 11 disquieting, distasteful, distressful, distressing 12 disagreeable, excruciating

pain in the neck 4 bane 6 bother 7 torment 8 headache, nuisance 9 annoyance 10 affliction

painstaking 5 fussy 7 careful, earnest, finicky, precise 8 diligent, exacting, thorough 9 assiduous, energetic, strenuous 10 meticulous, scrupulous 11 industrious, persevering, punctilious 13 conscientious, thoroughgoing

paint 4 coat, daub, draw, limn, swab, tint 5 adorn, brush, color, cover, horse, rouge, shade, stain 6 depict, enamel, makeup, opaque, sketch 7 pigment, portray, stipple, touch up 8 cosmetic, decorate, describe, variegate 9 delineate, represent

Painted Bird, The
author: 13 Jerzy Kosinski

painter 6 artist, drawer 8 sketcher 9 old master 10 delineator 11 illustrator, landscapist, miniaturist 13 watercolorist

Painter, Painter's Easel
constellation of: 6 Pictor

painting 3 art, oil 5 draft, mural, piece 6 canvas, design, tablet 7 cartoon, daubing, drawing, graphic, picture, tableau 8 panorama, portrait, seascape 9 depiction, landscape, still life 10 cerography, watercolor 11 perspective 12 illustration
colloidal: 7 tempera
method: 9 encaustic
on plaster: 5 secco 6 fresco
one-color: 8 monotint 10 monochrome
opaque: 7 gouache
religious: 5 Pieta
style: 5 genre
tool: 5 brush, easel, knife 6 canvas, roller, sponge 7 palette 8 spraygun

pair 3 duo 4 dyad, mate, span, team, yoke 5 brace, match, unite 6 couple 7 combine, doublet, match up, pair off, twosome

pair off 10 go two by two 11 form couples

Paiute
language family: 10 Shoshonean
tribe: 12 Mono-Paviosto, Snake Indians 13 Digger Indians 14 Northern Paiute, Southern Paiute
location: 4 Utah 5 Idaho 6 Nevada, Oregon 7 Arizona 10 California

Pakistan
name means: 13 Land of the Holy, Land of the Pure
capital: 9 Islamabad
largest city: 7 Karachi
others: 3 Dir, Sui 4 Mari, Sidi 5 Dacca, Qasim, Ralat 6 Chalna, Khulna, Lahore, Multan, Quetta 7 Larkana, Sialkot 8 Jamalpur, Lyallpur, Peshawar, Sargodha 9 Hyderabad 10 Gujranwala, Rawalpindi
school: 9 U of Punjab 10 U of Karachi 12 U of Hyderabad 16 Allama Iqbal Open U 22 Pakistan U of Agriculture 39 Pakistan Institute of International Affairs
division: 3 Dir 4 Sind, Swat 5 Hunza, Kalat 6 Bengal, Kharan, Punjab 7 Chitral 8 Khairpur, Peshawar 10 Bahawalpur, Waziristan 11 Baluchistan
empire: 5 Gupta, Mogul 6 Kushan, Maurya 7 British, Magadha
seceded state: 10 Bangladesh
monetary unit: 4 anna, pice 5 paisa, rupee
weight: 4 seer, tola 5 maund
mountain: 3 Pab, Pub 4 Salt 6 Makran 7 Kirthar 8 Himalaya, Safed Koh, Sulaiman 9 Hindu Kush, Karakoram 11 Makran Coast 13 Central Makran 14 Takht-i-Sulaiman
highest point: 9 Tirich Mir 12 Godwin Austin
river: 3 Nal 4 Bado, Beas, Ravi, Swat, Zhob 5 Dasht, Indus, Kabul 6 Chenab, Ganges, Jamuna, Jhelum, Kundar, Porali, Sutlej 7 Jamunna
sea: 7 Arabian
physical feature:
bay: 8 Soymiani
canal: 4 Nara 5 Rohri
cape: 5 Fasta, Jaddi 6 Jiwani
delta: 6 Ganges 11 Char-Manpura
desert: 4 Sind, Thal, Thar
mountain pass: 5 Bolan 6 Khyber
plateau: 11 Baluchistan
valley: 5 Kohat
people: 5 Sindi, Wazir 6 Afridi, Bengal, Mahsud, Pathan, Sindhi 7 Baluchi, Brahuis, Puktuns, Punjabi, Sherani 8 Khattack, Pushtuns, Shinwari, Yusefazi 11 Mohammedzai
leader: 6 Jinnah 7 Aly Khan 8 Ayub Khan, Zia Ul-Haq 9 Ali Bhutto, Yahya Khan 13 Benazir Bhutto, Mujibur Rahman 15 Mah-

mud of Ghaznbi
poet: 5 Igbal, Iqbal
language: 4 Urdu 6 Pushtu, Sindhi 7 Baluchi, Bengali, English, Punjabi
religion: 5 Hindu, Islam 8 Buddhism 12 Christianity
place:
dam: 6 Mangla 7 Tarbela
gardens: 8 Shalamar
mosque: 8 Badshahi
tomb: 15 Emperor Jahangir
feature:
clothing: 5 kurta, pugri, qamis 6 jinnah 7 dupatta, shalwar 8 sherwani 9 churidars
food:
bread: 8 chappati
dish: 5 kebab, pilaf 6 qormas, salans, sautes 10 vermicelli
yogurt: 4 dahi

Pakula, Alan
director of: 13 Sophie's Choice 19 All the President's Men

pal 4 chum, mate, pard 5 buddy, crony 6 cohort, friend 7 comrade, partner 8 alter ego, intimate, sidekick 9 associate, colleague, companion, confidant 10 accomplice, bosom buddy 13 boon companion

palace 5 villa 6 castle 7 chateau, mansion 8 hacienda
French: 6 palais
Italian: 7 palazzo

palais 6 palace 17 municipal building 18 government building

Palamedes
lieutenant of: 9 Agamemnon

pal around 7 consort, hang out 9 associate, be friends, run around 10 fraternize

palatable 5 tasty 6 savory 8 pleasant 9 agreeable, toothsome 10 appetizing

palatial 4 posh, rich 5 grand, noble, plush, regal, ritzy, showy 6 swanky 7 elegant, opulent, stately 8 imposing, splendid 9 grandiose, luxurious, sumptuous 10 monumental 11 magnificent

palaver 3 gab 4 chat, talk 5 prate 6 confer, gossip, parley 7 consult, discuss, prattle 8 chitchat, idle talk 10 chew the fat, chew the rag, conference, discussion

palazzo 6 palace

pale 3 pen, wan 4 fold, post 5 ashen, close, light, pasty, stake, white 6 anemic, blanch, paling, pallid, picket, sallow, whiten 7 closure, confine, deathly, ghastly, upright, whitish 8 bleached, palisade 9 bloodless, colorless, deathlike, enclosure, ghostlike 10 ash-colored, cadaverous, light-toned

Pale Horse, Pale Rider
author: 19 Katherine Anne Porter

paleness 6 pallor 7 wanness 8 dullness 9 whiteness 13 colorlessness

paleontology

study of: 18 correlation of parts
founder: 13 Georges Cuvier

Palermo
    capital of: 6 Sicily

Palestine see **6** Israel

Palestrina, Giovanni Pierluigi da
    born: 5 Italy **10** Palestrina
    composer of: 11 Stabat Mater **18** Missa Papae Marcelli

Paley, Grace
    author of: 26 The Little Disturbances of Man **30** Enormous Changes at the Last Minute

Palici
    origin: 5 Roman
    form: 4 gods **5** twins
    gods of: 14 sulphur springs

paling 4 pale, rail **5** fence, stake **6** picket

Palinurus
    steersman of: 6 Aeneas

palisade 5 close, fence **7** bulwark, rampart **8** stockade **9** enclosure

palisades 4 crag **5** ledge **6** bluffs, cliffs **10** escarpment, promontory

pall 4 cloy, haze, sate **5** gloom, weary **6** shadow, sicken **7** dimness, satiate **8** darkness **10** become dull, be tiresome, depression, desolation, melancholy, moroseness, oppression

Palladio, Andrea
    real name: 26 Andrea di Pietro della Gondola
    architect of: 12 Villa Rotunda (Vicenza Italy) **14** Teatro Olimpico (Vicenza) **19** Church of Il Redentore (Venice) **26** Church of San Giorgio Maggiore (Venice)
    style: 9 Palladian

Pallas see **6** Athena

Pallas Athena see **6** Athena

pallet 3 bed, cot **4** bunk, tick **5** berth **8** mattress, platform

palliate 4 calm, curb, ease, hush, lull, tame **5** abate, allay, check, quiet, sooth, still **6** lessen, modify, reduce, soften, subdue, temper **7** assuage, comfort, cushion, lighten, relieve **8** decrease, diminish, minimize, mitigate, moderate **9** alleviate **10** ameliorate

palliative 4 balm **6** solace **7** anodyne, comfort **10** comforting

pallid 3 wan **4** ashy, blah, dull, pale **5** ashen, bland, pasty, vapid, waxen **6** boring, chalky, peaked, sallow **7** ghostly, humdrum, insipid, tedious **8** blanched, lifeless **9** bloodless, colorless **10** monotonous **13** anemic looking, unimaginative, uninteresting

pallor 7 wanness **8** paleness **9** pastiness, whiteness **10** ashen color, pallidness **11** ghostliness **13** bloodlessness, colorlessness

palm
    varieties: 3 Fan, Ita, Key, Nut, Oil, Wax **4** Cane, Date, Doom, Doub, Doum, Fern, Hair, Hemp, King, Lady, Nipa, Nypa, Rock, Sago, Step, Tala, Wine **5** Areca, Areng, As sai, Betel, Black, Bread, Broom, Curly, Grass, Honey, Inaga, Ivory, Jelly, Latan, Manac, Nikau, Peach, Queen, Royal, Snake, Spine, Sugar, Syrup, Toddy, Yatay, Zombi **6** Bamboo, Barbel, Barrel, Bottle, Cherry, Cohune, Coyoli, Gebang, Gomuti, Gru-gru, Hesper, Kentia, Licuri, Manila, Mazari, Needle, Nibung, Parlor, Pignut, Raffia, Rattan, Ruffle, Sagisi, Sentry, Silver, Thatch, Thread, Yellow **7** Arikury, Cabbage, Calappa, Coconut, Coquito, Feather, Fiji fan, Funeral, Jaggery, Leopard, Mexican, Moriche, Overtop, Palmyra, Prickly, Spindle, Talipot, Weddell **8** Betel nut, Carnauba, Cucurite, Dwarf fan, Fishtail, Good luck, Ivory-nut, Mangrove, Pandanus, Peaberry, Princess, Roebelin, Umbrella, Wild date, Windmill **9** Alexander, Alexandra, Butterfly, Christmas, Desert fan, Gippsland, Guadalupe, Hurricane, India date, Macarthur, Ouricouri, Panama-hat, Petticoat, Piccabeen, Porcupine, Pygmy date, Silver saw, Solitaire, Spiny-club, Traveler's **10** African oil, Black-fiber, Canary date, Chinese fan, Cuban belly, Cuban royal, Everglades, Franceschi, Saw cabbage, Sealing-wax, Thatch-leaf, Washington **11** American oil, Chilean wine, European fan, Gingerbread, Mexican blue, Morass royal, Senegal date, Slender lady, Woolly butia **12** Caribee royal, Egyptian doum, Florida royal, Miniature fan, Walking stick **13** Australian fan, Australian ivy, Australian nut, Belmore sentry, Feather-duster, Florida silver, Florida thatch, Forster sentry, Golden feather, Miniature date, San Jose hesper **14** Common princess, East Indian wine, Puerto Rican hat, Tufted fish tail, Yellow princess **15** Burmese fishtail, Chinese fountain, Chinese windmill, Yellow butterfly **16** Hispaniolan royal, Northern bangalow, Puerto Rican royal **17** Australian cabbage, Clustered fishtail, Mexican Washington, Piccabeen bangalow **18** South American royal

Palm Beach Story, The
    director: 14 Preston Sturges
    cast: 9 Mary Astor **10** Joel McCrea, Rudy Vallee **15** William Demarest **16** Claudette Colbert

Palmer, Arnold
    sport: 4 golf
    noted for: 10 Arnie's Army

Palmer, Lilli
    real name: 17 Lillie Marie (Maria Lilli) Peiser
    born: 5 Posen **7** Germany
    husband: 11 Rex Harrison **14** Carlos Thompson
    roles: 11 Body and Soul
    autobiography: 22 Change Lobsters and Dance

Palmetto State
    nickname of: 13 South Carolina

Palm Sunday
    author: 12 Kurt Vonnegut

palmy 4 rosy **5** balmy, sunny **6** golden **7** booming, halcyon **8** blooming, pleasant, thriving **9** agreeable, bounteous, congenial **10** prosperous, successful **11** flourishing, pleasurable

Palmyra
    Biblical name: 6 Tadmor

palpable 5 clear, plain **7** evident, obvious, tactile, visible **8** apparent, definite, distinct, feelable, manifest, tangible **9** touchable **10** noticeable **11** discernible, perceivable, perceptible **12** recognizable, unmistakable

palpitate 4 beat **5** pound, shake, throb **6** quaver, quiver, shiver **7** flutter, tremble, vibrate **9** go pit-a-pat

palsied 7 quaking, shaking, spastic **9** trembling

palsy-walsy 5 close, palsy, thick **6** chummy **8** friendly, intimate **10** buddy-buddy **14** thick as thieves

paltriness 10 triviality **12** unimportance **14** insignificance **18** inconsequentiality

paltry 4 poor, puny **5** petty, sorry **6** measly, shabby **7** scrubby, trivial **8** inferior, picayune, piddling, trifling, wretched **11** unimportant **13** insignificant, of little value **14** inconsiderable **15** inconsequential

Pamela
    author: 16 Samuel Richardson
    character: 3 Mr B **9** Mrs Jervis, Mrs Jewkes **10** Lady Davers **13** Pamela Andrews

pamper 5 humor, spoil **6** coddle, cosset **7** cater to, indulge **8** give in to **11** mollycoddle

pampered 7 coddled, humored **8** indulged **9** catered to, cossetted

pamphlet 5 tract **6** folder **7** booklet, leaflet **8** brochure, bulletin, circular **9** monograph, throwaway

pan 3 boo, map, mug, pot **4** face, hiss **6** kisser **8** ridicule, saucepot **9** criticize

Pan
    also: 7 Sinoeis
    origin: 5 Greek
    form combined: 3 man **4** goat
    god of: 6 flocks **7** forests **8** pastures **9** shepherds
    father: 4 Zeus **6** Hermes
    loved: 4 Echo **5** Pitys **6** Syrinx
    invented: 5 pipes **6** syrinx
    corresponds to: 6 Faunus

panacea 6 elixir **7** cure-all, nostrum **13** universal cure

panache 4 dash, elan, tuft **5** flair, plume, style, verve **11** flamboyance

Panama
  capital/largest city: **10** Panama City
  others: **4** Daid **5** Ancon, Colon **6** Azuero, Balboa, Gamboa **8** Dos Bocas, Penonome, Santiago **9** Cristobal **10** Portobello
  division: **5** Cocle, Colon **6** Darien, Panama **7** Herrera **8** Chiriqui, Veraguas **9** Los Santos **12** Bocas del Toro
  measure: **7** celemin
  monetary unit: **4** cent **6** balboa **10** centesimos
  island: **5** Coiba, Pearl **6** Cebaco, Multas, Taboga **7** San Blas **10** Isla Del Rey **12** Bocas del Toro, Juan Gallegos **13** Barro Colorado
  lake: **5** Gatun
  mountain: **4** Baru, Maje **5** Chico, Gandi **6** Darien **7** Columan, San Blas, Veragua **8** Santiago, Tabasara **10** Costa Rican **14** Serrania de Sapo **15** Aspave Highlands **17** Cordillera Central
  highest point: **8** Chiriqui
  river: **5** Chepo, Sambu, Tuira **6** Bayano, Panugo **7** Chagres
  sea: **7** Pacific **9** Caribbean
  physical feature:
    bay: **5** Limon **6** Panama
    dam: **5** Gatun
    gulf: **6** Darien, Panama, Parita **7** Montijo, San Blas **8** Chiriqui **9** Mosquitos, San Miguel
    isthmus: **6** Darien, Panama **7** San Blas
    lagoon: **8** Chiriqui
    peninsula: **6** Azuero **8** Valjente
  people: **4** Cuna **5** Choco **6** Guaymi **7** mestizo
    canal builder: **7** Lesseps
    explorer: **6** Balboa **8** Bastidas, Columbus
    leader: **4** Royo **5** Arias **7** Noriega **8** Guerrero, Torrijos **9** Espriella **12** Simon Bolivar
    poet: **4** Miro **5** Korsi, Sinan
  language: **7** English, Spanish
  religion: **13** Roman Catholic
  place:
    church: **7** San Jose **15** Virgen del Carmen
    plaza: **13** Independencia
    ruins: **9** Old Panama
  feature:
    clothing: **7** montuno, pollera
    dance: **4** caja **7** pujador **9** tamborito
    tree: **4** yaya **5** maria, quira **6** alfaje, cativo
    US operation: **9** Just Cause
  food:
    meat: **6** tazajo
    soup: **8** sancocho

Panama City
  capital of: **6** Panama

pancake 4 blin **5** blini, crepe, kisra, latke, lefse **6** blintz, makeup **7** fritter, hotcake **8** flapjack, slapjack **11** griddlecake **12** silverdollar
  day: **13** Shrove Tuesday

Pancks
  character in: **12** Little Dorrit
  author: **7** Dickens

pancreas
  produces: **7** insulin

Pandareus
  father: **6** Lycaon, Merops
  daughter: **5** Aedon **6** Merope **9** Cleothera
  wounded: **8** Menelaus
  stole: **9** golden dog
  turned to: **5** stone
  killed by: **8** Diomedes

Pandarus
  character in: **18** Troilus and Cressida, Troilus and Criseyde
  author: **7** Chaucer **11** Shakespeare

Pandarus
  son: **7** Alcanor
  companion of: **6** Aeneas

pandemic 4 rife **7** rampant **8** epidemic **10** prevailing, widespread **21** dangerously contagious

pandemonium 3 din **5** chaos **6** bedlam, clamor, hubbub, racket, rumpus, tumult, uproar **7** turmoil **8** disorder **9** commotion **10** hullabaloo **11** disturbance

Pandemos
  epithet of: **9** Aphrodite

pander, panderer 4 mack, pimp **5** cadet **7** hustler **8** procurer **9** maquereau, souteneur **12** fleshpeddler

Pandion the Younger
  king of: **6** Athens
  later reigned in: **6** Megara

Pandora
  form: **10** first woman
  created by: **10** Hephaestus
  presented to: **10** Epimetheus
  daughter: **6** Pyrrha
  given by gods: **3** box
    box contained: **4** hope **5** evils

Pandrosos
  position: **9** priestess
  first priestess of: **6** Athena
  father: **7** Cecrops
  mother: **8** Agraulos

panegyric 6 eulogy, homage, praise **7** tribute **8** citation, encomium, good word **9** extolment, laudation **10** compliment **11** testimonial **12** commendation

panegyrize 4 laud **5** extol **6** praise **8** eulogize

panel 4 jury, pane **5** board, group, piece **6** insert **7** divider **8** bulkhead **9** committee, partition **10** round table **11** compartment, expert group, select group **13** advisory group

pang 4 ache, pain **5** agony, pinch, smart, stick, sting, throb **6** stitch, twinge **7** anguish **8** distress **9** suffering **10** discomfort

Pangloss
  character in: **7** Candide
  author: **8** Voltaire
  characteristic: **8** optimism

pang of conscience 5 demur, qualm **6** unease **7** remorse, scruple **9** misgiving **10** uneasiness **11** compunction

panhandle 3 beg, bum **5** cadge, mooch **6** hustle **7** solicit **9** importune

Panhandle State
  nickname of: **12** West Virginia

Panhellenius
  epithet of: **4** Zeus
  means: **14** god of all Greeks

panic 5 alarm, dread, go ape, scare **6** fright, horror, terror **7** anxiety **8** affright, hysteria **9** cold sweat, confusion, fall apart **10** go to pieces **11** nervousness, trepidation **12** apprehension, perturbation **13** consternation

panicky 6 scared **7** alarmed, anxious **9** terrified **10** frightened **13** panic-stricken, scared to death **14** terror-stricken

panic-stricken 6 afraid, scared **7** alarmed, anxious, fearful, panicky **9** terrified **13** scared to death **14** terror-stricken

Panjabi
  language family: **12** Indo-European
  branch: **11** Indo-Iranian
  group: **5** Indic
  spoken in: **5** (northern) India

Pankrits
  language family: **12** Indo-European
  branch: **11** Indo-Iranian
  form of: **5** Indic
  followed use of: **8** Sanskrit

pannier 3 bag **4** hoop **6** basket, dossel, pantry **7** corbeil, drapery **9** framework, overskirt
  literally: **11** breadbasket

Panoptes
  epithet of: **5** Argus
  means: **7** all eyes

panorama 5 scene, vista **6** survey **7** diorama, picture, scenery, tableau **8** long view, overview, prospect **10** scenic view **11** perspective **12** bird's-eye view

panoramic 3 ide **7** overall **8** bird's-eye, extended, sweeping **9** extensive **10** far-ranging **11** far-reaching **12** all-embracing, all-inclusive **15** all-encompassing

pansy 5 Viola
  varieties: **4** Wild **5** Field **6** Garden, Orchid **8** Japanese **9** Miniature **11** Monkey-faced **12** European wild

pant 4 blow, gasp, huff, puff **6** wheeze

pant after 4 seek **5** covet, crave **6** desire, pursue **7** hope for, long for, lust for, wish for **8** yearn for **9** hanker for, hunger for, lust after **11** thirst after, have a yen for **14** set one's heart on

Pantagruel *see* **22** Gargantua and Pantagruel

panther 3 cat **6** cougar **7** leopard

Pantomime Quiz
   host: **10** Mike Stokey **15** Pat Harrington Jr

pantry 5 ambry, store **6** closet, galley, larder **7** butlery, buttery, pannier, spicery **8** cupboard, scullery

pants 5 jeans **6** denims, shorts, slacks **7** drawers, panties **8** breeches, britches, knickers, trousers **9** bluejeans, dungarees **10** underpants **11** undershorts **12** underdrawers

pantywaist 4 wimp **5** sissy, softy **7** crybaby, milksop **8** mama's boy, weakling **10** namby-pamby, sissypants, weak sister **11** Milquetoast, mollycoddle **13** sissy-britches

Panurge
   character in: **22** Gargantua and Pantagruel
   author: **8** Rabelais

Panza, Sancho
   character in: **10** Don Quixote
   author: **9** Cervantes

pap 3 rot **4** bosh, junk, mash, mush, pulp, tosh **5** gruel, paste **6** cereal, drivel, l'ablum, trivia **7** rubbish, twaddle **8** soft food **10** balderdash, flapdoodle, triviality

papa 2 pa **3** dad, doc, paw, pop **5** daddy, poppy **6** father, priest **9** Hemingway
   mate: **4** mama

Papa Bear
   nickname of: **11** George Halas

Papago
   language family: **5** Piman **10** Uto-Aztecan
   location: **6** Mexico **7** Arizona
   related to: **4** Pima

papal 9 apostolic, of the pope **10** pontifical

paper 4 bond, deed, news, opus, pulp, work **5** daily, draft, essay, stock, theme **6** record, report, tissue, weekly **7** article, gazette, journal, monthly, tabloid, writing **8** document, gift wrap **9** cardboard, chronicle, newspaper, newsprint, onionskin **10** instrument, manuscript, paperboard, periodical, stationery, typescript **11** certificate, com position, publication

Paper Chase, The
   character: **10** James T Hart, Willis Bell **13** Asheley Brooks **14** Elizabeth Logan, Jonathan Brooks **15** Franklin Ford III **19** Thomas Craig Anderson **29** Professor Charles W Kingsfield Jr
   cast: **10** James Keane **11** Robert Ginty **12** Deka Beaudine, John Houseman **13** James Stephens, Jonathan Segal

14 Francine Tacker, Tom Fitzsimmons
   subject: **9** law school
   Kingsfield's specialty: **11** contract law

paper measure 4 ream **5** quire

Paper Moon
   director: **16** Peter Bogdanovich
   cast: **9** Ryan O'Neal **10** Tatum O'Neal **12** Madeline Kahn (Trixie Delight) **13** John Hillerman
   Oscar for: **17** supporting actress (O'Neal)

Papua New Guinea
   formerly: **16** British New Guinea
   capital: **11** Port Moresby
   town: **3** Thu, Lae **4** Ioma **6** Kikori, Madang
   province of: **9** Indonesia
   province: **9** West Irian
   monetary unit: **4** kina
   island: **6** Misima **10** New Britain
   archipelago: **8** Bismarck
   lake: **6** Murray
   river: **3** Fly **4** Ramu
   sea: **5** Coral **7** Solomon
   strait: **6** Torres
   people: **4** Hula, Kate **5** Kiwai, Kwoma **6** Banaro **7** Arapesh **10** Melanesian
   language: **7** English

papyrus 4 pith, reed **5** paper, sedge **6** scroll **7** bulrush **8** document **10** manuscript
   accordion pleated: **6** orihon
   genus: **7** Cyperus
   origin: **5** Egypt **9** Nile delta **10** Nile valley
   use: **3** mat **4** rope, shoe, sail **5** paper

par 5 level, usual **6** normal, parity **7** average, balance, the norm **8** equality, evenness, identity, sameness, standard **9** stability **11** equilibrium, equivalency **12** equal footing **13** identicalness

parable 4 myth, tale **5** fable, story **6** homily, legend **8** allegory, apologue, folk tale **9** folk story **12** morality tale

Paracelsus
   author: **14** Robert Browning

parade 4 line, pomp, show **5** array, march, strut, train, vaunt **6** column, defile, flaunt, review, string **7** caravan, cortege, display, show off **8** vaunting **9** cavalcade, flaunting, march past, motorcade, pageantry, put on airs, spectacle **10** exposition, grandstand, procession **11** progression **13** demonstration

paradigm 5 ideal, model **6** matrix, sample **7** example, paragon, pattern **8** exemplar, original, standard **9** archetype, criterion, prototype, yardstick

paradise 3 joy **4** Eden **5** bliss **6** heaven, utopia **7** delight, ecstasy, nirvana, rapture **8** pleasure **9** enjoyment, happiness, Shangri-la, transport **11** happy valley **12** Garden of Eden, sat-

isfaction **13** gratification, seventh heaven **15** Land of Cockaigne

Paradise
   also: **9** Paradisio
   part three of: **12** Divine Comedy
   author: **14** Dante Alighieri

Paradise Lost
   author: **10** John Milton
   character: **3** Eve, God **4** Adam **5** Satan **6** Christ **7** Lucifer

Paradise of the Pacific
   nickname of: **6** Hawaii

Paradise Regained
   author: **10** John Milton

paradisiacal 7 elysian, sublime **8** blissful, empyreal, empyrean, ethereal, heavenly **9** celestial, unearthly **12** otherworldly

paradox 5 poser **6** enigma, oddity, puzzle, riddle **7** anomaly **11** incongruity **13** inconsistency

paradoxical 9 ambiguous, enigmatic, equivocal **13** contradictory

paragon 4 norm **5** ideal, model **6** symbol **7** example, pattern **8** exemplar, paradigm, standard **9** archetype, criterion, prototype, yardstick **10** apotheosis

Paraguay
   capital/largest city: **8** Asuncion
   others: **3** Ita **4** Rica, Yuty **5** Belen, Luque, Pilar, Villa **7** Caacupe **8** Trinidad **9** Paraguari **10** Concepcion, Villarrica **11** Encarnacion **26** Puerto Presidente Stroessner
   division: **6** Guaira, Itapua, Olimpo **7** Caazapa **8** Boqueron **10** Concepcion
   measure: **3** pie **4** lino, lira, lire, vara **5** legua **6** cuadra, fanega
   monetary unit: **4** peso **7** guarani, centimo
   weight: **7** quintal
   island:
      floating island: **8** camalote
   lake: **4** Vera, Ypoa **8** Ypacarai
   river: **3** Apa **5** Guazu, Negro, Plata, Verde, Ypane **6** Acaray, Parana **7** Aguaray, Confuso **8** Paraguay **9** Aquidaban, Pilcomayo, Tebicuary, Tibiquare **10** Monte Lindo **14** Riacho Gonzales **15** Riacho Mosquitos
   physical feature:
      falls: **6** Guaira
      plains: **5** Chaco
      plateau: **6** Parana
   people: **6** Abipon, Moskoi **7** Guarani, mestizo **8** Guayaqui
      artist: **7** Bestard
      author: **3** Pla **4** Baez **6** Alcala, Bastos, Correa, O'Leary **7** Cervera **8** Casaccia
      composer: **8** Asuncion
      leader: **5** Lopez **7** Francia **10** Stroessner **16** Antequera y Castro
      sculptor: **8** Guggiari
   language: **6** German **7** Guarani, Spanish

religion: 9 Mennonite 13 Roman Catholic

place:

church: 10 Villarrica 11 Incarnation

dam: 6 Itaipu

memorial: 16 Pantheon of Heroes

museum: 5 Godoi

palace: 10 Government

feature:

animal: 4 puma 5 tapir 6 iguana, jaguar 7 peccary

bird: 6 toucan

clothing: 5 fajas, typoi 6 poncho 7 rebozos 9 bombachas 10 alpargatas

communes: 11 reducciones

dance: 7 Sante Fe 15 Paraguayan polka

fish: 7 piranha

lace: 7 nanduti

music: 8 quarania

townspeople: 9 comuneros

tree: 5 ceiba 7 lapacho 9 quebracho

food:

bread: 5 chipa, mbeyu

dish: 12 sopa paraguay

tea: 9 yerba mate

vegetable: 8 mandioca

parallel 4 akin, like, same, twin 5 alike, equal, match 6 follow 7 abreast, analogy, be alike, similar 8 analogue, likeness, relation 9 alongside, analogous, corollary, duplicate 10 collateral, comparable, comparison, concurrent, connection, equivalent, similarity 11 coextensive, coincidence, comparative, compare with, correlation, correlative, counterpart, equidistant, resemblance 12 correspond to 13 corresponding 14 correspondence

parallelism 8 affinity, likeness, sameness 9 agreement 10 comparison, similarity, similitude 11 resemblance 14 correspondence

parallelogram 5 rhomb 6 square 7 diamond, rhombus 8 rhomboid 9 rectangle 11 plane figure 13 quadrilateral

paralyze 4 stun 6 benumb, deaden, disarm, freeze, weaken 7 cripple, destroy, disable, petrify, stupefy, wipe out 8 demolish, enfeeble 10 debilitate, immobilize, neutralize 12 incapacitate

Paramaribo

capital of: 8 Suriname

paramount 4 main 5 chief 6 utmost 7 capital, highest, leading, premier, supreme 8 cardinal, dominant, foremost, greatest, peerless, superior 9 essential, principal, unmatched 10 preeminent 11 outstanding, predominant 12 incomparable, preponderant, transcendent

paramour 3 man 4 doxy 5 lover, Romeo 6 gigolo 7 Don Juan 8 Casanova, fancy man, lothario, loverboy, mistress 9 boyfriend, concubine, courtesan, inamorata, inamorato, kept woman 10 girlfriend, lady friend, sugar daddy

paranoid 4 wary 7 deluded 9 paranoiac 11 distrustful 14 oversuspicious

parapet 7 bulwark, rampart 8 abutment, palisade 9 barricade, earthwork 10 battlement, breastwork

paraphernalia 3 rig 4 gear 5 stuff 6 outfit, tackle, things 7 effects, harness, regalia 8 fittings, material, supplies, utensils 9 apparatus, equipment, trappings 10 belongings, implements, properties, provisions 11 accessories, furnishings 13 accoutrements

paraphrase 5 recap 6 rehash, reword 7 restate 8 rephrase 12 recapitulate

parasite 5 leech 6 beggar, cadger, loafer 7 moocher, shirker, slacker, sponger 8 deadbeat 9 goldbrick, scrounger 10 freeloader 11 bloodsucker

inside host: 12 endoparasite

outside host: 12 ectoparasite

parasol 5 shade 6 shadow 7 roundel 8 sunshade, umbrella

mushroom: 7 lepiota

par avion 5 by air

parboil 4 boil 5 scald 6 blanch 7 precook

Parca

origin: 5 Roman

member of: 6 Parcae

goddess of: 7 destiny 10 childbirth

Parcae see 5 Fates

parcel 3 lot 4 bale, pack, part, plot 5 allot, piece, tract 6 bundle, divide, packet 7 carve up, deal out, dole out, package, portion, section, segment, split up 8 allocate, dispense, disperse, division, fraction, fragment, property 9 allotment, allowance, apportion, partition 10 distribute 11 piece of land

parceling out 9 allotment, doling out, meting out 10 allocation, assignment, dealing out 12 distribution 13 apportionment

parcel out 5 allot 7 dole out, give out, mete out 8 allocate, dispense, divide up 9 apportion 10 distribute, portion out

parch 4 bake, burn, char, sear 5 dry up, singe 6 dry out, scorch, sun-dry, wither 7 blister, shrivel 9 dehydrate, dessicate, evaporate

parched 3 dry 4 arid 6 barren 8 withered 9 shriveled 10 dehydrated, desiccated

parchment 6 scroll, vellum 7 papyrus 8 goatskin 9 sheepskin

pardon 5 grace, mercy 6 excuse, wink at 7 absolve, amnesty, blink at, forbear, forgive, release, set free 8 overlook, reprieve, shrug off 9 discharge, disregard, exculpate, exonerate, remission, vindicate 10 absolution, indulgence 11 deliverance, exculpation, forbearance, forgiveness 12 grant amnesty 16 forgive and forget

Pardoner

character in: 18 The Canterbury Tales

author: 7 Chaucer

pare 3 cut, lop 4 clip, crop, dock, hull, husk, peel, skin, trim 5 lower, prune, shave, shear, shell, shuck, slash, strip 6 lessen, reduce, shrink 7 curtail, cut back 8 decrease, diminish 11 decorticate

pare down 3 cut 4 trim 5 shave 6 reduce 7 abridge, curtail, cut down, shorten 8 condense, cut short, diminish 10 abbreviate

parent 3 dam 4 sire 5 model 6 father, mother 7 creator 8 ancestor, begetter, exemplar, original, producer 9 precursor, prototype 10 antecedent, forerunner, originator, procreator, progenitor 11 predecessor

parentage 5 birth, roots, stock 6 family, origin, strain 7 descent, lineage 8 ancestry, forbears, heredity, pedigree 9 ancestors, genealogy 10 background, derivation, extraction, family tree 11 antecedents

Parentalia

origin: 5 Roman

event: 8 festival

parenthetical 5 aside 6 braced, casual 8 inserted 9 bracketed 10 extraneous, immaterial, incidental, interposed, irrelevant 11 impertinent, intervening, superfluous

par excellence 8 superior 10 preeminent

parfait d'amour

type: 7 liqueur

flavor: 7 violets

color: 6 purple

Paria

form: 5 nymph

loved by: 5 Minos

children: 7 Chryses 9 Eurymedon, Nephalion, Philolaus

pariah 5 exile, rover, stray 6 outlaw, roamer 7 outcast 8 vagabond, wanderer 10 expatriate 11 undesirable, untouchable

paring 4 chip, snip 5 scrap, shred, slice 6 sliver 7 cutting, peeling, shaving 8 fragment

pari passu 6 fairly 7 equably 10 side by side 13 equal progress 17 without partiality

Paris

airport: 4 Orly 9 Le Bourget 15 Charles de Gaulle

area: 5 Passy 6 Clichy, Marais, Ternes, Wagram 7 Auteuil 8 Chaillot, Gobelins, Left Bank, St Honore 9 Les Halles, Right Bank, St Germain 10 Montmartre, Rive Droite, Rive

Gauche, Val de Grace **11** Ile de la Cite **12** Hotel de Ville, Latin Quarter, Montparnasse
capital of: 6 France
city planner: 9 Haussmann
island: 10 Ile St Louis **11** Ile de la Cite
landmark: 8 Pantheon **9** Notre Dame **10** Paris Opera, Sacre Coeur **11** Eiffel Tower, La Madeleine, Palais Royal **12** Elysee Palace, Hotel de Ville, Place Vendome **13** Arc de Triomphe, Palais Bourbon **14** Bois de Boulogne, Place de l'Etoile, Pompidou Center, Sainte Chapelle, Tomb of Napoleon **15** Bois de Vincennes **16** Luxembourg Palace **17** Hotel des Invalides, Place de la Bastille, Place de la Concorde **18** Jardin des Tuileries **20** Place Charles de Gaulle
nickname: 11 city of light
river: 5 Seine
street: 9 Haussmann, Invalides **10** Grand Armee **11** Saint Michel **12** Montparnasse, Saint Germain **13** Champs Elysees **15** Charles de Gaulle
subway: 5 Metro
university: 8 Sorbonne

Paris
character in: 14 Romeo and Juliet
author: 11 Shakespeare

Paris
position: 6 prince
father: 5 Priam
mother: 6 Hecuba
brother: 6 Hector **9** Polydorus
sister: 9 Cassandra
wife: 6 Oenone
abducted: 5 Helen
judgment of: 14 apple of discord
awarded apple to: 9 Aphrodite
killed by: 11 Philoctetes

parish 4 fold **5** flock, shire **6** canton, county **7** diocese, section **8** brethren, district, precinct, province **9** community, pastorate **10** department **11** archdiocese **12** congregation, neighborhood

parity 7 balance **8** equality, sameness **10** coequality, uniformity **11** equivalence, equivalency **14** correspondence

park 4 lawn **5** field, green, grove, woods **6** common, meadow, square **7** grounds, reserve **8** parkland, preserve, woodland **9** grassland, sanctuary **10** public park, quadrangle

Parker, Dorothy
author of: 6 Resume **9** Big Blonde **10** Enough Rope **13** Death and Taxes **18** After Such Pleasures **19** Laments for the Living

parkway 6 avenue **7** thruway **9** boulevard **12** thoroughfare

parlance 4 talk **5** idiom, lingo **6** speech **16** manner of speaking

Parlement of Fowles, The
author: 15 Geoffrey Chaucer

parley 4 talk **6** confab, powwow, summit **7** council, meeting, palaver **8** conclave **9** discourse, mediation, peace talk **10** conference, discussion **11** arbitration, negotiation **12** conversation

parliament 4 diet **5** court, house, junta **6** fan-tan, senate, sevens **7** cabinet, council **8** assembly, congress **9** high court **11** legislature **12** three estates
Communist: 6 Soviet **9** politburo, presidium
estate: 12 House of Lords **14** House of Commons
Germanic: 9 Bundesrat, Bundestag, Bolksraad **11** Volkshammer
Greek: 5 Boule
Icelandic: 7 Althing
Israeli: 7 Knesset **8** Knesseth
Scandinavian: 7 Lagting, Riksdag **8** Lagthing, Storting **9** Odelsting, Storthing
Spanish: 6 Cortes

parlor 5 salon **6** saloon **8** best room **9** front room **10** living room **11** drawing room, sitting room

Parnopius
epithet of: 6 Apollo
means: 9 locust god

parochial 5 local, petty, small **6** church, little, narrow, parish **7** insular, limited **8** regional **9** hidebound, illiberal, religious, sectional, small-town **10** provincial, restricted **11** countrified **12** narrow-minded

parodos
from Greek drama: 9 choral ode

parody 5 mimic **6** satire **7** lampoon, takeoff **8** satirize, travesty **9** burlesque, take off on **10** caricature

Parolles
character in: 20 All's Well That Ends Well
author: 11 Shakespeare

paroxysm 3 fit **5** spasm, spell **7** seizure **10** convulsion

parrot 3 ape **4** bird, echo, lory **5** macaw, mimer, mimic **6** chorus, monkey **7** copycat, imitate **8** cockatoo, imitator, parakeet **9** reiterate

parry 4 duck, shun **5** avert, avoid, dodge, elude, repel **7** beat off, fend off, repulse, ward off **8** sidestep, stave off **10** circumvent, fight shy of

Parsifal
opera by: 6 Wagner
character: 6 Kundry **8** Amfortas, Klingsor **9** Gurnemanz

Parsifal Mosaic, The
author: 12 Robert Ludlum

parsimonious 5 close, tight **6** frugal, saving, stingy **7** miserly, sparing, thrifty **9** niggardly, penurious **10** economical, ungenerous **11** closefisted,

tightfisted **13** money-grubbing, penny-pinching

parsimony 6 thrift **7** economy **8** meanness **10** stinginess **13** niggardliness **15** tightfistedness

parsley 19 Petroselinum crispum
varieties: 5 Horse **7** Chinese, Italian **12** Turnip-rooted
related herb: 4 dill **5** cumin **6** fennel
garland worn by: 8 Hercules
gives speed to: 6 horses
use in: 11 fines herbes **12** bouquet garni

parson 5 clerk, padre **6** cleric, divine, father, pastor, priest, rector **7** dominie **8** minister, preacher, reverend, shepherd, sky pilot **9** clergyman
French: 4 abbe, cure

parsonage 5 glebe, manse **7** deanery, rectory, Vatican **8** vicarage **9** pastorate

part 2 go **3** bit, job **4** care, chip, duty, hunk, item, open, rend, role, slit, task, tear, unit **5** break, chore, crumb, guise, leave, piece, place, scrap, sever, shard, share, sherd, shred, slice, split **6** branch, charge, cleave, depart, detach, detail, divide, go away, member, morsel, region, sector, set out, sliver, sunder **7** concern, cutting, disjoin, element, portion, push off, section, segment, snippet **8** breakoff, business, capacity, disguise, disunite, division, fraction, fragment, function, separate, set forth, start out **9** character, component, disengage, go one's way **10** assignment, break apart, department, disconnect, get up and go, ingredient, mosey along, say good-bye **11** be on one's way, call it quits, constituent, subdivision

partake 5 enjoy, savor, share **6** join in, sample **7** share in **8** engage in **11** participate

part from 5 leave **9** break with **12** separate from

Parthenia
epithet of: 6 Athena
means: 6 virgin

Parthenopaeus
father: 10 Hippomenes
mother: 8 Atalanta
member of: 18 Seven against Thebes

partial 6 biased, unfair, unjust **7** limited, slanted **8** one-sided, partisan **9** factional **10** fractional, incomplete, interested, prejudiced, subjective, unbalanced, unfinished **11** fragmentary, inequitable, predisposed, uncompleted **12** inconclusive, prepossessed

partiality 4 bent, bias, love, tilt **5** fancy, slant, taste **6** choice, liking **7** leaning **8** affinity, fondness, penchant, tendency, weakness **9** prejudice **10** attraction, favoritism, preference, proclivity, propensity **11** inclination **12**

one-sidedness, partisanship, predilection 14 predisposition

partially 6 in part, partly 7 partway 8 somewhat 9 piecemeal 12 fractionally, incompletely

participant 4 ally 5 party 6 cohort, fellow, helper, member, player, sharer, worker 7 partner 8 confrere, partaker 9 accessory, associate, colleague, performer 10 accomplice 11 contributor, shareholder 12 collaborator, participator

participate 5 share 6 join in 7 partake, perform 8 engage in, take part 9 play a part

particle 3 bit, jot 4 atom, iota, mite, snip, whit 5 crumb, grain, scrap, shred, speck, trace 6 morsel, tittle, trifle 7 granule, modicum, smidgen, snippet 9 scintilla

parti-colored 4 pied 5 plaid 6 motley 7 checked, dappled, mottled 8 colorful 9 checkered 10 variegated 11 many-colored 12 multicolored

particular 4 sole 5 exact, fixed, fussy, picky 6 single, strict 7 express, finicky, special 8 concrete, critical, definite, detailed, distinct, especial, exacting, explicit, itemized, personal, separate, specific 9 demanding 10 fastidious, individual, meticulous, scrupulous 11 painstaking, persnickety, punctilious, well-defined 12 hard to please

particularize 6 detail 7 itemize, specify 9 enumerate

particularly 6 mainly 7 notably 8 markedly 9 eminently, expressly, specially, supremely, unusually 10 definitely, distinctly, especially, explicitly, strikingly 11 principally, prominently 13 exceptionally 15 extraordinarily

particulars 5 facts, items 6 events 7 details 9 specifics 13 circumstances

parti pris 15 position decided 20 preconceived attitude

partisan 3 fan 4 ally 6 backer, biased, rooter, zealot 7 booster, devotee, partial, slanted 8 adherent, advocate, champion, follower, one-sided, upholder 9 guerrilla, insurgent, irregular, jayhawker, supporter 10 bushwacker, enthusiast, prejudiced, subjective, unbalanced 11 sympathizer

partition 4 wall 5 allot, fence, panel 6 assign, divide, screen 7 barrier, deal out, divider, mete out, parting, split up 8 allocate, bulkhead, dispense, disperse, dividing, division, separate 9 allotment, apportion, parcel out, separator, severance, splitting, subdivide 10 allocation, assignment, distribute, separation 11 demarcation, segregation 12 distribution, dividing wall 13 apportionment

partly 6 in part 7 part way 8 somewhat 9 not wholly, partially, to a de-

gree 10 relatively 12 fractionally, incompletely 13 after a fashion, comparatively

partly open 4 ajar 5 agape 6 gaping 7 cracked 8 half- open, unclosed 9 squinting 10 half-closed

partner 3 aid, pal 4 ally, chum, mate, wife 5 aider, buddy 6 fellow, friend, helper, sharer, spouse 7 comrade, co-owner, husband 8 confrere, helpmate, partaker, sidekick, teammate 9 accessory, assistant, associate, colleague, companion, co-partner 10 accomplice, better half, joint owner 11 confederate, participant 12 collaborator

Parton, Dolly
 roles: 10 Nine to Five, Rhinestone 30 The Best Little Whorehouse in Texas

partridge
 group of: 5 covey

Partridge
 character in: 8 Tom Jones
 author: 8 Fielding

Partridge Family, The
 character: 13 Reuben Kinkaid 14 Danny Partridge, Keith Partridge, Tracy Partridge 15 Connie Partridge, Laurie Partridge 20 Christopher Partridge
 cast: 8 Susan Dey 11 David Madden 12 Brian Forster, David Cassidy, Shirley Jones 13 Danny Bonaduce, Suzanne Crough 14 Jeremy Gelbwaks
 song: 14 I Think I Love You

parturition 5 birth 8 delivery 10 childbirth 11 giving birth 12 childbearing

party 2 do 4 band, bash, body, crew, fete, gang, team, unit, wing 5 corps, force, group, squad 6 affair, at-home, league, soiree 7 accused, blow out, company, coterie, faction 8 alliance, claimant, conclave, litigant, wingding 9 appellant, coalition, defendant, festivity, gathering, plaintiff, reception 10 contestant, federation, petitioner, respondent 11 celebration, confederacy, get-together, participant, paticipator, perpetrator

party-pooper 4 drag 10 spoilsport, wet blanket

parvenu 4 snob 6 nobody 7 upstart 8 arrivist, mushroom 9 arriviste 12 nouveau riche

Pascal, Blaise
 nationality: 6 French
 invented: 7 syringe 13 adding machine 14 hydraulic press
 author of: 7 Pensees 19 Lettres provinciales 20 Essay pour les coniques

Pascin, Julius
 real name: 6 Pincas
 born: 5 Vidin 8 Bulgaria
 artwork: 6 Femmes 12 Les Deux Amies 17 Ginette et Mireille

Pasiphae

father: 6 Helios
 mother: 7 Perseis
 husband: 5 Minos
 daughter: 7 Ariadne, Phaedra 9 Acacallis
 became enamored of: 10 Cretan bull
 mother of: 8 Minotaur

Pasithea
 member of: 6 Graces

pass 2 go 3 cap, die, end, gap, hit, top, use, way 4 best, busy, fill, flow, give, go by, go on, hand, kick, lane, meet, toss 5 canal, exact, excel, gorge, gulch, leave, outdo, route, spend, throw, trail 6 accept, affirm, avenue, be over, canyon, convey, course, decree, depart, devote, elapse, employ, engage, exceed, expend, expire, finish, go away, go past, occupy, ordain, permit, pickle, plight, ratify, ravine, slip by, strait, take up, vanish 7 achieve, advance, approve, channel, confirm, consume, deliver, die away, eclipse, freebie, glide by, go ahead, let have, narrows, pathway, present, proceed, qualify, satisfy, slide by, surpass 8 blow over, dissolve, exigency, fade away, furlough, go beyond, go onward, hand over, juncture, legalize, melt away, outshine, outstrip, passaway, peter out, progress, quandary, sanction, transfer, transmit, turn over 9 authorize, disappear, evaporate, extremity, hand along, legislate, situation, terminate 10 accomplish, difficulty, free ticket, get through, move onward, over shadow, passageway 11 predicament, proposition 12 complication, run its course, solicitation, stand the test 13 authorization 15 amorous overture
 French: 13 laissez passer

passable 4 fair, open, so-so 5 clear 6 not bad 8 adequate, fordable, mediocre, middling 9 allowable, crossable, navigable, tolerable 10 acceptable, admissible, pretty good 11 presentable, respectable, traversable 12 unobstructed

passage 3 way 4 hall, pass, path, road, tour, trek, trip 5 aisle, canal, piece, route, verse 6 access, clause, column, course, junket, tunnel, voyage 7 channel, chapter, hallway, journey, passing, portion, section, transit 8 approach, approval, corridor, movement, sanction, sentence 9 enactment, excursion, paragraph, selection, ship's fare 10 acceptance, expedition, ordainment 11 affirmation, endorsement, legislation, progression 12 confirmation, legalization, ratification 13 authorization

passage out 4 exit 6 egress, outlet

Passages
 author: 10 Gail Sheehy

Passage to India, A

author: 9 E M Forster
character: 6 Dr Aziz **8** Mrs Moore **12** Adela Quested **13** Cecil Fielding, Ronald Heaslop **16** Professor Godbole
setting: 11 Chandrapore **12** Marabar Caves
director: 9 David Lean
cast: 9 Judy Davis **12** Alec Guinness **13** Peggy Ashcroft **15** Victor Bannerjee
Oscar for: 17 supporting actress (Ashcroft)
passageway 4 exit, hall, lane, path, walk **5** aisle **6** access, arcade, tunnel **7** doorway, gangway, gateway, hallway, passage **8** corridor, entrance, entryway, sidewalk **12** companionway
pass away 3 die **6** depart, expire, pass on, perish **7** decease **8** pass over **13** go to one's glory **14** give up the ghost
pass by 4 go by, pass **5** lapse **6** elapse, roll by, slip by **7** glide by, slide by **8** slip away
passe 4 past **5** faded, hoary, stale **6** demode, lapsed, quaint **7** ancient, antique, archaic, disused, outworn, retired **8** obsolete, outdated, outmoded **9** out-of-date **10** antiquated **11** prehistoric **12** antediluvian, old-fashioned, out of fashion **13** superannuated
passenger 4 fare **5** rider **8** commuter, stowaway, traveler, wayfarer
Passepartout
character in: 26 Around the World in Eighty Days
author: 5 Verne
pas seul
ballet: 9 solo dance
literally: 8 solo step
passim 12 here and there, repeated item
passing 5 brief, death, dying **6** demise, fickle **7** decease, passage **8** adequate, fleeting **9** enactment, ephemeral, momentary, temporary, transient **10** evanescent, expiration, not failing, short-lived, transitory **11** impermanent, legislating
passing the bounds of propriety
French: 5 outre
passion 4 fire, idol, love, lust, rage, urge **5** ardor, craze, fancy, flame, gusto, heart, mania **6** desire, fervor, hunger, thirst, warmth **7** beloved, craving, ecstasy, emotion, feeling, rapture **8** loved one **9** carnality, eagerness, inamorata, intensity, obsession, sentiment, transport, vehemence **10** carnal love, enthusiasm **11** amorousness, earnestness, infatuation
passionate 3 hot **4** sexy **5** fiery **6** ardent, carnal, erotic, fervid, fierce, heated, loving, raging **7** amorous, earnest, excited, feeling, fervent, furious, intense, lustful **8** desirous, ecstatic, inflamed, sensuous, vehement **9** emo-

tional, heartfelt, wrought-up **11** tempestuous **12** enthusiastic, intoxicating
passionfruit
type: 7 liqueur
origin: 6 Hawaii
flavor: 5 peach
passionless 4 calm, cold **6** placid, serene **7** passive **8** tranquil **9** apathetic, unfeeling **10** spiritless **11** emotionless, indifferent, unemotional
Passion Play
author: 13 Jerzy Kosinski
passive 5 inert **6** docile **7** dormant, patient, pliable **8** enduring, inactive, lifeless, listless, resigned, yielding **9** apathetic, compliant, impassive, quiescent, tractable **10** spiritless, submissive **11** acquiescent, unassertive, unresisting **12** nonresistant
passiveness 7 apathy **7** inertia **8** docility **10** quiescence **11** resignation **12** acquiescence, lifelessness **14** submissiveness **16** unresponsiveness
passivity 6 apathy **7** inertia **8** docility, meekness **11** resignation **12** complaisance, lifelessness **13** nonresistance **14** submissiveness
pass muster 2 do **5** serve **6** answer **8** be enough **10** be adequate **12** be sufficient **14** be satisfactory
pass on 3 die **6** depart, expire **7** decease **8** pass away **13** go to one's glory **14** give up the ghost, leave this world **15** breathe one's last
pass over 6 ignore, slight **7** neglect **8** overlook **10** brush aside
pass up 4 miss **6** ignore, refuse
password 3 key **4** word **6** by word, slogan **7** keyword, tessera **9** catchword, watchword **10** open sesame, secret word, shibboleth **11** countersign, passe-parole
Password
host: 11 Allen Ludden
past 2 by **4** gone **5** ended, prior **6** beyond, bygone, former, gone by **7** ancient, earlier, elapsed, expired, history, long ago, through **8** departed, finished, previous **9** antiquity, days of old **10** days gone by, days of yore, historical, olden times, passed away, yesteryear **11** dead and gone, former times, times gone by **12** ancient times
pasta 4 orzo, ziti **6** elbows, shells **7** gnocchi, lasagna, pastina, ravioli, rotelli **8** ditalini, linguini, macaroni, rigatoni, tortelli **9** canelloni, cavatelli, fettucine, manicotti, spaghetti **10** tortellini, vermicelli
ingredient: 3 egg **5** flour
pasta sauce 4 ragu **5** pesto, salsa **6** tomato **7** alfredo **8** mushroom, pomodoro **9** bolognese, carbonara
past due 4 late **5** tardy **7** belated, overdue **9** in arrears **10** behindhand
paste 3 gum, hit **4** glue, seal, sock **5**

affix, punch, stick **6** attach, cement **7** stickum **8** adhesive, mucilage
pastel 3 dim **4** pale, soft **5** chalk, faded, faint, light, muted **6** crayon **9** washed-out **13** coloring stick **14** coloring pencil
Pasternak, Boris
author of: 9 Dr Zhivago
Pasteur, Louis
field: 9 chemistry
nationality: 6 French
originated: 14 anti-rabies shot, pasteurization
founded: 12 microbiology
disproved: 21 spontaneous generation
pastime 3 fun **4** game, play **5** hobby, sport **9** amusement, avocation, diversion **10** relaxation **11** distraction **13** entertainment **14** divertissement
pastis
type: 7 liqueur
flavor: 8 licorice
substitute for: 8 absinthe
past one's prime 3 old **4** aged **5** aging **7** elderly **9** venerable **11** over the hill **12** in one's dotage
pastor 4 cure, dean **5** padre, vicar **6** cleric, father, parson, priest, rector **8** chaplain, minister, preacher **9** clergyman
pastoral 5 rural **6** rustic **7** bucolic, idyllic **8** arcadian, clerical, priestly **9** episcopal **10** sacerdotal **11** ministerial **14** ecclesiastical
Pastoral Symphony, The
author: 9 Andre Gide
pastorate 6 clergy **8** ministry, the cloth **10** priesthood
pastures
god of: 3 Pan **6** Dumuzi
pasty 3 wan **4** ashy, gray, pale **5** ashen, gluey, gooey, gummy, white **6** anemic, chalky, doughy, pallid, peaked, sallow, sticky **7** deathly, starchy **9** bloodless, colorless, ghostlike, glutinous, like paste **12** mucilaginous
pat 3 apt, dab, hit, pet, rap, tap **4** cake, daub, easy, glib, slap **5** exact, ideal, ready, slick, thump **6** caress, facile, fondle, simple, smooth, stroke, thwack **7** apropos, fitting, perfect, precise, reliant **8** flippant, suitable **9** contrived, pertinent, rehearsed
patch 3 fix, lot **4** area, darn, mend, plot, spot, zone **5** field, sew up, tract **6** garden, repair, stitch **7** expanse, stretch **8** clearing, insignia **9** reinforce **13** reinforcement
patchwork 4 hash, mess **6** jumble, medley, muddle, tangle **7** grab bag, melange, mixture **8** mishmash, mixed bag, pastiche, scramble **9** confusion, potpourri **10** hodgepodge, miscellany, salmagundi **11** gallimaufry **14** conglomeration, omnium-gatherum

pate 3 pie **4** brow, head **5** brain, crown, paste, pastry, patty, skull **6** noddle, noggin, noodle **9** meat paste

patella
bone of: **7** kneecap

patent 4 bald, bold, open, rank **5** clear, gross, overt, plain **6** permit **7** decided, evident, express, glaring, license, obvious **8** apparent, distinct, flagrant, manifest, palpable, registry, striking **9** copyright, downright, prominent **10** pronounced, unreserved **11** conspicuous, copyrighted, indubitable, self-evident, trademarked, transparent, unconcealed, undisguised **12** unmistakable **15** nonprescription

paterfamilias 6 father **17** father of the family, master of the family **20** master of the household

paternal 4 kind **6** tender **8** fatherly, parental, vigilant, watchful **9** concerned, indulgent **10** benevolent, fatherlike, interested, solicitous **11** patriarchal

Pater Patriae 18 father of his country

path 3 way **4** lane, plan, road, walk **5** byway, means, orbit, route, track, trail **6** access, by path, course **7** pathway, process, walkway **8** approach, footpath

pathetic 3 sad **6** moving, rueful, woeful **7** doleful, piteous, pitiful **8** dolorous, grievous, pitiable, poignant, touching, wretched **9** affecting, miserable, plaintive, sorrowful **10** deplorable, lamentable, to be pitied **11** distressing

Pathfinder, The
author: **19** James Fenimore Cooper
character: **9** Arrowhead, Dew-of-June **10** Charles Cap **11** Mabel Dunham, Natty Bumppo **12** Chingachgook **13** Jasper Western **14** Sergeant Dunham **18** Lieutenant Davy Muir

Pathfinders, The
author: **10** Gail Sheehy

pathogen 3 bug **4** germ **5** virus **7** microbe **8** bacillus **9** bacterium **13** microorganism

pathophobia
fear of: **7** disease

pathos 3 woe **5** agony **6** misery **7** anguish, feeling, sadness **8** distress **9** heartache, poignancy, sentiment **10** desolation **12** pitiableness **13** plaintiveness

Paths of Glory
director: **14** Stanley Kubrick
cast: **11** Kirk Douglas, Ralph Meeker **13** Adolphe Menjou

pathway 4 lane, path, road **5** alley, route, track **6** course **7** passage, walkway **8** footpath **10** passageway

patience 5 poise **7** stamina **8** industry, tenacity **9** composure, diligence, fortitude, restraint, tolerance **10** equanimity, resolution, sufferance **11** application, forbearance, longanimity, persistence, self-control **12** perseverance, tirelessness

Patience 8 operetta
by: **7** Gilbert, Sullivan

patient 4 case **6** dogged, serene **8** composed, diligent, enduring, resolute, tireless **9** dauntless, tenacious, undaunted **10** determined, forbearing, persistent, sick person, unflagging, unswerving, unwavering **11** industrious, persevering, unfaltering, unperturbed **13** indefatigable, long-suffering, uncomplaining

patio 4 deck **5** lanai, porch **6** piazza **7** terrace, veranda

patois 5 argot, idiom, lingo **6** jargon **7** dialect **10** vernacular

Paton, Alan
author of: **19** Too Late the Phalarope **20** Cry the Beloved Country **24** Ah but Your Land Is Beautiful

pat on the back 6 praise **7** plaudit **10** compliment **12** commendation

patriarch 5 elder, ruler **6** father, leader, old man **8** male head **9** chieftain **13** paterfamilias

patrician 4 lord, peer **5** noble **6** lordly **7** genteel, stately **8** highborn, imposing, noble man, princely, well-bred **9** blueblood, dignified, gentle man **10** aristocrat, upper- class **12** aristocratic, silk-stocking

patrimony 3 lot **5** dower, share **6** devise, estate, legacy **7** portion **8** bestowal, heritage, jointure **9** endowment **10** bequeathal, birthright **11** inheritance **12** hereditament

patriotism
Latin: **11** amor patriae

Patroclus
father: **9** Menoetius
mother: **8** Periapis
friend: **8** Achilles
killed by: **6** Hector

patrol 5 guard, scout, watch **6** ranger, sentry, warden **7** protect **8** sentinel **9** safe guard, walk a beat, watch man, watch over **10** stand watch

patron 5 angel, buyer **6** backer, client, friend, helper **7** habitue, shopper, sponsor, visitor **8** advocate, attender, champion, customer, defender, financer, promoter, upholder **9** protector, spectator, supporter **10** benefactor, encourager, frequenter, wellwisher **11** sympathizer **12** benefactress **14** philanthropist

patronage 3 aid **4** help **5** favor, plums, trade **6** buying, custom, spoils **7** backing, charity, clients, dealing, support **8** advocacy, auspices, business, commerce **9** clientele, customers, fosterage **10** assistance, friendship, pork barrel, protection, purchasing **11** benefaction, sponsorship **12** philanthropy **13** encouragement

patronize 5 humor **6** shop at **7** buy from **8** deal with, frequent **9** trade with **10** condescend

patsy 4 dupe, pawn, tool **7** cat's-paw, fall guy

patter 3 pad, pat, rap, tap **4** beat, drum **5** pound, thrum **6** tattoo **7** rat-a-tat, spatter, tapping **8** drumming, sprinkle

pattern 4 copy, form, mold, plan **5** draft, guide, ideal, mimic, model, motif, shape **6** design, follow, sample **7** emulate, example, fashion, imitate, paragon **8** exemplar, original, paradigm, parallel, simulate, specimen, standard **9** archetype, criterion, duplicate, prototype **10** apotheosis, stereotype **12** illustration

Patton
director: **17** Franklin Schaffner
cast: **10** Karl Malden (Omar Bradley) **12** George C Scott (George Patton), Stephen Young **13** Michael Strong
Oscar for: **5** actor (Scott), story **7** picture **8** director **10** screenplay (Francis Ford Coppola and Edmund H North)

Patton, George S
nickname: **15** Old Blood and Guts
served in: **3** WWI **4** WWII **11** World War One, World War Two
commander of: **9** Third Army
invasion of: **8** Normandy **11** North Africa
capture of: **6** Sicily
battle: **5** Bulge
wore: **21** ivory-handled revolvers
memoirs: **12** War As I Knew It

Patty Duke Show, The
character: **7** Richard **8** Ross Lane **9** Cathy Lane, Patty Lane **10** Martin Lane **14** Natalie Masters
cast: **9** Jean Byron, Patty Duke **10** Paul O'Keefe **14** Eddie Applegate **16** William Schallert

paucis verbis 10 by few words, in few words **12** with few words

paucity 4 lack **6** dearth **7** fewness, poverty **8** exiguity, poorness, puniness, scarcity, shortage, sparsity, thinness **10** deficiency, meagerness, scantiness, scarceness **13** insufficiency

Paul
former name: **4** Saul
birthplace: **6** Tarsus
teacher: **8** Gamaliel
companion: **5** Silas **7** Timothy **8** Barnabas, John Mark **9** Trophimus
cities visited: **4** Rome **5** Derbe, Perga, Troas **6** Lystra, Paphos **7** Antioch, Corinth, Ephesus, Iconium, Miletus, Salamis **8** Caesarea, Damascus, Neapolis, Philippi **9** Macedonia **12** Thessalonica
conversion place: **14** road to Damas-

cus
wrote: 8 epistles

Paul Bunyan
author: 12 James Stevens
character: 9 Shanty Boy **10** Hels Helson **11** King Bourbon **12** Sourdough Sam **13** Babe the Blue Ox **14** Hot Biscuit Slim **16** Johnny Inkslinger

Pauli, Wolfgang
field: 7 physics
researched: 13 quantum theory
established: 14 Pauli principle **18** exclusion principle
awarded: 10 Nobel Prize

Paulina
character in: 14 The Winter's Tale
author: 11 Shakespeare

Pauling, Linus Carl
field: 12 biochemistry
worked on: 8 proteins **18** molecular structure
advocated: 8 Vitamin C
awarded: 10 Nobel Prize
awarded for: 5 peace **9** chemistry

paunch 3 gut, pot **5** belly, tummy **7** abdomen, stomach **8** potbelly **9** bay window, beer belly, spare tire **10** midsection **11** breadbasket, corporation

pauper 6 beggar **7** almsman **8** bankrupt, indigent **9** insolvent, mendicant **10** poor person, starveling **11** charity case **12** down-and-outer

pause 3 gap **4** halt, rest, stop, wait **5** break, cease, delay, let up **6** hiatus **7** interim, time out **8** break off, hesitate, interval **9** cessation, interlude **10** deliberate, suspension **12** intermission, interruption

pave 3 tar **4** face **6** cement **7** asphalt, surface **8** black top **9** resurface **10** macadamize

pavement 4 slab **5** brick **6** cement, hearth, street, tarmac **7** asphalt, cobbles, macadam **8** concrete, driveway, flagging, sidewalk **9** flagstone

pavilion 4 tent, ward, wing **5** arbor, kiosk **6** gazebo **7** pergola **9** bandshell **11** summerhouse

Pavlov, Ivan Petrovich
nationality: 7 Russian
researched: 9 digestion
studied: 20 behavior conditioning **21** Pavlovian conditioning
awarded: 10 Nobel Prize

paw 2 pa **3** dad, pop, toe **4** feel, foot, grab, hand, maul, mitt, papa **5** daddy, flail, touch **6** caress, clutch, father, handle, scrape, strike **7** rough up **8** forefoot **9** mishandle
mate: 3 maw

pawn 4 bond, dupe, hock, tool **5** agent, patsy **6** flunky, lackey, pledge, puppet **7** cat's-paw **8** borrow on, creature, guaranty, henchman, hireling, security **9** assurance, guarantee, underling **10** instrument **12** raise money on **14** give as security

pawnbroker
French: 11 mont-de-piete

Pawnbroker, The
director: 11 Sidney Lumet
cast: 10 Rod Steiger (Sol Nazerman) **11** Brock Peters **12** Jaime Sanchez **19** Geraldine Fitzgerald
setting: 6 Harlem

Pawnee (Chahiksichhiks)
language family: 7 Caddoan
location: 5 Texas **8** Nebraska, Oklahoma **9** New Mexico
related to: 7 Arikara
god: 6 Tirawa

Pawtuxet
location: 13 Massachusetts
leader: 7 Squanto

Pax
origin: 5 Roman
goddess of: 5 peace
corresponds to: 5 Irene

pax vobiscum 14 peace be with you

pay 3 fee **4** foot, give, meet **5** grant, honor, remit, repay, serve, wages, yield **6** ante up, chip in, extend, income, profit, render, return, salary, settle **7** benefit, bring in, cough up, payment, present, proffer, stipend **8** be useful, earnings, paycheck, shell out **9** bear fruit, liquidate, reimburse **10** come across, compensate, make good on, recompense **12** compensation **13** reimbursement

payable 3 due **4** owed **5** owing **6** mature, unpaid **8** to be paid **9** in arrears, spendable **10** demandable, expendable, receivable **11** outstanding

pay attention 4 heed, note **6** attend, notice **7** observe

Payaya
language family: 12 Coahuiltecan
location: 5 Texas

pay back 5 repay **7** counter, get even **9** reimburse, retaliate **10** recompense, remunerate **15** make restitution

pay for 6 redeem **7** expiate **8** atone for **9** answer for, suffer for **10** compensate, recompense, remunerate **13** make amends for **17** make reparation for

pay heed 6 notice **8** consider **11** concentrate **12** pay attention **13** put one's mind to

pay homage 5 defer, honor **7** acclaim **10** pay tribute

paying back 9 repayment **11** getting even **12** making good on **13** reimbursement

paymaster 6 bursar, purser **7** cashier **10** cashkeeper

payment 3 fee, pay **4** debt **6** outlay, paying, salary **7** premium **8** defrayal, spending **9** allowance, discharge **10** recompense, remittance, settlement **11** expenditure, installment, liquidation **12** compensation, contribution, dis-

bursement, remuneration **13** reimbursement

pay no heed to 4 defy **6** ignore, slight **7** disobey, neglect, violate **8** overlook, pass over **9** disregard **10** brush aside, infringe on **14** shut one's eyes to **16** pay no attention to **17** transgress against

payoff 3 end **4** soap **5** bribe, graft **6** climax, crunch, finale, finish, grease, payola, result, upshot, windup **7** outcome **8** clincher **9** hush money **10** bottom line, conclusion, denouement, protection, resolution **11** culmination

pay off 5 bribe **6** buy off, suborn **13** grease the palm

payola 5 bribe, graft **6** grease, payoff

pay out 5 spend **6** expend, lay out **7** fork out **8** allocate, disburse, dispense, shell out **10** distribute

pay suit 3 woo **5** court **8** pay court

Payton, Walter
nickname: 9 Sweetness
sport: 8 football
position: 11 running back
team: 12 Chicago Bears

pay tribute to 4 laud, tout **5** boost, toast **6** praise, salute **7** applaud, commend **8** eulogize **10** compliment **16** sing the praises of

pea 5 Pisum **12** Pisum sativum
varieties: 4 Flat, Love, Snow, Wild **5** Beach, Caley, Chick, Congo, Coral, Field, Glory, Green, Heart, Heath, Hoary, No-eye, Rough, Sugar, Sweet **6** Angola, Canada, Desert, Garden, Marble, Pigeon, Rosary, Scurfy, Winged, Winter **7** Catjang, Darling, English, Rabbit's, Seaside **8** Earthnut, Egyptian, Princess, Shamrock **9** Asparagus, Black-eyed, Butterfly, Chaparral, Jerusalem, Partridge, Perennial **10** Australian, Singletary, Wild winter **11** Everlasting, Sturt desert, Two-flowered, Winter sweet **12** Edible-podded **14** Austrian winter **15** Australian flame

peace 4 calm, ease **5** amity, truce **6** accord, repose **7** concord, content, entente, harmony **8** serenity **9** agreement, armistice, composure, placidity **12** pacification, tranquillity **14** reconciliation
god of: 4 Frey **5** Freyr
goddess of: 3 Pax **9** Concordia
Hebrew: 6 shalom
Russian: 3 mir

peace be with you
Latin: 11 pax vobiscum

peaceful 4 calm **5** quiet, still **6** placid, serene, silent **7** pacific, restful **8** amicable, friendly, tranquil **9** agreeable, peaceable, peacetime **10** harmonious, nonviolent, nonwarring, pacifistic, untroubled **11** undisturbed

peacefulness 4 calm **7** concord, har-

peacemaker 8 diplomat, mediator, placater 9 go-between 10 ambassador, arbitrator, negotiator 11 adjudicator, conciliator, pacificator, peacekeeper, peacemonger 12 intermediary

peacemaking 9 pacifying, placating, placatory 11 reconciling 12 conciliating, conciliatory, pacification

peace offering 6 amends 11 appeasement 12 conciliation

peace of mind 8 security, serenity 11 tranquility 16 freedom from worry

peace to you
Hebrew: 14 shalom aleichem

peach 13 Prunus persica
varieties: 4 Muir, Peak, Sims, Vine, Wild 5 Gaume, Hiley, Pavie 6 Carmen, Crosby, Desert, Foster, J H Hale, Lovell, Orejon, Paloro, Peen-to, Salwey 7 Dixigem, Dixired, Elberta, Persian, Quadong 8 Champion, Crawford, Isabella, Redhaven, Russelet 9 Alexander, Freestone, Halehaven, Rochester, Southland 10 Clingstone, Goldeneast, Heath Cling, Summer Snow 12 Chinese Cling, Iron Mountain, Mountain Rose, Oldmixon Free 13 Golden Jubilee, Oldmixon Cling, Phillips Cling 14 Belle of Georgia
peach-like: 7 apricot 9 nectarine

Peach State
nickname of: 7 Georgia

Peachum, Polly
character in: 12 Beggar's Opera
author: 3 Gay

peachy 4 fine, keen 5 dandy, super, swell 9 excellent, marvelous, wonderful

peacock
group of: 6 muster

Peacock
constellation of: 4 Pavo

Peacock, Thomas Love
author of: 12 Headlong Hall 14 Crotchet Castle, Nightmare Abbey

Peacock Spring, The
author: 11 Rumer Godden

peak 3 tip, top 4 acme, apex 5 crest, crown, flood, prime 6 apogee, climax, summit, zenith 8 pinnacle 9 culminate 11 culmination

peaked 3 ill, wan 4 lean, pale, thin, weak 5 ashen, drawn, gaunt, spare, spiked, spiny, white 6 ailing, infirm, pallid, pointy, sallow, sickly, skinny, spiked 7 haggard, pinched, pointed, scrawny, tapered, wizened 9 emaciated, shriveled 11 debilitated

peal 3 din 4 boom, clap, ring, roar, roll, toll 5 blare, blast, clang, crack, crash, knell 6 rumble 7 clangor, resound, ringing 10 resounding 11 reverberate 13 reverberation 14 tintinnabulate 16 tintinnabulation

Peale, Charles Willson
born: 17 Queen Anne County MD
son: 9 Raphaelle, Rembrandt 12 Titian Ramsay
artwork: 26 The Exhumation of the Mastodon
portrait: 8 Franklin 9 Jefferson, John Adams 10 Washington

Peale, Raphaelle
born: 13 Bucks County PA
father: 14 Charles Willson
brother: 9 Rembrandt 12 Titian Ramsay
artwork: 12 After the Bath

Peale, Rembrandt
born: 13 Bucks County PA
father: 14 Charles Willson
brother: 9 Raphaelle 12 Titian Ramsay
artwork: 15 The Court of Death
portrait: 9 Jefferson 10 Washington

peal of bells 7 clangor, ringing 16 tintinnabulation

peanut 3 pod, tot 4 puny, seed 5 petty, small 6 goober, legume, measly, paltry 8 earthpea 9 little one
species: 15 Arachis hypogaea

Peanuts
creator: 14 Charles Schultz
character: 4 Lucy 5 Linus, Sally, Marcy 6 Pig Pen, Snoopy 9 Schroeder, Woodstock 11 Lucy Van Pelt 12 Linus Van Pelt, Charlie Brown 15 Peppermint Patty 19 Little Red Haired Girl
Halloween figure: 12 Great Pumpkin
Snoopy's plane: 12 Sopwith Camel
Snoopy's foe: 8 Red Baron
saying: 9 Good grief

pear 5 Pyrus 13 Pyrus communis
varieties: 4 Bosc, Sand 5 Anjou, Aslan, Blind, Melon, Smith 6 Balsam, Burrel, Butter, Comice, Common, Garber, Garlic, Orient, Seckel, Warden 7 Chinese, Kieffer, Prickly, Vinegar 8 Bartlett, Japanese, Oriental 9 Alligator, Evergreen, Muscadine 10 Beurre Bosc, Brandywine, Chaumontel 11 Birch-leaved, Bon Chretien, Paper-spined, Winter Nelis 12 Beurre d'Anjou, Easter Beurre, Sacred garlic, Willow-leaved 13 Flemish Beauty, Waite Bergamot 15 Doyenne du Comice 18 Duchesse d'Angouleme

pearl
grows in: 6 oyster
genus: 8 Pinctada
source: 6 Red Sea 9 Caribbean 11 Persian Gulf 12 South Pacific 16 Gulf of California
composed of: 5 nacre 9 aragonite 10 conchiolin 13 mother-of-pearl
quality: 6 luster 11 iridescence
color: 4 blue, rose 5 black, brown, cream, green, white 6 yellow
shape: 5 round 7 baroque
type: 8 cultured, Oriental (saltwater) 9 simulated 10 freshwater

Pearl-Fishers, The
also: 19 Les Pecheurs de Perles
opera by: 5 Bizet
setting: 6 Ceylon

Pearl of the Antilles see 4 Cuba

Pearly Gates 7 heaven
mentioned in: 10 Revelation

peasant 4 boor, esne, peon, serf 5 churl, knave, yokel 6 farmer, rustic, worker 7 laborer, lowlife, villein 10 countryman, dirt farmer
Arabic: 6 fellah
Indian: 4 ryot 5 kisan 6 raiyat
Irish: 4 kern
Russian: 5 kulak 6 muzhik
Scottish: 6 cotter

peasantlike 5 crude, rough 6 coarse, oafish, rustic, vulgar 7 boorish, loutish, uncouth 9 unrefined 10 unpolished

peccadillo 4 slip 5 lapse 6 boo-boo 7 blunder, faux pas, misdeed, misstep 8 petty sin, trespass 9 false move, wrong step 10 misconduct, wrongdoing 11 misdemeanor 13 transgression

peck 3 pat, rap, tap 4 buss, gobs, lots, mess 5 a slew, batch, bunch, heaps, scads, smack, snack, stack, thump 6 nibble, oodles, pick at, strike, stroke, worlds 8 light jab 9 abundance, light kiss 11 eight quarts
abbreviation of: 2 pk

Peck, Gregory
real name: 17 Eldred Gregory Peck
born: 9 La Jolla CA
roles: 8 Moby Dick 10 On the Beach, Spellbound 11 The Yearling 12 Duel in the Sun, Roman Holiday 15 The Paradine Case 16 Twelve O'Clock High 17 The Boys from Brazil, The Guns of Navarone 18 To Kill a Mockingbird (Oscar) 19 Gentleman's Agreement, The Keys of the Kingdom 21 The Snows of Kilimanjaro 26 The Man in the Gray Flannel Suit
autobiography: 12 An Actor's Life

Peckinpah, Sam
director of: 9 Straw Dogs 12 The Wild Bunch

Pecksniff
character in: 16 Martin Chuzzlewit
author: 7 Dickens

peculiar 3 odd 5 queer, weird 6 farout, quaint, unique 7 bizarre, curious, erratic, private, special, strange, typical, unusual 8 abnormal, distinct, freakish, personal, singular, specific 9 eccentric, exclusive, whimsical 10 capricious, individual, outlandish, particular 11 distinctive 13 idiosyncratic 14 characteristic, distinguishing, representative, unconventional

peculiarity 4 mark 5 badge, stamp,

trait **6** oddity **7** feature, quality **8** odd trait **9** attribute, queerness, weirdness **10** erraticism, uniqueness **11** abnormality, bizarreness, distinction, singularity, strangeness **12** eccentricity, freakishness, idiosyncrasy **13** particularity, unnaturalness **14** characteristic **21** distinguishing quality

pecuniary 6 fiscal **8** economic, monetary **9** budgetary, financial

pedagogic 7 bookish, donnish **8** academic, didactic, pedantic, tutorial **9** scholarly **11** educational **12** professorial **13** instructional

pedagogue, pedagog 5 tutor **7** teacher **8** academic, educator **9** professor **10** instructor, schoolmarm **12** educationist, schoolmaster **13** schoolteacher **14** schoolmistress

pedant 6 purist **8** bookworm **9** dogmatist **13** methodologist

pedantic 5 fussy **7** bookish, finicky, pompous, stilted **8** academic, didactic, dogmatic **10** nitpicking, scholastic **11** doctrinaire, punctilious **13** hairsplitting **14** overparticular

peddle 4 hawk, sell, vend **6** retail **7** deal out **8** dispense

Peder Victorious
  character in: **16** Giants of the Earth
  author: **7** Rolvaag

pedestal 4 base, foot **6** bottom, plinth **10** foundation

pedestrian 6 walker **7** mundane, prosaic, tedious, trekker **8** mediocre, ordinary, stroller **9** itinerant **10** ambulatory, for walking, unexciting **11** commonplace, peripatetic, unimportant **12** foot-traveler, run-of-the-mill **13** insignificant, perambulating, perambulatory, unimaginative **15** inconsequential

pedigree 4 line **6** family, strain **7** descent, lineage **8** ancestry **9** bloodline, parentage **10** derivation, extraction, family tree **13** line of descent

peek 3 pry **4** peep, peer **5** watch **6** glance **7** glimpse

peel 4 bark, hull, husk, pare, rind, skin, tear, zest **5** flake, scale, shuck, spade, strip **6** remove **7** undress **11** decorticate

peel off 6 remove **7** veer off **8** strip off

peep 4 peek, peer, skim, word **5** cheep, chirp, tweet **6** emerge, glance, murmur, mutter, squeak **7** chirrup, glimpse, peeping, peer out, twitter, whimper, whisper **9** come forth, quick look

peeper 3 eye **4** frog **6** voyeur **10** peeping Tom

peer 4 gape, gaze, look, lord, peek, peep **5** equal, noble, stare **6** appear, emerge, squint **7** compeer **8** nobleman **9** blue blood, gentleman, patrician **10** aristocrat

peerage 8 nobility **10** blue bloods, patricians **11** aristocracy

Peer Gynt
  author: **11** Henrik Ibsen
  character: **3** Ase **6** Anitra **7** Solveig **12** The Great Boyg **16** The Button Moulder
  suite composer: **5** Grieg

peerless 7 supreme **8** flawless **9** faultless, matchless, unequaled, unmatched, unrivaled **10** consummate, inimitable, preeminent, surpassing, unexcelled **11** superlative, unsurpassed **12** incomparable, transcendent

peeve 3 bug, eat, irk, vex **4** fret, gall, rile **5** annoy, chafe, eat at, frost, gripe **6** gnaw at, nettle **7** dislike, perturb, provoke **8** irritate, vexation **9** aggravate, annoyance, complaint, grievance **10** exasperate, irritation **11** aggravation, provocation **12** exasperation, give one a pain **13** pain in the neck **14** thorn in the side

peevish 4 mean **5** cross, huffy, sulky, surly, testy **6** crabby, cranky, grumpy **7** grouchy, pettish **8** churlish, petulant, snappish **9** fractious, irritable, querulous, splenetic **10** ill-humored, ill-natured **11** bad-tempered, ill-tempered, quarrelsome **12** cantankerous

peewee 4 tiny **5** dwarf, small, teeny **6** little, midget, minute **9** itsy-bitsy, itty-bitty, minuscule **10** diminutive, teeny-weeny **11** Lilliputian

Pee Wee
  nickname of: **11** Harold Reese

peg 3 pin **4** nail **5** cleat, dowel, spike, thole **6** skewer, toggle **8** fastener, tholepin

Pegasus
  form: **5** horse
  characteristic: **6** winged
  mother: **6** Medusa
  ridden by: **11** Bellerophon

Peggotty, Clara
  character in: **16** David Copperfield
  author: **7** Dickens

Pei, I M (Ieoh Ming)
  architect of: **12** East Building (National Gallery of Art), L'Enfant Plaza (Washington DC) **14** East-West Center (U of Hawaii), Mile High Center (Denver) **15** Place Ville Marie (Montreal) **16** John Hancock Tower (Boston) **18** Everson Museum of Art (Syracuse NY) **22** Kips Bay Plaza Apartments (NYC) **36** National Center for Atmospheric Research (Boulder CO)

peignoir 4 gown **6** kimono **8** negligee **9** nightgown **12** dressing gown

pejorative 7 mocking **8** debasing, negative, scornful **9** degrading, demeaning, slighting **10** belittling, derogatory, detracting, disdainful, ridiculing, unpleasant **11** deprecatory, disparaging, downgrading **12** contemptuous, depreciatory, disapproving **15** uncomplimentary

Peking
  also: **7** Beijing
  means: **15** northern capital
  capital of: **5** China
  landmark: **9** Bell Tower, Drum Tower, Ming Tombs **10** Pei-hai Park **12** Palace Museum **13** Forbidden City **14** Hall of Classics, Temple of Heaven **15** Marco Polo Bridge **17** Temple of Confucius **18** Old Legation Quarter **19** Temple of Agriculture **20** Great Hall of the People, Hall of Supreme Harmony **21** Mausoleum of Mao Tse-tung **22** Palace of Heavenly Purity **26** Monument to the People's Heroes **32** Revolutionary and Historical Museum
  mountain: **7** Taihang
  river: **3** Hai **7** Ch'ao-pai **8** Yungting
  square: **9** T'ien-an Men
  university: **8** Tsinghua
  walled city: **5** Inner, Outer, Tatar **7** Chinese

pelagic 6 marine **7** aquatic, oceanic **9** thalassic **11** sea-dwelling

Pele
  real name: **24** Edson Arantes do Nascimento
  sport: **6** soccer
  team: **13** New York Cosmos
  nationality: **9** Brazilian

Peleus
  king of: **6** Phthia **9** Myrmidons
  father: **6** Aeacus
  mother: **6** Endeis
  brother: **7** Telamon
  half-brother: **6** Phocus
  wife: **6** Thetis **8** Antigone
  son: **8** Achilles
  daughter: **8** Polydora

pelf 4 gain **5** booty, lucre, money **6** mammon, riches, spoils

Pelican State
  nickname of: **9** Louisiana

pelisse 4 cape, coat **5** cloak **6** mantle

Pelles (King Pelleas)
  character in: **16** Arthurian romance
  daughter: **6** Elaine

Pelleas and Melisande
  also: **18** Pelleas et Melisande
  opera by: **7** Debussy
  character: **6** Golaud, Yniold
  author: **18** Maurice Maeterlinck

pellet 3 pea **4** ball, bead, drop, pill **5** pearl, stone **6** marble, pebble, sphere **7** globule

pell-mell 6 rashly **7** hastily **8** slapdash **9** hurriedly, post haste **10** at half cock, carelessly, heedlessly, recklessly **11** hurry-scurry, impetuously, imprudently **12** incautiously **13** helter-skelter, precipitately, thoughtlessly

pellucid 5 clear, lucid **10** articulate **11** crystalline, translucent, transparent **12** intelligible **14** understandable

Pelops
father: 8 Tantalus
sister: 5 Niobe
son: 6 Atreus, Sciron **7** Letreus **8** Pittheus, Thyestes **9** Alcathous **10** Chrysippus
daughter: 7 Nicippe **8** Lysidice **9** Astydamia
resurrected by: 6 Hermes

pelt 3 fur, hit, rap **4** belt, coat, hide, skin, sock **5** pound, punch, whack **6** batter, buffet, fleece, pepper, pummel, strike, thrash, thwack **7** clobber

pen 3 sty **4** cage, coop, crib, fold **5** draft, hutch, pound, quill, stall, write **6** corral, pencil, scrawl **7** compose, paddock **8** compound, scribble, stockade **9** ballpoint, enclosure

penal 7 of jails **8** punitive **9** punishing **10** corrective, penalizing **11** castigatory, retributive **12** disciplinary

penalty 4 fine **7** forfeit **8** handicap **9** suffering **10** assessment, forfeiture, infliction, punishment **11** retribution **12** disadvantage

penance 9 atonement, expiation, hair shirt, penitence **10** contrition, repentance **12** propitiation **13** mortification

penates
protectors of: 4 home
companions: 5 lares

penchant 4 bent, bias, gift, turn **5** fancy, flair, knack, taste **6** liking, relish **7** leaning **8** affinity, fondness, tendency **9** prejudice, proneness, readiness **10** attraction, partiality, preference, proclivity, propensity **11** disposition, inclination **12** predilection **14** predisposition

pendant 3 fob **5** charm **6** locket **15** hanging ornament

Pendennis
author: 25 William Make peace Thackeray
character: 9 Laura Bell **10** Henry Foker **12** Blanche Amory **13** Emily Costigan **14** Helen Pendennis, Major Pendennis **15** Arthur Pendennis

pendent, pendant 7 hanging, jutting, pensile **8** dangling, swinging **9** extending, pendulous, suspended **10** projecting, protruding **11** overhanging, protuberant

pendente lite 16 during litigation **19** with a lawsuit pending

pending 8 imminent **9** undecided, unsettled **10** in suspense, unfinished, unresolved, up in the air **11** in the offing **12** undetermined

pendulous 7 hanging, pendent, pensile, sagging **8** dangling, drooping, swinging **9** suspended

pendulum
invented by: 7 Galileo

Penelope
father: 7 Icarius
mother: 8 Periboea
husband: 8 Odysseus **9** Telegonus
son: 6 Ifalus **10** Telemachus **11** Polyporthis
fended off: 7 suitors

penetrate 3 get **4** bore **5** catch, enter, prick **6** decode, fathom, invade, pierce, seep in **7** cut into, discern, pervade, unravel **8** decipher, perceive, permeate, puncture, saturate, traverse **9** figure out, perforate **10** comprehend, cut through, impregnate, infiltrate, see through, understand **11** pass through

penetrating 4 keen **5** acrid, alert, alive, aware, harsh, heady, sharp, smart **6** astute, biting, clever, shrewd, strong **7** caustic, pungent, reeking **8** piercing, redolent, stinging **9** pervading, pervasive, trenchant **10** discerning, perceptive, percipient, permeating, saturating, thoughtful **11** intelligent, sharp-witted **13** perspicacious

penetration 5 foray, grasp **6** access, boring **7** insight, passage **8** infusion, invasion, keenness, piercing **9** intrusion, quickness, sharpness **10** astuteness, cleverness, perception, puncturing, shrewdness **11** discernment, perforation **12** intelligence, perspicacity

penguin 8 great auk

Penguin Island
author: 13 Anatole France

peninsula 4 cape **5** point **8** headland **10** promontory

Peninsula State
nickname of: 7 Florida

penitence 6 regret, sorrow **7** penance, remorse **9** atonement, attrition, expiation **10** contrition, repentance **11** compunction, humiliation

penitent 5 sorry **6** rueful **7** atoning, devotee, pilgrim **8** contrite **9** regretful, repentant **10** remorseful

penitentiary 3 can, pen **4** jail, stir **5** joint **6** prison **7** slammer **8** big house

Penn, Arthur
director of: 12 Little Big Man **14** Bonnie and Clyde **16** The Miracle Worker

Penn, Sean
wife: 7 Madonna **11** Robin Wright
roles: 5 U-Turn **7** Bad Boys, The Game **11** Carlito's Way **12** She's So Lovely **14** Dead Man Walking **15** Shanghai Express **22** The Falcon and the Snowman **24** Fast Times at Ridgemont High

Pennacook (Merrimac)
language family: 9 Algonkian **10** Algonquian

location: 5 Maine **6** Quebec **7** New York, Vermont **10** New England **12** New Hampshire **13** Massachusetts
leader: 11 Wannalancet **12** Passaconaway
related to: 6 Abnaki

pen name
French: 10 nom de plume

pennant 4 flag, jack **6** banner, burgee, colors, ensign, pennon **7** bunting **8** ensignia, standard, streamer **9** banderole, oriflamme

penniless 4 poor **5** broke, needy **6** busted, ruined **8** bankrupt, indigent, strapped, wiped out **9** destitute, flat broke, insolvent, moneyless **10** down-and-out, pauperized **12** impoverished **15** poverty-stricken

pennon 4 flag, jack **6** banner, colors, ensign **7** pennant **8** standard, streamer

Pennsylvania
abbreviation: 2 PA **5** Penna
nickname: 8 Keystone
capital: 10 Harrisburg
largest city: 12 Philadelphia
others: 4 Erie, Etna, Plum, York **5** Avoca, Baden **6** Beaver, Bethel, Butler, Easton, Emmaus, Radnor, Ridley, Sharon **7** Altoona, Baldwin, Bristol, Chester, Ephrata, Hanover, Hershey, Lebanon, Reading **8** Abington, Braddock, Bradford, Bryn Mawr, Carlisle, Clairton, Harrison, Hazelton, Monessen, Scranton, Shamokin **9** Aliquippa, Allentown, Bethlehem, Charleroi, Haverford, Jeannette, Johnstown, Lancaster, Meadville, Mill Creek, Newcastle, Swissvale, Uniontown, Whitehall **10** Carbondale, Gettysburg, McKeesport, Norristown, Pittsburgh **11** Springfield, Wilkes Barre **12** State College, Williamsport
college: 3 PSU **4** Penn, Pitt **5** Gratz, Thiel **6** Drexel, Lehigh, Temple **7** Juniata, LaSalle, Ursinus **8** Alliance, Bryn Mawr, Bucknell, Duquesne, Lycoming **9** Dickinson, Lafayette, Penn State, St Josephs, Villanova **10** Pittsburgh, Swarthmore **12** Carnegie Tech **17** Pennsylvania State
feature:
battle site: 10 Gettysburg
bell: 7 Liberty
hall: 12 Independence
historical site: 11 Valley Forge
tribe: 6 Seneca **7** Shawnee **8** Delaware **11** Lenni- Lanape **13** Susquehannock
people: 5 Amish, Dutch **10** Stan Musial **11** Andrew Wyeth, Ethel Waters, Mary Cassatt, Stuart Davis **12** Andrew Mellon, Anthony Wayne, Margaret Mead, Martha Graham, Samuel Barber, Thomas Eakins **13** Clifford Odets, Gertrude Stein **14** George S Kaufman **15** Maxwell Anderson **19**

Stephen Vincent Benet
explorer: 5 Brule **6** Hudson **11** Hendrickson
lake: 4 Erie **7** Harveys **8** Conneaut **10** Pymatuning **13** Wallenpaupack
land rank: 11 thirty-third
mountain: 5 South **6** Pocono **11** Alleghenies
  highest point: 5 Davis
physical feature:
  peninsula: 11 Presque Isle
  valley: 5 Great
president: 13 James Buchanan
river: 4 Ohio **6** Lehigh **7** Clarion, Genesee, Juniata, Licking, Towanda **8** Caldwell, Delaware, Schrader **9** Allegheny **10** Schuylkill **11** Monongahela, Susquehanna
state admission: 6 second
state bird: 12 ruffed grouse
state fish: 10 brook trout
state flower: 14 mountain laurel
state motto: 28 Virtue Liberty and Independence
state tree: 7 hemlock
penny 3 sum **4** cent **5** cheap, pence **6** copper, stiver **7** trivial
penny-pinching 5 close, tight **6** stingy **7** miserly **8** grudging **9** niggardly, penurious **10** ungenerous **11** tight-fisted **12** parsimonious
Penny Serenade
director: 13 George Stevens
cast: 9 Cary Grant **10** Irene Dunne **11** Beulah Bondi **13** Edgar Buchanan
pennyweight
abbreviation of: 3 dwt
Penobscot
language family: 9 Algonkian **10** Algonquian
location: 5 Maine **13** Old Town Island
members of: 17 Abnaki Confederacy
Penrod
author: 15 Booth Tarkington
sequel: 12 Penrod and Sam **13** Penrod Jashber
character: 6 Herman, Verman **9** Sarah Crim **11** Rupe Collins **13** Marjorie Jones **15** Penrod Schofield
dog: 4 Duke
pensee 7 thought **10** reflection
Pensees
author: 12 Blaise Pascal
pension 5 grant **6** income, retire **7** annuity, stipend, subsidy **9** allowance **13** boardinghouse **14** retirement fund
pensive 3 sad **5** grave **6** dreamy, musing, solemn, somber **7** serious, wistful **8** dreaming **10** meditative, melancholy, reflective **11** day dreaming **13** contemplative, introspective **15** sadly thoughtful
Pentateuch 10 Law of Moses **28** first five books of Old Testament
see also **7** books of **12** Old Testament
Penthesilea

queen of: 7 Amazons
father: 4 Ares
mother: 6 Otrere
sister: 9 Hippolyta
killed by: 8 Achilles
Pentheus
king of: 6 Thebes
father: 6 Echion
mother: 5 Agave
grandfather: 6 Cadmus
pent-up 7 boxed-up, checked, stifled **8** hedged-in, held back, penned-in, penned-up, reined in, stored-up **9** bottled-up, repressed **10** restrained, suppressed
penurious 5 close **6** frugal, stingy **7** miserly, sparing **8** stinting **9** niggardly **12** parsimonious **13** penny-pinching
penury 4 need, want **7** poverty **9** indigence, privation **10** bankruptcy, insolvency **11** destitution **14** impoverishment
peon 4 pawn, serf **5** slave **6** drudge, menial, worker **7** footman, laborer, orderly, peasant, servant
peony 7 Paeonia
varieties: 4 Tree **7** Chinese, Tibetan **8** Majorcan **11** Chinese tree **12** Common garden
people 3 kin **5** folks **6** family, humans, the mob **7** kinfolk, mankind, mortals, the herd **8** citizens, humanity, populace, the crowd **9** ancestors, citizenry, commoners, human kind, relatives, the masses, the public, the rabble **10** population **11** Homo sapiens, human beings, individuals, inhabitants, John Q Public, men and women, the millions
People Are Funny
host: 13 Art Linkletter
pep 3 vim, zip **4** dash, life, snap **5** gusto, verve, vigor **6** energy, ginger, spirit **8** vitality, vivacity **9** animation **10** enthusiasm, get-up-and-go, liveliness
Pepe Le Moko
director: 14 Julien Duvivier
cast: 9 Jean Gabin **13** Gabriel Gabrio, Mireille Balin
remade as: 6 Casbah **7** Algiers
peperomia
varieties: 3 Ivy **6** Prayer, Vining **7** Ivy-leaf, Leather, Red-edge **8** Coin-leaf, Platinum **9** Flowering **10** Silver-edge, Silver-leaf, Watermelon **11** Green-ripple **13** Emerald-ripple, Little fantasy
Pepin
called: 8 the Short
king of: 6 Franks
son: 11 Charlemagne
Pepita
character in: 21 The Bridge of San Luis Rey
author: 6 Wilder
Peppard, George

born: 9 Detroit MI
wife: 15 Elizabeth Ashley
roles: 6 Tobruk **7** Banacek **8** The A-Team **16** The Carpetbaggers **19** Breakfast at Tiffany's
pepper 3 dot **6** shower, strafe **7** bombard **8** sprinkle **9** condiment, vegetable
pepper, peppercorn
botanical name: 5 Piper **7** Pnigrum **8** Capsicum **10** Piperaceae **11** C frutescens
color: 3 red **5** black, green, white
origin: 5 India **6** Brazil, Ceylon **7** Malabar, Sarawak, Sumatra **8** Alleppey, Pandjang, Sri Lanka **11** Tellicherry
varieties: 3 Red **4** Baby, Bell, Bird, Cone, Long, Wild **5** Betle, Black, Chili, Cubeb, Green, Japan, Sweet, White **6** Cherry **7** Cayenne, Celebes, Cluster, Tabasco **8** Capsicum **9** Mild water **10** Australian, Red cluster **12** Mountain long, Tabasco-sauce
French: 6 poivre
German: 7 pfeffer
Italian: 4 pepe
Latin: 5 piper
Persian: 5 biber **6** pilpil
Spanish: 8 pimienta
Swedish: 6 peppar
Sanskrit: 7 pippali
peppermint 6 Mentha
varieties: 4 Gray **5** Black, River, White **6** Silver, Sydney **9** Blackbutt **10** Robert- son's **11** Broad-leaved **15** Mount Wellington **17** Narrow-leaved black **19** Nichol's willow-leaved
peppermint schnapps
type: 7 liqueur
flavor: 4 mint
peppery 3 hot **5** fiery, sharp, spicy **7** burning, piquant, pungent **14** highly seasoned
peppy 4 spry **5** brisk, perky **6** active, bouncy, frisky, lively, snappy **7** dynamic **8** animated, spirited, vigorous **9** energetic, full of pep, sparkling, sprightly, vivacious **12** enthusiastic
pep up 4 fire **6** excite, vivify, wake up **7** animate, enliven, quicken **8** vitalize
Pepys, Samuel
author of: 10 Pepys' Diary
Pepys' Diary
author: 11 Samuel Pepys
Pequot
language family: 9 Algonkian **10** Algonquian
location: 11 Connecticut, Rhode Island
perambulate 4 pace, tour, walk **5** amble, mosey **6** ramble, stroll **7** meander, saunter **9** promenade
perceivable 7 visible **8** apparent, distinct **10** detectable, noticeable, observable **11** discernible, perceptible **13** ascertainable

perceive 3 get, see 4 feel, hear, know, note 5 grasp, savvy, sense, smell, taste 6 deduce, detect, gather, notice 7 discern, make out, observe, realize 8 conclude, discover 9 apprehend, be aware of, recognize 10 comprehend, understand 11 distinguish

perceptible 5 clear, plain 7 evident, notable, obvious, visible 8 apparent, distinct, manifest, palpable, tangible, unhidden 9 prominent 10 detectable, noticeable, observable 11 conspicuous, discernible, perceivable, unconcealed, well-defined 12 discoverable, unmistakable 13 ascertainable

perception 5 grasp, sense 7 faculty 8 judgment 9 awareness, detection 10 cognizance, conception 11 discernment, recognition 12 apprehension 13 comprehension, consciousness, understanding 14 discrimination

perceptive 4 keen 5 acute, aware, quick, sharp 6 astute, shrewd 8 sensible 9 sensitive 10 discerning, insightful, responsive 11 intelligent, penetrating, quick-witted 13 understanding

perch 3 sit 4 land, rest, seat 5 eyrie, light, roost 6 alight, settle

Percival, Perceval
   character in: 16 Arthurian romance
   also see Parsifal

percolate 4 boil, brew 6 bubble, seethe

percussion instrument 4 gong 5 anvil, bells, tabor 6 chimes, rattle 7 celesta, cymbals, marimba, taboret, timpani 8 bass drum, side drum, triangle 9 castanets, dulcitone, snare drum, tenor drum, typophone, xylophone 10 kettledrum, tambourine 12 Glockenspiel, tubular bells

Percy, Walker
   author of: 8 Lancelot 12 The Moviegoer 14 Love in the Ruins 15 The Second Coming 16 The Last Gentleman

Perdita
   character in: 14 The Winter's Tale
   author: 11 Shakespeare

perdition 4 Hell, ruin 8 hellfire 9 damnation, ruination 11 destruction 12 condemnation

Perdix
   also: 9 Polycaste
   brother: 8 Daedalus
   son: 5 Talus
   changed into: 9 partridge

pere 6 father, senior

Pere Goriot
   author: 14 Honore de Balzac
   character: 15 Monsieur Vautrin 17 Eugene de Rastignac, Madame de Beauseant 18 Victorine Taillefer 26 Countess Anastasie de Restaud, Baroness Delphine de Nucingen

peregrination 4 trip 5 jaunt, sally 6 hiking, junket, roving, travel 7 journey, roaming 8 rambling, trekking 9 excursion, wandering 10 expedition

Peregrine Pickle
   author: 14 Tobias Smollett

Pereira, William
   architect of: 13 Cape Canaveral 20 Transamerica Building (San Francisco)

Perelman, S J
   author of: 10 Eastward Ha 15 One Touch of Venus (with Ogden Nash and Kurt Weill) 16 The Road to Miltown 18 Strictly from Hunger 24 Under the Spreading Atrophy

peremptory 5 final 6 biased, lordly 8 absolute, decisive, dogmatic 9 assertive, imperious 10 aggressive, high-handed, imperative, obligatory, undeniable 11 dictatorial, domineering, irrevocable, opinionated, overbearing, unavoidable, unequivocal 12 closed-minded, irreversible 13 authoritative 14 unquestionable 16 incontrovertible

perennial 5 fixed 7 durable, lasting, undying 8 constant, enduring, timeless 9 ceaseless, continual, immutable, incessant, long-lived, permanent, perpetual, unceasing, unfailing 10 changeless, continuous, persistent, unchanging 11 everlasting, long-lasting, unremitting 12 imperishable 14 indestructible

Perez, Manuel Benitez
   nickname: 10 El Cordobes

perfect 4 pure, true 5 exact, ideal, whole 6 effect, entire, evolve, strict 7 achieve, develop, fulfill, precise, realize, sublime, supreme 8 absolute, accurate, complete, faithful, finished, flawless, peerless, thorough, unbroken, unerring 9 blameless, faultless, matchless, undamaged, unequaled, unrivaled, untainted 10 accomplish, consummate, immaculate, impeccable, scrupulous, unimpaired 11 superlative, unblemished, unmitigated, unqualified

perfection 6 purity 9 achieving, evolution, exactness, precision, sublimity 10 completion, excellence, ideal state 11 development, fulfillment, perfectness, realization, superiority 12 accurateness, consummation, flawlessness 13 faultlessness, impeccability 14 accomplishment

perfectly 5 fully, quite 6 purely, wholly 7 totally, utterly 8 entirely, superbly 9 downright, supremely 10 absolutely, altogether, completely, flawlessly, impeccably, infinitely, positively, thoroughly 11 faultlessly, wonderfully 12 consummately, preeminently, to perfection, without fault 13 without defect 14 to the nth degree, without blemish

perfidious 5 false, lying 6 shifty, sneaky 7 corrupt 8 cheating, disloyal, two-faced 9 deceitful, dishonest, faithless 10 traitorous, treasonous, unfaithful, untruthful 11 treacherous, treasonable 12 dishonorable, undependable, unscrupulous 13 double-dealing, untrustworthy

perfidy 6 deceit 7 treason 8 bad faith, betrayal 9 falseness, recreancy, treachery, two-timing 10 disloyalty, infidelity 11 double-cross, inconstancy 13 breach of faith, deceitfulness, double-dealing, faithlessness 14 unfaithfulness

perforate 4 bore, gash, hole, slit, stab 5 drill, prick, punch, slash, split, stick 6 pierce 8 puncture 9 lancinate, penetrate

perform 2 do 3 act 4 meet, play 5 enact 6 attain, depict, effect, finish, render, troupe 7 achieve, execute, fulfill, portray, present, pull off, realize 8 carry out, knock off 9 discharge, dispose of, polish off, represent 10 accomplish, bring about, consummate, perpetrate, take part in

performance 4 play, show 5 doing, opera 6 ballet 7 concert, conduct, recital 8 ceremony, dispatch, exercise 9 acquittal, discharge, execution, rendering, spectacle 10 attainment, completion, exhibition, performing, production 11 achievement, fulfillment, realization, transaction 12 consummation, effectuation, perpetration, presentation 13 entertainment 14 accomplishment

perfume 4 odor 5 aroma, scent, smell 7 bouquet, cologne, essence, extract, sweeten 9 aromatize, fragrance

perfumed 7 odorous, scented 8 aromatic, fragrant 11 odoriferous 12 sweet-scented 13 sweet-smelling

perfunctory 3 lax 5 hasty 6 casual 7 cursory, offhand, routine 8 careless, listless, lukewarm 9 apathetic, negligent 10 mechanical, spiritless, unthinking 11 halfhearted, inattentive, indifferent, passionless, superficial, unconcerned 13 disinterested

pergola 5 arbor, bower 6 ramada 7 balcony, trellis

Per Hanea
   character in: 16 Giants of the Earth
   author: 7 Rolvaag

perhaps 5 maybe 6 mayhap 8 peut-etre, possibly 9 perchance 10 God willing, imaginably 11 conceivably 12 peradventure

Periboea
   father: 9 Alcathous, Hipponous
   husband: 6 Oeneus 7 Polybus
   son: 6 Tydeus 7 Olenias, Pelegon 14 Telamonian Ajax
   foster son: 7 Oedipus

Perichole, La
   character in: 21 The Bridge of San

Luis Rey
author: 6 Wilder
Pericles, Prince of Tyre
author: 18 William Shakespeare
character: 5 Cleon **6** Marina, Thaisa
7 Dionyza **9** Antiochus **10** Lysimachus
Periclymenus
father: 6 Neleus **8** Poseidon
grandfather: 8 Poseidon
gift: 13 shape-changing
killed by: 8 Hercules
periderm 4 bark **8** covering **9** sheathing
peridot
species: 7 olivine
source: 5 Burma, Mogok **8** Zehirget
color: 11 yellow-green
perigee 5 depth, nadir **8** low point
Perikeiromene (The Rape of the Ringlets)
author: 8 Menander
peril 4 risk **6** danger, hazard, menace, threat **7** pitfall **8** jeopardy, unsafety **10** insecurity **11** uncertainty **13** cause for alarm, vulnerability
perilous 5 risky, shaky **6** chancy, unsafe, unsure **7** ominous **8** insecure, slippery, ticklish **9** dangerous, hazardous, uncertain **10** precarious, vulnerable **11** threatening, venturesome
perimeter 4 edge **6** border, bounds, margin **8** confines **9** periphery **10** borderline **13** circumference
period 3 age, end, eon, era **4** halt, stop, term, time **5** close, epoch, limit **6** finale, finish, season **7** curtain **8** duration, interval **9** cessation, interlude
French: 6 siecle
periodic, periodical 6 cyclic **7** regular, routine **8** frequent, repeated, seasonal **9** recurrent, recurring **12** intermittent
periodical 5 daily, paper **6** annual, review, weekly **7** journal, monthly **8** bulletin, magazine **9** newspaper, quarterly **10** newsletter **11** publication **12** newsmagazine
periodically 5 often **9** regularly, routinely **10** frequently, repeatedly **12** occasionally
peripatetic 6 roving **7** migrant, nomadic, roaming, walking **8** rambling, tramping **9** itinerant, migratory, traveling, wandering **10** ambulating, ambulatory **12** Aristotelian, gallivanting **13** peregrinating
periphery 4 edge **5** bound **6** border **7** fringes **8** boundary **9** outskirts, perimeter **13** circumference
perish 3 die **5** decay **6** expire, vanish **7** crumble **8** pass away **9** disappear **10** come to ruin, wither away **11** be destroyed
perishable 8 fleeting, unstable **9**

ephemeral **10** evanescent, short-lived, transitory **12** decomposable
perished 4 dead, died **7** expired **8** lifeless **10** passed away
periwinkle 5 Vinca **12** Catharanthus
varieties: 4 Rose **6** Common, Lesser **7** Greater **10** Madagascar
perjury 13 false swearing **14** lying under oath **20** giving false testimony
Perker
character in: 14 Pickwick Papers
author: 7 Dickens
Perkins, Anthony
born: 9 New York NY
roles: 6 Psycho **11** Norman Bates **14** Catch Twenty-Two **17** Look Homeward Angel **18** Desire Under the Elms, Friendly Persuasion
perk up 4 lift **5** cheer, rally, renew **6** buoy up, lift up, revive **7** animate, enliven, gladden **8** brighten, vitalize **9** stimulate **10** rejuvenate
perky 3 gay **4** pert **5** alert, brisk, happy, saucy, sunny **6** jaunty, lively **7** smiling **8** animated, cheerful, spirited **9** sprightly, vivacious **11** free and easy **12** full of spirit, lighthearted
permanent 3 set **4** perm, wave **6** stable **7** abiding, durable, endless, eternal, lasting, undying **8** constant, enduring, immortal, infinite, unending, unfading **9** deathless, immutable, long-lived, perpetual, unfailing **10** changeless, unyielding **11** everlasting, long-lasting, never-ending, unalterable **12** imperishable
permeate 4 fill **5** imbue **6** infuse **7** pervade **8** saturate **9** penetrate **11** pass through, seep through, soak through
per mensem 10 by the month
permissible 5 legal, licit **6** lawful **7** allowed, granted **8** licensed **9** allowable, permitted, tolerated **10** admissible, authorized, legitimate, sanctioned **12** unprohibited
permission 5 grant, leave **6** assent, permit **7** consent, license **8** approval, sanction **9** agreement, allowance **10** compliance, concession, indulgence **11** approbation, endorsement **12** acquiescence, dispensation **13** authorization
permissive 3 lax **7** lenient **8** allowing, granting, tolerant **9** assenting, easygoing, indulgent **10** consenting, forbearing, permitting **11** acquiescent **13** unprohibitive **14** unproscriptive
permit 2 OK **3** let **5** allow **6** endure, suffer **7** agree to, approve, condone, endorse, let pass, license, warrant **8** bear with, sanction, tolerate **9** authority, authorize, consent to, put up with **11** give leave to **12** give assent to **13** authorization
French: 13 laissez passer

permit to leave 4 free **5** let go **6** excuse **7** dismiss, release, set free **8** liberate **9** allow to go, discharge, send forth
pernicious 5 fatal, toxic **6** deadly, lethal, mortal **7** baneful, harmful, noxious, serious **8** damaging, venomous **9** dangerous, injurious, malignant, poisonous **10** disastrous **11** deleterious, destructive, detrimental
pernod
type: 8 aperitif
flavor: 5 anise
substitute for: 8 absinthe
with gin: 7 Dubarry
with orange juice: 9 Tiger Tail
with rum: 8 Shanghai
with rye: 3 TNT
peroration 6 sermon, speech, tirade **7** address, lecture, oration **8** diatribe, harangue, jeremiad **9** discourse, philippic **10** filibuster **11** declamation, exhortation
perpendicular 4 sine **5** erect, plumb, sheer, steep **7** upright **8** vertical **10** right angle
perpetrate 2 do **5** enact **6** commit, pursue **7** execute, inflict, perform, pull off **8** carry out, transact
perpetration 5 doing **9** committal **10** commission, committing, performing **11** carrying out, performance
perpetrator 9 performer **11** participant
perpetual 7 abiding, endless, eternal, lasting **8** constant, enduring, repeated, unending **9** ceaseless, continual, incessant, permanent, sustained, unceasing **10** continuous **11** everlasting, never ending, unremitting **12** interminable **13** inexhaustible, uninterrupted
perpetuate 4 save **7** sustain **8** continue, maintain, make last, preserve **10** eternalize **11** immortalize, memorialize
perpetuity 7 all time, forever **8** eternity, infinity **9** end of time **10** permanence **11** endlessness **12** perpetuation, timelessness **13** perdurability, perennialness
perplex 5 mix up, stump **6** baffle, boggle, muddle, puzzle, rattle **7** confuse, mystify, nonplus **8** befuddle, bewilder, confound **9** dumbfound
perplexed 7 anxious, amazed, baffled, bemused, muddled, puzzled **8** confused, doubtful, involved **9** befuddled, intricate, mystified **10** astonished, bewildered, nonplussed
perplexing 4 hard, mazy **6** thorny **7** complex **10** mysterious
riddle: 9 conundrum
perplexity 9 confusion **10** bafflement, puzzlement **12** bewilderment **13** mystification
perquisite 3 due **4** gift, perk **5** right **6**

reward **7** benefit, present **9** advantage, emolument, privilege **10** honorarium, inducement, recompense **13** fringe benefit

Perrine, Valerie
  born: 11 Galveston TX
  roles: 5 Lenny **8** Superman **18** Slaughterhouse Five

Perry, Matthew Calbraith
  served in: 10 Mexican War **19** War of Eighteen Twelve
  rank: 9 commodore
  helped establish: 7 Liberia
  commander of: 17 US African Squadron
  gained treaty with: 5 Japan

Perry, Oliver Hazard
  nickname: 14 Hero of Lake Erie
  served in: 13 Tripolitan War **19** War of Eighteen-Twelve
  battle: 8 Lake Erie
  commander of ship: 7 Niagara **8** Lawrence
  defeated: 7 British
  saying: 31 We have met the enemy and they are ours

Perry, William
  nickname: 12 Refrigerator
  sport: 8 football
  team: 12 Chicago Bears

Perry Como Show, The
  regulars: 8 Don Adams **9** Jack Duffy, Paul Lynde **10** Pierre Olaf **11** Kaye Ballard **12** Sandy Stewart **14** Fontane Sisters **17** Ray Charles Singers **18** Louis Da Pron Dancers **19** Peter Gennaro Dancers
  announcer: 9 Dick Stark, Ed Herlihy **11** Frank Gallop, Martin Block **12** Durward Kirby
  orchestra: 13 Mitchell Ayres
  theme: 16 Dream Along with Me

Perry Mason
  character: 6 Lt Drum **7** Lt Tragg **9** Paul Drake **10** Lt Anderson **11** Della Street **14** Hamilton Burger
  cast: 9 Wesley Lau **10** Ray Collins **11** Barbara Hale, Raymond Burr **13** William Hopper, William Talman **15** Richard Anderson

persecute 3 vex **4** bait **5** abuse, annoy, bully, harry, hound **6** badger, harass, harrow, hector, plague **7** oppress, torment **8** maltreat **9** tyrannize, victimize

Persephone
  also: 4 Cora, Kore **10** Perserpina, Proserpine
  queen of: 5 Hades
  father: 4 Zeus
  mother: 7 Demeter
  husband: 5 Hades
  abducted by: 5 Pluto
  ate seeds of: 11 pomegranate
  epithet: 11 Carpophorus
  corresponds to: 5 Brimo **6** Libera **8** Despoena

Persepolis
  capital of: 13 Persian Empire
  near modern-day: 10 Shiraz, Iran

Perseus
  father: 4 Zeus
  mother: 5 Danae
  grandfather: 8 Acrisius
  wife: 9 Andromeda
  son: 6 Mestor, Perses **7** Alcaeus, Heleius **9** Electryon, Sthenelus
  daughter: 10 Gorgophone
  saved: 9 Andromeda
  killed: 6 Gorgon, Medusa

perseverance 8 tenacity **10** doggedness, resolution **11** persistence **12** resoluteness **13** determination, steadfastness

persevere 6 hang on, keep on **7** persist **8** keep at it, plug away, work hard **9** not give up, stick to it **10** be resolute, be resolved, hammer away **11** be obstinate, be steadfast, hang in there

persevering 6 dogged **8** constant, diligent, resolute, sedulous **9** keeping on, steadfast, tenacious **10** determined, persistent, unflagging **11** hardworking, industrious, unremitting

Pershing, John J
  nickname: 9 Black Jack
  served in: 3 WWI **11** Philippines, World War One **18** Spanish-American War
  commander of: 21 Mexican border campaign
  trained: 27 American Expeditionary Forces
  battle: 10 Kettle Hill **11** San Juan Hill
  fought against: 5 Moros **11** Pancho Villa
  rank: 16 brigadier general **18** general of the armies
  memoirs: 26 My Experiences in the World War
    won: 13 Pulitzer Prize (for history)

Persia *see* **4** Iran

Persian Gulf War
  caused by: 4 Iraq **13** Saddam Hussein **14** Kuwait invasion
  took place in: 4 Iraq **6** Kuwait **10** Middle East **11** Saudi Arabia
  leaders:
    Allies: 11 Colin Powell **15** Khalid bin Sultan **18** H Norman Schwarzkopf
    Iraq: 13 Saddam Hussein
  operations: 11 Desert Storm **12** Desert Shield
  weapons: 4 Scud **5** AWACS **6** Abrams, Apache **7** Bradley, Patriot, Stealth **8** Tomahawk
  battle: 6 Khafji **18** mother of all battles

Persian Mythology
  god of light/truth: 7 Mithras

Persians, The
  author: 9 Aeschylus

character: 6 Atossa, Xerxes **13** Ghost of Darius

persist 4 go on, last, stay **6** endure, hang on, hold on, remain **7** hold out, survive **8** continue, keep at it, not yield **9** not give up, persevere, stand fast, stick to it **10** be resolute **11** be obstinate, be tenacious, hang in there, never say die

persistence 8 tenacity **9** diligence **11** application **12** perseverance **13** determination

persistent 6 dogged **7** abiding, endless, eternal, lasting **8** constant, enduring, obdurate, resolute, stubborn **9** continual, incessant, obstinate, perpetual, steadfast, sustained, tenacious, unceasing, unfailing **10** continuous, determined, persisting, relentless, unshakable, unswerving **11** persevering, unrelenting, unremitting **12** interminable **13** inexhaustible

persnickety 5 fussy **6** choosy **7** finical, finicky **8** picayune **10** fastidious, fuddy-duddy, meticulous, nitpicking, particular, pernickety **11** overprecise, punctilious **13** overdemanding

person 4 body, soul **5** being, human **6** mortal **8** creature **9** earthling **10** human being, individual, living body, living soul

persona 5 being **6** facade **9** character

personable 4 warm **7** affable, amiable, cordial, likable, tactful **8** amicable, charming, friendly, outgoing, pleasant, sociable **9** agreeable **10** attractive, diplomatic **11** complaisant, sympathetic **12** well-disposed, well-mannered

Personae
  author: 9 Ezra Pound

personage 3 VIP **5** nabob **6** bigwig **7** big name, big shot, notable **8** big wheel, luminary, somebody **9** celebrity, dignitary **11** heavyweight **12** leading light, public figure **13** highmuck-a-muck

persona grata 8 diplomat **16** acceptable person **34** acceptable diplomatic representative

personal 3 own **5** privy **6** bodily, inward, secret **7** private, special **8** intimate, physical **9** corporeal, exclusive **10** individual, particular, subjective **12** confidential

Personal Anthology, A
  author: 15 Jorge Luis Borges

personality 3 ego **4** self **5** charm **6** makeup, nature **8** charisma, identity **9** magnetism **10** affability, amiability **11** disposition, temperament **12** friendliness **13** agreeableness, individuality **15** distinctiveness

persona non grata 15 unwelcome person **18** unacceptable person **33** unwelcome diplomatic representative

Personification of
aging: 4 Elli
air: 4 Amen, Amon 5 Ammon 6 Aether
astronomy: 6 Urania
breath: 4 Amen, Amon 5 Ammon
chaos: 4 Nunu
choral song: 11 Terpsichore
comedy: 6 Thalia
confusion: 5 Chaos
conscience: 5 Aidos
courage: 5 Arete 6 Virtus
dance: 8 Polymnia 10 Polyhymnia 11 Terpsichore
death: 4 Mors 6 Namtar 8 Thanatos
desert: 3 Set 4 Seth
desire: 6 Pothos
divine punishment: 3 Ate 7 Nemesis
east wind: 5 Eurus 9 Volturnus
echo: 4 Echo
emulation: 5 Zelos
familial affection: 6 Pietas
fate: 4 Norn 5 Moira, Moras
fear: 6 Deimos
femininity: 5 Neith
fire: 4 Logi
force: 3 Bia
good faith: 5 Fides
grain blight: 7 Robigus
heaven: 6 Uranus
hostile nature: 8 Fomorian
idyllic poetry: 6 Thalia
liberty: 8 Libertas
longing: 6 Pothos
lotus: 8 Nefertem
meditation: 6 Melete
memory: 5 Mneme, Munin
moon: 4 Luna
nature: 7 Erlking
night: 3 Nox
north wind: 6 Boreas
order: 7 Eunomia
pain: 5 Oizys
past: 3 Urd
peace: 5 Irene
prayer: 5 Litae
present: 8 Verdandi
punishment: 5 Poena, Poine
recklessness: 3 Ate
retribution: 7 Nemesis
revenge: 5 Poena, Poine
Roman nation: 8 Quirinus
sacred music: 8 Polymnia 10 Polyhymnia
sea: 3 Ler, Lir 5 Nammu 6 Pontus 8 Thalassa
sky: 6 Aether, Hathor
soul: 6 Psyche
southeast wind: 5 Eurus 9 Volturnus
south wind: 5 Notus 7 Ninurta
strength: 6 Cratus
sun: 3 Sol
thought: 5 Hugin
tragedy: 9 Melpomene
truth: 7 Alethia
unavailing effort: 5 Ocnus
victory: 4 Nike
wealth: 6 Plutus

west wind: 8 Favonius, Zephyrus
wind: 7 Ninurta
zeal: 5 Zelos
personify 6 embody 7 express 9 exemplify, incarnate, represent, symbolize 11 externalize, incorporate, personalize 12 characterize
personnel 4 crew 5 staff 7 members, workers 8 manpower 9 employees, work force 10 associates
Person to Person
host: 13 Edward R Murrow 18 Charles Collingwood
perspective 4 view 5 scape, scene, vista 7 outlook 8 overview, prospect 9 broad view, viewpoint 12 bird's-eye view
perspicacious 4 keen 5 acute, alert, awake, sharp 6 astute, shrewd 9 clear-eyed, sagacious 10 discerning, perceptive 11 clearheaded, keen-sighted, penetrating, sharp-witted 12 clear-sighted
perspicacity 6 acumen 8 keenness, sagacity 9 acuteness, alertness, sharpness 10 astuteness, perception, shrewdness 11 discernment 14 discrimination
persuadable 7 willing 8 amenable, obliging 9 malleable, tractable 10 open-minded 16 open to suggestion
persuade 3 get 4 coax, lure, move, sway 5 tempt 6 cajole, entice, induce, prompt 7 wheedle, win over 8 convince, inveigle, motivate, talk into 9 influence
Persuasion
author: 10 Jane Austen
character: 7 Mrs Clay 8 Mrs Croft 11 Lady Russell 12 Admiral Croft 25 Captain Frederick Wentworth
Elliot family: 4 Anne 7 William 9 Elizabeth, Sir Walter
Musgrove family: 4 Mary 6 Louisa 7 Charles 9 Henrietta
persuasive 6 cogent 7 coaxing, logical, winning 8 alluring, credible, forceful, inviting 9 effective, plausible, seductive 10 believable, compelling, convincing 11 influential
pert 4 flip, spry 5 alert, brash, brisk, fresh, nervy, perky, quick, saucy 6 brassy, brazen, cheeky, lively, nimble 7 chipper 8 flippant, impolite, impudent, insolent 9 audacious, energetic, insulting, sprightly, wide-awake 11 impertinent, smart-alecky 12 discourteous
pertain 2 be 5 apply, touch 6 befall, belong, relate 7 concern, connect
Perth see Australia
pertinacious 6 dogged 8 stubborn 9 obstinate, tenacious 10 persistent, unyielding 11 persevering
pertinacity 9 obstinacy 10 mulishness 11 persistence, willfulness 12 contrari-

ness, obdurateness, perverseness, stubbornness 13 determination, inflexibility, intransigence, pigheadedness 14 bullheadedness, intractability
pertinence 9 relevance 11 germaneness 12 appositeness 13 applicability
pertinent 3 apt 4 meet 7 apropos, fitting, germane, related 8 apposite, material, relevant, suitable 9 befitting, concerned, congruent, connected 10 applicable, consistent, to the point
Latin: 5 ad rem
perturb 5 upset, worry 6 bother 7 disturb, fluster, trouble 8 disquiet, distress 10 discompose, disconcert
perturbation 5 alarm, upset, worry 6 dismay 7 anxiety, concern, turmoil 8 distress 9 agitation, commotion 10 excitement 11 disquietude, trepidation 12 apprehension, discomposure 13 consternation
perturbed 5 upset 7 annoyed, worried 8 agitated, troubled 9 disturbed 12 disconcerted
perturbing 6 vexing 7 irksome 8 annoying 9 vexatious 10 bothersome, irritating, unsettling 11 disquieting, distressing, troublesome 13 disconcerting
Peru
capital/largest city: 4 Lima
Inca capital: 5 Cuzco
others: 3 Ica 4 Puno 5 Cuzco, Paita, Pisco, Tacna 6 Callao, Talara 7 Huanuco, Iquitos 8 Arequipa, Castilla, Chiclayo, Chimbote, Mollendo, Pucallpa, Trujillo 9 Cajamarca 10 Yurimaguas
school: 8 Trujillo 8 San Marcos
division: 3 Ica 4 Lima, Puno 5 Cusco, Cuzco, Junin, Piura, Tacna 6 Ancash, Loreto, Tumbes
Inca empire: 13 Tahuantinsuyo
measure: 4 topo 5 galon 7 celemin
monetary unit: 3 sol 5 libra 6 dinero, reseta 7 centavo
weight: 5 libra 7 quintal
island: 6 Chinca 7 Chincha
lake: 8 Titicaca
mountain: 5 Andes 7 El Misti, Huamina 8 Coropuna
highest point: 9 Huascaran
river: 3 Ene, Ica, Ilo 4 Napo, Napu 5 Piura, Rimac 6 Amazon, Oroton, Pampas, Yaguas, Yavari 7 Curaray, Mantaro, Maranon, Pastaza, Tapiche, Ucayali 8 Apurimac, Huallaga, Urubamba 11 Madre de Dios, Paucartambo
sea: 7 Pacific
physical feature:
current: 6 el nino
desert: 5 Nazca 7 Atacama, Sechura
drizzling rain: 8 ilovizna
fog: 5 garua
gulf: 9 Guayaquil
plateau: 7 Tablazo

people: 4 Ande, Boro, Cana, Inca, Inka, Lama, Pano, Peba, Piro, Yutu **5** Campa, Carib, Chana, Colan, Colla, Jwaro, Moche, Nasca, Senci, Yagua, Yunca **6** Atalan, Aymara, Canchi, Chanca, Chanka, Chimer, Cholos, Cocama, Jibaro, Kechua, Omagua, Quiche, Quolla, Setibo, Sipibo **7** Changos, Chincha, Chuncho, Mestizo, Mochica **8** Amahuaca, Criollos, Mayoruma, Quechuia **9** Callawaya **10** Tiahuanaca, Tiatinagua **11** Chumpivilca

  artist: 4 Lazo **7** Montero, Sabogal, Szyszlo **8** Codesido

  author: 4 Vega **5** Palma, Prada **8** Caviedes **10** Mariategui

  explorer: 7 Pizarro

  Inca leader: 7 Huascar **9** Atahualpa **10** Manco Capac

  leader: 5 Balta, Pardo, Prado, Torre **7** Bolivar **8** Castilla, Fujimori **9** Santa Cruz **13** Belaunde Terry **15** Leguiay y Salcedo, Morales Bermudez

language: 6 Aymara **7** English, Quechua, Spanish

religion: 13 Roman Catholic

place:

  bullring: 11 Plaza de Acho

  center of Lima: 12 Plaza de Armas

  church: 10 La Compania

  open market/street: 9 Calle Real

  ruins: 5 Huaco **8** Chan-Chan **9** Cajamarca **11** Machu- Picchu **22** Fortress of Sacsayhuaman

feature:

  animal: 5 llama **6** alpaca, vicuna **7** guanaco

  commune: 6 ayllus

  dance: 5 cueca, kaswa **6** cachua

  farmers: 10 campesinos

  priest: 6 villac

  slums: 9 barriadas

  tree: 8 cinchona

food:

  dish: 3 aji, cuy **7** ceviche **10** anticuchos

  drink: 5 pisco **6** chicha **11** aguardiente

Perugino, Pietro

  real name: 14 Pietro Vannucci

  also called: 10 Il Perugino **14** Pier della Pieve

  born: 5 Italy **15** Citta della Pieve

  artwork: 24 The Crucifixion with Saints **26** Delivery of the Keys to St Peter **27** The Giving of the Keys to St Peter **32** Apparition of the Virgin to St Bernard, Christ Delivering the Keys to St Peter

perusal 5 study **6** review **7** reading **8** scanning, scrutiny **10** inspection, runthrough **11** examination, lookthrough **12** scrutinizing **13** contemplation

peruse 3 con **4** read, scan **5** study **6** search, survey **7** examine, inspect **10** scrutinize

pervade 4 fill **5** imbue **6** infuse **7** suffuse **8** permeate, saturate **9** penetrate **13** spread through **17** diffuse throughout

pervasive 4 rife **7** rampant **8** dominant **9** prevalent **10** ubiquitous **11** omnipresent, predominant

perverse 5 balky **6** dogged, mulish, ornery **7** wayward, willful **8** contrary, obdurate, stubborn **9** obstinate, pigheaded **10** hardheaded, headstrong, inflexible, rebellious **11** disobedient, intractable, wrongheaded

perversion 9 depravity **10** corruption, degeneracy, immorality **11** dissipation, dissolution

pervert 4 warp **5** abuse **6** debase, misuse **7** contort, corrupt, degrade, deprave, distort, falsify, subvert **8** misapply **9** desecrate **12** misrepresent

perverted 5 false **6** faulty, untrue, warped **7** corrupt, debased, deviant, twisted, unsound **8** aberrant, abnormal, degraded, depraved **9** contorted, distorted, erroneous, imperfect, unnatural **10** fallacious, unbalanced **12** misconceived, misconstrued **13** misunderstood

pesky 7 chafing, galling, irksome **8** annoying **9** maddening, obnoxious, offensive, vexatious **10** bothersome, disturbing, nettlesome **11** aggravating, distasteful, infuriating, pestiferous, troublesome **12** disagreeable, exasperating **13** objectionable

pessimism 5 gloom **7** despair **10** gloominess **12** hopelessness **13** gloomy outlook **14** discouragement **15** downheartedness

pessimist 7 kill-joy **8** sourpuss **9** Cassandra, defeatist, gloomy Gus **10** spoilsport, wet blanket **11** crepehanger **13** prophet of doom

pessimistic 6 gloomy **8** hopeless **10** despairing, dispirited **11** discouraged, downhearted

pest 4 bane **5** curse **6** blight, bother **7** scourge **8** nuisance, vexation **9** annoyance **10** irritation **13** pain in the neck

pester 3 irk, nag, vex **4** bait, fret **5** annoy, harry, taunt, worry **6** badger, bother, harass, hector, nettle, plague **7** disturb, provoke, torment, trouble **8** irritate

pesticide 3 DDT **7** biocide **8** fumigant **9** fungicide, germacide, vermicide **11** insecticide

  user: 12 exterminator

pestilence 6 blight, plague **7** disease **8** epidemic

  god of: 4 Irra

pesto sauce

ingredients: 5 basil **6** garlic **8** olive oil

pet 3 pat **4** baby, dear **6** caress, choice, fondle, stroke **7** beloved, darling, dearest, favored **8** favorite **9** cherished, preferred **10** sweetheart **14** apple of one's eye

pet activity 5 hobby **7** passion **8** interest **10** enthusiasm, hobbyhorse

Petain, Henri Philippe

  rank: 7 general, premier

  nationality: 6 French

  leader of government at: 5 Vichy

  convicted of: 7 treason

Peter 7 apostle

  means: 4 rock

  also called: 5 Simon **6** Cephas

  father: 4 John **5** Jonas

  brother: 6 Andrew

  birthplace: 9 Bethsaida

  hometown: 9 Capernaum

  disciple of: 5 Jesus

  companion: 4 John **5** James

  rebuked: 7 Ananias **8** Sapphira

  secretary: 8 Silvanus

  pertaining to: 7 Petrine

Peter and the Wolf

  composed by: 9 Prokofiev

Peter Grimes

  opera by: 7 Britten

  character: 11 Ellen Orford

Peter Heering, Cherry Heering

  type: 6 brandy **7** liqueur

  origin: 7 Denmark

  flavor: 6 cherry

  color: 3 red

Peter Ibbetson

  author: 15 George Du Maurier

peter out 3 ebb **7** decline, dwindle, fall off, give out **8** diminish

Peter Pan

  author: 11 James Barrie

  character: 4 John, Smee **7** Michael **9** Nurse Nana, Tiger Lily **10** Tinker Bell **11** Captain Hook **12** Wendy Darling

  locale: 14 Never-never Land

petiole 4 stem **5** spine, stalk, stipe **8** peduncle **9** leafstalk

petite 3 wee **4** tiny **5** small **6** little **9** miniature **10** diminutive

petition 3 ask, beg, sue **4** plea, pray, seek, suit, urge **5** press **6** appeal, invoke, orison, prayer **7** apply to, beseech, entreat **8** appeal to, call upon, entreaty, proposal **9** imploring, plead with, request of **10** invocation, supplicate **11** application, beseechment, requisition **12** solicitation, supplication

petitioner 6 suitor **8** claimant **9** solicitor, suppliant **10** supplicant

pet name 8 nickname **9** sobriquet **10** diminutive, endearment

pet phrase 5 maxim, motto **6** saying, slogan **9** catchword

Petre (Lord)

character in: 16 The Rape of the Lock
author: 4 Pope

petrified 4 hard **5** dense, solid, stony
6 frozen **8** hardened, rocklike **9** paralyzed **10** solidified **11** hard as a rock,
scared stiff **13** turned to stone

Petrified Forest, The
director: 10 Archie Mayo
based on play by: 14 Robert Sherwood
cast: 9 Dick Foran **10** Bette Davis **12**
Leslie Howard **14** Humphrey Bogart
(Duke Mantee)
setting: 7 Arizona

Petronius
author of: 9 Satyricon

Petruchio
character in: 19 The Taming of the
Shrew
author: 11 Shakespeare

Petticoat Junction
character: 10 Floyd Smoot, Sam
Drucker **11** Homer Bedloe, Kate
Bradley **12** Charlie Pratt, Dr Janet
Craig, Steve Elliott, Wendell Gibbs
14 Betty Jo Bradley, Uncle Joe Car-
son **15** Billie Jo Bradley, Bobbie Jo
Bradley
cast: 9 Frank Cady, Linda Kaye, Mike
Minor, Rufe Davis **10** Pat Woodell
11 Charles Lane **12** Bea Benaderet,
Byron Foulger, June Lockhart, Lori
Saunders **13** Edgar Buchanan,
Gunilla Hutton, Jeannine Riley **14**
Meredith MacRae, Smiley Burnette
setting: 11 Hooterville **14** Shady Rest
Hotel
train: 10 Cannonball

petto 5 chest **6** breast

petty 4 mean **5** minor, small **6** flimsy,
paltry, shabby, slight **7** ignoble, trivial
8 niggling, picayune, piddling, trifling
10 ungenerous **11** small minded, unimportant **12** narrow-minded **13** insignificant **14** inconsiderable **15** inconsequential

petulance 9 poutiness, sulkiness **11**
fretfulness, peevishness **12** irritability

petulant 4 sour **5** cross, gruff, huffy,
sulky, surly, testy **6** grumpy, sullen,
tetchy, touchy **7** bearish, crabbed,
fretful, grouchy, peevish, pettish, uncivil **8** snappish **9** crotchety, fractious,
irascible, irritable **10** ill-natured, out
of sorts, ungracious **11** complaining,
contentious, ill-tempered, quarrelsome, thin-skinned **12** cantankerous,
faultfinding

Petulia
director: 13 Richard Lester
cast: 10 Arthur Hill, Pippa Scott **12**
George C Scott, Joseph Cotten **13** Julie Christie, Shirley Knight **18** Richard Chamberlain
setting: 12 San Francisco

petunia
varieties: 4 Wild **7** Mexican, Seaside

10 Large white **12** Common garden
14 Violet-flowered

peu a peu 14 little by little

peu de chose 14 trifling matter **17** unimportant matter

pew 4 seat **5** bench **6** settle

Peychaud Bitters
type: 8 aperitif
origin: 10 New Orleans

Peyton Place
author: 14 Grace Metalious
character: 9 Rita Jacks (Harrington)
10 Hannah Cord, Steven Cord **12**
Matthew Swain **13** Betty Anderson
(Harrington Cord Harrington), Elliott
Carson, Julie Anderson **14** Dr Mi-
chael Rossi, Dr Robert Morton,
George Anderson **16** Allison Macken-
zie (Harrington), Leslie Harrington,
Norman Harrington, Rodney Harrington **18** Constance Mackenzie (Carson)
cast (television): 8 Ed Nelson **9** Kent
Smith, Mia Farrow, Ryan O'Neal **10**
Tim O'Connor **11** Kasey Rogers, Paul
Langton, Ruth Warrick **12** Henry
Beckman, James Douglas **13** Dorothy
Malone **14** Barbara Parkins, Patricia
Morrow, Warner Anderson **19** Christopher Connelly
director (movie): 10 Mark Robson
cast (movie): 9 Hope Lange **10** Lana
Turner, Lloyd Nolan **13** Arthur Kennedy
score: 11 Franz Waxman

Phaedo
author: 5 Plato

Phaedra
father: 5 Minos
mother: 8 Pasiphae
sister: 7 Ariadne
husband: 7 Theseus
son: 6 Acamas **8** Demophon
stepson: 10 Hippolytus
loved: 10 Hippolytus
death by: 7 hanging, suicide

Phaenna
origin: 5 Greek **7** Spartan
member of: 6 Graces

Phaethon
father: 6 Helios
mother: 7 Clymene

phalanx 6 column, parade **9** formation
13 ranks and files

Phallus
image of: 9 male organ
symbol of: 9 fertility
carried in: 6 comedy **9** festivals
associated with: 3 Pan **6** Hermes **7**
Demeter **8** Dionysus

phantasm 5 ghost, shade, spook **6** mirage, spirit, vision **7** fantasy, figment,
incubus, phantom, specter **8** delusion,
illusion, succubus **10** apparition

Phantasus
origin: 5 Greek
god of: 6 dreams

phantom 5 dream, ghost **6** mirage,
spirit, vision, wraith **7** chimera, specter **8** illusion, phantasm **10** apparition
13 hallucination

Phantom, The
creator: 7 Lee Falk **8** Ray Moore
nickname: 16 The Ghost Who Walks
mask: 5 black
costume: 6 purple

Phantom of the Opera, The
director:
1925 version: 12 Rupert Julian
1943 version: 11 Arthur Lubin
cast:
1925 version: 9 Lon Chaney **11**
Mary Philbin, Norman Kerry
1943 version: 10 Hume Cronyn,
Jane Farrar, Nelson Eddy **11**
Claude Rains **12** Edgar Barrier **13**
Susanna Foster
setting: 10 Paris Opera

Phaon
occupation: 7 boatman
location: 8 Mitylene
given: 5 youth **6** beauty
given by: 9 Aphrodite

pharos 5 light **6** beacon, signal **7** seamark **10** lighthouse, watchtower

phase 4 side, step, view **5** angle, facet,
guise, level, slant, stage **6** aspect, degree, period **7** feature **8** attitude, juncture **9** condition, viewpoint **10** appearance **11** development **12**
circumstance

pheasant
group of: 4 nest, nide

Phedre, Phaedra
author: 6 Racine
character: 6 Aricia **7** Theseus **10** Hippolytus

phenomenal 5 super **6** unique **7**
amazing, unusual **8** singular, superior,
uncommon **9** fantastic, marvelous,
unheard-of **10** incredible, miraculous,
prodigious, remarkable, stupendous,
surpassing **11** astonishing, exceptional, outstanding, sensational, spectacular **12** overwhelming, unparalleled
13 extraordinary, unprecedented

phenomenon 5 thing **6** marvel, rarity,
wonder **7** episode, miracle **8** incident,
occasion **9** actuality, curiosity, exception, happening, nonpareil, sensation
10 fact of life, occurrence, proceeding
11 contingency

phial 4 vial **6** bottle, vessel **9** container

Phidias
born: 6 Athens, Greece
artwork: 4 Zeus **6** Amazon **13** Lem-
nian Athene (Athena Lemnia) **15**
Apollo Parnopios, Athena Parthenos,
Athena Promachos

Philadelphia
baseball team: 8 Phillies
basketball team: 13 Seventy-Sixers
bay: 8 Delaware
football team: 5 Stars **6** Eagles

founded/planned by: 4 Penn
hockey team: 6 Flyers
landmark: 6 US Mint **8** City Hall **11** Liberty Bell **12** Christ Church, Congress Hall **13** Franklin Field, Roosevelt Park **14** Betsy Ross House, Carpenter's Hall **15** Gloria Dei Church, Veterans Stadium **16** Independence Hall
means: 19 city of brotherly love
museum: 5 Rodin **15** Fels Planetarium **16** Barnes Foundation **17** Franklin Institute
river: 8 Delaware **10** Schuylkill
university: 4 Penn **6** Drexel, Temple **9** Jefferson, St Joseph's **22** Curtis Institute of Music

Philadelphia Story, The
director: 11 George Cukor
based on play by: 11 Philip Barry
cast: 9 Cary Grant **10** Ruth Hussey **12** James Stewart **16** Katharine Hepburn
Oscar for: 5 actor (Stewart)
remade as: 11 High Society

philanderer 3 rip **4** rake, wolf **5** flirt **6** lecher, tomcat, wanton **7** dallier, Don Juan, gallant, swinger, trifler **8** lothario, lover boy, rakehell **9** adulterer, libertine, womanizer **10** ladykiller **11** woman-chaser

philanthropic, philanthropical 7 liberal **8** generous **9** bounteous **10** almsgiving, beneficent, benevolent, charitable, munificent **11** magnanimous **12** eleemosynary, humanitarian

philanthropist 5 donor, giver **8** dogooder **9** almsgiver **11** contributor **12** humanitarian **13** Good Samaritan

philanthropy 6 bounty **7** charity **8** goodness **10** almsgiving, generosity, liberality **11** beneficence, benevolence, munificence **13** unselfishness **14** charitableness, openhandedness **15** humanitarianism **16** largeheartedness **18** public-spiritedness

Philaster
author: 30 Francis Beaumont and John Fletcher
Philemon
friend: 4 Paul
slave: 8 Onesimus
wife: 6 Baucis
entertained: 4 Hera, Zeus
became: 12 temple priest
Philip
hometown: 9 Bethsaida
disciple of: 5 Jesus
Philippines
named for: 15 Philip II of Spain
capital/largest city: 6 Manila
others: 3 Iba **4** Agoa, Bogo, Cebu, Debu, Naga, Palo **5** Albay, Davao, Gapan, Iriga, Lanao, Laoag, Pasay, Vigan **6** Aparri, Baguio, Cavite, Ilagan, Iloilo, Tarlac **7** Bacolod, Basilan, Calapan, Dagupan, Legaspi **8** Batangas, Caloocan, Cotabato, Taclo-

ban **9** Zamboanga **10** Cabanutuan, Dumaguette, Quezon City
school: 10 Santo Tomas **14** Ateneo de Manila
division: 4 Abra, Cebu **5** Aklan, Albay, Bohol, Capiz, Davao, Lanao, Leyte, Rizal, Samar **6** Agusan, Bataan, Cavite, Iloilo, Laguna, Quezon, Tarlac **7** Isabela, Lepanto, Surigao
measure: 4 loan **5** braza, catty, cavan, chupa, fardo, ganta, picul, punto **6** apatan, balita, lachsa, quinon **7** quilate **8** chinanta
monetary unit: 4 peso **6** conant, peseta **7** centavo
weight: 5 catty, picul **6** lachsa **7** quilate **8** chinanta
island: 4 Cebu, Cuyo, Jolo, Poro, Sulu **5** Batan, Bohol, Leyte, Luzon, Panay, Samar, Ticao **6** Culion, Lubang, Negros **7** Babuyan, Batanes, Bisayan, Masbate, Mindoro, Palawan, Paragua, Polillo, Visoyan **8** Mindanao **10** Corregidor, Marinduque
lake: 4 Taal **5** Lanao
mountain: 3 Iba **4** Mayo, Taal **5** Albay, Askja, Hibok, Mayon, Pulog **6** Pagsan **7** Banahao, Canlaon
highest point: 3 Apo
river: 4 Abra, Agno **5** Magat, Pasig **6** Agusan, Laoang **7** Cagayan **8** Mindanao, Pampanga
sea: 4 Sulu **5** Samar **7** Celebes, Pacific, Visayan **10** Philippine, South China
physical feature:
  bay: 6 Manila
  falls: 9 Pagsanjan **14** Maria Christina
  gulf: 4 Moro **5** Albay, Davao, Leyte, Ragay **8** Lingayen
  hot springs: 8 Los Banos
  national park: 12 Mayon Volcano
  ocean trench: 8 Mindanao
  peninsula: 6 Bataan
  storm: 6 bagyos **7** monsoon, typhoon
  volcano: 8 Pinatubo
people: 3 Ati, Eta, Ita, Tao **4** Aeta, Ifil, Moro, Sulu, Tino **5** Abaca, Aripa, Batak, Batan, Bicol, Bikol, Busao, Lutao, Mundo, Sinay, Tagal, Vicol, Yakan **6** Apayao, Baluga, Bilaan, Biscol, Bontoc, Bontok, Busaos, Ibanag, Ibilao, Ifugao, Igalot, Igorot, Illano, Isinai, Lutayo, Manabo, Manobo, Montes, Sambal, Tagala, Timaua, Timawa, Zambal **7** Bagoboo, Bisayan, Cagayan, Ilocano, Itanega, Malanoa, Mangyan, Naboloi, Negrito, Tagalog, Tirurai, Visayan **8** Arupaata, Babaylan, Bukidono, Filipino, Igorotte, Manguian, Pampanga **9** Arupaatta, Dulangane, Macajambo, Pampangao, Tinguiane **10** Magindanao, Pangasinan **11** Calalangane
  author: 5 Rizal
  explorer: 7 Legazpe **8** Magellan **10**

Villalobos
leader: 5 Ramos **6** Aquino, Marcos, Osmena, Quezon **9** Aguinaldo, Bonifacio, Macapagal, Magsaysay **11** Roxas y Acuna
language: 4 Moro **5** Bicol, Bikol **6** Ibanag **7** Cebuano, English, Ilocano, Spanish, Tagalog, Visayan **8** Filipino, Pilipino **9** Pampangan **10** Samar-Leyte **13** Bamboo-English
religion: 7 animism **9** Aglipayan **10** Protestant **13** Roman Catholic **15** Iglesia ni Kristo
place:
  church: 14 Saint Augustine
  esplanade: 6 Luneta
  fort: 4 Cota, Gota, Kota **5** Lotta **10** Corregidor
  president's palace: 10 Malacanang
  street: 7 Escolta
  US bases: 5 Clark **8** Subic Bay
  walled city: 10 Intramuros
feature:
  animal: 7 carabao, tamarau, tarsier **9** mouse deer
  bird: 7 creeper
  clothing: 4 saya **6** camisa **10** balintawak **12** mestiza terno **13** barong tagalog
  dance: 9 tinikling
  drama: 8 moro-moro
  guerrilla fighter: 3 huk
  musicians: 12 musikongbuho
  naval base: 6 Cavite
  song: 8 kundiman
  village: 8 barangay
food:
  dish: 3 poi **4** baha, sabu, taro **5** balut
  drink: 4 beno, vino **5** bubud **6** tampoy **7** pangasi
philistine 5 yahoo **6** savage **7** Babbitt, lowbrow, prosaic **8** ignorant **9** barbarian, bourgeois, unrefined, untutored **10** conformist, uncultured, uneducated, uninformed, unlettered **11** commonplace **12** conventional, uncultivated **13** unenlightened **15** conventionalist **16** anti-intellectual

Philistine city 4 Gath
Philius
epithet of: 4 Zeus
means: 8 friendly
Phillotson, Richard
character in: 14 Jude the Obscure
author: 5 Hardy
Philoctetes
author: 9 Sophocles
character: 8 Heracles, Odysseus **11** Neoptolemus
inherits arms of: 8 Hercules
father: 5 Poeas, Poias
killed: 5 Paris
philodendron
varieties: 5 Dubia, giant **6** common **7** cut-leaf, red-leaf **8** blushing **9** blackgold, heart-leaf, horsehead, spade-

leaf, split-leaf **10** fiddle-leaf, variegated, velvet-leaf **11** leather-leaf

Philomela
  position: **8** princess
  realm: **6** Athens
  father: **7** Pandion
  sister: **6** Procne
  brother-in-law: **6** Tereus
  raped by: **6** Tereus
  transformed into: **7** swallow **11**
    nightingale

Philomelides
  king of: **6** Lesbos
  defeated by: **8** Odysseus

philosopher/theologian 4 sage **6** savant **7** thinker, wise man **8** logician,
reasoner **9** theorizer **11** rationalist,
truth seeker **12** dialectician **13** metaphysician
  Alsatian: 10 Schweitzer
  American: 4 Eddy **5** Dewey, James,
    Royce, Smith, Young **6** Mather,
    Peirce **7** Edwards, Niebuhr, Russell,
    Tillich **8** Williams **9** McPherson **14**
    Elijah Muhammad
  Austrian: 12 Wittgenstein
  British: 3 Fox **4** Hume, Inge, Knox,
    More, Owen **5** Bacon, Burke, Locke,
    Moore **6** Biddle, Cotton, Hobbes,
    Huxley, Newman, Wesley **7** Ben-
    tham, Bradley, Carlyle, Cranmer,
    Russell, Spencer **8** Berkeley, Wycliffe
    9 Whitehead **13** Thomas a Becket **14**
    William of Occam
  Chinese: 6 Lao tzu **9** Confucius
  Christian: 6 Calvin, Luther, Origen, St
    Paul **7** Abelard **8** St Anselm **9** St Pat-
    rick **10** Duns Scotus, St Benedict **11**
    St Augustine **14** William of Occam
    15 St Thomas Aquinas **16** St Alber-
    tus Magnus
  Czech: 3 Hus
  Danish: 11 Kierkegaard
  Dutch: 7 Erasmus, Spinoza
  El Salvadorian: 9 Masferrer
  French: 5 Comte **6** Calvin, Pascal,
    Sartre **7** Abelard, Bergson, Diderot **8**
    Maritain, Rousseau, Voltaire **9** Des-
    cartes, Levy-Bruhl, Montaigne **11**
    Montesquieu
  German: 4 Kant, Marx **5** Buber, He-
    gel **6** Boehme, Fichte, Herder, Luther
    7 Husserl, Jaspers, Leibniz **9** Heideg-
    ger, Nietzsche, Schelling **10** Muhlen-
    berg **11** Melanchthon **12** Schopen-
    hauer **13** Thomas a Kempis **14**
    Schleiermacher
  Greek: 5 Plato **6** St Paul, Thales **8**
    Socrates **9** Aristotle **10** Anaxagoras,
    Anaximenes, Heraclitus, Parmenides,
    Pythagoras **11** Anaximander
  Indian: 6 Buddha **16** Siddharta Gau-
    tama
  Islamic: 7 al Kindi **8** al-Farabi, Aver-
    roes, Avicenna **9** al Ghazali **10** Ibn
    Khaldun
  Italian: 5 Bruno **7** Aquinas, Mazzini
    10 St Benedict, Zeno of Elea **17** St

  Francis of Assisi
  Japanese: 6 Suzuki
  Jewish: 7 Spinoza **10** Maimonides
  Latin: 8 Plotinus **11** St Augustine
  Spanish: 8 Averroes **10** Maimonides
    13 Ortega y Gasset **16** Ignatius of
    Loyola
  Swedish: 10 Swedenborg
  Swiss: 7 Zwingli

Philosopher's Pupil, The
  author: **11** Iris Murdoch

philosophic, philosophical 4 calm **5**
quiet, stoic **6** serene **7** erudite,
learned, logical, patient, stoical **8** abstract, composed, rational, resigned,
tranquil **9** impassive, judicious, sagacious, unexcited, unruffled **10** complacent, fatalistic, reasonable, theorizing,
thoughtful **11** imperturbed, theoretical, unemotional **14** self-restrained

philosophy 4 calm, view **5** ideas, logic
6 reason **7** beliefs, opinion, thought **8**
doctrine, fatalism, patience, serenity,
stoicism, thinking **9** basic idea, composure, esthetics, principle, reasoning,
restraint, viewpoint **10** conception,
theorizing **11** complacency, convictions, forbearance, impassivity, metaphysics, rationalism, resignation
  means: **12** love of wisdom
  branch: **6** ethics **8** ontology **10** aes-
    thetics **11** metaphysics **12** epistemol-
    ogy
  term: **8** noumenon **9** causality, dialec-
    tic, solipsism
  school of: **7** Sophism **8** idealism, Mi-
    lesian, Stoicism **9** Epicurean, panthe-
    ism, Platonism **10** empiricism, prag-
    matism, Skepticism **11** rationalism
    12 Aristotelian, neoplatonism **13**
    Phenomenology, scholasticism **14** ex-
    istentialism **17** logical positivism

Phil Silvers Show, The
  character: **6** Fender **7** Col Hall, Hen-
    shaw **8** Doberman **9** Sgt Ritzik **12**
    Sgt Joan Hogan **13** Rocco Barbella,
    Sgt Ernie Bilko
  cast: **8** Joe E Ross, Paul Ford **10** Alan
    Melvin, Herbie Faye **13** Harvey Lem-
    beck **15** Elisabeth Fraser, Maurice
    Gosfield
  setting: **6** Kansas **10** Fort Baxter

phlegmatic 4 calm, cool, dull **6** serene
7 languid, passive, stoical **8** listless,
sluggish, tranquil **9** apathetic, impassive, lethargic, unfeeling **10** nonchalant, spiritless **11** indifferent, insensitive, unconcerned, unemotional,
unexcitable **12** unresponsive **13** imperturbable, unimpassioned **15** undemonstrative

phlox
  varieties: **4** blue, fall, moss, sand,
    star **6** annual, smooth **7** prickly **8**
    creeping, drummond, mountain,
    trailing **9** perennial, sword-leaf,
    thick-leaf **15** summer perennial

Phnom-Penh
  airport: **10** Pochentong
  also: **8** Pnom Penh
  capital of: **8** Cambodia **9** Kampuchea
  pagoda: **12** Preah Morokot
  river: **6** Mekong **8** Tonle Sap

phobia 5 dread **6** horror, terror **7** bugaboo, bugbear **8** aversion, loathing **12**
apprehension **16** unreasonable fear **19**
overwhelming anxiety
  fear of animals: **9** zoophobia
  fear of birds: **13** ornithophobia
  fear of blushing: **13** erythrophobia
  fear of bridges: **13** gephyrophobia
  fear of cats: **10** gatophobia **12** aelu-
    rophobia, ailurophobia
  fear of closed/confined spaces: **14**
    claustrophobia
  fear of crowds: **11** ochlophobia
  fear of darkness/the dark of night:
    11 nyctophobia
  fear of death: **13** thanatophobia
  fear of death/dead bodies: **11** nec-
    rophobia
  fear of dirt: **10** mysophobia
  fear of disease: **11** pathophobia
  fear of fire: **10** pyrophobia
  fear of flowers: **11** anthophobia
  fear of flying: **10** aerophobia
  fear of germs: **11** mikrophobia
  fear of hair: **12** trichophobia
  fear of heights: **10** acrophobia
  fear of insanity: **13** dementophobia
  fear of lightning: **11** astraphobia
  fear of men: **11** androphobia
  fear of mice: **10** murophobia
  fear of numbers: **12** numerophobia
  fear of open spaces: **11** agoraphobia
  fear of pain: **10** algophobia
  fear of people: **12** anthropophobia
  fear of reptiles: **13** herpetophobia
  fear of snakes: **13** ophidiophobia
  fear of speaking aloud: **11** pho-
    nophobia
  fear of spiders: **13** arachnophobia
  fear of strangers: **10** xenophobia
  fear of thunder: **12** brontophobia
  fear of the number thirteen: **17** tris-
    kaidekaphobia
  fear of vehicles/driving: **11** amax-
    ophobia
  fear of water: **10** aquaphobia **11** hy-
    drophobia
  fear of women: **10** gynophobia

Phoebe
  member of: **6** Titans
  father: **6** Uranus
  mother: **4** Gaea
  sister: **6** Themis
  daughter: **4** Leto **7** Asteria
  identified with: **4** moon
  corresponds to: **5** Diana **7** Artemis

Phoebus *see* **6** Apollo
Phoenicia *see* **7** Lebanon
Phoenician Mythology
  god of agriculture/earth: **5** Dagon
    corresponds to Mesopotamian: 5
    Dagan

bird: 6 Phenix **7** Phoenix
goddess of fertility/reproduction: 7 Astarte

Phoenissae (The Phoenician Maidens)
author: 9 Euripides
character: 5 Creon **7** Jocasta, Oedipus **8** Adrastus, Antigone, Eteocles, Tiresias **9** Polynices **10** Menoikieus

Phoenix
basketball team: 4 Suns **7** Mercury
capital of: 7 Arizona
event: 5 rodeo
feature: 10 Papago Park **22** Desert Botanical Gardens
football team: 9 Cardinals
hockey team: 7 Coyotes
river: 4 Salt

Phoenix
also: 6 Phenix
origin: 10 Phoenician
form: 4 bird
gift: 11 immortality
king of: 9 Dolopians
father: 7 Amyntor
mother: 8 Cleobule
brother: 6 Cadmus
sister: 6 Europa
foster son: 8 Achilles
ancestor of: 11 Phoenicians

Pholus
form: 7 centaur
guarded: 4 wine
wine a gift from: 8 Dionysus

phonograph 4 hi-fi **5** phono **6** stereo **8** Victrola **9** turntable **10** gramophone **12** record player

phonophobia
fear of: 13 speaking aloud

phony, phoney 4 fake, hoax, mock, sham **5** bogus, false, fraud, trick **6** forged, pseudo, unreal, untrue **7** forgery **8** specious, spurious **9** deceptive, imitation, pretended, synthetic **10** artificial, fraudulent, not genuine **11** counterfeit, make-believe, unauthentic

Phorcys
god of: 3 sea
sister: 4 Ceto
children: 5 Ladon **6** Graiae **7** Echidna, Gorgons **8** Phorcids
harbor in: 6 Ithaca

phosphorus
chemical symbol: 1 P

photograph 3 pic **4** film, snap **5** image, print, shoot, still **6** candid, glossy **7** mugshot, picture, tintype **8** likeness, portrait, snapshot **12** daguerrotype
bath: 5 fixer, toner **7** reducer **9** developer
book: 5 album

photographer
American: 4 Haas, Hine, Penn, Riis, Rose, Tice **5** (Ansel) Adams, Annan, Arbus, Brady, Evans, Hawes, Lange, Lynes, Smith, White **6** Avedon, Coburn, Eakins, Man Ray, Strand, Turner, Weston **7** Burrows, Eastman, Gardner, Jackson, Watkins **8** Bogardus, Davidson, Steichen **9** Muybridge, O'Sullivan, Rothstein, Stieglitz **10** Cunningham, Southworth **11** Bourke-White, Eisenstaedt, Turberville **13** Watson-Schutze
British: 5 Evans, Frith **6** Bailey, Beaton, Fenton, Mayall, Talbot **7** Cameron **8** Brewster, Robinson **9** Rejlander **10** MacPherson
French: 5 Marey, Nadar **6** Baldus, DuCamp, Le Secq, Newton, Niepce **7** Lumiere **8** Daguerre **12** Sabatier-Blot **14** Cartier-Bresson
German: 4 Hoch **5** Ernst **7** Hausman **8** Stelzner **13** Renger-Patzsch
Hungarian: 7 Kertesz **10** Moholy-Nagy
Japanese: 4 Ikko
Scottish: 4 Hill **7** Adamson
Spanish: 7 Picabia

photostat 4 copy **7** replica **9** duplicate, facsimile **12** reproduction

phrase 3 put, say **4** word **5** couch, idiom, maxim, state, utter, voice, words **6** cliche, dictum, impart, remark, saying, truism **7** declare, express, proverb **8** aphorism, banality, locution **9** enunciate, find words, platitude, utterance, verbalize, word group **10** articulate, expression **11** communicate

phraseology 5 style **7** diction, wording **13** choice of words **18** manner of expression

Phrixus
father: 7 Athamas
mother: 7 Nephele
stepmother: 3 Ino
sister: 5 Helle
wife: 9 Chalciope
son: 5 Argus, Melas **8** Phrontis **10** Cytissorus

physical 4 real **5** human, solid **6** actual, animal, bodily, carnal, living **7** fleshly, natural, sensual **8** apparent, concrete, corporal, existent, existing, external, material, palpable, tangible **9** corporeal, essential, of the body **11** substantive

physical checkup 4 exam **8** physical **11** examination **19** physical examination

physical condition 5 shape **7** fitness, stamina **12** constitution

physical disorder 6 malady **7** ailment, disease, illness **8** sickness **9** ill health, infirmity

physical training 3 gym **6** sports **8** exercise **9** athletics, shaping up **10** gymnastics, working out **12** conditioning

physician 2 GP, MD **3** doc **5** medic **6** doctor, medico **7** surgeon **8** sawbones **10** specialist **11** medicine man, pill peddler **13** medical doctor
Alsatian: 10 Schweitzer
American: 4 Long, Rush, Salk **5** Sabin **6** Dooley, Gorgas **7** Huggins, Whipple **8** Williams **9** Blackwell **11** Landsteiner
British: 5 Paget **6** Adrian, Harvey, Jenner, Lister
Canadian: 4 Best **7** Banting
Dutch: 7 Eijkman
French: 7 Charcot
German: 6 Mesmer **7** Fechner, Virchow **10** Blumenbach
Greek: 10 Herophilus **11** Hippocrates **12** Erasistratus
Italian: 8 Malpighi
Russian: 6 Pavlov
Scottish: 4 Lind
South African: 7 Barnard

Physician to Olympian gods 5 Paeon **6** Apollo

physicist
American: 4 Hess, Rabi **5** Bethe, Gamow, Pauli, Yalow **6** Bekesy, Teller, Townes, Watson **7** Feynman, Richter, Seaborg **8** Einstein, Lawrence, Van Allen **9** Michelson **11** Chamberlain, Oppenheimer
Austrian: 7 Doppler, Meitner
British: 4 Born **5** Bragg, Hooke, Joule **6** Kelvin **7** Gilbert, Thomson **8** Chadwick, Rayleigh **9** Cockcroft **10** Rutherford
Danish: 4 Bohr **7** Oersted
Dutch: 6 Zeeman **7** Lorentz
French: 6 Ampere **7** Broglie, Coulomb, Fresnel **8** Foucault **9** Becquerel **11** Joliot-Curie
German: 3 Ohm **5** Hertz, Stark **6** Planck **7** Rontgen, Wegener **8** Humboldt, Roentgen **9** Kirchhoff, Mossbauer **10** Fahrenheit, Fraunhofer
Indian: 5 Raman
Irish: 7 Tyndall **10** Fitzgerald
Italian: 5 Fermi
Russian: 6 Landau **8** Cerenkov, Sakharov
Scottish: 7 Rankine

Physics
author: 9 Aristotle

physiognomy 4 face **5** shape **6** facade, visage **7** contour, outline, profile **8** features **10** silhouette **11** countenance

physiology
founder: 13 William Harvey
study of: 8 function
study of nervous sytem: 15 neurophysiology

pianissimo
music: 8 very soft
abbreviation: 2 pp

pianist 4 Hess **5** Liszt, Watts **6** Busoni, Chopin, Gilels, Serkin **7** Cliburn, Hofmann, Richter **8** Backhaus, Horowitz, Schnabel, Schumann, Thalberg, von Bulow **9** Barenboim, Casadesus, Gieseking **10** Gottschalk, Rubinstein **12** Rachmaninoff

piano
  invented by: **10** Cristofori
  player piano: **9** Fourneaux
  forerunner: **6** spinet **10** clavichord **11** harpsichord
piano
  music: **4** soft
    abbreviation: **1** p
piazza **5** patio, porch **6** square **7** gallery, portico, veranda
Piazzi, Giuseppe
  field: **9** astronomy
  nationality: **7** Italian
  discovered: **5** Ceres
  catalogued: **5** stars
picaresque **6** daring **7** raffish, roguish, waggish **8** devilish, prankish, rascally, scampish **9** foolhardy **10** roistering **13** adventuresome **14** mischief-loving
Picasso, Pablo
  born: **5** Spain **6** Malaga
  artwork: **4** Dove **6** Guitar, Jester **7** Ma Jolie, Rooster, She-Goat **8** Guernica **9** Bull's Head, Notre Dame **11** Seated Woman, Woman Diving **12** Head of a Woman **13** Seated Bathers **14** Minotauromachy, Mother and Child, Women of Algiers **15** Ambroise Vollard, Man Holding a Lamb, The Charnel-House, The Large Profile, The Three Dancers **16** Nude in an Armchair **17** Girl Before a Mirror, The Glass of Absinth, The Three Musicians **20** Still Life with a Candle **22** Les Demoiselles d'Avignon **23** Portrait of Gertrude Stein
picayune, picayunish **5** dinky, petty, small **6** flimsy, little, measly, paltry, slight **7** trivial **8** niggling, nugatory, piddling, trifling **11** unimportant **13** insignificant **14** inconsiderable **15** inconsequential
Piccini, Nicola (Piccinni, Niccola)
  born: **4** Bari **5** Italy
  composer of: **5** Didon **6** Roland **11** The Good Girl **15** La buona figliola **18** Iphigenie en Tauride
pick **3** cut **4** crop **5** cream, elect, elite, pluck, prize **6** choice, choose, detach, flower, gather, opt for, select **7** collect, fix upon, harvest, pull off, pull out, the best **9** single out **10** decide upon, favored one, preference, settle upon
picket **4** pale, post **5** fence, go out, guard, hem in, pen in, stake, watch **6** corral, paling, patrol, sentry, shut in, strike, tether, wall in **7** boycott, enclose, hedge in, lookout, striker, upright, walk out **8** blockade, palisade, restrain, restrict, sentinel **9** blockader, boycotter, protester, restraint, stanchion
picketing **5** march **7** protest **8** marching, on strike, striking **10** protesting **12** protest march **13** demonstrating, demonstration

Pickett, George E
  served in: **8** Civil War **10** Mexican War
  side: **11** Confederate
  battle: **10** Gettysburg
  famous for: **6** charge
Pickford, Mary
  real name: **15** Gladys Mary Smith
  nickname: **18** America's Sweetheart
  born: **6** Canada **7** Toronto
  husband: **16** Douglas Fairbanks **18** Charles Buddy Rogers
  roles: **4** Rags **8** Coquette (Oscar) **9** Pollyanna **19** The Taming of the Shrew **21** The Poor Little Rich Girl **23** Rebecca of Sunnybrook Farm
  home: **8** Pickfair
  memoirs: **17** Sunshine and Shadow
  formed: **13** United Artists
    partners: **10** D W Griffith **14** Charlie Chaplin **16** Douglas Fairbanks
pickings **4** loot **5** booty **6** scraps, spoils **7** plunder, takings **9** leftovers
pickle **3** fix, jam **4** corn, dill, mess, sour **6** crisis, plight, scrape **7** dilemma, gherkin, mustard **8** cucumber, hot water, quandary **9** emergency, extremity, tight spot **10** difficulty, kosher dill, pretty pass **11** predicament **14** bread-and-butter
pickled **5** drunk **6** soused **8** powdered
pick on **5** annoy, bully **6** harass, jibe at **7** torment **8** browbeat
pick out **3** see **4** espy **6** choose, descry, detect, notice, select **7** discern, make out **8** perceive **12** catch sight of
pickup **4** rise **5** boost, truck **7** advance **9** impromptu **11** improvement **12** acceleration
pick up **3** buy, get **6** gather, lift up, look up, obtain, secure **7** acquire, develop, improve, procure **8** contract, retrieve **9** cultivate, get better
Pickwick Papers
  author: **14** Charles Dickens
  character: **6** Perker, Tupman, Wardle, Winkle **9** Sam Weller, Snodgrass **10** Mrs Bardell **11** Emily Wardle **12** Alfred Jingle, Rachel Wardle **13** Arabella Allen
picky **5** fussy **6** choosy **7** finicky **10** fastidious, particular **11** persnickety **14** discriminating
Picrochole
  character in: **22** Gargantua and Pantagruel
  author: **8** Rabelais
picture **3** see **4** copy, draw, film **5** fancy, flick, image, model, movie, paint, photo, study **6** cinema, depict, double, mirror, sketch **7** believe, drawing, essence, etching, feature, imagine, paragon, portray, tintype **8** envision, likeness, painting, snapshot **9** delineate, duplicate, facsimile, portrayal, represent **10** call to mind, carbon copy, conceive of, dead ringer,

embodiment, illustrate, photograph **11** delineation **12** illustration, see in the mind **13** daguerreotype, motion picture, moving picture, spitting image **14** representation **15** exemplification, personification
Picture of Dorian Gray, The
  author: **10** Oscar Wilde
  character: **9** James Vane, Sibyl Vane **13** Basil Hallward **15** Lord Henry Wotton
picturesque **6** exotic, quaint **7** unusual **8** artistic, charming, colorful, striking **9** beautiful, pictorial **10** attractive **11** distinctive, imaginative, interesting
Picus
  origin: **5** Roman **7** Italian
  god of: **11** agriculture
  father: **6** Saturn
  associated with: **10** woodpecker
  loved by: **5** Circe
  changed into: **10** woodpecker
  son: **6** Faunus
piddling **4** puny **5** petty, small **6** flimsy, little, measly, modest, paltry, skimpy, slight **7** trivial **8** picayune, trifling **9** niggardly **11** unimportant **13** insignificant **15** inconsequential
pie **4** tart **5** pastry, quiche **7** cobbler, dessert **8** turnover
  liner: **5** crust, shell
  top: **7** lattice **8** meringue
piebald **6** motley **7** dappled, flecked, mottled, spotted **8** many-hued, speckled **10** variegated **11** many-colored, varicolored **12** multicolored, particolored
piece **3** bit, cut, fix, pat **4** blob, case, hunk, item, lump, mend, part, play, unit, work **5** chunk, drama, essay, patch, scrap, shard, share, shred, slice, story, study, thing **6** amount, entity, length, member, paring, repair, review, sample, sketch, sliver, swatch **7** article, cutting, example, patch up, portion, restore, section, segment **8** creation, division, fraction, fragment, instance, quantity, specimen **9** component, selection **11** composition
piece de resistance **13** principal dish **14** principal event
piece goods **5** cloth, goods **6** fabric **8** dry goods, material **9** yard goods
piecemeal **9** gradually **10** fragmented, one at a time **14** little by little
piece of the action **3** cut, fee **5** piece **7** portion, rake-off **10** commission, percentage
pied **6** motley **7** checked, dappled, mottled, piebald **8** colorful **9** checkered **10** variegated **11** many-colored **12** parti-colored
pied-a-terre **17** temporary dwelling
  literally: **12** foot on ground
Pied Piper
  source: **6** German, legend

town: 7 Hamelin
plague: 4 rats
charmed by: 6 piping
led away: 4 rats **8** children
Pied Piper of Hamlin, The
author: 14 Robert Browning
pier 4 anta, dock, mole, quay, slip **5** jetty, levee, wharf **6** pillar **7** landing, support **10** breakwater
pierce 3 cut **4** hurt, pain, stab **5** drill, lance, prick, spear, spike, stick, sting, wound **6** grieve, impale **7** affront **8** distress, puncture **9** penetrate, perforate **10** cut through, run through
Pierce, Franklin
nickname: 29 Young Hickory of the Granite Hills
presidential rank: 10 fourteenth
party: 8 Democrat
state represented: 2 NH
defeated: 4 (John Parker) Hale **5** (Winfield) Scott
vice president: 4 (William Rufus Devane) King (died in office)
cabinet:
  state: 5 (William Learned) Marcy
  treasury: 7 (James) Guthrie
  war: 5 (Jefferson) Davis
  attorney general: 7 (Caleb) Cushing
  navy: 6 (James Cochran) Dobbin
  postmaster general: 8 (James) Campbell
  interior: 10 (Robert) McClelland
born: 14 Hillsborough (Hillsboro) NH
died/buried: 9 Concord NH
education:
  academy: 7 Hancock **11** Francestown
  college: 7 Bowdoin
  studied: 3 law
religion: 12 Episcopalian
political career: 8 US Senate **16** state legislature **24** US House of Representatives
civilian career: 6 lawyer
military service: 6 US Army **10** Mexican War **16** brigadier general
notable events of lifetime/term:
  Act: 6 Tariff (of 1857)
  bill: 14 Kansas-Nebraska
  civil war in: 6 Kansas
  first US: 10 World's Fair
  Manifesto: 6 Ostend
  Purchase: 7 Gadsden
  treaty of: 8 Kanagawa
father: 8 Benjamin
mother: 4 Anna (Kendrick)
siblings: 5 Henry, Nancy **7** Charles, Harriet **9** Charlotte **12** John Sullivan **16** Benjamin Kendrick
  half sister: 9 Elizabeth
wife: 4 Jane (Means Appleton)
children: 8 Benjamin, Franklin **11** Frank Robert
piercing 3 raw **4** keen, loud **5** angry, cruel, sharp **6** biting, bitter, fierce, shrill **7** caustic, cutting, furious, grat-ing, hurtful, intense, painful, probing **8** strident **9** agonizing, deafening, searching, shrieking, torturous **10** screeching **11** penetrating **12** earsplitting, excruciating **13** ear-shattering
Pierian
pertains to: 5 Muses
Pierian Spring
form: 8 fountain
Pierides *see* **5** Muses
Piero della Francesca (Piero dei Franceschi)
born: 5 Italy **16** Borgo San Sepolcro
artwork: 12 Duke of Urbino **15** The Resurrection **18** Federigo and His Wife **19** St John the Evangelist **20** Flagellation of Christ **23** The Compassionate Madonna, The Legend of the True Cross, The Old Age and Death of Adam **24** The History of the True Cross **45** The Madonna and Saints with Frederigo da Montefeltro
Piers Plowman
author: 15 William Langland
Pietas
personifies: 17 familial affection
piety 7 loyalty, respect **8** devotion, humility **9** godliness, piousness, reverence **10** devoutness **11** dutifulness, religiosity **13** religiousness
pig 3 hog **5** piggy, porky, swine **6** porker **7** glutton, guzzler **8** gourmand **9** chowhound **11** gormandizer
  male: 4 boar
  female: 3 sow
  young: 5 shoat **6** piglet **11** suckling pig
pigeon
  young: 5 squab **8** squeaker
pigeonhole 4 rank, rate, type **5** brand, cubby, group, label, niche **8** category, classify **9** cubbyhole **10** categorize **11** compartment
pigheaded 6 dogged, mulish **7** willful **8** contrary, obdurate, perverse, stubborn **9** insistent, obstinate, unbending **10** bullheaded, inflexible, refractory, unyielding **11** opinionated, wrongheaded
Piglet
  character in: 13 Winnie-the-Pooh
  author: 5 Milne
pigment 3 dye **4** tint **5** color **8** coloring, dyestuff **14** coloring matter
pigmentation 5 color **9** skin color **10** coloration
pigtail 5 braid, plait, queue **8** ponytail
pike 4 bill **5** lance, spear, spike **6** poleax **7** assegai, freeway, halberd, harpoon, highway, javelin, parkway, thruway **8** autobahn, hard road, speedway, toll road, turnpike **10** expressway, interstate, throughway **12** superhighway
  British: 12 King's Highway **13** Queen's highway
  German: 8 autobahn
piker 5 miser **7** niggard, trifler **8** tightwad **9** skinflint **10** cheapskate, pinchpenny **12** penny pincher
Pilar
  character in: 19 For Whom the Bell Tolls
  author: 9 Hemingway
pilaster 4 pier **6** column, pillar **7** support, upright **8** baluster
pile 3 nap **4** heap, mass, pier, post, shag, warp **5** amass, batch, fluff, grain, hoard, mound, plush, stack, store **6** fleece, gather, piling, pillar **7** collect, pyramid, support, surface, upright **8** assemble, quantity **9** abundance, amassment, profusion, stanchion **10** accumulate, assortment, collection, foundation **11** agglomerate, aggregation, fibrousness **12** accumulation
pile up 4 bank, heap **5** amass, hoard, mound, stack **7** collect **10** accumulate
pile-up 3 jam, mob **4** mass **5** snarl **8** crowding, gridlock **10** bottleneck, congestion **11** obstruction **12** overcrowding
pilfer 3 cop, rob **4** hook, lift **5** boost, filch, heist, pinch, steal, swipe **6** finger, pirate, snitch, thieve **7** purloin **8** shoplift **10** plagiarize
pilferer 5 thief **6** robber **7** burglar **10** shoplifter, sneak thief
pilgrim, Pilgrim 4 haji **5** exile, hadji **6** palmer **7** pioneer, Puritan, settler **8** newcomer, traveler, wanderer, wayfarer **9** foreigner
  father: 5 Alden
  founder: 10 Separatist
  interpreter: 7 Squanto
  leader: 8 Standish
  protector: 7 Templar
  ship: 9 Mayflower, Speedwell
Pilgrim, Billy
  character in: 18 Slaughterhouse Five
  author: 8 Vonnegut
pilgrimage 4 hadj, trek **6** ramble, roving, voyage **7** journey, roaming, sojourn **8** long trip **9** excursion, wandering **13** peregrination
  destination: 5 Mecca **10** Canterbury
Pilgrim's Progress, The
  author: 10 John Bunyan
  character: 7 Despair, Hopeful **8** Apollyon, Faithful **9** Christian, Ignorance **10** Evangelist **14** Worldly Wiseman
pill 3 rob **4** ball, pell **5** bolus **6** bullet, pellet, tablet, pilule **7** capsule **8** medicine **9** cigarette
pillage 3 rob **4** loot, raid, sack **5** booty, rifle, strip **6** fleece, maraud, piracy, ravage, spoils **7** despoil, looting, plunder, robbery **9** filchings **10** plundering

pillager 6 looter, vandal **7** brigand **9** despoiler, plunderer

pillar 3 VIP **4** pile, post, rock **5** shaft, wheel **6** column, piling **7** obelisk, support, upright **8** champion, mainstay, pilaster, somebody **9** colonnade, stanchion

Pillars of Society, The
  author: **11** Henrik Ibsen

pillow 3 pad **7** bolster, cushion **8** headrest

pilot 4 lead **5** flyer, guide, steer **6** airman, direct, escort, fly-boy, handle, leader, manage **7** aviator, birdman, conduct, control **8** aeronaut, coxswain, helmsman, navigate, wheelman **9** accompany, sky jockey, steersman

Pilot, The
  author: **19** James Fenimore Cooper

Pima (Aatam, Pima Alto)
  language family: **10** Uto-Aztekan
  location: **7** Arizona
  related to: **6** Papago
  descendants of: **7** Hohokam

Pima Alto *see* **4** Pima

pin 4 bind, clip, tine **5** affix, badge, clasp, dowel, medal, prong **6** brooch, fasten, pinion, secure, skewer **8** hold down, hold fast, restrain **10** decoration
  type: **3** hat **4** push **5** stick, thole **6** breast, common, diaper, safety **8** straight

pincer 4 claw **5** chela

pinch 4 bit, cop, jam, jot, nab, nip **4** bust, crib, grab, iota, lift, mite, pain, snip, spot **5** catch, cramp, crimp, crush, filch, run in, speck, steal, swipe, trace, trial, tweak **6** arrest, clutch, collar, crisis, misery, ordeal, pickle, plight, snatch, snitch, strait, tittle **7** capture, purloin, squeeze, tighten **8** compress, exigency, hardship **9** apprehend, emergency **10** affliction, difficulty, discomfort **11** predicament

Pinch, Tom
  character in: **16** Martin Chuzzlewit
  author: **7** Dickens

pinch hitter 5 proxy **7** stand-in **9** alternate **10** substitute

pinchpenny 5 miser **6** frugal, stingy **7** niggard, prudent, thrifty
  Dickensian: **7** Scrooge

Pindar
  author of: **4** Odes **8** Epinicea

pine 3 die, ebb **4** flag, long, sigh, wilt **5** covet, crave, droop, yearn **6** desire, expire, hanker, weaken, wither **7** decline, dwindle, pant for **8** languish **9** hunger for, waste away **11** have a yen for, thirst after **12** fail in health

pine 5 Pinus
  varieties: **3** air, nut, red **4** blue, chir, gray, hoop, Huon, Imou, Jack **5** beach, cedar, Cuban, Emodi, giant, house, Kauri, pitch, Scots, screw, scrub, shore, slash, stone, sugar, white **6** Aleppo, Apache, Bhutan, Bishop, celery, Dammar, digger, ground, Jersey, Korean, limber, Mallee, Norway, Parana, Pinyon, Scotch, spruce, Torrey, Totara, yellow **7** Amboina, Benguet, big-cone, Chilean, Chinese, cluster, Cypress, Formosa, Georgia, Gerard's, hickory, jointed, long-tag, poverty, prickly, prince's, running, Soledad **8** Austrian, Buddhist, cow's-tail, knob-cone, lacebark, Loblolly, longleaf, mahogany, Monterey, mountain, Nepal nut, oldfield, princess, umbrella **9** Brazilian, Calabrian, Chilghoza, Jerusalem, lodgepole, Oyster Bay, shortleaf, white-bark **10** Australian, Bunyabunya, dwarf stone, Macedonian, Moreton Bay, red cypress, Swiss stone, Tenasserim **11** African fern, bristlecone, common screw, Japanese red, Parry pinyon, Port Jackson, thatch screw, twisted-leaf, Veitch screw **12** black cypress, Canary Island, Chinese water, eastern white, frankincense, Italian stone, Mexican stone, Mexican white, two-leaved nut, western white **13** dwarf Siberian, Japanese black, Japanese white, Mexican yellow, New Caledonian, Norfolk Island, Swiss mountain, table mountain **14** Himalayan white, Rottnest Island, southern yellow **15** Mueller's cypress **16** Japanese umbrella, single-leaf pinyon **18** Rough-barked Mexican **19** Rocky Mountain yellow

Pine Tree State
  nickname of: **5** Maine

pin hope on 6 bank on **7** count on, long for, wish for **8** aspire to, yearn for **10** anticipate

pink 8 Dianthus
  varieties: **3** Sea **4** fire, moss, pine, rose, wild **5** cameo, clove, dairy, grass, marsh, swamp **6** button, ground, indian, Kirtle, maiden **7** cheddar, cottage, cushion, Mullein, rainbow **8** Childing, Deptford, election **11** cluster-head **13** fringed indian, spottle kirtle **16** California indian

pinnacle 3 cap, top **4** acme, apex, peak **5** crest, crown, spire, tower **6** belfry, height, summit, tiptop, vertex, zenith **7** steeple **9** bell tower, campanile

pinochle
  also known as: **7** binocle, pinocle **8** penuchle
  derived from: **7** bezique
  points/game: **11** one thousand
  lowest card: **4** nine

pinpoint 3 dot, jot **4** iota, spot **5** speck **6** detail **8** home in on, localize, zero in on **12** characterize

pint
  abbreviation of: **2** pt

pinxit 11 he painted it **12** she painted it

pioneer 5 found, start **6** create, father, herald, invent, leader **7** develop, founder **8** colonist, discover, explorer **9** be a leader, developer, establish, harbinger, innovator, precursor **10** antecedent, forerunner, lead the way, pathfinder, show the way **11** establisher, predecessor, trailblazer **12** first settler, frontiersman **13** blaze the trail **14** early immigrant, founding father
  Hebrew: **6** halutz **7** chalutz

Pioneers, The
  author: **19** James Fenimore Cooper
  character: **10** Indian John **11** Judge Temple, Natty Bumppo **13** Oliver Edwards **14** Hiram Doolittle **15** Elizabeth Temple

pious 4 holy **5** godly **6** devout, divine **7** sainted, saintly **8** faithful, reverent, unctuous **9** dedicated, insincere, pietistic, religious, spiritual **10** worshipful **11** reverential **12** hypocritical **13** rationalizing, sanctimonious, self-righteous **14** holier-than-thou

Pip
  character in: **17** Great Expectations
  author: **7** Dickens

pipe 4 duct, main, peep, sing, tube **5** cheep, chirp, trill, tweet **6** warble **7** conduit, twitter, whistle **8** conveyor **9** conductor **10** play a flute **12** play a bagpipe

Pippa Passes
  author: **14** Robert Browning

piquant 3 hot **4** acid, racy **5** peppy, salty, sharp, spicy, tangy, zesty **6** biting, bitter, bright, clever, lively, savory **7** mordant, peppery, pungent, rousing **8** animated, incisive, piercing, spirited, stinging, vigorous **9** sparkling, trenchant **11** interesting, provacative, stimulating **13** scintillating **14** highly seasoned, strong-flavored

pique 3 ire, irk, vex **4** gall, goad, miff, snit, spur, stir **5** annoy, peeve, rouse, spite **6** arouse, excite, grudge, kindle, malice, nettle, offend **7** affront, incense, perturb, provoke, quicken, umbrage **8** disquiet, irritate, vexation **9** annoyance, displease, stimulate **10** discomfort, exasperate, irritation, resentment **11** displeasure, humiliation, ill feelings, indignation **12** exasperation, hurt feelings **13** embarrassment, mortification, put one's back up **14** vindictiveness

piqued 5 angry, riled, vexed **6** galled, miffed, peeved **7** annoyed, aroused, excited, kindled, nettled, stirred **9** affronted, irritated **10** displeased, stimulated

Pirandello, Luigi
author of: 17 The Old and the Young 18 Tonight We Improvise 19 The Late Mattia Pascal 31 Six Characters in Search of an Author

pirate 3 rob 5 steal 6 raider, robber, sea dog 7 brigand, corsair, plunder 8 marauder 9 buccaneer, privateer 10 freebooter
flag: 9 blackjack 10 Jolly Roger
name: 4 Kidd 6 Morgan 7 Lafitte 10 Blackbeard

Pirate Coast *see* 18 United Arab Emirates

Pirates of Penzance, The
author: 9 W S Gilbert
comic opera by: 18 Gilbert and Sullivan
character: 4 Kate, Ruth 5 Edith, Mabel 6 Isabel 8 Frederic, Sergeant 10 Pirate King 14 General Stanley

pis aller 10 last resort 12 last resource

Pisan Cantos
author: 9 Ezra Pound

Pisanio
character in: 9 Cymbeline
author: 11 Shakespeare

Pisces
symbol: 4 fish
planet: 7 Jupiter, Neptune
rules: 7 secrets
born: 13 February-March

Pisistratus
tyrant of: 6 Athens
father: 11 Hippocrates
son: 7 Hippias 10 Hipparchus

Pissarro, Camille
born: 8 St Thomas 16 Danish West Indies
artwork: 8 Red Roofs 15 Morning Sunlight 21 Lower Norwood Snow Scene 28 Peasant Woman with a Wheelbarrow

pistol (revolver) 3 gat, gun, rod 4 colt, iron 5 luger 6 heater, mauser 7 firearm, sidearm 9 automatic, derringer 20 Saturday night special

pit 3 dip, nut 4 dent, hole, nick, pock, scar, seed 5 gouge, gully, match, notch, stone 6 cavity, crater, dimple, furrow, hollow, indent, kernel, oppose, trough 7 scratch 8 contrast, pockmark 9 concavity, juxtapose 10 depression, set against 11 indentation

Pit, The
author: 11 Frank Norris

Pit and the Pendulum, The
author: 13 Edgar Allan Poe

pitch 3 bob, dip, fix, lob, set, shy, top 4 apex, cant, cast, fall, fire, hurl, jerk, jolt, peak, rock, tone, toss 5 angle, chuck, crown, erect, fling, grade, heave, level, lurch, place, plant, point, raise, set up, shake, slant, sling, slope, sound, throw 6 degree, height, let fly, locate, plunge, propel, settle, summit, topple, tumble, zenith 7 bob-

bing, incline, rocking, station 8 delivery, harmonic, lurching, pinnacle, undulate 9 declivity, establish, oscillate 10 undulation 11 oscillation 12 fall headlong
speed of: 9 vibration

pitcher 3 jar, jug 4 ewer 6 carafe 8 decanter 9 container 10 spitballer
and catcher: 7 battery
award: 7 Cy Young
brother duo: 4 Dean 5 Perry 6 Niekro
Hall of Famer: 4 Dean, Ford, Wynn 5 Young 6 Hunter, Koufax, Palmer, Willis 7 Carlton, Fingers 8 Drysdale 9 Newhouser
left-hander: 8 southpaw
relief staff: 7 bullpen
reliever: 7 fireman

pitch in 5 begin 7 share in 8 take part 9 cooperate, get to work, join hands 10 act jointly, contribute, get started 11 collaborate, participate 12 make an effort, pull together, work together

pitch into 5 fly at 6 assail, have at 7 assault, set upon

piteous 3 sad 6 moving, woeful 7 pitiful 8 pathetic, pitiable, poignant, touching 9 affecting 10 deplorable 11 distressing 12 heart-rending 13 heartbreaking

pitfall 4 risk, trap 5 peril, snare 6 ambush, danger, hazard 7 springe 8 quagmire 9 booby trap, quicksand 14 stumbling block

pith 4 core, gist, meat 5 heart, point 7 essence, meaning 12 significance

pithy 5 terse 6 cogent 7 concise 8 forceful, succinct 9 effective, trenchant 10 expressive, meaningful, to the point 12 concentrated

pitiful 3 sad 4 poor 5 sorry 6 abject, measly, moving, paltry, shabby 7 doleful, forlorn, piteous 8 dreadful, god-awful, mournful, pathetic, pitiable, poignant, touching, wretched 9 miserable, plaintive, worthless 10 abominable, despicable, lamentable 11 distressing 12 arousing pity, contemptible, heartrending

pitiless 5 cruel 6 brutal 7 inhuman, unmoved 8 ruthless, uncaring 9 heartless, merciless, unpitying, unsparing, untouched 10 implacable, relentless, unmerciful 11 cold-blooded, hardhearted, indifferent, insensitive, unrelenting

pittance 4 mite 5 crumb 6 little, trifle 7 minimum, modicum, smidgen

Pittsburgh
baseball team: 7 Pirates
feature: 14 Fort Pitt Museum 15 Buhl Planetarium
football team: 8 Steelers
formerly: 8 Fort Pitt 12 Fort Duquesne
hockey team: 8 Penguins

noted for: 5 steel
river: 4 Ohio 9 Allegheny 11 Monongahela
university: 8 Duquesne 14 Carnegie-Mellon

Pittypat, Aunt
character in: 15 Gone With the Wind
author: 8 Mitchell

pituitary
located in: 5 brain
known as: 11 master gland

pity 5 mercy, shame 6 lament, lenity, regret 7 charity, feel for, weep for 8 bleed for, clemency, humanity, leniency, sad thing, sympathy 10 compassion, condolence, indulgence, kindliness, tenderness 11 crying shame, forbearance, magnanimity 12 feel sorry for 13 commiseration

piu
music: 4 more

pivot 4 axis, axle, hang, rely, spin, turn 5 focus, hinge, twirl, wheel, whirl 6 center, circle, depend, rotate, swivel 7 fulcrum, hinge on, revolve 9 pirouette

pivotal 5 vital 7 crucial 8 critical, decisive 9 climactic 11 determining

pivotal point 4 axis 12 turning point 13 crucial moment

pixie, pixy 3 elf 5 fairy 6 sprite 10 leprechaun

pizazz 5 flair, vigor, style 6 energy, spirit 8 vitality

pizzicato
music: 21 plucked instead of bowed
abbreviation: 4 pizz

placable 7 lenient 8 flexible, tolerant, yielding 9 indulgent, relenting 10 appeasable, forbearing 12 reconcilable

placard 4 bill, sign 6 notice, poster 8 bulletin 13 advertisement

placate 4 calm, lull 5 quiet 6 pacify, soothe 7 appease, assuage, mollify, win over 9 alleviate 10 conciliate, propitiate

placatory 9 appeasing, pacifying 10 mollifying 12 conciliatory 13 accommodative

place 3 fix, job, put, set 4 area, city, digs, duty, farm, firm, home, land, plot, post, rank, rest, shop, site, spot, town, zone 5 abode, affix, array, berth, house, lodge, niche, plant, point, ranch, space, stand, state, store, venue 6 assign, attach, county, harbor, invest, locale, locate, office, region, settle 7 appoint, borough, company, concern, country, deposit, install, quarter, shelter, situate, station, village 8 building, business, classify, district, domicile, dwelling, ensconce, find hire, function, identify, locality, location, lodgings, position, premises, property, province, quarters, remember, standing, township, vicin-

ity **9** recognize, residence, situation, territory **10** commission, get a job for, habitation **11** appointment, find work for, whereabouts **12** neighborhood **13** establishment
Latin: **4** situ

Place in the Sun, A
director: **13** George Stevens
based on novel by: **15** Theodore Dreiser (An American Tragedy)
cast: **14** Keefe Brasselle, Shelley Winters **15** Elizabeth Taylor, Montgomery Clift
Oscar for: **5** score **9** direction **10** screenplay

placement 8 grouping, location **10** assignment, employment **11** arrangement, disposition, positioning

place of residence 4 home **5** abode, house **7** address, lodging **8** domicile, dwelling **9** residence **10** habitation **14** living quarters

place to stand on
Greek: **6** pou sto

place upright 5 erect, raise **7** stand up

placid 4 calm, mild **5** quiet **6** gentle, poised, serene, smooth **7** pacific, restful **8** composed, peaceful, tranquil **9** collected, unexcited, unruffled **10** untroubled **11** undisturbed, unexcitable **13** imperturbable, self-possessed **15** undemonstrative

plague 3 irk, vex, woe **4** bane, evil, fret, gall, pain, pest **5** agony, chafe, curse, harry, haunt, peeve, worry **6** badger, blight, bother, burden, cancer, harass, misery, nettle **7** afflict, disturb, perturb, scourge, torment, trouble **8** aggrieve, calamity, disquiet, distress, hardship, pandemic **9** embarrass, persecute, suffering **10** affliction, Black Death, pestilence, visitation
French: **5** peste

Plague, The
author: **11** Albert Camus
character: **7** Rambert **10** Jean Tarrou **11** Joseph Grand **14** Father Paneloux, Raymond Cottard **15** Dr Bernard R Rieux

plain 4 bald, bare, open **5** blunt, clear, frank, naked, vivid **6** candid, common, direct, homely, honest, modest, simple **7** average, glaring, legible, obscure, obvious, plateau, prairie, sincere, visible **8** apparent, clear-cut, distinct, everyday, explicit, manifest, ordinary, palpable, specific, straight, striking, uncomely, unlovely **9** grassland, outspoken, prominent, tableland, unadorned, undiluted **10** forthright, pronounced, unaffected, unassuming, unhandsome, unreserved, well-marked **11** commonplace, conspicuous, discernible, not striking, open country, outstanding, plain-spoken, unambigu-

ous, undecorated, undisguised, unequivocal, ungarnished, unvarnished, well-defined **12** matter-of-fact, not beautiful, unattractive, unmistakable, unornamented **13** unembellished, unpretentious, without frills **14** comprehensible, understandable **15** straightforward, undistinguished

plainly 6 baldly, openly, simply **7** bluntly, clearly, frankly, visibly, vividly **8** candidly, directly, honestly, markedly, modestly **9** doubtless, obviously **10** apparently, definitely, distinctly, explicitly, manifestly, ordinarily, positively, strikingly, undeniably **11** beyond doubt, discernibly, prominently, undoubtedly **12** unaffectedly, unassumingly, unmistakably, without doubt **13** conspicuously, unambiguously, unequivocally **14** comprehensibly, unquestionably

plainness 10 homeliness, simplicity **12** ordinariness

plainspoken 4 open **5** bluff, blunt, frank, plain **6** candid, direct, honest **7** genuine, sincere **8** explicit, straight **9** open-faced, outspoken, unsparing **10** above board, forthright, point-blank **11** straight-out **15** straightforward

plaint 3 cry, sob **4** beef, moan, wail **5** gripe **6** charge, grouse, grudge, lament, regret, squawk **7** grumble, reproof **8** reproach **9** complaint, grievance, objection **10** accusation, resentment **12** remonstrance

plaintive 3 sad **6** rueful **7** doleful, moaning, piteous, pitiful, tearful **8** dolorous, grievous, mournful, pathetic, wretched **9** lamenting, sorrowful, woebegone **10** lugubrious, melancholy **12** heartrending

plait 5 braid, queue, twine, twist, weave **7** pigtail **10** intertwine

plan 3 aim, map, way **4** form, idea, plot **5** frame, shape **6** design, devise, intend, lay out, map out, method, scheme, sketch **7** diagram, outline, prepare, program, project, propose, purpose **8** block out, conceive, contrive, organize, proposal, strategy, think out **9** blueprint, fabricate, procedure, stratagem **10** conception, suggestion **11** proposition
French: **8** demarche

Planchet
character in: **18** The Three Musketeers
author: **5** Dumas (pere)

Planck, Max
field: **7** physics
nationality: **6** German
developed: **13** quantum theory **15** Planck's constant
awarded: **10** Nobel Prize

plane 3 jet **4** bird, flat **5** level, plumb **6** degree, status **7** regular, station **8** aircraft, airplane, position, standing **9**

condition, elevation
type: **4** jack **5** block

planet, planets 13 celestial body
first: **7** Mercury
second: **5** Venus
third: **5** Earth
  satellite: **4** Moon
fourth: **4** Mars
  satellite: **6** Deimos, Phobos
  nickname: **9** Red Planet
fifth: **7** Jupiter
  satellite: **2** Io **6** Europa **8** Amalthea, Callisto, Ganymede
  characteristic: **7** red spot
sixth: **6** Saturn
  satellite: **4** Rhea **5** Dione, Janus, Mimas, Titan **6** Phoebe, Tethys **7** Iapetus **8** Hyperion **9** Enceladus
  characteristic: **5** rings
seventh: **6** Uranus
  satellite: **5** Ariel **6** Oberon **7** Miranda, Titania, Umbriel
  color: **9** blue green
  characteristic: **5** rings
eighth: **7** Neptune
  satellite: **6** Nereid, Triton
  color: **5** green
ninth: **5** Pluto
  satellite: **6** Charon
asteroid/minor planet/planetoid: **4** Eros, Juno **5** Ceres, Vesta **6** Chiron, Hermes, Icarus, Pallas **7** Astraea, Hidalgo

planetary 6 astral **7** earthly **9** celestial **11** terrestrial **12** astronomical

Planet of the Apes
director: **18** Franklin J Schaffner
based on novel by: **12** Pierre Boulle
cast: **9** Kim Hunter **12** Maurice Evans **13** Roddy McDowall **14** Charlton Heston
script: **10** Rod Serling

plank 4 deal, deck, slab **5** board, shole, stone **8** platform

planned 7 devised, schemed **8** designed, expected, foreseen, intended, prepared **9** mapped out, organized, projected, rehearsed **10** calculated, purposeful, thought out **11** intentional, prearranged, prepared for **12** premeditated

planner 6 author, framer **7** creator, deviser **8** arranger, designer **9** architect, organizer

plant 4 bush, herb, mill, moss, shop, slip, tree, vine, weed, wort, yard **5** algae, flora, fungi, grass, set in, shrub, works **6** flower, foster, infuse, set out **7** factory, foundry, herbage, implant, inspire, instill, scatter, sow seed **8** business, engender, seedling **9** broadcast, cultivate, establish, inculcate, propagate, vegetable **10** transplant, vegetation **13** establishment, sow the seeds of **14** put in the ground

plaster 4 coat, daub, sand **5** grout, smear **6** bedaub, gypsum, lather,

stucco **7** overlay, spackle
mixture of: 4 lime **5** water **6** gypsum

plastered 5 drunk **6** coated, daubed, soused **7** covered, crocked, smeared, swacked **8** mortared, polluted, stuccoed **10** inebriated **11** intoxicated

plastic 4 soft **6** pliant, supple **7** ductile, elastic, pliable **8** flexible, formable, moldable, shapable, yielding **9** malleable, tractable

plate 4 dish **6** saucer **7** helping, platter, portion, serving **10** platterful **11** serving dish

plateau 4 mesa **5** table **6** upland **8** highland **9** tableland

platform 4 dais, goal, plan **5** creed, plank, stage, stand **6** podium, policy, pulpit, tenets **7** program, rostrum

Plath, Sylvia
author of: 5 Ariel **10** The Bell Jar

platinum
chemical symbol: 2 Pt

platitude 3 saw **6** cliche, old saw, truism **7** bromide **8** banality, chestnut **11** commonplace

platitudinous 5 banal, corny, stale, tired, trite, vapid **6** jejune **8** bromidic, ordinary **9** hackneyed **10** pedestrian, unexciting, unoriginal **12** cliche-ridden, conventional **13** unimaginative

Plato
author of: 4 Laws **5** Crito **6** Phaedo **7** Apology, Gorgias, Sophist, Timaeus **8** Philebus, Republic **9** Symposium **10** Parmenides

platoon 4 band, body, crew, team, unit **5** corps, force, group **10** detachment

platter 4 dish, disk, lanx **6** salver **7** record **8** trencher **9** recording

plaudit, plaudits 4 rave **5** cheer, kudos **6** hurrah, huzzah, praise **7** acclaim, bouquet, ovation **8** applause, approval, cheering **10** compliment, hallelujah **11** approbation **12** commendation

plauditory 8 admiring, praising **9** extolling, laudatory, praiseful **12** commendatory **13** complimentary

plausible 5 sound, valid **6** likely **7** logical, tenable **8** credible, feasible, possible, probable, rational, sensible **10** acceptable, believable, convincing, persuasive, reasonable **11** conceivable, justifiable

Plautus
author of: 7 Stichus **8** Mercator **9** Amphitruo, Menaechmi, Pseudolus **10** Amphitryon **14** Miles Gloriosus

play 3 act, fun, toy **4** jest, lark, romp, room, show **5** antic, caper, drama, enact, farce, frisk, revel, space, sport, sweep, swing **6** act out, cavort, comedy, frolic, gambol, leeway, trifle **7** disport, have fun, pageant, perform, skylark, tragedy, vie with **8** pleasure,

take part **9** amusement, diversion, elbowroom, enjoyment, make merry, melodrama, perform on, personify, represent, spectacle **10** recreation **11** impersonate, merrymaking

playboy 4 rake, wolf **5** Romeo, sheik **6** lecher **7** Don Juan, swinger **8** Casanova, hedonist, Lothario, party boy **9** jet-setter, ladies' man, partygoer, womanizer **10** lady-killer, profligate **14** pleasure seeker **15** good-time Charlie

Playboy of the Western World, The
author: 19 John Millington Synge
character: 8 Old Mahon **9** Widow Quin **10** Shawn Keogh **16** Christopher Mahon, Margaret Flaherty (Pegeen)

play down 9 underplay **11** de-emphasize

played out 4 beat **5** all in, spent, weary **6** bushed, done in, pooped **7** drained, wearied, worn out **8** depleted, dog tired, fatigued, tired out, unreeled **9** dead tired, exhausted

player 4 jock, mime **5** actor **6** mummer **7** actress, athlete, trouper **8** gamester, opponent, thespian **9** adversary, contender, performer **10** antagonist, competitor, contestant, team member **11** entertainer, participant

play false 4 dupe **5** trick **6** betray **7** deceive, two-time **10** be disloyal **12** be unfaithful **13** be treacherous

playfellow 3 pal **4** chum **5** buddy **6** friend **8** playmate

playful 6 frisky, impish, lively **7** amusing, coltish, jesting, waggish **8** humorous, mirthful, prankish, sportive **9** fun-loving, sprightly **10** capricious, frolicsome, rollicking **12** lighthearted
French: 8 espiegle

play host 4 host **9** entertain **10** give a party, have guests **13** keep open house

playing field 4 bowl **5** arena **7** diamond, stadium **8** gridiron **10** playground **12** amphitheater

playing piece 3 man **4** disk **5** piece **7** counter

play in water 3 dip **4** swim **6** dabble, paddle, splash

play Judas 6 betray **7** sell out, two-time **9** play false **11** double-cross

playmate 3 pal **4** chum **5** buddy **6** friend **10** playfellow

play of spirit
French: 10 jeu d'esprit

play on words
French: 3 pun **9** jeu de mots

plaything 3 toy **4** dupe **5** patsy, sport **6** bauble, trifle **9** diversion

play truant 3 cut **4** skip **8** be absent **9** play hooky

play with 5 bandy **7** torment, toy with **11** have fun with

playwright 6 author, writer **9** dramatist, scenarist **10** dramatizer, dramaturge, librettist, play doctor **12** dramatic poet, dramaturgist, scriptwriter **13** melodramatist

plea 4 suit **5** alibi **6** appeal, excuse, prayer **7** apology, begging, defense, pretext, request **8** argument, entreaty, petition **10** adjuration, beseeching **11** explanation, extenuation, vindication **12** solicitation, supplication **13** justification

plead 3 ask, beg **6** adjure, enjoin **7** beseech, entreat, implore, request, solicit **8** appeal to, petition **9** importune **10** supplicate

pleader 6 beggar **8** advocate, defender, implorer **9** apologist, beseecher **10** importuner, supplicant

plead with 3 beg **4** pray **6** adjure **7** beseech, implore **10** supplicate

Pleasance, Donald
born: 7 England, Worksop
roles: 12 The Caretaker **14** The Great Escape **16** You Only Live Twice **17** The Eagle Has Landed **24** The Greatest Story Ever Told

pleasant 4 fine, good, mild, nice, soft, warm **6** genial, gentle, lovely, polite **7** affable, amiable, cordial, likable, tactful **8** amicable, charming, cheerful, friendly, inviting, pleasing, sociable **9** agreeable, congenial, enjoyable **10** attractive, felicitous, gratifying, gregarious, satisfying **11** good-humored, good-natured, pleasurable **13** companionable

Pleasant Island *see* **5** Nauru

pleasantry 4 jape, jest, joke, quip **5** sally **6** bon mot **8** greeting **9** wisecrack, witticism **10** salutation

pleasant-tasting 4 mild **5** sweet, tasty **6** savory **8** luscious **9** delicious, palatable, succulent **10** appetizing, delectable **11** scrumptious **13** mouth-watering

please 3 opt **4** like, suit, want, will, wish **5** amuse, charm, elate, elect **6** choose, desire, divert, prefer, thrill, tickle **7** content, delight, gladden, gratify, satisfy **8** enthrall, entrance **9** enrapture, entertain, fascinate, make happy **10** be inclined **14** give pleasure to
French: 12 s'il vous plait
German: 5 bitte
Spanish: 8 por favor

pleased 4 glad **5** happy, proud **6** elated **8** thrilled **9** delighted, gratified

please reply
French: 4 rsvp **20** repondez s'il vous plait

pleasing 6 genial, polite **7** affable, amiable, amusing, likable, winning **8** charming, cheerful, friendly, inviting, mannerly **9** agreeable, congenial, diverting, enjoyable **10** attractive, delightful, gladdening, gratifying, satisfying **11** captivating, fascinating, good-humored, good- natured, pleasurable **12** entertaining, well-mannered

pleasing inactivity
Italian: **14** dolce far niente

pleasurable 8 pleasing **9** agreeable, enjoyable **10** delightful

pleasure 3 fun, joy **4** like, will, wish **5** bliss, cheer, mirth **6** choice, desire, gaiety, option **7** delight, elation, rapture **9** amusement, diversion, enjoyment, festivity, happiness, merriment, selection **10** exultation, jubilation, preference, recreation **11** high spirits, inclination **13** entertainment, gratification **15** beer and skittles **16** lightheartedness
goddess of: **8** Voluptas

pleasure-giving 7 amusing **8** pleasing **9** agreeable, enjoyable **10** delightful **11** pleasurable **12** entertaining

Pleasure of His Company, The
author: **19** Cornelia Otis Skinner

pleasure trip 4 tour **5** jaunt **6** outing **8** vacation **9** excursion

pleat 4 fold **5** crimp, frill **6** crease

pleated 6 fluted, folded **7** creased, crimped **10** corrugated

plebeian 3 low **4** base, mean **5** banal **6** coarse, common, vulgar **7** lowborn, lowbrow, popular **8** commoner, everyman, low-class, ordinary **9** bourgeois, common man, unrefined **10** average man, uncultured **11** bourgeoisie, commonplace, proletarian **12** uncultivated

plebs 5 demos **6** masses **7** commons **8** populace **9** commoners, hoi polloi, plebeians **11** bourgeoisie **12** common people

plecoptera
class: **8** hexapoda
phylum: **10** arthropoda
group: **8** stone fly

pledge 3 vow **4** bail, bond, oath, pact, pawn, word **5** swear, troth **6** assert, avowal, surety **7** compact, promise, warrant **8** contract, covenant, guaranty, security, warranty **9** agreement, assurance, guarantee **10** adjuration, collateral

Pleiades
father: **5** Atlas
mother: **7** Pleione
half-sisters: **6** Hyades
names: **4** Maia **6** Merope **7** Alcyone, Celaeno, Electra, Sterope, Taygete
number of daughters: **5** seven

plenary 4 full **6** entire **7** perfect **8** absolute, complete

plenitude 4 glut, heap, mass **5** flood **6** bounty, plenty, wealth **7** quality, surfeit, surplus **8** fullness, plethora, totality **9** abundance, amplitude, profu-

sion, repletion, wholeness **10** cornucopia, entireness, quantities **11** ample supply, copiousness, full measure, sufficiency **12** completeness **14** more than enough

plenteous 6 lavish **7** copious, profuse **8** abundant **9** bountiful, plentiful

plentiful 4 lush **5** ample, large **6** lavish **7** copious, liberal, profuse **8** abundant, generous, infinite, prolific **9** abounding, bounteous, bountiful, plenteous, unsparing, unstinted **11** overflowing **13** inexhaustible

plenty 4 gobs, lots, slew **5** scads **6** luxury, oceans, oodles, riches, wealth, worlds **8** opulence **9** abundance, affluence, good times, great deal, plenitude, profusion, well-being **10** prosperity **11** ample amount, good fortune, sufficiency **12** a full measure
goddess of: **3** Ops

plethora 4 glut **5** flood **6** excess, wealth **7** overage, surfeit, surplus **8** fullness **9** abundance, amplitude, plenitude, profusion **10** oversupply, redundancy, surplusage **11** superfluity **13** overabundance **14** more than enough, superabundance

pliable 5 lithe **6** limber, pliant, supple **7** elastic, plastic, springy, willing **8** flexible, yielding **9** adaptable, compliant, receptive, resilient, tractable **10** manageable, responsive, submissive **11** acquiescent **13** accommodating **14** easily bendable, impressionable

pliancy 8 docility, meekness, yielding **9** passivity **10** compliance, pliability, submission, suppleness **11** flexibility **12** complaisance

pliant 4 meek **6** supple **7** pliable **8** flexible, yielding **9** compliant **10** submissive **11** deferential

pliers
type: **10** fixed-joint **11** combination, needle-nosed, side- cutting **17** offset combination

plight 3 fix, jam **5** pinch, state, trial **6** crisis, muddle, pickle, scrape **7** dilemma, impasse, straits, trouble **8** distress, exigency **9** condition, emergency, extremity, situation **10** difficulty **11** predicament, tribulation, vicissitude **12** circumstance

Plisthenes
brother/half-brother: **8** Menelaus **9** Agamemnon
father: **6** Atreus
mother: **6** Cleola
sister/half-sister: **8** Anaxibia
sister-in-law: **12** Clytemnestra
uncle: **8** Thyestes

plod 4 drag, grub, moil, plug, slog, toil **5** grind, sweat, tramp **6** drudge, lumber, trudge, waddle **7** peg away, shuffle **8** struggle **9** persevere

plodding 4 dull **6** clumsy **8** trudging **9** laborious **10** pedestrian

plot 3 lot, map **4** area, draw, mark, plan, tale, yarn **5** chart, draft, field, patch, space, story, tract **6** action, design, scheme, sketch **7** collude, compute, diagram, outline, section **8** clearing, conspire, contrive, evil plan, intrigue, maneuver **9** blueprint, calculate, determine, incidents, narrative, story line, stratagem **10** conspiracy, secret plan **11** machination

plotting 4 wily **6** artful, crafty **7** cunning **8** scheming **9** conniving, designing **10** intriguing

Plough and the Stars, The
author: **10** Sean O'Casey

plover
group of: **4** wing **12** congregation

plow, plough 3 cut, dig **4** push, till, work **5** break, dig up, drive, forge, press, shove, spade **6** furrow, harrow, loosen, plunge, turn up **7** break up **8** bulldoze **9** cultivate
invented by:
cast iron: **7** Ransome
disc: **5** Hardy

plowable 6 arable **7** friable **8** farmable, tillable **10** cultivable

Plowright, Joan
born: **5** Brigg **7** England
husband: **15** Laurence Olivier
roles: **13** A Taste of Honey **14** The Entertainer

ploy 4 game, ruse, wile **5** trick **6** design, gambit, scheme, tactic **7** gimmick **8** artifice, maneuver, strategy **9** stratagem **10** subterfuge

pluck 4 draw, grab, grit, guts, jerk, pick, sand, yank **5** spunk, valor **6** daring, mettle, pull at, snatch, spirit, uproot **7** bravery, courage, pull off, pull out, resolve **8** boldness, temerity, tenacity **9** extirpate, fortitude **10** doggedness, resolution **11** persistence **12** perseverance **13** determination

pluck out 7 extract, pick out, pull out

plucky 4 bold, game **5** brave, gutsy **6** daring, spunky **7** doughty, valiant **8** fearless, intrepid, spirited, unafraid, valorous **9** audacious, dauntless, undaunted **10** courageous, mettlesome **11** lionhearted, unflinching **12** stouthearted

plug 4 bung, cork **5** close, stuff **6** fill up, stanch, stop up **7** shut off, stopper, stopple

plug up 3 dam **4** clog, plug **5** block, choke, dam up, stuff **6** stop up **7** congest **8** obstruct

plum
varieties: **3** hog **4** Coco, date, Duhr, gage, Java, sand, sloe, wild **5** beach, black, goose, Islay, Jaman, Lansa, Moxie, nanny, Natal, shore, Simon **6** August, Batoko, Canada, Cheney, cherry, common, Damson, ground, Indian, Jambul, Kaffir, Kelsey, Lomboy, Pigeon, Sapote, Sierra, Sisson **7**

apricot, Burbank, Cheston, Jambosa, Malabar, Orleans, Pacific, Spanish, Wickson **8** American, Assyrian, Burdekin, European, Hortulan, Jambolan, Japanese, Oklahoma, Prunello, Victoria **9** Allegheny, Chickasaw, Governor's, greengage, marmalade, Myrobalan, wild-goose **10** Madagascar **13** Queensland hog

plumb 4 lead, test, true **5** gauge, level, probe, sheer, sound **6** fathom **7** examine, measure, plummet **8** plumb bob, straight, vertical **9** penetrate

plume 3 pen **4** down **5** egret, pique, preen, pride, prize, quill **7** feather
military: **7** panache

Plumed Serpent, The
author: **10** D H Lawrence

Plummer, Christopher
real name: **28** Arthur Christopher Orme Plummer
born: **6** Canada **7** Toronto
wife: **11** Tammy Grimes **12** Elaine Taylor
roles: **14** Murder by Decree **15** The Sound of Music **18** Baron Georg von Trapp **20** The Man Who Would Be King **25** The Return of the Pink Panther

plummet 4 dive, fall **6** plunge, tumble **8** nosedive **12** fall headlong

plump 4 drop, firm, flop, plop, sink **5** blunt, buxom, obese, plunk, pudgy, solid, spill, stout **6** abrupt, chubby, direct, fleshy, portly, rotund, sprawl, stocky, tumble **7** rounded **8** collapse, outright **9** corpulent

plumpness
French: **10** embonpoint

plunder 3 rob **4** haul, loot, raid, sack, swag, take **5** booty, rifle, prize, strip **6** fleece, maraud, pilfer, ravage, spoils **7** despoil, pillage, ransack, takings **9** filchings **10** pilferings

plunderer 6 looter, vandal **7** brigand **8** pillager **9** despoiler

plunge 3 dip, fly, run **4** bolt, cast, dart, dash, dive, drop, duck, fall, jerk, roll, jump, leap, push, reel, rock, rush, sink, sway, tear, toss **5** douse, drive, heave, lunge, lurch, pitch, press, shoot, speed, surge, swarm, whisk **6** charge, hasten, hurtle, hustle, scurry, sprint, streak, thrust, tumble **7** descend, immerse, scuttle **8** scramble, submerge, submerse **12** fall headlong

plunk 4 pick, thud **5** pluck, plumb, strum, twang **6** dollar **7** exactly **8** squarely **9** precisely

plurality 4 bulk, most **8** majority **13** preponderance

plus 5 added, extra, other, spare **6** useful **7** helpful **9** auxiliary, desirable **10** additional, beneficial **12** advantageous, supplemental **13** supplementary

plush 4 lush, posh, rich **5** fancy, grand,

ritzy, swank, thick **6** classy, deluxe, lavish, snazzy, swanky **7** elegant, opulent **8** palatial **9** luxurious, sumptuous **11** extravagant

plushy 4 soft **5** cushy, swank **7** opulent, velvety **9** luxurious, sumptuous

Plutarch
author of: **13** Parallel Lives

Plutarch's Lives
author: **8** Plutarch

Pluto
also: **5** Hades
god of: **10** underworld
corresponds to: **3** Dis **5** Orcus **8** Dis Pater

Pluto
position: **5** ninth
satellite: **6** Charon

plutocrat 5 mogul **6** fat cat, tycoon **9** financier **10** capitalist

plutonic 7 abyssal, igneous **9** cimmerian, intrusive, vulcanian

plutonium
chemical symbol: **2** Pu

Plutus
author: **12** Aristophanes
character: **5** Cario **9** Chremylus **11** Blepsidemus
god of: **6** wealth

Plutus
personifies: **6** wealth
father: **6** Iasion
mother: **7** Demeter

Pluvius
epithet of: **7** Jupiter
realm: **4** rain

ply 3 fly, run **4** leaf, sail, work **5** layer, offer, plait, plate, press, sheet, slice, twist, wield **6** employ, follow, handle, lamina, pursue, sheath, strand, supply **7** besiege, carry on, labor at, operate, stratum, utilize **8** exercise, navigate, practice, put to use, urge upon **9** thickness **10** manipulate

poach 3 rob **4** cook **5** shirr, steal **6** plunge, simmer **7** trample **8** encroach, trespass

pocket 3 bag, get, pit **4** gain, lode, sack, vein **5** pouch, purse, pygmy, small, steal, strip, usurp **6** attain, bantam, cavity, come by, hollow, little, obtain, pilfer, strain, streak **7** chamber, compact, handbag, placket, receive **8** arrogate, envelope, portable **9** miniature **10** diminutive, receptacle **11** appropriate, compartment

Pocket, Herbert
character in: **17** Great Expectations
author: **7** Dickens

pocketbook 3 bag **5** pouch, purse **6** clutch, wallet **7** handbag, satchel **8** moneybag, notecase **9** coin purse **10** money purse **11** shoulder bag
French: **12** porte-monnaie

pocket flask 5 flask **6** bottle **7** canteen

pocket-sized 3 wee **4** tiny **5** dwarf, pygmy, small **6** bantam, little, midget, minute, petite **7** compact **9** miniature **10** diminutive, vest-pocket

poco
music: **6** little

Pocock, Mamie
character in: **14** The Ambassadors
author: **5** James

pod 4 case, hull, husk **5** shell **6** jacket, sheath **8** pericarp, seed case **10** seed vessel

Podgorica
capital of: **10** Montenegro
once called: Titograd

podium 4 dais, foot, wall **5** stipe **7** lectern **8** pedestal, platform **9** footstalk

Poe, Edgar Allan
author of: **6** Ligeia **7** Israfel, To Helen **8** The Bells, The Raven **10** Annabel Lee, The Gold Bug **18** The Purloined Letter **20** The Cask of Amontillado, The Pit and the Pendulum **22** The Masque of the Red Death **24** The Fall of the House of Usher, The Murders in the Rue Morgue **29** The Narrative of Arthur Gordon Pym

Poeas
also: **5** Poias
lit: **11** funeral pyre
  pyre of: **8** Hercules
son: **11** Philoctetes

poem 3 lay, ode **4** epic, song **5** elegy, idyll, lyric, rhyme, verse **6** ballad, jingle, sonnet **8** doggerel, limerick, madrigal

Poema del Cid see **6** The Cid

Poems Chiefly in the Scottish Dialect
author: **11** Robert Burns

poet 4 bard **5** maker **6** lyrist, rhymer, singer **7** reciter **8** lyricist, minstrel, verseman **9** balladeer, balladist, poetaster, rhymester, sonneteer, versifier **10** improviser, librettist, songwriter

poetaster 4 bard, poet **6** rhymer, writer **8** poetizer, rimester **9** rhymester, versifier

poetic, poetical 5 lyric **7** lilting, lyrical, melodic, musical **8** metrical, rhythmic, songlike **9** melodious **11** imaginative

Poetics
author: **9** Aristotle

poetizer 4 bard, poet **6** rhymer, writer **8** rhymster **9** poetaster, versifier

poetry 5 poesy, rhyme, verse **13** versification
god of: **4** Odin, Ogma **5** Brage, Bragi, Othin **6** Apollo **7** Phoebus, Pythius **9** Musagetes

Pogo
creator: **9** Walt Kelly
character: **9** Porkypine, Wiley Catt **10** Boll Weevil **12** PT Bridgeport **13**

Deacon Mushrat, Mole MacCarony
  alligator: 6 Albert
  fox: 11 Seminole Sam
  frog: 15 Moonshine Sonata
  hound: 18 Beauregard Bugleboy
  possum: 4 Pogo
  skunk: 16 Ma'm'selle Hepzibah
  snake: 7 Snavely
  sorcerer: 10 Howland Owl
  turtle/pirate captain: 14 Churchy
    La Femme
  place: 15 Okefenokee Swamp
Pohjola
  origin: 7 Finnish
  identified with: 7 Lapland
  location: 12 North Finland
poignant 3 sad **5** sharp **6** biting, moving, rueful, woeful **7** cutting, doleful, piquant, piteous, pitiful, pungent, tearful **8** grievous, pathetic, piercing, pitiable, touching **9** affecting, sorrowful, trenchant **10** lamentable **11** distressing, penetrating **12** heartrending
poilu
  slang: 13 French soldier
  in: 9 World War I
point 3 aim, end, hit, nib, run, tip, use **4** apex, bend, bode, core, game, gist, goal, item, mark, meat, pike, pith, spur, time, turn, unit **5** argue, cause, guide, heart, imply, level, limit, place, prong, prove, score, sense, slant, spike, stage, steer, tally, train, value **6** aspect, basket, degree, detail, direct, hint at, kernel, marrow, moment, number, object, reason **7** essence, feature, instant, portend, presage, purpose, quality, signify, suggest, testify **8** indicate, intimate, juncture, main idea, manifest, offshoot, position, sharp end **9** condition, extension, intention, objective, outgrowth **10** foreshadow, particular, projection, prominence, promontory **11** demonstrate **12** protuberance
point-blank 5 blunt **6** direct **10** forthright **11** plainspoken
Point Counter Point
  author: 12 Aldous Huxley
point d'appui 4 prop, stay **24** point of battle line support
pointed 5 acute, blunt, sharp **6** biting, direct, peaked, pointy **7** cutting, fitting, hinting, telling **8** accurate, incisive, piercing **9** aciculate, acuminate, cuspidate, pertinent, trenchant **10** emphasized, forthright **11** appropriate, conspicuous, insinuating, penetrating
pointer 3 arm, tip **4** hand, hint **5** arrow, guide, stick **6** needle **7** caution, warning **9** indicator **10** admonition, advisement, suggestion **13** piece of advice **14** recommendation
  dog breed: 16 German wirehaired **17** German shorthaired **25** wirehaired pointing griffon
pointless 4 dull **5** blunt **6** absurd, fu-

tile, obtuse, stupid **7** aimless, invalid, rounded, unedged, useless **8** bootless, worn down **9** fruitless, illogical, senseless, unpointed, worthless **10** irrational, irrelevant, ridiculous, unavailing **11** ineffectual, meaningless, purposeless, unsharpened **12** inapplicable, preposterous, unproductive, unprofitable, unreasonable
point of view 4 side **5** angle, slant **6** aspect **7** outlook **8** attitude **9** viewpoint **10** standpoint **11** frame of mind, perspective
point the way 5 guide, pilot, usher **6** direct **8** indicate, navigate **14** give directions
point to 5 argue, imply **6** denote **7** express **8** indicate
point up 6 stress **9** emphasize, underline **10** accentuate, underscore
Poirot, Hercule
  detective created by: 14 Agatha Christie
  nationality: 7 Belgian
  famed for: 10 moustaches
  phrase: 15 little grey cells
  played by: 11 David Suchet (PBS Mystery) **12** Peter Sellers
poise 4 calm **5** raise **6** aplomb **7** balance, elevate **8** presence **9** assurance, composure, hold aloft, sangfroid **10** equanimity **11** savoir faire, self-command, self-control **13** self-assurance **14** presence of mind, self-confidence **15** be in equilibrium
poised 7 assured **8** composed **9** confident **10** controlled **11** self-assured **13** self-possessed
poison 4 bane, evil, harm **5** curse, taint, toxin, venom **6** cancer, canker, debase, defile, impair, infect, plague, weaken **7** corrode, corrupt, degrade, disease, outrage, pollute **8** enormity, make sick **9** malignity **10** adulterate, corruption, debilitate, malignancy, pestilence **11** abomination, contaminate
poisonous 5 fatal, toxic **6** deadly, lethal, mortal **7** baneful, noxious **8** venomous, virulent **10** pernicious **11** deleterious **12** pestilential
Poitier, Sidney
  born: 7 Miami FL
  wife: 13 Joanna Shimkus
  roles: 11 Virgil Tibbs **12** A Patch of Blue, For Love of Ivy, Porgy and Bess **13** To Sir with Love **14** The Defiant Ones **15** A Raisin in the Sun **16** Lilies of the Field (Oscar) **17** They Call Me Mr Tibbs **19** In the Heat of the Night, The Blackboard Jungle, Uptown Saturday Night **23** Guess Who's Coming to Dinner?
Pokanoket *see* **10** Wampanoags
poke 3 dig, hit, jab **4** butt, drag, gore, idle, jolt, prod, push, stab **5** crawl, dally, delay, mosey, nudge, punch,

stick, thump **6** dawdle, fiddle, potter, thrust **7** meander, saunter, shamble, shuffle **8** hang back **10** dillydally **12** shilly-shally
poker
  derived from: 5 as nas, gilet **6** brelan **7** primero **11** brouillotte
  cards/hand: 4 five **5** seven
  bets: 4 ante **5** chips
  hand: 4 pair **5** flush **8** straight, two pairs **9** full house **10** royal flush **11** four of a kind **12** three of a kind **13** straight flush
  term: 4 ante, call, fold **5** check, raise **6** ante up **7** reraise
  variation: 4 draw, stud **5** jacks, Omaha **6** hold em, pai gow **8** jackpots **12** five-card draw **13** seven-card stud
poky, pokey 4 dull, jail, slow **5** dowdy, small **6** dreary, shabby, stodgy, stuffy **7** cramped **8** confined, dawdling, dilatory, frumpish **9** puttering **10** monotonous
  creature: 5 sloth, snail **6** turtle **8** slowpoke, tortoise
Poland
  other name: 6 Polska **17** the land of the plain
  capital/largest city: 6 Warsaw
    medieval capital: 6 Cracow, Krakow
  others: 3 Lwo **4** Kudz, Kolo, Lida, Lodz, Lvov, Lyck, Nysa, Oels, Pila **5** Brest, Bytom, Chelm, Dukla, Narev, Opole, Posen, Radom, Sroda, Torun, Vilna **6** Danzig, Elblag, Gdansk, Gdynia, Gnesen, Grodno, Kalisz, Kielce, Kracow, Lublin, Poznan, Tarnow, Zabrze **7** Beuthen, Breslau, Chorzow, Garocin, Gliwice, Litousk, Litovsk, Lyublin, Oleztyn, Stettin, Wroclaw **8** Fromboik, Gleiwitz, Katowice, Lidzbark, Liegnitz, Oswiecim, Przemysl, Szczecln, Tarnopol **9** Auschwitz, Bialogard, Bialystok, Bydgoszcz, Sosnowiec, Szcezecin, Walbrzych **11** Czestochowa
  school: 6 Warsaw **12** Jagiellonian
  division: 7 Galicia, Silesia **8** Podlesia, Volhynia **9** Lithuania, Pomerania
  measure: 3 cal **4** mila, pret **5** morga, sazen, vloka, wloka **6** cwierc, cwierk, kwarta, lokiec **7** garniec **9** kwarterka
  monetary unit: 4 abia **5** dalar, ducat, grosz, marka, zloty **6** fennig, groszy, gulden, halerz, ko rona **8** groschen
  weight: 3 lut **4** funt **6** kamian **7** skrupul
  island: 5 Wolin
  lake: 5 Goplo, Mamry **8** Niegocin, Sniardwy **13** Stettin Lagoon
  mountain: 5 Tatra **6** Beskid **7** Pieniny, Sudeten **9** Beshchady, High Tatra, Holy Cross **10** Carpathian
  highest point: 4 Rysy
  river: 3 Bug, San **4** Alle, Brda, Gwda,

Lyna, Nysa, Oder, Styr **5** Biala, Drana, Dwina, Narev, Narew, Notec, Podra, Seret, Warta, Wista **6** Neisse, Niemen, Nyeman, Pilica, Pripet, Prosna, Styrpa, Wieprz **7** Nemunas, Vistula, Wistoka **8** Dniester
sea: 6 Baltic
physical feature:
forest: 10 Bialowieza
gulf: 6 Danzig, Gdansk
lagoon: 7 Stettin **12** Frischeshaff
plain: 7 Silesia
plateau: 6 Lublin
people: 4 Pole, Slav **5** Mazur **8** Silesian
astronomer: 10 Copernicus
author: 7 Reymont **8** Zeromski **10** Mickiewicz, Wyspianski **11** Sienkiewicz
composer: 6 Chopin **10** Paderewski
dynasty: 5 Piast **7** Jagello
king: 7 Casimir **8** Augustus
leader: 5 Kania **6** Gierek **7** Gomulka, Mieszko **8** Boleslaw **9** Pilsudski, Stanislaw **10** Jaruzel ski, Kosciuszko, Lech Walesa
pope: 10 John Paul II **20** Cardinal Carol Wojtyla
queen: 7 Jadwiga
musician: 7 Kiepura **9** Landowska
scientist: 5 Curie
language: 6 Kaszub, Polish **10** Pomeranian
religion: 13 Roman Catholic
title: 3 pan **4** pani
place:
castle: 5 Wawel
church: 6 St John **10** Panna Maria
monastery: 9 Jasna Gora
monument: 17 Heroes of the Ghetto
national park: 5 Ojcow **10** Bialowieza
palace: 7 Casimir
feature:
folk dance: 5 polka **7** mazurka **9** krakowiak, polonaise
union: 10 Solidarity
food:
dish: 5 bigos **6** pirogi **7** borscht **7** kolduny
drink: 5 vodka **7** Krupnik
sausage: 8 kielbasa
soup: 7 barszca
Polanski, Roman
director of: 4 Tess **7** Macbeth **9** Chinatown **13** Rosemary's Baby
polar 3 icy **6** arctic, frigid, wintry **7** glacial, ice-cold **8** freezing **9** antarctic **11** nothernmost **12** southernmost
polaroid 6 camera
invented by: 4 Land
pole 3 rod **4** mast, spar **5** shaft, staff, stick **6** tongue **9** pikestaff
flax holder: 7 distaff
pertaining to: 5 nodal
sacred: 7 Asherah
Scottish: 5 caber

tribal: 5 totem
vehicular: 4 neap
police, police officer 4 cops, dick, fuzz, tidy **5** clean, guard **6** neaten, patrol, tidy up **7** clean up, control, marshal, officer, protect, sheriff **8** blue coat, flatfoot, gendarme, regulate, spruce up, troopers **9** gendarmes, men in blue, patrolmen **10** traffic cop **11** arm of the law, keep in order **12** constabulary, cop on the beat
French: 8 gendarme
Italian: 11 carabiniere
Police Woman
character: 9 (Det) Joe Styles, (Lt) Paul Marsh **11** (Det) Pete Royster, (Lt) Bill Crowley **12** (Sgt Suzanne) Pepper Martin
cast: 9 Ed Bernard **11** Val Bisoglio **12** Earl Holliman **14** Angie Dickinson, Charles Dierkop
policy 3 way **4** plan, rule **5** habit, style **6** custom, design, method, scheme, system **7** program, routine, tactics **8** behavior, platform, practice, strategy **9** principle, procedure
polish 3 oil, wax **4** buff, sand **5** class, emend, glaze, gloss, grace, rouge, rub up, shine **6** pumice, refine, smooth **7** burnish, correct, culture, enhance, finesse, improve, perfect, sauvity, touch up, varnish **8** abrasive, courtesy, elegance, round out, urbanity **9** gentility, politesse, sandpaper **10** politeness, refinement **11** cultivation, good manners
polished 4 able, deft, fine, oily **5** oiled, suave, waxed **6** buffed, expert, glassy, glazed, glossy, polite, rubbed, sanded, shined, urbane **7** capable, elegant, genteel, refined, skilled **8** cultured, finished, mannerly, masterly, skillful, smoothed **9** brilliant, burnished, courteous, masterful, practiced, varnished **10** cultivated, profi- cient **11** experienced **12** accomplished
polish off 6 finish **8** complete, get rid of **9** dispose of
polite 4 high **5** civil, elite **6** proper **7** courtly, elegant, gallant, genteel, refined **8** cultured, mannerly, polished, well-bred **9** civilized, courteous, diffident, patrician **10** cultivated, respectful **11** ceremonious, fashionable, gentlemanly, well-behaved **12** well-mannered
politeness 7 decorum **8** courtesy **9** gentility, propriety **10** refinement **11** good manners
Polites
character in: 7 Odyssey
brother: 5 Paris **6** Hector
companion: 8 Odysseus
father: 5 Priam
mother: 6 Hecuba
sister: 9 Cassandra

transformed by: 5 Aeaea, Circe
transformed into: 3 hog, pig **5** swine
politic 4 wily, wise **5** chary, suave **6** artful, astute, shrewd, subtle **7** mindful, prudent, tactful **8** cautious, discreet, scheming **9** designing, expedient, judicious, opportune **10** contriving, diplomatic **11** calculating, circumspect, machinating **13** Machiavellian
political party 3 GOP **4** Tory, Whig **5** Labor **7** faction **9** Communist, Greenback, Socialist **10** Democratic, Republican **11** Know-Nothing
political refugee 2 DP **5** exile **6** emigre **10** expatriate **15** displaced person
politician 8 politico **9** incumbent, statesman **10** campaigner, legislator **12** officeholder, office seeker **13** public servant
politics 10 government, statecraft **11** party policy **13** statesmanship **14** affairs of state
Politics
author: 9 Aristotle
Politic Would-Be, Lord and Lady
characters in: 7 Volpone
author: 6 Jonson
Polixenes
character in: 14 The Winter's Tale
author: 11 Shakespeare
Polk, James Knox
presidential rank: 8 eleventh
party: 8 Democrat
state represented: 2 TN
defeated: 4 (Henry) Clay **6** (James Gillespie) Birney
vice president: 6 (George Mifflin) Dallas
cabinet:
state: 8 (James) Buchanan
treasury: 6 (Robert John) Walker
war: 5 (William Learned) Marcy
attorney general: 5 (John Young) Mason **6** (Isaac) Toucey **8** (Nathan) Clifford
navy: 5 (John Young) Mason **8** (George) Bancroft
postmaster general: 7 (Cave) Johnson
born: 2 NC **17** Mecklenburg County
died/buried: 2 TN **9** Nashville
education: 11 prep schools **16** tutored privately
University: 13 North Carolina
religion: 9 Methodist
political career: 16 state legislature **17** Speaker of the House **24** US House of Representatives
governor of: 9 Tennessee
civilian career: 6 lawyer
notable events of lifetime/term:
boundary dispute: 9 Northwest
discovery in California of: 4 gold
Proviso: 6 Wilmot
treaty of: 16 Guadalupe Hidalgo
war: 7 Mexican

father: 6 Samuel
mother: 4 Jane
siblings: 7 John Lee **9** Jane Maria, Naomi Tate **10** Lydia Eliza **12** Marshall Tate, Samuel Wilson **14** William Hawkins **15** Franklin Ezekiel, Ophelia Clarissa
wife: 5 Sarah (Childress)
children: 4 none
polka 5 dance **10** round dance **13** Bohemian dance
poll 4 head, vote **5** count, tally **6** census, survey, voting **7** canvass, figures, returns **8** register, sampling **9** interview, nose count **10** count noses, voting list **11** voting place
Pollack, Sydney
director of: 11 Out of Africa (Oscar) **12** The Way We Were **15** Absence of Malice **23** They Shoot Horses Don't They?
Pollock, Jackson
born: 6 Cody WY
artwork: 5 Scent **9** Blue Poles **10** The She-Wolf **11** Convergence **12** Autumn Rhythm **13** Eyes in the Heat **17** Easter and the Totem **20** Guardians of the Secret
pollutant 5 fumes, smoke, waste **7** exhaust **8** emission, impurity
pollute 4 foul, soil **5** dirty, sully **6** befoul, debase, defile **7** deprave, profane **9** desecrate **10** adulterate, make filthy **11** contaminate
polluted 4 foul **5** dirty, drunk **6** impure, soiled **7** corrupt, profane, smashed, unclean **9** poisonous **12** contaminated
pollution 7 fouling, soiling **8** defiling, dirtying, foulness, impurity **9** befouling, pollutant **11** uncleanness **12** adulteration **13** contaminating, contamination
Pollux *see* **15** Castor and Pollux
Pollyanna
director: 10 David Swift
based on story by: 13 Eleanor Porter
cast: 9 Jane Wyman **10** Karl Malden **11** Hayley Mills, Richard Egan
polo
equipment: 6 mallet
period of play: 7 chukker
championship: 10 Camacho Cup **13** Coronation Cup **16** Cup of the Americas
Polonius
character in: 6 Hamlet
author: 11 Shakespeare
Polska *see* **6** Poland
poltergeist 5 ghost **6** spirit
literally: 10 noise-ghost
manifestation: 5 knock, noise, prank
Poltergeist
director: 10 Tobe Hooper
cast: 12 Craig T Nelson **14** Jobeth Williams **16** Beatrice Straight

co-writer/producer: 15 Steven Spielberg
poltroon 6 coward, craven **7** caitiff, chicken, dastard **11** yellow-belly
polygon 10 multiangle **11** plane figure
eight-sided: 7 octagon
equal angled: 6 isogon
five-sided: 8 pentagon
four-sided: 6 square **7** rhombus **8** tetragon **9** rectangle, trapezoid
nine-sided: 7 nonagon
seven-sided: 8 heptagon
six-sided: 7 hexagon
ten-sided: 7 decagon
three-sided: 8 triangle
twelve-sided: 9 dodecagon
Polyhymnia
also: 8 Polymnia
member of: 5 Muses
personifies: 5 dance **11** sacred music
mother: 9 Mnemosyne
polymer 5 dimer, nylon **6** hydrol **7** hexamer **8** oligomer
Polynesia
name means: 11 many islands
cities: 4 Apia **7** Papeete **8** Auckland, Pago Pago **9** Nukualofa
island: 4 Cook, Line **5** Samoa, Tonga **6** Easter, Ellice, Hawaii, Midway, Tahiti, Tubuai, Tuvalu **7** Austral, Maupiti, Phoenix, Society, Tokelau, Tuamotu **8** Pitcairn **9** Marquesas **10** New Zealand **15** French Polynesia
sea: 7 Pacific
people: 3 Ati **5** Maori **6** Kanaka, Nivean, Samoan, Tongan **9** Nesogaean **10** Polynesian
explorer: 4 Cook **6** Tasman, Wallis **8** Magellan **9** Roggeveen **12** Bougainville
language: 4 Niue, Uvea **5** Maori **6** Samoan, Tongan **7** Austral, Tagalog, Tokelau **8** Hawaiian, Tahitian **9** Marquesan, Tuamatuan **10** Mangarevan
religion: 12 Christianity
place:
legendary origin: 8 Hawaiiki
feature:
chief: 5 matai
clothing: 5 pareu **6** sarong **8** lava-lava
dance: 4 hula, siva
dwelling: 4 fale
family social unit: 4 aiga
priest: 7 kahunas
supernatural power: 4 mana
food:
dish: 3 kai, poi **4** taro **8** palusami
drink: 3 ava **4** kava, kawa
Polynices
also: 10 Polyneices
father: 7 Oedipus
mother: 7 Jocasta
uncle: 5 Creon
brother: 7 Oedipus **8** Eteocles
sister: 6 Ismene **8** Antigone
killed by: 8 Eteocles

polyp 5 coral, hydra, tumor **6** growth, isopod **7** octopod **10** sea anemone
Polyphemus
form: 7 Cyclops **12** one-eyed giant
father: 6 Elatus **8** Poseidon
mother: 6 Thoosa
joined: 9 Argonauts
killed: 4 Acis
blinded by: 8 Odysseus
loved: 7 Galatea
Polyphides
king of: 6 Sicyon
vocation: 4 seer
protected: 8 Menelaus **9** Agamemnon
polyphony 7 organum **8** faburden **11** fauxbourdon **12** counterpoint
Polypoetes
king of: 10 Thesprotia
father: 6 Apollo **8** Odysseus **9** Pirithous
mother: 6 Phthia **9** Callidice **10** Hippodamia
leader of: 6 Greeks
polysaccharide 6 insulin, starch **7** dextrin **8** galactin, lichenin **9** cellulose **12** carbohydrate
Polyxena
father: 5 Priam
mother: 6 Hecuba
loved by: 8 Achilles
Pomaria *see* **7** Algeria
Pomerania
capital: 7 Stettin
city: 5 Thorn, Torun **6** Anklam
country: 6 Poland **7** Germany
island: 5 Rugen **6** Usedom
province: 7 Pomorze
pommel, pummel 4 beat, hilt, horn, knob, pake **6** finial, strike **9** saddlebow
Pomona
origin: 5 Roman
goddess of: 10 fruit trees
pomp 4 show **5** front, glory, style **7** display **8** ceremony, flourish, grandeur, splendor **9** pageantry, showiness, solemnity, spectacle **10** brilliance **11** affectation, grandiosity, ostentation, pompousness **12** magnificence **14** stately display **15** pretentiousness
pompous 4 vain **5** proud **6** lordly, uppish **7** haughty **8** affected, arrogant, mannered, overdone, puffed-up, snobbish **9** conceited, egotistic, grandiose, imperious **10** blustering, swaggering **11** overbearing, patronizing, pretentious **12** ostentatious, presumptuous, supercilious, vainglorious **13** condescending, high and mighty, self-important
Ponchielli, Amilcare
born: 5 Italy **7** Cremona
composer of: 10 La Gioconda **15** Dance of the Hours
poncho 4 cape **5** cloak, shawl **6** mantle, serape

pond 4 pool, tarn **5** basin **6** lagoon **9** small lake, water hole

ponder 4 muse **5** study **6** wonder **7** examine, reflect **8** cogitate, consider, mull over, ruminate **9** brood over, cerebrate, reflect on, speculate, think over **10** deliberate, meditate on, puzzle over **11** contemplate

ponderous 3 big **4** dull **5** bulky, heavy, hefty, large, wordy **6** boring, bovine, dreary **7** awkward, droning, hulking, labored, lumpish, massive, tedious, weighty **8** cumbrous, enormous, sluggish, unlively, unwieldy **9** corpulent, graceless, lumbering, wearisome **10** burdensome, cumbersome, long-winded, lusterless, monotonous, unexciting, ungraceful **11** heavy-handed

pontiff 4 pope **6** bishop, priest **8** pontifex

pontifical 7 pompous **8** churchly, clerical, dogmatic, priestly **9** apostolic, episcopal, imperious **11** opinionated, overbearing, patronizing, pretentious **13** authoritarian, condescending **14** ecclesiastical

Pontus
  personifies: **3** sea
  father: **2** Ge
  son: **6** Nereus **7** Phorcys

pony 3 nag **4** crib, trot **5** glass, horse, pinto **7** mustang **9** racehorse
  breed: **6** Exmoor **8** Shetland

Pooh *See* **13** Winnie-the-Pooh

pooh-pooh 5 knock **7** disdain, put down, run down, sneer at **8** belittle **9** disparage

Pooka *see* **4** Puca

pool 3 pot **4** ally, bank, lake, mere, pond, tarn **5** group, kitty, merge, share, union, unite **6** puddle, splash, stakes **7** combine **8** alliance, fishpond, millpool **9** coalition **10** amalgamate, collective **11** association, consolidate, cooperative **13** confederation

Poole, Grace
  character in: **8** Jane Eyre
  author: **6** Bronte

poop 3 fag **4** bush, deck, do in, tire **7** exhaust, fatigue, wear out **8** enervate

pooped 4 beat **5** all in, spent, tired, weary **6** bushed, done in **7** drained, wearied, worn out **8** fatigued, tired out **9** dead tired, exhausted, played out

poor 3 sad **4** bare, dead, vain, worn **5** broke, empty, needy, sorry **6** barren, fallow, faulty, futile, hard up, in need, in want, meager, paltry, wasted **7** forlorn, sterile, unhappy, unlucky, wanting **8** badly off, bankrupt, beggarly, depleted, desolate, devoid of, grieving, indigent, inferior, pathetic, pitiable, strapped, unworthy, wretched **9** defective, deficient, destitute, exhausted, fruitless, imperfect, infertile, insolvent, in straits, miserable, moneyless, penniless, unfertile, worthless **10** distressed, inadequate, pauperized **11** impecunious, unfortunate **12** impoverished, uncultivable, unproductive, unprofitable **15** poverty-stricken

Poor People
  author: **16** Fyodor Dostoevsky

Poor Richard's Almanack
  author: **16** Benjamin Franklin

Poor White
  author: **16** Sherwood Anderson

pop 4 bang, boom, come, shot, snap, soda **5** arise, blast, burst, crack **6** appear, report **7** explode **8** detonate **9** discharge, explosion, soft drink **10** detonation

pope 3 Leo **4** John, Paul, Pius **5** Peter, Urban **6** Adrian, Eugene, Julius, Martin, Sixtus **7** Clement, Gregory **8** Benedict, Innocent, John Paul, Nicholas **9** Alexander, Callistus
  also: **12** Bishop of Rome **13** Vicar of Christ **14** Primate of Italy, Supreme Pontiff **16** Archbishop of Rome **18** Metropolitan of Rome, Patriarch of the West **25** Servant of the Servants of God
  office: **6** Papacy **7** Holy See **11** Seat of Peter
  elected by: **18** College of Cardinals
  elected in: **8** conclave
  signal that election is concluded: **10** white smoke
  resides: **4** Rome **10** the Vatican **11** Vatican City
  former residence: **13** Lateran Palace
  summer residence: **14** Castel Gondolfo
  papal land holding: **9** patrimony **21** patrimony of Saint Peter
  first pope: **10** Saint Peter
  pope who crowned Charlemagne: **6** Leo III
  pope who excommunicated Luther: **4** Leo X
  pope who authorized Michelangelo to paint Sistine Chapel: **8** Julius II
  "September Pope": **9** John Paul I
  original name of pope:
    Alexander VI: **15** Rodrigo de Borgia
    Callistus III: **15** Alfonso de Borgia
    Clement VII: **14** Giulio de' Medici
    John XXIII: **22** Angelo Giuseppe Roncalli
    John Paul I: **13** Albino Luciani
    John Paul II: **12** Karol Wojtyla **18** Archbishop of Krakow
    Leo X: **16** Giovanni de' Medici
    Pius XI: **12** Achille Ratti
    Pius XII: **35** Eugenio Maria Giuseppe Giovanni Pacelli
  popes of Avignon papacy: **6** Urban V **8** Clement V, John XXII **9** Clement VI, Gregory XI, Nicholas V **10** Innocent VI **11** Benedict XII
  popes during Great Western Schism:
    Avignon: **10** Clement VII **12** Benedict XIII
    Pisa: **9** John XXIII **10** Alexander V
    Rome: **7** Urban VI **10** Boniface IX, Gregory XII **11** Innocent VII
  papal bull/encyclical: **11** Unam sanctam **12** Humanae vitae, Rerum novarum, Vox in excelso **13** Pacem in terris **15** Mater et magistra **19** Populorum progressio **22** Sacerdotalis caelibatus

Pope, Alexander
  author of: **10** The Dunciad **12** An Essay on Man **15** Eloisa to Abelard **16** The Rape of the Lock **18** An Essay on Criticism **20** Epistle to Dr Arbuthnot

Pope, John Russell
  architect of: **17** Jefferson Memorial **20** National Gallery of Art **23** Temple of the Scottish Rite **24** National Archives Building

Popeye
  character in: **9** Sanctuary
  author: **8** Faulkner

Popeye
  cartoonist: **10** Elzie Segar
  character: **5** Bluto, Wimpy **7** Swee' Pea **8** Olive Oyl
  food: **7** spinach

popinjay 3 fop **4** beau **5** dandy **7** coxcomb

poplar 7 Populus **22** Liriodendron tulipifera
  varieties: **4** gray **5** black, downy, tulip, white **6** balsam, Eugene, yellow **8** Car- olina, Lombardy, necklace **10** Queensland **12** Chinese white, silver-leaved **13** Western balsam

poppy 7 Papaver
  varieties: **3** sea **4** blue, bush, corn, snow, tree, wind, wood **5**·field, opium, plume, satin, tulip, water, Welsh **6** arctic, desert, horned **7** Asiatic, flaming, Iceland, Mexican, prickly, Shirley, Western **8** Flanders, harebell, Matilija, oriental **9** Celandine **10** California, island tree **12** Mexican tulip **13** yellow Chinese **14** California tree
  drug: **5** opium **6** heroin **8** morphine

poppycock 3 rot **4** bosh, bunk, jive, tosh **5** froth, fudge, hooey, stuff, trash **6** drivel, humbug **7** baloney, blabber, blather, eyewash, fustian, garbage, hogwash, inanity, prattle, rubbish, twaddle **8** falderal, flummery, nonsense, tommyrot, wish-wash **9** absurdity, gibberish, moonshine, rigmarole **10** applesauce, balderdash, flapdoodle, hocus-pocus, mumbo-jumbo, rigamarole **11** abracadabra, jabberwocky **12** fiddlefaddle, gobble-dygook

poppy seed
  botanical name: **7** Papaver **11** P somniferum (sleep- bearing poppy)
  color: **4** blue **5** white

origin: 4 Asia **6** Europe
guards against: 9 creditors
use: 5 bread, cakes, rolls **6** sweets **10** vegetables **11** butter sauce

populace 4 folk **6** people, public **7** society **9** citizenry, community **10** population

popular 5 cheap, civic, civil, stock **6** famous, public, social **7** admired, current, general, in favor **8** accepted, approved, communal, familiar, favorite, in demand, national, orthodox **9** community, preferred, prevalent, well-known, well-liked **10** affordable, celebrated, democratic **11** established, fashionable, inexpensive, of the people, sought-after

popularity 4 fame, note **5** favor, glory, kudos, vogue **6** esteem, regard, renown, repute **7** acclaim, fashion **8** approval **9** celebrity, notoriety **10** acceptance, admiration, notability, reputation **11** acclamation

popular opinion
 Latin: 9 vox populi

popular whim 3 fad **4** rage **5** craze, mania **7** passion **11** infatuation

populate 6 occupy, people, settle **7** inhabit

populated 5 urban **7** peopled, settled **8** citified, occupied **9** inhabited

population 4 folk **6** people, public **8** citizens, populace **9** citizenry, habitancy, residents **11** body politic, commonality, inhabitants

populous 5 dense **6** jammed **7** crowded, peopled, teeming **8** swarming, thronged

porcelain 5 china **11** ceramic ware

porch 4 stoa **5** lanai, stoop **7** balcony, narthex, portico, veranda **8** solarium, verandah **9** colonnade, vestibule

pore 4 hole, read, scan **5** probe, study **6** outlet, peruse, ponder, review, search, survey **7** dig into, examine, explore, inspect, orifice **8** aperture, consider **9** delve into

Porfiry
 character in: 18 Crime and Punishment
 author: 10 Dostoevsky

Porgy
 author: 13 DuBose Heyward

Porgy and Bess
 opera by: 14 George Gershwin
 character: 4 Bess **5** Clara, Crown, Porgy **6** Serena **11** Sportin' Life
 setting: 10 Catfish Row

pornographic 4 blue, lewd **5** bawdy, dirty, gross **6** coarse, filthy, smutty, vulgar **7** obscene **8** indecent, off-color, prurient **9** salacious **10** lascivious, licentious

porous 4 lacy **6** spongy **7** riddled **8** cellular, pervious **9** absorbent, permeable, sievelike **10** penetrable **11** honeycombed

porpoise 4 leap **5** whale **6** palach, puffer, seahog **7** cowfish, dolphin, surface **8** cetacean
 genus: 8 Phocaena **9** Delphinus

porridge 4 pobs, samp **5** atole, brose, brout, gruel **6** cereal **7** crowdie, oatmeal, polenta **8** flummery

porringer 4 bowl, dish **6** vessel **9** container **10** receptacle

Porsena, Lars
 nationality: 8 Etruscan
 attacked: 4 Rome
 to reinstate: 7 Tarquin

port 4 dock, pier, quay **5** haven, wharf **6** harbor, refuge **7** dry dock, landing, mooring, seaport, shelter **9** anchorage, harborage **11** destination

port
 type: 4 wine **6** brandy
 origin: 8 Portugal
 variety: 4 ruby **5** tawny **7** vintage
 with brandy: 9 Betsy Ross
 with vermouth: 10 Broken Spur

portable 5 handy, light, small **6** bantam, pocket **7** compact, folding, movable **8** cartable, haulable, liftable **9** ready-to-go **10** convenient, conveyable, manageable, vest-pocket **11** pocket-sized

portal, portals 4 adit, arch, door, gate **5** entry **6** wicket **7** doorway, gateway, portico **8** approach, entrance **9** threshold, vestibule **10** portcullis **11** entranceway

Port-au-Prince
 capital of: 5 Haiti

porte-monnaie 5 purse **10** pocketbook **12** money-carrier

portend 4 bode **5** augur **6** denote, herald, warn of **7** bespeak, betoken, point to, predict, presage, signify, suggest **8** forebode, forecast, foretell, forewarn, prophesy **9** foretoken, prefigure **10** foreshadow

portent 4 omen, sign **5** token **6** augury, boding, threat **7** presage, warning **9** harbinger **10** foreboding **11** forewarning

portentous 6 superb **7** amazing, fateful, ominous, pompous **8** alarming, menacing **9** bombastic, grandiose, prophetic **10** foreboding, incredible, prodigious, remarkable, stupendous, surprising **11** astonishing, exceptional, frightening, pretentious, significant, superlative, threatening **12** inauspicious, intimidating, unpropitious

porter 4 brew **5** stout **6** bearer, coolie, redcap, skycap **7** carrier **8** conveyer **9** conductor

Porter, Katherine Anne
 author of: 11 Ship of Fools **12** Old Mortality **14** Flowering Judas **15** The Leaning Tower **18** Pale Horse Pale Rider

Porter, William Sidney
 real name of: 6 O Henry

portfolio 4 case, file **5** album **6** binder, folder **7** dossier **8** envelope **9** scrapbook **10** securities

Porthos
 character in: 18 The Three Musketeers
 author: 5 Dumas (pere)

Portia
 character in: 12 Julius Caesar **19** The Merchant of Venice
 author: 11 Shakespeare

portico 4 stoa **5** lanai **6** piazza **7** balcony, veranda, walkway

portion 3 cut, lot, sum **4** dole, doom, fate, luck, part **5** carve, cut up, moira, piece, sever, share, slice, split **6** amount, divide, kismet, parcel, ration, sector **7** break up, deal out, destiny, fortune, helping, measure, section, segment, serving **8** allocate, disperse, division, fraction, fragment, quantity, separate **9** allotment, allowance, demarcate, partition **10** allocation, distribute, percentage

portion out 5 allot **6** ration **7** dole out, mete out, prorate **8** allocate, dispense, divide up **9** apportion, parcel out **10** distribute, measure out

Portland
 basketball team: 12 Trail Blazers
 football team: 8 Breakers
 river: 8 Columbia **10** Willamette
 university: 4 Reed

Port Louis
 capital of: 9 Mauritius

portly 3 big, fat **4** full **5** beefy, burly, heavy, large, obese, plump, pudgy, round, stout, tubby **6** brawny, chubby, fleshy, rotund, stocky **9** corpulent

Portman, John
 architect of: 15 Peachtree Center (Atlanta)

portmanteau 3 bag **4** grip **5** cloak **6** mantle, valise **8** suitcase **9** gladstone

Port Moresby
 capital of: 9 New Guinea

Portnoy's Complaint
 author: 10 Philip Roth

Port of Spain
 capital of: 17 Trinidad and Tobago

Porto-Novo
 capital of: 5 Benin

portrait 5 cameo **6** sketch **7** drawing, picture **8** likeness, painting, vignette **9** depiction **10** impression, photograph **11** description

Portrait of a Lady, The
 author: 10 Henry James
 character: 11 Madame Merle, Pansy Osmond **12** Isabel Archer **13** Gilbert Osmond, Lord Warburton, Ralph

Touchett **14** Caspar Goodwood **18** Henrietta Stackpole

Portrait of the Artist as a Young Man
author: 10 James Joyce
character: 4 Emma **12** Simon Dedalus **14** Stephen Dedalus

portray 3 ape **4** draw, play **5** carve, enact, mimic, model, paint **6** depict, detail, figure, pose as, sketch **7** imitate, narrate, picture **8** describe, set forth, simulate **9** delineate, represent, sculpture **10** illustrate, photograph **11** impersonate **12** characterize

portrayal 7 picture **8** portrait **9** picturing **11** delineation, description **14** representation **16** characterization

ports
god of: 8 Portunus

Portugal
capital/largest city: 6 Lisbon
others: 4 Beja, Faro, Ovar **5** Braga, Evora, Olhao, Porto, Viseu **6** Aveiro, Guarda, Leiria, Oporto, Sintra **7** Algarve, Amadora, Bragama, Cascoes, Coimbra, Covilha, Estoril, Funchal, Granada, Setubal **8** Barreiro, Portimao **9** Lusitania **10** Portalegre **14** Vila Nova de Gaia
  Roman city: 10 Portus Cale
school: 5 Minho **6** Aveiro, Lisbon, Oporto **7** Coimbra
division: 3 Goa **4** Tejo, Tete **5** Beira, Evora, Macao, Minho, Timor **6** Azores, Loanda **7** Algarve, Madeira **8** Alemteho, Rebatejo **9** Cape Verde **10** Mozambique **11** Estremadura
  Roman district: 9 Lusitania
measure: 2 pe **4** bota, moio, vara **5** almud, fanga, geira, linha, milha **6** almude, covado **7** alquier, ferrado, selamin **8** alqueire
monetary unit: 3 avo, rei **4** peca, real **5** conto, crown, dobra, indio, justo, rupia **6** escudo, macuta, octave, pataca, testad, tostao, vintem **7** angalar, centavo, crusado, miereis, testone **8** equipaga, johannes
weight: 4 onca, once **5** libra, marco **6** arroba **7** arratel **9** excropulo
island: 6 Azores **7** Madeira **8** Terceira
mountain: 4 Acor, Lapa **5** Gerez, Marao, Mousa **6** Bornes, Peneda **7** Larouco **8** Caramulo **9** Caldeirao, Monchique **14** Serra da Estrela
highest point: 11 Pico da Serra
river: 3 Sor, Tua **4** Lima, Mino, Mira, Sado, Seda, Tago, Tajo, Tejo, Vara **5** Douro, Duero, Le goa, Micha, Minho, Sabar, Tagus, Vouga, Zatas **6** Cavado, Chanca, Quarto, Tamega, Zezere **7** Mondego, Selamin, Sorraia **8** Quadiana, Tonelada
ocean: 8 Atlantic
physical feature:
  bay: 7 Setubal
  cape: 4 Roca **7** Mondego **8** Espichel **9** St Vincent

  peninsula: 7 Iberian
  port: 4 Faro **6** Aveiro, Lisbon, Oporto **7** Leixoes
people: 4 Celt, Moor **7** Iberian **10** Portuguese
  artist: 7 Pereira **9** Goncalves **13** Soares dos Reis
  author: 5 Dinis **6** Camoes, Vieira **7** Garrett, Vicente **9** Deus-Ramos
  explorer: 3 Cam, Cao **4** Dias, Diaz **6** Cabral, Da Gama **7** Almeida **8** Magellan **11** Albuquerque **23** Prince Henry the Navigator
  king: 6 Manuel, Philip, Sancho **7** Alfonso **9** Ferdinand, Sebastian
  leader: 5 Eanes **6** Dombal, Soares **7** Caetano, Carmona, Salazar, Spinola
  queen: 5 Maria **9** Elizabeth
language: 10 Portuguese
religion: 13 Roman Catholic
place:
  church: 5 Jesus **6** Christ **11** Os Jeronimos, Sao Lourenco **12** Old Cathedral **13** Santa Engracia **16** Sao Vicente de Fora
  city square: 15 Praca do Comercio
  dam: 6 Belver, Idanha **13** Castelo do Bode
  fortress-church: 12 Leco do Bailio
  monastery: 8 Alcobaca **12** Hieronymites **20** Santa Maria da Victoira
  monument: 11 Discoveries
  museum: 13 Soares dos Reis
  palace: 6 Cintra
  shrine: 6 Fatima
colony: 5 Macad, Macao
  former colony: 3 Goa **5** Timor **6** Angola **7** Sao Tome **8** Principe, St Thomas **9** Cape Verde **10** Mozambique **12** Guinea Bissau
feature:
  song: 4 fado
food:
  dish: 8 bacalhau, bucellas **10** calcavella **11** carcavellos
  sausage: 8 linguica
  wine: 4 port **7** madeira

Portuguese Guinea *see* **12** Guinea-Bissau

Portuguese West Africa *see* **6** Angola

Portunus
origin: 5 Roman
god of: 5 ports **7** harbors

posada 3 inn **12** halting place

pose 3 air, set **4** cast, mien **5** group, order, state, style **6** line up, stance, submit **7** advance, arrange, bearing, bring up, posture, present, propose, show off, suggest **8** attitude, carriage, position, propound, set forth, throw out **9** mannerism, postulate **10** put forward

Poseidon
also: 9 Asphalius
origin: 5 Greek
god of: 3 sea

caused: 11 earthquakes
father: 6 Cronos
mother: 4 Rhea
brother: 4 Zeus
wife: 10 Amphitrite
lover: 2 Ge **6** Aethra, Medusa, Thoosa **7** Demeter
child: 5 Arion **6** Triton **7** Antaeus, Pegasus, Theseus **8** Chrysaor **10** Polyphemus
symbol: 5 horse **7** trident
epithet: 11 Ennosigaeus, Hippocurius **12** Prosclystius
corresponds to: 7 Neptune

poser 5 facer **6** puzzle **7** problem **8** examiner, stickler

posh 4 chic **5** fancy, ritzy, smart, swell **6** chi-chi, classy, deluxe, lavish, swanky **7** elegant, opulent, refined, stylish **9** high-class, luxurious **11** extravagant

position 3 fix, job, put, set **4** duty, pose, post, role, site **5** array, caste, class, locus, lodge, order, place, stand, state **6** career, charge, ground, locate, office, plight, stance, status **7** arrange, deposit, opinion, outlook, posture, situate, station, vantage **8** attitude, capacity, eminence, function, locality, location, prestige, standing **9** condition, elevation, establish, placement, situation, viewpoint **10** assignment, commission, importance, notability, prominence **11** appointment, consequence, disposition, distinction, frame of mind, point of view

position decided upon
French: 9 parti pris

positive 4 firm, good, real, sure **5** total **6** narrow, useful **7** assured, certain, gainful, helpful **8** absolute, cocksure, complete, decisive, definite, dogmatic, explicit, obdurate, salutary **9** assertive, confident, convinced, effective, immovable, practical, satisfied, veritable **10** applicable, autocratic, beneficial, conclusive, definitive, optimistic, undisputed, undoubting **11** affirmative, cooperative, dead certain, dictatorial, irrefutable, opinionated, overbearing, practicable, progressive, self-assured, serviceable, unequivocal, unqualified **12** confirmatory, constructive, contributory, unchangeable **13** corroborative, thoroughgoing **16** incontrovertible

positively 9 assuredly, certainly, decidedly, literally **10** absolutely, definitely **11** confidently, indubitably **12** emphatically, indisputably, unmistakably, without doubt **13** affirmatively, categorically, unqualifiedly **14** beyond question, unhesitatingly, unquestionably

possess 3 own **4** grab, have, hold **5** boast, enjoy **6** absorb, fixate, obsess, occupy **7** acquire, bedevil, bewitch, command, conquer, consume, control, enchant, overrun **8** dominate, maintain, take over, vanquish **9** fascinate, hypnotize, influence, mesmerize

Possessed, The
  author: 16 Fyodor Dostoevsky
  character: 5 Marya, Pyotr **6** Shatov **7** Nikolay **16** Varvara Stavrogin **17** Stepan Verhovensky

possession 4 hold **5** asset, poise, title **6** effect, owning **7** command, control, control, custody, tenancy **8** calmness, coolness, dominion, province, resource **9** belonging, composure, occupancy, ownership, placidity, sangfroid, territory **10** equanimity, even temper, occupation, possessing **11** equilibrium, self-control **12** accoutrement, protectorate

possibility 4 hope, odds, risk **6** chance, gamble, hazard **7** promise **8** prospect **9** prospects **10** likelihood **11** contingency, eventuality, feasibility, probability, workability **12** potentiality **14** practicability

possible 8 credible, feasible, workable **9** potential, thinkable **10** achievable, admissible, attainable, cognizable, compatible, contingent, imaginable, manageable, obtainable, reasonable **11** conceivable, performable, practicable **12** hypothetical

possibly 5 at all, maybe **6** mayhap **7** could be, perhaps **8** in any way, normally **9** at the most, perchance **10** by any means, God willing **11** conceivably

post 2 PX **3** fix, job, put, set **4** base, beat, camp, pale, part, pile, pole, role, seat, send, spot, work **5** brace, house, lodge, place, put up, round, shaft, stake **6** advise, column, inform, locate, notify, office, picket, report, settle, splint, tack up **7** apprise, declare, install, mission, publish, quarter, routine, situate, station, support, upright **8** acquaint, announce, capacity, disclose, exchange, fasten up, function, instruct, mainstay, position, proclaim **9** advertise, broadcast, circulate, enlighten, establish, make known, situation **10** assignment, settlement

postdate 6 follow **7** succeed **9** come after

poster 4 bill, sign **6** notice **7** placard **8** bulletin **13** advertisement

posterior 3 bum, can **4** back, butt, prat, rear, rump, seat, tail, tush **5** fanny, stern, tushy **6** behind, bottom, caudal, dorsal, hinder **7** keister **8** backside, buttocks, derriere, hindmost, rearward **9** aftermost

posterity 5 heirs, issue, young **6** family **7** descent, history, lineage, progeny **8** children **9** offspring **10** succession, successors **11** descendants

post hoc, ergo propter hoc 29 after

this therefore because of it
  describes: 14 logical fallacy

Posthumus, Leonatus
  character in: 9 Cymbeline
  author: 11 Shakespeare

Postman Always Rings Twice, The
  director: 10 Tay Garnett
  based on story by: 10 James M Cain
  cast: 10 Hume Cronym, Lana Turner **12** John Garfield **13** Cecil Kellaway

postpone 4 stay **5** defer, delay, table, waive **6** put off, remand, shelve **7** adjourn, lay over, reserve, suspend

postponement 4 stay **5** delay **6** recess **7** tabling **8** abeyance, deferral **9** deferment, extension **10** suspension

postscript 2 ps **5** rider **7** codicil **8** addendum **10** attachment

postulate 5 axiom, guess **6** assume, hazard, submit, theory **7** premise, presume, propose, surmise, theorem **8** put forth, theorize **9** speculate **10** assumption, conjecture, hypothesis, presuppose **11** hypothesize, presumption

posture 3 air, set **4** case, mien, mood, pose, post, tone **5** phase, place, shape, state, tenor **6** aspect, stance, status **7** bearing, contour, station **8** attitude, carriage, position, standing **9** condition, situation **11** predicament **12** circumstance

Postvorta
  form: 5 nymph
  member of: 7 Camenae
  knowledge of: 4 past

posy 5 bloom, motto **6** flower, phrase **7** blossom, bouquet, corsage, garland, nosegay

pot 3 pan **4** ruin **5** crock, kitty **6** vessel **9** container, marijuana **11** rack and ruin
  Spanish: 4 olla

potable 3 ale **5** clean, drink, water **6** liquor **8** beverage, quencher **9** drinkable

potage 4 soup **9** thick soup

potassium
  chemical symbol: 1 K

potato 16 Solanum tuberosum
  varieties: 3 air, yam **4** duck, swan, wild, Zulu **5** Idaho, Irish, Maine, rural, swamp, sweet, white **6** Russet **7** Burbank, epicure, prairie, Telinga
  dish: 4 chip **5** baked, salad **6** mashed **8** au gratin **9** lyonnaise, scalloped **11** french fries **12** baked stuffed

Potawatomi
  language family: 9 Algonkian **10** Algonquian
  location: 4 Ohio **6** Kansas **7** Indiana **8** Illinois, Michigan, Oklahoma **9** Wisconsin
  leader: 7 Pontiac
  united with: 6 Ojibwa, Ottawa **7** Ojibway

Potemkin

director: 17 Sergei Eisenstein
  cast: 14 Vladimir Barsky **16** Alexander Antonov **17** Grigori Alexandrov
  famous segment: 11 Odessa Steps

potency 3 vis **5** force, power **6** energy **8** efficacy, strength, virility, vitality

potent 5 solid, tough **6** mighty, strong **7** dynamic **8** forceful, forcible, powerful, vigorous **9** effective, operative **10** compelling, convincing, formidable, impressive, persuasive **11** efficacious, influential **12** overpowering

potentate 4 lord **5** chief, mogul, ruler **6** prince, satrap, sultan **7** emperor, monarch **8** overlord, suzerain **9** chieftain, sovereign

potential 6 covert, hidden, latent **7** dormant, lurking, passive **8** implicit, possible **9** concealed, quiescent, unexerted **10** unapparent, unrealized **11** conceivable, undisclosed, unexpressed

potentiality 7 ability **10** capability **13** possibilities

potentially
  Latin: 7 in posse

pother 3 ado **4** fuss, stir, to-do **6** bustle, flurry, hustle, tumult **8** activity **9** agitation, commotion

Pothos
  companion of: 9 Aphrodite
  personifies: 6 desire **7** longing

potion 4 brew, dram **5** draft, toddy **6** elixir **7** mixture, philter **8** libation, potation **10** concoction

Potlatch people see **8** Kwakiutl

Pot of Gold, The
  author: 7 Plautus

Potok, Chaim
  author of: 9 The Chosen **10** Wanderings **15** The Book of Lights

potpourri 4 hash, mess, olio, stew **6** jumble, medley, mosaic, motley **7** farrago, goulash, melange, mixture **8** mishmash, pastiche **9** patchwork **10** hodgepodge, miscellany, salmagundi **11** gallimaufry, olla podrida

pottage 4 soup, stew **6** brewis **8** porridge

Potter, Beatrix
  author of: 11 (The Tale of) Peter Rabbit **21** The Tailor of Gloucester

Potter, Muff
  character in: 9 Tom Sawyer
  author: 5 Twain

potter's field 8 boneyard, cemetery **9** graveyard **12** burial ground **13** burying ground

pottery 5 china **8** clayware, crockery **11** ceramic ware, earthenware

pouch 3 bag, kit, sac **4** sack **5** purse **6** pocket, wallet **7** handbag, satchel **8** carryall, ditty bag, reticule, rucksack **9** container **10** pocketbook, receptacle

Poulenc, Francis
  born: 5 Paris **6** France
  member of: 6 Les Six, The Six

composer of: 9 Les Biches **13** The Carmelites **22** Dialogues des Carmelites

poultice 7 plaster **8** dressing **10** medicament

poultry 3 hen **4** cock, duck, fowl, swan **5** capon, geese, goose, quail **6** grouse, layers, pigeon, turkey **7** chicken, peacock, rooster **8** pheasant **9** partridge **10** guinea fowl
breed: 6 Ancona, Bantam **7** Cornish, Dorking, Leghorn **9** Wyandotte **12** Plymouth Rock **14** Rhode Island Red
disease: 3 pip **4** roup, tick
farm: 7 hennery
house: 4 coop

pounce 4 jump, leap **5** fly at, swoop **6** ambush, dash at, jump at, plunge, snatch, spring **8** downrush, fall upon, surprise

Pounce, Peter
character in: 13 Joseph Andrews
author: 8 Fielding

pound 4 bang, beat, drub, drum, maul **5** clomp, clout, crush, grind, march, paste, smack, stomp, throb, thump, tramp **6** batter, bruise, cudgel, hammer, pummel, strike, thrash, thwack, wallop **7** clobber, crumble, pulsate, thunder, trounce **8** lambaste **9** fustigate, palpitate, pulverize **13** sixteen ounces
abbreviation: 2 lb

Pound, Ezra
author of: 6 Cantos **8** Personae **11** Exultations, Pisan Cantos

pound troy
abbreviation: 3 lb t

pour 3 tap **4** drip, drop, flow, gush, ooze, rain, seep, slop **5** drain, flood, issue, spill, spout **6** decant, deluge, drench, effuse, squirt, stream **7** cascade, draw off, dribble, lade out **15** rain cats and dogs **16** come down in sheets **17** come down in buckets

pourboire 3 tip **8** gratuity
literally: 11 for drinking

pourparler 29 informal preliminary conference
literally: 10 for talking

Poussin, Nicholas
born: 6 France **10** Les Andelys
artwork: 10 The Seasons **14** Birth of Bacchus, St John on Patmos **17** Bacchanalian Revel **18** The Burial of Phocion **19** The Poet's Inspiration **20** The Arcadian Shepherds **23** Landscape with Polyphemus, The Holy Family on the Steps **27** The Adoration of the Golden Calf

pou sto 14 place to stand on, where I may stand **16** base of operations

pout 4 crab, fret, fume, mope, sulk **5** brood, frown, lower, scowl **6** glower
French: 4 moue

poverty 4 lack, need, want **6** dearth, penury **7** beggary, deficit, paucity **8** scarcity, shortage **9** indigence, neediness, pauperism, privation **10** bankruptcy, deficiency, insolvency, meagerness, mendicancy **11** destitution **13** insufficiency, pennilessness **14** impoverishment

poverty-stricken 4 poor **5** broke, needy **8** indigent **9** destitute, penniless **10** down and out

powder 4 dust, talc **5** emery **6** pollen, talcum **7** crumble **9** pulverize
antiseptic: 6 formin **7** aristol
applier: 4 puff
cookery: 4 soda
cosmetic: 5 blush, rouge **7** compact
poisonous: 5 robin

powder-blue 5 azure **6** pastel **7** skyblue **8** pale-blue **9** light-blue, robin's egg

powdery 5 dusty, mealy **6** chalky, floury, grated, ground, milled **7** crushed, pestled **8** shredded **10** comminuted, pulverized, triturated

Powell, Dick
real name: 14 Richard E Powell
born: 14 Mountain View AR
wife: 11 June Allyson **12** Joan Blondell
costar: 10 Ruby Keeler
roles: 7 Mrs Mike **8** Cornered **12** Johnny O'Clock **13** Murder My Sweet **15** Footlight Parade **17** Fortysecond Street **32** Gold Diggers of Nineteen Thirty-three

Powell, Jane
real name: 12 Suzanne Burce
born: 10 Portland OR
roles: 5 Irene **12** Royal Wedding **13** A Date with Judy **27** Seven Brides for Seven Brothers

Powell, John
nickname: 4 Boog
sport: 8 baseball
team: 16 Baltimore Orioles

Powell, Michael
codirector: 17 Emeric Pressburger
director of: 11 The Red Shoes **14** Black Narcissus **16** Stairway to Heaven

Powell, SR
creator/artist of: 22 Sheena Queen of the Jungle

Powell, William
born: 12 Pittsburgh PA
wife: 13 Carole Lombard
costar: 8 Myrna Loy
roles: 10 Philo Vance, The Thin Man **11** Nick Charles **12** My Man Godfrey **13** Mister Roberts **14** Life with Father **16** The Great Ziegfeld **22** How to Marry a Millionaire

power 4 gift, sway **5** brawn, force, might, right, ruler, skill, vigor **6** energy, genius, muscle, status, talent **7** faculty, license, operate, potency, quality **8** activate, aptitude, capacity, energize, iron grip, pressure, prestige, property, strength, vitality **9** attribute, authority, endowment, influence, puissance **10** capability, competence
Latin: 3 vis

Power, Tyrone
born: 12 Cincinnati OH
wife: 9 Annabella **14** Linda Christian
roles: 10 Jesse James **12** Blood and Sand **13** The Razor's Edge **14** Nightmare Alley, The Mark of Zorro **15** The Sun Also Rises **18** Captain from Castile

powerful 5 hardy, husky, stout **6** brawny, cogent, mighty, moving, potent, robust, sturdy **7** intense, rousing **8** athletic, emphatic, exciting, forceful, incisive, muscular, stalwart, vigorous **9** effective, energetic, herculean, strapping **10** able-bodied, commanding, invincible

powerhouse 9 strongman **10** power plant **15** generating plant

powerless 4 weak **6** feeble, infirm **7** unarmed **8** crippled, disabled, feckless, helpless, impotent **9** incapable, pregnable, prostrate **10** impuissant, vulnerable, weaponless **11** debilitated, defenseless, immobilized **13** incapacitated

powerlessness 8 debility, weakness **9** impotence, inability, infirmity **10** enervation, feebleness, inadequacy, incapacity **12** helplessness, incapability, inefficiency **13** vulnerability

Power Politics
author: 14 Margaret Atwood

powers that be 9 higher-ups **10** government **11** authorities **13** establishment **14** administration

Powhatan
language family: 9 Algonkian **10** Algonquian
tribe: 11 Confederacy
location: 8 Atlantic, Maryland, Virginia
leader: 8 Powhatan **11** Opechancano **13** Wahunsonacock
member: 10 Pocahontas

powwow 4 meet, talk **5** forum **6** caucus, confer, huddle, parley **7** consult, convene, council, discuss, meeting, palaver **8** assembly, colloquy, conclave, congress **9** discourse, interview **10** colloquium, conference, convention, discussion, round table **12** consultation

Poyser, Martin
character in: 8 Adam Bede
author: 5 Eliot

practicable 6 doable, viable **8** feasible, possible, workable **9** practical **10** achievable, attainable, functional

practical 4 able **5** solid, sound **6** expert, useful, versed **7** skilled, trained, veteran, working **8** seasoned, sensible, skillful **9** efficient, judicious, practiced, pragmatic, qualified, realistic **10**

functional, hardheaded, instructed, proficient, systematic, unromantic **11** down-to-earth, experienced, pragmatical, serviceable, utilitarian **12** accomplished, businesslike, matter-of-fact **13** unsentimental

practical joke 4 jape **5** caper, prank, stunt, trick

practically 6 all but, almost, nearly **8** actually, in effect **9** basically, in the main, just about, virtually **11** essentially **13** fundamentally, substantially

practice 2 do **3** use, way **4** deed, mode, play, rule, ruse, ways, wont **5** apply, dodge, drill, habit, train, trick, usage **6** action, custom, device, effect, follow, manner, method, pursue, ritual, work at **7** conduct, fashion, perform, process, qualify, routine, utilize **8** carry out, engage in, exercise, live up to, maneuver, rehearse, tendency, training **9** execution, operation, perform in, procedure, rehearsal, seasoning, set to work, turn to use **10** discipline, observance, prepare for, repetition **11** application, be engaged in, performance, preparation

practiced 4 able, fine **5** adept **6** adroit, expert **7** capable, drilled, pursued, skilled, trained **8** masterly, polished, seasoned, skillful, worked at **9** competent, engaged in, masterful, qualified, rehearsed **10** cultivated, proficient **11** experienced, prepared for **12** accomplished

practice sorcery 5 charm **7** bewitch, conjure, enchant **9** work magic **10** cast a spell

Practicing History
author: **15** Barbara W Tuchman

practitioner 6 doctor **7** dentist **9** performer **12** professional

pragmatic 5 sober **8** sensible **9** hardnosed, practical, realistic **10** hardheaded, hard-boiled **11** down-to-earth, utilitarian **12** businesslike, matter-of-fact, unidealistic **13** materialistic, unsentimental

Praia
capital of: **9** Cape Verde

prairie 3 bay **5** llano, pampa, plain **6** camass, meadow, steppe **7** quamash **9** grassland
apple: **9** breadroot
berry: **9** trampillo
chicken: **6** grouse
dog: **6** gopher, marmot
schooner: **12** covered wagon
state: **8** Illinois
wolf: **6** coyote

Prairie, The
author: **19** James Fenimore Cooper
character: **4** Inez **9** Dr Battius, Ellen Wade, Hard-Heart, Paul Hover **10** Esther Bush **11** Abiram White, Ishmael Bush, Natty Bumppo **16** Captain Middleton

Prairie State
nickname of: **8** Illinois

praise 4 laud, tout **5** cheer, exalt, extol, honor **6** esteem, eulogy, hurrah, regard, revere **7** acclaim, applaud, approve, build up, commend, glorify, plaudit, respect, root for, tribute, worship **8** accolade, applause, approval, encomium, eulogize, venerate **9** adoration, celebrate, good words, laudation, panegyric **10** admiration, compliment, panegyrize **11** approbation, compliments, testimonial **12** appreciation, commendation, congratulate **14** congratulation
Hebrew: **6** hallel

praise be to God
Latin: **7** laus Deo

praiseful 8 praising **9** extolling, laudatory **10** plauditory **12** commendatory **13** complimentary

praiseworthiness 5 merit **10** excellence **12** admirability, desirability **14** commendability

praiseworthy 4 fine **6** worthy **8** laudable **9** admirable, estimable, excellent, exemplary **11** commendable, meritorious

pram, praam, prahm 4 boat **5** buggy **6** vessel **7** rowboat **8** carriage, stroller **12** perambulator

prance 4 jump, leap, romp, skip **5** bound, caper, dance, frisk, strut, vault **6** bounce, cavort, frolic, gambol, spring **7** swagger

prank 4 joke, lark **5** antic, caper, spoof, stunt, trick **6** gambol **8** escapade, mischief **9** horseplay **10** shenanigan, tomfoolery

prate 3 gab, yak **4** blah, brag, chat, crow, talk **5** boast **6** babble, gabble, jabber **7** blabber, chatter, prattle, twaddle, twattle

Prathet Thai see **8** Thailand

prattle 3 gab, yak **4** blab **5** prate **6** babble, gabble, hot air, jabber **7** blather, chatter, twaddle **8** cackling, chitchat, gabbling **9** gibbering, jabbering

Pravda 15 Soviet newspaper
literally: **5** truth

pray 3 beg, bid, sue **4** urge **5** cry to, plead **7** beseech, entreat, implore, request, solicit **8** call upon, invocate, petition **9** importune **10** supplicate

prayer 6 litany, orison, praise **7** worship **9** adoration **12** thanksgiving **13** glorification

prayerful 4 holy **5** godly, pious **6** devout, solemn **8** reverent **9** pietistic, religious, spiritual **10** worshipful **11** reverential

prayers 4 hope, plea, suit **5** dream **6** appeal **7** request **8** entreaty, petition **10** aspiration, invocation **11** beseechment **12** solicitation, supplication

prayer service 9 devotions **13** prayer meeting **14** worship service

pray for us
Latin: **11** ora pro nobis

pray to 3 beg **5** plead **7** address, entreat, worship **8** call upon, petition, venerate **10** supplicate

preach 4 urge **6** advise, exhort **7** counsel, declare, expound, profess **8** admonish, advocate, homilize, proclaim, stand for **9** discourse, hold forth, preachify, prescribe, pronounce, propagate, sermonize **10** evangelize, promulgate

preacher 5 vicar **6** curate, parson, pastor **8** chaplain, homilist, minister, reverend, sky pilot **9** churchman, clergyman **10** evangelist, prebendary, sermonizer **12** ecclesiastic **13** man of the cloth

preachy 8 didactic, pedantic **10** moralistic, moralizing

prearranged 7 planned **10** calculated, deliberate, purposeful **11** intentional **12** premeditated

pre-Cambrian 5 Azoic **6** Eozoic **7** primary **10** Archeozoic **11** Proterozoic

precarious 5 risky, shaky **6** chancy, unsafe **7** dubious **8** alarming, critical, doubtful, insecure, perilous, sinister, ticklish, unstable, unsteady **9** hazardous, uncertain **10** touch-and-go, unreliable, vulnerable **12** questionable, uncontrolled, undependable **13** problematical

precaution 4 care **7** caution, defense **8** prudence, security, wariness **9** foresight, provision, safeguard **10** protection **11** carefulness, forethought, heedfulness **12** anticipation **14** circumspection

precede 8 antecede, antedate, go before **9** go ahead of **10** come before

precedence, precedency 8 priority **10** importance, preference, prevalence **11** antecedence, preeminence **12** predominance, preexistence

precedent 5 model **7** example, pattern **8** standard **9** criterion, guideline

preceding 5 prior **6** former **7** earlier **8** anterior, previous **9** aforesaid, foregoing **10** antecedent, first-named, precursory **11** preexistent, preliminary **14** abovementioned, aforementioned, first-mentioned

precept 3 law **4** bull, code, rule **5** axiom, canon, edict, maxim, motto, tenet, truth, ukase **6** byword, decree, dictum **7** dictate, mandate, statute **8** standard, teaching **9** ordinance, principle, yard stick **10** regulation **11** commandment, declaration

preceptor 5 coach, tutor **6** mentor **7** advisor, teacher **8** director **9** admonitor, counselor, principal **10** headmaster **12** headmistress

precincts 7 suburbs 8 environs 9 districts, outskirts 10 boundaries 12 subdivisions 15 surrounding area

precious 4 dear, rare 5 fussy, sweet 6 adored, choice, costly, dainty, prissy, prized, valued 7 beloved, darling, finical, finicky, lovable 8 adorable, affected, uncommon, valuable 9 cherished, expensive, exquisite, priceless, treasured 10 fastidious, high-priced, invaluable, meticulous, particular 11 beyond price, inestimable, overrefined, pretentious

precipice 4 crag 5 bluff, cliff, ledge 8 headland, palisade 9 cliff edge, declivity 10 escarpment

precipitate 4 cast, hurl, rash, spur 5 drive, fling, hasty, throw 6 abrupt, hasten, launch, let fly, propel, rushed, speedy, thrust 7 advance, bring on, hurried, quicken, speed up 8 catapult, expedite, headlong, reckless 9 discharge, foolhardy, impetuous, imprudent, impulsive 10 accelerate, incautious 11 thoughtless

precipitation 4 hail, rain, rush, snow 5 haste, sleet 8 rainfall, rashness 9 hastiness 11 impetuously

precipitous 5 hasty, sharp, sheer, steep 6 abrupt 9 impetuous

precis 5 brief 6 apercu, digest, resume, sketch 7 epitome, outline, rundown, summary 8 abstract, synopsis 10 abridgment, compendium 12 condensation 14 recapitulation

precise 4 true 5 exact, fussy, rigid 6 strict 7 careful, express, finicky, literal 8 accurate, clear-cut, definite, distinct, explicit, incisive, specific 9 unbending 10 fastidious, inflexible, meticulous, particular, to the point 11 painstaking, unequivocal

precision 5 rigor 8 accuracy, fidelity 9 attention, exactness 11 factualness, preciseness 12 authenticity, truthfulness 14 meticulousness

preclude 3 bar, dam 4 balk, curb, foil, stop 5 avert, avoid, block, check, debar, deter 6 arrest, hamper, hinder, thwart 7 head off, inhibit, prevent 8 stave off 9 forestall, frustrate 11 nip in the bud

preclusion 9 exclusion, restraint 10 prevention

precocious 3 apt 5 quick, smart 6 bright, clever, gifted, mature 8 advanced 9 brilliant

preconception 4 bias 6 notion 9 fixed idea, prejudice 11 prejudgment, presumption 14 predisposition

precursor 4 mark, omen, sign 5 token, usher 6 herald 7 portent, symptom, warning 8 vanguard 9 harbinger, messenger 10 antecedent, forerunner 11 predecessor

precursory 5 prior 8 anterior, previous

9 precedent 10 antecedent 11 preexistent

predaceous, predacious 9 predatory, rapacious 10 meat-eating 11 carnivorous, flesh-eating

predate 7 precede 8 antecede, antedate, go before

predatory 8 thievish 9 larcenous, marauding, pillaging, piratical, rapacious, raptorial, vulturine 10 plunderous, predacious

predecessor 7 forbear 8 ancestor, forebear, foregoer 10 antecedent, forefather, forerunner

predestination 4 fate 6 kismet 7 destiny, fortune 8 God's will 10 providence 13 inevitability, preordination 16 predetermination

predetermined 5 fated 7 decided, planned 8 destined 10 calculated, deliberate, preplanned 11 intentional, prearranged, predestined 12 foreordained, premeditated

predicament 3 fix, jam 4 bind, mess 5 pinch 6 corner, crisis, pickle, plight, scrape, strait 7 dilemma, trouble 8 hot water, quandary 9 imbroglio, sad plight 10 difficulty, perplexity

predicate 4 base, real, rest, true 5 found, imply 6 affirm, assert 7 commend, connote, declare 8 proclaim

predict 4 omen 5 augur 6 divine 7 betoken, foresee, presage 8 envision, forecast, foretell, prophesy 10 anticipate 13 prognosticate

prediction 6 augury 7 portent 8 forecast, prophecy 10 divination 11 declaration, foretelling, soothsaying 12 announcement, anticipation, proclamation 13 crystal gazing 15 prognostication

predilection 4 bent, bias, love 5 fancy, favor, taste 6 desire, hunger, liking, relish 7 leaning 8 appetite, fondness, penchant, tendency 9 prejudice, proneness 10 attraction, partiality, preference, proclivity, propensity 11 inclination 13 prepossession 14 predisposition

predispose 4 bias, lure, sway, urge 5 tempt 6 entice, induce, prompt, seduce 7 dispose, incline, win over 8 persuade 9 encourage, influence, prejudice

predisposed 3 apt 5 given, prone 8 inclined

predisposition 7 leaning 8 tendency 11 inclination

predominance 7 command, control 8 currency 9 dominance, supremacy 10 ascendancy, importance, prevalence 11 preeminence, superiority 12 universality

predominant 4 main 5 chief, major 6 potent, ruling, strong 7 leading, supreme 8 dominant, forceful, powerful,

reigning, vigorous 9 ascendant, important, paramount, sovereign 11 controlling, influential 13 authoritative

predominate 4 lead 7 prevail 8 dominate

predominating 5 chief 6 ruling 8 dominant, superior 9 principal 10 commanding, prevailing 11 controlling, predominant 13 authoritative

preeminence 9 greatness, supremacy 10 ascendancy, importance, leadership, notability, prominence 11 distinction, superiority 12 predominance

preeminent 4 best 5 famed 6 famous 7 eminent, honored, supreme 8 dominant, foremost, greatest, peerless, renowned, superior 9 matchless, paramount, unequaled, unrivaled 10 celebrated, consummate 11 illustrious, predominant, unsurpassed 12 incomparable, second to none, unparalleled 13 distinguished
French: 13 par excellence

preempt 4 take 5 seize, usurp 8 arrogate, take over 10 commandeer, confiscate 11 appropriate, expropriate

preen 3 pin 4 perk, trim 5 adorn, dress, groom, plume, pride, primp, prink 6 brooch, smooth
wings: 4 whet

preexistent 5 prior 8 anterior, previous 9 precedent 10 antecedent, precursory

preface 4 open 5 begin, proem, start 6 launch 7 prelude 8 commence, foreword, initiate, lead into, overture, preamble, prologue 9 introduce 12 introduction

prefer 3 opt 4 file 5 adopt, elect, exalt, fancy, favor, lodge, offer 6 select, take to, tender 7 dignify, elevate, ennoble, fix upon, pick out, present, proffer, promote 8 graduate, set forth 9 single out

preference 4 bent, bias, pick 5 fancy 6 liking, option 7 leaning 8 favoring, priority 9 advantage, prejudice, proneness, selection, supremacy 10 ascendancy, partiality, precedence, proclivity, propensity 11 first choice, inclination 12 predilection 13 predomination 14 predisposition
French: 4 gout

prefigure 4 hint, type 6 shadow, typify 7 foresee, imagine, presage, suggest 9 adumbrate 10 foreshadow

pregnant 4 full, rich 6 fecund, filled, gravid 7 copious, fertile, fraught, replete, seminal, teeming, weighty 8 forceful, fruitful, prolific 9 abounding, expecting, gestating, important, luxuriant, momentous, plenteous, potential, with child, with young 10 impressive, life-giving, meaningful, parturient, productive, suggestive 11 having a baby, proliferous, provocative, signifi-

cant **12** fructiferous, in a family way
French: **8** enceinte

prehistoric 3 old **7** ancient **10** immemorial
continent: **8** Atlantis
epoch: **6** Eocene **7** Miocene **8** Plio-
cene **9** Oligocene, Paleocene **11**
Pleistocene
era: **8** Cenozoic, Mesozoic **9** Paleo-
zoic **10** Archeozoic **11** Proterozoic
implement: **4** celt **6** eolith
period: **7** Neogene, Permian **8** Cambrian, Devonian, Jurassic, Silurian,
Triassic **9** Paleogene **10** Cretaceous,
Ordovician, Quaternary
reptile: **8** dinosaur

prehistoric era 6 Ice Age **8** Cenozoic,
Jurassic, Mesozoic, Triassic **9** Paleo-
zoic **9** Cenomanian, Cretaceous **11**
Precambrian **15** Upper Cretaceous **16**
Pleistocene Epoch

prehistoric man *see* **8** early man

prejudice 3 ill, mar **4** bias, harm, hurt,
loss, sway **5** slant, spoil, taint **6** damage, impair, infect, injure, injury, poison **7** bigotry **8** jaundice **9** detriment
10 favoritism, impairment, partiality,
predispose, unfairness **11** contaminate, intolerance, prejudgment **12** disadvantage, one-sidedness, predilection
13 preconception **14** discrimination,
predisposition

prejudiced 6 biased, unfair, unjust **7**
bigoted, slanted **9** arbitrary **10** intolerant **11** close-minded, opinionated **12**
narrow-minded

prejudicial 3 bad **6** biased **7** harmful,
hurtful **8** damaging, inimical, sinister
9 injurious **11** deleterious, detrimental

prelate 5 abbot **6** bishop, cleric **9**
churchman, clergyman **12** ecclesiastic

preliminary 9 prelusive, prelusory **10**
initiatory, precursory, prefactory **11**
preparative, preparatory **12** introductory

prelude 7 opening, preface **8** overture,
preamble, prologue **9** beginning **11**
preliminary, preparation **12** introduction

premature 3 raw **5** green, hasty **6** callow, unripe **7** too soon, unready **8**
abortive, ill- timed, immature, previous, too early, untimely **9** embryonic,
overhasty, unfledged, unhatched, vestigial **10** incomplete, unprepared **11**
inopportune, precipitate, rudimentary,
undeveloped **12** unseasonable

premeditated 7 planned, plotted,
studied, willful **8** intended **9** conscious, contrived, voluntary **10** calculated, considered, deliberate, prede-
vised, purposeful **11** in cold blood,
intentional, prearranged, predesigned
13 predetermined **22** with malice
aforethought

premeditation 4 plan **6** design **7** pur-

pose **11** calculation, forethought, pre-
planning **12** deliberation

premier 3 bet **4** head **5** chief, first **6**
oldest **7** leading, supreme **8** earliest,
foremost **9** principal **13** prime minister

Preminger, Otto
director of: **5** Laura **11** Carmen Jones
16 Anatomy of a Murder

premise 6 theory **8** argument **9** postulate, principle **10** assumption, hypothesis **11** presumption, proposition, supposition **14** presupposition

premises 4 site **8** environs, property,
vicinity **9** precincts

premium 4 gain, gift **5** award, bonus,
prize **6** bounty, return, reward **7** benefit, payment **8** priority **9** high value,
incentive **10** great stock, recompense,
reparation **11** overpayment **12** appreciation, compensation, inflated rate,
remuneration **13** consideration, encouragement

premonition 4 omen, sign **5** hunch,
token **6** augury **7** auspice, feeling,
inkling, portent, presage **9** foretoken
10 foreboding, indication, prediction
11 forewarning **12** presentiment

Prendergast, Maurice Brazil
born: **6** Canada **7** St John's **12** Newfoundland
artwork: **6** Dieppe **8** Seashore **11** Picnic Grove **12** The Promenade **16**
Ponte della Paglia **17** Along the
Boulevard, Four Girls in Meadow **24**
Umbrellas in the Rain Venice

Prentice, John
creator/artist of: **8** Rip Kirby

preoccupation 9 immersion, obsession **10** absorption, detachment,
dreaminess, employment **11** abstraction, involvement **16** absentmindedness

preoccupied 6 absent, dreamy **8** absorbed, immersed, involved, obsessed
9 engrossed, wrapped up **10** abstracted, distracted **12** absent-minded

preoccupy 6 absorb, arrest, obsess,
take up, wrap up **7** engross, immerse
9 fascinate

preparation 8 prudence, readying **9**
foresight, preparing, provision, safeguard **10** precaution **11** expectation,
forethought **12** anticipation

preparations 5 plans **7** elixirs **8** guidance, measures, mixtures, training, tutelage **9** dressings, education, seasoning, tinctures **11** concoctions,
confections **12** arrangements **13**
preliminaries, prepared foods, pre-
scriptions **14** qualifications

prepare 3 fix **5** adapt, prime, ready **7**
arrange, be ready, provide **8** get ready
9 make ready, rearrange, take steps

prepared 4 done **5** fixed, ready **6**
cooked, primed **7** planned **8** arranged,

finished **9** made ready, rehearsed **11**
provided for

prepayment 6 credit **7** advance **9** allowance **11** downpayment

preponderance, preponderancy 4
bulk, glut, mass **6** excess **7** surfeit,
surplus **8** majority, plethora **9** dominance, plurality, profusion **10** domination, lion's share, oversupply, prevalence, redundance **12** predominance
14 superabundance

preponderant 3 key **4** main **5** chief,
first, major, prime **7** highest, leading,
primary, supreme **8** dominant, foremost, greatest **9** paramount, principal,
uppermost **10** prevailing **11** outstanding, predominant

prepossessing 4 nice **7** winsome **8** alluring, charming, engaging, inviting,
pleasant, striking **9** beguiling **10** attractive, bewitching, enchanting, entrancing, personable **11** captivating,
fascinating, tantalizing

preposterous 5 inane, outre, silly **6**
absurd, stupid **7** asinine, bizarre, fatuous, foolish, idiotic **9** imbecilic, laughable, ludicrous **10** irrational, outrageous, ridiculous **11** nonsensical,
unthinkable **12** unreasonable

prerequisite 4 need **6** demand **8** demanded, exigency, required **9** called
for, condition, de rigueur, essential,
mandatory, necessary, necessity, postulate, requisite **10** imperative, sine
qua non **11** requirement, stipulation
13 indispensable, qualification

prerogative 3 due **5** claim, grant,
right **6** choice, option **7** freedom, liberty, license, warrant **9** advantage, exemption, franchise, privilege **10** birthright

presage 4 bode, omen, osse, sign **5**
augur, token **6** augury, herald **7** betoken, portend, portent, predict **8** forecast, foreshow, foretell, indicate **9**
foresight **10** foreboding, foreshadow,
indication, prediction, prescience,
prognostic **11** premonition **12** presentiment

presbyter 5 elder **13** church officer

prescience 7 presage **9** foresight, prevision **13** foreknowledge

prescribe 3 fix, set **4** rule, urge **5** enact, order **6** assign, decree, demand,
direct, enjoin, impose, ordain, settle **7**
appoint, command, dictate, require,
specify **8** advocate, proclaim **9** authorize, establish, institute, legislate, recommend, stipulate

prescribed 3 set **5** fixed **6** thetic **9** for-
mulary

prescript 3 law **4** rule **5** order **7** precept, statute **10** regulation

prescriptive 7 binding **8** demanded,
dictated, didactic, required **9** customary, mandatory, requisite **10** compulsory, imperative, obligatory

presence 3 air 4 life, look, mien 5 being, curse, favor, ghost, group, midst 6 aspect, entity, figure, manner, shadow, spirit, vision, wraith 7 bearing, company, eidolon, phantom, specter 8 carriage, charisma, demeanor, features, phantasm, revenant, vitality 9 character, existence 10 apparition, attendance, deportment, expression, lineaments 11 reification, subsistence 12 neighborhood 13 manifestation

presence of mind 6 aplomb 8 calmness, coolness 9 composure, sangfroid 10 equanimity, steadiness 14 self-possession 16 imperturbability

present 2 in 3 fee, now, tip 4 alms, aver, boon, cite, gift, give, here, near, nigh, read, show, tell 5 about, award, frame, grant, offer, state, today 6 accord, allege, assert, at hand, bestow, bounty, call up, chip in, coeval, confer, donate, hand in, impart, legacy, nearby, on hand, recite, relate, render, rooted, submit, summon, supply, tender, turn in 7 advance, bequest, bring on, current, declare, deliver, display, dole out, exhibit, expound, give out, instant, largess, mete out, not away, produce, profess, proffer, propose, provide, recount, vicinal 8 donation, embedded, existent, existing, give away, give over, gratuity, hand over, nowadays, oblation, offering, propound, put forth 9 apprise of, attending, draw forth, endowment, ensconced, hold forth, immediate, implanted, in the room, introduce, make known, not absent, on-the-spot, prevalent, pronounce, surrender, the moment, unremoved 10 asseverate, come up with, contribute, here and now, liberality, perquisite, put forward 11 benefaction, communicate 12 accounted for, bring forward, contemporary, in attendance

presentable 4 chic, so-so 6 decent, modish, not bad, proper 7 stylish 8 becoming, passable, suitable 9 tolerable 10 acceptable, good enough 11 appropriate, fashionable, fit to be seen, respectable

presentation 3 fee, tip 4 boon, gift, show 5 favor, grant, offer 6 bounty 7 advance, display, exhibit, largess, present, proffer 8 bestowal, exposure, gratuity, oblation, offering, overture, proposal 9 unfolding 10 appearance, compliment, disclosure, exhibition, exposition, liberality, production, proffering, submission, unfoldment 11 benefaction, performance, proposition 13 demonstration

Present at the Creation
    author: 11 Dean Acheson

presentiment 7 feeling 10 foreboding 11 forewarning, premonition 12 apprehension

presently 3 now 4 anon, soon 7 shortly 8 directly, in a while, this week, this year 9 at present, currently, forth with 10 any time now, before long, pretty soon 11 after a while, at the moment 12 in a short time
    French: 11 tout a l'heure

preservation 6 saving 7 defense 9 salvation 10 protection 11 maintenance, safekeeping 12 conservation, safeguarding

preservative 4 salt 5 brine, spice 8 marinade 12 formaldehyde

preserve, preserves 3 can, dry, jam 4 corn, cure, park, salt, save, seal 5 guard, haven, jelly, nurse, put up, smoke, sweet 6 comfit, defend, embalm, foster, freeze, pickle, refuge, season, secure, shield 7 care for, compote, mummify, protect, reserve, shelter 8 conserve, insulate, keep safe, maintain, marinate 9 dehydrate, keep sound, marmalade, safeguard, sanctuary, sweetmeat, watch over 10 confection, keep intact, perpetuate 11 refrigerate, reservation

preside 4 boss, host, rule 5 chair, watch 6 direct, govern, manage 7 command, conduct, control, hostess, oversee 8 chairman, overlook, regulate 9 keep order, supervise 10 administer 11 superintend 12 administrate, take the chair

president, President 4 head 5 ruler 8 chairman 12 chief officer, chief of state, first citizen 14 chief executive 16 commander in chief, executive officer, head of government

President of the United States
    first: 16 George Washington
    second: 9 John Adams
    third: 15 Thomas Jefferson
    fourth: 12 James Madison
    fifth: 11 James Monroe
    sixth: 15 John Quincy Adams
    seventh: 13 Andrew Jackson
    eighth: 14 Martin Van Buren
    ninth: 20 William Henry Harrison
    tenth: 9 John Tyler
    eleventh: 10 James K Polk
    twelfth: 13 Zachary Taylor
    thirteenth: 15 Millard Fillmore
    fourteenth: 14 Franklin Pierce
    fifteenth: 13 James Buchanan
    sixteenth: 14 Abraham Lincoln
    seventeenth: 13 Andrew Johnson
    eighteenth: 13 Ulysses S Grant
    nineteenth: 16 Rutherford B Hayes
    twentieth: 14 James A Garfield
    twenty-first: 17 Chester Alan Arthur
    twenty-second: 15 Grover Cleveland
    twenty-third: 16 Benjamin Harrison
    twenty-fourth: 15 Grover Cleveland
    twenty-fifth: 15 William McKinley
    twenty-sixth: 17 Theodore Roosevelt
    twenty-seventh: 17 William Howard Taft
    twenty-eighth: 13 Woodrow Wilson
    twenty-ninth: 14 Warren G Harding
    thirtieth: 14 Calvin Coolidge
    thirty-first: 13 Herbert Hoover
    thirty-second: 18 Franklin D Roosevelt
    thirty-third: 12 Harry S Truman
    thirty-fourth: 17 Dwight D Eisenhower
    thirty-fifth: 12 John F Kennedy
    thirty-sixth: 14 Lyndon B Johnson
    thirty-seventh: 13 Richard M Nixon
    thirty-eighth: 11 Gerald R Ford
    thirty-ninth: 11 (James E) Jimmy Carter (Jr)
    fortieth: 12 Ronald Reagan
    forty-first: 10 George Bush
    forty-second: 11 (William Jefferson) Bill Clinton

President's Analyst, The
    director: 16 Theodore J Flicker
    cast: 8 Will Geer 11 James Coburn 12 Severn Darden 16 Godfrey Cambridge

preside over 5 chair, guide 6 direct, govern, manage 7 conduct 8 dominate 9 supervise 10 administer 11 superintend

Presley, Elvis Aron
    nickname: 7 The King 14 Elvis the Pelvis 15 King of Rock n Roll
    born: 6 Tupelo 11 Mississippi
    wife: 9 Priscilla
    daughter: 9 Lisa Marie
    father: 6 Vernon
    mother: 6 Gladys
    twin brother: 11 Jessie Garon
    manager: 16 Colonel Tom Parker
    home: 9 Graceland
    location: 7 Memphis 9 Tennessee
    song: 8 Hound Dog 10 All Shook Up 11 Don't Be Cruel 12 Love Me Tender 13 Jailhouse Rock 14 Blue Suede Shoes 15 Heartbreak Hotel 17 That's All Right Mama
    film: 7 G I Blues 9 Loving You 10 Blue Hawaii, King Creole 12 Love Me Tender, Viva Las Vegas 13 Jailhouse Rock

press 2 TV 3 beg, bug, dun, hit, hug, jam, mob, pet, tap, tax 4 army, body, cram, duty, heap, herd, host, iron, mash, mill, pack, prod, push, rush 5 beset, bunch, clasp, crowd, crush, drove, exact, flick, force, horde, hound, hurry, media, plead, radio, set on, steam, stuff, surge, swarm 6 appeal, bother, burden, caress, compel, duress, enjoin, exhort, extort, fondle, gather, huddle, legion, mangle, push in, reduce, smooth, strain, stress, throng 7 cluster, collect, depress, embrace, entreat, flatten, implore, newsmen, oppress, snuggle, squeeze, trouble 8 assemble, bear down, bear upon, calender, compress, condense, hot-press, insist on, pressure, printing, push down 9 annoyance, be hard put, constrain, constrict, final form, force down, force from, importune, multitude, reporters **10** compulsion, congregate, newspapers, obligation, supplicate, television, thrust down **11** journalists, periodicals, publication **12** bear down upon, broadcasting, come together, news services, newspapermen **14** Fourth Estate

press down 7 compact, depress **8** push down

press forward 5 drive **6** push on **7** advance **10** forge ahead

press home 6 stress **9** emphasize, underline **10** accentuate, underscore

pressing 5 vital **6** crying, needed, urgent **7** crucial, exigent, needful **8** critical **9** clamoring, demanding, essential, important, insistent, necessary **10** imperative **11** importunate **13** indispensable

pressing necessity 6 crisis **7** urgency **8** exigency **9** emergency

press on 9 move ahead, persevere **10** accelerate, forge ahead **11** move forward

pressure 4 bias, care, load, need, pull, sway, want **5** force, hurry, pinch, power, press, trial **6** burden, demand, strain, stress, weight **7** anxiety, density, gravity, potency, squeeze, straits, tension, trouble, urgency **8** coercion, distress, exigency, interest **9** adversity, grievance, heaviness, influence, necessity **10** affliction, compaction, compulsion, difficulty, oppression

pressure measurement 6 pascal **10** atmosphere

prestige 4 fame, mark, note **5** glory, honor **6** esteem, import, regard, renown, report, repute **7** account, respect **8** eminence **9** authority, celebrity **10** importance, notability, prominence, reputation **11** consequence, distinction, preeminence **12** significance

prestigious 5 famed **6** famous **7** eminent, honored, notable **8** esteemed, renowned **9** acclaimed, important, prominent, reputable, respected, well-known **10** celebrated **11** illustrious, outstanding **13** distinguished

Preston, Robert
    real name: **21** Robert Preston Meservey
    born: **17** Newton Highlands MA
    roles: **4** Mame **9** Semi-Tough **11** The Music Man **12** Junior Bonner **14** Victor Victoria **16** How the West Was Won

presumable 6 likely **8** apparent, probable **10** ostensible

presumably 6 likely **8** probably **9** assumably, doubtless **10** apparently, ostensibly **13** presumptively **14** unquestionably **15** in all likelihood **16** in all probability

presume 4 dare **5** fancy, guess, posit **6** assume, deduce, gather, have it, impose, take it **7** believe, imagine, suppose, surmise, suspect, venture **8** be so bold, conceive, make bold, make free **9** postulate, take leave **11** hypothesize, rely too much, think likely **12** take a liberty

presumed 7 assumed, deduced, posited **8** believed, imagined, supposed, surmised **9** suspected **10** postulated **13** took advantage **15** taken for granted

presumption 3 lip **4** gall **5** brass, cheek, guess, nerve, pride **6** belief, daring **7** egotism, premise, surmise **8** audacity, boldness, chutzpah, rudeness **9** arrogance, flippancy, impudence, insolence, postulate **10** assumption, conjecture, effrontery **11** forwardness, haughtiness, prejudgment, speculation, supposition **12** impertinence **13** preconception **14** presupposition

presumptuous 4 bold **5** brash, cocky, fresh, lofty, nervy, proud **6** brassy, brazen, daring, lordly **7** forward, haughty, pompous **8** arrogant, assuming, snobbish **9** audacious, imperious, shameless **10** disdainful **11** dictatorial, domineering, overbearing, patronizing **12** contemptuous, overfamiliar **13** overconfident

presuppose 6 assume **7** presume, suppose **9** speculate **10** conjecture **11** hypothesize

presupposed 7 assumed **8** presumed, supposed **10** speculated **11** conjectured

presupposition 7 premise **10** assumption **11** postulation, presumption

pretend 4 fake, sham **5** claim, fancy, feign, mimic, put on **6** affect, assume **7** imagine, imitate, playact, purport, suppose **8** simulate **9** dissemble **10** masquerade **11** counterfeit, dissimulate, impersonate, make believe

pretended
    French: **9** soi-disant

pretender 5 faker, fraud, phony **8** claimant, imposter

pretense 4 airs, fake, hoax, mask, sham, show **5** cloak, cover, feint, guile, trick, vaunt **6** deceit **7** bluster, bombast, display, pretext **8** boasting, bragging, disguise, trickery **9** deception, false show, imposture, invention, pomposity **10** camouflage, pretension, showing off, subterfuge **11** affectation, counterfeit, fabrication, fanfaronade, make-believe, ostentation **12** affectedness

pretension 4 airs, pomp, show **5** claim, right, title **7** bombast, display **8** ambition, pretense, snobbery **9** hypocrisy, pomposity, showiness **10** aspiration, showing off **11** affectation, os-

tentation **13** grandioseness **14** self-importance **16** ostentatiousness

pretentious 4 airy, smug **5** gaudy, lofty, showy, stagy **6** flashy, florid, garish, ornate, tawdry **7** blown-up, fatuous, pompous, stuck-up **8** affected, assuming, boastful, inflated, overdone, pedantic, puffed-up, snobbish **9** bombastic, flaunting, insincere, presuming, unnatural **10** hoity-toity, theatrical **11** exaggerated, extravagant, overbearing **12** ostentatious, self-praising **13** high-and-mighty, self-important

pretentiousness 4 cant **6** humbug **9** hypocrisy **11** insincerity **17** sanctimoniousness

preternatural 5 eerie, weird **6** arcane, occult **7** bizarre, strange, uncanny **8** esoteric, mystical **9** unearthly, unworldly **10** miraculous, mysterious, superhuman **11** hypernormal, preterhuman, supernormal **12** extramundane, metaphysical, supernatural, supranatural **14** transcendental

pretext 5 basis, bluff, feint **6** excuse, ground **8** pretense **9** semblance **10** pretension, subterfuge **11** vindication

pretty 4 fair **5** bonny **6** comely, dainty, fairly, goodly, lovely, rather **7** shapely, sightly, well-set **8** alluring, charming, delicate, engaging, fetching, graceful, handsome, somewhat, well-made **9** beauteous, beautiful **10** adequately, attractive, moderately, reasonably **11** captivating, good-looking, symmetrical, well-favored

pretty child 4 doll **5** cutie **10** living doll

prevail 3 win **4** rule **5** exist, reign **6** abound, obtain, win out **7** conquer, succeed, triumph **8** have sway, hold sway, overcome **9** be a winner, be current **11** be prevalent, be the victor, carry the day, gain the palm, predominate **12** be victorious, be widespread, preponderate

prevailing 3 set **4** main **5** fixed, usual **6** normal **7** current, general, in style, popular **8** definite, dominant **9** customary, prevalent, principal **10** accustomed, widespread **11** established, predominant **12** conventional, preponderant

prevail over 4 beat **5** outdo **6** defeat **7** eclipse, surpass **8** overcome

prevail upon 4 sway **8** convince, persuade **9** influence

prevalent 4 rife **5** usual **6** common, normal **7** general, popular, rampant **8** abundant, everyday, familiar, frequent, habitual, numerous **9** customary, extensive, pervasive, universal **10** prevailing, ubiquitous, widespread **11** commonplace **12** conventional

prevaricate 3 fib, lie **4** fake **6** palter **7** deceive, distort, falsify, mislead, perjure **8** hoodwink, misstate **9** be evasive, dissemble **10** equivocate, tell a story **11** counterfeit **12** be untruthful, misrepresent

prevarication 3 fib, lie **5** fable **7** fiction, untruth, whopper **9** fairy tale, falsehood, fish story, invention **11** fabrication **12** equivocation **16** cock-and-bull story **17** misrepresentation

prevent 3 bar, dam **4** balk, foil, halt, stop, veto **5** avert, avoid, block, deter **6** arrest, forbid, thwart **7** deflect, draw off, fend off, obviate, rule out, ward off **8** hold back, preclude, prohibit, stave off, turn away **9** forestall, frustrate, intercept, sidetrack, turn aside **10** anticipate, counteract **11** nip in the bud

prevention 6 defeat **8** stoppage **9** avoidance, hindrance, obviation, restraint, thwarting **10** deterrence, inhibition, preclusion **11** elimination, frustration **12** interception **13** forestallment

preview 5 sneak **6** sample, survey **8** futurama **9** foretaste **10** inspection

previous 5 early, prior **6** before, former **7** earlier **8** foregone **9** aforesaid, erstwhile, foregoing, preceding **10** antecedent **14** aforementioned

previously 4 once **6** before **7** earlier, long ago **8** back when, formerly **9** at one time, a while ago, earlier on **10** a while back, heretofore **11** in times past **12** sometime back

Prevost, Abbe
   author of: 12 Manon Lescaut

prey 3 eat **4** dupe, food, game, gull, kill **5** patsy, prize, quest **6** devour, infest, pigeon, quarry, sucker, target, victim **7** cat's-paw, consume, fall guy, live off **8** feed upon **9** feast upon **10** fasten upon, fatten upon, parasitize

Priam
   king of: 4 Troy
   father: 8 Laomedon
   brother: 8 Tithonus
   wife: 6 Hecuba
   son: 5 Paris **6** Hector **9** Polydorus
   daughter: 8 Polyxena **9** Cassandra
   number of sons: 5 fifty
   number of daughters: 5 fifty
   killed by: 11 Neoptolemus

Priamid
   father: 5 Priam

Priapus
   god of: 5 herds **7** gardens **9** fertility, male power **11** procreation
   father: 8 Dionysus
   mother: 9 Aphrodite
   corresponds to: 7 Mutinus

price 3 fee **4** cost, fine, rate **5** value, worth **6** amount, assess, charge, outlay **7** expense, penalty **8** appraise, evaluate, par value **9** face value, list price **10** forfeiture, punishment

Price, Fanny

character in: 13 Mansfield Park
   author: 6 Austen

Price, Vincent
   born: 9 St Louis MO
   wife: 11 Coral Browne **12** Edith Barrett
   roles: 6 The Fly **8** The Raven **10** House of Wax **13** Tower of London **15** The House of Usher **20** The Pit and the Pendulum **22** The Masque of the Red Death
   expert in: 3 art

Price Is Right, The
   host: 9 Bob Barker **10** Bill Cullen

priceless 4 dear, rare **6** costly, prized, valued **8** peerless, precious, valuable **9** cherished, expensive, treasured **10** high-priced, invaluable **11** beyond price **12** incomparable, without price **13** irreplaceable **17** worth a king's ransom

prick 5 stick **6** pierce **8** puncture

prickle 4 barb, itch **5** point, quill, smart, sting, thorn **6** tingle **7** barbule, bristle, spicule

prickly 5 itchy **6** coarse, thorny **8** scratchy, stinging **9** vexatious

pride 3 joy **4** airs, pomp, show **5** honor **6** egoism, parade, vanity **7** comfort, conceit, delight, dignity, display, egotism, swagger **8** pleasure, self-love, smugness **9** arrogance, be proud of, enjoyment, happiness, immodesty, pomposity, vainglory **10** pretension, self-esteem **11** haughtiness, ostentation, self-respect **14** self-importance

Pride and Prejudice
   author: 10 Jane Austen
   character: 7 Mr Darcy **9** Mr Bingley, Mr Collins, Mr Wickham **14** Charlotte Lucas **15** Caroline Bingley **21** Lady Catherine de Bourgh
      Bennet daughters: 4 Jane, Mary **5** Kitty, Lydia **9** Elizabeth
   director: 14 Robert Z Leonard
   cast: 10 Mary Boland **11** Edmund Gwenn, Greer Garson, Karen Morley **13** Ann Rutherford, Edna May Oliver **15** Laurence Olivier **16** Maureen O'Sullivan

Pride of the Yankees, The
   director: 7 Sam Wood
   cast: 8 Babe Ruth **9** Dan Duryea **10** Gary Cooper (Lou Gehrig) **12** Teresa Wright **13** Walter Brennan

priest 5 padre **6** cleric, father **8** minister, preacher **9** churchman **13** man of the cloth

priesthood 5 cloth **6** clergy **8** ministry, the cloth **9** pastorage

Priestley, J B
   author of: 9 Bright Day **11** Lost Empires **13** Angel Pavement **17** The Good Companions

Priestley, Joseph
   field: 9 chemistry

nationality: 7 British
   discovered: 6 oxygen **7** ammonia **13** nitrogen oxide
   invented: 11 carbonation

priestly 8 churchly, clerical **10** sacerdotal **14** ecclesiastical

prig 5 bigot, prude **6** pedant **7** puritan **8** bluenose **9** formalist, hypocrite, nitpicker, pretender **10** fuddy-duddy **11** faultfinder **12** bluestocking, precisionist, stuffed shirt **14** attitudinarian

priggish 4 prim, smug **6** stuffy **7** prudish **9** blue-nosed **10** tight-laced **11** puritanical, straitlaced **13** self-righteous, self-satisfied

prim 4 smug, tidy **5** fussy **6** prissy, proper, strict, stuffy **7** haughty, prudish **8** priggish, starched **9** squeamish, unbending **10** fastidious, fuddy-duddy, inflexible, no-nonsense, particular **11** overprecise, puritanical, stiff-necked, straitlaced

prima donna 4 diva, lead, star **6** singer **9** principal
   literally: 9 first lady

primarily 6 mainly, mostly **7** chiefly, largely **9** basically, generally, in the main **11** essentially, principally **13** fundamentally, predominantly **14** for the most part **16** first and foremost

primary 3 key **4** main, star **5** basal, basic, chief, first, prime, vital **6** innate, native, oldest, primal, ruling, utmost **7** highest, initial, leading, nascent, natural **8** cardinal, dominant, earliest, greatest, inherent, original, primeval **9** beginning, elemental, essential, important, necessary, primitive, principal, prominent **10** aboriginal, elementary, indigenous, primordial, rudimental **11** fundamental, predominant, preparatory, rudimentary **12** introductory

primary constituent 5 basic **9** basic need, essential, necessity, requisite **10** sine qua non

primate 3 ape, man **5** avahi, indri, lemur, loris, potto **6** aye-aye, baboon, bishop, galago, gibbon, mammal, monkey **7** gorilla, tamarin, tarsier **8** marmoset, simpoona **9** orangutan, tree shrew **10** archbishop, chimpanzee

prime 2 A1 **3** ace, fit **4** best, main, peak, pink **5** adapt, basal, basic, bloom, breed, brief, chief, coach, early, first, groom, guide, lucky, raise, ready, train, tutor, vital **6** adjust, choice, fill in, flower, Grade A, height, heyday, inform, innate, native, oldest, primal, prompt, ruling, school, seemly, select, timely, utmost, zenith **7** educate, fitting, highest, leading, maximal, natural, prepare, primary, quality, supreme, top-hole **8** best days, cardinal, crowning, earliest, get ready, greatest, inherent, instruct, maturity, original, peerless, suitable, superior **9** befitting, elemental, essential, expedient, important, intrinsic, make ready, matchless, necessary, opportune, paramount, preferred, principal, provident, top-drawer, top-flight, unmatched, well-timed **11** superlative, unsurpassed, without peer **12** unparalleled

prime example 5 model **7** classic **8** exemplar **9** archetype

prime mover 6 author **9** initiator, organizer **10** originator
   Latin: 12 primum mobile

Prime of Miss Jean Brodie, The
   author: 11 Muriel Spark

primer 3 cap **4** book **5** paint **6** manual, reader **8** hornbook, textbook **9** undercoat

primeval 5 early **6** oldest, primal **7** ancient, archaic **8** earliest, original **9** ancestral, legendary, primitive **10** aboriginal, indigenous, primordial **11** fundamental, prehistoric **12** antediluvian, mythological

primitive 4 bare **5** crude, early, first **6** native, simple **7** antique, archaic, artless, ascetic, austere, primary, Spartan **8** backward, earliest, original **9** beginning, unlearned, unrefined, unskilled **10** aboriginal, elementary **11** rudimentary, uncivilized, undeveloped

primordial 5 first **6** primal **7** initial **8** original, primeval **9** beginning, primitive **10** elementary **11** fundamental, prehistoric

primp 5 groom, plume, preen **6** doll up, make up **7** gussy up **8** prettify, spruce up

primrose 7 Primula **15** Primula vulgaris
   varieties: 4 baby, cape, star **5** fairy **6** German, poison **7** Chinese, English, evening **8** bird's-eye **9** buttercup **12** beach evening, white evening **13** desert evening **14** Mexican evening

primum mobile 10 prime mover **16** first moving thing

primus inter pares 16 first among equals

prince
   Italian: 8 principe
   Turkish: 3 beg, bey

Prince
   original name: 18 Prince Rogers Nelson
   alias: 9 The Artist **30** The Artist Formerly Known as Prince
   nickname: 12 Royal Badness
   born: 2 MN **11** Minneapolis
   recording: 6 For You, Parade, Prince **9** Dirty Mind **10** Purple Rain **11** Controversy, Crystal Ball **20** Around the World in a Day
   film: 10 Purple Rain **12** 3 Chains o' Gold **13** Sign o' the Times **14** Graffiti Bridge **18** Under the Cherry Moon

Prince, The
   author: 18 Niccolo Machiavelli

Prince and the Pauper, The
   author: 9 Mark Twain
   character: 4 Hugo **8** Tom Canty **9** John Canty **10** Hugh Hendon **11** Miles Hendon **19** Edward Prince of Wales

Prince Edward Island
   abbreviation: 3 PEI
   bay: 5 Rollo **6** Egmont **7** Bedeque **8** Cardigan, Malpeque **9** Cascumpec **12** Hillsborough
   capital: 13 Charlottetown
   gulf: 10 St Lawrence
   people: 4 Scot **5** Irish, Scots **6** French **7** English
      discoverer: 7 Cartier
   province of: 6 Canada
   river: 4 Dunk **5** Eliot, Yorke **12** Hillsborough
   strait: 14 Northumberland

Prince Igor
   also: 9 Kniaz Igor
   opera by: 7 Borodin
   character: 11 Khan Konchak
   contains: 17 Polovetsian dances

princely 3 big **5** noble, royal **8** generous **11** magnificent

prince of darkness 5 Satan **7** Lucifer **8** the Devil **9** Beelzebub

Prince of Peace 5 Jesus **6** Christ

Princess and the Pea, The
   author: 21 Hans Christian Andersen

Princess Casamassima
   author: 10 Henry James

Princess Daisy
   author: 12 Judith Krantz

Princesse de Cleves, La
   author: 14 Mme de LaFayette

Princess Flavia
   character in: 15 Prisoner of Zenda
   author: 4 Hope

Prince Valiant
   creator: 12 Harold Foster
   character: 5 Ilene **9** Prince Arn **10** King Arthur
      wife: 5 Aleta
   nickname: 3 Val

principal 4 dean, fund, main, star **5** basic, chief, first, money, prime **6** master **7** capital, leading, primary, supreme **8** cardinal, dominant, foremost, greatest, superior, ultimate **9** essential, paramount, preceptor, prominent **10** capital sum, headmaster, leading man, preeminent **11** fundamental, predominant, protagonist **13** most important

principal constituent 4 base **12** chief feature **14** main ingredient

principal dish of a meal
   French: 17 piece de resistance

principal event
   French: 17 piece de resistance

principality 5 angel **9** princedom **14** celestial being, heavenly spirit

principally 6 mainly, mostly **7** chiefly, largely **8** above all **9** basically, primarily **10** especially **12** particularly **13** fundamentally, predominantly **14** for the most part **16** first and foremost

principe 6 prince

principle 3 law **4** code, fact, rule, view **5** axiom, basis, canon, credo, creed, dogma, honor, maxim, tenet, truth **6** belief, dictum, ethics, morals, theory, virtue **7** element, formula, honesty, precept, probity, scruple, theorem **8** attitude, doctrine, goodness, morality, position, rudiment, scruples, teaching **9** direction, integrity, rectitude, standards **10** assumption, regulation **11** fundamental, proposition, uprightness

principled 6 honest **7** upright **9** honorable **10** aboveboard, forthright

Pringle, John
   real name of: 11 John Gilbert

prink 4 deck, fuss **5** adorn, preen, primp **6** spruce

print 3 die **4** copy, text, type **5** issue, plate, press, stamp, write **7** compose, edition, engrave, etching, gravure, impress, picture, publish, woodcut **10** lithograph, silkscreen **11** letterpress

printing press
   invented by:
      rotary: 3 Hoe
      web: 7 Bullock

prior 6 former **7** earlier **8** anterior, previous **9** aforesaid, erstwhile, foregoing, prefatory **10** antecedent, precursory **11** going before, preexistent, preexisting, preparatory **14** aforementioned

Prioress
   character in: 18 The Canterbury Tales
   author: 7 Chaucer

priority 7 urgency **9** immediacy, seniority **10** ascendancy, precedence, precedency, preference **11** antecedence, preeminence, superiority

priory 5 abbey **6** friary **7** convent, nunnery **8** cloister **9** hermitage, monastery

Prism, Letitia
   character in: 27 The Importance of Being Earnest
   author: 5 Wilde

prison 3 can, jug, pen **4** brig, gaol, jail, stir, tank **5** clink, joint, pokey, tower **6** cooler **7** dungeon, slammer **8** bastille, big house **9** calaboose, jailhouse

Prisoner of Zenda
   author: 11 Anthony Hope
   character: 14 Princess Flavia **17** Lady Rose Burlesdon, Rudolph Rassendyll **18** Antoinette de Mauban, Fritz von Tarlenhein **21** Michael Duke of Strelsau **22** Rudolph King of Ruritania
   director: 12 John Cromwell
   cast: 9 Mary Astor **10** David Niven **12** C Aubrey Smith, Ronald Colman

(Rudolf Rassendyll) **16** Madeleine Carroll **18** Douglas Fairbanks Jr (Rupert of Hentzau)
setting: 9 Ruritania

prissy 4 prim **5** fussy **6** proper, stuffy **7** finicky, prudish **8** overnice **9** sissified **10** effeminate **11** strait-laced

Prissy
character in: 15 Gone With the Wind
author: 8 Mitchell

pristine 4 pure **8** unmarred, virginal **9** undefiled, unspoiled, unsullied, untouched **10** unpolluted **11** untarnished **14** uncontaminated

Pritchett, V S
author of: 11 Midnight Oil **16** Collected Stories, The Spanish Temper **19** On the Edge of the Cliff

privacy 6 secret **7** privity, retreat, secrecy **8** security, solitude **9** integrity, isolation, seclusion **10** retirement, withdrawal **11** privateness **12** dissociation, solitariness **13** sequestration

private 4 dark **5** fixed, privy **6** buried, closed, covert, hidden, lonely, remote, secret **7** cryptic, express, limited, obscure, special **8** confined, desolate, esoteric, hush-hush, isolated, lonesome, personal, secluded, solitary **9** concealed, exclusive, inviolate, invisible, nonpublic, not public, reclusive **10** classified, indistinct, mysterious, restricted, undercover, under wraps, unofficial, unrevealed **11** clandestine, nonofficial, sequestered, underground, undisclosed **12** confidential, off-the-record, unfrequented

privateer 6 pirate **7** brigand, corsair **9** buccaneer

private eye 4 dick **6** shamus **7** gumshoe **9** detective **12** investigator

Private Life of Henry VIII, The
director: 14 Alexander Korda
cast: 11 Merle Oberon, Robert Donat **12** Binnie Barnes **14** Elsa Lanchester (Anne of Cleves) **15** Charles Laughton (Henry VIII)

Private Life of the Master Race, The
author: 13 Bertold Brecht

Private Lives
author: 10 Noel Coward
character: 10 Elyot Chase, Sibyl Chase **12** Amanda Prynne, Victor Prynne

Private Lives of Elizabeth and Essex, The
director: 13 Michael Curtiz
cast: 10 Bette Davis (Elizabeth I), Errol Flynn (Essex) **11** Donald Crisp **12** Vincent Price **13** Nanette Fabray **17** Olivia de Havilland
also known as: 17 Elizabeth the Queen

privately 7 sub rosa **8** in secret, secretly **9** between us, entre nous, in private **12** in confidence **14** confiden-

tially **15** between you and me **16** between ourselves **17** behind closed doors

privation 4 lack, need, want **5** pinch **6** misery, penury **7** beggary, poverty, straits **8** distress, exigency, hardship **9** indigence, neediness, pauperism **10** bankruptcy, mendicancy **11** destitution **14** impoverishment **15** impecuniousness

privilege 3 due **4** boon **5** allow, favor, grant, honor, power, right, title **6** patent, permit **7** benefit, charter, empower, entitle, freedom, liberty, license **8** pleasure **9** advantage, authority, franchise **10** birthright **11** entitlement, prerogative **12** prerequisite

privileged 4 free **6** exempt, immune **7** allowed, excused, granted, limited, special **8** entitled, licensed **9** empowered, not liable, permitted, warranted **10** authorized, sanctioned **13** unaccountable

prize 3 cup, gem, pip **4** like, lulu **5** award, catch, crown, dandy, honey, honor, jewel, medal, peach, pearl, value **6** admire, esteem, honors, regard, reward, ribbon, trophy **7** cherish, diamond, guerdon, honored, laurels, premium, respect, winning **8** accolade, champion, citation, hold dear, look up to, pure gold, treasure **9** humdinger, medallion **10** appreciate, blue ribbon, decoration, set store by **11** crackerjack, masterpiece

prized 4 dear **8** esteemed, precious **9** cherished, treasured

prizefight 2 go **4** bout **5** match **6** boxing **7** contest **10** fisticuffs

prizefighter 3 pug **5** boxer **7** slugger **8** pugilist **9** flyweight **11** heavyweight, lightweight **12** bantamweight, middleweight, welterweight **13** featherweight **16** light heavyweight

pro 3 for **5** forth **6** before, expert, master **8** favoring **9** authority **11** affirmative
opposite: 3 con **7** amateur

probability 4 odds **6** chance **10** likelihood

probable 6 likely **7** logical, seeming, tenable **8** apparent, assuring, credible, expected, possible, presumed, supposed **9** plausible, promising, thinkable **10** believable, in the cards, ostensible, presumable, reasonable **11** conceivable, encouraging, presumptive

probably 6 likely **10** most likely, presumably, supposedly **11** as like as not **15** in all likelihood

probe 4 hunt, quiz, seek, test **5** query, study, trial **6** pursue, review, search, survey **7** examine, fish for, inquest, inquire, inquiry, inspect, pry into, rummage **8** analysis, look into, question, research **9** penetrate **10** inspec-

tion, scrutinize **11** examination, exploration, interrogate, investigate **13** investigation

probity 5 honor **6** virtue **7** decency, honesty **8** goodness, morality **9** character, integrity, principle **11** uprightness **12** straightness **13** righteousness **14** high-mindedness **15** trustworthiness **16** incorruptibility

problem 5 poser, query **6** puzzle, riddle, unruly **8** question, stubborn **9** conundrum, difficult **10** difficulty **11** intractable **12** disagreement, hard to manage, incorrigible, unmanageable

problematic 7 dubious, unknown **8** doubtful, puzzling **9** difficult, enigmatic, uncertain, unsettled, worrisome **10** perplexing **11** paradoxical, troublesome **12** questionable, undetermined

pro bono publico 16 for the public good

proboscis 4 beak, nose **5** snoot, snout, trunk **6** siphon, sucker, syphon **7** rostrum
monkey: 4 kaha **5** kahua

procedure 2 MO **3** way **4** mode **6** course, manner, method **7** process, routine **8** approach, strategy **9** technique **11** methodology **13** modus operandi

proceed 2 go **3** act **4** come, flow, go on, grow, move, stem, work **5** arise, begin, ensue, issue, start **6** derive, follow, move on, push on, result, set out, spring **7** advance, carry on, emanate, go ahead, operate, press on, succeed **8** be caused, commence, continue, function, progress, take rise **9** be derived, go forward, move ahead, originate, undertake

proceedings 4 case, suit **5** cause, trial **6** doings, events, report **7** account, actions, affairs, lawsuit, matters, minutes, records, returns **8** activity, archives, goings on **9** incidents, memoranda **10** happenings, litigation, operations **11** occurrences **12** transactions

proceeds 3 net **4** gain, gate, pelf, take **5** gross, lucre, money, yield **6** assets, income, profit, reward **7** returns, revenue **8** earnings, pickings, receipts, winnings **9** box office

process 3 can, dry **4** fill, flow, flux, mode, plan, ship, step, writ **5** alter, candy, smoke, treat, usage **6** change, course, freeze, handle, manner, method, motion, policy, scheme, system **7** convert, measure, passage, prepare, project, summons **8** deal with, function, movement, practice, preserve, progress, subpoena **9** dehydrate, dispose of, freeze-dry, procedure, transform, unfolding **10** court order, proceeding

procession 4 file, line, rank **5** array, march, train **6** column, course, parade

7 caravan, cortege, pageant, passage **8** progress, sequence **9** cavalcade, motorcade **10** succession **11** progression

Procheneosaurus
  type: **8** dinosaur **10** ornithopod
  location: **6** Canada
  period: **10** Cretaceous

proclaim 3 cry **4** tell **5** blare, state, voice **6** affirm, assert, blazon, herald, report, reveal **7** call out, declare, divulge, give out, profess, publish, release, sing out, trumpet **8** announce, disclose, set forth **9** advertise, broadcast, circulate, enunciate, hawk about, make known, publicize **10** make public, promulgate

proclamation 5 edict, ukase **6** decree **12** announcement **13** pronouncement

proclivity 3 yen **4** bent, bias **5** taste **6** desire, liking **7** impulse, leaning **8** affinity, appetite, penchant, soft spot, tendency **9** affection, prejudice, proneness **10** partiality, propensity **11** disposition, inclination **12** predilection **14** predisposition

procrastinate 3 lag **5** dally, defer, delay, stall, tarry **6** dawdle, linger, loiter **7** adjourn **8** hang back, hesitate, hold back, kill time, postpone, put on ice **9** temporize, waste time **10** be dilatory, dillydally **11** play for time **12** drag one's feet

procrastinating 4 slow **5** tardy **6** remiss **8** dilatory **9** reluctant **12** footdragging **13** dillydallying

procreate 3 get **4** bear, sire **5** beget, breed, spawn **6** create, father, mother **7** produce **8** conceive, engender, generate, multiply **9** propagate, reproduce **10** bring forth **11** give birth to, proliferate

procreation
  god of: **7** Priapus

procreator 4 sire **6** father **8** begetter

procrustean 7 drastic **8** ruthless **19** conforming at any cost

Procrustes
  also: **5** giant **8** Damastes **9** Polypemon
  seized: **9** travelers
  killed by: **7** Theseus
  tied them to: **3** bed
  made them fit by: **10** stretching **14** cutting off their feet

procure 3 buy, get, win **4** earn, gain, take **5** evoke, seize **6** attain, come by, effect, elicit, gather, incite, induce, obtain, pick up, secure **7** achieve, acquire, receive **8** contrive, purchase **10** accumulate, bring about, commandeer, lay hands on **11** appropriate

procurement 4 gain **7** seizure **8** purchase **10** attainment, purchasing **11** achievement, acquirement, acquisition **12** accumulation **13** appropriation

prod 3 jab, nag **4** flog, goad, lash, move, poke, push, spur, stir, urge,

whip **5** egg on, impel, prick, rouse, shove, speed **6** excite, exhort, incite, needle, prompt, propel, stir up **7** actuate, animate, provoke, quicken **8** motivate, pressure **9** encourage, instigate, stimulate

prodigal 4 lush **5** ample **6** lavish, myriad, wanton **7** copious, profuse, replete, spender, teeming, wastrel **8** abundant, generous, numerous, reckless, swarming, wasteful **9** abounding, bounteous, bountiful, countless, excessive, exuberant, impetuous, luxuriant, plentiful, unthrifty **10** exorbitant, gluttonous, immoderate, inordinate, numberless, profligate, squanderer, thriftless **11** dissipating, extravagant, improvident, innumerable, intemperate, overliberal, precipitate, spendthrift **13** multitudinous

prodigality 10 imprudence, lavishness **12** extravagance, improvidence, overspending, wastefulness

prodigious 3 big **4** huge, rare, vast **5** grand, great, large **6** mighty, unique **7** amazing, immense **8** colossal, enormous, gigantic, renowned, singular, striking, terrific, uncommon, unwonted, wondrous **9** marvelous, monstrous, startling, wonderful **10** astounding, impressive, miraculous, monumental, noteworthy, remarkable, stupendous, surprising, tremendous **11** astonishing, exceptional, far-reaching, uncustomary, unthinkable **12** dumbfounding, overwhelming, unimaginable **13** extraordinary, inconceivable, unprecedented

prodigiously 10 enormously, incredibly, remarkably **12** inordinately, tremendously **13** astonishingly, exceptionally, extravagantly, outstandingly, spectacularly **14** overwhelmingly

prodigiousness 6 rarity **8** enormity, hugeness, vastness **10** uniqueness **11** singularity **12** extravagance

prodigy 4 whiz **6** expert, genius, marvel, master, rarity, wizard, wonder **7** stunner, whiz kid **8** rara avis **9** sensation **10** mastermind, phenomenon, wunderkind **11** wonder child

produce 4 bear, form, give, make, show **5** beget, bloom, cause, found, frame, hatch, set up, shape, yield **6** adduce, afford, create, devise, effect, evince, evolve, flower, fruits, greens, invent, reveal, sprout, supply, unmask, unveil **7** achieve, advance, bring in, compose, concoct, develop, display, divulge, exhibit, fashion, furnish, present, provide, staples, turn out, uncover **8** bring off, bring out, conceive, disclose, discover, generate, manifest, set forth **9** bear fruit, construct, fabricate, institute, make plain, originate, procreate, put on view, show forth **10** accomplish, bring

about, come up with, effectuate, foodstuffs, give life to, give rise to, put in force, vegetables **11** bring to pass, give birth to, manufacture, materialize **14** bring into being

Producers, The
  director: **9** Mel Brooks
  cast: **9** Dick Shawn **10** Gene Wilder, Zero Mostel **11** Kenneth Mars

production 4 film, play, show **5** drama, movie **6** cinema, circus, making **7** display, exhibit, musical, showing **8** building, carnival, creation **9** execution, formation, producing, stage show **10** appearance, disclosure, revelation **11** fabrication, fulfillment, manufacture, origination, performance **12** construction, effectuation, introduction, presentation **13** demonstration, entertainment, manifestation, manufacturing, motion picture **15** materialization

productive 4 busy, rich **6** active, fecund, paying, useful **7** causing, copious, dynamic, fertile, gainful, teeming **8** creating, creative, fruitful, prolific, valuable, vigorous, yielding **9** effectual, luxuriant, plenteous, plentiful, producing **10** invaluable, profitable, worthwhile **11** efficacious, moneymaking, proliferous **12** contributing, fructiferous, remunerative

profanation 9 sacrilege **10** defilement **11** desecration

profane 3 lay **4** evil, foul, lewd, mock, vile **5** abuse, bawdy, crude, nasty, scorn, waste **6** coarse, debase, filthy, ill-use, impure, misuse, offend, revile, ribald, sinful, unholy, vulgar, wicked **7** abusive, earthly, godless, impious, obscene, outrage, pervert, pollute, satanic, secular, ungodly, violate, worldly **8** agnostic, diabolic, off-color, temporal, unchaste, undevout, unseemly **9** atheistic, blaspheme, desecrate, hellbound, heretical, misemploy, shameless, unsaintly **10** irreverent, prostitute **11** blasphemous, contaminate, irreligious, terrestrial, unbelieving **12** nonreligious, sacrilegious

profanity 5 filth, oaths **7** cursing, cussing, impiety **8** swearing **9** blasphemy, obscenity, scatology **10** dirty words, execration, expletives, scurrility, swearwords **11** irreverence, obscenities, ungodliness **12** billingsgate **15** four-letter words

profess 3 act, own, say **4** aver, avow, fake, sham, tell **5** admit, claim, feign, offer, put on, state, vouch **6** affirm, allege, assert, assume, depose **7** advance, certify, confess, confirm, contend, declare, embrace, pretend, purport **8** announce, lay claim, maintain, practice, proclaim, propound, simulate **9** believe in, dissemble, enunciate, hold forth **10** asseverate, put forward **11** acknowledge, counterfeit, dissimulate

professed 6 avowed **7** alleged **8** admitted **9** confessed, purported **12** acknowledged, self-declared **14** self-proclaimed

profession 3 job, law, vow **4** line, post, word, work **5** claim, craft, field, trade, troth **6** avowal, career, metier, office, pledge, plight, sphere **7** calling, promise, pursuit, service **8** averment, business, endeavor, industry, medicine, position, practice, teaching, vocation **9** assertion, assurance, guarantee, situation, specialty, statement, testimony **10** allegation, confession, deposition, employment, line of work, occupation, walk of life **11** affirmation, attestation, declaration, undertaking, word of honor **12** announcement, confirmation **13** pronouncement **15** acknowledgement

professional 4 paid **5** adept **6** expert **9** authority, competent, practiced **10** specialist **11** experienced

professionalism 5 savvy, skill **7** know-how **9** expertise **10** expertness

professor 3 don **6** regent **7** adjoint, teacher **8** lecturer **10** instructor **retired: 8** emeritus

Professor, The
author: **15** Charlotte Bronte

professorial 6 teachy **7** bookish, donnish, preachy **8** academic, didactic, pedantic, teachery **11** pedagoguish **13** schoolmarmish **15** schoolmasterish **16** schoolteacherish

Professor's House, The
author: **11** Willa Cather

proffer 5 offer **6** extend, tender **7** advance, hold out, present

proficiency 5 knack, skill **6** acumen **7** ability, know-how **8** aptitude, capacity, deftness, facility **9** adeptness, dexterity, expertise, handiness **10** adroitness, capability, competence **13** qualification **14** accomplishment

proficient 3 apt **4** able, deft, good **5** adept, handy, quick, ready, sharp **6** adroit, clever, expert, gifted **7** capable, skilled, trained **8** masterly, polished, skillful, talented **9** competent, dexterous, effective, efficient, masterful, practiced, qualified, versatile **11** experienced **12** accomplished, professional

profile 4 form, side, tale **5** shape **6** figure, sketch **7** contour, drawing, outline, picture, skyline **8** half face, portrait, side view, vignette **9** biography **10** lineaments, silhouette **11** delineation **13** configuration

Profiles in Courage
author: **12** John F Kennedy

profit 3 pay, use **4** boon, earn, gain, good, help **5** avail, favor, money, serve, value **6** income, return **7** account, benefit, revenue, service, utility, utilize **8** earnings, interest, proceeds, receipts **9** advantage, make money **11** advancement

profitable 6 paying, useful **7** gainful **8** fruitful, salutary, valuable **9** favorable, lucrative, rewarding **10** beneficial, invaluable, productive, well-paying, worthwhile **11** moneymaking, serviceable **12** advantageous, remunerative

profitmaking 8 business **11** moneymaking **13** noncharitable

profits 4 gate, take **5** gains, yield **6** assets, income **7** returns, revenue **8** earnings, receipts

profligacy 10 lavishness **11** dissipation, dissolution, prodigality, unrestraint **12** extravagance, immoderation, improvidence, recklessness, wastefulness **13** excessiveness

profligate 4 evil, fast, rake, roue, wild **5** loose, satyr **6** erotic, lavish, sinful, sinner, wanton, wicked **7** corrupt, immoral, pervert, satyric, wastrel **8** degraded, depraved, prodigal, reckless, wasteful **9** abandoned, debauched, debauchee, dissolute, libertine, reprobate, sybaritic, unbridled, unthrifty, wrongdoer **10** degenerate, dissipated, dissipater, iniquitous, lascivious, licentious **11** extravagant, improvident, promiscuous, spendthrift **12** unprincipled, unrestrained

pro forma 15 according to form, as a matter of form

profound 4 deep, keen, sage, wise **5** acute, sober, utter **6** abject, hearty, moving, severe **7** decided, erudite, extreme, intense, knowing, learned, radical, serious, sincere **8** complete, educated, informed, piercing, positive, thorough **9** heartfelt, out-and-out, recondite, sagacious, scholarly **10** all-knowing, consummate, deep-seated, omniscient, pronounced, reflective, thoughtful **11** enlightened, far-reaching, penetrating **12** intellectual, soul-stirring **13** comprehensive, knowledgeable, philosophical, thoroughgoing

profundity 5 abyss, depth **6** wisdom **8** deepness, sagacity, sapience **9** erudition **11** learnedness, penetration **12** abstractness, abstruseness, profoundness **13** reconditeness, sagaciousness **16** impenetrableness

profuse 4 rich **5** ample, wordy **6** lavish, prolix **7** copious, diffuse, verbose **8** abundant, generous, prodigal, rambling, wasteful **9** bounteous, bountiful, excessive, garrulous, unthrifty **10** digressive, discursive, immoderate, inordinate, long-winded, loquacious, munificent **11** extravagant, improvident, intemperate, spendthrift

profuseness 9 abundance, diffusion, profusion, prolixity, verbosity, wordi-

ness **10** lavishness **11** copiousness, diffuseness

profusion 4 glut **5** waste **6** excess **7** surfeit, surplus **8** plethora **9** abundance, multitude **10** oversupply **11** superfluity **12** extravagance, multiplicity

progenitor 8 ancestor, forebear **10** forefather

progeny 3 kin, son **4** clan, heir, line, race, seed **5** blood, breed, child, heirs, issue, scion, stock, young **6** family **7** kindred, lineage **8** children, offshoot **9** offspring, posterity **10** descendant

prognosticate 7 predict, presage **8** forecast, foretell, prophesy **9** foretoken

prognostication 6 augury **8** forecast, prophecy **10** divination, prediction

prognosticator 4 seer **5** augur **7** prophet **9** predictor **10** forecaster

program 4 bill, book, card, list, plan, show **5** slate **6** agenda, design, docket, expect, intend, line up, notice, series, sketch **7** arrange, outline **8** bulletin, calendar, playbill, register, schedule, syllabus **9** timetable **10** curriculum, production, prospectus **12** presentation

progress 4 gain, grow, rise **5** climb, get on, mount, ripen **6** action, course, grow up, growth, mature, stride **7** advance, develop, headway, improve, proceed, process, success **8** get ahead, increase, movement **9** get better, go forward, move ahead, promotion, unfolding **10** betterment, enrichment, gain ground **11** achievement, advancement, development, enhancement, furtherance, improvement, make headway, make strides

progression 3 run **5** chain, climb, order **6** ascent, course, series, strain, string **7** advance **8** progress, sequence **10** succession **11** advancement, continuance, furtherance **12** continuation **14** continuousness **15** consecutiveness

progressive 7 dynamic, gradual, liberal, ongoing **8** activist, advanced, populist, up-to-date **9** advancing, enlarging, reformist, spreading, traveling **10** ameliorist **11** incremental **12** enterprising

prohibit 3 ban, bar **4** curb, deny, stay, stop, veto **5** block, check, delay, limit **6** enjoin, forbid, hamper, hinder, impede, negate **7** inhibit, obviate, prevent, repress **8** disallow, obstruct, preclude, restrain, restrict, suppress, withhold **9** proscribe

prohibited
German: **8** verboten

prohibition 3 ban **4** veto **5** edict **7** embargo, sanction **10** temperance **11** forbiddance **12** interdiction

prohibitive, prohibitory 9 enjoining, hindering **10** forbidding, inhibitive, injunction, preventative, repressive **11**

disallowing, obstructive, restraining, restrictive, suppressive **12** inadmissible, unacceptable **13** disqualifying **15** circumscriptive

project 3 aim, job **4** cast, emit, fire, goal, plan, send, task, work **5** draft, eject, expel, fling, frame, shoot, throw **6** beetle, design, devise, extend, hurtle, invent, jut out, launch, map out, propel, scheme **7** concoct, outline, propose **8** activity, ambition, bend over, contrive, forecast, overhang, protrude, stand out, stick out, throw out, transmit **9** calculate, discharge, ejaculate, intention, objective, plan ahead **10** assignment **11** extrapolate, undertaking **12** predetermine

projected 6 hurled **7** hurtled, planned **8** extended, forecast, launched, overhung, proposed, stood out, stuck out **9** mapped out, propelled, protruded **10** catapulted **11** conjectural

projectile 4 dart **5** arrow, spear **6** rocket **7** javelin, missile

projecting part 3 arm, ell, leg **4** eave, limb, tail **6** branch, feeler, member **7** antenna **8** tentacle **9** appendage

projection 4 brow, bump, eave **5** bulge, guess, jetty, jutty, ledge, ridge, shelf **8** estimate, forecast, overhang **9** extension, extrusion **10** estimation, prediction, prospectus, protrusion **11** guesstimate **12** protuberance **13** approximation, extrapolation

Prokofiev, Serge
 born: 6 Russia **9** Sontsovka
 composer of: 6 Lt Kije **10** Cinderella, The Gambler **11** War and Peace **13** Scythian Suite, The Fiery Angel **14** Lieutenant Kije, Romeo and Juliet, The Prodigal Son **15** Alexander Nevsky, Peter and the Wolf **17** Classical Symphony **22** The Love for Three Oranges **57** Cantata for the Twentieth Anniversary of the October Revolution

proletarian 6 worker **7** laborer **10** working man

proletariat 5 plebs **6** rabble, the mob **7** populus **8** canaille, laborers, populace **9** commonage, commoners, hoi polloi, the masses **10** commonalty **11** lower orders, rank and file, wage earners **12** lower classes, vulgus mobile, working class **15** the common people **16** the great unwashed

proliferate 4 teem **5** breed, hatch, spawn, swarm **8** increase, multiply **9** procreate, propagate, pullulate **10** regenerate **11** overproduce

prolific 4 lush **6** fecund **7** copious, fertile, profuse **8** abundant, breeding, creative, fruitful, yielding **9** luxuriant **11** germinative, multiplying, procreative, progenitive, proliferous, propagating **12** reproductive

prolix 5 wordy **7** verbose **10** long-winded

prolixity 9 verbosity, wordiness **11** profuseness **14** long-windedness

prologue 7 opening, preface, prelude **8** foreword, overture, preamble **9** beginning **12** introduction

prolong 5 delay **6** extend, retard **7** drag out, draw out, spin out, stretch, sustain **8** continue, elongate, lengthen, maintain, protract **9** attenuate **10** perpetuate

prolongation 5 delay **9** extending, extension **10** drawing out **11** attenuation, dragging out, lengthening, protraction, retardation **12** perpetuation **13** streching out

prolonged 7 lengthy **8** drawn-out, extended **9** continued, long-lived **10** continuing, lengthened, persistent, protracted **11** long-lasting

prom 3 hop **4** ball **5** dance **9** cotillion, promenade

promenade 3 hop **4** ball, prom, walk **5** dance **6** soiree, stroll **9** cotillion

Prometheus
 member of: 6 Titans
 father: 7 Iapetus
 mother: 6 Themis **7** Clymene
 brother: 5 Atlas **10** Epimetheus
 son: 9 Deucalion
 created mankind from: 4 clay
 stole: 4 fire
 punished by: 4 Zeus
 chained to: 4 rock
 released by: 8 Hercules

Prometheus Bound
 author: 9 Aeschylus
 character: 2 Io **3** Bia **6** Hermes, Kratos **7** Oceanus **10** Hephaestus

Prometheus Unbound
 author: 18 Percy Bysshe Shelley
 character: 4 Asia, Ione **5** Earth **7** Jupiter, Mercury, Panthea **8** Hercules **9** Demogoron

prominence 3 tor **4** bump, dune, fame, hill, hump, knob, lump, mark, mesa, name, node, peak, rise, spur **5** bluff, bulge, cliff, crest, honor, jetty, jutty, knoll, knurl, might, mound **6** credit, height, renown, rising, summit, weight **7** dignity, hillock, majesty, process **8** eminence, grandeur, mountain, nobility, outshoot, overhang, pinnacle, prestige, salience, splendor, swelling **9** celebrity, convexity, elevation, extension, extrusion, greatness, influence, notoriety, precipice **10** brilliance, importance, notability, popularity, projection, promontory, protrusion, reputation, tumescence **11** distinction, excrescence, excurvature, preeminence, superiority **12** protuberance, significance

prominent 6 convex, famous **7** bulging, eminent, evident, glaring, honored, jutting, leading, notable, ob-

vious, salient, staring, swollen **8** apparent, definite, excurved, extended, renowned, striking, swelling **9** arresting, important, respected, well-known **10** celebrated, easily seen, jutting out, noticeable, preeminent, projecting, pronounced, protruding, protrusive, remarkable **11** conspicuous, discernible, illustrious, outstanding, prestigious, protuberant **12** recognizable **13** distinguished

promiscuous 3 lax **4** fast, lewd, wild **5** loose, mixed **6** casual, impure, medley, motley, rakish, wanton **7** aimless, chaotic, diverse, immoral, jumbled, mingled, mixed-up, satyric **8** careless, confused, immodest, sweeping, unchaste **9** composite, desultory, dissolute, haphazard, perplexed, scrambled, wholesale **10** commingled, disordered, disorderly, dissipated, intermixed, lascivious, licentious, uncritical, undirected, unvirtuous, variegated **11** disarranged, incontinent, indifferent, intemperate, unselective **12** disorganized, of easy virtue, undiscerning **13** helter-skelter, heterogeneous, miscellaneous **14** indiscriminate

promise 3 vow **4** aver, avow, oath, word **5** agree, augur, imply, swear, troth, vouch **6** assure, avowal, hint of, parole, pledge, plight **7** be bound, betoken, suggest, warrant **8** covenant, indicate, warranty **9** agreement, assurance, guarantee, potential, undertake **11** declaration, stipulation, swear an oath, word of honor

Promised Land 6 Canaan
 nickname of: 10 California **6** Israel

promising 4 rosy **5** happy, lucky **6** bright, rising **7** hopeful **8** assuring, cheerful, cheering **9** advancing, favorable, fortunate, looking up **10** auspicious, of good omen, optimistic, propitious, reassuring **11** encouraging, inspiriting, up-and-coming

promissory note 3 IOU **4** bond, chit **6** pledge **7** promise **9** agreement **10** obligation **11** certificate

promontory 4 cape, hill, ness, spur **5** bluff, cliff, jetty, jutty, point **6** height **8** headland, overhang **9** peninsula, precipice **10** embankment, projection

promote 3 aid **4** abet, ease, help, plug, push **5** raise **6** assist, foster, prefer, refine **7** advance, develop, elevate, enhance, forward, further, support, upgrade, work for **8** advocate, expedite, graduate **9** advertise, cultivate, encourage, publicize

promoter 6 backer **8** advocate, champion **9** proponent, supporter

promotion 4 hype **5** raise **7** advance, fanfare, puffery **8** ballyhoo, boosting, progress **9** elevation, publicity, upgrading **10** preferment **11** advancement, advertising, furtherance **12**

promulgation 13 advertisement, encouragement

promotive 7 helpful **9** conducive **10** beneficial **12** contributive, contributory, instrumental

prompt 3 cue **4** goad, keen, move, prod, push, spur, stir **5** alert, alive, cause, drive, eager, force, impel, press, quick, ready, sharp **6** active, assist, bright, excite, incite, induce, intent, lively, on time, propel, remind, thrust, timely **7** actuate, animate, dispose, help out, incline, inspire, instant, on guard, provoke, zealous **8** activate, inspirit, motivate, occasion, open-eyed, persuade, punctual, vigilant, watchful **9** attentive, determine, efficient, immediate, influence, instigate, observant, open- eared, stimulate, wide-awake **10** on one's toes **12** jog the memory, unhesitating **13** instantaneous

prompting 6 cueing, urging **7** goading **8** egging on **10** motivation **11** exhortation

promptly 3 pat **4** anon, soon, tite **6** pronto **7** quickly, swiftly **10** punctually **11** immediately

promptness 5 haste **8** alacrity, celerity, dispatch **9** quickness, readiness, swiftness **11** punctuality **15** expeditiousness

promulgate 6 foster **7** explain, expound, present, promote, sponsor **8** instruct, set forth **9** elucidate, enunciate, interpret **11** communicate

promulgation 9 fostering, promotion **11** circulation, instruction, sponsorship **12** distribution, presentation, transmission **13** communication **14** interpretation

prone 3 apt **4** flat **5** level **6** liable, likely **7** subject, tending **8** disposed, face-down, inclined **9** prostrate, reclining, recumbent **10** accustomed, habituated, horizontal **11** predisposed, susceptible

proneness 4 bent, bias, turn **7** leaning **8** penchant, tendency **9** prejudice **10** proclivity, propensity **11** inclination **12** predilection **14** predisposition

prong 4 barb, hook, horn, spur, tine **5** point, spike, tooth **6** branch **10** projection

pronoun 2 he, it, me, my, us, we, ye **3** all, any, few, her, his, one, she, thy, who, you **4** hers, mine, ours, some, thee, them, they, that, this, thou, what, whom **5** no one, their, these, thine, those, which, whose, yours **6** anyone, itself, myself, nobody **7** anybody, herself, himself, nothing, someone, whoever **8** somebody, whomever **9** everybody, something, whosoever **10** everything, themselves
French: 2 il, je, tu **3** ils, lui, mes, moi **4** elle, vous

German: 2 er, es, du **3** ich, mir, sie **4** dein, mein, mich, sich
Italian: 2 io, me, mi, ti, tu, vi **3** cio, lei, lui, mio, tei, voi **4** egli, ella, essa, esse, essi, loro
Spanish: 2 el, la, lo, me, mi, tu, yo **4** ella, ello, suyo, tuyo **5** usted

pronounce 3 say **4** emit, form, rule **5** frame, judge, orate, sound, speak, state, utter, voice **6** decree **7** declare, enounce **8** announce, proclaim, vocalize **9** enunciate **10** articulate

pronounced 4 bold **5** broad, clear, plain, vivid **6** patent **7** decided, evident, obvious, visible **8** apparent, clear-cut, definite, distinct, manifest, positive, unhidden **9** arresting **10** noticeable **11** conspicuous, outstanding, undisguised, well-defined **12** recognizable, unmistakable **14** unquestionable

pronouncement 6 decree **11** declaration **12** announcement, proclamation

pronto 3 now **4** asap, fast, stat **5** quick **7** quickly **8** promptly **11** immediately

Pronuba
epithet of: **4** Juno

pronunciamento 5 edict **12** proclamation **13** pronouncement

pronunciation 6 accent **10** inflection **11** enunciation **12** articulation **16** manner of speaking

proof 4 test **5** essay, proof, sheet, trial **6** galley, ordeal **8** scrutiny, weighing **9** probation **10** assessment **11** attestation, examination **12** confirmation, ratification, verification **13** certification, corroboration, documentation **14** substantiation

proofreader's mark 3 cap, rom **4** dele, ital, stet **5** caret, space

prop 3 set **4** lean, rest, stay **5** brace, stand **6** hold up, pillar **7** bolster, shore up, support **8** buttress, mainstay, shoulder, underpin **9** stanchion, supporter, sustainer **13** reinforcement
French: 11 point d'appui

propaganda 6 hoopla **8** ballyhoo **9** party line, promotion, publicity **10** persuasion **11** advertising

propagandist 6 zealot **8** activist, exponent **9** apologist, proponent, publicist **12** spokesperson

propagate 3 air, sow **4** bear, tell **5** beget, breed, hatch, issue, rumor, spawn, spray **6** blazon, herald, impart, notify, preach, purvey, repeat, report, spread **7** bestrew, give out, implant, instill, make known, scatter, trumpet **8** disperse, engender, generate, increase, multiply, proclaim, put forth **9** broadcast, circulate, enunciate, give birth, inculcate, make known, procreate, publicize, reproduce

propagation 6 laying, siring **7** bearing **8** breeding, hatching, issuance, spawning, yielding **9** begetting, diffu-

sion, gestation, pregnancy, spreading **10** dispersion, generation **11** circulation, engendering, giving birth, procreation, publication **12** distribution, reproduction, transmission **13** dissemination

pro patria 14 for one's country

propel 4 cast, goad, hurl, poke, prod, push, send, toss **5** drive, eject, force, heave, impel, pitch, shoot, shove, sling, start **6** launch, thrust **7** project **8** catapult **9** discharge **11** precipitate, set in motion

propeller, screw
invented by: **7** Stevens **8** Ericsson

propensity 4 bent, bias, turn **5** fancy, favor, taste **6** liking **7** leaning **8** affinity, penchant, pleasure, sympathy, tendency, weakness **9** prejudice **10** attraction, partiality, preference, proclivity **11** disposition, inclination **12** predilection **14** predisposition

proper 3 apt, fit, own **4** meet, nice, true **5** per se, right **6** decent, marked, modest, polite, seemly **7** apropos, correct, express, fitting, germane, precise, typical **8** assigned, becoming, decorous, orthodox, peculiar, relevant, specific, suitable **9** befitting, courteous, pertinent **10** acceptable, applicable, individual, particular, respective **11** appropriate, conformable, distinctive **12** conventional **14** characteristic, distinguishing, representative
French: 11 comme il faut

properly 5 aptly, right **7** exactly **8** decently, politely, suitably **9** correctly, perfectly, precisely **10** acceptably, accurately, decorously, tastefully **12** without error **13** appropriately **14** conventionally

property 4 hold, land, mark **5** acres, badge, funds, goods, means, point, stock, title, trait **6** aspect, assets, estate, moneys, realty, wealth **7** acreage, capital, earmark, effects, estates, feature, grounds, quality **8** chattels, holdings, treasure **9** attribute, ownership, resources, territory **10** belongings, real estate **11** investments, peculiarity, possessions, singularity **12** appointments, idiosyncrasy **13** individuality, particularity **14** characteristic, proprietorship

prophecy 6 augury **7** portent **8** forecast **10** divination, prediction, revelation **15** prognostication
god of: **6** Apollo **7** Phoebus, Pythius **9** Musagetes

prophesy 4 warn **5** augur **6** divine **7** forbode, foresee, portend, predict, presage **8** forecast, foretell, forewarn, soothsay **9** apprehend, premonish **13** prognosticate

prophet 4 seer **5** augur, guide, sibyl **6** oracle **7** diviner, palmist, seeress **8** preacher, sorcerer **9** Cassandra, divinator, geomancer, predictor, sorceress **10** evangelist, forecaster, foreteller, prophesier, prophetess, soothsayer **11** clairvoyant, intercessor, interpreter **12** crystal gazer **13** fortune-teller **14** prognosticator

Prophet, major 6 Baruch, Daniel, Elijah, Isaiah **7** Ezekiel **8** Jeremiah

Prophet, minor 3 Gad **4** Amos, Joel **5** Hosea, Jonah, Micah, Nahum **6** Haggai, Nathan **7** Malachi, Obadiah **8** Habakkuk **9** Zechariah, Zephaniah

Prophetess 4 Anna **6** Miriam **7** Deborah **9** Cassandra

prophetic, prophetical 5 vatic **6** mantic **7** fateful, ominous **8** oracular **10** portentous, predictive, presageful

Prophetic Books
author: **12** William Blake

prophylactic 8 hygienic **10** preventive **13** contraceptive

propinquity 7 kinship **8** affinity, nearness, vicinity **9** closeness, proximity **10** similarity

propitiate 4 calm **5** allay **6** pacify, soothe **7** appease, assuage, mollify, placate **10** conciliate **11** accommodate

propitiation 8 soothing **11** appeasement **12** conciliation, pacification

propitious 3 fit **5** bonny, happy, lucky **6** benign, golden **8** suitable **9** agreeable, favorable, fortunate, opportune, promising, well-timed **10** auspicious, beneficial, felicitous **12** advantageous, providential

proponent 6 backer, friend, patron, votary **7** booster **8** advocate, champion, defender, endorser, espouser, exponent, partisan, upholder **9** apologist, spokesman, supporter **10** enthusiast, vindicator **14** representative

proportion 5 ratio **7** balance, harmony **8** evenness, symmetry **9** agreement **11** consistency, correlation, perspective **12** distribution, relationship **14** commensuration, correspondence

proportionate 5 equal **8** balanced **10** comparable, equivalent **12** commensurate **13** commensurable, corresponding

proportions 3 fit, lot **4** area, bulk, form, gear, mass, part, size, span **5** adapt, gauge, grade, match, order, poise, quota, range, ratio, scope, shape, share, width **6** amount, degree, equate, extent, spread, volume **7** balance, breadth, conform, correct, expanse, measure, portion, rectify, segment **8** capacity, division, equalize, fraction, graduate, modulate, regulate **9** amplitude, apportion, greatness, harmonize, magnitude **10** dimensions **12** measurements

proposal 3 bid **4** idea, plan, plot, suit **5** draft, offer **6** appeal, course, design, motion, scheme, sketch, theory **7** out-

line, proffer, program, project **8** overture, prospect **9** stratagem **10** conception, invitation, nomination, prospectus, resolution, suggestion **11** proposition **12** presentation **14** recommendation

propose 3 aim, woo **4** hope, mean, plan, plot **6** aspire, design, expect, intend, scheme, submit, tender **7** advance, present, proffer, purpose, suggest, venture **8** affiance, propound, put forth, set about, set forth **9** determine, have a mind, introduce, recommend, undertake **10** come up with, have in mind, have in view, put forward **11** contemplate **14** pop the question **21** offer for consideration

proposition 4 deal, pass, plan **5** issue, offer, point, topic **6** matter, scheme **7** advance, bargain, solicit, subject **8** contract, proposal, question **9** agreement, assurance, guarantee **10** resolution, suggestion **11** make a pass at, negotiation, stipulation, undertaking **14** recommendation

propound 4 pose **5** boost **6** assert **7** advance, profess, propose **8** put forth, set forth

proprieties 7 decorum, manners **8** protocol **9** amenities, etiquette **10** civilities **11** conventions

proprietor 5 owner **6** holder, master **7** manager **8** landlord **9** landowner, possessor **10** landholder **11** titleholder **12** proprietress

propriety 7 aptness, decorum, dignity, fitness **8** courtesy **9** etiquette, formality, rightness **10** seemliness **11** correctness, good manners, savoir faire **12** becomingness, decorousness, good behavior, suitableness **13** applicability **14** respectability **15** appropriateness

propulsion 6 launch, thrust **9** launching **10** propelling

prop up 5 brace **7** bolster, support **8** buttress

pro rata 12 in proportion

prorate 6 divide **9** apportion **10** distribute

prosaic 3 dry **4** blah, dull, flat **5** prosy, stale, trite, vapid, wordy **6** common, jejune **7** humdrum, tedious **8** ordinary, plebeian, tiresome **9** hackneyed **10** monotonous, pedestrian, spiritless, unpoetical **12** matter-of-fact **13** platitudinous, unimaginative, uninteresting

Prosclystius
epithet of: **8** Poseidon
means: **7** flooder

proscribe 3 ban **4** damn **5** curse, exile **6** banish, forbid, outlaw **7** boycott, censure, condemn **8** denounce, prohibit **9** interdict, repudiate **10** disapprove **12** anathematize **13** excommunicate

proscription 3 ban **7** barring, censure **8** anathema **9** interdict **11** forbid-

dance, prohibition **12** condemnation, denunciation, interdiction **15** excommunication

prose 3 dry **4** dull **5** novel **7** fiction, quality, tedious, writing **8** sequence **9** discourse **10** expression **11** commonplace **13** unimaginative

prosecute 3 sue, try **4** wage **6** direct, go with, handle, indict, manage, pursue **7** arraign, carry on, conduct, execute, go to law, perform, prolong, stick to, sustain **8** continue, deal with, follow up, maintain **9** discharge, persist in **10** administer, put on trial, see through **11** take to court **12** bring to trial **14** bring to justice

prosecution 4 suit **6** action **7** conduct, pursuit **11** performance **14** administration

Proserpina see **10** Persephone

prosit 11 may it do good
used as: **5** toast

prospect, prospects 4 hope, plan, seek, view **5** scene, vista **6** aspect, design, search, vision **7** chances, explore, go after, look for, outlook, picture, promise, scenery **8** ambition, panorama, proposal **9** candidate, foretaste, intention, landscape, work a mine **10** expectancy, likelihood **11** expectation, possibility, probability **12** anticipation **13** contemplation

prospective 4 to be **6** coming, future, in view, likely, to come **7** looming **8** destined, eventual, expected, foreseen, hoped-for, intended, possible **9** about to be, impending, in the wind, looked-for, potential, promising **10** in prospect **11** approaching, forthcoming, threatening

prosper 4 gain **5** get on **6** flower, thrive **7** advance, succeed **8** fare well, flourish, fructify, get ahead, grow rich, increase, make good, progress **9** bear fruit **15** make one's fortune

prosperity 4 ease, gain **6** luxury, plenty, profit, wealth **7** advance, success, welfare **8** good luck, progress **9** abundance, advantage, affluence, blessings, golden age, good times, palmy days, run of luck, well-being **11** advancement, good fortune
god of: **4** Frey **5** Freyr, Niord, Njord **12** Bonus Eventus
goddess of: **5** Salus

Prospero
character in: **10** The Tempest
author: **11** Shakespeare

prosperous 4 fair, good, rich, rosy **5** happy, lucky, sunny **6** bright, golden, timely **7** hopeful, moneyed, opulent, smiling, wealthy, well-off **8** affluent, cheering, pleasing, thriving, well-to-do **9** favorable, fortunate, opportune, promising **10** auspicious, heartening, of good omen, propitious, reassuring, successful **11** comfortable, encouraging, flourishing **12** on easy street

Pross, Miss
character in: **16** A Tale of Two Cities
author: **7** Dickens

prostitute 4 bawd, jade, slut, tart **5** abuse, hussy, lower, spoil, whore **6** chippy, debase, defile, demean, floozy, harlot, hooker, misuse **7** cheapen, corrupt, debauch, degrade, hustler, pervert, profane, sell out, trollop **8** call girl, misapply, strumpet **9** courtesan, desecrate, misdirect, misemploy **12** streetwalker **14** lady of the night

prostrate 4 deck, flat **5** abase, floor, prone, spent **6** fagged, kowtow **7** bow down, flatten, laid out, worn out **8** bowed low, overcome **9** bone weary, crouching, dead tired, exhausted, kneel down, lying flat, overthrow, recumbent **10** beseeching, horizontal **11** on one's knees **12** on bended knee, stretched out, supplicating **13** lying face down **15** fall to one's knees

prostration 3 bow, woe **5** grief **6** misery, sorrow **7** anguish, despair **8** distress, kneeling, weakness **9** abasement, dejection, heartache, impotence, lowliness, paralysis, weariness **10** depression, desolation, enervation, exhaustion, subjection, submission **11** desperation, despondency **12** genuflection, helplessness, wretchedness **13** depth of misery

prosy 4 dull, flat **5** banal, inane **6** stupid **7** humdrum, prosaic, tedious **9** wearisome **11** commonplace **13** uninteresting

protagonist 4 diva, hero, lead, star **7** heroine **9** headliner, principal, superstar, title role **10** leading man, prima donna **11** leading lady **12** danseur noble, jeune premier **13** jeune premiere, main character **14** prima ballerina **16** central character

protect 4 hide, keep, save, tend, veil **5** cover, guard **6** defend, harbor, screen, secure, shield **7** care for, shelter, sustain **8** conserve, maintain, preserve **9** look after, safeguard, watch over **10** take care of

protected 4 safe **5** saved **6** immune, secure **7** guarded, secured **8** anchored, defended, shielded **9** sheltered **10** inviolable **12** invulnerable

protection 3 aid **4** care, keep, wall **5** cover, fence, guard, haven, shade **6** asylum, buffer, charge, harbor, refuge, safety, saving, screen, shield **7** barrier, custody, defense, shelter, support **8** guarding, immunity, preserve, security **9** preserver, safeguard, sanctuary **10** assistance **11** safekeeping **12** championship, conservation, guardianship, preservation

protective 7 careful, heedful **8** fatherly, guarding, maternal, motherly, paternal, sisterly, vigilant, watchful **9** avuncular, brotherly, defensive, shielding **10** preventive, sheltering, solicitous **11** safekeeping **12** big-brotherly, safeguarding

protective covering 4 coat, husk, mail **5** armor, shell **6** shield **7** coating, plating **8** carapace **10** coat of mail **11** suit of armor **12** armor plating

protectorate 6 colony **7** mandate **8** province, dominion **9** satellite, territory **10** dependency, possession, settlement

protege 4 ward **5** pupil **6** charge **7** student, trainee **9** dependent

pro tempore 9 temporary **11** temporarily **15** for the time being

protest 3 vow **4** aver, avow, beef, deny, kick **5** gripe, march, offer, sit-in, speak, state **6** affirm, allege, assert, assure, attest, avouch, cry out, insist, object, oppose, strike **7** boycott, contend, declare, dispute, dissent, hold out, profess, testify **8** announce, complain, demurral, disagree, maintain, propound, put forth, set forth **9** enunciate, objection, picketing, pronounce **10** asseverate, contradict, controvert, disapprove, disclaimer, dissidence, opposition, put forward, resistance **11** beg to differ, deprecation **12** disaffection, disagreement, remonstrance, renunciation **13** contradiction, demonstration, remonstration, take exception **14** discountenance

Protestant 5 Amish **6** Mormon, Quaker, Shaker **7** Baptist, Puritan **8** Anglican, Huguenot, Lutheran **9** Adventist, Calvinist, Methodist, Unitarian **12** Episcopalian, Presbyterian **17** Congregationalist **18** Christian Scientist

protest meeting 5 rally, sit-in **13** demonstration

Proteus
character in: **20** Two Gentlemen of Verona
author: **11** Shakespeare

Proteus
god of: **3** sea
king of: **5** Egypt
father: **7** Oceanus
mother: **6** Tethys
wife: **8** Psamathe
son: **12** Theoclymenus
daughter: **7** Theonoe
gift: **8** prophesy **12** form-changing **13** shape-changing

Prothoenor
leader of: **9** Boeotians

protocol 5 usage **7** customs, decorum, manners **8** good form **9** amenities, etiquette, formality, standards **11** conventions, proprieties **14** code of behavior, court etiquette, diplomatic code **17** dictates of society

prototypal 5 model **7** classic **9** exemplary **10** archetypal, definitive **12** prototypical

prototype 5 model **7** example **8** original **9** archetype

protozoan 4 cell **5** ameba, cilia **6** amoeba **7** euglena **8** flagella, protista **9** eukaryote, pseudopod **10** paramecium, plasmodium **11** microscopic, unicellular **17** nonphotosynthetic

protract 6 extend, keep up **7** drag out, draw out, prolong, spin out **8** lengthen **9** keep going **10** stretch out

protracted 4 long **7** lengthy **8** drawn-out, extended **9** continued, long-lived, prolonged **10** lengthened, persistent **11** long-lasting

protraction 4 stay **7** lasting **9** extension **10** continuing, drawing out **11** continuance, dragging out, persistence **12** perseverance, prolongation

protrude 5 belly, bulge, swell **6** jut out **7** project **8** stand out, stick out **11** push forward

protrusion 4 bump, hump **6** hernia **8** swelling **9** extension **10** projection **12** prolongation, protuberance

protuberance 3 bow **4** bump, hump, knob, knot, lump, node, weal, welt **5** bulge, gnarl, ridge **6** rising **8** swelling **9** convexity, elevation, roundness **10** projection, prominence **11** excrescence, excurvature

protura
class: **8** hexapoda
phylum: **10** arthropoda
characteristic: **5** small **6** minute **7** eyeless **8** wingless

proud 4 fine, smug, vain **5** aloof, cocky, grand, great, happy, lofty, noble **6** august, lordly, snooty, snotty, strict, uppish, uppity **7** bloated, exalted, haughty, high-hat, pleased, pompous, revered, stately, storied, stuck-up, swollen **8** affected, arrogant, assuming, boastful, braggart, bragging, elevated, euphoric, glorious, inflated, insolent, majestic, prideful, puffed up, reserved, snobbish **9** admirable, cherished, conceited, contented, delighted, dignified, flaunting, gratified, honorable, imperious, know-it-all, satisfied, venerable **10** complacent, disdainful, high-minded, intolerant, principled, scrupulous **11** egotistical, independent, magnificent, overbearing, patronizing, punctilious **12** contemptuous, self-praising, supercilious, vainglorious **13** condescending, distinguished, high-and-mighty, self-important, self-satisfied **14** self-respecting, self-sufficient

Proudie, Dr
character in: **16** Barchester Towers
author: **8** Trollope

Proust, Marcel
author of: **23** Remembrance of

Things Past **24** A la Recherche du Temps Perdu

prove 3 try **4** test **5** check, end up, probe **6** affirm, attest, result, try out, uphold, verify, wind up **7** analyze, bear out, certify, confirm, examine, justify, support, sustain, warrant, witness **8** document, evidence, look into, make good, manifest, result in, validate **9** ascertain, establish, eventuate, testify to **11** corroborate, demonstrate **12** authenticate, substantiate

proved 5 known **6** proven, upheld **8** affirmed, attested, borne out, verified **9** certified, confirmed, supported, sustained, warranted, witnessed **10** documented **11** established **12** corroborated, demonstrable **13** authenticated, substantiated

prove false 5 belie **6** refute, reject **7** explode **8** disprove **9** discredit **10** invalidate

proven 5 known **6** proved, upheld **8** accepted, affirmed, attested, borne out, verified **9** certified, confirmed, supported, sustained, warranted, witnessed **10** documented, verifiable **11** established **12** corroborated, demonstrable **13** authenticated, substantiated

provender 3 hay **4** chow, corn, eats, feed, food, grub, oats **5** grain **6** fodder, forage, ration, viands **7** nurture **10** provisions **11** subsistence

proverb 3 mot, saw **5** adage, axiom, maxim, moral, motto **6** byword, cliche, dictum, saying, truism **7** bromide, epigram, precept **8** aphorism, apothegm **9** platitude **11** commonplace **13** accepted truth, popular saying

prove wrong 5 belie **6** expose, refute **7** explode **8** disprove **9** discredit

provide 3 arm, fit, pay **4** give, plan **5** allow, award, cater, equip, grant, offer, state, yield **6** accord, afford, bestow, confer, donate, impart, outfit, render, save up, submit, supply, tender **7** arrange, deliver, furnish, prepare, present, produce, require, specify **8** dispense, get ready **9** make plans, postulate, stipulate **10** accumulate, contribute

provide for 7 care for **8** attend to, wait upon **9** look after **10** minister to, take care of

providence 8 prudence **9** foresight, husbandry, provision **11** forethought **14** circumspection, farsightedness, forehandedness

provident 4 wary **5** chary, ready **6** frugal, saving **7** careful, prudent, thrifty **8** cautious, discreet, equipped, vigilant **9** farseeing, judicious **10** discerning, economical, farsighted, forehanded, foreseeing, thoughtful **11** circumspect, foresighted, precautious **12** parsimonious, well-prepared

province 3 job **4** area, duty, part, role, zone **5** field, place, state **6** canton, charge, county, domain, office, region, sphere **7** section, station **8** business, capacity, function **9** authority, bailiwick, territory **10** assignment, department **11** subdivision **12** jurisdiction **13** scope of duties **14** arrondissement, responsibility

provincial 4 rude **5** crude, gawky, local, rough, rural **6** clumsy, gauche, homely, narrow, oafish, rustic **7** awkward, boorish, bucolic, country, hayseed, insular, loutish **8** cloddish, clownish, down-home, homespun, regional, yokelish **9** backwoods, parochial, small-town, unrefined **10** unpolished **11** clodhopping, countrified, territorial **15** unsophisticated

provision 6 giving **8** donation **9** endowment, providing, supplying **10** furnishing

provisional 6 acting, pro tem **7** interim **9** surrogate, temporary, tentative **10** substitute **11** conditional **12** probationary **15** for the time being

provisions 4 feed, food, term **6** clause, fodder, forage, stores, string, viands **7** article, commons, edibles, proviso **8** eatables, supplies, victuals **9** condition, groceries, provender, readiness, requisite **10** limitation, obligation, precaution, sustenance **11** arrangement, comestibles, forethought, preparation, requirement, reservation, restriction, stipulation, wherewithal **12** anticipation, modification **13** qualification **14** forehandedness, prearrangement

proviso 5 rider **6** clause, string **8** addition **9** amendment, condition **10** limitation **11** requirement, restriction, stipulation **12** modification **13** qualification

provocation 4 goad, spur **5** cause, pique **6** insult, slight **7** affront, offense **8** prodding, stimulus, vexation **9** actuation, annoyance **10** excitation, incitement, irritation, motivation **11** aggravation, fomentation, instigation, stimulation **12** perturbation

provocative 4 sexy **6** vexing **7** irksome **8** alluring, annoying, arousing, exciting, inviting, tempting **9** beguiling, provoking, ravishing, seductive, thrilling, vexatious **10** attractive, bewitching, enchanting, entrancing, intriguing, irritating **11** aggravating, captivating, fascinating, stimulating, tantalizing **12** intoxicating, irresistible

provoke 3 irk, vex **4** fire, gall, move, rile, stir **5** anger, annoy, cause, chafe, evoke, grate, impel, pique, rouse **6** arouse, awaken, compel, create, effect, elicit, enrage, excite, foment, incite, induce, kindle, madden, prompt, put out, stir up **7** actuate, agitate, animate, bring on, incense, inflame, inspire, outrage, produce, quicken **8** generate, get to one, irritate, motivate **9** aggravate, call forth, establish, galvanize, infuriate, instigate, stimulate **10** bring about, exasperate, give rise to **11** get one's goat, put in motion **15** try one's patience **16** get under one's skin

prow 3 bow **4** stem **5** front **10** forward end

prowess 4 grit, guts **5** knack, might, nerve, power, skill, spunk, valor, vigor **6** daring, genius, mettle, spirit, talent **7** ability, bravery, courage, faculty, heroism, know-how, stamina **8** aptitude, boldness, strength **9** adeptness, derring-do, endurance, fortitude, gallantry, hardihood **10** competence, expertness **11** intrepidity, proficiency **12** fearlessness, skillfulness **13** dauntlessness **14** accomplishment

prowl 4 hunt, lurk, roam **5** creep, range, skulk, slink, snack, stalk, steal **6** ramble **8** scavenge

prowler 7 burglar **10** peeping Tom **16** suspicious person

proximate 4 near **5** close **6** beside, nearby, next to **8** adjacent, imminent, next-door **11** forthcoming

proximity 7 presence **8** locality, nearness, vicinity **9** closeness **10** contiguity **11** propinquity **12** togetherness

proximo see month

proxy 3 sub **4** vote **5** agent **6** ballot, deputy **7** stand-in **9** alternate **10** substitute

prude 4 prig **6** modest **7** puritan **9** hypocrite **10** goody-goody **13** prim and proper

prudence 4 care, tact **6** thrift, wisdom **7** caution, economy **9** austerity, foresight, frugality, parsimony **10** discretion, precaution **11** calculation, thriftiness **14** thoughtfulness

prudent 4 sage, sane, wary, wise **5** chary **6** frugal, saving, shrewd **7** careful, guarded, heedful, politic, sapient, sparing, thrifty **8** cautious, discreet, prepared, rational, sensible, vigilant **9** expedient, judicious, provident, sagacious, wideawake **10** discerning, economical, farsighted, prudential, reflecting, thoughtful **11** circumspect, considerate, foresighted, levelheaded, precautious, well-advised **13** self-possessed

Prud'hon, Pierre-Paul
born: **5** Cluny **6** France
artwork: **14** Venus and Adonis **15** The Rape of Psyche **16** Empress Josephine **33** Crime Pursued by Vengeance and Justice **38** Justice and Divine Vengeance Pursuing Crime

prudish 3 shy **4** prim, smug **5** timid **6** demure, modest, prissy, queasy, stuffy **7** finical, mincing, precise, stilted **8** pedantic, priggish, skittish, starched **9**

prude squeamish, Victorian 10 fastidious, old-maidish, overmodest, particular 11 punctilious, puritanical, straitlaced 13 sanctimonious, self-righteous

prudishness 8 primness 10 prissiness, puritanism 11 overmodesty 12 overdelicacy, priggishness 14 overrefinement

prudish phrase 9 euphemism 10 bowdlerism

prune 3 cut, lop 4 clip, crop, pull, snip, thin, trim 5 shear 6 reduce 7 abridge, clarify, curtail, shorten, thin out 8 condense, simplify 10 abbreviate

prunelle
  type: 7 liqueur
  origin: 6 France
  flavor: 4 plum

pruning 6 digest 8 clipping, snipping, synopsis, trimming 10 shortening 11 abridgement, cutting back, cut-down form 12 abbreviation, condensation

prurient 4 lewd, sexy 6 carnal 7 fleshy, goatish, immoral, lustful, obscene, priapic, satyric 9 lecherous, salacious 10 hot-blooded, lascivious, libidinous, licentious, lubricious, passionate 12 concupiscent

pry 4 butt, nose, peek, peer, poke, tear, work, worm 5 break, crack, delve, force, jimmy, lever, mix in, prize, probe, smoke, sniff, snoop, wrest, wring 6 butt in, ferret, horn in, meddle, search, winkle, wrench 7 explore, extract, inquire, intrude, squeeze 9 interfere, intervene 15 stick one's nose in

prying 4 busy, nosy 7 peering, raising, seeking 8 levering, snooping 9 searching 10 intrusive, meddling 11 inquisitive

Prynne, Hester
  character in: 16 The Scarlet Letter
  author: 9 Hawthorne

Pryor, Richard
  born: 8 Peoria IL
  roles: 6 The Wiz 9 Stir Crazy 12 Silver Streak 17 Lady Sings the Blues 19 Uptown Saturday Night

psalm 3 ode 4 hymn, poem, song 5 canon, chant, verse 6 praise 7 cantata, glorify, introit 8 canticle

Psalter 12 Book of Psalms

Psamathe
  member of: 6 Nereid
  form: 8 princess
  husband: 7 Proteus
  son: 5 Linus 6 Phocus 12 Theoclymenus
  daughter: 7 Theonoe

pseudo 4 fake, mock, sham 5 bogus, false, phony 6 forged 7 feigned 8 spurious 9 pretended, simulated, soidisant 10 fictitious, fraudulent, self-styled 11 counterfeit, make-believe 13 self-described

pseudonym 5 alias 6 anonym 7 pen name 8 cognomen, nickname 9 false name, sobriquet, stage name 11 assumed name 16 professional name
  French: 10 nom de plume 11 nom de guerre 12 nom de theatre

pseudonymous 7 assumed 10 fictitious 11 pseudonymic

psocoptera
  class: 8 hexapoda
  phylum: 10 arthropoda
  group: 8 booklice

psyche 2 id 3 ego 4 mind, self, soul 5 anima 6 bowels, make up, spirit 8 superego 10 penetralia 11 personality, unconscious 12 subconscious

Psyche
  personifies: 4 soul
  loved by: 4 Eros 5 Cupid
  persecutor: 5 Venus
  immortalized by: 7 Jupiter
  daughter: 8 Voluptas

psychic 5 augur 6 medium, mental, mystic, occult, voyant 7 diviner, prophet, voyante 8 cerebral 9 paragnost, sensitive, spiritual 10 soothsayer, telepathic 11 clairvoyant, telekinetic, telepathist 12 extrasensory, intellectual, spiritualist, supernatural, supersensory 13 preternatural

Psycho
  director: 15 Alfred Hitchcock
  cast: 9 John Gavin, Vera Miles 10 Janet Leigh 12 Martin Balsam 14 Anthony Perkins
  score: 15 Bernard Herrmann
  feature: 10 Bates Motel 11 shower scene

psychoanalysis 7 therapy 8 analysis 14 physchotherapy

psychoanalyst 6 shrink 7 analyst 12 headshrinker

psychologist/psychiatrist
  American: 4 Hall, Hull 5 Dewey, James, Lewin 6 Harlow, Horney, Miller, Rogers, Terman, Tolman, Watson, Witmer 7 Cattell, Chomsky, Erikson, Goddard, Guthrie, Johnson, Masters, Skinner 8 Brothers, Wechsler 9 Thorndike 10 Westheimer
  Austrian: 5 Adler, Freud, Reich
  British: 5 Ellis 7 Eysenck 9 Titchener
  French: 5 Binet
  German: 5 Wundt 6 Koffka, Kohler 7 Fechner 9 Helmholtz, Kraepelin 10 Ebbinghaus, Wertheimer 11 Krafft-Ebing
  Russian: 6 Pavlov
  Swiss: 4 Jung 6 Piaget

psychology 4 head, mind 6 makeup 7 feeling 8 attitude 15 mental processes
  problem/illness: 6 phobia 7 obesity, smoking 8 hysteria, neuroses, paranoia, schizoid 9 drug abuse, obsession, psychoses 10 alcoholism, compulsion, depression 11 sociopathic 13 schizophrenia 14 sexual deviance 15 anxiety reaction 17 passive-aggressive
  term: 2 id 3 ego 6 libido 7 empathy 8 neuroses, superego 9 catatonic, cognition, psychoses 10 inhibition, repression 11 behaviorism, unconscious 12 conditioning, transference 13 actualization, Rorschach test 14 identification, Oedipus complex 19 operant conditioning 20 behavior modification
  type: 6 social 7 Gestalt 8 abnormal, clinical 9 cognitive 10 industrial 11 educational 12 experimental 13 developmental, physiological, psychometrics, psychophysics

psychopomp
  conductor of spirits to: 5 Hades 10 otherworld
  epithet: 12 psychopompus
  epithet of: 6 Charon, Hermes

psychosis 8 dementia, insanity, neurosis, paranoia 9 paranomia, unreality 10 pathomania 12 hallucinosis 13 schizophrenia 14 mental disorder

psychotherapy 7 therapy 8 analysis 14 psychoanalysis

psychotic 3 mad, nut 4 kook, loon 5 crazy, kooky, loony, nutty 6 insane, madman, maniac 7 lunatic 8 demented, deranged 9 disturbed 10 psychopath 12 insane person, psychopathic 15 non compos mentis

Ptah
  origin: 8 Egyptian
  deity of: 17 universal creation
  worshiped at: 7 Memphis

Ptolemy
  author of: 8 Almagest 9 Geography

pub 3 bar, inn 5 local 6 bistro, saloon, lounge, tavern 7 bar room, ginmill, rummery, rum shop, taproom 8 alehouse, grogshop, pothouse 9 road house, speakeasy 10 beer parlor 11 public house

pubescent 7 teenage 8 immature, juvenile 10 adolescent

public 3 mob 4 folk, open 5 civic, civil, frank, overt, plain, state, trade 6 buyers, common, in view, masses, nation, patent, people, shared, social 7 evident, exposed, general, in sight, obvious, outward, patrons, popular, society, visible 8 apparent, audience, communal, divulged, everyone, manifest, national, passable, populace, revealed, societal, unbarred, unfenced 9 available, citizenry, clientele, community, disclosed, followers, following, free to all, hoi polloi, multitude, notorious, political, statewide, unabashed, unashamed, unbounded, used by all 10 accessible, attendance, nationwide, not private, observable, population, purchasers, recognized, supporters, unenclosed 11 body politic, bourgeoisie, commonality, conspicuous, countrywide, discernible, perceivable, proletariat, rank and file, unconcealed, undisguised **12** acknowledged, constituency, unobstructed, unrestricted **14** community-owned

publication 4 book, news **5** issue, paper **6** digest, report **7** edition, gazette, journal, tabloid **8** bulletin, magazine, pamphlet **9** broadcast, newspaper **10** periodical **11** circulation, information **12** announcement, notification

public disturbance 4 riot **6** fracas, ruckus, uproar **7** turmoil **9** commotion

public house 3 bar, pub **5** local **6** saloon, tavern **7** gin mill, taproom **8** alehouse **9** roadhouse

publicity 4 hype, plug, puff **5** blurb, flack **7** build-up, puffery, write-up **8** ballyhoo, currency **9** attention, notoriety, promotion **10** propaganda, publicness **11** advertising, circulation, information **12** promulgation, public notice, salesmanship

publicize 4 hype, plug, puff, push, sell **6** herald **7** acclaim, promote **8** announce, ballyhoo, emblazon, proclaim **9** advertise, broadcast, make known, propagate **10** make public, promulgate **11** circularize **12** propagandize

publicly
Latin: **11** coram populo

public matter
Latin: **10** res publica

public notice 5 edict, ukase **6** decree **8** bulletin **9** manifesto **12** proclamation **13** pronouncement **14** pronunciamento
French: **7** affiche

public speaking 7 oratory **9** lecturing **12** speechmaking

public-spirited 8 generous **10** altruistic, benevolent **12** humanitarian

publish 3 air **4** tell, vent **5** issue, print, utter **6** herald, impart, put out, spread **7** declare, diffuse, divulge, give out, placard, promote, release, trumpet **8** announce, bring out, disclose, proclaim **9** advertise, broadcast, circulate, make known, propagate, publicize **10** make public, promulgate, put to press **11** communicate, disseminate

Puca
also: **5** Pooka
origin: **5** Irish
form: **6** spirit
corresponds to: **4** Puck

Puccini, Giacomo
born: **5** Italy, Lucca
composer of: **5** Tosca **8** La Boheme, Turandot **12** Manon Lescaut **14** Gianni Schicchi, Madam Butterfly **15** Madama Butterfly **18** La Fan ciulla del West **22** The Girl of the Golden West

puce 3 red **7** dark red **13** purplish-brown

Puck
also: **15** Robin Goodfellow
character in: **21** A Midsummer Night's Dream
author: **11** Shakespeare
form: **6** spirit
characteristic: **11** mischievous
corresponds to: **4** Puca **5** Pooka

pucker 4 fold, tuck **5** pinch, pleat, purse **6** crease, gather, ruffle, rumple, shrink **7** crinkle, crumble, squeeze, wrinkle **8** compress, contract **12** draw together

puckered 6 pursed, rucked, tucked **7** creased, crinkly, pinched, pleated **8** crinkled, gathered, wrinkled **10** compressed, corrugated

puckish 5 elfin **6** impish **7** playful **8** annoying **9** whimsical **11** mischievous

pudding 5 jello **7** junket **8** custard, dessert, tapioca **8** pandowdy **9** charlotte, yorkshire **14** floating island

pudgy, podgy 3 fat **5** buxom, dumpy, obese, plump, squat, stout, tubby **6** chubby, chunky, fleshy, rotund, stocky, stubby **7** paunchy **8** roly-poly, thickset

Pueblo (Cliff Dwellers)
language family: **4** Tewa, Zuni **6** Queres, Tanoan **10** Shoshonean
tribe: **4** Hopi, Tiwa, Towa, Tusi **5** Acoma, Kiowa **6** Isleta
location: **4** Utah **7** Arizona **8** Colorado **9** New Mexico
noted for: **5** adobe **12** architecture
spirit: **7** Kachina **8** Katchina

puerile 3 raw **5** green, inane, petty, silly, vapid **6** callow, simple **7** babyish, foolish, trivial **8** childish, immature, juvenile, piddling **9** childlike, frivolous, infantile, senseless, worthless **10** irrational, ridiculous, sophomoric **11** harebrained, nonsensical

Puerto Rico
name means: **8** rich port
other name: **9** Borinquen **15** San Juan Bautista
capital/largest city: **7** San Juan
others: **5** Cayey, Coamo, Lares, Ponce **6** Caguas, Dorado, Manati, Utuado **7** Arecibo, Bayamon, Fajardo, Guanica, Guayama, Humacao **8** Adjuntas, Cabo Rojo, Mayaguez **9** Aquadilla **11** Santa Isabel
government: **32** self-governing commonwealth of the U S
measure: **6** cuerda **10** caballeria
island: **4** Mona **7** Culebra, Vieques **13** Caja de Muertos **15** Greater Antilles
lake: **5** Loiza **6** Carite **8** Dos Bocas **9** Caonillas, Guatajaca
mountain: **4** Toro **5** Cayey **6** Yunque **8** Guilarte, Luquilla **10** Torrecilla **17** Cordillera Central
highest point: **5** Punta
river: **5** Camuy, Canas, Loiza, Yauco **6** Anasco, Manati, Tanama **7** Are-

cibo, Fajardo, La Plata **9** Caonillas
sea: **8** Atlantic **9** Caribbean
physical feature:
bay: **5** Sucia **6** Rincon **8** Boqueron **9** Aquadilla **14** Phosphorescent
sound: **7** Vieques
people: **6** gibaro **10** borinqueno
explorer: **8** Columbus **11** Ponce de Leon
leader: **10** Munoz Marin
language: **7** English, Spanish
religion: **10** Protestant **13** Roman Catholic
place:
area of San Juan: **7** Hato Rey **10** Rio Piedras
beach: **7** Condado
cathedral: **15** San Juan Bautista
fortress: **7** El Morro **11** San Jeronimo **12** San Cristobal
governor's residence: **11** La Fortaleza
museum: **14** El Museo de Ponce
reservoir: **5** Loiza
tomb: **11** Ponce de Leon
feature:
bird: **4** rola **7** yeguita
festival: **6** Casals
housing development: **14** urbanizaciones
song: **9** aguinaldo
strolling musicians: **9** parrandas
tree: **4** mora **5** yafua, yaray **8** emajagua, guayrote **10** guaranguao
food:
dish: **4** sama, sisi **9** moreillas **11** lechon asado
drink: **3** rum **10** anis-golila

puff 3 bow **4** blow, draw, emit, gasp, hump, node, pant, plug, suck, wisp **5** bloat, blurb, bulge, heave, smoke, swell, whiff **6** blow up, breath, dilate, exhale, expand, extend, flurry, inhale, rising, wheeze **7** bluster, bombast, distend, inflate, puffery, stretch **8** ballyhoo, be winded, dilation, encomium, flattery, flummery, swelling **9** convexity, discharge, elevation, euphemism, extension, inflation, panegyric, publicity, sales talk **10** be inflated, distention, exhalation, overpraise, protrusion, tuberosity **11** be distended, breathe hard, excrescence, excurvature **12** exaggeration, inflammation, protuberance, protuberancy **13** overlaudation **16** overcommendation **17** misrepresentation

puffed 5 baggy **7** bulbous, swollen **9** ballooned

puffed up 4 vain **5** proud, puffy **7** swollen **8** inflated **9** conceited **11** swell-headed **12** vainglorious **13** self-important

puffery 4 hype **7** big talk, bluster, bombast **9** hyperbole **11** braggadocio

puff out 5 bloat, bulge, swell **6** billow, expand **7** balloon, distend, enlarge, inflate

puffy 3 fat **5** round **6** fleshy **7** bloated, bulging, swollen **8** enlarged, expanded, inflamed, inflated, puffed up **9** corpulent, distended

pugilist 3 pug **5** boxer **7** battler, bruiser, fighter **12** prizefighter

pugnacious 7 defiant, hostile, warlike **8** menacing, militant **9** bellicose, combative, fractious **10** aggressive, unfriendly **11** belligerent, contentious, quarrelsome, threatening **12** antagonistic, disputatious **13** argumentative

pugnacity 9 hostility **10** antagonism **12** belligerence **13** combativeness **14** aggressiveness, fighting spirit **15** contentiousness

puissance 5 force, might, power **6** energy **7** potency, prowess **8** strength

pulchritude 6 beauty **8** fairness **9** bonniness, good looks **10** comeliness, loveliness, prettiness **12** gorgeousness, handsomeness **13** beauteousness, exquisiteness **14** attractiveness, personableness

pulchritudinous 4 fair, fine **5** bonny **6** comely, lovely, pretty **8** gorgeous, handsome **9** beauteous, beautiful, ravishing **10** attractive **11** good-looking

Pulitzer
    author: 10 W A Swanberg

Pulitzer Prize
    originator: 14 Joseph Pulitzer
    administered by: 18 Columbia University
    awarded for: 4 play **5** drama, music, novel **6** poetry **7** cartoon, feature, fiction, history, letters **9** biography, criticism, editorial, reporting **10** commentary, journalism, literature, nonfiction **11** photography **13** autobiography

pull 2 go **3** lug, rip, tow, tug **4** drag, draw, grab, haul, jerk, lure, move, rend, rive, tear, yank **5** drive, sever, shake, split, trawl, troll, twist, wrest, wring **6** allure, appeal, detach, dig out, entice, remove, sprain, strain, uproot, wrench **7** attract, draw out, extract, gravity, stretch, weed out **8** withdraw **9** extirpate, influence, magnetism, take in tow **10** allurement, attraction, enticement **11** fascination **14** attractiveness

pull apart 3 rip, tug **4** drag, rend, tear **6** detach, wrench **7** extract **8** separate **9** criticize, disengage **10** disconnect

pull away 5 wrest **7** remove **8** drawback, withdraw

pull back 7 back off, retreat **8** fall back, withdraw

Pullman, George Mortimer
    nationality: 8 American
    developed: 9 (railroad) dining car **11** (railroad) sleeping car

pull off 4 pull **6** commit, effect **7** execute, perform **8** carry out **10** perpetuate **13** participate in

pull on 3 don **5** put on **7** get into

pull one's leg 3 kid **4** fool, hoax **5** tease, trick **7** deceive **9** make fun of

pull out 5 leave **7** draw out, extract **8** withdraw

pull over, pullover 4 cite, stop **5** shirt **6** arrest, jersey, slip on, ticket, t-shirt **7** maillot, sweater **8** slip over

pull together 4 join **5** unite **7** pitch in, share in **8** take part **9** cooperate, join hands **10** act jointly, join forces **11** collaborate, participate

pull to pieces 5 shred **4** rend **6** tear up **7** destroy **9** tear apart

pull up 4 halt, rein, stop, weed **5** check, hoist **6** arrest, uplift, uproot **7** extract, reprove

pulp 4 curd, mash, mush, pith **5** crush, flesh, paste, puree, slush, smash **6** squash, tissue **7** journal **8** magazine **9** masticate

pulsate 4 beat, tick, wave **5** pound, pulse, shake, throb, thump, waver **6** quaver, quiver, shiver **7** flutter, shudder, tremble, vibrate **8** undulate **9** alternate, come and go, oscillate, palpitate **10** ebb and flow **11** reverberate

pulse 4 beat **5** throb, thump **6** quiver, rhythm, stroke **7** cadence, pulsate, shudder, tremble, vibrate **9** oscillate, palpitate, pulsation, vibration **10** recurrence, undulation **11** oscillation, palpitation

pulverize 4 mash, mill **5** crumb, crush, grind, mince, pound **6** powder **7** atomize, crumble **9** comminate, granulate, triturate **12** reduce to dust

pulverized 6 ground, milled **7** crumbed, crushed, pounded **8** atomized, crumbled, crunched, powdered **10** granulated **12** ground to dust

pummel 4 beat, maul **5** pound **6** batter, thrash **7** trounce

pump 4 quiz, shoe, well **5** grill **7** inflate, slipper **8** question **9** draw water

Pump
    constellation of: 6 Antlia

Pump House Gang, The
    author: 8 Tom Wolfe

pumpkin 5 fruit, gourd, melon **6** squash **9** vegetable **12** jack o'lantern

pun
    French: 9 jeu de mots

punch 3 box, hit, jab **4** beat, blow, chop, clip, conk, cuff, pelt, plug, poke, slam, sock, swat **5** baste, clout, knock, paste, pound, smite, thump, whack **6** pummel, strike, stroke, thrust, thwack, wallop **7** clobber **8** haymaker **10** roundhouse

punchy 3 fat **5** dazed **6** stubby **8** confused, forceful **9** befuddled

punctilious 5 exact, fussy, picky, rigid **6** proper, strict **7** correct, finicky, precise **8** exacting, rigorous **9** demanding

10 meticulous, particular, scrupulous **11** painstaking

punctual 5 early, quick, ready **6** on time, prompt, steady, timely **7** instant, not late, regular **8** constant, on the dot **9** immediate, well-timed **10** in good time, seasonable **11** expeditious **13** instantaneous

punctuate 4 lace **5** break **6** pepper **7** scatter **8** separate, sprinkle **9** interrupt **11** intersperse

punctuation mark 4 dash **5** colon, comma, pause, point, slash **6** accent, ending, hyphen, parens, period, quotes **7** bracket **8** ellipsis **9** semicolon **10** apostrophe **11** parenthesis **12** question mark **13** quotation mark **16** exclamation point

puncture 3 cut **4** bite, hole, nick, pink **5** break, prick, stick, sting, wound **6** pierce **7** deflate, let down, opening, rupture **9** knock down, shoot down **10** depreciate **11** perforation

pundit 4 guru, sage **5** guide **6** critic, expert, master, mentor, savant, wizard **7** thinker **9** authority **13** learned person

pungent 3 hot **4** acid, keen, racy, sour, tart **5** acrid, acute, nippy, salty, sharp, smart, spicy, tangy, tasty, witty **6** biting, bitter, clever, savory, snappy, strong **7** acetous, caustic, cutting, mordent, peppery, piquant, pointed **8** incisive, piercing, poignant, smarting, stinging, stirring, vinegary, wounding **9** brilliant, flavorful, invidious, palatable, sarcastic, sparkling, trenchant **10** astringent, flavorsome, keen-witted **11** acrimonious, penetrating, provocative, stimulating, tantalizing **12** sharptasting **13** scintillating, sharp-smelling **14** highly flavored, highly seasoned

punish 4 beat, fine, flog, whip **6** avenge, rebuke **7** chasten, correct, reprove **8** admonish, chastise, imprison, penalize, sentence **9** castigate, dress down, retaliate **10** discipline, take to task **11** get even with, take revenge **14** bring to account **15** take vengeance on

punishing 5 harsh, penal **6** brutal, severe **7** abusive **8** scolding **9** torturing **10** chastizing, tormenting **11** castigating

punishment 4 fine **5** price **7** damages, deserts, flaying, forfeit, hanging, payment, penalty, penance, redress **8** flogging, punition, spanking, whipping **10** chastening, correction, crucifying, discipline, reparation **11** castigation, retribution **12** chastisement, penalization

punk 4 hood, lout, poor **5** bully, lousy, rowdy, tough **6** crummy, rotten **7** hoodlum, ruffian **8** hooligan **9** barbarian, roughneck **10** delinquent

Punt *see* **7** Somalia

Puntarvolo
   character in: 22 Every Man Out of
   His Humour
   author: 6 Jonson

punt e mes
   type: 8 aperitif
   origin: 5 Italy
   flavor: 6 orange
   color: 12 reddish-brown

puny 4 poor, thin, tiny, weak 5 frail,
   light, petty, runty, small 6 bantam,
   feeble, flimsy, infirm, little, meager,
   measly, paltry, sickly, slight, weakly 7
   fragile, shallow, tenuous, trivial 8 delicate, impotent, picayune, piddling,
   runtlike, sawed-off, trifling 9 emaciated, miniature, mite- sized, pint-
   sized, worthless 10 diminutive, inadequate, picayunish, under sized 11 unimportant 12 insufficient
   13 insignificant 14 inconsiderable, underdeveloped

pupa 3 egg 5 larva, nymph 6 cocoon 7
   wiggler 9 chrysalis 14 transformation

pupil 4 coed, tyro 5 tutee 6 novice 7
   learner, scholar, student, trainee 8 beginner, disciple, initiate 9 schoolboy
   10 apprentice, schoolgirl 11 probationer 13 undergraduate

puppet 3 toy 4 doll, dupe, pawn, tool
   6 flunky, lackey 7 cat's-paw, manikin,
   servant 8 creature, henchman, hireling 9 jackstraw, lay figure, underling
   10 figurehead, instrument, man of
   straw, marionette 11 subordinate

puppeteer 4 sarg 5 (Bil) Baird 8 Gep-
   petto 9 Jim Henson 10 Shari Lewis

puppy 3 dog, pet, pup 6 canine

Purcell, Henry
   born: 6 London 7 England
   composer of: 9 Fantasian 10 Bell Anthem, Dioclesian, King Arthur (The
   British Worthy), The Tempest 12
   Golden Sonata 13 Dido and Aeneas
   14 The Indian Queen

purchase 3 buy 4 edge, hold 6 buying,
   pay for, pick up 7 footing, support,
   toehold 8 foothold, leverage 9 advantage, influence 11 acquirement, acquisition

pure 4 full, mere, neat, true 5 basic,
   clean, fresh, moral, sheer, stark, utter,
   whole 6 chaste, decent, entire, higher,
   virgin 7 angelic, ethical, perfect, sincere, sinless, sterile, unmixed, upright
   8 absolute, abstract, complete, flawless, germfree, innocent, positive,
   purebred, sanitary, spotless, straight,
   thorough, unmarred, virginal, virtuous
   9 blameless, downright, faultless,
   guileless, guiltless, healthful, inviolate,
   out-and-out, pedigreed, righteous, unalloyed, undefiled, unmingled, unspoiled, unsullied, untainted, wholesome 10 antiseptic, immaculate,
   inviolable, sterilized, uninfected, unmodified, unpolluted 11 conjectural,

disinfected, fundamental, pureblooded, speculative, theoretical, unblemished, uncorrupted, unqualified,
untarnished 12 full-strength, hypothetical, thoroughbred 13 unadulterated,
unimpeachable 14 above suspicion,
uncontaminated

puree 4 bisk, pulp, soup 5 paste 6
   bisque

purely 4 only 5 fully 6 merely, simply,
   solely, wholly 7 cleanly, morally, pi-
   ously, totally 8 chastely, devoutly, entirely, worthily 9 admirably 10 absolutely, completely, flawlessly, in all
   honor, innocently, virginally, virtu-
   ously 11 essentially, faultlessly 13 in-
   corruptibly

Purgatory, Purgatorio
   part II of: 12 Divine Comedy
   author: 14 Dante Alighieri

purge 4 kill, oust 5 crush, expel 6 banish, emetic, pardon, physic, purify, remove, up- root 7 clean up, cleanse,
   cleanup, clyster, dismiss, expiate,
   purging, rout out, shake up 8 aperient, atone for, clean out, get rid of,
   laxative, sweep out, wash away 9 cathartic, discharge, eliminate, eradicate,
   liquidate, purgation, purgative 10 do
   away with 11 exterminate 12 obtain
   pardon (from), purification 15 obtain
   remission (from) 16 obtain absolution
   (from) 17 obtain forgiveness

purification 7 baptism 9 cleansing 13
   sterilization

purify 4 boil 5 clear 6 filter 7 clarify,
   distill 8 make pure, sanitize 9 disinfect, sterilize 10 chlorinate, pasteurize
   13 decontaminate

Purim 11 Feast of Lots
   celebrates: 11 deliverance
   heroine: 6 Esther
   villian: 5 Haman
   month: 4 Adar

Puritani, I
   also: 11 The Puritans
   opera by: 7 Bellini
   character: 14 Oliver Cromwell, Queen
   Henrietta 16 Lord Arthur Talbot

puritanical 4 prim 5 rigid, stiff 6 narrow, prissy, severe, strict, stuffy 7 ascetic, austere, bigoted, prudish, puritan, stilted 8 dogmatic, priggish 9
   bluenosed, fanatical 11 stiff-necked,
   straitlaced 13 sanctimonious

Puritan State
   nickname of: 13 Massachusetts

purity 5 honor, piety 6 virtue 7 clarity,
   decency, honesty, modesty 8 chastity,
   fineness, holiness, lucidity, morality,
   pureness, sanctity 9 cleanness, clearness, innocence, integrity, limpidity,
   plainness, rectitude, virginity 10 brilliance, chasteness, directness, excellence, immaculacy, simplicity, temperance, uniformity 11 cleanliness,
   homogeneity, saintliness, uprightness

12 virtuousness 13 guilelessness,
guiltlessness 14 immaculateness 15
clear conscience 16 incorruptibility

purlieu 4 area 5 haunt, limit 6 border,
   locale, region, resort 7 district, envi-
   ron 8 out- skirt 11 surrounding 12
   neighborhood

purloin 3 rob 5 steal 6 pilfer 11 appropriate, make off with

Purloined Letter, The
   author: 13 Edgar Allan Poe

purloiner 5 thief 6 robber 7 burglar 8
   pilferer

purple 4 plum, puce, racy 5 color,
   grape, lilac, lurid, mauve, royal 6
   florid, orchid, turgid, violet 7 crimson,
   flowery, furious, fuchsia, magenta 8
   amethyst, burgundy, imperial, lavender 9 gastropod

Purple Land see 7 Uruguay

Purple Rose of Cairo, The
   director: 10 Woody Allen
   cast: 9 Mia Farrow 11 Danny Aiello,
   Jeff Daniels

purport 3 aim, end 4 gist 5 claim,
   drift, point, sense, tenor, trend 6 allege, burden, design, import, intent,
   object, reason 7 bearing, meaning,
   profess, purpose 9 intention, objective, rationale, substance 11 implication 12 significance 13 signification

purpose 3 aim 4 goal, hope, mean,
   plan, will, wish 5 elect, point, sense 6
   aspire, choose, decide, design, desire,
   intend, intent, motive, object, reason,
   scheme, target 7 drive at, meaning,
   mission, persist, project, propose, resolve, think to 8 ambition, conclude,
   endeavor, function, proposal, set
   about 9 determine, intention, objective, persevere, rationale, undertake
   10 aspiration, motivation, resolution
   11 contemplate, disposition, expectation, fixed intent, have a mind to, raison d'etre 13 commit one self, determination

purposeful 7 decided, studied 8 resolute, resolved 9 committed, conscious
   10 calculated, considered, deliberate,
   determined 11 intentional 12 premeditated, strong-willed

purposefulness 7 purpose, resolve 10
   resolution 11 decidedness 12 decisiveness, resoluteness 13 determination

purposeless 6 random 7 aimless, useless 8 needless, plotless 9 desultory,
   driftless, haphazard, irregular, senseless, unplanned 11 meaningless 12
   functionless, undetermined, unprofitable

purposely 8 by design 9 advisedly, expressly, knowingly, on purpose, will-
   fully, wittingly 10 designedly, with intent 11 consciously, voluntarily 12
   calculatedly, deliberately 13 intention-
   ally

purse 3 bag 4 fold, fund, knit 5 award,

bunch, pinch, pleat, pouch, prize, stake **6** clutch, coffer, gather, pucker, wallet **7** handbag, sporran, wrinkle **8** contract, moneybag, proceeds, treasury, winnings **10** pocketbook **11** shoulder bag
French: **12** porte-monnaie

purser 6 bursar **7** cashier **9** paymaster **10** cashkeeper

pursue 4 seek **5** aim at, chase, track, trail **6** aim for, follow, try for **7** be after, carry on, go after, perform **8** aspire to, engage in, labor for, run after **9** race after, strive for **10** chase after, push toward

pursuer 5 pupil **6** seeker **7** devotee, student **8** disciple, follower, searcher **10** aficionado

pursuit 4 hunt **5** chase **6** search **7** pastime **8** activity **9** following **10** occupation

purvey 3 get **4** give, hand **5** cater, equip, yield **6** obtain, outfit, supply **7** deliver, furnish, procure, provide

purveyor 4 pimp **6** seller **8** procurer, provider, supplier

purview 3 ken **4** area **5** field, range, reach, realm, savvy, scope, sweep **6** domain, extent **7** compass, horizon, outlook **8** dominion, overview **9** territory, viewpoint **10** commission, experience **11** mental grasp **13** comprehension, understanding **14** responsibility

push 2 go **3** dun, ram **4** butt, goad, jolt, move, plug, prod, spur, sway, urge, work, worm **5** boost, drive, egg on, elbow, fight, foray, force, forge, harry, hound, impel, nudge, press, rouse, shove, stick, stuff, vigor, wedge **6** arouse, badger, coerce, compel, energy, exhort, harass, heckle, hustle, incite, induce, inroad, jostle, plunge, prompt, propel, thrust, wiggle **7** advance, animate, buffalo, inspire, promote, provoke, squeeze **8** ambition, browbeat, motivate, persuade, shoulder, struggle, vitality **9** advertise, constrain, encourage, importune, incursion, instigate, make known, publicize, stimulate, strong-arm **10** get-up-and-go **11** make one's way, prevail upon, vim and vigor **12** force one's way, propagandize **13** determination

pushcart 5 wagon **6** barrow **8** handcart **10** handbarrow **11** wheelbarrow

push forward 4 goad, prod, spur **5** drive, impel, press **9** urge along

Pushkin, Alexander (Aleksandr)
author of: 12 Boris Godunov, Eugene Onegin **16** The Queen of Spades **17** The Bronze Horseman **19** The Captain's Daughter

push through 6 hasten **7** advance, forward **8** dispatch, expedite **10** accelerate, facilitate

pushy 8 forceful **9** assertive, insistent **10** aggressive **11** domineering **12** strong-willed **13** self-assertive

pusillanimous 7 fearful **8** cowardly, timorous **10** spiritless **11** lily-livered **12** apprehensive, fainthearted, meanspirited

pusillanimousness 8 timidity **9** cowardice **12** yellow streak **13** yellow feather **16** faint heartedness **18** chickenheartedness

puss 3 cat, mug, pan **4** face **5** kitty **6** feline, kisser, kitten

pussyfoot 5 dodge, evade, hedge, sneak **6** tiptoe, weasel **8** sidestep **13** evade the issue **14** beg the question **15** walk on eggshells **16** straddle the fence

put 3 fix, lay, set **4** cast, pose, rest, word **5** bring, drive, force, heave, offer, pitch, place, state, throw **6** assign, employ, impute, phrase, submit **7** ascribe, deposit, express, present, propose **8** position **9** attribute, enunciate **10** articulate

put a damper on 4 cool, dull **7** depress, squelch **10** discourage, dishearten

put an edge on 4 hone, whet **6** excite **7** sharpen **9** stimulate

put an end to 4 halt, stop **5** annul, quash **6** cancel, finish, repeal, revoke **7** abolish, blot out, rescind, squelch, wipe out **8** abrogate, demolish, dispatch, stamp out **9** eliminate, eradicate, finish off **10** discourage, do away with, put a stop to **12** write finis to

put aside 5 table **6** forget **7** discard, lay away **10** relinquish

put away 3 eat **4** down, stow **5** stash **6** commit **7** confine, consume **9** drink down

put back 4 rout **5** delay **6** defeat, demote, impair, reject, return **7** replace, restore **9** reinstate

put down 4 note, post **5** crush, enter, knock, quash, quell **6** dispel, enlist, record, subdue **7** deposit, disdain, sneer at, squelch **8** belittle, derogate, laugh off, pooh-pooh, suppress **9** denigrate, disparage, humiliate, write down **10** deprecate

put forth 5 offer **6** extend, put out **7** proffer, send out

put forward 4 pose **6** assert **7** advance, profess, propose **8** propound

put in irons 5 chain **6** fetter **7** manacle, shackle **8** handcuff

put in motion 4 move **5** begin, start **6** arouse, launch **8** activate, carry out, commence, initiate **9** instigate, undertake

put in order 5 array **6** neaten, tidy up **7** arrange **8** organize **10** straighten

put in plain sight 4 show **6** set out **7** display, exhibit

put in shackles 6 fetter, hobble **7** enchain, enslave, manacle **8** handcuff, imprison

put into circulation 4 move **5** issue, print **7** publish **10** pass around

put into effect 6 effect **7** achieve, enforce, execute, fulfill, realize **8** carry out, complete **10** accomplish, administer, consummate, effectuate, perpetrate **12** carry through

put into words 5 voice **7** express **8** describe **9** verbalize **10** articulate **11** communicate

Putnam, Abbie
character in: 18 Desire Under the Elms
author: 6 O'Neill

put off 5 delay, repel, stall **6** offend, rebuff, recess **7** adjourn, repulse, set sail, suspend **8** hold back, launched, offended, postpone, rebuffed, repelled, repulsed **9** interrupt **11** discontinue **13** procrastinate

put off guard 4 lull **6** disarm **10** make unwary

put on 3 don **5** affix **6** attach **7** dress in, get into, stick on **8** fasten to

put-on 4 hoax, joke **8** pretense **11** affectation

put on guard 4 warn **5** alert **6** advise, tip off **7** caution **8** forewarn **9** make ready **10** precaution

put out 3 irk **5** annoy, issue **6** quench, retire **7** produce, publish **8** irritate **9** strike out **10** extinguish **11** manufacture **13** leave the shore

put out of order 5 mix up, upset **6** jumble, mess up, muddle **7** confuse, scatter **8** disarray, disorder, displace, put askew, scramble **10** disarrange **11** disorganize

putrefaction 3 rot **5** decay **7** rotting **8** spoilage, spoiling **10** rottenness **12** decompostion

putrefy 3 rot **4** turn **5** decay, spoil, taint **6** molder **8** putresce, stagnate **9** decompose **10** biodegrade **11** deteriorate **12** disintegrate

putrescent 4 foul, rank **5** fetid **6** smelly **7** rotting **8** decaying, spoiling, stinking **9** offensive **10** malodorous, putrefying **11** decomposing

putrid 3 bad **4** foul, rank **5** fetid **6** rancid, rotten, spoiled **7** tainted **8** decaying, polluted, purulent, stinking **9** putrefied **10** putrescent **11** decomposing **12** contaminated, putrefactive

putridity 5 decay, filth, taint **8** foulness, impurity **9** dirtiness, pollution, purulence, rancidity **10** rottenness **11** putrescence, uncleanness **13** contamination, decomposition

putsch 6 revolt **8** uprising

putter 4 fool, idle, laze, loaf, loll **5**

dally, drift **6** dawdle, diddle, fiddle, loiter, lounge, piddle, potter, tinker **8** golf club, lallygag **10** dillydally

put to death 4 do in, hang, kill, slay **5** slain **6** done in, hanged, killed, murder, poison, rub out **7** bump off, butcher, execute **8** dispatch, executed, massacre, murdered, poisoned, strangle **9** bumped off, butchered, finish off, massacred, strangled, suffocate **11** assassinate, electrocute, exterminate **12** assassinated, electrocuted, exterminated

put to flight 4 rout, shoo **5** chase **6** dispel **7** cast out, scatter **8** drive off, send away **11** send packing

put together 4 join **5** unite **7** combine **8** assemble

put to shame 6 ashame **7** chagrin, mortify **9** discomfit, embarrass, humiliate

put to sleep 4 lull **5** quiet **6** sedate **8** knock out **9** narcotize **11** anesthetize

put to use 3 use **5** apply **6** employ, engage, occupy **7** exploit, utilize **9** make use of

put under a spell 5 charm **7** bewitch, enchant **8** entrance **9** fascinate, mesmerize, spellbind

put up 3 can **4** hang **5** erect, house, lodge, raise, store **6** billet **7** shelter **8** preserve **11** accommodate **14** furnish room for

put up with 4 bear, take **5** abide, brave, brook, stand **6** endure, suffer **7** stomach, sustain, undergo **8** stand for, submit to, tolerate **9** withstand **11** countenance

Puvis de Chavannes, Pierre Cecile
born: **5** Lyons **6** France
artwork: **6** Summer **13** Shepherd's Song **14** Ludus pro patria **16** The Poor Fisher- man **17** Life of St Genevieve, The Inspiring Muses **21** Science Arts and Letters

Puzo, Mario
author of: **12** The Godfather

puzzle 4 foil, mull **5** brood, stump **6** baffle, enigma, outwit, ponder, riddle, wonder **7** confuse, dilemma, mystery, mystify, nonplus, perplex, problem **8** bewilder, confound, hoodwink **9** conundrum **10** bafflement, difficulty, perplexity **12** bewilderment, complication **13** mystification

puzzled 6 amazed **7** baffled **8** befogged, confused, troubled **9** astounded, befuddled, mystified, perplexed **10** bewildered, confounded, nonplussed

puzzling 7 elusive **8** baffling **9** confusing, enigmatic **10** mysterious, mystifying, perplexing **11** bewildering, confounding, enigmatical **12** unfathomable **16** hard to understand, incomprehensible

Pyanepsia
origin: **5** Greek **8** Athenian
event: **8** festival
honoring: **6** Apollo **7** harvest

Pygmalion
author: **17** George Bernard Shaw
character: **12** Henry Higgins **14** Eliza Doolittle
basis for: **10** My Fair Lady
director: **14** Anthony Asquith
cast: **11** Wendy Hiller (Eliza Doolittle) **12** Leslie Howard (Professor Henry Higgins) **13** Wilfrid Lawson

Pygmalion
king of: **6** Cyprus
avocation: **8** sculptor
statue named: **7** Galatea
loved: **7** Galatea
statue changed to: **5** woman
wife: **7** Galatea
daughter: **6** Paphos **8** Metharme

pygmy 3 elf, toy, wee **4** mite, runt, tiny **5** dwarf, elfin, short, small **6** bantam, midget, peewee, shrimp **7** manikin **8** dwarfish, half-pint, Tom Thumb **9** miniature, pipsqueak **10** diminutive, homunculus, undersized **11** Lilliputian

Pyncheon family
character in: **24** The House of the Seven Gables
members: **6** Phoebe **8** Clifford, Hepzibah **12** Judge Jaffrey
author: **9** Hawthorne

Pynchon, Thomas
author of: **1** V **15** Gravity's Rainbow **23** The Crying of Lot Forty-Nine

Pyongyang
capital of: **10** North Korea

Pyramus
form: **5** youth
location: **7** Babylon
loved: **6** Thisbe
died at tomb of: **5** Ninus

pyre 8 woodpile
rite: **7** funeral
method: **7** burning

Pyrigenes
epithet of: **8** Dionysus
means: **10** born of fire

Pyriphlegethon see **10** Phlegethon

pyromaniac 7 firebug **8** arsonist **10** incendiary **11** firestarter

Pyronia
epithet of: **7** Artemis
means: **11** fire goddess

pyrope
species: **6** garnet
color: **3** red

pyrophobia
fear of: **4** fire

pyrotechnics 9 fireworks **16** brilliant display **19** dazzling performance

Pyrrhus
king of: **6** Epirus
triumphed over: **5** Romans
result: **11** heavy losses
phrase: **14** Pyrrhic victory

Pythagoras
born: **5** Samos
vocation: **11** philosopher **13** mathematician
created: **7** theorem
of: **13** right triangle

Pythia
priestess of: **6** Apollo
location: **6** Delphi
delivered: **7** oracles

Pythias
friend: **5** Damon

Pythius see **6** Apollo

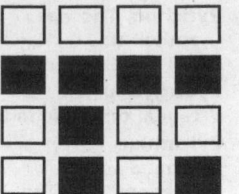  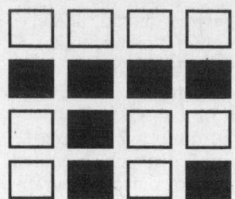

Qatar
  capital/largest city: 4 Doha **7** al-Dawha
  others: 3 Juh **5** Wagra **6** Dukhan, Umm-Bab **7** al-Khawr, Musayid, Umm Said
  government: 7 emirate
  head of state/government: 4 emir
  monetary unit: 5 riyal **6** dirham
  highest point: 13 Aba al-Bawl Hill
  physical feature:
      bay: 5 Salwa
      cape: 5 Rakan **6** Laffan **8** Ushayriq **9** al-Matbakh
      gulf: 7 Bahrain, Persian
      people: 4 Arab **6** Pushtu, Yemeni **7** Baluchi, Iranian **9** Pakistani
      rulers: 12 Great Britain, Ottoman Turks
      sheik/sheikh: 18 Ahmad bin Ali al-Thani **22** Khalifa bin Hamad al-Thani
  language: 6 Arabic
  religion: 5 Islam
      sect: 7 Wahhabi
  war: 4 Gulf **11** Desert Storm
QED 21 quod erat demonstrandum
quack 4 fake, sham **5** phony **6** pseudo **9** charlatan, pretender **10** fake doctor, fraudulent **11** counterfeit, quacksalver **15** medical impostor
quackery 5 bluff, guile **6** deceit **7** cunning **9** deception, duplicity **12** charlatanism
Quadrigesima 4 Lent **9** forty days
quaff 4 down, gulp, swig **5** drink, lap up, swill **6** guzzle, imbibe, tipple **7** swallow, toss off **8** belt down, chug-a-lug **9** knock back **11** drink deeply
quagmire 3 bog, fen, fix, jam **4** mess, mire, ooze, quag, sump **5** marsh, pinch, swamp **6** crisis, morass, muddle, pickle, plight, scrape, slough, sludge, strait **7** dilemma **8** hot water, quandary **9** imbroglio, intricacy, quicksand **10** difficulty, perplexity **11** Gordian knot, involvement, predicament **12** entanglement
quail 3 shy **5** cower, quake, shake **6** blanch, flinch, recoil, shrink **7** run away, shudder, tremble **8** fight shy, turn tail **9** lose heart **10** be cowardly, lose spirit, take fright **11** lose courage **12** have cold feet **16** shake in one's boots **17** shiver in one's shoes, show a yellow streak

quail
  group of: 4 bevy **5** covey
quaint 3 odd **4** rare **5** droll, queer **6** unique **7** antique, bizarre, curious, strange, unusual **8** charming, fanciful, old-timey, original, peculiar, singular, uncommon **9** eccentric, whimsical **10** antiquated, outlandish **11** out-of-the-way, picturesque **12** old-fashioned **13** extraordinary **14** unconventional
quake 4 wave **5** quail, shake, spasm, throb **6** blanch, quaver, quiver, ripple, shiver, thrill, tremor **7** shudder, tremble **9** trembling **10** earthquake **18** seismic disturbance
Quaker
  founder: 9 George Fox
  group: 7 friends
  pronoun: 4 thee, thou
qualification 4 gift **5** forte, skill **6** talent **7** ability, faculty, fitness, proviso **8** aptitude, bona fide, capacity, property, standard **9** attribute, condition, endowment, exception, exemption, objection, postulate, provision, requisite **10** capability, competency, credential, limitation **11** achievement, arrangement, eligibility, requirement, reservation, restriction, stipulation **12** escape clause, modification, prerequisite, suitableness **13** certification **14** accomplishment
qualified 3 fit **4** able, meet **5** adept, equal **6** expert, fitted, suited, versed **7** capable, guarded, hedging, knowing, limited, skilled, trained **8** eligible, equipped, licensed, reserved, skillful, talented **9** ambiguous, certified, competent, efficient, equivocal, practiced **10** authorized, indefinite, proficient, restricted **11** conditional, efficacious, experienced, provisional **12** accomplished
qualify 3 fit **4** ease **5** abate, adapt, alter, endow, equip, limit, ready, train **6** adjust, enable, ground, modify, narrow, permit, reduce, soften, temper **7** assuage, certify, empower, entitle, license, make fit, prepare **8** describe, diminish, mitigate, moderate, restrain, restrict, sanction **9** authorize, condition, give power, measure up **10** be accepted, be eligible, commission, legitimate **11** accommodate **12** characterize, circumscribe, make eligible

qualifying 9 tempering **10** mitigating **11** eligibility, extenuating, preparatory
quality 4 mark, rank **5** blood, class, grade, merit, trait, value, worth **6** aspect, family, nature **7** caliber, dignity, faculty, feature **8** capacity, eminence, position, property, standing **9** attribute, character **11** disposition, distinction, high station, temperament **12** constitution, social status **13** qualification **14** characteristic
Quality Street
  author: 12 James M Barrie
qualm 4 turn **6** nausea **7** scruple, vertigo **9** faintness, giddiness, misgiving **10** dizzy spell, hesitation, queasiness, reluctance, uneasiness **11** compunction, reservation, sick feeling **13** indisposition, unwillingness **14** disinclination **18** twinge of conscience
quandary 3 fix, jam **4** mire **5** pinch **6** crisis, morass, pickle, plight, scrape, strait **7** dilemma, impasse **8** hot water, quagmire **9** imbroglio **10** difficulty **11** involvement, predicament **12** entanglement, kettle of fish
quantities 4 lots, much **5** heaps, loads **7** amounts
quantity 3 sum **4** area, bulk, dose, mass, size **5** quota, share **6** amount, dosage, extent, length, number, volume **7** expanse, measure, portion **8** vastness **9** abundance, aggregate, allotment, amplitude, extension, greatness, magnitude, multitude **10** proportion **11** measurement **13** apportionment
quarantine 7 confine, isolate **9** isolation, segregate, sequester **13** sequestration **15** cordon sanitaire **18** medical segregation
Quare Fellow, The
  author: 12 Brendan Behan
quarrel 3 jar, nag, row **4** carp, feud, fuss, spat, tiff **5** argue, brawl, cavil, clash, fight, scrap **6** bicker, differ, strife **7** contend, discord, dispute, dissent, fall out, wrangle **8** argument, be at odds, conflict, squabble **9** altercate, bickering, complaint, find fault, have words, objection **10** contention, difference, dissension, dissidence, falling out **11** controversy **12** disagreement **13** breach of peace, contradiction, misunderstand **14** apple of discord

15 be at logger heads **16** bone of contention, misunderstanding

quarreling 6 strife **7** discord **8** clashing, conflict, disunity, friction **9** bickering, disputing, scrapping, wrangling **10** contention, dissension, dissidence, squabbling **11** discordance **12** disagreement

quarrelsome 7 peevish **8** captious, churlish, contrary, militant, petulant **9** bellicose, combative, fractious, irascible, querulous, truculent **10** pugnacious **11** belligerent, contentious **12** antagonistic, cantankerous, disagreeable, disputatious **13** argumentative

quarry 3 bed, dig, pit **4** game, lode, mine, prey **5** catch, stone **6** source, victim **8** excavate

quart
abbreviation: **2** qt

quarter, quarters 4 area, part, pity, post, side, spot, zone **5** board, house, lodge, mercy, place, put up, realm, rooms **6** billet, domain, fourth, locale, region, sphere **7** housing, install, lodging, shelter, station, terrain **8** clemency, district, humanity, leniency, locality, location, lodgings, position, precinct, province, sympathy **9** percent, direction, one-fourth, situation, territory **10** compassion, fourth part, indulgence, quadrisect **11** place to live, place to stay, three months **13** quarter dollar, specific place **14** accommodations **15** twenty-five cents

quarterstaff 4 pole **5** staff **6** cudgel

quartz
varieties: **4** sard **5** agate, topaz **8** amethyst **9** carnelian, tiger's-eye **11** rock crystal

quash 4 ruin, stop, undo, void **5** annul, crush, erase, quell, smash, wreck **6** cancel, delete, dispel, efface, quench, recall, revoke, squash, subdue, vacate **7** blot out, destroy, expunge, nullify, put down, repress, rescind, retract, reverse, squelch **8** abrogate, dissolve, override, overrule, overturn, set aside, suppress **9** devastate, eradicate, extirpate, overthrow, overwhelm, repudiate, strike out **10** annihilate, extinguish, invalidate, obliterate, put an end to **11** countermand, exterminate

quasi 4 near, part, semi **6** almost, ersatz **7** halfway, seeming, virtual **8** apparent, somewhat, so-called **9** imitation, synthetic **10** resembling

Quasimodo
character in: **23** The Hunchback of Notre Dame
author: **4** Hugo

Quatermain, Allan
character in: **17** King Solomon's Mines
author: **7** Haggard

quaver 4 beat, sway, wave **5** quake,

shake, throb, trill, waver **6** falter, quiver, shiver, teeter, totter, tremor, wobble, writhe **7** pulsate, shudder, tremble, tremolo, vibrate, vibrato, wriggle **9** oscillate, trembling, vibration **14** tremulous shake

quay 4 dock, mole, pier **5** basin, jetty, levee, wharf **6** marina **7** landing **10** waterfront

queasy 5 giddy, upset **6** uneasy **7** bilious, sickish **8** nauseous, qualmish, troubled **9** nauseated, sickening, uncertain **10** nauseating **13** uncomfortable **16** sick to the stomach

Quebec
borders: **7** Ontario **8** Labrador **9** Hudson Bay **12** Newfoundland, United States **13** Atlantic Ocean **16** Gulf of St Lawrence
cape: **5** Gaspe
city: **6** Quebec **8** Montreal **10** Chicoutimi, Sherbrooke **13** Trois Rivieres
highest point: **18** Mont Jacques Cartier
hockey team: **9** Canadiens, Nordiques
island: **9** Anticosti
lake: **5** Gouin **9** Bienville, Eau Claire, Saint Jean **10** Mistassini **11** Manicouagan
mineral: **4** gold, zinc **6** copper **7** iron ore **8** asbestos **9** limestone
mountain: **5** Otish **10** Laurentian, Shickshock **11** Appalachian **12** Monteregians
province of: **6** Canada

Quechua
tribe: **4** Inca

queen 5 ranee **7** czarina, empress **8** princess **13** female monarch
French: **5** reine
German: **7** Konigin
Latin: **6** regina
Spanish: **5** reina

queen/empress/princess
of Egypt: **9** Cleopatra, Nefertari, Nefertiti **10** Hatshepsut, Hetepheres
of England: **3** Mab **4** Anne, Bess, Jane, Mary **7** Eleanor **8** Boadicea, Victoria **9** Catherine, Charlotte, Elizabeth, Guinevere **10** Bloody Mary, Elizabeth I **11** Elizabeth II, Jane Seymour
of France: **7** Eugenie **9** Josephine **11** Marie Louise **14** Marie de Medicis **15** Marie Antoinette
of Italy/Rome: **7** Poppaea **9** Agrippina, Messalina **13** Livia Drusilla
of Monaco: **8** Caroline **9** Stephanie **10** Grace Kelly
of the Netherlands: **7** Beatrix, Juliana **10** Wilhelmina
of Poland: **7** Jadwiga
of Portugal: **5** Maria **9** Elizabeth
of Russia: **9** Alexandra, Catherine **17** Catherine the Great
of Scotland: **4** Mary **13** Saint Margaret **16** Mary Queen of Scots

of Spain: **8** Isabella **16** Elizabeth Farnese
of Sweden: **9** Christina
of Syria: **7** Zenobia
in folklore: **3** Mab **7** Titania

Queen Christina
director: **15** Rouben Mamoulian
cast: **8** Ian Keith **10** Greta Garbo, Lewis Stone **11** John Gilbert **12** C Aubrey Smith

Queen Mab
author: **18** Percy Bysshe Shelley

Queen of Amazons 9 Hippolyta, Hippolyte

Queen of Hearts
character in: **28** Alice's Adventures in Wonderland
author: **7** Carroll

Queen of Heaven 4 Hera, Mary **6** Ishtar **7** Mylitta

Queen of Spades, The
also: **12** Pikovaya Dama
opera by: **11** Tchaikovsky
character: **4** Lisa **6** Herman **8** Countess

Queen of Spades, The
author: **16** Alexander Pushkin

Queen of the Surf
nickname of: **14** Esther Williams

Queen's Necklace, The
author: **14** Alexandre Dumas (pere)
character: **5** Oliva **13** Count de Charny **15** Cardinal de Rohan, Count Cagliostro, Marie Antoinette **16** Andree de Taverney **18** Philippe de Taverney **21** Jeanne de la Motte Valois

Queequeg
character in: **8** Moby Dick
author: **8** Melville

queer 3 gay, odd **4** daft, harm, hurt, rare, ruin **5** crazy, dizzy, droll, faint, fishy, funny, giddy, shady, spoil, weird, woozy, wreck **6** absurd, damage, exotic, impair, injure, quaint, qualmy, queasy, thwart, unique **7** bizarre, comical, curious, disrupt, erratic, reeling, strange, touched, unusual **8** abnormal, bohemian, doubtful, fanciful, freakish, original, peculiar, uncommon, unhinged **9** eccentric, fantastic, grotesque, homosexual, irregular, laughable, ludicrous, unnatural **10** capricious, compromise, farfetched, irrational, outlandish, remarkable, ridiculous, suspicious, unbalanced, unexampled, unorthodox **11** astonishing, exceptional, light-headed, out of the way, slightly ill, vertiginous **12** preposterous, questionable, unparalleled **13** extraordinary, nonconforming, unprecedented **14** unconventional
French: **5** outre

quell 4 calm, dull, ease, hush, lull, rout, ruin, stay, stem **5** abate, allay, blunt, crush, quash, quiet, still, worst, wreck **6** becalm, deaden, defeat, pacify, quench, reduce, soften, soothe, subdue **7** appease, assuage, compose, conquer, destroy, mollify, put down, scatter, silence, squelch **8** beat down, disperse, mitigate, overcome, palliate, stamp out, suppress, vanquish **9** alleviate, overpower, overthrow, overwhelm, subjugate **10** extinguish **11** tranquilize

quench 4 cool, sate **5** allay, crush, douse, quell, slake **6** dampen, put out, stifle **7** appease, blow out, put down, satiate, satisfy, smother **8** stamp out, suppress **10** annihilate, extinguish

Quentin Durward
  author: 14 Sir Walter Scott
  character: 8 Isabelle **9** Le Balafre **10** Jacqueline **11** King Louis XI **12** Lady Hameline **13** Ludovic Lesley **15** Countess of Croye **16** William de la Marck **18** Hayraddin Maugrabin **20** King Louis the Eleventh **21** Charles Duke of Burgundy **23** Count Philip de Crevecoeur

querulous 4 sour **5** cross, fussy, testy, whiny **6** cranky, touchy **7** crabbed, finical, finicky, fretful, grouchy, peevish, pettish, waspish, whining **8** captious, exacting, petulant, shrewish **9** difficult, grumbling, irascible, irritable, long-faced, obstinate, resentful, splenetic **10** nettlesome **11** complaining, quarrelsome **12** disagreeable, discontented, disputatious, dissatisfied, faultfinding

query 3 ask **4** quiz **5** doubt, issue, quest **6** demand, impugn, search **7** dispute, examine, impeach, inquest, inquiry, inspect, problem, request, suspect **8** distrust, look into, mistrust, question, sound out **9** catechize, challenge, inquire of **10** controvert **11** examination, inquisition, interrogate, investigate, make inquiry **13** interrogation, investigation

quest 4 hunt, seek **6** pursue, search, voyage **7** crusade, journey, mission, pursuit, seeking **9** adventure **10** enterprise, pilgrimage **11** exploration

Quested, Adela
  character in: 15 A Passage to India
  author: 7 Forster

Quest for Fire
  director: 17 Jean-Jacques Annaud
  cast: 10 Ron Perlman **12** Rae Dawn Chong **13** Everett McGill

question 3 ask, rub **4** pump, quiz, test **5** doubt, drill, grill, issue, query **6** impugn, matter, motion, oppose **7** dispute, dubiety, examine, problem, subject, suspect **8** distrust, look into, mistrust, proposal, sound out **9** catechize, challenge, inquire of, misgiving, moot point, objection **10** difficulty, disbelieve **11** controversy, interrogate,

investigate, proposition, uncertainty **12** cross-examine **13** consideration

questionable 4 moot **5** fishy, shady **6** unsure **7** dubious, in doubt, suspect **8** arguable, doubtful, puzzling, unproven **9** ambiguous, confusing, debatable, enigmatic, equivocal, in dispute, uncertain, undecided **10** apocryphal, disputable, indefinite, mysterious, mystifying, perplexing, suspicious **12** hypothetical **13** controversial, problematical

queue 3 row **4** file, line, rank **5** chain, train **6** column, string

quibble 3 nag **4** carp, spar **5** argue, cavil, dodge, fence, fudge, shift **6** bicker, haggle, hassle, nicety, niggle, waffle **7** evasion, nitpick, shuffle **8** artifice, pretense, squabble, subtlety, white lie **9** be evasive, duplicity **10** equivocate, pick a fight, subterfuge **11** distraction **12** equivocation **13** dodge the issue, prevarication

quick 3 apt **4** able, deft, fast, keen, spry **5** acute, adept, agile, alert, brief, brisk, eager, fiery, fleet, hasty, rapid, sharp, smart, swift, testy **6** abrupt, active, adroit, astute, brainy, bright, clever, expert, facile, flying, frisky, lively, nimble, prompt, shrewd, speedy, sudden, touchy, winged **7** hurried, peppery, waspish **8** animated, choleric, headlong, petulant, skillful, snappish, spirited, vigilant, vigorous **9** dexterous, energetic, excitable, impatient, impetuous, impulsive, irascible, irritable, sagacious, splenetic, sprightly, vivacious, whirlwind, wideawake **10** discerning, high-strung, hot-blooded **11** accelerated, expeditious, hot-tempered, intelligent, light-footed, penetrating, precipitate **12** nimble-footed **13** perspicacious, temperamental

quicken 4 fire, goad, move, rush, spur, stir, urge **5** drive, egg on, hurry, impel, pique, press, rouse, speed **6** affect, arouse, excite, hasten, hustle, incite, kindle, propel, revive, vivify **7** actuate, advance, animate, enliven, further, hurry on, inspire, provoke, refresh, sharpen **8** activate, dispatch, energize, enkindle, expedite, inspirit, vitalize **9** galvanize, instigate, stimulate **10** accelerate, invigorate **11** precipitate

quick glance
  French: 9 coup d'oeil

quickly 4 anon, fast, soon **6** keenly, presto, pronto **7** briefly, hastily, rapidly, swiftly **8** promptly, speedily **9** instantly **11** immediately **12** lickety-split

Quickly, Mistress
  character in: 22 The Merry Wives of Windsor
  author: 11 Shakespeare

quickness 5 haste, speed **6** acuity

8 alacrity, celerity, keenness, rapidity **9** acuteness, alertness, dexterity, sharpness **10** cleverness, nimbleness, promptness **15** expeditiousness

quick-tempered 5 cross, testy **6** cranky, shirty, touchy **7** grouchy, peevish, waspish **8** choleric, churlish, shrewish, snappish **9** emotional, excitable, irascible, irritable **10** ill-humored **11** bad-tempered, hot-tempered, quarrelsome **12** cantankerous **13** temperamental

quick-witted 4 keen **5** acute, alert, aware, quick, ready, sharp, smart, witty **6** astute, bright, clever, shrewd **8** incisive **9** brilliant, wide-awake **10** discerning, perceptive **11** clearheaded, intelligent, penetrating **13** perspicacious

quid pro quo 4 swap **5** trade **8** exchange **9** tit for tat **21** something for something

quien sabe? 8 who knows?

quiescence 7 latency **8** dormancy, inaction **10** inactivity

quiescent 6 latent **7** dormant **8** inactive **10** in abeyance

quiet 3 low, mum **4** calm, curb, dull, ease, hush, lull, meek, mild, mute, rest, soft, stay, stop **5** abate, allay, blunt, check, fixed, inert, peace, plain, quell, still **6** arrest, at rest, deaden, docile, dozing, gentle, humble, hushed, lessen, mellow, modest, muffle, pacify, placid, repose, sedate, serene, settle, silent, simple, soften, soothe, stable, steady, stifle, subdue, weaken **7** assuage, clement, comfort, compose, dormant, halcyon, mollify, not busy, pacific, passive, patient, relieve, restful, silence, smother, subdued, suspend, unmoved **8** becalmed, calmness, comatose, composed, decrease, immobile, inactive, mitigate, moderate, muteness, not rough, not showy, palliate, peaceful, quietude, reserved, reticent, retiring, serenity, sleeping, stagnant, taciturn, tranquil **9** alleviate, collected, contented, easygoing, immovable, lethargic, makequiet, noiseless, not bright, peaceable, placidity, quietness, set at ease, soundless, stillness, temperate, terminate, unruffled, voiceless **10** coolheaded, gentleness, motionless, phlegmatic, put a stop to, relaxation, slumbering, speechless, stationary, stock-still, unassuming, untroubled **11** discontinue, tranquility, tranquilize, undisturbed, unexcitable, unobtrusive, unperturbed **12** bring to an end, even-tempered, inarticulate, peacefulness, tranquillity **13** at a standstill, dispassionate, imperturbable, noiselessness, soundlessness, unimpassioned, unpretentious **14** unostentatious, unpresumptuous

15 uncommunicative, undemonstrative

quietly 5 coyly **6** calmly, humbly, meekly, mildly, mutely, softly, tamely **8** demurely, modestly, placidly, serenely, silently **9** bashfully, inaudibly, patiently **10** composedly, moderately, peacefully, tranquilly **11** collectedly, contentedly, diffidently, noiselessly, pacifically, soundlessly, temperately, unexcitedly **12** speechlessly, unassumingly, unboastfully **13** unobtrusively, unperturbedly **15** dispassionately, unpretentiously, without ceremony **16** unostentatiously **17** undemonstratively

Quiet Man, The
director: **8** John Ford
author: **13** Liam O'Flaherty
cast: **9** John Wayne **12** Maureen O'Hara **14** Mildred Natwick, Victor McLaglen **15** Barry Fitzgerald
setting: **7** Ireland
score: **11** Victor Young
Oscar for: **8** director

quietness 5 peace, quiet **7** silence **8** softness **9** stillness **12** peacefulness

quietude 4 calm, rest **6** repose **8** easiness **9** composure

quill 3 pen **4** fold, hair, pick, seta, stem, tube **5** pluck, plume, spike, spine, spool **6** bobbin, needle **7** bristle, feather, spindle **9** toothpick

Quilp
character in: **19** The Old Curiosity Shop
author: **7** Dickens

quilt 5 cover **6** spread **7** blanket **8** coverlet **9** bedspread, comforter

Quin, Widow
character in: **24** Playboy of the Western World
author: **5** Synge

Quincy, M. E.
character: **3** Lee **5** Danny, (Sgt) Brill **11** Sam Fujiyama, (Dr) Robert Astin **12** (Lt) Frank Monahan
cast: **9** Robert Ito **10** John S Ragin **11** Jack Klugman, Joseph Roman, Val Bisoglio **12** Garry Walberg **13** Lynette Mettey
setting: **10** Los Angeles **11** Danny's Place

Quinn, Anthony
born: **6** Mexico **9** Chihuahua
wife: **16** Katherine DeMille
roles: **8** La Strada **10** Viva Zapata **11** Lust for Life **13** Zorba the Greek **17** The Guns of Navarone **22** Requiem for a Heavyweight, The Shoes of the Fisherman
autobiography: **14** The Original Sin

Quintana and Friends
author: **16** John Gregory Dunne

quintessence 4 core, gist, pith, soul **5** heart **6** elixir, marrow, nature **7** essence **8** exemplar, quiddity, sum total **9** substance **10** embodiment **12** distillation **15** personification, sum and substance

quip 3 gag, pun **4** barb, gibe, jape, jeer, jest, joke **5** crack, sally, spoof, taunt **6** banter, retort **7** epigram, put-down, riposte, sarcasm **8** badinage, raillery, repartee, wordplay **9** wisecrack, witticism
French: **6** bon mot **14** double entendre

Quirinus
origin: **5** Roman
god of: **3** war
personifies: **11** Roman nation
identified with: **7** Romulus

quirk 4 kink, turn, whim **6** fetish, foible, oddity, vagary, whimsy **7** caprice **8** crotchet, odd fancy **9** mannerism **10** aberration **11** abnormality, affectation, peculiarity, sudden twist **12** eccentricity, idiosyncrasy

quisling 6 puppet **7** traitor **12** collaborator **16** collaborationist

quit 3 end, rid **4** free, stop **5** cease, clear, forgo, leave, let go, waive, yield **6** depart, desist, disown, exempt, forego, give up, reject, resign, retire **7** abandon, disavow, drop out, forsake, take off **8** abdicate, absolved, forswear, renounce, withdraw **9** acquitted, foreswear, leave a job, surrender, terminate **10** discharged, exculpated, exonerated, relinquish **11** discontinue

quite 4 very **5** fully, truly **6** highly, hugely, indeed, in fact, in toto, really, surely, vastly, verily, wholly **7** exactly, in truth, totally, utterly **8** actually, entirely, outright **9** assuredly, certainly, extremely, in reality, out and-out, perfectly, precisely, unusually, veritably **10** absolutely, altogether, completely, enormously, positively, remarkably, throughout **11** exceedingly, excessively **12** considerably **13** exceptionally

Quito
capital of: **7** Ecuador

quiver 3 tic **4** jerk, jolt, jump, pant **5** quake, shake, spasm, throb **6** quaver, shiver, totter, tremor, twitch, wobble **7** flicker, flutter, pulsate, seizure, shudder, tremble, vibrate, wriggle **8** convulse **9** fluctuate, oscillate, palpitate, pulsation, quivering, twitching, vibration **10** convulsion **11** palpitation

Quiverful, Mr
character in: **16** Barchester Towers
author: **8** Trollope

quivering 7 shaking **9** agitating, quavering, shimmying, shivering, trembling, vibrating **10** flittering, fluttering, shuddering, twittering **11** palpitating

qui vive? 12 who goes there?

quixotic 4 wild **6** absurd, dreamy, madcap, poetic **7** utopian **8** fanciful, romantic **9** fantastic, impulsive, visionary, whimsical **10** chimerical, idealistic, ridiculous, starry-eyed **11** impractical, ineffective, sentimental, unrealistic **12** preposterous **13** inefficacious

quiz 3 ask, rib **4** exam, joke, mock, pump, test **5** prank, query, taunt, tease **6** banter **7** examine, inquest, inquiry **8** question, ridicule, sound out **9** catechism, eccentric, inquire of **11** examination, inquisition, interrogate, investigate, questioning **12** cross-examine **13** interrogation, investigation **16** cross-examination

Quiz Kids
host: **8** Joe Kelly **14** Clifton Fadiman

quizzical 3 coy **4** arch **6** joking **7** baffled, curious, mocking, puzzled, teasing **8** derisive, impudent, insolent **9** bantering, inquiring, perplexed, searching **11** inquisitive, questioning

quoad hoc 12 as much as this, to this extent

quod erat demonstrandum 17 which was to be shown **24** which was to be demonstrated
abbreviation: **3** QED

quod erat faciendum 16 which was to be done

quod vide 8 which see
abbreviation: **2** qv

quo jure? 11 by what right?

quo modo 3 how **9** in what way **19** in the same manner that

quondam 4 erst, late, once, past **6** bygone, former **8** formerly, sometime **9** erstwhile

quota 4 part **5** share **6** ration **7** measure, minimum, portion **8** quantity **9** allotment **10** allocation, assignment, percentage, proportion **12** distribution **13** apportionment

quotation 5 quote **7** cutting, excerpt, extract, passage **8** citation, clipping **9** reference, selection **12** illustration

quote 4 cite, name **6** adduce, recall, repeat, retell **7** excerpt, extract, refer to **8** instance **9** exemplify, recollect, reproduce **10** paraphrase

quoted passage 7 excerpt, extract **9** quotation

quotidian 5 daily **6** common **8** everyday, ordinary **11** commonplace

Quo Vadis?
author: **17** Henryk Sienkiewicz
character: **4** Nero **5** Chilo, Lygia, Peter **8** Vinitius **9** Petronius, Tigellius
director: **11** Mervyn LeRoy
cast: **7** Leo Genn **11** Deborah Kerr **12** Peter Ustinov, Robert Taylor
setting: **11** ancient Rome

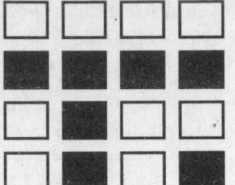
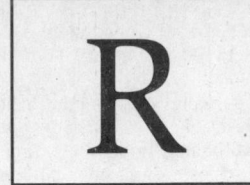
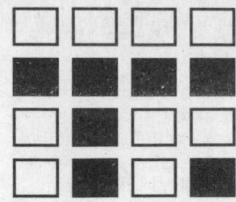

Ra
  also: 2 Re
  origin: 5 Greek 10 Heliopolis
  god of: 3 sun
  also worshipped by: 9 Egyptians
Rabat, Rabbat
  capital of: 7 Morocco
rabbi 6 master, rabbin 7 scholar, teacher 9 clergyman 15 spiritual leader
rabbinical, rabbinic 8 clerical
rabbit 4 cony, hare, jack, lure 5 bunny, coney, lapin 6 novice, rodent 8 beginner 10 cottontail, pacesetter
Rabbit Is Rich
  author: 10 John Updike
Rabbit Redux
  author: 10 John Updike
rabble 3 mob 5 swarm 7 the herd 8 populace, riffraff 9 commoners, hoi polloi, the masses 11 proletariat, rank and file 12 lower classes 15 disorderly crowd 16 the great unwashed
  French: 8 canaille
  German: 17 Lumpenproletariat
Rabelais, Francois
  author of: 22 Gargantua and Pantagruel
rabid 4 wild 6 ardent, crazed, raging 7 berserk, fervent, frantic, violent, zealous 8 deranged, frenzied, maniacal, wild-eyed 9 fanatical 11 hydrophobic 17 foaming at the mouth
race 3 fly, run 4 dart, dash, heat, rush 5 hurry 6 hasten, hustle 7 contest, operate 8 campaign 11 competition
racecourse 4 turf 5 track 6 course 9 racetrack
Rachel
  father: 5 Laban
  husband: 5 Jacob
  sister: 4 Leah
  son: 6 Joseph 8 Benjamin
  slave: 6 Bilhah
Rachmaninov (Rachmaninoff, Rakhmaninov), Sergei
  born: 6 Russia 8 Novgorod
  composer of: 15 Symphonic Dances 16 The Isle of the Dead 19 Second Piano Concerto 26 Rhapsody on a Theme by (of) Paganini
Racine, Jean Baptiste
  author of: 6 Phedre 7 Athalie 8 Berenice 10 Andromache 11 Britannicus
racism 7 bigotry 8 color bar 9 color line 10 race hatred, racial bias 11 segregation 15 racial prejudice 20 racial discrimination
rack 4 buck, gait, hurt, neck, pace, pain, path 5 agony, cloud, exert, frame, raise, track, trail, worry, wreck, wring 6 canter, holder, strain 7 afflict, agonize, draw off, oppress, stretch, torment, torture 8 distress 9 suffering 10 destruction, excruciate, iron maiden
racked 4 torn 5 paced 6 framed, pained, traced, walked 7 annoyed, tracked, trotted, wronged, worried 8 cantered, suffered, tortured 9 afflicted, anguished, destroyed, oppressed, tormented 10 persecuted
racket 3 din 4 game, line, roar, stir 5 babel 6 clamor, hubbub, rumpus, tumult, uproar 7 clangor, clatter, turmoil 8 business, shouting 9 commotion, loud noise 10 hullabaloo, hurly-burly, occupation, turbulence 11 disturbance, pandemonium 12 caterwauling, vociferation
racketeer 4 hood 5 crook 6 bagman, bandit, extort 7 hoodlum, mafioso, mobster 8 criminal, gangster 12 extortionist
racking 7 painful 9 agonizing, torturous 10 tormenting, unbearable 11 intolerable, unendurable 12 excruciating, insufferable
raconteur 8 fabulist, narrator, romancer 10 anecdotist 11 storyteller 13 teller of tales 14 spinner of yarns
racy 4 keen 5 bawdy, crude, heady, lurid, zesty 6 erotic, lively, ribald, risque, smutty, vulgar 7 buoyant, glowing, obscene, zestful 8 animated, exciting, immodest, indecent, off-color, prurient, spirited, vigorous 9 energetic, fast-paced, salacious, sparkling 10 suggestive 11 stimulating 12 exhilarating, pornographic
radar
  invented by: 4 Watt 6 Watson
Radcliffe, Mrs Ann
  author of: 10 The Italian 21 The Mysteries of Udolpho
raddle 3 rod 4 reed, scar, twig 5 fence, hedge, rouge, stick, weave 6 branch, ruddle 8 hematite, red ocher, red ochre 10 interweave
radiance, radiancy 3 joy 5 gleam, gleem, sheen 6 dazzle, luster 7 glitter, rapture, sparkle 8 lambency, splendor 9 animation, happiness 10 brightness, brilliance, brilliancy, effulgence, luminosity, refulgence 11 coruscation, iridescence 12 luminousness, resplendence 13 incandescence
  god of: 5 Baldr 6 Balder, Baldur
radiant 5 aglow, happy, sunny 6 bright, elated, joyous 7 beaming, glowing, pleased, shining 8 blissful, dazzling, ecstatic, flashing, gladsome, gleaming, luminous, lustrous 9 brilliant, delighted, effulgent, overjoyed, rapturous, refulgent, sparkling 10 glittering 12 incandescent 13 scintillating
radiate 4 beam, pour, shed 5 carry 6 spread 7 diffuse, diverge, give off, give out, scatter 8 disperse, emit heat, transmit 9 branch out, circulate, emit light, spread out 11 disseminate
radical 4 rash 5 basic, rebel 6 severe 7 drastic, extreme 8 left-wing, militant 9 extremist, firebrand 10 immoderate, inordinate 11 freethinker, fundamental, precipitate 13 revolutionary 22 antiestablishmentarian
radio
  invented by: 7 Donovan, Fleming, Marconi 8 De Forest, Nicolson 9 Armstrong, Fessenden 12 Alexanderson
radium
  chemical symbol: 2 Ra
radon
  chemical symbol: 2 Rn
raffish 3 low 4 fast, wild 5 cheap, rowdy, showy 6 common, flashy, rakish, tawdry, vulgar 7 boorish 8 rakehell 9 worthless 10 dissipated 12 devil-may-care, disreputable
raft 3 lot 4 mass 5 barge, float 6 plenty 7 carrier, pontoon 8 flatboat, platform, quantity 9 abundance, multitude
Raft, George
  real name: 11 George Ranft
  born: 9 New York NY
  roles: 8 Scarface 11 Johnny Angel 12 Guido Rinaldo 13 Some Like It Hot
rag 3 kid, rib 4 scap, song, tune, twit 5 cloth, taunt, taunt, tease 6 harass 7 torment 8 magazine 9 newspaper 11 ragtime tune 14 worn-out garment
ragamuffin 3 bum 4 hobo, waif

5 gamin, tramp **6** beggar, gamine, hoyden, sloven, urchin, wretch **7** vagrant **8** derelict, vagabond **9** itinerant, ragpicker **10** panhandler, street arab **11** guttersnipe **14** tatterdemalion

rage 3 fad, ire **4** boil, fume, fury, mode, rant, rave, roar **5** craze, furor, mania, pique, storm, vogue, wrath **6** blow up, choler, frenzy, seethe, spleen, temper **7** explode, fashion, ferment, flare up, madness, passion, rampage, umbrage **8** paroxysm, the thing **9** animosity, fulminate, raise cain, throw a fit, vehemence **10** bitterness, excitement, irritation, resentment, the ''in'' thing **11** displeasure, high dudgeon, indignation, the last word **12** current style, le dernier cri, perturbation, violent anger **13** temper tantrum **14** the latest thing **15** fly off the handle, froth at the mouth

ragged 4 rent, torn, worn **5** seedy, tacky **6** beat up, frayed, shabby, shaggy, shoddy **7** patched, run down, worn-out **8** battered, shredded, strained, tattered **9** overtaxed **10** aggravated, threadbare, worn to rags **11** exacerbated

ragging 5 chaff **6** banter **7** kidding, ribbing, teasing **8** chaffing, needling, raillery, taunting, twitting

raging 3 mad **4** wild **5** angry, livid, rabid, rough **6** fierce, raving, stormy **7** fervent, frantic, furious, rampant, violent **8** frenzied, incensed, storming **9** turbulent **10** blustering, ferocious, infuriated **11** tempestuous

Raging Bull
   director: 14 Martin Scorsese
   cast: 8 Joe Pesci **12** Frank Vincent, Robert De Niro (Jake La Motta) **13** Cathy Moriarty
   Oscar for: 5 actor (De Niro)

Ragnarok
   also: 15 Gotterdammerung **17** Twilight of the Gods
   origin: 12 Scandinavian
   event: 11 final battle
   battlefield: 6 Vigrid

ragout 4 hash, stew **7** borscht, goulash **9** fricassee

Ragtime
   author: 10 E L Doctorow

raid 4 bust **5** foray, onset, sally, storm **6** attack, inroad, invade, razzia, sortie **7** assault, round-up **8** invasion **10** pounce upon **14** surprise attack

Raiders of the Lost Ark
   director: 15 Steven Spielberg
   cast: 10 Karen Allen, Wolf Kahler **11** Paul Freeman **12** Harrison Ford
   sequel: 29 Indiana Jones and the Last Crusade **30** Indiana Jones and the Temple of Doom

rail 3 bar **4** rage, rant **5** scold, fence, train **6** blow up, scream, take on **7** barrier, carry on, declaim, inveigh, railing, railway, the cars **8** banister, railroad **9** fulminate **10** vituperate, vociferate **11** rant and rave **14** foam at the mouth

rail at 5 scold **6** berate **7** chew out **9** castigate **14** inveigh against

railing 3 bar **5** fence, grate, rails **6** fender **7** barrier, parapet, support **8** banister **9** enclosing **10** balustrade

raillery 5 chaff, sport **6** banter, japing, joking, satire **7** fooling, jesting, joshing, kidding, ragging, razzing, ribbing, teasing **8** badinage, chaffing, roasting, twitting **10** lampoonery, persiflage, pleasantry

railroad sleeping car
   French: 8 wagon-lit

railroad station 5 depot **8** terminal, terminus

railway 4 tube **5** track, train **6** cogway, subway **7** cogroad, trolley **8** elevated, monorail, railroad **9** streetcar

raiment 4 duds, togs **5** dress **6** attire **7** apparel, clothes, costume, threads **8** clothing, garments **11** habiliments

rain, rains 4 down, drop, mist, pour **5** spate **6** deluge, lavish, shower, squall **7** drizzle, monsoon, torrent **8** downpour, drencher, plethora, rainfall, send down, sprinkle **9** hurricane, rainstorm **10** cloudburst **13** precipitation, thundershower **15** rain cats and dogs **16** come down in sheets **17** come down in buckets
   god of: 4 Thor

Rainbow
   goddess of: 4 Iris

Rainbow, The
   author: 10 D H Lawrence
   character: 10 Anna Lensky **11** Lydia Lensky, Tom Brangwen **12** Will Brangwen **14** Ursula Brangwen **15** Anton Skrebensky

Rainbow Bridge *see* **7** bifrost

raincoat 3 mac **4** mack **6** poncho, ulster **7** oilskin, slicker **8** burberry **9** tarpaulin **10** mackintosh, trenchcoat, waterproof

rainless 3 dry **4** arid, sere **10** desert-like

Rains, Claude
   born: 6 London **7** England
   wife: 11 Isabel Jeans
   roles: 9 Notorious **10** Casablanca, Now Voyager **13** Mr Skeffington **14** Anthony Adverse **15** The Invisible Man **16** Lawrence of Arabia **17** Here Comes Mr Jordan **20** The Phantom of the Opera **23** Mr Smith Goes to Washington **24** The Adventures of Robin Hood

rain shower 6 shower **7** drizzle **8** sprinkle **12** thunderstorm

rainstorm 6 deluge, shower **8** downfall, downpour **10** cloudburst **12** thunderstorm

rainy 3 wet **4** damp **7** drizzly, showery **11** pouring rain **18** raining cats and dogs

raise 3 end **4** grow, hike, lift, rear, spur, urge **5** amass, boost, breed, build, erect, nurse, pique, put up, rouse, set up, spark **6** arouse, awaken, excite, foster, hike up, jack up, kindle, obtain, stir up **7** advance, bring in, bring up, canvass, collect, develop, elevate, inflame, inflate, inspire, nurture, procure, produce, sharpen, solicit **8** increase, summon up **9** construct, cultivate, elevation, promotion, stimulate, terminate **10** make higher, put forward **11** advancement

raise aloft 5 boost, hoist **6** lift up, uplift **7** elevate, upraise

raised 4 bred, grew **5** anted, built, grown **6** anteed, convex, jacked, lifted, reared, roused **7** aroused, erected, exalted, hoisted, honored, incited **8** elevated, embossed, leavened, mustered **9** brought up, collected **10** cultivated **11** resurrected

Raisin in the Sun, A
   director: 12 Daniel Petrie
   based on play by: 17 Lorraine Hansberry
   cast: 7 Ruby Dee **9** Ivan Dixon **10** Diana Sands **13** Claudia McNeil, Sidney Poitier
   setting: 7 Chicago

rake 4 comb, goat, roue **5** rogue, satyr, scour, sport **6** lecher, pepper, rascal **7** Don Juan, playboy, ransack, seducer, swinger **8** Casanova, Lothario, enfilade, prodigal, rakehell **9** debauchee, libertine, womanizer **10** immoralist, profligate, sensualist, voluptuary

rake-off 3 cut, fee **5** piece **10** percentage **16** piece of the action

Rake's Progress, The
   etchings by: 7 Hogarth
   opera by: 10 Stravinsky
   character: 10 Ann Trulove, Nick Shadow **11** Baba the Turk, Mother Goose, Tom Rakewell

rakish 4 airy **6** breezy, dapper, jaunty, sporty **7** dashing, gallant, immoral, lustful **8** cavalier, debonair, depraved, sporting **9** bumptious, debauched, dissolute, lecherous, libertine **10** dissipated, lascivious, profligate, sauntering, swaggering

rally 4 meet, rush **5** score, unite **6** caucus, gather, muster, pick up, powwow, revive **7** catch up, collect, get well, improve, recruit, reunite, revival **8** assemble, assembly, recovery **9** come round, gathering, get better, reconvene **10** assemblage, convalesce, convention, reassemble, recuperate **11** convocation, improvement, mass meeting, pull through, restoration **12**

call together, congregation, recuperation **13** convalescence

ram 3 hit, jam **4** beat, bump, butt,
dash, goat, slam **5** crash, drive, force,
smash **6** batter, hammer, hurtle,
strike, thrust **7** run into

Ram
    constellation of: 5 Aries

ramble 3 gad **4** hike, roam, rove, wind
5 amble, drift, range, snake, twist **6**
stroll, wander, zigzag **7** meander,
saunter, traipse **8** gad about, idle walk
9 gallivant **11** perambulate, peregrinate

rambling 6 prolix, uneven **7** diffuse
10 circuitous, digressive, discursive,
disjointed

rambunctious 4 wild **5** noisy, rowdy
6 active, unruly **7** raucous, untamed,
violent **9** irascible **10** boisterous, pugnacious **11** quarrelsome **14** uncontrollable

Rameau, Jean-Philippe
    born: 5 Dijon **6** France
    composer of: 6 Platee **8** Dardanus **13**
    Les Fetes d'Hebe **14** Castor et Pollux
    15 Castor and Pollux **16** Les Indes
    Galantes, The Indigo Suitors **17** Hip-
    polyte et Aricie **20** La Princesse de
    Navarre

ramification 3 arm **4** part, spur **5**
prong **6** branch **8** division, offshoot **9**
branching, outgrowth **10** divergence,
separation **11** consequence, subdivision

rampage 4 rage **5** storm **7** run amok,
run riot

rampant 4 rife **5** erect **6** raging **8** epidemic, pandemic **9** prevalent, un-
checked, universal **10** on hind legs,
standing up, widespread **12** ungovernable, unrestrained **14** uncontrollable

rampart 7 barrier, bastion, bulwark,
parapet **9** barricade, earthwork **10**
breastwork **13** defensive wall, fortification **14** protective wall

Ramsay, William
    field: 9 chemistry
    nationality: 7 British
    discovered: 4 neon **5** argon (in air) **6**
    helium **7** krypton
    awarded: 10 Nobel Prize

ramshackle 5 shaky **6** flimsy, shabby
7 rickety, run-down **8** decrepit, unstable, unsteady **9** crumbling, tottering
10 tumbledown **11** dilapidated **13** deteriorating

Ramtil *see* **5** Niger

ranch 4 farm **5** range **6** grange, spread
7 acreage, station **8** hacienda **10** plantation

rancher 6 cowboy, farmer, gaucho **7**
cowhand, cowpoke **8** herdsman,
sheepman, stockman **9** cattleman **10**
cowpuncher

rancid 3 old **4** foul, gamy, high, rank **6**

putrid, strong **8** mephitic, stinking **10**
malodorous

rancor 4 hate **5** spite **6** animus, enmity, hatred, malice, spleen **7** ill will
8 acrimony **9** animosity, antipathy,
hostility **10** antagonism, bitterness, ill
feeling, resentment **11** malevolence
12 spitefulness

rancorous 5 nasty **6** bitter **7** hostile **8**
churlish, spiteful, vengeful, venomous
9 splenetic **10** ill-natured **11** acrimonious **12** antagonistic

Rand, Ayn
    author of: 6 Anthem **13** Atlas
    Shrugged **15** The Fountainhead **17**
    Romantic Manifesto
    philosophy: 11 objectivism

Randall, Tony
    real name: 16 Leonard Rosenberg
    born: 7 Tulsa OK
    wife: 13 Heather Harlan
    roles: 9 Mr Peepers **10** Felix Unger,
    Pillow Talk **12** Harvey Weskit, The
    Odd Couple **13** Fatal Instinct, The
    Mating Game **20** The Seven Faces of
    Dr Lao **22** Hitler's SS: Portrait in Evil

random 5 stray **6** casual, chance **7**
aimless, offhand **9** haphazard, hit-or-
miss, unplanned **10** accidental, fortuitous, occasional, undesigned, unexpected, unintended **12** adventitious **13**
unintentional **14** unpremeditated

range 3 run **4** roam, rove **5** field,
gamut, limit, orbit, reach, ridge, scope
6 bounds, domain, extend, massif,
plains, radius, sierra, sphere, wander
7 explore, pasture, purview, stretch,
variety **8** province **9** selection **11**
grazing land **16** chain of mountains

Rangoon
    capital of: 5 Burma **7** Myanmar
    former name: 5 Dagon **6** Yangon
    founder: 10 Alaungpaya
    landmark: 10 Sule Pagoda **15** Shwe
    Dagon Pagoda
    name means: 11 end of strife
    river: 7 Rangoon
    square: 12 Independence

rangy 4 tall **5** broad, lanky **9** expansive, extensive

rank 3 row **4** bald, file, foul, line, lush,
rate, sort, tall, type, wild **5** class,
crass, dense, grade, gross, level,
nasty, order, sheer, stale, stand, total,
utter **6** arrant, coarse, column, estate,
filthy, jungly, lavish, rancid, status **7**
come out, echelon, glaring, profuse,
quality, rampart **8** absolute, complete,
flagrant, position, standing, tropical **9**
atrocious, be classed, come first,
downright, have place, luxuriant,
monstrous, overgrown **10** outrageous,
scurrilous **11** highgrowing, ill smelling, unmitigated **12** over abundant **14**
classification, social standing, strong
smelling

rank and file 6 troops **17** enlisted personnel, general membership

Rankine, William John Macquorn
    field: 7 physics
    nationality: 8 Scottish
    devised: 12 Rankine Cycle, Rankine
    Scale **26** Fahrenheit temperature
    scale
    author of: 22 Manual of the Steam
    Engine

rankle 4 gall, rile **5** chafe, gripe, pique
6 fester **8** irritate **10** not sit well

ransack 3 gut **4** comb, loot, raid, rake,
sack **5** rifle, scour, strip **6** ravage,
search **7** despoil, pillage, plunder **8**
lay waste **9** devastate, vandalize **14**
rummage through, turn upside down

ransom 3 buy **4** free, save **5** atone,
price **6** redeem, rescue **7** deliver, expiate, reclaim, recover, release **8** liberate, retrieve **10** liberation, redemption

Ransom, John Crowe
    member of: 12 the Fugitives
    author of: 14 I'll Take My Stand **16**
    Captain Carpenter **30** Bells for John
    Whiteside's Daughter

rant 4 fume, rage, rave, yell **5** orate,
scold, spout, storm **6** bellow **7** bluster, bombast, bravado, explode **8** harangue **11** declamation **12** exaggeration

rap 3 jaw, pan, tap **4** bang, chat, drum,
talk **5** blame, knock, roast, speak,
thump **6** dump on **7** clobber **8** converse **9** criticize **10** come down on **11**
communicate **14** responsibility, shoot
the breeze

rapacious 6 greedy **7** looting, wolfish
8 covetous, grasping, ravenous, thievish **9** marauding, mercenary, pillaging,
predatory, voracious **10** avaricious, insatiable, plundering, ransacking

rapacity 5 greed **7** avarice **10** greediness **12** covetousness, graspingness
13 mercenariness

Rape of Lucrece
    author: 18 William Shakespeare
    character: 7 Tarquin **9** Collatine

Rape of the Lock, The
    author: 13 Alexander Pope
    character: 5 Ariel **7** Belinda, Umbriel
    9 Lord Petre **10** Thalestris

Raphael 9 archangel

Raphael
    real name: 14 Raffaello Santi **15** Raff-
    aello Sanzio
    born: 5 Italy **6** Urbino
    artwork: 7 Disputa **8** Julius II **10** En-
    tombment **14** Sistine Madonna **17**
    The School of Athens, The Virgin
    and Child **18** Madonna di Casa
    Tempi, The Transfiguration **19** The
    Triumph of Galatea **21** Baldassare
    Castiglione **22** The Marriage of the
    Virgin **24** The Expulsion of Helio-
    dorus **28** The Madonna and Child
    with St John (La Belle Jardiniere)

architect of: 11 Villa Madama (Rome) **16** Pandolfini Palace (Florence) **22** Vidoni-Caffarelli Palace (Rome)

rapid 4 fast **5** brisk, fleet, hasty, quick, swift **6** active, flying, prompt, speedy **7** express, hurried, instant, rushing **8** agitated, feverish **9** galloping, unchecked **11** accelerated, expeditious, precipitate

rapidity 5 haste, speed **8** celerity, velocity **9** fleetness, quickness, swiftness **10** promptness

rapidly 4 fast **5** apace **7** briskly, hastily, quickly, swiftly **8** pell-mell, speedily **9** hurriedly, like a shot, overnight **10** in high gear **11** at full speed **13** expeditiously, helter-skelter

rapids 5 chute **7** current **10** white water

rapport 3 tie **4** link **10** connection, fellowship **11** affiliation, camaraderie **12** relationship **13** understanding **17** interrelationship

rapprochement 6 accord **7** detente, entente **9** agreement **10** adjustment, compromise, settlement **11** appeasement, arrangement **12** conciliation, pacification **13** accommodation, harmonization, reconcilement, understanding **14** reconciliation **16** mutual concession

rapscallion 5 knave, rogue, scamp **6** rascal **7** low-life, villain **8** scalawag **9** scoundrel **10** blackguard, ne'er-do-well, rascallion **14** good-for-nothing

rapt 6 dreamy, enrapt, intent **7** bemused, charmed **8** absorbed, ecstatic **9** attentive, bewitched, delighted, enchanted, engrossed, entranced, rapturous **10** captivated, enraptured, enthralled, fascinated, interested, moonstruck, spellbound **11** transported

rapture 3 joy **5** bliss **6** thrill **7** delight, ecstasy, elation **8** euphoria, felicity **9** beatitude

rapturous 4 rapt **8** beatific, blissful, ecstatic **10** enraptured, enthralled

rare 3 few **6** scarce, unique **7** unusual **8** uncommon **10** hard to find, infrequent **11** exceptional, seldom found **16** few and far between

rarefied 4 thin **6** dilute, purify, rarify, reduce, refine, subtle **7** inflate **8** diminish **9** attenuate, extenuate

rarely 6 hardly, seldom **8** not often **10** hardly ever, uncommonly **12** infrequently, scarcely ever **15** once in a blue moon, on rare occasions **17** once in a great while

raring 4 agog, avid, keen **5** eager **8** desirous **9** impatient **12** enthusiastic

rarity 6 oddity **7** anomaly **8** scarcity **11** unusualness **12** uncommonness **14** remarkableness

rascal 3 cad, imp **4** rake **5** devil, knave, rogue, scamp **7** villain **8** rakehell, scalawag **9** prankster, reprobate, scoundrel, trickster **10** blackguard, delinquent **11** rapscallion

rash 5 brash, hasty **6** abrupt **7** foolish **8** careless, headlong, heedless, reckless **9** foolhardy, impetuous, imprudent, impulsive, premature, unadvised, unchecked **10** incautious, indiscreet, ungoverned, unthinking **11** adventurous, harebrained, injudicious, precipitate, thoughtless **12** devil-may-care, uncontrolled **13** irresponsible

rashness 8 audacity, boldness **9** riskiness **12** heedlessness, indiscretion, recklessness **13** foolhardiness, impulsiveness **15** precipitousness, thoughtlessness

Rashomon
    author: 18 Ryunosuke Akutagawa
    director: 13 Akira Kurosawa

Raskolnikov
    character in: 18 Crime and Punishment
    author: 10 Dostoevsky

rasp 3 irk, nag, rub, vex **4** file **5** chafe, grate, worry **6** abrade, scrape, wheeze **7** grating, scraper, scratch **8** abrasive, irritate **9** huskiness **10** hoarseness

raspberry 11 Rubus idaeus
    varieties: 3 red **4** hill **5** black, dwarf **6** Mysore, purple **8** European **9** flowering, Mauritius **11** American red **13** Rocky Mountain **15** Purple-flowering **22** Rocky Mountain flowering
    brandy: 9 Framboise

rasping 5 harsh, raspy, rough **6** hoarse **7** chafing, grating, nagging **8** abrading, scraping, worrying **9** offensive **10** irritating

Rasselas
    author: 13 Samuel Johnson
    character: 5 Imlac **6** Pekuah **7** Nekayah
    Rasselas's title: 17 Prince of Abyssinia

rat 3 cad, cur **4** fink, heel **5** churl, knave, louse **6** betray, rascal, rotter, squeal, vermin **7** bounder, villain **8** informer, inform on **9** scoundrel **10** blackguard **11** stool pigeon

rate 3 fee **4** cost, deem, dues, levy, pace, rank, toll **5** class, count, price, speed, tempo **6** charge, figure, look on, regard, tariff **7** expense, measure **8** classify **10** assessment

rate highly 5 prize, value **6** admire, esteem **7** cherish, respect **8** treasure

Rathbone, Basil
    real name: 25 Philip St John Basil Rathbone
    born: 11 South Africa **12** Johannesburg
    roles: 6 Tybalt **7** Karenin **10** Dawn Patrol **11** Mr Murdstone **12** Anna Karenina **14** Romeo and Juliet, Sher-

lock Holmes, The Mark of Zorro **16** A Tale of Two Cities, David Copperfield **20** The Last Days of Pompeii **24** The Adventures of Robin Hood **25** The Hound of the Baskervilles

rather 4 a bit, very **5** quite **6** fairly, kind of, pretty, sort of **8** slightly, somewhat **10** moderately, more or less, relatively **13** comparatively

rathskeller 6 saloon **8** beer hall
    vessel: 4 Toby **5** stein **6** seidel **7** tankard **8** pilsener, schooner

ratification 2 OK **4** okay **7** consent **8** approval, sanction **10** validation **11** affirmation, endorsement **12** confirmation **13** authorization, corroboration **14** seal of approval

ratify 2 OK **4** okay **6** affirm, uphold **7** agree to, approve, certify, confirm, endorse, support **8** accede to, make good, sanction, validate **9** authorize, consent to, make valid **11** acknowledge **12** authenticate

rating 4 mark, rank **5** class, grade, ratio, value **6** degree, rebuke, sailor, seaman **7** ranking **8** standing **9** appraisal **10** assessment, evaluation, percentage **14** classification

ratio 8 equation **10** proportion **11** arrangement **12** distribution **13** apportionment, fixed relation **15** proportionality **17** interrelationship **20** proportional relation

ration, rations 3 due **4** dole, food **5** allot **6** stores **7** measure, mete out **8** allocate **9** allotment, apportion, food share, provender, provision **10** provisions **13** apportionment

rational 4 sage, sane, wise **5** lucid, solid, sound **6** normal **7** logical **8** all there, balanced, credible, feasible **9** advisable, judicious, plausible, sagacious **10** reasonable **11** clearheaded, responsible **12** compos mentis **13** perspicacious **15** in one's right mind

rationale 5 basis, logic **6** excuse, reason **7** grounds **9** reasoning **10** key concept, philosophy **11** explanation, foundations **16** underlying reason

rationalize 6 excuse **7** explain, justify **8** palliate **9** whitewash **10** account for **11** explain away **13** put a gloss upon **14** make excuses for **16** make allowance for

ratite 3 em(e)u, moa **4** kiwi, rhea **7** ostrich **9** cassowary

rattan 4 cane, lash, palm, whip **5** thong **6** switch, wicker

Ratti, Achille 10 Pope Pius XI

rattle 3 gab, jar **4** faze **5** clang, clank, clink, prate, shake, throw, upset **6** bounce, flurry, jangle **7** agitate, blather, chatter, clatter, confuse, disturb, fluster, maunder, nonplus, perturb **8** bewilder, clacking, distract **9** discomfit **10** discompose, disconcert **11** roll loosely

rattlebrained 4 dumb **5** silly **6** stupid **7** asinine, doltish, foolish, idiotic, moronic, witless **9** brainless, imbecilic **10** fool-headed, half-witted **11** harebrained, lamebrained

rattled 5 fazed, upset **7** annoyed **9** disturbed, flustered, perturbed, thrown off **10** distracted **11** discomposed **12** disconcerted

rattle on 3 gab **4** blab **5** prate, run on **6** babble, gabble **7** blabber, chatter, prattle **16** run off at the mouth

ratty 4 poor, worn **5** angry, cross, nasty, testy **6** cranky, shabby, touchy **7** tangled, unkempt **8** wretched **9** irascible, motheaten **11** dilapidated

raucous 4 loud **5** harsh, raspy, rough **6** hoarse, shrill **7** blaring, grating, jarring **8** grinding, jangling, piercing, strident **9** dissonant **10** discordant, stertorous **11** cacophonous **12** earsplitting, inharmonious

raunchy 4 lewd **5** dirty, gross **6** coarse, smutty, vulgar **8** off-color

Rauschenberg, Robert
   born: 12 Port Arthur TX
   artwork: 3 Bed **5** Barge **7** Jammers **8** Monogram **11** Retroactive

ravage 3 gut **4** loot, raid, rape, raze, ruin, sack **5** strip, waste, wreck **6** maraud **7** despoil, destroy, overrun, pillage, plunder, ransack, shatter **8** demolish, desolate, lay waste, spoliate **9** devastate **10** lay in ruins

rave 3 wax **4** fume, go on, gush, rage, rant **5** be mad, kudos, storm **6** babble, bubble, ramble **7** be angry, bluster, carry on, explode, flare up, run amok, sputter, thunder **8** flattery **9** be furious, expatiate, go on and on, good press, laudatory **10** effervesce, high praise, rhapsodize **11** blow one's top, compliments

ravel 4 undo **6** unknit **7** unravel, untwine, untwist

Ravel, Maurice
   born: 6 France **7** Ciboure
   composer of: 6 Bolero **7** La Valse, Mirrors **8** Jeux d'eau **9** Fountains **11** Mother Goose, Sheherazade **14** Daphnis et Chloe **15** Gaspard de la Nuit, L'Heure Espagnole **17** Rapsodie Espagnole, The Tomb of Couperin **20** Pavane for a Dead Infant **21** Don Quichotte a Dulcinee **22** L'Enfant et les Sortileges, Pavane for a Dead Princess **27** Pavane pour une infante de funte, Valses nobles et sentimentales

raven 3 jet **4** crow, dark, inky, rook **5** black, ebony, sable **6** devour **9** coalblack

Raven, The
   author: 13 Edgar Allan Poe
   woman 6 Lenore
   refrain: 9 nevermore

ravenous 6 greedy, hungry **7** piggish,

starved **8** covetous, famished, grasping, ravening, starving **9** insatiate, predatory, rapacious, voracious **10** avaricious, gluttonous, insatiable

ravine 3 gap **4** pass, rift, wadi **5** abyss, break, chasm, cleft, crack, gorge, gulch, gully, split **6** arroyo, breach, canyon, clough, divide, valley **7** fissure **8** crevasse

raving 3 mad **4** wild **6** insane **7** ranting **8** frenzied **9** delirious

ravish 4 rape **5** abuse, charm, cheer **6** defile, snatch, tickle **7** delight, enchant, gladden, outrage, overjoy, violate **8** deflower, enthrall, entrance, knock out **9** captivate, enrapture, fascinate, transport

ravishing 8 alluring, charming, gorgeous, smashing, splendid, striking **9** beautiful **10** bewitching, delightful, enchanting, entrancing **11** captivating, fascinating, sensational

raw 4 bare, cold, damp, rare **5** basic, bleak, crude, frank, fresh, green, harsh, plain, rough, young **6** biting, bitter, brutal, callow, chilly, rookie, unripe **7** cutting, natural, nipping, numbing, unbaked, untried **8** blustery, freezing, ignorant, immature, inexpert, piercing, pinching, uncooked, untaught, untested **9** inclement, underdone, undrilled, unfledged, unrefined, unskilled, untrained, windswept **10** amateurish, unprepared, unseasoned **11** not finished, undercooked, undeveloped, unexercised, uninitiated, unpracticed, unprocessed, unvarnished **13** inexperienced, undisciplined, unembellished **15** not manufactured

rawboned 4 lean **5** gaunt, lanky, spare **7** angular

Rawdon, Captain
   character in: 10 Bleak House
   author: 7 Dickens

Rawhide
   character: 5 Mushy **8** Gil Favor, Ian Cabot, Wishbone **9** Jim Quince, Pete Nolan **10** Rowdy Yates **11** Joe Scarlett, Solomon King **13** Clay Forrester **14** Hey Soos Patines
   cast: 10 Sheb Wooley **11** Charles Gray, David Watson, Eric Fleming, Robert Cabal, Rocky Shahan, Steve Raines **12** James Murdock, Paul Brinegar **13** Clint Eastwood **16** Raymond St Jacques

Rawlings, Marjorie Kinnan
   author of: 11 The Yearling

rawness 3 nip **4** bite **5** chill **8** rudeness **9** crudeness, greenness, roughness, sharpness, vulgarity **10** chilliness **12** inexperience

ray 3 arm **4** beam, fish, line **5** gleam, light, manta, shaft, shine, skate, trace **6** branch, streak, stream, stripe **7** radi-

ate **8** particle, plowfish, radiance **9** emanation, radiation

Ray, Man
   born: 14 Philadelphia PA
   artwork: 4 Gift (Le Cadeau) **7** Manikin **9** The Lovers **13** Observing Time **45** The Rope Dancer Accompanies Herself with Her Shadows

Rayleigh, John William Strutt
   field: 7 physics
   nationality: 7 British
   discovered: 5 argon
   awarded: 10 Nobel Prize

rayon
   invented by: 4 Swan

raze 4 fell, ruin **5** level, smash, wreck **6** reduce, remove, topple **7** destroy, flatten, wipe out **8** demolish, pull down, tear down **9** break down, dismantle, knock down **10** obliterate

razor
   invented by: 6 Schick **8** Gillette

Razorback State
   nickname of: 8 Arkansas

Re *see* **2** Ra

reach 3 get, hit **4** find, go to, grab, make, move **5** climb, enter, get to, grasp, seize, touch **6** attain, clutch, come to, extend, grab at, land at, secure, spread **7** contact, stretch **8** amount to, approach, arrive at **9** get hold of, set foot in **10** get as far as, outstretch, stretch out

reachable 6 at hand **8** possible **10** accessible, achievable, attainable, obtainable, procurable

reach the top 6 arrive **7** prosper, succeed **8** make good **13** hit the big time

react 4 work **6** answer, behave, resist, return **7** respond **11** reverberate

reaction 5 reply **6** answer, reflex **8** backlash, response **11** restoration **13** counteraction **14** chemical change **17** counterrevolution, right-wing comeback

reactionary 7 diehard **8** mossback, rightist **9** right-wing **10** regressive **11** right-winger **12** reversionary **17** ultraconservative **20** counterrevolutionary

react to 5 reply **6** answer **7** respond **11** acknowledge

read 2 go **3** say **4** note, scan, show **5** study, utter **6** adduce, peruse, recite **7** analyze, deliver, discern, explain, present **8** construe, decipher, indicate, perceive, pore over **9** apprehend, interpret, translate **10** comprehend, glance over, understand **11** extrapolate

Read, Piers Paul
   author of: 5 Alive **9** Polonaise **10** Monk Dawson, The Junkers, The Upstart **18** Professor's Daughter

Reade, Charles
   author of: 13 Peg Woffington **23** The Cloister and the Hearth

readily 6 at once, easily, freely, pronto **7** quickly **8** in no time, promptly, smoothly, speedily **9** expressly, hands down, instantly, willingly **10** graciously **11** immediately, straightway **12** effortlessly, ungrudgingly

readiness 8 alacrity, dispatch **9** alertness **10** promptness **12** preparedness

read the riot act 5 chide, scold **6** berate, rebuke **7** censure, chasten, correct, lecture, reprove **8** admonish **9** dress down, reprimand **10** take to task

ready 3 apt, fit, set **4** deft, keen, ripe, up to **5** acute, alert, eager, equip, handy, on tap, prone, sharp **6** adroit, all set, artful, astute, at hand, bright, clever, expert, facile, fit out, liable, mature, on hand, primed, prompt, shrewd, speedy **7** cunning, equal to, prepare, present, tending, willing **8** disposed, inclined, masterly, punctual, skillful **9** attentive, dexterous, fitted out, furnished, ingenious, in harness, versatile, wide-awake **10** accessible, discerning, perceptive, put in order **11** acquisitive, expeditious, predisposed, quick-witted, resourceful, serviceable

ready for use 5 handy, on tap **6** at hand, on hand **9** available **10** accessible, convenient **11** at one's elbow **14** at one's disposal

ready-made 10 off-the-rack **11** prêt-à-porter, ready-to-wear, store-bought

ready money 4 cash **8** currency **10** cash on hand

ready to go 5 peppy **9** full of pep **10** raring to go **17** full of vim and vigor **24** bright-eyed and bushy-tailed

Reagan, Ronald Wilson
  nickname: 5 Dutch **6** Ronnie
  presidential rank: 8 fortieth
  party:
    current: 10 Republican
    former: 10 Democratic
  state represented: 2 CA
  defeated: 6 (James Earl) Carter (Jr) **7** (Walter Frederick "Fritz") Mondale **8** (John Bayard) Anderson
  vice president: 4 (George Herbert Walker) Bush
  cabinet:
    state: 4 (Alexander M) Haig (Jr) **6** (George P) Shultz
    treasury: 5 (Donald T) Regan
    defense: 10 (Caspar W) Weinberger
    attorney general: 5 (William French) Smith
    interior: 4 (James) Watt **5** (William P) Clark
    agriculture: 5 (John R) Block
    commerce: 8 (Malcolm) Baldrige
    labor: 7 (Raymond J) Donovan
    health and human services: 7 (Margaret M) Heckler **9** (Richard S) Schweiker

  education: 4 (Terrel H) Bell
  HUD: 6 (Samuel R) Pierce (Jr)
  transportation: 4 (Elizabeth H) Dole **5** (Andrew L) Lewis (Jr)
  energy: 5 (Donald P) Hodel **7** (James B) Edwards
  born: 9 Tampico IL
  college: 6 Eureka
  religion: 17 Disciples of Christ
  interests: 2 TV **5** track **6** movies **8** football **9** chops wood **10** basketball, jelly beans **13** weightlifting **15** horseback riding
  vacation spot: 14 Rancho del Cielo (Santa Barbara CA)
  dog: 5 Lucky
  author: 18 Where Is the Rest of Me?
  political career:
    governor of: 10 California
  civilian career: 5 actor **17** radio sportscaster
    host: 15 Death Valley Days **22** General Electric Theater
    president of: 17 Screen Actors Guild
    roles: 8 King's Row **10** Brother Rat **13** John Loves Mary, The Hasty Heart **15** Bedtime for Bonzo **19** The Voice of the Turtle **20** Cattle Queen of Montana **21** The Girl from Jones Beach **22** Knute Rockne All American
  military service: 6 US Army **7** captain **10** World War II
  notable events of lifetime/term:
    approval of: 10 MX missiles
    assassination attempt on: 6 Reagan **14** Pope John Paul II
    attempted assassination on Reagan by: 15 John W Hinckley Jr
    bombing of: 5 Libya
    hostages freed in: 4 Iran
    invasion of: 7 Grenada
    marines sent to: 7 Lebanon
    nuclear disaster at: 9 Chernobyl
    Russians shot down: 14 Korean airliner
    scandal: 8 Irangate
  father: 10 John Edward
    nickname: 4 Jack
  mother: 5 Nelle (Wilson)
  siblings: 4 (John) Neil
  wife: 4 Jane (Wyman) **5** Nancy (Davis)
    Nancy Davis born: 18 Anne Frances Robbins
  children: 6 Ronald **7** Maureen, Michael (adopted) **8** Patricia
    Patricia also actress known as: 10 Patti Davis
  first lady:
    program: 9 Drug abuse, Just Say No **12** Alcohol abuse **18** Foster Grandparents

real 4 pure, true **5** solid, valid **6** actual, honest **7** certain, factual, genuine, sincere **8** absolute, bona fide, positive, rightful, tangible, truthful **9** authentic,

unalloyed, unfeigned, veracious, veritable **10** legitimate, unaffected **11** not affected, substantial, substantive, unvarnished **12** well-grounded **13** unadulterated **14** unquestionable

realistic 4 real **7** genuine, graphic, natural, precise **8** faithful, lifelike, truthful **9** authentic, depictive, objective, pragmatic **10** true-to-life **11** descriptive, down-to-earth **12** naturalistic **16** representational

reality 4 fact **5** truth **6** verity **9** actuality **11** materiality, tangibility **12** corporeality **14** substantiality **17** physical existence

realization 7 success **8** grasping **10** attainment, perception **11** achievement, culmination, fulfillment **12** appreciation, consummation **13** comprehension, understanding **14** accomplishment

realize 2 do **3** get, net **4** gain **5** clear, grasp **6** absorb, attain, fathom, gather, profit **7** achieve, acquire, cognize, discern, execute, fulfill, imagine, make out, perform, produce **8** carry out, complete, conceive, make good, perceive **9** actualize, apprehend, discharge, make money, penetrate, recognize **10** accomplish, appreciate, bring about, comprehend, consummate, effectuate, understand **11** bring to pass **12** carry through

realized 3 got **6** gained, netted, proved, proven **7** cleared, grasped, made out, saw into **8** absorbed, accepted, effected, executed, existing, fathomed, gathered, imagined, made good, profited **9** completed, conceived, discerned, fulfilled, perceived, performed **10** actualized, penetrated, recognized, understood **11** appreciated, apprehended, consummated, established **12** accomplished, comprehended

really 5 truly **6** indeed, in fact, surely, verily **8** actually **9** certainly, genuinely, literally, veritably **10** absolutely, positively, truthfully **13** categorically **14** unquestionably

realm 4 land **5** field, orbit, state **6** domain, empire, nation, region, sphere **7** country, demesne, kingdom **8** dominion, monarchy, province **11** royal domain

real McCoy, the 4 real **7** genuine **9** authentic **12** the real thing

Realpolitik 10 expediency **13** power politics

reap 3 get, win **4** earn, gain **5** glean, score **6** derive, gather, obtain, profit, secure, take in **7** acquire, bring in, harvest, procure, realize

rear 3 aft, end **4** back, heel **5** after, nurse, raise, stern, train **6** dorsal, foster **7** bring up, care for, cherish, develop, educate, nurture, postern, tail

end **8** back part, hind part, hindmost
9 aftermost, after part, at the back,
cultivate, in the back, posterior

Rear Window
 director: 15 Alfred Hitchcock
 based on story by: 15 Cornell Wool-
 rich
 cast: 10 Grace Kelly **11** Raymond
 Burr **12** James Stewart, Thelma Ritter, Wendell Corey

reason 3 wit **4** head **5** cause, logic,
 sense, solve **6** acumen, brains, figure,
 motive, sanity **7** grounds, insight **8** lucidity, occasion **9** awareness, faculties, intellect, normality, rationale,
 reasoning **10** perception **11** common
 sense, discernment, exhortation, explanation, penetration, rationality **12**
 apprehension, intelligence, perspicacity, think through **13** argumentation,
 comprehension, justification, mental
 balance, understanding **15** clearheadedness

reasonable 4 fair, just, sage, sane,
 wise **5** sound **6** likely, proper **7** fitting, knowing, lenient, logical, natural, patient, prudent **8** credible, moderate, possible, probable, rational,
 sensible, suitable, thinking **9** equitable, impartial, judicious, objective,
 plausible, temperate, tolerable **10** admissible, coolheaded, legitimate, not
 extreme, reflective, thoughtful **11** circumspect, intelligent, justifiable, levelheaded, not unlikely, of good sense,
 predictable, well-founded **12** not excessive, well-grounded **13** understanding **14** understandable **15** of sound
 judgment

reasonableness 5 logic **6** sanity, wisdom **8** fairness, prudence **9** good
 sense **10** moderation **11** credibility,
 objectivity, rationality **12** good judgment, impartiality, intelligence **13** judiciousness **14** circumspection,
 thoughtfulness **15** clearheadedness

reasonably 6 almost, fairly **8** passably, somewhat **10** moderately, more
 or less **13** approximately

reasoning 5 basis, logic **6** ground **7**
 thought **8** analysis, argument, thinking **9** deduction, inference, rationale
 10 cogitation, reflection **11** penetration **13** ratiocination **14** interpretation

reason out 8 mull over **10** deliberate
 12 think through

reassure 5 cheer **6** buoy up, uplift **7**
 bolster, comfort **8** inspirit **9** encourage
 13 inspire hope in

reassured 6 buoyed **9** bolstered, comforted, heartened **10** emboldened, encouraged, inspirited

reassuring 7 hopeful **10** auspicious,
 comforting, heartening **11** encouraging

Reb 2 Mr **5** Rabbi **6** Mister

rebate 6 refund **8** discount **9** abatement

Rebecca
 author: 15 Daphne du Maurier
 character: 10 Jack Favell, Mrs Danvers (Danny) **12** Frank Crawley **13**
 Colonel Julyan, Maxim de Winter
 house: 9 Manderley
 director: 15 Alfred Hitchcock
 cast: 10 Nigel Bruce **12** Joan Fontaine
 13 George Sanders **14** Judith Anderson (Mrs Danvers) **15** Laurence Olivier (Maxim de Winter)
 Oscar for: 7 picture

Rebecca
 character in: 7 Ivanhoe
 author: 5 Scott

Rebecca *see* **7** Rebekah

Rebecca of Sunnybrook Farm
 author: 17 Kate Douglas Wiggin
 character: 4 Cobb **8** Adam Ladd **11**
 Aunt Miranda **14** Rebecca Randall
 15 Emma Jane Perkins

Rebekah
 also: 7 Rebecca
 father: 7 Bethuel
 husband: 5 Isaac
 brother: 5 Laban
 son: 4 Esau **5** Isaac, Jacob

rebel 3 shy **4** riot **5** avoid, quail, react,
 wince **6** flinch, mutiny, recoil, revolt,
 rise up, shrink **7** seceder, traitor, upstart **8** deserter, maverick, resister,
 turncoat **9** anarchist, dissenter, insurgent **10** iconoclast, malcontent, separatist **12** secessionist **13** nonconformist, revolutionary, revolutionist **15**
 insurrectionist

rebellion 6 mutiny, putsch, revolt **8**
 defiance, sedition, upheaval, uprising
 9 coup d'etat **10** insurgency, revolution **12** insurrection

rebellious 6 unruly **7** defiant **8** contrary, mutinous, up in arms **9** alienated, fractious, insurgent, seditious,
 truculent, turbulent **10** disorderly,
 pugnacious, refractory **11** disobedient,
 intractable, quarrelsome **12** contumacious, recalcitrant, ungovernable, unmanageable **13** insubordinate, revolutionary **14** uncontrollable **15**
 insurrectionary

rebelliousness 8 defiance **9** rebellion
 12 disobedience

Rebel Without a Cause
 director: 11 Nicholas Ray
 cast: 8 Sal Mineo **9** James Dean, Jim
 Backus **11** Natalie Wood

Rebirth
 god of: 4 Gwyn

rebound 3 bob **6** bounce, recoil, re-
 echo **7** flounce **8** recovery, ricochet
 10 spring back

rebounding 7 rubbery, springy **9** resilient **11** ricocheting **12** bouncing back

rebuff 4 deny, snub **5** check, repel,
 spurn **6** ignore, put off, refuse, reject,
 slight **7** decline, put-down, refusal, repulse **8** turn down **9** disregard, rejec-

tion **10** putting off **12** cold shoulder
 13 slap in the face **15** keep at a distance

rebuke 5 blame, chide, scold, score **6**
 berate **7** censure, chew out, chiding,
 lecture, reproof, reprove, upbraid **8**
 admonish, berating, call down, reproach, reproval, scolding **9** dress
 down, reprimand **10** admonition,
 chewing out, take to task, upbraiding
 11 castigation, disapproval **12** admonishment, dressing down, remonstrance, reprehension, take down a
 peg **13** find fault with, tongue-lashing
 15 remonstrate with

rebuttal 5 reply **6** answer, denial, retort **7** defense, riposte **8** disproof, negation, response **9** disproval, rejoinder
 10 refutation **11** confutation **12** coun-
 terreply, disagreement, surrejoinder
 13 contradiction **15** counterargument

recalcitrant 5 balky **6** mulish, unruly
 7 willful **8** contrary, stubborn **9** obstinate, pigheaded, unwilling **10** bullheaded, headstrong, refractory **11** disobedient, intractable **12** unsubmissive

recall 5 place **6** memory, revive **8** call
 back, remember **9** reanimate, recognize, recollect **10** reactivate, remobil-
 ize **11** reinstitute, remembrance **12** recollection **17** ability to remember

recant 4 deny **5** unsay **6** abjure, disown, recall, renege, repeal, revoke **7**
 disavow, rescind, retract **8** disclaim,
 forswear, renounce, take back, withdraw **9** foreswear, repudiate **10** apos-
 tatize **12** eat one's words **14** change
 one's mind

recantation 6 denial **9** disavowal **10**
 refutation, retraction, revocation **11**
 repudiation **12** renunciation

recapitulate 5 recap, sum up **6** relate,
 repeat, reword **7** recount, restate **8** rephrase **9** epitomize, reiterate, summarize **15** repeat in essence

recapture 6 retake **7** reprise **15** experience again

recede 3 ebb **5** abate **6** back up, go
 back, retire, retreat, subside **7** regress,
 retreat, subside **10** retrogress

receipt 7 arrival, release, voucher **9**
 admission, discharge, receiving, reception **10** acceptance, admittance, possession, recipience **11** acquisition,
 transferral

receipts 3 pay **4** gain, gate, take **5**
 share, split, wages **6** income, recipe,
 return **7** formula, payment, profits,
 returns, revenue **8** earnings, proceeds
 9 emolument **10** net profits **12** remuneration **13** reimbursement

receive 3 get **4** meet **5** admit, greet,
 put up **6** accept, come by, obtain, regard, secure, suffer, take in **7** acquire,
 adjudge, approve, be given, react to,
 sustain, undergo, welcome **8** meet

with, submit to **9** encounter, entertain **10** experience **11** accommodate

receive willingly 6 accept **10** take gladly **16** accept with thanks **18** accept with open arms

receive with favor 6 praise **7** approve **10** appreciate

receive with open arms 6 invite **7** embrace, welcome **13** accept eagerly **19** roll out the red carpet

recent 3 new **4** late **5** fresh, novel **6** modern **8** up-to-date **9** latter-day **12** contemporary **13** up-to-the-minute

receptacle 3 bag, bin, box, can, jar **4** file, tray **6** basket, bottle, hamper, holder, hopper, vessel **7** carrier **8** receiver **9** container **10** depository, repository **11** compartment

reception 2 do **4** fete **5** party **6** affair, soiree **7** welcome **8** greeting **11** recognition **15** social gathering

receptive 8 amenable, friendly **10** accessible, hospitable, interested, openminded, responsive **11** susceptible **12** approachable **17** favorably disposed

recess 3 bay, gap **4** bend, cell, cove, fold, gulf, lull, nook, pass, rest, slot **5** break, cleft, gorge, inlet, letup, niche, pause **6** alcove, corner, harbor, hiatus, hollow **7** holiday, interim, respite, time out **8** interval, vacation **9** interlude **10** pigeonhole **11** coffee break, indentation **12** intermission **14** breathing spell

recessed 4 sunk **6** paused, sunken **7** delayed **8** deferred, extended, indented **9** adjourned, dissolved, postponed, prolonged, withdrawn **10** terminated
church wall: 5 ambry
wall: 6 alcove

recesses 6 depths **10** inmost part, penetralia

recession 10 depression **11** recessional **16** economic downturn

recherche 4 rare **5** prize **6** choice, exotic, scarce, select, unique **7** special, unusual **8** original, superior, uncommon, valuable **9** different, priceless **10** one of a kind **11** exceptional

recipe 2 Rx **4** cure, rule **5** axiom **6** elixir, remedy **7** formula, receipt **12** instructions, prescription

recipient 4 heir **5** donee, taker **6** getter **7** legatee **8** accepter, acquirer, obtainer, receiver **9** presentee **11** beneficiary

reciprocal 6 common, linked, mutual, shared **8** returned **9** bilateral, exchanged, one for one **10** equivalent **11** give-and-take **12** interchanged, interrelated **13** complementary, corresponding, given in return **14** interdependent **15** interchangeable

reciprocate 4 feel **6** return **7** requite, respond **9** retaliate **10** make return **11** act likewise, give and take, interchange **12** give in return **19** return the compliment

reciprocity 8 exchange **11** give and take, interchange

recital 4 talk **6** report **7** concert, telling **8** delivery, reciting **9** discourse, narration, narrative, rendition **10** recitation **11** description, particulars, performance **12** dissertation, oral exercise **13** public reading **14** graphic account, recapitulation

recite 4 tell **5** quote, speak **6** relate, repeat **7** declaim, deliver, narrate, perform, recount **10** say by heart **11** communicate

reckless 4 rash, wild **5** giddy, hasty **6** daring, fickle, madcap, unwary **7** flighty, foolish, unaware **8** careless, cavalier, heedless, mindless, unsteady, volatile **9** daredevil, desperate, foolhardy, imprudent, impulsive, negligent, oblivious, unheeding, unmindful **10** incautious, indiscreet, insensible, neglectful, regardless, unthinking, unwatchful **11** harebrained, inattentive, precipitate, thoughtless, unconcerned **12** devil-may-care, unsolicitous **13** inconsiderate, irresponsible, uncircumspect **14** scatterbrained

recklessly 4 fast **5** blind **6** rashly, wildly **7** hastily **8** headlong **9** headfirst **10** carelessly, heedlessly **11** audaciously, desperately, impetuously, impulsively **12** unmindfully **13** irresponsibly, unconcernedly

recklessness 7 abandon **8** rashness **9** disregard, unconcern **10** imprudence, profligacy **11** impetuosity **12** heedlessness, immoderation **13** foolhardiness **15** thoughtlessness **16** irresponsibility

reckon 3 add **4** bank, cope, deal, deem, plan, rank, rate **5** add up, class, count, fancy, guess, judge, tally, think, total, value **6** assess, decide, esteem, expect, figure, handle, regard **7** account, adjudge, balance, bargain, compute, imagine, presume, suppose, surmise **8** appraise, consider, estimate **9** calculate, determine, speculate

reckoning 3 tab **4** bill, doom **5** count, tally, total **6** adding, charge **7** account **8** estimate, judgment **9** appraisal, summation **10** estimation, evaluation **11** calculation, computation **13** final judgment **19** settling of an account

reclaim 6 reform, rescue **7** correct, recover, rectify, restore

reclame 9 notoriety, publicity

recline 4 lean, loll, rest **6** lounge, repose, sprawl **7** lie back, lie down **12** take one's ease

reclining 7 lolling, resting **8** lounging, reposing **9** lying down, recumbent

recluse 3 nun **4** monk **5** crank, loner **6** hermit, hidden, secret **7** ascetic, eremite, erratic, oddball **8** cenobite,

crackpot **9** eccentric **10** cloistered **11** sequestered **13** nonconformist

recognition 6 notice **9** discovery **10** acceptance, validation **13** comprehension, understanding **14** acknowledgment, identification **19** diplomatic relations

recognizable 5 clear, plain **8** distinct **10** detectable **11** discernable, perceivable, perceptible **12** identifiable, intelligible **13** ascertainable **14** comprehensible, understandable **15** distinguishable

recognizance 4 bond **6** pledge **10** obligation **11** recognition **15** acknowledgement

recognize 3 see **4** know, spot **5** admit, place, sight **7** discern, make out, pick out, realize, respect, yield to **8** identify, submit to **9** be aware of, concede to **10** appreciate, comprehend, understand **11** acknowledge **14** give the floor to

recognized 5 known **8** accepted, admitted, approved, familiar, realized **9** customary **10** accredited **11** traditional **12** acknowledged, conventional

recoil 4 fail, kick **5** blink, cower, demur, quail, shirk, start, wince **6** blench, cringe, falter, flinch, revolt **7** fly back, rebound, retreat **8** draw back, hang back, jump back **9** bound back **10** shrink back, spring back

recoil at 4 hate **5** abhor **6** detest, eschew, loathe **7** despise **9** abominate, shudder at **10** shrink from **12** be revolted by **14** view with horror **18** feel aversion toward

recoiling 7 wincing **9** flinching **10** rebounding **11** drawing back **13** shrinking back, springing back

recollect 5 place **6** recall **8** remember **10** call to mind

recollection 4 mind **6** memoir, memory, recall, record **11** remembrance **12** reminiscence **13** retrospection
French: 8 souvenir

recommend 4 urge **5** favor, order **6** advise **7** counsel, endorse, propose, suggest **8** advocate, vouch for **9** encourage, prescribe **10** put forward **11** speak well of

recommendable 9 advisable, favorable **10** worthwhile

recommendation 4 plug **6** behest, praise **8** approval, good word **9** reference **11** endorsement **12** commendation

recompense 3 pay **5** repay **6** return, reward **7** payment **9** reimburse, repayment **10** compensate, remunerate, reparation **12** compensation, remuneration **15** indemnification

reconcile 5 fix up **6** adjust, make up, resign, settle, square **7** correct, patch up, rectify, reunite, win over **8** per-

suade 9 harmonize **10** conciliate, propitiate **11** set straight

reconcile oneself 6 submit **9** acquiesce **13** resign oneself

reconciliation 8 fixing up, making up, settling, squaring **10** adjustment, correction, patching up, rectifying **11** resignation, winning over **12** cohciliation **13** justification, rectification **15** setting straight

recondite 4 deep **6** arcane, hidden **7** obscure **8** abstruse, esoteric **9** concealed **10** mysterious **16** incomprehensible

reconnaissance 6 survey **7** viewing **8** scouting, scrutiny **10** inspection **11** exploration, observation **12** surveillance **13** investigation **14** reconnoitering

reconnoiter 4 look **5** probe, scout **6** patrol, picket, survey **7** examine **8** remember, traverse

reconsider 5 amend **6** modify, ponder, review, revise **7** correct, rethink, sleep on **8** mull over, reassess **9** reexamine, think over **10** reevaluate **13** think better of **15** think twice about

reconstitute 7 restore **9** recompose **10** add water to **11** reconstruct

reconstruct 7 rebuild **8** make over, recreate **10** reassemble **11** reestablish **12** reconstitute

record 3 log **4** copy, file, list, memo, note, post, show, tape **5** admit, enter **6** annals, career, docket, enroll, report **7** account, archive, catalog, conduct, history, jot down, jotting, journal **8** document, indicate, register, take down **9** chronicle, introduce, write down **10** adventures, background, memorandum, transcribe **11** experiences, make an entry, performance, proceedings **12** unbeaten mark **14** top performance
   French: **11** compte rendu

record, phonograph 2 EP, LP **5** vinyl **7** platter
   invented by: **4** Bell **6** Edison **7** Tainter **8** Berliner **10** Goldenmark

recount 4 tell **6** detail, recite, relate **7** explain, narrate **8** describe **9** count over

recoup 5 atone **6** redeem, regain **7** recover, replace **8** make good, retrieve **9** make up for, reacquire **13** make amends for

recourse 6 choice, option, resort **11** alternative, other choice

recover 4 heal, mend **5** rally **6** offset, pick up, recoup, redeem, regain, retake, revive **7** balance, get back, get well, improve, reclaim, restore, win back **8** make good, retrieve, revivify **9** make up for, reacquire, recapture, reconquer, repossess **10** come around, compensate, convalesce, recuperate, rejuvenate **11** pull through, resuscitate

recovery 4 cure **5** rally **6** recoup, rescue, upturn **7** revival, salvage **8** comeback **9** retrieval **10** betterment, regainment **11** improvement, reclamation, reformation, restoration **12** recuperation **13** business cycle, convalescence

recreancy 8 apostasy **9** cowardice, desertion **10** cravenness, disloyalty, infidelity **13** faithlessness, pusillanimity **14** unfaithfulness

recreant 6 coward, craven, yellow **8** apostate, cowardly, deserter, disloyal, renegade **9** undutiful **10** unfaithful **11** lily-livered **12** dishonorable **13** pusillanimous, yellow-bellied

recreation 4 play **5** hobby, sport **7** pastime **9** amusement, avocation, diversion **10** relaxation **13** entertainment **15** leisure activity

recrimination 5 blame **6** charge **10** accusation **13** countercharge

recruit 4 hire **5** raise, renew **6** employ, enlist, enroll, muster, novice, recoup, revive, rookie **7** draftee, provide, recover, restore **8** beginner, newcomer **9** conscript **10** recuperate

rectangle 3 box **6** oblong, square **7** polygon **10** quadrangle **13** parallelogram, quadrilateral

rectangular 4 long **6** square **7** boxlike **11** right-angled **12** quadrangular **13** quadrilateral

rectification 6 fixing, reform **7** redress **8** righting, squaring **9** remedying, repairing **10** adjustment, correction, regulation **12** setting right **15** putting straight, putting to rights **16** straightening out

rectify 3 fix **4** cure, mend **5** amend, emend, focus, right **6** adjust, attune, reform, remedy, repair, revise, square **7** correct, redress **8** put right, regulate, set right **9** make right **10** straighten

rectitude 5 honor **7** decency, probity **8** morality **9** integrity, principle **11** uprightness **12** virtuousness **13** righteousness **14** high-mindedness **15** trustworthiness **16** incorruptibility **17** irreproachability

rector 6 cleric, parson, pastor, priest **8** minister, preacher **9** churchman, clergyman **12** ecclesiastic

recumbent 4 flat **5** prone **6** supine **7** leaning **8** couchant **9** lying down, prostrate, reclining **10** horizontal **12** stretched out

recuperate 4 heal, mend **7** get well, improve, recover **8** come back **9** get better **10** come around, convalesce **11** be on the mend, pull through **14** return to health **16** regain one's health

recuperation 8 recovery **11** restoration **13** convalescence

recuperative 11 restorative **15** health-restoring

recur 6 repeat, resume, return **7** persist **8** come back, continue, reappear **9** come again **10** occur again

recurrence 5 cycle, round **6** repeat, return **7** relapse, renewal, reprise, routine **8** iterance, rotation **10** continuity, repetition **11** periodicity **12** reappearance

recurrent 7 regular **8** frequent, periodic **9** recurring, repeating **10** repetitive **11** reappearing **12** intermittent **14** appearing again

red 4 pink, rose, rosy, ruby, wine **5** aglow, coral, flame, ruddy **6** auburn, cherry, florid, maroon **7** burning, crimson, flaming, flushed, glowing, scarlet **8** blooming, blushing, cardinal, inflamed, reddened, rubicund **9** rubescent, vermilion **12** blood-colored

Red and the Black, The (Le Rouge et le Noir)
   author: **8** Stendhal
   character: **6** Fouque **8** M de Renal **11** Julien Sorel **16** Mathilde de la Mole

Red Badge of Courage, The
   author: **12** Stephen Crane
   character: **6** Wilson **10** Jim Conklin **12** Henry Fleming

red-blooded 5 lusty, peppy, vital **6** ardent, robust, strong, sturdy **7** dynamic, intense **8** forceful, powerful, spirited, vigorous **9** energetic **10** hot-blooded, passionate

Red Branch
   origin: **5** Irish
   warriors of: **9** Conchobar

Redburn
   author: **14** Herman Melville

red-cheeked 4 rosy **5** ruddy **6** robust **8** blushing **12** apple-cheeked

Red Cross Knight
   character in: **15** The Faerie Queene
   author: **7** Spenser

redden 4 burn, glow **5** blush, color, flame, flush **9** go crimson **12** become florid

reddish 4 rosy, ruby **5** ruddy, rufus **6** flushy, rufous **7** roseate **8** rubicund

reddish-brown 4 rust **5** henna **6** auburn, copper, russet, sienna **8** chestnut, cinnamon

Red Earth People *see* **3** Fox

redeem 4 keep, save **5** cover **6** defray, ransom, recoup, reform, regain, rescue, settle **7** buy back, convert, fulfill, reclaim, recover, satisfy **8** atone for, make good, retrieve **9** discharge, make up for, repossess **10** evangelize, repurchase

redeemed 5 saved **7** claimed, rescued **8** made good, ransomed, reformed **9** atoned for, delivered, fulfilled, recovered **10** carried out, regenerate **11** repossessed

redemption 6 excuse, pardon, ransom, reform, rescue **7** salvage **8** recovery **9** amendment, atonement, exemption, expiation, salvation **10** conversion **11** deliverance, reformation

Redford, Robert
   real name: 20 Charles Robert Redford
   born: 13 Santa Monica CA
   roles: 8 The Sting **10** The Natural **11** Legal Eagles **12** The Candidate, The Way We Were **13** Downhill Racer **14** The Great Gatsby **15** Jeremiah Johnson **17** Barefoot in the Park **19** All the President's Men **20** Three Days of the Condor **29** Butch Cassidy and the Sundance Kid
   director: 8 Quiz Show **14** Ordinary People (Oscar) **17** The Horse Whisperer **19** A River Runs Through It

Redgrave, Corin
   born: 6 London **7** England
   sisters: 4 Lynn **7** Vanessa
   roles: 8 The Magus **17** A Man for All Seasons **20** In the Name of the Father **23** Four Weddings and a Funeral

Redgrave, Lynn
   born: 6 London **7** England
   father: 18 Sir Michael Redgrave
   sister: 15 Vanessa Redgrave
   roles: 10 Georgy Girl, Howard's End **13** The Bostonians **14** The Happy Hooker **26** Whatever Happened to Baby Jane
   author of: 7 Vanessa **16** Pussies and Tigers

Redgrave, Sir Michael
   born: 7 Bristol, England
   daughter: 4 Lynn **7** Vanessa
   roles: 11 Dan Peggotty **15** The Lady Vanishes **16** David Copperfield **22** Mourning Becomes Electra **27** The Importance of Being Earnest

Redgrave, Vanessa
   born: 6 London **7** England
   father: 18 Sir Michael Redgrave
   sister: 12 Lynn Redgrave
   husband: 14 Tony Richardson
   roles: 5 Julia, Yanks **6** Agatha, Blow-Up, Morgan **7** Camelot, Isadora **9** Guinevere **16** Mary Queen of Scots **17** The Lady from the Sea

red-hot 5 aglow, fiery **6** heated, raging **7** blazing, burning, glowing, intense **12** all-consuming

red-letter 5 happy, lucky **6** banner **10** auspicious, felicitous

redness 4 glow **5** blush, flush **8** rosiness **9** ruddiness **10** floridness

redolence 5 aroma, savor **7** bouquet **9** fragrance, good smell **12** pleasant odor

redolent 5 balmy, spicy **6** savory, smelly **7** mindful, odorous, reeking, scented **8** aromatic, fragrant, perfumed, stinking **9** evocative, odiferous

10 expressive, indicative, suggestive **11** odoriferous, reminiscent **13** sweet-smelling

Redon, Odilon
   born: 6 France **8** Bordeaux
   artwork: 10 In the Dream, The Cyclops **11** Le Vieil Ange **13** Flowers of Evil **15** Violette Heymann

redouble 7 augment, magnify **8** heighten, multiply **9** intensify

redoubtable 7 awesome **8** alarming, imposing **10** formidable **11** illustrious **12** awe-inspiring

redound 4 lead, tend **5** cause, surge **6** abound **7** conduce, incline **8** overflow **10** contribute **11** reverberate

redress 4 ease **5** amend, right **6** amends, reform, relief, remedy **7** correct, payment, rectify, relieve **8** easement, set right **9** make up for **10** recompense, reparation **11** restitution **12** compensation, satisfaction **13** compensate for, rectification **15** indemnification **18** make retribution for

Red River
   director: 11 Howard Hawks
   cast: 9 Joanne Dru, John Wayne **11** John Ireland **13** Walter Brennan **15** Montgomery Clift

Reds
   director: 12 Warren Beatty
   cast: 11 Diane Keaton (Louise Bryant), Paul Sorvino **12** Warren Beatty (John Reed) **13** Jack Nicholson, Jerzy Kosinski **14** Edward Herrmann **16** Maureen Stapleton
   Oscar for: 8 director **17** supporting actress (Stapleton)

Red Shoes, The
   author: 21 Hans Christian Andersen
   director: 13 Michael Powell **17** Emeric Pressburger
   cast: 12 Marius Goring, Moira Shearer **13** Anton Walbrook **14** Robert Helpmann

Red Skelton Show, The
   character: 8 Gertrude **10** Heathcliff **13** Mean Widdle Kid **14** San Fernando Red, Sheriff Deadeye, Willie Lump-Lump **16** Bolivar Shagnasty **17** Cauliflower McPugg **18** Clem Kadiddlehopper **20** Freddie the Freeloader
   saying: 7 I dood it
   closing line: 8 God bless

Red Sky at Morning
   author: 15 Richard Bradford

reduce 3 cut **4** bust, curb, diet, dull, ease, thin **5** abate, blunt, break, check, force, lower, slash, water **6** damage, demote, dilute, lessen, retard, soften, temper, weaken **7** assuage, atrophy, cripple, cut down, leave in **8** diminish, discount, enfeeble, mark down, minimize, mitigate, moderate, modulate, slim down, slow down, tone down, trim down **9** bring down, checkmate, undermine **10** debilitate,

devitalize, slenderize **11** lower in rank **12** incapacitate

reduced form 6 digest **7** summary **9** short form **11** abridgement, contraction **12** abbreviation, condensation

reduce speed 4 slow **5** brake **6** rein in **8** slow down **10** decelerate

reduce to nothing 5 erase **7** abolish, destroy, wipe out **8** lay waste **9** eradicate, liquidate **10** annihilate **11** exterminate

reductio ad absurdum 22 reduction to an absurdity

reduction 3 cut **5** break **8** decrease, discount **9** abatement, lessening **10** concession **11** abridgement, subtraction

reduction to an absurdity
   Latin: 18 reductio ad absurdum

redundancy 6 excess **7** surplus **8** verbiage **9** tautology **10** repetition **11** diffuseness, superfluity **13** overabundance **14** circumlocution, repetitiveness

redundant 5 extra **6** excess **7** surplus **10** pleonastic **11** dispensable, inessential, overflowing, repetitious, superfluous, unnecessary **12** tautological **13** superabundant

redwood 19 Adenanthera pavonina, Sequoia sempervirens
   varieties: 4 dawn **5** coast, giant **7** Madeira

reed
   varieties: 3 bur **4** vine **5** Burma, giant **6** common **14** Mauritania vine

reed 9 six cubits

Reed, Sir Carol
   director of: 6 Oliver (Oscar) **11** The Third Man

Reed, Walter S
   field: 12 bacteriology
   discovered cause of: 11 yellow fever

reef 3 bar **4** bank, flat, spit **5** shelf, shoal **7** sandbar, shallow

reek 4 fume **5** smell, smoke, steam, stink **6** stench **7** give off **9** effluvium, emanation

reel 4 rock, roll, spin, sway **5** lurch, pitch, swirl, waver, whirl **6** rotate, teeter, totter, wobble **7** revolve, stagger, stumble

reeling 5 dizzy, giddy, shaky **6** whirly **8** spinning, unsteady **10** staggering **11** vertiginous

Reese, Harold
   nickname: 6 Pee Wee
   sport: 8 baseball
   position: 9 shortstop
   team: 15 Brooklyn Dodgers

Reeve
   character in: 18 The Canterbury Tales
   author: 7 Chaucer

Reeve, Christopher
   born: 9 New York NY
   author of: 7 Still Me

roles: 8 Superman **9** Deathtrap **13** The Bostonians **15** Remains of the Day, Somewhere in Time **18** Village of the Damned

refer 2 go **4** cite, send, turn **6** advert, allude, direct, submit **7** consult, deliver, mention **8** hand over, transfer, transmit **9** pass along

referee 5 judge **6** decree, settle, umpire **7** arbiter, mediate **8** judgment, mediator, moderate **9** arbitrate, determine, intercede, intervene, moderator, pronounce **10** adjudicate, arbitrator **11** adjudicator, intercessor **12** intermediary

reference 4 hint **7** inkling, mention **8** allusion, good word, innuendo **10** deposition, intimation, suggestion **11** affirmation, credentials, endorsement, implication, testimonial **13** certification **14** recommendation

reference book 5 atlas, bible **6** manual **9** guidebook **10** dictionary **12** encyclopedia

refine 6 filter, purify, strain **7** cleanse, develop, improve, perfect, process **9** cultivate

refined 5 clean, suave **6** gentle, polite, urbane **7** courtly, elegant, genteel **8** cleansed, cultured, delicate, finished, graceful, ladylike, mannerly, polished, purified, well-bred **9** civilized, clarified, courteous **10** cultivated, fastidious **11** gentlemanly **14** discriminating

refinement 5 grace **6** finish, nicety, polish, step up **7** advance, culture, dignity, finesse, suavity **8** breeding, civility, cleaning, courtesy, delicacy, elegance, fineness, revision, urbanity **9** amendment, cleansing, gentility, propriety **10** betterment, filtration, gentleness, politeness **11** advancement, cultivation, development, discernment, enhancement, good manners, improvement, progression, savoir faire, step forward **12** amelioration, distillation, graciousness, purification, tastefulness **13** courteousness, rectification **14** discrimination, fastidiousness

refitting 8 adapting **10** adaptation, remodeling **11** reequipping, resupplying

reflect 4 cast, copy, muse, show, undo **5** image, study, think, throw **6** betray, evince, expose, mirror, ponder, reason, return, reveal **7** condemn, display, exhibit, express, imitate, present, rebound, uncover **8** cogitate, consider, disclose, give back, indicate, manifest, meditate, mull over, register, ruminate, send back, set forth **9** bring upon, cerebrate, dwell upon, represent, reproduce, speculate, throw back, undermine **10** deliberate **11** concentrate, contemplate, demonstrate

reflection 4 blot, idea, slur, view **5** image, study **6** insult, musing, notion **7** opinion, reproof, thought **8** reproach, thinking **9** attention, pondering, sentiment **10** cogitation, conviction, derogation, impression, imputation, meditation, rumination **11** cerebration, insinuation, mirror image, pensiveness **12** deliberation **13** concentration, consideration, disparagement

French: 6 pensee

reflective 7 pensive **8** thinking **9** judicious, pondering **10** meditative, ruminative, thoughtful **11** speculative **13** contemplative

reform 4 mend **5** amend, atone, emend **6** better, remedy, repair, repent, revise **7** convert, correct, improve, rebuild, rectify, remodel, restore **8** progress **9** amendment **10** correction **12** mend one's ways, rehabilitate **13** rectification **16** set straight again, turn over a new leaf

reformation 6 change, reform **9** amendment, reforming **10** alteration, conversion **11** improvement **12** modification **14** reorganization

refractory 5 balky **6** mulish, unruly **7** restive, wayward, willful **8** contrary, stubborn **9** fractious, obstinate, pigheaded **10** rebellious **11** disobedient, intractable **12** unmanageable

refrain 5 avoid, forgo **6** desist, eschew, forego, refuse, resist **7** abstain, forbear, hold off **8** leave off, renounce **11** curb oneself, keep oneself **12** stay one's hand **15** restrain oneself

refrain from 5 avoid, forgo **6** desist, eschew, forego **7** abstain, forbear **8** leave off, renounce

refresh 3 jog **4** prod **5** brace, renew, rouse **6** arouse, awaken, prompt, revive, stir up, vivify **7** cool off, freshen, quicken, recruit, restore **8** activate, energize, recreate **9** reanimate, stimulate **10** invigorate, rejuvenate, strengthen

refreshed 7 revived **8** animated, restored, vivified **9** enlivened, freshened **11** invigorated

refreshing 7 bracing **11** revivifying **12** invigorating **13** strengthening **15** thirst-quenching

refreshment 4 bite, eats **5** drink, snack **6** bracer **7** potable **8** beverage, cocktail, pick-me-up, potation **9** appetizer, drinkable, refresher **10** recreation, relaxation **11** hors d'oeuvre, nourishment, restoration, restorative **12** food and drink, invigoration, rejuvenation **14** reinvigoration, thirst quencher

refrigerate 4 cool **5** chill **6** freeze **7** congeal **8** keep cold, keep cool, put on ice **9** keep on ice

Refrigerator, The
nickname of: **12** William Perry

refuge 4 home **5** haven **6** asylum, harbor, resort **7** hideout, retreat, shelter **8** safehold **9** anchorage, harborage, sanctuary **10** protection **12** port in a storm **14** help in distress, place of shelter

refugee 2 DP **5** exile **6** bolter, eloper, emigre **7** escapee, evacuee, runaway **8** emigrant, fugitive **9** absconder **10** expatriate **15** displaced person

refulgent 6 bright, lucent **7** glowing, lambent, radiant, shining **8** luminous, relucent **9** brilliant

refund 5 remit, repay **6** rebate, return **7** pay back **9** reimburse, repayment **10** recompense, remittance, remunerate **12** amount repaid **13** give back money, reimbursement **18** make restitution for **19** make compensation for

refurbish 4 mend, redo **5** clean, fix up, renew **6** repair, tidy up **7** freshen, improve, remodel, restore **8** overhaul, renovate, spruce up **11** recondition

refusal 2 no **3** nay **4** veto **6** denial **7** regrets **8** turndown **9** declining, rejection **10** nonconsent **11** declination, disapproval **13** nonacceptance, noncompliance, unwillingness

refuse 2 no **4** deny, junk, veto **5** spurn, trash, waste **6** forbid, litter, reject **7** decline, garbage, rubbish, say no to **8** disallow, prohibit, turn down, withhold

refuse pile 4 dump **6** midden **11** rubbish heap

refuse to submit 4 defy **5** rebel **6** resist **7** disobey, hold out, violate **10** transgress **12** fail to comply

refutation 4 veto **6** denial **7** counter **8** negation, rebuttal **9** disavowal **11** confutation, repudiation **12** invalidation **13** contradiction

refutatory 8 contrary, opposing **10** discrepant **11** conflicting, disagreeing **12** antithetical, inconsistent **13** contradictory **14** countervailing, irreconcilable

refute 4 deny **5** rebut **6** answer **7** confute, counter **8** disprove **9** challenge **10** contradict, invalidate **12** give the lie to

regain 6 recoup, redeem, retake **7** get back, reclaim, recover, win back **8** gain anew, get again, retrieve **9** recapture, repossess

regal 5 grand, noble, proud, royal **6** august, kingly, lordly **7** queenly, stately **8** imposing, kinglike, majestic, princely, splendid **9** queenlike **10** princelike **11** magnificent **13** splendiferous

regale 3 ply **4** fete **5** amuse, feast **6** divert, please **7** banquet, delight, lionize **8** enthrall **9** entertain **10** serve nobly **11** wine and dine **15** feed sumptuously

Regan

character in: 8 King Lear
author: 11 Shakespeare

regard 3 eye, see **4** care, heed, hold, mind, note, rate, scan, view **5** judge, point, think, value, watch **6** accept, admire, aspect, behold, detail, esteem, follow, gaze at, look at, matter, notice, reckon, survey, take in **7** account, believe, concern, put down, respect, set down, subject, thought **8** consider, estimate, listen to, look upon, look up to, note well, relation **9** attention, hearken to, reference **10** admiration, connection, estimation, meditation, reflection, scrutinize **11** contemplate, observation, think well of **12** appreciation **13** cast the eyes on, consideration, think highly of **14** pay attention to

regardful 5 civil **6** polite **7** mindful **8** reverent **9** courteous, observant **10** respectful **11** deferential, reverential

regard highly 6 admire, esteem **7** respect **10** appreciate

regarding 4 in re **5** about, anent **7** apropos **10** concerning, respecting

regardless 6 anyhow, anyway **10** for all that **11** nonetheless **12** nevertheless **15** notwithstanding **19** in spite of everything

regard with repugnance 4 hate **5** abhor **6** detest, loathe **7** despise **8** execrate **9** abominate, can't stand, shudder at **10** recoil from, shrink from **11** can't stomach **12** be revolted by **13** be nauseated by, find repulsive **18** feel aversion toward

regard with suspicion 5 doubt **7** suspect **8** distrust, mistrust, question

regenerate 5 renew **6** redeem, reform, revive, uplift **7** restore **8** inspirit, reawaken, retrieve, revivify **9** enlighten, resurrect **10** rejuvenate **11** resuscitate **12** generate anew **13** give new life to, make a new man of

regent 4 king **5** queen, ruler **8** governor **9** protecter, protector

regime 4 rule **5** power, reign **7** command, control, dynasty **8** dominion **9** direction **10** government, leadership, management **12** jurisdiction **14** administration

regimen 4 diet, rule **6** system **10** government

regimentation 5 order, rigor **6** method, system **7** control, regimen **9** orthodoxy **10** discipline, regulation, uniformity **12** rigorousness **13** methodization **19** doctrinaire approach

Regin
  origin: 12 Scandinavian
  mentioned in: 8 Volsunga
  brother: 6 Fafnir
  raised: 6 Sigurd

region 4 area, land, zone **5** field, range, realm, space, tract **6** domain, sphere **7** country, expanse **8** district, locality, province, vicinity **9** territory **12** neighborhood

regional 5 areal, local, zonal **7** dialect **10** locational, provincial **11** territorial **12** geographical

register 3 log **4** dial, mark, roll, show **5** diary, gauge, meter, range, scale **6** betray, enlist, enroll, heater, ledger, record, sign up **7** betoken, check in, compass, counter, daybook, exhibit, express, logbook, point to, portray, set down **8** disclose, heat duct, heat vent, indicate, manifest, note down, radiator, recorder, registry, take down **9** indicator, write down **10** calculator, heat outlet, hot-air vent, record book **12** put in writing

regnat populus 16 let the people rule
  motto of: 8 Arkansas

regress 3 ebb **4** back, exit, fall **6** go back, recede, return, revert **7** relapse, retreat, reverse **8** fall back, pass back, withdraw **9** backslide **10** lose ground, retrogress **11** deteriorate **12** move backward

regressive 8 backward **9** declining, worsening **10** retrograde **13** retrogressive

regret 3 rue, woe **4** moan **5** grief, mourn, qualm **6** bemoan, bewail, lament, repent, sorrow, twinge **7** anguish, apology, deplore, eat crow, remorse, scruple **8** be rueful, grieve at, weep over **9** apologize, grievance, heartache, rue the day **10** be sorry for, contrition, repentance, ruefulness **11** be ashamed of, compunction, lamentation, reservation **12** be remorseful, eat humble pie, eat one's words, self-reproach **13** feel sorrow for, regretfulness, second thought **14** disappointment, feel remorse for, remorsefulness **15** dissatisfaction **16** feel distress over, pang of conscience, self-condemnation

regretful 6 rueful **8** contrite **9** sorrowful **10** apologetic, remorseful **15** self-reproachful

regrettable 6 woeful **7** unhappy **8** grievous, pitiable **10** calamitous, deplorable, lamentable **11** unfortunate

regular 3 set **4** even, fine, real **5** daily, fixed, plain, usual **6** common, normal, proper, smooth, steady, trusty **7** classic, correct, genuine, habitue, natural, typical, uniform **8** absolute, accepted, complete, constant, everyday, faithful, familiar, frequent, habitual, loyalist, ordinary, orthodox, periodic, stalwart, standard, thorough, true blue **9** customary, recurrent, recurring, unvarying **10** consistent, dependable, invariable, periodical, unchanging **11** commonplace, down-to-earth, established, old reliable, symmetrical, undeviating **12** well-balanced **16** well-proportioned

regulate 3 fix **5** guide **6** adjust, direct, govern, handle, manage **7** balance, control, monitor, oversee, rectify **8** moderate, modulate, organize **9** supervise **10** regularize **11** superintend

regulation 4 rule **5** edict, order **6** decree **7** command, control, dictate, statute **8** handling **9** adjusting, direction, ordinance **10** adjustment **11** commandment **13** standing order

regulator 5 guide **7** manager **8** director, governor, overseer **9** moderator, modulator **10** adjustment, supervisor **14** superintendent **15** adjusting device

regurgitate 4 barf **5** vomit **7** throw up **8** disgorge

rehabilitate 3 fix **4** save **6** redeem, remake **7** restore, salvage **8** make over, readjust, renovate **9** reeducate, refurbish, reinstate **11** recondition, reconstruct, resocialize, set straight **13** straighten out **16** restore to society

rehash 6 repeat, retell, reword **7** restate **8** rephrase **9** iteration, rechauffe

rehearsal 5 drill, recap **6** tryout **7** hearing, reading, test run **8** audition, exercise, practice, trial run **9** polishing **10** perfecting, repetition, run-through **11** preparation, reiteration, walk-through **14** recapitulation

rehearse 5 drill, ready, train **6** go over, polish, recite, relate, repeat, retell **7** narrate, prepare, recount **8** practice **9** reiterate **10** run through **13** read one's lines **14** give a recital of, study one's lines

rehoboam 18 oversize wine bottle

Rehoboth
  founder: 6 Nimrod

Reich, Charles
  author of: 20 The Greening of America

Reichsfuhrer 11 Reich leader
  chief of: 8 SS troops

reign 4 rule **6** govern, regime, regnum, tenure **7** command **8** dominion, hold sway, regnancy, tutelage **9** dominance, influence **10** government, incumbency **11** sovereignty, supervision **12** wear the crown **13** hold authority **14** have royal power, sit on the throne **15** occupy the throne **17** exercise authority **19** exercise sovereignty
  Hindu: 3 raj

reign over 4 rule **6** govern **7** command, control **8** dominate

reimburse 5 pay up, remit, repay **6** rebate, refund **7** pay back **8** square up **9** indemnify **10** compensate, recompense, remunerate **15** make restitution

reimbursement 6 refund **9** indemnity, repayment **12** compensation, remuneration

rein, reins 4 curb, hold **5** check, limit, watch **6** bridle **7** control, harness **8**

hold back, restrict, suppress **9** restraint **11** keep an eye on

Reiner, Carl
born: **7** Bronx NY
son: **9** Rob Reiner
roles: **15** Your Show of Shows **21** It's a Mad Mad Mad Mad World
created: **15** Dick Van Dyke Show
director of: **5** Oh God **7** The Jerk **8** The Comic **11** Where's Poppa?
novel: **13** Enter Laughing

Reiner, Rob
father: **10** Carl Reiner
roles: **8** Meathead **10** Mike Stivik **14** All in the Family
director of: **6** Misery **9** Stand By Me **11** A Few Good Men **15** This Is Spinal Tap **16** The Princess Bride **17** When Harry Met Sally

reinforce 4 prop **5** steel **7** bolster, brace up, fortify, support **8** buttress **10** strengthen **12** make stronger

reinforcement 4 stay **5** brace, strut **7** bracing, support **10** assistance **11** buttressing **13** strengthening

reinstate 5 renew **6** revive **7** readmit, restore **11** reestablish, reinstitute, reintroduce

reinstatement 7 renewal, revival **11** restoration **13** reinstitution **14** reintroduction **15** reestablishment

reiterate 5 resay **6** hammer, rehash, repeat, retell, reword, stress **7** iterate, reprise, restate **8** rephrase **11** pound away at **12** recapitulate **13** go over and over

reject 4 deny **5** repel, spurn **6** rebuff, refuse **7** castoff, decline, discard, disdain, dismiss, flotsam, repulse, say no to **8** castaway, disallow, shrug off, turn down, turn from **9** repudiate

rejected 6 denied, dumped, jilted **7** cast off, outcast, refused, spurned, unloved **8** disowned, forsaken, lovelorn **9** abandoned, discarded, disproved **10** unaccepted, repudiated **11** invalidated

rejection 6 rebuff **7** disdain, refusal **8** scorning, spurning **9** declining, dismissal, rebuffing, rejecting, ruling out

rejoice 5 exult, glory, revel **6** be glad **7** be happy, delight **8** be elated, jubilate **9** be pleased, celebrate, make merry **10** exhilarate, sing for joy **11** be delighted, be overjoyed **13** be transported

rejoice in 5 eat up, enjoy, savor **6** relish **7** revel in **9** delight in **13** be pleased with, get a kick out of **14** take pleasure in

rejoicing 5 mirth **6** gaiety **7** delight, ecstasy, elation, jollity, jubilee, revelry, triumph **8** cheering, gladness, pleasure, reveling **9** festivity, good cheer, happiness, jubilance, merriment **10** exultation, joyfulness, jubilation, liveliness **11** celebration, merrymaking

rejoin 6 answer, retort **7** respond

rejoinder 5 reply **6** answer, retort, return **7** riposte **8** backtalk, comeback, rebuttal, repartee, response **10** refutation **11** surrebuttal **12** counterblast, remonstrance, surrejoinder **13** countercharge **16** counterstatement

rejuvenate 6 revive **7** restore **8** revivify **9** reanimate **10** revitalize **12** reinvigorate **14** put new life into **17** make youthful again

relapse 4 fall **5** lapse **6** revert, worsen **7** decline, regress, reverse **8** fall back, sink back, slip back, turn back **9** backslide, reversion, worsening **10** degenerate, recurrence, regression, retrogress **11** backsliding, falling back **13** deterioration, retrogression **15** return to illness, turn for the worse

relate 3 say **4** link, tell **5** apply, refer, speak, state, utter **6** attach, belong, convey, detail, impart, recite, report, reveal **7** concern, connect, divulge, narrate, pertain, recount **8** describe, disclose **9** appertain, associate, feel close, make known **10** be relevant **11** communicate, have rapport **12** be responsive, interact well, recapitulate **13** be sympathetic, have reference, particularize **15** feel empathy with, give an account of

related 3 kin **4** akin, said, told **7** kindred, recited **8** narrated, reported **9** recounted **15** of the same family

related by blood 3 kin **4** akin **7** kindred **14** consanguineous, of the same stock **21** having a common ancestor

relation 3 kin, tie **4** bond, link **5** tie-in **6** regard, report **7** account, bearing, concern, kinsman, recital, telling, version **8** relative **9** narrating, narration, narrative, reference, relevance, retelling **10** connection, pertinence, recitation **11** affiliation, application, association, correlation, description **13** applicability, communication **17** interrelationship

relationship 3 kin **5** blood, union **6** affair **7** kindred, kinship, liaison, sibship, society **8** affinity, alliance **10** connection **11** affiliation, association, correlation **13** consanguinity

relative 3 kin **4** clan, kith **5** blood, folks, tribe **6** allied, cousin, family, people **7** cognate, germane, kinfolk, kinsman, related **8** relation, relevant **9** connected, dependent, kinswoman, pertinent, referable **10** affiliated, applicable, associated, comparable, connection, connective, correlated, kith and kin, pertaining, relational, respective **11** appropriate, comparative, correlative, not absolute **12** interrelated **13** flesh and blood **14** interconnected

relax 4 bend, calm, ease, idle, laze, loaf, rest **5** let up, slack **6** be idle, be lazy, ease up, loosen, soften, soothe, unbend, unwind **7** cool off, holiday,

make lax, slacken, take ten **8** decrease, loosen up, take five, vacation **9** lie around **10** take it easy **12** enjoy oneself **13** make less tense **14** make less severe, make less strict

relaxation 3 fun **5** games, hobby, sport **6** repose **7** bending, leisure, pastime **8** pleasure **9** abatement, amusement, avocation, diversion, enjoyment, loosening, remission **10** recreation, slackening **11** refreshment **12** rest from work **13** entertainment

relaxed 3 lax **4** calm, cool, easy, slow, soft **5** loose, slack **6** at ease, casual, gentle, remiss **7** flaccid, lenient **8** informal, laid back, unstrict **9** easygoing, leisurely, negligent, nerveless, unnervous **10** unstrained **11** free and easy, thoughtless
French: **6** degage

relaxed manner 4 ease **5** poise **6** aplomb **9** composure **10** confidence **11** naturalness **12** unconstraint **14** unaffectedness

relay 3 leg **4** race, tour **5** shift **6** length **8** transfer, transmit **9** conductor, regulator, satellite **10** retransmit
cylinder: **5** baton
part: **8** armature, receiver **11** transmitter **13** electromagnet
race: **6** medley **10** track event

release 4 free **5** let go, loose, untie **6** detach, let out, unbind **7** freeing, present, relieve, set free, unloose **8** liberate, set loose, unfasten **9** circulate, discharge, disengage, dismissal, extricate, letting go, releasing **10** distribute, liberating, liberation **11** circulation, communicate, extrication, publication, setting free **12** distribution, emancipation, set at liberty, setting loose

relegate 3 bar **5** eject, expel **6** assign, banish, charge, commit, demote, reject **7** cast out, consign, discard, dismiss, exclude, keep out, shut out **8** delegate **9** ostracize

relent 4 bend, melt **5** let up, relax, yield **6** give in, soften, unbend, weaken **7** give way **8** have pity **10** be merciful, capitulate, come around **11** give quarter, grow lenient **12** become milder **14** grow less severe

relentless 4 hard **5** harsh, rigid, stern, stiff **6** severe **7** adamant **8** pitiless, rigorous, ruthless **9** merciless **10** implacable, inexorable, inflexible, unyielding **11** remorseless, undeviating, unrelenting **14** uncompromising

relevance 7 aptness, fitness, meaning **9** propriety **10** pertinence **11** materiality, relatedness, suitability **12** significance **13** applicability **15** appropriateness

relevant 3 apt, fit **6** allied, suited, tied in **7** apropos, bearing, cognate, fitting, germane, related **8** apposite, material, suitable **9** connected, intrinsic, pertinent, referring **10** applicable, associated, concerning, to the point **11** appropriate, significant **12** on the subject, to the purpose

reliable 4 true **5** solid, sound **6** trusty **8** faithful **9** unfailing **10** dependable **11** responsible, trustworthy **12** tried and true **13** conscientious

reliance 5 faith, trust **6** belief, credit **8** credence **9** assurance **10** confidence, dependence

relic 5 scrap, token, trace **7** antique, memento, records, remnant, vestige **8** artifact, fragment, heirloom, keepsake, reminder, souvenir **11** remembrance

relief 4 balm, cure, dole, rest **5** break, cheer **6** remedy **7** anodyne, elation, panacea, respite, welfare **8** antidote, easement, lenitive **9** abatement, reduction **10** mitigation, palliation, palliative **11** alleviation, assuagement, peace of mind **12** amelioration **13** encouragement **16** public assistance **17** welfare assistance
Italian: **7** rilievo

relieve 3 aid **4** calm, ease, free, help, mark **5** abate, allay, cheer, spell **6** assist, let out, pacify, remove, set off, solace, soothe, subdue, succor, temper **7** appease, assuage, break up, comfort, console, lighten, mollify, release, replace, support, take out **8** contrast, mitigate, palliate, reassure **9** alleviate, encourage, interrupt, punctuate **12** free from fear

relieved 5 freed **6** calmed, exempt **7** cheered, excused, solaced **8** consoled **9** comforted, reassured **10** encouraged

religion 4 cult, sect **5** canon, creed, dogma, faith, piety **6** belief, church, homage **7** worship **8** devotion, theology **9** adoration, godliness, reverence **10** devoutness, persuasion, veneration **11** affiliation, belief in God **12** belief in gods, denomination, spirituality **13** system of faith **15** system of worship

religionist 8 believer

religiosity 5 piety **8** devotion **10** fanaticism **15** religious fervor

religious 3 nun **4** holy, monk **5** exact, friar, godly, rigid **6** ardent, devout, divine, priest, sacred **7** devoted, staunch **8** constant, faithful, unerring **9** spiritual, steadfast **10** devotional, fastidious, God-fearing, meticulous, scrupulous, unswerving **11** punctilious, theological, undeviating **12** wholehearted **13** conscientious **14** denominational **15** spiritual-minded

religious belief 5 canon, credo, creed, dogma, tenet **8** doctrine

religious fervor 5 piety **7** ecstasy **8** holiness **9** godliness **10** devoutness **12** religiousity, spirituality

religious group 4 sect **12** denomination

religious orders
Christian: **6** Jesuit **7** Cluniac, Templar **8** Capuchin, Theatine, Trappist, Ursuline **9** Carmelite, Dominican **10** Carthusian, Cistercian, Franciscan **11** Augustinian, Benedictine, Camaldolite **16** Sisters of Charity **20** Order of the Visitation
non-Christian: **4** Sufi **7** Jainism **8** Dasanami

relinquish 4 cede, deny, drop, quit, shed **5** forgo, leave, let go, waive, yield **6** forego, give up, resign, vacate **7** abandon, cast off, discard, dismiss, forbear, forsake, release **8** abdicate, break off, disclaim, hand over, lay aside, put aside, renounce, sign away **9** deliver up, repudiate, surrender

relinquishable 9 forgoable **10** expendable, foregoable **11** dispensable **12** renounceable

relinquished 5 ceded, let go **6** gave up **7** forgone, given up, yielded **8** cast away, foregone, forsaken **9** abandoned, given away, renounced **10** left behind

relinquishment 7 cession **8** giving up, yielding **9** letting go, rejection, surrender **10** abnegation **11** repudiation **12** renunciation

relish 3 dig **4** like, love, tang, want, wish, zest **5** enjoy, fancy, gusto, savor, spice, taste **6** accent, desire, dote on, flavor, liking, palate **7** delight, longing, stomach **8** appetite, fondness, groove on, penchant, piquancy, pleasure **9** condiment, delight in, enjoyment, hankering, rejoice in **10** appreciate, ebullience, enthusiasm, exuberance, partiality, propensity **11** luxuriate in **12** appreciation, be crazy about, predilection, satisfaction **13** gratification
type: **4** beef, corn **5** sweet **7** chutney **6** pickle, tomato **10** chili sauce, piccalilli **11** horseradish

reluctance 10 hesitation **13** unwillingness **14** disinclination

reluctant 3 shy **4** slow **5** loath **6** averse **7** laggard **8** hesitant **9** diffident, unwilling **10** indisposed **11** disinclined

rely 3 bet **4** bank, lean, rest **5** count, swear, trust **6** credit, depend, reckon **7** believe **10** feel sure of **11** be dependent **12** give credence

remain 4 go on, last, stay, wait **5** abide, stand **6** be left, endure, hang on, hold up, linger **7** not move, not stir, persist, prevail, stay put, subsist, survive **8** continue, stand pat **10** be left over, stay behind

remainder 4 rest **5** waste **6** excess, refuse **7** balance, overage, remains, remnant, residue, surplus, wastage **8** leavings, residual, residuum **9**

leftovers, scourings **10** surplusage **11** superfluity

remains 4 body **5** stiff **6** corpse, scraps **7** cadaver **8** dead body **9** leftovers

remark 3 say, see **4** espy, mark, mind, note, view, word **6** behold, look at, notice, regard, survey **7** comment, mention, observe, pay heed **8** perceive **9** attention **10** commentary, give heed to, make note of, reflection, take note of **11** contemplate, observation **12** fix the mind on, say in passing, take notice of **13** consideration **14** pay attention to

remarkable 6 signal **7** notable, unusual **8** singular, striking **9** memorable **10** impressive, noteworthy, phenomenal **11** conspicuous, exceptional, outstanding **13** distinguished, extraordinary, unforgettable

Remarque, Erich Maria
author of: **25** All Quiet on the Western Front

Rembrandt (Harmensz) van Rijn
born: **6** Leiden, Leyden **14** The Netherlands
artwork: **6** Balaam **9** Bathsheba **13** The Night Watch (The Sortie of the Company of Captain Banning Cocq) **14** The Jewish Bride **15** Old Woman Reading, The Bridal Couple **19** Blinding of Samson **20** Christ Healing the Sick **21** The Stoning of St Stephen **22** Man with the Golden Helmet, Self-Portrait with Saskia, The Descent from the Cross **24** The Anatomy Lesson of Dr Tulp, The Syndics of the Cloth Hall **36** Aristotle Contemplating the Bust of Homer

remedial 7 healing, helpful, mending **8** curative, salutary, sanative **10** beneficial, corrective **11** meliorative, reformative, restorative, therapeutic **12** advantageous, correctional, prophylactic

remedy 3 aid, fix **4** calm, cure, ease, heal, help, mend **5** amend, emend, right **6** relief, repair, soothe **7** assuage, correct, cure-all, improve, mollify, nostrum, panacea, rectify, redress, relieve, restore **8** make easy, medicine, mitigate, palliate, regulate, set right **9** alleviate, make sound, treatment **10** ameliorate, assistance, corrective, make better, medicament, medication, preventive **13** rectification **15** restore to health

remember 3 tip **6** recall, reward **9** not forget, recognize, recollect **10** appreciate, bear in mind, call to mind, have in mind, keep in mind, take care of, take note of **11** bring to mind **12** bear in memory

remember that thou must die
Latin: **11** memento mori

remembrance 5 favor, relic, token **6** memory, recall **7** memento **8** keepsake, memorial, reminder, souvenir **9** nostalgia **11** recognition, remembering **12** recognizance, recollection, reminiscence **13** commemoration

Remembrance of Things Past
   author: **12** Marcel Proust

Remembrance Rock
   author: **12** Carl Sandburg

Remick, Lee
   born: **8** Quincy MA
   roles: **16** Anatomy of a Murder, The Long Hot Summer **18** Days of Wine and Roses

remind 9 put in mind, suggest to **11** bring back to, bring to mind, put in memory **16** awaken memories of

reminder of death
   Latin: **11** memento mori

Remington, Frederic Sackrider
   born: **8** Canton NY
   artwork: **12** Bronco Buster **23** Roping Horses in the Corral **32** Cavalry Charge on the Southern Plains

reminisce 4 mull, muse **6** ponder **7** reflect **8** hark back, look back, remember **9** recollect, think back **12** tell old tales **16** exchange memories, swap remembrances

reminiscent 9 nostalgic, remindful, similar to **11** analogous to, remembering **12** recollecting **13** retrospective

remiss 3 lax **4** idle, lazy, slow **5** loose, slack **6** sloppy **7** laggard, loafing **8** careless, derelict, dilatory, inactive, indolent, slipshod, slothful, uncaring **9** do-nothing, forgetful, negligent, oblivious, shiftless, undutiful, unmindful **10** delinquent, neglectful, unthinking, unwatchful **11** inattentive, indifferent, thoughtless

remission 4 cure **5** lapse, pause **6** hiatus, pardon **7** respite, retreat **8** decrease **9** abatement, acquittal, cessation, reduction, shrinkage **10** absolution, diminution, hesitation, moderation, modulation, subsidence **11** exoneration, forgiveness, vindication

remit 3 pay **4** free, send, ship **5** clear, let go, relax, slack **6** excuse, let out, pardon, reduce **7** absolve, forgive, forward, release, set free, slacken **8** decrease, diminish, dispatch, liberate, make good, moderate, overlook, pass over, transmit **9** discharge, reimburse **10** compensate **11** put to rights **13** send in payment

remnant 3 bit **5** piece, relic, scrap, shred, token, trace **7** discard, remains, residue, vestige **8** fragment, leavings, leftover, monument, residuum, survival **9** remainder **11** odds and ends

remodel 4 redo **5** adapt, alter, fix up **6** change, modify **7** convert, reshape **8** overhaul, renovate **9** refashion, transform **11** recondition

remodeling 6 change **10** alteration,

conversion **12** modification **13** transmutation **14** transformation

remonstrance 6 rebuke **7** censure **8** reproach, scolding **9** criticism, reprimand **10** admonition

remonstrate 5 argue, chide, demur, scold **6** differ, object, rebuke **7** censure, chasten, contend, dispute, dissent, protest, reprove, upbraid **8** admonish, complain, reproach **9** criticize **10** take to task **11** expostulate **13** call to account

remorse 3 rue **4** pang **5** grief, guilt, qualm **6** regret, sorrow **7** anguish **9** penitence **10** contrition, repentance, ruefulness **11** compunction, lamentation, self-reproof **12** self-reproach **13** regretfulness **14** second thoughts

remorseful 8 contrite, penitent **9** chastened, regretful, repentant, sorrowful **10** apologetic **13** grief-stricken **18** conscience-stricken

remote 3 far **4** slim **5** alien, alone, aloof, faint, quiet **6** exotic, far-off, lonely, meager, slight **7** distant, dubious, faraway, foreign, removed, strange **8** detached, doubtful, isolated, secluded, separate, set apart, solitary, unlikely **9** withdrawn **10** far-removed, segregated **11** God-forsaken, implausible, out of the way, sequestered, standoffish

removal 6 moving, ouster **7** doffing **8** deletion, ejection **9** discharge, dismissal, expulsion, taking off, taking out **10** amputation, carting off, cutting away, dislodging, evacuation, lopping off **11** carrying off, chopping off, elimination, transferral **12** cancellation, displacement **14** transportation **15** transplantation

remove 4 doff, drop, fire, move, oust, quit **5** eject, erase, expel, leave, shift **6** cancel, change, cut off, delete, depart, go away, lop off, retire, unseat, vacate **7** blot out, boot out, cart off, chop off, cut away, dismiss, extract, kick out, retreat, take off, take out, wipe out **8** amputate, carry off, dislodge, displace, evacuate, get rid of, sweep out, take away, transfer, withdraw **9** discharge, eliminate, take leave, transport **10** make an exit, transplant

removed 3 off **4** away, took **5** alone, aloof, apart **6** remote **7** distant, faraway **8** abstract, detached, isolated, reticent, secluded **9** alienated, separate, unrelated, withdrawn **10** segregated, unsociable **11** interspaced, standoffish

remove from office 4 oust **6** depose, unseat **9** discharge

remunerate 3 pay **5** award, grant, repay **6** reward **7** requite, satisfy **9** indemnify, reimburse, vouchsafe **10**

compensate, recompense **15** make restitution

remuneration 7 payment **9** repayment **10** recompense, reparation **12** compensation **13** reimbursement **15** indemnification

Remus
   father: **4** Mars
   mother: **4** Ilia **9** Rea Silvia **10** Rhea Silvia
   twin brother: **7** Romulus
   raised by: **7** she-wolf

renaissance 7 rebirth, renewal, revival **10** rekindling, renascence, resurgence **11** reawakening, reemergence, restoration **12** regeneration, rejuvenation, resurrection, risorgimento **14** revitalization, revivification **15** reestablishment

rend 3 cut, rip **4** hurt, pain, rive, sear, tear **5** break, crack, sever, split, wound **6** cleave, divide, pierce, sunder **7** afflict, rupture, shatter **8** dissever, fracture, lacerate, polarize, splinter **12** disintegrate, fall to pieces **15** break into pieces

render 2 do **4** cede, give, make, play **5** allot, grant, remit, yield **6** accord, donate, give up, supply, tender **7** deal out, dole out, execute, hand out, pay back, perform, present, requite **8** construe, dispense, fork over, hand over, pay as due, shell out, turn over **9** cause to be, interpret, surrender, translate **10** relinquish **12** give in return, make requital **13** cause to become, make available, make payment of

render impotent 6 defuse, weaken **7** disable, unnerve **8** paralyze **9** undermine **10** devitalize, emasculate

render inoperable 6 damage, impair **7** cripple, disable **12** incapacitate

render null and void 4 void **5** annul **6** cancel, repeal, revoke **7** abolish, nullify, rescind, retract, reverse **8** abrogate, dissolve **10** invalidate

rendezvous 4 date **5** focus, haunt, mecca, tryst **6** gather, muster **7** retreat **8** assemble **9** encounter, tete-a-tete **10** engagement, focal point **11** appointment, assignation, get together **12** meeting place, watering hole **14** gathering place, stamping ground **15** agreement to meet **17** meet by appointment **18** prearranged meeting

rendition 7 edition, reading, version **9** depiction, portrayal, rendering **11** arrangement, performance, translation **14** interpretation

rend the air 3 cry **4** bawl, howl, wail **6** clamor, scream, shriek, squeal **7** screech **9** caterwaul

Renee Mauperin
   author: **24** Edmond and Jules de Goncourt

renegade 5 rebel **6** outlaw **7** heretic,

runaway, slacker, traitor **8** apostate, betrayer, defector, deserter, forsaker, fugitive, mutineer, mutinous, quisling, recreant, turncoat **9** dissenter, insurgent **10** backslider, traitorous, treasonist, unfaithful

renege 7 back out, fink out, pull out **8** back down, fall back, withdraw **9** repudiate, weasel out **11** get cold feet **12** turn one's back **13** break a promise, break one's word **16** go back on one's word

renew 4 save **6** extend, pick up, redeem, resume, retain, revive **7** prolong, refresh, restore, salvage **8** continue, maintain **9** make sound, reinstate, sign again **10** begin again, offer again, regenerate, rejuvenate, revitalize **11** reestablish, take up again **12** reinvigorate **16** put back into shape

renewal 7 revival **9** extension **10** redemption **11** restoration **12** regeneration **13** reinstatement **14** revitalization

Renoir, Pierre-Auguste
born: 6 France **7** Limoges
artwork: 4 Lise **6** La Loge **10** The Bathers **12** Margot Berard, The Umbrellas **14** La Grenouillere **19** Le Moulin de la Galette **28** Mme Charpentier and Her Children, The Luncheon of the Boating Party

renounce 4 cede, deny, quit **5** forgo, waive **6** abjure, disown, eschew, forego, give up, recant, reject, resign **7** abandon, cast off, disavow, discard, dismiss **8** abdicate, abnegate, abrogate, disclaim, forswear, lay aside, part with, put aside, turn from, write off **9** cast aside, foreswear, repudiate **10** relinquish **13** give up claim to **15** wash one's hands of

renovate 3 fix **4** mend **6** remake, repair, revamp **7** improve, remodel, restore **8** make over **9** modernize, refurbish **10** redecorate

renown 4 fame, mark, note **6** repute, status **7** acclaim **8** eminence **9** celebrity, notoriety **10** popularity, prominence, reputation **11** distinction

renowned 5 famed, noted **6** famous **7** eminent, notable, popular **9** acclaimed, prominent, well-known **10** celebrated, noteworthy **11** outstanding **13** distinguished

rent 3 fee, gap, let, rip **4** dues, gash, hire, hole, rift, slit, tear **5** break, chasm, chink, cleft, crack, lease, split **6** breach, hiatus, rental, schism, tatter, wrench **7** charter, fissure, opening, payment, rent out, rupture **8** cleavage, crevasse, division, fracture **11** buy the use of **12** sell the use of

rente 6 income **7** revenue **12** annual income

rentier 21 one who has a fixed income

renunciation 6 denial **7** refusal **8** for-going, spurning **9** disavowal, eschewing, foregoing, rejection, repulsion **10** abjuration, renouncing **11** abandonment, disclaiming, forswearing, repudiation **12** foreswearing **14** relinquishment

Renwick, James, Jr
architect of: 8 Main Hall (Vassar College) **11** Grace Church (NYC) **15** Corcoran Gallery (now Renwick Gallery, Washington, DC) **19** St Patrick's Cathedral (NYC) **22** Smithsonian Institution (Washington DC)
style: 13 Gothic Revival

reopen 7 restart **9** begin anew, reconvene, start anew **10** recommence, reinitiate **11** reestablish, reinstitute **12** reinaugurate

repair 2 go **3** fix **4** mend, move **5** amend, emend, patch, renew, shape, state **6** fixing, remedy, remove, retire **7** correct, mending, patch up, rebuild, rectify, redress, restore **8** make good, overhaul, patching, set right, withdraw **9** condition, make up for, refurbish, repairing **10** rebuilding **11** recondition **12** refurbishing **14** reconditioning

reparation 6 amends, return **7** damages, redress **8** requital **9** quittance **10** recompense **11** restitution **12** compensation, satisfaction **13** peace offering

repartee 6 banter, bon mot **7** riposte **8** badinage, chit chat, word play **10** persiflage, witty reply **11** witty retort **12** pleasantries **14** snappy comeback

repast 4 food, meal **5** board, feast, snack, table **6** spread **7** banquet **8** victuals **9** provision **11** nourishment, refreshment

repay 5 match **6** refund, return, reward **7** pay back, requite **9** get back at, indemnify, pay in kind, reimburse **10** recompense, remunerate **11** get even with, reciprocate **12** make requital **14** give in exchange, make a return for **15** make restitution, make retribution **19** return the compliment

repayment 10 paying back, recompense **12** compensation **13** reimbursement **17** making restitution

repeal 4 void **5** annul **6** cancel, revoke **7** abolish, nullify, rescind, voiding **8** abrogate, set aside **9** abolition, annulment **10** abrogation, invalidate, revocation **11** termination **12** cancellation, invalidation **13** nullification **18** declare null and void

repeat 4 echo, redo, tell **5** mimic, quote, rerun **6** pass on, recite, relate, retell **7** imitate, recount, restate, retread, say over **8** say again **9** duplicate, reiterate, reproduce **10** repetition **11** duplication, reiteration **12** perform again

repeated exercises 4 rote **5** drill **8** practice, training

repel 4 foil, rout **5** check **6** dispel, offend, oppose, put off, rebuff, resist, revolt, sicken **7** deflect, disgust, fend off, forfend, hold off, keep off, keep out, repulse, scatter, turn off, ward off **8** alienate, beat back, disperse, nauseate, push back, stave off, throw off **9** chase away, drive away, drive back, force back, frustrate, keep at bay, withstand

repellent 5 proof **9** abhorrent, loathsome, offensive, repelling, repugnant, repulsive, resisting, revolting, sickening **10** disgusting, nauseating **11** distasteful, impermeable

repent 3 rue **6** bemoan, bewail, lament, regret, repine **7** deplore **8** mea culpa, weep over **9** be ashamed **10** be contrite, be penitent **11** be regretful, feel remorse

repentance 5 grief, guilt **6** regret, sorrow **7** remorse **9** penitence **10** contrition **11** compunction **12** self-reproach **16** self-condemnation **17** pangs of conscience

repercussion 4 echo **6** effect, result **8** backlash, reaction **10** concussion, side effect **11** aftereffect, consequence **13** reverberation **15** boomerang effect

repetition 6 repeat **9** iteration, retelling **11** reiteration, restatement **14** recapitulation

repetitious 5 wordy **6** prolix **8** repeated **9** redundant **10** repetitive

Repin, Ilya Efimovich
born: 6 Russia **8** Chugeyev
artwork: 15 The Volga Boatmen **18** Zaporozhye Cossacks **19** They Did Not Expect Him **26** Ivan the Terrible Kills His Son

replace 5 spell **6** return **7** put back, restore, succeed **8** supplant **9** supersede

replaceable 10 disposable, expendable **11** dispensable

replenish 5 renew **6** refill, reload **7** refresh, reorder, replace, restock, restore

replenished 7 renewed **8** refilled, replaced, restored **9** restocked

replenishment 7 renewal **9** refilling **10** restocking **11** replacement, restoration

replete 4 full **5** sated **6** gorged, loaded **7** crammed, fraught, stuffed, teeming **8** brimming, satiated **9** abounding, jam-packed, surfeited **11** well-stocked

repletion 4 glut **6** excess **7** surfeit, surplus **9** abundance, plenitude, profusion, satiation **11** sufficiency

replica 4 copy **5** model **6** double **8** likeness **9** duplicate, facsimile, imitation **12** reproduction

reply 5 react **6** answer, rejoin, retort **7** counter, respond **8** reaction, response **9** rejoinder **14** acknowledgment

reply if you please
French: 4 rsvp 20 repondez s'il vous
plait

reply to 6 answer 7 counter, react to 8
retort to 9 respond to 11 acknowledge

repondez s'il vous plait 11 please
reply 16 reply if you please
abbreviation: 4 rsvp

report 4 bang, boom, note, talk, tell,
word 5 crack, noise, rumor, sound,
state, story 6 appear, detail, expose,
gossip, recite, record, relate, reveal,
show up, tell on 7 account, article,
check in, divulge, hearsay, message,
missive, recount, summary, version,
write-up 8 announce, denounce, describe, disclose, dispatch, relation
9 discharge, narration 10 communique, detonation, memorandum 11
communicate, description, information
French: 11 compte rendu

reporter 7 newshen, newsman 8
newshawk 9 anchorman, announcer,
columnist, newshound, newswoman
10 journalist, newscaster 11 commentator 12 newspaperman 13 correspondent 14 newspaperwoman

repose 3 lie 4 calm, ease, rest 5 quiet,
relax 6 be calm, settle 7 leisure, recline, respite 8 quietude 10 inactivity,
quiescence, relaxation 11 tranquility
12 peacefulness, tranquillity

repository 5 depot 8 magazine 9
warehouse 10 storehouse

reprehend 5 decry 7 censure, condemn, reprove 8 denounce, reproach
9 criticize 10 disapprove

reprehensible 3 bad 4 base, evil,
foul, vile 6 guilty, wicked 7 heinous,
ignoble 8 blamable, culpable, infamous, shameful, unworthy 9 nefarious 10 censurable, despicable, villainous 11 blameworthy, condemnable,
disgraceful, inexcusable, opprobrious
12 unpardonable 13 objectionable,
unjustifiable

reprehension 6 rebuke 7 censure, reproof 8 reproach 9 criticism 11 disapproval 12 condemnation, denunciation
14 disapprobation

represent 2 be 4 mean, show 5 enact,
equal, state 6 denote, depict, pose as,
sketch, typify 7 betoken, express, outline, picture, portray, present, serve as
8 appear as, describe, indicate, stand
for 9 delineate, designate, symbolize
10 illustrate 11 emblematize, impersonate 12 characterize

representation 5 image 6 effigy, emblem, symbol 7 epitome, essence, picture 8 likeness 9 depiction, portrayal
10 embodiment 12 illustration 15 exemplification 16 characterization

representative 2 MP 3 rep 5 agent,
envoy, proxy 6 deputy, varied 7 de-
puted, elected, proctor, typical 8 balanced, delegate, elective, emissary,

symbolic 9 delegated, exemplary,
spokesman, surrogate, typifying 10
delegatory, democratic, denotative,
emblematic, legislator, mouthpiece, republican, substitute, symbolical 11 assemblyman, congressman, delineative,
descriptive 12 exemplifying, illustrative 13 assemblywoman, congresswoman 14 characteristic, cross-
sectional

repress 4 curb, hide, mask, veil 5 box
up, check, cloak, cover, crush, pen
up, quash, quell 6 hold in, muffle,
shut up, squash, stifle, subdue 7 conceal, control, inhibit, put down, silence, smother, squelch 8 bottle up,
hold back, keep down, restrain, strangle, suppress

repression 8 muffling 9 holding in, restraint, retention 10 inhibition, throt-
tling 11 concealment, holding back,
suppression

reprieve 4 lull, stay 5 delay, pause 6
pardon, parole 7 amnesty, respite 8
breather 9 remission 10 moratorium,
suspension 11 adjournment 12 postponement 14 breathing spell

reprimand 4 trim 5 chide, scold 6 berate, rail at, rebuff, rebuke, revile 7
censure, chew out, chiding, lecture,
obloquy, tell off, upbraid 8 admonish,
berating, chastise, denounce, reproach, reproval, scolding, take down,
trimming 9 castigate, criticism, criticize, disparage, dispraise, dress down,
reprehend, reprobate 10 admonition,
chewing out, opprobrium, take to
task, upbraiding 11 castigation 12 admonishment, denunciation, dressing
down, remonstrance 13 disparagement 16 rap on the knuckles

reprisal 7 redress, revenge 8 requital 9
tit for tat, vengeance 11 counterblow,
retaliation, retribution 13 counterattack 16 counteroffensive
Latin: 10 quid pro quo

reproach 4 blot, slur, spot 5 blame,
chide, scold, shame, stain, taint 6
charge, insult, malign, rail at, rebuke,
revile, stigma, tirade, vilify 7 asperse,
blemish, censure, condemn, offense,
reproof, reprove, scandal, tarnish, upbraid 8 admonish, denounce, diatribe,
disgrace, dishonor, scolding 9 castigate, criticism, criticize, discredit, disparage, indignity, reprimand 10 stigmatize, take to task, tongue-lash,
upbraiding 11 degradation, humiliation 12 remonstrance 13 call to account, embarrassment

reprobate 3 bad, low 4 base, evil,
rake, roue, vile 5 scamp 6 pariah, rascal, rotter, sinner, wanton, wicked 7
corrupt, outcast 8 castaway, depraved, derelict, evildoer, prodigal,
rakehell 9 abandoned, dissolute, miscreant, shameless, wrongdoer 10

black sheep, degenerate, immoralist,
profligate, voluptuary 11 rapscallion,
untouchable 12 incorrigible, transgressor, wicked person

reproduce 4 copy, redo, sire 5 beget,
breed, match, spawn 6 mirror, repeat,
re-echo 7 imitate, reflect 8 generate,
multiply 9 duplicate, procreate, propagate, replicate, represent 11 counterfeit, proliferate

reproduction 4 copy 7 replica 8
breeding, likeness 9 duplicate, facsimile, imitation 10 carbon copy, generation, simulation 11 procreation, propagation 13 progeneration, proliferation
14 multiplication, representation
goddess of: 7 Astarte

reproductive system
component: 5 penis 6 testes, uterus,
vagina 7 ovaries

reproof 5 blame 6 rebuke 7 censure,
chiding 8 reproach, scolding 9 criticism, reprimand 10 admonition 12
condemnation, dressing-down, remonstrance

reprovable 7 at fault 8 blamable, culpable 10 censurable 11 blameworthy
12 reproachable

reprove 5 chide, scold 6 rebuke 7 censure, chasten 8 admonish, reproach 9
castigate, reprimand

reptile 3 asp, eft 4 newt, teju 5 agama, anole, gecko, skink, snake, viper
6 dragon, iguana, lizard, mugger, turtle 7 crawler, creeper, serpent, tuatara
8 basilisk, dinosaur, groveler, terrapin,
tortoise 9 alligator, chameleon, crocodile, pterosaur 10 salamander, vertebrate 11 Gila monster, pterodactyl

republic 9 democracy
Latin: 10 res publica

Republic
author: 5 Plato

Republican Party
also called: 3 GOP 13 Grand Old
Party
president belonging to: 4 Bush,
Ford, Taft 5 Grant, Hayes, Nixon 6
Arthur, Hoover, Reagan 7 Harding,
Lincoln, (Andrew) Johnson 8 Cool-
idge, Garfield, Harrison, McKinley 9
(Theodore) Roosevelt 10 Eisenhower
symbol: 8 elephant

Republic of China see 6 Taiwan

repudiate 4 deny, void 5 annul 6 cancel, desert, disown, reject, repeal, revoke 7 abandon, abolish, cast off, disavow, discard, forsake, nullify,
protest, rescind, retract, reverse 8 abrogate, disclaim, dissolve, renounce

repudiation 6 denial 9 disavowal, rejection 10 abrogation, disclaimer, retraction

repugnance 4 hate 5 odium 6 hatred
7 disgust 8 aversion, loathing 9 antipathy, revulsion 10 abhorrence 11
abomination, detestation

repugnant 4 foul, vile **5** nasty **6** odious **7** adverse, counter, hateful, opposed **8** contrary, unsavory **9** abhorrent, loathsome, obnoxious, offensive, repellent, repulsive, revolting, sickening **10** abominable, detestable, disgusting, nauseating, unpleasant **11** distasteful, uncongenial, undesirable, unpalatable **12** antipathetic, disagreeable, insufferable, unacceptable, unappetizing **13** objectionable

repulse 4 shun **5** avoid, repel, spurn **6** ignore, rebuff, refuse, reject **7** refusal **8** shunning, spurning **9** rejection

repulsion 6 hatred **7** disgust, dislike **8** aversion, distaste, loathing **9** antipathy **10** abhorrence, repugnance **11** abomination, detestation **13** indisposition **14** disinclination

repulsive 4 vile **5** nasty **6** odious **7** hateful **9** abhorrent, loathsome, obnoxious, offensive, repellent, repugnant, revolting **10** abominable, detestable, disgusting, nauseating **11** distasteful **12** disagreeable **13** objectionable

repulsiveness 8 ugliness **13** loathsomeness, offensiveness **14** disgustingness, unpleasantness **16** disagreeableness

reputable 7 honored **8** esteemed, reliable **9** respected **10** creditable **11** respectable, trustworthy

reputation 4 name **7** stature **8** standing

repute 3 say **4** deem, fame, hold, view **5** judge, think **6** esteem, reckon, regard, renown **7** account, believe, suppose **8** consider, estimate, standing **9** celebrity, notoriety **10** prominence **14** respectability

request 3 ask **4** seek **6** ask for, bid for, desire, sue for **7** call for, entreat, solicit **8** petition **9** importune **11** application **12** solicitation

requiem 5 dirge **6** lament **8** threnody

requiescat in pace 11 rest in peace **16** may he rest in peace **17** may she rest in peace

require 3 bid **4** lack, miss, need, want **5** crave, imply, order **6** charge, compel, desire, direct, enjoin, entail, oblige **7** command, dictate **9** constrain **11** necessitate

required 6 forced, needed **7** obliged **9** compelled, essential, necessary **10** compulsory, imperative, obligatory

requirement 4 must **8** standard **9** criterion, essential, guideline, requisite **12** prerequisite **13** specification
Latin: 10 sine qua non **11** desideratum

requisite 4 must, need **6** needed **8** required **9** essential, mandatory, necessary, necessity **10** compulsory, imperative, obligatory **11** requirement **12** prerequisite **13** indispensable

Latin: 10 sine qua non **11** desideratum

requisition 4 form **7** request **11** application

requital 7 redress **9** repayment **11** retaliation **12** compensation **15** indemnification

rescind 4 void **5** annul, quash **6** cancel, recall, repeal, revoke **7** abolish, discard, nullify, retract, reverse **8** abrogate, dissolve, override, overrule **10** invalidate **11** countermand **12** counterorder

rescinding 6 recall **7** voiding **8** recision **9** abolition **10** abrogation, retraction, revocation **11** abolishment, dissolution **12** cancellation, invalidation **13** nullification

rescue 4 save **6** ransom, saving **7** deliver, freeing, recover, release, salvage **8** liberate, recovery **9** extricate **10** liberation **11** deliverance, extrication

research 5 probe, study **7** delving, inquiry **8** analysis, scrutiny **10** inspection **11** examination, exploration, factfinding, investigate, scholarship **13** investigation

resemblance 7 analogy **8** affinity, likeness, parallel **10** congruence, similarity, similitude **14** correspondence

resemble 5 favor **6** be like **8** be akin to, look like, parallel **9** take after

resent 7 dislike

resentful 5 angry **6** bitter **7** annoyed **8** grudging, offended, provoked **10** displeased **12** dissatisfied

resentfulness 5 anger, spite **10** bitterness **15** dissatisfaction

resentment 3 ire **4** huff **5** anger, pique, spite **6** animus, malice, rancor **7** dudgeon, ill will, offense, umbrage **8** acerbity, acrimony, asperity, jealousy, soreness, sourness **9** animosity, crossness **10** bitterness, irritation **11** displeasure, indignation **12** irritability, vengefulness **14** vindictiveness

reservation 4 date **5** doubt **7** booking, proviso, scruple, strings **8** preserve **9** condition, hesitancy, provision **10** encampment, reluctance, settlement **11** appointment, compunction, stipulation, uncertainty **12** installation **13** accommodation, establishment, qualification **14** prearrangement

reserve 4 book, hold, keep, save **5** amass, delay, extra, hoard, lay up, spare, stock, table **6** backup, engage, retain, shelve, unused **7** husband, nest egg, savings **8** conserve, keep back, postpone, preserve, salt away, schedule, withhold **9** aloofness, reticence, stockpile **10** additional, prearrange

reserved 5 aloof, taken **6** booked, formal **7** distant, engaged **8** bespoken, retained, reticent, strained, unsocial **9**
inhibited, spoken for **10** restrained, unsociable **11** ceremonious, constrained, standoffish **12** unresponsive **15** uncommunicative, undemonstrative

reservoir 4 fund, pool, tank, well **5** basin, fount, hoard, stock, store **6** supply **7** backlog, cistern **8** millpond **9** container, stockpile **10** depository, receptacle, repository **12** accumulation

res gestae 5 deeds **10** things done **15** accomplishments

reshape 4 redo **5** adapt, alter, block **6** change, modify, reform, remold, rework **7** convert, reframe, remodel **9** refashion, transform

reside 3 lie **4** live, rest, room **5** dwell, exist, lodge **6** belong, occupy **7** inhabit, sojourn **9** domicile

residence 3 pad **4** digs, flat, home, room, stay **5** abode, house, place **7** address, lodging, sojourn **8** domicile, dwelling, quarters **9** apartment, homestead, household **10** habitation
French: 10 pied a terre

resident 5 local **6** lodger, tenant **7** citizen, denizen, dweller **8** occupant, townsman **9** sojourner **10** inhabitant **11** housekeeper

residual 5 extra **7** abiding, lasting, surplus **8** enduring, leftover **9** lingering, remaining **10** continuing **13** supplementary

residue 4 rest **5** dregs **6** scraps **7** balance, remains, remnant **8** leavings **9** remainder

resign 4 quit **5** leave **6** give up, submit **8** abdicate, disclaim, renounce **9** reconcile **10** relinquish

resignation 8 fatalism, patience, quitting, stoicism **9** departure **10** equanimity, retirement, submission, withdrawal **11** passiveness **12** acquiescence **13** nonresistance **14** submissiveness

resign oneself 5 yield **6** submit **9** acquiesce

resilience 6 recoil **7** rebound **8** buoyancy **10** elasticity **11** flexibility **12** adaptability **13** changeability, nonuniformity **16** lightheartedness

resilient 5 hardy **6** supple **7** buoyant, elastic, rubbery, springy **8** flexible **9** adaptable, expansive, resistant, tenacious **10** rebounding, responsive **13** irrepressible

resin 3 gum, lac, tar **5** amber, copal, elemi, epoxy, jalap, myrrh, pitch, rosin **6** balsam, guaiac, mastic **7** galipot, lacquer, shellac

resist 4 balk, foil, stem, stop **5** fight, repel **6** baffle, combat, oppose, refuse, reject, thwart **7** contest, counter, weather **8** beat back, turn down **9** frustrate, withstand **10** counteract

resistance 6 mutiny, rebuff **7** refusal **8**

defiance, struggle **9** obstinacy, rebellion, rejection **10** contention, insurgency, opposition **11** obstruction **12** insurrection **13** intransigence, noncompliance, recalcitrance

resolute 5 stern **6** dogged, steady **7** earnest, staunch, zealous **8** decisive, diligent, intrepid, stubborn, untiring, vigorous **9** assiduous, obstinate, purposive, steadfast, tenacious, unbending **10** deliberate, determined, inflexible, persistent, relentless, unflagging, unswerving, unwavering, unyielding **11** industrious, persevering, undeviating, unfaltering, unflinching **12** pertinacious, strong-minded, strong-willed **13** indefatigable **14** uncompromising

resoluteness 7 purpose, resolve **8** decision, tenacity **11** decidedness, persistence **12** decisiveness, perseverance **13** determination, steadfastness **14** purposefulness

resolution 3 aim **4** goal, plan, zeal **6** design, energy, intent, mettle, motion, object, spirit **7** promise, purpose, resolve **8** ambition, proposal, solution, tenacity **9** constancy, intention, objective, resolving, stability **10** resilience, steadiness **11** earnestness, persistence **12** perseverance, resoluteness **13** determination, steadfastness **14** aggressiveness **16** indefatigability

resolve 4 plan **6** answer, decide, design, intend, set out, settle, vote on **7** adjudge, clear up, explain, purpose **8** decision **9** determine, elucidate **10** commitment, resolution **12** resoluteness **13** determination **14** make up one's mind

resonant 4 full, rich **7** booming, orotund, ringing, vibrant **8** sonorous **9** bellowing **10** resounding, stentorian, thunderous **11** reverberant

resort 3 use **4** hope **5** apply, avail **6** chance, employ, take up **7** utilize **8** exercise, recourse **9** expedient

resound 4 echo, peal, ring **5** clang **6** re-echo **7** vibrate **11** reverberate **14** tintinnabulate

resounding 7 echoing, ringing **9** re-echoing **10** thundering, thunderous **13** reverberating

resource 8 recourse **9** expedient **11** wherewithal

resourceful 4 able **5** ready, sharp, smart **6** adroit, artful, bright, shrewd **7** capable, cunning **8** creative, original, skillful, talented **9** competent, effectual, ingenious, inventive **10** innovative, proficient **11** imaginative **12** enterprising

resourcefulness 9 ingenuity **10** creativity, enterprise **13** inventiveness

resources 5 funds, means, money **6** assets, income **7** capital, effects, revenue **10** belongings, collateral **11** possessions, wherewithal

respect 5 honor, point, sense **6** detail, esteem, matter, notice, praise, regard **7** bearing, feature, viewing **8** approval, courtesy, relation **9** affection, attention, deference, laudation, reference, relevance, reverence **10** admiration, connection, particular, veneration **11** point of view, recognition **12** appreciation, circumstance **13** consideration

respectability 7 decency, decorum **9** gentility, propriety **11** correctness, genteelness

respectable 4 fair **5** ample, civil, noble **6** decent, honest, polite, proper, worthy **7** correct, courtly, passing, refined, upright **8** becoming, decorous, moderate, polished **9** admirable, dignified, estimable, honorable, reputable **10** aboveboard, admissible, sufficient **11** presentable **12** considerable, praiseworthy, satisfactory

respected 6 valued, worthy **7** admired, honored, revered **8** esteemed **9** admirable, venerated

respectful 5 civil **6** formal, genial, polite **7** amiable, winning **8** admiring, decorous, gracious, mannerly, obliging, reverent **9** attentive, courteous, regardful **10** personable, solicitous **11** ceremonious, deferential, reverential **13** accommodating

respects 4 heed, obey **5** honor, prize, value **6** admire, esteem, fealty, follow, regard, revere **7** abide by, cherish, defer to, observe, regards, tribute **8** adhere to, consider, venerate **9** greetings **10** appreciate, understand **11** acknowledge, compliments **12** remembrances **13** consideration

Respighi, Ottorino
  born: 5 Italy **7** Bologna
  composer of: 8 La Fiamma, The Birds **14** The Pines of Rome **18** The Fountains of Rome **19** La Boutique Fantasque, The Fantastic Toyshop **27** Ancient Airs and Dances for Lute

respiration 9 breathing

respiratory system
  component: 4 lung, nose **6** larynx **7** pharynx, trachea **8** voice box, windpipe **9** bronchius, diaphragm
  action: 9 breathing

respire 7 breathe

respite 4 lull **5** break, delay, letup, pause **6** recess **8** reprieve **9** extension **12** intermission

resplendence 6 dazzle, luster **7** glitter **8** lambency, radiance **10** brilliance, luminosity, refulgence **12** circumstance, magnificence

resplendent 6 bright **7** beaming, blazing, glowing, lambent, radiant **8** dazzling, gleaming, luminous, lustrous, splendid **9** brilliant, refulgent, sparkling **10** glittering **11** coruscating

respond 5 react, reply **6** answer, rejoin

7 speak up **9** recognize **11** acknowledge

respond to 6 answer **7** act upon, react to, reply to **8** thank for **11** acknowledge

response 5 reply **6** answer, retort, return **7** riposte **8** comeback, feedback, reaction, rebuttal **9** rejoinder **10** impression **13** countercharge **14** acknowledgment **16** counterstatement

responsibility 4 duty, task **5** blame, order, trust **6** burden, charge **8** function **9** liability **10** obligation **11** culpability, reliability **13** answerability, dependability **14** accountability **15** trustworthiness

responsible 5 adult, of age **6** guilty, liable, mature **7** at fault, capable **8** culpable, reliable **9** demanding, executive, important **10** answerable, creditable, dependable **11** accountable, challenging, trustworthy **13** conscientious **14** administrative

responsive 5 alive, awake, sharp **8** reactive **9** receptive, sensitive **11** retaliative, retaliatory, susceptible, sympathetic **13** compassionate, understanding **14** impressionable

responsiveness 6 action **7** concern **8** interest **9** attention, awareness **11** sensitivity **13** understanding

res publica 8 republic, the state **12** commonwealth, public matter

rest 2 be **3** end, lay, lie, nap, set **4** base, ease, halt, hang, keep, laze, lean, loaf, loll, lull, prop, rely, stay, stop **5** break, death, exist, hinge, let up, pause, peace, place, quiet, relax, sleep, stand **6** demise, depend, holder, lounge, others, recess, remain, repose, reside, scraps, siesta, snooze, trivet **7** balance, be based, be found, be quiet, decease, deposit, holiday, leisure, lie down, recline, remains, remnant, residue, respite, set down, slumber, support **8** breather, platform, vacation **9** cessation, departure, leftovers, remainder, stillness **10** complement, quiet spell, relaxation, standstill, suspension **11** hibernation, take time out **12** intermission, interruption **13** take a breather
  Latin: 8 residuum

restaurant 5 diner **6** eatery **7** beanery, tearoom **9** cafeteria, chophouse, grillroom, hashhouse, lunchroom **11** coffeehouse **12** luncheonette
  French: 4 cafe **6** bistro **9** brasserie
  German: 11 rathskeller

restful 4 calm **5** quiet **6** placid, serene **7** pacific, relaxed **8** peaceful, soothing, tranquil **10** unagitated **11** comfortable, undisturbed

restfulness 4 ease **5** quiet **6** repose **8** serenity, softness **10** relaxation **11** tranquility **12** tranquillity

rest in peace
Latin: **16** requiescat in pace

restitution 6 amends **7** redress, replevy **8** replevin, requital, restoral **9** atonement, indemnity, repayment **10** recompense, reparation **11** restoration **12** compensation, remuneration, satisfaction **13** reimbursement, reinstatement **15** indemnification

restive 5 balky **6** mulish, ornery, unruly **7** fidgety, wayward, willful **8** contrary, stubborn **9** fractious, pigheaded **10** rebellious, refractory **11** disobedient, intractable **12** recalcitrant, unmanageable

restless 5 awake, jumpy **6** fitful, uneasy **7** anxious, fidgety, fretful, jittery, nervous, on the go, unquiet, wakeful, worried **8** agitated **9** excitable, impatient, incessant, insomniac, on the move, sleepless, transient, unsettled **10** disquieted, highstrung **11** hyperactive **13** uncomfortable

restoration 7 revival **8** recovery **12** recuperation **13** convalescence, reinstatement **14** rehabilitation, reintroduction, reinvigoration **15** reestablishment

restorative 5 tonic **6** elixir **7** bracing, healing **8** curative **10** beneficial, energizing, fortifying **11** revivifying **12** invigorating, revitalizing **13** strengthening

restore 3 fix **4** cure, dose, heal, mend **5** rally, renew, treat **6** do over, recoup, remedy, repair, rescue, return, revive **7** convert, get back, patch up, put back, rebuild, reclaim, recover, refresh, remodel, retouch, touch up **8** energize, give back, make over, make well, medicate, renovate, retrieve, revivify, recreate **9** reanimate, refurbish, reinstall, reinstate, stimulate **10** exhilarate, revitalize, strengthen **11** recondition, reconstruct, reestablish, reinstitute, resuscitate **12** rehabilitate, reinvigorate

restored 4 kept **5** saved **7** revived **8** replaced **9** conserved, pressured **11** replenished **13** rehabilitated

restrain 3 gag **4** bind, curb, hold, stop **5** check, leash, limit **6** arrest, bridle, fetter, muzzle, pinion, temper, tether **7** chasten, contain, curtail, harness, inhibit, prevent, shackle, trammel **8** handicap, hold back, restrict, suppress, withhold

restrained 4 cool **5** aloof **6** curbed **7** checked, distant **8** held back, reined in, reserved **10** controlled, unfriendly

restraint 4 curb **5** check **7** control **10** limitation

restrict 4 curb, hold **5** check, cramp, crimp, hem in, limit **6** hamper, impede, narrow, thwart **7** confine, inhibit, prevent, squelch **8** hold back,

obstruct, straiten, suppress **9** constrain, frustrate **12** circumscribe

restricted 7 cramped, limited **8** confined, hampered, held back **9** exclusive **10** suppressed **13** circumscribed

restriction 4 rule **7** control, curbing, proviso **9** condition, provision **10** limitation, regulation **11** requirement, reservation, stipulation **13** consideration, qualification

restrictive 8 limiting **9** confining, exclusive **12** constraining

result 4 stem **5** arise, end up, ensue, fruit, issue, owe to **6** derive, effect, happen, pan out, report, sequel, spring, upshot, wind up **7** finding, opinion, outcome, product, turn out, verdict **8** decision, judgment, reaction, solution **9** aftermath, culminate, eventuate, originate, outgrowth **10** resolution **11** aftereffect, consequence, development, eventuality **13** determination

resume 2 CV **3** bio **4** go on **5** brief **6** digest **7** epitome, proceed, summary **8** abstract, continue, reembark, synopsis **9** biography, summation **10** abridgment, recommence **11** reestablish **12** condensation
Latin: **15** curriculum vitae
French: **6** precis

resumption 11 recommenced, restora **12** continuation

resurgam 15 I shall rise again

resurgence 6 return **7** rebirth, renewal, revival **10** renascence **11** reemergence, renaissance **12** rejuvenation **13** recrudescence

ret 4 soak **6** dampen

retailer 5 store **6** dealer, seller, trader **8** merchant, provider, supplier **9** tradesman **10** wholesaler **11** distributor, storekeeper, tradeswoman **12** merchandiser
French: **9** vivandier **10** vivandiere

retain 4 hold, keep **5** grasp **6** absorb, recall **7** possess **8** hang on to, hold on to, maintain, memorize, remember **9** recollect

retainer 7 servant **8** employee **9** attendant

retainership 4 hire **6** employ **7** service **10** employment

retaliate 5 repay **6** avenge, pay off, return **7** counter, pay back, requite, revenge **11** reciprocate

retaliation 6 talion **7** deserts, revenge **8** reprisal, requital **9** vengeance **10** recompense **11** comeuppance, eye for an eye, interchange, just deserts, lex talionis, retribution **12** compensation **13** reciprocation **14** tooth for a tooth

retard 4 clog, drag **5** block, brake, check, delay **6** arrest, baffle, detain, fetter, hamper, hinder, hold up, impede, slow up **7** draw out, inhibit,

prevent, prolong, slacken **8** hold back, obstruct, slow down **10** decelerate

retarded 4 dull, slow **6** simple **7** idiotic, moronic, unsound **8** backward, disabled **9** imbecilic, mongoloid, subnormal **10** slow-witted **11** handicapped **12** simpleminded

reticent 3 shy **5** quiet **6** closed, silent **7** subdued **8** reserved, retiring, taciturn **9** diffident, withdrawn **10** restrained **11** tight-lipped **12** closemouthed **15** uncommunicative

retinue 5 court, staff, suite, train **6** convoy **9** courtiers, employees, entourage, followers, following, personnel, retainers **10** associates, attendance, attendants

retire 6 depart, go away, remove, resign, resort, secede, turn in **7** drop out, retreat **8** abdicate, flake out, withdraw

retired
French: **8** ci-devant

retiring 3 shy **4** meek **5** quiet, timid **6** demure, humble, modest **7** bashful **8** reserved, reticent, sheepish, timorous, unsocial **9** diffident, shrinking, withdrawn **10** unassuming **11** unassertive **12** self-effacing **13** inconspicuous, unpretentious **15** uncommunicative

retort 3 say **4** quip **5** rebut, reply **6** answer, rejoin, return **7** counter, respond, riposte **8** fire back, rebuttal **9** rejoinder

retract 4 deny **6** abjure, disown, draw in, recall, recant, recede, recoil, reel in, repeal, revoke **7** disavow, rescind, retreat, reverse **8** abnegate, abrogate, disclaim, draw back, forswear, peel back, pull back, renounce, take back, withdraw **9** foreswear, repudiate

retraction 6 recall **8** recision **9** disavowal **10** disclaimer, refutation, withdrawal

retreat 2 go **3** den **4** bolt, flee, port **5** haunt, haven, leave **6** asylum, depart, escape, flight, harbor, recoil, refuge, resort, retire, shrink **7** abscond, getaway, privacy, sanctum, shelter, shy away **8** back away, draw back, fall back, hideaway, move back, solitude, turn tail, withdraw **9** departure, isolation, reclusion, sanctuary, seclusion **10** evacuation, immurement, retirement, withdrawal **11** hibernation, rustication

retrench 5 slash **6** reduce, scrape, scrimp **7** curtail, cut back, cut down **8** conserve, cut costs **9** economize **15** tighten one's belt

retribution 6 amends, return, reward **7** justice, nemesis, penalty, redress, revenge **8** reprisal, requital **9** vengeance **10** punishment, recompense, reparation **11** just deserts, restitution, retaliation, vindication **12** satisfaction **13** reciprocation, recrimination

retrieve 4 snag 5 fetch 6 ransom, recoup, redeem, regain, rescue 7 get back, reclaim, recover, salvage 9 recapture, repossess

retriever
dog breed: 5 Irish 6 golden, Gordon 7 English 8 Labrador 10 flat-coated 11 curly-coated 13 Chesapeake Bay

retrograde 5 worse 6 worsen 7 inverse, retreat, reverse 8 backward 10 regressive 13 retrogressive

retrogress 6 worsen 9 backslide

retrogression 7 decline, setback 9 worsening 11 backsliding

retrogressive 8 backward 9 declining, worsening 11 backsliding

retrospect 6 review 9 flashback, hindsight 11 remembrance 12 afterthought, reminiscence 15 reconsideration

return 3 net 4 earn, gain 5 gross, recur, repay, yield 6 advent, come to, go back, income, profit, render, reseat, reward 7 arrival, benefit, produce, provide, put back, requite, restore, revenue 8 announce, come back, earnings, give back, hand down, interest, proceeds, reappear, recovery, restoral, send back 9 advantage, reinstall, reinstate, retrieval, reversion 10 homecoming, recurrence 11 reciprocate, reestablish, restoration 12 compensation, reappearance 13 reinstatement 15 reestablishment

Return of the Native
author: 11 Thomas Hardy
character: 11 Diggory Venn, Eustacia Vye 12 Damon Wildeve 13 Clym Yeobright 17 Thomasin Yeobright

Reuben
father: 5 Jacob
mother: 4 Leah
brother: 3 Dan, Gad 4 Levi 5 Asher, Judah 6 Joseph, Simeon 7 Zebulun 8 Benjamin, Issachar, Naphtali
sister: 5 Dinah
descendant of: 9 Reubenite

Reuben sandwich
ingredient: 3 rye 8 dressing 10 corned beef, sauerkraut 11 Swiss cheese

reunite 5 rewed 7 remarry 9 reconcile

reveal 4 bare, show 6 betray, expose, impart, let out, unfold, unmask, unveil 7 display, divulge, exhibit, give out, lay bare, publish, uncover, unearth 8 disclose, evidence, manifest, point out

revealed 4 open 5 clear, known 7 evident, obvious 8 manifest

revel 4 romp 5 caper, enjoy 6 bask in, frolic, gambol, relish 7 carouse, delight, indulge, rejoice, roister, skylark 8 wallow in 9 celebrate

revelation 6 expose, vision 7 shocker 8 exposure, prophecy 9 admission, bombshell, discovery, eyeopener, unveiling 10 apocalypse, confession, disclosure, divulgence 11 divulgation, divulgement

revelatory 10 expressive 11 informative 13 communicative

reveler 6 barfly, ranter, player 7 drinker 8 bacchant, carouser, drunkard 9 roisterer, rollicker, skylarker 10 merrymaker

revelry 5 spree 7 jollity 8 carnival, carousal, festival, jamboree 9 high jinks, merriment, rejoicing 10 exultation, roistering 11 celebrating, celebration, merrymaking 12 conviviality 13 jollification 14 boisterousness
god of: 5 Comus

revenge 5 repay 7 pay back, requite 8 reprisal, requital 9 repayment, retaliate, vengeance, vindicate 10 recompense 11 eye for an eye, reciprocate, retaliation, retribution 12 satisfaction

revenue 3 pay 4 take 5 gains, wages, yield 6 income, profit, return, salary 7 annuity, pension, subsidy 8 earnings, interest, pickings, proceeds, receipts 9 allowance, emolument 12 compensation, remuneration

revenue, annual
French: 5 rente

reverberate 4 boom, echo, ring 5 carry 6 rumble 7 resound, thunder, vibrate

reverberation 4 boom, echo 6 rumble 7 ringing, thunder 8 rumbling 9 vibration 10 resounding, thundering

revere 5 honor 6 esteem 7 defer to, respect 8 venerate

revered 6 adored 7 admired, honored 9 estimable, respected, venerated, worshiped 10 worshipped

reverence 3 awe 4 fear 5 honor, piety 6 esteem, homage, regard 7 respect, worship 8 devotion 9 adoration, deference 10 admiration, devoutness, observance, veneration 11 prostration, religiosity 12 genuflection

reverent 4 pure 5 pious 6 devout, humble, solemn 7 adoring, awesome, devoted 8 faithful 9 religious, spiritual 10 respectful, worshipful

reverential 4 awed 10 respectful, worshipful 11 deferential

reverie 5 dream, fancy 6 musing 7 fantasy 8 daydream 9 dreamland, quixotism 10 brown study, meditation 12 extravagance 13 woolgathering 14 fantasticality

reverse 4 back, rear, tail, undo, void 5 annul, upend, upset 6 cancel, change, defeat, invert, mishap, negate, recall, recant, repeal, revoke, unmake, upturn 7 counter, failure, nullify, rescind, retract, setback, trouble 8 abrogate, backward, contrary, converse, hardship, inverted, opposite, override, overrule, set aside, turn over, withdraw 9 adversity, mischance, posterior, transpose 10 antithesis, invalidate, misfortune 11 countermand, counterpart, frustration 14 disappointment

revert 5 lapse 6 go back, repeat, return 7 regress, relapse 9 backslide 10 recidivate, retrogress

review 4 show 5 study, sum up 6 notice, parade, rehash, survey 7 analyze, journal, retrace, run over 8 critique, evaluate, hash over, magazine, reassess, report on, scrutiny 9 criticism, criticize, reexamine, reiterate, summarize 10 commentary, evaluation, exhibition, exposition, procession, reconsider, reevaluate, reflection, scrutinize 11 examination 12 presentation, reassessment, recapitulate, reevaluation 13 demonstration, retrospection 14 recapitulation 15 reconsideration
French: 11 compte rendu

revile 4 slur 5 abuse, curse, scold, scorn 6 berate, defame, deride, malign, rebuke, vilify 7 bawl out, chew out, slander, upbraid 8 belittle, denounce, execrate, reproach, sail into 9 blaspheme, castigate, denigrate, disparage 10 vituperate

reviler 6 critic, curser 8 vilifier 9 backbiter, slanderer 10 blasphemer

revise 4 edit, redo 5 alter, amend, emend, fix up 6 change, doctor, modify, recast, redact, revamp, review, update 7 correct, rectify, rewrite 8 emendate, overhaul

revision 6 change 7 edition 9 amendment, recension 10 alteration, correction, emendation 11 improvement 12 modification

revival 7 renewal 11 restoration 13 reinstatement, reinstitution, resuscitation

revive 5 dig up, renew 6 drag up, repeat 7 freshen, refresh, restage 8 reawaken 9 reanimate, reproduce, resurrect 11 resuscitate

revived 7 renewed 8 animated, repeated, restaged 9 enlivened, freshened, refreshed 10 reanimated, reawakened, reproduced 11 invigorated, resurrected 12 resuscitated

revocation 6 repeal 8 recision 9 abolition, annulment 10 abrogation, retraction 11 abolishment, elimination, repudiation 12 cancellation 13 nullification

revoke 4 void 5 annul, erase, quash 6 abjure, cancel, negate, recall, repeal, vacate 7 abolish, dismiss, expunge, nullify, rescind, retract, reverse 8 abrogate, call back, disallow, disclaim, override, overrule, renounce, set aside, take back, withdraw 9 repudiate 10 invalidate 11 countermand

revolt 4 coup, rise 5 rebel, repel,

shock 6 appall, mutiny, offend, rise up, sicken 7 disgust, dissent, horrify, repulse 8 disorder, distress, nauseate, sedition, uprising 9 rebellion 10 insurgency, opposition, 12 factiousness, insurrection
German: 6 Putsch

revolting 4 foul, grim, vile 5 nasty 6 horrid, odious 7 hateful, noisome, noxious 8 dreadful, horrible, horrific, shocking, stinking 9 abhorrent, appalling, frightful, invidious, loathsome, obnoxious, offensive, repellent, repugnant, repulsive, sickening 10 abominable, disgusting, malodorous, nauseating 11 distasteful 12 disagreeable 13 objectionable

revolution 6 mutiny, revolt, rising 8 circling, gyration, rotation, uprising 9 rebellion 12 insurrection 14 circumrotation, circumvolution
French: 4 coup 6 coup d'etat
German: 6 Putsch

revolutionary 7 radical 8 mutinous 9 extremist, insurgent, seditious 10 dissenting, rebellious, subversive 13 superadvanced, unprecedented 15 insurrectionary

revolve 4 spin, turn 5 twist, wheel 6 circle, gyrate, rotate 12 circumrotate

revolver 3 gat, gun, rod 4 colt 6 pistol, weapon 7 firearm, handgun, rotator, sidearm 10 six-shooter 20 Saturday night special

revulsion 8 aversion, distaste, loathing 10 abhorrence, repugnance 11 detestation

reward 3 due 5 bonus, prize, repay, wages 6 bounty 7 deserts, guerdon, payment, premium, requite 9 reckoning 10 compensate, recompense, remunerate 12 compensation, remuneration 13 consideration
Latin: 10 quid pro quo

rewarding 8 pleasant, valuable 9 enjoyable 10 delightful, gratifying, satisfying 11 pleasurable

rework 4 redo 5 adapt, alter 6 modify 7 remodel, reshape 9 refashion, transform

rex 4 king

Reykjavik
capital of: 7 Iceland

Reynolds, Burt
born: 10 Waycross GA
wife: 9 Judy Carne, Loni Anderson
roles: 4 Bean 6 Shamus 9 Dan August, Semi-Tough, The Player 10 Striptease 11 Cop-and-a-half, Deliverance 12 Boogie Nights 14 The Longest Yard 18 Smokey and the Bandit

Reynolds, Debbie
real name: 19 Mary Frances Reynolds
born: 8 El Paso TX
husband: 11 Eddie Fisher
roles: 13 The Singing Nun, The Tender Trap 15 Singin' in the Rain 19

Tammy and the Bachelor 23 The Unsinkable Molly Brown

Reynolds, Sir Joshua
born: 7 England 8 Plympton
artwork: 14 Lord Heathfield, Miss Jane Bowles 15 Commodore Keppel 18 Mrs Francis Beckford 21 Mrs Abington as Miss Prue 25 Mrs Siddons as the Tragic Muse 38 Lady Sarah Bunbury Sacrificing to the Graces

Rhadamanthus, Rhadamanthys
father: 4 Zeus
mother: 6 Europa
brother: 5 Minos 6 Aeacus 8 Sarpedon
became a judge in: 5 Hades

rhapsodic 6 elated 7 beaming, excited 8 blissful, ecstatic, thrilled 9 delirious, overjoyed, rapturous 11 exhilarated, transported

Rhea
member of: 6 Titans
father: 6 Uranus
mother: 4 Gaea
brother: 6 Cronos, Cronus, Kronos
husband: 6 Cronos, Cronus, Kronos
son: 4 Zeus 5 Hades 8 Poseidon
daughter: 4 Hera 6 Hestia 7 Demeter
called: 10 Magna Mater
corresponds to: 3 Ops 6 Cybele 9 Dindymene 10 Berecyntia
epithet: 6 Antaea

Rhea Silvia
form: 12 vestal virgin
lover: 4 Mars
son: 5 Remus 7 Romulus

Rheingold see Ring des Nibelungen, Der

Rhesus
owned: 6 horses
horses captured by: 8 Diomedes, Odysseus

rhetoric 4 bunk, wind 5 hokum, hooey 6 bunkum, hot air 7 fustian, oratory 8 euphuism 9 discourse, elocution, eloquence, hyperbole 10 hocus-pocus 11 flamboyance 13 magniloquence 14 grandiloquence

Rhetoric
author: 9 Aristotle

rhetorical 5 showy, windy 6 florid, ornate, purple, verbal 7 aureate, flowery 8 eloquent, inflated 9 bombastic, grandiose, highflown, stylistic 10 decorative, discursive, euphuistic, expressive, flamboyant, linguistic, oratorical, ornamental 11 disputative, embellished, extravagant 12 disputatious, elocutionary, magniloquent 13 argumentative, grandiloquent

Rhoda
character: 8 Gary Levy 9 Joe Gerard 12 Benny Goodwin 14 Ida Morgenstern, Sally Gallagher 17 Brenda Morgenstern, Martin Morgenstern 22 Rhoda Morgenstern Gerard
cast: 9 Anne Meara, David Groh, Ron

Silver 11 Julie Kavner, Nancy Walker 12 Harold J Gould, Ray Buktenica 13 Valerie Harper

Rhode Island
abbreviation: 2 RI
nickname: 11 Little Rhody
capital/largest city: 10 Providence
others: 7 Bristol, Newport 8 Cranston, Kingston, Westerly 9 Pawtucket, Wakefield 10 Woonsocket
college: 5 Brown 6 Bryant 8 Pembroke 10 Barrington, Providence 11 Salve Regina 13 Mount St Joseph, Roger Williams 15 Johnson and Wales, Naval War College
feature: 7 Newport
tribe: 7 Niantic 9 Wampanoag 12 Narragansett
people: 8 Puritans 12 George M Cohan 13 Gilbert Stuart, Matthew C Perry, Roger Williams 15 Ambrose Burnside, Nathanael Greene 17 Oliver Hazard Perry
island: 5 Block, Rhode 8 Prudence 9 Aquidneck, Conanicut
lake: 8 Scituate
pond: 7 Wordens 8 Stafford, Watchaug
land rank: 8 fiftieth
mountain: 10 Durfee Hill
highest point: 12 Jerimoth Hill
physical feature:
bay: 12 Narragansett
sea: 8 Atlantic
sound: 11 Block Island
river: 7 Seekonk 8 Pawtuxet 9 Pawcatuck, Pawtucket, Potowomut 10 Blackstone, Providence
state admission: 10 thirteenth
state bird: 14 Rhode Island Red
state flower: 6 violet
state motto: 4 Hope
state song: 11 Rhode Island
state tree: 8 red maple

Rhodesia see 8 Zimbabwe

rhodium
chemical symbol: 2 Rh

rhododendron
varieties: 4 tree 5 Bluet 6 Indian, Yunnan 7 catawba, fringed, Lapland, silvery, Smirnow 8 Carolina, Chapman's, Fortune's, Fujiyama, piedmont 9 Caucasian, honey-bell, West Coast 11 leather-leaf 12 willow-leaved

rhodolite
species: 6 garnet

rhubarb 5 Rheum 16 Rheum rhabarbarum
varieties: 4 wild 5 monk's 6 garden, Sikkim 7 spinach 8 mountain

rhyme 3 pun 4 poem, rune, song 5 chime, clink, meter, poesy, verse 6 jingle, poetry, rhythm 7 measure, poetize, versify 8 assonate, doggerel 10 consonance 12 alliteration
game: 6 crambo

rhymer, rhymester 4 bard, poet **6** writer **8** minstrel, poetizer **9** poetaster, versifier **10** troubadour

Rhys, Jean
  author of: 7 Quartet **15** Voyage in the Dark, Wide Sargasso Sea

rhythm 4 beat, lilt, time **5** meter, pulse, swing, throb **6** accent, number, stress **7** cadence, measure **8** emphasis, movement **9** pulsation **10** recurrence **11** fluctuation, syncopation **12** accentuation

riant 3 gay **4** airy **5** jolly, merry **6** blithe, bright, jocund, jovial **7** smiling **8** cheer- ful, laughing, mirthful

rib 3 kid, rag **4** bait, bone, josh **5** chaff, costa, jolly, tease

ribald 4 lewd, racy, rude **5** bawdy, crude, gross **6** coarse, earthy, rakish, risque, vulgar, wanton **7** raffish, uncouth **8** improper, indecent, off-color, prurient, shocking **9** salacious, unrefined **10** lascivious, libidinous, licentious, suggestive

ribbon 3 bow, ray **4** band, sash **5** award, braid, prize, reins, strip **6** cordon, riband **7** binding, rosette **8** memorial, streamer **10** decoration

rice 5 Oryza **11** Oryza sativa
  varieties: 4 wild **6** Indian, pampas **7** basmati **8** mountain **9** Tennessee **10** annual wild
  dish: 5 grits, pilaf, pilau **7** pudding, risotto **8** porridge **9** jambalaya
  liquor: 4 sake

Rice, Anne
  lives: 10 New Orleans
  character: 6 Lestat **7** vampire
  author of: 11 Cry to Heaven **16** The Vampire Lestat **19** The Queen of the Damned **23** Interview with the Vampire

Rice, Elmer
  author of: 11 Street Scene **16** The Adding Machine

rich 4 dark, deep, fine, lush **5** flush, heavy, loamy, sweet, vivid **6** bright, costly, fecund, lavish, mellow **7** fertile, filling, intense, moneyed, opulent, wealthy, well-off **8** abundant, affluent, fruitful, in clover, precious, prodigal, resonant, sonorous, splendid, valuable, well-to-do **9** abounding, estimable, expensive, luxuriant, luxurious, priceless, sumptuous **10** euphonious, productive, propertied, prosperous **11** mellifluous **12** on easy street

Richard, Maurice
  nickname: 6 Rocket
  sport: 6 hockey
  position: 7 forward
  team: 17 Montreal Canadiens

Richard Cory
  author: 22 Edwin Arlington Robinson

Richard Diamond, Private Detective
  character: 3 Sam **6** Lt Kile **9** Lt Mc-

Gough **10** Karen Wells
  cast: 10 Russ Conway **11** Barbara Bain, Regis Toomey **12** David Janssen **13** Roxanne Brooks **14** Mary Tyler Moore
  viewers saw only Sam's: 4 legs

Richard I 11 Coeur de Lion, Lion-Hearted
  father: 7 Henry II
  mother: 8 Eleanor (of Aquitaine)
  brother: 4 John

Richard II
  author: 18 William Shakespeare
  character: 11 John of Gaunt **13** Edmund Langley, Thomas Mowbray **16** Henry Bolingbroke **20** Earl of Northumberland
  Duke of: 4 York **7** Aumerle, Norfolk **8** Hereford **9** Lancaster

Richard III
  author: 18 William Shakespeare
  character: 6 George **7** Richard **8** Edward IV, Lady Anne **10** Henry Tudor (Earl of Richmond) **11** Lord Stanley **12** Lord Hastings **13** Queen Margaret **14** Queen Elizabeth **15** Edward the Fourth **17** Sir William Catesby **19** Edward Prince of Wales
  Duke of: 4 York **8** Clarence **10** Buckingham, Gloucester

Richardson, Joely
  parents: 14 Tony Richardson **15** Vanessa Redgrave
  sister: 7 Natasha
  roles: 12 Event Horizon **13** 101 Dalmatians **14** Shining Through **17** Drowning By Numbers

Richardson, Henry Hobson
  architect of: 9 Sever Hall (Harvard) **11** Grace Church (West Medford MA) **13** Trinity Church (Boston) **23** State Asylum for the Insane (Buffalo NY) **27** Marshall Field Wholesale Store (Chicago)

Richardson, Natasha
  parents: 14 Tony Richardson **15** Vanessa Redgrave
  sister: 5 Joely
  roles: 11 Patty Hearst **12** The Handmaid's Tale **23** Every Picture Tells a Story

Richardson, Samuel
  author of: 6 Pamela (or Virtue Rewarded) **8** Clarissa (Harlowe) **19** Sir Charles Grandison

Richardson, Sir Ralph
  born: 7 England **10** Cheltenham
  roles: 6 Exodus **10** Oscar Wilde, Richard III, The Heiress **11** A Doll's House **12** Anna Karenina **13** Doctor Zhivago **15** Richard the Third **20** Little Lord Fauntleroy **24** Long Day's Journey into Night **26** Greystoke The Legend of Tarzan

Richardson, Tony
  wife: 15 Vanessa Redgrave
  daughter: 5 Joely **7** Natasha

director of: 7 Blue Sky **8** Tom Jones (Oscar) **14** The Entertainer **15** Look Back in Anger **36** The Loneliness of the Long Distance Runner

riches 4 pelf **5** lucre, means **6** assets, mammon, wealth **7** fortune **8** opulence, treasure **9** resources **10** prosperity **11** possessions

richness 6 wealth **8** fullness, lushness, opulence **9** amplitude, intensity **10** lavishness, mellowness **12** completeness **13** luxuriousness

Richter, Charles Francis
  field: 10 geophysics, seismology
  developed: 12 Richter scale **24** measurement of earthquakes

rickety 4 weak **5** frail, shaky **6** feeble, flimsy, infirm, wasted, weakly, wobbly **7** fragile **8** decrepit, unsteady, withered **9** tottering **10** brokendown, tumbledown **11** debilitated, dilapidated, weakjointed **12** deteriorated

rid 4 free **5** clear, purge **6** remove **8** disabuse, liberate, unburden **9** disburden, eliminate **11** disencumber

Ridd, John
  character in: 10 Lorna Doone
  author: 9 Blackmore

riddance 6 ouster, relief **7** freeing, removal **8** ejection **9** clearance, expulsion **11** deliverance, dislodgment

riddle 5 poser, rebus **6** enigma, puzzle, secret **7** mystery, problem, puzzler, stumper **9** conundrum

ride 4 move **5** annoy, carry, drive, harry, hound **6** badger, handle, harass, hector, manage, needle, travel **7** control, journey, support **8** progress **9** transport

rider 5 affix **6** suffix **7** adjunct, codicil **8** addendum, addition, appendix **9** amendment, appendage **10** attachment, supplement

ridge 3 bar, rib, rim **4** bank, fret, hill, hump, rise, wale, weal, welt **5** bluff, crest, crimp, knoll, mound, spine **6** ripple **7** crinkle, hillock, wrinkle **10** promontory **11** corrugation

ridicule 3 guy, rib **4** gibe, jeer, josh, mock, razz, ride, twit **5** mimic, scorn, taunt, tease **6** deride, gibe at, parody **7** lampoon, laugh at, mockery, ribbing, sarcasm, scoff at, sneer at, snicker, teasing **8** belittle, derision, sneering, travesty **9** aspersion, burlesque, disparage, humiliate, make fun of, poke fun at **10** caricature, derogation, lampoonery **13** disparagement
  god of: 5 Momos, Momus

ridiculous 3 odd **5** crazy, droll, funny, inane, nutty, queer, silly **6** absurd, screwy **7** amusing, asinine, bizarre, comical, fatuous, foolish, idiotic **8** farcical **9** fantastic, frivolous, grotesque, laughable, ludicrous, screwball, senseless **10** hysterical, incredible, irrational, outlandish **11** astonishing, nonsensical **12** preposterous, unreasonable

Rienzi
 author: **18** Edward Bulwer-Lytton
 composer: **6** Wagner

Riesling, Paul
 character in: **7** Babbitt
 author: **5** Lewis

rife 5 close, dense, solid, thick **6** common, packed **7** crowded, general, studded, teeming **8** epidemic, pandemic, populous, swarming **9** chockfull, extensive, plumbfull, prevalent, universal **10** prevailing, widespread **11** predominant

riffraff 3 mob **4** herd, scum **5** crowd, dregs, trash **6** masses, proles, rabble, vermin **9** peasantry **10** commonalty **11** proletariat
 French: **8** canaille

rifle 3 rob **4** loot, sack **6** ravage **7** despoil, pillage, plunder, ransack **8** spoliate **10** burglarize

rifle, repeating
 invented by: **7** Spencer

Rifleman, The
 character: **10** Lou Mallory, Mark McCain **11** Lucas McCain **14** Miss Milly Scott **20** Marshal Micah Torrance
 cast: **7** Paul Fix **10** Joan Taylor **12** Chuck Connors **13** Patricia Blair **14** Johnny Crawford
 setting: **9** New Mexico, North Fork

rift 3 cut, gap **4** gash, gulf, rent, slit **5** abyss, break, chasm, chink, cleft, crack, fault, gorge, gulch, gully, split **6** breach, cranny, ravine **7** breakup, crevice, fissure, quarrel, rupture **8** aperture, crevasse, division, fracture **12** disagreement **16** misunderstanding

rig 4 gear **5** equip **6** fit out, outfit **8** carriage **9** apparatus, equipment, machinery

Riga *see* **Latvia**

Rigaud
 character in: **12** Little Dorrit
 author: **7** Dickens

Rigg, Diana
 born: **7** England **9** Doncaster
 title: **4** Dame
 roles: **6** Helena **8** Emma Peel **10** Bleak House **11** Lady Dedlock, The Avengers **12** Julius Caesar **21** A Midsummer Night's Dream **26** On Her Majesty's Secret Service

right 2 OK **3** due **4** deed, fair, good, just, meet, nice, real, sane, true, well **5** amend, emend, exact, grant, honor, ideal, legal, licit, moral, power, solve, sound, valid **6** actual, at once, decent, honest, lawful, morals, normal, proper, remedy, seemly, square, virtue **7** certain, correct, ethical, exactly, factual, fitting, freedom, genuine, liberty, license, perfect, precise, probity, redress, regular, standup, warrant **8** accurate, becoming, clear-cut, definite,

directly, goodness, morality, promptly, properly, rational, sanction, straight, suitable, suitably, truthful, virtuous **9** allowable, authentic, authority, correctly, desirable, equitable, exemplary, favorable, favorably, honorable, integrity, nobleness, opportune, ownership, perfectly, precisely, presently, privilege, propriety, rectitude, veracious, veridical, vindicate **10** aboveboard, accurately, admissible, completely, convenient, infallible, legitimate, permission, preferable, reasonable, recompense, scrupulous, undisputed, unmistaken **11** inheritance, immediately, irrefutable, prerogative, punctilious **12** advantageous, jurisdiction, satisfactory **13** appropriately, authorization, incontestable, justification, unimpeachable **14** proprietorship, satisfactorily, unquestionable
 Latin: **3** jus

right beside 6 next to **8** abutting, adjacent, touching

righteous 4 fair, good, holy, just **5** godly, moral, pious **6** chaste, devout, honest **7** ethical **8** elevated, innocent, reverent, virtuous **9** blameless, equitable, honorable, incorrupt, religious, spiritual, unsullied

righteousness
 goddess of: **4** Maat

righteous person
 Hebrew: **6** zaddik

rightful 3 due **4** just, true **5** legal, valid **6** lawful, proper **7** allowed, condign, correct, fitting, merited **8** deserved **9** deserving, equitable **10** authorized, designated, legitimate, prescribed, sanctioned **11** appropriate, inalienable **14** constitutional

right hand 4 aide, ally **6** helper **7** partner **8** adjutant **9** assistant
 French: **10** aide-de-camp

right of blood
 Latin: **12** jus sanguinis

right of soil/land
 Latin: **7** jus soli

Right People, The
 author: **17** Stephen Birmingham

right side up 7 upright **10** on one's feet

Right Stuff, The
 director: **13** Philip Kaufman
 author: **8** Tom Wolfe
 cast: **8** Ed Harris **10** Sam Shepard
 Oscar for: **5** score

right-wing 7 old-line **10** nonliberal **11** reactionary **12** conservative **14** nonprogressive

right-winger 8 rightist **11** reactionary **12** conservative

rigid 3 set **4** firm, hard, taut **5** fixed, harsh, sharp, stern, stiff, tense **6** formal, severe, strict, strong, wooden **7** austere **8** exacting, obdurate, rigorous, stubborn, unpliant **9** inelastic, strin-

gent, unbending **10** inflexible, unyielding **11** puritanical, unrelenting **14** uncompromising

Rigoletto
 opera by: **5** Verdi
 character: **5** Gilda **9** Maddalena **11** Sparafucile **12** Duke of Mantua **15** Countess Ceprano **16** Count of Monterone

rigorous 5 exact, harsh, stern, tough **6** severe, strict, trying **7** austere, correct, precise **8** accurate, exacting **9** demanding, stringent **10** meticulous, scrupulous **11** challenging, punctilious

rig out 4 garb **5** array, dress **6** attire, clothe

rile 3 irk, vex **4** gall, miff, roil **5** anger, annoy, chafe, gripe, peeve, pique **6** bother, enrage, nettle, offend, plague **7** incense, inflame, provoke **8** irritate **9** aggravate, infuriate

Riley, James Whitcomb
 called: **11** Hoosier poet
 author of: **18** Little Orphant Annie **25** When the Frost Is on the Punkin

rilievo 6 relief

Rilke, Rainer Maria
 author of: **11** Book of Hours **12** Duino Elegies, Life and Songs **13** Divine Elegies **16** Sonnets to Orpheus **19** Letters to a Young Poet

rill 5 brook, cleft, creek **6** furrow, groove, runnel, stream **7** channel, rivulet **9** streamlet

rim 3 lip **4** edge, side **5** brink, ledge, verge **6** border, margin **9** outer edge

Rimbaud, Arthur
 born: **6** France
 author of: **12** Le Bateau Ivre **13** A Season in Hell **14** The Drunken Boat **16** Les Illuminations **17** Sonnet of the Vowels

rime 3 ice **4** hoar **5** chink, cleft, crack, crust, frost **7** crevice, fissure **9** hoarfrost

Rime of the Ancient Mariner, The
 author: **21** Samuel Taylor Coleridge
 character: **6** Hermit **9** Albatross **12** Wedding Guest **14** Ancient Mariner

Rimsky-Korsakov, Nikolai (Nicholas)
 born: **6** Russia **8** Novgorod
 member of: **7** The Five
 composer of: **5** Mlada, Sadko **6** Kitezh **10** Night in May, Snow Maiden, Tzar Saltan **11** Sheherazade **12** Christmas Eve, Scheherazade **16** Spanish Capriccio **17** Capriccio Espagnol, The Golden Cockerel **21** Russian Easter Overture **29** Russian Easter Festival Overture

rind 4 bark, hull, husk, peel, skin **5** crust, shell **6** cortex, fringe **7** epicarp, surface **8** exterior
 pork: **9** crackling

ring 4 aura, band, bloc, buzz, call,

echo, gang, hoop, loop, peal, toll, tone **5** cabal, chime, clang, knell, party, sound **6** cartel, circle, cordon, herald, jangle, jingle, league, signal, strike, summon, tinkle **7** besiege, circuit, combine, enclose, quality, resound, seal off, vibrate **8** announce, blockade, encircle, proclaim, striking, surround **9** broadcast, encompass, perimeter, resonance, syndicate, ting-a-ling, vibration **10** federation **11** reverberate **12** circumscribe **13** circumference, reverberation **14** tintinnabulate **16** tintinnabulation

Ring and the Book, The
  author: **14** Robert Browning
Ring des Nibelungen, Der
  also: **12** The Ring Cycle **20** The Ring of the Nibelung(s)
  opera by: **6** Wagner
  part one: **12** Das Rheingold, The Rhine Gold
  part two: **10** Die Walkure **11** The Valkyrie
  part three: **9** Siegfried
  part four: **15** Gotterdammerung **17** Twilight of the Gods
  character: **4** Erda, Mime **5** Freia, Hagen, Wotan **6** Fafner, Fasolt **7** Gunther, Gutrune, Hunding **8** Alberich, Siegmund **9** Siegfried, Sieglinde, Valkyries **10** Brunnhilde
ringleader 5 chief **6** master **10** mastermind
ringlet 4 curl **6** circle
ring-shaped 5 round **8** circular
Rin Tin Tin, The Adventures of
  character: **5** Rusty, (Cpl) Boone **9** (Sgt) Biff O'Hara **10** (Lt) Rip Masters
  cast: **8** Lee Aaker **9** Joe Sawyer **10** James Brown, Rand Brooks
Rio Bravo
  director: **11** Howard Hawks
  cast: **8** Ward Bond **9** John Wayne **10** Dean Martin **11** Ricky Nelson **13** Walter Brennan **14** Angie Dickinson
Rio de Janeiro
  airport: **6** Galeao
  architect: **5** Costa, Reidy **8** Niemeyer
  area: **4** Caju, Lapa **6** Catete, Gamboa, Gloria, Grajau, Tijuca **7** Catumbi, Ipanema **8** Botafogo **10** Copacabana, Vila Isabel **12** Sao Cristovao
  bay: **8** Botafogo, Jurujuba **9** Guanabara
  bridge: **11** Costa e Silva
  celebration: **8** Carnival **9** Mardi Gras
  discovered by: **6** Coelho
  former capital of: **6** Brazil
  island: **10** Governador
  lake: **16** Rodrigo de Freitas
  landmark: **10** Candelaria **14** Mount Corcovado **15** Maracana Stadium **17** Sugarloaf Mountain
    statue of: **17** Christ the Redeemer
  means: **14** river of January
  ocean: **8** Atlantic

people: **8** Cariocas
replaced as capital by: **8** Brasilia
slums: **7** favelas
suburb: **7** Niteroi
riot 4 rage **5** act up, arise, melee, rebel **6** fracas, mutiny, resist, revolt, rumpus, strife, tumult, uproar **7** rampage, run amok, trouble, turmoil **8** disorder, outburst, uprising, violence **9** commotion, confusion, rebellion **10** Donnybrook, turbulence **11** lawlessness, pandemonium **12** insurrection
rioting 6 tumult, uproar **7** turmoil **8** disorder, outbreak, violence **9** commotion **11** disturbance
riotous 4 loud, wild **5** arroar, noisy, randy **6** stormy, unruly, wanton **7** bacchic, rampant, violent **8** bacchian **9** debauched, dissolute, insurgent, plentiful, tumultuous, turbulent **10** boisterous, dissipated, licentious, rebellious **11** intemperate, overcopious **12** unrestrained **13** superabundant **15** insurrectionary
party: **4** orgy
rip 3 cut, gap **4** rend, rent, rift, rive, slit, tear **5** burst, sever, shred, slash, split **6** cleave **7** fissure, rupture **8** cleavage, cut apart, fracture, incision, tear open **10** laceration
ripe 3 due, fit **4** come **5** ideal, ready **6** mature, mellow, primed, timely **7** perfect **8** complete, finished, seasoned **9** maturated **10** consummate **12** accomplished
ripen 3 age **4** grow **5** bloom, fruit **6** flower, mature, mellow **7** develop
Rip Kirby
  creator: **11** Alex Raymond **12** John Prentice
Ripley, Robert L
  author of: **14** Believe It or Not
Rip Van Winkle
  author: **16** Washington Irving
rise 4 bank, defy, dune, face, gain, go up, grow, hill, lift, meet, soar **5** climb, get up, knoll, march, mount, rebel, ridge, spire, stand, surge, swell, tower **6** ascend, growth, mutiny, resist, revolt, rocket, strike, thrive **7** advance, balloon, burgeon, disobey, elevate, headway, improve, prosper, stand up, succeed, upswing **8** addition, flourish, increase, progress **9** expansion, extension **10** embankment **11** advancement, enlargement
Rise and Fall of the Third Reich, The
  author: **14** William L Shirer
Rise of Silas Lapham, The
  author: **18** William Dean Howells
  character: **5** Irene **8** Mr Rogers, Penelope, Tom Corey **9** Mrs Lapham
risible 4 rich **5** comic, droll, funny, merry, silly, witty **6** absurd, jocose, jovial **7** amusing, comical, jocular **8** farcical, humorous, mirthful **9** face-

tious, laughable, ludicrous, whimsical **10** ridiculous **11** nonsensical
rising sun
  god of: **5** Janus
risk 4 dare **5** peril **6** chance, danger, gamble, hazard **7** imperil, venture **8** endanger, jeopardy **9** speculate **10** jeopardize **11** imperilment, speculation, uncertainty **12** endangerment
risky 6 chancy, daring, unsafe **8** insecure, perilous, ticklish **9** dangerous, daredevil, haphazard, hazardous, hit or miss, uncertain **10** precarious **11** adventurous, unprotected, venturesome
risque 4 blue, lewd, racy **5** bawdy, dirty, gross, spicy **6** coarse, daring, ribald, smutty, vulgar **7** immoral, obscene **8** immodest, improper, indecent, off-color **9** offensive, salacious **10** indecorous, indelicate, lascivious, licentious, suggestive **12** pornographic
rite 6 ritual **7** liturgy, service **8** ceremony **9** formality, solemnity **10** ceremonial, observance
rite of passage 6 ritual **7** baptism **8** ceremony, marriage **10** bar mitzvah, bat mitzvah, initiation **11** christening **12** confirmation
Rites of Passage
  author: **14** William Golding
Ritt, Martin
  director of: **3** Hud **7** Sounder **8** Norma Rae, The Front **26** The Spy Who Came in From the Cold
Ritter, John
  born: **9** Burbank CA
  father: **9** Tex Ritter
  roles: **9** Hooperman **11** Americathon, Jack Tripper **13** Three's Company **14** Captain Avenger
Ritter, Thelma
  born: **10** Brooklyn NY
  roles: **10** Pillow Talk, Rear Window, The Misfits **11** All About Eve **15** The Mating Season **17** Birdman of Alcatraz **18** With a Song in My Heart **19** A Letter to Three Wives, Pickup on South Street **21** The Proud and the Profane **27** Miracle on Thirty-Fourth Street
ritual 4 rite **7** service **8** ceremony **10** observance
ritual bathing place
  Jewish Orthodox: **6** mikvah
ritualistic 6 formal, solemn **10** ceremonial **11** ceremonious
ritualize 7 observe **9** celebrate, solemnize **13** ceremonialize
ritzy 4 chic, posh, tony **5** sharp, swank **6** classy, snazzy, spiffy **7** elegant, stylish **9** high-class, high-toned, luxurious, sumptuous
rival 3 foe **5** enemy, equal, excel, fight, match, outdo, touch **6** strive **7** eclipse, surpass **8** approach, oppo-

nent, opposing, outshine **9** adversary, competing, contender, disputant **10** antagonist, competitor, contending, contestant

Rivals, The
　author: 23 Richard Brinsley Sheridan
　character: 8 Bob Acres **9** Faulkland **11** Mrs Malaprop **13** Julia Melville, Lydia Languish **17** Sir Lucius O'Trigger **18** Sir Anthony Absolute **19** Captain Jack Absolute (Ensign Beverley)

rive 4 rend **5** crack, split **6** cleave, detach, divide, sunder **7** shatter **8** fracture

riven 4 rent, torn **5** split **7** cleaved, cracked **8** sundered **9** fractured, shattered

River, The
　director: 10 Jean Renoir
　based on novel by: 11 Rumer Godden
　cast: 5 Radha **13** Adrienne Corri, Arthur Shields, Nora Swinburne **15** Patricia Walters
　setting: 5 India **6** Bengal

Rivera, Diego
　born: 6 Mexico **10** Guanajuato
　artwork: 5 Sleep **8** Creation **11** Mother Earth **14** The Fecund Earth **15** Detroit Industry **18** Man at the Crossroads **21** Carnival of Mexican Life **23** Life in Pre-Hispanic Mexico

river mouth 5 delta, didi **7** estuary

rivers
　god of: 6 Peneus, Simois **7** Inachus

Rivers, Reba
　character in: 9 Sanctuary
　author: 8 Faulkner

rivet 3 fix, pin **6** absorb, clinch, engage, fasten, occupy **7** engross **8** fastener **9** fascinate

Rivieres du Sud *see* **6** Guinea

rivulet 3 run **4** rill **5** brook, creek **6** stream **9** streamlet

Riyadh
　capital of: 11 Saudi Arabia

Rizzuto, Phil
　nickname: 7 Scooter
　position: 9 shortstop
　sport: 8 baseball
　team: 14 New York Yankees

road 3 via, way **4** lane, path **5** byway, route, trail **6** avenue, street **7** freeway, highway, parkway **8** turnpike **9** boulevard **10** expressway, throughway **12** thoroughfare

Road Not Taken, The
　author: 11 Robert Frost

roads
　god of: 6 Hermes

road safety
　god of: 6 Sancus **10** Semo Sancus

Road to Gandolfo, The
　author: 12 Robert Ludlum

roam 3 gad **4** rove **5** drift, jaunt,

prowl, range, stray, tramp **6** ramble, stroll, travel, wander **7** meander, traipse **8** divagate **9** gallivant **11** peregrinate

roan 5 horse **7** grayish, reddish, tannish **8** blackish, brownish

Roan Stallion
　author: 15 Robinson Jeffers

roar 3 bay, cry, din **4** bawl, boom, howl, roll, yell **5** blare, growl, grunt, noise, shout, snort **6** bellow, clamor, guffaw, outcry, racket, rumble, scream, shriek **7** bluster, resound, thunder **8** outburst **10** vociferate

roast 3 pan **4** bake **6** berate **7** scourge **8** barbecue **9** criticize

rob 4 bilk, lift, loot, raid, sack, skin **5** cheat, filch, heist, rifle, seize, steal **6** burgle, fleece, forage, hold up, pilfer, thieve **7** despoil, pillage, plunder, purloin, ransack, stick up, swindle **8** carry off, embezzle **9** bamboozle **10** burglarize **11** appropriate

Robards, Jason
　born: 9 Chicago IL
　wife: 12 Lauren Bacall
　roles: 5 Julia **7** Isadora **9** Dick Diver **10** Ben Bradlee **11** Jamie Tyrone **12** Hour of the Gun **15** A Thousand Clowns, Dashiell Hammett, Melvin and Howard, The Disenchanted **16** Tender Is the Night **19** All the President's Men **24** Long Day's Journey into Night

Robbe-Grillet, Alain
　author of: 8 Jealousy **9** The Voyeur **10** The Erasers **14** In the Labyrinth **19** Last Year at Marienbad

robber 4 yegg **5** crook, thief **6** bandit, con man, outlaw, pirate, raider **7** brigand, burglar, forager, rustler, sharper **8** Barabbas, marauder, swindler **9** buccaneer, despoiler, embezzler, larcenist, plunderer **10** highwayman, pickpocket

Robbins, Harold
　author of: 8 The Betsy **13** The Inheritors **14** Dreams Die First, The Adventurers **16** The Carpetbaggers **17** The Dream Merchants **18** Never Love a Stranger **20** A Stone for Danny Fisher **21** Seventy-Nine Park Avenue

Robbins, Jerome
　choreographer of: 8 Les Noces **9** Fancy Free, Interplay
　director of: 13 West Side Story (with Robert Wise, Oscar)

robe 4 gown **5** dress, habit, smock **6** duster **7** costume, garment **8** bathrobe, vestment **9** housecoat
　French: 8 negligee
　Japanese: 6 kimono

Robe, The
　author: 13 Lloyd C Douglas

robe-de-chambre 12 dressing-gown

Robert Kennedy and His Times
　author: 20 Arthur M Schlesinger Jr

Roberts, Kenneth
　author of: 16 Northwest Passage

Roberts, Rachel
　born: 5 Wales **8** Llanelly
　husband: 11 Rex Harrison
　roles: 8 Foul Play **10** Oh Lucky Man **16** This Sporting Life **24** Murder on the Orient Express **29** Saturday Night and Sunday Morning

Robertson, Cliff
　real name: 23 Clifford Parker Robertson
　born: 9 La Jolla CA
　wife: 11 Dina Merrill
　roles: 5 PT-109 **6** Charly (Oscar) **9** Obsession **11** Falcon Crest

Robertson, Oscar
　nickname: 7 The Big O
　sport: 10 basketball
　position: 5 guard
　team: 14 Milwaukee Bucks **16** Cincinnati Royals

Robeson, Paul
　born: 11 Princeton NJ
　roles: 7 Othello **8** Show Boat **11** Brutus Jones **15** The Emperor Jones **17** King Solomon's Mines **22** All God's Chillun Got Wings

Robin Hood's Adventures
　author: 7 unknown
　character: 9 Friar Tuck **10** Little John **11** Will Scarlet **14** Band of Merry Men **18** Sir Richard of the Lea **19** Sheriff of Nottingham

robin's-egg-blue 4 aqua **5** azure **7** sky-blue **8** cerulean **9** light blue **10** aquamarine, powder-blue

Robinson, Edward G
　real name: 18 Emmanuel Goldenberg
　born: 7 Romania **9** Bucharest
　roles: 8 Key Largo **12** Little Caesar, Rico Bandello **13** Scarlet Street **15** Double Indemnity, Flesh and Fantasy **16** House of Strangers **19** The Woman in the Window **20** A Dispatch from Reuters **21** Dr Ehrlich's Magic Bullet

Robinson, Edwin Arlington
　author of: 6 Merlin **8** Amaranth, Tristram **10** King Jasper **11** Richard Cory **12** Captain Craig **13** Miniver Cheevy, Mr Flood's Party

Robinson, Jackie
　sport: 8 baseball
　team: 15 Brooklyn Dodgers
　first black in: 12 major leagues

Robinson, Sugar Ray
　real name: 19 Walker Smith Robinson
　sport: 6 boxing
　class: 12 middleweight, welterweight

Robinson Crusoe
　author: 11 Daniel Defoe
　character: 6 Friday

Rob Roy

author: 14 Sir Walter Scott
character: 11 Diana Vernon **18** Sir Frederick Vernon **23** Rob Roy MacGregor Campbell
  Osbaldistone family: 5 Frank **7** William **9** Rashleigh **13** Sir Hildebrand

robust 3 fit **4** firm, hale, well, wiry **5** hardy, husky, lusty, sound, stout, tough **6** active, brawny, hearty, mighty, potent, rugged, sinewy, strong, sturdy, virile **7** healthy, staunch **8** athletic, forceful, muscular, powerful, stalwart, vigorous **9** energetic, healthful, strapping, wholesome **10** able-bodied **12** in fine fettle
French: 8 puissant

robustness 5 vigor **8** strength **10** good health, ruggedness, sturdiness **11** healthiness

Roche, Kevin
architect of: 13 Oakland Museum (CA) **14** Fine Arts Center (U of MA), Ford Foundation (NYC) **17** Knights of Columbus (New Haven CT) **21** One United Nations Plaza (NYC) **24** Union Carbide Headquarters (Danbury CT) **31** Power Center for the Performing Arts (U of Michigan)

Rochester
football team: 8 Panthers

Rochester, Edward
character in: 8 Jane Eyre
author: 6 Bronte

rock 3 bob, jar **4** crag, reef, roll, stun, sway, toss **5** cliff, flint, pitch, quake, shake, stone, swing, upset **6** gravel, marble, pebble, totter, wobble **7** agitate, bobbing, boulder, disturb, shaking **8** convulse, flounder, undulate, wobbling **9** limestone, oscillate, tottering **10** convulsion, undulation

rock & rye
type: 7 liqueur
flavor: 6 citrus
ingredient: 3 rye **9** rock candy

rock crystal
species: 6 quartz
color: 9 colorless

Rocket
nickname of: 14 Maurice Richard

rocket engine
invented by: 7 Goddard

Rockford Files, The
character: 10 John Cooper **11** Angel Martin, Jim Rockford **12** (Det) Dennis Becker **13** Beth Davenport, (Joseph) Rocky Rockford
cast: 9 Bo Hopkins, Joe Santos, Noah Beery **11** James Garner **14** Stuart Margolin **15** Gretchen Corbett

rock of Tarik see **9** Gibraltar

Rockwell, Norman
born: 9 New York NY
artwork:
  covers: 19 Saturday Evening Post
  mural: 15 Freedom of Speech

Rocky
director: 13 John G Avildsen
cast: 9 Burt Young **10** Talia Shire **11** Thayer David **12** Carl Weathers **15** Burgess Meredith **17** Sylvester Stallone (Rocky Balboa, the Italian Stallion)
setting: 12 Philadelphia
Oscar for: 7 editing, picture **8** director
sequel: 7 Rocky II, Rocky IV **8** Rocky III, Rocky Two **9** Rocky Four **10** Rocky Three

rod 4 cane, lash, mace, pale, pole, wand, whip **5** baton, birch, crook, staff, stake, stick **6** cudgel, rattan, switch **7** penalty, scepter, scourge **8** caduceus **9** stanchion **10** alpenstock, punishment **11** retribution **12** swagger stick

rod, Aaron's see **9** Aaron's rod

rodent 4 cavy, vole **5** coypu, gundi, hutia, mouse **6** agouti, beaver, cururo, gerbil, gopher, jerboa, nutria **7** blesmol, cane rat, hamster, lemming, mole-rat, rock rat **8** capybara, chipmunk, dormouse, pacarana, sewellel, spiny rat, squirrel, tucu-tuco, viscacha **9** chozchori, false paca, porcupine, woodchuck **10** chinchilla, prairie dog, springhare **11** kangaroo rat, pocket mouse, viscacha rat **13** kangaroo mouse **16** Speke's pectinator

Roderick Hudson
author: 10 Henry James

Roderick Random
author: 14 Tobias Smollett
character: 5 Strap **8** Narcissa **10** Tom Bowling **12** Miss Williams

Rodin, (Francois) Auguste Rene
born: 5 Paris **6** France
artwork: 7 The Kiss **10** Head of Iris, The Thinker, Victor Hugo, Walking Man **14** John the Baptist, The Age of Bronze, The Gates of Hell **16** Monument to Balzac **19** The Burghers of Calais **23** The Man with the Broken Nose

rodomontade 4 rant **5** boast **6** hot air **7** blather, bluster, bombast, fustian **8** bragging, folderol, nonsense, rhetoric **10** balderdash, doubletalk **11** braggadocio **12** boastfulness

roe 3 doe, elk, hen **4** buck, deer, eggs, fawn, fish, hart, hind, milt **5** spawn, sperm **6** caviar **8** fish eggs
of lobster: 5 coral

Roentgen, Rontgen, Wilhelm Konrad
field: 7 physics
nationality: 6 German
discovered: 5 X-rays
awarded: 10 Nobel Prize

Roethke, Theodore
author of: 9 Open House, The Waking **11** The Far Field **15** Straw for the Fire, Words for the Wind

Rogers, Ginger
real name: 23 Virginia Katherine McMath
born: 14 Independence MO
husband: 8 Lew Ayres **15** Jacques Bergerac, William Marshall
partner: 11 Fred Astaire
roles: 6 Top Hat **9** Stage Door **10** Hello Dolly, Kitty Foyle (Oscar) **12** Shall We Dance? **14** The Gay Divorcee **15** Flying Down to Rio, Tom Dick and Harry **17** Forty-Second Street **19** The Major and the Minor **21** The Barkleys of Broadway **30** The Story of Vernon and Irene Castle

Rogers, James Gamble
architect of: 22 Northwestern University (Chicago) **33** Columbia-Presbyterian Medical Center (NYC)

Rogers, Roy
real name: 11 Leonard Slye
born: 12 Cincinnati OH
wife: 9 Dale Evans
sidekick: 10 Gabby Hayes
singing group: 17 Sons of the Pioneers
horse: 7 Trigger
roles: 10 Apache Rose **11** Song of Texas **12** My Pal Trigger **13** Song of Arizona, Son of Paleface **17** Heart of the Rockies, Under Western Stars **18** Billy the Kid Returns **19** Tumbling Tumbleweeds **20** The Yellow Rose of Texas **22** Springtime in the Sierras

rogue 3 cur **5** devil, fraud, knave, scamp **6** bad man, rascal, rotter, varlet, wretch **7** bounder, hellion, villain **8** deceiver, evildoer, scalawag **9** miscreant, reprobate, scoundrel **10** blackguard, malefactor, mountebank, scapegrace **11** rapscallion **13** mischiefmaker **14** good-for-nothing **15** snake in the grass

Rogue Herries
author: 11 Hugh Walpole

roguish 3 sly **4** arch **5** saucy **8** devilish, rascally **11** mischievous

roil 3 irk, vex **4** mill, rile, stir **5** annoy, muddy **6** ruffle, seethe **7** agitate, disturb, perturb, provoke, turmoil **8** irritate **9** aggravate **10** exasperate

role 3 job **4** duty, part, pose, post, task, work **5** chore, guise **7** posture, service **8** capacity, function **9** character, portrayal **10** assignment **13** impersonation **14** representation **15** personification **16** characterization
Latin: 7 persona

roll 4 boom, coil, curl, echo, flip, flow, furl, knot, list, loop, reel, roar, rock, spin, sway, toss, tube, turn, wind **5** coast, crack, lurch, pitch, sound, spool, surge, swell, swing, swirl, throw, twirl, twist, wheel, whirl **6** billow, gyrate, muster, roster, rotate, rumble, scroll, tumble **7** booming, catalog, entwine, resound, revolve, rocking, thunder, tossing, turning **8** cylinder, drumbeat, drumming, rumbling, schedule, tumbling, undulate **9** inventory **10** undulation **11** reverberate **13** reverberation **15** turn over and over

Rolland, Romain
author of: **14** Jean-Christophe **16** The Soul Enchanted

rollicking 3 gay **5** happy, jolly, merry, sunny **6** bright, hearty, jocund, jovial, joyous, lively **7** gleeful, jocular, playful, romping **8** cheerful, mirthful, spirited **9** exuberant, gamboling, sparkling, sprightly **10** frolicking, frolicsome, hysterical, rip roaring **12** lighthearted

Rolvaag, Ole Edvart
author of: **15** Peder Victorious, Their Father's God **16** Giants in the Earth

roly-poly 3 fat **5** obese, plump, pudgy, round **6** chubby, rotund **9** corpulent

roman 5 novel **17** metrical narrative

Roman Catholic church
council/synod: **4** Pisa **5** Basel, Trent **6** Nicaea, Vienne, Whitby **7** Ephesus, Pistoia, Sardica **9** Chalcedon, Constance **12** First Vatican **13** Fourth Lateran, Second Vatican **14** Constantinople **15** Ferrara-Florence
official Vatican yearbook: **18** Annuario Pontificio
first Christian emperor: **11** Constantine
gift of territory/sovereignty to papacy: **15** Donation of Pepin **21** Donation of Constantine

romance 4 bosh, call, pull **5** amour, idyll, novel **6** affair, allure **7** fantasy, fiction **8** illusion **9** courtship, exoticism, fairy tale, fish story, invention, love story, melodrama, moonshine, tall story **10** attachment, concoction, flirtation, love affair **11** fabrication, fascination, imagination **12** exaggeration, relationship, self-delusion **13** flight of fancy, tender passion **16** affair of the heart

Romance language see **5** Latin

Romances sans paroles
author: **12** Paul Verlaine

Romancing the Stone
director: **14** Robert Zemeckis
cast: **11** Danny De Vito **14** Kathleen Turner, Michael Douglas
sequel: **17** The Jewel of the Nile

Roman Holiday
director: **12** William Wyler
cast: **11** Eddie Albert, Gregory Peck **13** Audrey Hepburn
Oscar for: **7** actress (Hepburn)

Romania
other name: **7** Rumania
capital/largest city: **9** Bucharest
others: **4** Aiud, Arad, Cluj, Deva, Iasi **5** Bacau, Balta, Cerna, Jassy, Neamt, Sibiu, Turnu, Yassy **6** Braila, Brasov, Brasso, Eforie, Galatz, Galeti, Lupeni,

Mamaia, Oradea, Sighet **7** Bendery, Craiova, Focsani, Giurgiu, Ploesti, Severin **8** Bloiesti, Cernavti, Chisinau, Irongate, Kishenef, Satu-Mare, Temesvar **9** Constanta, Kolozsvar, Timisoara **10** Czernowitz **11** Klausenburg
school: **4** Cuza
division: **4** Alba, Iasi **5** Banat, Bihor, Jassy **6** Ardeal **7** Dobruja **8** Bucovina, Bukovina, Dobrogea, Moldavia, Walachia **9** Maramures **10** Bessarabia **12** Transylvania
   Roman province: **5** Dacia
measure: **7** faltche
monetary unit: **3** ban, lei, leu, lev, ley **4** bani **5** uncia **6** triens
lake: **5** Sinoe **6** Snagov
mountain: **5** Banat, Bihor **6** Codrul, Rodnei **7** Apuseni, Balkans, Caliman, Fagaras **8** Pietrosu **9** Moldavian **10** Carpathian, Moldoveanu **17** Transylvanian Alps
highest point: **11** Moldoveanul
river: **3** Alt, Jui, Olt **4** Prut **5** Aluta, Arges, Buzdu, Moros, Mures, Oltul, Schyl, Sirct, Somes, Timis, Vedea **6** Crasna, Danube **7** Argesul **8** Bistrita, Ialomita, Iniester **9** Dimbovita, Jiul Mures
sea: **5** Black
physical feature:
   canal: **4** Bega
   forest: **6** Snagov **7** Baragan
   gorge: **8** Iron Gate
   peninsula: **6** Balkan
   plain: **5** Banat **6** Moldavian, Walachian **13** Prahova Valley
   plateau: **7** Dobruja
   wind: **6** crivat
people: **6** Dacian **8** Romanian, Rumanian
   artist: **8** Brancusi
   author: **7** Ionesco
   composer: **6** Enesco
   leader: **6** Carol I **7** Michael, Iliescu **8** Ioan Cuza **9** Ceausescu **12** Gheorghiu-Dej, Ion Antonescu
language: **6** French, Magyar **7** Russian **8** Romanian, Rumanian **9** Hungarian
religion: **7** Judaism **8** Lutheran **9** Calvinism, Unitarian **10** Protestant **13** Roman Catholic **16** Romanian Orthodox
place:
   castle: **4** Bran **7** Huniady
   church: **5** Golia **9** Mihaivoda **10** Cretulescu, Patriarchy **11** Curtea Veche, Stavropdeos, Trei Ierarhi
   monastery: **5** Humor **6** Arbore **7** Voronet **8** Sucerita **9** Moldovita
   museum: **11** Peles Castle
   palace: **9** mogosoaia
   park: **7** Baneasa
   resort: **5** Venus **6** Eforie, Mamaia, Neptun **7** Jupiter **10** Costinesti
feature:

community gathering: **9** sezatoare
game: **4** oina
food:
   dish: **6** ciorba **7** mititei, sarmala **8** mamaliga **11** imam bayildi
   plum brandy: **5** tuica
Roman measure 2 as **5** cubit, libra **6** pondus **7** stadium
Roman Mythology
collective name for gods: **6** Superi
goddess of anguish: **8** Angerona
goddess of agriculture: **5** Ceres **6** Dea Dia, Vacuna **13** Acca Laurentia
   Ceres corresponds to Greek: **7** Demeter
goddess of the arts: **7** Minerva
   corresponds to Greek: **6** Athena
goddess of baking: **6** Fornax
goddess of chastity: **5** Fauna **7** Bona Dea
goddess of childbirth: **5** Parca **6** Lucina, Matuta, Parcae **11** Mater Matuta
goddess of the dawn: **6** Aurora, Matuta **11** Mater Matuta
   Aurora corresponds to Greek: **3** Eos
goddess of destiny: **5** Parca **6** Parcae
goddess of discord: **9** Discordia
goddess of door hinges: **6** Cardea
goddess of the earth: **6** Tellus
   corresponds to Greek: **4** Gaea
goddess of the family: **6** Cardea
goddess of fertility: **5** Fauna **6** Libera, Tellus **7** Bona Dea
   Libera corresponds to Greek: **10** Persephone
   Tellus corresponds to Greek: **4** Gaea
goddess of flowers: **5** Flora
goddess of fortune: **7** Fortuna
   corresponds to Greek: **5** Tyche
goddess of fruit trees: **6** Pomona
goddess of gardens: **5** Venus
   corresponds to Greek: **9** Aphrodite
goddess of grain/protectress against grain blight: **6** Robigo
goddess of harbors: **6** Matuta **11** Mater Matuta
goddess of harmony: **9** Concordia
goddess of the hearth: **4** Caca **5** Salus, Vesta
   Salus corresponds to Greek: **6** Hygeia
goddess of heaven: **4** Juno
   corresponds to Greek: **4** Hera
goddess of hunting: **5** Diana
   corresponds to Greek: **6** Phoebe **7** Artemis
goddess of longevity: **11** Anna Perenna
goddess of love: **5** Venus
   corresponds to Greek: **9** Aphrodite
goddess of marriage: **4** Juno **6** Tellus
   corresponds to Greek: **4** Gaea, Hera
goddess of marshes: **6** Marica **9** Dea

Marica
goddess of the moon: 5 Diana
  corresponds to Greek: 6 Phoebe **7**
  Artemis
goddess of peace: 3 Pax **9** Concordia
  Pax corresponds to Greek: 5 Irene
goddess of pleasure: 8 Voluptas
goddess of plenty: 3 Ops **10** Magna
  Mater
goddess of prosperity: 5 Salus
  corresponds to Greek: 6 Hygeia
goddess of the sea: 6 Matuta **11** Mater Matuta
goddess of sleeping infants: 6 Cunina
goddess of the spring: 5 Venus
  corresponds to Greek: 9 Aphrodite
goddess of storms: 11 Tempestates
goddess of victory: 8 Victoria
  corresponds to Greek: 4 Nike
goddess of vineyards: 6 Libera
  corresponds to Greek: 10 Persephone
goddess of war: 7 Bellona
  corresponds to Greek: 5 Enyon
goddess of wine: 6 Libera
  corresponds to Greek: 10 Persephone
goddess of wisdom: 7 Minerva
  corresponds to Greek: 6 Athena
god of agriculture: 5 Picus **6** Saturn
  7 Eventus **12** Bonus Eventus
  corresponds to Greek: 6 Cronos,
  Cronus, Kronos
god of beginnings: 5 Janus
god of boundaries: 8 Terminus
god of commerce: 7 Mercury
  corresponds to Greek: 6 Hermes
god of the dead: 7 Veiovis
god of doorways: 5 Janus
god of drinking/revelry: 5 Comus
god of eloquence: 7 Mercury
  corresponds to Greek: 6 Hermes
god of farm boundaries: 8 Silvanus,
  Sylvanus
god of fertility: 7 Mutinus, Priapus **8**
  Lupercus, Picumnus
god of fire/metalworking: 6 Vulcan
  corresponds to Greek: 10 Hephaestus, Hephaistos
god of forest: 7 Virbius
god of gardens: 9 Vertumnus
god of good counsel: 3 Ops **6** Consus
**god of grain/protector against grain
  blight: 7** Robigus
god of healing: 11 Aesculapius
  corresponds to Greek: 9 Asclepius
god of heavens: 4 Jove **7** Jupiter
  corresponds to Greek: 4 Zeus
god of herds: 8 Silvanus, Sylvanus
god of horse racing: 3 Ops **6** Consus
god of hospitality: 6 Sancus **10** Dius
  Fidius, Semo Sancus
god of the house: 8 Silvanus, Sylvanus
god of hunting: 7 Virbius
god of international affairs: 6

Sancus **10** Dius Fidius, Semo Sancus
god of landmarks: 8 Terminus
god of light: 6 Apollo
god of love: 4 Amor **5** Cupid
  corresponds to Greek: 4 Eros
god of luck: 7 Eventus **12** Bonus
  Eventus
god of medicine: 11 Aesculapius
  corresponds to Greek: 9 Asclepius
god of music: 6 Apollo
god of oaths: 6 Sancus **10** Dius
  Fidius, Semo Sancus
god of orchards: 9 Vertumnus
god of ports/harbors: 8 Portunus
god of prosperity: 7 Eventus **12** Bonus Eventus
god of the rising sun: 5 Janus
god of science: 7 Mercury
  corresponds to Greek: 6 Hermes
god of sea: 7 Neptune
  corresponds to Greek: 8 Poseidon
god of seasons: 9 Vertumnus
god of the setting sun: 5 Janus
god of sleep: 6 Somnus
  corresponds to Greek: 6 Hypnos,
  Hypnus
god of springs: 4 Fons
gods of sulphur springs (twins): 6
  Palici
god of the sun: 3 Sol
  corresponds to Greek: 6 Helios **8**
  Hyperion
god of thievery: 7 Mercury
  corresponds to Greek: 6 Hermes
god of thunder: 7 Taranis
god of thunderstorms: 8 Summanus
god of the Tiber: 9 Tiberinus
god of uncultivated land: 8 Silvanus, Sylvanus
god of underworld: 3 Dis **5** Orcus **8**
  Dis Pater
  corresponds to Greek: 5 Pluto
god of war: 4 Mars **6** Mamers, Mavors **8** Quirinus
  corresponds to Greek: 4 Ares
god of weather: 4 Jove **7** Jupiter
god of weddings: 8 Talassio
  corresponds to Greek: 5 Hymen **9**
  Hymenaeus
god of the woods: 6 Faunus **8** Silvanus, Sylvanus
household gods: 5 lares **7** penates
**nymphs/deities with gift of proph-
  ecy: 7** Camenae
  names: 6 Egeria **8** Carmenta **9** Antevorta, Postvorta
  correspond to Greek: 5 Muses
protectress of childbirth: 8 Carmenta
protectress of cows/oxen: 6 Bubona
protector of flocks/shepherds: 5 Pa-
  les
protectress of military age men: 8
  Juventas
  corresponds to Greek: 4 Hebe
protectress of women: 5 Diana
  corresponds to Greek: 6 Phoebe **7**
  Artemis
protectress of women/marriage: 4

Juno
  queen of heaven: 4 Juno
  corresponds to Greek: 4 Hera,
  Here
staff of Mercury: 8 Caduceus
troublesome ghosts: 7 lemures
romantic 4 fond **5** mushy, soppy **6** ardent, dreamy, loving, tender, unreal **7**
  amorous, devoted, fervent, flighty,
  idyllic, utopian **8** enamored, fanciful,
  quixotic **9** fantastic, idealized, imaginary, sensitive, visionary, whimsical
  10 idealistic, improbable, passionate
  11 extravagant, impassioned, impractical, rhapsodical, sentimental, unrealistic, warmhearted **12** melodramatic,
  preposterous
Romantic Comedians, The
  author: 12 Ellen Glasgow
romanticize 8 idealize **9** embroider
Romantic Manifesto
  author: 7 Ayn Rand
Romany Rye, The
  author: 17 George Henry Borrow
Rome, ancient
  emperor: 4 Nero, Otho **5** Galba,
  Nerva, Titus **6** Trajan **7** Hadrian **8**
  Augustus, Caligula, Claudius, Commodus, Domitian, Tiberius **9** Caracalla, Vespasian, Vitellius **10** Diocletian **11** Constantine, Lucius Verus **13**
  Antoninus Pius **14** Marcus Aurelius
  emperor's bodyguard: 15 Praetorian
  Guard
  first citizen title: 8 princeps
  first triumvirate: 6 Caesar, Pompey **7**
  Crassus
  foe: 4 Gaul **5** Spain **6** Cimbri **7** Perseus, Philip V, Pyrrhus, Teutons **8**
  Carthage, Hannibal, Iberians, Jugurtha, Samnites, Tarentum, Umbrians
  9 Etruscans, Macedonia, Seleucids
  11 Latin League **12** Antiochus III **13**
  Achaean League, Hamilcar Barca
  general: 5 Sulla **6** Brutus, Marius,
  Pompey **7** Crassus **8** Octavian **10**
  Flamininus, Mark Antony **12** Julius
  Caesar **14** Caesar Augustus **20** Quintus Fabius Maximus, Scipio Africanus Major, Scipio Africanus Minor
  king: 12 Ancus Marcius **13** Numa
  Pompilius **16** Sextus Tarquinius **17**
  Tarquinius Priscus (Tarquin the Elder) **18** Tarquinius Superbus (Tarquin the Proud)
  reformer: 8 Gracchus
  republican ruler: 6 consul **7** senator,
  tribune **8** plebeian **9** optimates, patrician, populares **10** magistrate
  Roman peace: 9 Pax Romana
  second triumvirate: 6 Antony **7** Lepidus **8** Octavian (Caesar Augustus)
Rome, Roma
  airport: 8 Ciampino **15** Leonardo da
  Vinci
  area: 9 Cinecitta (Cinema City) **10**
  Trastevere **11** Vatican City

capital of: 5 Italy **6** Latium **11** Papal States, Roman Empire

church: 8 St Peter's **11** San Giovanni **18** Santa Maria Maggiore **19** San Paolo Fuori le Mura

Italian: 4 Roma

landmark: 5 Forum **7** Capitol **8** Pantheon **9** catacombs, Colosseum **12** Palazzo Doria **13** Circus Maximus, Lateran Palace, Sistine Chapel, Vatican Palace, Villa Borghese **14** Palazzo Corsini, Villa Farnesina **16** Baths of Caracalla, Castel Sant'Angelo, Palazzo Barberini **17** Arch of Constantine **19** Saint Peter's Basilica

legendary founders: 5 Remus **6** Aeneas **7** Romulus

nickname: 11 Eternal City

mountain: 8 Apennine

museum: 5 Doria **7** Colonna, Corsini, Vatican **8** Borghese, National **10** Capitoline

river: 5 Tiber

school: 33 Conservatorio di Musica Santa Cecilia

sea: 10 Tyrrhenian

seven hills: 7 Caelian, Viminal **8** Aventine, Palatine, Quirinal **9** Esquiline **10** Capitoline

square/piazza: 6 Popolo, Spagna **7** Colonna, Venezia **9** Quirinale **11** Campidoglio

state within: 11 Vatican City

street: 9 Appian Way, Emmanuele **11** Via del Corso **13** Corso Vittorio

subway: 13 Metropolitana

Romeo 4 beau **5** lover, sheik, swain, wooer **7** Don Juan, gallant **8** Casanova, cavalier, Lothario **9** boyfriend, Lochinvar

French: 8 paramour

Latin: 9 inamorato

Romeo and Juliet

author: 18 William Shakespeare

character: 5 Nurse, Paris **6** Tybalt **8** Benvolio, Mercutio **13** Friar Laurence

family: 7 Capulet **8** Montague

setting: 6 Verona

Romeo and Juliet

director:

  1936 version: 11 George Cukor

  1968 version: 16 Franco Zeffirelli

based on play by: 18 William Shakespeare

cast:

  1936 version: 12 Leslie Howard, Norma Shearer **13** Basil Rathbone, Edna May Oliver, John Barrymore

  1968 version: 9 Milo O'Shea **11** John McEnery, Michael York **12** Olivia Hussey **14** Leonard Whiting

score: 8 Nino Rota

Romeo and Juliet

symphony by: 7 Berlioz

opera by: 6 Gounod

orchestral piece by: 11 Tchaikovsky

ballet by: 9 Prokofiev

Romney, George

born: 7 England **15** Dalton-in-Furness

artwork: 5 Circe **9** Joan of Arc **11** Mrs Robinson, Sensibility **12** Mrs Davenport, Saint Cecilia **19** Mrs Carwardine and Son **22** The Death of General Wolfe **24** The Levenson-Gower Children **26** Sir Christopher and Lady Sykes

Romola

author: 11 George Eliot

character: 5 Bardo, Tessa **10** Tito Melema **15** Baldasarre Calvo

romp 3 hop **4** skip **5** caper, cut up, frisk, sport **6** frolic, gambol **7** disport, rollick

Romulus

father: 4 Mars

mother: 4 Ilia **9** Rea Silvia **10** Rhea Silvia

twin brother: 5 Remus

raised by: 7 she-wolf **9** Faustulus **12** Acca Larentia

first king of: 4 Rome

founder of: 4 Rome

Romus

father: 6 Aeneas **8** Ascanius

possible founder of: 4 Rome

Roncalli, Angelo Giuseppe 13 Pope John XXIII **22** Pope John the Twenty-Third

Ronsard, Pierre de

author of: 17 Sonnets pour Helene

member of: 7 Pleiade

roofing 4 tile, turf **5** slate, terne **6** thatch **7** asphalt, ceiling, pantile, shingle **8** housetop

Roof of the World *see* **5** Tibet

rook 3 gyp **4** bilk, crow, dupe, gull **5** cheat, cozen, raven, trick **6** castle, fleece **7** deceive, defraud, swindle **8** chessman **9** bamboozle, victimize

rookie 4 tyro **6** novice **8** beginner **9** fledgling, greenhorn **10** apprentice, tenderfoot

Rookies, The

character: 9 Jill Danko, (Officer) Mike Danko **10** (Lt) Eddie Ryker, (Officer) Chris Owens **12** (Officer) Terry Webster, (Officer) Willie Gillis

cast: 11 Kate Jackson, Sam Melville **14** Bruce Fairbairn, Michael Ontkean **16** Gerald S O'Loughlin **18** Georg Stanford Brown

room 4 area **5** range, scope, space **6** chance, extent, leeway, margin, volume **7** chamber, cubicle, expanse, lodging **9** allowance, provision, territory **11** compartment

French: 5 salle

Spanish: 4 sala

Room at the Top

director: 11 Jack Clayton

based on novel by: 10 John Braine

cast: 12 Heather Sears **14** Laurence Harvey, Simone Signoret **16** Hermione Baddeley

Oscar for: 7 actress (Signoret)

sequel: 11 Man at the Top **12** Life at the Top

Room 222

character: 6 Bernie **9** Pete Dixon **11** Liz McIntyre **12** Alice Johnson **14** Seymour Kaufman

cast: 11 Lloyd Haynes **13** David Jolliffe **14** Denise Nicholas, Karen Valentine **18** Michael Constantine

school: 15 Walt Whitman High

roomy 3 big **4** huge, long, vast, wide **5** ample, broad, large **7** immense, lengthy, sizable **8** generous, spacious **9** boundless, capacious, expansive, extensive, unlimited **10** commodious

Rooney, Mickey

real name: 9 Joe Yule Jr

born: 10 Brooklyn NY

wife: 10 Ava Gardner **13** Martha Vickers

co-star: 11 Judy Garland

roles: 4 Puck **8** Boys' Town **9** Andy Hardy **11** Sugar Babies **13** Mickey McGuire **14** Baby Face Nelson, National Velvet, The Human Comedy **21** A Midsummer Night's Dream **30** The Adventures of Huckleberry Finn

Roosevelt, Franklin Delano

presidential rank: 12 thirty-second

party: 10 Democratic

state represented: 2 NY

defeated: 5 (Jacob Sechler) Coxey, (John W) Aiken, (Thomas Edmund) Dewey, (William) Lemke **6** (Alfred Mossman) Landon, (Claude A) Watson, (David Leigh) Colvin, (Herbert Clark) Hoover, (Norman) Thomas, (Roger Ward) Babson, (William David) Upshaw, (William Hope) Harvey, (William Zebulon) Foster **7** (Earl Russell) Browder, (Wendell Lewis) Willkie **8** (Edward A) Teichert, (Verne L) Reynolds

vice president: 6 (Harry S) Truman, (John Nance) Garner **7** (Henry Agard) Wallace

cabinet:

  state: 4 (Cordell) Hull **10** (Edward Reilly) Stettinius (Jr)

  treasury: 6 (William Hartman) Woodin **10** (Henry) Morgenthau (Jr)

  war: 4 (George Henry) Dern **7** (Henry Lewis) Stimson **8** (Harry Hines) Woodring

  attorney general: 6 (Francis) Biddle, (Frank) Murphy **7** (Robert Houghwout) Jackson **8** (Homer Stille) Cummings

  navy: 4 (Frank) Knox **6** (Charles) Edison **7** (Claude Augustus) Swanson **9** (James Vincent) Forrestal

  postmaster general: 6 (Frank Comerford) Walker, (James Aloysius) Farley

  interior: 5 (Harold LeClaire) Ickes

  agriculture: 7 (Claude Raymond)

Wickard, (Henry Agard) Wallace
commerce: 5 (Daniel Calhoun) Roper, (Jesse Holman) Jones **7** (Henry Agard) Wallace, (Henry Lloyd) Hopkins
labor: 7 (Frances) Perkins (Wilson)
born: 10 Hyde Park NY
died: 13 Warm Springs GA **16** Little White House
buried: 10 Hyde Park NY
education:
  prep school: 6 Groton
  university: 7 Harvard
  law school: 8 Columbia
religion: 12 Episcopalian
interests: 3 art **4** polo **6** tennis, travel **7** fishing, hunting **8** shooting
vacation spot: 13 Warm Springs GA **16** Campobello Island (Canada)
dog: 4 Fala
author: 27 The Happy Warrior: Alfred E Smith
political career: 12 state senator
  assistant secretary of: 4 Navy
  governor of: 7 New York
civilian career: 6 lawyer **11** bank officer
notable events of lifetime/term: 4 D-Day, WWII **7** New Deal **10** atomic bomb, Depression, World War II **11** World War Two **13** United Nations **15** Atlantic Charter
  act: 9 Lend-Lease
  attack on: 11 Pearl Harbor
  conference: 5 Cairo, Yalta **7** Arcadia, Crimean, Teheran
  scandal: 11 Tammany Hall
quote: 24 A day that will live in infamy **31** Meet every day's troubles as they come **36** The only thing we have to fear is fear itself **50** This generation of Americans has a rendezvous with destiny **53** I pledge you I pledge myself to a new deal for the American people
father: 5 James
mother: 4 Sara (Delano)
siblings:
  half-brother: 5 James
wife: 7 (Anna) Eleanor (Roosevelt)
children: 5 James **7** Elliott **11** Anna Eleanor **13** John Aspinwell **14** Franklin Delano
first lady:
  author: 7 On My Own **13** This I Remember, This Is My Story **34** The Autobiography of Eleanor Roosevelt
  chairwoman: 25 UN Commission on Human Rights
  codirector: 23 Office of Civilian Defense
  member: 35 Democratic National Campaign Committee
  newspaper column: 5 My Day
  US delegate to: 2 UN
Roosevelt, Theodore
  nickname: 5 Teddy

presidential rank: 11 twenty-sixth
party: 10 Republican
state represented: 2 NY
succeeded: 8 McKinley
defeated (second term): 4 (Eugene Victor) Debs **6** (Alton Brooks) Parker, (Thomas Edward) Watson **7** (Austin) Holcomb, (Silas Comfort) Swallow **8** (Charles Hunter) Corregan
vice president: 4 none (1st term) **9** (Charles Warren) Fairbanks
cabinet:
  state: 3 (John Milton) Hay **4** (Elihu) Root **5** (Robert) Bacon
  treasury: 4 (Leslie Mortier) Shaw, (Lyman Judson) Gage **9** (George Bruce) Cortelyou
  war: 4 (Elihu) Root, (William Howard) Taft **6** (Luke Edward) Wright
  attorney general: 4 (Philander Chase) Knox **5** (William Henry) Moody **9** (Charles Joseph) Bonaparte
  navy: 4 (John Davis) Long **5** (William Henry) Moody **6** (Paul) Morton **7** (Victor Howard) Metcalf **8** (Truman Handy) Newberry **9** (Charles Joseph) Bonaparte
  postmaster general: 5 (Charles Emory) Smith, (George von Lengerke) Meyer, (Henry Clay) Payne, (Robert John) Wynne **9** (George Bruce) Cortelyou
  interior: 8 (James Rudolph) Garfield **9** (Ethan Allen) Hitchcock
  agriculture: 6 (James) Wilson
  commerce and labor: 6 (Oscar Solomon) Straus **7** (Victor Howard) Metcalf **9** (George Bruce) Cortelyou
born: 13 New York City NY
died/buried: 2 NY **9** Oyster Bay **10** Long Island
education:
  university: 7 Harvard
  law school: 8 Columbia (did not graduate)
religion: 13 Dutch Reformed
interests: 7 hunting (African game), writing **9** exploring (South America) **14** natural history
author: 11 Rough Riders **14** Oliver Cromwell **16** Gouverneur Morris, Thomas Hart Benton **17** African Game Trails, The New Nationalism **19** The Winning of the West **20** Letters to His Children **21** America and the World War **24** The Foes of Our Own Household **25** Fear God and Take Your Own Part **27** A Booklover's Holiday in the Open, Ranch Life and the Hunting Trail, The Naval War of Eighteen-Twelve **28** Hero Tales from American History **29** Through the Brazilian Wilderness **33** Life Histories of African Game Animals

political career: 13 Vice President **15** NY State Assembly **24** US Civil Service Commission
  assistant secretary: 4 Navy
  governor of: 7 New York
  organized party: 9 Bull Moose **11** Progressive
civilian career: 6 author **7** rancher **14** public lecturer
military service: 15 NY National Guard **18** Spanish- American War
  organized cavalry regiment: 11 Rough Riders
  led charge up: 11 San Juan Hill
notable events of lifetime/term: 5 Panic (of 1907) **10** Square Deal **15** Nobel Peace Prize **22** San Francisco earthquake
  Act: 11 Reclamation **14** Meat Inspection **15** Hepburn Railroad, Pure Food and Drug
  bureau of: 12 Corporations **28** Immigration and Naturalization
  first flight by: 14 Wright Brothers
  revolution: 6 Panama
  treaty: 13 Hay-Pauncefote **15** Hay-Bunau-Varilla
quotes: 25 Hasten forward quickly there **28** Speak softly and carry a big stick
father: 8 Theodore
mother: 6 Martha (Bulloch)
siblings: 4 Anna **7** Corinne, Elliott
wife: 5 Alice (Hathaway Lee), Edith (Kermit Carow)
children: 6 Kermit **7** Quentin **8** Alice Lee, Theodore **10** Ethel Carow **16** Archibald Bulloch
rooster
  young: 8 cockerel
root 3 fix, set **4** back, base, bind, bulb, clap, hail, nail, rise, stem **5** basis, boost, cheer, fount, radix, start, stick, tubes **6** bottom, fasten, ground, motive, origin, reason, second, source, spring **7** acclaim, applaud, bolster, cheer on, pull for, radicle, support **8** fountain, occasion, shout for **9** beginning, encourage, establish, inception, rationale **10** derivation, foundation, mainspring **11** fundamental **12** commencement, fountainhead
Root, John Wellborn
  partner: 14 Daniel H Burnham
  architect of: 10 The Rookery **12** Hotel Statler (Washington DC), Montauk Block **13** Hotel Tamanaco (Caracas) **17** Monadnock Building, Palmolive Building (Chicago) **19** Rand-McNally Building
root for 5 boost **6** urge on **7** cheer on, pull for
root out 5 dig up **6** remove **7** extract, pull out, uncover, unearth **8** discover **9** extirpate, ferret out **12** bring to light
Roots
  author: 9 Alex Haley
  character: 3 Tom **4** Ames, Bell, Noah

5 Binta, Fanta, Grill, Irene, Kizzy, Lewis, Mingo, Omoro **6** Justin, Martha, Ordell **7** Fiddler, Gardner, Nyo Boto **8** Kintango, Mathilda, Mrs Moore, Tom Moore **9** Evan Brent, Missy Anne **10** Brima Cesay, Capt Davies, Carrington, Jemmy Brent, Kadi Touray, Kunta Kinte, Sam Bennett, Sister Sara **11** Mrs Reynolds, Squire James **12** John Reynolds **13** Chicken George **14** Sir Eric Russell, Stephen Bennett **15** Ol' George Johnson, Third Mate Slater **17** Dr William Reynolds
cast: **8** Burl Ives, John Amos, Ren Woods **9** Ben Vereen, Brad Davis, Moses Gunn, O J Simpson, Vic Morrow **10** Billy Hicks, Ian McShane, John Schuck, Lynne Moody, Olivia Cole, Paul Shenar, Ralph Waite, Robert Reed **11** Beverly Todd, Cicely Tyson, Doug McClure, Edward Asner, Gary Collins, Harry Rhodes, Lane Binkley, LeVar Burton, Lorne Greene, Maya Angelou, Sandy Duncan **12** Carolyn Jones, Chuck Connors, Leslie Uggams, Lloyd Bridges **13** Louis Gosset Jr, Madge Sinclair, William Watson **14** George Hamilton, Lynda Day George, Macdonald Carey **15** Lillian Randolph, Scatman Crothers, Thalmus Rasulala **16** Raymond St Jacques, Richard Roundtree **18** Georg Stanford Brown **20** Lawrence Hilton-Jacobs

rope 3 gad, guy, tie, tow **4** bind, cord, fast, guss, hemp, line, lure, snag, trap, wire, yarn **5** cable, catch, chord, lasso, noose, riata, shank, strap, twine **6** corral, entice, hawser, lariat, seduce, string, tether **7** bobstay, cordage, halyard, lanyard, lashing, painter **8** dragline, restrain
fiber: **5** sisal

Rosaline
character in: **16** Love's Labour's Lost
author: **11** Shakespeare
rose 4 Rosa
varieties: **3** bog, dog, sun, tea, wax **4** baby, gold, moss, musk, rock, rush, sand, wood **5** briar, brier, China, fairy, field, malva, Ophir, pygmy, swamp **6** Alpine, Burnet, copper, cotton, damask, desert, French, ground, Karroo, Lenten, mallow, Nootka, Scotch, velvet **7** baby sun, Banksia, Bourbon, cabbage, cluster, Guelder, Manetti, pasture, prairie, rambler **8** Burgundy, Champney, Cherokee, chestnut, cinnamon, climbing, Japanese, Memorial, mountain, Noisette **9** Christmas, evergreen, hybrid tea, McCartney, Polyantha, Remontant, Turkestan **10** California, Chinquapin, shaggy-rock, underwater **11** confederate, giant velvet, hairy alpine **12** green Mexican, Hawaiian wood, Seven-sisters,

white Mexican **13** Himalayan musk, Hybrid Bourbon, Persian yellow, Stuart's desert **15** hybrid perpetual **16** York-and-Lancaster

Rose, Pete (Peter Edward)
nickname: **13** Charlie Hustle
sport: **8** baseball
position: **7** baseman **8** outfield
team: **14** Cincinnati Reds **20** Philadelphia Phillies
scandal: **8** gambling

Roseanne
former name: **4** Barr **6** Arnold
husband: **3** Tom **6** Thomas
television:
    show: **8** Roseanne
    husband: **3** Dan
    children: **2** DJ **5** Becky **7** Darlene
    sister: Jackie
    town: Lanford

Rosedale, Mr
character in: **15** The House of Mirth
author: **7** Wharton

Rosemary's Baby
director: **13** Roman Polanski
based on novel by: **8** Ira Levin
cast: **9** Mia Farrow **10** Ruth Gordon **14** John Cassavetes, Sidney Blackmer
Oscar for: **17** supporting actress (Gordon)

Rosenberg, Stuart
director of: **12** Cool Hand Luke

Rosenbloom, Maxie
nickname: **12** Slapsie Maxie
sport: **6** boxing
class: **16** light heavyweight

Rosencrantz
character in: **6** Hamlet
author: **11** Shakespeare

Rosenkavalier, Der
also: **18** The Knight of the Rose
opera by: **7** (Richard) Strauss
character: **6** Sophie **8** Octavian **9** Baron Ochs **11** Marschallin (Princess von Werderberg)

Rose of Sharon
character in: **16** The Grapes of Wrath
author: **9** Steinbeck

Rose Tattoo, The
director: **10** Daniel Mann
based on play by: **17** Tennessee Williams
cast: **11** Anna Magnani **13** Burt Lancaster
Oscar for: **7** actress (Magnani)
rosiness 5 bloom, blush, flush **7** redness **8** pinkness

Ross, Barney
real name: **14** Barnet Rosofsky
sport: **6** boxing
class: **12** welterweight

Ross, Herbert
director of: **14** The Goodbye Girl **15** The Turning Point

Ross, Katharine
born: **12** Los Angeles CA
aunt: **16** Katharine Hepburn

roles: **9** The Colbys **11** The Graduate **13** Stepford Wives **29** Butch Cassidy and the Sundance Kid

Rossellini, Roberto
director of: **6** Paisan **8** Open City **9** Stromboli **10** The Miracle **15** Germany Year Zero
wife: **13** Ingrid Bergman
daughter: **8** Isabella

Rossen, Robert
director of: **11** Body and Soul **14** All the King's Men

Rossetti, Dante Gabriel
author of: **17** The Blessed Damozel
born: **6** London **7** England
group: **14** Pre-Raphaelites
artwork: **12** Beata Beatrix **15** The Annunciation **17** Ecce Ancilla Domini

Rossini, Gioacchino Antonio
born: **5** Italy **6** Pesaro
composer of: **5** Moise **6** Otello **8** Tancredi **10** Le Comte Ory, Semiramide **11** William Tell **12** Mose in Egitto **13** Guillaume Tell, La Cenerentola **15** Barber of Seville **20** Il Barbiere di Siviglia **22** La Cambiale di Matrimonio

Rossner, Judith
author of: **11** Attachments **14** Ordinary People **19** Looking for Mr Goodbar

Rostand, Edmond
author of: **7** L'Aiglon **10** Chantecler **12** The Romancers **16** Cyrano de Bergerac

roster 4 list, roll **5** cadre, panel, slate **6** agenda, docket, muster, record **7** catalog, listing, posting **8** register, schedule **9** catalogue, directory

rostrum 4 dais **5** stage, stand, stump **6** podium, pulpit **7** lectern, soapbox **8** platform

rosy 4 pink **5** ruddy **6** bright, florid **7** flushed, glowing, hopeful, reddish **8** blooming, blushing, cheerful, cheering, flushing, inflamed, rubicund **9** confident, favorable, promising, reddening, rubescent **10** auspicious, felicitous, optimistic, propitious, reassuring **11** encouraging, high-colored, inspiriting **13** full of promise

Roszak, Theodore
born: **6** Poland, Poznan
artwork: **5** Raven, Surge **7** Anguish **9** Chrysalis, Scavenger, Sea Quarry **11** Sea Sentinel **12** Amorphic Form, Thorn Blossom **18** Specter of Kitty Hawk **20** The Whaler of Nantucket **27** Recollections of the Southwest

rot 3 mar **4** bosh, bull, bunk, harm, hurt, warp **5** decay, go bad, spoil, stain, taint, trash **6** damage, debase, defile, drivel, impair, infect, injure, jabber, molder, poison **7** blather, corrupt, crumble, deprave, inanity, pervert, pollute, putrefy, rubbish, twaddle **8** flummery, folderol, nonsense, putresce **9** absurdity, decompose, gibberish, moonshine, poppycock, purulence, putridity **10** balderdash, corruption, degenerate, flapdoodle **11** contaminate, deteriorate, putrescence **12** disintegrate, fiddle-faddle, gobbledygook, putrefaction **13** contamination, decomposition, deterioration **14** disintegration **16** stuff and nonsense

rotate 4 eddy, reel, roll, spin, turn **5** pivot, swirl, twirl, twist, wheel, whirl **6** change, circle, gyrate, swivel **7** revolve **9** alternate, circulate, pirouette **11** interchange

Roth, Philip
author of: 8 The Facts **15** Goodbye Columbus **16** The Anatomy Lesson, Zuckerman Unbound **17** Portnoy's Complaint

Rothko, Mark
born: 6 Dvinsk, Latvia, Russia **16** Daugavpils Latvia
artwork: 5 Light **12** Central Green, Earth and Blue **14** Four Darks in Red

rotten 3 bad **4** base, foul, rank **5** dirty, fetid, nasty, reeky, venal **6** filthy, putrid, rancid, scurvy **7** corrupt, crooked, decayed, devious, immoral, tainted, very bad, vicious **8** criminal, decaying, indecent, purulent, two-faced **9** deceitful, dishonest, dissolute, faithless, insincere, mercenary, moldering, putrefied, worm-eaten **10** decomposed, iniquitous, putrescent, scurrilous, unpleasant, villainous **11** decomposing, disgraceful, treacherous **12** contemptible, dishonorable, unforgivable, unscrupulous **13** double-dealing, untrustworthy

rotter 3 cad, cur, rat **4** heel **5** knave, louse, rogue **6** no-good, rascal **7** bounder, caitiff, villain **9** scoundrel

rotund 3 fat **5** obese, ovate, ovoid, plump, pudgy, round, stout, tubby **6** chubby, curved, fleshy, portly **7** bulbous, lumpish, rounded **8** circular, globular **9** corpulent, egg-shaped, spherical **10** potbellied **11** full-fleshed

Rouault, Georges
born: 5 Paris **6** France
artwork: 3 Mr X **5** Clown **8** Le Chahut, Miserere, Twilight **9** The Mirror **10** The Old King **11** Fleurs du mal, The Holy Face **12** Head of a Clown **13** Little Olympia **14** The Three Judges **19** Small Family of Clowns **22** Christ Mocked by Soldiers **26** Les Reincarnations du Pere Ubu **28** The Child Jesus among the Doctors

roue 3 cad, rip **4** rake, wolf **6** lecher, wanton **7** bounder, dallier, Don Juan, playboy, seducer, trifler **8** Casanova, debauche, Lothario, rakehell **9** libertine, womanizer **10** profligate **11** philanderer, skirt-chaser

Rouget de Lisle 17 French army officer

composer of: 14 La Marseillaise

rough 3 raw **4** beat, hard, rude, wild **5** bluff, blunt, bumpy, crude, cruel, draft, green, gruff, harsh, hasty, husky, quick, raspy, rocky, scaly, sharp, surly, tough, vague **6** abrupt, beat on, broken, brutal, callow, choppy, clumsy, coarse, craggy, crusty, gauche, hoarse, jagged, knotty, ragged, raging, roiled, rugged, savage, severe, stormy, thrash, turbid, uneven, vulgar **7** austere, awkward, bearish, boorish, brusque, chapped, coarsen, drastic, extreme, general, gnarled, grating, ill-bred, inexact, jarring, loutish, outline, rasping, raucous, scraggy, sketchy, stubbly, uncouth, unlevel, untamed, violent **8** agitated, churlish, rigorous, scabrous, scratchy, strident, ungentle, unsmooth **9** brutalize, difficult, ferocious, imperfect, imprecise, inelegant, irregular, manhandle, sketch out, stringent, turbulent, uncourtly, unfeeling, ungenteel, unmusical, unrefined **10** discordant, incomplete, indelicate, push around, tumultuous, unfinished, ungracious, unmannerly, unpleasant, unpolished **11** approximate, cacophonous, ill-mannered, preliminary, rudimentary, tempestuous, unluxurious **12** inharmonious **13** inconsiderate, uncomfortable, ungentlemanly

rough going 8 struggle **10** difficulty **11** arduousness **13** laboriousness

Roughing It
author: 9 Mark Twain
character: 12 Brigham Young, Hank Erickson **16** Slade the Terrible

rough it 4 camp **7** camp out

roughneck 4 hood, lout, punk **5** bully, rowdy, tough **6** vandal **7** hoodlum, ruffian **8** hooligan **9** barbarian **10** delinquent

roughness 7 crudity **8** acrimony, aviation, pungency, violence **9** gruffness, harshness, vulgarity **10** coarseness, inelegance, unevenness, unkindness **11** raucousness **12** irregularity, unsmoothness, unrefinement **13** undevelopment

Rough Riders see Roosevelt, Theodore

rough sketch 5 draft **7** cartoon, outline

rough-textured 5 harsh **6** coarse, nubbly, shaggy, tweedy **7** bristly, prickly **8** scratchy **9** bristling **10** sandpapery

round 3 fat **4** full, oval **5** cycle, obese, orbed, ovate, ovoid, plump, pudgy, stout, total, tubby, whole **6** chubby, circle, curved, entire, fluent, intact, portly, rotund, series, smooth **7** flowing, globoid, perfect, rounded **8** circular, complete, globular, resonant, sonorous, spheroid, thorough, unbroken

9 corpulent, egg-shaped, spherical, undivided **10** ball-shaped, elliptical, harmonious, pear-shaped, procession, succession **11** cylindrical, full-fleshed, mellifluent, progression

roundabout 5 wordy **6** random, zigzag **7** devious, erratic, oblique, sinuous, winding **8** indirect, rambling, tortuous, twisting **9** desultory **10** circuitous, discursive, meandering, serpentine **12** labyrinthine **14** circumlocutory

roundaboutness 9 wandering **10** digression, meandering **11** indirection **14** circuitousness, circumlocution

rounded 6 convex **7** curving **11** protuberant

rounding out 10 developing **12** augmentation **13** amplification

rounding-out 10 complement, completion, perfecting **12** consummation

rounds 4 beat **5** route, skirt, watch **7** circuit

roundup 6 muster, resume **7** meeting, summary **8** assembly **9** gathering **11** convocation

round up 6 gather, muster, summon **7** collect, convene, convoke, marshal **8** assemble **10** accumulate **12** call together

rouse 4 call, goad, move, prod, spur, stir, wake **5** arise, awake, get up, pique, rally, waken **6** awaken, excite, foment, kindle, incite, stir up, summon, turn on, wake up **7** animate, inflame, inspire, provoke, shake up **8** activate **9** galvanize, instigate, stimulate

roused 2 up **5** astir, awake **7** excited, incited, kindled, rallied, shook up **8** awakened, inflamed, inspired, out of bed, shaken up **9** stirred up **10** up and about

rousing 5 brisk, peppy **6** active, lively **8** animated, exciting, stirring, vigorous **9** awakening, inspiring **10** energizing, refreshing, remarkable **11** provocative, stimulating **12** exhilarating, intoxicating **13** extraordinary

Rousseau, Henri Julien Felix
nickname: 10 Le Douanier
born: 5 Laval **6** France
artwork: 3 War **8** The Dream **12** Child on Rocks, The Waterfall **13** The Hungry Lion **15** Carnival Evening, The Snake Charmer **16** Bouquet of Flowers, The Sleeping Gypsy **17** The Poet and his Muse

Rousseau, Jean Jacques
author of: 5 Emile **11** Confessions **17** La Nouvelle Heloise, The Social Contract

Rousseau, (Pierre Etienne) Theodore
born: 5 Paris **6** France
artwork: 7 Evening **12** After the Rain **15** Edge of the Forest, Under the

Birches **18** Descent of the Cattle, Oak Trees at Apremont **19** The Marsh in the Landes **20** The Valley of Tiffauges **21** Meadow Bordered by Trees

roust 4 bust **5** rouse **6** arrest, hassle **7** capture, seizure **12** apprehension

rout 4 beat, drub, lick, ruin, trim **5** chaos, cream, crush, panic, quell, repel, worst **6** defeat, subdue, thrash **7** beating, clobber, conquer, licking, repulse, scatter **8** drive off, drubbing, lambaste, overcome, vanquish **9** chase away, drive away, overpower, overthrow **11** put to flight **15** disorganization **18** throw into confusion

route 3 run **4** beat, pass, path, road, ship, tack **5** remit, round, track **6** artery, course, detour, direct **7** circuit, highway, parkway, passage, roadway **8** dispatch, transmit, turnpike **9** boulevard, itinerary **10** throughway **12** thoroughfare

Route 66
  character: 8 Linc Case **9** Tod Stiles **10** Buz Murdock
  cast: 12 Glenn Corbett, Martin Milner **13** George Maharis
  car: 8 Corvette

routine 4 dull **5** order, usual **6** boring, custom, method, normal, system **7** formula, regular, tedious, typical **8** habitual, ordinary, periodic, practice **9** customary, operation, technique **11** arrangement, predictable **12** conventional, run-of-the-mill **13** unexceptional

rove 4 roam **5** drift, prowl, range **6** ramble, stroll, travel, wander **7** meander, traipse **9** gallivant

roving 6 errant **7** aimless, gadding, migrant, nomadic, roaming, vagrant **8** errantry, rambling, restless **9** desultory, itinerant, traveling, uncertain, wandering **10** changeable, discursive, meandering, inconstant **11** peripatetic **14** discursiveness

row 4 file, line, rank, spat, tier, tiff **5** brawl, chain, melee, queue, range, scrap, set-to, train, words **6** column, fracas, scrape, series, string **7** echelon, quarrel, wrangle **8** argument, disorder, sequence, squabble **9** imbroglio, wrangling **10** difference, succession **11** altercation, contretemps

rowboat 3 gig **4** bark, dory **5** barge, canoe, dingy, scull, shell, skiff **6** barque, caique, dinghy, wherry
  seat: 4 taft

rowdy 6 unruly **7** lawless, raffish **9** roughneck **10** boisterous, disorderly **11** mischievous **12** obstreperous

Rowena, Lady
  character in: 7 Ivanhoe
  author: 5 Scott

rowing
  athlete: 10 James Dietz **14** Anthony Johnson

Rowlands, Gena
  real name: 23 Virginia Cathryn Rowlands
  born: 9 Cambria WI
  husband: 14 John Cassavetes
  roles: 5 Faces **12** Opening Night **23** A Woman Under the Influence

Roxana
  subtitle: 20 The Fortunate Mistress
  author: 11 Daniel Defoe

Roxane see Cyrano de Bergerac

royal 5 grand, regal **6** august, lavish, superb **7** stately **8** imposing, majestic, splendid **9** monarchal, sovereign **10** munificent **11** fit for a king, magnificent, resplendent

royalty 4 sway **7** command, majesty **8** dominion, hegemony, kingship, regality **9** queenship, supremacy **11** divine right, sovereignty

Royaume de Belgique see **7** Belgium

Roy Rogers Show, The
  regular: 8 Pat Brady **9** Dale Evans
  theme: 16 Happy Trails to You
  horse: 7 Trigger
  dog: 6 Bullet
  jeep: 10 Nellybelle
  ranch: 10 Double R Bar

Ruanda see **6** Rwanda

rub 4 buff, swab, wipe **5** annoy, braze, catch, chafe, clean, hitch, knead, pinch, scour, scrub, smear, thing, touch, trick **6** abrade, finger, handle, polish, secret, smooth, spread, strait, stroke **7** burnish, dilemma, massage, problem, rubdown, setback, slather, trouble **8** handling, hardship, kneading, obstacle, stroking **10** difficulty, impediment, manipulate **12** manipulation

Rubaiyat of Omar Khayyam, The
  author: 11 Omar Khayyam
  translator: 16 Edward FitzGerald

rubber, vulcanized
  invented by: 8 Goodyear

rubber plant 13 Ficus elastica
  varieties: 4 baby **5** dwarf **7** Chinese **8** American, creeping, Japanese **9** mistletoe **11** small-leaved **16** broadleaved India

rubberstamp 6 affirm **7** approve, endorse

rubber tree 10 Schefflera
  varieties: 4 Para **5** India **8** Castilla **11** West African

rubbery 5 tough **6** supple **7** elastic **8** flexible **9** resilient **11** stretchable

rubbing 7 chafing **8** abrading, scraping **12** manipulation

rubbish 3 rot **4** bosh, junk **5** dross, offal, trash, waste **6** babble, debris, drivel, idiocy, jetsam, litter, refuse, rubble **7** blather, garbage, inanity, twaddle **8** folderol, nonsense **9** gibberish, rigmarole, silliness **10** balderdash, flapdoodle, rigamarole

rubbish heap 4 dump **6** midden **10** refuse pile

rubble 4 junk, rock **5** brash, chalk, stent, stone, talus, trash **6** debris, refuse **7** rubbish **8** nonsense **9** fragments **11** foolishness

rube 3 oaf **4** boor, clod, hick **5** yokel **6** rustic **7** bumpkin, hayseed, peasant **10** clodhopper

Rube Goldberg 10 cartoonist
  known for: 23 complicated contraptions

rub elbows 3 mix **4** club **6** hobnob, mingle **7** consort, hang out **9** associate **10** fraternize

Rubens, Peter Paul
  born: 6 Siegen **10** Westphalia
  artwork: 8 Lion Hunt **10** The Rainbow **15** The Garden of Love **17** Laocoon and his Sons **18** Battle of the Amazons **20** The Raising of the Cross **21** Landscape with Het Steen **22** The Descent from the Cross **23** Altarpiece of St Aldefonso **26** The Adoration of the Shepherds **27** Marchesa Brigida Spinola-Doria, Mystic Marriage of St Catherine **29** Rape of the Daughters of Leucippus **34** Helene Fourment with Two of her Children

rubicund 3 red **4** rosy **5** ruddy **6** florid **7** flushed, reddish

rubidium
  chemical symbol: 2 Rb

rub out 4 do in, kill, slay **5** erase **6** efface, murder **7** bump off, destroy, execute, expunge **8** massacre **10** obliterate, put to death **11** assassinate, exterminate

ruby
  species: 8 corundum
  source: 5 Burma, India, Mogok **7** Bangkok, Kashmir **8** Sri Lanka, Thailand
  kind: 4 star
  color: 3 red

ruckus 3 row **4** fray, to-do **5** brawl, broil, clash, fight, melee **6** battle, fracas, rumpus, uproar **7** scuffle **9** imbroglio **10** donnybrook, free-for-all **11** embroilment

ruddy 3 red **4** rosy **6** florid **7** flushed, reddish, roseate, scarlet **8** blushing, rubicund, sanguine **11** rosy-cheeked

rude 3 raw **4** wild **5** blunt, crude, fresh, green, gross, gruff, rough, saucy, sulky, surly **6** abrupt, callow, clumsy, coarse, crusty, gauche, homely, rugged, rustic, sullen, uneven, vulgar **7** abusive, artless, awkward, boorish, brusque, brutish, illbred, loutish, profane, scraggy, uncivil, uncouth **8** churlish, homebred, ignorant, impolite, impudent, indecent, insolent, slapdash, untaught **9** inelegant, insulting, makeshift, primitive, roughhewn, uncourtly, ungallant, unlearned, unrefined, untrained, untutored **10** illiterate, indecorous, indelicate, peremptory, provincial, uncultured, uneducated, ungraceful, ungracious, unladylike, unmannerly, unpolished **11** bad-mannered, countrified, impertinent, uncivilized, uncourteous, undignified **12** discourteous, roughly built **13** disrespectful, inconsiderate, ungentlemanly

rudeness 9 bluntness, impudence, insolence, sauciness **10** bad manners, coarseness, disrespect, incivility **11** boorishness, discourtesy **12** impertinence, impoliteness **14** ungraciousness **17** inconsiderateness

rudimentary 5 basic **6** simple **7** initial, primary **8** immature **9** elemental, formative, imperfect, premature, primitive, vestigial **10** elementary, incomplete, prototypal **11** undeveloped

rudiments 6 basics **7** essence **8** elements **9** beginning **10** principles **12** fundamentals

Rudkus, Jurgis and Antanas
characters in: 9 The Jungle
author: 8 Sinclair

Rudolph, Paul
architect of: 16 Jewett Arts Center (Wellesley College) **24** Government Services Center (Boston) **28** School of Architecture Building (Yale)

rue 4 Ruta
varieties: 4 bush, lady, wall **5** goat's **6** common, meadow **10** tall meadow **11** early meadow **12** Alpine meadow

rue 5 mourn **6** bemoan, lament, regret, repent, repine **7** deplore

rueful 3 sad **5** sorry **6** woeful **7** doleful **8** contrite, mournful, dolorous, penitent, repining **9** depressed, plaintive, regretful, sorrowful, sorrowing **10** deplorable, lamentable, melancholy, remorseful, unpleasant

ruff 9 sandpiper
female: 3 ree

ruffian 4 hood, thug **5** brute, bully, crook, knave, rogue, rough, rowdy, tough **6** mugger **7** hoodlum, villain **8** gangster, hooligan **9** cutthroat, roisterer, roughneck, scoundrel **10** blackguard

ruffle 4 fold, muss, wave **5** frill, plait, pleat, ruche, upset **6** edging, excite, muss up, pucker, rimple, ripple, rumple **7** agitate, confuse, crinkle, disturb, flounce, perturb, roughen, trouble, wrinkle **8** dishevel, disorder, disquiet, furbelow, unsettle **9** aggravate, agitation, commotion, corrugate **10** disarrange, discompose, disconcert **11** disturbance

ruffled 5 upset, vexed **7** annoyed, frilled, nettled, pleated **8** agitated, flounced, troubled **9** nonplused, unsettled **10** nonplussed

ruffle one's feathers 3 vex **5** anger,

annoy, pique **6** enrage, madden, nettle **7** incense, outrage, provoke **9** displease, infuriate

Rugg
character in: 12 Little Dorrit
author: 7 Dickens

rugged 4 hale, hard, rude, wiry, worn **5** bumpy, hardy, harsh, husky, lined, rocky, rough, stern, tough **6** brawny, coarse, craggy, jagged, ridged, robust, severe, sinewy, sturdy, taxing, trying, uneven, virile **7** arduous, cragged, onerous, scraggy, uncouth **8** athletic, furrowed, muscular, stalwart, vigorous, wrinkled **9** difficult, graceless, irregular, laborious, masculine, roughhewn, strenuous, unrefined, weathered **12** uncultivated **13** weather-beaten

Ruggles of Red Gap
director: 10 Leo McCarey
cast: 9 ZaSu Pitts **10** Mary Boland **14** Charlie Ruggles **15** Charles Laughton
remade as: 10 Fancy Pants

ruin, ruins 3 gut, pot **4** doom, fall, fell, harm, raze, seed **5** break, crush, decay, level, quash, quell, shell, spoil, upset, wreck **6** beggar, defeat, ravage, squash **7** destroy, failure, remains, shatter, undoing **8** bankrupt, demolish, downfall, lay waste, make poor, overturn, remnants, wreckage **9** breakdown, devastate, disrepair, overthrow, pauperize **10** impoverish **11** destruction, devastation, dissolution **14** disintegration

ruination 4 ruin **5** wreck **6** fiasco **7** trouble **8** disaster **9** adversity, cataclysm **11** destruction, devastation **12** misadventure

ruinous 4 dire **5** fatal **6** deadly **7** adverse, baneful **8** damaging, ravaging **10** calamitous, disastrous, pernicious **11** cataclysmic, deleterious, destructive, devastating **12** catastrophic

Ruisdael, Jacob (Jakob) van
born: 7 Haarlem **14** The Netherlands
uncle: 18 Salomon van Ruysdael
artwork: 5 Dunes **12** The Waterfall **13** View of Haarlem **14** Bentheim Castle **15** Winter Landscape **17** The Jewish Cemetery **28** View on the Amstel near Amsterdam

rule 3 law, run **4** find, form, head, lead, sway **5** adage, axiom, canon, guide, judge, maxim, model, order, reign **6** custom, decide, decree, direct, empire, govern, manage, method, policy, regime, settle, system **7** adjudge, command, control, declare, formula, precept, prevail, resolve, routine **8** conclude, doctrine, dominate, domineer, dominion, pass upon, practice, regnancy, regulate, standard **9** authority, criterion, determine, direction, establish, guideline, influence, ordinance, precedent, principle,

pronounce, supremacy **10** adjudicate, administer, convention, domination, government, leadership, regulation, suzerainty **11** predominate, preside over, sovereignty **12** jurisdiction, prescription **14** administration
type: 5 bench **7** folding **9** steel tape
constellation: 5 Norma

rule out 4 omit **6** delete, except **7** exclude **9** eliminate

ruler 4 boss, czar, emir, head, khan, king, lord, shah, tsar, tzar **5** chief, judge, queen, rajah, sheik **6** dynast, leader, prince, satrap, shogun, sultan **7** arbiter, emperor, manager, measure, monarch, pharaoh, referee, viceroy **8** chairman, director, governor, suzerain **9** chieftain, commander, potentate, president, sovereign, yardstick **10** controller, supervisor **11** coordinator, crowned head, head of state, tape measure **12** straightedge **13** administrator

rules of conduct 6 ethics **9** moral code **10** principles **12** code of ethics

Rules of the Game
director: 10 Jean Renoir
cast: 10 Jean Renoir, Mila Parely, Nora Gregor **11** Marcel Dalio

ruling 6 decree **7** regnant **8** decision, dominant, reigning **9** enactment, governing, prescript **10** commanding, widespread **11** controlling, predominant **13** authoritative, predominating

ruling class 11 aristocracy **13** Establishment

Ruling Class, The
director: 10 Peter Medak
cast: 10 Arthur Lowe **11** Alastair Sim, Peter O'Toole **12** Harry Andrews

rum
drink: 4 Bolo, Grog **6** Mojito **7** Gauguin **8** Daiquiri, Navy Grog, Pina Fria **9** Borinquen, Hurricane **10** Pina Colada **12** Boston Cooler **13** Planter's Punch **14** Fish House Punch **15** Bacardi Cocktail **18** Barbados Rum Swizzle
ingredient: 8 molasses **9** sugar cane
origin: 10 West Indies
type: 4 dark **5** light
with apple brandy: 6 Bolero **8** Apple Pie
with apricot brandy: 11 Apricot Lady
with black coffee: 9 Black Rose
with bouillon: 6 Creole
with bourbon: 14 Artillery Punch
with brandy: 15 Quaker's Cocktail
with Cointreau: 8 Acapulco **10** Casa Blanca **11** Beachcomber **12** Blue Hawaiian
with cola: 9 Cuba Libre
with creme de cacao: 6 Panama
with curacao: 6 Mai-Tai **8** Blue Lady **12** Blue Hawaiian
with Dubonnet: 3 BVD **10** Bushranger

with Galliano: 9 Bossa Nova
with gin: 3 BVD
with guava: 8 Ocho Rios
with kahlua: 10 Black Maria
with milk: 6 Rum Cow **11** Tom-and-Jerry
with Pernod: 8 Shanghai
with sloe gin: 11 Shark's Tooth
with Tia Maria: 10 Black Maria
with vermouth: 6 Bolero **8** Apple Pie **10** Black Devil **11** Shark's Tooth

rumble 4 bang, boom, clap, roar, roll **7** booming, resound, thunder **8** drumming **9** resonance **11** reverberate **13** reverberation

Rumford, Benjamin Thomson
invented: 10 photometer **11** calorimeter

Rumina
protectress of: 14 nursing mothers

ruminant 3 cow, elk, yak **4** deer, oxen **5** bison, camel, llama, moose, sheep **6** alpaca, cattle, vicuna **7** buffalo, giraffe, pensive **8** antelope **10** chevrotain, meditative, thoughtful **13** contemplative

ruminate 4 mull, muse **5** brood, study, think, weigh **6** ponder **7** reflect **8** cogitate, consider, meditate, mull over **9** speculate, think over **10** deliberate, think about **11** contemplate

ruminating 6 musing **7** pensive **8** thinking **10** meditating, meditative, reflecting, reflective, thoughtful **11** chewing over, mulling over, speculative **13** contemplating, contemplative, introspective

rumination 5 study **6** musing **7** mulling, reverie, thought **8** brooding, thinking **9** pondering **10** cogitation, meditation, reflection **11** speculation **12** deliberation **13** consideration, contemplation **15** reconsideration

rummage 4 root **5** probe **7** examine, explore, ransack **10** disarrange, poke around **11** look through

rummy 3 sot **4** lush, soak **5** drunk, souse, toper **6** barfly, boozer **7** tippler **8** card game, drunkard **9** alcoholic **11** dipsomaniac
also known as: 3 gin, rum **4** rhum **5** romme **8** gin rummy
derived from: 8 conquien

rumor 4 talk **5** story **6** babble, gossip, report **7** hearsay, whisper **8** innuendo, intimate **9** circulate, insinuate **11** insinuation, scuttlebutt, supposition

rump 4 rear, seat **5** croup, stern **6** behind, bottom, breech, dorsum **7** rear end **8** backside, buttocks, derriere, haunches **9** posterior **12** hindquarters

Rumpelstiltskin
origin: 8 Germanic
form: 5 dwarf
spun: 4 flax
made: 4 gold

rumple 4 fold, muss **5** crimp, crush **6** crease, pucker, rimple, ruffle, tousle **7** crinkle, crumple, wrinkle **8** dishevel, disorder **9** corrugate **10** disarrange

rumpus 3 ado, row **4** fray, fuss, stir, to-do **5** brawl, melee, noise **6** affray, fracas, hubbub, pother, racket, ruckus, tumult, uproar **7** rhubarb, scuffle, tempest **8** brouhaha, upheaval **9** agitation, commotion, confusion, imbroglio **10** hullabaloo **11** disturbance, embroilment

run 2 be, go **3** fly, get, hie, jog, pen, ply **4** bolt, boss, cost, dart, dash, defy, flee, flow, go by, head, kind, last, meet, melt, pass, pour, push, race, roll, rush, sort, tear, tour, trip, trot, type, vary **5** bleed, bound, class, court, drift, drive, genre, glide, hurry, impel, incur, issue, leave, pilot, print, speed, spell, split, stand, surge, total, while **6** become, canter, course, decamp, direct, elapse, endure, escape, extend, gallop, hasten, hustle, invite, ladder, manage, motion, move on, outing, period, pierce, propel, scurry, series, sprint, streak, stream, thrust, vanish, voyage, wander **7** abscond, add up to, advance, bring on, compete, current, display, freedom, get past, journey, liquefy, meander, operate, oversee, passage, proceed, publish, running, scamper, stretch, take off, vamoose **8** amount to, campaign, continue, dissolve, duration, evanesce, maneuver, meet with, navigate, progress, scramble, separate, tendency **9** direction, disappear, enclosure, encounter, excursion, go quickly, lose color, penetrate, skedaddle, supervise **10** coordinate, pilgrimage **11** continuance **12** beat a retreat, continuation, perpetuation
baseball: 5 point, score, tally **17** circuit of the bases

run aground 7 founder **8** collapse

runaround 4 slip **5** dodge **6** bypass **7** evasion **8** shunning, sidestep **9** avoidance **11** elusiveness, evasiveness **12** equivocation

run around 7 consort, hang out **9** associate, pal around **10** fraternize

runaway 4 pure **6** bolter **7** escapee, perfect, refugee **8** absolute, complete, deserter, fugitive **9** out-and-out, unalloyed **10** skedaddler **11** unmitigated, unqualified

run away 3 fly **4** flee **5** elope **6** decamp, escape, run off **7** abscond, make off **8** sneak off **10** fly the coop, make a break, take flight **12** make a getaway

rundown 5 brief **6** digest, precis, resume, review, sketch **7** outline, summary **8** abstract, synopsis **12** capitulation, condensation

run-down 5 frail, seedy, tacky, tired, weary **6** ailing, beat-up, feeble, shabby, sickly **7** rickety, worn out **8** fatigued, tattered **9** crumbling, exhausted **10** broken-down, tumbledown **11** dilapidated **12** deteriorated

run down 4 scan **5** knock **6** slight **7** detract, put down, run over **8** belittle, derogate, ridicule **9** denigrate, deprecate, discredit, disparage, downgrade, enumerate, underrate **10** depreciate, undervalue

run-in 5 brush, set-to **6** battle, fracas **7** scuffle **8** skirmish **9** encounter **10** engagement

run into 4 meet **8** flow into **9** encounter **10** chance upon, meet up with **11** collide with

run off 3 fly **4** flee **5** elope **6** escape **7** abscond, make off, runaway **9** steal away **10** take flight **15** head for the hills

run off at the mouth 3 gab **5** prate **6** babble, gabble **8** rattle on **11** talk too much

run off with 5 seize **6** abduct, kidnap **7** bear off **8** carry off **9** elope with **11** abscond with, make off with

run-of-the-mill 4 dull, so-so **5** banal, stock, usual **6** common, modest **7** average, humdrum, mundane, routine, typical **8** everyday, mediocre, middling, ordinary, passable, standard **10** second-rate **11** commonplace, indifferent, nondescript **12** unimpressive **13** unimaginative **15** undistinguished

runt 3 elf **4** chit **5** dwarf, pygmy **6** midget, peewee, shrimp **8** half-pint, Tom Thumb **11** Lilliputian
Latin: 10 homunculus

run through 5 spend, waste **6** expend, pierce **7** deplete, exhaust **8** rehearse, squander

runty 5 short **6** bantam **7** dwarfed, squatty, stunted **9** pint-sized

Runyon, Damon
author of: 12 Guys and Dolls **16** Blue Plate Special

rupture 3 pop **4** part, rent, rift, snap **5** break, burst, clash, cleft, crack, split **6** breach, divide, schism, sunder **7** discord, disrupt, fissure **8** breaking, bursting, cleavage, dissever, disunion, disunite, fracture, friction, puncture **9** severance **10** dissension, falling out, separation **12** disagreement

R U R
author: 10 Karel Capek **22** Rossum's Universal Robots

rural 4 hick **6** rustic **7** bucolic, country **8** pastoral **10** provincial **11** countrified

rural area 6 sticks **7** boonies, country **8** farmland **9** backwater, backwoods, boondocks **10** hinterland **11** countryside

ruse 4 hoax **5** blind, dodge, feint, shift, trick **6** deceit, device, scheme **8** artifice, maneuver **9** deception, stratagem

10 subterfuge **11** contrivance, machination

rush 3 hie, run **4** dart, dash, goad, leap, push, race, spur, tear, urge, whip **5** drive, haste, hurry, press, speed, storm **6** charge, hasten, hustle, plunge, scurry, sprint, urgent **7** scamper, urgency **8** dispatch, expedite, pressure, scramble **9** emergency **10** accelerate **11** top priority

rush 6 Juncus

varieties: 3 bog **4** salt, soft, wood **5** spike **6** grassy **8** scouring **9** field wood, flowering **10** common wood, least spike **11** chair-maker's, greater wood, Japanese-mat **12** slender spike **13** dwarf scouring **14** common scouring **18** variegated scouring

Rush, Benjamin

field: 8 medicine

established first: 21 free medical dispensary

signer of: 25 Declaration of Independence

rush light 3 dip **5** torch **6** candle, tallow

Rushworth

character in: 13 Mansfield Park

author: 6 Austen

Ruskin, John

author of: 13 Fors Clavigera **14** Modern Painters **17** The Stones of Venice **27** The Seven Lamps of Architecture

Russell, Bertrand

author of: 19 Why I Am Not a Christian **20** Principia Mathematica (with Alfred North)

Russell, Jane

real name: 29 Ernestine Jane Geraldine Russell

born: 9 Bemidji MN

discovered by: 12 Howard Hughes

roles: 4 Waco **9** The Outlaw **13** The French Line **22** Gentlemen Prefer Blondes, The Revolt of Mamie Stover

Russell, Rosalind

born: 11 Waterbury CT

roles: 5 Gypsy **6** Picnic **8** The Women **9** Hired Wife **10** Auntie Mame **11** Sister Kenny **13** His Girl Friday **14** My Sister Eileen **22** Mourning Becomes Electra

russet 5 apple, umber **6** auburn, copper **10** terra-cotta **11** rust-colored **12** reddish-brown

Russia (includes constituent republics of the former USSR)

other name: 17 Russian Federation

former name: 4 USSR **11** Soviet Union **31** Union of Soviet Socialist Republics

member of: 3 CIS **31** Commonwealth of Independent States

capital/largest city: 6 Moscow

others: 4 Baku, Eisk, Kiev, Okha, Omsk, Poti, Riga **5** Anapa, Batum, Gorki, Gorky, Memel, Minsk, Sochi, Vilna, Yeisk **6** Batumi, Erevan, Frunze, Odessa, Rostov, Samara, Tiflis **7** Alma-Ata, Derbent, Donetsk, Kharkov, Liepaja, Petsamo, Pivonia, Saratov, Tallinn, Tbilisi, Yerevan **8** Dushanbe, Kishinev, Murmansk, Pechenga, Taganrog, Tashkent **9** Ashkhabad, Astrakhan, Balaklava, Kronstadt, Kuibyshev, Leningrad, Nikolayev, Petrograd, Ulyanovsk, Volgograd, Yaroslavl **10** Kronshtadt, Sevastopol, Stalingrad, Sverdlovsk **11** Chelyabinsk, Kaliningrad, Makhachkala, Novorossisk, Novosibirsk, Vladivostok **12** St Petersburg, Vladisvostok **14** Dnepropetrovsk

division/country: 6 Latvia **7** Armenia, Belarus, Estonia, Georgia, Moldova, Siberia, Ukraine **8** Moldavia **9** Kirghizia, Lithuania, Turkmenia **10** Azerbaijan, Belorussia, Kazakhstan, Kyrgyzstan, Tajikistan, Uzbekistan **12** Tadzhikistan, Turkmenistan

former: 4 Kiev **8** Novgorod

government:

legislature: 4 Duma, Rada **7** Zemstvo **8** Congress

measure: 3 fut, lof **4** duim, fass, loof, pood, quar, stof **5** duime, foute, korec, korek, ligne, osmin, pajak, stoff, stoof, vedro, verst **6** charka, liniya, osmina, paletz, sagene, stekar, tchast, tsarki, versta, verste **7** archine, arsheen, botchka, chkalik, garnetz, verchoc, verchok **8** boutylka, chetvert, krouchka, kroushka **9** chetverik **10** dessiatine **11** poługarnetz

monetary unit: 5 altin, bisti, copec, denga, grosh, kopek, ruble, shaur **6** abassi, copeck, grivna, kopeck, piatak, rouble **7** poltina, valiuta **8** auksinas, deneshka, imperial, polushka **9** poltinnik **10** altininink, chervonets

weight: 3 lof, lot **4** dola, funt, lana, last, loof, loth, once, pood, poud **5** dolia

island: 5 Kuril **7** Hiiumaa, Karagin, Shantar, Vaygach, Wrangel **8** Kolguyev, Saaremaa, Sakhalin **9** Andreanof **12** Novaya Zemlya **13** Komandorskiye **14** Franz Josef Land, Novosibirskiye **15** Severnaya Zemlya

lake: 3 Seg **4** Aral, Azov, Kola, Sego, Topo, Vigo **5** Chany, Elton, Erara, Ilmen, Lacha, Onega, Pskov, Vozhe **6** Baikal, Byeloe, Ladoga, Peipus, Selety, Taymyr, Tengiz, Zaysan **8** Balkhash **10** Caspian Sea

mountain: 5 Altai, Lenin, Sayan, Urals **6** Anadyr, Elbrus, Koryak, Pamirs, Pobedy **7** Belukha, Crimean, Khibiny, Stanovi, Zhiguli **8** Caucasus, Dzhughur, Stanavoi, Tien Shan **9** Kopet Dagh, Narodnaya, Pamir-Alai, Yablonovy **10** Carpathian **11** Sikhote-Alin, Verkhoyansk

highest point: 9 Communism

river: 3 Don, Ili **4** Amur, Lena, Neva, Ural **5** Dvina, Kuban, Neman, Volga **6** Kolyma, Moskva **7** Dnieper, Pechora, Yenisei **8** Amu Darya, Dniester, Ob-Irtysh, Syr Darya **9** Indigirka

sea: 4 Aral, Azov, Kara **5** Black, Japan, White **6** Arctic, Baltic, Bering, Laptev **7** Barents, Caspian, Chukchi, Okhotsk, Pacific

physical feature:

gulf: 4 Azov **5** Mezen **9** Kara-Bogaz, Shelikhov

peninsula: 4 Kola **5** Yamal **6** Crimea, Taymyr **7** Chukchi, Karelia **9** Kamchatka **10** Mangyshlak

strait: 5 Tatar **6** Bering **8** Bosporus **11** Dardanelles

people: 3 Jew **4** Slav **5** Ersar, Kulak, Tatar, Uzbec **6** Kazakh, Soviet, Velika **7** Chukchi, Cossack, Kirghiz, Latvian, Russian, Tadzhik, Turkmen **8** Armenian, Estonian, Georgian, Siberian **9** Moldavian, Ukrainian **10** Lithuanian **11** Azerbaijani, Belorussian

actor: 12 Stanislavsky

author: 5 Gogol **7** Nabokov, Pushkin, Tolstoy **8** Turgenev **9** Ehrenburg, Pasternak, Sholokhov **10** Dostoevsky **12** Solzhenitsyn

composer: 6 Glinka **7** Borodin **9** Prokofiev **10** Mussorgsky, Stravinsky **11** Tchaikovsky **12** Rachmaninoff, Shostakovich **14** Rimsky-Korsakov

cosmonaut: 11 Yuri Gagarin

czar/tsar/tzar: 4 Ivan, Paul **5** Peter **6** Alexis **7** Michael **8** Nicholas **9** Alexander **12** Boris Godunov

dancer: 7 Nureyev, Pavlova **8** Danilova, Nijinsky **11** Baryshnikov

dynasty: 7 Romanov

early people: 3 Hun **4** Goth **5** Tatar **6** Khazar, Mongol, Tartar **8** Norsemen, Scythian **9** Cimmerian, Sarmatian, Varangian

empress: 9 Alexandra, Catherine

hereditary noble: 5 boyar

leader: 5 Beria, Lenin **6** Stalin, Suslov **7** Gromyko, Kosygin, Molotov, Trotsky, Yeltsin **8** Andropov, Brezhnev, Bukharin, Bulganin, Kerensky, Malenkov, Podgorny **9** Chernenko, Gorbachev **10** Khrushchev

monk: 8 Rasputin

prince: 4 Oleg **5** Rurik **8** Vladimir

revolutionary: 9 bolshevik **10** Decembrist

ruler: 5 Tatar **6** Mongol **8** Batu Khan

scientist: 6 Pavlov **9** Mendeleev **11** Tsiolkovsky

language: 5 Evenk, Tatar, Uzbek **6** Buriat, Kalmyk, Kazakh **7** Finnish, Kirghiz, Latvian, Russian, Tadzhik, Turkmen **8** Armenian, Estonian, Georgian, Ossetian **9** Moldavian,

Ukrainian **10** Lithuanian **11** Belorussian
  alphabet: **8** cyrillic
religion: **5** Islam **7** Judaism **8** Buddhism, Lutheran **10** Protestant **13** Roman Catholic **15** Russian Orthodox **16** Armenian Orthodox, Georgian Orthodox
place: **7** Kremlin **9** Red Square
  art gallery: **9** Tretyakov
  castle: **8** Starosty
  cathedral: **5** Sobor **7** Zagorsk **8** St Basils
  cemetery: **11** Piskarevsky
  museum: **9** Hermitage **12** Petrodvorets **18** Cathedral of St Isaac
  palace: **6** Winter
  park: **5** Gorky
  ruins: **7** Bukhara **10** Echmiadzin **15** Gediminas Castle
  prison: **8** Lubyanka
  street: **11** Kreshchatik **14** Nevski Prospekt
  theater: **7** Bolshoi
feature:
  collective farm: **7** kolkhoz
  country house: **5** dacha
  dance: **4** kolo **5** gopac, hopak, saber **6** cossac, trepak **7** cosaque, ziganka **8** kozachok **9** tzazatski
  dance company: **5** Kirov **7** Bolshoi
  labor camp: **5** gulag
  musical instrument: **9** balalaika
  secret police: **3** KGB, MGB **4** NKVD, OGPU **5** Cheka
  state farm: **7** sovkhoz
food:
  caviar: **13** ikra zernistia
  cereal: **5** kasha
  sour cream: **7** smetana
  dessert: **8** vareniki
  dish: **4** plov **5** pirau **6** pelemo **8** osetina, shashlyk **16** kotleta po kievski
  drink: **4** kvas **5** kvass, vodka **6** chacha, kumiss
  filled pastries: **8** piroshki, pirozhki
  soup: **5** shchi **6** borshch **7** borscht, borsch
Russian village commune 3 mir
rust 3 rot **5** decay, stain **6** auburn, blight, russet **7** corrode, crumble, decline, oxidize **9** corrosion, oxidation **11** deteriorate **12** reddish-brown **13** reddish-yellow
rust-colored 5 henna **6** auburn, russet **8** cinnamon **12** reddish-brown
rustic 4 rube, rude **5** crude, plain, rough, rural, yokel **6** coarse, gauche, simple **7** awkward, boorish, bucolic, bumpkin, country, hayseed, loutish, peasant, uncouth **8** agrarian, churlish, cloddish, pastoral **9** inelegant, unrefined **10** clodhopper, countryman, provincial, uncultured, unpolished **11**

countrified **13** country person **15** unsophisticated
rustle 3 rub **4** hiss, stir **5** swish, whish **6** riffle
rustler 5 thief **6** bandit, outlaw **7** brigand **9** desperado
rusty 5 moldy, stiff **6** rotten, rusted **7** reddish, tainted **8** corroded, sluggish **11** rust-colored **13** out of practice
rut 3 cut **4** mark **5** ditch, habit, score, tread **6** furrow, groove, gutter, hollow, trench, trough **7** channel, depress, dig into, pattern **8** monotony **9** deep track **10** depression **11** dull routine
Ruth
  husband: **4** Boaz **6** Mahlon
  son: **4** Obed
  father-in-law: **9** Elimelech
  mother-in-law: **5** Naomi
  brother-in-law: **7** Chilion
Ruth, George Herman
  nickname: **4** Babe **12** Sultan of Swat
  sport: **8** baseball
  position: **8** outfield
  team: **14** New York Yankees
Rutherford, Dame Margaret
  born: **6** London **7** England
  roles: **7** The VIPs **10** Jane Marple **12** Blithe Spirit **27** The Importance of Being Earnest
Rutherford, Ernest
  field: **7** physics
  nationality: **7** British
  discovered: **6** proton **13** atomic nucleus, beta radiation **14** alpha radiation, gamma radiation
  awarded: **10** Nobel Prize
ruthless 5 cruel, harsh **6** brutal, deadly, savage **7** bestial, brutish, callous, inhuman, vicious **8** pitiless **9** barbarous, ferocious, heartless, merciless, murderous, unfeeling, unpitying, unsparing **10** relentless, sanguinary, unmerciful **11** cold-blooded, hardhearted, remorseless, unforgiving, unrelenting **12** bloodthirsty
ruthlessness 7 cruelty **9** barbarity, brutality, harshness **10** inhumanity, savageness **11** viciousness
Ruysdael, Salomon van
  born: **7** Naarden **14** The Netherlands
  nephew: **16** Jacob van Ruisdael
  artwork: **9** River Bank **10** River Scene **14** River Landscape **18** River with Ferry Boat
Rwanda
  other name: **6** Ruanda
  capital/largest city: **6** Kigali
  others: **6** Biumba, Butare, Kibuye, Nyanza **7** Astrida, Gisenyi, Kibungu **8** Cyangugu **9** Ruhengeri
  division:
    colonial: **12** Ruanda-Urundi

  monetary unit: **5** franc **7** centime
  lake: **4** Kivu **5** Ihema **6** Bufera, Bulera, Mohasi **7** Rugwero, Ruhnodo **8** Mugesera, Tshohoha
  mountain: **7** Mitumba, Virunga **8** Muhavura
  highest point: **9** Karisimbi
  river: **6** Kagera, Ruzizi **7** Akagera **8** Akanyaru **9** Luvironza **10** Nyawarongo
  physical feature:
    forest: **7** Nyungwe
    valley: **11** Western Rift
  people: **3** Twa **4** Hutu **5** Batwa, Pygmy, Tutsi **6** Bahutu, Watusi **7** Batutsi
    explorer: **5** Speke **6** Gotzen
    leader: **9** Kayibanda **11** Habyarimana
  language: **6** French **7** Swahili **11** Kinyarwanda
  religion: **7** animism **13** Roman Catholic
  place:
    game reserve: **6** Gabiro
    park: **6** Albert, Kagera **16** Virunga Volcanoes
  feature:
    clothing: **5** pagne
    king: **5** mwami
Ryan, Cornelius
  author of: **13** A Bridge Too Far, The Last Battle, The Longest Day
Ryan, Robert
  born: **9** Chicago IL
  roles: **6** Caught **8** The Set-Up **9** Billy Budd, Crossfire **12** Clash by Night, The Wild Bunch **13** Act of Violence, The Longest Day **14** About Mrs Leslie, God's Little Acre **17** Bad Day at Black Rock **18** The Woman on the Beach
Ryder, Albert Pinkham
  born: **12** New Bedford MA
  artwork: **12** The Race Track (Death on a Pale Horse) **15** Toilers of the Sea **27** Siegfried and the Rhine Maidens
rye 6 Secale
  varieties: **4** wild **5** giant **6** common **8** Aral wild, blue wild **9** Altai wild, giant wild, Volga wild **10** Canada wild **11** Chinese wild, Russian wild **12** Siberian wild, Virginia wild
  type: **6** liquor **7** whiskey
  origin: **7** Ireland **8** Scotland
  ingredient: **10** mash grains
  drink: **9** Cablegram **11** John Collins, Whiskey Sour
  with Cointreau: **10** Temptation
  with Pernod: **3** TNT
  with vermouth: **8** Brooklyn **9** Algonquin

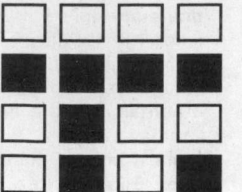  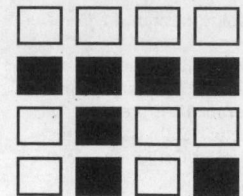

Saarinen, Eero
father: 5 Eliel
architect of: 11 St Louis Arch 20 Gateway to the West Arch (St Louis) 26 Trans World Airlines Terminal (NYC) 28 General Motors Technical Center (Warren MI) 39 Columbia Broadcasting Company Headquarters (NYC)
style: 13 International

Saarinen, Eliel
son: 4 Eero
architect of: 16 Cranbrook Academy (Bloomfield Hills MI) 18 Kleinhaus Music Hall (Buffalo) 19 Tanglewood Music Shed (MA) 20 Christ Lutheran Church (Minneapolis MN), First Christian Church (Columbus IN)

Saba *see* 5 Sheba

Sabbath 8 Lord's Day 9 day of rest

Sabbatical: A Romance
author: 9 John Barth

saber, sabre 3 cut 4 kill, stab 5 blade, sword, wound 6 cutlas, rapier, strike 7 cutlass, soldier 8 scimitar 10 broadsword

Sabin, Albert Bruce
field: 8 medicine
developed: 16 oral polio vaccine

sable 3 fur, jet 4 dark, inky 5 black, ebony, raven

sabotage 3 sap 6 retard 7 cripple, destroy, disable, disrupt, subvert 8 paralyze 9 undermine, vandalize 10 subversion 12 incapacitate

sabra 11 Israeli-born 14 native of Israel

Sabra
type: 7 liqueur
origin: 6 Israel
flavor: 6 orange 9 chocolate

Sac *see* 4 Sauk

saccharine 5 gooey, mushy, soppy, sweet 6 sugary, syrupy 7 candied, cloying, honeyed, maudlin, mawkish, sugared 9 offensive, oversweet, revolting, sickening 10 disgusting, nauseating 11 sentimental

sacerdotal 5 papal 8 clerical, pastoral, priestly 9 apostolic, canonical, episcopal 10 pontifical 11 ministerial 12 hierarchical 14 ecclesiastical

Sachs, Hans 13 Meistersinger

sack 3 bag, rob 4 loot, pack, raid 5 pouch, spoil, store, waste 6 duffel, maraud, rapine, ravage, tear up 7 despoil, pillage, plunder, ransack 8 spoliate 9 depredate, duffel bag, gunnysack, haversack, marauding 10 plundering, ravishment 11 depredation, devastation 12 despoliation

sackbut 18 medieval instrument
resembles: 8 trombone

sacrament 3 vow 4 rite 5 troth 6 pledge, plight, ritual 7 liturgy, promise, service 8 ceremony, contract, covenant 9 solemnity 10 ceremonial, obligation, observance 11 affirmation 12 ministration

sacramental 4 holy 6 ritual 7 blessed 10 ceremonial, liturgical

Sacraments, Seven 7 Baptism, Penance 9 Eucharist, Last Rites, Matrimony 10 Holy Orders 12 Confirmation 13 Holy Communion 14 Extreme Unction, Reconciliation 18 Anointing of the Sick

sacred 4 holy 6 church 7 blessed, revered 8 Biblical, hallowed, hieratic 9 religious, venerable 10 sanctified, scriptural 11 consecrated 14 ecclesiastical

Sacred and Profane Love Machine, The
author: 11 Iris Murdoch

Sacred writings 5 Bible 11 Bibliotheca

sacrifice 4 cede, loss 5 forgo, waive 6 forego, give up, homage 7 cession, forfeit, offer up 8 immolate, oblation, offering, renounce 9 surrender 10 concession, immolation, lustration, relinquish 12 renunciation 14 relinquishment

sacrilege 3 sin 7 impiety, mockery, outrage 8 iniquity 9 blasphemy, profanity, violation 10 irreligion, sinfulness, wickedness 11 desecration, impiousness, irreverence, profanation, profaneness

sacrilegious 7 impious, profane 10 irreverent 11 blasphemous, irreligious

sacrosanct 4 holy 5 godly 6 divine, solemn 8 hallowed, heavenly 9 celestial, inviolate, religious, spiritual 10 inviolable, unexamined 11 consecrated 12 unquestioned

sacrum
bone of: 11 base of spine

sad 3 low 4 blue, grim, hard, hurt 5 grave 6 dismal, solemn, taxing, tragic, trying, woeful 7 adverse, crushed, doleful, forlorn, grieved, joyless, maudlin, pitiful, serious, unhappy 8 dejected, desolate, downcast, grievous, mournful, pathetic, touching, troubled, wretched 9 cheerless, depressed, difficult, miserable, sorrowful 10 calamitous, chapfallen, despairing, despondent, dispirited, distressed, lachrymose, lamentable, melancholy 11 crestfallen, distressing, pessimistic, troublesome, unfortunate 12 disconsolate, heartrending, heavyhearted, inconsolable 13 brokenhearted, griefstricken, heartbreaking 14 down in the dumps, down in the mouth
French: 6 triste

Sadat, Anwar el-
president of: 5 Egypt
awarded: 15 Nobel Peace Prize
author of: 18 In Search of Identity

sadden 4 damp, dash 5 crush 6 burden, deject, grieve, sorrow, subdue 7 depress 8 aggrieve, dispirit 10 discourage, dishearten

saddle with 9 stick with 10 burden with 12 encumber with 18 make responsible for

Sade, Marquis de
author of: 7 Justine 8 Juliette 14 120 Days of Sodom 26 The Philosopher in the Bedroom

sadistic 6 brutal 7 vicious 8 fiendish, perverse 9 perverted 12 bloodthirsty

sadness
French: 9 tristesse

sad poem 5 elegy 6 lament

Sad Sack
creator: 11 George Baker

Saehrimnir
origin: 12 Scandinavian
form: 4 boar
served in: 8 Valhalla
feat: 12 regeneration

safe 4 firm, sure, wary 5 sound, vault, whole 6 intact, modest, secure, stable, steady, unhurt 7 certain, guarded, prudent 8 cautious, defended, discreet, harmless, reliable, unbroken, unharmed 9 innocuous, protected, undamaged, unexposed, unscathed 10 dependable, protecting 11 circumspect, impregnable, out of danger, trustworthy, unscratched 12 conservative, invulnerable, noncommittal

safeguard 4 ward **5** armor, charm **6** amulet, buffer, defend, harbor, screen, secure, shield **7** bulwark, defense, fortify, protect, shelter **8** conserve, garrison, preserve, security, talisman **10** precaution, protection

safekeeping 4 care **6** charge **7** custody **8** security **9** husbandry **10** protection **12** conservation, guardianship, preservation

Safety Net, The
author: **12** Heinrich Boll

saffron
botanical name: **13** Crocus sativus
also called: **6** Krokus
Moorish: **6** Zafran
of all spices most: **6** costly
color: **6** orange, yellow **12** yellow-orange
used as: **8** coloring, cosmetic, medicine **9** fabric dye
origin: **5** Egypt, Syria **8** Holy Land **9** Palestine
use: **4** rice **5** bread, rolls

sag 3 bow, dip **4** drop, fail, flag, flap, flop, keel, lean, list, sink, sway, tilt, tire **5** droop, pitch, slump, weary **6** billow, plunge, settle, weaken **7** decline, descend, give way **8** diminish

saga 4 epic, myth, tale, yarn **6** legend **7** history, romance **9** adventure, chronicle, narrative
French: **11** roman-fleuve

sagacious 4 foxy, wise **5** acute, canny, sharp, smart, sound **6** astute, brainy, clever, shrewd **7** cunning, knowing, prudent, sapient, tactful **8** discreet, rational, sensible **9** judicious, practical **10** diplomatic, discerning, perceptive **11** calculating, intelligent **13** perspicacious **14** discriminating

sagacity 6 acumen, brains, smarts, wisdom **8** sapience **9** canniness, smartness **10** astuteness, braininess, cleverness, shrewdness **11** discernment **12** intelligence, perspicacity **13** judiciousness **14** discrimination

Sagan, Carl
author of: **6** Cosmos **7** Contact **16** The Dragons of Eden

Sagan, Francoise
real name: **16** Francoise Quoirez
author of: **13** A Certain Smile **15** Aimez-vous Brahms **16** Bonjour Tristesse

sage 4 guru, wise **5** sound **6** astute, pundit, savant, shrewd **7** egghead, knowing, prudent, sapient, scholar, wise man **8** mandarin, sensible **11** intelligent, philosopher
French: **6** savant
Latin: **5** magus, solon

sage 6 Salvia **12** S officinalis
varieties: **3** bog **4** baby, blue, gray, rose, sand, wood **5** black, lilac, Texas, white **6** autumn, common, desert, garden, purple, silver, yellow **7** bladder, gentian, scarlet, Spanish, thistle, Vervain **8** creeping, gray ball, mealy-cup, rose-leaf **9** Bethlehem, Jerusalem **11** Mexican bush **16** pineapple-scented
means: **6** to heal, to save
strengthens: **6** memory, wisdom **8** prudence
makes men: **8** immortal
origin: **7** Albania **10** Yugoslavia **13** Mediterranean
use: **4** pork **6** breads, cheese **7** chicken, poultry, seafood **8** stuffing

Sage of Concord
nickname of: **17** Ralph Waldo Emerson

Sagittarius
symbol: **6** archer **7** centaur
planet: **7** Jupiter
rules: **10** philosophy **15** higher education
born: **8** November, December

Sagittary
form: **7** centaur
carried: **3** bow

said 5 above, quoth **6** quoted, spoken, stated **7** related, uttered **8** repeated

Saigon
capital of: **7** Vietnam
now: **13** Ho Chi Minh City

sail 3 fly **4** boat, scud, skim, soar **5** drift, float, glide, steam **6** course, cruise, voyage **8** navigate **9** excursion

sailboat 4 saic, yawl **5** craft, ketch, sloop, yacht **6** vessel **7** sunfish **8** schooner **9** catamaran
part: **4** boom, mast **6** canvas **7** rigging **9** mainsheet

sailcloth 4 duck **6** canvas

Sailing to Byzantium
author: **7** W B Yeats

sailor 3 gob, tar **4** salt **6** sea dog, seaman **7** mariner, voyager **8** deckhand, seafarer **9** navigator, yachtsman
terms: **3** yaw **4** ahoy, alee, conn, draw, fast, furl, heel, list, luff, moor, scud, tack, trim, wake **5** avast, belay, heave, hoist, lie to, pilot, pitch, weigh **6** aweigh **8** aweather, put about

sailors
patron saint: **4** Elmo

Sails (of Argo)
constellation of: **4** Vela

saint 6 martyr
Buddhist: **5** arhat **11** bodhisattva
Chinese: **8** immortal
Islamic: **3** pir
lives of the saints: **8** menology **9** hagiology **11** hagiography **13** acta sanctorum
process of becoming: **12** canonization
relic box: **6** chasse
remains: **5** relic
symbol: **4** halo

Saint, Eva Marie
born: **8** Newark NJ
roles: **6** Exodus **15** On the Waterfront **16** North by Northwest

saint, patron
acolytes: **13** John Berchmans
actors: **8** Genesius
artists: **4** Luke
astronomers: **7** Dominic
athletes: **9** Sebastian
authors: **14** Francis de Sales
aviators: **15** Our Lady of Loreto **16** Therese of Lisieux **17** Joseph of Cupertino
bakers: **8** Nicholas **18** Elizabeth of Hungary
bankers: **7** Matthew
barbers: **5** Louis **6** Cosmas, Damian
barren women: **9** Felicitas **14** Anthony of Padua
beggars/cripples: **5** Giles
blind: **6** Odilia **7** Raphael
bodily ills: **16** Our Lady of Lourdes
boy scouts: **6** George
brides: **14** Nicholas of Myra
builders: **13** Vincent Ferrer
butchers: **4** Luke **7** Hadrian **14** Anthony of Egypt
carpenters: **6** Joseph
cancer patients: **9** Peregrine
children: **10** Santa Claus **14** Nicholas of Myra
comedians: **5** Vitus
cooks: **6** Martha **8** Lawrence
deaf: **14** Francis de Sales
dying: **6** Joseph **7** Barbara
emigrants: **14** Frances Cabrini
England: **6** George
eye sufferers: **4** Lucy
falsely accused: **15** Raymond Nonnatus
farmers: **6** George **7** Isidore
fishermen: **5** Peter **6** Andrew
foreign missions: **13** Francis Xavier **16** Therese of Lisieux
foundlings: **13** Holy Innocents
France: **5** Denis
gardeners: **6** Fiacre, Phocas **7** Adelard, Dorothy, Tryphon
heart patients: **9** John of God
hospitals: **9** John of God **12** Jude Thaddeus **16** Camillus de Lellis
housewives: **4** Anne
hunters: **6** Hubert **10** Eustachius
invalids: **4** Roch
Ireland: **7** Patrick
Italy: **7** Anthony
laborers: **5** James **7** Isidore **9** John Bosco
lawyers: **3** Ivo **4** Ives **8** Genesius **10** Thomas More
librarians: **6** Jerome
lovers: **9** Valentine
mariners: **4** Elmo **7** Michael **19** Nicholas of Tolentino
mentally ill: **6** Dympna
merchants: **14** Nicholas of Myra **15** Francis of Assisi
metalworkers: **7** Eligius

miners: 7 Barbara
mothers: 6 Monica
musicians: 7 Cecilia, Dunstan **15** Gregory the Great
Norway: 4 Olaf, Olav
nurses: 6 Agatha **7** Alexius, Raphael **9** John of God **16** Camillus de Lellis
painters: 4 Luke
philosophers: 6 Justin **21** Catherine of Alexandria
physicians: 4 Luke **6** Cosmas, Damian **7** Raphael **9** Pantaleon
pilgrims: 5 James **7** Alexius
poets: 5 David **7** Cecilia
policemen: 7 Michael
poor souls: 19 Nicholas of Tolentino
postal workers: 7 Gabriel
priests: 19 Jean-Baptiste Vianney
printers: 8 Genesius **9** John of God **16** Augustine of Hippo
prisoners: 6 Dismas **7** Barbara **13** Joseph Cafasso
rheumatism: 15 James the Greater
sailors: 4 Elmo **7** Brendan, Erasmus, Eulalia **8** Cuthbert, Nicholas **11** Christopher **13** Peter Gonzales
scholars: 6 Brigid
scientists: 6 Albert
Scotland: 6 Andrew
sculptors: 6 Claude
seamen: 4 Elmo **14** Francis of Paolo
sick: 7 Michael **9** John of God **16** Camillus de Lellis
singers: 7 Cecilia, Gregory
skiers: 7 Bernard
shoemakers: 7 Crispin
soldiers: 6 George **7** Hadrian **8** Ignatius **9** Joan of Arc, Sebastian **13** Martin of Tours
Spain: 5 James **8** Santiago
students: 13 Thomas Aquinas **21** Catherine of Alexandria
surgeons: 6 Cosmas, Damian
tailors: 9 Homobonus
tax collectors: 7 Matthew
teachers: 15 Gregory the Great **21** Catherine of Alexandria, Jean Baptiste de la Salle
theologians: 9 Augustine **16** Alphonsus Liguori
throat sufferers: 6 Blaise
travelers: 7 Raphael **11** Christopher **14** Anthony of Padua, Nicholas of Myra
Wales: 5 David
winegrowers: 7 Vincent
workingmen: 6 Joseph
writers: 14 Francis de Sales
youth: 13 John Berchmans **15** Aloysius Gonzaga, Gabriel Possenti
Saint, The
author: 15 Leslie Charteris
character: 12 Simon Templar **26** Inspector Claude Eustace Teal
cast: 10 Roger Moore
Saint Anthony's fire 6 herpes **8** ergotism, shingles **10** erysipelas
Saint Elmo's fire 5 flame, hermo **6**

castor, corona, furole, helena **9** corposant **12** luminescence
Saint Esprit 9 Holy Ghost **10** Holy Spirit
Saint-Exupery, Antoine de
author of: 11 Night Flight **12** Southern Mail **15** The Little Prince **16** Wind Sand and Stars
Saint Francis
born: 6 Assisi
called: 9 Poverello
Saint-Gaudens, Augustus
born: 6 Dublin **7** Ireland
artwork: 7 Puritan **13** Mrs Henry Adams (Grief) **14** General Sherman **15** Admiral Farragut **16** President Lincoln
Saint Jack
author: 11 Paul Theroux
Saint Joan
author: 17 George Bernard Shaw
Saint John's bread 5 carob
Saint John's wort 5 amber **6** tutsan **7** ascyrum, cammock **9** androseme, hypericum, rosin-rose **10** broombrush **11** Aaron's-beard
saintliness 6 purity **8** goodness, holiness **9** beatitude, godliness **11** blessedness **12** spirituality
Saint Lucia, St Lucia
capital: 8 Castries
highest point: 5 Gimie
island group: 8 Windward **14** Lesser Antilles
language: 6 patois
location: 9 Caribbean
saintly 4 good, holy **5** godly, moral, pious **6** devout **7** angelic, blessed, exalted, sinless, upright **8** beatific, faithful, reverent, virtuous **9** believing, religious, righteous, spiritual **10** benevolent
Saint Paul
born: 6 Tarsus
companion: 4 Luke
epistle: 5 Titus **6** Romans **7** Hebrews, Timothy **8** Philemon **9** Ephesians, Galatians **10** Colossians **11** Corinthians, Philippians **13** Thessalonians
Saint Paul's Cathedral (London)
architect: 4 Wren
Saint Peter
called: 4 Rock **5** Simon **6** Cephas
brother: 6 Andrew
Saint-Saens, (Charles) Camille
born: 5 Paris **6** France
composer of: 12 Danse Macabre **14** Samson et Dalila **16** Samson and Delilah **18** La Jeunesse d'Hercule **20** Carnival of the Animals
Saints' lives
writer of: 12 hagiographer
Saint Vincent, St Vincent
capital: 9 Kingstown
highest point: 9 Soufriere
Indian: 5 Carib **6** Arawak

island group: 8 Windward **14** Lesser Antilles
islands: 10 Grenadines
language: 6 patois
location: 9 Caribbean
volcano: 9 Soufriere
Saint Vitus' dance 6 chorea
sake 3 end **4** care, gain, good **5** cause **6** behalf, object, profit, regard **7** account, benefit, concern, purpose, respect, welfare **8** interest **9** advantage **11** enhancement **13** consideration
sake
type: 4 wine **6** spirit
origin: 5 Japan
ingredient: 4 rice
Sakharov, Andrei Dimitrievich
field: 7 physics
nationality: 7 Russian
researched: 14 nuclear fission
defended: 12 civil liberty
exiled to: 5 Gorky
awarded: 10 Nobel Prize
Saki
real name: 7 H H Munro
author of: 8 Reginald **20** Beasts and Super-Beasts **21** The Chronicles of Clovis **23** The Unbearable Bassington
salaam 3 bow **6** homage **9** obeisance
Salacia
partner of: 7 Neptune
salacious 4 lewd, sexy **7** lustful, obscene **8** indecent **9** lecherous **10** lascivious, libidinous **12** pornographic
salad days 5 prime, youth **6** heyday **9** flowering
salamander 3 eft **4** newt **5** giant, siren, tiger **6** lizard, red eft **7** axolotl, urodela **8** congo eel, mudpuppy **9** amphibian, fire-eater, proteidae **10** hellbender, necturidae **14** red-spotted newt
Salamis
father: 6 Asopus
mother: 6 Metope
son: 8 Cychreus
Salammbo
author: 15 Gustave Flaubert
character: 5 Matho **8** Hamilcar, Spendius **9** Narr Havas
setting: 8 Carthage
salary 3 pay **5** wages **6** income **7** stipend **8** earnings **9** allowance, emolument **10** recompense **12** remuneration
sale 3 cut **7** auction, bargain, selling, special **8** discount, exchange, markdown, transfer **9** reduction
Salem
suburb of: 6 Boston
old site of: 11 witch trials
salesperson 5 agent, clerk **6** vendor **8** huckster
salient 6 arrant, marked **7** glaring, notable, obvious **8** flagrant, manifest, palpable, striking **9** egregious, important, prominent **10** noteworthy, no-

ticeable, pronounced, protruding, remarkable **11** conspicuous,
outstanding, substantial **12** considerable
Salii
also: **6** Salian
form: **7** priests
priests of: **4** Mars
guarded: **7** ancilia **13** sacred shields
saline 4 salt **5** briny, salty **8** brackish
Salinger, J D 7 recluse
author of: **11** Nine Stories **14** Franny
and Zooey **18** The Catcher in the
Rye
character: **4** Esme
Salisbury
capital of: **8** Zimbabwe
Salisbury, Harrison E
author of: **16** American in Russia **19**
A Journey for Our Times, Black
Night White Snow
Salish (Flatheads)
language family: **8** Salishan
location: **5** Idaho **6** Oregon **7** Montana **10** Washington **15** British Columbia
Salk, Jonas Edward
field: **8** medicine
developed: **12** (inactivated) polio
vaccine
salle a manger 10 dining room
literally: **13** hall for eating
sallow 3 wan **4** gray, pale **5** ashen,
livid **6** anemic, pallid, sickly, yellow **7**
bilious **9** jaundiced, washed-out, yellowish
sallowness 6 pallor **7** wanness **8** paleness **10** sickliness **11** biliousness **13**
colorlessness, yellowishness
Sallust
author of: **9** Histories **13** War of Jugurtha **20** Conspiracy of Catiline
sally 3 mot **4** flow, pour, quip, raid,
trip **5** erupt, foray, surge **6** attack,
banter, charge, outing, retort, sortie,
spring, thrust **7** debouch, journey **8**
badinage, repartee **9** excursion, wisecrack, witticism **10** expedition **13**
counterattack
Salmacis
form: **5** nymph
loved: **14** Hermaphroditus
joined with: **14** Hermaphroditus
became: **13** hermaphrodite **14** bisexual person
Salmagundi
author: **16** Washington Irving
salmon 4 fish, king **5** cohoe **6** silver
7 chinook, Pacific, quinnat, sockeye,
spawner **8** Atlantic, humpback
enclosure: **4** yair
female: **4** raun **6** baggit
genus: **12** Oncorhynchus
hatchling: **4** pink **6** alevin
male: **3** gib **4** buck, cock
post-spawning: **4** kelt **7** shedder

pre-spawning: **7** gilling, girling
young: **4** parr **7** essling
Salome
father: **11** Herod Philip
mother: **8** Herodias
husband: **7** Zebedee
opera by: **7** (Richard) Strauss
character: **5** Herod (the Tetrarch)
8 Herodias, Jokanaan (John the Baptist) **9** Narraboth
salon 4 hall **7** gallery **11** drawing room
13 establishment
saloon 3 bar, inn, pub **6** bistro, tavern
7 barroom, ginmill, taproom **8** alehouse **9** roadhouse, speakeasy
salt 3 wit **4** best, corn, cure, pick, save
5 brine, briny, cream, elect, humor,
savor, smack, souse, spice **6** choice,
flavor, pickle, saline, season, select **8**
brackish, marinate, piquancy, pungency **9** seasoning **12** quintessence
Salten, Felix
author of: **5** Bambi
saltwater 3 sea **5** brine, ocean
salty 4 racy **5** briny, funny, spicy,
terse, witty **6** corned, ribald, risque,
saline **7** pungent, zestful **8** brackish,
improper
salubrious 7 bracing, healthy **9** healthful, wholesome **10** beneficial, lifegiv-
ing **11** therapeutic **12** invigorating
salubriousness 11 healthiness **13**
healthfulness, wholesomeness
Salus
origin: **5** Roman
goddess of: **6** health **10** prosperity
corresponds to: **6** Hygeia
salutary 4 good **5** tonic **6** useful **7**
healing, healthy **8** curative, sanitary **9**
healthful, wholesome **10** beneficial,
profitable **12** advantageous
salutation 3 bow **5** hello, howdy,
toast **6** curtsy **7** address, welcome **8**
greeting **9** reception
Hawaiian: **5** aloha
Italian: **4** ciao
Latin: **3** ave
salute 3 ave **4** hail, kiss **5** bow to,
cheer, greet, honor, nod to, salvo **6**
accost, homage, praise, wave to **7** address, applaud, respect, welcome **8**
accolade, applause, greeting **9** laudation, reverence **11** acclamation, recognition **12** congratulate
Salvador
author: **10** Joan Didion
salvage 4 junk, save **5** scrap **6** debris,
rescue **7** recover, remains, restore **8**
recovery, retrieve **9** retrieval **11** reclamation **12** rehabilitate
salvation 4 rock **5** grace **6** rescue, saving **8** election, lifeline, mainstay, recovery, survival **9** retrieval **10** protection, redemption **11** deliverance,
reclamation **12** preservation
salve 4 aloe, balm, calm, ease, hail **5**

hello **6** lessen, lotion, pacify, reduce,
soothe, temper **7** anodyne, assuage,
mollify, relieve, unguent **8** dressing,
liniment, mitigate, moderate, ointment
9 alleviate, emollient, greetings **11** alleviative
salver 4 bowl, dish, tray **6** waiter **7**
coaster
salvia 4 herb, mint, sage **5** shrub **8**
mejorana **9** artemisia
salvo 5 burst **6** volley **7** barrage, battery **8** shelling **9** cannonade, fusillade
11 bombardment
sambuca
type: **7** liqueur
origin: **5** Italy
flavor: **5** anise **10** elderberry
same 4 like, twin, very **5** alike, equal **6**
on a par **7** similar, uniform **8** parallel
9 identical, unchanged **10** consistent,
equivalent, invariable **13** corresponding
same as previously given
Latin: **4** idem
sameness 6 parity **8** equality, evenness, likeness, monotony **10** similarity, uniformity **11** homogeneity **14** ho-
mogenousness
Samoa
capital:
American Samoa: **8** Pago Pago
Western Samoa: **4** Apia
studied by: **13** Margaret Mead
cities: **6** Utulei **7** Palauli **8** Fagatogo
division: **12** Western Samoa **13** American Samoa
monetary unit: **4** tala
island: **3** Ofu, Tau **4** Rose **5** Aunuu,
Manua, Namua, Upolu **6** Manono,
Nuulua, Savaii, Swains **7** Apolima,
Nuutele, Olosega, Tutuila **8** Nuusafee
mountain: **4** Vaea **5** Alava **6** Savaii **7**
Matafao **9** Rainmaker
highest point: **4** Fito **8** Silisili
sea: **12** South Pacific
physical feature:
bay: **5** Afono, Leone **6** Fagasa,
Falefa, Safata **7** Lafanga, Masefau,
Matautu **8** Massacre, Salealua **9**
Saluofata
people: **6** Samoan **10** Polynesian
explorer: **9** Roggeveen **12** Bougainville
language: **6** Samoan **7** English
religion: **6** Mormon **9** Methodist **13**
Roman Catholic **15** Latter Day Saints
19 Seventh-Day Adventist **26** Congregational Christianity
feature:
bird: **3** iao **4** lulu, lupe **6** manuao,
manuma, maomao **7** manuali **8**
manusina, manutagi
chief: **5** matai
chief's daughter: **5** taupo
cloth: **4** para, tapa
clothing: **5** pareu **8** lavalava, pu-
letasi

dance: 4 siva
dwelling: 4 fale
food:
    drink: 3 ava

Samoyed
language family: 6 Uralic
spoken in: 7 Siberia

sample 3 try **4** test **5** model, taste **7** dip into, examine, example, pattern, portion, segment **8** instance, paradigm, specimen **10** experience **12** cross section, illustration **14** representative **15** exemplification

Samson 11 Hebrew judge
father: 6 Manoah
feature: 4 hair **8** strength
weapon: 7 jawbone
mistress/betrayer: 7 Delilah
hometown: 5 Zorah
fate: 7 blinded
brought down: 4 Gaza

Samson Agonistes
author: 10 John Milton

Samuel 11 Hebrew judge
father: 7 Elkanah
mother: 6 Hannah
hometown: 5 Ramah
anointed: 4 Saul **5** David

Sana, Sanaa
capital of: 10 North Yemen

San Antonio
basketball team: 5 Spurs
football team: 11 Gunslingers
landmark: 8 The Alamo **9** River Walk

sanctification 8 blessing **9** hallowing **12** consecration
Hebrew: 7 Kiddush

sanctified 4 holy **6** sacred **7** blessed **8** hallowed **11** consecrated

sanctify 5 bless, exalt **6** anoint, hallow, purify, uphold **7** absolve, beatify, cleanse **8** dedicate, enshrine, make holy **10** consecrate, legitimate, legitimize **12** legitimatize

sanctimonious 6 solemn **7** canting, pompous, preachy **8** unctuous **9** overblown, pietistic **11** pharisaical, pretentious **14** holier-than-thou

sanctimoniousness 4 cant, sham **6** humbug **9** hypocrisy **11** insincerity **15** pretentiousness

sanction 5 allow, favor, leave **6** accept, assent, permit, ratify **7** agree to, approve, consent, endorse, liberty, license, penalty, support **8** approval, coercion, pressure **9** authority, authorize **10** legitimate, permission **11** countenance, endorsement **12** commendation, confirmation, ratification **13** authorization

sanctuary 4 park **5** cover, haven **6** asylum, chapel, church, refuge, safety, shrine, temple **7** reserve, retreat, shelter **8** preserve **10** protection

Sanctuary
author: 15 William Faulkner

character: 5 Tommy **6** Popeye **9** Ruby Lamar **10** Lee Goodwin, Reba Rivers **11** Temple Drake **12** Gowan Stevens, Horace Benbow

sanctum sanctorum 12 holy of holies

sanctus 4 holy

Sancus
also: 10 Semo Sancus
origin: 5 Roman
god of: 5 oaths **10** road safety **11** hospitality **20** international affairs
corresponds to: 8 Hercules **10** Dius Fidius

sand 4 grit, guts **5** pluck, spunk **6** mettle **7** bravery, courage, resolve **8** backbone **9** fortitude **10** resolution **12** resoluteness

Sand, George
real name: 14 Aurore Dudevant
protege: 6 Chopin
author of: 5 Lelia **7** Indiana **8** Consuelo **9** Valentine **13** Story of My Life **14** The Country Waif, The Haunted Pool **17** Fanchon the Cricket **18** Les Maitres Sonneurs **23** The Countess of Rudolstadt

sandal 4 clog, flat, shoe, zori **5** scuff, thong **6** loafer **7** slipper **8** flipflop, huarache, moccasin, overshoe **10** espadrille

sandalwood 5 Algum, Almug

sandbank 4 dune, reef **5** shelf, shoal **7** shallow

sandbar 4 bank, flat, reef, spit **5** shelf, shoal **7** shallow

Sandbox, The
author: 11 Edward Albee

Sandburg, Carl
author of: 3 Fog **7** Chicago **12** Harvest Poems **13** Smoke and Steel **14** Abraham Lincoln, The Cornhuskers **15** Remembrance Rock

Sanders, George
born: 6 Russia **12** St Petersburg
wife: 10 Benita Hume, Magda Gabor **11** Zsa Zsa Gabor
roles: 6 The Fan **7** Ivanhoe, Rebecca **8** The Saint **9** The Falcon **11** All About Eve **12** Forever Amber, The Gay Falcon **18** The Moon and Sixpence **20** Foreign Correspondent **22** The Picture of Dorian Gray **24** The House of the Seven Gables
autobiography: 25 Memoirs of a Professional Cad

San Diego
airport: 14 Lindbergh Field
area: 7 La Jolla, Old Town **8** Coronado **9** Point Loma **10** Balboa Park, Mission Bay **13** Mission Valley **14** Gaslamp Quarter
baseball team: 6 Padres
football team: 8 Chargers
founder: 13 Junipero Serra
landmark: 11 San Diego Zoo **14** Wild Animal Park **30** Scripps Institute of Oceanography

sandpiper 3 ree **4** bird, ruff **5** reeve, stint, wader **6** common, oxbird, plover **7** fiddler, haybird, spotted, tipbird **8** graybird, sandpeep, shadbird **10** beachrobin

Sands of Iwo Jima
director: 9 Allan Dwan
cast: 8 John Agar **9** Adele Mara, John Wayne **13** Forrest Tucker

sandwich 3 BLT, sub **4** club, deli, hero **5** hogie **6** burger, hoagie, insert **7** grinder, western **8** laminate **9** interpose, submarine **10** lamination **11** combination

sane 5 lucid, sober **7** logical **8** all there, balanced, credible, rational, sensible **9** judicious, plausible, sagacious **10** farsighted, reasonable **11** clearheaded, responsible
Latin: 12 compos mentis

Sanford and Son
character: 5 Bubba **6** Melvin **10** Aunt Esther **11** Donna Harris, Fred Sanford, Grady Wilson, Rollo Larson **12** Julio Fuentes, Officer Smith (Smitty) **13** Lamont Sanford
cast: 8 Redd Foxx **9** Don Bexley **11** Hal Williams, LaWanda Page, Slappy White, Whitman Mayo **12** Demond Wilson, Lynn Hamilton **13** Gregory Sierra **15** Nathaniel Taylor

San Francisco
baseball team: 6 Giants
bay: 12 San Francisco
county: 5 Marin **8** San Mateo **12** San Francisco
football team: 11 Forty-Niners
known as: 12 City by the Bay **19** City by the Golden Gate
landmark: 8 Alcatraz **16** Golden Gate Bridge
noted for: 8 cable car **9** earthquake (1906) **26** crookedest street in the world
street/section: 6 Market **7** Lombard, Nob Hill **8** Presidio **9** Chinatown **10** Montgomery **11** Embarcadero, Russian Hill

sangaree, sangria
flavor: 5 fruit, spice

sangfroid 5 poise **6** aplomb **7** balance **8** coolness **9** composure **10** confidence, equanimity **11** tranquility **12** tranquillity **16** imperturbability

sanguine 3 red **4** rosy **5** happy, ruddy, sunny **6** bright, elated, florid **7** buoyant, crimson, flushed, glowing, hopeful, reddish, scarlet **8** blooming, cheerful, inflamed, rubicund **9** confident **10** optimistic **12** lighthearted

Sanhedrin 7 council

sanitarium, sanitorium 8 hospital **11** institution
French: 13 maison de sante

sanitary 5 clean **7** aseptic, healthy, sterile **8** germ-free, hygienic **9** healthful, wholesome **10** salubrious, sterilized, uninfected, unpolluted **11** disinfected **12** prophylactic

sanitorium *see* **10** sanitarium

sanity 5 sense **6** reason **8** lucidity, saneness **9** coherence, normality **11** rationality **12** sensibleness **14** reasonableness **15** clearheadedness

San Jose
   capital of: **9** Costa Rica

San Juan
   capital of: **10** Puerto Rico

San Juan Bautista *see* **10** Puerto Rico

San Marino
   capital/largest city: **9** San Marino
   enclave in: **5** Italy
   others: **10** Serravalle **13** Borgo Maggiore
   division: **8** Castelli
   government:
      legislature: **22** Great and General Council
   monetary unit: **4** lira, lire **9** centesimi
   mountain: **9** Apennines
   highest point: **6** Titano
   people: **7** Italian **11** San Marinese
      founder: **7** Marinus
   language: **7** Italian
   religion: **13** Roman Catholic
   place: **13** Valloni Palace **17** Palazzo del Governo **19** Basilica of San Marino
   church: **5** Pieve **9** St Francis

San Salvador
   capital of: **10** El Salvador

sans doute 12 without doubt

Sansovino, Andrea
   real name: **14** Andrea Contucci
   born: **5** Italy **5** Monte San Savino
   artwork: **15** Baptism of Christ **20** Virgin Child and St Anne

Sansovino, Il
   real name: **11** Jacopo Tatti
   born: **5** Italy **7** Caprese
   artwork: **4** Mars **7** Bacchus, Logetta, Neptune **10** Old Library **15** Madonna del Parto **16** St John the Baptist

sans pareil 12 without equal

sans peur et sans reproche 29 without fear and without reproach

sans souci 8 carefree **11** without care

Santa Cruz de Tenerife
   capital of: **13** Canary Islands

Santayana, George
   author of: **14** The Last Puritan **16** The Realms of Being, The Sense of Beauty **24** Skepticism and Animal Faith

Santiago
   capital of: **5** Chile

Santiago
   character in: **18** The Old Man and the Sea
   author: **9** Hemingway

Santo Domingo
   capital of: **17** Dominican Republic

Santo Domingo *see* **5** Haiti

Sao Tome
   capital of: **18** Sao Tome and Principe

Sao Tome and Principe
   capital/largest city: **7** Sao Tome
   others: **8** Trindade **11** Porto Alegre **12** Santo Antonio
   monetary unit: **5** dobra **6** escudo **7** centavo
   highest point: **7** Sao Tome
   sea: **8** Atlantic
   physical feature:
      bay: **11** Ana de Chaves
      gulf: **6** Guinea
   people: **7** African **10** Portuguese **11** Cape Verdean
      explorer: **7** Escobar **8** Santarem
   language: **10** Portuguese
   religion: **7** animism **13** Roman Catholic **19** Seventh Day Adventist **21** Evangelical Protestant

sap 3 rob, tax **4** ruin, wear **5** bleed, drain **6** impair, reduce, weaken **7** afflict, cripple, deplete, destroy, disable, exhaust, subvert **8** enervate, enfeeble **9** devastate, undermine **10** debilitate, devitalize

sapient 4 wise **7** knowing **8** profound **9** sagacious **10** discerning, perceptive **11** intelligent **13** knowledgeable

sap one's energy 3 fag **4** bush, poop, tire **5** drain, weary **6** tucker, weaken **7** deplete, exhaust, fatigue, wash out **8** enervate, enfeeble **10** debilitate, devitalize

Sapphira
   husband: **7** Ananias
   lied to: **5** Peter

sapphire 3 gem **4** blue **5** azure, jewel **6** indigo
   species: **8** corundum
   source: **5** Burma, Mogul **6** Ceylon **7** Kashmir **8** Sri Lanka, Thailand **9** Australia
   kind: **4** star

Sappho
   author: **14** Alphonse Daudet

Sarah, Sarai
   father: **5** Asher
   former name: **5** Sarai
   husband: **7** Abraham
   son: **5** Isaac
   slave: **5** Hagar
   burial place: **9** Machpelah

sarcasm 3 rub **4** gibe, jeer, jest **5** irony, scorn, sneer, taunt **7** mockery **8** contempt, derision, ridicule, scoffing **13** disparagement

sarcastic 5 acerb **6** biting, bitter, ironic **7** caustic, cutting, mocking, mordant **8** derisive, piercing, sardonic, scornful, sneering, stinging, taunting **11** disparaging **12** contemptuous

sarcoma 5 tumor **6** cancer, growth **8** neoplasm **10** malignancy

sarcophagus 4 pall **6** coffin

sard
   species: **6** quartz

sardine 4 bang, cram, fish, lile, lour, pack **5** crowd **7** alewife, anchovy, herring **8** pilchard

Sardinia
   other name: **8** Sardegna
   capital: **8** Cagliari
   cities: **4** Bono, Bosa **5** Nuoro, Olbia **7** Alghero, Bonorva, Sassari, Thatari **8** Iglesias, Oristano **11** Porto Torres
   division: **5** Nuoro **7** Arborea, Gallura, Sassari **8** Cagliari, Logudoro
   government: **13** region of Italy
   monetary unit: **7** carline
   island: **7** Caprera **8** Tavolara **9** Maddalena
   lake: **6** Omodeo
   mountain: **4** Rasu **5** Ferry, Linas **7** Gallura, Limbara **8** Marghine, Serpeddi, Vittoria **11** Gennargentu
   river: **5** Mannu, Tirso **6** Lascia **8** Coghinas **10** Flumendosa
   sea: **13** Mediterranean
   physical feature:
      gulf: **6** Orosei, Palmas **7** Asinara **8** Cagliari, Oristano
      plain: **7** Sassari **9** Campidano
      strait: **9** Bonifacio
   people:
      king: **12** Charles Felix **13** Charles Albert **14** Victor Emmanuel
      leader: **6** Cavour
      ruler: **4** Pisa **5** Genoa, Spain **7** Austria, Vandals **9** Byzantium, Phoenicia **12** House of Savoy
   language: **7** Italian
   religion: **13** Roman Catholic
   feature:
      towers: **7** nuraghi
   food:
      cheese: **6** romano **8** pecorino

Sardius 8 gemstone

sardonic 6 biting **7** caustic, cynical, jeering, mocking, mordant, satiric **8** derisive, scornful, sneering, taunting **9** sarcastic **11** disparaging **12** contemptuous

sardonyx 8 gemstone

Sargent, John Singer
   born: **5** Italy **8** Florence
   artwork: **6** Madam X (Madame Gautreau) **7** El Jaleo **17** The Wyndham Sisters **20** Robert Louis Stevenson **21** Carnation Lily Lily Rose **22** Daughters of Edward D Boit **24** Oyster Gatherers of Cancale

Sargon
   captured: **5** Accad
   successor: **11** Sennacherib

Saroyan, William
   author of: **12** My Name Is Aram **14** The Human Comedy **17** The Time of Your Life **22** My Heart's in the Highlands

Sarton, May
   author of: **5** Anger **11** Kinds of Love

17 Plant Dreaming Deep **20** Faithful Are the Wounds **33** Mrs Stevens Hears the Mermaids Singing

Sartor Resartus
  author: **13** Thomas Carlyle

Sartre, Jean-Paul
  author of: **6** Nausea, No Exit **8** The Words **17** The Roads to Freedom **19** Being and Nothingness
  philosophy: **14** Existentialism
  quote: **17** Hell is other people

sash 3 tie **4** band, belt **5** frame, scarf, strip **6** casing, corset, girdle, ribbon, window **7** baldric **8** casement **9** doorframe, waistband **10** cummerbund **11** windowframe
  Japanese: **3** obi
  pulley weight: **5** mouse
  window: **5** chess

sashay 4 move, skip **5** glide, mince **6** chasse, travel

sashimi 7 raw fish **12** Japanese dish

Saskatchewan 5 river **8** province
  boundary: **7** Alberta, Montana **8** Manitoba **11** North Dakota **12** Old Northwest **20** Northwest Territories
  capital: **6** Regina
  city: **8** Moose Jaw **9** Saskatoon **12** Prince Albert, Swift Current
  country: **6** Canada
  Indian: **4** Cree **9** Chipewyan **10** Assiniboin
  lake: **8** Reindeer **9** Athabasca, Wollaston
  mountain: **7** Cypress, Pasquia **9** Porcupine **14** Missouri Coteau
  river: **9** Churchill, Frenchman
  river mouth: **12** Lake Winnipeg

Sassoon, Siegfried
  author of: **26** The Memoirs of a Fox-Hunting Man **26** The Memoirs of George Sherston **29** The Memoirs of an Infantry Officer

sassy 4 bark, bold, flip, rude, tree **5** brash, fresh, saucy **6** mouthy, snippy **7** forward **8** impolite, impudent, insolent **12** discourteous **13** disrespectful

Satan 6 Belial, Moloch **7** Lucifer, Old Nick **8** Apollyon, the Devil **9** Beelzebub **10** Old Scratch, the Evil One, the Tempter **11** fallen angel **12** the Foul Fiend **13** the Old Serpent **14** Mephistopheles **19** the Prince of Darkness

satanic 3 bad **4** evil, vile **5** cruel **6** wicked **7** demonic, heinous, hellish, inhuman, vicious **8** devilish, fiendish, infamous, infernal, sadistic **9** malicious, malignant **10** demoniacal, diabolical, malevolent

satchel, Satchel 3 bag **4** case, grip, sack **5** purse **6** valise **7** handbag **8** reticule, suitcase **9** carpetbag, Gladstone, schoolbag
  pitcher, Hall of Famer: **5** Paige

sate 4 cloy, fill, glut **5** gorge, stuff **7** surfeit

satellite 4 moon **5** crony, toady **6** menial, puppet, vassal **7** servant **8** disciple, follower, hanger-on, parasite, retainer **9** assistant, attendant, companion, sycophant, tributary, underling

satellite state 6 colony **8** dominion **10** possession **12** protectorate

satiate 4 bore, cloy, fill, glut, jade **5** slake, stuff, weary **6** overdo, quench, sicken **7** content, disgust, gratify, suffice, surfeit **8** nauseate, overfill, saturate

Satie, Erik
  born: **6** France **8** Honfleur
  composer of: **6** Parade **13** Pieces froides **16** The Three Gymnasts **19** Limp Preludes for a Dog **20** Pieces en forme de poire **23** Pieces in the Shape of a Pear

satiny 4 fine **5** shiny, silky **6** smooth

satire 5 irony **6** banter, parody, send up **7** lampoon, mockery, sarcasm, takeoff **8** acrimony, derision, raillery, ridicule, travesty **9** burlesque **10** caricature, persiflage

satirical 5 comic **6** biting, bitter **7** caustic, mocking, mordant **8** derisive, humorous, ironical, sardonic, scornful, sneering **9** malicious, sarcastic

satirize 4 mock **6** parody **7** lampoon **9** burlesque **10** caricature

satisfaction 5 pride **6** amends **7** comfort, content, damages, deserts, justice, payment, redress **8** pleasure, requital **9** answering, atonement, happiness, quittance, reckoning, repayment **10** correction, recompense, remittance, settlement **11** contentment, fulfillment, restitution **12** compensation, remuneration **13** gratification, rectification, reimbursement

satisfactory 2 OK **4** okay **8** adequate, all right, passable, suitable **9** competent **10** acceptable, sufficient

satisfied 5 happy **7** content, pleased **9** gratified **10** complacent **11** comfortable

satisfy 3 pay **4** fill, meet **5** annul, clear, remit, repay, serve, slake **6** answer, assure, pacify, pay off, please, quench, remove, settle **7** appease, content, delight, fulfill, gratify, mollify, requite, suffice **8** convince, persuade, reassure **9** discharge, reimburse **10** compensate, recompense

satisfying 8 pleasant, pleasing **9** agreeable, enjoyable, rewarding **10** delightful, fulfilling, gratifying **11** pleasurable

satori
  term in: **3** Zen
  means: **13** enlightenment

saturate 4 fill **5** cover, douse, imbue, souse **6** drench, infuse **7** immerse, pervade, suffuse **8** permeate, submerge **10** impregnate, infiltrate

saturated 3 wet **4** full **5** drunk, soggy, soppy **6** soaked, sodden **8** bursting

Saturday
  day of: **15** Biblical Sabbath
  French: **6** samedi
  from: **8** Saturnus
  German: **7** samstag
  heavenly body: **6** Saturn
  Italian: **6** sabato
  observance: **13** Jewish Sabbath **20** Seventh Day Adventists
  Spanish: **6** sabado

Saturday Night Fever
  director: **10** John Badham
  cast: **11** Barry Miller **12** John Travolta **15** Karen Lynn Gorney
  setting: **8** Brooklyn
  score: **7** Bee Gees
  sequel: **12** Staying Alive

Saturday Night Live, NBC's
  regular: **9** Mike Myers **10** Bill Murray, Chevy Chase, Dana Carvey, Dan Aykroyd, Jane Curtin **11** Eddie Murphy, Gilda Radner, John Belushi **13** Garrett Morris, Laraine Newman
  group: **27** Not Ready For Prime Time Players
  bits: **4** Bees **7** Samurai **9** Coneheads **10** Church Lady **13** Blues Brothers, Weekend Update **16** Pathological Liar **18** Rosanne Rosanna-Dana

Saturn
  origin: **5** Roman
  god of: **11** agriculture
  consort of: **3** Ops
  son: **5** Picus
  corresponds to: **6** Cronos, Cronus, Kronos

Saturn
  position: **5** sixth
  satellite: **4** Rhea **5** Dione, Janus, Mimas, Titan **6** Phoebe, Tethys **7** Iapetus **8** Hyperion **9** Enceladus
  characteristic: **5** rings

saturnalia, Saturnalia 4 orgy **5** revel, spree **7** carouse, debauch, revelry **8** carousal **9** bacchanal **10** debauchery
  origin: **5** Roman
  event: **8** festival
  honoring: **6** Saturn **13** sowing of crops

saturnine 4 dour, glum, grim **5** grave, staid, stern, sulky **6** gloomy, moping, morose, solemn, somber, sullen **7** austere, serious **8** dejected, downcast, reserved, sardonic, taciturn **9** apathetic, cheerless, withdrawn **11** downhearted **15** uncommunicative

satyr
  form: **4** faun **5** deity
  location: **8** woodland
  part: **3** man **4** goat
  attendant of: **7** Bacchus
  known for: **7** lechery

Satyricon
  author: **9** Petronius

character: 4 Gito **8** Ascyltus, Eumolpus **9** Encolpius **10** Trimalchio

sauce 3 dip **4** sass **5** booze, gravy, salsa **6** fillip, flavor **7** alcohol **8** dressing, pertness **9** condiment, flippancy **12** impertinence
  basil: 5 pesto
  fish: 4 alec
  hot: 7 Tabasco
  Indian: 5 curry
  salty: 3 soy

saucy 4 bold, pert, rude, trim **5** brash, cocky, fresh, natty, smart **6** brazen, cheeky, jaunty, lively, spruce **7** forward **8** flippant, impolite, impudent, insolent **9** audacious, barefaced, unabashed **11** impertinent, smart-alecky **12** discourteous **13** disrespectful

Saudi Arabia
  capital/largest city: 6 Riyadh
  others: 4 Abha, Hail, Taif **5** Hofuf, Hufuf, Jedda, Jidda, Yanbu, Yenbo **6** Anaiza, Dammam, Jiddah, Jubail **7** Alhofuf, Buraido, Dhahran **9** Ras Tanura
  holy city: 5 Mecca **6** Medina
  school: 5 Islam **13** King Abd al-Aziz **19** Imam Muhammad bin Saud **20** Petroleum and Minerals
  division: 4 Asir, Nejd **5** Hejaz **6** El Hasa
  government: 8 monarchy
  head of state/government: 4 king
  monetary unit: 5 girsh, gursh, pound, riyal
  weight: 3 oke
  mountain: 6 Tuwayq
  highlands: 4 Asir **5** Hejaz
  highest point: 5 Razih **10** Jebal Sawda
  sea: 3 Red
  physical features
    desert: 3 Red **5** Dahna, Nafud, Nefud, Nufud **6** al-Dahy, Dahana **10** Rub al Khali
    gulf: 5 Aqaba **7** Persian
    peninsula: 7 Arabian
    plain: 6 Tihama
    plateau: 4 Nejd
  people: 4 Arab **7** Bedouin
    king: 4 Fahd, Saud **6** Faisal, Khalid **7** Ibn Saud **9** Abdul Aziz
    religious leader: 8 Mohammed, Muhammad
  language: 6 Arabic
  religion: 5 Islam
    sect: 5 Sunni **6** Shiite **7** Wahhabi
  place:
    shrine: 5 Kaaba **10** Black Stone
  feature:
    annual pilgrimage: 4 hadj, hajj
    clothing: 3 aba **4** agal **5** thobe **6** ghutra
    kingdom: 5 Hejaz **7** Minaean, Ottoman, Sabaean **9** Himyarite
    laws of Islam: 6 sharia
    village school: 6 kuttab

war: 4 Gulf **11** Desert Storm **12** Desert Shield

Sauguet, Henri
  born: 6 France **8** Bordeaux
  composer of: 6 La Nuit **10** Les Forains, Les Mirages

Sauk, Sac
  family: 9 Algonkian **10** Algonquian
  tribe: 3 Fox, Sac **8** Kickapoo
  location: 4 Iowa, Ohio **6** Kansas **7** Indiana **8** Illinois, Michigan, Oklahoma **9** Wisconsin
  leader: 9 Blackhawk
  related to: 8 Kickapoo **9** Mesquakie **11** Potawatomie
  involved in: 12 Black Hawk War

Saul
  king of: 4 Edom **6** Israel
  father: 4 Kish
  daughter: 5 Merab **6** Michal
  son: 7 Abinoam **8** Jonathan **10** Ishbosheth
  anointed by: 6 Samuel
  hometown: 6 Gibeah **8** Rehoboth
  successor: 5 David

Saunders, Allen
  creator/artist of: 9 Mary Worth

saunter 4 roam **5** amble, mosey, stray **6** loiter, ramble, stroll, wander **7** meander, traipse **8** straggle **9** promenade

sausage 5 frank, gigot, wurst **6** hotdog, salami, weenie, wiener **7** baloney, bologna **8** kielbasa **9** bratwurst, pepperoni **10** liverwurst **11** frankfurter
  British: 6 banger

sauve qui peut 4 rout **8** stampede **18** every man for himself **23** let him save himself who can

savage 4 boor, wild **5** brute, cruel, feral, fiend, harsh, rough, yahoo **6** animal, bloody, brutal, fierce, maniac, native, rugged, unkind **7** brutish, hoodlum, ruffian, untamed, violent **8** barbaric, hooligan, pitiless, ruthless, sadistic **9** aborigine, barbarian, barbarous, ferocious, merciless, murderous, primitive **10** aboriginal, heathenish, relentless, uncultured, unmerciful **11** uncivilized **12** uncultivated **14** undomesticated

savagery 7 cruelty **8** ferocity **9** barbarism, barbarity, brutality **10** fierceness, inhumanity **12** pitilessness, ruthlessness

savanna, savannah 5 campo, plain **9** grassland

savant 6 genius **7** scholar **13** learned person

save 3 but **4** bank, free, help, hold, keep **5** amass, guard, hoard, lay by, lay up, put by, spare, stock, store **6** defend, except, garner, heap up, redeem, rescue, shield **7** deliver, deposit, husband, protect, put away, recover, reserve, salvage **8** conserve,

preserve, retrench, withhold **9** economize, safeguard **10** accumulate

save up 5 amass, hoard **7** collect, put away **8** salt away, sock away **10** accumulate **12** squirrel away

saving 5 close, tight **6** frugal, stingy **7** careful, miserly, prudent, sparing, thrifty **8** markdown, stinting **9** illiberal, niggardly, provident, redeeming, restoring **10** economical, reclaiming, redemptory, reparative **12** compensating, conservative

savings 3 IRA **5** hoard **7** nest egg, reserve

savior 5 freer **7** rescuer **8** champion, defender, guardian, redeemer **9** deliverer, liberator, preserver, protecter, protector, salvation **11** emancipator

Savior 5 Jesus **6** Christ **8** Redeemer **10** the Messiah **11** Jesus Christ, the Son of God **13** Prince of Peace

Savior anointed 5 Jesus

savoir-faire 4 tact **5** poise **6** aplomb, polish **7** finesse, know-how, suavity **8** presence, urbanity **9** assurance, composure **10** adroitness, discretion, smoothness **11** worldliness **12** complaisance, graciousness **14** self-possession

savoir-vivre 16 knowing how to live **19** knowledge of the world

savor 3 try **4** aura, gist, like, odor, soul, tang, zest **5** aroma, enjoy, scent, smack, smell, spice, taste, trait **6** flavor, nature, relish, sample, season, spirit **7** essence, quality **8** piquancy, property, pungency **9** character, fragrance, substance **10** appreciate, experience **11** peculiarity **13** particularity **14** characteristic

savory 5 tangy, tasty, yummy **6** honest **7** odorous, piquant, pungent **8** alluring, aromatic, charming, edifying, fragrant, luscious, tasteful **9** delicious, flavorous, palatable, reputable, toothsome **10** appetizing, attractive, delectable **11** inoffensive, respectable, scrumptious **13** mouth-watering

savory
  botanical name: 8 Satureia, S montana **10** S hortensis
  origin: 13 Mediterranean
  varieties: 6 summer, winter
  use: 4 eggs, meat **5** beans, salad **6** sauces **8** dressing **11** chicken soup

savvy 5 catch, get it **7** know-how **10** comprehend, understand **13** understanding

saw 3 cut **4** tool **5** adage, maxim, slash **6** saying **7** proverb **8** aphorism
  type: 3 jig, rip **4** back, band, hack **5** miter **6** coping **7** keyhole **8** circular, crosscut

sawfly
  varieties: 4 stem, wood **5** cedar **6** pergid **7** conifer **8** horntail **11** web spinning

saxophone
　type: **4** alto **5** tenor
say 2 do **4** hint, hold, read, tell, vote, word **5** bruit, claim, guess, imply, judge, mouth, rumor, speak, state, utter, voice **6** allege, assert, assume, chance, convey, phrase, reason, recite, remark, render, repeat, report, reveal, spread **7** comment, contend, declare, deliver, divulge, express, imagine, mention, perform, suggest, suppose, surmise **8** announce, disclose, intimate, maintain, rehearse, vocalize **9** circulate, franchise, insinuate, pronounce, verbalize **10** articulate, conjecture **11** communicate

Sayers, Dorothy L
　author of: **9** Whose Body **12** Strong Poison **14** Have His Carcase, The Nine Tailors, Unnatural Death **15** Clouds of Witness, Five Red Herrings **16** Busman's Honeymoon **19** Murder Must Advertise **30** Unpleasantness at the Bellona Club
　character: **6** Bunter **11** Harriet Vane **15** Lord Peter Wimsey

Say Hey Kid
　nickname of: **10** Willie Mays

saying 3 saw **5** adage, maxim, moral, motto **6** byword, dictum, truism **7** epigram, precept, proverb **8** aphorism, apothegm **10** expression

Sayonara
　director: **11** Joshua Logan
　author: **13** James Michener
　cast: **9** Miiko Taka **10** Red Buttons **11** James Garner, Martha Scott **12** Marlon Brando, Miyoshi Umeki **16** Ricardo Montalban
　score: **12** Irving Berlin
　Oscar for: **15** supporting actor (Buttons) **17** supporting actress (Umeki)

scabrous 5 dirty, rough, scaly **7** immoral, leprous **8** indecent, off-color **9** salacious **10** suggestive **12** pornographic

scalding 3 hot **5** harsh **7** boiling, caustic **8** seething, steaming **9** sarcastic

scale, scales 3 key, set **4** chip, film, husk, peel, rise, rule, skin **5** crust, flake, layer, mount, order, plate, range, ratio, scour, shave, shell, weigh **6** adjust, ascend, goupen, ladder, lamina, octave, rub off, scrape, series, spread **7** balance, chip off, clamber, climb up, coating, lamella, measure **8** escalade, membrane, register, regulate, spectrum, surmount **9** continuum, gradation, solfeggio **10** delaminate, graduation, proportion **11** calibration, progression **14** classification

scale down 4 trim **6** reduce **7** abridge, curtail, shorten **8** compress, condense, decrease, diminish, downsize, moderate **10** abbreviate

scale insects

varieties: 3 lac, pit, wax **5** giant **6** ensign **7** armored **8** mealybug, tortoise **12** ground pearls

scale note 2 do, fa, la, mi, re, so, ti **3** sol

Guido's: 3 ela

scamp 3 imp, rip **5** cut-up, knave, rogue, tease **6** rascal, rotter **7** bounder, villain **8** blighter, scalawag **9** miscreant, prankster, scoundrel **10** scapegrace **11** rapscallion **13** mischief-maker

scamper 3 fly, run, zip **4** dart, dash, flit, race, romp, rush, scud **5** frisk, hurry, scoot **6** frolic, gambol, hasten, scurry, sprint **7** scuttle **9** skedaddle **21** running about playfully

scan 4 skim **5** check, probe, scour, study, sweep **6** peruse, search, size up, survey **7** analyze, examine, explore, inspect **10** scrutinize

scandal 4 blot **5** abuse, libel, odium, shame, stain **6** expose, smirch, stigma **7** calumny, obloquy, outrage, slander **8** disgrace, dishonor, ignominy **9** aspersion, discredit, disesteem, sensation **10** debasement, detraction, opprobrium, revilement **12** vituperation **13** disparagement, embarrassment

scandalize 5 shock **6** appall, defame, insult, offend **7** horrify, outrage **10** calumniate

scandalmonger 6 gossip **8** busybody **10** talebearer, tattletale

scandalous 8 libelous, shameful, shocking **9** gossiping, offensive **10** defamatory, outrageous, scurrilous, slanderous **11** disgraceful **12** disreputable **13** reprehensible

Scandinavia 6 Norway, Sweden **7** Denmark, Faeroes, Iceland

Scandinavian (Norse)
　language family: **12** Indo-European
　branch: **8** Germanic
　group: **15** Western Germanic
　language: **6** Danish **7** Faroese, Swedish **9** Icelandic, Norwegian

scant 3 cut **4** bare **5** limit, short, small, stint **6** in need, meager, paltry, reduce, sparse **7** limited **8** exiguous, hold back **9** deficient **10** inadequate, incomplete **12** insufficient

scantiness 10 deficiency, inadequacy, meagerness, skimpiness **13** insufficiency

scanty 4 thin **5** short, small **6** meager, modest, paltry, skimpy, sparse **7** slender, stunted **9** deficient **10** inadequate, undersized **12** insufficient

scapegoat, Scapegoat 4 butt, dupe, gull **5** patsy **6** Azazel, victim **7** fall guy **11** whipping boy **13** laughingstock

scapolite
　source: **5** Burma, Mogok

scapula
　bone of: **13** shoulder blade

scar 3 cut, pit **4** dent, flaw, gash, hurt, mark, pock, seam **5** brand, wound **6** affect, bruise, damage, deface, defect, impair, mangle **7** blemish, scratch **8** cicatrix, lacerate, mutilate **9** disfigure, influence

Scaramouch(e) 6 coward, rascal **8** braggart, poltroon

scarce 4 rare **6** scanty, sparse **7** unusual, wanting **8** uncommon **9** deficient

scarcely 4 just **6** at most, barely, hardly **7** but just, faintly **8** slightly

scarcity 4 lack, want **5** stint **6** dearth, rarity **7** fewness, paucity **8** rareness, shortage, sparsity, thinness **10** deficiency, scantiness, sparseness **12** uncommonness **13** insufficiency

scare 4 turn **5** alarm, daunt, panic, shake, shock, start **6** harrow, shiver **7** horrify, jitters, startle, terrify **8** disquiet, frighten **9** terrorize **10** disconcert, dishearten, intimidate **11** nervousness, palpitation **13** consternation

scarecrow 6 effigy **8** straw man

Scarecrow
　character in: **13** The Wizard of Oz
　author: **4** Baum

scared 5 shaky, timid, upset **6** afraid **7** alarmed, fearful, nervous, spooked **8** startled, timorous **9** diffident, terrified, tremulous **10** frightened **12** apprehensive, fainthearted **13** panic-stricken

scarf 3 boa **4** sash, veil, wrap **5** ascot, shawl, stole **6** choker, cravat, tippet **7** foulard, muffler, overlay **8** babushka, bandanna, mantilla **11** neckerchief

Scarface
　director: **11** Howard Hawks
　cast: **8** Paul Muni **9** Ann Dvorak **10** George Raft **12** Boris Karloff

scarify 3 cut **6** incise, loosen **7** break up, scratch **8** lacerate **9** cultivate

Scarlatti, Alessandro
　born: **6** Sicily **7** Palermo
　composer of: **11** Stabat Mater **17** Mitridate Eupatore, The Triumph of Honor **18** Il Trionfo dell Onore **23** Gli equivoci nel sembiante

Scarlatti, Domenico
　born: **5** Italy **6** Naples
　composer of: **7** Sonatas **9** Cat's Fugue, Essercizi **18** Le Donne di Buon Umore **20** The Good-Humored Ladies **23** Ottavia risituita al trono

scarlet 3 red **6** cherry, claret **7** carmine **8** cardinal

Scarlet Letter, The
　author: **18** Nathaniel Hawthorne
　character: **5** Pearl **12** Hester Prynne **16** Arthur Dimmesdale **18** Roger Chillingworth

Scarlett see Gone With the Wind

scary 3 bad **5** awful, hairy **6** creepy **7**

fearful 8 alarming, menacing, shocking **9** difficult **10** disturbing, terrifying **11** frightening, goosepimply, hair-raising, threatening **12** discomfiting

scat 3 off, out **4** away, shoo **5** be off, leave, scram **6** beat it, be gone, depart, get out, go away **7** get lost, vamoose

scathing 4 keen, tart **5** sharp **6** biting, brutal, savage **7** caustic, cutting, hostile, mordant, pointed, searing **8** incisive, stinging, virulent **9** ferocious, rancorous, scorching, trenchant, vitriolic, withering **10** lacerating **11** acrimonious, excoriating

scatter 3 sow **4** cast, flee, rout **5** strew, throw **6** dispel **8** disperse, sprinkle **9** broadcast, circulate, dissipate **10** distribute **11** disseminate

scatterbrained 4 rash, wild, zany **5** crazy, dizzy, giddy, nutty, silly **6** madcap, stupid **7** flighty, foolish **8** careless, heedless, reckless, unstable, unsteady **9** foolhardy, forgetful, frivolous, imprudent **11** birdbrained, empty-headed, harebrained **12** absent-minded, muddleheaded **13** irresponsible

scattered 6 random, spotty **7** diffuse **9** irregular **10** infrequent, occasional

scattering 6 sowing **7** casting **8** strewing **9** dispersal **10** dispersing, sprinkling **12** broadcasting, distribution **13** dissemination

scavenger 5 hyena **6** magpie **7** vulture **8** salvager **9** collector

scenario 4 book, idea, plan **6** scheme **7** concept, outline, summary **8** abstract, game plan, synopsis, teleplay **10** conception, manuscript, screenplay **French: 6** precis

scene 3 act **4** fuss, part, show, site, spot, to-do, view **5** place, sight, vista **6** locale, region, survey, vision **7** display, episode, picture, scenery, setting **8** backdrop, division, locality, location, panorama, position, prospect, sequence **9** commotion, spectacle **10** background **11** whereabouts

scenery 4 sets, view **5** vista **7** terrain **9** backdrops, landscape, spectacle **11** backgrounds

Scenes from a Marriage
director: **13** Ingmar Bergman
cast: **10** Liv Ullmann **13** Bibi Andersson **15** Erland Josephson

scent 4 odor, path, wake, wind **5** aroma, smell, sniff, spoor, trace, track, trail **6** course, detect, inhale **7** bouquet, breathe, discern, essence, perfume, pursuit, suspect **9** aromatize, fragrance, get wind of, recognize **11** distinguish

scented 5 spicy **7** odorous, piquant, pungent **8** aromatic, fragrant, perfumed **9** odiferous **13** sweet-smelling

Schaffner, Franklin
director of: **6** Patton (Oscar) **15** Planet of the Apes

schedule 3 fix **4** book, list, plan, roll **5** fit in, slate, table **6** agenda **7** appoint, program, put down, set down **8** calendar **9** inventory, timetable

Scheele, Karl Wilhelm
field: **9** chemistry
nationality: **7** Swedish
discovered: **6** oxygen **8** chlorine **9** glycerine

Scheider, Roy
born: **8** Orange NJ
roles: **4** Jaws **11** All That Jazz, Blue Thunder, The Seven-Ups **14** Fifty-two Pickup **19** The French Connection

Schell, Maria
real name: **15** Margarete Schell
born: **6** Vienna **7** Austria
brother: **16** Maximilian Schell
roles: **8** Cimarron, Gervaise **11** End of Desire, White Nights **13** The Last Bridge **20** The Brothers Karamazov

Schell, Maximilian
born: **6** Vienna **7** Austria
sister: **11** Maria Schell
roles: **5** Julia **13** The Young Lions **19** Judgment at Nuremberg (Oscar) **21** The Man in the Glass Booth

scheme 3 map, way **4** plan, plot, ruse **5** cabal, chart, frame, means, shift, study **6** course, design, device, devise, layout, method, policy, sketch, system **7** complot, concoct, connive, drawing, network, outline, program, project, tactics **8** conspire, contrive, grouping, intrigue, maneuver, organize, strategy **9** machinate, procedure, stratagem **10** connivance, conspiracy **11** arrangement, contrivance, delineation, disposition, machination **12** organization

scheming 3 sly **4** arch, wily **6** artful, crafty, shrewd, tricky **7** cunning **8** slippery **9** conniving, designing, insidious **10** contriving, intriguing **11** calculating **13** Machiavellian

Schiller, (Johann) Friedrich von
author of: **8** Ode to Joy **9** Don Carlos **11** Maria Stuart, William Tell **17** The Bride of Messina **18** The Maiden of Orleans

schism 5 break, split **8** division **10** separation **14** disassociation

Schlegel family
characters in: **10** Howards End
members: **5** Helen **8** Margaret, Theobald
author: **7** Forster

schlepp 3 lug **4** cart, haul, tote **5** carry **6** convey **9** transport

Schlesinger, Arthur M, Jr
author of: **13** A Thousand Days **15** The Age of Jackson **21** The Imperial Presidency **24** Robert Kennedy and His Times

Schlesinger, John

director of: 7 Darling **14** Midnight Cowboy (Oscar) **22** The Falcon and the Snowman

Schlesinger, Leon
creator/artist of: **9** Bugs Bunny

schmaltz 4 corn **14** sentimentalism, sentimentality

Schmeling, Max (Maxmillian Adolph Otto Siegfried)
nickname: **10** Black Uhlan
sport: **6** boxing
class: **11** heavyweight

Schneider, Romy
real name: **20** Rosemarie Albach-Retty
born: **6** Vienna **7** Austria
roles: **8** The Trial **11** The Cardinal **16** Boccaccio Seventy

Schoenberg, Arnold
born: **6** Vienna **7** Austria
composer of: **9** Erwartung **11** De Profundis, Expectation, Gurrelieder **12** The Lucky Hand **13** Moses and Aaron, Ode to Napoleon **14** Verklarte Nacht **16** Die Glucklich Hand, Resplendent Night **17** Transfigured Night **19** A Survivor from Warsaw, Pelleas and Melisande **26** The Book of the Hanging Gardens

Schoenius
father: **7** Athamas
mother: **8** Themisto
wife: **7** Clymene
daughter: **8** Atalanta

scholar 4 coed, sage **5** brain, grind, pupil **6** pundit, savant **7** egghead, learner, student, studier, wise man **8** bookworm, humanist, mandarin **9** collegian, schoolboy **10** schoolgirl **11** matriculant **12** intellectual **13** undergraduate

scholarly 6 humane **7** erudite, learned, liberal **8** academic, educated, informed, lettered, literate, well-read **12** intellectual

scholarship 5 grant **7** stipend **8** learning **9** education, endowment, erudition **12** intelligence, thoroughness **13** enlightenment

scholastic 8 academic, pedantic **9** pedagogic **11** educational **12** professorial **13** instructional

school 3 ism **4** view **5** bunch, crowd, faith, order, style, teach, train **6** belief, lyceum, method, system, theory **7** academy, college, educate, faction, thought **8** doctrine, instruct, seminary **9** institute **10** persuasion, university **12** denomination, kindergarten

schoolbook 3 abc **4** text **5** atlas **6** manual, primer, reader **7** grammar, lessons, speller

School for Scandal, The
author: **23** Richard Brinsley Sheridan
character: **5** Maria **6** Rowley **10** Lady Teazle **13** Joseph Surface, Lady

Sneerwell **14** Charles Surface, Sir Peter Teazle **16** Sir Oliver Surface

School for Wives, The
  author: 7 Moliere
  character: 5 Agnes **6** Horace, Oronte **7** Enrique **8** Arnolphe **9** Chrysalde

schooling 5 drill **8** drilling, training **9** education **11** instruction, preparation **14** indoctrination

schoolmaster 4 head **5** tutor **7** dominie, pedagog, scholar, teacher **9** pedagogue, principal, professor **10** headmaster, instructor **12** disciplinarian
  fish: 7 snapper
  genus: 8 Lutianus
  species: 6 apodus

Schubert, Franz Peter
  born: 6 Vienna **7** Austria
  composer of: 6 Little (symphony), Tragic (symphony No 4) **8** Sad Waltz **9** Rosamunde **11** Winterreise **12** Trout Quintet **13** Mourning Waltz **17** Die Schone Mullerin **18** Unfinished Symphony (No 8) **24** Death and the Maiden Quartet, Symphony of Heavenly Length

Schulz, Charles
  creator/artist of: 7 Peanuts

Schuman, William
  born: 9 New York NY
  composer of: 8 Undertow **9** Credendum **14** The Mighty Casey **16** American Festival **18** New England Triptych

Schumann, Robert Alexander
  born: 7 Germany, Zwickau
  composer of: 6 Myrten, Spring (symphony No 1) **7** Rhenish (symphony No 3) **8** Arabeske, Carnival **9** Papillons **10** Novelettes **11** Blumenstuck, Butterflies, Nachtstucke, Nightpieces, Novelletten **12** Bunte Blatter, Dichterliebe, Flower Pieces, Kinderscenen, Kreisleriana, Motley Leaves **14** Fantasiestucke **16** David's Band Dances, Symphonic Studies **18** Davidsbundlertanze **19** Frauenliebe und Leben

Schwann, Theodor
  field: 7 biology
  nationality: 6 German
  established: 10 cell theory

Schwarzenegger, Arnold
  roles: 5 Twins **7** Red Heat **8** Commando, Predator, Red Sonja, True Lies **11** Total Recall **13** The Terminator **15** Kindergarten Cop **17** Conan the Barbarian, Conan the Destroyer
  wife: 12 Maria Shriver

Schweitzer, Albert
  field: 8 medicine
  worked in: 5 Gabon **6** Africa
  founded: 17 Lambarene Hospital
  awarded: 15 Nobel Peace Prize

Schwitters, Kurt
  born: 7 Germany **8** Hannover

  artwork: 7 Merzbau
  collages called: 10 Merzbilden

science 3 art **5** skill **6** method **7** finesse **8** aptitude, facility **9** technique **10** discipline **11** acquirement
  god of: 7 Mercury

scintilla 3 dot, jot **4** atom, iota **5** shred, spark, speck, trace **7** glimmer **10** smithereen

scintillate 4 joke, snap **5** amuse, charm, flash, gleam, glint, shine, spark **7** glimmer, glisten, glitter, shimmer, sparkle, twinkle **9** coruscate **10** effervesce

scintillating 5 witty **6** bright, lively **8** animated, charming, dazzling **9** brilliant, ebullient, exuberant, sparkling **10** glittering **11** stimulating **12** effervescent

scion 3 son **4** heir, seed **5** child, issue **7** heiress, progeny **8** daughter, offshoot **9** offspring, posterity, successor **10** descendant **11** progeniture

scissors 5 snips **6** blades, cutter, shears **7** clipper, snipper, trimmer
  French: 8 secateur

scoff 4 jeer, mock, razz **5** flout, knock, taunt **6** deride, rail at, revile **7** condemn, laugh at, put down, run down **8** belittle, ridicule

Scofield, Paul
  real name: 13 David Scofield
  born: 7 England **14** Hurstpierpoint
  roles: 8 King Lear **13** Sir Thomas More **17** A Man for All Seasons (Oscar)

scold 3 nag **5** chide, shrew **6** berate, carp at, nagger, rail at, rebuke, virago **7** censure, reprove, upbraid **9** castigate, criticize, dress down, reprehend, reprimand, termagant **10** complainer
  Yiddish: 6 kvetch

scolding 7 chiding, reproof **8** berating, rebuking **9** reprimand, talking-to **10** admonition, upbraiding **11** castigation **12** admonishment **13** tongue-lashing

sconce 7 bracket **11** candlestick **12** candleholder

scoop 4 bail, beat **5** clean, clear, gouge, ladle, spoon **6** burrow, dig out, dipper, hollow, shovel, trowel **7** dish out, lade out, lift out **8** excavate

scoop out 3 dig **5** gouge **8** excavate

scoot 3 run **4** dash, rush **6** scurry, sprint

Scooter
  nickname of: 11 Phil Rizzuto

scope 3 aim **4** area, goal, rein, room, span, vent **5** field, force, grasp, range, reach **6** bounds, effect, margin, motive, spread, vision **7** bearing, compass, freedom, liberty, purpose, stretch **8** ambition, confines, latitude **9** extension, influence, intention **10** competence **11** application, destination **13** determination

scorch 3 dry **4** char, sear **5** parch, singe **6** dry out, scathe, wither **7** blacken **8** discolor **9** dehydrate

score, scores 3 cut, mar, run, tab, win **4** bill, debt, gain, gash, goal, lots, make, mark, nick, slit **5** amass, count, facts, grade, hosts, judge, notch, point, slash, tally, truth **6** basket, charge, damage, deface, droves, groove, grudge, masses, pile up, strike, swarms, twenty **7** account, achieve, arrange, legions, reality, scratch, throngs **8** evaluate, incision, register **9** grievance **10** amount owed, difference, multitudes, obligation **11** orchestrate

scoria 4 slag **5** dross **6** cinder, refuse

scorn 5 spurn **6** ignore, rebuff, refuse, reject, slight **7** condemn, despise, disdain, mockery, repulse, sarcasm **8** contempt, derision, ridicule, scoffing, spit upon **9** arrogance, contumely, disregard, ostracize **10** look down on, opprobrium **11** haughtiness

scorned 7 derided, refused **8** despised, rebuffed, rejected, repulsed **9** disdained **10** deprecated, disparaged

scornful 6 lordly **7** cynical **8** arrogant, derisive, insolent, sardonic, scoffing, sneering **9** sarcastic **10** disdainful, ridiculing **11** disparaging **12** contemptuous, supercilious

Scorpio, Scorpius
  symbol: 8 scorpion
  planet: 4 Mars **5** Pluto
  rules: 5 death **7** passion
  born: 7 October **8** November

Scorpion 4 whip **7** scourge
  constellation of: 8 Scorpius

Scorsese, Martin
  director of: 6 Casino, Kundun **8** Cape Fear **9** Good Fellas **10** After Hours, Raging Bull, Taxi Driver **11** Mean Streets **12** The Last Waltz **14** Mad Dog and Glory **25** The Last Temptation of Christ

scotch 4 foil, kill, stop **5** crush, quash **6** thwart **7** destroy **8** confound, obstruct, sabotage, suppress **9** undermine **11** nip in the bud

scotch
  type: 6 whisky **7** whiskey **10** single-malt
  origin: 8 Scotland
  ingredient: 12 cereal grains
  drink: 10 Scotch Mist **14** Highland Cooler
  with amaretto: 9 Godfather
  with cherry brandy: 12 Blood and Sand
  with Drambuie: 9 Rusty Nail
  with gin: 12 Barbary Coast
  with vermouth: 6 Rob Roy **8** Affinity **10** Bobby Burns
  brands: 5 J and B **7** Dewars **10** White Horse **11** Chivas Regal, Wild Grouse **12** Johnny Walker

Scotia
  poetic: **8** Scotland
Scotland
  Roman name: **9** Caledonia
  capital: **9** Edinburgh
  symbol: **7** thistle
  poetic: **6** Scotia
  largest city: **7** Glasgow
    others: **3** Ayr **4** Duns, Oban **5** Alloa, Banff, Brora, Burgh, Cupar, Ellon, Leith, Perth, Salen, Troon **6** Dundee, Girvan, Hawick **7** Airdrie, Alloway, Dunkeld, Falkirk, Frunock, Mallaig, Paisley, Renfrew **8** Aberdeen, Dumfries, Greenock, Hamilton, Kirkwall, Rothesay, Stirling **9** Clydebank, Dumbarton, Greenlock, Inverness, Kirkcaldy, Peter head, St Andrews **10** Coatbridge, Kilmarnock, Motherwell **11** Dunfermline, Grangemouth
    school: **7** Glasgow **8** Aberdeen **9** Edinburgh **12** Saint Andrew's
    division: **3** Ayr **4** Bute, Fife, Ross **5** Angus, Banff, Moray, Nairn, Perth **6** Argyll, Lanark, Orkney **7** Berwick, Kinross, Lothian, Peebles, Renfrew, Selkirk, Wigtown **8** Aberdeen, Ayrshire, Cromarty, Dumfries, Roxburgh, Shetland, Stirling **9** Buteshire, Caithness, Dumbarton **10** Kincardine, Midlothian, Sutherland **11** Clackmannan, Kincudbight **12** Renfrewshire **13** Stirlingshire
      kingdom: **8** Dalriada **11** Northumbria, Strathclyde
    government: **13** United Kingdom
    measure: **3** cop **4** boll, cran, fall, mile, peck, pint, rood, rope, span **5** crane, lippy **6** audlet, davach, firlot, lippie, noggin **7** chalder, choppin **8** mutchkin, stimpart, stimpert **9** particate, shaftment, shathmont
    monetary unit: **3** ecu **4** demy, dolt, lion, mark, rial, ryal **5** bodle, broad, groat, plack, rider, turne **6** bawbee, folles **7** unicorn **8** atchison, hardhead **9** halfpenny **11** bonnetpiece
    weight: **4** boll, drop **5** trone **6** bushel
    island: **3** Rum **4** Aran, Bute, Eigg, Fair, Inch, Iona, Jura, Lona, Muck, Mull, Rhum, Skye **5** Arran, Barra, Islay, Lewis **6** Harris, Orkney, Staffa **7** St Kilda **8** Berneray, Cumbraes, Hebrides, Shetland **9** North Uist, South Uist
    lake/loch: **3** Awe, Dee, Lin, Tay **4** Earn, Fyne, Gair, Gare, Linn, Ness, Oich, Ryan, Sloy **5** Duich, Leven, Lochy, Lough, Morar, Maree, Nevis **6** Laggan, Linnhe, Lomond **7** Katrine, Rannoch, St Mary's
    mountain: **4** Hope **5** Attow, Dearg, Nevis, Tinto, Wyvis **7** Cheviot, Macdhui, Merrick **8** Grampian **9** Ben Lomond, Cairngorm, Highlands, Trossachs
      hills: **5** Ochil **6** Calton, Sidlaw **7** Cheviot
    highest point: **8** Ben Nevis
    river: **3** Ayr, Dee, Don, Esk, Tay **4** Doon, Glen, Nith, Norn, Spey **5** Afton, Annan, Clyde, Forth, Garry, North, Tweed, Ythan **6** Affric, Teviot, Tummel **7** Deveron **8** Findhorn
    sea: **5** Irish, North **8** Atlantic, Hebrides
    physical feature:
      bay: **5** Scapa
      canal: **10** Caledonian
      channel: **5** Minch, North
      firth: **3** Tay **4** Kyle, Lorn **5** Clyde, Forth, Lorne, Moray **6** Linnhe, Solway **7** Comarty, Dornoch **8** Pentland
      glen: **8** Glen More **9** Great Glen
      hillside: **4** brae
      moor: **7** Rannoch
      valley: **8** Trossach
    people: **4** Gael, Pict, Scot **5** Norse
      artist: **7** Raeburn
      author: **5** Burns, Scott **6** Barrie, Cronin, Dunbar **7** Barbour, Douglas **8** Henryson **9** Stevenson **10** Conan-Doyle, MacDiarmid, Macpherson
      economist: **5** Smith
      historian: **7** Carlyle
      inventor: **4** Bell
      king: **5** David, James **6** Duncan **7** Kenneth, Macbeth, Malcolm, Stuarts, William **9** Alexander **14** Robert the Bruce
      landowner: **5** laird
      philosopher: **4** Hume
      prime minister: **9** Macdonald, MacMillan **11** Douglas-Home
      prince: **19** Bonnie Prince Charlie
      queen: **4** Mary **13** Saint Margaret
      religious leader: **8** John Knox
      scientist: **7** Fleming
      patronymic: **3** Mac
      patron saint: **6** Andrew
    language: **4** Erse **6** Celtic, Gaelic, Keltic, Lallan **7** English, Lalland
    religion: **12** Episcopalian, Presbyterian **13** Roman Catholic
    place:
      abbey: **5** Kelso **7** Melrose **8** Dryburgh, Jedburgh
      castle: **8** Stirling **9** Edinburgh **11** Eilean Donan
      church/kirk: **7** St Giles **11** St Cuthbert's
      coronation site: **12** Stone of Scone
      royal residence: **8** Balmoral
      Scott's home: **10** Abbotsford
      street: **7** Prince's **9** Royal Mile **11** Sauchiehall
    feature:
      bird: **3** bae, cae **4** hern, muir, smeu **6** grouse, smeuth, snabby **7** jackdaw **8** throstle **9** swinepipe
      clothing: **3** tam **4** kilt **6** tartan **7** filibeg **12** Harris tweeds **13**

Shetland knits **15** Fair Isle sweater
      dance: **3** bob **4** reel **7** walloch **9** ecossaise **10** petronella **11** strathsprey **12** gilliecallum **13** Highland fling
      game: **4** golf **12** caber tossing
      holiday: **8** Hogmanay
      monster: **6** Nessie **8** Loch Ness
      musical instrument: **7** bagpipe
      symbol: **7** thistle
    food:
      bread: **5** scone
      cheese: **7** crowdie
      dish: **6** haggis **12** finnan haddie **15** kippered herring
      drink: **12** Scotch whisky
      soup: **11** cock-a-leekie
    football team: **6** Oilers
Scott, George C
  born: **6** Wise VA
  wife: **14** Trish Van Devere **15** Colleen Dewhurst
  roles: **4** Rage **6** Patton (Oscar, refused) **8** Jane Eyre **16** The New Centurions **18** The Day of the Dolphin
Scott, Sir Walter
  author of: **6** Rob Roy **7** Ivanhoe, Marmion **8** The Abbot, Waverley **10** Kenilworth **11** The Talisman **12** Guy Mannering, Old Mortality, The Antiquary **14** Quentin Durward **16** The Lady of the Lake **20** The Bride of Lammermoor, The Heart of Midlothian **23** The Lay of the Last Minstrel
Scottish Mythology
  spirit/horse: **6** kelpie
scoundrel 3 cad, cur **5** crook, knave, rogue, scamp, thief **6** rascal, rotter, varlet, weasel **7** bounder, ruffian, sharper, varmint, villain **8** scalawag, swindler, turncoat **9** miscreant, trickster **10** blackguard, copperhead, mountebank, ne'er-do-well **11** fourflusher, rapscallion **12** carpetbagger
scoundrelly 3 low **4** mean **7** debased **8** rascally **10** degenerate, despicable, villainous **12** contemptible, disreputable **13** reprehensible
Scoundrel Time
  author: **14** Lillian Hellman
scour 4 buff, comb, rake, scan **5** scrub, shine **6** abrade, polish, scrape **7** burnish, cleanse, ransack, rummage **8** brighten, traverse
scourge 3 rod **4** bane, beat, cane, flog, lash, whip **5** birch, blast, curse, flail, strap **6** punish, switch, terror, thrash **7** censure, chasten **8** chastise, scorpion, vexation **9** castigate, excoriate **10** affliction, discipline, flagellate **11** troublement **13** cat-o'-nine-tails
scout 3 spy **4** case **5** guide, pilot **6** escort, spy out, survey **7** lookout, observe **8** outrider, point man, vanguard **9** recruiter **11** reconnoiter **13** reconnoiterer

scowl 4 pout 5 frown, glare, lower 6 glower 7 grimace

scrabble 3 paw 4 claw, rake 5 climb 6 drudge, jostle, scrape, scrawl 7 clamber, grapple, scratch 8 struggle

scram 3 out 4 scat, shoo 5 be off, leave 6 beat it, begone, depart, get out, go away 7 get lost, vamoose 10 make tracks

scramble 3 run, vie 4 race, rush 5 clash, fight, mix up, scrap, upset 6 battle, combat, engage, garble, jostle, jumble, mess up, scurry, strive, tussle 7 collide, confuse, disturb, scatter, scuffle, shuffle 8 disorder, struggle, unsettle 9 scrimmage 10 disarrange, free-for-all 11 competition, disorganize

scramble up 5 climb, mount, scale 7 clamber

scrap 3 bit, dab, jot, row 4 atom, drop, iota, junk, spat 5 brawl, crumb, fight, grain, melee, speck, trace, trash 6 fracas, morsel, refuse, ruckus, sliver 7 abandon, glimmer, minimum, modicum, quarrel, snippet 8 brouhaha, fraction, fragment, jettison, molecule, particle, squabble 10 free-for-all, smattering, sprinkling

scrapbook 5 album 9 portfolio 11 memorabilia, miscellanea

scrape 3 dig 4 buff, gash, mark, rasp, save, skin 5 amass, clean, fight, glean, gouge, grate, graze, grind, plane, run-in, score, scour, scuff, stint 6 abrade, bruise, forage, gather, groove, obtain, pick up, plight, scrimp, secure, smooth, tussle 7 acquire, burnish, dilemma, procure, rub hard, scratch, scuffle, straits 8 abrasion 9 economize, tight spot 10 difficulty 11 predicament 13 confrontation

scratch 3 cut, mar, rub 4 claw, etch, gash, nick, omit, rasp 5 dig at, erase, grate, graze, grind, score 6 cancel, delete, incise, remove, rub out, scrape, scrawl, streak, strike 7 blemish, blot out, exclude, expunge, rule out 8 abrasion, cross out, lacerate, scribble, withdraw 9 eliminate 10 laceration

scratchy 5 rough 6 coarse 7 bristly, prickly 9 irritated 10 irritating

scrawl 4 draw 5 write 6 doodle 7 scratch, writing 8 scrabble, scribble, squiggle 10 penmanship 11 handwriting

scrawniness 8 lankness, leanness, slimness, thinness 10 skinniness, slightness 11 slenderness

scrawny 4 bony, lank, lean, puny 5 drawn, gaunt, lanky, runty, spare 6 sinewy, skinny, wasted 7 angular, scraggy, spindly, stunted 8 rawboned, skeletal 9 emaciated, fleshless 10 attenuated, undersized 11 underweight

screak 4 rasp 5 grate, grind 6 shriek, squeak 7 screech

scream 4 howl, loud, roar, wail, yell,

yelp, yowl 5 shout, whine 6 bellow, cry out, holler, outcry, shriek, squawk, squeal 7 screech 11 lamentation

screech 3 cry 4 howl, rasp 6 screak, scream, shriek 9 caterwaul

screen 3 see, web 4 cull, mask, mesh, rate, show, sift, sort, veil, view 5 class, cloak, cover, eject, films, grade, grate, group, guard, order, shade, sieve 6 buffer, cinema, defend, filter, mantle, movies, secure, shield, shroud, sifter, size up, strain, winnow 7 arrange, conceal, curtain, defense, discard, lattice, present, preview, project, protect, secrete, shelter, shutter, weed out 8 colander, coverage, evaluate, jalousie, separate, strainer, withhold 9 eliminate, partition, safeguard 10 protection 11 concealment

screw 4 bolt, join, knot, turn, warp 5 clamp, exact, force, gnarl, rivet, twist, wrest, wring 6 adjust, attach, deform, driver, extort, fasten, garble, wrench 7 contort, distort, pervert, squeeze, tighten 8 fastener, misshape 9 propeller

screwball 3 nut 4 kook 5 flake, freak 6 looney 7 lunatic 8 crackpot 9 character, eccentric

screwdriver
type: 6 rachet 11 spiral-drive 12 Phillips-head

screwy 3 odd 4 daft 5 batty, dotty, flaky, funny, kinky, kooky, nutty, queer, wacky, weird 6 weirdo 7 oddball 8 peculiar 9 eccentric 10 unbalanced

Scriabin, Aleksandr (Scriabine, Skryabin)
born: 6 Moscow, Russia
composer of: 7 Mystery 10 Prometheus 12 Vers la flamme 13 Poem of Ecstasy, The Divine Poem, The Poem of Fire

scribble 4 tear 5 squib 6 doodle, scrawl 7 scratch 8 squiggle 9 pull apart
fiber: 4 wool
procedure: 7 carding

scribe, Scribe 3 cut 4 mark, tool 5 clerk, score 6 author, copier, penman, writer 7 copyist, teacher 8 recorder 9 archivist, scrivener, secretary 10 amanuensis, translator 12 newspaperman, stenographer 13 calligraphist
Biblical: 4 Ezra 6 Esdras
French dramatist: 8 Augustin
Palestinian: 5 sofer 6 sopher

scribe of gods 5 Thoth

scrimp 4 save 5 hoard, pinch, skimp, stint 8 begrudge 9 besparing 12 pinch pennies

scrimping 6 frugal 7 sparing 10 economical 11 economizing 12 cheeseparing 15 pinching pennies

scrip 5 paper 8 document 11 certificate

scripsit 7 he wrote 8 she wrote

script 4 book, hand 5 lines, score 6 dialog 7 cursive 8 dialogue, libretto, longhand, scenario 10 manuscript, penmanship 11 calligraphy, chirography, handwriting

Scriptures, the 5 Bible 6 the Law, oracle 8 holy writ, the Bible, the Torah 10 the Gospels 11 The Good Book 12 New Testament, Old Testament, the Word of God 13 the Pentateuch, the Septuagint 14 sacred writings *see also* 5 Bible

scroll of the Torah
Hebrew: 11 Sepher Torah

Scrooge, Ebenezer
character in: 15 A Christmas Carol
author: 7 Dickens

scrub 4 swab 5 brush, scour 8 scouring 9 brushwood, scrubbing

scrubby 4 base 6 brushy 7 stunted 8 inferior 10 undersized

scrumptious 5 juicy, tasty 6 savory, tender 8 luscious, pleasant, pleasing 9 agreeable, delicious, enjoyable, flavorful, succulent, toothsome 10 appetizing, delectable, delightful, flavorsome 13 mouth-watering

scruple 3 shy 4 balk, care, halt 5 demur, pause, qualm, waver 6 blench, ethics, falter 7 anxiety, concern, refrain 8 hesitate 9 fluctuate, misgiving, principle 10 conscience, hesitation 11 compunction, fearfulness, uncertainty 12 apprehension, doubtfulness, protestation 13 squeamishness 17 conscientiousness

Scruples
author: 12 Judith Krantz

scrupulous 5 exact 6 honest 7 careful, dutiful, precise, upright 8 cautious, exacting, sedulous 9 honorable 10 deliberate, fastidious, meticulous, principled 11 painstaking, punctilious 13 conscientious

scrupulousness 4 care 5 pains 9 exactness 14 meticulousness 17 conscientiousness

scrutinize 4 scan 5 probe, study 6 peruse, search, survey 7 explore, inspect, observe 11 investigate

scrutiny 5 study, watch 7 inquiry, perusal 9 attention 10 inspection 11 examination 12 surveillance 13 investigation

scuffle 3 row 4 spar 5 brawl, clash, fight, melee, scrap 6 fracas, jostle, rumpus, tussle 8 squabble, struggle 9 commotion, imbroglio 10 donnybrook, free-for-all

sculpsit 10 he carved it 11 she carved it 12 he engraved it 13 she engraved it 14 he sculptured it 15 she sculptured it

sculptor 6 artist, carver, caster, imager, molder 7 marbler, modeler 8

chiseler, engraver
constellation: 19 Apparatus Sculptoris
French: 5 Rodin
Greek: 7 Phidias **10** Praxiteles
Irish-American: 12 Saint-Gaudens
Italian: 7 Cellini **12** Michelangelo
tool: 6 chisel, graver **7** spatula **9** ebauchoir

sculpture 3 cut **4** bust, cast, head, work **5** cameo, carve, erode, model, mould **6** chisel, relief, statue **7** carving, erosion, faience **8** intaglio, statuary **9** cloissone, medallion, statuette
medium: 4 clay **5** china, stone **6** bronze, enamel, marble **7** ceramic **9** porcelain **10** terra cotta **11** earthenware

scum 4 film, slag **5** crust, dregs, dross, trash **6** rabble, refuse **7** deposit, rubbish, surface **8** riffraff

scurrility 5 abuse **8** rudeness **9** indecency, obscenity, profanity **13** offensiveness, salaciousness

scurrilous 3 low **5** gross **6** coarse, vulgar **7** obscene **8** churlish, derisive, indecent, reviling **9** insulting, offensive, shameless **10** derogatory, detracting, indelicate, slanderous **11** disparaging, foulmouthed **12** contemptuous

scurry 3 hie **4** race, rush, skim **5** haste, hurry, scoot, speed **6** bustle, hasten, hustle, spring **7** rushing, scamper, scuttle **8** hurrying, scooting, scramble **9** confusion, dispersal **10** scattering

scurvy 3 low **4** base, mean, vile **6** shabby **7** ignoble **9** worthless **10** despicable **12** contemptible, dishonorable

scuttle 4 sink **5** abort, hurry, scrap, speed, wreck **6** hasten, scurry **7** destroy, discard, scamper **8** dispatch, scramble

scuttlebutt 4 talk **5** rumor **6** gossip **7** hearsay, prattle, scandal **8** chitchat

Scylaceus
origin: 6 Lycian
ally of: 7 Trojans
death by: 7 stoning

Scylla
form: 5 nymph **7** monster
location: 3 sea **16** Straits of Messina **20** Whirlpool of Charybdis
father: 7 Phorcys
mother: 6 Hecate
loved by: 8 Poseidon
rival: 10 Amphitrite

Scyphius
first: 5 horse
created by: 8 Poseidon

sea 3 bay, ton **4** deep, gulf, host, lake, leap, lots, main, mass, slew, wave **5** bight, flock, flood, ocean, scads, spate, surge, swarm, swell, waves **6** legion, roller, scores, waters **7** breaker **9** abundance, multitude, profusion
French: 3 mer
god of: 5 Aegir, Memir **6** Nereus, Tri-

ton **7** Glaucus, Neptune, Phorcys, Proteus **8** Poseidon **9** Asphalius
goddess of: 3 Ino, Ran **6** Graeae, Graiae, Matuta **8** Dictynna, Menannan **9** Leucothea **10** Amphitrite

Sea, the Sea, The
author: 11 Iris Murdoch

Sea Around Us, The
author: 13 Rachel L Carson

seaboard 5 coast **9** shoreline

Seaborg, Glen Theodore
field: 7 physics
worked with: 14 actinide series **19** transuranic elements
headed: 3 AEC **22** Atomic Energy Commission
awarded: 10 Nobel Prize

seacoast 5 beach, coast, shore **7** seaside **8** littoral **9** coastland, coastline, shoreline, waterside
French: 4 cote
Italian: 4 lido **7** riviera

seafarers 4 tars **5** salts **7** sailors, seadogs **8** mariners

Seagull, The
author: 12 Anton Chekhov
character: 5 Masha **6** Polina **10** Pyotr Sorin **11** Yevgeny Dorn **12** Ilya Shamraev, Irina Arkadin **13** Boris Trigorin, Nina Zaretchyn **16** Semyon Medvedenko **17** Konstantin Treplev

Seah 15 Biblical measure

Sea Hawk, The
director: 13 Michael Curtiz
cast: 10 Errol Flynn **11** Claude Rains, Donald Crisp **14** Brenda Marshall
score: 21 Erich Wolfgang Korngold

seal 2 OK **3** dam, fix **4** cork, lock, mark, plug, shut, stop **5** brand, close, stamp **6** accept, affirm, emblem, fasten, figure, ratify, secure, settle, shut up, signet, stop up, symbol, verify **7** approve, certify, confirm, endorse, imprint **8** colophon, conclude, fastener, hallmark, insignia, sanction, validate **9** determine, establish, trademark **10** impression **12** authenticate
Latin: 10 imprimatur

seal
young: 3 pup
group of: 3 pod

sea lion
young: 3 pup

seam 3 gap **4** line, lode, mark, scar, vein **5** break, chink, cleft, crack, joint, layer, notch **6** breach, furrow, incise, suture **7** crevice, fissure, joining, opening, rupture, stratum, wrinkle **8** junction, juncture **9** interface

seaman 3 gob, tar **4** hand, mate, salt **5** bosun, middy **6** lubber, merman, sailor, sea dog **7** mariner **9** boatswain **10** bluejacket, midshipman

seamark 5 light **6** beacon, pharos, signal **10** lighthouse, watchtower

sea monster 6 dragon **9** Leviathan

seamstress 10 dressmaker
French: 9 midinette **10** couturiere

seamy 3 raw **4** dark **5** dirty, nasty, rough **6** coarse, sordid **7** squalid, unclean **10** unpleasant **11** unwholesome **12** disagreeable

Sea of Grass, The
author: 13 Conrad Richter

sear 4 burn, char, scar **5** blast, singe, steel **6** harden, scorch **7** blister **9** cauterize **10** caseharden

search 4 comb, drag, fish, hunt, look, seek, sift **5** check, frisk, probe, quest, rifle, scour, snoop, study **6** survey, tracer **7** dragnet, examine, explore, inquiry, inspect, pry into, pursuit, ransack, rummage **8** overhaul, scrutiny **10** inspection, scrutinize **11** examination, exploration **13** investigation

Search, The
director: 13 Fred Zinnemann
cast: 9 Ivan Jandl **13** Aline MacMahon **14** Jarmila Novotna **15** Montgomery Clift
setting: 6 Berlin

Searchers, The
director: 8 John Ford
cast: 8 Ward Bond **9** John Wayne, Vera Miles **11** Natalie Wood **13** Jeffrey Hunter

searching 4 dour, keen, nosy **5** sharp **6** prying, shrewd, snoopy **7** curious, groping **8** exacting, piercing, rigorous, thorough **9** observant, quizzical, unsparing **11** inquisitive, penetrating **13** investigative

Seascape
author: 11 Edward Albee

seashore 5 beach, coast

seasick 3 ill **5** barfy, dizzy, faint, giddy, woozy **6** queasy **8** qualmish, vomitous **9** nauseated, squeamish **11** vertiginous

seasickness
French: 8 mal de mer

seaside 5 beach, coast, shore **9** shoreline

season 3 age, dry **4** fall, lace, tame, term **5** adapt, color, drill, inure, prime, ripen, shape, spell, spice, stage, train **6** accent, autumn, finish, flavor, inform, leaven, mature, mellow, period, refine, soften, spring, summer, temper, winter **7** enhance, enliven, prepare, quarter, stretch **8** accustom, duration, heighten, interval, ornament, practice **9** condition, cultivate, embellish **10** discipline

seasoned 6 herbed, inured, salted, spiced **7** veteran **8** flavored, hardened, peppered **9** competent, qualified **10** acclimated, accustomed, habituated **11** experienced **12** familiarized

seasoning 4 dill, herb, mace, sage, salt, zest **5** aging, basil, clove, gusto, onion, spice, thyme **6** drying, garlic, ginger, nutmeg, pepper, relish **7** oregano, paprika, parsley **8** allspice, cinnamon, marjoram, practice, ripening, rosemary, training **9** condiment, flavoring **10** maturation **11** orientation, preparation **15** familiarization

seasons
　god of: 9 Vertumnus
　goddess of: 5 Horae, Hours

seat 3 box, hub **4** axis, core, home, rump, site, sofa **5** abode, bench, chair, couch, croup, divan, fanny, heart, house, locus, place **6** behind, bottom, center, locale, settle **7** address, capital, cushion, habitat, housing, nucleus, rear end, situate **8** backside, buttocks, derriere, domicile, dwelling, haunches, location, quarters **9** posterior, residence **10** incumbency, membership **12** hindquarters

seat of justice 5 bench, court **8** tribunal **9** judiciary **10** courthouse

Seattle
　baseball team: 8 Mariners
　basketball team: 11 Supersonics
　bay: 7 Elliott
　football team: 8 Seahawks
　lake: 10 Washington
　landmark: 11 Space Needle
　site of: 10 World's Fair
　sound: 5 Puget

Sea Wolf, The
　author: 10 Jack London

Sebastian
　character in: 12 Twelfth Night
　author: 11 Shakespeare

Seberg, Jean
　born: 14 Marshalltown IA
　husband: 10 Romain Gary
　roles: 6 Lilith **7** Airport **9** Saint Joan **10** Breathless **16** Bonjour Tristesse

Secchi, Angelo
　field: 9 astronomy
　nationality: 7 Italian
　classified: 5 stars

secede 4 quit **5** leave **6** resign, retire **7** forsake **8** withdraw **12** disaffiliate

secession 10 separation, withdrawal **14** disaffiliation

seclude 4 hide **6** retire **7** isolate **8** separate **9** sequester **10** dissociate

secluded 6 covert, cut off, lonely, remote, shut in **7** private **8** closeted, confined, isolated, shut away, solitary **9** reclusive, sheltered, unvisited, withdrawn **10** cloistered **11** out-of-the-way, sequestered **12** unfrequented

seclusion 5 exile **6** asylum, hiding **7** retreat **8** cloister, hideaway, solitude **9** hermitage, isolation, reclusion, sanctuary **10** quarantine, retirement, withdrawal **11** concealment **13** sequestration

second 3 aid **4** abet, back, help, wink **5** agent, favor, flash, jiffy, other, proxy, trice **6** assist, back up, deputy, fill-in, helper, minute, moment, up-

hold **7** advance, another, endorse, further, instant, one more, outdone, promote, stand by, stand-in, support **8** advocate, delegate, exceeded, inferior **9** alternate, assistant, attendant, encourage, surpassed, twinkling **10** additional, lieutenant, substitute, understudy **11** alternating, subordinate **14** representative
abbreviation: 1 s **3** sec

secondary 5 lower, minor, other **6** backup, lesser **7** smaller **8** inferior, mediocre, middling **9** alternate, ancillary, auxiliary, following, resultant **10** consequent, subsequent, subsidiary **11** subordinate

second childhood 6 dotage **8** senility

secondhand 4 used **8** indirect **10** derivative, hand me down

second-in-command 6 deputy **8** adjutant **9** assistant **10** lieutenant **13** vice president

second-rate 3 bad **4** poor, so-so **5** cheap, tacky **6** shabby **7** average **8** everyday, inferior, mediocre, middling **9** imperfect **10** inadequate, outclassed, pedestrian **11** commonplace, substandard **15** undistinguished

Second Sex, The
　author: 16 Simone de Beauvoir

second-story man 5 thief **6** robber **7** burglar **9** cracksman **10** cat burglar

second string 4 subs **5** bench **11** substitutes

second team 5 bench **11** substitutes

secrecy 6 hiding **7** mystery, privacy, private, silence, stealth **8** muteness, solitude **9** closeness, seclusion **10** covertness **11** concealment, furtiveness **13** sequestration **15** clandestineness, confidentiality, underhandedness **17** surreptitiousness **19** uncommunicativeness

secret 3 key, mum **4** dark **6** arcane, covert, enigma, hidden, mystic, occult, puzzle, recipe, unseen **7** formula, furtive, mystery, private, unknown **8** discreet, esoteric, hush-hush, secluded, stealthy **9** concealed, disguised, invisible, secretive **10** confidence, mysterious, undercover, unrevealed **11** camouflaged, clandestine, undisclosed, unpublished **12** confidential, unrevealable **13** surreptitious

Secret Agent
　character: 9 John Drake
　cast: 15 Patrick McGoohan
　theme: 14 Secret Agent Man

secretary 4 aide, desk **5** clerk **6** scribe **7** officer **8** recorder **10** amanuensis **12** stenographer
　French: 10 escritoire

secret council 8 conclave

secrete 4 hide, veil **5** cache, cloak, cover, stash **6** screen, shroud **7** conceal, curtain **8** disguise

secretive 3 mum, sly **4** mute **6** covert, silent **7** cryptic, evasive, furtive, laconic, private **8** discreet, reserved, reticent, stealthy, taciturn **9** enigmatic, withdrawn **10** mysterious **11** tight-lipped, underhanded, unrevealing **13** surreptitious **15** uncommunicative

secretiveness 7 mystery, stealth **9** reticence **11** furtiveness **14** inscrutability, mysteriousness **19** uncommunicativeness

Secret Life of Walter Mitty, The
　author: 12 James Thurber
　cast: 10 Danny Kaye

sect 4 camp, cult **7** faction **8** division **10** persuasion **11** affiliation **12** denomination

sectarian 6 narrow **7** limited **8** clannish **9** exclusive, parochial **10** provincial, restricted

section 4 area, part, side, unit, ward, zone **5** piece, range, share, slice **6** region, sample, sphere **7** chapter, cutting, measure, passage, portion, segment, terrain **8** district, division, province, specimen, vicinity **9** allotment, increment, territory **10** department, proportion **11** installment **12** neighborhood

sector 4 area, zone **7** theater **8** district

secular 3 lay **4** laic **6** carnal **7** earthly, fleshly, mundane, profane, sensual, worldly **8** material, temporal **9** nonsacred **11** nonclerical **12** nonreligious, nonspiritual **17** nonecclesiastical

secundum 11 according to

secure 3 get, set **4** bind, easy, safe, sure **5** fixed, tight **6** at ease, defend, ensure, fasten, immune, insure, obtain **7** acquire, assured, certain, protect, shelter, tie down **8** absolute, carefree, composed, defended, definite, in the bag, positive, surefire **9** confident, guarantee, protected, reassured, safeguard, sheltered **10** guaranteed **11** impregnable **12** invulnerable, unassailable, unattackable, unthreatened

securities 5 bonds, title **6** stocks **12** certificates

security 4 bond, care, hope, keep **5** faith, trust **6** guards, pledge, police, safety, surety, troops **7** defense, deposit, promise, support **8** reliance, sureness, warranty **9** assurance, certainty, guarantee **10** collateral, confidence, conviction, protection, safeguards **11** maintenance, safekeeping **12** absoluteness, decisiveness, definiteness, positiveness, preservation

sedate 4 calm, cool **5** grave, quiet, sober, staid, still **6** poised, serene, solemn, steady **7** serious, subdued **8** composed, decorous, reserved **9** collected, dignified, impassive, unexcited, unruffled **10** cool-headed **11** level-headed **13** imperturbable **15** undemonstrative

sedateness 7 decorum, dignity, gravity, reserve **8** calmness **9** composure, soberness, solemnity **11** impassivity, seriousness

sedative 6 easing, opiate **7** anodyne, calming **8** allaying, lenitive, narcotic, relaxing, soothing **9** analgesic, assuasive, calmative, composing, mitigator, soporific **10** comforting, palliative **11** alleviative **12** tranquilizer **13** tranquilizing

sedentary 5 fixed, inert, still **6** seated **7** resting, sitting **8** inactive, unmoving **9** quiescent **10** stationary, unstirring

sedge 4 reed **5** grass **10** marsh grass

sediment 4 lees, scum, slag **5** dregs, dross, waste **6** debris, sludge **7** grounds, remains, residue **8** leavings **9** settlings

sedition 6 mutiny, revolt **7** treason **8** defiance, uprising **9** rebellion **10** disloyalty, insurgency, subversion, unruliness **11** lawlessness **12** disobedience, insurrection **14** rebelliousness, subversiveness

Sedley, Amelia and Joseph
characters in: 10 Vanity Fair
author: 9 Thackeray

seduce 4 lure, ruin **5** abuse, charm, tempt **6** allure, defile, entice, ravish **7** attract, conquer, corrupt, debauch, deprave, pervert, violate, win over **8** deflower, disgrace, dishonor, persuade **9** captivate

seducer 3 cad **4** wolf **5** letch, Romeo **7** defiler, Don Juan, playboy **8** Casanova, Lothario, lover-boy, ravisher, violater **9** corrupter, debaucher, womanizer **10** deflowerer **11** philanderer **12** heartbreaker
French: 4 roue

seductive 4 sexy **8** alluring, charming, enticing, tempting **9** beguiling, disarming **10** attractive, bewitching, come-hither, enchanting, voluptuous **11** captivating, provocative

seductress 4 vamp **5** siren **7** charmer, Jezebel, Lorelei, mantrap **9** temptress **11** adventuress, enchantress
French: 7 cocotte **11** femme fatale

sedulous 6 dogged **8** diligent, thorough **9** assiduous, steadfast **10** determined, persistent **11** industrious, painstaking, persevering **13** conscientious, indefatigable

sedulousness 4 zeal **8** industry, tenacity **9** assiduity, diligence **11** persistence **12** perseverance

see 3 dig, eye, spy, woo **4** date, espy, know, meet, mind, spot, view **5** court, grasp, sight, visit, watch **6** attend, behold, descry, escort, fathom, notice, regard, survey **7** consult, discern, glimpse, observe, picture, realize, receive, undergo, witness **8** conceive, consider, discover, envision, meditate, perceive, register, ruminate **9** accom-

pany, apprehend, ascertain, determine, encounter, entertain, interview, recognize, visualize **10** appreciate, comprehend, experience, understand **11** contemplate, distinguish
Latin: 4 vide

see above
Latin: 9 vide supra

see after
Latin: 8 vide post

see before
Latin: 8 vide ante

see below
Latin: 9 vide infra

seed 3 pit, sow **4** germ **5** basis, grain, heirs, issue, ovule, plant, stone **6** embryo, origin, source **7** progeny **8** children **9** beginning, offspring, posterity **11** descendants

seedy 4 worn **5** dingy, faded, lousy, mangy, ratty, spent, tacky **6** scuffy, shabby **7** haggard, sickish, squalid **8** slovenly **10** threadbare **11** debilitated

see fit 5 deign **6** choose, please

seek 3 try **4** hunt **5** court, essay, trace **6** demand, invite, pursue **7** attempt, examine, explore, inspect, request, solicit, venture **8** endeavor **9** undertake **10** scrutinize **11** investigate

seek out 4 find **6** pursue **7** embrace, look for, solicit

seem 4 look **6** appear

seeming 7 evident, obvious, surface **8** apparent, presumed, putative, supposed **10** ostensible **11** superficial

seemly 3 due **5** right **6** decent, polite, proper **7** correct, fitting, prudent, refined **8** becoming, decorous, suitable, tasteful, well-bred **9** befitting, courteous **10** acceptable, felicitous **11** appropriate **12** conventional
French: 11 comme il faut

seep 4 drip, leak, ooze, soak **7** diffuse, dribble, suffuse, trickle **8** permeate **9** penetrate

seepage 4 ooze **5** flour, issue **7** leakage, outflow **9** discharge, dribbling, secretion, trickling

seer 4 sage **5** augur **6** medium, oracle **7** diviner, prophet, psychic **8** conjurer, sorcerer **9** sorceress, stargazer **10** astrologer, soothsayer **11** clairvoyant, necromancer **13** fortuneteller **14** prognosticator

seesaw 5 waver **6** teeter **9** alternate, fluctuate, up-and-down, vacillate **12** teeter-totter

seethe 4 boil, brew, cook, fume, rage, rant, rave, roil, stew **5** churn, storm **6** blow up, bubble, simmer **7** bluster, smolder

seething 3 mad **7** boiling **8** agitated, bubbling, frenzied **10** distraught

see through 3 get **6** detect, effect, finish **7** achieve, execute, perform **8** carry out, complete, conclude **9** catch

onto, figure out, penetrate **10** comprehend, understand

Segal, Erich
author of: 9 Love Story **12** Oliver's Story **16** Man Woman and Child

Segal, George
born: 9 New York NY
roles: 11 Blume in Love, Where's Poppa? **13** A Touch of Class **18** Fun with Dick and Jane **25** Who's Afraid of Virginia Woolf?

segment 3 leg **4** part **5** cut up, piece, stage **6** cleave **7** disjoin, portion, section, split up **8** disunite, division, separate **9** increment **11** installment

segmented 5 cut up **7** split up **9** sectioned, separated

segregate 6 cut off, detach, divide **7** divorce, isolate, seclude, sort out **8** disunite, insulate, separate **9** sequester **10** disconnect, quarantine

seine 3 net **4** drag, fish **5** trawl **7** dragnet

Seinfeld
Network: 3 NBC
cast: 11 Wayne Knight (Newman) **13** Jerry Seinfeld (Jerry) **14** Jason Alexander (George) **15** Michael Richards (Kramer) **17** Julia Louis-Dreyfus (Elaine)
characters: 6 Newman **11** Elaine Benes, Cosmo Kramer **13** Jerry Seinfeld **14** George Costanza
episodes/themes: 8 Man Hands, Soup Nazi **9** Marble Rye **10** The Contest **11** Junior Mints **12** masturbation, yada-yada-yada **16** Master of My Domain

seism 5 quake, shock **6** tremor **8** temblor, upheaval **10** earthquake

seize 3 bag, nab **4** grab, read **5** catch, glean, grasp, pinch, pluck, usurp **6** arrest, clutch, collar, gather, snatch **7** capture, embrace, impound, possess, utilize **8** arrogate **9** apprehend, overpower, overwhelm **10** commandeer, comprehend, confiscate, understand **11** appropriate

seize the day
Latin: 9 carpe diem

seizure 3 fit **5** onset, spell, throe **6** access, arrest, attack, crisis, stroke, taking **7** capture, episode **8** grasping, paroxysm **9** abduction, snatching **10** convulsion, kidnapping, possession, usurpation, visitation **11** impressment **12** apprehension, confiscation **13** appropriation, commandeering

Sekhmet
origin: 8 Egyptian
goddess of: 4 evil

seldom 6 rarely **8** scarcely **10** uncommonly **12** infrequently, occasionally, sporadically

select 3 tap **4** A-one, pick, posh **5** elect, elite, fancy **6** choice, choose, chosen, opt for, picked, prefer **8** four-star, superior, top-notch **9** exclusive, first-rate, preferred **10** first-class, privileged

selection 4 pick **5** range **6** choice, medley, option **7** program, variety **8** choosing, decision **9** potpourri **10** collection, miscellany, preference

selective 5 fussy, picky **6** choosy **7** careful, finicky **8** cautious **10** discerning, fastidious, meticulous, particular **14** discriminating

Selene
  goddess of: **4** moon
  father: **8** Hyperion
  mother: **5** Theia
  brother: **6** Helios
  sister: **3** Eos
  loved: **8** Endymion
  daughter: **5** Herse **6** Pandia
  corresponds to: **5** Diana **7** Artemis

self 3 ego **6** person, psyche **8** identity **10** individual **11** homogeneity, personality
  inner: **5** anima **6** animus
  Universal: **5** Atman

self-abnegation 7 modesty **8** humility **10** diffidence **11** bashfulness

self-absorbed 4 vain **8** egoistic **9** egotistic **10** egocentric **11** egotistical **12** narcissistic

self-absorption 6 egoism, vanity **7** conceit **11** egocentrism, selfishness **16** self-centeredness

self-admiration 6 vanity **7** conceit, egotism **8** smugness **9** immodesty, vainglory

self-assertive 4 bold **7** dynamic **8** forceful **9** ambitious, confident **10** aggressive

self-assuming 4 vain **8** arrogant, egoistic **9** conceited **10** egoistical **11** egotistical

self-assurance 6 aplomb **9** brashness **12** cocksureness
  French: **9** sangfroid

self-assured 5 brash, cocky **8** cocksure **9** confident

self-centered 4 vain **8** egoistic, immodest **9** conceited, egotistic **10** egocentric **11** egotistical, swellheaded **12** narcissistic

self-centeredness 6 egoism, vanity **7** conceit **10** narcissism **11** egocentrism

self-composure 5 poise **6** aplomb **8** calmness **10** equanimity

self-confidence 5 nerve, pluck **6** mettle, spirit **8** boldness, gameness **9** cockiness **10** resolution **12** cocksureness

self-conscious 7 awkward **8** affected **9** chagrined, ill at ease, unnatural **11** discomposed, embarrassed **12** disconcerted

self-consciousness 7 modesty, reserve, shyness **8** timidity **9** abashment, hesitancy, reticence **10** con-

straint, demureness, diffidence **11** bashfulness, fearfulness **12** apprehension, sheepishness

self-control 5 poise **6** aplomb **8** firmness, patience, sobriety **9** composure, soberness, soundness, stability, willpower **10** temperance **11** forbearance **14** cool-headedness, unexcitability **15** levelheadedness **16** imperturbability
  French: **9** sangfroid **11** savoir faire

self-critical 6 humble, modest **9** diffident **13** perfectionist

self-criticism 7 modesty **8** humility **10** diffidence **13** perfectionism

self-deception 7 fantasy **8** delusion, illusion **13** hallucination

self-declared 5 sworn **6** avowed **8** admitted **9** confessed, professed **12** acknowledged

self-denial 8 eschewal **10** abnegation, abstention, abstinence, continence **11** forbearance **12** renunciation **14** abstemiousness

self-deprecation
  also: **16** self-depreciation **7** modesty **8** humility, meekness **10** humbleness

self-doubt 11 uncertainty

self-effacement 7 modesty, shyness **8** humility, meekness **10** diffidence **11** bashfulness

self-esteem 5 pride **10** confidence

self-evident 5 plain **6** patent **7** glaring, obvious **8** apparent, distinct, explicit, manifest, palpable **10** unarguable, undeniable **11** unambiguous, unequivocal **12** unmistakable **16** incontrovertible

self-explanatory 5 clear, lucid, plain **7** obvious **8** manifest **12** intelligible **15** straightforward

self-governing 4 free **9** sovereign **10** autonomous **11** independent

self-government 8 autonomy, home rule **11** sovereignty **12** independence

self-gratifying 11 intemperate

self-importance 6 egoism, vanity **8** smugness **9** arrogance, immodesty, pomposity, vainglory **11** egocentrism

self-important 4 smug, vain **7** pompous **8** egoistic, immodest **10** egocentric **11** egotistical **12** vainglorious

self-indulgence 12 extravagance, incontinence, intemperance

self-indulgent 9 libertine, sybaritic **10** hedonistic, voluptuous **11** extravagant, incontinent, intemperate

selfish 4 mean **5** tight, venal **6** greedy, stingy **7** miserly **8** covetous, egoistic, grasping, grudging **9** egotistic, illiberal, mercenary, rapacious **10** avaricious, egocentric, ungenerous **11** egotistical **12** parsimonious, uncharitable

self-love 6 egoism, vanity **7** conceit, egotism **9** vainglory **10** narcissism **11** complacency, egocentrism, haughtiness **13** conceitedness **15** swellhead-

edness
  French: **11** amour propre

self-possessed 4 calm, cool **6** poised **7** assured, courtly, refined **8** balanced, composed, polished, resolute **9** collected, confident **12** aristocratic **13** distinguished

self-possession 5 poise **6** aplomb **7** dignity **8** calmness, coolness **9** composure **10** confidence, equanimity, steadiness **16** imperturbability
  French: **9** sangfroid

self-praise 6 vanity **7** conceit, egotism **8** bragging, smugness **9** arrogance, immodesty, vainglory **12** boastfulness
  Italian: **11** braggadocio

self-propelling 9 automatic

self-questioning 10 uneasiness **13** soul-searching

self-reliance 8 sureness **9** assurance **12** independence

Self-Reliance
  author: **17** Ralph Waldo Emerson

self-reliant 5 hardy **6** plucky **7** assured **8** resolute, spirited **10** mettlesome **11** independent **12** enterprising

self-reproachful 8 contrite **9** regretful **10** apologetic, remorseful

self-respecting 5 proud **7** upright **8** decorous **9** dignified, honorable **10** upstanding **11** circumspect **13** distinguished

self-restraint 9 willpower **10** continence **11** forbearance

self-righteous 4 smug **5** pious **7** pompous **9** insincere, pietistic **10** complacent, moralizing **11** pharisaical, pretentious **12** hypocritical, mealy-mouthed **13** sanctimonious **14** holier-than-thou

self-sacrificing 6 heroic **7** gallant **9** unselfish **10** altruistic, martyrlike

self-satisfaction 5 pride **6** vanity **8** smugness **9** complacency

self-satisfied 4 smug, vain **8** cocksure, priggish **9** overproud **10** complacent **11** egotistical **12** narcissistic, vainglorious **13** overconfident

self-secure 4 smug **7** content **9** contented **10** complacent

self-seeking 6 greedy **8** covetous

self-styled
  French: **9** soi-disant

self-willed 8 obdurate, stubborn **9** obstinate, pigheaded **10** headstrong, refractory **11** intractable **12** ungovernable, unmanageable

sell 4 dump, hawk, vend **6** barter, betray, deal in, enlist, handle, market, peddle, unload **7** deceive, trade in, win over **8** convince, dispense

Selleck, Tom
  roles: **8** Lassiter, Magnum PI **12** Thomas Magnum **15** High Road to China **16** Three Men and A Baby

seller 6 dealer, jobber, monger, trader, vendor **7** peddler **8** merchant, retailer, salesman **9** middleman, salesgirl, saleslady, tradesman **10** saleswoman, shopkeeper, wholesaler **11** salesperson, storekeeper

Sellers, Peter
real name: 19 Richard Henry Sellers
born: 7 England **8** Southsea
wife: 11 Britt Ekland
roles: 10 Being There **12** Casino Royale **13** Dr Strangelove, Murder by Death **14** A Shot in the Dark, The Pink Panther **16** What's New Pussycat? **17** Inspector Clouseau **18** The Mouse that Roared **21** The World of Henry Orient

Selli
priests of: 4 Zeus

sell out 6 betray **11** double-cross

semblance 3 air **4** cast, copy, look, show **5** image **6** aspect **7** bearing, replica **8** likeness, pretense **9** duplicate, facsimile **10** simulacrum **11** counterpart **12** reproduction **14** representation
French: 4 mien

Semele
also: 6 Thyone
father: 6 Cadmus
mother: 8 Harmonia
loved by: 4 Zeus
son: 8 Dionysus
sister: 3 Ino **5** Agave **7** Autonoe

seminal 7 primary **8** creative, fruitful, germinal, original **9** formative **10** generative, productive **11** germinative, originating

Seminole
language family: 9 Muskogean
tribe: 8 Cow Creek, Mikasaki
location: 6 Mexico **7** Florida, Georgia **10** Everglades
leader: 7 Osceola, Wild Cat **10** Coacoochie

Semiramis
queen of: 7 Assyria
husband: 5 Ninus
founder of: 7 Babylon

Semitic
language family: 11 Afro-Asiatic **13** Hamito-Semitic
eastern branch: 8 Akkadian, Assyrian **10** Babylonian
western branch: 4 Geez **5** Tigre **6** Arabic, Gurage, Harari, Hebrew, Minean, Sabean, Syriac **7** Amharic, Aramaic, Argobba, Moabite **8** Ethiopic, Tigrinya, Ugaritic **9** Canaanite **10** Himyaritic, Phoenician, Qatabanian
southwest branch: 6 Minean, Sabean **7** Amharic **10** Himyaritic, Qatabanian **11** North Arabic **19** South Arabic-Ethiopic

Semo Sancus see **6** Sancus

senatus consultum 17 Roman senate decree

send 4 cast, emit, head, hurl, lead, show, toss **5** drive, fling, guide, refer, relay, shoot, throw **6** convey, direct, launch, propel **7** conduct, deliver, forward, give off, project **8** dispatch, transmit **9** broadcast, cause to go, discharge **11** disseminate

send away 4 oust, rout, shoo **5** chase, evict

send forth 4 emit, gush **5** erupt, expel, issue, let go **7** dismiss, release **8** disgorge, dispatch **9** discharge

send off 4 post **7** forward **8** dispatch, disperse, transmit

send out 4 beam, emit **8** dispatch, transmit **9** discharge

send packing 3 axe, can **4** fire, oust, rout, sack, shoo **5** evict **6** bounce **7** cast out, dismiss

send to Coventry 3 cut **5** eject, expel **6** banish, ignore **7** cast out, exclude **9** ostracize

Seneca
language family: 9 Iroquoian
location: 7 New York **15** Canandaigua Lake
leader: 9 John Abeel, John O'Bail **11** Cornplanter
member: 19 League of the Iroquois

Senegal
capital/largest city: 5 Dakar
others: 5 Bakel, Matam, Thies **7** Bignona, Kaolack, Kaollak **8** Diourbel, Kedougou, Linguere, Rufisque **10** Saint-Louis, Ziguinchor **11** Richard-Toll, Tambacounda
division: 7 Sudanic **8** Sahelian **9** Casamance
  empire: 4 Mali **5** Jolof **6** Tekrur
monetary unit: 5 franc **7** centime
island: 5 Goree
lake: 6 Guiers
mountain: 6 Gounou
highest point: 12 Fouta Djallon
river: 4 Sine **6** Faleme, Gambia, Saloum **7** Senegal **9** Casamance
sea: 8 Atlantic
physical feature:
  desert: 5 Ferlo
  peninsula: 9 Cape Verde
people: 4 Lebu, Peul, Soce **5** Diola, Dyola, Foula, Laobe, Peulh, Serer, Wolof **6** Fulani, Serere **7** Bambara, Malinke, Tukuler, Tukulor **8** Mandingo
  leader: 7 Senghor
language: 5 Wolof **6** French
religion: 5 Islam **7** animism **13** Roman Catholic
feature:
  musical instrument: 4 kora
  tree: 6 acacia, baobab **7** juniper, oil palm **10** raffia palm

Senhor, Senhora 2 sr **3** man, sra **5** madam (Portuguese)

senile 6 doting, infirm **7** foolish **8** decrepit **9** doddering, senescent **13** superannuated

senior, Senior 4 head, over **5** above, chief, doyen, elder, older **6** better **7** veteran **8** superior

seniority 6 tenure **9** longevity **10** precedence
French: 4 pere

senor 2 Mr **3** don **5** title **6** mister **8** Spaniard

senora 3 Mrs, sra **4** lady, wife **5** madam, woman **8** mistress

senorita 4 lass, miss
abbreviation: 4 srta

senorita 6 wrasse
genus: 8 Oxyjulis
species: 11 californica

sensation 3 hit **4** stir, to-do **6** thrill, uproar **7** feeling, scandal **9** agitation, awareness, commotion, detection **10** impression, perception

sensational 5 cheap, lurid **6** superb **8** dramatic, exciting, galvanic, shocking, striking **9** emotional, excellent, thrilling **10** electrical, scandalous **11** exaggerated, exceptional, extravagant, outstanding, spectacular **12** meretricious **13** extraordinary **14** heartthrobbing

sensationalism 7 scandal **9** luridness, melodrama **13** grandstanding **15** blood and thunder **16** yellow journalism

sense 3 see, use **4** aura, espy, feel, good, mind, note **5** grasp, guess, point, sight, smell, taste, touch, value, worth **6** descry, detect, divine, reason, regard, take in, wisdom **7** benefit, discern, faculty, feeling, hearing, meaning, purpose, realize, suspect **8** efficacy, function, judgment, perceive, sagacity **9** apprehend, awareness, intuition, recognize **10** atmosphere, comprehend, definition, denotation, impression, understand **11** connotation, premonition, realization, recognition **12** appreciation, intelligence, perspicacity, practicality, presentiment **13** consciousness, signification, understanding **14** reasonableness

Sense and Sensibility
author: 10 Jane Austen
character: 10 Lucy Steele **13** Edward Ferrars, Robert Ferrars **14** Colonel Brandon, John Willoughby **16** Sir John Middleton
  Dashwood family: 4 John **5** Fanny **6** Elinor **8** Marianne

senseless 4 dumb, idle, numb **5** crazy, inane, nutty, silly **6** stupid, unwise **7** aimless, foolish, stunned, useless, witless **8** comatose, deadened **9** brainless, foolhardy, illogical, insensate, pointless **10** groundless, ill-advised, insensible, irrational, ridiculous **11** harebrained, meaningless, purposeless, unconscious **12** unreasonable **13** irresponsible

sense of duty 15 moral obligation **21** sense of responsibility

sensibilities 8 feelings, sore spot, thin skin **12** Achilles' heel **14** susceptibility

sensibility 7 feeling **10** perception **11** temperament **14** responsiveness

sensible 4 just, sage, sane, wise **5** aware, plain, sound **7** evident, knowing, logical, obvious, prudent, visible **8** apparent, apprised, credible, discreet, informed, palpable, possible, rational, tangible **9** cognitive, cognizant, conscious, judicious, plausible, sagacious **10** detectable, discerning, farsighted, noticeable, perceiving, perceptive, reasonable, responsive, thoughtful **11** discernible, enlightened, intelligent, perceptible, susceptible **13** perspicacious **14** discriminating

sensitive 4 fine, keen, sore **5** acute, exact **6** tender, touchy **7** painful, precise **8** accurate, delicate, faithful, sentient **10** perceptive, responsive **11** susceptible, thin-skinned **14** impressionable

sensitiveness 8 delicacy **10** touchiness

sensual 4 lewd, sexy **6** carnal, earthy, erotic **7** fleshly, lustful **9** lecherous **10** hedonistic, licentious, voluptuous

sensualist 8 hedonist, sybarite **9** libertine **10** voluptuary

sensuous 9 delicious, exquisite **10** delightful

sententious 7 orotund, pompous, preachy, stilted **8** didactic, pedantic **9** grandiose, high-flown, pietistic **10** judgmental, moralistic **13** sanctimonious

sentient 5 aware **7** alert to, alive to, awake to, mindful **8** sensible **9** conscious

sentiment, sentiments 4 idea **5** heart **6** notion **7** emotion, feeling, opinion, romance, thought **8** attitude **9** nostalgia, viewpoint **10** tenderness **11** romanticism **12** emotionalism **15** softheartedness

sentimental 5 mushy, weepy **7** maudlin, mawkish, tearful **8** pathetic, romantic **9** emotional, nostalgic **10** lachrymose **12** melodramatic, romanticized

Sentimental Education, A
author: **15** Gustave Flaubert
character: **6** Arnoux **9** Dambreuse, Rosanette **11** Des Lauriers, Louise Roque **14** Frederic Moreau

sentimentalism 4 corn, mush **5** slush **6** bathos, pathos **8** schmaltz **9** mushiness, soppiness **10** maudlinism, slushiness **11** mawkishness

sentimentality 4 mush **5** heart **6** bathos, pathos **10** sloppiness **11** mawk-

ishness, temperament **12** emotionalism

Yiddish: 6 kitsch

Sentimental Journey, A
author: **14** Laurence Sterne
character: **5** Maria **6** Yorick **7** La Fleur

sentinel 4 ward **5** guard, scout, watch **6** patrol, picket, ranger **7** lookout **8** guardian, watchman **9** guardsman

sentry 5 guard, watch **7** lookout, vedette, vidette **8** sentinel, watchman
greeting: **4** halt

Seoul
capital of: **10** South Korea

separate 3 cut **4** cull, fork, part, sift **5** break, crack, sever, split **6** bisect, detach, divide, ramify, remove, single, spread, sunder **7** crumble, disjoin, diverge, diverse, divorce, isolate, radiate **8** detached, discrete, distinct, disunite **9** bifurcate, break away, come apart, different, disunited, partition, segregate, subdivide **10** autonomous, disconnect, dissimilar, divaricate, individual **11** distinguish, independent

separated 6 cut off **7** severed **8** detached **10** disengaged **12** disconnected, disentangled

separate from 5 apart, leave

separately 5 apart **6** singly **7** asunder **9** severally **12** individually

Separate Tables
director: **11** Delbert Mann
based on play by: **15** Terence Rattigan
cast: **10** David Niven **11** Deborah Kerr, Wendy Hiller **12** Rita Hayworth **13** Burt Lancaster
Oscar for: **5** actor (Niven) **17** supporting actress (Hiller)

separation 3 gap **4** fork **5** break, space, split **6** breach, divide, schism **7** divider, divorce, good-bye, opening, parting, removal, sorting **8** boundary, distance, disunion, division, farewell, interval **9** branching, isolation, partition, severance **10** detachment, divergence **11** bifurcation, disjunction, segregation **12** estrangement **13** disconnection, disengagement **14** disassociation

Sepharvite god 10 Anammelech **11** Adrammelech

Sepher Torah 16 scroll of the Torah
literally: **9** book of law

September
characteristic: **11** harvest moon
event: **14** aurora borealis, Northern lights **15** autumnal equinox
flower: **5** aster **12** morning glory
French: **9** Septembre
gem: **8** sapphire **12** star sapphire
German: **9** September
holiday: **8** Labor Day (1st Monday) **10** Michaelmas (29) **15** Grandparents' Day

Italian: **9** Settembre
number of days: **6** thirty
origin of name: **6** septum (Latin meaning seven)
place in year:
Gregorian: **5** ninth
Roman: **7** seventh
Spanish: **10** Septiembre
Zodiac sign: **5** Libra, Virgo

septentrional 6 arctic **8** northern **11** hyperborean

Septuagint
abbreviation: **3** LXX
author: **10** the Seventy

sepulcher 4 tomb **5** crypt, grave, vault **7** ossuary **8** cenotaph **9** mausoleum, reliquary **10** necropolis

sepulchral 6 hollow **7** charnel **8** funereal, mournful, tomblike **10** lugubrious

sequel 3 end **6** finish, result, upshot **7** outcome, product **8** addendum, epilogue, follow-up, offshoot **9** aftermath, corollary, outgrowth **10** conclusion, postscript **11** consequence, culmination **12** continuation
French: **10** denouement

sequence 3 run **4** flow **5** chain, cycle, order, round, train **6** course, parade, series, string **7** routine **8** schedule **9** cavalcade **10** procession, succession **11** arrangement, progression **14** successiveness **15** consecutiveness

sequester 6 banish, lock up, retire **7** confine, isolate, seclude **8** separate, withdraw **9** segregate **10** quarantine

sequestered 8 closeted, confined, isolated, secluded **9** insulated, sheltered, withdrawn **10** cloistered **11** dissociated

sequin 4 coin, disk **5** ducat **7** spangle **8** ornament
French: **9** paillette

seraglio 3 oda **5** harem, serai **6** zenana **9** gynaeceum

serape 4 cape **5** shawl **6** mantle, poncho

seraph 5 angel

seraphic 7 angelic **8** beatific, ethereal, heavenly **9** celestial

Seraphim 6 angels

Serapis
origin: **5** Greek **8** Egyptian
form: **5** deity
combination of: **4** Apis, Hapi **6** Osiris

Serbia see **10** Yugoslavia

sere 3 dry **4** arid **6** barren **7** parched, wizened **8** droughty, scorched, withered **9** shriveled, unwatered, waterless **10** dehydrated, desiccated **12** dehumidified, moistureless

serene 4 calm, cool, fair **5** clear, quiet, still **6** bright, limpid, placid, poised, sedate, smooth **7** halcyon **8** composed, peaceful, pellucid, tranquil **9** dignified, unruffled **10** nonchalant, unobscured, untroubled **11** undisturbed, unexcitable, unperturbed **13** unimpassioned

serenity 7 dignity **8** calmness, coolness, quietude **9** composure, placidity **10** equanimity, quiescence **11** complacence, nonchalance, tranquility **12** peacefulness, tranquillity **13** collectedness
French: 9 sangfroid

serf 6 cotter, thrall, vassal **7** bondman, peasant, villein

serfdom 4 yoke **6** thrall **7** bondage, slavery **9** servitude, thralldom, vassalage **11** enslavement, subjugation

Sergeant York
director: 11 Howard Hawks
cast: 10 Gary Cooper, Joan Leslie **12** George Tobias **13** Walter Brennan
Oscar for: 5 actor (Cooper)

Sergestus
origin: 6 Trojan
companion to: 6 Aeneas

serial 7 regular **9** continued, piecemeal, recurring **10** continuous, sequential, successive **11** consecutive, incremental

series 3 set **5** chain, cycle, group, order **6** course, number, parade, string **8** sequence **10** procession, succession **11** progression

serious 3 bad, sad **4** grim **5** grave, heavy, sober, staid **6** rueful, sedate, severe, solemn, somber **7** crucial, decided, earnest, fateful, harmful, pensive, sincere, weighty **8** alarming, critical, dejected, downcast, frowning, perilous, resolute, resolved **9** crippling, dangerous, important, momentous, saturnine **10** determined, portentous, purposeful, thoughtful **13** consequential **14** incapacitating

seriousness 7 gravity **8** severity **9** sincerity, soberness, solemnity **10** importance **11** earnestness

sermon 6 homily, rebuke, tirade **7** lecture, reproof **8** diatribe, harangue **9** preaching **10** admonition, preachment **11** exhortation

serpent, Serpent 3 asp **5** cheat, devil, rogue, Satan, snake, viper **7** reptile, traitor **8** deceiver **9** trickster
constellation of: 7 Serpens

Serpent Holder
constellation of: 9 Ophiuchus

serpentine 4 mazy **6** spiral, zigzag **7** coiling, crooked, devious, sinuous, snaking, winding **8** flexuous, tortuous, twisting **10** circuitous, convoluted, meandering, round about, undulating **12** labyrinthine

Serpico
director: 11 Sidney Lumet
based on story by: 9 Peter Maas
cast: 8 Al Pacino **9** Jack Kehoe **12** John Randolph
setting: 11 New York City

serrate 5 notch **6** jagged, pinked, ridged **7** dentate, grooved, notched, toothed **10** sawtoothed

serration 5 notch, ridge, teeth, tooth **8** notching, sawtooth

servant 3 man **4** cook, girl, help, maid **5** valet **6** butler, flunky, helper, lackey, menial, minion, slavey **7** footman **8** domestic, employee, factotum, henchman, hired man, retainer, scullion **9** attendant, chauffeur, hired girl, hired help, man Friday, underling **10** girl Friday **11** housekeeper

serve 2 do **3** act, aid **4** help, pass, suit, tend, work **5** avail, spend, treat **6** assist, attend, be used, do duty, oblige, supply, wait on **7** content, deliver, further, perform, present, promote, satisfy, suffice, work for **8** carry out, complete, function, hand over, minister **9** officiate **11** fill the bill

service, services 3 aid, use **4** help, mend, rite **5** avail, labor **6** adjust, agency, bureau, effort, employ, profit, repair, ritual, system **7** benefit, support, utility, waiting **8** ceremony, facility, maintain, military **9** advantage, provision, treatment **10** assistance, attendance, ceremonial, department, employment, observance, usefulness **11** celebration, convenience, maintenance **12** ministration **13** accommodation

serviceable 5 tough **6** rugged, strong, sturdy, usable, useful **7** durable, lasting **8** workable **9** effective, operative, practical **10** functional **11** utilitarian

serviceman 6 marine, sailor **7** soldier **9** repairman

servile 4 oily **6** abject, humble, menial **7** fawning, in bonds, slavish **8** cringing, scraping, toadying, unctuous **9** groveling, truckling **10** obsequious, submissive **11** bootlicking, subservient, sycophantic

serving 6 acting **7** dishful, helping, portion, waiting **8** plateful **9** assisting, attending, sufficing **11** ministering

serving counter 3 bar **6** buffet **9** sideboard

servitude 5 bonds **6** chains **7** bondage, fetters, serfdom, slavery **8** shackles **9** thralldom, vassalage **10** oppression **11** enslavement, subjugation **12** enthrallment, imprisonment

Servius Tullius
also: 7 Tullius
king of: 4 Rome
daughter: 6 Tullia
son-in-law: 7 Tarquin
killed by: 6 Tullia **7** Tarquin

sesame
also called: 10 benne seeds
botanical name: 14 Sesamum indicum
fairy tale: 10 "open sesame" **25** Ali Baba and the Forty Thieves

high in: 7 protein
former/mythical use: 3 oil **8** medicine **10** opens locks **11** lighting oil **16** discovers secrets **21** discovers secret places
use: 5 bread **6** salads **10** casseroles
use like: 8 nutmeats **11** chopped nuts

Sesame Street
character: 4 Bert, Elmo **5** Ernie, Herry, Oscar **6** Snuffy **7** Barkley, Big Bird, Muppets **8** the Count **12** Telly Monster **13** Cookie Monster **15** Mr Snuffleupagus

Sesostris
king of: 5 Egypt

session 4 bout, term **5** round, synod **6** course, period **7** meeting, quarter, sitting **8** assembly, conclave, semester **10** conference, convention

set 3 cut, fit, fix, gel, kit, lay, put, sic **4** club, drop, firm, line, make, plop, post, rate, sink, stud, suit **5** adapt, align, array, banal, bunch, crowd, embed, fixed, group, imbed, order, place, plunk, ready, rigid, scene, stale, stiff, stock, style, trite, usual **6** adjust, assess, assign, attach, common, confer, create, decree, frozen, harden, line up, locale, locate, ordain, outfit, studio **7** arrange, bearing, complex, congeal, decided, faction, install, jellify, machine, prepare, profile, regular, release, routine, scenery, service, setting, situate, station, thicken, unleash **8** arranged, assembly, backdrop, carriage, definite, estimate, everyday, familiar, firmness, habitual, hardened, location, ornament, position, prepared, regulate, rigidity, solidify, stubborn **9** apparatus, calibrate, customary, determine, establish, hackneyed, immovable, obstinate, prescribe, represent, steadfast **10** accustomed, assortment, collection, inflexible **11** anticipated, commonplace, consolidate, established, prearranged **12** conventional
French: 6 clique **7** coterie

Set
also: 4 Seth
origin: 8 Egyptian
form: 6 animal
personifies: 6 desert
brother: 6 Osiris
killed: 6 Osiris

set about 5 begin **6** assume **9** undertake **10** surrounded

set against 8 alienate, estrange

set apart 5 allot **6** detach, divide **7** earmark, isolate **8** allocate, separate **9** apportion, segregate **11** appropriate

set aside 4 kill **5** allot, annul **6** abjure, cancel, repeal, revoke **7** abandon, abolish, call off, destroy, discard, earmark, nullify, put away, rescind, retract, reverse **8** abrogate, allocate,

override, overturn **9** designate, repudiate **10** invalidate **11** discontinue

set at ease 5 cheer **6** please **7** appease, comfort, content, gratify

set at liberty 4 free **5** let go **6** parole **7** manumit, release, unchain **8** liberate, unfetter **9** unshackle **10** emancipate

setback 4 flop, loss, snag **5** hitch, slump **6** defeat, mishap, rebuff **7** failure, relapse, reverse, undoing **8** reversal **9** adversity, mischance, worsening **10** misfortune, regression **13** retrogression **14** disappointment

set down 6 record **7** deposit

set forth 2 go **5** be off, leave **6** assert, avouch, depart **7** advance **8** advocate, propound **10** sally forth

set free 5 let go, loose, untie **6** acquit, loosen, pardon, parole, unbind, uncage, unlock **7** deliver, release **8** liberate, unfetter **9** discharge, disengage, extricate **10** emancipate

Seth *see* **3** Set

Seth
  means: 12 compensation
  father: 4 Adam
  mother: 3 Eve
  son: 4 Enos

set in 5 arise, ensue, occur **6** arrive

set in motion 5 begin, start **6** launch **8** initiate **9** instigate, originate **10** inaugurate

set in order 4 rank, sort **5** align **6** line up **7** arrange, marshal **8** classify, organize **9** methodize **11** systematize

set of beliefs 5 credo, creed, dogma, ethos **6** ethnic, tenets **8** doctrine **10** philosophy, principles **11** convictions

set off 6 depart **7** explode, go forth **8** detonate, start out **10** sally forth

set on fire 4 burn **5** light **6** ignite, kindle

set out 4 pose **5** array, begin, be off, place, range **6** deploy, embark, intend **7** arrange, display **9** undertake

set right 7 correct **8** disabuse

set store by 5 prize, value **6** esteem **7** respect **8** treasure

set straight 5 edify **6** advise, inform **7** educate **8** disabuse **9** enlighten

settee 4 seat, sofa **5** bench

setting 5 scene **6** fixing, locale **7** jelling **8** aligning, ambiance, locating, location, mounting **9** adjusting, arranging, decreeing, hardening, ordaining **10** congealing, regulating, thickening **11** arrangement, determining, environment, prescribing, solidifying **12** establishing, surroundings
  French: 6 milieu **11** mise-en-scene

setting sun
  god of: 5 Janus

settle 3 fix, pay, sag **4** calm, drop, land, sink **5** agree, allay, clear, droop,

light, lodge, perch, quiet **6** alight, choose, decide, locate, move to, pacify, people, soothe **7** arrange, clarify, clear up, compose, inhabit, rectify, resolve, satisfy, sit down, situate **8** colonize, make good, populate, take root **9** determine, discharge, establish, reconcile **11** precipitate

settled 4 sure **7** certain, decided

settlement 3 sum **4** camp, post **6** amount, colony, hamlet **7** bequest, outpost, payment, village **8** clearing, peopling **9** clearance, discharge **10** adjustment, colonizing, encampment, resolution **11** acquittance, arrangement, liquidation **12** amortization, colonization, compensation, satisfaction **14** reconciliation

settler 7 pioneer **8** colonist, squatter **9** colonizer, immigrant **11** homesteader **12** frontiersman

settle upon 6 bestow **7** consign **8** bequeath

settlings 4 lees **5** dregs **7** deposit, grounds, remains, residue **8** leavings

set-to 4 spat **5** brush, clash, run-in **6** battle, fracas **7** dispute, quarrel, scuffle **8** argument, skirmish, squabble **10** engagement, falling out **12** disagreement **13** confrontation
  French: 11 contretemps

setup 4 plan **6** scheme, system **8** practice **9** apparatus **11** arrangement **12** organization

set up 3 rig **5** erect, found **7** arrange, install **9** construct, establish, institute **10** inaugurate, prearrange

set upon 3 mug **5** beset, fly at **6** assail, attack **7** besiege, lunge at **9** pitch into

Seurat, Georges Pierre
  born: 5 Paris **6** France
  artwork: 9 The Chahut, The Circus, The Models, The Parade, The Uproar **10** The Bathers **12** Le Grand Jatte, The Yoked Cart **19** Une Baignade Asnieres **23** A Bathing Scene at Asnieres, The Bec du Hoc at Grand champ **40** Sunday Afternoon on the Island of La Grand Jatte

Seuss, Dr
  real name: 19 Theodore Seuss Geisel
  author of: 12 If I Ran the Zoo **14** The Cat in the Hat **15** Green Eggs and Ham, Horton Hears a Who, If I Ran the Circus **19** Horton Hatches the Egg **23** Mister Brown Can Moo Can You? **26** Thidwick The Big-Hearted Moose, How the Grinch Stole Christmas

Seve
  nickname of: 20 Severiano Ballesteros

Seven Against Thebes
  author: 9 Aeschylus
  character: 6 Ismene **8** Antigone, Eteocles **9** Polynices **11** Theban Women

seven heroes: 6 Tydeus **8** Adrastus, Capaneus **9** Polynices **10** Amphiaraus, Hippomedon **13** Parthenopaeus

Seven Beauties
  director: 14 Lina Wertmuller
  cast: 11 Fernando Rey **13** Shirley Stoler **17** Giancarlo Giannini

Seven Brides for Seven Brothers
  director: 12 Stanley Donen
  cast: 9 Tammy Rall **10** Howard Keel, Jane Powell **11** Julie Newmar (Newmeyer), Russ Tamblyn **12** Jeff Richards **14** Virginia Gibson
  score: 11 Saul Chaplin **12** Johnny Mercer
  choreography: 11 Michael Kidd

Seven Pillars of Wisdom
  author: 10 T E Lawrence

Seven Samurai
  director: 13 Akira Kurosawa
  cast: 11 Yoshio Inaba **13** Toshiro Mifune **14** Takashi Shimura
  remade as: 19 The Magnificent Seven

seven seas 6 Arctic, Indian **9** Antarctic **12** North Pacific, South Pacific **13** North Atlantic, South Atlantic

Seven Sisters colleges 5 Smith **6** Vassar **7** Barnard **8** Bryn Mawr **9** Radcliffe, Wellesley **12** Mount Holyoke

Seventeen
  author: 15 Booth Tarkington
  character: 7 Genesis **9** Miss Pratt, Mrs Baxter **10** Jane Baxter, May Parcher **21** William Sylvanus Baxter

Seventh Seal, The
  director: 13 Ingmar Bergman
  cast: 9 Nils Poppe **11** Max von Sydow **13** Bibi Andersson **17** Gunnar Bjornstrand

Seventy-seven Sunset Strip
  character: 6 J R Hale, Kookie (Gerald Lloyd Kookson III), Roscoe **7** Suzanne **11** Jeff Spencer, Rex Randolph **12** Stuart Bailey
  cast: 9 Edd Byrnes **10** Louis Quinn, Roger Smith **11** Richard Long, Robert Logan **14** Jacqueline Beer **16** Efrem Zimbalist Jr
  Kookie's sayings: 10 a dark seven **12** the ginchiest **13** piling up the Z's **14** lend me your comb **15** play like a pigeon **17** headache grapplers **22** keep the eyeballs rolling

seven wonders of the ancient world 8 pyramids (Egypt) **12** Olympian Zeus (sculpted by Phidias) **15** Temple of Artemis (at Ephesus) **16** Colossus of Rhodes **22** Lighthouse (Pharos) at Alexandria **23** hanging gardens of Babylon (of Semiramis) **24** Mausoleum at Halicarnassus

Seven Year Itch, The
  director: 11 Billy Wilder
  cast: 8 Tom Ewell **10** Sonny Tufts **11** Evelyn Keyes, Victor Moore **13** Mari-

lyn Monroe
setting: 11 New York City

sever 3 saw 4 part, rend, rive, tear 5 slice, split 6 bisect, cleave, cut off, lop off 7 disjoin, rupture, split up 8 amputate, break off, cut in two, dissolve, disunite, separate, truncate 9 dismember, terminate 10 disconnect 11 discontinue

several 3 own 4 a few, some 6 divers, single, sundry 7 certain, diverse, express, private, special 8 assorted, distinct, peculiar, personal, separate, specific 9 different, exclusive 10 individual, particular, respective 11 distinctive, independent

severe 4 cold, dour, grim, wild 5 cruel, grave, harsh, plain, rough, sober, stern, stiff 6 biting, bitter, brutal, chaste, fierce, fuming, raging, savage, sedate, simple, somber, strict, taxing 7 austere, cutting, drastic, extreme, furious, intense, painful, serious, uniform, violent 8 piercing, rigorous, ruthless, stinging, vigorous 9 dangerous, demanding, difficult, draconian, merciless, saturnine, turbulent, unadorned, unsparing 10 forbidding, restrained, tumultuous 11 distressing, undecorated, unrelenting 12 conservative

severed 6 cut off 8 detached 9 uncoupled, unhitched 10 unfastened 11 unconnected 12 disconnected

Severini, Gino
born: 5 Italy 7 Cortona
artwork: 9 Harlequin 15 The Armored Train 25 Dancer Sea and Vase of Flowers 32 Dynamic Hieroglyph of the Bal Tabarin

severity 5 rigor 7 cruelly 8 acrimony, violence 9 austerity, gruffness, harshness, sternness 10 asceticism, difficulty, strictness, stringency 11 seriousness 12 grievousness

Seville
former name: 8 Hispalis
landmark: 7 Alcazar, Giralda
plain: 9 Andalusia
river: 12 Guadalquivir
ruler: 5 Moors 6 Romans 7 Vandals 8 Abbasids, Almohads, Iberians 9 Visigoths 10 Almoravids
Spanish: 7 Sevilla

sew 3 hem 4 mend, seam, tack 5 unite 6 fasten, ground, stitch, suture 10 run aground
loosely: 5 baste

sewage 5 waste 6 efflux, refuse 8 effluent 9 effluence

Seward, Dr
character in: 7 Dracula
author: 6 Stoker

sewing machine
invented by: 4 Howe

sex 4 Eros, love 6 coitus, gender, libido 7 coition 8 maleness 10 copulation,

femaleness, femininity, generation, lovemaking 11 masculinity, procreation 12 reproduction

Sexton, Anne
author of: 15 All My Pretty Ones 22 To Bedlam and Part Way Back 23 The Awful Rowing Toward God

sexual 6 coital, erotic 7 amatory, genital, marital, sensual 8 conjugal, intimate, venereal 10 copulatory, generative, libidinous 11 procreative 12 reproductive

sexually stimulating 3 hot 4 sexy 6 erotic, risque 9 salacious 10 suggestive 12 pornographic

sexy 4 lewd 5 bawdy 6 erotic 8 prurient 9 seductive 10 come-hither, coquettish, suggestive, voluptuous 11 flirtatious, provocative

Seychelles
capital/largest city: 8 Victoria
monetary unit: 4 cent 5 rupee
island: 4 Mahe 7 Aldabra, La Digue, Praslin 8 Farquhar 9 Desroches 10 Silhouette
highest point: 16 Morne Seychellois
sea: 6 Indian
people: 5 Asian 6 Creole, French, Indian 7 African, Chinese
    leader: 4 Rene 7 Mancham
language: 6 Creole, French 7 English
religion: 8 Anglican 13 Roman Catholic

sforzando
music: 12 sudden accent

Shabbas 7 Sabbath

shabby 3 low 4 mean, poor, torn, worn 5 cheap, dirty, mangy, raggy, ratty, seedy, sorry, tatty, tight 6 frayed, meager, ragged, sordid, unfair 7 ignoble, rundown, scruffy 8 beggarly, decaying, inferior, slovenly, unworthy, wretched 9 illiberal, miserable, neglected 10 ramshackle, threadbare, tumbledown, ungenerous 11 dilapidated 12 contemptible, deteriorated, dishonorable, impoverished

shabby bar 4 dive 5 joint 7 gin mill 9 honky-tonk

shack 3 hut 5 cabin 6 lean-to, shanty

shackle 3 bar, tie 4 balk, bind, cuff, curb, foil, rein 5 block, bonds, chain, check, cramp, cuffs, deter, irons, limit, stall 6 chains, fetter, hamper, hinder, hobble, hogtie, impede, pinion, retard, secure, tether, thwart 7 inhibit, manacle, prevent 8 encumber, handcuff, restrict 9 forestall, frustrate, hamstring, handcuffs 12 circumscribe

shackled 7 chained, in irons 8 in chains, manacled 10 handcuffed

shadchan, schatchen 10 matchmaker 14 marriage broker

Shaddai 3 God

shade 3 bit, dim, hue, jot 4 atom, cast, hint, hood, iota, tint, tone, veil, whit

5 blind, color, drape, tinge, touch, trace 6 awning, canopy, darken, screen, shadow, shield 7 curtain, modicum, shadows, shutter 8 darkness, particle, semidark 9 scintilla 10 suggestion
French: 7 soupcon
form: 6 spirit
location: 5 Hades

shadow, shadows 3 bit, dog 4 blot, hint, tail 5 cloud, ghost, hound, shade, smear, stain, stalk, taint, tinge, touch, trace, track, trail 6 blight, follow, pursue, smirch, smudge, threat 7 blemish, specter, whisper 8 penumbra 10 reflection, silhouette, suggestion

Shadow of a Doubt
director: 15 Alfred Hitchcock
cast: 10 Hume Cronyn 12 Joseph Cotten, Teresa Wright 14 Macdonald Carey 16 Patricia Collinge
remade as: 16 Step Down to Terror

Shadows on the Rock
author: 11 Willa Cather

shadowy 3 dim 5 shady 6 gloomy, unreal 7 obscure 8 illusory 9 tenebrous 10 indistinct 13 insubstantial

Shadrach
former name: 8 Hananiah
friend: 6 Daniel
companion: 7 Meshach 8 Abednego

shady 5 fishy 7 crooked, devious, dubious, shadowy 9 dishonest, unethical 10 suspicious 11 underhanded 12 disreputable, questionable 13 untrustworthy

shady dealings 5 fraud, graft 7 bribery 10 corruption, dishonesty

shaft 3 cut, pit, ray 4 barb, beam, dart, duct, flue, gibe, hilt, stem, vent, well 5 abyss, arrow, chasm, gleam, lance, patch, pylon, quill, shank, spear, spire, stalk, tower, trunk 6 cavity, column, funnel, handle, insult, pillar, streak, stream 7 affront, chimney, conduit, minaret, obelisk, spindle, steeple 8 brickbat, monolith, pilaster 9 aspersion 10 excavation

shaggy 5 bushy, downy, fuzzy, hairy, nappy, piled, wooly 6 tufted, woolly 7 bearded, hirsute, shagged, unshorn 9 whiskered 11 bewhiskered

shah 4 king 5 ruler 7 emperor, monarch 8 autocrat 9 sovereign

Shahaptian
tribe: 6 Numipu 8 Nez Perce

Shahn, Ben
born: 6 Kaunas 9 Lithuania
artwork: 5 Epoch 8 Handball 12 Seurat's Lunch, The Physicist 16 Pacific Land scape 18 Willis Avenue Bridge 28 The Passion of Sacco and Vanzetti

shake 3 jar, jog, mix 4 jerk, jolt, move, stir, stun, sway, wave 5 elude, quake, swing, touch 6 affect, bounce, jiggle, joggle, jostle, jounce, quaver, quiver, rattle, ruffle, shimmy, shiver, slough, totter, twitch, wobble **7** agitate, disturb, flicker, flutter, perturb, quaking, shudder, stagger, startle, tremble, unnerve, vibrate **8** brandish, disquiet, distress, flourish, frighten, throw off, unsettle, unstring **9** quivering, shivering, trembling **10** discompose, flickering, fluttering

shakedown 6 extort, payoff, search, tryout **7** testing **8** thorough **9** blackmail, extortion, hush money

Shakespeare, William
also: 10 bard of A/on **12** immortal bard
author of: 6 Hamlet, Henry V **7** Henry IV, Henry VI, Macbeth, Othello, Sonnets **8** King John, King Lear, Pericles (Prince of Tyre) **9** Cymbeline, Henry VIII, Richard II **10** Coriolanus, Richard III, The Tempest **11** As You Like It **12** Julius Caesar, Twelfth Night **13** Rape of Lucrece, Timon of Athens **14** Romeo and Juliet, The Winter's Tale, Venus and Adonis **15** Titus Andronicus **16** Love's Labour's Lost **17** Measure for Measure, The Comedy of Errors **18** Antony and Cleopatra, Troilus and Cressida **19** Much Ado About Nothing, The Merchant of Venice, The Taming of the Shrew **20** All's Well That Ends Well **21** A Midsummer Night's Dream **22** The Merry Wives of Windsor **23** The Two Gentlemen of Verona
birthplace: 15 Stratford-on-Avon
theater: 4 Swan **5** Globe
wife: 12 Anne Hathaway

shakeup 5 purge **7** cleanup **8** turnover **10** clean sweep **11** realignment **13** rearrangement, redisposition, restructuring **14** redistribution, reorganization

shake up 3 mix **4** stir **5** churn **7** agitate, disturb

shakiness 6 tremor **10** insecurity **11** instability, uncertainty **12** unsteadiness

shaky 4 weak **5** frail, jumpy **6** flimsy, unsafe, unsure, wobbly **7** dubious, fidgety, fragile, halting, jittery, nervous, teetery **8** hesitant, insecure, unstable, unsteady, wavering **9** faltering, hazardous, quivering, teetering, tottering, trembling, tremulous, uncertain, undecided **10** inconstant, irresolute, precarious, unreliable, unresolved **11** vacillating **12** undependable

shallow 5 shoal **6** frothy, slight **7** surface, trivial **8** knee-deep, skin-deep, trifling **9** frivolous **11** meaningless, superficial, unimportant **13** insubstantial **15** inconsequential

shalom 5 hello, peace **7** goodbye

shalom aleichem 10 peace to you

sham 3 act **4** copy, fake **5** bogus, false, feign, fraud, phony, put on, trick **6** affect, assume, forged **7** feigned, forgery, imitate, pretend **8** pretense, simulate, spurious **9** imitation, pretended, simulated, synthetic **10** artificial, fraudulent **11** counterfeit, make-believe

Shamash
origin: 8 Akkadian
god of: 3 sun

shamble, shambles 4 limp **5** hitch, lurch, stall **6** hobble **7** shuffle **8** butchery **14** slaughterhouse

shame 5 guilt, odium **6** humble, stigma **7** chagrin, mortify, remorse, scandal **8** contempt, disgrace, dishonor, ignominy **9** disrepute, embarrass, humiliate **10** debasement, disrespect **11** degradation, humiliation, self-disgust **12** unworthiness **13** embarrassment, mortification **14** disappointment

shamed be the one who thinks evil of it
Latin: 20 honi soit qui mal y pense

shamefaced 5 sorry **7** abashed, crushed, humbled, put-down **8** blushing, sheepish **9** chagrined, disgraced, mortified **10** humiliated, remorseful **11** embarrassed

shameful 3 low **4** base, mean, vile **6** odious **7** heinous, ignoble **8** shocking, unworthy **9** dastardly, degrading **10** deplorable, despicable, inglorious, iniquitous, outrageous, villainous **11** disgraceful, ignominious, opprobrious **12** contemptible, dishonorable **13** reprehensible

shameless 4 pert **5** brash, saucy **6** brazen, wanton **7** forward, immoral **8** degraded, flagrant, immodest, impudent, indecent **9** abandoned, audacious, barefaced, boldfaced, dissolute, unabashed **10** indecorous, unblushing, unreserved **11** disgraceful **12** dishonorable

shamelessness 4 gall **5** brass, cheek **8** audacity **10** brazenness, effrontery **11** forwardness, presumption

shamus 3 tec **7** gumshoe **9** detective **10** private eye **12** investigator

Shane
director: 13 George Stevens
cast: 8 Alan Ladd **9** Van Heflin **10** Jean Arthur **11** Jack Palance **12** Elisha Cook Jr **13** Edgar Buchanan **14** Brandon de Wilde

Shanghai
area: 23 International Settlement
landmark: 13 Long Hua Temple **17** People's Opera House **28** Shanghai Industrial Exhibition
river: 6 Wusung **7** Huang-P'u, Yangtze

Shangri-La *see* **5** Nepal

shanty 3 hut **5** cabin, hovel, shack **6** lean-to

shape 4 form, make, mold, trim **5** array, build, frame, guide, model, order **6** create, fettle, figure, health **7** contour, develop, fashion, outline, profile **8** physique **9** condition, construct, determine **10** silhouette **12** conformation **13** configuration

shapeless 5 baggy **8** formless **9** amorphous, irregular

shapely 3 fit **4** neat, trim **6** comely, gainly **11** symmetrical

shaper 9 architect, innovator **10** instigator, prime mover

Shapley, Howard
field: 9 astronomy
studied: 6 galaxy

Shardik
author: 12 Richard Adams

share 3 cut **4** dole, part **5** allot, cut up, quota, split **6** ration **7** deal out, divvy up, mete out, percent, portion **8** allocate **9** allotment, allowance, apportion **10** percentage **13** apportionment

shared 5 joint **6** common, public **7** general **8** communal **10** collective

share one's sorrow 7 condole **10** sympathize **11** commiserate

Sharif, Omar
real name: 15 Michael Shalhoub
born: 5 Egypt **10** Alexandria
roles: 3 Che **9** Dr Zhivago, Funny Girl, Funny Lady **11** Genghis Khan **12** Nick Arnstein **16** Lawrence of Arabia
expert on: 6 bridge

shark 3 ace **4** fish **5** cheat **6** expert, usurer, wizard **8** predator **9** trickster **12** extortionist

sharp 3 sly **4** acid, curt, fine, foxy, high, keen, sour, tart, wily **5** acrid, acute, alert, angry, awake, blunt, clear, cruel, edged, gruff, harsh, nippy, piked, quick, rapid, salty, sheer, spiny, steep **6** abrupt, artful, astute, barbed, biting, bitter, clever, crafty, crusty, fierce, keenly, marked, pointy, severe, shrewd, shrill, strong, sudden, thorny, tricky, unkind **7** acutely, alertly, angular, bearish, bristly, brusque, caustic, closely, crabbed, cunning, cutting, drastic, exactly, extreme, galling, intense, nipping, piquant, pointed, prickly, quickly, raucous, toothed, violent **8** abruptly, distinct, on the dot, piercing, promptly, scathing, serrated, spiteful, stinging, strident, suddenly, venomous, vertical, vigilant, vinegary **9** conniving, deceptive, excessive, on the nose, precisely, rancorous, unethical, vitriolic **10** contriving, discerning, immoderate, inordinate, perceptive, punctually **11** attentively, calculating, on the button, penetrating, precipitous **12** unprincipled, unscrupulous **13** precipitously
French: 5 juste
Spanish: 7 en punto

Sharp, Becky
character in: **10** Vanity Fair
author: **9** Thackeray

sharp-cornered 6 jagged **7** angular

sharp dresser 3 fop **4** dude **5** dandy **12** Beau Brummell, clotheshorse, fashion plate

sharpen 4 edge, hone, whet **5** grind, strop

sharply pointed 4 keen **5** acute **6** spiked **7** tapered **8** piercing **10** rapierlike **11** needle-nosed

sharpness 3 nip, wit **4** edge, tang **6** acuity, acumen **7** acidity, insight **8** acerbity, acridity, acrimony, keenness, pungency, saliency, tartness **9** acuteness, alertness, quickness **10** causticity, craftiness **12** perspicacity

sharp pain 4 pang, stab **5** cramp **6** twinge

sharpshooter
French: **10** tirailleur

sharp-sighted 5 acute **6** shrewd **8** piercing **9** far-seeing **10** discerning, perceptive **11** penetrating **13** perspicacious

sharp-witted 4 keen **5** acute, alert, canny, quick, smart **6** astute, brainy, clever

Shatner, William
born: **6** Canada **8** Montreal
roles: **8** Star Trek, T J Hooker **17** Captain James T Kirk

shatter 4 rive, ruin **5** break, burst, crack, crash, crush, quash, smash, split, spoil, upset, wreck **6** squash, sunder, topple **7** crumble, destroy, explode, scuttle **8** demolish, fracture, overturn, splinter **9** devastate, pulverize

shattered 6 broken, dashed **7** crushed, smashed **8** crumbled, decrepit **9** flustered **10** demolished, fragmented, splintered, tumbledown **11** crestfallen, demoralized **13** disillusioned, disintegrated

shave 3 cut, lop, mow **4** clip, crop, dock, pare, skin, snip, trim **5** brush, graze, prune, shear **6** barber, cut off, fleece, glance, scrape **7** scissor

Shaw, George Bernard
author of: **7** Candida **9** Pygmalion, Saint Joan **12** Major Barbara **13** Arms and the Man **14** Man and Superman **15** Heartbreak House **16** Back to Methuselah **17** The Devil's Disciple, The Doctor's Dilemma **18** Caesar and Cleopatra **19** Androcles and the Lion **20** Mrs Warren's Profession
member of: **13** Fabian Society

Shaw, Irwin
author of: **12** Top of the Hill **13** The Young Lions **14** Beggarman Thief, Rich Man Poor Man

Shaw, Robert
born: **7** England **12** Westhoughton
wife: **7** Mary Ure
roles: **4** Jaws **7** The Deep **8** The Sting **12** Swashbuckler **13** The Caretakers **17** A Man for All Seasons **20** Force Ten from Navarone **28** The Taking of Pelham One-Two-Three
author of: **14** The Hiding Place **21** The Man in the Glass Booth

Shawabti
origin: **8** Egyptian
form: **8** figurine
where used: **6** burial

shawl 4 wrap **5** scarf **6** mantle **7** paisley **10** fascinator
Mexican: **6** serape
Spanish: **8** mantilla

Shawnee
language family: **9** Algonkian **10** Algonquian
location: **4** Ohio **6** Kansas **8** Missouri, Oklahoma **9** Tennessee **12** Pennsylvania **13** South Carolina
leader: **8** Tecumseh **11** Tenskwatawa
related to: **8** Delaware

She
author: **13** H Rider Haggard
character: **6** Ayesha

shear 3 cut, lop **4** clip, crop, snip, trim **5** prune, shave **6** fleece, remove **7** deprive, relieve, scissor

Shearer, Norma
born: **6** Canada **8** Montreal
husband: **14** Irving Thalberg
roles: **8** The Women **9** A Free Soul **11** The Divorcee (Oscar) **14** Romeo and Juliet, Their Own Desire **15** Marie Antoinette **26** The Barretts of Wimpole Street

shears 5 clips, trims **6** prunes **7** pruners **8** clippers, scissors, trimmers

sheath 3 pod **4** case, coat, skin **6** casing, jacket **7** capsule, coating, wrapper **8** covering, envelope, membrane, scabbard, slipcase, wrapping **9** container **10** receptacle

sheathing 6 casing, siding **8** covering

Sheba
also: **4** Saba
visited: **7** Solomon
father: **6** Bichri, Joktan, Raamah **7** Jokshan
grandfather: **4** Cush **7** Keturah
people of: **7** Sabeans

Shebat 19 eleventh Hebrew month

she carved it
Latin: **8** sculpsit

shed 3 hut **4** cast, doff, drop, emit, molt **5** exude, hovel, shack, spill, strew, throw **6** lean-to, shanty, shower, slough, spread **7** cast off, discard, let fall, let flow, radiate, scatter **8** disperse, lose hair, toolshed **9** broadcast, discharge, tool house **10** distribute **11** disseminate, outbuilding

she died
Latin: **5** obiit

shed light on 7 clarify, explain **9** elucidate, explicate, make clear, make plain **10** illuminate

She Done Him Wrong
director: **13** Lowell Sherman
cast: **7** Mae West (Diamond Lil) **9** Cary Grant, Noah Beery **13** Gilbert Roland

shed tears 3 cry, sob **4** bawl, weep **6** boohoo **7** blubber

Sheehy, Gail
author of: **8** Passages **14** The Pathfinders

Sheeler, Charles
born: **14** Philadelphia PA
artwork: **9** Landscape, Upper Deck **11** Incantation **12** City Interior, Rolling Power **15** Bucks County Barn, River Rouge Plant **31** American Landscape Nineteen Thirty

sheen 4 glow **5** glaze, gleam, glint, gloss, shine **6** luster, patina, polish **7** burnish, glister, glitter, shimmer **8** radiance **9** shininess **10** brightness, brilliance, effulgence, glossiness, luminosity, refulgence **12** luminousness, resplendence

Sheen, Martin
real name: **12** Ramon Estevez
born: **8** Dayton OH
son: **12** Charlie Sheen **13** Emilio Estevez
roles: **5** Spawn **8** Badlands **12** The Believers **13** Apocalypse Now **14** Catch Twenty-two **18** The Subject Was Roses **20** The American President **27** The Execution of Private Slovik

Sheena, Queen of the Jungle
creator: **8** SR Powell **13** W Morgan Thomas
character: **3** Bob **4** Chim

she engraved it
Latin: **8** sculpsit

sheep
breed: **5** Iraqi **6** Hirrik, Merino, Panama, Romney, Somali **7** Cheviot, Karakul, Lincoln, Suffolk, Targhee **8** Columbia, Cotswold, Tatarian **9** Montadale, Romeldale, Southdown **10** Corriedale, Dorset Down, Dorset Horn, Shropshire, Sikkim Bera **11** Rambouillet **13** Hampshire Down **15** Border Leicester
female: **3** ewe
family: **7** Bovidae
genus: **4** Ovis
group of: **5** drove, flock **6** cosset
meat: **4** lamb **6** mutton
oil from: **7** lanolin
wild: **5** urial **6** argali **7** bighorn, mouflon
young: **4** lamb **7** lambkin **8** yearling

sheepish 3 shy **4** meek **5** timid **6** docile, guilty, humble **7** abashed, ashamed, bashful, fearful, hangdog, passive, servile **8** blushing, obedient, obeisant, timorous, yielding **9** chagrined, chastened, diffident, mortified, shrinking, tractable **10** shamefaced, submissive **11** embarrassed, subservient, unassertive, unresisting

sheepishness 7 chagrin **8** docility, meekness **10** diffidence **11** bashfulness **12** tractability **13** embarrassment **14** submissiveness **15** unassertiveness

Sheep Well, The
also: **13** Fuente Ovejuna
author: **10** Lope de Vega

sheer 4 fine, pure, thin **5** bluff, filmy, gauzy, plumb, sharp, steep, total, utter **6** abrupt **7** perfect, unmixed **8** absolute, complete, gossamer, vertical **9** out and out, unalloyed, unbounded, unlimited **10** consummate, diaphanous **11** precipitous, transparent, unmitigated, unqualified **12** unrestrained **13** perpendicular, unadulterated, unconditional

sheet 3 top **4** coat, film, leaf, pane, slab **5** layer, panel, piece, plate **6** sheath, square **7** blanket, coating, overlay **8** bed sheet, covering, membrane **9** rectangle

shegetz 12 non-Jewish boy, non-Jewish man

Sheldon, Sidney
author of: **9** Bloodline **12** Rage of Angels, The Naked Face **15** If Tomorrow Comes **20** A Stranger in the Mirror **22** The Other Side of Midnight

shelf 4 bank, prop, reef, slab **5** ledge, shoal **6** mantel, mantle **7** bedrock, bracket, stratum **9** supporter **11** mantelpiece, mantlepiece

shell 3 pod **4** bomb, case, hulk, hull, husk, shot **5** pound, round, shuck **6** bullet, fire on, pepper, rocket **7** barrage, bombard, grenade, missile **8** carapace, skeleton **9** cartridge, framework **10** projectile

shellac 4 beat, drub, lick, whip **7** clobber, lacquer, trounce, varnish

Shelley, Mary Wollstonecraft
father: **13** William Godwin
husband: **18** Percy Bysshe Shelley
author of: **12** Frankenstein

Shelley, Percy Bysshe
author of: **7** Adonais, Alastor **8** Queen Mab, The Cenci **10** To a Skylark **16** A Defence of Poetry, Ode to the West Wind **17** Prometheus Unbound

shellfish 4 clam, crab **5** prawn **6** cockle, mussel, oyster, shrimp **7** abalone, lobster, mollusk, scallop **8** barnacle, crawfish, crayfish **9** trunkfish **10** crustacean **13** softshell crab
spawn: **4** spat

shell out 3 pay **6** expend **8** allocate, disburse, dispense **10** contribute

shelter 5 cover, guard, haven, house, lodge **6** asylum, defend, harbor, ref-

uge, safety, shield, take in **7** care for, housing, lodging, protect **8** quarters, security **9** safeguard, sanctuary **10** protection

Sheltered Life
author: **12** Ellen Glasgow

shelve 5 defer, table **6** put off **7** suspend **8** lay aside, postpone, put aside, put on ice, set aside **10** pigeonhole

Shem
father: **4** Noah
brother: **3** Ham **7** Japheth
son: **8** Arphazed
descendant of: **6** Semite

shenanigans 5 sport **6** antics, capers, hijinx, pranks, stunts, tricks **8** deviltry, mischief, nonsense **9** highjinks, horseplay, silliness **10** buffoonery, tomfoolery **11** roguishness **12** monkeyshines, sportiveness **14** monkey business **15** mischievousness

she painted it
Latin: **6** pinxit

shepherd 4 herd, lead, show, tend **5** guard, guide, pilot **6** direct, escort, herder, keeper, patron, shield **7** protect, shelter **8** champion, defender, guardian, herdsman, provider **9** custodian, protector, safeguard **10** benefactor

Shepherdess and the Sweep, The
author: **21** Hans Christian Andersen

shepherds
god of: **3** Pan **6** Tammuz

sherbet 3 ade, ice **6** sorbet **7** dessert

Shere Khan
character in: **14** The Jungle Books
author: **7** Kipling

Sheridan, Ann
real name: **16** Clara Lou Sheridan
nickname: **9** Oomph Girl
born: **8** Denton TX
husband: **10** Scott McKay **11** George Brent **12** Edward Norris
roles: **8** King's Row **11** Silver River **12** Nora Prentiss **16** Wings for the Eagle **20** Angels with Dirty Faces

Sheridan, Philip H
served in: **8** Civil War **10** Indian Wars
side: **5** Union
commander of: **19** Army of the Shenandoah
rank: **22** general in chief of US army
battle: **9** Five Forks **10** Cedar Creek, Winchester **11** Chattanooga, Chickamauga, Fisher's Hill **12** Sayler's Creek **18** Wilderness Campaign

Sheridan, Richard Brinsley
author of: **9** The Critic, The Duenna, The Rivals **18** A Trip to Scarborough **19** The School for Scandal

sheriff 7 officer **9** constable
men: **5** posse

Sheriff of Nottingham
character in: **9** Robin Hood

Sherman, William Tecumseh
nickname: **4** Cump
served in: **8** Civil War **10** Mexican War
side: **5** Union
battle: **6** Shiloh **7** Atlanta, Bull Run **8** Savannah **9** Vicksburg **11** Chattanooga **15** Kenesaw Mountain
fought against: **8** Johnston
rank: **20** general in chief of army
famous for: **13** march to the sea (Georgia)
established: **29** Command and General Staff College
saying: **9** War is hell

sherry
type: **4** wine **6** brandy
origin: **5** Jeres, Spain, Xerez
varieties: **4** fino (dry) **5** cream **7** amoroso (sweet), oloroso (medium dry) **10** Manzanilla **11** Amontillado
drink: **6** Adonis, Bamboo **9** Andalusia
with gin: **11** Renaissance
with vermouth: **6** Brazil

Sherwood, Robert E
author of: **13** Idiot's Delight **15** Reunion in Vienna **18** The Petrified Forest **19** Roosevelt and Hopkins, There Shall Be No Night **20** Abe Lincoln in Illinois
screenplay: **22** The Best Years of Our Lives

she sculptured it
Latin: **8** sculpsit

she speaks
Latin: **8** loquitur

She Stoops to Conquer
author: **15** Oliver Goldsmith
character: **6** Marlow **8** Hastings **10** Sir Charles **11** Tony Lumpkin **12** Mr Hardcastle **13** Mrs Hardcastle **14** Kate Hardcastle **16** Constance Neville

she wrote (it)
Latin: **8** scripsit

shibah, shivah 14 mourning period
literally: **9** seven days

shibboleth 6 byword, saying, slogan **8** apothegm **9** catchword

Shibboleth 17 Gileadite password

shield 4 keep, star **5** aegis, badge, cover, guard, house, shade **6** buffer, button, emblem, ensign, fender, harbor, screen, secure **7** buckler, defense, protect, shelter **8** insignia, keep safe, preserve **9** medallion, protecter, protector, safeguard **10** escutcheon, protection

Shield (of Sobieski)
constellation of: **6** Scutum

shielded 6 hidden **7** guarded **9** concealed, protected, sheltered

Shields, Brooke
real name: **20** Christa Brooke Shields
born: **9** New York NY
roles: **10** Pretty Baby **11** Endless Love **13** The Blue Lagoon, Suddenly Susan
husband: **11** Andre Agassi

shift 2 go **4** move, slip, vary, veer **5** hitch, stint **6** change, swerve, switch **7** chemise, turning, veering **8** exchange, straight, transfer **9** deviation, transpose, variation **10** alteration, assignment, reposition **11** alternating, fluctuation, interchange **12** modification
French: 8 camisole

shiftless 3 lax **4** idle, lazy **8** careless, inactive, indolent, slothful **10** ne'er-do-well **13** lackadaisical **14** good-for-nothing **15** unconscientious

shifty 4 foxy, wily **6** crafty, sneaky, tricky **7** cunning, evasive **8** scheming, slippery **9** conniving, deceitful, dishonest **10** contriving, unreliable **11** maneuvering, treacherous **13** untrustworthy

Shikasta
  author: 12 Doris Lessing

shiksa 14 non-Jewish woman

shillelagh 4 club **5** stick **6** cudgel **9** truncheon

shilly-shally 5 stall, waver **6** dawdle, dither, falter, seesaw **8** hesitate **9** fluctuate, hem and haw, oscillate, vacillate

shilly-shallying 8 dawdling, wavering **9** uncertain, undecided **10** indecision, indecisive, irresolute **11** vacillation

Shimazaki Toson
  author of: 5 Hakai **20** The Broken Commandment

shimmer 4 beam, glow **5** blink, dance, flash, gleam, quake, shine, waver **6** quiver, shiver **7** flicker, flutter, glisten, sparkle, tremble, twinkle, vibrate **8** blinking **9** coruscate **11** scintillate **12** phosphoresce

shindig 3 hop **4** ball, bash, prom **5** dance, party **6** affair, shindy **7** blowout, revelry **9** barn dance, festivity, record hop **10** masked ball, the dansant
French: 4 fete, gala **6** soiree **9** bal masque **10** bal costume

shine 3 wax **4** beam, buff, glow **5** blink, flash, glare, gleam, glint, gloss, light, rub up, sheen **6** dazzle, luster, polish, waxing **7** buffing, burnish, flicker, glimmer, glisten, glister, glitter, radiate, shimmer, sparkle, twinkle **8** brighten, radiance **9** coruscate, irradiate, polishing **10** brightness, brilliance, burnishing, luminosity **11** scintillate **12** illumination, luminousness **13** incandescence

shininess 5 gleam, glint, gloss, sheen **6** luster, polish **7** shimmer

shining 5 aglow **6** glossy **7** glowing, radiant **8** gleaming, luminous, lustrous **9** brilliant, effulgent **11** illustrious **12** incandescent

Shining, The
  author: 11 Stephen King

shiny 6 bright, glossy **7** glaring, glowing, radiant **8** gleaming, luminous, lustrous, polished **9** brilliant, burnished, effulgent, sparkling **10** glistening, glittering, shimmering **12** incandescent **13** scintillating

ship 4 crew, send **5** craft, liner, route, tramp, yacht **6** packet, tanker, vessel **7** carrier, cruiser, forward, steamer **8** dispatch **9** destroyer, freighter, steamship, transport **10** ocean liner

Ship of Fools
  author: 19 Katherine Anne Porter
  director: 13 Stanley Kramer
  cast: 9 Jose Greco, Lee Marvin **10** Jose Ferrer **11** George Segal, Oscar Werner, Vivien Leigh **14** Simone Signoret **15** Elizabeth Ashley

shipshape 4 neat, snug, taut, tidy, trip, trim **5** tight **6** spruce **7** orderly

Shirer, William L
  author of: 28 The Collapse of the Third Republic **29** The Rise and Fall of the Third Reich

shirk 4 duck, shun **5** avoid, dodge, elude, evade **6** escape, eschew, ignore **7** goof off, neglect **8** malinger, sidestep **9** goldbrick

shirker 5 piker **6** dodger, evader, loafer, rotter, truant **7** deserter, quitter, slacker **9** goldbrick **10** backslider, malingerer

Shirley Temple
  ingredient: 9 ginger ale, grenadine
  also called: 9 Roy Rogers

shirr 5 crimp, smock **6** gather, pucker **8** bake eggs

shirt 3 top **4** sark **5** frock, waist **6** blouse, bodice **10** underwaist

shirty 5 angry, irked, testy, vexed **7** annoyed **9** irritated **11** disgruntled

Shittimwood 12 Biblical tree

shiver 5 quake, shake **6** quaver, shimmy **7** shudder, tremble

shivers 3 bit **5** piece, shard **6** sliver **8** fragment

shivery 3 icy, raw **4** cold, cool **5** brisk, chill, crisp, nippy **6** arctic, biting, bitter, chilly, frigid, frosty, wintry **7** quaking, trembly **8** chilling **9** quivering **11** penetrating

shoal 3 bar **4** bank, flat **5** crowd, shelf **6** school **7** sand bar, shallow **8** sand bank

shock 3 jar, mat, mop **4** blow, bush, cock, crop, daze, jolt, mane, mass, pile, rick, rock, stun, turn **5** scare, shake, sheaf, stack, start, upset **6** appall, bundle, dismay, impact, offend, revolt, thatch, trauma **7** astound, disgust, disturb, horrify, outrage, perturb, stagger, startle, stupefy **8** astonish, bowl over, disquiet, distress, paralyze, surprise, unsettle **9** collision, overwhelm **10** concussion, discompose,

disconcert **11** disturbance **13** consternation

shocking 4 foul **5** awful **6** grisly, horrid, odious **7** ghastly, hideous, jarring, jolting **8** gruesome, horrible, indecent, terrible, wretched **9** abhorrent, appalling, frightful, monstrous, offensive, repellent, repugnant, revolting, startling, upsetting **10** abominable, astounding, detestable, disgusting, disturbing, horrifying, outrageous, perturbing, scandalous, staggering, stupefying, surprising, unsettling **11** astonishing, disgraceful, disquieting **12** insufferable, overwhelming **13** disconcerting, reprehensible

shoddy 3 low **4** base, mean, poor **5** dirty, nasty, tacky **6** shabby, sloppy, stingy **7** low-down, miserly **8** careless, inferior, slipshod **9** haphazard, negligent, niggardly **10** second-rate, ungenerous **11** inefficient **12** contemptible **13** inconsiderate, reprehensible

shoe
  French: 9 chaussure

shoemaker 7 cobbler **9** bootmaker

Shoemaker's Holiday, The
  author: 12 Thomas Dekker

Shoes of the Fisherman, The
  author: 11 Morris L West

Shogun
  author: 12 James Clavell

Sholokhov, Mikhail
  author of: 19 And Quiet Flows the Don **21** The Virgin Soul Upturned

shoo 3 out **4** away, oust, rout, scat **5** be off, chase, leave, scram **6** beat it, be gone, depart, get out, go away **7** cast out, get lost, vamoose

shoot 3 bud, fly, hit **4** bolt, cast, dart, dash, drop, fell, fire, hurl, jump, kill, leap, nick, pelt, plug, race, rain, rush, stem, tear, toss, twig, wing **5** eject, fling, go off, hurry, shell, sling, speed, spray, sprig, spurt, sweep, throw, waste **6** charge, launch, let fly, pepper, propel, riddle, shower, spring, sprout **7** bombard, explode, pick off, tendril **8** catapult, detonate, open fire **9** discharge

Shootist, The
  director: 9 Don Siegal
  cast: 9 John Wayne, Ron Howard **10** Hugh O'Brien **11** Harry Morgan, Sheree North **12** James Stewart, Lauren Bacall, Richard Boone **13** John Carradine **15** Scatman Crothers

Shoot the Piano Player
  director: 16 Francois Truffaut
  cast: 11 Marie Dubois **12** Nicole Berger **14** Michele Mercier **15** Charles Aznavour
  setting: 5 Paris

shop 3 buy **4** hunt, look, mart, mill **5** plant, store, works **6** browse, market, studio **7** factory **8** emporium, purchase, workshop **9** patronize **10** win-

dowshop **13** establishment
French: **7** atelier **8** boutique

shopkeeper 6 dealer, monger, trader, vendor **8** merchant, purveyor, retailer **9** tradesman

shopworn 5 banal, corny, faded, stale, tired, trite, vapid **6** jejune **10** threadbare

shore 4 bank, hold, land, prop **5** beach, brace, brink, coast **6** hold up, margin, strand **7** bolster, bulwark, seaside, support, sustain **8** buttress, mainstay, seaboard, seacoast, underpin **9** reinforce, riverbank, waterside **10** strengthen
Latin: **10** terra firma

shorebird 3 auk **4** rail, sora **5** snipe, stilt, wader **6** avocet, curlew, plover, puffin **7** lapwing **8** woodcock **9** guillemot, sandpiper **13** oyster catcher

shore up 4 prop **5** brace **6** prop up **7** bolster, support **8** buttress **9** reinforce

short 3 low **4** curt, lean, slim, thin **5** brief, cross, elfin, fleet, gruff, hasty, pygmy, quick, runty, scant, sharp, small, squat, terse, testy, tight **6** abrupt, bantam, little, meager, scanty, scarce, skimpy, slight, sparse, stubby **7** brusque, compact, concise, cursory, lacking, limited, not long, not tall, slender, stunted, summary, wanting **8** abridged, abruptly, dwarfish, fleeting, impolite, snappish, succinct, suddenly, unawares **9** condensed, curtailed, deficient, impatient, momentary, niggardly, pint-sized, truncated **10** by surprise, diminutive, short-lived **11** abbreviated, ill-tempered, Lilliputian, pocket-sized **12** insufficient **13** precipitously **14** without warning

shortage 4 lack, want **6** dearth **7** deficit **8** leanness, scarcity, sparsity **9** shortfall **10** deficiency, inadequacy, scantiness, sparseness **13** insufficiency

shortcoming 4 flaw **5** fault **6** defect, foible **7** blemish, failing, failure, frailty **8** drawback, handicap, weakness **10** deficiency, inadequacy **12** imperfection

shorten 3 cut **4** clip, pare, trim **5** prune, shave, shear **6** lessen, reduce **7** abridge, curtail, cut down **8** condense, contract, cut short, decrease, diminish **10** abbreviate

shortening 3 fat, oil **4** lard, oleo **6** butter, digest **7** cutting, summary **8** abstract, synopsis, trimming **9** hemming up, margarine, reduction **11** abridgement, compression, contraction, curtailment **12** abbreviation, condensation

short form 6 digest, precis **7** summary **8** abstract, synopsis **11** abridgement, contraction **12** abbreviation, condensation

Short Happy Life of Francis Ma-

comber, The
author: **15** Ernest Hemingway

short journey 5 jaunt **6** outing **7** day trip **9** excursion

short-lived 5 brief **7** passing **8** fleeting **9** ephemeral, momentary, temporary, transient **10** evanescent, transitory, unenduring **11** impermanent **24** here today and gone tomorrow

shortly 4 anon, soon **7** by and by **8** directly, in a trice, promptly **9** forthwith, presently **10** before long **11** immediately

short narrative 5 essay, story **6** sketch **8** anecdote **10** short story

shortsighted 4 rash **6** myopic **7** foolish **8** careless, heedless, purblind, reckless, weak-eyed **9** amblyopic, imprudent **10** ill-advised, incautious, unthinking **11** improvident, injudicious, nearsighted, thoughtless **12** undiscerning **13** uncircumspect

short-tempered 4 curt **5** cross, huffy, sharp, testy **6** abrupt, cranky, crusty, grumpy, shirty, touchy **7** bearish, grouchy, peevish, waspish **8** choleric, snappish **9** irascible, irritable, splenetic **10** ill-humored, out of sorts, short-fused **11** hot-tempered, ill-tempered **12** cantankerous

Shosha
author: **19** Isaac Bashevis Singer

Shoshone (Snake)
language family: **10** Shoshonean
location: **4** Utah **5** Idaho **6** Nevada **7** Wyoming
translator: **9** Sacagawea

Shoshonean
tribe: **4** Hopi, Moki **5** Snake **6** Hopitu, Paiute **7** Bannock **8** Comanche, Shoshoni

Shostakovich, Dmitri (Dimitri)
born: **6** Russia **12** St Petersburg
composer of: **7** The Nose **9** Leningrad (symphony No 7) **11** May the First **12** The Golden Age **17** Katerina Ismailova **19** Lady Macbeth of Mzensk

shot 2 go **3** hit, try **4** dose, move, play, toss **5** balls, blast, crack, drive, essay, guess, salvo, slugs, throw **6** beat-up, archer, bowman, chance, report, ruined, shabby, stroke, volley **7** attempt, bullets, gunfire, shooter, surmise, worn-out **8** decrepit, marksman, rifleman **9** discharge, explosion, fusillade, injection **10** ammunition, conjecture, detonation **11** dilapidated, projectiles **12** falling apart, sharpshooter

shot in the arm 4 lift **5** boost **6** uplift **8** stimulus **13** encouragement

shot in the dark 5 guess **6** notion, theory **9** guesswork, suspicion **10** assumption, conjecture, hypothesis

shoulder 3 rim **4** bank, bear, brow, bump, edge, push, side, take **5** brink, carry, crest, elbow, lunge, shove,

skirt, verge **6** assume, border, jostle, margin, take on, thrust, uphold **7** scapula, support, sustain **8** clavicle **9** undertake

shoulder blade 7 scapula **8** omoplate **9** bladebone

shout 3 cry **4** bawl, call, hoot, howl, roar, yell, yelp **5** burst, cheer, hollo, whoop **6** bellow, chorus, clamor, cry out, holler, hurrah, huzzah, outcry, scream, shriek **7** call out, exclaim, screech, thunder **8** outburst **9** hue and cry **10** hullabaloo

shout down 3 boo **4** hiss **6** hoot at, revile **7** catcall, condemn **8** denounce, drown out

shove 4 bump, butt, jolt, prod, push **5** boost, crowd, drive, elbow, force, impel, nudge **6** joggle, jostle, propel, thrust **8** shoulder

show 4 bare, bill, fair, give, lead, mark, play, pomp, pose, sham, sign **5** argue, coach, drama, endow, favor, front, grant, guide, movie, opera, prove, teach, token, tutor, usher **6** appear, attest, ballet, bestow, comedy, direct, effect, evince, expose, hint at, impart, inform, lavish, reveal, school, tender, unveil **7** bear out, bespeak, certify, conduct, confirm, display, exhibit, explain, lay bare, musical, picture, pretext, proffer, program, suggest, uncover **8** ceremony, delusion, disclose, dispense, evidence, illusion, indicate, instruct, intimate, manifest, operetta, point out, pretense, vaunting **9** establish, make clear, make known, represent, spectacle **10** appearance, disclosure, distribute, exhibition, exposition, expression, impression, indication, pretension, production, revelation **11** affectation, attestation, corroborate, counterfeit, demonstrate, performance, testimonial **12** bring to light, substantiate **13** demonstration, entertainment, manifestation, motion picture

Show Boat
author: **10** Edna Ferber

showcase 7 cabinet, counter, display, exhibit, vitrine

showdown 3 war **6** battle, climax, combat, crisis **7** face-off **8** clashing, conflict **9** collision, encounter **13** confrontation

shower 3 wet **4** fall, pour, rain, rush **5** flood, salvo, spray, surge **6** deluge, lavish, splash, stream, volley, wealth **7** barrage, bombard, drizzle, torrent **8** downpour, plethora, sprinkle **9** profusion **10** cloudburst, inundation **11** bombardment

showiness 5 eclat **7** glitter **8** splendor **9** jazziness **10** flashiness **11** ostentation **14** grandiloquence

Show-me State
nickname of: **8** Missouri

show-off 6 egoist 7 boaster, egotist, windbag 8 braggart, fanfaron, flaunter, strutter 9 extrovert, swaggerer 11 braggadocio 13 cock of the walk, exhibitionist 14 life of the party

showpiece 3 gem 5 jewel, pearl, pride, prize 6 rarity, wonder 7 classic, paragon 8 treasure 10 masterwork 11 chef d'oeuvre, masterpiece, prizewinner 17 piece de resistance

show up 4 come 5 outdo 6 appear, arrive, attend, crop up, expose, loom up, reveal, turn up 9 be present 11 come to light, make a fool of 12 come into view 13 become visible

showy 4 loud 5 gaudy, vivid 6 flashy, florid, garish, ornate 7 pompous 8 colorful, gorgeous, imposing, splendid, striking 9 brilliant 11 magnificent, pretentious 12 ostentatious

shred 3 bit, ion, jot, rag 4 atom, band, hair, iota, spot, whit 5 grain, piece, scrap, speck, strip, trace 6 morsel, ribbon, sliver, tatter 7 snippet 8 fragment, molecule, particle 9 scintilla

shrew 3 hag, nag 5 harpy, scold, vixen, yenta 6 kvetch, virago 7 shewolf 8 battle-ax, fishwife, harridan, spitfire 9 termagant, Xanthippe

shrewd 3 sly 4 foxy, keen, wily, wise 5 acute, cagey, canny, quick, sharp, slick, smart 6 artful, astute, clever, crafty, shifty, smooth, tricky 7 careful, cunning, knowing, probing, prudent 8 cautious, piercing, scheming, sensible, slippery 9 designing, farseeing, sagacious 10 contriving, discerning, farsighted, perceptive 11 calculating, circumspect, intelligent, penetrating, quick-witted, self-serving, sharp-witted 12 disingenuous 13 Machiavellian, perspicacious

shrewdness 6 acumen 7 cunning, slyness 8 foxiness, keenness, wiliness 9 acuteness, cageyness, sharpness, slickness, smartness 10 artfulness, astuteness, cleverness, craftiness, smoothness, trickiness 11 carefulness, discernment 12 slipperiness 16 disingenuousness

shriek 3 cry 4 call, hoot, howl, peal, yell, yelp 5 shout, whoop 6 cry out, holler, out-cry, scream, squawk, squeak, squeal 7 screech

shrift 7 penance 9 atonement, expiation 10 confession

shrill 4 high, loud 6 piping 7 blaring, raucous 8 piercing, strident 9 clamorous 10 screeching 11 high-pitched, penetrating

shrimp 5 prawn 6 scampi 8 cocktail

shrine 5 altar 6 chapel, church, temple 7 sanctum 8 monument 9 sanctuary

shrink 3 ebb, shy 4 balk, duck, wane 5 cower, demur, dry up, quail, stick, wince 6 blench, bridle, cringe, flinch, lessen, pucker, recoil, reduce, refuse,
retire 7 curtail, decline, deflate, dwindle, retreat, shorten, shrivel, shudder 8 compress, condense, contract, decrease, diminish, draw back, hang back, make less, withdraw 9 constrict 11 make smaller 12 draw together 13 become smaller

shrink from 4 hate, shun 5 abhor, evade 6 balk at, detest, eschew, loathe, resist 7 despise 8 recoil at 9 abominate, shudder at 12 be revolted by 13 find repulsive

shrinking 3 shy 5 timid 6 ebbing, waning 7 bashful 8 reticent, retiring, timorous 9 declining, dwindling 10 decreasing, shriveling 11 contraction, diminishing

shrive 6 pardon 7 absolve, forgive

shrivel 5 dry up, parch, wizen 6 pucker, scorch, shrink, wither 7 wrinkle

Shropshire Lad, A
  author: 9 A E Housman

shroud 4 hide, pall, veil, wrap 5 cloak, cloud, cover, sheet 6 clothe, mantle, screen, swathe 7 blanket, conceal, envelop 8 covering 9 cerecloth, cerements 11 burial cloth 12 graveclothes, winding sheet

shrub 4 bush 5 brush 8 beverage 10 fruit drink

shrubbery 4 bush 5 brush 6 bushes, shrubs 9 brushwood 10 underbrush 11 undergrowth

shuck 4 husk, peel, shed 5 chaff, shell, strip

shudder 4 jerk, pang 5 quake, shake, spasm, throb 6 quaver, quiver, shimmy, shiver, tremor, twitch 7 flutter, tremble 8 paroxysm 9 pulsation, trembling 10 convulsion

shudder at 4 hate 5 abhor 6 detest, loathe 8 recoil at 9 abominate, can't stand 10 recoil from, shrink from

shuffle 3 mix 4 drag, gimp, limp, step 5 scuff, slide 6 clumsy, jumble, scrape 7 shamble 8 scramble 9 rearrange 10 disarrange 11 interchange

shul, schul 9 synagogue

shun 5 avoid, dodge, elude, evade, forgo 6 eschew, forego, ignore, refuse, reject 7 boycott, disdain 10 circumvent, fight shy of, shrink from 11 keep clear of, shy away from 12 have no part of, keep away from, steer clear of, turn away from

shut 3 box 4 cage, coop, draw, fold, lock, snap 5 clasp, close, drawn, latch 6 closed, closet, corral, draw to, fasten, intern, locked, lock in, secure 7 confine, drawn to, enclose, fence in, impound, latched, secured 8 cloister, closed up, fastened, imprison 9 barricade, constrain 11 incarcerate

shut down 4 halt, stop 5 cease 7 suspend 9 close down, interrupt 11 discontinue

Shute, Nevil
  author of: 10 On the Beach

shut in 4 cage 5 caged, pen in 6 coop up, encage, lock up 7 confine, encaged, enclose 8 confined, cooped up, enclosed, locked up, restrain, restrict 10 restrained, restricted

shut one's eyes to 5 allow 6 ignore, wink at 8 overlook 9 connive in, disregard 11 pay no heed to 14 turn one's back on

shut out 3 bar 5 debar 6 defeat 7 exclude 8 obstruct, prohibit

shutter 5 blind, close, shade 6 screen 7 curtain

shut the door on 3 ban, bar 6 forbid, refuse, reject 7 exclude, keep out, shut out 8 prohibit

shut up 4 cage, coop, hush, lock, pent 5 close, pen in 6 immure 7 be quiet, confine, silence 8 imprison 11 incarcerate

shy 4 balk, meek, wary 5 chary, cower, dodge, leery, minus, coant, short, timid, under, wince 6 blench, demure, flinch, in need, modest, shrink, swerve 7 anxious, bashful, careful, fearful, lacking, needing, nervous, wanting 8 cautious, draw back, jump back, reserved, reticent, skittish, timorous 9 deficient, diffident, shrinking, tremulous 10 suspicious 11 distrustful 12 apprehensive 13 self-conscious

shy away from 4 duck, shun 5 avoid, dodge, spurn 6 balk at, refuse, reject 10 shrink from 12 steer clear of

Shylock
  character in: 19 The Merchant of Venice
  author: 11 Shakespeare

shyness 8 meekness, timidity 9 reticence 10 diffidence, insecurity 11 bashfulness 12 sheepishness, timorousness 14 self-effacement 15 unassertiveness

shyster 5 rogue 6 lawyer 8 attorney 10 mouthpiece 11 pettifogger 15 ambulance chaser

si 3 yes

Siam *see* 8 Thailand

Sibelius, Jean
  born: 7 Finland 10 Tavastehus
  composer of: 6 En Saga 7 Karelia, Legends, Tapiola, The Band 8 Kalevala 9 Finlandia 10 The Tempest 12 The Oceanides, Voces Intimae 14 Ride and Sunrise

Siberia 8 disfavor 10 punishment 14 undesirability
  city: 4 Omsk 5 Chita, Tomsk 6 Kurgan 7 Irkutsk, Yakutsk
  conqueror: 9 Timafeyev 11 Genghis Khan
  continent: 4 Asia

gulf: 2 Ob

inhabitant: 4 Yaku **5** Sagai, Tatar **6** Tartar **7** Yukagir **8** prisoner **17** political prisoner

mountain range: 4 Ural **5** Altai, Altay

river: 2 Ob **3** Ket, Ili, Taz **4** Amga, Amur, Lena, Onon **5** Ishim, Tobol **6** Olekma

sea: 4 Kara **6** Laptev **7** Okhotsk

sibling 6 sister **7** brother

problem: 7 rivalry

sibyl 4 seer **5** augur **6** oracle **7** diviner **9** predictor, sorceress **10** forecaster, prophetess, soothsayer **13** fortune teller **14** prognosticator

Sibyls

form: 10 prophetess

inspired by: 5 deity **6** Apollo

names: 6 Libyan **7** Cumaean **10** Erythraean

prophecies: 14 Sibylline Books

sic 2 so **4** thus

Sicilian Vespers, The

also: 20 Les Vepres Siciliennes

opera by: 5 Verdi

character: 5 Elena **6** Arrigo **7** Procida **8** Monforte

Sicily

other name: 7 Sicilia **9** Trinacria, Triquetra

capital/largest city: 7 Palermo

others: 3 Aci **4** Enna, Noto **6** Ragusa **7** Augusta, Catania, Marsala, Messina, Trapani **8** Syracuse **10** Montelepre

division: 4 Enna **6** Ragusa **7** Catania, Messina, Palermo, Trapani **8** Siracusa, Syracuse **9** Agrigento **13** Caltanissetta

government: 13 region of Italy

measure: 5 salma **7** caffiso

monetary unit: 5 litra, oncia, uncia **6** carlin **7** carline, oncetta

island: 5 Egadi **6** Lipari, Ustica **7** Pelagie **11** Pantelleria

lake: 7 Pergusa **8** Camarina

mountain: 4 Erei, Moro, Sori **5** Atlas, Erici, Hybla, Iblei, Ibrei **7** Nebrodi, Vulcano **9** Apennines, Le Madonie, Stromboli **10** Peloritani

highest point: 4 Etna **5** Aetna

river: 4 Acis **5** Salso, Torto **6** Belice, Simeto **7** Mazzaro, Platani

sea: 6 Ionian **10** Tyrrhenian **13** Mediterranean

physical feature:

cape: 4 Boeo, Faro **7** Lilibeo, Passaro, Passero, Pelorus

gulf: 4 Noto **7** Catania

strait: 7 Messina

wind: 7 sirocco

people: 5 Elymi, Sican, Sicel **6** Sicani, Siculi

author: 9 Lampedusa **10** Pirandello

composer: 7 Bellini

king: 4 Eryx **5** Bomba, Henry, Peter, Roger **7** Charles, Cocalus,

Leontes **9** Ferdinand, Frederick

ruler: 4 Rome **5** Arabs, Goths, Spain **6** Greeks **7** Germans, Normans, Vandals, Vikings **8** Carthage, Saracens **9** Aragonese, Byzantium, Egyptians, Phoenicia **15** Holy Roman Empire

language: 7 Italian

religion: 13 Roman Catholic

place:

cathedral: 8 Monreale

resort: 4 Enna **8** Taormina

ruins: 14 Villa Imperiale **15** Temple of Concord **18** Valley of the Temples

feature:

brigands: 5 Mafia

evening stroll: 11 passeggiata

sick 3 ill **4** weak **5** frail, tired, weary **6** ailing, infirm, laid up, poorly, queasy, sickly, uneasy, unwell **7** crushed, grieved, invalid, unsound **8** delicate, stricken, troubled, wretched **9** afflicted, bored with, disturbed, miserable, nauseated, perturbed, suffering, unhealthy **10** disquieted, distressed, indisposed **11** discomposed, heartbroken **15** under the weather

sicken 5 repel, shock, upset **6** offend, revolt **7** disgust, horrify, make ill, repulse **8** nauseate **14** turn the stomach

sickening 4 foul, vile **5** nasty **7** noisome **8** horrible, unsavory **9** abhorrent, loathsome, offensive, repellent, repugnant, repulsive, revolting **10** disgusting, nauseating **11** distasteful

sickly 3 ill, wan **4** drab, flat, lame, pale, sick, weak **5** ashen, faint, frail, silly **6** ailing, feeble, flimsy, guilty, infirm, leaden, peaked, poorly, sneaky, torpid, unwell **7** insipid, invalid, unsound **8** delicate, smirking **9** afflicted, apathetic, bloodless, simpering, unhealthy **10** cadaverous, lackluster, namby-pamby, snickering, spiritless, uninspired, wishy-washy **11** ineffective **12** unconvincing **13** self-conscious

sickness 6 malady, nausea **7** ailment, disease, illness **8** debility, disorder, vomiting **9** complaint, frailness, ill health, infirmity **10** affliction, disability, invalidism, poor health, queasiness **11** unsoundness **12** qualmishness **13** indisposition

sic passim 12 so throughout

sic semper tyrannis 19 thus always to tyrants

motto of: 8 Virginia

sic transit gloria mundi 33 thus passes away the glory of this world

Siddhartha

author: 12 Hermann Hesse

story of: 6 Buddha

siddur 16 Jewish prayer book

literally: 5 order

side 3 hem, rim **4** area, body, brim,

edge, half, hand, part, sect, team, view **5** angle, bound, cause, facet, flank, group, house, light, limit, minor, party, phase, skirt, slant, stand, stock **6** allied, aspect, behalf, belief, border, circle, clique, fringe, lesser, margin, region, sector, strain **7** askance, coterie, faction, lateral, lineage, oblique, opinion, postern, quarter, related, section, segment, surface **8** alliance, attitude, boundary, division, indirect, marginal, position, skirting **9** accessory, bloodline, coalition, on one side, perimeter, periphery, secondary, territory, viewpoint **10** collateral, contingent, federation, incidental, standpoint, subsidiary **11** affiliation, association, unimportant **13** insignificant

Side

origin: 5 Irish

form: 7 fairies

owner: 14 Tuatha De Danann

sideboard 6 buffet **8** credenza

side by side 7 abreast **8** abutting, together **9** adjoining **11** cheek by jowl, in proximity

Latin: 9 pari passu

Side Effects

author: 10 Woody Allen

sidekick 3 pal **4** aide **5** buddy **6** deputy, friend **9** assistant **10** lieutenant

sideline 5 bench, hobby **8** boundary **9** avocation **14** put out of action

sidestep 4 duck **5** avert, avoid, dodge, elude, evade, skirt **6** bypass, escape **10** circumvent, fight shy of **12** steer clear of

sidestepping 7 dodging, ducking, eluding, evasion **8** skirting **9** avoidance **13** circumvention

sidewalk 4 curb **8** footpath, pavement **9** promenade

sideways, sideway 6 aslant **7** askance, lateral, oblique **8** crabwise, edgeways, edgewise, sidelong, sideward, sidewise **9** cross wise, laterally, obliquely, to the side **11** from one side

side with 5 agree **7** stand by, stick by, support **8** champion **12** take one's part

sidle 4 cant, edge, skew, veer **10** lateralize

Sidney, Sir Philip

author of: 7 Arcadia **15** Defence of Poesie, Defence of Poetry **18** Apologie for Poetrie, Astrophel and Stella

Sidney, Sylvia

real name: 11 Sophia Kosow

born: 7 Bronx NY

husband: 11 Luther Adler **12** Bennett A Cerf

roles: 4 Fury **7** Dead End **11** Street Scene **13** Les Miserables **15** Madame Butterfly **17** An American Tragedy **24** Summer Wishes Winter Dreams

Sidrophel
  character in: **8** Hudibras
  author: **6** Butler
siecle 3 age **6** period **7** century
Siegel, Jerry
  creator/artist of: **8** Superman
Siegfried
  origin: **8** Germanic
  mentioned in: **14** Nibelungenlied
  father: **7** Sigmund
  mother: **9** Sieglinde
  wife: **9** Kriemhild
  killed by: **5** Hagen
  same as: **6** Sigurd
  killed: **6** Fafnir
  won for Gunther: **10** Brunnhilde
  stole: **9** Tarnkappe
Sieg Heil 13 hail to victory
  salute used by: **5** Nazis
Sieglinde
  origin: **8** Germanic
  mentioned in: **14** Nibelungenlied
  husband: **7** Sigmund
  son: **9** Siegfried
Sienkiewicz, Henryk
  author of: **8** Quo Vadis?
Sierra Leone
  name means: **12** lion mountain
  other name: **9** Gold Coast **10** Grain
    Coast, Ivory Coast
  capital/largest city: **8** Freetown
  others: **2** Bo **5** Hepel, Kissi, Lungi,
    Pepel **6** Bonthe, Kenema, Makeni,
    Shenge, Sulima
  school: **6** Njala U **9** Fourah Bay
  measure: **4** load **6** kettle
  monetary unit: **4** cent **5** leone
  island: **4** York **6** Banana, Turtle **7**
    Sherbro
  mountain: **4** Loma **10** Tingi Hills
  highest point: **9** Bintimani
  river: **3** Moa **4** Jong, Mano, Meli,
    Ribi, Sewa, Taia **5** Bagbe, Mongo,
    Morro, Rokel **6** Mabole, Rokkel,
    Scarcy, Waanje **13** Great Scarcies
    14 Little Scarcies
  sea: **8** Atlantic
  physical feature:
    bay: **5** Yawri **7** Sherbro
    cape: **8** Shilling **11** Sierra Leone
    peninsula: **7** Turners **11** Sierra
      Leone
    wind: **9** harmattan
  people: **3** Vai **4** Kono, Loko, Susu **5**
    Bulom, Kissi, Limba, Mende, Mendi,
    Temne **6** Creole, Fulani, Syrian **7**
    Gallina, Koranko, Kuranko, Sherbro,
    Yalunka, Lebanese, Mandingo
    explorer: **6** Cintra
    leader: **6** Margai **7** Stevens
  language: **4** Krio **5** Limba, Mende,
    Mendi, Temne **6** Creole **7** English
  religion: **5** Islam **7** animism **12** Christianity
  place:
    wharf: **10** King Jimmys
  feature:

  cloth: **5** garra
  clothing: **5** lappa **6** caftan
  secret society: **4** poro
  food:
    dish: **4** fufu **7** cassava
    sauce: **7** palaver
siesta 3 nap **4** rest **5** break, sleep **6** cat
  nap, snooze **10** forty winks
sieve 4 sift **6** filter, riddle, screen,
  sorter, strain **7** tattler **8** colander,
  strainer **9** separator **12** blabbermouth
sift 4 sort **5** drift, probe, study **6** filter,
  review, screen, search, winnow **7** analyze, inspect, scatter, sort out **8** separate **10** scrutinize **11** distinguish, investigate **12** discriminate
Siggeir
  origin: **12** Scandinavian
  king of: **5** Goths
  wife: **5** Signy
  causes death of: **7** Volsung
sigh 3 sob **4** hiss, long, moan, pine,
  weep **5** brood, groan, mourn, whine,
  yearn **6** grieve, lament, sorrow
sight 3 ken, see, spy **4** bead, espy,
  gaze, spot, view **5** image, scene, vista
  6 behold, seeing, survey, vision **7** display, exhibit, eyeshot, glimpse, observe, pageant, scenery, viewing **8**
  eyesight, perceive, prospect, scrutiny
  9 peepsight, sighthole, spectacle **10**
  appearance, visibility
sighted 3 saw **4** seen **6** seeing **8** not
  blind, observed
sightless 5 blind **8** unseeing **9** unsighted
sightly 4 fair **6** lovely, pretty **8** handsome, pleasing **9** appealing, beautiful
  10 attractive
Sigmund
  origin: **8** Germanic **12** Scandinavian
  mentioned in: **8** Volsunga **14** Nibelungenlied
  king of: **11** Netherlands
  father: **7** Volsung
  mother: **4** Liod, Ljod **5** Hliod
  wife: **7** Hiordis, Hjordis **8** Borghild **9**
    Sieglinde
  sister: **5** Signy
  lover: **5** Signy
  son: **6** Sigurd **9** Siegfried, Sinfiotli
sign 3 nod **4** clue, hint, mark, note,
  omen, wave **5** badge, brand, index,
  stamp, token, trait **6** emblem, ensign,
  figure, herald, motion, signal, symbol
  7 earmark, endorse, feature, gesture,
  go-ahead, placard, portent, presage,
  symptom, warning **8** evidence, forecast, inscribe, neon sign, road sign,
  signpost **9** autograph, billboard,
  guidepost, harbinger, indicator, nameplate, trademark **10** indication, intimation, prognosis, suggestion, underwrite **11** forewarning **13** manifestation
  14 characteristic see also **6** zodiac
signal 3 cue, nod **4** sign **6** beckon, famous, motion, unique **7** command,

eminent, gesture, guiding, honored,
notable, warning **8** high sign, password, pointing, renowned, singular,
striking **9** arresting, directing, direction, important, indicator, memorable,
momentous, prominent, watchword
10 commanding, impressive, indicating, indication, noteworthy, one of-a-kind, remarkable **11** conspicuous, distinctive, exceptional, illustrious, outstanding, significant **12** considerable
13 consequential, distinguished, extraordinary, unforgettable
significance 3 aim **4** note **5** drift,
  force, merit, sense, value, worth **6** import, intent, moment, object, virtue,
  weight **7** concern, gravity, meaning,
  portent, purpose **8** eminence, interest,
  priority **9** authority, direction, influence, intention, relevance **10** excellence, importance, notability, prominence **11** consequence, distinction,
  implication
significant 4 main **5** chief, grave,
  great, major, prime, vital **6** cogent,
  signal **7** eminent, knowing, notable,
  serious, telling, weighty **8** critical, distinct, eloquent, eventful, material,
  pregnant, symbolic **9** important, momentous, paramount, principal, prominent **10** emblematic, expressive, indicative, meaningful, noteworthy,
  portentous, remarkable, suggestive **11**
  exceptional, influential, outstanding,
  substantial, symptomatic **12** considerable **13** consequential, demonstrative
  14 representative
signify 4 mean, omen, show, tell **5** argue, augur, imply **6** convey, denote,
  evince, herald, hint at, import, reveal,
  typify **7** bespeak, betoken, connote,
  declare, exhibit, express, portend, predict, presage, promise, suggest **8** announce, disclose, evidence, forebode,
  foretell, indicate, intimate, manifest,
  proclaim, set forth, stand for **9** be a
  sign of, designate, represent, symbolize **10** foreshadow **11** communicate,
  demonstrate
signing up 7 joining **9** enlisting, enrolling **10** enlistment, enrollment **11** registering **12** registration **13** matriculating, matriculation
Sign of Four, The
  author: **19** Sir Arthur Conan Doyle
  character: **11** Mary Morstan **12** Dr
    John Watson **13** Jonathan Small **14**
    Sherlock Holmes, Thaddeus Sholto
Signoret, Simone
  real name: **32** Simone-Henriette-Charlotte Kaminker
  born: **7** Germany **9** Wiesbaden
  husband: **11** Yves Montand **12** Yves
    Allegret
  roles: **10** Madame Rosa **11** Ship of
    Fools **12** Room at the Top (Oscar)
    14 Is Paris Burning?

autobiography: 27 Nostalgia Isn't What It Used to Be

sign up 4 join **6** enlist, enroll, join up **8** register **9** volunteer **11** matriculate

Sigurd
origin: 12 Scandinavian
mentioned in: 8 Volsunga
father: 7 Sigmund
mother: 7 Hiordis, Hjordis
wife: 6 Gudrun, Kudrun **7** Guthrun
killed: 6 Fafnir
acquired treasure of: 8 Andavari
won for Gunnar: 8 Brynhild

Sigyn
origin: 12 Scandinavian
husband: 4 Loki

Sikes, Bill
character in: 11 Oliver Twist
author: 7 Dickens

Sikkim
capital/largest city: 7 Gangtok
others: 6 Dikchu, Lachen, Namchi, Rangpo, Rumtek **7** Lachung **9** Chungtang
government: 12 state of India
mountain: 7 Dongkya, Donkhya **9** Himalayas, Singalili **10** Darjeeling **12** Kanchenjunga
river: 5 Tista **6** Ranjit **9** Lachen Chu **10** Lachung Chu
physical feature:
  mountain pass: 6 Natu La **7** Jelep La
  storm: 7 monsoon
people: 4 Rong **5** Bhote **6** Bhotia, Bhutia, Indian, Lepcha **7** Tibetan **8** Nepalese **9** Mongoloid
king: 7 chogyal
religion: 5 Hindu **7** Lamaism **15** Tibetan Buddhism

Sikorsky, Igor
nationality: 7 Russian **8** American
invented: 10 helicopter

Silas Marner
author: 11 George Eliot
profession: 6 weaver
character: 5 Eppie **11** Dunstan Cass, Godfrey Cass **13** Aaron Winthrop, Nancy Lammeter

silence 3 gag **4** calm, curb, halt, hush, kill, rout, stop **5** allay, check, crush, peace, quash, quell, quiet, still **6** banish, deaden, defeat, muffle, muzzle, repose, squash, stifle, subdue **7** conquer, nullify, put down, quieten, repress, reserve, squelch **8** choke off, dumbness, muteness, overcome, serenity, suppress, vanquish **9** lay to rest, placidity, quietness, reticence, stillness, tongue-tie **10** extinguish, placidness, put an end to, strike dumb **11** taciturnity, tranquility **12** tranquillity **13** noiselessness, secretiveness, soundlessness **14** speechlessness **16** closemouthedness **19** uncommunicativeness

silent 3 mum **4** calm, dumb, idle, mute

5 inert, muted, quiet, still, tacit **6** covert, hidden, hushed, placid, serene, unsaid **7** dormant, implied, muffled **8** discreet, implicit, inactive, inferred, lifeless, peaceful, reserved, reticent, taciturn, tranquil, unspoken, wordless **9** concealed, intimated, noiseless, quiescent, secretive, soundless, suggested, unsounded, unwritten **10** insinuated, mysterious, speechless, tongue-tied, undeclared, understood, unrevealed, unstirring, untalked-of **11** close-lipped, tight-lipped, unexpressed, unmentioned, unpublished, untalkative, unvocalized **12** closemouthed, unpronounced **15** uncommunicative

Silent Spring
author: 13 Rachel L Carson

Silenus
god of: 6 forest
oldest: 5 satyr
father: 3 Pan **6** Hermes
foster father of: 8 Dionysus
teacher of: 8 Dionysus
companion of: 8 Dionysus
sons: 6 Sileni

silicon
chemical symbol: 2 Si

silk
fabric: 4 crin **5** crepe, ninon, satin, surah, tulle **6** faille, pongee, sendal, tussah **7** chiffon, foulard, organza, raw silk, taffeta **8** organzie, paduasoy **10** peau de soie **12** crepe de chine
lining: 7 sarsnet **8** sarcenet
measure: 6 denier
raw silk: 5 grege **6** greige **8** marabout
source: 6 cocoon **9** silkworms
waste: 4 noil **5** floss
watered: 5 moire
yarn/thread: 4 tram **5** floss

silk-stocking 6 uptown **8** highborn, highbred, wellborn **9** patrician **10** upper-class **11** blue-blooded **12** aristocratic

Silk Stockings
director: 15 Rouben Mamoulian
cast: 10 Janis Paige, Peter Lorre **11** Cyd Charisse, Fred Astaire
setting: 5 Paris
score: 10 Cole Porter
remake of: 9 Ninotchka

silky 4 fine, soft **6** satiny, smooth **11** fine-grained

silliness 5 folly **6** drivel, idiocy **7** inanity **9** absurdity, asininity, frivolity **10** buffoonery, tomfoolery **11** foolishness **13** pointlessness **14** playing the fool, ridiculousness

Sillitoe, Alan
author of: 10 Her Victory **29** Saturday Night and Sunday Morning **36** The Loneliness of the Long-Distance Runner

silly 3 mad **4** dumb **5** crazy, giddy, insane **6** absurd, frothy, insane, stupid,

unwary, unwise **7** aimless, asinine, fatuous, foolish, idiotic, shallow, witless **8** childish, farcical **9** brainless, foolhardy, frivolous, laughable, ludicrous, pointless, senseless **10** ill-advised, irrational, ridiculous **11** empty-headed, harebrained, meaningless, nonsensical, purposeless **12** muddleheaded, preposterous, simple-minded, unreasonable **13** inappropriate, irresponsible, muddlebrained, rattlebrained **14** featherbrained **15** inconsequential

Silmarillion, The
author: 10 J R R Tolkien

silo 3 pit **5** tower
storage of: 6 fodder **7** missile

Silone, Ignazio
real name: 17 Secondo Tranquilli
author of: 9 Fontamara **12** Bread and Wine **26** The Story of a Humble Christian

Silvanus
also: 8 Sylvanus
god of: 5 herds, house, woods **12** farm boundary **16** uncultivated land

silver 5 coins, plate **6** argent, change **7** jewelry **8** argentum, platinum **9** argentine **10** silverware
chemical symbol: 2 Ag

Silver
horse of: 10 Lone Ranger

Silver, Long John
character in: 14 Treasure Island
author: 9 Stevenson

Silver, Mattie
character in: 10 Ethan Frome
author: 7 Wharton

Silvers, Phil
real name: 17 Philip Silversmith
born: 10 Brooklyn NY
roles: 9 Top Banana **13** Sergeant Bilko **15** High Button Shoes **22** A Guide for the Married Man **37** A Funny Thing Happened on the Way to the Forum
autobiography: 14 The Laugh Is on Me

s'il vous plaît 6 please **11** if you please

Simenon, Georges
author of: 8 The Train **12** Act of Passion **14** The Little Saint **15** Maigret's Memoirs **28** The Strange Case of Peter the Lett
character: 21 Inspector Jules Maigret

Simeon
father: 5 Jacob
mother: 4 Leah
brother: 3 Dan, Gad **4** Levi **5** Asher, Judah **6** Joseph, Reuben **7** Zebulun **8** Benjamin, Issachar, Naphtali
sister: 5 Dinah
canticle: 12 nunc dimittis
descendant of: 9 Simeonite

similar 4 akin, like, twin **5** close **6** allied **7** cognate, kindred **8** agreeing, matching, parallel **9** analogous, duplicate **10** comparable, equivalent, resembling **11** approximate, correlative, much the same, nearly alike **13** correspondent, corresponding

similarity 7 harmony, kinship, oneness **8** affinity, likeness, nearness, sameness **9** agreement, closeness, congruity, semblance **10** congruence, similitude **11** concordance, conformance, equivalence, parallelism, reciprocity, resemblance **13** comparability **14** conformability, correspondence

similarly 4 thus **5** alike **7** equally **8** likewise **11** furthermore, identically **15** correspondingly

similitude 7 analogy **8** likeness, sameness **10** similarity **11** parallelism, resemblance

simmer 4 boil, burn, foam, fume, stew **5** chafe, smart **6** bubble, burble, gurgle, seethe, sizzle

simmer down 7 cool off **8** calm down **14** collect oneself, compose oneself

Simmons, Jean
born: **6** London **7** England
husband: **13** Richard Brooks **14** Stewart Granger
roles: **4** Trio **6** Hamlet **7** Desiree, Ophelia, The Robe **9** Spartacus, Young Bess **11** Elmer Gantry **12** Guys and Dolls **14** The Happy Ending **17** Great Expectations **19** Androcles and the Lion

Simon
also known as: **5** Peter
son: **13** Judas Iscariot
disciple of: **5** Jesus

Simon, Neil
author of: **10** Chapter Two, Plaza Suite **11** Biloxi Blues **12** The Odd Couple **15** The Sunshine Boys **16** Come Blow Your Horn **17** Barefoot in the Park **21** Last of the Red Hot Lovers **25** The Prisoner of Second Avenue

Simon & Simon
character: **7** AJ Simon **9** Rick Simon **12** Cecilia Simon **13** Downtown Brown
cast: **7** Tim Reid **10** Mary Carver **13** Gerald McRaney, Jameson Parker
setting: **8** San Diego

Simon Boccanegra
opera by: **5** Verdi
setting: **5** Genoa
character: **5** Maria, Paolo **6** Andrea, Fiesco, Pietro **14** Amelia Grimaldi, Gabriele Adorno

Simon Legree 8 overseer **11** slave-driver
in: **14** Uncle Tom's Cabin

Simonov, Konstantin
author of: **13** Days and Nights

Simon Templar *see* Saint, The

simpatico 7 likable **9** agreeable, congenial, gemutlich

simper 5 smirk **6** giggle, tee-hee, titter **7** snicker, snigger

simple 4 bare, dull, dumb, easy, open, slow, soft, true **5** basic, blunt, dense, frank, green, homey, naive, naked, plain, quiet, sheer, stark, thick **6** callow, candid, common, direct, honest, modest, obtuse, rustic, stupid **7** artless, foolish, natural, sincere **8** absolute, innocent, not fancy, ordinary, peaceful, straight, workaday **9** downright, elemental, guileless, ingenuous, out-and-out, unadorned, unfeigned, untrimmed, unworldly **10** elementary, manageable, not complex, unaffected, uninvolved **11** commonplace, fundamental, plain-spoken, rudimentary, thick-witted, undecorated, unvarnished **12** not difficult, not elaborate, uncompounded **13** inexperienced, uncomplicated, unembellished, unpretentious **15** straightforward, unsophisticated

simple house 3 cot, hut **5** shack **6** chalet **7** cottage **8** bungalow

simpleminded 4 dull, dumb, slow **5** dense, silly, thick **6** stupid **7** asinine, fatuous, foolish, idiotic, moronic, witless **8** retarded **9** brainless, dim-witted, imbecilic **10** dull-witted, half-witted **11** empty-headed, harebrained, lamebrained **12** feeble-minded

simpleton 3 ass, oaf **4** dolt, dope, fool, hick, jerk, rube **5** booby, dummy, dunce, goose, idiot, ninny, stupe **6** donkey, rustic **7** dullard, jackass **8** dumbbell, imbecile, numskull **9** blockhead, greenhorn, ignoramus, numbskull **10** nincompoop

simplicity 6 candor, purity **7** clarity, honesty, naivete **8** easiness, openness, serenity **9** austerity, clearness, innocence, plainness, restraint, sincerity **10** directness **11** artlessness, cleanliness, naturalness, obviousness **12** truthfulness **13** guilelessness, unworldliness **19** straightforwardness

simply 7 clearly, lucidly, plainly, starkly **8** directly, modestly **9** naturally **10** explicitly **11** ingenuously **12** intelligibly, unaffectedly **15** uncomplicatedly, unpretentiously **17** straightforwardly

Simpson, O J (Orenthal James)
nickname: **5** Juice
sport: **8** football
position: **11** running back
team: **10** USC Trojans **12** Buffalo Bills **23** San Francisco Forty-Niners
film: **11** The Naked Gun

Simpsons, The
creator: **12** Matt Groening
roles: **3** Apu, Moe **4** Bart, Lisa, Otto **5** Homer, Marge **6** Barney **7** Mr Burns **8** Smithers **11** Chief Wiggum **12** Mrs. Karbappel

simulate 3 act, ape **4** copy, fake, play,

pose, sham **5** feign, mimic, put on **6** affect, assume, invent **7** imitate, play-act, pretend **9** dissemble, fabricate **11** counterfeit, make believe

simulated 4 fake, sham **5** phony **6** forged **7** manmade, pretend **9** imitation, synthetic **10** artificial, fabricated **11** counterfeit, make-believe

simultaneous 6 coeval **10** coexistent, coexisting, coincident, concurrent, synchronal, synchronic **11** concomitant, synchronous **12** accompanying, contemporary **15** contemporaneous

sin 3 err **4** evil, fall, slip, vice **5** crime, error, lapse, shame, stray, wrong **6** breach, do evil, offend **7** do wrong, misdeed, offense, scandal **8** disgrace, evil deed, iniquity, trespass, villainy **9** violation **10** infraction, transgress, wrongdoing **13** transgression

Sin
origin: **8** Akkadian
god of: **4** moon

Sinatra, Frank
real name: **20** Francis Albert Sinatra
nickname: **8** The Voice **11** Old Blue Eyes **18** Chairman of the Board
born: **9** Hoboken NJ
wife: **9** Mia Farrow **10** Ava Gardner
daughter: **12** Nancy Sinatra
son: **14** Frank Sinatra Jr
leader of: **7** Rat Pack
roles: **8** Tony Rome **12** Angelo Maggio, Guys and Dolls, The Detective **14** The Joker Is Wild **17** The First Deadly Sin **18** From Here to Eternity **22** The Man with the Golden Arm

Sinbad the Sailor
character in: **27** Arabian Nights' Entertainments

since 2 as **3** ago, for, yet **4** ergo, from **5** after, hence, later **6** thence, whence **7** because, whereas **8** in as much **9** therefore **10** afterwards **11** accordingly, considering **12** subsequently
archaic: **4** sith
prefix: **3** cis
Scottish: **4** syne

sincere 4 real **5** frank **6** candid, honest **7** artless, earnest, genuine, natural, serious **8** truthful **9** authentic, guileless, heartfelt, ingenuous, unfeigned **10** forthright, unaffected **11** in good faith, undeceitful **12** wholehearted **15** straightforward

sincerely 5 truly **6** really **8** honestly **9** earnestly, genuinely, seriously **10** truthfully **14** wholeheartedly

sincerity 6 candor **7** honesty, probity **8** openness **9** frankness, good faith **11** artlessness, earnestness, genuineness, seriousness **12** truthfulness **13** guilelessness, ingenuousness **14** forthrightness, unaffectedness **16** wholeheartedness **19** straightforwardness

Sinclair, Upton
author of: **9** The Jungle, World's End

12 Dragon's Teeth
character: **9** Lanny Budd

Sindhi
language family: **12** Indo-European
branch: **11** Indo-Iranian
group: **5** Indic
spoken in: **13** Northern India

sine die 17 without fixing a day (for future action or a future meeting)
literally: **13** without the day

sine prole 14 without progeny **16** without offspring

sine qua non 15 without which not **18** something essential **22** indispensable condition

sinew, sinews 4 grit, thew **5** fiber, nerve, power, vigor **6** muscle, tendon **7** stamina **8** ligament, strength, virility, vitality **10** resilience, strengthen

sinewy 4 wiry **5** beefy, nervy, thewy, tough **6** brawny, robust, strong **7** fibrose, stringy **8** muscular, powerful, vigorous

sinful 3 bad **4** evil, vile **5** wrong **6** errant, unholy, wicked **7** corrupt, heinous, immoral, impious, ungodly, wayward **8** criminal, depraved, shameful **9** miscreant **10** degenerate, despicable, iniquitous, profligate, villainous **11** disgraceful, irreligious, unrighteous

sing 3 hum **4** lilt, pipe **5** carol, chant, chirp, croon, trill, tweet **6** intone, warble **7** chir rup, whistle **8** melodize

Sing Along with Mitch
regulars: **10** Diana Trask **11** Mitch Miller **12** Leslie Uggams, Louise O'Brien, Sandy Stewart **13** Gloria Lambert, Sing Along Gang, Sing Along Kids

Singapore
other name: **8** Singa Pur
name means: **13** city of the lion
capital/largest city: **9** Singapore
others: **4** Tuas **6** Changi, Jurong **7** Nee Soon **9** Paya Lebar, Woodlands **10** Bukit Timah, Queenstown **12** Bukit Panjang **15** Toa Payoh New Town
  medieval town: **7** Temasek
school: **7** Nanyang **8** National **9** Singapore
monetary unit: **4** cent **6** dollar
island: **4** Ubin **5** Brani, Bukum, Pesek **7** Semakau **8** Merlimau, Southern **10** Ayer Chawan, Ayer Merbau **11** Blakang Mati, Tekong Besar **12** Tekong Kechil
mountain: **6** Mandai **7** Panjang
highest point: **10** Bukit Timah
river: **6** Jurong, Sungei **7** Kallang, Seletar **9** Singapore
sea: **6** Indian **10** South China
physical feature:
  harbor: **6** Keppel **9** Serangoon
  strait: **6** Johore, Pandan **8** Sembilan **9** Singapore

people: 5 Malay **6** Indian **7** Chinese **9** Malaysian, Pakistani, Sri Lankan
founder: **7** Raffles
leader: **10** Lee Kwan Yew
language: **5** Malay, Tamil **7** Chinese, English **8** Mandarin
religion: **4** Sikh **5** Hindu, Islam **6** Taoism **8** Buddhism **12** Christianity, Confucianism
place:
  amusement park: **8** New World **10** Great World, Happy World
  aquarium: **8** Van Kleef
  cathedral: **9** St Andrews
  gardens: **7** Botanic
  hall: **16** Victoria Memorial
  industrial park: **6** Jurong
  mosque: **6** Sultan
  park: **6** Farber **7** Merlion **12** Raffles Place
  street: **16** Raffles Boulevard
  temple: **17** One Thousand Lights
feature:
  boat: **4** junk **6** sampan
  clothing: **4** sari

singe 4 burn, char, sear **5** brand **6** scorch

singer 4 alto, bard, bass, diva, lark **5** tenor **6** canary **7** crooner, soprano **8** baritone, minstrel, songbird, songster, vocalist **9** chanteuse, chantress, contralto **10** cantatrice, songstress, troubadour **11** nightingale **12** countertenor, mezzo-soprano

Singer, Isaac Bashevis
author of: **6** Shosha **7** Old Love **8** The Manor **9** The Estate **13** Gimpel the Fool **15** The Family Moskat **16** In My Father's Court **24** The Spinoza of Market Street

singing group 4 trio **5** choir, nonet, octet **6** chorus, sextet **7** quartet, quintet **8** glee club **13** choral society **17** barbershop quartet

Singin' in the Rain
director: **9** Gene Kelly **12** Stanley Donen
cast: **9** Gene Kelly, Jean Hagen **11** Cyd Charisse **13** Donald O'Connor **14** Debbie Reynolds
song: **11** Make 'em Laugh

single 3 one **4** lone, sole **5** unwed **6** maiden **7** only one **8** bachelor, singular, solitary, spinster, wifeless **9** unmarried **10** individual, spouseless **11** husbandless

single file 8 one by one **10** Indian file, one at a time **13** in a single line **16** one behind another

single-handedly 5 alone **7** unaided **9** by oneself, on one's own **10** unassisted **11** without help

single-minded 4 firm **6** dogged **7** devoted, intense, staunch, zealous **8** resolved, tireless, untiring **9** dedicated, steadfast, tenacious **10** determined, inflexible, persistent, relentless, un-

swerving, unwavering **11** persevering, unflinching

singleness 12 bachelorhood, spinsterhood **14** unmarried state **17** single blessedness

single out 4 pick, take **6** choose, opt for, select **7** call out, extract, fix upon, pick out **8** decide on, set apart, settle on **11** distinguish

sing the praises of 4 hail, laud, tout **5** boost, cheer, exalt, extol, honor **6** praise **7** acclaim, applaud, approve, commend **8** eulogize **9** celebrate **10** compliment

singular 3 odd **4** rare **5** queer **6** choice, quaint, select, unique **7** bizarre, curious, strange, unusual **8** aberrant, abnormal, atypical, freakish, peculiar, peerless, superior, uncommon, unwonted **9** anomalous, different, eccentric, fantastic, marvelous, matchless, unequaled, unnatural, wonderful **10** noteworthy, outlandish, prodigious, remarkable, surpassing, unfamiliar **11** exceptional, uncustomary **12** unparalleled **13** extraordinary, unaccountable, unprecedented **14** unconventional **16** out-of-the-ordinary

Sinhalese
language family: **12** Indo-European
branch: **11** Indo-Iranian
group: **5** Indic
spoken in: **6** Ceylon **8** Sri Lanka

sinister 4 dark, dire, evil, foul, rank, vile **5** black **6** cursed, malign, wicked **7** adverse, fearful, hellish, ominous, unlucky **8** accursed, alarming, damnable, devilish, infernal, menacing, rascally **9** dismaying, insidious, malignant **10** despicable, detestable, diabolical, disturbing, malevolent, perfidious, villainous **11** disquieting, frightening, threatening, treacherous, unfavorable, unpromising **12** blackhearted, inauspicious, unpropitious **13** Machiavellian, reprehensible

sink 3 dig, dip, ebb, lay, sag, set **4** bore, bowl, bury, drop, fall, seep, slip, soak, tilt, wane **5** basin, drill, drive, droop, drown, gouge, lower, slant, slope, slump, stoop, yield **6** engulf, go down, lessen, plunge, reduce, shrink, worsen **7** decline, descend, give way, go to pot, go under, put down, regress, subside, succumb **8** diminish, excavate, languish, lavatory, scoop out, submerge, submerse, washbowl **9** hollow out, wash basin **10** degenerate, depreciate, go downhill, retrogress **11** deteriorate, go to the dogs

sinless 4 good, holy, pure **6** chaste **7** upright **8** innocent, spotless, virtuous **9** reputable, righteous

sinner 8 apostate, evildoer, offender **9** miscreant, misfeasor, reprobate, wrongdoer **10** backslider, malefactor, malfeasant, recidivist, trespasser **12** transgressor

Sinon
pretended to be: **13** Greek deserter
told Trojans of: **11** Trojan Horse

Sino-Tibetan
language branch: **7** Sinitic **12** Tibeto-Burman
includes: **4** Naga **5** Karen **7** Burmese, Chinese **8** Kuki-Chin, Mandarin

Sins, Seven 4 envy, lust **5** anger, pride, sloth **8** gluttony **12** covetousness

sinuosity 10 slinkiness **11** convolution, sinuousness **12** tortuousness

sinuous 6 curved, folded, volute, zigzag **7** bending, coiling, curving, twisted, winding **8** indirect, mazelike, rambling, tortuous, twisting **9** wandering **10** circuitous, convoluted, meandering, roundabout, serpentine, undulating **12** labyrinthine

sinuousness 9 sinuosity **10** slinkiness **11** convolution **12** tortuousness

Siouan
tribe: **4** Crow, Iowa **5** Ioway, Omaha, Osage, Sioux **6** Dakota, Mandan **7** Hidatsa **8** Minitari, Wazhazhe **10** Assiniboin, Gros Ventre **11** Assiniboine

Sioux *see* **6** Dakota

Sioux State
nickname of: **11** North Dakota

sip 3 lap, nip, sup **4** dram, drop **5** drink, savor, taste **6** sample **7** soup con, swallow **10** thimbleful

siphon 4 tube **5** drain **7** draw off

siphonaptera
class: **8** hexapoda
phylum: **10** arthropoda
group: **4** flea

Sippar residents 11 Sepharvites

Siqueiros, David Alfaro
born: **6** Mexico **9** Chihuahua
artwork: **12** New Democracy **13** Echo of a Scream **14** Trial of Fascism **15** Ascent of Culture, Burial of a Worker **16** Towards the Cosmos **17** Death to the Invader **18** Polyforum Siqueiros **22** March of Humanity on Earth **24** Cuauhtemoc Against the Myth

sir *see* **6** mister

sire 4 king, lord **5** beget, breed **6** create, father **7** creator **9** originate **10** originator, progenitor

siren, Siren 4 horn, vamp **5** alarm, nymph, witch **6** sexpot **7** charmer, whistle **8** deceiver, sea nymph **9** temptress **10** seductress **11** enchantress **13** warning signal **15** bewitching woman
French: **11** femme fatale
form: **5** nymph
location: **3** sea
lured sailors by: **7** singing

Sir Gawain and the Green Knight
author: **7** unknown

character: **10** King Arthur **22** Sir Bernlak de Hautdesert
horse: **9** Gringalet

Sirian Experiments, The
author: **12** Doris Lessing

sissified 6 prissy **7** unmanly **8** womanish **10** effeminate

sissy 6 coward **8** weakling **9** fraidy-cat **10** scaredy-cat

sister 3 nun, kin, sib **5** nurse **6** female **7** sibling **8** feminist, relation, relative
nautically: **6** secure **10** strengthen
society: **8** sorority

Sister Carrie
author: **15** Theodore Dreiser
character: **11** G W Hurstwood **12** Carrie Meeber **13** Charles Drouet

Sister Woman
character in: **16** Cat on a Hot Tin Roof
author: **8** Williams

Sisyphean 4 hard **5** tough **6** uphill **7** arduous, onerous **8** toilsome **9** demanding, difficult, strenuous, wearisome **10** exhausting

Sisyphus
king of: **7** Corinth
father: **6** Aeolus
mother: **7** Enarete
brother: **9** Salmoneus
wife: **6** Merope
son: **5** Almus **7** Glaucus **8** Ornytion **10** Thersander
founded: **6** Ephyra **7** Corinth
rolled: **11** stone uphill

sit 3 lie **4** loll, meet, mind, rest, rule, stay **5** abide, chair, nurse, perch, reign, roost, squat, stand, teach, watch **6** attend, endure, gather, govern, linger, remain, reside, settle, sprawl **7** baby-sit, care for, convene, preside **8** assemble, be placed, be seated, chaperon **9** have a seat, officiate **10** deliberate **11** be in session

site 4 area, post, spot, zone **5** field, locus, place, point, scene **6** ground, locale, region, sector **7** section, setting, station **8** district, locality, location, position, province **9** territory **11** whereabouts

sit in judgment 5 judge **6** decide, settle **7** adjudge, mediate **9** arbitrate, reconcile **10** adjudicate **12** bring to terms

situ 5 place

situate 3 put, set **4** post **5** build, house, lodge, place, plant, stand **6** billet, locate, settle **7** install, station **8** ensconce, position **9** construct, establish

situation 3 fix, job **4** case, duty, post, role, seat, site, spot, work **5** berth, place, state **6** locale, office, plight, status **7** dilemma, posture, station **8** capacity, function, locality, location, position, quandary **9** condition **10** assignment, livelihood **11** predicament **13** circumstances **14** state of affairs

sit upon 5 brood, cover, hatch **8** incubate

Sivan 16 third Hebrew month

Six Characters in Search of an Author
author: **15** Luigi Pirandello

six cubits 4 reed

Six Million Dollar Man
character: **11** Dr Rudy Wells, (Col) Steve Austin **12** Oscar Goldman
cast: **9** Lee Majors **13** Martin E Brooks **15** Alan Oppenheimer, Richard Anderson
spinoff: **11** Bionic Woman

Sixty Minutes
correspondent: **9** Dan Rather, Ed Bradley **10** Andy Rooney, Steve Kroft **11** Diane Sawyer, Leslie Stahl, Mike Wallace, Morley Safer **13** Harry Reasoner

sizable 5 ample, broad, large, roomy **7** immense **8** spacious **9** capacious, good-sized

size 3 sum **4** area, bulk, mass, sort **5** array, grade, group, scope, total **6** amount, extent, spread, volume **7** arrange, bigness, content, expanse, stretch **8** capacity, classify, quantity, totality **9** aggregate, amplitude, greatness, largeness, magnitude **10** dimensions **11** measurement, proportions

sizzle 3 fry **4** hiss, spit **7** crackle, frizzle, hissing, sputter **8** splutter **10** sputtering

skate 3 nag, ray **4** skid, skim, slip **5** blade, coast, glide, horse, slide **6** rotter
female: **4** maid
genus: **4** Raja
mark: **4** cusp

skein 4 coil, hank, reel, yarn **5** twist **6** tangle, thread **9** filaments, twistings
members: **4** fowl **5** ducks, flock, geese **6** flyers

skeletal 4 bony, thin **5** gaunt **6** wasted **9** emaciated **10** cadaverous

skeleton 4 hulk **5** bones, frame, shell **9** framework
purpose: **7** support **8** protects **9** framework

Skelton, Red
real name: **21** Richard Bernard Skelton
born: **11** Vincennes IN
roles: **7** I Dood It **8** Ship Ahoy **12** Panama Hattie **16** Neptune's Daughter **17** The Fuller Brush Man **18** Clem Kadiddlehopper, Whistling in the Dark **20** Freddie the Freeloader

skeptic, sceptic 7 atheist, doubter, scoffer **8** agnostic **10** questioner, unbeliever **14** doubting Thomas

skeptical, sceptical 6 unsure **7** cynical, dubious **8** doubtful, doubting, scoffing **9** uncertain **11** incredulous, questioning, unbelieving, unconvinced **12** disbelieving **13** hypercritical

skepticism 5 doubt **7** dubiety **8** distrust, mistrust, unbelief **9** disbelief, suspicion **11** agnosticism, incredulity **12** doubtfulness **13** faithlessness

sketch 3 map **4** draw, plot, skit **5** chart, draft, graph, scene **6** depict, digest, precis, satire **7** drawing, lampoon, mark out, outline, picture, portray, summary, takeoff **8** abstract, rough out, synopsis, vignette **9** blueprint, burlesque, delineate, short play, summarize **11** preliminary **16** characterization

Sketch Book, The
  author: **16** Washington Irving

sketchy 4 bare, hazy **5** brief, crude, light, rough, short, vague **6** meager, skimpy, slight **7** cursory, outline, shallow, slender **9** essential, rough-hewn, unrefined **10** incomplete, undetailed, unfinished, unpolished **11** preliminary, preparatory, provisional, superficial

skewed 5 slued **6** veered, warped **7** oblique, sheered, slanted, swerved, twisted **9** distorted

skewer 3 pin, rod **4** spit, stab **5** truss **6** pierce, skiver **7** impale **9** brochette **10** run through

skid 3 ski **4** drag, dray, skim, skip, sled, slip **5** coast, glide, skate, slide **6** runner, sledge **7** skitter **8** glissade, platform, sideslip

Skidbladnir
  origin: **12** Scandinavian
  ship of: **4** Frey **5** Freyr
  feature: **11** collapsible

Skidmore, Owings, and Merrill
  partners: **13** John Merrill Sr, Louis Skidmore **15** Nathaniel Owings
  architects of: **10** Lever House (NYC) **11** AEC town site (Oak Ridge TN) **13** Banque Lambert (Brussels) **16** John Hancock Tower (Chicago) **17** Terrace Plaza Hotel (Cincinnati), US Air Force Academy (CO) **18** Mauna Kea Beach Hotel (Kamuela HI) **19** Istanbul Hilton Hotel (Turkey) **23** Beinecke Rare Book Library (Yale) **26** Chase Manhattan Bank Building (NYC) **33** American Republic Insurance Building (Des Moines IA)
    world's tallest building: **10** Sears Tower (Chicago)

skiff 4 boat **6** dinghy **7** rowboat

skiing
  athlete: **9** Phil Mahre **11** Bill Johnson, Cindy Nelson **13** Gustavo Thoeni, Robert Cochran **14** Marilyn Cochran, Martha Rockwell **15** Debbie Armstrong, Ingemar Stenmark, Jean Claude Killy **16** Michael Gallagher **17** Barbara Ann Cochran **20** Annemarie Proell Moser

skill 4 gift **5** craft, knack **6** acumen, tal-

ent **7** ability, cunning, faculty, knowhow, mastery, prowess **8** artistry, capacity, deftness, facility **9** adeptness, dexterity, expertise, handiness, ingenuity **10** adroitness, cleverness, competence, experience, expertness **11** proficiency **12** skillfulness **13** inventiveness

skilled 6 adroit, expert **7** trained **8** skillful **9** competent, masterful, practiced **10** proficient **12** accomplished

skilled worker 7 artisan **9** craftsman **10** technician **15** master craftsman

skillful 3 apt **4** able, deft, keen **5** adept, handy, sharp, slick **6** adroit, clever, expert, facile, gifted **7** capable, cunning, skilled, trained, veteran **8** masterly, talented **9** competent, dexterous, ingenious, masterful, practiced, qualified **10** proficient, well-versed **11** experienced **12** accomplished, professional

skim 3 fly **4** flip, ream, sail, scan, scud, skid, skip **5** coast, float, glide, skate, sweep **6** bounce, scrape **7** dip into **8** glissade **10** glance over **11** leaf through, move lightly **12** thumb through

skimp 5 pinch, stint **6** scrimp, slight **8** be frugal, be stingy, hold back, withhold **9** economize **11** cut expenses, scrape along

Skimpole, Harold
  character in: **10** Bleak House
  author: **7** Dickens

skimpy 5 close, scant, small, spare, tight **6** frugal, meager, modest, scanty, slight, sparse, stingy **7** miserly, scrimpy, sparing, wanting **8** exiguous, grudging, smallish, stinting **9** illiberal, niggardly, penurious, scrimping **10** inadequate, incomplete, too thrifty **11** close fisted, tightfisted **12** insufficient, parsimonious **13** pennypinching **14** inconsiderable

skin 3 fur, pod **4** bark, case, coat, flay, hide, hull, husk, peel, pelt, rind **5** shell **6** abrade, casing, fleece, jacket, scrape, sheath **7** lay bare **9** epidermis **10** complexion, integument **12** body covering, outer coating
  outer layer: **9** epidermis
  contains: **3** fat **4** hair, pore, root **5** nerve **6** vessel **8** oil gland **10** sweat gland
  body's largest: **5** organ
  sense of: **4** cold, heat, pain **5** touch **8** pressure, tickling

skinflint 5 miser **7** hoarder, niggard, scrooge **8** tightwad **10** pinchpenny **12** penny pincher

Skinner, Cornelia Otis
  author of: **23** The Pleasure of His Company (with Samuel Taylor) **24** Our Hearts Were Young and Gay (with Emily Kimbrough)

skinny 4 lank, lean, thin, wiry **5** gaunt,

gawky, lanky, spare **6** slight **7** angular, scraggy, scrawny, slender, spindly **8** gangling, rawboned, shrunken, skeletal **9** emaciated

Skin of Our Teeth, The
  author: **14** Thornton Wilder

skip 3 bob, cut, hop **4** flee, flit, jump, leap, miss, omit, romp, shun, trip **5** bound, caper, dodge, elude, evade **6** bounce, escape, eschew, gambol, ignore, prance, spring **7** abscond, make off, neglect **8** leap over, leave out, overlook, pass over **9** disappear, disregard, do without, play hooky, skedaddle **10** fly the coop **12** be absent from

skirmish 4 fray, tilt **5** brush, clash, joust, run-in, scrap, set-to **6** action, affray, battle, fracas, tussle **7** scuffle **8** struggle **9** encounter, firefight, scrimmage **10** engagement

skirt 3 hem, rim **4** edge, gird, kilt, maxi, mini, ring, shun **5** avoid, evade, flank, hem in, verge **6** border, bounds, circle, dirndl, fringe, girdle, margin **7** enclose, envelop **8** boundary, encircle, go around, lie along **9** crinoline, outer area, perimeter, periphery **10** circumvent, fight shy of **12** circumscribe, detour around

skittish 3 shy **4** wary **5** chary, jumpy, leery, shaky, timid **6** fitful, unsure **7** bashful, fearful, fidgety, flighty, guarded, jittery, nervous, restive **8** cautious, restless, unstable, unsteady, volatile **9** demurring, excitable, impulsive, mercurial, reluctant **10** suspicious **11** distrustful

skittles
  equipment: **4** pins **6** cheese
  also called: **5** closh **6** cloddy **8** rolypoly **10** Dutch bowls
  tabletop version: **15** Enfield skittles

Skrymir
  also: **10** Utgardloki
  origin: **12** Scandinavian
  form: **5** giant
  took to Jotunheim: **4** Loki, Thor **7** Thialfi

Skuld 4 Norn
  origin: **12** Scandinavian
  form: **5** dwarf
  personifies: **6** future
  developed from: **5** Urdar
  companions: **3** Urd **8** Verdandi

skulduggery, skullduggery 7 knavery **8** trickery **9** chicanery, deception **10** dirty trick **12** pettifoggery

skulk 4 hide, lurk **5** cower, creep, prowl, slink, sneak **9** pussyfoot

skull
  contains: **5** brain

Skull place 7 Calvary **8** Golgotha

sky 5 space **9** firmament **10** atmosphere, outer space, the heavens **12** arch of heaven

goddess of: 3 Fri, Nut 5 Frigg, Frija 6 Frigga

sky blue 5 azure 8 cerulean, pale blue 9 clear blue, light blue

Sky King
character: 5 Penny 7 Clipper
cast: 10 Kirby Grant 11 Ron Haggerty 13 Gloria Winters
ranch: 11 Flying Crown
plane: 8 Songbird

skylarking 5 sport 6 antics 7 hijinks, romping 10 frolicking

skypilot 5 padre, rabbi 6 cleric, parson, priest 8 chaplain, minister 9 clergyman

skyward 2 up 6 upward 8 to the sky 10 heavenward 12 to the heavens

slab 3 wad 4 hunk, slat 5 block, board, chunk, plank, slice, wedge 10 thick slice

slack 3 lax 4 dull, easy, free, lazy, limp, slow, soft 5 baggy, loose, quiet, relax 6 easily, flabby, freely, limply, loosen, pliant, remiss, slowly, untied 7 flaccid, let up on, loosely, not busy, not firm, not taut, offhand, relaxed, slacken 8 careless, dilatory, flexible, heedless, inactive, indolent, listless, not tight, slapdash, slipshod, slothful, sluggish 9 leisurely, lethargic, negligent, slow-paced, unmindful, untighten 10 neglectful, nonchalant, permissive, slow-moving, sluggishly, unexacting, unfastened, unthinking 11 inattentive, indifferent, thoughtless, unconcerned, undemanding

slacken 4 curb, ease, flag, free, slow 5 abate, check, let go, let up, limit, loose, relax, slack 6 arrest, go limp, lessen, loosen, reduce, retard, soften, temper, weaken 7 dwindle, inhibit, release 8 decrease, diminish, keep back, mitigate, moderate, restrain, slow down, taper off 9 untighten

slacker 5 idler 6 dodger, loafer, truant 7 dallier, dawdler, goof-off, laggard, quitter, shirker 9 do-nothing, goldbrick 10 malingerer 14 good-fornothing, procrastinator

slag 5 dross 6 cinder, scoria 8 clinkers

slake 4 calm, cool, curb, ease, hush, sate 5 allay, quell, quiet, still 6 modify, quench, soothe, subdue, temper 7 appease, assuage, compose, gratify, mollify, relieve, satiate, satisfy 8 decrease, mitigate, moderate 9 alleviate 11 tranquilize 14 take the edge off

slake off 4 wane 5 abate 6 lessen, reduce, weaken 7 decline, subside 8 diminish, fade away, slack off

slam 3 hit 4 bang, bump, slap 5 crash, smack, smash, throw

slammer 3 jug, pen 4 jail, stir 5 clink 6 cooler, lockup, prison 8 big house, hoosegow 9 calaboose, jailhouse 12 penitentiary

Slammin' Sammy
nickname of: 8 Sam Snead

slander 4 soil 5 libel, smear, sully 6 defame, malign, revile, vilify 7 calumny 8 besmirch 9 falsehood 10 defamation, distortion 12 vilification 14 false statement 17 misrepresentation

Slaney, Mary *see* 10 Mary Decker

slang 4 cant, jive 5 argot, idiom, lingo 6 jargon 7 dialect

slant 4 bias, lean, list, rake, tilt, view 5 angle, color, pitch, slope 7 distort, incline, leaning 8 attitude 9 prejudice, viewpoint

slanted 4 awry 6 biased, tilted 7 colored, crooked, leaning, pitched, sloping 8 inclined 9 on an angle, on the bias 10 prejudiced

slanting 4 bias 5 alean, atilt 7 oblique, sloping 8 diagonal, glancing, inclined 10 distorting

slap 3 cut, hit 4 blow, clap, cuff, snub, swat 5 smack, whack 6 insult, rebuff, strike, wallop 9 rejection

slapdash 6 casual, sloppy 8 careless, slipshod, slovenly 9 haphazard

Slapsie Maxie
nickname of: 15 Maxie Rosenbloom

slash 3 cut, rip 4 drop, gash, mark, pare, rend, rent, slit, tear 5 lower, slice 6 reduce, stroke 8 decrease, lacerate, lowering 9 reduction 10 laceration

slate 4 list 6 ballot, tablet, ticket 10 blackboard, chalkboard

slattern 4 drab, slob, slut 5 bitch, frump 6 harlot, sloven 7 trollop

slatternly 6 frowsy, frumpy, sloppy, untidy 7 unkempt 8 slipshod, slovenly

slaughter 4 kill, slay 6 pogrom 7 butcher, destroy, killing, wipe out 8 decimate, massacre 9 bloodbath 10 annihilate, butchering, mass murder 11 exterminate

Slaughterhouse Five
author: 12 Kurt Vonnegut
character: 12 Billy Pilgrim
setting: 7 Dresden

Slav 4 Pole, Serb, Sorb, Wend 5 Croat, Czech 6 Bulgar, Slovak 7 Russian, Serbian, Slovene, Sorbian 8 Bohemian, Croatian, Moravian 9 Bulgarian, Ruthenian, Slavonian, Slovadian, Ukrainian

slave 4 prey, serf, toil 6 addict, drudge, menial, thrall, toiler, vassal, victim 7 chattel, plodder 8 bondsman 9 workhorse 11 bond servant

slaver 5 drool 6 drivel 7 slobber

slavery 4 toil 5 grind, labor, sweat 6 strain 7 bondage, serfdom, travail 8 drudgery, struggle 9 captivity, treadmill, vassalage 11 enslavement, impressment, subjugation 12 enthrallment

Slavic
language family: 12 Indo-European
group: 11 Balto-Slavic
subgroup: 12 Old Bulgarian 13 Eastern Slavic, Western Slavic 14 Southern Slavic 15 Old Church Slavic

slavish 5 exact 6 strict 7 literal, servile 9 imitative, slavelike 10 derivative, obsequious, submissive, unoriginal 11 subservient 13 unimaginative

slay 4 do in, kill 6 murder 7 destroy, execute 8 massacre 9 slaughter 10 annihilate

slayer 6 hit man, killer 7 butcher 8 assassin, murderer 11 executioner 12 exterminator

slaying 6 murder 7 killing 8 homicide 9 execution

sleazy 5 cheap, tacky 6 flimsy, shabby, shoddy, trashy, vulgar 7 schlock 13 insubstantial

sleek 4 oily 5 shiny, silky, slick, suave 6 glossy, satiny, smooth 7 fawning, velvety 8 lustrous, unctuous 12 ingratiating

sleep 3 nap 4 doze, rest 5 death, peace 6 repose, snooze 7 slumber
god of: 6 Hypnos, Hypnus, Somnus

sleeping 6 asleep, dozing 7 dormant, napping, resting 8 snoozing 9 quiescent, somnolent 11 hibernating 19 in the arms of Morpheus

Sleeping Beauty, The
composer: 11 Tchaikovsky

sleeping car (railroad)
invented by: 7 Pullman

sleeping infants
goddess of: 6 Cunina

sleeping place 3 bed, cot 4 bunk 5 berth 6 pallet 7 bedroom 9 dormitory 10 bedchamber

sleepless 5 alert 7 wakeful 8 restless, watchful 9 insomniac, wide awake 11 industrious

sleeplessness 8 insomnia 9 alertness, attention 11 wakefulness 12 restlessness

sleep lightly 3 nap, nod 4 doze 6 catnap, snooze 15 catch forty winks

sleepy 4 dull 5 quiet, tired, weary 6 drowsy 8 fatigued, inactive 9 exhausted

sleigh 4 dray, sled 6 cutter, sledge, troika 8 transport

Sleipnir
origin: 12 Scandinavian
horse of: 4 Odin 5 Othin
legs: 5 eight

slender 4 lean, poor, slim, thin, weak 5 faint, scant, small, spare 6 feeble, little, meager, narrow, remote, skinny, slight 7 willowy 8 delicate

Slender
character in: 22 The Merry Wives of Windsor
author: 11 Shakespeare

Sleuth
 director: **17** Joseph L Mankiewicz
 based on play by: **14** Anthony Shaffer
 cast: **12** Michael Caine **15** Laurence Olivier

slew 3 lot, ton **4** gang, heap, load, lots, peck, pile, raft **5** batch, did in **6** killed **8** murdered **12** assassinated

Slezak, Walter
 born: **6** Vienna **7** Austria
 father: **9** Leo Slezak
 roles: **5** Fanny **8** Lifeboat **11** Dr Coppelius

slice 3 cut **4** pare **5** carve, piece, sever, shave **6** cut off, divide **7** portion, section, segment, whittle **8** separate **9** dismember

slick 3 sly **4** coat, film, foxy, oily, scum, waxy, wily **5** sharp, shiny, sleek **6** clever, glassy, glossy, greasy, satiny, smooth, tricky **7** coating, cunning **8** slippery **10** make glossy **11** fast-talking **13** smooth-talking

slicker 8 raincoat **9** sou'wester **10** mackintosh, waterproof

slide 4 fall, pass, ramp, skid, slip, veer **5** chute, coast, glide, lapse, slope **7** slither **8** sideslip **11** diapositive **12** transparency

slide by 4 go by **5** lapse **6** elapse, roll by, slip by **7** glide by **8** slip away

slight 3 cut **4** lean, slap, slim, snub, thin, tiny **5** frail, small, spare **6** insult, little, modest, rebuff **7** fragile, limited, slender **8** moderate **10** incivility, negligible, restricted **11** unimportant **13** imperceptible, inappreciable, infinitesimal

slight amount 3 bit **4** dash, drop **5** pinch, touch, trace **6** little **7** smidgen, smidgin, soupcon **8** smidgeon **9** little bit **10** smattering

slightly 6 feebly, rarely **8** meagerly, scantily, scarcely, somewhat **10** negligibly **13** superficially **15** insignificantly

slim 4 lean, thin **5** faint, small **6** meager, remote, skinny, slight, svelte **7** distant, slender, thready, willowy **10** negligible

slime 3 mud **4** mire, muck, ooze **6** sludge

slimy 4 foul, vile **5** gummy, mucky, nasty **6** creepy, putrid, sticky **7** viscous **9** glutinous, loathsome, obnoxious, offensive, repulsive

sling 3 net **4** cast **5** fling, throw **9** slingshot **10** arm support

Slingin' Sammy
 nickname of: **10** Sammy Baugh

slingshot 5 sling **8** catapult

slink 4 slip **5** creep, prowl, skulk, sneak, steal **6** tiptoe

slip 3 put **4** dock, drop, fail, fall, leak, pass, sink, skid **5** berth, error, glide, lapse, scrap, shoot, shred, slide, sneak, sprig, steal, strip **6** escape, sprout, ticket, worsen **7** blunder, chemise, cutting, decline, faux pas, receipt, sapling, voucher **9** petticoat, stripling, youngling, youngster **10** be revealed, get clear of, imprudence, underdress **12** indiscretion

slip away 4 go by **5** lapse **6** elapse, escape **7** run away, slide by **8** creep off **9** tiptoe off

slip by 4 go by, pass **5** lapse **6** elapse, pass by, roll by **7** glide by, slide by

slip of the tongue, a
 Latin: **13** lapsus linguae

slipper 4 mule, shoe **5** scuff **6** sandal

slippery 4 foxy, oily, waxy, wily **5** slick, soapy **6** crafty, glassy, greasy, shifty, smooth, sneaky, tricky **7** devious **9** deceitful **10** contriving, unreliable **11** treacherous **13** untrustworthy

slipshod 3 lax **5** loose, messy **6** casual, sloppy, untidy **7** offhand **8** careless, slovenly **11** thoughtless

slip-up 4 flub, goof **5** botch, error, gaffe, lapse **6** boo-boo, bungle, foul-up, mess-up, miscue **7** blooper, blunder, clinker, faux pas, mistake, screw-up **9** oversight

slit 3 cut **4** gash **5** crack, slash **7** crevice, fissure **8** incision

slither 5 glide, slide **25** move with a side-to-side motion

sliver 5 crumb, shred, slice, snick **6** morsel **8** splinter

slivovitz
 type: **6** brandy **7** liqueur
 origin: **10** Yugoslavia
 flavor: **4** plum

Sloan, John F
 born: **11** Lock Haven PA
 artwork: **12** McSorley's Bar **14** Wake of the Ferry **18** Hairdresser's Window **25** Backyards Greenwich Village

slob 6 sloven **8** slattern

slobber 4 slop **5** drool **6** drivel, slaver **7** dribble, sputter **8** salivate, splutter

sloe gin
 type: **7** liqueur
 flavor: **9** sloe berry **15** blackthorn berry
 drink: **11** Sloe Gin Fizz
 with bourbon: **9** Black Hawk
 with rum: **11** Shark's Tooth
 with vermouth: **10** Blackthorn

slogan 5 motto **6** byword **9** battle cry, catchword, watchword

sloop 4 boat, brig, ship **5** smack **8** sailboat, schooner

slop 3 mud **4** mire, muck, ooze **5** filth, slosh, slush, spill, swash, swill, waste **6** refuse, sludge, splash **7** garbage, spatter **8** splatter

Slop, Dr
 character in: **14** Tristram Shandy
 author: **6** Sterne

slope 3 tip **4** bank, bend, lean, tilt **5** angle, pitch, slant **7** descent, incline **9** downgrade **11** inclination

sloping 5 alean, steep **6** aslant **7** leaning, oblique, tilting **8** diagonal, inclined, on a slant, slanting **9** slantways **11** declivitous

sloppiness 5 chaos, mix-up, upset **6** jumble **7** clutter **8** disarray, disorder, shambles **9** messiness **10** disharmony, untidiness **12** dishevelment **14** disarrangement **15** disorganization

sloppy 3 wet **5** dirty, messy, muddy **6** marshy, sloshy, slushy, sodden, soiled, swampy, untidy, watery **7** unclean **10** disorderly

sloppy person 4 slob **6** sloven

slosh 3 lap **4** drop, mire, stir **5** slush, spill, swash **6** splash **8** flounder

slot 3 gap **4** slit **5** crack, niche, notch
 machine: **14** one-armed bandit

sloth 6 phlegm, torpor **7** languor **8** idleness, laziness, lethargy **9** indolence, lassitude, torpidity **12** listlessness, sluggishness **13** do-nothingness, shiftlessness

slothful 3 lax **4** idle, lazy **5** inert **6** drowsy, otiose, supine, torpid **8** indolent, listless, sluggish **9** do-nothing, lethargic, negligent, shiftless **10** sluggardly **11** unambitious

slouch 4 bend **5** droop, hunch, idler, slump, stoop **6** loafer **7** laggard, shirker, slacker **8** sluggard **9** goldbrick, lazybones

Slovakia
 formerly part of: **14** Czechoslovakia
 capital/largest city: **10** Bratislava
 others: **6** Kosice
 head of state: **9** president
 government: **8** republic
 monetary unit: **5** crown **6** koruna
 mountain: **7** Sudetes **8** Low Tatra **9** High Tatra, Slovak Ore **10** Carpathian, Nizke Tatry **11** Visoke Tatry **15** White Carpathian
 river: **2** Uh **3** Vah **4** Hron **5** Nitra, Slana **6** Danube, Hornad, Ondava, Poprad **7** Laborec **8** Latorica
 people: **5** Czech **6** Slavik, Slovak **9** Hungarian
 language: **6** Slavik, Slovak
 religion: **9** Christian **13** Roman Catholic

Slovenia
 capital/largest city: **9** Ljubljana
 others: **5** Celje, Koper, Kranj **7** Maribor
 head of state: **9** president
 government: **8** republic
 monetary unit: **5** tolar
 river: **4** Sava **5** Drava
 sea: **8** Adriatic
 people: **8** Slovenes
 language: **7** Slovene
 religion: **13** Roman Catholic

slovenly 5 dirty, dowdy, messy **6**

frowzy, sloppy, untidy **7** unclean, unkempt **8** careless, slapdash, slipshod **10** disorderly, slatternly **11** indifferent, unconcerned

slow 3 dim, off **4** curb, dull, dumb, flag, late, long **5** brake, check, dense, heavy, loath, quiet **6** averse, boring, falter, hinder, hold up, impede, obtuse, retard, stupid, torpid **7** belated, delayed, laggard, lumpish, not busy, overdue, tedious, unhasty **8** backward, cautious, dawdling, dilatory, dragging, drawn out, extended, hesitant, inactive, obstruct, sluggish, tarrying **9** dim-witted, leisurely, lingering, ponderous, prolonged, reluctant, snaillike, unhurried **10** behind time, decelerate, deliberate, dull-witted, indisposed, protracted, unexciting, unpunctual

slowdown 4 curb, flag **5** brake, delay, letup, slump **6** ease-up, falter, hinder, impede, lessen, retard, slow-up **7** decline, fall off, letdown, setback, slowing, subside **8** diminish, downturn, flagging **9** grind down **10** decelerate, slackening, stagnation **11** reduce speed, retardation **12** deceleration

slow-moving 4 poky **5** pokey **6** idling **8** crawling, creeping, dawdling, sluggish **9** leisurely, snaillike **10** turtlelike **12** tortoiselike
    creature: 4 slug **5** loris, sloth, snail **6** turtle **8** tortoise

slowness 6 tedium **8** dullness **9** torpidity **10** snail's pace **12** backwardness, sluggishness

slow-paced 4 easy **7** gradual, laggard **8** sluggish **9** leisurely, lethargic, unhurried **10** deliberate

slowpoke 4 slug **5** idler, snail **7** dallier, dawdler, laggard, lie-abed, plodder **8** lingerer, slugabed, tortoise **9** saunterer, straggler **11** foot-dragger

slow to learn 4 dull **5** dense, inapt **6** stupid **8** retarded **10** slow-witted

slow up 4 stem **5** delay **6** detain, hinder, impede, retard **8** slow down

slow-witted 4 dull **5** dense **7** doltish, idiotic, moronic **8** backward, retarded **9** imbecilic

sludge 3 mud **4** mire, muck, ooze, slop **5** dregs, slime, slush **8** sediment

slug 3 bat, hit **4** bash, belt, sock **5** baste, clout, pound, punch, smite, thump, whack, whale **6** batter, strike, wallop **7** clobber **8** lambaste

sluggard 4 lazy **5** drone, idler, sloth, snail **6** loafer, truant, turtle **7** dawdler, laggard, loiterer, slothful, slowpoke, tortoise **9** do-nothing, lazybones **11** couch potato **12** lounge lizard **13** stick-in-the-mud

sluggish 4 lazy, slow **5** inert **6** torpid **7** languid **8** inactive, indolent, lifeless, listless, slothful **9** leisurely, lethargic,

soporific, unhurried **10** phlegmatic, protracted, spiritless

sluggishness 6 torpor **7** inertia **8** lethargy, slowness **9** lassitude **10** inactivity **12** listlessness

slum
    Portuguese: 6 favela

slumber 3 nap **4** doze **5** sleep **6** snooze **8** vegetate **9** hibernate **10** be inactive, lie dormant

slump 3 dip, sag **4** drop, fall, slip **5** droop, lapse **6** plunge, slouch, tumble **7** decline, give way, reverse, setback **8** collapse

slur 3 cut, dig **4** mark, skip, spot **5** smear, stain, sully, taint **6** defame, ignore, insult, malign, mumble, mutter, slight **7** affront, blacken, blemish, let pass **8** mumbling, overlook, pass over **9** disregard, gloss over, muttering **11** run together

slush 4 slop **6** bathos **9** soppiness **11** mawkishness, melting snow **14** sentimentalism, sentimentality

slushiness 5 slush **10** sponginess **11** mawkishness **14** sentimentalism, sentimentality

slut 4 doxy, jade **5** bimbo, frump, hussy, tramp, wench, whore **6** floozy, harlot, sloven, wanton **7** jezebel, trollop **8** slattern, strumpet **10** prostitute

sly 4 foxy, wily **6** artful, covert, crafty, secret, shrewd, sneaky, tricky **7** cunning, furtive, playful, private **8** stealthy **9** conniving **11** dissembling, mischievous **12** confidential

Slye, Leonard
    real name of: 9 Roy Rogers

slyness 5 craft **7** cunning, stealth **8** archness, foxiness, subtlety, wiliness **10** artfulness, craftiness, shrewdness, trickiness **11** furtiveness **15** underhandedness

smack 3 bit, hit, rap **4** blow, buss, clap, cuff, dash, hint, kiss, slap **5** savor, smell, smite, spank, taste, tinge, touch, trace, whack **6** buffet, flavor **7** suggest

small 4 mean, tiny, weak **5** faint, minor, petty, scant **6** feeble, lesser, little, meager, modest, narrow, petite, slight **7** bigoted, fragile, ignoble, trivial **8** not great, trifling **10** diminutive, provincial, undersized **11** of no account, opinionated, superficial, unimportant **13** insignificant **15** inconsequential

Small, Lennie
    character in: 12 Of Mice and Men
    author: 9 Steinbeck

small details
    Latin: 8 minutiae

smaller 4 less **5** lower **6** lesser, tinier **7** dinkier, littler, pettier, reduced, shorter **8** inferior

smallest 5 least **6** lowest **7** tiniest **8** dinkiest, pettiest, shortest **9** slightest

Small House at Allington, The
    author: 15 Anthony Trollope

small intestine
    part of: 15 digestive system
    lined with: 5 villi

small-minded 4 mean **5** petty **6** narrow **7** bigoted **9** parochial **10** prejudiced **12** mean-spirited

smallness 8 meanness, tininess **9** pettiness **10** meagerness, triviality **12** dwarfishness **14** insignificance **18** inconsequentiality

small piece 3 bit, dab **4** chip, drop, snip **5** crumb, grain, piece, pinch, scrap, shred, speck **6** dollop, morsel **7** granule, smidgen, smidgin **8** fragment, particle, smidgeon

small quantity 3 bit, dab, few **5** touch **7** smidgen, smidgin, soupcon **8** smidgeon **9** little bit

small round window
    French: 11 oeil-de-boeuf

small spot 3 dab, dot **5** fleck, speck

small talk 6 banter, gossip **7** chatter, prattle **8** chitchat, idle talk, repartee **9** bavardage, prattling **12** tittle-tattle

smart 4 ache, burn, chic, hurt, keen, neat, trim **5** brash, brisk, quick, sassy, sharp, sting, wince, witty **6** astute, blench, brainy, bright, clever, flinch, modish, shrewd, suffer **7** elegant, stylish **8** feel pain, vigorous **9** be painful, energetic **10** smart-aleck **11** fashionable, intelligent

smart aleck 6 smarty **7** show-off, windbag, wiseass, wise guy **8** blowhard, braggart, saucebox, wiseacre **9** know-it-all **11** smarty-pants **12** grandstander **13** exhibitionist

smarten up 7 dress up, improve **8** beautify, spruce up

smartness 6 acumen, wisdom **8** keenness, sagacity **9** acuteness **10** astuteness, cleverness, perception, shrewdness **12** intelligence, perspicacity

smash 3 hit **4** bang, bash, beat, blow **5** break, clout, crack, crash, crush **6** batter, strike, winner **7** clobber, crack-up, destroy, shatter, success, triumph **8** accident, demolish, splinter **9** collision, sensation **12** disintegrate

smash against 4 beat, lash **5** crash, pound, smite **6** batter, buffet **7** break on

smashed 5 drunk **6** soused, wasted, zapped, zonked **7** crashed, crushed **8** squashed **9** plastered, shattered **10** inebriated **11** intoxicated **17** under the influence **20** three sheets to the wind

smashing 5 great, super **6** superb **8** fabulous, terrific **9** fantastic, marvelous, wonderful **10** stupendous **11** magnificent, sensational **13** extraordinary

smashup 5 crash, wreck **7** crackup **8** accident **9** collision **12** fender bender

smattering 3 bit, dab 4 dash, drop 5 scrap 7 smidgen, smidgin, snippet 8 smidgeon 10 sprinkling

smear 3 mar, rub 4 blur, coat, daub, soil 5 cover, lay on, libel, stain 6 blotch, injure, malign, smirch, smudge, spread, streak 7 blacken, blemish, degrade, slander, splotch, tarnish 8 besmirch, besmudge 9 denigrate 10 accusation, obliterate

smell 4 feel, nose, odor, reek 5 aroma, fetor, scent, sense, sniff, stink 6 detect, stench 7 bouquet, perfume, suspect 8 perceive 9 emanation, fragrance, get wind of

smelly 4 rank 5 fetid 6 putrid 7 noisome, odorous, reeking 8 stinking 10 malodorous

Smerdyakov
    character in: 20 The Brothers Karamazov
    author: 10 Dostoevsky

Smetana, Bedrich
    born: 7 Bohemia 8 Litomysl 11 Leitomischl 14 Czechoslovakia
    composer of: 7 Ma Vlast 9 My Country 10 From My Life 11 Czech Dances 12 The Two Widows 16 The Bartered Bride

smidgen, smidgin, smidgeon 3 bit, dab 4 mite, snip 5 crumb, pinch, scrap, shred, speck, trace 6 dollop, morsel

Smike
    character in: 16 Nicholas Nickleby
    author: 7 Dickens

smile 4 beam, grin 5 favor, shine, smirk 6 simper

Smiles of a Summer Night
    director: 13 Ingmar Bergman
    cast: 11 Eva Dahlbeck 13 Ulla Jacobsson 15 Margit Carlquist 16 Harriet Andersson
    remade as: 17 A Little Night Music

Smiley's People
    author: 11 John Le Carre

Smintheus
    epithet of: 6 Apollo

smirch 4 blot, mark, soil, spot 5 dirty, smear, stain, sully, taint 6 blotch, damage, smudge, stigma 7 begrime, blacken, blemish, slander, tarnish 8 besmirch, besmudge, dishonor 9 discredit

smirk 4 grin, leer 5 sneer 6 simper 7 grimace

Smirke, Sir Robert
    architect of: 12 King's College (U of London) 13 British Museum (London) 19 Covent Garden Theater (London)
    style: 12 Greek Revival

smite 3 hit 4 swat 5 knock, smack, whack 6 enamor, strike, wallop 7 clobber

Smith, Adam
    author of: 18 The Wealth of Nations

Smith, Al
    creator/artist of: 11 Mutt and Jeff

Smith, Betty
    author of: 20 A Tree Grows in Brooklyn

Smith, Charles Aaron
    nickname: 5 Bubba
    sport: 8 football
    team: 14 Baltimore Colts

Smith, David
    born: 8 Decatur IN
    artwork: 3 Zig 4 Cubi 6 Oculus 8 Agricola, Main View, Sentinel, Star Cage 9 Australia, Royal Bird, Tank Totem 10 The Banquet 12 Detroit Queen 15 Lectern Sentinel 17 Medals for Dishonor 20 Hudson River Landscape 23 Song of an Irish Blacksmith

Smith, Harriet
    character in: 4 Emma
    author: 6 Austen

Smith, Lillian
    author: 12 Strange Fruit

Smith, Maggie
    born: 6 Ilford 7 England
    husband: 14 Robert Stephens
    roles: 7 Othello 15 California Suite, The Pumpkin Eater 17 Travels with My Aunt 24 The Prime of Miss Jean Brodie (Oscar)

Smith, Winston
    character in: 18 Nineteen Eighty-Four
    author: 6 Orwell

smithereen 3 bit 4 atom 5 crumb, shard 8 fragment, particle 9 scintilla

Smithson, James
    field: 9 chemistry
    nationality: 7 British
    discovered: 11 smithsonite 13 zinc carbonite
    funded: 22 Smithsonian Institution

smitten 8 enamored 9 bewitched 10 enraptured, infatuated

smoke 4 draw, fume, pipe, puff, reek, suck 5 cigar, fumes 6 billow, inhale 7 light up, smolder 9 cigarette, have a drag

Smoke
    author: 12 Ivan Turgenev
    character: 5 Irina 7 Potugin 13 Tanya Shestoff 16 General Ratmiroff, Grigory Litvinoff 18 Kapitolina Shestoff

smoke screen 4 ruse 5 cover, dodge, front 6 screen 9 deception 10 camouflage, subterfuge

smoky 5 dingy, grimy, sooty 6 fuming, smudgy 7 reeking 10 smoldering

smolder 4 burn, fume, rage 5 smoke 6 seethe

Smollett, Tobias George
    author of: 14 (The Expedition of) Humphry Clinker, Roderick Random 15 Peregrine Pickle

smooch 3 pet 4 buss, kiss, neck 5 smack, spoon 7 make out

smooth 4 calm, ease, easy, even, flat, glib, help, mild, open, pave 5 allay, level, silky, sleek, suave 6 facile, mellow, placid, polish, refine, serene, soften, soothe, steady 7 appease, assuage, flatten, mollify, orderly, perfect, prepare, velvety 8 civilize, composed, make even, mitigate, peaceful, pleasant 9 collected, cultivate, easygoing, make level 10 facilitate, flattering, harmonious, methodical, uneventful 11 well-ordered 12 ingratiating 13 self-possessed, well-regulated

smoothness 8 evenness, fineness, flatness 9 silkiness, sleekness

smooth the feathers 4 calm 6 pacify, soothe 7 appease, assuage, mollify, placate 10 conciliate

smooth-tongued 4 glib 5 suave 6 fluent 8 unctuous 10 flattering 11 fast-talking 12 hypocritical, ingratiating

smother 4 hide, mask, wrap 5 choke, quash, snuff 6 deaden, quench, shower 7 conceal 8 keep down, strangle, suppress, surround 9 choke back, envelop in, suffocate 10 asphyxiate, extinguish

Smothers Brothers Comedy Hour, The
    regulars: 10 Don Novello, Pat Paulsen 11 Bob Einstein, Leigh French, Steve Martin, Tom Smothers 12 Betty Aberlin, Dick Smothers, John Hartford, Nino Senporty, Spencer Quinn 13 Mason Williams 14 Jennifer Warren, Sally Struthers 16 Anita Kerr Singers 17 Jimmy Joyce Singers 18 Louis DaPron Dancers 19 Marty Paich Orchestra 20 Denny Vaughn Orchestra, Ron Poindexter Dancers 21 Nelson Riddle Orchestra

smudge 4 blot, mark, soil, spot 5 dirty, smear, stain 6 smutch

smudgy 5 dirty, messy 6 filthy, grubby, smeary 7 sullied 8 befouled, unwashed 9 besmeared

smug 8 superior, virtuous 10 complacent 13 self-righteous, self-satisfied

smuggle 5 sneak 15 export illegally, import illegally

smuggled goods 10 contraband 14 illegal exports, illegal imports 18 prohibited articles

smuggler 6 runner 9 gunrunner, rumrunner 10 bootlegger 13 contrabandist

smugness 7 egotism 9 immodesty 11 superiority 12 virtuousness 16 self-satisfaction 17 self-righteousness

smut 4 dirt, porn, soot 5 filth, grime 6 smudge 9 obscenity, scatology 11 pornography

smutty 4 lewd 5 dirty, grimy, sooty 6

filthy, soiled, vulgar **7** obscene **8** indecent **12** pornographic

Smyrna *see* **6** Myrrha

Smythe, Reginald
  creator/artist of: **8** Andy Capp

snack 3 eat, tea **4** bite, nosh **5** munch **6** nibble, tidbit **7** take tea **8** lap lunch, munchies, nibblies, pick-me-up, snackies **9** collation, crunchies, elevenses **10** finger food, light lunch **11** cassecroute, coffee break, light repast, refreshment

snag 3 bar, rip **4** grab, stub, tear **5** block, catch, hitch, stump **7** barrier **8** obstacle **9** hindrance **10** difficulty, impediment, projection, protrusion **11** encumbrance, obstruction **14** stumbling block

snail
  French: **8** escargot

snake 5 sneak, viper **7** reptile, serpent, traitor **8** ophidian **9** reptilian
  combining form: **4** ophi **5** ophio, ophis **6** herpes **7** herpeto
  expert: **13** herpetologist
  fear of: **13** herpetophobia
  genus: **7** Ophidia
  kind: **3** asp, boa, sea **4** file, habu, wart, whip **5** aboma, adder, cobra, coral, krait, mamba, tiger, viper **6** bongar, elapid, garter, gopher, python, taipan **7** rattler, sunbeam **8** anaconda, cerastes, moccasin, pit viper, ringhals **9** boomslang, colubrina, mole viper, puff adder **10** black mamba, bushmaster, copperhead, fer-de-lance, sidewinder **11** cottonmouth, diamond back, Gaboon viper, rattlesnake **12** slender blind **13** elephant-trunk, water moccasin **14** boa constrictor
  shedding: **7** ecdysis **8** moulting
  skin: **6** exuvia
  snake killer: **8** mongoose

Snake *see* **8** Shoshone

Snake, the
  nickname of: **10** Ken Stabler

Snake Pit, The
  author: **12** Mary Jane Ward, Sigrid Undset

snap 3 nip, pop **4** bark, bite, grab, lock, yelp **5** break, catch, cinch, clasp, click, close, crack, growl, hasty, latch, quick, snarl, spell **6** breeze, period, secure, snatch, sudden **8** careless, fastener, fracture **9** impulsive **11** thoughtless

snapdragon 11 Antirrhinum
  varieties: **4** wild **5** dwarf **6** common, garden, lesser **7** spurred **8** withered

snappish 4 edgy **5** cross, huffy, surly, testy **6** crabby, cranky, shirty, touchy **7** grouchy, huffish, peevish, waspish **8** captious, petulant **9** irascible, irritable, querulous **10** ill-humored, ill-natured, out of sorts **11** hot-tempered

12 cantankerous **13** quick-tempered, short-tempered

snappy 4 fast, tony **5** hasty, quick, rapid, ritzy, sharp, smart, swank, swift, swish **6** classy, dapper, jaunty, speedy, spiffy **7** stylish **12** lickety-split

snare 3 net **4** bait, hook, lure, ruse, trap **5** catch, decoy, noose, seize, trick **6** entrap **7** capture, ensnare, pitfall **9** deception **12** entanglement

snarl 3 mat **4** bark, clog, kink, knot, mess, snap **5** chaos, growl, ravel, twist **6** hinder, impede, jumble, muddle, tangle **7** confuse, lash out **8** disorder, entangle **9** confusion

snatch 3 bit, nab **4** grab, part, pull, take **5** catch, grasp, piece, pluck, seize, wrest **7** snippet **8** fragment

Snead, Sam
  nickname: **12** Slammin' Sammy
  sport: **4** golf
  won: **7** Masters

sneak 3 sly **4** slip **5** creep, knave, rogue, scamp, steal **6** lurker, rascal, secret, spirit **7** bounder, furtive, skulker, slinker, smuggle **8** scalawag, surprise **9** miscreant, scoundrel, secretive, underhand **11** rapscallion **13** surreptitious

sneak attack 4 raid **6** ambush **7** assault **9** ambuscade, incursion

sneakers
  brands: **4** Avia, Fila, Keds, Nike, Puma **5** Asics **6** Adidas, Reebok **7** Saucony **10** New Balance

sneak off 5 elope **6** decamp **7** abscond **9** steal away

sneaky 3 sly **4** mean **7** devious, furtive, vicious **9** malicious, secretive, underhand **10** traitorous **11** treacherous

sneer 4 jeer, leer, mock **5** scoff, scorn, smirk **6** deride, rebuff **7** disdain **8** belittle, ridicule

sneer at 5 knock, scorn **6** deride, malign **7** disdain, put down, run down **8** pooh-pooh **16** cast aspersions on

Sneerwell, Lady
  character in: **19** The School for Scandal
  author: **8** Sheridan

snicker 5 snort **6** cackle, giggle, simper, titter **7** snigger

snide 5 nasty **7** mocking **8** scoffing **9** malicious, sarcastic **11** insinuating **12** contemptuous

Snider, Edwin
  nickname: **4** Duke
  sport: **8** baseball
  position: **7** fielder
  team: **15** Brooklyn Dodgers

sniff 4 jeer, mock, odor **5** aroma, scoff, smell, snort, snuff, whiff **6** snivel **7** disdain, sniffle, snuffle **9** disparage

snip 3 bit, bob, cut, lop **4** brat, clip, crop, punk, snap, trim **5** clack, click,

piece, prune, scrap, shear, twerp **6** sample, shrimp, swatch **7** cutting **8** fragment

snippy 4 curt, rude **5** sassy, saucy, short **6** cheeky, snotty **7** brusque **8** flippant, impudent, insolent, snippety **11** ill- mannered, impertinent, smart-alecky

snivel 3 cry **5** sniff, whine **6** boohoo **7** sniffle **8** complain

sniveler 6 coward, whiner **7** crybaby **10** complainer

snob 7 elitist **13** social climber

snobbish 4 vain **6** snooty, snotty **7** haughty, high-hat, stuck-up **8** arrogant, superior **10** disdainful **11** overbearing, patronizing, pretentious **13** condescending

Snodgrass
  character in: **14** Pickwick Papers
  author: **7** Dickens

snoop 3 pry **7** meddler, Paul Pry **8** busybody **10** Nosy Parker **12** eavesdropper

Snoopy 6 beagle
  brother: **5** Spike
  creator: **6** Schulz
  friend: **9** Woodstock
  master: **12** Charlie Brown

snooze 3 nap **4** doze **5** sleep **6** catnap, drowse, siesta **7** slumber **10** forty winks

Snopes family
  characters in: **9** The Hamlet
  members: **2** Ab **4** Flem, Mink **5** Isaac
  author: **8** Faulkner

snort 4 blow, gasp, huff, jeer, pant, puff, rage **5** blast, grunt, scoff, sneer, storm

snout 3 neb **4** beak, bill, nose **5** snoot, spout **6** muzzle, nozzle **9** proboscis

Snow, C P (Charles Percy Snow, Lord Snow)
  author of: **9** The New Men **10** Last Things, The Masters **14** A Coat of Varnish **16** Corridors of Power **20** Strangers and Brothers

snowfall 4 firn, neve **6** flurry **8** blizzard
  Scottish: **6** onding

Snow Leopard, The
  author: **16** Peter Matthiessen

Snow Queen, The
  author: **21** Hans Christian Andersen

Snows of Kilimanjaro, The
  author: **15** Ernest Hemingway

snow-white 4 pure **5** snowy **9** lily-white, pure white **11** white as snow

Snow White and the Seven Dwarfs
  character: **3** Doc **5** Dopey, Happy, Queen **6** Grumpy, Sleepy, Sneezy, mirror **7** Bashful **14** Prince Charming

snowy 4 pure **5** white **7** nievous **8** pristine, spotless **9** blizzardy

snub 3 cut **5** blunt, check, scorn, short

dain 9 retrousse **11** repudiation **12** cold shoulder **16** turn up one's nose at **19** give the cold shoulder

snuff 5 scent, smell, sniff, whiff **7** sniffle, snuffle

snuff out 5 crush **8** suppress **10** extinguish, put an end to

snug 4 cozy, neat, safe **5** close, tight **6** secure **7** compact **8** tranquil **9** sheltered, skin-tight **11** comfortable **12** close-fitting, tight-fitting **13** well-organized

snuggle 3 hug **4** nest **6** cuddle, curl up, enfold, nestle, nuzzle

so
    Latin: **3** sic

soak 3 wet **4** seep **5** bathe, enter, steep **6** absorb, drench, sink in, take in, take up **7** immerse, pervade **8** permeate, saturate **9** penetrate

soaked 5 soggy **6** sodden, soused **7** sopping **8** drenched **9** saturated **11** waterlogged, wringing wet

soak up 4 blot **6** absorb, take up **8** sponge up

soak up warmth 4 bask **11** warm oneself **12** toast oneself

Soames Forsyte
    character in: **14** The Forsyte Saga
    author: **10** Galsworthy

Soap
    character: **5** Major **6** Benson **9** Billy Tate **10** Eunice Tate **11** Chester Tate, Corrine Tate, Danny Dallas, Jessica Tate, Jodie Dallas **12** Burt Campbell **18** Mary Dallas Campbell
    cast: **7** Ted Wass **9** Jimmy Baio **11** Diana Canova **12** Billy Crystal, Cathryn Damon, Jennifer Salt, Robert Mandan **14** Arthur Peterson **15** Richard Mulligan, Robert Guillaume **16** Katherine Helmond

soar 3 fly **4** rise, wing **5** climb, float, glide, mount, tower **8** take wing

soave
    music: **6** gentle

sob 3 cry **4** howl, wail, weep **6** lament, plaint, snivel **7** blubber, whimper

so be it 4 amen **7** let it be **9** let it be so

sober 3 dry, sad **4** cool, drab, dull, grim, sane **5** grave, sound, staid **6** dreary, sedate, solemn, somber, steady **7** joyless, prudent, serious, subdued **8** moderate, not drunk, rational **9** judicious, realistic, sorrowful, temperate **10** abstemious **11** level-headed **13** dispassionate

So Big
    author: **10** Edna Ferber

sobriety 10 abstention, abstinence, continence, temperance **13** nonindulgence **14** abstemiousness

sobriquet 7 epithet, pet name **8** nickname **11** appellation

so-called
    French: **9** soi-disant

soccer
    athlete: **4** Pele **11** Johan Cruyff
    players/team: **6** eleven
    position: **6** goalie **7** forward **8** fullback, halfback **10** goalkeeper
    championship: **8** World Cup **11** European Cup, National Cup **13** Cup Winner's Cup
    violation: **5** hands **7** hacking, offside **11** obstructing
    gaining control of ball: **4** trap

sociable 6 social **7** affable, cordial **8** friendly, gracious, outgoing **9** agreeable, congenial, convivial **10** gregarious, neighborly **11** extroverted **13** companionable

social 2 in **5** smart **7** stylish **8** friendly, pleasant, sociable **9** agreeable **10** gregarious, neighborly **11** cooperative, fashionable **14** interdependent

Social Contract, The
    author: **19** Jean-Jacques Rousseau

social order
    goddess of: **4** Hour **5** Horae

society 4 body, club **5** elite, group **6** circle, gentry, league **7** mankind **8** alliance, humanity, nobility **9** community, humankind **10** blue bloods **11** aristocracy, association, high society, social order **12** organization **14** the four hundred **16** the general public

sociologist
    American: **4** Mead, Park, Ward **5** Coser, Gerth, Mills, Small, Wirth **6** Bendix, Cooley, Merton, Speier, Sumner, Thomas **7** Parsons, Sorokin **8** Eberhard **10** Lazarsfeld
    British: **4** Webb **8** Hobhouse, Mannheim **12** Carr-Saunders
    Danish: **6** Geiger
    French: **4** Aron **5** Comte **8** Durkheim, Gurvitch **9** Friedmann
    German: **5** Konig, Weber, Wiese **6** Simmel **8** Habermas, Luckmann **10** Dahrendorf, Horkheimer
    Hungarian: **6** Lukacs **8** Mannheim
    Israeli: **5** Buber **10** Eisenstadt
    Norwegian: **6** Aubert **7** Galtung
    Swedish: **8** Carlsson

sociopathic 9 alienated **10** antisocial, rebellious

sock 3 box, hit, sox **4** belt, blow, slap **5** punch, smack, smash **6** strike, wallop **7** clobber **8** knee sock **9** ankle sock **13** short stocking

Socrates
    born: **6** Athens
    taught using: **5** irony **6** method
    disciple: **5** Plato **8** Xenophon
    wife: **9** Xanthippe
    death potion: **7** hemlock

sod 4 soil, turf **5** divot, earth, grass, sward **10** greensward

soda 3 pop **4** base, cola **5** tonic **6** bicarb, sodium **7** barilla, seltzer **8** bev-

erage, root beer **9** ginger ale, soft drink **11** bicarbonate **12** sarsaparilla

ash: 6 alkali

in faro: 9 first card

maker: 4 jerk

sodden 4 dull **5** heavy, lumpy, mushy, pasty, soggy, soppy **6** doughy, soaked **7** sopping **8** besotted, drenched, dripping, listless **9** saturated **10** wet through **14** expressionless

Soddy, Frederick
    field: **9** chemistry
    nationality: **7** British
    discovered: **8** isotopes
    worked with: **13** William Ramsay **16** Ernest Rutherford
    awarded: **10** Nobel Prize

sodium
    chemical symbol: **2** Na

Sodom
    destroyed with: **5** Admah **6** Zeboim **8** Gomorrah

sofa 5 couch, divan **6** canape, lounge, settee **8** love seat **9** davenport **12** chesterfield

Sofia
    Roman name: **12** Ulpia Serdica
    Byzantine name: **9** Triaditsa
    capital of: **8** Bulgaria
    landmark: **13** Buyuk Dzhamiya **16** Saint Sofia Church **17** Saint George Church **24** Alexander Nevsky Cathedral **32** Cyril and Methodius National Library

soft 4 easy, kind, mild, pale, weak **5** downy, faint, furry, muted, quiet, silky, sleek **6** feeble, gentle, hushed, pliant, satiny, shaded, silken, smooth, supple, tender **7** lenient, not hard, pitying, pliable, restful, subdued, velvety **8** delicate, not sharp, shadowed, tolerant, tranquil, twilight **9** malleable, not strong **10** harmonious **11** sentimental, sympathetic **12** easily molded, low intensity **13** compassionate, pleasantly low **16** easily penetrated **19** having a breathy sound **21** requiring little effort **25** incapable of great endurance

soften 4 lower **6** lessen, subdue, temper **7** cushion, mollify **8** make soft, mitigate, moderate, palliate, tone down, turn down **10** ameliorate, make softer

softhearted 4 kind, soft, warm **6** benign, gentle, humane, kindly, tender **8** generous **9** forgiving, indulgent **10** benevolent **11** considerate, kindhearted, sympathetic, warmhearted **13** compassionate, tenderhearted

softly 6 easily, gently, mildly, weakly **7** quietly

softness 8 mildness **9** downiness, silkiness **10** fluffiness, gentleness, smoothness, tenderness **11** tranquility **12** tranquillity

soft soap 7 blarney **8** cajolery, flattery **10** persuasion

sogginess 7 wetness **8** dampness **9** mushiness **10** soddenness

soggy 5 heavy, mushy, pasty, soppy **6** doughy, soaked, sodden **7** sopping **8** drenched, dripping **9** saturated

Sogliardo
character in: **22** Every Man out of His Humour
author: **6** Jonson

Soglow, Otto
creator/artist of: **13** The Little King

soi-disant 8 so-called **9** pretended **10** self-styled **18** calling oneself thus

soigne, soignee 4 chic, neat, tidy **5** sleek, smart **6** classy, modish **7** elegant **11** well-groomed

soil 4 dirt, foul, land, loam, ruin, soot, spot **5** dirty, earth, grime, humus, muddy, smear, stain, sully **6** debase, defile, ground, region, smudge **7** blacken, country, tarnish **8** disgrace

soiled 5 dirty, grimy, messy **6** filthy, grubby, smudgy **7** muddied, sullied, unclean **8** begrimed, unwashed **9** besmeared

soiree 4 ball, prom **5** dance, party **9** cotillion, promenade

sojourn 4 stay **5** abide, pause, visit **6** stay at **7** holiday, layover **8** stay over, stopover, vacation

sojourner 6 lodger, tenant **7** pilgrim, tourist, visitor **8** traveler **9** transient, weekender **10** daytripper, vacationer

Sol
origin: **5** Roman
form: **3** god
personifies: **3** sun
corresponds to: **6** Helios **7** Mithras **8** Hyperion

sola, solus 5 alone **9** by oneself

solace 4 calm **5** cheer **6** soothe **7** assuage, comfort, console **8** reassure **10** help in need **11** consolation, reassurance **18** relief in affliction

solder 4 fuse, join, weld **5** braze, stick

soldier 2 GI **3** PFC **5** GI Joe, major **6** worker, zealot **7** captain, colonel, dogface, general, private, servant, trooper, veteran, warrior **8** corporal, follower, partisan, sergeant **10** lieutenant, serviceman, specialist **11** enlisted man, military man **14** militant leader **16** brigadier general

Soldier of Orange
director: **13** Paul Verhoeven
based on novel by: **13** Erik Hazelhoff
cast: **10** Peter Faber **11** Derek De Lint, Eddy Habbema, Rutger Hauer **12** Jeroen Krabbe **15** Susan Penhaligon
setting: **14** The Netherlands

Soldier's Embrace, A
author: **14** Nadine Gordimer

soldiery 4 army **6** legion, troops **7** legions, militia **8** military, soldiers **11** fighting men

sole 4 lone, only **6** single **8** solitary **9** exclusive

solely 5 alone **6** merely, purely, singly **8** uniquely **11** exclusively **14** single-handedly

solemn 4 dark, drab, grim, holy **5** grave, sober, staid **6** formal, gloomy, sacred, sedate, somber **7** earnest, serious, sincere **8** absolute **9** dignified, religious, spiritual, steadfast **10** ceremonial, depressing, determined **11** ceremonious **12** awe-inspiring

solemnity 3 awe **7** dignity **8** ceremony **9** formality, reverence **11** seriousness **12** circumstance

solemnize 4 mark **5** honor **6** hallow **7** observe **9** celebrate **10** consecrate **11** commemorate

solicit 3 ask **4** seek **5** plead **7** entreat, request **9** appeal for, importune

solicitation 6 appeal **7** request **8** entreaty **11** importuning

solicitor 6 beggar, lawyer **7** counsel **8** salesman **10** supplicant

solicitous 4 avid, keen **5** eager **6** ardent, intent **7** anxious, intense, longing, mindful, zealous **8** desirous **9** attentive, concerned, regardful **10** thoughtful **12** enthusiastic

solicitude 4 care, zeal **5** worry **7** anxiety, avidity, concern **9** attention **10** enthusiasm, inquietude, uneasiness **11** disquietude, fearfulness, overconcern **12** apprehension

solid 4 firm, hard, pure, real **5** dense, massy, sober, sound, tough **6** rugged, stable, steady, strong, sturdy **7** durable, genuine, lasting, unmixed **8** complete, concrete, constant, rational, reliable, sensible, tangible, thorough, unbroken **9** not hollow, unalloyed, unanimous, undivided, well-built **10** continuous, dependable, solidified **11** impermeable, levelheaded, substantial, trustworthy **12** impenetrable **13** uninterrupted **15** well- constructed

solidarity 5 union, unity **7** harmony **9** closeness **11** cooperation, unification

solidify 3 fix, gel, set **4** cake, jell **6** cement, harden **7** congeal, stiffen, thicken **9** coagulate **11** crystallize **12** agglomerate

soliloquy 9 monologue **10** solo speech

Solinus
character in: **17** The Comedy of Errors
author: **11** Shakespeare

solitariness 8 solitude **9** aloneness, seclusion **13** reclusiveness

solitary 4 lone **6** hidden, lonely, remote, single **8** desolate, isolated, lonesome, secluded **9** concealed **10** cloistered **11** out-of-the-way, uninhabited **13** companionless

solitude 9 aloneness, isolation, seclu-

sion, wasteland **10** desolation, loneliness, remoteness, wilderness

solo 5 alone **8** solitary **9** by oneself **10** unattended **12** singlehanded **13** unaccompanied
operatic: **4** aria

solo dance
ballet: **7** pas seul

Solomon
father: **5** David
mother: **9** Bathsheba
wife: **6** Naamah
son: **8** Rehoboam
brother: **5** Amnon **7** Absalom, Chileab **8** Adonijah
sister: **5** Tamar
visitor: **5** Sheba
wrote: **8** Proverbs **12** Ecclesiastes **13** Song of Solomon
built: **6** temple

Solomon Islands
capital/largest city: **7** Honiara
others: **4** Aukl, Bina, Gizo, Luti **5** Kieta, Munda **6** Tulagi **7** Yandina **8** Kira Kira **9** Tangarare **10** Sasamungga
head of state: **14** British monarch **15** governor-general
member of: **14** Spearhead Group
monetary unit: **4** cent **6** dollar
island: **4** Buka, Gizo, Savo **5** Ndeni, Ulawa **6** Tulagi **7** Malaita, Rennell, Solomon, Vangunu **8** Choiseul, Sikaiana, Vanikoro **9** Santa Cruz **10** New Georgia, Ontong Java **11** Guadalcanal, Santa Isabel **12** Bougainville, San Cristobal
mountain: **5** Balbi
highest point: **11** Popomanasiu
ocean: **7** Pacific
physical feature:
gulf: **4** Huon, Kula
sound: **10** New Georgia
strait: **13** Indispensable
people: **7** Chinese **8** European **10** Melanesian, Polynesian
explorer: **14** Mendana de Neyra
leader: **8** Mamaloni **9** Kenilorea
language: **7** English **13** Pidgin English **16** Melanesian pidgin
religion: **8** Anglican **13** Roman Catholic

so long
Spanish: **12** hasta la vista

solution 3 key **5** blend **6** answer, cipher **7** mixture, solving **8** emulsion **9** resolving **10** resolution, suspension, unraveling **11** explanation

solve 7 resolve, unravel, work out **8** decipher, unriddle, untangle **9** figure out **10** find the key **13** find the answer

solvent 7 diluent, soluble **9** dilutable **10** dissoluble, dissolvent **11** dissolvable **16** financially sound

Solymi

origin: 9 Asia Minor
occupation: 8 warriors

Solzhenitsyn, Aleksandr
author of: 13 The Cancer Ward **14** The First Circle **19** The Gulag Archipelago **22** August Nineteen-Fourteen **31** One Day in the Life of Ivan Denisovich

Somalia
other name: 4 Punt **10** Somaliland **12** Horn of Africa
capital/largest city: 9 Mogadishu **10** Mogadiscio
others: 5 Burao, Merca **6** Mereka **7** Berbera, Galkayu, Kismayu **8** Belet Uen, Hargeisa **9** Chisimaio
division: 6 Hawiya **9** Mijirtein **10** Midjertein
  colonial: 17 British Somaliland, Italian Somaliland
measure: 3 top **4** caba **5** chela, darat, tabla **6** cubito **8** parsalah
monetary unit: 4 besa **6** somalo **8** shilling **9** centesimi
weight: 8 parsalah
mountain: 5 Guban **11** Migiurtinia, Ogo Highland
highest point: 7 Surud Ad
river: 4 Juba **5** Daror, Nogal **9** Nugaaleed **11** Webi Shebeli **13** Webi Shabeelle
sea: 6 Indian
physical feature:
  bay: 5 Negro
  cape: 9 Guardafui
  desert: 4 Aror
  gulf: 4 Aden
  plateau: 3 Ogo **4** Haud
people: 3 Sab **4** Asha **5** Galla **6** Hawiya, Isbaak, Somali **7** Danakil, Hamitic, Marehan, Samaale, Shuhali **8** Rahanwin
  leader: 9 Siad Barre **12** Ali Shermarke
language: 6 Arabic, Somali **7** English, Italian
religion: 5 Islam
feature:
  boat: 4 dhow
  cloth: 7 banadir
  clothing: 4 futa, toga **6** sarong
  tree: 6 acacia, baobab **7** incense

Somaliland *see* **7** Somalia

somber 4 dark, drab, gray, grim **5** grave, sober **6** dreary, gloomy, solemn **7** serious **8** funereal, mournful, toneless **9** cheerless **10** depressing, melancholy

Some Like It Hot
director: 11 Billy Wilder
cast: 9 Joe E Brown, Pat O'Brien **10** George Raft, Jack Lemmon, Tony Curtis **13** Marilyn Monroe

Somers Islands *see* **7** Bermuda

something essential
Latin: 10 sine qua non

something for something
Latin: 10 quid pro quo

Something Happened
author: 12 Joseph Heller

sometime 4 late, once **5** later **6** former **7** quondam **8** formerly, previous **9** erstwhile **10** occasional

sometimes 7 at times **10** now and then, on occasion **12** occasionally, once in a while

somewhat 6 fairly, kind of, partly, sort of **8** passably **9** tolerably **10** moderately, more or less, reasonably **13** approximately

somnolent 4 dozy, dull **5** dopey **6** drowsy, groggy, sleepy, torpid **7** languid, nodding, out of it, yawning **8** hypnotic, sluggish **9** half-awake, lethargic, soporific **10** half-asleep, slumberous **11** heavy-lidded **13** semiconscious

Somnus
origin: 5 Roman
god of: 5 sleep
mother: 3 Nyx
brother: 4 Mors
corresponds to: 6 Hypnos, Hypnus

son
French: 4 fils

sone
unit of: 8 loudness

song 4 call, poem, tune **5** ditty, lyric, verse **6** ballad, melody, number, piping
French: 7 chanson

songbird 4 chat, lark, wren **5** robin, veery, vireo **6** canary, singer, thrush **7** warbler **11** nightingale

Song of Bernadette, The
author: 11 Franz Werfel
character: 13 Dean Peyramale **18** Sister Marie Therese **19** Bernadette Soubirous
director: 9 Henry King
cast: 8 Lee J Cobb **12** Vincent Price, William Eythe **13** Jennifer Jones **15** Charles Bickford
Oscar for: 7 actress (Jones)

Song of Hiawatha *see* **8** Hiawatha

Song of Roland, The *see* **15** Chanson de Roland

Song of Solomon
author: 12 Toni Morrison

Song of Solomon
bride: 9 Shulamite

Song of Songs, The
author: 16 Hermann Sudermann

Song of the Lark, The
author: 11 Willa Cather

Songs of Experience
author: 12 William Blake

Songs of Innocence
author: 12 William Blake

Sonnets from the Portuguese
author: 24 Elizabeth Barrett Browning

Sonnets to Orpheus
author: 16 Rainer Maria Rilke

Sonny
nickname of: 13 Charles Liston

Son of the Morning
author: 15 Joyce Carol Oates

sonorous 4 deep, rich **6** florid **7** ringing, vibrant **8** eloquent, resonant **9** full-toned, grandiose **10** flamboyant, impressive, resounding **13** reverberating

Sons and Lovers
author: 10 D H Lawrence
character: 10 Clara Dawes **11** Baxter Dawes **13** Miriam Leivers
  Morel family: 4 Paul **5** Annie **6** Arthur, Walter **7** William **8** Gertrude

Sons of thunder 4 John **5** James
also: 9 Boanerges

Soo
canals at: 13 Sault Ste. Marie

soon 4 anon **6** pronto **7** betimes, by and by, early on, ere long, quickly, shortly **8** directly **9** any minute, forthwith, instantly, presently, right away **10** before long **12** without delay **14** in a little while

sooner 6 before, in time **7** earlier **9** before now, in advance **10** beforehand **11** ahead of time

sooner or later 6 one day **7** finally, someday **8** in the end, sometime **10** eventually, ultimately **17** in the course of time, sometime or another

Sooner State
nickname of: 8 Oklahoma

soot 4 dirt, smut **5** crock, grime **6** carbon, smudge, smutch **7** residue **9** lampblack

soothe 4 calm, ease **6** lessen, pacify **7** appease, comfort, console, mollify, placate, relieve **8** mitigate, moderate **9** alleviate **11** tranquilize

soothing 4 mild **7** calming, healing, salving **9** appeasing, consoling, emollient, pacifying, placating **10** comforting, mitigating **13** tranquilizing

soothsayer 4 seer **5** sibyl **7** diviner, prophet **10** forecaster **13** fortune-teller

soothsaying 6 augury **8** divining, prophecy **10** divination, predicting, prediction **11** foretelling, prophesying

sooty 4 inky **5** black, dingy, dirty, grimy **6** smudgy, smutty **9** coal-black

sop 3 dip, tip, wet **4** dunk, soak **5** bribe **6** absorb, drench, payoff, payola, take up **8** gratuity, saturate **9** baksheesh, become wet, hush money

Sophie's Choice
author: 13 William Styron

Sophisms
author: 9 Aristotle

sophisticate 8 civilize **11** cosmopolite, disillusion, make worldly **12** cosmopolitan

sophisticated 6 subtle **7** complex,

studied, worldly **8** advanced, cultured, highbrow, mannered, precious, seasoned **9** difficult **10** artificial, cultivated **11** complicated, experienced, worldly-wise **12** cosmopolitan, intellectual

sophistry 6 deceit **7** fallacy **8** subtlety **9** casuistry, chicanery, deception **10** distortion **12** speciousness

Sophocles
author of: **4** Ajax **7** Electra, Oedipus **8** Antigone **10** Oedipus Rex, Trachiniae **11** Philoctetes **16** Oedipus at Colonus **18** The Trachinian Women

sophomoric 6 callow **7** foolish, puerile **8** childish, immature, juvenile **9** infantile **10** adolescent **12** schoolboyish

soporific 4 lazy **5** balmy, heavy **6** drowsy, sleepy **8** hypnotic, sedative, sluggish **9** lethargic, somnolent **10** slumberous **11** somniferous **12** sleep-inducer **13** sleep-inducing

soppiness 4 corn, mush **5** slush **6** bathos **7** wetness **9** mushiness **10** slushiness **11** mawkishness **14** sentimentalism, sentimentality

sopping 3 wet **5** soggy, soppy **6** soaked, sodden **8** drenched, dripping **9** saturated **10** bedraggled, soaking wet

sorcerer 5 witch **6** shaman, wizard **7** warlock **8** magician **11** medicine man

sorceress 5 siren, witch **11** enchantress

sorcery 8 witchery, wizardry **9** shamanism **10** black magic, necromancy, witchcraft **11** enchantment

Sordello
author: **14** Robert Browning

sordid 3 low **4** base, rank, vile **5** dirty, gross **6** filthy, putrid, rotten, vulgar, wicked **7** corrupt, ignoble, squalid, unclean **8** degraded, depraved **9** debauched **12** disreputable

Sordido
character in: **22** Every Man out of His Humour
author: **6** Jonson

sordino, con
music: **11** with the mute

sore 4 hurt **5** acute, angry, great, harsh, irked, sharp, upset, wound **6** aching, pained, severe, tender **7** bruised, extreme, grieved, hurting, painful **8** agonized, critical, grievous, smarting, sorespot, wounding **9** agonizing, desperate, indignant, irritated, sensitive **10** distressed, unbearable **11** distressing **12** inflammation

So Red the Rose
author: **10** Stark Young

Sorel, Julien
character in: **17** The Red and the Black
author: **8** Stendhal

sorely 5 badly **7** greatly **8** severely **9** extremely **10** critically **11** desperately

soreness 4 ache, pain **10** discomfort, irritation, tenderness

sorrel 3 bay **4** herb, roan, weed **5** brown, plant, Rumex **8** chestnut **12** reddish-brown
varieties: **3** red **4** dock, tree, wood **5** lady's, sheep **6** common, French, garden, Indian **7** redwood **8** Jamaican, mountain **10** violet wood **12** European wood

Sorrel, Hetty
character in: **8** Adam Bede
author: **5** Eliot

sorrow 3 woe **4** loss, weep **5** be sad, mourn, trial **6** grieve, lament **7** despair, sadness, travail, trouble **8** disaster, hardship **9** affliction, bad fortune, misfortune **11** catastrophe, unhappiness
French: **9** tristesse

sorrowful 3 sad **6** woeful **7** unhappy **8** affected, grieving, mournful **9** lamenting

Sorrows of Young Werther, The
author: **6** Goethe
character: **6** Albert **9** Charlotte (Lotte)

sorry 3 sad **6** woeful **7** grieved, pitiful, unhappy **8** contrite, pathetic, pitiable, wretched **9** miserable, regretful, repentant, sorrowful **10** deplorable, melancholy, remorseful, ridiculous **11** crestfallen **13** brokenhearted

sort 4 kind, list, make, sift, type **5** brand, class, grade, group, index, order **6** divide, person **7** arrange, catalog, species, variety **8** classify, organize, separate, take from **9** segregate **10** categorize, individual **11** systematize **14** classification

sortie 4 rush **5** onset **6** attack, charge **7** assault **8** storming **9** onslaught

sortilege 6 augury **7** auspice, sorcery **10** divination, witchcraft

sorting 8 dividing, grouping **9** arranging **10** organizing **11** classifying **12** categorizing

so-so 4 blah, fair **5** ho-hum **6** casual, modest **7** average, humdrum **8** adequate, bearable, mediocre, middling, ordinary, passable **9** tolerable **10** second-rate **11** commonplace, indifferent **12** run-of-the-mill **13** unexceptional **15** undistinguished

sot 4 lush, soak **5** drunk, rummy, souse, toper **8** drunkard, rumhound **9** alcoholic, inebriate **11** dipsomaniac

Soter
epithet of: **4** Zeus
means: **6** savior

Sothern, Ann
real name: **13** Harriette Lake
born: **12** Valley City ND
husband: **10** Roger Pryor **14** Robert Sterling

roles: **6** Maisie **8** Cry Havoc **10** Lady Be Good **16** Private Secretary **19** A Letter to Three Wives

so throughout
Latin: **9** sic passim

sotto voce
music: **11** in a low voice **13** in an undertone, under the voice

sought 6 hunted **7** pursued, quested **9** attempted, looked for **10** endeavored

soul 5 being, force **6** person, spirit **7** essence **8** creature, vitality **9** inner core **10** embodiment, individual, vital force **11** inspiration **12** quintessence

soul-searching 10 discontent, insecurity, uneasiness **15** dissatisfaction, self-questioning

soul-stirring 7 rousing **8** electric, exciting, stirring **9** inspiring, thrilling **11** galvanizing

sound 3 fit **4** deep, firm, good, seem, tone, wise **5** drift, hardy, noise, range, sober, solid, tenor, utter, voice **6** intact, robust, severe, signal, stable, strong, sturdy **7** durable, earshot, healthy, lasting, perfect, solvent **8** announce, rational, reliable, sensible, thorough, unmarred **9** come off as, competent, enunciate, pronounce, undamaged, well-built **10** articulate, dependable, make a noise, reasonable, suggestion, untroubled **11** implication, penetrating, responsible, substantial **13** thoroughgoing **15** hearing distance, well-constructed

Sound and the Fury, The
author: **15** William Faulkner
character: **6** Dilsey **17** Sydney Herbert Head
Compson family: **5** Jason **7** Candace (Caddy), Quentin **8** Benjamin (Benjy)

Sounder
director: **10** Martin Ritt
cast: **8** Taj Mahal **10** Kevin Hooks **11** Cicely Tyson **12** Paul Winfield **13** Carmen Mathews
sequel: **13** Sounder Part II

sound measure 7 decibel

sound mind in a sound body
Latin: **21** mens sana in cor pore sano

soundness of mind 6 reason, sanity **9** normality **12** mental health

Sound of Music, The
director: **10** Robert Wise
cast: **9** Peggy Wood **12** Julie Andrews (Maria Von Trapp) **13** Eleanor Parker **18** Christopher Plummer
setting: **7** Austria
score: **21** Rodgers and Hammerstein
Oscar for: **7** picture **8** director
song: **5** Maria **6** Do-Re-Mi **9** Edelweiss **16** My Favorite Things

sound out 3 ask **8** approach **15** make a proposal to, make overtures to, put out feelers to

soup
  clear: 5 broth **8** bouillon, consomme
  server: 6 tureen
  spoon: 5 ladle
  thick: 5 cream, gumbo **6** bisque, potage **7** chowder **10** minestrone
soupcon 3 bit, dab, jot, tad **4** clue, dash, drop, hint **5** pinch, shade, taint, taste, tinge, touch, trace, whiff **6** little, trifle **7** smidgen, smidgin, vestige **8** smidgeon **9** little bit, suspicion **10** smattering, sprinkling, suggestion **12** slight amount
Soupy Sales
  character: 9 White Fang **10** Black Tooth **13** Herman the Flea, Hippy the Hippo, Pookie the Lion, Willie the Worm **14** Marilyn Monwolf
sour 3 bad **4** acid, dour, keen, tart, turn **5** nasty, sharp, spoil, surly, tangy, testy **6** crabby, cranky, curdle, rancid, sullen, turned **7** acerbic, bilious, crabbed, curdled, ferment, grouchy, peevish, spoiled, turn off, uncivil, waspish **8** alienate, choleric, embitter, jaundice, petulant, unsavory, vinegary **9** acidulous, clabbered, fermented, irritable, jaundiced, offensive, prejudice, repugnant **10** astringent, ill-dispose, ill-humored, unpleasant **11** bad-tempered, distasteful, ill-tempered **12** disagreeable
sourball 4 crab **5** crank, grump **6** grouch **9** hard candy **10** curmudgeon
source 4 font, head, root **5** basis, cause, fount **6** author, father, origin, rising, spring **8** begetter, fountain **9** authority, beginning, headwater **10** antecedent, derivation, foundation, prime mover, wellspring
source and origin
  Latin: 11 fons et origo
Sourdough State
  nickname of: 6 Alaska
sourness 7 acidity, vinegar **8** acerbity, acrimony, ill humor, pungency, tartness **9** acridness, greenness **10** bitterness
sourpuss 4 bear, crab **5** crank, grump **6** griper, grouch **7** grouser, killjoy **8** grumbler, sorehead **10** bellyacher, complainer, crosspatch, curmudgeon, spoilsport
Sousa, John Philip
  born: 12 Washington DC
  composer of: 9 El Capitan **14** Washington Post **25** The Stars and Stripes Forever
souse 3 dip, sot **4** duck, dunk, lush, soak **5** douse, drunk, rummy, steep, toper **6** barfly, boozer, drench, pickle **7** immerse, tippler **8** drunkard, inundate, marinate, saturate, submerge **9** alcoholic, inebriate **11** dipsomaniac
soused 5 drunk **6** dunked, potted, zapped, zonked **7** pickled, sloshed, smashed **8** immersed **9** plastered **10**

inebriated **11** intoxicated **17** under the influence **20** three sheets to the wind
South Africa
  capital: 8 Cape Town, Pretoria **12** Bloemfontein
  largest city: 12 Johannesburg
  others: 3 Aus **4** Mara, Stad **6** Benoni, Bononi, Braker, Durban, Garies, Severn, Soweto, Umtata, Untata **7** Brakpan, Kokstad **8** Kaapstad, Mafeking, Modjadji **9** Germiston, Kimberley **10** East London, Oudtshoorn **11** Krugersdorp, Vereeniging **13** Port Elizabeth **16** Pietermaritzburg
  school: 5 Natal **8** Capetown **13** Witwatersrand **15** Orange Free State
  division: 5 Natal **8** Backveld **9** Transvaal **10** Basutoland **12** Cape Province **14** Cape of Good Hope **15** Orange Free State
    independent homelands: 5 Venda **6** Ciskei **8** Transkei **10** bantustans **14** Bophuthatswana
  goverment:
    legislature: 4 Raad
  measure: 4 vara
  monetary unit: 4 cent, pond, rand **5** pound **6** florin **7** daalder **9** krugerand
  mountain: 3 Aux, Kop **5** Table **7** Kathkin **9** Stormberg **10** Devil's Peak, Sneeuwberg **11** Drakensberg **12** Giant's Castle **13** Witwatersrand **14** Mont-aux-Sources **15** Great Escarpment
  highest point: 8 Injasuti
  river: 3 Hex **4** Vaal **5** Nosob **6** Modder, Molopo, Orange, Tugela **7** Caledon, Kurumam, Limpopo **8** Olifants **9** Crocodile, Great Fish
  ocean: 6 Indian **8** Atlantic
  physical feature:
    bay: 5 Algoa, False, Table **6** Mossel, Walvis **7** Walfish **8** Richard's, Saldanha **11** Saint Helena
    cape: 7 Agulhas **8** Good Hope
    current: 8 Benguela
    desert: 5 Namib **8** Kalahari
    plateau: 6 Karroo
    region: 8 Highveld, Zululand **9** Kaffraria **11** Great Karroo **12** Little Karroo
  people: 3 San **4** Boer, Yosa, Zulu **5** Asian, Bantu, Namas, Nguni, Pondo, Sotho, Swazi, Tembu, Venda, Xhosa **6** Damara, Kaffir **7** African, British, Bushmen, English, Swahili **8** Bechuana, Khoikhoi **9** Afrikaner, Hottentot
    author: 5 Paton **7** Luthuli **8** Gordimer
    civil rights advocate: 6 Gandhi
    explorer: 8 Riebeeck
    leader: 4 Biko, Tutu **5** Botha, Malan, Smuts, Tomba **6** Kruger, Rhodes **7** de Klerk, Hertzog, Mandela, Vorster **8** Verwoerd **9** Buthelezi, Pretorius
  language: 4 Taal, Zulu **5** Bantu,

Hindi, Nguni, Sotho, Swazi, Tamil, Venda, Xhosa **6** Telegu, Thonga **7** English, Khoisan, Ndebele, Sesotho **8** Bujarati, Fanakalo **9** Afrikaans
  religion: 5 Hindu, Islam **7** animism, Judaism **8** Anglican **9** Methodist **12** Episcopalian, Presbyterian **13** Dutch Reformed, Roman Catholic
  place:
    Cecil Rhodes' estate: 11 Groote Shuur
    game reserve: 5 Mkuze **6** Kruger **8** Hluhluwe
    monument: 11 Voortrekker
  feature:
    bird: 4 taha
    bride price: 6 lobolo
    flower: 5 coral **6** clivia, protea **7** cowslip, fuchsia **9** phygelius **10** lachenalia
    oganization: 3 ANC **7** Inkatha **23** African National Congress
    segregation: 9 apartheid
    tree: 7 assagai **9** jacaranda
  food:
    corn: 6 mealie
    drink: 9 sundowner
    meat: 7 biltong **8** sosaties **9** boerewors
South America
  bird: 5 macaw **7** seriema, tinamou **8** caracara
  cape: 4 Horn
  country: 4 Peru **5** Chile **6** Brazil, Guyana **7** Bolivia, Ecuador, Surinam, Uruguay **8** Colombia, Paraguay **9** Argentina, Venezuela **12** French Guiana
  desert: 7 Atacama
  explorer: 16 Francisco Pizarro **18** Pedro Alvares Cabral
  hero: 12 Simon Bolivar **15** Jose de San Martin **16** Bernardo O'Higgins **18** Antonio Jose de Sucre
  highest mountain: 9 Aconcagua
  islands: 8 Falkland **9** Galapagos
  lake: 8 Titicaca **9** Maracaibo
  mountain range: 5 Andes
  native: 2 Ge **3** Ona **4** Inca **5** Carib, Mayan **7** Quechua **10** Araucanian
  plain: 5 llano, pampa
  region: 9 Patagonia
  river: 3 Apa **5** Plata **6** Amazon **7** Orinoco
South Carolina
  abbreviation: 2 SC
  nickname: 7 Calinky **8** Palmetto
  capital/largest city: 8 Columbia
  others: 5 Aiken, Greer, Union **6** Belton, Camden, Cheraw, Conway, Dillon, Seneca, Sumter **7** Bamberg, Laurens, Manning **8** Beaufort, Florence, Newberry, Rock Hill, Walhalla **9** Greenwood **10** Charleston, Greenville, Orangeburg **11** Spartanburg
  college: 5 Allen, Coker **6** Furman, Lander **7** Claflin, Clemson, Erskine, Wofford **8** Benedict, Bob Jones, Co-

lumbia, Winthrop **13** Francis Marion **15** Citadel Military

explorer: 6 Ayllon, Ribaut

feature:
  beach: 6 Myrtle
  dam: 6 Saluda
  fort: 6 Sumter
  gardens: 7 Cypress

tribe: 5 Pedee, Sewee **6** Cusabo, Santee, Waxhaw, Yamasi **7** Catawba, Shawnee, Sugeree, Wateree **8** Congaree

people: 11 James Byrnes **12** Althea Gibson, John C Calhoun **13** Bernard Baruch, Francis Marion **14** Dizzy Gillespie

island: 3 Sea **6** Parris **10** Hilton Head

lake: 6 Marion, Murray **7** Catawba, Wateree **8** Hartwell, Moultrie **9** Clark Hill

land rank: 8 fortieth

mountain: 5 Kings **6** Little **9** Blue Ridge, Sassafras

physical feature:
  bay: 8 Carolina
  plateau: 8 Piedmont

president: 13 Andrew Jackson

river: 5 Broad **6** Edisto, Pee Dee, Saluda, Santee **7** Ashepoo **8** Savannah

state admission: 6 eighth

state bird: 12 Carolina wren

state flower: 13 yellow jasmine **17** Carolina Jessamine

state motto: 18 While I Breathe I Hope **26** Prepared in Mind and Resources

state song: 8 Carolina

state tree: 8 palmetto

South Dakota

abbreviation: 2 SD **4** S Dak

nickname: 6 Coyote **8** Blizzard, Sunshine

capital: 6 Pierre

largest city: 10 Sioux Falls

others: 4 Lead, Leap **5** Huron **6** Custer, Eureka, Lemmon, Miller, Winner **7** Sturgis, Webster, Yankton **8** Aberdeen, Deadwood, Sisseton **9** Brookings, Rapid City **10** Vermillion

college: 5 Huron **7** Yankton **9** Augustana **10** Mount Marty, Sioux Falls **14** Dakota Wesleyan

explorer: 8 Varennes **13** Lewis and Clark

feature: 8 Deadwood
  battlefield: 11 Wounded Knee
  dam: 4 Oahe
  mine: 9 Homestake
  monument: 13 Mount Rushmore
  national park: 8 Badlands, Wind Cave

tribe: 5 Brule, Sioux **6** Dakota, Sutaio **8** Cheyenne

people: 10 Crazy Horse **11** Sitting Bull **14** George McGovern, Hubert Humphrey

lake: 4 Oahe **5** Sharp **8** Big Stone, Traverse **11** Francis Case **13** Lewis and Clark

land rank: 9 sixteenth

mountain: 4 Bear **5** Sheep, Table **6** Crook's, Moreau
  highest point: 6 Harney
  hills: 5 Black **7** Prairie

physical feature:
  butte: 7 Thunder **9** Deer's Ears **10** Castle Rock
  cave: 5 Jewel

river: 3 Bad **5** Grand, James, White **6** Moreau **8** Big Sioux, Cheyenne, Missouri **10** Vermillion

state admission: 8 fortieth **11** thirtyninth (with North Dakota)

state bird: 18 ring-necked pheasant

state flower: 12 pasqueflower

state animal: 6 coyote

state motto: 21 Under God the People Rule

state song: 15 Hail South Dakota

state tree: 11 white spruce **16** Black Hills spruce

southeast wind
  associated with: 5 Eurus **9** Volturnus

Southern Comfort
  type: 7 liqueur
  origin: 10 New Orleans
  flavor: 5 peach
  base: 7 bourbon
  drink: 13 Scarlett O'Hara **15** Plantation Punch
  with bourbon: 14 Blended Comfort

Southern Cross
  constellation of: 4 Crux

Southern Crown
  constellation of: 15 Corona Australis

Southerner, The
  director: 10 Jean Renoir
  cast: 10 Betty Field **11** Beulah Bondi **12** Zachary Scott **13** Bunny Sunshine

Southern Fish
  constellation of: 15 Piscis Austrinus

Southern Fly
  constellation of: 5 Musca

Southern Rhodesia *see* **8** Zimbabwe

Southern Slavic
  language family: 12 Indo-European
  group: 11 Balto-Slavic
  branch: 6 Slavic
  language: 7 Slovene **9** Bulgarian **10** Macedonian **13** Serbo-Croatian

Southern Triangle
  constellation of: 18 Triangulum Australe

South Korea *see* **5** Korea

South Vietnam *see* **7** Vietnam

South West Africa *see* **7** Namibia

south wind
  associated with: 5 Notus

South Wind
  author: 13 Norman Douglas

South Yemen *see* **5** Yemen

souvenir 4 scar **5** relic, token **6** emblem, memory, trophy **7** memento **8** keepsake, reminder **11** remembrance

sovereign 4 czar, free, king, lord, main, tsar **5** chief, major, prime, queen, regal, royal **6** kingly, potent, prince, ruling, utmost **7** emperor, highest, leading, monarch, queenly, supreme **8** absolute, autocrat, dominant, foremost, imperial, overlord, powerful, princely, reigning **9** chieftain, governing, paramount, potentate, prepotent, principal, uppermost **10** autonomous, self-ruling **11** allpowerful, crowned head, independent, monarchical **12** supreme ruler **13** selfdirecting, self-governing

sovereignty 4 sway **5** crown, power **6** throne **7** command, control, freedom, primacy, scepter **8** autonomy, dominion, home rule, kingship, lordship, self-rule **9** authority, supremacy **10** ascendancy **11** paramountcy **12** independence, jurisdiction, predominance **14** self-government **17** selfdetermination

Soviet Union *see* **6** Russia

sow 4 cast, seed **5** lodge, plant, set in, strew **6** inject, spread **7** implant, instill, scatter **8** disperse, sprinkle **9** broadcast, establish, introduce **11** disseminate

space 3 gap, sky **4** area, part, rank, room, seat, span, spot, term, time **5** berth, blank, break, chasm, ether, field, order, place, range, reach, scope, sweep, swing, width **6** hiatus, lacuna, line up, margin, period, set out, spread **7** arrange, breadth, compass, expanse, mark out, the void **8** distance, duration, infinity, interval, latitude, omission, organize, schedule, separate **9** amplitude, emptiness, keep apart, territory **10** distribute, interspace, interstice, outer space, separation, the heavens **11** nothingness, reservation, the universe **12** interruption, the firmament **13** accommodation

Space
  author: 13 James Michener

spacecraft 4 ship **6** rocket **7** orbiter, shuttle **9** satellite **10** rocketship

space flight
  US mission: 6 Apollo, Gemini, Skylab **7** Mercury
  US rocket: 5 Atlas, Titan **6** Saturn **8** Redstone
  US space shuttle: 8 Columbia **9** Discovery **10** Challenger
  Soviet mission: 5 Soyuz **6** Salyut, Vostok **7** Voskhod
  Soviet astronaut:
    first man in space: 11 Yuri Gagarin
    first woman in space: 19 Valentina Tereshkova
    first space walk by: 13 Aleksei Leonov

American astronaut: 9 John Glenn, John Young **11** Alan Shepard, Edward White, Edwin Aldrin, Frank Borman, James Lovell **12** Roger Chaffee, Wally (Walter) Schirra **13** Charles Conrad, L Gordon Cooper, Virgil (Gus) Grissom **14** Scott Carpenter, Thomas Stafford
  first man on moon: 13 Neil Armstrong
  Challenger seven: 12 Michael Smith, Ronald McNair **13** Francis Scobee, Gregory Jarvis, Judith Resnick **14** Ellison Onizuka **16** Christa McAuliffe

Spacek, Sissy
  real name: 19 Mary Elizabeth Spacek
  born: 9 Quitman TX
  roles: 6 Carrie **7** Missing **8** Badlands, The River **10** Raggedy Man **16** Crimes of the Heart **18** Coal Miner's Daughter (Oscar)

spacious 4 vast, wide **5** ample, broad, large, roomy **7** immense, sizable **8** enormous **9** capacious, expansive, extensive, uncrowded **10** commodious

spaciousness 9 amplitude, largeness, roominess **13** capaciousness **14** commodiousness

Spade, Sam
  character in: 16 The Maltese Falcon
  author: 7 Hammett

Spain
  other name: 6 Iberia **8** Hispania
  capital/largest city: 6 Madrid
  others: 4 Adra, Aspe, Baza, Elda, Horo, Irun, Jaen, Leon, Noya, Olot, Reus, Rota, Sama, Vigo **5** Baena, Bejar, Cadiz, Cieza, Cueta, Ecija, Eibar, Elche, Gades, Gadir, Gijon, Ibiza, Jerez, Jodar, Liego, Lorca, Oliva, Palma, Palos, Ronda, Siero, Ubeda, Xeres, Yecla, Zafra **6** Abdera, Aviles, Azuaga, Bilbao, Burgos, Coruna, Duenca, Gandia, Gerona, Getafe, Guadix, Hellin, Huelva, Huesca, Jativa, Lerida, Lucena, Malaga, Mataro, Merida, Murcia, Orense, Oviedo, Termel, Toledo, Utrera, Zamora **7** Almeria, Badajos, Cordoba, Daimiel, Granada, Jumilla, Linares, Logrono, Manresa, Segovia, Sevilla, Seville, Tarrasa, Vitoria **8** Alicante, Badalona, Figueras, Pamplona, Sabadell, Santiago, Torrente, Valencia, Zaragoza **9** Barcelona, Las Palmas, Saragossa
  school: 6 Ciudad, Madrid
  division: 4 Jaen, Leon, Lugo **5** Alava, Avila, Cadiz, Soria **6** Basque, Burgos, Coruna, Cuenca, Gerona, Huelva, Huesca, Lerida, Madrid, Malaga, Murcia, Orense, Oviedo, Teruel, Toledo, Zamora **7** Almeria, Caceres, Cordoba, Granada, Logrono, Navarra, Segovia, Sevilla, Vizcaya, Zadajoz **8** Albacete, Alicante, Baleares, Palencia, Valencia, Zaragoza **9** Cata-

lonia
  kingdom: 4 Leon **6** Aragon **7** Castile, Galicia, Granada, Navarre **8** Asturias **9** al-Andalus, Catalonia **12** Spanish March
government: 8 monarchy
  legislature: 6 Cortes
head of state: 4 king
measure: 3 pie **4** codo, dedo, paso, vara **5** braza, cahiz, carga, legua, medio, palmo, sesma **6** cordel, cuarta, fanega, racion, yugada **7** azumbre, celemin, estadel, pulgada **8** fanegada
monetary unit: 3 cob **4** duro **5** dobla **6** cuarto, dinero, escudo, peseta **7** alfonso, centimo, pistole **8** doubloon
weight: 4 onza **5** frail, libra, marco, tomin **6** arroba, dinero, dracma **7** arienzo, quilate, quintal **8** tonelada
island: 5 Ceuta, Ibiza, Iviza, Palma **6** Canary, Gomera, Hierro **7** Alboran, Majorca, Melilla, Minorca **8** Balearic, Mallorca, Tagomago, Tenerife **9** Lanzarote **13** Fuerteventura
lake: 4 lago **8** Albufera
mountain: 4 Gata **5** Aneto, Rouch **6** Cuenca, Estats, Europa, Gredos, Magina, Morena, Nethou, Nevada, Teleno, Toledo **7** Alcaraz, Banuelo, Catalan, Cerredo, Demanda, Iberian, La Sagra, Moncayo, Perdido **8** Almanzor, Asturias, Galician, Maladeta, Monegros, Montseny, Penalara, Pyrenees **10** Albarracin, Cantabrian, Guadarrama, Torrecilla
highest point: 5 Teide **8** Mulhacen
river: 3 Sil, Ter **4** Cega, Ebro, Esla, Lima, Mino, Muga, Tajo, Ulla **5** Adaja, Cinca, Douro, Duero, Genil, Jalon, Jucar, Navia, Odiel, Riaza, Segie, Tagus, Tinto, Turia **6** Alagon, Aragon, Eresma, Huerva, Jarama, Orbigo, Segura, Torote **7** Almeria, Almonte, Arlanza, Barbate, Cabriel, Gallego, Henares, Mijares, Perales **8** Duration, Guadiana **12** Guadalquivir
sea: 8 Atlantic, Balearic **13** Mediterranean
physical feature:
  bay: 5 Bahia **6** Biscay
  cape: 9 Trafalgar
  gulf: 5 Cadiz **8** San Jorge, Valencia
  peninsula: 7 Iberian
  plateau: 6 meseta
  strait: 9 Gibraltar
people: 5 Diego, Gente, Latin **6** Basque, Espana **7** Catalan, Espanol, Iberian **8** Galician, Gallegos, Maragato
  architect: 5 Gaudi
  artist: 4 Dali, Goya, Gris, Miro **6** Ribera **7** El Greco, Murillo, Picasso **8** Zurbaran **9** Velazquez
  author: 4 Cela, Vega **5** Barea, Cueva, Rojas **6** Aleman, Alonso, Azorin, Baroja, Castro, Encina, Felipe, Ibanez, Miguel **7** Alarcon,

Becquer, Cernuda, Ercilla, Gongora, Guillen, Jimenez, Machado, Unamuno **8** Montalvo, Zorrilla **9** Benavente, Cervantes, Goytisola **10** Aleixandre, Espronceda, Lope de Vega, Pardo Bazan **11** Garcia Lorca **12** Lopez de Ayala **13** Tirso de Molina **17** Calderon de la Barca
  cellist: 6 Casals
  composer: 7 Albeniz **8** Granados, Victoria **13** Manuel de Falla
  converted Moslem: 7 morisco
  dynasty: 7 Almohad, Umayyad **9** Almoravid
  explorer: 6 Balboa, Cortes **7** Pizarro **8** Columbus
  Jesuit founder: 14 Ignatius Loyola
  king: 6 Pelayo, Philip, Ramiro, Sancho, Witiza **7** Alfonso, Charles **8** al-Mansur, Reccared, Roderick **9** Ferdinand, Leovigild **10** Juan Carlos **11** Abd al-Rahman, Reccosvinth
  leader: 4 Prim **5** Godoy **6** Franco **7** Canovas **11** Calvo Sotelo **13** Primo de Rivera **14** Suarez-Gonzalez
  queen: 8 Isabella **16** Elizabeth Farnese
  ruler: 4 Rome **5** Celts, Moors **6** Greece **7** Almeria, Vandals **8** Carthage **9** Phoenicia, Visigoths
  scholar: 8 Averroes
  singer: 7 Domingo **8** Iglesias
  warrior: 14 El Cid Campeador
language: 6 Basque **7** Catalan, Spanish **8** Balearic, Galician **9** Castilian, Valencian
expressions: 5 adios **10** buenos dias **11** que sera sera **12** hasta la vista
religion: 7 Judaism **10** Protestant **13** Roman Catholic
place:
  aqueduct: 7 Segovia
  bridge: 7 Cordoba
  castle: 7 Alcazar **12** Santa Barbara
  cathedral bell tower: 7 Giralda
  center of Madrid: 12 Puerto del Sol
  church/cathedral: 4 Leon **6** Burgos, Gerona, Toledo **7** Seville **9** Barcelona, San Isidro **10** Santa Maria **14** Sagrada Familia
  fountain: 6 Cibele
  library: 8 Columbus
  minaret: 7 Seville
  mosque: 11 Great Mosque **19** Santo Cristo de la Cruz
  museum: 5 Prado **15** Museo de Pinturas
  palace: 7 Granada, Naranco **8** Alhambra, Escorial **9** Real Mayor
  park: 6 Retiro
  resort: 8 Marbella **10** Costa Brava **12** Torremolinos
  shrine: 32 Saint James at Santiago de Compostela
  street: 7 Ramblas **13** Paseo del Prado **16** Plaza de la Cibeles **19**

Paseo de la Castellana
synagogue: 10 El Transito
theater: 6 Merida
wall paintings/caves: 8 Altamira
possession: 5 Ceuta **6** Melill
feature:
　bar: 6 tascas
　dance: 5 tango **8** fandango, flamenco
　estate: 10 latifundia
　matador's suit: 12 traje de luces
　political party: 7 Falange
food:
　dish: 6 cocido, paella **8** zarzuela
　soup: 8 gazpacho
span 4 arch, area, last, term, wing **5** cover, cross, range, reach, scope, spell, sweep, vault **6** bridge, endure, extent, length, period **7** archway, breadth, measure, stretch, survive, trestle **8** distance, duration, interval **9** extension, reach over, territory **10** bridge over, dimensions **11** proportions, reach across, stretch over **12** extend across
spangle 4 star **5** bedew **6** sequin **7** glisten, glitter, shimmer, twinkle **9** bugle head, coruscate, paillette
spaniel
　dog breed: 5 field **6** cocker, Sussex **7** clumber, Tibetan **8** Brittany **10** Irish water **13** American water, English cocker, Welsh springer **15** English springer **19** Cavalier King Charles
Spanish (language, person) 7 espanol
Spanish Guinea see **16** Equatorial Guinea
Spanish Sahara see **13** Western Sahara
Spanish Tragedy, The
　author: 9 Thomas Kyd
　character: 7 Horatio, Lorenzo, Villupo **9** Alexandro, Balthazar, Hieronimo **10** Bel Imperia **16** Ghost of Don Andrea
spank 3 hit, tan **4** beat, belt, blow, cane, flog, hide, lick, slap, whip, whop **5** birch, strap, whale **6** paddle, strike, switch, thrash, wallop **8** paddling **10** flagellate
spanking 4 very **5** brisk, fresh **7** beating **8** paddling, whipping **9** extremely, thrashing **10** punishment **12** chastisement
spanking new 5 fresh **6** unused **8** brand new **9** untouched
spar 4 boom, mast, pole **5** argue, fight, sprit **6** bicker **7** dispute, quarrel, wrangle **8** crossbar **10** crosspiece
spare 3 odd **4** bony, cede, free, give, keep, lank, lean, save, thin **5** amass, extra, forgo, gaunt, grant, guard, hoard, lanky, lay up, limit, pinch, rangy, scant, stint, weedy **6** acquit, afford, defend, donate, excess, exempt, forego, let off, meager, not use, par-

don, scanty, shield, skimpy, skinny, slight, unused **7** forgive, haggard, husband, let go of, protect, release, relieve, reserve, scraggy, scrawny, shelter, skimp on, slender, surplus **8** conserve, hold back, leftover, liberate, part with, reprieve, set aside, skeletal, withhold **9** auxiliary, emaciated, exonerate, fleshless, safeguard, show mercy **10** additional, extraneous, relinquish, substitute, unconsumed **11** economize on, have mercy on, superfluous, unnecessary, use frugally **12** be merciful to, dispense with, supplemental **13** supernumerary, supplementary
spared 5 freed **6** exempt, immune **7** excused **8** absolved, excepted, relieved
sparing 4 near **5** close, scant **6** frugal, meager, saving, scanty, stingy **7** careful, miserly, thrifty **8** grudging, stinting **9** niggardly, penurious **10** economical, ungenerous **11** closefisted, tightfisted **12** parsimonious
spark 3 bit, jot **4** atom, beam, fire, iota, life **5** brand, ember, flash, gleam, pique, trace **6** arouse, excite, incite, spirit **7** flicker, glimmer, glitter, inspire, provoke, sparkle **8** vitality **9** animation, instigate, stimulate **10** get-up-and-go
Spark, Muriel
　author of: 11 Memento Mori **14** The Driver's Seat, The Only Problem **17** The Mandelbaum Gate, Territorial Rights **19** Loitering with Intent **21** A Far Cry from Kensington **24** The Prime of Miss Jean Brodie
sparkle 3 pep, pop, vim **4** dash, elan, fizz, foam, glow, life **5** be gay, brand, cheer, ember, flash, froth, gleam, glint, light, shine, verve **6** bubble, dazzle, fizzle, gaiety, spirit **7** be witty, flicker, glimmer, glisten, glitter, jollity, rejoice, shimmer, twinkle **8** radiance, vitality, vivacity **9** alertness, animation, briskness, coruscate, quickness **10** be cheerful, brilliance, ebullience, effervesce, effulgence, exuberance, liveliness, luminosity **11** be vivacious, scintillate **12** cheerfulness, exhilaration, luminousness **13** effervescence, scintillation
sparkling 5 fizzy **6** bubbly **7** fizzing, twinkly **8** bubbling, dazzling, glittery **9** twinkling **10** glistening, glittering **11** coruscating **12** effervescent **13** scintillating
Sparky Lyle
　nickname of: 16 Albert Walter Lyle
sparse 3 few **4** thin **5** scant, spare **6** meager, scanty, scarce, skimpy, spotty, strewn **7** diffuse **8** exiguous, sporadic **9** dispersed, scattered, spaced-out, uncrowded **10** infrequent **16** few and far between

sparseness 7 paucity **8** sparsity, thinness **10** meagerness, scantiness
Sparsit, Mrs
　character in: 9 Hard Times
　author: 7 Dickens
Spartacus
　director: 14 Stanley Kubrick
　cast: 8 Nina Foch **9** John Gavin **10** Tony Curtis **11** Jean Simmons, Kirk Douglas **12** Peter Ustinov **15** Charles Laughton, Laurence Olivier
　setting: 4 Rome
　score: 9 Alex North
spartan 4 hard **5** plain, stark, stern, stiff **6** frugal, severe, simple, strict **7** ascetic, austere **8** exacting, rigorous **9** stringent **10** abstemious, inexorable, inflexible, restrained, restricted **11** disciplined, self-denying **15** self-disciplined
Sparti
　occupation: 8 warriors
spasm 3 fit, tic **4** grip, jerk, pang **5** burst, cramp, crick, flash, onset, spell, spurt, start, storm, throe **6** access, attack, frenzy, twitch **7** seizure, shudder, tempest **8** eruption, paroxysm **9** explosion **10** convulsion
spasmodic 6 fitful **7** erratic, flighty **8** fleeting, periodic, sporadic **9** desultory, irregular, mercurial, transient **10** capricious, inconstant, occasional **12** intermittent **13** discontinuous
spat 4 tiff **5** argue, fight, scrap, set-to **6** bicker, differ **7** contend, dispute, dissent, quarrel, wrangle **8** disagree, squabble **10** difference **11** altercation **12** disagreement **16** misunderstanding
spatter 4 slop, soil, spot **5** fleck, plash, spray, spurt, stain, swash **6** mottle, shower, splash **7** speckle, stipple **8** splatter, sprinkle
spawn 4 eggs, seed, teem **5** beget, breed, brood, fruit, yield **7** lay eggs, produce, product **8** engender, generate, multiply **9** offspring, propagate, reproduce **10** bring forth, give rise to **11** deposit eggs, give birth to, proliferate
speak 3 air, say **4** call, chat, deal, talk, tell **5** imply, orate, refer, shout, sound, state, treat, voice **6** advise, confer, convey, cry out, dilate, impart, mumble, murmur, mutter, preach, recite, relate, remark, report, reveal **7** bespeak, comment, consult, declaim, declare, discuss, divulge, expound, express, lecture, mention, suggest, whisper **8** announce, converse, disclose, harangue, indicate, proclaim, vocalize **9** discourse, enunciate, expatiate, hold forth, make known, pronounce, sermonize **10** articulate **11** communicate, give a speech
speakeasy 3 bar **6** saloon, tavern **7** gin mill **14** cocktail lounge
speaker 5 voice **6** orator, reader, talker

7 reciter **8** advocate, lecturer, preacher **9** declaimer, spokesman **10** discourser, monologist, mouthpiece, sermonizer **11** rhetorician, speechmaker, spokeswoman **13** valedictorian

speak highly of 4 laud **5** exalt, extol **6** praise **7** commend **8** eulogize **10** compliment **16** sing the praises of

speak ill of 4 slur **5** curse, knock, libel **6** defame, insult, malign, vilify **7** slander **8** bad-mouth **9** criticize, denigrate, discredit, disparage **13** find fault with **14** inveigh against

speak loudly 3 cry **4** bawl, call, hail, roar, yell **5** shout **6** bellow, clamor, cry out, halloo, holler **7** call out, speak up

speak of 7 mention, refer to **8** allude to **9** talk about, touch upon

speak to 6 talk to **7** address, lecture

speak together 3 gab, jaw, rap **4** chat, chin, talk **6** confer **7** chatter, palaver **8** chitchat, converse **10** chew the fat, chew the rag **11** communicate, confabulate

speak well of 4 laud **5** boost, extol **6** praise **7** acclaim, approve, commend, flatter, root for **8** eulogize **9** sweet talk **10** compliment, stick up for **13** speak highly of **16** sing the praises of **17** put in a good word for

spear 4 bolt, dart, gaff, gore, pike, spit, stab **5** lance, prick, shaft, spike, stick **6** impale, pierce **7** harpoon, javelin **8** puncture, transfix **9** penetrate **10** run through

spearhead 4 iron, lead **5** begin, found, start **6** launch, leader **7** creator, develop, founder, pioneer **8** begetter, conceive, initiate **9** establish, initiator, institute, originate, spokesman **10** inaugurate, instituter, prime mover **11** establisher, inaugurator, spokeswoman **12** avant-gardist

special 4 fast, good, rare **5** close, great, novel **6** ardent, proper, select, signal, unique **7** bargain, certain, devoted, endemic, feature, staunch, typical, unusual **8** distinct, especial, intimate, peculiar, personal, sale item, singular, specific, uncommon **9** headliner, high point, highlight, important, momentous, specialty, steadfast **10** attraction, individual, noteworthy, particular, remarkable **11** distinctive, exceptional, outstanding, specialized **12** extravaganza **13** distinguished, extraordinary **14** representative, unconventional **16** out of the ordinary **17** piece de resistance

specialist 4 buff **5** adept, maven **6** expert, master **9** authority **10** past master **11** connoisseur

specialization 5 focus, forte, major **6** metier **8** province **10** speciality **13** concentration

specialize 5 adapt, focus, major **6** pursue **10** narrow down **11** concentrate

specialty 4 bent, mark, turn **5** badge, focus, forte, hobby, major, stamp **6** genius, talent **7** earmark, faculty, feature, pursuit, special **8** aptitude **9** endowment, trademark **10** competence, profession **11** claim to fame, distinction

species 4 form, kind, make, sort, type **5** breed, class, genre, group, order **6** kidney, nature, stripe **7** variety **8** category, division **11** designation, subdivision **14** classification

specific 5 exact, fixed **6** minute, stated, unique **7** bounded, certain, endemic, limited, pointed, precise, special, typical **8** clear-cut, concrete, confined, definite, detailed, especial, peculiar, personal, relevant, singular, tied-down **9** intrinsic, pertinent, specified **10** individual, particular, pinned-down, restricted **11** categorical, determinate, distinctive, unequivocal **13** circumscribed **14** characteristic

specification 6 detail **7** clarity **9** condition, precision, substance **11** enumeration, itemization, requirement, stipulation **12** concreteness **13** particularity, qualification **17** particularization

specifics 4 cure, fact, item **5** datum **6** detail, physic **10** medication, particular **12** circumstance

specify 4 cite, name **5** order **6** adduce, define, denote, detail **7** call for, focus on, itemize **8** describe, indicate, set forth **9** designate, enumerate, stipulate **13** particularize

specimen 4 case, type **5** model **6** sample **7** example **8** exemplar, instance **9** prototype **14** representative **15** exemplification

specious 5 false **6** faulty, tricky, untrue **7** dubious, in valid, unsound **8** slippery, spurious **9** casuistic, deceptive, illogical, incorrect, unfounded **10** fallacious, inaccurate, misleading **11** sophistical **12** questionable **15** unsubstantiated

speck 3 bit, dot, jot, pin **4** drop, hair, iota, mark, mite, mote, spot, whit **5** fleck, grain, pinch, trace **6** shadow, trifle **7** glimmer, modicum, speckle **8** farthing, flyspeck, particle **9** scintilla

speckled 4 pied **6** dotted **7** flecked, spotted, studded **8** freckled, peppered **9** sprinkled

spectacle 5 scene, sight **6** marvel, parade, rarity, wonder **7** display, exhibit, pageant **9** curiosity, rare sight **10** exhibition, exposition, phenomenon, production **12** extravaganza, presentation **13** demonstration

spectacles 6 lenses, shades **7** glasses **8** bifocals, pince-nez **10** eyeglasses

spectacular 4 gala, rich **5** grand, showy **6** daring **7** jeweled, opulent, stately **8** dramatic, fabulous, glorious, gorgeous, splendid, striking **9** daredevil, elaborate, marvelous, spectacle, sumptuous, thrilling **10** astounding, bespangled, eye-filling, impressive, theatrical **11** ceremonious, hairraising, magnificent, sensational **12** extravaganza, overwhelming **16** ostentatious show **19** elaborate production

spectator 3 fan **5** house **6** viewer **7** gallery, witness **8** audience, beholder, kibitzer, observer, onlooker **9** bystander, sightseer **10** aficionado, eyewitness **11** afficionado, theatergoer **12** rubbernecker

Spectator, The author: 13 Joseph Addison, Richard Steele

specter 5 demon, ghost, ghoul, shade, spook **6** spirit, sprite, vision, wraith **7** banshee, fantasy, phantom **8** phantasm, presence, revenant **9** hobgoblin **10** apparition

spectral 4 airy **5** eerie, weird **6** creepy, spooky, unreal **7** ghastly, ghostly, phantom, shadowy, uncanny **8** ethereal, gossamer, vaporous **9** unearthly **10** chimerical, phantasmal, wraithlike **11** incorporeal **12** otherworldly, supernatural **13** insubstantial

speculate 4 muse **5** brood, dream, fancy, guess, study, think, wager **6** chance, gamble, hazard, ponder, reason, wonder **7** imagine, reflect, suppose, surmise, venture **8** cogitate, consider, meditate, ruminate, theorize **10** conjecture, deliberate, excogitate, play a hunch **11** contemplate, hypothesize, take a chance **13** play the market

speculation 4 risk **7** venture **8** gambling **9** guesswork **10** conjecture, estimation **11** supposition

speculative 4 iffy **5** dicey, risky **6** chancy **8** academic **11** conjectural, theoretical **12** experimental, hypothetical **13** suppositional

speculator 7 gambler, plunger **8** investor, operator, theorist **10** adventurer, arbitrager **11** arbitrageur

speech 4 talk **5** idiom, lingo, slang, voice **6** appeal, gossip, homily, jargon, sermon, tirade, tongue **7** address, chatter, comment, dialect, diction, lecture, oration, palaver, prattle, remarks, talking **8** chitchat, colloquy, converse, dialogue, diatribe, harangue, language, parlance, rhetoric, speaking **9** discourse, elocution, monologue, soliloquy, statement, utterance **10** discussion, expression, recitation, salutation **11** declamation, declaration, enunciation, exhortation, observation, valedictory **12** articulation, conversation, dissertation, vocalization **13** col-

loquialism, confabulation, pronouncement, pronunciation, verbalization

speechless 3 mum **4** dumb, mute **6** silent **7** aphonic **8** wordless **9** stupefied
10 tongue-tied

speed 3 aid, hie, run, zip **4** dart, dash,
help, race, rate, rush, tear, zoom **5**
boost, favor, gun it, haste, hurry, impel, speed, tempo **6** assist, barrel, gallop, hasten, hurtle, hustle, pick up,
plunge, propel, scurry, step up **7** advance, further, hurry up, promote,
quicken, tear off **8** alacrity, celerity,
dispatch, expedite, high tail, make
time, momentum, rapidity, step on it,
velocity **9** bowl along, briskness, fleetness, give a lift, hastiness, make
haste, move along, quickness, rapid-
ness, swiftness **10** accelerate, expedition, get a move on, go hell-bent, lose
no time, promptness, spurt ahead
11 push forward **12** acceleration **13**
burn up the road

speedily 4 fast **5** apace, quick **6**
pronto **7** hastily, rapidly, swiftly **8** in
no time, promptly **9** post haste, right
away, summarily **11** on the double **12**
lickety-split

speed up 4 rush **5** hurry **6** hasten,
step up **7** hop to it, quicken **8** expedite, multiply, step on it **9** encourage,
intensify **10** accelerate, facilitate, get a
move on **12** step on the gas

speedy 4 fast **5** brisk, early, fleet,
hasty, quick, rapid, ready, swift **6** abrupt, lively, sudden **7** express, hurried, running, summary **8** headlong **9**
quick-fire, rapid-fire **10** not delayed
11 precipitate

Spelaites
epithet of: 6 Hermes
means: 9 of the cave

spell 2 go **3** hit, hex **4** bout, free, lull,
mean, omen, snap, term, time, tour,
turn, wave **5** augur, break, charm,
hitch, imply, magic, pause, round,
stint, trick, while **6** allure, course, denote, herald, hoodoo, make up, period, recess, tenure, typify, voodoo **7**
bespeak, betoken, connote, glamour,
portend, presage, promise, purport,
rapture, release, relieve, respite, signify, sorcery, stretch, suggest **8**
amount to, cover for, duration, forebode, forecast, foretell, indicate, interval, stand for, witchery **9** form a
word, influence, interlude, represent,
symbolize **10** assignment, invocation,
mumbo jumbo, open-sesame **11** abracadabra, bewitchment, enchantment,
fascination, incantation, pinch-hit for,
take over for **12** magic formula

spellbind 5 charm **7** bewitch, enchant
8 enthrall, entrance, intrigue, transfix
9 enrapture, fascinate, hypnotize,
mesmerize, transport

spellbound 4 rapt **5** agape **7** charmed

8 wordless **9** awestruck, bewitched,
enchanted, entranced, possessed **10**
breathless, dumbstruck, enraptured,
enthralled, fascinated, hypnotized,
mesmerized, speechless, tongue-tied,
transfixed **11** openmouthed, transported

Spellbound
director: 15 Alfred Hitchcock
cast: 9 John Emery **11** Gregory Peck,
Leo G Carroll **13** Ingrid Bergman **14**
Michael Chekhov
score: 11 Miklos Rosza
Oscar for: 5 score
dream sequences by: 12 Salvador
Dali

spell out 6 define, detail **7** clarify,
clear up, explain, expound, specify **8**
describe **9** delineate, designate, elucidate, explicate, interpret, make plain
10 illustrate

Spemann, Hans
field: 7 zoology
nationality: 6 German
worked in: 20 embryonic development
awarded: 10 Nobel Prize

Spencer, Sir Stanley
born: 7 Cookham, England **9** Berkshire
artwork: 22 Resurrection of Soldiers,
The Resurrection Cookham **31** Christ
Preaching at Cookham Regatta **43**
Double Nude Portrait the Artist and
his Second Wife

spend 3 pay, use **4** dole, fill, give, pass
5 drain, empty, use up, waste **6** devote, employ, expend, invest, occupy,
outlay, pay out, take up **7** burn out,
consume, deplete, destroy, exhaust,
fork out, scatter, wear out **8** allocate,
disburse, dispense, shell out, squander
9 dissipate, while away **10** impoverish

spendable 9 available **10** expendable
13 discretionary

spend foolishly 5 waste **8** misspend,
squander **9** dissipate, throw away **11**
fritter away

spendthrift 6 lavish, waster **7** wastrel
8 prodigal, spend-all, wasteful **10** big
spender, profligate, squanderer **11** extravagant, improvident **12** overgenerous

Spengler, Oswald
author of: 19 The Decline of the
West

Spenlow, Dora
character in: 16 David Copperfield
author: 7 Dickens

Spenser, Edmund
author of: 8 Amoretti **12** Epithalamion **15** The Faerie Queene **22** The
Shephearde's Calendar

spent 4 beat, done, weak **5** faint,
weary **6** bushed, done in, used up **7**
laid low, wearied, worn out **8** drooping, fatigued, tired out **9** enfeebled,

exhausted, fagged out, played out,
powerless, prostrate **11** debilitated,
ready to drop **12** strengthless **14** on
one's last legs

Sperry, Elmer Ambrose
invented: 11 gyrocompass **22** airplane automatic pilot

spew 5 eject, expel, heave, vomit **6**
cast up **7** spit out **8** disgorge, throw
out **11** regurgitate

spew up 4 spew **5** eject, expel, spout,
vomit **6** cast up **7** cough up, throw up
8 disgorge **11** regurgitate

sphere 3 orb **4** area, ball, beat, pale **5**
globe, orbit, range, realm, scope **6** domain **7** compass, globule **8** province,
spheroid **9** bailiwick, round body, territory **10** experience

spherical 5 orbic, round **6** global, rotund **7** globate, globose, orbical **8**
globular **9** orbicular **11** globe-shaped
nearly: 8 obrotund

spheroid 3 orb **4** ball **5** globe **6** sphere
7 globule

spherule 4 ball, bead, drop **6** pellet **7**
droplet, globule

Sphinx
form: 7 monster
bust of: 5 woman
body of: 4 lion
father: 6 Typhon **7** Orthrus
mother: 7 Echidna **8** Chimaera
proposed: 7 riddles
location: 4 Giza **6** Thebes
answered by: 7 Oedipus

spice 3 zip **4** herb, kick, snap, tang,
zest **5** savor **6** accent, flavor, relish,
stacte **7** pizzazz **8** piquancy, pungency **9** condiment, flavoring, seasoning **10** excitement

spicule 4 barb **5** point, spine **7** prickle

spicy 3 hot **4** keen, racy **5** acute,
bawdy, fiery, nippy, pithy, salty,
sharp, tangy, witty, zippy **6** clever,
ribald, risque, snappy, strong **7** gingery, peppery, piquant, pungent **8** aromatic, improper, incisive, indecent,
off-color, piercing, redolent, spirited **9**
sparkling, trenchant **10** indelicate,
scandalous, suggestive **11** provocative
12 questionable **13** scintillating

spider
black widow marking: 9 hourglass
class: 9 Arachnida
combining form: 6 arachn **7** arachno
family: 7 Attidae **9** Drassidae **10** Citi-
gradae, Pisauridae
famous: 9 Charlotte
fear of: 13 arachnophobia
kind: 4 crab, wolf **5** taint **7** jumping
8 trap-door **9** orb weaver, solpugida,
tarantula **10** black widow **13** daddy
longlegs
mythology: 7 Arachne
nest: 5 nidus
order: 7 Araneae
part: 4 claw, coxa **5** femur, tibia **6**

tarsus **7** abdomen, mammula, patella, pedicel, scopula **9** chelicera, protarsis, spinneret **10** pedipalpus, trochanter **11** calamistrum **13** cephalothorax
study of: 10 araneology **11** arachnology
young: 11 spiderlings

Spielberg, Steven
wife: 11 Kate Capshaw
former wife: 9 Amy Irving
company: 13 Dreamworks SKG
director of: 4 Jaws **7** Amistad **11** Poltergeist **12** Jurassic Park, The Lost World **14** Schindler's List (Oscar), The Color Purple **19** Raiders of the Lost Ark **21** ET The Extra Terrestrial **29** Close Encounters of the Third Kind, Indiana Jones and the Last Crusade **30** Indiana Jones and the Temple of Doom

spike 3 peg, pin **4** barb, nail, spur, tine **5** briar, point, prong, rivet, spine, stake, thorn **6** needle, skewer **7** bramble, bristle, hobnail **8** spikelet

spill 3 run **4** blab, drip, drop, dump, fall, flow, shed, slop, tell, toss **5** slosh, throw, waste **6** reveal, splash **7** let flow, pour out **8** disclose, overflow, overturn

Spillane, Mickey
real name: 13 Frank Morrison
author of: 8 I the Jury **12** Kiss Me Deadly **14** The Girl Hunters **15** The Death Dealers
character: 10 Mike Hammer

spin 4 roll, tell, turn **5** swirl, twirl, wheel, whirl **6** gyrate, invent, relate, render, rotate, unfold **7** concoct, narrate, recount, revolve **8** rotation, spinning **9** fabricate, pirouette

spinach 3 rot **4** bull, bunk **5** hokum, hooey, stuff **6** bunkum, hot air, humbug **7** baloney, blather, hogwash, potherb **8** claptrap, nonsense, tommyrot **9** poppycock, vegetable **10** applesauce **11** foolishness **16** stuff and nonsense

spinach 16 Spinacia oleracea
varieties: 4 wild **5** Cuban **6** Indian **7** Malabar **8** mountain **10** New Zealand **11** round-seeded **13** prickly-seeded

spinal column 4 back **5** spine **8** backbone

spindly 4 puny **5** frail, leggy **6** skinny **7** scraggy **8** skeletal

spine 4 barb, horn, spur **5** briar, point, prong, quill, spike, thorn **6** needle **7** bramble, bristle, prickle **8** backbone **9** vertebrae **12** spinal column

spinel
source: 5 Burma, Mogok
color: 3 red **5** mauve

spineless 4 weak **5** timid **7** fearful **8** cowardly, cowering, cringing, timorous, wavering **10** indecisive, irresolute, spiritless, weak-willed **11** lily-livered, vacillating **12** fainthearted **13** pusillanimous **14** chickenhearted

spinelessness 8 timidity, weakness **9** cowardice **10** indecision **11** fearfulness **12** cowardliness, irresolution **13** pusillanimity

spine-tingling 7 rousing **8** exciting **9** thrilling **11** hair-raising, sensational **12** breathtaking, electrifying

spinning jenny
invented by: 10 Hargreaves

spinoff 5 issue **6** result **7** ad junct, outcome **8** offshoot **9** byproduct, outgrowth **10** descendant, side effect, supplement **11** aftereffect, consequence

spin out 4 skid **7** draw out **8** lengthen **9** attenuate

spinster 6 virgin **7** old maid **14** unmarried woman

spinsterhood 8 celibacy **9** virginity **11** old maidhood

spiral 4 coil, curl, gyre **5** helix, screw, whirl, whorl **6** coiled, curled **7** helical, ringlet, spiroid, whorled, winding **8** curlicue, twisting **9** corkscrew **11** screw-shaped

Spiral Staircase, The
director: 13 Robert Siodmak
based on story by: 14 Ethel Lina White (Some Must Watch)
cast: 9 Kent Smith **11** George Brent **13** Rhonda Fleming **14** Dorothy McGuire, Ethel Barrymore

spire 3 cap, tip **4** apex, cone, peak **5** crest, point, shaft, tower **6** belfry, summit, turret, vertex **7** minaret, obelisk, steeple **8** pinnacle **9** bell tower, campanile

spirit 3 elf **4** mind, soul, urge, will **5** fairy, ghost, ghoul, heart, shade, spook **6** animus, dybbuk, goblin, psyche, sprite, wraith **7** banshee, bugaboo, bugbear, impulse, phantom, resolve, specter **8** phantasm, presence **9** hobgoblin, intellect **10** apparition, motivation, resolution
German: 5 Geist

spirited 4 bold **5** fiery, nervy **6** frisky, lively, plucky **8** fearless, intrepid **10** courageous, mettlesome

spiritless 4 dull, limp, tame **6** abject **8** cowardly, lifeless, listless **9** apathetic, spineless **10** unanimated, world-weary **11** passionless

spirit of the time
German: 9 Zeitgeist

spirits 3 aim, vim **4** bond, elan, fire, gist, glow, grit, guts, mood, sand, tone, vein, zeal, zest **5** ardor, drive, humor, pluck, sense, spunk, tenor, valor, verve, vigor **6** daring, effect, elixir, energy, fervor, intent, liquor, mettle, morale, stripe, temper, warmth **7** alcohol, avidity, bravery, courage, essence, extract, feeling, loyalty,

meaning, purport, purpose, sparkle **8** attitude, audacity, backbone, boldness, devotion, emotions, feelings, tincture, vitality, vivacity **9** animation, eagerness, fortitude, intention, sentiment, stoutness, substance **10** allegiance, attachment, enterprise, enthusiasm, liveliness **11** disposition, doughtiness, staunchness **12** fearlessness, significance **13** dauntlessness, sprightliness **16** stoutheartedness **17** alcoholic solution

spiritual 4 holy **5** godly, inner, moral, pious **6** divine, mental **7** blessed, churchy, ghostly, phantom, psychic **8** cerebral, hallowed, heavenly, platonic, priestly, spectral, supernal **9** celestial, Christian, innermost, of the soul, religious, unearthly, unfleshly, unworldly **10** devotional, immaterial, intangible, sacrosanct, sanctified **11** consecrated, incorporeal **12** metaphysical, otherworldly, supernatural **13** insubstantial, psychological **14** ecclesiastical

spirituality 5 piety **8** devotion, holiness **9** godliness, reverence **10** devoutness

spirituous 4 hard **6** strong **9** alcoholic, distilled **12** intoxicating

spit 3 bar, pop, rod **4** foam, hiss, reef, spew **5** atoll, drool, eject, fling, froth, shoal, throw **6** saliva, shower, shriek, skewer, slaver, sputum **7** dribble, scatter, slobber, spatter, spittle, sputter **8** headland, sandbank, turnspit **9** brochette, peninsula **10** promontory **11** expectorate

spite 3 irk, vex **4** gall, hate, hurt, pain **5** annoy, odium, sting, venom, wound **6** animus, enmity, grudge, harass, hatred, injure, malice, misuse, nettle, put out, rancor **7** ill will, mortify, provoke **8** bad blood, ill-treat, irritate, loathing, meanness **9** animosity, antipathy, hostility, humiliate, malignity, nastiness, vengeance **10** bitterness, resentment **11** detestation, malevolence **12** vengefulness **13** maliciousness, slap in the face **14** revengefulness, vindictiveness

spiteful 4 evil **5** nasty **6** bitter, malign, wicked **7** caustic, envious, hateful, hostile, vicious **8** grudging, vengeful, venomous **9** malicious, merciless, rancorous, resentful, sarcastic, splenetic **10** ill-natured, malevolent, vindictive **11** acrimonious, unforgiving **12** antagonistic

spitting image (spit and image) 4 copy, mate, twin **6** double **9** duplicate **15** perfect likeness

splash 3 ado, hit **4** cast, dash, daub, soil, stir, toss, wash **5** bathe, break, fling, plash, slosh, smack, smear, stain, strew, surge, swash **6** batter, blazon, buffet, effect, impact, paddle, plunge, shower, spread, streak, strike, uproar, wallow, welter **7** bestrew, scatter, spatter, splotch **8** besmirch, discolor, disperse, splatter, sprinkle **9** bespatter, broadcast, commotion, sensation **10** spattering **11** splattering

splashy 5 jazzy, showy **6** flashy **10** glittering **11** spectacular **12** ostentatious

splatter 4 dash **6** splash **7** spatter

splay 4 awry **5** askew, broad **6** aslant, clumsy, extend, tilted, warped **7** awkward, crooked, fanlike, slanted, sloping, turn out **8** inclined, slanting **9** distorted, fan-shaped, irregular, outspread, spread out **10** stretch out

spleen 4 bile, gall **5** anger, spite, venom **6** animus, enmity, hatred, malice, rancor **7** ill will **8** acrimony, ill humor, vexation **9** animosity, bad temper, hostility **10** bitterness, resentment **11** malevolence, peevishness **12** irritability, spitefulness

splendid 4 fine, high, rare, rich **5** grand, lofty, noble, regal, royal **6** august, costly, ornate, superb **7** elegant, eminent, exalted, stately **8** dazzling, elevated, flashing, gleaming, glorious, gorgeous, imposing, majestic, palatial, peerless, terrific **9** admirable, beautiful, brilliant, effulgent, estimable, excellent, marvelous, sumptuous, wonderful **10** glittering, preeminent, remarkable, surpassing **11** exceptional, illustrious, magnificent, outstanding, resplendent, splendorous **12** transcendent **13** distinguished, splendiferous

Splendid Splinter
 nickname of: 11 Ted Williams

splendor 4 fire, pomp **5** gleam, glory, light, sheen, shine **6** beauty, dazzle, luster, renown **7** burnish, glitter **8** grandeur, nobility, opulence, radiance **9** intensity, sublimity **10** augustness, brilliance, effulgence, irradiance, luminosity **11** preeminence, stateliness **12** gorgeousness, luminousness, magnificence, resplendence **13** incandescence

Splendor in the Grass
 director: 9 Elia Kazan
 based on story by: 11 William Inge
 cast: 9 Pat Hingle **11** Natalie Wood **12** Sean Garrison, Warren Beatty **14** Audrey Christie

splenetic 5 cross, nasty, surly, testy **6** cranky, malign **7** bilious, hostile, peevish **8** choleric, spiteful, venomous **9** irascible, rancorous **11** acrimonious, ill-tempered **12** cantankerous, disagreeable

splice 3 wed **4** join, knit **5** graft, merge, plait, unite **7** connect **8** dovetail **9** interlace **10** intertwine, interweave **12** interconnect

splinter 4 chip **5** smash, split **6** needle, shiver, sliver **7** break up, crumble, explode, shatter **8** fly apart, frac-

ture, fragment **9** pulverize **12** disintegrate

split 3 hew **4** deal, dole, dual, mete, part, rent, rift, rive, snap, tear, torn **5** allot, break, burst, cleft, crack, halve, mixed, riven, sever, share **6** bisect, breach, broken, cleave, differ, divide, ripped, schism, shiver, sunder, varied **7** be riven, cracked, diverge, divided, divorce, divvy up, fissure, give way, opening, portion, quarrel, rupture, severed, twofold **8** alienate, allocate, cleavage, disagree, dispense, disperse, dissever, disunion, disunite, division, fracture, ruptured, splinter **9** apportion, fractured, parcel out, partition, segmented, segregate, separated, set at odds, subdivide, undecided **10** alienation, ambivalent, break apart, difference, dissension, disseR vered, distribute, divergence, falling out, separation, splintered **11** come between, part company, tear asunder **12** disagreement, estrangement

split off 7 deviate, diverge **8** separate **9** draw apart

split the difference 5 agree **6** settle **9** make a deal **10** compromise **11** come to terms, meet halfway **14** strike a bargain

splitting off 9 diverging **10** separating **12** drawing apart

splitting up 8 dividing **9** divorcing **10** breaking up, separating **11** subdividing **12** partitioning

splotch 4 blot, daub, mark, spot **5** smear, stain **6** blotch, smudge **13** discoloration

splurge 5 binge, spree **6** bender **8** live it up **10** indulgence, showing off **12** showy display **13** be extravagant, shoot the works **14** indulge oneself, self-indulgence **21** throw caution to the winds

splutter 4 hiss, spew, spit **5** burst, spray **6** gibber, jabber, mumble, seethe **7** bluster, slobber, spatter, sputter, stammer, stumble, stutter **9** hem and haw **11** expectorate

spoil 3 mar, rot **4** baby, flaw, harm, mold, ruin, sour, turn **5** addle, botch, decay, go bad, humor, taint **6** blight, bungle, coddle, damage, deface, foul up, impair, injure, mess up, mildew, muddle, pamper **7** blemish, destroy, disrupt, putrefy **8** mutilate **9** decompose, disfigure **11** deteriorate, mollycoddle, overgratify, overindulge

spoiled 3 bad, off **6** putrid, rotten, ruined **7** coddled, corrupt, decayed, gone bad, went bad **8** indulged, overripe, pampered **9** putrefied **10** decomposed, frustrated **12** deteriorated **15** rotten to the core

spoiler 6 vandal **8** underdog **9** deflector

spoils 4 haul, loot, swag, take **5** booty

6 bounty, prizes, quarry **7** plunder, profits **8** benefits, comforts, pickings **9** amenities, patronage **11** perquisites **12** acquisitions

spoilsport 4 drag **10** wet blanket **11** party-pooper

spoken 4 oral, said **5** parol **6** verbal, voiced **7** uttered **8** expressed **10** pronounced **11** articulated

spokesman 5 agent, PR man, proxy **6** backer, deputy **7** speaker **8** delegate, promoter **9** middleman, proponent, supporter, surrogate **10** mouthpiece, negotiator, press agent **11** protagonist

sponge 3 bum, dry, mop, rub **4** blot, swab, wash **5** cadge, clean, leech, mooch, towel **6** borrow, live on **7** cleanse, moisten **8** freeload, impose on, scrounge **9** panhandle

sponger 5 leech **6** cadger, sponge **7** moocher **8** barnacle, borrower, deadbeat **9** scrounger **10** freeloader **11** bloodsucker

sponsor 4 back **5** angel, set up **6** backer, patron, uphold **7** finance, promote, support **8** advocate, champion, defender, financer, guardian, partisan, promoter, start out, upholder, vouch for, warranty **9** guarantee, financier, guarantor, proponent, protecter, protector, supporter **10** advertiser, stand up for, underwrite

sponsorship 5 aegis **7** support **8** advocacy, auspices **9** patronage **12** championship

spontaneity 7 freedom **11** impetuosity, naturalness **12** unconstraint **13** impulsiveness, offhandedness **18** extemporaneousness

spontaneous 4 free **5** ad lib **7** natural, offhand, willing **8** unbidden **9** automatic, extempore, impetuous, impromptu, impulsive, ingenuous, unplanned, unstudied, voluntary **10** gratuitous, improvised, off the cuff, unprompted **11** independent, instinctive, uncontrived **12** unhesitating **13** unconstrained **14** extemporaneous, unpremeditated

spoof 3 kid **4** joke, josh, twit **6** parody, satire, sendup **7** joshing, kidding, lampoon, mockery, ribbing, takeoff **8** satirize, travesty **9** burlesque, take off on **10** caricature

spook 5 alarm, bogey, ghost, haunt, scare, shade **6** goblin, shadow, spirit **7** disturb, phantom, specter, startle, terrify, unnerve **8** disquiet, frighten, unsettle **9** hobgoblin, terrorize **10** apparition, intimidate

spooky 5 eerie, jumpy, scary, weird **6** creepy **7** ghostly, nervous **8** skittish **10** mysterious

sporadic 3 few **4** rare, thin **6** fitful, meager, random, scarce, sparse, spotty **8** isolated, periodic, uncommon **9** haphazard, irregular, scattered,

spasmodic 10 infrequent, now and then, occasional **11** fragmentary **12** intermittent, widely spaced **13** discontinuous **16** few and far between

sport 3 fun, toy **4** bear, butt, game, goat, jest, joke, lark, play, romp, trip **5** abuse, caper, carry, chaff, dally, frisk, hobby, mirth, revel **6** antics, cavort, frolic, gaiety, gambol, misuse, monkey, take in, trifle **7** buffoon, contest, display, disport, exhibit, gambler, jesting, jollity, kidding, mockery, rollick, show off, skylark **8** badinage, derision, fair game, flourish, hilarity, illtreat, raillery, ridicule, scoffing, trifling **9** amusement, athletics, daredevil, diversion, festivity, joviality, make merry, play games, scapegoat **10** persiflage, pleasantry, recreation, relaxation, skylarking **11** competition, distraction, merrymaking **12** depreciation **13** entertainment, laughingstock **14** divertissement

sporting house 4 stew **5** house **6** bagnio, bordel **7** brothel **8** bordello, cathouse **10** bawdy house, fancy house, whorehouse **14** house of ill fame **16** house of ill repute **19** house of prostitution

sportive 6 blithe, frisky **7** playful **8** animated **10** frolicsome

sportsman 6 hunter **9** fisherman

Sportsman's Notebook, A
  author: 12 Ivan Turgenev

sporty 6 casual, flashy, jaunty **8** informal

spot 3 dot, fix, see, spy **4** area, bind, blot, daub, espy, flaw, mark, part, seat, site, slur, soil **5** brand, fleck, grime, locus, patch, place, point, smear, space, speck, stain, sully, taint, tract **6** blotch, defect, detect, locale, locate, plight, region, sector, smirch, smudge, splash, stigma **7** blemish, dilemma, discern, light on, pick out, quarter, section, spatter, speckle, splotch, station **8** discolor, discover, disgrace, district, flyspeck, locality, location, position, premises, reproach, sprinkle **9** aspersion, discredit, recognize, situation, territory **10** difficulty, imputation **11** predicament **12** bad situation, neighborhood **13** discoloration

spotless 4 pure **5** clean, snowy **7** perfect, shining **8** flawless, gleaming, pristine, unflawed, unmarred, unsoiled **9** faultless, stainless, unspotted, unstained, unsullied, untainted **10** immaculate, impeccable **11** unblemished, untarnished **14** irreproachable **15** unexceptionable

spotted 3 saw **6** dotted, espied, soiled **7** dappled, located, mottled, stained **8** detected, speckled **9** blemished, discerned, spattered **10** discovered **13** caught sight of

spotty 6 fitful, pimply, random, une-

ven **7** blotchy, dappled, erratic, flecked, mottled, spotted **8** episodic, freckled, splotchy, sporadic, unsteady, variable, wavering **9** broken out, desultory, irregular, spasmodic, uncertain **10** capricious, inconstant, unreliable, variegated **11** full of spots **12** disorganized, intermittent, undependable, unmethodical, unsystematic

spouse 4 mate, wife **7** consort, husband, partner **8** helpmate **10** better half

spout 3 jet, lip **4** beak, flow, go on, gush, nose, pipe, rant, spew, tube, vent, well **5** eject, erupt, expel, exude, issue, mouth, shoot, snout, spray, spurt, surge, vomit **6** nozzle, outlet, sluice, squirt, stream, trough **7** bluster, carry on, channel, conduit, pour out **8** disgorge, fountain, harangue **9** discharge, hold forth **10** waterspout **11** pontificate **12** emit forcibly **14** speak pompously

sprawl 4 flop, lean, loll, wind **5** slump **6** branch, extend, lounge, slouch **7** gush out, meander, recline **8** languish, reach out, straggle **9** spread out **10** stretch out **11** spread-eagle

spray 4 coat, mist, posy, twig **5** bough, burst, shoot, sprig, treat, vapor **6** dampen, nozzle, shower, splash, switch, volley **7** atomize, barrage, blossom, bouquet, drizzle, moisten, nosegay, scatter, spatter, sprayer, syringe **8** atomizer, disperse, droplets, moisture, sprinkle **9** discharge, fusillade, sprinkler, vaporizer

spread 3 air, lay **4** area, cast, coat, open, pave, shed, span, vent **5** apply, bruit, cloak, cover, feast, field, issue, range, reach, scope, smear, spray, story, strew, sweep, table, tract, width **6** bedaub, beshed, blazon, extend, extent, herald, length, notice, repeat, report, unfold, unfurl, unroll **7** account, advance, article, banquet, besmear, bestrew, breadth, circuit, compass, declare, diffuse, divulge, expanse, overlay, overrun, pervade, plaster, publish, radiate, scatter, spatter, stretch, suffuse, trumpet, untwine, write-up **8** announce, coverage, disperse, distance, increase, permeate, proclaim, sprinkle **9** broadcast, circulate, diffusion, expansion, extension, make known, penetrate, pervasion, propagate, publicize, radiation, spreading, suffusion, ventilate **10** dispersion, distribute, make public, permeation, promulgate, stretch out **11** communicate, disseminate, noise abroad, proliferate **13** amplification, dissemination, proliferation

spread out 5 broad, widen **6** expand, extend **7** broaden, diffuse, enlarge, radiate, stretch **8** expanded, extended, open wide **9** dispersed, outspread, scattered **10** distribute, unhampered

11 unconfirmed **12** unrestricted **14** unconcentrated

spree 4 bout, orgy, toot **5** binge, drunk, fling, revel **6** bender **7** carouse, debauch, revelry, splurge, wassail **8** carousal **9** bacchanal **10** saturnalia

sprightliness 8 buoyancy, spryness, vivacity **9** animation, briskness **10** breeziness, liveliness **16** lightheartedness

sprightly 3 gay **4** keen, spry **5** agile, alive, brisk, jolly, merry **6** active, blithe, breezy, cheery, jaunty, jovial, lively, nimble **7** buoyant, chipper, dashing, dynamic, playful **8** animated, cheerful, spirited, sportive **9** energetic, vivacious **10** blithesome, frolicsome **12** lighthearted

spring 3 hop, jet, pop, spa **4** come, dart, flow, gush, jump, kick, leap, loom, pool, pour, rise, rush, stem, well **5** arise, baths, begin, bound, caper, ensue, fount, issue, lunge, shoot, spout, spurt, start, surge, vault **6** appear, bounce, derive, gambol, recoil, reflex, result, sprout, stream **7** burgeon, crop out, descend, emanate, proceed, release, shoot up, start up, stretch, trigger **8** buoyancy, commence, fountain, mushroom **9** come forth, entrechat, germinate, originate, saltation, waterhole **10** break forth, burst forth, elasticity, resiliency **11** flexibility
  goddess of: 4 Hebe **5** Venus

spring back 6 bounce, recoil **7** rebound **8** ricochet

spring flowers
  goddess of: 6 Thallo

springlike 4 mild, soft, warm **5** balmy

springs
  god of: 4 Fons **6** Palici
  goddess of: 4 Idun **5** Idura, Ithun **6** Ithunn

spring up 4 grow, rise **5** arise, occur, pop up **6** crop up, emerge, happen, sprout **9** originate **10** burst forth

springy 6 bouncy, spongy, supple **7** elastic **9** resilient **10** rebounding

sprinkle 4 dash, dust, rain **5** spray, strew, water **6** powder, shower, splash, spread, squirt **7** bestrew, diffuse, drizzle, moisten, scatter, spatter **8** splatter

sprinkling 4 dash, drop, hint **5** pinch, touch **7** droplet, minimum, modicum, soupcon **8** sprinkle **10** smattering

sprint 3 run **4** dart, dash, kick, race, rush, tear, whiz **5** burst, shoot, spurt, whisk **7** scamper

sprit 3 bar **4** spar **8** crossbar **10** crosspiece

sprite 3 elf **5** fairy, pixie **10** leprechaun

sprout 3 bud, wax **4** grow **5** bloom, shoot, sprig **6** come up, flower, spread, thrive **7** blossom, burgeon **8** multiply, offshoot, put forth, spring up **9** germinate, outgrowth

spruce 4 chic, neat, tidy, trim **5** kempt, natty, sharp, smart **6** dapper **7** conifer, elegant **9** evergreen, shipshape **11** well-groomed **12** spick-and-span **French: 6** soigne

spruce 5 Picea
  varieties: 3 bog, cat, red **4** blue **5** black, Hondo, Sitka, snake, white, Yeddo **6** double, Norway **7** Alberta, big-cone, Finnish, hemlock **8** Colorado, Sakhalin, Siberian **9** Himalayan, tiger-tail **10** Black Hills **12** Colorado blue, Japanese bush

spry 4 deft, hale **5** agile, brisk, quick **6** active, frisky, hearty, jaunty, lively, nimble, supple **7** buoyant, chipper, playful **8** animated, spirited, sportive, vigorous **9** energetic, sprightly, vivacious **11** lightfooted

spunk 4 fire, grit, guts, salt, sand **5** heart, nerve, pluck **6** daring, ginger, mettle, pepper, spirit **7** bravery, courage **8** backbone, boldness, gumption **10** feistiness

spur 3 arm, leg **4** fork, goad, prod, whet, whip, wing **5** prick **6** branch, feeder, fillip, hasten, motive, siding **7** impetus, impulse **8** excitant, stimulus **9** boot spike, encourage, incentive, stimulant, stimulate, tributary **10** incitement, inducement **11** instigation, provocation, stimulation **13** encouragement

spurge 9 Euphorbia **11** Pachysandra
  varieties: 5 caper, leafy, melon **6** ipecac, myrtle, tramp's **7** cypress, mottled, seaside, slipper **8** fiddler's, Japanese **9** Allegheny, flowering **10** Indian tree

spurious 4 fake, mock, sham **5** bogus, false, phony **6** faulty, forged, hollow **7** feigned, unsound **8** specious **9** imitation, simulated **10** fallacious, fraudulent, not genuine **11** counterfeit, make-believe, unauthentic **12** illegitimate

spurn 4 mock, snub **5** flout, repel, scorn **6** rebuff, refuse, reject, slight **7** condemn, decline, disdain, dismiss, repulse, scoff at, sneer at **8** turn down **9** cast aside, disparage, repudiate **12** coldshoulder, look down upon **16** turn up one's nose at

spur-of-the-moment 5 ad-lib **7** offhand **9** extempore, impromptu **10** improvised, unprepared **11** extemporary, spontaneous, unrehearsed **14** extemporaneous, unpremeditated

spurt 3 jet **4** dart, dash, emit, flow, gush, gust, rush, tear, whiz **5** burst, flash, issue, lunge, scoot, shoot, speed, spout, spray, surge **6** access, spring, sprint, squirt, stream **7** pour out **8** disgorge, ejection, eruption, fountain, outbreak, outburst **9** discharge, explosion, spring out **10** outpouring

spy 3 pry, see **4** find, peep, spot, view **5** scout, sight, snoop **6** behold, descry, detect, notice, shadow **7** discern, glimpse, make out, observe **8** discover, informer, Mata Hari, perceive, saboteur **9** keep watch, operative, recognize **11** reconnoiter, secret agent **12** catch sight of **13** undercover man, watch secretly **14** espionage agent, fifth columnist **16** agent provocateur **17** intelligence agent
  famous: 4 Abel, Hale **5** Andre, Caleb, Pitts **6** Arnold, Dulles, Philby, Powers, Smiley **8** Mata Hari **9** James Bond, Nicholson, Philbrick, Pinkerton, Rosenberg

Spy, The
  author: 19 James Fenimore Cooper

Spy Who Came In from the Cold, The
  director: 10 Martin Ritt
  based on novel by: 11 John LeCarre
  cast: 11 Claire Bloom, Oskar Werner **12** Peter Van Eyck **13** Richard Burton

Spy Who Loved Me, The
  author: 10 Ian Fleming
  director: 12 Lewis Gilbert
  cast: 10 Bernard Lee (M), Roger Moore (James Bond) **11** Barbara Bach, Curt Jurgens (Stromberg), Richard Kiel (Jaws)

squabble 3 row, war **4** spat, tiff **5** argue, brawl, clash, fight, run-in, scrap, set-to, words **6** battle, bicker, differ **7** contend, contest, dispute, quarrel, wrangle **8** argument **9** have words, lock horns **10** bandy words, contention, difference, dissension **11** altercation, controversy **12** disagreement

squadron 5 fleet **6** armada **8** flotilla **9** naval unit **10** escadrille **11** cavalry unit **12** military unit

squalid 4 foul, mean **5** dirty, nasty **6** abject, filthy, horrid, rotten, shabby, sloppy, sordid **7** decayed, reeking, run-down, unclean **8** battered, degraded, slovenly, wretched **9** miserable **10** broken-down, disheveled, ramshackle, slatternly, tumbledown **11** dilapidated **12** deteriorated

squalor 4 dirt **5** filth **6** misery **7** neglect, poverty **8** foulness, meanness, ugliness **9** dinginess, dirtiness, nastiness, seediness **10** abjectness, grubbiness, sordidness **11** squalidness, uncleanness **12** wretchedness **13** uncleanliness

squander 4 blow **5** spend, waste **6** lavish, misuse **7** consume, deplete, exhaust **8** misspend **9** dissipate, throw away **10** run through **11** fritter away **14** spend like water

squanderer 6 waster **7** wastrel **8**

prodigal **10** dissipater, profligate **11** spendthrift

squandering 7 wasting **8** prodigal, wasteful **9** imprudent **10** profligate **11** dissipating, extravagant, improvident, spendthrift **12** overspending, throwing away **14** frittering away **17** spending like water

square 3 box, fit **4** even, fogy, heal, hick, jerk, jibe, just, mend, park, prig **5** agree, align, blend, block, close, equal, green, match, place, plane, plaza, prude, tally **6** accord, adjust, candid, circus, cohere, common, concur, even up, fall in, honest, pay off, settle, smooth **7** arrange, balance, clear up, compose, conform, even out, flatten, mediate, patch up, rectify, resolve **8** block out, cornball, make even, quadrate, set right, settle up, truthful **9** arbitrate, discharge, equitable, harmonize, liquidate, make level, reconcile **10** clodhopper, correspond, quadrangle, straighten **11** marketplace **12** apple knocker, conservative **13** quadrilateral, stick-in-the- mud **15** straightforward
  type: 1 T **3** try **11** combination

Square
  character in: 8 Tom Jones
  author: 8 Fielding

Square
  constellation of: 5 Norma

square centimeter
  abbreviation: 4 sq cm

square decimeter
  abbreviation: 4 sq dm

square dekameter
  abbreviation: 5 sq dam

square foot
  abbreviation: 4 sq ft

square hectometer
  abbreviation: 4 sq hm

square inch
  abbreviation: 4 sq in

square kilometer
  abbreviation: 4 sq km

square meter
  abbreviation: 3 sq m

square mile
  abbreviation: 4 sq mi

square millimeter
  abbreviation: 4 sq mm

square rod
  abbreviation: 4 sq rd

square yard
  abbreviation: 4 sq yd

squash 3 jam **4** cram, mash, pulp **5** crowd, crush, level, quash, quell, smash, upset **6** dispel, squish **7** compact, destroy, flatten, put down, ram down, repress, squeeze, squelch, trample **8** compress, suppress **9** dissipate, overthrow, prostrate, undermine **10** annihilate, obliterate **11** concentrate

squash 9 Cucurbita
  varieties: 4 bush 5 acorn 6 autumn, banana, summer, turban, winter 7 Hubbard, scallop 8 pattypan, zucchini 9 cocozelle, crookneck 12 Boston marrow 13 sweet dumpling 15 Canada crookneck, summer crookneck, winter crookneck

squat 5 cower, dumpy, dwell, kneel, pudgy 6 chunky, cringe, crouch, encamp, hunker, lie low, locate, move in, shrink, square, stocky, stubby, stumpy 8 thickset

squawk 5 blare, croak, gripe 6 scream, squall 7 grumble, protest, screech 8 complain

squeak 3 cry 4 peep, yelp 5 cheep, chirp, creak, grate 6 shriek, shrill, squeal 7 screech

squeal 3 cry 4 bawl, blab, fink, peep, sing, wail, yelp, yelp 5 cheep, whine 6 inform, scream, shriek, shrill, squeak 7 screech

squealer 3 pig, rat 4 fink 6 canary, piglet, snitch 7 stoolie, tattler, traitor 8 informer 10 tattletale 11 stool pigeon 12 blabbermouth

squeamish 3 coy 4 prim, sick 5 fussy 6 demure, modest, proper, queasy 7 finical, finicky, mincing, prudish, sickish 8 delicate, nauseous, priggish, qualmish 9 finicking 10 fastidious 11 puritanical, straitlaced 13 sanctimonious

Squeers, Wackford
  character in: 16 Nicholas Nickleby
  author: 7 Dickens

squeeze 3 hug, jam, pry, ram 4 butt, cram, edge, grip, hold, pack, push 5 clasp, cramp, crowd, drive, elbow, grasp, press, shove, stuff, wedge, wrest, wring 6 clutch, coerce, compel, defile, elicit, extort, jostle, thrust, wrench 7 compact, draw out, embrace, extract, passage, pull out, tear out 8 compress, crowding, crushing, force out, pinching, press out, pressure, shoulder, withdraw 9 extricate, narrowing, stricture 10 bottleneck 11 compression, concentrate, consolidate 12 constriction

squelch 4 hush 5 abort, crush, quash, quell, quiet, smash 6 retort, squash 7 put down, riposte, silence 8 silencer, suppress

squire 4 date, take 5 court 6 attend, escort 7 consort, gallant, planter 8 cavalier, chaperon 9 accompany, attendant, boyfriend, chauffeur, companion, landowner 14 lord of the manor 16 country gentleman

Squire
  character in: 18 The Canterbury Tales
  author: 7 Chaucer

squirm 4 bend, jerk, toss, turn 5 pitch, shift, smart, sweat, twist, wince 6 blench, fidget, flinch, shrink, twitch,
wiggle, writhe 7 agonize, contort, wriggle 8 flounder

squirt 3 jet 4 dash, gush, punk, runt 5 piker, shoot, spout, spray, spurt 6 shower, splash, stream 7 spatter 8 sprinkle 9 discharge, pipsqueak 10 besprinkle

Sri Lanka
  other name: 6 Ceylon 8 Serendib 9 Taprobane
  capital/largest city: 7 Colombo
    ancient capital: 11 Polonnaruwa 12 Anuradhapura
  others: 3 Uva 5 Galle, Kandy 6 Jaffna, Mannar, Matale, Matara 7 Badulla, Kegalle, Negombo 8 Kalutara, Mankulem, Moratuwa, Puttalam 9 Ratnapura 10 Batticaloa, Mullaitivu 11 Ambalangoda, Trincomalee
  division: 8 Dambulla, Sri Lanka 9 Taprobane
  measure: 4 para, seer 5 parah 6 amunam, parrah
  monetary unit: 4 cent 5 rupee
  island: 5 Delft 6 Mannar 8 Sri Lanka
  mountain: 5 Pedro 7 Sri Pada 9 Adam's Peak
  highest point: 14 Pidurutalagala
  river: 4 Kala 6 Deduru, Gal Ova 8 Aruvi Aru 9 Deburu Ova 11 Kelani Ganga 13 Mahaweli Ganga
  sea: 6 Indian
  physical feature:
    bay: 6 Bengal 8 Koddiyar
    falls: 8 Lazapana
    gulf: 6 Mannar
    peninsula: 6 Jaffna
    plateau: 6 Hatton
    strait: 4 Palk
  people: 5 Malay, Tamil, Vedda 6 Veddah, Weddah 7 Burgher, Mahinda, Malabar 8 Eurasian 9 Cingalese, Dravidian, Sinhalese 10 Singhalese
    leader: 11 Jayawardene 12 Bandaranaike
    ruler: 5 Dutch 7 British, Chinese 10 Portuguese
  language: 4 Pali 5 Tamil 7 English 9 Sinhalese
  religion: 5 Hindu, Islam 8 Buddhism
  place:
    fortress: 8 Sigiriya
    gardens: 8 Hakgalle 10 Peradiniya
    national park: 6 Ruhuna 8 Wilpattu
    temple: 5 Tooth 6 Gal Oya 7 Kelanya 8 Runaweli 9 Ruanvelli 10 Dankahlaka 12 Asokharamaya
  feature:
    animal: 5 loris 12 wild elephant
    clothing: 4 sari 5 camba 6 sarong 7 cambaya 8 sherwani
    dancer: 7 Kandyan
    drama: 5 kolam 7 nadagam
    festival: 8 Perahera
    shrine: 6 dagoba
    tree: 4 doon, hora, palu, tala 5
domba, ebony 7 talipot 8 halmilla, ironwood 9 satinwood 11 allaeanthus 12 shimohabodhi

SS-GB
  author: 11 Len Deighton
SS troops, chief of 12 Reichsfuhrer

stab 2 go 3 cut, jab, try 4 ache, bite, gash, gore, hurt, pain, pang, pass, shot, spit 5 essay, gouge, knife, lance, lunge, prick, qualm, slash, spear, spike, stick, sting, trial, wound 6 cleave, dagger, effort, impale, pierce, shiver, stroke, thrill, thrust, twinge 7 attempt, bayonet 8 endeavor, lacerate, transfix 10 laceration, run through

stability 5 poise 6 aplomb, fixity 7 balance 8 evenness, firmness, security, solidity 9 constancy, fixedness, solidness, soundness 10 continuity, durability, permanence, stableness, steadiness, sturdiness 11 abidingness, equilibrium, reliability 13 steadfastness 14 changelessness 16 unchangeableness

stabilize 7 balance 8 hold firm, make firm 10 hold steady, make steady

stabilizer 7 balance, ballast 8 additive 9 equipoise, gyroscope 10 ballasting 12 airplane part 14 counterbalance

stable 4 barn, byre, even, firm, mews, safe, true 5 fixed, loyal, solid, sound 6 moored, secure, steady, sturdy 7 abiding, durable, staunch, uniform 8 anchored, constant, cowhouse, cowshed, enduring, faithful, reliable, resolute, stalwart 9 immovable, steadfast 10 dependable, persisting, stationary, unchanging, unwavering 11 established, unfaltering 12 indissoluble, unchangeable

Stabler, Ken
  nickname: 8 the Snake
  sport: 8 football
  position: 11 quarterback
  team: 13 Houston Oilers 14 Oakland Raiders

staccato
  music: 12 disconnected 16 each note separate

stack 4 bank, flue, heap, load, lump, mass, pile, rick 5 amass, batch, bunch, clump, hoard, mound, sheaf 6 bundle, funnel, gather 7 chimney 8 assemble, mountain 9 amassment 10 accumulate 11 aggregation 12 accumulation

Stack, Robert
  born: 12 Los Angeles CA
  roles: 9 Eliot Ness 13 Name of the Game 15 The Untouchables 16 Written on the Wind 19 The High and the Mighty 24 The Bullfighter and the Lady

Stackpole, Henrietta
  character in: 18 The Portrait of a Lady
  author: 5 James

Stacte 5 spice

stadium 4 bowl, park **5** arena, field, stade **6** circus **8** ballpark, coliseum **9** palaestra **10** hippodrome **12** amphitheater

Stael, Madame de
author of: **7** Corinne **8** Delphine **9** On Germany **35** The Influence of Literature upon Society

staff 3 bat, man, rod **4** cane, crew, help, pole, team, tend, wand, work **5** cadre, force, group, stave, stick **6** crutch, cudgel, manage **7** retinue, scepter, service, support **8** advisors, bludgeon, flagpole **9** billy club, employees, flagstaff, personnel **10** alpenstock, assistants, shillelagh **12** walking stick

staff member 4 aide **6** worker **8** employee

stage 3 act **4** dais, play, spot, step **5** arena, drama, grade, level, phase, put on, sight, stump **6** acting, locale, period, podium, pulpit **7** perform, present, produce, rostrum, setting, show biz, soapbox, theater **8** bearings, locality, location, position, scaffold **9** dramatize, the boards

Stagecoach
director: **8** John Ford
cast: **9** John Wayne **10** Andy Devine **11** Louise Platt **12** Claire Trevor **13** John Carradine **14** George Bancroft, Thomas Mitchell
Oscar for: **15** supporting actor (Mitchell)

stagecraft 5 drama **7** theater **9** theatrics **10** dramaturgy **11** thespianism **12** dramatic arts

Stage Door
author: **10** Edna Ferber **14** George S Kaufman
director: **13** Gregory La Cava
cast: **11** Andrea Leeds, Gail Patrick **12** Ginger Rogers **13** Adolphe Menjou **16** Katharine Hepburn

stage setting
French: **11** mise en scene

stagger 3 jar **4** jolt, reel, stun, sway **5** amaze, lurch, shake, shock, waver **6** hobble, totter, wobble **7** astound, blunder, nonplus, overlap, shamble, startle, stumble, stupefy **8** astonish, bewilder, bowl over, confound, flounder, unsettle **9** alternate, dumbfound, give a turn, overwhelm, spread out **10** disconcert, knock silly, strike dumb **11** cause to reel, cause to sway, consternate, flabbergast, take in turns **12** make unsteady **15** throw off balance

staggering 7 amazing **8** shocking, stunning **9** startling **10** astounding **11** astonishing **12** breathtaking

stagnant 4 dead, dull, foul, lazy, slow **5** close, inert, quiet, slimy, stale, still **6** filthy, leaden, putrid, static, supine, torpid **7** dormant, dronish, languid,

tainted **8** inactive, lifeless, listless, polluted, sluggish, standing **9** lethargic, ponderous, putrefied, quiescent **10** monotonous, motionless, not flowing, not running, stationary, unstirring, vegetative **13** uncirculating

stagnate 7 go to pot, lie idle, putrefy **8** go to seed, lie still, vegetate **10** stand still **11** cease to flow, deteriorate, stop growing **14** become inactive, become polluted, become sluggish

stagy 5 phony **8** affected, mannered **9** unnatural **10** artificial, factitious, theatrical

staid 5 grave, quiet, sober, stiff **6** decent, demure, proper, sedate, seemly, solemn, somber **7** earnest, prudish, serious, settled, subdued **8** decorous, priggish, reserved **9** dignified **10** complacent **15** undemonstrative

stain 3 dye, mar **4** blot, daub, flaw, foul, mark, ruin, slur, soil, spot, tint **5** brand, color, dirty, grime, libel, patch, shame, smear, speck, spoil, sully, taint **6** befoul, blotch, debase, defile, impair, malign, smirch, smudge, stigma, vilify **7** blacken, blemish, pigment, slander, splotch, subvert, tarnish **8** besmirch, coloring, discolor, disgrace, dishonor, dyestuff, tincture **9** denigrate, discredit, disparage, undermine **10** imputation, stigmatize **13** discoloration

stainless 5 clean, moral **6** chaste, decent **8** spotless, unsoiled **9** exemplary, unspotted, unsullied, untainted **11** unblemished

Stairway to Heaven
director: **13** Michael Powell **17** Emeric Pressburger
cast: **9** Kim Hunter **10** David Niven **12** Roger Livesey **13** Raymond Massey
original title: **21** A Matter of Life and Death

stake 3 bar, bet, peg, pot, rod **4** ante, back, grab, haul, lash, loot, moor, pale, pawn, pile, play, pole, post, prop, risk, stay, take **5** booty, brace, hitch, kitty, prize, purse, share, spike, stand, stick, treat, wager **6** chance, column, define, fasten, fetter, hazard, hold up, marker, picket, pillar, reward, secure, spoils, tether **7** delimit, finance, jackpot, mark off, mark out, outline, peg down, returns, sponsor, support, trammel, venture **8** interest, make fast, pickings, standard, winnings **9** delineate, demarcate, speculate, subsidize **10** investment, jeopardize, underwrite **11** involvement, speculation

Stalag 17
director: **11** Billy Wilder
cast: **9** Don Taylor **11** Peter Graves **12** Neville Brand **13** Harvey Lem-

beck, Otto Preminger, Richard Erdman, Robert Strauss, William Holden
Oscar for: **5** actor (Holden)

stale 4 dull, flat **5** banal, close, fusty, musty, trite, vapid **6** common **7** humdrum, insipid, prosaic, tedious, worn-out **8** mediocre, not fresh, ordinary, stagnant, unvaried **9** hackneyed, savorless, tasteless **10** monotonous, pedestrian, threadbare **11** commonplace **13** unimaginative, uninteresting

stalemate 3 tie **4** draw, halt **7** dead end, impasse **8** blockage, cul-de-sac, dead heat, deadlock, standoff **10** standstill

stalk 4 hunt, lurk, stem **5** haunt, march, prowl, shaft, spire, stamp, steal, stomp, strut, track, tramp, trunk **6** column, menace, stride **7** pedicel, pervade, swagger **8** hang over, threaten **9** creep up on, go through, sneak up on

stall 3 box, pen **4** cell, coop, halt, shed, shop, stop **5** block, booth, check, delay, kiosk, stand **6** arcade, arrest, hobble, impede, pull up, put off **7** bed down, confine, cubicle, disable, trammel **8** obstruct, paralyze, postpone **9** be evasive, interrupt, stop short, temporize **10** equivocate **11** compartment, play for time, stop running **12** incapacitate **13** orchestra seat

Stallone, Sylvester
born: **9** New York NY
nickname: **3** Sly
roles: **4** FIST **5** Rambo, Rocky (Oscar) **7** Copland **10** First Blood, Judge Dredd, Rhinestone **11** Cliffhanger **18** The Lords of Flatbush

stalwart 4 bold, firm, hale **5** beefy, brave, hardy, hefty, husky, manly, sound **6** brawny, gritty, heroic, mighty, plucky, robust, rugged, spunky, stable, strong, sturdy **7** gallant, staunch, valiant **8** constant, intrepid, muscular, powerful, resolute, valorous, vigorous **9** steadfast, strapping, unbending, undaunted **10** able-bodied, courageous, persistent, unflagging, unshakable, unswerving, unwavering, unyielding **11** indomitable, lionhearted, undeviating, unfaltering, unflinching, unshrinking **12** intransigent, stouthearted, strong-willed **14** uncompromising

stamina 4 pith **5** vigor **6** energy **8** vitality **9** endurance, hardiness, stoutness **10** ruggedness, sturdiness **12** perseverance, staying power

stammer 6 falter, fumble, mumble **7** sputter, stumble, stutter **8** splutter **9** hem and haw

stamp
block: **4** pane
collecting: **9** philately
first: **10** Penny Black
issued by: **12** Great Britain

inscribed with: 8 One Penny **picture of: 13** Queen Victoria **first-day hand stamper: 6** cachet **hole measurer: 16** perforation gauge **mounting paper: 5** hinge **not perforated: 11** imperforate **paper design: 9** watermark **rolls: 4** coil **tear holes: 12** perforations **tear slit: 8** roulette **unseparated group: 5** block **used mark: 8** postmark **12** cancellation **value suspended: 11** demonetized

stamp, stamp out 2 OK **3** die, tag **4** cast, kind, make, mark, mint, mold, seal, sort, type **5** brand, breed, clump, crush, erase, genre, label, march, order, print, pound, punch, quash, smash, stalk, stomp, strut, thump, tramp **6** banish, betray, emblem, expose, matrix, nature, put out, reveal, rub out, signet, step on, strain, stride, trudge **7** abolish, blot out, display, engrave, exhibit, impress, imprint, put down, squelch, trample, variety, voucher **8** get rid of, hallmark, identify, inscribe, intaglio, manifest, suppress, typecast **9** character, eliminate, engraving, eradicate, personify, signature, trademark **10** annihilate, do away with, extinguish, imprimatur, stigmatize, validation **11** attestation, certificate, demonstrate, distinguish, endorsement, exterminate, **12** characterize, official mark, ratification **13** certification **14** authentication, characteristic, identification

stampede 4 bolt, dash, flee, race, rout, rush **5** chaos, flood, panic **6** engulf **7** overrun, retreat, scatter **8** inundate **10** take flight **11** crowd around, pandemonium **12** beat a retreat **French: 12** sauve qui peut

stanchion 4 post, prop, stay **5** brace, strut **7** support, upright

stand 2 be **3** put, set **4** draw, face, hold, last, move, rank, rear, rest, rise, stay, step, take, tent **5** abide, argue, booth, brook, erect, exist, get up, hoist, honor, kiosk, mount, place, put up, raise, shift, stall, treat **6** bear up, effort, endure, obtain, pay for, policy, remain, remove, stance, suffer, uphold **7** carry on, commend, counter, defense, endorse, finance, hold out, opinion, persist, posture, prevail, provide, stick up, stomach, support, survive, sustain, undergo, weather **8** advocate, be placed, champion, continue, pavilion, position, sanction, submit to, tolerate **9** be located, be present, be upright, persevere, put up with, sentiment, undertake, viewpoint **10** resistance, set upright **11** be permanent, countenance, disposition, point of view **13** remain in force, take a position

Stand, The author: 11 Stephen King **standard 3** leg **4** base, flag, foot, jack, post **5** basic, canon, guide, ideal, stock, usual **6** banner, column, common, ensign, normal, pillar **7** measure, pennant, regular, support, typical, upright **8** accepted, ordinary, streamer **9** criterion, customary, guideline, principle, prototype, stanchion, universal, yardstick **10** foundation, touchstone **11** requirement **13** specification

stand behind 4 back **7** endorse, support **8** champion, vouch for **9** recommend

standby 6 backup **9** alternate, available **10** substitute, understudy **11** old reliable **12** tried-and-true

stand by 4 keep **5** cling **6** adhere, be true, defend, hold to, keep to **7** be loyal, stick by **8** cleave to, maintain **10** be constant, be faithful, stick up for

stand fast 4 hold **6** resist **8** stand pat

stand for 4 bear **5** abide, favor, stand **6** embody **7** signify **8** advocate, submit to, tolerate **9** personify, put up with, represent, symbolize

stand-in 3 sub **5** agent, proxy **6** backup, deputy, double, fill-in, second **9** alternate, assistant, surrogate **10** substitute, understudy **11** pinch hitter, replacement

standing 3 age **4** life, rank, term, time **5** erect, fixed, grade, inert, order, place, still **6** at rest, static, status, tenure **7** dormant, footing, lasting, station, upended, upright **8** duration, inactive, position, stagnant, vertical **9** immovable, permanent, perpetual, quiescent, renewable **10** continuing, importance, motionless, reputation, stationary, unstirring **11** continuance **13** perpendicular

standoff 7 impasse **8** deadlock

standoffish 4 cool **5** aloof **6** formal, remote **7** distant, haughty **8** detached, reserved, solitary, taciturn **9** reclusive, withdrawn **10** antisocial, restrained, unfriendly, unsociable **12** inaccessible, misanthropic, unresponsive **14** unapproachable **15** uncommunicative, uncompanionable

standpoint 4 side **5** angle, slant **6** aspect **9** viewpoint **11** point of view

standstill 3 end **4** halt, stop **5** pause, hiatus **7** dead end, impasse **8** abeyance, deadlock, dead stop, full stop **9** breakdown, cessation, stalemate **10** suspension **11** termination **14** discontinuance

stand up for 4 back **5** boost **6** defend **7** further, promote, support **8** advocate, champion

stand up to 4 defy, face **5** brave **6** resist **8** confront **9** challenge

Stant, Charlotte character in: 13 The Golden Bowl **author: 5** James

Stan the Man nickname of: 10 Stan Musial

Stanton, Adam character in: 14 All the King's Men **author: 6** Warren

Stanwyck, Barbara real name: 11 Ruby Stevens **born: 10** Brooklyn NY **husband: 8** Frank Fay **12** Robert Taylor **roles: 9** Big Valley, The Colbys **10** Ball of Fire, The Lady Eve **11** Meet John Doe **12** Stella Dallas **15** Double Indemnity **16** Sorry Wrong Number **20** Cattle Queen of Montana **22** Christmas in Connecticut

staple 3 key **4** main **5** basic, chief, major, prime, vital **6** leader **7** feature, primary, product **8** resource, vendible **9** commodity, essential, necessary **11** fundamental, raw material **13** indispensable

Stapleton, Jean real name: 12 Jeanne Murray **born: 9** New York NY **roles: 7** Dingbat **11** Edith Bunker **14** All in the Family

Stapleton, Maureen born: 6 Troy NY **roles: 7** Airport **9** Interiors **12** Lonelyhearts **13** The Rose Tattoo **18** A View from the Bridge

star, stars 3 god, sun, VIP **4** diva, fate, hero, idol, lead, lion, name **5** comet, excel, giant, great, omens, shine **6** big wig, do well, galaxy, meteor, nebula, planet **7** destiny, feature, fortune, goddess, heroine, notable, soloist, starlet, succeed, top draw **8** asteroid, cynosure, eminence, immortal, luminary, mainstay, Milky Way, portents, showcase, stand out, virtuoso **9** celebrity, headliner, meteoroid, principal, satellite, top banana **10** prima donna **11** All-American, drawing card, play the lead, protagonist **12** famous person, gain approval, heavenly body **13** celestial body, constellation **14** main attraction, predestination, prima ballerina **brightest: 6** Sirius **brightness measure: 9** magnitude **10** luminosity **color: 3** red **4** blue **5** black, white **6** orange, yellow **distance measure: 6** parsec **9** light year **double star: 6** binary **exploding star: 4** nova **9** supernova **French: 6** etoile **name: 4** Mira, Ross, Vega, Wolf **5** Cygni, Deneb, Rigel, Spica **6** Altair, Luyten, Pollux **7** Antares, Canopus, Capella, Lalande, Polaris, Procyon,

Regulus, Tau Ceti **8** Achernar, Arcturus, Barnard's, Lacaille, Pleiades **9** Aldebaran, Fomalhaut **10** Beta Crucis, Betelgeuse **11** Delta Cephei, Epsilon Indi, Groombridge **12** Beta Centauri **14** Epsilon Eridani

nearest: 13 Alpha Centauri

position/motion: 7 azimuth **8** parallax **11** declination

type: 5 dwarf, giant **6** pulsar **7** cluster, neutron **8** variable **9** black hole, collapsed

Starbuck

character in: 8 Moby Dick

author: 8 Melville

starch 5 vigor **6** sizing **8** backbone, gumption **10** stiffening

starched 5 crisp, sized, stiff **7** starchy **9** stiffened

starchy 5 rigid, stiff **6** formal, proper **7** correct **10** meticulous

stare 3 eye **4** gape, gawk, gaze, ogle, peep, peer **5** glare, lower, watch **6** gaping, glower, goggle, ogling, regard **7** staring **8** once-over, scrutiny **9** fixed look **10** inspection, rubberneck

stare at 3 eye **4** ogle **5** watch **6** behold, gaze at, look at, regard **7** inspect, observe **10** scrutinize **11** contemplate

Star Is Born, A

director:

    1937 version: 14 William Wellman
    1954 version: 11 George Cukor
    1976 version: 12 Frank Pierson

cast:

    1937 version: 11 Janet Gaynor **13** Adolphe Menjou, Frederic March
    1954 version: 10 Jack Carson, James Mason **11** Judy Garland **15** Charles Bickford
    1976 version: 9 Gary Busey **11** Oliver Clark **15** Barbra Streisand **17** Kris Kristofferson

Oscar for:

    1937 version: 5 story

song:

    1954 version: 17 The Man That Got Away

stark 4 bare, bold, cold, grim, pure **5** bleak, blunt, clean, empty, fully, gross, harsh, naked, plain, plumb, quite, sheer, total, utter **6** arrant, barren, chaste, patent, severe, simple, vacant, wholly **7** austere, evident, forlorn, glaring, obvious, staring, utterly **8** absolute, complete, deserted, desolate, entirely, flagrant, forsaken, outright, palpable **9** abandoned, downright, out-and-out, unadorned, unalloyed, veritable **10** absolutely, altogether, completely, consummate **11** conspicuous, unmitigated **12** unmistakable

Stark, Johannes

field: 7 physics

nationality: 6 German

described: 11 Stark Effect **14** dispersed light

awarded: 10 Nobel Prize

Stark, Willie

character in: 14 All the King's Men

author: 6 Warren

starlet 7 actress, ingenue **9** bit player, pinup girl

Starsky and Hutch

character: 5 Hutch (Ken Hutchinson) **7** (Dave) Starsky **9** Huggy Bear **11** (Capt) Harold Dobey

cast: 9 David Soul **13** Antonio Fargas **14** Bernie Hamilton **17** Paul Michael Glaser

car: 10 Ford Torino

start 3 aid, shy **4** dawn, drop, edge, form, gush, jerk, jolt, jump, lead, leap, odds, rush, turn **5** beget, begin, birth, blink, bound, eject, erupt, evict, flush, forge, found, issue, leave, leg up, onset, rouse, set up, shoot, spasm, spurt, wince **6** blench, broach, chance, create, depart, embark, emerge, fall to, father, flinch, ignite, kindle, launch, origin, outset, pop out, propel, recoil, set off, set out, spring, take up, twitch **7** advance, backing, disturb, genesis, make off, opening, push off, scatter, set sail, support, take off, turn out, usher in **8** advocacy, commence, creation, dis place, embark on, engender, generate, get going, initiate, organize, priority, set about, set going, touch off **9** advantage, beginning, establish, fabricate, first step, inception, institute, introduce, originate, propagate, undertake, venture on **10** assistance, break forth, bring about, buckle down, burst forth, give rise to, inaugurate, initiation, plunge into, sally forth, venture out **11** break ground, put in motion, set in action **12** commencement, inauguration, introduction **14** set in operation

starting point 5 onset, start **8** zero hour **9** beginning

Latin: 12 terminus a quo

startle 3 jar **4** faze **5** alarm, scare, shake, shock, upset **7** perturb, unnerve **8** disquiet, frighten, surprise, unsettle **9** give a turn **10** discompose, disconcert, intimidate

Star Trek

character: 4 Sulu **5** Uhura **6** Scotty (Engineer Montgomery Scott), (Ensign Pavel) Chekov **7** Mr Spock **10** (Captain) James T Kirk, (Yeoman) Janice Rand **12** (Dr) Leonard McCoy **15** (Nurse) Christine Chapel

cast: 11 George Takei, James Doohan **12** Leonard Nimoy, Majel Barrett, Walter Koenig **13** DeForest Kelly **14** William Shatner **15** Grace Lee Whitney, Nichelle Nichols

ship: 10 (USS) Enterprise

aliens: 8 Klingons, Romulans

Spock's planet: 6 Vulcan

pet: 7 tribble

starve 3 yen **4** burn, deny, fast, gasp, long, lust, pine **5** crave, raven, yearn **6** aspire, cut off, famish, hunger, refuse, thirst **7** deprive **8** be hungry, go hungry, languish

Star Wars

director: 11 George Lucas

cast: 10 Kenny Baker, Mark Hamill (Luke Skywalker) **12** Alec Guinness, Carrie Fisher (Princess Leia), Harrison Ford (Han Solo), Peter Cushing **14** Anthony Daniels

    voice of Darth Vader: 14 James Earl Jones

score: 12 John Williams

Oscar for: 5 score

sequel: 15 Return of the Jedi **20** The Empire Strikes Back

stasimon 9 choral ode

literally: 8 standing

state 3 put **4** form, land, mind, mode, mood, pass, pomp **5** guise, offer, phase, realm, shape, stage **6** aspect, luxury, morale, nation, people, plight, recite, relate, report, ritual, status **7** comfort, country, declare, explain, expound, express, kingdom, narrate, posture, present, recount, spirits **8** attitude, ceremony, describe, dominion, monarchy, official, position, propound, republic, set forth **9** condition, elucidate, formality, full dress, high style, situation, structure **10** ceremonial, government **11** body politic, frame of mind, predicament, state of mind **12** commonwealth, constitution, governmental, principality **13** circumstances

state abbreviations

Alabama: 2 AL **3** Ala

Alaska: 2 AK **4** Alas

Arizona: 2 AZ **4** Ariz

Arkansas: 2 AR **3** Ark

California: 2 CA **3** Cal **5** Calif

Colorado: 2 CO **4** Colo

Connecticut: 2 CT **4** Conn

Delaware: 2 DE **3** Del

Florida: 2 FL **3** Fla

Georgia: 2 GA

Hawaii: 2 HI

Idaho: 2 ID **3** Ida

Illinois: 2 IL **3** Ill

Indiana: 2 IN **3** Ind

Iowa: 2 IA

Kansas: 2 KS **4** Kans

Kentucky: 2 KY

Louisiana: 2 LA

Maine: 2 ME

Maryland: 2 MD

Massachusetts: 2 MA **4** Mass

Michigan: 2 MI **4** Mich

Minnesota: 2 MN **4** Minn

Mississippi: 2 MS **4** Miss

Missouri: 2 MO

Montana: 2 MT

Nebraska: 2 NE **4** Nebr

Nevada: **2** NV **3** Nev
New Hampshire: **2** NH
New Jersey: **2** NJ
New Mexico: **2** NM **4** N Mex
New York: **2** NY
North Carolina: **2** NC **4** N Car
North Dakota: **2** ND **4** N Dak
Ohio: **2** OH
Oklahoma: **2** OK **4** Okla
Oregon: **2** OR **4** Oreg
Pennsylvania: **2** PA **4** Penn **5** Penna
Rhode Island: **2** RI
South Carolina: **2** SC
South Dakota: **2** SD **4** S Dak
Tennessee: **2** TN **4** Tenn
Texas: **2** TX **3** Tex
Utah: **2** UT
Vermont: **2** VT
Virginia: **2** VA
Washington: **2** WA **4** Wash
West Virginia: **2** WV **3** W Va
Wisconsin: **2** WI **3** Wis
Wyoming: **2** WY **3** Wyo

state admittance
first: **8** Delaware
second: **12** Pennsylvania
third: **9** New Jersey
fourth: **7** Georgia
fifth: **11** Connecticut
sixth: **13** Massachusetts
seventh: **8** Maryland
eighth: **13** South Carolina
ninth: **12** New Hampshire
tenth: **8** Virginia
eleventh: **7** New York
twelfth: **13** North Carolina
thirteenth: **11** Rhode Island
fourteenth: **7** Vermont
fifteenth: **8** Kentucky
sixteenth: **9** Tennessee
seventeenth: **4** Ohio
eighteenth: **9** Louisiana
nineteenth: **7** Indiana
twentieth: **11** Mississippi
twenty-first: **8** Illinois
twenty-second: **7** Alabama
twenty-third: **5** Maine
twenty-fourth: **8** Missouri
twenty-fifth: **8** Arkansas
twenty-sixth: **8** Michigan
twenty-seventh: **7** Florida
twenty-eighth: **5** Texas
twenty-ninth: **4** Iowa
thirtieth: **9** Wisconsin
thirty-first: **10** California
thirty-second: **9** Minnesota
thirty-third: **6** Oregon
thirty-fourth: **6** Kansas
thirty-fifth: **12** West Virginia
thirty-sixth: **6** Nevada
thirty-seventh: **8** Nebraska
thirty-eighth: **8** Colorado
thirty-ninth/fortieth: **11** North
Dakota, South Dakota
forty-first: **7** Montana
forty-second: **10** Washington
forty-third: **5** Idaho
forty-fourth: **7** Wyoming

forty-fifth: **4** Utah
forty-sixth: **8** Oklahoma
forty-seventh: **9** New Mexico
forty-eighth: **7** Arizona
forty-ninth: **6** Alaska
fiftieth: **6** Hawaii

state capitals
Alabama: **10** Montgomery
Alaska: **6** Juneau
Arizona: **7** Phoenix
Arkansas: **10** Little Rock
California: **10** Sacramento
Colorado: **6** Denver
Connecticut: **8** Hartford
Delaware: **5** Dover
Florida: **11** Tallahassee
Georgia: **7** Atlanta
Hawaii: **8** Honolulu
Idaho: **5** Boise
Illinois: **11** Springfield
Indiana: **12** Indianapolis
Iowa: **9** Des Moines
Kansas: **6** Topeka
Kentucky: **9** Frankfort
Louisiana: **10** Baton Rouge
Maine: **7** Augusta
Maryland: **9** Annapolis
Massachusetts: **6** Boston
Michigan: **7** Lansing
Minnesota: **6** St Paul
Mississippi: **7** Jackson
Missouri: **13** Jefferson City
Montana: **6** Helena
Nebraska: **7** Lincoln
Nevada: **10** Carson City
New Hampshire: **7** Concord
New Jersey: **7** Trenton
New Mexico: **7** Santa Fe
New York: **6** Albany
North Carolina: **7** Raleigh
North Dakota: **8** Bismarck
Ohio: **8** Columbus
Oklahoma: **12** Oklahoma City
Oregon: **5** Salem
Pennsylvania: **10** Harrisburg
Rhode Island: **10** Providence
South Carolina: **8** Columbia
South Dakota: **6** Pierre
Tennessee: **9** Nashville
Texas: **6** Austin
Utah: **12** Salt Lake City
Vermont: **10** Montpelier
Virginia: **8** Richmond
Washington: **7** Olympia
West Virginia: **10** Charleston
Wisconsin: **7** Madison
Wyoming: **8** Cheyenne

State Fair
author: **9** Phil Stong
movie composers: **7** Rodgers **11**
Hammerstein
state in detail 7 explain, expound **8**
describe, spell out **9** explicate **16** give
a full account
stateliness 7 dignity, majesty **10** augustness
stately 5 grand, lofty, noble, proud, regal, royal **6** august, formal, lordly **7**

awesome, elegant, eminent **8** glorious,
imperial, imposing, majestic **9** dignified, grandiose **10** ceremonial, impressive **11** magnificent
statement 3 tab **4** bill **5** check, claim,
count, tally **6** avowal, charge, record,
remark, report, speech **7** account,
comment, invoice, mention, recital **8**
relation, sentence **9** assertion, manifesto, reckoning, testimony, utterance,
valuation **10** accounting, allegation,
communique, exposition, profession,
recitation **11** declaration, delineation,
explanation, observation **12** announcement, balance sheet **13** pronouncement, specification
state of affairs 5 state **6** status **9**
condition, situation **13** circumstances
State of the Union
director: **10** Frank Capra
cast: **10** Van Johnson **12** Spencer
Tracy **13** Adolphe Menjou **14** Angela
Lansbury **16** Katharine Hepburn
stateroom 5 cabin **8** quarters **11** compartment
statesman 8 diplomat **15** political
leader
statesmanship 9 diplomacy **19** political leadership
static 5 fixed, inert, still **8** immobile,
inactive, stagnant, unmoving **9** crackling, suspended **10** changeless, motionless, stationary, unchanging **12** interference
station 4 post, rank, site, spot, stop **5**
caste, class, depot, grade, level, place
6 assign, degree, locate, sphere, status
7 footing, install **8** ensconce, facility,
location, position, prestige, terminal,
terminus **9** condition, firehouse, place
ment **10** dispensary, guardhouse, importance **11** emplacement, whistle-
stop **12** headquarters
stationary 4 even, firm **5** fixed, inert
6 intact, moored, stable, steady **7** riveted, uniform **8** constant, immobile,
standing **9** dead-still, immovable, immutable, unchanged, unvarying **10**
motionless, stock-still, transfixed **11**
not changing, undeviating **12** unchangeable **13** standing still
Statius
author of: **6** Silvae **10** The Thebaid
12 The Achilleid
statue 8 monument **9** sculpture **14**
representation
statuesque 5 regal **7** stately **8** majestic **9** dignified
stature 4 rank, size **5** place **6** height,
regard **8** eminence, position, prestige,
standing, tallness **9** elevation **10** importance, prominence, reputation **11**
distinction
status 4 rank **5** caste, class, grade,
place, state **6** degree **7** caliber, footing, station **8** eminence, position,

prestige, standing **9** condition, situation **10** estimation **11** distinction

statute 3 law **7** precept **9** prescript

statute law
Latin: **10** lex scripta

staunch, stanch 3 dam **4** firm, stem, true **5** check, loyal, solid, sound, stout **6** impede, rugged, steady, strong, sturdy **7** contain, zealous **8** constant, faithful, hold back, obstruct, resolute, stalwart **9** steadfast, well-built **10** watertight **11** substantial

stave off 7 beat off, fend off, keep off, ward off **9** keep at bay

stay 3 aim, guy, rib, rod **4** bunk, curb, foil, halt, live, pole, prop, rest, room, stem, stop **5** abide, block, brace, check, delay, dwell, lodge, quell, shore, stick, tarry, visit **6** endure, keep in, linger, rein in, remain, reside, splint, stifle, thwart **7** carry on, hold out, holiday, last out, persist, sojourn, support, ward off **8** abeyance, buttress, continue, hold back, mainstay, postpone, reprieve, restrain, standard, stopover, suppress, vacation, withhold **9** deferment, frustrate, persevere, staunchion **10** hang around, see through, suspension **12** postponement, reinforcement

stay put 4 stay **6** remain **8** stand pat

St Clare, Eva
character in: **14** Uncle Tom's Cabin
author: **5** Stowe

steadfast 4 keen, rapt **5** fixed **6** direct, intent, steady **8** resolute **9** attentive, obstinate, tenacious, undaunted **10** deep-rooted, deep-seated, inflexible, unchanging, unflagging, unwavering, unyielding **11** indomitable, persevering, unalterable, undeviating, unfaltering, unflinching **12** intransigent, single-minded, unchangeable, undistracted **14** uncompromising

steadfastness 8 tenacity **10** resolution **11** persistence **12** perseverance, resoluteness **13** determination

Steadfast Tin Soldier, The
author: **21** Hans Christian Andersen

steadiness 4 care **5** poise **6** aplomb **8** calmness, coolness, evenness, firmness **9** composure, sangfroid, stability **10** equanimity, resolution **11** carefulness, persistence, self-control, tranquility **12** resoluteness, tranquillity **13** dependability, steadfastness **14** presence of mind, self-possession **16** imperturbability

steady 4 even, firm, sure **5** sober **6** secure, stable **7** balance, careful, devoted, regular, serious, staunch **8** constant, faithful, frequent, habitual, hold fast, reliable, resolute, unending, untiring **9** ceaseless, confirmed, dedicated, immovable, incessant, stabilize, steadfast, tenacious, unceasing **10** continuing, continuous, coolheaded,

deliberate, dependable, methodical, persistent, unflagging, unwavering **11** levelheaded, persevering, substantial, undeviating, unfaltering, unremitting **12** single-minded **13** conscientious

steal 3 buy, cop **4** copy, crib, flit, flow, lift, slip, take **5** creep, drift, filch, glide, pinch, skulk, slide, slink, sneak, swipe, usurp **6** borrow, elapse, escape, extort, filter, pilfer, pocket, rip off, snatch, snitch, thieve **7** bargain, defraud, diffuse, good buy, imitate, purloin, swindle **8** abstract, embezzle, good deal, liberate **10** burglarize, plagiarize **11** abscond with, appropriate, make off with **14** misappropriate

steal away 3 fly **4** bolt, flee, skip **5** elope **6** escape **7** get away, make off, slip out **8** creep off, slip away, sneak off **9** break free, tiptoe out **10** break loose, fly the coop **12** make a getaway

stealth 7 secrecy, slyness **10** covertness, sneakiness, subterfuge **11** furtiveness **12** stealthiness **13** secretiveness **15** unobtrusiveness **17** surreptitiousness

stealthy 3 sly **5** shady **6** covert, shifty, sneaky **7** devious, furtive **8** slippery, sneaking **9** secretive, underhand **11** clandestine, underhanded **12** huggermugger **13** surreptitious

steamboat
invented by: **6** Fulton **9** Symington

steamed up 5 angry, het up, irate **6** raging **7** enraged, furious, riled up **8** heated up, inflamed **10** infuriated **12** mad as a wet hen **14** hot and bothered **17** hot under the collar

steamer 4 boat, clam, ship **5** liner, trunk **10** paddleboat **11** side wheeler **12** stern-wheeler **13** paddle-wheeler

steel 4 dirk, foil, gird **5** blade, brace, knife, nerve, saber, sword **6** dagger, rapier **7** bayonet, cutlass, fortify, machete **8** falchion, scimitar **10** broadsword
process invented by: **8** Bessemer

Steele, Sir Richard
pseudonym: **16** Isaac Bickerstaff
author of: **9** The Tatler (with Joseph Addison) **10** The Funeral **12** The Spectator (with Joseph Addison) **13** The Lying Lover **16** The Tender Husband **18** The Conscious Lovers

steely 4 hard **5** stony **6** flinty **9** heartless, unfeeling **10** forbidding **11** coldhearted

Steen, Jan
born: **6** Leiden, Leyden **14** The Netherlands
artwork: **7** Cabaret **11** The Egg Dance **12** Merry Company **14** Garden of the Inn **15** The Doctor's Visit, The Rhetoricians **16** The Morning Toilet **17** The Skittle Players **18** The World

Topsy-Turvy, Young Woman Dressing

Steenburgen, Mary
roles: **10** Cross Creek **12** Dead of Winter **13** Time After Time **22** Attic: Hiding of Anne Frank

steep 4 brew, bury, fill, soak **5** imbue, sharp, sheer, souse **6** abrupt, drench, engulf, infuse, plunge **7** immerse, pervade, suffuse **8** marinate, saturate, submerge **10** impregnate **11** precipitous

steeple 5 spire, tower **6** belfry **9** campanile

steer 3 aim, lay, run **4** bear, head, lead, make, sail **5** coach, guide, pilot **6** direct, govern, manage **7** conduct, proceed **8** navigate **9** supervise

steer clear of 4 shun **5** avert, avoid, dodge, evade, forgo, skirt **6** escape, eschew, forego **8** sidestep **9** keep shy of **11** abstain from, refrain from **16** give a wide berth to

Steerforth
character in: **16** David Copperfield
author: **7** Dickens

Steffens, Lincoln
author of: **19** The Shame of the Cities

Steiger, Rod
real name: **20** Rodney Stephen Steiger
born: **13** Westhampton NY
wife: **11** Claire Bloom
roles: **8** Waterloo **13** The Longest Day, The Pawnbroker, W C Fields and Me **15** On the Waterfront **19** In the Heat of the Night (Oscar)

Stein, Clarence S
architect of: **13** Temple Emanu-El (NYC)

Stein, Gertrude
author of: **10** Three Lives **13** Tender Buttons **20** The Making of Americans **27** Autobiography of Alice B Toklas
coined phrase: **14** lost generation

Steinbeck, John
author of: **8** The Pearl **10** Cannery Row, East of Eden, The Red Pony **12** Of Mice and Men, Tortilla Flat **15** In Dubious Battle **16** The Grapes of Wrath **18** Travels with Charley **24** The Winter of Our Discontent

Steinmetz, Charles P
field: **11** engineering
developed: **2** AC **18** alternating current

Stella, Frank
born: **8** Malden MA
artwork: **4** Jill **5** Itata **14** Jasper's Dilemma **15** Guadalupe Island

Stella, Joseph
born: **5** Italy **6** Naples
artwork: **8** Full Moon (Barbados) **9** Sunflower, The Bridge **14** Brooklyn Bridge **16** Pittsburgh Winter **18** New

York Interpreted **28** Battle of the Lights Coney Island

Stella Dallas
director: 9 King Vidor
cast: 9 John Boles **11** Anne Shirley **12** Barbara O'Neil **15** Barbara Stanwyck

stellar 6 astral, starry **7** leading **8** starring **9** brilliant, celestial, principal **11** outstanding

stem 3 dam **4** buck, cane, come, curb, grow, halt, rise, stay, stop **5** arise, block, check, deter, ensue, issue, quell, shank, shoot, speak, spire, stalk, stall, stock, trunk **6** arrest, derive, hinder, impede, oppose, resist, result, retard, spring, stanch, thwart **7** counter, pedicel, petiole, prevent, proceed, tendril **8** hold back, obstruct, peduncle, restrain, surmount **9** leafstalk, originate, withstand

stem from 5 arise, begin, start **6** derive **9** originate

stench 4 odor, reek **5** fetor, stink **8** bad smell **9** fetidness

Stendhal (Henri Marie Beyle)
author of: 17 The Red and the Black **18** Memoirs of an Egotist **22** The Charterhouse of Parma

Stengel, Charles Dillon
nickname: 5 Casey
sport: 8 baseball
position: 7 manager
team: 11 New York Mets **14** New York Yankees **15** Brooklyn Dodgers

Stentor
vocation: 6 herald
characteristic: 10 loud-voiced
voice as loud as: 8 fifty men

step 3 act **4** clip, gait, move, pace, rank, rung, span, walk **5** notch, phase, point, riser, stage, stair, strut, track, tramp, tread **6** action, degree, hobble, period, remove, stride **7** footing, measure, process, shamble, shuffle, swagger, trample **8** footfall, foothold, maneuver, purchase **9** footprint, gradation, procedure **10** proceeding

step down 4 quit **5** leave **6** resign, retire

Stephens, James
author of: 7 Deirdre **14** The Crock of Gold **21** The Charwoman's Daughter

Stephenson, George and Robert
nationality: 7 English
developed: 15 steam locomotive

Steppenwolf
author: 12 Hermann Hesse
character: 5 Maria, Pablo **7** Hermine **11** Harry Haller

Steps
author: 13 Jerzy Kosinski

step up 4 spur **6** come up **7** quicken, speed up **8** approach, escalate, expedite, increase **9** intensify **10** accelerate

stereotype 4 type **6** cliche **7** formula

8 typecast **10** categorize, pigeonhole **13** preconception

stereotyped 5 stale, trite **9** hackneyed **11** commonplace **13** unimaginative

sterile 4 bare, pure, vain **5** empty **6** barren, fallow, futile **7** aseptic, useless **8** abortive, bootless, impotent, infecund, sanitary **9** childless, fruitless, infertile, worthless **10** antiseptic, profitless, sterilized, unavailing, unfruitful, uninfected **11** disinfected, ineffective, ineffectual, unrewarding **12** unproductive, unprofitable **13** free from germs **14** uncontaminated

sterilize 6 purify **9** autoclave, disinfect **13** decontaminate

sterling 4 pure, true **5** noble **6** silver, superb, worthy **7** genuine, perfect **8** flawless, superior **9** admirable, estimable, first-rate, honorable **10** invaluable **11** meritorious, superlative

stern 4 cold, grim, hard **5** cruel, grave, harsh, rigid, sharp, stiff **6** brutal, gloomy, severe, somber, strict, unkind **7** austere, serious **8** coercive, despotic, frowning, pitiless, rigorous, ruthless, ungentle **9** reproving, stringent, unfeeling **10** forbidding, implacable, ironfisted, ironhanded, tyrannical, unmerciful **11** admonishing, coldblooded, reproachful **12** unreasonable **13** unsympathetic **14** unapproachable

Sterne, Laurence
author of: 14 Tristram Shandy **19** A Sentimental Journey
character: 9 Uncle Toby **12** Parson Yorick, Walter Shandy

sternum
bone of: 6 breast

Steve Canyon
creator: 12 Milton Caniff
character: 7 Cheetah **9** Madam Lynx **10** Doe Redwood, Miss Mizzou **11** Savannah Gay **13** Copper Calhoun **14** Herself Muldoon **17** Princess Sun Flower
  wife: 6 Summer
  ward/cousin: 12 Poteet Canyon
  Summer's son: 13 Leigh ton Olson

Stevens, George
director of: 5 Giant (Oscar), Shane **8** Gunga Din **9** Swing Time **13** I Remember Mama, Penny Serenade **14** A Place in the Sun (Oscar), Woman of the Year **16** The Talk of the Town **19** The Diary of Anne Frank

Stevens, Gowan
character in: 9 Sanctuary
author: 8 Faulkner

Stevens, James
author of: 10 Paul Bunyan

Stevens, Wallace
author of: 7 The Rock **9** Harmonium **13** Sunday Morning **17** Transport to Summer **23** Peter Quince at the Clavier, The Idea of Order at Key West, The Man with the Blue Guitar

Stevenson, Robert
director of: 8 Jane Eyre **10** Back Street **11** Mary Poppins

Stevenson, Robert Louis
author of: 9 Kidnapped **13** The Black Arrow **14** Treasure Island **18** Travels with a Donkey **21** A Child's Garden of Verses, Doctor Jekyll and Mr Hyde, The Master of Ballantrae

St Evremond, Marquis
character in: 16 A Tale of Two Cities
author: 7 Dickens

stew 4 fret, fume, fuss **5** chafe, gripe, steep, tizzy, worry **6** grouse, ragout, seethe, simmer **7** agonize, fluster, flutter, grumble, mixture **10** miscellany

steward 5 agent, proxy **6** deputy, factor, waiter **7** bailiff, manager, trustee **8** executor, overseer **10** controller, supervisor **11** comptroller **13** administrator **14** representative, ship's attendant **15** flight attendant

Stewart, James
born: 9 Indiana PA
roles: 4 Rope **6** Harvey **7** Vertigo **10** Rear Window, Shenandoah **11** Elwood P Dowd **14** Cheyenne Autumn **16** Anatomy of a Murder, Destry Rides Again, The Stratton Story **17** Bell Book and Candle, It's a Wonderful Life **18** It's a Wonderful World, The Spirit of St Louis **19** The Glenn Miller Story **20** The Philadelphia Story (Oscar), You Can't Take It with You **22** The Greatest Show on Earth **23** Mr Smith Goes to Washington

Stewart, Mary
real name: 22 Florence Rainbow Stewart
author of: 11 Crystal Cave **14** The Hollow Hills **15** The Moon-Spinners **16** My Brother Michael, The Gabriel Hounds **18** Airs Above the Ground, The Last Enchantment

St George's
capital of: 7 Grenada

stick 3 bar, bat, cue, dig, fix, jab, pin, put, rod, set **4** balk, bind, cane, club, curb, fuse, glue, hold, join, last, mire, nail, pink, poke, pole, seal, snag, stab, stop, tack, twig, wand, weld **5** abide, affix, baton, billy, block, catch, check, fagot, leave, lodge, paste, place, plant, prick, punch, shift, snarl, spear, spike, staff, stall, stake, stand, stave, stump **6** adhere, attach, boggle, branch, burden, cement, cudgel, detain, endure, fasten, hamper, hinder, hog-tie, impede, insert, pierce, puzzle, scotch, skewer, stymie, switch, thrust, thwart **7** confuse, crosier, inhibit, perplex, shackle, trammel **8** bewilder, bludgeon, caduceus, continue, obstruct, puncture **9** checkmate, constrain, perforate, truncheon, victimize **10** immobilize, shillelagh

stick fast 4 hold **5** cling, stick **6** adhere, cleave

stickler 3 bug, nut **5** crank, poser **6** enigma, purist, puzzle, riddle, zealot **7** devotee, dilemma, fanatic, mystery, stumper **8** martinet **10** enthusiast, monomaniac

sticks 4 skis **5** bonds, glues, twigs **6** pastes, Podunk **7** adheres, boonies, catches, cements, country **8** kindling **9** backwoods, boondocks, golf clubs, provinces **10** hicksville, hinterland **11** countryside, hinterlands

stick together 4 bind, fuse, glue, hold, join **5** cling, stick, unite **6** cement, cohere

stick-to-itiveness 8 tenacity **9** endurance **10** resolution **11** persistence **12** perseverance, resoluteness **13** determination, tenaciousness

stickum 3 gum **4** glue **5** paste **6** cement **8** adhesive, mucilage **12** rubber cement

stick up for 5 boost **6** defend **7** root for **11** speak well of **17** put in a good word for

stick with 4 stay **5** abide **6** keep at **7** stand by **9** accompany, persevere

sticky 3 wet **4** damp, dank **5** gluey, gooey, gummy, humid, moist, muggy, pasty, tacky **6** clammy, clingy, steamy, sultry, viscid **7** viscous **8** adherent, adhesive, clinging, cohesive, sticking **9** glutinous, tenacious **10** gelatinous **12** mucilaginous

stiff 4 body, cold, cool, firm, grim, hard, high, iron, keen, prim, sore, taut **5** aloof, awful, brave, brisk, crisp, cruel, dense, fixed, gusty, harsh, heavy, rigid, sharp, smart, solid, steep, stern, tense, thick, tight, tough, undue **6** bitter, brutal, chilly, clumsy, corpse, dogged, forced, formal, raging, severe, steady, steely, strong, uneasy, viscid, wooden **7** austere, awkward, cadaver, clotted, decided, distant, drastic, extreme, fearful, intense, jellied, labored, precise, remains, settled, starchy, stately, staunch, steeled, stilted, uptight, valiant, violent, viscous **8** affected, constant, dead body, exacting, forceful, grievous, mannered, pitiless, pounding, powerful, resolute, resolved, rigorous, ruthless, spanking, stubborn, ungainly, unlimber, unshaken, vigorous **9** difficult, draconian, excessive, graceless, inelastic, inelegant, laborious, merciless, obstinate, resistant, steadfast, stringent, tenacious, unnatural **10** artificial, courageous, determined, exorbitant, formidable, gelatinous, immoderate, inflexible, inordinate, persistent, solidified, unswerving, unyielding **11** ceremonious, constrained, extravagant, indomitable, straitlaced, unfaltering, unflinching, unwarranted **12**

strong-willed, unreasonable **14** uncompromising

stiff-necked 6 mulish **7** will ful **8** contrary, obdurate, stubborn **9** obstinate, pigheaded, unbending **10** bullheaded, refractory, self-willed, unshakable, unyielding **11** intractable **12** intransigent, pertinacious

stiffness 7 tension **8** firmness, rigidity **9** aloofness, formality, tenseness, tightness **10** constraint **11** starchiness

stifle 3 gag **4** curb **5** check, choke **6** muffle, subdue **7** garrote, inhibit, repress, smother, squelch, swelter **8** keep back, restrain, strangle, suppress, throttle **9** suffocate **10** asphyxiate

stifling 3 hot **6** stuffy **7** airless **10** overheated

stigma 4 blot, flaw, mark, scar **5** brand, odium, shame, stain, taint **6** smirch, smudge **7** blemish, tarnish **8** disgrace, dishonor **11** mark of shame **12** besmirchment

stigmatize 5 brand, smear **6** debase, defame, smirch **7** villify **9** discredit, disparage

still 4 calm, hush **5** inert, quiet **6** at rest, hushed, pacify, settle, silent **7** appease, as suage, gratify, put down, repress, silence, turn off **8** immobile, overcome, restrain, suppress, unmoving **9** noiseless, soundless **10** motionless, put an end to, stationary, unstirring

stillness 4 calm, hush **5** quiet **6** repose **7** silence **8** calmness, inaction, quietude **9** composure **10** immobility, inactivity, quiescence **11** tranquility **12** tranquillity

Stillness at Appomattox, A
author: 11 Bruce Catton

stilted 4 cold, prim **5** rigid, stiff **6** forced, formal, stuffy, wooden **7** awkward, labored, pompous, starchy, studied, uptight **8** mannered, priggish, starched **9** graceless, unnatural **10** artificial **11** ceremonious, constrained

Stilwell, Joseph W
nickname: 10 Vinegar Joe
served in: 3 WWI **4** WWII
chief of staff for: 13 Chiang Kai-shek
driven out of: 5 Burma

stimulant 5 tonic, upper **6** bracer **8** excitant **9** energizer

stimulate 3 fan **4** spur, stir, wake **5** alert, rouse **6** arouse, awaken, excite, incite, prompt, vivify **7** actuate, animate, inflame, inspire, quicken, sharpen **8** activate, enkindle, initiate, inspirit

stimulating 5 tonic **7** piquing **8** arousing, exciting, spurring, stirring, whetting **9** animating, provoking **10** energizing, refreshing **11** interesting, provocative

stimulus 4 goad, spur, whet **5** tonic **6** bracer, fillip, motive **7** impetus **8** excitant **9** activator, energizer, incentive, quickener, stimulant **10** incitement, inducement **11** provocation **13** encouragement

sting 3 cut, nip, rub, vex **4** ache, barb, bite, blow, burn, fire, gall, gnaw, goad, grip, hurt, itch, lash, move, pain, prod, rack, rasp, rile, sore, spur, stab, whip **5** anger, chafe, cross, egg on, grate, impel, pinch, pique, prick, shake, shock, smart, venom, wince, wound **6** arouse, awaken, excite, harrow, incite, insult, kindle, madden, nettle, offend, pierce, prompt, propel, stir up, tingle, twinge **7** actuate, agonize, disturb, incense, inflame, prickle, provoke, quicken, scourge, stinger, torment, torture **8** irritate, motivate, vexation **9** infuriate, instigate, penetrate **10** affliction, irritation

Sting, The
director: 13 George Roy Hill
cast: 10 Paul Newman, Ray Walston, Robert Shaw **13** Eileen Brennan, Robert Redford **14** Charles Durning
score: 11 Scott Joplin
Oscar for: 7 picture **8** director

stinginess 6 penury **9** parsimony **11** miserliness **13** niggardliness, penny-pinching **15** tight-fistedness

stinging 4 acid **5** harsh, sharp **6** biting, bitter **7** burning, caustic, cutting, pungent **8** piercing **9** sarcastic, satirical **10** astringent

stingy 4 lean, mean, thin **5** close, scant, small, tight **6** frugal, meager, modest, paltry, scanty, skimpy, sparse **7** miserly, scrimpy, slender, sparing **8** piddling, stinting **9** illiberal, niggardly, penurious **10** inadequate, ungenerous **11** closefisted, tightfisted **12** cheeseparing, insufficient, parsimonious **13** penny-pinching

stink 4 odor, reek **5** fetor **6** stench **8** bad smell **17** smell to high heaven

stint 3 job **4** curb, duty, part, save, task, term, turn **5** check, chore, limit, quota, shift **6** reduce, scrimp **8** hold back, restrain, restrict, withhold **9** constrain, cut down on, economize **10** assignment, engagement **12** circumscribe, pinch pennies

stipend 5 grant, wages **6** income, salary **7** pension **8** fixed pay **9** allowance, emolument **10** honorarium, recompense **11** scholarship **12** compensation, remuneration

stipulate 4 cite, name **5** agree, allow, grant, state **6** assure, insure, pledge **7** promise, provide, specify, warrant **8** indicate, set forth **9** designate, guarantee

stipulation 4 term **7** proviso **9** condition **10** limitation **11** requirement, restriction

stipulative 7 limited **9** qualified, tentative **10** contingent, restricted **11** conditional, provisional **16** with reservations

stir 3 act, mix **4** beat, fire, goad, jolt, move, prod, rush, spur, to-do, whip **5** blend, rouse, shake, sough, start **6** arouse, awaken, bustle, commix, excite, flurry, hasten, hustle, kindle, mingle, mixing, moving, pother, quiver, rustle, shiver, tumult, twitch, uproar, vivify, work up **7** agitate, animate, enflame, flutter, inspire, provoke, quicken, scamper **8** energize, inspirit, intermix, mingling, movement, prodding, rustling, scramble, stirring **9** agitation, commingle, commotion, electrify, stimulate **10** get a move on, step lively **11** set in motion **12** exert oneself, make an effort

stirred up 5 riled, upset **7** aroused, excited, kindled, ruffled **8** agitated, inflamed **9** disturbed **10** stimulated

stirring 5 astir, awake **6** moving **7** rousing **8** electric, exalting, exciting, in motion, spirited **9** inspiring, thrilling **10** up and about **11** galvanizing, stimulating **12** electrifying

stir up 5 upset **6** arouse, awaken, excite, kindle, ruffle **7** agitate, disturb **9** call forth, stimulate **10** antagonize

stir vigorously 3 mix **4** beat, whip **7** agitate

stitch 3 bit, jot, sew **4** ache, iota, kink, mend, pain, pang, seam, tack **5** baste, cramp, crick, piece, scrap, shoot, shred **6** suture, tingle, twinge, twitch **7** article, garment **8** particle **9** embroider **12** charley horse

St John's
  capital of: 17 Antigua and Barbuda

St Louis
  baseball team: 9 Cardinals
  football team: 9 Cardinals
  founded by: 13 Pierre Laclede
  hockey team: 5 Blues
  landmark: 11 Gateway Arch
  newspaper: 12 Post-Dispatch
  river: 11 Mississippi
  site of: 10 Exposition (1904)
  university: 10 Washington

stock 4 butt, clan, form, fund, haft, herd, hold, kind, line, pull, race, root, type **5** array, basic, birth, blood, breed, broth, cache, caste, equip, goods, grasp, hoard, house, offer, shaft, store, tribe, wares **6** cattle, family, fit out, formal, handle, origin, people, shares, source, staple, strain, supply **7** appoint, capital, descent, dynasty, furnish, lineage, provide, regular, reserve, routine **8** accoutre, ancestry, bouillon, heredity, pedigree, pro forma, quantity, standard **9** forebears, genealogy, inventory, livestock, ownership, parentage, provision, reservoir, selection **10** assortment, background, extraction, family tree, investment **11** merchandise, nationality, progeniture **12** accumulation **13** capital shares

Stockhausen, Karlheinz
  born: 7 Germany, Modrath
  composer of: 5 Cycle, Tempi **6** Groups, Hymnen, Mantra, Zyklus **7** Anthems, Gruppen, Momente **8** Attuning, Gold Dust, Kontakte, Stimmung **9** Goldstaub, Zeitmasze **10** Procession, Prozession **12** Kontrapunkte **13** Klavierstucke **16** From the Seven Days **17** Aus den Sieben Tagen

Stockholm
  nickname: 16 Venice of the North
  capital of: 6 Sweden
  sea: 6 Baltic
  lake: 7 Malaren
  section: 8 Norrmalm **9** Sodermalm **11** Gamla Staden
  landmark: 7 Skansen **8** City Hall **11** Great Church
  site of: 10 Nobel Prize

stockpile 5 cache, hoard, stock, store **10** accumulate

stocky 5 dumpy, husky, pudgy, solid, squat, stout **6** blocky, chunky, stubby, stumpy, sturdy **8** thickset

stodgy 4 dull, flat **5** dated, heavy, lumpy, passe, staid, thick **6** boring, clumsy, dreary, narrow, prolix, stuffy **7** humdrum, pompous, prosaic, serious, starchy, tedious **8** lifeless, pedantic, tiresome **9** laborious, lumbering, wearisome **10** antiquated, inflexible, monotonous **12** indigestible, old-fashioned **13** uninteresting

stoic 4 calm **8** detached, fatalist, quietist, tranquil **9** impassive, unruffled **11** philosophic **13** dispassionate, imperturbable, unimpassioned

stoicism 8 fatalism **9** fortitude **11** impassivity, tranquility **12** tranquillity **16** imperturbability

Stoker, Bram
  author of: 7 Dracula

stole 3 fur **4** cape, robe, took, wrap **5** crept, orary, scarf **6** swiped **7** filched, pinched, sneaked, tiptoed **8** mantilla, pilfered, snatched, vestment **9** embezzled, purloined

stolen 3 hot **5** taken **6** swiped **7** filched, pinched **8** pilfered, snatched **9** embezzled, ill-gotten, purloined

stolid 4 dull **5** dense **6** bovine, obtuse **7** lumpish **8** sluggish **9** apathetic, impassive, lethargic **10** phlegmatic **11** insensitive, unemotional

stolidity 6 apathy **8** lethargy **9** inertness **11** impassivity **12** sluggishness

stomach 3 maw, pot **4** bear, bent, bias, craw, crop, guts, mind, take **5** abide, belly, brook, fancy, humor, stand, taste, tummy **6** desire, endure, hunger, liking, middle, paunch, relish, retain, suffer, temper, thirst **7** abdo-

men, gizzard, leaning, midriff, swallow **8** affinity, appetite, bear with, keenness, overlook, pass over, pleasure, potbelly, sympathy, tolerate **9** put up with **10** attraction, midsection, partiality, proclivity, propensity **11** breadbasket, countenance, disposition, inclination **12** predilection

stone 3 gem, nut, pip, pit **4** rock, seed **5** bijou, jewel **6** kernel, pebble **9** brilliant **10** throw rocks

Stone, Edward Durell
  architect of: 9 US Embassy **17** Museum of Modern Art **33** Kennedy Center for the Performing Arts

Stone, Irving
  author of: 9 The Origin **11** Lust for Life **12** Those Who Love **17** Sailor on Horseback, The President's Lady **19** Adversary in the House **21** The Agony and the Ecstasy

Stone, Oliver
  born: 9 New York NY
  profession: 6 writer **8** director
  films: 3 JFK **5** Nixon, U-Turn **7** Platoon (Oscar) **10** Wall Street **12** Patriot Games **14** Heaven and Earth **15** Midnight Express **18** Natural Born Killers **21** Born on the Fourth of July

stonefly
  varieties: 5 giant, green **6** spring, winter **8** perlodid **9** roachlike **11** green-winged **12** rolled-winged

Stone of Scone
  location: 8 Scotland
  purpose: 12 crowning king
  moved to: 16 Westminster Abbey

stoneware 5 china **7** ceramic, pottery **8** crockery

stony 3 icy **4** cold **5** blank, bumpy, chill, rocky, rough, stern **6** coarse, craggy, flinty, frigid, jagged, marble, pebbly, rugged, severe, steely, stolid, uneven **7** austere, callous, granite, lithoid, stoical **8** concrete, deadened, gravelly, hardened, indurate, obdurate, ossified, pitiless, rocklike, soulless, uncaring **9** bloodless, heartless, merciless, petrified, unfeeling, untouched **10** ada mantine, forbidding, fossilized, hard-boiled, inexorable, insensible, unaffected, unyielding

stool 5 bench **7** cricket, has sock, ottoman

stool pigeon 3 rat, spy **4** fink **5** decoy, patsy **6** snitch **7** peacher, stoolie, tattler **8** informer, squealer **10** talebearer, tattletale

stoop 3 bow, sag **4** bend, fall, sink **5** deign, droop, porch, slump, steps, yield **6** resort, slouch, submit **7** concede, descend, succumb **8** doorstep **9** acquiesce **10** condescend **11** entranceway **19** round-shoulderedness

stooped 4 bent **5** bowed **7** deigned, hunched **9** contorted **12** condescended

stop 3 ban, bar, end **4** curb, fill, halt, hold, idle, plug, quit, rest, seal, stay, stem, wait **5** abide, block, brake, break, caulk, cease, check, close, depot, deter, dwell, lapse, lodge, pause, put up, spell, stall, stand, tarry, visit **6** alight, arrest, cut off, desist, draw up, expire, falter, finish, hamper, hiatus, hinder, pull up, recess, rein in, repose, run out, stanch, stop up, thwart **7** close up, halting, layover, occlude, prevent, respite, sojourn, station, suspend **8** abeyance, break off, conclude, cut short, hold back, intermit, interval, leave off, obstruct, pass away, peter out, postpone, preclude, restrain, suppress, surcease, terminal, terminus, wind down **9** cessation, frustrate, interlude, stand fast, terminate **10** desistance, drop anchor, put an end to, standstill, suspension **11** come to a halt, come to an end, destination, discontinue, prohibition, termination **12** intermission, interruption **17** come to a standstill **18** bring to a standstill

stopgap 7 stand-by **9** contrived, emergency, expedient, impromptu, makeshift, temporary, tentative **10** improvised, substitute **11** provisional
Latin: 5 ad hoc **6** pro tem

stop in 4 call **5** visit **6** drop in, look in

stop off 4 call **5** visit **6** drop in, look in, stop by

stoppage 4 halt **5** check, ticup **6** arrest **7** barrier, embargo, staying **8** blockage, checking, clogging, gridlock, obstacle **9** checkmate, hindrance, restraint, stricture **10** disruption, impediment **11** curtailment, obstruction **12** interruption

Stoppard, Tom
   author of: **10** Travesties **33** Rosencrantz and Guildenstern Are Dead

stopper 3 lid **4** bung, cock, cork, plug **5** spile

Stopping by Woods on a Snowy Evening
   author: **11** Robert Frost

Stop the Music
   host: **9** Bert Parks
   orchestra: **11** Harry Salter
   vocalist: **9** June Valli **11** Jaye P Morgan, Jimmy Blaine **12** Marion Morgan **13** Betty Ann Grove, Estelle Loring

stop up 3 jam **4** clog **5** block, choke **8** obstruct

store 3 lot **4** fund, hold, host, keep, mart, pack, pile, save, shop **5** amass, array, cache, faith, hoard, lay by, lay in, lay up, stash, stock, trust, value, wares **6** credit, esteem, gather, heap up, legion, market, plenty, regard, riches, scores, supply, volume, wealth **7** deposit, effects, husband, put away, reserve, satiety **8** emporium, lay

aside, overflow, plethora, quantity, reliance, richness, salt away, sock away, stow away **9** abundance, inventory, multitude, profusion, provision, reservoir, stockpile **10** accumulate, confidence, cornucopia, dependence, estimation, exuberance, luxuriance **11** copiousness, full measure, prodigality, supermarket **12** accumulation **13** establishment

storehouse 4 bank, silo **5** depot, vault **7** arsenal, granary **8** elevator, magazine, treasury **9** stockroom, warehouse **10** depository, repository

storied 4 epic **6** fabled **8** fabulous **9** legendary

Stories and Texts for Nothing
   author: **13** Samuel Beckett

storm 3 ado, row **4** blow, fume, fuss, gale, rage, rant, rave, roar, rush, stir, tear, to-do **5** burst, furor, snarl, stalk, stamp, stomp, tramp **6** assail, attack, charge, clamor, deluge, flurry, hubbub, pother, ruckus, squall, strike, tumult, uproar **7** assault, besiege, bluster, carry on, cyclone, rampage, tempest, tornado, torrent, turmoil, twister, typhoon **8** blizzard, brouhaha, downpour, eruption, fall upon, outbreak, outburst, upheaval **9** agitation, commotion, explosion, fulminate, hurricane, raise hell **10** cloudburst, hullabaloo **11** blow one's top, disturbance **12** blow one's cool, vent one's rage

storm and stress
   German: **13** Sturm und Drang
   name of 18th century: **16** literary movement

storm troopers
   German: **14** Sturmabteilung

stormy 4 foul, wild **5** rainy, rough, snowy, windy **6** raging, rugged **7** howling, roaring, squally, violent **8** blustery **9** inclement, turbulent **10** blustering **11** tempestuous

story 3 fib, lie **4** news, plot, tale, word, yarn **5** alibi, fable, piece **6** excuse, legend, report, sketch **7** account, article, parable, romance, tidings, version **8** allegory, anecdote, argument, dispatch, news item, white lie **9** falsehood, narrative, statement, testimony **10** allegation **11** fabrication, information **13** prevarication

Story of a Bad Boy, The
   author: **19** Thomas Bailey Aldrich

Story of G I Joe, The
   director: **14** William Wellman
   cast: **13** Freddie Steele, Robert Mitchum **15** Burgess Meredith (Ernie Pyle)

Story of Louis Pasteur, The
   director: **15** William Dieterle
   cast: **8** Paul Muni (Pasteur) **11** Anita Louise **19** Josephine Hutchinson
   Oscar for: **5** actor (Muni)

stout 3 big, fat, fit **4** able, bold, firm,

true **5** brave, bulky, burly, hardy, heavy, hefty, husky, large, obese, plump, pudgy, round, solid, tough, tubby **6** brawny, chubby, daring, fleshy, heroic, mighty, plucky, portly, robust, rotund, rugged, spunky, steady, stocky, strong, sturdy **7** doughty, gallant, staunch, valiant **8** athletic, constant, enduring, faithful, fearless, intrepid, leathery, muscular, resolute, resolved, stalwart, thickset, untiring, valorous, vigorous **9** confident, corpulent, dauntless, steadfast, strapping **10** able-bodied, courageous, determined, inflexible, unshakable, unswerving, unwavering **11** indomitable, lionhearted, unfaltering, unflinching, unshrinking

Stout, Rex
   author of: **10** Fer-de-Lance **12** Too Many Cooks **16** If Death Ever Slept
   character: **5** Fritz **9** Nero Wolfe **13** Archie Goodwin

stouthearted 4 bold **5** brave, gutsy, hardy **6** heroic, plucky, spunky **7** valiant **8** fearless, intrepid, resolute, spirited, stalwart, unafraid, valorous **9** dauntless, undaunted **10** courageous **11** indomitable, lionhearted, unblenching, unflinching

stouteartedness 4 grit, guts, sand **5** nerve, pluck, spunk, valor **6** daring, mettle **7** bravery, courage **8** boldness **12** fearlessness **13** dauntlessness

stoutness
   French: **10** embonpoint

stow 3 jam, put, set **4** cram, load, pack, tuck **5** cache, crowd, place, stash, store, stuff, wedge **7** deposit, squeeze **8** ensconce, salt away

Stowe, Harriet Beecher
   author of: **4** Dred **12** Oldtown Folks **14** Uncle Tom's Cabin

Strachey, Lytton
   author of: **13** Queen Victoria **17** Elizabeth and Essex, Eminent Victorians
   member of: **15** Bloomsbury Group

strafe 7 bombard **8** fire upon **10** machine-gun

straggle 4 rove **5** drift, stray **6** sprawl, wander **7** deviate, meander **8** divagate

straight 4 even, neat, tidy, true **5** clear, frank, right, solid, sound **6** candid, direct, evenly, honest, square, unbent **7** aligned, erectly, in order, orderly, upright **8** accurate, adjusted, arranged, directly, on a level, reliable, squarely, truthful, unbroken **9** ceaseless, forthwith, incessant, instantly, not curved, shipshape, sorted out, sustained, veracious **10** aboveboard, continuous, forthright, four-square, methodical, persistent, straightly, successive, unrelieved, unswerving, unwavering **11** consecutive, coordinated, immediately, trustworthy, undeviating **13** uninterrupted

straighten 4 tidy **5** align **6** adjust, neaten, unbend **7** even out **8** level out, square up **9** put in line **10** put in order, stand erect

straightening 7 tidying **9** adjusting, alignment, evening up, unbending **10** evening out **11** leveling out **13** putting in line **14** putting in order

straighten out 6 unbend **7** realign **8** redirect **10** discipline

straighten up 4 tidy **5** align, clean, order **6** neaten, tidy up **7** arrange, stand up **8** organize

straightforward 4 open **5** blunt, frank **6** candid, direct, honest, square **7** ethical, upright **8** straight **9** guileless, honorable **10** aboveboard, creditable, forthright, scrupulous **11** plainspoken, trustworthy

straightforwardness 6 candor **7** honesty **12** truthfulness **14** forthrightness

straight from the shoulder 4 open **5** frank **6** candid, direct, openly **7** bluntly, frankly, sincere **8** candidly, directly **9** downright

straightness 7 honesty **8** evenness **10** directness **11** uprightness

strain 3 air, tax, tug **4** kind, line, pull, sift, song, sort, toil, tune, type, vein **5** blood, breed, drain, force, grain, grind, group, heave, labor, people, press, sieve, streak, stock, trait, twist **6** burden, drudge, effort, extend, family, filter, genius, injure, injury, melody, overdo, purify, refine, screen, sprain, stress, weaken, winnow, wrench **7** descent, distend, exhaust, fatigue, lineage, overtax, species, stretch, tension, tighten, try hard, variety, wear out **8** ancestry, bear down, elongate, exertion, hardship, heredity, make taut, overwork, pressure, protract, struggle, tendency **9** draw tight, make tense, overexert, parentage **10** buckle down, derivation, extraction, overburden **11** disposition, huff and puff, inclination **12** do double duty, drive oneself, exert oneself **14** predisposition, work like a horse, work like a slave

strained 5 tense **6** touchy **8** volatile **9** explosive **10** precarious

strait 7 channel, narrows, passage

straitened 5 broke, needy **6** hard-up **7** pinched **8** bank rupt, indigent, strapped, wiped-out **9** destitute, penniless, penurious **10** distressed, pauperized, restricted **11** embarrassed **12** impoverished **15** poverty-stricken

Strait Is the Gate
    author: **9** Andre Gide

straitlaced 4 prim **5** rigid, stiff **6** formal, narrow, proper, severe, strict **7** austere, prudish, uptight **8** reserved **9** inhibited **11** puritanical **14** overscrupulous **15** undemonstrative

straits 3 fix **4** hole **6** pickle, plight **8** distress **9** extremity **10** difficulty **11** predicament **13** embarrassment

strand 4 bank, cord, lock, rope **5** beach, braid, coast, fiber, leave, shore, tress, twist **6** desert, ground, maroon, string, thread **8** filament, necklace, seacoast, seashore **9** component, go aground, riverside, shipwreck **10** ingredient, run aground **15** leave high and dry, leave in the lurch

stranded 5 stuck **6** ashore **7** aground, beached **8** grounded **9** foundered **11** shipwrecked **14** left high and dry, left in the lurch

strange 3 new, odd **4** lost **5** alien, queer **6** uneasy, unused **7** awkward, bizarre, curious, erratic, foreign, unknown, unusual **8** aberrant, abnormal, freakish, peculiar, singular, uncommon **9** alienated, anomalous, eccentric, estranged, fantastic, ill at ease, irregular, unnatural **10** bewildered, farfetched, out of place, outlandish, unexplored, unfamiliar **11** discomposed, disoriented, out-of-theway **12** unaccustomed, undiscovered, unhabituated **13** extraordinary, unaccountable, uncomfortable **14** unconventional

Strange Fruit
    author: **12** Lillian Smith

Strange Interlude
    author: **12** Eugene O'Neill

strangeness 7 anomaly, oddness **9** queerness **10** aberration **11** abnormality, peculiarity **12** eccentricity, idiosyncrasy, irregularity, unconformity **13** nonconformity

stranger 5 alien **8** newcomer, outsider **9** auslander, foreigner, immigrant, outlander

Stranger, The
    author: **11** Albert Camus

Strangers on a Train
    director: **15** Alfred Hitchcock
    cast: **9** Ruth Roman **11** Leo G Carroll, Marion Lorne **12** Robert Walker **13** Farley Granger **17** Patricia Hitchcock
    remade as: **20** Once You Kiss a Stranger

strange to say
    Latin: **13** mirabile dictu

strangle 3 gag **4** stop **5** burke, check, choke, crush, quell **6** muzzle, stifle **7** garrote, put down, repress, smother, squelch **8** choke off, snuff out, suppress, throttle **9** suffocate **10** asphyxiate, extinguish

strangulate 8 choke off, compress, strangle **9** constrict

strap 3 tie **4** band, beat, belt, bind, cord, flog, lash, whip **5** flail, leash, thong, truss **6** tether, thrash **7** scourge

strapped 8 bankrupt, wiped out **9** insolvent, penniless **12** impoverished, without funds

strapping 5 burly, hardy, husky, stout **6** brawny, robust, strong, sturdy **8** muscular, powerful, stalwart

stratagem 4 game, plan, plot, ploy, ruse, wile **5** blind, dodge, feint, trick **6** deceit, device, scheme, tactic **8** artifice, intrigue, maneuver, trickery **9** deception **10** subterfuge **11** contrivance, machination

strategic 3 key **4** wary **5** vital **6** clever **7** careful, crucial, cunning, guarded, planned, politic, prudent, turning **8** cautious, critical, decisive, military, tactical, vigilant **9** important, momentous, principal **10** calculated, deliberate, diplomatic **11** significant **13** consequential, precautionary

strategy 4 game **5** craft, wiles **6** policy, scheme **7** cunning, devices, tactics **8** artifice, art of war, game plan, plotting **9** war policy **10** artfulness, craftiness **11** grand design, machination, maneuvering **12** military plan **15** military science

stratosphere 3 sky **5** ozone **7** heavens **8** upper air **12** high altitude **14** wild blue yonder

stratum 4 band, belt, seam, zone **5** layer

Strauss, Johann (the Elder)
    composer of: **13** Radetzky March

Strauss, Johann (the Younger)
    composer of: **6** The Bat **13** Die Fledermaus, The Gipsy Baron **16** Der Zigeunerbaron
    waltz: **12** Emperor Waltz **13** The Blue Danube **23** Tales from the Vienna Woods

Strauss, Joseph
    composer of: **17** Music of the Spheres **27** The Village Swallows in Austria

Strauss, Levi
    make of: **5** jeans **9** dungarees

Strauss, Richard
    born: **6** Munich **7** Germany
    composer of: **6** Salome **7** Don Juan, Elektra **8** Arabella **9** Capriccio **10** Don Quixote **14** Ein Heldenleben **15** Ariadne auf Naxos **16** Der Rosenkavalier, Domestic Symphony, Till Eulenspiegel **19** Die Frau ohne Schatten **20** Die Aegyptische Helena, Thus Spake Zarathustra **21** Also Sprach Zarathustra **23** Death and Transfiguration

Stravinsky, Igor Feodorovich
    born: **6** Russia **11** Oranienbaum
    composer of: **4** Agon **6** Threni **7** Orpheus **8** The Flood **9** Card Party, Fireworks **10** Oedipus Rex, Petrouchka, Petruschka, Pulcinella **11** Jeu de Cartes, The Firebird **13** Dumbarton Oaks, Psalm Symphony **14** The Nightingale **15** Abraham and Isaac, The Rite of Spring **16** Requiem

Canticles, The Rake's Progress **18** Le Sacre du Printemps

straw 3 hay **4** tube **5** chaff **7** pipette

strawberry 8 Fragaria
  varieties: **4** mock **5** beach **6** barren, Dunlap, garden, Indian **7** sow-teat **8** Klondike, Rosacean, Virginia, woodland
  liqueur: **13** creme de fraise

Straw Dogs
  director: **12** Sam Peckinpah
  cast: **9** T P McKenna **11** Susan George **12** Peter Vaughan **13** Dustin Hoffman

straw man 6 effigy **9** scapegoat, scarecrow

stray 4 lost, roam, rove, waif **5** drift **6** random, wander **7** digress, drifter **8** go astray, sepa rate, set apart, straggle, straying, vagabond, wanderer **9** itinerant, misplaced, scat tered, straggler **10** lost animal, lost person **11** lose one's way

straying 5 lapse **8** drifting, rambling **9** departure, deviation, wandering **10** abberation, digression, divergence

streak 3 bar, bed, fly **4** band, blot, blur, cast, dart, dash, daub, line, lode, race, rush, seam, tear, vein, whiz, zoom **5** layer, level, plane, smear, speed, strip, touch **6** blotch, hurtle, smirch, smudge, strain, stripe **7** portion, splotch, stratum

stream 3 jet, run **4** blow, file, flow, flux, gush, pour, race, rill, rush, teem, tide, wall, wave **5** brook, burst, creek, float, flood, issue, river, shoot, spate, spill, spout, spurt, surge **6** abound, branch, course, deluge, extend, feeder, onrush, sluice **7** current, flutter, freshet, rivulet, torrent **8** effusion, fountain, overflow **9** profusion, tributary **11** watercourse

streamer 4 flag **6** banner, burgee **7** pennant

streamlet 3 run **4** rill **5** brook, creek **7** rivulet

streamlined 4 racy **5** clean, sleek **7** compact **8** up-to-date **9** organized **10** futuristic, modernized, simplified **11** aerodynamic

stream of abuse 6 tirade **8** diatribe, harangue **9** contumely, invective **12** vituperation

Streep, Meryl
  real name: **16** Mary Louise Streep
  born: **14** Basking Ridge NJ
  roles: **8** Ironweed, Silkwood **11** Out of Africa **13** Falling in Love, Sophie's Choice (Oscar), The Deer Hunter **14** Before and After, Kramer vs Kramer **20** Postcards from the Edge, The House of the Spirits **25** The Bridges of Madison County, The French Lieutenant's Woman

street 3 way **4** lane, mews, road **5** alley, block, route **6** avenue **7** highway,

roadway, terrace, thruway **8** turnpike **9** boulevard **10** expressway **12** thoroughfare

Streetcar Named Desire, A
  author: **17** Tennessee Williams
  director: **9** Elia Kazan
  cast: **9** Kim Hunter (Stella Dubois Kowalski) **10** Karl Malden **11** Vivien Leigh (Blanche Dubois) **12** Marlon Brando (Stanley Kowalski)
  setting: **10** New Orleans
  score: **9** Alex North
  Oscar for: **7** actress (Leigh) **15** supporting actor (Malden) **17** supporting actress (Hunter)

Streets of San Francisco, The
  character: **9** (Det Lt) Mike Stone **10** (Inspector) Dan Robbins **11** (Inspector) Steve Keller
  cast: **10** Karl Malden **12** Richard Hatch **14** Michael Douglas

strega
  type: **7** liqueur
  origin: **5** Italy
  flavor: **6** spices **10** orange peel
  with brandy: **10** Strega Flip

Streisand, Barbra
  real name: **20** Barbara Joan Streisand
  born: **10** Brooklyn NY
  husband: **11** Elliot Gould
  roles: **5** Yentl **9** Funny Girl (Oscar), Funny Lady **10** Fanny Brice, Hello Dolly, What's Up Doc? **11** A Star Is Born **12** The Main Event, The Way We Were **13** The Prince of Tides **20** The Mirror Has Two Faces
  recordings: **10** The Concert **11** A Star Is Born **23** The Barbra Streisand Album

strength 4 beef, grit, kick, pith, sand, size **5** brawn, force, forte, might, pluck, power, sinew, spice, vigor **6** anchor, mettle, number, purity, spirit, succor, virtue **7** bravery, muscles, potency, stamina, support **8** backbone, buttress, efficacy, firmness, mainstay, security, solidity, tenacity, vitality **9** endurance, fortitude, hardiness, intensity, lustiness, puissance, stoutness, toughness, viability **10** robustness, sturdiness, sustenance **13** concentration, effectiveness **16** stoutheartedness
  Latin: **3** vis

strengthen 4 prop **5** brace, renew, steel **6** harden **7** build up, enhance, fortify, improve, restore, shore up, support, sustain **8** buttress **9** reinforce

strength of character 4 grit, guts **5** pluck, spunk **6** mettle **7** resolve **8** backbone **9** fortitude **10** resolution **12** resoluteness **13** steadfastness

strenuous 4 hard **5** eager **6** active, ardent, dogged, taxing, uphill **7** arduous, dynamic, earnest, intense, zealous **8** animated, diligent, sedulous, spirited, untiring, vigorous **9** assiduous, difficult, energetic, laborious,

punishing **10** exhausting, on one's toes **11** hardworking, industrious, painstaking **12** enterprising **13** indefatigable

stress 4 beat, mark **5** force, value, worth **6** accent, affirm, assert, burden, moment, repeat, strain, weight **7** anxiety, concern, feature, gravity, meaning, sawdust, tension, urgency **8** emphasis, pressure **9** emphasize, necessity, underline **10** accentuate, importance, insist upon, oppression, prominence, underscore **11** consequence, seriousness **12** accentuation, significance **13** consideration

stretch 4 span, term, tire **5** cover, reach, spell, stint, tract, while, widen **6** burden, deepen, expand, extend, period, sprawl, spread, spring, strain **7** distend, draw out, expanse, fatigue, lie over, over tax, pull out **8** distance, draw taut, duration, elongate, interval, lengthen, overtask, over work, protract, put forth, reach out, tautness, traverse **9** be elastic, draw tight, make tense, make tight, overexert **10** elasticity, exaggerate, overburden, overcharge, overstrain, push too far, resiliency **11** carry too far **12** be expandable, be extendable **14** push to the limit

stretchable 7 elastic, rubbery **8** flexible **9** resilient

stretching 9 extending, extension **10** drawing out, elongation **11** attenuation, enlargement, lengthening, protraction **12** prolongation **13** amplification

stretching out 8 outreach **9** expansion, extending, extension **10** elongation **11** attenuation, lengthening **12** prolongation

stretch out 6 expand, extend **7** amplify, augment, draw out **8** elongate, lengthen, protract

Strether
  character in: **14** The Ambassadors
  author: **10** Henry James

strew 3 sow **6** litter **7** scatter **8** disperse **9** broadcast **11** disseminate

stricken 3 ill **4** hurt, sick **7** injured, smitten, wounded **8** blighted, diseased **9** afflicted, taken sick **13** incapacitated

strict 4 nice **5** exact, rigid, stern **6** severe **7** austere, perfect **8** absolute, complete, exacting, rigorous, unerring **9** stringent **10** fastidious, inflexible, meticulous, scrupulous, unyielding **13** authoritarian, conscientious **14** uncompromising

strictly required
  French: **9** de rigueur

stride 4 gait, lope, pace, step **5** march, stalk **7** advance, headway **8** long step, progress **11** advancement, improvement **13** take long steps

strident 5 harsh **6** shrill **7** grating, jarring, rasping, raucous **8** clashing, grinding, jangling, piercing, twanging **9** dissonant **10** discordant, screeching **11** cacophonous, high-pitched

Striebel, John H
creator/artist of: **10** Dixie Dugan

strife 6 unrest **7** discord, trouble, turmoil, warfare **8** conflict, disquiet, fighting, struggle, upheaval, violence **10** contention, convulsion, disharmony, dissension **11** altercation, disturbance

Strife
author: **14** John Galsworthy

strike 3 bat, box, hit, run, tap **4** bang, beat, belt, bump, clap, clip, club, come, cuff, drub, find, flog, lash, make, meet, pelt, ring, slam, slap, slug, sock, toll, whip, wipe **5** chime, clout, erase, flail, knell, knock, light, pound, punch, reach, smash, smite, sound, thump, tie-up, whack, whale **6** affect, arrive, assail, attack, batter, buffet, cancel, chance, charge, cudgel, delete, effect, fold up, hammer, pommel, remove, seem to, thrash, wallop **7** achieve, arrange, assault, boycott, impress, occur to, protest, put away, ram into, run into, scourge, scratch, stumble, unearth, walk out **8** appear to, bump into, come upon, cross out, dawn upon, discover, fall upon, lambaste, pull down, take down **9** burst upon, devastate, eliminate, encounter, eradicate, knock into, take apart **10** come across, flagellate, meet head-on **11** beat against, collide with, dash against **12** labor dispute, work stoppage

strike a bargain 5 agree **6** settle **9** make a deal **10** compromise **11** come to terms, meet halfway **18** split the difference **20** reach an understanding

strike back 7 counter, get even, hit back, pay back, riposte **9** fight back, retaliate **13** counterattack

strike dumb 4 daze, stun **5** amaze, shock **7** astound, stagger, stupefy **8** astonish, dumfound **9** dumbfound, electrify **11** flabbergast

strike noisily 4 bang, beat, clap, slam **5** thump

strike out 6 delete, fan out, set off, set out **7** take out **10** sally forth

strike sharply 3 rap **4** slap **5** crack

striking 6 marked **7** notable **9** prominent **10** astounding, impressive, noteworthy, noticeable, remarkable, surprising **11** conspicuous, outstanding **13** extraordinary

Strindberg, August
author of: **9** Miss Julie, The Father **10** A Dream Play **12** The Creditors **14** The Ghost Sonata **15** The Dance of Death

string 3 row **4** cord, file, line, rope **5** chain, queue, train, twine **6** column,

extend, parade, series, spread, strand, thread **7** binding, stretch **8** necklace, sequence **10** procession, succession

stringent 5 close, harsh, spare, stern, stiff, tight **6** cogent, frugal, severe, strict **7** sparing **8** exacting, forceful, rigorous **9** demanding, effectual, unbending **10** inflexible, unyielding **14** uncompromising

strip 3 rob **4** band, flay, loot, peel, raid, sack, skin, slip, tear **5** field, flake, rifle, shave **6** denude, divest, length, ravage, remove, ribbon, stripe, unwrap **7** deprive, despoil, disrobe, draw off, lay bare, measure, plunder, pull off, ransack, uncover, undrape, undress **8** airstrip, desolate, lay waste, spoliate, unclothe **9** steal from **11** disencumber

stripe 3 bar **4** band, line, tape **5** braid, strip, swath **6** ribbon, streak **7** chevron **8** insignia **9** striation

stripling 3 boy, lad **5** minor, youth **8** teenager, young man **9** schoolboy, youngster **10** adolescent

stripped 4 bare, nude **5** naked **6** peeled, unclad **7** denuded, exposed, unrobed **8** disrobed, divested **9** unclothed, uncovered, undressed

strive 3 vie **4** push **5** essay, fight, labor **6** battle, strain **7** contend, try hard **8** endeavor, struggle **9** take pains, undertake **10** do one's best **12** apply oneself, do one's utmost, exert oneself, spare no pains **15** work like a Trojan **18** move heaven and earth **20** leave no stone unturned

striving 4 toil **5** exert, labor **6** effort, strain **7** toiling, travail **8** exertion, struggle **9** straining **10** struggling

stroke 3 bat, hit, pat, pet, tap **4** blow, chop, coup, deed, feat, poke, slap, sock, swat **5** brush, chime, fluke, punch, whack **6** caress, chance, wallop **7** massage, ringing, seizure, tolling **8** accident, apoplexy, flourish, movement, sounding, striking **11** achievement, coincidence, piece of luck, transaction **15** brain hemorrhage

stroll 4 tour, turn, walk **5** amble, mosey **6** ramble, wander **7** meander, saunter **9** poke along, promenade **14** constitutional

stroller 4 pram **5** buggy **6** ambler, walker **7** rambler **8** carriage **9** itinerant, pushchair, saunterer **10** promenader **12** perambulator

strong 3 hot **4** able, bold, deep, keen, tart **5** burly, clear, close, fiery, hardy, nippy, sharp, solid, sound, stout, tangy, tough, vivid **6** ardent, biting, brawny, bright, cogent, fervid, fierce, gritty, hearty, mighty, moving, plucky, potent, robust, savory, severe, sinewy, sturdy **7** buoyant, capable, devoted, earnest, fervent, healthy, intense, piquant, pungent, skilled, violent, zeal-

ous **8** animated, athletic, definite, diligent, distinct, emphatic, faithful, forceful, muscular, powerful, puissant, sedulous, spirited, stalwart, tireless, vehement, vigorous **9** assiduous, competent, confirmed, effective, energetic, herculean, resilient, tenacious, undiluted **10** compelling, convincing, courageous, deep-seated, persistent, proficient **11** impassioned, persevering, resourceful **12** advantageous, concentrated, highly spiced, high-spirited, unmistakable **13** indefatigable, well-qualified **14** highly flavored, highly seasoned
Spanish: **5** macho

Strong
character in: **7** Erewhon
author: **6** Butler

strong-arm 3 cow **5** bully, force **6** coerce, compel **8** browbeat, threaten **10** intimidate

strong feeling 4 fear, hate, heat, love, zeal **5** anger, ardor **6** fervor, sorrow, warmth **7** despair, emotion, passion, sadness **8** jealousy **9** happiness, vehemence **12** satisfaction

stronghold 4 fort, hold, home, keep **6** bunker, center, locale, refuge **7** bastion, bulwark, citadel, rampart, redoubt **8** fastness, fortress, safehold, stockade **10** battlement, blockhouse **13** fortification

strongly committed 4 true **5** loyal **6** ardent **7** devoted, staunch, zealous **8** adhering, faithful **9** dedicated, steadfast **10** passionate, unwavering

strong point 5 forte **6** anchor **8** mainstay, strength

strong-willed 5 pushy **8** forceful, positive **9** assertive **10** aggressive **11** domineering, self-assured **13** self-assertive

structural support 3 bar **4** beam, prop, stud **5** brace, joist **6** girder, rafter, timber **7** trestle **12** underpinning

structure 4 form, plan **6** design, makeup **7** arrange, edifice, pattern **8** assemble, building, conceive, organize **9** construct, formation **11** arrangement, composition, put together **12** conformation, construction, organization **13** configuration

struggle 3 vie, war **4** duel, feud, pull, push, spar, tilt **5** argue, brawl, brush, clash, fight, grind, joust, labor, match, scrap, trial **6** action, battle, combat, differ, effort, engage, jostle, oppose, resist, strain, stress, strife, strive, tussle **7** compete, contend, contest, grapple, quarrel, scuffle **8** conflict, endeavor, exertion, long haul, skirmish, work hard **9** encounter, lock horns, take pains **10** engagement **11** altercation, cross swords **15** work like a Trojan **18** move heaven and earth **20** leave no stone unturned

strut 4 sail 6 parade, sashay 7 peacock, swagger 9 promenade

Struthiomimus
type: 8 dinosaur, theropod
known as: 15 ostrich dinosaur
period: 10 Cretaceous
characteristic: 9 toothless

Stryver
character in: 16 A Tale of Two Cities
author: 7 Dickens

Stuart, Gilbert
born: 15 North Kingston RI
artwork: 16 George Washington

Stuart, J E B
served in: 8 Civil War
side: 11 Confederate
commander of: 7 cavalry
battle: 7 Bull Run 8 Antietam 10 Gettysburg 14 Fredericksburg 16 Chancellorsville 18 Peninsular campaign

Stuart Little
author: 7 E B White

stub 3 end 4 bump, butt, dock, tail 5 crush, knock, snuff, stump 6 fag end, scrape 7 receipt, remains, tamp out, voucher 10 extinguish, torn ticket 11 counterfoil

stubble 5 beard 6 stumps 8 bristles, whiskers 9 cut stalks 16 five-o'clock shadow

stubborn 6 dogged, mulish, strong, sturdy 7 willful 8 forceful, obdurate, perverse, resolute 9 concerted, immovable, obstinate, pigheaded, resistant, tenacious, unbending, unmovable 10 bullheaded, headstrong, inflexible, persistent, purposeful, refractory, self-willed, unshakable, unyielding 11 indomitable, intractable, opinionated, uncompliant 12 hard to handle, recalcitrant, ungovernable, wholehearted

stubbornness 10 mulishness, obstinancy, resistance 11 willfulness 13 intransigence, pigheadedness

stubby 5 dumpy, pudgy, squab, squat, tubby 6 chubby, chunky, stocky, stodgy, stumpy 7 squatty 8 thickset

Stubtoe State
nickname of: 7 Montana

stuck 3 dug, put 4 held 5 bound, fixed, fused, glued, mired, poked 6 balked, curbed, jabbed, joined, nailed, pasted, pinned, placed, sealed, spiked, tacked, thrust, welded 7 adhered, affixed, boggled, impeded, planted, pricked, punched, saddled, snarled, speared, stabbed, stalled, stumped, stymied 8 attached, burdened, cemented, fastened, inserted 9 punctured 10 obstructed, perforated 11 immobilized

stuck-up 4 vain 5 cocky 6 snooty, uppish, uppity 7 haughty, high-hat 8 arrogant, snobbish 9 bigheaded, conceited 10 disdainful, egocentric, hoity-toity 11 overbearing, swellheaded 13 self-important, self-satisfied

stud 3 dot 4 beam, buck, dude, sire 5

board, rivet 6 button 7 upright 8 fastener, macho man, nailhead

student 4 coed 5 pupil 6 reader 7 analyst, learner, scholar, watcher 8 disciple, examiner, follower, observer, reviewer 9 collegian, schoolboy, spectator 10 schoolgirl 11 commentator, interpreter, matriculant 13 undergraduate

studied 8 measured 10 calculated, deliberate, purposeful 11 intentional 12 premeditated

studious 6 brainy, intent 7 bookish, earnest, erudite 8 academic, cerebral, diligent, literate, well-read 9 laborious, scholarly 10 determined, purposeful, scholastic 11 painstaking 12 intellectual

Studs Lonigan
series includes: 11 Judgment Day 12 Young Lonigan 29 The Young Manhood of Studs Lonigan
author: 13 James T Farrell

study 3 den 4 cram, read 5 grind, probe 6 office, peruse, review, search, studio, survey 7 examine, explore, inquiry, library, observe, reading 8 analysis, consider, learning, pore over, read up on, research, scrutiny 9 delve into, education 10 glance over, inspection, scrutinize 11 examination, exploration, hit the books, inquire into, instruction, investigate, read closely, reading room, scholarship 13 consideration, investigation, school oneself, search through

Study in Scarlet, A
author: 19 Sir Arthur Conan Doyle
character: 12 Dr John Watson 13 Jefferson Hope, Tobias Gregson 14 Sherlock Holmes 17 Inspector Lestrade

Study of History, A
author: 14 Arnold J Toynbee

stuff 3 act, bit, jam, pad, wad 4 best, bosh, bunk, cram, fill, gear, heap, load, pack, pile, sate, stow 5 cache, crowd, gorge, hokum, hooey, stash, store, thing, trash, wedge 6 burden, fill up, humbug, matter, staple, tackle, things, thrust, tricks, utmost 7 effects, essence, hogwash, overeat, rubbish, satiate, spinach, twaddle 8 darndest, falderal, material, nonsense 9 component, empty talk, substance 10 balderdash, belongings, gluttonize, ingredient, make a pig of 11 constituent, foolishness, overindulge, performance, possessions, raw material 12 quintessence 13 paraphernalia

stuff-and-nonsense 3 rot 4 bosh, bull, bunk 5 hokum, hooey, trash 6 bunkum, drivel, humbug 7 baloney, hogwash, spinach, twaddle 8 buncombe, claptrap, nonsense, tommyrot 9 poppycock 10 applesauce, balder-

dash, tomfoolery 11 foolishness 12 fiddlesticks 13 horsefeathers

stuffed 4 full 6 filled, jammed, loaded, packed, rammed, wadded 7 crammed, crushed, replete 8 overfull, satiated, squeezed 10 sandwiched

stuff in 4 cram, pack 6 devour 8 bolt down, compress, gobble up, wolf down

stuffing 5 farce 7 filling, packing, padding, wadding 8 dressing 9 forcemeat

stuffy 4 cold, smug 5 close, fusty, heavy, muggy, musty, staid 6 stodgy, sultry 7 airless, pompous 8 reserved, stagnant, stifling 9 clogged-up, congested, high-flown, stopped-up, stuffed-up 10 old-fogyish, oppressive, sweltering 11 pretentious, straitlaced, suffocating 12 supercilious, unventilated 13 ill-ventilated, self-satisfied, stale-smelling

stultify 4 balk 6 hinder, impair, impede, thwart 7 cripple, inhibit, nullify, vitiate 8 suppress 9 frustrate, hamstring 11 make useless

stumble 3 hit 4 fall, reel, roll, sway, trip 5 botch, lurch, pitch, spill 6 bungle, falter, happen, hash up, hobble, mess up, slip up, sprawl, topple, totter 7 blunder, misstep, shamble, stagger 8 flounder 10 take a spill 12 come by chance, make mistakes, pitch forward

stumble upon 4 find 7 learn of 8 come upon, discover 10 chance upon, happen upon 14 find by accident

stumbling block 3 bar, rub 4 snag 5 block, catch, hitch 6 hamper, hurdle 7 barrier, problem 8 drawback, obstacle 9 detriment, hindrance 10 difficulty, impediment 11 obstruction 12 complication, interference

stump 3 end 4 butt, foil, stub, thud 5 befog, clomp, clonk, clump, clunk, stamp, stomp, tramp 6 baffle, nubbin, stymie 7 confuse, mystify, nonplus, perplex 8 bewilder, confound, dumfound, footfall, stomping, tramping 9 bamboozle, dumbfound

stun 4 daze, numb 5 amaze, shock 7 astound, stagger, startle, stupefy 8 astonish, dumfound 9 dumbfound 11 flabbergast

stunner 4 doll 5 beaut, Venus 6 beauty, eyeful 8 knockout 9 dreamboat 10 good-looker

stunning 6 dazing, lovely 7 amazing, numbing 8 shocking, striking 9 beautiful, exquisite, startling 10 astounding, staggering, stupefying 11 astonishing, dumfounding 12 dumbfounding, electrifying 14 flabbergasting

stunt 3 act 4 curb, feat 5 abort, check, cramp, dwarf, limit, stint, trick 6 impede, number, stifle **7** curtail, delimit **8** restrain, restrict, suppress

stunted 5 dumpy, runty **6** bantam **7** dwarfed, squatty, wizened **9** pint-sized **13** foreshortened

Stunt Man, The
director: **11** Richard Rush
cast: **9** Alex Rocco **11** Peter O'Toole (Eli Cross) **13** Allen Goorwitz, Sharon Farrell **14** Barbara Hershey, Steve Railsback

stupefaction 5 shock **8** numbness, surprise **9** amazement **12** astonishment

stupefied 5 dazed **6** amazed **7** shocked, stunned **8** benumbed **10** dumbstruck, dumfounded **11** dumbfounded **13** flabbergasted, thunderstruck

stupefy 4 daze, stun **5** amaze, shock **7** astound, nonplus, stagger **8** astonish, confound, dumfound, surprise **9** dumbfound, overwhelm **11** flabbergast

stupefying 8 shocking, stunning **11** dumfounding **12** dumbfounding, electrifying, overwhelming **14** flabbergasting

stupendous 3 big **4** huge, vast **5** giant, great, jumbo **6** mighty **7** amazing, immense, mammoth, massive, titanic, unusual **8** colossal, enormous, fabulous, gigantic, imposing, stunning, terrific **9** cyclopean, herculean, marvelous, monstrous, very great, very large, wonderful **10** astounding, gargantuan, incredible, monumental, phenomenal, prodigious, remarkable, surprising, tremendous, unexpected **11** astonishing, elephantine **13** extraordinary

stupid 4 dull, dumb **5** dense, inane, inept, silly **6** absurd, oafish, obtuse, simple, unwise **7** aimless, asinine, boorish, doltish, fatuous, foolish, idiotic, moronic, witless **8** backward, childish, heedless, mistaken, reckless, tactless **9** brainless, cretinous, dimwitted, duncelike, foolhardy, ill-judged, imbecilic, imprudent, pointless, senseless **10** half-witted, ill-advised, indiscreet, irrelevant, weak-minded **11** empty-headed, meaningless, nonsensical, purposeless, thoughtless **12** absentminded, muddleheaded, preposterous, simpleminded, slow-learning, unreasonable **13** ill-considered, inappropriate, irresponsible, rattlebrained, unintelligent

stupor 4 daze **5** faint **6** apathy, torpor **7** inertia **8** blackout, lethargy, numbness **9** inertness **10** somnolence **12** stupefaction **13** insensibility

sturdy 4 able, firm **5** brave, burly, gutsy, hardy, heavy, solid, sound, stout, tough **6** daring, dogged, gritty, heroic, mighty, plucky, robust, rug-

ged, secure, sinewy, spunky, strong **7** defiant, doughty, durable, gallant, lasting, valiant **8** enduring, fearless, forceful, intrepid, muscular, powerful, resolute, spirited, stalwart, stubborn, vigorous, well-made **9** dauntless, strapping, unabashed, undaunted, well-built **10** courageous, determined, invincible **11** indomitable, substantial, unshrinking **12** high-spirited, stouthearted **15** well-constructed

Sturges, John
director of: **14** The Great Escape **19** The Magnificent Seven

Sturges, Preston
director of: **10** The Lady Eve **16** Sullivan's Travels **17** The Palm Beach Story, Unfaithfully Yours **21** Hail the Conquering Hero **24** The Miracle of Morgan's Creek

Sturmabteilung 13 storm troopers

Sturm und Drang 22 German literary movement (18th century)
literally: **14** storm and stress

stygian 3 dim **4** dark **5** black, murky **6** dreary, gloomy, somber **7** hellish **8** funereal, infernal, starless **9** tenebrous, unlighted

style 3 fad **4** call, elan, kind, mode, name, pomp, rage, sort, type **5** charm, class, craze, favor, flair, grace, model, taste, trend, vogue **6** design, luxury, manner, polish **7** arrange, comfort, fashion, pattern **8** currency, elegance **9** affluence, designate **10** smoothness **11** savoir faire
French: **4** gout

stylish 3 hip, new **4** chic **5** natty, smart, swank **6** dapper, latest, modern, modish, with-it **7** a la mode, elegant, in vogue, voguish **8** up-to-date **9** in fashion **11** fashionable **13** sophisticated, up-to-the-minute

stymie 4 balk **5** block, check, stump **6** baffle, hinder, puzzle, thwart **7** confuse, mystify **8** confound, obstruct **9** frustrate

Styracosaurus
type: **8** dinosaur **10** ceratopsid
location: **12** North America
period: **10** Cretaceous
characteristic: **6** horned

Styron, William
author of: **12** The Long March **13** Sophie's Choice **15** Darkness Visible **17** Lie Down in Darkness **18** Set This House on Fire **25** The Confessions of Nat Turner

Styx
form: **5** river
location: **5** Hades **10** underworld
father: **7** Oceanus
ferryman: **6** Charon

suave 6 silken, smooth, urbane **7** affable, elegant, politic **8** charming, gracious, mannerly, polished, unctuous **9**

civilized **10** diplomatic, flattering **12** ingratiating **13** smooth-tongued

sub 5 below, proxy, under **6** backup, deputy, second **7** beneath, standby, stand-in **9** alternate, submarine, surrogate **10** substitute, understudy **11** pinch-hitter

subaltern 4 aide **6** helper **9** assistant **10** lieutenant **11** subordinate

subconscious 3 dim **7** dawning **9** intuitive **10** subliminal **11** instinctive

subdivide 6 divide **7** split up **8** separate **9** partition

subdivision 3 arm **4** wing **6** branch **7** chapter, section **8** offshoot **11** development **12** neighborhood

subdue 3 bow **4** calm, curb, down, drub, ease, foil, mute, rout, trim, whip **5** allay, break, check, crush, floor, quell, salve, smash, still **6** deaden, defeat, master, mellow, muffle, reduce, soften, soothe, temper, thrash **7** appease, assuage, conquer, mollify, oppress, overrun, put down, relieve, slacken, subject, trample **8** mitigate, moderate, overcome, palliate, surmount, tone down, vanquish **9** meliorate, overpower, overwhelm, quiet down, soft-pedal, subjugate **10** ameliorate **11** triumph over **12** tranquillize

subdued 4 dull **5** cowed, muted, quiet **7** abashed, crushed, humbled, muffled, quelled **8** deadened, overcame **10** humiliated, indistinct, lackluster **11** intimidated, overpowered

subduer 6 victor, winner **9** conqueror, overcomer **10** subjugator, vanquisher **11** intimidator

subject 4 bare, case, gist, open, pith, text **5** field, issue, liege, motif, prone, study, theme, topic **6** affair, expose, liable, matter, submit, thesis, vassal **7** bound by, citizen, concern, exposed, lay open **8** business, disposed, follower, obedient, question **9** dependent, subjected, substance **10** answerable, discipline, in danger of, make liable, put through, vulnerable **11** stipulatory, subordinate, subservient, susceptible

subjection 11 subjugation **12** subservience **13** regimentation, subordination

subjective 5 inner **6** biased **7** partial **8** partisan, personal **9** emotional **10** individual, prejudiced **12** nonobjective

subjoin 5 add on, affix, annex **6** append, attach, tack on

subjugate 4 tame **5** crush, quell **6** subdue **7** conquer, put down **8** dominate, suppress, vanquish **10** over master

subjugation 6 chains, thrall **7** bondage, slavery **9** dominance, mastering, servitude, thralldom **10** conquering, domination **11** enslavement, vanquishing

subjugator 6 master, victor 7 subduer 9 conqueror, dominator 10 vanquisher 11 slavemaster

sublimate 4 turn 5 exalt, shift 6 divert, purify 7 channel, convert, elevate, ennoble 8 redirect, transfer 9 transform, transmute 12 spiritualize

sublime 4 high 5 grand, great, lofty, noble 6 superb 7 exalted, stately 8 elevated, imposing, majestic, splendid, terrific, very good 9 estimable, excellent, marvelous, wonderful 12 awe-inspiring, praiseworthy

submarine
　　invented by: 7 Holland
　　even keel: 4 Lake
　　torpedo: 8 Bushnell

submerge 4 dive, sink 5 douse, drown, flood, souse 6 deluge, engulf, go down, plunge 7 go under, immerse 8 inundate, pour over, submerse

submerse 5 drown 6 engulf 7 immerse 8 inundate, submerge

submersion 7 sinking 8 drowning 9 immersion 10 inundation 11 submergence

submission 8 giving in, meekness, tameness, yielding 9 handing in, obedience, passivity, surrender, tendering 10 compliance, remittance, submitting 11 passiveness 12 acquiescence, capitulation, presentation, subservience, tractability 13 nonresistance 14 submissiveness

submissive 4 meek, mild 6 docile, humble, pliant 7 dutiful, fawning, passive, servile, slavish 8 crawling, obedient, toadying, yielding 9 compliant, malleable, tractable, truckling 10 obsequious 11 acquiescent, bootlicking, complaisant, deferential, subservient, unassertive 12 capitulating, ingratiating, nonresisting 13 accommodating

submissiveness 8 docility, meekness 9 passivity 10 compliance 11 resignation 12 complaisance, tractability

submit 3 bow 4 bend, cede 5 agree, argue, claim, defer, kneel, offer, stoop, yield 6 accede, assert, commit, comply, give in, give up, resort, tender 7 contend, hold out, present, proffer, propose, succumb, suggest 8 back down, put forth 9 acquiesce, surrender, volunteer 10 capitulate, put forward 12 knuckle under

submit an offer 3 bid 6 tender 7 proffer, propose

submit to 4 bear, take 5 abide, brave, brook, stand 6 endure, suffer 7 stomach, undergo 8 stand for, tolerate 9 put up with

subnormal 3 bad, low 5 seedy, sorry 6 crummy, dismal, shabby, sleazy, subpar 7 abysmal 8 below par, inferior, mediocre, wretched 9 defective, deficient 10 inadequate, second-rate 11 below normal, substandard 12 insufficient

subordinate 4 help 5 lower 6 junior, lackey, lesser, menial, worker 7 servant, subject 8 hireling, inferior 9 ancillary, assistant, attendant, auxiliary, dependent, of low rank, outranked, secondary, subaltern, underling 10 subsidiary 11 subservient

subordination 10 subjection 11 inferiority, subjugation 12 subservience 13 regimentation

suborn 5 bribe 6 buy off, pay off

sub rosa 8 covertly, in secret, on the sly, secretly 9 in private, privately 12 off-the-record 14 confidentially 15 behind-the-scenes 17 behind closed doors

subscribe 4 help, sign 6 assent, chip in, donate 7 consent, endorse, support 8 hold with 9 undersign 10 contribute

subsequent 4 next 7 ensuing 9 following, proximate 10 consequent, succeeding, successive

subsequently 2 so 5 after, later, since 9 afterward, following 10 succeeding 12 consequently

subservient 6 docile, menial 7 fawning, servile, slavish, subject 8 cringing, toadying 9 accessory, ancillary, auxiliary, prostrate, truckling 10 obsequious, subsidiary 11 bootlicking, subordinate, sycophantic 12 contributory, ingratiating

subside 3 ebb, sag 4 calm, drop, ease, sink, wane 5 abate, let up 6 cave in, lessen, recede, settle, shrink 7 descend, dwindle 8 decrease, diminish, level off, melt away, moderate

subsidence 5 letup 6 easing, ebbing, waning 7 calming 9 abatement, dwindling, lessening, recession, shrinking 10 decreasing, inactivity, moderation 12 diminishment

subsidiary 5 extra, lower, minor 6 branch, junior, lesser 7 adjunct 8 addition, division, inferior 9 accessory, affiliate, auxiliary, secondary 10 additional, supplement 11 subordinate 12 supplemental 13 supplementary

subsidy 3 aid 4 gift 5 award, grant 7 backing, support 9 allotment, provision 10 fellowship, grant-in-aid, honorarium, subvention 11 scholarship, sponsorship 13 appropriation, assistantship

subsist 4 live 5 exist 7 survive 9 stay alive 11 feed oneself, support life 12 make ends meet 23 keep body and soul together

subsistence 6 living, upkeep 7 support 8 survival 10 livelihood, sustenance 11 maintenance, nourishment

substance 4 body, core, germ, gist, pith, soul 5 force, heart, means, money, sense, stuff 6 burden, import, intent, marrow, matter, riches, thrust, wealth 7 element, essence, keynote, purport, reality 8 backbone, material, property, solidity 9 actuality, affluence, basic idea, main point 10 ingredient 11 connotation, constituent, corporality 12 corporeality, quintessence 13 corporealness

substandard 3 bad 4 poor 5 awful, lousy 6 crummy, shoddy 8 below par, inferior, terrible 9 imperfect 10 second-rate 11 second-class 12 below average

substantial 3 big 4 firm, full 5 ample, bulky, large, massy, solid, sound 7 massive, sizable 8 abundant 9 plenteous, plentiful 10 monumental 12 considerable

substantiate 5 prove 6 verify 7 confirm, support, sustain 11 corroborate, demonstrate 12 authenticate

substantiated 6 proved, proven 7 factual 8 verified 9 supported 11 well-founded 12 corroborated, demonstrated, well-grounded 13 authenticated

substantiation 5 proof 8 evidence 11 affirmation 12 verification 13 corroboration, demonstration, documentation 14 authentication

substitute 3 act 6 backup, change, ersatz, fill in, switch 7 standby, stand in, stopgap 8 deputize, exchange, pinch-hit, take over 9 alternate, makeshift, surrogate, temporary 10 understudy 11 alternative, pinch hitter, replacement

substitution 5 shift 6 change, switch 8 exchange, swapping 9 variation 10 alteration 11 replacement

substructure 4 base 6 ground 10 foundation, groundwork 12 underpinning

subsume 5 cover 6 assume, deduce 7 explain, include, involve 8 consider 13 subcategorize

subterfuge 4 ruse, sham, wile 5 blind, dodge, guile, shift, trick 6 scheme 7 evasion 8 artifice, intrigue, pretense, scheming 9 casuistry, chicanery, deception, duplicity, imposture, sophistry, stratagem 10 camouflage, sneakiness 11 deviousness, evasiveness, game-playing, machination, make-believe, smoke screen

subtle, subtile 3 sly 4 cagy, deft, fine, foxy, keen, wily 5 light, quick, sharp, slick 6 artful, astute, clever, crafty, expert, shifty, shrewd, tricky 7 cunning, devious, elusive, refined 8 delicate, indirect, masterly, skillful 9 deceptive, designing, ingenious, underhand 10 discerning 11 understated 13 perspicacious, sophisticated 14 discriminating

Subtle

character in: 12 The Alchemist
author: 6 Jonson

subtleties 7 nuances **10** fine points **11** refinements **12** distinctions

subtract 6 deduct, detach, lessen, reduce, remove **8** decrease, diminish, take away, withdraw

subtraction 7 removal **8** decrease **9** deduction, lessening, reduction **10** diminution, taking away, withdrawal **11** diminishing

suburbs 8 environs, vicinity **9** outskirts, periphery, precincts

sub verbo 12 under the word **15** under the heading

subversion 4 fall, ruin **6** defeat, mutiny **8** disorder, sabotage **9** overthrow, rebellion **10** corruption, disruption **11** destruction

subversive 7 traitor **8** quisling **9** insurgent, seditious **10** incendiary, traitorous, treasonous **11** seditionary **12** collaborator **13** revolutionary **14** fifth columnist **15** insurrectionary **16** collaborationist

subvert 3 mar **4** ruin, undo **5** smash, spoil, upset, wreck **6** defile, poison, ravage **7** despoil, destroy, disrupt, shatter **8** demolish, overturn **9** devastate, overthrow, undermine **11** contaminate

sub voce 21 under the specified word
literally: 13 under the voice

subway 2 El **4** tube **5** metro, train **11** underground
New York City line: 3 BMT, IND, IRT
San Francisco: 4 BART

succeed 3 hit, win **5** avail, catch, click **6** accede, do well, follow, move up **7** inherit, prevail, prosper, replace, triumph **8** make a hit, make good, supplant, take over **9** bear fruit, strike oil

succeed at 2 do **6** attain **7** execute, fulfill, perform, realize **8** carry out **9** make a go of **10** accomplish

succeeding 5 later **6** coming, future **7** ensuing **8** oncoming **9** following, impending, posterior **10** consequent, subsequent, successive

succeed to 6 follow **7** inherit **15** ascend the throne

succes d'estime 15 critical success

success 3 hit **4** fame **5** smash **7** triumph, victory **8** conquest **9** affluence **10** ascendancy, attainment, prosperity **11** achievement, advancement, fulfillment, good fortune

successful 4 rich **6** proven **7** perfect, wealthy, well-off **8** achieved, affluent, complete, fruitful, thriving **9** effective **10** prosperous, triumphant **11** efficacious, flourishing **12** accomplished, acknowledged

successful completion 7 success, victory, winning **9** execution **10** making good **11** achievement, culmina-

tion, fulfillment, realization **12** consummation **14** accomplishment

succession 3 run **5** chain, cycle, round, train **6** course, series **8** sequence **9** accession **10** assumption, procession, stepping-up, taking over **11** inheritance, progression

successive 7 ensuing **10** continuous, succeeding **11** consecutive

successor 4 heir **5** donee **7** devisee, heiress, heritor, legatee **8** follower, parcener **9** heritress, joint heir **10** co-parcener, substitute **11** beneficiary, replacement, reversioner **12** heir apparent

succinct 4 neat **5** brief, crisp, pithy, short, terse, tight **6** direct, gnomic **7** clipped, compact, concise, summary **9** condensed **10** aphoristic, to the point **12** epigrammatic

succinctness 7 brevity **9** crispness, terseness **11** compactness, conciseness **12** condensation

succor 3 aid **4** help **5** nurse **6** assist, back up, relief, shield, wait on **7** comfort, nurture, protect, relieve, support, sustain **8** befriend **10** assistance, minister to, sustenance, take care of **11** helping hand, lend a hand to, maintenance **13** accommodation

succulent 5 juicy **6** fleshy **9** toothsome **10** appetizing

succumb 3 die **5** yield **6** accede, expire, give in, submit **7** defer to, give way, go under **8** pass away **9** surrender **10** capitulate, comply with **12** fall victim to

such as
Latin: 2 eg **13** exempli gratia

such is life
French: 9 c'est la vie

sucker 3 sap **4** boob, butt, dupe, fool, goat, gull, jerk, mark **5** chump, patsy **6** pigeon, victim **7** cat's-paw, fall guy **8** easy mark, fair game, pushover **9** schlemiel, soft touch **11** sitting duck

Sucker State
nickname of: 8 Illinois

suck up 6 absorb, soak up **7** drink in **8** sponge up **9** swallow up

Sucre
legal capital of: 7 Bolivia

Sudan
capital/largest city: 8 Khartoum
others: 3 Waw, Yei **4** Juba **5** Kosti, Meroe, Nyala, Obeid, Opari, Segon **6** Atbara, Suakin **7** Aluboyd, Elobeid, Geneina, Kassala, Malakal **8** El-fasher, Omdurman **9** al-Ubayyid, El-geneina, Port Sudan, Wad Medani
division: 7 Jonglei **9** Upper Nile **12** Bahr el Ghazal **16** Eastern Equatoria, Western Equatoria
  ancient kingdom: 4 Alwa, Funj, Kush **7** Maqurra
measure: 2 ud

monetary unit: 5 pound **8** piastres
weight: 5 habba
lake: 2 No **4** Chad, Toad **6** Nasser
mountain: 4 Nuba **7** Imatong **9** Dongotona **10** Jabal Marra, Jebel Marra **18** Ethiopian Highlands
highest point: 7 Kinyeti
river: 4 Nile **5** Sobat **6** Atbara **8** Blue Nile **9** White Nile **10** Bahr el-Arab **11** Bahr el-Jebel **12** Bahr el-Ghazal
sea: 3 Red
physical feature:
  desert: 6 Libyan, Nubian
  gum forest: 8 Kordofan
  plain: 6 Gezira
  sandstorm: 6 haboob
  plateau: 8 Kordufan
  swamp: 4 Sudd
people: 3 Bor, Dor, Fur **4** Arab, Bari, Beri, Bobo, Daza, Egba, Fula, Golo, Nuba, Nuer, Poul, Sere **5** Anuak, Bongo, Dinka, Fulah, Hausa, Joluo, Junje, Mosgu, Mossi, Negro, Tibbu, Volta **6** Acholi, Azande, Gurusi, Hamite, Lotuho, Makari, Nilote, Nubian, Senufo, Surhai, Tuareg **7** Balante, Baqqara, Gubayna, Jaaliin, Nilotes, Shilluk, Songhai, Songhay, Songhoi, Sourhai **8** Kababish, Mandingo, Menkiera **9** Sarakille **10** Gurmantshi, Shaiquiyya
  leader: 5 Mahdi **9** al-Nimeiry **10** Mehemet Ali **22** Jaafar Mohammed al-Nemery
language: 2 Ga **3** Efe, Ewe, Ibo, Kru, Vak, Vei **4** Efik, Mole, Tshi **6** Arabic, Nubian, Yoruba **7** English **8** Mandango, Mandingo **9** Ta Bedawie
religion: 5 Islam **7** animism **12** Christianity
place:
  canal: 7 Jonglei
  dam: 6 Sennar **8** Roseires **10** Jebel Aulia
  temple: 4 Lion
  tomb: 5 Mahdi
feature:
  boat: 6 murkab
food: 4 dura **5** dukhn, kisra

Sudanese Republic see **4** Mali

sudden 4 rash **5** hasty, quick, rapid **6** abrupt, speedy **7** instant **9** immediate, impetuous **10** surprising, unexpected, unforeseen **11** precipitate, unlooked-for **13** instantaneous, unanticipated, unforeseeable

suddenly 7 quickly **8** abruptly, in no time **9** all at once, instantly, on the spot **11** in an instant **12** all of a sudden, unexpectedly **13** at short notice **14** without warning **21** in the twinkling of an eye

sudden movement 4 dart, jolt **5** flash, spurt

sudden noise 3 pop **4** bang, clap, slam **5** burst, crash **6** report **9** explosion

Sudermann, Hermann

author of: 5 Honor **8** Dame Care **14** The Song of Songs

suds 3 ale **4** beer, brew, foam **5** draft, froth, lager **10** malt liquor

sue 3 beg **4** pray **5** plead **6** appeal **7** beseech, entreat, implore **8** petition **9** importune **10** supplicate

Sue, Eugene (Marie-Joseph)
author of: 15 The Wandering Jew **19** The Mysteries of Paris

suffer 4 ache, bear, hurt, pine **5** stand **6** endure, grieve, lament **7** agonize, despair, drop off, fall off, stomach, sustain, undergo **8** bear with, feel pain, tolerate **9** go through, put up with, withstand **10** be impaired **11** deteriorate

suffer for 6 pay for **8** atone for **9** answer for

suffering 3 woe **4** ache, care, hurt, pain, pang **5** agony, dolor, grief, throe, trial **6** misery, sorrow, twinge **7** anguish, anxiety, torment, torture, travail **8** distress, soreness **9** heartache **10** affliction, discomfort, heavy heart, irritation **11** tribulation

suffice 2 do **4** last, meet, pass **5** avail, get by, serve **6** answer, make do **7** fulfill, qualify, satisfy

sufficiency 6 enough, plenty **7** surfeit **8** adequacy **9** abundance, ampleness, profusion

sufficient 5 ample **6** enough, plenty **7** copious, minimal **8** abundant, adequate **9** plenteous, plentiful **11** up to the mark **12** satisfactory

suffocate 3 gag **5** choke **6** quench, stifle **7** garrote, smother **8** snuff out, strangle, throttle **10** asphyxiate, extinguish

suffuse 4 fill, soak **5** cover, steep **6** infuse **7** diffuse, overrun, pervade **8** overflow, permeate, saturate **9** transfuse **10** impregnate, infiltrate, overspread

Sugar State
nickname of: 9 Louisiana

sugary 5 mushy, sweet **6** syrupy **7** cloying, fulsome, gushing, honeyed, mawkish **8** cajoling, unctuous **10** flattering, saccharine

suggest 3 bid **4** move, urge **5** imply, posit **6** advise, hint at, submit **7** advance, counsel, propose **8** advocate, indicate, intimate, propound **9** give a clue, recommend **16** lead one to believe

suggested 6 hinted **7** implied, oblique **8** implicit, indirect, possible, proposed

suggestion 3 dab, tip **4** dash, hint, tint **5** grain, shade, taste, tinge, touch, trace **6** advice, urging **7** counsel, feeling, pointer, soupcon **9** prompting, suspicion **10** intimation, sprinkling **11** exhortation **14** recommendation

suggestive 4 lewd, racy **5** bawdy, loose 6** risque, sexual, wanton **8** allusive, improper, indecent, off-color, prurient, unseemly **9** evocative, remindful, seductive, shameless **10** expressive, indelicate, licentious **11** provocative, reminiscent, stimulating

sui generis 6 unique **10** one of a kind
sui juris 14 of one's own right
suit 3 fit **4** duds, garb, plea, togs **5** befit, court, getup, habit, match **6** appeal, attire, become, beseem, follow, livery, oblige, outfit, please, prayer, wooing **7** apparel, begging, clothes, content, costume, delight, gladden, gratify, raiment, satisfy, uniform **8** clothing, entreaty, jell with, make glad, petition **9** addresses, agree with, conform to, courtship, do one good, overtures, tally with, trappings **10** accord with, attentions, comply with, fall in with, habiliment, lovemaking, square with **11** accommodate, go along with **12** be becoming to, blandishment, correspond to, dovetail with, solicitation, supplication **13** accoutrements, be agreeable to, harmonize with **14** be acceptable to, be convenient to **15** be appropriate to **16** be appropriate for

suitable 3 apt, fit **4** meet **5** right **6** proper, seemly, worthy **7** apropos, fitting, germane **8** adequate, becoming, relevant **9** befitting, congruous, cut out for, pertinent, qualified **10** applicable, seasonable **11** appropriate **12** commensurate

suitcase 3 bag **4** grip **6** valise **7** satchel **8** knapsack, rucksack **9** duffel bag, gladstone, two-suiter **11** portmanteau **12** overnight bag, traveling bag

suite 3 set **4** flat **5** chain, court, group, rooms, round **6** convoy, series **7** company, cortege, retinue **8** servants **9** apartment, followers, following **10** attendants **11** progression

suited 3 fit **7** adapted, attired, clothed, dressed, good for, matched **8** adjusted, agreeing, becoming **9** agreeable **11** appropriate, harmonizing

suit of armor 4 mail **5** armor **9** chain mail **10** coat of mail

suitor 4 beau, love **5** flame, lover, swain, wooer **6** fellow **7** admirer, gallant **8** young man **9** boyfriend **10** sweetheart

sulfur
chemical symbol: 1 S

sulk 4 crab, fret, fume, mope, pout **5** brood, chafe, frown, grump, scowl **6** glower, grouch **7** grumble **8** be in a pet, be miffed, be put out, be sullen, look glum **9** be in a huff **11** be resentful **12** be out of humor

sulky 6 morose, sullen **7** pouting **8** petulant

sullen 4 blue, dark, glum, grim, sore, sour **5** cross, heavy, moody, sulky, surly **6** crabby, dismal, dreary, gloomy, grumpy, morose, somber, touchy **7** crabbed, doleful, forlorn, grouchy, peevish **8** brooding, desolate, dolorous, funereal, mournful, petulant, scowling **9** cheerless, glowering, resentful, saturnine, splenetic, unamiable **10** depressing, foreboding, ill-humored, ill-natured, melancholy, out of humor, out of sorts, unsociable **11** ill-tempered **13** temperamental
French: 8 farouche

sullied 5 dirty **6** impure, soiled **7** defiled, stained, unclean **9** tarnished

Sullivan, John L (Lawrence)
nickname: 15 Boston Strong Boy
sport: 6 boxing
class: 11 heavyweight
fought: 12 bareknuckled

Sullivan, Louis H
architect of: 16 Guaranty (now Prudential) Building (Buffalo NY) **18** Auditorium Building (Chicago), Wainwright Building (St Louis MO) **21** Carson Pirie Scott Store (Chicago), Stock Exchange Building (Chicago), Merchants' National Bank (Grinnell, IA), National Farmers' Bank (Owatonna, MN)
principle: 21 "form follows function"
student: 16 Frank Lloyd Wright

Sullivan, Pat
creator/artist of: 11 Felix the Cat

Sullivan's Travels
director: 14 Preston Sturges
cast: 10 Joel McCrea **12** Veronica Lake **13** Robert Warwick **15** William Demarest

sully 4 ruin, soil, spot **5** dirty, spoil, stain **6** befoul, defame, defile, smudge **7** begrime, besmear, blemish, corrupt, pollute, tarnish **8** disgrace, dishonor **10** adulterate **11** contaminate

Sully, Thomas
born: 7 England **10** Horncastle
artwork: 13 Queen Victoria **23** The Passage of the Delaware **28** Colonel Thomas Handasyd Perkins **29** Washington Crossing the Delaware

sultan 4 king **5** ruler **7** emperor, monarch **9** sovereign

sultana 5 grape **6** raisin **7** empress **11** sultan's wife

sultry 3 hot **4** sexy **5** close, humid, muggy **6** erotic, stuffy, sweaty **7** sensual **8** stifling **10** oppressive, sweltering, voluptuous **11** provocative, suffocating

sum 4 cash, coin, jack **5** bread, bucks, dough, funds, score, tally, whole **6** amount, moolah **7** lettuce, measure **8** currency, entirety, quantity, sum total, totality **9** aggregate, summation

sumac 4 Rhus
varieties: 5 dwarf, lemon, scrub, sugar, swamp **6** desert, laurel, poi-

son, smooth, velvet **7** scarlet, shining, tanner's, tobacco, wing-rib **8** fragrant, lemonade, Sicilian, staghorn, Venetian **9** elm-leaved, evergreen, Virginian **11** small-leaved **12** sweet-scented

sum and substance 4 core, crux, gist, guts, meat **5** heart **7** essence **10** brass tacks **11** nitty-gritty

Sumatra
   chevrotain: **4** napu
   city: **5** Medan **6** Padang **9** Palembang
   country: **9** Indonesia
   crop: **3** tea **6** coffee, rubber
   currency: **6** rupiah
   empire: **9** Srivijaya
   highest point: **10** Mt Kerintji
   inhabitant: **5** Batak, Malay **11** Minangkabau
   mountain range: **7** Barisan
   river: **4** Musi, Siak **6** Asahan
   squirrel shrew: **4** tana
   strait: **5** Sunda **7** Malacca

Sumerian Mythology *see* **19** Babylonian Mythology

summa cum laude 17 with highest praise

summarily 6 at once **7** quickly **8** directly, promptly, speedily **9** forthwith, on the spot **11** arbitrarily, immediately, straightway **12** straightaway, with dispatch, without delay **13** at short notice, precipitately

summarize 5 sum up **6** digest **7** abridge, outline **8** abstract, compress, condense **9** capsulize, epitomize, synopsize **10** abbreviate **11** concentrate **12** recapitulate

summary 4 curt **5** brief, hasty, rapid, short, terse, token **6** apercu, digest, precis, resume, sketch, sudden, survey **7** concise, cursory, epitome, hurried, rundown **8** abridged, abstract, analysis, succinct, syllabus, synopsis **9** breakdown, condensed **10** abridgment, peremptory **11** perfunctory **12** abbreviation, condensation, short version **13** instantaneous

Summa Theologiae
   author: **13** Thomas Aquinas

summation 5 total **6** review **7** summary **8** addition **9** reckoning **19** concluding statement

Summer and Smoke
   author: **17** Tennessee Williams
   director: **14** Peter Glenville
   cast: **9** Una Merkel **10** Rita Moreno **12** Earl Holliman **13** Geraldine Page **14** Laurence Harvey

summerhouse 5 arbor, cabin, kiosk **6** cabana, gazebo, pagoda **7** cottage

Summerson, Esther
   character in: **10** Bleak House
   author: **7** Dickens

Summertime
   director: **9** David Lean
   based on story by: **14** Arthur Lau-

rents (The Time of the Cuckoo)
   cast: **10** Isa Miranda **13** Darren McGavin, Rossano Brazzi **16** Katharine Hepburn
   setting: **6** Venice

summery 3 hot **4** warm **5** balmy, close, humid, muggy, sunny **6** stuffy, sultry, torrid, vernal **8** aestival, roasting, stifling, sunshiny **9** scorching, temperate **10** oppressive, summerlike

summit 3 tip, top **4** acme, apex, peak **5** crest, crown **6** apogee, climax, height, vertex, zenith **8** pinnacle **11** culmination **12** highest point **13** crowning point

summon 4 call **5** rouse **6** beckon, call on, draw on, gather, invoke, muster, strain **7** call for, call out, command, send for **8** activate, subpoena **9** call forth **12** call together

summons 4 call **8** citation, subpoena **12** notification

summon up 4 stir **5** evoke **6** arouse, excite **7** collect, marshal, provoke **8** assemble **9** call forth, stimulate

summum bonum 9 chief good **11** highest good

sumptuous 4 dear, posh, rich **5** grand, plush, regal **6** costly, deluxe, lavish, superb **7** elegant **8** splendid **9** elaborate, expensive, luxurious **10** exorbitant, munificent **11** extravagant, magnificent, spectacular

sumptuousness 4 luxe **6** luxury **8** elegance, grandeur, richness, splendor **12** magnificence **13** expensiveness, luxuriousness

sum total 6 amount **8** totality **9** aggregate **11** final result

sum up 3 add **5** tally, total, tot up **6** reckon **7** compute, count up **9** calculate, enumerate, summarize

sun
   god of: **2** Ra, Re **3** Sol, Utu **5** Horus **6** Apollo, Helios **7** Shamesh **8** Hyperion

Sun Also Rises, The
   author: **15** Ernest Hemingway
   character: **10** Bill Gorton, Jake Barnes, Robert Cohn **11** Pedro Romero **15** Lady Brett Ashley, Michael (Mike) Campbell

sunbathe 3 tan **4** bask **12** soak up the sun **13** catch some rays

Sunday
   means: **11** day of the sun
   heavenly body: **3** sun
   day of: **4** rest **7** worship **8** blue laws
   observance: **16** Christian Sabbath
   French: **8** dimanche
   Italian: **8** domenica
   Spanish: **7** domingo
   German: **7** sonntag

Sunday best 6 finery **8** glad rags **11** fine clothes **16** best bib and tucker

sunder 4 rend, rive **5** crack, sever **6**

cleave, divide **8** separate **9** tear apart **10** break in two **11** break in half

sundown 4 dusk **6** sunset **7** evening **8** eventide, twilight **9** nightfall

Sundowners, The
   director: **13** Fred Zinnemann
   cast: **11** Deborah Kerr, Dina Merrill, Glynis Johns **12** Peter Ustinov **13** Robert Mitchum
   setting: **9** Australia

sundry 4 many **5** mixed **6** divers, motley, myriad, varied **7** diverse, several, various **8** assorted, manifold, numerous **9** different **12** multifarious **13** heterogeneous, miscellaneous

sun-filled 4 fair **5** clear, sunny **6** bright, cheery **8** cheerful **9** cloudless

sunfish 5 dwarf, perch, pigmy, sunny **6** redear **7** lepomis, longear, teleost **8** bluegill, sailboat **9** blackband **10** Sacramento **11** bluespotted, centrarchid, pumpkinseed, yellowbelly

sunflower 10 Helianthus **12** Balsamorhiza
   varieties: **4** ashy **5** giant, showy, stiff, swamp **6** common, desert, Oregon **7** dark-eye, Mexican **8** thin-leaf **10** Maximilian **12** cucumber-leaf

Sunflower State
   nickname of: **6** Kansas

sunless 4 dark, dull, gray, hazy **5** bleak, foggy, misty, murky, rainy **6** cloudy, dismal, dreary, gloomy, leaden, somber **8** overcast **9** cheerless **10** depressing

sunny 4 fair, fine **5** clear, happy, jolly, merry **6** blithe, breezy, bright, cheery, genial, jovial, joyful, joyous, sunlit **7** affable, amiable, buoyant, shining, smiling **8** cheerful, sunshiny **9** brilliant, cloudless, sparkling, unclouded **10** optimistic **12** lighthearted

sunrise 4 dawn **5** sunup **6** aurora **7** dawning **8** cockcrow, daybreak, daylight **10** break of day, crepuscule, newborn day **15** dawn's early light **16** rosy-fingered dawn

sunset 4 dusk **7** sundown **8** blue hour, eventide, gloaming, twilight **9** nightfall **10** close of day, crepuscule

Sunset Boulevard
   director: **11** Billy Wilder
   cast: **8** Jack Webb **9** Fred Clark **11** Hedda Hopper **12** Buster Keaton **13** Cecil B DeMille, Gloria Swanson (Norma Desmond), William Holden **16** Erich von Stroheim

Sunset State
   nickname of: **6** Oregon

sunshade 3 hat **5** visor **6** awning **7** parasol, roundel **8** sombrero, umbrella

Sunshine State
   nickname of: **7** Florida **9** New Mexico

sunstone
   species: **8** feldspar

suntan 3 tan 5 brown 6 bronze 7 sunburn

suo jure 14 in one's own right

suo loco 14 in one's own place 19 in one's rightful place

Suomen Tasavalta *see* 7 Finland

Suomi *see* 7 Finland

sup 3 eat, sip 4 dine, feed 5 drink, feast, supra 6 absorb, supper, supply 7 consume 8 superior 10 supplement 11 superlative 13 supplementary

super 4 A-one, fine 5 grand, great, prime, prize, swell 6 grade-A, superb, tip-top 7 capital 8 peerless, superior, terrific, top-notch 9 excellent, fantastic, first-rate, marvelous, matchless, non pareil, superfine, wonderful 10 first-class, tremendous, unexcelled, world-class 11 outstanding, superlative 12 incomparable 13 extraordinary

superabound 4 teem 5 swarm 6 thrive 7 burgeon 8 be rich in, flourish, overflow

superabundance 4 glut, riot 5 flood, spate 6 deluge, excess, plenty 7 surfeit, surplus 8 overdose, overflow, pleonasm, plethora 9 avalanche 10 inundation, oversupply, redundance 11 superfluity 12 extravagance 13 overabundance 14 more than enough **French:** 19 embarras de richesses

superabundant 4 lush 6 lavish 7 copious, profuse, teeming 8 swarming, thriving 9 exuberant, luxuriant 10 burgeoning 11 flourishing, overflowing

superb 4 A-one, rare, rich 5 elect, grand, regal 6 choice, costly, deluxe, golden, lordly, select, tip-top 7 elegant, stately 8 gorgeous, imposing, laudable, majestic, peerless, precious, princely, splendid, top-notch, very fine 9 admirable, excellent, expensive, exquisite, first-rate, luxurious, marvelous, matchless, priceless, sumptuous, top-drawer 10 first-class 11 crackerjack, magnificent 12 breathtaking, praiseworthy 15 of the first water

Super Bowl
1967:
    winner: 15 Green Bay Packers
    loser: 16 Kansas City Chiefs
    site: 8 Coliseum 10 Los Angeles
1968:
    winner: 15 Green Bay Packers
    loser: 14 Oakland Raiders
    site: 5 Miami 10 Orange Bowl
1969:
    winner: 11 New York Jets
    loser: 14 Baltimore Colts
    site: 5 Miami 10 Orange Bowl
1970:
    winner: 16 Kansas City Chiefs
    loser: 16 Minnesota Vikings
    site: 10 New Orleans 13 Tulane Stadium
1971:

    winner: 14 Baltimore Colts
    loser: 13 Dallas Cowboys
    site: 5 Miami 10 Orange Bowl
1972:
    winner: 13 Dallas Cowboys
    loser: 13 Miami Dolphins
    site: 10 New Orleans 13 Tulane Stadium
1973:
    winner: 13 Miami Dolphins
    loser: 18 Washington Redskins
    site: 8 Coliseum 10 Los Angeles
1974:
    winner: 13 Miami Dolphins
    loser: 16 Minnesota Vikings
    site: 7 Houston 11 Rice Stadium
1975:
    winner: 18 Pittsburgh Steelers
    loser: 16 Minnesota Vikings
    site: 10 New Orleans 13 Tulane Stadium
1976:
    winner: 18 Pittsburgh Steelers
    loser: 13 Dallas Cowboys
    site: 5 Miami 10 Orange Bowl
1977:
    winner: 14 Oakland Raiders
    loser: 16 Minnesota Vikings
    site: 8 Pasadena, Rose Bowl
1978:
    winner: 13 Dallas Cowboys
    loser: 13 Denver Broncos
    site: 9 Superdome 10 New Orleans
1979:
    winner: 18 Pittsburgh Steelers
    loser: 13 Dallas Cowboys
    site: 5 Miami 10 Orange Bowl
1980:
    winner: 18 Pittsburgh Steelers
    loser: 14 Los Angeles Rams
    site: 8 Pasadena, Rose Bowl
1981:
    winner: 14 Oakland Raiders
    loser: 18 Philadelphia Eagles
    site: 9 Superdome 10 New Orleans
1982:
    winner: 23 San Francisco Forty-Niners
    loser: 17 Cincinnati Bengals
    site: 7 Pontiac 10 Silverdome
1983:
    winner: 18 Washington Redskins
    loser: 13 Miami Dolphins
    site: 8 Pasadena, Rose Bowl
1984:
    winner: 17 Los Angeles Raiders
    loser: 18 Washington Redskins
    site: 12 Tampa Stadium
1985:
    winner: 23 San Francisco Forty-Niners
    loser: 13 Miami Dolphins
    site: 8 Palo Alto 15 Stanford Stadium
1986:
    winner: 12 Chicago Bears
    loser: 18 New England Patriots
    site: 9 Superdome 10 New Orleans

1987:
    winner: 13 New York Giants
    loser: 13 Denver Broncos
    site: 8 Pasadena, Rose Bowl
1988:
    winner: 18 Washington Redskins
    loser: 13 Denver Broncos
    site: 8 San Diego 17 Jack Murphy Stadium
1989:
    winner: 23 San Francisco Forty-Niners
    loser: 17 Cincinnati Bengals
    site: 5 Miami 16 Joe Robbie Stadium
1990:
    winner: 23 San Francisco Forty-Niners
    loser: 13 Denver Broncos
    site: 9 Superdome 10 New Orleans
1991:
    winner: 13 New York Giants
    loser: 12 Buffalo Bills
    site: 5 Tampa 12 Tampa Stadium
1992:
    winner: 18 Washington Redskins
    loser: 12 Buffalo Bills
    site: 9 Metrodome 11 Minneapolis
1993:
    winner: 13 Dallas Cowboys
    loser: 12 Buffalo Bills
    site: 8 Pasadena, Rose Bowl
1994:
    winner: 13 Dallas Cowboys
    loser: 12 Buffalo Bills
    site: 7 Atlanta 11 Georgia Dome
1995:
    winner: 23 San Francisco Forty-Niners
    loser: 16 San Diego Chargers
    site: 5 Miami 9 Joe Robbie
1996:
    winner: 13 Dallas Cowboys
    loser: 18 Pittsburgh Steelers
    site: 5 Tempe 8 Sun Devil
1997:
    winner: 15 Green Bay Packers
    loser: 18 New England Patriots
    site: 9 Superdome 10 New Orleans
1998:
    winner: 13 Denver Broncos
    loser: 15 Green Bay Packers
    site: 8 San Diego
1999:
    winner: 13 Denver Broncos
    loser: 14 Atlanta Falcons
    site: 5 Miami 9 Pro Player

supercilious 5 proud 6 lordly, snooty, uppity 7 haughty, pompous, stuck-up 8 arrogant, prideful, snobbish 10 disdainful 11 egotistical, magisterial, overbearing, patronizing 12 vainglorious 13 condescending, high-and-mighty, self-important

superciliousness 4 airs 7 hauteur 8 snobbery 9 arrogance, pomposity 10 lordliness, snootiness 11 haughtiness 12 snobbishness 14 disdainfulness

superficial 4 slim 5 faint, outer, silly, trite 6 flimsy, hollow, myopic, slight 7 cursory, minimal, nodding, partial, passing, shallow, summary, surface 8 exterior, mindless, skin-deep 9 desultory, frivolous 10 incomplete 11 empty-headed, perfunctory 12 lacking depth, narrow-minded, on the surface

superficiality 6 myopia 9 frivolity 11 cursoriness, shallowness 13 desultoriness 16 narrow-mindedness, short-sightedness

superfine 4 A-one 6 choice, grade-A, superb, tip-top 8 superior, top-notch 9 excellent, extra fine, first-rate 10 first-class 11 outstanding, overrefined, superlative 13 extraordinary

superfluity 3 fat 5 extra, frill 6 excess, luxury 7 greater, surfeit, surplus 8 overflow, overmuch, plethora 11 gingerbread 12 extravagance 13 embellishment 14 superabundance

superfluous 5 extra, spare 6 excess 7 surplus 8 needless 9 excessive, redundant 10 extraneous, gratuitous, pleonastic 11 inessential, unnecessary 12 nonessential, overgenerous 13 superabundant, supernumerary 14 supererogatory

superhuman 4 epic 5 great 6 divine, heroic 7 godlike, supreme 8 superior 9 herculean, unearthly 10 miraculous, omnipotent 12 otherworldly, supermundane, supernatural, supranatural, transcendent 13 preternatural

superintend 3 run 4 boss 6 direct, govern, manage 7 oversee 8 supervise, watch over 10 administer 12 administrate, have charge of

superintendence 6 charge 7 bossing, running 9 direction, governing 10 leadership, management, overseeing 12 jurisdiction 14 administration

superintendent 4 boss, head 5 chief 6 warden 7 foreman, headman, manager, proctor, steward 8 director, guardian, overseer 9 custodian 10 supervisor

superior 4 boss, fine 5 chief 6 better, choice, deluxe, leader, lordly, senior 7 greater, haughty, notable 8 arrogant, foremost, higher-up, peerless, snobbish 9 commander, excellent, first-rate, imperious, matchless, nonpareil, unrivaled 10 inimitable, noteworthy, preeminent, supervisor 11 exceptional, illustrious, patronizing 12 incomparable, more advanced, vainglorious 13 condescending, distinguished, high-and-mighty
French: 13 par excellence

superlative 4 best 5 crack, prime 6 expert 7 supreme 8 foremost, greatest, peerless, superior 9 exquisite, first-rate, matchless, nonpareil, paramount, unequaled, unmatched, unrivaled 10 consummate, preeminent,

surpassing 11 magnificent, unsurpassed 12 incomparable, transcendent, unparalleled 15 of the first water 17 of the highest order

superman
German: 10 Ubermensch
Superman
artist: 11 Jerry Siegel
creator: 10 Joe Shuster
character: 4 Lara 5 Jor-el, Kal-el 8 Eben Kent, Lois Lane, Sy Horton 9 Clark Kent 10 Jimmy Olsen, Martha Kent, Perry White 22 Inspector Bill Henderson 23 Professor JJ Pepperwinkle
place: 7 Krypton 10 Metropolis, Smallville 14 telephone booth
nickname: 10 Man of Steel
director: 13 Richard Donner
cast: 9 Glenn Ford, Ned Beatty 11 Gene Hackman 12 Jackie Cooper, Margot Kidder (Lois Lane), Marlon Brando 14 Valerie Perrine 16 Christopher Reeve

supernatural 6 mystic, occult 7 psychic 9 spiritual, unearthly 10 miraculous, paranormal 12 otherworldly, supranatural 13 preternatural, superphysical 14 transcendental

superpatriotism 8 jingoism 10 chauvinism 11 nationalism

supersede 7 discard, replace, succeed 8 displace, set aside, supplant

supervise 4 boss, head 5 guide 6 direct, govern, handle, manage, survey 7 conduct, control, oversee 8 regulate 9 look after, watch over 10 administer 11 preside over, superintend 12 have charge of

supervision 6 orders 7 control 8 guidance 9 direction 10 governance, government, management, regulation 12 surveillance 15 superintendence

supervisor 4 boss, head 5 chief 7 foreman, manager, steward 8 director, overseer 9 commander 13 administrator 14 superintendent

supper club 4 cafe 6 bistro 7 cabaret 9 nightclub, night spot

supplant 6 depose 7 replace 8 displace 9 supersede 14 take the place of

supple 5 lithe 6 limber, pliant 7 elastic, lissome, plastic, pliable 8 amenable, bendable, flexible, graceful, yielding 9 adaptable, compliant, malleable, tractable 10 submissive 11 acquiescent, complaisant, coordinated

supplement 5 add to, annex, extra, rider 6 extend, insert 7 adjunct, augment, codicil, section 8 addendum, addition, appendix, increase 9 added part, corollary, extension 10 attachment, complement, postscript 12 augmentation

supplementary 5 added, extra 6 backup 7 added on, reserve 8 appended, attached, expanded, extended

9 ancillary, auxiliary, enlarging, secondary 10 additional, amplifying, augmenting 11 subordinate 13 complementary

suppliant 5 asker 6 beggar, cadger, seeker, suitor 7 almsman 8 claimant 9 almswoman, appellant, beseecher, entreater, mendicant 10 petitioner, supplicant 11 supplicator
Suppliants, The
author: 9 Aeschylus
character: 6 Danaus 8 Pelasgus 19 Fifty Sons of Aegyptus 20 Fifty Maiden Daughters
Suppliants, The
author: 9 Euripides
character: 6 Aethra, Evadne 7 Theseus 8 Adrastus

supplicate 3 ask, beg 4 pray 5 plead 6 ask for 7 entreat 8 appeal to, call upon, petition

supplication 3 cry 4 plea, suit 6 appeal, orison, prayer 7 bumming, cadging, request 8 entreaty, mooching, petition 10 invocation 11 application, beseechment, imploration, imprecation, panhandling 12 solicitation

supplies 4 gear 5 goods, items 8 material 9 equipment, foodstuff, trappings 10 provisions 13 accoutrements

supply 4 fund, give 5 cache, equip, grant, quota, stock, store, yield 6 bestow, outfit, render 7 deal out, deliver, furnish, present, provide, reserve 9 providing, provision, reservoir 10 allocation, come up with, contribute, furnishing 12 provisioning

support 3 aid 4 base, bear, help, hold, keep, lift, pile, post, prop, stay 5 abide, boost, brace, brook, carry, favor, means, shore, stand 6 assist, back up, bear up, clinch, column, defend, endure, foster, hold up, pay for, pillar, ratify, second, succor, suffer, uphold, upkeep, verify 7 backing, bear out, bolster, comfort, confirm, defense, endorse, espouse, finance, further, keeping, nurture, shore up, sustain, warrant 8 abutment, accredit, advocacy, advocate, buttress, champion, espousal, maintain, pedestal, pilaster, sanction, strength, tolerate, vouch for 9 establish, guarantee, patronage, patronize, promotion, put up with, reinforce, stanchion, subsidize 10 assistance, livelihood, provide for, stand up for, stick up for, strengthen, sustenance, underwrite 11 buttressing, consolation, corroborate, countenance, furtherance, go along with, involvement, maintenance, subsistence 12 substantiate, underpinning 13 encouragement

supportable 9 endurable 10 defensible, verifiable 11 sustainable 12 demonstrable, maintainable

supporter 4 ally 6 backer, helper, pa-

tron 8 adherent, advocate, champion, defender, disciple, follower, partisan, upholder 10 benefactor, well-wisher 11 sympathizer

supposable 8 credible 9 thinkable 10 believable, imaginable 11 conceivable, perceivable

suppose 5 fancy, guess, judge, posit 6 assume, divine, gather, reckon 7 believe, imagine, presume, surmise, suspect 8 conceive, consider 9 predicate 11 hypothesize 14 take for granted

supposed 5 given 7 alleged, assumed 8 probable, putative 9 imaginary 11 conjectural, speculative, theoretical 12 hypothetical

supposition 4 idea, view 5 given, guess 6 belief, notion, theory, thesis 7 opinion, surmise 9 guesswork, postulate, suspicion 10 assumption, conjecture, hypothesis 11 predication, presumption, proposition, speculation

suppress 4 bury, curb, hide 5 check, crush, quash, quell, still 6 keep in, muffle, quench, squash, stifle, subdue 7 conceal, control, cover up, inhibit, put down, repress, silence, smother, squelch 8 hold back, keep back, overcome, restrain, restrict, snuff out, withhold 9 overpower 10 extinguish, keep secret, put an end to 11 hold in leash, keep private 12 put a damper on 13 put under wraps

suppressant 4 curb 5 brake 7 control 9 restraint

suppressed feelings 7 reserve 9 restraint 10 constraint, diffidence

supremacy 5 power 7 mastery, primacy 10 ascendancy, domination, precedence 11 omnipotence, paramountcy, preeminence, sovereignty, superiority 13 transcendency

supreme 4 tops 5 chief, first, prime 6 ruling 7 extreme, highest, leading, perfect, topmost 8 absolute, dominant, foremost, peerless 9 matchless, nonpareil, paramount, principal, sovereign, unequaled, unlimited, unmatched, unrivaled, uppermost 10 commanding, consummate, unexcelled 11 all-powerful, superlative, unqualified, unsurpassed 12 front-ranking, immeasurable, incomparable, second to none, unparalleled

Supreme Court
  Chief Justices: 3 Jay (John) 4 Taft (William Howard) 5 Chase (Salmon), Stone (Harlan Fiske), Taney (Roger Brooke), Waite (Morrison), White (Edward) 6 Burger (Warren), Fuller (Melville), Hughes (Charles Evans), Vinson (Frederick), Warren (Earl) 8 Marshall (John), Rutledge (John) 9 Ellsworth (Oliver), Rehnquist (William)
  Associate Justices: 5 Black (Hugo), Story (Joseph), White (Byron) 6

Breyer (Stephen), Fortas (Abe), Holmes (Oliver Wendell), Powell (Lewis), Scalia (Antonin), Souter (David), Thomas (Clarence) 7 Brennan (William), Cardozo (Benjamin), Douglas (William O), Kennedy (Anthony), O'Connor (Sandra Day), Stevens (John), Stewart (Potter) 8 Blackmun (Harry), Brandeis (Louis), Ginsburg (Ruth Bader), Goldberg (Arthur), Marshall (Thurgood) 11 Frankfurter (Felix)
  Cases: 15 Marbury v Madison 17 Gideon v Wainwright 18 McCulloch v Maryland 20 Griswold v Connecticut
    abortion: 8 Roe v Wade
    antitrust: 8 E C Knight 11 Standard Oil 15 Swift and Company 22 American Tobacco Company
    civil rights: 9 Bakke Case 15 Plessy v Ferguson 30 Brown v Board of Education of Topeka
    Japanese internment: 22 Korematsu v United States 24 Hirabayashi v United States
    rights of accused: 15 Miranda v Arizona 17 Escobedo v Illinois
    slavery: 13 Dred Scott Case 14 Scott v Sandford

surcease 4 quit, rest, stop 5 abate, cease, pause 7 die away, respite 8 conclude, leave off 11 come to an end, discontinue 17 come to a standstill

surcharge 3 tax 4 levy 6 excise, impost

surcingle 4 band, belt 5 girth 6 girdle 8 cincture

sure 4 fast, firm, true 5 solid, sound 6 stable, steady 7 assured, certain 8 accurate, fail-safe, faithful, flawless, positive, reliable, surefire, unerring 9 confident, convinced, unfailing 10 dependable, infallible, undoubting 11 trustworthy 12 never-failing

sure bet 4 fact 5 cinch 7 reality 9 actuality, certainty, sure thing 13 inevitability 14 inescapability

surely 7 no doubt 8 of course, to be sure 9 assuredly, certainly, doubtless 10 by all means, definitely, for certain, infallibly, positively 11 come what may, indubitably, undoubtedly, without fail 12 emphatically, without doubt 14 unquestionably

sureness 6 surety 9 assurance, certainty, certitude 10 confidence 11 assuredness 12 positiveness 13 self-assurance 14 conclusiveness, self-confidence, self-possession

sure thing 4 fact 5 cinch 7 reality, sure bet 9 actuality, certainty 13 inevitability 14 inescapability

surety 4 bail, bond 8 sureness 9 certainty, certitude, guarantee 10 confidence 12 positiveness

surface 3 top 4 coat, face, skin 5

crust, shell 6 facade, finish, veneer 7 coating, outside 8 covering, exterior 11 superficies

Surface family
  characters in: 19 The School for Scandal
  member: 6 Joseph 7 Charles 9 Sir Oliver
  author: 8 Sheridan

surfeit 4 cloy, glut, sate 5 gorge, stuff 6 excess 7 satiate, satisfy, surplus 8 overmuch, plethora 9 plenitude, profusion, repletion, satiation 10 oversupply, surplusage 11 exorbitance, overindulge, prodigality, superfluity 12 extravagance 13 overabundance 14 more than enough, superabundance 15 supersaturation

surfeited 4 full 5 sated 6 gorged 7 glutted, replete, stuffed 8 overfull, satiated 9 satisfied

surge 4 rush, wave 5 flood, swell 7 torrent

Suriname
  other name: 7 Surinam 11 Dutch Guiana
  capital/largest city: 10 Paramaribo
  others: 6 Albina 7 Totness 9 Groningen 10 Brokopondo, Onverwacht 13 Nieuw Nickerie 14 Nieuw Amsterdam
  measure: 7 ketting
  monetary unit: 4 cent 7 guilder
  lake: 14 Van Blommestein
  mountain: 4 Emma 6 Kayser, Oranje 10 Tumuc Humac, Wilhelmina 13 Eilerts II Haan, Van Ach Van Wyck 15 Guiana Highlands
  highest point: 10 Julianatop
  river: 6 Maroni 7 Surinam 8 Nickerie, Suriname 9 Coppename 10 Courantijn, Courantyne, Tapanahoni
  ocean: 8 Atlantic
  physical feature:
    falls: 7 Kaiteur
  people: 4 Boni, Bush, Trio 5 Djuka, Dutch 6 Creole, Wayana 7 African, Chinese 10 Amerindian, Boschneger, West Indian 11 Asian Indian
    settler: 22 Lord Willoughby of Parham
  language: 5 Carib, Dutch, Hindi 6 Arawak 7 English 8 Javanese, Taki-Taki 10 Hindustani 11 Sranan Tongo 12 Sranang Tongo
  religion: 5 Hindu, Islam 10 Protestant 13 Roman Catholic
  feature:
    canoe: 6 corial
    clothing: 4 sari 5 dhoti 6 kamisa, sarong 10 kotomissie
    hat: 3 fez
    hut: 5 benab
    scarf: 9 selendong
    tree: 4 dali, lana, mora 5 dalli, genip, icica 7 acuyari, quassia 9 bethabara

food:
  drink: **7** paiwari

surliness 8 ill humor, rudeness **9** bad temper **11** discourtesy, grouchiness **12** irascibility

surly 4 rude, sour **5** cross, gruff, harsh, testy **6** abrupt, crusty, grumpy, sullen, touchy **7** bearish, crabbed, grouchy, hostile, peevish, uncivil, waspish **8** choleric, churlish, insolent, petulant, snappish, snarling **9** irascible, splenetic, unamiable **10** ill-humored, ill-natured, unfriendly **11** bad-tempered **12** discourteous

surmise 4 deem, idea **5** guess, infer, judge, opine, posit, think **6** belief, notion **7** believe, imagine, opinion, presume, suppose, suspect, thought **8** conclude, consider, theorize **9** suspicion **10** assumption, conjecture, hypothesis, presuppose **11** hypothesize, presumption, speculation, supposition **13** shot in the dark

surmount 3 top **4** best **5** clear, climb, scale, worst **6** defeat, master **7** conquer, get over **8** overcome, vanquish **11** prevail over, triumph over **14** get the better of

surpass 3 top **4** beat, best **5** excel, outdo **6** exceed, outrun **7** eclipse **8** go beyond, outclass, outshine, outstrip, override **9** rise above, transcend **10** overshadow **11** go one better, leave behind, outdistance, triumph over **12** be better than, be superior to **13** have it all over

surplus 4 glut **5** extra **6** excess **7** overage, surfeit **8** leftover, overflow, plethora, residual **10** oversupply, surplusage **11** superfluity, superfluous **14** overproduction

surprise 4 stun **5** amaze, shock **6** ambush, wonder **7** astound, nonplus, set upon, stagger, startle, stupefy **8** astonish, confound, discover, dumfound, fall upon **9** amazement, bombshell, burst in on, dumbfound, take aback **10** defy belief, pounce upon, revelation, wonderment **11** flabbergast, incredulity, astonishment, take unawares **13** boggle the mind

surprise attack
  French: **10** coup de main

surrender 4 cede **5** forgo, let go, waive, yield **6** accede, forego, give up, render, submit, vacate **7** abandon, concede, forsake **8** delivery, forgoing, give over, giving up, hand over, part with, renounce, turn over, yielding **9** deliver up, foregoing **10** capitulate, relinquish, submission **11** lay down arms **12** capitulation, renunciation **14** relinquishment **15** throw in the towel **16** show the white flag

surreptitious 6 covert, hidden, secret, veiled **7** furtive **8** hush-hush, stealthy **9** concealed, secretive **10** undercover

surrogate 6 acting, deputy **7** interim, stand-in **9** temporary **10** substitute **11** provisional

surround 4 belt, ring **5** hedge, hem in **6** circle, enfold, engird, girdle, shut in **7** close in, compass, enclose, envelop, fence in, hedge in **8** encircle **9** encompass **12** circumscribe

surrounding area 7 suburbs **8** environs, vicinity **9** outskirts, precincts

surroundings 5 scene **6** milieu **7** habitat, setting **8** ambience, environs **10** atmosphere, conditions **11** environment **13** circumstances
  French: **11** mise en scene

surveillance 5 vigil, watch **8** scrutiny, trailing **11** observation **13** eavesdropping

survey 4 plot, poll, scan **5** gauge, graph, plumb, probe, scout, study **6** fathom, review **7** canvass, delimit, examine, inspect, measure, observe **8** analysis, block out, consider, look over, overview **10** scrutinize **11** contemplate, reconnoiter **12** pass in review **13** investigation

survival 5 relic **6** living **7** atavism, vestige **8** hangover **9** carry-over, throwback **11** subsistence **12** continuation, keeping alive

survive 4 last **5** abide, exist **6** endure, hang on, live on **7** hold out, outlast, outlive, persist, prevail, subsist **8** be extant, continue **9** keep alive **11** live through

surviving 6 extant **7** abiding, lasting **8** enduring, existent, existing, living on **9** hanging on, outliving, to be found **10** continuing, holding out, outlasting, persistent, persisting, subsisting **11** in existence **13** living through

Susann, Jacqueline
  author of: **14** The Love Machine **15** Once Is Not Enough **16** Valley of the Dolls

Susanna
  husband: **6** Joakim
  accused of: **8** adultery
  saved by: **6** Daniel

susceptible 4 open **5** prone **7** alive to, subject **8** liable to, sensible **9** sensitive **10** disposed to, responsive, vulnerable **11** conducive to, receptive to, sensitive to, sympathetic

suspect 5 doubt, fancy, guess, judge, opine, posit, think **7** believe, imagine, presume, suppose, surmise **8** distrust, misdoubt, mistrust, question, theorize **9** speculate **10** conjecture **11** hypothesize, wonder about **14** alleged culprit, be suspicious of **19** have one's doubts about

suspend 4 halt, hang, quit, stay, stop **5** cease, check, defer, delay, sling, swing, table **6** append, arrest, dangle, put off, shelve **7** reserve **8** break off, cut short, leave off, postpone, with-

hold **9** interrupt, stop short **10** put an end to **11** discontinue **12** bring to a stop **18** bring to a standstill

suspenders 6 braces, straps **7** gallows, garters, hangers **8** elastics, galluses **10** supporters

suspense 7 anxiety, tension **8** edginess **9** curiosity **10** indecision **11** expectation, incertitude, uncertainty **12** anticipation **15** indetermination

suspenseful 7 anxious **8** dramatic, exciting **9** climactic, uncertain

suspension 4 stay **5** pause **6** hiatus, recess **7** tabling **8** abeyance, deferral **12** postponement **14** discontinuance

suspicion 4 idea **5** guess, hunch **6** notion **7** feeling, surmise **8** distrust, mistrust **10** conjecture, hypothesis **11** supposition

Suspicion
  director: **15** Alfred Hitchcock
  cast: **9** Cary Grant **10** Nigel Bruce **12** Joan Fontaine **13** Dame May Whitty **15** Cedric Hardwicke
  Oscar for: **7** actress (Fontaine)

suspicious 4 wary **5** shady **7** dubious, suspect **8** doubtful, doubting, slippery **9** ambiguous **10** untrusting **11** distrustful, incredulous, mistrustful, open to doubt **12** disbelieving, questionable **13** untrustworthy

sustain 4 bear, feed, prop **5** abide, brave, brook, stand **6** bear up, endure, hold up, keep up, suffer, uphold **7** nourish, nurture, prolong, support, undergo **8** maintain, protract, tolerate, underpin **9** keep alive, withstand **10** experience **12** carry on under **14** hold out against

sustenance 4 food, gear **5** bread, means **6** living **7** aliment, support **9** provender **10** provisions **11** maintenance, nourishment, subsistence
  heaven-sent: **5** manna

sustineo alas 16 I sustain the wings
  motto of: **10** US Air Force

Sutherland, Donald
  born: **6** Canada, St John **12** New Brunswick
  roles: **4** MASH **5** Klute **13** Hawkeye Pierce **14** Eye of the Needle, Ordinary People **16** Fellini's Casanova **17** The Eagle Has Landed **26** Invasion of the Body Snatchers

Sutpen, Colonel Thomas
  character in: **14** Absalom Absalom
  author: **8** Faulkner

Suva
  capital of: **4** Fiji

Suzanne
  character in: **19** The Marriage of Figaro
  author: **12** Beaumarchais

svelte 4 fine, lean, neat, slim, thin, trim **5** lithe, spare **7** elegant, lissome, shapely, slender, willowy **8** graceful **9** sylphlike

Svengali
  character in: 6 Trilby
  author: 9 Du Maurier

Sverige *see* **6** Sweden

swab 3 dab, mop **4** daub, lout, wipe **5** clean, cloth, patch, scrub **6** cotton, sponge **7** cleanse **8** specimen
  brand name: 4 Q-tip

swagger 5 strut, sweep **6** parade, sashay, stride **7** saunter **11** swashbuckle

swaggerer 6 gascon **7** boaster, bragger **8** blowhard, braggart, strutter **11** braggadocio

swain 4 beau **6** fellow, suitor **7** admirer, gallant **8** cavalier, young man **9** boyfriend **10** sweetheart

swallow 3 bit, nip, sip **4** down, gulp, swig **5** drink, quaff, swill, taste **6** credit, devour, gobble, guzzle, hold in, imbibe, ingest, tipple **7** believe, fall for, repress **8** gulp down, hold back, keep back, mouthful, suppress, withhold

swallow up 5 drown, eat up, swamp **6** absorb, engulf **7** consume, envelop **8** inundate **9** overwhelm **10** assimilate

swallow words 6 mumble, mutter

swamp 3 bog, fen **4** fill, mire, moor, ooze, quag, sink, slew, slue **5** bayou, beset, flood, marsh, swale **6** deluge, engulf, morass, slough **7** besiege, bottoms, envelop **8** inundate, quagmire, submerge, wash over **9** everglade, marshland, overwhelm, snow under, swallow up

swamped 7 deluged, flooded, glutted, overrun **9** inundated **11** overwhelmed

Swan
  constellation of: 6 Cygnus

swan
  young: 6 cygnet
  group of: 4 bevy

swank 4 airs **5** ritzy **6** la-di-da, snooty, swanky **9** high-class, top-drawer **11** pretensions, pretentious **12** affectations, ostentatious **15** pretentiousness **16** superciliousness

swanky 4 chic, posh, rich **5** fancy, grand, jazzy, plush, ritzy, sharp, showy, smart, swank **6** flashy, snazzy, spiffy, sporty **7** dashing, elegant, splashy, stylish **9** sumptuous **11** fashionable

Swan Lake
  composer: 11 Tchaikovsky

Swanson, Gloria
  real name: 25 Gloria Josephine Mae Swenson
  born: 9 Chicago IL
  husband: 12 Wallace Beery
  roles: 13 Sadie Thompson, The Trespasser **15** Sunset Boulevard

swap 5 trade **6** barter, dicker, switch **7** bargain **8** exchange **11** give and take

sward 3 sod **4** lawn, rind, skin, turf **5** grass

swarm 4 herd, host, mass, rush, teem **5** cloud, crowd, drove, flock, horde, press, surge **6** abound, legion, myriad, stream, throng **7** cluster, overrun **8** stampede **9** multitude

swarthy 4 dark **5** dusky, swart, tawny **6** brunet **8** brunette **11** dark-skinned **12** brown-colored, brown-skinned, olive-skinned **14** dark-complected **16** dark-complexioned

swashbuckler 9 buccaneer, daredevil **10** adventurer

swashbuckling 4 bold **7** dashing **8** boasting **9** audacious, daredevil

swat 3 hit, tap **4** bash, belt, slam, slap, slug, sock **5** clout, knock, smack, smite, whack **6** buffet, strike, thwack, wallop **7** clobber

swathe 4 bind, wrap **5** cloak, cover **6** encase, enfold, enwrap **7** envelop, sheathe, swaddle

sway 4 bend, grip, hold, lead, list, move, reel, rock, roll, rule, spur, vary, wave **5** alter, clout, impel, power, reign, rouse, shift, swing, waver **6** change, domain, incite, induce, prompt, swerve, totter, waving, wobble **7** command, control, dispose, mastery, stagger, swaying **8** hesitate, iron hand, motivate, persuade, swinging, to-and-fro, undulate **9** authority, direction, encourage, fluctuate, influence, oscillate, pendulate, pulsation, stimulate, vacillate **10** domination, government, predispose, suzerainty, undulation **11** fluctuation, oscillation **12** back and forth, dictatorship, jurisdiction, manipulation

Swaziland
  capital/largest city: 7 Mbabane
  others: 5 Bunya, Hluti, Mpaka, Nsoko, Stegi **6** Gollel, Mhlume **7** Big Bend, Lobamba, Manzini **8** Havelock, Malkerns **9** Geodgegun, Hlatikulu, Mankaiana, Mankayana, Nhlangano, Pigg's Peak, Rocklands
  government: 22 constitutional monarchy
  head of state: 4 king
  monetary unit: 4 rand **9** lilangeni
  mountain: 8 Highveld **11** Drakensberg
  highest point: 7 Emlembe
  river: 5 Usutu **6** Komati, Lomati **8** Mhlatuze, Ngwavuma, Umbeluzi, Umbuluzi
  physical feature:
    forest: 5 Usutu
    plateau: 7 Lebombo, Lubombo
  people: 5 Asian, Bantu, Swazi **11** Eurafricans
    king: 3 Kbe **5** Nyama **6** Mswati **7** Sobhuza
    prince: 6 Sozisa
  language: 5 Ngumi **7** English, Siswati

  9 Afrikaans **10** Portuguese
  religion: 7 animism **10** Protestant **13** Roman Catholic
  feature:
    bride payment: 6 lobolo
    god: 14 Mkhulumngcandi
    ritual dance: 7 Incwala

swear 3 vow **4** aver, avow, cuss **5** curse, vouch **6** adjure, assert, attest, pledge **7** certify, promise, warrant **9** blaspheme **10** take an oath, utter oaths **11** bear witness

swear by 7 believe, count on **9** believe in **10** put faith in

sweat 4 ooze, toil **5** exude, worry **6** effort **7** agonize **8** drudgery, hard work, perspire **9** exudation **12** perspiration

sweaty 3 wet **6** clammy, sticky **10** perspiring

Sweden
  other name: 7 Sverige
  capital/largest city: 9 Stockholm
  others: 4 Lund, Umea **5** Boden, Boras, Edane, Falun, Gavle, Lulea, Malmo, Pitea, Visby **6** Arvika, Kiruna, Orebro **7** Uppsala **8** Goteborg, Jokkmokk, Vasteras **9** Jonkoping, Linkoping, Sundsvall **10** Eskilstuna, Gottenburg, Norrkoping, Skelleftea **11** Halsingborg
  school: 4 Lund **7** Uppsala **8** Goteborg **9** Stockholm
  division: 3 Lan **4** Laen **5** Skane **6** Kalmar, Orebro **7** Dalarna, Gotland, Lapland **8** Alvsborg, Blekinge, Elfsborg, Gotaland, Jamtland, Malmohus, Norrland, Svealand
  government: 22 constitutional monarchy
    legislature: 7 Riksdag
  head of state: 4 king
  measure: 3 aln, fot, ret **4** alar, amar, famn, kapp, last, stop **5** carat, foder, kanna, linje, nymil, spann **6** fathom, jumfru **7** oxhuvud, tunland **8** fjarding, koltunna, tunnland
  monetary unit: 3 ore **5** krona, krone **7** carolin **8** skilling **9** rigsdaler
  weight: 3 ass, lod **4** last, mark, sten **5** carat **6** nylast **7** centner, lispund **8** skalpund, skeppund **9** shippound
  island: 5 Oland **7** Gotland
  lake: 4 Ster **5** Asnen, Malar, Silja, Vaner **6** Vanern, Vetter, Wenner **7** Hielmar, Malaren, Vattern **8** Dalalven **9** Hjalmaren
  mountain: 4 Sarv **5** Ammar **6** Helags, Kjolen, Ovniks, Sarjek **7** Kjollen
  highest point: 5 Kebne **10** Kebnekaise
  river: 3 Dal **4** Gota, Klar, Lule, Pite, Umea **5** Indal, Kalix, Lulea, Pitea, Ranea, Torne **6** Lainio, Muonio **7** Ljusnan **8** Angerman
  sea: 6 Baltic **8** Atlantic
  physical feature:
    canal: 4 Gota
    gulf: 7 Bothnia

sound: 6 Kalmar
strait: 7 Oresund **8** Kattegat **9** Skagerrak
people: 4 Lapp **5** Norse, Swede **6** Viking
  actress: 9 Liv Ullman **10** Greta Garbo **13** Ingrid Bergman
  astronomer: 7 Celsius **8** Angstrom
  author: 8 Lagerlof **10** Lagerkvist, Strindberg
  diplomat: 12 Hammarskjold
  director: 13 Ingmar Bergman **14** Arne Sucksdorff
  inventor: 5 Nobel
  king: 4 Vosa, Wasa **5** Oscar **6** Gustav **8** Gustavus **10** Carl Gustav **12** Gustav Adolph **13** Charles Gustav **22** Jean Baptiste Bernadotte
  philosopher/scientist: 10 Swedenborg
  queen: 9 Christina
  scientist: 8 Linnaeus
language: 4 Lapp **7** Swedish
religion: 19 Evangelical Lutheran
place:
  castle: 9 Gripsholm
  center of Stockholm: 11 Gamla Staden
  park: 7 Skansen **12** Millesgarden
  theater: 18 Drottningholm Court
  walled city: 5 Visby
food: 11 smorgasbord
  cheese: 7 fontina **8** jarlberg **9** jarlsberg
  dish: 10 kottbullar
  drink: 5 glogg **7** aquavit

Swedish Punch
  type: 7 liqueur
  origin: 6 Sweden
  base: 3 rum
  with gin: 5 Biffy
  with vermouth: 9 Grand Slam

Sweeney Among the Nightingales
  author: 7 T S Eliot

sweep 3 arc, fly **4** dart, dash, race, rush, scud, tear, zoom **5** hurry, spell, swing, swish, swoop, whisk **6** charge, gather, scurry, stroke **7** stretch **8** distance

sweeping 5 broad **7** blanket, radical **9** extensive, out-and-out, wholesale **10** exhaustive, large-scale, widespread **11** far-reaching, wide-ranging **12** all-inclusive **13** comprehensive, thoroughgoing

sweepings 4 dirt, dust **6** refuse

sweep off one's feet 7 enchant **8** bedazzle **9** captivate, overpower, overwhelm

sweet 4 dear, kind, nice **5** candy, fresh **6** dulcet, mellow, smooth, sugary **7** amiable, cloying, darling, dessert, lovable, nonsalt, not salt, tuneful **8** fragrant, pleasant, pleasing **9** agreeable, melodious, sweetmeat, wholesome **10** attractive, confection, euphonious, saccharine **11** good-natured, melliflu-

ous, silver-toned, sympathetic **12** nonfermented

Sweet Bird of Youth
  director: 13 Richard Brooks
  based on play by: 17 Tennessee Williams
  cast: 8 Ed Begley **10** Paul Newman **13** Geraldine Page, Shirley Knight **17** Madeleine Sherwood
  Oscar for: 15 supporting actor (Begley)

sweetheart 4 beau, dear, love **5** flame, honey, lover, swain **6** fiance, old man, steady, suitor **7** beloved, darling, fiancee, old lady **8** ladylove, mistress, true love **9** boyfriend, inamorata, valentine **10** girlfriend, lady friend **15** gentleman friend
  French: 6 cherie

sweet life
  Italian: 9 dolce vita

Sweet Mama Stringbean
  nickname of: 11 Ethel Waters

sweetmeats 5 candy **6** sweets **7** bonbons **10** sugar candy **11** confections **13** confectionery

sweet-natured 5 sweet **6** benign, gentle, kindly **7** likable, lovable **8** pleasant **13** compassionate

sweetness
  French: 7 douceur

sweet roll 3 bun **6** Danish **7** cruller **8** doughnut **10** coffee cake **11** cinnamon bun

sweets 5 candy **7** goodies **8** desserts **10** sugar candy, sweetmeats **11** confections **13** confectionery

sweet-scented 8 aromatic, fragrant, perfumed, redolent

sweet-smelling 5 spicy **7** scented **8** aromatic, fragrant, perfumed, redolent **9** odiferous

sweet talk 6 cajole, praise **7** blarney, flatter **8** cajolery, flattery, soft soap **10** compliment **11** endearments, loving words **13** blandishments **14** fond utterances

Sweetwater
  nickname of: 16 Nathaniel Clifton

sweet words 7 blarney **8** flattery, soft soap **9** sweet talk **12** honeyed words

swell 3 fop, wax **4** A-one, fine, good, grow, okay, puff, rise, wave **5** bloat, bulge, dandy, great, heave, mount, super, surge, throb, widen **6** billow, blow up, comber, expand, extend, fatten, puff up **7** amplify, breaker, burgeon, distend, inflate, stretch, thicken **8** fabulous, heighten, increase, lengthen, splendid, terrific **9** excellent, first-rate, intensify, marvelous, spread out **10** delightful, first-class, tremendous, undulation **11** pleasurable **12** clotheshorse, fashion plate, smart dresser

swell-headed 8 egoistic, puffed up **9**

conceited **10** egoistical **11** egotistical **12** vainglorious **13** self-important

swelling 4 bump, lump **5** bulge, swell **8** dilation **9** puffiness **10** distension **11** enlargement **12** protuberance

swell out 5 bloat, bulge **6** billow, expand **7** distend, inflate, puff out

swelter 3 fry **4** boil, cook **5** be hot, broil, sweat **8** languish, perspire

sweltering 3 hot **5** humid, muggy **6** sultry, torrid **7** burning **8** sweating **10** oppressive, perspiring

sweltry 3 hot **4** dank **5** humid, muggy **6** baking, clammy, steamy, sticky, sultry, torrid **7** boiling **8** broiling, roasting, sizzling, stifling **9** scorching **10** blistering **11** suffocating

Swept Away
  subtitle: 38 by an unusual destiny in the blue sea of August
  director: 14 Lina Wertmuller
  cast: 16 Mariangela Melato **17** Giancarlo Giannini

swerve 3 shy, yaw **4** tack, turn, veer **5** avert, dodge, sheer, shift, stray **6** careen, change **7** deviate, digress, diverge **9** turn aside

swift 4 fast **5** brisk, fleet, hasty, quick, rapid **6** abrupt, flying, prompt, speedy **8** headlong **9** immediate **11** expeditious, precipitate

Swift, Jonathan
  author of: 11 A Tale of a Tub **15** A Modest Proposal **16** Battle of the Books, Gulliver's Travels
  fictional places: 6 Laputa **8** Lilliput **11** Brobdingnag
  character: 6 Yahoos **10** Houyhnhnms **14** Lemuel Gulliver

swiftness 5 haste, speed **8** alacrity, celerity, dispatch, rapidity **9** quickness

swill 4 mash, slop, swig **5** quaff, waste **6** guzzle, refuse, scraps, soak up, tipple **7** garbage **8** chugalug, gulp down

swimming
  athlete: 9 Diana Nyad, John Naber, Mark Spitz **10** Dawn Fraser, Kim Linehan, Linda Jezek **11** Claudia Kolb, Debbie Meyer, John Hencken **12** Brian Goodell, Bruce Furniss, Greg Louganis, John Kinsella **13** Jim Montgomery, Kornelia Ender, Michael Burton, Tracy Caulkens **14** Charles Hickcox, Duke Kahanamoku, Esther Williams, Gertrude Ederle **15** Cynthia Woodhead **16** Shirley Babashoff **17** Johnny Weissmuller

Swinburne, Algernon Charles
  author of: 16 Hymn to Perserpine **17** Atalanta in Calydon **18** Songs Before Sunrise

swindle 2 do **3** con, gyp **4** bilk, dupe, gull, hoax, rook **5** cheat, cozen, fraud, mulct, steal, trick **6** delude, fleece, racket, rip-off **7** con game, deceive, defraud **8** embezzle, hoodwink **9**

bamboozle, defalcate **12** embezzle-ment **14** confidence game

swindler 3 gyp **5** cheat, crook, faker, fraud **6** con man **7** sharper **8** chiseler, deceiver **9** charlatan, embezzler **10** mountebank **12** rip-off artist

swine 3 cad, cur, rat **4** pigs **5** beast, brute **6** animal
  group of: 5 drift **7** sounder

Swineherd, The
  author: 21 Hans Christian Andersen

swing 4 drop, hang, loop, move, rein, rock, sway, turn **5** pivot, rally, scope, sweep, whirl **6** dangle, decide, han-dle, manage, rotate, seesaw, stroke, wangle **7** compass, extract, freedom, inveigh, liberty, license, listing, pull off, rocking, rolling, suspend, swaying **8** maneuver, pitching, undulate **9** de-termine, influence, oscillate **10** accom-plish, manipulate **11** be suspended, oscillation

Swing Time
  director: 13 George Stevens
  cast: 9 Eric Blore **11** Fred Astaire, Victor Moore **12** Betty Furness, Gin-ger Rogers **14** Helen Broderick
  score: 10 Jerome Kern **13** Dorothy Fields
  Oscar for: 4 song
  song: 12 A Fine Romance **14** Pick Yourself Up **20** The Way You Look Tonight

swirl 4 howl, eddy, reel, roll, spin, swim, turn **5** churn, twirl, twist, wheel, whirl **6** gyrate, rotate **7** re-volve

Swiss Family Robinson
  director: 10 Ken Annakin
  cast: 9 John Mills **10** Janet Munro **14** Dorothy McGuire, James MacArthur, Sessue Hayakawa
  author: 16 Johann Rudolf Wyss
  character: 13 Emily Montrose
    Robinson family: 4 Jack **5** Fritz **6** Ernest **7** Francis

switch 3 box, rod, tan **4** cane, jerk, lash, move, whip **5** birch, lever, shift, shunt, stick, swing, trade, whisk **6** button, change, handle **8** exchange **9** sidetrack **11** alternation

Switzerland
  also: 6 Suisse (French) **7** Schweiz (German) **8** Helvetia (Latin)
  capital: 4 Bern(e)
  largest city: 6 Zurich
  others: 3 Zug **4** Bale, Bern, Biel, Brig, Chur, Nyon, Sion, Thun **5** Basel, Basle, Berne, Coire, Surat, Vevey **6** Geneva, Geneve, Glarus, Lugano, Sarnen, Schwyz **7** Altdorf, Fyzabad, Herisau, Locarno, Lucerne, Luzerne, Zermatt **8** Lausanne, Montreux, St Moritz **9** Neuchatel, Solothurn **10** Bellinzona, Interlaken, Winterthur **12** Schaffhausen
  school: 4 Bern **5** Basel **8** Catholic,

Lausanne **28** Federal Institute of Technology
  division: 3 Uri, Zug **4** Bern, Chur, Nyon, Vaud **5** Aarau, Basel, Basle, Berne, Sankt, Waadt **6** Aargau, can-ton, Gallen, Geneva, Geneve, Glaris, Glarus, Luzern, Obwald, Schwyz, St Gall, Tessin, Ticino, Valais, Wallis, Zurich **7** Atldorf, Grisons, Lucerne, Nidwald, Thurgau **8** Fribourg, Ob-walden, St Gallen **9** Appenzell, Neu-chatel, Neuenberg, Solothurn **10** Graubunden **11** Unterwalden **12** Schaffhausen
  measure: 3 imi, pot **4** aune, fuss, muid, pied, zoll **5** lieue, linie, maass, pouce, staab, toise **6** perche, strich **7** klafter, viertel **9** quarteron **10** hol-zlafter **11** holzklafter
  monetary unit: 5 franc, rappe **6** hal-lar, rappen **7** centime, duplone **8** baetzner
  weight: 4 fund **5** pfund **7** centner, quintal **12** zugthierlast
  lake: 3 Uri, Zug **4** Biel, Thon, Thun **5** Ageri, Leman, Morat **6** Bienne, Bri-enz, Geneva, Lugano, Sarnen, Wal-len, Zurich **7** Hallwil, Lucerne, Lung-ern **8** Maggiore, Viervald **9** Bielersee, Constance, Neuchatel, Sarnersee, Thunersee
  mountain: 3 Dom **4** Alps, Jura, Rigi, Rosa, Todi **5** Adula, Blanc, Cenis, Eiger, Genis, Karpf, Righi **6** Linard, Pinela, Santis **7** Bernina, Beverin, Grimsel, Pilatus, Rotondo **8** Balm-horn, Jungfrau **9** Weisshorn **10** Diablerets, Matterhorn, St Gotthard, Wetterhorn **11** Burgenstock **12** Du-fourspitze **13** Rheinwaldhorn **14** Fin-steraarhorn
    mountain pass: 5 Cenis, Furka, Gemmi **6** Albula, Kinzig, Maloja, Unteri **7** Bernina, Brenner, Grim-sel, Simplon, Splugen **8** Lotschen **10** St Gotthard
  highest point: 12 Dufourspitze
  river: 2 Po **3** Aar, Inn **4** Aare, Arve, Thur, Toss **5** Broye, Doubs, Linth, Reuss, Rhine, Rhone, Saane **6** Lim-mat, Maggia, Safane, Sarine, Ticino **8** Engadine, Pratigau
  physical feature:
    glacier: 5 Rhone
    plateau: 5 Swiss
  people: 5 Swiss
    artist: 4 Klee
    author: 5 Hesse, Spyri **6** Keller **8** Gotthelf, Rousseau **10** Durrenmatt
    educational reformer: 10 Pesta-lozzi
    hero: 4 Tell
    psychologist: 4 Jung **6** Piaget
    religious leader: 6 Calvin **7** Zwingli
    scientist: 9 Bernoulli
  language: 5 Ladin **6** French, German **7** Italian **8** Romansch **14**

Switzerdeutsch
  religion: 9 Calvinism **10** Protestant **13** Roman Catholic
  place:
    castle: 7 Chillon
    fountain: 7 Jet d'Eau
    playhouse: 6 Zurich
    resort: 5 Arosa, Davos **6** Gstaad **7** Zermatt **8** St Moritz **9** Schwagalp **10** Interlaken
    street: 14 Bahnhofstrasse
    tower: 5 Clock
  feature:
    animal: 4 ibex **7** chamois
    flower: 9 edelweiss
    pageant: 9 Alpenfest
  food:
    cheese: 6 bagnes, sbrinz **7** Gruyere **10** Emmentaler **11** Appenzeller
    dish: 5 rosti **6** fondue **8** raclette **11** grisons beef **14** bundnerfleisch
    drink: 11 cheri-suisse **14** marmot-chocolat

Swiveller, Dick
  character in: 19 The Old Curiosity Shop
  author: 7 Dickens

swollen 5 puffy **7** bloated, bulging, swelled **8** inflated, puffed-up **9** dis-tended

swoon 5 faint **8** collapse, keel over **13** fall prostrate **17** become unconscious

swoop 4 dive, drop, rush **5** pitch, sweep **6** plunge, pounce, spring **7** de-scend, plummet **8** nosedive, swoop-ing **9** sweep down **12** rush headlong

sword 4 epee, foil **5** blade, saber, steel **6** rapier **7** cutlass **8** scimitar **10** broadsword

sybarite 8 hedonist **10** sensualist, vo-luptuary

sybaritic 4 rich **6** lavish **7** sensual **9** dissolute, epicurean, luxurious **10** dis-sipated, hedonistic, voluptuous **12** luxury-loving, pleasure-bent **13** self-indulgent **14** pleasure loving **15** pleas-ure-seeking

sycamore 8 Platanus **18** Acer pseudo-platanus
  varieties: 7 eastern **8** Egyptian

sycophant 4 tool **5** slave, toady **6** fawner, flunky, jackal, lackey, puppet, stooge, yes-man **7** cat's-paw **8** hang-er-on, parasite, truckler **9** brown-nose, flatterer **10** bootlicker **11** lickspittle, rubber stamp **13** apple-polisher

Sydney
  bay: 5 Walsh **11** Rushcutter's **13** Woolloomooloo
  capital of: 13 New South Wales
  cove: 4 Farm
  founder: 7 Phillip
  harbor: 7 Darling **11** Port Jackson
  island: 4 Goat **6** Garden
  landmark: 10 Opera House **11** Wyn-yard Park **13** Harbour Bridge **14** Fitzroy Gardens **15** Mitchell Library

16 Australian Museum, Hyde Park Barracks, Saint James Church **18** Rushcutter's Bay Park **21** Royal Botanical Gardens
  river: 10 Parramatta
  university: 9 Macquarie **13** New South Wales

sylvan 5 bushy, leafy, woody **6** wooded, woodsy **8** arcadian, forested, timbered, woodland **9** luxuriant, overgrown **10** forestlike

Sylvanus *see* **8** Silvanus

Sylvia
  character in: 20 Two Gentlemen of Verona
  author: 11 Shakespeare

symbol 4 mark, sign **5** badge, token **6** emblem, figure, signal **10** indication **14** representation **15** exemplification

symbolize 4 mean **5** imply **6** denote, embody, symbol **7** betoken, connote, express, signify **8** stand for **9** emblemize, exemplify, personify, represent, signalize **10** allegorize **11** emblematize

symmetrical 7 orderly, regular **8** balanced **9** congruent **12** well-balanced **16** well-proportioned

symmetry 4 form **5** order **7** balance, harmony **9** congruity **10** conformity, regularity **11** equilibrium, orderliness, parallelism, shapeliness **15** proportionality

sympathetic 6 benign, humane, kindly **7** feeling, pitying **8** friendly, merciful **9** agreeable, approving, benignant, sensitive **10** benevolent, comforting **11** soft-hearted, warmhearted **12** sympathizing, welldisposed **13** commiserative, compassionate, tenderhearted, understanding

sympathize 4 back, pity, side **5** agree, favor **7** approve, feel for, go along, support **8** sanction **9** empathize **10** appreciate, be in accord, be sorry for **11** condole with, have pity for, stand behind

sympathy 4 pity **5** amity, favor, grief **6** accord, regard, sorrow **7** concern, concert, concord, empathy, feeling, harmony, rapport, support **8** advocacy, affinity, approval, sanction **9** agreement, communion, patronage, unanimity **10** compassion, consonance, fellowship, friendship, tenderness **11** well-wishing **12** congeniality, partisanship **13** commiseration, fellow feeling, understanding

Symplegades
  form: 5 rocks
  location: 8 Bosporus **9** Euxine Sea
  characteristic: 8 clashing, dark-blue

symposium 5 forum, synod **6** debate, parley, powwow **7** meeting **8** colloquy, congress **10** conference, discussion, round table **12** deliberation **15** panel discussion

Symposium
  author: 5 Plato
  character: 7 Agathon **8** Phaedrus, Socrates **9** Pausanias **10** Alcibiades **11** Aristodemus **12** Aristophanes

symptom 4 mark, sign **5** token **6** signal **7** earmark, warning **8** evidence, giveaway **10** indication **15** prognostication

synagogue
  Yiddish: 4 shul **5** schul

synchronal 11 concomitant, synchronous **12** contemporary, simultaneous

synchronous 10 synchronal **11** concomitant **12** contemporary, simultaneous

syndicalist 5 rebel **9** anarchist, insurgent **13** revolutionary

syndicate 5 group, trust, union **6** cartel, league, merger **7** combine **8** alliance **9** coalition **10** consortium, federation **11** association

Synge, John Millington
  author of: 14 Riders to the Sea **19** Deirdre of the Sorrows **20** In the Shadow of the Glen **27** The Playboy of the Western World

synod 4 diet **13** governing body **15** advisory council **21** ecclesiastical council

synonym 8 analogue **10** equivalent **11** another name

synonymous 4 like, same **5** alike, equal **7** coequal **10** equivalent

synopsis 5 brief **6** apercu, digest, precis, resume **7** epitome, outline, rundown, summary **8** abstract, argument **11** abridgement

synopsize 6 digest **7** abridge, outline **8** abstract, condense **9** summarize

Synoptist 12 Gospel writer

synthesize 3 mix **4** fuse **5** blend **7** combine **8** compound **10** amalgamate

synthetic 4 fake, sham **5** phony **6** ersatz **7** man-made **9** unnatural **10** artificial **11** counterfeit **12** manufactured

Syria
  other name: 4 Aram
  capital/largest city: 8 Damascus
  others: 4 Hama, Homs, Nawa **5** Busra, Calno, Derra, Emesa, Halab, Hamah, Idlib, Jerud, Raqqa **6** Aleppo, Calneh, Dumeir, Fajami, Tadmor, Ugarit **7** Antioch, Latakia, Palmyra **8** Seleucia **9** Ghabaghib
  school: 6 Aleppo, Syrian **11** Arab Academy
  measure: 5 makuk **6** garava
  monetary unit: 4 lira **5** pound **6** talent **7** piaster
  weight: 4 cola **5** artal, ratel **6** talent
  lake: 5 Merom **7** Djeboid **8** Tiberias
  mountain: 6 Carmel **7** Alawite, Libanus **10** Nusairiyya **11** Anti-Lebanon
  highest point: 6 Hermon
  river: 3 Asi **6** Balikh, Barada, Jordan, Khabur, Yarmuk **7** Orontes **9** Asi Knabur, Euphrates
  sea: 13 Mediterranean
  physical feature:
    desert: 5 Hamad **6** Hauran, Syrian
    heights: 5 Golan
  people: 4 Arab, Kurd, Turk **5** Alawi, Aptal, Druse, Druze **6** Afshar, Aissor, Aushar, Avshar, Awshar **7** Amorite, Ansarie, Bedouin, Nosaris, Saracen, Shemite **8** Ansarieh, Armenian **9** Ansariyah **10** Circassian **12** Khachaturian
    king: 5 Rezin **6** Faisal, Hazael **8** Benhadad **9** Antiochus
    leader: 10 T E Lawrence **12** Hafiz al-Assad **16** Lawrence of Arabia
    queen: 7 Zenobia
    ruler: 4 Rome **5** Arabs **6** France, Greeks, Persia **7** Mongols **8** Abbasids **9** Mamelukes, Phoenicia, Seleucids **11** Seljuk Turks **12** Ottoman Turks
  language: 6 Arabic, French, Syriac **7** Aramaic, English, Kurdish, Turkish **8** Armenian
  religion: 5 Druze, Islam **7** Alawite **12** Christianity **13** Greek Orthodox **23** Eastern Rite Christianity
  place:
    dam: 5 Tabqa **9** Euphrates
    ruins: 7 Palmyra
    square: 7 Martyrs'
  feature:
    animal: 9 dromedary
    clothing: 3 aba **4** abah **7** abayyah **8** kafiyyah
    marketplace: 4 souk
    tent: 8 bayt shar
    village common: 6 maidan

Syrinx
  form: 5 nymph
  location: 8 mountain
  transformed into: 4 reed
  transformed by: 3 Pan
  made into: 7 panpipe
  pipes called: 6 syrinx

system 4 body, unit **5** setup **6** method, scheme, theory **7** program, regimen, routine **8** organism **9** procedure, structure **10** hypothesis **11** arrangement **12** constitution, organization **13** modus operandi **15** mode of operation

systematic 4 neat, tidy **7** ordered, orderly, planned, precise, regular **8** constant **9** organized **10** methodical **12** businesslike, systematized **13** wellorganized, well-regulated

systematization 5 order **8** ordering **9** gradation **10** organizing **11** arrangement **12** categorizing, codification, organization **13** methodization **14** categorization, classification

systematize 5 order **7** arrange **8** classify, organize **9** methodize

systematized 7 ordered **8** arranged, codified **9** organized **10** classified, methodized, systematic

  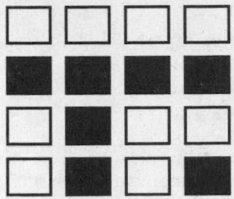

tab 3 lip **4** bill, cost, flap, loop **5** check, PC key, price, strip, tally **6** tongue **7** eyehole **10** projection

tabard 4 cape, coat **5** cloak, tunic

Tabard Inn
starting point in: 18 The Canterbury Tales

tabernacle 6 church, temple **14** house of worship

Tabeth 16 tenth Hebrew month

Tabitha
also called: 6 Dorcas
revived by: 5 Peter
hometown: 5 Joppa

table 4 fare, list, roll **5** board, chart, index **6** record, roster, shelve, spread **7** catalog **8** lay aside, postpone, put aside, register, schedule, syllabus, synopsis **9** inventory **10** tabulation

Table
constellation of: 5 Mensa

tableau 4 view **5** scene **7** pageant, picture, setting **8** grouping **9** depiction, spectacle, still life **11** arrangement, delineation **12** illustration **13** picturization

tableau vivant 13 living picture

tablespoon
abbreviation: 3 tbs **4** tbsp

tablet 3 pad **4** leaf **5** bolus, panel, sheet, wafer **6** pellet, plaque, troche **7** lozenge, memo pad, surface **8** flat cake, thin slab **9** tablature **10** pad of paper, writing pad

tableware 5 china **6** dishes, plates **7** cutlery **8** crockery, utensils **9** chinaware, glassware **10** dinnerware, silverware **14** cups and saucers

taboo, tabu 3 ban **4** no-no **6** banned **8** anathema, outlawed, verboten **9** forbidden, social ban **10** in bad taste, prohibited, proscribed **11** disapproved, prohibition, unthinkable **12** interdiction, proscription, religious ban, unacceptable **13** unmentionable

tabulate 4 file, list, rank, rate, sort **5** chart, grade, group, index, order, range **6** codify **7** arrange, catalog, compute, diagram, sort out **8** classify, organize **9** methodize **10** categorize, make a table **11** systematize

tace
music: 6 silent

tacit 7 assumed, implied **8** implicit, inferred, unspoken, unstated, wordless **10** undeclared, understood **11** unexpressed **15** taken for granted

taciturn 5 aloof, quiet **6** silent **7** laconic **8** reserved, reticent **9** secretive **11** tight-lipped **12** close-mouthed **15** uncommunicative

tack 3 add, peg, pin, way **4** clap, nail, slap, veer **5** affix, sheer, shift, spike, thole **6** append, attach, change, fasten, method, swerve, switch, zigzag **7** go about **8** approach, tholepin **9** short nail **12** change course **14** course of action

tackle 3 try **4** gear, lift **5** assay, begin, crane, hoist, jenny, throw, tools, winch **6** accept, assume, attack, take on, take up **7** attempt, capstan, derrick, embrace, go about, halyard, rigging **8** endeavor, engage in, material, set about, windlass **9** apparatus, enter upon, equipment, trappings, undertake **10** appliances, embark upon, implements **11** instruments **12** appointments **13** accoutrements, paraphernalia

tack on 3 add **5** annex **6** adjoin, append, attach **7** stick on, subjoin **8** fasten to

tacky 5 dowdy, gluey, gooey, gucky, gummy, messy, ratty, seedy, tatty **6** grubby, shabby, shoddy, sloppy, sticky, untidy, viscid **7** stringy, unkempt, viscous **8** adhesive, frazzled, slipshod, slovenly **10** disordered

tact 7 finesse, suavity **8** delicacy **9** diplomacy, suaveness **10** discretion **11** savoir faire, sensibility **13** consideration **14** circumspection
French: 11 savoir-faire

tactful 5 suave **6** polite, smooth, subtle **7** politic **8** decorous, delicate, discreet, mannerly **9** sensitive **10** diplomatic, thoughtful **11** considerate

tactic 3 way **4** line, plan, tack **6** method, policy, scheme **8** approach **9** stratagem **14** course of action

tactics 9 maneuvers **18** battle arrangements, military operations

tactless 4 curt, rude **5** blunt, brash, rough **6** abrupt, clumsy, gauche, stupid **7** boorish **8** impolite **9** hamhanded, impolitic, imprudent, untactful **10** blundering, indelicate, indiscreet **11** insensitive, thoughtless **12** undiplomatic **13** ill-considered, inconsiderate
French: 6 gauche

tactlessness 8 curtness **9** bluntness, gaucherie **10** abruptness, clumsiness, indelicacy **13** insensitivity, tastelessness

taedium vitae 5 ennui **12** tedium of life **22** feeling life is wearisome

Taft, William Howard
presidential rank: 13 twenty-seventh
party: 10 Republican
state represented: 2 OH
defeated: 4 (Eugene Victor) Debs **5** (William Jennings) Bryan **6** (Daniel Braxton) Turney, (Eugene Wilder) Chafin, (Thomas Edward) Watson, (Thomas Louis) Hisgen **8** (August) Gillhaus
vice president: 7 (James Schoolcraft) Sherman
cabinet:
state: 4 (Philander Chase) Knox
treasury: 8 (Franklin) MacVeagh
war: 7 (Henry Lewis) Stimson **9** (Jacob McGavock) Dickinson
attorney general: 10 (George Woodward) Wickersham
navy: 5 (George von Lengerke) Meyer
postmaster general: 9 (Frank Harris) Hitchcock
interior: 6 (Walter Lowrie) Fisher **9** (Richard Achilles) Ballinger
agriculture: 6 (James) Wilson
commerce and labor: 5 (Charles) Nagel
born: 12 Cincinnati OH
died: 12 Washington DC
buried: 25 Arlington National Cemetery
education:
university: 4 Yale
law school: 10 Cincinnati
religion: 9 Unitarian
interests: 4 golf
author: 22 Four Aspects of Civic Duty **23** The United States and Peace **30** Our Chief Magistrate and His Powers **33** The Anti-Trust Act and the Supreme Court **65** The Presidency: Its Duties Its Powers Its Opportunities and Its Limitation
political career: 18 US Solicitor General
judge: 19 Federal Circuit Court
president of: 21 Philippines

Commission
  civil governor of: 11 Philippines
  secretary of: 3 War
  US Supreme Court: 12 Chief Justice
civilian career:
  law professor: 4 Yale
  president: 22 American Bar Association
notable events of lifetime/term: 19
Postal Savings System
  Act: 10 Webb-Kenyon **11** Mann-Elkinst **12** Payne-Aldrich
  sinking of: 7 Titanic
father: 8 Alphonso
mother: 6 Louisa (Maria Torrey)
siblings: 5 Fanny **11** Henry Waters **12** Horace Dutton **15** Samuel Davenport
  half-brothers: 11 Peter Rawson **13** Charles Phelps
wife: 5 Helen (Herron)
  nickname: 6 Nellie
children: 11 Helen Herron **13** Charles Phelps **14** Robert Alphonso
first lady:
  author: 24 Recollections of Full Years

tag 3 add, dog, tab **4** card, heel, mark, name, slip, stub, tail, term **5** add on, affix, annex, hound, label, title, trail **6** append, attach, attend, fasten, follow, handle, join to, marker, shadow, tack on, ticket **7** earmark, moniker, pendant **8** cognomen, identify, nickname **9** accompany, appendage, sobriquet

Tahiti
artist: 7 Gauguin
author: 9 Stevenson
capital: 7 Papeete
formerly: 8 Otaheite
island group: 7 Society
isthmus: 7 Taravao
ocean: 7 Pacific
volcano: 5 Roniu **7** Orohena

tail 3 dog **4** butt, seat **5** fanny, stalk, track, trail **6** follow, shadow **7** back end, rear end **8** buttocks

tail end, tail-end 4 back, butt, rear, rump, tail **6** caudal **7** hind end, rear end **8** backside, buttocks, last part **9** posterior

tailor 3 fit, sew **4** make, redo **5** adapt, alter, build, shape **6** change, create, design, devise, modify **7** convert, fashion, produce **8** clothier, costumer **9** construct, couturier, fabricate, transform **10** dressmaker, seamstress

taint 3 mar, rot **4** blot, flaw, ruin, soil, spot, turn **5** dirty, fault, go bad, smear, spoil, stain, sully **6** damage, debase, defect, defile, smudge, stigma **7** blemish, putrefy, tarnish **8** besmirch **12** imperfection

tainted 5 dirty **6** impure, rotten **7** spoiled, stained, unclean **9** blemished, tarnished **10** besmirched

Taipei
capital of: 6 Taiwan
Taiwan
name means: 11 terraced bay
other name: 7 Formosa **11** Ilha Formosa **15** Republic of China
capital/largest city: 6 Taipei
others: 4 Suao **5** Shoka, Takao **6** Tainan **7** Chilung, Hualien, Keelong, Keelung, Taoyuan **8** Fengshan, Kaohiung, Taichung **9** Kaohsiung
school: 7 Soochow, Tunghai **14** National Taiwan
monetary unit: 4 yuan **6** dollar
island: 5 Matsu **6** Lan Hsu, Penghu, Quemoy, Taiwan **7** Hungtou, Huoshao **10** Pescadores
mountain: 5 Tatun **6** Tzukao **7** Taitung **15** Chungyang Shanmo
highest point: 6 Yu Shan **8** Morrison **10** Sinkao Shan **11** Hsin-Kao Shan
river: 5 Wuchi **6** Tachia **7** Choshui, Hualien, Tanshui
sea: 7 Pacific **9** East China **10** Philippine, South China
physical feature:
  cape: 7 Olwanpi
  channel: 5 Bashi
  gorge: 6 Taroko
  storm: 7 monsoon, typhoon
  strait: 6 Taiwan **7** Formosa
people: 4 Yami **5** Hakka, Hoklo **7** Chinese, Malayan **9** Fukienese, Taiwanese **10** Indonesian, Polynesian **12** Kwangtungese
  goddess: 5 Matsu
  leader: 7 Koxinga **9** Sun Yat-sen **10** Yen Chia-Kan **13** Chiang Kai-shek **14** Cheng Cheng-Kung, Chiang Ching-kuo
language: 4 Amon, Amoy **5** Hakka, Kuo Yu **6** Minnan **9** Taiwanese **15** Mandarin Chinese
religion: 6 Taoism **7** animism **8** Buddhism **12** Christianity, Confucianism
place:
  museum: 14 National Palace
  square: 12 Presidential
feature:
  festival: 5 Ghost
  political party: 10 Kuomintang
food:
  feast: 6 pai-pai

Tajikistan
other name: 12 Tadzhikistan
capital/largest city: 8 Dushanbe
head of state: 9 president
government: 8 republic
monetary unit: 5 ruble
mountain: 13 Communism Peak
people: 5 Tajik, Uzbek **7** Tadzhik
language: 7 Tadzhik
religion: 11 Sunni Muslim
Taj Mahal 4 tomb **9** mausoleum
location: 4 Agra **5** India
built by: 9 Shah, Jahan
for: 4 wife

take 3 buy, get, lug, nab, net, see, use

4 bear, bilk, deem, draw, feel, gain, grab, grip, haul, have, heed, hire, hold, know, lead, loot, mark, mind, move, need, obey, read, rent, sack, tote, work **5** bring, brook, carry, catch, cheat, claim, clasp, filch, grasp, gross, guide, infer, lease, seize, stand, steal, use up, usher, usurp **6** accept, assume, attain, clutch, convey, deduce, deduct, demand, derive, divest, employ, endure, escort, fleece, follow, look on, obtain, pilfer, pocket, profit, regard, remove, secure, snatch, suffer **7** acquire, agree to, believe, call for, capture, conduct, consume, deliver, make out, observe, pillage, plunder, purloin, receive, require, respect, stomach, succeed, suppose, undergo **8** accede to, assent to, conceive, conclude, consider, listen to, perceive, proceeds, purchase, shoulder, submit to, subtract, take away, tolerate, transfer **9** ascertain, be ruled by, consent to, deprive of, eliminate, get hold of, interpret, lay hold of, put up with, respond to, transport, undertake **10** commandeer, comply with, comprehend, confiscate, experience, lay hands on, take effect, understand **11** appropriate, begin to work, go along with, necessitate **13** help oneself to **14** avail oneself of, misappropriate

take aback 5 amaze **7** astound **8** astonish, surprise **9** overwhelm
take a crack at 3 try **5** essay **6** hazard, tackle, take on **7** attempt, venture **9** have a go at, undertake **11** make a stab at
take advantage of 3 use **5** avail **7** exploit, utilize **10** profit from
take after 4 copy, echo **6** follow, repeat **7** imitate **8** resemble, simulate **9** duplicate, reproduce
take apart 7 destroy **8** demolish **9** dismantle, knock down **11** disassemble
take a powder 4 blow, exit **5** go out, leave, scram, split **6** cut out, depart, escape **8** withdraw
take away 5 seize **6** lessen, reduce **7** abridge, bear off, curtail, detract **8** carry off, decrease, subtract **9** deprive of **11** make off with
take a whack at 3 try **5** essay **6** hazard, tackle **7** attempt, venture **8** give a try **9** have a go at **10** give a whirl **12** take a crack at
take back 6 abjure, recall, recant, renege **7** disavow, retract, reverse **8** forswear, withdraw
take captive 3 bag **4** snag, take, trap **5** catch, seize, snare **7** capture, ensnare **9** apprehend, lay hold of **12** take prisoner
take care 6 beware, be wary **9** be careful **10** be cautious **17** look before you leap
take care of 4 tend **6** assume **7** nur-

ture **8** attend to, shoulder **10** minister to

take exception 5 demur **6** object, resent **11** look askance

take flight 3 fly **4** flee **6** escape, run off **7** abscond, fly away, run away, run free, take off **9** make a dash **10** fly the coop **12** make a getaway

take for granted 6 assume **10** undervalue

take heed 4 mind **6** beware **7** look out **8** take care, watch out **11** take warning

take hold 4 bite, grab, grip **5** grasp **6** clutch **7** catch on

take in stride 12 not skip a beat **13** be unperturbed

take into custody 3 bag, nab **4** book, bust, hold **5** catch, pinch, seize **6** arrest, collar, detain, secure **7** capture **9** apprehend **12** take prisoner

take into service 4 hire **6** employ, engage, retain, secure, take on

take issue 5 demur **6** differ **8** disagree **12** be at variance, stand opposed

take no notice of 6 ignore **9** disregard **11** pay no heed to **15** fail to recognize **16** pay no attention to **17** fail to acknowledge

take notice
  Latin: **8** nota bene

take notice of 3 see **4** heed, mark, note **6** call on, regard **7** observe **8** call upon **9** recognize **10** get a load of **11** acknowledge **14** pay attention to

take nourishment 3 eat **4** feed **10** break bread **14** take sustenance

takeoff 5 spoof **6** parody, satire **7** lampoon **9** burlesque **10** caricature

take off 4 doff, lift **5** leave **6** decamp, depart, detach, remove **7** lift off, peel off, run away **8** strip off **14** leave the ground

take off guard 5 catch **8** surprise **14** take by surprise

take on 4 bear, hire **6** accept, assume, engage **8** shoulder **9** undertake

take one's breath away 4 daze, stun **5** shock **7** stupefy **8** astonish, dumfound **9** dumbfound, electrify **11** flabbergast **15** make one's eyes pop

take out 4 date **5** court **6** delete, escort, remove **7** extract, isolate **8** abstract, separate, take home, withdraw **9** strike out

take over 4 take **5** seize **6** assume, take on, take up **8** shoulder **10** commandeer, confiscate **11** appropriate, expropriate, gain control

take pains 6 strive **7** attempt, try hard **8** endeavor, go all out **10** do one's best **11** give one's all **12** make an effort **15** knock oneself out **16** give one's best shot

take pleasure in 4 like, love **5** adore,

eat up, enjoy, fancy, savor **6** dote on, relish, relish **7** revel in **9** rejoice in **10** appreciate **13** be pleased with, get a kick out of

take possession of 5 claim **10** confiscate **11** appropriate, expropriate

take prisoner 3 bag, nab **4** book, bust **5** catch, pinch, seize **6** arrest, collar **7** capture **9** apprehend **11** take captive **15** take into custody

take sick 3 ail **6** sicken **8** collapse **9** become ill **10** be stricken

take stock of 5 audit, check **6** assess, review, survey **7** examine, inspect **8** look over **9** inventory

take sustenance 3 eat **4** feed **10** break bread **15** take nourishment

take the cake 5 excel **7** beat all, surpass **12** beat the devil, win hands down

take the edge off 6 lessen, pacify, soothe, temper **7** appease, assuage, lighten, mollify **8** tone down

take the first step 5 begin, start **6** launch, set out **8** commence, embark on, initiate **9** undertake **10** inaugurate

take the place of 7 replace **8** displace, supplant **9** supersede

take to be 4 deem, hold **5** count, judge, think **6** assume, regard, view as **7** account, believe **8** consider **10** look upon as

take to heart 4 heed, mind **6** attend **8** consider **9** hearken to **12** give thought to **14** pay attention to

take to one's heels 3 fly **4** flee **6** escape **7** get away, run away **10** fly the coop, make a break, take flight **12** make a getaway **15** head for the hills

take to task 5 chide, scold **6** accuse, berate, charge, rail at, rebuke **7** bawl out, censure, chasten, chew out, reprove, upbraid **8** admonish, chastise, reproach **9** castigate, criticize, dress down, reprimand **10** tongue-lash **11** remonstrate **13** call to account

take turns 5 share **6** rotate **9** alternate

take under one's wing 6 assist, defend **7** protect **8** befriend **9** look after

take unfair advantage of 5 abuse **6** misuse **7** exploit

take up 4 lift **6** absorb, accept, assume, occupy, pick up, resume, soak up, suck up **7** discuss, drink in **8** consider, continue, sponge up, talk over **9** cultivate, swallow up

taking a siesta 6 dozing **7** napping **8** snoozing **10** taking a nap **18** catching forty winks

takings 4 loot **5** booty **6** spoils **7** plunder **8** pickings

Talaria
  form: **7** sandals
  owner: **6** Hermes **7** Mercury
  characteristic: **6** winged

tale 3 fib, lie **4** epic, myth, saga, yarn

5 fable, novel, rumor, story **6** legend, report **7** account, fiction, hearsay, recital, romance, scandal, untruth **8** anecdote **9** falsehood, fish story, narration, narrative, tall story **10** short story **11** fabrication, scuttlebutt **12** tittle-tattle **13** falsification, piece of gossip **16** cock-and-bull story

talebearer 6 gossip **7** blabber, reciter, tattler **8** busybody, informer, reporter, telltale **10** newsmonger, tattletale **11** storyteller **12** blabbermouth **13** scandalmonger

talent 4 bent, gift, turn **5** flair, forte, knack, skill **6** genius **7** faculty **8** aptitude, capacity, facility, strength **9** endowment **10** capability **11** proficiency

Talent 14 Biblical weight

talented 4 able **5** adept **6** expert, gifted **7** born for, capable, endowed, skilled **8** artistic, polished **9** brilliant, competent **10** proficient **11** well-endowed **12** accomplished

Tale of a Tub, A
  author: **9** Ben Jonson **13** Jonathan Swift

Tale of Genji
  author: **19** Lady Murasaki Shikibu

Tale of Two Cities, A
  author: **14** Charles Dickens
  character: **7** Gaspard, Stryver **9** Dr Manette, Miss Pross **11** Jarvis Lorry, John Barstad **12** Lucie Manette, Sydney Carton **13** Charles Darnay, Jerry Cruncher, Madame Defarge **10** Marquis St Evremonde
  director: **10** Jack Conway
  cast: **12** Blanche Yurka, Isabel Jewell, Reginald Owen, Ronald Colman (Sydney Carton) **13** Basil Rathbone, Edna May Oliver **14** Elizabeth Allan
  setting: **16** French Revolution

Tales Before Midnight
  author: **19** Stephen Vincent Benet

Talese, Gay
  author of: **14** Honor Thy Father **16** Thy Neighbor's Wife

Tales of a Fourth Grade Nothing
  author: **9** Judy Blume

Tales of a Wayside Inn
  author: **24** Henry Wadsworth Longfellow

Tales of Hoffmann, The
  also: **18** Les Contes d'Hoffmann
  opera by: **9** Offenbach
  character: **6** Stella **7** Antonia, Olympia **9** Dr Miracle, Giulietta **11** E T A Hoffmann **14** mechanical doll

Tales of Manhattan
  author: **16** Louis Auchincloss

talisman 4 tiki **5** charm **6** amulet, fetish, grigri **10** lucky piece

Talisman, The
  author: **14** Sir Walter Scott
  character: **7** Conrade, El Hakim **10** Sir Kenneth **15** Queen Berengaria

19 Theodorick of Engaddi **20** Lady Edith Plantagenet **21** Richard the Lion-Hearted **31** Grand Master of the Knights Templars

talk 3 gab, jaw, rap, say **4** cant, chat, word **5** argot, idiom, lingo, noise, prate, rumor, slang, speak, state, utter **6** babble, bunkum, confab, confer, gossip, hot air, intone, jargon, parley, patois, powwow, preach, report, sermon, speech, take up, tirade **7** address, blarney, blather, chatter, consult, declare, deliver, dialect, discuss, express, hearsay, lecture, oration, palaver, prattle, twaddle **8** chitchat, colloquy, converse, dialogue, harangue, language, proclaim, rattle on, verbiage **9** discourse, enunciate, negotiate, pronounce, tete-a-tete, utterance **10** bandy words, conference, discussion, rap session, recitation, speak about **11** declamation, exhortation, pontificate, scuttlebutt **12** blatherskite, consultation, conversation, tittle-tattle **13** confabulation

talkative 5 gabby, talky, windy, wordy **6** babbly, chatty, prolix **7** gossipy, verbose, voluble **8** effusive **9** garrulous **10** long-winded, loquacious

talk big 4 brag, crow **5** boast, vaunt **13** puff oneself up **15** blow one's own horn **19** pat oneself on the back

talk down to 9 patronize **10** condescend

talker 6 gabber, gossip, magpie, orator **7** babbler, speaker, windbag **8** lecturer, prattler **9** chatterer, converser **10** chatterbox, mouthpiece **11** rumormonger, speechifier, speechmaker **12** blatherskite, spokesperson **13** scandalmonger **17** conversationalist

talk nonsense 6 babble, drivel, ramble

Talk of the Town, The
 director: **13** George Stevens
 cast: **9** Cary Grant **10** Jean Arthur **12** Ronald Colman **13** Edgar Buchanan, Glenda Farrell

talk out of 4 balk **6** thwart **8** dissuade **10** discourage

talk over 6 confer, review **7** consult, discuss, hash out

Talk-show hosts 5 Leeza **7** Jay Leno, Geraldo **8** Cristina **9** Ricki Lake **10** Jenny Jones **11** Phil Donahue, Conan O'Brian, Arsenio Hall, Maury Povich **12** Johnny Carson, Oprah Winfrey **13** Rosie O'Donnell, Jerry Springer **14** David Letterman, Montel Williams, Regis & Kathy Lee **17** Sally Jessy Raphael

talk to 7 address, lecture, speak to **12** converse with

talk together 4 talk **6** confer **7** discuss **8** converse **9** discourse

tall 3 big **4** high **5** lanky, lofty, rangy **6** absurd **7** soaring, stringy **8** elevated, gangling, towering **10** incredible, long-limbed **11** embellished, exaggerated, implausible **12** preposterous, unbelievable **13** hard to believe, hard to swallow

tallow 3 fat, tip **5** taper **6** bougie, candle, cierge **9** rushlight

Tall State
 nickname of: **8** Illinois

tall story 3 fib, lie **4** yarn **5** fable **7** fiction, untruth, whopper **9** fairy tale, falsehood, fish story, invention **11** fabrication **16** cock-and-bull story

tally 3 add, sum **4** jibe, list, mark, poll, post **5** agree, count, match, score, sum up, total **6** accord, census, concur, muster, reckon, record, square **7** catalog, compute, conform **8** coincide, mark down, register, scorepad, tabulate **9** calculate, harmonize, reckoning, scorecard **10** correspond **11** enumeration

talon 4 claw, nail, spur

Talos
 form: **5** youth **7** monster
 calling: **8** inventor
 made of: **5** brass **6** bronze
 made by: **10** Hephaestus
 guarded: **5** Crete
 destroyed by: **5** Medea
 uncle: **8** Daedalus
 killed by: **8** Daedalus
 because of: **8** jealousy

talus
 bone of: **5** ankle
 connected to: **5** tibia **6** fibula

Tamar
 father: **5** David
 mother: **6** Maacah
 husband: **2** Er **4** Onan **5** Judah, Uriah
 brother: **5** Amnon **7** Absalom, Chileab, Solomon **8** Adonijah
 son: **5** Zarah **6** Pharez
 daughter: **8** Maachiah
 father-in-law: **5** Judah

Tamburlaine the Great
 author: **18** Christopher Marlowe
 character: **6** Cosroe **7** Mycetes, Orcanes **8** Bajazeth **9** Callepine, Techelles, Zenocrate **10** Theridamas, Usumcasane

tame 4 curb, damp, dull, flat, meek, mild, rein **5** break, check, quiet, timid, train **6** boring, bridle, broken, docile, gentle, govern, manage, master, placid, pliant, serene, subdue **7** conquer, control, pliable, prosaic, repress, subdued, tedious **8** amenable, domestic, dominate, lifeless, overcome, regulate, restrain, suppress, timorous, tranquil **9** tractable **10** make docile, submissive, unexciting **11** complaisant, domesticate, unresisting **12** domesticated **13** uninteresting

tameness 8 docility **9** placidity **10** gentleness, insipidity **12** complaisance, tractability **13** domestication **14** submissiveness

Taming of the Shrew, The
 author: **18** William Shakespeare
 character: **6** Bianca, Gremio, Tranio **8** Baptista, Lucentio **9** Hortensio, Katharina, Petruchio, Vincentio
 director: **16** Franco Zeffirelli
 cast: **11** Michael York, Natasha Pyne **13** Richard Burton (Petruchio) **14** Michael Hordern **15** Elizabeth Taylor (Katharina), Vernon Dobtcheff
 score: **8** Nino Rota

Tammuz
 origin: **8** Sumerian
 god of: **9** shepherds
 Hebrew month: **6** fourth

Tam O'Shanter
 author: **11** Robert Burns

Tampa Bay
 football team: **7** Bandits **10** Buccaneers
 baseball team: **9** Devil Rays

tamper 3 mix **4** muck **6** butt in, fiddle, horn in, meddle, tinker **7** intrude, obtrude **9** interfere, intervene **10** fool around, mess around **12** monkey around

tamper with 5 alter **6** change, doctor **7** falsify

tan 4 roan **5** beige, brown, khaki, sandy, tawny **6** bronze, sorrel, suntan **7** bronzed **8** brownish, cinnamon, sunburnt **9** sunburned, suntanned **10** light brown **11** yellow-brown

Tanah Airkita see **9** Indonesia

Tan, Amy
 author of: **14** The Joy Luck Club **18** The Kitchen God's Wife **22** The Hundred Secret Senses

Tananarive, Antananarivo
 capital of: **10** Madagascar

Tanaquil
 origin: **5** Roman
 form: **5** queen
 husband: **7** Tarquin **17** Tarquinius Priscus

Tandy, Jessica
 born: **6** London **7** England
 husband: **10** Hume Cronyn **11** Jack Hawkins
 roles: **8** The Birds **10** The Gin Game **12** Forever Amber **16** Driving Miss Daisy (Oscar) **21** A Streetcar Named Desire

tang 3 bit **4** bite, hint, odor, reek **5** aroma, punch, savor, scent, smack, smell, sting, tinge, touch, trace **6** flavor **8** acridity, piquancy, pungency, tartness **9** acridness, sharpness, spiciness **10** suggestion

Tange, Kenzo
 architect of: **11** Press Center (Kofu) **16** Shizuoka Building (Tokyo) **19** Olympic Sports Stadia (Tokyo) **24** Kagawa Prefectural Offices (Takama-

tsu) **30** Imabara Municipal Office Building

tangibility 11 materiality, palpability **12** touchability

tangible 4 real **5** solid **6** actual **7** obvious **8** clear-cut, concrete, manifest, material, palpable, physical, positive **9** corporeal, touchable **10** verifiable **11** indubitable, substantial

tangle 3 fix, net, web **4** knot, maze, mesh, muss **5** ravel, skein, snarl, twist **6** jumble, jungle, ruffle, rumple, tousle **7** impasse, network **8** dishevel, disorder **9** labyrinth **10** disarrange

tangled 6 knotty **7** chaotic, complex, jumbled, mixed-up, snarled **11** complicated, intertwined

Tanguy, Yves
 born: 5 Paris **6** France
 artwork: 4 Fear **17** Mama Papa is Wounded, Untitled Landscape **18** Rose of the Four Winds **20** Slowly Toward the North **22** Four O'Clock in Summer Hope, Indefinite Divisibility **23** Multiplication of the Arcs **25** Extinction of Useless Lights

tank 3 vat **6** boiler **7** cistern **8** aquarium, fish tank **9** container, reservoir **10** armored car, receptacle **11** storage tank

Tannhauser and the Tournament of Song at Wartburg
 opera by: 6 Wagner
 also: 41 Tannhauser und der Sangerkrieg auf dem Wartburg
 character: 5 Venus **7** Wolfram **9** Elizabeth

Tanoan
 tribe: 4 Tuei **5** Kiowa **6** Isleta

tantalize 4 bait **5** charm, taunt, tease, tempt **6** entice, lead on **7** bewitch, provoke, torment **8** intrigue **9** captivate, fascinate, titillate **15** whet the appetite **18** make one's mouth water

tantalizing 7 teasing **8** inviting, tempting **9** appealing, leading on **10** intriguing **11** fascinating

Tantalus
 king of: 4 Pisa **7** Phrygia
 father: 8 Thyestes
 wife: 12 Clytemnestra
 son: 6 Pelops
 daughter: 5 Niobe
 punishment in Hades: 6 hunger, thirst

tantamount 4 like **5** equal **9** analogous **10** comparable, equivalent, on a par with **12** commensurate **13** commensurable

tantrum 3 fit **5** storm **7** flare-up, rampage **8** outburst, paroxysm **9** explosion **12** fit of passion **13** burst of temper, conniption fit

Tanzania
 other name: 12 isle of cloves
 capital/largest city: 11 Dar es Salaam
 new capital: 6 Dodoma

 others: 4 Wete, **5** Kilwa, Lindi, Moshi, Tanga, Ujiji **6** Arusha, Kigoma, Mwadui, Mwanza, Tabora **7** Korogwe, Mtawara **8** Morogoro, Zanzibar **12** Kwasemangube, Zanzibar Town
 division: 8 Zanzibar **17** union of Tanganyika
 monetary unit: 4 cent **8** shilling
 weight: 8 farsalah
 island: 5 Mafia, Pemba **6** Latham **8** Zanzibar
 lake: 5 Eyasi, Nyasa, Rukwa **6** Malawi, Natron, Nyassa **7** Manyara **8** Victoria **10** Tanganyika
 mountain: 4 Kibo, Mero **8** Usambara
 highest point: 11 Kilimanjaro
 river: 4 Lupa, Ruvu, Wami **5** Ruaha **6** Kagera, Luwegu, Mbaesa, Rufiji, Rungwa, Ruvuma **7** Nkululu, Pangani **8** Mbenkuru **11** Mbarangandu
 sea: 6 Indian
 physical feature:
  crater: 10 Ngorongoro
  gorge: 7 Olduvai
  national park: 9 Serengeti
  plains: 9 Serengeti
  steppe: 5 Masai **8** Iwembere
  valley: 9 Great Rift
 people: 2 Ila **4** Arab, Gogo, Goma, Haya, Hehe **5** Asian, Bantu, Masai **6** Arusha, Chagga, Sukuma, Wagogo, Wagoma **7** African, Makonde, Sambara, Sandawe, Shirazi, Swahili, Wabunga, Zongora **8** Nyakyusa, Nyamwezi
  early man: 13 zinjanthropus
  explorer: 6 Da.Gama **7** Rebmann **11** Livingstone
  leader: 5 Sayid **6** Karume **7** Nyerere **16** Sultan of Zanzibar
 language: 5 Bantu **6** Arabic **7** English, Khoisan, Nilotic, Swahili **8** Cushitic, Gujarati
 religion: 5 Islam **7** animism **12** Christianity
 feature:
  animal: 6 dik-dik
  cattle barn: 4 byre
  clothing: 4 sari **6** bui bui
  fly: 6 tsetse
  holiday: 8 Saba Saba
  homestead: 8 manyatta
 food:
  dish: 5 ugali

Tao Te Ching
 author: 6 Lao-tzu

Taotieh
 origin: 7 Chinese
 form: 6 animal

tap 3 pat, rap, use **4** cock, drum, peck, thud **5** spout, touch, valve **6** broach, employ, faucet, hammer, spigot, stroke, uncork, unplug **7** draw off, exploit, utilize **8** draw upon, stopcock **9** put to work, unstopper

taper 3 dip, wax **4** wick **5** light **6** candle, cierge, narrow **8** decrease **9** nar-

 rowing **10** diminution **12** come to a point

taper off 4 wane **5** abate **6** weaken **7** slacken, subside **8** decrease, diminish, fade away, slack off

tapestry 3 rug **5** arras, tapis **6** Bruges, fabric, mosaic **7** Gobelin, hanging, montage, weaving **8** Aubusson **12** wallcovering

Tapley, Mark
 character in: 16 Martin Chuzzlewit
 author: 7 Dickens

Tappertit, Simon
 character in: 12 Barnaby Rudge
 author: 7 Dickens

Taprobane *see* **8** Sri Lanka

taproom 3 bar, pub **6** lounge, saloon, tavern **8** alehouse **11** bar and grill, public house **14** cocktail lounge

Taras Bulba
 author: 12 Nikolai Gogol
 character: 5 Ostap **6** Andrii, Yankel **26** Daughter of the Polish Waiwode

Tarascans, Tarascos
 location: 6 Mexico **9** Michoacan **14** Central America
 leader: 8 Zincicha **9** Tangaxoan, Tariacuri

Tarawa
 capital of: 8 Kiribati

Tar Baby
 author: 12 Toni Morrison

Tarchetius
 king of: 9 Alba Longa

tardy 4 late, slow **5** slack **6** remiss **7** belated, languid, overdue **8** crawling, creeping, dilatory, slowpoke, sluggish **9** leisurely, not on time, reluctant, slow-paced, snail-like **10** behindhand, behind time, unpunctual **14** slow as molasses **15** procrastinating

tare 12 Biblical weed **15** weight deduction

target 3 aim, end **4** butt, dupe, goal, goat, gull, mark, plan, prey **5** patsy **6** design, intent, object, pigeon, victim **7** purpose **8** ambition **9** intention, objective **13** laughingstock

Targitaus
 father: 4 Zeus
 first inhabitant of: 7 Scythia

Tar Heel State
 nickname of: 13 North Carolina

tariff 3 fee **4** cost, duty, fare, levy, rate, rent **5** price **6** charge, excise, impost **7** expense **8** input tax **9** excise tax, export tax **10** assessment, commission, freightage

Tarkington, Booth
 author of: 6 Penrod **9** Seventeen **10** Alice Adams **13** Kate Fennigate **14** The Man from Home **17** Monsieur Beaucaire **19** The World Does Not Move **23** The Magnificent Ambersons

Tarleton, Stuart and Brent

characters in: 15 Gone With the Wind
author: 8 Mitchell

tarnish 3 dim **4** blot, dull, foul, soil, spot **5** dirty, erode, stain, sully, taint **6** befoul, darken, defame, defile, smirch, vilify **7** blacken, blemish, corrode, degrade, oxidize **8** besmirch, discolor, disgrace, dishonor **9** denigrate, discredit **10** lose luster, stigmatize **17** drag through the mud

tarnished 5 dirty **6** soiled **7** stained, sullied **8** oxidized **10** discolored

Tarnkappe
origin: 8 Germanic
mentioned in: 14 Nibelungenlied
form: 5 cloak
gives wearer: 8 strength **12** invisibility
stolen by: 9 Siegfried
stolen from: 8 Niblungs **9** Nibelungs

tarot
Italian: 6 naibes **7** attutti **8** tarocchi
German: 5 tarok
French: 5 tarau, tarot
cards/deck: 12 seventy-eight
division: 11 major arcana, minor arcana **12** lesser arcana **13** greater arcana
suit: 3 cup **4** coin, wand **5** baton, money, sword **6** cudgel **8** pentacle
face card: 4 king, page **5** knave, queen, valet **6** knight
major arcana: 4 Fool, Moon **5** Death **7** Justice **8** Judgment **9** Hanged Man **14** Wheel of Fortune

tarpaulin 4 tarp **6** canvas **9** dropcloth **15** waterproof cover

Tarpeia
form: 12 vestal virgin
father: 15 Spurius Tarpeius
betrayed: 4 Rome
betrayed to: 7 Sabines
killed by: 7 Sabines

Tarquin
king of: 4 Rome
origin: 8 Etruscan
also called: 17 Tarquinius Priscus **18** Tarquinius Superbus
wife: 8 Tanaquil

tarragon
botanical name: 20 Artemisia dracunculus
means: 6 dragon **12** little dragon
Arab: 7 tarkhum
French: 8 estragon
origin: 7 Siberia
used as: 8 purifier
flavor: 8 licorice
use: 4 fish **5** salad, sauce **10** mayonnaise **14** Bearnaise sauce

tarry 3 lag **4** bide, rest, stay, wait **5** abide, dally, delay, pause, stall **6** dawdle, linger, put off, remain **7** be tardy **8** hang back, postpone, stave off, take time **9** temporize **10** hang

around **13** cool one's heels, procrastinate

tarsal
bone of: 5 ankle

tart 3 pie **4** acid, sour **5** acerb, acrid, sharp, spicy, tangy **6** acetic, barbed, biting, bitter, crusty **7** caustic, cutting, piquant, pungent, sourish **8** vinegary **10** astringent **11** pastry shell

tartan
fabric: 6 woolen
pattern: 5 plaid
identifies: 4 clan
in: 8 Scotland **9** Highlands
skirt: 4 kilt
trousers: 5 trews

Tartarean *see* **8** infernal

Tartarin of Tarascon
author: 14 Alphonse Daudet

Tartarus
form: 5 abyss
below: 5 Hades
imprisoned: 6 Titans

tartness 7 acidity, sarcasm **8** acerbity **9** sharpness **11** astringency

Tartuffe
author: 7 Moliere
character: 5 Damis, Orgon **6** Dorine, Elmire, Valere **7** Cleante, Mariane **14** Madame Pernelle

Tarzan
author: 18 Edgar Rice Burroughs
character: 3 Boy **4** Jane **7** Cheetah
Tarzan also called: 15 Lord of Greystoke, Lord of the Jungle
comic strip creator: 9 Hal Foster **12** Burme Hogarth
played by: 6 Ron Ely **9** Lex Barker **11** Elmo Lincoln **12** Buster Crabbe **17** Johnny Weissmuller

task 3 job **4** duty, work **5** chore, labor, stint **6** charge, errand **7** mission **8** business **10** assignment **11** undertaking **14** responsibility

Task, The
author: 13 William Cowper

taskmaster 4 boss **6** despot, master, tyrant **7** foreman, headman, manager **8** director, martinet, overseer, stickler **10** supervisor **11** Simon Legree, slave driver **14** disciplinarian, superintendent

Tasmania
bay: 5 Storm **6** Oyster
capital: 6 Hobart
city: 10 Launceston
country: 9 Australia
formerly: 14 Van Diemen's Land
island: 4 Echo **6** Sorell
mountain: 4 Ossa **6** Cradle
river: 3 Esk
strait: 4 Bass
birthplace of: 10 Errol Flynn

Tasso, Torquato
author of: 6 Aminta **7** Rinaldo **18** Jerusalem Delivered

taste 3 bit, nip, sip, try, yen **4** bent, bite, feel, meet, tang, test, whim **5** crumb, enjoy, fancy, savor, smack **6** desire, flavor, hunger, liking, morsel, relish, sample, thirst **7** craving, decorum, discern, forkful, insight, leaning, longing, savor of, smack of, swallow, undergo **8** appetite, delicacy, fondness, judgment, mouthful, penchant, piquancy, spoonful, yearning **9** encounter, hankering, partake of, propriety **10** experience, partiality, propensity, take a sip of **11** correctness, discernment, disposition, inclination, take a bite of **12** eat a little of, predilection **14** discrimination, drink a little of
French: 4 gout

tasteful 7 elegant, refined **8** artistic, becoming, cultured, esthetic, handsome, suitable **9** beautiful, exquisite **10** attractive, well-chosen

tasteless 3 low **4** flat, mild, rude, weak **5** bland, cheap, crass, crude, gaudy, gross, tacky **6** coarse, common, flashy, garish, ribald, watery **7** insipid, uncouth **8** improper, indecent, unseemly **9** inelegant, offensive, unrefined **10** disgusting, flavorless, indecorous, indelicate, uncultured, unesthetic, unflavored, unsuitable **11** distasteful, insensitive

tastemakers 7 leaders **10** avant-garde, innovators **12** stylesetters, trendsetters

tasty 3 hot **5** spicy, tangy, yummy **6** savory **7** piquant, zestful **8** luscious **9** delicious, flavorful, palatable, toothsome **10** appetizing, delectable, flavorsome **11** good-tasting, scrumptious **12** full-flavored, well-seasoned

Tatar, Mr
character in: 22 The Mystery of Edwin Drood
author: 7 Dickens

Tatius
also: 5 Titus
co-ruler with: 7 Romulus

Tatler, The
author: 13 Joseph Addison, Richard Steele

tattered 4 torn **6** broken, ragged, ripped, shabby, shaggy **10** disheveled **11** dilapidated

tatters 4 rags **6** shreds **7** patches

tattle 3 rat **4** blab **5** prate **6** gabble, gossip, snitch, squeal, tell on **7** blather, chatter, hearsay, prattle, twaddle **8** inform on **9** loose talk **11** mudslinging **12** tittle-tattle **13** tonguewagging

tattletale 3 rat **4** fink **5** sneak **6** gossip, snitch **7** ratfink, stoolie, tattler **8** betrayer, busybody, informer, squealer, telltale **8** informer **10** newsmonger, talebearer **11** rumormonger, stool pigeon **12** blabbermouth, troublemaker **13** scandalmonger

Tatum, Edward Lawrie
    field: **8** genetics **12** biochemistry
    discovered: **19** gene characteristics
    awarded: **10** Nobel Prize
taunt 3 guy, rag **4** gibe, jeer, jive,
    mock, slur, twit **5** scoff, sneer, tease **6**
    deride, harass, insult, jeer at **7** pro-
    voke, ragging, sneer at, snigger, tor-
    ment **8** chaffing, derision, ridicule **9**
    make fun of, poke fun at, snigger at
    10 harassment, make game of, tor-
    menting **11** provocation
Taura
    form: **3** cow
    attribute: **6** sacred
taurobolium
    rite of: **7** baptism
Taurog, Norman
    director of: **6** Skippy (Oscar) **8** Boys
    Town
Taurus
    symbol: **4** bull
    planet: **5** Venus
    rules: **5** money **9** resources
    born: **3** May **5** April
taut 4 neat, snug, tidy, trig, trim **5**
    rigid, smart, tense, tight **6** spruce **7**
    orderly **8** not loose, not slack **9** ship-
    shape, unbending, unrelaxed **10**
    drawn tight, inflexible, no-nonsense
    11 under strain **12** businesslike **13**
    well-regulated **15** well-disciplined
tavern 3 bar, pub **4** dive **6** bistro, sa-
    loon **7** barroom, gin mill, taproom **8**
    alehouse, drinkery, grogshop **9** beer
    joint, brasserie, honky-tonk, road-
    house **10** restaurant **11** public house
    12 watering hole **14** cocktail lounge
    French: **7** auberge
    German: **8** Brauhaus
tawdry 4 loud **5** cheap, crass, gaudy,
    showy, tacky **6** flashy, garish, tinsel,
    vulgar **7** raffish **8** gimcrack **9** inele-
    gant, obtrusive, tasteless **10** flamboy-
    ant **11** conspicuous, pretentious **12**
    meretricious, ostentatious
tawny 3 tan **4** fawn **5** beige, dusky, ol-
    ive, sandy **6** bronze **7** swarthy **8**
    brownish **10** light brown **14** yellow-
    ish-brown
tax 3 sap, try **4** duty, lade, levy, load,
    tire, toll **5** drain, weigh **6** assess, bur-
    den, charge, custom, impost **7** deplete,
    exhaust, stretch, wear out **8** exertion,
    overwork **10** assessment, obligation,
    overburden
    kind: **4** city **5** sales, state **6** county,
    excise, income, luxury **8** property
    11 inheritance **12** excess profit
Taxi
    character: **9** John Burns, Tony Banta
    10 Alex Rieger **11** Elaine Nardo,
    Latka Gravas **12** Bobby Wheeler,
    Louie De Palma
    cast: **9** Carol Kane, Tony Danza **10**
    Judd Hirsch **11** Andy Kaufman,

Danny DeVito, Jeff Conaway
    12 Marilu Henner **13** Randall Carver
    company: **11** Sunshine Cab
taxicab 4 hack **6** jitney **7** droshky,
    hackney **8** hired car, rickshaw **10** au-
    tomobile **11** jinrickshaw
Taxi Driver
    director: **14** Martin Scorsese
    cast: **10** Peter Boyle **11** Jodie Foster
    12 Albert Brooks, Harvey Keitel, Ro-
    bert De Niro **13** Leonard Harris **14**
    Cybill Shepherd
    setting: **11** New York City
    score: **15** Bernard Herrmann
    script: **12** Paul Schrader
taxon 5 class, genus, order **6** family,
    phylum **7** kingdom, species
taxonomy
    study of: **17** structure contrast **19**
    structure comparison
Taylor, Elizabeth
    born: **6** London **7** England
    husband: **8** Mike Todd **10** John
    Warner **11** Eddie Fisher, Nicky Hil-
    ton **13** Richard Burton **14** Michael
    Wilding
    roles: **5** Giant **7** Ivanhoe **9** Cleopatra
    11 Little Women **12** The Sandpiper
    14 A Place in the Sun, National Vel-
    vet, Raintree County **16** Butterfield
    Eight (Oscar), Cat on a Hot Tin Roof,
    Father of the Bride **18** Suddenly Last
    Summer **19** The Taming of the
    Shrew **25** Who's Afraid of Virginia
    Woolf (Oscar)
Taylor, Robert
    real name: **22** Spangler Arlington
    Brugh
    wife: **12** Ursula Thiess **15** Barbara
    Stanwyck
    roles: **7** Camille, Ivanhoe **8** Quo Vadis
    11 Billy the Kid **14** Waterloo Bridge
    20 Magnificent Obsession
Taylor, Zachary
    nickname: **18** Old Rough and Ready
    presidential rank: **7** twelfth
    party: **4** Whig
    state represented: **2** LA
    defeated: **4** (Lewis) Cass **8** (Martin)
    Van Buren
    vice president: **8** (Millard) Fillmore
    cabinet:
        state: **7** (John Middleton) Clayton
        treasury: **8** (William Morris) Mere-
        dith
        war: **8** (George Walker) Crawford
        attorney general: **7** (Reverdy)
        Johnson
        navy: **7** (William Ballard) Preston
        postmaster general: **8** (Jacob) Col-
        lamer
        interior: **5** (Thomas) Ewing
    born: **12** Montebello VA **12** Orange
    County
    died: **12** Washington DC
    buried: **12** Louisville KY
    education: **9** no college **16** privately

tutored
    religion: **12** Episcopalian
    political career: **21** none prior to
    presidency
    civilian career: **7** planter, soldier
    military service: **6** US Army **12** major
    general
        War: **7** Mexican **9** Black Hawk **19**
        War of Eighteen-Twelve **14** Sec-
        ond Seminole
    notable events of lifetime/
    presidency:
        treaty: **13** Clayton-Bulwer
    father: **7** Richard
    mother: **5** Sarah (Dabney Strother)
    siblings: **6** George **7** Hancock **11**
    Sarah Bailey **12** Elizabeth Lee, Emily
    Richard **13** Joseph Pannill **21** Wil-
    liam Dabney Strother
    wife: **8** Margaret (Mackall Smith)
    children: **7** Richard **9** Sarah Knox **10**
    Ann Mackall **13** Margaret Smith,
    Mary Elizabeth, Octavia Panill
Tchad see **4** Chad
**Tchaikovsky, Peter (Piotr Ilyich
    Chaikovsky)**
    born: **6** Russia **8** Votkinsk
    composer of: **7** Manfred, Mazeppa **8**
    Iolanthe, Pathetic (symphony No 6),
    Swan Lake **9** Joan of Arc **10** Nut-
    cracker **12** Eugene Onegin, Winter
    Dreams **14** Italian Caprice, Romeo
    and Juliet, The Enchantress **16** The
    Queen of Spades **17** Francesca da
    Rimini, The Sleeping Beauty **22**
    Eighteen-Twelve Overture
tea 10 Camellia sinensis
    varieties: **4** chai **5** Assam, Bohea,
    China, green, pekoe, Yerba **6** Ceylon,
    Oolong, Oswego, Tisane **7** African,
    Arabian, cambric, crystal, Lapsang,
    Mexican, redroot, Spanish **8** berga-
    mot, camomile, Earl Grey, Labrador,
    mountain, Paraguay, Siberian, Sou-
    chong, Woodrull **9** gunpowder,
    lemon balm, New Jersey, sassafras
    10 Darjeeling, Philippine **11** Appala-
    chian, Orange Pekoe **14** Irish break-
    fast **16** English breakfast
teach 5 coach, drill, edify, prime, tutor
    6 inform, school **7** educate, implant,
    prepare **8** exercise, instruct **9** en-
    lighten, inculcate **10** discipline **12** in-
    doctrinate
Teach
    character in: **21** The Master of Bal-
    lantrae
    author: **9** Stevenson
teacher 3 don **5** coach, tutor **6** master,
    mentor **7** maestro, trainer **8** educator
    9 preceptor, professor **10** instructor,
    schoolmarm **12** schoolmaster **13**
    schoolteacher **14** schoolmistress
teaching 5 dogma, tenet **6** belief **7**
    nurture, precept **8** doctrine, pedagogy,
    training, tutelage, tutoring **9** educa-
    tion, principle, schooling **10** convic-

tion, philosophy **11** inculcation, instructing, instruction, preparation **14** indoctrination

tea dance
    French: 10 the dansant

teal
    group of: 5 ducks
    color: 4 blue **5** green

team 3 rig, set **4** ally, band, crew, five, gang, join, nine, pair, side, unit, yoke **5** force, group, merge, party, squad, staff, unify, unite **6** circle, clique, couple, eleven, league, tandem **7** combine, company, coterie, faction **8** alliance, federate **9** coalition, cooperate **10** amalgamate, federation, sports team, yoked group **11** association, consolidate, get together, incorporate **12** band together, join together **13** confederation

teammate 4 ally **7** partner **8** coplayer, coworker **9** associate, colleague, co-partner **11** confederate **12** collaborator

team spirit 10 group pride, solidarity **13** esprit de corps

team up 4 ally **5** unite **9** cooperate **10** join forces **11** collaborate

tear 3 fly, gap, hie, rip, run **4** bolt, dart, dash, grab, hole, mist, pull, race, rend, rent, rift, rive, rush, scud, slit, snag, swim, whiz, yank **5** abuse, break, crack, fault, pluck, scoot, seize, sever, shoot, shred, speed, split, spurt, sweep, whisk **6** breach, cleave, damage, divide, gallop, hasten, hustle, injury, plunge, ravage, scurry, snatch, sprint, sunder, wrench **7** disrupt, fissure, hard use, opening, rupture, scamper, scuttle **8** disunite, teardrop, scramble, splinter **9** come apart, hotfoot it, pull apart, skedaddle **10** impairment, make tracks **11** destruction **12** pull to pieces

tear down 4 raze **5** level, smash, wreck **7** destroy, flatten **8** demolish **9** dismantle, take apart

tearful 5 teary, weepy **6** crying **7** bawling, crushed, sobbing, wailing, weeping **8** mournful **9** lamenting, sniveling **10** blubbering, lachrymose, whimpering **11** heartbroken **12** inconsolable **13** brokenhearted

tear off 5 sever **6** detach, rip off **7** pull off **8** break off, separate **10** wrench away

Teasdale, Sara
    author of: 8 Love Song **11** Helen of Troy **13** Dark of the Moon **14** Flame and Shadow, Rivers to the Sea, Strange Victory

tease 3 guy, irk, nag, rag, vex **4** bait, gall, gibe, goad, haze, jeer, josh, mock, pest, rile, twit **5** annoy, chafe, harry, mimic, pique, scoff, sneer, taunt, worry **6** bad- ger, bother, harass, hazing, heckle, hector, mocker,

needle, pester, plague, teaser **7** bedevil, chafing, laugh at, needler, provoke, razzing, snigger, taunter, torment, worrier **8** derision, heckling, irritate, needling, ridicule **9** aggravate, make fun of, mimicking, persecute, tantalize, tormentor **10** harassment, tantalizer **11** persecution

teaspoon
    abbreviation: 3 tsp

Teazle, Sir Peter and Lady
    characters in: 19 The School for Scandal
    author: 8 Sheridan

technical 5 trade **10** mechanical, vocational **11** complicated, nonacademic **13** technological

technique 3 art, way **4** form **5** craft, knack, style **6** manner, method, system **7** formula, know-how **8** approach, facility **9** procedure **10** adroitness, expertness, technology **11** proficiency **12** skillfulness

tedious 3 dry **4** drab, dull, long, slow **5** vapid **6** boring, dismal, dreary, jejune, tiring **7** humdrum, insipid, irksome, onerous, prosaic **8** drawn-out, lifeless, tiresome, wearying **9** fatiguing, laborious, wearisome **10** burdensome, exhausting, monotonous, oppressive, unexciting **13** time-consuming, unimaginative, uninteresting

tediousness 5 ennui **7** boredom **8** dullness, monotony

tedium 3 rut **5** ennui **7** boredom **8** drabness, dullness, monotony, sameness **10** dreariness **11** routineness **12** tiresomeness

tedium of life
    Latin: 12 taedium vitae

teem 4 brim, gush **5** swarm **6** abound **8** be full of, overflow **9** be overrun **15** burst at the seams

teeming 4 full **7** crowded **8** swarming **9** abounding, bounteous **11** overflowing

teeny-weeny 3 wee **4** tiny **5** dwarf **6** little, minute, petite **9** miniature, minuscule **10** diminutive, pocket-size **11** lilliputian, microscopic, pocket-sized

teeter 4 reel, sway **5** lurch, waver **6** seesaw, totter, wobble **7** stagger **8** hesitate **9** vacillate

teetotaler 3 dry **9** abstainer **10** nondrinker **14** prohibitionist

Tegucigalpa
    capital of: 8 Honduras

Tegyrius
    king of: 6 Thrace

Tehani
    character in: 17 Mutiny on the Bounty
    authors: 4 Hall **8** Nordhoff

Tehran, Teheran
    capital of: 4 Iran

    landmark: 10 Melaat Park **12** Marble Palace, Marmar Palace **14** Azadai Monument, Gulestan Palace, Saadabad Palace **15** Freedom Monument, Hosseineh Mosque, Shahyad Monument **23** Center for Islamic Studies
    means: 9 warm place
    mountain: 6 Elburz **8** Demavend
    ruler: 8 Khomeini **23** Muhammad Reza Shah Pahlavi

Telamon
    king of: 7 Salamis
    member of: 9 Argonauts
    father: 6 Aeacus
    mother: 6 Endeis
    brother: 6 Peleus
    half-brother: 6 Phocus
    wife: 6 Glauce **7** Eriboea
    son: 4 Ajax **6** Teucer
    friend: 8 Hercules

Telegonus
    father: 7 Proteus **8** Odysseus
    mother: 5 Circe
    wife: 2 Io **8** Penelope
    killed: 8 Odysseus
    killed by: 8 Hercules

telegraph
    invented by: 5 Morse, Woods **6** Edison **7** Marconi

Telemachus
    father: 8 Odysseus
    mother: 8 Penelope
    son: 7 Latinus

Telemann, Georg Philipp
    born: 7 Germany **9** Magdeburg
    composer of: 9 Fantasias **10** Times of Day **12** Don Quichotte **14** Die Tageszeiten, Musique de Table

Telemus
    vocation: 4 seer
    father: 7 Eurymus
    warned: 10 Polyphemus

telepathy 3 ESP **10** sixth sense **11** second sight **12** clairvoyance **19** spirit communication, thought transference **22** extrasensory perception

telephone
    invented by: 4 Bell
    type: 3 cell, pay, TDD **6** mobile, rotary **8** cellular, portable, princess, wireless **9** extension, touch-tone **10** push-button

Telephone, The
    opera by: 7 Menotti

telescope
    invented by: 7 Galileo **10** Lippershey
    astronomical: 6 Kepler

telesterion
    form: 8 building
    purpose: 8 religion **11** celebration

television
    invented by: 5 Baird **8** Zworykin **10** Farnsworth

tell 3 ask, bid, own, say, see **4** blab **5** bruit, count, order, speak, spout, state, utter, weigh, write **6** advise, babble, betray, blazon, depict, detail, direct, figure, impart, inform, number, recite, reckon, relate, report, reveal, sketch, unfold **7** apprise, command, compute, confess, declare, discern, divulge, express, find out, mention, narrate, portray, predict, publish, recount, request **8** acquaint, count off, describe, disclose, estimate, forecast, foretell, identify, instruct, perceive, register, set forth **9** apprehend, ascertain, broadcast, calculate, chronicle, enumerate, enunciate, influence, make known, pronounce, recognize **10** take effect **11** communicate, distinguish **12** discriminate **17** breathe a word about

Teller, Edward
field: **7** physics
developed: **8** atom bomb **12** hydrogen bomb

telling 5 solid, valid **6** cogent, potent **7** decided, weighty **8** decisive, definite, forceful, material, positive, powerful, striking **9** effective, effectual, important, momentous, trenchant **10** conclusive, definitive, impressive **11** efficacious, influential, significant **13** consequential

telltale 6 gossip **7** tattler **8** busybody, giveaway, informer, squealer **9** affirming, betraying, divulging, revealing, verifying **10** confirming, disclosing, newsbearer, talebearer, tattletale **11** informative **12** blabbermouth, enlightening **13** scandalmonger

Tellus
called: **10** Terra Mater
origin: **5** Roman
goddess of: **5** earth **8** marriage **9** fertility **11** agriculture
corresponds to: **4** Gaea

temerity 4 gall **5** brass, cheek, nerve **8** audacity, boldness, chutzpah, rashness **9** brashness, freshness, impudence, insolence, pushiness, sauciness **10** brazenness, effrontery **11** forwardness **12** impertinence, indiscretion **13** foolhardiness, intrusiveness

Temin, Howard Martin
field: **8** genetics, oncology
discovered: **20** reverse transcriptase
awarded: **10** Nobel Prize

temper 3 ire **4** bile, calm, fury, gall, mood, rage **5** allay, anger, humor, pique, quiet, still, wrath **6** animus, anneal, choler, dander, harden, pacify, soften, soothe, spleen **7** appease, balance, compose, dudgeon, emotion, ferment, passion, toughen, umbrage **8** acrimony, bad humor, calmness, mitigate, moderate, palliate, vexation **9** annoyance, composure, huffiness **10** irritation, strengthen **11** displeasure, disposition, equilibrium, frame of mind, indignation, peevishness, tranquilize **12** churlishness, irascibility, irritability

temperament 4 bent, cast, mood,

soul, tone **5** humor, tenor **6** makeup, nature, spirit, temper **7** leaning, quality **8** tendency **9** character **10** complexion **11** disposition, frame of mind, personality

temperamental 5 fiery, moody **6** fickle **7** erratic, peppery, willful **8** unstable, volatile **9** emotional, excitable, explosive, hotheaded, mercurial, sensitive, turbulent **10** capricious, headstrong, high-strung, hysterical, mettlesome, passionate, unreliable **11** tempestuous, thin-skinned **12** undependable **13** unpredictable

temperance 8 prudence, sobriety **9** restraint **10** abstention, abstinence, discretion, moderation, self-denial **11** forbearance, prohibition, self-control, teetotalism **14** abstemiousness, self-discipline

temperate 4 calm, cool, even, mild, sane, soft, warm **5** balmy, sober, sunny **6** gen- tle, mellow, sedate, steady **7** clement, patient, sparing **8** composed, moderate, pleasant, rational, tranquil **9** collected, easygoing, unruffled **10** coolheaded, reasonable **11** levelheaded **13** dispassionate, self-possessed, unextravagant, unimpassioned **14** self-controlled, self-restrained

temperature measurement 6 degree, Kelvin **7** Celsius **10** Fahrenheit

tempest 5 chaos, furor, storm **6** hubbub, tumult, uproar **8** brouhaha, outbreak, upheaval **9** agitation, cataclysm, commotion **10** hurly-burly, turbulence **11** disturbance

Tempest, The
author: **18** William Shakespeare
character: **5** Ariel **6** Alonso **7** Antonio, Caliban, Gonzalo, Miranda **8** Prospero **9** Ferdinand, Sebastian

Tempestates
origin: **5** Roman
goddesses of: **6** storms

tempestuous 3 hot **5** fiery **6** raging, stormy **7** excited, frantic, furious, violent **8** agitated, feverish, frenzied **9** emotional, explosive, turbulent, wrought-up **10** hysterical, passionate, tumultuous **11** impassioned, overwrought

Templar, Simon
character in: **8** The Saint
author: **9** Charteris

temple 4 fane, kirk **6** chapel, church, mosque, pagoda, priory, shrine **7** convent **8** basilica, pantheon **9** cathedral, joss house, monastery, sanctuary, synagogue **10** house of God, tabernacle **12** meeting house

Temple, Shirley
married name: **18** Shirley Temple Black
born: **13** Santa Monica CA
roles: **5** Heidi **10** Bright Eyes **15** Wee

Willie Winkie **16** Little Miss Marker, The Little Colonel, The Littlest Rebel **18** Poor Little Rich Girl **21** Susannah of the Mounties **23** Rebecca of Sunnybrook Farm

tempo 4 clip, gait, pace, rate, time **5** meter, speed **6** pacing, stride, timing **8** momentum, velocity

tempo giusto
music: **10** strict time

temporal 3 lay **5** civil **6** mortal **7** mundane, passing, profane, secular, worldly **8** day-to-day, fleeting, fugitive **9** ephemeral, temporary, transient **10** evanescent, noneternal **11** impermanent, nonclerical **12** nonspiritual **17** nonecclesiastical

temporary, temporarily 5 brief, fleet **7** interim, passing, stopgap **8** fleeting, fugitive **9** ephemeral, momentary, provisory, transient **10** evanescent, short-lived, transitory **11** impermanent, provisional **13** flash-in-the-pan
Latin: **10** pro tempore

temporary dwelling
French: **10** pied-a-terre

temporize 5 delay, hedge, stall, tarry, waver **8** hang back, maneuver **9** hem and haw, vacillate **10** equivocate **11** play for time **12** drag one's feet, tergiversate **13** procrastinate

tempt 3 try, woo **4** bait, draw, goad, lure, pull, risk **5** charm, decoy, prick, rouse **6** allure, arouse, entice, incite, invite, seduce **7** attract, bewitch, provoke **8** appeal to, intrigue, inveigle **9** captivate, tantalize **12** put to the test **13** take one's fancy **14** fly in the face of **15** whet the appetite

temptation 4 bait, draw, lure, pull, urge **5** charm, snare, spell **8** stimulus, tempting **9** incentive, seduction **10** allurement, attraction, enticement, incitement, inducement **11** captivation, fascination, provocation

tempter 5 Satan **7** enticer, seducer **8** the Devil

temptress 4 vamp **5** Circe, flirt, siren **7** charmer, Delilah, Jezebel, Lorelei, vampire **8** coquette **9** odalisque, sorceress **10** seductress **11** enchantress, femme fatale

tempus fugit 9 time flies

Ten (10)
director: **12** Blake Edwards
cast: **7** Bo Derek **11** Dudley Moore **12** Julie Andrews

tenable 6 viable **8** arguable, rational, sensible, workable **9** excusable **10** condonable, defendable, defensible, vindicable **11** justifiable, warrantable **12** maintainable

tenacious 3 set **4** fast, firm, hard, iron **6** dogged, mulish **7** adamant, staunch **8** clinging, constant, obdurate, resolute, stalwart, stubborn **9** immovable, obstinate, pigheaded, steadfast, un- bending **10** determined, inexorable, inflexible, persistent, relentless, un- swerving, unwavering, unyielding **11** persevering, undeviating, unfaltering, unremitting **12** intransigent, un- changeable **14** uncompromising

tenaciousness 8 tenacity **9** endurance **10** resolution **11** persistence **12** perse- verance, resoluteness **13** determina- tion **16** stick-to-itiveness

tenacity 8 strength **9** toughness **10** resolution **11** persistence **12** cohesive- ness, perseverance, resoluteness **13** determination, tenaciousness **16** stick- to-itiveness

tenant 6 lessee, lodger, renter, roomer **7** boarder, denizen, dweller **8** occu- pant, resident **10** inhabitant **11** house- holder, leaseholder, paying guest

Tenant of Wildfell Hall, The
   author: 10 Anne Bronte
Tenants, The
   author: 14 Bernard Malamud
Ten Commandments
   also: 9 Decalogue
   given to: 5 Moses
   where given: 10 Mount Sinai
   inscribed on: 12 stone tablets
   first: 32 Thou shalt have no other Gods before me
   second: 37 Thou shalt not bow down before graven images
   third: 44 Thou shalt not take the name of the Lord thy God in vain
   fourth: 34 Remember the Sabbath Day and keep it holy
   fifth: 26 Honor thy father and thy mother
   sixth: 16 Thou shalt not kill
   seventh: 26 Thou shalt not commit adultery
   eighth: 17 Thou shalt not steal
   ninth: 46 Thou shalt not bear false witness against thy neighbor
   tenth: 17 Thou shalt not covet
Ten Commandments, The
   director: 13 Cecil B DeMille
   cast: 8 Nina Foch **9** John Derek **10** Anne Baxter, Debra Paget, Yul Bryn- ner **11** Martha Scott **12** Vincent Price **13** John Carradine, Yvonne De Carlo **14** Charlton Heston (Moses), Judith Anderson **15** Cedric Hardwicke, Edward G Robinson

tend 3 aim **4** bear, head, lead, lean, mind, move **5** be apt, guide, nurse, point, watch **6** extend, foster, man- age, wait on **7** care for, nurture **8** at- tend to, be liable, be likely **9** bid fair to, gravitate, look after, supervise, watch over **10** minister to, predispose, take care of **11** keep an eye on
tendency 3 aim, set **4** bent **5** drift, drive, habit, trend **6** course **7** head- ing, impulse, leaning, turning **8** pen- chant **9** direction, proneness, readi-

ness **10** proclivity, propensity **11** disposition, gravitation, inclination **14** predisposition
tender 3 raw **4** fond, give, good, kind, soft, sore, weak **5** frail, green, place, young **6** aching, benign, callow, car- ing, dainty, extend, feeble, gentle, hand in, loving, prefer, submit, weakly **7** advance, fragile, hold out, painful, present, proffer, propose, sug- gest, swollen **8** delicate, generous, im- mature, inflamed, juvenile, merciful, propound, underage, youthful **9** lay before, sensitive, volunteer **10** benev- olent, put forward, thoughtful, vulner- able **11** considerate, sentimental, soft- hearted, sympathetic, warmhearted **12** affectionate **13** compassionate, inexpe- rienced, understanding **14** impression- able **15** unsophisticated
tenderfoot 4 tyro **6** novice, rookie **8** beginner, neophyte **9** fledgling, green- horn **10** apprentice
tenderhearted 4 mild **6** benign, gen- tle, humane **8** generous, merciful **10** altruistic, benevolent, responsive, thoughtful **11** considerate, kind- hearted, softhearted, sympathetic, warmhearted **13** compassionate, un- derstanding
tenderheartedness 4 pity **5** heart **7** empathy **8** sympathy **10** compassion
tendering 6 giving **8** offering **9** ad- vancing, extending, proposing **10** holding out, preferring, proffering, submitting, suggesting **11** propound- ing **12** volunteering
Tender Is the Night
   author: 16 F Scott Fitzgerald
   character: 8 Abe North **9** Dick Diver **11** Nicole Diver, Tommy Barban **12** Rosemary Hoyt
tenderness 4 love **6** aching, warmth **7** rawness **8** delicacy, fondness, good- ness, humanity, kindness, mildness, smarting, softness, soreness, sympathy **9** affection **10** compassion, gentleness, humaneness, kindliness, lovingness **11** beneficence, benevolence, painful- ness, sensitivity **12** mercifulness **14** loving kindness
tendon 4 cord **5** sinew
   connects: 4 bone **6** muscle
tendril 4 coil, curl **5** crook, shoot, sprig, twist **6** winder **7** climber, ring- let
tenebrous 3 dim **4** dark **5** murky **6** gloomy **7** obscure, shadowy **8** dark- ened, obscured **13** unilluminated
tenet 4 rule, view **5** canon, credo, creed, dogma, maxim **6** belief, thesis **7** opinion **8** doctrine, ideology, posi- tion, teaching **9** principle **10** convic- tion, persuasion
Tennessee
   abbreviation: 2 TN **4** Tenn
   nickname: 7 Big Bend **9** Volunteer **11**

Old Franklin
   capital: 9 Nashville
   largest city: 7 Memphis
   others: 5 Alcoa, Paris **6** Camden, Sparta **7** Bristol, Dickson, Pulaski **8** Franklin, Gallatin, Oak Ridge **9** Ce- dar Hill, Cleveland, Inglewood, Kingsport, Knoxville, Lexington **10** Greenbrier, Morristown, Old Hickory **11** Chattanooga, Clarksville, Spring- field **12** Fayetteville, Murfreesboro **14** Hendersonville
   college: 4 Fisk, Lane **5** Bryan, Siena **6** Bethel **7** Belmont, Lambuth, Le- moyne **8** Milligan, Tusculum **10** Vanderbilt **12** Southwestern **13** Da- vid Lipscomb **14** Meharry Medical **17** Tennessee Wesleyan
   feature: 12 The Hermitage
      dam: 6 Norris, Wilson **7** Douglas
      fort: 5 Henry **8** Donalson, Nash- boro
      national park: 6 Shiloh **13** Cum- berland Gap **19** Great Smoky Mountains (with North Carolina)
      national parkway: 12 Natchez Trace
   tribe: 7 Shawnee **8** Cherokee **9** Chickasaw
   people: 7 Sequoya **8** John Bell **9** James Agee **10** Grace Moore **11** Bes- sie Smith, Cordell Hull **12** Davy Crockett **18** Carey Estes Kefauver **23** Alvin Cullum "Sergeant" York **32** Er- nest Jennings "Tennessee Ernie" Ford
      explorer: 6 Arthur, De Soto **7** Jol- liet, La Salle, Needham **9** Mar- quette
   lake: 7 Douglas **8** Barkeley, Cherokee, Reelfoot, Watts Bar **10** Center Hill **11** Chickamauga
   land rank: 12 thirty-fourth
   mountain: 5 Guyot **7** Lookout, Smo- kies **9** Blue Ridge **10** Cumberland, Great Smoky
      highest point: 13 Clingman's Dome
   physical feature:
      basin: 9 Nashville
      highlands: 11 Appalachian
      plain: 7 Coastal
      plateau: 10 Cumberland
   president: 10 James K Polk **13** An- drew Jackson, Andrew Johnson
   river: 3 Elk **4** Duck **5** Caney, Obion, Stone **6** Clinch **7** Hatchie, Holston **8** Hiwassee **9** Tennessee **10** Cumber- land **11** French Broad, Mississippi **15** Little Tennessee
   state admission: 9 sixteenth
   state bird: 11 mockingbird
   state flower: 4 flag, iris **6** maypop **13** passion flower
   state motto: 16 America at Its Best **22** Agriculture and Commerce
   state song: 11 My Tennessee **17** The Tennessee Waltz **19** My Homeland

Tennessee **26** When It's Iris Time in Tennessee
state tree: 11 tulip poplar **12** yellow poplar
tennis
  athlete: 8 Don Budge, Jan Kodes, Rod Laver, Tom Okker **9** Bjorn Borg, Ivan Lendl, Stan Smith **10** Arthur Ashe, Bill Tilden, Jack Kramer, Maria Bueno, Pam Shriver, Roy Emerson, Steffi Graf **11** Alice Marble, Andre Agassi, Boris Becker, Edward Dibbs, Ilie Nastase, John McEnroe, Ken Rosewall, Monica Seles, Pete Sampras, Tracy Austin **12** Althea Gibson, Darren Cahill, Francois Durr, Jimmy Connors, John Newcombe, Mats Wilander, Roscoe Tanner, Virginia Wade **13** Dennis Ralston, Harold Solomon, Manuel Orantes, Manuel Santana, Martina Hingis, Martin Riessen, Wendy Turnbull **14** Brian Gottfried, Guillermo Vilas, Hana Mandlikova, Pancho Gonzalez, Rosemary Casals **15** Charles Pasarell, Chris Evert Lloyd, Maureen Connolly, Richard Stockton, Vitas Gerulaitis **17** Donald Schollander, Nancy Richey Gunter **18** Margaret Smith Court, Martina Navratilova **20** Helen Wills Moody Roark **21** Billie Jean Moffitt King, Evonne Goolagong Cawley
  cup: 5 Davis
Tennyson, Alfred, Lord
  author of: 4 Maud **7** Mariana, Ulysses **10** Enoch Arden, In Memoriam (A H H) **12** Locksley Hall, Morte d'Arthur **16** The Lady of Shalott **18** The Idylls of the King **26** The Charge of the Light Brigade
tenor 4 gist **5** drift, sense, trend **6** course, import, intent, nature, object **7** content, essence, meaning, purport, purpose **8** argument, tendency **9** direction, intention, substance **11** connotation, implication **12** significance
tense 4 taut **5** brace, drawn, rigid, shaky, stiff, tight **6** braced, draw up, on edge, uneasy **7** anxious, excited, fearful, fidgety, jittery, nervous, restive, stiffen, uptight **8** agitated, make taut, restless, strained, timorous **9** tighten up, tremulous, wrought-up **10** high-strung, inflexible, unyielding **12** apprehensive
tension 5 dread **6** spring, strain, stress **7** anxiety, pulling, tugging **8** bad vibes, exertion, pressure, rigidity, tautness, traction **9** hostility, misgiving, stiffness, straining, tightness **10** stretching **11** fearfulness, nervousness, restiveness, trepidation **12** apprehension, elastic force, perturbation **13** bad vibrations, combativeness
tent 3 pup **4** care, hard **5** gauze, probe, tepee **6** bigtop, canvas, search, teepee, wigwam **7** shelter **8** pavilion **10** tabernacle

tentacle 3 arm **6** feeler **9** appendage
tentative 4 iffy **5** trial **6** acting **8** not final, proposed **9** ad interim, temporary, undecided, unsettled **10** contingent, indefinite, not settled **11** conditional, probational, provisional, speculative, unconfirmed **12** experimental, probationary **15** subject to change **18** under consideration
tentative procedure 4 test **5** flier, trail **6** feeler, tryout **7** venture **10** experiment **12** trial balloon
tenuous 4 slim, thin, weak **5** frail, shaky **6** flimsy, paltry, slight **7** fragile, shallow, slender **8** delicate, gossamer **9** uncertain **10** indefinite **11** halfhearted, unsupported **12** unconvincing **13** unsubstantial
tenure 4 rule, term, time **5** reign **7** tenancy **9** occupancy, retention **10** incumbency, occupation, permanency, possession **11** entitlement, job security **14** administration
tepee, teepee 4 chum, tent **5** lodge **6** wigwam **7** wickiup
tepid 4 cool, mild **7** languid, warmish **8** lukewarm, moderate **9** apathetic, impassive, temperate **10** nonchalant, phlegmatic **11** halfhearted, indifferent, unemotional **13** lackadaisical **14** unenthusiastic
tequila
  type: 6 spirit
  origin: 6 Mexico
  made from: 5 agave **6** maguey
  used with: 4 lime, salt **5** lemon
  drink: 7 Chapala **8** El Diablo
  with creme de cacao: 8 Toreador
  with kahlua: 9 Brave Bull
  with orange juice: 7 Sunrise
  with Tia Maria: 9 Brave Bull
  with triple sec: 9 Margarita
Teraphim
  origin: 6 Hebrew
  form: 4 idol
Ter Borch, Gerard
  born: 6 Zwolle **14** The Netherlands
  artwork: 8 Flea Hunt **10** The Concert **14** Peace of Munster **21** The Parental Admonition
Terbrugghen, Hendrick
  born: 8 Deventer **14** The Netherlands
  artwork: 14 The Flute Player **19** Liberation of St Peter **21** The Calling of St Matthew
Tereshkova, Valentina
  first: 12 woman in space
terete 7 tapered **11** cylindrical
tergal 4 back **6** dorsal
Terkel, Studs
  author of: 4 Race **7** Working **9** Hard Times **10** "The Good War" **14** American Dreams
term, terms 3 age, dub, era, tag **4** call, cite, item, name, span, time, word **5** catch, cycle, epoch, idiom,

reign, spell, stage, state, style, while **6** clause, course, detail, period, phrase, status, string **7** dynasty, footing, proviso **8** duration, interval, position, standing **9** condition, designate, provision, relations, requisite **10** expression, span of time **11** appellation, designation, requirement, stipulation **12** characterize, circumstance, prerequisite **14** administration
termagant 3 nag **4** fury **5** scold, shrew, vixen **6** ogress, virago **7** hellcat, hellion, she-wolf, tigress **8** battle-ax, fishwife, harridan, spitfire **9** Xanthippe
Termagant
  character in: 21 medieval morality plays
terminal 3 end **4** last **5** depot, fatal, final, stand **6** deadly, lethal, mortal **7** station **8** terminus **10** concluding
terminate 3 end **4** stop **5** cease, close, lapse **6** expire, finish, run out, wind up **8** complete, conclude **11** come to an end, discontinue **12** bring to an end
termination 3 end **4** halt **5** close, finis, lapse **6** ending, finale, finish, windup **7** closing **8** stoppage **9** cessation **10** completion, concluding, conclusion, expiration **15** discontinuation
terminus 3 end **4** stop **5** depot, limit **6** ending **7** extreme, station **8** boundary, last stop, terminal **9** extremity **10** conclusion
Terminus
  origin: 5 Roman
  god of: 9 landmarks **10** boundaries
terminus ad quem 10 end to which, final limit **11** ending point
terminus a quo 9 beginning **12** end from which **13** starting point
termite
  variety: 6 desert **7** dry wood **8** damp wood **10** powderpost, rotten wood **11** soldierless **12** subterranean
Terms of Endearment
  director: 12 James L Brooks
  based on novel by: 13 Larry McMurtry
  cast: 11 Debra Winger **13** Jack Nicholson **15** Shirley MacLaine
  Oscar for: 7 actress (MacLaine), picture **8** director **15** supporting actor (Nicholson)
Terpsichore
  member of: 5 Muses
  personifies: 7 dancing **10** choral song
Terra
  goddess of: 5 Earth
  Greek: 4 Gaea
  mother: 5 Chaos
  offspring: 6 Pontus, Titans, Uranus **7** Erinyes, Oceanus **8** Cyclopes **9** mountains **13** Hecatonchires
terrace 4 roof **5** level, patio, plane, porch **6** street **7** balcony, plateau **9**

esplanade, promenade **10** embankment

Terraced Bay *see* **6** Taiwan

terra-cotta 4 clay **6** russet **8** brownish **12** reddish-brown **14** brownish-orange

terrain 4 area, zone **5** tract **6** ground, milieu, region **7** setting **8** district **9** territory **10** topography **11** countryside, environment **12** surroundings

terra incognita 11 unknown land **14** unexplored land, unknown subject **16** unknown territory

terrapin 3 box **4** emyd, emys **6** slider, turpin, turtle **8** tortoise **11** diamond back
family: 8 Emydidae
female: 6 heifer
male: 4 bull

terrestrial 4 land **6** earth's, global, ground **7** earthly, mundane, worldly **8** riparian **10** earthbound

terrible 3 bad **4** dire, huge **5** awful, great, harsh, rough, scary **6** brutal, fierce, horrid, odious, severe, strong **7** beastly, extreme, fearful, ghastly, hateful, heinous, hideous, intense **8** alarming, dreadful, enormous, fearsome, horrible, shocking, terrific **9** appalling, excessive, harrowing, monstrous, obnoxious, offensive, repulsive, revolting, upsetting **10** disturbing, formidable, horrifying, immoderate, inordinate, terrifying, tremendous, unpleasant **11** distasteful, distressing, frightening, intolerable **12** insufferable **13** objectionable

terrier
dog breed: 3 fox **4** bull, Skye **5** Cairn, Irish, Welsh **6** border, Boston **7** Norfolk, Tibetan, wire fox **8** Airedale, Lakeland, Scottish, Sealyham **9** Kerry Blue **10** Australian, Bedlington, Manchester **13** Dandie Dinmont **17** soft-coated wheaten, Staffordshire bull, West Highland white **18** miniature schnauzer **21** American Staffordshire

terrific 3 fab **4** fine, good, huge **5** awful, great, harsh, marvy, scary, super **6** bang-up, fierce, severe, superb **7** extreme, fearful, intense, sensash **8** alarming, dreadful, enormous, fabulous, fearsome, smashing, splendid, terrible **9** excellent, excessive, fantastic, harrowing, marvelous, monstrous, upsetting, wonderful **10** disturbing, horrifying, immoderate, inordinate, remarkable, stupendous, superduper, terrifying, tremendous **11** distressing, exceptional, frightening, sensational **13** extraordinary **14** out of this world

terrified 6 afraid, scared **7** alarmed, panicky **9** petrified **10** frightened **11** scared stiff **13** panic-stricken **14** terror-stricken **17** frightened to death

terrify 3 cow **5** abash, alarm, daunt, panic, scare, unman, upset **6** appall,

dismay **7** agitate, disturb, horrify, overawe, petrify **8** disquiet, frighten **10** intimidate **17** make one's skin crawl **20** make one's blood run cold **22** make one's hair stand on end

terrifying 5 awful, dread **7** fearful **8** alarming, dreadful **9** frightful **11** frightening, hair-raising

territory 4 area, land, pale, zone **5** clime, realm, state, tract **6** bounds, colony, domain, empire, limits, locale, nation, region, sector **7** acreage, kingdom, mandate, terrain **8** confines, district, dominion, province **9** bailiwick **10** dependency **11** countryside **12** commonwealth, principality, protectorate

terror 3 awe **4** fear **5** alarm, dread, panic **6** dismay, fright, horror **7** anxiety **8** affright, disquiet **9** agitation **11** disquietude, trepidation **12** apprehension, perturbation **13** consternation **16** fear and trembling

terrorize 3 cow **5** abash, force **6** menace **7** terrify **8** browbeat, bulldoze, threaten **10** intimidate

terror-stricken 6 afraid, scared **7** alarmed, panicky **9** horrified, petrified, terrified **11** scared green, scared stiff **13** panic-stricken, scared to death

Terry and the Pirates
creator: 12 Milton Caniff
character: 7 Pat Ryan **8** Terry Lee **10** Dragon Lady

terse 4 curt, neat **5** brief, clear, crisp, pithy, short **6** abrupt **7** clipped, compact, concise, laconic, pointed, summary **8** clearcut, incisive, succinct **9** axiomatic, condensed, trenchant **10** compressed **11** unambiguous **12** epigrammatic **18** brief and to the point

terseness 7 brevity **8** curtness **9** crispness **10** abruptness **11** compactness, conciseness **12** succinctness

Tesman family
characters in: 11 Hedda Gabler
members: 5 Hedda **6** George **7** Juliana
author: 5 Ibsen

Tess (of the D'Urbervilles)
author: 11 Thomas Hardy
director: 13 Roman Polanski
cast: 8 John Bett **10** Peter Firth, Tom Chadbon **14** Rosemary Martin **15** Nastassia Kinski (Tess)

test 4 exam, quiz **5** check, final, flyer, probe, proof, prove, trial **6** dry run, feeler, try out, verify **7** analyze, confirm, examine, midterm **8** analysis, validate **9** catechism **11** corroborate, examination, investigate, questioning **12** confirmation, substantiate, verification **13** comprehensive, corroboration, investigation, questionnaire

Testament 5 Bible **7** the Book **10** Scriptures **12** New Testament, Old Testament

testament 6 legacy **7** bequest **10** settlement

tester 6 canopy **8** examiner **10** questioner

testify 4 show **5** prove, swear **6** affirm, attest, evince **7** declare, signify **8** evidence, indicate, manifest **11** bear witness, demonstrate **12** give evidence

testimonial 5 medal **6** ribbon, trophy **7** tribute **8** citation, memorial, monument **9** affidavit, reference **10** deposition **11** certificate, endorsement **12** commendation **14** recommendation

testimony 5 proof **6** avowal **7** witness **8** averment, evidence **9** affidavit, statement **10** deposition, indication, profession **11** affirmation, attestation, endorsement **12** confirmation, verification **13** certification, corroboration, demonstration, documentation, manifestation **14** acknowledgment

testy 5 cross, moody **6** crabby, cranky, crusty, filthy, grumpy, snappy, sullen, touchy **7** fretful, peevish, waspish **8** captious, caviling, choleric, churlish, perverse, petulant, snappish, snarling **9** fractious, impatient, irascible, irritable, splenetic **10** ill-humored **11** acrimonious, contentious **12** cantankerous, faultfinding, sharp-tongued **13** quick-tempered, temperamental

tete-a-tete 4 chat, talk **6** parley **9** interview **12** conversation **13** confabulation

tether 3 tie **4** cord, rein, rope **5** chain, leash **6** fasten, halter, hobble, secure

Tethys
member of: 6 Titans
father: 6 Uranus
mother: 4 Gaea
husband: 7 Oceanus
mother of: 8 Oceanids **9** river gods
daughters: 13 three thousand
foster child: 4 Hera

Tetragrammaton
consonants in: 10 name for God **4** JHVH, IHVH, JHWH, YHVH, YHWH

Teutonic 5 Dutch **6** German, Gothic, Nordic **7** British, English **8** Germanic **12** Scandinavian
alphabet character: 4 rune
demon: 3 alp
goddess of death: 3 Hel, Ran
goddess of peace: 7 Nerthus
god of peace: 6 Balder
god of thunder: 4 Thor
god of war: 3 Tiu, Tyr
god of wisdom: 4 Odin

Teutonic Mythology *see* **17** Germanic Mythology

Texas
abbreviation: 2 TX **3** Tex
nickname: 8 Lone Star
capital: 6 Austin
largest city: 7 Houston
others: 4 Gail, Rice, Vega, Waco **5** Bryan, Marfa, Ozona, Pampa, Tyler,

Wiley **6** Baylor, Borger, Dallas, Denton, El Paso, Kileen, Laredo, Odessa, Quanah, Sonora **7** Abilene, Denison, Lubbock **8** Amarillo, Beaumont, Floydada **9** Fort Worth, Galveston **10** San Antonio **13** Corpus Christi
college: 3 SMU, TCU **4** Rice **5** Lamar, Wiley **6** Austin, Baylor **7** St Mary's, Trinity **10** Texas A and M **12** Southwestern **14** Texas Christian **16** Abilene Christian **17** Southern Methodist
feature:
  fort: 5 Alamo
  national park: 7 Big Bend **18** Guadalupe Mountains
  national seashore: 11 Padre Island
  state park: 10 San Jacinto
tribe: 4 Adar, Waco **5** Caddo, Lipan **6** Apache, Biloxi, Jumano, Kichai, Shuman, Tejano **7** Alabama, Hasinai, Tonkawa **8** Comanche, Querecho **9** Coushatta, Karankawa
people: 10 James S Hogg **12** Edward M House, Thomas C Clark **13** John B Connally, Samuel Houston **14** Chester W Nimitz, Mirabeau B Lamar, Samuel T Rayburn, Stephen F Austin, William B Travis **15** John Nance Garner, Thomas T Connally **19** Katherine Anne Porter
  explorer: 4 Vaca **7** La Salle
island: 5 Padre
lake: 6 Falcon, Sabine, Texoma **7** Amistad
river: 3 Red **5** Pecos **6** Brazos, Neches, Nueces, Sabine **7** Trinity **8** Colorado **9** Rio Grande **10** San Jacinto
land rank: 12 second
physical feature:
  bay: 13 Corpus Christi
  port: 7 Houston **9** Galveston **13** Corpus Christi
president: 14 Lyndon B Johnson **17** Dwight D Eisenhower
  Republic of Texas: 10 Sam Houston
state admission: 12 twenty-eighth
state bird: 11 mockingbird
state flower: 10 bluebonnet, yellow rose
state motto: 10 Friendship
state song: 13 Texas Our Texas
state tree: 5 pecan
baseball team: 7 Rangers
text 5 motif, theme, topic, verse, words **6** manual, primer, sermon, thesis **7** content, passage, subject, wording **8** argument, sentence, textbook, workbook **9** paragraph, quotation **10** schoolbook **13** subject matter
textile 4 yarn **5** cloth, fiber **6** fabric **8** filament, material **9** yard goods **10** piece goods
texture 3 nap **4** feel, look **5** grain, touch, weave **6** makeup **7** quality, surface **8** fineness **9** character, structure **10** coarseness **11** composition
Tey, Josephine

real name: 19 Elizabeth MacKintosh
author of: 10 Brat Farrar **15** Miss Pym Disposes, The Singing Sands **17** The Daughter of Time **19** A Shilling for Candles
character: 9 Alan Grant
Thackeray, William Makepeace
author of: 9 Pendennis **10** Vanity Fair **11** Barry Lyndon, Henry Esmond, The Newcomes **13** The Virginians
Thaddeus of Arimathea *see* **5** Judas
Thai-Austronesian
language branch: 9 Thai-Kadai **12** Austronesian
includes: 5 Batak, Malay **6** Fijian, Samoan **7** Tagalog **8** Hawaiian, Javanese **15** Bahasa Indonesia
spoken in: 4 Fiji, Java **5** China, Samoa **6** Hawaii, Taiwan **7** Sumatra **9** Indonesia, Polynesia **10** Madagascar **11** Philippines **12** Easter Island
Thailand
name means: 13 land of the free
other name: 4 Siam **11** Prathet Thai
capital/largest city: 6 Bankok **7** Bangkok
  old capital: 8 Thonburi **9** Ayutthaya
others: 4 Ubon **5** Puket **6** Nakhon, Ranong **7** Ayudhya, Ayuthea, Lampang, Lamphur, Lopburi, Rahaeng, Singora, Songkla **8** Khonkaen, Kiangmai, Songkhla, Sukhotai, Thonburi **9** Ayutthaya, Chiangmai, Chiengmai **10** Ratchasima **11** Phitsanulok **14** Ubonratchthani
kingdom: 5 Funan **6** Khymer **8** Thonburi **9** Ayutthaya, Chiang Mai, Dvaravati, Sukhothai **12** Subarnabhumi
school: 9 Thammasat **13** Chulalongkorn
head of state: 4 king
measure: 2 can, ken, niv, rai, sat, sok, wah **4** cohi, keup, niou, tang **5** kwien, leeng, sesti, vouah **6** kabiet, kanahn **7** chalmcu **8** chan gawn **9** anukabiet
monetary unit: 2 at **3** att **4** baht **5** cutty, fuang **6** pynung, salung **11** bullet money
weight: 3 bat, hap, pay, sen, sok **4** baht, haph, kati, klam **5** catty, chang, fuang, picul, pilul, tical **6** fluang, graini, salung, **7** tamlung
island: 2 Ko **3** Kut, Tao **4** Chan, Rawi **5** Chang, Lanta, Samui, Thalu **6** Libong, Phuket **7** Phangan, Terutao
lake: 9 Nong Lahan
mountain: 5 Dawna, Khieo **6** Phanom **8** Dang Raek, Kao Prawa, Maelamun **9** Khao Luang **11** Bilauktaung
highest point: 8 Inthanon **11** Doi Inthanon
river: 3 Chi, Mun, Nan, Yom **4** Ping **5** Menam **6** Mekong, Meping **7** Sal-

ween **10** Chaophraya
sea: 7 Andaman
physical feature:
  gulf: 4 Siam **8** Thailand
  isthmus: 3 Kra
  pass: 12 Three Pagodas
  peninsula: 5 Malay
  plateau: 5 Korat **6** Khorat
people: 3 Lao, Mon **4** Lawa, Shan, Thai **5** Malay **6** Indian, Khymer **7** Chinese, Siamese **9** Cambodian **10** Vietnamese
  king: 4 Rama **7** Chakkri, Mongkut **10** Chao Phraya **12** Prahjadhipok **13** Chulalongkorn **17** Bhumibol Adulyadej
  leader: 9 Phraruang **12** Kukrit-Pramoj
language: 3 Lao, Tai **4** Ahom, Shan, Thai **5** Kadai, Malay **7** Bangkok, Chinese, English **9** Krung Thep
religion: 5 Islam **8** Buddhism **12** Christianity, Confucianism **17** Theravada Buddhism
place:
  dam: 8 Bhumibol
  palace: 5 Grand
  ruins: 7 Ayuthia **9** Ayutthaya
  street: 7 Yawarai
  temple: 4 Dawn **7** Trimlu **10** Wat Phra Keo **11** Royal Chapel **13** Emerald Buddha
feature:
  canal: 5 klong
  clothing: 6 panung, sarong **12** saffron robes
  festival: 12 Surin Round Up
  houseboat: 6 sampan
  temple: 3 wat
  tree: 4 teak
food:
  fruit: 5 camut **6** durian, litchi, pomelo **8** rambutan **10** mangosteen
Thais
author: 13 Anatole France
character: 8 Athanael
composer: 8 Massenet
Thalassa
personifies: 3 sea
thalassic 6 marine **7** aquatic, deep-sea, neritic, oceanic, pelagic
Thales
field: 11 mathematics
nationality: 5 Greek
discovered: 18 geometry principles
predicted: 11 sun's eclipse
Thalestris
character in: 16 The Rape of the Lock
author: 4 Pope
Thalia
member of: 5 Muses **6** Graces
personifies: 6 comedy **13** idyllic poetry
lover: 4 Zeus
killed by: 5 Erato
Thallo

member of: **5** Horae
goddess of: **13** spring flowers

Thamyris
vocation: **4** poet **8** musician
father: **9** Philammon
mother: **7** Argiope
punished for: **9** arrogance
punished by: **5** Muses
punishment: **7** maiming **8** blinding

thanatophobia
fear of: **5** death

Thanatos
personifies: **5** death

thank 5 bless **12** be grateful to **13** be much obliged **18** express gratitude to

thankful 7 obliged **8** beholden, grateful **10** indebted to **12** appreciative, full of thanks **16** feeling gratitude **22** expressing appreciation

thankfulness 6 thanks **9** gratitude **12** appreciation, gratefulness

thankless 4 vain **7** ingrate, useless **8** bootless, caviling, critical, heedless **9** fruitless, unmindful, unwelcome **10** profitless, ungracious, ungrateful, uninviting, unpleasant, unrewarded, unthankful **11** distasteful, thoughtless, undesirable, unrewarding **12** disagreeable, faultfinding **13** inconsiderate, unappreciated **14** unacknowledged, unappreciative

thanks 5 grace **8** blessing **9** gratitude **11** benediction **12** appreciation, gratefulness

thanks be to God
Latin: **10** Deo gratias

thanksgiving 6 thanks **8** blessing

Thanksgiving
started by: **8** Bradford, Pilgrims
traditional food: **4** corn, yams **6** turkey **10** pumpkin pie **13** sweet potatoes **14** cranberry sauce
symbol: **9** ear of corn **12** horn of plenty

thank you
French: **5** merci
German: **5** danke
Spanish: **7** gracias
Italian: **6** grazie
Japanese: **4** domo

Thank You, Jeeves
author: **11** P G Wodehouse

thank you very much
French: **9** merci bien **13** merci beaucoup
German: **10** danke schon
Japanese: **11** domo arigato
Spanish: **13** muchas gracias

That Certain Feeling
author: **12** Kingsley Amis

Thatcher, Becky
character in: **9** Tom Sawyer
author: **5** Twain

Thatcher, Judge
character in: **15** (The Adventures of)

Huckleberry Finn
author: **5** Twain

That Girl
character: **8** Ann Marie, Lou Marie **10** Helen Marie, Ruth Bauman **11** Jerry Bauman **12** Don Hollinger, Judy Bessemer **14** Dr Leon Bessemer
cast: **9** Lew Parker **10** Ted Bessell **11** Alice Borden, Bonnie Scott, Marlo Thomas **12** Bernie Kopell **13** Dabney Coleman **14** Carolyn Daniels, Rosemary DeCamp

that is
Latin: **2** ie **5** id est

that is to say
Latin: **3** viz **9** videlicet

that's life
French: **9** c'est la vie

thaw 4 melt, warm **5** relax **6** soften, unbend, warm up **7** liquefy, melting, thawing **8** dissolve **11** break the ice

Thea
companion of: **7** Artemis
ravished by: **6** Aeolus
changed into: **4** mare
mare named: **6** Euippe

Theale, Milly
character in: **17** The Wings of the Dove
author: **5** James

theater 4 site **5** arena, drama, house, movie, odeum, place, scene, stage **6** cinema, lyceum **7** gallery, setting **8** assembly, audience, coliseum **9** colosseum, music hall, playhouse **10** assemblage, auditorium, movie house, spectators **11** histrionics, lecture hall, theatricals **12** amphitheater, show business

theatrical 4 film **5** hammy, movie, showy, stage, stagy **6** flashy **7** fustian, show-biz, stilted **8** affected, dramatic, mannered, thespian **9** grandiose, unnatural **10** artificial, histrionic **11** exaggerated, extravagant, pretentious, spectacular **12** magniloquent, ostentatious, show-business **13** entertainment, grandiloquent **14** larger-than-life

theatrical trick
French: **13** coup de theatre

Thebaid
author: **7** Statius
character: **4** Atys **5** Creon **6** Ismene, Tydeus **7** Jocasta, Theseus **8** Antigone, Capaneus, Eteocles, Opheltes, Tiresias **9** Menoeceus, Polynices **10** Amphiaraus, Hippomedon, Melanippus

the bottle 5 booze, drink, sauce **6** liquor **7** alcohol **8** demon rum

the dansant 8 tea dance

thee therefore
Latin: **8** te igitur

theft 5 fraud **7** larceny, looting, robbery **8** burglary, filching, rustling,

stealing, thievery **9** hijacking, pilfering, swindling **10** purloining **11** shoplifting **12** embezzlement
god of: **6** Hermes **7** Mercury

Theia
also: **4** Thia
member of: **6** Titans
father: **6** Uranus
mother: **4** Gaea
brother: **8** Hyperion
mother of: **8** Cercopes
son: **6** Helios
daughter: **3** Eos **6** Selene

the life of the land is maintained by righteousness
Hawaiian: **52** ua mau ke ea o ka aina i ka pono
motto of: **6** Hawaii

Them
author: **15** Joyce Carol Oates

theme 3 air **4** song, text, tune **5** essay, focus, motif, point, topic, tract **6** melody, report, review, strain, thesis **7** keynote, premise, subject **8** argument, critique, question, treatise **9** discourse, leitmotif, monograph **10** commentary **11** composition, proposition **12** dissertation

Then Again, Maybe I Won't
author: **9** Judy Blume

thence 6 whence **9** from there, therefore **11** accordingly, in due course **13** from that place

the next world 6 Heaven **8** eternity, paradise **12** the hereafter **14** the world to come

the norm 7 the mean, the rule **9** the median **10** the average **14** the common thing

the Occident 7 the West **20** the western hemisphere

theologian see **22** philosopher/theologian

theological 4 holy **6** sacred **8** Biblical, dogmatic **9** apostolic, canonical, doctrinal, religious, spiritual **10** scriptural **14** ecclesiastical

theology 5 dogma **8** divinity, doctrine, religion

Theophane
bore: **3** ram
fleece of ram: **6** golden

theoretical 8 abstract, academic, putative **11** conjectural, postulatory, speculative **12** hypothetical, nonpractical **13** suppositional

theorize 5 infer, posit, think **6** assume **7** imagine, presume, propose, suppose, surmise **8** propound **9** formulate, postulate, predicate, speculate **10** conjecture **11** hypothecate, hypothesize

theory 3 law **4** idea, view **5** guess **6** belief, notion, thesis **7** concept, opinion, science, surmise, thought **8** doctrine, ideology, judgment **9** deduction, postulate, principle **10** conclusion, conjecture, hypothesis, persuasion, philosophy **11** presumption, speculation, supposition

therapeutic, therapeutical 7 healing **8** curative, remedial, salutary, sanative **11** restorative **12** ameliorative

therapy 7 healing **9** treatment **14** rehabilitation

thereafter 5 later **9** after that, afterward **10** afterwards, from then on **11** thenceforth **12** subsequently **14** from that time on

therefore 2 so **4** ergo, thus **5** hence **11** accordingly **12** consequently, on that ground **13** for that reason, in consequence, on that account **14** for which reason

there is no disputing about tastes
  Latin: **27** de gustibus non est disputandum

there it is
  French: **5** voila

Therese Raquin
  author: **9** Emile Zola
  character: **7** Camille, Laurent

There Shall Be No Night
  author: **15** Robert E Sherwood

thereupon 4 then **6** at once / thereon **8** directly, suddenly, upon that **9** forthwith, in a moment, upon which **11** immediately **12** straightaway, without delay

thermometer
  invented by: **7** Galileo, Reaumur
    mercury: **10** Fahrenheit

Thero
  nurse of: **4** Ares

theropod
  type of: **8** dinosaur
  member: **10** Allosaurus, Antrodemus **11** Coelophysis, Gorgosaurus **13** Albertosaurus, Compsognathus, Struthiomimus, Tyrannosaurus

Theroux, Paul
  author of: **9** Saint Jack **16** The Mosquito Coast **20** Riding the Iron Rooster **21** The Great Railway Bazaar **23** The Old Patagonian Express

Thersites
  mentioned in: **5** Iliad
  origin: **5** Greek
  characteristics: **4** ugly **8** deformed **11** quarrelsome
  accused Agamemnon of: **5** greed
  accused Achilles of: **9** cowardice
  fought in: **9** Trojan War
  killed by: **8** Achilles

the same as 4 like **7** equal to **9** a match for **12** comparable to, equivalent to, tantamount to **16** commensurate with

thesaurus 8 synonymy **10** word finder **11** synonymicon **12** word treasury **13** synonym finder **17** synonym dictionary **18** semantic dictionary

Thescelosaurus
  type: **8** dinosaur **10** ornithopod
  location: **6** Canada **12** United States
  period: **10** Cretaceous

These Three
  director: **12** William Wyler
  based on play by: **14** Lillian Hellman (The Children's Hour)
  cast: **10** Alma Kruger, Joel McCrea **11** Merle Oberon **13** Miriam Hopkins **15** Bonita Granville, Catherine Doucet

Theseus
  king of: **6** Athens
  father: **6** Aegeus **8** Poseidon
  mother: **6** Aethra
  wife: **7** Phaedra
  consort: **9** Hippolyta
  lover: **7** Ariadne
  son: **6** Acamas **8** Demophon **10** Hippolytus, Melanippus
  helmsman: **10** Nausithous
  killed: **5** Sinis **6** Sciron **8** Minotaur **10** Cretan bull, Procrustes

thesis 5 essay, paper, tract **6** notion, theory **7** article, concept, surmise **8** argument, critique, proposal, treatise **9** discourse, monograph, postulate, term paper **10** commentary, conjecture, hypothesis **11** composition, proposition, speculation, supposition **12** disquisition, dissertation

Thesmia
  epithet of: **7** Demeter
  means: **12** goddess of law

Thesmophorus
  epithet of: **7** Demeter
  means: **8** lawgiver

thespian 3 ham **4** star **5** actor, extra **6** co-star, player, walk-on **7** actress, ingenue, trouper **8** juvenile **9** bit-player, guest star, performer, tragedian **10** leading man **11** leading lady, stage player

Thespis 9 Greek poet
  originator of: **12** Greek tragedy

Thessalus
  king of: **8** Thessaly
  father: **5** Jason **8** Hercules
  mother: **5** Medea **9** Chalciope

the state
  Latin: **10** res publica

Thetis
  member of: **7** Nereids
  husband: **6** Peleus
  sister: **8** Eurynome
  son: **8** Achilles

the very words
  Latin: **14** ipsissima verba

the world over 10 every place, everywhere, far and wide, near and far **11** in all places

They Shoot Horses, Don't They?
  director: **13** Sydney Pollack
  cast: **8** Gig Young **9** Bruce Dern, Jane Fonda **10** Red Buttons **12** Susannah York **13** Bonnie Bedelia **15** Michael Sarrazin

  Oscar for: **15** supporting actor (Young)

They Won't Forget
  director: **11** Mervyn LeRoy
  cast: **10** Lana Turner, Otto Kruger **11** Allyn Joslyn, Claude Rains **12** Elisha Cook Jr **13** Gloria Dickson

thiasus
  also: **7** thiasos
  group worshipping: **11** patron deity
  followers of: **8** Dionysus
    followers called: **6** satyrs **7** maenads

thick 3 big, fat **4** deep, dull, dumb, slow, wide **5** broad, bulky, close, dense, fuzzy, great, heavy, husky, piled, solid **6** chummy, heaped, hoarse, lavish, obtuse, packed, strong, stupid, viscid, wooden **7** blurred, clotted, compact, copious, crowded, decided, devoted, doltish, extreme, intense, liberal, muffled, profuse, teeming, throaty, viscous **8** abundant, familiar, friendly, generous, guttural, intimate, profound, sisterly, swarming **9** brotherly, condensed, fatheaded, glutinous, plenteous, unstinted **10** coagulated, dull-witted, gelatinous, indistinct, munificent, pronounced, slow-witted **11** inseparable, overflowing **12** concentrated, impenetrable, inarticulate

thicken 3 set **4** cake, clot, jell **5** muddy **6** darken, deepen, muddle **7** compact, congeal, jellify **8** condense **9** coagulate, intensify **10** gelatinize

thicket 4 bush, wood **5** brake, brush, copse, grove, scrub **6** bushes, covert, forest, shrubs **7** bracken **9** shrubbery **10** underbrush **11** undergrowth

thickheaded 4 dull, dumb, slow **5** blank, dense, dopey, thick **6** obtuse, stupid **8** ignorant **9** dim-witted, fatheaded **10** boneheaded, dull-witted, half-witted, slow-witted **11** blockheaded, thick-witted **12** dunderheaded, thick-skulled **13** chuckleheaded, knuckleheaded

thickset 5 bulky, close, dense, dumpy, husky, solid, squat, stout, tubby **6** chunky, packed, stocky, stubby, stumpy, sturdy **8** close-set, heavyset, roly-poly

thickskinned 4 hard **5** horny, tough **6** inured **7** callous **8** callused, hardened **9** unfeeling, unmovable **10** impervious, insensible **11** insensitive, unconcerned **13** imperturbable, unsusceptible **14** pachydermatous

thick-skulled 4 dull **5** dense **6** stupid **11** thickheaded **12** dunderheaded

thick-witted 4 dull, slow **5** dense **6** stupid **7** idiotic, moronic **9** dim-witted, imbecilic **11** thickheaded **12** dunderheaded, simple-minded

thief 5 crook **6** bandit, mugger, robber **7** burglar, filcher, rustler **8** hijacker, pilferer, swindler **9** defrauder, embezzler, holdup man, larcenist, purloiner, racketeer **10** highwayman, pickpocket, shoplifter **12** housebreaker, kleptomaniac **13** confidence man, pursesnatcher **14** second-story man

Thief of Bagdad, The
  director: 9 Tim Whelan **12** Ludwig Berger **13** Michael Powell
  cast: 4 Sabu **9** Rex Ingram **10** John Justin, June Duprez **11** Conrad Veidt

Thieves' Carnival
  also: 15 Le Bal des Voleurs
  author: 11 Jean Anouilh

thievish 3 sly **6** sneaky **7** furtive **8** stealthy, thieving **9** dishonest, larcenous, secretive, thieflike **13** lightfingered, surreptitious **14** stickyfingered

thigh 3 ham, leg **4** hock **5** femur, flank, ilium **6** gammon
  pain: 8 meralgia

Thimbu, Thimphu
  capital of: 6 Bhutan

thin 4 fine, lank, lean, slim, weak **5** faint, gaunt, lanky, prune, runny, scant, sheer, spare, water **6** dilute, feeble, narrow, not fat, reduce, skinny, slight, sparse, watery **7** curtail, diluted, fragile, scrawny, slender, spindly **8** delicate, diminish, finespun **9** emaciated, water down **10** inadequate, threadlike **11** transparent **12** insufficient **13** unsubstantial

thin-blooded 3 wan **4** pale, weak **6** anemic, sickly

thing, things 3 act **4** deed, feat, gear, item **5** event, gizmo, goods, point **6** action, affair, aspect, detail, dingus, entity, gadget, matter, object, person **7** article, clothes, concern, effects, feature, thought **8** business, clothing, creature, movables **9** doohickey, equipment, happening, statement **10** belongings, human being, occurrence, particular, proceeding **11** eventuality, living being, possessions, thingamabob, thingamajig, transaction **12** circumstance **13** paraphernalia

Thing
  legislative body of: 11 Scandinavia

thing already done
  French: 12 fait accompli

thingamajig 5 gizmo **6** doodad, gadget **11** contraption, contrivance, thingamabob **15** whatchamacallit

thing of no value
  Latin: 5 nihil

things done
  Latin: 9 res gestae

think 4 deem, mean, plan **5** brood, fancy, guess, judge **6** design, expect, intend, ponder, reason, recall, reckon **7** believe, dwell on, imagine, presume, propose, purpose, reflect, suppose, surmise **8** cogitate, conceive, conclude, contrive, meditate, mull

over, remember, ruminate **9** recollect, speculate **10** anticipate, deliberate, have in mind, keep in mind **11** contemplate, use one's mind, use one's wits **13** rack one's brain

thinkable 8 knowable **10** imaginable **11** conceivable, perceivable

think about 4 mull **6** debate, ponder **7** reflect **8** consider, mull over **10** deliberate

think alike 5 agree **11** be of one mind, see eye to eye

thinker 4 sage **6** savant, wizard **7** egghead, scholar **9** intellect **10** mastermind **11** mental giant, philosopher **13** metaphysician

Thinker, The
  by: 5 Rodin

think fit 4 deem **5** deign, stoop **7** consent **10** condescend

think highly of 5 favor, honor, value **6** admire, esteem, revere **7** approve, respect **8** look up to, venerate **10** set store by

think ill of 4 hate **5** decry **6** detest **7** condemn, deplore, despise, dislike **8** object to **9** abominate, disparage, frown upon **10** disapprove **13** look askance at **14** discountenance **15** take exception to **16** find unacceptable, view with disfavor

thinking 4 view **5** smart, stand, study **6** belief, bright **7** concept, surmise, thought **8** cultured, educated, judgment, position, rational, studious **9** brainwork, deduction, inference, reasoning **10** conclusion, cultivated, impression, meditation, meditative, reflection, reflective, rumination, thoughtful **11** intelligent, speculation **12** deliberation **13** consideration, contemplation, contemplative, philosophical, sophisticated, using one's head **15** paying attention

Thinking Reed, The
  author: 15 Dame Rebecca West

think over 5 study, weigh **8** cogitate, consider, mull over **11** reflect upon **12** deliberate on

think through 5 weigh **6** ponder **7** analyze **8** appraise, consider, evaluate

think up 5 frame, hatch **6** create, invent **7** concoct, dream up **8** conceive, contrive

think well of 4 like **6** admire **8** look up to **10** appreciate

Thin Man, The
  author: 15 Dashiell Hammett
  character: 4 Asta (pet terrier) **7** Morelli **11** Nick Charles, Nora Charles **13** Arthur Nunheim, Mimi Jorgensen **15** Herbert Macaulay **18** Christian Jorgensen
    Wynant family: 5 Clyde **7** Dorothy, Gilbert
  director: 11 W S Van Dyke II

  cast: 4 Asta **8** Myrna Loy (Nora Charles) **13** William Powell (Nick Charles)
  thin man is: 6 victim
  sequel (film): 14 Another Thin Man **15** After the Thin Man **16** Song of the Thin Man **18** The Thin Man Goes Home

Thin Mountain Air, The
  author: 10 Paul Horgan

thin out 5 prune **6** dilute, reduce, weaken **7** weed out **9** water down **10** adulterate

thinskinned 5 cross, huffy, sulky, testy **6** grumpy, sullen, touchy **7** crabbed, peevish **8** petulant, snappish **9** irascible, irritable, sensitive, squeamish **11** ill-tempered, quarrelsome, susceptible **12** cantankerous **13** oversensitive **14** hypersensitive

third estate
  French: 9 tiers etat

Third Man, The
  director: 9 Carol Reed
  based on story by: 12 Graham Greene
  cast: 10 Alida Valli **11** Orson Welles (Harry Lime) **12** Joseph Cotten, Trevor Howard **16** Wilfrid Hyde-White
  setting: 6 Vienna

Third Wave, The
  author: 12 Alvin Toffler

thirst 3 yen **4** itch, lust, pant **5** ardor, covet, crave, yearn **6** desire, fervor, hunger, relish **7** craving, passion, stomach **8** appetite, keenness, voracity, yearning **9** hanker for, hankering **11** thirstiness

thirsty 3 dry **4** avid **5** eager **7** parched **9** thirsting

Thirteen O'Clock
  author: 19 Stephen Vincent Benet

Thirty-Nine Steps, The (The 39 Steps)
  author: 10 John Buchan
  director: 15 Alfred Hitchcock
  cast: 11 Robert Donat **13** Godfrey Tearle, Lucie Mannheim, Peggy Ashcroft **16** Madeleine Carroll

This Above All
  author: 10 Eric Knight

Thisbe
  loved: 7 Pyramus
  location: 7 Babylon
  death by: 7 suicide
  death at tomb of: 5 Ninus

this is
  Latin: 6 hoc est

This Is Your Life
  host: 12 Ralph Edwards
  announcer: 9 Bob Warren

thistle 7 Cirsium
  varieties: 3 Oat **4** Bull, Holy, Milk, Star **5** Glove, Plume, White **6** Canada, Cotton, Golden, Scotch, Silver

7 Blessed, St Mary's **8** Fishbone, Mountain, Plumless **9** Argentine, Thornless **10** Great globe, Small globe **11** Mountain sow **14** Acanthus-leaved
emblem of: 8 Scotland

Thomas 7 apostle
means: 4 twin
also called: 7 Didymus, Doubter **8** Doubting

Thomas, Ambroise
born: 4 Metz **6** France
composer of: 6 Mignon

Thomas, Danny
real name: 16 Amos Muzyad Jacobs
born: 11 Deerfield MI
daughter: 11 Marlo Thomas
roles: 13 The Jazz Singer **16** Make Room for Daddy **19** I'll See You in My Dreams

Thomas, Dylan
author of: 8 Fern Hill **13** Under Milk Wood **23** A Child's Christmas in Wales

Thomas, George H
nickname: 20 The Rock of Chickamauga
served in: 8 Civil War **10** Mexican War
side: 5 Union
commander of: 19 Army of the Cumberland
battle: 9 Nashville **11** Chattanooga, Chickamauga

Thomas, Marlo
real name: 14 Margaret Thomas
born: 9 Detroit MI
father: 11 Danny Thomas
husband: 11 Phil Donahue
roles: 8 That Girl

Thomas, W Morgan
creator/artist of: 22 Sheena Queen of the Jungle

Thomas a Kempis
author of: 20 The Imitation of Christ

Thomson, Joseph John
field: 7 physics
nationality: 7 British
discovered: 8 electron
awarded: 10 Nobel Prize

Thomson, Thomas John
born: 6 Canada **9** Claremont
artwork: 9 Spring Ice **11** The Jack Pine **12** Northern Lake **13** Northern River

Thomson, Virgil
born: 12 Kansas City MO
composer of: 9 Portraits **16** The Mother of Us All **21** Four Saints in Three Acts

thong 4 band **5** strap, strip **6** sandal **7** binding **8** swimsuit **9** underwear

Thor
origin: 12 Scandinavian
god of: 4 rain **7** farming, thunder
rode: 7 chariot
chariot pulled by: 5 goats

wielded: 6 hammer **7** Miolnir
father: 4 Odin **5** Othin

thorax 5 chest, trunk **6** breast, cavity **8** forebody

Thoreau, Henry David
author of: 6 Walden (Life in the Woods) **17** Civil Disobedience

thorium
chemical symbol: 2 Th

thorn 2 th **4** rune

thorn 3 woe **4** bane, barb, care, gall, spur **5** cross, curse, spike, spine, sting **6** plague **7** prickle, scourge, torment, trouble **8** nuisance, vexation **9** annoyance, sore point **10** affliction, bitter pill, infliction, irritation

thorn 9 Crataegus
varieties: 3 Box **4** Lily, Pear **5** Camel, Hedge, White **6** Christ, Karroo, Mysore, Sallow, Sickle, Winter **7** Thirsty **8** Cockspur, Egyptian, Kangaroo, Quick-set **9** Jerusalem, Paper-bark **10** Washington **11** Crucifixion **13** Yellow-fruited

Thornbirds, The
author: 17 Colleen McCullough

Thornburg, Betty June
real name of: 11 Betty Hutton

Thornfield
house in: 8 Jane Eyre
author: 6 Bronte

Thornhill, Squire
character in: 19 The Vicar of Wakefield
author: 9 Goldsmith

thorn in the side 4 bane **7** torment **9** annoyance **10** irritation

thorny 4 dire, hard **5** spiny, tough **6** barbed, spiked, sticky, trying **7** arduous, brambly, complex, crucial, irksome, prickly **8** annoying, critical, involved, ticklish **9** bristling, dangerous, difficult, vexatious **10** formidable, nettlesome, perplexing **11** complicated, troublesome

thorough 4 full, pure **5** sheer, total, utter **6** entire **7** careful, perfect, uniform **8** absolute, complete, of a piece **9** downright, out-and-out **10** consistent, definitive, exhaustive, meticulous **11** painstaking, unmitigated, unqualified **12** all-embracing, all-inclusive

thoroughbred 7 unmixed **8** purebred **9** blueblood, pedigreed, racehorse **10** aristocrat **11** full-blooded, pureblooded **12** silkstocking

thoroughfare 4 road **6** avenue, street **7** freeway, highway, parkway, roadway, thruway **8** main road, turnpike **9** boulevard, concourse **10** expressway, interstate **12** superhighway **13** through street

thoroughgoing 5 utter **6** arrant **7** extreme **8** outright **9** confirmed, notorious, out-and-out **11** undisguised, unmitigated

thoroughly 5 fully **7** totally, utterly **8** entirely **9** carefully, downright, out-and-out, perfectly, uniformly **10** absolutely, completely, throughout **11** inclusively **12** consistently, exhaustively, meticulously **13** in all respects **15** from top to bottom **17** through and through **18** from beginning to end

Thorpe, Isabella
character in: 15 Northanger Abbey
author: 6 Austen

Thorpe, Jim (James Francis)
sport: 8 football **13** track and field
won: 8 Olympics
named: 11 All-American

Thorvaldsen, Albert Bertel
born: 7 Denmark **10** Copenhagen
artwork: 4 Hope **9** Lord Byron **14** Cupid and Psyche **16** The Lion of Lucerne **22** Cupid and the Three Graces **24** Jason with the Golden Fleece

Thoth
origin: 8 Egyptian
god of: 5 magic **6** wisdom **8** learning
scribe of: 4 gods
inventor of: 6 letter **7** numbers
corresponds to: 6 Hermes
head of: 3 dog **4** ibis

though 3 tho, yet **4** even, that **5** still **6** albeit, even if **7** granted **8** although, granting **9** admitting **12** nevertheless **15** notwithstanding

thought 3 aim, end **4** goal, idea, plan, view **5** credo, dogma, fancy, tenet **6** belief, caring, design, intent, musing, notion, object, regard, scheme **7** concept, concern, opinion, purpose, reverie, surmise **8** doctrine, judgment, kindness, thinking **9** attention, intention, objective, sentiment **10** brown study, cogitation, conception, conclusion, meditation, reflection, rumination **11** expectation, imagination, speculation, supposition **12** anticipation, deliberation **13** consideration, contemplation, introspection
French: 6 pensee

thoughtful 4 kind **6** caring, loving, musing **7** pensive, probing, serious, wistful **8** thinking **9** attentive **10** meditative, neighborly, reflective, solicitous **11** considerate, kindhearted **13** contemplative, introspective

thoughtfulness 7 probing, thought **8** kindness, thinking **10** meditation, reflection **11** questioning **13** attentiveness, consideration, contemplation **14** solicitousness **15** kindheartedness

thoughtless 4 dumb, rash, rude **5** silly **6** stupid, unkind **7** foolish **8** careless, heedless, impolite, reckless **9** imprudent **10** ill-advised, indiscreet, neglectful, unthinking **11** harebrained, improvident, inadvertent, inattentive, insensitive **12** absent-minded, unre-

flecting **13** ill-considered, inconsiderate, rattlebrained **14** scatterbrained

thoughtlessness 7 neglect **8** rashness, rudeness **9** oversight, unconcern
10 imprudence, negligence, unkindness **11** inattention **12** carelessness,
heedlessness, impoliteness, recklessness **13** insensitivity **15** inattentive-
ness **16** absentmindedness

Thousand Clowns, A
   director: 7 Fred Coe
   based on play by: 11 Herb Gardner
   cast: 11 Barry Gordon **12** Jason Robards, Martin Balsam **13** Barbara
   Harris
   setting: 11 New York City
   Oscar for: 15 supporting actor (Balsam)

Thousand Days, A
   author: 20 Arthur M Schlesinger Jr

thou too
   Latin: 8 tu quoque

thrall 4 serf **5** slave **6** chains **7** bondage, serfdom, servant, slavery **9** servitude **11** enslavement, subjugation

thralldom 6 chains **7** bondage, serfdom, slavery **9** servitude **11** enslavement, subjugation

thrash 4 beat, cane, drub, flog, jerk,
lash, maul, toss, whip **5** birch, flail,
heave, solve, spank, strap **6** jiggle,
joggle, plunge, pommel, squirm,
switch, thresh, tumble, wiggle, writhe
7 flounce, resolve, scourge, trounce **8**
argue out, lambaste **9** thresh out **10**
flagellate

threadbare 4 dull, worn **5** banal,
stale, stock, tacky, trite **6** boring,
frayed, jejune, ragged, shabby **7** cliched, humdrum, napless, prosaic, rav-
eled, routine, worn-out **8** bromidic,
everyday, pileworn **9** hackneyed,
well-known **11** commonplace, stereotyped **12** conventional, overfamiliar
15 the worse for wear

threads 4 duds, togs **6** attire **7** apparel, clothes, strands, strings **8** clothing, garments **9** filaments

threat 4 omen, risk **5** peril **6** danger,
hazard, menace **7** ill omen, portent,
warning **8** jeopardy **10** foreboding **11**
commination, premonition **12** intimidation

threaten 3 cow **4** warn **6** impend,
menace **7** imperil **8** endanger, forewarn, hang over **9** terrorize **10** be imminent, intimidate, jeopardize

threatening 4 grim **7** baleful, ominous, warning **8** alarming, imminent,
menacing, sinister **9** ill-omened, impending **10** forbidding, foreboding **11**
approaching, forewarning, terrorizing
12 inauspicious, intimidating, unpropitious

three
   French: 5 trois

Three-Cornered Hat, The
   author: 21 Pedro Antonio de Alarcon

Three Faces of Eve, The
   director: 15 Nunnally Johnson
   cast: 8 Lee J Cobb **9** Nancy Kulp **10**
   David Wayne **12** Vince Edwards **14**
   Joanne Woodward
      narration by: 13 Alistair Cooke
   Oscar for: 7 actress (Woodward)

Three Lives
   includes: 9 Melanctha **11** The Good
   Anna **13** The Gentle Lena
   author: 13 Gertrude Stein

Three Men in a Boat
   author: 13 Jerome K Jerome

Three Musketeers, The
   author: 14 Alexandre Dumas (pere)
   director: 13 Richard Lester
   character: 5 Athos **6** Aramis **7**
   Porthos **8** Planchet **9** D'Artagnan **12**
   Lady de Winter **17** Cardinal Richelieu **18** Constance Bonacieux
   cast: 10 Oliver Reed **11** Faye
   Dunaway (Milady), Michael York
   (D'Artagnan), Raquel Welch **12**
   Frank Findlay **14** Charlton Heston,
   Christopher Lee **16** Geraldine Chaplin **18** Richard Chamberlain
   sequel: 17 The Four Musketeers

Threepenny Opera, The
   author: 6 Brecht
   composer: 5 Weill
   based on: 15 The Beggar's Opera
   by: 7 John Gay
   song: 11 Mack the Knife

three R's 6 'riting **7** reading **9** 'rithma-
.tic

Three's Company
   character: 5 Larry **9** Janet Wood **10**
   Helen Roper **11** Chrissy Snow, Jack
   Tripper **12** Stanley Roper
   cast: 10 John Ritter, Norman Fell **11**
   Joyce DeWitt **12** Audra Lindley,
   Richard Kline **13** Suzanne Somers

Three Sisters
   director: 10 John Sichel **15** Laurence
   Olivier
   author: 12 Anton Chekhov
   character: 13 Fyodor Kuligin **14**
   Baron Tusenbach, Vassily Solyony
   17 Alexandr Vershinin
      Prozorov family: 4 Olga **5** Irina,
      Masha **6** Andrey **7** Natasha
   cast: 9 Alan Bates **11** Derek Jacobi,
   Jeanne Watts **13** Joan Plowright,
   Louise Purnell **15** Laurence Olivier

Three Soldiers
   author: 13 John Dos Passos

threnody 5 dirge, elegy **6** lament **7**
requiem

threshold 4 dawn, door, edge, sill **5**
brink, limen, onset, start, verge **6** portal **7** doorway, gateway, opening,
prelude **8** doorsill, entrance **9** beginning, groundsill, inception **10** groundsill **11** entranceway **12** commencement **13** starting point

thrift 7 economy **8** prudence **9** frugality, husbandry, parsimony **10** moderation **11** sparingness, thriftiness **14** reasonableness **15** closefistedness **16**
parsimoniousness

thriftiness 5 tight **6** thrift **7** economy
8 prudence **9** frugality, parsimony **13**
penny-pinching **15** closefistedness,
tightfistedness **16** parsimoniousness

thriftless 6 lavish **8** feckless, prodigal,
wasteful **11** extravagant, improvident

thrifty 5 frugal, saving, stingy **7** sparing **9** niggardly, penny-wise **10** economical **11** closefisted, economizing,
tightfisted **12** parsimonious **13** penny-
pinching

thrill 4 fire, glow, kick, stir **5** flush,
rouse, throb **6** arouse, excite, quiver,
tickle, tingle, tremor **7** delight, impress, inspire, tremble **9** adventure,
electrify, enrapture, galvanize, stimulate, transport **12** satisfaction

thrilled 4 agog **7** excited **9** delighted,
overjoyed **11** transported

thrilling 7 awesome **8** engaging, exciting, riveting, stirring **9** absorbing, exquisite **10** delightful **11** fascinating,
pleasurable, provocative, sensational,
tantalizing, titillating **12** electrifying

thrip
   variety: 6 banded **10** tube tailed **11**
   heterothrip, merothripid

thrive 3 wax **4** boom **5** bloom, get on
6 fatten **7** burgeon, prosper, succeed
8 flourish, get ahead, grow rich

thriving 4 busy, lush, rank, rich **7**
wealthy, well-off **8** blooming, in clover, vigorous, well-to-do **9** flowering,
luxuriant **10** blossoming, prospering,
prosperous, succeeding, successful **11**
flourishing

throat 3 maw **4** craw, gula, neck **5**
gorge **6** gullet **7** chamber, jugulum,
passage, pharynx
   lozenge: 6 pastil
   nautical: 3 jaw **4** jaws, nock
   part: 6 fauces, larynx, tonsil **7** glottis,
   trachea
   pertaining to: 5 gular
   seizing: 4 knot **5** hitch **12** cuckold's
   knot
   swelling: 6 goiter

throaty 3 dry, low **4** base, deep **5**
gruff, husky, thick **6** hoarse **7**
cracked, grating, rasping **8** croaking,
guttural, resonant, sonorous **9** full-
toned

throb 4 beat, jerk, pant **5** heave, pulse,
shake **6** quiver, tremor, twitch **7** beating, flutter, pulsate, shaking, tremble,
vibrate **9** palpitate, pulsation, quivering, throbbing, trembling, vibration **10**
fluttering **11** oscillation, palpitation **13**
reverberation

throes 5 agony, chaos, pangs **6** ordeal,
spasms, tumult **7** anguish, turmoil **8**
disorder, paroxysm, upheaval **9** confu-

sion, paroxysms **10** convulsion, disruption

thrombus 4 clot **9** blood clot **11** coagulation

throng 3 jam **4** army, cram, herd, host, mass, mill, pack, rush **5** bunch, crowd, crush, flock, flood, horde, press, surge, swarm **6** deluge, gather, huddle, stream **7** cluster, collect **8** assemble, converge **9** multitude **10** assemblage, congregate

thronged 4 full **6** jammed, mobbed, packed **7** crammed, crowded, flocked, swarmed, teeming **8** swarming **9** congested, jampacked **11** overflowing

throttle 3 gag, gas **4** stop **5** block, burke, check, choke **6** stifle **7** garrote, seal off, shut off, silence, smother **8** choke off, gas pedal, strangle **9** fuel lever, fuel valve **11** strangulate

through, thru 4 done, past **5** ended **6** direct **7** express **8** finished, from A to Z, to the end **9** all the way, completed, concluded **10** terminated **12** long-distance **15** from first to last **18** from beginning to end **20** from one end to the other

through and through 5 total **6** wholly **7** totally, utterly **8** complete **10** completely, thoroughly **15** from top to bottom **18** from beginning to end **20** from one end to the other

through my fault
  Latin: **8** mea culpa

throughout 7 all over **10** all the time, everywhere **11** in every part **16** all the way through **18** from beginning to end

Through the Looking Glass
  sequel to: **28** Alice's Adventures in Wonderland
  author: **12** Lewis Carroll
  character: **4** Gnat, Lion **5** Alice, Dinah **7** Red King, Unicorn **8** Red Queen **9** Red Knight, White King **10** Tweedledee, Tweedledum, White Queen **11** Black Kitten, White Kitten, White Knight **12** Humpty Dumpty

throw 3 lob, pit, put, shy **4** cast, hurl, shot, toss **5** chuck, fling, floor, heave, impel, pitch, place, put in, put on, sling **6** hurtle, launch, let fly, propel, unseat **7** project **8** delivery **9** knock down, put around

throw away 7 cast off, discard **8** get rid of

throw down 5 let go **8** drop hard, hurl down, toss down **9** fling down

throw into disorder 5 upset **7** agitate, disrupt **10** disarrange

throw off 4 emit, gush **5** exude **7** abandon, cast off, mislead **8** get rid of, shake off, shrug off **9** cast aside, discharge, give forth, pour forth

throw off the scent 7 confuse, mis-

lead **8** confound **19** throw out a red herring

throw out 4 beam, emit, oust **5** eject, evict, expel, exude **6** banish, bounce, remove **7** discard, dismiss, toss out **8** get rid of, jettison **9** cast aside, throw away

throw overboard 4 dump **7** cast off, discard **8** jettison, toss over

throw suspicion upon 11 cast doubt on **17** bring into question

throw up 4 barf, spew **5** eject, expel, spout, vomit **6** cast up, spew up **7** cough up **8** disgorge **9** discharge **11** regurgitate

thrust 3 jab, jam, ram **4** butt, pass, poke, prod, push, raid, stab **5** boost, drive, foray, force, impel, lunge, press, sally, shove, swipe **6** attack, charge, pierce, plunge, propel, sortie, strike, stroke **7** assault, impetus, impulse, riposte **8** momentum **9** incursion **10** aggression

thrust aside 4 dump **6** shelve **7** discard **8** get rid of, throw off, throw out **9** cast aside, dispose of, throw away

thrust at 6 assail, attack **7** lunge at **8** strike at

thrust out 4 spew, spit **5** eject, expel, vomit **6** extend, propel **7** protrude

Thucydides
  author of: **28** History of the Peloponnesian War

thud 4 bang **5** clunk, knock, smack, thump

thug 4 hood **6** bandit, gunman, hit man, killer, mugger, robber **7** hoodlum, mobster, ruffian **8** assassin, gangster, murderer **9** cutthroat

thumb 5 hitch **6** finger, handle **9** hitchhike **10** catch a ride, hitch a ride **11** flip through, leaf through

Thumbelina
  author: **21** Hans Christian Andersen

thumbnail 5 brief, short **7** compact, concise

thump 3 hit, jab, rap **4** bang, beat, clip, cuff, poke, slam, slap, swat, thud **5** clout, clunk, knock, pound, punch, smack, whack **6** batter, bounce, buffet, pommel, strike, thwack **8** collapse, lambaste

thunder 4 boom, clap, echo, peal, roar, roll **5** crack, crash **6** rumble **7** explode, resound **8** rumbling **9** discharge, explosion **11** reverberate, thunderbolt, thunderclap
  god of: **4** Thor **5** Donar **7** Taranis

thunderbolt 4 dart **5** flash, shaft **6** stroke

Thunderstorms, god of 8 Summanus

thunderstruck 4 agog, awed **5** agape **6** aghast, amazed **8** confused, overcome **9** astounded, awestruck, perplexed, surprised **10** astonished, be-

wildered **11** dumbfounded **13** flabbergasted

Thunder-ten-Tronckh
  character in: **7** Candide
  author: **8** Voltaire

Thurber, James
  author of: **12** The New Yorker **14** Is Sex Necessary (with E B White), The Catbird Seat **16** The Owl in the Attic **18** My Life and Hard Times, The Thurber Carnival **26** The Secret Life of Walter Mitty

Thurber Carnival, The
  author: **12** James Thurber

Thurio
  character in: **20** Two Gentlemen of Verona
  author: **11** Shakespeare

Thursday
  French: **5** jeudi
  from: **4** Thor
  German: **10** donnerstag
  heavenly body: **4** Jove **7** Jupiter
  Italian: **7** giovedi
  Latin: **9** Dies Jovis
  observance: **12** Holy Thursday, Thanksgiving **13** Corpus Christi **14** Maundy Thursday **17** Ascension Thursday
  Scandinavian: **7** torsdag
  Spanish: **6** jueves

thus 2 so **4** ergo **5** hence **6** like so **8** like this **9** as follows, in this way, therefore, wherefore **11** accordingly **12** consequently, in this manner **13** for this reason
  Latin: **3** sic

thus always to tyrants
  Latin: **17** sic semper tyrannis
  motto of: **8** Virginia

thus passes away the glory of this world
  Latin: **21** sic transit gloria mundi

Thus Spake Zarathustra
  also: **21** Also Sprach Zarathustra
  author: **18** Friedrich Nietzsche

thwack 3 box, hit, rap **4** bang, blow, slam, slap **5** baste, clout, knock, smack, thump, whack **6** buffet, paddle, strike, wallop

Thwackum
  character in: **8** Tom Jones
  author: **8** Fielding

thwart 3 bar **4** balk, foil, stop **5** check, cross **6** baffle, hinder, oppose **7** inhibit, prevent, ward off **8** obstruct, stave off **9** frustrate **10** contravene

Thyestean banquet
  meal of: **10** human flesh

Thyestes
  author: **6** Seneca

Thyestes
  father: **6** Pelops
  mother: **10** Hippodamia
  brother: **6** Atreus
  half-brother: **10** Chrysippus

sister-in-law: 6 Aerope
son: 9 Aegisthus
daughter: 7 Pelopia
Thyiad *see* **9** bacchante
Thymbraeus
  father: 7 Laocoon
thyme
  botanical name: 6 Thymus **9** T vulgaris
  varieties: 4 Wild **5** Basil, Lemon, Water **6** Common, Garden, Golden **7** Caraway, Spanish
  symbol of: 8 activity
  attracts: 4 bees
  conjures: 9 fairy folk
  use: 4 fish **7** poultry **8** stuffing **10** Creole food **21** New England clam chowder
Thyrus
  staff of: 8 Dionysus
  tipped with: 8 pine cone
  twined with: 3 ivy **5** vines
thysanoptera
  class: 8 hexapoda
  phylum: 10 arthropoda
  group: 5 thrip
thysanura
  class: 8 hexapoda
  phylum: 10 arthropoda
  group: 8 firebrat **10** silverfish **11** bristletail
Tia Maria
  type: 6 brandy **7** liqueur
  origin: 7 Jamaica
  flavor: 6 coffee
  with rum: 10 Black Maria
  with tequila: 9 Brave Bull
  with vodka: 12 Black Russian
tiara 4 band **5** crown, miter **6** diadem **7** coronet **8** frontlet, ornament **9** headdress
Tibet
  other name: 3 Bod **4** Bhot **5** Tobet **8** Hsitsang **10** Land of Snow **14** Roof of the World
  capital: 5 Lassa, Lhasa
  city: 3 Noh **5** Karak **6** Chamdo, Gartok **7** Changtu, Totling **8** Gyangtse, Jihkatse, Shigatse **9** Chiangtzu
  government: 23 autonomous region of China
  monetary unit: 5 tanga
  lake: 3 Aru, Bam, Bun, Nam **4** Mema, Tosu **5** Jagok, Tabia **6** Dagtse, Garhur, Kashun, Nam Iso, Seling, Tangra, Yamdok **7** Kyaring, Teriman, Tsaring, Zilling **8** Jiggitai **9** Tengrinor **11** Manasarowar
  mountain: 5 Kamet, Sajum **6** Kailas, Kunlun **7** Bandala **8** Himalaya **9** Karakoram
  highest point: 7 Everest
  river: 3 Nak, Nau, Sak **4** Song **5** Hwang, Indus **6** Mekong, Sutlej, Yellow **7** Hwang Ho, Matsang, Melsang, Salween, Tsangpo, Yangtze **11** Brahmaputra

  physical feature:
    plain: 4 Kham **9** Chang Tang
    valley: 7 Tsangpo
  people: 5 Asian, Balti, Bodpa, Drupa **6** Bhotia, Champa, Drokpa, Khamba, Khambu, Panaka, Sherpa, Tangut **7** Bhotiya, Bhutani, Gyarung, Taghlik, Tibetan **9** Mongoloid
    patron god: 14 Avalokitesvara
    ruler: 4 Yuan **6** Mongol **9** dalai lama **13** Songtsan Gampo
  language: 5 Balti **6** Ladkhi **7** Bhutani, Bodskad **8** Sanskrit **9** Bhutanese
  religion: 5 Bonko **7** Lamaism
  place:
    Indian border: 11 McMahon Line
    palace: 7 Potalaf
    temple: 7 Jokhang **10** Tashi Lumpo **11** Tashi Lhunpo
  feature:
    animal: 3 dzo, yak **5** kiang **7** mastiff **8** musk deer **10** giant panda
    clothing: 5 chuba
    dance: 4 cham **9** achelhamo
    dog: 9 lhasa apso
    leader: 9 dalai lama
    legend: 4 yeti **17** abominable snowman
    monastery: 8 lamasery
    monk: 4 lama
  food:
    dish: 6 tsamba, tsampa
    drink: 5 chang
tibia
  bone of: 4 shin
tic 5 spasm **6** twitch **12** facial twitch **13** tic douloureux **19** trigemi nal neuralgia
tick 3 dot, tap **4** beat, line, list, mark, nick, note **5** blaze, check, clack, click, enter, notch, swing, throb **6** record, slight, stroke **7** scratch, vibrate **8** mark down, register, ticktock **9** checkmark, chronicle, oscillate, pulsation, vibration
ticket 3 tag **4** card, mark, pass, slip, stub **5** label, slate **6** ballot, coupon, marker, roster **7** sticker, voucher **14** list of nominees, traffic summons
  type: 4 trip **7** parking, traffic **9** admission
  free: 11 Annie Oakley
tickle 4 itch **5** amuse, cheer, prick, sting, throb **6** divert, please, regale, stroke, thrill, tingle, twitch **7** delight, enchant, enliven, gladden, gratify, prickle, rejoice **8** enthrall, entrance **9** captivate, fascinate, titillate **12** scratchiness **15** do one's heart good
ticklish 4 hard **5** itchy, tough **6** knotty, thorny, tickly, touchy, tricky **7** awkward, prickly **8** critical, delicate, scratchy, tingling **9** difficult, intricate, sensitive, uncertain **11** complicated
tidal basin 3 bay **5** inlet, sound **6** lagoon **7** estuary **11** arm of the sea

tidbit 3 bit **4** item **5** treat **6** morsel **8** delicacy, mouthful **9** choice bit
tide 4 flow, neap, wave **5** drift, state **7** current **8** movement, tendency, undertow **9** direction **10** ebb and flow, wax and wane **11** rise and fall
tidings 4 news, word **6** advice, notice, report **8** good word **11** declaration, information **12** announcement, intelligence, notification
tidy 4 neat, trig, trim **5** ample, array, clean **6** goodly, neaten, tidy up **7** arrange, careful, clean up, orderly, precise, regular, sizable **8** neaten up, spotless, spruce up **9** organized, regulated, shipshape **10** immaculate, methodical, meticulous, put in order, straighten, systematic **11** substantial **12** businesslike, considerable, straighten up **15** in apple-pie order
tidy up 5 clean **6** neaten **9** freshen up **10** put in order, straighten
tie 3 rod **4** ally, band, beam, belt, bind, bond, cord, draw, duty, join, knot, lash, line, link, rope, sash, yoke **5** brace, ca- ble, cinch, limit, marry, match, truss, unite **6** attach, bow tie, clinch, couple, cravat, engage, fasten, girdle, hamper, hinder, ribbon, secure, string, tether **7** confine, connect, kinship, necktie, support **8** affinity, cincture, dead heat, make a bow, make fast, relation, restrain, restrict, tied vote **9** constrain, crossbeam, fastening **10** allegiance, connection, cummerbund, obligation **11** affiliation, come out even **12** relationship **13** connecting rod **15** divide the honors
Tiepolo, Giovanni Battista (Giambattista)
  born: 5 Italy **6** Venice
  artwork: 10 Kaisersaal (salon) **11** Treppenhaus (staircase) **14** The Crucifixion **16** Ronaldo and Armida **20** Madonna of Mount Carmel **21** The Communion of St Lucia, The Triumph of Aphrodite **24** St Thekla and the Pestilence **28** Apotheosis of Francesco Barbaro **28** The Worship of the Bronze Serpent
tier 3 row **4** bank, file, line, rank, step **5** layer, level, range, story **7** stratum **14** stratification
Tierney, Gene
  born: 10 Brooklyn NY
  husband: 11 Oleg Cassini
  roles: 5 Laura **10** Belle Starr **11** Tobacco Road **13** A Bell for Adano **16** Leave Her to Heaven **18** The Ghost and Mrs Muir
tiers etat 11 third estate
  in French politics: 7 commons
tie-up 3 jam **4** snag **5** block, hitch, snarl **6** slow-up **7** failure **8** blockage, gridlock, stop page **9** breakdown **10** bottleneck, disruption **11** malfunction **13** embouteillage

tie up 3 tie **4** bind, gird, lash, rope **5** hitch, snarl, strap, truss **6** engage, fasten, hinder, impede, occupy, secure, tangle **8** entangle

tiff 4 huff, miff, rage, snit, spat **5** clash, run-in, scrap, tizzy, words **6** hassle **7** dispute, quarrel, rhubarb, wrangle **8** argument, ill humor, squabble **10** difference **11** altercation **12** disagreement **16** misunderstanding

tiger 3 cat **6** cougar, jaguar **7** fighter, wildcat
 young: 5 whelp

Tiger Joy
 author: 19 Stephen Vincent Benet

tiger's-eye
 species: 6 quartz

Tigger
 character in: 13 Winnie-the-Pooh
 author: 5 Milne

tight 4 busy, firm, full, hard, high, snug, taut **5** blind, close, dense, drunk, exact, happy, harsh, lit up, rigid, scant, solid, stern, stiff, tense, tipsy, tough **6** firmly, frugal, gorged, hard-up, jammed, juiced, loaded, scarce, secure, severe, skimpy, sloppy, soused, stewed, stingy, stoned, strict, trying, zonked **7** austere, closely, com- pact, crammed, crowded, drunken, miserly, onerous, pickled, pie-eyed, smashed, solidly, sparing, stuffed **8** grudging, rigorous, securely, too small **9** deficient, difficult, illiberal, jam-packed, niggardly, penurious, plastered, skintight, stringent, worrisome **10** burdensome, compressed, glassy-eyed, impassable, inadequate, inebriated, inflexible, in one's cups, nip-and-tuck, nose-to-nose, tyrannical, ungenerous, unyielding **11** closefisted, constricted, dictatorial, impermeable, intoxicated, troublesome, well-matched **12** closefitting, impenetrable, insufficient, parsimonious **13** closely fitted, feeling no pain **14** fitting closely, uncompromising **20** three sheets to the wind

tighten 5 pinch **6** anchor, fasten, narrow, secure **7** squeeze **8** contract, make fast, make taut **9** constrict **14** take up the slack

tighten one's belt 4 save **5** skimp, stint **6** scrimp **8** conserve, cut costs **9** economize **11** cut expenses **12** pinch pennies

tightfisted 5 cheap, mingy, tight **6** greedy, stingy **7** miserly **9** illiberal, niggardly, penurious **10** avaricious **11** closefisted **12** cheeseparing, parsimonious **13** penny-pinching

tightfistedness 6 penury **9** parsimony **10** stinginess **11** miserliness **13** niggardliness, penny-pinching

tight-fitting 4 snug **5** tight **8** too small **9** skintight **11** constricted **12** constricting **15** like a second skin

tight-laced 4 prim **6** prissy, stuffy **7** prudish **8** priggish **9** inhibited, repressed, Victorian **11** puritanical, standoffish, straitlaced **13** self-righteous

tight-lipped 3 mum **4** curt **5** brief, quiet, short, terse **8** discreet, reserved, reticent, taciturn **10** unsociable **11** untalkative **12** close-mouthed **15** uncommunicative

tightly packed 5 dense **6** jammed **7** compact, crammed, stuffed **10** compressed **12** concentrated

tightwad 5 miser, piker **7** niggard, Scrooge **9** lickpenny, skinflint **10** cheapskate, pinchpenny **12** money-grubber

Tiki
 Polynesian: 8 first man **6** amulet

till 3 sow **4** even, farm, plow, seed, tray, unto up to **6** before, coffer, drawer, harrow, plough **7** as far as, develop, prepare **8** moneybox, treasury **9** cultivate **12** cash register
 geological: 5 drift

tillable 6 arable **8** farmable, plowable **10** cultivable

tillage 7 farming, plowing **11** agriculture, cultivation

Till Eulenspiegel
 also: 16 Tyll Eulenspiegel
 origin: 8 Germanic
 means: 14 practical joker

Tillie the Toiler
 creator: 12 Russ Westover
 character: 3 Mac **7** Mr Chase

Tilney, Henry
 character in: 15 Northanger Abbey
 author: 6 Austen

tilt 3 row, tip **4** cant, lean, list, rake, spar, tiff **5** brawl, fence, fight, grade, joust, pitch, slant, slope **6** affray, battle, combat, oppose **7** content, dispute, incline, quarrel **8** argument, skirmish, squabble **9** encounter **10** tournament **11** altercation

Timaeus
 author: 5 Plato

Timandra
 father: 9 Tyndareus
 mother: 4 Leda
 brother: 6 Castor, Pollux
 sister: 5 Helen **12** Clytemnestra
 husband: 7 Echemus, Phyleus
 son: 5 Meges
 cursed by: 9 Aphrodite

timber 4 bush, logs, wood **5** copse, trees, woods **6** boards, forest, lumber **7** thicket

timberland 5 woods **6** forest, sticks **8** woodland

timbre 4 tone **5** pitch **9** resonance

time, times 3 age, day, eon, era **4** beat, days, hour, term, week, year **5** clock, cycle, epoch, event, match, month, phase, spell, stage, tempo, while, years **6** adjust, chance, decade, moment, period, rhythm, season **7** century, episode, freedom, instant, liberty, measure, stretch **8** duration, incident, interval, occasion **10** experience, generation **11** opportunity, synchronize

time flies
 Latin: 11 tempus fugit

time-honored 6 common, normal **7** regular, revered **8** accepted, standard **9** customary, respected, universal

timeless 7 abiding, durable, endless, eternal, lasting, undying **8** enduring, immortal, infinite, unending **9** boundless, ceaseless, deathless, immutable, incessant, permanent, perpetual **10** continuous, persistent **11** everlasting, never-ending **12** interminable, unchangeable **13** never-stopping **14** indestructible

timely 6 prompt **8** punctual **9** opportune, well-timed **10** convenient, felicitous, seasonable **12** providential

Time Machine, The
 author: 7 H G Wells
 character: 4 Eloi **5** Weena **8** Morlocks **12** Time Traveler

Time of Your Life, The
 author: 14 William Saroyan
 director: 8 H C Potter
 cast: 8 Ward Bond **11** James Cagney, Wayne Morris **12** Jeanne Cagney **13** William Bendix **17** Broderick Crawford

timepiece 5 clock, watch **8** horologe **11** chronometer

Time Remembered
 author: 11 Jean Anouilh

Timerman, Jacobo
 author of: 38 Prisoner Without a Name Cell Without a Number

timesaving 5 quick **6** speedy **9** efficient **11** expeditious

time without end 7 forever **8** eternity, infinity

timeworn 3 old **4** aged, worn **5** dated, hoary, passe, stale, trite **6** age-old, beat-up, old-hat, shabby **7** ancient, antique **8** battered, dog-eared, obsolete, overused **9** hackneyed, out of date, venerable, weathered **10** antiquated **12** antediluvian

timid 3 coy, shy **6** afraid, humble, modest, scared **7** bashful, fearful **8** cowardly, retiring, sheepish, timorous **9** diffident, shrinking, spineless, weak-kneed **10** unassuming **12** apprehensive, fainthearted **13** pusillanimous

timidity 7 modesty, shyness **8** cold feet, humility **9** cowardice, timidness **10** diffidence **11** bashfulness, fearfulness, trepidation **12** sheepishness, timorousness **13** spinelessness **16** faint-heartedness

timidness 7 shyness **8** meekness, timidity **10** diffidence, insecurity **11** bashfulness **12** timorousness **14** submissiveness **15** unassertiveness **16** faintheartedness

Timon of Athens
   author: **18** William Shakespeare
   character: **6** Lucius **7** Flavius **8** Lucullus **9** Apemantus, Ventidius **10** Alcibiades, Sempronius

Timor
   capital: **4** Dili
   country: **8** Portugal **9** Indonesia
   islands: **5** Sunda **11** Lesser Sunda
   strait: **5** Ombai

timorous 3 shy **4** meek **5** timid **6** afraid **7** anxious, bashful, fearful **8** retiring **9** shrinking **10** submissive **12** fainthearted

timorousness 7 shyness **8** cold feet, meekness, timidity **9** cowardice **11** fearfulness, trepidation **16** faintheartedness

Timothy
   mother: **6** Eunice
   grandmother: **4** Lois
   companion: **4** Paul **8** Silvanus

tin
   chemical symbol: **2** Sn

tincture 6 elixir **7** essence, extract, spirits **8** solution **11** concentrate

Tinder Box, The
   author: **21** Hans Christian Andersen

Tin Drum, The
   author: **11** Gunter Grass
   director: **17** Volker Schlondorff
   character: **8** Oskar Matzerath
   cast: **10** Mario Adorf **12** David Bennent (Oskar) **13** Angela Winkler **16** Daniel Olbrychski **17** Katharina Tahlbach
   Oscar for: **11** foreign film

tine 3 die, tip **4** barb, lose, tyne **5** point, prong, spike **6** bodkin, branch, perish, skewer **7** destroy, forfeit

tinge 3 dye **4** cast, dash, hint, lace, tint, tone, vein **5** color, imbue, shade, smack, stain, taste, touch, trace **6** flavor, infuse, nuance, season **7** instill, soupcon **9** suspicion

tingle 5 sting, throb **6** thrill, tickle, tremor **7** flutter, prickle **9** prickling, pulsation **11** palpitation

Tinker, Tailor, Soldier, Spy
   author: **11** John Le Carre

Tinker Bell
   character in: **8** Peter Pan
   author: **6** Barrie

tinkle 4 ding, peal, ping, ring **5** chime, chink, clank, clink, plink **6** jingle **9** ting-a-ling

tin lizzie 3 car **4** auto, heap **5** motor **6** jalopy, wheels **7** flivver, machine, vehicle **8** motorcar **10** automobile **12** motor vehicle

Tin Man, Tin Woodsman

character in: **13** The Wizard of Oz
   author: **4** Baum

tinsel 4 sham, show **5** gloss **6** sequin **7** glitter, spangle **8** pretense **9** gaudiness **10** camouflage, decoration, masquerade **11** affectation, false colors, make-believe, ostentation

tint 3 dye, hue **4** hint, tone, wash **5** color, frost, shade, stain, tinge, touch, trace **6** nuance **7** pigment **8** coloring, tincture **10** suggestion

Tintern Abbey
   author: **17** William Wordsworth

tintinnabulate 4 peal, ring, toll **5** chime, clang, knell, sound **6** jingle, tinkle

tintinnabulation 4 gong, peal, ring, toll **5** chime, knell **6** jingle **7** clangor, pealing, ringing **8** clanging, ding-dong, jingling, tinkling **11** peal of bells

Tintoretto, Jacopo
   real name: **13** Jacopo Robusti
   born: **5** Italy **6** Venice
   artwork: **8** Paradise **13** The Last Supper **14** The Crucifixion **16** The Road to Calvary **17** Bacchus and Ariadne **18** Apotheosis of St Roch, The Flight into Egypt **20** Susannah and the Elders **21** The Temptation of Christ **26** St Mark Frees a Christian Slave **27** The Finding of the Body of St Mark **32** The Miracle of St Mark Rescuing a Slave

tiny 3 wee **5** pygmy, runty, small, teeny **6** bantam, little, midget, minute, petite **8** dwarfish **9** itsy-bitsy, miniature, minuscule, pint-sized **10** diminutive, teeny-weeny, undersized **11** Lilliputian, microscopic, pocket-sized **12** teensy-weensy

Tiny Alice
   author: **11** Edward Albee

Tiny Tim
   character in: **15** A Christmas Carol
   author: **7** Dickens

tip 3 cap, pat, tap, top **4** acme, apex, barb, brow, cant, clue, head, hint, hook, lean, list, peak, rake, tilt **5** crest, crown, pitch, point, prong, slant, slope, spike, upend, upset **6** advice, reward, stroke, summit, tip-off, topple, upturn, vertex, zenith **7** capsize, incline, leaning, lowdown, pointer, sharpen, tilting, tipping, warning **8** gratuity, over turn, pinnacle, slanting **9** baksheesh, lagniappe **10** admonition, inside dope, perquisite, suggestion, turn turtle **11** forewarning **13** word to the wise
   French: **7** douceur

tipcart 4 cart **8** dumpcart, pushcart

Tiphys
   member of: **9** Argonauts
   occupation: **9** steersman

tip off 3 tip **4** warn **5** alert **6** caveat **7** caution, warning **8** forewarn **11** forewarning

tip over 5 upend, upset **7** capsize **8** flip over, keel over, overturn, turn over **10** turn turtle

Tippett, Michael Kemp
   born: **6** London **7** England
   composer of: **9** King Priam **13** The Knot Garden **15** A Child of Our Time **20** The Midsummer Marriage **22** The Vision of St Augustine **32** Concerto for Double String Orchestra

tipple 5 drink, quaff **6** guzzle, imbibe, liquor **8** beverage

tippler 3 sot **4** lush, soak, wino **5** drunk, rummy, souse, toper **6** bibber, boozer, sponge **7** guzzler, imbiber, swiller, tosspot **8** drunkard **9** alcoholic, inebriate **10** booze hound **11** dipsomaniac

tipsy 4 high **5** awash, blind, drunk, happy, lit-up, stiff, tight **6** juiced, loaded, sloppy, sodden, soused, stewed, stoned **7** drunken, pickled, pie-eyed, smashed **9** inebriate, plastered **10** glassy-eyed, inebriated, in one's cups **11** intoxicated **12** half seas over **13** feeling no pain **20** three sheets to the wind

tip-top 4 A-one **5** elite, super **7** supreme **8** very fine **10** consummate **11** exceptional, superlative **13** extraordinary

tirade 5 curse **6** screed **7** lecture **8** diatribe, harangue, jeremiad, scolding **9** invective, reprimand **11** castigation, fulmination **12** condemnation, denunciation, dressing-down, vilification, vituperation

tirailleur 10 skirmisher **12** sharpshooter

Tirane, Tirana
   capital of: **7** Albania

tire 3 fag, irk **4** bore **5** annoy, weary **6** bother, tucker **7** disgust, exhaust, fatigue, wear out **8** be sick of **10** make sleepy **11** be fed up with **12** lose interest, lose patience

tire
   invented by: **6** Dunlop **7** Thomson

tired 4 beat **5** all in, weary **6** bushed, drowsy, fagged, pooped, sleepy **7** wearied, worn out **8** dog-tired, fatigued, tuckered **9** enervated, exhausted, played out

tireless 6 steady **7** devoted, staunch **8** constant, faithful, resolute, untiring **9** steadfast, unceasing, unwearied **10** determined, unflagging, unswerving **11** hard-working, industrious, never-tiring, persevering, unfaltering, unremitting **13** indefatigable

Tiresias
   also: **9** Teiresias
   vocation: **4** seer **7** prophet
   father: **6** Everes
   mother: **8** Chariclo
   grandfather: **6** Udaeus
   home: **6** Thebes

struck: 5 blind
character in: 7 Odyssey **10** Oedipus Rex
characteristic: 9 blind seer

tiresome 4 drab, dull, hard **6** boring, deadly, dismal, tiring, trying, vexing **7** arduous, fagging, humdrum, irksome, tedious, wearing **8** annoying, wearying **9** difficult, fatiguing, laborious, wearisome **10** bothersome, exhausting, monotonous **13** uninteresting

Tishri 18 seventh Hebrew month

Tisiphone
member of: 6 Furies

'Tis Pity She's a Whore
author: 8 John Ford
character: 6 Donado, Florio, Putana **7** Soranzo, Vasques **8** Bergetto, Giovanni, Grimaldi **9** Annabella, Hippolita **11** Richardetto **16** Friar Bonaventura

tissue
kind: 4 bone, skin **5** nerve **6** muscle

titan 5 giant, great, mogul **7** magnate

Titan
race of: 4 gods
father: 6 Uranus
mother: 2 Ge **4** Gaea
names: 5 Coeus, Crius **6** Cronus **7** Iapetus, Oceanus **8** Hyperion
sisters: 8 Titaness
  names of sisters: 4 Rhea **5** Theia **6** Phoebe, Tethys, Themis **9** Mnemosyne

Titan, The
sequel to: 12 The Financier
author: 15 Theodore Dreiser
character: 13 Peter Laughlin **15** Berenice Fleming, Stephanie Platow **16** Aileen Cowperwood **23** Frank Algernon Cowperwood

Titan, the see **6** Helios

Titaness see **5** Titan

Titania
character in: 21 A Midsummer Night's Dream
author: 11 Shakespeare

titanic 4 huge, vast **5** giant, great, stout **6** mighty, strong **7** immense, mammoth **8** colossal, enormous, gigantic, whopping **9** herculean, humongous, monstrous **10** gargantuan, monumental, prodigious, stupendous

titanium
chemical symbol: 2 Ti

tit for tat 8 exchange **10** quid pro quo **13** an eye for an eye

Titian
real name: 15 Tiziano Vecellio
born: 5 Italy **13** Pieve di Cadore
artwork: 5 Pieta **12** The Bacchanal, Tribute Money **13** Noli Me Tangere **15** Diana and Actaeon, The Rape of Europa **16** The Pesaro Madonna, The Venus of Urbino **17** Bacchus and Ariadne, The Death of Actaeon, The

Girl in a Fur Wrap, The Three Ages of Man **18** Charles V at Muhlberg, The Adrian Bacchanal, The Young Englishman **19** Francis I Roi de France **20** Sacred and Profane Love **21** Venus and the Lute Player **23** The Madonna of the Cherries **24** Pope Paul III and his Nephews, The Assumption of the Virgin

titillate 5 charm, rouse, tease, tempt **6** allure, arouse, excite, seduce, tickle, turn on **7** attract, provoke **8** entrance **9** captivate, fascinate, stimulate **15** whet the appetite

titillating 8 alluring, exciting, tempting **9** seductive **10** suggestive **11** provocative

title 3 dub **4** deed, name, rank, term **5** claim, crown, grade, label, place, right **6** status, tenure **7** entitle, epithet, station **8** christen, nobility, position **9** condition, designate, ownership **10** legal right, lordly rank, noble birth, possession **11** appellation, designation **12** championship

titled 5 named, noble, regal, royal **6** called, lordly **7** courtly **8** entitled **10** designated **11** blue-blooded **12** aristocratic

Titograd 9 Podgorica
capital of: 10 Montenegro

titter 5 chirp, smirk **6** cackle, giggle, simper, teehee **7** chuckle, snicker, snigger

tittle 3 bit, dot, jot **4** atom, iota, mite **5** speck **8** particle

Tittle, Y A (Yelberton Abraham)
sport: 8 football
position: 11 quarterback
team: 13 New York Giants **14** Baltimore Colts **23** San Francisco Forty-Niners

titular 7 known as, nominal **8** so called **10** in name only, ostensible **11** in title only

Titus
surname: 6 Justus
hometown: 7 Corinth
companion: 4 Paul

Titus see **6** Tatius

Titus Andronicus
author: 18 William Shakespeare
character: 5 Aaron **6** Chiron, Marcus, Tamora **7** Alarbus, Lavinia **9** Bassianus, Demetrius **10** Saturninus

Tiu
Germanic god of: 3 sky, war
Norse: 3 Tyr
eponym of: 7 Tuesday

tizzy 4 snit **6** dither, swivet **7** dudgeon **8** tailspin
British: 8 sixpence

Tjaden
character in: 25 All Quiet on the Western Front
author: 8 Remarque

to 2 ad, on **3** for **4** into, near, unto, upon, with **5** about, until **6** at hand, closed, toward **7** against, forward **8** together **10** concerning, included in **11** contained in
prefix: 2 ac, ad
Scottish: 3 tae

toad
group of: 4 knot

toady 4 fawn **6** fawner, flunky, stooge, yes-man **8** hanger-on, kowtow to, parasite, truckler **9** flatterer, sycophant **10** bootlicker, curry favor **11** apple-polish, lickspittle **13** apple-polisher, backscratcher

To Althea, From Prison
author: 15 Richard Lovelace

to a man 3 all **8** every one **9** one and all **10** completely **12** to the last man

To a Skylark
author: 18 Percy Bysshe Shelley

toast 3 dry **4** heat, warm **5** brown, grill, honor **6** salute, warm up **9** celebrate **10** compliment **11** commemorate **12** browned bread, clink glasses **15** drink one's health

tobacco
varieties: 4 tree, wild **6** Indian **7** jasmine, Turkish **9** broadleaf, flowering, Nicotiana **12** long-flowered **16** Nicotiana rustica, Nicotiana tabacum

Tobacco Road
author: 15 Erskine Caldwell
character: 3 Ada **4** Dude **5** Pearl **6** Bessie **8** Ellie May **9** Lov Bensey **12** Jeeter Lester

To Be or Not To Be
director: 13 Ernst Lubitsch
cast: 9 Jack Benny **11** Robert Stack **12** Lionel Atwill **13** Carole Lombard, Felix Bressart
setting: 6 Poland

To Catch a Thief
director: 15 Alfred Hitchcock
cast: 9 Cary Grant **10** Grace Kelly **12** John Williams **17** Jessie Royce Landis
setting: 13 French Riviera

Tocqueville, Alexis de
author of: 18 Democracy in America

tocsin 4 bell **5** alarm **7** warning

today 3 now **7** this day, this era **8** nowadays, this time **9** in this era, on this day, this epoch **10** the present **11** in this epoch, modern times **13** in modern times, the present age, the present day **15** in this day and age

Todd, Richard
real name: 27 Richard Andrew Palethorpe-Todd
born: 6 Dublin **7** Ireland
roles: 13 The Hasty Heart, The Longest Day **14** The Virgin Queen **15** A Man Called Peter

toddle 6 waddle, wobble **14** take short steps, walk unsteadily

toddler 3 tot 4 babe, baby, tyke 5 child 6 infant 9 little one

to-do 3 ado 4 fuss, stir 5 furor, noise 6 bustle, flurry, hubbub, hustle, pother, racket, ruckus, rumpus, tumult, uproar 7 turmoil 8 activity 9 agitation, commotion 10 excitement, hullabaloo, hurly-burly 11 disturbance

Toe, The
    nickname of: 8 Lou Groza

to err is human
    Latin: 16 errare humanum est

toff 3 nob 4 beau 5 dandy, swell 10 young blood

Toffler, Alvin
    author of: 11 Future Shock 12 The Third Wave

toga 3 aba 4 garb, gown, robe 6 trabea 7 garment 12 outergarment
    virilis: 9 white robe 11 manhood robe

Togo
    other name: 14 French Togoland
    capital/largest city: 4 Lome
    others: 5 Badon, Kpeme 6 Anecho, Ansoho, Blitta, Klonto, Nuatja, Palime, Sokode 7 Bassari, Dopango, Pagonda 8 Atakpame, Tabligbo 10 Niamtougou
    school: 5 Benin 6 Mawull
    monetary unit: 5 franc 7 centime
    mountain: 4 Togo 7 Atakora, Koronga
    highest point: 7 Baumann
    river: 3 Oti 4 Anie, Haho, Mono, Ogou
    sea: 8 Atlantic
    physical feature:
        bight: 5 Benin
        gulf: 6 Guinea
        plain: 4 Mono
    people: 3 Ana, Ewe, Twi 4 Mina 5 Hausa 6 Akposa, Kabrai 7 Bassari, Cabrais, Kabrais, Ouatchi 8 Konkomba, Kotokoli, Lotokoli
        leader: 7 Eyadema 15 Sylvanus Olympio 16 Nicolas Grunitzky
    language: 3 Ana, Ewe, Twi 4 Mina 5 Hausa 6 French, Kabrai, Kabrie 7 Bassari, Dagomba, Ouatchi 8 Kotokoli, Lotocoli
    religion: 5 Islam 7 animism 12 Christianity

togs 4 duds 6 attire, outfit 7 apparel, clothes, threads 8 clothing, garments

To Have and Have Not
    director: 11 Howard Hawks
    based on novel by: 15 Ernest Hemingway
    cast: 12 Dolores Moran, Lauren Bacall 13 Walter Brennan 14 Humphrey Bogart 15 Hoagy Carmichael
    remade as: 13 The Gunrunners 16 The Breaking Point

To His Coy Mistress
    author: 13 Andrew Marvell

toil 4 grub, moil, work 5 grind, labor, pains, slave, sweat 6 drudge, effort 7 travail 8 drudgery, exertion, hardship, hard work, industry, struggle, work hard 11 application, elbow grease 12 apply oneself, exert oneself 14 work like a horse

toiler 4 peon, serf, swot 5 navvy, prole, slave 6 drudge, flunky, menial, slavey, worker 7 grubber, laborer, servant, slogger 9 workhorse 10 wage earner 11 galley slave

toilet 2 WC 3 can, loo 4 john 5 privy 7 commode, latrine 8 facility, lavatory, men's room, outhouse, rest room, washroom 10 ladies' room 11 convenience, water closet

toilet water 5 scent 7 cologne, essence, perfume 9 fragrance

toilsome 4 hard 5 tough 6 tiring, uphill 7 arduous, onerous, tedious 8 wearying 9 difficult, effortful, fatiguing, herculean, laborious, strenuous, wearisome 10 burdensome, exhausting 12 backbreaking

To Jerusalem and Back
    author: 10 Saul Bellow

token 4 mark, sign 5 index, proof 6 jetton, symbol 7 for show, memento, minimal, nodding, nominal, passing 8 evidence, keepsake, reminder, souvenir, symbolic 9 vestigial 10 expression, indication 11 perfunctory, remembrance, superficial, testimonial 13 manifestation

To Kill a Mockingbird
    director: 14 Robert Mulligan
    based on novel by: 9 Harper Lee
    cast: 9 John Megna 10 Mary Badham 11 Gregory Peck 12 Philip Alford
    Oscar for: 5 actor (Peck)

Tokyo
    airport: 6 Haneda
    capital of: 5 Japan
    district: 5 Ginza 6 Keihin 7 Chiyoda 8 Yokohama 10 Marunouchi 18 Tama New Town Project
    former name: 3 Edo
    island: 6 Honshu
    landmark: 8 Ueno Park 11 Meiji Shrine 12 National Diet 14 Imperial Palace, Kitanomaru Park 19 Komazawa Olympic Park
    means: 14 Eastern capital

tolerable 4 fair, so-so 7 allowed, average 8 abidable, accepted, adequate, bearable, mediocre, middling, ordinary, passable 9 allowable, endurable, innocuous, permitted 10 acceptable, admissible, fairly good, sufferable 11 commonplace, indifferent, permissible 12 run-of-the-mill 14 fair-to-middling

tolerance 7 charity 8 fairness, goodwill, patience, sympathy 9 endurance 10 compassion, sufferance 11 forbearance 13 brotherly love, fair treatment, fellow feeling, power to endure 15 lack of prejudice

tolerant 4 easy, fair, soft 7 lenient, liberal, patient, sparing 8 moderate 9 easygoing, forgiving, indulgent, unbigoted 10 charitable, forbearing, permissive 11 broad-minded, kindhearted, softhearted, sympathetic 12 unprejudiced 13 compassionate, uncomplaining, understanding

tolerate 3 let 4 bear, take 5 abide, admit, allow, brook, stand 6 endure, permit, suffer, wink at 7 indulge, stomach, undergo 8 be easy on, be soft on, sanction, submit to 9 consent to, put up with, recognize, vouchsafe

To Let
    author: 14 John Galsworthy

to life
    Hebrew: 7 lehayim 8 lechayim

Tolkien, J R R
    author of: 9 The Hobbit 15 The Silmarillion 17 The Lord of the Rings
    creature: 3 ent orc
    fictional setting: 11 Middle Earth

toll 3 fee, tax 4 duty, levy, loss 6 charge, impost, tariff 7 payment, penalty, tribute, undoing 8 exaction 9 depletion, sacrifice 10 assessment, disruption, extinction 11 destruction 12 annihilation 13 extermination

Tolstoy, Leo
    author of: 11 War and Peace 12 Anna Karenina, Resurrection 17 The Kreutzer Sonata 18 Death of Ivan Ilyitch

Toltec
    city: 4 Tula
    preceded: 5 Aztec
    tribe: 4 Itza

To Lucasta, Going to the Wars
    author: 15 Richard Lovelace

tom 3 cat 6 tomcat 10 male turkey

tomato 12 Lycopersicon 24 Lycopersicon lycopersicum
    varieties: 4 Husk, Pear, Tree 6 Cherry 7 Currant 10 Gooseberry, Strawberry 11 Mexican husk
    soup: 8 gazpacho
    sauce: 6 catsup 7 ketchup

tomb 5 crypt, grave, vault 8 monument 9 mausoleum, sepulcher 11 burial place 12 resting place 13 burial chamber

tomboy 3 meg 4 girl, romp 5 rowdy 6 female, gamine, hoiden, hoyden, tomrig 8 strumpet

Tom Brown's School Days
    author: 12 Thomas Hughes

tombs
    god of: 6 Anubis

tomcat 3 cat, tom 9 womanizer

tomfoolery 4 play 6 antics 8 drollery, nonsense 9 high jinks, horseplay, silliness 10 goofing off, skylarking 11 foolishness 12 lollygagging, monkeyshines, prankishness 13 fooling around, messing around, playing around

Tom Jones
  also: **29** The History of Tom Jones Foundling
  author: **13** Henry Fielding
  character: **6** Square **7** Bridget, Western **8** Mrs Honor, Thwackum **9** Mrs Miller, Partridge **11** Black George, Nightingale **12** Master Blifil **13** Lady Bellaston, Sophia Western **15** Squire Allworthy
  director: **14** Tony Richardson
  cast: **11** Joyce Redman **12** Albert Finney, Diane Cilento, Hugh Griffith, Susannah York **14** Dame Edith Evans
  score: **11** John Addison
  Oscar for: **5** score **7** picture **9** direction **10** screenplay

Tomlin, Lily
  real name: **14** Mary Jean Tomlin
  born: **9** Detroit MI
  roles: **7** Laugh-In **8** Edith Ann **9** Ernestine, Nashville, The Player **11** The Late Show **14** Moment By Moment **20** Flirting with Disaster **27** The Incredible Shrinking Woman

tommyrot 3 rot **4** bosh, bull, bunk, crap, tosh **5** bilge, hokum, hooey, trash **6** bunkum, drivel, humbug **7** baloney, hogwash, spinach, rubbish, twaddle **8** buncombe, claptrap, folderol, malarkey, nonsense **9** poppycock **10** applesauce, balderdash, tomfoolery **11** foolishness **12** bullfeathers, fiddle-faddle **13** horsefeathers **16** stuff-and-nonsense

tomorrow 9 the future, the morrow **11** in the future **12** in days to come **16** the day after today **17** the next generation
  Spanish: **6** manana

Tom Sawyer
  author: **9** Mark Twain
  character: **8** Huck (Huckleberry) Finn, Injun Joe **9** Aunt Polly, Joe Harper **10** Muff Potter **13** Becky Thatcher

Tom Thumb the Great
  author: **13** Henry Fielding

ton
  abbreviation: **1** t

tone 3 hue **4** cast, lilt, mood, note, tint **5** color, pitch, shade, sound, style, tenor, tinge **6** accent, chroma, firm up, manner, soften, spirit, stress, subdue, temper **7** cadence, quality **8** attitude, harmonic, make firm, moderate, modulate, overtone, tonality **10** inflection, intonation, make supple, modulation

Tone, Franchot
  real name: **27** Stanislas Pascal Franchot Tone
  born: **14** Niagara Falls NY
  wife: **11** Jean Wallace **12** Joan Crawford **13** Barbara Payton **15** Dolores Dorn-Heft
  roles: **10** Uncle Vanya **11** Phantom

Lady **13** Three Comrades **16** Advise and Consent **17** Five Graves to Cairo, Mutiny on the Bounty **23** The Lives of a Bengal Lancer

tone up 7 make fit, shape up **9** condition **10** put in shape

Tonga
  other name: **15** Friendly Islands
  capital/largest city: **9** Nukualofa
  others: **3** Mua, Pea **6** Neiafu **7** Haakame, Kolonga, Kolovai **8** Fuaamotu
  division: **5** Vavau **6** Haapai **9** Tongatapu
  government: **8** monarchy
  head of state: **4** king
  monetary unit: **6** paanga, seniti
  island: **3** Eua, Kao, Ono **4** Kotu **5** Tofua, Vavau **6** Haapai, Lifuke, Nomuka **7** Otu Tolu **9** Tongatapu
  highest point: **3** Kao
  sea: **7** Pacific
  people: **10** Polynesian
    explorer: **4** Cook **5** Bligh **6** Tasman
    king: **11** George Tupou **14** Taufaahau Tupou
    missionary: **12** Shirley Baker
    queen: **6** Salote
  language: **6** Tongan **7** English
  religion: **9** Methodist **12** Christianity **25** Wesleyan Free Church of Tonga
  feature:
    fabric: **4** tapa
    spiritual king: **8** tui tonga

tongue 3 lap **4** flap, lick, spit **5** point, shaft **6** lingua, patois, speech **7** dialect, lingula **8** language **10** promontory, vernacular, vocabulary **13** organ of speech, power of speech, style of speech
  tastes: **4** salt, sour **5** sweet **6** bitter

tongue-lash 5 scold **6** berate, rail at, rebuke **7** bawl out, chew out, reprove, upbraid **8** reproach **9** castigate, reprimand **10** take to task

tongue-lashing 6 rebuke **7** censure, chiding, reproof **8** reproach, scolding **9** reprimand **10** bawling-out, chewing-out, upbraiding **11** castigation, reprobation **12** dressing-down, remonstrance

tonic 6 bracer, pickup **7** keynote **8** pick-me-up **9** analeptic, refresher, stimulant **10** invigorant **11** restorative

Tono-Bungay
  author: **7** H G Wells

tonsure 3 cut **4** trim **8** bald spot **11** shaven patch

too
  French: **4** trop

tool 4 dupe, pawn **5** agent, means **6** device, medium, puppet, stooge **7** cat's-paw, machine, utensil, vehicle **8** hireling **9** apparatus, appliance, implement, mechanism **10** instrument **11** contrivance, wherewithal **12** intermediary **15** instrumentality

carpenter's: 3 adz, awl, bit, peg, saw **4** adze, nail, rasp, vise **5** auger, brace, edger, gouge, knife, lathe, plane, ruler, screw **6** bodkin, chisel, gimlet, hammer, pliers, router, sander **7** bradawl, scraper **9** hand drill, try square **11** screwdriver
  cutting/shaping: **2** ax **3** adz, axe, saw **4** adze, burr, file, froe, frow, rasp **5** burin, croze, gouge, knife, plane, razor, shave, wedge **6** chisel, sander, shears, trepan **7** hatchet, scraper **8** scissors
  drilling/boring: **3** awl, bit, zax **4** pick **5** chuck, drill **6** gimlet, wimble **7** bradawl **11** countersink
  farmer's: **2** ax **3** axe, hoe **4** plow, rake **5** spade **6** cradle, harrow, pickax, plough, scythe, seeder, shovel, sickle, tiller, trowel **7** hayfork **9** plowshare **10** cultivator
  gripping/turning: **6** pliers, wrench **11** screwdriver
  holding: **4** vise **5** clamp
  measuring: **4** rule **5** gauge, level **6** square **7** caliper **8** dividers **10** micrometer
  mechanic's: **3** awl, zax **4** burr, file, vise **5** bevel, lathe **6** bodkin, pliers **7** bradawl, crowbar **8** calipers **9** jackscrew **11** screwdriver **12** monkey wrench
  pounding/striking: **4** maul **5** punch, wedge **6** hammer, mallet

too little 4 lack **6** dearth, scanty, scarce **7** paucity **8** scarcity, shortage **9** deficient, not enough, scantiness **10** deficiency, inadequacy, inadequate **12** insufficient **13** insufficiency

too many
  French: **6** de trop

too much 4 glut **5** flood **6** excess **7** profuse, surfeit, surplus **8** fullness, overflow, plethora **9** avalanche, excessive, profusion, repletion **10** inundation, oversupply **12** overabundant **13** overabundance **14** superabundance
  French: **4** trop

Toonerville Folks
  creator: **11** Fontaine Fox
  character: **7** skipper **13** Aunt Eppie Hogg **15** Little Scorpions, Powerful Katrina, Suitcase Simpson **20** Mickey Himself McGuire **22** Terrible Tempered Mr Bang
  rode on: **7** trolley

to one side 4 over **5** aloof, apart, aside **6** aslant **14** on the sidelines

to one's liking 7 fitting **8** pleasant, pleasing, suitable **9** agreeable **10** acceptable, gratifying **11** appropriate, to one's taste **12** satisfactory

toot 4 blow, honk **5** binge, blare, blast, spree **6** bender **7** trumpet **8** wingding

tooth 3 cog, nib **4** barb, cusp, fang, spur, tang, tine, tusk **5** molar, point, spike, thorn **6** canine, cuspid **7**

grinder, incisor **8** bicuspid, sprocket **9** serration

toothed 6 fanged, tusked **7** dentate, notched, serrate, virgate

toothsome 6 savory **8** luscious **9** delicious, palatable **10** appetizing

Toots
   character in: **12** Dombey and Son
   author: **7** Dickens

top 3 cap, lid, van **4** acme, apex, best, brow, cork, fore, head, lead, peak **5** chief, cover, crest, crown, excel, front, noted, outdo, upper **6** better, exceed, famous, summit, tiptop, vertex, zenith **7** eclipse, eminent, highest, notable, put over, stopper, surpass, topmost **8** complete, fore most, greatest, outshine, outstrip, pinnacle, renowned **9** paramount, principal, put a top on, transcend, uppermost, upper part **10** celebrated, first place, overshadow, preeminent

topaz
   color: **4** blue **5** brown **6** yellow
   source: **5** Japan **6** Brazil, Mexico, Saxony **13** Ural Mountains **18** Cairngorm Mountains
   month: **8** November

Topaz
   director: **9** Hitchcock
   book by: **4** Uris

Topaze
   author: **12** Marcel Pagnol

topaz quartz
   species: **6** quartz
   color: **4** blue, pink **5** brown, green **6** sherry

toper 3 sot **4** lush, soak **5** drunk **6** boozer **7** tippler **8** drunkard **9** alcoholic **11** dispomaniac

Top Hat
   director: **12** Mark Sandrich
   cast: **9** Eric Blore **11** Fred Astaire **12** Ginger Rogers **14** Helen Broderick **19** Edward Everett Horton
   score: **12** Irving Berlin
   song: **12** Cheek to Cheek **22** Top Hat White Tie and Tails

topic 4 text **5** theme **6** thesis **7** keynote, subject

topical 5 local **6** timely **7** current, limited **9** localized, parochial **10** particular, restricted **12** contemporary

Topkapi
   director: **11** Jules Dassin
   cast: **12** Peter Ustinov, Robert Morley **14** Melina Mercouri **16** Maximilian Schell
   book by: **6** Ambler
   setting: **8** Istanbul
   Oscar for: **15** supporting actor (Ustinov)

topknot 4 comb, tuft **5** crest **9** cockscomb, headdress, headpiece

topmost 3 top **4** head **5** chief **7** highest, leading, supreme **8** foremost **9**

paramount, principal, uppermost **10** preeminent

topnotch 3 ace **4** best **5** prime **6** choice, finest, tip-top **7** supreme **8** superior, very fine **9** excellent, first-rate, nonpareil, unequaled, unrivaled **10** preeminent **11** outstanding, unsurpassed **12** incomparable, unparalleled

top of the head 4 dome, pate **5** crown **6** noggin, noodle

Topper
   director: **13** Norman Z McLeod
   based on novel by: **11** Thorne Smith
   cast: **9** Cary Grant **11** Alan Mowbray, Billie Burke, Hedda Hopper, Roland Young **16** Constance Bennett
   sequel: **13** Topper Returns **16** Topper Takes a Trip

topple 4 fall **5** crush, quash, quell, smash, upset **6** defeat, sprawl, tumble **7** abolish, shatter, tip over **8** fall over, over come, overturn, turn over, vanquish **9** bring down, overpower, overthrow **12** pitch forward

tops 4 aces, A-one, fine **5** great, prime, super, swell **6** choice, grade-A, superb, tip-top **7** capital **8** peerless, sterling, superior, terrific, top-notch **9** excellent, first-rate, marvelous, matchless, superfine, wonderful **10** first-class, inimitable, out-of-sight, tremendous **11** outstanding, superlative **12** incomparable **13** extraordinary

top-secret 5 privy **7** private **8** eyesonly, hush-hush **12** confidential

topsoil 4 dirt, loam **5** earth

Topsy
   character in: **14** Uncle Tom's Cabin
   author: **5** Stowe

topsy-turvy 5 messy **6** untidy **7** chaotic **8** confused, inverted, reversed **9** confusing, inside out **10** disorderly, upside down **11** disarranged, wrong side up **12** disorganized

Torah 10 law of Moses

torch 7 brand **7** cresset **8** arsonist, flambeau **8** firebrand **9** set fire to **10** flashlight

torment 3 nag, vex **4** bane, pain, rack **5** agony, annoy, curse, worry **6** harass, harrow, misery, pester, plague **7** afflict, agonize, anguish, despair, scourge, torture, trouble **8** distress, irritate **9** annoyance, persecute, suffering **10** irritation

tormenter 5 bully, tease **6** despot, tyrant **7** coercer **9** oppressor **10** browbeater **11** intimidator

tormenting 7 painful, racking **9** agonizing, torturous **10** unbearable **11** unendurable **12** excruciating, insufferable

torn 4 rent, slit **5** split **6** ragged, ripped **8** ruptured, shredded **9** unraveled

tornado 4 wind **5** storm **6** funnel, squall, vortex **7** cyclone, twister, ty-

phoon **8** outburst **9** hurricane, whirlwind, windstorm **10** waterspout **12** thunderstorm
   belt: **7** Midwest
   cloud: **4** tuba

torn apart 4 rent **6** ripped **7** asunder **8** in pieces, in shreds, shredded

toro 4 bull

Toronto
   baseball team: **8** Blue Jays
   bay: **6** Humber
   football team: **9** Argonauts
   former name: **4** York
   harbor: **5** Inner
   hockey team: **10** Maple Leafs
   lake: **7** Ontario
   landmark: **7** CN Tower **12** Ontario Place, O'Keefe Centre **13** Dufferin Grove **14** Dominion Centre **15** Roy Thompson Hall **16** Maple Leaf Stadium, St Lawrence Centre **17** Commerce Court West **18** Royal Ontario Museum **20** Nathan Phillips Square
      park: **7** Chorley, Stanley, Trinity **8** Winthrow **9** Cedarvale **12** Center Island **16** Winston Churchill
   street: **5** Yonge
   university: **4** York

torpedo 4 sink **5** wreck **7** destroy, missile, scuttle **9** explosive **10** projectile

torpedo (marine)
   invented by: **6** Fulton

torpid 4 dull, lazy **5** inert **6** drowsy, sleepy **7** dormant, languid, passive **8** inactive, indolent, listless, sluggish **9** apathetic, lethargic, somnolent **10** half asleep, languorous, slow-moving, spiritless **12** slow-thinking **13** lackadaisical

torpor, torpidity 6 apathy **7** inertia, languor **8** dullness, laziness, lethargy **9** indolence, lassitude **10** drowsiness, inactivity, sleepiness, somnolence **11** languidness, passiveness **12** listlessness, sluggishness

torrent 4 gush, rain, rush **5** burst, flood, salvo **6** deluge, rapids, stream, volley **7** barrage, cascade, Niagara **8** cataract, downpour, effusion, eruption, outburst **9** discharge, heavy rain, rapid flow, waterfall **10** cloudburst, outpouring, white water

Torrey, John
   field: **6** botany
   developed: **16** botanical library

Torricelli, Evangelista
   nationality: **7** Italian
   discovered concept leading to development of: **9** barometer

torrid 3 hot **4** sexy **5** fiery **6** ardent, erotic, fervid, heated, sexual, sultry **7** amorous, boiling, burning, excited, fervent, intense, lustful **8** broiling, desirous, parching, sizzling, spirited, tropical, vehement **9** hot and dry,

scorching 10 passionate, sweltering **11** hot and heavy, impassioned

torte 4 cake **7** dessert **9** layer cake

tortilla 7 tostada **8** corncake **11** Mexican cake
griddle: 5 comal

Tortilla Flat
author: **13** John Steinbeck

tortuous 4 bent **5** snaky **6** spiral, zigzag **7** crooked, devious, sinuous, turning, winding, wriggly **8** indirect, involved, twisting, wrongful **9** ambiguous **10** circuitous, convoluted, meandering, roundabout, serpentine **11** complicated **12** full of curves, hard to follow, labyrinthine

tortuousness 9 sinuosity **11** indirection, sinuousness **12** convolutions **14** circuitousness

torture 4 pain, rack **5** abuse, agony, prick, smite, trial, wring **6** harrow, ordeal **7** anguish, cruelty, torment **8** distress, maltreat, mistreat **9** brutality, suffering **10** infliction, punishment **11** tribulation **12** put to the rack

torturous 5 cruel **7** galling, irksome, painful, racking **8** annoying **9** agonizing, anguished, harrowing, miserable, tormented, torturing **10** anguishing, distressed, tormenting, unpleasant **11** distressful, distressing **12** disagreeable, excruciating

tory 8 loyalist, royalist **12** conservative

Tosca
opera by: **7** Puccini
character: **7** Scarpia **9** Angelotti **11** Floria Tosca **16** Mario Cavaradossi

To Sir With Love
director: **12** James Clavell
cast: **4** Lulu **10** Judy Geeson **11** Suzy Kendall **13** Sidney Poitier **16** Christian Roberts
setting: **6** London

toss 3 lob **4** cast, flip, hurl, jerk, rock, roll, sway **5** churn, fling, heave, pitch, shake, sling, throw **6** joggle, let fly, propel, tumble, wiggle, writhe **7** agitate, flounce, wriggle **8** flourish, undulate **9** oscillate

toss about 4 roil **5** bandy **6** jostle, jounce

toss back and forth 5 bandy **8** exchange

total 3 add, sum **4** full **5** add up, gross, sheer, solid, sum up, utter, whole **6** entire, figure, reckon, tote up **7** add up to, compute, perfect, total up **8** absolute, combined, complete, entirety, figure up, integral, outright, sum total, sweeping, thorough, totality **9** aggregate, calculate, down right, out-and-out, unlimited, wholesale **10** full amount, undisputed, unmodified **11** unqualified, whole amount **13** comprehensive, unconditional

totaling 8 addition, coming to **9** reckoning **10** adding up to

totalitarian 7 fascist **8** despotic **9** fascistic, tyrannous **10** autocratic, tyrannical **11** dictatorial **12** undemocratic **16** unrepresentative

totally 7 solidly, utterly **8** entirely **9** downright, out-and-out, perfectly **10** absolutely, completely, thoroughly, throughout **15** unconditionally **18** from beginning to end **20** without qualification

tote 3 lug **4** bear, cart, drag, haul, move, pack, pull **5** carry, fetch **6** convey **7** schlepp **9** transport

to the city and the world
Latin: **10** urbi et orbi
form of address used on: **10** papal bulls

to the four winds 7 all over **10** everywhere, far and wide **26** to the four corners of the world

to the letter 5 exact, right **7** correct, precise **8** accurate, explicit, specific **9** on the nose

To the Lighthouse
author: **13** Virginia Woolf
character: **4** Prue **5** James **7** Camilla **8** Mr Ramsey **9** Mr Tansley, Mrs Ramsey **11** Lily Briscoe **12** Mr Carmichael

to the point 6 direct **7** apropos, germane **8** explicit, relevant **9** pertinent **12** to the purpose

to the rear 3 aft **4** back **5** abaft **6** astern, behind **8** backward, rearward **9** backwards, sternward **10** to the stern **14** toward the stern

to the stern 6 astern, behind **8** rearward **9** sternward **10** to the stern

to the word
Latin: **8** ad verbum

to this extent
Latin: **8** quoad hoc

Toto
dog in: **13** The Wizard of Oz
author: **4** Baum

totter 4 reel, rock, sway **5** lurch, shake, waver **6** falter, teeter, waddle, wobble **7** shuffle, stagger, stumble **9** oscillate, vacillate

tottering 5 shaky **6** wobbly **7** rickety, shaking **8** insecure, topheavy, unstable, unsteady, wobbling **9** doddering, quivering, trembling **10** ramshackle, staggering

Toucan
constellation of: **6** Tucana

touch 3 art, bit, paw, pet, rub, use **4** abut, cite, dash, feel, fire, form, gift, hand, hint, join, meet, melt, move, note, stir, sway, tint, work **5** equal, flair, match, pinch, rival, rouse, skill, smack, speck, style, taste, thumb, tinge, trace, unite **6** adjoin, affect, arouse, border, broach, caress, excite,

finger, finish, fondle, handle, hint at, manner, method, pawing, polish, sadden, soften, strike, stroke, thrill **7** concern, consume, contact, feeling, finesse, impress, inflame, inspire, mastery, mention, quality, refer to, soupcon, surface, texture, utilize **8** allude to, artistry, bear upon, come near, come up to, converge, deal with, deftness, fineness, fondling, handling, inspirit, resort to, thumbing **9** awareness, direction, electrify, fingering, influence, palpation, pertain to, suspicion, technique **10** adroitness, intimation, manipulate, perception, sprinkling, suggestion, virtuosity **11** be in contact, compare with, familiarity, guiding hand, realization **12** acquaintance, manipulation **13** communication, comprehension, understanding

touched 3 mad **4** daft, felt, nuts **5** crazy, moved, nutty **6** insane, joined **7** abutted, cracked, handled **8** demented, deranged, unhinged **10** unbalanced **12** mad as a hatter **13** off one's rocker, out of one's head **14** off one's trolley **15** mad as a March hare

Touchett, Ralph
character in: **18** The Portrait of a Lady
author: **5** James

touching 3 sad **6** moving, tender **7** pitiful **8** dramatic, pathetic, poignant, stirring **9** affecting, emotional, heartfelt, saddening, sorrowful **11** distressing, sentimental **12** heartrending **13** heartbreaking

touch me not
Latin: **13** noli me tangere

Touch of Evil
director: **11** Orson Welles
cast: **10** Janet Leigh, Ray Collins **11** Joanna Moore, Orson Welles, Zsa Zsa Gabor **12** Akim Tamiroff, Dennis Weaver **13** Joseph Calleia **14** Charlton Heston
cameo: **15** Marlene Dietrich **19** Mercedes McCambridge

touch off 5 shoot **6** set off **7** explode, fire off, trigger **8** activate, detonate **9** discharge

touch on 4 pose **6** broach, submit **7** advance, bring up, mention, propose, suggest **9** introduce

touchstone 4 norm, rule **5** basis, gauge, guide, model, proof **7** example, measure, pattern **8** standard **9** benchmark, criterion, guideline, precedent, principle, yardstick

Touchstone
character in: **11** As You Like It
author: **11** Shakespeare

touch upon 7 apply to, concern, mention, refer to **8** allude to, bear upon, relate to **9** appertain

touchy 5 cross, huffy, surly, testy **6**

bitter, crabby, grumpy **7** awkward, fragile, grouchy, peevish, waspish **8** captious, critical, delicate, petulant, snappish, ticklish **9** concerned, difficult, irascible, irritable, querulous, resentful, sensitive **10** precarious **11** thinskinned **12** cantankerous **13** quick-tempered

tough 4 cold, firm, hard, hood, lout, mean, punk, wily **5** bully, cagey, canny, cruel, hardy, rigid, rough, rowdy, solid, stern **6** brutal, crafty, dogged, knotty, mulish, rugged, savage, strict, strong, sturdy, thorny, trying **7** adamant, arduous, callous, complex, durable, hoodlum, inhuman, irksome, lasting, onerous, ruffian, vicious **8** baffling, barbaric, enduring, exacting, grievous, hooligan, involved, leathery, obdurate, perverse, pitiless, puzzling, ruthless, stubborn, ticklish, toilsome **9** barbarian, confusing, difficult, enigmatic, heartless, heavy-duty, intricate, laborious, obstinate, pigheaded, resistant, roughneck, strenuous, unbending, unfeeling **10** bullheaded, delinquent, exhausting, formidable, hardheaded, inflexible, perplexing, unyielding **11** bewildering, calculating, cold-blooded, complicated, hardhearted, hard-to-solve, infrangible, insensitive, troublesome **12** bloodthirsty, impenetrable **13** unsympathetic **14** uncompromising

toughen 4 firm **5** inure, steel **6** firm up, harden, season, temper **7** fortify, stiffen **8** accustom **9** acclimate, habituate **10** discipline, strengthen **11** acclimatize

Toulouse-Lautrec, Henri Marie Raymond de
  born: **4** Albi **6** France **8** Albigois
  artwork: **7** Friends **13** The Inspection **16** At the Moulin Rouge **24** Au Salon de la Rue des Moulins **27** Jane Avril at the Jardin de Paris **29** Cirque Fernando The Equestrienne **29** In the Parlor at the Rue des Moulins **29** The English Girl at Le Star Le Havre **30** La Goulue Entering the Moulin Rouge

toupee 3 rug, wig **6** carpet, peruke **7** periwig **9** hairpiece

tour 4 trek, trip **5** jaunt, visit **6** junket, safari, travel, voyage **7** inspect, journey **8** sightsee **9** excursion, itinerary

tourist 7 pilgrim, tripper, voyager **8** traveler, vagabond, wanderer, wayfarer **9** journeyer, sightseer **10** rubberneck **12** excursionist, globetrotter

tourmaline
  color: **3** red **4** blue, pink **5** green

tournament 4 game **5** event, match **7** contest, rivalry, tourney **11** competition

tourney 4 game **5** event, joust, match **7** contest, rivalry **10** tournament **11** competition

tousled 5 messy **6** mussed, untidy **7** rumpled, tangled, unkempt **8** mussed-up, uncombed **10** disheveled, disordered

tout 4 plug, push **5** boost, exalt, extol, vaunt **6** praise, talk up **7** acclaim, commend, glorify, promote, tipster **8** ballyhoo, eulogize, give a tip **9** advertise, brag about, celebrate, publicize, recommend **10** aggrandize, noise about

tout a fait 8 entirely
  literally: **12** wholly to fact

tout a l'heure 7 just now **8** very soon **9** presently **14** just a moment ago
  literally: **15** wholly to the hour

tout de suite 6 at once **11** immediately
  literally: **19** wholly consecutively

tout ensemble 11 all together

tout le monde 8 everyone **9** everybody **13** the whole world

tovarich 7 comrade

tow 3 lug **4** drag, draw, haul, lift, pull **5** hoist, trail

toward the end
  Latin: **5** ad fin

toward the front 5 ahead **6** before **7** forward **9** to the fore **13** in the vanguard **14** in the forefront

toward the rear 4 back **6** astern **8** backward, rearward **9** sternward

toward the stern 6 astern **8** rearward **9** sternward **10** to the stern

tower 4 keep, loom, rock, soar **5** mount, outdo, spire, surge **6** ascend, belfry, castle, column, exceed, pillar, refuge, turret **7** bulwark, eclipse, minaret, obelisk, overtop, shoot up, steeple, surpass **8** mainstay, outclass, outshine, overhang, rise high **9** bell tower, rise above, transcend **10** foundation, overshadow, skyscraper, stronghold, wellspring **12** fountainhead

towering 4 high, tall **5** lofty **6** alpine **7** soaring, sublime, supreme **8** dominant, foremost, mounting, peerless, snowclad, superior **9** ascending, matchless, paramount, principal, unequaled, unmatched, unrivaled **10** cloud-swept, preeminent, surpassing, unexcelled **11** cloud-capped, overhanging **12** incomparable, second to none, transcendent, unparalleled **13** extraordinary

Tower of London, The
  author: **24** William Harrison Ainsworth

tower over 5 dwarf **7** surpass **8** dominate **9** rise above

Townes, Charles Hard
  field: **7** physics

  invented: **5** maser
  awarded: **10** Nobel Prize

town hall
  German: **7** Rathaus

town house 8 row house **10** brownstone, pied-a-terre **13** city residence

township 4 town **7** village **11** subdivision **12** municipality

toxic 5 fatal **6** deadly, lethal, mortal **7** noxious **8** poisoned, venomous **9** poisonous, unhealthy **10** pernicious

toxin 4 bane **5** venom **6** poison **8** pathogen

toy 4 play, tiny, yoyo **5** dally, pygmy, sport **6** bantam, bauble, fiddle, gadget, gewgaw, little, midget, trifle **7** dwarfed, for play, stunted, trinket **8** gimcrack **9** miniature, plaything, small-size **10** diminutive, small-scale **11** Lilliputian

Toy Bulldog
  nickname of: **12** Mickey Walker

Toynbee, Arnold
  author of: **15** A Study of History

to your health
  French: **11** a votre sante

toy with 8 play with **9** flirt with **10** trifle with **16** amuse oneself with

trace 3 bit, jot, map **4** draw, drop, find, hint, hunt, iota, mark, seek, sign **5** dig up, relic, shade, tinge, token, touch, track, trail **6** depict, flavor, trifle **7** diagram, hunt for, look for, mark out, nose out, outline, remains, uncover, unearth, vestige **8** describe, discover, draw over, evidence **9** delineate, ferret out, footprint, light upon, little bit, search for, suspicion, track down **10** come across, indication, suggestion **11** small amount

trace to 6 credit **7** ascribe **8** charge to **9** attribute

Trachiniae
  author: **9** Sophocles
  characters: **4** Iole **6** Hyllus, Nessus **8** Deianira, Heracles

track 3 way **4** mark, path, rail, sign, tack **5** dirty, route, scent, spoor, trace, trail **6** course, follow **9** footprint, guide rail

track and field
  athlete: **7** Jim Ryun, Ray Ewry **8** Al Oerter, Lee Evans, Zola Budd **9** Ben Jonson, Bob Beamon, Carl Lewis, Henry Rono, Jim Thorpe **10** Bob Mathias, Bob Seagren, Edwin Moses, Grete Waitz, James Hines, Jesse Owens, John Carlos, Lasse Viren, Mac Wilkins, Paavo Nurmi, Peter Snell, Steve Ovett, Wyomia Tyus **11** Bill Rodgers, Bruce Jenner, Marty Liouri, David Wottle, Dick Fosbury, Doug Padilla, Emil Zatopek, Joni Huntley, Ralph Boston, Randy Matson, Tommie Smith **12** Dwight Stones, Frank Shorter, Harvey Glance, Jay Silvester,

Kathy Hammond, Maren Seidler, Rafer Johnson, Sebastian Coe, Willie B White, Wilma Rudolph **13** Allan Feurbach, Arnie Robinson, Janice Merrill, Kathy McMillan, Kipchoge Keino, Rodney Milburn, Ronny Ray Smith, Rosalyn Bryant, William Toomey **14** Alberto Salazar, Francie Larrieu, Roger Bannister **15** Martha Rae Watson, Renaldo Nehemiah, Willie Davenport **16** Madeleine Manning, Mary Decker Slaney, Richard Wohlhuter, Steve Prefontaine **17** Alberto Juantoreno **18** Jackie Joyner-Kersee, Stephanie Hightower **21** Babe Didrikson Zaharias **22** Florence Griffith-Joyner

tract 3 lot **4** area, plot, zone **5** essay **6** parcel, region **7** booklet, expanse, leaflet, quarter, stretch **8** brochure, district, pamphlet, treatise **9** monograph, territory **12** disquisition

tractable 4 tame **6** docile **8** amenable, obedient, yielding **9** compliant, teachable, trainable **10** governable, manageable, submissive **12** controllable, easy to manage **13** easy to control

tractate 8 treatise **9** discourse, monograph **12** disquisition, dissertation

Tracy, Spencer
born: **11** Milwaukee WI
costar: **16** Katharine Hepburn
roles: **7** Desk Set **8** Adam's Rib, Boys Town (Oscar) **10** Pat and Mike **12** San Francisco, Tortilla Flat **13** The Last Hurrah **14** Cass Timberlane, Inherit the Wind, Woman of the Year **15** State of the Union **16** Father of the Bride, Keeper of the Flame **17** Bad Day at Black Rock **18** Captains Courageous (Oscar), The Old Man and the Sea **19** Judgment at Nuremberg **23** Guess Who's Coming to Dinner

Traddles
character in: **16** David Copperfield
author: **7** Dickens

trade 3 buy **4** deal, line, shop, swap **5** craft **6** barter, buyers **7** calling, patrons, pursuit **8** business, commerce, exchange, shoppers, vocation **9** clientele, customers, patronize **10** buy and sell, do business, employment, handicraft, line of work, occupation, profession **12** transactions **13** merchandising **16** business dealings, buying and selling

trade commodity 5 goods, wares

trademark 6 emblem **7** feature **8** property **9** specialty **11** peculiarity **14** characteristic

trade off 4 swap **5** trade **6** barter **8** exchange

trader 6 dealer, monger, seller **7** drummer **8** merchant, retailer **10** shopkeeper, trafficker, wholesaler **11** sales-

person, storekeeper **12** merchandiser, tradesperson **14** businessperson

tradesman 6 dealer, seller **8** merchant, retailer **9** craftsman **10** shopkeeper **11** storekeeper

tradition 4 lore, myth, saga, tale **5** habit, usage **6** custom, legend **8** folklore, practice **10** convention **12** superstition

traditional 3 old **5** fixed, usual **7** typical **8** habitual, historic **9** ancestral, customary **10** accustomed, inveterate **11** established **12** acknowledged, conventional

traduce 5 abuse, libel, smear, sully **6** defame, malign, vilify **7** run down, slander **8** backbite, bad-mouth, besmirch **9** deprecate, disparage **10** calumniate

traffic 4 cars, deal **5** buses, ships, trade **6** barter, doings, planes, riders, trains, trucks **7** bootleg, contact, freight, smuggle **8** business, commerce, dealings, exchange, tourists, voyagers **9** commuters, relations, smuggling, travelers **10** buy and sell, enterprise, passengers **11** bootlegging, intercourse, pedestrians, proceedings **12** transactions, vacationists **13** excursionists

tragedy 3 woe **4** blow **5** grief **6** misery, sorrow **7** anguish, setback **8** accident, calamity, disaster, reversal, sad thing **9** heartache **10** affliction, heartbreak **11** catastrophe

tragic 3 sad **4** dire **5** awful, fatal **6** deadly, dreary, woeful **7** piteous, pitiful, ruinous, serious, unhappy **8** dramatic, dreadful, grievous, horrible, mournful, pathetic, pitiable, shocking, terrible **9** appalling, frightful **10** calamitous, deplorable, disastrous, lamentable **11** destructive, devastating, unfortunate **12** catastrophic **13** heartbreaking

trail 3 dog, tow, way **4** drag, draw, fall, flow, hunt, mark, path, poke, sign, tail **5** float, hound, scent, spoor, trace, track **6** be down, course, dangle, dawdle, follow, lessen, shrink, stream **7** dwindle, pathway, subside **8** decrease, diminish, footpath, grow weak, hand down, peter out, taper off **9** drag along, grow faint, grow small, lag behind **10** bridle path, drag behind, footprints, move slowly **11** beaten track **14** bring up the rear

trailblazers 7 leaders **8** pioneers **10** avant-garde, innovators **11** forerunners, originators, tastemakers **12** trendsetters

train 2 el **3** aim, set **4** line **5** break, chain, drill, focus, level, point, queue, sight, teach, trail, tutor **6** column, direct, escort, school, series, subway **7** caravan, cortege, educate, prepare, retinue **8** elevated, exercise, instruct,

practice, rehearse, sequence **9** afterpart, appendage, entourage, followers **10** attendants, discipline, get in shape, procession, succession **11** bring to bear, domesticate, progression **12** continuation

Train, The
director: **17** John Frankenheimer
cast: **10** Albert Remy **11** Michel Simon **12** Jeanne Moreau, Paul Scofield **13** Burt Lancaster

trained 4 able **6** expert, master **7** capable, skilled **8** schooled, seasoned **9** competent, qualified **11** experienced **12** accomplished

trainee 4 boot **5** cadet **6** rookie **7** private, rookie, student **9** greenhorn **10** apprentice

trainer 5 coach, tutor **7** teacher **16** athletic director

training 5 drill **8** coaching, drilling, practice, teaching **9** education, schooling **10** discipline **11** preparation **14** apprenticeship, indoctrination

traipse 3 gad **4** roam, walk **5** range, tramp, tread **6** stroll, trapes, wander **7** meander, saunter **8** gadabout **9** gallivant

trait 4 mark **5** quirk **7** earmark, feature, quality **8** hallmark **9** attribute, mannerism **11** peculiarity **12** idiosyncrasy **14** characteristic

traitor 3 rat **5** Judas, rebel **6** ratter **7** ratfink, serpent **8** apostate, betrayer, deceiver, deserter, mutineer, quisling, renegade, turncoat **9** hypocrite **11** false friend **12** double-dealer **13** double-crosser, revolutionary **14** fifth columnist **15** snake in the grass **20** wolf in sheep's clothing

traitorous 5 false **7** corrupt **8** disloyal, renegade **9** betraying, faithless **10** perfidious, treasonous, unfaithful **11** treacherous

tramp 3 bum **4** hike, hobo, roam, rove, slog, trek, walk **5** march, prowl, stamp, stomp **6** ramble, trudge, wander **7** floater, meander, traipse, trample, vagrant **8** derelict **9** gallivant, itinerant **10** panhandler **11** perambulate, peregrinate **15** knight-of-the-road

trample 5 crush, stamp, stomp **6** squash **7** flatten, run over **14** grind under foot **15** step heavily upon

trance 4 coma, daze **5** dream, spell **6** stupor, vision **7** reverie **8** daydream, hypnosis **9** pipe dream **10** absorption, brown study **11** abstraction **12** sleepwalking **13** concentration, preoccupation, woolgathering

tranquil 4 calm, cool, mild **5** quiet, still **6** gentle, placid, serene **7** halcyon, restful **8** composed, peaceful **9** unexcited, unruffled **11** undisturbed, unperturbed **13** self-possessed

tranquility 4 calm, hush **5** peace, quiet **6** repose **7** concord, harmony **8**

quietude, serenity **9** composure, placidity, stillness **11** restfulness **12** peacefulness

tranquilize 4 calm, drug, lull **5** allay, quiet, relax, still **6** becalm, pacify, sedate, settle, soothe **7** appease, assuage **9** alleviate

transact 2 do **5** exact **6** handle, manage, settle **7** achieve, carry on, conduct, execute, perform **8** carry out, exercise **9** discharge **10** accomplish, take care of **12** carry through

transaction 4 deal **6** affair **7** bargain, dealing, venture **8** exchange **9** operation **10** enterprise, settlement **11** negotiation **15** business dealing, piece of business

transcend 5 excel, outdo **6** exceed **7** eclipse, outrank, surpass **8** go beyond, outrival, outshine, outstrip, overleap, overstep, surmount **9** rise above **10** overshadow **11** outdistance

transcendence 5 merit **8** eminence **9** exceeding, greatness **10** exaltation, excellence, surpassing **11** distinction, preeminence, superiority

transcendental 5 great **6** mental **7** supreme, unusual **8** elevated, peerless, superior, uncommon **9** exceeding, intuitive, matchless, spiritual, unequaled, unrivaled **10** surpassing **11** unsurpassed **12** incomparable, metaphysical **13** extraordinary

transfer 4 cede, deed, move, send **5** bring, carry, shift **6** change, convey, moving, remove **7** consign, deeding, removal, sending **8** bringing, carrying, hand over, make over, relegate, relocate, shifting, shipment, transmit, turn over **9** conveying, transport **10** delivering, relegation, relocating, relocation **11** consignment, transmittal **12** transporting **14** transportation

transferable 8 catching **10** contagious, infectious **12** communicable **13** transmissible, transmittable

transferal 8 delivery, transfer **10** giving over **11** handing over, transmittal **12** transmission

transference 5 shift **6** change **7** passage, removal **9** transport **11** transmittal **12** dislodgement, displacement, transmission **13** transmittance

transfiguration 10 conversion **13** metamorphosis, transmutation **14** transformation

transfigure 6 change **9** transform **12** metamorphose

transfix 3 pin **4** hold, stab, stun **5** rivet, spear, spike, stick **6** absorb, impale, pierce, skewer **7** astound, bewitch, enchant, engross, fix fast, terrify **8** astonish, hold rapt, intrigue **9** captivate, fascinate, hypnotize, mesmerize, penetrate, spellbind **10** run through

transform 4 turn **5** alter **6** change, re-

cast, remold **7** convert, remodel **8** make over **9** refurbish, transmute **11** reconstruct, transfigure **12** metamorphose, transmogrify

transformation 6 change **9** restyling **10** alteration, conversion, remodeling **13** metamorphosis, transmutation **15** transfiguration

transgress 3 err, sin **4** slip **5** break, cross, fault, lapse, wrong **6** exceed, impose, offend **7** digress, infract, violate **8** infringe, trespass

transgression 3 sin **5** crime, error, lapse, wrong **6** breach **7** misdeed, offense **8** evil deed, iniquity, trespass **9** violation **10** immorality, infraction, wrongdoing **11** lawbreaking **12** encroachment, infringement, overstepping **13** contravention

transgressor 6 felon **7** culprit **8** criminal, evildoer, offender, violator **9** miscreant, wrongdoer **10** lawbreaker, malefactor, trespasser

transience 7 brevity **11** evanescence **12** ephemerality, impermanence

transient 5 brief **7** passing **8** fleeting, soon past, temporal **9** ephemeral, momentary, short-term, temporary **10** evanescent, perishable, short-lived, transitory, unenduring **11** impermanent **14** passing through **24** here today and gone tomorrow

transistor
invented by: 7 Bardeen **8** Brattain, Shockley

transition 4 jump, leap **6** change **7** passage, passing **8** shifting **9** gradation, variation **10** alteration, changeover, conversion, graduation **11** progression **13** transmutation **14** transformation

transitory 5 brief **7** passing **8** fleeting, fugitive **9** ephemeral, temporary, transient **10** evanescent, not lasting, short-lived, unenduring **11** impermanent **24** here today and gone tomorrow

translate 4 turn **5** alter, apply **6** change, decode, recast, render, reword **7** clarify, convert, explain **8** decipher, rephrase, simplify, spell out **9** elucidate, interpret, make clear, transform, transmute **10** paraphrase

translucence 7 clarity **8** lucidity **10** luminosity **12** transparency **16** semitransparency

translucent 8 pellucid **10** semiopaque, translucid **15** semitransparent

transmissible 8 catching **10** contagious, infectious **12** communicable, transferable **13** transmittable

transmission 4 note **7** message, passage, passing, sending **8** delivery, dispatch, transfer **9** broadcast **10** conveyance, forwarding, remittance **11** handing over, transmittal **12** transfer-

ence, transferring **13** communication **14** transportation

transmit 4 send, ship **5** carry, issue, relay, remit **6** convey, pass on, spread **7** deliver, forward **8** dispatch, televise, transfer **9** broadcast **11** communicate, disseminate

transmittable 8 catching **10** contagious, infectious **12** communicable, transferable

transmittal 7 sending **8** delivery, transfer **10** giving over, transferal **11** handing over **12** transmission

transmutation 6 change **10** conversion **13** metamorphosis **14** transformation **15** transfiguration

transmute 5 alter **6** change **7** convert **9** transform **12** metamorphose

transparency 6 purity **7** clarity **8** lucidity **9** clearness, sheerness **11** obviousness **14** diaphanousness

transparent 4 thin **5** clear, gauzy, lucid, plain, sheer **6** glassy, limpid, patent **7** evident, obvious, visible **8** apparent, clear-cut, distinct, explicit, manifest, palpable, peekaboo, pellucid **10** diaphanous, see-through **11** perceptible, self-evident, translucent, unambiguous, unequivocal **12** crystal-clear, unmistakable

transpire 5 arise, occur **6** appear, befall, chance, crop up, evolve, happen, turn up **7** come out, leak out **9** be met with, eventuate, take place **10** be revealed, come to pass, make public **11** become known, be disclosed, come to light, show its face

transplant 5 graft, repot, shift **7** replant **8** displace, relocate, resettle, transfer **9** transport, transpose

transport 3 bus, lug **4** bear, cart, lift, move, send, ship, take, tote **5** bring, carry, charm, fetch, train, truck **6** convey, moving, remove, thrill **7** bearing, bewitch, carting, delight, deliver, enchant, freight, removal, sending, vehicle **8** airplane, carrying, delivery, dispatch, enthrall, entrance, shipment, shipping, transfer, transmit, trucking **9** captivate, cargo ship, carry away, conveying, electrify, enrapture, freighter, overpower **10** cargo plane, conveyance **12** freight train

transportation 7 cartage, haulage, portage, removal, transit **8** delivery, dispatch, movement, shipment **9** transport **10** conveyance, transferal **12** transference, transmission **13** transmittance

transported 5 moved **6** lifted **7** charmed **8** ecstatic, thrilled, uplifted **9** bewitched, entranced **10** captivated, enthralled **11** carried away, electrified **13** beside oneself

transverse 5 cross **6** across **7** athwart, oblique, transom **8** crossbar, crossing, diagonal, traverse **9** crosswise **10** crosspiece, horizontal

transversely 9 crossways, crosswise, laterally

Transylvania
  region of: 7 Romania
  city: 4 Cluj
  fictional home of: 7 Dracula

trap 3 net, pit **4** lure, ploy, ruse, seal, stop, wile **5** catch, feint, snare, trick **6** ambush, device, enmesh, entrap, lock in **7** ensnare, pitfall, springe **8** artifice, entangle, hold back, hunt down, maneuver **9** booby trap, stratagem **11** machination **16** compartmentalize

trappings 4 garb, gear **5** array, dress **6** attire, outfit, things **7** apparel, clothes, costume, effects, raiment, vesture **8** adjuncts, clothing, fittings **9** ornaments, trimmings **10** adornments, habiliment, investment **11** decorations **13** accoutrements, paraphernalia **14** embellishments

trash 3 rot **4** bums, crap, junk, scum **5** dregs, dross, tripe, waste **6** debris, drivel, idlers, litter, refuse, rubble, tramps **7** garbage, hogwash, loafers, residue, rubbish, twaddle **8** castoffs, leavings, nonsense, riffraff **9** poppycock, sweepings **10** balderdash **11** foolishness, ne'er-do-wells, odds and ends **15** good-for-nothings, unsavory element

trashy 4 vile **5** cheap, inane, junky, tacky **6** flashy, flimsy **7** rubbish, trivial, useless **8** riff-raff, trumpery, wasteful **9** worthless **13** insignificant

trauma 4 hurt **5** shock, wound **6** injury, stress

travail 4 pain, toil **5** labor, worry **6** strain, stress **7** anguish **8** delivery, distress, drudgery, exertion, hard work, hardship **9** suffering **10** birth pains, childbirth, labor pains **11** parturition **12** accouchement

travel 2 go **4** be on, move, roam, rove, sail, tour, trek, wend **5** cross, drive, range, visit **6** cruise, junket, voyage, wander **7** journey, proceed **8** pass over, progress, sightsee, traverse **9** globetrot, hitchhike, take a trip **11** pass through, press onward

traveler 5 gypsy, nomad, rover **7** drummer, migrant, pilgrim, tourist, trekker, tripper, voyager **8** vagabond, wanderer, wayfarer **9** itinerant, journeyer, sightseer **10** vacationer **12** excursionist, globetrotter

Traveller Without Luggage
  author: 11 Jean Anouilh

Travels With a Donkey
  author: 20 Robert Louis Stevenson
  donkey: 9 Modestine

Travels With My Aunt
  author: 12 Graham Greene

travel through 2 do **5** cover, cross, visit **8** traverse **9** negotiate **11** pass through

traverse 4 span **5** cross **6** bridge, travel **8** go across, move over, overpass **9** cross over, cut across, intersect, move along, negotiate, reach over **10** extend over, run through, travel over **11** move through, pass through, reach across

travesty 4 sham **5** farce, spoof **6** parody, satire **7** lampoon, mockery, takeoff **8** disgrace **9** burlesque **10** caricature, distortion, perversion **17** misrepresentation

Traviata, La
  also: 9 The Misled **23** The Woman Who Was Led Astray
  opera by: 5 Verdi
  based on a story by: 14 Alexandre Dumas (fils)
    called: 7 Camille **17** La Dame aux Camelias
  character: 8 Violetta **14** Alfredo Germont

Travolta, John
  born: 11 Englewood NJ
  roles: 6 Carrie, Grease **7** Face/Off, Mad City **9** Get Shorty **10** Tony Manero **11** Pulp Fiction, Urban Cowboy **12** She's So Lovely, Staying Alive **13** Primary Colors **14** Moment By Moment **15** Vinnie Barbarino **17** Welcome Back Kotter **18** Saturday Night Fever

trawl 3 net **4** drag, fish, haul, line **5** seine, troll **6** dredge **7** dragnet

Treacher, Arthur
  real name: 11 Arthur Veary
  born: 7 England **8** Brighton
  roles: 11 Mary Poppins **14** National Velvet, Thank You Jeeves **16** David Copperfield **20** Magnificent Obsession

treacherous 5 false, risky **6** tricky, unsafe, untrue **7** devious **8** disloyal, perilous, two-faced **9** dangerous, deceitful, deceptive, faithless, hazardous **10** misleading, perfidious, precarious, traitorous, treasonous, unfaithful **12** falsehearted **13** untrustworthy

treachery 5 guile **6** deceit **7** perfidy, treason **8** apostasy, betrayal, trickery **9** deception, duplicity, falseness **10** disloyalty, infidelity **11** double cross **13** breach of faith, deceitfulness, double-dealing, faithlessness **15** underhandedness **17** untrustworthiness

tread 4 gait, hike, pace, roam, rove, step, walk **5** prowl, range, stamp, stomp, tramp **6** step on, stride, stroll, trudge, walk on **7** trample **8** footfall, footstep

treason 6 mutiny, revolt **7** perfidy **8** apostasy, betrayal, sedition **9** duplicity, rebellion, treachery **10** conspiracy, disloyalty, insurgence, revolution, sub-

version **11** lese majesty **12** insurrection

treasonable 9 faithless, seditious **10** perfidious, subversive, traitorous **11** treacherous

treasure 3 gem **4** gold **5** hoard, jewel, prize, store, value **6** esteem, jewels, regard, revere, riches, silver **7** cherish, deposit, paragon **8** bank upon, dote upon, gold mine, hold dear **11** pride and joy **14** apple of one's eye **17** pearl of great price

treasure chest 3 box **4** case **5** chest, trunk **6** coffer

treasured 4 dear **5** loved **6** adored, valued **7** beloved **8** precious **9** cherished

Treasure Island
  author: 20 Robert Louis Stevenson
  character: 7 Ben Gunn **8** Smollett **9** Dr Livesey **10** Jim Hawkins **14** Long John Silver **15** Squire Trelawney
  director:
    1934 version: 13 Victor Fleming
    1950 version: 11 Byron Haskin
  based on novel by: 20 Robert Louis Stevenson
  cast:
    1934 version: 10 Lewis Stone **12** Jackie Cooper (Jim Hawkins), Wallace Beery (Long John Silver) **15** Lionel Barrymore
    1950 version: 11 Basil Sydney **12** Robert Newton (Long John Silver) **13** Bobby Driscoll (Jim Hawkins) **16** Walter Fitzgerald

Treasure of the Sierra Madre, The
  director: 10 John Huston
  cast: 7 Tim Holt **12** Bruce Bennett, Walter Huston **13** Alfonso Bedoya, Barton MacLane **14** Humphrey Bogart
  Oscar for: 8 director **10** screenplay **15** supporting actor (Huston)

treasurer 6 banker, bursar, purser, teller **7** auditor, cashier **9** financier **10** accountant, bookkeeper, cash-keeper, controller **16** financial officer **17** minister of finance **22** secretary of the treasury **24** Chancellor of the Exchequer

Treasure State
  nickname of: 7 Montana

treasury 4 bank, safe, till **5** funds, purse, vault **6** coffer **8** money box **9** anthology, exchequer, strongbox, thesaurus **10** collection, compendium, depository, repository, storehouse **11** bank account, compilation

treasury note 4 bill **8** bank note **9** greenback **12** currency note **17** silver certificate

treat 3 joy **4** blow, coat, give **5** apply, cover, favor, grant, imbue, stand **6** attend, divert, doctor, handle, manage, remedy, spring, thrill **7** comfort, delight, discuss, patch up, take out **8** consider, deal with, look upon, medicate, pleasure, relate to **9** act toward, small gift, try to cure, try to heal **10** impregnate, minister to, speak about, write about **12** prescribe for, satisfaction **13** gratification

treat as inferior 7 disdain **9** patronize **12** condescend to **18** look down one's nose at **19** discriminate against

treatise 4 text **5** essay, study, tract **6** manual, memoir, report, thesis **8** textbook, tractate **9** discourse, monograph **12** dissertation

treatment 3 way **4** cure **6** course, remedy **7** conduct, process, regimen, therapy **8** antidote, approach, handling, treating **9** doctoring, operation, procedure **10** management, medication **11** application, medical care **12** manipulation

treaty 4 deal, pact **6** accord **7** bargain, compact, entente **8** covenant **9** concordat **13** understanding **15** formal agreement **22** international agreement

tree 3 ash, elm, fir, oak **4** bush, palm, pine, wood **5** beech, birch, chase, maple, plane, plant, scrub, staff, stake, stick **6** corner, cudgel, redbud, spruce, timber, willow **7** gallows, lineage, live oak, sapling **8** ancestry, chestnut, hardwood, mahogany, pedigree, seedling **9** ailanthus, evergreen **10** cottonwood, eucalyptus

Tree Grows in Brooklyn, A
  author: 10 Betty Smith
  character:
    Nolan family: 5 Katie **6** Neeley **7** Francie, Johnnie
  director: 9 Elia Kazan
  cast: 9 James Dunn **10** Lloyd Nolan **12** Joan Blondell **14** Dorothy McGuire, Peggy Ann Garner
  Oscar for: 7 special (Garner) **15** supporting actor (Dunn)

treeless 4 bald, bare **6** barren **7** denuded **8** unwooded **10** unforested

Treeplanters State
  nickname of: 8 Nebraska

tref 9 not kosher

trek 4 hike, plod, roam, rove, sail, slog, trip **5** jaunt, march, range, tramp **6** junket, outing, travel, trudge, voyage, wander **7** journey, odyssey, passage **8** traverse **9** excursion, migration **10** expedition, pilgrimage **11** peregrinate **13** peregrination

trellis 5 arbor, bower, cross, frame, grill, trail **6** gazebo, screen **7** lattice, network, pergola **8** espalier **10** interweave **11** summerhouse

tremble 5 quail, quake, shake, waver **6** quaver, quiver, shiver **7** flutter, pulsate, shudder **9** palpitate

trembling 5 shaky **7** quaking, shaking **8** unsteady **9** doddering, quavering, quivering, shivering **10** shuddering **11** palpitating

tremblor 5 quake, seism, shock **6** tremor **8** upheaval **10** earthquake

tremendous 4 fine, huge, vast **5** giant, great, major **7** amazing, awesome, immense, mammoth, sizable, titanic, unusual **8** colossal, enormous, fabulous, gigantic, terrific, towering, uncommon **9** excellent, fantastic, first-rate, humongous, important, marvelous, monstrous, wonderful **10** formidable, gargantuan, incredible, noteworthy, stupendous **11** elephantine, exceptional **12** considerable **13** consequential, extraordinary

tremolo
  music: 9 trembling, vibrating **30** rapid reiteration of a single pitch

tremor 3 jar **4** jolt **5** quake, shake, shock, spasm, throb, waver **6** quiver, shiver **7** flutter, shaking, shudder, tremble **8** paroxysm **9** pulsation, quavering, quivering, shivering, trembling, vibration **10** convulsion **11** palpitation

tremulous 5 jumpy, shaky, timid **6** wobbly **7** aquiver, excited, fearful, jittery, keyed-up, nervous, panicky, quaking **8** aflutter, agitated, atremble, hesitant, restless, wavering, worked-up **9** faltering, impatient, quivering, trembling, uncertain **10** irresolute, stimulated **13** on tenterhooks, panic-stricken

trench 3 cut, rut **4** scar **5** canal, ditch, drain, fosse, slash, slice **6** dugout, furrow, gutter, trough **7** channel, wrinkle **8** aqueduct **9** earthwork **10** depression

trenchant 4 acid, keen, tart **5** crisp **6** bitter **7** acerbic, caustic, concise, mordant, probing **8** clear-cut, distinct, incisive, scathing **9** sarcastic, scorching **10** razor-sharp **11** acrimonious, penetrating, well-defined

trend 4 bent, flow, mode **5** drift, style **7** fashion, impulse, leaning **8** movement, tendency **9** direction **10** proclivity, propensity **11** inclination

trendsetters 7 leaders **8** trendies, vanguard **10** avant-garde, innovators **11** pacesetters, tastemakers **12** advance guard, stylesetters, trailblazers

trendy 2 in **4** chic, tony **5** swank **6** modern, modish, with-it **7** current, faddish, popular, stylish, voguish **8** up-to-date **10** all the rage **11** fashionable **13** up-to-the-minute

Trenor, Gus and Judy
  characters in: 15 The House of Mirth
  author: 7 Wharton

Trent, Little Nell
  character in: 19 The Old Curiosity Shop
  author: 7 Dickens

trepidation 4 fear **5** alarm, dread, panic, worry **7** anxiety, jitters **8** cold feet, disquiet **10** uneasiness **11** butterflies, disquietude, jitteriness, nervousness **12** apprehension **13** consternation

trespass 3 sin **5** error, wrong **6** invade **7** impinge, intrude, misdeed, offense **8** encroach, infringe, iniquity, invasion **9** evildoing, intrusion, violation **10** immorality, infraction, misconduct, wrongdoing **11** delinquency, misbehavior **12** encroachment, infringement, overstepping **13** transgression, unlawful entry, wrongful entry

tress 4 curl, hair, lock, mane **5** braid, plait **6** strand **7** ringlet, wimpler **8** spitcurl

trestle 4 beam **5** board, brace, frame, table **6** timber **9** framework

trial 2 go **3** try, woe **4** care, pain, shot, test **5** agony, essay, flyer, whirl, worry **6** burden, effort, misery, ordeal, trying, tryout **7** anguish, attempt, bad luck, hearing, testing, test run, torment, trouble, venture **8** accident, distress, endeavor, hardship, vexation **9** adversity, court case, heartache, suffering **10** affliction, litigation, misfortune **11** cross to bear **12** misadventure, wretchedness

Trial, The
  author: 10 Franz Kafka
  character: 4 Leni **7** Joseph K **9** Titorelli **11** The Advocate

trial and error 10 experiment **13** investigation **15** experimentation **20** process of elimination

tribe *see* **11** ethnic group

Tribes of Israel *see* **6** Israel

tribulation 3 woe **4** care, pain **5** agony, grief, trial, worry **6** misery, ordeal, sorrow **7** anguish, bad luck, torment, trouble **8** distress, hardship, vexation **9** adversity, heartache, suffering **10** affliction, ill fortune, misfortune **11** unhappiness **12** wretchedness

Tribulation Wholesome
  character in: 12 The Alchemist
  author: 6 Jonson

tribunal 3 bar **5** bench, court, forum **6** judges **9** authority, judiciary **10** ruling body **11** judge's bench, judge's chair **14** seat of judgment

tributary 6 branch, feeder, source, stream **7** helping, subject **8** affluent **9** ancillary, auxiliary, confluent, secondary **10** subjugated, subsidiary **11** subordinate **12** contributing, contributory

tribute 3 tax **4** duty, levy, toll **5** bribe, honor, kudos **6** esteem, eulogy, excise, impost, payoff, praise, ransom **7** payment, respect **8** accolade, encomium, memorial **9** extolling, gratitude, laudation, panegyric **10** assessment, blood money, compliment, settlement **11** recognition, testimonial **12** commendation, pound of flesh **13**

consideration, peace offering **14** acknowledgment

trice 3 sec **4** jiff, wink **5** blink, flash, jiffy, shake **6** minute, moment, second **7** instant **9** coup d'oeil, twinkling **11** split second

trichophobia
  fear of: **4** hair

trichoptera
  class: **8** hexapoda
  phylum: **10** arthropoda
  group: **3** fly **6** caddis

trick 3 art, gag **4** bait, dupe, feat, gift, gull, have, hoax, joke, ploy, ruse, trap, wile **5** antic, blind, bluff, caper, cheat, dodge, feint, fraud, knack, prank, put-on, skill, stunt **6** deceit, device, number, outfox, outwit, resort, secret, take in **7** deceive, gimmick, know-how, mislead, swindle **8** artifice, deftness, flimflam, hoodwink, maneuver **9** bamboozle, chicanery, deception, dexterity, imposture, sophistry, stratagem, technique **10** adroitness, hocus-pocus, manipulate, subterfuge **11** contrivance, machination, outmaneuver **13** practical joke, sleight of hand **16** prestidigitation

trickery 5 guile **6** bunkum, deceit **8** artifice, flimflam, pretense, quackery, wiliness **9** chicanery, deception, duplicity, imposture, rascality, stratagem **10** artfulness, craftiness, hocus-pocus, shiftiness **11** crookedness, deviousness **12** charlatanism, skullduggery, slipperiness **13** deceitfulness

trickiness 6 deceit **7** cunning, slyness **8** trickery **9** duplicity **10** craftiness **15** underhandedness

trickle 4 drip, leak, ooze, seep **5** exude **7** dribble, seepage **9** percolate

trickster 5 cheat, joker **6** dodger, rascal **8** deceiver, impostor, sleeveen **9** prankster

tricky 3 sly **4** foxy, wily **5** risky **6** artful, crafty, shifty, unsafe **7** cunning, devious **8** rascally, slippery, unstable **9** dangerous, deceptive, difficult, hazardous **10** touch-and-go, unreliable **11** complicated, underhanded **12** hard to handle, undependable **13** temperamental, unpredictable

trident
  form: **5** spear
  number of prongs: **5** three
  scepter of: **7** Neptune **8** Poseidon

trifle 3 bit, dab, jot, nip, toy **4** dash, drop, idle, iota, mite, play **5** crumb, dally, pinch, scrap, speck, tinge, touch, trace **6** bauble, dawdle, gewgaw, linger, little, morsel, sliver **7** modicum, nothing, trinket **8** fragment, gimcrack, kill time **9** bagatelle, plaything, waste time **10** dillydally, knickknack, sprinkling, triviality **11** deal lightly, small matter **12** amuse oneself, treat lightly **13** small quantity

trifler 5 flirt, idler **6** coquet **7** dabbler, dallier **8** coquette **10** dilettante

trifling 4 puny **5** petty, small, sorry, token **6** paltry, slight **7** nominal, trivial **8** beggarly, niggling, nugatory, picayune, piddling **9** worthless **10** negligible **11** unimportant **13** beneath notice, inappreciable, insignificant **14** inconsiderable **15** inconsequential

trifling circumstances
  Latin: **8** minutiae

trifling matter
  French: **10** peu de chose

trigger 5 shoot **6** set off **7** fire off **8** activate, detonate, touch off **9** discharge

trikerion 11 candelabrum, candlestick **12** candleholder

Trilby
  author: **15** George du Maurier
  character: **5** Gecko, Sandy, Taffy **8** Svengali **12** Little Billee **14** Trilby O'Ferrall

trill
  music: **7** shaking, tremolo **9** quavering

trim 3 cut, fit, lop **4** clip, crop, deck, form, lean, pare, slim, thin **5** adorn, array, lithe, prune, shape, shave, shear, shift, sleek, state **6** adjust, bedeck, border, change, fettle, kilter, limber, paring, piping, supple, svelte **7** arrange, balance, bedizen, compact, cutting, fitness, furbish, garnish, lissome, pruning, shapely, slender, willowy **8** athletic, beautify, clipping, cropping, decorate, equalize, ornament, shearing, trick out, trimming **9** adornment, condition, embellish, embroider, shipshape **10** decoration, distribute **11** streamlined **13** embellishment, ornamentation

Trim, Corporal
  character in: **14** Tristram Shandy
  author: **6** Sterne

trimming 4 trim **5** frill **7** cutting, pruning, slicing **8** clipping **9** adornment **10** decoration, shortening, truncation **11** abridgement, contraction, curtailment **12** abbreviation **13** embellishment

Trinacria see **6** Sicily

Trinidad and Tobago
  capital/largest city: **11** Port of Spain
  others: **4** Debe, Toco **5** Arima **6** Canaan, Coryal, Labrea **7** San Juan, Siparia **8** Rio Claro, Tunapuna **10** Roxborough **11** San Fernando, Scarborough **12** Princess Town, Sangre Grande **14** Charlotteville
  school: **6** Fatima **7** St Mary's **11** Queen's Royal
  head of state: **14** British monarch **15** governor general
  monetary unit: **4** cent **6** dollar
  island: **12** Chacachacare, Little Tobago **14** Bird of Paradise

  lake: **5** Pitch
  mountain:
    hills: **7** Trinity **10** Montserrat **12** Three Sisters
  highest point: **5** Aripo
  river: **6** Caroni **7** Ortoire **8** Oropuche, Trinidad
  sea: **8** Atlantic **9** Caribbean
  physical feature:
    bay: **5** Cocos, Guapo **6** Matura, Mayaro
    channel: **12** Dragon's Mouth **13** Serpent's Mouth
    gulf: **5** Paria
    point: **5** Radix **6** Arenal, Galera **7** Chupara, Galeota **8** Columbus
  people: **5** Irish **6** French, Syrian **7** African, Chinese, English, Spanish **8** European, Lebanese **10** East Indian, Portuguese, Venezuelan **11** Asian Indian **13** Latin American
    explorer: **8** Columbus
    leader: **8** Williams
  language: **6** French **7** Chinese, English, Spanish **10** Portuguese **12** French Patois
  religion: **5** Hindu, Islam **8** Anglican **10** Protestant **12** Christianity **13** Roman Catholic
  place:
    asphalt lake: **9** Pitch Lake
    mansions: **16** Magnificent Seven
    park: **18** Queen's Park Savannah
  feature:
    bird: **7** oilbird **8** cocorico
    clothing: **4** sari **5** dhoti
    dancer: **6** Dragon, Shango
    festival: **6** Hosein, Lights
    fish: **5** guppy
    music: **7** calypso, goombay
    tree: **4** mora
  food:
    drink: **16** Angostura Bitters

Trinity
  author: **8** Leon Uris

trinket 3 toy **5** bijou, charm, jewel **6** bauble, gewgaw, notion, trifle **8** gimcrack, ornament **9** bagatelle, plaything **10** knickknack

trip 3 bob, err **4** flip, flub, fool, muff, pull, skip, slip, tour, trek, undo **5** caper, catch, dance, fluff, foray, jaunt, outdo, throw, upset **6** bungle, cruise, frolic, gambol, junket, outfox, outing, prance, safari, set off, slip up, voyage **7** blunder, commute, confuse, flounce, journey, misstep, release, scamper, stumble **8** activate, fall over, flounder, hoodwink, throw off **9** excursion **10** disconcert, expedition, pilgrimage **11** step lightly

Triple Crown 7 Belmont **9** Preakness **13** Kentucky Derby
  winner: **5** Omaha **7** Assault **8** Affirmed, Citation **9** Sir Barton, Whirlaway **10** Count Fleet, Gallant Fox, War Admiral **11** Seattle Slew, Secretariat

Triple Sec *see* 9 Cointreau
Tripoli
    capital of: 5 Libya
Triptolemos, Triptolemus
    favorite of: 7 Demeter
    inventor of: 4 plow 5 wheel
    patron of: 11 agriculture
Triquetra *see* 6 Sicily
triskaidekaphobia
    fear of: 14 number thirteen
Trismegistus *see* 5 Thoth
Tristan and Isolde
    also: 16 Tristan und Isolde
    opera by: 6 Wagner
    character: 5 Melot 8 Brangane, Kurwenal 18 King Mark of Cornwall
triste 3 sad 10 melancholy
tristesse 6 sorrow 7 sadness 10 melancholy
Tristram
    author: 22 Edwin Arlington Robinson
    character in: 16 Arthurian romance
Tristram Shandy
    author: 14 Laurence Sterne
    character: 6 Dr Slop 8 Mr Yorick 10 Toby Shandy 11 Widow Wadman 12 Corporal Trim, Walter Shandy
trite 5 banal, silly, stale 6 common 7 cliched, humdrum, routine, shallow, worn-out 8 bromidic, everyday, ordinary, overdone, shopworn 9 frivolous, hackneyed 10 pedestrian, threadbare 11 commonplace, oft-repeated, stereotyped, unimportant 12 run-of-the-mill 13 platitudinous
Tritogeneia *see* 6 Athena
Triton
    god of: 3 sea
    father: 8 Poseidon
    mother: 10 Amphitrite
    shape: 6 merman
    trumpet: 10 conch-shell
triumph 3 hit, win 4 best, coup 5 smash 6 subdue 7 conquer, mastery, prevail, succeed, success, surpass, victory 8 conquest, overcome, smash hit, vanquish 9 overwhelm 10 ascendancy, attainment, gain the day 11 achievement, superiority 12 come out on top, take the prize 14 accomplishment, get the better of
triumphal 5 proud 6 joyous 8 exultant 9 ascendant, rewarding 10 fulfilling, gratifying, successful, triumphant, victorious 11 spectacular
triumphant 6 elated, joyful 7 winning 8 exultant, jubilant 9 rejoicing 10 conquering, first-place, successful, victorious 11 celebrating 12 prizewinning
Triumph of Death, The
    author: 17 Gabriele D'Annunzio
trivia
    Latin: 8 minutiae
trivial 4 idle, puny, slim 5 banal, petty, small, trite 6 common, flimsy, little,

meager, paltry, slight, two-bit 7 foolish 8 beggarly, everyday, niggling, nugatory, ordinary, picayune, piddling, trifling 9 rinky-dink, worthless 10 incidental, pedestrian 11 commonplace, meaningless, unessential, unimportant 13 inappreciable, insignificant, of little value 14 inconsiderable 15 inconsequential
triviality 5 frill 6 trifle 9 frivolity 10 paltriness 12 nonessential, unimportance 14 insignificance 18 inconsequentiality
troglodyte 5 brute 6 hermit 9 barbarian 11 cave dweller
Troilus
    father: 5 Priam
    mother: 6 Hecuba
Troilus and Cressida
    author: 18 William Shakespeare
    character: 4 Ajax 5 Priam 6 Hector 7 Ulysses 8 Achilles, Diomedes, Pandarus 9 Agamemnon
Troilus and Criseyde
    author: 15 Geoffrey Chaucer
    character: 8 Diomedes, Pandarus
trois 5 three
Trojan Horse
    made of: 4 wood
    made by: 7 Epeiosk
    contained: 8 Odysseus, warriors
Trojans, The
    also: 10 Les Troyens
    opera by: 7 Berlioz
    part one: 14 La Prise de Troie 16 The Capture of Troy
    part two: 19 Les Troyens a Carthage 20 The Trojans in Carthage
    character: 4 Dido 6 Aeneas, Hector
Trojan War
    length: 8 ten years
    combatants: 6 Greeks 7 Trojans
    cause: 5 Helen, Paris 14 Apple of Discord
Trojan Women, The
    author: 9 Euripides
    character: 5 Helen 6 Hecuba 8 Astyanax, Menelaus, Odysseus, Polyxena 9 Agamemnon, Cassandra 10 Andromache, Talthybius 11 Neoptolemus
troll 3 imp 4 ogre 5 dwarf, gnome 6 goblin
    origin: 12 Scandinavian
    form: 12 supernatural
    inhabits: 10 subterrain
trollop 4 doxy, slut 5 bitch, doxie, frump, hussy, trull, whore 6 floozy, harlot, wanton 7 baggage 8 slattern, strumpet 10 prostitute
Trollope, Anthony
    author of: 9 Orley Farm, The Warden 15 The Way We Live Now 16 Barchester Towers, Framley Parsonage
    character: 11 Phineas Finn
troop, troops 4 army, band, file, gang, herd, step, unit 5 bunch,

crowd, crush, drove, flock, horde, march, press, swarm, tramp 6 parade, stride, throng, trudge 7 cavalry, company, militia 8 infantry, soldiers, soldiery, troopers 9 aggregate, gathering 10 armed force, assemblage 11 cavalry unit, fighting men, police force 12 congregation 13 military force
trop 3 too 7 too many, too much
Trophonius
    vocation: 7 builder
    father: 7 Erginus
    brother: 8 Agamedes
    god of: 5 earth
    killed: 8 Agamedes
    became: 6 oracle
        oracle called: 14 Zeus Trophonius
trophy 4 palm 5 award, booty, honor, kudos, medal, prize, relic, spoil 6 wreath 7 laurels, memento 8 citation, souvenir 9 loving cup 10 blue ribbon 11 testimonial
tropical 5 muggy 6 sultry, torrid 8 stifling 10 sweltering 11 hot and humid
troppo, non
    music: 10 not too much
Tros
    king of: 4 Troy
    father: 12 Erichthonius
    mother: 8 Astyoche
    wife: 10 Callirrhoe
    son: 4 Ilus 8 Ganymede 9 Assaracus
trot 3 jog 9 go briskly 11 step quickly, walk smartly
troth 8 fidelity 9 betrothal 10 affiancing, engagement 12 faithfulness
Trotwood, Betsey
    character in: 16 David Copperfield
    author: 7 Dickens
trouble 3 fix, row, vex, woe 4 blow, care, fuss, heed, mess, pain, pass, snag, work 5 agony, annoy, grief, harry, labor, pains, pinch, think, trial, upset, worry 6 affect, attend, badger, bother, burden, crisis, defect, dismay, effort, grieve, harass, misery, ordeal, pester, pickle, plague, pother, put out, scrape, sorrow, strain, strait, stress, strife, unrest 7 afflict, agitate, ailment, attempt, concern, depress, dilemma, discord, disturb, ferment, ill wind, oppress, perturb, reverse, setback, torment 8 disaster, disorder, disquiet, distress, disunity, exertion, hardship, hot water, quandary, rainy day, struggle, take time, unsettle, vexation 9 adversity, agitation, annoyance, attention, breakdown, challenge, commotion, deep water, hard times, suffering 10 affliction, convulsion, difficulty, disability, discommode, discompose, disconcert, discontent, dissension, irritation, make uneasy, misfortune, opposition 11 competition, disturbance, embroilment, instability, malfunction, predicament, tribulation 12 entanglement, exert oneself

13 inconvenience, make the effort **14** discontentment **15** dissatisfaction

troubled 5 upset **7** worried **8** bothered, careworn **9** disturbed, perturbed **10** distressed **12** heavyhearted

troublemaker 6 gossip **7** inciter **8** agitator, fomenter, provoker **9** miscreant **10** incendiary, instigator **11** rumormonger, scaremonger **12** rabble-rouser **13** mischief-maker, scandalmonger **16** agent provocateur

troublesome 4 hard **5** heavy, pesky, tough **6** cursed, knotty, taxing, thorny, tiring, trying, vexing **7** arduous, irksome, onerous, tedious **8** annoying, tiresome, unwieldy **9** demanding, difficult, fatiguing, harassing, herculean, laborious, wearisome, worrisome **10** bothersome, burdensome, cumbersome, disturbing, irritating, oppressive, tormenting, unpleasant **11** disobedient, distressing **12** disagreeable, exasperating, inconvenient, uncontrolled **13** undisciplined

troublesomeness 5 trial **10** difficulty **11** arduousness **13** inconvenience, laboriousness, vexatiousness, worrisomeness **14** bothersomeness

Trouble with Harry, The
 director: 15 Alfred Hitchcock
 cast: 11 Edmund Gwenn **12** John Forsythe **14** Mildred Dunnock, Mildred Natwick **15** Shirley MacLaine

troubling 6 vexing **8** worrying **9** worrisome **10** bothersome, disturbing, unsettling

trough 4 duct, moat, race, tray **5** canal, ditch, flume, gorge, gully **6** furrow, hollow, ravine, trench **7** channel **8** aqueduct **10** depression

trounce 4 beat, drub, lick, trim, whip **5** cream, skunk **6** humble **7** clobber **8** vanquish **9** overpower, overwhelm **10** take care of **11** carry the day **14** get the better of

troupe 4 band, cast **5** group, troop **6** actors **7** company, players **10** performers **11** road company

trouper 5 actor **7** actress **8** thespian **9** performer **13** touring player **15** repertory player

trousers 5 jeans, pants **6** chinos, slacks **7** drawers **8** breeches, britches, jodhpurs, knickers, overalls **9** dungarees **10** pantaloons **11** bellbottoms **12** pedal pushers **14** knickerbockers

Trovatore, Il
 also: 13 The Troubadour
 opera by: 5 Verdi
 character: 7 Azucena, Leonora, Manrico **11** Count di Luna

Troy
 abducted queen: 5 Helen
 archaeologist: 6 Blegen **8** Dorpfeld **10** Schliemann
 defender: 5 Eneas **6** Aeneas

Greek name: 5 Ilion
 hero: 6 Hector
 king: 5 Priam
 Latin name: 5 Ilium
 modern name: 9 Hissarlik
 mountain: 3 Ida
 neighboring city in NY: 6 Albany **10** Watervliet
 river: 6 Hudson
 city in: 7 Alabama, New York **8** Michigan
 story: 5 Iliad **7** Odyssey
 surrounding region: 5 Troad, Troas

Troy, Sergeant
 character in: 22 Far From the Madding Crowd
 author: 5 Hardy

truancy 3 cut **7** absence **11** absenteeism, nonpresence **12** playing hooky **13** nonappearance, nonattendance **14** cutting classes, skipping school

truant 4 gone **5** idler **6** absent, dodger, evader, loafer, no show **7** drifter, goof-off, missing, not here, shirker, slacker, vagrant **8** absentee, deserter, layabout **9** goldbrick **10** delinquent, malingerer, nonpresent, not present **11** boondoggler, hooky-player **12** nonattendant, playing hooky

truce 4 halt, lull, rest, stay, stop **5** break, pause **7** respite **9** armistice, cease-fire **12** interruption **14** breathing spell, discontinuance **23** suspension of hostilities

Trucial Oman, Trucial States *see* **18** United Arab Emirates

truck 3 rig, van **5** lorry **15** eighteen-wheeler
 type: 5 panel **6** pickup **7** trailer **8** delivery

truckle 3 bow **4** fawn **5** court, defer, yield **6** grovel, pander, submit **7** flatter **8** bootlick, butter up, suck up to **9** shine up to **10** curry favor, take orders **11** apple-polish, fall all over **12** knuckle under **17** ingratiate oneself

truculence 8 defiance, ill humor **9** hostility, ill temper, pugnacity, surliness **10** fierceness **11** bellicosity **12** belligerence, churlishness **14** aggressiveness

truculent 4 rude, sour **5** cross, nasty, sulky, surly **6** fierce, touchy **7** defiant, hostile, peevish **8** churlish, insolent, petulant, snappish, snarling **9** bellicose **10** aggressive, ill-humored, ill-natured, pugnacious, ungracious **11** bad-tempered, belligerent, ill-tempered

Trudeau, Garry
 creator/artist of: 10 Doonesbury

Trudeau Pierre
 home: 6 Canada
 office: 13 prime minister

trudge 4 drag, limp, plod **5** clump, march, tramp **6** hobble, lumber **7** shamble

true 4 even, firm, full, just, pure, real **5**

exact, legal, loyal, right, usual, valid **6** actual, lawful, normal, proper, steady, strict, trusty **7** correct, devoted, factual, genuine, literal, precise, regular, staunch, typical **8** absolute, accurate, bona fide, constant, faithful, official, positive, reliable, rightful, true-blue, truthful **9** authentic, simon-pure, steadfast **10** dependable, legitimate, unswerving, unwavering **11** trustworthy **14** unquestionable

true being 4 core, soul **6** nature, psyche, spirit **7** essence

True Grit
 director: 13 Henry Hathaway
 based on novel by: 13 Charles Portis
 cast: 8 Kim Darby **9** John Wayne **11** Jeremy Slate **12** Glen Campbell, Robert Duvall **14** Strother Martin
 Oscar for: 5 actor (Wayne)

Truffaut, Francois
 director of: 11 Day for Night, Jules and Jim **19** Shoot the Piano Player, The Four Hundred Blows

truism 3 saw **5** adage, axiom **6** cliche, dictum, saying **9** platitude

truly 6 indeed, in fact, really, surely, verily **7** exactly, in truth, no doubt **8** actually, honestly, to be sure **9** assuredly, certainly, correctly, factually, genuinely, literally, precisely, sincerely **10** absolutely, accurately, definitely, faithfully, positively, truthfully, upon my word **11** beyond doubt, in actuality, indubitably, so help me God **12** indisputably **13** incontestably, unequivocally **14** beyond question, unquestionably **15** all kidding aside, without question

Truman, Harry S
 nickname: 15 Give Em Hell Harry
 presidential rank: 11 thirty-third
 party: 10 Democratic
 state represented: 8 Missouri
 succeeded upon death of: 9 Roosevelt
 defeated: 5 (Farrell) Dobbs, (Thomas Edmund) Dewey **6** (Claude A) Watson, (Norman) Thomas **7** (Henry Agard) Wallace **8** (Edward A) Teichert, (James Strom) Thurmond
 vice president: 7 (Alben William) Barkley
 cabinet:
  state: 6 (James Francis) Byrnes **7** (Dean Gooderham) Acheson **8** (George Catlett) Marshall **10** (Edward Reilly) Stettinius (Jr)
  treasury: 6 (Frederick Moore) Vinson, (John Wesley) Snyder **10** (Henry) Morgenthau (Jr)
  war: 6 (Kenneth Claiborne) Royall **7** (Henry Lewis) Stimson **9** (Robert Porter) Patterson
  defense: 6 (Robert Abercrombie) Lovett **7** (Louis Arthur) Johnson **8** (George Catlett) Marshall **9** (James Vincent) Forrestal

attorney general: 5 (Thomas Campbell) Clark **6** (Francis) Biddle **7** (James Howard) McGrath **9** (James Patrick) McGranery
navy: 9 (James Vincent) Forrestal
postmaster general: 6 (Frank Comerford) Walker **8** (Robert Emmet) Hannegan **9** (Jesse Monroe) Donaldson
interior: 4 (Julius Albert) Krug **5** (Harold LeClaire) Ickes **7** (Oscar Littleton) Chapman
agriculture: 7 (Charles Franklin) Brannan, (Claude Raymond) Wickard **8** (Clinton Presba) Anderson
commerce: 6 (Charles) Sawyer **7** (Henry Agard) Wallace **8** (William Averell) Harriman
labor: 5 (Maurice Joseph) Tobin **7** (Frances), Perkins (Wilson) **13** (Lewis Baxter) Schwellenbach
born: 2 MO **5** Lamar **8** Missouri
died: 2 MO **8** Missouri **10** Kansas City
buried: 2 MO **8** Missouri **12** Independence
education:
law school: 21 Kansas City School of Law (did not graduate)
religion: 7 Baptist
interests: 5 piano **7** history
vacation spot: 2 FL **7** Florida, Key West
author: 14 Year of Decision **19** Years of Trial and Hope
political career: 8 US Senate **13** Vice President
presiding judge of: 13 Jackson County
civilian career: 6 farmer
owned: 9 men's store **12** haberdashery
military service: 5 major **9** World War I **15** MO National Guard **18** Army Reserve colonel
notable events of lifetime/term: 4 NATO **5** V-E Day **8** Fair Deal **9** Korean War **17** iron-curtain speech **20** assassination attempt **31** North Atlantic Treaty Organization
act: 11 Taft-Hartley **12** Bretton-Woods
airlift to: 6 Berlin
conference: 7 Potsdam
dropping of first: 5 A-bomb **8** atom bomb
plan: 8 Marshall **9** Point Four
signing of: 9 UN charter
Treaty of: 12 Rio de Janeiro
trial of: 9 Alger Hiss
father: 12 John Anderson
mother: 6 Martha (Ellen Young)
siblings: 8 Mary Jane **10** John Vivian
wife: 9 Elizabeth (Virginia Wallace)
nickname: 4 Bess
children: 12 Mary Margaret
Trumbull, John
born: 9 Lebanon CT

artwork: 21 The Battle of Bunker Hill **26** The Resignation of Washington **28** The Declaration of Independence **29** The Surrender of General Burgoyne **32** The Capture of the Hessians at Trenton **38** The Surrender of Lord Cornwallis at Yorktown **46** The Death of General Montgomery in the Attack of Quebec, The Death of General Warren at the Battle of Bunker Hill
trumpery 5 showy, trash **6** deceit, trashy, trivia **7** rubbish, twaddle, useless **8** frippery, nonsense, trifling **9** deception, worthless **11** nonsensical
trumpet 4 honk, horn **5** blare, bugle **6** cornet **7** clarion **8** proclaim **10** hearing aid
Trumpet of the Swan, The
author: 7 E B White
trump up 4 fake **6** invent, make up **7** concoct, falsify **9** fabricate
truncate 3 bob, lop, nip **4** clip, crop, dock, snub, trim **5** prune **7** abridge, curtail, shorten **8** amputate, condense, cut short **10** abbreviate
truncheon 3 bat **4** club **5** baton, billy, stick **6** cudgel **8** bludgeon **9** billyclub
trunker 3 box, die **4** body, bole, dado, line, main **5** chief, pants, shaft, snout, stock, torso **6** coffer, engine, locker, shut up, thorax **7** baggage, close in
truss 3 tie **4** beam, bind, prop, stay **5** brace, hitch, shore, strap, tie up **6** bind up, fasten, girder, pinion, secure **7** confine, support **8** make fast **9** constrict, framework, stanchion **12** underpinning
trust 4 care, duty, hope **5** faith, hands **6** accept, assume, belief, charge, credit, expect, look to, rely on **7** believe, count on, custody, keeping, presume, swear by **8** credence, feel sure, reliance, sureness **9** certainty, certitude, count upon **10** anticipate, confidence, conviction, depend upon, obligation, protection **11** assuredness, contemplate, have faith in, safekeeping, subscribe to, take on faith, take stock in **12** guardianship **14** give credence to, responsibility, take for granted
trusted 6 trusty **8** reliable **9** unfailing **10** dependable **11** trustworthy
trustee 8 guardian **9** caretaker, custodian, protector
trusteeship 4 care **6** charge **7** custody **10** protection **11** safekeeping **12** guardianship
trusting 8 gullible, trustful **9** believing, credulous **12** unsuspicious
trustworthy 4 true **5** loyal **6** honest **7** ethical, trusted, upright **8** faithful, reliable, true-blue **9** honorable, steadfast **10** aboveboard, dependable, scrupulous **11** responsible **12** tried and true

13 incorruptible, unimpeachable **14** high-principled
trusty 7 trusted **8** reliable **9** unfailing **10** dependable **11** trustworthy
trusty companion 3 pal **5** buddy, crony **6** friend **8** intimate, sidekick **9** confidant **10** bosom buddy, confidante
truth 3 law **4** fact **5** facts **6** verity **7** reality **8** accuracy, fidelity, trueness, veracity **9** actuality, exactness, integrity **11** reliability **12** authenticity, faithfulness, truthfulness **15** proven principle, trustworthiness
Russian: 6 Pravda
also name of: 9 newspaper
god of: 7 Mithras
truth conquers all things
Latin: 18 vincit omnia veritas
truthful 4 open, true **5** exact, frank **6** candid, honest **7** artless, correct, factual, precise, sincere **8** accurate, faithful, reliable **9** authentic, guileless, veracious **10** aboveboard, meticulous, scrupulous **11** trustworthy, undeceitful, unvarnished **13** unadulterated **15** straightforward
truthfulness 6 candor **7** honesty **8** veracity
Truth or Consequences
host: 10 Jack Bailey, Steve Dunne **12** Ralph Edwards
try 2 go **3** aim, use **4** risk, seek, shot, test, turn **5** crack, essay, fling, prove, trial, whack **6** effort, sample, strain, strive, tackle **7** adjudge, attempt, venture **8** endeavor **9** have a go at, partake of, undertake **10** adjudicate, deliberate, put to a test **11** opportunity **12** have a fling at, make an effort, take a crack at
trying 4 hard **5** pesky, tough **6** taxing, vexing **7** arduous, irksome, onerous, tedious **8** tiresome **9** difficult, fatiguing, harrowing, wearisome **10** bothersome, burdensome, exhausting, irritating **11** aggravating, distressing, troublesome **12** exasperating
tryout 4 test **5** trial **7** hearing **8** audition **10** experiment
try out 3 fry **6** render **7** compete **8** audition **9** give a test **11** performance
tryst 4 date **7** meeting, vis-a-vis **9** tete-a-tete **10** engagement, rendezvous **11** appointment, assignation
try the patience of 5 annoy **7** provoke **8** irritate **10** exasperate
try to equal 5 rival **7** compete, emulate
Tuatha De Danann 4 gods
origin: 5 Irish
mother: 4 Danu
tub 3 keg, kit, pot, tun, vat **4** bath, boat, butt, cask, ship, tank, tram, wash **5** barge, bathe, fatso, fatty, keeve, tramp **6** barrel, bucket, firkin, ore car, vessel **7** cistern, tankard **8**

cauldron, slow boat **9** container, freighter

tube 4 duct, hose, pipe **7** conduit **8** cylinder

tuber 3 anu, yam **4** beet, bulb, corm, eddo, root, taro **5** jalop, shoot **6** potato, turnip **8** rutabaga, swelling **11** enlargement

Tuchman, Barbara W
  author of: **14** A Distant Mirror, The First Salute **15** The Guns of August, The March of Folly **17** Practicing History

tuck 3 put **4** cram **5** pleat, shove, stick, stuff **6** enwrap, gather, insert, pucker, roll up, ruffle, shroud, swathe, thrust **7** crinkle, swaddle

tucker 3 fag **4** bush, poop, tire **5** weary **7** exhaust, fatigue

tuckered out 5 all in, tired, weary **6** bushed, done in, pooped **8** fatigued **9** exhausted, fagged out

Tudor
  dynasty of: **7** England
  rulers: **8** Henry VII **9** Henry VIII **8** Edward VI **5** Mary I **10** Elizabeth I

Tudor, Antony
  choreographer of: **11** Lilac Garden **12** Pillar of Fire

tuebor 11 I will defend

Tuei see **6** Isleta

Tuesday
  from: **3** Tiw
  heavenly body: **4** Mars
  French: **5** mardi
  Italian: **7** martedi
  Spanish: **6** martes
  German: **8** dienstag

tuft 4 wisp **5** batch, brush, bunch, clump, crest, plume, sheaf **6** bundle, tassel **7** cluster, topknot

tug 3 lug, tow **4** drag, draw, haul, jerk, pull, yank **6** wrench **7** wrestle

tulip 6 Tulipa
  varieties: **4** lady, star **5** globe **7** Turkish **9** butterfly, guinea-hen, waterlily **10** Sierra star **11** golden globe, purple globe **16** common late garden **17** common early garden

Tulkinghorn
  character in: **10** Bleak House
  author: **7** Dickens

Tullia
  father: **14** Servius Tullius
  husband: **7** Tarquin

Tullius see **14** Servius Tullius

Tulsa
  football team: **7** Outlaws

tumble 3 mix **4** dive, drop, fall, flip, roll, toss **5** whirl **6** bounce, jumble, plunge, stir up, topple **7** descend, shuffle, stumble **9** cartwheel **10** somersault

tumbledown 5 shaky **7** rickety, rundown **8** decaying, decrepit, unstable **9** crumbling, tottering **10** broken-down,

jerry-built, ramshackle **11** dilapidated, falling-down **14** disintegrating

tumbler 3 cog, dog **5** drier, glass, lever **6** goblet, vessel **7** acrobat, athlete, gymnast, juggler **12** somersaulter

tumbrel 4 cart **5** wagon **7** tipcart **8** dumpcart

tumbril
  French: **7** fourgon

tumid 5 puffy **6** turgid **7** bloated, bulging, dilated, pompous, swollen **8** enlarged, expanded, inflated **9** bombastic, distended, edematous, tumescent **11** protuberant **12** magniloquent **13** grandiloquent

tummy 3 gut **5** belly **6** paunch, tumtum **7** abdomen, midriff, stomach **9** bay window **11** breadbasket

tumor 3 wen **4** cyst, lump, wart **5** pride **6** cancer, growth **7** bombast, sarcoma **8** hematoma, neoplasm, swelling, tubercle **9** carcinoma, papilloma, pomposity **11** tumefaction

tumult 3 ado, din **6** bedlam, bustle, clamor, hubbub, racket, uproar **7** turmoil **8** disorder, upheaval **9** agitation, commotion, confusion **10** excitement, hullabaloo **11** disturbance, pandemonium

tumultuous 4 loud **5** noisy, rough, rowdy **6** stormy, unruly **7** chaotic, furious, lawless, raucous, riotous, violent **8** agitated, confused **9** clamorous, disturbed, turbulent **10** boisterous, disorderly, uproarious **11** tempestuous

tun 3 keg, tub, vat **4** butt, cask, drum **6** barrel **8** hogshead

tune 3 air **4** aria, line, song, step **5** adjust, ditty, motif, pitch, theme **6** accord, adjust, melody, number, strain, unison **7** concert, concord, harmony **9** agreement **10** conformity

tuneful 6 catchy, dulcet **7** lyrical, musical **9** melodious

tungsten
  chemical symbol: **1** W

tunic 4 robe **5** cloak **6** jacket, mantle, poncho, tabard **7** garment, surcoat

Tunica
  tribe: **10** Chitimacha

Tunis
  capital of: **7** Tunisia

Tunisia
  other name: **8** Carthage **9** Ifriqiyah
  capital/largest city: **5** Tunis
  others: **4** Beja, Sfax, Susa **5** Gabes, Gofsa **6** Djerba, Mateur, Nabeul, Remada, Sousse, Tozeur **7** Bizerte, Kairwan **8** Carthage, Jendouba, Kairouan, Monastir, Tebourba, Zaghouan **9** Grombalia **10** Ferryville
  empire: **8** Carthage **13** Barbary States
  school: **5** Tunis **16** Pasteur Institute
  measure: **3** saa **4** saah **5** cafiz **6** mettar **8** milerole
  monetary unit: **5** dinar **6** dollar **7**

millime
  weight: **3** saa **4** rotl **5** artal, ratel, uckia
  island: **6** Djerba, Galite
  lake: **6** Achkel, Djerid **7** Bizerte
  mountain: **5** Atlas **6** Mrhila **7** Tebessa **8** High Tell, Zaghouan **12** Northern Tell **17** Dorsale Tunisienne
  highest point: **6** Chambi
  river: **8** Medjerda, Mellegue
  sea: **13** Mediterranean
  physical feature:
    cape: **3** Bon **5** Blanc **8** Rasaddar
    desert: **6** Sahara
    gulf: **5** Gabes, Tunis **8** Hammamet
    oasis: **5** Gabes, Gafsa, Nefta **6** Djerba, Tozeur **9** El Oudiane **13** El Hamma Djerid
    plains: **5** Sahel
    salt lake: **11** Chott Djerid, Shatt Djerid
    valley: **8** Medjerda
    wind: **5** chile **6** chilli **7** sirocco
  people: **3** Jew **4** Arab **6** Berber
    artist: **5** Gorgi, Turki
    dynasty: **6** Hafsid **7** Fatimid **8** Aghlabid, Almohade **10** Husseinite
    leader: **6** Ben Ali **9** Bourguiba
  language: **6** Arabic, Berber, French
  religion: **5** Islam **7** Judaism **12** Christianity
  place:
    center of Tunis: **13** Place d'Afrique
    mosque: **5** Great **7** Zitouna
    museum: **5** Bardo, Kouba **6** Sousse
    palace: **14** Dar Ben Abdallah
    ruins: **8** Carthage
    street: **14** Habib Bourguiba
  feature:
    cap: **7** chechia
    clothing: **5** jebba **7** safasri **9** babbouche
    market: **4** souk
  food:
    dish: **7** mesfouf **8** couscous
    drink: **4** lban **5** legmi
    fruit: **12** deglet en nour

Tunney, Gene
  real name: **17** James Joseph Tunney
  nickname: **14** Fighting Marine
  sport: **6** boxing
  class: **11** heavyweight

Tuonela
  also: **6** Manala
  origin: **7** Finnish
  name of: **10** afterworld
  form: **6** island
  lacked: **3** sun **4** moon

Tupman
  character in: **14** Pickwick Papers
  author: **7** Dickens

tu quoque 7 thou too

Turandot
  opera by: **7** Puccini
  character: **3** Liu **4** Pang, Ping, Pong **5** Calaf, Timur **8** Turandot (Princess of China)

turbid 5 muddy, murky **6** cloudy,

opaque, roiled **7** clouded, unclear **8** agitated **9** disturbed, stirred up, unsettled

turbulence 4 fury **6** frenzy, hubbub, tumult, unrest, uproar **7** ferment, rioting, torrent, turmoil **8** disorder, violence **9** agitation, commotion **10** excitement, unruliness **11** disturbance

turbulent 5 rowdy **6** fierce, raging, stormy, unruly **7** chaotic, furious, riotous, violent **8** agitated, restless **9** clamorous, disturbed **10** blustering, boisterous, disorderly, tumultuous, uproarious **11** tempestuous

tureen 4 bowl, dish **9** casserole, container **10** receptacle

turf 3 sod **4** area, peat, plot, soil **5** divot, grass, haunt, sward, track **7** verdure **9** racetrack, territory **10** greensward

Turgenev, Ivan
author of: 5 Smoke **9** First Love **10** Virgin Soil **14** Fathers and Sons **18** A Month in the Country **19** A Sportsman's Notebook, A Sportsman's Sketches, The Torrents of Spring

turgid 5 puffy, showy **6** florid, ornate **7** flowery, pompous, swollen **8** inflated, puffed up **9** bombastic, grandiose, overblown **10** hyperbolic

Turkey
capital: 6 Angora, Ankara
largest city: 8 Istanbul
others: 4 Enos, Troy, Urfa **5** Adana, Bursa, Izmir, Konya, Maras, Siirt, Sivas **6** Aintab, Edessa, Edirne, Elaziz, Marash, Samsun, Smyrna **7** Antakya, Antioch, Erzurum, Kayseri, MMersin, Scutari, Trabzon, Uskudar **8** Stamboul **9** Byzantium, Eskisehir, Gaziantep **10** Adrianople **14** Constantinople
school: 6 Aegean, Ankara **8** Istanbul
division: 4 Pera, Sert **5** Siirt, Troad **6** Angora, Eyalet, Thrace **7** Anadolu, Beyoglu, Cilicia **8** Anatolia **9** Asia Minor, Kurdistan
measure: 3 dra, oka, pik **4** draa, khat, kile, zira **5** berri, kileh, zirai **6** arshin, chinik, fortin, halebi **7** nocktat
monetary unit: 4 lira, para **5** akcha, asper, kurus, pound, rebia **6** akcheh, zequin **7** aetilik, beshlik, piaster **8** medjidie
weight: 3 oka, oke **4** aqui, dram, rotl **5** artal, cheke, kerat, obolu, ratel **6** batman, dirhem, kantar, maunch, miskal **7** drachma, quintal, yusdrum
island: 6 Cyprus, Kibris
lake: 3 Tuz, Van **7** Egridir **8** Beysehir
mountain: 2 Ak **3** Ala **4** Alai, Dagh, Kara **5** Hasan, Hinis, Honaz, Murat, Murit **6** Ala Dag, Bingol, Bolgar, Pontic, Suphan, Taurus **7** Aladagh, Erciyas **8** Karacali **10** Kackar Dagi
highest point: 6 Ararat
river: 4 Aras, Kura **5** Araks, Dicle,

Firat, Gediz, Goksu, Halys, Irmak, Kizil, Mesta, Murat, Sarus **6** Araxes, Ceyhan, Seihun, Seyhan, Seylan, Tigris **7** Kurucay, Muradsu, Orontes, Sakarya **8** Granicus, Macestus, Maeander, Menderes **9** Euphrates **13** Buyukmenderes
sea: 4 Aral **5** Black **6** Aegean **7** Marmara **13** Mediterranean
physical feature:
  cape: 4 Baba, Ince **5** Bafra **6** Anamur, Helles, Hinzir **7** Karatas, Kerempe
  gulf: 3 Cos **5** Izmir **7** Antalya
  inlet: 10 Golden Horn
  peninsula: 9 Anatolian, Gallipoli
  plateau: 9 Anatolian
  strait: 8 Bosporus **9** Bosphorus **11** Dardanelles
people: 4 Arab, Kurd, Turk **6** Seljuk
  king: 8 Mausolus
  leader: 5 Inonu, Osman **6** Ecevit **7** Demirel **8** Menderes, Suleiman **12** Kemal Ataturk
  poet: 5 Homer
language: 6 Arabic **7** Kurdish, Turkish
religion: 5 Islam **7** Judaism **12** Christianity **13** Greek Orthodox, Roman Catholic
place:
  bridge: 6 Galata
  dam: 8 Gokcekaya
  mosque: 4 Blue, Yeni **8** Selimiye **11** Hagia Sophia, Sultan Ahmed
  museum: 7 Topkapi
  ruins: 4 Troy **7** Ephesus **8** Pergamum
  tomb: 12 Kemal Ataturk
feature:
  cap: 3 fez **6** calpac **7** calpack
  clothing: 6 caftan, dolman, jelick **7** yashrak **8** charshaf, maharmah, shakseer
  goat hair: 6 mohair
  grill: 6 mangal
  harem: 5 serai **8** seraglio
  musical instrument: 5 canum, kanum **6** canoon, johnie, kussir, zither **8** crescent, jingling
  pipe: 10 meerschaum
food:
  dish: 5 halva, pilaw **10** doner kebab, shish kebab
  drink: 4 boza, raki **5** airan, pasha, rakee **6** mastic
  pastry: 7 baklava
  turkey: 4 hind

Turkic
language family: 6 Altaic
group: 5 Kazak, Nogai, Uigur, Uzbek, Yakut **7** Chuvash, Kirghiz **8** Turkoman **10** Karakalpak **11** Azerbaijani **14** Osmanli Turkish

Turkmenistan
capital/largest city: 9 Ashkhabad
head of state: 9 president
government: 8 republic

monetary unit: 5 ruble
river: 8 Amu Darya
sea: 7 Caspian
physical feature: 13 Kara Kum Desert
people: 7 Turkmen **10** Turkmenian
language: 6 Turkic **10** West Turkic
religion: 11 Sunni Muslim
feature: 9 Altyn Depe

turmeric
botanical name: 12 Curcuma longa
also called: 7 tumeric **13** Crocus indicus, Indian saffron
family: 6 ginger
color: 6 yellow
used as: 3 dye **6** amulet **8** cosmetic, medicine
origin: 4 Asia **9** Caribbean, East India
charm against: 5 ghost **10** tree spirit

turmoil 4 mess **5** chaos **6** tumult, uproar **7** ferment **8** disorder **9** agitation, commotion, confusion **10** convulsion **11** disturbance, pandemonium
French: 14 bouleversement

turn 2 do, go **3** act, arc, lie, put **4** bend, coil, come, deed, flex, hang, look, loop, make, rest, ride, roll, send, shot, sour, spin, time, veer, walk, wing **5** alter, apply, crack, curve, drive, eject, fling, hinge, pivot, round, scare, shift, shock, spell, spoil, start, stint, swing, throw, twist, whack, wheel, whirl **6** action, become, chance, change, curdle, depend, direct, effort, fright, gyrate, invert, period, reside, rotate, sprain, stroll, swerve, swivel, wrench, zigzag **7** acidify, attempt, convert, deliver, execute, ferment, perform, reverse, revolve, service, winding **8** gyration, overturn, roll over, rotation, surprise **9** cause to go, deviation, discharge, transform **10** accomplish, alteration, revolution

turn a deaf ear to 6 ignore, slight **9** disregard

turn aside 5 avert **6** divert **7** deflect, deviate **8** turn away

turn away 5 avert **6** give up **8** alienate, estrange, send away **9** turn aside **12** turn one's back

turnback 4 fold, quit, tack **5** repel **6** defect, desert, return, revert **7** forsake, regress, relapse, repulse, retrace, retreat, reverse **9** backslide

turncoat 5 Judas **6** bolter **7** traitor **8** apostate, betrayer, defector, deserter, quisling, renegade **12** double-dealer

turn down 5 spurn **6** refuse, reject **14** lower the volume, refuse to accept

Turner, Joseph Mallord William
born: 6 London **7** England
artwork: 12 The Shipwreck, The Slave Ship, Tintern Abbey **17** Dawn After the Wreck **20** Dido Building Carthage **22** Venice S Giorgio Maggiore **24** The Sun of Venice Going to Sea **25** The Thames near Walton

Bridge, Ulysses Deriding Polyphemus **30** Burning of the Houses of Parliament **32** Snowstorm Hannibal Crossing the Alps **32** The Falls of the Rhine at Schaffhausen **34** The Bay of Baiae with Apollo and the Sibyl **37** Fighting Temeraire Tugged to her Last Berth **47** The Parting of Hero and Leander from the Greek of Musaeus **50** The Shipwreck Fishing Boats Endeavoring to Rescue the Crew

Turner, Kathleen
  roles: **8** Body Heat **9** Serial Mom **12** Prizzi's Honor **13** The Real Blonde, War of the Roses **17** Romancing the Stone, The Jewel of the Nile **18** Peggy Sue Got Married

Turner, Lana
  real name: **29** Julia Jean Mildred Frances Turner
  nickname: **11** Sweater Girl
  born: **9** Wallace ID
  discovered at: **16** Schwab's Drugstore
  husband: **9** Artie Shaw, Lex Barker **10** Bob Topping **12** Stephen Crane
  roles: **7** Madame X **11** Peyton Place **15** By Love Possessed, Imitation of Life **26** The Postman Always Rings Twice

turning 4 bend **5** curve **7** bending, curving, winding **8** pivoting, rotating, spinning, twisting, whirling **9** revolving, swiveling

turnip 12 Brassica rapa
  group: **8** Rapifera
  varieties: **6** Indian **7** Italian, Swedish **8** rutabaga, seven-top

turn off 4 bore, exit **5** douse, leave, repel **6** revolt, sicken **7** disgust, repulse **8** alienate, turn away **9** switch off **10** deactivate

turn of phrase 5 idiom **8** locution, phrasing **10** expression **11** phraseology

Turn of the Screw, The
  author: **10** Henry James
  character: **5** Flora, Miles **7** Mr Quint **8** Mrs Grose **10** Miss Jessel **12** The Governess

turn on 5 start, tempt **6** allure, attack, entice, excite **7** actuate, attract **8** activate, energize, interest, switch on

turn one's stomach 6 revolt, sicken **7** disgust **8** nauseate

turnout 5 crowd **6** output, throng **8** assembly, audience **9** gathering **10** assemblage, production

turn out 4 garb, oust **5** array, dress, eject, end up, evict, exile, expel **6** appear, attend, attire, banish, clothe, evolve, fit out, invest, rig out, show up, unfold **7** cast out, come out, costume, develop, kick out **8** drive out, send away **9** switch off **11** come to light

turn over 4 flip **5** upset **6** bestow, ro-

tate **7** deliver **8** flipflop, give over, hand over, overturn **9** surrender **10** relinquish, somersault

turn pale 4 fade **6** blanch, whiten **7** lighten

turn tail 4 flee **7** retreat, run away **8** back away **12** beat a retreat

turn to account 7 exploit, utilize **8** profit by, put to use **9** make use of **12** capitalize on

turn topsy turvy 5 upset **7** capsize, confuse, tip over **8** flip-flop, overturn, put askew **10** disarrange, turn turtle **11** disorganize

turn turtle 5 upset **7** capsize, tip over **8** flip over, keel over, overturn, turn over **14** turn upside down

turn up 4 come **6** appear, arrive, crop up, drop in, emerge, loom up, show up **7** develop, surface **11** come to light

Turpentine State
  nickname of: **13** North Carolina

turpitude 4 evil, vice **8** baseness, lewdness, vileness **9** depravity **10** corruption, debauchery, defilement, degeneracy, immorality, perversion, sinfulness, wickedness, wrongdoing **13** dissoluteness **14** licentiousness

turquoise 4 aqua **5** stone **7** mineral, sky-blue **10** aquamarine **12** greenish-blue, Prussian-blue
  source: **12** United States

turret 5 tower **6** belfry, cupola, garret, gazebo, louver, terret **7** minaret, rotator, steeple **8** gunhouse, gunmount **9** belvedere, pepperbox **10** watchtower
  tool: **5** lathe

turtle 3 box **4** musk, wood **6** slider **7** painted, reptile, snapper, spotted **8** slowpoke, terrapin, tortoise **10** turtle-dove **11** leatherback
  dorsal shell: **8** carapace
  nautical: **5** upset **6** pocket **7** capsize **8** overturn
  order: **8** Chelonia
  ventral shell: **8** plastron
  young: **7** turtlet

Turveydrop
  character in: **10** Bleak House
  author: **7** Dickens

tussle 4 fray **5** brawl, fight, melee, scrap, set-to **6** battle, fracas **7** grapple, scuffle, wrestle **8** conflict, struggle **10** donnybrook, free-for-all **11** altercation

tussock 4 hair, tuft **5** brush, bunch, clump, grass, sedge **7** bulrush, cluster, thicket **8** feathers

tutelage 8 coaching, guidance, teaching, training, tutoring **9** direction, education, schooling **10** discipline **11** inculcation, instruction, supervision, trusteeship **12** guardianship **14** indoctrination

tutor 4 guru **5** coach, drill, teach **6** master, mentor, school **7** prepare,

teacher **8** instruct **10** instructor **11** give lessons

tutorial 5 class **8** didactic, edifying **11** educational, instructive **12** prescriptive

tutti
  music: **3** all **18** all players together, all singers together

Tuvalu
  other name: **13** Ellice Islands, Lagoon Islands
  capital: **8** Funafuti
  head of state: **14** British monarch **15** governor general
  monetary unit: **4** cent **6** dollar
  island: **3** Nui **6** Niutao **7** Nanumea, Vaitupu **8** Funafuti **9** Nanumanga, Niulakita, Nukufetau **10** Nukulaelae
  highest point: **5** Nuwak
  sea: **7** Pacific
  people: **6** Samoan **10** Polynesian
  leader: **5** Lauti
  language: **6** Samoan **7** English **8** Tuvaluan **10** Polynesian
  religion: **10** Protestant **12** Tuvalu Church

twaddle 3 rot **4** bosh, bunk **5** trash, tripe **6** babble, drivel, gabble, jabber, piffle **7** chatter, prattle, rubbish **8** claptrap, idle talk, nonsense, tommy rot **9** jabbering, silly talk **10** balderdash **16** stuff-and-nonsense

Twain, Mark
  real name: **13** Samuel Clemens
  author of: **9** Tom Sawyer **10** Roughing It **12** A Tramp Abroad, The Gilded Age **15** (Adventures of) Huckleberry Finn **18** The Innocents Abroad **20** Life on the Mississippi **21** The Mysterious Stranger, The Prince and the Pauper **29** The Man That Corrupted Hadleyburg **36** A Connecticut Yankee in King Arthur's Court **41** The Celebrated Jumping Frog of Calaveras County

twang 9 resonance, vibration **10** nasal sound **13** reverberation

Tweedledee
  character in: **22** Through the Looking Glass
  author: **7** Carroll

Tweedledum
  character in: **22** Through the Looking Glass
  author: **7** Carroll

tweet 4 peep **5** cheep, chirp **7** chirrup, chitter, twitter

Twelfth Night
  author: **18** William Shakespeare
  character: **5** Feste, Maria, Viola (Cesario) **6** Olivia, Orsino **7** Antonio **8** Malvolio **9** Sebastian **12** Sir Toby Belch **18** Sir Andrew Aguecheek

Twelve Angry Men
  director: **11** Sidney Lumet
  cast: **8** Ed Begley, Lee J Cobb **10** E G Marshall, Henry Fonda, Jack Warden

11 Jack Klugman, John Fiedler 12 Martin Balsam

Twelve O'Clock High
director: 9 Henry King
cast: 10 Dean Jagger 11 Gary Merrill, Gregory Peck, Hugh Marlowe 15 Millard Mitchell
Oscar for: 15 supporting actor (Jagger)

Twentieth Century
director: 11 Howard Hawks
based on play by:.8 Ben Hecht 16 Charles MacArthur
cast: 11 Roscoe Karns 13 Carole Lombard, John Barrymore 14 Walter Connolly

Twentieth Century, The
narrator: 14 Walter Cronkite

twenty-one *see* 9 blackjack

Twenty Questions
host: 10 Bill Slater, Jay Jackson
panelist: 11 Herb Polesie 12 Bobby McGuire 13 Johnnie McPhee 14 Dickie Harrison, Florence Rinard 15 Fred Van De Venter

Twenty Thousand Leagues Under the Sea
author: 10 Jules Verne
character: 7 Conseil, Ned Land 11 Captain Nemo 22 Professor Pierre Aronnax
submarine: 8 Nautilus

Twenty Years After
author: 14 Alexandre Dumas (pere)

Twice-Told Tales
author: 18 Nathaniel Hawthorne

Twightwee *see* 5 Miami

twilight 3 ebb, eve 4 dusk 6 sunset 7 decline, evening, sundown 8 eventide, gloaming, moonrise 9 half-light, last phase, nightfall 14 edge of darkness

Twilight of the Gods 8 Ragnarok
German: 15 Gotterdammerung

Twilight Zone, The
host: 10 Rod Serling

twin 4 dual, like 5 alike 6 double, paired 7 matched, twofold 9 duplicate, identical

Twin 6 Thomas

twine 4 coil, cord, rope, wind 5 braid, cable, plait, twist, weave 6 string, thread 7 binding, entwine 9 interlace 10 intertwine

twinge 4 pain, pang, stab 5 cramp, spasm, throb 6 stitch, tingle, twitch

twinkle 4 glow 5 blaze, flare, flash, gleam, shine 7 flicker, glimmer, glisten, shimmer, sparkle 11 scintillate

Twinkleton, Miss
character in: 22 The Mystery of Edwin Drood
author: 7 Dickens

Twins
constellation of: 6 Gemini

twirl 4 spin 5 pivot, twine, wheel,

whirl 6 gyrate, rotate 7 revolve 9 pirouette

twist 3 arc, way 4 bend, coil, curl, idea, kink, knot, pull, roll, spin, turn, veer, wind, wrap, yank 5 curve, pivot, ravel, slant, snake, swing, twine, whirl, wrest 6 change, method, notion, rotate, spiral, sprain, swerve, swivel, system, tangle, wrench, zigzag 7 contort, distort, entwine, meander 8 approach, rotation, surprise 9 corkscrew, interlace, treatment 10 intertwine, involution 11 convolution, development

twisted 4 bent 6 warped 7 crooked, gnarled 8 deformed 9 contorted, distorted, misshapen

twisting 7 crooked, curving, turning 9 contorted, revolving, spiraling, swiveling

twist out of shape 4 warp 6 deform 7 contort, distort

twitch 3 tic 4 jerk 5 shake, spasm, throb 6 quaver, quiver, squirm, tremor, wiggle, writhe 7 tremble 8 paroxysm 10 convulsion

twitter 4 fuss, peep, stew 5 cheep, chirp, tizzy, tweet, whirl 6 bustle, flurry, pother, uproar, warble 7 chatter, chirrup, ferment, fluster, flutter 8 chirping 10 turbulence 11 chirrupping

two-faced 5 false 7 devious 8 slippery 9 deceitful, deceptive, dishonest, insincere 10 perfidious 11 dissembling, double-faced, duplicitous, forktongued, treacherous, underhanded 12 dishonorable, disingenuous, falsehearted, hypocritical 13 doubledealing, untrustworthy

twofold 4 dual 6 double 7 two-part

Two Gentlemen of Verona, The
author: 18 William Shakespeare
character: 5 Julia 6 Silvia, Thurio 7 Proteus 9 Valentine 11 Duke of Milan

Two Lands, The *see* 5 Egypt

two of a kind 4 pair 5 twins 6 couple 7 doublet

two-part 4 dual, twin 6 double, paired 9 bipartite

twosome 3 duo 4 pair 5 brace 6 couple

2001: A Space Odyssey
author: 13 Arthur C Clarke
director: 14 Stanley Kubrick
character: 4 Dave 5 Steve
computer: 3 HAL
cast: 3 HAL 10 Keir Dullea 12 Gary Lockwood 16 William Sylvester
song: 20 Thus Spake Zarathustra (Richard Strauss)
sequel: 24 Two Thousand Ten: Odyssey Two

two-time 6 betray 10 be disloyal 11 double-cross 12 be unfaithful 13 be

treacherous, play false with 14 break faith with

two-timing 5 false 6 tricky 7 perfidy 8 bad faith, betrayal, disloyal, trickery 9 deceiving, deception, duplicity, falseness, treachery 10 disloyalty, perfidious 11 double-cross, duplicitous, treacherous 13 breach of faith, double-dealing, faithlessness 14 doublecrossing

two-wheeler 4 bike 5 cycle 7 bicycle

Two Years Before the Mast
author: 18 Richard Henry Dana Jr

Tybalt
character in: 14 Romeo and Juliet
author: 11 Shakespeare

Tyche
origin: 5 Greek
goddess of: 7 fortune
corresponds to: 7 Fortuna

tycoon 4 boss 5 mogul, nabob 6 big gun, bigwig 7 big shot, magnate 8 big wheel 9 potentate 12 entrepreneur 13 industrialist 17 captain of industry

tyke 3 kid, tad, tot 5 child 6 shaver, squirt, wee one 9 little one

Tyler, John
presidential rank: 5 tenth
party: 4 Whig 20 Democratic-Republican
state represented: 2 VA 8 Virginia
defeated: 5 no-one
  succeeded upon death of: 8 Harrison
vice president: 4 none
cabinet:
  state: 6 (Abel Parker) Upshur 7 (Daniel) Webster, (John C) Calhoun
  treasury: 4 (George Mortimer) Bibb 5 (Thomas) Ewing 7 (John Canfield) Spencer, (Walter) Forward
  war: 4 (John) Bell 7 (John Canfield) Spencer, (William) Wilkins
  attorney general: 6 (Hugh Swinton) Legare, (John) Nelson 10 (John Jordan) Crittenden
  navy: 5 (John Young) Mason 6 (Abel Parker) Upshur, (George Edmund) Badger, (Thomas Walker) Gilmer
  postmaster general: 7 (Francis) Granger 9 (Charles Anderson) Wickliffe
born: 2 VA 8 Greenway, Virginia 17 Charles City County
died/buried: 2 VA 8 Richmond, Virginia
education: 14 William and Mary
religion: 12 Episcopalian
vacation spot: 2 VA 7 Hampton 8 Virginia
political career: 8 US Senate 12 State Council 13 vice president 24 US House of Representatives
  delegate to: 13 State Assembly
  governor of: 8 Virginia

civilian career: 6 farmer, lawyer
military service: 19 War of Eighteen Twelve
notable events of lifetime/term:
  act: 6 Tariff (of 1842)
  annexation of: 5 Texas
  treaty: 16 Webster-Ashburton
father: 4 John
mother: 4 Mary (Marott Armistead)
siblings: 7 William **8** Wat Henry **10** Maria Henry **12** Anne Contesse **14** Christina Booth **15** Martha Jefferson **18** Elizabeth Armistead
wife: 5 Julia (Gardiner) **7** Letitia (Christian)
children: 4 John, Mary **5** Alice, Julia, Pearl **6** Robert **7** Lachlan, Letitia **8** Tazewell **9** Elizabeth **12** Anne Contesse, Lyon Gardiner **13** David Gardiner, John Alexander **16** Robert FitzWalter

Tyll Eulenspiegel *see* **16** Till Eulenspiegel

Tyndall, John
  field: 7 physics
  nationality: 5 Irish
  studied diffusion of: 5 light

Tyndareus
  wife: 4 Leda
  daughter: 6 Phoebe **8** Philonoe, Timandra **12** Clytemnestra

Tyndaridae *see* **15** Castor and Pollux

typo 4 font, kind, race, sort **5** brand, class, genus, group, model, order, print **6** design, family, phylum, sample **7** pattern, species, variety **8** category, division, specimen, typeface **9** archetype, prototype **10** typography

type, movable
  invented by: 9 Gutenberg

Typee
  author: 14 Herman Melville
  character: 3 Tom (Melville) **4** Toby **6** Marnoo, Mehevi **7** Fayaway **8** Kory-Kory

typewriter

invented by: 5 Soule **6** Sholes **7** Glidden

Typhoeus
  form: 7 monster
  father: 8 Tartarus
  mother: 2 Ge
  number of heads: 10 one hundred

typhoon 4 gale, gust, wind **5** storm **7** cyclone, tempest, tornado, twister **9** hurricane, whirlwind

Typhoon
  author: 12 Joseph Conrad

typical 5 model, stock, usual **6** normal **7** average, regular **8** ordinary, orthodox, standard **9** exemplary, in keeping **10** individual, prototypal, true to type **11** distinctive, in character **12** conventional, to be expected **14** characteristic, representative

typify 5 sum up **6** embody **7** betoken, connote, pass for **8** instance, stand for **9** epitomize, exemplify, incarnate, personify, represent **10** illustrate **12** characterize

typography measure 2 em, en **4** pica **5** point

Tyr
  origin: 12 Scandinavian
  god of: 7 victory
  father: 4 Odin **5** Othin
  mother: 3 Fri **5** Frigg, Frija **6** Frigga
  killed by: 4 Garm

tyrannical 7 fascist **8** despotic **9** imperious **10** oppressive **11** dictatorial, domineering **13** authoritarian

tyrannize 7 oppress **8** domineer, overlord **10** slave drive

tyrannized 9 exploited, oppressed **11** downtrodden, subservient **12** harshly ruled

Tyrannosaurus
  type: 8 dinosaur, theropod
  location: 7 Montana **12** North America
  period: 10 Cretaceous

tyrannous 8 despotic **9** imperious **10** iron-handed, oppressive, repressive, tyrannical

tyranny 7 cruelty, fascism **8** coercion, iron fist, iron hand, iron rule, severity **9** despotism, harshness **10** domination, oppression, repression **11** persecution **12** dictatorship **13** reign of terror **15** totalitarianism

tyrant 5 bully **6** despot **8** dictator, martinet **10** persecutor, taskmaster **11** cruel master, slave driver

Tyre
  king of: 5 Hiram

tyro 6 intern, novice, rookie **7** learner, recruit, trainee **8** beginner, initiate, neophyte, newcomer **9** greenhorn **10** apprentice, tenderfoot

Tyro
  father: 9 Salmoneus
  loved by: 8 Cretheus, Poseidon
  son: 5 Aeson **6** Neleus, Pelias
  grandson: 5 Jason **6** Nestor

Tyrrheus
  occupation: 8 shepherd

Tyson, Cicely
  born: 9 New York NY
  roles: 5 Roots **7** Sounder **33** The Autobiography of Miss Jane Pittman

Tyson, Mike
  original name: 7 Michael
  nickname: 8 Iron Mike
  born: 2 NY **8** Brooklyn **17** Bedford-Stuyvesant
  wife: 11 Robin Givens
  manager: 9 Cus D'Amato **10** Bill Cayton **11** Jimmy Jacobs
  trainer: 12 Angelo Dundee
  promoter: 7 Don King
  boxing title: 3 IBF, WBA, WBC **11** heavyweight
  defeated: 6 Holmes, Spinks, Thomas, Tillis, Tucker **7** Berbick
  defeated by: 7 Douglas (Buster)
  convicted of: 4 rape

tzimmes 4 fuss **6** uproar **10** hullabaloo
  literally: 4 stew **9** mixed dish

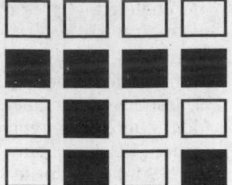  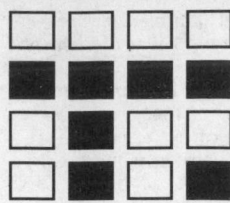

U

Ubangi-Shari *see* **22** Central African Republic

Ubermensch 8 superman

ubiquitous 7 allover **9** pervading, pervasive, prevalent, universal, worldwide **10** everywhere, widespread **11** everpresent, omnipresent **12** all-pervading

ubiquitously 10 everywhere **11** extensively

ubi supra 19 where mentioned above

Ucalegon
  counselor to: **5** Priam

Uccello, Paolo
  real name: **11** Paolo di Dono
  born: **5** Italy **8** Florence
  artwork: **8** The Flood **12** The Night Hunt **15** Sir John Hawkwood **18** The Rout (Battle) of San Romano **20** St George and the Dragon

Udall, Nicholas
  author of: **19** Ralph Roister Doister

Uganda
  capital/largest city: **7** Kampala
  others: **4** Arua, Gulu, Lira **5** Atiak, Jinja, Mbale, Mengo **6** Kasese, Kiboga, Kitgum, Masaka, Moroto, Pajule, Soroti, Tororo **7** Entebbe, Kachung, Kilembe, Mbarara, Mombasa **8** Kyenjojo **11** Port Masindi
  school: **8** Makerere
  division: **4** Toro **6** Ankole, Busoga **7** Buganda, Bunyoro
  monetary unit: **4** cent **8** shilling
  island: **4** Sese
  lake: **5** Kioga, Kyoga **6** Albert, Edward, George **8** Victoria
  mountain: **4** Oboa **5** Elgon **7** Virunga **9** Mufumbiro, Ruwenzori **18** Mountains of the Moon
  highest point: **10** Margherita
  river: **4** Aswa, Kafu **5** Pager **7** Katonga **9** White Nile **10** Albert Nile **12** Victoria Nile
  physical feature:
    falls: **5** Owens **8** Kabalega **9** Murchison
    plateau: **6** Ankole **11** East African
    valley: **9** Great Rift
  people: **4** Alur, Gisu, Soga, Teso **5** Ateso, Bantu, Chiga, Ganda, Langi, Lango, Nkole, Pygmy **6** Acholi, Ankole, Bagisu, Bakega, Basiga, Batoro **7** Baganda, Banyoro, Bunyoro, Hamitic, Lugbara, Nilotic, Sudanic **9** Nyoro-Toro **10** Banyankole, Karamojong
    explorer: **5** Baker, Speke **7** Stanley
    king: **6** Mutesa, Mwanga **8** Kabarega
    leader: **5** Obote **6** Mutesa **7** Omukama **11** Idi Amin Dada
  language: **5** Ateso, Ganda **7** English, Luganda, Swahili
  religion: **5** Islam **7** animism **8** Anglican **10** Protestant **13** Roman Catholic
  place:
    airport: **7** Entebbe
    dam: **10** Owens Falls
    national park: **6** Kidepo **14** Murchison Falls, Queen Elizabeth
  feature:
    clothing: **7** busuuti
    council of chiefs: **6** lukiko
    dance group: **17** Heart Beat of Africa
    king: **6** kabaka
  food:
    drink: **6** waragi

ugliness 8 ill-favor **9** grossness **10** homeliness **11** hideousness, monstrosity **12** unseemliness **13** frightfulness, grotesqueness, monstrousness, repulsiveness, unsightliness **14** unpleasantness **16** unattractiveness

ugly 4 foul, mean, vile **5** nasty **6** homely, horrid, odious **7** hideous, hostile, ominous **8** dreadful, horrible, menacing, unseemly **9** abhorrent, dangerous, difficult, frightful, grotesque, monstrous, obnoxious, offensive, repellent, repugnant, repulsive, sickening, unsightly **10** abominable, disgusting

ugly as sin 7 hideous **9** frightful, grotesque, monstrous, repulsive

Ugly Duckling, The
  author: **21** Hans Christian Andersen

ukase 4 fiat **5** edict, order **6** decree, dictum, ruling **7** command, mandate, statute **9** directive, manifesto, ordinance **10** injunction **12** proclamation **13** pronouncement

Ukraine
  capital/largest city: **4** Kiev
  others: **4** Lviv (Lvov), **6** Odessa **7** Donetsk, Kharkov, Lugansk (Voroshilovgrad) **8** Mariupol (Zhdanov) **9** Krivoi Rog, Zaporozhe **14** Dnepropetrovsk
  head of state: **9** president
  government: **8** republic
  monetary unit: **6** grivna **10** karbovanet
  mountain: **7** Crimean **10** Carpathian
  river: **3** Bug **6** Donets **7** Dnieper
  sea: **5** Black
  people: **7** Russian **9** Ukrainian
  language: **9** Ukrainian
  religion: **17** Ukrainian Catholic, Ukrainian Orthodox
  feature: **25** Askaniya Nova Nature Reserve

Ulan Bator
  capital of: **8** Mongolia

ulcer 4 sore **6** canker

Uller
  also: **4** Ullr
  origin: **8** Teutonic
  god of: **12** winter sports
  stepfather: **4** Thor

Ullmann, Liv
  born: **5** Japan, Tokyo
  nationality: **9** Norwegian
  roles: **7** Persona **10** Face to Face **11** Forty Carats, Lost Horizon **12** The Emigrants **16** Cries and Whispers **19** Scenes from a Marriage

ulna
  bone of: **8** lower arm
  neighbor: **6** radius

ulterior 6 covert, hidden, secret **7** selfish **9** concealed **10** undivulged, unrevealed **11** self-serving, undisclosed, unexpressed **13** opportunistic

ultimate 3 end **4** acme, apex, last, peak **5** final **6** height, utmost **7** extreme, maximum, supreme **8** crowning, eventual, greatest, terminal **9** at the peak, high point, last straw, long-range, resulting **10** conclusive, definitive
  French: **7** dernier

Ultima Thule 12 far-off region **15** uttermost degree

Ultor
  epithet of: **7** Jupiter
  means: **7** avenger

ultra 7 extreme **9** excessive, extremist

ultramodern 8 advanced, brand-new **10** avant-garde, newfangled **13** in the vanguard, up-to-the-minute

ulu 5 knife
  used by: **11** Eskimo women

ululate 4 hoot, howl, wail **6** lament

Ulysses
  author: **10** James Joyce

character: 10 Molly Bloom **12** Blazes Boylan, Buck Mulligan, Leopold Bloom **14** Stephen Dedalus

Ulysses *see* **8** Odysseus

umber 5 brown **7** pigment **9** dark-brown **14** yellowish-brown

umbilicus 5 navel **11** belly button

umbrage 5 pique, shade **6** leaves, shadow **7** foliage, offense, outrage **10** resentment

umbrella 6 brolly **7** parasol **11** bumbershoot

Umbrellas of Cherbourg, The
director: **11** Jacques Demy
cast: **10** Anne Vernon **15** Nino Castelnuovo **16** Catharine Deneuve
score: **13** Michel Legrand

Umbrian
language family: **12** Indo-European
branch: **6** Italic

umpire 5 judge **7** arbiter, mediate, referee **8** mediator, moderate **9** arbitrate, go-between, moderator **10** adjudicate, arbitrator, negotiator **11** adjudicator, intercessor

umpteen 4 many, slew **5** loads (of)

Una
character in: **15** The Faerie Queene
author: **7** Spenser

unabbreviated 5 uncut **8** complete, undocked, unpruned **9** uncropped, unreduced, unsnipped, untrimmed **10** full-length, unabridged **11** uncondensed, uncurtailed, unshortened **12** uncompressed, unexpurgated

unable 5 unfit **6** cannot **8** helpless, impotent **9** incapable **10** inadequate, unequipped **11** incompetent, unqualified
to tell pitch: **8** tone deaf

unabridged 5 uncut **6** entire, intact **8** complete **10** full-length **11** uncondensed

unacceptable 8 below par, improper, unseemly, unworthy **9** deficient, out of line, unwelcome **10** disallowed, inadequate, unsuitable **11** displeasing, intolerable **12** inadmissible, not allowable, not up to snuff **13** insupportable **14** unsatisfactory **15** not up to standard

unacceptableness 8 disfavor, disgrace, ignominy **18** unsatisfactoriness

unaccommodating 4 rude **8** churlish **9** difficult, unhelpful **10** inflexible, intolerant, unyielding **11** disobliging **13** inconsiderate

unaccompanied 4 lone, solo **5** alone, apart **6** single, singly **8** isolated, lonesome, separate, solitary **9** a cappella, by oneself **10** unattended, unescorted **12** all by oneself **13** companionless

unaccountable 3 odd **4** free **5** clear, queer, weird **6** exempt, immune **7** bizarre, curious, excused, strange, unusual **8** baffling, innocent, peculiar **9** blameless, not liable, unheard-of

10 inculpable, intriguing, mysterious, surprising **11** astonishing, unexplained **12** inexplicable, unfathomable **13** extraordinary, inexplicable, not responsible **16** incomprehensible

unaccustomed 3 new, odd **4** rare, wild **5** green, new to, novel, queer **6** quaint, unique, unused **7** amazing, bizarre, curious, foreign, not used, strange, ungiven, untried, unusual **8** original, peculiar, singular, uncommon **9** fantastic, startling, unheard-of **10** remarkable, surprising, unfamiliar, unversed in **11** astonishing, out-of-the-way, unpracticed **12** unacquainted, unhabituated, unimaginable **13** extraordinary, inexperienced **14** unfamiliar with **16** out of the ordinary

unacknowledged 9 anonymous **10** unanswered **11** disregarded **12** unidentified, unrecognized

unadorned 4 bald, bare **5** naked, plain, stark **6** simple **7** austere **11** undecorated **12** unornamented **13** unembellished **15** straightforward

unadulterated 4 pure, true **5** clear, uncut **7** genuine **9** unalloyed, untainted **14** untampered-with

unadventurous 5 chary, timid **7** careful **8** cautious, hesitant **11** circumspect

unadvisable 5 silly **6** stupid, unwise **8** unseemly **9** imprudent **11** inadvisable, inexpedient, injudicious, undesirable **15** disadvantageous

unaesthetic 9 tasteless **10** inartistic **11** insensitive **16** undiscriminating

unaffected 4 open **5** frank, naive, plain **6** candid, direct, honest, simple **7** genuine, natural, sincere, unmoved **8** innocent **9** childlike, guileless, ingenuous, unfeeling, unstirred, untouched, unworldly, wholesome **10** impervious, unbothered, unreserved **11** indifferent, insensitive, openhearted, plain-spoken, unconcerned, undesigning, undisturbed **12** unresponsive **13** unsympathetic **15** straightforward, unsophisticated

unaffectedness 4 ease **11** naturalness **12** unconstraint

unafraid 4 bold **5** brave **6** daring, heroic, plucky **7** valiant **8** fearless, intrepid, stalwart, valorous **9** audacious, daredevil, dauntless **10** courageous **11** indomitable, lionhearted, venturesome **12** stouthearted **13** adventuresome

unaggressive 3 shy **4** meek **5** timid **7** passive **8** peaceful, timorous **9** peaceable, shrinking **11** unambitious **14** unenterprising

unagitated 4 calm **6** gentle, placid, serene **8** composed, tranquil **9** collected, unexcited, unruffled **10** untroubled **11** undisturbed, unperturbed **13** self-possessed

unalloyed 4 pure **7** unmixed **11** unqualified **13** unadulterated

unalterable 5 fixed, rigid **6** stable **8** constant **9** immutable, indelible, obstinate, permanent, perennial **10** inflexible, persistent **11** irrevocable **12** indissoluble, unchangeable **13** irretrievable

unambitious 4 easy, lazy **6** humble, modest, simple **8** slothful **10** unaspiring **12** unaggressive **14** unenterprising

unamiable 4 sour **5** cross, surly, testy **6** sullen **7** grouchy, hostile, peevish **8** churlish **9** irascible **10** ill-humored, unfriendly, unpleasant, unsociable **11** bad-tempered, uncongenial **12** disagreeable

unamorous 4 cold, cool **6** frigid **8** unloving **11** passionless

unanimated 4 dull, flat, limp **5** inert, vapid **7** insipid **8** lifeless **10** insentient **11** unconscious

unanimity 6 accord **7** concord, harmony **9** agreement, consensus **11** concordance, concurrence **17** meeting of the minds

unanimous 6 allied, united **9** accordant, consonant, of one mind **10** harmonious, like-minded

unannounced 6 secret, sudden **8** surprise, withheld **10** suppressed, unheralded **11** undisclosed, unlooked for, unpublished **12** unadvertised **13** unanticipated

unanticipated 6 sudden **8** surprise **10** unexpected, unforeseen, unheralded **11** unannounced, unlooked-for, unpredicted

unappealing 10 disgusting, uninviting, unpleasant **11** displeasing **12** disagreeable, unappetizing, unattractive

unappetizing 6 horrid **7** insipid **10** bad-tasting, disgusting, uninviting **11** unpalatable **12** disagreeable

unapproachable 4 cold, cool **5** aloof **6** remote, unique **7** austere, awesome, distant, supreme **8** foremost, peerless, superior **9** matchless, nonpareil, unequaled, unrivaled **10** forbidding, inimitable, preeminent **11** beyond reach, stand-offish, unreachable **12** inaccessible, incomparable, intimidating, second to none, unattainable, unparalleled **13** beyond compare

unasked 6 wanton **8** unbidden, unsought, unwanted **9** uninvited, unwelcome **10** gratuitous **11** uncalled-for, undesirable, unrequested, unsolicited

unassertive 3 shy **5** timid **6** humble, modest **7** bashful **8** sheepish **9** diffident, shrinking

unassertiveness 7 modesty, shyness **8** docility, timidity **9** timidness **10** diffidence, humbleness **11** bashfulness **12** sheepishness

unassuming 5 muted, plain **6** homely, modest, simple **7** natural **9** easygoing

11 unassertive, unobtrusive **13** unpretentious **14** unostentatious

unattached 5 apart, split **6** single **8** detached, separate **9** separated **11** unconnected **12** disconnected

unattractive 4 dull, ugly **5** plain **6** homely **8** frumpish **11** unappealing, undesirable **12** unappetizing

unauthentic 4 fake, mock, sham **5** bogus, false, phony **6** untrue **7** dubious **8** doubtful **9** imitation, synthetic **10** fraudulent **11** counterfeit **12** questionable

unauthenticated 8 disputed **10** apocryphal, unverified **15** unsubstantiated

unauthorized 6 banned, covert **7** furtive **8** outlawed, unlawful **9** concealed, unallowed, underhand **10** prohibited, unapproved, unofficial **11** clandestine, uncertified, unpermitted, unwarranted **12** unaccredited, unsanctioned **13** under-the-table

unavailable 5 taken **6** scarce **7** lacking, married **9** not at hand **10** nonpresent **11** nonexistent

unavailing 4 idle, vain, weak **5** empty, inept **6** futile, no good **7** invalid, useless **8** bootless, impotent **9** fruitless, worthless **11** ineffective, ineffectual **12** unproductive, unsuccessful

unavoidable 4 sure **5** fated, fixed **7** certain **9** necessary, requisite **10** compulsory, imperative, inevitable, obligatory **11** inescapable **13** unpreventable **14** uncontrollable

unaware 8 heedless, ignorant, unwarned **9** in the dark, unalerted, unknowing, unmindful **10** unapprised **11** incognizant, unconscious **12** off one's guard, unacquainted, unsuspecting **13** unenlightened

unawares 8 abruptly, by chance, suddenly **9** by mistake **10** by accident, by surprise, mistakenly **11** unknowingly, unwittingly **12** accidentally, out of nowhere, unexpectedly, unthinkingly **13** inadvertently, involuntarily, unconsciously **14** without warning **15** unintentionally **16** like a thunderbolt **20** like a bolt from the blue, like a thief in the night

unbalanced 3 mad **4** daft, loco **5** batty, nutty, wacky **6** crazed, uneven, warped **7** bonkers, cracked, leaning, unequal, unglued, unsound **8** demented, deranged, lopsided, unhinged, unpoised, unstable, unsteady **9** disturbed, illogical, psychotic, unsettled **10** irrational, unadjusted **11** not all there **12** psychopathic

unbearable 11 intolerable, unendurable, unthinkable **12** inadmissible, insufferable, unacceptable **13** insupportable

unbecoming 4 ugly **6** homely, vulgar **8** improper, unfitted, unseemly,

unsuited **9** offensive, tasteless, unsightly **10** indecorous, unsuitable **11** unappealing, unbefitting **12** unattractive **13** inappropriate

unbelief 5 doubt **7** dubiety **9** disbelief **10** skepticism **11** incredulity **12** doubtfulness

unbelievable 5 false **6** absurd, insane **7** amazing, asinine, idiotic **10** astounding, farfetched, incredible, irrational, remarkable, ridiculous **11** astonishing **12** preposterous, unimaginable, unreasonable **13** hard to swallow

unbeliever 7 atheist, heathen infidel, skeptic **8** apostate **10** godless one **11** disbeliever, nonbeliever

unbelieving 7 dubious **8** doubting **9** quizzical, skeptical **10** suspicious **11** distrustful, incredulous, questioning, unconvinced **12** disbelieving, nonbelieving

unbend 5 relax **6** relent, unflex **10** straighten **12** straighten up **13** straighten out

unbending 4 firm **5** rigid, stiff, tough **6** severe, strict **8** stubborn **9** obstinate **10** inflexible, stone-faced, unyielding **11** hard as nails **14** uncompromising

unbent 5 erect **7** relaxed, unbowed, upright, yielded **8** relented, straight, uncurved, unflexed **9** unstooped **12** straightened

unbiased 4 fair, just **7** liberal, neutral **8** detached, tolerant **9** impartial, unbigoted **10** fair-minded, open-minded, undogmatic **11** broad-minded **12** uninfluenced, unprejudiced **13** disinterested, dispassionate

unbigoted 8 tolerant, unbiased **10** open-minded **11** broad-minded **12** unprejudiced

unbind 4 free, undo **5** loose, untie **6** detach, loosen, ungird **7** deliver, release, undress **8** let loose, unfasten

unblamable 5 clear **8** innocent **9** blameless, guiltless, not guilty **10** inculpable, not at fault **14** not responsible

unblemished 4 pure **7** perfect **8** flawless, spotless, unmarred, unsoiled **9** unsullied **10** immaculate, unvitiated **11** white as snow **13** unadulterated **14** uncontaminated **15** clean as a whistle

unblock 4 free, open **5** unbar, unjam **6** unclog, unstop

unborn 5 fetal, later **6** coming, future, to come **7** in utero **9** embryonic **10** subsequent, succeeding **11** prospective

unbosom oneself 7 confess, confide, lay bare **15** unburden oneself

unbound 4 free **5** freed, loose **6** loosed, untied **8** detached, let loose,

loosened, released **10** unconfined, unfastened **12** unrestrained

unbounded 8 absolute **9** boundless, unbridled, unlimited **12** uncontrolled, unrestrained, unrestricted **13** unconditional, unconstrained

unbreakable 5 tough **6** strong

unbroken 5 whole **6** entire, intact **7** endless **8** complete **9** ceaseless, continual, incessant, uncracked, undivided, unsmashed **10** continuous, sequential, successive, unruptured **11** consecutive, progressive, unremitting, unshattered **12** undiminished **13** uninterrupted

unbuckle 4 undo **6** loosen **7** release, unhitch, unstrap **8** uncouple, unfasten

unburden 4 free **6** reveal **7** confess, confide, relieve, unbosom **8** disclose **9** disburden **10** unencumber **11** disencumber **15** get off one's chest **18** get out of one's system

unbusinesslike 6 casual, sloppy **8** informal **11** impractical, inefficient

uncalculated 9 unplanned **10** accidental, unintended **11** inadvertent **14** unpremeditated

uncalled-for 6 wanton **7** unasked **8** needless, unneeded, unsought, unwanted **9** redundant, uninvited **10** gratuitous, unprompted **11** unjustified, unnecessary, unsolicited **12** nonessential **13** supererogatory

uncanny 5 eerie, weird **6** spooky **7** curious, strange **8** inspired **9** fantastic, intuitive, marvelous, unearthly, unheard-of, unnatural **10** incredible, mysterious, prodigious, remarkable, unexampled **11** astonishing, exceptional **12** unbelievable, unimaginable **13** extraordinary, uncomfortable

uncanonical 12 unauthorized, unscriptural

Uncas
 character in: **20** The Last of the Mohicans
 author: **6** Cooper

unceasing 7 endless, eternal **8** constant **9** continual, incessant, perpetual, sustained **10** continuous, persistent, without end

uncelebrated 6 unsung **7** obscure, unknown **9** anonymous **14** uncommemorated

unceremonious 4 curt, rude **5** hasty, rough **6** abrupt **7** brusque **8** informal **11** precipitate

uncertain 4 hazy **6** fitful, unsure **7** dubious, erratic, not sure, obscure, unclear **8** doubtful, hesitant, nebulous, not fixed, variable, wavering **9** debatable, undecided, unsettled **10** disputable, indefinite, indistinct, in question, irresolute, unresolved, up in the air **11** conjectural, fluctuating, not definite, speculative, unconfirmed, vacillating

12 not confident, questionable, undetermined **13** indeterminate, unpredictable

uncertainty 4 odds, risk **5** doubt **6** chance, gamble **8** quandary **9** ambiguity, confusion, hesitancy, vagueness **10** hesitation, indecision, perplexity, unsureness **11** ambivalence, vacillation **12** equivocation, irresolution, shilly-shally **14** indefiniteness

unchain 4 free **7** release, set free **8** liberate, unfetter **9** unshackle

unchangeable 5 rigid **6** stable **7** uniform **8** stubborn **9** immutable, obstinate, permanent **10** inflexible, invariable **11** unalterable **12** intransigent

unchanging 4 fast, firm **5** fixed **6** stable, static **7** abiding, durable, lasting **8** constant **9** immutable, permanent, steadfast **10** monotonous **11** everlasting **12** indissoluble

unchaperoned 10 unattended, unescorted **12** unsupervised **13** unaccompanied

uncharacteristic 8 atypical **12** out of keeping **16** unrepresentative

uncharitable 5 tight **6** stingy, unkind **7** miserly **9** illiberal, niggardly, unfeeling **10** unfriendly, ungenerous, ungracious **11** closefisted, insensitive, tightfisted **12** parsimonious **13** unsympathetic **15** uncompassionate

unchaste 4 lewd **5** loose **6** erotic, impure **7** corrupt, immoral **8** immodest **9** abandoned, debauched **10** dishonored

unchecked 4 free **5** loose **6** unruly **7** liberal, rampant **8** reinless, unreined **9** out of hand, unbridled, unmuzzled **10** unhindered **12** out of control, unrestrained, unsuppressed

uncial 6 script
   form: **5** large, round
   used in: **5** Greek, Latin

unciform 10 hook-shaped

uncivil 4 curt, rude **5** blunt, surly **6** abrupt, gauche **7** boorish, brusque **8** impolite **10** ungracious **11** ill-mannered **12** disagreeable, discourteous

uncivilized 4 rude **6** savage, vulgar **7** boorish, brutish, ill-bred, uncouth, untamed **8** barbaric, churlish **9** barbarous, obnoxious, ungenteel **10** uncultured, unpolished **12** uncultivated

unclad 4 bare, nude **5** naked **7** exposed, unrobed **8** disrobed, in the raw, starkers, stripped **9** in the nude, unclothed, uncovered, undressed **10** stark naked **15** in the altogether

unclean 4 evil, foul, tref, vile **5** dirty, dusty, grimy, messy, muddy, sooty **6** filthy, impure, soiled **7** defiled, immoral, obscene, smutted, stained **8** polluted, unchaste **9** blemished **10** besmirched

unclear 3 dim **4** hazy **5** blear, faint, foggy, fuzzy, misty, vague **6** bleary, cloudy, vapory **7** clouded, obscure, shadowy **8** shrouded, vaporous **9** ambiguous, uncertain **10** indefinite, indistinct

Uncle Remus
   author: **18** Joel Chandler Harris

Uncle Sam
   personification of: **7** America

Uncle Tom's Cabin
   author: **19** Harriet Beecher Stowe
   character: **5** Eliza, Topsy **10** Eva St Clare **11** Simon Legree

Uncle Vanya
   author: **12** Anton Chekhov
   character: **6** Marina **12** Mihail Astrov **13** Ivan Voynitsky (Uncle Vanya) **14** Marya Voynitsky **15** Sonya Andreyevna **16** Yelena Andreyevna **19** Alexandr Serebryakov

unclose 4 open **6** reveal, unclog, unfold, unshut, unstop, unwrap **7** unblock
   poetic: **3** ope

unclothed 4 bare, nude **5** naked **6** unclad **7** exposed, unrobed **8** stripped **9** in the nude, uncovered, undressed

unclouded 5 clear, light, sunny **6** bright, serene **10** unobscured

uncollected 4 owed **5** owing, upset **6** shaken **8** agitated, troubled **9** disturbed, perturbed **11** discomposed, outstanding

uncolored 4 bald, bare, true **5** plain, stark **6** simple **9** unadorned **11** unvarnished **12** unelaborated **13** unembellished **15** straightforward

uncombed 5 messy **6** blowsy, frowzy, matted, mussed, untidy **7** ruffled, rumpled, snarled, tangled, tousled, unkempt **11** disarranged

uncomfortable 4 edgy **5** tense, upset **6** on edge, uneasy **7** awkward, keyed up, nervous, painful **8** confused, strained, troubled **9** ill at ease **10** bothersome, disquieted, irritating, out of place **11** discomfited, discomposed, distressful **13** on tenterhooks

uncommitted 9 unpledged **11** undedicated

uncommon 4 rare **5** novel **6** scarce, unique **7** bizarre, curious, notable, supreme, unusual **8** peculiar, peerless, superior **9** matchless, unmatched **10** infrequent, remarkable, unexcelled, unfamiliar **11** exceptional, outstanding, superlative **12** incomparable, unparalleled **13** extraordinary **14** unconventional **15** once in a lifetime **16** few and far between

uncommunicative 3 mum, shy **4** dumb, mute **5** quiet **6** silent **8** reserved, reticent, retiring, taciturn **9** secretive, withdrawn **10** speechless, tongue-tied, unsociable **11** untalkative **12** close-mouthed, inexpressive

uncomplicated 4 easy **5** clear, plain **6** simple **10** uninvolved

uncomplimentary 8 critical, derisive, negative **9** insulting **10** unadmiring **11** disparaging **12** disapproving, unflattering

uncompromising 4 firm **5** rigid, stiff **6** strict **8** exacting, hardline, obdurate **9** immovable, unbending, unvarying **10** inexorable, inflexible, scrupulous, unyielding **11** unrelenting

unconcealed 4 bald, bare, open **5** overt **6** in view **7** exposed, in sight, obvious, visible **8** apparent, manifest, revealed **9** uncovered **11** discernible, perceivable, perceptible **12** in plain sight, out in the open

unconcentrated 4 weak **7** diffuse, diluted, thinned **9** dispersed, scattered, spread out **11** watered down

unconcern 10 dispassion **11** insouciance, nonchalance **12** indifference

unconcerned 4 cold **5** aloof **6** serene **7** distant, unaware, unmoved **8** composed, uncaring **9** apathetic, oblivious, unfeeling, unmindful **10** impervious, nonchalant, uninvolved, untroubled **11** indifferent, insensitive, passionless, unperturbed **12** unresponsive **13** unsympathetic

unconditional 5 utter **6** entire **8** absolute, complete, outright **9** downright, unlimited **10** conclusive **11** categorical, unqualified **12** unrestricted **13** thoroughgoing

unconfident 3 shy **5** timid **7** bashful **8** reticent, retiring, timorous **9** diffident, shrinking, uncertain

unconfirmed 7 dubious **8** unproved **10** unapproved, unverified **11** unvalidated **12** questionable **14** uncorroborated **15** unsubstantiated

unconformity 7 anomaly **9** deviation **10** aberration, divergence **11** abnormality, peculiarity **12** eccentricity, idiosyncrasy, irregularity **13** nonconformity

uncongenial 9 ill-suited, unamiable **10** dissimilar, unfriendly, unpleasant **12** disagreeable, incompatible **13** unsympathetic

unconnected 7 severed **8** detached, discrete, separate **9** uncoupled, unhitched, unrelated **12** disconnected

unconquerable 6 innate **9** ingrained **10** inveterate, invincible, unbeatable **12** impenetrable, invulnerable, undefeatable **14** insurmountable, unvanquishable

unconscionable 7 extreme **9** excessive **10** immoderate, inordinate, outrageous **11** inexcusable, unjustified, unwarranted **12** indefensible, preposterous, unforgivable, unpardonable, unreasonable **13** unjustifiable

unconscious 3 out **6** latent **7** in a

coma, out cold **8** comatose, in a faint **9** insensate, senseless, unknowing, unmindful **10** suppressed, unrealized **11** incognizant **12** unsuspecting **14** dead to the world

unconstitutional 7 illegal **8** unlawful **12** unauthorized

unconstrained 4 bold, easy **7** natural, relaxed **8** unforced **9** abandoned **10** unaffected **11** spontaneous, uninhibited
French: **6** degage

unconstraint 4 ease **7** abandon **8** boldness, free will, openness **9** frankness **11** naturalness, spontaneity

uncontrollable 6 unruly **7** wayward **12** ungovernable, unmanageable

uncontrolled 4 free, wild **8** absolute **9** abandoned, unlimited **10** ungoverned **12** unrestrained

unconventional 3 odd **4** rare **5** crazy, kinky, nutty, queer, wacky, weird **6** far-out, quaint, unique **7** bizarre, curious, offbeat, strange, unusual **8** aberrant, atypical, bohemian, freakish, original, peculiar, singular, uncommon **9** different, eccentric, fantastic, irregular **10** newfangled, outlandish, unorthodox **11** exceptional **12** unaccustomed **13** extraordinary, idiosyncratic, nonconforming, nonconformist **15** individualistic

unconvinced 7 dubious **8** doubtful **9** skeptical, uncertain, unsettled

unconvincing 5 false, fishy **7** dubious, suspect **10** suspicious **11** implausible **12** questionable, unbelievable

uncooked
French: **9** au naturel

uncooperative 6 ornery **7** selfish **8** perverse, stubborn **9** difficult, unhelpful, unwilling **11** intractable **12** intransigent

uncoordinated 6 clumsy **7** awkward **8** ungainly **9** graceless

uncouple 4 undo **6** detach, loosen, unhook **7** release, unhitch **8** unbuckle

uncoupled 8 detached, loosened **9** separated, unhitched **10** disengaged **11** unconnected **12** disconnected

uncourageous 5 timid **8** cowardly, timorous **9** dastardly, shrinking **13** pusillanimous

uncourtly 7 ill-bred, uncivil, uncouth **9** ungallant **10** ill- behaved, ungracious, unmannerly **11** uncourteous **12** discourteous **13** ungentlemanly

uncouth 4 rude **5** crass, crude, gross, rough **6** callow, coarse **7** boorish, brutish, ill-bred, loutish, uncivil **8** barbaric, churlish, impolite **9** unrefined **10** indelicate, uncultured, unmannerly **11** ill-mannered, uncivilized **12** uncultivated

uncover 4 bare, undo **5** dig up, strip **6** denude, dig out, expose, reveal,

unmask, unveil, unwrap **7** disrobe, lay bare, uncloak, undrape, undress, unearth **8** disclose, unclothe **9** make known, unsheathe **11** make visible **12** bring to light

uncovered 4 bare **5** bared, dug up, naked **7** exposed, noticed **8** detected, revealed **9** disclosed, made known **10** discovered **13** brought to view **14** brought to light

uncovering 8 exposure **9** divulging, unmasking **10** disclosure, divulgence, laying open, revelation **15** bringing to light **20** bringing out in the open

uncritical 4 dull, dumb **6** casual, obtuse, stupid **7** inexact, offhand, shallow **8** careless, ignorant, slipshod **9** imprecise, untutored **10** inaccurate, uneducated, unschooled, unthinking **11** perfunctory, superficial **12** unreflecting **16** undiscriminating

unctuous 4 oily, smug **6** smarmy **7** fawning, honeyed, servile **8** slippery, too suave **9** pietistic, too smooth **10** flattering, obsequious **11** sycophantic **12** honey- tongued, ingratiating **13** sanctimonious, self-righteous

uncultivated 3 raw **4** wild **7** uncouth **8** unfarmed, unplowed, untilled **9** unrefined **10** unimproved **11** undeveloped

uncultivated land
god of: **8** Silvanus, Sylvanus

uncultured 5 crass **6** coarse, common, vulgar **7** low-bred **9** inelegant, unrefined **10** unpolished **12** uncultivated

uncustomary 4 rare **6** unique **7** amazing, unusual **8** singular, uncommon, unwonted **9** unheard-of **10** incredible, unexpected **11** astonishing, exceptional **12** unaccustomed, unbelievable **13** extraordinary, unanticipated

undaunted 5 brave **6** gritty, heroic, plucky **7** unfazed, valiant **8** fearless, intrepid, resolute, stalwart, valorous **9** not put off **10** courageous, undismayed **11** indomitable, unflinching, unperturbed, unshrinking **12** stouthearted **13** undiscouraged

undeceive 8 disabuse **10** disenchant **11** disenthrall, disillusion **12** open one's eyes **13** break the spell **15** burst one's bubble **19** bring one down to earth **20** shatter one's illusions

undecided 4 open **5** vague **6** unsure **7** dubious, pending **8** not final, wavering **9** tentative, uncertain, unsettled **10** indecisive, indefinite, in abeyance, in a dilemma, irresolute, of two minds, open-minded, unresolved, up in the air **11** fluctuating, vacillating **12** undetermined, unformulated **16** hemming and hawing **17** blowing hot and cold **20** going around in circles

undecorated 4 bare **5** blank, plain, stark **6** simple **7** austere **9** unadorned **13** unembellished

undedicated 11 indifferent, uncommitted

undefiled 4 pure **5** clean **6** chaste, intact, virgin **7** natural **8** innocent, spotless **9** stainless, unsullied **10** unpolluted

undemanding 4 easy **6** low-key, simple **7** patient, relaxed **9** easygoing **10** submissive **12** easy to please, laissez-faire **14** live-and-let-live

undemonstrative 3 shy **4** cold **5** aloof **7** distant, stoical **8** reserved **9** impassive **11** unemotional **12** inexpressive, unresponsive **14** self-controlled

undeniable 4 sure **6** patent, proven **7** certain, obvious **8** decisive, manifest **10** conclusive **11** established, indubitable, irrefutable **12** beyond a doubt, demonstrable, indisputable **13** incontestable **14** unquestionable **16** incontrovertible

undeniably 6 surely **9** certainly **10** decisively, definitely **11** irrefutably **12** conclusively, demonstrably, indisputably **13** incontestably **14** beyond question, unquestionably **16** incontrovertibly

undependable 6 fickle **7** erratic, flighty **8** unstable, variable, wavering **10** capricious, changeable, inconstant, unreliable **13** irresponsible, unpredictable, untrustworthy

under 3 sub **5** below, lower, neath, short **7** beneath, sedated **8** inferior, less than **9** because of **11** subordinate, unconscious

undercover 3 sly **6** covert, hidden, secret **7** furtive, sub rosa **8** hush-hush, stealthy **9** concealed, disguised, incognito **10** unrevealed **11** clandestine, undisclosed **12** confidential **13** surreptitious
French: **8** a couvert

undercurrent 4 aura, hint, mood **5** sense, tinge, vibes **7** quality, riptide **8** undertow **9** undertone **10** atmosphere, intimation, suggestion, vibrations **12** crosscurrent

undercut 9 discredit, undermine, undersell **10** compromise

underestimate 7 dismiss, put down **8** belittle, minimize, misjudge **9** deprecate, discredit, disparage, disregard, sell short, underrate, undersell **10** depreciate, undervalue **11** detract from **12** miscalculate

undergarment 3 bra **4** BVDs, slip **5** pants, shift, teddy, thong **6** boxers, corset, girdle, shorts **7** chemise, panties **8** bloomers, camisole, knickers, lingerie, skivvies **9** brassiere, petticoat, union suit **12** jockey shorts

undergo 5 brave, stand **6** endure, suffer **7** sustain, weather **8** submit to **9** encounter, go through, withstand **10** experience

undergraduate 4 coed, soph **5** frosh, plebe **6** junior, senior **7** scholar, student **8** freshman **9** sophomore, undegreed **10** degreeless, nondegreed **13** underclassman, upperclassman

underground 6 buried, covert, secret **7** sub-rosa **10** undercover **11** belowground, clandestine **12** subterranean **13** surreptitious **15** below the surface

underground chamber 4 tomb **5** crypt, vault **6** cellar **8** catacomb **9** sepulcher

underhand, underhanded 6 covert, crafty, sneaky, tricky **7** corrupt, crooked, cunning, devious, evasive, furtive, illegal **8** sneaking, stealthy **9** conniving, dishonest, unethical **10** fraudulent **12** unprincipled, unscrupulous **13** surreptitious

underhandedness 5 guile **6** deceit **7** slyness **8** trickery **9** chicanery, deception, duplicity **10** sneakiness, trickiness **13** secretiveness

underline 6 accent, stress **7** dwell on, point up **9** emphasize, press home **10** accentuate, underscore **15** bring into relief

underling 4 serf **6** flunky, lackey, menial, minion, thrall, vassal **7** servant, subject **8** employee, hireling, inferior **9** attendant, hired hand **11** subordinate

underlying 5 basic **6** covert **7** beneath, radical **8** implicit **9** elemental, essential **10** subtending **11** fundamental

undermine 4 foil, ruin **5** erode **6** injure, riddle, scotch, thwart, weaken **7** cripple, destroy, subvert, torpedo **8** sabotage **9** eat away at, frustrate, hamstring **10** neutralize **11** burrow under, tunnel under

underneath 5 below, lower **6** bottom, hidden **9** disguised, subject to **14** misrepresented

undernourished 8 starving, underfed **12** malnourished

under obligation 5 bound **6** liable **7** obliged **8** beholden, indebted **9** obligated **10** answerable, in one's debt **11** accountable, responsible

underpart 4 sole **5** belly, tails **6** bottom **9** lower side, underside

underpin 4 bear **7** bolster, support **10** strengthen **12** substantiate

underpinning 4 base **5** basic **6** ground **7** support **9** essential **10** foundation, groundwork **11** fundamental **12** substructure

underplay 8 play down **11** deemphasize

underprivileged 4 poor **5** needy **6** in need **7** hapless, unlucky **8** badly-off, deprived, ill-fated, indigent **9** destitute, penniless, penurious **10** ill-starred, pauperized **11** handicapped,

unfortunate **12** impoverished **13** disadvantaged **22** in adverse circumstances

underrate 6 slight **8** belittle, derogate, minimize **9** denigrate, deprecate, disparage **10** depreciate, undervalue **13** underestimate

underscore 4 mark **6** accent, deepen, play up, stress **7** feature, point up **8** heighten **9** emphasize, intensify, press home, underline **10** accentuate **15** draw attention to

underscoring 6 stress **8** emphasis **11** underlining

underside 4 back, sole **5** belly, tails **6** bottom **7** reverse **9** lower side, underpart

undersized 4 tiny **5** elfin, short, small **6** little, petite, slight **7** stunted **8** dwarfish **10** diminutive **11** lilliputian

underskirt 4 slip **7** pannier **9** crinoline, hoopskirt, petticoat

understand 3 dig, get, see **4** hear, know, read, use **5** grasp, learn **6** absorb, accept, assume, can see, fathom, gather, take it **7** be aware, discern, make out, presume, realize **8** conclude, perceive **9** apprehend, interpret, recognize **10** appreciate, comprehend, take to mean **14** sympathize with, take for granted

understandable 8 apparent **12** recognizable, unmistakable **14** comprehensible

understanding 4 pact **5** grasp **7** empathy, insight, knowing **8** sympathy, tolerant **9** agreement, awareness, intuition, knowledge, sensitive **10** cognizance, compassion, compromise, discerning, perception, perceptive, responsive **11** concordance, sensitivity, sympathetic **12** appreciation, appreciative, apprehension **13** compassionate, comprehension **17** meeting of the minds

understate 8 minimize **11** deemphasize

understated 9 minimized **10** restrained **12** conservative, deemphasized

understatement 7 litotes **10** minimizing **20** conservative estimate

understudy 3 sub **6** backup, double, fill-in, relief **7** stand-by, stand-in **9** alternate, surrogate **10** substitute **11** pinch hitter, replacement

undertake 3 try **5** begin, essay, start **6** assume, strive, tackle, take on **7** attempt **8** commence, embark on, endeavor, set about, shoulder **9** agree to do, enter upon **11** promise to do **13** get involved in

undertaking 3 job **4** task **6** effort **7** concern, project, pursuit, venture **8** endeavor **10** commitment, enterprise

Under the Greenwood Tree
author: **11** Thomas Hardy

under the influence 5 drunk **6** sodden, soused, wasted, zapped, zonked **7** smashed **8** besotted **9** plastered **10** inebriated **11** intoxicated **20** three sheets to the wind

under the weather 3 bad, ill **4** sick **6** ailing, sickly, unwell **9** unhealthy **10** indisposed

undertone 4 aura, hint, mood **5** scent, sense, tinge, trace **6** flavor, mumble, murmur, nuance **7** feeling, inkling, low tone, quality, whisper **8** coloring **10** atmosphere, intimation, suggestion **11** connotation, implication **12** subdued voice, undercurrent

undervalue 6 slight **8** belittle, derogate **9** discredit, disparage, underrate **10** depreciate **13** underestimate

underwear 3 bra **4** BVDs, slip **5** pants, teddy, thong **6** boxers, briefs, corset, girdle, shorts **7** chemise, panties **8** bloomers, camisole, knickers, lingerie, skivvies **9** brassiere, petticoat, union suit **12** jockey shorts, smallclothes **14** unmentionables

underweight 4 bony, lank **5** gaunt, lanky **6** skinny **7** scrawny, spindly **8** skeletal, underfed **9** emaciated **12** skin-and-bones **13** hollow-cheeked **14** spindle-shanked, undernourished

underworld 4 Hell **5** Hades, limbo **6** the mob **8** mobsters, the Mafia **9** criminals, gangsters, purgatory **10** Cosa Nostra **11** shades below **12** the syndicate **13** bottomless pit, nether regions **14** organized crime **15** criminal element, infernal regions **16** abode of the damned
god of: **3** Dis **5** Hades, Orcus, Pluto **8** Dis Pater

under wraps 6 hidden, secret **9** concealed **10** suppressed, under cover

underwrite 3 aid **4** back **7** approve, endorse, finance, sponsor, support, warrant **8** invest in, sanction, validate **9** guarantee, subsidize **11** countersign

underwriter 5 angel **6** backer, patron **7** sponsor **8** investor **9** financier, guarantor

undeserving 3 bad **8** inferior, unworthy

undesirable 5 unfit **8** disliked, improper, unbidden, unsavory, unseemly, unwanted, unworthy **9** offensive, unpopular **10** unbecoming, uninviting, unsuitable, unwelcomed **11** distasteful, unbefitting, unwished-for **12** disagreeable, inadmissible, unacceptable, unattractive **13** inappropriate, objectionable **14** unsatisfactory

undetectable 12 unnoticeable, unobservable **13** imperceptible, unsubstantial

undetermined 6 chance **7** unfixed, unknown **8** unproved, unproven

9 uncertain, undecided **10** indefinite, irresolute **13** indeterminate, unascertained

undeveloped 3 raw **5** crude, green **6** callow, unripe **8** immature, inchoate, unformed **9** embryonic, half-baked **10** unfinished **11** rudimentary, unexploited **12** uncultivated

undignified 3 low **7** boorish **8** improper, shameful, unseemly, unworthy **9** degrading, inelegant, tasteless, unrefined **10** beneath one, indecorous, indelicate, in bad taste, unbecoming, unladylike, unsuitable **11** unbefitting **13** discreditable, inappropriate, ungentlemanly **18** beneath one's dignity **Latin: 8** infra dig **15** infra dignitatem

undiluted 4 neat, pure **5** sheer **7** unmixed **8** straight **11** unfortified **12** full-strength **13** unadulterated

Undine
form: 6 spirit
location: 5 water
sex: 6 female

undiscerning 11 insensitive **12** unperceptive **14** indiscriminate

undisciplined 4 wild **6** fickle, fitful **7** erratic, wayward, willful **8** unsteady, untaught **9** mercurial, untrained, untutored **10** capricious, changeable, inconstant, uneducated, unfinished, unreliable, unschooled **11** unpracticed **12** obstreperous, uncontrolled, undependable, unrestrained **13** unpredictable

undisclosed 6 hidden, secret **7** private **9** concealed **10** unrevealed **12** confidential

undisguised 4 open **5** clear, utter **7** evident, obvious **8** complete, distinct, manifest, unhidden **9** out-and-out **10** plain as day, pronounced, unreserved **11** unconcealed **12** unmistakable, wholehearted **13** thoroughgoing **24** plain as the nose on one's face

undismayed 7 uncowed **8** unafraid, unscared **9** confident, unabashed, unalarmed, undaunted **12** unfrightened **13** undiscouraged, unintimidated

undisputed 4 sure **7** certain, granted **8** accepted **9** undoubted **10** conclusive, undeniable **11** beyond doubt, indubitable, irrefutable, past dispute, uncontested **12** acknowledged, indisputable, unchallenged, unquestioned **13** a matter of fact, incontestable **14** beyond question, freely admitted, unquestionable **15** without question **16** incontrovertible

undistinguished 5 plain, usual **6** common **7** prosaic **8** everyday, mediocre, ordinary **10** pedestrian, unexciting **11** commonplace **12** run-of-the-mill, unremarkable **13** unexceptional **18** nothing to rave about

undistracted 4 calm **6** serene, stolid

7 unfazed **9** impassive, unruffled **10** untroubled **11** undisturbed

undisturbed 4 calm, cool **5** quiet **6** placid, serene, steady **7** equable, unmoved **8** composed, peaceful, tranquil **9** collected, inviolate, unexcited, unruffled, untouched **10** of solitude, unagitated, unbothered, untroubled **11** left in order, unperturbed **13** imperturbable, self-possessed, uninterrupted

undivided 5 solid, whole **6** entire, united **7** unified, unsplit **8** complete **9** of one mind, unanimous **10** not divided, unstinting **12** wholehearted

undo 3 end **4** free, open, ruin, void **5** annul, erase, loose, quash, untie **6** cancel, defeat, loosen, offset, repair, unbind, unfold, unhook, unknot, unlace, unlock, unwrap **7** destroy, nullify, rectify, reverse, subvert, unchain, unravel, wipe out **8** demolish, overturn, unbutton, unfasten **9** disengage, eliminate, make up for, undermine **10** counteract, invalidate, neutralize **11** disentangle **13** compensate for **14** counterbalance

undogmatic 7 liberal **8** flexible, tolerant **10** open-minded **11** broad-minded

undoing 4 doom, jinx, ruin **5** upset **6** defeat **7** erasure, nemesis **8** collapse, downfall, negation, reversal, weakness **9** annulment, breakdown, overthrow, ruination, thwarting, wiping out **11** cause of ruin, destruction **12** Achilles' heel, cancellation, invalidation **13** counteraction, nullification **14** neutralization

undomesticated 4 wild **5** feral **6** ferine, savage **7** untamed **8** barbaric **9** barbarous **11** uncivilized

undone 6 ruined **9** come apart, destroyed **10** incomplete, unfastened **12** not completed

undoubted 4 sure **5** utter **7** certain **8** absolute, complete, definite, positive **11** indubitable, unequivocal **12** indisputable **13** unimpeachable **14** unquestionable

undoubtedly 6 surely **7** no doubt **9** assuredly, certainly, decidedly, doubtless **10** absolutely, definitely, positively, undeniably **11** indubitably **12** beyond a doubt, unmistakably, without doubt **13** unequivocally **14** beyond question, unquestionably **15** without question

undress 5 strip **6** nudity **7** disrobe, uncover, undrape **8** disarray, unclothe **9** nakedness **10** dishabille **18** take off one's clothes

undressed 4 bare, nude **5** naked **6** unclad **7** denuded, exposed, unrobed **8** disrobed, stripped, undraped **9** unclothed, uncovered

Undset, Sigrid
author of: 6 The Axe **20** Kristin Lavransdatter, The Master of Hestviken

undue 6 unmeet **8** impolite, improper, needless, overmuch, too great, unseemly, unworthy **9** excessive, tasteless **10** ill-advised, indiscreet, in bad taste, inordinate, not fitting, unbecoming, unsuitable **11** superfluous, uncalled-for, unjustified, unnecessary, unwarranted **13** inappropriate, objectionable

undulate 4 coil **5** slink, weave **9** fluctuate **11** rise and fall

undulating 4 wavy **5** bumpy **6** uneven

undulation 7 coiling **8** slinking, twisting **10** contortion **11** convolution **16** rising and falling

undutiful 6 remiss **8** disloyal **11** disobedient

undying 6 steady **7** abiding, endless, eternal, lasting **8** constant, enduring, immortal, unending, unfading, untiring **9** continual, deathless, incessant, perennial, permanent, perpetual, unceasing **10** continuing **11** everlasting, never-ending, unfaltering, unrelenting, unremitting **12** imperishable, never-failing, undiminished **13** uninterrupted **14** indestructible

unearth 4 find, show **5** dig up **6** dig out, exhume, expose, reveal **7** display, divulge, exhibit, root out, uncover **8** disclose, discover, disinter, dredge up, excavate **9** disentomb, ferret out **10** come across, come up with **12** bring to light

unearthly 5 awful, eerie, weird **6** absurd **7** extreme, ghostly, phantom, strange, uncanny, ungodly, unusual **8** abnormal, ethereal, spectral, terrible **10** horrendous, unpleasant **11** disembodied, incorporeal, unspeakable **12** disagreeable, extramundane, supernatural **13** extraordinary, preternatural

unease 5 worry **7** tension **8** disquiet **9** misgiving **10** discomfort, uneasiness **11** disquietude **12** apprehension

uneasiness 5 dread **6** dismay **7** anxiety **9** agitation, misgiving **10** discomfort, foreboding **11** disquietude, distraction, nervousness **12** apprehension, discomfiture, discomposure, perturbation **16** apprehensiveness

uneasy 4 edgy **5** nervy, tense, upset **6** on edge, queasy, unsure **7** awkward, irksome, nervous, uptight, worried **8** strained, troubled, worrying **9** disturbed, ill at ease, perturbed, upsetting **10** bothersome, disquieted, disturbing, unpleasant **11** constrained, disquieting **12** apprehensive **13** uncomfortable

uneatable 8 inedible **11** not fit to eat

uneconomical 4 dear **6** costly **8** wasteful **9** expensive **10** exorbitant, high-priced, immoderate, overpriced **11** extravagant **12** unreasonable

uneducated 8 ignorant, untaught **9** unlearned, untrained, untutored **10** illiterate, uncultured, unlettered, unschooled **12** uncultivated, uninstructed **13** unenlightened

unelaborated 4 bald, bare **5** plain, stark **6** simple **8** essential, unadorned, uncolored **11** fundamental, unvarnished **13** unembellished **15** straightforward

unembellished 4 bald, bare **5** naked, plain, stark **7** austere **9** unadorned **11** undecorated **12** unornamented

unemotional 4 cold, cool **6** formal, remote **7** distant **8** lukewarm, reserved **9** apathetic, impassive, unfeeling **11** indifferent, passionless, unconcerned **12** unresponsive **15** undemonstrative

unemployed 4 axed, idle **5** fired **6** canned, sacked, unused **7** bounced, jobless, laid-off **8** workless **9** at leisure, at liberty, booted-out, dismissed, on the dole, on welfare, out of a job, out of work **10** discharged, unoccupied **11** pink-slipped

unencumbered 4 free **6** vacant **7** unladen **8** expedite **10** unburdened, unhindered **13** unhandicapped

unending 6 steady **7** endless, eternal, lasting **8** constant, enduring **9** continual, incessant, perennial, permanent, perpetual, unceasing **10** continuous, unwavering **11** everlasting, never-ending, unremitting **12** undiminished **13** uninterrupted

unendurable 7 racking **9** agonizing, torturous **10** tormenting, unbearable **11** intolerable **12** excruciating, insufferable

unenlightened 8 ignorant **9** in the dark, unlearned **10** uneducated, uninformed **11** uninitiated **12** uninstructed

unenterprising 4 lazy **11** unambitious **12** unaggressive

unenthusiastic 8 lukewarm **10** unspirited **11** halfhearted, indifferent **13** unimpassioned

unequal 6 biased, uneven, unfair, unjust, unlike **7** bigoted, partial **9** different, disparate, unmatched **10** dissimilar, not uniform, prejudiced **11** inequitable

unequaled 7 supreme **8** peerless **9** matchless, paramount, unmatched, unrivaled **10** consummate, unexcelled **11** ne plus ultra, unsurpassed **12** incomparable, second to none, unapproached, unparalleled **13** beyond compare **16** beyond comparison

unequivocable 4 bald **5** utter **8** outright **9** out-and-out **11** categorical, unqualified

unequivocal 5 clear, final **7** certain **8** absolute, clear-cut, decisive, definite, emphatic **11** unambiguous **12** indis-

putable **13** incontestable **16** incontrovertible

unequivocally 7 clearly **9** certainly, downright **10** completely, decisively, definitely, thoroughly **12** emphatically, indisputably, unmistakably **13** incontestably **14** unquestionably, wholeheartedly **16** incontrovertibly

unerring 4 sure **7** certain, precise **8** constant, faithful, reliable **9** faultless, unfailing **10** infallible, unchanging

unessential 8 nonvital **9** accessory, extrinsic **10** disposable, expendable **11** dispensable, superfluous, unimportant, unnecessary **12** nonessential

unethical 5 dirty, shady, wrong **6** shoddy, unfair **7** devious **8** unworthy **9** dishonest, underhand **10** unladylike **12** dishonorable, disreputable, questionable, unprincipled **13** ungentlemanly **14** unconscionable

uneven 4 awry, bent **5** bumpy, lumpy, rough **6** angled, coarse, craggy, curved, jagged, tilted, unfair, unjust, unlike **7** crooked, not flat, slanted, sloping, unequal **8** lopsided, not level, not plumb, one-sided, unsmooth **9** different, disparate **10** dissimilar, ill-matched, unbalanced

unevenness 7 oddness **9** bumpiness, lumpiness, roughness **10** jaggedness, ruggedness **11** crookedness **12** irregularity **14** changeableness

uneventful 4 dull **5** quiet, usual **6** boring **7** average, humdrum, prosaic, routine, tedious **8** ordinary, standard, tiresome **10** monotonous **11** commonplace **12** conventional **13** insignificant, unexceptional, uninteresting

unexcelled 7 supreme **8** flawless, peerless, superior, unbeaten **9** faultless, matchless, unequaled, unmatched, unrivaled **10** consummate **11** unsurpassed **12** incomparable, second to none, transcendent, unapproached, unparalleled **13** beyond compare

unexceptional 5 usual **6** normal **7** mundane, typical **8** ordinary, standard **9** customary **12** conventional, run of the mill

unexcited 4 calm, cool **6** placid, serene **7** unmoved **8** composed, detached **9** collected, unruffled **11** undisturbed, unemotional **13** dispassionate, unimpassioned

unexciting 4 dull, flat **5** vapid **6** boring **7** insipid **10** lackluster

unexpected 6 sudden **9** startling, unplanned **10** accidental, surprising, undesigned, unforeseen, unintended **11** astonishing, unlooked-for, unpredicted **12** out of the blue **13** unanticipated, unintentional

unextinguished 5 alive **10** unquenched **12** still burning

unfaded 5 fresh **6** bright **8** undimmed **10** unwithered

unfailing 4 true **5** loyal **6** steady **7** endless **8** constant, enduring, faithful, reliable **9** continual **10** continuous, dependable, infallible, unchanging, unwavering **12** never-failing **13** inexhaustible

unfair 4 foul **5** dirty **6** biased, unjust **7** corrupt, crooked, partial, unequal **8** not right, onesided, partisan **9** dishonest, underhand, unethical **10** not cricket, prejudiced **11** inequitable **12** dishonorable, unprincipled, unreasonable, unscrupulous **14** unconscionable

unfaithful 5 false **6** faulty, untrue **7** inexact **8** disloyal, unchaste **9** deceitful, distorted, erroneous, faithless, imperfect **10** adulterous, inaccurate, inconstant, perfidious **11** not accurate, treacherous **12** falsehearted **13** untrustworthy

Unfaithfully Yours
director: **14** Preston Sturges
cast: **10** Rudy Vallee **11** Rex Harrison **12** Edgar Kennedy, Linda Darnell **15** Barbara Lawrence

unfaithfulness 7 falsity, perfidy **9** falseness, treachery **10** disloyalty, fickleness, infidelity **11** inconstancy **13** faithlessness **14** perfidiousness

unfaltering 4 firm, sure **6** steady **8** enduring, resolute **9** obstinate, steadfast, unfailing **10** dependable, persistent, unflagging, unswerving, unwavering **11** persevering, undeviating **12** never-failing, wholehearted

unfamiliar 3 new **5** novel **6** exotic, unique **7** curious, foreign, strange, unknown, unusual **9** different **10** ignorant of, unversed in **11** a stranger to, little known, out-of-the-way, unexposed to, uninitiated, unskilled in **12** not well-known, unacquainted, unconversant **13** not acquainted, unpracticed in **14** unaccustomed to **15** inexperienced in, uninformed about **18** unenlightened about

unfamiliarity 9 ignorance **11** strangeness **12** inexperience **15** lack of knowledge

unfashionable 5 dated, dowdy, passe **6** frumpy, old-hat **8** outmoded **9** out-of-date, unstylish **12** old-fashioned

unfasten 4 undo **5** unpin, untie **6** detach, unbind, unbolt, unhook, unlace, unlash, unlink, unlock **7** unclose, unhitch, unlatch, unstick **8** unbutton, uncouple

unfastened 5 apart, undid **6** undone, untied **7** severed, unlaced, unstuck **8** detached, unhooked **9** unbuckled, uncoupled, unhitched **11** unconnected **12** disconnected

unfathomable 4 deep, vast **6** arcane, remote, subtle **7** complex, extreme, obscure **8** abstract, abstruse, esoteric, profound, puzzling **9** enigmatic **10** bottomless, perplexing **16** hard to understand, incomprehensible

unfavorable 3 bad **4** poor **7** adverse, unhappy **8** unsuited, untimely **9** ill-suited **10** ill-favored, regretable **11** inopportune, regrettable, unfortunate, unpromising **12** inauspicious, inconvenient, infelicitous, unpropitious, unseasonable **15** disadvantageous

unfeasible 10 impossible, infeasible, unsuitable, unworkable **11** impractical **12** unachievable **13** impracticable

unfeeling 4 cold **5** cruel **9** heartless **11** hardhearted, insensitive **13** unsympathetic

unfeigned 4 real, true **7** genuine, sincere **10** unaffected

unfetter 4 free **7** release, set free, unchain **8** liberate **9** unshackle

unfilled 4 open **5** blank, empty **6** hollow, vacant **7** drained **9** available **10** unoccupied

unfinished 5 crude, rough **6** undone **7** lacking, sketchy, wanting **8** immature **9** deficient, imperfect, unnatural, unpainted, unrefined, unstained **10** incomplete, unexecuted, unpolished **11** uncompleted, unfulfilled, unlacquered, unvarnished

unfit 4 sick, weak **5** frail **6** infirm, not fit, sickly **7** not up to, unequal, unready, unsound, useless **8** delicate, disabled, unsuited **9** incapable, not suited, unhealthy, unskilled, untrained **10** inadequate, ineligible, not equal to, unequipped, unprepared, unsuitable **11** debilitated, ill-equipped, incompetent, ineffective, inefficient, not designed, unqualified **12** ill-contrived, not cut out for **13** inappropriate, incapacitated

unflagging 4 firm **5** fixed **6** steady **7** staunch **8** constant, enduring, resolute, tireless, unshaken, untiring **9** steadfast, tenacious, undaunted **10** determined, persistent, relentless, undrooping, unswerving, unwavering, unyielding **11** indomitable, persevering, undeviating, unfaltering, unremitting **13** indefatigable **14** uncompromising

unflappable 4 calm, cool **6** placid, serene **8** composed **9** collected **10** coolheaded **11** unexcitable **13** imperturbable, self-possessed

unflinching 4 firm, game **6** gritty, plucky, steady, strong **7** staunch **8** fearless, resolute, stalwart, unshaken **9** steadfast, tenacious, unabashed, undaunted **10** persistent, unswerving, unwavering, unyielding **11** indomitable, unfaltering, unshrinking **12** unhesitating

unfold 4 bare, show, tell **6** open up, reveal, unfurl, unroll, unveil, unwrap **7** divulge, explain, expound, lay open,

open out, present, recount, uncover **8** describe, disclose, set forth **9** elucidate, explicate, make known, spread out **10** stretch out

unfolding 4 rise **5** birth, start **9** beginning, evolution, inception, unfurling **10** revelation **11** development

unforced 4 easy **5** frank **6** candid, casual **7** natural, relaxed **8** informal **9** easygoing **10** unaffected **13** unconstrained

unforeseen 6 abrupt, sudden **8** surprise **9** unplanned **10** accidental, surprising, unexpected, unintended **11** unlooked-for, unpredicted **12** out of the blue **13** unanticipated

unforeseen danger 7 pitfall **8** exigency **9** emergency **11** contingency

unforgettable 7 notable **8** eventful, exciting **9** important, memorable, thrilling **10** noteworthy **11** significant

unfortunate 5 sorry **6** cursed, jinxed, woeful **7** hapless, unblest, unhappy, unlucky **8** ill-fated, ill-timed, luckless, untimely, wretched **10** disastrous, ill-advised, ill-starred **11** inopportune, regrettable, unfavorable **12** inauspicious, infelicitous, unpropitious, unprosperous, unsuccessful

unfounded 4 idle **5** false **6** untrue **8** baseless, spurious **9** erroneous **10** fabricated, groundless

unfrequented 5 empty **6** lonely **7** remote, uncouth **8** isolated, solitary **9** unvisited **11** out-of-the-way **16** off the beaten path

unfriendly 4 cold **5** aloof **6** at odds, chilly **7** distant, haughty, hostile, warlike **8** inimical, snobbish **9** on the outs, reclusive, withdrawn **10** ungracious, unsociable **11** belligerent, contentious, quarrelsome, uncongenial **12** antagonistic, disagreeable, disputatious, inhospitable **13** at loggerheads, at sword's point, unsympathetic

unfruitful 4 vain **6** barren, fallow, futile **7** useless, worn-out **8** infecund **9** fruitless **10** unavailing **11** purposeless, unrewarding **12** impoverished, unproductive, unprofitable **14** unremunerative

unfulfilled 8 thwarted **10** frustrated, unrealized **11** unsatisfied
French: 6 manque

unfurl 4 open **6** expand, spread, unfold, unroll **7** develop, roll out **8** shake out **9** spread out

ungainly 5 stiff **6** clumsy, klutzy **7** awkward **9** lumbering, maladroit **10** ungraceful **13** uncoordinated

ungallant 4 rude **7** boorish, uncivil, uncouth **8** impolite **9** uncourtly **10** ill-behaved, ungracious, unmannerly **11** ill-mannered, uncourteous **12** discourteous **13** ungentlemanly

ungenerous 4 mean, near **5** close,

cruel, petty, small, venal **6** greedy, shabby, sordid, stingy **7** miserly, selfish, sparing **8** churlish, covetous, cowardly, grudging **9** illiberal, mercenary, niggardly, penurious, rapacious **10** avaricious **11** small-minded **12** narrow-minded, parsimonious, uncharitable

ungifted 8 mediocre **9** unskilled **10** amateurish, unskillful, untalented **14** unaccomplished

unglue 6 unseal **7** peel off, unstick **9** pull apart

ungodly 4 base, vile **5** awful **6** rotten, sinful, wicked **7** corrupt, ghastly, godless, heinous, immoral, impious **8** depraved, dreadful, terrible **9** dissolute **10** degenerate, horrendous, iniquitous, outrageous, villainous **11** blasphemous **12** dishonorable, unreasonable

ungovernable 6 unruly **7** defiant, froward, naughty, wayward **8** contrary, mutinous, perverse, stubborn **9** fractious, obstinate **10** disorderly, rebellious, refractory **11** disobedient, intractable **12** noncompliant, recalcitrant, unmanageable, unsubmissive

ungraceful 5 inept **6** clumsy **7** awkward **9** inelegant

ungracious 4 rude **5** bluff, blunt, gruff, harsh, short **6** abrupt, coarse, crusty, vulgar **7** boorish, brusque, loutish, uncivil, uncouth **8** churlish, grudging, impolite **9** uncourtly, ungallant **10** ill-behaved, unladylike, unmannerly **11** bad-mannered, ill-mannered, impertinent, uncourteous **12** disagreeable, discourteous, inhospitable **13** disrespectful, ungentlemanly

unguarded 6 unwary **8** careless, tactless, too frank **9** imprudent, unmindful, unwatched **10** incautious, indiscreet, undefended **11** defenseless, unpatrolled, unprotected **12** undiplomatic, unrestrained **13** ill-considered, uncircumspect

unguent 4 balm **5** cream, salve **6** lotion **8** ointment **9** emollient

ungula 4 hoof, nail

ungulate 2 ox **3** cow, gnu, hog, pig, yak **4** boar, calf, deer, goat, ibex **5** camel, daman, horse, llama, tapir **6** hoofed, vicuna **7** buffalo, caribou, giraffe, peccary **8** antelope, elephant, hooflike, ruminant **9** dromedary **10** hartebeest, rhinoceros, wildebeest **12** hippopotamus

unhampered 4 free **8** expedite **9** unimpeded **10** unconfined **12** unencumbered, unrestrained, unrestricted

unhandy 5 inept **6** clumsy, gauche, klutzy **7** awkward **8** bumbling, fumbling, inexpert, unwieldy **9** all thumbs, ham-handed, maladroit, unskilled **10** cumbersome, unskillful

11 inefficient **12** inconvenient, unmanageable **14** butterfingered

unhappiness 3 woe **5** grief **6** misery, sorrow **7** anguish, sadness **8** distress **9** heartache

unhappy 3 bad, sad **4** blue, poor **5** inapt, sorry **6** gloomy, somber, unwise **7** adverse, awkward, doleful, foolish, forlorn, hapless, joyless, unlucky **8** dejected, downcast, luckless, unseemly **9** depressed, imprudent, longfaced, sorrowful, woebegone **10** despondent, dispirited, ill-advised, melancholy, unbecoming, unsuitable **11** crestfallen, injudicious, regrettable, unbefitting, unfortunate **12** heavyhearted, infelicitous, unsuccessful **13** inappropriate **14** down in the mouth

unharmed 5 whole **6** unhurt **9** uninjured, unscathed, untouched **10** in one piece, unaffected **14** with a whole skin

unhealthy 3 bad **4** sick, weak **6** ailing, feeble, infirm, morbid, poorly, sickly, unwell **7** harmful, hurtful, invalid, not well, noxious, unsound **8** depraved, diseased, negative, perilous **9** dangerous, degrading, hazardous **10** corrupting, indisposed, morally bad **11** destructive, detrimental, undesirable, unhealthful, unwholesome **12** demoralizing, in poor health, insalubrious **13** contaminating

unheard-of 3 odd **4** rare **6** unique **7** amazing, curious, unknown, unusual **8** freakish, original, singular, uncommon **9** irregular, matchless **10** incredible, outlandish, outrageous, phenomenal, unexpected **11** exceptional **12** incomparable, preposterous, unbelievable, unparalleled, unreasonable **13** extraordinary, inconceivable, unprecedented

unheated 3 icy **4** cold **6** chilly, drafty, frosty **7** ice-cold **8** unwarmed

unheeding 7 ignored **8** mindless **12** disregarding

unhelpful 7 of no use, useless **8** in the way **9** hindering **11** disobliging **13** inconsiderate, uncooperative

unheralded 6 unsung **10** unexpected, unforeseen **11** unacclaimed, unannounced, unlooked-for **12** unproclaimed, unpublicized, unrecognized **13** unanticipated

unhesitating 5 eager, quick, ready **6** direct, prompt **9** immediate **10** unreserved **11** unflinching **12** wholehearted, without delay **13** instantaneous **18** without reservation

unhinge 6 detach **7** disrupt **8** separate, unsettle **9** disengage, dislocate, disorient, unbalance **10** disconnect **13** disarticulate

unhitch 6 detach **8** separate, uncouple, unfasten **9** disengage **10** disconnect

unhitched 8 detached **9** uncoupled **10** unfastened **12** disconnected

unholy 4 base, evil, vile **5** awful **6** rotten, sinful, wicked **7** corrupt, heinous, immoral, ungodly **8** depraved, dreadful, shocking **9** dishonest **10** horrendous, iniquitous, outrageous, villainous **12** dishonorable, unreasonable

Unholy Loves
  author: **15** Joyce Carol Oates

unhurried 4 easy, slow **7** gradual **9** leisurely **10** deliberate, slow-moving

unicorn
  form: **5** horse
  feature: **4** horn
  symbolizes: **6** purity **8** chastity
  constellation of: **9** Monoceros

unidentified 5 vague **7** unknown, unnamed **8** nameless **9** anonymous, unlabeled **11** unspecified **12** undesignated, unrecognized

unification 5 union, unity **6** fusion, merger **7** uniting **8** alliance, junction **9** coalition, combining **11** coalescence, combination, confederacy **12** amalgamation **13** confederation, consolidating, consolidation, incorporation

uniform 4 even, garb **5** alike, array, at one, dress, equal, habit **6** attire, in line, in step, livery **7** apparel, costume, regalia, regular, similar, the same **8** agreeing, constant, in accord, of a piece, unvaried, vestment **9** consonant, identical, of one mind, unaltered, unvarying **10** conforming, consistent, harmonious, unchanging **11** regimentals, undeviating

uniformity 8 equality, monotony, sameness **10** consonance **11** consistency, equivalency, homogeneity **15** standardization

unify 3 wed **4** ally, fuse, join **5** blend, merge, unite **6** couple, link up **7** combine **8** coalesce, federate **10** amalgamate **11** confederate, consolidate, form into one, incorporate **12** lump together **13** bring together

unilluminated 3 dim **4** dark **5** murky, unlit **6** gloomy **7** obscure **8** darkened **9** lightless, unlighted

unimaginable 10 incredible **12** unbelievable **13** inconceivable **16** incomprehensible

unimaginative 4 dull **5** stale, stock, trite, usual, vapid **6** dreary **7** cliched, humdrum, prosaic, routine, tedious **8** everyday, mediocre, ordinary **9** hackneyed **10** pedestrian, uncreative, unexciting, uninspired, unoriginal, unromantic **11** commonplace, predictable **12** run-of-the-mill, unremarkable **13** uninteresting

unimpaired 4 good **5** clear, sound **6** intact, unhurt **8** unbroken, unharmed **9** uninjured, unscathed, unspoiled **10** undeformed

unimpassioned 4 calm, cool **6** placid,

serene, stolid **7** unmoved **8** detached, unloving **9** apathetic, impassive, objective, unexcited **11** indifferent, unemotional **13** dispassionate

unimpeachable 4 pure **5** clean, solid **7** perfect **8** reliable, spotless, unmarred **9** blameless, faultless, inviolate, stainless, undefiled, untainted **10** immaculate, impeccable, inculpable, infallible **11** trustworthy, unblemished **12** unassailable **13** above reproach, totally honest **14** beyond question, irreproachable, unquestionable **15** beyond criticism, unchallengeable

unimportant 5 minor **6** lesser, meager, paltry, slight **7** trivial **8** inferior, mediocre, not vital, nugatory, piddling, trifling **10** immaterial, irrelevant, low-ranking, negligible, of no moment, second-rate **11** subordinate **12** nonessential, not important **13** insignificant **14** inconsiderable **15** inconsequential, of no consequence

uninformed 6 unread **7** unaware **8** ignorant **9** in the dark, not with it, unadvised, unknowing, unlearned **10** uneducated, unschooled **12** unconversant, uninstructed **13** unenlightened

uninhabited 5 empty **6** vacant **8** deserted, forsaken **9** abandoned, unlived in, unpeopled, unsettled **10** unoccupied, untenanted **11** unpopulated

uninhibited 4 fast, free, open, rash **5** frank **6** candid, daring, madcap, not shy, unwary **8** careless, heedless, immodest, reckless, uncurbed, unreined **9** abandoned, impetuous, impulsive, outspoken, unbridled, unchecked, unguarded, unimpeded, unstopped **10** capricious, flamboyant, forthright, headstrong, incautious, indiscreet, unhampered, unhindered, unreserved **11** instinctive, plainspoken, spontaneous **12** free-spirited, uncontrolled, unobstructed, unrestrained, unrestricted **13** unconstrained **15** straightforward, unself-conscious

uninjured 5 whole **6** intact, unhurt **8** unharmed **9** unscathed, untouched **10** in one piece **14** with a whole skin

uninspired 4 dull **5** stale, stock, trite, vapid **7** cliched, humdrum, prosaic, unmoved **8** ordinary **9** hackneyed, unexcited, unstirred, untouched **10** pedestrian, unaffected, unexciting, unoriginal **11** commonplace, indifferent, predictable, unemotional, unimpressed **12** run-of-the-mill, uninfluenced, unstimulated **13** unimaginative, uninteresting

uninspiring 4 dull **5** bland, stale **6** boring **7** insipid, prosaic **10** lackluster **13** uninteresting

uninstructive 6 barren **9** unhelpful **10** unedifying **12** unproductive **13** uninformative

unintelligent 4 dull, dumb, slow

5 blank, dense, dopey, thick **6** obtuse, stupid **7** asinine, doltish, idiotic, moronic **8** retarded **9** cretinous, dimwitted, imbecilic **10** dull- witted, half-witted, slow-witted **11** blockheaded, thickheaded **12** simpleminded

unintelligible 8 baffling, puzzling **9** confusing, illegible, insoluble **10** incoherent, perplexing **11** meaningless **12** impenetrable, inarticulate, unfathomable **14** undecipherable **16** incomprehensible

unintentional 9 unplanned, unwitting **10** accidental, fortuitous, undesigned, unintended, unthinking **11** inadvertent, involuntary, unconscious **14** unpremeditated

uninterested 5 aloof, blase **6** remote **8** heedless, listless, uncaring **9** apathetic, incurious, unmindful **10** above it all, uninvolved **11** indifferent, unconcerned **13** unimpressible

uninteresting 3 dry **4** drab, dull **5** trite, vapid **6** boring, dreary, jejune **7** humdrum, insipid, prosaic, tedious **8** lifeless, ordinary, tiresome, unmoving **9** colorless, wearisome **10** monotonous, pedestrian, uneventful **11** uninspiring **12** unsatisfying **13** insignificant

uninterrupted 8 unbroken **9** ceaseless, continual, incessant **10** continuous **11** unremitting

uninviting 8 annoying **9** offensive **10** unalluring, unpleasant, untempting **11** displeasing, distasteful, unappealing, undesirable, unwelcoming **12** disagreeable, unappetizing, unattractive

uninvolved 4 easy **5** clear **6** simple **7** neutral, obvious, outside **8** detached **9** impartial **10** unaffected **13** disinterested, dispassionate, uncomplicated

union 5 blend, guild, unity **6** fusion, league, merger **7** amalgam, joining, mixture, oneness, uniting, wedding **8** alliance, marriage, unifying **9** synthesis **10** federation, fraternity **11** affiliation, association, combination, corporation, partnership, unification **12** amalgamation **13** confederation, consolidation
   type: 5 craft, labor, trade

Union of Soviet Socialist Republics
   abbr: 4 CCCP, USSR
   see **Russia**

unique 8 by itself, peerless, singular **9** matchless, nonpareil, unequaled, unmatched, unrivaled **10** inimitable, one of a kind, surpassing, unexampled, unexcelled **11** distinctive, unsurpassed **12** incomparable, unapproached, unparalleled

unit 4 part **5** group, whole **6** entity, member **7** element, measure, package, section, segment **8** category, division, quantity **9** component **10** detachment

11 constituent, measurement **12** denomination

Unitas, Johnny
   nickname: 7 Johnny U
   sport: 8 football
   position: 11 quarterback
   team: 14 Baltimore Colts

unite 4 ally, fuse, join, pool **5** blend, merge, unify **6** couple **7** combine **8** coalesce, federate, lock arms, organize **10** amalgamate, homogenize, join forces **11** confederate, consolidate, incorporate **12** join together, lump together **13** stand together

united 3 one **5** fused **6** allied, joined, merged, pooled **7** blended, coupled, leagued, unified **8** combined **9** federated, of one mind, unanimous **10** collective **11** amalgamated, in agreement **12** consolidated, incorporated **14** joined together, lumped together

United Arab Emirates
   other name: 11 Pirate Coast, Trucial Oman **13** Trucial States
   capital/largest city: 8 Abu Dhabi
   others: 5 Ajman, Dubai, Kalba, Tarif **6** Sharja **7** Fujaira **11** Ras al Khaima **12** Umm al Qaiwain
   division: 5 Ajman, Dibai, Dubai **6** Sharja **7** Fujaira, Sharjah **8** Abu Dhabi, Fujairah **11** Ras al Khaima, Umm al Qaiwan **12** Ral al Khaimah, Umm al-Qaiwain
   monetary unit: 3 fil **6** dirham
   highest point: 5 Hafit
   physical feature:
     desert: 10 Rub al Khali
     gulf: 4 Oman **7** Persian
     oasis: 7 Buraimi **9** Al Buraymi
     peninsula: 7 Arabian
   people: 4 Arab **6** Indian **7** African, Iranian **9** Pakistani **10** South Asian
     leader: 22 Zaid Bin Sultan al-Nahayan
   language: 5 Farsi **6** Arabic **7** English, Persian
   religion: 5 Islam
   war: 4 Gulf **11** Desert Storm

United Arab Republic 3 UAR
   onetime union of: 5 Egypt, Syria

United Kingdom
   union of: 12 Great Britain **15** Northern Ireland

United States
   capital: 12 Washington DC
   largest city: 11 New York City
   others: 4 Nome **5** Miami **6** Boston, Dallas, El Paso **7** Chicago, Detroit, Houston, Memphis, Phoenix, San Jose, Seattle **8** Columbus, Honolulu, San Diego **9** Anchorage, Baltimore, Cleveland, Milwaukee **10** Los Angeles, New Orleans, San Antonio **12** Indianapolis, Jacksonville, Philadelphia, Salt Lake City, San Francisco
   school: 3 MIT **4** Penn, Yale **5** Brown **6** Baylor, Drexel, Vassar **7** Amherst,

Colgate, Cornell, Fordham, Harvard, Oberlin **8** Bryn Mawr, Columbia, Stanford, Wesleyan **9** Dartmouth, Princeton, Radcliffe **10** Bennington **12** Johns Hopkins, Mount Holyoke
   division: 4 Iowa, Ohio, Utah **5** Idaho, Maine, Texas **6** Alaska, Hawaii, Kansas, Nevada, Oregon **7** Alabama, Arizona, Florida, Georgia, Indiana, Montana, New York, Vermont, Wyoming **8** Arkansas, Colorado, Delaware, Illinois, Kentucky, Maryland, Michigan, Missouri, Nebraska, Oklahoma, Virginia **9** Louisiana, Minnesota, New Jersey, New Mexico, Tennessee, Wisconsin **10** California, Puerto Rico, Washington **11** Connecticut, Mississippi, North Dakota, Rhode Island, South Dakota **12** New Hampshire, Pennsylvania, West Virginia **13** Massachusetts, North Carolina, South Carolina **18** District of Columbia
   island: 4 Guam, Long, Maui, Oahu **5** Block, Ellis, Kauai, Lanai, Umnak **6** Hawaii, Kodiak, Niihau, Unimak, Virgin **7** Baranof, Key West, Long Key, Molokai, Nunivak, Sanibel **8** Aleutian, Hawaiian, Key Largo, Shumagin, Unalaska **9** Atka Amlia, Canal Zone, Chichagof, Kahoolawe, Nantucket, Snipe Keys **10** Islamorada, Oyster Keys, Puerto Rico, St. Lawrence **11** Longboat Key **12** Santa Barbara **13** American Samoa, Marquesas Keys, Prince of Wales, Santa Catalina, Summerland Key **15** Martha's Vineyard **16** Cantout Enderbury **26** Trust Territory of the Pacific
   lake: 4 Erie, Mead **5** Huron, Tahoe **6** Cayuga, Finger, George, Itasca, Oneida, Seneca **7** Iliamma, Ontario **8** Michigan, Superior **9** Champlain, Great Salt, Salton Sea, Teshekpuk, Winnebago **10** Okeechobee **11** Yellowstone **13** Pontchartrain, Wallenpaupack, Winnipesaukee **14** Lake of the Woods
   mountain: 4 Hood **5** Coast, Green, Kenai, Ozark, Rocky, White **6** Alaska, Brooks, DeLong, Elbert, Helena, Mesabi, Pocono, Shasta **7** Cascade, Chugach, Foraker, Harvard, Kilauea, Massive, Olympic, Olympus, Rainier, St Elias, Whitney **8** Catskill, Davidson, Endicott, Katahdin, Mauna Loa, Mitchell, Ouachita, St Helens, Wrangell **9** Allegheny, Blue Ridge, Kuskokwim, North Peak, Pikes Peak **10** Black Hills, Blanca Peak, Grand Teton, Washington, Williamson **11** Appalachian, Santa Monica **12** Sierra Nevada **14** Berkshire Hills
   highest point: 6 Denali **8** McKinley
   river: 3 New, Red **4** Gila, Iowa, Milk, Ohio, Rock **5** Black, Cedar, Coosa, Flint, Grand, Green, James, Neuse, Osage, Pearl, Pecos, Snake, White, Yukon **6** Brazos, Hudson, Neches,

Neosho, Nueces, Owybee, Pee Dee, Platte, Powder, Sabine, Salmon, Wabash **7** Alabama, Big Horn, John Day, Klamath, Potomac, Roanoke, San Juan, St Johns, Trinity **8** Arkansas, Big Black, Canadian, Cheyenne, Cimarron, Colorado, Columbia, Delaware, Humboldt, Illinois, Kentucky, Kootenay, Missouri, Niabrana, Ouachita, Savannah **9** Allegheny, Deschutes, Des Moines, Minnesota, Rio Grande, Smoky Hill, St Francis, Tennessee, Tombigbee, Wisconsin **10** Cumberland, Republican, Sacramento, San Joaquin, St Lawrence, Tallapoosa **11** Connecticut, Mississippi, North Platte, South Platte, Susquehanna, Yellowstone **12** Tallahatchie **14** Little Colorado, Little Missouri

sea: 6 Arctic, Bering **7** Pacific **8** Atlantic, Beaufort

physical feature:

  bay: 5 Tampa **7** Bristol, Prudhoe **8** Biscayne, Monterey **9** Apalachee **10** Chesapeake **12** San Francisco

  desert: 4 Gila **6** Mojave **7** Painted **8** Colorado, Vizcaino **9** Black Rock **11** Death Valley

  falls: 7 Niagara

  gulf: 6 Alaska, Mexico **10** California

  plain: 5 Great

  plateau: 8 Colorado, Piedmont **10** Cumberland **11** Appalachian

  strait: 6 Bering **7** Florida

people:

  architect: 4 Root **5** Davis **6** Upjohn, Wright **7** Burnham, Downing, Furness, Gilbert, Gropius, Latrobe **8** Bogardus, Holabird, Sullivan **9** Bullfinch, Jefferson **10** Richardson **14** Mies van der Rohe

  artist: 5 Henri, Homer, Leutz, Moses, Peale, Wyeth **6** Copley, Durand, Millet, Rothko, Stuart **7** Audubon, Cassatt, O'Keeffe, Pollock, Sargent **8** Whistler

  author: 3 Poe **4** Grey, Inge, Loos, Lurp, West, Wouk **5** Aiken, Albee, Beach, Benet, Crane, Eliot, Frost, Guest, Harte, Hecht, James, Lewis, Oates, Odets, O'Hara, Paine, Pound, Stowe, Twain, Vidal, Welty, Wolfe, Wylie **6** Bellow, Bierce, Bryant, Cabell, Capote, Cather, Cooper, Cullen, Ferber, Holmes, Hughes, Irving, Kilmer, Lanier, London, Lowell, Mather, Millay, Miller, Norris, O'Neill, Porter, Styron, Updike, Wilder **7** Angelou, Baldwin, Clemens, Costain, Dreiser, Emerson, Gallico, Hammett, Hellman, Howells, Jeffers, Kerouac, Lardner, Malamud, Nabokov, Roethke, Stevens, Thoreau, Webster, Wharton, Whitman **8** Anderson, Bradbury, Caldwell,

Cummings, Faulkner, Macleish, McCarthy, Melville, Michener, Mitchell, Morrison, Rawlings, Robinson, Sandburg, Schwartz, Sherwood, Sinclair, Teasdale, Whittier, Williams **9** Burroughs, Dickinson, Dos Passos, Hawthorne, Hemingway, McCullers, Steinbeck **10** Fitzgerald, Longfellow, Tarkington

  composer: 4 Ives, Kern **5** Cohan, Loewe, Sousa **6** Berlin, Foster, Joplin, Lerner, Porter **7** Copland, Gilbert, Rodgers **8** Gershwin, Sullivan **9** Bernstein **11** Hammerstein

  explorer: 4 Byrd, Pike **5** Boone, Cabot, Clark, Lewis, Perry **6** Hudson, Joliet **7** Jolliet **8** Columbus **9** Marquette **10** Eric the Red

  leader: 3 Jay **4** Clay, King, Penn **5** Bryan, Davis, Henry, Paine **6** Revere, Sumner **7** Stevens, Webster **8** Franklin, Humphrey **9** Goldwater

  military leader: 3 Lee **4** Pike **5** Clark, Gates, Grant, Meade, Tyler **6** Austin, Custer, Marion, Patton **7** Bradley, Houston, Jackson, Sherman **8** Marshall, Pershing **9** MacArthur, Roosevelt, Stillwell **10** Eisenhower, Vandenburg, Washington **11** Schwarzkopf

  president: 4 Bush, Ford, Polk, Taft **5** Adams, Grant, Hayes, Nixon, Tyler **6** Arthur, Carter, Hoover, Monroe, Pierce, Reagan, Taylor, Truman, Wilson **7** Clinton, Harding, Jackson, Johnson, Kennedy, Lincoln, Madison **8** Buchanan, Coolidge, Fillmore, Garfield, Hamilton, Harrison, McKinley, Van Buren **9** Cleveland, Jefferson, Roosevelt **10** Eisenhower, Washington

  sculptor: 4 Rush **6** Calder, French, Rogers **7** Borglum **9** Greenough, Remington **12** Saint-Gaudens

language: 7 English, Spanish

religion: 5 Amish **6** Mormon **7** Baptist, Judaism, Shakers **8** Lutheran **9** Methodist **10** Protestant **11** Pentacostal **12** Episcopalian, Presbyterian **13** Roman Catholic **14** Church of Christ, Congregational **15** Eastern Orthodox, Latter Day Saints **19** Seventh Day Adventist

place:

  national park: 4 Zion **5** Platt **6** Acadia **7** Big Bend, Glacier, Olympic, Redwood, Sequoia **8** Wind Cave, Yosemite **9** Haleakala, Mesa Verde, Multnomah **10** Crater Lake, Everglades, Grand Teton, Hot Springs, Isle Royale, Shenandoah **11** Bryce Canyon, Canyonlands, Grand Canyon, Kings Canyon, Mammoth Cave, Yellowstone **12** Mount Rainier **13** Mount McKinley, Virgin Islands **14** Lassen Volcanic, Rocky Mountains **15** Carls-

bad Caverns, Petrified Forest **19** Great Smoky Mountains

  possession: 4 Guam **10** Puerto Rico **13** American Samoa, Virgin Islands **14** Mariana Islands **15** Caroline Islands, Marshall Islands

feature:

  colony: 7 Roanoke **8** Plymouth **9** Jamestown **11** Rhode Island **12** New Amsterdam, New Hampshire **14** New Netherlands **16** Massachusetts Bay

  festival: 9 Mardi Gras

  national symbol: 9 bald eagle

  tree: 7 redwood, sequoia

unity 5 peace, union **6** accord, entity, fusion, league, merger **7** concord, harmony, joining, oneness, rapport **8** alliance, goodwill **9** synthesis, unanimity, wholeness **10** federation, fellowship, friendship **11** affiliation, association, cooperation, partnership, unification **12** amalgamation, amicableness **13** compatibility, confederation, consolidation, understanding **14** likemindedness

universal 7 general **9** worldwide **10** ubiquitous, widespread **11** omnipresent **12** affecting all, all-embracing, all-inclusive **13** international

Universal creator
  Egyptian: 4 Ptah

universality 8 currency **10** prevalence **12** predominance **17** comprehensiveness

universe
  god of: 6 Amen Ra, Amon Ra

university 6 campus, school **7** academy, college **11** institution
  English: 6 Oxford **9** Cambridge
  Cambridge: 7 Harvard
  former: 9 alma mater
  French: 8 Sorbonne
  Hanover: 9 Dartmouth
  lecturer: 9 prelector
  New Haven: 4 Yale
  New Jersey: 9 Princeton
  New York: 8 Columbia
  Providence: 5 Brown
  session: 4 term **7** seminar **8** semester
  Wit: 4 Lyly, Nash **5** Peele **6** Greene

unjust 6 biased, unfair, warped **7** partial **8** one-sided, partisan, wrongful **9** unmerited **10** prejudiced, unbalanced, undeserved **11** inequitable, unjustified, unwarranted

unjustifiable 11 inexcusable **12** indefensible

unjustly 7 falsely, wrongly **8** unfairly **10** wrongfully **11** dishonestly, faithlessly, inequitably **12** undeservedly

unkempt 5 messy **6** sloppy, untidy **7** rumpled, tousled **8** mussed-up, slovenly, uncombed **9** ungroomed **10** disheveled, disordered **11** disarranged

unkind 4 mean **5** nasty **7** abusive **8** uncaring **9** malicious, unfeeling

10 unfriendly, ungenerous, ungracious **11** insensitive, thoughtless **12** inhospitable, uncharitable **13** inconsiderate, unsympathetic

unknot 5 untie **7** unsnarl **8** untangle **11** disentangle

unknowable 12 inaccessible **13** inconceivable

unknown 7 obscure, unnamed **8** nameless **9** anonymous, unheard-of **10** unrenowned **12** uncelebrated, undesignated, undetermined, undiscovered, unidentified

unknown authors
 abbr.: 4 anon
 author of: 4 Edda (elder) **7** Beowulf **8** Everyman, King Horn, Stasimon **10** Cinderella **11** Poema del Cid **12** Panchatantra, Vercelli Book, Volsunga Saga **14** Gesta Romanorum, Sibylline Books **15** Chanson de Roland, The Forty Thieves, The Song of Roland **16** Grettir the Strong **17** The Nibelungenlied **20** Aucassin and Nicolette, Robin Hood's Adventures **23** The Dream of the Red Chamber, The Thousand and One Nights **26** Sir Gawain and the Green Knight **29** Collection of Ten Thousand Leaves **29** The Arabian Nights' Entertainment

unladylike 4 rude **6** coarse, common, vulgar **7** ill-bred, uncouth **8** impolite **10** unmannerly **12** discourteous

unlawful 7 illegal, illegit, illicit, lawless **8** criminal **9** forbidden **10** prohibited, unlicensed, unofficial **12** unauthorized **13** against the law **16** unconstitutional

unlawful act 5 crime **6** felony **10** wrongdoing **11** lawbreaking, malfeasance, misdemeanor

unleash 4 free **5** let go **7** release, set free **8** let loose, liberate **12** give free rein

unlettered 8 ignorant, untaught **9** unlearned, untutored **10** illiterate, uneducated, unschooled **11** unscholarly

unlighted 3 dim **4** dark **5** murky, unlit **6** gloomy **7** stygian, sunless **8** moonless **9** lightless **13** unilluminated

unlikable, unlikeable 7 hateful **9** offensive, unlovable **10** hard to like, unloveable, unpleasant **11** displeasing, unappealing **12** disagreeable

unlike 7 diverse, unalike, unequal **9** different, disparate **10** dissimilar

unlikelihood 12 doubtfulness, unlikeliness **13** improbability

unlikely 8 hopeless **10** improbable **11** unpromising **12** questionable, unbelievable, unpropitious **19** scarcely conceivable

unlikeness 8 contrast, variance **9** disparity, variation **10** difference, divergence **13** dissimilarity, dissimilitude

unlimited 4 huge, vast **5** total **7** end-

less, immense **8** absolute, complete, infinite **9** boundless, limitless, unbounded, unchecked **11** unqualified **12** immeasurable, totalitarian, uncontrolled, unrestrained, unrestricted **13** comprehensive, inexhaustible, unconstrained **15** all- encompassing

unload 4 dump **7** off-load **8** get rid of, unburden **9** dispose of **10** unencumber

unlooked for 6 sudden **7** unasked **8** surprise **10** unexpected, unforeseen, unheralded **11** unannounced, uncalled for, unpredicted, unsolicited **13** serendipitous, unanticipated

unlovable, unloveable 7 hateful **9** unlikable **10** hard to like, unlikeable, unpleasant **11** displeasing, unappealing **12** disagreeable

unloving 4 cold, cool **6** frigid **11** indifferent, passionless **13** unimpassioned

unlucky 6 cursed, jinxed **7** hapless, unhappy **8** ill-fated, luckless, untoward **9** ill-omened **10** ill-starred **11** star- crossed, unfortunate **12** inauspicious, misfortunate

unman 7 unnerve **8** castrate **10** discourage, emasculate

unmanageable 5 balky, bulky **6** mulish, unruly **7** awkward, unhandy, wayward, willful **8** ungainly, unwieldy **9** fractious, pigheaded **10** cumbersome, rebellious, refractory **11** disobedient, intractable, troublesome **12** incorrigible **14** uncontrollable

unmanly 5 timid **6** yellow **8** cowardly, sissyish, womanish **9** sissified, weakkneed **10** effeminate **11** lily-livered, unmasculine, weakhearted **12** fainthearted **13** pusillanimous **14** chickenhearted

unmannerly 5 crude, gross, surly **6** coarse **7** boorish, ill- bred, loutish, uncivil, uncouth **8** impolite **10** ungracious, unladylike **11** ill-mannered **12** badly behaved, discourteous **13** ungentlemanly

unmarked 5 clean, clear **9** undamaged, undefaced, unnoticed **10** unobserved **11** unblemished **15** undistinguished

unmarried 4 free **5** unwed **6** maiden, single **7** old maid, widowed **8** bachelor, divorced, spinster, unwedded, virginal, wifeless **9** available, fancy free **10** spouseless, unattached **11** husbandless **21** footloose and fancy-free

unmarried girl
 French: 10 jeune fille
 German: 8 fraulein
 Spanish: 8 senorita

Unmarried Woman, An
 director: 12 Paul Mazursky
 cast: 9 Alan Bates **11** Cliff Gorman **13** Jill Clayburgh, Michael Murphy

unmask 4 bare, show **6** betray, expose, reveal, unveil **7** lay open,

uncover **8** disclose, discover **12** bring to light

unmasking 6 baring **8** betrayal, exposure **9** discovery, unveiling **10** disclosure, laying open, revelation, uncovering **15** bringing to light

unmatched 6 unlike **7** diverse, supreme, unequal **8** peerless, variable **9** differing, disparate, matchless, unequaled **10** dissimilar **12** second to none, unparalleled **13** beyond compare

unmerciful 4 cold, evil **5** cruel, harsh **6** brutal, severe, unkind **7** brutish, extreme, inhuman **8** inhumane, pitiless, ruthless **9** excessive, heartless, inclement, merciless, unfeeling, unpitying, unsparing **10** malevolent, relentless **11** hardhearted **14** unconscionable

unmindful 3 lax **6** remiss **7** unaware **8** careless, derelict, heedless **9** forgetful, negligent, oblivious, unheeding **11** thoughtless, unconscious

unmistakable 5 clear, plain **6** patent **7** evident, glaring, obvious **8** apparent, distinct, manifest, palpable **9** prominent **10** pronounced, undeniable **11** conspicuous, unequivocal **12** indisputable **14** unquestionable

unmistakably 7 clearly, plainly **8** palpably, patently **9** certainly, decidedly, downright, evidently, glaringly, obviously **10** definitely, distinctly, manifestly, positively, thoroughly, undeniably **11** prominently **12** indisputably **13** conspicuously, unequivocally **14** unquestionably **17** beyond all question

unmitigated 6 arrant **8** absolute, unabated, unbroken **9** downright, out-and-out **10** persistent, unrelieved **11** unqualified **12** unalleviated **13** uninterrupted

unmixed 4 neat, pure **5** sheer **6** simple **8** straight **9** unalloyed, unblended, undiluted, unmingled **13** unadulterated

unmoved 4 calm, cold, firm **5** aloof **6** dogged **7** devoted, staunch **8** resolute, resolved, uncaring, unshaken **9** dedicated, obstinate, steadfast, unfeeling, unpitying, unstirred, untouched **10** determined, inflexible, not shifted, persistent, relentless, unaffected, unswerving, unwavering **11** indifferent, unconcerned, undeviating, undisturbed, unfaltering **12** stonyhearted, uninterested, unresponsive **14** uncompromising

unmoving 4 dead, dull **5** fixed, inert, still **6** boring, serene **8** immobile **9** powerless **10** motionless, stationary **11** emotionless **13** at a standstill

unnamed 8 nameless, unsigned **9** anonymous, incognito **10** innominate, uncredited, unreported, unrevealed **11** undisclosed, unspecified **12** pseudonymous, undesignated, undiscovered, unidentified **14** unacknowledged

unnatural 4 fake **5** phony, put-on **6** forced **7** assumed, stilted, studied, unusual **8** aberrant, abnormal, affected, freakish, mannered, peculiar **9** anomalous, contrived **10** artificial, theatrical **13** self-conscious

unnecessary 5 extra **6** excess **7** surplus **8** needless, overmuch **9** auxiliary, excessive **10** expendable, gratuitous, unrequired **11** dispensable, superfluous, uncalled- for, unessential **13** supplementary

unnerve 5 daunt, scare, upset **7** agitate, unhinge **8** frighten, unsettle **10** intimidate

unnerving 5 scary **8** daunting **9** upsetting **10** enervating, unsettling **11** frightening

unnoticeable 3 dim **5** faint **6** hidden **7** obscure **9** concealed **10** indistinct, unassuming, unemphatic, unobserved **11** unobtrusive **12** undetectable **13** imperceptible, inconspicuous, insignificant, undiscernible **14** unostentatious

unnoticed 6 unfelt, unseen **7** unheard, unnoted **8** unheeded, untasted **10** not smelled, overlooked, unobserved **11** disregarded, unperceived **12** undiscovered

unobservant 4 dull **5** blind **8** unseeing **9** unmindful **11** incognizant

unobstructed 4 fair, free, open **5** clear **8** apparent **9** unimpeded **10** unhampered, unhindered **11** unprevented

unobtainable 9 hard to get **10** impossible, out of reach, out of touch **11** unavailable, unreachable **12** improcurable, inaccessible

unobtrusive 3 shy **6** humble, modest **7** bashful **8** reserved, reticent, retiring **9** diffident **10** unassuming **11** unassertive **13** inconspicuous, unpretentious **14** unostentatious

unoccupied 4 idle **5** empty **6** vacant **8** unfilled **9** abandoned, unengaged **10** untenanted **11** uninhabited

unofficial 8 informal **12** unauthorized

unorganized 5 loose **6** casual, random **7** aimless, chaotic **8** confused **9** haphazard, orderless, unordered **10** disjointed, unarranged, undirected **11** harum-scarum **12** unclassified, unsystematic **13** helter-skelter **14** unsystematized

unornamented 4 bald, bare **5** blank, naked, plain, stark **6** simple **7** austere **9** unadorned **11** undecorated **13** unembellished

unorthodox 7 erratic **9** eccentric, irregular **14** unconventional

unostentatious 3 shy **5** plain, quiet **6** humble, modest, simple **9** unadorned, unaffected **10** unassuming **11** con-

strained **13** inconspicuous, unpretentious **14** unpresumptuous

unpaid 3 due **4** owed **5** owing **9** in arrears **11** outstanding

unpaid debt 5 debit **7** arrears **9** liability **10** balance due, obligation **12** indebtedness

unpalatable 5 nasty **8** inedible, unsavory **9** repellent, repulsive **10** badtasting, unpleasant **11** displeasing, distasteful **12** disagreeable, unappetizing **13** hard to swallow

unparalleled 4 best, rare **5** alone, crack, elect **6** unique **8** gilt-edge, peerless, singular **9** matchless, superfine, unequaled, unmatched, unrivaled **10** crackajack, inimitable, unimitated **11** unsurpassed **12** unapproached **13** unprecedented **15** of the first water

unperceptive 5 blind **9** unfeeling **11** insensitive, unobservant **12** imperceptive, imperceptient **13** unsympathetic

unperturbed 4 calm, cool **6** poised **8** composed, tranquil **9** collected, unexcited, unruffled **10** coolheaded, nonchalant, unagitated, undismayed, untroubled **11** levelheaded, undisturbed **13** unimpassioned

unplanned 9 impromptu **10** accidental, fortuitous, improvised, unexpected, unforeseen **11** spontaneous **12** uncalculated **13** unintentional **14** extemporaneous, unpremeditated **15** spur-of-the-moment

unpleasant 5 nasty, pesky **7** irksome, noisome **8** annoying, churlish **9** obnoxious, offensive, repugnant, repulsive, unlikable, vexatious **10** illhumored, ill-natured **11** displeasing, distasteful **12** disagreeable, unattractive **13** objectionable

unpleasantness 8 ugliness **9** ill nature, nastiness **12** churlishness **13** obnoxiousness, offensiveness, repulsiveness **15** distastefulness **16** disagreeableness, unattractiveness

unpointed 4 dull **5** blunt **6** dulled **11** unsharpened

unpolished 3 raw **5** gawky, inept, rough **6** cloudy, clumsy **7** amateur, awkward, unwaxed **8** inexpert, unbuffed, unglazed, unshined **9** inelegant, unrefined, unskilled **10** uncultured, unfinished, unskillful **11** unburnished, unpracticed **12** uncultivated **13** inexperienced **14** unaccomplished **15** unsophisticated

unpopular 7 snubbed **8** disliked, rebuffed, rejected, slighted, unwanted **9** disdained, neglected, unwelcome **10** unaccepted **11** disapproved, undesirable **12** looked down on, unacceptable

unpopulated 5 rural **9** backwoods, unpeopled, unsettled

unprecedented 5 novel **6** unique **9** unheard-of **10** unexampled **11** excep-

tional **12** unparalleled **13** extraordinary **15** hitherto unknown

unpredictable 6 fitful **7** erratic **8** fanciful, unstable, variable **9** arbitrary, eccentric, impulsive, mercurial, uncertain, whimsical **10** capricious, changeable, inconstant

unprejudiced 4 fair, just **8** unbiased, unswayed **9** impartial, objective, unbigoted **10** even-handed, fair-minded, open-minded, undogmatic **11** broad-minded **12** uninfluenced **13** disinterested

unpremeditated 5 ad-lib **9** impetuous, impromptu, impulsive, unplanned **10** accidental, improvised, unintended **11** involuntary, spontaneous **12** uncalculated, unthought-out **13** unintentional **14** extemporaneous **15** spur-of-the-moment

unprepared 5 ad-lib **7** offhand, unready **8** off guard **9** extempore, impromptu **10** flat-footed, improvised **11** spontaneous, unrehearsed **14** extemporaneous **15** spur-of-the-moment

unprepossessing 4 grim **5** seedy **10** ill-favored, ill- looking **12** unattractive

unpressed 5 baggy **6** mussed, sloppy **7** creased, rumpled **8** unironed, wrinkled **9** shapeless, uncreased

unpretentious 5 plain **6** homely, humble, modest, simple **10** unassuming, unimposing **11** unelaborate, unobtrusive **14** unostentatious

unprincipled 6 amoral **12** unscrupulous **14** conscienceless, unconscionable

unproductive 4 poor **6** barren **7** sterile, useless **8** bootless **9** infertile **10** unfruitful, unyielding **11** ineffective, ineffectual, inefficient **12** unprofitable

unprofessional 6 shoddy, sloppy **7** amateur **8** bungling, careless **9** negligent, unethical **10** amateurish **11** incompetent, inefficient, unpracticed **12** unprincipled **13** inexperienced, undisciplined, unworkmanlike **14** unbusinesslike

unprofitable 4 vain **7** useless **8** bootless **11** ineffective, ineffectual

unprogressive 7 diehard **8** backward, standpat, stubborn **9** benighted, right-wing **11** reactionary, reactionist **12** conservative **17** ultraconservative

unprolific 6 barren **7** sterile **9** infertile, unfertile **10** nonbearing **12** unproductive

unpromising 5 bleak **9** ill-omened **10** forbidding **11** unfavorable **12** inauspicious, unpropitious

unpropitious 7 adverse **8** contrary **9** unfitting **10** unsuitable **11** unfavorable **12** antagonistic, inauspicious, infelicitous

unprotected 4 open **5** naked **6** unsafe **7** exposed, unarmed **8** helpless, insecure, perilous **9** dangerous, hazardous, unguarded **10** undefended, vulnerable **11** defenseless

unproven 7 in doubt **8** arguable, doubtful **10** indefinite, in question, up in the air **11** open to doubt, unconfirmed **12** experimental, inconclusive, questionable **13** unestablished **14** open to question

unpunctual 4 late **5** tardy **7** belated **10** behindhand, behindtime

unqualified 5 total, unfit, utter **8** absolute, complete, inexpert, positive, thorough, unsuited **9** downright, out-and-out, unskilled, untrained **10** consummate, undisputed, uneducated, unprepared, unschooled **11** ill-equipped, incompetent **13** inexperienced, unconditional

unquenched 8 unslaked **11** unsatisfied **14** unextinguished

unquestionable 4 sure **5** clear, plain **6** proven **7** certain, evident, obvious, perfect **8** definite, flawless **9** blameless, errorless, faultless **10** impeccable, undeniable **11** beyond doubt, irrefutable, self-evident, unequivocal **12** indisputable, uncensurable **13** uncontestable, unimpeachable **14** irreproachable

unquestionably 6 surely **7** totally **9** certainly, doubtless **10** absolutely, completely, definitely, positively, unarguably **12** conclusively, indisputably, without doubt **13** unequivocally

unravel 4 undo **5** feaze, solve **6** unfold, unfurl, unknit **7** clear up, resolve **8** decipher, separate, untangle **9** pull apart **10** disinvolve **11** disentangle

unreachable 10 impossible, out of touch **11** out of the way, unavailable, unrealistic **12** inaccessible, unobtainable **14** unapproachable

unreal 4 airy **5** dream **6** dreamy **7** ghostly, not real, phantom, shadowy **8** ethereal, illusive, illusory, imagined, spectral **9** dreamlike, fantastic, imaginary, legendary **10** chimerical, fictitious, idealistic, intangible **11** nonexistent **13** insubstantial **16** phantasmagorical

unrealistic 4 wild **5** crazy, silly **6** absurd **7** asinine, foolish **8** crackpot, delusory, fanciful **9** illogical **10** idealistic, improbable, infeasible, starry-eyed **11** impractical **12** unreasonable

unrealized 8 thwarted **10** frustrated, incomplete **11** nonexistent, unfulfilled, unsatisfied **14** unaccomplished

unreasonable 5 undue **6** absurd, biased, mulish, unfair **7** bigoted **8** obdurate, stubborn, too great **9** excessive, fanatical, illogical, obstinate, pigheaded, senseless, unbending **10** bullheaded, exorbitant, far-fetched, headstrong, immoderate, inflexible, inordinate, irrational, prejudiced, un-

yielding **11** extravagant, intractable, nonsensical, opinionated, uncalled-for, unwarranted **12** closed-minded, preposterous, ungovernable, unmanageable **13** unjustifiable

unreasoning 8 careless, heedless **9** impulsive **10** irrational, unthinking **11** thoughtless **13** unintelligent

unrecognizable 9 disguised, incognito **10** in disguise **11** camouflaged **14** unidentifiable

unrecognized 6 unsung **7** cryptic, unknown **9** incognito, unnoticed

unrefined 3 raw **5** crude, rough **6** coarse, vulgar **7** boorish, low-bred **9** inelegant

unrehearsed 7 offhand **8** informal **9** extempore, impromptu, impulsive, unplanned, unstudied **10** improvised, off-the-cuff, unprepared **11** extemporary, spontaneous **14** extemporaneous, unpremeditated **15** improvisational, spur-of-the-moment **19** off the top of one's head

unrelated 6 not kin, unlike **7** foreign **8** unallied **10** dissimilar, extraneous, irrelevant, non-germane **11** unconnected **12** inapplicable, incompatible, unassociated **13** inappropriate

unrelenting 5 rigid **6** steady **7** adamant, endless **8** constant, unabated, unbroken **9** ceaseless, incessant, tenacious, unbending **10** implacable, inexorable, inflexible, relentless, unrelieved, unswerving, unwavering, unyielding **11** undeviating, unremitting **14** uncompromising

unreliable 4 fake **5** false, phony **6** fickle **8** fallible, mistaken, unstable **9** deceitful, erroneous, uncertain **10** capricious, changeable, inaccurate, inconstant **12** questionable, undependable **13** irresponsible, untrustworthy

unremarkable 5 usual **6** common **7** average **8** everyday, mediocre, ordinary **11** commonplace **12** unimpressive, unsurprising **13** insignificant, unexceptional **15** undistinguished

unremitting 6 dogged **8** constant, tireless, untiring **9** ceaseless, continual, incessant, unceasing **10** continuous, persistent **11** persevering

unrepentant 7 callous **8** hardened, obdurate, unatoned **9** unashamed **10** uncontrite, unexpiated **11** remorseless **12** incorrigible, unregenerate

unrepressed 4 free, open **7** liberal **8** effusive, outgoing **9** expansive, exuberant **11** extroverted, uninhibited **12** unrestrained

unreserved 4 full, open **5** frank **6** entire **11** unqualified **12** wholehearted

unresolved 4 moot **5** vague **7** pending **8** doubtful, unsolved **9** tentative, uncertain, undecided, unsettled **10** disputable, unanswered **11** contestable, speculative **12** questionable, undeter-

mined **13** problematical, unascertained

unresponsive 4 cold, cool, dull, limp **5** inert **6** frigid **7** passive **8** lifeless **9** apathetic, unfeeling **11** cold-blooded, inattentive, indifferent, unemotional **13** dispassionate, unsympathetic

unresponsiveness 6 apathy **7** inertia **9** lassitude, passivity **11** inattention, passiveness **12** indifference

unrest 5 chaos **6** tumult **7** anarchy, discord, ferment, protest, turmoil **8** disorder, disquiet, upheaval **9** agitation, rebellion **10** discontent, turbulence **12** restlessness **15** dissatisfaction

unrestrained 8 uncurbed **9** abandoned, boundless, excessive, unbridled, unchecked, unlimited **10** immoderate, inordinate, unfettered, ungoverned, unhampered, unhindered, unreserved **11** extravagant, intemperate, uninhibited, unrepressed **12** uncontrolled, unrestricted, unsuppressed **13** irrepressible

unrestraint 6 excess **7** abandon **9** uncontrol **10** unruliness **12** extravagance, immoderation, recklessness **13** excessiveness, impulsiveness

unrestricted 8 absolute, complete **9** out-and-out, unbounded, unlimited **11** unqualified **12** unrestrained **13** unconditional

unrigid 3 lax **4** easy, limp, soft **5** loose **6** giving, limber, mobile, pliant, supple **7** elastic, lenient, plastic, pliable **8** flexible, informal, merciful, tolerant, yielding **9** indulgent, malleable **11** conformable

unrigorous 4 easy **5** loose, slack **6** casual, sloppy **7** inexact **8** careless, slapdash **9** imprecise

unripe 5 green **8** immature **10** unseasoned **11** undeveloped **14** underdeveloped

unrivaled 8 superior, topnotch **9** unequaled **10** undisputed **11** unsurpassed

unroll 6 reveal, uncoil, unfold, unfurl, unwind **7** display, lay open, play out **9** spread out

unruffled 4 calm, cool, even, mild **5** quiet, still **6** placid, serene, smooth **8** composed, tranquil **9** collected **10** coolheaded, nonchalant, unagitated, untroubled **11** undisturbed, unperturbed **13** self-possessed

unruly 4 wild **5** rowdy **7** restive, wayward, willful **8** contrary, perverse **9** fractious, unbridled **10** boisterous, disorderly, headstrong, refractory **11** disobedient, intractable **12** obstreperous, ungovernable, unmanageable **13** undisciplined **14** uncontrollable

unsafe 5 risky **7** exposed **8** insecure, perilous **9** dangerous, hazardous, unguarded **10** undefended, unreliable,

vulnerable 11 defenseless, treacherous, unprotected **13** untrustworthy

unsatisfactory 4 poor **5** inept, unfit **8** below par, inferior, unworthy **9** deficient **10** inadequate, ineligible, unsuitable **12** inadmissible, unacceptable **13** inappropriate

unsavory 3 bad **4** flat, foul **5** nasty **7** insipid, tainted **9** tasteless **10** badtasting, nauseating, unpleasant **11** distasteful, unpalatable **12** disagreeable, unappetizing

unscathed 5 sound, whole **6** entire, intact, unhurt **7** perfect **8** unharmed **9** uninjured, untouched **10** unimpaired **11** unscratched **13** all in one piece

unscholarly 8 ignorant **9** unlearned **10** illiterate, uneducated, uninformed **11** ill-informed **13** unintelligent

unschooled 3 raw **5** green **6** callow **8** ignorant, untaught **9** unlearned **10** illiterate, uneducated, uninformed, unlettered, unseasoned **11** uninitiated **13** inexperienced

unscrupulous 5 sharp **6** amoral **7** crooked, devious, immoral **9** unethical **12** dishonorable, unprincipled

unseasonable 6 too hot **7** too cold, too warm **8** abnormal, untimely

unseasoned 3 raw **5** bland, green, plain **6** callow **7** untried **8** immature **13** inexperienced

unseeing 5 blind **7** unaware **9** oblivious, sightless **11** unobservant

unseemly 4 rude **5** crude, gross **6** coarse, vulgar **7** boorish, loutish **8** churlish, improper, indecent, unworthy **9** incorrect, offensive, tasteless **10** indecorous, indelicate, out of place, unbecoming, unladylike, unsuitable **11** distasteful, ill-mannered, unbefitting, undignified **12** discourteous, disreputable **13** discreditable, inappropriate, reprehensible, ungentlemanly

unselfconscious 7 artless **10** unaffected **13** unpretentious

unselfish 7 liberal **8** generous, handsome, princely, selfless **10** altruistic, benevolent, big-hearted, charitable, open-handed **11** considerate, magnanimous, magnificent **12** humanitarian **13** philanthropic **15** self-sacrificing

unserviceable 7 useless **8** unusable

unsettle 5 upset **6** bother, rattle, ruffle **7** agitate, confuse, disturb, fluster, perturb, trouble, unhinge **8** bewilder, confound, disorder **9** unbalance **10** disconcert **13** throw off guard

unsettled 5 fazed **7** anxious, nervous, ruffled **8** agitated, confused, doubtful **9** disturbed, nonplused, perturbed, undecided **10** disquieted, distracted, nonplussed, up in the air **11** discomfited **12** disconcerted **16** at sixes and sevens

unshackle 4 free **7** release, set free, unchain **8** liberate, unfetter

unshakable 4 fast **6** stable **7** abiding, staunch **8** constant, enduring **9** dauntless, permanent, steadfast, unruffled **10** changeless, inflexible, unsinkable, unwavering **11** levelheaded, unflappable **13** imperturbable

unshaken 4 calm, cool **6** poised, serene, stable **7** staunch, unmoved **8** composed, constant, resolved **9** steadfast, tenacious, undaunted, unexcited, unruffled **10** controlled, determined, inflexible, relentless, unaffected, unswerving, untroubled, unwavering **11** levelheaded, undeviating, undisturbed, unemotional, unfaltering, unflinching, unperturbed **13** self-possessed **14** uncompromising

unshapely 5 baggy **9** amorphous, shapeless

unshaven 5 hairy **7** bearded, bristly, hirsute, stubbly, unkempt **9** whiskered **11** bewhiskered

unsheathe 4 bare **6** expose **7** pull out **8** withdraw

unsightly 4 ugly **6** horrid, odious **7** hideous **u 9** obnoxious, offensive, repellent, repulsive, revolting, sickening **11** distasteful **12** unattractive

unsigned 9 anonymous **13** bearing no name

unskilled 5 green, inept **7** untried **9** untrained **10** amateurish, apprentice **11** incompetent, unqualified **13** inexperienced

unskillful 5 inept **6** clumsy, unable **7** awkward **8** inexpert **9** incapable, maladroit, untrained **10** amateurish **11** incompetent, ineffective, unpracticed **13** inexperienced

unsmiling 3 sad **4** glum, grim **5** grave **6** dismal **7** austere, joyless, serious **9** cheerless, grim-faced

unsociable 7 haughty **9** withdrawn **10** antisocial, unfriendly, ungracious **11** introverted **14** unapproachable

unsoiled 4 pure **5** clean, fresh, white **6** chaste **8** innocent, pristine, spotless **9** unstained, unsullied **10** immaculate **11** unblemished, untarnished

unsolicited 4 free **8** unforced, unsought, unwanted **9** undesired, uninvited, unwelcome, voluntary **10** gratuitous, unasked for **11** spontaneous, unnecessary, unrequested, unwished for, volunteered

unsophisticated 4 open **5** green, naive **6** candid **7** artless, natural **8** homespun, innocent, trusting **9** ingenuous, unstudied, unworldly **10** unaffected, unassuming **11** uncontrived **13** undissembling, unpretentious **15** straightforward

unsound 3 mad, off **4** weak **5** risky, shaky, unfit, wrong **6** absurd, ailing,

faulty, feeble, flawed, infirm, insane, marred, sickly, unsafe **7** foolish, invalid, rickety, tottery **8** confused, crippled, decrepit, deranged, diseased, drooping, impaired, insecure, not solid, not valid, perilous, specious, spurious, unhinged, unstable, unsteady **9** blemished, dangerous, defective, erroneous, hazardous, illogical, imperfect, incorrect, senseless, uncertain, unfounded, unhealthy, unsettled, untenable **10** disordered, fallacious, groundless, irrational, precarious, unbalanced, unreliable **11** languishing, mentally ill **12** in poor health **13** off one's rocker, unsubstantial

unsoundness 7 frailty **8** delicacy, weakness **9** fragility, frailness, shakiness **11** decrepitude, derangement, instability **12** unsteadiness

unsparing 4 full **6** giving, lavish **7** copious, liberal, profuse **8** abundant, generous **9** bountiful, plenteous, plentiful, unlimited **10** big-hearted, munificent, ungrudging, unstinting **11** extravagant, magnanimous, unqualified **13** unconditional

unspeakable 4 huge, vast **5** awful, great **6** odious **7** fearful, immense **8** enormous, shocking **9** abhorrent, frightful, loathsome, monstrous, repellent, repulsive, revolting, sickening, unheard-of **10** abominable, disgusting, incredible, nauseating, prodigious **11** astonishing, unutterable **12** overwhelming, unimaginable **13** extraordinary, inconceivable, inexpressible, undescribable

unspecified 5 vague **7** general, unnamed **9** undefined, unsettled **10** indefinite **11** unannounced, unindicated, unmentioned **12** undesignated, undetermined, unpublicized, unstipulated

unspoiled 4 open **7** artless, natural, perfect **8** pristine, spotless, trusting, unharmed, unmarred **9** preserved, undamaged, unscarred, unspotted, unstudied, unworldly **10** unaffected, unassuming, unimpaired, unpampered **11** unblemished, uncorrupted **13** unpretentious **15** unself-conscious, unsophisticated

unspoken 5 tacit **6** silent **7** implied **8** implicit **9** ineffable, not voiced, unuttered **10** understood **11** unexpressed

unspotted 5 clean **8** spotless, unsoiled **9** undefiled, unstained, unsullied **11** unblemished

unstable 4 weak **5** frail, shaky, tippy **6** fickle, fitful, flimsy, wobbly **7** erratic, fragile, rickety **8** changing, insecure, shifting, unsteady, volatile **9** emotional, mercurial, tottering **10** capricious, changeable, fly-by-night, irrational **11** fluctuating, vacillating **12** inconsistent **13** irresponsible, unpredictable, unsubstantial

unstained 5 clean 8 spotless 9 unspotted, unsullied, untainted 11 unblemished, uncorrupted

unsteady 6 fickle, wobbly 7 rickety 8 doubtful, unstable 10 unreliable 12 questionable, undependable 13 untrustworthy

unstinting 11 unqualified 12 enthusiastic, unrestrained, wholehearted

unstooped 5 erect 6 unbent 7 upright 8 straight, vertical

unstudied 4 glib 6 casual 7 artless, natural 8 informal, unforced, unversed 9 guileless, unuttered 10 unaffected 11 spontaneous 12 uncalculated

unsubmissive 6 unruly 7 defiant, froward, naughty, wayward 8 contrary, mutinous, perverse, stubborn 9 fractious, insurgent, obstinate, seditious, undutiful 10 disorderly, rebellious, refractory, unyielding 11 disobedient, intractable 12 noncompliant, recalcitrant, ungovernable, unmanageable 13 insubordinate

unsubstantial 4 airy, weak 5 filmy 6 feeble, flimsy 7 unsound 8 ethereal, fanciful, illusory 9 idealized, imaginary 10 jerrybuilt 11 lightweight 12 undetectable 13 imperceptible 17 indistinguishable

unsubstantiated 8 disputed 10 unverified 15 unauthenticated

unsuccessful 4 poor, vain 6 foiled, futile, hard up 7 baffled, hapless, unlucky, useless 8 abortive, badly off, luckless, strapped, thwarted 9 fruitless, moneyless, penniless 10 illstarred, profitless, unavailing, unfruitful 11 ineffectual, unfortunate 12 unproductive, unprofitable, unprosperous 14 unremunerative

unsuitability 9 unfitness, wrongness 11 impropriety, uselessness 12 unseemliness 13 inconsistency 15 incompatibility, unacceptability 17 inappropriateness

unsuitable 5 inapt, unfit 7 unhappy, useless 8 improper, unseemly 9 unfitting, worthless 10 inadequate, indecorous, out of place, unbecoming, unsuitable 11 incongruous, unbefitting 12 inadmissible, incompatible, inconsistent, infelicitous, out of keeping, unacceptable 13 inappropriate

unsuited 5 inapt, wrong 9 unfitting 10 out of place 13 inappropriate

unsullied 5 clean 8 spotless, unsoiled 9 undefiled, uninjured, untainted 10 unpolluted 11 unblackened, unblemished, uncorrupted, untarnished 14 uncontaminated

unsupportable 6 faulty 9 unfounded, untenable 12 indefensible

unsure 3 shy 5 timid 7 bashful 8 hesitant, insecure, reserved 9 unassured, uncertain, undecided 11 in a quan-

dary, unconfi- dent, unconvinced 12 self-doubting 15 self-distrustful

unsurpassed 4 best 7 highest, supreme 8 greatest, peerless, superior 9 matchless, nonpareil, paramount, unequaled, unmatched, unrivaled 10 consummate, unexcelled 11 exceptional 12 incomparable, transcendent, unparalleled

unsuspecting 5 naive 6 unwary 7 unaware 8 gullible, off guard, trusting 9 believing, credulous 12 overtrustful, unsuspicious 13 overcredulous

unsuspicious 5 naive 8 gullible, trustful, trusting 9 credulous 12 unsuspecting 13 unquestioning

unswerving 4 firm 6 steady, strong 7 devoted, staunch 8 faithful, resolute, resolved, unshaken, untiring 9 dedicated, steadfast, undaunted 10 determined, inflexible, unflagging, unwavering, unyielding 11 undeviating, unfaltering, unflinching, unremitting 12 single-minded 14 uncompromising

unsympathetic 7 callous 8 pitiless, uncaring 9 heartless, repellent, repugnant, unfeeling, unlikable 10 hardboiled, unlikeable, unmerciful, unpleasant 11 coldhearted, displeasing, hardhearted, indifferent, uncongenial 12 antipathetic, unattractive 15 uncompassionate

unsystematic 6 sloppy 7 chaotic, jumbled, muddled 8 confused 9 haphazard, unplanned 10 disordered, disorderly 12 disorganized, unmethodical

untainted 4 pure 5 clear 9 unsullied 11 uncorrupted 13 unadulterated

untalented 5 inept 8 mediocre, ungifted 9 unskilled 10 amateurish, unskillful 14 unaccomplished

untamed 4 wild 5 feral 6 savage 9 unsubdued 11 uncivilized 12 uncultivated

untangle 5 solve 7 clear up, unravel, unsnarl, untwist 9 extricate 11 disentangle 13 straighten out

untarnished 6 bright 7 perfect, shining 8 flawless, polished, spotless, unsoiled 9 faultless, undefiled, unstained, unsullied, untainted 10 immaculate, impeccable, undisputed, unoxidized 11 unblackened, unblemished 12 unbesmirched 13 unimpeachable

untaught 6 unread 7 natural 8 ignorant 9 untutored 10 illiterate, uneducated, unlettered, unschooled 11 spontaneous 12 uninstructed

untenable 4 weak 6 faulty, flawed 7 invalid, unsound 8 baseless, specious, spurious 9 debatable, erroneous, illogical 10 fallacious, groundless, unreliable 11 contestable 12 indefensible, questionable 13 insupportable, unjustifiable, unsustainable 14 unmaintainable

unthinkable 11 unwarranted 12 unimaginable 13 inconceivable, insupportable, unjustifiable 16 incomprehensible, out of the question

unthinking 7 witless 8 careless, heedless, mindless, tactless 9 imprudent, negligent, senseless 11 inadvertent, insensitive, thoughtless 12 undiplomatic 13 inconsiderate, uncircumspect

untidiness 5 chaos, mix-up, upset 6 jumble 7 clutter 8 disarray, disorder, scramble, shambles 9 confusion, messiness 10 sloppiness 12 dishevelment 14 disarrangement 15 disorganization

untidy 5 dowdy, messy 6 frowsy, mussed, sloppy 7 chaotic, rumpled, tousled, unkempt 8 careless, confused, littered, mussed up, slipshod, slovenly 9 cluttered 10 bedraggled, disarrayed, disheveled, disorderly, slatternly, topsy-turvy 12 unmethodical 13 helter-skelter

untie 4 free, undo 5 loose 6 loosen, unbind, unlace 7 unchain, unstrap 8 make free, unfasten 11 disentangle

untilled 6 fallow 8 unplowed 12 uncultivated

until we meet again
French: 5 adieu 8 au revoir
German: 14 auf Wiedersehen
Hawaiian: 5 aloha
Italian: 4 ciao 5 addio 11 arrivederci
Japanese: 8 sayonara
Spanish: 5 adios

untimely 5 inapt 7 unhappy 8 illtimed, mistimed, unseemly 9 imprudent, premature, unfitting 10 illadvised, malapropos, out of place, unbecoming, unexpected, unsuitable 11 inopportune, unbefitting, unfortunate 12 inconvenient, infelicitous 13 inappropriate

untiring 5 fresh 6 steady 7 devoted, earnest, patient, staunch, zealous 8 constant, diligent, resolute, sedulous, tireless 9 assiduous, dedicated, steadfast, tenacious, unceasing, unwearied 10 determined, persistent, relentless, unflagging 11 never tiring, persevering, unfaltering, unremitting 12 wholehearted 13 indefatigable

untold 6 myriad, secret, unsaid 7 endless, private, unknown 8 hushed up, infinite, numerous, unspoken, withheld 9 concealed, countless, limitless, unbounded, uncounted, unrelated 10 numberless, suppressed, unnumbered, unreported, unrevealed 11 innumerable, undisclosed, unexpressed, unpublished 12 immeasurable, incalculable, undetermined

Untouchables, The
character: 7 Rossman 9 Eliot Ness, Lee Hobson 10 Cam Allison, Frank Nitti 11 Enrico Rossi 14 Martin Flaherty 18 William Youngfellow

cast: 10 Jerry Paris **11** Bruce Gordon, Paul Picerni, Robert Stack, Steve London **13** Abel Fernandez, Anthony George, Nick Georgiade
narrator: 14 Walter Winchell

untouched 3 new **4** pure **5** alone **6** intact, virgin **8** pristine, unharmed **9** uninjured **10** unaffected, unmolested

untoward 5 amiss **6** unruly **7** adverse **8** contrary **9** difficult **11** unfavorable **12** inauspicious, unpropitious

untrainable 6 unruly **11** intractable, unteachable **12** ungovernable

untrained 3 raw **5** green **7** untried **9** unskilled **11** unqualified **13** inexperienced

untried 3 raw **5** green **6** callow **8** immature, untested **10** unseasoned **13** inexperienced

untroubled 4 calm **6** placid, serene **7** halcyon, relaxed **8** carefree, careless, peaceful, tranquil **9** easygoing, unworried **10** unbothered **11** free-and-easy, undisturbed, unperturbed **12** happy-go-lucky, lighthearted

untrue 4 fake, sham **5** false **6** made up **7** not true **8** disloyal, spurious, unchaste **9** dishonest, erroneous, faithless, falsified, incorrect, unfounded **10** adulterous, fallacious, fictitious, fraudulent, groundless, inaccurate, inconstant, perfidious, unfaithful, untruthful **11** promiscuous, treacherous **12** meretricious **13** double-dealing

untrustworthy 5 false **6** fickle, shifty, untrue **7** corrupt, crooked, devious **8** disloyal, fallible, slippery, two-faced **9** corrupted, deceitful, dishonest, faithless, insincere, uncertain, unethical **10** capricious, inconstant, perfidious, unfaithful, unreliable, untruthful **11** treacherous **12** dishonorable, disreputable, questionable, undependable, unprincipled, unscrupulous **13** irresponsible **15** unauthenticated

untruth 3 fib, lie **4** hoax, tale, yarn **5** fable, story **6** canard, humbug **8** flimflam **9** deception, falsehood, fish story, invention **11** fabrication **12** equivocation **13** falsification, prevarication **16** cock-and-bull story **17** misrepresentation

untruthful 5 false, lying **8** specious, spurious **9** deceptive, dishonest **10** fraudulent, mendacious

untutored 5 naive **6** native, unread **8** ignorant, untaught **10** illiterate, uneducated, unlettered, unschooled **12** uninstructed **15** unsophisticated

untypical 3 odd **4** rare **5** alien **7** bizarre, deviant, strange, unusual **8** aberrant, abnormal, atypical, uncommon **9** anomalous, irregular, unnatural **10** unfamiliar **16** unrepresentative

unused 3 new **7** strange, untried **8** left over, not given, pristine, unopened **9**

remaining, untouched **10** unemployed **12** unaccustomed, unacquainted, unhabituated

unusual 4 rare **5** novel **6** unique **7** curious, offbeat, strange **8** atypical, peculiar, singular, uncommon **9** unequaled, unheard-of, unmatched, untypical **10** noteworthy, one of a kind, phenomenal, remarkable, surprising, unfamiliar **11** exceptional **12** incomparable, unparalleled **13** extraordinary, unprecedented **16** out of the ordinary

unvaried 4 even **5** fixed **6** steady **7** regular, uniform **8** all alike, constant **9** identical, unchanged **10** all the same, invariable, monotonous, unchanging **11** homogeneous, unalterable, undeviating

unvarnished 3 raw **4** bald, bare **5** blunt, crude, frank, naked, plain, stark **6** candid, direct, honest, simple **7** sincere **8** straight **9** unadorned, uncolored **10** unfinished **11** fundamental, undisguised **13** unembellished **15** straightforward **23** straight-from-the-shoulder

unvarying 4 even **6** steady **7** regular, uniform **8** constant **10** unwavering

unveil 4 bare **6** reveal **7** divulge, publish, uncloak, uncover **8** announce, disclose **9** broadcast, make known, unsheathe **12** bring to light

unveiled 5 bared **8** divulged, laid bare, revealed **9** announced, broadcast, disclosed, made known, published, uncovered **14** brought to light

unveiling 4 show **5** array **7** display, exhibit, showing **10** exhibition, exposition **13** demonstration

unverified 7 alleged, rumored **8** disputed **15** unauthenticated, unsubstantiated

unwarranted 7 illegal **8** culpable, unlawful **9** arbitrary, unfounded **10** censurable, groundless, unapproved **11** inexcusable, uncalled-for, unjustified **12** indefensible, unauthorized, unreasonable, unsanctioned

unwary 4 rash **5** hasty **7** unalert **8** careless, headlong, heedless, reckless **9** imprudent, unguarded **10** incautious, indiscreet, unwatchful **11** precipitate **12** disregardful **13** uncircumspect

unwashed 4 foul **5** dirty, grimy, muddy **6** filthy, grubby, smudgy, soiled **7** unclean **8** begrimed

unwasteful 6 frugal **7** thrifty **9** effective, effectual, efficient **10** productive

unwavering 4 firm **6** steady, strong **7** staunch **8** faithful, resolute, unshaken, untiring **9** dedicated, steadfast, tenacious **10** determined, persistent, unflagging, unswerving **11** persevering, undeviating, unfaltering, unflinching,

unremitting **12** single-minded **14** uncompromising

unwelcome 7 outcast **8** excluded, rejected, unwanted **9** thankless, uninvited, unpopular **10** uncared for, unpleasant, unrequired **11** displeasing, distasteful, undesirable, unessential, unnecessary, unwished for **12** disagreeable, unacceptable

unwell 3 ill, low **4** sick **5** frail **6** ailing, infirm, laid up, poorly, queasy, sickly **7** run-down **8** delicate, qualmish **10** indisposed **11** off one's feed **15** under the weather

unwholesome 3 bad **4** evil, foul **5** toxic **6** deadly, filthy, sinful, wicked **7** baneful, harmful, hurtful, immoral, noxious, ruinous **8** depraved, venomous **9** corrupted, dangerous, degrading, poisonous, polluting, unhealthy **10** corrupting, pernicious **11** deleterious, detrimental, undesirable, unhealthful **12** demoralizing, dishonorable, insalubrious, unnourishing **13** contaminating

unwieldy 5 bulky, heavy **6** clumsy **7** awkward, weighty **8** not handy **10** burdensome, cumbersome **12** hard to handle, incommodious, inconvenient **13** uncomfortable

unwilled 6 reflex **9** automatic **11** involuntary, unconscious **12** uncontrolled **13** nonvolitional

unwilling 5 loath **6** averse **7** against, opposed **9** demurring, reluctant, resistant **10** dissenting, indisposed, undesirous **11** disinclined **12** not in the mood, recalcitrant **14** unenthusiastic

unwillingness 8 aversion **10** opposition, reluctance, resistance **13** indisposition **14** disinclination

unwise 4 dumb **5** crazy, silly **6** stupid **7** foolish, unsound **8** reckless **9** foolhardy, imprudent, senseless **10** ill-advised **11** improvident, inadvisable, injudicious **12** shortsighted, unreasonable **13** irresponsible, unintelligent

unwitting 7 unaware, unmeant **9** unknowing, unplanned **10** accidental, undesigned, unexpected, unthinking **11** inadvertent, involuntary **12** unconsenting **13** unintentional **14** unpremeditated

unwonted 4 rare **7** unusual **8** atypical, uncommon **10** infrequent, remarkable, unexpected, unfamiliar **11** exceptional **12** unaccustomed **13** extraordinary

unworkmanlike 6 clumsy, sloppy **11** inefficient

unworldly 4 holy, pure **5** godly, green, moral, naive, pious **6** callow, devout, divine, sacred, solemn **7** ethical **8** ethereal, heavenly, innocent, trusting **9** aesthetic, celestial, religious, spiritual, unearthly **10** idealistic, immaterial, provincial **12** intellectual, metaphysical, overtrusting **13** inexperienced, philosophical **14** transcendental **15** unsophisticated

unworried 4 calm **6** serene **7** relaxed **8** carefree, composed, peaceful, tranquil **9** easygoing, unruffled **10** untroubled

unworthy 5 unfit **7** ignoble **8** improper, shameful, unseemly **9** degrading, unethical **10** unbecoming, unsuitable **11** unbefitting **12** dishonorable, disreputable, unacceptable **13** discreditable, inappropriate, objectionable

unwrap 4 open **6** loosen, unbind **7** uncover

unwrinkled 4 even, flat **6** ironed, smooth **7** unlined **8** smoothed **9** uncreased, unrumpled

unwritten 4 oral **5** tacit, vocal **7** assumed, implied **8** implicit, inferred, unstated **9** customary **10** spoken only, understood, unrecorded **11** traditional, unexpressed **12** unformulated, unregistered **13** by word of mouth

unwritten law
Latin: **13** lex non scripta

unyielding 4 firm, hard **5** rigid, stiff, stony, tough **6** wooden **8** resolute, rocklike, stubborn **9** obstinate, steadfast, unbending, unpliable **10** determined, inexorable, inflexible, persistent, unswerving, unwavering **11** undeviating **14** uncompromising

up 4 atop, lift, over, rear **5** about, above, aloft, along, aside, astir, at bat, built, close, equal, erect, raise **6** apiece, ascend, higher, lifted **7** abreast, batting, forward, promote, skyward, through **8** advanced, cheerful, increase, out of bed, overhead, standing, together, windward **9** northward **10** optimistic **11** constructed

up and about 5 afoot, astir **6** active, mobile, roused **7** walking **8** out of bed **10** ambulatory, on one's feet

up-and-down 6 fitful, seesaw, uneven **7** bobbing **8** jouncing, wavering **11** alternating, fluctuating, vacillating

upbraid 5 scold **6** berate, rebuke, revile **7** bawl out, censure, chew out, reprove **8** admonish, chastise, denounce, reproach **9** castigate, dress down, reprimand **10** tongue-lash

upbringing 7 rearing **8** breeding, training **10** background

upcoming 6 coming, nearby **7** looming, nearing, pending **8** imminent **9** impending, momentary **11** approaching, drawing nigh, forthcoming, in the offing, prospective

update 5 amend, emend, renew **6** recast, revamp, revise, rework **7** restore, touch up, upgrade **8** overhaul, renovate **9** refurbish **10** rejuvenate, reorganize, streamline

up for grabs 4 open **9** available

upgrade 5 raise, slope **6** ascent, better **7** advance, dignify, elevate, incline, inflate, promote **8** gradient

upheaval 5 flood, quake **6** blowup, tumult **7** turmoil **8** disorder, upthrust **9** cataclysm, explosion, tidal wave **10** disruption, earthquake, revolution **11** catastrophe, disturbance

uphill 4 hard **5** tough **6** rising, taxing, tiring, upward **7** arduous, onerous **8** toilsome, wearying **9** ascending, difficult, fatiguing, strenuous, wearisome **10** burdensome, enervating, exhausting **12** backbreaking

uphill work 8 struggle, tough job **10** difficulty, rough going **11** arduousness **12** hard sledding **13** laboriousness

uphold 4 bear, prop **5** brace, carry, raise, shore **6** defend, hold up, prop up **7** approve, bolster, confirm, elevate, endorse, protect, shore up, support, sustain **8** advocate, buttress, champion, maintain, preserve, underpin **9** encourage **10** stand up for, underbrace **11** acknowledge, corroborate

upholder 7 devotee **8** adherent, advocate, defender, partisan **9** supporter

up in the clouds 6 elated, joyful, joyous **8** ecstatic, euphoric **9** exuberant, rapturous **11** on cloud nine **15** in seventh heaven

Upis
goddess of: **10** childbirth

Upjohn, Richard
architect of: **13** Trinity Church (NYC)
style: **13** Gothic Revival

upkeep 4 keep **6** living **7** support **8** expenses, overhead **10** management, sustenance **11** maintenance, subsistence **12** conservation, preservation

upland 4 high, rise **5** ridge **6** height **7** plateau **8** eminence, highland **9** elevation, high place, high point **10** prominence

uplift 5 edify, raise **6** better, refine **7** advance, bracing, elevate, improve, inspire, lifting, shoring, support, upgrade **8** civilize, propping **9** cultivate, elevation **10** betterment, bolstering, enrichment, refinement **11** advancement, buttressing, cultivation, edification, enhancement, improvement **12** underpinning

uplifting 9 elevating, elevation, improving, inspiring **11** improvement **12** enlightening **13** enlightenment, inspirational

upon 2 at, on **4** atop **5** about **6** toward **7** against, thereon **9** by means of, thereupon **10** after which, thereafter

upper 3 top **4** high **5** major **6** higher, inland **7** eminent, greater, topmost **8** elevated, northern, superior **9** important

upper-case letter 7 capital **9** majuscule **13** capital letter

upper class 5 elite **6** gentry, uptown **7** (high) society **8** highborn, highbred, wellborn **9** beau monde, haut monde, high-class, patrician, top drawer **10** upper crust **11** aristocracy, blue-blooded **12** aristocratic, silk-stocking **14** creme de la creme, to the manor born **15** to the manner born

upper crust 5 elite **6** gentry **7** (high) society **9** beau monde, haut monde, top drawer **10** upper class **11** aristocracy **14** creme de la creme

upper hand 4 edge, sway **5** power **7** command, control, mastery **8** whip hand **9** advantage, authority, supremacy **10** domination **12** predominance

upper house 6 Senate **12** House of Lords

uppermost, upmost 3 top **4** main **5** chief, first, major, prime **7** highest, leading, primary, supreme, topmost **8** crowning, dominant, foremost, greatest, loftiest **9** essential, paramount, principal **10** preeminent **11** predominant **12** transcendent **13** most important

Upper Volta
other name **11** Burkina Faso (Fasso)
capital/largest city: **11** Ouagadougou
others: **4** Kaya **7** Banfora **9** Koudougou **10** Ouahigouya
division: **7** Yatenga **9** Tenkodogo **11** Fada Ngourma
monetary unit: **5** franc **7** centime
mountain: **4** Tema
highest point: **8** Nakourou **10** Tenakourou, Tenekourou
river: **5** Komoe **6** Mekrou, Sourou **8** Pendjari, Red Volta **10** Black Volta, White Volta
physical feature:
  plateau: **5** Sahel **7** Sikasso, Voltaic
  wind: **9** harmattan
people: **4** Bobo, Lobi, Samo **5** Bella, Bissa, Dyula, Fulbe, Hausa, Mande, Marka, Mossi, Puehl **6** Fulani, Senufo, Tuareg **7** Grunshi, Voltaic, Yatenga **8** Mandingo **9** Gourounsi **15** Bunsansi Gambaga
  French governor: **7** Hesling
  god: **4** Wuro **5** Tenga
  king: **4** Naba **5** Mogho
  leader: **5** Oubri, Zerbo **7** Yameogo **8** Lamizana **9** Mogho Naba
language: **4** Bobo, Lobi, More, Samo **5** Dyula, Mande, Mossi **6** French
religion: **5** Islam **7** animism **12** Christianity
place:
  game reserve: **11** Arlyand Pama
feature:
  animal: **5** hyena **6** duiker, jackal **7** gazelle, warthog **10** hartebeest
  tree: **4** shea **6** acacia, baobab, karite, locust

upright 3 rib 4 fair, good, just, pale, pier, pile, pole, post, prop 5 erect, moral, shaft, stake, strut 6 column, honest, picket, pillar 7 ethical, support, upended 8 reliable, standard, vertical 9 honorable, righteous, stanchion 10 aboveboard, high-minded, principled, standing-up, upstanding 11 trustworthy 12 on the up-and-up 13 perpendicular

uprightness 5 honor 7 dignity, honesty 8 morality 9 integrity 13 righteousness 15 trustworthiness

uprising 4 riot 6 mutiny, revolt 8 outbreak 9 rebellion 10 insurgence, revolution 12 insurrection

uproar 3 ado 4 stir, to-do 5 furor 6 clamor, tumult 7 turmoil 9 agitation, commotion 11 disturbance, pandemonium 16 state of confusion

uproarious 4 loud, wild 5 noisy 6 raging, stormy 7 furious, intense, riotous 9 clamorous, hilarious, turbulent, very funny 10 boisterous, disorderly, hysterical, tumultuous 11 tempestuous 13 sidesplitting

uproot 6 banish 7 abolish, cast out, destroy, root out, wipe out 8 dislodge, displace, force out 9 eliminate, extirpate 10 annihilate, do away with 11 exterminate

upset 3 ire, irk, mad, vex 4 beat 5 anger, annoy, crush, irked, messy, mix up, pique, quash, smash, upend, vexed, worry 6 bother, cancel, change, defeat, enrage, grieve, invert, jumble, muddle, mussed, rattle, thrash, untidy 7 agitate, angered, annoyed, capsize, chaotic, confuse, conquer, disturb, enraged, fluster, furious, grieved, incense, jumbled, mixed-up, perturb, reverse, tip over, trouble, trounce, unnerve, upended, worried 8 agitated, bothered, capsized, confused, demolish, disorder, distress, incensed, inverted, overcome, overturn, slovenly, troubled, turn over, unnerved, upturned, vanquish 9 discomfit, disturbed, infuriate, overpower, overthrow, overwhelm, perturbed 10 discompose, disconcert, disheveled, disordered, disorderly, disquieted, distressed, hysterical, overturned, tipped over, topple over, topsy-turvy, turned over, upside-down 11 disarranged, disorganize, overwrought, wrong side up 12 disorganized 13 make miserable 14 turn topsy-turvy

upsetting
French: 14 bouleversement

upshot 3 end 6 effect, payoff, result, sequel 7 outcome 8 offshoot 9 aftermath, outgrowth 10 conclusion 11 aftereffect, consequence, culmination, eventuality 16 final development

upside down 7 chaotic 8 reversed 10

disorderly 11 topsy turvey 12 bottomside up 16 at sixes and sevens

upstairs 2 up 11 above stairs, second floor

upstanding 4 good, tall, true 5 erect, moral, on end 6 honest 7 ethical, upright 8 straight, truthful, vertical, virtuous 9 honorable, righteous 11 trustworthy 13 incorruptible, perpendicular

upstart 4 snip, snob, snub 6 nobody 7 bounder, parvenu 8 mushroom 9 conceited, newly-rich 12 adventurer 12 nouveau riche 13 self-assertive

upsurge 4 gain, push, rise 5 spurt 6 pickup, thrust, upturn 7 advance, upswing 8 increase 11 improvement

upswing 4 rise 6 pickup 7 upsurge 11 improvement, upward trend

uptight 5 tense 7 anxious, fearful, nervous, worried, wound up 8 insecure, neurotic, troubled 9 unbending 10 unyielding 12 apprehensive

up-to-date 2 in 3 new 5 today 6 modern, modish, timely, trendy, with-it 7 current, stylish 9 in fashion 12 contemporary 13 up-to-the-minute
French: 9 au courant

upturn 4 gain, push 6 thrust 7 advance, upsurge 8 increase 9 expansion 11 improvement

upward 4 high, more 5 above, aloft 7 skyward 9 ascending, uppermost

upward movement 4 rise 5 climb 6 ascent, rising, upturn 7 scaling, takeoff 8 climbing, mounting 9 ascension

upward trend 4 rise 5 boost 6 pickup 7 advance, upsurge, upswing 8 increase 11 improvement

uraeus
figure of: 3 asp 5 cobra
on: 9 headdress
of: 7 pharoah

Uralic
language branch: 7 Samoyed 10 Finno-Ugric

Urania
member of: 5 Muses
personifies: 9 astronomy

uranium
chemical symbol: 1 U

Uranus
mother: 4 Gaea
wife: 4 Gaea
father of: 6 Giants, Titans 8 Cyclopes 10 Titanesses 13 Hecatonchires
castrated by: 6 Cronos, Cronus Kronos

Uranus
position: 7 seventh
satellite: 5 Ariel 6 Oberon 7 Miranda, Titania, Umbriel
color: 9 blue-green
characteristic: 5 rings

Urartu see 7 Armenia

urban 4 city, town 5 civic 8 citified 9

municipal 11 worldly- wise 12 cosmopolitan, metropolitan 13 sophisticated

urban area 3 urb 4 city 9 inner city 10 metropolis 11 megalopolis 16 metropolitan area

urbane 5 civil, suave 6 polite, smooth 7 courtly, elegant, gallant, genteel, politic, refined, tactful 8 debonair, gracious, mannerly, polished, wellbred 9 civilized, courteous 10 chivalrous, cultivated, diplomatic 11 gentlemanly 12 cosmopolitan, wellmannered 13 sophisticated

urchin 3 boy, imp, lad 4 brat, waif 5 gamin, stray, whelp, youth 6 gamine, laddie 8 young pup 9 stripling, young punk, youngster 10 young rogue, young tough 11 guttersnipe

Urd 4 Norn
origin: 12 Scandinavian
form: 8 giantess
personifies: 4 past
developed from: 5 Urdar
companion: 5 Skuld 8 Verdandi

Urey, Harold Clayton
field: 9 chemistry
isolated: 9 deuterium
awarded: 10 Nobel prize

urge 3 yen 4 back, coax, goad, itch, poke, prod, push, spur, sway, wish 5 drive, egg on, fancy, force, press, prick, speed 6 advise, desire, exhort, hasten, hunger, motive, reason, thirst 7 beseech, counsel, craving, dictate, entreat, implore, impulse, longing, passion, push for, quicken, request, solicit, suggest 8 advocate, appeal to, argue for, champion, convince, persuade, petition, pressure, stimulus, yearning 9 hankering, importune, incentive, plead with, prescribe, prompting, recommend 10 accelerate, inducement, motivation, supplicate 11 prevail upon, provocation

urgency 4 need, urge, want 5 press 6 stress 8 exigency, pressure 9 necessity 10 importance, insistence 11 persistence 14 imperativeness 15 importunateness

urgent 5 grave 6 ardent 7 crucial, earnest, fervent, intense, serious, weighty, zealous 8 critical, pleading, pressing, required, spirited 9 demanding, essential, heartfelt, important, insistent, momentous, necessary 10 beseeching, compelling, compulsory, imperative, obligatory, passionate 12 wholehearted 13 indispensable

urge on 4 push 5 boost 7 cheer on, pull for, root for

urging 7 bidding, counsel, goading 8 egging on 9 prompting 11 exhortation

Uri 6 canton
in: 11 Switzerland
home of: 11 William Tell

Uriah
father: 7 Shemiah

wife: 9 Bathsheba
served: 5 David
urinary system
 component: 6 kidney, ureter **7** bladder, urethra
 rids body of: 5 salts, waste, water **8** minerals
Uris, Leon
 author of: 5 Topaz **6** Exodus **7** Trinity **9** Battle Cry **10** Armageddon
urn 3 jar, pig **4** ewer, kist, tomb, vase **5** grave, steen **6** teapot **7** samovar **9** coffeepot
 botanical: 7 capsule **11** spore-bearer
 in keno: 5 goose
Ursa Major 9 Great Bear
 contains: 9 Big Dipper
Ursa Minor 10 Little Bear
 contains: 7 Polaris **12** Little Dipper
Uruguay
 other name: 10 Purple Land
 capital/largest city: 10 Montevideo
 others: 4 Fray, Melo **5** Minas, Rocha, Salto **6** Bentos, Rivera **7** Artigas, Colonia, Dolores, Durazno, Florida, San Jose **8** Mercedes, Paysandu, Trinidad **9** Maldonado **10** Las Piedras, Santa Lucia, Tacuarembo **12** Treinta y Tres **13** San Jose de Mayo
 measure: 4 vara **6** cuadra, suerte
 monetary unit: 4 peso **9** centesimo, centisimo
 weight: 7 quintal
 island: 5 Lobos
 lake: 5 Merin, Mirim **18** Embalse del Rio Negro
 mountain: 6 Animas **10** Grand Hills **14** Cuchilla Grande
 highest point: 15 Mirador Nacional
 river: 4 Malo **5** Mirim, Negro, Plata **6** Parana, Ulimar **7** Cuareim, Queguay, Uruguay **8** Yaguaron **9** Cebollati **10** Tacaurembo
 sea: 8 Atlantic
 physical feature:
  estuary: 5 Plata
 people: 4 Yaro **5** Swiss **6** Indian **7** Italian, mestizo, Russian, Spanish **8** Charruas
  artist: 6 Figari
  author: 4 Rodo **5** Reyes **6** Onetti **7** Sanchez **9** San Martin **10** Ibarbourou
  leader: 5 Oribe **6** Rivera **7** Artigas **9** Lavelleja **10** Bordaberry **14** Batlle y Ordonez
 language: 7 Italian, Spanish
 religion: 13 Roman Catholic
 place:
  resort: 12 Punta del Este
  square: 13 Independencia
 feature:
  animal: 4 puma **6** jaguar **8** capybara **9** armadillo
  bird: 4 rhea **5** nandu **7** hornero, ostrich
  cattle ranch: 8 estancia
  cowboy: 6 gaucho

 dance: 5 tango **7** milonga
 festival: 8 Carnival **13** Semana Criolla
 lasso: 10 boleadoras
 metal straw: 8 bombilla
 music: 9 candomble
 musical drama: 7 tablado
 ruling class: 10 Patriciado
 food:
  barbecue: 5 asado
  dish: 7 puchero **9** churrasco **13** asado con cuero
  drink: 4 mate
U S A
 author: 13 John Dos Passos
 character: 10 Ben Compton, Mary French **11** Joe Williams **12** Margo Dowling **13** Fainy McCreary (Mac), Janey Williams **14** J Ward Morehouse **15** Charley Anderson, Eleanor Stoddard, Eveline Hutchins **18** Anne Elizabeth Trent **22** Richard Ellsworth Savage
usable 5 handy **6** useful **9** adaptable **10** functional **11** serviceable
usage 3 use **4** care, mode **5** habit **6** custom, manner, method, system **7** control **8** good form, habitude, handling, practice **9** etiquette, operation, tradition, treatment **10** convention, employment, management **12** manipulation
use 3 aid, ply, sap **4** good, help, work **5** apply, avail, drain, exert, spend, treat, usage, value, waste, wield, worth **6** devour, employ, expend, handle, profit **7** benefit, consume, deplete, exhaust, exploit, operate, service, utilize **8** deal with, exercise, function, handling, profit by, put to use, resort to, squander **9** act toward, advantage, dissipate, enjoyment, make use of, operation, swallow up, throw away **10** employment, manipulate, run through, usefulness **11** application, convenience, fritter away, utilization **12** behave toward, capitalize on **13** make the most of **14** serviceability
used 3 old **5** eaten, spent **7** applied, treated **8** actuated, consumed, depleted, employed, occupied, operated, utilized **9** customary, exercised, exhausted, exploited, practiced **10** accustomed, habituated, secondhand **11** implemented, manipulated
used up 4 beat, shot **5** all in, spent **6** wasted **7** worn out **8** depleted, tired out **9** exhausted
useful 5 handy, utile **7** helpful **8** valuable **9** effective, practical, rewarding **10** beneficial, convenient, functional, profitable, time-saving, worthwhile **11** serviceable, utilitarian **12** advantageous
usefulness 5 avail, value, worth **6** profit **7** benefit, purpose, utility **9** advantage **11** convenience, helpfulness,

 suitability **12** adaptability, practicality **13** effectiveness **14** serviceability
useless 4 vain **6** futile **7** of no use **8** bootless, unusable **9** fruitless, unhelpful, worthless **10** inadequate, profitless, unavailing **11** incompetent, ineffectual, inefficient **12** unproductive **13** impracticable, inefficacious, nonfunctional, unserviceable
uselessness 6 vanity **8** futility, idleness **9** inutility **10** inefficacy **13** fruitlessness, worthlessness
Uses of Enchantment, The
 author: 15 Bruno Bettelheim
use sparingly 4 save **5** hoard, stint **6** scrimp **7** cut back, dole out **8** conserve, not waste, preserve
use to advantage 7 exploit **8** profit by **12** capitalize on **13** turn to account
use up 5 drain, spend **6** expend, finish **7** consume, deplete, exhaust **9** dissipate **10** run through
Ushant
 author: 11 Conrad Aiken
usher 4 lead, show **5** guide, steer **6** attend, convoy, direct, escort, herald, launch, leader, porter, ring in, squire **7** conduct, precede, preface **8** announce, director, proclaim **9** conductor, introduce **10** doorkeeper, gatekeeper, inaugurate
Usnech see **6** Usnach
USSR see **6** Russia
Ustinov, Peter
 born: 6 London **7** England
 roles: 7 Topkapi **8** Quo Vadis? **9** Billy Budd, Spartacus **12** We're No Angels
usual 5 stock, trite **6** common, normal, wonted **7** popular, regular, routine, typical **8** expected, familiar, habitual, ordinary, orthodox, standard **9** customary, hackneyed **10** accustomed, prescribed, threadbare **11** commonplace, established, oft-repeated, traditional **12** conventional, run-of-the-mill **15** well-established
usurer 9 loan shark **11** money lender
usurp 4 grab **5** steal **7** preempt **8** arrogate **10** commandeer **11** appropriate **12** encroach upon, infringe upon
usurpation 6 taking **7** seizure **8** grabbing, stealing **10** arrogation, preemption **13** appropriation
Utah
 abbreviation: 2 UT
 nickname: 6 Mormon **7** Beehive
 capital/largest city: 12 Salt Lake City
 others: 3 Roy **4** Moab, Orem **5** Delta, Heber, Kanab, Logan, Magna, Manti, Nepli, Ogden, Price, Provo **6** Beaver, Eureka, Kearns, Layton, Murray, Tooele, Vernal **7** Bingham **8** American **9** Bountiful **11** Brigham City
 college: 5 Weber **11** Westminster **12** Brigham Young

feature:
  bridge: 7 Rainbow
  dam: 6 Hoover **10** Glen Canyon
  gorge: 7 Flaming
  national historic site: 11 Golden
    Spike
  national monument: 8 Dinosaur
    14 Natural Bridges
  national park: 4 Zion **6** Arches **11**
    Bryce Canyon, Canyonlands, Capi-
    tal Reef
  reef: 7 Capital
tribe: 3 Ute **5** Piute, Uinta(h), Yampa
  6 Navajo, Paiute **7** Gosiute **8** Pavio-
  tso, Shoshoni
people: 7 Mormons **10** Maude Adams
  11 Karl G Maeser **12** Brigham Young
  13 John M Browning **15** Latter-Day
  Saints **16** George Sutherland **19** Daniel Cowan Jackling
  explorer: 9 Dominguez, Escalante
lake: 4 Mead, Swan, Utah **6** Powell,
  Sevier **9** Great Salt
land rank: 8 eleventh
mountain: 4 Lena, Lion, Waas **5** Cedar, Henry, Hogup, Peale, Rocky,
  Trail, Uinta **6** Frisco, Navajo,
  Swasey, Wahwah **7** Granite, Griffin,
  Hawkins, Pennell, Terrace, Wasatch
  8 Linnaeus **9** Confusion
  highest point: 9 Kings Peak
physical feature:
  basin: 5 Great
  canyon: 4 Echo
  desert: 6 Sevier
  plateau: 7 Wasatch **8** Colorado,
    Tavaputs
river: 4 Bear **5** Grand, Green, Weber
  6 Jordan, Sevier, Virgin **7** San Juan
  8 Colorado
basketball team: 4 Jazz **6** Starzz
state admission: 10 forty-fifth
state bird: 7 seagull
state flower: 8 sego lily
state motto: 8 Industry
state song: 14 Utah We Love Thee
state tree: 10 blue spruce
utensils 4 gear **5** tools **6** outfit, silver,

tackle **8** flatware **9** apparatus **10** implements, silverware **11** instruments
13 paraphernalia

utilitarian 5 handy **6** usable, useful **8**
sensible, valuable, workable **9** effective, efficient, practical, pragmatic **10**
beneficial, convenient, functional,
profitable **11** serviceable **12** advantageous

utility 3 aid, gas, use **4** help **5** avail,
extra **6** backup **7** benefit, reserve,
service **8** function **9** accessory, advantage, alternate, auxiliary, secondary,
surrogate, telephone **10** additional,
substitute, usefulness **11** convenience,
electricity **12** availability, supplemental **13** public service **14** serviceability

utilization 3 use **10** employment **11**
application **12** exploitation

utilize 3 use **6** employ **7** exploit **8**
profit by, put to use, resort to **9** make
use of **12** capitalize on **13** bring into
play, make the most of, turn to account **14** avail oneself of, have recourse to, put into service **15** take advantage of

utmost, uttermost 4 acme, best,
main, peak, tops **5** chief, first, major,
prime **6** tiptop, zenith **7** capital, highest, leading, maximum, primary, supreme, the most **8** cardinal, foremost,
greatest, last word, ultimate **9** paramount, principal, sovereign **10** preeminent **11** predominant

Uto-Aztecan (Nahuatl)
  tribe: 4 Pima **5** Aatam, Aztec, Nahua
  6 Mexica, Papago **8** Pima Alto

utopia 4 Eden **6** heaven **7** Erewhon **8**
paradise **9** ideal life, Shangri-la **12**
perfect bliss, perfect place **13** seventh
heaven

utopian 9 visionary **10** idealistic, unfeasible, unworkable **11** unrealistic **12**
otherworldly, unattainable, unrealiza-
ble **13** impracticable, insubstantial,
unfulfillable

Utrillo, Maurice

  born: 5 Paris **6** France
  mother: 14 Suzanne Valadon
  artwork: 16 The Church at Deuil, The
    Church of Blevy **17** Church at St Hi-
    laire **19** La Petite Communiante **22**
    Sacre Coeur de Montmartre
ut supra 7 as above
utter 3 say **4** emit, pure, talk, tell, yell
  5 sheer, shout, speak, state, total,
  voice **6** entire, mutter, reveal **7** declare, deliver, divulge, exclaim, express, perfect, whisper **8** absolute,
  complete, disclose, outright, proclaim,
  thorough, vocalize **9** downright, enunciate, out-and-out, pronounce, unchecked **10** articulate, unmodified,
  unrelieved **11** categorical, unequivocal, unmitigated, unqualified
utterance 4 talk, word **6** answer, remark, speech **7** opinion **9** discourse,
  statement **10** expression **11** declaration, exclamation **12** articulation,
  proclamation, vocalization **13** pronouncement, verbalization
utterly 4 just **5** fully **6** wholly **7** totally
  8 entirely, outright **9** downright,
  extremely, perfectly **10** absolutely,
  completely, thoroughly **14** to the nth
  degree
uttermost 6 utmost **7** extreme, maximum, supreme **9** outermost, sovereign
  12 extreme limit
uxorious
  doting on: 8 one's wife
  from Latin: 4 uxor, wife
Uzbekistan
  capital/largest city: 8 Tashkent
  others: 9 Samarkand
  head of state: 9 president
  government: 8 republic
  monetary unit: 5 ruble
  river: 8 Amu Darya, Syr Darya
  sea: 4 Aral
  people: 5 Uzbek
  language: 5 Uzbek
  religion: 5 Islam **11** Sunni Muslim
Uzi 10 Israeli gun, machine gun

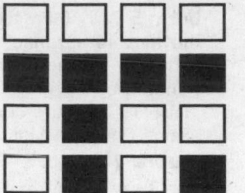  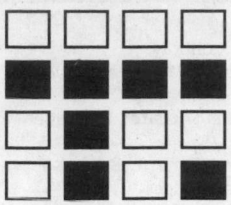

V

vacancy 3 gap **4** hole, void **5** abode, place **6** breach, cavity, hollow **7** crevice, fissure, housing, lodging, opening **9** emptiness, situation **10** empty space, vacantness **11** room for rent **12** house for rent

vacant 4 dull, free, idle, open **5** aloof, blank, blase, clear, empty, vapid **6** unused, wooden **7** deadpan, for rent, leisure, vacuous **8** deserted, detached, for lease, forsaken, not in use, unfilled **9** abandoned, apathetic, incurious, oblivious, poker-face, unengaged **10** tenantless, unemployed, unoccupied, untenanted **11** indifferent, unconcerned, unfurnished, uninhabited **12** unencumbered **14** expressionless **15** uncomprehending

vacate 4 quit **5** empty, leave **6** give up, resign **8** abdicate, evacuate, hand over **9** surrender **10** depart from, relinquish

vacate the throne 4 cede, flee, quit **5** yield **6** give up, resign, retire **7** abandon **8** abdicate **10** relinquish

vacation 4 rest **5** leave, R and R **6** recess **7** holiday **8** furlough, holidays **10** sabbatical **12** intermission **13** take a vacation **14** leave of absence **17** rest-and-recreation
French: 8 vacances

vaccine 5 serum **8** antitoxin
inventor: 4 Salk **5** Sabin **6** Jenner **7** Pasteur

vacillate 4 reel, rock, roll, sway, toss **5** pitch, shift, waver **6** falter, teeter, totter, wobble **7** flutter, vibrate **8** hesitate **9** fluctuate, hem and haw, oscillate **12** shilly-shally **14** blow hot and cold

vacillating 7 swaying **8** wavering **9** diffident, uncertain, vibrating **10** hesitating, irresolute, on the fence **11** fluctuating, uncertainty **12** irresolution **15** shilly-shallying

vacillation 7 swaying **8** wavering **9** faltering, vibration **10** indecision **11** fluctuation, uncertainty **12** irresolution **15** shilly-shallying

Vacuna
origin: 6 Sabine
goddess of: 11 agriculture

vacuous 4 dull, idle, void **5** blank, empty, inane, silly **6** stupid, vacant **7** fatuous, foolish **8** indolent, unfilled **9** senseless **11** empty-headed, purposeless

Vaduz
capital of: 13 Liechtenstein

vae victis 18 woe to the vanquished

vagabond 4 hobo **5** gypsy, nomad, rover, tramp **6** roamer, roving **7** drifter, floater, migrant, nomadic, rambler, roaming, vagrant **8** bohemian, carefree, homeless, rambling, wanderer, wayfarer **9** footloose, itinerant, transient, traveling, wandering, wayfaring **10** journeying **11** beachcomber

Vagabond Lover
nickname of: 10 Rudy Vallee

vagary 4 kink, whim **5** fancy, humor, quirk **6** notion, oddity, whimsy **7** caprice, fantasy, impulse **8** crotchet, daydream **10** brainstorm, erraticism **11** peculiarity **12** eccentricity, idiosyncrasy, passing fancy

vagrant 3 bum **4** hobo **5** nomad, rover, tramp **6** beggar, loafer, roamer, roving **7** floater, migrant, nomadic, roaming **8** homeless, rambling, vagabond, wanderer **9** itinerant, transient, wandering **10** panhandler **11** peripatetic **15** knight-of-the-road

vague 4 hazy **5** fuzzy, loose **6** casual, random, unsure **7** general, unclear **8** confused, nebulous **9** imprecise, uncertain, unsettled **10** ill-defined, indefinite, inexplicit, undetailed, unspecific **11** not definite, unspecified **12** undetermined

vaguely 5 dimly **6** hazily **7** loosely **8** dreamily, slightly, vacantly **9** obscurely, sketchily **10** nebulously **11** ambiguously **12** indistinctly

vagueness 8 haziness **9** ambiguity, confusion, fuzziness **11** uncertainty **13** lack of clarity **14** indefiniteness

vain 4 idle **5** cocky, proud, silly **6** futile **7** foolish, pompous, stuck-up, useless **8** arrogant, boastful, bootless, dandyish, egoistic, nugatory, puffed-up, trifling **9** conceited, egotistic, fruitless, pointless, worthless **10** disdainful, profitless, swaggering, unavailing **11** egotistical, ineffective, ineffectual, superficial, time-wasting **12** selfadmiring, supercilious, unprofitable, unsuccessful, vainglorious **13** selfimportant, self-satisfied

Vainamoinen
origin: 7 Finnish
hero of: 8 Kalevala
form: 8 magician
opposes: 5 Louhi **11** Joukahainen

vainglorious 5 cocky **7** haughty, pompous, stuck-up **8** affected, arrogant, boastful, bragging, insolent **9** conceited **10** egoistical, pretentious, swaggering **11** egotistical, swellheaded **12** narcissistic, supercilious **13** full of oneself, self-important

vainglory 6 vanity **7** conceit, swagger **9** cockiness **10** pretension **11** braggadocio **14** self-importance **16** overbearing pride

vale 6 good-by **8** farewell

valedictory 4 last **5** final **7** parting **8** farewell, terminal, ultimate **9** departing **10** conclusive **11** leavetaking **14** farewell speech **19** commencement address

Valentine
character in: 20 Two Gentlemen of Verona
author: 11 Shakespeare

Valentino, Rudolph
real name: 16 Rodolfo (Alfonzo Raffaele Pierre Philibert) Guglielmi
born: 5 Italy **12** Castellaneta
wife: 9 Jean Acker **14** Natasha Rambova
roles: 8 The Sheik **12** Blood and Sand **16** The Son of the Sheik **17** Monsieur Beaucaire **30** The Four Horsemen of the Apocalypse

valerian 9 Valeriana
varieties: 3 red **5** Greek **6** common **7** African **8** American **11** long-spurred

Valery, Paul
author of: 7 Cahiers, Charmes **12** The Young Fate **13** Le Jeune Parque **16** Sketch of a Serpent **20** The Graveyard by the Sea

Valhalla
origin: 8 Teutonic
hall of: 4 Odin **5** Othin

valiant 4 bold **5** brave, noble **6** daring, heroic **7** gallant **8** fearless, intrepid, knightly, resolute, stalwart, unafraid, valorous **9** audacious, dauntless, undaunted **10** chivalrous, courageous **11** lionhearted, unflinching **12** boldspirited, great-hearted, stouthearted

valid 4 good **5** legal, licit, sound

6 lawful, proper, strong **7** fitting, genuine, logical, weighty **8** accurate, decisive, forceful, official, powerful, suitable, truthful **9** authentic, effective, legalized, realistic **10** acceptable, applicable, compelling, convincing, legitimate **11** substantial, well- founded **12** well-grounded **13** authoritative, being in effect **14** constitutional, legally binding

validate 5 enact, prove, stamp **6** ratify, verify **7** certify, confirm, sustain, warrant, witness **8** legalize, sanction **9** authorize, make legal, make valid **10** make lawful **11** corroborate, countersign **12** authenticate, make official, substantiate

validation 8 sanction **12** confirmation, legalization, ratification **13** authorization, certification

validity 5 force, logic, power, right **6** weight **7** grounds, potency **8** accuracy, legality, strength **9** authority, soundness, substance **10** legal force, legitimacy, properness **11** suitability **12** authenticity, truthfulness **13** acceptability, applicability, effectiveness **14** conclusiveness, convincingness

valise 3 bag **4** grip **7** handbag, luggage, satchel **8** suitcase **9** briefcase, Gladstone **11** portmanteau

Valjean, Jean
    character in: **13** Les Miserables
    author: **4** Hugo

Valkyrie
    origin: **8** Teutonic
    home: **8** Valhalla
    attendant of: **4** Odin **5** Othin
    queen: **8** Brunhild, Brynhild **10** Brunnhilde

Vallee, Rudy
    real name: **17** Hubert Prior Vallee
    nickname: **16** The Vagabond Lover
    born: **13** Island Point VT
    played: **9** saxophone
    wife: **9** Jane Greer
    roles: **16** The Vagabond Lover **17** The Palm Beach Story, Unfaithfully Yours **41** How to Succeed in Business Without Really Trying

Valletta
    capital of: **5** Malta

valley 3 cut, dip, gap **4** dale, dell, glen, vale **5** basin, chasm, glade, gorge, gulch, gully **6** bottom, canyon, divide, hollow, ravine **8** water gap

Valley Forge
    author: **15** Maxwell Anderson

Valley of Horses, The
    author: **9** Jean M Auel

Valley of the Dolls
    author: **16** Jacqueline Susann

valor 4 grit, guts **5** nerve, pluck, spunk **6** daring, mettle **7** bravery, courage, heroism **8** boldness, chivalry **9** fortitude, gallantry **11** intrepidity **12** fearlessness **13** dauntlessness

valorous 4 bold **5** brave, gutsy **6** heroic, plucky **7** valiant **8** fearless, intrepid, stalwart, unafraid **9** dauntless **10** courageous **11** indomitable, lionhearted **12** stouthearted

valse 5 waltz

valuable 4 dear, good **6** costly, prized, useful, valued **7** admired, helpful **8** esteemed, fruitful, precious **9** expensive, important, priceless, respected, treasured **10** beneficial, high-priced, invaluable, profitable, worthwhile **11** serviceable, significant, utilitarian **12** advantageous

valuation 9 appraisal **10** assessment, evaluation **14** estimated value

value, values 3 use **4** cost, help, rate **5** assay, count, judge, merit, price, prize, rules, weigh, worth **6** admire, amount, assess, charge, esteem, ideals, profit, reckon, revere, size up **7** beliefs, benefit, cherish, compute, customs, respect, service, utility **8** appraise, evaluate, prestige, treasure **9** advantage, appraisal, greatness, moral code, practices, standards **10** admiration, appreciate, assessment, estimation, excellence, importance, set store by, usefulness **11** conventions, market price, superiority **12** code of ethics, institutions, significance

valued 6 prized **7** revered **8** esteemed **9** cherished, respected, treasured **11** appreciated **14** highly regarded

valueless 7 trivial, useless **9** worthless **11** of no account, unimportant **13** insignificant **14** good for nothing **15** inconsequential

vamoose 3 out **4** away, scat, shoo **5** be off, leave, scram **6** beat it, begone, depart, get out, go away **7** get lost

vamp 5 siren **9** temptress **10** seductress **11** enchantress, femme fatale **12** introduction

Vamp
    nickname of: **9** Theda Bara

vampire 3 bat **7** Dracula **11** bloodsucker

van 4 cart, dray, head **5** lorry, scout, truck, wagon **6** camper, picket **7** trailer **8** sentinel, vanguard **9** first line, forefront, front rank **10** avantgarde, large truck **12** advance guard, covered truck **13** front of an army **16** foremost division
    french: **7** fourgon

Van, Bobby
    real name: **10** Robert King
    born: **9** New York NY
    roles: **10** Kiss Me Kate, On Your Toes **11** No No Nanette **12** It's Only Money, The Ladies' Man **13** Small Town Girl **23** The Affairs of Dobie Gillis

van Alen, William
    architect of: **16** Chrysler Building (NYC)

Van Allen, James Alfred
    field: **7** physics
    invented: **18** radio proximity fuse
    discovered: **22** Van Allen radiation belts

Van Buren, Martin
    nicknames: **9** The Red Fox **17** The Little Magician **18** The Careful Dutchman
    presidential rank: **6** eighth
    party: **8** Democrat
    state represented: **7** New York
    defeated: **5** (Hugh Lawson) White **6** (William Person) Mangum **7** (Daniel) Webster **8** (William Henry) Harrison
    vice president: **7** (Richard Mentor) Johnson
    cabinet:
        state: **7** (John) Forsyth
        treasury: **8** (Levi) Woodbury
        war: **8** (Joel Roberts) Poinsett
        attorney general: **6** (Benjamin Franklin) Butler, (Felix) Grundy, (Henry Dilworth) Gilpin
        navy: **8** (James Kirke) Paulding **9** (Mahlon) Dickerson
        postmaster general: **5** (John Milton) Niles **7** (Amos) Kendall
    born/died/buried: **12** Kinderhook NY
    education:
        Academy: **10** Kinderhook
        college: **4** none
        studied: **3** law
    religion: **13** Dutch Reformed
    vacation:
        toured: **6** Europe (1853-1855)
    author: **64** Inquiry into the Origin and Course of Political Parties in the United States
    political career: **8** US Senate **11** state Senate **13** vice presi dent **20** state Attorney General
        governor of: **7** New York
        secretary of: **5** State
        minister: **12** Great Britain
    civilian career: lawyer
    notable events of lifetime/term: **5** Panic (of 1837)
        treaty: **16** Webster-Ashburton
        war: **9** Aroostook
    father: **7** Abraham
    mother: **5** Maria (Hoes Van Alen)
    siblings: **6** Derike, Hannah **7** Abraham **8** Lawrence
    wife: **6** Hannah (Hoes)
    children: **4** John **6** Martin **7** Abraham **13** Smith Thompson

Vance, Vivian
    real name: **11** Vivian Jones
    born: **12** Cherryvale KS
    roles: **9** I Love Lucy **10** Ethel Mertz

Vancouver
    hockey team: **7** Canucks

vandal 6 looter, raider **7** ravager, wrecker **8** marauder, pillager, saboteur **9** barbarian, despoiler, destroyer, plunderer **10** demolisher

vandalism 6 damage **10** de facement **11** destruction **17** malicious mischief

vandalize 3 mar **5** trash, wreck **6** damage, deface **7** despoil, destroy

Vanderlyn, John
born: **10** Kingston NY
artwork: **14** Ariadne on Naxos **20** The Death of Jane McCrea **28** Marius Amid the Ruins of Carthage **31** Ariadne Asleep on the Island of Naxos

Van Dyck, Sir Anthony
born: **7** Antwerp **8** Flanders
artwork: **8** Charles I (in Hunting Dress) **11** Iconography **18** Madonna of the Rosary **19** Blessed Herman Joseph, Cardinal Bentiroglio **20** Ecstasy of St Augustine **21** Marchesa Elena Grimaldi

Van Dyke, Dick
born: **12** West Plains MO
roles: **11** Mary Poppins **12** Bye Bye Birdie **15** Diagnosis Murder, Dick Van Dyke Show
brother: **5** Jerry
son: **5** Barry

Vane, Sutton
author of: **12** Outward Bound

Vanessa
author: **11** Hugh Walpole

Van Gogh, Vincent
born: **12** GrootZundert **14** The Netherlands
artwork: **10** Pere Tanguy **11** Cafe at Night, L'Arle sienne **13** The Olive Grove **14** The Starry Night **15** The Potato Eaters **16** The Bridge at Arles **18** Portrait of Dr Gachet, The Chair and the Pipe **22** Cornfield with Cypresses

vanguard 3 van **7** leaders **8** forerank **9** first line, forefront, front line, front rank, spearhead **10** avant-garde, innovators, leadership, modernists **11** pacesetters, tastemakers **12** advance guard, trailblazers, trendsetters

Van Helsing, Dr
character in: **7** Dracula
author: **6** Stoker

vanish 3 die, end **5** cease **6** die out, expire, perish **7** die away **8** dissolve, fade away, melt away, pass away **9** disappear, evaporate, terminate **13** dematerialize **15** become invisible

vanished 4 dead, gone, lost **7** defunct, died out, extinct **11** disappeared

vanishing 8 dying out **10** ex tinction, fading away **11** passing away **12** disappearing **13** disappearance **15** dematerializing

vanitas vanitatum 16 vanity of vanities

vanity 4 sham **5** folly, pride **6** mirage **7** compact, conceit, egotism, falsity, inanity **8** de lusion, futility, idleness, self- love **9** emptiness, powder box, vainglory, vanity bag **10** hollowness, narcissism, self-praise, vanity case

11 makeup table, mirror table, self-conceit, uselessness **13** dressing table, fruitlessness, worthlessness **14** self-admiration, superficiality

Vanity Fair
author: **25** William Makepeace Thackeray
character: **10** Becky Sharp **11** Miss Crawley **12** Amelia Sedley, Joseph (Jos) Sedley **13** George Osborne, Rawdon Crawley **14** Sir Pitt Crawley **20** Captain William Dobbin

vanity of vanities
Latin: **16** vanitas vanitatum

vanquish 4 beat, best, drub, lick, rout **5** crush **6** defeat, master, subdue, thrash **7** conquer **8** overcome **9** overpower, overthrow, overwhelm, subjugate **11** triumph over

vanquisher 6 master, victor, winner **7** subduer **8** champion **9** conqueror **10** subjugator

vanquishment 6 defeat **7** mastery, triumph, victory, winning **8** conquest **10** conquering, overcoming

Van Slyke, Helen
author of: **10** No Love Lost **15** A Necessary Woman, The Heart Listens **18** Always Is Not Forever

Van Tassel, Katrina
character in: **23** The Legend of Sleepy Hollow
author: **6** Irving

Vanuatu
other name: **11** New Hebrides
capital/largest city: **4** Vila
others: **5** Santo **6** Forari **10** Luganville
school: **7** Malapoa
monetary unit: **5** franc **7** centime
island: **3** Api, Epi **4** Aoba, Gaua, Malo, Tana, Vate **5** Banks, Efate, Maewo, Santo, Tanna **6** Ambrym, Mabrim, Torres **8** Anei tyum, Malekula **9** Erromanga, Pentecost, Vanua Lava **13** Espiritu Santo
mountain: **6** Lopevi
highest point: **11** Tabwemasana
sea: **7** Pacific
people: **8** European **10** Melanesian, Polynesian **11** Micronesian
  explorer: **4** Cook **7** Queiros
  leader: **4** Lini
language: **6** French **7** Bislama, English **16** Melanesian Pidgin
religion: **7** animism **8** Anglican, John Frum **10** Protestant **12** Presbyterian **13** Roman Catholic
feature:
  cult: **5** cargo

vapid 4 dull, flat, lame, tame **5** bland, empty, stale **7** insipid **8** lifeless **9** colorless, pointless **10** flavorless, wishy-washy **11** meaningless, uninspiring **12** unsatisfying **13** characterless

vapor 3 dew, fog **4** haze, mist, smog

5 fumes, smoke, steam **6** miasma **8** moisture

vaporize 5 dry up **7** distill **8** condense, melt away **9** dissipate, evaporate

Varden, Gabriel/Dolly
character in: **12** Barnaby Rudge
author: **7** Dickens

Vargas Llosa, Mario
author of: **13** The Green House **16** The Time of the Hero **26** Conversation in the Cathedral **27** Aunt Julia and the Scriptwriter **34** Captain Pantoja and the Special Service

variable 6 fickle, fitful, uneven, unlike **7** diverse, mutable **8** changing, shifting, unstable, wavering **9** alterable, different, spasmodic, unsettled **10** capricious, changeable, inconstant, indefinite **11** fluctuating

variance 4 odds **6** change **7** dispute, quarrel **9** deviation, disparity **10** contention, difference, dissension, divergence, unlikeness **11** discrepancy, incongruity **12** disagreement, modification **13** dissimilarity, inconsistency

variant 7 altered, derived, take off **8** modified **9** departure, different, divergent, variation **10** alteration **11** transformed **12** modification **14** transformation

variation 6 change **7** variant, variety **8** mutation, variance **9** departure, deviation, diversity **10** aberration, alteration, difference, divergency, innovation **11** discrepancy **12** disagreement, modification **13** metamorphosis **14** transformation

varicolored 6 calico, motley, tartan **7** dappled, flecked, marbled, mottled, piebald **9** multi-hued **10** iridescent, opalescent, variegated **11** rainbowlike, technicolor **12** multicolored, particolored **13** polychromatic

varied 5 mixed **6** motley, sundry **7** diverse, various **8** assorted **9** different **10** variegated **11** diversified **13** heterogeneous, miscellaneous

variegated 4 pied **6** motley **7** checked, dappled, mottled, piebald **9** checkered **12** parti-colored

variety 4 hash, kind, race, sort, type **5** brand, breed, class, genre, genus, group, stock, tribe **6** change, family, jumble, medley, motley, strain **7** melange, mixture, species **8** category, division, pastiche **9** diversity, patchwork, variation **10** assortment, collection, difference, hodgepodge, innovation, miscellany, subspecies **11** subdivision **12** denomination, multiplicity, unconformity **13** dissimilarity, heterogeneity, nonuniformity **14** classification, omnium-gatherum **15** diversification

various 3 few **4** many, some **5** other **6** divers, myriad, sundry, varied

7 diverse, several **8** assorted, manifold, numerous **9** countless, different **10** dissimilar **11** innumerable **12** multifarious **13** miscellaneous, multitudinous

varlet 3 cur **6** rascal, wretch **7** villain **9** scoundrel **10** blackguard

Varner, Will
character in: **9** The Hamlet
author: **8** Faulkner

varnish 4 gilt **5** adorn, cover, gloss, stain **6** excuse, soften **7** conceal, lacquer **8** disguise, mitigate **9** embellish, gloss over **10** smooth over

vary 4 veer **5** alter, shift **6** change, depart, differ, modify **7** deviate, dissent, diverge **8** be unlike, contrast, disagree **9** alternate, disaccord, diversify, fluctuate

vase 3 jar, jug, pot, urn **5** crock, diota **8** canister **9** container **10** jardiniere

Vashti
husband: **9** Ahasuerus
replaced by: **6** Esther

vassal 4 serf **5** helot, liege, slave **6** tenant, thrall **7** bondman, servant, subject, villein **8** retainer **9** bondslave, bondwoman, dependent **11** subordinate

vassalage 4 yoke **7** bondage, serfdom, slavery **9** servitude **11** enslavement

vast 4 huge, wide **5** great, jumbo **7** endless, immense, titanic, very big **8** colossal, enormous, far-flung, gigantic, infinite, spacious **9** boundless, capacious, extensive, limitless, monstrous, unbounded, unlimited, very large **10** monumental, prodigious, stupendous, tremendous, voluminous, widespread **11** far-reaching, measureless, significant, substantial **12** immeasurable, interminable

vastness 7 bigness **8** enormity, hugeness **9** immensity, largeness **12** enormousness

Vatican City 10 papal state
enclave in: **4** Rome
includes: **7** Vatican **13** Sistine Chapel **16** St. Peter's Basilica
retreat: **14** Castel Gandolfo
statue: **7** Laocoon

Vaughan Williams, Ralph
born: **7** Britain **10** Down Ampney
composer of: **3** Job **8** The Wasps **9** Flos Campi **10** Antarctica (symphony No 7), **11** Old King Cole **12** A Sea Symphony **13** Hugh the Drover, On Wenlock Edge, Sir John in Love, Songs of Travel **14** Riders to the Sea, The House of Life, The Sons of Light **15** A London Symphony, The Poisoned Kiss **16** The Lark Ascending **17** A Pastoral Symphony **18** Five Tudor Portraits, Sinfonia Antarctica **19** The Pilgrim's Progress **22** Toward the Unknown Region

Vaughn, Robert

born: **9** New York NY
roles: **7** Bullitt **12** Napoleon Solo **15** The Man from UNCLE **19** The Magnificent Seven **22** The Young Philadelphians

vault 4 arch, dome, jump, leap, safe, tomb **5** bound, clear, crypt **6** arcade, cupola, hurdle, spring **7** ossuary **8** catacomb, jump over, leapfrog, leap over, wall safe **9** mausoleum, polevault, sepulcher, strongbox **10** arched roof, spring over, strongroom **13** arched ceiling, burial chamber

vaunt 5 strut **6** brag of, flaunt **7** exult in, show off, swagger **9** crow about, gasconade, gloat over **10** boast about

vaunted 7 exalted, praised **11** gloated over, overpraised **12** boasted about

veer 3 yaw **4** jibe, tack, turn **5** curve, dodge, drift, shift, wheel **6** swerve, zigzag **7** go about **9** come round, turn aside **15** change direction

Vegas
character: **5** Angie **6** Binzer **8** Beatrice, Dan Tanna **10** Bernie Roth **11** (Sgt) Bella Archer
cast: **10** Tony Curtis **11** Judy Landers, Robert Urich **12** Naomi Stevens, Phyllis Davis **13** Bart Braverman

vegetable 3 pea **4** bean, beet, corn **6** carrot, greens, legume, squash, turnip **7** cabbage, lettuce, parsnip, produce, spinach **8** broccoli, eggplant, lima bean, rutabaga, zucchini **10** string bean **11** cauliflower

vegetarian 5 vegan **8** meatless **9** herbivore **11** herbivorous

vegetation 5 flora, grass, sloth, weeds **6** leaves, plants, torpor **7** foliage, herbage, languor, loafing, verdure **8** dormancy, idleness, lethargy **9** flowerage, indolence, plant life, shrubbery **10** inactivity **11** hibernation, languidness, rustication **12** sluggishness
god of: **6** Dumuzi

vehemence 4 heat, zeal **5** ardor **6** fervor, warmth **7** passion **9** intensity

vehement 3 hot **4** wild **5** eager, fiery, rabid **6** ardent, fervid, fierce, heated, stormy **7** earnest, excited, fanatic, fervent, furious, intense, violent, zealous **8** agitated, forceful, frenzied, vigorous **9** emotional, fanatical, hotheaded **10** passionate **11** impassioned, tempestuous **12** enthusiastic

vehemently 5 hotly **6** wildly **7** eagerly **8** ardently, fiercely, strongly **9** earnestly, excitedly, fervently, furiously, intensely, violently, zealously **10** vigorously **11** emotionally, fanatically **12** passionately **13** tempestuously **16** enthusiastically

vehicle 3 bus, car **4** tool **5** agent, means, organ, plane, train, truck **6** agency, device, medium **7** bicycle **9** mechanism **10** automobile, conveyance, instrument, motorcycle, rocket

ship **12** intermediary **14** transportation

veil 3 dim **4** hide, mask **5** cloak, cloud, cover **6** enwrap, mantle, screen, shroud **7** blanket, conceal, curtain, envelop, obscure **8** covering **10** camouflage

veiled 3 dim **5** murky **6** draped, hidden **7** muffled **8** obscured, shrouded **9** concealed, covered up, disguised, enveloped, enwrapped **11** camouflaged

veiling 3 net **4** mesh **8** cloaking, covering **9** obscurity **10** concealing

vein 3 rib, web **4** bent, hint, line, lode, mark, mood, seam, tone **5** fleck, layer, stria, style, touch **6** furrow, manner, marble, nature, strain, streak, stripe, temper, thread **7** stratum **8** tendency **9** capillary, character **10** complexion, propensity **11** blood vessel, disposition, inclination, temperament **12** predilection **14** predisposition

Velazquez (Velasquez), Diego Rodriguez de Silva y
born: **5** Spain **7** Seville
artwork: **8** Philip IV **10** Las Meninas **13** Luis de Gongora, Pope Innocent X, Venus and Cupid **14** Cardinal Borgia **17** Don Gaspar de Guzman, Isabella of Bourbon **18** Adoration of the Magi, The Tapestry Weavers **19** The Infanta Margarita, The Surrender of Breda **20** Infanta Maria Theresia **21** An Old Woman Cooking Eggs **22** Portrait of a Court Jester, Portrait of Juan de Pareja **23** The Immaculate Conception **30** Prince Balthasar Carlos at the Hunt

veloce
music: **4** fast

velocity 4 pace **5** haste, speed **8** alacrity, celerity, rapidity **9** fleetness, quickness, swiftness **10** expedition, speediness

venal 5 shady **6** greedy **7** corrupt, crooked, selfish **8** bribable, covetous, grasping **9** dishonest, mercenary, rapacious **10** avaricious **11** corruptible **12** unprincipled, unscrupulous **13** money-grubbing

venality 7 avarice **10** corruption **11** bribe-taking **13** mercenariness, money-grubbing

vend 4 hawk, sell **5** trade **6** barter, deal in, market, peddle, retail **7** auction, trade in **8** huckster **11** merchandise

Vendetta, La
author: **14** Honore de Balzac

vendor, vender 6 dealer, hawker, monger, seller, trader **7** peddler **8** huckster, merchant, purveyor, retailer, salesman, supplier **9** tradesman **10** wholesaler **12** merchandiser **13** street peddler

veneer 4 coat, mask, show **5** front, layer **6** casing, facade, facing, jacket, sheath **7** coating, overlay, wrapper **8** covering, envelope, pretense **10** outer layer

venerable 3 old **4** aged **5** hoary **6** august **7** admired, ancient, elderly, honored, revered **8** esteemed **9** respected, venerated **11** patriarchal, white-haired

venerate 5 adore, extol, honor **6** admire, esteem, hallow, revere **7** cherish, glorify, idolize, respect, worship **8** look up to **9** reverence **11** pay homage to

venerated 4 holy **5** loved **6** adored, sacred **7** honored, revered **8** hallowed **9** respected **10** reverenced, worshipped **12** paid homage to

veneration 3 awe **5** honor **6** esteem, homage, wonder **7** respect, worship **8** devotion **9** adoration, adulation, reverence **10** admiration, exaltation **11** idolization **13** glorification

venereal 6 carnal, sexual **7** genital

Venezuela
name means: 12 little Venice
capital/largest city: 7 Caracas
others: 4 Aroa, Coro **6** Atures, Cumana, Merida **7** Barinas, Barines, Cabello, Guaware, Maracay, Maturin **8** Asuncion, Carupano, La Guaira, La Gyayra, Tacupita, Valencia **9** Barcelona, Maracaibo, Tacarigua **12** Barquisimeto, Puerto La Cruz, San Cristobal **13** Ciudad Bolivar, Puerto Cabello **18** Santo Tome de Guayana
division: 4 Lara **5** Apure, Sucre, Zulia **6** Aragua, Falcon, Merida **7** Barinas, Bolivar, Cojedes, Guarico, Monagas, Tachira, Yaracuy **8** Carabobo, Trujillo
measure: 5 galon **6** fanega **7** estadel
monetary unit: 4 peso **5** medio **6** fuerte **7** bolivar, centimo **8** morocota **10** venezolano
weight: 3 bag **5** libra
island: 4 Aves **7** Cubagua, Tortuga **9** La Orchila, Los Roques, Margarita **11** Los Hermanos **12** La Blanquilla
lake: 9 Maracaibo, Tacarigua
mountain: 3 Pao **4** Pava, Yair **5** Andes, Duida, Icutu **6** Concha, Cuneva, Merida, Parima, Sierra, Yumari **7** Imutaca, Masaiti, Roraima **8** Gurupira **9** Pacaraima **10** Auyan-Tepui **11** Turimiquire **18** Cordillera del Norte
highest point: 7 Bolivar
river: 3 Oro, Pao **4** Meta **5** Apure, Caura, Negro, Suata, Tigre, Unare, Zulia **6** Amazon, Arauca, Caroni, Cuyuni **7** Guanare, Guanipa, Guarico, Orinoco, Oritueo, Paragua, Suapure, Vichada, Yuruari **8** Guaviare, Manapire, Ventuari **9** Cuchivero **10** Casiquiare, Portuguesa
sea: 8 Atlantic **9** Caribbean
physical feature:

falls: 5 Angel
gulf: 5 Paria **6** Triste **9** Venezuela
highlands: 6 Guiana **7** Guayana, Segovia
plains: 6 Llanos
people: 4 Bare, Pume **5** Bello, Carib, pardo, zambo **6** Arawak, Creole, Timote **7** Charoya, Guahibo, Kaliana, mestizo, mulatto, Otomaca, Timotex **8** Caquetio, Guarauno, Matilone **11** Maquiritare
artist: 7 Marisol
author: 5 Bello **8** Gallegos **13** Diaz-Rodriguez
explorer: 8 Columbus
god: 5 Tsuma
leader: 4 Paez **5** Gomez, Leoni **6** Castro **7** Bolivar, Miranda **10** Betancourt **12** Guzman Blanco **14** Herrera Campins
language: 4 Pume **7** Spanish
religion: 5 Islam **7** Judaism **10** Protestant **13** Roman Catholic
feature:
animal: 4 puma **5** sloth **6** jaguar, ocelot **7** manatee, peccary **8** anteater, capybara **9** armadillo
cowboy: 7 llanero
dance: 6 joropo **16** diablos danzantes
folk entertainment: 10 burriquita
musical instrument: 6 cuatro **7** maracas
street performance: 8 parranda
food:
black beans: 8 caraotas
bread: 5 arepa
dish: 7 hallaca **8** cachapos, pabellon
soup/stew: 8 sancocho

vengeance 7 revenge **8** avenging, reprisal, requital **11** malevolence, retaliation, retribution **12** ruthlessness **13** an eye for an eye, implacability **14** revengefulness, vindictiveness **15** a tooth for a tooth

veni, vidi, vici 19 I came I saw I conquered
author: 12 Julius Caesar

venial 5 minor **6** slight **7** trivial **9** allowable, excusable **10** defensible, forgivable, not serious, pardonable **11** justifiable, unimportant, warrantable

Venice
art exhibition: 8 Biennale
artist: 7 Bellini, Codussi **8** Fabriano, Longhena, Mantegna, Palladio, Scamozzi, Veronese **9** Canaletto, Carpaccio, Giorgione, Sansovino **10** Tintoretto
capital of: 6 Veneto **15** Venezia province
church: 18 San Giorgio Maggiore, Santa Maria dei Frari **19** Santi Giovanni e Paolo
Italian: 7 Venezia
landmark: 6 Ca' d'Oro **9** Campanile **10** Grand Canal **11** Doge's Palace

13 Bridge of Sighs **15** Libreria Vecchia **16** Palazzo Rezzonico, Saint Mark's Church **20** Accademia di Belle Arti **21** Palazzo dei Procuratori **22** Scuola Grande di San Rocco **23** Palazzo Vendramin-Calergi
port: 8 Marghera
resort: 9 Lido Beach
sea: 8 Adriatic
small canal: 3 rii
tomb: 5 Titan
traveler: 9 Marco Polo

Venn, Diggory
character in: 17 Return of the Native
author: 5 Hardy

venom 3 ire **4** gall, hate **5** anger, spite, toxin, virus **6** choler, enmity, grudge, hatred, malice, poison, rancor, spleen **7** ill will **8** acrimony, savagery **9** animosity, barbarity, brutality, hostility **10** bitterness, resentment **11** malevolence **12** spitefulness **13** maliciousness, rancorousness

venomous 5 cruel, fatal, toxic **6** bitter, brutal, deadly, lethal, malign, savage **7** abusive, caustic, hostile, noxious, vicious **8** spiteful, virulent **9** malicious, malignant, poisonous, rancorous, resentful **10** malevolent **11** illdisposed **12** bloodthirsty

vent 3 air, tap **4** bare, drip, emit, flue, gush, hole, ooze, pipe **5** exude, spout, utter, voice **6** effuse, escape, faucet, let out, outlet, reveal, spigot **7** air hole, chimney, debouch, declare, divulge, express, opening, orifice, release **8** aperture, disclose, exposure, venthole **9** discharge, let escape, pour forth, utterance **10** disclosure, expression, revelation, smoke stack, ventilator **11** communicate, declaration

ventilate 3 air, sow **5** voice **6** aerate, air out, report, review, spread **7** analyze, declare, discuss, dissent, divulge, examine, express **9** broadcast, circulate, comment on, criticize, oxygenate, publicize, talk about **10** bandy about **11** disseminate, noise abroad

ventilator 3 fan **4** flue **7** aera tor **10** exhaust fan, smoke stack **14** air conditioner

venture 2 go **3** bet, try **4** dare, risk **5** flyer, offer, wager **6** chance, gamble, hazard, plunge, submit, tender, travel **7** advance, attempt, hold out, presume, proffer, project **8** endeavor, make bold **9** adventure, risk going, strive for, undertake, volunteer **10** enterprise, put forward, take a flyer **11** speculation, uncertainty, undertaking

venturesome, adventuresome 4 bold, rash **5** risky **6** daring, tricky, unsafe, unsure **7** dubious **8** doubtful, insecure, perilous, reckless, ticklish **9** ambitious, audacious, dangerous, daredevil, energetic, foolhardy, hazardous, impetuous, impulsive, uncertain **10** aggressive, precarious **11** adventurous, speculative **12** enterprising, questionable

venturesomeness 6 daring **8** audacity, boldness **9** derring-do **11** impetuosity **12** recklessness

Venus
  origin: 5 Roman **7** Italian
  goddess of: 4 love **6** beauty, spring **7** gardens
  son: 6 Aeneas
  grandson: 5 Iulus
  epithet: 7 Erycina **8** Gene trix **10** Erticordia
  also see Aphrodite

Venus and Adonis
  author: 18 William Shakespeare

veracious 4 true **6** honest **7** sincere **8** accurate, faithful, truthful **10** scrupulous **11** punctilious

veracity 5 truth **6** candor, verity **7** honesty, probity **8** accu racy, openness **9** exactness, frankness, integrity, sincerity **10** exactitude **11** correctness **12** truthfulness **13** guileless ness, ingenuousness **14** verisimilitude

Vera-Ellen
  real name: 13 Vera-Ellen Rohe
  born: 12 Cincinnati OH
  roles: 9 On the Town **14** White Christmas

veranda
  Hawaiian: 5 lanai

verbal 4 oral, said **5** vocal **6** spoken, voiced **7** in words, of verbs, of words, uttered **9** expressed, unwritten

verbal exchange 6 dialog **8** dialogue **10** discussion **12** conversation

verbalize 5 speak, utter, voice **7** express **10** articulate **12** put into words

verbal thrust 3 dig **4** gibe, jeer **5** taunt **13** cutting remark

verbatim 5 exact **7** exactly, literal, precise **8** accurate, faith ful **9** literally, literatim, precisely **10** accurately, faithfully **11** to the letter, word for word **15** chapter and verse, letter for letter
  Latin: 14 ipsissima verba

verbatim et literatim 21 in exactly the same words **29** word for word and letter for letter

verbena
  varieties: 4 moss, rose, sand **5** clump, lemon, shrub **7** red sand **8** pink sand **9** beach sand **10** desert sand, Mojave sand, yellow sand **12** common garden

verbiage 9 logorrhea, loquacity, prolixity, verbosity, wordiness **10** volubility **11** verboseness **12** effusiveness **14** circumlocution, grandiloquence, longwindedness

verbose 5 gabby, wordy **6** prolix **7** voluble **8** effusive **9** garrulous, talka-

tive **10** longwinded, loquacious **13** grandiloquent **14** circumlocutory

verbosity 9 diffusion, prolixity, talkiness, wordiness **11** diffuseness **13** talkativeness **14** long-windedness

verboten 9 forbidden **10** prohibited

Verdandi 4 Norn
  origin: 12 Scandinavian
  form: 3 elf
  personifies: 7 present
  developed from: 5 Urdar
  companions: 3 Urd **5** Skuld

verdant 4 lush **5** green, leafy, shady, turfy **6** grassy **7** meadowy **8** blooming, thriving **9** luxuriant **10** burgeoning, springlike **11** flourishing

Verdi, Giuseppe
  born: 5 Italy **7** Busseto
  composer of: 4 Aida **6** Otello **7** Macbeth, Nabucco, Othello **8** Falstaff **9** Don Carlos, Il Corsaro, Rigoletto, The Misled **10** La Traviata **11** Il Trovatore **13** The Troubadour **14** Manzoni Requiem **15** Simon Boccanegra

verdict 6 answer, decree, ruling **7** finding, opinion **8** decision, judgment, sentence **9** valuation **10** assessment, estimation **11** arbitrament, arbitration **12** adjudication **13** determination

Vere, Captain
  character in: 9 Billy Budd
  author: 8 Melville

Vereen, Ben
  born: 7 Miami FL
  roles: 5 Roots **6** Pippin **13** Chicken George **20** Jesus Christ Superstar

verge 3 end, hem, lip, rim **4** brim, edge **5** bound, brink, ledge, limit, skirt **6** be near, border, flange, fringe, margin **7** confine, extreme **8** up proach, boundary, frontier, terminus **9** threshold **11** approximate **12** be on the brink

verge upon 4 abut **5** flank **6** adjoin, border **8** be next to **10** neighbor on

Vergil, Virgil
  author of: 6 Aeneid **8** Bucolics, Eclogues, Georgics

verification 5 proof **7** support **9** guarantee **10** validation **12** confirmation **13** accreditation, certification, corroboration, documentation **14** authentication, substantiation

verify 5 prove **7** certify, confirm, support, sustain, witness **8** accredit, attest to, document, validate, vouch for **9** establish, guarantee, testify to **11** corroborate **12** authenticate, substantiate

verily 4 amen **5** truly **6** really **9** certainly, yes indeed **10** positively

veritable 4 real, true **5** utter, valid **6** actual **7** genuine, literal **8** absolute, bona fide, complete, positive, true-blue **9** authentic **13** incontestable, unimpeachable **14** unquestionable **17** through-and-through

Verlaine, Paul
  author of: 6 Wisdom **7** Sagesse **8** Langueur **17** Songs Without Words **19** Romances sans Paroles

Vermeer, Jan
  born: 5 Delft **7** Holland
  artwork: 11 View of Delft **12** The Lace Maker, The Procuress **13** Drinking Scene **14** A Street in Delft, The Head of a Girl **15** Alle gory of Faith, Girl with a Red Hat **16** The Artist's Studio **18** Girl Reading a Letter, Girl with a Wine glass **19** A Girl Asleep at a Table, A Painter in his Studio **20** A Woman Weighing Pearls **22** Maidservant Pouring Milk **23** Young Woman with a Water Jug **24** A Soldier and a Laughing Girl **31** Christ in the House of Mary and Martha

vermilion 3 red **7** scarlet **8** cinnabar **9** bright red **15** mercuric sulfide

vermin 4 ants, lice, mice, owls, rats **5** crows, fleas, foxes, pests **6** snakes, wolves **7** bed bugs, coyotes, roaches, spiders, weasels **8** termites, varmints **9** water bugs **10** centipedes, silverfish **11** birds of prey **18** pestiferous insects

Vermont
  abbreviation: 2 VT
  nickname: 13 Green Mountain **20** Four-Season Recreation
  capital: 10 Montpelier
  largest city: 10 Burlington
  others: 5 Barre, Stowe **7** Grafton, Newfane, Newport, Rutland **8** St Albans, Winooski **9** Bountiful, Vergennes **10** Bennington **11** Brattleboro
  college: 7 Goddard, Norwich, Trinity, Windham **8** Marlboro **10** Bennington, Middlebury, St Michaels
  feature:
    covered bridge: 5 Scott
    house: 15 Old Constitution
    monument: 6 Battle
  people: 9 John Deere, John Dewey **10** Ethan Allen **12** Brigham Young **13** Warren R Austin **15** Stephen A Douglas
  lake: 7 Caspian, Dunmore, Seymour **8** Bomoseen **9** Champlain **10** Willoughby **12** Memphremagog
  land rank: 10 forty-third
  mountain: 5 Green, White **7** Bromley, Hogback, Taconic **8** Prospect, Stratton
    highest point: 9 Mansfield
  physical feature:
    uplands: 10 New England
    valley: 9 Champlain
  president: 14 Calvin Coolidge, Chester A Arthur
  river: 4 West **5** Otter, White **7** Saxtons **8** Lamoille, Nulhegan, Winooski **10** Missisquoi **11** Connecticut
  state admission: 10 fourteenth
  state bird: 12 hermit thrush
  state animal: 11 Morgan horse
  state flower: 9 red clover

state motto: 15 Freedom and Unity
state song: 11 Hail Vermont
state tree: 10 sugar maple

vermouth
type: 4 wine **6** brandy **8** aperitif
origin: 5 Italy **6** France
varieties: 3 dry **5** sweet
drink: 9 Boomerang **11** Bittersweet
with bourbon: 9 Allegheny
with brandy: 3 BVD
with Dubonnet: 3 BVD
gin: 5 Bijou, Bronx, Tango **6** Caruso **7** Bermuda, Caberet, Martini **10** Bloodhound
with rum: 6 Bolero **8** Apple Pie **10** Black Devil **11** Shark's Tooth
with rye: 8 Brooklyn **9** Algonquin
with scotch: 8 Affinity **10** Bobby Burns
with sherry: 6 Bamboo, Brazil
with sloe gin: 10 Blackthorn
with vodka: 8 Kangaroo **9** Corkscrew
with whiskey: 9 Manhattan

vernacular 4 cant **5** idiom, lingo, slang **6** jargon, patois **7** dialect **8** parlance, shoptalk **9** the vulgar **12** common speech, native tongue **13** natural speech **14** informal speech, native language

vernal 3 new **5** fresh, green **6** spring **8** youthful **10** springlike

Verne, Jules
author of: 19 Five Weeks in a Balloon **21** From the Earth to the Moon **26** Around the World in Eighty Days **32** Twenty Thousand Leagues Under the Sea
character: 11 Captain Nemo, Phineas Fogg **12** Passepartout

Veronese, Paolo (Cagliari)
born: 5 Italy **6** Verona
artwork: 12 Book of Esther **13** The Last Supper **14** Supper at Emmaus **15** The Rape of Europa, Triumph of Venice **17** Mary with the Saints, The Finding of Moses, The Marriage at Cana, Wisdom and Strength **19** Martyrdom of St George, The Choice of Hercules **21** Esther before Ahasuerus **22** Feast at the House of Simon **24** Mars and Venus United in Love, The Feast in the House of Levi, The Temptation of St Anthony **31** Jesus and the Centurion of Capernaum **32** The Family of Darius before Alexander

Verrocchio, Andrea del
real name: 31 Andrea di Michele di Francesco Cione
born: 5 Italy **8** Florence
artwork: 5 David **15** Boy with a Dolphin **17** Christ and St Thomas **18** The Baptism of Christ **19** Bartolommeo Colleoni **23** Christ and Doubting Thomas **25** Beheading of John the Baptist

versatile 3 apt **4** able **5** handy

6 adroit, clever, expert, gifted **7** protean **8** talented **9** adaptable, all-around, ingenious, many-sided **10** proficient **11** many-skilled, resourceful **12** accomplished, multifaceted

verse 4 poem **5** meter, rhyme, stave **6** jingle, poetry, stanza **7** measure, strophe

versed 4 able **5** adept **6** expert, taught **7** erudite, learned, skilled, tutored **8** lettered, schooled, skillful, well-read **9** competent, practiced, scholarly **10** at home with, instructed, proficient **11** enlightened, experienced **12** accomplished, familiar with, well-informed **14** acquainted with, conversant with

versifier 4 bard **6** rhymer, writer **8** minstrel, poetizer, poetling, rhymster **9** poetaster, rhymester **10** rhymesmith, troubadour, versemaker, versesmith **11** versemonger **12** balladmonger

version 4 side **5** story **6** report **7** account **9** depiction, rendering **10** adaptation, paraphrase, re-creation **11** description, re statement, translation **14** interpretation

vers libre 9 free verse

vertebral column
bone of: 5 spine **8** backbone

vertex 3 cap, tip **4** apex, peak **5** crown **6** summit, zenith **8** pinnacle **12** highest point **13** crowning point

vertical 5 plumb, sheer **7** up right **12** ninety-degree **13** perpendicular

vertiginous 5 dizzy, giddy, shaky **6** whirly **7** reeling **11** lightheaded

vertigo 7 reeling **8** fainting **9** dizziness, giddiness **12** unsteadiness **15** lightheadedness

Vertigo
director: 15 Alfred Hitchcock
cast: 8 Kim Novak **12** James Stewart **16** Barbara Bel Geddes
setting: 12 San Francisco
score: 15 Bernard Herrmann

verve 3 vim, zip **4** dash, elan, fire, zeal **5** ardor, drive, force, gusto, punch, vigor **6** energy, fervor, relish, spirit, warmth **7** abandon, feeling, passion, rapture, sparkle **8** vitality, vivacity **9** animation, eagerness, vehemence **10** enthusiasm, liveliness

Verver, Maggie
character in: 13 The Golden Bowl
author: 5 James

very 4 bare, mere, most, much, pure **5** exact, extra, plain, quite, sheer, truly **6** deeply, highly, hugely, mighty, really, simple, vastly **7** awfully, exactly, fitting, greatly, notably, perfect, precise, totally **8** actually, entirely, markedly, specific, suitable, terribly **9** assuredly, certainly, decidedly, eminently, essential, extremely, immensely, intensely, necessary, obviously, perfectly, precisely, unusually,

veritably **10** abnormally, absolutely, abundantly, completely, defi nitely, especially, particular, profoundly, remarkably, strikingly, thoroughly, uncommonly, undeniably **11** appropriate, exceedingly, excessively **12** emphatically, surpassingly, tremendously **13** exceptionally, significantly **14** unquestionably

very best
French: 14 creme de la creme

Very Easy Death, A
author: 16 Simone de Beauvoir

very great 4 huge **6** severe **7** extreme, intense, mammoth, titanic **8** colossal, enormous, gigantic **9** excessive, monstrous **10** gargantuan, immoderate, inordinate, prodigious **11** magnificent, spectacular **14** Brobdingnagian

very nearly 6 almost **7** close to **9** just about **10** more or less, not far from **13** approximately

very old 4 aged **6** primal **7** ancient, antique, archaic **8** primeval **10** antiquated, primordial **11** prehistoric **12** antediluvian

very soon
French: 11 tout a l'heure

vessel 3 cup, jar, jug, keg, mug, pot, tub, vat **4** boat, bowl, butt, cask, dish, duct, scow, ship, tube, vase, vein **5** barge, craft, crock, flask, glass, liner, plate, yacht **6** artery, barrel, beaker, carafe, flagon, goblet, packet, tanker, whaler **7** caldron, collier, cruiser, platter, tankard, trawler, tugboat, tumbler, utensil **8** decanter, paquebot, sailboat **9** capillary, container, ferry boat, freighter, houseboat, steamboat, steamship **10** ocean liner, receptacle

vest 3 rig **4** garb, robe **5** array, drape, dress **6** attire, clothe, enwrap, fit out, jacket, jerkin **7** apparel, deck out, doublet, envelop **8** accouter **9** waistcoat

Vesta
origin: 5 Roman
goddess of: 6 hearth
festival: 8 Vestalia
corresponds to: 4 Caca **6** Hestia

vestal 4 pure **6** chaste, maiden, simple, virgin **8** maidenly, virginal, virtuous **9** pure woman, undefiled, unmarried, unworldly **10** immaculate **15** unsophisticated

vested 5 fixed **7** settled **8** absolute, complete **9** permanent **10** guaranteed **11** established, inalienable **12** indisputable **14** unquestionable

vestibule 4 hall **5** entry, foyer, lobby **6** lounge **7** hallway, passage **8** anteroom, corridor **10** passageway **11** antecham ber, entrance way, waiting room **12** entrance hall

vestige 4 sign **5** relic, token, trace

6 record 7 memento, remnant 8 evidence, souvenir

vestment 3 alb 4 garb, gear 5 amice, dress 6 livery, outfit 7 apparel, clothes, costume, raiment, regalia, uniform 8 clothing 9 trappings 13 accoutrements

vesture 4 robe 5 robes 7 apparel, clothes, garment, raiment 8 clothing, garments 9 vestments

vetch 5 Vicia
  varieties: 3 cow 4 bard, bird, milk 5 crown, hairy, Sitka 6 bitter, common, kidney, purple, smooth, spring, tufted, winter 8 Narbonne 9 horseshoe, Hungarian, woolly-pod 12 large Russian

veteran 3 vet 6 expert, master 7 old hand 8 old-timer, seasoned 9 ex-soldier 10 campaigner, old soldier, war veteran 11 experienced 12 ex-serviceman 13 long- practiced

veto 4 deny, void 6 denial, enjoin, forbid, negate, reject 7 nullify, prevent, refusal 8 disallow, prohibit, turn down 9 rejection 10 prevention 11 disallowing, prohibition 12 disallowance 16 turn thumbs down on

vex 3 bug, irk 4 fret, gall, miff, pain, rile 5 anger, annoy, chafe, harry, pique, upset, worry 6 badger, bother, grieve, harass, hassle, nettle, pester, plague, ruffle 7 chagrin, disturb, provoke, torment, trouble 8 distress, irritate 9 displease 10 exasperate 18 ruffle one's feathers

vexation 5 pique, trial 6 hassle 7 torment 8 headache, nuisance 9 annoyance 10 affliction, harassment, irritation 11 aggravation 13 pain in the neck

vexatious 5 pesky 6 thorny, vexing 8 annoying, nettling 9 badgering, harassing, hectoring, provoking, troubling, worrisome 10 bothersome, irritating 11 disquieting, pestiferous, troublesome

vexed 5 irked, riled, testy 6 galled, miffed, piqued 7 annoyed, nettled, peevish 8 provoked 9 irritated 11 disgruntled, exasperated

viable 6 usable 8 feasible, workable 9 adaptable, practical 10 applicable 11 practicable

viaduct 4 ramp, span 8 overpass

vial 5 ampul, flask, phial 7 ampoule

via media 10 a middle way

viands 4 cate, diet, eats, fare, food 7 cuisine, edibles, vittles 8 victuals 9 provender 10 foodstuffs, provisions

vibrancy 4 fire 5 ardor 7 elation 8 vitality, vivacity 9 animation 10 enthusiasm 11 high spirits

vibrant 4 deep, loud 5 alive, eager, vital, vivid 6 ardent, bright, florid, lively 7 fervent, glowing, intense,

orotund, pealing, pulsing, radiant, ringing 8 animated, bell-like, colorful, forceful, luminous, lustrous, resonant, sonorous, spirited, vehement 9 brilliant, deep-toned, energetic, quivering, thrilling, throbbing, vibrating, vivacious 10 fluttering, glittering, resounding, shimmering 11 full of vigor, resplendent, reverber ant 12 electrifying, enthusiastic

vibrate 4 beat, sway 5 quake, swing, throb, waver 6 quaver, quiver, ripple, wobble 7 flut ter, pulsate, tremble 8 undulate 9 oscillate, palpitate, pendulate 11 reverberate

vibration 5 quake 6 quiver, tremor 7 quaking 9 quivering, throbbing, trembling

vicar 6 cleric, parson, pastor 8 preacher 9 churchman, clergyman 12 ecclesiastic

vicarious 6 mental 7 by proxy 8 imagined, indirect 9 imaginary, surrogate 10 empathetic, fantasized, secondhand 11 at one remove, sympathetic

Vicar of Wakefield, The
  author: 15 Oliver Goldsmith
  character: 6 George, Olivia, Sophia 7 Deborah 10 Dr Primrose, Mr Burchill 14 Arabella Wilmot 15 Squire Thornhill 19 Sir William Thornhill

vice 4 flaw 5 fault 6 defect 7 blemish, failing, frailty 8 iniquity, weakness 9 depravity, weak point 10 corruption, debauchery, degeneracy, profligacy, wantonness, wickedness 11 shortcoming 12 imperfection 14 licentiousness

vice president
  resigned: 10 Spiro Agnew 12 John C Calhoun
  accused of treason: 9 Aaron Burr 17 John C Breckinridge
  youngest elected: 17 John C Breckinridge
  elected by Senate: 14 Richard Johnson
  elected but did not serve: 11 William King
  rejected nomination: 11 Frank Lowden, Silas Wright
  lived longest: 15 John Nance Garner
  succeeded to presidency: 9 John Tyler 10 Gerald Ford 12 Harry S Truman 13 Andrew Johnson 14 Calvin Coolidge, Chester A Arthur, Lyndon B Johnson 15 Millard Fillmore 17 Theodore Roosevelt

vice versa 9 in reverse 10 conversely 12 contrariwise 16 the other way round 18 in the opposite order

vicinity 4 area 6 region 8 environs, locality, vicinage 9 adjoining, precincts, proximity 11 environment, precinct 12 neighborhood, surroundings

vicious 3 bad 4 base, evil, foul, mean, vile, wild 5 awful, cruel, gross, nasty, surly 6 brutal, fierce, horrid, savage,

sullen, wicked 7 hateful, heinous, hellish, immoral, inhuman, untamed, violent 8 churlish, depraved, fiendish, libelous, shocking, spiteful, terrible, venomous 9 abhorrent, atrocious, barbarous, dangerous, ferocious, invidious, malicious, monstrous, nefarious, offensive, predatory, rancorous 10 abominable, defamatory, diabolical, ill-humored, ill-natured, malevolent, pernicious, slanderous, villainous, vindictive 11 acrimonious, ill-tempered, treacherous 12 bloodthirsty

viciousness 4 evil 6 malice 7 cruelty 8 ferocity, savagery, villainy, violence 9 barbarity, brutality, ill nature 10 fierceness, wickedness 11 heinousness

vicissitude 6 change 8 mutation 9 variation 10 difficulty, mutability, succession 11 fluctuation

Vicomte of Bragelonne, The
  author: 14 Alexandre Dumas (pere)

victim 4 butt, dead, dupe, gull, mark, pawn, prey, tool 5 patsy 6 pigeon, quarry, sucker, target 7 injured, wounded 8 casualty, fatality, innocent 9 scapegoat

victimize 3 con 4 dupe, gull, hoax 5 bully, cheat, cozen 6 betray, delude 7 deceive, defraud 8 hoodwink 9 bamboozle

victor 6 winner 8 champion, medalist 9 conqueror 10 vanquisher 11 prizewinner

Victoria, Queen
  realm: 13 British Empire
  House of: 7 Hanover
  Prince Consort: 6 Albert
  son; successor: 9 Edward VII

Victoria
  capital of: 8 Hong Kong 10 Seychelles

Victoria
  origin: 5 Roman
  goddess of: 7 victory
  corresponds to: 4 Nike

Victorian 4 prim, smug 6 narrow, proper, stuffy 7 insular, prudish 8 priggish 9 pietistic 10 tight-laced 11 puritanical, straitlaced 12 conventional, hypocritical 13 sanctimonious

victorious 7 winning 8 champion 10 conquering, successful, triumphant 11 vanquishing 12 championship, prizewinning

Victor Victoria
  director: 12 Blake Edwards
  cast: 10 Alex Karras 11 James Garner 12 Julie Andrews 13 Robert Preston 14 John Rhys-Davies 15 Lesley Ann Warren
  setting: 5 Paris

victory 7 laurels, success, the palm, triumph 8 conquest, the prize 9 supremacy 10 ascendancy 11 superiority
  god of: 3 Tyr
  goddess of: 4 Nike 8 Victoria

Victory
author: **12** Joseph Conrad
character: **4** Lena, Wang **5** Jonas, Pedro **8** Davidson **9** Axel Heyst, Schomberg **13** Martin Ricardo

victuals 4 chow, diet, eats, fare, feed, food, grub, meat **5** meals **6** fodder, forage, repast, stores, viands **7** cooking, cuisine, edibles, rations, vittles **8** supplies **9** groceries, provender **10** foodstuffs, provisions **11** comestibles, nourishment, refreshment

Vidal, Gore
author of: **4** Burr **5** Kalki **6** Julian **8** Creation **16** Myra Breckinridge **18** Eighteen Seventy-Six, The Judgment of Paris **19** Visit to a Small Planet

Vidar
origin: **12** Scandinavian
father: **4** Odin **5** Othin
killed: **6** Fenrir, Fenris

vide 3 see

vide ante 9 see before

vide infra 8 see below

videlicet 6 namely **11** that is to say
abbreviation: **3** viz

vide post 8 see after **10** see further

vide supra 8 see above

vide ut supra 10 see as above **16** see as stated above

Vidor, King
director of: **8** The Crowd **12** Stella Dallas, The Big Parade **16** Northwest Passage

vie 4 life **5** fight **6** strive **7** compete, contend, contest **8** be a rival, struggle, tilt with **9** challenge

Vienna
airport: **9** Schwechat
area: **11** Innere Stadt
capital of: **7** Austria
early name: **4** Wena **9** Vindobono
German: **4** Wien
landmark: **6** Prater **7** Hofburg **10** Stadtsoper **13** Saint Stephen's **15** Albertina Museum, Belvedere Palace **16** Historical Museum, Schonbrunn Palace
river: **6** Danube
ruler: **8** Hapsburg
street: **11** Ringstrasse

Vientiane, Viengchan
capital of: **4** Laos

vi et armis 20 with force and with arms

Vietnam
other name: **5** Annam **15** French Indochina
capital: **5** Hanoi **6** Saigon
largest city: **6** Saigon **13** Ho Chi Minh City
others: **3** Hue, Ron **4** Ngai, Vinh **5** Dalat, Hoa Da, Hoian **6** Annhon, Cholon, Danang, Hongay **7** Bacninh, Cam Ranh, Caobang, Donghoi, Hoabinh, Namdinh, Quinhon, Songoan, Tayninh, Viettri, Vinhloi **8** Binhdinh, Haiphong, Nhatrang, Panthiet, Phan Rang, Quangtri, Quangyen, Thanhhoa, Vinhlong **9** Haiphoang, Longxuyen **11** Dienbienphu
school: **3** Hue **5** Hanoi **9** Ho Chi Minh
division: **5** Annam, North, South **6** Tonkin **11** Cochin China
measure: **4** gang, phan, thon
monetary unit: **2** xu **4** dong **7** piaster
weight: **3** can, yet **4** uyen
mountain: **6** Badinh, Badink **7** Nindhoa, Ninhhoa **8** Fansipan, Knontran, Ngoklinh, Ngoolink, Tchepone, Tclepore **18** Annamese Cordillera
highest point: **8** Fan Si Pan
river: **2** Bo, Ca, Da, Lo, Ma **3** Chu, Gam, Koi, Red **4** Chay **5** Nhiha **6** Mekong **7** Dongnai
sea: **10** South China
physical feature:
   delta: **6** Mekong **8** Red River
   gulf: **4** Siam **6** Tonkin **7** Tonking **8** Thailand
   peninsula: **11** Indochinese
people: **3** Hoa, Man, Meo, Tai, Tay **4** Cham, Kinh, Nung, Thai **5** Khmer, Malay, Muong **7** Chinese **8** Annamese, Annamite **9** Cambodian **10** montagnard, Vietnamese
   leader: **5** Le Loi **8** Le Duc Tho **9** Ho Chi Minh **11** Ngo Dinh Diem, Pham Van Doug **14** Nguyen Van Thieu
language: **3** Yue **4** Cham **5** Khmer, Rhade **6** French **7** Chinese, English **9** Cantonese **10** Vietnamese
religion: **6** Cao Dai, Hoa Hao, Taoism **7** animism **8** Buddhism **12** Christianity, Confucianism **13** Roman Catholic
place:
   ruins: **10** Nguyen tomb
feature:
   army: **4** ARVN **5** COSVN **8** Communsi, Viet Cong, Viet Minh
   clothing: **5** ao dai
   new year: **3** Tet

view 3 eye, ken, see **4** gaze, look, note, peek, peep, scan **5** judge, scene, sight, study, vista, watch **6** behold, belief, gaze at, glance, look at, notion, regard, survey, take in, theory, vision **7** diorama, examine, explore, feeling, glimpse, inspect, observe, opinion, outlook, picture, scenery, thought, witness **8** attitude, consider, glance at, judgment, panorama, perceive, pore over, prospect **9** landscape, sentiment, spectacle **10** conception, conviction, scrutinize, think about **11** contemplate, perspective

view as 4 deem, hold **5** count, judge, think **6** regard **7** account, believe **8** consider, take to be **10** look upon as

viewpoint 4 bias, side **5** angle, slant **6** aspect, belief **7** feeling, opinion **8** attitude, position **9** sentiment **10** conviction, standpoint **11** orientation, perspective **12** vantage point **16** frame of reference

view with disfavor 7 condemn, dislike **8** object to **9** frown upon **10** disapprove, think ill of **13** look askance at, regard as wrong **14** discountenance **15** take exception to

view with horror 5 abhor **6** eschew **8** sicken at **9** abominate, shudder at **10** recoil from, shrink from

vif
music: **6** lively

vigilance 4 care, heed **7** caution, concern **8** prudence **9** alertness, attention **10** precaution **11** carefulness, forethought, guardedness, heedfulness **12** cautiousness, watchfulness **14** circumspection

vigilant 4 wary **5** alert, chary **7** careful, guarded, heedful, on guard, prudent **8** cautious, watchful **9** attentive, observant, wide-awake **10** on one's toes, on the alert **11** circumspect, on one's guard **12** on the lookout, on the qui vive

vigor 3 pep, vim, zip **4** dash, elan, fire, zeal **5** ardor, drive, force, might, power, verve **6** energy, fervor, spirit **7** passion, stamina **8** haleness, strength, vitality, vivacity **9** animation, hardiness, intensity, vehemence **10** enthusiasm, liveliness, robustness **11** earnestness **12** forcefulness

vigorous 4 bold, hale **5** hardy, lusty, vital **6** active, ardent, brawny, lively, mighty, robust, strong, sturdy, virile **7** dynamic, intense, vibrant **8** forceful, muscular, powerful, spirited **9** assertive, energetic **10** aggressive

vigorously 4 hard **7** briskly, lustily **8** actively, cogently, forcibly, robustly, strongly, sturdily **9** with force **10** forcefully, powerfully **11** strenuously **13** energetically

Vigrid
origin: **12** Scandinavian
final battlefield of: **4** gods

Viking, viking 4 Dane **6** pirate **7** mariner **8** Norseman, Northman, searover **9** plunderer **12** Scandinavian
boat: **8** long ship
burial: **9** ship grave
chieftain: **4** jarl
exploration: **5** Italy, Spain **6** France, Russia **7** England, Germany, Iceland, Ireland, Vinland **9** Greenland
famous: **4** Eric **8** Eirikson, Ericsson **10** Eric the Red **11** Leif Ericson
governing council: **4** Ting **5** Thing **8** Folkmoot
legend: **4** Edda, saga
origin: **6** Norway, Sweden **7** Denmark, Finland
warrior: **7** beserk **9** berserker
writing: **4** rune

Vila
 capital of: **7** Vanuatu
vile 3 bad, low **4** base, evil, foul, lewd, mean, ugly **5** aw ful, gross, nasty **6** coarse, filthy, odious, sinful, smutty, sordid, vulgar, wicked **7** beastly, hateful, heinous, ignoble, immoral, obscene, vicious **8** depraved, shameful, shocking, wretched **9** abhorrent, degrading, execrable, invidious, loathsome, nefarious, obnoxious, offensive, perverted, repellent, repugnant, repulsive, revolting, salacious **10** abominable, degenerate, despicable, detestable, disgusting, iniquitous, unpleasant, villainous **11** disgraceful, foul mouthed, humiliating **12** contemptible **13** objectionable

Vile Bodies
 author: **11** Evelyn Waugh
vileness 4 evil **8** foulness, iniquity, villainy **9** depravity, nastiness **10** immorality, odiousness **11** degradation, heinousness, viciousness **12** wretchedness **13** offensiveness

Vili
 origin: **12** Scandinavian
 brother: **4** Odin **5** Othin
vilification 5 libel **7** calumny, slander **10** defamation **13** disparagement
vilifier 5 scold **6** carper, critic **7** reviler **9** backbiter
vilify 5 abuse **6** defame, revile **7** slander **8** bad-mouth, dis honor **9** criticize, disparage **14** inveigh against
vilifying 7 abusive **8** libelous **9** malignant **10** calumnious, defamatory, slanderous
villa, Villa 5 aldea, dacha **6** castle, Pancho **7** chateau, mansion **9** residence **13** coun try estate
village 4 burg **6** hamlet, suburb **8** hick town **9** smalltown **11** whistlestop **12** municipality

Village, A
 author: **10** Sholem Asch
villain 3 cad, cur, rat **5** knave, louse, rogue **6** rascal, rotter, varlet **7** caitiff, stinker **8** evil doer, scalawag **9** miscreant, scoundrel **10** blackguard, malefactor **11** rapscallion **12** transgressor, wicked person **15** snake in the grass
villainous 4 base, evil, foul, vile **6** wicked **7** caddish, heinous **8** horrible, infamous **9** monstrous, nefarious **10** abominable, despicable, detestable, maleficent **12** blackguardly **13** reprehensible
villainy 4 evil **8** vileness **9** depravity, rascality **10** wickedness **11** viciousness, maleficence

Villa-Lobos, Heitor
 born: **6** Brazil **12** Rio de Janeiro
 composer of: **6** Choros **20** Bachianas Brasileiras

Villefort

character in: 21 The Count of Monte Cristo
 author: **5** Dumas (pere)
villein 4 carl, esne, serf **5** ceorl, churl, slave **6** drudge **7** bondman, peasant **9** bondwoman

Villette
 author: **15** Charlotte Bronte
Villon, Francois
 author of: **9** The Legacy **16** Le grand testament, Le petit testament
 quote: **25** Mais ou sont les neiges d'antan **31** But where are the snows of yesteryear

Villuppo
 character in: **17** The Spanish Tragedy
 author: **3** Kyd
vim 2 go **3** pep, zip **4** dash, fire, snap, zeal **5** ardor, drive, force, might, power, punch, verve, vigor **6** energy, fervor, spirit **7** passion, potency **8** strength, vitality, vivacity **9** animation, intensity, vehemence **10** enthusiasm, liveliness
vin, vino 4 wine
Vincentio
 character in: **17** Measure for Measure
 author: **11** Shakespeare
vincit omnia veritas 16 truth conquers all **22** truth conquers all things
vindicate 4 free **5** clear **6** acquit, assert, defend, excuse, uphold **7** absolve, bear out, bolster, justify, support **8** advocate, champion, maintain **9** discharge, exculpate, exonerate **11** corroborate **12** substantiate
vindication 6 excuse **7** apology, defense **11** explanation **13** justification
vindictive 6 bitter, malign **8** avenging, punitive, spiteful, vengeful **9** malicious **10** malevolent, revengeful **11** retaliative, retaliatory, unforgiving
vinegarish 4 acid, sour, tart **5** harsh **6** acidic, biting **7** acerbic, pungent **9** acidulous **10** astringent
vin ordinaire 12 ordinary wine **20** inexpensive table wine
vintage 3 era, old **4** aged, date, fine, rare **5** epoch, great, prime, prize **6** choice, period **7** ancient, antique **8** sterling, superior **9** excellent, out-of-date, wonderful **11** outstanding **12** old-fashioned

Viola (Cesario)
 character in: **12** Twelfth Night
 author: **11** Shakespeare
violate 4 rape **5** abuse, break **6** defile, invade, ravish **7** disobey, outrage, profane **8** dishonor, infringe, trespass **9** blaspheme, desecrate, disregard, trample on **10** contravene, transgress **12** encroach upon
violation 5 abuse **6** breach **8** trespass **9** sacrilege **10** defilement, infraction **11** desecration, dishonoring **12** en-

croachment, infringement **13** contravention, nonobservance, transgression
violence 4 fury, rage **5** force, might, power **6** impact **7** out rage **8** ferocity, savagery, severity **9** brutality, intensity, onslaught **10** bestiality, fierceness **11** desecration, profanation **13** ferociousness, physical force **16** bloodthirstiness
violent 3 hot **4** wild **5** cruel, fiery **6** brutal, fierce, insane, raging, savage, severe, strong, unruly **7** berserk, furious, intense, rampant **8** maniacal, vehement **9** explosive, ferocious, hotheaded, murderous, unbridled **10** passionate **11** full of force, intractable, tempestuous **12** ungovernable **14** uncontrollable

Violent Bear It Away, The
 author: **15** Flannery O'Connor
Violent Land, The
 author: **10** Jorge Amado
violet 5 Viola
 varieties: **3** dog, red **4** bush, pale, pine, rock, tree, wood **5** coast, cream, dame's, false, flame, green, marsh, pansy, sweet, water **6** Alaska, alpine, Canada, garden, German, horned, plains, stream **7** African, English, Mexican, Olympic, Persian, redwood, scarlet, striped, two-eyed **8** bird-foot, crowfoot, dog-tooth, florist's, hook-spur, Labrador, larkspur, Missouri, trailing **9** early blue, evergreen, ivy-leaved, marsh blue, sage brush, tall white **10** Australian, great basin, Philippine, sweet white, western dog, woolly blue, yellow wood **11** Alpine marsh, American dog, arrow-leaved, Confederate, downy yellow, early yellow, lance-leaved, long spurred, northern bog, strap-leaved **12** eastern water, great-spurred, kidney-leaved, northern blue, smooth yellow **13** common African, Halberd-leaved, northern downy, northern white, purple prairie, southern coast, white dog-tooth, yellow prairie **14** primrose-leaved, triangle-leaved **16** California golden, large-leaved white **17** round-leaved yellow, western sweet white **18** western round-leaved

violin family
 instruments: **3** kit **5** cello, rebec, viola **7** baryton **8** bass viol, lyra viol, violetta **10** hurdy-gurdy **11** viola d'a more, violoncello **12** tromba marina, viola pomposa **13** lira da braccio **14** violino piccolo **15** hardanger fiddle
viper 3 asp, boa **5** adder, krait **9** puff adder **10** copperhead, fer-de-lance **11** rattlesnake
 group of: **4** nest

Viper's Tangle, The
 author: **15** Francois Mauriac
virago 3 nag **4** fury **5** harpy, scold,

shrew, vixen **6** dragon, gorgon **7** she-wolf **8** battle-ax, fishwife, harridan **9** termagant, Xanthippe

Virbius
origin: **5** Roman
god of: **6** forest **7** hunting

Virchow, Rudolf
field: **8** medicine **9** pathology
nationality: **6** German
completed formulation of: **10** cell theory

Virgil *see* **8** Vergil

virgin 4 girl, lass, maid, Mary, pure **6** chaste, damsel, maiden, unused **7** unmixed **8** pristine **9** unalloyed, undefiled, unsullied, untouched **10** unpolluted **13** unadulterated **14** uncontaminated
constellation of: **5** Virgo

Virgin *see* **4** Mary

Virginia
abbreviation: **2** VA
nickname: **11** Old Dominion
capital: **8** Richmond
largest city: **7** Norfolk
others: **5** Galax, Luray, Salem **6** Marion **7** Bedford, Bristol, Emporia, Fairfax, Pulaski, Roanoke **8** Danville, Hopewell, Manassas, Staunton, St Albans, Tazewell, Yorktown **9** Arlington, Lexington, Lynchburg **10** Alexandria, Appomattox, Petersburg, Portsmouth, Waynesboro, Winchester **11** Newport News **12** Hampton Roads, Martinsville, Williamsburg **13** Virginia Beach **14** Fredericksburg **15** Charlottesville
college: **3** Lee **7** Hampton, Madison, Radford **8** Longwood, Richmond **10** Washington **11** Mary Baldwin, Old Dominion **13** Randolph Macon **14** Averett Hollins, Mary Washington, William and Mary
feature:
 battle site: **7** Bull Run **8** Fair Oaks, Manassas, Richmond, Yorktown **10** Petersburg, Seven Pines, Wilderness **12** Spotsylvania **14** Fredericksburg **16** Chancellorsville
 dam: **4** Kerr
 historical site: **10** Monticello **11** Mount Vernon **12** Williamsburg **13** Stratford Hall
 national monument: **26** George Washington Birthplace
 national park: **10** Shenandoah **26** Colonial National Historical
tribe: **6** Saponi, Tutelo **7** Monacan **8** Manahoac, Meherrin, Nottaway, Pamunkey, Powhatan **9** Matchotic **10** Appomuttoc
people: **9** Henry Clay, John Rolfe, John Smith **10** Robert E Lee, Walter Reed **11** George Mason **12** John Marshall, Patrick Henry **13** Samuel Houston **14** Cyrus McCormick **15** Meriwether Lewis **17** Booker T Washington, Richard Evelyn Bird

18 Light-Horse Harry (Henry) Lee
lake: **4** Kerr **5** Smith
land rank: **11** thirty-sixth
mountain: **5** Cedar **6** Clinch, Elliot **8** Baldknob **9** Allegheny, Blueridge
 highest point: **6** Rogers
physical feature:
 bay: **10** Chesapeake
 bridge: **7** Natural
 caverns: **5** Luray
 port: **7** Norfolk **8** Richmond **10** Portsmouth **11** Newport News
 tunnel: **7** Natural
 valley: **10** Shenandoah
president: **9** John Tyler **11** James Monroe **12** James Madison **13** Woodrow Wilson, Zachary Taylor **15** Thomas Jefferson **16** George Washington **20** William Henry Harrison
river: **3** Dan **4** York **5** James **7** Potomac, Rapidan, Roanoke **10** Appomattox, Shenandoah **12** Rappahannock
state admission: **5** tenth
state bird: **8** cardinal
state flower: **16** flowering dogwood
state motto: **17** Thus Ever To Tyrants
state song: **24** Carry Me Back to Old Virginia
state tree: **7** dogwood

Virginian, The
author: **10** Owen Wister
character: **5** Betsy, Randy, Steve **6** Shorty **7** Trampas **9** Molly Wood **10** Judge (Henry) Garth
cast: **8** Lee J Cobb **10** Gary Clarke, James Drury, Pippa Scott, Randy Boone **11** Doug McClure **12** Roberta Shore
setting: **11** Shiloh Ranch **16** Wyoming Territory

Virginians, The
author: **25** William Makepeace Thackeray

Virgin Mary
ingredient: **11** tomato juice

Virgin Soil
author: **12** Ivan Turgenev

Virgo
symbol: **6** virgin
planet: **7** Mercury
rules: **7** service
zodiac: **5** sixth
born: **6** August **9** September

virile 4 bold **5** brave, hardy, husky, lusty, macho, manly **6** brawny, heroic, manful, mighty, potent, robust, strong **7** valiant **8** fearless, forceful, muscular, powerful, resolute, stalwart, vigorous **9** audacious, masculine, masterful, strapping, undaunted **10** courageous **12** stouthearted

virtual 5 tacit **7** implied **8** implicit, indirect **9** essential, practical **11** substantial

virtually 8 in effect **9** in essence **11** essentially, in substance, practically

13 substantially **14** for the most part **23** for all practical purposes, to all intents and purposes

virtue 5 honor, value **6** purity, reward **7** benefit, decency, honesty, modesty, probity **8** chastity, goodness, morality, strength **9** advantage, good point, innocence, integrity, principle, rectitude, virginity **11** strong point, uprightness

virtuosity 7 mastery **8** artistry, wizardry **14** accomplishment

virtuoso 4 whiz **6** expert, genius, master, wizard **7** artiste, prodigy **10** master hand

virtuous 4 good, just, pure **5** moral **6** chaste, decent, modest **7** ethical, upright **8** innocent, laudable, virginal **9** continent, exemplary, honorable, righteous, unsullied **11** commendable, meritorious **12** praiseworthy **14** high-principled

virtuous person
Hebrew: **6** zaddik

Virtus
personifies: **7** courage

virtute et armis 15 by virtue and arms
motto of: **11** Mississippi

virulent 5 toxic **6** bitter, deadly, lethal, malign **7** harmful, hostile, hurtful, noxious, vicious **8** spiteful, venomous **9** injurious, malicious, poisonous, rancorous, resentful, unhealthy **10** malevolent, pernicious **11** acrimonious, deleterious

virus 3 bug **4** germ **7** microbe **11** computer bug **13** microorganism

vis 5 force, power **8** strength

visage 3 air **4** face, look, mien **5** image **6** aspect **7** profile **8** demeanor, features **9** semblance **10** appearance **11** countenance, physiognomy

vis-a-vis 8 eye to eye, together **9** in company, privately, tete-a-tete **10** face-to-face, side by side **11** as opposed to **12** in contrast to **14** as compared with, confidentially **19** as distinguished from

viscera 4 guts **6** bowels **7** innards, insides **8** entrails **10** intestines

visceral 3 gut **5** crude **6** earthy **11** instinctive

viscous 5 gluey, gooey, gummy, slimy, tacky, thick **6** sticky, syrupy, viscid **9** glutinous

Vishnu
in trinity of: **4** Siva **5** Shiva **6** Brahma
religion: **8** Hinduism
called: **9** Preserver
avatar: **7** Krishna

visibility 7 ceiling, clarity, horizon **10** definition, prominence **11** range of view **12** distinctness **14** perceptibility **15** conspicuousness, discernibleness

visible 4 open **5** clear, plain **6** in view,

marked, patent **7** blatant, evident, glaring, in focus, in sight, obvious, pointed, salient, seeable **8** apparent, distinct, manifest, palpable, revealed **9** prominent **10** noticeable, observable, pronounced **11** conspicuous, discernible, inescapable, perceivable, perceptible, well-defined **12** unmistakable

vision 4 idea **5** dream, fancy, ghost, sight **6** notion **7** concept, fantasy, phantom, specter **8** daydream, eyesight, illusion **9** foresight **10** apparition, conception, perception, revelation **11** discernment, imagination **15** materialization

visionary 4 seer **6** dreamy, unreal, zealot **7** dreamer, fanatic, fancied, utopian **8** delusive, fanciful, idealist, illusory, romantic, theorist **9** imaginary, unfounded **10** chimerical, daydreamer, idealistic, starry-eyed **11** imaginative, impractical **13** insubstantial

Vision of Judgement, The
 author: 9 Lord Byron

visit 4 call, stay **5** haunt, smite **6** affect, assail, attack, befall, call on, punish **7** afflict, assault, go to see, sojourn **8** drop in on, frequent, happen to, look in on, stay with **9** sojourn at **10** be a guest of

Visit, The
 author: 19 Friedrich Durrenmatt

visitant 5 alien **7** arrival, visitor

visitor 5 guest **6** caller **7** company, tourist, tripper, voyager **8** traveler **9** journeyer, sightseer, sojourner, transient **10** houseguest, vacationer

vista 4 view **5** scene **6** vision **7** outlook, picture, scenery **8** panorama, prospect **9** landscape **11** perspective

visual 5 optic **6** ocular **7** optical, seeable, visible **9** for the eye **10** noticeable, observable, ophthalmic **11** perceptible

visualize 5 fancy, image **7** dream of, foresee, imagine, picture **8** envision **10** conceive of, daydream of **16** see in the mind's eye

vita 3 bio **6** resume **9** biography **13** autobiography **15** curriculum vitae

vital 4 life, live **5** alive, basic, chief, quick **6** lively, living, urgent, viable **7** animate, crucial, dynamic, primary, serious, vibrant **8** animated, cardinal, critical, existing, forceful, foremost, material, pressing, spirited, vigorous **9** breathing, energetic, essential, important, necessary, paramount, requisite, vivifying **11** fundamental, significant **13** indispensable

vitality 3 pep, vim, zip **4** zeal, zest **5** verve, vigor **6** energy **8** dynamism, strength, vivacity **9** animation, life force **10** ebullience, enthusiasm, exuberance, liveliness **13** animal spirits

vitalize 6 excite, vivify **7** animate, quicken **8** activate, energize **9** stimu-

late **10** invigorate, strengthen **11** bring to life

vital part 9 essential, necessity, requisite **10** key element, sine qua non **11** requirement

Vital Parts
 author: 12 Thomas Berger

vital principle 5 blood **6** source **9** lifeblood **10** sine qua non

vitals 5 belly **6** bowels **10** intestines **11** vital organs **14** liver and lights

Vita Nuova
 author: 14 Dante Alighieri

vitiate 3 mar **4** thin, undo, void **5** spoil, taint **6** blight, cancel, debase, defile, dilute, impair, infect, injure, poison, weaken **7** abolish, corrupt, pervert, pollute **8** sabotage **9** discredit, undermine **10** adulterate, depreciate, invalidate, make faulty, obliterate **11** contaminate

vitriolic 4 acid **5** acerb, nasty, sharp **6** biting **7** abusive, acerbic, caustic, cutting **8** sardonic, scathing **9** sarcastic, satirical, withering **11** acrimonious **13** hypercritical

vituperate 5 abuse **6** carp at, defame, malign, rail at, rebuke, revile, vilify **7** censure **9** castigate **10** speak ill of **14** inveigh against

vituperation 5 abuse, blame, scorn **6** insult, rebuke, tirade **7** censure, obloquy, slander **8** acrimony, scolding **9** invective **10** defamation, revilement, scurrility **11** castigation, deprecation **12** calumniation, denunciation, faultfinding, vilification **13** tongue-lashing

vituperative 5 harsh **7** abusive **8** scornful **9** insulting, maligning, vilifying **10** censorious, defamatory, scurrilous, slanderous **11** acrimonious, deprecatory

vivace
 music: 5 quick **9** vivacious

vivacious 3 gay **5** jolly, merry, sunny, vital **6** active, bright, bubbly, cheery, genial, lively **7** buoyant **8** animated, bubbling, cheerful, spirited **9** convivial, ebullient, sparkling, sprightly **10** frolicsome, full of life **12** effervescent, lighthearted

vivacity 3 zip **4** dash, elan **5** gaity, verve, vigor **6** energy, spirit **8** buoyancy, vitality **9** animation **10** ebullience, liveliness **13** effervescence

Vivaldi, Antonio
 born: 5 Italy **6** Venice
 composer of: 10 Gloria Mass **14** L'Estro Armonico, The Four Seasons **16** Judith Triumphant **17** Juditha Triumphans, Le Quattro Stagioni **19** Harmonic Inspiration

viva voce 5 aloud **6** orally

Viva Zapata!
 director: 9 Elia Kazan
 cast: 10 Jean Peters **12** Anthony

Quinn, Marlon Brando
 Oscar for: 15 supporting actor (Quinn)
 script: 13 John Steinbeck

vive 8 long live (whomever)
 opposite: 4 a bas

vive valeque 15 live and keep well

Vivian
 also: 16 The Lady of the Lake
 character in: 16 Arthurian romance
 lover: 6 Merlin

Vivian Grey
 author: 16 Benjamin Disraeli

vivid 3 gay **4** deep, loud, rich **5** clear, shiny, showy **6** bright, florid, garish, lively, moving, strong **7** glowing, graphic, in tense, radiant, shining **8** colorful, definite, distinct, dramatic, emphatic, forceful, lifelike, luminous, lustrous, powerful, stirring, striking, true-life, vigorous **9** brilliant, effulgent, energetic, marvelous, memorable, pictorial, realistic **10** astounding, expressive, impressive, remarkable **11** astonishing, conspicuous, descriptive, inescapable, luminescent, picturesque, resplendent **12** unmistakable **13** extraordinary

vividness 9 intensity **10** brightness, brilliance

vivified 7 revived **8** animated, awakened **9** enlivened, quickened, vitalized **11** invigorated

vivify 6 revive, wake up **7** animate, enliven, quicken **8** vitalize **10** invigorate

vixen 4 fury **5** scold, shrew, witch **6** virago **8** fishwife, harridan, spitfire **9** female fox, termagant

Vladimir
 character in: 15 Waiting for Godot
 author: 7 Beckett

Vlaminck, Maurice de
 born: 5 Paris **6** France
 artwork: 8 Red Trees, The Storm **15** Hamlet in the Snow, Winter Landscape **17** The Bridge at Chatou **18** Picnic in the Country, Street at Marly-le-Roi **21** Landscape with Red Trees

vocabulary 4 cant **5** argot, idiom, lingo, slang, style **6** jargon, patois, speech, tongue **7** dialect, lexicon **8** language, glossary, phrasing **9** word stock **10** vernacular **11** phraseology, terminology

vocal 4 open, oral, sung **5** blunt, frank, lyric **6** candid, choral, direct, spoken, voiced **7** uttered, voluble **8** operatic, viva-voce **9** outspoken, vocalized **10** forthright, of the voice **11** articulated, plainspoken

vocalize 3 air, say **4** sing, vent **5** speak, utter **7** express **9** ventilate **10** articulate **12** put into words

vocation 3 job **4** line, post, role, task

5 berth, field, stint, trade **6** career, estate, metier **7** calling, pursuit, station **8** business, lifework **9** situation **10** assignment, employment, line of work, occupation, profession

vocational 3 job **5** trade **6** career **9** technical **11** specialized **12** occupational

vociferate 4 howl, yell, yelp **5** shout, shout **6** bellow, clamor, cry out, holler, shriek, squeal **7** bluster, call out, exclaim, screech **9** ejaculate **11** make a racket **12** raise a rumpus

vociferation 3 cry **4** howl, yell, yelp **5** noise, shout **6** bellow, clamor, outcry, shriek, squeal, uproar **7** screech **11** ejaculation, exclamation

vociferous 4 loud **5** noisy, vocal **6** shrill **7** blatant **8** piercing, shouting, strident, vehement **9** clamorous, outspoken **10** boisterous, loud-voiced, uproarious **11** importunate

vodka
  origin: 6 Poland, Russia
  drink: 10 Moscow Mule **12** Cosmopolitan
  with amaretto: 9 Godmother
  with bouillon: 8 Bullshot
  with cider: 15 Brewster Special
  with Cognac: 7 Cossack
  with cranberry juice: 10 Cape Codder
  with creme de cacao: 7 Barbara **9** Ninotchka **11** Russian Bear **12** Velvet Hammer, White Russian
  with curacao: 8 Aqueduct
  with Galliano: 16 Harvey Wallbanger
  with gin: 15 Russian Cocktail
  with kahlua or Tia Maria: 12 Black Russian
  with kirsch: 12 Volga Boatman
  with orange juice: 11 screwdriver
  with tomato juice: 10 Bloody Mary
  with vermouth: 8 Kangaroo **9** Corkscrew

vogue 3 fad **4** mode, rage **5** craze, style, trend **6** custom **7** fashion **8** currency, practice, the thing **10** acceptance, popularity **11** the last word **12** popular favor **14** the latest thing **15** prevailing taste

voguish 4 chic **5** smart **6** modish **7** faddish, stylish **11** fashionable

voice 3 air, say **4** alto, bass, part, role, tone, vent, vote, will, wish **5** speak, state, tenor, utter **6** choice, desire, option, reveal, singer, speech **7** declare, divulge, express, opinion, singers, soprano **8** announce, baritone, delivery, disclose, proclaim, vocalize **9** contralto, enunciate, pronounce, ventilate **10** articulate, intonation, modulation, preference, vocal sound **11** communicate **12** articulation, mezzo-soprano **13** participation, power of speech

voiceless 3 mum **4** deaf, mute, surd **6** silent **7** anaudia, aphonic, spirate

voice of the people
  Latin: 9 vox populi

void 4 bare, emit, free, null, pass **5** annul, blank, clear, drain, eject, empty, purge **6** barren, cancel, devoid, recant, repeal, revoke, vacant, vacuum **7** abolish, drained, emptied, exhaust, invalid, lacking, nullify, pour out, rescind, reverse, vacuity, wanting **8** depleted, evacuate, nugatory, renounce, throw out **9** destitute, discharge, emptiness, exhausted, repudiate **10** empty space, invalidate, not in force **11** countermand, inoperative

voidance 7 voiding **8** ejection, emission **9** discharge, expulsion

Voight, Jon
  born: 9 Yonkers NY
  roles: 7 Joe Buck **8** The Champ **10** Coming Home (Oscar) **11** Deliverance **13** The Odessa File **14** Catch Twenty-Two, Midnight Cowboy

voila 3 see **4** look **9** there it is

volatile 4 rash, wild **5** brash, giddy, moody **6** fickle, fitful **7** erratic, flighty, gaseous **8** eruptive, reckless, unstable, unsteady, vaporous, variable **9** explosive, frivolous, mercurial, spasmodic, unsettled **10** capricious, changeable, evaporable, inconstant, irresolute, vaporizing **12** undependable **13** temperamental, unpredictable

volition 4 will **6** choice, option **8** choosing, decision, free will **10** discretion, resolution **13** determination

volley 5 burst, salvo **6** shower **7** barrage **8** outbreak, outburst **9** broadside, discharge, fusillade **10** outpouring

Volpone (The Fox)
  author: 9 Ben Jonson
  character: 5 Celia, Mosca **7** Bonario, Corvino, Voltore **9** Corbaccio, Peregrine **18** Lady Politic Would-Be, Lord Politic Would-Be

Volsung
  origin: 12 Scandinavian
  mentioned in: 8 Volsunga
  grandfather: 4 Odin **5** Othin
  son: 7 Sigmund
  daughter: 5 Signy

Volsunga
  origin: 9 Icelandic **12** Scandinavian
  form: 4 saga
  time: 17 thirteenth century
  subject: 8 Volsungs

Volta, Alessandro, Count
  nationality: 7 Italian
  invented: 15 electric battery
  discovered: 10 methane gas

Voltaic
  also: 3 Gur
  language family: 16 Niger-Kordofanian
  group: 10 Niger-Congo
  includes: 5 Mossi

Voltaire, Francois
  real name: 19 Francois Marie Arouet

  author of: 5 Zadig, Zaire **6** Alzire, Merope **7** Candide, L'Ingenu, Mahomet **11** The Henriade **16** The Maid of Orleans **23** Philosophical Dictionary
  member of: 11 Philosophes

Volturnus
  origin: 5 Roman
  personifies: 4 wind **8** east wind **13** southeast wind

voluble 4 glib **5** wordy **6** chatty, fluent **7** twining **8** effusive, flippant, rotating, twisting **9** garrulous, talkative **10** loquacious

volume 4 book, bulk, heap, mass, size, tome **5** folio, sound, tract **6** amount, extent, quarto **7** measure **8** capacity, loudness, quantity, treatise, vastness **9** abundance, aggregate, magnitude, monograph **10** dimensions

voluminous 5 ample, large **7** copious, massive, sizable **8** abundant **9** extensive

Volund see **7** Wayland

voluntary 6 willed **8** free-will, intended, optional, unforced **10** deliberate **11** intentional, volunteered **13** discretionary, noncompulsory

volunteer 5 offer **6** extend, tender, unpaid **7** advance, present, proffer, recruit **8** enlistee **9** voluntary **10** put forward **11** step forward **12** unpaid worker **13** charityworker

Volunteer State
  nickname of: 9 Tennessee

Voluptas
  origin: 5 Roman
  goddess of: 8 pleasure

voluptuary 4 rake, roue **7** epicure, gourmet, seducer **8** gourmand, hedonist, sybarite **9** bon vivant, debauchee, high liver, libertine, womanizer **10** gastronome, sensualist **14** pleasure seeker

voluptuous 4 soft **6** carnal, erotic, sexual, smooth, wanton **7** fleshly, lustful, sensual **8** sensuous **9** debauched, dissolute, luxurious, sybaritic **10** dissipated, hedonistic, lascivious, licentious, profligate **13** self-indulgent **14** pleasure-loving **15** pleasure-seeking

vomit 4 barf, emit, puke **5** eject, expel, heave, retch **7** bring up, throw up, upchuck **8** disgorge **9** discharge, spew forth **10** belch forth **11** regurgitate **15** toss one's cookies

Vonnegut, Kurt, Jr
  author of: 8 Jailbird **9** Slapstick **10** Cat's Cradle, Palm Sunday **11** Player Piano **18** Slaughterhouse Five **20** Breakfast of Champions **22** Happy Birthday Wanda June

Von Sternberg, Josef
  director of: 12 The Blue Angel

Von Sydow, Max

real name: 18 Carl Adolph von Sydow
born: 4 Lund **6** Sweden
roles: 12 The Emigrants **14** The Seventh Seal **15** The Virgin Spring **16** Wild Strawberries **24** The Greatest Story Ever Told

voracious 6 greedy **7** hoggish **8** edacious, ravenous **10** gluttonous, insatiable, omnivorous

vortex 4 eddy **7** cyclone, twister **9** maelstrom, whirlpool, whirlwind

votary 3 fan **4** buff **6** zealot **7** admirer, devotee, fanatic, habitue **8** adherent, champion, disciple, follower, partisan **10** aficionado, enthusiast **11** afficionado

vote 3 say **4** poll **5** voice **6** ballot, choice, option, ticket **8** approval, decision, election, judgment, suffrage **9** franchise, selection **10** plebiscite, preference, referendum **11** cast a ballot **13** determination

vouch 4 back **6** affirm, attest, back up, uphold, verify **7** certify, confirm, endorse, support, sustain, swear to, warrant, witness **8** attest to, maintain **9** guarantee **11** corroborate **12** authenticate

voucher 4 chit, chit **5** check, proof **6** surety, ticket **7** receipt, warrant **8** warranty **9** affidavit, debenture **10** credential **11** certificate **12** verification **14** authentication

vouchsafe 4 give **5** allow, deign,

favor, grant **6** bestow, convey, tender **7** concede **10** condescend

vow 4 oath, word **5** swear, troth, vouch **6** affirm, assert, assure, parole, pledge, plight, stress **7** declare, promise, resolve **8** contract **9** emphasize **11** word of honor **13** solemn promise

vox populi 14 popular opinion **16** voice of the people

voyage 4 sail **6** cruise **7** passage **8** crossing, navigate **9** ocean trip **10** sea journey

Voyage of the Beagle, The
    author: 13 Charles Darwin

voyager 5 rover **7** cruiser, pilgrim, rambler, tourist **8** traveler, wayfarer **9** jet-setter, journeyer, sightseer **10** adventurer **12** excursionist, globe-trotter, peregrinator **13** world traveler

Voyage to the Bottom of the Sea
    character: 6 Doctor **8** Kowalsky, Stu Riley, (Cdr/Capt) Lee Crane **9** Patterson **10** (Lt Cdr) Chip Morton **11** (Chief Petty Officer) Curley Jones **12** Chief Sharkey **14** (Adm) Harriman Nelson
    cast: 9 Allan Hunt, Del Monroe **10** Henry Kulky, Paul Trinka **11** Richard Bull, Terry Becker **12** David Hedison **13** Robert Dowdell **15** Richard Basehart
    submarine: 7 Seaview
    explorer: 7 Sea Crab
    mini-sub: 10 Flying Fish

Vronsky, Count Alexei

    character in: 12 Anna Karenina
    author: 7 Tolstoy

Vulcan
    origin: 5 Roman
    god of: 4 fire **12** metalworking
    epithet: 8 Mulciber
    corresponds to: 10 Hephaestus, Hephaistos

vulgar 3 low **4** base, rude **5** crude, dirty, gross, rough **6** coarse, common, filthy, ribald, risque, smutty **7** boorish, ill-bred, lowbrow, obscene, uncouth **8** impolite, indecent, off-color, ordinary, plebeian **9** offensive, tasteless, unrefined **10** suggestive **11** ill-mannered, proletarian **12** pornographic, uncultivated

vulgarian 3 oaf **4** boor, lout **5** brute, yahoo **7** Babbitt **9** ignoramus **10** philistine **16** anti-intellectual

vulgarity 8 bad taste, rudeness **9** crudeness, grossness, indecency, indecorum, obscenity **10** coarseness, ill manners, indelicacy, smuttiness **11** boorishness, pornography **12** impoliteness **13** tastelessness

vulnerable 4 weak **7** exposed **8** helpless, insecure **9** sensitive, unguarded **10** easily hurt, undefended **11** defenseless, susceptible, thin-skinned, unprotected

Vye, Eustacia
    character in: 17 Return of the Native
    author: 5 Hardy

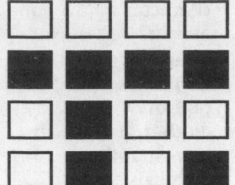  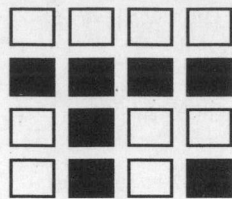

wacky, whacky 3 odd **4** nuts **5** crazy, kooky **6** cuckoo, insane, kookie **7** cracked, foolish, touched **9** eccentric, senseless **10** irrational **12** crackbrained

wad 3 bat, pad **4** cram, head, heap, lump, mass, tuft **5** money, stuff **6** bundle, riches, stop up **7** fortune **8** bankroll, plumbago

waddle 3 wag **4** sway **6** hobble, toddle, totter, wobble

wade 4 ford, plod, plow, toil, trek **5** labor **6** drudge, trudge **9** walk in mud **11** walk in water

wafer 4 chip **5** candy, flake **6** cookie **7** cracker **15** unleavened bread

waft 4 blow, puff **5** drift, float

wag 3 bob, wit **4** card, move, stir, wave **5** clown, droll, flick, joker, shake **6** jester, jiggle, switch, twitch, waggle, wiggle, wigwag **7** buffoon, farceur, flicker, flutter **8** comedian, humorist, jokester **9** oscillate **11** wisecracker **14** life of the party

wage 3 fee, pay **6** income, salary **7** carry on, conduct, payment, revenue, stipend **8** earnings, engage in, maintain, practice **9** emolument, undertake **10** recompense **12** compensation, remuneration

wage earner 6 worker **8** employee **9** job holder **12** hourly worker

wager 3 bet, pot **4** ante, pool, risk **5** fancy, guess, stake **6** assume, gamble, hazard **7** imagine, jackpot, presume, suppose, surmise, venture **8** make a bet, theorize **10** speculate **10** conjecture, take a flyer **11** speculation, try one's luck **12** tempt fortune **15** hazard an opinion

wages 3 bet, fee, pay **4** gage, hire **6** fights, reward, return, salary **7** engages, payment, stipend **8** conducts, earnings **9** emolument **10** prosecutes, recompense **12** remuneration

wage war 5 fight **6** combat **7** contend, make war **8** do battle **12** march against

waggery 5 chaff **6** banter, riding **7** joshing, kidding, ragging, ribbing **8** chaffing, drollery, raillery, twitting **French: 8** badinage

waggish 5 droll, funny **7** comical, puckish **8** humorous

waggle 4 wave **5** wield **8** brandish

Wagner, Honus
  real name: 15 John Peter Wagner
  nickname: 14 Flying Dutchman
  sport: 8 baseball
  position: 9 shortstop
  team: 17 Pittsburgh Pirates

Wagner, Richard
  born: 7 Germany, Leipzig
  composer of: 5 Faust **6** Rienzi **7** Die Feen **8** Parsifal **9** Lohengrin **10** Tannhauser, The Fairies **14** Siegfried Idyll **16** The Mastersingers, Tristan and Isolde, Wesendonck Lieder **17** The Flying Dutchman **20** Der Ring des Nibelungen, The Ring of the Nibelungs **27** Die Meistersinger von Nurnberg
    the Ring Cycle Part 1: 12 Das Rheingold, The Rhine Gold
    the Ring Cycle Part 2: 10 Die Walkure **11** The Valkyrie
    the Ring Cycle Part 3: 9 Siegfried
    the Ring Cycle Part 4: 15 Gotterdammerung **17** Twilight of the Gods

Wagner, Robert
  born: 9 Detroit MI
  wife: 11 Natalie Wood
  roles: 6 Switch **10** Hart to Hart **13** It Takes a Thief, Prince Valiant, The Longest Day **24** All the Fine Young Cannibals

wagon 3 car, van **4** cart, dray, tram, wain **5** coach, lorry, tonga, truck **7** caisson **10** automobile, battleship
  covered: 15 prairie schooner
  maker: 10 wainwright
  police: 10 Black Maria
  Russian: 6 telega
  sideless: 6 rolley
  track: 3 rut

Wagon Train
  character: 9 Bill Hawks **11** Barnaby West, Cooper Smith, Duke Shannon **14** Charlie Wooster, Major Seth Adams **15** Christopher Hale, Flint McCullough
  cast: 8 Ward Bond **11** Scott Miller, Terry Wilson **12** Frank McGrath, John McIntire, Michael Burns, Robert Fuller, Robert Horton

waif 5 gamin, stray **6** gamine, urchin **7** mudlark **9** foundling **10** ragamuffin, street arab **11** guttersnipe **13** homeless child **14** tatterdemalion

wail 3 cry **4** bawl, howl, keen, moan, roar, weep, yell **5** groan, shout, whine **6** bellow, bemoan, bewail, cry out, lament, outcry, plaint **7** keening, moaning, wailing **9** caterwaul **10** rend the air **11** lamentation

waist 3 top **5** shirt **6** blouse, bodice, middle **7** midriff **9** mid-region, waistband, waistline **10** middle part, midsection, shirtwaist

waistband 4 belt, sash **5** cinch **6** girdle

waistcoat 4 vest **5** benjy **6** jacket, jerkin, veskit, vestee, weskit **7** singlet **French:** gilet

wait 4 halt, stay, stop **5** dally, delay, pause, tarry **6** linger, put off **7** suspend **8** postpone, stopover **9** deferment **10** suspension **11** continuance **12** postponement

wait for 6 expect **10** anticipate

Waiting for Godot
  author: 13 Samuel Beckett
  character: 8 Estragon, Vladimir

wait on 5 serve **6** assist, attend

waive 4 stay **5** defer, forgo, let go, table, yield **6** give up, not use, put off, shelve **7** forbear, lay over **8** disclaim, forswear, postpone, renounce **9** surrender

waiver 9 dismissal **10** abdication, disclaimer **11** abandonment **12** renunciation **14** relinquishment

wake 4 fire, path, stir, wash **5** rally, rouse, trail, train, vigil **6** arouse, course, excite, kindle, revive **7** enliven, provoke, quicken **8** backwash **9** galvanize, stimulate **11** resuscitate

wakeful 4 wary **5** alert, astir **7** careful, heedful **8** cautious, restless, vigilant, watchful **9** insomniac, observant, sleepless **10** unsleeping **11** circumspect

wake up 4 rise **5** arise **6** vivify **7** animate, enliven **8** vitalize **9** stimulate

Walcott, Joe
  real name: 18 Arnold Raymond Cream
  nickname: 9 Jersey Joe
  sport: 6 boxing
  class: 11 heavyweight

Walden, or Life in the Woods
  author: 17 Henry David Thoreau

Wales
  other name: 5 Cymru **7** Cambria
  part of: 13 United Kingdom

title of British heir apparent: 13
Prince of Wales
capital: 7 Cardiff
cities: 4 Rhyl, Ross **5** Flint, Towyn **6**
Amlwch, Bangor, Brecon, Sidney **7**
Cwmbran, Herford, Newport, Rhon-
dda, Swansea **8** Aberdare, Caerleon,
Holyhead, Pembroke **9** Fishguard,
Glamorgan **10** Caernarvon, Caerphilly, Carmarthen **11** Aberystwyth
12 Milford Haven **13** Kidderminster,
Merthyr-Tydfil
division: 5 Clwyd, Dyfed, Flint,
Cwent, Powys **6** Radnor **7** Denbigh,
Gwynedd **8** Anglesey, Cardigan,
Monmouth, Pembroke **9** Brecknoch,
Glamorgan, Merioneth **10** Caernarvon, Carmarthen, Montgomery
emblem: 4 leek
government: 29 constituent part of
Great Britain
measure: 5 cover **7** cantred, crannoc,
listred
island: 4 Mona **5** Caldy **8** Anglesey,
Holyhead
lake: 4 Bala **6** Vyrnwy
mountain: 6 Berwyn **8** Cambrian **9**
Prescelly **13** Brecon Beacons
highest point: 7 Snowdon
river: 3 Dee, Usk, Wye **4** Alun, Taff,
Tawe, Teme, Towy **5** Clwyd, Conwy,
Dovey, Neath, Teifi **6** Conway, Severn, Vyrnwy
sea: 5 Irish **8** Atlantic
physical feature:
    bay: 7 Swansea **8** Cardigan, Trema-
    doc, Tremadog
    channel: 7 Bristol **9** St George's
    hills: 7 Malvern
    peninsula: 5 Lleyn
    strait: 5 Menai
    valley: 7 Rhondda
people: 4 Celt, Kelt **5** Cymry, Kymry,
Welsh **7** Brython, Silures, Taffies **8**
Awabokal, Cambrian **9** Siluridan
    actor: 6 Burton **8** Williams **13**
    Richard Burton, Emlyn Williams
    artist: 4 John
    author: 3 Map **5** Jones, Lewis,
    Mapes, Parry **6** Machan, Thrale **9**
    Llewellyn **11** Dylan Thomas **14**
    Dafydd ap Gwylym
    god: 3 Deu, Dew **4** Bran, Gwyn **5**
    Dylan **7** Gwydion
    leader: 5 Bevan **6** Rhodri **8** Hywel
    Dwa **11** Cadwallader **12** Bishop
    Morgan **13** Owen Glendower **16**
    David Lloyd George **18** Llewelyn
    ap Gruffydd
language: 5 Welsh **6** Celtic, Cymric,
Keltic, Kymric **7** Cymraeg, English
religion: 8 Anglican **9** Methodist **10**
Protestant **12** Presbyterian
place:
    bridge: 6 Severn
    castle: 6 Conway **7** Harlech **9**
    Beaumaris **10** Caernarvon, Caer-
    philly **11** Aberystwyth

feature:
    festival: 10 Eisteddfod
    stories: 10 Mabinogion
food:
    dish: 8 flummery
Walesa, Lech
born: 6 Poland
leader of: 10 Solidarity
voted: 7 premier
wander aimlessly 5 amble, stray **6**
ramble, stroll **7** meander, saunter
wandering 5 lapse **8** rambling, straying **9** deviation **10** aberration, digressive, discursive, maundering, meandering, roundabout **11** abnormality **12**
idiosyncrasy **13** nonconformity **14** circumlocutory
Wandering Jew, The
    author: 9 Eugene Sue
Wanderings
    author: 10 Chaim Potok
wane 3 ebb **4** fade, sink **5** abate,
droop, waste **6** ebbing, fading, lessen,
weaken, wither **7** abating, decline,
dwindle, subside **8** decrease, diminish, fade away **9** dwindling, lessening,
recession, subsiding, weakening, withering
wangle 4 worm **5** trick **6** jockey,
scheme **7** finagle, wheedle **8** engineer,
intrigue, maneuver **9** machinate **10**
manipulate
wanness 6 pallor **8** grayness, paleness
9 ashenness **10** sallowness, sickliness
13 colorlessness
want 4 hunt, lack, need, seek, wish **5**
covet, crave, fancy **6** dearth, demand,
desire, hunger, penury **7** be needy,
craving, hope for, long for, paucity,
pine for, poverty, require, wish for **8**
scarcity, shortage, yearn for, yearning
9 indigence, necessity, pauperism, privation, requisite **10** deficiency, insolvency **11** destitution, requirement **13**
impecuniosity, insufficiency, pennilessness **14** impoverishment
Wanted: Dead or Alive
    character: 11 Josh Randall
    cast: 12 Steve McQueen
    job: 12 bounty hunter
    gun: 8 Mare's Leg
wanting 5 short **6** absent **7** lacking,
missing **9** defective, deficient, imperfect **10** inadequate **11** substandard **12**
insufficient
wanton 4 bawd, fast, jade, lewd, rake,
roue, slut, tart **5** gross, hussy, loose,
satyr, whore **6** chippy, harlot, lecher
7 bestial, immoral, lustful, obscene,
seducer, trollop, willful **8** careless,
heedless, mindless, needless, strumpet, sybarite, unchaste **9** abandoned,
adulterer, concubine, debauched, debauchee, dissolute, lecherous, libertine,
malicious, senseless, womanizer **10**
deliberate, fornicator, groundless, licentious, malevolent, profligate,

prostitute, sensualist, unprovoked, voluptuary **11** fornicatrix, promiscuous,
unjustified, whoremaster **13** inconsiderate, irresponsible
wapiti 3 elk **4** deer **11** American elk
female: 3 cow
literally: 9 white rump
male: 4 bull
species: 16 Cervus canadensis
Wapshot Chronicle
    author: 11 John Cheever
war 5 clash, fight **6** attack, battle, combat, invade **7** contend **8** conflict,
fighting, struggle **10** opposition **11**
hostilities
    god of: 4 Ares, Odin **5** Othin **8** Quiri-
    nus
    goddess of: 4 Enyo **6** Athena,
    Athene, Inanna, Ishtar, Pallas, Saitis
    7 Bellona, Mylitta **11** Tritogeneia **12**
    Pallas Athena **18** Alalcomencan
    Athena
War and Peace
    author: 10 Leo Tolstoy
    character: 7 Kutuzov **8** Napoleon **13**
    Natasha Rostov, Nikolay Rostov, Pi-
    erre Bezuhov **14** Anatole Kuragin **15**
    Andrey Bolkonsky **19** Ellen Kuragin
    Bezuhov **22** Princess Marva Bolkon-
    sky
War and Remembrance
    author: 10 Herman Wouk
warble 4 lump, purl, sing **5** carol,
larva, trill, tumor, yodel **6** growth,
quaver, ripple **7** twitter, vibrate, whistle
war cry 6 slogan **8** Geronimo
ward 4 zone **5** avert, block, repel **6**
charge, thwart **7** beat off, fend off,
prevent, quarter **8** pavilion, precinct,
stave off, turn away **9** dependent,
forestall
    French: 7 protege
warden 5 guard **6** keeper, ranger, sentry **7** curator, manager **8** guardian,
watchman **9** protector **14** superintendent
Warden, The
    author: 15 Anthony Trollope
ward off 5 avert **7** prevent
wardrobe 4 togs **5** chest **6** attire,
closet, outfit **7** apparel, clothes **8**
clothing, garments **10** cedar chest **12**
clothespress
    French: 6 bureau **7** armoire, com-
    mode **10** chiffonier **11** habillement
wares 4 line **5** stock **7** staples **8** supplies **9** inventory **11** commodities,
merchandise
warfare 5 fight **6** battle, combat **8**
conflict, fighting **11** hostilities
Warhol, Andy
born: 14 Philadelphia PA
artwork: 9 Brillo Box, Liz Taylor **13**
Marilyn Monroe **16** Campbell's Soup

Can **20** Green Coca-Cola Bottles
protegee: 12 Edie Sedgwick

wariness 7 caution **9** alertness, suspicion, vigilance **11** carefulness, guardedness, heedfulness **12** watchfulness **14** circumspection

warlike 7 hostile, martial, valiant **8** inimical, militant, military **9** bellicose, combative **10** unfriendly **11** belligerent, contentious, threatening
Indian: 8 Arapahoe

warlike attitude 9 hostility, pugnacity **11** bellicosity **12** belligerence, belligerency **13** combativeness **14** aggressiveness

warm 3 hot **4** cook, heat, kind, melt, thaw **5** cheer, happy, sunny, tepid, vivid **6** bright, heated, heat up, joyful, joyous, kindly, lively, loving, simmer, tender **7** affable, cordial, earnest, fervent, glowing, intense **8** animated, cheerful, friendly, gracious, outgoing, pleasant, spirited, vehement, vigorous **9** brilliant **10** passionate **11** kindhearted, sympathetic **12** affectionate, enthusiastic **13** compassionate, tenderhearted

warmhearted 4 kind **6** genial, kindly, loving **7** cordial **10** solicitous **11** sympathetic **12** affectionate **13** compassionate

warm-hued 3 red **4** rosy **5** ruddy, vivid **6** golden, orange, yellow **7** crimson, roseate, scarlet **8** blushing

warmish 5 tepid **7** cooling

warm oneself 4 bask **12** soak up warmth, toast oneself

warmth 3 joy **4** fire, heat, zeal **5** ardor, cheer, verve, vigor **6** fervor, spirit **7** hotness, passion **8** kindness, sympathy **9** animation, happiness, intensity, vehemence **10** affability, compassion, cordiality, enthusiasm, excitement, joyfulness, kindliness, liveliness, lovingness, tenderness **11** earnestness **12** cheerfulness, friendliness, graciousness **15** kindheartedness **17** tenderheartedness

warn 5 alert **6** advise, inform, notify, signal **7** apprise, caution, counsel **8** admonish

warning 4 hint, omen, sign **5** alarm, token **6** advice, notice, signal **7** portent, presage **8** apprisal **9** foretoken **10** intimation **12** notification

War of the Worlds, The
author: 7 H G Wells
invasion by: 8 Martians

war of words 7 dispute, quarrel **8** argument **11** altercation, controversy **12** disagreement

warp 4 bend, bent, bias **5** quirk, twist **6** debase, deform, infect **7** contort, corrupt, distort, leaning, mislead, pervert **8** misguide, misshape, tendency **9** prejudice, proneness **10** contortion, distortion, partiality, proclivity,

propensity **11** deformation, disposition, inclination **14** predisposition

warrant 3 vow **4** aver, avow **5** swear **6** affirm, assert, assure, attest, permit, pledge **7** certify, declare, justify, license, promise **9** authorize, guarantee **10** asseverate, permission **13** authorization

warranty 6 pledge **9** agreement **11** certificate

Warren, Robert Penn
author of: 5 Flood **7** Audubon **8** Promises **10** Now and Then **12** Incarnations **14** All the King's Men **18** World Enough and Time
member of: 12 the Fugitives

warring 7 hostile **8** battling, clashing, fighting, opposing **9** combatant **10** contending **11** belligerent, conflicting, contentious

warrior 7 fighter, soldier, veteran **9** combatant, man-at-arms **10** campaigner **11** legionnaire

Warsaw
area: 11 Stare Miasto
capital of: 6 Poland
landmark: 14 Kazimierzowski **25** Palace of Culture and Science
Polish: 8 Warszawa
river: 7 Vistula
square: 5 Rynek

warship 5 Maine, U-boat **6** corvet **7** Alabama, cruiser, frigate, gunboat, Monitor **8** Bismarck, corvette, Graf Spee, ironclad, man-of-war **9** destroyer, ironsides, Merrimack, submarine **11** dreadnought, torpedo boat **12** Constitution, Old Ironsides **13** Constellation **15** aircraft carrier **16** superdreadnought
fleet: 6 armada
part: 6 turret
plating: 5 armor

War Within and Without
author: 19 Anne Morrow Lindbergh

wary 5 alert **7** careful, guarded, heedful, mindful, prudent, wakeful **8** cautious, discreet, vigilant, watchful **10** suspicious **11** circumspect

wash 3 mop, rub, wet **4** bath, lave, soak, swab, wipe **5** bathe, clean, float, flood, rinse, scour, scrub **6** drench, shower, sponge **7** cleanse, immerse, launder, laundry, moisten, mopping, shampoo **8** ablution, cleaning, inundate, irrigate, lavation, scouring **9** cleansing **10** laundering

washbasin 3 tub **4** bowl **5** laver **6** lavabo **8** lavatory

washed out 4 drab, dull, pale **5** dingy, faded, white **6** dreary, grayed **8** bleached **9** colorless

washed up, washed-up 4 lost, shot **6** bathed, broken, ruined, undone **7** done for, preened, through **8** bankrupt, done with, fatigued, finished, scrubbed **9** played out, showered

washing 6 laving **7** bathing, laundry, purging, rinsing, soaking **8** cleaning, scouring **9** ablutions, drenching, scrubbing, showering **10** laundering, shampooing

Washington
abbreviation: 2 WA **4** Wash
nickname: 7 Chinook **9** Evergreen
capital: 7 Olympia
largest city: 7 Seattle
others: 4 Omak **5** Pasco **6** Renton, Tacoma, Yakima **7** Ephrata, Everett, Hoquiam, Othello, Pullman, Spokane **8** Aberdeen, Bellevue, Longview, Puyallup, Richland **9** Anacortes, Bremerton, Kennewick, Vancouver, Wenatchee **10** Bellingham, Burlington, Walla Walla **11** Port Angeles
college: 7 Gonzaga, Seattle, Whitman **9** Evergreen, Whitworth **10** Puget Sound **14** Seattle Pacific **15** Pacific Lutheran
feature:
  dam: 10 Bonneville, **11** Grand Coulee
  fort: 5 Lewis
  national park: 7 Olympic **12** Mount Rainier **13** North Cascades
tribe: 3 Hoh **5** Lummi, Makah, Twana **6** Cayuse, Samish, Skagit, Yakima **7** Chinook, Clallam, Clatsop, Cowlitz, Dwamish, Nooksak, Palouse, Quaitso, Sanpoil, Spokane, Squaxon, Tulalip **8** Chehalis, Chimakum, Colville, Nespelim, Nez Perce, Okanagon, Pishquow, Puyallup, Quileute, Quinault, Sahaptin, Salishan, Sinkiuse **9** Nisqually, Quinaielt, Semiahmoo, Skokomish, Swinomish **10** Senijextee, Shoalwater **11** Shahaptaine
people: 7 Seattle **10** Bing Crosby **11** Hank Ketcham **12** Elisha P Ferry **13** Marcus Whitman **15** William O Douglas **19** Isaac Ingalls Stevens
  explorer: 4 Cook, Gray **6** Heceta **9** Vancouver **13** Lewis and Clark
lake: 4 Soap **5** Moses, Union **6** Chelan, Ozette **7** Cle Elum, Cushman, Kachess **8** Crescent, Quinault **9** Keechelus, Wenatchee **10** Washington
land rank: 9 twentieth
mountain: 4 Blue, Jack, Tunk **5** Adams, Baker, Lemei, Logan, Moses, Sloan **6** Kettle, Quartz, Simcoe, Stuart **7** Shuksan **8** Cascades, Olympics, St Helens **11** Kettle River
  highest point: 7 Rainier
physical feature:
  falls: 10 Snoqualmie
  port: 6 Tacoma **7** Everett, Seattle **10** Bellingham
  sound: 5 Puget **7** Rosario
river: 5 Snake, White **6** Yakima **7** Spokane **8** Columbia, Quinault **9** Snohomish **10** Snoqualmie **11** Pend Oreille
state admission: 11 forty-second

state bird: 15 willow goldfinch
state fish: 14 steelhead trout
state flower: 17 coast rhododendron
19 western rhododendron
state motto: 7 By and By (Alki)
state song: 16 Washington My Home
state tree: 14 western hemlock

Washington, George
nickname: 18 Father of His Country
presidential rank: 5 first
party: 10 Federalist
state represented: 2 VA
elected: 11 unanimously
vice president: 5 (John) Adams
cabinet:
  state: 9 (Thomas) Jefferson
  treasury: 8 (Alexander) Hamilton
  war: 4 (Henry) Knox **7** (James)
  McHenry **9** (Timothy) Pickering
  attorney general: 3 (Charles) Lee
  8 (Edmund Jennings) Randolph,
  (William) Bradford
born: 2 VA **9** Wakefield **18** Westmoreland County
died/buried: 11 Mount Vernon
religion: 12 Episcopalian
interests: 7 fishing, hunting, theater
17 scientific farming
vacation: 11 Mount Vernon
author: 33 The Journal of Major
George Washington
political career: 9 president **16** House
of Burgesses **24** First Continental
Congress **25** Second Continental
Congress
signed: 12 Constitution
civilian career: 6 farmer **8** surveyor
military service:
  war: 13 Revolutionary **15** French
  and Indian
notable events of lifetime/term: 18
  American Revolution
  crossed: 13 Delaware River
  rebellion: 7 Whiskey
  winter at: 11 Valley Forge
father: 9 Augustine
mother: 4 Mary (Ball)
siblings: 5 Betty **6** Samuel **7** Charles,
Mildred **13** John Augustine
  half-brother: 6 Butler **8** Lawrence
  9 Augustine
  half-sister: 4 Jane
wife: 6 Martha (Dandridge Custis)
children:
  stepchildren: 15 John Parke Custis
  17 Martha Parke Custis

Washington DC
airport: 6 Dulles **8** National
basketball team: 7 Mystics, Wizards
capital of: 12 United States
designed by: 7 L'Enfant
football team: 8 Redskins
hockey team: 8 Capitals
landmark: 4 Mall **7** Capitol, Ellipse **8**
Pentagon **10** White House **11** National Zoo **12** Ford's Theatre, Franklin Park, Supreme Court **13** Lafayette
Park, Rock Creek Park **14** Farragut

Square, Reflecting Pool, Watergate
Hotel **15** Lincoln Memorial, McPher-
son Square **16** National Archives **17**
Jefferson Memorial, Library of Congress, National Arboretum **18** Washington Monument **21** Frederick
Douglass Home, Robert F Kennedy
Stadium **22** Smithsonian Institution
23 National Sculpture Garden **25** Arlington National Cemetery **33** Kennedy Center for the Performing Arts
museum: 5 Freer **7** Renwick **8** Corcoran **9** Hirshhorn **10** African Art **11**
Smithsonian **13** Dumbarton Oaks **15**
National Gallery **17** Folger Shakespeare **18** Phillips Collection **23** National Portrait Gallery
river: 7 Potomac **9** Rock Creek
street/avenue: 4 Ohio **7** New York,
Potomac **12** Constitution, Independence, Pennsylvania **13** Massachusetts
university: 6 Howard **8** American,
Catholic **10** Georgetown **11** George
Mason **16** George Washington

Washington Square
author: 10 Henry James

wash one's hands of 4 deny, quit **6**
give up **7** abandon, decline, disavow,
forsake **8** abnegate, cast away, disclaim, forswear, renounce **9** repudiate
10 relinquish

washout 6 fiasco, fizzle **7** failure, letdown **8** disaster **14** disappointment

wash out 4 fade, fail **6** bleach **7** deplete, fatigue **8** enervate, enfeeble **10**
debilitate, devitalize

wasp 5 vespa **6** vespid
variety: 5 paper **6** cuckoo, ensign,
hornet, potter, spider **12** yellow
jacket

waspish 5 huffy, testy **6** crabby,
cranky, ornery, shirty **7** bearish, fretful, peevish, pettish **8** petulant, snappish **9** crotchety, fractious, irascible,
irritable, querulous **12** cantankerous

Wasps, The
author: 12 Aristophanes
character: 10 Bdelycleon, Philocleon
  dog: 5 Labes

wassail 5 drink, punch, revel, toast **6**
liquor, tipple **7** carouse, revelry **8**
beverage, carousal

waste 3 die, ebb, rob **4** fade, loot,
melt, rape, raze, ruin, sack, sink,
void, wane **5** abate, crush, decay,
drain, dregs, droop, empty, offal,
smash, spoil, strip, trash, wreck **6**
barren, burn up, debris, devour, litter,
misuse, ravage, razing, refuse, scraps,
steppe, tundra, weaken, wither **7**
crumble, decline, deplete, despoil, destroy, dwindle, exhaust, garbage, looting, pillage, plunder, rubbish, shatter,
subside **8** badlands, decrease, demolish, diminish, leavings, misapply, misspend, needless, prey upon, remnants,
squander, wrecking **9** devastate, dis-

appear, dissipate, emptiness, evaporate, excrement, leftovers, misemploy,
ruination, sweepings **10** demolition,
plundering, remainders, wilderness **11**
destruction, devastation, dissipation,
expenditure, fritter away, prodigality,
squandering **12** despoliation, extravagance **14** misapplication

waste away 4 fail, rust **7** corrode, decline, eat into

wasted 5 spent **6** used-up **7** ravaged **9**
emaciated, exhausted **12** unproductive

wasteful 8 prodigal **9** unthrifty **10**
thriftless **11** extravagant, improvident,
spendthrift, squandering **12** uneconomical

wastefulness 10 imprudence, lavishness **11** prodigality, squandering **12**
extravagance, improvidence

wasteland 6 desert

Waste Land, The
author: 7 T S Eliot
editor: 9 Ezra Pound

waste time 5 dally **6** dawdle, loiter
10 dillydally

watch 3 eye, see **4** heed, look, mark,
mind, note, ogle, save, tend **5** alert,
guard, scout, stare **6** attend, be wary,
gaze at, guards, look at, look on, notice, patrol, peep at, peer at, picket,
regard, sentry, survey, tend to **7** be
chary, care for, examine, lookout, observe, oversee, protect, stare at **8** pore
over, preserve, sentinel, sentries, take
heed **9** attention, patrolman, vigilance
10 observance, scrutinize **11** contemplate, observation, superintend, supervision **15** superintendence

watch fire 6 beacon
kinds: 4 bale **6** signal

watchful 4 wary **5** alert, aware,
canny, chary **6** shrewd **7** careful,
guarded, heedful, mindful, prudent **8**
cautious, open-eyed, vigilant **9** attentive, observant **11** circumspect

watchfulness 4 care, heed **9** attention, diligence, vigilance **13** attentiveness

watchman 5 guard, scout **6** patrol,
picket, sentry **7** lookout **8** sentinel **9**
patrolman

Watch on the Rhine
director: 13 Herman Shumlin
based on play by: 14 Lillian Hellman
cast: 9 Paul Lukas **10** Bette Davis **19**
Geraldine Fitzgerald
Oscar for: 5 actor (Lukas)

watch over 5 guard **6** attend **7** oversee, protect **11** superintend

watchtower 6 beacon, pharos, signal
7 seamark **8** landmark **10** lighthouse

watchword 5 motto **6** byword, slogan

water 3 cut, dip, sea, wet **4** damp,
lake, pond, pool, soak, tear, thin **5**
douse, flood, H two O, ocean, river,
souse **6** dampen, deluge, dilute,

drench, lagoon, splash, stream **7** immerse, moisten **8** inundate, irrigate, sprinkle, submerge **10** adulterate
goddess of: 4 Enki

Water Carrier (Water Bearer)
constellation of: 8 Aquarius

watercolor
French: 9 aquarelle

watercourse 5 canal, river **6** strait **7** channel, conduit, narrows, passage **8** aqueduct

water down 3 cut **6** censor, dilute, weaken **7** thin out **9** expurgate **10** adulterate

watered down 4 weak **6** dilute **7** diluted **8** weakened **11** adulterated

waterfall 7 cascade, Niagara **8** cataract

waterfront 4 dock, mole, pier, quay **5** basin, jetty, levee, wharf **6** marina **7** landing

waterless 3 dry **4** arid, sere **6** barren **7** parched, thirsty **10** desertlike

Waterloo Bridge
director: 11 Mervyn LeRoy
cast: 11 Vivien Leigh **12** Lucile Watson, Robert Taylor **13** Virginia Field
remade as: 4 Gaby

Water Monster (Sea Serpent)
constellation of: 5 Hydra

water of life
Latin: 9 aqua vitae

Waters, Ethel
nickname: 19 Sweet Mama Stringbean
born: 9 Chester PA
roles: 5 Pinky **6** Beulah **21** The Member of the Wedding

Watership Down
author: 12 Richard Adams

Water Snake
constellation of: 6 Hydrus

watertight 9 nonporous **10** impervious **11** impermeable

waterway 5 canal, inlet, river, route **6** gutter, strait, strake, stream **7** channel

Water Wonderland
nickname of: 8 Michigan

watery 3 wet **4** damp, thin, weak **5** fluid, moist, teary **6** liquid, rheumy **7** aqueous, diluted, tearful, tearing **11** adulterated

Watling, Belle
character in: 15 Gone With the Wind
author: 8 Mitchell

Watt, James
nationality: 8 Scottish
developed: 11 steam engine **12** piston engine

Watteau, Jean Antoine
born: 6 France **12** Valenciennes
artwork: 6 Gilles **8** Mezzetin **9** La Finette **10** La Toilette **12** Joys of Living, L'indifferent **13** La Gamme d'Amour **16** Company in the Park, La Lecon de Musique **18** Enseigne de

Gersaint, Gersaint's Signboard, La Comedie Francaise, La Concert de Famille **20** Le Dejeuner en plein air, L'assemblee dans un parc **21** Harlequin and Columbine **23** Embarquement pour Cythere, Italian and French Theater, Jupiter Surprises Antiope, Les Amusements Champetres **24** Conversation in the Open Air, The Embarkation for Cythera

wattle 6 Acacia
varieties: 5 black, broom, cedar, glory, green, hairy, oven's, Sally, swamp **6** frosty, golden, mudgee, orange, silver, sticky **7** bramble, buffalo, coastal, prickly, weeping, Wyalong **8** blue-leaf, cinna- mon, graceful, screw-pod, sunshine **9** red-leaved **10** golden-rain, needle-bush **11** Cootamundra, Mount Morgan, Wallangarra **12** Sydney golden **14** Peppermint-tree **16** Queensland silver

Watts, Sir George Frederic
born: 6 London **7** England
artwork: 4 Hope **14** Physical Energy **17** Paolo and Francesca **19** Anastasio degl'Onesti **45** Caractacus Led in Triumph Through the Streets of Rome **54** Alfred Inciting his Subjects to Prevent the Landing of the Danes

Waugh, Evelyn
author of: 9 Men at Arms **10** Vile Bodies **11** The Loved One **13** Black Mischief, Edmund Campion **14** A Handful of Dust, Decline and Fall **15** A Little Learning **19** Brideshead Revisited **20** Officers and Gentlemen **22** Unconditional Surrender

wave 4 coil, curl, file, flap, line, rank, rise, roll, rush, sway, tier **5** curve, flood, pulse, shake, surge, swell, swing, train, twirl, wield **6** billow, column, comber, deluge, motion, quiver, ripple, roller, signal, spiral, string **7** breaker, flutter, gesture, pulsate, tremble, vibrate, winding **8** brandish, flourish, increase, undulate, whitecap **9** advancing, oscillate, pulsation, vibration **10** salutation, undulation **11** gesticulate, heightening **13** gesticulation

wave at 4 hail **6** signal **7** gesture

wave on 6 beckon, signal **7** gesture **11** gesticulate

waver 4 flap, reel, sway, vary **5** pause, shake, swing, weave **6** careen, change, falter, quiver, totter, wobble **7** flutter, stagger, tremble **8** hesitate, undulate **9** fluctuate, vacillate **10** dillydally **12** shilly-shally

wavering 8 hesitant, waffling **9** undecided **10** hesitating, indecisive, irresolute **11** vacillating

Waverley
author: 14 Sir Walter Scott
character: 12 Flora MacIvor **14** Don-

ald Bean Lean, Edward Waverley **15** Rose Bradwardine **16** Baron Bradwardine **17** Evan Dhu MacCombich **24** Fergus MacIvor Vich Ian Vohr **25** Prince Charles Edward Stuart

wavy 4 onde, unde **5** curly **6** coiled, curved **7** rolling, sinuous, winding **8** mazelike, rippling, tortuous **10** meandering, serpentine, undulating **11** curvilinear **12** labyrinthine

wax 4 grow **5** swell, widen **6** become, blow up, dilate, expand, extend, thrive **7** balloon, develop, enlarge, fill out, inflate, puff out **8** increase

way 3 far, off **4** area, form, lane, pass, path, road, room, wont **5** habit, means, route, space, trail, usage **6** course, custom, far off, manner, method, nature, region, system **7** conduct, passage, pathway, process **8** behavior, distance, practice, remotely, vicinity **9** direction, procedure, technique **12** neighborhood

wayfarer 8 traveler, wanderer **9** sojourner

Wayfaring Stranger
nickname of: 8 Burl Ives

way in 4 door, gate **5** entry **6** access, portal **7** doorway, gateway, ingress **8** approach, entrance

Wayland
also: 6 Volund **7** Wieland
origin: 8 European
king of: 5 elves

waylay 4 lure **5** decoy **6** ambush, assail, attack, entrap **7** assault, ensnare, set upon **8** inveigle

Wayne, Anthony
nickname: 10 Mad Anthony
served in: 10 Indian Wars **16** Revolutionary War
captured: 10 Stony Point
battle: 10 Brandywine, Germantown **13** Fallen Timbers

Wayne, David
real name: 13 Wayne McMeekan
born: 14 Traverse City MI
roles: 6 Sakini **8** Adam's Rib **12** The Front Page **13** Mister Roberts, Tonight We Sing **15** Huckleberry Finn **16** Portrait of Jennie **26** The Teahouse of the August Moon

Wayne, John
real name: 21 Marion Michael Morrison
nickname: 4 Duke
born: 11 Winterset IA
roles: 5 Hondo **6** Chisum **8** Ringo Kid, Rio Bravo, The Alamo, True Grit (Oscar) **9** McLintock, Rio Grande **10** Stagecoach **11** The Quiet Man, The Shootist **12** The Searchers **14** Rooster Cogburn, The Green Berets **16** How the West Was Won **17** The Sands of Iwo Jima **27** The Man Who Shot Liberty Valance

Way of All Flesh, The

author: 12 Samuel Butler
character: 9 Mr Overton
　Pontifex family: 5 Ellen **6** Althea, Ernest, George **8** Theobald **9** Christina

Way of the World, The
author: 15 William Congreve
character: 6 Foible **7** Fainall, Witwoud **8** Mirabell, Waitwell **10** Mrs Fainall, Mrs Marwood **12** Lady Wishfort, Mrs Millamant **17** Sir Wilfull Witwoud

way of thinking 7 beliefs **9** principle **10** conviction **11** persuasions

way out 4 exit **6** egress, escape, outlet

Ways of Escape
author: 12 Graham Greene

wayward 5 balky **6** fickle, fitful, mulish, unruly **7** erratic, restive, willful **8** contrary, perverse, stubborn, variable **9** mercurial, obstinate, whimsical **10** capricious, changeable, headstrong, inconstant, rebellious, refractory, self-willed **11** disobedient, fluctuating, intractable, troublesome **12** inconsistent, incorrigible, recalcitrant, undependable, ungovernable, unmanageable **13** insubordinate

Wazhazhe *see* **5** Osage

weak 4 lame, poor, puny, soft, thin **5** faint, frail, shaky, spent **6** feeble, flimsy, unsafe, wasted, watery **7** brittle, diluted, exposed, fragile, insipid, lacking, unmanly **8** cowardly, delicate, helpless, timorous, unsteady, wide open **9** breakable, enervated, exhausted, frangible, powerless, spineless, tasteless, unguarded, untenable **10** assailable, effeminate, irresolute, namby-pamby, vulnerable, wishy-washy **11** adulterated, debilitated, defenseless, ineffective, ineffectual, inefficient, unprotected, unsupported **12** unconvincing **13** inefficacious, unsubstantial, untrustworthy **14** unsatisfactory

weaken 3 sap **4** fade, fail, flag, thin, wane **5** abate, droop, lower, unman, waste **6** dilute, expose, impair, lessen, soften **7** cripple, dwindle, exhaust, thin out **8** diminish, enervate, mitigate, moderate **9** undermine **10** devitalize, emasculate

weakened 5 frail **6** dilute, faulty, flawed, watery **7** diluted **8** delicate, disabled **9** enfeebled **10** undermined **11** adulterated, debilitated, watered down

weakling 4 twit, wimp **5** mouse, sissy **6** coward **7** chicken, milksop **9** cream puff, jellyfish **10** namby-pamby, pantywaist **11** milquetoast, mollycoddle

weak-minded 4 daft, dull **7** foolish **8** backward, mindless **10** irresolute **11** addleheaded, vacillating **12** feebleminded, muddleheaded, thick-skulled

weakness 4 bent, bias **5** fault **6** defect, hunger, thirst **7** failing, frailty, leaning, passion **8** appetite, debility, fondness, lameness, penchant, tendency **9** prejudice, proneness, shakiness **10** deficiency, feebleness, flimsiness, proclivity, propensity **11** inclination **12** debilitation, imperfection, unsteadiness **13** vulnerability **14** susceptibility **15** ineffectiveness **16** unconvincingness, unsubstantiality **17** untrustworthiness

weak point 4 flaw **5** break, crack, fault **6** defect **10** deficiency **11** shortcoming **12** Achilles heel

weak position 8 handicap **12** disadvantage

weak-willed 8 hesitant, wavering **10** hesitating, indecisive, irresolute

wealth 4 fund, mine **5** goods, means, money, store **6** assets, bounty, estate, luxury, mammon, riches **7** capital, fortune **8** chattels, fullness, opulence, property, richness **9** abundance, affluence, amplitude, plenitude, profusion, resources **10** easy street, prosperity **11** copiousness **12** independence **13** luxuriousness

wealthy 4 rich **5** flush **6** loaded **7** moneyed, well-off **8** affluent, well-to-do **9** well-fixed **10** prosperous, well-heeled

weapon 3 arm **5** guard, means **6** attack, resort **7** bulwark, defense, measure, offense **8** armament, resource, security **9** offensive, safeguard **10** protection **14** countermeasure

weaponry 4 arms, guns **8** armament, materiel, ordnance

wear 3 don, tax, use **4** duds, fray, last, tire, togs, wrap **5** drain, erode, put on, shred, weary **6** abrade, attire, damage, endure, injury, shroud, slip on, swathe **7** apparel, clothes, corrode, dress in, eat away, exhaust, fatigue, frazzle, rub away, service, swaddle, utility **8** clothing, costumes, garments, overwork, wash away **9** disrepair **10** employment, overburden **11** application, consumption, utilization **12** dilapidation **13** deterioration **14** disintegration

wear away 4 rust **5** erase, erode **7** corrode, eat into

weariness
French: 5 ennui

wearing apparel 4 duds, garb, rags, togs, wear **5** dress **6** attire, finery **7** clothes, costume, raiment, regalia, threads **8** clothing, ensemble, garments, wardrobe
French: 11 habillement

wearing away 7 erosion **8** abrasion, friction, grinding, scraping **9** corrosion

wearing down 6 tiring **7** eroding, erosion **8** abrasion, friction, grinding, scraping **10** overcoming

wearisome 4 dull **6** boring, dreary, tiring, trying **7** arduous, irksome, tedious **8** annoying, tiresome, toilsome **9** fatiguing, laborious, vexatious **10** bothersome, burdensome, exhausting, irritating, monotonous, oppressive

wear out 4 tire **7** exhaust, fatigue **8** enervate, enfeeble **10** debilitate

weary 3 fag **4** beat, dull, tire **5** all in, blase, bored, fed up, jaded, spent, tired **6** boring, bushed, done in, drowsy, pooped, sleepy, tiring, tucker **7** annoyed, drained, exhaust, fatigue, humdrum, overtax, play out, routine, tedious, tire out, worn-out **8** dog tired, fatigued, overwork, tiresome **9** disgusted, exhausted, fatiguing, impatient, soporific, wearisome **10** dispirited, exhausting, monotonous, overburden **11** somniferous **12** discontented, dissatisfied

weather 3 dry, tan **4** face, rust **5** brave, clime, stand **6** bleach, season **7** climate, oxidize, toughen **8** confront, windward **9** withstand **11** temperature
god of: 4 Jove **7** Jupiter

weather line 6 isobar

weave 4 fuse, join, knit, lace, link, loom, meld, wind **5** blend, braid, curve, plait, snake, twist, unify, unite **6** mingle, writhe, zigzag **7** combine, entwine, meander, texture **9** interlace **10** crisscross, intertwine **11** incorporate

Weaver, Earl
nickname: 15 Earl of Baltimore
sport: 8 baseball
position: 7 manager
team: 16 Baltimore Orioles

Weaver, Dennis
born: 8 Joplin MO
roles: 7 Chester, McCloud **8** Gunsmoke **9** Gentle Ben **13** Kentucky Jones

Weaver, Sigourney
born: 12 Los Angeles CA
roles: 5 Alien **6** Aliens **10** Eyewitness **12** Ghostbusters **17** Gorillas in the Mist **26** The Year of Living Dangerously

web 3 net **4** maze, mesh, trap **5** snare **6** screen, tangle, tissue **7** complex, netting, network **8** gossamer **9** labyrinth, screening

Web and the Rock, The
author: 11 Thomas Wolfe
character: 10 Esther Jack **12** George Webber

Webb, Jack
born: 13 Santa Monica CA
wife: 11 Julie London
roles: 6 The Men **7** Dragnet **9** Joe Friday **15** Sunset Boulevard

Webber, George
character in: 16 The Web and the Rock **18** You Can't Go Home Again
author: 5 Wolfe

Webb family

characters in: 7 Our Town
member: 5 Emily, Wally
author: 6 Wilder

Weber, Karl Maria Friedrich Ernst von
born: 6 Lubeck **7** Germany
composer of: 6 Oberon **9** Euryanthe **13** Der Freischutz **20** Invitation to the Dance

Weber, Max
born: 6 Russia **9** Bialystok
artwork: 11 The Geranium **17** Chinese Restaurant **18** Adoration of the Moon

Webfoot State
nickname of: 6 Oregon

Webster
character: 6 George **7** Webster **9** Katherine
cast: 10 Alex Karras, Susan Clark **13** Emmanuel Lewis

Webster, John
author of: 13 The White Devil **17** The Duchess of Malfi

we cannot
Latin: 11 non possumus

we command
Latin: 8 mandamus

wed 3 tie **4** bind, fuse, link, mate, meld **5** blend, hitch, marry, merge, unify, unite, weave **6** attach, commit, couple, devote, pledge, splice **7** combine, espouse, make one, win over **8** dedicate **11** incorporate

wedded 4 tied **5** bound, fused **6** joined, linked, melded, merged, united **7** blended, devoted, marital, married, pledged, unified **9** committed, connected **12** incorporated

wedding 8 marriage, nuptials

wedding anniversaries
first: 5 clock, paper
second: 6 china **6** cotton
third: 5 glass **7** crystal, leather
fourth: 4 silk **5** linen **20** electrical appliances
fifth: 4 wood **10** silverware
sixth: 4 iron, wood
seventh: 4 wool **6** copper **8** desk sets **16** pen and pencil sets
eighth: 4 lace **6** bronze, linens
ninth: 5 china **7** leather, pottery
tenth: 3 tin **8** aluminum **14** diamond jewelry
eleventh: 5 steel **11** accessories **14** fashion jewelry
twelfth: 4 silk **6** pearls **11** colored gems
thirteenth: 4 furs, lace **8** textiles
fourteenth: 5 ivory **11** gold jewelry
fifteenth: 7 crystal, watches
twentieth: 5 china **8** platinum
twenty-fifth: 6 silver **21** sterling silver jubilee
thirtieth: 5 pearl **7** diamond
thirty-fifth: 4 jade **5** coral
fortieth: 4 ruby

forty-fifth: 8 sapphire
fiftieth: 4 gold **13** golden jubilee
fifty-fifth: 7 emerald
sixtieth: 7 diamond

weddings
god of: 8 Talassio

wedge 3 jam, ram **4** cram, pack, rend, rive **5** chock, chunk, crowd, force, press, split, stuff **6** cleave **7** squeeze

wedlock 8 marriage **9** matrimony

Wednesday
Dutch: 8 woensdag
French: 8 mercredi
German: 8 mittwoch
heavenly body: 7 Mercury
Italian: 9 mercoledi
name comes from: 4 Odin **5** Woden
observance: 12 Ash Wednesday
Spanish: 9 miercoles
Swedish: 6 onsdag

wee 4 tiny **5** dwarf, scant, teeny **6** little, minute, petite, scanty **9** itty-bitty, miniature, minuscule **10** diminutive, teeny-weeny, undersized **11** Lilliputian, microscopic

weed 3 bur, hoe, nag, pot **4** burr, butt, cull, dock, hemp, rake **5** cigar, joint, vetch **6** darnel, harrow, pull up, root up, uproot **7** tobacco **8** nuisance, plantain, purslane, toadflax **9** cigarette, crabgrass, cultivate, dandelion, eliminate, extirpate, marijuana **12** mourning band

weed out 6 banish **7** abolish, discard **8** get rid of, throw out **9** eliminate

Weena
character in: 14 The Time Machine
author: 5 Wells

weeny 3 wee **4** tiny **5** frank, small, teeny **6** hotdog, little, teensy, wiener **11** frankfurter

weep 3 cry, orp, sob **4** bawl, bend, drip, leak, lerm, ooze, shed, tear, wail **5** exude, mourn **6** bewail, boohoo, lament, shower **7** blubber, lapwing, whimper **8** sweating **9** exudation
genus: 8 Vanellus

weep over 5 mourn **6** bemoan, bewail, lament

weevil
variety: 4 boll, rice

Wegener, Alfred L
field: 10 geophysics **11** meteorology
nationality: 6 German
theory of: 16 continental drift

Wegg
character in: 15 Our Mutual Friend
author: 7 Dickens

weigh 4 lift **5** count, hoist, raise, scale **6** burden, charge, ponder, regard **7** balance, compare, measure **8** consider, encumber, evaluate, ruminate **11** contemplate **12** counterbalance

weigh anchor 4 sail **7** cast off, set sail, ship out

weigh down 4 load **6** anchor, burden

7 oppress **8** encumber, obligate, overload

weight 3 tax **4** heft, load, mass **5** value **6** burden, import, saddle, strain, stress **7** ballast, concern, oppress, tonnage, urgency **8** emphasis, encumber, poundage, pressure **9** heaviness, influence, magnitude **10** importance **11** consequence **12** significance **13** consideration, ponderousness

weight, unit of
of Afghanistan: 3 pau, paw, ser, sir
of Algeria: 4 rotl
of Argentina: 4 last **5** grano, libra **7** quintal **8** tonelada
of Austria: 4 marc, saum, unze **5** denat, karch, pfund, stein **7** centner, pfennig **8** vierling **9** quantchen
of Belgium: 4 last **5** carat, livre, pound **6** charge **7** chariot **9** esterling
of Bolivia: 5 libra, marco
of Borneo: 4 para **6** chapah
of Brazil: 3 bag **4** onca, onza **5** libra **6** arroba, oitava **7** arratel, quilate, quintal **8** tonelada
of Bulgaria: 3 oka, oke **5** tovar
of Cambodia: 4 mace, tael
of Chile: 5 grano, libra **7** quintal
of China: 3 fan, fen, hao, kin, ssu, tan, yin **4** chee, chin, dong, shih, tael, tsin **5** catty, chien, picul, tchin, tsien **6** kungli **7** haikwan, kungfen, kungssu, kungtun **8** kungchin **9** candareen **10** kupingtael
of Colombia: 3 bag **4** saco **5** carga, libra **7** quilate, quintal
of Costa Rica: 3 bag **4** caja **5** libra
of Cuba: 5 libra **6** tercio
of Ecuador: 5 libra
of Egypt: 3 kat, ket, oka, oke **4** dera, heml, khar, okia, rotl **5** artal, artel, deben, kerat, minae, minas, okieh, pound, ratel, uckia **6** hamlah, kantar **7** drachma, quintal
of El Salvador: 3 bag **4** caja **5** libra
of England: 3 bag, kip, tod, ton **4** keel, last, mast, maun **5** barge, fagot, grain, maund, pound, score, stand, stone, truss **6** bushel, cental, fangot, firkin, fother, fotmal, pocket **7** quarter, quintal, sarpler
of Estonia: 4 lood, nael, puud
of Ethiopia: 3 pek **4** kasm, natr, oket, rotl **5** alada, artal, mocha, neter, ratel, wakea **6** wogiet **8** farasula **9** mutagalla
of France: 3 sol **4** gros, kilo, marc, once **5** carat, livre, pound, tonne, uckia **6** gramme, passir **7** tonneau **8** esterlin **9** esterling
of Greece: 3 mna, oka, oke **4** mina, obol **5** litra, livre, maneh, pound **6** diobol, dramme, kantar, obolos, obolus, stater, talent **7** chalcon, chalque, drachma **8** diobolon, talanton
of Guatemala: 4 caja **5** libra
of Guinea: 4 akey, piso, uzan **5** benda, seron **6** quinto **8** aguirage

of Hungary: 7 vamfont **8** vammazsa

of Iceland: 4 pund **5** pound, tunna **6** smjors

of India: 3 mod, pai, ser, vis **4** dhan, drum, hoen, kona, myat, pala, pank, pice, raik, ruay, tael, tali, tank, tola, wang, yava **5** adpad, bahar, hubba, masha, maund, tical **6** abucco, karsha **8** mangelin

of Indonesia: 5 catty, ounce, thail **6** soekoe

of Iran: 3 ser **4** dram, dung, rotl, sang, seer **5** abbas, artel, maund, pinar, ratel **6** dirhem, gandum, karwar, miscal, nakhod, nimman **7** abbassi **8** tcheirek

of Italy: 5 carat, libra, oncia, pound **6** carato, denaro, libbra, ottava

of Japan: 2 mo **3** fun, kin, kon, rin, shi **4** kati, kwan, niyo **5** carat, catty, momme, picul **6** kwamme **8** hiyakkin

of Java: 4 amat, pond, tali **5** pound **6** soekel

of Korea: 3 won

of Latvia: 9 liespfund

of Libya: 3 pik, saa **4** kele **5** teman, uckia **6** gorraf, misura **7** mattaro, termino **8** kharouba

of Malaysia: 4 chee, mace, tael, wang **7** tampang

of Mexico: 3 bag **4** onza **5** carga, libra, marco **6** adarme, arroba, ochava, tercio **7** quintal

of Mongolia: 3 lan

of Morocco: 4 rotl **5** artal, artel, gerbe, ratel **6** dirhem, kintar **7** quintal

of Myanmar: 2 ta **3** can, mat, moo, pai, vis **4** binh, dong, kyat, ruay, viss **5** bahar, behar, candy, tical, ticul **6** abucco **7** peiktha

of the Netherlands: 3 ons **4** last, lood, pond **5** bahar, grein **6** korrel **7** wichtje **8** esterlin

of Nicaragua: 3 bag **4** caha, caja **8** tonelada

of Norway: 3 lod **4** mark, pund **9** skaalpund **10** bismerpund

of Pakistan: 4 seer, tola **5** maund

of Paraguay: 7 quintal

of Peru: 5 libra **7** quintal

of the Philippines: 5 catty, fardo, picul, punto **6** lachsa **7** quilate **8** chinanta

of Poland: 3 lut **4** funt **5** uncya **6** kamian **7** centner, skrupul

of Portugal: 4 grao, onca, once **5** libra, marco **6** arroba, oitava **7** arratel, quintal **9** excropulo

of Russia: 3 lof, lot **4** dola, funt, lana, last, loof, loth, once, pood, poud **5** dolia

of Saudi Arabia: 3 oke

of Scotland: 4 boll, drop **5** trone **6** bushel

of Somalia: 8 parsalah

of Spain: 4 onza **5** frail, grano, libra,

marco, tomin **6** adarme, arroba, dinero, dracma, ochava **7** arienzo, quilate, quintal **8** caracter, tonelada

of Sudan: 5 habba

of Sweden: 3 ass, lod, ort **4** last, mark, sten **5** carat **6** nylast **7** centner, lispund **8** skalpund, skeppund **9** shippound

of Switzerland: 4 fund **5** pfund **7** centner, quintal **12** zugthierlast

of Syria: 4 cola, rotl **5** artal, artel, ratel **6** talent

of Tanzania: 8 farsalah

of Thailand: 3 bat, hap, pai, pay, sen, sok **4** baht, haph, kati, klam, klom **5** catty, chang, coyan, fuang, picul, pilul, tical **6** fluang, graini, salung, sompay **7** tamlung

of Tunisia: 3 saa **4** rotl **5** artal, artel, ratel, uckia **6** kantar

of Turkey: 3 oka, oke **4** aqui, dram, kile, rotl **5** artal, artel, cheke, kerat, obolu, ratel **6** batman, dirhem, kantar, maunch, miskal **7** drachma, quintal, yusdrum

of Uruguay: 7 quintal

of Venezuela: 3 bag **5** libra

of Vietnam: 3 can, yet **4** uyen

of Yugoslavia: 3 oka **5** dramm, tovar, wagon **7** satlijk

weightlessness 8 buoyancy **9** lightness **11** zero gravity

weighty 5 grave, heavy, hefty, vital **6** solemn, taxing, trying, urgent **7** arduous, crucial, earnest, massive, onerous, serious **8** critical, crushing, cumbrous, pressing **9** difficult, essential, important, ponderous **10** burdensome, cumbersome, oppressive **11** significant, substantial, troublesome **12** considerable **13** consequential

Weill, Kurt
  born: 6 Dessau **7** Germany
  composer of: 8 Happy End **13** Lady in the Dark **15** Down in the Valley **18** The Lindbergh Flight, The Threepenny Opera **19** Die Dreigroschenoper **31** Rise and Fall of the City of Mahagonny **32** Aufstieg und Fall der Stadt Mahagonny

Weir, Peter
  director of: 7 Witness **9** Gallipoli **11** The Last Wave **26** The Year of Living Dangerously

weird 3 odd **4** wild **5** crazy, eerie, kooky, nutty, queer **6** far-out, mystic, spooky **7** bizarre, curious, ghostly, magical, strange, unusual **8** abnormal, freakish, peculiar **9** eccentric, grotesque, irregular, unearthly, unnatural **10** mysterious, outlandish, phantasmal, unorthodox **12** supernatural **14** unconventional

weirdo 3 nut **4** kook **5** flake, freak **6** looney **7** lunatic, oddball **8** crackpot, original **9** character, eccentric, screwball **10** one-of-a-kind

Weird sisters 5 Fates, Norns

Weisenfreund, Muni
  real name of: 8 Paul Muni

Weismuller, Johnny
  real name: 20 Peter John Weissmuller
  born: 9 Windbar PA
  Olympic sport: 8 swimming
  Olympic gold medals: 4 five
  wife: 9 Lupe Velez
  roles: 6 Tarzan **9** Jungle Jim

Weiss, Peter
  author of: 10 Marat/Sade **14** Vanishing Point

welcome 4 meet **5** admit, greet **6** at home, salute, wanted **7** embrace, receive, usher in, winning **8** accepted, admitted, charming, engaging, enticing, greeting, inviting, pleasant, pleasing **9** agreeable, entertain, reception **10** delightful, gratifying, salutation **11** comfortable

Weld, Tuesday
  real name: 12 Susan Ker Weld
  born: 9 New York NY
  husband: 11 Dudley Moore
  roles: 12 I Walk the Line **14** Play It as It Lays **16** The Cincinnati Kid, Wild in the Country **19** Looking for Mr Goodbar

welfare 4 good **6** health, profit, relief **7** benefit, success, the dole **9** advantage, happiness

well 3 jet, run **4** flow, fund, good, gush, hale, mine, ooze, pool, pour, rise **5** amply, fount, fully, issue, lucky, right, shaft, sound, spout, spurt, store, surge **6** easily, fairly, hearty, justly, kindly, nicely, proper, robust, source, spring, stream, strong, warmly **7** chipper, fitting, healthy, readily, rightly **8** famously, fountain, laudably, properly, suitably, very much, vigorous **9** agreeably, capitally, carefully, correctly, favorable, favorably, fortunate, promising, quite well **10** abundantly, acceptably, adequately, auspicious, completely, familiarly, felicitous, intimately, personally, prosperous, splendidly, successful, thoroughly **11** approvingly, commendably **12** advantageous, auspiciously, considerably, propitiously, satisfactory, successfully, sufficiently **13** substantially **14** advantageously, satisfactorily **15** sympathetically **16** enthusiastically
  hole drilled in ground for: 3 gas, oil **5** water

well-adjusted 6 normal, secure **8** sensible

Welland, May
  character in: 17 The Age of Innocence
  author: 7 Wharton

well-behaved 6 polite, sedate **8** decorous

well-being 4 ease, good, luck, weal **6** health, profit **7** benefit, comfort, fortune, success, welfare **8** felicity, good luck **9** advantage, affluence, happiness **10** prosperity

wellborn 8 highbred **9** patrician **10** upper-class **12** aristocratic, silk-stocking

Wellbred
character in: **19** Every Man in His Humour
author: **6** Jonson

well-bred 5 civil, suave **6** polite, urbane **7** elegant, gallant, genteel, refined **8** cultured, ladylike, mannerly, polished **9** civilized, courteous **10** cultivated **11** gentlemanly **13** sophisticated

well-chosen 3 apt **4** fine **5** prize **6** choice, seemly, select **7** apropos, correct, fitting, special **8** superior **9** excellent **11** appropriate

well-considered 7 careful, prudent **8** cautious **10** thoughtful **11** circumspect

well-coordinated 6 smooth **8** graceful **9** dexterous **10** effortless

well-defined 5 clear, plain **8** clear-cut, definite, distinct, palpable **10** pronounced

well-dressed 4 chic **5** natty, smart **6** dapper **11** fashionable

well-educated 7 erudite, learned **8** cultured, literate **9** scholarly **10** cultivated **13** knowledgeable

Weller, Sam
character in: **14** Pickwick Papers
author: **7** Dickens

Welles, Orson
real name: **17** George Orson Welles
born: **9** Kenosha WI
wife: **9** Paola Mori **12** Rita Hayworth
formed: **14** Mercury Theatre
radio show: **14** War of the Worlds
roles: **8** Jane Eyre **11** Citizen Kane, The Third Man, Touch of Evil
director of: **7** Macbeth, Othello **8** Falstaff **11** Citizen Kane, The Stranger, Touch of Evil **23** The Magnificent Ambersons

well-favored 4 fair **5** bonny **6** comely, pretty **7** sightly, winsome **8** fetching, handsome **9** beautiful **10** attractive **11** good looking

well-fed 5 hefty, plump, stout **6** portly, rotund **9** corpulent

well-fixed 4 rich **7** moneyed, wealthy **8** affluent **10** prosperous

well-founded 7 factual **9** supported **12** corroborated **13** substantiated

well-groomed 4 neat, tidy **5** natty **6** spruce **10** impeccable

well-grounded 5 valid **7** factual **8** reliable **9** supported **10** undeniable, undisputed, unshakable **11** irrefutable **12** corroborated, indisputable **13** incontestable, substantiated **16** incontrovertible

well-heeled 4 rich **7** moneyed, wealthy **8** affluent **10** in the chips, in the money, prosperous

Wellington
capital of: **10** New Zealand

Wellington, Duke of
also: **15** Arthur Wellesley
nickname: **6** Hookey **12** The Great Duke
nationality: **7** British
served in: **5** India **14** Napoleonic Wars
battle: **6** Assaye **7** Vitoria **8** Talavera, Waterloo **9** Salamanca
served as: **13** prime minister
memoirs: **20** Wellington Dispatches

well-kept 4 heat, neat, tidy **7** orderly **9** organized **10** systematic **11** disciplined, uncluttered

well-known 4 open **5** famed, noted **6** common, famous **7** big-time, eminent, evident, leading, obvious, popular **8** familiar, infamous, renowned **9** important, notorious, prominent **10** celebrated, scandalous, understood **11** established, illustrious, outstanding

well-lighted 5 lit up **6** ablaze, bright **11** illuminated

well-made 4 fine **7** perfect **8** executed, flawless **9** faultless **11** beautifully

Wellman, William
director of: **5** Wings **9** Beau Geste **11** A Star Is Born **13** Nothing Sacred **15** The Story of GI Joe **16** The Ox-Bow Incident

well-mannered 6 polite **7** genteel, refined **8** cultured, decorous, ladylike, polished **9** courteous, dignified **10** cultivated **11** gentlemanly

well-matched 5 close **10** nip-and-tuck

well-off 4 rich **5** flush **6** loaded **7** moneyed, wealthy **8** affluent **10** prosperous **11** comfortable

well-padded 5 plump, stout **6** chubby, fleshy, portly, rotund **9** corpulent

well-proportioned 7 classic, elegant, shapely **8** graceful **11** symmetrical

well-read 7 erudite, learned **8** cultured, literate **9** scholarly **10** cultivated

well-reasoned 4 wise **10** perceptive, thoughtful **11** intelligent

well-rehearsed 6 smooth **7** planned **8** prepared **9** practiced

Wells, H G (Herbert George)
author of: **5** Kipps **10** Tono-Bungay **11** Ann Veronica **14** The Time Machine **15** The Invisible Man **16** Outline of History **17** Love and Mr Lewisham, The War of the Worlds **19** The History of Mr Polly **22** The Shape of Things to Come **23** Mr Britling Sees It Through

wellspring 4 font **6** origin, source **9** beginning **10** birthplace **12** fountainhead

well-stocked 4 full **11** overflowing

well-suited 6 proper **7** correct, fitting **8** suitable **9** congenial, congruous **10** compatible, harmonious **11** appropriate

well-to-do 4 rich **7** moneyed, wealthy **8** affluent **10** in the chips, in the money, prosperous

well up 4 boil, rise **6** bubble **7** surface

well-ventilated 4 airy **5** windy **6** breezy, drafty

well-versed 7 knowing **9** qualified **10** conversant **11** experienced **13** knowledgeable
French: **9** au courant

well-wisher 6 friend **8** advocate, champion **9** supported

Welsh Mythology
goddess: **3** Don
goddess of fire/fertility/agriculture/ household/wisdom: **6** Brigit
king: **4** Bran, Llud, Ludd, Nudd
magician: **5** Lloyd
paradise: **5** Annwn **6** Annfwn
prince: **5** Pwyll **7** Kilwich
princess: **5** Olwen
romantic tales: **10** Mabinogian

welt 4 bump, lump, mark, wale, weal **6** bruise, streak, stripe **8** swelling **9** contusion

Weltanschauung 25 manner of looking at the world

Weltansicht 9 world view

Weltschmerz 6 sorrow **9** world pain **10** melancholy **20** sentimental pessimism

Welty, Eudora
author of: **12** Delta Wedding, Golden Apples **13** Losing Battles **14** The Ponder Heart **15** A Sweet Devouring **19** The Robber Bridegroom **20** The Optimist's Daughter

wench 4 doxy, girl, lass, maid, slut **5** whore **6** damsel, lassie, maiden **8** strumpet **10** prostitute

Wend 4 Slav, Sorb
in: **7** Germany

wend 4 make **5** hie to

went 3 ran **4** flew, left **5** faded, got on **6** flew by, lapsed, passed **7** elapsed, sallied **8** departed, filed off, passed by, took wing, vanished **9** proceeded, took leave **10** shuffled on, took flight **11** disappeared, forged ahead **12** sallied forth **13** pressed onward

Wentworth, Captain Frederick
character in: **10** Persuasion
author: **6** Austen

Werfel, Franz
author of: **9** Mirror Man **19** Forty Days of Musa Dagh, The Song of Bernadette

Werle, Gregers

character in: **11** The Wild Duck
author: **5** Ibsen

Werner, Oskar
real name: **24** Oskar Josef Bschliess-mayer
born: **6** Vienna **7** Austria
roles: **11** Jules and Jim, Ship of Fools **17** Voyage of the Damned **22** Fahrenheit Four Fifty One, The Shoes of the Fisherman **26** The Spy Who Came in from the Cold

Wertmuller, Lina
director of: **9** Swept Away (by an unusual destiny in the blue sea of August) **13** Seven Beauties

Wescott, Glenway
author of: **14** The Grandmother, The Pilgrim Hawk **16** The Apple of the Eye **17** Apartment in Athens

Wessex
fictional place created by: **5** Hardy

West, Benjamin
born: **13** Springfield PA
artwork: **17** Death on a Pale Horse **19** Death of General Wolfe **22** Saul and the Witch of Endor

West, Dame Rebecca
real name: **28** Cicily Isabel Fairfield Andrews
author of: **8** The Judge **11** Harriet Hume **13** Birds Fall Down **15** The Thinking Reed **19** The Strange Necessity **20** The Fountain Overflows **21** The Return of the Soldier **22** Black Lamb and Grey Falcon

West, Jessamyn
author of: **11** Leafy Rivers **13** A Matter of Time **18** Except for Me and Thee **21** The Friendly Persuasion **22** The Massacre at Fall Creek

West, Mae
born: **10** Brooklyn NY
roles: **3** Sex **8** Sextette **9** I'm No Angel **10** Diamond Lil **13** Klondike Annie **14** Go West Young Man **15** Night After Night, She Done Him Wrong **16** Myra Breckinridge **17** My Little Chickadee
autobiography: **28** Goodness Had Nothing To Do With It
quote: **18** Beulah peel me a grape **22** Come up and see me sometime

West, Morris L
author of: **7** Proteus **9** Harlequin **13** The Salamander **14** The Clowns of God **15** The Tower of Babel **17** The Devil's Advocate **22** The Shoes of the Fisherman

West, Nathanael
author of: **12** A Cool Million **16** Miss Lonelyhearts **17** The Day of the Locust

Westcott, Edward Noyes
author of: **10** David Harum

Westenra, Lucy
character in: **7** Dracula
author: **6** Stoker

Western, Sophia
character in: **8** Tom Jones
author: **8** Fielding

Western Sahara
other name: **13** Spanish Sahara
capital: **6** Al Aiun **7** El Aaiun
city: **3** Zug **5** Daora, Smara **6** Aargub, Dakhla, Tichla **9** Asqueimat, Bir Gandus **10** Bir Enzaran **12** Guelta Zemmur
government: **33** disputed territory claimed by Morocco
river: **7** Uad Atui **8** Uad Assag **13** Saguia el Hamra
sea: **8** Atlantic
physical feature:
    cape: **6** Barbas **7** Bojador
    desert: **6** Sahara
    wind: **5** leste **6** gibleh
people: **4** Arab **6** Berber
language: **16** Hassaniyya Arabic
religion: **5** Islam
feature:
    political group: **14** Polisario Front

Western Samoa
other name: **17** Navigator's Islands
capital/largest city: **4** Apia
others: **6** Safotu, Sataua **7** Faleolo, Palauli, Poutasi, Tuasivi **8** Fagamalo, Falelima, Lufilufi **9** Falealupo, Mulifanua **10** Samalaeulu, Satupaitea
monetary unit: **4** sene, tala
island: **5** Upolu **6** Manono, Savaii **7** Apolima
mountain: **4** Fito, Vaea
highest point: **13** Mauga Silisili
sea: **7** Pacific
physical feature:
    bay: **4** Asau, Salu **6** Safata **7** Lafanga, Matautu **8** Fangaloa, Salealua **9** Saluofata
    strait: **7** Apolima
people: **6** Samoan **10** Melanesian, Polynesian
    author: **20** Robert Louis Stevenson (Tusitala, Teller of Tales)
    explorer: **6** Wilkes **9** Roggeveen **12** Bougainville
language: **6** Samoan **7** English
religion: **9** Methodist **10** Protestant **13** Roman Catholic **14** Congregational
place:
    observatory: **4** Apia
    tomb: **9** Stevenson
feature:
    chief: **5** matai
    clothing: **5** pareu **8** lavalava, puletasi
    dance: **4** siva
    daughter of chief: **5** taupo
    house: **4** fale
food:
    dish: **8** palusami
    drink: **3** ava

Western Star
author: **19** Stephen Vincent Benet

Westhus, Haie

character in: **25** All Quiet on the Western Front
author: **8** Remarque

West Indies 11 archipelago
Associated States: **7** Antigua, Grenada, St Lucia **8** Anguilla, Dominica **12** St Kitts-Nevis
bird: **4** tody **6** mucaro
channel: **7** Jamaica **9** Old Bahama
component: **4** Cuba **5** Haiti **6** Tobago **7** Bahamas, Jamaica **8** Barbados, Trinidad **10** Hispaniola, Puerto Rico **13** Virgin Islands **14** Leeward Islands, Lesser Antilles **15** Greater Antilles, Windward Islands **17** Dominican Republic
crop: **6** coffee **9** sugarcane
fish: **4** pega **5** pelon
formerly: **10** federation
fruit: **5** papaw **6** pawpaw **7** genipap
islands: **5** Turks **6** Caicos, Cayman, Virgin **7** Bahamas, Leeward **8** Windward
kale: **7** malanga
lizard: **6** arbalo
music: **7** calypso
passage: **4** Mona **8** Windward
rodent: **5** hutia
sea: **9** Caribbean
shark: **4** gata
sorcery: **3** obi **5** obeah
tree: **5** genip **6** aralie
tribesman: **5** Carib **6** Arawak **7** Ciboney
vessel: **6** droger, drogher
volcano: **5** Pelee

Westinghouse, George
nationality: **8** American
invented: **8** air brake **12** railroad frog **20** railroad signal system

Westlake, Donald E
author of: **8** Bank Shot **10** The Hot Rock **13** Dancing Aztecs **15** Brothers Keepers
    as Richard Stark: **9** The Hunter **10** The Seventh
    as Tucker Coe: **19** Murder Among Children

Westover, Russ
creator/artist of: **15** Tillie the Toiler

West Side Story
director: **10** Robert Wise **13** Jerome Robbins
cast: **10** Rita Moreno **11** Natalie Wood, Russ Tamblyn **13** Richard Beymer **14** George Chakiris
score: **15** Stephen Sondheim **16** Leonard Bernstein
Oscar for: **7** picture **8** director **15** supporting actor (Chakiris) **17** supporting actress (Moreno)

West Virginia
abbreviation: **2** WV **3** W Va
nickname: **8** Mountain **9** Panhandle
capital: **10** Charleston
largest city: **10** Huntington
others: **5** Logan **6** Elkins, Keyser, Ripley, Vienna, Weston **7** Beckley,

Grafton, Spencer, Weirton **8** Fairmont, Wheeling **10** Clarksburg **11** Moundsville, Parkersburg
college: 5 Salem **7** Bethany, Concord **8** Marshall, Wheeling **9** Bluefield **10** Charleston **14** Davis and Elkins **16** Alderson Broaddus **20** West Virginia Wesleyan
feature:
   historical site: 12 Harper's Ferry
   national road: 10 Cumberland
tribe: 7 Moneton
people: 9 Pearl Buck **14** Arthur I Boreman **19** Walter Philip Reuther **24** Thomas "Stonewall" Jackson
   explorer: 12 Morgan Morgan
island: 14 Blennerhassett
lake: 4 Lynn
land rank: 10 forty-first
mountain:
   highest point: 10 Spruce Knob
physical feature:
   cavern: 6 Seneca
   plateau: 9 Allegheny
   rock: 6 Seneca
   spring: 8 Berkeley **12** White Sulphur
river: 3 Elk **4** Ohio **6** Gauley **7** Kanawha, Potomac, Tug Fork **8** Big Sandy, Guyandot **11** Monongahela
state admission: 11 Thirty-fifth
state bird: 8 cardinal
state fish: 10 brook trout
state flower: 11 great laurel **15** big rhododendron **17** great rhododendron
state motto: 25 Mountaineers Are Always Free
state song: 17 West Virginia Hills **20** This Is My West Virginia **27** West Virginia My Home Sweet Home
state tree: 10 sugar maple

Westward Ho!
author: 15 Charles Kingsley

west wind
associated with: 8 Favonius, Zephyrus

wet 3 dip **4** damp, dank, rain, soak **5** humid, moist, rainy, soggy, steep, storm, water **6** clammy, dampen, drench, liquid, shower, soaked, sodden, splash, stormy, watery **7** immerse, moisten, showery, soaking, sopping, squishy, wetness **8** dampened, dampness, dankness, drenched, dripping, inundate, irrigate, moisture, sprinkle, submerge **9** exudation, liquified, moistness, rainstorm **10** clamminess **11** waterlogged **12** condensation **13** precipitation

wet blanket 4 drag **6** damper **10** spoilsport **11** party-pooper

wet down 5 spray **6** dampen **7** moisten **8** sprinkle

wettish 4 damp **5** moist **6** clammy

we who are about to die salute thee

Latin: 19 morituri te salutamus
said by: 15 Roman gladiators
said to: 13 Roman emperors

whack 2 go **3** box, hit, rap, try **4** bang, belt, blow, cuff, slam, slap, slug, sock, stab, turn **5** baste, clout, crack, knock, pound, punch, smack, smite, thump, trial **6** strike, wallop **7** attempt, venture **8** endeavor

whale 4 beat, cane, drub, flog, orca, whip **6** baleen, thrash **9** bastinado
constellation of: 5 Cetus
group of: 3 gam, pod
swallowed: 5 Jonah
Melville: 8 Moby Dick

whammy 3 hex **4** jinx **5** curse **7** evil eye **9** evil spell

wharf 3 key **4** dock, pier, quai, quay, slip **5** jetty **6** marina **7** landing **10** breakwater

Wharton, Edith
author of: 10 Ethan Frome, The Old Maid **15** The House of Mirth **17** The Age of Innocence **21** The Custom of the Country

Whatever Happened to Baby Jane?
director: 13 Robert Aldrich
cast: 10 Bette Davis **11** Victor Buono **12** Joan Crawford **15** Marjorie Bennett

What Every Woman Knows
author: 12 James M Barrie
character: 9 John Shand **15** Charles Venables **18** Comtesse de la Briere, Lady Sybil Tenterden
   Wylie family: 5 Alick, David, James **6** Maggie

what it takes 5 knack, skill **7** ability, know-how, mastery **9** expertise **10** capability, competence, expertness **11** proficiency **13** the right stuff

What Mrs McGillicuddy Saw!
author: 14 Agatha Christie

What Price Glory?
author: 15 Maxwell Anderson

What's Happening!!
character: 5 Rerun **6** Dwayne **7** Shirley **9** Dee Thomas, (Mama) Mrs Thomas **11** Roger (Raj) Thomas
cast: 9 Fred Berry, Mabel King **12** Ernest Thomas **13** Haywood Nelson **15** Danielle Spencer, Shirley Hemphill

What's My Line?
host: 8 John Daly
panelist: 8 Hal Block **9** Fred Allen **10** Steve Allen **11** Bennett Cerf **13** Arlene Francis **15** Louis Untermeyer **16** Dorothy Kilgallen

wheat 8 Triticum
varieties: 4 club, rice **5** durum, dwarf, India, river **6** Alaska, common, German, Polish, starch **7** English, poulard **8** hedgehog **10** one-grained, two-grained **13** Mediterranean

product: 4 bran **5** bread, flour, pasta **6** cereal **8** macaroni **9** spaghetti

Wheat State
nickname of: 6 Kansas

wheedle 4 coax, lure **5** charm **6** cajole, entice, induce **7** beguile, flatter **8** butter up, inveigle, persuade, soft soap

wheel 4 disk, drum, hoop, ring, roll, spin **5** pivot, round, swirl, twirl, whirl **6** caster, circle, gilgal, gyrate, roller, rotate, swivel **7** revolve **9** pirouette

Wheel of Fortune
host: 8 Pat Sajak
assistant: 10 Vanna White

wheels 3 car **4** auto, heap **5** motor **6** jalopy **7** flivver, vehicle **8** motorcar **9** tin lizzie **10** automobile

wheeze 4 gasp, hiss, pant, puff **7** panting, whistle

whelp 3 boy, cub, kid, lad, pup **4** brat **5** child, puppy, youth **6** urchin **9** stripling, youngster **14** whippersnapper

whence 9 from where **10** antecedent **14** from what source

Where Eagles Dare
director: 12 Brian G Hutton
based on novel by: 15 Alistair MacLean
cast: 7 Mary Ure **12** Robert Beatty **13** Clint Eastwood, Patrick Wymark, Richard Burton **14** Michael Hordern

wherefore 2 so **3** why **7** because **13** for what reason

where I may stand
Greek: 6 pou sto

where mentioned above
Latin: 8 ubi supra

whereupon 8 upon what **10** after which **14** upon which point

wherewithal 4 cash **5** funds, means **6** assets **7** capital **9** financing, resources

whet 4 edge, hone, stir **5** grind, pique, strop, tempt **6** allure, arouse, awaken, entice, excite, induce, kindle **7** animate, provoke, quicken, sharpen **9** stimulate **11** put an edge on

whether willing or not
Latin: 12 nolens volens

which see
Latin: 2 qv **8** quod vide

which was to be demonstrated
Latin: 3 QED **21** quod erat demonstrandum

which was to be done
Latin: 17 quod erat faciendum

which was to be shown
Latin: 3 QED **21** quod erat demonstrandum

whiff 4 hint, odor, puff **5** aroma, draft, scent, smell, sniff, trace **6** breath, breeze, zephyr **7** bouquet
French: 7 soupcon

Whig Party

president belonging to: 5 Tyler **6** Taylor **8** Fillmore, Harrison

while 2 as **3** yet **4** idle, till, time, when **5** until **6** during, effort, whilst **7** filling, interim, trouble, whereas **8** although, occasion

whim 4 urge **5** fancy, quirk **6** notion, vagary **7** caprice, conceit, impulse **8** crotchet **11** inspiration **12** eccentricity

whimper 3 sob **4** pule **5** whine **6** snivel **7** blubber, sniffle, sobbing **9** cry softly, sniveling **11** sob brokenly **16** whine plaintively

whimsical 5 droll **6** fickle, fitful, quaint **7** amusing, erratic, waggish **8** fanciful, notional, quixotic **9** eccentric **10** capricious, changeable, chimerical **12** inconsistent

whimsy, whimsey 4 bent, wish **5** fancy, humor, prank, quirk **6** notion, vagary **7** caprice, fantasy **8** escapade, drollery **11** make-believe

whine 3 cry, sob **4** fret, mewl, moan, wail **6** grouse, murmur, mutter, snivel **7** grumble, whimper **8** complain **9** complaint **11** gripe meekly **12** plaintive cry **14** cry plaintively

whip 3 rod **4** beat, cane, drub, flap, flog, jerk, jolt, lash, lick, maul, rout **5** birch, flick, spank, strap, thong, whisk **6** rattan, snatch, switch **7** cowhide, rawhide, scourge, trounce **8** birch rod, vanquish **9** horsewhip, toss about **10** blacksnake, flagellate **13** cat-o'-nine-tails, defeat soundly, move violently **14** beat decisively, beat into a froth

Whip 8 scorpion

whip hand 4 sway **5** power **7** control, mastery **9** advantage, authority, dominance, supremacy, upper hand **10** ascendancy, domination

whipped 5 caned, waled **6** beaten, darted, flayed, frothy, lashed, roused **7** flogged, frothed, incited, revived, spanked, subdued, swished, whisked **8** defeated, overlaid, punished, scourged, switched **9** chastised **10** vanquished

whir 3 hum **4** buzz, purr **5** drone **7** whisper

whirl 2 go **3** try **4** reel, spin, stab, turn **5** crack, fling, pivot, swirl, trial, twirl, whack, wheel **6** circle, dither, flurry, gyrate, rotate **7** attempt, revolve, turning **8** circling, gyration, pivoting, rotation, spinning, swirling, twirling, wheeling **9** feel dizzy, feel giddy, pirouette, revolving, turn round **10** dizzy round, rapid round, revolution **12** merry-go-round **17** state of excitement **18** dizzying succession

whirlpool 4 eddy **5** swirl, whirl **6** vortex **9** maelstrom **15** whirling current

whirlwind 4 rash **5** hasty, quick, rapid, short, swift **7** cyclone, tornado, twister **8** headlong **9** breakneck, impetuous, impulsive **10** waterspout

whirly 5 dizzy, giddy, shaky **7** reeling **8** spinning **11** vertiginous

whisk 3 fly, zip **4** beat, bolt, dart, dash, race, rush, tear, whip, whiz **5** bound, brush, flick, hurry, scoot, shoot, speed, spurt, sweep **6** hasten, scurry, spring, sprint
type: 4 wire **6** French **8** omelette

whiskbroom 5 brush

whiskered 5 bushy, hairy **6** shaggy **7** bearded, bristly, hirsute **8** unshaven **11** bewhiskered, mustachioed

whiskers 3 awn **5** beard **7** stubble **8** bristles

whiskey, whisky 3 gin, rum, rye **4** corn, shot **5** booze, hooch, Irish, juice, vodka **6** liquor, red eye, rotgut, Scotch **7** alcohol, aquavit, blended, bourbon, spirits **8** eau-de-vie **9** aquavitae, firewater, moonshine, unblended **10** sneaky pete, usquebaugh **11** mountain dew **14** John Barleycorn, white lightning
type: 3 rye **6** Scotch **7** bourbon
drink: 8 hot toddy **14** Klondike Cooler
with beer: 11 Boilermaker
with Benedictine: 10 Frisco Sour
with Cointreau: 16 Canadian Cocktail
with vermouth: 9 Manhattan

whisper 3 hum **4** blab, buzz, hint, purr, sigh, tell **5** blurt, bruit, drone, rumor **6** gossip, murmur, mutter, reveal, rustle **7** breathe, confide, divulge, inkling **8** disclose, innuendo, intimate **9** undertone **10** suggestion **11** insinuation

whist
derived from: 8 triomphe
descendant: 6 bridge
number of players: 4 four
six tricks: 4 book

Whistle
author: 10 James Jones

Whistler, James Abbott McNeill
born: 8 Lowell MA
artwork: 6 Etudes **9** Harmonies, Nocturnes **10** Rosa Corder **12** Arrangements, The White Girl **13** Thomas Carlyle **15** Cicely Alexander, Wapping-on-Thames **24** Venetian Palaces Nocturnes **28** Arrangement in Grey and Black No 1 (The Artist's Mother) **29** Chelsea Nocturne in Blue and Green **31** Princess of the Land of the Porcelain **35** Falling Rocket Nocturne in Black and Gold **37** Cremorne Lights Nocturne in Blue and Silver

whistle-stop 5 stump **8** campaign **11** electioneer

whit 3 dab, dot, jot **4** chip, dash, drop, iota, mite, snip **5** crumb, grain, pinch, speck **6** morsel, tittle, trifle **7** modicum, smidgen **8** fragment, particle, splinter **9** scintilla

white 3 wan **4** ashy, fair, gray, pale, pure **5** ashen, blond, clean, filmy, hoary, ivory, milky, pasty, pearl, smoky, snowy **6** benign, chalky, chaste, cloudy, frosty, leaden, pallid, pearly, sallow, silver **7** ghostly, silvery **8** blanched, bleached, grizzled, harmless, innocent, spotless, virtuous **9** alabaster, bloodless, Caucasian, colorless, stainless, undefiled, unspotted, unstained, unsullied **10** cadaverous, immaculate **11** translucent, unblemished, unmalicious

White, E B (Elwyn Brooks)
author of: 11 One Man's Meat **12** Stuart Little **13** Charlotte's Web **14** Is Sex Necessary? (with James Thurber) **19** The Trumpet of the Swan
column: 13 Talk of the Town

White, Stanford see **17** Mead McKim and White

White, T H (Terence Hanbury)
author of: 15 The Book of Merlyn **16** The Ill-Made Knight **17** The Witch in the Wood **18** The Candle in the Wind, The Sword in the Stone **20** The Once and Future King

White Album
author: 10 Joan Didion

White Company, The
author: 19 Sir Arthur Conan Doyle

White Heat
director: 10 Raoul Walsh
cast: 11 James Cagney **12** Edmond O'Brien, Virginia Mayo **16** Margaret Wycherly

White-Jacket
author: 14 Herman Melville

whiten 4 pale **5** clean, frost **6** blanch, bleach, silver **7** lighten

whiteness 6 pallor **7** wanness **8** paleness **9** snowiness **10** sallowness **13** colorlessness

White Nights
director: 14 Taylor Hackford
cast: 12 Gregory Hines **18** Mikhail Baryshnikov
choreographer: 10 Twyla Tharp

White Rabbit
character in: 28 Alice's Adventures in Wonderland
author: 7 Carroll

whitewash 6 excuse **7** absolve, cover up, justify **8** downplay, minimize, play down **9** calcimine, exonerate, vindicate
paint made by mixing: 12 lime and water

Whitewater
author: 10 Paul Horgan

whitish 4 buff, pale **6** chalky, creamy **7** grayish

Whitman, Bert
creator/artist of: 14 The Green Hornet

Whitman, Walt
author of: 12 Song of Myself **13** Leaves of Grass **18** Oh Captain My

Captain 33 When Lilacs Last in the Dooryard Bloom'd

Whitmore, James
born: 13 White Plains NY
roles: 4 Them 5 Bully 8 Oklahoma 9 Battlecry 10 Will Rogers 11 Black Like Me 12 Battleground, Harry S Truman, Tora Tora Tora 15 Command Decision, Give 'em Hell Harry 19 The Next Voice You Hear

Whitney, Eli
nationality: 8 American
invented: 9 cotton gin
pioneered use of: 14 mass production

Whittier, John Greenleaf
author of: 9 Snow-Bound 10 Maud Muller 14 The Barefoot Boy 16 Barbara Frietchie

whittle 3 cut 4 clip, pare 5 carve, shave, slash 7 curtail, shorten 8 decrease

whiz 3 fly, hum, zip 4 bolt, buzz, dart, dash, hiss, race, rush, scud, tear, whir, zoom 5 adept, drone, scoot, shark, shoot, speed, spurt, sweep, swish, whine, whisk 6 expert, genius, hasten, master, scurry, sizzle, sprint, wizard 7 prodigy, scuttle, whistle 11 crackerjack

who goes there?
French: 7 qui vive

who knows?
Spanish: 9 quien sabe

whole 4 body, bulk, full, hale, unit, well 5 sound, total, uncut 6 entire, intact, robust, system 7 essence, healthy, perfect 8 complete, ensemble, entirety, totality, unbroken, unharmed, vigorous 9 aggregate, undivided, uninjured 10 assemblage, unabridged 12 completeness, quintessence, undiminished

wholehearted 4 true 7 earnest, serious, sincere, zealous 8 complete, emphatic 9 unfeigned 10 unreserved, unstinting 12 enthusiastic

wholesome 4 hale, nice, pure, well 5 clean, fresh, hardy, moral, sound 6 decent, honest, worthy 7 chipper, dutiful, ethical, healthy, upright 8 blooming, hygienic, innocent, sanitary, vigorous, virtuous 9 exemplary, healthful, honorable, uplifting 10 nourishing, nutritious, principled 11 meritorious, responsible 12 invigorating 13 strengthening

whole world, the
French: 11 tout le monde

wholly 5 fully, quite 7 totally, utterly 8 as a whole, entirely 9 perfectly 10 altogether, completely, thoroughly
Latin: 6 in toto

whoop 3 cry 4 hoot, howl, roar, yell 5 cheer, hollo, shout 6 bellow, cry out, holler, hurrah, outcry, scream, shriek 7 screech 9 hue and cry

whopper 3 fib, lie 6 big one 7 fiction 9 falsehood, fish story, tall story 16 cock-and-bull story

whopping 4 huge 5 giant, large 8 thumping, whacking, whapping 10 incredible 13 extraordinary

whore 3 pro 4 bawd, doxy, jade, slut, tart 5 hussy, tramp 6 chippy, harlot, hooker, prosty, wanton 7 demirep, hustler, trollop 8 call girl, mistress, strumpet 9 concubine 10 prostitute 12 streetwalker
French: 9 courtesan 12 demimondaine

whorl 4 coil, curl, roll 5 helix 6 circle, spiral 9 corkscrew 11 convolution

Who's Afraid of Virginia Woolf?
author: 11 Edward Albee
director: 11 Mike Nichols
cast: 11 George Segal, Sandy Dennis 13 Richard Burton 15 Elizabeth Taylor
Oscar for: 7 actress (Taylor) 17 supporting actress (Dennis)

Who Said That?
host: 8 John Daly 11 Robert Trout 13 Walter Kiernan
panelist: 9 Bill Henry 12 Bob Considine, H V Kaltenborn, June Lockhart 14 John Mason Brown, Morey Amsterdam 17 John Cameron Swayze

Who's on First?
comedy routine by: 6 Abbott 8 Costello
first base: 3 who
second base: 4 what
third base: 9 I don't know
shortstop: 9 I don't care
catcher: 5 today
pitcher: 8 tomorrow
left field: 3 why
center field: 7 because

Who's on First?
author: 17 William F Buckley Jr

wicked 3 bad, low 4 base, evil, foul, vile 5 acute, awful, gross, rowdy 6 cursed, fierce, impish, raging, severe, sinful 7 corrupt, extreme, fearful, galling, heinous, hellish, immoral, intense, knavish, naughty, painful, rampant, Satanic, serious, vicious 8 depraved, devilish, dreadful, fiendish, infamous, rascally, shameful 9 atrocious, malicious, monstrous, nefarious 10 abominable, bothersome, degenerate, iniquitous, malevolent, scandalous, villainous 11 disgraceful, mischievous, troublesome 12 blackhearted, dishonorable, incorrigible 13 reprehensible

wickedness 4 evil 6 infamy 8 baseness, foulness, iniquity, vileness 9 depravity, malignity 10 immorality, sinfulness 11 malevolence 13 maliciousness, nefariousness

Wicked Witch of the West

character in: 13 The Wizard of Oz
author: 4 Baum

Wickfield, Agnes
character in: 16 David Copperfield
author: 7 Dickens

Wickford Point
author: 13 John P Marquand

Wickham, Mr
character in: 17 Pride and Prejudice
author: 6 Austen

wide 4 vast 5 ample, broad, fully, great, large, roomy 7 dilated, immense 8 expanded, extended, spacious 9 boundless, capacious, distended, extensive, outspread 10 commodious, completely

wide-awake 2 up 5 alert, aware, quick 8 vigilant, watchful 9 attentive, insomniac, observant, sleepless

widely 3 far 5 broad 6 abroad 7 broadly, greatly, largely 10 by and large, far and near 11 extensively

widely known 5 famed, noted 6 common 7 popular 8 familiar 9 universal, worldwide

widen 6 expand, extend, spread 7 broaden, enlarge, stretch

widened 7 swelled, swollen 8 enlarged, expanded, extended 9 broadened, distended, stretched

wide open 4 ajar, vast 5 agape 6 gaping 7 exposed, yawning 8 extended, unfenced 9 cavernous, expansive, outspread, unbounded 12 outstretched, unobstructed

wide open spaces 7 boonies, country 9 boondocks 11 countryside, hinterlands

wide-ranging 5 broad 7 immense 8 sweeping 9 extensive, universal, unlimited 10 exhaustive 11 diversified, far-reaching 12 encyclopedic 13 comprehensive

Wide Sargasso Sea
author: 8 Jean Rhys

widespread 5 broad 9 extensive, outspread, pervasive, worldwide 10 nationwide 11 far-reaching

Widmark, Richard
born: 9 Sunrise MN
roles: 4 Coma 7 Madigan 8 The Alamo 11 Kiss of Death 12 The Long Ships 16 Halls of Montezuma, How the West Was Won 19 Judgment at Nuremberg

Widow Douglas
character in: 15 (The Adventures of) Huckleberry Finn
author: 5 Twain

wie geht's 9 how are you?

wield 3 ply, use 4 wave 5 apply, exert, swing 6 employ, handle, manage 7 display, utilize 8 brandish, exercise, flourish 10 manipulate

wife 3 rib 4 mate 5 bride, squaw, woman 6 missus, spouse 7 consort,

old lady **8** helpmate, helpmeet **9** companion
French: 5 femme
German: 4 frau
Wife of Bath
　character in: **18** The Canterbury Tales
　author: **7** Chaucer
Wifey
　author: **9** Judy Blume
wig 3 rug **4** fall **6** carpet, peruke, switch, topper, toupee, wiglet **7** periwig **9** hairpiece
Wiggin, Kate Douglas
　author of: **23** Rebecca of Sunnybrook Farm
wiggle 3 wag **4** jerk **5** shake, twist **6** quiver, squirm, twitch, writhe **7** flutter **8** writhing **9** squirming
wigwam, Wigwam 3 hut **4** tent, tipi **5** hogan, lodge, tepee **6** teepee **7** weekwam, wickiup **11** Tammany Hall
Wilcox family
　characters in: **10** Howard's End
　members: **4** Paul, Ruth **5** Henry **7** Charles
　author: **7** Forster
wild, wilds, the wild 3 mad **4** bush, rash **5** bleak, feral, giddy, madly, nutty, rabid, rough, waste **6** choppy, crazed, fierce, insane, madcap, raging, raving, rugged, savage, unruly, wooded **7** berserk, bizarre, flighty, frantic, furious, howling, lawless, natural, untamed, violent **8** barbaric, blustery, demented, desolate, fanciful, forested, frenzied, insanely, maniacal, reckless, unbroken, unhinged **9** abandoned, fanatical, fantastic, ferocious, furiously, illogical, lawlessly, naturally, overgrown, primitive, rampantly, screwball, turbulent, violently, wasteland **10** disorderly, maniacally, uninformed **11** harebrained, impractical, tempestuous, uncivilized, uninhabited **12** uncultivated, ungovernable, unrestrained **13** rattlebrained, undisciplined **14** undomesticated
wild animal 5 beast, brute
Wild Ass's Skin
　author: **14** Honore de Balzac
Wild Bunch, The
　director: **12** Sam Peckinpah
　cast: **10** Ben Johnson, Robert Ryan **11** Warren Oates **12** Edmond O'Brien **13** William Holden **14** Ernest Borgnine
wildcat 3 cat **4** lynx **6** ocelot
Wild Duck, The
　author: **11** Henrik Ibsen
　character: **5** Werle **8** Old Ekdal **9** Gina Ekdal **12** Gregers Werle, Hjalmar Ekdal **13** Hedvig Relling
Wilde, Cornel
　real name: **19** Cornelius Louis Wilde
　born: **9** New York NY
　wife: **11** Jean Wallace
　roles: **9** Maracaibo **11** Omar Khayyam

12 Forever Amber, The Naked Prey **15** A Song to Remember **21** A Thousand and One Nights **22** The Greatest Show on Earth
Wilde, Oscar
　author of: **6** Salome **17** The Critic as Artist **18** Lady Windermere's Fan **22** The Ballad of Reading Gaol, The Picture of Dorian Gray **27** The Importance of Being Earnest
Wilder, Billy
　director of: **11** One Two Three **12** The Apartment (Oscar) **13** Some Like It Hot **14** The Lost Weekend (Oscar) **15** Double Indemnity, Stalag Seventeen, Sunset Boulevard **16** The Seven Year Itch **18** Love in the Afternoon **24** Witness for the Prosecution
Wilder, Gene
　real name: **14** Jerry Silberman
　born: **11** Milwaukee WI
　roles: **12** Silver Streak, The Producers **14** Blazing Saddles, Bonnie and Clyde **17** Young Frankenstein **22** The World's Greatest Lover **27** Start the Revolution Without Me **43** The Adventures of Sherlock Holmes' Smarter Brother
Wilder, Laura Ingalls
　author of: **26** The Little House on the Prairie
Wilder, Thornton
　author of: **7** Our Town **9** The Cabala **13** The Matchmaker **14** The Ides of March **16** The Woman of Andros **17** The Skin of Our Teeth **20** Heaven's My Destination **21** The Bridge of San Luis Rey
wilderness 4 bush **5** waste **6** barren, desert, forest, plains, tundra **7** barrens **8** badlands, wasteland **9** mountains
Wildeve, Damon
　character in: **17** Return of the Native
　author: **5** Hardy
Wild Is the River
　author: **14** Louis Bromfield
Wild Kingdom
　host/narrator: **9** Jim Fowler, Stan Brock **13** Marlin Perkins
Wild One, The
　director: **12** Laslo Benedek
　cast: **9** Lee Marvin **10** Mary Murphy **12** Marlon Brando
Wild Strawberries
　director: **13** Ingmar Bergman
　cast: **12** Ingrid Thulin **13** Bibi Andersson **14** Victor Sjostrom **17** Gunnar Bjornstrand
Wild Wild West
　character: **10** James T West **13** Artemus Gordon
　cast: **10** Ross Martin **12** Robert Conrad
　traveled by: **5** train
wile, wiles 4 coax, lure, ploy, ruse, trap **5** charm, guile **6** cajole, entice, gambit, seduce **7** cunning **8** artifice,

maneuver, persuade, subtlety, trickery **9** chicanery, expedient, stratagem **10** artfulness, craftiness, subterfuge **11** contrivance, machination
Wilfer, Bella
　character in: **15** Our Mutual Friend
　author: **7** Dickens
Wilhelm, Kate
　author of: **10** City of Cain, Fault Lines **11** The Planners **14** The Infinity Box **16** The Clewiston Test **19** More Bitter than Death **26** Where Late the Sweet Birds Sang
Wilhelm Meister
　author: **6** Goethe
Wilhelm Tell
　also: **11** William Tell
　author: **17** Johann von Schiller
wiliness 5 guile **7** cunning, slyness **8** artifice, foxiness, scheming, trickery **10** artfulness, craftiness **11** machination
Wilkes family
　characters in: **15** Gone With the Wind
　members: **4** John **5** Honey, India **6** Ashley **15** Melanie Hamilton
　author: **8** Mitchell
will 4 want, wish **5** endow **6** bestow, confer, desire **7** craving, feeling, longing, resolve, wish for **8** attitude, bequeath, pleasure, yearning **9** hankering, testament **10** conviction, preference, resolution **11** disposition, inclination **12** resoluteness **13** determination
Willard, Frank
　creator/artist of: **11** Moon Mullins
Willet, John
　character in: **12** Barnaby Rudge
　author: **7** Dickens
willful 6 mulish, unruly **7** planned, studied **8** designed, intended, obdurate, perverse, stubborn **9** obstinate, pigheaded **10** bullheaded, deliberate, determined, headstrong, inflexible, persistent, purposeful, unyielding **11** intentional, intractable **12** contemplated, premeditated, ungovernable **13** undisciplined **14** uncompromising
Williams, Esther
　nickname: **13** Mermaid Tycoon **14** Queen of the Surf **17** Hollywood's Mermaid
　born: **12** Los Angeles CA
　husband: **13** Fernando Lamas
　roles: **13** Bathing Beauty **15** Jupiter's Darling, Ziegfeld Follies **16** Dangerous When Wet, Neptune's Daughter **20** Million Dollar Mermaid
Williams, Janey
　character in: **3** USA
　author: **9** Dos Passos
Williams, Robin
　born: **9** Chicago IL
　roles: **6** Popeye **12** Mork and Mindy **15** Good Will Hunting (Oscar)

18 Good Morning Vietnam **23** The World According to Garp

Williams, Ted
nickname: **6** the Kid **16** Splendid Splinter
sport: **8** baseball
position: **8** outfield
team: **12** Boston Red Sox

Williams, Tennessee
author of: **10** Camino Real **13** The Rose Tattoo **14** Summer and Smoke **16** Cat on a Hot Tin Roof, Night of the Iguana, Sweet Bird of Youth **17** Orpheus Descending, The Glass Menagerie **18** Small Craft Warnings, Suddenly Last Summer **21** A Streetcar Named Desire **24** The Roman Spring of Mrs Stone

Williams, William Carlos
author of: **7** Tempers **8** Paterson **9** White Mule **11** Al Que Quiere **20** Pictures from Brueghel

William Tell
also: **13** Guillaume Tell
opera by: **7** Rossini
character: **6** Arnold **7** Gessler

William the Conqueror
also: **17** William of Normandy **21** William I King of England
fought against: **8** Harold II
battle: **8** Hastings
succeeded by: **6** Henry I **9** William II

Willie and Joe
creator: **11** Bill Mauldin

willing 4 game **5** ready **7** content **8** amenable **9** agreeable, compliant, not averse **10** responsive

willingly 4 gain, lief, soon **6** freely, gladly, liefly **7** eagerly, happily, readily **8** by choice **10** cheerfully, graciously **11** voluntarily **12** with pleasure

willingness 4 zeal **8** alacrity **9** eagerness, readiness **10** enthusiasm **11** inclination

Willoughby, John
character in: **19** Sense and Sensibility
author: **6** Austen

willow 5 Salix
varieties: **3** bay, red **4** bush, goat, gray, seep **5** black, crack, false, Niobe, Pekin, pussy, silky, water, white **6** Arctic, arroyo, basket, desert, golden, laurel, puzzle, woolly, yellow **7** brittle, prairie, sandbar, scouler, shining, weeping **8** creeping, florist's, polished, Virginia **9** bayleaved, bearberry, flowering, sprouting **10** cricket- bat, dragon-claw, large pussy, small pussy **11** greenscaled, heart-leaved, peach-leaved, Port Jackson **13** halberd-leaved **16** Wisconsin weeping

willowy 5 lithe **6** limber, pliant, supple, svelte **7** lissome **8** flexible **9** sylphlike

Wills, Chill

born: **12** Seagoville TX
group: **26** Chill Wills and the Avalon Boys
voice of: **21** Francis the Talking Mule
roles: **5** Giant **8** The Alamo **10** Way Out West **11** The Yearling **15** Meet Me in St Louis

Wills, Garry
author of: **14** Nixon Agonistes, Reagan's America **16** Inventing America

Will Scarlet
character in: **9** Robin Hood

willy-nilly 8 perforce **10** helplessly, inevitably **11** inescapably, unavoidably **12** compulsively, irresistibly **14** uncontrollably
Latin: **12** nolens volens

Wilmer
character in: **16** The Maltese Falcon
author: **7** Hammett

Wilson, Edmund
author of: **11** Axel's Castle **19** To the Finland Station

Wilson, Myrtle
character in: **14** The Great Gatsby
author: **10** Fitzgerald

Wilson, Sloan
author of: **26** The Man in the Gray Flannel Suit

Wilson, Woodrow
name at birth: **19** Thomas Woodrow Wilson
nickname: **5** Tommy
presidential rank: **12** twenty-eighth
party: **10** Democratic
state represented: **2** NJ
defeated: **4** (Eugene Victor) Debs, (William Howard) Taft **5** (James Franklin) Hanly **6** (Allen Louis) Benson, (Arthur Edward) Reimer, (Charles Evans) Hughes, (Eugene Wilder) Chafin **9** (Theodore) Roosevelt
vice president: **8** (Thomas Riley) Marshall
cabinet:
    state: **5** (Bainbridge) Colby, (William Jennings) Bryan **7** (Robert) Lansing
    treasury: **5** (Carter) Glass **6** (William Gibbs) McAdoo **7** (David Franklin) Houston
    war: **5** (Newton Diehl) Baker **8** (Lindley Miller) Garrison
    attorney general: **6** (Alexander Mitchell) Palmer **7** (Thomas Watt) Gregory **10** (James Clark) McReynolds
    navy: **7** (Josephus) Daniels
    postmaster general: **8** (Albert Sidney) Burleson
    interior: **4** (Franklin Knight) Lane **5** (John Barton) Payne
    agriculture: **7** (David Franklin) Houston **8** (Edwin Thomas) Meredith
    commerce: **8** (William Cox) Red-

field **9** (Joshua Willis) Alexander
    labor: **6** (William Bauchop) Wilson
born: **2** VA **8** Staunton
died/buried: **2** DC **10** Washington
education:
    college: **8** Davidson **18** College of New Jersey (later known as Princeton U)
    law school: **20** University of Virginia
    university: **12** Johns Hopkins
religion: **12** Presbyterian
author: **8** The State **16** George Washington **18** Division and Reunion **27** A History of the American People **28** More Literature and Other Essays **34** An Old Master and Other Political Essays **41** President Wilson's Case for the League of Nations **47** Congressional Government: A Study in American Politics
political career:
    governor ot: **9** New Jersey
civilian career: **6** lawyer
    professor of history: **15** Bryn Mawr College **18** Wesleyan University
    professor of jurisprudence: **9** Princeton
    president of: **9** Princeton
notable events of lifetime/term: **14** Fourteen Points **15** League of Nations
    Act: **7** Adamson **8** Sedition **9** Espionage **10** Child Labor **11** Liberty Loan, Panama Canal **14** Federal Reserve **15** Federal Farm Loan **16** Clayton Antitrust, Selective Service **22** Federal Trade Commission
    conference: **3** ABC **10** Paris Peace
    18th Amendment: **11** Prohibition
    program: **10** New Freedom
    sinking of: **9** Lusitania
    Treaty: **10** Versailles
    won: **15** Nobel Peace Prize
quote: **34** The world must be made safe for democracy
father: **13** Joseph Ruggles
mother: **5** Janet (Woodrow)
siblings: **13** Joseph Ruggles **14** Annie Josephson **16** Marion Williamson
wife: **5** Edith (Bolling Galt), Ellen (Louise Axson)
children: **13** Jessie Woodrow **15** Eleanor Randolph, Margaret Woodrow

wilt 3 die, ebb, sag **4** fade, flag, sink, wane **5** droop **6** recede, weaken, wither **7** decline, dwindle, shrivel, subside **8** decrease, diminish, languish **10** degenerate **11** deteriorate

Wilt the Stilt
nickname of: **15** Wilt Chamberlain

wily 3 sly **4** foxy **5** alert, sharp **6** artful, crafty, shifty, shrewd, tricky **7** crooked, cunning, devious **8** guileful, scheming **9** deceitful, deceptive, designing, underhand **10** intriguing **11** calculating, treacherous

Wimbledon
  suburb of: 6 London
  site of: 16 tennis tournament
  court surface: 5 grass

win 3 bag, get, net **4** earn, gain, sway **6** attain, induce, master, obtain, pick up, secure **7** achieve, acquire, collect, conquer, convert, prevail, procure, realize, receive, success, triumph, victory **8** conquest, convince, overcome, persuade, vanquish **9** influence **10** accomplish

win acceptance 9 establish **10** ingratiate

wince 5 cower, quail **6** cringe, flinch, recoil, shrink **7** grimace, shudder **8** cowering, cringing, draw back, quailing **9** shrinking

wind 3 air, lap **4** bend, blow, clue, coil, curl, fold, gale, gust, hint, loop, news, puff, roll **5** blast, bluff, curve, draft, scent, smell, snake, twine, twirl, twist, whiff **6** breath, breeze, hot air, ramble, report, wander, zephyr, zigzag **7** bluster, bombast, cyclone, entwine, inkling, meander, sinuate, tempest, tidings, tornado, twaddle, twister, typhoon, whisper **8** boasting, idle talk **9** aerophone, hurricane, knowledge, whirlwind **10** intimation, suggestion **11** braggadocio, fanfaronade, information **12** intelligence
  god of: 5 Eurus, Niord, Njord, Notus **6** Aquilo, Auster, Boreas **8** Favonius, Zephyrus
  father: 8 Astraeus
  mother: 3 Eos

windfall 7 bonanza

Windhoek
  capital of: 7 Namibia

Wind in the Willows, The
  author: 14 Kenneth Grahame
  character: 4 Mole, Toad **6** Badger **8** Water Rat

windless 4 calm **5** still **8** stifling

window 3 bay **5** oriel **6** dormer **7** opening, orifice, transom **8** aperture, casement, porthole, skylight

Winds of War, The
  author: 10 Herman Wouk

windstorm 4 gale **6** squall **7** cyclone, tempest, tornado, twister, typhoon **9** hurricane, whirlwind

windswept 4 bare **5** bleak **6** barren **8** desolate **13** weatherbeaten

windup 3 end **5** close **6** ending, finish **10** completion, conclusion, expiration **11** termination

wind up 3 end **4** halt, stop **5** cease, close **6** finish, settle **8** complete, conclude **9** terminate

windy 5 blowy, empty, gabby, gusty, wordy **6** breezy **7** verbose **8** blustery, rambling **9** bombastic, garrulous, talkative **10** loquacious, meandering, rhetorical **13** grandiloquent

wine
  French: 3 vin
  Italian: 4 vino
  god of: 7 Bacchus
  goddess of: 6 Libera

wine-colored 6 claret **8** burgundy, cardinal

winemaking
  god of: 9 Aristaeus

Winesburg, Ohio
  author: 16 Sherwood Anderson

Winfrey, Oprah
  born: 12 Kosciusko MS
  host of: 19 The Oprah Winfrey Show
  author of: 17 Make the Connection **20** Oprah An Autobiography **21** In the Kitchen with Rosie
  Roles: 7 Beloved **14** The Color Purple **23** The Women of Brewster Place

wing 3 ala, fly, set **4** band, clip, flap, knot, nick, soar, zoom **5** annex, graze, group **6** circle, clique, pennon, pinion **7** adjunct, aileron, coterie, faction, section, segment **8** addition, coulisse **9** appendage, extension **10** fraternity

Winged Horse
  constellation of: 7 Pegasus

Winger, Debra
  husband: 13 Timothy Hutton
  roles: 10 Black Widow, Cannery Row **11** Urban Cowboy **17** Terms of Endearment **22** An Officer and a Gentleman

Wingert, Dick
  creator/artist of: 6 Hubert

Wingfield family
  characters in: 17 The Glass Menagerie
  member: 3 Tom **5** Laura **6** Amanda
  author: 8 Williams

Wings
  director: 15 William A Wellman
  cast: 8 Clara Bow **10** Gary Cooper **12** Richard Arlen **18** Charles Buddy Rogers
  Oscar for: 7 picture

Wings of the Dove, The
  author: 10 Henry James
  character: 8 Kate Croy, Lord Mark **9** Mrs Lowder **11** Milly Theale **12** Mrs Stringham **13** Merton Densher, Sir Luke Strett

wink at 6 ignore **7** condone, let pass **8** overlook **9** disregard

Winkle
  character in: 14 Pickwick Papers
  author: 7 Dickens

winner 5 champ **6** master, victor **8** champion **9** conqueror **10** vanquisher

Winnie-the-Pooh
  author: 7 A A Milne
  character: 3 Owl **5** Kanga **6** Eeyore, Piglet, Rabbit, Tigger **7** Baby Roo **16** Christopher Robin

winning 7 amiable **8** charming, engag-

ing, pleasing **9** appealing, beguiling, disarming **10** attractive, bewitching, entrancing **11** captivating **12** ingratiating, irresistible

Winnipeg
  hockey team: 3 Jets

win over 4 beat, best **5** charm **6** defeat, seduce **7** convert **8** overcome, vanquish **9** captivate, overpower

winsome 5 sweet **6** comely **7** amiable, likable, lovable **8** charming, cheerful, engaging, pleasing **9** agreeable, appealing, endearing **10** attractive, bewitching, delightful

Winter, Lady de
  character in: 18 The Three Musketeers
  author: 5 Dumas (pere)

Winter, Maxim de
  character in: 7 Rebecca
  author: 9 Du Maurier

Winterbourne
  character in: 11 Daisy Miller
  author: 5 James

Winter of Our Discontent, The
  author: 13 John Steinbeck

Winters, Shelley
  real name: 14 Shirley Schrift
  born: 9 St Louis IL
  husband: 13 Tony Franciosa **15** Vittorio Gassman
  roles: 11 A Double Life **12** A Patch of Blue **14** A Place in the Sun **16** A House Is Not a Home **19** The Diary of Anne Frank **20** The Poseidon Adventure

Winterset
  author: 15 Maxwell Anderson

winter sports
  god of: 4 Ullr **5** Uller

Winter's Tale, The
  author: 18 William Shakespeare
  character: 7 Camillo, Leontes, Paulina, Perdita **8** Florizel, Hermione **9** Autolycus, Polixenes

Winter Wonderland
  nickname of: 8 Michigan

wintry 3 icy, raw **4** cold **5** bleak, chilly, harsh, polar, snowy, stark **6** arctic, chilly, dreary, frigid, frosty, frozen, gloomy, stormy **7** glacial **8** Siberian **9** cheerless

wipe 3 dry, mop, rub **4** swab **5** apply, brush, clean, erase, rub on, scour, scrub, swipe, towel **6** banish, remove, rub off, sponge, stroke

wiped out 5 broke **6** failed, ruined **8** bankrupt, indigent, strapped **9** destitute, insolvent, penniless **12** impoverished

wipe out 4 ruin **5** erase **7** abolish, destroy, eclipse **8** bankrupt **9** devastate, eliminate, eradicate, extirpate, liquidate **10** annihilate, obliterate **11** exterminate

wiping out 7 erasing **9** eclipsing, expunging **10** abolishing, destroying **11** eliminating, eradicating **12** annihilating, obliterating

wire 5 cable **8** filament, telegram **9** cablegram, telegraph

wiry 4 lean **5** agile, kinky, lanky, spare, stiff **6** limber, pliant, sinewy **7** brittle

Wisconsin
> **abbreviation: 2** WI **3** Wis
> **nickname: 6** Badger
> **capital: 7** Madison
> **largest city: 9** Milwaukee
> **others: 5** Ripon **6** Antigo, Beloit, Cudahy, Neenag, Racine, Wausau **7** Ashland, Baraboo, Bloomer, Kenosha, Menasha, Oshkosh, Portage, Shawano **8** Appleton, Boscobel, Green Bay, Lacrosse, Superior, Waukesha **9** Eau Claire, Fond du Lac, Sheboygan, Shorewood, Wauwatosa, West Allis **10** Brookfield, Janesville **12** Steven's Point
> **college: 5** Ripon **6** Beloit **7** Alverno, Carroll, Viterbo **8** Carthage, Lawrence **9** Marquette, Northland
> **feature:**
>> **fort: 6** Howard **8** Crawford **9** Winnebago
>> **national lakeshore: 14** Apostle Islands
> **tribe: 3** Fox, Sac **4** Sauk **5** Huron **6** Oneida, Ottawa **8** Chippewa, Kickapoo **9** Winnebago **10** Potawatomi
> **people: 11** Orson Welles **12** Fredric March, Harry Houdini, Spencer Tracy **13** Hamlin Garland **14** Joseph McCarthy, Georgia O'Keeffe, Thornton Wilder **16** Frank Lloyd Wright **17** Robert M LaFollette
>> **explorer: 6** Joliet **7** Allouez, Nicolet **8** Radisson **9** Marquette **12** Groseilliers
> **island: 8** Madeline
> **lake: 6** Geneva, Poygan **7** Kenosha, Mendota, Wissota **8** Michigan, Superior **9** Winnebago
> **land rank: 11** twenty-sixth
> **mountain: 7** Baraboo **9** Sugarbush **10** Blue Mounds
>> **highest point: 9** Timm's Hill
> **physical feature:**
>> **glacial hills: 13** Kettle Moraine
>> **rock formations: 8** The Dells
> **river: 3** Fox **4** Wolf **7** St Croix **8** Chippewa **9** Black Rock, Wisconsin **11** Mississippi
> **state admission: 9** thirtieth
> **state bird: 5** robin
> **state fish: 11** muskellunge
> **state flower: 5** pansy **6** violet **10** wood violet
> **state motto: 7** Forward
> **state song: 11** On Wisconsin
> **state tree: 10** sugar maple

wisdom 6 brains **8** sagacity **9** teachings **10** philosophy, principles, profundity **11** discernment, penetra-

tion **12** apperception, intelligence **13** comprehension, judiciousness, understanding

> **god of: 2** Ea **4** Enki, Odin **5** Othin, Thoth
> **goddess of: 6** Athena, Athene, Brigit, Pallas, Saitis **7** Minerva **11** Tritogeneia **12** Pallas Athena **18** Alalcomenean Athena

wise 3 way **4** sage **6** manner **7** knowing, respect, sapient **8** profound **9** judicious, sagacious **10** discerning, perceptive **11** intelligent **13** knowledgeable, perspicacious, understanding

Wise, Robert
> **director of: 11** I Want to Live **13** West Side Story (with Jerome Robbins, Oscar) **15** The Sound of Music (Oscar)

wiseacre 4 fool, sage **5** idiot **7** tomfool **9** know-it-all, simpleton **10** smart aleck

Wise Blood
> **author: 15** Flannery O'Connor

wisecrack 4 jest, joke, quip **5** flash, sally **8** cut jokes **9** witticism **11** smart saying

Wise men see **4** Magi

wise up 5 edify **6** advise, in form **7** apprise **9** enlighten, make aware

wish 3 yen **4** hope, long, love, pine, want, whim, will **5** crave, yearn **6** aspire, desire, hunger, thirst **7** command, craving, leaning, longing, request **8** ambition, appetite, fondness, penchant, yearning **10** aspiration, partiality **11** inclination **12** predilection

wishes 11 compliments **13** felicitations **15** congratulations

wish for 4 want **5** covet, crave **6** desire

Wishfort, Lady
> **character in: 16** The Way of the World
> **author: 8** Congreve

wishful 4 avid **5** eager **6** keen on, pining **7** anxious, craving, hopeful, longing, wanting, wistful **8** aspiring, bent upon, desirous, fanciful, yearning **9** ambitious, expectant

wish well 10 felicitate **12** congratulate

wishy-washy 4 blah, dull, weak **5** inane, vapid, wimpy **6** jejune **7** insipid **8** wavering **10** indecisive, irresolute **11** ineffective, ineffectual, vacillating **12** equivocating, noncommittal **14** tergiversating **15** shilly-shallying

wisp 4 lock, tuft **5** bunch, shred, torch, twist **6** bundle, rumple **8** fragment **10** whisk broom **11** ignis fatuus **13** friar's lantern

wispy 4 thin **5** frail **6** slight **8** fleeting, nebulous

wistaria, wisteria

varieties: 4 pink, wild **5** silky, water **7** Chinese **8** Japanese **9** Rhodesian

Wister, Owen
> **author of: 12** The Virginian

wistful 3 sad **6** musing, pining **7** craving, doleful, forlorn, longing, pensive **8** desirous, mournful, yearning **9** hankering, sorrowful, woebegone **10** meditative, melancholy, reflective **12** disconsolate **13** contemplative, introspective

wit 3 wag **4** gags **5** comic, humor, joker, jokes, quips, sense **6** acumen, banter, brains, jester, joking, levity, wisdom **7** cunning, funster, gagster, insight, punster, sparkle, waggery **8** comedian, drollery, humorist, jokester, judgment, raillery, sagacity, satirist, vivacity **9** funniness, intellect **10** astuteness, brightness, cleverness, jocularity, perception, shrewdness, witticisms **11** discernment, penetration, wisecracker **12** intelligence, perspicacity **13** comprehension, epigrammatist, sagaciousness, understanding
> **French: 8** badinage **9** bel-esprit **10** persiflage

witch 3 hag **4** fury **5** crone, scold, shrew, vixen **6** beldam, ogress, virago **7** seeress **8** battle-ax, harridan **9** sorceress, temptress, termagant **10** prophetess **11** enchantress

witchcraft 5 obeah **6** hoodoo, voodoo **7** sorcery **8** black art, witchery, wizardry **9** diabolism, fetishism, voodooism **10** black magic, divination, necromancy **11** conjuration, enchantment

with
> **French: 4** avec, chez

with a grain of salt
> **Latin: 13** cum grano salis

with a lawsuit pending
> **Latin: 12** pendente lite

with authority
> **Latin: 10** ex cathedra

withdraw 2 go **5** leave, split **6** depart, go away, recall, recant, remove, retire **7** extract, rescind, retract, retreat, take off, vamoose **9** disappear, unsheathe

withdrawal 4 exit **6** egress **7** leaving, retreat **9** departure **10** retirement, retraction **14** discontinuance

withdrawn 3 shy **5** quiet **8** reserved, retiring, unsocial **9** reclusive **10** unfriendly **11** introverted **15** uncommunicative

wither 4 fade, wilt **5** abash, blast, droop, dry up, shame **7** cut down, mortify, shrivel **9** dehydrate, desiccate, humiliate

withered 3 dry **4** arid, sere **5** dried, faded **6** shrunk, wilted **7** decayed, dried up, drooped, stunned, wizened **9** petrified, shriveled **10** languished

withering 6 biting **7** caustic **8** scathing **9** shrinkage, shrinking, wrinkling

10 shriveling **11** contracting, contraction, devastating

with few words
Latin: **12** paucis verbis

with force and with arms
Latin: **9** vi et armis

with great praise
Latin: **13** magna cum laude

withheld 4 kept **7** checked, forbore, refused, starved **8** kept back **9** boycotted, refrained

with highest praise
Latin: **13** summa cum laude

withhold 4 hide, keep **6** hush up, retain **7** conceal, cover up **8** suppress

withhold from 4 deny **6** refuse

within 2 on **4** into **5** inner **6** during, inside **7** indoors **8** inwardly
combining form: **3** eso **4** endo
prefix: **5** intra

within an inch of 4 near **6** all but, almost, nearly

with-it 7 current **8** up-to-date
French: **9** au courant

with one's own two hands 7 oneself, unaided **10** unassisted

without 4 save **5** minus **6** beyond, except, unless **7** lacking, nowhere, outside, wanting **8** exterior, external, free from, outdoors **9** excepting **10** externally
appointment: **7** sine die
care: **8** sine cure
charge: **4** free **6** gratis **8** sine cure
combining form: **4** ecto
doubt: **9** sine dubio
feet: **4** apod **6** apodal
French: **4** sans
horns: **7** acerous
Latin: **4** sine
law: **8** anarchic
light: **7** aphotic
life: **5** amort **9** inanimate
luster: **3** mat **5** matte
offspring: **9** sine prole
prefix: **2** in
roads: **7** invious
saddles: **8** asellate, bareback
subcalyx leaves: **9** bractless
teeth: **5** morne **8** edentate
this: **7** sine hoc
tongue, teeth, or claws: **5** morne
which not: **10** sine qua non
wings: **7** apteral **8** apterous

without a doubt 6 surely **8** of course **9** certainly **10** absolutely, positively **11** indubitably **12** indisputably **14** unquestionably

without basis 7 unsound **9** unfounded **10** groundless, ungrounded **11** unjustified, unsupported **15** unsubstantiated

without care
French: **9** sans souci

without charge 4 free **10** gratuitous,

on the house **13** complimentary
Latin: **6** gratis

without doubt
French: **9** sans doute

without end 7 endless, eternal, forever **8** immortal, infinite, timeless, unending **9** ceaseless, continual, endlessly, eternally, perpetual **10** immortally, infinitely, timelessly, unendingly **11** ceaselessly, continually, everlasting, never-ending **13** everlastingly **14** lasting forever

without equal
French: **10** sans pareil

without error 4 true **5** exact, right **7** correct, perfect, precise, sinless **8** accurate, truthful, unerring **9** faultless **10** infallible

without exception 5 never **6** always, wholly **8** entirely **10** absolutely, completely, invariably, positively

without fear and without reproach
French: **22** sans peur et sans reproche

Without Feathers
author: **10** Woody Allen

without funds 5 broke **6** ruined **8** bankrupt, indigent, strapped, wiped out **9** destitute, flat broke, insolvent, penniless **10** stone broke **12** impoverished

without light 3 dim **4** dark **5** black, dusky, murky, shady **6** opaque **7** obscure, shadowy, stygian, sunless

without limit
Latin: **11** ad infinitum

without limitation 6 wholly **7** totally, utterly **8** entirely **9** endlessly **10** absolutely, completely, definitely, positively, thoroughly **11** boundlessly **13** unequivocally **15** unconditionally
French: **12** carte blanche

without notice 5 ad-lib **9** impromptu **10** improvised **11** extemporary **14** extemporaneous
Latin: **9** extempore

without offspring, without progeny
Latin: **9** sine prole

without the day
Latin: **7** sine die

without which not
Latin: **10** sine qua non

with praise
Latin: **8** cum laude

withstand 4 bear, defy **5** brave **6** endure, resist, suffer **7** weather **8** confront, cope with, tolerate

witless 3 mad **5** crazy **6** insane, stupid **7** fatuous, foolish, unaware **9** slaphappy

witness 3 see **4** mark, note, sign, view **5** proof **6** attend, behold, look on, notice, verify **7** bear out, certify, confirm, endorse, initial, observe **8** attester, attest to, beholder, deponent,

document, evidence, looker-on, observer, onlooker, perceive, validate, vouch for **9** establish, spectator, testifier, testimony **10** validation **11** corroborate, countersign **12** authenticate, confirmation, substantiate, verification **13** corroboration, documentation **14** authentication, substantiation

Witness for the Prosecution
director: **11** Billy Wilder
based on play by: **14** Agatha Christie
cast: **11** Tyrone Power **14** Elsa Lanchester **15** Charles Laughton, Marlene Dietrich

wits 4 mind **6** sanity **9** composure **14** coolheadedness

witticism 4 jest, joke, quip **5** sally **7** epigram
French: **6** bon mot **10** jeu d'esprit

witty 5 comic, droll, funny **6** bright, clever, jocose **7** amusing, jocular, waggish **8** humorous, mirthful **9** brilliant, sparkling, whimsical **11** quickwitted **13** scintillating

witty saying 4 jest, quip **6** bon mot **7** epigram **9** witticism **13** clever comment

Witwoud, Sir Wilfull
character in: **16** The Way of the World
author: **8** Congreve

wizard 4 sage, seer, whiz **5** adept, shark **6** expert, genius, oracle **7** diviner, prodigy, wise man **8** conjurer, magician, sorcerer, virtuoso **9** enchanter **10** soothsayer **11** clairvoyant, necromancer

Wizard of Id, The
creator: **10** Johnny Hart **11** Brant Parker
character: **4** King **5** Spook **6** jester, Rodney, Tyrant

Wizard of Oz, The
director: **13** Victor Fleming
author: **10** L Frank Baum
cast: **4** Toto **8** Bert Lahr (Zeke, Cowardly Lion) **9** Jack Haley (Hickory, Tin Woodsman), Ray Bolger (Hunk, Scarecrow) **11** Billie Burke (Good Witch of the North), Frank Morgan (wizard), Judy Garland (Dorothy Gale) **13** Clara Blandick **15** Charley Grapewin **16** Margaret Hamilton (Almira Gulch, Wicked Witch of the West), The Singer Midgets (Munchkins)
other roles: **6** Aunt Em **10** Uncle Henry
score: **9** E Y Harburg **11** Harold Arlen
remade as: **6** The Wiz
place: **6** Kansas **8** Land of Oz **11** Emerald City
Dorothy wore: **8** red shoes

wizened 3 dry **5** dried **7** dried up **8** shrunken, withered, wrinkled **9** shriveled

WKRP in Cincinnati

character: 10 Andy Travis, Herb Tarlek, Les Nessman **12** Venus Flytrap **13** Arthur Carlson, Dr Johnny Fever **14** Bailey Quarters **15** Jennifer Marlowe

cast: 7 Tim Reid **9** Gary Sandy **10** Gordon Jump **11** Frank Bonner, Jan Smithers **12** Loni Anderson **14** Howard Hesseman, Richard Sanders

wobble 4 reel, sway **5** quake, shake, waver **6** shimmy, teeter, totter **7** quaking, shaking, stagger, swaying **8** wavering **9** shimmying, teetering, tottering **12** unsteadiness

wobbly, Wobbly 5 loose, shaky **7** doubtful **8** hesitant, insecure, unstable, unsteady, wavering **9** quavering, trembling **11** vacillating
union: 17 Industrial Workers

Wodehouse, P G (Pelham Grenville)
author of: 8 Full Moon **14** Thank You Jeeves **15** The Mating Season
character: 6 Jeeves, Psmith **13** Bertie Wooster

Woden
origin: 10 Anglo-Saxon
chief of: 4 gods

woe 5 agony, gloom, grief, trial, worry **6** misery, sorrow **7** anguish, anxiety, despair, torment, torture, trouble **8** calamity, distress **9** adversity, dejection, heartache, suffering **10** affliction, depression, melancholy, misfortune **11** tribulation **12** wretchedness

woebegone 3 sad **4** glum **6** gloomy **7** doleful, forlorn **8** dejected, funereal, mournful, tortured, troubled, wretched **9** agonizing, anguished, miserable, sorrowful, suffering **10** distressed

woeful 3 bad, sad **5** awful, cruel **6** tragic **7** doleful, painful, unhappy **8** crushing, dreadful, grievous, hopeless, horrible, terrible, unlikely, wretched **9** agonizing, appalling, miserable, sorrowful **10** calamitous, deplorable, depressing, disastrous, lamentable **11** distressing, unpromising **12** catastrophic, heartrending **13** disheartening, heartbreaking

woe to the vanquished
Latin: 9 vae victis

Wofford, Chloe Anthony
real name of: 12 Toni Morrison

Wojtyla, Karol
real name of: 14 Pope John Paul II **18** Archbishop of Krakow

wolf 4 bolt, gulp **5** scarf **6** devour, gobble **7** consume
constellation of: 5 Lupus
group of: 4 pack

Wolf, The
author: 11 Frank Norris

Wolfe, Nero see Stout, Rex

Wolfe, Thomas
author of: 14 The Hills Beyond **16** The Web and the Rock **17** Look Homeward Angel, Of Time and the River **18** You Can't Go Home Again
character: 10 Eugene Gant **12** George Webber

Wolfe, Tom
author of: 11 Radical Chic **13** The Right Stuff **14** The Painted Word **16** The Pump House Gang **21** From Bauhaus to Our House **23** The Bonfire of the Vanities **24** Mau-mauing the Flak Catchers **26** The Electric Kool-Aid Acid Test **43** The Kandy Kolored Tangerine Flake Streamline Baby

Wollstonecraft, Mary
husband: 13 William Godwin
daughter: 25 Mary Wollstonecraft Shelley
author of: 30 A Vindication of the Rights of Women

Wolverine State
nickname of: 8 Michigan

woman 4 girl, lady, maid, wife **5** flame, lover **6** damsel, maiden, matron **7** beloved, darling, dowager, females, fiancee, sweetie **8** ladylove, mistress **9** charwoman, concubine **10** girlfriend, hand maiden, sweetheart, sweetie pie **11** chambermaid, housekeeper, maidservant
French: 5 femme **8** paramour
Latin: 9 inamorata

Woman, first 3 Eve **5** Embla **7** Pandora

Woman in White, A
author: 13 Wilkie Collins

womanish 7 unmanly **8** feminine, ladylike **9** sissified **10** effeminate

womanlike 8 feminine **10** effeminate

womanly 8 feminine, matronly

Woman of Substance, A
author: 21 Barbara Taylor Bradford

Woman of the Year
director: 13 George Stevens
cast: 10 Fay Bainter **12** Reginald Owen, Spencer Tracy **16** Katharine Hepburn

Woman's Life, A
author: 15 Guy de Maupassant

Women, The
director: 11 George Cukor
based on play by: 15 Clare Boothe Luce
cast: 11 Hedda Hopper **12** Joan Crawford, Joan Fontaine, Marjorie Main, Norma Shearer **15** Paulette Goddard, Rosalind Russell
remade as: 14 The Opposite Sex

Women in Love
director: 10 Ken Russell
based on novel by: 10 DH Lawrence
character: 11 Gerald Crich **12** Rupert Birkin **14** Gudrun Brangwen, Ursula Brangwen
cast: 9 Alan Bates **10** Oliver Reed **11** Eleanor Bron **12** Jennie Linden **13** Glenda Jackson
Oscar for: 7 actress (Jackson)

wonder 3 awe **4** gape **5** sight, stare **6** marvel, ponder, rarity **7** miracle **8** cogitate, meditate, question **9** amazement, spectacle, speculate **10** conjecture, phenomenon **11** fascination **12** astonishment, stupefaction

wonder child
German: 10 wunderkind

wonderful 4 fine, good **5** great, super **6** divine, superb, tiptop, unique **7** amazing, capital **8** fabulous, singular, smashing, striking, terrific **9** admirable, excellent, fantastic, marvelous **10** astounding, incredible, miraculous, phenomenal, staggering, surprising **11** astonishing, crackerjack, fascinating, magnificent, sensational, spectacular **13** extraordinary

Wonderland State
nickname of: 5 Maine

wonderstruck 4 agog **6** amazed **8** thrilled **9** astounded, stupefied **10** astonished, enthralled, spellbound **11** dumbfounded **13** flabbergasted

Wonder Woman
character: 9 (Corp) Etta Candy **11** Diana Prince, Joe Atkinson, (Maj) Steve Trevor **13** Gen Blankenship
cast: 11 Lynda Carter **12** Lyle Waggoner **13** Beatrice Colen, Normann Burton **14** Richard Eastham

wont 3 apt, use **4** used, vain **5** habit, haunt, usage **6** custom, desire **8** accustom, inclined, practice **10** accustomed

wonted 3 apt **5** prone **6** likely **7** given to **10** accustomed, habituated

woo 3 sue **5** chase, court **6** cajole, pursue **7** address, entreat, solicit **8** petition **9** importune

wood 3 log **4** bush **5** brake, brush, copse, grove **6** boards, forest, lumber, planks, siding, timber **7** thicket **8** firewood, kindling **9** clapboard, wallboard **10** timberland

Wood, Grant
born: 9 Anamosa IA
artwork: 12 Spring in Town **13** Stone City Iowa **14** American Gothic **15** Woman with Plants **16** Parson Weems' Fable **18** Dinner for Threshers, John B Turner Pioneer **21** Daughters of Revolution

Wood, John, Sr
architect of: 6 Circus (Bath)

Wood, Natalie
real name: 13 Natasha Gurdin
born: 14 San Francisco CA
husband: 12 Robert Wagner
roles: 5 Gypsy **10** Brainstorm **12** The Great Race, The Searchers **13** West Side Story **17** Inside Daisy Clover **18** Rebel Without a Cause, Splendor in the Grass **19** Sex and the Single Girl **23** This Property Is Condemned **25**

Love with the Proper Stranger **27** Miracle on Thirty- fourth Street

wooded 5 treed **8** forested

wooden 4 dull **5** frame, rigid, stiff **6** clumsy, vacant **7** awkward, deadpan **8** lifeless, ungainly **9** impassive, unbending **10** inflexible, ungraceful **11** unemotional **14** expressionless

Woodhouse, Emma
character in: **4** Emma
author: **6** Austen

woodland 5 copse, grove, treed **6** forest **7** coppice, thicket **8** forested

wood of life
Latin: **11** lignum vitae

woods
god of: **8** Silvanus, Sylvanus

Woods, Sara
real name: **13** Sara Bowen-Judd
author of: **11** Done to Death **12** My Life Is Done **13** Yet She Must Die **15** A Show of Violence, Knives Have Edges **16** And Shame the Devil **17** The Third Encounter, Trusted Like the Fox **18** Bloody Instructions
character: **15** Anthony Maitland

Woodstock
also called: **11** The Cavalier
author: **14** Sir Walter Scott

Woodstock
director: **15** Michael Wadleigh
cast: **6** The Who **7** Santana **8** Joan Baez **9** Joe Cocker **12** Richie Havens **13** John Sebastian, Ten Years After **17** Jefferson Airplane **19** Crosby Stills and Nash **20** Country Joe and the Fish, Sly and the Family Stone
Oscar for: **11** documentary

Woodward, Bob
author of: **4** Veil **19** All the President's Men (with Carl Bernstein)

Woodward, Joanne
born: **13** Thomasville GA
husband: **10** Paul Newman
roles: **12** A Fine Madness, Rachel Rachel **15** Three Faces of Eve (Oscar) **16** The Long Hot Summer **43** The Effect of Gamma Rays on Man-in-the-Moon Marigolds

woodwind instrument 4 oboe **5** flute **7** bassoon, piccolo **8** clarinet **9** bass flute **10** cor anglais **12** bass clarinet **13** double bassoon

wooer 4 beau, love **5** flame, lover, swain **6** adorer, suitor **7** admirer, courter **8** para mour **10** sweetheart

wool
fabric: **4** felt **5** crepe, llama, serge, tweed, twill **6** alpaca, angora, boucle, covert, faille, melton, vicuna, woolen **7** challis, doeskin, Donegal, worsted **8** cashmere, homespun, shetland **9** Astrakhan, camelhair, gabardine, sharkskin **10** hopsacking **11** Harris tweed, herringbone

Woolf, Virginia
author of: **7** Orlando **8** The Waves, The Years **10** Jacob's Room **11** Mrs Dalloway **14** A Room of One's Own **15** To the Lighthouse
member of: **15** Bloomsbury Group

wool-gather 8 daydream, muse idly

woolly, wooly 5 downy, furry, fuzzy, hairy, sheep, vague **6** fleecy, lanate, lanose **7** blurred, muddled, unclear **8** confused, floccose, peronate **10** flocculent, indistinct **12** disorganized

woozy 4 hazy **5** dizzy, faint, foggy, fuzzy, giddy, shaky **6** punchy **7** muddled **9** befuddled **11** light-headed

word, words 3 vow **4** chat, dirt, news, poop, term **5** edict, order, rumor, set-to, voice **6** advice, avowal, decree, gossip, letter, notice, phrase, pledge, remark, report, ruling, signal **7** command, comment, dictate, dispute, explain, express, hearsay, lowdown, mandate, message, promise, quarrel, summons, tidings **8** argument, audience, bulletin, chitchat, colloquy, decision, describe, dialogue, dispatch, locution, telegram **9** assertion, assurance, bickering, direction, discourse, interview, sobriquet, ultimatum, utterance, wrangling **10** articulate, communique, conference, contention, discussion, expression **11** altercation, appellation, declaration, designation, information, scuttlebutt **12** consultation, intelligence, tittle-tattle **13** communication, pronouncement
French: **9** tete-a-tete

word for word and letter for letter
Latin: **19** verbatim et literatim

wordiness 9 diffusion, prolixity, verbosity **11** diffuseness, profuseness

wording 8 language, phrasing **11** phraseology

wordless 4 dumb, mute **5** tacit **6** silent **8** implicit, taciturn **10** speechless **11** unexpressed

word of honor 3 vow **4** oath **6** pledge **9** assurance

word play 6 banter **7** jesting, kidding
French: **8** badinage, repartee

Words, The
author: **14** Jean-Paul Sartre

Wordsworth, William
author of: **7** Michael **9** Ode to Duty **10** The Prelude **12** Tintern Abbey **14** Lyrical Ballads (with Coleridge) **16** The Ruined Cottage **24** Intimations of Immortality **25** Resolution and Independence
home: **11** Dove Cottage

wordy 5 windy **6** prolix, turgid **7** fustian, gushing, verbose **8** effusive, mumbling **9** bombastic, garrulous, redundant, talkative **10** discursive, loquacious, rhetorical, roundabout **12** tautological **13** grandiloquent

work, works 2 do, go **3** act, job, run, win **4** book, deed, duty, feat, form, gain, line, make, mill, mold, move, shop, song, task, toil, yard **5** beget, cause, chore, craft, enact, labor, opera, piece, plant, shape, slave, solve, sweat, trade **6** drudge, effect, effort, office, output **7** achieve, calling, drawing, execute, exploit, factory, fashion, foundry, innards, insides, operate, perform, produce, product, pursuit, succeed, trouble **8** building, business, concerto, contents, creation, drudgery, endeavor, engender, exertion, function, industry, maneuver, painting, progress, symphony, transmit, vocation **9** originate, sculpture, structure **10** assignment, employment, enterprise, manipulate, occupation, production, profession **11** achievement, composition, performance, transaction
Latin: **4** opus **5** opera
French: **6** metier

work, artistic or literary
French: **6** oeuvre

workaday 5 plain **6** common **7** humdrum, prosaic, routine **8** ordinary **10** unexciting **11** commonplace

work at 3 try **5** essay **6** tackle **7** attempt **8** endeavor

workbench 5 board, table **7** counter

work conquers all
Latin: **16** labor omnia vincit
motto of: **8** Oklahoma

worker 4 doer, hand **5** grind **6** drudge, toiler **7** artisan, hustler, laborer, plodder **8** achiever, employee, producer **9** craftsman, performer **11** breadwinner, eager beaver, proletarian

work for 6 assist **7** support **8** champion

working 3 job **4** duty, toil **5** labor, tasks **6** action, chores, fluent, usable, useful **8** business, drudgery, employed, exertion, industry, laboring **9** effective, operation, operative, practical **10** employment, occupation, profession **11** assignments, functioning, performance

Working
author: **11** Studs Terkel

working-class 5 labor **8** plebian **10** blue-collar **11** proletarian

working class 4 Non-U **9** commoners, common man **10** lower class **11** blue collars, proletariat
Greek: **9** hoi polloi

workmanlike 5 adept **8** skillful **9** efficient **10** productive

workmanship 5 skill **9** handcraft, handiwork, technique **10** handicraft **11** manufacture **12** construction

work out 5 solve, train **6** figure, reckon **7** compute, resolve **8** exercise, practice **9** ascertain, calculate, determine

Works and Days
   author: **6** Hesiod

work saver 9 appliance **11** convenience

work-saving 4 easy **6** simple **9** efficient

worktable 4 desk **5** bench, board, table **7** counter

work together 5 unite **7** pitch in, share in **8** take part **9** cooperate **11** collaborate, participate

work toward 3 try **4** seek **6** aim for **7** attempt **8** aspire to, endeavor, reach for

work up 4 goad, urge **5** upset **6** excite **7** agitate, ferment, provoke

work with 5 coach, drill, teach, train **6** assist **8** exercise, instruct **9** cooperate **11** collaborate

world 3 age, era, orb **4** gobs, lots, star **5** class, Earth, epoch, globe, group, heaps, realm, times **6** domain, nature, oodles, people, period, planet, sphere, system **7** mankind, society **8** creation, division, duration, everyone, humanity, industry, universe **9** everybody, humankind, macrocosm **10** profession
   Latin: **6** cosmos
   Russian: **3** mir

World According to Garp, The
   author: **10** John Irving
   director: **13** George Roy Hill
   cast: **10** Glenn Close, Hume Cronyn **11** John Lithgow **12** Jessica Tandy, Mary Beth Hurt **13** Robin Williams

World Enough and Time
   author: **16** Robert Penn Warren

worldly 5 blase **6** astute, shrewd, urbane **7** callous, earthly, fleshly, knowing, mundane, profane, secular **8** material, physical, temporal **9** corporeal, mercenary **11** experienced, terrestrial **12** cosmopolitan **13** sophisticated

world pain
   German: **11** Weltschmerz

world view
   German: **11** Weltansicht

world-weary 5 blase, bored, jaded **9** unexcited

worldwide 4 rife **6** global **8** catholic, ecumenic, globular, planetal, sweeping **9** universal

worm 4 edge, inch **5** crawl, creep, steal **6** writhe **7** wriggle **9** penetrate **10** infiltrate
   kinds: **4** inch, tape **5** angle, earth

worn 4 weak **5** dingy, drawn, faded, seedy, spent, tired, weary **6** frayed, shabby, wasted **7** abraded, haggard, pinched, rickety, wearied **8** battered, decrepit, dog-tired, drooping, fatigued **9** enfeebled, exhausted **10** threadbare, tumbledown **11** debilitated, dilapidated

worn-out 4 dead, shot **5** spent, tired **6** beat-up, effete, shabby, used-up **7**

run-down **9** exhausted **10** threadbare **11** dilapidated **12** deteriorated

worn thin 9 motheaten **10** threadbare **11** dilapidated

worried 6 afraid, scared **7** anxious, fearful **9** concerned **10** distressed **12** apprehensive

worrisome 5 fussy, pesty **6** trying, uneasy, vexing **7** anxious, fretful, irksome **8** annoying **10** bothersome, despairing, disturbing, irritating, tormenting **11** aggravating, troublesome **12** apprehensive

worry 3 vex, woe **4** care, fret, stew **5** agony, beset, dread, grief, harry, upset **6** badger, bother, dismay, harass, hector, misery, pester, plague **7** agitate, agonize, anguish, anxiety, bugaboo, concern, despair, disturb, perturb, problem, torment, trouble **8** distress, vexation **9** misgiving, persecute **10** difficulty, uneasiness **12** apprehension **13** consternation

worsen 4 fail, slip **5** erode, lapse, slide **7** decline **10** degenerate, retrogress **11** deteriorate **12** disintegrate

worsening 7 setback **9** inflaming **10** increasing, regressing, regression **11** aggravating, heightening **12** exacerbating, intensifying **13** retrogressing, retrogression

worship 5 adore, exalt, extol **6** admire, esteem, praise, pray to, revere **7** adulate, glorify, idolize, lionize **8** dote upon, venerate **9** adoration, reverence **10** exaltation, veneration **11** devotionals

worshipful 5 pious **6** devout **8** reverent

worshiping 7 adoring **8** exalting **9** adoration, adulation, adulating, idolizing, reverence **10** exaltation, glorifying, magnifying, venerating, veneration **11** idolization **13** glorification, magnification

worst 3 bad **4** beat, best, rout **5** floor, outdo **6** defeat, lowest, outwit **7** conquer, poorest, triumph **8** inferior, overcome, vanquish **9** discomfit **10** overmaster, unpleasant

worth 3 use **4** cost, good **5** merit, price, value **6** assets, estate, wealth **7** benefit, effects, utility **8** holdings **9** appraisal, resources, valuation **10** importance, usefulness **11** consequence, possessions

worth having 8 valuable **9** desirable

Worthing, Jack
   character in: **27** The Importance of Being Earnest
   author: **5** Wilde

worthless 6 futile, paltry **7** trivial, useless **8** bootless, piddling, unusable **9** fruitless, meritless, pointless **10** unavailing **11** ineffectual, undeserving, unimportant **12** meretricious, unpro-

ductive **13** insignificant **14** good-for-nothing

worthless objects 4 junk **5** trash **7** garbage, rubbish **8** discards **11** odds and ends

worthwhile 4 good **6** usable, useful **8** valuable **9** rewarding **10** beneficial, profitable

worthy 3 fit, VIP **4** good, name **5** moral, noble **6** bigwig, decent, honest, leader, proper **7** big shot, ethical, fitting, notable, upright **8** big wheel, great man, immortal, laudable, luminary, official, reliable, suitable, virtuous **9** admirable, befitting, deserving, dignitary, estimable, excellent, honorable, personage, reputable **10** creditable **11** appropriate, commendable, meritorious, respectable

worthy of imitation 5 model **9** emulative, exemplary

Wotan
   origin: **8** Germanic
   chief of: **4** gods
   corresponds to: **4** Odin **5** Othin

Wouk, Herman
   author of: **13** The Winds of War **14** The Caine Mutiny **17** War and Remembrance **19** Marjorie Morningstar
   character: **12** Captain Queeg

wound 3 cut **4** gash, harm, hurt, pain, slit, tear **5** slash, sting **6** bruise, damage, grieve, injure, injury, lesion, offend, pierce, trauma **7** anguish, mortify, torment **8** distress, lacerate, vexation **9** contusion **10** affliction, irritation, laceration **11** provocation

wounded 3 cut **4** hurt **6** mauled **7** damaged, injured, pierced, stabbed **8** impaired, ruptured, stricken **11** traumatized

wrack 4 kelp, ruin **5** ruins, trash **6** clouds, refuse **7** destroy, seaweed, torment **8** downfall, eelgrass, wreckage **9** cloud rack **11** destruction, storm clouds

wraith 5 ghost, shade, spook **6** spirit **7** phantom, specter **8** phantasm **10** apparition **15** materialization
   Irish: **7** banshee
   German: **12** doppelganger
   French: **8** revenant

wrangle 4 tiff **5** argue, brawl **6** bicker **7** dispute, quarrel **8** squabble

wrangling 6 strife **7** arguing, discord **8** clashing, friction **9** bickering **10** contention **11** quarrelling

wrap 4 bind, cape, coat, fold, gird, hide, mask, veil, wind **5** cloak, cover, scarf, shawl, stole **6** bundle, clothe, encase, enfold, girdle, jacket, mantle, shroud, swathe **7** conceal, en close, envelop, sweater **8** surround

wrapper, wrapping paper 4 case **6** casing, jacket, sheath **8** covering, envelope, slipcase **9** container

wrapping 6 caping, hiding 7 veiling 8 cerement, bundling, swathing 9 embracing, packaging, shrouding 10 engrossing, enswathing, enveloping 11 enshrouding, surrounding

wrap up 3 end 4 pack 6 finish, wind up 7 engross, envelop, involve, package 8 bundle up, complete, conclude 9 polish off 11 dress warmly

wrath 3 ire 4 bile, fury, gall, rage 5 anger 6 animus, choler, rancor, spleen 8 vexation 9 animosity, hostility 10 irritation, resentment 11 displeasure, indignation 13 irritableness

wrathful 3 mad 5 angry, irate 6 bitter, raging 7 furious 8 incensed, virulent

wreak 4 vent, work 5 visit 7 execute, indulge, inflict, unleash

wreak vengeance 6 avenge 7 get even, revenge 9 retaliate

wreath 5 crown 6 diadem, laurel 7 chaplet, coronet, festoon, garland
Hawaiian: 3 lei

wreathe 4 bend, coil, wind 5 curve, twist 7 entwine, envelop 8 encircle 10 intertwine, interweave

wreck 3 end 4 mess, raze, ruin 5 break, crash, death, level, ruins, smash, total, up set 6 finish, ravage, wretch 7 breakup, crack-up, destroy, shatter, undoing 8 demolish, derelict 9 devastate, over throw 10 disruption 11 destruction, devastation, dissolution 12 annihilation

wreckage 4 ruin 5 ruins 6 jet sam 7 flotsam, remains 8 shambles 11 destruction

Wren, P C
author of: 9 Beau Geste

wrench 3 rip 4 jerk, pull, tear, warp 5 force, twist, wrest, wring 6 sprain, strain 7 distort, pervert 12 misrepresent
type: 6 monkey, socket 7 spanner

wrest 3 get, rip 4 earn, gain, grab, jerk, make, pull, take, tear 5 force, glean, twist, wring 6 attain, obtain, secure, wrench 7 achieve, extract, squeeze

wrestle 4 toil 5 labor 6 battle, strive, tussle 7 contend, grapple, scuffle 8 struggle 10 struggling

wrestling
athlete: 8 Dan Gable

wretch 3 cur, pig, rat 4 hobo, waif, worm 5 knave, louse, rogue, swine, tramp 6 misfit, rascal, rotter, varlet 7 castoff, outcast, stinker, villain 8 derelict, scalawag, sufferer, vagabond 9 scoundrel 10 blackguard 11 unfortunate

wretched 3 low 4 base, mean, vile 5 awful, lousy, sorry 6 abject, gloomy, rotten, shabby, sleazy 7 crushed, doleful, forlorn, hapless, pitiful, scruffy, unhappy, worried 8 dejected, downcast, dreadful, hopeless, inferior, pathetic, pitiable, terrible 9 cheerless, depressed, miserable, nig gardly, sorrowful, woebegone, worthless 10 abominable, despairing, despicable, despondent, melancholy 11 crestfallen, unfortunate 12 contemptible, disconsolate, disheartened, inconsolable 13 brokenhearted

wretchedness 4 pain 6 misery, sorrow 7 despair, torment, trouble 8 distress, hardship 9 adversity 10 affliction, melancholy, misfortune 11 un happiness 12 hopelessness

wriggle 5 twist 6 squirm, wangle, writhe 7 meander

Wright, Frank Lloyd
architect of: 8 Taliesin (Spring Green WI) 10 Robie House (Chicago) 11 Martin House (Buffalo NY), Unity Church (Oak Park IL) 12 Fallingwater (Kaufmann House Bear Run PA), Taliesin West (near Phoenix AZ) 13 Imperial Hotel (To kyo) 16 Guggenheim Museum (NYC) 22 Marin County Civic Center (CA) 35 Larkin Company Administration Building (Buffalo NY) 45 S C Johnson and Son Wax Company Administration Center (Racine WI)
style: 6 Modern 7 Organic, Prairie

Wright, Orville and Wilbur
invented: 8 airplane
first plane: 6 Flyer I 9 Kitty Hawk

Wright, Richard
author of: 8 Black Boy 9 Native Son 17 Uncle Tom's Children

wring 4 hurt, pain, rend, stab 5 choke, force, press, twist, wrest 6 coerce, grieve, pierce, sadden, wrench 7 agonize, extract, squeeze, torture 8 compress, distress

wrinkle 4 fold, idea 5 crimp, fancy, pleat, slant, trick 6 crease, device, furrow, gather, notion, pucker, rimple, rumple 7 crumple, gimmick 9 crow's-feet, viewpoint 11 corrugation

wrinkled 3 old 4 aged 5 lined 6 folded, ridged, rucked, rugate, rugose, rugous, seamed 7 creased, crimped, rimpled, rippled, ruckled, rumpled 8 crimpled, furrowed, puckered 9 shriveled

writ 10 court order 11 sealed order 14 mandatory order

write 3 pen 4 copy, show 5 draft 6 author, draw up, record, scrawl 7 compose, dash off, jot down, make out, produce, set down, turn out 8 inscribe, scribble 10 transcribe

write down 3 jot 4 note, post 5 enter 6 record

write in full 5 add to 6 expand, extend, pad out 7 amplify, augment, stretch 9 expatiate

write out 6 expand, extend 7 amplify, enlarge, stretch 8 lengthen

writer 4 hack, poet 6 author, critic, penman, scribe 7 copyist 8 essayist, novelist, reporter, reviewer, scrawler 9 columnist, dramatist, scribbler 10 journalist, librettist, playwright, songwriter 11 penny-a-liner 12 calligrapher, newspaperman 13 correspondent 14 newspaperwoman
French: 11 litterateur

write to 7 address 8 send word 9 drop a line, send a card, send a note 10 correspond 11 send a letter

write-up 4 item 5 piece, story 7 article

write up 5 cover 6 report

writhe 4 jerk 5 flail 6 squirm, thrash, thresh, wiggle 7 contort, wriggle

writing 4 book, play, poem, tome, work 5 diary, essay, novel, print, story 6 column, letter, report, script, volume 7 article, copying, journal, penning 8 critique, document, drafting, libretto, longhand 9 authoring, composing, editorial, recording 10 inscribing, manuscript, penmanship 11 calligraphy, composition, publication 12 transcribing
Latin: 4 opus

writings
Hebrew: 7 Ketubim

written agreement 6 treaty 7 compact 8 contract

written law
Latin: 10 lex scripta

written-out form 9 extension 12 augmentation 13 amplification

wrong 3 bad, sin 4 awry, bilk, evil, harm, hurt, ruin, vice 5 abuse, amiss, cheat, crime, false, inapt, kaput, unfit 6 faulty, fleece, injure, injury, ruined, sinful, unfair, unjust, untrue, wicked 7 crooked, defraud, illegal, illicit, immoral, inexact, inverse, misdeed, offense, reverse, swindle, unhappy, unsound 8 criminal, dishonor, evil deed, ill-treat, immodest, improper, iniquity, maltreat, mistaken, mistreat, opposite, trespass, unlawful, unseemly, villain 9 dishonest, erroneous, felonious, illogical, incorrect, injustice, unethical, unfitting 10 dishonesty, fallacious, illegality, immorality, inaccurate, indecorous, indelicate, iniquitous, malapropos, mistakenly, sinfulness, unbecoming, unfairness, unsuitable, wickedness, wrongdoing 11 blameworthy, erroneously, incongruous, incorrectly, inexcusable, unbefitting, undesirable, unwarranted 12 dishonorable, inaccurately, infelicitous, unlawfulness 13 inappropriate, reprehensible, transgression, unjustifiable 15 unrighteousness

wrongdoer 5 crook, felon, knave, rogue 6 rascal, sinner 7 culprit, misdoer, villain 8 evildoer, offender 9 miscreant, scoundrel 10 blackguard, delinquent, lawbreaker, malefactor, trespasser **11** perpetrator **12** transgressor

wrongdoing 3 sin **4** evil, vice **5** crime **8** misdeeds **10** misconduct **11** delinquency, malfeasance, misbehavior

wrongful 3 bad **6** unfair, unjust **7** illegal **8** criminal, unlawful **10** iniquitous, inequitable **12** illegitimate
    act: **4** tort
    dispossession: **6** ouster

wrongheaded 3 wry **8** perverse, stubborn **9** misguided

wrong side out 9 backwards **10** topsy-turvy

wrought 4 made **6** beaten, formed, worked **7** crafted **8** hammered **9** fashioned **11** constructed, handcrafted

wrought-up 7 excited **8** agitated **9** emotional **10** hysterical

wry 3 dry **5** askew, droll **6** bitter, ironic, warped **7** amusing, caustic, crooked, cynical, satiric, twisted **8** perverse, sardonic **9** contorted, distorted, sarcastic

Wunderkind 11 wonder child **12** child prodigy

Wurster, William
    architect of: **13** Cowell College (UC Berkeley) **17** Ghirardelli Square (San Francisco CA)

Wuthering Heights
    character: **9** Ellen Dean **10** Heathcliff, Mr Lockwood **11** Edgar Linton **14** Isabella Linton **15** Catherine Linton, Frances Earnshaw, Hareton Earnshaw, Hindley Earnshaw **16** Linton Heathcliff **17** Catherine Earnshaw
    director: **12** William Wyler
    author: **11** Emily Bronte
    cast: **10** David Niven **11** Donald Crisp, Flora Robson, Leo G Carroll, Merle Oberon (Cathy) **15** Laurence Olivier (Heathcliff) **19** Geraldine Fitzgerald

Wyatt, James
    architect of: **8** Pantheon (London) **9** Lee Priory (Kent) **10** Stoke Poges (Buckinghamshire) **13** Fonthill Abbey (Wiltshire) **14** Dodington House Gloucestershire) **15** Heveningham Hall (Suffolk) **16** Sandleford Priory (Berkshire)
    style: **13** Gothic Revival

Wyatt, Jane
    born: **9** Campgaw NJ

roles: **9** Boomerang **11** Lost Horizon **15** Father Knows Best **17** Great Expectations **19** Gentleman's Agreement **21** None But the Lonely Heart

Wyatt Earp, The Life and Legend of
    character: **10** Morgan Earp, Virgil Earp **11** Ben Thompson, Doc Holliday **12** Bat Masterson, Bill Thompson **13** Old Man Clanton
    cast: **9** Hal Baylor **10** Denver Pyle, Dirk London, Hugh O'Brien **12** John Anderson **13** Douglas Fowley **14** Trevor Bardette **20** Mason Alan Dinehart III
    setting: **8** OK Corral **9** Dodge City, Ellsworth, Tombstone
    Wyatt's pistols: **15** Buntline Special

Wyeth, Andrew Newell
    born: **2** PA **10** Chadds Ford
    father: **7** N C Wyeth
    artwork: **9** Grape Wine, River Cove **12** Nick and Jamie **14** Christina Olson, Distant Thunder **15** Christina's World **22** Winter Nineteen Forty-six

Wyler, William
    director of: **6** Ben Hur (Oscar) **7** Jezebel **9** Dodsworth, Funny Girl, The Letter **10** Mrs Miniver (Oscar), The Heiress, These Three **12** Roman Holiday **14** The Little Foxes **15** Counsellor-at-Law **16** Wuthering Heights **18** Friendly Persuasion **22** The Best Years of Our Lives (Oscar)

Wylie, Philip
    author of: **13** Opus Twenty-one **19** A Generation of Vipers

Wyman, Jane
    real name: **14** Sarah Jane Fulks
    born: **10** St Joseph MO
    husband: **12** Ronald Reagan
    daughter: **13** Maureen Reagan
    son: **13** Michael Reagan
    roles: **5** So Big **9** Pollyanna **11** Falcon Crest, The Blue Veil, The Yearling **13** Johnny Belinda (Oscar) **14** Angela Channing, The Lost Weekend **17** The Glass Menagerie **20** Magnificent Obsession

Wyndham, John
    real name: **16** John Beynon Harris
    author of: **14** The Kraken Wakes **15** Consider Her Ways **17** The Midwich Cuckoos, Trouble with Lichen **19** The Day of the Triffids

Wyoming

abbreviation: **2** WY **3** Wyo
nickname: **8** Equality
capital: **8** Cheyenne
largest city: **6** Casper
others: **4** Cody, Lusk **7** Bighorn, Buffalo, Laramie, Rawlins, Worland **8** Gillette, Greybull, Kemmerer, Riverton, Sheridan, Sundance **11** Rock Springs
feature:
    center: **11** Buffalo Bill
    dam: **8** Shoshone
    fort: **7** Laramie
    historical preserve: **11** Fort Bridger
    national grassland: **11** Tunder Basin
    national monument: **11** Devil's Tower, Fossil Butte
    national park: **10** Grand Teton **11** Yellowstone
    reservoir: **12** Flaming Gorge
    tribe: **4** Crow **5** Kiowa, Sioux **7** Arapaho, Bannock **8** Cheyenne
    people: **11** Buffalo Bill **14** Jackson Pollock **16** Nellie Tayloe Ross **18** Francis Emroy Warren
        explorer: **6** Colter, Stuart **7** Bridger **10** Bonneville
    lake: **7** Jackson **11** Yellowstone
    land rank: **5** ninth
    mountain: **3** Elk **5** Cloud, Moran **6** Absaro, Hoback, Tetons **7** Bighorn, Fremont, Laramie, Rockies **8** Atlantic, Sheridan **9** Wind River **10** Black Hills **11** Rattlesnake
        highest point: **11** Gannett Peak
    physical feature: **11** Jackson Hole
        basin: **7** Wyoming
        cave: **8** Shoshone
        hot springs: **11** Thermopolis
        plains: **5** Great
    river: **4** Bear, Wind **5** Green, Snake **6** Platte, Powder, Tongue **7** Bighorn **8** Cheyenne, Shoshone **10** Sweetwater **11** Yellowstone **12** Belle Fourche
state admission: **11** forty-fourth
state bird: **17** western meadowlark
state flower: **10** painted cup **16** Indian paintbrush
state motto: **11** Equal Rights
state song: **7** Wyoming
state tree: **10** cottonwood

Wyss, Johann Rudolf
    author of: **22** The Swiss Family Robinson
        inspired by: **14** Robinson Crusoe

Xanthippe, Xantippe 3 hag 4 fury 5 scold, shrew, vixen 6 dragon, virago 7 scolder 8 spitfire 9 termagant
husband: 8 Socrates

Xanthus and Balius
horses of: 8 Achilles
trait: 8 immortal

Xenia
epithet of: 6 Athena
means: 10 hospitable

xeno- 6 prefix 7 foreign, strange

Xenoclea
form: 9 priestess

xenon
chemical symbol: 2 Xe

xenophobia
fear of: 9 strangers

xerox 4 copy

Xerxes *000* 9 Ahasuerus

X-Files
Creator: 11 Chris Carter
director: 11 Chris Carter
characters: 3 Mr. X (Steven Williams) 9 Fox Mulder (David Duchovny) 10 Alex Krycek (Nick Lea), Dana Scully (Gillian Anderson), Deep Throat (Jerry Hardin) 13 Walter Skinner (Mitch Pileggi) 19 Cigarette-Smoking Man (William B. Davis)

x-ray 9 radiogram 10 radiograph 13 roentgenogram 14 roentgenograph

X-ray tube
invented by: 8 Coolidge

yacht 4 boat, race, sail, ship, yawl 5 ketch, sloop 6 cruise, cutter 7 catboat 8 schooner
race: 11 America's Cup

yachting
athlete: 9 Ted Turner 11 Lowell North

yahoo 4 lout 5 brute, yokel 7 lowbrow 9 barbarian, ignoramus, vulgarian

Yahoos
fictional people in: 16 Gulliver's Travels
author: 5 Swift

Yahweh 3 God 4 Lord 5 Jahve, Jahwe, Yahve 6 Author, I am I am, Jahveh 7 Creator, Eternal, Jehovah 8 Absolute, Almighty, Infinite
component: 2 he 3 yod, vav
pronunciation: 6 Adonai, Elohim 9 forbidden
transliteration: 4 YHVH

Yale, Linus, Jr
invented: 12 cylinder lock 27 dial-operated combination lock

Yalta
in: 7 Ukraine
conference participant: 6 Stalin 9 Churchill, Roosevelt

yam 9 Dioscorea 14 Ipomoea batatas
varieties: 4 wild 5 Negro, water, white 6 Attoto, potato, yellow 7 Chinese 11 sweet potato

Yamasaki, Minoru
architect of: 14 St Louis Airport (MO) 16 World Trade Center (NYC) 21 Woodrow Wilson Building (Princeton NJ)

yammer 3 cry 4 carp, harp, howl, wail, yell 5 whine 7 grumble, whimper 8 complain

yank 3 tug 4 jerk, pull 5 pluck, wrest 6 snatch, wrench 7 draw out, extract, pull out

Yankee, Yank 2 GI 5 teddy 6 gringo 8 American, doughboy 10 Northerner
Spanish: 6 yanqui

Yankee Doodle Dandy
director: 13 Michael Curtiz
cast: 10 Joan Leslie 11 James Cagney (George M Cohan) 12 Irene Manning, Walter Huston
Oscar for: 5 actor (Cagney)

yanqui 6 Yankee 9 US citizen

Yaounde
capital of: 8 Cameroon

yap 3 yip 4 blab, gush, rave, talk, yawp, yelp 5 scold 6 babble, gabble, gossip, jabber, rave on, tattle 7 blather, chatter, lecture, palaver, prattle 8 complain, converse

Yaqui
language family: 6 Cahita
location: 6 Mexico, Sonora 7 Arizona

yard 4 lawn 5 close, court 6 garden 7 confine, grounds, pasture 8 compound 9 enclosure, three feet
abbreviation: 2 yd

yardbird 3 con 5 felon 7 convict 8 prisoner

yard goods 5 cloth 6 fabric 8 material, textiles

Yard of Sun
author: 14 Christopher Fry

yardstick 4 rule 7 measure 8 standard 9 criterion

Yaren District
capital of: 5 Nauru

yarn 4 tale 5 story 7 account 8 anecdote 9 adventure, narrative 10 experience

Yastrzemski, Carl
nickname: 3 Yaz
sport: 8 baseball
team: 12 Boston Red Sox

Yates, Peter
director of: 7 Bullitt 12 Breaking Away

yawn 3 gap 4 bore, gape 5 chasm 8 open wide, oscitate

yawp 4 roar, yelp 5 noise 6 clamor, squawk, yammer

Yaz
nickname of: 15 Carl Yastrzemski

Yazoo
author: 12 Willie Morris

year, years 3 age, era 4 time 5 cycle, epoch 6 period
abbreviation: 2 yr

Yearling, The
director: 13 Clarence Brown
author: 22 Marjorie Kinnan Rawlings
cast: 9 Jane Wyman 10 Chill Wills 11 Gregory Peck 14 Claude Jarman Jr
character: 9 Ora Baxter 10 Jody Baxter 11 Oliver Hutto, Penny Baxter 12 Grandma Hutto 14 Twink Weatherby 19 Fodder-Wing Forrester

yearn 4 ache, long, pine, sigh, want, wish 5 crave 6 hanker, hunger, thirst 8 languish

yearning 3 yen 4 ache, want, wish 5 fancy 6 desire, hunger, thirst 7 craving, longing, passion 9 hankering 10 aspiration 11 inclination

Year of Living Dangerously, The
director: 9 Peter Weir
cast: 9 Linda Hunt (Billy Kwan), Mel Gibson 15 Sigourney Weaver
setting: 7 Jakarta
Oscar for: 17 supporting actress (Hunt)

year of wonders
Latin: 14 annus mirabilis

Yeats, William Butler
author of: 7 A Vision 8 The Tower 9 Last Poems 14 Leda and the Swan 15 The Winding Stair 18 Sailing to Byzantium 19 Among School Children, The Wild Swans at Coole 21 Easter Nineteen Sixteen 22 The Lake Isle of Innisfree 29 An Irish Airman Foresees His Death

yegg 6 bomber **9** cracksman **11** safe-cracker

yell 3 boo, cry **4** bawl, hoot, howl, roar, yowl **5** cheer, hollo, shout, whoop **6** bellow, clamor, cry out, holler, hurrah, huzzah, outcry, scream, shriek, squall, squeal **7** screech

yellow 4 gold **5** blond, lemon, ocher **6** afraid, canary, craven, flaxen **7** chicken, fearful, saffron **8** cowardly, timorous **10** frightened **12** apprehensive, fainthearted **13** pusillanimous **14** chickenhearted

yellow-belly 6 coward **7** caitiff, chicken, dastard **8** poltroon

Yellowhammer State
  nickname of: 7 Alabama

yellowish 4 buff **5** blond, cream **6** blonde, creamy, flaxen

Yellow Kid, The
  creator: 10 R F Outcault
  trademark: 10 nightshirt
  place: 5 slums **11** Hogan's Alley
  coined term: 16 yellow journalism
  first: 10 comic strip

yelp 3 yap, yip **4** bark, howl **5** shout **6** clamor, holler, scream, shriek, squeal **7** screech

Yemen, North
  other name: 4 Sana
  capital/largest city: 4 Sana **5** Sanaa
  others: 4 Moka, Taiz **5** Dahhi, Damar, Jibla, Mocha, Mukha, Taizz, Umram **7** Hodeida, Hudayda
  monetary unit: 4 fils, rial **5** riyal
  island: 5 Zugar **6** Hanish
  highest point: 6 Shuayb
  river: 5 Abrad, Zabid **6** al-Jawf, Surdud
  sea: 3 Red
  physical feature:
    desert: 10 Rub al Khali
    gulf: 4 Aden
    lowlands: 6 Tihama
    peninsula: 7 Arabian
    strait: 11 Bab el Mandeb
  people: 4 Arab **5** Zaidi **6** Shafai, Yemeni **8** Yemenite
    leader: 16 Ali Abdallah Saleh **19** Abd al-Aziz Abd al-Ghani
  language: 6 Arabic
  religion: 5 Islam
  place:
    ruins: 5 Marib
  feature:
    dagger: 7 jambiya
    king: 4 imam
    kingdom: 4 Saba **5** Sheba **11** Arabia Felix
    tree: 3 fig **5** carob, mango, myrrh
  food:
    coffee: 5 mocha

Yemen, South
  capital: 4 Aden **14** Madinat al-Shaab
  largest city: 4 Aden
  others: 5 Ahwar, Shihr, Tarim **6** Balhaf, Damqut, Seiyun, Shabwa, Shibam, Zamakh **7** Mukalla
  monetary unit: 4 fils **5** dinar
  island: 5 Perim **7** Kamaran, Socotra
  mountain: 7 Djehaff
  highest point: 6 Thamir
  river: 4 Bana **6** Tibban **7** Masilah **9** Hadramaut
  sea: 6 Indian **7** Arabian
  physical feature:
    desert: 10 Rub al Khali **12** Empty Quarter
    gulf: 4 Aden
    peninsula: 7 Arabian
    valley: 9 Hadramawt
  people: 4 Arab
  language: 6 Arabic
  religion: 5 Islam
  feature:
    animal: 4 ibex, oryx
    clothing: 4 futa

yen 4 ache, long, pine, sigh, want, wish **5** crave, fancy, yearn **6** aching, desire, hanker, hunger, relish, thirst **7** craving, longing, passion **8** appetite, languish, yearning **9** hankering **10** aspiration **11** inclination

yenta 3 hen **6** gossip **8** busybody **12** blabbermouth

Yentl
  director: 15 Barbra Streisand
  based on story by: 19 Isaac Bashevis Singer
  cast: 13 Mandy Patinkin **15** Barbra Streisand

Yeobright, Thomasin and Clym
  characters in: 17 Return of the Native
  author: 5 Hardy

yeoman 4 chap, exon **5** churl, clerk, swain **6** farmer, fellow **7** granger, plowman, servant **8** graycoat, retainer **9** beefeater **10** freeholder **12** petty officer

Yerby, Frank
  author of: 8 Fair Oaks **10** Health Card **11** Griffin's Way **12** Pride's Castle **16** The Foxes of Harrow **21** Hail the Conquering Hero

yes 3 aye, yea **4** amen, okay, true **5** truly **6** assent, indeed, it is so, just so, really, so be it, surely, verily **7** consent, exactly, granted, no doubt **8** approval, of course, to be sure **9** agreement, assuredly, certainly, doubtless, precisely **10** acceptance, positively **11** affirmation, undoubtedly **12** acquiescence, emphatically **13** affirmatively, authorization
  French: 3 oui
  German: 2 ja
  Spanish: 2 si

yesterday 7 the past **10** bygone days, days of yore, olden times, time gone by **11** former times **13** the recent past **14** the good old days **17** the day before today **22** on the day preceding today

yet 3 but **4** also, even, then, up to **5** again, still, while, until **6** no less, though **7** besides, earlier, even now, further, however, thus far **8** although, hitherto, moreover **9** presently **10** eventually, ultimately **12** nevertheless **15** notwithstanding

yew 5 Taxus
  varieties: 4 plum **5** Irish **6** golden **7** Chinese, English, Florida, Western **8** American, Japanese, Southern **11** Chinese plum, Plum-fruited **12** Japanese plum, Prince Albert **14** Harrington plum

Yggdrasil
  also: 9 Iggdrasil
  origin: 12 Scandinavian
  kind of tree: 12 evergreen ash
  roots: 5 three
  binds: 6 Asgard **7** Midgard **8** Niflheim **10** Mithgarthr

yield 3 pay, sag **4** bear, crop, earn, gain, give **5** beget, break, burst, defer, droop, forgo, grant, spawn, split, waive **6** accede, cave in, give in, give up, kowtow, ren- der, return, submit, supply **7** bow down, concede, forbear, furnish, give way, harvest, pay ment, premium, produce, product, provide, revenue, succumb, truckle **8** collapse, cry uncle, earnings, generate, interest, proceeds, renounce **9** acquiesce, gleanings, procreate, surrender **10** capitulate, relinquish

yielding 3 lax **4** soft **6** ceding, spongy **7** sagging **8** flexible, obedient **9** compliant **11** complaisant **13** accommodating

Yigdal 22 Jewish liturgical prayer
  literally: 12 becomes great

Yizkor 33 Jewish service to commemorate the dead
  literally: 9 be mindful

Ymir
  origin: 12 Scandinavian
  progenitor of: 6 giants
  earth made from: 5 flesh
  water made from: 5 blood
  heavens made from: 5 skull

yoga, yogi 5 Hindu **6** mystic **7** ascetic

Yogi Bear
  creator: 12 Hanna-Barbera
  character: 6 BooBoo
  setting: 14 Jellystone Park

yoke 3 tax **4** bond, join, link, load, pair, span, team **5** brace, clasp, hitch, trial, unite **6** at tach, burden, collar, couple, fasten, strain, weight **7** bondage, coupler, harness, serfdom, slavery **8** distress, pressure, troubles **9** servitude, thralldom, vassalage **10** oppression **11** enslavement, tribulation

yokel 4 clod, hick, rube **7** bumpkin, hayseed, peasant, plowboy **10** clodhopper, provincial

yolk 6 yellow

yonder 3 yon **5** there **6** far-off **7** faraway, farther, thither

Yorick
  skull in: **6** Hamlet
  author: **11** Shakespeare
Yorick, Mr
  character in: **14** Tristram Shandy
  author: **6** Sterne
York, Michael
  born: **6** Fulmer **7** England
  roles: **6** Tybalt **7** Cabaret **11** Lost Ho-
    rizon **14** Four Musketeers, Romeo
    and Juliet, The Forsyte Saga **15**
    Three Musketeers **19** The Island of
    Dr Moreau **24** The Last Remake of
    Beau Geste
York, Susannah
  real name: **23** Susannah Yolande
    Fletcher
  born: **6** London **7** England
  roles: **5** Freud **6** Images **8** Jane Eyre,
    Tom Jones **12** The Awakening
  author of: **18** In Search of Unicorns
Yossarian
  character in: **14** Catch Twenty-two
  author: **6** Heller
You Asked for It
  host: **8** Art Baker **9** Jack Smith
You Bet Your Life
  host: **11** Groucho Marx
  announcer: **14** George Fenneman
You Can't Go Home Again
  author: **11** Thomas Wolfe
  character: **10** Esther Jack **11** Lloyd
    McHarg **12** George Webber **13** Else
    von Kohler **14** Foxhall Edwards
You Can't Take It With You
  author: **8** Moss Hart **14** George S
    Kaufman
  director: **10** Frank Capra
  cast: **10** Jean Arthur, Mischa Auer **12**
    Edward Arnold, James Stewart **15** Li-
    onel Barrymore
  Oscar for: **7** picture **8** director
young 3 cub, pup **4** baby, kids **5** child,
    issue, minor, whelp **6** boyish, callow,
    junior, kitten, youths **7** budding, girl-
    ish, growing, progeny, puerile, teen-
    age **8** childish, children, immature,
    juvenile, underage, youthful **9** beard-
    less, infantile, juveniles, offspring,
    teenagers **10** adolescent, descendant,
    sophomoric, youngsters **11** adoles-
    cents, undeveloped **13** inexperienced
  god of: **7** Angus Og
  goddess of: **4** Hebe
Young, Chic
  creator/artist of: **7** Blondie
Young, Denton True
  nickname: **2** Cy **7** Cyclone
  sport: **8** baseball
  position: **7** pitcher
  team: **12** Boston Braves, Boston Red
    Sox **16** Cleveland Indians, St Louis
    Cardinals
Young, Loretta
  real name: **13** Gretchen Young
  husband: **12** Grant Withers
  roles: **13** Cause for Alarm **14** The

  Bishop's Wife **15** Come to the Stable
    18 The Farmer's Daughter (Oscar)
    20 Rachel and the Stranger
Young, Robert
  born: **9** Chicago IL
  roles: **10** Relentless **11** H M Pulham
    Esq **13** Marcus Welby M D **15** Fa-
    ther Knows Best **16** Strange Interlude
Young Adventure
  author: **19** Stephen Vincent Benet
Young Frankenstein
  director: **9** Mel Brooks
  cast: **8** Teri Garr **10** Gene Wilder, Pe-
    ter Boyle **11** Gene Hackman **12**
    Madeline Kahn, Marty Feldman **14**
    Cloris Leachman
  score: **10** John Morris
young girl
  French: **10** jeune fille
young lady
  German: **8** fraulein
Young Lonigan
  author: **13** James T Farrell
Young Manhood of Studs Lonigan
  author: **13** James T Farrell
youngster 3 boy, kid, tot **4** baby, girl
    5 child, minor, youth **7** progeny **8** ju-
    venile, teenager **9** fledgling, offspring
    10 adolescent
young Turks 6 rebels **8** radicals, up-
    starts **9** activists **10** insurgents **15** re-
    volutionaries
young woman
  French: **10** demoiselle
you're welcome
  German: **5** bitte
Your Show of Shows
  regular: **9** Bill Hayes, Jerry Ross, Sid
    Caesar **10** Carl Reiner **11** Imogene
    Coca **12** Howard Morris, Nellie
    Fisher **13** James Starbuck, Robert
    Merrill **16** Marguerite Piazza
youth 3 boy, kid, lad **4** kids **5** bloom,
    child, minor, prime, teens **6** heyday **7**
    boyhood **8** children, girlhood, juve-
    nile, minority, teenager **9** childhood,
    fledgling, juveniles, schoolboy, strip-
    ling, teenagers, youngster **10** adoles-
    cent, pubescence, youngsters **11** ado-
    lescence, adolescents
youthful 5 fresh, young **6** boyish, cal-
    low **7** girlish, puerile, teenage **8** child-
    ish, immature, juvenile **10** adolescent,
    sophomoric **12** enthusiastic, light
    hearted **13** inexperienced
yowl 3 bay, cry **4** bawl, roar, wail,
    yelp **5** shout, whine **6** bellow, holler,
    scream, shriek, squeal **7** screech **9**
    caterwaul
Ypres
  in: **7** Belgium
  WWI: **10** battle site
yuan
  currency of: **5** China
yucca 5 agave

  varieties: **4** blue **6** banana **9** San An-
    gelo, spineless **11** twisted-leaf
Yugoslavia
  other name: **8** Dalmatia **34** Kingdom
    of the Serbs Croats and Slovenes
  capital/largest city: **7** Beograd **8** Bel-
    grade
  others: **3** Nis **4** Pola, Pula, Savo, Zara
    5 Agram, Bosna, Budva, Fiume, Ko-
    tor, Pirot, Rieka, Rtanj, Senta, Split,
    Tuzla, Uskub, Zadar **6** Bitola, Bitolj,
    Ca Haro, Maglaj, Morava, Mostar,
    Osijek, Prilep, Ragusa, Rijeka,
    Skopje, Trogir, Visoko, Zagreb **7** Ce-
    tinje, Laibach, Maribor, Novisad,
    Skoplje, Spalato **8** Monastir, Pristina,
    Sarajevo, Subotica, Titograd **9** Banja
    Luka, Dubrovnik, Ljubljana, Podgo-
    rica, Smederevo
  divisioin/former division: **6** Bosnia,
    Serbia **7** Croatia **8** Crna Gora, Slove-
    nia **9** Macedonia, Vojvodina, Voy-
    vodina **10** Montenegro **11** Hercego-
    vina, Herzegovina **14** Kosovo-
    Metohija
  measure: **3** oka, rif **4** akov, ralo **5**
    donum, khvat, lanaz, plaze, stopa **6**
    motyka, ralico **9** danoranja
  monetary unit: **4** para **5** dinar
  weight: **3** oka **5** dramm, tovar,
    wagon **7** satlijk
  island: **3** Rab **4** Arbe, Brac, Cres,
    Hvar, Pago **5** Mljet, Solta, Susac, Su-
    sak **7** Korcula
  lake: **4** Bled **5** Ohrid **6** Prespa **7**
    Ochrida, Scutari
  mountain: **5** Karst **6** Balkan **7** Rhod-
    ope **8** Crna Gora, Durmitor **9** Sar-
    Pindus **10** Karawanken
    Alps: **6** Carnic, Julian **7** Dinaric **9**
      Slovenian **16** Northern Albanian
  highest point: **7** Triglav
  river: **3** Una **4** Drim, Drin, Ibar, Krka,
    Kupa, Sava, Tisa **5** Anube, Bosna,
    Cazma, Drava, Drina, Raska, Tamis,
    Timok, Tisza, Vrbas **6** Danube, Mo-
    rava, Vardar, Velika **7** Neretva **9**
    Vojvodina
  sea: **8** Adriatic
  physical feature:
    bay: **5** Kotor
    cave: **8** Postojna
    channel: **7** Narento
    gulf: **5** Kotor **7** Kvarner, Trieste
    hot springs: **16** Krapinske Toplice
    peninsula: **6** Balkan **7** Istrian
  people: **4** Serb, Slav **5** Croat **7** Slo-
    vene **8** Albanian **10** Macedonian **11**
    Montenegrin
    author: **6** Andric, Djilas, Krleza **7**
      Dedijer
    leader: **4** Tito **5** Dusan, Pasic **6** Dji-
      las **7** Nemanja **9** Milosevic, Obre-
      novic **13** Mikhailovitch
    ruler: **5** Peter **9** Hapsburgs **12** Otto-
      man Turks
    sculptor: **9** Mestrovic
  language: **7** Bosnian, Slovene **8** Alba-

nian, Croatian **9** Hungarian, Slovenian **10** Macedonian **11** Montenegrin **13** Herzegovinian, Serbo-Croatian
  alphabet: 5 Latin **8** Cyrillic
  religion: 5 Islam **13** Roman Catholic **15** Eastern Orthodox, Serbian Orthodox
  place:
    amphitheater: 4 Pula
    bridge: 9 Stari Most
    fortress: 10 Kalemedgan
    monastery: 8 Sopocani
    mosque: 6 Begova **15** Bajrakli Dzamija
    ruins: 14 Hadrjan's Palace
    square: 8 Republic
  feature:
    coffee house: 7 kafanas
    fields: 5 polje
    military governor: 7 vojvodi
    musical instrument: 5 gusla
    poems: 5 pesme
    slippers: 6 opanki
  food:
    dessert: 4 pita
    drink: 5 rakia **6** rakija **7** maraska **9** slivovitz **10** sljivovice **13** Turkish coffee
    meat: 7 shaslik **9** cevapcici **10** culbastija
    soup: 6 corbas
Yuit *see* **6** Eskimo
Yukon Territory
  border: 6 Alaska **15** British Columbia, Selwyn Mountains **18** Mackenzie Mountains
  capital: 10 Whitehorse
  country: 6 Canada
  event: 8 gold rush (1897)
  Indian: 4 Dene **6** Eskimo **7** Kutchin **8** Loucheux **9** Athabasca
  lake: 6 Kluane **9** Great Bear
  mineral: 4 gold **6** silver
  mountain: 3 Joy **5** Logan **6** Harper **7** Kennedy **8** Campbell
  region: 8 Klondike
  river: 5 Pelly **9** Porcupine
  sea: 8 Beaufort
  town: 4 Elsa, Faro, Mayo, Snag **5** Rocky **6** Dawson **8** Franklin, Wernecke **9** Mackenzie
yule 4 Noel **9** Christmas
Yule, Joe, Jr
  real name of: 12 Mickey Rooney
Yuman
  tribe: 6 Mohave, Mojave **8** Hualapai
Zachariah
  father: 4 Babi, Elam **9** Barachias
  wife: 9 Elizabeth
  son: 3 Abi **14** John the Baptist
  succeeded: 8 Jeroboam
  visitor: 7 Gabriel
zaddik 14 virtuous person **15** righteous person
Zadkine, Ossip
  born: 6 Russia **8** Smolensk
  artwork: 4 Stag **6** Christ **7** Orpheus

9 Musicians **10** The Prophet **13** Woman with a Fan **14** Mother and Child **16** The Destroyed City
Zadok
  father: 5 Baana, Immer **6** Ahitub
  son: 7 Shallum
  daughter: 7 Jerusha
  served: 5 David
zaftig 5 buxom, plump **6** bosomy
Zagreus
  form: 5 child, deity
  father: 4 Zeus
  mother: 6 Semele **10** Persephone
Zaire
  other name: 5 Congo **12** Belgian Congo **13** Congo-Kinshasa **17** Congo-Leopoldville
  capital/largest city: 8 Kinshasa
  others: 4 Baya, Boma, Lebo **5** Aketi, Ilebo **6** Banana, Kamina, Kasaji, Kikwit, Matadi, Sandoa **7** Butembo, Kananga, Kolwezi **8** Bakwanga, Yangambi **9** Kisangani **10** Lubumbashi, Luluabourg, Mutshatsha **12** Port-Francqui, Stanleyville **14** Elisabethville
  school: 5 Zaire **8** Lovanium
  division: 4 Kivu **5** Kasai, Shaba **7** Equator, Katanga **8** Oriental
  monetary unit: 5 zaire **6** makuta
  lake: 4 Kivu **5** Mweru, Tumba **6** Albert, Edward, Upemba **9** Mai-Ndombe **10** Tanganyika
  mountain: 7 Crystal, Mitumba, Virunga **9** Ruwenzori **10** Nyaragongo **18** Mountains of the Moon
  highest point: 10 Margherita
  river: 4 Ruki, Uele **5** Congo, Dengu, Ibina, Kasai, Lindi, Zaire **6** Likati, Lomami, Lukuga, Ubangi **7** Aruwimi, Lualaba, Lulonga
  sea: 8 Atlantic
  physical feature:
    falls: 4 Kivu **6** Tshopo **7** Stanley
    forest: 5 Ituri
    valley: 9 Great Rift
  people: 4 Kuba, Luba, Yaka **5** Bantu, Bashi, Bemba, Kongo, Lulue, Lunda, Mongo, Pygmy **6** Azande, Baluba, Watusi **7** Bakongo, Nilotes, Tshokwe **8** European, Mangbetu, Sudanese
    explorer: 3 Cao **7** Stanley
    leader: 6 Mobutu (Sese Seko) **7** Lumumba, Tshombe **8** Kasavubu
    ruler: 7 Belgium, Leopold
  language: 5 Bantu **6** French **7** Chiluba, Kikongo, Lingala, Swahili **8** Sudanese, Tshiluba
  religion: 5 Islam **7** animism, Kimbang **10** Protestant **13** Roman Catholic
  place:
    dam: 4 Inga **9** Le Marinee **10** Del Commune
    national park: 6 Albert, Upemba **7** Garamba
  feature:
    animal: 5 hyena, okapi **7** giraffe,

gorilla **10** rhinoceros
    fish: 11 electric eel
Zambia
  other name: 16 Northern Rhodesia
  capital/largest city: 6 Lusaka
  others: 4 Kafu **5** Choma, Isoka, Kabwe, Kitwe, Mansa, Mbala, Mongu, Mpika, Mumba, Ndola **6** Mwenda **7** Chipata, Luapula, Mankoya **8** Balovale, Chingola, Luanshya, Mazabuka, Mufulira, Mulobezi **11** Livingstone
  division: 7 Puapula **10** Copperbelt **11** Barotseland
  monetary unit: 5 ngwee **6** kwacha
  lake: 5 Mweru **6** Kariba **9** Bangweulu **10** Tanganyika
  mountain: 8 Muchinga
  highest point: 12 Mafinga Hills
  river: 5 Congo, Kafue **7** Luangwa, Luapula, Zambezi **8** Chambezi **9** Chambeshi
  physical feature:
    cave: 5 Nsalu **14** Chifabwa Stream
    falls: 7 Kalambo **8** Victoria
    gorge: 6 Kariba
    plateau: 7 Zambian
    swamp: 7 Lukanga **9** Bangweulu **12** Mweru Wantipa
    valley: 8 Chambezi **9** Great Rift
  people: 4 Lozi **5** Bantu, Bemba, Ngoni, Tonga
    developer: 6 Rhodes
    explorer: 11 Livingstone
    hero: 11 Chitimukulu
    leader: 6 Kaunda
  language: 4 Lozi **5** Bemba, Lunda, Tonga **6** Luvale, Nyanja **7** English **9** Afrikaans
  religion: 5 Hindu, Islam **7** animism **10** Protestant **13** Roman Catholic
  place:
    botanical garden: 10 Munda Wanga
    dam: 5 Kafue **6** Kariba
    game reserve: 6 Valley
    library: 20 Hammerskjold Memorial
    museum: 11 Livingstone
    national park: 5 Kafue, Sumbu **12** South Luangwa
  feature:
    canoe: 10 nalikwanda
    king: 7 litunga
    king's aide: 5 sungu, twite **8** inabanza
    taxi: 6 zamcab
zany 3 nut **4** wild **5** balmy, batty, booby, buffo, clown, comic, crazy, cutup, daffy, dizzy, goofy, inane, nutty, silly, wacky **6** jester, nitwit, screwy, weirdo **7** buffoon, half-wit, lunatic **8** bonehead, clownish, imbecile, lunkhead, numskull **9** blockhead, eccentric, harlequin, ludicrous, pantaloon, simpleton, slapstick **10** nincompoop, noodlehead, outlandish **11** nonsensical person
French: 7 farceur

Zapotec
  language family: 5 Otomi **6** mixtec
  location: 6 Mexico, Oaxaca

zapped 5 drunk **6** killed, soused,
  wasted, zonked **7** smashed **9** destroyed, plastered **10** inebriated **11**
  annihilated, intoxicated

zeal 4 fire, zest **5** ardor, gusto, verve,
  vigor **6** fervor, relish **7** passion **8** devotion, industry **9** animation, eagerness, intensity, vehemence **10** enthusiasm, fanaticism, fierceness,
  intentness **11** earnestness

zealot 3 fan, nut **4** buff **5** bigot, crank
  6 pusher **7** devotee, fanatic, hustler **8**
  believer, champion, crackpot, go- getter, livewire, partisan **9** extremist **10**
  enthusiast

zealous 5 eager, rabid **6** ardent, fervid,
  fierce, gung ho, raging, raving **7** devoted, earnest, fanatic, fervent, intense **8** animated, vehement, vigorous
  10 passionate **11** impassioned, industrious **12** enthusiastic

Zebedee
  wife: 6 Salome
  son: 4 John **5** James

Zeboim
  destroyed with: 5 Admah, Sodom **8**
  Gomorrah

Zebulun
  father: 5 Jacob
  mother: 4 Leah
  brother: 3 Dan, Gad **4** Levi **5** Asher,
  Judah **6** Joseph, Reuben, Simeon **8**
  Benjamin, Issachar, Naphtali
  sister: 5 Dinah
  descendant of: 10 Zebulunite

Zechariah
  father: 5 Bebai, Hosah **6** Jehiel,
  Pashur **7** Issiliah **8** Iehoiada, Jonathan **9** Berechiah **11** Jeberechiah,
  Meshelemiah
  grandfather: 4 Iddo
  mother: 6 Merari
  son: 8 Jahaziel
  daughter: 6 Abijah

Zeffirelli, Franco
  director of: 14 Romeo and Juliet **19**
  The Taming of the Shrew **20** Brother
  Sun Sister Moon

Zeitgeist 18 the spirit of the time

Zelos
  origin: 5 Greek
  personifies: 4 zeal **9** emulation
  father: 11 Titan Palles
  mother: 4 Styx
  brother: 3 Bia **6** Cratus
  sister: 4 Nike

Zemeckis, Robert
  director of: 15 Back to the Future **17**
  Romancing the Stone

zenith 4 acme, apex, best, peak **6** apogee, climax, summit, vertex **7** maximum **8** pinnacle **11** culmination

Zenobia (Zeena)

character in: 10 Ethan Frome
  author: 7 Wharton

zephyr 8 west wind **9** puff of air **10**
  gentle wind **11** breath of air, light
  breeze

Zephyrus
  personifies: 8 west wind
  father: 8 Astraeus
  mother: 3 Eos
  loved: 10 Hyacinthus
  son: 6 Balius **7** Xanthus

Zeppelin, Ferdinand Graf von
  nationality: 6 German
  invented: 9 dirigible **21** rigid dirigible
  airship
  famous ship: 10 Hindenberg

zero 2 no **3** nil, zip **5** aught, nadir,
  zilch **6** cipher, naught **7** nothing **8**
  goose egg **11** nonexistent, nothingness

zero hour 5 onset, start **7** liftoff **9** beginning **12** commencement

zest 3 joy, zip **4** salt, tang, zeal, zing **5**
  gusto, savor, spice, taste, verve **6** flavor, relish, thrill **7** delight, passion **8**
  appetite, piquancy, pleasure **9** eagerness, flavoring, seasoning **10** enthusiasm, excitement **12** exhilaration, satisfaction

zestful 6 active, lively **7** dynamic, vibrant **8** animated, spirited, vigorous **9**
  vivacious **12** invigorating

zesty 5 spicy, tangy **7** piquant

Zeus
  also: 7 Cenaean **9** Atabyriam, Ithoma-
  tas **10** Anchesmius **11** Panomphaeus
  12 Cithaeronian
  birthplace: 5 Crete
  brother: 5 Hades **8** Poseidon
  corresponds to: 4 Amen, Amon, Jove
  5 Ammon **6** Amen Ra, Amon Ra **7**
  Jupiter
  daughter: 4 Hebe **6** Athene **10**
  Eileithyia, Persephone
  epithet: 5 Areus, Arius, Sotor **6**
  Aqueus, Nemean, Philus **7** Alastor,
  Apemius, Ctesius, Lycacus, Polieus,
  Stenius **8** Agoraeus, Aphesius, Apomyius, Catharius, Chthonius, Coccygius, Hecalcius, Lecheates, Mechaneus **10** Catiebates, Coryphaeus,
  Homagyrius, Laphystius, Meilichius
  11 Eleutherius **12** Panhellenius
  father: 6 Cronus
  form: 5 deity
  god of: 7 heavens
  lover: 4 Leto **6** Demeter
  mother: 4 Rhea
  position: 7 supreme
  sister: 4 Hera **6** Hestia **7** Demeter
  son: 4 Ares **6** Apollo, Hermes
  wife: 4 Hera **5** Metis

zigzag 4 awry, tack **6** angles, forked,
  jagged **7** chevron, crankle, crooked,
  notched, sinuous, stagger **8** crotched,
  serrated, sideling, traverse **9** bifurcate
  10 circuitous, deflection

Zilpah

slave of: 4 Leah
  concubine of: 5 Jacob
  son: 3 Gad **5** Asher

Zimbabwe
  other name: 8 Rhodesia **16** Southern
  Rhodesia
  capital/largest city: 6 Harare **9** Salisbury
  others: 5 Gwelo, Gweru **6** Kariba,
  KweKwe, Mutare, QueQue, Umtali **7**
  Gatooma, Rusambo, Selukwe, Sha-
  bani **8** Bulawayo, Zimbabwe **10** Beit-
  bridge
  monetary unit: 4 cent **6** dollar
  lake: 4 Kyle **6** Kariba
  mountain: 5 Vumba **6** Manica **7** Inyanga **11** Chimanimani, Matopo Hills
  highest point: 9 Inyangani
  river: 4 Sabi, Save **5** Lundi **6** Shashi
  7 Limpopo, Umniati, Zambezi
  physical feature:
    falls: 8 Victoria
    grassland: 4 veld
    plateau: 8 Highveld **11** Mashona-
    land
  people: 3 Ila **4** Sena **5** Asian, Bantu,
  Bemba, Sotho, Tongo, White **6** Indian **7** Barotse, Chinese, English,
  Mashoma, Mashona, Ndebele **8** Coloured, Japanese, Matabele **9** Afrikaner **10** Balokwakwa
    developer: 6 Rhodes
    explorer: 11 Livingstone
    king: 9 Lobengula, Mzilikaze
    leader: 5 Nkomo **6** Mugabe **7**
    Sithole **8** Muzorewa **9** Ian D Smith
  language: 3 Ila **5** Bantu, Shona **7**
  English, Ndebele
  religion: 7 animism **8** Anglican **12**
  Christianity, Presbyterian **13** Dutch
  Reformed, Roman Catholic
  place:
    dam: 6 Kariba
    national park: 6 Hwange, Wankie
    7 Matopos **9** Inyan gani
    13 Victoria Falls
    ruins: 5 Khami **6** Temple **8** Zim-
    babwe **9** Acropolis **13** Valley of
    Ruins
  feature:
    cattle pen: 5 kraal
    game: 5 tsoro **7** mandani
    hut: 4 kaia
    kingdom: 5 Rozwi **10** Monomotapa
    tree: 4 teak **6** baobab, mopani

Zimbalist, Efrem, Jr
  born: 9 New York NY
  father: 14 Efrem Zimbalist
  mother: 9 Alma Gluck
  daughter: 18 Stephanie Zimbalist
  roles: 3 FBI **13** Wait Until Dark **15** By
  Love Possessed **16** The Chapman Report **23** Seventy-seven Sunset Strip

zinc
  chemical symbol: 2 Zn

zing 3 pep, vim, zap, zip **4** dash, snap,
  tang, whiz, zest **5** gusto, speed, vigor,
  whine **6** energy, spirit **7** liven up

8 satirize, vitality **9** animation, criticize **10** enthusiasm, liveliness

zingara, zingaro 5 gypsy

Zinnemann, Fred
director of: **5** Julia **8** High Noon, Oklahoma **9** The Search **12** The Nun's Story **13** The Sundowners **17** A Man for All Seasons (Oscar) **18** From Here to Eternity (Oscar)

Zion 6 utopia **9** city of God **11** City of David **13** ancient Israel
hill in: **9** Jerusalem
built on the hill: **6** Temple

zip 3 fly, nil, pep, run, vim **4** buzz, dart, dash, hiss, life, nada, rush, zero, zest **5** aught, close, drive, force, gusto, hurry, power, punch, speed, verve, vigor, whine, zilch **6** cipher, energy, impact, naught, spirit, streak **7** nothing, whistle **8** goose egg, strength, vitality, vivacity **9** animation, intensity **10** enthusiasm, exuberance, liveliness **13** effervescence

zipper
invented by: **6** Judson

Zipporah
father: **5** Reuel **6** Jethro
husband: **5** Moses
son: **7** Eliezer, Gershom

zircon
source: **5** Burma **6** Ceylon **8** Cambodia, Sri Lanka **9** Kampuchea

zirconium
chemical symbol: **2** Zr

zloty
currency of: **6** Poland

zodiac 4 belt, zone **5** stars **7** circuit
fire sign: **3** Leo **5** Aries **11** Sagittarius
earth sign: **5** Virgo **6** Taurus **9** Capricorn
air sign: **5** Libra **6** Gemini **8** Aquarius
water: **6** Cancer, Pisces **7** Scorpio
division: **4** sign **5** decan **6** trigon
number of houses: **6** twelve
falling between two signs: **4** cusp

Zola, Emile
author of: **4** Nana **7** The Soil **8** Germinal **10** L'Assommoir **11** The Downfall, The Dram Shop **13** Therese Raquin **14** The Human Animal **20** The Experimental Novel

zone 4 area, belt, ward **5** tract **6** region, sector **7** quarter, section, terrain **8** district, locality, location, precinct **9** territory

zonked 5 drunk **6** soused, wasted, zapped **7** smashed **9** plastered **10** inebriated **11** intoxicated

zoo 8 vivarium **9** menagerie

zoom 3 fly, zip **4** buzz, race, rise, soar **5** climb, flash, shoot, speed **6** ascend, rocket, streak **7** advance, take off **9** skyrocket

zoophobia
fear of: **7** animals

Zophar
friend: **3** Job **5** Elihu **6** Bildad **7** Eliphaz

Zorba the Greek
director: **17** Michael Cacoyannis
based on the story by: **11** Kazantzakis
cast: **9** Alan Bates **11** Irene Pappas, Lila Kedrova **12** Anthony Quinn
score: **16** Mikis Theodorakis
Oscar for: **17** supporting actress (Kedrova)

zori 14 Japanese sandal

zucchini 5 gourd **6** squash **12** summer squash

Zuckerman Unbound
author: **10** Philip Roth

Zurich
festival: **12** Sechselauten
landmark: **8** Rietberg **9** Kunsthaus **15** CG Jung Institute **17** Centre Le Corbusier, Fraumunster Kirche **21** Grossmunster Cathedral
religious figure: **7** Zwingli **9** Bullinger
river: **6** Limmat
Roman name: **7** Turicum

Zweig, Arnold
author of: **7** Claudia **24** The Case of Sergeant Grischa